*The Wordsworth Dictionary of Phrase and Fable*

# *The Wordsworth Dictionary of*
# *Phrase and Fable*

*Based on the original book by*

E. C. BREWER

*Wordsworth Reference*

In loving memory of
MICHAEL TRAYLER
the founder of Wordsworth Editions

2

Readers who are interested in other titles from Wordsworth Editions are invited to visit our website at www.wordsworth-editions.com

For our latest list and a full mail-order service, contact Bibliophile Books, 5 Thomas Road, London E14 7BN
TEL: +44 (0)20 7515 9222 FAX: +44 (0)20 7538 4115
E-MAIL: orders@bibliophilebooks.com

First published in 2001 by
Wordsworth Editions Limited
8B East Street, Ware, Hertfordshire SG12 9HJ
Reset 2006

ISBN 13: 978 1 84022 310 1

Copyright © Wordsworth Editions Limited 2001 and 2006

Wordsworth® is a registered trademark of Wordsworth Editions Limited

All rights reserved. This publication may not be reproduced, stored in a retrieval system or transmitted in any form or by any means, electronic, mechanical, photocopying, recording or otherwise, without the prior permission of the publishers.

Typeset in Great Britain by Antony Gray
Printed and bound by Clays Ltd, St Ives plc

# A

**A.** The form of this letter is modified from the Egyptian hieroglyph which represents the eagle. The Phoenician (Hebrew) symbol was א (*aleph* = an ox), which has been thought, probably erroneously, to represent an ox-head in outline. The Greek A (*alpha*) was the symbol of a bad augury in the sacrifices.

***A*** in logic denotes a universal affirmative. *A* asserts, *E* denies. Thus, syllogisms in *bArbArA* (*q.v.*) contain three universal affirmative propositions.

**A1** means first-rate – the very best. In Lloyd's Register of British and Foreign Shipping, the character of the ship's hull is designated by *letters*, and that of the anchors, cables, and stores by *figures*. A1 means hull first-rate, and also anchors, cables, and stores; A2, hull first-rate, but fittings second-rate. Vessels of an inferior character are classified under the letters AE, E and I.

> She is a prime girl she is; she is A1. Sam Slick

**Aaron.** The name of the patriarch of the Jewish priesthood, possibly connected with *ha'aron*, 'the ark'.

**Aaron's Beard.** The popular name of many wild plants, including Great St John's Wort (Rose of Sharon), the Ivy-leaved Toadflax, Meadowsweet, Saxifrage Sarmentosa, etc.

**Aaron's Rod.** The name given (with reference to Num. 17:8) to various flowering plants, including Golden Rod, Great Mullein, and others.

**Aaron's Serpent.** Something so powerful as to eliminate minor powers.

> And hence one master passion in the breast,
> Like Aaron's serpent swallows up the rest.
> Pope, *Essay on Man*, ii, 131

The allusion is to Exod. 7:10–12.

**A.B.** *See* Able-bodied.

**Ab.** ***Ab ovo***. From the very beginning. Stasinus, in his *Cypria*, a poem in 11 books belonging to the Homeric cycle and forming an introduction to the *Iliad*, does not rush (as does the *Iliad* itself) *in medias res*, but begins with the eggs of Leda, from one of which Helen was born. If Leda had not laid this egg, Helen would never have been born, therefore Paris could not have eloped with her, therefore there would have been no Trojan War, etc. The English use of the phrase probably derives from the line in Horace's *De Arte Poetica*:

> Nec gemino bellum Troianum orditur ab ovo.

[illegible] Roman banquet began with an appetiser, which consisted of eggs and salt fish (*promulsis*), and ended with dessert, at which *mala* (i.e. apples, pears, quinces, pomegranates, and so on) formed the most conspicuous part. Hence the phrase is applied to the monopolising of the conversation during the whole of a dinner or at any other time. *See* Horace, *Sat*. I, iii, 6:

> Si collibuisset, ab ovo
> Usque ad mala citaret 'io Bacche'.

**Abacus.** A primitive calculating machine, consisting of a small frame with wires stretched across it in one direction, each wire having threaded on it ten balls which can be shifted backwards or forwards. It is used to teach children addition and subtraction and was employed by the Greeks and Romans for calculations, as a modification of it still is by the Chinese. The word is derived from the Greek, ἄβαξ, a cyphering table (a slab covered with sand). In Turkish schools this method is still used for teaching writing. The multiplication table invented by Pythagoras is called *Abacus Pythagoricus*.

In architecture the *abacus* is the topmost member of a capital.

**Abaddon.** The angel of the bottomless pit (Rev. 9:11), from Heb. *abad*, he perished.

> The angell of the bottomlesse pytt, whose name
> in the hebrew tonge is Abadon. Tindale

> All hell beneath
> Made me boil over. Devils pluck'd my sleeve;
> Abaddon and Asmodeus caught at me.
> Tennyson, *St Simeon Stylites*

Milton uses the name for the bottomless pit itself:

> In all her gates Abaddon rues
> Thy bold attempt. *Paradise Regained*, iv, 624

**Abaris.** A mythical Greek sage of the 6th century BC (surnamed 'the Hyperborean') mentioned by Herodotus, Pindar, etc. Apollo gave him a magic arrow which rendered him invisible, cured diseases, gave oracles, and on which he could ride through the air. Abaris gave it to Pythagoras, who, in return, taught him philosophy. Hence *the dart of Abaris*.

> The dart of Abaris carried the philosopher wheresoever he desired it. Willmott

**Abatement** (O. Fr., *abatre*, to beat down). In heraldry, a mark of depreciation annexed to coat armour, whereby the honour of it is abated. It is at least doubtful whether abatements were ever in regular use by heralds, and the marks of illegitimacy are the only ones that have survived.

**Abaton** (Gr., α, not; βαίνω, I go). *As inaccessible as Abaton.* A name given to various places of antiquity difficult of access. (1) A statue erected by Artemisia to commemorate her conquest of Rhodes, which was looked upon by the Rhodians after they had recovered their liberty as a kind of palladium, and was therefore surrounded with a fortified enclosure. (2) An island difficult of access in the fens of Memphis (according to Lucan). (3) That part of the temple of Asclepius at Epidaurus in Argolis to which invalids used to retire to sleep and to await visions in the hope of emerging cured in the morning.

**Abbassides** (3 syl.). A dynasty of thirty-seven caliphs who reigned over the Mohammedan Empire from 750 to 1258. They were descended from Abbas, uncle of Mahomet. Haroun al-Raschid (born 765, reigned 786–808), of the *Arabian Nights*, was one of their number.

**Abbey-lubber.** An idle, lazy monk. Father Dominic, in Dryden's *Spanish Friar*, may be taken as the type. The term came to be applied to any well-fed dependant or loafer.

> It came into a common proverbe to call him an *Abbay-lubber*, that was idle, wel fed, a long, lewd, lither loiterer, that might worke and would not.
>
> *The Burnynge of Paules Church*, 1563

**Abbot of Misrule.** *See* King of Misrule.

**Abbotsford.** The name given by Sir Walter Scott to Clarty Hole, on the south bank of the Tweed, after it became his residence in 1812. Sir Walter devised it from the fancy that the *abbots* of Melrose Abbey used to pass over the *fords* of the Tweed near by.

**ABC** An abbreviation having a number of meanings that can be decided only by the context. Thus, 'So-and-so doesn't know his ABC' means that he is intensely ignorant; 'he doesn't understand the ABC of engineering' means that he has not mastered its rudiments. So, an *ABC Book*, or *Absey Book*, is a primer which used to be used as a child's first lesson book and contained merely the alphabet and a few rudimentary lessons often set in catechism form, as is evident from Shakespeare's lines:

> That is question now;
> And then comes answer like an Absey book.
>
> *King John*, 1, 1

Quarles alludes figuratively to the Absey Book in his lines:

> Man is man's ABC. There is none can
> Read God aright unless he first spell man
>
> *Hieroglyphics of the Life of Man*

***ABC*** may also stand for the Aerated Bread Company, or for one of their tea-shops in London; while a farmer speaking of the *ABC process* would be referring to an obsolete method of making artificial manure, said to be named from the initials of Alum, Blood, and Clay, the three chief ingredients.

**Abd** in Arabic = slave or servant, as Abdiel (*q.v.*) and Abd-Allah (*servant of God*), Abd-el-Kader (*servant of the Mighty One*), Abd-ul-Latif (*servant of the Gracious One*), etc.

**Abdael.** In Dryden's *Absalom and Achitophel* stands for George Monk, first Duke of Albemarle.

> Brave Abdael o'er the prophets' school was placed;
> Abdael with all his father's virtues graced;
> A hero, who while stars look'd wond'ring down,
> Without one Hebrew's blood, restored the crown.

**Abdallah.** The father of Mahomet. He died shortly before his famous son was born, and is said to have been so beautiful, that when he married Amina, 200 virgins broke their hearts from disappointed love. – *See* Washington Irving's *Life of Mahomet*.

**Abdals.** The name given by Mohammedans to certain mysterious persons whose identity is known only to God, and through whom the world is able to continue in existence. They number 70, 40 of whom are always living in Syria. When one of the 70 dies another is secretly appointed by God to fill the vacant place. The word is an Arab plural meaning 'the Substitutes'.

**Abdera.** A maritime town of Thrace (said to have been founded by Abdera, sister of Diomede), so overrun with rats that it was abandoned, and the inhabitants migrated to Macedonia. The *Abderites*, or *Abderitans*, were proverbial for stupidity, yet the city gave birth to some of the wisest men of Greece, among them being Democritus (the laughing philosopher, from whom we get the phrases *Abderitan laughter*, meaning 'scoffing laughter', and an *Abderite*, or 'scoffer'), Protagoras (the great sophist), Anaxarchos (the philosopher and friend of Alexander), and Hecataeus (the historian).

**Abdiel** (Arab., *the servant of God*; cf. Abd). In Milton's *Paradise Lost* (v, 805, 896, etc.) the faithful seraph who withstood Satan when he urged the angels to revolt.

> [He] adheres, with the faith of Abdiel, to the ancient form of adoration. Sir W. Scott

**Abecedarian.** Usually, one who teaches or is learning his ABC; but also the name of a 16th-century sect of Anabaptists who regarded the teaching of the Holy Spirit (as extracted by them from the Bible) as sufficient for every purpose in life, and hence despised all learning of every kind, except so much of the ABC as was necessary to enable them to read. The sect was founded in 1520 by Nicholas Stork, a weaver of Zwickau; hence they are also spoken of as 'the *Zwickau prophets*'.

**Abecedarian Hymns.** Hymns the lines or other divisions of which are arranged in alphabetical order. In Hebrew the 119th Psalm is abecedarian. *See* Acrostic Poetry.

**Abel.** *See* Cain.

**Abelites,** *Abelians*, or *Abelonians*. A Christian sect of the 4th century mentioned by St Augustine as living in North Africa. They married but remained virgin, as they affirm Abel did – on the assumption that because no children of his are mentioned in Scripture he had none. The sect was maintained by adopting the children of others.

**Abessa,** typification of superstition in Spenser's *Faerie Queene*, Bk I, iii. She is the daughter of Corceca (blindness of heart).

**Abhorrers.** *See* Petitioners.

**Abidhamma.** The third pitaka of the three Pali texts (Tripitaka) which together form the sacred canon of the Buddhists. The Abidhamma contains 'the analytical exercises in the psychological system on which the doctrine is based', in seven treatises. *See* Tripitaka.

**Abigail.** A lady's maid. *Abigail*, wife of Nabal and afterwards of David, is a well-known Scripture heroine (1 Sam. 25:3). Marlowe called the daughter of Barrabas, his *Jew of Malta*, by this name, and it was given by Beaumont and Fletcher to the 'waiting gentlewoman' in *The Scornful Lady*. Swift, Fielding, and other novelists of the period employ it in their novels, and it was further popularised by the notoriety of Abigail Hill, better known as Mrs Masham, the waiting-woman to Queen Anne.

**Abimelech.** A Canaanitish regal title probably meaning 'Melech, the divine king, is father'. Besides the two of this name in the Bible (Gen. 26 and Judges 9) it occurs as that of a prince of Arvad in the Annals of Assurbanipal, and in the Amarna tablets as that of an Egyptian governor of Tyre.

**Abingdon Law.** *See* Cupar Justice.

**Able-bodied Seaman, An,** or, *an able seaman*, is a skilled seaman, a sailor of the first class. A crew is divided into three classes: (1) skilled seamen, termed A.B. (Able-Bodied); (2) ordinary seamen; and (3) boys, which include 'green hands', or inexperienced men, without regard to age or size.

**Aboard.** (*See also* Board.) *He fell aboard of me* – he disagreed with me, quarrelled with me. A ship is said to fall aboard another when it runs against it.

***To go aboard*** is to embark, to go on the board or deck.

***Aboard main tack*** is an old sea-term meaning to draw one of the lower corners of the mainsail down to the chess tree. Figuratively, 'to keep to the point'.

**Abolla.** An ancient military garment worn by the Greeks and Romans, opposed to the *toga* or robe of peace. The abolla, being worn by the lower orders, was affected by philosophers in the vanity of humility.

**Abomination of Desolation, The,** mentioned in Dan. (chs 9, 11, and 12), and in Matt. 24:15, probably refers to some statue set up in the Temple by either the heathens or the Romans. The subject is very obscure, the best Hebrew and Greek scholarship leaving the actual thing intended unidentified, Dr Cheyne concluding that 'the "abomination" which thrusts itself into the "holy place" has for its nature "desolation" – i.e. finds its pleasure in undoing the divine work of a holy Creator'.

**Abou-Bekr** (571–634), called *Father of the Virgin*, i.e. Mahomet's favourite wife. He was the first caliph, or successor of Mahomet, of the Sunni Moslems, and reigned for only two years.

**Abou Hassan.** A rich merchant (in *The Arabian Nights*), transferred during sleep to the bed and palace of the Caliph Haroun al-Raschid. Next morning he was treated as the caliph, and every effort was made to make him forget his identity (*The Sleeper Awakened*). The same story, localised to Shakespeare's own Warwickshire, forms the Induction to *The Taming of the Shrew*, where a tinker, Christopher Sly, takes the place of

Abou Hassan, and the incident is said by Burton (*Anatomy of Melancholy*, II, iv) actually to have occurred during the wedding festivities of Philip the Good of Burgundy (about 1440). *The Ballad of the Frolicsome Duke, or the Tinker's Good Fortune* in the *Percy Reliques*, and another version in Calderon's play, *Life's a Dream* (*c.*1633), go to show how popular and widely spread was this oriental fable.

**Abou ibn Sina,** commonly called *Avicenna* from his birthplace, Afshena, near Bokhara. A great Persian physician whose canons of medicine were founded on those of Galen, Hippocratés, and Aristotle, and whose teaching had great influence on western mediaeval medicine. He died in 1037.

**Above-board.** In a straightforward manner. Conjurers place their hands *under* the table when they are preparing their tricks, but *above* when they show them. 'Let all be above-board' means 'let there be no *under*-hand work, but let us see everything'.

**Above par.** A commercial term meaning that the article referred to is more than its nominal value. *See* Par, at.

***Above your hook.*** *See* Hook.

**Abracadabra.** A cabalistic charm, said to be made up from the initials of the Hebrew words Ab (Father), Ben (Son) and Ruach ACadsch (Holy Spirit), and formerly used as a powerful antidote against ague, flux, toothache, etc. The word was written on parchment, and suspended from the neck by a linen thread, in the following form:

A B R A C A D A B R A
A B R A C A D A B R
A B R A C A D A B
A B R A C A D A
A B R A C A D
A B R A C A
A B R A C
A B R A
A B R
A B
A

**Abracax.** *See* Abraxas.

**Abraham.** *Mohammedan mythology* adds the following legends to those told us in the Bible concerning the patriarch. His parents were Prince Azar and his wife, Adna. As King Nimrod had been told that one shortly to be born would dethrone him, he proclaimed a 'massacre of the innocents', and Adna retired to a cave where Abraham was born. He was nourished by sucking two of her fingers, one of which supplied milk and the other honey. At the age of fifteen months Abraham was equal in size to a lad of 15, and was so wise that his father introduced him to the court of King Nimrod.

Other Mohammedan traditions relate that Abraham and his son 'Ismail' rebuilt for the fourth time the Kaaba over the sacred stone at Mecca; that Abraham destroyed the idols manufactured and worshipped by his father, Terah; and that the mountain (called in the Bible 'Mount Moriah') on which he offered up his son was 'Arfaday'.

The Ghebers say that the infant Abraham was thrown into the fire by Nimrod's order, but the flame turned into a bed of roses, on which he went to sleep. Hence Moore's allusion in *Lalla Rookh*:

> Sweet and welcome as the bed
> For their own infant prophet spread,
> When pitying Heaven to roses turned
> The death-flames that beneath him burned.
>
> *Fire Worshippers*

***To sham Abraham.*** *See* Abram-Man.

***Abraham's Bosom.*** The repose of the happy in death –

> The sons of Edward sleep in Abraham's bosom.
>
> Shakespeare, *Richard III*, 4, 3

The allusion is to Luke 16:22, and refers to the ancient custom of allowing a dear friend to recline on your bosom, as did John on the bosom of Jesus.

***There is no leaping from Delilah's lap into Abraham's bosom*** – i.e. those who live and die in notorious sin must not expect to go to heaven at death. Boston, *Crook in the Lot*.

**Abraham Newland, An.** A banknote. So called from the name of the chief cashier at the Bank of England from 1782 to 1807, without whose signature no Bank of England notes were genuine.

> I have heard people say *Sham Abram* you may,
> But must not sham Abraham Newland.
>
> T. Dibdin *or* Upton

> Trees are notes issued from the bank of Nature, and as current as those payable to Abraham Newland.
>
> G. Colman, Junr, *The Poor Gentleman*, i, 2 (1801)

**Abrahamic Covenant.** The covenant made by God with Abraham (Gen. 12:2, 3, and 17), interpreted to mean that the Messiah should spring from his seed. This promise was given to Abraham, because he left his father's house to live in a strange land, as God told him.

**Abrahamites** (4 syl.). Certain Bohemian deists, so called because they professed to believe what

Abraham believed before he was circumcised. All they acknowledged as Holy Scripture was the Decalogue and the Lord's Prayer. The sect was suppressed by Joseph II in 1783.

**Abram-colour.** 'Abram' here is a corruption of *aulburn*. In *Coriolanus*, 2, 3, the word is so printed in the first three folios –

> Our heads are some brown, some black, some Abram, some bald.

But in the fourth folio (1685) and in later editions *auburn* is given. Kyd's tragedy, *Soliman and Perseda* (1588) has:

> Where is the eldest son of Priam, the Abram-coloured Trojan ?

And Middleton, in *Blurt, Master Constable* (1601), mentions:

> A goodly, long, thick Abram-coloured beard.

**Abram-Man,** or **Abraham Cove.** A pretended maniac who, in Tudor and early Stuart times, wandered about the country as a begging impostor; a Tom o' Bedlam (*q.v.*); hence the phrase, *to sham Abraham*, meaning to pretend illness or distress, in order to get off work.

Inmates of Bedlam (*q.v.*) who were not dangerously mad were kept in the 'Abraham Ward', and were allowed out from time to time in a distinctive dress, and were permitted to supplement their scanty rations by begging. This gave an opportunity to impostors, and large numbers availed themselves of it. Says *The Canting Academy* (Richd Head, 1674), they

> 'used to array themselves with party-coloured ribbons, tape in their hats, a fox-tail hanging down, a long stick with streamers', and beg alms; but 'for all their seeming madness, they had wit enough to steal as they went along'.

There is a good picture of them in *King Lear* 2, 3; and see also Beaumont and Fletcher's *Beggar's Bush*, ii, i.

> Come, princes of the ragged regiment
> And these, what name or title e'er they bear,
> *Jarkman* or *Patrico*, *Cranke* or *Clapper-dudgeon*,
> *Frater* or *Abram-man*, I speak to all
> That stand in fair election for the title
> Of King of Beggars.

**Abraxas.** A cabalistic word used by the Gnostics to denote the Supreme Being, the source of 365 emanations, the sum of the numbers represented by the Greek letters of the word totalling 365. It was frequently engraved on gems (hence known as *abraxas stones*), that were used as amulets or talismans. *See* Basilidians. By some authorities the name is given as that of one of the horses of Aurora.

**Abroach.** *To set mischief abroach* is to set it afoot:

> Alack, what mischiefs might be set abroach
> In shadow of such greatness!
>
> Shakespeare, *2 Henry IV*, 4, 2

The figure is from a cask of liquor, which is broached that the liquor may be drawn from it, in which sense Tennyson uses it in *The Cup* (I, ii):

> Not set myself abroach
> And run my mind out to a random guest.

(Fr. *brocher*, to pierce.)

**Abroad. *The schoolmaster is abroad.*** Education is spreading. The phrase was coined by Brougham; it was first used by him at the opening meeting of the London Mechanics' Institution in 1825, and afterwards in the House of Commons when opposing the succession of the Duke of Wellington to the premiership, 29 Jan., 1828.

***You are all abroad.*** Wide of the mark; not at home with the subject.

The word really means, 'In all directions'.

> Eftsoones he gan to gather up around
> His weapons which lay scattered all abroad.
>
> Spenser, *Faerie Queene*, IV, iv, 23

**Abrogate.** When the Roman senate wanted a law to be passed, they asked the people to give their votes in its favour. The Latin for this is *rogare legem* (to solicit or propose a law). If they wanted a law repealed, they asked the people to vote against it; this was *abrogare legem* (to solicit against the law).

**Absalom.** *See* Absalom and Achitophel.

**Absalom and Achitophel.** A political satire published in 1681, the first part by Dryden and the second by Nahum Tate and revised by Dryden. Of the principal characters, many of whom are separately noted in this book, *David* stands for Charles II; *Absalom* for his natural son James, Duke of Monmouth (handsome and rebellious); *Achitophel* for Lord Shaftesbury; *Zimri* for the Duke of Buckingham; and *Abdael* for Monk. The accommodation of the biblical narrative to contemporary history is so skilfully made that the story of David seems to repeat itself. Of Absalom, Dryden says (Part i):

> Whate'er he did was done with so much ease,
> In him alone 'twas natural to please;
> His motions all accompanied with grace,
> And paradise was opened in his face.

**Absent.** 'Out of mind as soon as out of sight'. This is the form in which the proverb is given by Fulke Greville, Lord Brooke (d.1628) in his *56th Sonnet*; but it appears with its more usual wording – 'Out of sight, out of mind', as the title of one of Barnabe Googe's *Eclogs* (1563).

***The absent are always wrong.*** The translation of the French proverb, *Les absents ont toujours tort*, which implies that if convenient one will readily sacrifice the interests of those who do not happen to be present.

**Absolute.** *A Captain Absolute*, a bold, despotic man, determined to have his own way, so called from the character in Sheridan's *Rivals*.

**Absquatulate.** To run away or abscond. An artificial American word, possibly from Lat. *ab*, from and *squat*, a squatting being a tenement taken in some unclaimed part, without purchase or permission. It seems to have been first used in 1833, in *The Kentuckian*, a play by W. B. Bernard.

**Abstract Numbers** are numbers considered without reference to anything else: 1, 2, 3; if we say 1 year, 2 feet, 3 men, etc., the numbers are no longer abstract, but *concrete*.

Things are said to be *taken in the abstract* when they are considered absolutely, that is, without reference to other matters or persons. Thus, in the abstract, one man may be as good as another, but is yet not so socially and politically.

***An abstract of title*** is a legal expression, meaning an epitome of the evidences of ownership.

**Abstraction.** Prof. Bain, in *The Senses and the Intellect*, defines abstraction as 'the generalising of some property, so as to present it to the mind, apart from the other properties that usually go along with it in nature'; or it is, as Pocke put it: 'Nothing more than leaving out of a number of resembling ideas what is peculiar to each'. This process is apt to result in what we call *an empty abstraction*, a mere ideality, of no practical use, and sooner or later we turn away from such unsatisfying ideas, as did Wordsworth:

> Give us, for our abstractions, solid facts;
> For our disputes, plain pictures.
>
> *Excursion*, v, 636

Gladstone furnished an excellent illustration of the meaning of the term when he said, 'Laws are abstractions until they are put into execution.'

**Absurd** meant originally 'quite deaf' (Lat. *ab*, intensive, and *surdus*, deaf); but the Lat. compound *absurdus* had the meaning, 'out of time', 'discordant', hence 'harsh' or 'rough', and hence the figurative (and now common) meaning 'irrational', 'silly' or 'senseless'.

***Reductio ad absurdum.*** *See* Reductio.

**Abudah,** Thackeray's allusion:

> Like Abudah, he is always looking out for the Fury, and knows that the night will come with the inevitable hag with it.

is to a story in Ridley's *Tales of the Genii* of a merchant of Bagdad who is haunted every night by an old hag.

**Abundant Number, An.** A number the sum of whose aliquot parts is greater than itself. Thus 12 is an abundant number, because its divisors, 1, 2, 3, 4, 6 = 16, which is greater than 12. *Cp.* Deficient Number, Perfect Number.

**Abus.** An old name of the river Humber. *See* Spenser's *Faerie Queene*, II, x, 16:

> He [Locrine] then encountred, a confused rout,
> Forbye the River that whylome was hight
> The ancient Abus ...
> And forst their Chiefetaine, for his safeties sake,
> (Their Chiefetaine Humber named was aright)
> Unto the mightie streame him to betake,
> Where he an end of battell and of life did make.

*See* Geoffrey of Monmouth's *Chronicles*, Bk ii, 2.

**Abyla.** *See* Calpe.

**Abyssinian Christians.** A branch of the Coptic Church. *See* Copts.

**Acacetus.** One who does nothing badly; an epithet given by Homer to Hermes (*Il.* 16, 185; *Od.* 24, 10), and by Hesiod to Prometheus. (Gr. *a*, not; *kakos*, bad.)

**Academy.** Originally the proper name of a garden near Athens (from *Academos*, the reputed founder) where Plato taught; hence, the philosophical school or system of Plato, and, later, a place where the arts and sciences, etc. are taught, and a society or institution for their cultivation.

Plato's Academy was divided into the *Old*, his own philosophic teaching, and that of his immediate followers Xenocrates, Crates, and others; the *Middle*, a modified Platonic system, founded by Arcesilaus about 244 BC; and the *New*, the half-sceptical school of Carneades, founded about 160 BC. *See* Platonism.

The principal modern Academies are:

The *French Academy* (*Académie française*), formally established in 1635 by Cardinal Richelieu, its principal function being:

> To labour with all the care and diligence possible, to give exact rules to our language, to render it capable of treating the arts and sciences.

The English *Royal Academy of Arts*, founded in 1768 by George III for the establishment of an art school and the holding of annual exhibitions of works by living artists. The following is a complete list of the Presidents of the Royal Academy:

1768 Sir Joshua Reynolds
1792 Benjamin West

1820 Sir Thos. Lawrence
1830 Sir Martin Archer Shee
1850 Sir Charles Eastlake
1866 Sir Francis Grant
1878 Lord Leighton
1896 Sir John Millais
1896 Sir Edward Poynter
1919 Sir Aston Webb

The *Royal Spanish Academy* was founded at Madrid in 1713 for purposes similar to those of the French Academy. There is also a *Royal Academy of Science* at Berlin (founded 1700), at Stockholm (the *Royal Swedish Academy*, founded 1739), and at Copenhagen (founded 1742). The *Imperial Academy of Sciences* at Petrograd was established by Catherine I in 1725.

**Academy Figures.** Drawings in black and white chalk, on tinted paper, usually about half life-size and from the nude.

**Acadia.** The early name of Nova Scotia, introduced to Europe by the Florentine explorer, Verazzani, who reported in 1524 that it was known by that name to the inhabitants. In 1621 Sir Wm Alexander obtained a grant of the land, and its name was changed to Nova Scotia. The old French inhabitants refused to take the oath of allegiance to the British crown and were in a state of constant rebellion, so in 1755 they were driven into exile by order of George II. Longfellow's *Evangeline* tells of the resulting sufferings.

**Acadine.** A Sicilian fountain mentioned by Diodorus Siculus as having magic properties. Writings were thrown into it for the purpose of being tested; if genuine they floated, if spurious they sank to the bottom.

**Acanthus.** The conventionalised representation of the leaf of *Acanthus mollis* used as a decoration in the capitals of Corinthian and composite columns. The story is that an acanthus sprang up around a basket of flowers that Callimachus had placed on his daughter's grave, and that this so struck the fancy of the architect that he introduced the design into his buildings.

**Accents.** *See* Typographical Signs.

**Acceptance.** A commercial term denoting a person's agreement to a contract or other arrangement submitted to him for approval. It often refers to the acceptance of a bill of exchange, and hence has come to be applied to the bill itself, which is accepted by the drawee writing on it 'accepted', and signing his name. The person who accepts it is called the 'acceptor'.

**Accessory.** ***Accessory before the fact*** is one who is aware that another intends to commit an offence, but is himself absent when the offence is perpetrated.

***Accessory after the fact*** is one who screens a felon, aids him in eluding justice, or helps him in any way to profit by his crime. Thus, the receiver of stolen goods, knowing or even suspecting them to be stolen, is an accessory *ex post facto*.

**Accident.** ***A logical accident*** is some property or quality which a substance possesses, the removal or change of which would not necessarily affect the substance itself, as the height of our bodies, the redness of a brick, the whiteness of paper, etc. Theologians explain the doctrine of transubstantiation by maintaining that the *substance* of the bread and wine is changed into that of the body and blood of Christ, but their *accidents* (flavour, appearance, and so on) remain the same as before.

**Accidental Colours.** *See* Colours.

**Accidentals** in music are signs indicating sharps, flats, naturals, and double sharps and flats, other than those sharps and flats prescribed by the key-signature.

**Accius Naevius.** A legendary Roman augur in the reign of Tarquin the Elder. When he forbade the king to increase the number of centuries (i.e. divisions of the army) instituted by Romulus without consulting the augurs, Tarquin asked him if, according to the augurs, the thought then in his mind was feasible. 'Undoubtedly,' said Accius, after consultation. 'Then cut through this whetstone with the razor in your hand.' The priest gave a bold cut, and the block fell in two (Livy, i, 36).

**Accolade** (3 syl.). The touch of a sword on the shoulder in the ceremony of conferring knighthood; originally an embrace or touch by the hand on the neck (Lat. *ad collum*, on the neck). In music the brace ( { ) that connects two or more staves in the score is called an accolade.

**Accommodation.** In commercial use, a loan of money.

***Accommodation note*** or ***bill.*** A bill of exchange for which value has not been received, used for the purpose of raising money on credit.

***Accommodation ladder.*** A flight of steps hung over the side of a ship at the gangway.

**Accord** means 'heart to heart'. (Lat. *ad corda*.) If two persons like and dislike the same things, they are heart to heart with each other.

Similarly, 'concord' means heart with heart; 'discord', heart divided from heart; 'record' – i.e. *re-cordare* – properly means to bring again to the mind or heart, and secondarily to set this down in writing.

**Accost** means to 'come to the side' of a person for the purpose of speaking to him. It used to be written, and pronounced, *accoast*. (Lat. *ad costam*, to the side.)

**Account.** ***To open an account,*** to enter a customer's name on your ledger for the first time. (Lat. *accomputare*, to calculate.)

***To keep open account.*** Merchants are said to keep open account when they agree to honour each other's bills of exchange.

***A current account*** or 'account current', *a/c*. A commercial term, meaning the account of a customer who does not pay for goods received at time of purchase.

***On account.*** A commercial phrase implying 'in part payment for'.

***To cast accounts.*** To give the results of the debits and credits entered, balancing the two, and carrying over the surplus.

***The account*** on the Stock Exchange means: the credit allowed on dealings for the fortnightly settlement, or the fortnightly settlement itself, which is also called *account-day*, or *settling-day*.

***To be sent to one's account.*** To have final judgment passed on one. The Ghost in *Hamlet* uses the phrase as a synonym for death:

> Sent to my account
> With all my imperfections on my head.
>
> *Hamlet*, 1, 5

***We will give a good account of them*** – i.e. we will give them a thorough good drubbing.

**Accusative.** Calvin was so called by his college companions. An 'accusative age' is an obsolete expression denoting an age that is *searching*, one that eliminates error by *accusing* it.

> This hath been a very accusative age.
>
> Sir E. Dering (16th cent.)

**Ace.** The unit of cards or dice, from *as*, which was the Latin unit of weight.

***Within an ace.*** Within a hair's breadth of; he who wins within an ace wins within a single mark. *See* Ambs-as.

***To bale an ace*** is to make an abatement, or to give a competitor some start or other advantage, in order to render the combatants more equal. *See* Bolton. Taylor, the water poet (1580–1654), speaking of certain women, says –

> Though bad they be, they will not bate an ace
> To be cald Prudence, Temp'rance, Faith, and Grace.

**Aceldama.** The 'field of blood' near Jerusalem, mentioned at Matt. 27:8, and Acts 1:19. It was appropriated as a cemetery for strangers, and was used as a burial-place by Christians during the Crusades and even as late as the 17th century. The name, which is Aramaic and means 'the field of blood', is figuratively used for any place of great slaughter.

**Acephalites** (Gr. *a-kephale*, without a head). The name given to various rebellious and discontented groups of early Christians, principally to (1) A faction among the Monophysites who seceded from the authority of Peter. (2) Certain bishops of the Eastern Church exempt from the jurisdiction and discipline of their patriarch. (3) A party of English levellers in the reign of Henry I, who acknowledged no leader.

The name is also given to the monsters described in various legends and mediaeval books of travel as having no head, their eyes and mouth being placed elsewhere.

**Acestes.** ***The arrow of Acestes.*** In a trial of skill Acestes, the Sicilian, discharged his arrow with such force that it took fire. (*Aeneid*, V, 525.)

> Acestes … shooting upward, sends his shaft to show
> An archer's art, and boast his twanging bow;
> The feathered arrow gave a dire portent –
> And latter augurs judge from this event –
> Chafed by the speed, it fired, and as it flew
> A trail of following flames ascending drew.
>
> Dryden, *Aen.*, V, 687

**Achaean League.** The first Achaean League was a religious confederation of the twelve towns of Achaea, lasting from very early times till it was broken up by Alexander the Great. The second was a powerful political federation of the Achaean and many other Greek cities, formed to resist Macedonian domination in 280 BC, and dissolved by the Romans in 147 BC.

**Achates.** A *fidus Achates*. A faithful companion, a bosom friend. Achates in Virgil's *Aeneid* is the chosen companion of the hero in adventures of all kinds.

> He has chosen this fellow for his *fidus Achates*.
>
> Sir Walter Scott

**Achemon.** According to Greek fable Achemon and his brother Basalas were two Cercopes (*q.v.*) forever quarrelling. One day they saw Hercules asleep under a tree and insulted him, but Hercules tied them by their feet to his club and walked off with them, heads downwards, like a brace of hares. Everyone laughed at the sight, and it became a proverb among the Greeks, when two men were seen quarrelling – 'Look out for Melampygos!' (i.e. Hercules).

Ne insidas in Melampygum.

**Acheron.** A Greek word meaning 'the River of Sorrows'; the river of the infernal regions into which Phlegethon and Cocytus flow: also, the lower world (Hades) itself.

They pass the bitter waves of Acheron
Where many souls sit wailing woefully.
Spenser, *Faerie Queene*, I, v, 33

**Acherontian Books.** *See* Tages.

**Acherontis Pabulum.** Food for the churchyard; said of a dead body.

**Acherusia.** A cavern on the borders of Pontus, through which Hercules dragged Cerberus to earth from the infernal regions.

**Achillea.** A genus of herbaceous plants of the aster family, including the common yarrow (*Achillea millefolium*), so called from Achilles. The tale is, that when the Greeks invaded Troy, Telephus, son-in-law of Priam, attempted to stop their landing; but, Bacchus causing him to stumble, Achilles wounded him with his spear. The young Trojan was told by an oracle that 'Achilles (meaning milfoil or yarrow) would cure the wound'; instead of seeking the plant he applied to the Grecian chief, and promised to conduct the host to Troy if he would cure the wound. Achilles consented to do so, scraped some rust from his spear, and from the filings rose the plant milfoil, which, being applied to the wound, had the desired effect. It is called by the French the *herbe aux charpentiers* – i.e. carpenter's wort, because it was supposed to heal wounds made by carpenters' tools.

**Achilles.** In Greek legend, the son of Peleus and Thetis and grandson of Eacus, king of the Myrmidons (in Thessaly), and hero of the *Iliad* (*q.v.*). He is represented as being brave and relentless; but, at the opening of the poem, in consequence of a quarrel between him and Agamemnon, commander-in-chief of the allied Greeks, he refused to fight. The Trojans prevailed, and Achilles sent Patroclus to oppose them. Patroclus fell; and Achilles, rushing into the battle, killed Hector (*q.v.*). He himself, according to later poems, was slain at the Scaean gate, before Troy was taken, by an arrow in his heel. *See* Achilles Tendon.

**Achilles.**

*Death of*: It was Paris who wounded Achilles in the heel with an arrow (a post-Homeric story).

*Horses*: Balios and Xanthos (*see* Horse).

*Mistress in Troy*: Hippodamia, surnamed Briseis (*q.v.*).

*Tomb*: In Sigoeum, over which no bird ever flies.
Pliny, x, 29

*Tutors*: First, Phoenix, who taught him the elements; then Chiron the centaur, who taught him the uses and virtues of plants.

*Wife*: Deidamia (*q.v.*).

***The English Achilles.*** John Talbot, first Earl of Shrewsbury (1388?–1453).

***Achilles of England.*** The Duke of Wellington (1769–1852).

***Achilles of Germany.*** Albert Elector of Brandenburg (1414–86).

**Achilles of Lombardy.** In Tasso's *Jerusalem Delivered*, the brother of Sforza and Palamedes, brothers in the allied army of Godfrey. Achilles of Lombardy was slain by Corinna.

***Achilles of Rome.*** Lucius Sicinius Dentatus, tribune of the Roman plebs, 454 BC put to death 450 BC also called the *Second Achilles*.

***Achilles of the West.*** Roland the Paladin; also called 'The Christian Theseus'.

***Achilles and the tortoise.*** The allusion is to the following paradox proposed by Zeno: In a race Achilles, who can run ten times as fast as a tortoise, gives the latter 100 yards start; but it is impossible for him to overtake the tortoise and win the race; for, while he is running the first hundred yards the tortoise runs ten, while Achilles runs that ten the tortoise is running one, while Achilles is running one the tortoise runs one-tenth of a yard, and so on *ad infinitum*.

***Achilles' spear.*** Shakespeare's lines:

That gold must round engirt these brows of mine
Whose smile and frown, like to Achilles' spear,
Is able with the change to kill and cure.
*2 Henry VI*, 5, 1

is an allusion from the story told above (*s.v.* Achillea) of the healing of Telephus. It is also referred to by Chaucer:

speche of Thelophus the king,
And of Achilles with his queynte spere,
For he coude with it bothe hele and dere (*harm*).
*Squieres Tale*, 238

***Achilles tendon.*** A strong sinew running along the heel to the calf of the leg. The tale is that Thetis took her son Achilles by the heel, and dipped him in the river Styx to make him invulnerable. The water washed every part, except the heel in his mother's hand. It was on this vulnerable point the hero was slain; and the sinew of the heel is called, in consequence, *tendo Achillis*. A post-Homeric story.

***The heel of Achilles.*** The vulnerable or weak point in a man's character or of a nation.

**Aching Void, An.** That desolation of heart which arises from the recollection of some cherished endearment no longer possessed.

> What peaceful hours I once enjoy'd
> How sweet their memory still
> But they have left an aching void
> The world can never fill.
>
> Cowper, *Walking with God*

**Achitophel.** Achitophel was David's traitorous counsellor, who deserted to Absalom; but his advice being disregarded, he hanged himself (2 Sam. 15). The Achitophel of Dryden's satire (*see* Absalom and Achitophel) was the Earl of Shaftesbury:

> Of these (*the rebels*) the false Achitophel was first;
> A name to all succeeding ages curst;
> For close designs and crooked counsels fit;
> Sagacious, bold, and turbulent of wit;
> Restless, unfix'd in principles and place;
> In power unpleased, impatient in disgrace
>
> I, 150

**Achor.** Said by Pliny to be the name of the deity prayed to by the Cyreneans for the averting of insect pests. *See* Flies, God of.

**Acid Test.** A test, or trial, that will finally decide the value, worth, or reliability of anything, just as the application of acid is a certain test of gold. It is a phrase often used of measures to be taken during political, social, economic, or other crises.

**Acis.** In *Greek mythology*, the son of Faunus, in love with Galatea. His rival, Polyphemus, the Cyclop, crushed him to death under a huge rock.

**Ack emma.** *See* Pip emma.

**Acme** (Gr. a point). The highest pitch of perfection; the term used by old medical writers for the crisis of a disease. They divided the progress of a disease into four periods: the *ar-che*, or beginning; the *anab-asis*, or increase; the *acme*, or term of its utmost violence; and the *pa-racme*, or decline.

**Acoemetae.** A monastic order instituted *c.*430 by Alexander, a Syrian monk. The twenty-four hours were divided into eight-hour 'shifts', and the order into three parts, so that one-third of the order was incessantly at worship, day and night. (Gr. *watchers*, or *the sleepless ones.*)

**Acolyte.** A subordinate officer in the Catholic Church, whose duty is to light the lamps, prepare the sacred elements, attend the officiating priests, etc. (Gr. *a follower.*)

**Aconite.** The herb Monkshood or Wolfsbane. Classic fabulists ascribe its poisonous qualities to the foam which dropped from the mouths of the three-headed Cerberus, when Hercules, at the command of Eurystheus, dragged the monster from the infernal regions. (Gr. ἀκόνιτον; Lat. *aconitum.*)

> Lurida terribiles miscent Aconita novercae.
>
> Ovid, *Metamorphoses*, i, 147

**Acrasia.** In Spenser's *Faerie Queene* (Bk II, ca. 12), an enchantress, mistress of the 'Bower of Bliss'. She transformed her lovers into monstrous shapes, and kept them captives. Sir Guyon captures her, frees her victims, destroys the bower, and sends her in chains of adamant to the Faerie Queene. She is the personification of Intemperance, the name signifying 'lack of self-control'.

**Acrates.** The typification of self-indulgence in the *Faerie Queene* (Bk II. ca. 4), father (by Despite) of Cymochles and Pyrochles.

**Acre.** O.E. *aecer*, is akin to the Lat. *ager* and Ger. *acker* (a field). *God's Acre*, a cemetery or churchyard. Longfellow calls this an 'ancient Saxon phrase', but as a matter of fact it is a modern borrowing from Germany.

**Acre-fight.** A 'ghost-word', i.e. a word having no real existence; it is said to denote a duel in the open field, originally between Scotch and English Borderers. It first appears in John Cowel's *Law Dictionary* (1607), and, according to the OED, 'seems to be merely transliterated by him from a mediaeval Latin phrase *acram committere* in the Annals of Burton, 1237, where *acram* (for *pugnam*) is a bad translation of O.E. *camp*, combat, confused with Lat. *campus*, Fr. *champ*, and so with Eng. *acre*. The word has never been in use outside the dictionaries.

**Acre-shot.** An obsolete name for a land tax. 'Shot' is *scot. See* Scot and Lot.

**Acres, Bob.** A coward by character in Sheridan's *The Rivals*, whose courage always 'oozed out at his fingers' ends'. Hence, a man of this kind is sometimes called 'a regular Bob Acres'.

**Acroamatics,** or **Acroatics.** Esterical lectures; the lectures of Aristotle, which none but his chosen disciples were allowed to attend. Those given to the public generally were called *exoteric*.

(Gr. *delivered to an audience*; ακροάσθαι, to hear lectures.)

**Acrobat** means one who *goes on his extremities*, or uses only the tips of his fingers and toes in moving about. (It is from Gr. *akros*, the point, or extremity, *baino*, to go.)

**Acropolis** (Gk. *akros*, point, height, *polis*, city). An elevated citadel, especially of ancient Athens, where was built in the 5th century BC the Parthenon, the Erechtheum, and the Propylaea or monumental gate.

**Acrostic** (Gr. *akros*, extremity, *stichos*, row, line of verse). A piece of verse in which the initial letters of each line read downwards consecutively form a word; if the final letters read in the same way also form a word it is a *double acrostic*; if the middle letters as well it is a *triple acrostic*. The term was first applied to the excessively obscure prophecies of the Erythraean sibyl; they were written on loose leaves, and the initial letters made a word when the leaves were sorted and laid in order. (*Dionys*. iv, 62.)

**Acrostic Poetry** among the Hebrews consisted of twenty-two lines or stanzas beginning with the letters of the alphabet in succession (*cp*. Abecedarian Hymns). There are acrostics in the Greek Anthology and in the comedies of Plautus, and among the English Elizabethans they were by no means uncommon.

**Act** and **Opponency.** An 'Act', in our University language, consists of a thesis publicly maintained by a candidate for a degree, with the 'disputation' thereon. The person 'disputing' with the 'keeper of the Act' is called the 'opponent', and his function is called an 'opponency'. In some degrees the student is required to keep his Act, and then to be the opponent of another disputant. This custom has long been given up at Oxford, but at Cambridge the thesis and examination for the doctor's degree in Divinity, Law, and Medicine is still called an 'Act'.

**Act of Faith.** *See* Auto da fé.

**Act of God.** Loss arising from the action of forces uncontrollable by man, such as a hurricane, lightning, etc., is said to be due to the 'act of God', and hence has no legal redress. A Devonshire jury once found – 'That deceased died by the act of God, brought about by the flooded condition of the river'.

**Actaeon.** In *Grecian mythology* a huntsman who, having surprised Diana bathing, was changed by her into a stag and torn to pieces by his own hounds. A stag being a horned animal, he became a representative of men whose wives are unfaithful. *See* Horn.

> Like Sir Actaeon he, with Ringwood at thy heel.
>
> Shakespeare, *Merry Wives*, 2, 1

> The Emperors themselves did wear Actaeon's badge.
>
> Burton, *Anatomy of Melancholy* (1621)

**Actian Games.** The games celebrated at Actium in honour of Apollo. They were reinstituted by Augustus to celebrate his naval victory over Antony, 31 BC, and were held every five years.

**Action Sermon.** A sacramental sermon (in the Scots Presbyterian Church).

> I returned home about seven, and addressed myself towards my Action Sermon.
>
> E. Irving (in Mrs Oliphant's *Life*)

**Active.** *Active verbs*, verbs which act on the noun governed.

***Active capital.*** Property in actual employment in a given concern.

***Active commerce.*** Is commerce that is carried to and fro in one's own ships, as opposed to *passive commerce*, which is that carried in foreign vessels.

**Acton.** A taffeta, or leather-quilted dress, worn under the habergeon to keep the body from being chafed or bruised. (Fr. *hoqueton*, cotton-wool, padding.)

**Actresses.** Coryat, in his *Crudities* (1611), says, 'When I went to a theatre (in Venice) I observed certain things that I never saw before; for I saw women acte ... I have heard that it hath sometimes been used in London,' but the first public appearance of a woman on the stage in England was on 8 Dec., 1660, when Margaret Hughes, Prince Rupert's mistress, played Desdemona in *Othello* at a new theatre in Clare Market, London. Previous to that female parts had always been taken by boys; Edward Kynaston (d.1706) seems to have been the last male actor to play a woman on the English stage, in serious drama.

> Whereas, women's parts in plays have hitherto been acted by men in the habits of women ... we do permit and give leave for the time to come that all women's parts be acted by women, 1662.
>
> Charles II

**Acu tetigisti.** *See* Rem acu.

**Ad Kalendas Graecas** (Lat.). (Deferred) to the Greek Calends – i.e. for ever. (It shall be done) on the Greek Calends – i.e. never – for the Greeks had no Calends (*q.v.*). Suetonius tells us that this used to be the reply of Augustus to the question when he was going to pay his creditors.

**Ad inquirendum** (Lat.). A judicial writ commanding an inquiry to be made into some complaint.

**Ad libitum** (Lat.). To choice, at pleasure, without restraint.

**Ad rem** (Lat.). To the point in hand; to the purpose.

**Ad valorem** (Lat.). According to the price charged. A commercial term used in imposing customs duties according to the value of the goods imported. Thus, if teas pay duty *ad valorem*, the high priced tea will pay more duty per pound than the lower priced tea.

**Ad vitam aut culpam** (Lat.). A phrase, meaning literally 'to lifetime or fault', used in Scotch law of the permanency of an appointment, unless forfeited by misconduct.

**Adam.** The Talmudists say that Adam lived in Paradise only twelve hours, and account for the time thus:

I God collected the dust and animated it.
II Adam stood on his feet.
IV He named the animals.
VI He slept and Eve was created.
VII He married the woman.
X He fell.
XII He was thrust out of Paradise.

Mohammedan legends add to the Bible story the tradition that –

> God sent Gabriel, Michael, and Israfel one after the other to fetch seven handfuls of earth from different depths and of different colours for the creation of Adam (thereby accounting for the varying colours of mankind), but that they returned empty-handed because Earth foresaw that the creature to be made from her would rebel against God and draw down his curse on her, whereupon Azrael was sent. He executed the commission and for that reason was appointed to separate the souls from the bodies and hence became the Angel of Death. The earth he had taken was carried into Arabia to a place between Mecca and Tayef, where it was kneaded by the angels, fashioned into human form by God, and left to dry for either forty days or forty years. It is also said that while the clay was being endowed with life and a soul, when the breath breathed by God into the nostrils had reached as far as the navel, the only half-living Adam tried to rise up and got an ugly fall for his pains. Mohammedan tradition holds that he was buried on Aboucais, a mountain of Arabia. (*See* Adam's Peak; Eblis.)

***Old as Adam.*** Generally used as a reproof for stating as news something well known. 'That's as old as Adam,' it was known as far back as the days of Adam.

***The old Adam. The offending Adam,*** etc.

> Consideration, like an angel, came
> And whipped the offending Adam out of him.
> Shakespeare, *Henry V*, 1, 1

Adam, as the head of unredeemed man, stands for 'original sin', or 'man without regenerating grace'.

***The second Adam. The new Adam,*** etc. Jesus Christ is so called.

> The Tempter set
> Our second Adam, in the wilderness,
> To show him all earth's kingdoms and their glory.
> *Paradise Lost*, xi, 383

Milton probably derived the idea from Rom. 6:6, or 1 Cor. 15:22:

> For as in Adam all die, even so in Christ shall all be made alive.

Compare the address of God to the Saviour in *Paradise Lost*, iii:

> Be thou in Adam's room
> The head of all mankind, though Adam's son.
> As in him perish all men, so in thee,
> As from a second root, shall be restored
> As many as are restored.

In the same way Milton calls Mary our 'second Eve' (*Paradise Lost*, v, 387, and x, 183).

***When Adam delved.***

> When Adam delved and Eve span,
> Who was then the gentleman?

This, according to the *Historia Anglicana* of Thos. Walsingham (d.1422), was the text of John Ball's speech at Blackheath to the rebels in Wat Tyler's insurrection (1381). It seems to be an adaptation of some lines by Richard Rolle of Hampole (d.*c.*1349):

> When Adam dalfe and Eve spanne
> To spire of thou may spede,
> Where was then the pride of man,
> That now marres his meed?

Shakespeare has an echo of the saying in *2 Henry VI*, 4, 2:

> *Stafford*: Villain, thy father was a plasterer;
> And thou thyself a shearman, art thou not?
> *Cade*. And Adam was a gardener.
> *Bro*. And what of that?

The French equivalent of the saying is:

> Au temps passé, Berthe filait.

'Berthe' being Bertha (d.783), wife of Pepin and mother of Charlemagne. *Cp.* Jack's as good as his master, under Jack (*phrases*).

***Adam Bell.*** *See* Clym of the Clough.

***Adam Cupid*** – i.e. Archer Cupid, probably alluding to Adam Bell. In all the early editions the line in *Romeo and Juliet* (2, 1, 13): 'Young Adam Cupid, he that shot so trim', reads 'Young *Abraham* Cupid', etc. The emendation was suggested by Steevens.

***Adam's ale.*** Water: because the first man had nothing else to drink. In Scotland sometimes called *Adam's Wine*.

***Adam's apple.*** The protuberance in the forepart of the throat, the anterior extremity of the thyroid cartilage of the larynx; so called from the superstition that a piece of the forbidden fruit stuck in Adam's throat.

***Adam's needle.*** Gen. 3:7, tells us that Adam and Eve 'sewed fig leaves together'; needles were (presumably) not then obtainable, but certain plants furnish needle-like spines, and to some of these the name has been given. The chief is the Yucca, a native of Mexico and Central America.

***Adam's Peak.*** A mountain in Ceylon where, according to Mohammedan legend, Adam bewailed his expulsion from Paradise, standing on one foot for 200 years to expiate his crime; when Gabriel took him to Mount Arafath, where he found Eve.

> In the granite is a curious impression resembling a human foot, above 5 feet long by $2^1/2$ broad; the Hindûs, however, assert that it was made by Buddha when he ascended to heaven.

***Adam's profession.*** Gardening or agriculture is sometimes so called – for obvious reasons.

> There is no ancient gentlemen but gardeners, ditchers, and grave-makers; they hold up Adam's profession.
>
> Shakespeare, *Hamlet*, 5, 1

***Parson Adams.*** The type of a benevolent, simple-minded, eccentric country clergyman; ignorant of the world, bold as a lion for the truth, and modest as a girl. Fielding's *Joseph Andrews*.

**Adamant** (from Gr. *a*, not, *damao*, I tame), a word used for any stone or mineral of excessive hardness (especially the diamond, which is really the same word); also for the magnet or loadstone; and, by poets, for hardness or firmness in the abstract. Thus, in Zech. 7:12, we have 'they made their hearts as an adamant stone', and Virgil (*Aen.* vi, 552) speaks of 'adamantine pillars', meaning that they were strong and solid. Milton frequently uses the word in the same way. Thus, in *Paradise Lost*, ii, 436, he says the gates of hell were made 'of burning adamant'; Satan, he tells us (vi, 110):

> Came towering armed in adamant and gold.

And at vi. 255 he speaks of –

> the rocky orb
> Of ten fold adamant, his ample shield,
> A vast circumference.

In *Midsummer Night's Dream*, 2, 1,

> You draw me, you hard-hearted adamant;
> But yet you draw not iron, for my heart
> Is true as steel.

we have an instance of the use of the word in both senses. *Adamant* as a name for the loadstone, or magnet, seems to have arisen through an erroneous derivation of the word by early mediaeval Latin writers from Late Lat., *adamare*, to take a liking for, to have an attraction for. So, Chaucer has:

> Right as betwixen adamauntes two
> Of even might, a pece of iren y-set,
> That hath no might to meve to ne fro.
>
> *Parlement of Foules*, 148

And Shakespeare's:

> As true as steel, as plantage to the moon,
> As sun to day, as turtle to her mate,
> As iron to adamant.
>
> *Troilus and Cressida*, 3, 2

Bacon in his *Essay*, *Of Travel*, says:

> When he stayeth in one city or town, let him [the traveller] change his lodging from one end and part of the town to another, which is a great adamant of acquaintance.

And in *Sir John Mandeville's Travels* (ch. xiv) we come across the 'adamant' as a test for the diamond:

> ... Men take the Ademand, that is the Schipmannes Ston. that drawethe the Nedle to him, and men leyn the Dyamand upon the Ademand, and leyn the Nedle before the Ademand; and if the Dyamand be gode and vertuous, the Ademand drawethe not the Nedle to him, whils the Dyamand is there present.

Pliny (xxxvii, 15) tells us there are six unbreakable stones, but the classical *adamas* (gen. *adamant-is*) is generally supposed to mean the diamond.

**Adamastor.** The spirit of the stormy Cape (Good Hope), described by Camoëns in the *Lusiad* as a hideous phantom that appears to Vasco da Gama and prophesies disaster to all seeking to make the voyage to India.

**Adamites.** The name given to various heretical sects who supposed themselves to attain to primitive innocence by rejecting marriage and clothing. There was such a sect in North Africa in the 2nd century; the *Abelites* (*q.v.*) were similar; the heresy reappeared in Savoy in the 14th century, and spread over Bohemia and Moravia in the 15th and 16th. One Picard, of

Bohemia, was the leader in 1400, and styled himself 'Adam, son of God'. There are references to the sect in James Shirley's comedy *Hyde Park* (II, iv) (1632), and in *The Guardian*, No. 134 (1713).

**Adams, Abraham.** *See* Parson Adams.

**Addison of the North.** A sobriquet of Henry Mackenzie (1745–1831), author of the *Man of Feeling*.

**Addison's Disease.** A state of anaemia, languor, irritable stomach, etc., associated with disease of the suprarenal capsules: so named from Dr Thomas Addison, of Guy's Hospital (d.1860), who first described it.

**Addisonian Termination.** The name given by Bishop Hurd to the construction which closes a sentence with a preposition, such as – 'which the prophet took a distinct view of'. Named, of course, from Joseph Addison, who frequently employed it.

**Addle** is the Old English *adela*, mire, or liquid filth; hence rotten, putrid, worthless.

***Addle egg.*** An egg which has no germ; also one in which the chick has died. Hence, fig., *addle-headed*, *addle-pate*, empty-headed. As an addle-egg produces no living bird, so an addle-pate lacks brains.

***The Addled Parliament.*** The second Parliament of James I, 5th April to 7th June, 1614. It refused to grant supplies until grievances had been redressed, and is so called because it did not pass a single measure.

**Adelantado.** A bigwig, the great boss of the place. Spanish for 'his excellency' (from *adelantar*, to promote), and is given to the governor of a province.

> Open no door. If the adelantado of Spain were here he should not enter.
>
> Ben Jonson, *Every Man out of his Humour*, v, 4

Middleton, in *Blurt*, *Master Constable* (IV, iii), uses *lantedo* as an abbreviation of this word.

**Adept** means one who has attained (Lat. *adeptus*, participle of *adipisci*). The alchemists applied the term *vere adeptus* to those persons who professed to have 'attained to the knowledge of' the elixir of life or of the philosopher's stone.

> Alchemists tell us there are always 11 adepts, neither more nor less. Like the sacred chickens of Compostella, of which there are only 2 and always 2 – a cock and a hen.

> In Rosicrucian lore as learn'd
> As he that *vere adeptus* earn'd.
>
> Butler, *Hudibras*, I, i, 546

**Adessenarians** (Lat. *adesse*, to be present). A branch of the Sacramentarians (*q.v.*) who held the real presence of Christ's body in the eucharist, but that the bread and wine do not lose any of their original properties.

**Adeste Fideles** ('O come, all ye faithful'). A Christmas hymn composed by John Reading (d.1692), organist at Winchester and author of 'Dulce Domum'.

**Adiaphorists** (Gr., indifferent). Followers of Melanchthon; moderate Lutherans, who held that some of the dogmas of Luther are matters of indifference. They accepted the Interim of Augsburg (*q.v.*).

**Adieu** (Fr. to God). An elliptical form for *I commend you to God* (*cp.* Good-bye).

**Adjective Colours** are those which require a mordant before they can be used as dyes.

**Adjourn** (Fr. *à-journer*). To put off to another day.

> Lady, un-to that court thou me ajourne
> That cleped is thy bench.
>
> *Chaucer's ABC* (*c.*360)

**Adjournment of the House.** *See under* Move.

**Admirable, The.** Abraham ben Meir ibn Ezra, a celebrated Spanish Jew (1092–1167), was so called. He was noted as a mathematician, philologist, poet, astronomer, and commentator on the Bible.

***The Admirable Crichton.*** James Crichton (1560–85?), Scottish traveller, scholar, and swordsman. So called by Sir Thomas Urquhart.

***Admirable Doctor*** (*Doctor mirabilis*). Roger Bacon (1214?–94), the English mediaeval philosopher.

**Admiral,** corruption of Arabic *Amir* (lord or commander), with the article *al*, as in *Amir-al-ma* (commander of the water), *Amir-al-Omra* (commander of the forces), *Amir-al-Muminim* (commander of the faithful).

Milton uses the old form for the ship itself; speaking of Satan, he says:

> His spear – to equal which the tallest pine
> Hewn on Norwegian hills, to be the mast
> Of some great ammiral, were but a wand –
> He walked with. *Paradise Lost*, i, 292

In England there are now four grades of Admiral, viz. *Admiral of the Fleet*, *Admiral*, *Vice-Admiral*, and *Rear-Admiral*. There used to be three classes, named from the colour of their flag – *Admiral of the Red*, *Admiral of the White*, and *Admiral of the Blue*, who, in engagements, held the centre, van, and rear respectively. The distinction was abolished in 1864.

***Admiral of the Blue*** (*see above*), used facetiously for a butcher who dresses in blue to conceal blood stains, or a tapster, from his blue apron.

As soon as customers begin to stir
The Admiral of the Blue cries, 'Coming, Sir!'
*Poor Robin*, 1731

***Admiral of the Red*** (*see above*), facetiously applied to a winebibber whose face and nose are very red.

**Admonitionists,** or **Admonitioners.** Certain Puritans who in 1571 sent an *admonition* to the Parliament condemning everything in the Church of England which was not in accordance with the doctrines and practices of Geneva.

**Adonai** (Heb. pl. of *adon*, lord). A name given to the Deity by the Hebrews, and used by them in place of Yahweh (Jehovah), the 'ineffable name', wherever this occurs. In the Vulgate, and hence in the Wyclif, Coverdale, and Douai versions, it is given for Jehovah in Exod. 6:3, where the A.V. reads:

And I appeared unto Abraham, unto Isaac, and unto Jacob, by the name of God Almighty, but by my name Jehovah was I not known to them.

Thus James Howell says of the Jews:

… they sing many tunes, and *Adonai* they make the ordinary name of God: Jehovah is pronounced at high Festivals.
*Letters*, Bk i, sec. vi, 14 (3 June, 1633)

**Adonais.** The poetical name given by Shelley to Keats in his elegy on the death of the latter (1821), probably in allusion to the mourning for Adonis.

**Adonia.** The feast of Adonis, celebrated in Assyria, Alexandria, Egypt, Judaea, Persia, Cyprus, and Greece, for eight days. Lucian gives a long description of these feasts, which were generally held at midsummer and at which the women first lamented the death and afterwards rejoiced at the resurrection of Adonis – a custom referred to in the Bible (Ezek. 8:14), where Adonis appears under his Phoenician name, Tammuz (*q.v.*).

**Adonis.** In *Greek mythology* a beautiful youth who was beloved by Venus, and was killed by a boar while hunting. Hence, usually ironically, any beautiful young man, as in Massinger's *Parliament of Love*, II, 2:

Of all men
I ever saw yet, in my settled Judgment …
Thou art the ugliest creature; and when trimm'd up
To the height, as thou imagin'st, in mine eyes,
A leper with a clap-dish (to give notice
He is infectious), in respect of thee
Appears a young Adonis.

And Leigh Hunt, it will be remembered, was sent to prison for libelling George IV when Regent, and calling him 'a corpulent Adonis of 50' (*Examiner*, 1813).

***The Adonis Flower,*** according to Bion, the rose; Pliny (i, 23) says it is the anemone; others, the field poppy; but now generally used for the pheasant's eye, called in French *goute-de-sang*, because in fable it sprang from the blood of the gored hunter.

***Adonis Garden.*** A worthless toy, a very perishable good.

Thy promises are like Adonis' gardens
That one day bloom'd and fruitful were the next.
Shakespeare, *1 Henry VI*, 1, 6

The allusion is to the baskets or pots of earth used at the Adonia (*q.v.*), in which quick-growing plants were sown, tended for eight days, allowed to wither, and then thrown into the sea or river with images of the dead Adonis.

In Spenser's *Faerie Queene* (Bk III, ca. vi) the Garden of Adonis is where –

All the goodly flowres,
Wherewith dame Nature doth her beautifie
And decks the girlonds of her paramoures,
Are fetcht: there is the first seminarie
Of all things that are borne to live and die,
According to their kindes.

It is to these gardens that Milton also refers in *Paradise Lost* (ix, 440):

Spot more delicious than those gardens feigned
Or of revived Adonis, or renowned
Alcinous, host of old Laertes' son.

***Adonis River.*** A stream which flows from Lebanon to the sea near Byblos which runs red at the season of the year when the feast of Adonis was held.

Thammuz came next behind,
Whose annual wound in Lebanon allured
The Syrian damsels to lament his fate
In amorous ditties all a summer's day,
While smooth Adonis from his native rock
Ran purple to the sea, supposed with blood
Of Thammuz yearly wounded.
Milton, *Paradise Lost*, i, 446

**Adonists.** Those Jews who maintain that the vowels of the word Adonai (*q.v.*) are not the vowels necessary to make the tetragrammaton (*q.v.*), JHVH, into the name of the Deity. *See also* **Jehovah**.

**Adoption.** ***Adoption by arms.*** An ancient custom of giving arms to a person of merit, which laid him under the obligation of being your champion and defender.

***Adoption by baptism.*** Being godfather or godmother to a child. The child by baptism is your godchild.

***Adoption by hair.*** Boson, King of Provence (879–89), is said to have cut off his hair and to have given it to Pope John VIII as a sign that the latter had adopted him.

**Adoption Controversy.** Elipand, Archbishop of Toledo, and Felix, Bishop of Urgel (in the 8th century), maintained that Christ in his *human* nature was the son of God by adoption only (Rom. 8:29), though in his pre-existing state he was the 'begotten Son of God' in the ordinary catholic acceptation. Duns Scotus, Durandus, and Calixtus were among the Adoptionists who supported this view, which was condemned by the Council of Frankfort in 794.

**Adoptive Emperors.** In Roman history, the five Emperors, Nerva, Trajan, Hadrian, Antoninus Pius, and Marcus Aurelius, each of whom (except Nerva, who was elected by the Senate) was the adopted son of his predecessor. Their period (96–180) is said to have been the happiest in the whole history of Rome.

**Adoration of the Cross.** *See* Andrew, St.

**Adrammelech.** A Babylonian deity to whom, apparently, infants were burnt in sacrifice (2 Kings 17:31). Possibly the sun god worshipped at Sippar (i.e. Sepharvaim).

**Adrastus.** (i) A mythical Greek king of Argos, leader of the expedition of the 'Seven Against Thebes' (*see under* Seven). (ii) In Tasso's *Jerusalem Delivered* (Bk xx), an Indian prince who aided the King of Egypt against the crusaders. He was slain by Rinaldo.

**Adrian, St.** The patron saint of the Flemish brewers is represented in art with an anvil and a sword or axe close by it. He had his limbs cut off on a smith's anvil, and was afterwards beheaded.

**Adriel,** in Dryden's *Absalom and Achitophel*, is John Sheffield, third Earl of Mulgrave.

> Sharp-judging Adriel, the muses' friend,
> Himself a muse: in Sanhedrin's debate
> True to his prince, but not a slave of state
> Whom David's love with honours did adorn,
> That from his disobedient son were torn.
>
> *Part* I, 877

**Adrift.** *I am all adrift. He is quite adrift. To turn one adrift.* Sea phrases. A ship is said to be adrift when it has broken from its moorings, and is driven at random by the winds. *To be adrift* is to be wide of the mark, or not in the right course. *To turn one adrift* is to turn him from house and home to go his own way.

**Adroit** means 'according to right, rightly' (Fr. *à droite*). The French call a person who is not adroit *gauche* (left-handed), meaning awkward, boorish.

**Adsidelae.** In the ritual of *Roman mythology* the table at which the priests or flamens sat during sacrifice.

**Adullamites.** The adherents of Lowe and Horsman, seceders in 1866 from the Reform Party. John Bright said of these members that they retired to the cave of Adullam, and tried to gather round them all the discontented. The allusion is to David, who, in his flight from Saul –

> Escaped to the cave Adullam; and every one that was in distress, and every one that was in debt, and every one that was discontented, gathered themselves unto him. 1 Sam. 22:1, 2

**Adulterous Bible.** *See* Bible, Specially Named.

**Advent** (Lat. *ad-ventus*, the coming to). The four weeks immediately preceding Christmas, commemorating the first and second coming of Christ; the first to redeem, and the second to judge the world. The season begins on St Andrew's Day (30th Nov.), or the Sunday nearest to it.

**Adversary, The.** A name frequently given in English literature to the Devil (from 1 Pet. 5:8).

**Advocate** (Lat. *ad*, to, *vocare*, to call). One called to assist pleaders in a court of law.

***The Devil's Advocate.*** A carping or adverse critic. From the *Advocatus diaboli*, the person appointed to contest the claims of a candidate for canonisation before a papal court. He advances all he can against the candidate, and is opposed by the *Advocatus dei* (God's Advocate), who says all he can in support of the proposal.

**Advocates' Library,** in Edinburgh, was founded 1682, by Sir George Mackenzie of Rosehaugh, Dean of the *Faculty of Advocates*, i.e. the body of members of the Scottish bar. It is one of the libraries to which books must be sent for purposes of copyright (*q.v.*).

**Advowson** (Lat. *advocatio*, a calling to, a summons: *cp.* Advocate), originally the obligation to be the *advocate* of a benefice or living and to defend its rights, the word now means the right of appointing the incumbent of a church or ecclesiastical benefice.

The different advowsons are:

***Advowson appendant.*** A right of presentation which belongs to and passes with the manor. This usually had its origin in the ownership of the advowson by the person who built or endowed the church; after a time they became regular 'commercial property', and advertisements of their sale can still be seen from time to time in the public journals.

***Advowson collative.*** In which the bishop himself is patron and, as he cannot 'present' to himself, does by the act of 'collation' (Lat., *conferre*, to confer) or conferring the benefice all that is done in other cases by presentation and institution.

***Advowson donative.*** In which a secular patron (usually the Crown) has the right of disposing of the benefice to any legally qualified person without institution or induction or examination by the bishop or ordinary. This form of advowson is now very rare.

***Advowson in gross.*** An advowson which has become legally separated from the manor to which it was appendant. *See* Gross.

***Advowson presentative.*** In which the patron (who may be a layman) presents to the bishop who, unless he is satisfied that there is sufficient legal or ecclesiastical disability, must 'institute' the clerk and send a mandate to the archdeacon to 'induct' him.

Should the patron be a Jew his right of presentation lapses to the Archbishop of Canterbury; if he is a Roman Catholic it goes to the University of Oxford or Cambridge according to the locality of the living.

**Adytum** (Gr. *a-duton*, not to be entered; *duo*, to go). The Holy of Holies in the Greek and Roman temples, into which the general public were not admitted; hence, a sanctum.

**Aediles.** Those who, in ancient Rome, had charge of the public buildings (*aedes*), such as the temples, theatres, baths, aqueducts, sewers, including roads and streets also.

**Aegeus.** A fabulous king of Athens who gave the name to the Aegean Sea. His son, Theseus, went to Crete to deliver Athens from the tribute exacted by Minos. Theseus said, if he succeeded he would hoist a white sail on his home-voyage, as a signal of his safety. This he neglected to do; and Aegeus, who watched the ship from a rock, thinking his son had perished, threw himself into the sea.

This incident is repeated in the tale of Tristram and Isolde. *See* Tristram.

**Aeginetan Sculptures.** Sculptures discovered by a party of German, Danish, and English excavators in 1811 at the temple of Pallas Athene, in the little island of Aegina. They consist of two groups of five and ten figures representing exploits of Greek heroes at Troy, and probably date from about 500 BC, i.e. a little before Phidias. They were restored by Thorwaldsen, and have long been the most remarkable ornaments of the Glyptothek, at Munich.

**Aegir.** In *Norse mythology* the god of the ocean, husband of Ran. They had nine daughters (the billows), who wore white robes and veils.

**Aegis** (Gr. goat skin). The shield of Jupiter made by Vulcan and covered with the skin of the goat Amalthaea, who had suckled the infant Zeus. It was sometimes lent to Athena, daughter of Zeus, and when in her possession carried the head of the Gorgon. By the shaking of his aegis Zeus produced storms and thunder; in art it is usually represented as a kind of cloak fringed with serpents; and it is symbolical of divine protection – hence the modern use of the word in such phrases as *I throw my aegis over you*, I give you my protection.

**Aegrotat** (Lat. he is ill). In university parlance, a medical certificate of indisposition to exempt the bearer from attending chapel and college lectures.

**A E I**, a common motto on jewellery, is Greek, and stands for 'for ever and for aye'.

**A. E. I. O. U.** The device adopted by Frederick V, Archduke of Austria, on becoming the Emperor Frederick III in 1440. They had been used by his predecessor, Albert II, and then stood for –

Albertus Electus Imperator Optimus Vivat.

The meaning that Frederick gave them was –

Archidux Electus Imperator Optime Vivat.

Many other versions are known, including –

Austriae Est Imperare Orbi Universo.
Alles Erdreich 1st Oesterreich Unterthan.
Austria's Empire Is Overall Universal.

To which wags added after the war of 1866 –

Austria's Emperor Is Ousted Utterly.

Frederick the Great is said to have translated the motto thus:

Austria Erit In Orbe Ultima (*Austria will be lowest in the world*).

**Aeneas.** The hero of Virgil's epic, son of Anchises, king of Dardanus, and Aphrodite. According to Homer he fought against the Greeks in the Trojan War and after the sack of Troy reigned in the Troad. Later legends tell how he carried his father Anchises on his shoulders from the flames of Troy, and after roaming about for many years, came to Italy, where he founded a colony which the Romans claim as their origin. The epithet applied to him is *pius*, meaning 'dutiful'.

**Aeneid.** The epic poem of Virgil (in twelve books). So called from *Aeneas* and the suffix *-is*, plur. *ides* (belonging to).

The story of Sinon (says Macrobius) and the taking of Troy is borrowed from Pisander.

The loves of Dido and Aeneas are taken from those of Medea and Jason, in Apollonius of Rhodes.

The story of the Wooden Horse and burning of Troy is from Arctinus of Miletus.

**Aeolian Harp.** The wind harp. A box on which strings are stretched. Being placed where a draught gets to the strings, they utter musical sounds.

> Awake, Aeolian lyre, awake,
> And give to rapture all thy trembling strings.
>
> Gray, *Progress of Poesy*

> Like an Aeolian harp that wakes
> No certain air, but overtakes
> Far thought with music that it makes.
>
> Tennyson, *The Two Voices*

**Aeolian Mode,** in *Music*, the ninth of the church modes, also called the Hypodorian, the range being from A to A, the dominant F or E, and the mediant E or C. It is characterised as 'grand and pompous though sometimes soothing'.

**Aeolian Rocks.** A geological term for those rocks the formation and distribution of which has been due more to the agency of wind than to that of water. Most of the New Red Sandstones, and many of the Old Red, are of Aeolian origin.

**Aeolic Digamma.** The sixth letter of the early Greek alphabet (*F*), sounded like our *w*. Thus *oinos* with the digamma was sounded *woinos*; whence the Latin *vinum*, our *wine*. Gamma, or *g*, was shaped thus Γ, hence digamma = double *g*; it was early disused as a letter, but was retained as the symbol for the numeral 6. True Aeolic was the dialect of Lesbos.

**Aeolus,** in *Roman mythology*, was 'god of the winds'.

**Aeon** (Gr. *aion*). An age of the universe, an immeasurable length of time; hence the personification of an age, a god, any being that is eternal. Basilides reckons there have been 365 such Aeons, or gods; but Valentinius restricts the number to 30.

**Aërated Bread.** Bread made from dough which has been raised by means of carbon dioxide instead of yeast.

**Aërated Waters.** Effervescent waters charged (either artificially or naturally) with carbon dioxide.

**Aerians.** Followers of the 4th-century Arian reformer, Aerius, a presbyter of Sebastia (Asia Minor), who maintained that there is no difference between the authority of bishops and of priests, rejected prayers for the dead, church fasts, etc.

**Aeschylus** (525–456 BC), the father of the Greek tragic drama. Titles of seventy-two of his plays are known, but only seven are now extant. Fable has it that he was killed by a tortoise thrown by an eagle (to break the shell) against his bald head, which it mistook for a stone.

***Aeschylus of France.*** Prosper Jolyot de Crébillon (1674–1762).

**Aesculapius.** The Latin form of the Greek Asklepios, god of medicine and of healing. Now used for 'a medical practitioner'. The usual offering to him was a cock, hence the phrase 'to sacrifice a cock to Aesculapius' – to return thanks (or pay the doctor's bill) after recovery from an illness.

> When men a dangerous disease did scape,
> Of old, they gave a cock to Aesculape.
>
> Ben Jonson, *Epigram*

Legend has it that he assumed the form of a serpent (*q.v.*) when he appeared at Rome during a pestilence; hence it is that the goddess of Health bears in her hand a serpent.

> O wave, Hygeia, o'er Britannia's throne
> Thy serpent-wand, and mark it for thine own.
>
> Darwin, *Economy of Vegetation*, iv

**Aesir.** The collective name of the celestial gods of Scandinavia, who lived in Asgard (*q.v.*). We are told that there were twelve gods and twenty-six goddesses, but it would be hard to determine who they were, for, like Arthur's knights, the number seems variable. The following may be mentioned: (1) Odin, the chief; (2) Thor (his eldest son, god of thunder); (3)Tiu (another son, god of wisdom); (4) Balder (another son, Scandinavian Apollo); (5) Bragi (god of poetry); (6) Vidar (god of silence); (7) Höder the blind (slayer of Balder); (8) Hermoder (Odin's son and messenger); (9) Hoenir (a minor god); (10) Odnir (husband of Freyja, the Scandinavian Venus); (11) Loki (the god of mischief); (12) Vali (Odin's youngest son).

*Wives of the Aesir.* Odin's wife was Frigga; Thor's wife was Sif (beauty); Balder's wife was Nanna (daring); Bragi's wife was Iduna; Loki's wife was Siguna.

The important deities mentioned above are more fully treated under their several names. *See also* Vanir.

**Aeson's Bath.**

> I perceive a man may be twice a child before the days of dotage; and stands in need of *Aeson's* Bath before three score.
>
> Sir Thos Browne, *Religio Medici, Section* 42

The reference is to Medea renovating Aeson, father of Jason, with the juices of a concoction made of sundry articles. After Aeson had imbibed these juices, Ovid says:

> Barba comaeque,
> Canitie posita, nigrum rapuere, colorem.
>
> *Metamorphoses*, vii, 288

**Aesop's Fables** are traditionally ascribed to Aesop, a deformed Phrygian slave of the 6th century ; but many of them are far older, some having been discovered on Egyptian papyri of 800 or 1,000 years earlier.

> Almost all Greek and Latin fables are ascribed to Aesop, as our Psalms were all ascribed to David.

Babirus, probably an Italian, compiled a collection of 137 of the fables in choliambic verse about AD 230, and this version was for long used in the mediaeval schools.

Pilpay (*q.v.*) has been called *the Aesop of India*.

**Aetion** in Spenser's *Colin Clout's Come Home Again* typifies Michael Drayton, the poet.

**Aetites** (Gr., *aetos*, an eagle).. Eagle-stones: hollow stones composed of several crusts, having a loose stone within, which were supposed at one time to be found in eagles' nests, to which medicinal virtues were attributed, and which were supposed to have the property of detecting theft. *See* Pliny x, 4, and xxx, 44; also Lyly's *Euphues* (1578) –

> The precious stone Aetites which is found in the filthy nests of the eagle.

Another account is given by Epiphanius, who says (*De duodecim geminis*), 'In the interior of Scythia there is a valley inaccessible to man, down which slaughtered lambs are thrown. The small stones at the bottom of the valley adhere to these, and eagles, when they carry away the flesh to their nests, carry the stones with it.' The story of Sindbad in the Valley of Diamonds will occur to the readers.

**Aetolian Hero, The.** Diomede, who was king of Aetolia. *Ovid.*

**Affable** (Lat. *ad fari*, to speak to). An *affable* person is 'one easy to be spoken to'. *Ineffable* expresses the opposite meaning – *the ineffable name*, the name (among the Jews, *Jehovah*) that was not to be uttered:

> Therefore to whom turn I but to thee, the ineffable Name?
> Builder and maker, thou, of houses not made with hands.
>
> Browning, *Abt Vogler*

**Affront**, from Lat. *affrontare*, from *ad frontem*, to the face; it came into English through the Old French *affronter*, meaning to strike or slap the face; hence, to insult one to his face. In savage nations opposing armies, before they begin hostilities, by grimaces, sounds, words, and all conceivable means, try to provoke and terrify their *vis-à-vis*. When this 'affronting' is over, the adversaries rush against each other, and the fight begins in earnest.

**Afraid.** *He who trembles to hear a leaf fall should keep out of the wood.* This is a French proverb: '*Qui a peur de feuilles, ne doit aller au bois.*' Our corresponding English proverb is, 'He who fears scars shouldn't go to the wars.' The timid should not voluntarily expose themselves to danger.

> Little boats should keep near shore,
> Larger ones may venture more. Proverb, Ray

**Afoot.** On the way, in progress. *See* Game's Afoot.

> Mischief, thou art afoot,
> Take thou what course thou wilt.
>
> Shakespeare, *Julius Caesar*, 3, 2

**Afreet, Afrit.** In Mohammedan mythology the most powerful but one (Marids) of the five classes of Jinn, or devils. They are of gigantic stature, very malicious, and inspire great dread. Solomon, we are told, once tamed an Afreet, and made it submissive to his will.

**Africa.** *Teneo te, Africa.* When Caesar landed at Adrumetum, in Africa, he tripped and fell – a bad omen; but, with wonderful presence of mind, he pretended that he had done so intentionally, and kissing the soil, exclaimed, 'Thus do I take possession of thee, O Africa'. The story is told also of Scipio, and of Caesar again at his landing in Britain, and of others in similar circumstances.

*Africa semper aliquid novi affert.* 'Africa is always producing some novelty.' A Greek proverb quoted (in Latin) by Pliny, in allusion to the ancient belief that Africa abounded in strange monsters.

**African Sisters, The.** The Hesperides (*q.v.*), who lived in Africa.

**Aft.** The hinder part of a ship.

***Fore and aft.*** The entire length (of a ship), from stem to stern.

**After-cast.** An obsolete expression for something done too late; literally, a throw of the dice after the game is ended.

Ever he playeth an after-cast
Of all that he shall say or do. Gower

**After-clap.** A catastrophe or misfortune after an affair is supposed to be over, as in thunderstorms one may sometimes hear a 'clap' after the rain subsides, and the clouds break.

What plaguy mischief and mishaps
Do dog him still with after-claps.
Butler, *Hudibras*, Pt i, 3

**After meat, mustard.** A phrase meaning doing a thing, or offering service when it is too late, or when there is no longer need thereof. In Latin, *Post bellum, auxilium.* We have also, 'After death, the doctor', which is the German, *Wann der kranke ist todt, so kommt der arztnei* (when the patient's dead, comes the physic). To the same effect is 'When the steed is stolen, lock the stable door.'

**After me, the Deluge;** *après moi le déluge*, 'I care not what happens when I am dead and gone.' So said Mdme de Pompadour, mistress of Louis XV (1721–64). Metternich, the Austrian statesman (1773–1859) also used the expression, but his meaning was that when his guiding hand was removed, things would probably go to rack and ruin.

**Aft-meal.** An extra meal; a meal taken after and in addition to the ordinary meals.

At aft-meals who shall pay for the wine ?
Thynne, *Debate* (*c.*1608)

**Agag,** in Dryden's *Absalom and Achitophel*, is Sir Edmondbury Godfrey, the magistrate before whom Titus Oates made his declaration, and who was afterwards found barbarously murdered in a ditch near Primrose Hill. Agag was hewed to pieces by Samuel (1 Sam. 15).

And Corah (*Titus Oates*) might for Agag's murder call
In terms as coarse as Samuel used to Saul.
I, 675–6

**Agamemnon.** In Greek legend, the King of Mycenae, son of Atreus, and leader of the Greeks at the siege of Troy.

Goodly Agamemnon ...
The glorie of the stock of Tantalus,
And famous light of all the Greekish hosts,
Under whose conduct most victorious,
The *Dorick* flames consumed the *Iliack* posts.
Spenser, *Virgil's Gnat*

His *brother* was Menelaos.
His *daughters* were Iphigenia, Electra, Iphianassa, and Chrysothemis (*Sophocles*).
He was *grandson* of Pelops.
He was *killed* in a bath by his wife Clytemnestra, after his return from Troy.
His *son* was Orestes, who slew his mother for murdering his father, and was called Agamemnonides.
His *wife* was Clytemnestra, who lived in adultery with Egistheus. At Troy he fell in love with Cassandra, a daughter of King Priam.

***Vixere fortes ante Agamemnona:*** a quotation from Horace (*Od.* IV, ix) translated by Conington as:

Before Atrides men were brave:
But ah! oblivion, dark and long,
Has lock'd them in a tearless grave,
For lack of consecrating song ——

And paraphrased by Byron in *Don Juan* (I, v):

Brave men were living before Agamemnon
And since, exceeding valorous and sage,
A good deal like him too, though quite the same none;
But then they shone not on the poet's page,
And so have been forgotten.

**Aganice,** or **Aglaonice,** the Thessalian, being able to calculate eclipses, she pretended to have the moon under her command, and to be able when she chose to draw it from heaven. Her secret being found out, her vaunting became a laughing-stock, and gave birth to the Greek proverb cast at braggarts, 'Yes, as the Moon obeys Aganice.'

**Aganippe.** In Greek legend a fountain of Boeotia at the foot of Mount Helicon, dedicated to the Muses, because it had the virtue of imparting poetic inspiration. Prom this fountain the Muses are sometimes called Aganippides.

**Agape.** A love-feast (Gr. *agape*, love). The early Christians held a love-feast before or after communion when contributions were made for the poor; they became a scandal, and were condemned at the Council of Carthage, 397.

**Agape** is also the name given by Spenser to the fairy mother of Priamond, Diamond, Triamond, and Cambina. *Faerie Queene*, IV, ii, 41 ff.

**Agapemone.** An association of men and women followers of one Prince, who founded a sect in the 1860s, holding the theory that the time of prayer was past and the time of grace come. They lived on a common fund at an Agapemone, or Abode of Love, at Charlynch, near Bridgwater, Somersetshire, and were constantly in trouble with the authorities. In the early years of the present century the 'Agapemonites' again attracted a lot of attention in the newspapers and police-courts: they have a flourishing church in the North of London.

**Agapetae** (Gr. beloved.) A group of 3rd century ascetic women who, under vows of virginity, contracted spiritual marriage with the monks and attended to their wants. Owing to the scandals occasioned the custom was condemned by St Jerome and suppressed by various Councils.

**Agate.** So called, says Pliny (xxxvii. 10), from Achates or Gagates, a river in Sicily, near which is found in abundance.

> These, these are they, if we consider well,
> That saphirs and the diamonds doe excell.
> The pearle, the emerauld, and the turkesse bleu.
> The sanguine corrall, amber's golden hiew,
> The christall, jacinth, *achate*, ruby red.
>
> Taylor, *The Waterspout* (1630)

Agate is supposed to render a person invisible, and to turn the sword of foes against themselves.

A very small person has been called an agate, from the old custom of carving the stone with diminutive figures for use as seals. Shakespeare speaks of Queen Mab as no bigger than an agate-stone on the forefinger of an alderman.

> I was never manned with an agate till now.
>
> Shakespeare, *2 Henry IV*, 1, 2

For the same reason the very small type between nonpareil and pearl, known in England as 'ruby', is called agate in America.

**Agatha, St,** was tortured and martyred in Sicily during the Decian persecution of 251. She is sometimes represented in art with a pair of shears or pincers, and holding a salver on which are her breasts, these having been cut off.

**Agave,** named from Agave, daughter of Cadmus (*q.v.*), or 'American aloe', a Mexican plant, naturalised in many parts of Europe, and fabled by English gardeners to bloom only once in a hundred years. It was introduced into Spain in 1561, and is used in Mexico, Switzerland, Italy, and elsewhere for fences. The Mohammedans of Egypt regard it as a charm and religious symbol; and pilgrims to Mecca hang a leaf of it over their door as a sign of their pilgrimage and as a charm against evil spirits.

**Agdistes.** The name given by Spenser in the *Faerie Queene* (II, xii, 48) to the Porter of the Bower of Bliss.

> He of this Gardin had the governall
> And Pleasure's Porter was devized to be.

The name is that of a Phrygian deity connected with the symbolic worship of the powers of Nature and by some identified with Cybele. He was hermaphrodite, and sprang from the stone Agdus, parts of which were taken by Deucalion and Pyrrha to cast over their shoulders for re-peopling the world after the flood.

**Age.** A word used of a long but more or less indefinite period of history, human and pre-human, distinguished by certain real or mythical characteristics and usually named from these characteristics or from persons connected with them, as the *Golden Age* (*q.v.*), the *Middle Ages*, the *Dark Ages* (*qq.v.*), the *Age of the Antonines* (from Antoninus Pius, 138, to Marcus Aurelius, 180), the *Prehistoric Age*, etc. Thus, Hallam calls the 9th century the *Age of the Bishops*, and the 12th, the *Age of the Popes*.

Varro (*Fragments*, p. 219, Scaliger's edition, 1623) recognises three ages:

> From the beginning of mankind to the Deluge, a time wholly unknown.
> From the Deluge to the First Olympiad, called the mythical period.
> From the first Olympiad to the present time, called the historic period.

Shakespeare's passage on the seven ages of man (*As You Like It*, 2, 7) is well known; and Titian symbolised the three ages of man thus:

> An infant in a cradle.
> A shepherd playing a flute.
> An old man meditating on two skulls.

According to Lucretius also there are three ages, distinguished by the materials employed in implements (v. 1282), viz.:

> *The age of stone*, when celts or implements of stone were employed.
> *The age of bronze,* when implements were made of copper or brass.
> *The age of iron,* when implements were made of iron, as at present.

The term *Stone Age* as now used includes the *Eolithic*, *Palaeolithic*, and *Neolithic Ages* (*qq.v.*).

Hesiod names five ages, viz.:

> The *Golden* or patriarchal, under the care of Saturn.
> The *Silver* or voluptuous, under the care of Jupiter.
> The *Brazen* or warlike, under the care of Neptune.
> The *Heroic* or renaissant, under the care of Mars.
> The *Iron* or present, under the care of Pluto.

Fichte names five ages also:

> The antediluvian, post-diluvian, Christian, Satanic and millennian.

***Age of Animals.*** An old Celtic rhyme, put into modern English, says:

> Thrice the age of a dog is that of a horse;
> Thrice the age of a horse is that of a man;
> Thrice the age of a man is that of a deer;
> Thrice the age of a deer is that of an eagle.

**_Age of Women._** The age of only one woman mentioned in the Bible (Sarah, Abraham's wife) is recorded, and that to show that at her advanced age she would become the mother of Isaac.

Elizabeth, the mother of the Baptist, we are told by St Luke, was 'well stricken in age'.

**Age hoc.** 'Attend to this'. In sacrifice the Roman crier perpetually repeated these words to arouse attention. In the Common Prayer Book the attention of the congregation is frequently aroused by the exhortation, 'Let us pray,' though nearly the whole service is that of prayer.

**Agelasta** (Gr. joyless). The stone on which Ceres rested when worn down by fatigue in searching for her daughter, Persephone.

**Agenor.** A son of Neptune, and founder of a nation in Phoenicia. His descendants, Cadmus, Perseus, Europa, etc., are known as the *Agenorides*.

**Agent.** ***Is man a free agent?*** This is a question of theology, which has long been mooted. The point is this: If God foreordains all our actions, they must take place as he foreordains them, and man acts as a watch or clock; but if, on the other hand, man is responsible for his actions, he must be free to act as his inclination leads him. Those who hold the former view are called *necessitarians*; those who hold the latter, *libertarians*.

**Agglutinate Language.** A language the chief characteristic of which is that its words are simple or root words combined into compounds without loss of original meaning. Thus, *inkstand* and *cowshed* are agglutinate words. Agglutination is a feature of most Turanian languages: it implies that the root words are *glued* together to form other words, and may be 'unglued' so as to leave the roots distinct.

**Aghast.** Frightened, horror-struck, has nothing to do with *ghost*, and should really be spelt 'gast' the 'h' having appeared first in Scotch in the early 15th century. It is from A. S. *gaestan*, to frighten, and 'ghost' from A. S. *gast*, a spirit.

**Agio** (Ital. ease, convenience). A commercial term denoting the percentage of charge made for the exchange of paper money into cash.

**Agis.** King of Sparta, 338–30 BC. He tried to deliver Greece from the Macedonian yoke and was slain in the attempt.

The generous victim to that vain attempt
To save a rotten state – Agis, who saw
Even Sparta's self to servile avarice sink.

Thomson, *Winter*, 488–9

**Agist.** To take in cattle to graze at a certain sum. The pasturage of these beasts is called *agistment*. The words are from the French *agister* (to lie down).

**Aglaia.** One of the three Graces (*see* Graces).

**Aglaos.** The poorest man in Arcadia, pronounced by Apollo to be far happier than Gyges, because he was 'contented with his lot'.

Poor and content is rich enough;
But riches endless are as poor as winter
To him who ever fears he shall be poor.

Shakespeare, *Othello*, 3, 3

**Agnes.** *She is an Agnes* (*elle fait l'Agnès*) – i.e. she is a sort of female 'Verdant Green', who is so unsophisticated that she does not even know what love means: from a character in Molière's *L'Ecole des Femmes*.

**Agnes, St,** was martyred in the Diocletian persecution (about 303) at the age of 13. She was tied to a stake, but the fire went out, and Aspasius, set to watch the martyrdom, drew his sword, and cut off her head. There is a picture of the incident by Domenichino. St Agnes is the patron of young virgins. She is commemorated on the 21st January. Upon St Agnes' night, says Aubrey in his *Miscellany*, though he should have said St Agnes' *Eve*, you take a row of pins, and pull out every one, one after another. Saying a paternoster, stick a pin in your sleeve, and you will dream of him or her you shall marry; and in the beautiful poem by Keats, *The Eve of St Agnes*, we are told

how, upon St Agnes' Eve,
Young virgins might have visions of delight,
And soft adorings from their loves receive
Upon the honey'd middle of the night,
If ceremonies due they did aright;
As, supperless to bed they must retire.

**Agnoites** (Gr. *a*, not, *gignoskein*, to know).

(1) Certain heretics in the fourth century who maintained that God had no certain knowledge of the future. God did *not know* everything.

(2) Another sect, in the 6th century, who maintained that Christ did not know the time of the day of judgment.

**Agnostic** (Gr. *a*, not, *gignoskein*, to know). A term coined by Prof. Huxley in 1869 (with allusion to St Paul's mention of an altar to 'the Unknown God') to indicate the mental attitude of those who withhold their assent to whatever is incapable of proof, such as an unseen world, a First Cause, etc. Agnostics neither dogmatically accept nor reject such matters, but simply say *Agnosco* – I do not know – they are not capable of proof. *Cp.* Theist.

**Agnus Bell.** *See* Agnus Dei.

**Agnus-castus.** *See* Vitex.

**Agnus Dei.** A cake of wax or dough stamped with the figure of a lamb supporting the banner of the Cross, and distributed by the Pope on the Sunday after Easter. This is a relic of the ancient custom of collecting and distributing to the worshippers the wax of the Paschal candle, which was stamped with the lamb. The part of the Roman Catholic Mass and English communion service beginning with the words *Agnus Dei, qui tollis peccata mundi* (O Lamb of God, that takest away the sins of the world), is also known as the *Agnus Dei*. In Catholic services it is introduced by the ringing of the *Agnus bell*.

**Agog.** *He is all agog*, in nervous anxiety, on the *qui vive*. The word is connected with the Old French phrase *en gogues*, meaning 'in mirth': the origin of O.F. *gogue* and Norman *goguer*, to be mirthful, is unknown.

**Agonistes.** This word in *Samson Agonistes* (the title of Milton's drama) is Greek for 'champion', so the title means simply 'Samson the Champion.' *Cp.* Agony.

**Agonistics.** A fanatical sect of peripatetic ascetics, adherents to the Donatist schismatics of the early 4th century. They gave themselves this name ( = 'Champions', or 'Soldiers', of the Cross); the Catholics called them the *Circumcelliones*, from their wandering about among the houses of the peasants (*circum, cellas*).

**Agony,** meaning great pain or anguish, is derived through French from the Greek word *agonia*, from *agon*, which meant first 'an assembly', then 'an arena for contests', and hence the 'contest' itself; so *agonia*, meaning first a struggle for mastery in the games, came to be used for any struggle, and hence for mental struggle or anguish.

**Agony Column.** A column in a newspaper containing advertisements of missing relatives and friends; indicating great distress of mind in the advertiser.

**Agrarian Law** (Lat. *ager*, land). In *Roman history*, a law regulating landed property or the division of conquered territory; hence, a law for making land the common property of a nation, and not the particular property of individuals. In a modified form, a redistribution of land, giving to each citizen a portion.

**Agrimony.** A common English plant, called by Pliny *argemonia*, possibly from the Greek *argemos*, a white speck on the eye, which this plant was supposed to cure.

**Ague,** from Lat. *acuta*, sharp, is really an adjective, as in French *fièvre aigue*. English folklore gives a number of curious charms for curing ague, and there was an old superstition that if the fourth book of the *Iliad* was laid under the head of a patient it would cure him at once. This book tells how Pandarus wounds Menelaus, and contains the cure of Menelaus by Machaon, 'a son of Aesculapius'.

**Aguecheek.** ***Sir Andrew Aguecheek,*** a straight-haired country squire, stupid even to silliness, self-conceited, living to cat, and wholly unacquainted with the world of fashion. The character is in Shakespeare's *Twelfth Night*.

**Agur's Wish** (Prov. 30:8). 'Give me neither poverty nor riches'.

**Ahead.** *The wind's ahead* – i.e. blows in the direction towards which the ship's head points; in front. If the wind blows in the opposite direction (i.e. towards the stern) it is said to be astern. When one ship is ahead of another, it is *before* it, or farther advanced. 'Ahead of his class', means at the head. Ahead in a race, means before the rest of the runners.

***To go ahead*** is to go on without hesitation, as a ship runs ahead of another.

**Ahithophel.** A treacherous friend and adviser. Ahithophel was David's counsellor, but joined Absalom in revolt, and advised him 'like the oracle of God' (2 Sam. 16:20–23). *See* Achitophel.

**Ahmed, Prince,** in the *Arabian Nights* is noted for the tent given him by the fairy Pari-banou, which would cover a whole army, but might be carried in one's pocket; and for the apple of Samarcand, which would cure all diseases. The qualities ascribed to the magic tent are the common property of many legends and romances. *See* Carpet and Skidhbladhnir.

**Aholah** and **Aholibah** (Ezek. 23). Personifications of prostitution. Used by the prophet to signify religious adultery or running after false faiths. These Hebrew names signify 'she in whom are tents', and have reference to the worship at the high places. Swinburne has a poem *Aholibah* (*Poems and Ballads*, 1*st Series*), in which occurs the verse:

God called thy name Aholibah,
His tabernacle being in thee,

A witness through waste Asia:
Thou wert a tent sown cunningly
With gold and colours of the sea.

The great difficulty in exposing the immoralities of this Aholibah is that her [acts] are so revolting. *Papers on the Social Evil*, 1885

**Aholibamah.** In the Bible, the name of one of Esau's wives (Gen. 36:2) and of a 'duke' that came of Esau (Gen. 36:41), but in Byron's *Heaven and Earth*, daughter of Cain's son, loved by the seraph Samiasa. She is a proud, ambitious, queen-like beauty, a female type of Cain. When the flood came, her angel-lover carried her off to 'a brighter world than this'.

**Ahriman.** In the dual system of Zoroaster, the spiritual enemy of mankind, also called *Angra Mainyn*, and *Druj* (deceit). He has existed since the beginning of the world, and is in eternal conflict with Ahura Mazda, or Ormuzd (*q.v.*)

Their evil principle, the demon Ahriman, might be represented as the rival or as the creature of The God of Light.
Gibbon, *Decline and Fall*, ch. ii

**Ahura Mazda.** *See* Ormuzd.

**Aide toi et le Ciel t'aidera.** A line from La Fontaine (vi, 18), meaning 'God will help those who help themselves', taken as the motto of a French political society, established in 1824. The society intended to induce the middle classes to resist the Government; it aided in bringing about the Revolution of 1830, and was dissolved in 1832. Guizot was at one time its president, and *Le Globe* and *Le National* its organs.

**Aigrette.** French for the Egret, or Lesser White Heron, the beautiful crest of which has been worn by ladies as a hat decoration, as a tuft for military helmets, etc. The French call any jewelled or feathery head-ornament, as well as the tuft of birds, *aigrette*.

**Aim.** ***To give aim.*** A term in archery, meaning to *give* the archers information how near their arrows fall to the mark *aimed at*; hence, to give anybody inside information.

But, gentle people, give me aim awhile,
For nature puts me to a heavy task.
Shakespeare, *Titus Andronicus*, 5, 3

***To cry aim.*** To applaud, encourage. In archery it was customary to appoint certain persons to cry '*Aim!*' for the sake of encouraging those who were about to shoot.

All my neighbours shall cry aim.
Shakespeare, *Merry Wives of Windsor*, 3, 2

***Aim-crier.*** An abettor, one who encourages. In archery, the person employed to 'cry aim'.

Thou smiling aim-crier at princess' fall.
Gervaise Markham, *English Arcadia* (1638)

**Air.** Held by Anaxagoras to be the primary form of matter, and given by Aristotle as one of the four elements. *See* Element.

The *air of the court*, the *air of gentility*; *a good air* (manner, deportment) means the pervading habit; hence, *to give oneself airs* – to assume in manner, appearance, and tone, a superiority to which you have no claim.

The plural is essential in this case; air, in the singular, is generally complimentary, but in the plural conveys censure. In Italian, we find the phrase, *Si da dell arie*.

***Air*** (in music) is that melody which predominates and gives its character to the piece.

***Hot air.*** *See* Hot.

***To air one's opinion.*** To state opinions openly, in an *airy* manner (i.e. in a light way, or in one that is really or apparently not based on true thought).

***Air-brained.*** An uneducated misspelling of Hare-brained (*q.v.*).

***Air-line.*** A direct line, taken – as a crow flies – through the air. *Cp.* Bee-line.

**Airships.** Formerly an epithet applied to any kind of balloon, but now restricted to a large aerial vehicle, depending for flotation upon gases contained in a balloon or in a series of enclosed ballonets, and, instead of being at the mercy of the winds, capable of being steered by mechanism.

**Aisle.** The north and south wings of a church, from the Lat., *ala* (*axilla*, *ascella*), through the French, *aile*, a wing. The intrusive 's' did not take root till the middle of the 18th century, and is probably due to a confusion with 'isle'. In some church documents the aisles are called *alleys* (walks); the choir of Lincoln Cathedral used to be called the 'Chanters' alley'; and Olden tells us that when he came to be church-warden, in 1638, he made the Puritans 'come up the middle alley on their knees to the raile'.

**Aitch-bone.** Corruption of 'naitch-bone', i.e. the haunch-bone (Lat. *nates*, a haunch or buttock). For other instances of the coalescence of the 'n' of 'an' with an initial vowel (or the coalescence of the 'n' with the article), *see* Apron, Newt.

**Ajax.** (1) *The Greater*. The most famous hero of the Trojan War after Achilles; king of Salamis, a man of giant stature, daring, and self-confident, son of Telamon. When the armour of Hector was awarded to Ulysses instead of to himself, he turned mad from vexation and stabbed himself. – Homer and later poets.

(2) *The Less.* Son of Oileus, King of Locris, in Greece. The night Troy was taken, he offered violence to Cassandra, the prophetic daughter of Priam; in consequence of which his ship was driven on a rock, and he perished at sea. – Homer and later poets.

**Akbar.** An Arabic title, meaning 'Very Great'. Akbar Khan, the 'very great Khan', is applied especially to the great Mogul emperor in India who reigned 1556–1605. His tomb at Secundra, a few miles from Agra, is one of the wonders of the East.

**Akuan.** One of the giants slain by the Persian mythological hero, Rustam.

**Alabama.** The name of this state of the USA is the Indian name of a river in the state, the meaning of which is 'here we rest'.

**Alabaster.** A stone of great purity and whiteness, used for ornaments. The name is said by Pliny (*Nat. Hist.*, xxxvi, 8) to be from an Egyptian town, Alabastron; but nothing is known of this town, or of the ultimate origin of the Greek word.

**Aladdin,** in the *Arabian Nights*, obtains a magic lamp, and has a splendid palace built by the genius of the lamp. He marries the daughter of the sultan of China, loses his lamp, and his palace is transported to Africa. Sir Walter Scott says, somewhat incorrectly:

> Vanished into air like the palace of Aladdin.

* The palace did not vanish into air, but was transported to another place.

***Aladdin's lamp.*** The source of wealth and good fortune. After Aladdin came to his wealth and was married, he suffered his lamp to hang up and get rusty.

> It was impossible that a family, holding a document which gave them access to the most powerful noblemen in Scotland, should have suffered it to remain unemployed, like Aladdin's rusty lamp. Senior

***Aladdin's ring,*** given him by the African magician, was a 'preservative against every evil'.

***Aladdin's window. To finish Aladdin's window*** – i.e. to attempt to complete something begun by a great genius, but left imperfect. The palace built by the genius of the lamp had twenty-four windows, all but one being set in frames of precious stones; the last was left for the sultan to finish; but after exhausting his treasures, the sultan was obliged to abandon the task as hopeless.

**Alans.** Large dogs, of various species, used for hunting. They were introduced to this country from Spain, whither they are said to have been brought by the Alani, a Caucasian tribe which invaded Western Europe in the 4th century. They were used in war as well as for hunting, and Chaucer, in his *Knight's Tale*, describes Lycurgus on his throne, guarded by white 'alauntes, twenty or mo, as grete as any steer', wearing muzzles, and golden collars. Scott, in the *Talisman* (ch. vi), speaks of three –

> Skins of animals slain in the chase were stretched on the ground ... and upon a heap of these lay three *alans*, as they were called, i.e., wolf greyhounds of the largest size.

**Al Araf** (Arab. the partition, from *'arafa*, to divide). A region, according to the Koran, between Paradise and Jahannam (hell), for those who are neither morally good nor bad, such as infants, lunatics, and idiots. Others regard it as a place where those whose good and evil deeds were about equally balanced can await their ultimate admission to heaven, a kind of 'limbo' (*q.v.*).

**Alarum Bell.** 'Alarum' is a variant of 'alarm', produced by rolling the 'r' in prolonging the final syllable. In feudal times a'larum bell was rung in the castle in times of danger to summon the retainers to arms.

> Awake! awake!
> Ring the alarum bell! Murder and treason!
> Shakespeare, *Macbeth*, 2, 3

The word is now used only (except sometimes in poetry) for the peal or chime of a warning bell or clock, or the mechanism producing it.

**Alasnam.** *Alasnam's lady*. In the *Arabian Nights* Alasnam has eight diamond statues, but had to go in quest of a ninth more precious still, to fill the vacant pedestal. The prize was found in the lady who became his wife, at once the most beautiful and the most perfect of her race.

> There is wanting one pure and perfect model, and that one, wherever it is to be found, is like Alasnam's lady, worth them all.
> Sir Walter Scott

***Alasnam's mirror.*** The 'touchstone of virtue', given to Alasnam by one of the Genii. If he looked in this mirror it informed him whether a damsel would remain to him faithful or not. If the mirror remained unsullied so would the maiden; if it clouded, the maiden would prove faithless.

**Alastor.** The evil genius of a house; a Nemesis. Cicero says: 'Who meditated killing himself that he might become the *Alastor* of Augustus, whom he hated'. Shelley has a poem entitled *Alastor, or*

*The Spirit of Solitude*. The word is Greek (*alastor*, the avenging god, a title applied to Zeus); the Romans had their Jupiter Vindex; and we read in the Bible, 'Vengeance is mine; I will repay, saith the Lord' (Rom. 12:19).

**Alauda.** A Roman legion raised by Julius Caesar in Gaul, and so called because they carried a *lark's tuft* on the top of their helmets.

**Alawy.** The Nile is so called by the Abyssinians. The word means 'the giant'.

**Alb** (Lat. *albus*, white). A long white vestment worn by priests under the chasuble and over the cassock when saying Mass. It is emblematical of purity and continence.

**Alban, St,** like St Denis and many other saints, is sometimes represented as carrying his head in his hands. His attributes are a sword and a crown.

Ss. Aphrodisius, Aventine, Desiderias, Chrysolius, Hilarian, Leo, Lucanus, Lucian, Proba, Solangia, and several other martyrs, are represented in the same way: it is the conventional symbol adopted by the artist to show that the martyr met death by beheading.

**Albano Stone** or Peperino, used by the Romans in building; a volcanic tufa quarried at Monte Albano.

**Albany, Albainn,** or **Albin.** An ancient name applied to the northern part of Scotland, called by the Romans 'Caledonia', and inhabited by the Picts. From Celtic *alp* or *ailpe*, a rock or cliff. The name Albany survives in Breadalbane, the hilly country of Albainn, i.e. western Perthshire.

In Spenser's *Faerie Queene* (II, x, 14, etc.) northern Britain is called *Albania*.

**Albati.** An order of hermits who were prominent in Italy about 1400, so called because they dressed in white. They were suppressed by Boniface IX.

**Albatross.** Tho largest of web-footed birds, called by sailors the *Cape Sheep*, from its frequenting the Cape of Good Hope. Many fables are told of the albatross; it is said to sleep in the air, because its flight is a gliding without any apparent motion of its long wings, and sailors say that it is fatal to shoot one. Coleridge's *Ancient Mariner* is founded on this superstition.

**Alberich.** The all-powerful king of the dwarfs in *Scandinavian mythology*. In Wagner's version of the *Nibelungenlied* he appears as a hideous gnome and steals the magic gold (*Das Rheingold*) guarded by the Rhine Maidens. With it he fashions himself the magic Ring, by means of which he becomes ruler of Nibelheim and possessor of much treasure. Later he is captured by the gods, and is forced to give up all he has in return for his freedom. He begs to be allowed to keep the Ring; but this is refused, and as Wotan snatches it from his finger he lays a curse on it and declares that it will for ever bring death and disaster on its possessor. It ultimately passes to Siegfried, leads indirectly to the Downfall of the Gods (*Die Götterdämmerung*), which puts an end to Alberich as well as the gods, and the curse is not removed till it has again fallen into the hands of the Rhine Maidens.

**Albert, An.** A chain from the waistcoat pocket to a button in front of the waistcoat. So called from Prince Albert, the consort of Queen Victoria. When he went to Birmingham, in 1849, he was presented by the jewellers of the town with such a chain, and the fashion took the public fancy.

**Albigenses.** A common name for a number of anti-sacerdotal sects in southern France during the 13th century; so called from the Albigeois, inhabitants of the district which now is the department of the Tarn, the capital of which was Albi, Languedoc, where their persecution began, under Innocent III in 1208.

**Albin.** *See* Albany.

**Albino** (Lat. *albus*, white). A term originally applied by the Portuguese to those negroes who were mottled with white spots; but now to those who, owing to the congenital absence of colouring pigment, are born with red eyes and white hair and skin. Albinos are found among white people as well as among negroes. The term is also applied to beasts and plants, and even, occasionally, in a purely figurative way: thus, Oliver Wendell Holmes, in the *Autocrat of the Breakfast Table* (ch. viii), speaks of Kirke White as one of the 'sweet Albino poets', whose 'plaintive song' he admires; apparently implying some deficiency of virility, and possibly playing upon the name.

**Albion.** An ancient and poetical name for Great Britain: thought to have been so called from the white (Lat. *albus*) cliffs that face Gaul, but possibly from the Celtic *alp*, *ailp* (*see* Albany), a rock, cliff, mountain. 'Albion' or 'Albany' may have been the Celtic name of all Great Britain, but was subsequently restricted to Scotland, and then to the Highlands of Scotland.

It was Napoleon who called England *Perfide Albion*!

**Al Borak.** *See* Borak.

**Album.** A blank book for photographs, stamps, autographs, miscellaneous jottings, scraps, and so on. The Romans applied the word to certain tables overlaid with gypsum, on which were inscribed the annals of the chief priests, the edicts of the praetors, and rules relating to civil matters. In the Middle Ages, 'album' was the general name of a register or list; so called from being kept either on a white (*albus*) board with black letters, or on a black board with white letters.

**Alcade,** or **Alcalde.** The name of a magistrate in Spain and Portugal; it is the Arabic *al cadi* (the judge).

**Alcaic Verse** or ***Alcaïcs.*** A Greek lyrical metre, so called from *Alcaeos*, a lyric poet, who is said to have invented it. Alcaic measure is little more than a curiosity in English poetry; probably the best example is Tennyson's:

O migh | ty-mouthed | in | ventor of | harmonies,
O skilled | to sing | of | Time or E | ternity.
God-gift | ed or | gan-voice | of Eng | land,
Milton, a | name to re | sound for | ages.

**Alcantara, Order of.** A military and religious order instituted in 1213 (on the foundation of the earlier order of San Juan del Pereyro, which had been created about 1155 to fight the Moors) by Alfonso IX, King of Castile, to commemorate the taking of Alcantara from the Moors. In 1835 the Order, which had been under the Benedictine rule, ceased to exist as a religious body, but it remains as a civil and military order under the Crown.

**Alceste.** The hero of Molière's *Misanthrope*. He is not unlike Shakespeare's character of Timon, and was taken by Wycherley for the model of his Manly (*q.v.*).

**Alchemilla.** A genus of plants of the rose family; so called because alchemists collected the dew of its leaves for their operations. Also called 'Lady's Mantle', from the Virgin Mary, to whom the plant was dedicated.

**Alchemy.** The derivation of this word is obscure: the *al* is the Arabic article, *the*, and *kimia* the Arabic form of Greek *chemeia*, which seems to have meant Egyptian art; hence 'the art of the Egyptians'. Its main objects were the transmutation of baser metals into gold, the universal solvent (alkahest, *q.v.*), the panacea (*q.v.*), and the elixir of life.

**Alcimedon.** A generic name for a first-rate carver in wood.

Pocula ponam
Fagina, coelatum divini opus Alcimedontis.

Virgil, *Eclogue*, iii, 36

**Alcina.** The personification of carnal pleasure in *Orlando Furioso*; the *Circe* of classic fable, and *Labe* of the Arabians. She enjoyed her lovers for a time, and then changed them into trees, stones, fountains, or beasts, as her fancy dictated.

**Alcinoo poma dare** (to give apples to Alcinous). To carry coals to Newcastle. The gardens of Alcinous, the legendary king of the Phaeacians on the island of Scheria, by whom Odysseus was entertained, were famous for their fruits. Thus, Milton speaks of Eden as a:

Spot more delicious than those gardens feigned
Or of revived Adonis, or renowned
Alcinous, host of old Laertes' son.

*Paradise Lost*, ix, 4, 9

**Alcion.** *See* Giants of Mythology.

**Alcmena.** In *Greek mythology*, daughter of Electryon, king of Mycenae, wife of Amphitryon, and mother (by Zeus) of Hercules. The legend is that at the conception of Hercules Zeus, for the additional pleasure of Alcmena, made the night the length of three ordinary nights.

**Alcofribas Nasier.** The anagrammatic pseudonym of François Rabelais, adopted as the name of the author of his first two books, viz. *Gargantua* and *Pantagruel.*

**Aldebaran** (Arab. *al*, the, *dabarân*, the follower, because its rising follows that of the Pleiades). A red star of the first magnitude, α Tauri, one of the brightest in the heavens. It forms the bull's eye in the constellation Taurus.

**Alderman.** A senior or elder: now applied to certain magistrates in corporate towns. In the City of London aldermen were first appointed by a charter of Henry III in 1242; there are 25 (or, counting the Lord Mayor, or chief magistrate, 26), and they are elected for life, one for each ward. In the London County Council there are 20 aldermen, who are elected and hold office for six years; they have no magisterial functions.

In slang use *alderman* may mean a *turkey*, both from its presence at aldermanic feasts, and also because of the brilliant colours about the head and neck, which make it a sort of alderman of the poultry-yard. An *alderman in chains*, by a similar effort of wit, is a turkey hung with sausages.

The name *alderman* is also given to a burglar's crowbar for forcing safes, perhaps from the high rank it holds with burglars, a heavier jemmy being known as a *Lord Mayor*. It is also a cant term for half a crown, possibly because as a half-crown may be looked on as a half king, so an alderman may be looked on as half a king in his own ward.

**Aldgate Pump.** ***A draught on Aldgate Pump.*** A worthless cheque or bill. The pun is on the word draught which may mean either an order on a bank or a sup of liquor.

**Aldibo-ronte-phosco-phornio.** A courtier in Henry Carey's burlesque, *Chronon-hoton-thologos* (1734).

**Aldine Editions.** Editions of the Greek and Latin classics, published and printed under the superintendence of Aldo Manuzio, his father-in-law Andrea of Asolo, and his son Paolo, from 1490 to 1597; most of them are in small octavo, and all are noted for their accuracy. The father invented the type called *italics*, once called *Aldine*, and first used in printing *Virgil*, 1501.

**Aldingar, Sir.** The story of Sir Aldingar is told in Percy's *Reliques*; he is steward to a Queen Eleanor, wife of a king Henry. He impeached her fidelity, and submitted to a combat to substantiate his charge; but an angel, in the shape of a child, established the queen's innocence. The story is common to the ballad literature of most European countries.

**Ale** is the Anglo-Saxon *ealu*, connected with the Scandinavian *öl*, and Lithuanian *alus*. Beer is the Anglo-Saxon *beor* (M.E., *bere*), connected with the German *bier* and Icelandic *bjorr*. A beverage made from barley is mentioned by Tacitus and even Herodotus. Hops were introduced from Holland and used for brewing about 1524, but their use was prohibited by Act of Parliament in 1528 – a prohibition which soon fell into disuse. Ale is made from pale malt, whence its light colour; porter and stout from malt more highly dried. The word *beer* is of general application; and in many parts of England it includes ale, porter, and stout. In some parts *ale* is used for the stronger malt liquors and *beer* for the weaker, while in others the terms are reversed.

> Called ale among men; but by the gods called beer.
> *The Alvismál* (10th cent. Scandinavian poem)

*See also* Church-ale.

***Aleberry.*** A corruption of ale-bree. A drink made of hot ale, spice, sugar, and toast. Burns speaks of the barley-bree (A.S. *bríw*, broth).

> Cause an aleberry to be made for her, and put into it powder of camphor. *The Pathway to Health*

***Ale-dagger.*** A dagger used in self-defence in alehouse brawls.

> He that drinkes with cutters must not be without his ale-dagger. *Pappe with a Hatchet* (1589)

***Ale-draper.*** The keeper of an alehouse. *Ale-drapery*, the selling of ale, etc.

> No other occupation have I but to be an ale-draper. Chettle, *Kind-harts' Dreame*, 1592

***Ale knight.*** A tippler, a sot.

***Ale-silver.*** Formerly, the annual fee paid to the Lord Mayor for the privilege of selling ale within the City of London.

***Ale-stake.*** The pole set up before alehouses by way of sign, often surmounted by a bush or garland. Thus, Chaucer says of the Somnour:

> A garland had he set upon his head
> As great as it were for an ale-stake.
> *Cant. Tales*, *Prol.*, 666

***Ale-wife.*** The landlady of an ale-house. In America a fish of the herring kind, only rather larger, is known as the *ale-wife*. Some think it is a corruption of a North American Indian name, *aloofe*, and some of the French *alose*, a shad.

**Alec** and **Sandle.** Contractions of Alexander; the one being Alex' and the other 'xander.

**Alecto.** In *Classical mythology*, one of the three Furies (*q.v.*); her head was covered with snakes.

> Then like Alecto, terrible to view,
> Or like Medusa, the Circassian grew.
> Hoole, *Jerusalem Delivered*, Bk vi

**Alectorian Stone** (Gr. *alector*, a cock). A stone, fabled to be of talismanic power, found in the stomach of cocks. Those who possess it are strong, brave and wealthy. Milo of Crotona owed his strength to this talisman. As a philtre it has the power of preventing thirst or of assuaging it.

**Alectryomancy.** Divination by a cock. Draw a circle, and write in succession round it the letters of the alphabet, on each of which lay a grain of corn. Then put a cock in the centre of the circle, and watch what grains he eats. The letters will prognosticate the answer. Libanius and Jamblicus thus discovered who was to succeed the emperor Valens. The cock ate the grains over the letters t, h, e, o, d = Theod[orus].

**Alert.** On the watch. Originally a military term, borrowed from Italian through French. From the Latin *erectus*, past part. of *erigere*, to set upright; Italian, *erta*, Old French, *erte*, a watch-tower. Hence the Italian *stare all' erta*, the Spanish *estar alerta*, and the Old French *être aerte* (now, *être alerte*), to be on the watch.

**Alexander and the Robber.** The story is that the pirate Diomedes, having been captured and brought before Alexander, was asked how he dared to molest the seas. 'How darest *thou* molest the earth?' was the reply. 'Because I am master only of a single galley I am termed a robber; but you who oppress the world with huge squadrons are called a king.' Alexander was so struck by this reasoning that he made Diomedes rich, a prince, and a dispenser of justice. *See* the *Gesta Romanorum*, cxlvi.

***You are thinking of Parmenio, and I of Alexander*** – i.e. you are thinking what you ought to receive, and I what I ought to give; you are thinking of those castigated or rewarded, but I of my position, and what reward is consistent with my rank. The allusion is to the tale that Alexander said to Parmenio, 'I consider not what Parmenio should receive, but what Alexander should give.'

***Only two Alexanders.*** Alexander said, 'There are but two Alexanders – the invincible son of Philip, and the inimitable painting of the hero by Apelles'.

***The continence of Alexander.*** Having gained the battle of Issus (333 BC) the family of Darius III fell into his hand; but he treated the women with the greatest decorum. A eunuch, having escaped, reported this to Darius, and the king could not but admire such nobility in a rival. *See* Continence.

***Alexander,*** so Paris, son of Priam, was called by the shepherds who brought him up.

***Alexander of the North.*** Charles XII of Sweden (1682–1718), so called from his military achievements. He was conquered at Pultowa (1709), by Peter the Great.

> Repressing here
> The frantic Alexander of the North.
>
> Thomson, *Winter*

***Alexander the Corrector.*** The self-assumed nickname of Alexander Cruden (1701–70), compiler of the *Concordance to the Bible*. After being, on more than one occasion, confined in a lunatic asylum he became a reader for the Press, and later developed a mania for going about constantly with a sponge to wipe out the licentious, coarse, and profane chalk scrawls which met his eye.

***Alexander's beard.*** A smooth chin, no beard at all. An Amazonian chin (*q.v.*).

> I like this trustie glasse of Steele ...
> Wherein I see a Sampson's grim regarde
> Disgraced yet with Alexander's bearde.
>
> Gascoigne, *The Steele Glas*

**Alexandra.** So Cassandra, daughter of Priam, is called. The two names are mere variants of each other.

**Alexandra Limp.** In the 1860s Queen Alexandra (then Princess of Wales) had a slight accident which for a time caused her to walk with an almost imperceptible limp. In a spirit of servile imitation many of the women about the court adopted this method of walking, which hence became known as the 'Alexandra limp'.

**Alexandrian.** Anything from the East was so called by the old chroniclers and romancers, because Alexandria was the depot from which Eastern stores reached Europe.

> Reclined on Alexandrian carpets (i.e., *Persian*).
>
> Rose, *Orlando Furioso*, x, 37

***Alexandrian Codex.*** A Greek MS of the Scriptures written (probably in the 5th century) in uncials on parchment, which is supposed to have originated at Alexandria. In 1628 it was presented to Charles I by Cyril Sucar, patriarch of Constantinople, and in 1753 was placed in the British Museum. It contains the Septuagint version (except portions of the Psalms), a part of the New Testament, and the Epistles of Clemens Romanus.

***Alexandrian Library.*** Founded by Ptolemy Soter, in Alexandria, in Egypt. The tale is that it was burnt and partly consumed in 391; but when the city fell into the hands of the calif Omar, in 642, the Arabs found books sufficient to 'heat the baths of the city for six months'. It is said that it contained 700,000 volumes, and the reason given by the Mohammedan destroyer for the destruction of the library was that the books were unnecessary in any case, for all knowledge that was necessary to man was contained in the Koran, and that any knowledge contained in the library that was not in the Koran must be pernicious.

***Alexandrian School.*** An academy of learning founded about 310 BC by Ptolemy Soter, son of Lagus, and Demetrius of Phaleron, especially famous for its grammarians and mathematicians. Of the former the most noted are Aristarchus (*c.*220–145 BC, Eratosthenes, (*c.*275–195 BC) and Harpocration (2nd cent. AD); and of its mathematicians Claudius Ptolemaeus (2nd cent. AD), and Euclid (*c.*300 BC), the former an astronomer, and the latter the geometer whose *Elements* are still very generally used.

**Alexandrine.** In *prosody*, an iambic or trochaic line of twelve syllables or six feet with, usually, a caesura (break) at the sixth syllable. So called either from the 12th-century French metrical romance, *Alexander the Great* (commenced by

Lambert-li-Cort and continued by Alexandre de Bernay), or from the old Castilian verse chronicle, *Poema de Alexandro Magno*, both of which are written in this metre. The final line of the Spenserian stanza is an Alexandrine.

> A needless Alexandrine ends the song,
> Which, like a wounded snake, – drags its slow length along. Pope, *Essay on Criticism*, ii, 356

***Alexandrine Age.*** From about AD 323 to 640, when Alexandria, in Egypt, was the centre of science, philosophy, and literature.

***Alexandrine Philosophy.*** A system of philosophy which flourished at Alexandria in the early centuries of the Christian era, characterised by its attempt to combine Christianity and Greek philosophy. It gave rise to Gnosticism and Neoplatonism.

**Alexandrite.** A variety of chrysoberyl found in the mica-slate of the Urals. So named from Alexander I of Russia.

**Alexis, St.** Patron saint of hermits and beggars. The story goes that he lived on his father's estate as a hermit till death, but was never recognised. It is given at length in the *Gesta Romanorum* (Tale xv).

He is represented in art with a pilgrim's habit and staff. Sometimes he is drawn as if extended on a mat, with a letter in his hand, dying.

**Alfadir** (father of all). In *Scandinavian mythology*, one of the epithets of Odin (*q.v.*).

**Alfana.** *See* Horse.

**Alfheim.** One of the heavenly mansions in *Scandinavian mythology*. It is inhabited by Freyr and the light elves.

**Alfonsin, *Alfonsine Fables.*** *See* Alphonsin, etc.

**Alfred's Scholars.** When Alfred the Great set about the restoration of letters in England he founded a school and gathered around him learned men from all parts; these became known as 'Alfred's scholars'; the chief among them are: Werfrith, Bishop of Worcester; Ethelstan and Werwulf, two Mercian priests; Plegmund (a Mercian), afterwards Archbishop of Canterbury; Asser, a Welshman; Grimbald, a French scholar from St Omer, and John the Old Saxon.

**Algarsife.** In Chaucer's unfinished *Squire's Tale*, son of Cambuscan, and brother of Cambalo, who 'won Theodora to wife'.

> This noble king, this Tartre Cambuscan,
> Had two sones by Elfeta his wife, –
> Of which the eldest sone highte Algarsife,
> That other was ycleped Camballo.
> A doghter had this worthy king also,
> That youngest was, and highte Canace.

Hence the reference in Milton's *Il Penseroso*:

> Call him up that left half told
> The story of Cambuscan bold,
> Of Camball, and of Algarsife,
> And who had Canace to wife.

**Algebra** is the Arabic *al jebr* (the equalisation), 'the supplementing and equalising (process)'; so called because the problems are solved by equations, and the equations are made by supplementary terms. Fancifully identified with the Arabian chemist Gebir. *See also* Whetstone of Witte.

**Algrind.** In Spenser's *Shepherd's Calendar* is Edmund Grindal, who became Bishop of London in 1558, and was Archbishop of Canterbury, 1576–83. He was a Puritan, and a Marian exile.

> The hills where dwellëd holy saints
> I reverence and adore:
> Not for themselves, but for the saints,
> Which had been dead of yore.
> And now they been to heaven forewent
> Their good is with them go;
> Their sample to us only lent,
> That als we mought do so.
>
> Shepherds they weren of the best,
> And lived in lowly leas,
> And sith their souls be now at rest,
> Why done we them disease?
> Such one he was (as I have heard
> Old Algrind often saine),
> That whilome was the first shepherd,
> And lived with little gain.
> *Shepherd's Calendar*, July

**Alhambra.** The citadel and palace built at Granada by the Moorish kings in the 13th century. The word is the Arabic *al-hamra*, or at full length *kal'-at al hamra* (the red castle).

**Ali.** Cousin and son-in-law of Mahomet, the beauty of whose eyes is with the Persians proverbial; insomuch that the highest term they employ to express beauty is *Ayn Hali* (eyes of Ali).

**Alias.** 'You have as many aliases as Robin of Bagshot,' said to one who passes under many names. The phrase is from Gay's *Beggar's Opera*: Robin of Bagshot, one of Macheath's gang, was *alias* Gordon, *alias* Bluff Bob, *alias* Carbuncle, *alias* Bob Booty.

**Alibi** (Lat. elsewhere). A plea of having been at another place at the time that an offence is alleged to have been committed. A clock which strikes an hour, while the hands point to a different time, the real time being neither one nor the other, has been humorously called *an alibi clock*.

> Never mind the character, and stick to the alley bi. Nothing like an alley bi, Sammy, nothing.
> Dickens, *Pickwick Papers*

**Aliboron.** The name of a jackass in La Fontaine's *Fables*; hence Maître Aliboron = Mr Jackass. *See* Gonin.

**Alichino** (wing-drooped). A devil, in *The Inferno* of Dante.

**Alicon.** The name, according to some accounts, of the seventh of the Mohammedan heavens, to which Azrael conveys the spirits of the just.

**Alien Priory, An.** A priory which is dependent upon and owes allegiance to another priory in a foreign country. A sub-priory, like Rufford Abbey, Notts, which was under the prior of Rievaulx in Yorkshire, has sometimes been erroneously called an alien priory.

**Alifanfaron.** Don Quixote attacked a flock of sheep, and declared them to be the army of the giant Alifanfaron. Similarly Ajax, in a fit of madness, fell upon a flock of sheep, which he mistook for Grecian princes.

**Al Kadr** (the Divine decree). A particular night in the month Ramadhan, when Mohammedans say that angels descend to earth, and Gabriel reveals to man the decrees of God. – *Al Koran*, ch. xcvii.

**Alkahest.** The hypothetical universal solvent of the alchemists. The word was invented, on Arabic models, by Paracelsus.

**All and Some.** An old English expression meaning 'one and all', confused sometimes with 'all and *sum*', meaning the whole total. It appears in the early 14th-century romance, *Coeur de Lion*:

> They that wolde nought Crystene become,
> Richard lect sleen hem alle and some.

**All and Sundry.** An English phrase dating from at least the 14th century, meaning 'every single person', 'all without exception'.

> He invited all and sundry to partake freely of the oaten cake and ale. Hall Caine

**All cannot do all.** Virgil (*Eclogues*, viii, 63) says, *Non omnia possumus omnes*. German proverb, *Ein jeder kann nicht alles*. All are not equally clever. Or rather, 'Be not surprised that I cannot do what you can do, for we are not all exactly alike.'

**All Fools' Day** (April 1st). *See* April Fool.

**All Fours.** A game of cards; so called from the four points that are at stake, viz. High, Low, Jack, and Game.

***To go on all fours*** is to crawl about on all four limbs, like a quadruped or an infant. The phrase used to be (more correctly) *all four*, as in Lev. 11:42, 'whatsoever goeth upon all four'.

***It does not go on all fours*** means it does not suit in every particular; it limps as a quadruped which does not go on all its four legs. Thus, the Latin saying, *Omnis comparatio claudicat* (All similes limp) was translated by Macaulay as 'No simile can go on all fours'.

**All-hallown Summer.** Another name for St Martin's Summer (*see* Summer), because it sets in about All Hallows; also called St Luke's Summer (St Luke's Day is Oct. 18th), and the Indian summer (*q.v.*). Shakespeare uses the term –

> Farewell, thou latter spring: farewell, All-hallown Summer! *I Henry IV*, 1, 2

**All-Hallows' Day.** All Saints' Day (Nov. 1st), 'hallows' being the Old English *hálig*, a holy (man), hence, a saint. The French call it *Toussaint*.

**All-Hallows' Eve.** Many old folklore customs are connected with All Hallows' Eve (Oct. 31st), such as bobbing for apples, cracking nuts (mentioned in the *Vicar of Wakefield*), finding by various 'tests' whether one's lover is true, etc. Burns's *Halloween* gives a good picture of Scottish customs; and there is a tradition in Scotland that those born on All Hallows' Eve have the gift of double sight, and commanding powers over spirits. Mary Avenel, on this supposition, is made to see the White Lady, invisible to less gifted visions.

> Being born on All-hallows' Eve, she (Mary Avenel) was supposed to be invested with power over the invisible world.
> Scott, *The Monastery*, ch. xiv

**All in all.** *He is all in all to me*, that is, the dearest object of my affection. *God shall be all in all* (*see* 1 Cor. 15:28) means all creation shall be absorbed or gathered into God. The phrase is also used adverbially, meaning altogether, as:

> Take him for all in all,
> I shall not look upon his like again.
> Shakespeare, *Hamlet*, 2, 2

**All is lost that is put in a riven dish.** In Latin, *Perlusum quicquid infunditur in dolium perit*. (It is no use helping the insolvent.)

**All is not gold that glitters.** Trust not to appearances. In Latin, *Nulla fides fronti*.

> Not all that tempts your wand'ring eyes
> And heedless hearts is lawful prize;
> Nor all that glisters gold.
> Gray, *On the Death of a Favourite Cat*

**All my Eye** (and) **Betty Martin.** All nonsense. Joe Miller says that a Jack Tar went into a foreign church, where he heard someone uttering these words – *Ah! mihi, beate Martine* (Ah! grant me, Blessed Martin). On giving an account of his adventure, Jack said he could not make much out of it, but it seemed to him very like 'All my eye and Betty Martin'; but there is no prayer known that fits this description, and the story is, on other grounds as well, absurd as an explanation. The shortened phrase, 'All my eye', is very common.

**All one.** The same in effect. Answers the same purpose.

**All-overish.** A familiar expression meaning *ill at ease all over.* 'I feel all-overish,' not exactly ill, but uncomfortable all over.

> The elder of the brothers gave a squeal,
> All-overish it made me for to feel.
>
> Sir W. S. Gilbert, *Prince Agib*

**All Saints' Day,** or **All-Hallows.** Between 603 and 610 the Pope (Boniface IV) changed the heathen Pantheon into a Christian church, and dedicated it to the honour of all the martyrs. The festival of All Saints was first held on May 1st, but in the year 834 it was changed to November 1st.

**All serene** (Sp. *seréna*). In Cuba the word was used as a countersign by sentinels, and is about equivalent to our 'All right', or 'All's well'. In the late 19th century it was a colloquial catch-word, and during the 1880s, when Sir Garnet Wolseley had become 'our only general' and was winning his battles in Egypt, it gave rise to the alternative 'all Sir Garnet', meaning 'everything is going well'.

**All Souls' Day.** The 2nd of November, so called because Catholics on that day seek by prayer and almsgiving to alleviate the sufferings of souls in purgatory. It was instituted in the monastery of Cluny in 993.

According to tradition, a pilgrim, returning from the Holy Land, was compelled by a storm to land on a rocky island, where he found a hermit, who told him that among the cliffs was an opening into the infernal regions through which huge flames ascended, and where the groans of the tormented were distinctly audible. The pilgrim told Odilo, abbot of Cluny, of this; and the abbot appointed the day following, which was November 2nd, to be set apart for the benefit of souls in purgatory.

**All there.** Said of a sharp-witted person. *Not all there*, said of one of weak intellect. The one has all his wits about him, the other has not.

**All this for a song!** Said to be Burleigh's remark when Queen Elizabeth ordered him to give £100 to Spenser as a royal gratuity.

**All to break** (Judges. 9:53). 'A certain woman cast a piece of millstone upon Abimelech's head, and all to brake his skull' does not mean for the sake of breaking his skull, but that she wholly smashed his skull. The *to* either belongs to the verb, and the passage should be printed 'all to-brake', or to the adverb (*all-to*), as in *all to pieces*, *altogether*. Probably the former is the correct reading, the *to* being an intensifying prefix (as is *zu* in German), and the *all* coming in as a natural addition. It is common among our early writers, as witness Chaucer's –

> Al is to-broken thilke regioun.
>
> *Knight's Tale*, 2759

And Gower's *Confessio Amantis*, I –

> Whereof the sheep ben al to-tore.

Later, Milton has in *Comus* (1. 380) 'Her wings ... were all to-ruffled and sometimes impaired'; but here the original and early editions had no hyphen: this was inserted by Warton, and it gives the sense that Milton probably intended.

**All work.** *A maid of all work.* A general servant who does all the work of a house; at once nursemaid, housemaid, and cook.

**Allah.** The Arabic name of the Supreme Being from *al*, the, *illah*, god. *Allah il Allah*, the Mohammedan war-cry, and also the first clause of their confession of faith, is a corruption of *la illah illa allah*, meaning 'there is no God but the God'. Another Mohammedan war-cry is *Allah akbar*, 'God is most mighty'.

**Allan-a-Dale.** A minstrel in the Robin Hood ballads, who appears also in Scott's *Ivanhoe*. He was assisted by Robin Hood in carrying off his bride, when on the point of being married against her will to a rich old knight.

**Alleluiah.** *See* Hallelujah.

**Allemand.** The French have a proverb, *une querelle d'Allemand*, meaning a quarrel about nothing; much as we call pot valour 'Dutch courage'.

***Gare la queue des Allemands.*** Before you quarrel, count the consequences.

**Alley, The.** An old name for Change Alley in the City of London, where dealings in the public funds, etc. used to take place.

> John Rive, after many active years in the Alley, retired to the Continent, and died at the age of 118.
>
> *Old and New London*, p. 476

**Alliensis, Dies.** June 16th, 390 BC, when the Romans were cut to pieces by the Gauls near the banks of the river Allia. It was ever after held to be a *dies nefastus*, or unlucky day.

**Alligator.** When the Spaniards first saw this reptile in the New World, they called it *el lagarto* (the lizard). Sir Walter Raleigh called these creatures *lagartos*; in the 1st 4to of *Romeo and Juliet*, (5, 1) the animal is called an *aligarta*, and in Ben Jonson's *Bartholomew Fair* an *alligarta*.

> To the present day the Europeans in Ceylon apply the term alligator to what are in reality crocodiles.
>
> J. E. Tennent, *Ceylon* (vol. I, pt 2, chap, iii, p. 186)

The chief physical differences between an alligator and a crocodile are that in the former the head is shorter and broader, there are recesses in the upper jaw which receive the points of the first and fourth lower jaw teeth, and the jaws cannot open to so great an extent.

**Alligator Pear.** The name given to the fruit of the West Indian tree, *Persea gratissima*. It is a corruption either of the Carib *aouacate*, called by the Spanish discoverers *avocado* or *avigato*, or of the Aztec *abuacath*, which was transmitted through the Fr. *avocat* and Sp. *aguacate*. In any case the fruit has nothing to do with the animal.

**Alliteration.** The rhetorical device of commencing adjacent accented syllables with the same letter or sound, as in Quince's ridicule of it in *Midsummer Night's Dream*, (5, 1):

> With *b*lade, with *b*loody *b*lameful *b*lade,
> He *b*ravely *b*roached his *b*oiling *b*loody *b*reast.

Alliteration was almost a *sine qua non* in Anglo-Saxon and early English poetry, and in modern poetry it is frequently used with great effect, as in Coleridge's:

> The fair *b*reeze *b*lew, the white *f*oam *f*lew,
> The *f*urrow *f*ollowed *f*ree. *Ancient Mariner*

And Tennyson's:

> The *m*oan of doves in i*mm*e*m*orial el*ms*,
> And *m*ur*m*uring of innu*m*erable bees.
>
> *Princess*, vii

Many fantastic examples of excessive alliteration are extant, and a good example from a parody by Swinburne will be found under the heading Amphigouri. Hugbald, for instance, composed an alliterative poem on Charles the Bald, every word of which begins with *c*, and Henry Harder a poem of 100 lines, in Latin hexameters, on cats, each word beginning with *c*, called *Canum cum Catis certamen carmine compositum currente calamo C Catulli Caninii*. The first line is –

> Cattorum canimus certamina clara canumque.

Tusser, who died 1580, has a rhyming poem of twelve lines, every word of which begins with *t*; and in the 1890s there was published a *Serenade* of twenty-eight lines, 'sung in M flat by Major Marmaduke Muttinhead to Mademoiselle Madeline Mendoza Marriott', which contained only one word – in the line, 'Meet me *by* moonlight, marry me' – not beginning with M.

The alliterative alphabetic poem beginning –

> An Austrian army awfully arrayed,
> Boldly by battery besieged Belgrade;
> Cossack commanders, cannonading come,
> Dealing destruction's devastating doom; ...

is well known. Published in 'The Trifler', May 7, 1817, ascribed to Rev. B. Poulter, later revised by Alaric A. Watts, though claimed for others.

Anothor attempt of the same kind begins thus:

> About an age ago, as all agree,
> Beauteous Belinda, brewing best Bohea
> Carelessly chattered, controverting clean,
> Dublin's derisive, disputatious dean ...

**Allodials.** (Med. Lat. from Old Frankish *al*, all, *od*, estate). Lands held by absolute right, without even the burden of homage or fidelity; opposed to feudal.

**Allopathy** is in opposition to *Homoeopathy* (*q.v.*). It is from the Greek, *allo pathos*, a different disease. In homoeopathy the principle is that 'like is to cure like'; in allopathy the disease is to be cured by its 'antidote'.

**Alls.** Tap-droppings. The refuse of all sorts of spirits drained from the glasses, or spilt in drawing. The mixture is sold in gin-houses at a cheap rate.

**Alls, The Five.** A public-house sign, several of which still exist. It has five human figures, with a motto to each:

| | | |
|---|---|---|
| (1) A king in his regalia | motto | *I govern all.* |
| (2) A bishop, in his pontificals | | *I pray for all.* |
| (3) A lawyer, in his gown. | | *I plead for all.* |
| (4) A soldier in regimentals | | *I fight for all.* |
| (5) A labourer, with his tools | | *I pay for all.* |

**Allworthy,** in Fielding's *Tom Jones*, is designed for the author's friend. Ralph Allen, the philanthropist of Bristol.

> Let humble Allen, with an awkward shame,
> Do good by stealth, and blush to find it fame.
>
> Pope, *Epilogue to Sat.* 1, 135, 136

**Alma** (Ital. soul, spirit, essence), in Prior's poem of this name typifies the mind or guiding principles of man. Alma is queen of 'Body Castle', and is beset by a rabble rout of evil desires, foul imaginations, and silly conceits for seven years (*the Seven Ages*). In Spenser's *Faerie*

*Queene* (II, ix-xi) Alma typifies the soul. She is mistress of the House of Temperance, and there entertains Prince Arthur and Sir Guyon.

**Alma Mater.** A collegian so calls the university of which he is a member. The words are Latin for 'fostering mother', and in ancient Rome the title was given to several goddesses, especially Ceres and Cybele.

They are also used for other 'fostering mothers', as in –

> You might divert yourself, too, with Alma Mater, the Church. Horace Walpole, *Letters*, 1778

**Almack's.** A suite of assembly rooms in King Street, St James's (London), built in 1765 by William Almack, an ex-valet, who a short time previously had founded the club now known as Brooks's, and who died in 1781. Balls, presided over by a committee of ladies of the highest rank, used to be given here; and to be admitted was almost as great a distinction as to be presented at Court. After 1840 they became known as Willis's Rooms, from the name of the then proprietor, and were used chiefly for large dinners. They were closed in 1890.

**Almagest.** The English form of the Arabic name given to Ptolemy's *Mathematike syntaxis*, the great astronomical treatise composed during the 2nd century AD, of which an Arabic translation was made about 820. It is in the third book of this work (which contains thirteen books in all) that the length of the year was first fixed at 365¼ days.

**Almain,** or **Alman,** a German, as in *Othello*, 2, 3. In Peele's *Arraignment of Paris* (ii, 2) –

> Knights in armour, treading a war-like Almain.

it is a dance of some kind.

The Fr. *Allemand*, a German, which, of course, is the classic *Alamani* or *Alamanni*. Similarly, Almany = Germany, Mod. Fr. *Allemagne*.

> Chonodomarius and Vestralpus, Aleman kings ... sat them downe neere unto Argentoratum
> Holland, *Ammianus Marcellius*
>
> Now Fulko comes ... And dwelt in Almany.
> Harrington, *Orlando Furioso*, iii, 30

**Almanac.** A mediaeval Latin word for a table of days and months with astronomical data, etc., and is supposed to be derived from Arabic though no Arabic original has yet been discovered. Some early almanacs are –

*Before the invention of printing*:

| | |
|---|---|
| By Solomon Jarchi | in and after 1150 |
| Peter de Dacia about | 1300 |
| Walter de Elvendene | 1327 |
| John Somers, Oxford | 1380 |
| Nicholas de Lynna | 1386 |
| Purbach | 1150–1461 |

*After invention of printing*:

| | |
|---|---|
| First printed by Gutenberg, at Mentz | 1457 |
| By Regiomontanus, at Nuremberg | 1474 |
| Zainer, at Ulm | 1478 |
| Richard Pynson (*Sheapeheard's Kalendar*) | 1497 |
| Stoffler, in Venice | 1499 |
| Poor Robin's Almanack | 1652 |
| Francis Moore's Almanack between | 1698 and 1713 |
| Almanach de Gotha, first published | 1764 |
| Whitaker's Almanack, first published | 1868 |

***The Man i' the Almanac stuck with pins*** (Nat. Lee), is a man marked with points referring to signs of the zodiac, and intended to indicate the favourable and unfavourable times of letting blood.

**Almesbury.** It was in a sanctuary at Almesbury that Queen Guenever, according to Malory, took refuge, after her adulterous passion for Lancelot was revealed to the king (Arthur). Here she died; but her body was buried at Glastonbury.

**Almeyda.** *See* Benbow.

**Almighty Dollar.** Washington Irving seems to have been the first to use this expression:

> The almighty dollar, that great object of universal devotion throughout our land. ...
> W. Irving, *Wolfert's Roost*, *Creole Village* (1837)

Ben Jonson in his *Epistle to Elizabeth, Countess of Rutland*, speaks of 'almighty gold'.

**Almond Tree.** Grey hairs: from Eccl. 12:5, 'and the almond tree shall flourish', which has been interpreted to mean 'grey hairs on a bald pate'.

**Almonry.** The place where the almoner resides, or where alms are distributed. An almoner is a person whose duty it is to distribute alms, which, in ancient times, consisted of one-tenth of the entire income of a monastery.

The word has become confused with *Ambry* (*q.v.*), and the Close in Westminster now known as 'Ambry Close' used to be called 'Almonry Close'.

Almonry is from the Latin *eleemosynarium*, a place for alms.

> The place wherein this Chapel or Almshouse stands was called the 'Elemosinary' or Almonry, now corrupted into Ambrey, for that the alms of the Abbey are there distributed to the poor. Stow, *Survey*

**Alms.** (O.E. *aelmysse*, ultimately from Lat. *elemosina* from Gr. *eleemosyne*, compassion); gifts to the poor.

Dr Johnson says the word has no *singular*, Todd and Dr Murray say it has no *plural*. It is a singular word which, like *riches* (from Fr. richesse), has in modern usage become plural. In the Bible we have 'he asked *an* alms' (Acts 3:3), but Dryden gives us 'alms *are* but the vehicles of prayer'.

(*Hind and the Panther*, iii, 106)

**Alms Basket** (in *Love's Labour's Lost*, 5, 1). *To live on the alms basket*. To live on charity.

**Alms-drink.** Leavings; the liquor which a drinker finds too much, and therefore hands to another; also, liquor left over from a feast and sent to the alms-people. *See Antony and Cleopatra*, 2, 7.

**Alms-fee.** Peter's pence (*q.v.*).

**Almshouse.** A house where paupers are supported at the public expense; a poorhouse. Also a house set apart for the aged poor free of rent.

Only alas! the poor, who had neither friends nor attendants,
Crept away to die in the almshouse, home of the homeless. Longfellow, *Evangeline*, pt ii, 5, 2

**Alms-man.** One who lives on alms.

**Alnaschar Dream, An.** Counting your chickens before they are hatched. Alnaschar, the barber's fifth brother (in the *Arabian Nights* story), invested all his money in a basket of glassware, on which he was to make a profit which, being invested, was to make more, and this was to go on till he grew rich enough to marry the vizier's daughter. Being angry with his imaginary wife he gave a kick, overturned his basket, and broke all his wares.

Psha! what an Alnaschar I am because I have made five pounds by my poems.

Thackeray, *Pendennis*, ch. xxxii

**Aloe** (Gr. *aloe*), A very bitter plant; hence the line in Juvenal's sixth satire (181), *Plus aloes quam mellis habet*, 'He has in him more bitters than sweets,' said of a writer with a sarcastic pen. The French say, *'La côte d'Adam contient plus d'aloès que de miel*,' where *côte d'Adam*, of course, means woman or one's wife.

**Alombrados.** *See* Illuminati.

**Along-shore Men** or **Longshoremen.** Stevedores; men employed to load and unload vessels.

**Alonzo of Aguilar.** When Fernando, King of Aragon, was laying siege to Granada in 1501, he asked who would undertake to plant his banner on the heights. Alonzo, 'the low-most of the dons', undertook the task, but was cut down by the Moors. His body was exposed in the wood of Oxijera, and the Moorish damsels, struck with its beauty, buried it near the brook of Alpuxarra. The incident is the subject of a number of ballads.

**Aloof.** A sea term, *to stand aloof*, meaning originally to bear to windward, or *luff*. The *a* is the same prefix as in *afoot* or *asleep*, and means *on*; *loof* is the Dutch *loef*, windward. *To hold aloof* thus means literally 'to keep to the windward', and as one cannot do that except by keeping the head of the ship *away*, it came to mean 'to keep away from' as opposed to 'to approach'.

**Aloros.** The first of the ten mythical kings of Babylon, who reigned before the Flood.

**À l'outrance.** An incorrect English version of the French *à outrance*. To the uttermost.

A champion has started up to maintain *à l'outrance* her innocence of the great offence.

*Standard*

**Alp.** The leading character in Byron's *Siege of Corinth*. He is a renegade who forswore the Christian faith to become a commander in the Turkish army, and was shot during the siege. He loved the daughter of the governor of Corinth, but she died of a broken heart because he was a traitor and apostate.

**Alph.** The sacred river in Xanadu, which ran 'through caverns measureless to man' (Coleridge, *Kubla Khan)*.

**Alpha.** '*I am Alpha and Omega, the first and the last*' (Rev.1:8). 'Alpha' is the first, and 'Omega' (Ω) the last letter of the Greek alphabet. *Cp.* Tau.

**Alphabet.** This is the only word of more than one syllable compounded solely of the names of letters. The Greek *alpha* (a) *beta* (b); our A B C (book), etc.

* The number of letters in an alphabet varies in different languages. Thus there are

| | |
|---|---|
| 21 | letters in the Italian alphabet. |
| 22 | Hebrew and Syriac alphabet. |
| 23 | Latin |
| 24 | Greek |
| 25 | French |
| 26 | English, German, Dutch |
| 27 | Spanish |
| 28 | Arabic |
| 32 | Coptic |
| 36 | Russian |
| 38 | Armenian |
| 39 | Georgian |
| 40 | Slavonic |
| 45 | Persian (Zend) |
| 49 | Sanskrit |

* The Chinese have no alphabet, but about 20,000 syllabic characters. The Japanese have seventy-two syllabic sounds, with forty-eight characters to express them.

Ezra 7:21, contains all the letters of the English language, presuming *I* and *J* to be identical.

Even the Italian alphabet is capable of more than seventeen trillion combinations; that is, 17 followed by eighteen other figures, as –

17,000,000,000,000,000,000;

while the English alphabet will combine into more than twenty-nine thousand quatrillion combinations; that is, 29 followed by twenty-seven other figures, as –

29,000,000,000,000,000,000,000,000,000

Yet we have no means of differentiating our vowel-sounds; take *a*, we have *fate*, *fat*, *Thames*, *war*, *orange*, *ware*, *abide*, *calm*, *swam*, etc. So with *e*, we have *era*, *the*, *there*, *prey* (*a*), *met*, *England*, *sew*, *herb*, *clerk*, etc. The other vowels are equally indefinite.

*See* Letter.

**Alpheus and Arethusa.** The Greek legend is that a youthful hunter named Alpheus was in love with the nymph Arethusa; she fled from him to the island of Ortygia on the Sicilian coast and he was turned into a river of Arcadia in the Peloponnesus. Alpheus pursued her under the sea, and, rising in Ortygia, he and she became one in the fountain hereafter called Arethusa. The myth seems to be designed for the purpose of accounting for the fact that the course of the Alpheus is for some considerable distance underground.

**Alphonsin.** An old surgical instrument for extracting bullets from wounds. So called from Alphonse Ferri, a surgeon of Naples, who invented it (1552).

**Alphonsine Tables.** A revision of the Ptolemaic planetary tables made at the command of Alphonsus X of Castile – himself a noted astronomer – by a body of 50 or more of the most learned astronomers of the time. They were completed in 1252.

**Alpieu** (Ital. *al più*, for the most). In the game of Basset, doubling the stake on a winning card.

What pity 'tis those conquering eyes,
Which all the world subdue.
Should, while the lover gazing dies,
Be only on alpieu.

Etherege, *Basset*

**Alquife.** A famous enchanter, introduced into the old romances, especially those relating to Amadis of Gaul.

**Al Rakim.** The dog in the legend of the Seven Sleepers of Ephesus.

**Alruna-wife, An.** The Alrunes were the *lares* or *penates* of the ancient Germans; and an Alruna-wife, the household goddess.

She (Hypatia) looked as fair as the sun, and talked like an Alruna-wife.

Kingsley, *Hypatia*, ch. xii

**Alsatia.** The Whitefriars district of London, which from early times till the abolition of all privileges in 1697 was a sanctuary for debtors and lawbreakers. It was bounded on the north and south by Fleet Street and the Thames, on the east and west by the Fleet River (now New Bridge Street) and the Temple; and was so called from the old Latin name of Alsace, which was for centuries a debatable frontier ground and a refuge of the disaffected. Scott, in his *Fortunes of Nigel*, described the life and state of this rookery; he borrowed largely from *The Squire of Alsatia* (1688), a comedy by Shadwell, who had been the first to use the name in literature.

**Al-Sirat** (Arab. the path). In *Mohammedan mythology*, the bridge leading to paradise; bridge over mid-hell, no wider than the edge of a sword, across which all who enter heaven must pass.

**Alsvidur.** *See* Horse.

**Altar** (Lat. *altus*, high; a high place). The oblong block or table, made of wood, marble, or stone, consecrated, and used in Christian churches for the celebration of the Holy Eucharist. The shape is probably derived from that of the tombs of the martyrs in the catacombs of Rome, which were used as altars.

The altar appears frequently in emblematical Christian art. St Stephen (the Pope), and Thomas à Becket are represented as immolated before one; Canute is pictured lying before one, and St Charles Borromeo as kneeling before an altar. In the paintings of St Gregory (the Pope) he is shown offering sacrifice at the altar; and the attribute of St Victor is an altar overthrown, in allusion to his throwing down a Roman altar in the presence of the Emperor Maximian.

***Led to the altar.*** Married. Said of a lady, who, as a bride, is led up the aisle to the altar-rail where marriages are solemnised.

***The north side of the altar.*** The side on which the Gospel is read. The north is the dark part of the earth, and the Gospel is the light of the world which shineth in darkness – '*illuminare his qui in tenebris et in umbra mortis sedent*'.

**Alter ego** (Lat. other I, other self). One's double; one's intimate and thoroughly trusted friend; one who has full powers to act for another. *Cp.* 'One's second self' *under* Second.

**Althaea's Brand,** a fatal contingency. Althaea's son, Meleager, was to live so long as a log of wood, then on the fire, remained unconsumed. With her care it lasted for many years, but being angry one day with Meleager, she pushed it into the midst of the fire; it was consumed in a few minutes and Meleager died in great agony at the same time. Ovid, *Metamorphoses*, viii, 4.

The fatal brand Althaea burned.
Shakespeare, *2 Henry VI*, 1, 1

**Althea.** The divine Althea of Richard Lovelace was Lucy Sacheverell, also called by the poet, 'Lucasta'.

When Love with unconfinëd wings
Hovers within my gates,
And my divine Althea brings
To whisper at the grates.

Lovelace was thrown into prison by the Long Parliament for his petition in favour of the king; hence the grates referred to.

**Altis.** The sacred precinct of Zeus at Olympia, containing the great temple and oval altar of Zeus, the Pelopium (grave of Pelops), the Heraeum, with many other buildings and statues. It was connected by an arched passage with the Stadium, where the Olympian games were held.

**Alto relievo.** Italian for 'high relief'. A term used in sculpture for figures in wood, stone, marble, etc., so cut as to project at least one-half from the tablet.

**Alumbrado,** a perfectionist; so called from a Spanish sect which arose in 1575, and claimed special illumination. (Spanish meaning 'illuminated', 'enlightened'.)

**Alvina weeps,** or 'Hark! Alvina weeps,' i.e. the wind howls loudly, a Flemish saying. Alvina was the daughter of a king, who was cursed by her parents because she married unsuitably. From that day she roamed about the air invisible to the eye of man, but her moans are audible.

**A.M.** or **M.A.** When the Latin form is intended the A comes first, as *Artium Magister*: but where the English form is meant the M precedes, as *Master of Arts*.

The abbreviation 'A.M.' also stands, of course, for *ante meridiem* (Lat.), before noon, and *anno mundi*, in the year of the world.

**Amadis of Gaul.** The hero of a prose romance of the same title, supposed to have been written by the Portuguese, Vasco de Loberia (d.1403), with additions by the Spaniard Montalvo, and by many subsequent romancers, who added exploits and adventures of other knights and thus swelled the romance to fourteen books. The romance was referred to as early as 1350 (in Egidis Colonna's *De Regimine Principium*); it was first printed in 1508, became immensely popular, and exerted a wide influence on literature far into the 17th century.

Amadis, called the 'Lion-knight', from the device on his shield, and 'Beltenebros' (*darkly beautiful*), from his personal appearance, was a love-child of Perion, King of Gaula (which is Wales), and Elizena, Princess of Brittany. He was cast away at birth and becomes known as the *Child of the Sea*, and after many adventures including wars with the race of Giants, a war for the hand of his lady-love, Oriana, daughter of Lisuarte, King of Greece, the Ordeal of the Forbidden Chamber, etc., he and the heroine, Oriana, are wed. He is represented as a poet and musician, a linguist and a gallant, a knight-errant and a king, the very model of chivalry.

Other names by which Amadis was called were the *Lovely Obscure*, the *Knight of the Green Sword*, the *Knight of the Dwarf*, etc.

**Amadis of Greece.** A Spanish continuation of the seventh book of *Amadis of Gaul* (*q.v.*), supposed to be by Feliciano de Siva. It tells the story of Lisuarte of Greece, a grandson of Amadis.

**Amaimon** (3 syl.). One of the chief devils in mediaeval demonology; king of the eastern portion of hell. Asmodeus is his chief officer. He might be bound or restrained from doing hurt from the third hour till noon, and from the ninth hour till evening.

Amaimon sounds well; Lucifer well.
Shakespeare, *Merry Wives of Windsor*, 2, 2

**Amalfitan Code.** The oldest existing collection of maritime laws, compiled in the 11th century at Amalfi, then an important commercial centre.

**Amalthaea.** In *Greek mythology*, the nurse of Zeus (*see* Amalthea's Horn). In Roman legend Amalthea is the name of the Sibyl who sold the Sibylline Books (*q.v.*) to Tarquin.

**Amalthea's Horn.** The cornucopia or 'horn of plenty' (*q.v.*). The infant Zeus was fed with goats' milk by Amalthea, one of the daughters of Melisseus, King of Crete. Zeus, in gratitude, broke off one of the goat's horns, and gave it to Amalthea, promising that the possessor should always have in abundance everything desired. *See* Aegis.

When Amalthea's horn
O'er hill and dale the rose-crowned Flora pours,
And scatters corn and wine, and fruits and flowers.
Camoens, *Lusiad*, Bk ii

**Amarant.** A cruel giant slain in the Holy Land by Guy of Warwick. *See Guy and Amarant,* in Percy's *Reliques.*

**Amaranth** (Gr. *amarantos*, everlasting). The name given by Pliny to some real or imaginary fadeless flower. Clement of Alexandria says – *Amarantus flos, symbolum est immortalitatis.* Among the ancients it was the symbol of immortality, because its flowers retain to the last much of their deep blood-red colour.

The best known species are 'Love lies bleeding' (*Amarantus caudalus*), and 'Prince's feather' (*Amarantus hypochondriacus*).

Immortal amarant, a flower which once
In Paradise, fast by the Tree of Life,
Began to bloom, but, soon for man's offence
To heaven removed where first it grew, there grows
And flowers aloft, shading the Fount of Life ...
With these, that never fade, the Spirits elect
Bind their resplendent locks.
Milton, *Paradise Lost*, iii, 353

Spenser mentions 'sad Amaranthus' as one of the flowers 'to which sad lovers were transformed of yore' (*Faerie Queene*, III, vi, 45), but there is no known legend to this effect.

In 1653 Christina, Queen of Sweden, instituted the order of the *Knights of the Amaranth*, but it ceased to exist at the death of the Queen.

**Amaryllis.** A rustic sweetheart. The name is borrowed from a shepherdess in the pastorals of Theocritos and Virgil.

To sport with Amaryllis in the shade.
Milton, *Lycidas*, 68

In Spenser's *Colin Clout's Come Home Again*, Amaryllis is intended for Alice Spenser, Countess of Derby.

**Amasis, Ring of.** Herodotus tells us (iii, 40) that Polycrates, tyrant of Samos, was so fortunate in everything that Amasis, king of Egypt, fearing such unprecedented luck boded ill, advised him to part with something which he highly prized. Polycrates accordingly threw into the sea a ring of great value. A few days afterwards, a fish was presented to the tyrant, in which the ring was found. Amasis now renounced friendship with Polycrates, as a man doomed by the gods; and not long afterwards, a satrap put the too fortunate despot to death by crucifixion.

**Amati.** A violin made by the Amati family which flourished at Cremona (*q.v.*) in the 16th and 17th centuries.

**Amaurote** (Gr. the shadowy or unknown place), the chief city of Utopia (*q.v.*) in the political romance of that name by Sir Thomas More. Rabelais, in his *Pantagruel*, introduces Utopia and 'the great city of the Amaurots' (Bk II, ch. xxiii). He had evidently read Sir Thomas More's book.

To add to the verisimilitude of the romance, More says he could not recollect whether Hythlodaye had told him it was 500 or 300 paces long; and he requested his friend Peter Giles, of Antwerp, to put the question to the adventurer. Swift, in *Gulliver's Travels*, uses very similar means of throwing dust in his reader's eyes. He says:

I cannot recollect whether the reception room of the Spaniard's Castle in the Air is 200 or 300 feet long. I will get the next aeronaut who journeys to the moon to take the exact dimensions for me, and will memorialise the learned society of Laputa. *Gulliver's Travels*

**Amazement.** *Not afraid with any amazement* (I Pet. 3:6), introduced at the close of the marriage service in the Book of Common Prayer. The meaning is, you will be God's children so long as you do his bidding, and are not drawn aside by any sort of bewilderment or distraction. Shakespeare uses the word in the same sense:

Behold, distraction, frenzy and amazement,
Like witless antics one another meet
*Troilus and Cressida*, 5, 3

**Amazon.** A Greek word meaning *without breast*, or rather, 'deprived of a pap'. According to Herodotus there was a race of female warriors, or *Amazons*, living in Scythia, and other Greek stories speak of a nation of women in Africa of a very warlike character. There were no men in the nation; and if a boy was born, it was either killed or sent to its father, who lived in some neighbouring state. The girls had their right breasts burnt off, that they might the better draw the bow. The term is now applied to any strong, brawny woman of masculine habits.

She towered, fit person for a Queen
To lead those ancient Amazonian files;
Or ruling Bandit's wife among the Grecian isles.
Wordsworth, *Poems of the Imagination*, xviii

**Amazonia.** An old name for the regions about the river Amazon in South America, which was so called because the early Spanish explorers (1541), under Orellana, thought they saw female warriors on its banks.

**Amazonian Chin.** A beardless chin, like that of a woman warrior.

When with his Amazonian chin he drove
The bristled lips before him.
Shakespeare, *Coriolanus*, 2, 2

**Ambassador.** The name given to a practical joke played on greenhorns aboard ship. A tub full of water is placed between two stools, and the whole being covered with a green cloth, a sailor sits on each stool, to keep the cloth tight. The two sailors represent Neptune and Amphitrite, and the greenhorn, as ambassador, is introduced to their majesties. He is given the seat of honour between them; but no sooner does he take his seat than the two sailors rise, and the greenhorn falls into the tub, amidst the laughter of the whole crew.

**Amber.** A yellow, translucent, fossilised vegetable resin, the name of which originally belonged to ambergris (*q.v.*). Beaumont and Fletcher use it as a verb meaning to perfume with ambergris:

Be sure
The wines be lusty, high, and full of spirit,
And amber'd all. *Custom of the Country*, III, ii

Legend has it that amber is a concretion, the tears of birds who were the sisters of Meleager and who never ceased weeping for the death of their brother. – Ovid, *Metamorphoses*, viii, 270.

Around thee shall glisten the loveliest amber
That ever the sorrowing sea-bird hath wept
T. Moore, *Fire Worshippers*

Insects, small leaves, etc. are often preserved in amber; hence such phrases as 'preserved for all time in the imperishable amber of his genius'.

Pretty! in amber, to observe the forms
Of hairs, or straws, or dirt, or grubs, or worms,
The things, we know, are neither rich nor rare,
But wonder how the devil they got there.
Pope, *Ep. to Arbuthnot*, 169–72

**Amber,** meaning a repository, is an obsolete spelling of *ambry* (*q.v.*).

**Amberabad.** Amber-city, one of the towns of Jinnistan, or Fairy Land.

**Ambergris.** A waxy, aromatic substance found floating on tropical seas and in the intestines of the cachalot. It is a marbled ashy grey in colour and is used in perfumery. Its original name was simply *amber* (*see* Amber) from Fr. *ambre*, which denoted only this substance; when it came to be applied to the fossil resin (Fr. *ambre jaune*, yellow amber), this grey substance became known as *amber gris* (grey amber).

**Ambi-dexter** properly means both hands right hands, and so one who can use his left hand as deftly as his right; in slang use a double-dealer: a juror who takes money from both parties for his verdict.

**Ambition,** strictly speaking, means 'the going from house to house' (Lat. *ambitio*, going about canvassing). In Rome the candidates for election went round to the different dwellings to solicit votes; those who did so were *ambitious* of office.

**Ambree, Mary.** An English heroine, immortalised by her valour at the siege of Ghent in 1584. See the ballad in Percy's *Reliques*:

When captains couragious, whom death cold not daunte,
Did march to the siege of the citty of Gaunt,
They mustred their souldiers by two and by three,
And the formost in battle was Mary Ambree.

Her name is proverbial for a woman of heroic spirit.

My daughter will be valiant,
And prove a very Mary Ambry i' the business.
Ben Jonson, *Tale of a Tub*, i, 4

**Ambrose, St,** represented in Christian art in the robes of a bishop. His attributes are (1) a *beehive*, in allusion to the legend that a swarm of bees settled on his mouth when he was lying in his cradle; (2) a *scourge*, by which he expelled the Arians from Italy.

The penance he inflicted on the Emperor Theodosius has been represented by Rubens, a copy of which, by Vandyck, is in the National Gallery. The incident is described in Gibbon's *Decline and Fall*, ch. xxvii; *see also* Ruskin's *Stones of Venice*, vol. i, ch. xx, 13.

**Ambrosia** (Gr. *a* privative, *brotos*, mortal). The food of the gods, so called because it made them immortal. Anything delicious to the taste or fragrant in perfume is so called from the notion that whatever is used by the celestials must be excellent.

... So fortunate
Whom the Pierian sacred sisters love
That ... with the Gods, for former vertues meede,
On nectar and Ambrosia do feede.
Spenser, *Ruines of Time*, 393

Husband and wife must drink from the cup of conjugal life; but they must both taste the same ambrosia, or the same gall.
R. C. Houghton, *Women of the Orient*, pt iii

**Ambrosian Chant.** The choral music introduced from the Eastern to the Western Church by St Ambrose, Bishop of Milan, in the 4th century. It was used till Gregory the Great introduced the Gregorian.

**Ambrosian Library.** A library in Milan founded by Count Federigo Borromeo, Cardinal Archbishop of Milan, in 1609; so called in compliment to St Ambrose, the patron saint.

**Ambrosio.** Hero of Lewis's romance, *The Monk*; abbot of the Capuchins at Madrid. The temptations of Matilda overcome his virtue, and he proceeds from crime to crime, till at last he sells his soul to the devil. Ambrosio, being condemned to death by the Inquisition, is released by Lucifer; but no sooner is he out of prison than he is dashed to pieces on a rock.

**Ambrosius Aurelianus.** A semi-mythical champion of the British race. The story is that he was a descendant of the Emperor Constantine, that he lived in the 5th century, and that he led the Romanised Britons against the Saxon invaders under Hengist. He is mentioned by Gildas as 'the last of the Romans', and he may have been a Count of the Saxon Shore. William of Malmesbury says of him:

> When Vortimer died, the British strength decayed, and all hope fled trom them; and they would soon have perished altogether, had not Ambrosius, the sole survivor of the Romans, who became monarch after Vortigern, quelled the presumptuous barbarians by the powerful aid of the warlike Arthur.

**Ambry** (Old Fr. *armarie*, from Lat. *armaria*, chest or cupboard, from *arma*, tools, gear). A cupboard, locker or recess. The ambry in a church is a closed recess in the wall which is used for keeping books, vestments, the sacramental plate, consecrated oil, and so on (*cp.* Almonry).

> Avarice hath almaries,
> And yren-bounden cofres.
>
> *Piers Plowman*, xiv, 494

**Ambsas** or **Ambes-ace** (Lat. *amboasses*, both or two aces). Two aces, the lowest throw in dice; figuratively, bad luck.

> I had rather be in this choice than throw ames-ace for my life.
>
> *All's Well*, 2, 3

It was also the name of a card-game, and was sometimes spelt aums-ace.

**Ambuscade.** From the Italian *imboscata*, concealed in a wood.

**Âme damnée** (Fr.), literally, a damned, or lost, soul; hence one's familiar or tool, one blindly devoted to another's wishes; and, sometimes, a scapegoat.

> He is the *âme damnée* of everyone about the court – the scapegoat, who is to carry away all their iniquities.
>
> Sir Walter Scott, *Peveril of the Peak*, ch. 48

**Amedians.** 'Friends of God'; a religious body in the Church of Rome, founded about 1400. They wore no breeches, but a grey cloak girded with a cord, and were shod with wooden shoes. About 1570 they were united by Pius V with the Cistercians.

**Amelia.** A model of conjugal affection, in Fielding's novel of that name. It is said that the character is intended for his own wife.

**Amen Corner,** at the west end of Paternoster Row, London, is where the monks used to finish the *Pater Noster* as they went in procession to St Paul's Cathedral on Corpus Christi Day. They began in *Paternoster* Row with the Lord's Prayer in Latin, which was continued to the end of the street; then said *Amen*, at the corner or bottom of the Row; then turning down *Ave Maria* Lane, commenced chanting the 'Hail, Mary!' then crossing Ludgate, they entered *Creed* Lane chanting the *Credo*.

**Amen-Ra.** The supreme King of the Gods among the ancient Egyptians, usually figured as a man with two long plumes rising straight above his head, but sometimes with a ram's head, the ram being sacred to him. He was the patron of Thebes; his oracle was at the oasis of Jupiter Ammon, and he was identified by the Greeks with Zeus.

**Amende honorable.** An anglicised French phrase signifying a full and frank apology. In mediaeval France the term was applied to a degrading punishment inflicted on traitors, parricides, and sacrilegious persons, who were brought into court with a rope round their neck, stripped to the shirt, and made to beg pardon of God, the king, and the court.

**A mensa et thoro.** *See* A vinculo.

**Amenthes.** The Egyptian Hades; the abode of the spirits of the dead who were not yet fully purified.

**American Flag.** The American Congress resolved (June 14, 1777) that the flag of the United States should have thirteen stripes, alternately red and white, to represent the thirteen States of the Union, together with thirteen white stars, on a blue ground. In 1818 it was decided by Congress that on the 4th July following the date of admission a new star should be added for each new State.

> However, before the separation the flag contained thirteen stripes of alternate red and white to indicate the thirteen colonies; and the East India Company flag, as far back as 1704, had thirteen stripes. The Company flag was cantoned with St George's Cross, the British American flag with the Union Jack.

**American States.** Specifically, the following eight states which retain the Indian names of the chief rivers: Alabama, Arkansas, Illinois, Kentucky, Mississippi, Missouri, Ohio, and Wisconsin.

*American States,* nicknames of inhabitants. The Americans are rich in nicknames. Every state has, or has had, its sobriquet. The people of

| | | |
|---|---|---|
| *Alabama* | are | lizards. |
| *Arkansas* | | toothpicks. |
| *California* | | gold-hunters. |
| *Colorado* | | rovers. |
| *Connecticut* | | wooden nutmegs. |
| *Dakota* | | squatters. |
| *Delaware* | | musk rats, *or* blue-hen's chickens. |
| *Florida* | | fly-up-the-creeks. |
| *Georgia* | | buzzards. |
| *Idaho* | | fortune-seekers, *or* cut-throats. |
| *Illinois* | | suckers. |
| *Indiana* | | hoosiers. |
| *Iowa* | | hawk-eyes. |
| *Kansas* | | jay-hawkers. |
| *Kentucky* | | corn-crackers. |
| *Louisiana* | | creoles. |
| *Maine* | | foxes. |
| *Maryland* | | clam-humpers. |
| *Massachusetts* | | Bay-State boys. |
| *Michigan* | | wolverines. |
| *Minnesota* | | gophers. |
| *Mississippi* | | tadpoles. |
| *Missouri* | | pukes. |
| *Nebraska* | | bug-eaters. |
| *Nevada* | | sage-hens. |
| *New Hampshire* | | granite-boys. |
| *New Jersey* | | Blues *or* clam-catchers. |
| *New Mexico* | | Spanish Indians. |
| *New York* | | knickerbockers. |
| *North Carolina* | | tar-boilers *or* Tuckoes. |
| *Ohio* | | buck-eyes. |
| *Oregon* | | web-feet *or* hard cases. |
| *Pennsylvania* | | Penamites *or* Leatherheads. |
| *Rhode Island* | | gun-flints. |
| *South Carolina* | | weasels. |
| *Tennessee* | | whelps. |
| *Texas* | | beef-heads. |
| *Vermont* | | green-mountain boys. |
| *Utah* | | polygamists. |
| *Virginia* | | beagles. |
| *Wisconsin* | | badgers. |

**Ames-ace.** *See* Ambs-as.

**Amethea.** *See* Horse.

**Amethyst** (Gr. *a*-, not, *methuein*, to be drunken). A violet-blue variety of crystalline quartz supposed by the ancients to prevent intoxication.

Drinking-cups made of amethyst were a charm against inebriety; and it was the most cherished of all precious stones by Roman matrons, from the superstition that it would preserve inviolate the affection of their husbands.

**Amiable** or **Amicable Numbers.** Any two numbers either of which is the sum of the aliquots of the other: thus, the aliquots of 220 are 1, 2, 4, 5, 10, 11, 20, 22, 44, 55, 110, the sum of which is 284; and the aliquots of 284 are 1, 2, 4, 71, 142, the sum of which is 220; so 220 and 284 are amicable numbers.

**Amicus curiae** (Lat. a friend to the court). One in court who is not engaged in the trial or action, but who is invited or allowed to assist with advice or information.

*Amicus Plato, sed magis amica veritas* (Plato I love, but I love Truth more). A free rendering of a noble dictum from Aristotle's *Nicomachean Ethics*, I, vi, 1.

**Amiel.** In Dryden's *Absalom and Achitophel*, is meant for Edward Seymour, Speaker of the House of Commons.

> Who can Amiel's praise refuse?
> Of ancient race by birth, but nobler yet
> In his own worth, and without title great:
> The Sanhedrin long time as chief he ruled,
> Their reason guided and their passion cooled.
>
> *Absalom and Achitophel*, 1, 899

The name is an anagram of Eliam ( = God is kinsman). Eliam in 2 Sam. 23:34, is son of Ahitophel the Gilonie, and one of David's heroes; in 2 Sam. 11:3, it is given as the name of Bathsheba's father, which, in 1 Chron. 3:5, appears as 'Ammiel'.

**Aminadab.** A Quaker. The Scripture name has a double *m*, but in old comedies, where the character represents a Quaker, the name has generally only one. *Obadiah* is used, also, to signify a Quaker, and *Rachel* a Quakeress.

**Amine** (3 syl.). Wife of Sidi Nouman, who ate her rice with a bodkin, and was in fact a ghoul. 'She was so hard-hearted that she led about her three sisters like a leash of greyhounds.' – *Arabian Nights.*

**Amiral** or **Ammiral.** An early form of the word 'admiral' (*q.v.*).

**Amis** and **Amile.** *See* Amys.

**Ammon.** The Libyan Jupiter; the Greek form of the name of the Egyptian god, Amun (*q.v.*).

*Son of Ammon.* Alexander the Great, who, on his expedition to Egypt, was thus saluted by the priests of the Libyan temple.

> Ammon's great son one shoulder had too high.
>
> Pope, *Epistle to Dr Arbuthnot*, 117

His father, Philip, claimed to be a descendant of Hercules, and therefore of Jupiter.

**Ammonites.** Fossil molluscs allied to the nautilus and cuttlefish. So called because they resemble the horn upon the ancient statues of Jupiter Ammon. *See above.*

Also the people of Ammon; that is, the descendants of Lot by the son of his younger daughter, Ben-ammi (Gen. 19:38), who are frequently mentioned in the Old Testament.

**Amoret,** in Spenser's *Faerie Queene*, is the daughter of Chrysogone, sister of Belphoebe, wife of Scudamore, and was brought up by Venus in the courts of love. She is the type of female loveliness – young, handsome, gay, witty, and good; soft as a rose, sweet as a violet, chaste as a lily, gentle as a dove, loving everybody and by all beloved; a living, breathing virgin, with a warm heart, and beaming eye, and passions strong, and all that man can wish and woman want. In her relations with Timias (typifying Raleigh) she stands for Elizabeth Throgmorton. She falls a prey to Corflambo (sensual passion) but is rescued by Timias and Belphoebe.

**Amoret.** An obsolete term for a sweetheart, love-song, love-knot, or love personified.

> He will be in his amorets, and his canzonets, his pastorals, and his madrigals.
>
> Heywood, *Love's Mistress*

> For not icladde in silke was he,
> But all in flouris and flourettes,
> I-paintid all with amorettes.
>
> *Romance of the Rose*, 892

**Amorous, The.** Philippe I of France; so called because he divorced his wife Berthe to espouse Bertrade, who was already married to Foulques, count of Anjou (1060–1108).

**Amour propre** (Fr.). One's self-love, vanity, or opinion of what is due to self. *To wound one's amour propre*, is to gall his good opinion of himself – to wound his vanity.

**Ampersand.** The character '&' for *and.* In the old horn books, after giving the twenty-six letters, the character & was added (… X, Y, Z, &), and was called 'Ampersand', a corruption of 'and per-se &' (and by itself, and). The symbol is an adaptation of the written *et* (Lat. *and*), the transformation of which can be traced if we look at the italic ampersand – *&* – where the 'e' and the cross of the 't' are clearly recognisable. *See* Tironian.

> Any odd shape folks understand
> To mean my Protean amperzand.
>
> *Punch* (17 April, 1869)

**Amphialus.** In Sidney's *Arcadia* the valiant and virtuous son of the wicked Cecropia, in love with Philoclea; he ultimately married Queen Helen of Corinth.

**Amphictyonic Council** (Gr. *amphictiones*, dwellers round about). In *Greek history*, the council of the Amphictyonic League, a confederation of twelve tribes, the deputies of which met twice a year, alternately at Delphi and Thermopylae. Throughout the whole of ancient Greek history it exercised paramount authority over the oracles of the Pythian Apollo and conducted the Pythian games.

**Amphigouri.** A verse composition which, while sounding well, contains no sense or meaning. A good example is Swinburne's well-known parody of his own style, *Nephelidia*, the opening lines of which are:

> From the depth of the dreamy decline of the dawn through a notable nimbus of nebulous moonshine.
> Pallid and pink as the palm of the flag-flower that flickers with fear of the flies as they float,
> Are they looks of our lovers that lustrously lean from a marvel of mystic miraculous moonshine,
> These that we feel in the blood of our blushes that thicken and threaten with throbs through the throat?

Here there is everything that goes to the making of poetry – except sense; and that is absolutely (and, of course, purposely) lacking.

> A kind of overgrown amphigouri, a heterogeneous combination. *Quarterly Review*, i, 50,1809

**Amphion.** The son of Zeus and Antiope who, according to Greek legend, built Thebes by the music of his lute, which was so melodious that the stones danced into walls and houses of their own accord.

> The gift to king Amphion
> That walled a city with its melody
> Was for belief no dream.
>
> Wordsworth, *Poems of the Imagination; On the Power of Sound*

**Amphitrite.** In *classic mythology*, the goddess of the sea; wife of Poseidon, daughter of Nereus and Doris. (Gr. *amphi-trio* for *tribo*, rubbing or wearing away [the shore] on all sides.)

> His weary chariot sought the bowers
> Of Amphitrite and her tending nymphs.
>
> Thomson, *Summer* (l. 1625)

**Amphitryon.** *Le véritable Amphitryon est l'Amphitryon où l'on dine* (Molière). That is, the person who *provides the feast* (whether master of the house or not) is the real host. The tale is that Jupiter assumed the likeness of Amphitryon for the purpose of visiting his wife, Alcmena (*q.v.*), and gave a banquet at his house; but Amphitryon came home, and claimed the honour of being the master of the house. As far as the servants and guests were concerned, the dispute was soon decided – 'he who gave the feast was to them the host'.

**Amphrysian Prophetess** (*Amphrysia Vates*). The Cumaen sibyl; so called from Amphrysus, a river of Thessaly, on the banks of which Apollo fed the herds of Admetus.

**Ampoulle, La Sainte.** The vessel containing oil used in anointing the kings of France, and said to have been brought from heaven by a dove for the coronation service of St Louis. It was preserved at Rheims till the first Revolution, when it was destroyed.

**Amram's Son.** Moses. (Exod. 6:20)

> As when the potent rod
> Of Amram's son, in Egypt's evil day,
> Waved round the coast.
>
> Milton, *Paradise Lost*, i, 338

**Amri.** In Dryden's *Absalom and Achitophel* is designed for Heneage Finch, Earl of Nottingham and Lord Chancellor.

> Our list of nobles next let Amri grace,
> Whose merits claimed the Abethdin's (*Lord Chancellor's*) high place ...
> To whom the double blessing does belong,
> With Moses' inspiration, Aaron's tongue.
>
> ii, 1013

**Amrita** (Sanskrit). In *Hindu mythology*, the elixir of immortality, the soma-juice, corresponding to the ambrosia (*q.v.*) of classical mythology.

> Lo, Krishna! lo, the one that thirsts for thee!
> Give him the drink of amrit from thy lips.
>
> Sir Edwin Arnold, *Indian Song of Songs*

**Amuck.** A Malay adjective, *amoq*, meaning, engaging in combat furiously or in a state of frenzy. Hence, to *run amuck* means, figuratively, to talk or write on a subject of which you are wholly ignorant; to run foul of.

> Satire's my weapon, but I'm too discreet
> To run amuck and tilt at all I meet.
>
> Pope, *Satires*, i, 69–70

**Amulet.** Something worn, generally round the neck, as a charm. The word was formerly connected with the Arabic *himalah*, the name given to the cord that secured the Koran to the person and was sometimes regarded as a charm; but it has nothing to do with this, and is from the Latin *amuletum*, a preservative against sickness, through French *amulette*.

The early Christians used to wear amulets called *Ichthus* (*q.v.*). *See also* Notarikon.

**Amun.** An Egyptian deity, usually represented with a ram's head with large curved horns, and a human body, or as a human figure with two long upright plumes springing from the head and holding a sceptre and the symbol of life. An immense number of temples were dedicated to him, and he was identified by the Greeks with Zeus. His oracle was in the oasis of Jupiter Ammon. *See* Ammon.

**Amyclaean Silence.** Amyclae was a Laconian town in the south of Sparta, ruled by the mythical Tyndareus. The inhabitants had so often been alarmed by false rumours of the approach of the Spartans, that they made a decree forbidding mention of the subject. When the Spartans actually came no one durst give warning, and the town was taken. Hence the proverb, *more silent than Amyclae*.

Castor and Pollux were born at Amyclae, and are hence sometimes referred to as the Amyclaean Brothers.

**Amyris plays the fool.** An expression used of one who assumes a false character with an ulterior object, like Junius Brutus. Amyris was a Sybarite sent to Delphi to consult the Oracle, who informed him of the approaching destruction of his nation; he fled to Peloponnesus and his countrymen called him a fool; but, like the madness of David, his 'folly' was true wisdom, for thereby he saved his life.

**Amys and Amylion.** A French romance of the 13th century telling the story of the friendship between two heroes of the Carlovingian wars, the Pylades and Orestes of mediaeval story. The story culminates in Amylon's sacrifice of his children to save his friend. It is of Greek or Oriental origin; an English version is given in Weber's *Metrical Romances* and in Ellis's *Specimens*.

**Anabaptists.** Originally, a Christian sect which arose in Germany about 1521, the members of which did not believe in infant baptism and hence were baptised *over again* (Gr. *ana* = over again) on coming to years of discretion.

Applied in England as a nickname, and more or less opprobriously, to the Baptists, a body of Dissenters holding similar views.

**Anacharsis.** ***Anacharsis among the Scythians.*** Proverbial for a wise man amongst fools. Anacharsis was renowned for his wisdom, but he was a Scythian by birth, and the Scythians were proverbial for their uncultivated state and great ignorance.

The opposite proverb is 'Saul amongst the prophets', i.e. a fool amongst wise men.

**Anacharsis Clootz.** Jean Baptiste Clootz (1755–94), a Prussian who was brought up in Paris, where he adopted revolutionary principles, took the name Anacharsis, and also the title, and called himself *The Orator of the Human Race*.

**Anaclethra.** Another name for the *ágelasta* (*q.v.*).

**Anacreon.** A Greek lyric poet, who wrote chiefly in praise of love and wine (about 563–478 BC).

***Anacreon of the Twelfth Century.*** Walter Mapes (about 1140–1210), also called 'The Jovial Toper'. His best-known piece is the famous drinking-song, 'Meum est propositum in taberna mori', translated by Leigh Hunt.

***Anacreon Moore.*** Thomas Moore (1779–1852), who not only translated Anacreon into English, but also wrote original poems in the same style.

***Anacreon of Painters.*** Francesco Albano, a famous painter of beautiful women (1578–1660).

***Anacreon of the Guillotine.*** Bertrand Barère de Vieuzac (1755–1841), president of the National Convention; so called from the flowery language and convivial jests used by him towards his miserable victims.

***Anacreon of the Temple.*** Guillaume Amfrye (1639–1720), abbé de Chaulieu; the 'Tom Moore' of France.

***The French Anacreon.*** Pontus de Thiard, one of the Pleiad poets (1521–1605); also P. Laujon (1727–1811).

***The Persian Anacreon.*** Hafiz (d. about 1390).

***The Scotch Anacreon.*** Alexander Scot, who flourished about 1550.

***The Sicilian Anacreon.*** Giovanni Meli (1740–1815).

**Anachronism** (Gr. *ana chronos*, out of time). An event placed at a wrong date; as when Shakespeare, in *Troilus and Cressida*, makes Nestor quote Aristotle.

**Anagram** (Gr. *ana graphein*, to write over again). A word or phrase formed by transposing and writing over again the letters of some other word or phrase. Among the many famous examples are:

Dame Eleanor Davies (prophetess in the reign of Charles I) = *Never so mad a lady*.
Gustavus = *Augustus*.
Horatio Nelson = *Honor est a Nilo*.
Queen Victoria's Jubilee Year = *I require love in a subject*.
Quid est Veritas (John 18:38)? = *Vir est qui odest*.
Marie Touchet (mistress of Charles IX, of France) = *Je charme tout* (made by Henri IV).
Voltaire is an anagram of *Arouet l(e) j(eune)*.

These are interchangeable words:

Alcuinus and Calvinus; Amor and Roma; Eros and Rose; Evil and Live; and many more.

**Anah.** In Byron's *Heaven and Earth*, a tender-hearted, pious creature, granddaughter of Cain, and sister of Aholibamah. Japhet loved her, but she had set her heart on the seraph Azaziel, who carried her off to some other planet when the flood came.

**Anamnestes.** *See* Eumnestes.

**Ananas** (Peruvian *nanas*). The pineapple. Through the final 's' having been mistaken for the sign of the plural, an erroneous singular, *anana*, is sometimes used:

Witness thou, best Anana! thou the pride
Of vegetable life. Thomson, *Summer*, 685

**Anastasia, St.** A saint martyred in the reign of Nero, and commemorated on April 15. Her attributes are a stake and faggots, with a palm branch in her hand.

**Anathema.** A denunciation or curse. The word is Greek, and means 'a thing devoted' – originally, a thing devoted to any purpose, e.g. to the gods, but later only a thing devoted to evil, hence, an accursed thing. It has allusion to the custom of hanging in the temple of a patron god something devoted to him. Thus Gordius hung up his yoke and beam; the shipwrecked hung up their wet clothes; retired workmen hung up their tools; cured cripples their crutches, etc.

**Anatomy.** ***He was like an anatomy*** – i.e. a mere skeleton, very thin, like one whose flesh had been anatomised or cut off. Shakespeare uses *atomy* as a synonym. Thus in 2 *Henry* IV, 5, 4, Quickly says to the Beadle: 'Thou atomy, thou!' and Doll Tearsheet caps the phrase with, 'Come, you thin thing; come, you rascal'.

**Anaxarete.** In Greek legend, a maiden of Cyprus who was changed into stone for despising the love of Iphis, who hung himself. – Ovid, *Metamorphoses*, xiv.

**Anaxarte.** A knight whose adventures form a supplement of *Amadis of Gaul* (*q.v.*), added by Feliciano de Silva.

**Ancaeus.** Helmsman of the ship *Argo*, after the death of Tiphys. He was told by a slave that he would never live to taste the wine of his vineyards. When a bottle made from his own grapes was set before him, he sent for the slave to laugh at his prognostications; but the slave made answer, 'There's many a slip 'twixt the cup and the lip.' At this instant a messenger came in, and told Ancaeus that the Calydonian boar was laying his vineyard waste, whereupon he set down his cup, went out against the boar, and was killed in the encounter.

**Anchor, The.** In Christian symbolism the anchor is the sign of hope, in allusion to Heb. 6:19, 'Hope we have as an anchor of the soul.' In art it is an attribute of Clement of Rome and Nicolas of Bari. Pope Clement, in AD 80, was bound to an anchor and cast into the sea; Nicolas of Bari is the patron saint of sailors.

***The anchor is apeak.*** That is, the cable of the anchor is so tight that the ship is drawn completely over it.

***The anchor comes home.*** The anchor has been dragged from its hold. Figuratively, the enterprise has failed, notwithstanding the precautions employed.

***To weigh anchor.*** To haul in the anchor, that the ship may sail away from its mooring. Figuratively, to begin an enterprise which has hung on hand.

***Anchor watch.*** A watch of one or two men, while the vessel rides at anchor, in port.

*See* Bower Anchor, Sheet Anchor.

**Ancien Régime** (Fr.). The old order of things; a phrase used during the French Revolution for the old Bourbon monarchy, or the system of government, with all its evils, which existed prior to that great change.

**Ancient.** A corruption of *ensign* – a flag and the officer who bore it. Pistol was Falstaff's 'ancient'.

> Ten times more dishonourable ragged than an old-faced ancient. Shakespeare, *1 Henry IV*, 4, 2
>
> My whole charge consists of ancients, corporals, lieutenants, gentlemen of companies ...
>
> *1 Henry IV*, 4, 2

**Ancient Mariner.** The story in Coleridge's *Rime of the Ancient Mariner* (first published in the *Lyrical Ballads*, 1798) is founded partly on a dream told by the author's friend, Mr Cruickshank, and partly on passages in various books that he had read. Shelrocke's *Voyages* gave the hint for the albatross; Thomas James's *Strange and Dangerous Voyage* (1683) is thought to have suggested some of the more eerie episodes, while the *Letter of St Paulinus to Macarius, in which he relates astounding wonders concerning the shipwreck of an old man* (1618), giving a story of how there is only one survivor of a crew and how the ship was navigated by angels and steered by 'the Pilot of the World', may have furnished the basis of part of the *Rime*.

**Ancient of Days.** A scriptural title of the Deity (Dan. 7:9).

**Ancile.** The Palladium of Rome; the sacred buckler said to have fallen from heaven in the time of Numa. To prevent its being stolen, he caused eleven others to be made precisely like it, and confided them to the twelve Salii, dancing priests of Mars (*see* Saliens), who bore them in procession through the city every year at the beginning of March.

**And, '*&*'.** *See* Ampersand.

**Andiron.** A fire-dog; that is, a contrivance consisting of a short horizontal bar projecting from an upright stand or rod, the whole usually of iron (though in Shakespeare's *Cymbeline*, 2, 4, they are of silver), for the purpose of holding up the ends of logs in a wood fire. Though the contrivance is made of iron the word originally had nothing to do with the metal, any more than the word *wormwood* (*q.v.*) has to do with *wood*. It is from the Old French *andier*, after the late Latin *andedus*, *andena*, or *anderius*, the ultimate origin of which is obscure. The '-iron' in the English form seems to be due partly to confusion, and partly to analogy with the Anglo-Saxon name for this article, *brand-isen*, literally, 'brand-iron'. The English form of the word – like the Latin – has, even in modern times, had many variations, such as *end-iron* and *hand-iron*. Thus, the marginal note to Ezek. 40:43, which, in the original A.V. of 1611, read *andirons*, in modern editions is given *endirons*, and in Quarles's *Judgment and Mercy* (1644) we read, 'Let heavy cynics ... be *handirons* for the injurious world to work a heat upon.' Andirons are also known as *dogs*, or *fire-dogs*.

**Andrea Ferrara.** A sword, also called, from the same cause, an *Andrew* and a *Ferrara*. All these expressions are common in Elizabethan literature. So called from a famous 16th- century sword-maker of the name.

> We'll put in bail, my boy; old Andrea Ferrara shall lodge his security.
>
> Scott, *Waverley*, ch. 50

**Andrew,** a name used in old plays for a valet or manservant. *See* Merry Andrew.

**Andrew, St,** depicted in Christian art as an old man with long white hair and beard, holding the Gospel in his right hand, and leaning on a cross like the letter **X**, termed St Andrew's cross. The great pictures of St Andrew are his *Flagellation* by Domenichino, and the *Adoration of the Cross* by Guido, which has also been depicted by Andrea Sacchi, in the Vatican at Rome. Both the *Flagellation* and the *Adoration* form the subjects of frescoes in the chapel of St Andrea, in the church of San Gregorio, at Rome. His day is November 30th. It is said that he suffered martyrdom in Patrae (AD 70). *See* Rule, St.

The 'adoration of the cross' means his fervent address to the cross on which he was about to Suffer. 'Hail, precious cross, consecrated by the body of Christ! I come to thee exulting and full of joy. Receive me into thy dear arms'. The 'flagellation' means the scourging which always preceded capital punishments, according to Roman custom.

**Andrew's Cross, St.** is represented in the form of an **X** (white on a blue field). The cross, however, on which the apostle suffered was of the ordinary shape, if we may believe the relic in the convent of St Victor, near Marseilles. The error rose from the way in which that cross is exhibited, resting on the end of the cross-beam and point of the foot.

Legend has it that a cross of this shape appeared in the heavens to Achaius, King of the Scots, and Hungus, King of the Picts, the night before their engagement with Athelstane. As they were the victors, they went barefoot to the kirk of St Andrew, and vowed to adopt his cross as the national emblem. *Cp.* Constantine's Cross *under* Cross.

**Andrew Macs, The.** A slang name for the crew of HMS *Andromache*. Similarly, the *Bellerophon* was called by English sailors 'Billy ruffian', and the *Achilles* the 'Ash heels'. These corruptions are similar to some of those given under Beef-eater (*q.v.*).

**Androcles and the Lion.** An oriental apologue on the benefits to be expected as a result of gratitude; told in Aesop, by Aulus Gellius, in the *Gesta Romanorum*, etc., but of unknown antiquity.

Androcles was a runaway slave who took refuge in a cavern. A lion entered, and instead of tearing him to pieces, lifted up his fore paw that Androcles might extract from it a thorn. The slave being subsequently captured, was doomed to fight with a lion in the Roman arena. It so happened that the same lion was let out against him, and recognising his benefactor, showed towards him every demonstration of love and gratitude.

**Android.** An old name for an automaton figure (*q.v.*) resembling a human being (Gr. *andros-eidos*, a man's likeness).

**Andromeda.** Daughter of Cepheus and Cassiopeia. Her mother boasted that the beauty of Andromeda surpassed that of the Nereids; so the Nereids induced Neptune to send a sea-monster on the country, and an oracle declared that Andromeda must be given up to it. She was accordingly chained to a rock, but was delivered by Perseus, who married her and, at the wedding, slew Phineus, to whom she had been previously promised, with all his companions. After death she was placed among the stars.

**Anent** (from the O.E. *on efn*, or *on emn*, meaning on even [ground] with, on a level with). Over against; concerning, with reference to. The term is common in Scottish legal phraseology, and is hence sometimes used, more or less archaically, by English writers.

**Angel.** In post-canonical and apocalyptic literature angels are grouped in varying orders, and the hierarchy thus constructed was adapted to Church uses by the early Christian Fathers. In his *De Hierarchia Celesti* the pseudo-Dionysius (early 5th cent.) gives the names of the nine orders; they are taken from the Old Testament, Eph. 1:21, and Col. 1:16, and are as follows:

(i) Seraphim, Cherubim, and Thrones, in the first circle.
(ii) Dominions, Virtues, and Powers, in the second circle.
(iii) Principalities, Archangels, and Angels, in the third circle.

'In heaven above,
The effulgent bands in triple circles move.'

Tasso, *Jerusalem Delivered*, xi, 13

Botticelli's great picture, *The Assumption of the Virgin*, in the National Gallery well illustrates the mediaeval conception of the 'triple circles'.

The seven holy angels are – Michael, Gabriel, Raphael, Uriel, Chamuel, Jophiel, and Zadkiel. Michael and Gabriel are mentioned in the Bible, Raphael in the Apocrypha, and all in the apochryphal book of Enoch (8:2).

Milton (*Paradise Lost*, Bk i, 392) gives a list of the fallen angels.

Mohammedans say that angels were created from pure, bright *gems*; the genii, of *fire*; and man, of *clay*.

**_Angel._** An obsolete English coin, current from the time of Edward IV to that of Charles I, its full name being the Angel-noble, as it was originally a reissue of the noble (*q.v.*), bearing the figure of the archangel Michael slaying the dragon. Its value varied from 6*s.* 8*d.* in 1465 (when first coined) to 10*s.* under Edward VI. It was the coin presented to persons touched for the King's Evil (*q.v.*).

**_Angel._** *See* Public-house Signs.

**_Angel of the Schools._** St Thomas Aquinas. *See* Angelic Doctor.

**_On the side of the Angels._** *See* Side.

**Angel-beast.** A 17th-century card game. Five cards were dealt to each player, and three heaps formed – one for the king, one for play, and the third for Triolet. The name of the game was *la bête* (beast), and an angel was a usual stake; hence the full name, much as we speak of 'halfpenny nap', or 'shilling auction'.

> This gentleman offers to play at Angel-beast, though he scarce knows the cards.
>
> Sedley, *Mulberry Garden* (1668)

**Angel Visits.** Delightful intercourse of short duration and rare occurrence.

> Visits
> Like those of angels, short and far between.
>
> Blair, *Grave*, ii, 586
>
> Like angel visits, few and far between.
>
> Campbell, *Pleasures of Hope*, ii, 378

These lines are both reminiscent of John Norris's:

> Like angels' visits, short and bright.

(In *The Parting*, which preceded *The Grave* and *The Pleasures of Hope* by some years.)

**Angel-water.** An old Spanish cosmetic, made of roses, trefoil, and lavender. So called because it was originally made chiefly of angelica.

> Angel-water was the worst scent about her.
>
> Sedley, *Bellam*

**Angelic Brothers.** A sect of Dutch Pietists founded in the 16th century by George Gichtel. Their views on marriage were similar to those held by the Abelites and Adamites (*qq.v.*).

**Angelic Doctor.** Thomas Aquinas was so called, because he discussed the knotty points in connexion with the being and nature of angels. An example is, *Utrum Angelus moveatur de loco ad locum transeundo per medium?* The Doctor says that it depends upon circumstances.

* It is said that one of his questions was: 'How many angels can dance on the point of a pin?'

**Angelic Hymn, The.** The hymn beginning with *Glory be to God on high*, etc. (Luke 2:14); so called because the former part of it was sung by the angel host that appeared to the shepherds of Bethlehem.

**Angelic Salutation, The.** The Ave Maria (*q.v.*).

**Angelical Stone.** The speculum of Dr Dee. He asserted that it was given him by the angels Raphael and Gabriel. It passed into the possession of the Earl of Peterborough, thence to Lady Betty Germaine, by whom it was given to the Duke of Argyll, whose son presented it to Horace Walpole. It was sold in 1842, at the dispersion of the curiosities of Strawberry Hill.

**Angelites.** A sect of Sabellian heretics at the end of the 5th century; so called from Angelius, in Alexandria, where they used to meet.

**Angelus, The.** A Roman Catholic devotion in honour of the Incarnation, consisting of three texts, each said as versicle and response and followed by the Ave Maria, and a prayer. So called from the first words, 'Angelus Domini' (The angel of the Lord, etc.).

The prayer is recited three times a day, at 6 A.M., noon, and 6 P.M., at the sound of a bell called the *Angelus*.

> Sweetly over the village the bell of the Angelus sounded.
>
> Longfellow, *Evangeline*

**Anger.** Athenodorus, the Stoic, told Augustus the best way to restrain unruly anger was to repeat the alphabet before giving way to it. *See* Dander.

> The sacred line he did but once repeat,
> And laid the storm, and cooled the raging heat.
>
> Tickell, *The Horn Book*

**Angevin Kings of England.** The early Plantagenet kings, from Henry II to John. Anjou first became connected with England in 1127, when Matilda, daughter of Henry I, married Geoffrey V, Count of Anjou; their son became Henry II of England (and Count of Anjou), and until 1205 Anjou was united to the English crown. *Cp.* Plantagenet.

**Angle. _A dead angle._** A term applied in old books on fortification to the ground before an angle in a wall which can neither be seen nor defended from the parapet.

**_To angle with a silver hook._** To buy fish at market; said of an angler who, having been unsuccessful, purchases fish that will enable him to conceal his failure.

**Angling.** *The father of angling*, Izaak Walton (1593–1683). *See* Gentle Craft, The.

**Angoulaffre,** called 'of the Broken Teeth'. In Croquemitaine (*q.v.*), a giant who was descended from Goliath, and who assumed the title of 'Governor of Jerusalem'. He had the strength of 30 men, and some say the Tower of Pisa lost its perpendicularity by the giant resting himself against it. He was slain by Roland in single combat at the Fronsac.

**Angra Mainyu.** *See* Ahriman.

**Angurvadel.** Frithiof's sword, inscribed with runic letters, which blazed in time of war, but gleamed with a dim light in time of peace. *See* Sword.

**Anima Mundi** (the soul of the world), with the oldest of the ancient philosophers, meant 'the source of life'; with Plato, it meant 'the animating principle of matter', inferior to pure spirit; with the Stoics, it meant 'the whole vital force of the universe'.

Stahl (1710) taught that the phenomena of animal life are due to an immortal *anima*, or vital principle distinct from matter.

**Animal.** *To go the entire animal*, a facetious euphuism for 'To go the whole hog'. *See* Hog.

***Animals in Heaven.*** According to Mohammedan legend the following ten animals have been allowed to enter paradise:

(1) Jonah's *whale*; (2) Solomon's *ant*; (3) the *ram* caught by Abraham and sacrificed instead of Isaac; (4) the *lapwing* of Balkis; (5) the *camel* of the prophet Saleh; (6) Balaam's *ass*; (7) the *ox* of Moses; (8) the *dog* Kratim of the Seven Sleepers; (9) Al Borak, Mahomet's ass; and (10) Noah's *dove*.

***Animals in Art.*** Some animals are appropriated to certain saints: as the calf or ox to *St Luke*; the cock to *St Peter*; the eagle to *St John the Divine*; the lion to *St Mark*; the raven to *St Benedict*, etc.

***Animals sacred to special Deities.*** To Apollo, the *wolf*, the *griffon*, and the *crow*; to Bacchus, the *dragon* and the *panther*; to Diana, the *stag*; to Aesculapius, the *serpent*; to Hercules, the *deer*; to Isis, the *heifer*; to Jupiter, the *eagle*; to Juno, the *peacock* and the *lamb*; to the Lares, the *dog*; to Mars, the *horse* and the *vulture*; to Mercury, the *cock*; to Minerva, the *owl*; to Neptune, the *bull*; to Tethys, the *halcyon*; to Venus, the *dove*, the *swan*, and the *sparrow*; to Vulcan, the *lion*, etc.

***Animals in Symbolism.*** The lamb, the pelican, and the unicorn, are symbols of Christ

The dragon, serpent, and swine symbolise Satan and his crew.

The ant symbolises *frugality* and *prevision*; ape, *uncleanness*, *malice*, *lust*, and *cunning*; ass, *stupidity*; bantam cock, *pluckiness*; *priggishness*; bat, *blindness*; bear, *ill-temper, uncouthness*; bee, *industry*; beetle, *blindness*; bull, *strength, straightforwardness*; bulldog, *pertinacity*; butterfly, *sportiveness, living in pleasure*; camel, *submission*; cat, *deceit*; calf, *lumpishness, cowardice*; cicada, *poetry*; cock, *vigilance, overbearing insolence*; crow, *longevity*; crocodile, *hypocrisy*; cuckoo, *cuckoldom*; dog, *fidelity, dirty habits*; dove, *innocence, harmlessness*; duck, *deceit* (French, *canard*, a hoax); eagle, *majesty, inspiration*; elephant, *sagacity, ponderosity*; fly, *feebleness, insignificance*; fox, *cunning, artifice*; frog and toad, *inspiration*; goat, *lasciviousness*; goose, *conceit, folly*; gull, *gullibility*; grasshopper, *old age*; hare, *timidity*; hawk, *rapacity, penetration*; hen, *maternal care*; hog, *impurity*; horse, *speed, grace*; jackdaw, *vain assumption, empty conceit*; jay, *senseless chatter*; kitten, *playfulness;* lamb, *innocence, sacrifice*; lark, *cheerfulness*; leopard, *sin*; lion, *noble courage*; lynx, *suspicious vigilance*; magpie, *garrulity*; mole, *blindness, obtuseness*; monkey, *tricks*; mule, *obstinacy*; nightingale, *forlornness*; ostrich, *stupidity*; ox, *patience, strength*, and *pride*; owl, *wisdom*; parrot, *mocking verbosity*; peacock, *pride*; pigeon, *cowardice* (pigeon-livered); pig, *obstinacy, dirtiness*; puppy, *empty-headed conceit*; rabbit, *fecundity*; raven, *ill luck*; robin redbreast, *confiding trust*; serpent, *wisdom*; sheep, *silliness, timidity*; sparrow, *lasciviousness*; spider, *wiliness*; stag, *cuckoldom*; swallow, *a sunshine friend*; swan, *grace*; swine, *filthiness, greed*; tiger, *ferocity*; tortoise, *chastity*; turkey-cock, *official insolence*; turtle-dove, *conjugal fidelity*; vulture, *rapine*; wolf, *cruelty, savage ferocity*, and *rapine*; worm, *cringing*; etc.

***Animals, Cries of.*** To the cry, call, or voice of many animals a special name is given; to apply these names indiscriminately is always wrong and frequently ludicrous. Thus, we do not speak of the 'croak' of a dog or the 'bark' of a bee. Apes *gibber*; asses *bray*; bees *hum*; beetles *drone*; bears *growl*; bitterns *boom*; blackbirds and thrushes *whistle*; bulls *bellow*; cats *mew, purr, swear*, and *caterwaul*; calves *bleat*; chaffinches *chirp* or *pink*; chickens *peep*; cocks *crow*; cows *moo* or *low*; crows *caw*; cuckoos cry *cuckoo*; deer *bell*; dogs *bark, bay, howl*, and *yelp*; doves *coo*; ducks *quack*; eagles, vultures, and peacocks *scream*; falcons *chant*; flies *buzz*; foxes *bark* and *yelp*; frogs *croak*; geese *cackle* and *hiss*; grasshoppers *chirp* and *pitter*; guineafowls cry '*Come back*'; and guineapigs and hares *squeak*; hawks *scream*; hens *cackle* and *cluck*; horses *neigh* and *whinny*; hyenas *laugh*; jays and magpies *chatter*; kittens *mew*; linnets *chuckle* in their call; lions and tigers *roar* and *growl*; mice *squeak* and *squeal*; monkeys *chatter* and *gibber*; nightingales *pipe* and *warble* – we also speak of its 'jug-jug'; owls *hoot* and *screech*; oxen *low* and *bellow*; parrots *talk*; peewits cry *pee-wit*; pigeons *coo*; pigs *grunt*, *squeak*, and *squeal*; ravens *croak*; rooks *caw*; screech-owls *screech* or *shriek*; sheep and lambs *baa* or *bleat*; snakes *hiss*; sparrows *chirp*; stags *bellow* and *call*; swallows *twitter*; swans *cry* and are said to *sing* just before death (*see* Swan); turkey-cocks *gobble*; wolves *howl*. Most birds, besides many of those here mentioned, *sing*, but we speak of the *chick-chick* of the black-cap, the *drumming* of the grouse, and the *chirr* of the whitethroat.

**Animosity** meant originally animation, spirit, as the fire of a horse, called in Latin *equi animositas*. Its present exclusive use in a bad sense is an instance of the tendency which words originally neutral have to assume a bad meaning. *Cp. churl, villain.*

**Animula vagula,** etc. The opening of a poem to his soul, ascribed by his biographer, Aelius Spartianus, to the dying Emperor Hadrian:

> Animula, vagula, blandula,
> Hospes, comesque corporis;
> Quae nunc abibis in loca,
> Pallidula, rigida, nudula;
> Nec ut soles, dabis jocos!

It was Englished by Byron:

> Ah! gentle, fleeting, wavering sprite,
> Friend and associate of this clay!
> To what unknown region borne,
> Wilt thou now wing thy distant flight?
> No more with wonted humour gay,
> But pallid, cheerless, and forlorn.

**Ann, Mother,** Ann Lee (1736–84), the founder and 'spiritual mother' of the Shakers (*q.v.*).

**Annabel,** in Dryden's *Absalom and Achitophel*, is designed for Anne Scott, Duchess of Monmouth and Countess of Buccleuch, the richest heiress in Europe. The duke was faithless to her, and after his death, the widow, still handsome, married again.

> To all his [Monmouth's] wishes, nothing he [David] denied:
> And made the charming Annabel his bride.
> i, 33

**Anna Matilda, An.** An ultra-sentimental girl. Mrs Hannah Cowley used this pen-name in her responses in the *World* to 'Della Crusca'. *See* Della Cruscans.

**Annates** (Lat. *annus*, a year). One entire year's income claimed by the Pope on the appointment of a bishop or other ecclesiastic in the Catholic Church, also called the *first fruits*. By the Statute of Recusants (25 Hen. VIII, c. 20, and the Confirming Act), the right to English Annates and Tenths was transferred to the Crown; but, in the reign of Queen Anne, annates were given up to form a fund for the augmentation of poor livings. *See* Queen Anne's Bounty.

**Anne's Great Captain.** The Duke of Marlborough (1650–1722).

**Annie Laurie** was eldest of the three daughters of Sir Robert Laurie, of Maxwellton, born December 16, 1682. William Douglas, of Fingland (Kirkcudbright), wrote the popular song, but Annie married, in 1709, James Fergusson, of Craigdarroch, and was the grandmother of Alexander Fergusson, the hero of Burns's song called *The Whistle*.

> William Douglas was the hero of the song 'Willie was a wanton wag'.

**Anno Domini** (Lat.). In the year of our Lord; i.e. in the year since the Nativity: generally abbreviated to 'AD'. It was Dionysius Exiguus who fixed the date of the Nativity; he lived in the early 6th century, and his computation is probably late by some three to six years.

The phrase is sometimes used as a slang synonym for old age; thus, 'Anno Domini is his trouble', means that he is suffering from senile decay.

**Annunciation, The Day of the.** The 25th of March, also called *Lady Day*, on which the angel announced to the Virgin Mary that she would be the mother of the Messiah.

***Order of the Annunciation.*** An Italian order of military knights, founded as the Order of the Collar by Amadeus VI of Savoy in 1362, and dating under its present name from 1518. It has on its collar the letters FERT. *Fert* (Lat. he bears) is an ancient motto of the House of Savoy; but the letters have also been interpreted as standing for the initials of *Fortitudo Ejus Rhodum Tenuit*, in allusion to the succour rendered to Rhodes by Savoy in 1310; *Faedere et Religione Tenemur*, on the gold doubloon of Victor Amadeus I (1718–30); or, *Fortitudo Ejus Rempublicam Tenet.*

***Sisters of the Annunciation.*** *See* Franciscans.

**Annus Luctus** (Lat. the year of mourning). The period during which a widow is supposed to remain unmarried. If she marries within about nine months from the death of her husband and a child is born, a doubt might arise as to its paternity. Such a marriage is not illegal, but it is inexpedient.

**Annus Mirabills.** The year of wonders, 1666, memorable for the great fire of London and the successes of our arms over the Dutch. Dryden wrote a poem with this title, in which he described both these events.

**Anodyne Necklace, An.** An anodyne is a medicine to relieve pain, and the anodyne necklace was an amulet supposed to be efficacious against various diseases. In Johnson's *Idler*, No. 40, we read:

> The true pathos of advertisements must have sunk deep into the heart of every man that remembers the zeal shown by the seller of the *anodyne necklace*, for the ease and safety of poor toothing infants.

The term soon came to be applied to the hangman's noose, and we have George Primrose saying:

> May I die by an anodyne necklace, but I had rather be an under-turnkey than an usher in a boarding-school.
>
> Goldsmith, *Vicar of Wakefield*, ch. xx

**Anomoeans** (Gr. *anomoios*, unlike). A 4th-century Arian sect which maintained that the essence of the Son is wholly *unlike* that of the Father. They were Pure Arians, as distinguished from the Semi-Arians, who acknowledged a *likeness* of nature but denied *consubstantiality*.

**Anon.** The O.E. *on ane*, in one (state, mind, course, body, etc.), the present meaning – *soon, in a little while* – being a misuse of the earlier meaning – *straightway, at once* – much as *directly* and *immediately* are misused. Mark 1:30, gives an instance of the old meaning:

> But Simon's wife's mother lay sick of a fever, and anon they tell him of her –

this is the Authorised Version; the Revised Version gives *straightway*. Wordsworth's

> Fast the churchyard fills: anon
> Look again, and they all are gone.
>
> *White Doe of Rylstone*, i, 31

exemplifies the later meaning. The word also was used by servants, tapsters, etc., as an interjectory reply meaning 'Coming, sir!'

**Ansar** (Auxiliaries). The name given to the early converts to Mohammedanism at Medina, distinguishing them from the Muhajirun, who were those who accompanied Mahomet from Mecca to Medina.

**Answer** is the O.E. *and-swaru*, verb *and-swarian* or *swerian*, where *and* is the preposition = the Lat. *re* in *respond-eo*. To *swear* (*q.v.*) means literally 'to affirm something', and to **an-swear** is to 'say something' by way of rejoinder; but figuratively both the 'swer' and the 'answer' may be made without words.

> '... My story being done, ...
> She [*Desdemona*] swore [*affirmed*] 'twas strange, ...
> 'Twas pitiful, 'twas wondrous pitiful'.
>
> Shakespeare, *Othello*, 1, 3

***To answer its purpose.*** To carry out what was expected or what was intended. Celsus says, *Medicina saepius respondet, interdum tamen fallit.*

***To answer like a Norman,*** that is, evasively.

> We say, in France, 'Answering like a Norman', which means to give an evasive answer, neither yes nor no.
>
> Max O'Rell, *Friend M'Donald*, ch. v

***To answer more Scotico.*** To divert the direct question by starting another question or subject.

> 'Hark you, sirrah,' said the doctor, 'I trust you remember you are owing to the laird 4 stone of barleymeal and a bow of oats ...'
>
> 'I was thinking,' replied the man *more Scotico*, that is, returning no direct answer on the subject on which he was addressed, 'I was thinking my best way would be to come down to your honour, and take your advice, in case my trouble should come back.' Scott, *The Abbot*, ch. xxvi

***To answer the bell,*** is to go and see what it was rung for.

***To answer the door,*** is to go and open it when a knock or ring has been given.

In both the last two instances the word is 'answering to a summons'.

**Antaeus,** in *Greek mythology*, a gigantic wrestler (son of Earth and Sea, Ge and Poseidon), whose strength was invincible so long as he touched the earth; and when he was lifted from it, it was renewed by touching it again. *Cp.* Maleger.

> As once Antaeus, on the Libyan strand,
> More fierce recovered when he reached the sand.
>
> *Hoole's Ariosto*, Bk iv

It was Hercules who succeeded in killing this charmed giant. He

> Lifts proud Antaeus from his mother's plains,
> And with strong grasp the struggling giant strains;
> Back falls his panting head and clammy hair,
> Writhe his weak limbs and flits his life in air.
>
> Darwin, *Economy of Vegetation*

Plutarch says that he was 60 cubits (from 90 to 105 ft) in height, and that his tomb was discovered by Serbonius. *See* Giants.

**Antediluvian.** Before the Deluge. The word is colloquially used in a disparaging way for anything that is very out of date or old fashioned.

**Anthony the Great, St.** The patron saint of swineherds; he lived in the 4th century, and was the founder of the fraternity of ascetics who lived in the deserts. The story of his temptations by the devil is well known in literature and art. His day is 17th January. Not to be confused with **St Anthony of Padua,** who was a Franciscan of the 13th century, and is commemorated on 13th June. *See also* Tantony.

***St Anthony's cross.*** The tau-cross. **T**; used as a sacred symbol and in heraldry.

***St Anthony's fire.*** Erysipelas is so called from the tradition that those who sought the intercession of St Anthony recovered from the pestilential erysipelas called the *sacred fire*, which proved so fatal in 1089.

***St Anthony's pig.*** A pet pig, the smallest of the litter, also called the 'tantony pig' (*q.v.*); in allusion to St Anthony being the patron saint of swineherds.

The term is also used of a sponger or hanger-on. Stow says that the officers of the market used to silt the ears of pigs unfit for food. One day one of the proctors of St Anthony's Hospital tied a bell about a pig whose ear was slit, and no one would ever hurt it. The pig would follow like a dog anyone who fed it.

**Anthroposophus.** The nickname of Thomas Vaughan (1622–66), the alchemist, twin-brother of Henry Vaughan, the Silurist. He was rector of St Bridget's in Brecknockshire, and was so called from his *Anthroposophia Teomagica* (1650), a book written to show the condition of man after death.

**Anti-Christ.** The many legends connected with Antichrist, or the *Man of Sin*, expected by some to precede the second coming of Christ, that were so popular in the Middle Ages are chiefly founded on 2 Thess. 2:1–12, and Rev. 13. In ancient times Antichrist was identified with Caligula, Nero, etc., and there is little doubt that in 2 Thess. 2:7, St Paul was referring to the Roman Empire. Mahomet was also called Antichrist, and the name has been given to many disturbers of the world's peace, even to Napoleon and to William II of Germany (*see* Number of the Beast). The Mohammedans have a legend that Christ will slay the Antichrist at the gate of the church at Lydda, in Palestine.

**Antigone.** The subject of a tragedy by Sophocles; daughter of Oedipus by his mother, Jocasta. In consequence of disobeying an edict of Creon she was imprisoned in a cave, where she slew herself. She was famed for her devotion to her brother, Polynices, hence the Duchess of Angoulême (1778–1851), sister and constant companion of Louis XVII, was sometimes called *the Modern Antigone.*

**Antimony.** A word of unknown, but (as it was introduced through alchemy) probably of Arabian, origin. 'Popular etymology' has been busy with this word, and Johnson – copying earlier writers – in his Dictionary derives it from the Greek *antimonachos* (bad for monks), telling the story that a prior once gave some of this mineral to his convent pigs, who thrived upon it, and became very fat. He next tried it on the monks, who died from its effects.

**Antinomian.** (Gr. *anti-nomos*, exempt from the law). One who believes that Christians are not bound to observe the 'law of God', but 'may continue in sin that grace may abound'. The term was first applied to John Agricola by Martin Luther, and was given to a sect that arose in Germany about 1535.

**Antinous.** A model of manly beauty. He was the page of Hadrian, the Roman Emperor.

**Anti-pope.** A pope chosen or nominated by temporal authority in opposition to one canonically elected by the cardinals; or one who usurps the popedom: the term is particularly applied (by the opposite party) to those popes who resided at Avignon during the Great Schism of the West, 1309–76.

**Antiquarian.** A standard size of drawing paper measuring 53 in. by 31 in.

**Antisthenes.** Founder of the Cynic School in Athens, born about 444 BC, died about 370. He wore a ragged cloak, and carried a wallet and staff like a beggar. Socrates, whose pupil he was, wittily said he could 'see rank pride peering through the holes of Antisthenes' rags'.

**Antoninus. *The Wall of Antoninus.*** A wall of regularly laid sods resting on a stone pavement, built by the Romans about 100 miles north of Hadrian's Wall, from Dumbarton on the Clyde to Carriden on the Forth, under the direction of Lollius Urbicus, governor of the province under Antoninus Pius, about AD 140. It was probably about 14 ft thick at the base and about the same height; it was fortified at frequent intervals, and was fronted by a deep ditch.

**Antony.** *See* Anthony.

**Antrustions** (O.Fr., from O.H.Ger. *trôst*, trust, fidelity). The chief followers of the Frankish kings, who were specially trusty to them.

None but the king could have antrustions.

Stubbs, *Constitutional History*, I. ix

**Anubis.** In *Egyptian mythology*, similar to the Hermes of Greece, whose office it was to take the souls of the dead before the judge of the infernal regions. Anubis was the son of Osiris the judge, and is represented with a human body and jackal's head.

**Anvil.** *It is on the anvil*, under deliberation; the project is in hand. Of course, the reference is to a smithy.

> She had another arrangement on the anvil.
> Le Fanu, *The House in the Churchyard*

**Anyhow,** i.e. in an irregular manner. 'He did it anyhow', in a careless, slovenly manner. 'He went on anyhow', in a wild, reckless manner.

***Anyhow, you must manage it for me.*** By hook or crook; at all events.

**Aonian.** Poetical, pertaining to the Muses. The Muses, according to *Grecian mythology*, dwelt in Aonia, that part of Boeotia which contains Mount Helicon and the Muses' Fountain. Milton speaks of 'the Aonian mount' (*Paradise Lost*, i, 15), and Thomson calls the fraternity of poets

> The Aonian hive
> Who praiséd are, and starve right merrily.
> *Castle of Indolence*, ii, 2

**À outrance.** *See* À l'outrance.

**Apache.** The name of a tribe of North American Indians, given to – or adopted by – the hooligans and roughs of Paris about the opening of the present century. The use of the name for this purpose has a curious parallel in the Mohocks (*q.v.*) of the 17th century.

**Ape.** *The buffoon ape*, in Dryden's *The Hind and the Panther*, means the Freethinkers.

> Next her [*the bear*] the buffoon ape, as atheists use,
> Mimicked all sects, and had his own to choose.
> Part i, 39

***He keeps them, like an ape, in the corner of his jaw; first mouthed, to be last swallowed*** (*Hamlet* 4, 2). Most of the Old World monkeys have cheek pouches, which they use as receptacles for food.

***To lead apes in hell.*** It is an old saying (frequent in the Elizabethan dramatists) that this is the fate of old maids. Hence, *ape-leader*, an old maid.

> I will even take sixpence in earnest of the bear-ward, and lead his apes into hell.
> Shakespeare, *Much Ado about Nothing*, 2, 1
>
> Women, dying maids, lead apes in hell.
> *The London Prodigal*, i, 2
>
> I will rather hazard my being one of the Devil's Ape-leaders, than to marry while he is melancholy.
> Brome, *The Jovial Crew*, ii

***To play the ape,*** to play practical jokes; to play silly tricks; to make facial imitations, like an ape.

***To put an ape into your hood*** (or) ***cap*** – i.e. to make a fool of you. Apes were formerly carried on the shoulders of fools and simpletons.

***To say an ape's paternoster,*** is to chatter with fright or cold, like an ape. One of the books in Rabelais' 'Library of St Victor' is called 'The Ape's Paternoster'.

**Apelles.** A famous Grecian painter, contemporary with Alexander the Great. He was born at Colophon, on the coast of Asia Minor, and is known as the *Chian painter* –

> The Chian painter, when he was required
> To portrait Venus in her perfect hue,
> To make his work more absolute, desired
> Of all the fairest maids to have the view.
> Spenser, *Dedicatory Sonnets*, 17

**Apemantus.** A churlish philosopher, in *Timon of Athens*.

> The cynicism of Apemantus contrasted with the misanthropy of Timon. Sir Walter Scott

**A-per-se.** An A1; a person or thing of unusual merit. 'A' all alone, with no one who can follow, *nemo proximus aut secundus*.

Chaucer calls Cresseide 'the floure and A-per-se of Troi and Greek'.

> London, thou art of townës *A-per-se*.
> Dunbar (1501)

**Apex.** The topmost height, summit, or tiptop; originally the pointed olive-wood spike on the top of the cap of a Roman flamen; also the crest or spike of a helmet.

**Aphrodite** (Gr. *aphros*, foam). The Greek Venus; so called because she sprang from the foam of the sea.

***Aphrodite's girdle.*** The cestus (*q.v.*).

**Apicius.** A gourmand. Marcus Gabius Apicius was a Roman gourmand of the time of Augustus and Tiberius, whose income being reduced by his luxurious living to only ten million sesterces (about £80,000), put an end to his life, to avoid the misery of being obliged to live on plain diet.

**A-pigga-back.** *See* Pick-a-back.

**Apis.** In *Egyptian mythology*, the bull of Memphis, sacred to Osiris of whose soul it was supposed to be the image. The sacred bull had to have natural spots on the forehead forming a triangle, and a half-moon on the breast. It was not suffered to live more than twenty-five years, when it was sacrificed and buried with great pomp. Cambyses, King of Persia (529–22 BC), and conqueror of Egypt, slew the sacred bull of

Memphis with his own hands, and is said to have become mad in consequence.

**Aplomb** (Fr. *à plomb*, according to the plummet). True to the plumbline; that self-possession which arises from perfect self-confidence. We talk of a dancer's aplomb, meaning that he has perfect mastery of his art.

> Here exists the best stock in the world ... men of aplomb and reserve, of great range and many moods, of strong instincts, yet apt for culture.
>
> Emerson, *English Traits*, p. 130

**Apocalyptic Number.** 666. *See* Number of the Beast.

**Apocrypha** (Gr. *apokrupto*, hidden); hence, of unknown authorship: the explanation given in the Preface to the Apocrypha in the 1539 Bible that the books are so called 'because they were wont to be read not openly ... but, as it were, in secret and apart' is not tenable. Those books included in the Septuagint and Vulgate versions of the Old Testament, but which, at the Reformation, were excluded from the Sacred Canon by the Protestants, mainly on the grounds that they were not originally written in Hebrew, and were not looked upon as genuine by the Jews. They are not printed in Protestant Bibles in ordinary circulation, but in the Authorised Version, as printed in 1611, they are given immediately after the Old Testament. The books are as follows:

| | |
|---|---|
| 1 and 2 Esdras. | Baruch, with the Epistle of Jeremiah. |
| Tobit. | The Song of the Three Children. |
| Judith. | The Story of Susanna. |
| The rest of Esther. | The Idol Bel and the Dragon. |
| Wisdom. | 1 and 2 Maccabees. |
| Ecclesiasticus. | |

The New Testament also has a large number of apocryphal books more or less attached to it: these consist of later gospels and epistles, apocalypses, etc., as well as such recently discovered fragments as the *Logia* (sayings of Jesus) of the Oxyrhynchus papyrus. The best known books of the New Testament apocrypha are:

- Protevangelium, or the Book of James.
- Gospel of Nicodemus, or the Acts of Pilate.
- The Ascents of James.
- The Acts of Paul and Thecla.
- Letters of Abgarus to Christ.
- Epistles of Paul to the Laodiceans, and to the Alexandrines, and the Third Epistle to the Corinthians.
- The Teaching of the Apostles (Didaché).
- The three Books of the Shepherd of Hermas.

**Apollinarians.** An heretical sect founded in the middle of the 4th century by Apollinaris, a presbyter of Laodicea. They denied that Christ had a human soul, and asserted that the *Logos* supplied its place. The heresy was condemned at the Council of Chalcedon, the fourth General Council, 451.

**Apollo.** In *Greek* and *Roman mythology*, son of Zeus and Leto (Latona), one of the great gods of Olympus, typifying the sun in its light- and life-giving as well as in its destroying power; often identified with Helios, the sun-god. He was god of music, poetry, and the healing art, the latter of which he bestowed on his son, Aesculapius. He is represented in art as the perfection of youthful manhood.

> The fire-robed god,
> Golden Apollo.
>
> Shakespeare, *Winter's Tale*, 4, 4

> Apollo with the plectrum strook
> The chords, and from beneath his hands a crash
> Of mighty sounds rushed forth, whose music shook
> The soul with sweetness, and like an adept
> His sweeter voice a just accordance kept.
>
> Shelley, *Homer's Hymn to Mercury*, lxxxv

***A perfect Apollo.*** A model of manly beauty, referring to the Apollo Belvidere (*q.v.*).

> A young Apollo, golden-haired,
> Stands dreaming on the verge of strife.
> Magnificently unprepared
> For the long littleness of life.
>
> Mrs Cornford, *Epigram on Rupert Brooke*

***The Apollo of Portugal.*** Luis Camoëns (*c.*1524–80), author of the *Lusiad*; he was god of poetry in Portugal, but was allowed to die in the streets of Lisbon like a dog, literally of starvation. Our own Otway suffered a similar fate.

***Apollo Belvidere.*** An ancient marble statue, supposed to be a Roman-Greek copy of a bronze votive statue set up at Delphi in commemoration of the repulsion of an attack by the Gauls on the shrine of Apollo in 279 BC. It represents the god holding the remains of a bow, or (according to some conjectures) an aegis, in his left hand, and is called Belvidere from the Belvidere Gallery of the Vatican, where it stands. It was discovered in 1495, amidst the ruins of Antium, and was purchased by Pope Julius II.

**Apollodoros.** Plato says: 'Who would not rather be a man of sorrows than Apollodoros, envied by all for his enormous wealth, yet nourishing in his heart the scorpions of a guilty conscience?' (*The Republic*). This Apollodoros was the tyrant of Cassandrea. He obtained the supreme power

379 BC, exercised it with the utmost cruelty, and was put to death by Antigonos Gonatas.

**Apollonius of Tyre.** *See* Pericles.

**Apollyon.** The Greek name of Abaddon (*q.v.*), king of hell and angel of the bottomless pit (Rev. 9:11). His introduction by Bunyan into the *Pilgrim's Progress* has made his name familiar.

**Aposiopesis.** *See* Quos ego.

**Apostate, The.** Julian, the Roman emperor (331–63). He was brought up as a Christian, but on his accession to the throne (361) he announced his conversion to paganism and proclaimed the free toleration of all religions.

**A posteriori** (Lat. from the latter). An *a posteriori* argument is proving the cause from the effect. Thus, if we see a watch we conclude there was a watchmaker. Robinson Crusoe inferred there was another human being on the desert island, because he saw a human footprint in the wet sand. It is thus the existence and character of Deity is inferred from His works. *See* A priori.

**Apostles.** In the preamble of the statutes instituting the Order of St Michael, founded in 1469 by Louis XI, the archangel is styled 'my lord', and is created a knight. The apostles had been already ennobled and knighted. We read of 'the Earl Peter', 'Count Paul', 'the Baron Stephen', and so on. Thus, in the introduction of a sermon upon St Stephen's Day, we have these lines:

> Contes vous vueille la patron
> De St Estieul le baron.

The Apostles were gentlemen of bloude … and Christ … might, if He had esteemed of the vayne glorye of this world, have born coat armour. *The Blazon of Gentrie*

The badges or symbols of the fourteen apostles (i.e. the twelve original apostles with Matthias and Paul).

Andrew, an X-*shaped cross*, because he was crucified on one.

Bartholomew, *a knife*, because he was flayed with a knife.

James the Great, *a scallop-shell*, *a pilgrim's staff*, or *a gourd bottle*, because he is the patron saint of pilgrims. *See* Scallop-Shell.

James the Less, *a fuller's pole*, because he was killed by a blow on the head with a pole, dealt him by Simeon the fuller.

John, *a cup with a winged serpent flying out of it*, in allusion to the tradition about Aristodemos, priest of Diana, who challenged John to drink a cup of poison. John made the sign of a cross on the cup, Satan like a dragon flew from it, and John then drank the cup which was quite innocuous.

Judas Iscariot, *a bag*, because he had the bag and 'bare what was put therein' (John, 7:6).

Jude, *a club*, because he was martyred with a club.

Matthew *a hatchet* or *halberd*, because he was slain at Nadabar with a halberd.

Matthias, *a battleaxe*, because he was first stoned, and then beheaded with a battleaxe.

Paul, *a sword*, because his head was cut off with a sword. The convent of La Lisla, in Spain, boasts of possessing the very instrument.

Peter, *a bunch of keys*, because Christ gave him the 'keys of the kingdom of heaven'. *A cock*, because he went out and wept bitterly when he heard the cock crow (Matt. 26:75).

Philip, *a long staff surmounted with a cross*, because he suffered death by being suspended by the neck to a tall pillar.

Simon, *a saw*, because he was sawn to death, according to tradition.

Thomas, *a lance*, because he was pierced through the body, at Meliapour, with a lance.

*See* Evangelists.

***Apostles, where buried.*** According to Catholic legend, seven of the Apostles are buried at Rome. These seven are distinguished by a star (*).

Andrew lies buried at Amalfi (Naples).

Bartholomew,* at Rome, in the church of Bartholomew Island, on the Tiber.

James the Great was buried at St Jago de Compostella, in Spain.

James the Less,* at Rome, in the church of SS Philip and James.

John, at Ephesus.

Jude,* at Rome.

Matthew, at Salerno (Naples).

Matthias,* at Rome, under the altar of the Basilica.

Paul, somewhere in Italy.

Peter,* at Rome, in the church of St Peter.

Philip,* at Rome.

Simon or Simeon,* at Rome.

Thomas, at Ortona (Naples). (? Madras.)

The supposed remains of Mark the Evangelist were buried at Venice, about 800.

Luke the Evangelist is said to have been buried at Padua.

N.B. – Italy claims thirteen of these apostles or evangelists – Rome seven, Naples three, Mark at Venice, Luke at Padua, and Paul.

***Apostles of***

*Abyssinians*, St Frumentius. (Fourth century.)

*Alps*, Felix Neff. (1798–1829.)

*Andalusia*, Juan de Avila. (1500–69.)

*Ardennes*, St Hubert. (656–727.)

*Armenians*, Gregory of Armenia, 'The Illuminator'. (256–331.)

*Brazil*, José de Anchieta, a Jesuit missionary. (1533–97.)

*English*, St Augustine. (Died 604.) St George.
*Ethiopia*. *See* Abyssinians.
*Free Trade*. Richard Cobden. (1804–65.)
*French*, St Denis. (Third century.)
*Frisians*, St Willibrord. (657–738.)
*Gauls*, St Irenaeus (130–200); St Martin of Tours (338–401).
*Gentiles*, St Paul.
*Germany*, St Boniface. (680–755.)
*Highlanders*, St Columba. (521–97.)
*Hungary*, St Anastatius. (954–1044.)
*Indians* (*American*), Bartolomé de Las Casas (1474–1566); John Eliot (1604–90).
*Indies* (*East*), St Francis Xavier. (1506–52.)
*Infidelity*, Voltaire. (1694–1778.)
*Ireland*, St Patrick. (373–463.)
*North*, St Ansgar or Anscarius, missionary to Scandinavia (801–64); Bernard Gilpin, Archdeacon of Durham, evangelist on the Scottish border. (1517–83.)
*Peru*, Alonzo de Barcena, a Jesuit missionary. (1528–98.)
*Picts*, St Ninian. (Fifth century.)
*Scottish Reformers*, John Knox. (1505–72.)
*Slavs*, St Cyril, (*c*.820–69.)
*Spain*, St James the Great. (Died 62.)
*The Sword*, Mahomet. (570–632.)
*Temperance*, Father Mathew. (1790–1856.)
*Yorkshire*, Paulinus, bishop of York and Rochester. (Died 644.)
*Wales*, St David. (Died about 601.)

***The Cambridge Apostles.*** *See* Cambridge.

***Prince of the Apostles.*** St Peter (Matt. 16:18, 19).

***The Twelve Apostles.*** The last twelve names on the poll or list of ordinary degrees were so called, when the list was arranged in order of merit, and not alphabetically, as now; they were also called the *Chosen Twelve*. The last of the twelve was designated 'St Paul', from a play on the verse 1 Cor. 15:9. The same term was later applied to the last twelve in the Mathematical Tripos.

***Apostle Spoons.*** Spoons having the figure of one of the apostles at the top of the handle, formerly given at christenings. Sometimes twelve spoons, representing the twelve apostles; sometimes four, representing the four evangelists; and sometimes only one, was presented. Occasionally a set occurs containing in addition the 'Master Spoon' and the 'Lady Spoon'.

***The Apostles' Creed.*** A church creed supposed to be an epitome of doctrine taught by the apostles. It was received into the Latin Church, in its present form, in the 11th century; but a formula somewhat like it existed in the 2nd century. Items were added in the 4th and 5th centuries, and verbal alterations much later.

**Apostolic Fathers.** Christian authors born in the 1st century, when the apostles lived. John is supposed to have died about AD 99, and Polycarp, the last of the Apostolic Fathers, born about 69, was his disciple. Clement of Rome (died about 100), Ignatius (died about 115), Polycarp (about 69–155), St Barnabas, to whom an apocryphal epistle (now usually assigned to the 2nd century) was ascribed by Clemens Alexandrinus and Origen (martyred, 61), Hermas (author of *The Shepherd of Hermas*, and possibly identical with the Hermas of Rom. 16:14), and Papias, a bishop of Hierapolis, mentioned by Eusebius.

**Apostolic Majesty.** A title borne by the former emperors of Austria, as kings of Hungary. It was conferred by Pope Sylvester II on the King of Hungary in 1000. *Cp.* Religious.

**Apostolicals.** An heretical sect founded by Gerard Sagarelli of Parma in the 13th century, later called Dulcinists (*q.v.*).

**Apparel.** One meaning of this word used to be 'ornament' or 'embellishment', especially the embroidery on ecclesiastical vestments. In the 19th century it was revived, and applied to the ornamental parts of the alb at the lower edge and at the wrists. Pugin says:

> The albe should be made with apparels worked in silk or gold, embroidered with ornaments.
>
> *Glossary of Ecclesiastical Ornament* (1844)

**Appeal to the Country, To.** To ask the nation to express their opinion of some moot question. In order to obtain such public opinion Parliament must be dissolved and a general election held.

**Appiades.** Five divinities whose temple stood near the fountains of Appius, in Rome. Their names are Venus, Pallas, Concord, Peace, and Vesta. They were represented on horseback, like Amazons.

**Appian Way.** The oldest and best of all the Roman roads, leading from Rome to Brundisium (Brindisi) by way of Capua. This 'queen of roads' was commenced by Appius Claudius, the decemvir, 313 BC.

**Apple. *Newton and the apple.*** The well-known story originated with Voltaire, who tells us that Mrs Conduit, Newton's niece, told him that Newton was at Woolsthorpe (visiting his mother) in 1666, when, seeing an apple fall, he was led into the train of thought which resulted in his establishment of the law of gravitation (1685).

***The Apple of Discord.*** A cause of dispute; something to contend about. At the marriage of

Thetis and Peleus, where all the gods and goddesses met together, Discord (Eris), who had not been invited, threw on the table a golden apple 'for the most beautiful'. Juno, Minerva, and Venus put in their separate claims; the point was referred to Paris (*q.v.*), who gave judgment in favour of Venus. This brought upon him the vengeance of Juno and Minerva, to whose spite the fall of Troy is attributed.

*The 'apple' appears more than once in Greek story; *see* Atalanta's Race; Hesperides.

Of course, the story of Eve and the apple will be familiar to every reader of this dictionary, but it is a mistake to suppose that the apple is mentioned in the Bible story. We have no further particulars than that it was 'the fruit of that forbidden tree', and the Mohammedans leave the matter equally vague, though their commentators hazard the guess that it may have been an ear of wheat, or the fruit of the vine or the fig. The apple is a comparatively late conjecture.

For the story of William Tell and the apple, *see* Tell.

***Prince Ahmed's apple.*** In the *Arabian Nights* story of Prince Ahmed, a cure for every disorder. The prince purchased it at Samarcand.

***Apples of Istakhar*** are 'all sweetness on one side, and all bitterness on the other'.

***Apples of Paradise,*** according to tradition, had a bite on one side, to commemorate the bite given by Eve.

***The apples of perpetual youth.*** In *Scandinavian mythology*, the golden apples of perpetual youth, in the keeping of Idhunn, daughter of the dwarf Svald, and wife of Bragi. It is by tasting them that the gods preserve their youth.

***Apples of Pyban,*** says Sir John Mandeville, fed the pigmies with their odour only.

***Apples of Sodom.*** Thevenot says – 'There are apple-trees on the sides of the Dead Sea which bear lovely fruit, but within are full of ashes.' Josephus, Strabo, Tacitus, and others speak of these apples, and are probably referring to the gall-nuts produced by the insect *Cynips insana*. The phrase is used figuratively for anything disappointing.

> You see, my lords, what goodly fruit she seems;
> Yet like those apples travellers report
> To grow where Sodom and Gomorrah stood,
> I will but touch her, and straight you will see
> She'll fall to soot and ashes.
>
> Webster, *Vittoria, Corombona*

***The apple of the eye.*** The pupil, because it was anciently supposed to be a round solid ball like an apple. Figuratively applied to anything extremely dear or extremely sensitive.

> He kept him as the apple of his eye.
>
> Deut. 32:10

**Apple-jack.** An apple-turnover is sometimes so called in East Anglia. In the United States the name is given to a drink distilled from fermented apple juice – like cider, but spirituous.

**Apple-john.** An apple so called from its being at maturity about St John's Day (Dec. 27th). We are told that apple-johns will keep for two years, and are best when shrivelled.

> I am withered like an old apple-john.
>
> Shakespeare, 1 *Henry IV*, 3, 3

Sometimes called the Apples of King John, which, if correct, would militate against the notion about 'St John's Day'.

> There were some things, for instance, the Apples of King John, ... I should be tempted to buy.
>
> Bigelow, *Life of B. Franklin*

**Apple-pie Bed.** A bed in which the sheets are so folded that a person cannot get his legs down; perhaps a corruption of 'a *nap-pe-pli* bed', from the Fr. *nappe pliée*, a folded sheet.

**Apple-pie Order.** Prim and precise order.

The origin of this phrase is still doubtful. Some suggest *cap-à-pie*, like a knight in complete armour. Some tell us that apples made into a pie are quartered and methodically arranged when the cores have been taken out. Perhaps the suggestion made above of *nap-pe-pli* (Fr. *nappes pliées*, folded linen, neat as folded linen) is nearer the mark. It has also been suggested that it may be a corruption of *alpha, beta*, meaning as orderly as the letters of the alphabet; and another guess is that it is connected with the old alphabet rhyme, 'A was an apple pie,' etc., the letters of the alphabet being there all 'in apple-pie order'.

**Après moi le déluge.** *See* After me.

**April.** The month when trees unfold and the womb of Nature opens with young life. (Lat. *aperire*, to open.)

> The old Dutch name was *Gras-maand* (grass-month); the old Saxon, *Easter-monath* (orient or pascal-month). In the French Republican calendar it was called *Germinal* (the time of budding, March 21st to April 19th).

**April Fool.** Called in France *un poisson d'Avril* (*q.v.*), and in Scotland a *gowk* (cuckoo). In Hindustan similar tricks are played at the Huli Festival (March 31st). So that it cannot refer to the uncertainty of the weather, nor yet to the mockery trial of our Redeemer, the two most popular explanations. A better solution is this: As March 25th used to be New Year's Day, April 1st was its octave, when its festivities culminated and ended.

It may be a relic of the Roman 'Cerealia', held at the beginning of April. The tale is that Proserpina was sporting in the Elysian meadows, and had just filled her lap with daffodils, when Pluto carried her off to the lower world. Her mother, Ceres, heard the echo of her screams, and went in search of 'the voice'; but her search was a fool's errand, it was hunting the gowk, or looking for the 'echo of a scream'.

Of course this fable is an allegory of seed-time.

**April Gentleman.** A man newly married, who has made himself thus 'an April fool'.

**April morn.** One's wedding day; the day when one was made a fool of. The allusion is obvious.

**April Squire.** A *novus homo*: a successful parvenu who has retired into the country, where his money may give him the position of a squire.

**A priori** (Lat. from an antecedent). An *a priori* argument is one in which a fact is deduced from something antecedent, as when we infer certain effects from given causes. All mathematical proofs are of the *a priori* kind, whereas judgments in the law courts are usually *a posteriori* (*q.v.*); we infer the *animus* from the act.

**Apron** (O.Fr. *napperon*). Originally *napron* in English, this word is representative of a considerable number that have either lost or gained an 'n' through coalescence – or the reverse – with the article 'a' or 'an'. *A napron* became *an apron*. Other examples are *adder* for *a nadder*, *auger* for *a nauger*, and *umpire* for *a numpire*. The opposite coalescence may be seen in *newt* for *an ewt*, *nickname* for *an ekename*, and the old *nuncle* for *mine uncle*. *Cp.* Nonce.

A bishop's apron represents the short cassock which, by the 74th canon, all clergymen were enjoined to wear.

***Apron-string tenure.*** A tenure held in virtue of one's wife.

***Tied to his mother's apron-string.*** Completely under his mother's thumb. Applied to a big boy or young man who is still under mother rule.

**A propos de bottes.** *See* Bottes.

**Aqua Regia** (Lat. royal water). A mixture of one part of nitric acid, with from two to four of hydrochloric acid; so called because it dissolves gold, *the king of metals*.

**Aqua Tofana.** A poisonous liquid containing arsenic, much used in Italy in the 17th century by young wives who wanted to get rid of their husbands. It was invented about 1690 by a Greek woman named Tofana, who called it the *Manna of St Nicholas of Bari*, from the widespread notion that an oil of miraculous efficacy flowed from the tomb of that saint. In Italian called also *Aquella di Napoli*.

**Aqua Vitae** (Lat. *water of life*). Brandy; any spirituous liquor; also, formerly, certain ardent spirits used by the alchemists. Ben Jonson terms a seller of such an 'aqua-vitae man' (*Alchemist*, i. 1). The 'elixir of life' (*q.v.*) was made from these spirits. *See* Eau-de-Vie.

**Aquarians.** A sect in the early Christian Church which insisted on the use of water instead of wine in the Lord's Supper.

**Aquarius** (Lat. the water-bearer). The eleventh of the twelve zodiacal constellations, representing the figure of a man with his left hand raised and with his right pouring from a ewer a stream of water; it is the eleventh division of the ecliptic, which the sun enters on January 21st, and which does not now coincide with the constellation.

**Aqueous Rocks.** Rocks deposited by the agency of water, such as bedded limestones, sandstones, and clays; in short, practically all the geological rocks which are arranged in layers or strata. *Cp.* Aeolian Rocks.

**Aquila non captat muscas** (Lat.). 'An eagle does not hawk at flies': a proverbial saying implying that little things are beneath a great man's contempt.

**Aquiline.** Raymond's matchless steed. *See* Horse.

**Aquinian Sage, The.** Juvenal is so called because he was born at Aquinum, a town of the Volscians.

**Arabesque.** An adjective and noun applied to the Arabian and Moorish style of decoration and architecture, such as can best be studied at the Alhambra, near Granada. One of its chief features is that no representation of animal forms is admitted. During the Spanish wars in the reign of Louis XIV, arabesque decorations were profusely introduced into France.

**Arabia.** It was Ptolemy who was the author of the threefold division into *Arabia Petraea*, 'Stony Arabia'; *Arabia Felix* (*Yemen*), 'Fertile Arabia', i.e. the south-west coast; and *Arabia Deserta*, 'Desert Arabia'.

**Arabian Bird, The.** The phoenix; hence, figuratively, a marvellous or unique person.

All of her that is out of door most rich!
If she be furnish'd with a mind so rare,
She is alone the Arabian bird.

Shakespeare, *Cymbeline*, 1, 6

**Arabian Nights Entertainments, The.** A collection of ancient Oriental tales, first collected in its present form about 1450, probably in Cairo. The first European translation was the French one by Antoine Galland (12 vols, 1704–8), which is a free rendering of the oldest known MS (1548). There are English translations founded on this by R. Heron (4 vols, 1792), W. Beloe (4 vols., 1795), and others. In 1840 E. W. Lane published an entirely new translation (3 vols), made from the latest Arabic edition (Cairo, 1835); John Payne's translation appeared in 4 vols, 1882–4, and Sir Richard Burton's monumental version was issued to subscribers only, by the Kamashastra Society of Benares, in 10 vols, 1885–6, followed by 6 vols of *Supplemental Nights* in 1886–8. The standard French translation is that by J. C. Mardrus, 16 vols, 1899–1904.

**Arabians.** A name given to the early Nestorians and Jacobites in Arabia; also to an heretical Arabian sect of the 3rd century, which maintained that the soul dies with the body; and to a sect which believed that the soul died and rose again with the body.

**Arabic Figures.** The figures 1, 2, 3, 4, etc. So called because they were introduced into Europe (Spain) by the Moors or Arabs (about the end of the 10th century), who brought them from India about 250 years earlier. They were not generally adopted in Europe till after the invention of printing. Far more important than the characters, is the decimalism of these figures: 1 figure = units, 2 figures = tens, 3 figures = hundreds, and so on *ad infinitum*. *Cp.* Numerals.

The figures i, ii, iii, iv, v, vi, vii, viii, ix, x, etc., are called Roman figures.

**Arabs. *Street Arabs.*** Children of the houseless poor; street children. So called because, like the Arabs, they are nomads or wanderers with no settled home.

**Arachne's Labours.** Spinning and weaving. Arachne, in Greek legend, was so skilful a spinner that she challenged Minerva to a trial of skill, and hanged herself because the goddess beat her. Minerva thEn changed her into a spider. Hence **arachnida**, the scientific name for spiders, scorpions, and mites.

Arachne's labours ne'er her hours divide,
Her noble hands nor looms nor spindles guide.

*Hoole's Jerusalem Delivered*, Bk ii

And over them Arachne high did lift
Her cunning web, and spread her subtle net.

Spenser, *Faerie Queene*, II, vii, 28

**Aratus.** A Greek statesman and general (271–13 BC), famous for his patriotism and devotion to freedom. He liberated his native Sicyon from the usurper Nicocles, and would not allow even a picture of a king to exist. He was poisoned by Philip of Macedon.

Aratus, who awhile relumed the soul
Of fondly-lingering liberty in Greece.

Thomson, *Winter*, 491, 492

**Arbaces.** A Mede and Assyrian satrap, who conspired against Sardanapalus, and founded the empire of Media on the ruins of the Assyrian kingdom. (Byron, *Sardanapalus.*)

**Arbor Day.** A day set apart in Canada and the United States for planting trees. It was first inaugurated about 1885 in Nebraska.

**Arbor Judae.** *See* Judas-tree.

**Arcades ambo** (Lat.). From Virgil's seventh Eclogue: '*Ambo florentes aetatibus, Arcades ambo*' (Both in the flower of youth, Arcadians both), meaning 'both poets or musicians', now extended to two persons having tastes or habits in common. Byron gave the phrase a whimsical turn:

Each pulled different ways with many an oath,
'Arcades ambo' – *id est*, blackguards both.

*Don Juan*, IV, xciii

**Arcadia.** A district of the Peloponnesus which, according to Virgil, was the home of pastoral simplicity and happiness. The name was taken by Sidney as the title of his romance (1590), and it was soon generally adopted in English. Hence, *arcadian*.

And Fancy sped
To scenes Arcadian, whispering, through soft air,
Of bliss that grows without a care,
And happiness that never flies.

Wordsworth, *The Gleaner*

**Arcadian Beasts.** An old expression, to be found in Plautus, Pliny, etc. *See Persius*, iii, 9:

Arcadiae pecuaria rudere credas

and *Rabelais*, V, vii. So called because the ancient Arcadians were renowned as simpletons. *Juvenal* (vii, 160) has *arcadicus juvenis*, meaning a stupid youth.

**Arcas.** *See* Calisto.

**Archangel.** In Christian legend, the title is usually given to Michael, the chief opponent of Satan and his angels and the champion of the Church of Christ on earth. In the mediaeval hierarchy (*see* Angel) the Archangels comprise the second order of the third division.

According to the Koran, there are four archangels. *Gabriel*, the angel of revelations, who writes down the divine decrees; *Michael*, the champion, who fights the battles of faith; *Azrael*, the angel of death; and *Israfel*, who is commissioned to sound the trumpet of the resurrection.

**Archers.** The best archers in British history and story are Robin Hood and his two comrades Little John and Will Scarlet.

The famous archers of Henry II were Tepus his bowman of the Guards, Gilbert of the white hind, Hubert of Suffolk, and Clifton of Hampshire.

Nearly equal to these were Egbert of Kent and William of Southampton. *See also* Clym of the Clough.

Domitian, the Roman emperor, we are told, could shoot four arrows between the spread fingers of a man's hand.

Tell, who shot an apple set on the head of his son, is a replica of the Scandinavian tale of Egil, who, at the command of King Nidung, performed a precisely similar feat.

Robin Hood, we are told, could shoot an arrow a mile or more.

**Arches, Court of.** The ecclesiastical court of appeal for the province of Canterbury, which was anciently held in the church of St Mary-le-Bow (*S. Maria de Arcubus*), Cheapside, London.

**Archeus.** The immaterial principle which, according to the Paracelsians, energises all living substances. There were supposed to be numerous *archei*, but the chief one was said to reside in the stomach.

**Archilochian Bitterness** Ill-natured satire, so named from Archilochus, the Greek satirist (fl. 690 BC).

**Archimage.** The name given by Thomson to the 'demon Indolence'. Archimagus is the title borne by the High Priest of the Persian Magi.

'I will,' he cried, 'so help me God! destroy
That villain Archimage.'

Thomson, *Castle of Indolence*, c. ii

**Archimago.** The enchanter in Spenser's *Faërie Queene* (Bks I and II), typifying hypocrisy and false religion. He assumes the guise of the Red Cross Knight, and deceives Una; but Sansloy sets upon him, and reveals his true character. When the Red Cross Knight is about to be married to Una, he presents himself before the King of Eden, and tells him that the Knight is betrothed to Duessa. The falsehood being exposed, Archimago is cast into a vile dungeon (Bk i). In Book ii the arch-hypocrite is loosed again for a season, and employs Braggadocchio to attack the Red Cross Knight. These allegories are pretty obvious: thus the first incident means that Truth (*Una*), when Piety (the *Red Cross Knight*) is absent, is in danger of being led astray by Hypocrisy; but any Infidel (*Sansloy*) can lay bare religious hypocrisy.

Such whenas Archimago them did view
He weenéd well to worke some uncouth wyle.

Spenser, *Faerie Queene*, II, 1, st. 8

* Sometimes Spenser employs the alternative form 'Archimage'.

**Archimedean Principle.** The quantity of water displaced by any body immersed therein will equal in bulk the bulk of the body immersed. This scientific fact was noted by the philosopher Archimedes of Syracuse (*c*.287–12 BC). *See* Eureka.

**Archimedean Screw.** An endless screw, used for raising water, etc., invented by Archimedes.

**Architect of his Own Fortune.** Appius says, '*Fabrum suoe esse quemque fortunae. Cp.* Régnier's '*Chacun est artisan de sa bonne fortune*' (*Sat.* 13), Steele's 'Every man is the maker of his own fortune' (*Tatler, No.* 52), Longfellow's 'All are architects of fate' (*The Builders*), and W. E. Henley's 'I am the master of my fate' (*To R. J. H. B.*). The sentiment is almost as common as it is true.

**Architecture, Orders of.** These five are the classic orders: *Tuscan*, *Doric*, *Ionic*, *Corinthian*, and *Composite*.

In ancient times the following was the *usual* practice:

Corinthian, for temples of Venus, Flora, Proserpine, and the Water Nymphs.

Doric, for temples of Minerva, Mars, and Hercules.

Ionic, for temples of Juno, Diana, and Bacchus.

Tuscan, for grottoes and all rural deities.

**Archon.** In Dryden's poem, *Albion and Albanius*, stands for George Monk, Duke of Albemarle. *See also* Archontics.

**Archontics.** A sect of Gnostics of the 2nd century who held a number of idle stories about creation, which they attributed to a number of agents called 'archons'. In ancient Greece the **archon** was a chief magistrate; the Gnostics applied the word as a subordinate power (analogous, perhaps, to the angels), who, at the bidding of God, made the world.

**Arcite.** A young Theban knight, made captive by Duke Theseus, and imprisoned with Palamon at Athens. Both captives fell in love with Emily, the duke's sister, sister-in-law, or daughter (according to different versions), and after they had gained their liberty Emily was promised by the duke to the victor in a tournament. Arcite won, but, as he was riding to receive the prize, he was thrown from his horse and killed. Emily became the bride of Palamon. *See* Chaucer's *Knight's Tale*, and Dryden's version, *Palamon and Arcite*; also Fletcher and Shakespeare's *Two Noble Kinsmen.* Chaucer derived the story from Boccaccio's *Teseide.* The Arcite of his *Compleynte of Faire Anelida and False Arcite* is a different person altogether. Chaucer says he found the story 'in Latyn', but the original has not been discovered.

**Arcos Barbs.** War steeds of Arcos, in Andalusia, very famous in Spanish ballads. *See* Barb.

**Arctic Region** means the region of *Arcturos* (the Bear stars), from Gr. *arktos*, meaning both the animal and the constellation, and *arktikos*, pertaining to the bear, hence, northern. *Arcturus* (the bear-ward) is the name now given to the brightest star in Boötes that can be readily found by following the curve of the Great Bear's tail; but in Job 38:32, it means the Great Bear itself.

**Arden, Enoch.** The story in Tennyson's poem of this name, first published in 1864 (of a husband who mysteriously and unwillingly disappears, and returns years later to find that his wife – who still loves his memory – is married to another), was, he says –

> founded on a theme given me by the sculptor Woolner. I believe that his particular story came out of Suffolk, but something like the same story is told in Brittany and elsewhere.

It is not uncommon, either in fact or fiction. Tennyson said that several similar true stories had been sent to him since its publication, and four years before it appeared Adelaide Anne Procter's *Homeward Bound*, to which *Enoch Arden* bears a strong resemblance, was published in her *Legends and Lyrics* (1858). Mrs Gaskell's *Manchester Marriage* has a similar plot.

**Area-sneak.** A boy or girl who sneaks about areas to commit petty thefts.

**Areopagus** (Gr. the hill of Mars, or Ares). The seat of a famous tribunal in Athens; so called from the tradition that the first cause tried there was that of Mars or Ares, accused by Neptune of the death of his son Halirrhothius.

> Then Paul stood in the midst of Mars' Hill.
> Acts 17:22

**Ares.** The god of war in *Greek mythology*, son of Zeus and Hera. In certain aspects he corresponds with the Roman Mars.

**Aretinian Syllables.** *Ut*, *re*, *mi*, *fa*, *sol*, *la*, used by Guido d'Arezzo in the 11th century for his hexachord, or scale of six notes. They are the first syllables of some words in the opening stanza of a hymn for St John's Day (*see* Doh). *Si*, the seventh note, was not introduced till the 17th century.

**Argand Lamp.** A lamp with a circular wick, through which a current of air flows, to supply oxygen to the flame, and increase its brilliancy. Invented by Aimé Argand, 1789.

**Argante.** A giantess of unbridled licentiousness, in Spenser's *Faërie Queene*.

> That geauntesse Arganté is behight,
> A daughter of the Titans …
> Her sire Typhoeus was … Bk iii, 7, st. 47

**Argantes.** A Circassian of high rank and matchless courage, but fierce to brutality. He was sent as an ambassador from Egypt to King Aladine, and was slain by Rinaldo. (Tasso, *Jerusalem Delivered.*)

> Bonaparte stood before the deputies like the Argantes of Italy's heroic poet, and gave them the choice of peace and war, with the air of a superior being, capable at once of dictating their fate. Sir Walter Scott

**Argenis.** A political allegory by John Barclay, written originally in Latin and published in 1621. It is apparently a romance of gallantry and heroism, and it contains double meanings throughout. 'Sicily' is France, 'Poliarchus' (with whom Argenis is in love), Henry IV, 'Hyanisbe', Queen Elizabeth, and so on. It deals with the state of Europe, and more especially of France, during the time of the league.

**Argentile** and **Curan.** A story printed from Warner's *Albion's England* (1586) in Percy's *Reliques.* Argentile was daughter of King Adelbright, who, on his deathbed, committed her in charge to King Edel. Edel kept her a close prisoner, under hope of getting her lands and dominion. Curan, son of a Danske king, in order to woo her became a kitchen hand in Edel's household, and Edel resolved to marry Argentile to this drudge, but she fled. Curan now turned shepherd, and fell in love with a neatherd's maid, who turned out to be Argentile. The two were married, and Curan claiming his wife's dominions, became King of Northumberland, and put Edel to death.

**Argentine, The.** The name originally given to the river was Rio de la Plata; this was translated by English mariners as 'the Plate', or the River of Silver; and the Latin for silver is *argentum*.

**Argo** (Gr. *argos*, swift). The galley of Jason that went in search of the Golden Fleece.

> The wondred Argo, which in venturous peece,
> First through the Euxine seas bore all the flower of Greece. Spenser, *Faerie Queene*, II, xii, 44

The story is told by Apollonius of Rhodes. Hence, a ship sailing on any specially adventurous voyage, and figuratively.

> Such an Argo, when freighted with such a fleece, will unquestionably be held in chase by many a pirate. Brooke, *Fool of Quality*

**Argonauts.** The sailors of the ship *Argo*, who sailed from Greece to Colchis in quest of the Golden Fleece. The name is also given to the paper nautilus, a cephalopod mollusc.

**Argosy.** Originally a merchant ship built at, or sailing from, Ragusa in Dalmatia. The word is particularly interesting as an early example of the adaptation of a place-name to ordinary use; it was frequent in the 16th-century English.

> He hath an argosy bound to Tripolis, another to the Indies … a third to Mexico, a fourth to England.
> Shakespeare, *Merchant of Venice*, 1, 3

**Argot.** Slang or flash language. The word is French, and was formerly used only for the canting jargon of thieves, rogues, and vagabonds.

**Argus-eyed.** Jealously watchful. According to *Grecian fable*, the fabulous creature, Argus, had 100 eyes, and Juno set him to watch Io, of whom she was jealous. Mercury, however, charmed Argus to sleep and slew him; whereupon Juno changed him into a peacock with the eyes in the tail (*cp.* Peacock's Feather). Hence the name *Argus* for a genus of Asiatic pheasants.

> Return to your charge, be Argus-eyed,
> Awake to the affair you have in hand.
> Ben Jonson, *Staple of News*, III, ii
>
> So praysen babes the Peacocks spotted traine,
> And wondren at bright Argus blazing eye.
> Spenser, *Shepherd's Calendar*, October

**Argyle,** of whom Thomson says, in his *Autumn* (928–30) –

> On thee, Argyle,
> Her hope, her stay, her darling, and her boast,
> Thy fond, imploring country turns her eye –

was John, the *great duke*, who lived only two years after he succeeded to the dukedom. Pope (*Ep. Sat.* ii, 86, 87) says –

> Argyle the state's whole thunder born to wield,
> And shake alike the senate and the field.

*God bless the Duke of Argyle.* A humorous phrase, supposed to be addressed to Highlanders when they scratched themselves. All Highlanders were supposed to be to some extent infested with lice, and the story is that a Duke of Argyle caused posts to be erected in a treeless portion of his estates so that his cattle might have the opportunity of rubbing themselves against them and so easing themselves of the 'torment of flies'. It was not long before the herdsmen discovered the efficacy of the practice, and as they rubbed their itching backs against the posts they thankfully muttered the above words.

**Ariadne.** In *Greek mythology*, daughter of the Cretan king, Minos. She helped Theseus to escape from the labyrinth, and later went with him to Naxos, where he deserted her and she became the wife of Bacchus (*q.v.*).

**Arians.** The followers of Arius, a presbyter of the church of Alexandria, in the 4th century. He maintained (1) that the Father and Son are distinct beings; (2) that the Son, though divine, is not equal to the Father; (3) that the Son had a state of existence previous to His appearance on earth, but not from eternity; and (4) that the Messiah was not real man, but a divine being in a case of flesh. Their tenets varied from time to time and also among their different sections. The heresy was formally anathematised at the Council of Nice (325), but the sect was not, and never has been, wholly extinguished. *See* Anomoeans.

**Ariel.** The name of a spirit. Used in cabalistic angelology, and in Heywood's *Hierarchie of the Blessed Angels* (1635) for one of the seven angelic 'princes' who rule the waters; by Milton for one of the rebel angels (*Paradise Lost*, vi, 371); by Pope (*Rape of the Lock*) for a sylph, the guardian of Belinda; but especially by Shakespeare, in the *Tempest*, for 'an ayrie spirit'.

> He was enslaved to the witch Sycorax, who overtasked him; and in punishment for not doing what was beyond his power, shut him up in a pine-rift for twelve years. On the death of Sycorax, Ariel became the slave of Caliban, who tortured him most cruelly. Prospero liberated him from the pine-rift, and the grateful fairy served him for sixteen years, when he was set free.

**Aries.** The Ram. The sign of the Zodiac in which the sun is from March 21st to April 20th; the first portion of the ecliptic, between 0° and 30° longitude.

> At last from Aries rolls the bounteous sun.
> Thomson, *Spring*, 20

***The first point of Aries*** is the spot in the celestial equator occupied by the sun at the spring equinox. It is in celestial mensuration what the meridian of Greenwich is in terrestrial.

**Arimanes.** The same as Ahriman (*q.v.*). In *Manfred* Byron introduces him under this name, seated 'on a Globe of Fire, surrounded by the Spirits'.

**Arimaspians.** A one-eyed people of Scythia (spoken of in Lucan's *Pharsalia*, iii, 280, by Pliny, Herodotus, and others), who adorned their hair with gold. They were constantly at war with the gryphons who guarded the gold mines.

As when a gryphon, through the wilderness ...
Pursues the Arimaspian, who by stealth
Had from his wakeful custody purloined
The guarded gold.

Milton, *Paradise Lost*, ii, 943

Rabelais (IV, lvi, and V, xxix) uses the name for the peoples of Northern Europe who had accepted the Reformation, the suggestion being that they had lost one eye – that of faith.

**Arioch.** In *Paradise Lost* (vi, 371) one of the fallen angels. The word means *a fierce lion*; Milton took it from Dan. 2:14, where it is the name of a man.

**Arion.** A Greek poet and musician who flourished about 700 BC, and who, according to legend, was cast into the sea by mariners, but carried to Taenaros on the back of a dolphin.

She would often climb
The steepest ladder of the crudded rack
Up to some beakèd cape of cloud sublime,
And like Arion on the dolphin's back
Ride singing through the shoreless air.

Shelley, *Witch of Atlas*, lv

**Arion.** The horse given by Hercules to Adrastus. *See* Horse.

**Ariosto of the North.** So Byron called Sir Walter Scott (*Childe Harold*, iv, 40).

**Aristeas.** An early Greek poet of about the 8th century BC, of whom fable relates that he was a magician who rose many times after death. A kind of 'wandering Jew'.

**Aristides.** An Athenian statesman and general, who died about 468 BC, and was surnamed 'The Just'. He was present at the battles of Marathon and Salamis, and was in command at Plataea.

Then Aristides lifts his honest front,
Spotless of heart; to whom the unflattering voice
Of Freedom gave the noblest name of 'Just'.

Thomson, *Winter*, 459

***The British Aristides.*** Andrew Marvell, the poet and satirist (1621–78).

***The French Aristides.*** François Paul Jules Grévy, president of the Third Republic from 1879 till he was compelled to resign in 1887 in consequence of a scandal connected with the sale of offices and honours, was so called.

**Aristippus.** A Greek philosopher (fl. 375 BC), pupil of Socrates, and founder of the Cyrenaic school of hedonists. *See* Hedonism.

**Aristocracy** (Gr. *aristo-cratia*, rule of the best born). Originally, the government of a state by its best citizens. Carlyle uses the term in this sense in his *Latter-day Pamphlets* (iii, 41): 'The attainment of a truer and truer Aristocracy, or Government again by the Best.' The word is today generally applied to the patrician order, or to a class that is, or is supposed to be, specially privileged by reason of birth or wealth.

**Aristophanes.** The greatest of the Greek comic dramatists. He was born about 450 BC and died about 380 BC, and is specially notable as a satirist.

***The English*** or ***modern Aristophanes.*** Samuel Foote (1720–77).

***The French Aristophanes.*** Molière (1622–73).

**Aristotelian Philosophy.** Aristotle maintained that four separate causes are necessary before anything exists: the material cause, the formal, the final, and the moving cause. The first is the antecedents from which the thing comes into existence; the second, that which gives it its individuality; the moving or efficient cause is that which causes matter to assume its individual forms; and the final cause is that for which the thing exists. According to Aristotle, matter is eternal.

**Aristotelian Unities.** *See* Dramatic Unities.

**Aristotle.** The greatest of the Greek philosophers, pupil of Plato, and founder of the Peripatetic School. *See* Peripatetics.

**Ark.** *You must have come out of the ark*, or *you were born in the ark*; because you are so old-fashioned, and ignorant of current events.

**Arm** (*see also* Arms). This word, with the meaning of the limb, has given rise to a good many common phrases, such as:

***To arm a magnet.*** To put an armature on a loadstone.

***Arm in arm.*** Walking in a friendly way with arms linked.

***An arm of the sea.*** A narrow inlet.

***Which arm of the service.*** Navy, army or air-force?

***The secular arm.*** Civil, in contradistinction to ecclesiastical jurisdiction.

> The relapsed are delivered to the secular arm.
>
> Priestley, *Corruption of Christianity*

***To chance your arm.*** *See* Chance.

***At arm's length.*** At a good distance; hence, with avoidance of familiarity.

***An infant in arms*** is one that cannot yet walk and so has to be carried, but *a nation in arms* is one in which all the people are prepared for war.

***With open arms.*** Cordially; as persons receive a dear friend when they open their arms for an embrace.

**Arms** (*see also* Arm). The word 'arm' is almost always plural nowadays when denoting implements or accoutrements for fighting, etc., and also in heraldic usage. Among common phrases are:

***A passage of arms.*** A literary controversy; a battle of words.

***An assault at arms*** (or *of arms*). An attack by fencers; a hand-to-hand military exercise.

***Small arms.*** Those which do not, like artillery, require carriages.

***To appeal to arms.*** To determine to decide a litigation by war.

***To arms.*** Make ready for battle.

> 'To arms!' cried Mortimer,
> And couched his quivering lance.
>
> Gray, *The Bard*

***To lay down their arms.*** To cease from armed hostility; to surrender.

***Under arms.*** Prepared for battle; in battle array.

***Up in arms.*** In open rebellion: figuratively, roused to anger.

In heraldic terminology *arms* is the name given to the various insignia or devices, or groups of the same, each of which has a special meaning or a special ownership.

***King of Arms.*** *See* Heralds.

***The right to bear arms.*** The right to use an heraldic device, which can be obtained only by direct grant from the College of Heralds (and the payment of certain fees), or by patrimony, i.e. direct descent from one on whom the grant has been conferred. In either case a small annual licence must be paid if the coat of arms is used in any way, such as on one's carriage, silver, or stationery. A person having such right is said to be *armigerous*.

***The Royal Arms of England.*** The three lions passant gardant were introduced by Richard Coeur de Lion after his return from the third Crusade; the lion rampant in the second quarter is from the arms of Scotland, it having first been used in the reign of Alexander II (1214–49); and the harp in the fourth quarter represents Ireland; it was assigned to Ireland in the time of Henry VIII; before that time her device was three crowns. The lion supporter is English, and the unicorn Scotch; they were introduced by James I. The crest, a lion statant gardant first appears on the Great Seal of Edward III.

The correct emblazoning of the arms of the United Kingdom of Great Britain and Ireland is:

> Quarterly, first and fourth gules, three lions passant gardant in pale, or, for England; second or, a lion rampant within a double tressure flory-counterflory gules, for Scotland; third, azure, a harp or, stringed argent, for Ireland; all surrounded by the Garter. *Crest.* – Upon the royal helmet, the imperial crown proper, thereon a lion statant gardant or, imperially crowned proper. *Supporters.* – A lion rampant gardant, or, crowned as the crest. Sinister, a unicorn argent, armed, crined, and unguled proper, gorged with a coronet composed of crosses patée and fleur de lis, a chain affixed thereto passing between the forelegs, and reflexed over the back, also or. *Motto.* – 'Dieu et mon Droit' in the compartment below, the shield, with the Union rose, shamrock, and thistle engrafted on the same stem.

**Armada.** Originally Spanish for 'army', the word is now used, from the *Spanish Armada*, for any fleet of large size or strength. Formerly spelt *armado*.

> At length resolv'd t'assert the wat'ry ball,
> He [Charles II] in himself did whole Armadoes bring;
> Him aged seamen might their master call,
> And choose for general, were he not their king.
>
> Dryden, *Annus Mirabilis*, xiv

***The Spanish Armada.*** The fleet assembled by Philip II of Spain, in 1588, for the conquest of England.

**Armageddon.** The name given in the Apocalypse (Rev. 16:16) to the site of the last great battle that is to be between the nations before the Day of Judgment; hence, any great battle or scene of slaughter.

> We seemed to see our flag unfurled,
> Our champion waiting in his place
> For the last battle of the world,
> The Armageddon of the race.
>
> Whittier, *Rantoul*

The place the author of the Apocalypse had in mind was probably the mountainous district near Megiddo, generally identified with the modern Lejjun, about 54 miles due north of Jerusalem.

**Arme Blanche** (Fr. white arm). Steel weapons – the sword, sabre, bayonet, or spear – in contradistinction to firearms.

**Armenian Church, The.** Said to have been founded in Armenia by St Bartholomew. Its members are to be found in Armenia, Persia, Syria, Poland, Asia Minor, etc.; they attribute only one nature to Christ and hold that the Spirit proceeds from the Father only, enjoin the adoration of saints, have some peculiar ways of administering baptism and the Lord's Supper, and communicate infants; they do not maintain the doctrine of purgatory.

**Armida.** In Tasso's *Jerusalem Delivered* a beautiful sorceress, with whom Rinaldo fell in love, and wasted his time in voluptuous pleasure. After his escape from her, Armida followed him, but not being able to allure him back, set fire to her palace, rushed into the midst of a combat, and was slain.

> In 1806, Frederick William of Prussia declared war against Napoleon, and his young queen rode about in military costume to arouse the enthusiasm of the people. When Napoleon was told of it, he wittily said of her, 'She is Armida, in her distraction setting fire to her own palace.'

**Arminians.** Followers of Jacobus Harmensen, or Arminius (1560–1609), a Protestant divine in Leyden. They were an offshoot of Calvinism, and formulated their creed (called the *Remonstrance*) in 1610, in five points. They asserted that God bestows forgiveness and eternal life on all who repent and believe; that He wills all men to be saved; and that His predestination is founded on His foreknowledge.

**Armory.** Heraldry is so called, because it first found its special use in direct connexion with military equipments, knightly exercises, and the *mêlée* of actual battle.

> Armory is an Art rightly prescribing the true knowledge and use of Armes.
>
> *Guillim's Display of Heraldrie* (1610)

**Armour Coat**, or **a Coat of Arms**, was originally a drapery of silk or other rich stuff worn by a knight over his armour and embroidered in colours with his distinguishing device.

**Armoury.** The place where armour and arms are kept.

> The sword
> Of Michael from the armoury of God
> Was given him. Milton, *Paradise Lost*, vi, 320

The word may also mean armour collectively, as in *Paradise Lost*, iv, 553:

> nigh at hand
> Celestial armoury, shields, helms, and spears,
> Hung high, with diamond flaming and with gold.

**Arnauts** (Turk. brave men). Albanian mountaineers

> Stained with the best of Arnaut's blood.
>
> Byron, *The Giaour*

**Arnoldists.** The partisans of Arnold of Brescia, who raised his voice against the abuses and vices of the papacy in the 12th century. He was burnt alive by Pope Adrian IV.

**Arod.** In Dryden's *Absalom and Achitophel* is designed for Sir William Waller.

> But in the sacred annals of our plot
> Industrious Arod never be forgot,
> The labours of this midnight magistrate
> May vie with Corah's [Titus Oates] to preserve the state. Part ii

**Aroint thee.** A phrase that first appears in Shakespeare's *Macbeth* (1, 3, 6) and *King Lear* (3, 4, 129), on both occasions in connection with witches. It signifies 'get ye gone', 'be off'; and its origin is quite unknown. The Brownings made a verb of it, Mrs Browning in her *To Flush* – 'Whiskered cats arointed flee', and Browning in *The Two Poets of Croisic*, and elsewhere.

**Arondight.** The sword of Sir Launcelot of the Lake. *See* Sword.

> It is the sword of a good knight,
> Though homespun was his mail,
> What matter if it be not hight,
> Joyeuse, Colada, Durindale,
> Excalibar, or Aroundight? Longfellow

**Arras.** Tapestry; the cloth of Arras, in Artois, formerly famed for its manufacture. When rooms were hung with tapestry it was easy for persons to hide behind it; thus Hubert hid the two villains who were to put out Arthur's eyes behind the arras, Polonius was slain by Hamlet while concealed behind the arras, Falstaff proposed to hide behind it at Windsor, etc.

**Arria.** The wife of Caecina Paetus, who, being accused of conspiring against the Emperor Claudius, was condemned to death by suicide. As he hesitated to carry out the sentence Arria stabbed herself, then presenting the dagger to her husband said; 'Paetus, it gives no pain' (*non dolet*) (AD 42). *See* Pliny, vii.

**Arrière ban.** *See* Ban.

**Arrière pensée** (Fr. 'behind-thought'). A hidden or reserved motive, not apparent on the surface.

**Arrow, Broad.** *See* Broad Arrow: Jonathan's Arrows.

**Arrowroot,** or **Arrow-root.** The starch extracted from the tubers of *Maranta arundinacea*, which were formerly used in the West Indies to extract the poison left in wounds made by poisoned arrows.

**Artaxerxes,** called by the Persians Artakhshathra, and surnamed the long handed (*Longimanus*), because his right hand was longer than his left, was the first Persian king of that name, and reigned from 465 to 425 BC. He was the son of Xerxes, and is mentioned in the Bible in connection with the part he played in the restoration of Jerusalem after the Captivity. *See* Ezra 4, 6, and 7, and Neh. 2, 5, and 13.

**Artegal,** or **Arthegal, Sir.** The hero of Bk v of Spenser's *Faërie Queene*, lover of Britomart, to whom he is made known by means of a magic mirror. He is emblematic of Justice, and in many of his deeds, such as the rescue of Irena (Ireland) from Grantorto, is typical of Arthur, Lord Grey of Wilton, who went to Ireland as Lord Lieutenant in 1580 with Spenser as his secretary. *See* Elidure.

**Artemis.** *See* Diana.

**Artesian Wells.** So called from *Arteis*, the Old French name for Artois, in France, where they were first bored.

**Artful Dodger.** A young thief in Dickens's *Oliver Twist*, pupil of Fagin. His name was John Dawkins, and he became a most perfect adept in villainy, up to every sort of dodge.

**Arthegal.** *See* Artegal.

**Arthur.** A shadowy British chieftain of the 6th century, first mentioned by Nennius, a Breton monk of the 10th century. He fought many battles and is said to have been a king of the Silures, a tribe of ancient Britons, to have been mortally wounded in the battle of Camlan (537), in Cornwall, during the revolt of his nephew, Modred (who was also slain), and to have been taken to Glastonbury, where he died.

*His wife* was Guinevere, who committed adultery with Sir Launcelot of the Lake, one of the Knights of the Round Table.

He was the natural *son* of Uther and Igerna (wife of Gorlois, duke of Cornwall), and was brought up by Sir Ector.

He *was born* at Tintagel Castle, in Cornwall.

His chief *home* and the seat of his *court* was Caerleon, in Wales; and he was buried at Avalon (*q.v.*).

His *sword* was called Excalibur; his *spear*, Rone; and his *shield*, Pridwin. His *dog* was named Cavall. *See* Round Table, Knights of the.

**Arthurian Romances.** The stories that centre round the legendary King Arthur owe their inception in English literature to the *Historia Regum Brittaniae* (*c.*1148) of Geoffrey of Monmouth (d.1154), which drew partly from the work of Nennius (*see* Arthur), partly – according to the author – from an ancient British (? or Breton) book (lost, if ever existing) lent him by Walter, Archdeacon of Oxford, and partly from sources which are untraced, but the originals of which are probably embedded in Welsh or Celtic legends, most of them being now nonextant. The original Arthur was a very shadowy warrior; Geoffrey of Monmouth, probably at the instigation of Henry I and for the purpose of providing the new nation with a national hero, made many additions; the story was taken up in France and further expanded; Wace, a French poet (who is the first to mention the Round Table – *q.v.*), turned it into a metrical chronicle of some 14,000 lines (*Brut d'Angleterre*, *c.*1155); Celtic and other legends, including those of the Grail (*q.v.*) and Sir Tristram, were superadded, and in about 1205 Layamon, the Worcestershire priest, completed his *Brut* (about 30,000 lines), which included Wace's work and amplifications such as the story of the fairies at Arthur's birth, who, at his death, wafted him to Avalon, as well as Sir Gawain and Sir Bedivere. In France the legends were worked upon by Robert de Borron (fl.1215), who first attached the story of the Grail (*q.v.*) to the Arthurian Cycle and brought the legend of Merlin into prominence, and Chrestien de Troyes (*c.*1140–90), who is responsible for the presence in the Cycle of the tale of Enid and Geraint, the tragic loves of Launcelot and Guinevere, the story of Perceval, and other additions for many of which he was indebted to the Welsh *Mabinogion*. Many other legends in the form of ballads, romances, and Welsh and Breton songs and lays were popular, and in the 15th century the whole *corpus* was collected, edited, and more or less worked into a state of homogeneity by Sir Thomas Malory (d.1471), his *Le Morte d'Arthur* being printed by Caxton in 1485. For the different heroes, sections, etc., of this great Cycle of Romance, *see* the various names throughout this Dictionary.

The six following clauses may be considered almost as axioms of the Arthurian romances:

(1) There was no braver or more noble king than Arthur.
(2) No fairer or more faithless wife than Guinevere.
(3) No truer pair of lovers than Tristan and Iseult (or Tristram and Ysolde).
(4) No knight more faithful than Sir Kaye.
(5) None so brave and amorous as Sir Launcelot.
(6) None so virtuous as Sir Galahad.

**Arthur's Seat.** A hill overlooking Edinburgh from the east. The name is not connected with King Arthur; it is a corruption of the Gaelic *Ard-na-said*, the height of the arrows, hence, a convenient ground to shoot from.

**Articles of Roup.** The conditions of sale at a roup (*q.v.*), as announced by a crier.

**Artists, The Prince of.** Albert Dürer (1471–1528) was so called by his countrymen.

**Artotyrites** (Gr. *artos*, bread, *turos*, cheese). Certain Montanist heretics of the early church, so called because they used bread and cheese in the Eucharist. They admitted women to the priesthood.

**Arts. *Degrees in Arts*.** In the mediaeval ages the full course consisted of the three subjects which constituted the *Trivium*, and the four subjects which constituted the *Quad rivium*:

The *Trivium* was grammar, logic, and rhetoric.

The *Quadrivium* was music, arithmetic, geometry, and astronomy.

The *Master of Arts* was the person qualified to teach or be the master of students in arts; as the *Doctor* was the person qualified to teach theology, law, or medicine.

**Arundel.** *See* Horse.

**Arundelian Marbles.** A collection of ancient sculptures made at great expense by Thomas Howard, Earl of Arundel, and presented to the University of Oxford in 1667 by his grandson, Henry Howard, afterwards Duke of Norfolk. They contain tables of ancient chronology, especially that of Athens, from 1582 to 264 BC, engraved in old Greek capitals, and the famous 'Parian Chronicle', said to have been executed in the island of Paros about 263 BC.

**Arvakur.** *See* Horse.

**Arval Brothers.** An ancient Roman college of priests, revived by Augustus. It consisted of 12 priests (including the Emperor), whose sole duty was to preside at the festival of Dea Dia in May; they worshipped in the groves of that goddess on the Via Campana, 5 miles from Rome.

**Aryans.** The parent stock of what is called the Indo-European family of nations. Their original home is quite unknown, authorities differing so widely as between a locality enclosed by the river Oxus and the Hindu-kush mountains, and the shores of the Baltic or Central Europe. The Aryan family of languages include the Persian and Hindu, with all the European except Basque, Turkish, Hungarian, and Finnic. Sometimes called the Indo-European, sometimes the Indo-Germanic, and sometimes the Japhetic.

Sanskrit, Zend, Latin, Greek, and Celtic are, of course, included.

**Arzina.** A river that flows into the North Sea, near Wardhus, where Sir Hugh Willoughby's three ships were ice-bound, and the whole crew perished of starvation.

In these fell regions, in Arzina caught,
And to the stony deep his idle ship
Immediate sealed, he with his hapless crew ...
Froze into statues.
Thomson, *Winter*, 930

**Asaph.** In the Bible, a famous musician in David's time (1 Chron. 25:1, 2). There was probably no such person, but in post-exilic times there were two hereditary choirs that superintended the musical services of the Temple, one of which was *b'ne Asaph*, and the other *b'ne Korah*. The Asaph mentioned in *Chronicles* is the supposed founder of the first named.

Tate, who wrote the second part of *Absalom and Achitophel*, lauds Dryden under this name.

While Judah's throne and Sion's rock stand fast,
The song of Asaph and the fame shall last.
*Absalom and Achitophel*, Pt ii, 1063

**Asbolos.** One of Actaeon's dogs. The word means *soot-coloured*.

**Ascalaphus.** In *Greek mythology*, an inhabitant of the underworld who, when Pluto gave Proserpine permission to return to the upper world if she had eaten nothing, said that she had partaken of a pomegranate. In revenge Proserpine turned him into an owl by sprinkling him with the water of Phlegethon.

**Ascapart.** In the romance of Bevis of Hampton, a giant conquered by Sir Bevis. He was thirty feet high, and the space between his eyes was twelve inches. This mighty giant, whose effigy figures on the city gates of Southampton, could carry under his arm Sir Bevis with his wife and horse.

Each man an Ascapart, of strength to toss
For quoits, both Temple bar and Charing-cross.
Pope, *Donne's IVth Satire Versified*

**Ascendant.** In casting a horoscope the point of the ecliptic or degree of the zodiac which is just rising at the moment of birth is called the ascendant, and the easternmost star represents the house of life (*see* House), because it is in the act of ascending. This is a man's strongest star, and when his outlook is bright, we say *his star is in the ascendant*.

***The House of the Ascendant***, includes five degrees of the zodiac above the point just rising, and twenty-five below it. Usually, the point of birth is referred to.

***The Lord of the Ascendant*** is any planet within the 'house of the Ascendant'. The house and lord of the Ascendant at birth were said by astrologers to exercise great influence on the future life of the child. Deborah referred to the influence of the stars when she said 'the stars in their courses fought against Sisera' (Judges 5:20).

**Ascension Day,** or **Holy Thursday** (*q.v.*). The day set apart by the Christian Churches to commemorate the ascent of our Lord from earth to heaven. It is the fortieth day after Easter. *See* Bounds, Beating the.

**Asclepiads,** or **Asclepiadic Metre.** A term in Greek and Latin prosody denoting a verse (invented by Asclepiades) which consists of a spondee, two (or three) choriambi, and an iambus, usually with a central caesura, thus:

—|—⏑ —‖—⏑⏑—|⏑—

The first ode of Horace is Asclepiadic. The first and last two lines may be translated in the same metre, thus:

Dear friend, patron of song, sprung from the race of kings;

Thy name ever a grace and a protection brings ...
My name, if to the lyre haply you chance to wed,
Pride would high as the stars lift my exalted head.
*E. C. B.*

**Ascodrogites.** Certain heretics of the 2nd century who said 'they were vessels full of new wine' (Gr. *askos*), meaning the Gospel (Matt. 9:17).

**Ascot Races.** A very fashionable 'meet', run early in June on Ascot Heath, Berkshire (6 miles from Windsor). They were instituted early in the 18th century. The best horses of all England compete, and at a somewhat more advanced age than at the great 'classic races' (*q.v.*).

**Ascraean Poet,** or **Sage.** Hesiod, the Greek didactic poet, born at Ascra in Boeotia. Virgil (*Eclogues*, vii, 70) calls him the 'Old Ascraeon'.

**Asgard** (*As*, a god, *gard* or *gardh* an enclosure, garth, yard). The realm of the *Aesir* or the Northern gods, the Olympus of *Scandinavian mythology*. It is said to be situated in the centre of the universe, and accessible only by the rainbow-bridge (*Bifrost*). It contained many regions and mansions, such as Gladsheim and Valhalla.

**Ash Tree,** or **Tree of the Universe.** *See* Yggdrasil.

**Ash Wednesday.** The first Wednesday in Lent, so called from an ancient Roman Catholic custom of sprinkling on the heads of the priests and people assembled the ashes of the palms that were consecrated on the Palm Sunday of the previous year which themselves had been consecrated at the altar. The custom, it is said, was introduced by Gregory the Great.

**Ashes. *Ashes to ashes, dust to dust.*** A phrase from the English Burial Service, used sometimes to signify total finality. It is founded on various scriptural texts, such as 'Dust thou art, and unto dust thou shalt return' (Gen. 3:19), and 'I will bring thee to ashes upon the earth in the sight of all them that behold thee' (Ezek. 28:18).

Ashes to ashes and dust to dust,
If God won't have him the Devil must.

According to Sir Walter Scott (*see* his edition of Swift's *Journal to Stella*, March 25th, 1710–11), this was the form of burial service given by the sexton to the body of Guiscard, the French refugee who, in 1711, attempted the life of Harley.

***To recover the ashes.*** A bit of cricketing slang, the 'ashes' being the mythical prize contended for at the matches between England and Australia. When the English were beaten in 1882 a humorous epitaph on English cricket appeared in a sporting journal, and it wound up with the remark that 'the body will be cremated and the ashes taken to Australia'.

**Ashmolean Museum.** Presented to the University of Oxford in 1682 by Elias Ashmole. Sometimes called the Tradescant, because the collections had been bequeathed to Ashmole by the Tradescant family. The building was erected by Sir Christopher Wren.

**Ashtoreth.** The goddess of fertility and reproduction among the Canaanites and Phoenicians, called by the Babylonians *Ishtar* (Venus), and by the Greeks *Astarte* (*q.v.*). She may possibly be the 'queen of heaven' mentioned by Jeremiah (7:18, 44:17, 25). Formerly she was supposed to be a moon-goddess, hence Milton's reference in his *Ode on the Nativity*.

Moonëd Ashtaroth,
Heaven's queen and mother both.

**Ashur.** *See* Asshur.

**Asinego** (Port.). A young ass, a simpleton.

> Thou hast no more brain than I have in mine elbows; an asinego may tutor thee –
> Shakespeare, *Troilus and Cressida*, 2, 1

**Asinus. *Asinus asinum fricat*** (Lat. 'one ass rubs another'), that is, we fraternise with persons like ourselves; or, in other words, 'Birds of a feather flock together.' The allusion needs no explanation.

**Asir.** *See* Aesir.

**Ask.** The vulgar and dialectical *ax* was the common literary form down to about the end of the 16th century. The word comes from the O.E. *ascian*, which, by metathesis, became *acsian*, and so *axian*. Chaucer has:

> How sholde I axen mercy of Tisbe
> Whan I am he that have yow slain, allas!
> *Legend of Good Women*, 835

and the Wyclif version of Matt. 7:7–10, reads:

> Axe ye and it schal be gyven to you; seke yee, and yee schulen fynde; knocke ye: and it schal be openid to you. For ech that axith, takith, and he that sekith, fyndith: and it schal be opened to him that knockith. What man of you is, that if his sone axe him breed: whether he wole take him a stoon? Or if he axe fish, whether he wole give him an Eddre?

**Asmodeus.** The 'evil demon' who appears in the Apocryphal book of *Tobit*, borrowed (and to some extent transformed) from Aeshma, one of the seven archangels of *Persian mythology*. The name is probably the Zend *Aeshmo daeva* (the demon Aeshma), and is not connected with the Heb. *samad*, to destroy. The character of Asmodeus is explained in the following passage from *The Testament of Solomon* –

> I am called *Asmodeus* among mortals, and my business is to plot against the newly-wedded, so that they may not know one another. And I sever them utterly by many calamities; and I waste away the beauty of virgins, and estrange their hearts.

In *Tobit* Asmodeus falls in love with Sara, daughter of Raguel, and causes the death of seven husbands in succession, each on his bridal night. After her marriage to Tobias, he was driven into Egypt by a charm, made by Tobias of the heart and liver of a fish burnt on perfumed ashes, and being pursued was taken prisoner and bound.

> Better pleased
> Than Asmodeus with the fishy fume
> That drove him, though enamoured, from the spouse
> Of Tobit's son, and with a vengeance sent
> From Media post to Egypt, there fast bound.
> Milton, *Paradise Lost*, iv, 167

Le Sage gave the name to the companion of Don Cleofas in his *Devil on Two Sticks*.

***Asmodeus flight***. Don Cleofas, catching hold of his companion's cloak, is perched on the steeple of St Salvador. Here the foul fiend stretches out his hand, and the roofs of all the houses open in a moment, to show the Don what is going on privately in each respective dwelling.

> Could the reader take an Asmodeus-flight, and, waving open all roofs and privacies, look down from the roof of Notre Dame, what a Paris were it! Carlyle, *French Revolution*, Bk vi, ch. vi

**Asoka.** An Indian king of the Maurya dynasty of Magadha, 263–26 BC, who was converted to Buddhism by a miracle and became its 'nursing father', as Constantine was of Christianity. He is called 'the king beloved of the gods'.

**Aspasia.** A Milesian woman (fl. 440 BC), celebrated for her beauty and talents, who lived at Athens as mistress of Pericles, and whose house became the centre of literary and philosophical society. She was the most celebrated of the Greek Hetaerae, and on the death of Pericles (429 BC) lived with the democratic leader, Lysicles.

**Aspatia**, in the *Maid's Tragedy*, of Beaumont and Fletcher, is noted for her deep sorrows, her great resignation, and the pathos of her speeches. Amyntor deserts her, women point at her with scorn, she is the jest and by-word of everyone, but she bears it all with patience.

**Aspen.** The aspen leaf is said to tremble, from shame and horror, because our Lord's cross was made of this wood. The fact is, of course, that owing to the shape of the leaf, and its long, flexible leaf-stalk, it is peculiarly liable to be acted on by the least breath of air.

**Aspen Leaf.** Metaphorically, a chattering tongue, especially a woman's.

> Those aspen leaves of theirs never leave wagging.
> Sir T. More, *The Second Parte of the Confutacyon of Tindale's Answere*.

**Aspersions** properly means 'sprinklings' or 'scatterings'. Its present meaning is base insinuations or slanders.

> No sweet aspersion [*rain*] shall the heavens let fall
> To make this contract grow.
> Shakespeare, *The Tempest*, 4, 1

***Casting aspersions on one***, i.e. sprinkling with calumnies, slandering or insinuating misconduct.

> I defy all the world to cast a just aspersion on my character. Fielding, *Tom Jones*

**Asphaltic Lake.** The Dead Sea, where asphalt abounds both on the surface of the water and on the banks. Asphalt is a bitumen.

> There was an asphaltic and Bituminous nature in that Lake before the fire of Gomorrah.
>
> Sir Thos Browne, *Religio Medici*, i, 19

There is a bituminous, or asphalt, lake in Trinidad.

**Ass.** *See* Golden Ass.

***Ass.*** The dark stripe running down the back of an ass, crossed by another at the shoulders, is, according to tradition, the cross that was communicated to the creature when our Lord rode on the back of an ass in His triumphant entry into Jerusalem.

***Till the ass ascends the ladder*** – i.e. never. A rabbinical expression. The Romans had a similar one, *Cum asinus in tegulis ascenderit* (When the ass climbs to the tiles).

***That which thou knowest not perchance thine ass can tell thee.*** An allusion to Balaam's ass.

***Ass, deaf to music.*** This tradition arose from the hideous noise made by 'Sir Balaam' in braying. *See* Ass-eared.

***An ass in a lion's skin.*** A coward who hectors, a fool that apes the wise man. The allusion is to the fable of an ass that put on a lion's hide, but was betrayed when he began to bray.

***To make an ass of oneself.*** To do something very foolish. To expose oneself to ridicule.

***Sell your ass.*** Get rid of your foolish ways.

***The ass waggeth his ears.*** This proverb is applied to those who lack learning, and yet talk as if they were very wise; men wise in their own conceit. The ass, proverbial for having no 'taste for music', will nevertheless wag its ears at a 'concord of sweet sounds', just as if it could well appreciate it.

***An ass with two panniers.*** Said of a man walking the streets with a lady on each arm, a form of bad manners which well merits the reproach. The Italian equivalent is a *pitcher with two handles*, and formerly it was called in London walking *bodkin* (*q.v.*). Our expression is from the French *faire le panier à deux anses*, a colloquialism for walking with a lady on each arm.

***Ass's bridge.*** *See* Pons Asinorum.

***Well, well! honey is not for the ass's mouth.*** Persuasion will not persuade fools. The gentlest words will not divert the anger of the unreasonable.

***Wrangle for an ass's shadow.*** To contend about trifles. The tale told by Demosthenes is, that a man hired an ass to take him to Megara; and at noon, the sun being very hot, the traveller dismounted, and sat himself down in the shadow of the ass. Just then the owner came up and claimed the right of sitting in this shady spot, saying that he let out the ass for hire, but there was no bargain made about the ass's shade. The two men then fell to blows to settle the point in dispute. A passer-by told the traveller to move on, and leave the owner of the beast to walk in the ass's shadow as long as he thought proper.

***Asses as well as pitchers have ears.*** Children, and even the densest minds, hear and understand many a word and hint which the speaker supposed would pass unheeded.

***Feast of Asses.*** *See* Fools.

***Asses that carry the mysteries*** (*asini portant mysteria*). A classical knock at the Roman clergy. The allusion is to the custom of employing asses to carry the *cista* which contained the sacred symbols, when processions were made through the streets. (Warburton, *Divine Legation*, ii, 4.)

**Ass-eared.** Midas had the ears of an ass. The tale says Apollo and Pan had a contest, and chose Midas to decide which was the better musician. Midas gave sentence in favour of Pan; and Apollo, in disgust, changed his ears into those of an ass.

> Avarice is as deaf to the voice of virtue, as the ass to the voice of Apollo. *Orlando Furioso*, xvii

**Assassins.** A sect of Oriental fanatics of a military and religious character, founded in Persia in 1090 by Hassan ben Sabbah, better known as the *Old Man* (or *Sheikh*) *of the Mountains* (*see* under Mountain), because the sect migrated to Mount Lebanon and made it its stronghold. This band was the terror of the world for two centuries, and, to the number of 50,000 strong, offered formidable opposition to the Crusaders. Their religion was a compound of Magianism, Judaism, Christianity, and Mohammedanism, and their name is derived from *haschisch* (bang), an intoxicating drink, with which they are said to have 'doped' themselves before perpetrating their orgies of massacre. They were finally put down by the Sultan Bibars, about 1272.

**Assay,** or *Essay* (through O. Fr. from Lat. *exagium*, to weigh). To try or test; to determine the amount of different metals in an ore, etc.; and, formerly, to taste food or drink before it is offered to a sovereign; hence, *to take the assay* is to taste wine to prove it is not poisoned.

The aphetic form of the word, 'say', was common down to the 17th century, and Edmund, in *King Lear*, (5, 5), says to Edgar, 'Thy tongue, some *say* of breeding breathes'; i.e. thy speech gives indication of good breeding – it savours of it.

Assay, as a noun, means a test or trial, as in –

> [He] makes vow before his uncle never more
> To give the assay of arms against your majesty.
> Shakespeare, *Hamlet*, 2, 2

But for the last three hundred years the spelling *essay* has been adopted (from French) for the noun, in all uses except those connected with the assaying of metals.

**Assaye Regiment.** The 74th Foot, so called because they first distinguished themselves in the battle of Assaye, where 2,000 British and 2,500 Sepoy troops under Wellington defeated 50,000 Mahrattas, commanded by French officers, in 1803. This regiment is now called 'the 2nd Battalion of the Highland Light Infantry'. The first battalion was the old No. 71.

**Asshur.** The chief god of the Assyrian pantheon, perhaps derived from the Babylonian god of heaven, Anu. His symbol was the winged circle in which was frequently enclosed a draped male figure carrying three horns on the head and with one hand stretched forth, sometimes with a bow in the hand. His wife was Belit (i.e. the Lady, *par excellence*), who has been identified with the Ishtar (*see* Ashtoreth) of Nineveh.

> Out of that land went forth Asshur, and builded Nineveh. Gen. 10:11

**Assiento Treaties** (Sp. *asiénto*, agreement). Contracts entered into by Spain with Portugal, France, and England to supply her South American colonies with negro slaves. England joined in 1713, after the peace of Utrecht, and kept the disgraceful monopoly (with a few breaks) till 1750.

**Assumption, Feast of the.** August 15th, so called in honour of the Virgin Mary, who (according to one legend) was taken to heaven that day (AD 45) in her corporeal form, being at the time seventy-five years of age.

> This seems very improbable, if Christ were crucified AD 33. It would make Mary survive her son twelve years, and to have been thirty years old at his birth instead of about fifteen.

Another legend has it that the Virgin was raised soon after her death, and assumed to glory by a special privilege before the general resurrection.

**Assurance.** Audacity, brazen self-confidence. 'His assurance is quite unbearable.'

***To make assurance double sure.*** To make security doubly secure.

> But yet I'll make assurance double sure,
> And take a bound of fate.
> Shakespeare, *Macbeth*, 4, 1

In business circles the difference between *assurance* and *insurance* is that the former is properly used in connection with *life* (*life assurance*), and the latter in connection with *fire*, *burglary*, *marine insurance*, etc. The distinction is not, however, uniformly kept.

**Astarte.** The Greek name for Ashtoreth (*q.v.*), sometimes thought to have been a moon-goddess. Hence Milton's allusion:

> With these in troop
> Came Astoreth, whom the Phoenicians called
> Astarte, queen of heaven, with crescent horns.
> *Paradise Lost*, i, 437

Byron gave the name to the lady beloved by Manfred in his drama, *Manfred*. In order to see and speak to her, the magician entered the hall of Arimanes, and the spirits called up the girl's phantom, which told the count that 'tomorrow would end his earthly ills'. When Manfred asked her if she still loved him, she sighed 'Manfred,' and vanished.

It has been suggested that Astarte was drawn from the poet's sister, Augusta (Mrs Leigh), whom Byron has been accused of loving with more than a brotherly affection.

**Astolat.** This town, mentioned in the Arthurian legends, is generally identified with Guildford, in Surrey.

***The Lily Maid of Astolat.*** Elaine (*q.v.*).

**Astolpho.** ***It came upon them like a blast from Astolpho's horn*** – i.e. it produced a panic. In Ariosto's *Orlando Furioso* Logistilla gave Astolpho (an English duke who joined Charlemagne against the Saracens) a magic horn, and whatever man or beast heard its blast was seized with panic, and became an easy captive (Bk viii).

***Like Astolpho's book, it told you everything.*** The same fairy gave Astolpho a book, which would not only direct him aright in his journeys, but would tell him anything he desired to know (Bk viii).

**Astoreth.** *See* Ashtoreth.

**Astraea.** Equity, innocence. During the Golden Age this goddess dwelt on earth, but when sin began to prevail, she reluctantly left it, and was metamorphosed into the constellation *Virgo*.

When hard-hearted interest first began
To poison earth, Astraea left the plain.
Thomson, *Castle of Indolence*, I, xi

Pope gave the name to Mrs Aphra Behn (1640–89), a writer of numerous and indecent plays, and some novels.

The stage how loosely does Astrea tread.
*Satires*, v, 290

**Astral Body.** In theosophical parlance, the phantasmal or spiritual appearance of the physical human form, that is existent both before and after the death of the material body, though during life it is not usually separated from it; also the 'kamarupa' or body of desires, which retains a finite life in the astral world after bodily death.

**Astral Spirits.** The spirits of the dead that occupy the stars and the stellar regions, or astral world. According to the occultists, each star has its special spirit; and Paracelsus maintained that every man had his attendant star, which received him at death, and took charge of him till the great resurrection.

**Astrology.** The ancient and mediaeval so-called 'science' that professed (and even, in some quarters, professes) to foretell events by studying the position of the stars and discovering their occult influence on human affairs. It is one of the most ancient superstitions; it prevailed from earliest times among the Chaldeans, Egyptians, Etruscans, Hindus, Chinese, etc., and had a powerful influence in the Europe of the Middle Ages. *Natural Astrology* – i.e. the branch that dealt with meteorological phenomena and with time, tides, eclipses, the fixing of Easter, etc. – was the forerunner of the science of Astronomy; what is now known as 'astrology' was formerly differentiated from this as *Judicial Astrology*, and dealt with star divination and the occult planetary and sidereal influences upon human affairs. *See* Houses, Astrological; Horoscope; Microcosm.

**Astronomers Royal.** (1) Flamsteed, 1675; (2) Halley, 1719; (3) Bradley, 1742; (4) Bliss, 1762; (5) Maskelyne, who originated the Nautical Almanack, 1765; (6) Pond, 1811; (7) Airy, 1835; (8) Christie, 1881; (9) Sir F. W. Dyson, 1910.

**Astrophel.** Sir Philip Sidney (1554–86). 'Phil. Sid.' being a contraction of Philos Sidus, and the Latin *sidus* being changed to the Greek *astron*, we get *astron-philos* (star-lover). The 'star' that he loved was Penelope Devereux, whom he called *Stella* (star), and to whom he was betrothed. Spenser wrote a pastoral called *Astrophel*, to the memory of his friend and patron, who fell at the battle of Zutphen.

**Asur.** The national god of the ancient Assyrians; the supreme god over all the gods. *See* Asshur.

**Asura.** In *Hindu mythology*, the opposers of the gods.

The Asuras and the Spirits of the damned
Acclaim their hero.
Southey, *Curse of Kehama*, vi, xiii

**Asurbanipal.** *See* Sardanapalus.

**Asylum** means, literally, a place where pillage is forbidden (Gr. *a*, not, *sulon*, right of pillage). The ancients set apart certain places of refuge, where the vilest criminals were protected, both from private and public assaults.

**Asynja.** The goddesses of Asgard; the feminine counterpart of the Aesir.

**At Home.** *See* Home.

**Atalanta's Race.** Atalanta, in Greek legend, was a daughter of Iasus and Clymene. She took part in the Calydonian hunt and, being very swift of foot, refused to marry unless the suitor should first defeat her in a race. Milanion overcame her at last by dropping, one after another, during the race, three golden apples that had been given him for the purpose by Venus. Atalanta was not proof against the temptation to pick them up, and so lost the race and became a wife. In the Boeotian form of the legend Hippomenes takes the place of Milanion.

**Atargatis.** A fish-goddess of the Phoenicians. Her temple at Carnaim is mentioned in the Apocryphal book of *Maccabees* (2, xii, 26), and she had another at Ascalon.

**Ate.** In *Greek mythology*, the goddess of vengeance and mischief; she was driven out of heaven, and took refuge among the sons of men.

With Atë by his side come hot from hell …
Cry 'Havoc' and let slip the dogs of war.
Shakespeare, *Julius Caesar*, 3, 1

In Spenser's *Faërie Queene* (IV, i, iv, ix, etc.), the name is given to a lying and slanderous hag, the companion of Duessa.

**Atellanae,** or **Atellan Farces.** Licentious interludes in the Roman theatres, introduced from Atella, in Campania. The characters of Macchus and Bucco are the forerunners of our Punch and Clown.

**Athanasian Creed.** One of the three creeds accepted by the Roman and Anglican Churches; so called because it embodies the opinions of Athanasius respecting the Trinity. It was compiled in the 5th century by Hilary, Bishop of Arles.

In the Episcopal Prayer Book of America this creed is omitted.

**Atheist.** *See* Theist.

**Athelstane.** The 'thane of Coningsburgh' in Scott's *Ivanhoe*. He was surnamed 'The Unready' (i.e. impolitic, unwise).

**Athenaeum.** A famous academy or university situated on the Capitoline Hill at Rome, and founded by Hadrian about AD 133. So called in honour of Athene. As now used the name usually denotes a literary or scientific institution.

The Athenaeum Club in London was established in 1824; the review of this name was founded by James Silk Buckingham in 1828.

**Athene.** The goddess of wisdom and of the arts and sciences in *Greek mythology*: the counterpart of the Roman Minerva (*q.v.*).

**Athenian Bee.** Plato (429–327 BC), a native of Athens, was so called because, according to tradition, when in his cradle a swarm of bees alighted on his mouth, and in consequence his words flowed with the sweetness of honey. The same tale is told of St Ambrose, and others. *See* Bee. Xenophon (444–359 BC) is also called 'the Bee of Athens', or 'the Athenian Bee'.

**Athens.** When the goddess of wisdom disputed with the sea-god which of them should give name to Athens, the gods decided that it should be called by the name of that deity which bestowed on man the most useful boon. Athene (the goddess of wisdom) created the olive tree, Poseidon created the horse. The vote was given in favour of the olive tree, and the city called Athens. An olive branch was the symbol of *peace*, and was also the highest prize of the victor in the Olympic games. The horse, on the other hand, was the symbol of *war*, and peace is certainly to be preferred to war.

***Athens of Ireland.*** Belfast.

***Athens of the New World.*** Boston, noted for its literary merit and institutions.

***Athens of the West.*** Cordova, in Spain, was so called in the Middle Ages.

***The Modern Athens.*** Edinburgh. Willis says that its singular resemblance to Athens, approached from the Piraeus, is very striking.

> An imitation Acropolis is commenced on the Calton Hill, and has the effect of the Parthenon. Hymettus is rather more lofty than the Pentland hills, and Pentelicus is farther off and grander than Arthur's Seat; but the old Castle of Edinburgh is a noble feature, superbly magnificent. *Pencillings*

**Athole Brose** (Scotch). A compound of oatmeal, honey, and whisky.

**Atin.** In Spenser's *Faërie Queene* (Bk ii), the squire of Pyrochles, typifying strife.

**Atkins.** *See* Tommy Atkins.

**Atlantean Shoulders.** Shoulders able to bear a great weight, like those of Atlas (*q.v.*).

> Sage he stood,
> With Atlantean shoulders, fit to bear
> The weight of mightiest monarchies.
> Milton, *Paradise Lost*, Bk ii, 305

**Atlantes.** Figures of men, used in architecture as pillars. So called from Atlas (*q.v.*). Female figures are called Caryatides (*q.v.*). *See also* Telamones.

**Atlantic Ocean.** The ocean is so called either from the Atlas mountains, the great range in north-west Africa which, to the ancients, seemed to overlook the whole ocean, or from Atlantis (*q.v.*).

**Atlantis.** A mythic island of great extent which was anciently supposed to have existed in the Atlantic Ocean. It is first mentioned by Plato (in the *Timaeus* and *Critias*), and Solon was told of it by an Egyptian priest, who said that it had been overwhelmed by an earthquake and sunk beneath the sea 9,000 years before his time. *Cp.* Lemuria; Lyonesse.

***The New Atlantis.*** An allegorical romance by Bacon (written between 1614 and 1618) in which he describes an imaginary island where was established a philosophical commonwealth bent on the cultivation of the natural sciences. *See* Utopia, City of the Sun.

Mrs Manley, in 1709, published a scandalous chronicle, in which the names of contemporaries are so thinly disguised as to be readily recognised, under the same title.

**Atlas.** In *Greek mythology*, one of the Titans condemned by Zeus for his share in the War of the Titans to uphold the heavens on his shoulders. He was stationed on the Atlas mountains in Africa, and the tale is merely a poetical way of saying that they prop up the heavens, because they are so lofty.

> Bid Atlas, propping heaven, as poets feign,
> His subterranean wonders spread!
> Thomson, *Autumn*, 797

We call a book of maps an 'Atlas', because the figure of Atlas with the world on his back was employed by Mercator on the title-page of his collection of maps in the 16th century. In the paper trade *Atlas* is a standard size of drawing paper measuring 26 x 34 in.

**Atli.** *See* Etzel.

**Atman,** in Buddhist philosophy, is the noumenon of one's own self. Not the Ego, but the ego divested of all that is objective; the 'spark of heavenly flame'. In the Upanishads the Atman is regarded as the sole reality.

> The unseen and unperceivable, which was formerly called the soul, was now called the self, Atman. Nothing could be predicated of it except that it was, that it perceived and thought, and that it must be blessed.
>
> Max Muller, *Nineteenth Century*, May, 1893, p. 777

**Atom.** *See* Atomic Theory.

**Atomic Philosophy.** The hypothesis of Leucippus, Democritus, and Epicurus, that the world is composed of a concourse of atoms, or particles of matter so minute as to be incapable of further diminution. *Cp.* Corpuscular Philosophy.

**Atomic Theory.** The doctrine that all elemental bodies consist of aggregations of *atoms* (i.e. the smallest indivisible particles of the element in question), not united fortuitously, but according to fixed proportions. The four laws of Dalton are – constant proportion, reciprocal proportion, multiple proportion, and compound proportion.

> These laws have nothing to do with the atomic philosophy of Leucippus. It merely means that gases and other elements always combine in certain known ratios or units.

**Atomic Volume.** The space occupied by a quantity of an element compared with, or in proportion to, atomic weight.

**Atomic Weight.** The weight of an atom of an element, compared with an atom of hydrogen, the standard of unity.

**Atomy.** *See* Anatomy.

**Atossa.** Sarah, Duchess of Marlborough, so called by Pope (*Moral Essays*, ii), because she was the friend of Lady Mary Wortley Montagu, whom he calls *Sappho*. Herodotus says that Atossa, the mother of Xerxes, was a follower of Sappho.

**A-trip.** The anchor is *a-trip* when it has just been drawn from the ground in a perpendicular direction. A sail is *a-trip* when it has been hoisted from the cap, and is ready for trimming.

**Attaint** (etymologically the same word as *attain*, through Fr. from Lat. *ad*, to, *tangere*, to touch). An old term in chivalry, meaning to strike the helmet and shield of an antagonist so firmly with the lance, held in a direct line, as either to break the lance or overthrow the person struck. Hence, to convict, condemn; hence, to condemn one convicted of treason to loss of honours and death. The later development of the word was affected by its fanciful association with *taint*.

**Attercop.** An ill-tempered, malignant person, who mars all sociability; from the Old English name for the spider, which was supposed to be poisonous. (O.E. *atter*, poison, and *cop*, which is from either *coppa*, the top, or *copp*, a cup; or perhaps *coppa* meant 'spider'; *cp. cop-web*, the old form of 'cob-web'.)

**Attic.** *The Attic Bee*, Sophocles (495–05 BC), the tragic poet, a native of Athens; so called from the great sweetness of his compositions. *See also* Athenian Bee.

***The Attic Bird.*** The nightingale; so called either because Philomel was the daughter of the King of Athens, or because of the great abundance of nightingales in Attica.

> Where the Attic bird
> Trills her thick-warbled notes the summer long.
>
> Milton, *Paradise Regained*, iv, 245

***The Attic Boy.*** Cephalos, beloved by Aurora or Morn; passionately fond of hunting.

> Till civil-suited Morn appear,
> Not tricked and frounced, as she was wont
> With the Attic boy to hunt,
> But kerchiefed in a comely cloud.
>
> Milton, *Il Penseroso*

***Attic Faith.*** Inviolable faith, the very opposite of Punic faith. *See* Punica Fides.

***The Attic Muse.*** Xenophon (444–356 BC), the historian, a native of Athens; so called because the style of his composition is a model of elegance.

***Attic Order,*** in *architecture*, a small square pillar or pilaster of any of the five orders. *See* Orders.

***Attic Salt.*** Elegant and delicate wit. Salt, both in Latin and Greek, was a common term for wit, or sparkling thought well expressed; thus Cicero says, *Scipio omnes sale superabat* (Scipio surpassed all in wit). The Athenians were noted for their wit and elegant turns of thought.

***Attics, Attic Storey.*** Attics are the rooms in the attic storey, which is an extra storey made in the roof. In the Roman and Renaissance styles of architecture the low storey above the cornice or entablature is called the 'Attic', because it was usually constructed of small pilasters instead of columns. *See* Attic Order.

Humorously, the *attic* or *attic storey* is the head; the body being compared to a house, the head is the highest storey.

Here a gentleman present, who had in his attic
More pepper than brains, shrieked: 'The man's a
fanatic.' Lowell, *Fable for Critics*, 50

***He's got rats in the attic.*** Said of a harmless lunatic or silly monomaniac.

***Ill furnished in the attic storey.*** Not clever, dull.

***Queer in the attic storey.*** Fuddled, partially intoxicated, or 'not quite right in the head'.

**Atticus.** The most elegant and finished scholar of the Romans, and a bookseller (109–32 BC). His admirable taste and sound judgment were so highly thought of that even Cicero submitted several of his treatises to him.

***The Christian Atticus.*** Reginald Heber (1783–1826), Bishop of Calcutta.

***The English Atticus.*** Joseph Addison (1672–1719), so called by Pope (*Prologue to Satires*), on account of his refined taste and philosophical mind.

***The Irish Atticus.*** George Faulkner (1700–75), bookseller, publisher, and friend of Swift; so called by Lord Chesterfield when Viceroy of Ireland.

**Attila.** *See* Etzel.

**Attingians.** Heretics of the 8th century, who solemnised baptism with the words, 'I am the living water.'

**Attis.** *See* Atys.

**Attorney** (Fr. *atourner*, to attorn, or turn over to another). One legally qualified to manage matters in law for others, and to prosecute or defend others, as the case may be. A *solicitor* is one who solicits or petitions in Courts of Equity on behalf of his clients. At one time solicitors belonged to Courts of Equity, and attorneys to the other courts.

From and after Act 36, 37 Vict. lxvi, 87, 'all persons admitted as solicitors, attorneys, or proctors ... empowered to practise in any court, the jurisdiction of which to hereby transferred to the High Court of Justice, or the Court of Appeal, shall be called Solicitors of the Supreme Court' (1873).

***Power of Attorney.*** Legal authority given to another to collect rents, pay wages, invest money, or to act in matters stated in the instrument on your behalf, according to his own judgment. In such cases *quod aliquis facit per aliquem, facit per se*.

***Warrant of Attorney.*** The legal instrument which confers on another the 'Power of Attorney'.

**Atys.** The Phrygian counterpart of the Greek Adonis and Phoenician Tammuz. He was beloved by Cybele, the mother of the gods, but died in youth at a pine tree, and violets sprang from his blood. A three days' festival was held in his honour every spring; great grief and mourning was expressed, he was sought for on the mountains, and on the third day brought back to the shrine of Cybele amid great rejoicing.

**Au courant** (Fr.), 'acquainted with' (literally, in the current [of events]). To keep one *au courant* of everything that passes, is to keep one familiar with, or informed of, passing events.

**Au fait** (Fr.). Skilful, thorough master of; as, He is quite *au fait* in those matters, i.e. quite master of them or conversant with them.

**A.U.C.** Abbreviation of the Lat. *Anno Urbis Conditae*, 'from the foundation of the city' (Rome). It is the starting point of the Roman system of dating events, and corresponds with 753 BC.

**Au pied de la lettre** (Fr.). *Literatim et verbatim*; according to the strict letter of the text.

Arthur is but a boy, and a wild, enthusiastic young fellow whose opinions one must not take *au pied de la lettre*. Thackeray, *Pendennis*, i, 11

**Au revoir** (Fr.). 'Goodbye for the present.' Literally, *till seeing you again*.

**Aubaine.** *See* Droit d'Aubaine.

**Aubry's Dog.** *See* Dog.

**Audeanism.** The doctrine of Audeus of Mesopotamia, who lived in the 4th century. He held various heretical beliefs, among which was one to the effect that Gen. 1:26 justifies the belief that God has a sensible form.

**Audhumla.** In *Scandinavian mythology*, the cow created by Surtr to nourish Ymir (*q.v.*). She supplied him with four rivers of milk. Through her licking the salty stones Buri arose; his son, Borr, was the father of Odin.

**Audley.** *We will John Audley it.* A theatrical phrase meaning to abridge, or bring to a conclusion, a play in progress. It is said that in the 18th century a travelling showman named Shuter used to lengthen out his performance till a goodly number of newcomers were waiting for admission. An assistant would then call out, 'Is John Audley here?' and the play was brought to an end as soon as possible.

**Audrey.** In Shakespeare's *As You Like It*, an awkward country wench, who jilted William for Touchstone. *See also* Tawdry.

**Augean Stables.** The stables of Augeas, the mythological king of Elis, in Greece. In these stables he had kept 3,000 oxen, and they had not been cleansed for thirty years. One of the labours of Hercules (*q.v.*) was to cleanse them, and he did so by causing two rivers to run through them. Hence the phrase, *to cleanse the Augean stables*, means to clear away an accumulated mass of corruption, moral, religious, physical, or legal.

**Augsburg Confession.** The chief standard of faith in the Lutheran Church, drawn up by Melancthon and Luther in 1530, and presented to Charles V and the Diet of the German Empire, which was sitting at Augsburg.

*The Interim of Augsburg.* A Concordat drawn up by Charles V in 1548 to allay the religious turmoil of Germany. It was a provisional arrangement, based on the Augsburg Confession, and was to be in force till some definite decision could be pronounced by the General Council to be held at Trent.

The *Interim of Ratisbon* was a similar temporary arrangement, resulting from the Diet of Ratisbon (1541).

**Augury** (probably from Lat. *avis*, a bird, and *garrire*, to talk), means properly the function of an augur, i.e. a religious official among the Romans who professed to foretell future events from omens derived chiefly from the actions of birds. The augur, having taken his stand on the Capitoline Hill, marked out with his wand the space of the heavens to be the field of observation, and divided it from top to bottom. If the birds appeared on the left of the division the augury was unlucky, but if on the right it was favourable.

> 'Hail, gentle bird, turn thy wings and fly on my right hand!' but the bird flew on the left side. Then the cat grew very heavy, for he knew the omen to be unlucky. *Reynard the Fox*, iii

This form of divination may have been due to the earliest sailors, who, if they ever got out of sight of land, would watch the flight of birds for indications of the shore. *Cp.* Inaugurate; Sinister.

**August.** This month was once called *sextilis*, as it was the sixth from March, with which the year used to open, but was changed to *Augustus* in compliment to Augustus (63 BC–AD 14), the first Roman Emperor, whose 'lucky month' it was. *Cp.* July. It was the month in which he entered upon his first consulship, celebrated three triumphs, received the oath of allegiance from the legions which occupied the Janiculum, reduced Egypt, and put an end to the civil wars.

The old Dutch name for August was *Oost-maand* (harvest-month); the old Saxon *Weod-monath* (weed-month), where weed signifies vegetation in general. In the French Republican calendar it was called *Thermidor* (hot-month, July 19th to August 17th).

**Augusta.** The Roman name for their town that occupied the site of the City of London.

> Oft let me wander o'er the dewy fields,
> ... or ascend
> Some eminence, Augusta, in thy plains,
> And see the country far diffused around.
> Thomson, *Spring*, 102, 107–9

**Augustan Age.** The best literary period of a nation; so called from Augustus (*see* August), whose period was the most fruitful and splendid time of Latin literature. Horace, Ovid, Propertius, Tibullus, Virgil, etc., flourished in his reign (27 BC–AD 14).

*Augustan Age of English Literature.* The period of Pope, Addison, Steele, Thomson, and the classical writers of the time of Queen Anne and George I.

**Augustan History.** A series of histories of the Roman Empire from Hadrian to Numerianus (117–285), of unknown authorship and date, but ascribed to Aelius Spartianus, Julius Capitolinus, Aelius Lampridius, Vulcatius Gallicanus, Trebellius Pollio, and Flavius Vopiscus.

**Augustine, The Second.** Thomas Aquinas, the *Angelic Doctor* (*q.v.*).

**Augustinian Canons.** An order of monks founded in the 11th century by Ivo, Bishop of Chartres, and following the traditionary rule of Augustine, Bishop of Hippo (d.430). They came to England in the reign of Henry I, and had houses at Oxford, Bristol, Carlisle, Walsingham, Newstead, etc.

**Augustinian,** or **Austin, Friars.** A mendicant order founded by Innocent IV in 1250; they came to England two years later. *See* Begging Friars.

**Augustus.** A title conferred in 27 BC upon Caius Julius Caesar Octavianus, the first Roman Emperor, meaning *reverend*, or *venerable*, and probably in origin *consecrated by augury*. In the reign of Diocletian (284–313) the two emperors each bore the title, and the two viceroys that of *Caesar*. Prior to that time Hadrian limited the latter to the heir presumptive.

**Augustus.** Philippe II of France; so called because he was born in the month of August (1165, 1180–1223.)

Sigismund II of Poland. (1520, 1548–72.)

**Auld Brig** and **New Brig,** of Robert Burns, refers to the bridges over the river Ayr, in Scotland.

**Auld Hornie.** After the establishment of Christianity, the heathen deities were degraded by the Church into fallen angels; and Pan, with his horns, crooked nose, goat's beard, pointed ears, and goat's feet, was transformed to his Satanic majesty, and called Old Horny.

> O thou, whatever title suit thee,
> Auld Hornie, Satan, Nick, or Clootie. Burns

**Auld Reekie.** Edinburgh old town; so called because it generally appears to be capped by a cloud of 'reek' or smoke.

**Aulic Council** (Lat. *aula*, a court). The council of the Kaiser in the Holy Roman Empire, from which there was no appeal. It was instituted in 1501, and came to an end with the extinction of the Empire in 1806, though the name was afterwards given to the Emperor of Austria's Council of State.

**Aums-ace.** *See* Ambsas.

**Aunt Sally.** A game in which sticks or cudgels are thrown at a wooden head mounted on a pole, the object being to hit the nose of the figure, or break the pipe stuck in its mouth. The word *aunt* was anciently applied to any old woman; thus, in Shakespeare, Puck speaks of

> The wisest aunt telling the saddest tale.
> *Midsummer Night's Dream*, 2, 1

**Aureole.** Strictly speaking, the same as the *vesica piscis* (*q.v.*), i.e. an elliptical halo of light or colour surrounding the whole figure in early paintings of the Saviour and sometimes of the saints. Now, however, frequently used as though synonymous with *nimbus* (*q.v.*).

> Du Cange inform us that the aureola of nuns is *white*, of martyrs *red*, and of doctors *green*.
>
> Herself shall bring us, hand in hand,
> To Him round whom all souls
> Kneel, the clear-ranged, unnumbered heads
> Bowed with their aureoles:
> And angels meeting us shall sing
> To their citherns and citoles.
> Rossetti, *The Blessed Damozel*

**Auri sacra fames.** A Latin 'tag' from the *Aeneid* (III, 57), meaning, the cursed hunger for wealth. It is applied to that restless craving for money which is almost a monomania.

**Aurora.** Early morning. According to *Grecian mythology*, the goddess Aurora, called by Homer 'rosy-fingered', sets out before the sun, and is the pioneer of his rising.

> The Orator hath yoked
> The Hours, like young Aurora, to his car.
> Wordsworth, *Prelude*, vii, 501

*Aurora's tears.* The morning dew.

**Aurora Borealis.** The electrical lights occasionally seen in the northern part of the sky; also called 'Northern Lights', and 'Merry Dancers'. *See* Derwentwater. The similar phenomenon that occurs in the south and round the South Pole is known as the *Aurora Australis*, or *Septentrionalis*,

**Ausonia.** An ancient name of Italy; so called from Auson, son of Ulysses, and father of the Ausones.

> England, with all thy faults, I love thee still ...:
> I would not yet exchange thy sullen skies,
> And fields without a flower for warmer France
> With all her vines; nor for Ausonia'a groves
> Of golden fruitage, and her myrtle bowers.
> Cowper, *The Task*, ii, 206–15

**Auspices.** In ancient Rome the *auspex* (pl. *auspices*, from *avis*, a bird and *specere*, to observe) was one who observed the flight of birds and interpreted the omens. *Cp.* Augury.

Only the chief in command was allowed to take the auspices of war, and if a subordinate gained a victory, he was said to win it 'under the good auspices' of his superior. Hence our modern use of the term.

**Auster** (Gr. *austeros*, hot, dry). A wind pernicious to flowers and health. In Italy one of the *South* winds was so called; its modern name is the *Sirocco*. In England it is a damp wind, generally bringing wet weather.

> Whan the wode wexeth rody of rosene floures, in the first somer sesoun, thorugh the brethe of the winde Zephirus that wexeth warm, yif the cloudy wind Auster blowe felliche, than goth awey the fairnesse of thornes.
> Chaucer, *Boethius*, II, iii

**Austin Friars.** *See* Augustinian Friars. The narrow lane in the City of London of this name is so called because it is on part of the site of an Augustinian priory, the church of which still remains.

**Aut Caesar aut nullus** (Lat. either a Caesar or a nobody). Everything or nothing; all or not at all. Caesar used to say, 'he would sooner be first in a village than second at Rome'. The phrase was used as a motto by Caesar Borgia (1478–1507), the natural son of Pope Alexander VI.

**Authentic Doctor.** A title bestowed on the scholastic philosopher, Gregory of Rimini (d.1358).

**Authorised Version, The.** *See* Bible, the English.

**Auto da Fé** (Port. an act of faith). A day set apart by the Inquisition for the examination of heretics, or for the carrying into execution of the sentences imposed by it. Those who persisted in their heresy were delivered to the secular arm and usually burnt. The reason why inquisitors *burnt* their victims was, because they are forbidden to 'shed blood'; an axiom of the Roman Catholic Church being, *Ecclesia non novit sanguinem* (The Church is untainted with blood).

**Autogenes.** *See* Barbeliots.

**Autolycus.** In *Greek mythology*, son of Mercury, and the craftiest of thieves. He stole the flocks of his neighbours, and changed their marks; but Sisyphus outwitted him by marking his sheep under their feet, a device which so tickled the rogue that he instantly 'cottoned' to him. Shakespeare uses his name for the rascally pedlar in *The Winter's Tale*, and says:

> My father named me Autolycus; who being, as I am, littered (i.e. born) under Mercury, was likewise a snapper-up of unconsidered trifles.
>
> *Winter's Tale*, 4, 2

**Automedon.** A coachman. He was, according to Homer, the companion and the charioteer of Achilles, but according to Virgil the brother-in-arms of Achilles' son, Pyrrhus.

**Autumn.** The third season of the year; *astronomically*, from September 21st to December 21st, but *popularly* comprising (in England) August, September, and October.

*Figuratively* the word may mean the fruits of autumn, as in Milton's:

> Raised of grassy turf
> Their table was, and mossy seats had round,
> And on her ample square, from side to side,
> All autumn piled. *Paradise Lost*, v, 391

or, a season of maturity or decay, as in Shelley's:

> His limbs were lean; his scattered hair,
> Sered by the autumn of strange suffering,
> Sung dirges in the wind. *Alastor*, 248

*He is come to his Autumn.* A colloquialism, which may mean either that he has entered on his period of (natural or induced) decay, or to his fall, 'fall' being formerly in England and still in America a synonym of autumn (short for 'the fall of the leaf').

**Avalanche** (Fr. descent; from *à val*, to the valley). A mass of snow mixed with earth, ice, and stones, which slips down a mountain-side to the lower ground. Metaphorically, we speak of an 'avalanche of applause', an 'avalanche of bouquets' showered on the stage, etc., and of anything overwhelming:

> Here Penury oft from misery's mount will guide
> Ev'n to the summer door his icy tide,
> And here the avalanche of Death destroy
> The little cottage of domestic Joy.
>
> Wordsworth, *Descriptive Sketches*, 600

**Avalon.** A Celtic word meaning 'the island of apples', and in *Celtic mythology* applied to the Island of Blessed Souls, an earthly paradise set in the western seas. In the Arthurian legends it is the abode and burial-place of Arthur, who was carried hither by Morgan le Fay. Its identification with Glastonbury (*q.v.*) rests on etymological confusion. Ogier le Dane and Oberon also held their Courts at Avalon.

**Avant-courier.** An Anglicised form of Fr. *avant-coureur*, a messenger sent before, one who is to get things ready for a party of travellers, soldiers, etc., or to announce their approach. Figuratively, anything said or done to prepare the way for something more important; a feeler, a harbinger.

**Avant-garde** (Fr.). The advanced guard of an army, usually nowadays cut down to *vanguard*.

**Avars.** *See* Banat.

**Avatar** (Sans. *avatara*, descent; hence, incarnation of a god). In *Hindu mythology*, the advent to earth of a deity in a visible form. The ten avataras of Vishnu are by far the most celebrated. 1st advent (the Matsya), in the form of a fish; 2nd (the Kurma), in that of a tortoise; 3rd (the Varaha), of a boar; 4th (the Narasinha), of a monster, half man and half lion; 5th (the Vamana), in the form of a dwarf; 6th (Parashurama), in human form, as Râma with the axe; 7th (Ramachandra), again as Râma; 8th, as Krishna (*q.v.*); 9th, as Buddha. These are all past. The 10th advent will occur at the end of four ages, and will be in the form of a white horse (Kalki) with wings, to destroy the earth.

> In Vishnu land what avatar?
> Or who in Moscow, towards the czar?
>
> Browning

The word is used metaphorically to denote a manifestation or embodiment of some idea or phase:

> I would take the last years of Queen Anne's reign as the zenith, or palmy state, of Whiggism, in its divinest avatar of common sense.
>
> Coleridge, *Table-talk*

**Ave atque vale.** *See* Vale.

**Ave Maria** (Lat. Hail, Mary!). The first two words of the angel's salutation to the Virgin Mary (Luke 1:28). In the Roman Catholic Church the phrase is applied to an invocation to the Virgin beginning with those words; and also to the smaller beads of a rosary, the larger ones being termed *pater-nosters*.

**Avenel.** Name of a family, a number of members of which appear in Scott's *Monastery* and *Abbot.* The *White Lady of Avenel* is a tutelary spirit in the *Monastery*.

**Avenger of Blood, The.** The man who, in the Jewish polity, had the right of taking vengeance on him who had slain one of his kinsmen (Josh. 20:5, etc.). The Avenger in Hebrew is called *goël*.

> Cities of refuge were appointed for the protection of homicides, and of those who had caused another's death by accident. (Numb. 35:12.) The Koran sanctions the Jewish custom.

**Aver.** *See* Avoirdupois.

**Avernus** (Gr. *a-ornis*, 'without a bird'). A lake in Campania, so called from the belief that its sulphurous and mephitic vapours caused any bird that attempted to fly over it to fall into its waters. *Latin mythology* placed the entrance to the infernal regions near it; hence Virgil's lines:

> Facilis decensus Averno
> Noctes atque dies patet atri janua Ditis;
> Sed revocare gradum, superasque evadere ad auras,
> Hoc opus, hic labor est. *Aeneid*, vi, 126

English by Dryden as follows:

> Smooth the descent and easy is the way;
> (The Gates of Hell stand open night and day)
> But to return, and view the cheerful skies,
> In this the task and mighty labour lies.

Bad habits are easily acquired, but very hard to be abandoned.

**Avesta.** The Zoroastrian and Parsee Bible, dating in its present form from the last quarter of the 4th century, AD, collected from the ancient writings, sermons, etc., of Zoroaster (fl. before 800 BC), oral traditions, etc. It is only a fragment, and consists of (1) the Yasna, the chief liturgical portion, which includes *Gathas*, or hymns; (2) the Vispered, another liturgical work; (3) the Vendidad, which, like our Pentateuch, contains the laws; (4) the Yashts, dealing with stories of the different gods; together with prayers and other fragments.

The books are sometimes erroneously called the Zend-Avesta; this is a topsy-turvy misunderstanding of the term 'Avesta-Zend', which means simply 'text and commentary'.

**Aveugle** (Fr. the blind one). The name given by Spenser to the father of Sansfoy, Sansjoy, and Sansloy (*Faërie Queene*, Bk I, ca. v).

**Avianus.** A writer of imitations of Aesop's fables in the decline of the Roman empire. In the Middle Ages they were used as a first lesson book in schools.

**Avicenna.** *See* Abou ibn Sina.

**A vinculo matrimonii** (Lat.). A total divorce from marriage ties. A divorce *a mensa et thoro* (i.e. from table and bed – from bed and board) is partial, because the parties may, if they choose, come together again; but a divorce *a vinculo matrimonii* is granted in cases in which the 'marriage' was never legal owing to a precontract (bigamy), consanguinity, or affinity.

**Avoid Extremes.** A traditional saying of Pittacus of Mitylene (652–569 BC), one of the seven Wise Men of Greece. It is echoed in many writers and literatures. Compare the advice given by Phoebus to Phaethon when he was preparing to drive the chariot of the sun:

> Medio tutissimus ibis (You will go more safely in the middle). Ovid, *Met*, ii, 137

**Avoirdupois.** Fr. *avoir*, *aver* or *avier*, goods in general, and *poise* = *poids* (weight). Not the verb, but the noun *avoir*. Properly *avoir de poids* (goods having weight), goods sold by weight. There is an obsolete English word *aver*, meaning goods in general, hence also cattle; whence such compounds as *aver-corn*, *aver-penny*, *aver-silver* and *aver-land*.

**Awar.** One of the sons of Eblis (*q.v.*).

**A-weather.** A sailor's term; towards the weather, or the side on which the wind strikes, the reverse of *a-lee*, which is in the *lee* or shelter, and therefore opposite to the wind side.

**Awkward.** Not dexterous, *gauche*. From an O.E. adjective, *awk*, meaning turned the wrong way round, back-handed, or from the left hand.

**Awkward Squad.** Military recruits not yet fitted to take their place in the ranks.

> A 'squad' is a small body of soldiers under a sergeant; the word is a contraction of 'squadron'. A squadron of cavalry is the unit of a regiment, as a rule four going to a regiment. In the Navy a squadron is a section of a fleet.

**Awl.** ***'I'll pack up my awls and be gone,'*** i.e. all my goods. The play is on *awl* and *all*.

**Axe.** ***To hang up one's axe.*** To retire from business, to give over a useless project. The allusion is to the battle-axe, formerly devoted to the gods and hung up when fighting was over. *See* Ask.

***He has an axe to grind.*** Some selfish motive in the background; some personal interest to answer. Franklin tells of a man who wanted to grind his axe, but had no one to turn the grindstone. Going to the yard where he saw young Franklin, he asked the boy to show him how the machine worked, and kept praising him till his axe was ground, and then laughed at him for his pains.

***To put the axe on the helve.*** To solve a difficulty. To hit the right nail on the head.

***To send the axe after the helve.*** To spend money in the hope of recovering bad debts.

***Where the chicken got the axe.*** *See To get it in the neck*, under Neck.

**Axinomancy.** A method of divination practised by the ancient Greeks with a view to discovering crime. An agate, or piece of jet, was placed on a red-hot axe, and indicated the guilty person by its motion. (Gr. *axine manteia.*)

**Ayah.** Now an Anglo-Indian word, but originally Portuguese. A native Hindu nurse or lady's maid.

**Ayeshah.** Mahomet's second and favourite wife. He married her when she was only nine years old, and died in her arms. She was born about 611 and died about 678.

**Aymon, The Four Sons of.** A mediaeval French romance belonging to the Charlemagne cycle. Aymon is a semi-mythical hero, and was father of Reynaud (or Rinaldo, *q.v.*), Guiscard, Alard, and Richard, all of whom were knighted by Charlemagne. The earliest version was probably compiled by Huon de Villeneuve from earlier chansons in the 13th century. The brothers, and their famous horse Bayard (*q.v.*), appear in many poems and romances, including Tasso's *Jerusalem Delivered*, Pulci's *Morgante Maggiore*, Boiardo's *Orlando Innamorato*, Ariosto's *Orlando Furioso*, etc., and it formed the basis of a number of French chap-books.

**Ayrshire Poet.** Robert Burns (1759–96), who was born near the town of Ayr.

**Azazel.** In Lev. 16 we read that among other ceremonies the high priest, on the Day of Atonement, cast lots on two goats; one lot was *for the Lord*, and the other lot *for Azazel*; the goat on which the latter lot fell was the scapegoat (*q.v.*). No satisfactory explanation of the word *Azazel* has been forthcoming; it may have referred to the scapegoat itself, or the place to which it was sent, or (which seems most likely) to an evil spirit inhabiting the desert. Milton uses the name for the standard-bearer of the rebel angels (*Paradise Lost*, i, 534). In Mohammedan legend, Azazel is a jinn of the desert; when God commanded the angels to worship Adam, Azazel replied, 'Why should the son of fire fall down before a son of clay?' and God cast him out of heaven. His name was then changed to *Eblis* (*q.v.*), which means 'despair'.

**Azaziel.** In Byron's *Heaven and Earth*, a seraph who fell in love with Anah, a granddaughter of Cain. When the flood came, he carried her under his wing to another planet.

**Azor's Mirror.** Zémire is the name of the lady, and Azor that of the beast, in Marmontel's tale of *Beauty and the Beast*. Zémire entreats the kind monster to let her see her father, if only for a few moments; so drawing aside a curtain, he shows him to her in a magic mirror, which, like a telescope, rendered distant objects distinctly visible.

**Azoth** (Arab.). The alchemist's name for mercury; also the panacea or universal remedy of Paracelsus. Browning, in his poem *Paracelsus* (Bk v), gives the name to Paracelsus's sword.

> Last, my good sword; ah, trusty Azoth, leapest
> Beneath thy master's grasp for the last time?

**Azrael.** In Mohammedan legend, the angel that watches over the dying, and takes the soul from the body; the angel of death. He will be the last to die, but will do so at the second trump of the archangel. *See* Adam.

***The Wings of Azrael.*** The approach of death; the signs of death coming on the dying.

**Azrafil.** *See* Israfil.

**Aztecs.** A branch of the Nahuatl Indians who came (probably) from the north-west and settled in the valley of Mexico about the 11th or 12th century, and ultimately subjugated the aborigines. Their power was put to an end by the Spaniards under Cortes between 1519 and 1530.

**Azure.** Sky blue. Represented in royal arms by the planet Jupiter, in noblemen's by the sapphire. The ground of the old shield of France was azure. Emblem of fidelity and truth. Represented in heraldic devices by horizontal lines. Ultimately Arabic or Persian, and connected with 'lapis *lazuli*', for which the word 'azure' used to stand. The blue colour in coats of arms; represented in engraving by horizontal lines. Also used as a synonym for the clear, blue sky.

**Azuriel.** *See* Kensington Garden.

**Azymites** (Gr. *azumos*, unleavened). The Roman Catholics are so called by the Greek Church, because the holy wafers used by them in the Eucharist are made of unleavened bread.

# B

**B.** The form of the Roman capital 'B' can be traced through early Greek to Phoenician and Egyptian hieratic; the small 'b' is derived from the cursive form of the capital. The letter is called in Hebrew *beth* (a house); in Egyptian hieroglyphics it was represented by the crane.

**B** in *Roman notation* stands for 300; with a *line above*, it denotes 3,000.

For *Becarre* and *Bemol* (French for B sharp and B flat) *see* Becarre.

***Marked with a B.*** In the Middle Ages, and as late as the 17th century (especially in America), this letter was branded on the forehead of convicted blasphemers. In France *être marqué au 'b'* means to be either one-eyed, hump-backed, or lame (*borgne*, *bossu*, *boiteux*); hence, a poor, miserable sort of creature.

***Not to know B from a battledore,*** or ***from a bull's foot.*** To be quite illiterate, not to know even one's letters. Conversely, *I know B from a bull's foot*, means 'I'm a sharp, knowing person; you can't catch *me*!' *Cp.* Hawk and Handsaw.

**B.C.** In dates an abbreviation for 'Before Christ', before the Christian era.

***Marked with B.C.*** When a soldier disgraced himself by insubordination he was formerly marked with 'B.C. (bad character) before he was drummed out of the regiment.

**B. and S.** Brandy and soda.

**B. K. S.** A humorous abbreviation of BarracKS, which formerly used to be given as an address by officers in mufti who did not wish to give their own address.

**B Flats.** Bugs; which obnoxious insects are characterised by their flatness. *See also* Norfolk-Howards. *Cp.* F. Sharp.

**B's.** ***Four B's essential for social success.*** Blood, brains, brass, brads (money). (Amer.)

**B. of B. K.** Some mysterious initials applied to himself in his diary by Arthur Orton, 'the Tichborne Claimant'. Supposed to denote 'Baronet of British Kingdom'.

**Baal.** A Semitic word meaning *proprietor* or *possessor*, primarily the title of a god as lord of a place (e.g. *Baal-peor*, lord of Peor), or as possessor of some distinctive characteristic or attribute (e.g. *Baal-zebub*, or *Beelzebub*, *q.v.*). The worship of the Baals – for they were legion – was firmly established in Canaan at the time of the Israelites' incursion; the latter adopted many of the Canaanitish rites, and grafted them on to their own worship of Jehovah, Jehovah becoming – especially when worshipped at the 'high places' – merely the national Baal. It was this form of worship that Hosea and other prophets denounced as heathenism. Bel (*q.v.*) is the Assyrian form of the name. *See also* Belphegor.

**Baalbec.** *See* Chilminar.

**Babel.** ***A perfect Babel.*** A thorough confusion. 'A Babel of sounds'. A confused uproar, in which nothing can be heard but hubbub. The allusion is to the confusion of tongues at Babel (Gen. 11).

God ... comes down to see their city,
... and in derision sets
Upon their tongues a various spirit, to raze
Quite out their native language, and instead
To sow a jangling noise of words unknown.
Forthwith a hideous gabble rises loud
Among the builders; each to other calls
Not understood ... Thus was the building left
Ridiculous, and the work Confusion named.

Milton, *Paradise Lost*, xii, 48–62

**Babes in the Wood.** *See* Children. The phrase has been humorously applied to (1) simple trustful folks, never suspicious, and easily gulled; (2) insurrectionary hordes that infested the mountains of Wicklow and the woods of Enniscorthy towards the close of the 18th century; and (3) men in the stocks or in the pillory.

**Babes, Protecting Deities of.** According to Varro, Roman infants were looked after by Vagitanus, the god who caused them to utter their first *cry*; Fabulinus, who presided over their *speech*; Cuba, the goddess who protected them in their cots; and Domiduca, who brought young children safe home, and kept guard over them when out of their parents' sight.

**Babies in the Eyes.** Love in the expression of the eyes. Love is the little babe Cupid, and hence the conceit, originating from the miniature image of oneself in the pupil of another's eyes.

In each of her two crystal eyes
Smileth a naked boy [Cupid]. Lord Surrey

She clung about his neck, gave him ten kisses,
Toyed with his looks, looked babies in his eyes.

Heywood, *Love's Mistress*

**Baboon, Lewis.** *See* Lewis.

**Babouin.** *Taisez-vous, petite babouin; laissez parlez votre mère, qui est plus sage que vous.* The tale or fable is this: A girl one day went to make an offering to Venus, and prayed the goddess to give her for husband a young man on whom she had fixed her affections. A young fellow happened at the time to be behind the image of Cupid, and hearing the petition, replied, 'So fine a gentleman is not for such as you.' The voice seemed to proceed from the image, and the girl replied, 'Hold your tongue, you little monkey; let your mother speak, for she is wiser than you.'

**Babylon.** ***The Modern Babylon.*** So London is sometimes called, on account of its wealth, luxury, and dissipation; also (with allusion to Babel) because of the many nationalities that meet, and languages that are spoken there.

***The hanging gardens of Babylon.*** *See* Hanging.

***The whore of Babylon.*** An epithet bestowed on the Roman Catholic Church by the early Puritans and some of their descendants. The allusion is to Rev. 17–19. (*Cp.* Scarlet Woman). In the book of the *Revelation* Babylon stands for the city of the Antichrist (*q.v.*).

**Babylonian Captivity.** The seventy years that the Jews were captives in Babylon. They were made captives by Nebuchadnezzar, and released by Cyrus (536 BC).

**Babylonian Numbers.** *Nec Babylonios temptaris numeros* (Horace, *Odes*, Bk i, xi, 2). Do not pry into futurity by astrological calculations and horoscopes. Do not consult fortune-tellers. The Chaldeans were the most noted of astrologers.

**Babylonish Garment, A.** *Babylonica vestis*, a garment woven with divers colours. Pliny, viii, 74.

> I saw among the spoils a goodly Babylonish garment. Josh. 7:21

**Baca, The Valley of.** An unidentified place mentioned in Ps. 84:6, meaning the Valley of Weeping, and so translated in the Revised Version. Baca trees were either mulberry trees or balsams.

> Our sources of common pleasure dry up as we journey on through the vale of Bacha.
>
> Scott, *The Antiquary*

**Bacbuc.** A Chaldean or Assyrian word for an earthenware pitcher, cruse, or bottle, taken by Rabelais as the name of the Oracle of the Holy Bottle (and of its priestess), to which Pantagruel and his companions made a famous voyage. The question to be proposed was whether or not Panurge ought to marry. The Holy Bottle answered with a click like the noise made by a glass snapping. Bacbuc told Panurge the noise meant *trinc* (drink), and that was the response, the most direct and positive ever given by the oracle. Panurge might interpret it as he liked, the obscurity would always save the oracle. *See* Oracle.

**Bacchanalia.** The triennial festivals held at night in Rome in honour of Bacchus, called in Greece *Dionysia*, Dionysus being the Greek equivalent of Bacchus. In Rome, and in later times in Greece, they were characterised by drunkenness, debauchery, and licentiousness of all kinds; but originally they were very different from this, and are of greater importance than are any other ancient festivals on account of their connection with the origin and development of the drama; for in Attica, at the Dionysia choragic literary contests were held, and from these both tragedy and comedy originated. Hence *bacchanalian*, drunken. The terms are now applied to any drunken and convivial orgy on the grand scale.

**Bacchanals** (*see also* Bag o' Nails), *Bacchants, Bacchantes.* Priests and priestesses, or male and female votaries, of Bacchus; hence, a drunken roysterer.

> The ivy falls with the Bacchanal's hair
> Over her eyebrows, hiding her eyes;
> The wild vine slipping down leaves bare
> Her bright breast shortening into sighs.
>
> Swinburne, *Atalanta in Calydon*

A female wine-bibber; so called from the 'bacchantes', or female priestesses of Bacchus. They wore fillets of ivy.

**Bacchus.** In *Roman mythology*, the god of wine, the Dionysus of the Greeks, son of Zeus and Semele. He is represented in early art as a bearded man and completely clad, but after the time of Praxiteles as a beautiful youth with black eyes, golden locks, flowing with curls about his shoulders, and filleted with ivy. In peace his robe was purple, in war he was covered with a panther's skin. His chariot was drawn by panthers.

In the famous statue at the Borghese Palace he has a bunch of grapes in his hand and a panther at his feet. Pliny tells us that, after his conquest of India, Bacchus entered Thebes in a chariot drawn by elephants, and, according to some accounts, he married Ariadne after Theseus had deserted her in Naxos.

The name 'Bacchus' is a corruption of Gr. *Iacchus* (from *Iache*, a shout), and was originally merely an epithet of Dionysus as the noisy or rowdy god.

> As jolly Bacchus, god of pleasure,
> Charmed the wide world with drink and dances,
> And all his thousand airy fancies. Parnell

***Bacchus sprang from the thigh of Zeus.*** The tale is that Semele, at the suggestion of Juno, asked Zeus to appear before her in all his glory, but the foolish request proved her death. Zeus saved the child which was prematurely born by sewing it up in his thigh till it came to maturity.

***What has that to do with Bacchus?*** i.e. what has that to do with the matter in hand? When Thespis introduced recitations in the vintage songs, the innovation was suffered to pass, so long as the subject of recitation bore on the exploits of Bacchus; but when, for variety sake, he wandered to other subjects, the Greeks pulled him up with the exclamation, 'What has that to do with Bacchus?' *Cp.* Moutons.

***Bacchus a noyé plus d'hommes que Neptune.*** The ale-house wrecks more men than the ocean.

***A priest,*** or ***son, of Bacchus.*** A toper.

> The jolly old priests of Bacchus in the parlour make their libations of claret.
>
> J. S. Le Fanu, *The House in the Churchyard*, p. 113

**Bacchus,** in the *Lusiad*, is the evil demon or antagonist of Jupiter, the lord of destiny. As Mars is the guardian power of Christianity, Bacchus is the guardian power of Mohammedanism.

**Bachelor.** A man who has not been married. This is a word whose ultimate etymology is unknown; it is from O.Fr. *bacheler*, which is from a late Latin word *baccalaris*. This last may be merely a translation of the French word, as it is only of rare and very late occurrence, but it may be allied to *baccalarius*, a late Latin adjective applied to farm labourers, the history of which is very doubtful.

In the Prologue to the *Canterbury Tales* (1. 80), Chaucer uses the word in its old sense of a knight not old enough to display his own banner, and so following that of another.

> With him ther was his sone, a young Squyer,
> A lovyere, and a lusty bacheler.

*Cp.* Knights Bachelors.

***Bachelor of Arts.*** A student who has passed his examinations and has taken the first or lowest degree at a university, but is not yet of standing to be a master.

***The Bachelor of Salamanca.*** The last novel of Le Sage (published in 1736); the hero is a bachelor of arts, Don Chérubin de la Ronda; he is placed in different situations of life, and associates with all classes of society.

***Bachelor's buttons.*** Several flowers are so called. Red bachelor's buttons, the double red campion; yellow, the upright crowfoot; white, the white ranunculus, or white campion.

> The similitude these flowers have to the jagged cloath buttons anciently worne … gave occasion … to call them Bachelour's Buttons.
>
> Gerard, *Herbal*

Or else from a custom still sometimes observed by rustics of carrying the flower in their pockets to know how they stand with their sweethearts. If the flower dies, it is a bad omen; but if it does not fade, they may hope for the best; hence, to *wear bachelor's buttons*, to remain a bachelor.

***Bachelor's fare.*** Bread and cheese and kisses.

***Bachelor's porch.*** An old name for the north door of a church. Menservants and poor men used to sit on benches down the north aisle, and maidservants and poor women on the south side. After service the men formed one line and the women another, down which the clergy and gentry passed.

***A bachelor's wife.*** A hypothetical ideal or perfect wife.

> Bachelors' wives and maids' children be well taught. Heywood, *Proverbs*

**Back, To.** To support with money, influence, or encouragement; as to 'back a friend'; to lay money on a horse in a race, 'backing' it to win or for a place.

A commercial term, meaning to *endorse*. When a merchant backs or endorses a bill, he guarantees its value.

Falstaff says to the Prince:

> You care not who sees your back. Call you that backing of your friends? A plague upon such backing! Shakespeare, *1 Henry IV*, 2, 4

***At the back of.*** Behind, following close after. Figure from following a leader.

> With half the city at his back. Byron, *Don Juan*

***At the back of beyond.*** Ever so far away; at some very out-of-the-way place.

***Back the oars,*** or ***back water,*** is to row backwards, that the boat may move the reverse of its ordinary direction.

***Back and edge.*** Entirely, heartily, tooth and nail, with might and main. The reference is, perhaps, to a wedge driven home to split wood.

> They were working back and edge for me.
>
> Boldrewood, *Robbery under Arms*, ch. ii

***Behind my back.*** When I was not present. When my back was turned.

***Laid on one's back.*** Laid up with chronic ill-health; helpless.

***Thrown on his back.*** Completely worsted. A figure taken from wrestling.

***To back and fill.*** A nautical phrase, denoting a mode of tacking when the tide is with the vessel and the wind against it. Metaphorically, to be irresolute.

***To back out.*** To withdraw from an engagement, bargain, etc.; to retreat from a difficult position.

***To back the field.*** To bet on all the horses bar one. A sporting term.

***To back the sails.*** So to arrange them that the ship's way may be checked.

***To back up.*** To uphold, to support. As one who stands at your back to support you.

***To break the back of.*** To finish the hardest part of one's work.

***To get one's back up.*** To be irritated. The allusion is to a cat, which sets its back up when attacked by a dog or other animal.

***To go back on one's word.*** To withdraw what one has said; to refuse to perform what one has promised. *To go back on a person* is to betray him.

***To have his back at the wall.*** To act on the defensive against odds. One beset with foes tries to get his back against a wall that he may not be attacked by foes behind.

> He planted his back against a wall, in a skilful attitude of fence, ready with his bright glancing rapier to do battle with all the heavy fierce unarmed men some six or seven in number.
>
> Mrs Gaskell, *The Poor Clare*, iii

***To see his back; to see the back of anything.*** To get rid of a person or thing; to see it leave.

***To take a back seat.*** To withdraw from a position one has occupied or attempted to occupy; to retire into obscurity, usually as a confession of failure. The phrase was originally American.

***To the back.*** To the backbone, entirely.

***To turn one's back on another.*** To leave, forsake, or neglect him. To leave one by going away.

**Backbite, To.** To slander behind one's back.

> The only thing in which all parties agreed was to backbite the manager.
>
> W. Irving, *Traveller*, *Buckthorne*, p. 193

**Backbone, The.** The main stay.

> Sober … practical men … constitute the moral backbone of the country.
>
> W. Booth, *In Darkest England* (Pt i, 2, p. 17)

***To the backbone.*** Thoroughly, as true to the backbone.

> A union man, and a nationalist to the backbone.
>
> T. Roosevelt, *T. H. Benton*, ch. v, p. 113

**Backgammon.** The A.S. *bac gamen* (back game), so called because the pieces (in certain circumstances) are taken up and obliged to go back to enter at the table again.

**Background.** *Placed in the background*, i.e. made of no consequence. Pictures have three distances, called grounds: the foreground, where the artist is supposed to be; the middle ground, where the most salient part of the picture is placed; and the background or distance, beyond which the eye cannot penetrate.

**Back-hander.** A blow with the back of the hand. Also one who takes *back* the decanter in order to *hand* himself another glass before the decanter is passed on.

> I'll take a back-hander, as Clive don't seem to drink.
>
> Thackeray, *The Newcomes*, ch. xliii

**Back-slang.** A species of slang which consists in pronouncing the word as though spelt backwards. Thus *police* becomes *ecilop* (hence the term *slop* for a policeman), *parsnips*, *spinsrap*, and so on. It was formerly much used by London costermongers.

**Back-speir, To.** To cross-examine. (Scotch.)

> He has the wit to lay the scene in such a remote … country that nobody should be able to back-speir him.
>
> Scott, *The Betrothed* (Introd.)

**Backstairs Influence.** Private or unrecognised influence, especially at Court. Royal palaces have more than one staircase, and those who sought the sovereign upon private matters would use one in an unobtrusive position; it was, therefore, highly desirable to conciliate the servants or underlings in charge of the 'back stairs'.

Hence, *backstairs gossip*, tittle-tattle obtained from servants; *backstairs plots*, underground or clandestine intrigue.

**Backward Blessing.** A curse. To say the Lord's Prayer backwards was to invoke the devil.

**Backwardation.** A Stock Exchange term denoting the sum paid by a speculator on a 'bear account' (i.e. a speculation on a *fall* in the price of certain stock), in order to postpone the completion of the transaction till the next settling day. *Cp.* Contango.

**Bacon.** ***To baste your bacon.*** To strike or scourge one. Bacon is the outside portion of the sides of pork, and may be considered generally as the part which would receive a blow.

Falstaff's remark to the travellers at Gadshill, 'On, bacons, on!' (*1 Henry IV*, 2, 2) is an allusion to the fact that formerly swine's flesh formed the staple food of English rustics; hence such terms as *bacon-brains* and *chaw-bacon* for a clownish blockhead.

***To save one's bacon.*** To save oneself from injury; to escape loss. The allusion may be to the care taken by our forefathers to save from the numerous dogs that frequented their houses the bacon which was laid up for winter.

> But as he rose to save his bacon,
> By hat and wig he was forsaken.
> Coombe, *Dr Syntax's Tour in Search of the Picturesque*, vi, 240

***He may fetch a flitch of bacon from Dunmow.*** He is so amiable and good-tempered he will never quarrel with his wife. The allusion is to the Dunmow Flitch. *See* Dunmow.

**Baconian Philosophy.** A system of philosophy based on principles laid down by Francis Bacon, Lord Verulam, in the 2nd book of his *Novum Organum*. It is also called inductive philosophy.

**Baconian Theory.** The theory that Lord Bacon wrote the plays attributed to Shakespeare.

**Bacon's Brazen Head.** *See* Brazen.

**Bactrian Sage.** Zoroaster, or Zarathusthra, the founder of the Perso-Iranian religion, who is supposed to have flourished in Bactria (the modern Balkh) before 800 BC.

**Bad.** Among rulers surnamed 'The Bad' are William I, King of Sicily from 1154 to 1166, Albert, Landgrave of Thuringia and Margrave of Meissen (d.1314), and Charles II, King of Navarre (1332–87).

***Bad blood.*** Vindictiveness, ill-feeling; hence, *to make bad blood*, or *to stir up bad blood*, to create or renew ill-feeling and a vindictive spirit.

***Bad books. You are in my bad books.*** *See* Black Books.

***Bad debts.*** Debts not likely to be paid.

***Bad form,*** not *comme il faut*. Not in good taste.

***The Bad Lands.*** In America, the *Mauvaises Terres* of the early French settlers west of Missouri; extensive tracts of sterile, alkali hills, rocky, desolate, and almost destitute of vegetation, in South Dakota.

***A bad lot.*** A person of bad moral character, or one commercially unsound. Also a commercial project or stock of worthless value. Perhaps from auctioneering slang, meaning a lot which no one will bid for. So an inefficient soldier is called one of the King's *bad bargains*.

***A bad shot.*** A wrong guess. A sporting phrase; a bad shot is one which does not bring down the bird shot at, one that misses the mark.

***He is gone to the bad.*** Has become a ruined man, or a depraved character. He is mixing with bad companions, has acquired bad habits, or is (usually implying 'through his own fault') in bad circumstances.

***To the bad.*** On the wrong side of the account; in arrears.

**Badaud.** A booby. *C'est un franc badaud*, he is a regular booby. *Le badaud de Paris*, a French cockney. From Lat. *badare*, to gaze in the air, to stare about one. *Cp.* Badinage.

**Badge-men.** Licensed beggars, or almshouse men; so called because they wore some special dress, or other badge, to indicate that they belonged to a particular foundation.

> He quits the gay and rich, the young and free,
> Among the badge-men with a badge to be.
> Crabbe, *Borough*

In former times those who received parish relief also had to wear a badge. It was the letter P, with the initial of the parish to which they belonged, in red or blue cloth, on the shoulder of the right sleeve. *See* Dyvour.

**Badger, A.** A hawker, huckster, or itinerant dealer, especially in corn, but also in butter, eggs, fish, etc. The word is still in use in some dialects; its derivation is not certainly known, but it is not in any way connected with a badge worn. Fuller derived it from Lat. *bajulare*, to carry, but there is no substantiation for this. The modern hawker's licence dates from the licences that badgers had to obtain from a Justice under Act 5 and 6 Edw. VI, c. 14, §7.

> Under Dec. 17,1565, we read of 'Certain persons upon Humber side who … by great quantities of corn, two of whom were authorised badgers.'
> *State Papers* (*Domestic Series*)

***To badger.*** To tease, annoy, or persistently importune, in allusion to badger-baiting. A badger was kennelled in a tub, where dogs were set upon him to worry him out. When dragged from his tub the poor beast was allowed to retire to it till he recovered from the attack. This process was repeated several times.

It is a vulgar error that the legs of a badger are shorter on one side than on the other.

> I think that Titus Oates was as uneven as a badger.
> Lord Macaulay

***Drawing a badger,*** is drawing him out of his tub by means of dogs.

In the USA *badger* is the slang name of an inhabitant of Wisconsin.

**Badinage.** Playful raillery, banter (Fr.), from the verb *badiner*, to joke or jest. This is from *badin*, a fool, a simpleton, which has the same origin as *badaud* (*see above*), viz. Lat. *badare*, to gape.

**Badinguet.** A nickname given to Napoleon III. It is said to be the name of the workman whose clothes he wore when he contrived to escape from the fortress of Ham, in 1846.

> If Badinguet and Bismarck have a row together let them settle it between them with their fists, instead of troubling hundreds of thousands of men who … have no wish to fight.
>
> Zola, *The Downfall*, ch. ii

**Badminton.** The country seat of the Dukes of Beaufort in Gloucestershire. It has given its name to a drink and a game. The drink is a claret-cup made of claret, sugar, spices, soda-water, and ice. In pugilistic parlance blood, which is sometimes called 'claret' (*q.v.*), is also sometimes called 'badminton', from the colour.

The game badminton is a predecessor of, and is similar to, lawn tennis; it is played with shuttle-cocks instead of balls.

**Baffle.** Originally a punishment meted out to a recreant or traitorous knight by which he was degraded and thoroughly disgraced, part of which seems to have consisted in hanging him or his effigy by the heels from a tree and loudly proclaiming his misdeeds. *See* Spenser's *Faerie Queene*, VI, vii, 26:

> Letting him arise like abject thrall
> He gan to him object his haynous crime,
> And to revile, and rate, and recreant call,
> And lastly to despoyle of knightly bannerall
> And after all, for greater infamie,
> He by the heeles he hung upon a tree.
> And baffuld so, that all which passed by,
> The picture of his punishment might see,
> And by the like ensample warned bee
> How ever they through treason doe trespasse.

**Bag and Baggage,** as 'Get away with you, bag and baggage.' i.e. get away, and carry with you all your belongings. Originally a military phrase signifying the whole property and stores of an army and of the soldiers composing it. Hence *the bag and baggage policy*. In 1876 Gladstone, speaking on the Eastern question, said, 'Let the Turks now carry away their abuses in the only possible manner, namely, by carrying away themselves … One and all, *bag and baggage*, shall, I hope, clear out from the province they have desolated and profaned.' This was for a time known as 'the bag and baggage policy'. *See also* Baggage.

***To bag.*** Secure for oneself; probably an extension of the sporting use of the word, meaning, to put into one's bag what one has shot, caught, or trapped. Hence, *a good bag*, a large catch of game, fish, or other animals sought after by sportsmen.

**Bag-man, A.** A commercial traveller, who carries a bag with samples to show to those whose custom he solicits. In former times commercial travellers used to ride a horse with saddle-bags sometimes so large as almost to conceal the rider.

**Bags.** Slang for 'trousers', which may be taken as the bags of the body. When the pattern was very staring and 'loud', they once were called *howling-bags*.

In Stock Exchange nomenclature *Bags* is the name of the bonds of the *B*uenos *A*yres *G*reat *S*outhern Railway; so called from the initials.

***Bags of mystery.*** Slang for sausages or saveloys; the allusion is obvious.

***Bag o' Nails.*** Many years ago there stood in the Tyburn Road, Oxford Street, a public-house called *The Bacchanals* – the sign was Pan and the Satyrs. The jolly god, with his cloven hoof and his horns, was called 'the devil'; and the word Bacchanals soon got corrupted into 'Bag o' Nails'. The *Devil and the Bag o' Nails* is a sign not uncommon even now in the midland counties.

***A bag of bones.*** Very emaciated; generally 'A mere bag of bones'.

***A bag of tricks,*** or ***a whole bag of tricks.*** Numerous expedients. In allusion to the fable of the *Fox and the Cat*. The fox was commiserating the cat because she had only one shift in the case of danger, while he had a thousand tricks to evade it. Being set upon by a pack of hounds, the fox was soon caught, while puss ran up a tree and was quite secure.

***The bottom of the bag.*** The last expedient, having emptied every other one out of his bag; a trump card held in reserve.

***To empty the bag.*** To tell the whole matter and conceal nothing (Fr. *vider le sac*, to expose all to view).

***To give the bag,*** now means the same as *to give the sack* (*see* Sack), but it seems originally to have had the reverse meaning; a servant or employee leaving without having given notice was said to have given his master 'the bag'.

***To let the cat out of the bag.*** *See under* Cat.

**Baga de Secretis.** Records in the Record Office of trials for high treason and other State offences from the reign of Edward IV to the close of the reign of George III. These records contain the proceedings in the trials of Anne Boleyn, Sir Walter Raleigh, Guy Fawkes, the regicides, and of the risings of 1715 and 1745. (*Baga* = Bag.)

**Bagatelle, A.** A trifle; a thing of no consideration. 'Oh! nothing. A mere bagatelle.' In French, *Il* *dépense tout son argent en bagatelles*, means, he squanders his money on trash. *Il ne s'amuse qu'à des bagatelles*, he finds no pleasure except in frivolities. Bagatelle! as an exclamation, means Nonsense! as *Vous dites qu'il me fera un procès. Bagatelle!* (fiddlesticks!).

> He considered his wife a bagatelle, to be shut up at pleasure [i.e.., a toy to be put away at pleasure].
> *The Depraved Husband*

**Baggage.** A playful, but in earlier times a contemptuous, term for a woman, so-called because soldiers used to send their wives in the baggage wagons, and they were consequently too often treated as mere baggage.

In England the word used to have the same meaning as 'luggage', personal property taken with one when travelling; and in the United States luggage is still called 'baggage', and the luggage-van the 'baggage-car'.

**Bahr Geist** (Ger. *bahr*, bier, *geist*, ghost). A banshee or spectre.

> Know then (said Eveline) it [the Bahr Geist] is a spectre, usually the image of the departed person, who, either for wrong suffered, sustained during life, or through treasure hidden … haunts the spot from time to time, becomes familiar to those who dwell there, and takes an interest in their fate.
> Scott, *The Betrothed*, ch. 15

**Bail** (Fr. *bailler*, to deliver up). Security given for the temporary release of an accused person pending his trial or the completion of his trial; also the person or persons giving such security. *See also* Leg-bail.

***Common bail*, or *bail below*.** A bail given to the sheriff to guarantee the appearance of the defendant in court at any day and time the court demands.

***Special bail*, or *bail above*.** A bail which includes, besides the guarantee of the defendant's appearance, an undertaking to satisfy all claims made on him.

***Bail up!*** The Australian bushranger's equivalent for the highwayman's 'Stand and deliver!'

**Bailey** (probably in ultimate origin from O.Fr. *baillier*, to enclose). The external wall of a mediaeval castle, forming the first line of defence; also the outer court of the castle, the space immediately within the outer wall. The entrance was over a drawbridge, and through the embattled gate. When there were two courts they were distinguished as the outer and inner bailey. Subsequently the word included the court and all its buildings; and when the court was abolished, the term was attached to the castle, as the Old Bailey (London) and the Bailey (Oxford).

**Bailiff.** *See* Bumbailiff.

**Bailleur.** *Un bon bâilleur en fait bâiller deux* (Fr.). Yawning is catching.

**Baillif, Herry** (Harry Bailey). Mine host of the Tabard Inn, Southwark, in Chaucer's *Canterbury Tales*. When the poet began the second 'Fit' of the *Tale of Sir Thopas*, 'Herry Baillif' interrupts him with unmitigated contempt:

> 'No more of this, for goddes dignitee!'
> Quod oure hoste, 'for thou makest me
> So wery of the verray lewednesse
> That, also wisly god my soule blesse,
> Myn eres aken of thy drasty speche.'
> *Prologue to Melibeus*

**Baily's Beads.** *See* Bead.

**Bain Marie.** The French name for a double saucepan like a glue-pot. The term is sometimes used in English kitchens. It appears earlier (as in Mrs Glasse's *Cookery Book*, 1796) under its Latin name, *Balneum Mariae*, hence the 'St Mary's bath' of Ben Jonson's *Alchemist*, II, iii. The name is supposed to be due to the gentleness of this method of heating.

**Bairam.** The name given to two great Mohammedan feasts. The *Lesser* begins on the new moon of the month Shawwal, at the termination of the fast of Ramadan, and lasts three days. The *Greater* ('Idu'l-Kabir) is celebrated on the tenth day of the twelfth month (Dhul Hijja), lasts for four days, and forms the concluding ceremony of the pilgrimage to Mecca. It comes seventy days after the Lesser Bairam.

**Bait** (connected both with the Old Norman *beita*, food, and with Eng. bite). Food to entice or allure, as *bait for fish*. Also used for a 'feed' by way of refreshment taken *en passant* by travellers and (more usually) their horses.

**Bajadere.** *See* Bayadere.

**Bajan, Bajanella.** *See* Bejan.

**Baked.** *Half baked.* Imbecile, of weak mind, 'soft'. The allusion is to half-baked food.

**Baked Meats,** or **bake-meats.** Meat pies. 'The funeral baked meats did coldly furnish forth the marriage tables' (*Hamlet*, 1, 2); i.e. the hot meat pies served at the funeral and not eaten were served cold at the marriage banquet.

**Baker, The.** Louis XVI was called 'The Baker', the queen was called 'the baker's wife' (or *La Boulangère*), and the dauphin the 'shop boy'; because they gave bread to the mob of starving men and women who came to Versailles on October 6th, 1789.

> The return of the baker, his wife, and the shop-boy to Paris [after the king was brought from Versailles] had not had the expected effect. Flour and bread were still scarce.
>
> A. Dumas, *The Countess de Charny*, ch. ix

**Baker's Dozen.** Thirteen for twelve. When a heavy penalty was inflicted for short weight, bakers used to give a surplus number of loaves, called the *inbread*, to avoid all risk of incurring the fine. The 13th was the 'vantage loaf'.

***To give one a baker's dozen,*** in slang phraseology, is to give him a sound drubbing – i.e. all he deserves and one stroke more.

**Baker's Knee.** Knock-knee. Bakers were said to be particularly liable to this deformity owing to the constrained position in which they have to stand when kneading bread.

**Bakha.** The sacred bull of Hermonthis in Egypt. He changed colour every hour of the day, and is supposed to have been an incarnation of Menthu, the Egyptian personification of the heat of the sun.

**Baksheesh.** A Persian word for a gratuity. These gifts are insolently demanded by all sorts of officials in Turkey, Egypt, and Asia Minor, more as a claim than a gratuity.

> I was to give the man, too, a '*baksheish*', that is a present of money, which is usually made upon the conclusion of any sort of treaty.
>
> Kinglake, *Eothen*

**Balaam.** (1) In Dryden's *Absalom and Achitophel*, the Earl of Huntingdon, one of the rebels in Monmouth's army.

(2) The 'citizen of sober fame', who lived hard by the Monument, in Pope's *Moral Essays*, *Ep*. iii, was drawn, in part, from Thomas Pitt ('Diamond Pitt', *see* Pitt, Diamond), grandfather of the Earl of Chatham. He 'was a plain, good man; religious, punctual, and frugal'; he grew rich; got knighted; seldom went to church; became a courtier; 'took a bribe from France'; was hanged for treason, and all his goods were confiscated to the State.

**Balaam.** Matter kept in type for filling up odd spaces in periodicals. Lockhart, in his *Life of Scott* (ch. lxx) tells us:

> Balaam is the cant name for asinine paragraphs about monstrous productions of nature and the like, kept standing in type to be used whenever the real news of the day leaves an awkward space that must be filled up somehow.

Hence *Balaam basket* or *box*; the printer's slang term for the receptacle for such matter, and also (in America) for the place where stereotyped 'fill-ups' are kept.

**Balafré, Le** (Fr. the gashed). Henri, second Duke of Guise (1550–88). In the Battle of Dormans he received a sword-cut which left a frightful scar on his face. Henri's son, François, third Duke of Guise, also earned – and was awarded – the same title; and it was given by Scott (in *Quentin Durward*) to Ludovic Lesly, an old archer of the Scottish Guard.

**Balak.** In the second part of *Absalom and Achitophel* (*q.v.*), stands for Dr Gilbert Burnet (1643–1715), Bishop of Salisbury and historian.

**Balan.** The name of a strong and courageous giant in many old romances. In *Fierabras* (*q.v.*) the 'Sowdan of Babylon', father of Fierabras, ultimately conquered by Charlemagne. In the Arthurian cycle, brother of Balin (*q.v.*).

**Balance, The.** 'Libra', an ancient zodiacal constellation between Scorpio and Virgo; also the 7th sign of the zodiac, which now contains the constellation Virgo, and which the sun enters a few days before the autumnal equinox.

According to *Persian mythology*, at the last day a huge balance, as big as the vault of heaven, will be displayed; one scale pan will be called that of light, and the other that of darkness. In the former all good will be placed, in the latter all evil; and everyone will receive his award according to the verdict of the balance.

In commercial parlance one's *balance* is the total money remaining over after all assets are realised and all liabilities discharged. Hence the phrases:

***To balance an account.*** To add up the debit and credit sides and subtract the less of the two from the greater.

***He has a good balance at his banker's.*** His credit side shows a large balance in his favour.

***To strike a balance.*** To calculate the exact difference, if any, between the debit and credit side of an account.

***Balance of trade.*** The money-value difference between the exports and imports of a nation.

***Balance of power.*** Such an adjustment of power among sovereign States as results in no one nation having such a preponderance as could enable it to endanger the independence of the rest.

**Balclutha.** A fortified town on the banks of the Clutha (i.e. the Clyde) mentioned in *Carthon*, one of the Ossian poems. It was captured and burnt by Fingal's father, Comhal, in one of his forays against the Britons.

**Bald. *Charles le Chauve.*** Charles I of France (823, 840–77), son of Louis le Débonnaire, was surnamed 'the Bald' (*le Chauve*).

**Baldachin.** The daïs or canopy under which, in Roman Catholic processions, the Holy Sacrament is carried: also the canopy above an altar. It is the Ital. *baldacchino*, so called from Baldacco (Ital. for Bagdad), where the cloth was originally made.

**Balder.** Son of Odin and Frigga; the Scandinavian god of light, who dwelt at Breidhablik, one of the mansions of Asgard. He is the central figure of many myths, the chief being connected with his death. He is said to have been slain by his rival Hodhr while fighting for possession of the beautiful Nanna, Hodhr having obtained Miming's sword, by which alone Balder could be wounded. Another legend tells that Frigga bound all things by oath not to harm him, but accidentally omitted the mistletoe. Loki learnt this, and armed his blind brother Hodhr with a mistletoe twig, with which, after everything had been tried, Balder was slain. His death brought general consternation to the gods, and formed the prelude to their final overthrow.

**Balderdash.** A word of uncertain origin, formerly meaning froth, also a mixture of incongruous liquors (such as wine and beer or beer and milk), but now denoting nonsensical talk, ridiculous poetry, jumbled ideas, etc. It may be connected with the Dan. *balder*, noise, clatter; but in view of the earlier senses of the word this is, at least, doubtful.

**Baldwin.** (1) In the Charlemagne romances, nephew of Roland and the youngest and comeliest of Charlemagne's paladins.

(2) Brother of Godfrey of Bouillon, whom he succeeded (1100) as King of Jerusalem. He figures in Tasso's *Jerusalem Delivered* as the restless and ambitious Duke of Bologna, leader of 1,200 horse in the allied Christian army. He died in Egypt, 1118.

(3) In *Reynard the Fox*, an Anglicised form of Boudewyn (*q.v.*).

**Bale.** ***When bale is highest, boot is nighest.*** An old Icelandic proverb that appears in Heywood and many other English writers. It means, when things have come to the worst they must needs mend. *Bale* means 'evil', and is common to most Teutonic languages; *boot* (*q.v.*) is the M.E. *bote*, relief, remedy.

**Balfour of Burley, John.** Leader of the Covenanters in Scott's *Old Mortality*. His prototype in real life was John Balfour of Kinloch. Scott seems to have confused him with John, Lord Balfour of Burleigh, who died in 1688 and was not a Covenanter.

**Balin.** Brother to Balan in the Arthurian romances. They were devoted to each other, but they accidentally met in single combat and slew each other, neither knowing until just before death who was his opponent. At their request they were buried in one grave by Merlin. The story is told in Malory, Bk ii. Tennyson gives a much altered version in the *Idylls of the King*.

**Balios.** *See* Horse.

**Balisarda.** *See* Sword.

**Balistraria** (mediaeval Lat.). Narrow apertures in the form of a cross in the walls of ancient castles, through which crossbow-men discharged their arrows.

**Balk.** Originally a ridge or mound on the ground (O.E. *balca*), then the ridge between two furrows left in ploughing, the word came to be figuratively applied to any obstacle, stumbling-block, or check on one's actions; as in billiards, the balk (or *baulk*) is the part of the table behind the *baulk-line* from which one has to play when, in certain circumstances, one's freedom is checked. So, also, *to balk* is to place obstacles in the way of.

***A balk of timber*** is a beam running across the ceiling, etc., like a ridge.

***To make a balk.*** To miss a part of the field in ploughing. Hence, to disappoint, to withhold deceitfully.

**Balker.** One who from an eminence on shore directs fishermen where shoals of herrings have gathered together. Probably from the Dutch *balken*, to shout, and connected with the O.E. *baelcan*, with the same meaning.

**Balkis.** The Mohammedan name for the Queen of Sheba, who visited Solomon.

**Ball.** 'Ball', the spherical body, is a Middle English and Old Teutonic word; 'ball', the dancing assembly, is from O.Fr. *baler*, to dance, from late Lat. *balare*. The two are in no way connected.

***To keep the ball a-rolling.*** To continue without intermission. To keep the fun, or the conversation, etc., alive; to keep the matter going. A metaphor taken from several games played with balls.

***To have the ball at your feet.*** To have a thing in one's power. A metaphor from football.

***To take the ball before the bound.*** To anticipate an opportunity; to be over-hasty. A metaphor from cricket.

***The ball is with you.*** It is your turn now.

***A ball of fortune.*** One tossed, like a ball, from pillar to post; one who has experienced many vicissitudes of fortune.

> Brown had been from infancy a ball for fortune to spurn at. Scott, *Guy Mannering*, ch. xxi

***To open the ball.*** To lead off the first dance at a ball.

***To strike the ball under the line.*** To fail in one's object. The allusion is to tennis, in which a line is stretched in the middle of the court, and the players standing on each side have to send the ball *over* the line.

**Ballad.** Originally a song to dance-music, or a song sung while dancing. It is from late Lat. *ballare*, to dance (as 'ball', the dance), through Provençal *balada*, and O.Fr. *balade*.

***Let me make the ballads, and who will may make the laws.*** Andrew Fletcher of Saltoun, in Scotland, wrote to the Marquis of Montrose, 'I knew a very wise man of Sir Christopher Musgrave's sentiment. He believed, if a man were permitted to make all the ballads, he need not care who should make the laws' (1703).

**Ballambangjan, The Straits of.** A sailor's joke for a place where he may lay any wonderful adventure. These straits, he will tell us, are so narrow that a ship cannot pass through without jamming the tails of the monkeys which haunt the trees on each side of the strait; or any other rigmarole which his fancy may conjure up at the moment.

**Ballast, A man of no.** Not steady; not to be depended on. Unsteady as a ship without ballast. A similar phrase is, 'The man wants ballast.'

**Ballet.** A theatrical representation of some adventure, intrigue, or emotional phase by pantomime and dancing. Baltazarini, director of music to Catherine de Medici, is said to have been the inventor of ballets as presented in modern times: for long they were an integral part of Italian opera.

**Balliol College,** Oxford, founded in 1263, by Sir John de Baliol (father of Baliol, King of Scotland) and his wife, Devorguilla.

**Balloon, A pilot.** Metaphorically, a feeler, something put forth to ascertain public opinion.

**Balls, The Three Golden.** The well known sign of the pawnbroker; originally the cognizance of the great Lombard family of the Medici, the Lombards being the first recognised money-lenders in England. They are said to have represented three gilded pills, in allusion to the *Medicis*' old profession of *medicine*; but *see* Mugello.

Also the emblem of St Nicholas of Bari, who is said to have given three purses of gold to three virgin sisters to enable them to marry.

**Balm** (Fr. *baume*; a contraction of *balsam*). An aromatic, resinous gum exuding from certain trees, and used in perfumery and medicine; hence, a soothing remedy or alleviating agency.

***Is there no balm in Gilead?*** (Jer. 8:22) Is there no remedy, no consolation? 'Balm' in this passage is the Geneva Bible's translation of the Heb. *son* which probably means mastic, the resin yielded by the mastic tree, *Pistacia Lentiscus*, which was formerly an ingredient used in many medicines. In Wyclif's Bible the word is translated 'gumme', and in Coverdale's 'triacle'. *See* Treacle.

The gold-coloured resin now known as 'Balm of Gilead' is that from the *Balsomodendron Gileadense*, an entirely different tree.

**Balmawhapple.** A stupid, obstinate Scottish laird in Scott's *Waverley*.

**Balmung.** One of the swords of Siegfried, forged by Wieland (*q.v.*).

**Balmy.** '*I am going to the balmy*' – i.e. to 'Balmy sleep'; one of Dick Swiveller's pet phrases (Dickens, *Old Curiosity Shop*).

For *balmy* in the sense of silly, or mildly idiotic, *see* Barmy.

**Balnibarbi.** A land occupied by projectors (Swift, *Gulliver's Travels*).

**Balthazar.** One of the kings of Cologne – i.e. the three Magi. *See* Melchior.

**Baltic Sea.** Scandinavia used to be known as *Baltia*. There is a Lithuanian word, *baltas*, meaning 'white', from which the name may be derived; but it may also be from Scand. *balba*, a strait or *belt*, and the Baltic would then be the sea of the 'belts'.

**Baltic, The,** in commercial parlance, is the familiar name of the *Baltic Mercantile and Shipping Exchange*, which was founded in the 17th century. It deals with chartering of ships, freights, marine insurance, etc., all over the world.

**Balwhidder, Rev. Micah.** A Scotch Presbyterian minister in Gait's *Annals of the Parish*, full of fossilised national prejudices, but kind-hearted and sincere.

**Bamberg Bible, The.** *See* Bible, specially named.

**Bambino.** An image of the infant Jesus, swaddled. The most celebrated is that in the church of Sta Maria, in the Ara Coeli of Rome. The word is Italian.

**Bambocciades.** Pictures of scenes in low life, such as country wakes, penny weddings, and so on, so called from the Ital. *bamboccio*, a cripple, a nickname given to Pieter van Laar (*c.*1613–*c.*74). a noted Dutch painter of such scenes. *See* Michael-Angelo des Bamboches.

**Bamboozle.** To cheat by cunning, or daze with tricks. It is a slang term of uncertain origin which came into use about the end of the 17th century.

> The third refinement observable in the letter I send you, consists of the choice of certain words invented by some pretty fellows, such as *banter*, bamboozle ... and *kidney* ... some of which are now straggling for the vogue, and others are in possession of it.
>
> Swift, *The Tatler* (Sept. 28,1710)

***To bamboozle into*** (doing something). To induce by trickery.

***To bamboozle one out of something.*** To get something by trickery.

**Bampton Lectures.** Founded by the Rev. John Bampton, canon of Salisbury, who, in 1751, left £120 per annum to the university of Oxford, to pay for eight divinity lectures on given subjects, to be preached yearly at Great St Mary's, and printed afterwards. MAs of Oxford or Cambridge are eligible as lecturers, but the same person may never be chosen twice. *Cp.* Hulsean Lectures.

**Ban** (A.S. *bannan*, to summon, O.Teut. to proclaim). Originally meaning to summon, the verb came to mean to imprecate, to anathematise, to pronounce a curse upon; and the noun from being a general proclamation was applied specifically to an ecclesiastical curse or denunciation, a formal prohibition, a sentence of outlawry, etc. *Banish* and Bandit (*q.v.*), as well as Banns (*q.v.*), are from the same root.

***Lever le ban et l'arrière ban*** (Fr.). To levy the *ban* was to call the king's vassals to active service; to levy the *arrière ban* was to levy the vassals of a suzerain or under-lord.

> Le mot *ban*, qui signifie bannière, se disait de l'appel fait par le seigneur à ses vassaux pour les convoquer sous son étendard. On distinguait le *ban* composé des vasseaux immédiats, que étaient convoqués par le *roi* lui-même, et l'*arrière ban*, composé des vasseaux convoqués par leurs *suzerains*.
>
> Bouillet, *Dictionnaire d'Histoire, etc.*

**Ban, King.** In the Arthurian legends, father of Sir Launcelot du Lac. He died of grief when his castle was taken and burnt through the treachery of his seneschal.

**Banagher, That beats.** Wonderfully inconsistent and absurd – exceedingly ridiculous. Banagher is a town in Ireland, on the Shannon, in King's County. It formerly sent two members to Parliament, and was, of course, a famous pocket borough. When a member spoke of a family borough where every voter was a man employed by the lord, it was not unusual to reply, 'Well, that beats Banagher.'

Grose, however, gives another explanation. According to him Banagher (or Banaghan) was an Irish minstrel famous for telling wonderful stories of the Munchausen kind.

> 'Well,' says he, 'to gratify them I will. So just a morsel. But, Jack, this beats Bannagher [*sic*].'
>
> W. B. Yeats, *Fairy Tales of the Irish Peasantry*, p. 196

**Banat.** A territory under a *ban* (Persian for lord, master), particularly certain districts of Hungary and Croatia. The word was brought into Europe by the Avars, a Ural-Altaic people allied to the Huns, who appeared on the Danube and settled in Dacia in the latter half of the 6th century.

**Banbury.** A town in Oxfordshire, proverbially famous for its Puritans, its 'cheese-paring', and its cakes. Hence a *Banbury man* is a Puritan or bigot. The term is common in Elizabethan literature: Zeal-of-the-land-busy, in Jonson's *Bartholomew Fair*, is described as a 'Banbury man', and Braithwaite's lines in *Drunken Barnabee's Journal* (1638) are well known:

> In my progresse travelling Northward,
> Taking my farewell oth' Southward,
> To *Banbery* came I, O prophane one!
> Where I saw a Puritane one,
> Hanging of his Cat on Monday,
> For killing of a Mouse on Sunday.

***As thin as Banbury cheese.*** In Marston's *Jack Drum's Entertainment* (1600) we read, 'You are like a Banbury cheese, nothing but paring'; and Bardolph compares Slender to Banbury cheese (*Merry Wives*, 1, 1). The Banbury cheese is a rich milk cheese about an inch in thickness.

**Banco.** A commercial term denoting bank money of account as distinguished from currency; it is used principally in exchange business, and in cases where there is an appreciable difference between the actual and the nominal value of money.

***In banco.*** A late Latin legal phrase, meaning 'on the bench'; it is applied to sittings of the Superior Court of Common Law in its own bench or court, and not on circuit, or at *Nisi Prius* (*q.v.*).

***Mark Banco.*** The mark of fixed value employed as an invariable standard in the old Bank at

Hamburg, and used by the Hanseatic League. Deposits in gold and silver were credited in *Mark Banco*, and all banking accounts were carried on in *Mark Banco*, so that it was a matter of no moment how exchange varied.

**Bancus Regius.** The king's or queen's bench. *Bancus Communis*, the bench of common pleas.

**Bandana** or **Bandanna.** An Indian word (*bandhnu*, a mode of dyeing, in which portions of the material are tied up to prevent the dye affecting them), properly applied to silk goods treated in this manner, but now usually restricted to handkerchiefs of either silk or cotton having a dark ground of Turkey red or blue, with white or yellow spots.

**Bandbox, He looks as if he were just out of a.** He is so neat and precise, so carefully got up in his dress and person, that he looks like some company dress, carefully kept in a bandbox.

***Neat as a bandbox.*** Neat as clothes folded and put by in a bandbox.

***The Bandbox Plot.*** Rapin (*History of England*, iv, 297) tells us that a bandbox was sent to the lord-treasurer, in Queen Anne's reign, with three pistols charged and cocked, the triggers being tied to a pack-thread fastened to the lid. When the lid was lifted, the pistols would go off and shoot the person who opened the lid. He adds that Dean Swift happened to be by at the time the box arrived, and seeing the pack-thread, cut it, thereby saving the life of the lord-treasurer.

> Two ink-horn tops your Whigs did fill
> With gunpowder and lead;
> Which with two serpents made of quill,
> You in a bandbox laid;
> A tinder-box there was beside,
> Which had a trigger to it,
> To which the very string was ty'd
> That was designed to do it.
>
> *Plot upon Plot* (about 1713)

**Bande Noire** (Fr. black band). The name given to certain speculators who, during the French Revolution, bought up confiscated Church property; they recklessly pulled down ancient buildings and destroyed relics of great antiquity.

**Bandit,** plural *banditti* or *bandits*. The Ital. *bandito*, which is from the same Lat. root as *ban* (*q.v.*). An outlaw, one who is 'banned' or proscribed; hence, a brigand. The name is given specially to members of organised bands of desperadoes infesting the mountainous parts of south and south-east Europe.

**Bands.** ***Clerical bands*** are a relic of the ancient *amice*, a square linen tippet tied about the neck of priests during the administration of Mass. They are rarely worn in England nowadays, but are still used by clerics on the Continent.

***Legal bands*** are a relic of the wide falling collars which formed a part of the ordinary dress in the reign of Henry VIII, and which were especially conspicuous in the reign of the Stuarts. In the showy days of Charles II the plain bands were changed for lace ends.

> The eighth Henry, as I understand,
> Was the first prince that ever wore a band.
>
> John Taylor, the Water Poet (1580–1654)

**Bandy.** ***I am not going to bandy words with you*** – i.e. to wrangle. The metaphor is from the old game, bandy (the precursor of hockey), in which each player has a stick with a crook at the end to strike a wooden or other hard ball. The ball is bandied from side to side, each party trying to beat it home to the opposite goal. The derivation of the word is quite uncertain. It was earlier a term in tennis, as is shown by the passage in Webster's *Vittoria Corombona* (IV, iv), where the conspirators regret that the handle of the racket of the man to be murdered had not been poisoned –

> That while he had been bandying at tennis,
> He might have sworn himself to hell, and strook
> His soul into the hazard.
>
> The bat was called a bandy from its being bent.
>
> Brand, *Popular Antiquities* (article 'Golf', p. 538)

**Bane** really means ruin, death, or destruction (A.S. *bana*, a murderer); and 'I will be his bane,' means I will ruin or murder him. Bane is, therefore, a mortal injury.

> My bane and antidote are both before it.
> This [sword] in a moment brings me to an end.
> But this [Plato] assures me I shall never die.
>
> Addison, *Cato*

**Bangorian Controversy.** A theological paper-war stirred up by a sermon preached March 31st, 1717, before George I, by Dr Hoadley, Bishop of Bangor, on the text, 'My kingdom is not of this world', the argument being that Christ had not delegated His power or authority to either king or clergy. The sermon was printed by royal command; it led to such discord in Convocation that this body was prorogued, and from that time till 1852 was allowed to meet only as a matter of form.

**Bang-up.** A slang synonym for first-rate, thumping, or striking. It is almost obsolete, but was quite common in the last century.

> His hat set jauntily on one side, his spotted neckcloth knotted in *bang-up* mode.
>
> Chas Lever, *Jack Hinton*, ch. vii

**Banian** or **Banyan.** A loose coat (Anglo-Indian).

> His coat was brownish black perhaps of yore,
> In summer time a banyan loose he wore.
>
> Lowell, *FitzAdam's Story*

'Banian' is probably the name given to Hindu traders, especially those in Gujerat; also (in Bengal) a native broker. It is from Sansk. *vanij*, a merchant.

**Banian Days.** A sailor's expression for days when no meat is served to the crew. The Hindu Banians were vegetarians.

**Bank.** The original meaning was 'bench' or 'shelf'; in Italy the word (*banco*) was applied specially to a tradesman's counter, and hence to a money-changer's bench or table, which gives the modern meaning of an establishment which deals in money, investments, etc.

**Bank of a River.** Stand with your back to the source, and face to the sea or outlet: the *left* bank is on your left, and *right* bank on your right hand.

***Sisters of the bank.*** *See* Bankside.

**Bankrupt.** In Italy, when a money-lender was unable to continue business, his bench or counter (*see* Bank) was broken up, and he himself was spoken of as a *bancorotto* – i.e. a bankrupt. This is said to be the origin of our term.

**Bankside.** Part of the borough of Southwark on the right bank of the Thames, between Blackfriars and Waterloo Bridges. In Shakespeare's time it was noted for its theatres, its prison, and its brothels. Hence, *Sisters of the Bank*, an old term for prostitutes.

> Come I will send for a whole coach or two of Bankside ladies, and we will be jovial.
>
> Randolph, *The Muses' Looking Glass*, II, iv

**Banks's Horse.** A horse trained to do all manner of tricks, called Marocco, and belonging to one Banks about the end of the reign of Queen Elizabeth. One of his exploits is said to have been the ascent of St Paul's steeple. He is frequently mentioned in contemporary literature.

**Bannatyne Club.** A literary club, named from George Bannatyne (d. about 1608), to whose industry we owe the preservation of much early Scottish poetry. It was instituted in 1823 by Sir Walter Scott, and had for its object the publication of rare works illustrative of Scottish history, poetry, and general literature. The club was dissolved in 1859.

**Banner.** The word comes to us through the late Lat. *bandum* or *bannum*, a standard, from the Gothic *bandwa*, a sign or token.

> An emperor's banner should be sixe foote longe, and the same in breadth; a king's banner five foote; a prince's and a duke's banner four foote; a marquys's, an erle's, a viscount's, a baron's, and a banneret's banner shall be but three foote square.
>
> Park

**Banner of the Prophet, The** (i.e. Mahomet). What purports to be the actual standard of Mahomet is preserved in the Eyab mosque of Constantinople. It is called *Sinjaqu'sh-shamif* and is 12 feet in length. It is made of four layers of silk, the topmost being green, embroidered with gold. In times of peace the banner is guarded in the hall of the 'noble vestment', as the dress worn by the Prophet is styled. In the same hall are preserved the sacred teeth, the holy beard, the sacred stirrup, the sabre, and the bow of Mahomet.

**Banner of France, The sacred,** was the *Oriflamme* (*q.v.*).

**Banneret.** One who leads his vassals to battle under his own banner. Also an order of knighthood formerly conferred for deeds of valour done on the field of battle. The first knight-banneret to be made seems to have been John de Copeland, who, in 1346, captured King David Bruce at Neville's Cross. The order was allowed to become extinct soon after the first creation of baronets, in 1611.

**Banners in Churches.** These are suspended as thank offerings to God. Those in St George's Chapel, Windsor, Henry VII's Chapel, Westminster, etc., are to indicate that the knight whose banner is hung up avows himself devoted to God's service.

**Bannière.** *Cent ans bannière, cent ans civière.* The ups and downs of life. A grand seigneur who has had his banner carried before him for a century may come to drive his hand-barrow through the streets as a costermonger.

**Bannière.** *Il faut la croix et la bannière pour l'avoir.* If you want to have him, you must make a great fuss over him – you must go to meet him with cross and banner, '*aller au devant de lui avec un croix et la bannière*'.

**Banns of Marriage.** The publication in the parish church for three successive Sundays of an intended marriage. It is made after the Second Lesson of the Morning Service. To announce the intention is called 'Publishing the banns', from the words 'I publish the banns of marriage between ...' The word is from the same root as Ban (*q.v.*).

***To forbid the banns.*** To object to the proposed marriage.

> And a better fate did poor Maria deserve than to have a banns forbidden by the curate of the parish who published them.
>
> Sterne, *Sentimental Journey*

**Banquet** used at one time to have, besides its present meaning the meaning of dessert. Thus, in the *Pennyless Pilgrimage* (1618) John Taylor, the Water Poet, says: 'Our first and second course being three-score dishes at one boord, and after that, always a banquet.' The word is from Ital. *banco* (*see* Bank), a bench or table; we use 'table' also for a meal, as in 'bad manners at table'.

**Banquo.** In Shakespeare's *Macbeth*, the thane of Lochaber and general in the king's army, slain by order of Macbeth because the witches had foretold that his descendants would reign over Scotland. His ghost afterwards appears to Macbeth at the banquet, though it is invisible to the others present. Banquo's name is given in many old genealogies of the Scottish kings, but there is no reason for supposing he ever existed.

**Banshee.** The domestic spirit of certain Irish or Highland Scottish families, supposed to take an interest in its welfare, and to wail at the death of one of the family. The word is the Old Irish *ben side*, a woman of the elves or fairies.

**Bantam.** *A little bantam cock.* A plucky little fellow that will not be bullied by a person bigger than himself. The bantam cock will encounter a dunghill cock five times his own weight, and is therefore said to 'have a great soul in a little body'. The bantam originally came from Bantam, in Java.

**Banting.** *Doing banting.* Reducing superfluous fat by living on meat diet, and abstaining from beer, farinaceous food, and vegetables, according to the method adopted by William Banting (1797–1878), a London cabinet-maker, once a very fat man. The word was introduced about 1864. *Cp.* Lessian.

**Bantling.** A child, a brat; usually with a depreciatory sense, or meaning an illegitimate child. It is from Ger. *bänkling*, a bastard, from *bank*, a bench; hence, a child begotten casually, as on a bench, instead of in the marriage-bed. The word has been confused with *bandling*, taken to mean a little one in swaddling clothes.

**Banyan.** *See* Banian.

**Baphomet.** An imaginary idol or symbol, which the Templars were said to worship in their mysterious rites. The word is a corruption of Mahomet. (Fr. *Baphomet*; O. Sp. *Matomat*.)

**Baptes.** Priests of the goddess Cotytto, the Thracian goddess of lewdness, whose midnight orgies were so obscene that they disgusted even the goddess herself. They received their name from the Greek verb *bapto*, to wash, because of the so-called ceremonies of purification connected with her rites (*Juvenal*, ii, 91).

**Baptist.** *John the Baptist.* His symbol is a sword, the instrument by which he was beheaded.

**Bar.** The whole body of barristers; as *bench* means the whole body of bishops. The bar is the partition separating the seats of the benchers from the rest of the hall, and, like the rood-screen of a church, which separates the chancel from the rest of the building, is due to the old idea that the laity form an inferior order of beings.

> A dinner was given to the English Bar.
>
> *The Times*

***Bar,*** excepting. In racing phrase a man will bet 'Two to one, bar one', that is, two to one against any horse in the field with one exception. The word means 'barring out', shutting out, debarring, as in Shakespeare's:

> Nay, but I bar tonight: you shall not gage me by what we do tonight. *Merchant of Venice*, 2, 2

***Bar.*** An honourable ordinary, in heraldry, consisting of two parallel lines drawn across the shield and containing a fifth part of the field.

> A barre ... is drawne overthwart the escochon ... it containeth the fifth part of the Field.
>
> Gwillim, *Heraldry*

***At the bar.*** As the prisoner at the bar, the prisoner in the dock before the judge.

***A bar sinister*** in an heraldic shield means one drawn the reverse way; that is, not from left to right, but from right to left. Popularly but erroneously supposed to indicate bastardy.

***To be called to the bar.*** To be admitted a barrister. Students having attained a certain status used to be called from the body of the hall within the bar, to take part in the proceedings of the court. To disbar means to expel a barrister from his profession.

***To be called within the bar.*** To be appointed king's counsel.

***Trial at Bar.*** By a full court of judges; the King's Bench division. These trials are for very difficult causes, before special juries, and occupy the attention of the four judges in the superior court, instead of at *Nisi Prius*.

**Baralipton.** A mnemonic word, coined by the Schoolmen and first used in mediaeval Latin, to denote the first indirect mood of the first figure of syllogisms, indicating by the first three vowels that the premises are universal affirmatives, and the conclusion a particular affirmative. The *memoria technica* is:

bArbArA cElArEnt dArII fErIO bArAlIpton.

**Barataria.** Sancho Panza's island-city, in *Don Quixote*, over which he was appointed governor. The table was presided over by Doctor Pedro Rezio de Aguero, who caused every dish set upon the board to be removed without being tasted – some because they heated the blood, and others because they chilled it; some for one ill effect, and some for another; so that Sancho was allowed to eat nothing. The word is from Span. *barato*, cheap.

> The meat was put on the table, and whisked away like Sancho's inauguration feast at Barataria.
>
> Thackeray

**Barathron,** or **Barathrum.** A deep ditch behind the Acropolis of Athens into which malefactors were thrown; somewhat in the same way as criminals at Rome were cast from the Tarpeian Rock. Sometimes used figuratively, as in Massinger's *New Way to Pay Old Debts*, where Sir Giles Overreach calls Greedy a 'barathrum of the shambles' (III, ii), meaning that he was a sink into which any kind of food or offal could be thrown.

> *Mercury*: Why, Jupiter will put you all into a sack together, and toss you into Barathrum, terrible Barathrum.
>
> *Carion*: Barathrum? What's Barathrum?
>
> *Mer.*: Why, Barathrum is Pluto's boggards [privy]: you must be all thrown into Barathrum.
>
> Randolph, *Hey for Honesty*, v, i (*c*.1630)

**Barb** (Lat. *barba*, a beard). Used in early times in England for the beard of a man, and so for similar appendages such as the feathers under the beak of a hawk; but its first English use was for a curved back instrument such as a fish-hook (which has one backward curve, or *barb*), or an arrow (which has two). The *barb* of an arrow is, then, the metal point having two iron 'feathers', which stick out so as to hinder extraction, and does not denote the feather on the upper part of the shaft.

**Barb.** A Barbary steed, noted for docility, speed, endurance, and spirit, formerly also called a Barbary, as in Ben Jonson's:

> You must … be seen on your barbary often, or leaping over stools for the credit of your back.
>
> *Silent Woman*, IV, i

*Cp.* also Barbary Roan.

**Barbara.** In logic, a mnemonic term designating the first mood of the first figure of syllogisms, the three a's indicating that the major and minor premises and the conclusion are all universal affirmatives. Sir Thos Browne (*Pseud. Ep.* I, iii) speaks of certain people to whom an apologue of Aesop is of more weight than 'a syllogism in Barbara', meaning that to them logical proof was of no consequence. *Cp.* Baralipton.

**Barbara, St.** The patron saint of arsenals and powder magazines. Her father delivered her up to Martian, governor of Nicomedia, for being a Christian. After she had been subjected to the most cruel tortures, her unnatural father was about to strike off her head, when a lightning flash laid him dead at her feet. Hence, St Barbara is invoked against lightning.

**Barbari.** ***Quod non fecerunt barbari, fecerunt Barberini***, i.e. What the barbarians left standing, Barberini contrived to destroy. A saying current in Rome at the time when Pope Urban VIII (Barberini) converted the bronze fittings of the Pantheon – which had remained in splendid condition since 27 BC – into cannon (1635).

**Barbarian.** The Greeks and Romans called all foreigners *barbarians* (babblers; men who spoke a language not understood by them); the word was probably merely imitative of unintelligible speech, but may have been an actual word in some outlandish tongue. The reproachful meaning crept in from the natural egotism of man. It is not very long ago that an Englishman looked with disdainful pity on a foreigner, and among other nations the feeling is not altogether unknown.

> If then I know not the meaning of the voice [*words*], I shall be to him that speaketh a barbarian [*a foreigner*], and he that speaketh will be a barbarian unto me. 1 Cor. 14:11

**Barbarossa** (*Red-beard*, similar to *Rufus*). The surname of Frederick I of Germany (1121–90). *Khaireddin Barbarossa*, the famous corsair, became Bey of Algiers in 1518, and in 1537 was appointed high admiral of the Turkish fleet. With Francis I he captured Nice in 1543; he died at Constantinople three years later.

**Barbary Roan,** the favourite horse of Richard II. *See* Horse.

> O, how it yearned my heart when I beheld
> In London streets that coronation day,
> When Bolingbroke rode on roan Barbary!
> That horse that thou [Rich. II] so often hast bestrid.
> That horse that I so carefully have dressed.
>
> Shakespeare, *Richard II*, 5, 5

*Cp.* Barbed Steeds.

**Barbason.** A fiend mentioned by Shakespeare in the *Merry Wives of Windsor*, 2, 2, and in *Henry V*, 2, 1.

> Amaimon sounds well, Lucifer well, Barbason well, yet they are … the names of fiends.
>
> *Merry Wives*

The name seems to have been obtained from Scot's *Discoverie of Witchcraft* (1584), where we are told of 'Marbas, alias Barbas', who –

> is a great president, and appeareth in the forme of a mightie lion; but at the commandement of a conjuror cummeth up in the likenes of a man, and answereth fullie as touching anie thing which is hidden or secret.

**Barbecue** (Sp. *barbacoa*, a wooden framework set on posts). A term used in America formerly for a wooden bedstead, and also for a kind of large gridiron upon which an animal could be roasted whole. Hence, an animal, such as a hog, so roasted; also the feast at which it is eaten, and the process of roasting it.

> Oldfield, with more than harpy throat subdued,
> Cries, 'Send me, ye gods, a whole hog barbecued!'
>
> Pope, *Satires*, ii, 25

**Barbed Steed.** A horse in armour. *Barbed* should properly be *barded*; it is from the Fr. *barde*, horse-armour. Horses' 'bards' were the metal coverings for the breast and flanks.

> And now, instead of mounting barbed steeds
> To fright the souls of fearful adversaries,
> He capers nimbly in a lady's chamber,
> To the lascivious pleasing of a lute.
>
> Shakespeare, *Richard III*, 1, 1

**Barbel.** The fish of this name is so called from the two fleshy filaments, or *barbels* (from late Lat. *barbellus*, a little beard, diminutive of *barba*, *see* Barb), hanging from its mouth.

**Barbeliots.** A sect of early Gnostics. Their first immortal son they called Barbeloth, omniscient, eternal, and incorruptible. He engendered light by the instrumentality of Christ, author of Wisdom. From Wisdom sprang Autogenes, and from Autogenes, Adam (male and female), and from Adam, matter. The first angel created was the Holy Ghost, from whom sprang the first prince, named Protarchontes, who married Arrogance, whose offspring was Sin.

**Barber.** ***Every barber knows that.***

> Omnibus notum tonsoribus.
>
> Horace, *1 Satires*, vii, 3

In ancient Rome, as in modern England, the barber's shop was a centre for the dissemination of scandal, and the talk of the town.

***Barber Poet.*** Jacques Jasmin (1798–1864), a Provençal poet, who was also known as 'the last of the Troubadours', was so called. He was a barber.

***Barber's pole.*** This pole, painted spirally with two stripes of red and white, and displayed outside barbers' shops as a sign, is a relic of the days when the callings of barber and surgeon were combined; it is symbolical of the winding of a bandage round the arm previous to blood-letting. The gilt knob at its end represents a brass basin, which is sometimes actually suspended on the pole. The basin has a curved gap cut in it to fit the throat, and was used for lathering customers before shaving them. The Barber-Surgeons' Company was founded in 1461 and was re-incorporated in 1540. In 1745 it was decided that the businesses or trades of barber and surgeon were really independent of each other and the two branches were separated; but the ancient company, or guild, was allowed to retain its charter, and its hall still stands in Monkwell Street, Cripplegate. The last barber-surgeon in London is said to have been one Middleditch, of Great Suffolk Street in the Borough, who died 1821.

> To this year (1541), (says Wornum) … belongs the Barber-Surgeons' picture of Henry (VIII) granting a charter to the Corporation. The barbers and surgeons of London, originally constituting one company, had been separated, but were again, in the 32 Henry VIII, combined into a single society, and it was the ceremony of presenting them with a new charter which is commemorated by Holbein's picture, now in their hall in Monkwell Street.

**Barbican.** The outwork intended to defend the drawbridge in a fortified town or castle (Fr. *barbacane*). Also an opening or loophole in the wall of a fortress, through which guns may be fired. The street of this name in London is built partly on the site of a barbican that was in front of one of the old city gates.

**Barcarole.** Properly, a song sung by Venetian boatmen, as they row their gondolas (It. *barcaruolo*, a boatman).

**Barcelona.** A fichu, piece of velvet for the neck, or small necktie, made at Barcelona, and common in England in the early 19th century. Also a neckcloth of some bright colour, as red with yellow spots.

> Now on this handkerchief so starch and white
> She pinned a Barcelona black and tight.
>
> Peter Pindar, *Portfolio* (*Dinah*)

> A double Barcelona protected his neck.
>
> Scott, *Peveril of the Peak* (*Prefatory Letter*)

**Barclayans.** *See* Bereans.

**Barcochebah** or **Barchochebas** (Shimeon). An heroic leader of the Jews against the Romans AD 132. He took Jerusalem in 132, and was proclaimed king, many of the Jews believing him to be the Messiah, but in 135 he was overthrown with great slaughter, Jerusalem was laid in ruins, and he himself slain. It is said that he gave himself out to be the 'Star out of Jacob' mentioned in Numb. 24:17. (Bar Cochba in *Hebrew* means 'Son of a star'.)

> Shared the fall of the Antichrist Barcochebah.
>
> Professor Seeley, *Ecce Homo*

**Bard.** The minstrel of the ancient Celtic peoples, the Gauls, British, Welsh, Irish, and Scots; they celebrated the deeds of gods and heroes, incited to battle, sang at royal and other festivities, and frequently acted as heralds. The oldest bardic compositions that have been preserved are of the 5th century.

***Bard of Avon.*** Shakespeare (1564–1616), who was born and buried at Stratford-upon-Avon.

***Bard of Ayrshire.*** Robert Burns (1759–96), a native of Ayrshire.

***Bard of Hope.*** Thomas Campbell (1777–1844), author of *The Pleasures of Hope*.

***Bard of the Imagination.*** Mark Akenside (1721–70), author of *Pleasures of the Imagination*.

***Bard of Memory.*** Samuel Rogers (1763–1855), author of *The Pleasures of Memory*.

***Bard of Olney.*** Cowper (1731–1800), who resided at Olney, in Bucks, for many years.

***The Bard of Prose.*** Boccaccio (1313–75), author of the *Decameron*.

> The Bard of Prose, creative spirit! he
> Of the Hundred Tales of Love.
>
> Byron, *Childe Harold*, IV, lvi

***The Bard of Rydal Mount.*** William Wordsworth (1770–1850); so called because Rydal Mount was his mountain home.

***Bard of Twickenham.*** Alexander Pope (1688–1744), who resided at Twickenham.

**Bardesanists.** Followers of Bardesanes, of Edessa, founder of a Gnostic sect in the 2nd century. They believed that the human body was ethereal till it became imbruted with sin. Milton, in his *Comus*, refers to this:

> When Lust
> By unchaste looks, loose gestures, and foul talk,
> But most by lewd and lavish acts of sin,
> Lets in defilement to the inward parts,
> The soul grows clotted by contagion,
> Imbodies and imbrutes.

**Bardiet.** The ancient German chant, which incited to war. Klopstock wrote patriotic dramas, incorporating ancient bardic hymns, to which he gave this name.

**Bardolph.** One of Falstaff's inferior officers. Falstaff calls him 'the knight of the burning lamp', because his nose was so red, and his face so 'full of meteors'. He is a low-bred, drunken swaggerer, without principle, and poor as a church mouse. (*Merry Wives*; *Henry IV*, 1, 2)

> We must have better assurance for Sir John than Bardolf's. We like not the security.
>
> Lord Macaulay

**Barebones Parliament, The.** The Parliament convened by Cromwell in 1653; so called from Praise-God Barebones, a fanatical leader, who was a prominent member. Also called the *Little Parliament*, because it comprised under 150 members.

**Barefaced.** The present meaning, *audacious*, *shameless*, *impudent*, is a depreciation of its earlier sense, which was merely *open* or *unconcealed*. A 'bare face' is, of course, one that is beardless, one the features of which are in no way hidden. The French equivalent is *à visage découvert*, with uncovered face.

**Barefooted.** Certain monks and nuns (some of whom use sandals instead of shoes), particularly the reformed section of the Order of Carmelites that was founded by St Theresa in the 16th century. These are known as the *Discalced Carmelites* (Lat. *calceus*, a shoe). The practice is defended by the command of our Lord to His disciples: 'Carry neither purse, nor scrip, nor shoes' (Luke 10:4). The Jews and Romans used to put off their shoes in mourning and public calamities, by way of humiliation.

**Bare Poles, Under.** A nautical term implying that on account of rough weather and high winds the ship carries no sails on the masts. Figuratively applied to a man reduced to the last extremity.

> We were scudding before a heavy gale, under bare poles. Capt. Marryat

**Bargain.** ***Into the bargain.*** In addition thereto; besides what was bargained for

***To make the best of a bad bargain.*** To bear bad luck, or bad circumstances, with equanimity.

***To stand to a bargain.*** To abide by it; the Lat. *stare conventis*, *conditionibus stare*, *pactis stare*, etc.

**Barisal guns.** A name given to certain mysterious booming sounds heard in many parts of the world as well as Barisal (Bengal), generally on or near water. They resemble the sound of distant cannon, and are probably of subterranean origin. At Seneca Lake, New York, they are known as *Lake guns*, on the coast of Holland and Belgium as *mistpoeffers*, and in Italy as *bombiti*, *baturlio marina*, etc.

**Bark.** Dogs in their wild state never bark; they howl, whine, and growl, but do not bark. Barking is an acquired habit.

***Barking dogs seldom bite.*** Huffing, bouncing, hectoring fellows rarely possess cool courage. Similar proverbs are found in Latin, French, Italian, and German.

***To bark at the moon.*** To rail uselessly, especially at those in high places, as a dog thinks to frighten the moon by baying at it. There is a superstition that when a dog does this it portends death or ill-luck.

> I'd rather be a dog, and bay the moon,
> Than such a Roman.
>
> Shakespeare, *Julius Caesar*, 4, 3

***His bark is worse than his bite.*** He scolds and abuses roundly, but does not bear malice, or do mischief.

***Barking up the wrong tree.*** To be wasting energy, to be on the wrong scent. The metaphor is from a dog chasing a cat.

**Barker.** A pistol, which barks or makes a loud report.

**Barkis is willin'.** The message sent by Barkis to Peggotty by David Copperfield, expressing his desire to marry. It has passed into a proverbial expression indicating willingness or consent. (Dickens, *David Copperfield*, ch. 5).

**Barlaam and Josaphat.** An Eastern romance telling how Barlaam, an ascetic monk of the desert of Sinai, converted Josaphat, son of a Hindu king, to Christianity. Probably written in the first half of the 7th century, it seems to have been put into its final form by St John of Damascus, a Syrian monk of the 8th century; it became immensely popular in the Middle Ages, and includes (among many other stories) the Story of the Three Caskets, which was used by Shakespeare in the *Merchant of Venice*. A poetical version of the romance was written by Rudolf von Ems (13th cent.).

**Barley.** *To cry barley.* To ask for truce (in children's games). Probably a corruption of *parley*, from Fr. *parler*, to speak.

> A proper lad o' his quarters, that will not cry barley in a brulzie. Scott, *Waverley*, xiii

**Barley-break.** An old country game like the modern 'Prisoners' Base', having a 'home' which was called 'hell'. Herrick has a poem, *Barley-break, or Last in Hel.*

**Barley-bree.** Ale; malt liquor brewed from barley, also called *barley-broth*.

> The cock may craw, the day may daw,
> And aye we'll taste the barley-bree.
>
> Burns, *Willie Brew'd a Peck o' Maut*

**Barley Cap.** *To wear the barley cap.* To be top-heavy or tipsy with barley-bree.

**Barleycorn.** *John* or *Sir John Barleycorn.* A personification of malt liquor. The term was made popular by Burns.

> Inspiring bold John Barleycorn,
> What dangers thou canst make us scorn!
>
> Burns, *Tam o' shanter*, 105, 106

**Barley-mow.** A heap or stack of barley. (A.S. *muga; cp.* Icel. *muge*, a swathe.) *See* Mow.

***Here's health to the Barley-mow!*** *See* Nipperkin.

**Barley Sugar.** Sugar boiled in a decoction of barley. It is not now made with barley, but usually with saffron, oil of citron, orange or lemon.

**Barmecide's Feast.** An illusion: particularly one containing a great disappointment. The reference is to the Story of the Barber's Sixth Brother in the *Arabian Nights.* A prince of the great Barmecide family in Bagdad, wishing to have some sport, asked Schacabac, a poor, starving wretch, to dinner, and set before him a series of empty plates. 'How do you like your soup?' asked the merchant. 'Excellently well'. replied Schacabac. 'Did you ever see whiter bread?' 'Never, honourable sir'. was the civil answer. Illusory wine was later offered him, but Schacabac excused himself by pretending to be drunk already, and knocked the Barmecide down. The latter saw the humour of the situation, forgave Schacabac, and provided him with food to his heart's content.

> Tomorrow! the mysterious unknown guest
> Who cries aloud, 'Remember Barmecide!
> And tremble to be happy with the rest.'
>
> Longfellow

**Barmy.** Empty-headed, 'dotty', light-headed. Sometimes spelt 'balmy', but properly as above, as from 'barm', froth, ferment. Burns has:

> Just now I've taen the fit o' rhyme.
> My barmie noddle's working prime.
>
> *To James Smith*, 19

Hence, in prison slang *to put on the barmy stick* is to feign insanity; and the 'Balmy Ward' is the infirmary in which the insane, real or feigned, are confined.

**Barnabas.** *St Barnabas' Day*, June 11th. St Barnabas was a fellow-labourer of St Paul. His symbol is a rake, because June 11th is the time of hay harvest.

**Barnabites.** An Order of regular clerks of St Paul, founded 1533, so called because the church of St Barnabas, in Milan, was given to them to preach in.

**Barnaby Bright.** An old provincial name for St Barnabas' Day (June 11th). Before the reform of the calendar it was the longest day, hence the jingle in Ray's *Collection of Proverbs* –

> Barnaby bright! Barnaby bright!
> The longest day and the shortest night.

**Barnaby Lecturers.** Four lecturers in the University of Cambridge, elected annually on St Barnabas' Day (June 11th), to lecture on mathematics, philosophy, rhetoric, and logic.

**Barnacle.** A species of wild goose allied to the brent goose, also the popular name of the Cirripedes, especially those which are attached by a stalk to floating balks of timber, the bottoms of ships, etc. In medieval times it was thought that the two were different forms of the same animal (much as are the frog and the tadpole), and as late as 1636 Gerard speaks of 'broken pieces of old ships on which is found certain spume or froth, which in time breedeth into shells, and the fish which is hatched therefrom is in shape and habit like a bird'.

The origin of this extraordinary belief is very obscure, but it is probably due to the accident of the identity of the name coupled with the presence in the shell-fish of the long feathery cirri which protrude from the shells and, when in the water, are very suggestive of plumage. In England the name was first attached to the bird. It is thought to be a diminutive of the M.R. *bernake*, a species of wild goose, though another suggestion (Max Müller) is that it is a corruption of *aves Hibernicae*, Irish birds, or rather *aves Hiberniculae*. The name of the shell-fish, on the other hand, may be from a diminutive (*pernacula*) of the Lat. *perna*, a mussel or similar shell-fish, though no such diminutive has been traced. With an identity of name it was, perhaps, natural to look for an identity of nature in the two creatures.

The name is given figuratively to close and constant companions, hangers on, or sycophants; also to placemen who stick to their offices but do little work, like the barnacles which stick to the bottoms of ships but impede their progress.

> The redundants would be 'Barnacles' with a vengeance ... and the work be all the worse done for these hangers-on.
>
> *Nineteenth Century* (August, 1888, p. 280)

**Barnacles.** Spectacles; especially those of a heavy or clumsy make or appearance. A slang term, from their supposed resemblance in shape to the twitches or 'barnacles' formerly used by farriers to keep under restraint unruly horses during the process of bleeding, shoeing, etc. This instrument consisted of two branches joined at one end by a hinge, and was employed to grip the horse's nose. The word is probably a diminutive of the O.Fr. *bernac*, a kind of muzzle for horses.

**Barnard's Inn.** One of the old Inns of Chancery, formerly situated on the south side of Holborn, east of Staple Inn. It was once known as 'Mackworth's Inn', because Dean Mackworth of Lincoln (d.1454) lived there.

**Barn-burners.** Destroyers, who, like the Dutchman of story, would burn down their barns to rid themselves of the rats.

**Barnstormer.** A slang term for a strolling player, and hence for any second-rate actor, especially one whose style is of an exaggerated declamatory kind. From the custom of itinerant troupes of actors giving their shows in village barns when better accommodation was not forthcoming.

**Barnwell, George.** The chief character in *The London Merchant, or the History of George Barnwell*, a prose tragedy by George Lillo, produced in 1731. It is founded on a popular 17th century ballad which is given in Percy's *Reliques*. Barnwell was a London apprentice who was seduced by Sarah Millwood, a disappointed and repulsive woman of the town, to whom he gave £200 of his master's money. He next robbed and murdered his pious uncle, a rich grazier at Ludlow. Having spent the money, Sarah turned him out; each informed against the other, and both were hanged. The popularity of the story is shown by James Smith's parody in the *Rejected Addresses* and Thackeray's caricature, *George de Barnwell*.

**Baron** is from late Lat. *baro* (through O.Fr. *barun*), and meant originally 'a man', especially opposed to something else, as a freeman to a slave, a husband to a wife, etc., and also in relation to someone else, as 'the king's man'. From the former comes the legal and heraldic use of the word in the phrase *baron and feme*, husband and wife; from the latter the more common use, the king's 'man' or 'baron' being his vassal holding tenure of the king by military or other service. Today a baron is a member of the lowest order of nobility; he is addressed as 'Lord', and by the Sovereign as 'Our right trusty and well beloved'. The premier English barony is that of De Ros, dating from 1264.

**Baron Bung.** Mine host, master of the beer bung.

**Baron Munchausen.** *See* Munchausen.

**Baron of Beef.** Two sirloins left uncut at the backbone. The *baron* is the backpart of the ox, called in Danish, the *rug*. Jocosely, but wrongly, said to be a pun upon *baron* and *sir* loin.

**Baronet.** An hereditary titled order of commoners, ranking next below barons and next above knights, using (like the latter) the title 'Sir' before the Christian name, and the contraction 'Bt' after the surname. The degree, as it now exi sts, was instituted by James I, and the title was sold to gentlemen possessing not less than £1,000 per annum for the purpose of raising funds for the plantation of Ulster, in allusion to which the Red Hand of Ulster (*see under* Hand) is the badge of Baronets of England, the United Kingdom, and of Great Britain, also of the old Baronets of Ireland (created prior to the Union in 1800).

The premier baronetcy is that of Bacon of Redgrave, originally conferred in 1611 on Nicholas, half-brother of Sir Francis Bacon, Viscount St Albans.

**Barrabas.** The hero of Marlowe's tragedy, *The Jew of Malta*.

> A mere monster, brought in with a large painted nose, … He kills in sport, poisons whole nunneries, invents infernal machines …
>
> C. Lamb

**Barrack Hack.** A term used in garrison towns for young women who attend barrack fêtes, balls, etc., year after year and are always ready to dance attendance on officers.

**Barrack, To.** To jeer at, to receive with derisive applause; hence *barracking*, derisive cheers and shouts. Introduced during the visit of the Australian cricketers in 1899, the term is said to be from a native word.

**Barracks.** Soldiers' quarters of a permanent nature. The word was introduced in the 17th century from Ital. *baracca*, a tent, through Fr. *baraque*, a barrack.

**Barrage** (Fr.). One of the words which, like Tank (*q.v.*) and a few others, acquired a new meaning during the Great War. In pre-war days it meant only an artificial dam or 'bar' built across a river to deepen the water on one side of it, as the great barrage on the Nile at Assouan; but during the war it was applied to the storm of projectiles from great guns that was made to fall like a curtain in front of advancing troops, raiding squadrons of aircraft, etc., or as a shield to offensive operations, etc.

**Barratry.** A legal term denoting (1) the offence of vexatiously exciting or maintaining lawsuits, and (2) – the commoner use – fraud or criminal negligence on the part of the master or crew of a ship to the detriment of the owners. Like many of our legal terms, it is from Old French.

**Barrel Fever.** Slang for intoxication or illness from intemperance in drink.

**Barrell's Blues.** The 4th Foot; so called from the colour of their facings, and William Barrell, colonel of the regiment (1734–9). Now called 'The King's Own (Royal Lancaster Regiment)'. They were called 'Lions' from their badge, the Lion of England.

**Barrette.** ***Parler à la barrette*** (Fr.). To give one a thump o' the head. The word *barrette* means the cap worn by the lower orders.

> Et moi, je pourrais hien parler à ta barrette.
>
> Molière, *L'Avare*

It is also used to signify the ordinary *birretta* of ecclesiastics and (probably) of French lawyers. *Il a reçu le chapeau* or *la barrette*. He has been made a cardinal.

> Le pape lui envoyait la barrette, mais elle ne servit qu'à le faire mourir cardinal.
>
> Voltaire, *Siècle de Louis XIV*, ch. xxxix

**Barricade.** To block up a street, passage, etc. The term rose in France in 1588, when Henri de Guise returned to Paris in defiance of the king's order. The king sent for his Swiss Guards, and the Parisians tore up the pavement, threw chains across the streets, and piled up barrels (Fr. *barriques*) filled with earth and stones, behind which they shot down the Swiss.

*The day of the Barricades* –

(1) May 12th, 1588, when the people forced Henry III to flee from Paris.

(2) August 5th, 1648, the beginning of the Fronde (*q.v.*).

(3) July 27th, 1830, the first day of *la grande semaine* which drove Charles X from the throne.

(4) February 24th, 1848, which resulted in the abdication of Louis Philippe.

(5) June 25th, 1848, when Affre, Archbishop of Paris, was shot in his attempt to quell the insurrection.

(6) December 2nd, 1851, the day of the *coup d'état*, when Louis Napoleon made his appeal to the people for re-election to the Presidency for ten years.

**Barrier Treaty.** A treaty fixing frontiers; especially that of November 15th, 1715, signed by Austria, Great Britain, and the Netherlands, by which the Low Countries were guaranteed to the House of Austria, and the Dutch were to garrison certain fortresses. The treaty was annulled at Fontainebleau in 1785.

**Barrikin.** Jargon, words not understood. The French word for 'gibberish' is *baragouin*, which was originally applied to the Lower Breton patois, and later to any unintelligible talk. It is from the Breton words *bara*, bread, and *gwen*, white; as these words occurred very frequently in conversation between the French and the Lower Bretons, they came to be applied to the latter as a nickname.

**Barrister.** One admitted to plead at the bar; one who has been 'called to the bar'. *See* Bar. They are of two degrees, the lower order being called simply 'barristers', or formerly 'outer' or 'utter' barristers; the higher 'King's Counsel'. Until 1880 there was a superior order known as 'Serjeants-at-Law' (*q.v.*). The King's Counsel (K.C.) is a senior, and when raised to this position he is said to 'take silk', he being privileged to wear a silk gown and, on special occasions, a full-bottomed wig. The junior counsel, or barristers, wear a plain stuff gown and a short wig.

***A Revising Barrister.*** One appointed to revise the lists of electors for members of parliament.

***A Vacation Barrister.*** Formerly one newly called to the bar, who for three years had to attend in 'Long Vacation'. The practice (and consequently the term) is now obsolete.

**Barristers' Bags.** *See* Lawyers.

**Barristers' Gowns.** 'Utter barristers wear a stuff or bombazine gown, and the puckered material between the shoulders of the gown is all that is now left of the purse into which, in early days, the successful litigant … dropped his … pecuniary tribute … for services rendered' (*Notes and Queries*, March 11th, 1893, p. 124). The fact is that the counsel was supposed to appear merely as a friend of the litigant. Even now he cannot recover his fees by legal process.

**Barry Cornwall,** poet. The *nom de plume* of Bryan Waller Procter (1787–1874). It is an anagram of his name.

**Barsanians.** Heretics who arose in the 6th century. Their sacrifices consisted in taking wheat flour on the tip of their first finger, and carrying it to their mouth. Also called *Gradanaites*, and *Semidulites*.

**Bar-sur-Aube.** *See* Castle of Bungay.

**Bartholomew, St.** The symbol of this saint is a knife, in allusion to the knife with which he was flayed alive. He is commemorated on August 24th, and is said to have been martyred in Armenia, AD 44.

**Bartholomew Doll.** A tawdry, over-dressed woman; like a flashy, bespangled doll offered for sale at Bartholomew Fair.

**Bartholomew Fair.** A fair held for centuries from its institution in 1133 at Smithfield, London, on St Bartholomew's Day: after the change of the calendar in 1752 it was held on September 3rd; in 1810 it was removed to Islington, and was suppressed in 1855, the licentious revelry and rioting that went on having entirely changed its character, which originally was that of a market for cloth and other goods. Ben Jonson wrote a comedy satirising the Puritans under this name.

**Bartholomew, Massacre of St.** The slaughter of the French Huguenots in the reign of Charles IX, begun on St Bartholomew's Day, August 24th, 1572, at the instigation of Catherine de' Medici, the mother of the young king. It is said that 30,000 persons fell in this dreadful persecution.

**Bartholomew Pig.** A very fat person. At Bartholomew Fair one of the chief attractions used to be a pig, roasted whole, and sold piping hot. Falstaff calls himself –

> A little tidy Bartholomew boar-pig.
>
> *2 Henry IV*, 2, 4

**Barthram's Dirge** (in Sir Walter Scott's *Border Minstrelsy*). Sir Noel Paton, in a private letter, says:

> The subject of this dirge was communicated to Sir Walter as a genuine fragment of the ancient *Border Muse* by his friend Mr Surtees, who is in reality its author. The ballad has no foundation in history; and the fair lady, her lover, and the nine brothers, are but the creation of the poet's fancy.

Sir Noel adds:

> I never painted a picture of this subject, though I have often thought of doing so. The engraving which appeared in the *Art Journal* was executed without my concurrence from the oil sketch, still, I presume, in the collection of Mr Pender, the late M.P. by whom it was brought to the Exhibition of the Royal Scottish Academy here (at Edinburgh) November 19th, 1866.

**Bartolist.** One skilled in law or, specifically, a student of Bartolus. Bartolus (1314–57) was an eminent Italian lawyer who wrote extensive commentaries on the Corpus Juris Civilis, and did much to arouse and stimulate interest in the ancient Roman law.

**Barzillai.** In Dryden's satire, *Absalom and Achitophel*, the Duke of Ormonde, friend and adherent of Charles II. The allusion is to Barzillai, who assisted David when he was expelled by Absalom from his kingdom (2 Sam. 17, 27–29).

Barzillai crowned with honours and with year …
In exile with his godlike prince he mourned,
For him he suffered, and with him returned.
*Absalom and Achitophel*, i, 817–24

**Bas Bleu.** *See* Blue Stocking.

**Base.** The adjective 'base', meaning 'low', both actually and figuratively, and the noun 'base', meaning 'the lowest part on which anything rests, the bottom of anything, groundwork, etc.', are etymologically separate words. The first is through Fr. *bas* from *bassus*, which in classical Latin was a cognomen signifying 'short and fat', and in late Latin was an ordinary word meaning 'low in height'. The noun is Fr. *base*, from Lat. and Gr. *basis*, a stepping, or that on which one steps, from the Gr. verb *bainein*, to go, step, or stand. **Bass,** in music, the lowest part in harmonised compositions, is from the *adjective* 'base'.

**Base Tenure.** Originally, tenure not by *military*, but by *base*, service, such as a serf or villein might give: later, a tenure in fee-simple that was determinate on the fulfilment of some contingent qualification.

**Base of Operations.** In military parlance, the protected place from which operations are conducted, where magazines of all sorts are formed, and upon which (in case of reverse) the army can fall back. The line from such a base to the object aimed at is called 'the Line of Operation'.

**Bashaw.** An arrogant, domineering man; a corruption of the Turkish *pasha*, a viceroy or provincial governor.

***A three-tailed Bashaw.*** A begler-beg or prince of princes among the Turks, who has a standard of three horse-tails borne before him. The next in rank is the bashaw with two tails, and then the bey, who has only one horse-tail.

**Bashi-bazouk.** A savage and brutal ruffian. The word is Turkish and means literally 'one whose head is turned'; it is applied in Turkey to non-uniformed irregular soldiers who make up in plunder for what they do not get in pay. It came into prominence at the time of the Crimean War, and again in that of the Bulgarian atrocities of 1876.

**Basilian Monks.** Monks of the Order of St Basil, who lived in the 4th century. It is said that the Order has produced 14 popes, 1,805 bishops, 3,010 abbots, and 11,085 martyrs.

**Basilica** (Gr. *basilikos*, royal). Originally a royal palace, but afterwards (in Rome) a large building with nave, aisles, and an apse at one end, used as a court of justice and for public meetings. By the early Christians they were easily adapted for purposes of worship; the church of St John Lateran at Rome was an ancient basilica.

**Basilics.** The legal code of the Eastern Empire, being a digest of the laws of Justinian and others prepared by the order of the Byzantine emperor Basilius, and completed by his son Leo towards the end of the 9th century.

**Basilidians.** A sect of Gnostic heretics, followers of Basilides, an Alexandrian Gnostic of about AD 125, who taught that from the unborn Father 'Mind' was begotten; from Mind proceeded 'The Word'; from the Word or *Logos* proceeded 'Understanding'; from Understanding 'Wisdom' and 'Power'; from Wisdom and Power 'Excellencies', 'Princes', and 'Angels', the agents which created heaven. Next to these high mightinesses come 365 celestial beings, the chief of whom is Abraxas (*q.v.*), and each of whom has his special heaven. He whom we call Christ is what the Basilidians term *The first-begotten 'Mind'*.

**Basilisco.** A cowardly, bragging knight in Kyd's tragedy, *Solyman and Perseda* (1588). Shakespeare (*King John*, 1, 1) makes the Bastard say to his mother, who asks him why he boasted of his ill-birth, 'Knight, knight, good mother, Basilisco-like' – i.e. my boasting has made me a knight. In the earlier play Basilisco, speaking of his name, adds, 'Knight, good fellow, knight, knight!' and is answered, 'Knave, good fellow, knave, knave!'

**Basilisk.** The king of serpents (Gr. *basileus*, a king), a fabulous reptile, also called a *cockatrice* (*q.v.*), and alleged to be hatched by a serpent from a cock's egg: supposed to have the power of 'looking anyone dead on whom it fixed its eyes'.

The Basiliske …
From powrefull eyes close venim doth convay
Into the lookers hart, and killeth farre away.
Spenser, *Faerie Queene*, IV, viii, 37

Also the name of a large brass cannon in use in Elizabethan times.

Thou hast talk'd
Of sallies and retires, of trenches, tents,
Of palisadoes, frontiers, parapets,
Of basilisks, of cannon.
Shakespeare, *1 Henry IV*, 2, 3

**Basket.** ***To be left in the basket.*** Neglected or uncared for. Left in the waste-basket.

***To give a basket.*** To refuse to marry. In Germany it was an old custom to fix a basket to the roof of one who had been jilted.

***To go to the basket.*** Old slang for to go to prison: referring to the dependence of the lowest grade of poor prisoners (those in the 'Hole') for their sustenance upon what passers-by put in the basket for them.

**Basochians.** An old French term for Clerks of the Parlements, hence, lawyers. The chief of the basochians was called *Le roi de la basoche*, and had his court, coin, and grand officers. He reviewed his 'subjects' every year, and administered justice twice a week. The *basoche* was responsible for public amusements, the presentation of farces, *soties*, and moralities, etc. Henri III suppressed the 'king', and transferred all his functions and privileges to the Chancellor.

Hence *monnaie de Basoche*, worthless money, from the coins at one time made and circulated by the lawyers of France, which had no currency beyond their own community.

**Bass** (in music). *See* Base.

**Bass.** The inner bark of the lime tree, or linden, properly called *bast*, a Teutonic word the ultimate origin of which is unknown. It is used by gardeners for packing, tying up plants, protecting trees, etc.; also for making mats, light baskets, hats, and (in Russia) shoes, while in parts of Central Europe a cloth is woven from it.

**Bast.** *See* Bubastis.

**Bastard.** An illegitimate child; a French word, from the Old French and Provençal *bast*, a pack-saddle. The pack-saddles were used by muleteers as beds; hence, as *bantling* (*q.v.*) is a 'bench-begotten' child, so is *bastard*, literally, one begotten on a pack-saddle bed.

The name was formerly given to a sweetened Spanish wine (white or brown) made of the bastard muscadine grape.

> I wil pledge you willingly in a cup of bastard.
>
> Sir Walter Scott, *Kenilworth*, ch. iii

**Baste.** *I'll baste your jacket for you*, i.e. cane you. *I'll give you a thorough basting*, i.e. beating. (A word of uncertain origin.)

**Bastille** means simply a building (O.Fr. *bastir*, now *bâtir*, to build). The famous state prison in Paris was commenced by Charles V as a royal château in 1370, and it was first used as a prison by Louis XI. It was seized and sacked by the mob in the French Revolution, July 14th, 1789, and on the first anniversary its final demolition was commenced and the Place de la Bastille laid out on its site.

**Bastinado.** A beating (Sp. *bastonada*, from *baston*, a stick). The Chinese, Turks, and Persians give the bastinado on the soles of the feet. The Turks call the punishment *zarb*.

**Bastion.** A fortification having two faces and two flanks, all the angles of which are *salient*, that is, pointing outwards. The line of rampart which joins together the flanks of two bastions is technically called a curtain.

Bastions in fortifications were invented in 1480 by Achmet Pasha; but San Michaeli of Verona, in 1527, is said by Maffei and Vasari to have been the real inventor.

**Bat.** Harlequin's lath wand (Fr. *batte*, a wooden sword).

***Off his own bat.*** By his own exertions; on his own account. A cricketer's phrase, meaning runs won by a single player.

***To carry out one's bat*** (in cricket). Not to be 'out' when the time for drawing the stumps has arrived.

***To get along at a great bat.*** Here the word means *beat*, *pace*, rate of speed.

**Batman.** A military officer's soldier-servant; but properly a soldier in charge of a *bat-horse* (or pack-horse) and its load. From Fr. *bât*, a pack-saddle (O.Fr. *bast*; *see* Bastard).

**Batavia.** The Netherlands; so called from the Batavi, a German tribe which in Roman times inhabited the modern Holland.

> Flat Batavia's willowy groves.
>
> Wordsworth, *Descriptive Sketches*, 520

**Bate me an Ace.** *See* Bolton.

**Bath.** *Knights of the Bath.* This name is derived from the ceremony of bathing, which used to be practised at the inauguration of a knight, as a symbol of purity. The last knights created in this ancient form were at the coronation of Charles II in 1661. G.C.B. stands for *Grand Cross of the Bath* (the first class); K.C.B. *Knight Commander of the Bath* (the second class); C.B. *Companion of the Bath* (the third class).

**Bath Brick.** Alluvial matter compressed to the form of a brick, and used for cleaning knives, polishing metals, etc. It is made at Bridgwater, the material being dredged from the river Parrett, which runs through Bridgwater.

**Bath Chair.** A chair mounted on wheels and used for invalids. First used at Bath, which for long has been frequented by invalids on account of its hot springs.

***There, go to Bath with you!*** Don't talk nonsense. Insane persons used to be sent to Bath for the benefit of its mineral waters. The implied reproof is, what you say is so silly, you ought to go to Bath and get your head shaved.

**Bath, King of.** Richard Nash (1674–1761), generally called Beau Nash, a celebrated master of the ceremonies at Bath for fifty-six years. He was ultimately ruined by gambling.

**Bath King-of-Arms.** *See* Heraldry (*College of Arms*).

**Bath Metal.** An alloy like pinchbeck (*q.v.*) consisting of about sixteen parts copper and five of zinc.

**Bath Post.** A letter paper with a highly glazed surface, used by the ultra-fashionable visitors of Bath when that watering-place was at its prime. *See* Post-paper.

**Bath Shillings.** Silver tokens coined at Bath in 1811–12, and issued by various tradespeople, with face values of 4*s*., 2*s*., and 1*s*.

**Bath Stone.** A limestone used for building, and found in the Lower Oolite, near Bath. It is easily wrought in the quarry but hardens on exposure to the air.

**Bath, St Mary's.** *See* Bain-Marie.

**Bathia.** The name given in the Talmud to the daughter of Pharaoh who found Moses in the ark of bulrushes.

**Bath-kol** (daughter of the voice). A sort of divination common among the ancient Jews after the gift of prophecy had ceased. When an appeal was made to *Bath-kol*, the first words uttered after the appeal were considered oracular. *See* Ray's *Three Physico-Theological Discourses*, iii, 1693.

**Bathos** (Gr. *bathos*, depth). A ludicrous descent from grandiloquence to commonplace.

> The Taste of the Bathos is implanted by Nature itself in the soul of man.
>
> Pope, *Art of Sinking*, ii (1727)

A good example is the well-known couplet given by Pope:

> And thou, Dalhousie, the great god of war,
> Lieutenant-general to the earl of Mar.
>
> *Art of Sinking*, ix

**Bathsheba.** In Dryden's *Absalom and Achitophel*, intended for the Duchess of Portsmouth, a favourite of Charles II. The allusion is to the wife of Uriah the Hittite, beloved by David (2 Sam. 11). The Duke of Monmouth says:

> My father, whom with reverence yet I name
> Charmed into ease, is careless of his fame;
> And, bribed with petty sums of foreign gold,
> Is grown in Bathsheba's embraces old.
>
> *Absalom and Achitophel*, i, 707–10

**Bathyllus.** A beautiful boy of Samos, greatly beloved by Polycrates the tyrant, and by the poet Anacreon. (Horace, *Epistle* xiv, 9.)

> To them [i.e. the aesthetic school] the boyhood of Bathyllus is of more moment than the manhood of Napoleon.
>
> Mallock, *The New Republic*, Bk iv, ch. i

**Batiste.** A kind of cambric (*q.v.*), so called from Baptiste of Cambrai, who first manufactured it in the 13th century.

**Bâton de commandement** (Fr., literally 'commander's truncheon'). The name given by archaeologists to a kind of rod, usually of reindeer horn, pierced with one or more round holes, and sometimes embellished with carvings. It belongs to the Magdalenian age; but its use or purpose is quite unknown.

**Batrachomyomachia.** A storm in a puddle; much ado about nothing. The word is the name of a mock heroic Greek epic, supposed to be by Pigres of Caria, but formerly attributed to Homer. It tells, as its name imports, of a *Battle between the Frogs and Mice*.

**Bats, The Parliament of.** The parliament held at Nottingham in 1426 during the quarrel between the Duke of Gloucester and Cardinal Beaufort, so called because its members, being forbidden to carry swords, came armed with cudgels, or 'bats'. Also called 'the Club Parliament'.

**Batta.** An Anglo-Indian term for perquisites. Properly, an extra allowance to troops when in the field or on special service. Sometimes spelt *batty*.

> He would rather live on half-pay in a garrison that could boast of a fives-court, than vegetate on full batta where there was none.
>
> G. R. Gleig, *Thomas Munro*, vol. i, ch. iv, p. 227

**Battels.** At Oxford University the accounts for board and provisions, etc., provided by the kitchen and also (more loosely) one's total accounts for these together with fees for tuition, membership of clubs, etc., for the term. The word has also been used for the provisions or rations themselves; which is the earlier use has never been decided, and the derivation of the word is still a matter for conjecture.

**Battersea.** *You must go to Battersea to get your simples cut.* A reproof to a simpleton, or one who makes a very foolish observation. The market gardeners of Battersea used to grow simples (medicinal herbs), and the London apothecaries went there to select or cut such as they wanted.

**Battle above the Clouds.** *See* Clouds.

**Battle of the Books.** A satire, by Swift (written 1697, published 1704), on the literary squabble as to the comparative value of ancient and modern authors. In the battle the ancient books fight against the modern books in St James's Library. *See* Boyle Controversy.

**Battle of the Frogs and Mice.** *See* Batrachomyomachia.

**Battle of the Giants.** *See* Giants.

**Battle of the Herrings.** *See* Herrings.

**Battle of the Kegs, The.** A humorous ballad heroic by Francis Hopkinson (1737–91), published in 1778, and telling of the alarm felt by the British over certain machines, in the form of kegs charged with gunpowder, which were floated down the Delaware.

**Battle of the Moat.** *See* Moat.

**Battle of the Nations.** *See* Nations.

**Battle of the Poets, The.** A satirical poem (1725) by John Sheffield, Duke of Buckingham, in which the versifiers of the time are brought into the field.

**Battle of the Spurs.** *See* Spurs.

**Battle of the Standard.** *See* Standard.

**Battle of the Three Emperors.** *See* Three Emperors.

**Battle-painter, The,** or **Delle Battaglie.** Michael Angelo Cerquozzi (1600–60), a Roman artist noted for his battle-scenes, was so called.

**Battle Royal.** A certain number of cocks, say sixteen, are pitted together; the eight victors are then pitted, then the four, and last of all the two; and the winner is victor of the battle royal. Metaphorically, the term is applied to chess, etc.

***A close battle.*** Originally a naval fight at 'close quarters'. in which opposing ships engage each other side by side.

***Line of battle.*** The position of troops drawn up in battle array. At sea, the formation of the ships in a naval engagement. A *line of battle ship* was a capital ship fit to take part in a main attack. *Frigates* did not join in a general engagement.

***A pitched battle.*** A battle which has been planned, and the ground pitched on or chosen beforehand.

***The Fifteen Decisive Battles of the World.*** *See* Fifteen.

***Half the battle.*** Half determines the battle. Thus, 'The first stroke is half the battle'. that is, the way in which the battle is begun determines what the end will be.

***Trial by battle.*** The submission of a legal suit to a combat between the litigants, under the notion that God would defend the right.

***Wager of battle.*** One of the forms of ordeal or appeal to the judgment of God, in the old Norman courts of the kingdom. It consisted of a personal combat between the plaintiff and the defendant, in the presence of the court itself. Abolished by 59 Geo. III, c. 46.

**Battle, Sarah.** A celebrated character in one of Lamb's *Essays of Elia*, who considered whist the business of life and literature one of the relaxations. When a young gentleman, of a literary turn, said to her he had no objection to unbend his mind for a little time by taking a hand with her, Sarah was indignant, and declared it worse than sacrilege to speak thus of her noble occupation. Whist 'was her life business; her duty; the thing she came into the world to do, and she did it. She unbent her mind afterwards over a book.'

**Battledore.** Originally the wooden bat used in washing linen. The etymology of the word is not at all certain, but there is an old Provençal *batedor*, meaning a washing-beetle.

**Battledore Book.** A name sometimes formerly given to a horn-book (*q.v.*), because of its shape. Hence, perhaps, the phrase 'Not to know B from a battledore'. *See* B.

**Battue.** A French word meaning literally 'a beating', used in English as a sporting term to signify a regular butchery of game, the 'guns' being collected at a certain spot over which the birds are driven by the beaters who 'beat' the bushes, etc., for the purpose. Hence, a wholesale slaughter, especially of unarmed people.

**Batty.** *See* Batta.

**Baturlio marina.** *See* Barisal guns.

**Baubee.** *See* Bawbee.

**Bauble.** ***A fool should never hold a bauble in his hand.*** ''Tis a foolish bird that fouls its own nest.' The bauble was a short stick, ornamented with ass's ears, carried by licensed fools. (O.Fr. *babel*, or *baubel*, a child's toy; perhaps confused with the M.E. *babyll* or *babulle*, a stick with a thong, from *bablyn*, to waver or oscillate.)

***If every fool held a bauble, fuel would be dear.*** The proverb indicates that the world contains a vast number of fools, a sentiment referred to by Carlyle in his often misquoted saying:

> A Parliament speaking through reporters to Buncomb and the twenty-seven millions, mostly fools. *Latter Day Pamphlet*, No. 6 (1850)

***To deserve the bauble.*** To be so foolish as to be qualified to carry the fool's emblem of office.

**Baucis.** *See* Philemon.

**Bauld Wullie.** *See* Belted Will.

**Baulk.** *See* Balk.

**Baviad, The.** A merciless satire by Gifford on the Della Cruscan poetry, published 1794, and republished the following year with a second part called *The Maeviad*. Bavius and Maevius were two minor poets pilloried by Virgil (*Eclogue*, iii, 9).

He may with foxes plough, and milk he-goats,
Who praises Bavius or on Maevius dotes.
*E. C. B.*

And their names are still used for inferior versifiers.

May some choice patron bless each grey goose quill,
May every Bavius have his Bufo still.
Pope, *Prologue to Satires*, 249

**Bavieca.** The Cid's horse.

**Bavius.** *See* Baviad.

**Bawbee.** A debased silver coin representing six Scots pennies and about equal in value to a halfpenny English, first issued in 1541, in the reign of James V.

The etymology of the word is uncertain, and many fantastic theories have been put forth to account for it. A Fifeshire tradition, for which there seems to be no authority, says:

> When one of the infant kings of Scotland, of great expectation, was shown to the public, for the preservation of order, the price of admission was in proportion to the rank of the visitant. The eyes of the superior classes being feasted, their retainers and the mobility were admitted at the rate of six pennies each. Hence this piece of money being the price of seeing the royal *Babie*, it received the name of *Babie*.

But this story, and others saying that the first bawbees were stamped with the head of an infant king, are discounted by the facts that at the time of the first issue the king was 30 years old, and, further, that the earliest bawbees bore no head at all. The word is probably derived from the laird of Sillebawby, a contemporary mint-master, as appears from the Treasurer's account, September 7th, 1541, '*In argento receptis a Jacobo Atzinsone, et Alexandro Orok de Sillebawby respective.*'

***Jenny's bawbee.*** Her marriage portion.

Wha'll hire, wha'll hire, wha'll hire me?
Three plumps and a wallop for ae bawbee.

An old rhyme embodying a reflection on the supposed parsimony and poverty of the Scots. The tradition is that the people of Kirkmahoe were so poor, they could not afford meat for their broth. A 'cute cobbler bought four sheep-shanks, and for the payment of one bawbee would 'plump' one of them into the boiling water, and give it a 'wallop' or whisk round. The sheep-shank was called a *gustin bone*, and was supposed to give a rich 'gust' to the broth.

**Bawtry.** *Like the saddler of Bawtry, who was hanged for leaving his liquor* (Yorkshire proverb). It was customary for criminals on their way to execution to stop at a certain tavern in York for a 'parting draught'. The saddler of Bawtry refused to accept the liquor and was hanged. If he had stopped a few minutes at the tavern, his reprieve, which was on the road, would have arrived in time to save his life.

**Baxterians.** Followers of Richard Baxter (1615–91), a noted English nonconformist. The chief points are – (1) That Christ died in a spiritual sense for the elect, and in a general sense for all; (2) that there is no such thing as reprobation; (3) that even saints may fall from grace. He thus tried to effect a compromise between the 'heretical' opinions of the Arminians and the Calvinists.

**Bay.** (1) The shrub was anciently supposed to be a preservative against lightning, because it was the tree of Apollo. Hence, according to Pliny, Tiberius and other Roman emperors wore a wreath of bay as an amulet, especially in thunder-storms.

Reach the bays –
I'll tie a garland here about his head;
'Twill keep my boy from lightning
Webster, *Vittoria Corumbona*, v, 1

The bay being sacred to Apollo is accounted for by the legend that he fell in love with, and was rejected by, the beautiful Daphne, daughter of the river-god Peneos, in Thessaly, who had resolved to pass her life in perpetual virginity. She fled from him and sought the protection of her father, who changed her into the bay tree, whereupon Apollo declared that henceforth he would wear bay leaves instead of the oak, and that all who sought his favour should follow his example.

The withering of a bay tree was supposed to be the omen of a death. Holinshed refers to this superstition:

> In this yeare [1399] in a manner throughout all the realme of England, old baie trees withered, and, afterwards, contrarie to all mens thinking, grew greene againe; a strange sight, and supposed to impart some unknown event. III, 496, 2, 66

Shakespeare makes use of this note in his *Richard II*, 2, 4:

'Tis thought the king is dead. We'll not stay –
The bay trees in our country are withered.

***Crowned with bays.*** A reward of victory: from the custom that obtained in ancient Rome of so crowning a victorious general.

**Bay.** (2) A reddish-brown colour, generally used of horses. The word is the Fr. *bai*, from Lat. *badius*, a term used by Varro in his list of colours appropriate to horses. Bayard (*q.v.*) means 'bay-coloured'.

***The Queen's Bays.*** The 2nd Dragoon Guards; so called because they are mounted on bay horses; often known, 'for short', as *The Queen's*.

**Bay the Moon, To.** *See* Bark.

**Bay Salt.** Coarse-grained salt, formerly obtained by slow evaporation of sea-water and used for curing meat, etc. Perhaps so called because originally imported from the shores of the *Bay* of Biscay. 'Bay'. in this case, does not signify the colour.

**Bay State, The.** Massachusetts. In Colonial days its full title was 'The Colony of Massachusetts Bay': hence the name.

**Bayadere.** A Hindu dancing girl employed both for religious dances and for private amusements. The word is a French corruption of the Portuguese *bailadeira*, a female dancer.

**Bayard.** A horse of incredible swiftness, given by Charlemagne to the four sons of Aymon. *See* Aymon. If only one of the sons mounted, the horse was of the ordinary size; but if all four mounted, his body became elongated to the requisite length. He is introduced in Boiardo's *Orlando Innamorato*, Ariosto's *Orlando Furioso*, and elsewhere, and legend relates that he is still alive and can be heard neighing in the Ardennes on Midsummer Day. The name is used for any valuable or wonderful horse, and means a 'high bay-coloured horse.'

***Bold as Blind Bayard.*** Foolhardy. If a blind horse leaps, the chance is he will fall into a ditch. Grose mentions the following expression, *To ride Bayard of ten toes* – 'Going by the marrow-bone stage' – i.e. walking.

***Keep Bayard in the stable.*** Keep what is of value under lock and key.

**Bayard, The Chevalier de.** Pierre du Terrail (1475–1524), a celebrated French knight and national hero, distinguished in the Italian campaigns of Charles VIII, Louis XII, and François I. Of him it was said that he was *le chevalier sans peur et sans reproche*.

***The Bayard of the East,*** or ***of the Indian Army.*** Sir James Outram (1803–63).

***The British Bayard.*** Sir Philip Sidney (1554–86).

***The Polish Bayard.*** Prince Joseph Poniatowski (1762–1813).

**Bayardo.** The famous steed of Rinaldo (*q.v.*), which once belonged to Amadis of Gaul. *See* Horse.

***Bayardo's Leap.*** Three stones, about thirty yards apart, near Sleaford. It is said that Rinaldo was riding on his favourite steed, when the demon of the place sprang behind him; but Bayardo in terror took three tremendous leaps and unhorsed the fiend.

**Bayes.** A character in the *Rehearsal*, by the Duke of Buckingham (1671), designed to satirise Dryden. The name, of course, refers to the laureateship.

**Bayes's Troops.** *Dead men may rise again, like Bayes's troops, or the savages in the Fantocini.* In the *Rehearsal* a battle is fought between foot-soldiers and great hobby-horses. At last Drawcansir kills all on both sides. Smith then asks how they are to go off, to which Bayes replies, 'As they came on – upon their legs'; upon which they all jump up alive again.

**Bayeux Tapestry.** A strip of linen 231 ft long and 20 in. wide on which is represented in tapestry the mission of Harold to William, Duke of Normandy (William the Conqueror), and all the incidents of his history from then till his death at Hastings in 1066. It is preserved at Bayeux, and is supposed to be the work of Matilda, wife of William the Conqueror. A replica is shown at the Victoria and Albert Museum, South Kensington.

> In the tapestry, the Saxons fight on foot with javelin and battle-axe, and bear shields with the British characteristic of a boss in the centre. The men were moustached.
>
> The Normans are on horseback, with long shields and pennoned lances. The men are not only shaven, but most of them have a complete tonsure on the back of the head, whence the spies said to Harold, 'There are more priests in the Norman army than men in Harold's'.

**Bayonet.** The etymology of this word is doubtful, but it is much more likely than not that it is from the French city, *Bayonne*, where it may have been first made or first used. It was known quite early in the 17th century.

**Bayonets.** A synonym of 'rank and file'. that is, privates and corporals of infantry. As, 'the number of bayonets was 25,000'.

> It is on the bayonets that a Quartermaster-General relies for his working and fatigue parties.
>
> Howitt, *Hist. of Eng.* (year 1854, p. 260)

**Bayou State.** The State of Mississippi; so called from its numerous bayous. A bayou is a creek, or sluggish and marshy overflow of a river or lake. The word may be of native American origin, but is probably a corruption of Fr. *boyau*, gut.

**Bead.** From A.S. *-bed* (in *gebed*), a prayer, *biddan*, to pray. 'Bead', thus originally meant simply 'a prayer'; but as prayers were 'told' (i.e. account kept of them) on a 'paternoster', the word came to be transferred to the small globular perforated body a number of which, threaded on a string, composed this paternoster or 'rosary'.

***To count one's beads.*** To say one's prayers. *See* Rosary.

***To draw a bead on.*** *See* Draw.

***To pray without one's beads.*** To be out of one's reckoning.

***Baily's beads.*** When the disc of the moon has (in an eclipse) reduced that of the sun to a thin crescent, the crescent assumes the appearance somewhat resembling a string of beads. This was first described in detail by Francis Baily in 1836, whence the name of the phenomenon, the cause of which is the sun shining through the depressions between the lunar mountains.

***St Cuthbert's beads.*** Single joints of the articulated stems of encrinites. They are perforated in the centre, and bear a fanciful resemblance to a cross; hence, they were once used for rosaries (*q.v.*). St Cuthbert was a Scottish monk of the 6th century, and may be called the St Patrick of the Border. Legend relates that he sits at night on a rock in Holy Island and uses the opposite rock as his anvil while he forges the beads.

> On a rock of Lindisfarn
> St Cuthbert sits, and toils to frame
> The sea-born beads that bear his name.
>
> Scott, *Marmion*

***St Martin's beads.*** Flash jewellery. St Martins-le-Grand was at one time a noted place for sham jewellery.

**Bead-house.** An almshouse for beadsmen.

**Bead-roll.** A list of persons to be prayed for; hence, also, any list.

**Beadle.** A person whose duty it is to *bid* or cite persons to appear to a summons; also a church servant, whose duty it is to *bid* the parishioners to attend the vestry, or to give notice of vestry meetings. It is ultimately a Teutonic word (Old High Ger. *bitel*, one who asks, whence the A.S. *bedan*, to bid, and *bydel*, a herald), but it came to us through the O.Fr. *badel*, a herald. *See* Bedel.

**Beadsman** or **Bedesman.** Properly, one who prays; hence, an inmate of an almshouse, because most charities of this class were instituted so that the inmates might 'pray for the soul of the founder'. *See* Bead.

> Seated with some grey beadsman.
>
> Crabbe, *Borough*

**Beak.** Slang for a police magistrate, but formerly (16th and 17th cents) for a constable. Various fanciful derivations have been suggested, but the etymology of the word is quite unknown.

**Beaker.** A drinking-glass; a rummer; a wide-mouthed glass vessel with a lip, used in scientific experiments. A much-travelled word, having come to us by way of the Scandinavian *bikkar*, a cup (Dut. *beker*; Ger. *becher*), from Greek *bikos*, a wine-jar, which was of Eastern origin. Our *pitcher* is really the same word.

> O for a beaker full of the warm South,
> Full of the true, the blushful Hippocrene.
>
> Keats, *Ode to a Nightingale*

**Beam. *Thrown on my beam-ends.*** Driven to my last shift. A ship is said to be on her beam-ends when she is laid by a heavy gale completely on her side, i.e. the part where her *beams end*. Not unfrequently the only means of righting her in such a case is to cut away her masts.

***On the starboard beam.*** A distant point out at sea on the right-hand side, and at right angles to the keel.

***On the port beam.*** A similar point on the left-hand side.

***On the weather beam.*** On that side of a ship which faces the wind.

***To kick the beam.*** *See* Kick.

**Beam** (*of a stag*). The main trunk of the horn, the part that bears the branches (A.S. *béam*, a tree).

**Bean. *Every bean has its black.*** *Nemo sine vitiis nascitur* (Everyone has his faults). The bean has a black eye. (*Ogni grano ha la sua semola.*)

***He has found the bean in the cake.*** He has got a prize in the lottery, has come to some unexpected good fortune. The allusion is to twelfth cakes in which a bean is buried. When the cake is cut up and distributed, he who gets the bean is the twelfth-night king. *See* Bean-king.

***Jack and the bean-stalk.*** *See* Jack (vi).

***Old bean.*** A slang expression of good-natured familiarity that became very common during the Great War. 'My dear old bean' corresponds roughly to 'My dear old chap', 'My dear fellow'.

**Bean-feast.** Much the same as wayz-goose (*q.v.*). A feast given by an employer to those he employs. Probably so called because either beans or a bean-goose used to be a favourite dish on such occasions.

**Bean-goose.** A migratory bird which appears in England in the autumn; so named from a mark on its bill like a horse-bean. It is next in size to the grey lag-goose.

**Bean-king.** *Rey de Habas*, the child appointed to play the part of king on twelfth-night. *See* Bean: *He has found the bean.* Twelfth-night was sometimes known as *the Bean-king's festival.*

**Beans.** Slang for property, money; also for a sovereign, and (formerly) a guinea. In this sense it is probably the O.Fr. cant, *biens*, meaning property; but in such phrases as *not worth a bean*, the allusion is to the bean's small value.

> Like a beane [alms-money] in a monkeshood.
>
> Cotgrave

***Blue beans.*** Bullets or shot; hence, 'Three blue beans in a blue bladder', a rattle for children.

> *Fort.*: (Of his purse). Hark! dost rattle?
>
> *Strad.*: Yes, like three blue beans in a blue bladder, rattle bladder, rattle; your purse is like my belly, th' one's without money, th' other without meat. Dakker, *Old Fortunatus*, I, ii

Three small bullets or large shot in a bladder would make a very good rattle for a child.

***Beans are in flower.*** A catch-phrase said to one by way of accounting for his being so silly. Our forefathers imagined that the perfume of the flowering bean made men silly or light-headed.

***He knows how many beans make five.*** He is 'up to snuff'; he is no fool; he is not to be imposed upon. The reference is to an old trap. Everyone knows that five beans make five, and on this answer being correctly given the questioner goes on, 'But you don't know how many blue beans make five white ones.' The complete answer to this is, 'Five – *if peeled.*'

***Full of beans.*** Said of a fresh and spirited horse; hence, in good form; full of health and spirits.

***I'll give him beans.*** I'll give him a licking, a jolly good hiding. A very common phrase. Hence, *to get beans*, to incur chastisement or reproof. Probably from the French proverb, *S'il me donne des pois, je lui donnerai des fèves* (i.e. If he gives me peas I will give him beans), I will give him tit for tat, a Roland for an Oliver.

In ancient times Pythagoras forbade the use of beans to his disciples – not the use of beans as food, but for political elections. Magistrates and other public officers were elected by beans cast by the voters into a helmet, and what Pythagoras advised was that his disciples should not interfere with politics or 'love beans' – i.e. office. But according to Aristotle the word *bean* implied venery, and that the prohibition to 'abstain from beans' was equivalent to 'keeping the body chaste'.

**Bear.** In the phraseology of the Stock Exchange, a speculator for a fall. (*Cp.* Bull.) Thus, *to operate for a bear*, or *to bear the market*, is to use every effort to depress prices, so as to buy cheap and make a profit on the rise. Such a transaction is known as a *Bear account.*

The term is of some antiquity, and was current at least as early as the South Sea Bubble, in the 18th century. Its probable origin will be found in the proverb, 'Selling the skin before you have caught the bear'.

> So was the huntsman by the bear oppressed.
> Whose hide he sold before he caught the beast.
>
> Waller, *Battle of the Summer Islands*, c. ii

**The Bear.** Albert, margrave of Brandenburg (1106–70). He was so called from his heraldic device.

***The bloody bear***, in Dryden's *The Hind and the Panther*, means the Independents.

> The bloody bear, an independent beast,
> Unlicked to form, in groans her hate expressed.
>
> Pt i, 35, 36

In mediaeval times it was popularly supposed that bear-cubs were born as shapeless masses of flesh and fur, and had to be literally 'licked into shape' by their mothers. Hence the reference in the above quotation, and the phrase '*to lick into shape*' (*q.v.*).

***The Great Bear***, and ***Little Bear.*** These constellations were so named by the Greeks, and their word, *arktos*, a bear, is still kept in the names Arcturus (the bear-ward, *oures*, guardian) and Arctic (*q.v.*). The Sanskrit name for the Great Bear is from the verb *rakh*, to be bright, and it has been suggested that the Greeks named it *arktos* as a result of confusion between the two words. *Cp.* Charles's Wain; Northern Wagoner.

> The wind-shaked surge, with high and monstrous mane,
> Seems to cast water on the burning bear
> And quench the guards of th' ever-fixed pole.
>
> Shakespeare, *Othello*, 2, 1

The *guards* referred to in the above extract are β and γ of Ursa Minor. They are so named, not from any supposed guarding that they do, but from the Sp. *guardare*, to behold, because of the great assistance they were to mariners in navigation.

The classical fable is that Calisto, a nymph of Diana, had two sons by Jupiter, which Juno changed into bears, and Jupiter converted into constellations.

'Twas here we saw Calisto's star retire
Beneath the waves, unawed by Juno's ire.
Camoens, *Lusiad*, Bk v

***The Bear,*** or ***Northern Bear.*** Russia.

France turns from her abandoned friends afresh,
And soothes the bear that growls for patriot flesh.
Campbell, *Poland*, st. 5

***A bridled bear.*** A young nobleman under the control of a travelling tutor. *See* Bear-leader.

***The bear and ragged staff.*** A crest of the Nevilles and later Earls of Warwick, often used as a public-house sign. The first earl is said to have been Arth or Arthgal, of the Round Table, whose cognizance was a *bear*, *arth* meaning a bear (Lat. *urs*'). Morvid, the second earl, overcame, in single combat, a mighty giant, who came against him with a club consisting of a tree pulled up by the roots, but stripped of its branches. In remembrance of his victory over the giant he added 'the ragged staff'.

***The bear and the tea-kettle.*** Said of a person who injures himself by foolish rage. The story is that one day a bear entered a hut in Kamschatka, where a kettle was on the fire. Master Bruin smelt at it and burnt his nose; greatly irritated, he seized it with his paws, and squeezed it against his breast. This, of course, made matters worse, for the boiling water scalded him terribly, and he growled in agony till some neighbours put an end to his life with their guns.

***A bear sucking his paws.*** It used to be believed that when a bear was deprived of food it sustained life by sucking its paws. The same was said of the badger. The phrase is applied to industrious idleness.

***As savage as a bear with a sore head.*** Unreasonably ill-tempered.

As a bear has no tail,
For a lion he'll fail.

The same as *Ne sutor supra crepidam* (Let not the cobbler aspire above his last). Robert Dudley, Earl of Leicester, a descendant of the Warwick family, is said to have changed his own crest, 'a green lion with two tails', for the Warwick 'bear and ragged staff'. When made governor of the Low Countries, he was suspected of aiming at absolute supremacy, or the desire of being the monarch of his fellows, as the lion is monarch among beasts. Some wit wrote under his crest the Latin verse, *Ursa caret cauda non queat esse leo*, i.e. –

Your bear for lion needs must fail,
Because your true bears have no tail.

***To take the bear by the tooth.*** To put your head into the lion's mouth; needlessly to run into danger.

**Bear, To.** ***Come, bear a hand!*** Come and render help. In French, *Donner un coup à quelqu'un.* Bring a hand, or bring your hand to bear on the work going on.

***To bear arms.*** To do military service.

***To bear away*** (nautical). To keep away from the wind.

***To bear one company.*** To be one's companion.

His faithful dog shall bear him company.
Pope, *Essay on Man*, epistle i,112

***To bear down.*** To overpower; to force down.

Fully prepared to bear down all resistance.
Cooper, *The Pilot*, ch. xvii

***To bear down upon*** (nautical). To approach from the weather side.

***To bear in mind.*** Remember; do not forget. Carry in your recollection.

'To learn by heart' means to learn *memoriter.* Mind and heart stand for memory in both phrases.

***To bear out.*** To corroborate, to confirm.

***To bear up.*** To support; to keep the spirits up.

***To bear with.*** To show forbearance; to endure with complacency.

How long shall I bear with this evil congregation?
Numb. 14:27

***To bear the bell.*** *See* Bell.

**Bear of Bradwardine, The.** In Scott's *Waverley*, a wine goblet made, according to Scott, by command of St Duthac, Abbot of Aberbrothoc, to be presented to the Baron of Bradwardine for services rendered in defence of the monastery. Inscribed upon it was the motto: 'Beware the bear.'

**Bear Account.** *See* Bear (Stock Exchange).

**Bear Garden.** *This place is a perfect bear garden* – that is, full of confusion, noise, tumult, and quarrels. In Elizabethan and Stuart times the gardens where bears were kept and baited for public amusement were famous for all sorts of riotous disorder.

**Bear-leader.** A common expression in the 18th century denoting a travelling tutor who escorted a young nobleman, or youth of wealth and fashion, on the 'Grand Tour'. From the old custom of leading muzzled bears about the streets, and making them show off in order to attract notice and money.

> Bear! [said *Dr Pangloss* to his pupil]. Under favour young gentleman, I am the bear-leader, being appointed your tutor.
>
> G. Colman, *Heir-at-Law*

**Beard.** Among the Jews, Turks, and Eastern nations generally the beard has long been regarded as a sign of manly dignity. To cut it off wilfully was a deadly insult, and the Jews were strictly forbidden to cut it off ceremonially, though shaving it was a sign of mourning. No greater insult could be offered to a man than to pluck or even touch his beard, hence the phrase *to beard one*, to defy him, to contradict him flatly, to insult him. By touching or swearing by one's own beard one's good faith was assured.

The dyeing of beards is mentioned by Strabo, and Bottom the Weaver satirises the custom when he undertakes to play Pyramus, and asks, 'what beard were I best to play it in?'

> I will discharge it in either your straw-colour beard, your orange-tawny beard, your purple-in-grain beard, or your French-crown-colour beard (your perfect yellow).
>
> Shakespeare, *Midsummer Night's Dream*, 1, 2

***To beard the lion in his den.*** Vehemently to contradict one either on some subject he has made his hobby, or on his own premises; to defy personally or face to face.

> Dar'st thou, then,
> To beard the lion in his den,
> The Douglas in his hall?
>
> Scott, *Marmion*, vi, 14

***To make one's beard.*** To have one wholly at your mercy, as a barber has when holding a man's beard to dress it, or shaving the chin of a customer. So, to be able to do what one likes with one, to outwit or delude him.

> Though thou preye Argus, with his hundred yën,
> To be my warde-cors, as he can best,
> In feith, he shal nat kepe me but me lest;
> Yet coude I make his berd, so moot I thee.
>
> Chaucer, *Wife of Bath's Prologue*, 358

***I told him to his beard.*** I told him to his face, regardless of consequences; I spoke to him openly and fearlessly.

***Maugre his beard.*** In spite of him.

***''Tis merry in hall when beards wag all'*** – i.e. when feasting goes on.

> Then was the minstrel's harp with rapture heard;
> The song of ancient days gave huge delight;
> With pleasure too did wag the minstrel's beard,
> For Plenty courted him to drink and bite.
>
> Peter Pindar, *Elegy to Scotland*

***To laugh at one's beard.*** To attempt to make a fool of a person – to deceive by ridiculous exaggeration.

> 'By the prophet! but he laughs at our beards.' exclaimed the Pacha angrily. 'These are foolish lies.'
>
> Marryat, *Pacha of Many Tales*

***To laugh in one's beard.*** To laugh up one's sleeve, that is, surreptitiously.

***To run in one's beard.*** To offer opposition to a person; to do something obnoxious to a person before his face. The French say, *à la barbe de quelqu'un* (under one's very nose).

***With the beard on the shoulder*** (Sp.). In the attitude of listening to overhear something; with circumspection, looking in all directions for surprises and ambuscades.

> They rode, as the Spanish proverb expresses it, 'with the beard on the shoulder', looking round from time to time, and using every precaution ... against pursuit.
>
> Scott, *Peveril of the Peak*, ch. vii

***Tax upon beards.*** Peter the Great imposed a tax upon beards. Everyone above the lowest class had to pay 100 roubles, and the lowest class had to pay a copeck, for enjoying this 'luxury'. Clerks were stationed at the gates of every town to collect the beard tax.

**Bearded.** ***Bearded Master*** (*Magister barbatus*). So Persius styled Socrates, under the notion that the beard is the symbol of wisdom.

***The bearded.*** A surname or nickname (*Pogonatus*) given to Constantine IV, Emperor of the East, 668–85; also to Baldwin IV, Count of Flanders, 988–1036, Geoffrey the Crusader, Bouchard of the house of Montmorency, and St Paula. *See* Bearded Women.

**Bearded Women.** St Paula the Bearded, a Spanish saint of uncertain date of whom it is said that when being pursued by a man she fled to a crucifix and at once a beard and moustache appeared on her face, thus disguising her and saving her from her would-be ravisher. A somewhat similar story is told of St Wilgefortis, a mythical saint supposed to have been one of seven daughters born at a birth to a king of Portugal; also of the English saint, St Uncumber.

Many bearded women are recorded in history; among them may be mentioned:

Bartel Graetjë, of Stuttgard, born 1562.

Charles XII had in his army a woman whose beard was a yard and a half long. She was taken prisoner at the battle of Pultowa, and presented to the Czar, 1724.

Mlle Bois de Chêne, born at Geneva in 1834, and exhibited in London in 1852–3; she had a profuse head of hair, a strong black beard, large whiskers, and thick hair on her arms and back.

Julia Pastrana, found among the Digger Indians of Mexico, was exhibited in London in 1857; died, 1862, at Moscow; was embalmed by Professor Suckaloff; and the embalmed body was exhibited at 191, Piccadilly.

**Bearings.** ***I'll bring him to his bearings.*** I'll bring him to his senses. A sea term. The bearings of a ship is that part of her hull which is on the water-line when she is in good trim. To bring a ship to her bearings is to get her into this trim.

***To lose one's bearings.*** To become bewildered; to get perplexed as to which is the right road.

***To take the bearings.*** To ascertain the relative position of some object.

**Béarnais, Le.** Henri IV of France (1553–1610); so called from *Le Béarn*, his native province.

**Beast.** *The Number of the Beast. See* Number.

**Beat** (A.S. *betan*). The first sense of the word was that of striking; that of overcoming or defeating followed on as a natural extension. A track, line, or appointed range. A walk often trodden or beaten by the feet, as a *policeman's beat*. The word means a beaten path.

***Not in my beat.*** Not in my line; not in the range of my talents or inclination.

***Off his beat.*** Not on duty; not in his appointed walk; not his speciality or line.

> Off his own beat his opinions were of no value.
>
> Emerson, *English Traits*, ch. i

***On his beat.*** In his appointed walk; on duty.

***Out of his beat.*** In his wrong walk; out of his proper sphere.

***Dead beat.*** So completely beaten or worsted as to have no leg to stand on. Like a dead man with no fight left in him; quite tired out.

> I'm dead beat, but I thought I'd like to come in and see you all once more.
>
> Roe, *Without a Home*, p. 32

***Dead beat escapement*** (of a watch). One in which there is no reverse motion of the escape-wheel.

***That beats Banagher. Termagant.*** *See* Banagher; Termagant.

***To beat about.*** A nautical phrase, meaning to tack against the wind.

***To beat about the bush.*** To approach a matter cautiously or in a roundabout way; to shilly-shally; perhaps because one goes carefully when beating a bush to find if any game is lurking within.

***To beat an alarm.*** To give notice of danger by beat of drum.

***To beat a retreat*** (Fr. *battre en retraite*); ***to beat to arms; to beat a charge.*** Military terms similar to the above.

***To beat down.*** To make a seller 'abate' his price.

***To beat*** or ***drum a thing into one.*** To repeat as a drummer repeats his strokes on a drum.

***To beat hollow,*** or ***to a mummy, a frazzle, to ribbons, a jelly,*** etc. To beat wholly, utterly, completely.

***To beat the air.*** To strike out at nothing, merely to bring one's muscles into play, as pugilists do before they begin to fight; to toil without profit; to work to no purpose.

> So fight I, not as one that beateth the air.
>
> 1 Cor. 9:26

***To beat the booby.*** *See* Booby.

***To beat the bounds.*** *See* Bounds.

***To beat the bush.*** To allow another to profit by one's exertions; 'one beat the bush and another caught the hare'. 'Other men laboured, and ye are entered into their labours' (John 4:48). The allusion is to beaters, whose business it is to beat the bushes and start the game for a shooting party.

***To beat the devil's tattoo.*** *See* Tattoo.

***To beat the Dutch.*** To draw a very long bow; to say something very incredible. *To beat the band* means the same thing.

> Well! if that don't beat the Dutch!

***To beat time.*** To mark time in music by beating or moving the hands, feet, or a wand.

***To beat up against the wind.*** To tack against an adverse wind; to get the better of the wind.

***To beat up someone's quarters.*** To hunt out where one lives; to visit without ceremony. A military term, signifying to make an unexpected attack on an enemy in camp.

> To beat up the quarters of some of our less-known relations. Lamb, *Essays of Elia*

***To beat up recruits*** or ***supporters.*** To hunt them up or call them together, as soldiers are by beat of drum.

***To beat one with his own staff.*** To confute one by his own words. An *argumentum ad hominem.*

> Can High Church bigotry go farther than this? And how well have I since been beaten with mine own staff. J. Wesley
>
> [He refers to his excluding Rolzius from communion because he had not been canonically baptised].

**Beati Possidentes.** Blessed are those who have (for they shall receive). 'Possession is nine points of the law.'

**Beatific Vision.** The sight of the Deity, or of the blessed in the realms of heaven, especially that granted to the soul at the instant of death. *See* Is. 6:1–4, and Acts 7:55, 56.

**Beatrice.** Dante's Beatrice, celebrated by him in the *Vita Nuova* and the *Divina Commedia*, was born 1266 and died in 1290, under twenty-four years old. She was a native of Florence, of the Portinari family, and married Simone de' Bardi in 1287. Dante married Gemma Donati about two years after her death.

**Beau.** The French word, which means 'fine', or 'beautiful', has, in England, often been prefixed to the name of a man of fashion or a fop as an epithet of distinction. The following are well known:

***Beau Brummell.*** George Bryan Brummell (1778–1840).

***Le Beau D'Orsay.*** Father of Count D'Orsay, and called by Byron *Jeune Cupidon*.

***Beau Feilding.*** Robert Feilding (d.1712), called 'Handsome Feilding' by Charles II. He died in Scotland Yard, London, after having been convicted of bigamously marrying the Duchess of Cleveland, a former mistress of Charles II. He figures as Orlando in Steele's *Tatler* (Nos 50 and 51).

***Beau Hewitt.*** The model for 'Sir Fopling Flutter', hero of Etheredge's *Man of Mode*.

***Beau Nash.*** Richard Nash (1674–1761). Son of a Welsh gentleman, a notorious diner-out. He undertook the management of the bathrooms at Bath, and conducted the public balls with a splendour and decorum never before witnessed.

***Beau Didapper***, in Fielding's *Joseph Andrews*, and *Beau Tibbs*, noted for his finery, vanity, and poverty in Goldsmith's *Citizen of the World*, may also be mentioned.

**Beau Ideal.** Properly, the ideal Beautiful, the abstract idea of beauty, *idéal* in the French, being the adjective, and *beau*, the substantive: but in English the parts played by the words are usually transposed, and thus have come to mean the ideal type or model of anything in its most consummate perfection.

**Beau Monde.** The fashionable world; people who make up the coterie of fashion.

**Beau Trap.** An old slang expression for a loose paving-stone under which water lodged, and which squirted up filth when trodden on, to the annoyance of the smartly dressed.

**Beauclerc** (*good scholar*). Applied to Henry I (1068, 1100–35), who had clerk-like accomplishments, very rare in the times in which he lived.

**Beaumontague** or **Beaumontage.** Material used for filling in accidental holes in wood- or metal-work, repairing cracks, disguising bad joinery, etc. Said to be so called from the celebrated French geologist, Elie de Beaumont (1798–1874), who also gave his name to *beaumonlite*, a silicate of copper.

**Beauseant.** The battle-cry of the Knights Templar. *See* Templar.

**Beautiful.** *Beautiful* or *fair as an angel*. Throughout the Middle Ages it was common to associate beauty with virtue, and ugliness with sin; hence the expressions given above, and the following also – 'Seraphic beauty', 'Cherubic loveliness'. 'Ugly as sin', etc.

**Beautiful Parricide.** Beatrice Cenci, daughter of Francesco Cenci, a dissipated and passionate Roman nobleman, who, with her brothers, plotted the death of her father because of his unmitigated cruelty to his wife and children. She was executed in 1599, and at the trial her counsel, with the view of still further gaining popular sympathy for his client, accused the father, probably without foundation, of having attempted to commit incest with her. Her story has been a favourite theme in poetry and art; Shelley's tragedy *The Cenci* is particularly noteworthy.

**Beauty.** *Tout est beau sans chandelles. 'La nuit tous les chats sont gris.'*

***Beauty is but skin deep.***

> O formose puer, nimium ne crede colori.
>
> Virgil, *Eclogues*, ii
>
> (O my pretty boy, trust not too much to your pretty looks.)

**Beauty and the Beast.** The hero and heroine of the well-known fairy tale in which Beauty saved the life of her father by consenting to live with the Beast; and the Beast, being disenchanted by Beauty's love, became a handsome prince, and married her. *See* Azor's Mirror.

The story is found in Straparola's *Piacevola Notti* (1550), and it is from this collection that Mme le Prince de Beaumont probably obtained it when it became popular through her French version (1757). It is the basis of Grétry's opera *Zémire et Azor* (1771).

> The story of a handsome and wealthy prince being compelled by enchantment to assume the appearance and character of a loathsome beast

or formidable dragon until by the pure love of one who does not suspect the disguise is of great antiquity and takes various forms. Sometimes, as in the story of Lamia, and the old ballads *Kempion* and *The Laidley Worm of Spindle stoneheugh*, it is the woman – the 'Loathly Lady' of the romances – who is enchanted into the form of a serpent and is only released at the kiss of a true knight.

**Beauty of Buttermere.** Mary Robinson, married in 1802 to John Hatfield, a heartless impostor, and already a bigamist, who was executed for forgery at Carlisle in 1803. She was the subject of many dramas and stories.

Here, too, were 'forms and pressures of the time'.
Rough, bold, as Grecian comedy displayed
When Art was young; dramas of living men,
And recent things yet warm with life; ...
I mean, O distant Friend! a story drawn
From our own ground – The Maid of Buttermere –
And how, unfaithful to a virtuous wife
Deserted and deceived, the Spoiler came
And wooed the artless daughter of the hills,
And wedded her, in cruel mockery
Of love and marriage bonds.

Wordsworth, *Prelude*, vii, 288

**Beauty Sleep.** Sleep taken before midnight. Those who habitually go to bed, especially during youth, after midnight, are usually pale and more or less haggard.

Would I please to remember that I had roused him up at night ... [in] his beauty sleep.

Blackmore, *Lorna Doone*, ch. 64

**Beaux Esprits** (Fr.). Men of wit or genius (singular, *Un bel esprit*, a wit, a genius).

**Beaux Yeux** (Fr.). Beautiful eyes or attractive looks. 'I will do it for your *beaux yeux*' (because you are so pretty, or because your eyes are so attractive).

The poor fellow is mad for your *beaux yeux*, I believe. Thackeray, *Pendennis*, ch. 26

**Beaver.** The lower and movable part of a helmet; so called from Fr. *bavière*, which meant a child's bib, to which this part had some resemblance. It is not connected with *bever* (*q.v.*), the afternoon draught in the harvest-field.

*Hamlet*: Then you saw not his face?
*Horatio*: O yes, my lord; he wore his beaver up.

Shakespeare, *Hamlet*, 1, 2

*Beaver* is also an old name for a man's hat; because they used to be made of beaver fur.

**Bécarre, Bémol.** *Sauter de becarre en bemol* (Fr.), to jump from one subject to another without regard to pertinence; *Sauter du coq a l'ane* from *Genesis* to *Revelation*. Literally, to jump from sharps to flats. *Bécarre* is the Latin *B quadratum* or *B quarré*. In the harmonic system of Guido d'Arezzo b sharp was expressed by a square b, and b flat by a round b. *Bémol* is b flat – b *mollis*, soft.

**Bécasse.** French for a woodcock and also for a booby or 'softy'. The word is sometimes used in the latter sense in English.

**Bed.** ***The great bed of Ware.*** A bed eleven feet square, and capable of holding twelve persons; assigned by tradition to the Earl of Warwick, the king-maker. It is now in Rye House, Hertfordshire.

Although the sheet were big enough for the bed of Ware in England.

Shakespeare, *Twelfth Night*, 3, 2

***As you make your bed you must lie on it.*** Everyone must bear the consequences of his own acts. 'As you sow, so must you reap.' 'As you brew, so must you bake.'

***To bed out.*** To plant what are called 'bedding-out plants' in a flower-bed.

• Bedding-out plants are reared in pots, generally in a hothouse, and are transferred into garden-beds early in the summer. Such plants as geraniums, marguerites, fuchsias, pentstemons, petunias, verbenas, lobelias, calceolarias, etc., are meant.

***To make the bed.*** To arrange it and make it fit for use. In America this sense of 'make' is much more common than it is with us. 'Your room is made.' arranged in due order. To make it all right.

***You got out of bed the wrong way,*** or ***with the left leg foremost.*** Said of a person who is patchy and ill-tempered. It was an ancient superstition that it was unlucky to set the left foot on the ground first on getting out of bed. The same superstition applies to putting on the left shoe first, a 'fancy' not yet wholly exploded. Augustus Caesar was very superstitious in this respect.

***Bed of justice.*** *See* Lit.

***A bed of roses.*** A situation of ease and pleasure.

***A bed of thorns.*** A situation of great anxiety and apprehension.

**Bed-post.** *In the twinkling of a bed-post* or *bed-staff.* As quickly as possible. In old bed-frames it is said that posts were placed in brackets at the two sides of the bedstead for keeping the bed-clothes from rolling off, and movable staves were used as we now use iron laths; there was also in some cases a staff used to beat the bed and clean it. In the reign of Edward I, Sir John Chichester had a mock skirmish with his servant (Sir John with his rapier and the servant with the bed-staff), in which the servant was accidentally killed. Wright, in his *Domestic Manners*, shows us a chambermaid of the 17th century using a bed-staff to beat up the bedding. 'Twinkling' is from A.S. *twinclian*, a frequentative verb connected with *twiccan*, to twitch, and connotes rapid or tremulous movement.

> I'll do it instantly, in the twinkling of a bed-staff.
> Shadwell, *Virtuoso*, I, i (1676)

The phrase is probably due to the older and more readily understandable one, *in the twinkling of an eye*, in the smallest thinkable fraction of time:

> We shall all be changed in a moment, in the twinkling of an eye, at the last trump.
> 1 *Cor*. 15:51, 52

**Bedel,** or **Bedell.** Old forms of the word *beadle* (*q.v.*), still used at Oxford and Cambridge in place of the modern spelling for the officer who carries the mace before the Vice-Chancellor and performs a few other duties. At Oxford there are four, called *bedels*, at Cambridge there are two, called *bedells*, or *esquire-bedells*.

**Beder.** (1) A village between Medina and Mecca famous for the first victory gained by Mahomet over the Koreshites (AD 624). In the battle he is said to have been assisted by 3,000 angels, led by Gabriel, mounted on his horse Haïzum.

(2) In the *Arabian Nights*, a King of Persia who married Giauharê, daughter of the most powerful of the under-sea emperors. Queen Labê tried to change him into a horse, but he changed her into a mare instead.

**Bedesman.** *See* Beadsman.

**Bedford Level.** The large tract of marshy land about 60 miles in breadth and 40 in length which lies in the counties of Norfolk, Suffolk, Cambridge, Huntingdonshire, Northamptonshire, and Lincolnshire, and includes the Isle of Ely and the whole of the Fen district. So called from Francis, fourth Earl of Bedford, who undertook the draining of the Fens in 1634.

**Bedfordshire.** ***I am off to Bedfordshire.*** To the land of Nod, to bed. The language abounds with these puns, e.g. 'the marrowbone stage', 'A Dunse scholar', 'Knight of the beer-barrel', 'Admiral of the blue', 'Master of the Mint' (*q.v.*), 'Master of the Rolls' (*q.v.*), etc. And the French even more than the English.

**Bedivere,** or **Bedver.** In the Arthurian romances, a knight of the Round Table, butler and staunch adherent of King Arthur. It was he who, at the request of the dying king, threw Excalibur into the Lake, and afterwards bore his body to the ladies in the barge which was to take him to Avalon.

**Bedlam.** A lunatic asylum or madhouse; a contraction for *Bethlehem*, the name of a religious house in London, converted into a hospital for lunatics.

> St Mary of Bethlehem was founded as a *priory* in 1247 and in 1547 it was given to the mayor and corporation of London, and incorporated as a royal foundation for lunatics.

***Bedlamite.*** A madman, a fool, an inhabitant of a Bedlam. *See* Abram-Man.

***Bedlam, Tom o'.*** *See* Tom.

**Bednall Green.** *See* Beggar's Daughter.

**Bedouins.** French (and hence English) form of an Arabic word meaning 'a dweller in the desert', given indiscriminately by Europeans to the nomadic tribes of Arabia and Syria, and applied in journalistic slang to gypsies, or the homeless poor of the streets. In this use it is merely a further extension of the term 'street Arab', which means the same thing.

**Bedreddin Hassan.** In the *Arabian Nights*, the son of Nureddin Ali, in the story of *Noureddin and his Son*.

> Comparing herself to Bedreddin Hassan, whom the vizier … discovered by his superlative skill in composing cream-tarts without pepper in them. Scott, *Heart of Midlothian*

**Bed-rock.** American slang for one's last shilling. A miner's term for the hard basis rock which is reached when the mine is exhausted. 'I'm come down to the bed-rock,' i.e. my last dollar.

> 'No, no!' continued Tennessee's partner, hastily, 'I'll play this yer hand alone. I've come down to the bed-rock: it's just this; Tennessee, thar, has played it pretty rough and expensive, like, on a stranger … . Now what's the fair thing? Some would say more, and some would say less. Here's seventeen hundred dollars in coarse gold and a watch – it's about all my pile – and call it square.' Bret Harte, *Tennessee's Partner*

**Bedver.** *See* Bedivere.

**Bee.** Legend has it that Jupiter was nourished by bees in infancy, and Pindar is said to have been nourished by bees with honey instead of milk.

The Greeks consecrated bees to the moon. With the Romans a flight of bees was considered a bad omen. Appian (*Civil War*, Bk ii) says a swarm of bees lighted on the altar and prognosticated the fatal issue of the battle of Pharsalia.

The coins of Ephesus had a bee on the reverse.

When Plato was an infant, bees settled on his lips when he was asleep, indicating that he would become famous for his honeyed words.

> And as when Plato did i' the cradle thrive,
> Bees to his lips brought honey from their hive.
>
> W. Browne, *Britannia's Pastorals*, ii

The same story is told of Sophocles, Pindar, St Chrysostom, and others, including St Ambrose, who is represented with a beehive.

*See also* Animals in Symbolism.

***The Athenian Bee.*** *See* Athenian.

***The Bee of Athens.*** *See* Athenian and Attic Bee.

The name *bee* is given, particularly in America, to a social gathering for some useful work, the allusion being to the social and industrious character of bees. The name of the object of the gathering generally precedes the word, as a *spelling-bee* (for a competition in spelling), *apple-bees*, *husking-bees*, etc. It is an old Devonshire custom, carried across the Atlantic in Stuart times, but the *name* appears to have originated in America.

***To have your head full of bees,*** or ***to have a bee in your bonnet.*** To be cranky; to have an idiosyncrasy; to be full of devices, crotchets, fancies, inventions, and dreamy theories. The connection between bees and the soul was once generally maintained: hence Mahomet admits bees to Paradise. Porphyry says of fountains, 'they are adapted to the nymphs, or those souls which the ancients called bees'. *Cp.* Maggot.

**Beef.** This word, from the O.Fr. *boef* (mod. Fr. *boeuf*), an ox, is, like *mutton* (Fr. *mouton*), a reminder of the time when, in the years following the Norman Conquest, the Saxon was the downtrodden servant of the conquerors: the Normans had the cooked meat, and when set before them used the word they were accustomed to; the Saxon was the herdsman, and while the beast was under his charge called it by its Saxon name.

> Old Alderman Ox continues to hold his Saxon title while he is under the charge of serfs and bondsmen; but becomes *Beef*, a fiery French gallant, when he arrives before the worshipful jaws that are destined to consume him.
>
> Scott, *Ivanhoe*

***Weaver's beef of Colchester,*** i.e. sprats, caught abundantly in the neighbourhood. (Fuller, *Worthies.*)

**Beefeaters.** The popular name of the Yeomen of the Guard in the royal household, appointed, in 1485, by Henry VII, to form part of the royal train at banquets and on other grand occasions; also of the Yeomen Extraordinary of the Guard, who were appointed as Warders of the Tower of London by Edward VI, and wear the same Tudor-period costume as the Yeomen of the Guard themselves.

There is no evidence whatever for the old guess that the word is connected with the French *buffet*, and signifies 'an attendant at the royal buffet, or sideboard'; on the contrary, every indication goes to show that it means exactly what it says, viz. 'eaters of beef'. That 'eater' was formerly used as a synonym for 'servant' is clear, not only from the fact that the O.E. *hláf-aeta* (literally, 'loaf-eater') meant 'a menial servant', but also from the passage in Ben Jonson's *Silent Woman* (1609), where Morose, calling for his servants, shouts,

> Bar my doors! bar my doors! Where are all my eaters? My mouths, now? Bar up my doors, you varlets!
>
> Act III, ii

Sir S. D. Scott, in his *The British Army* (i, 513), quotes an early use of the word from a letter of Prince Rupert's dated 1645, and shows (p. 517) that the large daily allowance of beef provided for their table makes the words in their literal meaning quite appropriate.

There is plenty of evidence to show that in the 17th century there was little doubt of the meaning of the word: *see*, e.g., Cartwright's *The Ordinary* (1651):

> Those goodly Juments of the guard would fight
> (As they eat beef) after six stone a day. Act II, i

and in 1741 Baron Bielfield, a visitor to England, described them as:

> Une Troupe d'Anglo-Suisses, qu'on nomme Yomen of the Gard, et par derision *Roast-beef* ou *Beef-eaters*, c'est à dire, Mangeurs de Boeuf, remplissent la Salle des Gardes et en font les fonctions. (Tom. I. lett. xxix)

*Cp.* Buphagos.

**Beef-steak Club.** The present Beef-steak Club dates from 1876, but the original club of this name was founded about 1707. Its badge was a gridiron, and it was said to comprise 'the chief wits and great men of the nation'. In 1735 the 'Sublime Society of the Steaks', which has sometimes been confused with this, but which scorned to be called a club, was inaugurated through a chance dinner taken by Lord Peterborough in the scene-room of Rich, over Covent Garden Theatre. His lordship was so delighted with the steak provided and cooked by the actor that he proposed repeating the entertainment every Saturday. The 'Sublime Society', which was then founded, continued to meet at Covent Garden till the fire of 1808, and, after various vicissitudes, was finally dissolved in 1867. The original gridiron on which Rich broiled the peer's steak is still in existence.

**Beefington, Milor.** A character in Canning's *The Rovers*, a burlesque (in the *Anti-Jacobin*) on the sentimental German dramas of the period. Casimere is a Polish emigrant, and Beefington an English nobleman, exiled by the tyranny of King John.

**Bee-line.** The shortest distance between two given points; such as a bee is supposed to take in making for its hive. *Air-line* is another term for the same thing.

> Our footmarks, seen afterwards, showed that we had steered a bee-line to the brig.
>
> Kane, *Arctic Explorations*, vol. i, ch. xvii

**Beelzebub.** The name should be spelt *Beelzebul* (or, rather, *Baalzebul*, *see* Baal), and means 'lord of the high house'; but, as this title was ambiguous and might have been taken as referring to Solomon's Temple, the late Jews changed it to *Beelzebub*, which has the meaning 'lord of flies'. Beelzebub was the particular Baal worshipped originally in Ekron and afterwards far and wide in Palestine and the adjacent countries. To the Jews he came to be the chief representative of the false gods, and he took an important place in their hierarchy of demons. He is referred to in Matt. 12:24, as 'the prince of the devils', and hence Milton places him next in rank to Satan.

> One next himself in power, and next in crime,
> Long after known in Palestine, and named
> Beelzebub. *Paradise Lost*, i, 79

**Beer.** *See* Ale.

***He does not think small beer of himself.*** *See* Small Beer.

***Life is not all beer and skittles***, i.e. not all eating, drinking, and play; not all pleasure; not all harmony and love.

> Sport like life, and life like sport,
> Isn't all skittles and beer.

**Beerocracy.** A satirical or humorous name for the powerful and wealthy brewing interest in politics and society. A burlesque on the word 'aristocracy' (Gr. *kratria*, from *kratos*, power).

**Beeswing.** The second crust, or film, composed of shining scales of tartar, which forms in good port and some other wines after long keeping, and which bears some resemblance to the wings of bees. A port drinker is very particular not to 'break the beeswing' by shaking the bottle, or turning it the wrong way up.

**Beetle, To.** To overhang, to threaten, to jut over. The word seems to have been first used by Shakespeare:

> Or to the dreadful summit of the din,
> That beetles o'er his base into the sea.
>
> *Hamlet*, 1, 4

It is formed from the adjective, *beetle-browed*, having prominent or shaggy eyebrows; and it is not the case, as has sometimes been stated, that the adjective was formed from the verb. The derivation of *beetle* in this use is not quite certain, but it probably refers to the tufted antennae which, in some beetles, stand straight out from the head.

**Beetle-crusher.** A large, flat foot. The expression was first used in *Punch*, in one of Leech's caricatures.

**Befana.** The good fairy of Italian children, who is supposed to fill their stockings with toys when they go to bed on Twelfth Night. Someone enters the children's bedroom for the purpose, and the wakeful youngsters cry out, '*Ecco la Befana.*' According to legend, Befana was too busy with house affairs to look after the Magi when they went to offer their gifts, and said she would wait to see them on their return; but they went another way, and Befana, every Twelfth Night, watches to see them. The name is a corruption of *Epiphania*.

**Before the Lights.** *See* Lights.

**Before the Mast.** *See* Mast.

**Beg.** A Turkish chief or governor. *See* Bey.

**Beg the Question, To.** To assume a proposition which, in reality, involves the conclusion. Thus, to say that parallel lines will never meet because they are parallel, is simply to assume as a fact the very thing you profess to prove. The phrase is the common English equivalent of the Latin term, *petitio principii*.

**Beggar.** ***A beggar may sing before a pickpocket.*** *Cantabit vacuus coram latrone viator* (Juvenal, x, 22). A beggar may sing in the presence of thieves because he has nothing in his pocket to lose.

***Beggar of Bednall Green.*** *See* Beggar's Daughter.

***Beggars should not be choosers.*** Beggars should take what is given them, and not dictate to the giver what they like best. They must accept and be thankful.

***Beggars' Barm.*** The thick foam which collects on the surface of ponds, brooks, and other pieces of water where the current meets stoppage. It looks like barm or yeast, but, being unfit for use, is only beggarly barm at best.

***Beggars' Bullets.*** Stones.

***Beggars' Bush.*** *To go by beggar's bush*, or *Go home by beggar's bush* – i.e. to go to ruin. Beggar's bush is the name of a tree which once stood on the left hand of the London road from Huntingdon to Caxton; so called because it was a noted rendezvous for beggars. These punning phrases and proverbs are very common.

***Beggar's Daughter, Bessee, the beggar's daughter of Bednall Green,*** the heroine of an old ballad given in Percy's *Reliques*, and introduced by Chettle and Day into their play *The Blind Beggar of Bednal Green* (1600). Sheridan Knowles also has a play on the story (1834). Bessee was very beautiful, and was courted by four suitors at once – a knight, a gentleman of fortune, a London merchant, and the son of the innkeeper at Romford. She told them that they must obtain the consent of her father, the poor blind beggar of Bethnal Green. When they heard that, they all slunk off except the knight, who went to ask the beggar's leave to wed the 'pretty Bessee'. The beggar gave her £3,000 for her dower, and £100 to buy her wedding gown. At the wedding feast he explained to the guests that he was Henry, son and heir of Sir Simon de Montfort. At the battle of Evesham the barons were routed, Montfort slain, and himself left on the field for dead. A baron's daughter discovered him, nursed him with care, and married him; the fruit of this marriage was 'pretty Bessee'. Henry de Montfort assumed the garb of a beggar to escape the vigilance of King Henry's spies.

***King of the beggars.*** Bampfylde Moore Carew (1693–1770), a famous English vagabond who was elected King of the Gypsies.

***Set a beggar on horseback, and he'll ride to the de'il.*** There is no one so proud and arrogant as a beggar who has suddenly grown rich.

> Such is the sad effect of wealth – rank pride –
> Mount but a beggar, how the rogue will ride!
>
> Peter Pindar, *Epistle to Lord Lonsdale*

Lat. *Asperius nihil est humili cum surgit in altum* (Claudianus: *In Eutropium*).

Fr. *Il n'est orgueil que de pauvre enrichi.*

Ital. *Il vilan nobilitado non connosce il parentado* (a beggar ennobled does not know his own kinsmen).

Sp. *Quando el villano está en ei mulo, non conoze á dios, ni al mundo* (when a beggar is mounted on a mule, he knows neither gods nor men).

**Begging Friars.** *See* Mendicant Orders.

**Beghards.** A monastic fraternity which rose in the Low Countries in the 12th century, so called from Lambert le Begue, a priest of Liège, who also founded a sisterhood. They took no vows, and were free to leave the society when they liked. In the 17th century, those who survived the persecutions of the popes and inquisition joined the Tertiarii of the Franciscans. *See* Béguines.

**Beglerbeg.** *See* Bashaw.

**Begorra.** An Irish form of the English minced oath 'begad', for 'By God'.

**Béguines.** A sisterhood founded in the 12th century by Lambert le Begue (*see* Beghards). The Béguines were at liberty to quit the cloister and to marry; they formerly flourished in the Low Countries, Germany, France, and Italy; and there are still communities with this name in Belgium. The cap called a *béguin* was named from this sisterhood.

**Begum.** A lady, princess, or woman of high rank in India; the wife of a *nawab*. *See* Nabob.

**Behemoth.** The animal described under this name in Job 40:15 *et seq.*, is, if an actual animal were intended, almost certainly the hippopotamus; but modern scholarship rather tends to the opinion that the reference is purely mythological. The English poet Thomson, apparently took it to be the rhinoceros:

> Behold! in plaited mail,
> Behemoth rears his head.
>
> *The Seasons: Summer*, 709

The word is generally pronounced Be'hemoth; but Milton, like Thomson, places the accent on the second syllable.

> Scarce from his mold
> Behemoth, biggest born of earth, upheaved
> His vastness. *Paradise Lost*, vii, 471

**Behmenists.** A sect of theosophical mystics, so called from Jacob Behmen, or Böhme (1575–1624), their founder. The first Behmenist sect in England was founded under the name of *Philadelphists* by a certain Jane Leade, in 1697.

**Behram.** The most holy kind of fire, according to Parseeism (*q.v.*). *See also* Guebres.

**Bejan.** A freshman or greenhorn. This term was introduced into some of the Scottish Universities from the University of Paris, and is a corruption of Fr. *bec jaune*, yellow beak, with allusion to a nestling or unfledged bird. At Aberdeen a woman student is called a *bajanella* or *bejanella*.

In France *béjaune* is still the name for the repast that the freshman is supposed to provide for his new companions.

> His grandmother yielded, and Robert was straightway a bejan or yellow-beak.
>
> Macdonald, *Robert Falconer*

**Bel.** The name of two Assyrio-Babylonian gods; it is the same word as Baal (*q.v.*). The story of Bel and the Dragon, in which we are told how Daniel convinced the king that Bel was not an actual living deity but only an image, was formerly part of the *Book of Daniel*, but is now relegated to the Apocrypha.

**Bel Esprit** (Fr.). Literally, fine mind, means, in English, a vivacious wit; one of quick and lively parts, ready at repartee (pl. *beaux esprits*).

**Belamour.** Anyone, man or woman, loved by one of the opposite sex; from Fr. *bel amour*, fair love. Also, some unidentified white flower:

> Her lips did smell like unto Gilly flowers,
> Her ruddy cheekes like unto Roses red;
> Her snowy browes like budded Bellamoures.
>
> Spenser, *Amoretti*, lxiv

**Belch, Sir Toby.** A reckless, roistering, jolly fellow: from the knight of that name in Shakespeare's *Twelfth Night.*

**Belcher.** A pocket-handkerchief – properly, one with white spots on a blue ground; so called from Jim Belcher (1781–1811), the pugilist, who adopted it.

**Beldam.** An old woman. This is not from the French *belle dame*, but from English *dam*, a mother, and *bel-*, a prefix expressing relationship as does *grand-* in *grandmother*, *god-* (i.e. *good*) in *godfather*, etc. *Belfather* is an old term for *grandfather*.

> Old men and beldames in the streets
> Do prophesy upon it dangerously.
>
> Shakespeare, *King John*, 4, 2

**Belfast Regiment, The.** The old 35th Foot, raised in Belfast in 1701. There is no such regiment now in the British Army. What used to be called No. 35 is now called the 1st battalion of the Royal Sussex, the 2nd battalion being the old No. 107.

**Bel-fires.** *See* Beltane.

**Belford.** A friend of Lovelace in Richardson's *Clarissa Harlowe*. These 'friends' made a covenant to pardon every sort of liberty which they took with each other.

**Belfry.** A military tower, pushed by besiegers against the wall of a besieged city, that missiles may be thrown more easily against the defenders. (From O.Fr. *berfrei*, *berfroi*, Mid. High Ger. *bercfrit* – *berc*, shelter, *fride*, peace – a protecting tower.) A church steeple is called a belfry from its resemblance to these towers, and not because bells are hung in it.

> Alone, and warming his five wits,
> The white owl in the belfry sits.
>
> Tennyson, *The Owl*, stanza i

**Belial** (Heb.). The worthless or lawless one, i.e. the devil.

> What concord hath Christ with Belial?
>
> 2 Cor. 6:15

Milton, in his pandemonium, makes him a very high and distinguished prince of darkness.

> Belial came last – than whom a spirit more lewd
> Fell not from heaven, or more gross to love
> Vice for itself *Paradise Lost*, bk i, 490

***Sons of Belial.*** Lawless, worthless, rebellious people.

> Now the sons of Eli were sons of Belial.
>
> 1 Sam. 2:12

**Belinda.** The heroine of Pope's mock heroic poem, the *Rape of the Lock* (*q.v.*).

**Belisarius.** *Belisarius begging for an obolus.* Belisarius (d.565), the greatest of Justinian's generals, being accused of conspiring against the life of the emperor, was deprived of all his property. The tale is that his eyes were put out, and that when living as a beggar in Constantinople he fastened a bag to his roadside hut, with the inscription, 'Give an obolus to poor old Belisarius.' This tradition is of no historic value.

**Belit.** *See* Asshur.

**Bell.** ***As the bell clinks, so the fool thinks,*** or, ***As the fool thinks, so the bell clinks.*** The tale says when Whittington ran away from his master, and had got as far as Highgate Hill, he was hungry, tired, and wished to return. Bow Bells began to ring, and Whittington fancied they said, 'Turn again, Whittington, Lord Mayor of London.' The bells clinked in response to the boy's thoughts. Dickens has the same idea in his *Christmas Chimes*.

***At three bells, at five bells,*** etc. A term on board ship pretty nearly tantamount to our expression *o'clock*. Five out of the seven watches last four hours, and each half-hour is marked by a bell, which gives a number of strokes corresponding to the number of half-hours passed. Thus, 'three bells' denotes the third half-hour of the watch, 'five bells' the fifth half-hour of the watch, and so on. The two short watches, which last only two hours each, are from four to six and six to eight in the afternoon. 'Eight bells' is rung at noon, four, and eight o'clock, and is the signal for the beginning of a new watch. *See* Watch.

> Do you there hear? Clean shirt and a shave for master at five bells. *Basil Hall*

***Bells, Eight.*** *See* At Three Bells, *above*.

***Bell, Book, and Candle.*** In the greater excommunication, introduced into the Catholic

Church in the 8th century, after reading the sentence a *bell* is rung, a *book* closed, and a *candle* extinguished. From that moment the excommunicated person is excluded from the sacraments and even from divine worship. The form of excommunication closed with the words 'Doe to the book, quench the candle, ring the bell!'

> Bell, book, and candle shall not drive me back.
>
> Shakespeare, *King John*, 3, 3

Hence, *in spite of bell, book, and candle*, signifies in spite of all the opposition which even the Christian hierarchy can offer.

***Give her the bells and let her fly.*** Don't throw good money after bad; make the best of the matter, but do not attempt to bolster it up. The metaphor is from falconry; when a hawk was worthless the bird was suffered to escape, even at the expense of the bells attached to her.

***I'll not hang all my bells on one horse.*** I'll not leave all my property to one son. The allusion is manifest.

***Like sweet bells jangled, out of tune and harsh*** (Hamlet, 3, 1). A metaphor for a deranged mind, such as that of Ophelia, or of Don Quixote.

***Passing bell.*** The hallowed bell which used to be rung when persons were *in extremis*, to scare away evil spirits which were supposed to lurk about the dying ready to pounce on the soul while *passing* from the body. It is a very ancient custom, and the Athenians used to beat on brazen kettles at the moment of a decease to scare away the Furies. A secondary object was to announce to the neighbourhood the fact that all good Christians might offer up a prayer for the safe *passage* of the soul into Paradise. The bell rung at a funeral is sometimes improperly called the 'passing bell'.

The Koran says that bells hang on the trees of Paradise, and are set in motion by wind from the throne of God, as often as the blessed wish for music.

> Bells as musical
> As those that, on the golden-shafted trees
> Of Eden, shook by the eternal breeze.
>
> T. Moore, *Lalla Rookh*, pt 1

***Ringing the hallowed bell.*** Consecrated bells were believed to be able to disperse storms and pestilence, drive away devils (*see* Passing Bell, *above*), and extinguish fire. In France in quite recent times it was by no means unusual to ring church bells to ward off the effects of lightning, and as lately as 1852 it is said that the Bishop of Malta ordered the church bells to be rung for an hour to 'lay a gale of wind'.

> Funera plango, fulgura frango, sabbata pango,
> Excito lentos, dissipo ventos, paco cruentos.
>
> *A Helpe to Discourse* (1668)
>
> (Death's tale I tell, the winds dispel, ill-feeling quell,
> The slothful shake, the storm-clouds break, the Sabbath wake. E. C. B.)

The legend on the Münster bell, cast at Basle in 1486, known as Schiller's bell because it furnished him with the idea for his *Lied von der Glocke*, reads:

> Vivos · Voco · Mortuos · Plango · Fulgura · Frango.

***Ringing the bells backwards***, is ringing a muffled peal. *Backwards* is often used to denote 'in a reverse manner', as, 'I hear you are grown rich –' 'Yes, backwards', meaning 'quite the reverse'. A muffled peal is a peal of sorrow, not of joy, and was formerly sometimes employed as a tocsin, or notice of danger.

> Beacons were lighted upon crags and eminences; the bells were rung backwards in the churches; and the general summons to arm announced an extremity of danger.
>
> Scott, *The Betrothed*, ch. iii

***Sound as a bell.*** Quite sound. A cracked bell is useless as a bell.

> Blinde Fortune did so happily contrive,
> That we as sound as bells, did safe arive
> At Dover. *Taylor's Workes*, ii, 22 (1630)

***Tolling the bell for church.*** The 'church-going bell', as Cowper called it (*Alexander Selkirk*) was in pre-Reformation days rung, not as an invitation to church, but as an Ave Bell, to invite worshippers to a preparatory prayer to the Virgin.

***To bear*** or ***carry away the bell.*** To be first fiddle; to carry off the palm; to be the best. The leader of the flock, the 'bell-wether', bore the bell; hence the phrase; but it has been confused with an old custom of presenting to winners of horse-races, etc., a little gold or silver bell as a prize.

> Jockey and his horse were by their masters sent
> To put in for the bell ...
> They are to run and cannot miss the bell.
>
> North, *Forest of Varieties*

***Warwick shakes his bells.*** Beware of danger, for Warwick is in the field. Trojans beware, Achilles has donned his armour. A metaphor from falconry, the bells being those of a hawk.

> Neither the king, nor he that loves him best,
> Dares stir a wing, if Warwick shakes his bells.
>
> Shakespeare, *3 Henry VI*, 1, 1

***Who is to bell the cat?*** Who will risk his own life to save his neighbours? Anyone who encounters great personal hazard for the sake of others undertakes to 'bell the cat'. *See* Bell-the-Cat.

**Bell rope.** A humorous name for a curl worn by a man – a 'rope' for the 'belles' to play with. *Cp.* Bow-catcher.

**Belladonna.** The Deadly Nightshade. The name is Italian, and means 'beautiful lady'; it is not certainly known why it should have been given to the plant. One account says that it is from a practice once common among ladies of touching their eyes with it to make the pupils large and lustrous; but another has it that it is from its having been used by an Italian poisoner, named Leucota, to poison beautiful women.

**Bellarmine.** A large Flemish gotch, or stone beer-jug, originally made in Flanders in ridicule of Cardinal Bellarmine (1542–1621), the great persecutor of the Protestants there. They carried a rude likeness of the cardinal. *Cp.* Greybeard.

> … like a larger jug, that some men call
> A bellarmine …
> Whereon the lewder hand of pagan workmen,
> Over the proud ambitious head, hath carved
> An idol large, with beard episcopal,
> Making the vessel look like tyrant Eglon.
>
> Cartwright, *The Ordinary*

Another, and quite incorrect, origin for the name is given in the following extract:

> One of the Fellows of Exeter [College], when Dr Prideaux was rector, sent his servitor, after nine o'clock at night, with a large bottle to fetch some ale from the alehouse. When he was coming home with it under his gown the proctor met him, and asked him what he did out so late, and what he had under his gown? The man answered that his master had sent him to the stationers to borrow *Bellarmine*, which book he had under his arm; and so he went home. Whence a bottle with a big belly is called a Bellarmine to this day, 1667.
>
> *Oxoniana*, vol. i, p. 232

**Belle** (Fr.). A beauty. *The Belle of the room.* The most beautiful lady in the room.

***La belle France.*** A common French phrase applied to France, as 'Merrie England' is to our own country.

***La Belle Sauvage.*** *See* La.

**Belles Lettres.** Polite literature; poetry, and standard literary works which are not scientific or technical: the study or pursuit of such literature. The term – which, of course, is French – has given birth to the very ugly words *bellelettrist* and *bellettristic*.

**Bellerophon.** The Joseph of *Greek mythology*; Antaea, the wife of Proetus, being the 'Potiphar's wife' who tempted him, and afterwards falsely accused him. Her husband, Proetus, sent Bellerophon with a letter to Iobates, the King of Lycia, his wife's father, recounting the charge, and praying that the bearer might be put to death. Iobates, unwilling to slay him himself, gave him many hazardous tasks (including the killing of the Chimaera, *q.v.*), but as he was successful in all of them Iobates made him his heir. Later Bellerophon is fabled to have attempted to fly to heaven on the winged horse Pegasos, but Zeus sent a gadfly to sting the horse, and the rider was overthrown.

The phrase *Letters of Bellerophon* is sometimes applied to documents that are dangerous or prejudicial to the bearer; as also is *Letters of Uriah*, from the similar piece of treachery on the part of David (2 Sam. 11:14).

Pausanias, the Spartan, also sent messengers from time to time to King Xerxes, with similar letters; the discovery by one of the bearers proved the ruin of the traitor.

*Bellerophon* has frequently been used for the name of a ship in the British Navy. The most famous took part in the Battle of the Nile, Trafalgar, etc., and was the vessel on which Napoleon surrendered himself to the British and which brought him to England. It was corrupted by sailors, etc., to 'Billy Ruffian', 'Bully-ruffran', 'Belly-ruffron', etc.

> Why, she and the Belly-ruffron seem to have pretty well shared and shared alike.
>
> Captain Marryat, *Poor Jack*, ch. xiii

**Bellerus.** The name of a giant invented by Milton by way of accounting for 'Bellerium', the old Roman name for the Land's End district of Cornwall:

> Sleep'st by the fable of Bellerus old.
>
> Milton, *Lycidas*, 160

Milton had originally written 'Corineus' (*q.v.*), a name already well known in British legend.

**Bellicent.** Daughter of Gorloise and Igerna, half-sister of King Arthur. According to Tennyson, she was the wife of Lot, King of Orkney; but in *Le Morte d'Arthur* Lot's wife is Margause.

**Bellin.** The ram, in the tale of *Reynard the Fox*. His wife was Olewey.

**Bellisant.** The mother of Valentine and Orson in the romance of that name, sister to King Pepin of France, wife of Alexander, Emperor of Constantinople. Being accused of infidelity, the emperor banished her.

**Bellman.** A town-crier. Before the present police force was established, watchmen or bellmen used to parade the streets at night, and at Easter a copy of verses was left at the chief houses in the hope of obtaining an offering. These verses were the relics of the old incantations sung or said by the bellman to keep off elves and hobgoblins.

**Bellona.** In *Roman mythology*, the goddess of war and wife (or sometimes sister) of Mars. She was probably in origin a Sabine deity.

**Bellows.** Slang for the lungs; hence, a *bellowser* is a blow on the pit of the stomach, one which takes a man's wind, or breath, away.

***Sing old rose and burn the bellows***. *See* Sing.

**Bell-rope.** *See* Lovelock.

**Bell Savage.** *See* La Belle Sauvage.

**Bell-the-Cat.** Archibald Douglas, fifth Earl of Angus (d.1514), was so called. James III made favourites of architects and masons. One mason, named Cochrane, he created Earl of Mar. The Scotch nobles held a council in the church of Lauder for the purpose of putting down these upstarts, when Lord Gray asked, 'Who will bell the cat?' 'That will I.' said Douglas, and he fearlessly put to death, in the king's presence, the obnoxious minions. The allusion is to the fable of the cunning old mouse (given in *Piers Plowman* and elsewhere), who suggested that they should hang a bell on the cat's neck to give notice to all mice of her approach. 'Excellent.' said a wise young mouse, 'but who is to undertake the job?'

**Bell-wavering.** Vacillating, swaying from side to side like a bell. A man whose mind jangles out of tune from delirium, drunkenness, or temporary insanity, is said to have his wits gone bell-wavering.

> I doubt me his wits have gone bell-wavering by the road. Scott, *The Monastery*, ch. vii

**Bellwether of the flock.** A jocose and rather deprecatory term applied to the leader of a party. Of course the allusion is to the wether or sheep which leads the flock with a bell fastened to its neck.

**Belly.** ***The belly and its members,*** The fable of Menenius Agrippa to the Roman people when they seceded to the *Sacred Mount:* 'Once on a time the members refused to work for the lazy belly; but, as the supply of food was thus stopped, they found there was a necessary and mutual dependence between them.' The fable is given by Aesop and by Plutarch, whence Shakespeare introduces it in his *Coriolanus*, 1, 1.

***The belly has no ears.*** A hungry man will not listen to advice or arguments. The Romans had the same proverb, *Venter non habet aures*; and in French, *Ventre affame n'a point d'oreilles.*

***Belly-timber.*** Food. The term is quite an old one, and was not originally slang. It is used seriously by Massinger and other Elizabethan dramatists, and is given by Cotgrave (1611) as a translation of the French *Carrelure de ventre* (literally, a re-soling, or re-furnishing, of the stomach).

> And now, Dame Peveril, to dinner, to dinner. The old fox must have his belly-timber, though the hounds have been after him the whole day.
> Scott, *Peveril of the Peak*, ch. 48

**Belomancy** (Gr.). Divination by arrows. Labels being attached to a given number of arrows, the archers let them fly, and the advice on the label of the arrow which flies farthest is accepted and acted on. Sir Thos Browne describes a method of belomancy in *Pseudodoxia Epidemica*, v, 23, and says that it –

> hath been in request with Scythians, Alanes, Germans, with the Africans and Turks of Algier.

**Beloved Disciple.** St John. (John 13:23, etc.).

**Beloved Physician.** St Luke. (Col. 4:14.)

**Below the Belt.** *See* Belt.

**Belphegor.** The Assyrian form of 'Baal-Peor' (*see* Baal), the Moabitish god to whom the Israelites became attached in Shittim (Numb. 25:3).

The name was given in a mediaeval Latin legend to a demon who was sent into the world from the infernal regions by his fellows to test the truth of certain rumours that had reached them concerning the happiness – and otherwise – of married life on earth. After a thorough trial, the details of which are told with great intimacy, he fled in horror and dismay to the happy regions where female society and companionship was non-existent. Hence, the term is applied both to a misanthrope and to a nasty, licentious, obscene fellow.

> The story is found in Machiavelli's works and became very popular. Its first appearance in English is in Barnabe Rich's *Farewell to the Military Profession* (1581); and it either forms the main source of, or furnishes incidents to, many plays including *Grim, the Collier of Croydon* (1600), Jonson's *The Devil is an Ass* (1616), and John Wilson's *Belphegor, or the Marriage of the Devil* (1691).

**Belphoebe.** The huntress-goddess in Spenser's *Faërie Queene*, daughter of Chrysogone and sister of Amoret, typifies Queen Elizabeth as a model of chastity. She was of the Diana and Minerva type; cold as an icicle, passionless, immovable, and, like a moonbeam, light without warmth.

**Belt.** ***To hit below the belt.*** To strike unfairly. It is prohibited in prize-fighting to hit below the waist-belt.

To make a slanderous report which is not actionable, or to take away a man's character in anyway where self-defence is impossible, is 'hitting him below the belt'.

***To hold the belt.*** To be the champion. In pugilism, a belt always forms part of the prize in big events, and is typical of the championship.

**Beltane.** In Scotland, old May-day, the beginning of summer; also the festival that was held on that day, a survival of the ancient heathen festival inaugurating the summer, at which the Druids lit two 'bel-fires' between which the cattle were driven, either preparatory to sacrifice or to protect them against disease. The word is Gaelic, and means literally 'the blaze-kindling'.

**Belted Will.** Lord William Howard (1563–1640), a Border chief, son of the fourth Duke of Norfolk, and warden of the western marches. He was so called by Scott. To his contemporaries he was known as 'Bould Wullie'. His wife was called 'Bessie with the braid apron'.

His Bilboa blade, by marchmen felt,
Hung in a broad and studded belt;
Hence, in rude phrase, the borderers still
Called noble Howard *Belted Will.* Scott

**Beltenebros.** Amadis of Gaul so calls himself after he retires to the Poor Rock. His lady-love is Oriana. (*Amadis of Gaul*, ii, 6.)

**Belvedere.** A sort of pleasure-house built on an eminence in a garden, from which one can survey the surrounding prospect, or a look-out on the top of a house. The word is Italian, and means a *fine sight*.

**Belvidera.** The heroine of Otway's *Venice Preserved* (1682). Scott says, 'More tears have been shed for the sorrows of Belvidera and Monimia than for those of Juliet and Desdemona.'

And Belvidera pours her soul in love.
Thomson, *Winter*

**Bémol.** *See* Bécarre.

**Ben.** In theatrical slang, a 'benefit performance'; i.e. a performance the profits of which go to some specified actor or theatrical or other charity.

***Big Ben.*** *See* Big.

**Ben-Jochanan.** In Dryden's *Absalom and Achitophel*, is meant for a Rev. Samuel Johnson (1649–1703), who suffered much persecution for his defence of the right of private judgment.

A Jew [*Englishman*] of humble parentage was he;
By trade a Levite [*clergyman*], though of low degree. Pt ii, 354

**Ben trovato** (Ital.). Well found, well invented; a happy discovery or invention. The full phrase is *se non è vero, è ben trovato*, if it is not true it is well invented: said of a plausible story.

**Benaiah.** In Dryden's *Absalom and Achitophel* is meant for George Edward Sackville, called General Sackville, a gentleman of family, and a zealous partisan of the Duke of York. Benaiah was captain in David's army, and was made by Solomon generalissimo (1 Kings 2:35).

Nor can Benaiah's worth forgotten lie,
Of steady soul when public storms were high:
Whose conduct, while the Moors fierce onsets made,
Secured at once our honour and our trade.
Pt ii, 19

**Benbow.** A name almost typical of a brave sailor, from John Benbow (1653–1702), a noted English Admiral. It is told of him that in an engagement with the French near St Martha, on the Spanish coast, in 1701, his legs and thighs were shivered into splinters by a chain-shot, but, supported in a wooden frame, he remained on the quarter deck till morning, when Du Casse bore away. Almeyda, the Portuguese governor of India, in his engagement with the united fleet of Cambaya and Egypt, had his legs and thighs shattered in a similar manner; but, instead of retreating, had himself bound to the ship's mast, where he 'waved his sword to cheer on the combatants', till he died from loss of blood.

Whirled by the cannon's rage, in shivers torn,
His thighs far shattered o'er the waves are borne;
Bound to the mast the god-like hero stands,
Waves his proud sword and cheers his woeful bands;
Though winds and seas their wonted aid deny,
To yield he knows not but he knows to die.
Camoens, *Lusiad*, Bk x

Somewhat similar stories are told of Cynaegiros and Jaafer (*qq.v.*).

**Bench.** Originally the same word as Bank, it means, properly, a long wooden seat, hence the official seat of judges in Court, bishops in the House of Lords, aldermen in the council chamber, etc.; hence, by extension judges, bishops, etc., collectively, the court or place where they administer justice or sit officially, the dignity of holding such an official status, etc. Hence *Bench of bishops.* The whole body of prelates, who sit in the House of Lords.

***To be raised to the bench.*** To be made a judge.

***To be raised to the Episcopal bench.*** To be made a bishop.

***King's*** (or ***Queen's***) ***Bench.*** *See* King's.

***Bench and Bar.*** Judges and barristers. *See* Bar: Barrister.

**Benchers.** Senior members of the Inns of Court. They exercise the function of calling students to the bar (*q.v.*), and have powers of expulsion.

**Bend.** In heraldry, an ordinary formed by two parallel lines drawn across the shield from the dexter chief (i.e. the top left-hand corner when looking at the shield) to the sinister base point (i.e. the opposite corner). It is said to represent the sword-belt.

***Bend sinister.*** A bend running across the shield in the opposite direction, i.e. from right to left. It is an indication of bastardy (*cp.* Bar sinister); hence the phrase '*he has a bend sinister*', he was not born in lawful wedlock.

***Beyond my bend,*** i.e. my means or power. The phrase is probably a corruption of *beyond my bent* (*see* Bent), but it may be in allusion to a bow or spring, which, if strained beyond its bending power, breaks.

**Bendemeer.** A river that flows near the ruins of Chilminar or Istachar, in the province of Chusistan in Persia.

> There's a bower of roses by Bendemeer's stream,
> And the nightingale sings round it all the day long.
> T. Moore, *Lalla Rookh*, Pt 1

**Bender.** A sixpenny-piece; perhaps because it can be bent without much difficulty. Also (in schoolboy slang) a 'licking' with the cane, the culprit being in a bent position. In Scotland it is an old term for a hard drinker, and in the United States it is still given to a drinking bout.

**Bendigo.** The nickname (said to be a corruption of 'Abednego') of William Thompson (1811–89), a well known pugilist. He left his nickname to a township in Victoria, Australia, and also to a rough fur cap. The Australian town changed its name to Sandhurst some years ago, but it has since officially reverted to its original appellation.

**Bendy, Old.** One of the numerous euphemistic names of the devil, who is willing to bend to anyone's inclination.

**Benedicite.** The 2nd pers. pl. imperative of the Latin verb, *benedicere*, meaning 'bless you', or 'may you be blessed'. In the first given sense it is the opening word of many old graces ('Bless ye the Lord', etc.); hence, a grace, or a blessing.

> The wandering pilgrim, or the begging friar answered his reverent greeting with a paternal benedicite.
> Scott, *Quentin Durward*, ch. ii

The second sense accounts for its use as an interjection or expression of astonishment, as in Chaucer's

> The god of love, A benedicite,
> How myghty and how great a lord is he!
> *Knight's Tale*, 927

**Benedick.** A sworn bachelor caught in the snares of matrimony: from Benedick in Shakespeare's *Much Ado about Nothing*.

> Let our worthy Cantab be bachelor or Benedick, what concern is it of ours.
> Mrs Edwards, *A Girton Girl*, ch. xv

Benedick and Benedict are used indiscriminately, but the distinction should be observed.

**Benedict.** A bachelor, not necessarily one pledged to celibacy, but simply a man of marriageable age, not married. St Benedict was a most uncompromising stickler for celibacy.

> Is it not a pun? There is an old saying, 'Needles and pins; when a man marries his trouble begins.' If so, the unmarried man is *benedictus*.
> *Life in the West* (1843)

**Benedictine.** A liqueur which used to be made at the Benedictine monastery at Fécamp, France.

**Benedictines.** Monks who follow the rule of St Benedict, viz. implicit obedience, celibacy, abstaining from laughter, spare diet, poverty, the exercise of hospitality, observance of canonical hours, feasts, and fasts, and unremitting industry. They are known as the 'Black Monks' (the Dominicans being the *Black Friars*). The Order was founded by St Benedict at Subiaco and Monte Cassino, Italy, about 530, and its members have from the earliest times been renowned for their learning.

**Benefice.** Under the Romans certain grants of lands made to veteran soldiers were called *beneficia*, and in feudal times an estate held for life in return for military or other service *ex mero beneficio* of the donor was called 'a benefice'. When the popes assumed the power of the feudal lords with reference to ecclesiastical patronage the name was retained for a 'living'.

**Benefit.** *See* Ben.

**Benefit of Clergy.** Originally, the privilege of exemption from trial by a secular court enjoyed by the clergy if arrested for felony. In time it comprehended not only the ordained clergy, but all who, being able to write and read, were capable of entering into holy orders. It seems to have been based on the text, 'Touch not mine anointed, and do my prophets no harm' (1 Chron. 16:22), and it was finally abolished in the reign of George IV (1827). *Cp.* Neck-verse.

**Benen-geli.** *See* Cid Hamet.

**Benevolence.** A means of raising money by forced loans and without the instrumentality of Parliament, first resorted to in 1473 by Edward IV. It seems to have been used for the last time by James I in 1614, but it was not declared illegal till the passing of the Bill of Rights in 1689.

> Royal benevolences were encroaching more and more on the right of parliamentary taxation.
> Green, *History of the English People*, bk vi, ch. i

**Bengal Tigers.** The old 17th Foot, whose badge, a royal tiger, was granted them for their services in India (1802–23). Now the Leicester Regiment.

**Bengodi.** A 'land of Cockaigne' (*q.v.*) mentioned in Boccaccio's *Decameron* (viii, 3), where 'they tie the vines with sausages, where you may buy a fat goose for a penny and have a gosling into the bargain; where there is also a mountain of grated Parmesan cheese, and people do nothing but make cheesecakes and macaroons. There is also a river which runs Malmsey wine of the very best quality'; etc., etc.

**Benicia Boy.** John C. Heenan, the American pugilist, who challenged and fought Tom Sayers for 'the belt' in 1860; so called from Benicia in California, his birthplace.

**Benjamin.** The pet, the youngest; in allusion to Benjamin, the youngest son of Jacob (Gen. 35:18). Also (in early and mid 19th cent.), an overcoat; so called from a tailor of the name, and rendered popular by its association with Joseph's 'coat of many colours'.

***Benjamin's mess.*** The largest share. The allusion is to the banquet given by Joseph, viceroy of Egypt, to his brethren. 'Benjamin's mess was five times so much as any of theirs' (Gen. 43:34).

***Benjamin tree.*** A tree of the Styrax family that yields benzoin, of which the name is a corruption, and so used by Ben Jonson in *Cynthia's Revels* (V, ii), where the Perfumer says:

> Taste, smell; I assure you, sir, pure benjamin, the only spirited scent that ever awaked a Neapolitan nostril.

**Bennet Fink, St.** *See* Finch Lane.

**Benshee.** *See* Banshee.

> How oft has the Benshee cried! [How busy death has been of late with our notables.]
> T. Moore, *Irish Melodies*, No. ii

**Bent.** Inclination; talent for something. *Out of my bent*, not in my way, not in the range of my talent. *Bent on it*, inclined to it. As a thing bent is inclined, so a bent is an inclination or bias. Genius or talent is a bent or bias.

> Whatever is done best, is done from the natural bent and disposition of the mind.
> Hazlitt, *Table Talk*

***They fool me to the top of my bent,*** i.e. to the limit – as far as a bow can be bent without snapping. (*Hamlet*, 3, 2) *See* Bend.

**Benvolio.** Nephew to Montague in Shakespeare's *Romeo and Juliet*; a testy, litigious gentleman, who would 'quarrel with a man that had a hair more or a hair less in his beard than he had'.

**Beowulf.** The hero of the ancient Anglo-Saxon epic poem of the same name, of unknown date and authorship, but certainly written before the coming of the Saxons to England, and modified subsequent to the introduction of Christianity.

The scene is laid in Denmark or Sweden: the hall (Heorot) of King Hrothgar is raided nightly by Grendel (*q.v.*), whom Beowulf mortally wounds after a fierce fight. Grendel's dam comes next night to avenge his death. Beowulf pursues her to her lair under the water and ultimately slays her with a magic sword. Beowulf in time becomes king, and fifty years later meets his death in combat with a dragon, the guardian of an immense hoard, his faithful Wiglaf being his only follower at the end.

The epic as we know it dates from the 8th century, but it probably represents a gradual growth which existed in many successive versions. In any case, it is not only the oldest epic in English, but the oldest in the whole Teutonic group of languages.

**Beppo.** The contraction of Giuseppe, and therefore equal to our Joe. In Byron's poem of this name Beppo is husband of Laura, a Venetian lady. He was taken captive in Troy, turned Turk, joined a band of pirates, grew rich, and, after several years' absence, returned to his native land, where he discovered his wife at a carnival ball with her *cavaliero servente*. He made himself known to her, and they lived together again as man and wife.

**Berchta.** A fairy (*the white lady*) of Southern Germany, corresponding to Hulda (*the gracious lady*) of Northern Germany. After the introduction of Christianity, when pagan deities were represented as demons, Berchta lost her former character, and became a bogy to frighten children.

**Bereans.** Followers of John Barclay, of Kincardineshire, who seceded from the Scotch Kirk in 1773. They believed that all we know of God is from revelation; that all the Psalms refer to Christ; that assurance is the proof of faith; and that unbelief is the unpardonable sin. They took their name from the Bereans, mentioned in Acts 27:11, who 'received the Word with all readiness of mind, and searched the Scriptures daily'.

**Berecynthian Hero.** Midas, the mythological king of Phrygia; so called from Mount Berecyntus, in Phrygia.

**Berengarians.** Followers of Berenger (998–1088), archdeacon of Angers, the learned opponent of Lanfranc. He held heretical opinions on the doctrines of transubstantiation and the real presence, and, in consequence, was condemned by many Synods and many times recanted.

**Berenice.** The sister-wife of Ptolemy Euergetes, king of Egypt (247–22 BC). She vowed to sacrifice her hair to the gods, if her husband returned home the vanquisher of Asia. She suspended her hair in the temple of Arsinoë at Zephyrium, but it was stolen the first night, and Conon of Samos told the king that the winds had wafted it to heaven, where it still forms the seven stars near the tail of Leo, called *Coma Berenices.*

**Bergelmir.** One of the frost-giants of *Scandinavian mythology*. When Ymir was slain by Odin and others, and the whole race of frost-giants was drowned in his blood, Bergelmir alone escaped, and he thereupon founded a second dynasty of giants.

**Bergomask.** A rustic dance (*see Midsummer Night's Dream*, 5, 1); so called from Bergamo, a Venetian province, the inhabitants of which were noted for their clownishness. Also, a clown or merry-andrew.

**Berkshire.** From the A.S. *Berrocshyre*, either from its abundance of *berroc* (box trees), or the *bare-oak-shire*, from a polled oak common in Windsor Forest, where the Britons used to hold meetings.

**Berlin.** An old-fashioned four-wheeled carriage with a hooded seat behind. It was introduced into England by a German officer about 1670.

**Berlin Decree.** A decree issued at Berlin by Napoleon I in November, 1806, forbidding any of the nations of Europe to trade with Great Britain, proclaiming her to be in a state of blockade, declaring all English property forfeit, and all Englishmen on French soil prisoners of war. This may be taken as the first step to the great man's fall.

**Bermoothes.** The name of the island in the *Tempest*, feigned by Shakespeare to be enchanted and inhabited by witches and devils.

> From the still-vexed Bermoothes, there she's hid.
>
> Shakespeare, *The Tempest*, 1, 2

Shakespeare almost certainly had the recently discovered Bermudas in his mind, but some sort of case has also been made out for the island of Lampedusa between Malta and the coast of Tunis.

**Bermudas.** The Bermudas was an old slang name for a district of London – thought to have been the narrow alleys in the neighbourhood of Covent Garden, St Martin's Lane, and the Strand – which was an Alsatia (*q.v.*), where the residents had certain privileges against arrest. Hence, *to live in the Bermudas*, to skulk in some out-of-the-way place for cheapness or safety.

**Bernard, St.** Abbot of the monastery of Clairvaux in the 12th century (b.1091, d.1153). His fame for wisdom was very great, and few church matters were undertaken without his being consulted.

***Bonus Bernardus non videt omnia.*** We are all apt to forget sometimes; events do not always turn out as they are planned beforehand.

> Poor Peter was to win honours at Shrewsbury school, and carry them thick to Cambridge; and after that a living awaited him, the gift of his godfather, Sir Peter Arley; but *Bonus Bernardus non videt omnia*, and Poor Peter's lot in life was very different to what his friends had planned.
>
> Mrs Gaskell, *Cranford*, ch. vi

***St Bernard Soup.*** *See* Stone Soup.

***Petit Bernard.*** Solomon Bernard, engraver of Lyons (16th century).

***Poor Bernard.*** Claude Bernard, of Dijon, philanthropist (1588–1641).

***Lucullus Bernard.*** Samuel Bernard, a famous French capitalist (1651–1739).

***Le gentil Bernard.*** Pierre Joseph Bernard, the French poet (1710–75).

**Bernardine.** A monk of the Order of St Bernard of Clairvaux; a Cistercian (*q.v.*).

**Bernardo,** in Dibdin's *Bibliomania* (a romance), is meant for Joseph Hazlewood, antiquary and critic (1811).

**Bernardo del Carpio.** A semi-mythical Spanish hero of the 9th century, and a favourite subject of the minstrels, and of Lope de Vega who wrote many plays around his exploits. He is credited with having defeated Roland at Roncesvalles.

**Bernesque Poetry.** Serio-comic poetry; so called from Francesco Berni (1498–1535), of Tuscany, who greatly excelled in it. Byron's *Beppo* is a good example of English bernesque; and concerning it Byron wrote to John Murray, his publisher:

> Whistlecraft is my immediate model, but Berni is the father of that kind of writing.

**Berserker.** In *Scandinavian mythology*, a wild, ferocious, warlike being who was at times possessed of supernatural strength and fury. The origin of the name is doubtful; one account says that it was that of the grandson of the eight-handed Starkader and the beautiful Alfhilde, who was called *baer-serce* (bare of mail) because he went into battle unharnessed. Hence, any man with the fighting fever on him.

Another disregards this altogether and holds that the name means simply 'men who have assumed the form of bears'. It is used in English both as an adjective denoting excessive fury and a noun denoting one possessed of such.

> Let no man awaken it, this same Berserker rage!
> Carlyle, *Chartism*

> You say that I am berserker. And ... baresark I go tomorrow to the war.
> Kingsley, *Hereward the Wake*

**Berth.** ***He has tumbled into a nice berth.*** A nice situation or fortune. The place in which a ship is anchored is called its berth, and the sailors call it a *good* or *bad* berth as they think it favourable or otherwise. The space also allotted to a seaman for his hammock is called his berth.

***To give a wide berth.*** Not to come near a person; to keep a person at a distance; literally, to give a ship plenty of room to swing at anchor.

**Bertha, Frau.** A German impersonation of the Epiphany, corresponding to the Italian Befana (*q.v.*). She is a white lady, who steals softly into nurseries and rocks infants asleep in the absence of negligent nurses, but is the terror of all naughty children. Her feet are very large, and she has an iron nose.

**Berthas.** The Stock Exchange name for London, Brighton & South Coast Railway Deferred Stock.

**Berthe au Grand Pied.** Mother of Charlemagne, and great-granddaughter of Charles Martel; so called because she had a club-foot. She died at an advanced age in 783.

**Bertram, Henry.** A character in Scott's *Guy Mannering* suggested by James Annesley, Esq., rightful heir of the earldom of Anglesey, of which he was dispossessed by his uncle Richard. He died in 1743.

**Bertram, Count of Rousillon,** beloved by Helena, the hero of Shakespeare's *All's Well that Ends Well.*

> I cannot reconcile my heart to Bertram, a man noble without generosity, and young without truth; who marries Helena as a coward, and leaves her as a profligate. Dr Johnson

**Berwicks.** The Stock Exchange name for the ordinary stock of the North-Eastern Railway. The line runs to Berwick.

**Besaile.** A word formerly used in England for a great-grandfather; it is the French *bisaieul.*

***Writ of besaile.*** An old legal term meaning:

> A writ that lies for the heire, where his great grandfather was seized the day that he died, or died seised of Land in fee-simple, and a stranger enters the day of the death of the great grandfather, or abates after his death, the heire shall have his writ against such a disseisor or abator.
> *Termes de la Ley*, 1641

**Besant.** *See* Bezant.

**Besom.** *To hang out the besom.* To have a fling when your wife is gone a visit. To be a quasi bachelor once more. *Cp.* the French colloquialism, *rôtir le balai.*

(Literally, 'to roast the besom'), which means 'to live a fast life' or 'to go on the razzle-dazzle'.

***Jumping the besom.*** Omitting the marriage service after the publication of banns, and living together as man and wife.

In Southern Scotch, *besom* is a contemptuous name applied to a prostitute or woman of low character, but it is by no means certain that the word is connected with either of the above usages.

**Bespeak night.** A theatrical term for a 'benefit'. *See* Ben.

**Bess, Good Queen.** Queen Elizabeth (1533, 1558–1603).

**Bess o' Bedlam.** A female lunatic vagrant. *See* Bedlam.

**Bess of Hardwick.** Elizabeth Talbot, Countess of Shrewsbury (1518–1608), to whose charge, in 1569, Mary Queen of Scots was committed. The countess treated the captive queen with great harshness, being jealous of the earl her husband. Bess of Hardwick married four times: Robert Barlow (when she was only fourteen); Sir William Cavendish; Sir William St Loe, Captain of Queen Elizabeth's Guard; and lastly, George, sixth Earl of Shrewsbury. She built Hardwick Hall, and founded the wealth and dignity of the Cavendish family.

**Bessee of Bednall Green.** *See* Beggar's Daughter.

**Bessemer Process.** The conversion of cast iron to steel by oxidising the carbon by passing currents of air through the molten metal, patented by Sir Henry Bessemer in 1856.

**Bessie Bell and Mary Gray.** A ballad relating how two young ladies of Perth, to avoid the plague of 1666, retired to a rural retreat called the Burnbraes, near Lynedock, the residence of Mary Gray. A young man, in love with both, carried them provisions, and they all died of the plague and were buried at Dornock Hough.

**Bessie with the braid apron.** *See* Belted Will.

**Bessus.** A cowardly, bragging captain, a sort of Bobadil (*q.v.*), in Beaumont and Fletcher's *A King and no King*.

**Best.** ***At best*** or ***At the very best.*** Looking at the matter in the most favourable light. Making every allowance.

> Man is a short-sighted creature at best.
>
> Defoe, *Colonel Jack*

***At one's best.*** At the highest or best point attainable by the person referred to.

***For the best.*** With the best of motives; with the view of obtaining the best results.

***I must make the best of my way home.*** It is getting late and I must use my utmost diligence to get home as soon as possible.

***To best somebody.*** To get the better of him; to outwit him and so have the advantage.

***To have the best of it,*** or, ***To have the best of the bargain.*** To have the advantage or best of a transaction.

***To make the best of the matter.*** To submit to ill-luck with the best grace in your power.

**Best Man.** The bridegroom's chosen friend who waits on him at the wedding, as the bride's maids wait on the bride.

**Bestiaries** or **Bestials.** Books very popular in the 11th, 12th, and 13th centuries, containing accounts of the supposed habits and peculiarities of animals, which, with the legendary lore connected with them, served as texts for devotional homilies. They were founded on the old *Physiologi*, and those in English were, for the most part, translations of Continental originals. The *Bestiaires* of Philippe de Thaon, Guillaume le Clerc, and *Le Bestiaire d'Amour*, by Richard de Fournival, were among the most popular.

**Bête Noire** (Fr. black beast). The thorn in the side, the bitter in the cup, the spoke in the wheel, the black sheep, the object of aversion. A black sheep has always been considered an eyesore in a flock, and its wool is really less valuable. In times of superstition it was looked on as bearing the devil's mark.

> The Dutch sale of tin is the *bête noire of* the Cornish miners. *The Times*

**Beth Gelert,** or 'the Grave of the Greyhound'. A ballad by the Hon. William Robert Spencer. The tale is that one day Llewellyn returned from hunting, when his favourite hound, covered with gore, ran to meet him. The chieftain ran to see if anything had happened to his infant son, found the cradle overturned, and all around was sprinkled with blood. Thinking the hound had eaten the child, he stabbed it to the heart. Afterwards he found the babe quite safe, and a huge wolf under the bed, dead; Gelert had killed the wolf and saved the child. The story is of very old origin and very widespread: with variations it is found in Sanskrit and in most ancient literatures.

> It is told of Tsar Piras of Russia, and in the *Gesta Romanorum*, of Folliculus a knight, but instead of a wolf the dog is said to have killed a serpent. The story occurs again in the *Seven Wise Masters*. In the Sanskrit version the dog is called an ichneumon and the wolf a 'black snake'. In the *Hilopadesa* (iv, 3) the dog is an otter; in the Arabic a weasel; in the Mongolian a polecat; in the Persian a cat, etc.

**Bethlehemites.** An order of reformed Dominicans, the friars of which wore a star upon the breast in memory of the Star of Bethlehem, introduced into England about 1257. Also a branch of the Augustinians, founded in Guatemala in 1653 by Peter Betancus, a native of the Canaries, for spreading the Gospel and serving the sick in Spanish America. Its members wore a shield on the right shoulder, on which was shown the manger at Bethlehem.

**Bethlemenites.** Followers of John Huss, so called because he used to preach in the church called Bethlehem of Prague.

**Bethnal Green.** *See* Beggar's Daughter.

**Better.** ***Better off.*** In more easy circumstances.

***For better for worse.*** For ever. From the English marriage service, expressive of an indissoluble union.

***My better half.*** A jocose way of saying my wife. As the twain are one, each is half. Horace calls his friend *animae dimidium meae* (*Odes* 1, iii, 8).

> 'Polly heard it,' said Toodle, jerking his hat over his shoulder in the direction of the door, with an air of perfect confidence in his better half.
>
> Dickens, *Dombey and Son*

***To be better than his word.*** To do more than he promised.

***To think better of the matter.*** To give it further consideration; to form a more correct opinion respecting it.

**Bettina.** The name taken by Elizabeth Brentano. Countess von Arnim (1785–1859), in her publication, *Letters to a Child*, in 1835. The letters purported to be her correspondence with Goethe (1807–11), but they are largely spurious.

**Betty.** A name of contempt given to a man who interferes with the duties of female servants, or occupies himself in female pursuits. *Cp.* Molly. Also burglar's slang for a skeleton key (the servant of a picklock), and sometimes for a jemmy (*q.v.*).

**Between.** ***Between hay and grass.*** Neither one thing nor yet another; a hobbledehoy, neither a man nor yet a boy.

***Between cup and lip.*** *See* Slip.

***Between Scylla and Charybdis.*** *See* Charybdis.

***Between two fires.*** Between two dangers. An army fired upon from opposite sides is in imminent danger.

***Between two stools you come to the ground.*** The allusion is to a practical joke played at sea (*see* Ambassador), in which two stools are set side by side, and it is arranged that the victim shall unexpectedly fall between them. Compare:

> Like a man to double business bound,
> I stand in pause where I shall first begin,
> And both neglect. Shakespeare, *Hamlet*, 3, 3
> He who hunts two hares leaves one and loses the other.
> Simul sorbere ac flare non possum.

***Between you and me*** (Fr. *entre nous*). In confidence be it spoken. Sometimes, *Between you and me and the gate-post* (or *bed-post*). These phrases, for the most part, indicate that some ill-natured remark or slander is about to be made of a third person, but occasionally they refer to some offer or private affair. *Between ourselves* is another form of the same phrase.

**Betwixt.** ***Betwixt and between.*** Neither one nor the other, but somewhere between the two. Thus, grey is neither white nor black, but betwixt and between the two.

***Betwixt wind and water.*** A nautical phrase denoting that part of the hull that is below the water-line except when the ship heels over under pressure of the wind. It is a most dangerous place for a man-of-war to be shot in; hence a 'knock-out' blow is often said to have caught the victim betwixt wind and water.

**Beulah.** *See* Land of Beulah.

**Bever.** A 'snack' or light repast (originally a drink) between meals; through O.Fr. *beivre* (Mod. Fr. *boire*) from Lat. *bibere*, to drink – *beverage* has the same ancestry. At Eton they used to have 'Bever days', when extra beer and bread were served during the afternoon in the College Hall to scholars, and any friends whom they might bring in. *Cp.* Nuncheon.

> He is none of these same ordinary eaters, that will devour three breakfasts, and as many dinners without any prejudice to their bevers, drinkings, or suppers.
> Beaumont and Fletcher, *Woman Hater*, i, 3

Chapman, in the *Odyssey*, however, uses the word for 'supper':

> 'So chance it, friend,' replied Telemachus,
> 'Your bever taken, go. In first of day
> Come and bring sacrifice the best you may.'
> Bk xvii, 794

**Bevil.** A model gentleman in Steele's *Conscious Lovers*.

> Whate'er can deck mankind,
> Or charm the heart, in generous Bevil showed.
> Thomson, *Winter*, 654–5

**Bevis.** Marmion's horse. *See* Horse.

***Sir Bevis of Hamtown***. A mediaeval chivalric romance, slightly connected with the Charlemagne cycle, which (in the English version) tells how the father of Bevis was slain by the mother, and how, on Bevis trying to avenge the murder, she sold him into slavery to Eastern merchants. After many adventures he converts and carries off Josian, daughter of the Soldan, returns to England, gets his revenge, and all ends happily. 'Hamtown' is generally taken as meaning 'Southampton', but it is really a corruption of *Antona*, for in the original Italian version the hero is called 'Beuves d'Antone', which, in the French, became 'Beuves d'Hantone'. Drayton tells the story in his *Polyolbion*, Song ii, lines 260–384.

**Bevoriskius,** whose *Commentary on the Generations of Adam* is referred to by Sterne in the *Sentimental Journey*, was Johan van Beverwyck (1594–1647), a Dutch medical writer and author of a large number of books.

**Bevy.** A throng or company of ladies, roebucks, quails, or larks. The word is the Italian *beva*, a drink, but it is not known how it acquired its present meaning. It may be because timid, gregarious animals, in self-defence, go down to a river to drink in companies.

> And upon her deck what a bevy of human flowers – young women, how lovely! – young men, how noble! De Quincey, *Dream-fugue*

**Bey.** A Turkish word for the governor of a town or province; also a title conferred by the Sultan, and a courtesy title given to the sons of Pashas. *See* Bashaw; Beglerbeg; Begum; and *cp.* Dey.

**Bezaliel.** In Dryden's *Absalom* and *Achitophel* is meant for Henry Somerset, 3rd Marquis of Worcester and 1st Duke of Beaufort (1629–1700). He was an adherent of Charles II.

Bezaliel with each grace and virtue fraught,
Serene his looks, serene his life and thought;
On whom so largely Nature heaped her store,
There scarce remained for arts to give him more.
Pt ii. 947

**Bezant** (from *Byzantium*, the old name of Constantinople). A gold coin of greatly varying value struck at Constantinople by the Byzantine Emperors. It was current in England till the time of Edward III. In *heraldry*, the name is given to a plain gold roundel borne as a charge, and supposed to indicate that the bearer had been a Crusader.

**Bezonian.** A new recruit; applied originally in derision to young soldiers sent from Spain to Italy, who landed both ill-accoutred and in want of everything (Ital. *besogni*, from *bisogno*, need; Fr. *besoin*). 'Under which king, bezonian? Speak or die' (*2 Hen. IV*, 5, 3). Choose your leader or take the consequences.

Great men oft die by vile bezonians.
Shakespeare, *2 Henry VI*, 4, 1

Base and pilfering besognios and marauders.
Scott, *Monastery*, xvi

**Bianchi.** The political faction in Tuscany to which Dante belonged. It and the Neri, both being branches of the Guelph family, engaged in a feud shortly before 1300 which became very violent in Florence and the neighbouring cities, and eventually the Bianchi joined the Ghibellines, the opponents of the Guelphs. In 1301 the Bianchi, including Dante, were exiled from Florence.

**Bias.** The weight in bowls which makes them deviate from the straight line; hence any favourite idea or pursuit, or whatever predisposes the mind in a particular direction.

Bowls are not now loaded, but the bias depends on the shape of the bowls. They are flattened on one side, and therefore roll obliquely.

Your stomach makes your fabric roll
Just as the bias rules the bowl. Prior, *Alma*, iii

**Biberius Caldius Mero.** The punning nickname of Tiberius Claudius Nero (the Roman Emperor, Tiberius, who reigned from AD 14 to 37). Biberius [Tiberius], drink-loving, Caldius Mero [Claudius Nero], by metathesis for *calidus mero*, hot with wine.

**Bible, The English.** The principal versions of the English Bible are:

***The Authorised Version.*** This, the version in general use in England, was made by a body of scholars working at the command of King James I (hence sometimes called 'King James's Bible') from 1604 to 1611, and was published in 1611. The modern 'Authorised Version' is, however, by no means an exact reprint of that authorised by King James; a large number of typographical errors which occurred in the first edition have been corrected, the orthography, punctuation, etc., has been modernised, and the use of italics, capital letters, etc., varied. The Bishops' Bible (*q.v.*) was used as the basis of the text, but Tyndale's, Matthew's, Coverdale's, and the Geneva translations were also followed when they agreed better with the original.

***The Bishops' Bible.*** A version made at the instigation of Archbishop Parker (hence also called 'Matthew Parker's Bible'), to which most of the Anglican bishops were contributors. It was a revision of the Great Bible (*q.v.*), first appeared in 1568, and by 1602 had reached its eighteenth edition. It is this edition that forms the basis of our Authorised Version. *See* Treacle Bible *below*.

***Coverdale's Bible.*** The first complete English Bible to be printed, published in 1535 as a translation out of Douche (*i.e.* German) and Latin by Myles Coverdale. It consists of Tyndale's translation of the Pentateuch and New Testament, with translations from the Vulgate, a Latin version (1527–8) by the Italian Catholic theologian, Sanctes Pegninus, Luther's German version (1534) and the Swiss-German version of Zwingli and Leo Juda (Zurich, 1527–9). The first edition was printed at Antwerp, but the second (Southwark, 1537) was the first Bible printed in England. Matthew's Bible (*q.v.*) is largely based on Coverdale's. *See* Bug Bible *below*.

***Cranmer's Bible.*** The name given to the Great Bible (*q.v.*) of 1540. It, and later issues, contained a prologue by Cranmer, and on the woodcut title-page (by Holbein) Henry VIII is shown seated while Cranmer and Cromwell distribute copies to the people.

***Cromwell's Bible.*** The Great Bible (*q.v.*) of 1539. The title-page (*see* Cranmer's Bible *above*) includes a portrait of Cromwell.

***The Douai Bible.*** A translation of the Vulgate, made by English Catholic scholars in France for the use of English boys designed for the Catholic priesthood. The New Testament was published at Rheims in 1582, and the Old Testament at Douai in 1609; hence sometimes called the Rheims-Douai version. *See* Rosin Bible *below*; Douai.

***The Geneva Bible.*** A revision of great importance in the history of the English Bible, undertaken by English exiles at Geneva during the Marian persecutions and first published in 1560. It was the work of William Whittingham, assisted by Anthony Gilby and Thomas Sampson. Whittingham had previously (1557) published a translation of the New Testament. The Genevan version was the first English Bible to be printed in roman type instead of black letter, the first in which the chapters are divided into verses (taken by Whittingham from Robert Stephen's Greek-Latin Testament of 1537), and the first in which italics are used for explanatory and connective words and phrases (taken from Beza's New Testament of 1556). It was immensely popular; from 1560 to 1616 no year passed without a new edition, and at least two hundred are known. In every edition the word 'breeches' occurs in Gen. 3:7; hence the Geneva Bible is popularly known as the 'Breeches Bible'. *See* Goose Bible, Placemakers' Bible, *below*.

***The Great Bible.*** Coverdale's revision of his own Bible of 1535 (*see* Coverdale's Bible *above*), collated with Tyndale's and Matthew's, printed in Paris by Regnault, and published by Grafton and Whitchurch in 1539. It is a large folio, and a splendid specimen of typography. It is sometimes called 'Cromwell's Bible', as it was undertaken at his direction, and it was made compulsory for all parish churches to purchase a copy. The Prayer Book version of the Psalms comes from the November, 1540, edition of the Great Bible. *See also* Cranmer's Bible.

***King James's Bible.*** The Authorised Version (*q.v.*).

***Matthew Parker's Bible.*** The Bishops' Bible (*q.v.*).

***Matthew's Bible.*** A pronouncedly Protestant version published in 1537 as having been 'truly and purely translated into Englysh by Thomas Matthew', which was a pseudonym, adopted for purposes of safety, of John Rogers, an assistant of Tyndale. It was probably printed at Antwerp, and the text is made up of the Pentateuch from Tyndale's version together with his hitherto unprinted translation of Joshua to 2 Chronicles inclusive and his revised edition of the New Testament, with Coverdale's version of the rest of the Old Testament and the Apocrypha. It was quickly superseded by the Great Bible (*q.v.*), but it is of importance as it formed the starting-point for the revisions which culminated in the Authorised Version. *See* Bug Bible *below*.

***The Revised Version,*** A revision of the Authorised Version commenced under a resolution passed by both Houses of Convocation in 1870 by a body of twenty-five English scholars (assisted and advised by an American Committee), the New Testament published in 1881, the complete Bible in 1885, and the Apocrypha in 1895.

***Rheims-Douai Version.*** *See* Douai Bible *above*.

***Taverner's Bible.*** An independent translation by a Greek scholar, Richard Taverner, printed in 1539 (the same year as the first Great Bible) by T. Petit for T. Berthelet. It had no influence on the Authorised Version, but is remarkable for its vigorous, idiomatic English, and for being the first English Bible to include a third Book of Maccabees in the Apocrypha.

***Tyndale's Bible.*** This consists of the New Testament (printed at Cologne, 1525), the Pentateuch (Marburg, Hesse, 1530 or 1531), Jonah, Old Testament lessons appointed to be read in place of the Epistles, and a MS translation of the Old Testament to the end of Chronicles which was afterwards used in Matthew's Bible (*q.v.*). His revisions of the New Testament were issued in 1534 and 1535. Tyndale's principal authority was Erasmus's edition of the Greek Testament, but he also used Erasmus's Latin translation of the same, the Vulgate, and Luther's German version. Tyndale's version fixed the style and tone of the English Bible, and subsequent Protestant versions of the books on which he worked should – with one or two minor exceptions – be looked upon as revisions of his, and not as independent translations.

***Wyclif's Bible.*** The name given to two translations of the Vulgate, one completed in 1380 and the other a few years later, in neither of which was Wyclif concerned as a translator. Nicholas of Hereford made the first version as far as Baruch 3:20; who was responsible for the remainder is unknown. The second version has been ascribed to John Purvey, a follower of Wyclif. The Bible of 1380 was the first complete version in English; as a whole it remained unprinted until 1850, when the monumental edition of the two versions by Forshall and Madden appeared, but in 1810 an edition of the New Testament was published by H. H. Baber, an assistant librarian at the British Museum.

**Bible, Specially named editions.** The following Bibles are named either from typographical errors or archaic words that they contain, or from some special circumstance in connection with them:

***Adulterous Bible.*** The 'Wicked Bible' (*q.v.*).

***Bamberg Bible.*** The 'Thirty-six Line Bible' (*q.v.*).

***The Bear Bible.*** The Spanish Protestant version printed at Basle in 1569; so called because the woodcut device on the title-page is a bear.

***Bedell's Bible.*** A translation of the Authorised Version into Irish carried out under the direction of Bedell (d.1642), Bishop of Kilmore and Ardagh.

***The Breeches Bible.*** The Genevan Bible (*see above*) was popularly so called because in it Gen. 3:7 was rendered, 'The eyes of them bothe were opened … and they sowed figge tree leaves together, and made themselves breeches.' This reading occurs in every edition of the Genevan Bible, but not in any other version, though it is given in the then unprinted Wyclif MS ('ya sewiden ye levis of a fige tre and madin brechis'), and also in the translation of the Pentateuch given in Caxton's edition of Voragine's *Golden Legend* (1483).

***The Brothers' Bible.*** The 'Kralitz Bible' (*q.v.*).

***The Bug Bible.*** Coverdale's Bible (*q.v.*), of 1535, is so called because Ps. 91:5, is translated, 'Thou shalt not nede to be afrayed for eny bugges by night.' The same reading occurs in Matthew's Bible (*q.v.*) and its reprints; the Authorised and Revised Versions both read 'terror'.

***Complutensian Polyglot.*** The great edition, in six folio volumes, containing the Hebrew and Greek texts, the Septuagint, the Vulgate, and the Chaldee paraphrase of the Pentateuch with a Latin translation, together with Greek and Hebrew grammars and a Hebrew Dictionary, prepared and printed at the expense of Cardinal Ximenes, and published at Alcala (the ancient Complutum) near Madrid, 1513–17.

***The Discharge Bible.*** An edition printed in 1806 containing *discharge* for *charge* in 1 Tim. 5:21: 'I discharge thee before God,… that thou observe these things, etc.'

***The Ears to Ear Bible.*** An edition of 1810, in which Matt. 13:43, reads: 'Who hath ears to *ear*, let him hear.'

***The Ferrara Bible.*** The first Spanish edition of the Old Testament, translated from the Hebrew in 1553 for the use of the Spanish Jews. A second edition was published in the same year for Christians.

***The Forty-two Line Bible.*** The 'Mazarin Bible' (*q.v.*).

***The Goose Bible.*** The editions of the Genevan Bible (*q.v.*) printed at Dort; the Dort press had a goose as its device.

***Gutenberg's Bible.*** The 'Mazarin Bible' (*q.v.*).

***The He Bible.*** In the two earliest editions of the Authorised Version (both 1611) in the first (now known as 'the He Bible') Ruth 3:15, reads: 'and *he* went into the city'; the other (known as 'the She Bible') has the variant '*she*'. 'He' is the correct translation of the Hebrew, but nearly all modern editions – with the exception of the Revised Version – perpetuate the confusion and print 'she'.

***The Idle Bible.*** An edition of 1809. in which 'the idole shepherd' (Zech. 11:17) is printed 'the idle shepherd'. In the Revised Version the translation is 'the worthless shepherd'. *See* Idol Shepherd.

***The Kralitz Bible.*** The Bible published by the United Brethren of Moravia (hence known also as the *Brothers' Bible*) at Kralitz, 1579–93.

***The Leda Bible.*** The third edition (second folio) of the Bishops' Bible (*q.v.*), published in 1572, and so called because the decoration to the initial at the *Epistle to the Hebrews* is a startling and incongruous woodcut of Jupiter visiting Leda in the guise of a swan. This, and several other decorations in the New Testament of this edition, were from an edition of Ovid's *Metamorphoses*; they created such a storm of protest that they were never afterwards used.

***The Leopolita Bible.*** A Polish translation of the Vulgate by John of Lemberg (anc. Leopolis) published in 1561 at Cracow.

***The Mazarin Bible.*** The first printed Bible (an edition of the Vulgate), and the first large book to be printed from movable metal type. It contains no date, but was printed probably in 1455, and was certainly on sale by the middle of 1456. It was printed at Mainz, probably by Fust and Schoeffer, but as it was for long credited to Gutenberg – and it is not yet agreed that he was not responsible – it is frequently called the *Gutenberg Bible*. By bibliographers it is usually known as the *Forty-two Line Bible* (it having 42 lines to the page), to differentiate it from the Bamberg Bible of 36 lines. Its popular name is due to the fact that the copy discovered in the Mazarin Library, Paris, in 1760, was the first to be known and described. Copies are extant both on paper and on a vellum; it is very scarce, and, while it is not the scarcest Bible, or book, it has fetched the largest sum ever paid for a book, viz. $50,000, at the Hoe sale in New York, 1911.

***The Murderers' Bible.*** An edition of 1801 in which the misprint *murderers* for *murmurers* makes Jude, 16, read: 'These are murderers, complainers, walking after their own lusts, etc.'

***The Old Cracow Bible.*** The 'Leopolita Bible' (*q.v.*).

***The Ostrog Bible.*** The first complete Slavonic edition; printed at Ostrog, Volhynia, Russia, in 1581.

***Pfister's Bible.*** The 'Thirty-six Line Bible' (*q.v.*).

***The Place-makers' Bible.*** The second edition of the Geneva Bible (*q.v.*), 1562; so called from a printer's error in Matt. 5:9, 'Blessed are the placemakers [peacemakers], for they shall be called the children of God.' It has also been called the 'Whig Bible'.

***The Printers' Bible.*** An edition of about 1702 which makes David pathetically complain that 'printers [princes] have persecuted me without a cause' (Ps. 119:161).

***The Proof Bible*** (*Probe-Bibel*), The revised version of the first impression of Luther's German Bible. A final revised edition appeared in 1892.

***Rebecca's Camels Bible.*** An edition printed in 1823 in which Gen. 24:61 tells us that 'Rebecca arose, and her camels', instead of 'her damsels'.

***The Rosin Bible.*** The Douai Bible (*q.v.*), 1609, is sometimes so called because it has in Jer. 8:22: 'Is there noe rosin in Galaad.' The Authorised Version translates the word by 'balm', but gives 'rosin' in the margin as an alternative. *Cp.* Treacle Bible *below*.

***Sacy's Bible.*** A French translation, so called from Louis Isaac le Maistre de Sacy, director of Port Royal, 1650–79. He was imprisoned for three years in the Bastille for his Jansenist opinions, and there translated, 1667, completing the Bible a few years later, after his release.

***Schelhorn's Bible.*** A name sometimes given to the 'Thirty-six Line Bible' (*q.v.*).

***The September Bible.*** Luther's German translation of the New Testament, published anonymously at Wittenberg in September, 1522.

***The She Bible.*** *See* He Bible.

***The Standing Fishes Bible.*** An edition of 1806 in which Ezek. 47:10, reads: 'And it shall come to pass that the fishes (instead of *fishers*) shall stand upon it, etc.'

***The Thirty-six Line Bible.*** A Latin Bible of 36 lines to the column, probably printed by A. Pfister at Bamberg in 1460. It is also known as the Bamberg, and Pfister's, Bible, and sometimes as Schelhorn's, as it was first described by the German bibliographer J. G. Schelhorn, in 1760.

***The To-remain Bible.*** In a Bible printed at Cambridge in 1805 Gal. 4:29, reads: 'Persecuted him that was born after the spirit to remain, even so it is now.' The words 'to remain' were added in error by the compositor, the editor having answered a proof-reader's query as to the comma after 'spirit' with the pencilled reply 'to remain' in the margin. The mistake was repeated in the first 8vo edition published by the Bible Society (1805), and again in their 12mo edition dated 1819.

***The Treacle Bible.*** A popular name for the Bishops' Bible (*q.v.*), 1568, because in it Jer. 8:22, reads: 'Is there no tryacle in Gilead, is there no phisition there?' *Cp.* Rosin Bible *above*. In the same Bible 'tryacle' is also given for 'balm' in Jer. 46:11, and Ezek. 27:17. Coverdale's Bible (1535) also uses the word 'triacle'. *See* Treacle.

***The Unrighteous Bible.*** An edition printed at Cambridge in 1653, containing the printer's error, 'Know ye not that the unrighteous shall inherit [for "shall not inherit"] the Kingdom of God?' (1 Cor. 6:9). The same edition gave Rom. 6:13, as: 'Neither yield ye your members as instruments of righteousness unto sin,' in place of 'unrighteousness'. This is also sometimes known as the 'Wicked Bible'.

***The Vinegar Bible.*** An edition printed at Oxford in 1717 in which the chapter heading to Luke 20 is given as 'The parable of the Vinegar' (instead of 'Vineyard').

***The Whig Bible.*** Another name for the 'Placemakers' Bible' (*q.v.*).

***The Wicked Bible.*** So called because the word *not* is omitted in the seventh commandment, making it, 'Thou shalt commit adultery'. Printed at London by Barker and Lucas, 1632. The 'Unrighteous Bible' (*q.v.*) is also sometimes called by this name.

***The Wife-hater Bible.*** An edition of 1810 in which the word 'life' in Luke 14:26 is printed 'wife'.

***Wuyck's Bible.*** The Polish Bible authorised by the Roman Catholics and printed at Cracow in 1599. The translation was made by the Jesuit, Jacob Wuyck.

***The Zurich Bible.*** A German version of 1530 composed of Luther's translation of the New Testament and portions of the Old, with the remainder and the Apocrypha by other translators.

**Bible, Statistics of the.** The following statistics are those given in the *Introduction to the Critical Study and Knowledge of the Bible*, by Thos Hartwell Horne, D.D., first published in 1818. They apply to the English Authorised Version.

| | O.T. | N.T. | Total. |
|---|---|---|---|
| Books | 39 | 27 | 66 |
| Chapters | 929 | 260 | 1,189 |
| Verses | 23,214 | 7,959 | 31,173 |
| Words | 593,493 | 181,253 | 774,746 |
| Letters | 2,728,100 | 838,380 | 3,566,480 |

*Apocrypha*. Books, 14; chapters, 183; verses, 6,031 words, 125,185; letters, 1,063,876

| | O.T. | N.T. |
|---|---|---|
| Middle book | Proverbs | 2 Thess. |
| Middle chapter | Job 29 | Rom.13 and 14 |
| Middle verse | 2 Chron. 20:17–18 | Acts 17:17 & 18 |
| Shortest verse | 1 Chron. 1:25 | John 11:35 |
| Shortest chapter | Psalm 117 | |
| Longest chapter | Psalm 119 | |

Ezra 7:21, contains all the letters of the alphabet except j.

2 Kings 19, and Isaiah 37, are exactly alike.

The last two verses of 2 Chron. and the opening verses of Ezra are alike.

Ezra 2, and Nehemiah 7, are alike.

The word *and* occurs in the O.T. 35,543 times, and in the N.T. 10,684 times.

The word *Jehovah* occurs 6,855 times, and *Lord* 1,855 times.

About 30 books are mentioned in the Bible but not included in the canon.

**Bible-backed.** Round-shouldered, like one who is always poring over a book.

**Bible-carrier.** A vagrant's term for an itinerant vendor of ballads who does not sing them; also a scornful term for an obtrusively pious person.

> Some scoffe at such as carry the scriptures with them to church, terming them in reproach *Bible-carriers*.
>
> Gouge, *Whole Armour of God*, p. 318 (1616)

**Bible Christians.** An evangelical sect founded in 1815 by William O. Bryan, a Wesleyan, of Cornwall; also called Bryanites.

**Bible-Clerk.** A sizar of certain colleges at Oxford who formerly got advantages for reading the Bible at chapel.

**Biblia Pauperum** (*the poor man's Bible*). A picture-book, widely used by the illiterate in the Middle Ages in place of the Bible. It was designed to illustrate the leading events in the salvation of man, and later MSS as a rule had a Latin inscription to each picture. These *Biblia* were probably the earliest books to be printed, first from blocks and later with movable type. *See* Mirror of Human Salvation.

**Bibliomancy.** Divination by means of the Bible. *See* Sortes Biblicae.

**Bibulus.** Colleague of Julius Caesar, a mere cipher in office, whence his name has become proverbial for one in office who is a mere *faineant*.

**Bickerstaff, Isaac.** A name assumed by Dean Swift in a satirical pamphlet against Partridge, the almanack-maker. This produced a paper war so diverting that Steele issued the *Tatler* under the editorial name of 'Isaac Bickerstaff, Esq., Astrologer' (1709). Later there was an actual Isaac *Bickerstaffe*, a playwright, born in Ireland in 1735.

**Bicorn.** A mythical beast, fabled by the early French romancers to grow very fat and well-favoured through living on good and enduring husbands. It was the antitype to Chichevache (*q.v.*).

> Chichevache (or *lean cow*) was said to live on good women; and a world of sarcasm was conveyed in always representing Chichevache as very poor – all ribs, in fact – her food being so scarce as to keep her in a wretched state of famine. Bycorne, on the contrary, was a monster who lived on good men: and he was always bursting with fatness, like a prize pig.
>
> Sidney Lanier, *Shakespere and his Forerunners*, ch. vi

Of course, *bi-corn* (two-horns) contains an allusion familiar to all readers of our early literature.

**Bid.** The modern verb, 'to bid', may be from either of the two Anglo-Saxon verbs, (1) *beodan*, meaning to stretch out, offer, present, and hence to inform, proclaim, command, or (2) *biddan*, meaning to importune, beg, pray, and hence also, command. The two words have now become very confused, but the four following examples are from (1), *beodan*:

***To bid fair.*** To seem likely; as 'He bids fair to do well'; 'It bids fair to be a fine day.'

***To bid for*** (votes). To promise to support in Parliament certain measures, in order to obtain votes.

***To bid against one.*** To offer or promise a higher price for an article at auction.

***I bid him defiance.*** I offer him defiance; I defy him.

The examples next given are derived from (2), *biddan*:

***I bid you good-night.*** I wish you good-night, or I pray that you may have a good-night. 'Bid him welcome.'

> Neither bid him God speed. 2 John 10:11

***To bid one's beads.*** To tell off one's prayers by beads. *See* Beads.

***To bid the (marriage) banns.*** To ask if anyone objects to the marriage of the persons named. '*Si quis*' (*q.v.*).

***To bid to the wedding.*** In the New Testament is to ask to the wedding feast.

**Bid-ale.** An entertainment at which drinking formed the excuse for collecting people together so that they could subscribe money for the benefit of some poor man or other charity. Bid-ales frequently developed into orgies.

> The ordinary amusements in country parishes (in 1632) were church-ales, clerk-ales, and bid-ales … consisting of drinking and sports, particularly dancing.
>
> T. V. Short, D.D., *History of the Church of England*, p. 392
>
> Denham, in 1634, issued an order in the western circuit to put an end to the disorders attending church-ales, bid-ales, clerk-ales, and the like.
>
> Howitt, *History of England* (Charles I, ch. iii, p. 159)

**Bidding-Prayer** (A.S. *biddan*; *see* Bid). This term, now commonly applied to a prayer for the souls of benefactors said before the sermon, is due to its having been forgotten after the Reformation that when the priest was telling the congregation who or what to remember in 'bidding their prayers' he was using the verb in its old sense of 'pray', i.e. 'praying their prayers'. Hence, in Elizabeth's time the 'bidding of prayers' came to signify 'the directing' or 'enjoyning' of prayers; and hence the modern meaning.

**Biddy** (i.e. Bridget). A generic name for an Irish servant-maid, as Mike is for an Irish labourer. These generic names are very common: for example, Tom Tug, a waterman; Jack Pudding, a buffoon; Cousin Jonathan, a citizen of the United States; Cousin Michel, a German; John Bull, an Englishman; Moll and Betty, English female servants of the lower order; Colin Tompon, a Swiss; Nic Frog, a Dutchman; Mossoo, a Frenchman; John Chinaman, and many others.

In Arbuthnot's *John Bull* Nic Frog is certainly a Dutchman; and Frogs are called 'Dutch Nightingales'. As the French have the reputation of feeding on frogs the word has been transferred to them, but, properly, Nic Frog is a Dutchman.

**Bideford Postman.** Edward Capern (1819–94), the poet, so called from his former occupation and abode.

**Bidpai.** *See* Pilpay.

**Biforked Letter of the Greeks.** So Longfellow called the Greek capital U (upsilon), made thus Υ, which resembles a bird flying.

> [The birds] flying, write upon the sky
> The biforked letter of the Greeks.
>
> *The Wayside Inn, Prelude*

**Bifrost** (Icel. *bifa*, tremble, *rost*, path). In *Scandinavian mythology*, the bridge between heaven and earth, Asgard and Midgard; the rainbow may be considered to be this bridge, and its various colours are the reflections of its precious stones.

The keeper of the bridge is Heimdall (*q.v.*).

**Big.** ***To look big.*** To assume a consequential air.

***To look as big as bull beef.*** To look stout and hearty, as if fed on bull beef. Bull beef was formerly recommended for making men strong and muscular.

***To talk big.*** To boast or brag.

> The archdeacon waxed wroth, talked big, and looked bigger.
>
> Trollope, *The Warden*, ch. xx

**Big Ben.** The name given to the large bell in the Clock Tower (or St Stephen's Tower) at the Houses of Parliament. It weighs 13½ tons, and is named after Sir Benjamin Hall, Chief Commissioner of Works in 1856, when it was cast.

**Big Bird.** ***To get the big bird*** (i.e. the goose). To be hissed; to receive one's congé; originally purely a theatrical expression. Today the more usual phrase is 'to get the bird'.

**Big-endians.** In Swift's *Gulliver's Travels*, a party in the empire of Lilliput, who made it a matter of conscience to break their eggs at the *big end*; they were looked on as heretics by the orthodox party, who broke theirs at the *little end*. The *Bigendians* typify the Catholics, and the *Little-endians* (*q.v.*) the Protestants.

**Big Gooseberry Season, The.** The 'silly season', the dead season, when Parliament is not assembled, and 'everybody' is out of town. It is at such times that newspapers are glad of any subject to fill their columns and amuse their readers; monster gooseberries, or the sea-serpent, will do for such a purpose.

**Bigaroon.** A white-heart cherry. (Fr. *bigarreau*, variegated; Lat. *bis varellus*, double-varied, red and white mixed.)

**Bight.** ***To hook the bight*** – i.e. to get entangled. A nautical phrase; the bight is the bend or doubled part of a rope, and when the fluke of one anchor gets into the 'bight' of another's cable it is 'hooked'.

**Bigot.** A person unreasonably and intolerantly devoted to a particular creed, system, or party. It is an old French word, but its original meaning and its derivation are quite unknown.

**Big-wig.** A person in authority, a 'nob'. Of course, the term arises from the custom of judges, bishops, and so on, wearing large wigs. Bishops no longer wear them.

**Bilbo.** A rapier or sword. So called from Bilbao, in Spain, once famous for its finely-tempered blades. Falstaff says to Ford:

> I suffered the pangs of three several deaths; first, an intolerable fright, to be detected ... next, to be compassed, like a good bilbo ... hilt to point, heel to head; and then ...' *Merry Wives*, 3, 5

**Bilboes.** A bar of iron with fetters annexed to it, by which mutinous sailors or prisoners were linked together. The word is probably derived, as the preceding, from Bilbao, in Spain, where they may have been first made. Some of the bilboes taken from the Spanish Armada are still kept in the Tower of London.

> Now a man that is marry'd, has as it were, d'ye see, his feet in the bilboes, and mayhap mayn't get 'em out again when he would.
>
> Congreve, *Love for Love*, iii, 6

**Bile.** ***It rouses my bile.*** It makes me angry or indignant. In Latin, *biliosus* (a bilious man) meant a choleric one. According to the ancient theory, bile is one of the humours of the body, black bile is indicative of melancholy, and when excited abnormally bile was supposed to produce choler or rage.

> It raised my bile
> To see him so reflect their grief aside.
>
> Hood, *Plea of Midsummer Fairies*, stanza 54

**Bilge-water.** Stale dregs; bad beer; any nauseating drink. Slang from the sea; the bilge is the lowest part of a ship, and, as the rain or sea-water which trickles down to this part is hard to get at, it is apt to become foul and very offensive.

In journalistic slang *bilge* is any worthless or sickly sentimental stuff: almost equivalent to 'tripe' (*q.v.*).

**Bilk.** Originally a word used in cribbage, meaning to spoil your adversary's score, to *balk* him; perhaps the two words are mere variants.

The usual meaning now is to cheat, to obtain goods and decamp without paying for them; especially to give a cabman less than his fare, and, when remonstrated with, give a false name and address. The usual method is for the 'bilker' to get out and say, 'Cabby, I shall be back in a minute.' and not return.

In the United States a 'bilk' is a person who habitually sponges on others and never pays or does anything in return for the hospitality received.

> The landlord explained it by saying that 'a bilk' is a man who never misses a meal and never pays a cent.
>
> A. K. McClure, *Rocky Mountains*, letter xxii, p. 211

**Bill.** The nose, also called the beak. Hence, 'Billy' is slang for a pocket-handkerchief.

> Lastly came Winter, clothed all in frize,
> Chattering his teeth for cold that did him chill;
> Whilst on his hoary beard his breath did freeze;
> And the dull drops that from his purpled bill,
> As from a limbeck did adown distill.
>
> Spenser, *Faërie Queene*, VII, vii, 31

**Bill, A.** The draft of an Act of Parliament. When a Bill is passed and has received the royal sanction it becomes an Act.

***A public bill*** is the draft of an Act affecting the general public.

***A private bill*** is the draft of an Act for the granting of something to a company, corporation, or certain individuals.

***A true bill.*** Under the old judicial system before a case went to the criminal Assizes it was examined by the Grand Jury whose duty it was to decide whether or not there was sufficient evidence to justify a trial. If they decided that there *was* they were said 'to find a true bill'; if, on the other hand, they decided there was *not* sufficient evidence they were said 'to ignore the bill'. Hence *to find a true bill* is a colloquial way of saying that after proper examination one can assert that such and such a thing is true.

***Bill of Attainder.*** A legislative Act, introduced and passed exactly like any other Bill, declaring a person or persons attainted. It was originally used only against offenders who fled from justice, but was soon perverted to the destruction of political opponents, etc. The last Bill of Attainder in England was that passed in 1697 for the attainting and execution of Sir John Fenwick for participation in the Assassination plot.

***Bill of exchange.*** An order transferring a named sum of money at a given date from the debtor ('drawee') to the creditor ('drawer'). The drawee having signed the bill becomes the 'acceptor', and the document is then negotiable in commercial circles just as is money itself.

> We discovered, many of us for the first time, that the machinery of commerce was moved by

> bills of exchange. I have seen some of them – wretched, crinkled, scrawled over, blotched, frowsy – and yet these wretched little scraps of paper moved great ships, laden with thousands of tons of precious cargo, from one end of the world to the other. What was the motive power behind them? The honour of commercial men.
>
> Lloyd George, *Speech to London Welshmen*, Sept. 19th, 1914

***Bill of fare.*** A list of the dishes provided, or which may be ordered, at a restaurant, etc.; a menu.

***Bill of health.*** A document, duly signed by the proper authorities, to certify that when the ship set sail no infectious disorder existed in the place. This is a *clean* bill of health, and the term is frequently used figuratively.

***A foul bill of health*** is a document to show that the place was suffering from some infection when the ship set sail. If a captain cannot show a *clean bill*, he is supposed to have a foul one.

***Bill of lading.*** A document signed by the master of a ship in acknowledgement of goods laden in his vessel. In this document he binds himself to deliver the articles in good condition to the persons named in the bill, certain exceptions being duly provided for. These bills are generally in triplicate – one for the sender, one for the receiver, and one for the master of the vessel.

***Bill of Pains and Penalties.*** A legislative Act imposing punishment (less than capital) upon a person charged with treason or other high crimes. It is like a Bill of Attainder (*q.v.*), differing from it in that the punishment is never capital and the children are not affected.

***Bill of quantities.*** An abstract of the probable cost of a building, etc.

***Bill of Rights.*** The declaration delivered to the Prince of Orange on his election to the British throne, and accepted by him, confirming the rights and privileges of the people. (Feb. 13th, 1689.)

***Bill of sale.*** When a person borrows money and delivers goods as security, he gives the lender a 'bill of sale', that is, permission to sell the goods if the money is not returned on a stated day.

**Bills of Mortality.** In 1592, when a great pestilence broke out, the Company of Parish Clerks, representing 109 parishes in and round London, began to publish weekly returns of all deaths occurring; these later included births or baptisms, but continued to be known as 'bills of mortality'. The term is now used for those abstracts from parish registers which show the births, deaths, and baptisms of the district.

***Within the Bills of Mortality*** = within the district covered by the 109 parishes mentioned above.

***Bills payable.*** Bills of exchange, promissory notes, or other documents promising to pay a sum of money.

***Bills receivable.*** Promissory notes, bills of exchange, or other acceptances held by a person to whom the money stated is payable.

**Billet-doux** (Fr., sweet note). A love-letter, a sweet or affectionate letter.

**Billiards.** From the Fr. *billard*, which formerly meant only the cue (a little *bille*, or stick), but afterwards came to mean the table and then the game itself. The singular form is used only in combination, as billiard-cue: billiard-marker, etc.

> Similar plural forms are bowls, cards, dominoes, marbles, skittles, etc.

**Billings, Josh.** The *nom de plume* of Henry Wheeler Shaw (1818–85), an American humorist. For many years he published an annual known as *Josh Billings' Farmers' Allminax*.

**Billingsgate.** The site of an old passage through that part of the city wall that protected London on the river side: so called from the Billings, who were the royal race of the Varini, an ancient tribe mentioned by Tacitus. Billingsgate has been the site of a fish-market for many centuries, and its porters, etc. were famous for their foul and abusive language at least three hundred years ago.

> Parnassus spoke the cant of Billingsgate.
>
> Dryden, *Art of Poetry*, c. 1

***To talk Billingsgate.*** To slang; to use foul, abusive language; to scold in a vulgar, coarse style.

***You are no better than a Billingsgate fish-fag.*** You are as rude and ill-mannered as the women of Billingsgate fish-market.

***Billingsgate pheasant.*** A red herring; a bloater.

**Billy.** A policeman's staff, which is a little bill or billet.

A pocket-handkerchief (*see* Bill). 'A blue billy' is a handkerchief with blue ground and white spots.

In Australia, a bushman's tea-pot or saucepan.

**Billy Barlow.** A street droll, a merry-andrew; so called from a half-idiot of the name, who fancied himself some great personage. He was well known in the East of London in the early half of last century, and died in Whitechapel workhouse. Some of his sayings were really witty, and some of his attitudes really droll.

**Billycock Hat.** A round, low-crowned, soft felt hat with a wide brim. One account says that the name is the same as 'bully-cocked', that is, cocked in the manner of a bully, or swell, a term which was applied to a hat in the description of an Oxford dandy in Amherst's *Terrae Filius* (1721). Another account says that it was first used by Billy Coke (Mr William Coke) at the great shooting parties at Holkham about 1850; and old-established hatters in the West End still call them 'Coke hats'.

**Bi-metallism.** The employment for coinage of two metals, silver and gold, which would be of fixed relative value. Gold is the only standard metal in England and some other countries; silver coins, like copper, are mere tokens; but a gold sovereign is always of one fixed legal value. The object is to minimise the fluctuations in the value of money.

**Binary Arithmetic.** Arithmetic in which the base of the notation is 2 instead of 10, a method suggested for certain uses by Leibniz. The unit followed by a *cipher* signifies two, by another *unit* it signifies three, by *two ciphers* it signifies four, and so on. Thus, 10 signifies 2, 100 signifies 4; while 11 signifies 3, etc.

**Binary Theory.** A theory which supposes that all acids are a compound of hydrogen with a simple or compound radicle, and all salts are similar compounds in which a metal takes the place of hydrogen.

**Bingham's Dandies.** The 17th Lancers; so called from their colonel, the Earl of Lucan, formerly Lord Bingham. The uniform is noted for its admirable fit and smartness. Now called 'The Duke of Cambridge's Own Lancers'.

**Binnacle.** The case of the mariner's compass, which used to be written *bittacle*, a corruption of the Span. *bitacula*, from Lat. *habitaculum*, an abode.

**Birchin Lane.** *I must send you to Birchin Lane*, i.e. whip you. The play is on *birch* (a rod).

***A suit in Birchin Lane.*** Birchin Lane was once famous for all sorts of apparel; references to second-hand clothes in Birchin Lane are common enough in Elizabethan books.

> Passing through Birchin Lane amidst a camp-royal of hose and doublets, I took ... occasion to slip into a captain's suit – a valiant buff doublet stuffed with points and a pair of velvet slops scored thick with lace.
>
> Middleton, *Black Book* (1604)

**Bird.** This is the Middle English and Anglo-Saxon *brid* (occasionally *byrde* in M.E.), which meant only the *young* of feathered flying animals, *foul*, *foule*, or *fowel* being the M.E. corresponding to the modern *bird*.

An endearing name for girl.

> And by my word, your bonnie bird
> In danger shall not tarry;
> So, though the waves are raging white,
> I'll row you o'er the ferry.
>
> Campbell, *Lord Ullin's Daughter*

This use of the word is probably connected with *burd* (*q.v.*), a poetic word for a lady which has long been obsolete, except in ballads. In modern slang 'bird' has not quite the same significance; here it is a rather contemptuous term for a young woman (perhaps connected with 'flapper'), and conveys the suggestion that she is, to say the least, on the 'fast' side.

***A bird in the hand is worth two in the bush; a pound in the purse is worth two in the book.*** Possession is better than expectation.

> *Italian*: E meglio aver oggi un uovo, che domani una gallina.
>
> *French*: Un, Tiens vaut, ce dit-on, mieux que deux Tu l' auras.
>
> L'un est sur, l'autre ne l'est pas.
>
> *La Fontaine*, v, iii
>
> *German*: Ein vogel in der hand ist besser als zehn über land.
>
> Besser ein spatz in der hand, als ein storch auf dem dache.
>
> *Latin*: Certa amittimus dum incerta petimus (*Plautus*).
>
> On the other side we have 'Qui ne s'aventure, n'a ni cheval ni mule'. 'Nothing venture, nothing have'. 'Give a sprat to catcha mackerel'. 'Chi non s'arrischia non guadagna'.

***A bird of ill-omen.*** A person who is regarded as unlucky; one who is in the habit of bringing ill news. The phrase dates from the time of augury (*q.v.*) in Greece and Rome, and even today many look upon owls, crows, and ravens as unlucky birds, swallows and storks as lucky ones.

Ravens, by their acute sense of smell, can locate dead and decaying bodies at a great distance; hence, perhaps, they indicate death. Owls screech when bad weather is at hand, and as foul weather often precedes sickness, so the owl is looked on as a funeral bird.

***A bird of passage.*** A person who shifts from place to place; a temporary visitant, like a cuckoo, the swallow, starling, etc.

***A little bird told me so.*** From Eccles. 10:20: 'Curse not the king, no not in thy thought, ... for a bird of the air shall carry the voice, and that which hath wings shall tell the matter'.

***Birds of a feather flock together.*** Persons associate with those of a similar taste and station as themselves. Hence, *of that feather*, of that sort.

I am not of that feather to shake off
My friend, when he must need me.
Shakespeare, *Timon of Athens*, 1, 1

Fr., *Qui se ressemble s'assemble*. Cicero says, '*Similes similibus gaudent, pares cum paribus facillime congregantur*'. '*Ne nous associons qu'avec nos égaux*' (La Fontaine).

***Fine feathers make fine birds.*** *See* Feather.

***Old birds are not to be caught with chaff.*** Experience teaches wisdom.

***One beats the bush, another takes the bird.*** The workman does the work, master makes the money. *See* Beat.

***The Arabian bird.*** The phoenix (*q.v.*).

***The bird of Juno.*** The peacock. Minerva's bird is either the cock or the owl; that of Venus is the dove.

***The bird of Washington.*** The American or bald-headed eagle.

The well-known bald-headed eagle, sometimes called the Bird of Washington. Wood

***Thou hast kept well the bird in thy bosom.*** Thou hast remained faithful to thy allegiance or faith. The expression was used of Sir Ralph Percy (slain in the battle of Hedgeley Moor in 1464) to express his having preserved unstained his fidelity to the House of Lancaster.

***'Tis the early bird that catches the worm.*** It's the energetic man who never misses an opportunity who succeeds.

Early to bed and early to rise.
Makes a man healthy, wealthy, and wise.

***To get the bird.*** To be hissed; to meet with a hostile reception. *See* Big Bird.

***To kill two birds with one stone.*** To effect two objects with one outlay of trouble.

**Birds** (protected by superstitions).

***Choughs*** were protected in Cornwall, because the soul of King Arthur was fabled to have migrated into a chough.

***The Hawk*** was held sacred by the Egyptians, because it was the form assumed by Ra or Horus; and the *Ibis* because it was said that the god Thoth escaped from the pursuit of Typhon disguised as an Ibis.

***Mother Carey's Chickens,*** or Storm Petrels, are protected by sailors, from a superstition that they are the living forms of the souls of deceased sailors.

***The Robin*** is protected, both on account of Christian tradition and nursery legend. *See* Robin Redbreast.

***The Stork*** is a sacred bird in Sweden, from the legend that it flew round the cross, crying *Styrka, Styrka*, when Jesus was crucified. *See* Stork.

***Swans*** are superstitiously protected in Ireland from the legend of the Fionnuala (daughter of Lir), who was metamorphosed into a swan and condemned to wander in lakes and rivers till Christianity was introduced. Moore wrote a poem on the subject.

**Bird's-eye View.** A mode of perspective drawing in which the artist is supposed to be *over* the objects delineated, in which case he beholds them as a *bird* in the air would see them. A general view.

**Birdcage Walk** (St James's Park, London); so called from an aviary that used to be there for the amusement of Charles II.

**Birler.** In Cumberland, a *birler* is the master of the revels at a bidden-wedding, who is to see that the guests are well furnished with drink. To *birl* is to carouse or pour out liquor (A.S. *byrelian*).

**Birmingham Poet.** John Freeth, who died at the age of seventy-eight in 1808. He was wit, poet, and publican, who not only wrote the words and tunes of songs, but sang them also, and sang them well.

**Birthday Suit.** *He was in his birthday suit*. Quite nude, as when born.

**Bis.** *Bis dat, qui cito dat* (he gives twice who gives promptly) – i.e. prompt relief will do as much good as twice the sum at a future period (*Publius Syrus Proverbs*).

**Biscuit.** The French form of the Lat. *bis coctum*, i.e. twice baked. In English it was formerly spelt as pronounced – *bisket* – the irrational adoption of the foreign spelling without the foreign pronunciation is comparatively modern.

In pottery, earthenware or porcelain, after it has been hardened in the fire, but has not yet been glazed, is so called.

**Bise.** A keen, dry wind from the north, sometimes with a bit of east in it, that is prevalent in Switzerland and the neighbouring parts.

The Bise blew cold.
Rogers, *Italy*, pt 1, div. ii, stanza 4

**Bishop** (A.S. *biscop*, from Lat. *episcopus*, and Gr. *episkopos*, an inspector or overseer). One of the higher order of the Christian priesthood who presides over a diocese (either actually or formally) and has the power of ordaining and confirming in addition to the rights and duties of the inferior clergy.

The name is given to one of the men in chess (formerly called the 'archer'), to the ladybird (*see*

Bishop Barnabee *below*), and to a drink made by pouring red wine (such as claret or burgundy), either hot or cold, on ripe bitter oranges, the liquor being sugared and spiced to taste. Similar drinks are *Cardinal*, which is made by using *white* wine instead of red, and *Pope*, which is made by using *tokay*.

> When I was at college, *Cup* was spiced audit ale; *Bishop* was 'cup' with wine (properly claret or burgundy) added; *Cardinal* was 'cup' with brandy added. All were served with a hedgehog [i.e. a whole lemon or orange bristling with cloves] floating in the midst. Each guest had his own glass or cup filled by a ladle from the common bowl (a large silver one).

*See also* Boy Bishop.

***The bishop hath put his foot in it.*** Said of milk or porridge that is burnt, or of meat over-roasted. Tyndale says, 'If the porage be burned to, or the meate ouer rosted, we saye the byshope hath put his fote in the potte'. and explains it thus, 'because the bishopes burn who they lust'. Such food is also said to be *bishopped*.

***To bishop.*** There are two verbs, 'to bishop', both from proper names. One is obsolete and meant to murder by drowning: it is from a man of this name who, in 1831, drowned a little boy in Bethnal Green and sold his body to the surgeons for dissection. The other is slang, and means to conceal a horse's age by 'faking' his teeth.

***Bishop Barnabee.*** The May-bug, ladybird, etc.

There is an old Sussex rhyme:

> Bishop, Bishop Barnabee
> Tell me when my wedding shall be;
> If it be tomorrow day,
> Ope your wings and fly away.

***Bishop in Partibus.*** *See* In Partibus.

***The Bishops' Bible.*** *See* Bible, The English.

**Bissextile.** Leap-year (*q.v.*). We add a day to February in leap-year, but the Romans counted February 24th twice. Now, February 24th was called by them '*dies bissextus*' (*sexto calendas Martias*), the sextile or sixth day before March 1st; and this day being reckoned twice (*bis*) in leap-year, was called '*annus bissextus*'.

**Bisson.** Shakespeare (*Hamlet*, 2, 2) speaks of *bisson rheum* (blinding tears), and in *Coriolanus* 2, 1, 'What harm can your bisson conspectuities glean out of this character?' This is the M.E. *bisen* and O.E. *bisene*, purblind. The ultimate origin of the word is unknown, but there was an A.S. *sten*, power of seeing, and it may be from this with the privative prefix *be-*, as in *behead*.

**Bistonians.** The Thracians; so called from Biston, son of Mars, who built Bistonia on the Lake Bistonis.

> So the Bistonian race, a maddening train,
> Exult and revel on the Thracian plain;
> With milk their bloody banquets they allay,
> Or from the lion rend his panting prey;
> On some abandoned savage fiercely fly,
> Seize, tear, devour, and think it luxury.
>
> Pitt, *Statius*, bk ii

**Bit.** A piece, a morsel. Really the same word as *bite* (A.S. *bitan*), meaning a piece bitten off, hence a piece generally; it is the substantive of *bite*, as *morsel* (Fr. *morçeau*) is of *mordre*.

Also used for a piece of money, as a 'threepenny-bit', a 'two-shilling bit', etc. *Bit* is old thieves' slang for money generally, and a coiner is known as a 'bit-maker'; but in Spanish North America and the West Indies it was the name of a small silver coin representing a portion, or 'bit', of the dollar.

***A bit of my mind,*** as 'I'll tell him a bit of my mind'. I'll reprove him.

***Bit by bit.*** A little at a time; piecemeal.

***Not a bit,*** or ***Not the least bit.*** Not at all; not the least likely.

**Bit** (*of a horse*). *To take the bit in* (or *between*) *his teeth.* To be obstinately self-willed; to make up one's mind not to yield. When a horse has a mind to run away, he catches the bit 'between his teeth', and the driver has no longer control over him.

**Bite.** A cheat; one who *bites* us. 'The biter bit' explains the origin. We say 'a man was bitten' when he 'burns his fingers' meddling with something which promised well but turned out a failure. Thus, Pope says, 'The rogue was bit', he intended to cheat, but was himself taken in. 'The biter bit' is the moral of Aesop's fable called *The Viper and the File*; and Goldsmith's mad dog, which, 'for some private ends, went mad and bit a man', but the biter was bit, for 'The man recovered of the bite, the dog it was that died'.

***Bites and Bams.*** Hoaxes and quizzes: humbug.

> [His] humble efforts at jocularity were chiefly confined to ... bites and bams.
>
> Scott, *Guy Mannering*, ch. 3

***To bite one's thumb at another.*** To insult; to provoke to a quarrel.

> *Gregory*: I will frown as I pass by: and let them take it as they list.
> *Sampson*: Nay, as they dare. I will bite my thumb at them: which is a disgrace to them, if they bear it.
>
> Shakespeare, *Romeo and Juliet*, 1, 1

***To bite the dust,*** or ***the ground.*** To be slain in battle.

***To bite the lip,*** indicative of suppressed chagrin, passion, or annoyance.

> She had to bite her lips till the blood came in order to keep down the angry words that would rise in her heart. Mrs Gaskell, *Mary Barton*, ch. xi

***To bite upon the bridle.*** To champ the bit, like an impatient or restless horse.

**Biteluus.** *See* Byteluys.

**Biting.** ***A remark more biting than Zeno's.*** Nearchos ordered Zeno the philosopher to be pounded to death in a mortar. When he had been pounded sometime, he told Nearchos he had an important secret to communicate to him; but, when the tyrant bent over the mortar to hear what Zeno had to say, the dying man bit off his ear.

> That would have been a biting jest.
> Shakespeare, *Richard III*, 2, 4

**Bitt.** *To bill the cable* is to fasten it round the 'bitt' or frame made for the purpose, and placed in the fore part of the vessel. *See* Bitter end.

**Bitter as Gall,** as soot, as wormwood. Absinthe is made of wormwood. *See* Similes.

**Bitter End, The.** *A outrance*; with relentless hostility; also applied to affliction, as, 'she bore it to the bitter end', meaning to the last stroke of adverse fortune. Perhaps 'bitter end' in this phrase is a sea term meaning the end of a rope, or that part of the cable which is 'abaft the bitts'. When there is no windlass the cables are fastened to bitts, that is, wooden posts fixed in pairs on the deck; and when a rope is paid out until all of it is let out and no more remains, the end at the bitts – hence, the *bitter* end, as opposed to the other end – is reached. In Captain Smith's *Seaman's Grammar* (1627) we read:

> A Bitter is but the turne of a Cable about the Bits, and veare it out by little and little. And the Bitters end is that part of the Cable doth stay within boord.

However, we read in Prov. 5:4, 'Her end is bitter as wormwood'. which, after all, may be the origin of the phrase.

**Bittock.** A little bit; -ock as a diminutive is preserved in bull-ock, hill-ock, butt-ock, etc. 'A mile and a bittock' is a mile and a little bit.

> A mile an' a bittock, a mile or twa,
> Abüne the burn' avont the law,
> Davie an' Dona an' Cherlie an' a'
> An' the müne was shinin' clearly!
> Stevenson, *Underwoods*, iv

**Biz.** A slang corruption of 'business'. *Good biz* means good business of any sort. It was originally an Americanism, but is now common in England. *See* Business.

**Black** for mourning was a Roman custom (Juvenal, x, 245) borrowed from the Egyptians. Mutes at funerals, who wore black cloaks, were sometimes known as the *blacks*, and sometimes as the Black Guards. *Cp.* Blackguards.

> I do pray ye
> To give me leave to live a little longer.
> You stand about me like my Blacks.
> Beaumont and Fletcher, *Monsieur Thomas*, III, 1

In several of the Oriental nations it is a badge of servitude, slavery, and low birth. Our word *blackguard* (*q.v.*) seems to point to this meaning, and the Lat. *niger*, black, also meant *bad*, *unpropitious*. *See under* Colours for its symbolism, etc.

***The Black and Tans.*** Members of the irregular force enlisted in 1920 for service in Ireland as auxiliaries to the Royal Irish Constabulary. So called because their original uniform was the army khaki with the black leather accoutrements of the R.I.C.

***Black as a crow,*** etc. Among the many common similes used in connection with 'black' are Black as a crow, a raven, a raven's wing, ink, hell, hades, death, the grave, your hat, a thundercloud, Egypt's night, a Newgate knocker (*q.v.*), ebony, a wolf's mouth, a coal-pit, coal, pitch, soot, etc. Most of these are self-explanatory.

***Beaten black and blue.*** So that the skin is black and blue with the marks of the beating.

***Black in the face.*** Extremely angry. The face discoloured with passion or distress.

> Mr Winkle pulled … till he was black in the face.
> Dickens, *Pickwick Papers*
>
> He swore himself black in the face.
> *Peter Pindar* (Wolcott)

***I must have it in black and white,*** i.e. in plain writing; the paper being white and the ink black.

> O, he has basted me rarely, sumptuously! but I have it here in black and white [*pulls out the warrant*], for his black and blue shall pay him.
> Jonson, *Every Man in His Humour*, IV, ii

***To say black's his eye,*** i.e. to vituperate, to blame. The expression, *Black's the white of his eye*, is a modern variation. To say the eye is black or evil, is to accuse a person of an evil heart or great ignorance.

> I can say black's your eye though it be grey. I have connived at this.
> Beaumont and Fletcher, *Love's Cure*, ii, 1

***To swear black is white.*** To swear to any falsehood no matter how patent it is.

**Black Act.** An Act passed in 1722 (9 Geo. I, c. 22) imposing the death penalty for certain offences against the Game Laws, and specially directed against the Waltham deer-stealers, who blackened their faces and, under the name of *Blacks*, committed depredations in Epping Forest. This Act was repealed in 1827.

**Black Art.** The art practised by conjurors, wizards, and others who professed to have dealings with the devil; so called from the idea that necromancy (*q.v.*) was connected with the Lat. *niger*, black.

> Wi' deils, they say, L – d safe's! colleaguin'
> At some black art.
> Burns, *On Grose's Peregrinations*

**Black Assize.** July 6th, 1577, when a putrid pestilence broke out at Oxford during the time of assize. The chief baron, the sheriff, and a large number of the Oxford gentry (some accounts say 300) died.

**Blackamoor. *Washing the blackamoor white*** – i.e. engaged upon a hopeless and useless task. The allusion is to one of Aesop's fables so entitled.

**Black-balled.** Not admitted to a club, or suchlike; the candidate proposed is not accepted as a member. In voting by ballot, those who accepted the person proposed used to drop a white or red ball into the box, but those who would exclude the candidate dropped into it a black one.

**Blackbeetles.** *See* Misnomers.

**Blackbirds.** Slang for negro slaves or indentured labourers. Hence *black-birding*, capturing or trafficking in slaves. *Cp.* Black cattle.

**Black Books. *To be in my black books.*** In bad odour; in disgrace; out of favour. A *black book* is a book recording the names of those who are in disgrace or have merited punishment. Amherst, in his *Terrae Filius, or the Secret History of the Universities of Oxford* (1726), speaks of the Proctor's black book, and tells us that no one can proceed to a degree whose name is found there. It also appears that each regiment keeps a black book or record of ill-behaviour.

***Black Book of the Admiralty.*** An old navy code, said to have been compiled in the reign of Edward III.

***Black Book of the Exchequer.*** An official account of the royal revenues, payments, perquisites, etc., in the reign of Henry II. Its cover was black leather. There are two of them preserved in the Public Record Office.

**Black Brunswickers.** A corps of 700 volunteer hussars under the command of Frederick William, Duke of Brunswick, who had been forbidden by Napoleon to succeed to his father's dukedom. They were called 'Black' because they wore mourning for the deceased Duke. Frederick William fell at Quatre-Bras, 1815. One of Millais's best-known pictures is called 'The Black Brunswicker'.

**Black Cap.** This is worn by a judge when he passes sentence of death on a prisoner; it is part of the judge's full dress, and is also worn on November 9th, when the new Lord Mayor takes the oath at the Law Courts. Covering the head was a sign of mourning among the Israelites, Greeks, Romans, and Anglo-Saxons. *Cp.* 2 Sam. 15:30.

**Black Cattle.** Negro slaves. *Cp.* Blackbirds, and *see* Black Ox.

> She was chartered for the West Coast of Africa to trade with the natives, but not in black cattle, for slavery was never our line of business.
> J. Grant, *Dick Rodney*, ch. xi

**Black Country, The.** The crowded manufacturing district of the Midlands of which Birmingham is the centre. It includes Wolverhampton, Walsall, Redditch, etc., and has been blackened by its many coal and iron mines, and smoking factory shafts.

**Black Death.** A plague which ravaged Europe in 1348–51; it was a putrid typhus, in which the body rapidly turned black. It reached England in 1349, and is said to have carried off twenty-five millions in Europe alone, while in Asia and Africa the mortality was even greater.

**Black Diamonds.** Coals. Coals and diamonds are both forms of carbon.

**Black Dog.** *See* Dog.

A common name in the early 18th century for counterfeit silver coin. It was made of pewter double washed. 'Black', as applied to bad money, was even then an old term.

***To blush like a black dog.*** *See* Dog.

**Black Doll.** The sign of a marine store shop. The doll was a dummy dressed to indicate that cast-off garments were bought. *See* Dolly shop.

**Black Douglas.** *See* Douglas.

**Blackfeet.** The popular name of two North American Indian tribes, one an Algonkian nation calling themselves the *Siksika*, and coming originally from the Upper Missouri district, the other, the *Sihasapa*.

**Blackfellow.** The name given to the aborigines of Australia. Their complexion is not really black, but a dark coffee colour.

**Black Flag.** The pirate's flag; the 'Jolly Roger'.

Pirates of the Chinese Sea who opposed the French in Tonquin were known as 'the Black Flags'. as also were the troops of the Caliph of Bagdad because his banner – that of the Abbasides – was *black*, while that of the Fatimites was *green* and the Ommiades *white*. It is said that the black curtain which hung before the door of Ayeshah, Mahomet's favourite wife, was taken for a national flag, and is still regarded by Mussulmans as the most precious of relics. It is never unfolded except as a declaration of war.

A black flag is run up over a prison immediately after an execution has taken place within its walls.

**Blackfoot.** A Scottish term for a matchmaker, or an intermediary in love affairs; if he chanced to play the traitor he was called a *white-foot*.

In the first half of the 19th century the name was given to one of the Irish agrarian secret societies:

> And the Blackfoot who courted each foeman's approach. Faith! 'tis hot-foot he'd fly from the stout Father Roach. Lover

**Black Friars.** The Dominican monks; so called from their black cloaks. The district of this name in the City of London is the site of a large monastery of Dominicans who used to possess rights of sanctuary, etc.

**Black Friday.** December 6th, 1745, the day on which the news arrived in London that the Pretender had reached Derby; also May 10th, 1886, when widespread panic was caused by Overend, Gurney and Co., the bankers, suspending payment.

**Black Game.** Heath-fowl; in contradistinction to red game, as grouse. The male bird is called a blackcock.

**Black Genevan.** A black preaching gown, formerly used in many Anglican churches, and still used by Nonconformists. So called from Geneva, where Calvin preached in such a robe.

**Blackguards.** The origin of this term, which for many years has been applied to low and worthless characters generally, and especially to roughs of the criminal classes, is not certainly known. It may be from the link-boys and torch-bearers at funerals, who were called by this name, or from the scullions and kitchen-knaves of the royal household who, during progresses, etc., had charge of the pots and pans and accompanied the wagons containing these, or from an actual body, or guard, of soldiers wearing a black uniform. The following extract from a proclamation of May 7th, 1683, in the Lord Steward's office would seem to bear out the second suggestion:

> Whereas ... a sort of vicious, idle, and masterless boyes and rogues, commonly called the Black guard, with divers other lewd and loose fellows ... do usually haunt and follow the court ... Wee do hereby strictly charge ... all those so called,... with all other loose, idle ... men ... who have intruded themselves into his Majesty's court and stables ... to depart upon pain of imprisonment.

**Black Hole of Calcutta.** A dark cell in a prison into which Suraja Dawlah thrust 146 British prisoners on June 20th, 1756. Next morning only twenty-three were found alive.

The punishment cell or lock-up in barracks is frequently called the 'black hole'.

**Black Horse.** The 7th Dragoon Guards, or 'the Princess Royal's Dragoon Guards'. Their 'facings' are black. Also called 'Strawboots', 'The Blacks'.

**Black Jack.** A large leather *gotch*, or can, for beer and ale, so called from the outside being tarred.

> He hath not pledged one cup, but looked most wickedly
> Upon good Malaga; flies to the black-jack still,
> And sticks to small drink like a water-rat.
>
> Middleton, *The Witch*, I, i

> Fill, fill the goblet full with sack!
> I mean our tall black-jerkin Jack,
> Whose hide is proof 'gainst rabbe Rout
> And will keep all ill weather out.
>
> Robt Heath, *Song in a Siege* (1650)

In Cornwall the miners call blende or sulphide of zinc 'Black Jack', the occurrence of which is considered by them a favourable indication. Hence the saying, *Black Jack rides a good horse*, the blende rides upon a lode of good ore.

**Black Joke.** An old tune, now called *The Sprig of Shillelagh*. Tom Moore adapted words to the tune, beginning, 'Sublime was the warning which Liberty spoke'.

**Blacklead.** *See* Misnomers.

**Black-leg.** An old name for a swindler, especially in cards and races; now used almost solely for a non-union workman, one who works for less than trade-union wages, especially during a strike, with the object of breaking it.

**Black Letter.** The Gothic or German type which, in the early days of printing, was the type in commonest use. The term came into use about 1600, because of its heavy, black appearance in comparison with roman type.

***Black letter day.*** An unlucky day; one to be recalled with regret. The Romans marked their unlucky days with a piece of black charcoal, and their lucky ones with white chalk, but the allusion here is to the old liturgical calendars in which the saints' days and festivals are distinguished by being printed in red.

**Black List.** A list of persons in disgrace, or who have incurred censure or punishment; a list of bankrupts for the private guidance of the mercantile community. *See* Black Books.

**Black Looks.** Looks of displeasure. *To look black*. To look displeased. The figure is from black clouds indicative of foul weather.

**Blackmail.** 'Mail' here is the Old English and Scottish word meaning rent, tax, or tribute. In Scotland *mails* and *duties* are rents of an estate in money or otherwise. Blackmail was originally a tribute paid by the Border farmers to freebooters in return for protection or for immunity from molestation. Hence the modern signification – any payment extorted by intimidation or pressure.

**Black Maria.** The van which conveys prisoners from the police courts to jail. There is an unsupported tradition that the term originated in America. Maria Lee, a negress of great size and strength, kept a sailors' boarding house in Boston, and when constables required help it was a common thing to send for 'Black Maria', who soon collared the refractory and led them to the lock-up.

During the Great War *Black Maria* was one of the names given to large enemy shells that emitted dense smoke on bursting.

**Black Monday.** Easter Monday, April 14th, 1360, was so called. Edward III was with his army lying before Paris, and the day was so dark, with mist and hail, so bitterly cold and so windy, that many of his horses and men died. Monday after Easter holidays is called 'Black Monday', in allusion to this fatal day. Launcelot says:

> It was not for nothing that my nose fell a-bleeding on Black Monday last, at six o'clock i' the morning. Shakespeare, *Merchant of Venice*, 2, 5

February 27th, 1865, was so called in Melbourne from a terrible sirocco from the N.N.W., which produced dreadful havoc between Sandhurst and Castlemain; and schoolboys give the name to the first Monday after the holidays are over, when lessons begin again.

**Black Money.** *See* Black dog *above*.

**Black Monks.** The Benedictines (*q.v.*).

**Black Ox.** *The black ox has trod on his foot* – i.e. misfortune has come to him. Black oxen were sacrificed to Pluto and other infernal deities.

**Black Pope.** *See* Pope.

**Black Prince.** Edward, Prince of Wales (1330–76), eldest son of Edward III. Froissart says he was 'styled black by terror of his arms' (*c.*169). Strutt confirms this saying: 'for his martial deeds surnamed Black the Prince' (*Antiquities*). Meyrick says there is not the slightest proof that he ever wore black armour, and, indeed, there is indirect proof against the supposition. Thus, there was a picture on the wall of St Stephen's Chapel, Westminster, in which the prince was clad in *gilt* armour; Stothard says 'the effigy is of copper gilt'; and in the British Museum is an illumination of Edward III granting to his son the duchy of Aquitaine, in which both figures are represented in silver armour with gilt joints. The first mention of the term 'Black Prince' occurs in a parliamentary paper of the second year of Richard II; so that Shakespeare has good reason for the use of the word in his tragedy of that king:

> Brave Gaunt, thy father and myself
> Rescued the Black Prince, that young Mars of men,
> From forth the ranks of many thousand French.
> *Richard II*, 2, 3
>
> That black name, Edward Black Prince of Wales.
> *Henry V*, 2, 4

**Black Rod.** The short title of a Court official, who is styled fully 'Gentleman Usher of the Black Rod', so called from his staff of office – a black wand surmounted by a golden lion. He is the Chief Gentleman Usher of the Lord Chamberlain's Department, and also Usher to the House of Lords and the Chapter of the Garter.

**Black Rood of Scotland.** The 'piece of the true cross' or *rood*, set in an *ebony* crucifix, which St Margaret, the wife of King Malcolm Canmore, left to the Scottish nation at her death in 1093. It fell into the hands of the English at the battle of Neville's Cross (1346), and was deposited in St Cuthbert's shrine at Durham Cathedral, but was lost at the Reformation.

**Black Russia.** A name formerly given to Central and Southern Russia, from its black soil.

**Blacks, The.** The 7th Dragoon Guards. *See* Black Horse.

**Black Saturday.** August 4th, 1621; so called in Scotland, because a violent storm occurred at the very moment the Parliament was sitting to enforce episcopacy on the people.

**Black Sea, The.** Formerly called the Euxine (*q.v.*), this sea probably was given its present name by the Turks who, accustomed to the Aegean with its many islands and harbours, were terrified by the dangers of this larger stretch of water which was destitute of shelter and was liable to sudden and violent storms and thick fogs.

**Black Sheep.** A disgrace to the family or community; a *mauvais sujet*. Black sheep are looked on with dislike by some shepherds, and are not so valuable as white ones. *Cp.* Bête noire.

**Blacksmith.** A smith who works in black metal (such as iron), as distinguished from a white-smith, who works in tin or other white metal. *See* Harmonious, Learned, *and* Village Blacksmith.

**Black Strap.** Bad port wine. A sailor's name for any bad liquor. In North America, 'Black-strap' is a mixture of rum and molasses, sometimes vinegar is added.

> The seething blackstrap was pronounced ready for use. Pinkerton, *Molly Maguires* (1882)

**Black Swan.** *See* Rara Avis.

**Blackthorn Winter.** The cold weather which frequently occurs when the blackthorn is in blossom. *See* Ice-saints.

**Black Thursday.** February 6th, 1851; so called in Victoria, Australia, from a terrible bush-fire which then occurred.

**Black Tom.** The Earl of Ormonde, Lord Deputy of Ireland in the reign of Elizabeth; so called from his ungracious ways and 'black looks'.

> He being very stately in apparel, and erect in port, despite his great age, yet with a dark, dour, and menacing look upon his face, so that all who met his gaze seemed to quake before the same.
> Hon. Emily Lawless, *With Essex in Ireland*, p. 105

**Black Watch.** Originally companies employed about 1725 by the English government to watch the Islands of Scotland. They dressed in a 'black' or dark tartan. They were enrolled in the regular army as the 42nd regiment under the Earl of Crawford, in 1737. Their tartan is still called 'The Black Watch Tartan'. The regiment is now officially 'The Royal Highlanders', but is still called 'The Black Watch'.

**Bladamour.** The friend of Paridel (*q.v.*) in Spenser's *Faerie Queene*. He typifies both inconstancy and the Earl of Northumberland, one of the leaders in the northern insurrection of 1569.

**Bladder of Lard.** A humorous, but vulgar, slang term signifying a bald head or a bald-headed person.

**Blade.** *A knowing blade*, a sharp fellow; *a regular blade*, a buck or fop. As applied to a man the word originally carried the sense of a somewhat bullying bravo, a fierce and swaggering man, and he was probably named from the sword that he carried – just as a regiment is said to consist of so many 'rifles' or 'bayonets', meaning 'men'.

**Bladud.** A mythical king of England, father of King Lear. He built the city of Bath, and dedicated the medicinal springs to Minerva. Bladud studied magic, and, attempting to fly, fell into the temple of Apollo and was dashed to pieces. (*Geoffrey of Monmouth.*)

**Blanchefleur.** The heroine of the Old French metrical romance, *Flore et Blanchefleur*, which was used by Boccaccio as the basis of his prose romance, *Il Filocopo*. The old story tells of a young Christian prince who falls in love with the Saracen slave-girl with whom he has been brought up. They are parted, but after many adventures he rescues her unharmed from the harem of the Emir of Babylon. It is a widespread story, and is substantially the same as that of Dorigen and Aurelius by Chaucer, and that of Dianora and Ansaldo in the *Decameron*. *See* Dorigen.

**Blandiman.** The faithful manservant of fair Bellisant (*q.v.*), who attended her when she was divorced. (*Valentine and Orson.*)

**Blank.** *To draw blank*. *See* Draw.

**Blank Cartridge.** Cartridge with powder only, that is, without shot, bullet, or ball. Used in drill and in saluting. Figuratively, empty threats.

**Blank Cheque.** A cheque duly signed, but without specifying any sum of money; the amount to be filled in by the payee.

***To give a blank cheque*** is, figuratively, to give *carte blanche* (*q.v.*).

**Blank Verse.** Rhymeless verse in continuous decasyllables with iambic or trochaic rhythm, first used in English by the Earl of Surrey in his version of the *Aeneid*, about 1540. There is other unrhymed verse, but it is not usual or advisable to extend to such poems as Collins's *Ode to Evening*, Whitman's *Leaves of Grass*, or the *vers libre* of today, the name blank verse.

**Blanket.** ***The wrong side of the blanket.*** An illegitimate child is said to come of the wrong side of the blanket.

> He grew up to be a fine waule fallow, like mony ane that comes o' the wrang side o' the blanket.
> Scott, *The Antiquary*, ch. xxiv

***A wet blanket.*** A discouragement; a marplot or spoil-sport. A person is a wet blanket who discourages a proposed scheme. 'Treated with a wet blanket', discouraged. 'A wet blanket influence', etc. A wet blanket is used to smother fire, or to prevent one escaping from a fire from being burnt.

**Blanketeers.** The name given to a body of some 5,000 working men out of employment who assembled on St Peter's Field, Manchester, March 10th, 1817, and provided themselves with blankets intending to march to London, to lay before the Prince Regent a petition of grievances. Only six got as far as Ashbourne Bridge, when the expedition collapsed.

In more recent times journalists have applied the name to similar bodies of unemployed, both in Great Britain and in America.

**Blarney.** Soft, wheedling speeches to gain some end; flattery, or lying, with unblushing effrontery. Blarney is a village near Cork. Legend has it that Cormack Macarthy held its castle in 1602, and concluded an armistice with Carew, the Lord President, on condition of surrendering the fort to the English garrison. Day after day his lordship looked for the fulfilment of the terms, but received nothing but soft speeches, till he became the laughing-stock of Elizabeth's ministers, and the dupe of the Lord of Blarney.

***To kiss the Blarney Stone.*** In the wall of the castle at Blarney, about twenty feet from the top and difficult of access, is a triangular stone containing this inscription: 'Cormac Mac Carthy *fortis me fieri fecit*, ad 1446'. Tradition says that to whomsoever can kiss this is given the power of being able to obtain all his desires by cajolery. As it is almost impossible to reach, a substitute has been provided by the custodians of the castle, and it is said that this is in every way as efficacious as the original.

Among the criminal classes of America 'to blarney' means to pick locks.

**Blasé.** Surfeited with pleasure. A man *blasé* is one who has had his fill of all the pleasures of life, and has no longer any appetite for any of them. A worn out *debauchée* (Fr. *blaser*, to exhaust with enjoyment).

**Blasphemous Balfour.** Sir James Balfour, the Scottish judge, was so called because of his apostasy. He died 1583. He is said to have served, deserted, and profited by all parties.

**Blast**. To strike by lightning; to make to wither. The 'blasted oak'. This is the sense in which the word is used as an expletive.

> If it [the ghost] assume my noble father's person,
> I'll cross it, though it blast me.
>
> Shakespeare, *Hamlet*, 1, 1

*In full blast.* In the extreme; 'all out'. 'When she came to the meeting in her yellow hat and feathers, wasn't she *in full blast*?' A metaphor from the blast furnace in full operation.

**Blatant Beast.** In Spenser's *Faerie Queene* 'a dreadful fiend of gods and men, ydrad'; the type of calumny or slander. He was begotten of Cerberus and Chimaera, and had a hundred tongues and a sting; with his tongues he speaks things 'most shameful, most unrighteous, most untrue'; and with his sting 'steeps them in poison'. Sir Calidore muzzled the monster, and drew him with a chain to Faërie Land. The beast broke his chain and regained his liberty. The word 'blatant' seems to have been coined by Spenser, and he never uses it except as an epithet for this monster, who is not mentioned till the twelfth canto of the fifth book. It is probably derived from the provincial word *blate*, meaning to bellow or roar.

**Blayney's Bloodhounds.** The old 89th Foot; so called because of their unerring certainty, and untiring perseverance in hunting down the Irish rebels in 1798, when the corps was commanded by Lord Blaney.

This regiment was later called 'the Second Battalion of the Princess Victoria's Irish Fusiliers'. The *first* battalion is the old 87th Foot.

**Blaze.** A white mark in the forehead of a horse, and hence a white mark on a tree made by chipping off a piece of bark and used to serve as an indication of a path, etc. The word is not connected with the *blaze* of a fire, but is from Icel. *blesi*, a white star on the forehead of a horse, and is connected with Ger. *blasz*, pale.

***To blaze a path.*** To notch trees as a clue. Trees so notched are called in America 'blazed trees', and the white wood shown by the notch is called 'a blaze'.

***To blaze abroad.*** To noise abroad. 'Blaze' here is the Icel. *blasa*, to blow, from O.Teut. *blaesan*, to blow, and is probably ultimately the same as Lat. *flare*. Dutch *blazen* and Ger. *blasen* are cognate words. *See* Blazon.

> He began to publish it much and to blaze abroad the matter.
>
> Mark 1:45

**Blazer.** A brightly coloured jacket, used in boating, cricket, and other summer sports. Originally applied to those of the Johnian crew (Camb.), whose boat jackets are the brightest possible scarlet.

> A blazer is the red flannel boating jacket worn by the Lady Margaret, St John's College, Cambridge, Boat Club.
>
> *Daily News*, August 22nd, 1889

**Blazon.** To blazon is to announce by a blast or blow (*see* Blaze abroad *above*) of a trumpet, hence the Ghost in *Hamlet* says, 'But this eternal blazon must not be to ears of flesh and blood', i.e. this talk about eternal things, or things of the other world, must not be made to persons still in the flesh. Knights were announced by the blast of a trumpet on their entrance into the lists; the flourish was answered by the heralds, who described aloud the arms and devices borne by the knight; hence, to blazon came to signify to 'describe the charges borne'; and blazonry is 'the science of describing or deciphering arms'. *See* Heraldry.

**Blé de Mars.** *See* Bloody Mars.

**Bleed.** ***To make a man bleed*** is to make him pay dearly for something; to victimise him. Money is the life-blood of commerce.

***It makes my heart bleed.*** It makes me very sorrowful.

> She found them indeed,
> But it made her heart bleed. *Little Bo-Peep*

**Bleeding Heart, Order of the.** One of the many semi-religious orders instituted in the Middle Ages in honour of the Virgin Mary, whose 'heart was pierced with many sorrows'.

> When he was at Holyrood who would have said that the young, sprightly George Douglas would have been content to play the locksman here in Lochleven, with no gayer amusement than that of turning the key on two or three helpless women? A strange office for a Knight of the Bleeding Heart. Scott, *The Abbot*, xxiii

Scott called Ellen Douglas the 'Lady of the Bleeding Heart', from the cognizance of the family (*Lady of the Lake*, ii, 10).

**Bleeding of a Dead Body.** It was at one time believed that, at the approach of a murderer, the blood of the murdered body gushed out. If in a dead body the slightest change was observable in the eyes, mouth, feet, or hands, the murderer was supposed to be present. The notion still survives in some places.

**Bleeding the Monkey.** The same as *Sucking the monkey*. *See* Monkey.

**Blefuscu.** An island in Swift's *Gulliver's Travels*, severed from Lilliput by a channel 800 yards wide, inhabited by pigmies. In describing it Swift satirised France.

**Blemmyes.** An ancient nomadic Ethiopian tribe mentioned by Roman writers as inhabiting Nubia and Upper Egypt. They were fabled to have no head, their eyes and mouth being placed in the breast. *Cp.* Acephalites; Caora.

**Blenheim Palace.** The mansion near Woodstock, Oxfordshire, given by the nation to the Duke of Marlborough, for his victory over the French at Blenheim, Bavaria, in 1704.

> When Europe freed confessed the saving power
> Of Marlborough's hand, Britain, who sent him forth,
> Chief of confederate hosts, to fight the cause
> Of liberty and justice, grateful raised
> This palace, sacred to the leader's fame.
> Lord Geo. Lyttelton, *Blenheim*

The building was completed in 1716, and the architect was Sir John Vanbrugh, for whom the epitaph was written:

> Lie heavy on him, Earth, for he
> Laid many a heavy load on thee.

And of all his buildings Blenheim was probably the heaviest.

The Palace has given its name to a small dog, the *Blenheim Spaniel*, a variety of King Charles's Spaniel, and to a golden-coloured apple the *Blenheim Orange*.

**Blenheim Steps.** *Going to Blenheim Steps* meant going to be dissected, or unearthed from one's grave. There was an anatomical school, over which Sir Astley Cooper presided at Blenheim Steps, Bond Street. Here 'resurrectionists' were sure to find a ready mart for their gruesome wares, for which they received sums of money varying from £3 to £10, and sometimes more.

**Bless.** *He has not a sixpence to bless himself with,* i.e. in his possession; wherewith to make himself happy. This expression may perhaps be traced to the time when coins were marked with a deeply-indented cross; silver is still used by gypsy fortune-tellers and so on for crossing one's palm for good luck. *Cp.* 'to keep the devil out of one's pocket'.

**Blessing.** Among Greek and Roman ecclesiastics the thumb and first two fingers, representing the Trinity, are used in ceremonial blessing in the name of the Father, and of the Son, and of the Holy Ghost. The thumb, being strong, represents the *Father*; the long or second finger, *Jesus Christ*; and the first finger, the *Holy Ghost*, which proceedeth from the Father and the Son. Some bishops of the Anglican Church use this gesture while pronouncing the benediction.

**Blest.** ***I'll be blest if I do it.*** I am resolved not to do it. A euphemism for *cursed* or *curst*.

**Blighter.** Slightly contemptuous but good-natured slang for a man, a fellow; generally with the implication that he is a bit of a scamp or, at the moment, somewhat obnoxious.

**Blighty.** Soldiers' slang for England or the homeland. It came into popular use during the Great War, but was well known to soldiers who had served in India long before. It is the Urdu Vilayati or Bilati, an adjective meaning provincial, removed at some distance; hence adopted by the military for England.

**Blimey.** One of the numerous class of mild oaths or expletives whose real meaning is little understood by those who use them. This is a corruption of 'blind me!'

**Blind.** A pretence; something ostensible to conceal a covert design. The metaphor is from window-blinds, which prevent outsiders from seeing into a room.

As an adjective *blind* is one of the many euphemisms for 'drunk' – short for 'blind drunk', i.e. so drunk as to be unable to distinguish things clearly.

> Landlady, count the lawin,
> The day is near the dawin;
> Ye're a' blind drunk, boys,
> And I'm but jolly fou. Burns

***Blind as a bat.*** A bat is not blind, but when it enters a well lighted room it cannot see, and blunders about. It sees best, like a cat, in the dusk.

***Blind as a beetle.*** Beetles are not blind, but the dor-beetle or hedge-chafer, in its rapid flight, will occasionally bump against one as if it could not see.

***Blind as a mole.*** Moles are not blind, but as they work underground, their eyes are very small. There is a mole found in the south of Europe, the eyes of which are covered by membranes, and probably this is the animal to which Aristotle refers when he says, 'the mole is blind'.

***Blind as an owl.*** Owls are not blind, but being night birds, they see better in partial darkness than in the full light of day.

***Blind leaders of the blind.*** Those who give advice to others in need of it, but who are, themselves, unfitted to do so. The allusion is to Matt. 15:14.

***To go it blind.*** To enter upon some undertaking without sufficient forethought, enquiry, or preparation. The phrase is from card-games such as 'blind poker' (*see below*).

***When the devil is blind.*** A circumlocution for 'never'. For similar phrases *see* Never.

***You came on his blind side.*** His soft or tender-hearted side. Said of persons who wheedle some favour out of another. He yielded because he was not wide awake to his own interest.

**Blind Alley, A.** *A cul de sac*, an alley with no outlet. It is blind because it has no 'eye' or passage through it.

**Blind Beggar of Bethnal Green.** *See* Beggar's Daughter. There is a public-house of this name in the Whitechapel Road.

**Blind Department, The.** In Post Office parlance, a colloquialism for the 'Returned Letter Office' (formerly known also as the 'Dead Letter Office'), the department where letters with incoherent, insufficient, or illegible addresses are examined, and, if possible, put upon the proper track for delivery. The clerk in charge was called 'The Blind Man'.

> One of these addresses was 'Santlings, Hilewite' (St Helen's, Isle of Wight). Dr Brewer had one from France addressed, 'A. Mons. E. Cobham. brasseur, Angleterre', and it reached him. Another address was 'Haselfeach in no famtshere' (Hazelbeach, Northamptonshire).

**Blind Ditch.** One which cannot be seen. Here blind means obscure, or concealed, as in Milton's 'In the blind mazes of this tangled wood' (*Comus*, 181).

**Blind Half-hundred, The.** An old name for the 50th Regiment of Foot. Many of them suffered from ophthalmia in the Egyptian campaign of 1801.

**Blind Harper, The.** John Parry, who died 1782. He lived at Ruabon, and published collections of Welsh music.

**Blind Harry.** A Scottish minstrel of the 15th century. He died about 1492 and left in MS an epic on Sir William Wallace which runs to 11,858 lines.

**Blind Hedge.** A ha-ha (*q.v.*).

**Blind Magistrate, The.** Sir John Fielding, knighted in 1761, was born blind. He was in the commission of the Peace for Middlesex, Surrey, Essex, and the liberties of Westminster.

**Blind Man.** *See* Blind Department.

**Blind Old Man of Scio's Rocky Isle.** Homer is so called by Byron in his *Bride of Abydos*.

**Blind poker.** A form of the card-game in which certain bets are made or stakes laid in ignorance of what one's hand consists. When one makes such bets one is said *to go it blind*.

**Blindman's Buff.** A very old-established name for an old and well-known children's game. 'Buff' here is short for 'buffet', and is an allusion to the three buffs or pats which the 'blind man' gets when he has caught a player.

**Blindman's Holiday.** The hour of dusk, when it is too dark to work, and too soon to light candles. The phrase was in common use at least as early as Elizabethan times.

**Blindmen's Dinner, The.** A dinner unpaid for, the landlord being made the victim. Eulenspiegel (*q.v.*) being asked for alms by twelve blind men, said, 'Go to the inn; eat, drink, and be merry, my men; and here are twenty florins to pay the bill'. The blind men thanked him; each supposing one of the others had received the money. Reaching the inn, they told the landlord of their luck, and were at once provided with food and drink to the amount of twenty florins. On asking for payment, they all said, 'Let him who received the money pay for the dinner'; but none had received a penny.

**Blindworm.** *See* Misnomers.

**Blinkers.** Slang for the eyes; also for spectacles; the allusion is to a horse's blinkers.

**Block.** ***To block a Bill.*** In parliamentary language means to postpone or prevent the passage of a Bill by giving notice of opposition, and thus preventing its being taken after half-past twelve at night.

***A chip of the old block.*** *See* Chip.

***To cut blocks with a razor.*** *See* Cut.

**Blockhead.** A stupid person; one without brains. The allusion is to a wig-maker's dummy or *tête à perruque*, on which he fits his wigs.

> Your wit will not so soon out as another man's will; 'tis strongly wedged up in a blockhead.
>
> Shakespeare, *Coriolanus*, 2, 3

**Blood.** In figurative use, *blood*, being treated as the typical component of the body inherited from parents and ancestors, came to denote members of a family or race as distinguished from other families and races, hence family descent generally, and hence one of noble or gentle birth, which latter degenerated into a buck, or aristocratic rowdy.

> A blood or dandy about town.
>
> Thackeray, *Vanity Fair*, ch. x

***A blood horse.*** A thoroughbred; a horse of good parentage or stock.

***A prince of the blood.*** One of the Royal Family. *See* Blood Royal.

***Bad blood.*** Anger, quarrels; as, *It stirs up bad blood*. It provokes to ill-feeling and contention.

***Blood and iron policy*** – i.e. war policy. No explanation needed.

***Blood is thicker than water.*** Relationship has a claim which is generally acknowledged. It is better to seek kindness from a kinsman than from a stranger. Water soon evaporates and leaves no mark behind; not so blood. So the interest we take in a stranger is thinner and more evanescent than that which we take in a blood relation. The proverb occurs in Ray's Collection (1672) and is probably many years older.

> Weel! blude's thicker than water. She's welcome to the cheeses and the hams just the same.
>
> Scott, *Guy Mannering*

***Blood money.*** Money paid to a person for giving such evidence as shall lead to the conviction of another; money paid to the next of kin to induce him to forgo his 'right' of seeking blood for blood, or (formerly) as compensation for the murder of his relative; money paid to a person for betraying another, as Judas was paid blood-money for his betrayal of the Saviour.

***Blood relation.*** One in direct descent from the same father or mother; one of the same family stock.

***Blue blood.*** *See* Blue.

***In cold blood.*** Deliberately; not in the excitement of passion or of battle.

***It makes one's blood boil.*** It provokes indignation and anger.

***It runs in the blood.*** It is inherited or exists in the family or race.

> It runs in the blood of our family.
>
> Sheridan, *The Rivals*, iv, 2

***Laws written in blood.*** Demades said that the laws of Draco were written in blood, because every offence was punishable by death.

***My own flesh and blood.*** My own children, brothers, sisters, or other near kindred.

***The blood of the Grograms.*** Taffety gentility; make-believe aristocratic blood. Grogram is a coarse silk taffety stiffened with gum (Fr. *gros grain*).

> Our first tragedian was always boasting of his being 'an old actor', and was full of the 'blood of the Grograms'.
>
> C. Thomson, *Autobiography*, p. 200

***The field of blood.*** Aceldama (Acts 1:19), the piece of ground purchased with the blood-money of our Saviour, and set apart for the burial of strangers.

The field of the battle of Cannae, where Hannibal defeated the Romans, 216 BC, is also so called.

***Young blood.*** Fresh members; as, 'To bring young blood into the concern'. The term with the article, '*a* young blood', signifies a young rip, a wealthy young aristocrat of convivial habits.

***Blood Royal.*** The royal family or race; also called simply 'the blood', as 'a prince of the blood'.

***Man of blood.*** Any man of violent temper. David was so called in 2 Sam. 16:7 (Rev. Ver.), and the Puritans applied the term to Charles I.

***Man of Blood and Iron.*** An epithet bestowed on Bismarck (1815–98), for many years Chancellor of Prussia and Germany, on account of his war policy and his indomitable will.

**Bloodhound.** Figuratively, one who follows up an enemy with pertinacity. Bloodhounds used to be employed for tracking wounded game by the blood spilt; subsequently they were employed for tracking criminals and slaves who had made their escape, and were hunters of blood, not hunters *by* blood. The most noted breeds are the African, Cuban, and English.

**Bloodstone.** *See* Heliotrope.

**Bloodsucker.** An animal like the leech, or the fabled vampire which voraciously sucks blood and which, if allowed, will rob a person of all vitality. Hence, a sponger, a parasite, or one intent upon another's material ruin.

The 63rd Regiment of Foot are nicknamed 'the Bloodsuckers'.

**Bloody.** This senseless, ugly, and far too common expletive, used in such phrases as 'A bloody fool', 'Bloody drunk', etc., probably arose from associating folly and drunkenness, etc., with what are called 'Bloods', or aristocratic rowdies. 'Bloody drunk' thus meant 'as drunk as a blood' (*cp*. the modern 'as drunk as a lord'); and the word, partly owing to its unpleasant, violent, and lurid associations, easily became applied as an intensive in a general way.

> It was bloody hot walking today.
>
> Swift, *Journal to Stella*, letter xxii

As a title the adjective has been bestowed on Otto II, Emperor of the Holy Roman Empire, 973–83, and the English Queen Mary (1553–58), has been called 'Bloody Mary' on account of the religious persecutions which took place in her reign.

***The Bloody Eleventh.*** The old 11th Foot, 'The Devonshire Regiment', was so called from their having been several times nearly annihilated, as at Almanza, Fontenoy, Roucoux, Ostend, and Salamanca (1812), in capturing a French standard.

**Bloody Assizes.** The infamous assizes held by Judge Jeffreys in 1685. Three hundred were executed, more whipped or imprisoned, and a thousand sent to the plantations for taking part in Monmouth's rebellion.

**Bloody Bill.** The 31 Henry VIII, c. 14, which denounced death, by hanging or burning, on all who denied the doctrine of transubstantiation.

**Bloody-bones.** A hobgoblin: generally 'Raw-head and Bloody-Bones'.

**Bloody Butcher.** *See* Butcher.

**Bloody Hand.** A term in old Forest Law denoting a man whose hand was bloody, and was therefore presumed to be the person guilty of killing the deer shot or otherwise slain. In *heraldry*, the 'bloody hand' is the badge of a baronet, and the armorial device of Ulster. In both uses it is derived from the O'Neils. *See* Red Hand, and Hand, the Red.

**Bloody Mars.** A local English name for a variety of wheat. It is a corruption of the French *blé de Mars*, March grain.

**Bloody-nose.** The popular name of the common wayside beetle, *Timarcha laevigata*, which can emit a reddish liquid from its joints when disturbed.

**Bloody Pots, The.** *See* Kirk of Skulls.

**Bloody Thursday.** The Thursday in the first week in Lent used to be so called.

**Bloody Wedding.** The massacre of St Bartholomew in 1572 is so called because it took place during the marriage feast of Henri (afterwards Henri IV) and Marguerite (daughter of Catherine de Medici).

**Bloomers.** A female costume consisting of a short skirt and loose trousers gathered closely round the ankles, so called from Mrs Amelia Bloomer, of New York, who tried in 1849 to introduce the fashion. Nowadays 'bloomers' is usually applied only to the trousers portion of the outfit.

**Blooming.** A meaningless intensive, used as a euphemism for the objectionable 'bloody'. 'A blooming fool' and 'a bloody fool' mean much the same thing, but the former is accounted as rather more suitable to ears polite.

**Blouse.** A short smock-frock of a blue colour worn commonly by French workmen. *Bleu* is French argot for *manteau*.

> A garment called *bliaut* or *bliaus*, which appears to have been another name for a surcoat ... In this *bliaus* we may discover the modern French *blouse*, a ... smock-frock. Planche, *British Costume*

**Blow.** The English spelling *blow* represents three words of different origin, viz. –

(1) To move as a current of air, to send a current of air from the mouth, etc., from the A.S. *blawan*, cognate with the Mod. Ger. *blahen* and Lat. *flare*.

(2) To blossom, to flourish, from A.S. *blowan*, cognate with *bloom*, Ger. *blühen*, and Lat. *florera*; and

(3) A stroke with the fist, etc., which is most likely from an old Dutch word, *blau*, to strike.

In the following phrases, etc., the numbers refer to the group to which each belongs.

***A blow out*** (1). A 'tuck in', or feast which swells out the paunch.

***At one blow*** (3). By one stroke.

***Blow me tight*** (1). A mild oath or expletive.

If there's a soul will give me food, or find me in employ,
By day or night, then blow me tight! (he *was* a vulgar boy).
Ingoldsby Legends, *Misadventures at Margate*

***Blown*** (1), in the phrase 'fly-blown', is a legacy from pre-scientific days, when naturalists thought that maggots were actually blown on to the meat by blow-flies.

***Blown herrings*** (1). Herrings bloated, swollen, or cured by smoking; another name for bloaters.

***Blown upon*** (1). Made the subject of a scandal. *His reputation has been blown upon*, means that he has been the subject of talk wherein something derogatory was hinted at or asserted. Blown upon by the breath of slander.

***Blow-point*** (1). A game similar to pea-puffing, only instead of peas small wooden skewers or bits of pointed wood were puffed through the tube. The game is alluded to by Florio, Strutt, and several other authors.

***It will soon blow over*** (1). It will soon be no longer talked about; it will soon come to an end, as a gale or storm blows over or ceases.

***I will blow him up sky high*** (1). Give him a good scolding. *A regular blowing up* is a thorough jobation. The metaphor is from blasting by gunpowder.

***The first blow is half the battle*** (3). Well begun is half done. Pythagoras used to say, 'The beginning is half the whole'. '*Incipe: Dimidium facti est caepisse*' (Ausonius). '*Dimidium facti, qui caepit, habet*' (Horace). '*Ce n'est que le premier pas qui coute*'.

***To blow a cloud*** (1). To smoke a cigar, pipe, etc. This term was in use in Queen Elizabeth's reign.

***To blow a trumpet*** (1). To sound a trumpet.

But when the blast of war blows in our ears,
Let us be tigers in our fierce deportment.
Shakespeare, *Henry V*, 3, 1

***To blow great guns*** (1). Said of a wind which blows so violently that its noise resembles the roar of artillery.

***To blow hot and cold*** (1). To be inconsistent. The allusion is to the fable of a traveller who was entertained by a satyr. Being cold, the traveller blew his fingers to warm them, and afterwards blew his hot broth to cool it. The satyr, in great indignation, turned him out of doors, because he blew both hot and cold with the same breath.

***To blow off steam*** (1). To get rid of superfluous energy. The allusion is to the forcible escape of superfluous steam no longer required.

***To blow the gaff*** (1). To let out a secret; to inform against a companion; to 'peach'. Here *gaff* is a variant of *gab* (*q.v.*).

***To blow up*** (1). To inflate, as a bladder; to explode, to burst into fragments; to censure severely. *See I will blow him up*, above.

***Without striking a blow.*** Without coming to a contest.

***You be blowed*** (1). A mild imprecation or expletive.

Don't link yourself with vulgar folks, who've got no fixed abode,
Tell lies, use naughty words, and say 'they wish they may be blow'd!'
Ingoldsby Legends, *Misadventures at Margate*

**Blowzelinda.** A common 18th century name applied to a rustic girl. *See* Gay's *Shepherd's Week*:

Sweet is my toil when Blowzelind is near;
Of her bereft, 'tis winter all the year ...
Come, Blowzelinda, ease thy swain's desire,
My summer's shadow and my winter's fire.
Pastoral i

A *blouze* was a ruddy fat-cheeked wench –

Sweet blowze, you are a beauteous blossom, sure.
Shakespeare, *Titus Andronicus*, 4, 2

**Blowzy.** Coarse, red-faced, bloated; applied to women. The word is allied to blush, blaze, etc.

Oh, it's sweet to sweat through stables, sweet to empty kitchen slops.
And it's sweet to hear the tales that troopers tell,
To dance with blowzy housemaids at the regimental hops
And thrash the cad who says you waltz too well.
Kipling, *Gentlemen Rankers*

**Blubber** (M.E. *bloberen*, probably of imitative origin). To cry like a child, with noise and slavering; *cp. slobber*, *slaver*.

I play the boy, and blubber in thy bosom.
Otway, *Venice Preserved*, i, 1

The word is also used attributively, as in blubber-lips, blubber-cheeks, fat flabby cheeks, like whale's blubber.

**Bluchers.** Half boots; so called after Field-Marshal von Blucher (1742–1819).

**Blue** or *Azure* is the symbol of Divine eternity and human immortality. Consequently, it is a mortuary colour – hence its use in covering the coffins of young persons. When used for the garment of an angel, it signifies faith and fidelity. As the dress of the Virgin, it indicates modesty. In *blazonry*, it signifies chastity, loyalty, fidelity, and a spotless reputation, and seems frequently to represent silver; thus we have the *Blue Boar* of Richard III, the *Blue Lion* of the Earl of Mortimer, the *Blue Swan* of Henry IV, the *Blue Dragon*, etc.

The *Covenanters* wore blue as their badge, in opposition to the scarlet of royalty. They based their choice on Numb. 15:38, 'Speak unto the children of Israel, and bid them that they make them fringes in the borders of their garments ... and that they put upon the fringe ... a *ribband of blue*'.

*See* Colours for its symbolisms.

***A blue,*** or a 'staunch blue', descriptive of political opinions, for the most part means a Tory, for in most counties the Conservative colour is blue. *See* Blue-Coat School, Blue Stocking, True Blue.

Also, at Oxford and Cambridge, a man who has been chosen to represent his 'Varsity in rowing, cricket, etc. Some sports, such as hockey and lacrosse, come in a lower category, and for these a 'half blue' is awarded.

***A dark blue.*** An Oxford man or Harrow boy.

***A light blue.*** A Cambridge man or Eton boy.

***True blue will never stain.*** A really noble heart will never disgrace itself. The reference is to blue aprons and blouses worn by butchers, which do not show blood-stains.

***True as Coventry blue.*** The reference is to a blue cloth and blue thread made at Coventry, noted for its permanent dye.

***'Twas Presbyterian true blue*** (*Hudibras*, i, 1). The allusion is to the blue apron which some of the Presbyterian preachers used to throw over their preaching-tub before they began to address the people. In one of the Rump songs we read of a person going to hear a lecture, and the song says –

> Where I a tub did view,
> Hung with an apron blue;
> 'Twas the preacher's, I conjecture.

***To look blue.*** To be disconcerted. *He was blue in the face*. Aghast with wonder. The effect of fear and wonder is to drive the colour from the cheeks, and give them a pale bluish tinge.

**Blue-apron Statesman.** A lay politician, a tradesman who interferes with the affairs of the nation. The reference is to the blue apron once worn by almost all tradesmen, but now restricted to butchers, poulterers, fishmongers, and so on.

**Blue bag.** *A priest of the blue bag*. A cant name for a barrister. *See* Lawyer's Bag.

> He [O' Flynn] had twice pleaded his own cause without help of attorney, and showed himself as practised in every law quibble ... as if he had been a regularly ordained priest of the blue bag.
> C. Kingsley, *Alion Locke*, ch. xx

**Blue Beans.** Bullets. Lead is blue.

> Many a valiant Gaul had no breakfast that morning but what the Germans call 'blue beans', i.e. bullets.
> W. Maccall, *My School Days*, 1885

*Three blue beans in a blue bladder. See* Beans.

**Bluebeard.** A bogy, a merciless tyrant, in Charles Perrault's *Contes du Temps* (1697). The tale of Bluebeard (Chevalier Raoul) is known to every child, but many have speculated on the original of this despot. Some say it was a satire on Henry VIII, of wife-killing notoriety. Dr C. Taylor thinks it is a type of the castle lords in the days of knight-errantry. Holinshed calls Giles de Retz, Marquis de Laval, the original Bluebeard; he lived at Machecoul, in Brittany, was accused of murdering six of his seven wives, and was ultimately strangled and burnt in 1440.

> The Bluebeard chamber of his mind, into which no eye but his own must look. *Carlyle*

Campbell has a Bluebeard story in his *Tales of the Western Highlands*, called *The Widow and her Daughters*; it is found also in Strapola's *Nights*, the *Pentamerone*, and elsewhere. *Cp*. the *Story of the Third Calender* in *The Arabian Nights*.

**Bluebeard's Key.** When the blood stain of this key was rubbed out on one side, it appeared on the opposite side; so prodigality being overcome will appear in the form of meanness; and friends, over-fond, will often become enemies.

**Blue Billy.** A blue neckcloth with white spots. *See* Billy.

**Blue Blood.** High or noble birth or descent; it is a Spanish phrase, and refers to the fact that the veins shown in the skin of the pure-blooded Spanish aristocrat, whose race had suffered no Moorish or other admixture, were more blue than those of persons of mixed, and therefore inferior, ancestry.

**Blue Boar.** A public-house sign; the cognisance of Richard III. In Leicester is a lane in the parish of St Nicholas, called the *Blue Boar Lane*, because Richard slept there the night before the battle of Bosworth Field.

The bristly boar, in infant gore,
Wallows beneath the thorny shade.
Gray, *The Bard*

**Blue Bonnets,** or **Blue Caps.** The Highlanders of Scotland, or the Scots generally. So called from the blue woollen cap at one time in very general use in Scotland, and still far from uncommon.

He is there, too, ... and a thousand blue caps more. Shakespeare, *1 Henry IV*, 2, 4

England shall many a day
Tell of the bloody fray,
When the blue bonnets came over the border.
Sir W. Scott

**Blue Books.** In England, parliamentary reports and official publications presented by the Crown to both Houses of Parliament. Each volume is in folio, and is covered with a blue wrapper.

Short Acts of Parliament, etc., even without a wrapper, come under the same designation.

The official colour of Spain is *red*, of Italy *green*, of France *yellow*, of Germany and Portugal *white*.

In America the 'Blue Books' (like our 'Red Books') contain lists of those persons who hold government appointments.

**Blue Bottle.** A constable, a policeman; also, formerly, an almsman, or anyone whose distinctive dress was blue.

You proud varlets, you need not be ashamed to wear blue when your master is one of your fellows. Dekker, *The Honest Whore* (1602)

Shakespeare makes Doll Tearsheet denounce the beadle as a 'blue-bottle rogue'.

I'll have you soundly swinged for this, you blue-bottle rogue. Shakespeare, *2 Hen. IV*, 5, 4

**Blue Caps.** *See* Blue Bonnets.

**Blue-coat School.** Christ's Hospital is so called because the boys there wear a long *blue coat* girded at the loins with a leather belt. Some who attend the mathematical school are termed *King's boys*, and those who constitute the highest class are *Grecians*.

Founded by Edward VI in the year of his death. There are several other blue-coat schools in England besides Christ's Hospital, and boys at them are generally called 'blues'.

**Blue Devils,** or *A fit of the blues*. A fit of spleen, low spirits. Roach and Esquirol affirm, from observation, that indigo dyers are especially subject to melancholy; and that those who dye scarlet are choleric. Paracelsus also asserts that blue is injurious to the health and spirits. There may, therefore, be more science in calling melancholy *blue* than is generally allowed. The Ger. *blei* (lead), which gives rise to our slang word *blue* or *bluey* (lead), seems to bear upon the 'leaden downcast eyes' of melancholy.

**Blue-eyed Maid.** Minerva, the goddess of wisdom, is so called by Homer.

Now Prudence gently pulled the poet's ear,
And thus the daughter of the Blue-eyed Maid,
In flattery's soothing sounds, divinely said,
'O Peter, eldest-born of Phoebus, hear'.
Peter Pindar, *A Falling Minister*

**Blue Fish, The.** The shark, technically called *Carcharias glaucus*, the upper parts of which are blue.

**Blue Flag.** *He has hoisted the blue flag.* He has turned publican or fishmonger, in allusion to the blue apron at one time worn by publicans, and still worn by fishmongers.

**Blue Gown.** A harlot. Formerly a blue gown was a dress of ignominy for a prostitute who had been arrested and placed in the House of Correction.

The bedesmen, to whom the kings of Scotland distributed certain alms, were also known as *blue gowns*, because their dress was a cloak or gown of coarse blue cloth. The number of these bedesmen was equal to that of the king's years, so that an extra one was added at every returning birthday. These paupers were privileged to ask alms through the whole realm of Scotland. *See* Gaberlunzie.

**Blue Guards.** So the Oxford Blues, now called the Royal Horse Guards, were called during the campaign in Flanders (1742–5).

**Blue Hen's Chickens.** The nickname for inhabitants of the State of Delaware. It is said that in the Revolutionary War a certain Captain Caldwell commanded, and brought to a high state of efficiency, a Delaware regiment. He used to say that no cock could be truly game whose mother was not a blue hen. Hence the Delaware regiment became known as 'Blue Hen's Chickens', and the name was transferred to the inhabitants of the State generally.

**Bluejackets.** Sailors; so called because the colour of their jackets is blue.

**Blue John.** A blue fluor-spar, found in the Blue John mine near Castleton, Derbyshire; so called to distinguish it from the Black Jack, an ore of zinc. Called John from John Kirk, a miner, who first noticed it.

**Blue Laws.** Puritanical laws, being extremely rigid codes passed at various times and places in the 17th and 18th centuries in America, especially those passed in 1732, at New Haven, Connecticut. Their object was to stamp out 'heresy', enforce a strict observance of the Sunday, and regulate every kind of social intercourse between the sexes, and even kissing between husbands and wives.

**Blue-light Federalists.** A name given to those Americans who were believed to have made friendly ('blue-light') signals to British ships in the war of 1812.

**Bluemantle.** One of the four English Pursuivants (*q.v.*) attached to the College of Arms, or Heralds' College, so called from his official robe.

**Blue Monday.** The Monday before Lent, spent in dissipation. It is said that dissipation gives everything a blue tinge. Hence 'blue' means gypsy. *Cp.* Blue Devils.

**Blue Moon.** *Once in a blue moon.* Very rarely indeed.

**Blue Murder.** *To shout blue murder.* Indicative more of terror or alarm than of real danger. It appears to be a play on the French exclamation *morbleu*; there may also be an allusion to the common phrase 'blue ruin'.

**Blue-noses.** The Nova Scotians.

> 'Pray, sir'. said one of my fellow-passengers, 'can you tell me the reason why the Nova Scotians are called "Blue-noses"?'
>
> 'It is the name of a potato'. said I, 'which they produce in the greatest perfection, and boast to be the best in the world. The Americans have, in consequence, given them the nickname of *Blue Noses*'. Haliburton, *Sam Slick*

**Blue Peter.** A flag with a blue ground and white square in the centre, hoisted as a signal that the ship is about to sail. It has been suggested that 'peter' is here a corruption of the French *partir* (leave or notice of departure); according to Falconer, it is a corruption of the 'blue repeater'; but these are both guesswork.

In whist, the *blue Peter* is a 'call for trumps'; that is, laying on your partner's card a higher one than is required.

***To hoist the blue Peter.*** To leave.

> 'When are you going to sail?'
>
> 'I cannot justly say. Our ship's bound for America next voyage ... but I've got to go to the Isle of Man first ... And I may have to hoist the blue Peter any day'.
>
> Mrs Gaskell, *Mary Barton*, ch. xiii

**Blue Pigeon Flyer.** A man who steals the lead off of a house or church. 'Bluey' is slang for lead, so called from its colour. To 'pigeon' is to gull, cheat, or fub. Hence, blue-pigeon, one who cheats another of his lead, or fubs his lead.

**Blue Ribbon.** The *blue ribbon* is the Garter, the badge of the highest and most coveted Order of Knighthood in the gift of the British Crown; hence the term is used to denote the highest honour attainable in any profession, walk of life, etc. The blue ribbon of the Church is the Archbishopric of Canterbury, that in law is the office of Lord Chancellor. *See* Cordon Bleu.

*The Blue Ribbon of the Turf.* The Derby. Lord George Bentinck sold his stud, and found to his vexation that one of the horses sold won the Derby a few months afterwards. Bewailing his ill-luck, he said to Disraeli, 'Ah! you don't know what the Derby is'. 'Yes, I do'. replied Disraeli; 'it is the blue ribbon of the turf'. alluding to the term *cordon bleu* (*q.v.*); or else to the blue garter, the highest of all orders.

A weal from a blow has had the term 'blue ribbon' applied to it, because a bruise turns the skin blue.

> 'Do you want a blue ribbon round those white sides of yours, you monkey?' answered Orestes; 'because, if you do, the hippopotamus hide hangs ready outside'. Kingsley, *Hypatia*, ch. iv

**Blue Ribbon Army.** The Blue Ribbon Army was a teetotal society founded in the early eighties of the last century by Richard Booth in the USA, and soon extending to Great Britain. The members were distinguished by wearing a piece of narrow blue ribbon in the buttonhole of the coat. From this symbol the phrase Blue Ribbon Army came in time to be applied to the body of teetotallers generally, whether connected with the original society or not.

**Blue Ruin.** Gin; especially gin of bad quality. Called *blue* from its tint, and *ruin* from its effects.

**Blue Squadron.** One of the three divisions of the British Fleet in the 17th century. *See* Admiral of the Blue.

**Blue Stocking.** A female pedant. In 1400 a society of ladies and gentlemen was formed at Venice, distinguished by the colour of their stockings, and called *della calza*. It lasted till 1590, when it appeared in Paris and was the rage among the lady *savantes*. From France it came to England in 1780, when Mrs Montague displayed the badge of the Bas-bleu club at her evening assemblies. Mr Benjamin Stillingfleet was a constant attendant of the *soirées*. The last of the clique was Miss Monckton, afterwards Countess of Cork, who died 1840, but the name has survived.

> You used to be fond enough of books ... a regular blue-stocking Mr Bland called you.
>
> E. S. Phelps, *The Gates Ajar*, ch. iv

**Blue Talk.** Indecent conversation. The term is perhaps derived from the French, *Bibliothèque Bleu*, the name of a collection of more or less obscene books; or from the dress of imprisoned prostitutes. *See* Blue Gown.

**Blue Wonder.** The German *Blaues Wunder*, which means 'a queer story', as *Du sollst dein blaues Wunder sehen*, You will be filled with amazement (at the queer story I have to relate). A 'blue wonder' is a cock and bull story, an improbable tale, something to make one stare. The French, *contes bleus*.

**Blue and Yellow, The.** The *Edinburgh Review*; so called from its yellow and blue cover. The back is yellow, the rest of the cover is blue.

**Blues.** *See* Blue Devils.

***The Oxford Blues.*** The Royal Horse Guards were so called in 1690, from the Earl of Oxford their commander and the blue facings. Wellington, in one of his dispatches, writes – 'I have been appointed colonel of the Blues'.

> It was also known as the 'Blue Guards' during the campaign in Flanders (1742–45).
>
> Trimen, *Regiments of the British Army*

**Bluey.** *See* Blue Pigeon Flyer.

**Bluff, To.** In *Poker* and other card-games, to stake on a bad hand. This is a dodge resorted to by players to lead an adversary to throw up his cards and forfeit his stake rather than risk them against the 'bluffer'.

> The game proceeded. George, although he affected no ignorance of the ordinary principles of poker, played like a novice – that is to say, he bluffed extravagantly on absurdly low hands.
>
> *Queer Stories from Truth*

**Bluff Harry** or **Hal.** Henry VIII, so called from his bluff and burly manners (1491, 1509–47).

**Blunderbore.** A nursery-tale giant, brother of Cormoran, who put Jack the Giant Killer to bed and intended to kill him; but Jack thrust a billet of wood into the bed, and crept under the bedstead. Blunderbore came with his club and broke the billet to pieces, but was much amazed at seeing Jack next morning at breakfast-time. When his astonishment was abated he asked Jack how he had slept. 'Pretty well'. said the Cornish hero, 'but once or twice I fancied a mouse tickled me with its tail'. This increased the giant's surprise. Hasty pudding being provided for breakfast, Jack stowed away such huge stores in a bag concealed within his dress that the giant could not keep pace with him. Jack cut the bag open to relieve 'the gorge', and the giant, to effect the same relief, cut his throat and thus killed himself.

**Blunderbuss.** A short gun with a large bore. (Dut. *donderbus*, a thunder-tube.)

**Blunt.** Ready money; a slang term, the origin of which is unknown.

> To get a Signora to warble a song,
> You must fork out the blunt with a haymaker's prong!
>
> Hood, *A Tale of a Trumpet*

**Blurt Out, To.** To tell something from impulse which should not have been told. To speak incautiously, or without due reflection. Florio makes the distinction, to 'flurt with one's fingers, and blurt with one's mouth'.

**Blush.** ***At the first blush.*** At the first glance, the first time the thought has flashed into your mind; speaking off-hand without having given the subject mature deliberation. The allusion is to blushing at something sudden or unexpected.

***To blush like a blue dog.*** *See* Dog.

***To put to the blush.*** To make one blush with shame, annoyance, or confusion.

> England might blush in 1620, when Englishmen trembled at a fool's frown, but not in 1649, when an enraged people cut off his son's head.
>
> Wendell Phillips, *Orations*, p. 419

**Bo.** ***You cannot say Bo! to a goose*** – i.e. you are a coward who dare not say bo! even to a fool. It is said that once when Ben Jonson was introduced to a nobleman, the peer was so struck with his homely appearance that he exclaimed, 'What! are you Ben Jonson? Why, you look as if you could not say Bo! to a goose'. 'Bo!' exclaimed the witty dramatist, turning to the peer and making his bow. (*Cp.* Lat. *bo-are*; Gr. *boa-ein*, to cry aloud.)

**Bo-tree.** The pipal tree, or *Ficus religiosa*, of India, allied to the banyan, and so called from Pali *Bodhi*, perfect knowledge, because it is under one of these trees that Gautama attained enlightenment and so became the Buddha. At the ruined city of Anuradhapura in Ceylon is a bo-tree that is said to have been grown from a cutting sent by King Asoka in 288 BC.

**Boa.** Pliny (*Natural History*, VIII, xiv) says the word is from Lat. *bos* (a cow), and arose from the supposition that the boa sucked the milk of cows.

**Boan.** *See* Jambuscha.

**Boanerges.** A name given to James and John, the sons of Zebedee, because they wanted to call down 'fire from heaven' to consume the Samaritans for not 'receiving' the Lord Jesus. It is said in the Bible to signify 'sons of thunder', but 'sons of tumult' would probably be nearer its meaning (Luke 9:54; *see* Mark 3:17).

**Boar, The.** Richard III. *See* Blue Boar.

> The wretched, bloody, and usurping boar
> That spoiled your summer fields and fruitful vines:
> ... This foul swine ... lies now ...
> Near to the town of Leicester, as we learn.
>
> Shakespeare, *Richard III*, 5, 3

***Buddha and the boar.*** A Hindu legend relates that Buddha died from eating boar's flesh dried. The third avatar of Vishnu was in the form of a boar, and in the legend 'dried boar's flesh' probably typifies esoteric knowledge prepared for popular use. None but Buddha himself must take the responsibility of giving out occult secrets, and he died while preparing for the general esoteric knowledge. The protreptics of Jamblicus are examples of similar interpretations.

***The bristled Baptist boar.*** So Dryden denominates the Anabaptists in his *Hind and Panther*.

> The bristled Baptist boar, impure as he [*the ape*],
> But whitened with the foam of sanctity,
> With fat pollutions filled the sacred place,
> And mountains levelled in his furious race.
>
> Pt i, 43

***The Calydonian boar.*** In *Greek legend*, Oeneus, king of Calydon, in Aetolia, having neglected to sacrifice to Artemis, was punished by the goddess sending a ferocious boar to ravage his lands. A band of heroes collected to hunt the boar, who was eventually slain by Meleager after he had been first wounded by Atalanta.

***The wild boar of the Ardennes.*** Guillaume, Comte de la Marck (d.1485), so called because he was fierce as the wild boar, which he delighted to hunt. Introduced by Scott in *Quentin Durward*.

**Boar's Head.** The Old English custom of serving this as a Christmas dish is said to derive from *Scandinavian mythology*. Freyr, the god of peace and plenty, used to ride on the boar Gullinbursti; his festival was held at Yuletide (*winter solstice*), when a boar was sacrificed to his honour.

The head was carried into the banqueting hall, decked with bays and rosemary on a gold or silver dish, to a flourish of trumpets and the songs of the minstrels. Many of these carols are still extant (*see* Carol), and the following is the first verse of that sung before Prince Henry at St John's College, Oxford, at Christmas, 1607:

> The Boar is dead,
> So, here is his head;
> What man could have done more
> Than his head off to strike,
> Meleager like
> And bring it as I do before?

*The Boar's Head Tavern.* Made immortal by Shakespeare, this used to stand in Eastcheap, on the site of the present statue of William IV. The sign was the cognisance of the Gordons, the progenitor of which clan slew, in the forest of Huntley, a wild boar, the terror of all the Merse (1093).

**Board.** In all its many senses, this word is ultimately the same as the A.S. *bord*, a board, plank, or table; but the verb, *to board*, meaning to attack and enter a ship by force, hence to embark on a ship, and figuratively to accost or approach a person, is short for Fr. *aborde*, from *aborder*, which itself is from the same word, *bord*, as meaning the side of a ship. In *starboard*, *larboard*, *on board* and *overboard* the sense 'the side of a ship' is still evident.

> I'll board her, though she chide as loud
> As thunder.
>
> Shakespeare, *Taming of the Shrew*, 1, 2

***A board.*** A council which sits at a board or table; as 'Board of Directors'. 'Board of Guardians', 'School Board', 'Board of Trade', etc.

***The Board of Green Cloth.*** A Court that used to form part of the English Royal Household, and was presided over by the Lord Steward. It was so called because it sat at a table covered with green cloth. It existed certainly in the reign of Henry I, and probably earlier, and was abolished in 1849.

> Board of Green Cloth, June 12th, 1681. Order was this day given that the Maides of Honour should have cherry-tarts instead of gooseberry-tarts, it being observed that cherrys are threepence a pound.

In modern slang *the board of green cloth* is the card-table or billiard-table.

***Board School.*** An undenominational elementary school managed by a School Board as established by the Elementary Education Act in 1870, and supported by a parliamentary grant collected by a rate. When the School Boards were abolished by the Education Act of 1902 and the County Councils were given their duties, the name *Board School* was dropped and the schools became known as County Schools.

***He is on the boards.*** He is an actor by profession.

***To sweep the board.*** To win and carry off all the stakes in a game of cards, or all the prizes at some meeting.

***To board.*** To feed and lodge together, is taken from the custom of the university members, etc., dining together at a common table or board.

***Boarding school.*** A school where the pupils are fed and lodged as well as taught. By the criminal classes the term is sometimes applied to 'prison'. *I am going to boarding school*, going to prison to be taught good behaviour.

***Board wages.*** Wages paid to servants which includes the cost of their food. Servants 'on board wages' provide their own victuals.

***Board,*** in many sea phrases, is all that space of the sea which a ship passes over in tacking.

***To go by the board.*** To go for good and all, to be quite finished with, thrown overboard. Here *board* means the side of the ship.

***To make a good board.*** To make a good or long tack in beating to windward.

***To make a short board.*** To make a short tack. 'To make short boards', to tack frequently.

***To make a stern board.*** To sail stern foremost.

***To run aboard of.*** To run foul of another ship. *See also* Aboard.

**Boast of England, The.** A name given to 'Tom Thumb' or 'Tom-a-lin' by Richard Johnson, who in 1599 published a 'history of this ever-renowned soldier, the Red Rose Knight, surnamed The Boast of England, showing his honourable victories in foreign countries, with his strange fortunes in Faëry Land, and how he married the fair Angliterra, daughter of Prester John …'

**Boat.** ***Both in the same boat.*** Both treated alike; both placed in the same conditions. The reference is to the boat launched when a ship is wrecked.

***To burn one's boats.*** *See* Burn.

**Boatswain.** The officer who has charge of the boats, sails, rigging, anchors, cordage, cables, and colours. Swain is the old Scand. *sveinn*, a boy, servant, attendant; hence the use of the word in poetry for a shepherd and a sweetheart. The word is pronounced 'bos'n', as the following quotation shows:

> The merry Bosun from his side
> His whistle takes. Dryden, *Albion and Albanius*

**Boaz.** *See* Jachin.

**Bob.** Slang for a shilling. The origin of the word is unknown; but it may be connected with *bawbee* (*q.v.*).

***Bob.*** A term used in campanology denoting certain changes in the long peals rung on bells. A *bob minor* is rung on six bells, a *bob triple* on seven, a *bob major* on eight, a *bob royal* on ten, and a *bob maximus* on twelve.

***To give the bob to anyone.*** To deceive, to balk. Here *bob* is from M.E. *bobben*, O.Fr. *bober*, to befool.

> With that, turning his backe, he smiled in his sleeve, to see howe kindely hee had given her the bobbe. Greene, *Menaphon* (1589)

***To bob*** for apples or cherries is to try and catch them in the mouth while they swing backwards and forwards. *Bob* here means to move up and down buoyantly; hence, the word also means 'to curtsy', as in the Scottish saying, *If it isn't weel bobbit we'll bob it again*, signifying, if it is not well done we'll do it again.

***To bob*** for eels is to fish for them with a *bob*, which is a bunch of lob-worms like a small mop. Fletcher uses the word in this sense:

> What, dost thou think I fish without a bait, wench?
> I bob for fools: he is mine own, I have him.
> I told thee what would tickle him like a trout;
> And, as I cast it, so I caught him daintily.
> *Rule a Wife and Have a Wife*, II, iv

To bob means also to thump, and a *bob* is a blow.

> He that a fool doth very wisely hit,
> Doth very foolishly, although he smart,
> Not to seem senseless of the bob.
> Shakespeare, *As You Like It*, 2, 7

***Bear a bob.*** Be brisk. The allusion is to bobbing for apples, in which it requires great agility and quickness.

***A bob wig.*** A wig in which the bottom locks are turned up into bobs or short curls.

***Bobbed hair*** is hair that has been cut short – docked – like a bobtailed horse's tail.

**Bobadil.** A military braggart of the first water. Captain Bobadil is a character in Ben Jonson's *Every Man in his Humour*. This name was probably suggested by Bobadilla, first governor of Cuba, who sent Columbus home in chains.

> Bobadil is the author's best invention, and is worthy to march in the same regiment with Bessus and Pistol, Parolles, and the Copper Captain. B. W. Procter

**Bobbery,** as *Kicking up a bobbery*, making a squabble or tumult, kicking up a shindy. It is much used in India, and Colonel Yule says it is of Indian origin.

**Bobbish.** *Pretty bobbish.* Pretty well (in spirits and health), from *bob*, as in the phrase *bear a bob* above.

**Bobby.** A policeman; this slang word is either derived from Sir *Robert* Peel, or became popular through his having in 1828 remodelled the Metropolitan Police Force. *Cp.* Peeler.

> But oh! for the grip of the bobby's hand
> Upon his neck that day. *Punch*, July 26, 1884

**Boccus, King.** *See* Sidrac.

**Bockland** or *Bookland*. Land severed from the *folk-land* (i.e. the common land belonging to the people and held either communally or in severally, and converted into a private estate of perpetual inheritance by a written *boc* (or *book*), i.e. a deed.

The common place-name *Buckland* is derived from this word.

**Boden-See.** The German name for the Lake of Constance; so called because it lies in the Boden, or low country at the foot of the Alps.

**Bodkin.** A word of uncertain origin, originally signifying a small dagger. In the early years of Elizabeth's reign it was applied to the stiletto worn by ladies in the hair. In the *Seven Champions*, Castria took her silver bodkin from her hair, and stabbed to death first her sister and then herself, and it is probably with this meaning that Shakespeare used the word in the well-known passage from *Hamlet*, 'When he himself might his quietus make with a bare bodkin'.

*To ride bodkin.* To ride in a carriage between two others, the accommodation being only for two. There is no ground for the suggestion that *bodkin* in this sense is a contraction of *bodykin*, a little body. The allusion to something so slender that it can be squeezed in anywhere is obvious.

> If you can bodkin the sweet creature into the coach. Gibbon

> There is hardly room between Jos and Miss Sharp, who are on the front seat, Mr Osborne sitting bodkin opposite, between Captain Dobbin and Amelia. Thackeray, *Vanity Fair*

**Bodle.** A Scotch copper coin, worth about the sixth of a penny; said to be so called from Bothwell, a mintmaster.

> Fair play, he car'd na deils a boddle.
> Burns, *Tam o' Shanter*, 110

*To care not a bodle* = our English phrase, 'Not to care a farthing'.

**Bodleian Library** (Oxford). So called because it was restored by Sir Thomas Bodley in 1597. It was originally established in 1455 and formally opened in 1488, but it fell into neglect in the course of the next century. It is now, in size and importance, second only to the library of the British Museum, and is one of the five libraries to which a copy of all copyright books must be sent.

**Body** (A.S. *bodig*).

***A compound body***, in old chemical phraseology, is one which has two or more *simple* bodies or *elements* in its composition, as water.

A *regular body*, in geometry, means one of the five regular solids, called 'Platonic' because first suggested by Plato. *See* Platonic Bodies.

***The heavenly bodies.*** The sun, moon, stars, and so on.

***The seven bodies*** (of alchemists). The seven metals supposed to correspond with the seven 'planets'.

| *Planets.* | *Metals.* |
|---|---|
| 1. Apollo, or the Sun | Gold. |
| 2. Diana, or the Moon | Silver. |
| 3. Mercury | Quicksilver. |
| 4. Venus | Copper. |
| 5. Mars | Iron. |
| 6. Jupiter | Tin. |
| 7. Saturn | Lead. |

***To body forth.*** To give mental shape to an ideal form.

> Imagination bodies forth
> The forms of things unknown.
> Shakespeare, *Midsummer Night's Dream*, 5, 1

***To keep body and soul together.*** To sustain life; from the notion that the soul gives life. The Latin *anima*, and the Greek *psyche*, mean both soul and life; and, according to *Homeric mythology* and the common theory of 'ghosts', the departed soul retains the shape and semblance of the body. *See* Astral Body.

***Body colour.*** Paint containing body or consistency. Water-colours are made opaque by mixing with white lead.

***Body corporate.*** An aggregate of individuals legally united into a corporation.

***Body politic.*** A whole nation considered as a political corporation; the state. In Lat., *totum corpus reipublicae*.

**Body-snatcher.** One who snatches or purloins bodies, newly buried, to sell them to surgeons for dissection. The first instance on record was in 1777, when the body of Mrs Jane Sainsbury was 'resurrected' from the burial ground near Gray's Inn Lane. The 'resurrection men' (*q.v.*) were imprisoned for six months.

By a play on the words, a bumbailiff was so called, because his duty was to snatch or capture the body of a delinquent.

**Boeotia.** The ancient name for a district in central Greece, probably so called because of its abundance of cattle, but, according to fable, because Cadmus was conducted by an ox (Gr. *bous*) to the spot where he built Thebes.

**Boeotian.** A rude, unlettered person, a dull blockhead. The ancient Boeotians loved agricultural and pastoral pursuits, so the Athenians used to say they were dull and thick as their own atmosphere; yet Hesiod, Pindar, Corinna, Plutarch, Pelopidas, and Epaminondas, were all Boeotians.

***Boeotian ears.*** Ears unable to appreciate music or rhetoric.

> Well, friend, I assure thee thou hast not got Boeotian ears [*because you can appreciate the beauties of my sermons*].
>
> Le Sage, *Gil Blas*, vii, 3

**Bogey, Colonel.** *See* Bogy.

**Bogomili.** An heretical sect which seceded from the Greek Church in the 12th century. Their chief seat was Thrace, and they were so called from a Bulgarian priest, Bogomil, a reformer of the 10th century. Their founder, Basilius, was burnt by Alexius Comnenus in 1118; they denied the Trinity, the institutions of sacraments and of priests, believed that evil spirits assisted in the creation of the world, etc.

**Bog-trotters.** Irish tramps; so called from their skill in crossing the Irish bogs, from tussock to tussock, either as guides or to escape pursuit.

**Bogus.** An adjective applied to anything spurious, sham, or fraudulent, as *bogus currency*, *bogus transactions*. The word came from America, and is by some connected with *bogy*; but there are other suggestions. One is that it is from an Italian named *Borghese* who, about 1837, was remarkably successful in amassing a fortune in the Western States by means of forged bills, fictitious cheques, etc.; another, that ten years before this the name was given to an apparatus for coining false money; while Lowell (*Biglow Papers*) says, 'I more than suspect the word to be a corruption of the French *bagasse*'.

**Bogy.** A hobgoblin; a person or object of terror; a bugbear. The word appeared only in the early 19th century, and is probably connected with the Scottish *bogle*, and so with the obsolete *bug*. *See* Bugbear.

***Colonel Bogy.*** A name given in golf to an imaginary player whose score for each hole is settled by the committee of the particular club and is supposed to be the lowest that a good average player could do it in. *Beating Bogy* or *the Colonel*, is playing the hole in a fewer number of strokes.

**Bohemia, The Queen of.** This old public-house sign is in honour of Elizabeth, daughter of James I, who was married to Frederick, elector palatine, for whom Bohemia was raised into a separate kingdom. It is through her that the Hanoverians succeeded to the throne of Great Britain.

**Bohemian.** A slang term applied to literary men and artists of loose and irregular habits, living by what they can pick up by their wits. Originally the name was applied to the gypsies, from the belief that before they appeared in western Europe they had been denizens of Bohemia, or because the first that arrived in France came by way of Bohemia (1427). When they presented themselves before the gates of Paris they were not allowed to enter the city, but were lodged at La Chapelle, St Denis. The French nickname for gypsies is *cagoux* (unsociables).

**Bohemian Brethren.** A religious sect formed out of the remnants of the Hussites. They arose at Prague in the 15th century, and are the forerunners of the modern Moravians.

**Bohort, Sir.** A knight of Arthur's Round Table, brother of Sir Lionel, and nephew of Lancelot of the Lake. Also called Sir Bors.

**Boiling-point.** *He was at boiling-point.* Very angry indeed. Properly the point of heat at which water, under ordinary conditions, boils (212° Fahrenheit, 100° Centigrade, 80° Réaumur).

**Boisserean Collection.** A collection of early specimens of German art, made by the brothers Boisserée, and sold to the king of Bavaria in 1836, who housed them in the *Pinakothek* at Munich. Sulpiz Boisserée died in 1854, and his brother Melchior in 1851; both were born at Cologne.

**Bold.** ***Bold as Beauchamp.*** It is said that Thomas Beauchamp, Earl of Warwick, with one squire and six archers, overthrew 100 armed men at Hogges, in Normandy, in 1346.

This exploit is not more incredible than that attributed to Captal-de-Buch, who, with forty followers, cleared Meaux of the insurgents called *La Jacquerie*, 7,000 of whom were slain by this little band, or trampled to death in the narrow streets as they fled panic-struck (1358).

***Bold as brass.*** Downright impudent; without modesty. Similarly we say 'brazen-faced'.

***I make bold to say.*** I take the liberty of saying; I venture to say. (A colloquialism not used by educated persons.)

**Bolerium Promontory.** Land's End; the Bellerium (*see* Bellerus) of the Romans.

**Bolero.** A Spanish dance; so called from the name of the inventor.

**Bolingbroke.** Henry IV of England; so called from Bolingbroke, in Lincolnshire, where he was born. (1367, 1399–1413.)

**Bollandists.** Editors of the *Acta Sanctorum* begun by John Bollandus, Dutch Jesuit martyrologist (1596–1665); the first two volumes were published in 1643; these contain the saints commemorated in January. The work is not yet finished, but the sixty-first folio volume was published in 1875.

**Bollen.** Swollen. The past participle of the obsolete English verb, *bell*, to swell. Hence 'joints bolne-big' (*Golding*), and 'bolne in pride' (*Phaer*). The seed capsule or pod of flax is called a 'boll'.

> The barley was in the ear, and the flax was bolled.
>
> Exod. 9:31

**Bologna Stone.** A sulphate of baryta found in masses near Bologna. After being heated, powdered, and exposed to the light it becomes phosphorescent.

**Bolognese School.** There were three periods to the Bolognese School in painting – the Early, the Roman, and the Eclectic. The first was founded by Marco Zoppo, in the 15th century, and its best exponent was Francia. The second was founded in the 16th century by Bagnacavallo, and its chief exponents were Primaticio, Tibaldi, and Nicolo dell' Abate. The third was founded by the Carracci, at the close of the 16th century, and its best masters have been Domenichino, Lanfranco, Guido, Schidone, Guercino, and Albani.

**Bolshevik** or (less correctly) **Bolshevist.** Properly, a member of the Russian revolutionary party that seized power under Lenin in 1917, declared war on capitalism and the *bourgeoisie* in all lands, and aimed at the establishment of supreme rule by the proletariat. The Bolshevik government was so called because it professed to act in the name of the majority (*bolshe* is the comparative of the adjective *bolshoi*, big, large, and *bolsheviki* = majority). In England the name *bolshevist*, or *bolshie*, is applied to those who are, or who are suspected of being, kind of 'superanarchists' who wish to overthrow the whole basis of society.

**Bolt.** Originally meaning a short, thick arrow with a blunt head, is an Anglo-Saxon word, and must not be confused with the old word *bolt* (O.Fr. *bulter*, connected with Lat. *burra*, a coarse cloth) meaning a sieve, or to sieve. This latter word is almost obsolete, but is used by Browning:

> The curious few
> Who care to sift a business to the bran
> Nor coarsely bolt it like the simpler sort.
>
> *Ring and the Book*, i, 923

From meaning an arrow *bolt* came to be applied to the door fastening, which is of a similar shape, and these meanings (a missile capable of swift movement, and a fastening) have given rise to combinations and phrases of very separated meaning, as will be seen from the following.

***Bolted arrow.*** A blunt arrow for shooting young rooks with a cross-bow; called 'bolting rooks'. A gun would not do, and an arrow would mangle the little things too much.

***Bolt upright.*** Straight as an arrow.

> Winsinge she was, as is a jolly colt,
> Long as a mast, and upright as a bolt.
>
> Chaucer, *Miller's Tale*, 77

***I must bolt.*** Be off like an arrow.

***The fool's bolt is soon spent.*** A foolish archer shoots all his arrows so heedlessly that he leaves himself no resources in case of need.

***The horse bolted.*** The horse shot off like a bolt or arrow.

***To bolt food.*** To swallow it quickly without waiting to chew it; hence, *To bolt a Bill*, a political phrase used of Bills that are passed whole before proper time or opportunity has been given for their consideration.

***To bolt out the truth.*** To blurt it out; also *To bolt out*, to exclude or shut out by bolting the door.

***A bolt from the blue.*** A sudden and wholly unexpected catastrophe or event, like a 'thunderbolt' from the blue sky, or flash of lightning without warning and wholly unexpected. Here 'bolt' is used for lightning, though, of course, in strict language, a meteorite, not a flash of lightning, is a thunderbolt.

> Namque Diespiter
> Igni corusco nubila dividens,
> Plerumque, per purum tenantes
> Egit equos volucremque currum.
>
> Horace, *1 Ode* xxxiv, 5, etc.

**Bolt in Tun.** In heraldry, a bird-bolt, in pale, piercing through a tun, often used as a public-house sign. The punning crest of Serjeant Bolton, who died 1787, was 'on a wreath a tun erect proper, transpierced by an arrow fesseways or'. Another family of the same name has for crest 'a tun with a bird-bolt through it proper'. A third, harping on the same string, has 'a bolt gules in a tun or'. The device was adopted as a public-house sign in honour of some family who own it as a coat of arms.

**Bolton. *Bate me an ace, quoth Bolton*.** Give me some advantage. What you say must be qualified, as it is too strong. Ray says that a collection of proverbs were once presented to the Virgin Queen, with the assurance that it contained all the proverbs in the language; but the Queen rebuked the boaster with the proverb, 'Bate me an ace, quoth Bolton'. a proverb omitted in the compilation. John Bolton was one of the courtiers who used to play cards and dice with Henry VIII, and flattered the king by asking him to allow him an *ace* or some advantage in the game.

**Bolus.** Properly, a rather large-sized pill; so called from a Greek word meaning a roundish lump of clay. Apothecaries are so called because they administer *boluses*. Similarly Mrs Suds is a washerwoman; Boots is the shoeblack of an inn, etc.

George Colman adopted the name for his apothecary who wrote his labels in rhyme, one of which was –

When taken,
To be well shaken;

but the patient being shaken, instead of the mixture, died.

**Bomb.** A metal shell filled with an explosive. From the Gr. *bombos*, any deep, especially humming, noise (ultimately the same word as *boom*).

**Bombshell.** A word used figuratively in much the same way as *bolt* in *a bolt from the blue*.

**Bomba.** *King Bomba.* A nickname given to Ferdinand II, King of Naples, in consequence of his cruel bombardment of Messina in 1848, in which the slaughter and destruction of property was most wanton.

Bomba II was the nickname given to his son Francis II for bombarding Palermo in 1860. He was also called *Bombalino* (Little Bomba).

**Bombast** literally means the produce of the bombyx, or silk-worm (Gr. *bombux*); formerly applied to cotton-wool used for padding, and hence to inflated language.

We have received your letters full of love …
And in our maiden council rated them …
As bombast and as lining to the time.

Shakespeare, *Love's Labour's Lost*, 5, 2

**Bombastes Furioso.** One who talks big or in an ultra-bombastic way. From the hero of a burlesque opera so called by William Barnes Rhodes, produced in 1810 in parody of *Orlando Furioso*.

**Bombastus.** Butler in the following lines refers to Paracelsus (1493–1541), whose name was originally Theophrastus Bombastus von Hohenheim.

Bombastus kept a devil's bird
Shut in the pommel of his sword,
That taught him all the cunning pranks
Of past and future mountebanks.

*Hudibras*, pt ii, 3

**Bombiti.** *See* Barisal Guns.

**Bon Gaultier Ballads.** Parodies of contemporary poetry by W. E. Aytoun and Sir Theodore Martin. They first appeared in *Tait's*, *Fraser's*, and *Blackwood's Magazines* in the forties, and were published in volume form in 1855.

**Bon gré mal gré** (Fr.). Willing or unwilling, willy nilly, *nolens volens*. Literally, 'good will bad will'.

**Bon mot** (Fr.). A good or witty saying; a pun; a clever repartee.

**Bon ton** (Fr). Good manners or manners accredited by good society.

**Bon vivant** (Fr.). A free liver; one who indulges in the 'good things of the table'. *Bon viveur* means much the same, but is rather stronger, suggesting one who makes a pursuit of other pleasures besides those of the table.

**Bona fide** (Lat.). Without subterfuge or deception; really and truly. Literally, *in good faith*. *To produce one's bona fides* is to produce one's credentials, to give proof that one is what he appears to be or can perform that which he says he can.

**Bona-roba** (from Ital. *buona roba*, good stuff, fine gown, fine woman). A courtesan; so called from the smartness of their robes or dresses.

We knew where the bona-robas were.

Shakespeare, *2 Henry IV*, 3, 2

**Bonduca.** One of the many forms of the name of the British Queen, which in Latin was frequently (and in English is now usually) written *Boadicea*, but which should properly be *Bonduca*. Fletcher wrote a fine tragedy with this name (1616), the principal characters being Caractacus and Bonduca.

**Bone.** Old thieves' slang for 'good', 'excellent'. From the Fr. *bon*. The lozenge-shaped mark chalked by tramps and vagabonds on the walls of houses where they have been well received is known among the fraternity as a 'bone'.

Also slang for dice and counters used at cards; and the man who rattles or plays the bones (a castanet-like instrument) in nigger troupes is known as 'Uncle Bones'.

**Bone, To.** To filch, as, *I boned it*. Shakespeare (*2 Henry VI*, 1, 3) says, 'By these ten bones, my lord …' meaning the ten fingers; and (*Hamlet*, 3, 2) calls the fingers 'pickers and stealers'. So 'to bone' may mean to finger, that is, 'to pick and steal'.

Other suggested explanations of the origin of the term are that it is in allusion to the way in which a dog makes off with a bone, and that it is a corruption of the slang 'bonnet' (*q.v.*).

You thought that I was buried deep
Quite decent-like and chary,
But from her grave in Mary-bone,
They've come and boned your Mary!

Hood, *Mary's Ghost*

***A bone of contention.*** A disputed point; a point not yet settled. The metaphor is taken from the proverb about 'Two dogs fighting for a bone', etc.

***Bred in the bone.*** A part of one's nature. 'What's bred in the bone will come out in the flesh'. A natural propensity cannot be repressed. *Naturam furca expellas, autem usque redibit.*

***I have a bone in my throat.*** I cannot talk; I cannot answer your question.

***I have a bone in my leg.*** An excuse given to children for not moving from one's seat. Similarly, 'I have a bone in my arm'. and must be excused using it for the present.

***Napier's bones.*** *See* Napier.

***One end is sure to be bone.*** It won't come up to expectation. 'All is not gold that glitters'. An American expression.

***To give one a bone to pick.*** To throw a sop to Cerberus; to give a lucrative appointment to a troublesome opponent or a too zealous ally in order to silence him and keep him out of the way. It is a method frequently resorted to in political life; one whose presence is not convenient in the House of Commons is sent to the Lords, given a Colonial appointment, or a judgeship, etc.

***To have a bone to pick with one.*** To have an unpleasant matter to discuss and settle. This is another allusion from the kennel. Two dogs and one bone invariably forms an excellent basis for a fight.

***To make no bones about the matter.*** To do it, say it, etc., without hesitation; to offer no opposition, present no difficulty or scruple. Dice are called 'bones', and the Fr. *flatter le dé* (to mince the matter) is the opposite of our expression. To make no bones of a thing is not to flatter, or 'make much of', or humour the dice in order to show favour. Hence, *without more bones.* Without further scruple or objection.

**Bone-grubber.** A person who grubs about dustbins, gutters, etc., for refuse bones, which he sells to bone-grinders, and other dealers in such stores; also a resurrectionist (*q.v.*).

**Bone-lace.** Lace woven on bobbins made of trotter-bones.

**Bone-shaker.** An 'antediluvian', dilapidated four-wheel cab; also an early type of bicycle in use before rubber tyres, the chain drive, spring saddles, etc., were thought of.

**Bonfire.** Originally a *bone-fire*, that is, a fire made of *bones*; *see* the *Festyvall* of 1493, printed by Wynkyn de Worde in 1515: 'In the worship of St John, the people ... made three manner of fires: one was of clean bones and no wood, and that is called a bonefire; another of clean wood and no bones, and that is called a wood-fire ... and the third is made of wood and bones, and is called "St John's fire"'; and:

> In some parts of Lincolnshire ... they make fires in the public streets ... with bones of oxen, sheep, etc. ... heaped together ... hence came the origin of bonfires. Leland, 1552

**Bonhomie** (Fr.). Kindness, good nature; free and easy manners; the quality of being 'a good fellow'.

> I never knew a more prepossessing man. His *bonhomie* was infectious.
>
> C. D. Warner, *Little Journey*, ch. vi

**Bonhomme.** A French peasant *See* Jacques Bonhomme.

**Boniface.** A sleek, good-tempered, jolly landlord. From Farquhar's comedy of *Beaux' Stratagem* (1707).

***St Boniface.*** The apostle of Germany, an Anglo-Saxon whose original name was *Winifrid* or *Winfrith.* (680–750.)

***St Boniface's cup.*** An extra cup of wine; an excuse for an extra glass. Pope Boniface, we are told in the *Ebrietatis Encomium*, instituted an indulgence to those who drank his good health after grace, or the health of the Pope of the time being. This probably refers to Boniface VI, an abandoned profligate who was elected Pope by the mob in 896 and held the position for only fifteen days. The only *Saint* Boniface to be Pope was Boniface I, who died in 422.

**Bonne Bouche** (Fr.). A delicious morsel; a titbit (tid-bit).

> This man was capable of speaking the truth even to a woman, not as a luxury and a *bonne bouche*, but as matter of habit.
>
> Marion Crawford, *Mr Isaacs*, ch. iv

**Bonnet.** A player at a gaming-table, or bidder at an auction, to lure others to play or bid, so called because he blinds the eyes of his dupes, just as if he had struck their bonnet over their eyes.

***Braid bonnet.*** The old Scotch cap, made of milled woollen, without seam or lining.

***Glengarry bonnet.*** The Highland bonnet, which rises to a point in front.

***He has a green bonnet.*** Has failed in trade. In France it used to be customary, even in the 17th century, for bankrupts to wear a green *bonnet* (cloth cap).

***He has a bee in his bonnet.*** *See* Bee.

**Bonnet Lairds.** Local magnates or petty squires of Scotland, who wore the braid bonnet, like the common people.

**Bonnet-piece.** A gold coin of James V of Scotland, the king's head on which wears a bonnet.

**Bonnet Rouge.** The red cap of liberty worn by the leaders of the French revolution. It is the emblem of Red Republicanism.

**Bonnie Dundee.** John Graham, of Claverhouse, Viscount Dundee. Born about 1649, he became a noted soldier in the Stuart cause, and was killed at the Battle of Killiecrankie in 1689.

**Bonnivard.** *See* Chillon.

**Bonny-clabber.** Sour buttermilk used as a drink. (Irish, *bainne*, milk; *claba*, thick or thickened.)

It is against my freehold, my inheritance,
My Magna Charta, *cor laetificat*,
To drink such balderdash or bonny-clabber!
Give me good wine!

Ben Jonson, *The New Inn*, I, i

**Bono Johnny.** John Bull is so called in the East Indies.

**Bontemps.** *Roger Bontemps* (Fr.). The personification of 'Never say die'. The phrase is from Béranger.

Vous pauvres, pleins d'envie;
  Vous riches, desireux;
Vous, dont le char dévie
  Après un cours heureux;
Vous, qui perdrez peut-être
  Des titres éclatans,
Eh! gai! prenez pour maitre
  Le gros Roger Bontemps.

Béranger

Ye poor, with envy goaded:
  Ye rich, for more who long;
Ye who by fortune loaded
  Find all things going wrong
Ye who by some disaster
  See all your cables break
From henceforth for your master
  Bluff Roger Bontemps take.

E. C. B.

**Bonus.** Something 'extra'; something over and above what was expected, due, or earned; something 'to the good' (Lat. *bonus*, good). An extra dividend paid to shareholders out of surplus profits is called a bonus; so is the portion of profits distributed to certain insurance-policy-holders; and also – as was the custom in the case of Civil Servants and others – a payment made to clerks, workmen, etc., over and above that stipulated for to meet some special contingency that had been unprovided for when the rate was fixed.

**Bonze.** The name given by Europeans to the Buddhist clergy of the Far East, particularly of Japan. In China the name is given to the priests of the Fohists.

**Booby.** A spiritless fool, who suffers himself to be imposed upon.

Ye bread-and-butter rogues, do ye run from me?
An my side would give me leave, I would so hunt ye,
Ye porridge-gutted slaves, ye veal-broth boobies!

Beaumont and Fletcher, *Humorous Lieutenant*, III, vii

The player who comes in last in whist-drives, etc.; the lowest boy in the class.

Also a species of Gannet, whose chief characteristic is that it is so tame that it can often be taken by hand.

***A booby will never make a hawk.*** The booby, that allows itself to be fleeced by other birds, will never become a bird of prey itself.

***To beat the booby.*** A sailor's term for warming the hands by striking them under the armpits.

**Booby-prize.** The prize – often one of a humorous or worthless kind – given to the 'booby' at whist-drives, etc., i.e. to the player who makes the lowest score.

**Booby-trap.** A pitcher of water, book, or something else, balanced gingerly on the top of a door set ajar, so that when the booby or victim is enticed to pass through the door, the pitcher or book falls on him.

**Boojum.** *See* Snark.

**Book** (A.S. *boc*; Dan. *beuke*; Ger. *buche*, a beech tree). Beech-bark was employed for carving names on before the invention of printing.

Here on my trunk's surviving frame,
Carved many a long-forgotten name …
As love's own altar, honour me:
Spare, woodman, spare the beechen tree.

Campbell, *Beech Tree's Petition*

In betting the *book* is the record of bets made by the *bookmaker* with different people on different horses. The bookmaker who knows his business can generally arrange this by means of balancing, cross-betting, etc., so that it is practically impossible for him to lose.

In whist, bridge, etc., the *book* is the first six tricks taken by either side. The whole pack of cards is sometimes called a 'book' – short for 'the Devil's picture-book'.

***Bell, book and candle.*** *See* Bell.

***Beware of a man of one book.*** Never attempt to controvert the statement of anyone in his own special subject. A shepherd who cannot read will know more about sheep than the wisest bookworm. This caution is given by St Thomas Aquinas.

***He is in my books,*** or ***in my good books.*** The former is the older form; both mean to be in favour. The word book was at one time used more widely, a single sheet, or even a list being called a book. To be in my books is to be on my list of friends.

> I was so much in his books, that at his decease he left me his lamp. Addison
>
> If you want to keep in her good books, don't call her 'the old lady'. Dickens

***He is in my black*** (or ***bad***) ***books.*** In disfavour. *See* Black Books.

***On the books.*** On the list of a club, the list of candidates, the list of voters, or any official list. At Cambridge University they say 'on the boards'.

***Out of my books.*** Not in favour; no longer in my list of friends.

***The battle of the books.*** The Boyle controversy (*q.v.*).

***That does not suit my book.*** Does not accord with my arrangements. The reference is to betting-books, in which the bets are formally entered.

***The Book of Books.*** The Bible; also called simply 'the Book', or 'the good Book'.

***The Book of Life,*** or ***of Fate.*** In Bible language, a register of the names of those who are to inherit eternal life (Phil. 4:3; Rev. 20:12).

***To book it.*** To take down an order; to make a memorandum; to enter in a book.

***To bring him to book.*** To make him prove his words; to call him to account. Make him show that what he says accords with what is written down in the indentures, the written agreement, or the book which treats of the subject.

***To kiss the book.*** *See* Kiss.

***To know one's book.*** To know one's own interest; to know on which side one's bread is buttered. Also, to have made up one's mind.

***To speak by the book.*** To speak with meticulous exactness. To speak *literatim*, according to what is in the book.

***To speak like a book.*** To speak with great precision and accuracy; to be full of information. Often used of a pedant.

***To speak without book.*** To speak without authority; from memory only, without consulting or referring to the book.

***To take one's name off the books.*** To withdraw from a club. In the passive voice it means to be excluded, or no longer admissible to enjoy the benefits of the institution. *See On the books, above.*

**Book-keeper.** Used humorously for one who borrows books and does not return them, but properly for a clerk who keeps the accounts in merchant's offices, etc. *Book-keeping* is the system of keeping debtor and creditor accounts in books provided for the purpose, either by single or by double entry. In the first named each debit or credit is entered only once into the ledger, either as a debit or credit item, under the customer's or salesman's name; in *double entry*, each item is entered twice into the ledger, once on the debit and once on the credit side.

***Waste book.*** A book in which items are not posted under heads, but as each transaction occurred.

***Day book.*** A book in which are set down the debits and credits which occur day by day. These are ultimately 'posted' in the ledger (*q.v.*).

**Bookland.** *See* Bockland.

**Bookmaker.** A professional betting man who makes a 'book' (*see above*) on horse-races, etc. Also called a *bookie*.

**Booksellers' Row.** *See* Holywell Street.

**Bookworm.** One always poring over books; so called in allusion to the maggot that eats holes in books, and lives both in and on its leaves.

**Boom.** A sudden and great demand of a thing, with a corresponding rise in its price. This usage of the word seems to have arisen in America, probably with allusion to the suddenness and rush with which the shares 'go off', the same word being used for the rush of a ship under press of sail. The word arises from the sound of booming or rushing water, and the sound made by the bittern is known as *booming*.

> The boom was something wonderful. Everybody bought, everybody sold.
>
> Mark Twain, *Life on the Mississippi*, ch. 57

**Boom,** a spar on board ship, or the chained line of spars, balks of timber, etc., used as a barrier to protect harbours, is the Dutch *boom*, meaning a tree or pole, our *beam*.

**Boom-passenger.** A convict on board a transport ship, who was chained to the boom when made to take his daily exercise.

**Boon Companion.** A convivial companion. A *bon vivant* is one fond of good living. 'Who leads a good life is sure to live well'. (Fr. *bon*, good.)

**Boot.** An instrument of torture made of four pieces of narrow board nailed together, of a length to fit the leg. The leg being placed therein, wedges were inserted till the victim confessed or fainted.

All your empirics could never do the like cure upon the gout as the rack in England or your Scotch boots. Marston, *The Malcontent*

***Boot and saddle.*** The order to cavalry for mounting. It is a corruption of the Fr. *boute selle*, put on the saddle, and is nothing to do with boots.

***I measure five feet ten inches without my boots.*** The allusion is to the chopine (*q.v.*) or high-heeled boot, worn at one time to increase the stature.

***Like old boots.*** Slang for vigorously; 'like anything'. 'I was working like old boots' means 'I was doing my very utmost'.

***Seven-leagued boots.*** The boots worn by the giant in the fairy tale, called *The Seven-leagued Boots*. A pace taken in them measured seven leagues.

***The boot is on the other leg.*** The case is altered; you and I have changed places, and whereas before *I* appeared to be in the wrong *you* are now shown to be.

***The order of the boot.*** 'The sack'; notice of dismissal from one's employment.

***To go to bed in his boots.*** To be very tipsy.

***To have one's heart in one's boots.*** To be utterly despondent; a humorous way of saying to be as *down*-hearted, or *low*-spirited, as possible.

**Boot.** *I will give you that to boot*, i.e. in addition. The A.S. *bot* (Gothic *bôta*) means advantage, good, profit; as in Milton's 'Alas, what boots it with uncessant care' (*Lycidas*), Alas, what profit is it ...?

It also meant compensation paid for injury; reparation. *Cp.* House-bote.

As anyone shall be more powerful ... or higher in degree, shall he the more deeply make boot for sin, and pay for every misdeed.
*Laws of King Ethelred*

***Bootless errand.*** An unprofitable or futile message.

I sent him
Bootless home and weather-beaten back.
Shakespeare, *1 Henry IV*, 3, 1

***When bale is highest boot is nighest.*** *See* Bale.

**Boot-jack.** *See* Jack.

**Boötes.** Greek for 'the ploughman'; the name of the constellation which contains the bright star, Arcturus (*q.v.*). *See also* Icarius. According to ancient mythology, Boötes invented the plough, to which he yoked two oxen, and at death, being taken to heaven with his plough and oxen, was made a constellation. Homer calls it 'the wagoner', i.e. the wagoner of 'Charles's Wain', the Great Bear.

Wide o'er the spacious regions of the north,
That see Boötes urge his tardy vain.
Thomson, *Winter*, 834

**Boots.** A servant at inns, etc., whose duty it is to clean the boots. Dickens has a Christmas Tale (1855) called *The Boots of the Holly-tree Inn*.

The bishop with the shortest period of service in the House of Lords, whose duty it is to read prayers, is colloquially known as the 'Boots', perhaps because he walks into the House in a dead man's shoes or boots, i.e. he was not there till some bishop died and left a vacancy.

**Booty.** ***Playing booty***. A trick of dishonest jockeys – appearing to use every effort to come in first, but really determined to lose the race.

Mr Kemble [in the *Iron Chest*] gave a slight touch of the jockey, and 'played booty'. He seemed to do justice to the play, but really ruined its success. George Colman the Younger

**Boozed.** Partly intoxicated. Though generally regarded as slang, this is the Mid.E. *bousen*, to drink deeply, probably connected with Dut. *buizen*, and Ger. *bousen*, to drink to excess. Spenser uses the word in his description of Gluttony:

Still as he rode, he somewhat still did eat,
And in his hand did beare a bouzing can,
Of which he supt so oft, that on his seat
His drunken corse he scarse upholden can.
Faerie Queene, 1, iv, 22

**Bor.** A familiar term of address in East Anglia to a lad or young man; as, 'Well, bor, I saw the mauther you spoke of' – i.e. 'Well, sir, I saw the lass ...' It is connected with the Dut. *boer*, a farmer, and with the *-bour* of neighbour.

**Bor** (in *Scandinavian mythology*). *See* Bohr.

**Borachio.** Originally a Spanish wine bottle made of goat-skin; hence a drunkard, one who fills himself with wine.

A follower of Don John, in *Much Ado About Nothing*, is called Borachio; he thus plays upon his own name:

I will like a true drunkard [*borachio*] utter all to thee. Act 3, 5

**Borak** or **Al Borak** (the lightning). The animal brought by Gabriel to carry Mahomet to the seventh heaven, and itself received into Paradise. It had the face of a man, but the cheeks of a horse; its eyes were like jacinths, but brilliant as the stars; it had the wings of an eagle, spoke with the voice of a man, and glittered all over with radiant light.

... the Prophet's ascent to the third heaven on the horse Borak, with a peacock's tail and a woman's face (I mean the horse).
T. Hope, *Anastasius*, vol. i, p. 197 (1820)

**Bordar.** In Anglo-Saxon England, a villein of the lowest rank who did menial service for his lord in return for his cottage; the *bordars*, or *bordarii*, were the labourers, and the word is the Med. Lat. *bordarius*, a cottager.

**Border, The.** The frontier of England and Scotland, which, from the 11th to the 15th century, was the field of constant forays, and a most fertile source of ill blood between North and South Britain.

> March, march, Ettrick and Teviotdale:
> Why the deil dinna ye march forward in order?
> March, march, Eskdale and Liddesdale –
> All the Blue Bonnets are bound for the border.
> Scott, *The Monastery*

**Border Minstrel.** Sir Walter Scott (1771–1832), because he sang of the border.

**Border States, The.** The five 'slave' states (Delaware, Maryland, Virginia, Kentucky, and Missouri) which lay next to the 'free states' were so called in the American Civil War, 1861–65.

**Bore, A.** A person who bestows his tediousness on you, one who wearies you with his prate, his company, or his solicitations.

The derivation of the word is uncertain; in the 18th century it was used as an equivalent for *ennui*; hence, for one who suffers from *ennui*, and afterwards for that which, or one who, causes *ennui*.

In racing terminology *to bore* is to ride so that another horse is thrust or pushed off the course, a sense in which it is also used of boats in rowing; in pugilistic language it is to force one's opponent on to the ropes of the ring by sheer weight.

> Their fighting code stood in great need of revision, as empowering them not only to bore their man to the ropes, but ... also to hit him when he was down. Dickens, *Edwin Drood*, ch. xvii

**Boreas.** In *Greek mythology*, the god of the north wind, and the north wind itself. He was the son of Astraeus, a Titan, and Eos, the morning, and lived in a cave of Mount Haemus, in Thrace.

> Cease, rude Boreas! blustering railer.
> Geo. Alex. Stevens

Hence *boreal*, of or pertaining to the north.

> In radiant streams,
> Bright over Europe, bursts the Boreal morn.
> Thomson, *Autumn*, 98

**Born. *Born in the purple*** (a translation of Gr. *porphyrogenitus*). The infant of royal parents in opposition to one *born in the gutter*, or the child of beggars. This refers to the chamber lined with porphyry by one of the Byzantine empresses for her accouchement, and has nothing to do with the purple robes of royalty.

> Zoe, the fourth wife of Leo VI, gave birth to the future Emperor Constantine Porphyrogenitus in the purple chamber of the imperial palace.
> Finlay, *Byzantine and Greek Empires*, vol. i

***Born with a silver spoon in one's mouth.*** Born to good luck; born with hereditary wealth. The reference is to the usual gift of a silver spoon by the godfather or godmother of a child. The lucky child does not need to wait for the gift, for it is born with it in its mouth or inherits it at birth. A phrase with a similar meaning is *born under a lucky star*; this, of course, is from astrology.

***In all my born days.*** Ever since I was born; in all my experience.

***Not born yesterday.*** Not to be taken in; worldly wise.

***Poets are born, not made.*** One can never be a poet by mere training or education if one has been born without the 'divine afflatus'. A translation of the Latin phrase *Poeta nascitur non fit*, of which an extension is *Nascimur poetae fimus oratores*, we are born poets, we are made orators.

**Borough English.** A custom by which real estate passes to the *youngest* instead of the *eldest* son. It is of English, as opposed to French, origin, and was so called to distinguish it from the Norman custom.

If the father has no son, then the youngest daughter is sole heiress. If neither wife, son, nor daughter, the youngest brother inherits; if no brother, the youngest sister; if neither brother not yet sister, then the youngest next of kin. *See* Cradle-holding, and *cp.* Gavelkind.

> The custom of Borough English abounds in Kent, Sussex, Surrey, the neighbourhood of London and Somerset. In the Midlands it is rare, and north of the Humber ... it does not seem to occur.
> F. Pollock, *Macmillan's Magazine*, xlvi (1882)

**Borowe.** *See* Borrow.

**Borr.** In *Scandinavian mythology*, the son of Buri (*see* Audhumla) and father of Odin, Ville, Ve, and Hertha or Earth. The priests claimed descent from him.

**Borre.** The name given to the Bull in Caxton's version of *Reynard the Fox*.

**Borrow.** Originally a noun (A.S. *borg*) meaning a pledge or security, the modern sense of the verb depended on the actual giving in pledge of something as security for the loan; a security is not now essential in a borrowing transaction, but the idea that the loan is the property of the lender and must be returned someday is always present. The noun sense is seen in the old oath *St George to borowe*, which is short for 'I take St George as pledge'. or 'as witness'; also in:

> Ye may retain as borrows my two priests.
>
> Scott, *Ivanhoe*, ch. xxxiii

***Borrowed*** or ***borrowing days.*** The last three days of March are said to be 'borrowed from April', as is shown by the proverb in Ray's *Collection* – 'March borrows three days of April, and they are ill'. The following is an old rhyme on the same topic:

> March said to Aperill,
> I see 3 hoggs [*hoggets, sheep*] upon a hill;
> And if you'll lend me dayes 3
> I'll find a way to make them dee [*die*].
> The first o' them was wind and weet,
> The second o' them wus snaw and sleet,
> The third o' them wus sic a freeze
> It froze the birds' nebs to the trees,
> But when the Borrowed Days were gane
> The 3 silly hoggs came hirpling [*limping*] hame.

February also (in Scotland) has its 'borrowed' days. They are the 12th, 13th and 14th, which are said to be borrowed from January. If these prove stormy the year will be favoured with good weather; but if fine, the year will be foul and unfavourable. They are called by the Scots *Faoilteach*, and hence *faoilteach* means execrable weather.

**Bors, Sir.** *See* Bohort.

**Borstall** (A.S. *beork*, a hill, and *steall*, place, or *stigol*, stile). A narrow roadway up the steep ascent of hills or downs. The word has given the name to the village of Borstal, near Rochester (Kent), and hence to the *Borstal system*, a method of treating youthful offenders against the law by technical instruction and education in order to prevent their drifting into the criminal classes. The first reformatory of this kind was instituted at Borstal in 1902.

**Bos in lingua.** A Latin proverbial saying, meaning literally 'an ox on the tongue', but figuratively implying that there is a weighty reason (generally bribery) for keeping silence about something.

> Thus have some been startled at the proverb, *Bos-in lingua*, confusedly apprehending how a man should be said to have an Oxe in his tongue that would not speak his mind; which was no more than that a piece of money had silenced him: for by the Oxe was onely implied a piece of coin stamped with that figure, first currant with the *Athenians*, and after among the *Romans*.
>
> Sir Thos Browne, *Pseudodoxia Epidemica*

**Bosh.** A Persian word meaning worthless. It was popularised by James Morier, author of *Adventures of Hajji Baba of Ispahan* (1824), and other eastern romances.

> I always like to read old Darwin's *Love of the Plants*: bosh as it is in a scientific point of view.
>
> Kingsley, *Two Years Ago*, ch. x

**Bosky.** On the verge of drunkenness. This is a slang term, and it is possibly connected with the legitimate *bosky* meaning bushy, or covered with thickets, as in Shakespeare's:

> And with each end of thy blue bow dost crown
> My bosky acres and my unshrubb'd down.
>
> *Tempest*, 4, 1, 81

As 'bosky acres' were overshadowed or obscured, so can a 'bosky man' be said to be.

**Bosom Friend.** A very dear friend. Nathan says, 'It lay in his bosom, and was unto him as a daughter' (2 Sam. 12:3). Bosom friend, *ami de coeur*. St John is represented in the New Testament as the 'bosom friend' of Jesus.

**Bosom Sermons.** Sermons committed to memory and learnt by heart; not extempore ones or those delivered from notes.

> The preaching from 'bosom sermons', or from writing, being considered a lifeless practice before the Reformation.
>
> Blunt, *Reformation in England*, p. 179

**Bosporus** (incorrectly written **Bosphorus**) is a Greek compound meaning 'the ford of the ox', or 'Oxford'. Legend says that Zeus greatly loved Io, and changed her into a white cow or heifer from fear of Hera; to flee from whom Io swam across the strait, which was thence called *bos poros*, the passage of the cow. Hera discovered the trick, and sent a gadfly to torment Io, who was made to wander, in a state of frenzy, from land to land. The wanderings of Io were a favourite subject of story with the ancients. Ultimately, the persecuted Argive princess found rest on the banks of the Nile.

**Boss**, a master, is the Dut. *baas*, head of the household. Hence the great man, chief, an overseer.

The word is of much more widely extended use in the United States than in England, it having been attached to political leaders, financial magnates, etc., who – generally by dubious methods – seek to obtain a preponderating influence. Hence *boss-rule*, and the verb *to boss*, which has become common in England also.

**Boss-eyed.** Slang for having one eye injured, or a bad squint, or for having only one eye in all. Hence, *boss one's shot*, to miss one's aim, as a person with a defective eye might be expected to do; and *a boss*, a bad shot. *Boss-backed*, a good old word for 'hump-backed', is in no way connected with this. *Boss* here is a protuberance or prominence, like the bosses on a bridle or a shield.

**Bostal.** *See* Borstall.

**Botanomancy.** Divination by leaves. One method was by writing sentences on leaves which were exposed to the wind, the answer being gathered from those which were left; another was through the crackling made by the leaves of various plants when thrown on the fire or crushed in the hands.

**Bothie.** An Irish or Gaelic word for a hut or cottage. The *bothie system* is a custom common in Scotland of housing the unmarried menservants attached to the farm in a large, one-roomed bothie.

> The bothie system prevails, more or less, in the eastern and north-eastern districts.
>
> J. Begg, D.D.

**Botley Assizes.** The joke is to ask a Botley man, 'When are the assizes coming on?' The reference is to the tradition that the men of Botley once hanged a man because he could not drink so deep as his neighbours.

**Bottes.** *A propos de bottes* (Fr.). Literally, 'touching the matter of boots'; used in the middle of a conversation as an introduction to a sudden irrelevancy or change of subject.

> That venerable personage [the Chaldaean Charon], not only gives Izdubar instructions how to regain his health, but tells him, somewhat *à propos de bottes* ... the long story of his perfidious adventure.
>
> *Nineteenth Century*, June, 1891, p. 911

**Bottle.** ***A three bottle man.*** A toper who can drink three bottles of port at a sitting without being drunk and incapable.

***Brought up on the bottle.*** Said of a baby which is artificially fed instead of being nursed at the breast.

***Hang me in a bottle.*** *See* Cat.

***Looking for a needle in a bottle of hay.*** Looking for a very small article amidst a mass of other things. Bottle is a diminutive of the Fr. *botte*, a bundle; as *botte de foin*, a bundle of hay.

***To bottle up one's feelings, emotions, etc.*** To suppress them; to hold them well under control.

***To put new wine into old bottles.*** A saying founded on Matt. 9:17; typical of incongruity.

**Bottle-chart.** A chart of ocean surface currents to show the track of sealed bottles thrown from ships into the sea.

**Bottle-holder.** One who gives moral but not material support. The allusion is to boxing or prize-fighting, where the attendant on each combatant, whose duty it is to wipe off blood, refresh him with water, and do other services to encourage his man to persevere and win, is called 'the bottle-holder'.

> Lord Palmerston considered himself the bottle-holder of oppressed States ... He was the steadfast partisan of constitutional liberty in every part of the world. *The Times*

**Bottle-washer.** Chief agent; the principal man employed by another; a factotum. The full phrase – which usually is applied more or less sarcastically – is 'head cook and bottle-washer'.

**Bottled Moonshine.** Social and benevolent schemes, such as Utopia, Coleridge's Pantisocracy, the dreams of Owen, Fourier, St Simon, the New Republic, and so on.

> Godwin! Hazlitt! Coleridge! Where now are their 'novel philosophies and systems'? Bottled moonshine, which does not improve by keeping.
>
> Birrell, *Obiter Dicta*

The idea was probably suggested by Swift's Laputan philosopher, in *Gulliver's Travels*, who

> Had been eight years upon a project of extracting sunbeams out of cucumbers, which were to be put into phials hermetically sealed, and let out to warm the air in raw inclement summers.

**Bottom.** In nautical language the keel of a ship, that part of the hull which is below the waves; hence, the hull itself, and hence extended to mean the whole ship, especially in such phrases as *goods imported in British bottoms* or *in foreign bottoms*.

A vessel is said to have a *full bottom* when the lower half of the hull is so disposed as to allow large stowage, and a *sharp bottom* when it is capable of speed.

***Never venture all in one bottom*** – i.e. 'do not put all your eggs into one basket', has allusion to the marine use of the word.

> My ventures are not in one bottom trusted.
>
> Shakespeare, *Merchant of Venice*, 1, 1

***At bottom.*** Radically, fundamentally: as, the young prodigal lived a riotous life, but was good at bottom, or below the surface.

***At the bottom.*** At the base or root.

> Pride is at the bottom of all great mistakes.
>
> Ruskin, *True and Beautiful*, p. 426

***From the bottom of my heart.*** Without reservation.

> If one of the parties ... be content to forgive from the bottom of his heart all that the other hath trespassed against him. *Common Prayer Book*

***He was at the bottom of it.*** He really instigated it, or prompted it.

***To have no bottom.*** To be unfathomable.

***To get to the bottom of the matter.*** To ascertain the entire truth; to bolt a matter to its bran.

***To knock the bottom out of anything.*** *See* Knock.

***To stand on one's own bottom.*** To be independent. 'Every tub must stand on its own bottom'.

***To touch bottom.*** To reach the lowest depth.

***A horse of good bottom*** means of good stamina, good foundation.

**Bottom, the Weaver.** A man who fancies he can do everything, and do it better than anyone else. Shakespeare has drawn him as profoundly ignorant, brawny, mock heroic, and with an overflow of self-conceit. He is in one part of *Midsummer Night's Dream* represented with an ass's head, and Titania, queen of the fairies, under a spell, caresses him as an Adonis.

The name is very appropriate, as one meaning of *bottom* is a ball of thread used in weaving, etc. Thus in Clark's *Heraldry* we read, 'The coat of Badland is *argent*, three bottoms in fess *gules*, the thread *or*'.

**Bottomless Pit, The.** Hell is so called in the book of *Revelation.* The expression had previously been used by Coverdale in Job 36:16.

William Pitt was humorously called *the bottomless Pitt*, in allusion to his remarkable thinness.

**Bottomry.** A nautical term implying a contract by which in return for money advanced to the owners a ship, or *bottom* (*q.v.*), is, in a manner, mortgaged. If the vessel is lost the lender is not repaid; but if it completes its voyage he receives both principal and interest

**Botty.** Conceited. The frog that tried to look as big as an ox was a 'botty' frog (*Norfolk*).

**Boudewyn.** The name given to the Ass in Caxton's version of *Reynard the Fox*.

**Boudoir.** Properly speaking, a room for sulking in (Fr. *bouder*, to sulk). When the word was introduced into England in the last quarter of the 18th century it was as often applied to a man's sanctum as to a woman's retiring room; now, however, it is used only for a private apartment where a lady may retire, receive her intimate friends, etc.

**Bought and Sold,** or **Bought, Sold, and Done For.** Ruined, done for, outwitted.

> Jocky of Norfolk, be not too bold,
> For Diccon, thy master, is bought and sold.
> Shakespeare, *Richard III*, 5, 3
>
> It would make a man mad as a buck to be so bought and sold. *Comedy of Errors*, 3, 1

**Bougie.** A wax candle; so called from Biayah, in Algeria, whence the wax was imported. Also, a thin, flexible instrument used in surgery for dilating strictures, removing obstructions, etc.

**Boule Work.** A kind of marquetry, consisting of inlay of gold, brass, tortoiseshell, etc.; so called from André Charles Boule (1642–1732), a cabinet-maker, to whom Louis XIV gave apartments in the Louvre. It is more commonly, though incorrectly, spelt *Buhl*, which seems to be a Germanised form of the French name.

**Bounce.** Brag, swagger; boastful and mendacious exaggeration.

> He speaks plain cannon, fire, and smoke, and bounce. Shakespeare, *King John*, 2, 2

***On the bounce.*** Ostentatiously swaggering. Trying to effect some object 'on the bounce' is trying to attain one's end through making an impression on one that is unwarrantable.

***That's a bouncer.*** A gross exaggeration, a braggart's lie. A *bouncing* lie is a *thumping* lie, and a *bouncer* is a *thumper*.

**Bounds, Beating the.** An old custom, still kept up in many English parishes, of going round the parish boundaries on Holy Thursday, or Ascension Day. The school-children, accompanied by the clergymen and parish officers, walked through their parish from end to end; the boys were switched with willow wands all along the lines of boundary, the idea being to teach them to know the bounds of their parish.

> Many practical jokes were played even during the first quarter of the nineteenth century, to make the boys remember the delimitations: such as 'pumping them', pouring water clandestinely on them from house windows, beating them with thin rods, etc.

Beating the bounds was called in Scotland *Riding the marches* (bounds), and in England the day is sometimes called *gang-day*.

**Bounty.** *See* Queen Anne's Bounty.

**Bouquet.** French for nosegay, bunch of flowers. The word is used in English also for the flavour or aroma of wine, a jewelled spray, and a large flight of rockets or of pheasants which have been driven by the beaters.

**Bourbon.** The Bourbon Kings of France were Henry IV, Louis XIII, XIV, XV, and XVI (1589–1793). The family is so named from the castle and seigniory of Bourbon, in the old province of Bourbonnais, in Central France, and is a branch of the Capet stock, through the marriage of Beatrix, heiress of the Bourbons, to Robert, Count of Clermont, sixth son of Louis IX, in 1272. Henry IV was tenth in descent from Louis IX and the twentieth king to succeed him.

Bourbons also reigned over Naples and the two Sicilies, and the present royal house of Spain is Bourbon, being descended from Philippe, Duke of Anjou, a grandson of Louis XIV, who became King of Spain in 1700.

**Bourgeois** (Fr.). Our burgess; a member of the class between the 'gentleman' and the peasantry. It includes merchants, shopkeepers, and what we call the 'middle class'.

In *typography*, *bourgeois* (pronounced burjois) is the name of a size of type between long primer and brevier.

**Bourgeoisie** (Fr.). The merchants, manufacturers, and master-tradesmen considered as a class.

> The Commons of England, the Tiers-Etat of France, the bourgeoisie of the Continent generally, are the descendants of this class [artisans] generally. Mill, *Political Economy*

In recent years, particularly since the Russian Revolution, when this class was held to be chiefly responsible for the continuance of privilege and for all sorts of abuses during the old regime and the early part of the new, the word *bourgeoisie* has acquired a new and sinister signification.

**Bouse.** *See* Boozed.

**Boustrapa.** A nickname of Napoleon III; in allusion to his unsuccessful attempts at a *coup d'état* at *Bou*logne (1840) and *Stra*sburg (1836) and the successful one at *Pa*ris (1851).

**Boustrophedon.** A method of writing or printing, alternately from right to left and left to right, like the path of oxen in ploughing. (Gr. *bous-strepho*, ox-turning.)

**Bouts-rimés** (Fr. *rhymed-endings*). A parlour game which, in the 18th century, had a considerable vogue in literary circles as a test of skill. A list of words that rhyme with one another is drawn up; this is handed to the competitors, and they have to make a poem to the rhymes, each rhyme-word being kept in its place on the list.

**Bovey Coal.** A lignite found at Bovey Tracy, in Devonshire.

**Bow** (to rhyme with *flow*). (A.S. *boga*; connected with the O.Teut. *beugan*, to bend.)

***Draw not your bow till your arrow is fixed.*** Have everything ready before you begin.

***He has a famous bow up at the castle.*** Said of a braggart or pretender.

***He has two strings to his bow.*** Two means of accomplishing his object; if one fails, he can try the other. The allusion is to the custom of bowmen carrying a reserve string in case of accident.

***To be too much of the bow-hand.*** To fail in a design; not be sufficiently dexterous. The *bow-hand* is the left hand; the hand which holds the bow.

***To draw a bow at a venture.*** To attack with a random remark; to make a random remark which may hit the truth.

> A certain man drew a bow at a venture and smote the King of Israel. 1 Kings, 22:34

***To draw the longbow.*** To exaggerate. The longbow was the famous English weapon till gunpowder was introduced, and it is said that a good archer could hit between the fingers of a man's hand at a considerable distance, and could propel his arrow a mile. The tales told about longbow adventures, especially in the Robin Hood stories, fully justify the application of the phrase.

***To unstring the bow will not heal the wound*** (Ital.). René of Anjou, king of Sicily, on the death of his wife, Isabeau of Lorraine, adopted the emblem of a bow with the string broken, and with the words given above for the motto, by which he meant, 'Lamentation for the loss of his wife was but poor satisfaction'.

**Bow** (to rhyme with *now*). The fore-end of a boat or ship. (A.S. *bog* or *boh*, connected with Dan. *boug*, Icel. *bogr*, a shoulder.)

*On the bow.* Within a range of 45° on one side or the other of the prow.

**Bow Bells.** *Born within sound of Bow bells.* Said of a true cockney. St Mary-le-Bow has long had one of the most celebrated bell-peals in London. John Dun, mercer, gave in 1472 two tenements to maintain the ringing of Bow bell every night at nine o'clock, to direct travellers on the road to town; and in 1520 William Copland gave a bigger bell for the purpose of 'sounding a retreat from work'. Bow Church, in Cheapside, is very near the centre of the City. (This *bow* rhymes with *flow*.)

**Bow-catcher.** A corruption of 'Beau catcher', a love-curl, termed by the French an *accroche coeur*. A love-curl worn by a man is a *Bell-rope*, i.e. a rope to pull the *belles* with.

**Bow-street Runners.** Detectives who scoured the country to find criminals, before the introduction of the police force. Bow Street, near Covent Garden, is where the principal London police-court stands. (This *bow* rhymes with *flow*.)

**Bow-window in Front, A.** A big corporation.

He was a very large man, ... with what is termed a considerable bow-window in front.
Capt. Marryat, *Poor Jack*, i

**Bow-wow Word.** A word in imitation of the sound made, as hiss, cackle, murmur, cuckoo, etc. Hence *the bow-wow school*, a term applied in ridicule to philologists who sought to derive speech and language from the sounds made by animals. The terms were first used by Max Müller.

**Bowden.** *Not every man can be vicar of Bowden.* Not everyone can occupy the first place. Bowden is one of the best livings in Cheshire.

**Bowdlerise.** To expurgate a book. Thomas Bowdler, in 1818, gave to the world an edition of Shakespeare's works 'in which nothing is added to the original text; but those words and expressions are omitted which cannot with propriety be read aloud in a family'. This was in ten volumes. Bowdler subsequently treated Gibbon's *Decline and Fall* in the same way. Hence the words Bowdlerist, Bowdleriser, Bowdlerism, Bowdlerisation, etc.

**Bowels of Mercy.** Compassion, sympathy. The affections were at one time supposed to be the outcome of certain secretions or organs, as the bile, the kidneys, the heart, the head, the liver, the bowels, the spleen, and so on. Hence such words and phrases as *melancholy* (black bile); the Psalmist says that his *reins*, or kidneys, instructed him (Ps. 10:7), meaning his inward conviction; the *head* is the seat of understanding; the *heart* of affection and memory (hence 'learning by heart'), the *bowels* of mercy, the *spleen* of passion or anger, etc.

***His bowels yearned over, upon,*** or ***towards him.*** He felt a secret affection for him.

Joseph made haste, for his bowels did yearn upon his brother. Gen. 43:30; *see also* 1 Kings, 3:26

**Bower.** A lady's private room. (A.S. *bur*, a chamber.)

She's at the window many an hour
His coming to discover:
And he look'd up to Ellen's bower
And she look'd on her lover.
Campbell, *Earl March*

Hence, *bower-woman*, a lady's maid and companion.

'This maiden'. replied Eveline, 'is my bower-woman, and acquainted with my most inward thoughts. I beseech you to permit her presence at our conference'. Scott, *The Betrothed*, ch. xi

***Bower,*** the term used in euchre, is an entirely different word. It is *bauer*, a peasant or knave.

But the hands that were played
By that heathen Chinee,
And the points that he made,
Were quite frightful to see –
Till at last he put down a right bower
Which the same Nye had dealt unto me.
Bret Harte, *Plain Language from Truthful James*

The *right bower* is the knave of trumps; the *left bower* is the other knave of the same colour.

**Bower Anchor.** An anchor carried at the bow of a ship. There are two: one called the *best bower*, and the other the *small bower*.

Starboard being the best bower, and port the small bower. Smyth, *Sailor's Word-book*

**Bower of Bliss.** In Spenser's *Faerie Queene* (Bk II) the beautiful enchanted home of Acrasia on the Wandering Isle. It was destroyed by Sir Guyon (ca. xii). *See* Gryll.

**Bowie Knife.** A long, stout knife with a horn handle and a curved blade some 15 in. long and 1¼ wide at the hilt, carried by hunters in the Western States of America. So called from Colonel James Bowie (d.1836), one of the most daring characters in the States.

**Bowing.** We uncover the head when we wish to salute anyone with respect; but the Jews, Turks, Siamese, etc., uncover their feet. The reason is this: With us the chief act of investiture is crowning or placing a cap on the head; but in the East it is putting on the slippers. To take off our symbol of honour is to confess we are but 'the humble servant' of the person whom we thus salute.

**Bowled.** *To be bowled out.* To be detected in a false statement and so to have one's plans frustrated; to be defeated or overcome. The allusion is to cricket.

**Bowling, Tom.** The type of a model sailor; from the character of that name in Smollett's *Roderick Random*.

The Tom Bowling referred to in Dibdin's famous sea-song was Captain Thomas Dibdin, brother of Charles Dibdin (1768–1833), who wrote the song, and father of Thomas Frognall Dibdin, the bibliomaniac.

Here a sheer hulk lies poor Tom Bowling,
The darling of the crew.

**Bowls.** *They who play bowls must expect to meet with rubbers.* Those who touch pitch must expect to defile their fingers. Those who enter upon affairs of chance, adventure, or dangerous hazard must make up their minds to encounter crosses, losses, or difficulties. The *rubber* is the final game which decides who is the winner.

**Bowse.** *See* Browse.

**Bowyer God.** The 'archer god', usually Cupid, but in his translation of the *Iliad* Bryant (I, v, 156) applies the epithet to Apollo.

**Box.** ***I've got into the wrong box.*** I am out of my element, or in the wrong place. Lord Lyttelton used to say that whenever he went to Vauxhall and heard the mirth of his neighbours, he used to fancy pleasure was in every box but his own. Wherever he went for happiness, he somehow always got into the wrong box.

***To be in the same box.*** To be in the same predicament as somebody else; to be equally embarrassed.

***To box Harry.*** A phrase in use among commercial travellers; applied to one who avoids the *table d'hôte* and takes something substantial for tea, in order to save expense; also, to cut down one's expenditure after a bout of extravagance. To box a tree is to cut the bark to procure the sap, and these travellers drain the landlord by having a cheap tea instead of an expensive dinner. To 'box the fox' is to rob an orchard.

***To box the compass.*** A nautical phrase meaning to name the thirty-two points of the compass in their correct order. Hence, a wind is said 'to box the compass' when in a short space of time it blows from every quarter in succession; hence, the figurative use of the term – to go right round, in political views, etc., or in direction, and to end at one's starting-place.

**Box Days.** In the Scottish Court of Session, two days in spring and autumn, and one at Christmas, during vacation, in which pleadings may be filed. This custom was established in 1690, for the purpose of expediting business. Each judge has a private box with a slit, into which informations may be placed on box days, and the judge, who alone has the key, examines the papers in private.

**Boxers.** A secret society in China which took a prominent part in the rising against foreigners in 1900 which was suppressed by joint European action. The Chinese name was *Gee Ho Chuan*, signifying 'righteousness, harmony, and fists', and implying training as in athletics, for the purpose of developing righteousness and harmony.

**Boxing-Day.** *See* Christmas Box.

**Boy.** In a number of connections 'boy' has no reference to age. In India, the colonies, and America, for instance, a native or negro servant or labourer of whatever age is called a boy, and among sailors the word refers only to experience in seamanship. A crew is divided into able seamen, ordinary seamen, and boys or greenhorns. A 'boy' is not required to know anything about the practical working of the vessel, but an 'able seaman' must know all his duties and be able to perform them.

***Boy*** is a slang name for champagne; its origin is uncertain.

> He will say that port and sherry his nice palate always cloy;
> He'll nothing drink but 'B. and S'. and big magnums of 'the boy'. *Punch*, 1882

***Boy in Buttons.*** *See* Buttons.

**Boy Bishop.** St Nicholas of Bari was called 'the Boy Bishop' because from his cradle he manifested marvellous indications of piety; the custom of choosing a boy from the cathedral choir, etc., on his day (December 6th), as a mock bishop, is very ancient. The boy possessed episcopal honour for three weeks, and the rest of the choir were his prebendaries. If he died during his time of office he was buried *in pontificalibus*. Probably the reference is to Jesus Christ sitting in the Temple among the doctors while He was a boy. The custom was abolished in the reign of Henry VIII.

***Naked boy.*** *See* Naked.

**Boycott.** *To boycott a person* is to refuse to deal with him, to take any notice of him, or even to sell to him. The term arose in 1881, when Captain Boycott, an Irish landlord, was thus ostracised by the Irish agrarian insurgents.

> One word as to the way in which a man should be boycotted. When any man has taken a farm from which a tenant has been evicted, or is a grabber, let everyone in the parish turn his back on him; have no communication with him; have no dealings with him. You need never say an unkind word to him; but never say anything at all to him. If you must meet him in fair, walk away from him silently. Do him no violence, but have no dealings with him. Let every man's door be closed against him; and make him feel himself a stranger and a castaway in his own neighbourhood.
>
> J. Dillon, M.P. (*Speech to the Land League*, Feb. 26, 1881)

**Boyle Controversy.** A book-battle between Charles Boyle, fourth Earl of Orrery, and the famous Bentley, respecting the *Epistles of*

*Phalaris*, which were edited by Boyle in 1695. Two years later Bentley published his celebrated *Dissertation*, showing that the epistles (*see* Phalaris) were spurious, and in 1699 published another rejoinder, utterly annihilating the Boyle partisans. Swift's *Battle of the Books* (*q.v.*) was one result of the controversy.

**Boyle's Law.** The volume of a gas is inversely proportional to the pressure if the temperature remain constant. If we double the pressure on a gas, its volume is reduced to one-half; if we quadruple the pressure, it will be reduced to one-fourth; and so on; so called from the Hon. Robert Boyle (1627–91).

**Boyle Lectures.** A course of eight sermons on natural and revealed religion delivered annually at St Mary-le-Bow Church, London. They were instituted by the Hon. Robert Boyle, and began in 1692, the year after his death.

**Boz.** Charles Dickens (1812–70).

> Boz, my signature in the *Morning Chronicle*, he tells us, was the nickname of a pet child, a younger brother, whom I had dubbed Moses, in honour of the *Vicar of Wakefield*, which, being pronounced *Bozes*, got shortened into *Boz*.
>
> Who the dickens 'Boz' could be
> Puzzled many a learned elf;
> But time revealed the mystery,
> For 'Boz' appeared as Dickens' self.
>
> *Epigram in the Carthusian*

**Bozzy.** James Boswell, the biographer of Dr Johnson (1740–95).

**Brabançonne.** The national anthem of Belgium, composed by Van Campenhout in the revolution of 1830, and so named from Brabant, of which Brussels is the chief city.

> Qui l'aurait cru? de l'arbitraire,
> Consacrant les affreux projets …

**Braccata.** *See* Gens Braccata: Gallia.

**Brace of Shakes.** *See* Shakes.

**Brads.** Slang for money. *See* B Flats.

**Bradshaw's Guide** was started in 1839 by George Bradshaw, printer, in Manchester. The *Monthly Guide* was first issued in December, 1841, and consisted of thirty-two pages, giving tables of forty-three lines of English railway.

**Brag.** A game at cards; so called because the players brag of their cards to induce the company to make bets. The principal sport of the game is occasioned by any player *bragging* that he holds a better hand than the rest of the party, which is declared by saying 'I brag', and staking a sum of money on the issue. (*Hoyle*.)

***Brag is a good dog, but Holdfast is a better.*** Talking is all very well, but doing is far better.

> Trust none;
> For oaths are straws, men's faiths are wafer-cakes,
> And hold-fast is the only dog, my duck.
>
> Shakespeare, *Henry V*, 2, 3

***Jack Brag.*** A vulgar, pretentious braggart, who gets into aristocratic society, where his vulgarity stands out in strong relief. The character is in Theodore Hook's novel of the same name.

> He was a sort of literary Jack Brag.
>
> T. H. Burton

**Braggadochio.** A braggart; one who is valiant with his tongue but a great coward at heart *Cp.* Erythynus. The character is from Spenser's *Faerie Queene*, and a type of the 'Intemperance of the Tongue'. After a time, like the jackdaw in borrowed plumes, Braggadochio is stripped of all his glories: his shield is claimed by Sir Marinell; his lady is proved by the golden girdle to be the false Florimel; his horse is claimed by Sir Guyon; Talus shaves off his beard and scourges his squire; and the pretender sneaks off amidst the jeers of everyone. It is thought that the poet had the Duke d'Alençon, a suitor of Queen Elizabeth, in his eye when he drew this character (*Faerie Queene*, ii, 3; iii, 5, 8, 10; iv, 2, 4; v, 3; etc.).

**Bragi.** In *Scandinavian mythology* the son of Odin and Frigga, and the god of poetry; represented as an old man with a long white beard. His wife was Iduna.

***Bragi's apples*** were an instant cure of weariness, decay of power, ill temper, and failing health; the supply was inexhaustible, for immediately one was eaten another took its place.

***Bragi's cup.*** To each new king before he ascended the high-seat of his fathers Bragi's cup was handed, and he had to make a pledge by it and drain it.

***Bragi's story.*** Always enchanting, but never coming to an end.

> But I have made my story long enough; if I say more, you may fancy that it is Bragi who has come among you, and that he has entered on his endless story. Keary, *Heroes of Asgard*, p. 224

**Brahma.** In Hinduism Brahma, properly speaking, is the Absolute, or God conceived as entirely impersonal; this theological abstraction was later endowed with personality, and became the Creator of the universe, the first in the divine Triad, of which the other partners were Vishnu, the maintainer, and Siva (or Shiva), the destroyer. As such the Brahmins claim Brahma as the founder of their religious system.

> Whate'er in India holds the sacred name
> Of piety or lore, the Brahmins claim;
> In wildest rituals, vain and painful, lost,
> Brahma, their founder, as a god they boast.
>
> Camoens, *Lusiad*, Bk vii

**Brahmin.** A worshipper of Brahma, the highest caste in the system of Hinduism, and of the priestly order. *See* Caste.

**Brahmo Somaj** (Sanskrit, 'the Society of Believers in the One God'). A monotheistic sect of Brahmins, founded in 1818 in Calcutta by Ramohun Roy (1744–1833), a wealthy and well educated Brahmin who wished to purify his religion and found a National Church which should be free from idolatry and superstition. In 1844 the Church was reorganised by Debendro Nath Tagore, and since that time its reforming zeal and influence has gained it many adherents. In recent years the Brahmo Somaj has become more and more political, and it is now looked upon as one of the chief factors in the movement for complete nationalisation and autonomy.

**Brain-wave.** A sudden inspiration; what used to be called 'a happy thought'.

**Bran.** *If not Bran, it is Bran's brother.*

> 'Mare Bran, is e a brathair' (if it be not Bran, it is Bran's brother) was the proverbial reply of Maccombich. Scott, *Waverley*, ch. xlv

If not the real 'Simon Pure', it is just as good. A complimentary expression. Bran was Fingal's dog, a mighty favourite. *See also* Brennus.

**Bran-new** or **Brand-new** (A.S. *brand*, a torch). Fire new. Shakespeare, in *Love's Labour's Lost*, 1, 1, says, 'A man of fire-new words'. And again in *Twelfth Night*, 3, 2, 'Fire-new from the mint'; and again in *King Lear*, 5, 3, 'Fire-new fortune'; and again in *Richard III*, 1, 3, 'Your fire-new stamp of honour is scarce current'. Originally applied to metals and things manufactured in metal which shine. Subsequently applied generally to things quite new.

**Brand.** *The Clicquot brand*, etc., *the best brand*, etc. That is the merchant's or excise mark branded on the article itself, the vessel which contains the article, the wrapper which covers it, the cork of the bottle, etc., to guarantee its being genuine, etc.

***He has the brand of villain in his looks.*** It was once customary to brand convicted persons with a red-hot iron; thus, in the reign of William III child-stealers (*comprachios*) were branded with R (rogue) on the shoulders, M (manslayer) on the right hand, and T (thief) on the left; and felons were branded on the cheek with an F. The custom was abolished by law in 1822.

**Brandan, St,** or **Brendan.** A semi-legendary Irish saint, said to have died and been buried at Clonfert (at the age of about 94), in 577, where he was abbot over 3,000 monks.

He is best known on account of the very popular mediaeval story of his voyage in search of the Earthly Paradise, which was supposed to be situated on an island in mid-Atlantic. The voyage lasted for seven years, and the story is crowded with marvellous incidents, the very birds and beasts they encountered being Christians and observing the fasts and festivals of the Church!.

> And we came to the Isle of a Saint who had sailed with St Brendan of yore,
> He had lived ever since on the Isle and his winters were fifteen score.
>
> Tennyson, *Voyage of Maeldune*

**Brandenburg.** ***Confession of Brandenburg.*** A formulary or confession of faith drawn up in the city of Brandenburg in 1610, by order of the elector, with the view of reconciling the tenets of Luther with those of Calvin, and to put an end to the disputes occasioned by the Confession of Augsburg.

**Brandon.** An obsolete form of *brand*, a torch. *Dominica de brandonibus* (St Valentine's Day), when boys used to carry about brandons (Cupid's torches).

**Brandy.** ***Brandy is Latin for goose.*** Here is a pun on *anser*, a goose, and *answer*, to reply. What is the Latin for goose? Answer, brandy; because *anser* is the Latin for 'goose', which brandy followed as surely and quickly as an answer follows a question. The joke occurs in Swift's *Polite Conversation*, ii. *Cp.* Tace.

***Brandy Nan.*** Queen Anne, who was very fond of brandy. On her statue in St Paul's Churchyard a wit once wrote:

> Brandy Nan, Brandy Nan, left in the lurch,
> Her face to the gin-shop, her back to the church.

A 'gin palace' used to stand at the south corner of St Paul's Churchyard.

**Brank.** A Scotch word for a gag for scolds. It consisted of an iron framework fitting round the head, with a piece projecting inwards which went into the mouth and prevented the 'tongue-wagging'. One is preserved in the vestry of the church of Walton-on-Thames. It is dated 1633, and has the inscription:

> Chester presents Walton with a bridle
> To curb women's tongues that talk too idle.

**Brant-goose.** *See* Brent-goose.

**Brasenose** (Oxford). Over the gate is a brass nose, the arms of the college; but the word is a corruption of *brasenhuis*, a brasserie or brewhouse, the college having been built on the site of an ancient brewery. For over 550 years the original nose was at Stamford, for in the time of Edward III the students, in search of religious liberty, migrated thither, taking the brazen nose with them. They were soon recalled, but the nose remained on their Stamford gateway till 1890, when, the property coming into the market, it was acquired by the College.

**Brass.** Impudence, effrontery. A lawyer said to a troublesome witness, 'Why, man, you have brass enough in your head to make a teakettle'. 'And you, sir'. replied the witness, 'have water enough in yours to fill it'.

***Brass hats.*** Soldier slang for staff-officers. Like many similar phrases, it became widely popular during the Great War, but it was in army use many years earlier.

***The Man of Brass.*** Talus, the work of Vulcan. He traversed Crete to prevent strangers from setting foot on the island, threw rocks at the Argonauts to prevent their landing, and used to make himself red-hot, and then hug intruders to death.

> That portentous Man of Brass
> Hephaestos made in days of yore,
> Who stalked about the Cretan shore.
>
> Longfellow, *The Wayside Inn*

**Brat.** A child, especially in contempt. The origin of the word is unknown, but it may be from the Welsh *breth*, swaddling clothes, or Gaelic *brat*, an apron.

> O Israel! O household of the Lord!
> O Abraham's brats! O brood of blessed seed!
>
> Gascoigne, *De Profundis*

**Brave.** *The Brave.*

Alfonso IV of Portugal (1290, 1324–1357).

John Andr. van der Mersch, patriot, *The brave Fleming* (1734–92).

**Bravery.** Finery is the Fr. *braverie*. The French for courage is *bravoure*.

> What woman in the city do I name
> When that I say the city woman bears
> The cost of princes on unworthy shoulders?
> Who can come in and say that I mean her?
> Or what is he of basest function
> That says his bravery is not of my cost?
>
> Shakespeare, *As You Like It*, 2, 7

**Bravest of the Brave.** Marshal Ney (1769–1815). So called by the troops of Friedland (1807), on account of his fearless bravery. Napoleon said of him, 'That man is a lion'.

**Brawn.** *The test of the brawn's head.* A little boy one day came to the court of King Arthur, and, drawing his wand over a boar's head, declared, 'There's never a cuckold's knife can carve this head of brawn'. No knight in the court except Sir Cradock was able to accomplish the feat. (Percy's *Reliques*.)

**Bray.** *See* Vicar.

**Brazen Age.** The age of war and violence. It followed the silver age.

> To this next came in course the brazen age,
> A warlike offspring, prompt to bloody rage,
> Not impious yet. Hard steel succeeded then,
> And stubborn as the metal were the men.
>
> Dryden, *Metamorphoses*, i

**Brazen-faced.** Bold (in a bad sense), without shame.

> What a brazen-faced varlet art thou!
>
> Shakespeare, *King Lear*, 2, 2

**Brazen Head.** The legend of the wonderful head of brass that could speak and was omniscient is common property to early romances, and is of Eastern origin. In *Valentine and Orson*, for instance, we hear of a gigantic head kept in the castle of the giant Ferragus (*q.v.*), of Portugal. It told those who consulted it whatever they required to know, past, present, or to come; but the most famous in English legend is that fabled to have been made by the great Roger Bacon.

It was said if Bacon heard it speak he would succeed in his projects; if not, he would fail. His familiar, Miles, was set to watch, and while Bacon slept the Head spoke thrice: 'Time is'; half an hour later it said, 'Time was'. In another half-hour it said, 'Time's past'. fell down, and was broken to atoms. Byron refers to this legend.

> Like Friar Bacon's brazen head, I've spoken,
> 'Time is'. 'Time was'. 'Time's past'.
>
> *Don Juan*, i, 217

References to Bacon's Brazen Head are frequent in literature; among them may be mentioned:

> Bacon trembled for his brazen head.
>
> Pope, *Dunciad*, iii, 104

> Quoth he, 'My head's not made of brass,
> As Friar Bacon's noddle was'.
>
> Butler, *Hudibras*, ii, 2

*See also* Speaking Heads.

**Brazen out, To.** To stick to an assertion knowing it to be wrong; to outface in a shameless manner; to disregard public opinion.

**Breaches,** meaning *creeks* or *small bays*, is to be found in Judges 5:17. Deborah, complaining of the tribes who refused to assist her in her war with Sisera, says that Asher remained 'in his breaches', that is, creeks on the seashore.

Spenser uses the word in the same way:

> The heedful Boateman strongly forth did stretch
> His brawnie armes and, all his body straine,
> That th' utmost sandy breach they shortly fetch.
> *Faerie Queene*, II, xii, 21

In Coverdale's version of the Bible the passage is rendered:

> Asser sat in the haven of the see, and tarled in his porcions.

**Bread. *Cast thy bread upon the waters; for thou shalt find it after many days*** (Eccles. 11:1). When the Nile overflows its banks the weeds perish and the soil is disintegrated. The rice-seed being cast into the water takes root, and is found in due time growing in healthful vigour.

***Don't quarrel with your bread and butter.*** Don't foolishly give up the pursuit by which you earn your living.

***To break bread.*** To partake of food. Common in Scripture language.

> Upon the first day of the week, when the disciples came together to break bread, Paul preached to them. Acts 20:7

***Breaking of bread.*** The Eucharist.

> They continued … in breaking of bread, and in prayer. Acts 2:42 and 46

***He took bread and salt,*** i.e. he took his oath. In Eastern lands bread and salt were formerly eaten when an oath was taken.

> They have looked each other between the eyes, and there they have found no fault,
> They have taken the Oath of the Brother-in-Blood on leavened bread and salt.
> Kipling, *Ballad of East and West*

***To know which side one's bread is buttered.*** To be mindful of one's own interest.

***To take the bread out of one's mouth.*** To forestall another; to say something which another was on the point of saying; to take away another's livelihood.

**Breadalbane.** *See* Albany.

**Bread-basket.** The stomach.

**Bread and Cheese.** The barest necessities of life.

**Break of Day.** Daybreak.

> At break of day I will come to thee again.
> Wordsworth, *Pet Lamb*, stanza 15

**Break, To.** To become bankrupt (*q.v.*).

***To break a bond.*** To dishonour it.

***To break a butterfly on a wheel.*** To employ superabundant effort in the accomplishment of a small matter.

> Satire or sense, alas! can Sporus feel,
> Who breaks a butterfly upon a wheel.
> Pope, *Epistle to Dr Arbuthnot*, 307–8

***To break a journey.*** To stop before the journey is accomplished, with the intention of completing it later.

***To break a matter to a person.*** To be the first to impart it, and to do so cautiously and by piecemeal.

***To break bread.*** *See* Bread.

***To break cover.*** To start forth from a hiding-place.

***To break down.*** To lose all control of one's feelings; to collapse, to become hysterical. A *break-down* is a temporary collapse in health; it is also the name given to a wild kind of negro dance.

***To break faith.*** To violate one's word or pledge; to act traitorously.

***To break ground.*** To commence a new project. As a settler does.

***To break in.*** To interpose a remark. To train a horse to the saddle or to harness, or to train any animal or person to a desired way of life.

***To break one's fast.*** To take food after long abstinence; to eat one's breakfast after the night's fast.

***To break one's neck.*** To dislocate the bones of one's neck.

***To break on the wheel.*** To torture on a 'wheel' by breaking the long bones with an iron bar. *Cp.* Coup de Grâce.

***To break out of bounds.*** To go beyond the prescribed limits.

***To break the ice.*** To prepare the way; to cause the stiffness and reserve of intercourse with a stranger to relax; to impart to another bit by bit distressing news or a delicate subject.

***To break your back.*** To make you bankrupt; to reduce you to a state of impotence. The metaphor is from carrying burdens on the back.

***To break up.*** To discontinue classes at the end of term time and go home; to separate. Also, to become rapidly decrepit or infirm. 'Old So-and-so is breaking up; he's not long for this world'.

***To break up housekeeping.*** To discontinue keeping a separate house.

***To break with one.*** To cease from intercourse.

> What cause have I given him to break with me?
> Florence Marryat

**Breakers Ahead.** Hidden danger at hand. Breakers in the open sea always announce sunken rocks, sandbanks, etc.

**Breaking a Stick.** Part of the marriage ceremony of certain North American Indians, as breaking a wineglass is part of the marriage ceremony of the Jews.

In one of Raphael's pictures we see an unsuccessful suitor of the Virgin Mary breaking his stick. This alludes to the legend that the several suitors were each to bring an almond stick, which was to be laid up in the sanctuary over-night, and the owner of the stick which budded was to be accounted the suitor which God approved of. It was thus that Joseph became the husband of Mary.

In Florence is a picture in which the rejected suitors break their sticks on Joseph's back.

**Breast.** *To make a clean breast of it.* To make a full confession; concealing nothing.

**Breath.** ***All in a breath.*** Without taking breath (Lat. *continenti spiritu*).

***It takes one's breath away.*** The news is so astounding it causes one to hold his breath with surprise.

***Out of breath.*** Panting from exertion; temporarily short of breath.

***Save your breath to cool your porridge.*** Don't talk to me, it is only wasting your breath.

> You might have saved your breath to cool your porridge.
>
> Mrs Gaskell, *Libbie Marsh* (Era 111)

***To catch one's breath.*** To check suddenly the free act of breathing.

> 'I see her'. replied I, catching my breath with joy.
>
> Capt. Marryat, *Peter Simple*

***To hold one's breath.*** Voluntarily to cease breathing for a time.

***To take breath.*** To cease for a little time from some exertion in order to recover from exhaustion of breath.

***Under one's breath.*** In a whisper or undertone of voice.

**Breathe.** ***To breathe one's last.*** To die.

**Brèche de Roland.** A deep defile in the crest of the Pyrenees, some three hundred feet in width, between two precipitous rocks. The legend is that Roland, the paladin, cleft the rock in two with his sword Durandal, when he was set upon by the Gascons at Roncesvalles.

> Then would I seek the Pyrenean Breach
> Which Roland clove with huge two-handed sway.
>
> Wordsworth, *Aix-la-Chapelle*

**Breeches.** ***To wear the breeches.*** Said of a woman who usurps the prerogative of her husband. Similar to *The grey mare is the better horse*. *See* Grey.

The phrase is common to the French, Dutch, Germans, etc., as *Elle porte les braies. Die vrouw die hosen anhaben. Sie hat die Hosen.*

**Breeches Bible, The.** *See* Bible, specially named.

**Breeze,** meaning a light gale or strongish wind (and, figuratively, a slight quarrel) is from the Fr. *brise*, and Span. *brisa*, the north-east wind. *Breeze*, the small ashes and cinders used in burning bricks, is the Fr. *braise*, older form *brese*, meaning glowing embers, or burning charcoal, and is connected with Swed. *brasa*, fire, and our *brazier*. *Breeze* in *breeze-fly*, a name of the gadfly, is A.S. *briosa*. So the three words, *breeze*, are in no way connected.

***The breeze-fly.*** The gad-fly; so called from its sting (A.S. *briosa*; Gothic, *bry*, a sting).

**Breezy.** A breezy person is one who is open, jovial, perhaps inclined to be a little boisterous.

**Breidablik** (*wide-shining*). The palace of Baldur, which stood in the Milky Way. (*Scandinavian mythology*.)

**Brendan, St** *See* Brandan.

**Brennus.** The name of the Gaulish chief who over-ran Italy and captured Rome about 390 BC is the Latin form of the Celtic word *Brenhin*, king or war-chief. *Bran*, a name of frequent occurrence in Welsh history, is the same word.

**Brent.** Without a wrinkle. Burns says of Jo Anderson, in his prime of life, his 'locks were like the raven', and his 'bonnie brow was brent'.

***Brent-hill*** means the eyebrows. *Looking* or *gazing from under brent-hill*, in Devonshire means 'frowning at one'; and in West Cornwall *to brend* means to wrinkle the brows.

**Brent-goose.** Formerly in England, and still in America, called properly a *brant-goose*, the *branta bernicla*, a brownish-grey goose of the genus *branta*.

> For the people of the village
> Saw the flock of brant with wonder.
>
> Longfellow, *Hiawatha*, pt xvi, stanza 32

**Brentford.** *Like the two kings of Brentford smelling at one nosegay*. Said of persons who were once rivals, but have become reconciled. The allusion is to *The Rehearsal* (1672), by the Duke of Buckingham. 'The two kings of Brentford enter hand in hand'. and the actors, to heighten the absurdity, used to make them enter 'smelling at one nosegay' (act ii, s. 2)

**Bressummer,** or *Breast-summer* (Fr. *sommier*, a lintel or bressummer). A beam supporting the whole weight of the building above it; as, the beam over a shop-front, the beam extending over an opening through a wall when a communication between two contiguous rooms is required; but properly applied only to a bearing beam in the face of a building. *Summer*, here, is the O.Fr. *somier*, for Lat. *sagmarius* (late Lat. *saumarius*), a packhorse, also a beam on which a weight can be laid.

**Bretwalda.** The name given to Egbert and certain other early English kings who exercised a supremacy – often rather shadowy – over the kings of the other English states. *See* Heptarchy. It means 'ruler' or 'overlord of the Brets' or 'Britons'.

> The office of Bretwalda, a kind of elective chieftainship, of all Britain, was held by several Northumbrian kings, in succession.
>
> Earle, *English Tongue*, p. 26

**Brevet Rank.** Titular rank without the pay that usually goes with it. A brevet major has the title of major, but the pay of captain, or whatever his *substantive* rank happens to be. (Fr. *brevet*, dim. of *bref*, a letter, a document.)

**Breviary.** A book containing the daily 'Divine Office', which those in orders in the Roman Catholic Church are bound to recite. The Office consists of psalms, collects, readings from Scripture, and the life of some saint or saints.

**Brew.** *Brew me a glass of grog*, i.e. mix one for me. *Brew me a cup of tea*, i.e. make one for me. *The tea is set to brew*, i.e. to draw. The general meaning of the word is to boil or mix; the restricted meaning is to make malt liquor.

***As you brew, so you will bake.*** As you begin, so you will go on; you must take the consequences of your actions; as you make your bed, so you will lie in it.

> *Nick*: Boy, have they appointed to fight?
> *Boy*: Ay, Nicholas; wilt not thou go see the fray?
> *Nick*: No, indeed; even as they brew, so let them bake. I will not thrust my hand into the flame, an I need not ... they that strike with the sword shall be beaten with the scabbard.
>
> Porter, *Two Angry Women of Abington* (1599)

**Brewer.** *The Brewer of Ghent.* Jakob van Artevelde (d.1345); a popular Flemish leader who, though by birth an aristocrat, was a member of the Guild of Brewers.

**Briareus,** or **Aegeon.** A giant with fifty heads and a hundred hands. Homer says the gods called him Briareus, but men called him Aegeon (*Iliad*, i, 403). He was the offspring of Heaven and Earth and was of the race of the Titans, with whom he fought in the war against Zeus.

> He [Ajax] hath the joints of everything, but everything so out of joint that he is a gouty Briareus, many hands and no use, or purblind Argus, all eyes and no sight.
>
> Shakespeare, *Troilus and Cressida*, 1, 2

***The Briareus of languages.*** Cardinal Mezzofanti (1774–1849), who knew fifty-eight different tongues. Byron called him 'a walking polyglot; a monster of languages; a Briareus of parts of speech'.

***Bold Briareus.*** Handel (1685–1759), so called by Pope:

> Strong in new arms, lo! giant Handel stands,
> Like bold Briareus, with a hundred hands;
> To stir, to rouse, to shake the soul he comes,
> And Jove's own thunders follow Mars's drums.
>
> Pope, *Dunciad*, iv, 65

**Briar-root Pipe.** A tobacco-pipe made from the root-wood of the large heath (*bruyère*), which grows in the south of France.

**Briboci.** Inhabitants of part of Berkshire and the adjacent counties referred to by Caesar in his *Commentaries*.

**Bric-à-brac.** Odds and ends of curiosities. In French, a *marchand de bric-à-brac* is a seller of rubbish, as old nails, old screws, old hinges, and other odds and ends of small value; but we employ the phrase for odds and ends of vertu. *Bricoler* in archaic French means *Faire toute espèce de metier*, to be Jack of all trades. *Brac* is the ricochet of *bric*, as fiddle-faddle and scores of other double words in English. Littré says that it is formed on the model of *de bric et de broc*, by hook or by crook.

> A man with a passion for bric-a-brac is always stumbling over antique bronzes, intaglios, mosaics, and daggers of the time of Benvenuto Cellini. Aldrich, *Miss Mehetable's Son*, ch. ii

**Brick.** ***A regular brick.*** A jolly good fellow; perhaps because a brick is solid, four-square, plain, and reliable.

> A fellow like nobody else, and, in fine, a brick.
>
> George Eliot, *Daniel Deronda*, Bk ii, ch. 16

***To make bricks without straw.*** To attempt to do something without having the necessary material supplied. The allusion is to the Israelites in Egypt, who were commanded by their taskmasters so to do (Ex. 5:7).

**Brick-and-mortar Franchise.** A Chartist phrase for the £10 household system, long since abolished.

**Brickdusts.** The 53rd Foot; so called from the brickdust-red colour of their facings. Also called *Five-and-thre'pennies*, a play on the number and the old rate of daily pay of the ensigns or subalterns.

Now called the 1st battalion of the 'King's Shropshire Light Infantry'. The 2nd battalion is the old 85th.

**Brick Tea.** The inferior leaves of the tea-plant mixed with a glutinous substance (sometimes bullock's or sheep's blood), pressed into cubes, and dried. These blocks used to be made in Central Asia and Mongolia for import into Russia, and were frequently used as a medium of exchange.

**Bride.** *The bridal wreath* is a relic of the *corona nuptialis* used by the Greeks and Romans to indicate triumph.

**Bride-ale.** *See* Church-ale. It is from this word that we get the adjective *bridal*.

**Bride Cake.** A relic of the Roman *confarreatio*, a mode of marriage practised by the highest class in Rome. It was performed before ten witnesses by the Pontifex Maximus, and the contracting parties mutually partook of a cake made of salt, water, and flour (*far*). Only those born in such wedlock were eligible for the high sacred offices.

**Bride** or **Wedding Favours** represent the *true lover's knot*, and symbolise union.

**Bride of the Sea.** Venice; so called from the ancient ceremony of the wedding of the sea by the doge, who threw a ring into the Adriatic, saying, 'We wed thee, O sea, in token of perpetual domination'. This took place each year on Ascension Day, and was enjoined upon the Venetians in 1177 by Pope Alexander III, who gave the doge a gold ring from his own finger in token of the victory achieved by the Venetian fleet at Istria over Frederick Barbarossa, in defence of the pope's quarrel. At the same time his Holiness desired that the doges should throw a similar one into the sea on each succeeding Ascension Day, in commemoration of the event. *See* Bucentaur.

> What, they lived once thus at Venice where the merchants were the kings,
> Where St Mark's is, where the Doges used to wed the sea with rings?
>
> Browning, *A Toccata of Galuppi's*

**Bridegroom.** In O.E. this word was *bridegome* (A.S. *bryd-guma*), from Gothic *guma*, a man. In M.E. times the *-gome* became corrupted into *grome*, and owing to this confusion and the long loss of the archaic *guma*, the word became connected with *grom*, or *grome*, a lad (which gives our *groom*), and hence the modern *bridegroom*.

**Bridegroom's Men.** In the Roman marriage by *confarreatio*, the bride was led to the Pontifex Maximus by bachelors, but was conducted home by married men. Polydore Virgil says that a married man preceded the bride on her return, bearing a vessel of gold and silver. *See* Bride Cake.

**Bridewell.** A generic term for a house of correction, or prison, so called from the City Bridewell, Bridge Street, Blackfriars, which was built as a hospital on the site of a former royal palace over a holy well of medical water, called St Bride's (Bridget's) Well. After the Reformation, Edward VI chartered this hospital to the City. Christ Church (Christ's Hospital) was given to the education of the young; St Thomas's Hospital to the cure of the sick; and Bridewell was made a penitentiary for unruly apprentices and vagrants. Most of it was demolished in 1863.

**Bridge.** A variety of whist, said to have originated in Russia, in which one of the hands ('dummy') is exposed. *Auction bridge* is a modification of bridge, in which there are greater opportunities for gambling.

**Bridge of Gold.** According to a German tradition, Charlemagne's spirit crosses the Rhine on a golden bridge at Bingen, in seasons of plenty, to bless the vineyards and cornfields.

> Thou standest, like imperial Charlemagne,
> Upon thy bridge of gold. Longfellow, *Autumn*

***Made a bridge of gold for him,*** i.e. enabling a man to retreat from a false position without loss of dignity.

**Bridge of Jehennam.** Another name for Al Sirat (*q.v.*).

**Bridge of Sighs.** Over this bridge, which connects the palace of the doge with the state prisons of Venice, prisoners were conveyed from the judgment-hall to the place of execution.

> I stood in Venice on the Bridge of Sighs,
> A palace and a prison on each hand.
>
> Byron, *Childe Harold's Pilgrimage*, iv, 1

Waterloo Bridge, in London, used, some years ago, when suicides were frequent there, to be called *The Bridge of Sighs*, and Hood gave the name to one of his most pathetic poems:

> One more Unfortunate,
> Weary of breath,
> Rashly importunate,
> Gone to her death!

**Bridgewater Treatises.** Instituted by the Rev. Francis Henry Egerton, Earl of Bridgewater, in 1829. He left the interest of £8,000 to be given to the author of the best treatise on 'The power, wisdom, and goodness of God, as manifested in the Creation'. The money was divided between the following eight authors: Dr Chalmers, Dr John Kidd, Dr Whewell, Sir Charles Bell, Dr Peter M. Roget, Dean Buckland, the Rev W. Kirby, and Dr William Prout.

**Bridle.** ***To bite on the bridle*** is to suffer great hardships. Horses bite on the bridle when trying, against odds, to get their own way.

***Bridle road*** or ***way.*** A way for a riding-horse, but not for a horse and cart.

***To bridle up.*** In Fr. *se rengorger*, to draw in the chin and toss the head back in scorn or pride. The metaphor is to a horse pulled up suddenly and sharply.

**Bridport.** ***Stabbed with a Bridport dagger***, i.e. hanged. Bridport, in Dorsetshire, was once famous for its hempen goods, and monopolised the manufacture of ropes, cables, and tackling for the British navy. The hangman's rope being made at Bridport gave birth to the proverb. (Fuller, *Worthies.*)

**Brief.** In legal parlance, a summary of the relevant facts and points of law given to a counsel in charge of a case. Hence, a *briefless barrister*, a barrister with no briefs, and therefore no clients.

***Brief*** is also the name given to a papal letter of less serious or important character than a bull (*q.v.*); and, in the paper trade, to foolscap ruled with a marginal line, and either thirty-six or forty-two transverse lines, also to the size of a foolscap sheet when folded in half.

**Brig.** *See* Brigandine.

**Brigador.** *See* Guyon, Sir.

**Brigand.** A French word, from the Ital. *brigante*, pres. part. of *brigare*, to quarrel. In England *brigands* were originally light-armed, irregular troops, like the Bashi-Bazouks, and, like them, were addicted to marauding. The *Free Companies* of France were brigands.

**Brigandine.** The armour of a brigand, consisting of small plates of iron on quilted linen, and covered with leather, hemp, or something of the kind. The word occurs twice in Jeremiah (46:4; 51:3), and in both of these passages the Revised Version reads 'coats of mail', while for the first Coverdale gives 'breastplates'. In the Geneva Version Goliath's coat of mail is called a 'brigandine'.

In course of time the Ital. *brigante* came to mean a robber or pirate; hence the use of *brigandine*, later *brigantine*, for a light pinnace; and hence the modern word *brig*, a square-rigged vessel with two masts.

**Bright's Disease.** A degeneration of the tissues of the kidneys into fat, first investigated by Dr Bright (1789–1858). The patient under this disease has a flabby, bloodless appearance, is always drowsy, and easily fatigued.

**Brigians.** The Castilians; so called from their mythical king, Brix or Brigus, said by monkish fabulists to be the grandson of Noah.

> Edward and Pedro, emulous of fame …
> Thro' the fierce Brigians hewed their bloody way,
> Till in a cold embrace the striplings lay.
>
> Camoens, *Lusiad*, v

**Brilliant Madman, The.** Charles XII of Sweden. (1682, 1697–1718.)

> Macedonia's madman or the Swede.
>
> Johnson, *Vanity of Human Wishes*

**Bring.** ***To bring about.*** To cause a thing to be done.

***To bring down the house.*** To cause rapturous applause in a theatre.

***To bring into play.*** To cause to act, to set in motion.

***To bring round.*** To restore to consciousness or health; to cause one to recover (from a fit, etc.).

***To bring to.*** To restore to consciousness; to resuscitate. Many other meanings.

> 'I'll bring her to'. said the driver, with a brutal grin; 'I'll give her something better than camphor'. Mrs Stowe, *Uncle Tom's Cabin*

***To bring to bear.*** To cause to happen successfully.

***To bring to book.*** To detect one in a mistake.

***To bring to pass.*** To cause to happen.

***To bring to the hammer.*** To offer or sell by public auction.

***To bring under.*** To bring into subjection.

***To bring up.*** To rear from birth or an early age. Also numerous other meanings.

**Briny.** ***I'm on the briny***. The sea, which is salt like brine.

**Brioche.** A kind of sponge-cake made with flour, butter, and eggs. When Marie Antoinette was talking about the bread riots of Paris during October 5th and 6th, 1789, the Duchesse de Polignac naïvely exclaimed, 'How is it that these silly people are so clamorous for *bread*, when they can buy such nice brioches for a few sous?' It is said that our own Princess Charlotte avowed 'that she would for her part *rather eat beef than starve*'. and wondered that the people should be so obstinate as to insist upon having bread when it was so scarce.

**Briseis.** The patronymic name of Hippodamia, daughter of Briseus. She was the cause of the quarrel between Agamemnon and Achilles, and when the former robbed Achilles of her, Achilles refused any longer to go to battle, and the Greeks lost ground daily. Ultimately, Achilles sent his friend Patroclus to supply his place; he was slain, and Achilles, towering with rage, rushed to battle, slew Hector, and Troy fell.

**Brisingamen.** *In Scandinavian mythology*, the magic necklace made by four dwarfs and obtained by Freyja, wife of Odin, as payment for her submission to the will of the dwarfs and her infidelity to her husband.

**Brissotins.** A nickname given to the advocates of reform in the French Revolution, because they were 'led by the nose' by Jean Pierre Brissot. The party was subsequently called the Girondists (*q.v.*).

**Bristol Board.** A stiff drawing-paper with a smooth surface, or a fine quality of cardboard composed of two or more sheets pasted together, the substance of board being governed by the number of sheets. Said to have been first made at Bristol.

**Bristol Boy, The.** Thomas Chatterton (1752–70), who was born at Bristol, and there composed his *Rowley Poems*. *See* Rowley.

> The marvellous boy,
> The sleepless soul that perished in his pride.
> Wordsworth, *Resolution and Independence*

**Bristol Diamonds.** Brilliant crystals of colourless quartz found in St Vincent's Rock, Clifton, near Bristol.

Spenser refers to them as 'adamants':

> But Avon marched in more stately path,
> Proud of his Adamants, with which he shines
> And glisters wide, as als of wondrous Bath,
> And Bristowe faire. *Faerie Queene*, IV, xi, 31

**Bristol Fashion, In.** Methodical and orderly. More generally *Shipshape and Bristol fashion.* A sailor's phrase; said in Smyth's *Sailor's Word Book* to refer to the time 'when Bristol was in its palmy commercial days ... and its shipping was all in proper good order'.

**Bristol Milk.** Sherry sack, at one time given by the Bristol people to their friends.

> This metaphorical milk, whereby Xeres or
> Sherrysack is intended. Fuller, *Worthies*

**Bristol Waters.** Mineral waters of Clifton, near Bristol, with a temperature not exceeding 74°; formerly celebrated in cases of pulmonary consumption. They are very rarely used now.

**Britain.** The derivation of this word is not certainly known, but its first recorded use is by the Greeks, who probably obtained it through the Greek colony at Massilia (Marseilles). According to Isaac Taylor it

> is derived from that family of languages of which the Lapp and Basque are the sole living representatives; and hence, we reasonably infer the earliest knowledge of the island, which was possessed by any of the civilised inhabitants of Europe, must have been derived from the Iberic mariners of Spain, who ... coasted along to Brittany, and thence crossed to Britain, at some dim prehistoric period.
> *Words and Places*, ch. iv

***Itan,*** or ***etan,*** in Basque signifies a district or country; the root appears in many names, e.g. Aqu*itan*ia, Lus*itan*ia, Maur*etan*ia.

Another suggestion is that it is from the Cymric-Celtic root, *brith*, meaning 'to paint'. with allusion to woad-painting of their bodies by the aborigines.

***Great Britain*** consists of 'Britannia prima' (England), 'Britannia secunda' (Wales), and 'North Britain' (Scotland), united under one sway. The term first came into use in 1604, when James I was proclaimed 'King of Great Britain'.

***Greater Britain.*** The whole British Empire, i.e. Great Britain and the Colonies. India is not generally comprised in the term, which seems to have become popular through a book of travels in English-speaking countries published with this title by (Sir) Charles Dilke in 1868.

**Britannia.** The first known representation of Britannia as a female figure sitting on a globe, leaning with one arm on a shield, and grasping a spear in the other hand, is on a Roman coin of Antoninus Pius, who died AD 161. The figure reappeared on our copper coin in the reign of Charles II, 1665, and the model was Miss Stewart, afterwards created Duchess of Richmond. The engraver was Philip Roetier, 1665.

> The King's new medall, where, in little, there is Mrs Stewart's face, ... and a pretty thing it is, that he should choose her face to represent Britannia by. *Pepys' Diary*

**British Lion, The.** The pugnacity of the British nation, as opposed to the *John Bull*, which symbolises the substantiality, solidity, and obstinacy of the people, with all their prejudices and national peculiarities.

***To rouse the British lion*** is to flourish a red flag in the face of John Bull; to provoke him to resistance even to the point of war.

***To twist the tail of the British lion*** used to be a favourite phrase in America for attempting to annoy the British people and government by abuse and vituperation. This was usually resorted to with the object of currying favour with citizens of Irish birth and getting their votes.

**Britomart.** In Spenser's *Faerie Queene*, a female knight, daughter of King Ryence of Wales. She is the impersonation of chastity and purity; encounters the 'savage, fierce bandit and mountaineer' without injury, and is assailed by 'hag and unlaid ghost, goblin, and swart fairy of the mine', but 'dashes their brute violence into sudden adoration and blank awe'. She finally marries Artegall.

> She charmed at once and tamed the heart,
> Incomparable Britomart. Scott

Spenser got the name, which means 'sweet maiden', from Britomartis, a Cretan nymph of *Greek mythology*, who was very fond of the chase. King Minos fell in love with her, and persisted in his advances for nine months, when she threw herself into the sea.

**Briton.** ***To fight like a Briton*** is to fight with indomitable courage.

***To work like a Briton*** is to work hard and perseveringly.

Certainly, without the slightest flattery, dogged courage and perseverance are the strong characteristics of John Bull. A similar phrase is 'To fight like a Trojan'.

**Brittany, The Damsel of.** Eleanor, daughter of Geoffrey, second son of Henry II of England, and Constance, daughter of Conan IV of Brittany. At the death of Prince Arthur (1203) she was heir to the English throne, but John confined her in Bristol castle, where she died in 1241.

**Broach.** *To broach a new subject.* To start one in conversation. The allusion is to beer barrels, which are tapped by means of a peg called a *broach*. So 'to broach a subject' is to introduce it, to bring it to light, as beer is drawn from the cask after the latter has been *broached*.

> I did broach this business to your highness.
> Shakespeare, *Henry VIII*, 2, 4

**Broad Arrow.** The representation of an arrowhead placed on Government stores by the Board of Ordnance. It was the cognizance of Henry, Viscount Sydney, Earl of Romney, master-general of the ordnance, 1693–1702.

**Broad as long.** *'Tis about as broad as it is long.* One way or the other would bring about the same result.

**Broad Bottom Ministry.** An administration formed by a coalition of parties in 1744. Pelham retained the lead; Pitt supported the Government; Bubb Doddington was treasurer of the navy. It held office till 1754.

**Broadcloth.** The best cloth for men's clothes. So called from its great breadth. It required two weavers, side by side, to fling the shuttle across it. Originally two yards wide, now about fifty-four inches; but the word is now used to signify a fine, plain-wove, black cloth.

> An honest man, close-button'd to the chin,
> Broadcloth without, and a warm heart within.
> Cowper, *Epistle to Joseph Hill*

**Broadside.** A large sheet of paper printed on one side only; strictly, the whole should be in one type and one measure, i.e. must not be divided into columns. It is also called a *broadsheet*.

> Pamphlets and broadsides were scattered right and left. Fiske, *American History*, ch. vii, p. 341

In naval language, a *broadside* means the whole side of a ship; and to 'open a broadside on the enemy' is to discharge all the guns on one side at the same moment.

**Brobdingnag.** In Swift's *Gulliver's Travels*, the country of gigantic giants, to whom Gulliver was a pigmy 'not half so big as a round little worm plucked from the lazy finger of a maid'. Hence the adjective, *Brobdingnagian*, colossal, gigantic.

> You high church steeple, you gawky stag,
> Your husband must come from Brobdingnag.
> Kane O'Hara, *Midas*

**Brocken.** *See* Spectre.

**Brogue.** An Irish word, *brog*, a shoe, connected with A.S. *broc*, breeches, and hence with *breeches*. A *brogue* is, properly, a stout, coarse shoe of rough hide; and secondarily hose, trousers. The use of *brogue* for the dialect or manner of speaking may be from this – i.e. 'brogue' is the speech of those who wear 'brogues'; but it is by no means certain.

**Broken Music.** In Elizabethan England this term meant (*a*) part, or concerted music, i.e. music performed on instruments of different classes, such as the 'consorts' given in Morley's *Consort Lessons* (1599), which are written for the treble lute, cithern, pandora, flute, treble viol, and bass viol, and (*b*) music played by a string orchestra, the term in this sense probably originating from harps, lutes, and such other stringed instruments as were played without a bow, not being able to sustain a long note. It is in this sense that Bacon uses the term:

> Dancing to song is a thing of great state and pleasure. I understand it that the song be in quire, placed aloft and accompanied with some broken music.
> Essays, *Of Masques and Triumphs*

Shakespeare two or three times makes verbal play with the term:

*Pand.*: What music is this?
*Serv.*: I do but partly know, sir; it is music in parts . . .
*Pand.*: . . . Fair Prince, here is good broken music.
*Paris*: You have broke it, cousin; and by my life, you shall make it whole again.

*Troilus and Cressida*, 3, 1

**Broken on the Wheel.** *See* Break.

**Broker.** *Broaches* wine, one who draws it from the cask and sells it; hence, one who buys to sell again, a retailer, a second-hand dealer, a middleman. The word is formed in the same way as *tapster*, one who *taps* a cask. In modern use some restricting word is generally prefixed: as bill-broker, cotton-broker, ship-broker, stock-broker, etc.

**Brontes.** A blacksmith personified; in *Greek mythology*, one of the Cyclops. The name signifies *Thunder*.

Not with such weight, to frame the forky brand,
The ponderous hammer falls from Brontes' hand.

Hoole, *Jerusalem Delivered*, Bk xx

**Bronzomarte.** *See* Horse.

**Brooks of Sheffield.** An imaginary individual mentioned in *David Copperfield* to put little David off the scent that he was being referred to:

'Quinnion', said Mr Murdstone, 'take care, if you please. Somebody's sharp'.
'Who is?' asked the gentleman, laughing.
I looked up quickly; being curious to know.
'Only Brooks of Sheffield'. said Mr Murdstone.
I was quite relieved to find it was only Brooks of Sheffield; for, at first, I really thought it was I.

Ch. ii

*Cp.* Harris, Mrs.

**Broom.** A broom is hung at the masthead of ships about to be sold – to be 'swept away'. The idea is popularly taken from Admiral van Tromp (*see* Pennant); but probably this allusion is more witty than true. The custom of hanging up something special to attract notice is very common; thus an old piece of carpet from a window indicates household furniture for sale; a wisp of straw indicates oysters for sale; a bush means wine for sale, etc. etc.

***New brooms sweep clean.*** Those newly appointed to an office find fault and want to sweep away old customs.

**Brosier.** An Eton term for a boy who has spent all his pocket-money.

***Brosier-my-dame.*** A phrase used at Eton for eating one out of house and home. When a dame keeps an unusually bad table, the boys agree together on a day to eat, pocket, or waste everything eatable in the house. The censure is well understood, and the hint is generally effective. (Gr. *broso*, to eat.)

**Brother.** A fellow-member of a religious order. *Friar*, from Lat. *frater*, and Fr. *frère*, is really the same word.

Also used as the official title of certain members of livery companies, of the members (always known as 'Elder Brethren') of Trinity House (*q.v.*), and the official mode of address of one barrister to another.

***Brother*** used attributively with another substantive denotes a fellow-member of the same calling, order, corporation, etc. Thus *brother birch*, a fellow-schoolmaster, *brother-blade*, a fellow-soldier or companion in arms, *brother bung*, a fellow licensed victualler, *brother mason*, a fellow freemason, etc. etc.

**Brother Jonathan.** When Washington was in want of ammunition, he called a council of officers, but no practical suggestion could be offered. 'We must consult brother Jonathan'. said the general, meaning His Excellency Jonathan Trumbull, governor of the State of Connecticut. This was done, and the difficulty was remedied. 'To consult Brother Jonathan' then became a set phrase, and Brother Jonathan became the 'John Bull' of the United States.

**Brother Sam.** The brother of Lord Dundreary (*q.v.*), the hero of a comedy based on a German drama, by John Oxenford, with additions and alterations by E. A. Sothern and T. B. Buckstone.

**Browbeat.** To beat or put a man down with sternness, arrogance, insolence, etc.; from knitting the brows and frowning on one's opponent.

**Brown.** A copper coin, a penny; so called from its colour. Similarly a sovereign is a 'yellow boy'.

***To be done brown.*** To be deceived, taken in; to be 'roasted'. This is one of many similar expressions connected with cooking. *See* Cooking.

**Brown Bess.** A familiar name for the old flintlock musket formerly in use in the British Army. In 1808 a process of browning was introduced, but the term was common long before this, and probably referred to the colour of the stock. *Bess* is unexplained; but may be a kind of counterpart to *Bill* (*see below*).

**Brown Bill.** A kind of halbert used by English foot-soldiers before muskets were employed. They were staff weapons, with heads like billhooks but furnished with spikes at the top and back. The *brown* probably refers to the rusty condition in which they were kept; though, on the other hand, it may stand for *burnished* (Dut. *brun*, shining), as in the old phrases 'my bonnie brown sword', 'brown as glass', etc. Keeping the weapons *bright*, however, is a modern fashion; our forefathers preferred the honour of blood stains. In the following extract the term denotes the soldiers themselves:

> Lo, with a band of bowmen and of pikes,
> Brown bills and targetiers.
>
> Marlowe, *Edward II*, 1, 1324

**Brown, Jones, and Robinson.** The typification of middle-class Englishmen; from the adventures of three Continental tourists of these names which were told and illustrated in *Punch* in the 1870's by Richard Doyle. They hold up to ridicule the gaucherie, insular ideas, vulgarity, extravagance, conceit, and snobbism that too often characterise the class.

**Brown Study.** Absence of mind; apparent thought, but real vacuity. The corresponding French expression explains it – *sombre réverie*. *Sombre* and *brun* both mean sad, melancholy, gloomy, dull.

> Invention flags, his brain grows muddy,
> And black despair succeeds brown study.
>
> Congreve, *An Impossible Thing*

**Brownie.** The house spirit in Scottish superstition. He is called in England *Robin Goodfellow*. At night he is supposed to busy himself in doing little jobs for the family over which he presides. Farms are his favourite abode. Brownies are brown or tawny spirits, in opposition to fairies, which are fair or elegant ones. *See* Fairies.

> It is not long since every family of considerable substance was haunted by a spirit they called Browny, which did several sorts of work; and this was the reason why they gave him offerings … on what they called 'Browny's stone'.
>
> Martin, *Scotland*

**Brownists.** Followers of Robert Brown, of Rutlandshire, a vigorous Puritan controversialist in the time of Queen Elizabeth. The later 'Independents' held pretty well the same religious tenets as the Brownists. Sir Andrew Aguecheek says:

> I'd as lief be a Brownist as a politician.
>
> Shakespeare, *Twelfth Night*, 3, 2

**Browns.** ***To astonish the Browns***. To do or say something regardless of the annoyance it may cause or the shock it may give to Mrs Grundy.

**Brownyng.** One of the names given to the bear in Caxton's version of *Reynard the Fox*. *Cp*. Bruin.

**Browse his Jib, To.** A sailor's phrase, meaning to drink till the face is flushed and swollen. The *jib* means the face, and to *browse* here means 'to fatten'. A piece of slang formed on the nautical phrase 'to bowse the jib', which means to haul the sail taut; the metaphor signifies that the man is 'tight'.

**Bruce and the Spider.** *See* Spider.

**Bruin.** In Butler's *Hudibras*, one of the leaders arrayed against the hero. His prototype in real life was Talgol, a Newgate butcher who obtained a captaincy for valour at Naseby. He marched next Orsin (Joshua Gosling, landlord of the bear-gardens at Southwark).

***Sir Bruin.*** The bear in the famous German beast-epic, *Reynard the Fox*. *Cp*. Brownyng.

**Brumaire.** The month in the French Republican Calendar from October 23rd to November 21st. It was named from *brume*, fog (Lat. *bruma*, winter). The celebrated 18th Brumaire (November 9th, 1799) was the day on which the Directory was overthrown and Napoleon established his supremacy.

**Brummagem.** Worthless or very inferior metallic articles made in imitation of better ones. The word is a local form of the name *Birmingham*, which is the great mart and manufactory of gilt toys, cheap jewellery, imitation gems, and suchlike.

**Brums.** In Stock Exchange phraseology, London and North-western Railway *stock*. This line was originally the London and Birmingham Railway (*see above*). Brum, i.e. the Birmingham line.

**Brunehild.** Daughter of the King of Issland (i.e. Isalaland, in the Low Countries), beloved by Günther, one of the two great chieftains in the *Nibelungenlied*. She was to be carried off by force, and Günther asked his friend Siegfried to help him. Siegfried contrived the matter by snatching from her the talisman which was her protector, but she never forgave him for his treachery.

**Brunel.** The name given to the goose in Caxton's version of *Reynard the Fox*.

**Brunswicker.** *See* Black Brunswicker.

**Brunt.** ***To bear the brunt.*** To bear the stress, the heat, and collision. The 'brunt of a battle' is the hottest part of the fight. *Cp*. Fire-brand.

***Brunt*** is partly imitative (like *dint*), and is probably influenced by the Icel. *bruna*, to advance with the speed of fire, as a standard in the heat of battle.

**Brush.** The tail of a fox or squirrel, which is brush-like and bushy.

***He brushed by me.*** He just touched me as he went quickly past. Hence also *brush*, a slight skirmish.

***Give it another brush.*** A little more attention; bestow a little more labour on it; return it to the file for a little more polish.

***To brush up.*** To renovate or revive: to bring again into use what has been neglected, as, 'I must brush up my French'.

**Brut.** A rhyming chronicle of British history beginning with the mythical *Brut*, or *Brute* (*q.v.*), and so named from him. Wace's *Le Roman de Brut*, of *Brut d'Angleterre*, written in French about 1150, is a rhythmical version of Geoffrey of Monmouth's *History* with additional legends. It is here that first mention is made of Arthur's Round Table. Wace's work formed the basis of Layamon's *Brut* (early 13th cent.), a versified history of England from the fall of Troy to AD 689. Layamon's poem contains 32,250 lines; Wace's rather over 14,000. *See* Arthur.

**Brute** or **Brutus.** In the mythological history of England, the first king of the Britons, was son of Sylvius (grandson of Ascanius and great-grandson of Aeneas). Having inadvertently killed his father, he first took refuge in Greece and then in Britain. In remembrance of Troy, he called the capital of his kingdom Troy-novant (*q.v.*), now London.

**Brutum fulmen** (Lat.). A noisy but harmless threatening; an innocuous thunderbolt.

The phrase is from Pliny's '*Bruta fulmina et vana, ut quae nulla veniant ratione naturae*' (II, xliii, 113) – Thunderbolts that strike blindly and harmlessly, being traceable to no natural cause.

> The Actors do not value themselves upon the Clap, but regard it as a mere *Brutum fulmen*, or empty Noise, when it has not the sound of the Oaken Plant in it.
>
> Addison, *Spectator*, 29 Nov. 1711

**Brutus, Junius.** In legend, the first consul of Rome, fabled to have held office about 509 BC. He condemned to death his own two sons for joining a conspiracy to restore to the throne the banished Tarquin. He was –

> The public father who the private quelled,
> And on the dread tribunal sternly sat.
>
> Thomson, *Winter*

***The Spanish Brutus.*** Alphonso Perez de Guzman (1258–1320). While he was governor, Castile was besieged by Don Juan, who had revolted from his brother, Sancho IV. Juan, who held in captivity one of the sons of Guzman, threatened to cut his throat unless Guzman surrendered the city. Guzman replied, 'Sooner than be a traitor, I would myself lend you a sword to slay him'. and he threw a sword over the city wall. The son, we are told, was slain by the father's sword before his eyes.

**Brutus, Marcus** (85–42 BC). Caesar's friend, who joined the conspirators to murder him because he made himself a king.

> And thou, unhappy Brutus, kind of heart,
> Whose steady arm, by awful virtue urged,
> Lifted the Roman steel against thy friend.
>
> Thomson, *Winter*, 524–6

***Et tu, Brute.*** What! does my own familiar friend lift up his heel against me? The reference is to the exclamation of Julius Caesar when he saw that his old friend was one of the conspirators against him.

**Bryanites.** *See* Bible Christians.

**Bub.** Drink; particularly strong beer.

> Drunk with Helicon's waters and double-brewed bub.
>
> Prior, *To a Person who wrote ill*

**Bubastis.** Greek name of Bast, or Pasht, the Diana of *Egyptian mythology*; she was daughter of Isis and sister of Horus, and her sacred animal was the cat. *See* Cat.

**Bubble,** or **Bubble Scheme.** A project or scheme of no sterling worth and of very ephemeral duration – as worthless and frail as a bubble. *See* Mississippi: South Sea.

***The Bubble Act.*** An Act of George I, passed in 1719, its object being to punish the promoters of bubble schemes. It was repealed in 1825.

**Bubble and Squeak.** Cold boiled potatoes and greens fried up together, sometimes with bits of cold meat as well. They first bubbled in water when boiled, and afterwards hissed or squeaked in the frying-pan.

**Bucca.** A goblin of the wind, supposed by the ancient inhabitants of Cornwall to foretell shipwrecks; also a sprite fabled to live in the tin-mines.

**Buccaneer.** Properly, a seller of smoke-dried meat, from the Brazilian word *boucan*, a gridiron or frame on which flesh was barbecued, which was adopted in France, and *boucanier* formed from it. *Boucanier* was first applied to the French settlers in Hayti, whose business it was to hunt animals for their skins and who frequently combined with this business that of a marauder and pirate. *Buccaneer* thus became applied to any desperate, lawless, piratical adventurer.

**Bucentaur.** The name of the Venetian state-galley employed by the Doge when he went on Ascension Day to wed the Adriatic. The word is Gr. *bous*, ox, and *centauros*, centaur; and the original galley was probably ornamented with a man-headed ox.

> The spouseless Adriatic mourns her lord
> And, annual marriage now no more renew'd,
> The Bucentaur lies rotting unrestored,
> Neglected garment of her widowhood.
>
> Byron, *Childe Harold*, iv, 9

The last *Bucentaur*, third of the name, was destroyed by the French in 1798. *See* Bride of the Sea.

**Bucephalos** (*bull-headed*). A horse. Strictly speaking, the favourite charger of Alexander the Great.

> True, true; I forgot your Bucephalus.
>
> Scott, *The Antiquary*

**Buchanites.** A sect of fanatics who appeared in the west of Scotland in 1783. They were named after Mrs or Lucky Buchan, their founder, who called herself 'Friend Mother in the Lord', claiming to be the woman mentioned in Rev. 12, and maintaining that the Rev. Hugh White, a convert, was the 'man-child'.

> I never heard of alewife that turned preacher, except Luckie Buchan in the West.
>
> Scott, *St Ronan's Well*, c. ii

**Buck.** A dandy; a gay and spirited fellow; a fast young man.

> A most tremendous buck he was, as he sat there serene, in state, driving his greys.
>
> Thackeray, *Vanity Fair*, ch. vi

**Buck-basket.** A linen-basket. To buck is to wash clothes in lye. When Cade says his mother was 'descended from the Lacies', two men overhear him, and say, 'She was a pedlar's daughter, but not being able to travel with her furred pack, she washes bucks here at home' (*2 Henry VI*, 4, 2). The word is probably connected with Ger. *beuche*, clothes steeped in lye, and Fr. *buer*, to steep in lye; and perhaps with A.S. *buc*, a pitcher.

**Buck-bean.** The popular name of *Menyanthes trifoliata*, a water-plant; an Elizabethan translation of the Flemish name *bocks boonen* (Mod. Dut. *bocksboon*), goat's beans. The name *bog-bean*, also given to this plant, is considerably later.

**Bucket, To.** An obsolete slang term for to cheat.

***To give the bucket, to get the bucket.*** To give (or receive) notice of dismissal from employment. Here *bucket* is synonymous with *sack* (*q.v.*).

***To kick the bucket.*** To die. *Bucket* here is a beam or yoke (O.Fr. *buquet*, Fr. *trébuchet*, a balance), and in East Anglia the big frame in which a newly slaughtered pig is suspended by the heels is still called a 'bucket'. An alternative theory is offered that the bucket was a pail kicked away by a suicide, who stood on it the better to hang himself.

**Bucket-shop.** A term (probably from the old slang 'to bucket', *above*) which originated in America, denoting the office of an 'outside' stockbroker, i.e. one who is not a member of the official Stock Exchange. As these offices are largely used for the sole purpose of *gambling*, in stocks and shares as apart from making *investments*, and as many of them have been run by very shady characters, the name is rarely used except with a bad significance.

**Buckhorn.** *See* Stockfish.

**Buckhorse.** A severe blow or slap on the face. So called from John Smith, a pugilist of about 1740, whose nickname it was. 'Buckhorse' was so insensible to pain that, for a small sum, he would allow anyone to strike him on the side of the face with all his force.

**Buckingham.** Fuller, in his *Worthies*, speaks of the beech trees as the most characteristic feature of this county, and the name is derived from the *Bocingas*, or dwellers among the beech trees (A.S. *boc*), a tribe which anciently inhabited that county.

***Off with his head! so much for Buckingham!*** A famous line, often searched for in vain in Shakespeare's *Richard III*. It is not to be found there, but is in Act iv, Sc. iii, of Colley Cibber's *The Tragical History of Richard III*, altered from Shakespeare (1700).

**Buck-rider.** A dummy fare who enables a cabman to pass police-constables who prevent empty cabs loitering at places where they will be likely to be required, as at theatres, hotels, etc.

**Buckle.** ***I can't buckle to.*** I can't give my mind to work. The allusion is to buckling on one's armour or belt.

***To cut the buckle.*** To caper about, to heel and toe it in dancing. In jigs the two feet buckle or twist into each other with great rapidity.

> Throth, it wouldn't lave a laugh in you to see the parson dancin' down the road on his way home, and the ministher and methodist praicher cuttin' the buckle as they went along.
>
> W. B. Yeats, *Fairy Tales of the Irish Peasantry*, p. 98

***To talk buckle.*** To talk about marriage.

**Buckler.** *See* Shields.

**Bucklersbury** (London) was at one time the noted street for druggists and herbalists; hence Falstaff says:

> I cannot cog, and say thou art this and that, like a many of these lisping hawthorn buds, that come like women in men's apparel, and smell like Bucklersbury in simple time.
>
> Shakespeare, *Merry Wives of Windsor*, 3, 3

Stow tells us that 'the Peperers and Grocers' had their shops there.

**Buckmaster's Light Infantry.** The 3rd West India Regiment was so called from Buckmaster, the tailor, who used to issue 'Light Infantry uniforms' to the officers of the corps without any authority from the Commander-in-Chief.

**Buckram.** A strong coarse kind of cloth stiffened with gum; perhaps so called (like *Astrakhan*, from the Eastern city) from Bokhara. In the Middle Ages the name was that of a valuable fabric that came from the East.

***Men in buckram.*** Hypothetical men existing only in the brain of the imaginer. The allusion is to the vaunting tale of Falstaff to Prince Henry (Shakespeare, *1 Henry IV*, 2, 4). Hence, 'a buckram army', one the strength of which exists only in the imagination.

**Buckshish.** *See* Baksheesh.

**Buck-tooth.** A large projecting front-tooth; formerly also called a *butter-tooth*.

**Buckwheat.** A corruption of *beechwheat* (A.S. *boc*, beech; *see* Buckingham), so called because its seeds are triangular, like beech-mast. The botanical name is *Fagopyrum* (beech-wheat).

> The buckwheat
> Whitened broad acres, sweetening with its flowers
> The August wind.
>
> Bryant, *The Fountain*, stanza 7

**Buddha** (Sanskrit, 'the Enlightened'). The title given to Prince Siddhartha or Gautama (*q.v.*), also called (from the name of his tribe, the Sakhyas) Sȧkya-muni, the founder of Buddhism, who lived from about 623 BC to 543 BC.

**Buddhism.** The system of religion inaugurated by the Buddha in India in the 6th century BC. The general outline of the system is that the world is a transient reflex of deity; that the soul is a 'vital spark' of deity; and that after death it will be bound to matter again till its 'wearer' has, by divine contemplation, so purged and purified it that it is fit to be absorbed into the divine essence.

The four sublime verities of Buddhism are as follows:

(1) Pain exists.

(2) The cause of pain is 'birth sin'. The Buddhist supposes that man has passed through many previous existences, and all the heaped-up sins accumulated in these previous states constitute man's 'birth sin'.

(3) Pain is ended only by Nirvana.

(4) The way that leads to Nirvana is – right faith, right judgment, right language, right purpose, right practice, right obedience, right memory, and right meditation (eight in all).

The abstract nature of the religion, together with the overgrowth of its monastic system and the superior vitality and energy of Brahminism, caused it to decline in India itself; but it spread rapidly in the surrounding countries and took so permanent a hold that it is computed that at the present time it has some 140,000,000 adherents, of whom 10 millions are in India, and the rest principally in Ceylon, Tibet, China, and Japan.

***Esoteric Buddhism.*** *See* Theosophy.

**Bude** or **Gurney Light.** A very bright light obtained by supplying an argand gas-jet with oxygen, invented by Sir Goldsworthy Gurney about 1834, and first used in a lighthouse at Bude, Cornwall.

**Budge.** Lambskin with the wool dressed outwards, worn on the edge of capes, bachelors' hoods, and so on. Hence the word is used attributively and as an adjective to denote pedantry, stiff formality, etc.

> O foolishness of men! that lend their ears
> To those budge-doctors of the stoic fur.
>
> Milton, *Comus*, 706

Budge Bow, Cannon Street, is so called because it was chiefly occupied by budge-makers.

***Budge Bachelors.*** A company of men clothed in long gowns lined with budge or lambs' wool, who used to accompany the Lord Mayor of London at his inauguration.

**Budget.** The statement which the Chancellor of the Exchequer lays annually before the House of Commons, respecting the national income and expenditure, taxes and salaries. The word is the old Fr. *bougette*, a wallet, and the present use arose from the custom of bringing to the House the papers pertaining to these matters in a leather bag, and laying them on the table. Hence, *to budget*, to prepare a budget or estimate.

***A budget of news.*** A bagful of news, a large stock of news.

***Cry Budget.*** A watchword or shibboleth; short for Mumbudget (*q.v.*). Slender says to Shallow:

We have a nay-word how to know one another. I come to her in white and cry *mum*: she cries *budget*: and by that we know one another.

Shakespeare, *Merry Wives of Windsor*, 5, 2

**Buff.** Properly, soft, stout leather prepared from the skin of the *buffalo*; hence, any light-coloured leather; and hence the figurative use, the bare skin. 'To stand in buff' is to stand without clothing in one's bare skin. 'To strip to the buff' is to strip to the skin.

***To stand buff.*** To stand firm, without flinching. Here *buff* means a blow or buffet. *Cp.* Blindman's Buff.

And for the good old cause stood buff,
'Gainst many a bitter kick and cuff.

Butler, *Hudibras's Epitaph*

I must even stand buff and outface him.

Fielding

The phrase also occurs as *to stand bluff.*

Sheridan, in his *School for Scandal*, ii, 3, says:

That he should have stood bluff to old bachelor so long, and sink into a husband at last.

Here the allusion is probably nautical; a 'bluff shore' is one with a bold and almost perpendicular front.

**Buffer.** A chap, a silly old fellow. In M.E. *buffer* meant a stutterer, and the word is used in Is. 22:4, in Wyclif's version, where the Authorised Version reads, 'And the tongue of the stammerers shall be ready to speak plainly'.

***Buffer*** of a railway carriage is an apparatus to *rebuff* or deaden the force of collision.

***Buffer State.*** A small, self-governing State separating two larger States, and thus tending to prevent hostilities between the two. The term seems to have originated on the north-west frontiers of India.

**Buffoon.** Properly, one who puffs out his cheeks, and makes a ridiculous explosion by causing them suddenly to collapse (Ital. *buffone*, from *buffare*, to puff out the cheeks, hence, to jest).

**Buffs.** The old 3rd regiment of foot soldiers, now the East Kents. The men's coats were lined and faced with buff; they also wore buff waistcoats, buff breeches, and buff stockings. These are the 'Old Buffs', raised in 1689.

At one time called the Buff Howards, from Howard their colonel (1737–49).

The 'Young Buffs' are the old 31st Foot raised in 1702; now called the 'Huntingdonshire Regiment', whose present uniform is scarlet with buff facings.

***The Rothshire Buffs.*** The old 78th, now the second battalion of the Seaforth Highlanders.

**Bug.** An old word for goblin, sprite, bogy; probably from Welsh *bwg*, a ghost. The word is used in Coverdale's Bible, which is hence known as the 'Bug Bible' (*see* Bible, Specially Named), and survives in *bogle*, *bogy*, and in *bugaboo*, a monster or goblin, introduced into the tales of the old Italian romancers, and *bugbear*, a scarecrow, or sort of hobgoblin in the form of a bear.

For all that here on earth we dreadfull hold,
Be but as bugs to fearen babes withall.

Spenser, *Faerie Queene*, II, xii, 25

Warwick was a bug that feared us all.

Shakespeare, *3 Henry IV*, 5, 3

To the world no bugbear is so great
As want of figure and a small estate.

Pope, *Satires*, iii, 67–68

Making believe
At desperate doings with a bauble-sword,
And other bugaboo-and-baby-work.

Browning, *Ring and the Book*, v, 949

***A big bug.*** A person of importance – especially in his own eyes; a swell; a pompous or conceited man. There is an old adjective *bug*, meaning pompous, proud.

Dainty sport toward, Dalyall! sit, come sit,
Sit and be quiet: here are kingly bug-words.

Ford, *Perkin Warbeck*, III, ii

**Buhl-work.** *See* Boule-work.

**Build,** for make, as, *A man of strong build*, a man of robust make. *Not so bad a build after all*, not badly made. The metaphor is evident.

**Bulbul.** An Eastern bird of the thrush family, noted for its beautiful singing; hence applied to the nightingale. The word is Persian, and was familiarised by Tom Moore.

'Twas like the notes, half-ecstasy, half pain,
The bulbul utters.

Moore, *Lalla Rookh* (*Veiled Prophet*, i, 14)

**Bull.** A blunder, or inadvertent contradiction of terms, for which the Irish are proverbial. *The British Apollo* (No. 22, 1708) says the term is derived from one Obadiah Bull, an Irish lawyer of London, in the reign of Henry VII, whose blundering in this way was notorious, but there is no corroboration of this story, which must be put down as *ben trovato.* There was a M.E. verb *bull*, to befool, to cheat, and there is the O.Fr. *boule* or *bole*, fraud, trickery; the word may be connected with one of these.

Slang for a five-shilling piece. 'Half a bull' is half a crown. Possibly from *bulla* (*see* Pope's bull *below*); but, as *bull's eye* was an older slang term for the same thing, this is doubtful. Hood, in one of his comic sketches, speaks of a crier who, being apprehended, 'swallowed three hogs (shillings) and a bull'.

In Stock Exchange phraseology, a bull is a speculative purchase for a rise; also a buyer who does this, the reverse of a *bear* (*q.v.*). A bull-account is a speculation made in the hope that the stock purchased will rise before the day of settlement.

In astronomy, the English name of the northern constellation (Lat. *Taurus*) which contains Aldebaran and the Pleiades; also the sign of the zodiac that the sun enters about April 22nd and leaves a month later. It is between Aries and Gemini. The time for ploughing, which in the East was performed by oxen or bulls.

At last from Aries rolls the bounteous sun,
And the bright Bull receives him.

Thomson, *Spring*, 26

***The Pope's bull.*** An edict or mandate issued by the Pope, so called from the heavy leaden seal (Lat. *bulla*) appended to the document. *See* Golden Bull.

***Bull*** is also the name given to a drink made from the swillings of empty spirit-casks. *See* Bulling the Barrel.

***A bull in a china shop.*** A maladroit hand interfering with a delicate business; one who produces reckless destruction.

***A brazen bull.*** An instrument of torture. *See* Phalaris.

***He may bear a bull that hath borne a calf*** (Erasmus, *Proverbs*) – 'He that accustometh hymselfe to lytle thynges, by lytle and lytle shal be able to go a waye with greater thynges' (Taverner).

***To score a bull.*** See *To make a bull's-eye* under Bull's-eye *below*.

***To take the bull by the horns.*** To attack or encounter a threatened danger fearlessly; to go forth boldly to meet a difficulty. The figure is taken from bullfights, in which a strong and skilful matador will grasp the horns of a bull about to toss him and hold it prisoner.

***John Bull.*** *See* John Bull.

**Bull and Gate. Bull and Mouth.** Public-house signs. A corruption of Boulogne Gate or Mouth, adopted out of compliment to Henry VIII, who took Boulogne in 1544. The public-house sign consisting of a plain (or coloured!) bull is usually with reference to the cognizance of the house of Clare. The bull and the boar were signs used by the partisans of Clare, and Richard, Duke of Gloucester (Richard III).

**Bulldog.** A man of relentless, savage disposition is sometimes so called. A 'bulldog courage' is one that flinches from no danger. The 'bulldog' was the dog formerly used in bull-baiting.

In University slang the 'bulldogs' are the two myrmidons (*q.v.*) of the proctor, who attend his heels like dogs, and are ready to spring on any offending undergraduate.

***Boys of the bulldog breed.*** Britishers; especially with reference to their pugnacity. The phrase comes from the song, 'Sons of the sea, all British born', that was immensely popular at the close of the 19th century.

**Bullet.** *Every bullet has its billet.* Nothing happens by chance, and no act is altogether without some effect. 'There's a divinity that shapes our ends, rough-hew them as we will'. Another meaning is this: an arrow or bullet is not discharged at random, but at some mark or for some deliberate purpose.

**Bulletin.** An official report of an officer to his superior, or of medical attendants respecting the health of persons of notoriety. The word is borrowed from the French, who took it from the Ital. *bulletino*, a passport or lottery ticket, from *bulla* (*see* Pope's bull *above*), because they were authenticated by an official *bulla* or seal.

**Bulling the barrel.** Pouring water into a rum cask, when it is nearly empty, to prevent its leaking. The water, which gets impregnated with the spirit and is frequently drunk, is called *bull*.

Seamen talk of *bulling the teapot* (making a second brew), *bulling the coffee*, etc.

**Bullion.** Gold or silver in the mass as distinguished from manufactured articles or coined money: also, a fringe made of gold or silver wire. The word is from the Fr. *bouillon*, boiling, and seems to refer to the 'boiling', or melting, of the metal before it can be utilised.

**Bull-ring.** In Spain, the arena where bullfights take place; in England, the place where bulls used to be baited. The name still survives in many English towns, as in Birmingham. *See* Mayor of the Bull-Ring.

**Bull's-eye.** The inner disk or centre of a target.

A black, globular sweetmeat with whitish streaks, usually strongly flavoured with peppermint.

Also a small cloud suddenly appearing, seemingly in violent motion, and expanding till it covers the entire vault of heaven, producing a tumult of wind and rain (1 Kings 18:44).

Also, a thick disk or boss of glass. Hence, a *bull's-eye lantern*, also called a *bull's-eye*.

***To make a bull's-eye,*** or ***to score a bull.*** To gain some signal advantage; a successful *coup*. To fire or shoot an arrow right into the centre disk of the target.

**Bully.** To overbear with words. *A bully* is a blustering menacer. The original meaning of the noun was 'sweetheart', as in:

> I kiss his dirty shoe, and from heart-string
> I love the lovely bully.
>
> Shakespeare, *Henry V*, 4, 1
>
> O sweet bully Bottom.
>
> *Midsummer Night's Dream*, 4, 4

It is probably to be derived from Dut. *boel*, a lover; and the later meaning may have been influenced by Dut. *bul*, a bull, also a clown, and *bulderen*, to bluster.

**Bully-beef.** Tinned, compressed beef; well known to all soldiers. Probably from Fr. *bouilli*, boiled meat.

**Bully-rag.** To intimidate; *bully-ragging* is abusive intimidation. According to Halliwell, a *rag* is a scold, and hence a 'ragging' means a scolding.

**Bully-rook.** Shakespeare uses the term (*Merry Wives*, 1, 3, 2) for a jollycompanion, but it later came to mean a bravo, a hired ruffian.

**A *bully rake*** is 'one who fights for fighting's sake'.

**Bum-bailiff.** The Fr. *pousse-cul* seems to favour the notion that *bum*-bailiff is no corruption. These officers are frequently referred to as *bums*.

> Scout me for him at the corner of the orchard, like a bum-bailiff.
>
> Shakespeare, *Twelfth Night*, 3, 4

**Bum-boat.** A small wide boat to carry provisions to vessels lying off shore. Also called 'dirt-boats', being used for removing filth from ships lying in the Thames.

**Bumble.** A beadle. So called from the officious, overbearing beadle in Dickens's *Oliver Twist*; hence *bumbledom*, fussy officialism, especially on the part of the parish officers; also parochial officials collectively.

**Bummarees.** A class of middlemen or fish-jobbers in Billingsgate Market, whose business is *bummareeing*, i.e. buying parcels of fish from the salesmen, and then retailing them. The etymology of the word is unknown, but it has been suggested that it is a corruption of *bonne marée*, good fresh fish, *marée* being a French term for all kinds of fresh sea-fish.

**Bumper.** A full glass, generally connected with a 'toast'. It may be so called because the surface of the wine 'bumps up' in the middle, but it is more likely from the notion that it is a 'bumping' or 'thumping', i.e. a large glass.

**Bumpkin.** A loutish person. Dut. *boomken*, a little tree, a small block; hence, a blockhead.

**Bumpo, Natty.** *See* Natty Bumpo, Deerslayer, Leatherstocking.

**Bumpologist.** A humorous name for a phrenologist, i.e. one who attempts to tell characters and state a person's capabilities from an examination of the *bumps* or prominences on the skull. Also called a *bumposopher*.

**Bumptious.** Arrogant, full of mighty airs and graces; apt to take offence at presumed slights. A humorous formation from *bump*, probably modelled on *presumptuous*.

**Bun.** A tail. *See* Bunny.

***Bun.*** 'Hot cross buns' on Good Friday were supposed to be made of the dough kneaded for the host, and were marked with the cross accordingly. As they are said to keep for twelve months without turning mouldy, some persons still hang up one or more in their house as a 'charm against evil'.

It may be remarked that the Greeks offered to Apollo, Diana, Hecate, and the Moon, cakes with 'horns'. Such a cake was called a *bous*, and (it is said) never grew mouldy. The round bun represented the full moon, and the 'cross' symbolised the four quarters.

> Good Friday comes this month: the old woman runs
> With one a penny, two a penny 'hot cross buns'.
>
> Whose virtue is, if you believe what's said,
> They'll not grow mouldy like the common bread.
>
> *Poor Robin's Almanack*, 1733

**Bunce.** A slang term for money; particularly for something extra or unexpected in the way of profit. Thought to be a corruption of *bonus* (*q.v.*).

**Bunch, Mother.** A noted London ale-wife of the late Elizabethan period, on whose name have been fathered many jests and anecdotes, and who is mentioned more than once in Elizabethan drama, e.g.

> Now, now, mother Bunch, how dost thou? What, dost frowne, Queene Gwyniver, dost wrinckle?
>
> Dekker, *Satiromastix*, III, i

In 1604 was published *Pasquil's Jests, mixed with Mother Bunches Merriments*; and in the 'Epistle to the Merrie Reader' is given a humorous description of her:

> ... She spent most of her time in telling of tales, and when she laughed, she was heard from Aldgate to the Monuments at Westminster, and all Southwarke stood in amazement, the Lyons in the Tower, and the Bulls and Beares of Parish Garden roar'd louder than the great roaring Megge ... She dwelt in Cornhill, neere

> the Exchange, and sold strong Ale ... and lived an hundreth, seventy and five yeares, two dayes and a quarter, and halfe a minute.

Other books were named after her, such, for instance, as *Mother Bunch's Closet newly Broke Open*, containing rare secrets of art and nature, tried and experienced by learned philosophers, and recommended to all ingenious young men and maids, teaching them how to get good wives and husbands.

**Bunch of Fives.** Slang for the hand or fist.

**Buncombe** *See* Bunkum.

**Bundle.** *Bundle off.* Get away. *To bundle a person off*, is to send him away unceremoniously. Similar to *pack off*. The allusion is obvious.

**Bundle of Sticks.** Aesop, in one of his fables, shows that sticks one by one may be readily broken; not so when several are bound together in a bundle. The lesson taught is that 'Union gives strength'.

**Bundschuh.** German, a *highlow*, i.e. a shoe consisting of a sole strapped to the foot. It was the symbol and name of the peasant's confederation during the Peasant's War (*q.v.*).

**Bung.** A cant term for a publican; also for a toper. 'Away, ... you filthy bung'. says Doll to Pistol (*2 Henry IV*, 2, 4).

**Bung up.** Close up, as a bung closes a cask.

**Bungalow.** Originally, the house of a European in India, generally of one floor only with a veranda all round it, and the roof thatched to keep off the hot rays of the sun. A *dâk-bungalow* is a caravansary or house built by the Government for the use of travellers. (Hindustani, *bangla*, of Bengal.)

**Bungay.** *See* Friar Bungay.

***Go to Bungay with you!*** i.e. get away and don't bother me, or don't talk such stuff. Bungay, in Suffolk, used to be famous for the manufacture of leather breeches, once very fashionable. Persons who required new ones, or to have their old ones new-seated, went or sent to Bungay for that purpose. Hence rose the cant saying, 'Go to Bungay, and get your breeches mended'. shortened into 'Go to Bungay with you!'

***My castle of Bungay.*** *See* Castle.

**Bunkum.** Claptrap. A representative at Washington being asked why he made such a flowery and angry speech, so wholly uncalled for, made answer, 'I was not speaking to the House, but to Buncombe'. which he represented (North Carolina).

> America, too, will find that caucuses, stump-oratory, and speeches to Buncombe will not carry men to the immortal gods.
>
> Carlyle, *Latter-day Pamphlets*

**Bunny.** A rabbit. So called from the provincial word *bun*, a tail, especially of a hare, which is said to 'cock her bun'. Bunny, a diminutive of bun, applied to a rabbit, means the animal with the 'little tail'.

> Bunny, lying in the grass,
> Saw the shiny column pass.
>
> Bret Harte, *Battle Bunny*

**Bunting.** In Somersetshire *bunting* means sifting flour. Sieves were at one time made of a strong gauzy woollen cloth, which was tough and capable of resisting wear. It has been suggested that this material was found suitable for flags, and that the name for the stuff of which they are now made is due to this.

A 'bunt-mill' is a machine for sifting corn.

**Buphagos.** Pausanias (viii, 24) tells us that the son of Japhet was called Buphagos (glutton), as Hercules was called Adephagus, because on one occasion he ate a whole ox (*Athenaeos* x).

**Burbon.** In Spenser's *Faerie Queene* (Bk v) the lover of Fleurdelis (France), typifying Henry of Navarre. He is assailed by a rabble rout, who batter his shield to pieces, and compel him to cast it aside. The rabble rout is the Roman Catholic party that tried to throw him off; the shield he is compelled to abandon is *Protestantism*; his carrying off Fleurdelis is his obtaining the kingdom by a *coup* after his renunciation of the Protestant cause.

**Burd.** A poetic word for a young lady (*cp.* Bird), obsolete except in ballads. Burd Helen, who is a heroine of Scottish ballad, is a female impersonation of the Fr. *preux* or *prud'homme*, with this difference, that she is discreet, rather than brave and wise.

**Burden of a Song.** A line repeated at intervals so as to constitute a refrain or chorus. It is the Fr. *bourdon*, the big drone of a bagpipe, or double-diapason of an organ, used in forte parts and choruses.

***Burden of Isaiah.*** 'The burden of Babylon, which Isaiah the son of Amoz did see'. *Burden*, here, is a literal translation of the Heb. *massa* (rendered in the Vulgate by *onus*), which means 'lifting up' either a burden or the voice; hence 'utterance', hence a prophecy announcing a calamity, or a denunciation of hardships on those against whom the burden is uttered.

***The burden of proof.*** The obligation to prove something.

> The burden of proof is on the party holding the affirmative [because no one can prove a negative, except by *reductio ad absurdum*].
>
> Greenleaf, *On Evidence*, vol. i, pt 2, ch. iii

**Bureaucracy.** A system of government in which the business is carried on in bureaux or departments. Hence, *bureaucrat*, the head of a department in a bureaucracy. The Fr. *bureau* means not only the office of a public functionary, but also the whole staff of officers attached to the department. During the Great War, Great Britain was almost necessarily in the hands of a bureaucracy; and afterwards it was found to be extremely difficult to get back to normal conditions of government. As a word of reproach, bureaucracy has much the same meaning as Dickens's *red-tapeism* (*q.v.*).

**Burgundian.** ***A Burgundian blow***, i.e. decapitation. The Duc de Biron, who was put to death for treason by Henri IV, was told in his youth, by a fortune-teller, 'to beware of a Burgundian blow'. When going to execution, he asked who was to be his executioner, and was told he was a man from Burgundy.

**Burgundy Pitch.** *See* Misnomers.

**Burial of an Ass.** No burial at all.

> He shall be buried with the burial of an ass, drawn and cast forth beyond the gates of Jerusalem.
>
> Jer. 22:19

**Buridan's Ass.** A man of indecision; like one 'on double business bound, who stands in pause where he should first begin, and both neglects'. Buridan was a French scholastic philosopher who died about 1360. He is incorrectly reputed to be the father of the well-known sophism:

> If a hungry ass were placed exactly between two haystacks in every respect equal, it would starve to death, because there would be no motive why it should go to one rather than to the other.

**Burke.** To murder by smothering. So called from Burke, an Irishman, who used to suffocate his victims and sell the bodies to surgeons for dissection. Hanged at Edinburgh, 1829.

***To burke a question.*** To smother it in its birth. *The publication was burked*, suppressed before it was circulated.

**Burlaw.** *See* Byrlaw.

**Burleigh.** ***As significant as the shake of Lord Burleigh's head.*** In Sheridan's *Critic* is introduced a mock tragedy called *The Spanish Armada*. Lord Burleigh is supposed to be too full of State affairs to utter a word; he shakes his head, and Puff explains what the shake means.

**Burler.** *See* Birler.

**Burlesque.** *Father of burlesque poetry.* Hipponax of Ephesus (6th cent. BC).

**Burn.** *His money burns a hole in his pocket.* He cannot keep it in his pocket, or forbear spending it.

***The burnt child dreads the fire.*** Once caught, twice shy. 'What! wouldst thou have a serpent sting thee twice?'

***To burn one's boats.*** To cut oneself off from all means or hope of retreat. The allusion is to Julius Caesar and other generals, who burned their boats or ships when they invaded a foreign country, in order that their soldiers might feel that they must either conquer the country or die, as retreat would be impossible.

***To burn one's fingers.*** To suffer loss by speculation or interference. The allusion is to taking chestnuts from the fire.

***To burn the Thames.*** To set the Thames afire. *See* Thames.

***You cannot burn the candle at both ends.*** You cannot do two opposite things at one and the same time; you cannot exhaust your energies in one direction, and yet reserve them unimpaired for something else. If you go to bed late you cannot get up early. You cannot eat your cake and have it too. You cannot serve God and Mammon. You cannot serve two masters.

***We burn daylight.*** We waste time in talk instead of action. (Shakespeare, *Merry Wives of Windsor*, 2, 1.)

**Burning Crown.** A crown of red-hot iron set on the head of regicides.

> He was adjudged
> To have his head seared with a burning crown.
>
> *Tragedy of Hoffmann* (1631)

**Burnt Candlemas.** The name given by the Scots to the period around Candlemas Day (*q.v.*), 1355–6, when Edward III marched through the Lothians with fire and sword. He burnt to the ground Edinburgh and Haddington, and then retreated through lack of provisions.

**Bursa** (Gr., a hide). So the citadel of Carthage was called. The tale is that when Dido came to Africa she bought of the natives 'as much land as could be encompassed by a bull's hide'. The agreement was made, and Dido cut the hide into thongs, so as to enclose a space sufficient for a citadel. *Cp.* Doncaster.

The following is a similar story: The Yakutsks granted to the Russian explorers as much land as they could encompass with a cow's hide; but the Russians, cutting the hide into strips, obtained land enough for the port and town of Yakutsk.

The Indians have a somewhat similar tradition. The fifth incarnation of Vishnu was in the form of a dwarf called Vamen. Vamen obtained permission to have as much land as he could measure in three paces to build a hut on. The request was laughed at but freely granted; whereupon the dwarf grew so prodigiously that, with three paces, he strode over the whole world.

**Burst.** To inform against an accomplice. Slang variety of 'split' (turn king's evidence, impeach). The person who does this *splits* or breaks up the whole concern.

***I'm bursting to tell you so-and-so.*** I'm all agog to tell you; I can't rest till I've told you.

***On the burst.*** *See* Bust.

**Bury the Hatchet.** Let bygones be bygones. The 'Great Spirit' commanded the North American Indians, when they smoked the calumet or peace-pipe, to bury their hatchet, scalping knives, and war-clubs, that all thought of hostility might be put out of sight.

> Buried was the bloody hatchet;
> Buried was the dreadful war-club;
> Buried were all warlike weapons,
> And the war-cry was forgotten;
> Then was peace among the nations.
>
> Longfellow, *Hiawatha*, xiii

**Burying at Cross Roads.** *See* Cross-Roads.

**Bus.** A contraction of *omnibus* (*q.v.*). The word is used by airmen and motorists in a humorous, almost affectionate, way for their conveyances.

**Busby.** A frizzled wig; also the tall cap of a hussar, artilleryman, etc., which hangs from the top over the right shoulder. It is not known what the word is derived from; Doctor Busby, master of Westminster school from 1638 to 1695, did not wear a frizzled wig, but a close cap, somewhat like a Welsh wig. *See* Wig.

**Bush. *One beats the bush, but another has the hare.*** *See* Beat the Bush.

***Good wine needs no bush.*** A good article will make itself known without being puffed. An ivy-bush (anciently sacred to Bacchus) was once the common sign of taverns, and especially of private houses where beer or wine could be obtained by travellers.

> Some ale-houses upon the road I saw,
> And some with bushes showing they wine did draw.
> *Poor Robin's Perambulations* (1678)

The proverb is Latin, and shows that the Romans introduced the custom into Europe. '*Vino vendibili hedera non opus est*' (*Columella*). It was also common to France. '*Au vin qui se vend bien, il ne faut point de lierre*'.

> If it be true that good wine needs no bush, 'tis true that a good play needs no epilogue.
> Shakespeare, *As You Like It* (Epilogue)

***To take to the bush.*** To become bushrangers, like runaway convicts, who live by plunder. An Australian term; the 'bush' means what the Dutch call *bosch*: the uncleared land as opposed to towns and clearings.

**Bushel. *To measure other people's corn by one's own bushel.*** To make oneself the standard of right and wrong; to appraise everything as it accords or disagrees with one's own habits of thought and preconceived opinions; to be extremely bigoted and self-opinionated.

***Under a bushel.*** Secretly; in order to hide it.

> Neither do men light a candle and put it under a bushel, but on a candlestick. Matt. 5:15

**Bushman** (Dut. *Boschjesman*). Natives of South Africa who live in the 'bush'; the aborigines of the Cape; dwellers in the Australian 'bush'; a bush farmer.

> Bushmen ... are the only nomads in the country. They never cultivate the soil, nor rear any domestic animal save wretched dogs.
> Livingstone, *Travels*, ch. ii

**Bushmaster.** A large and very poisonous South American snake – *Lachesis mutus*.

**Bushrangers.** Escaped convicts who took refuge in the Australian 'bush', and subsisted by plunder.

> The bushrangers at first were absentees [i.e. escaped convicts] who were soon allured or driven to theft and violence. So early as 1808 they had, by systematic robbery, excited feelings of alarm. West, *Tasmania*

**Business.** A.S. *bisigness*, from *bisigian*, to occupy, to worry, to fatigue. In theatrical parlance 'business' or 'biz' means by-play. Thus, Hamlet trifling with Ophelia's fan, Lord Dundreary's hop, and so on, are the special 'business' of the actor of the part. As a rule, the 'business' is invented by the actor who creates the part, and it is handed down by tradition.

***Business Tomorrow.*** When the Spartans seized upon Thebes they placed Archias over the garrison. Pelopidas, with eleven others, banded together to put Archias to the sword. A letter containing full details of the plot was given to the Spartan pole-march at the banquet table; but Archias thrust the letter under his cushion, saying, 'Business tomorrow'. But long ere that sun arose he was numbered with the dead.

***Good business.*** *See* Biz.

***Mind your own business.*** Don't get poking your nose into *my* affairs; your advice is not needed. A rather rude rejoinder.

> He who doeth his own business defileth not his fingers. *Fielding's Proverbs*

***The business end.*** The end of the tool, etc., with which the work is done. The 'business end of a tin-tack' is its point; of a revolver, its muzzle; and so on.

***To do one's business for one.*** To ruin him, to settle him for ever; kill him.

***To mean business.*** To be determined to carry out one's project; to be in earnest.

**Busirane.** An enchanter bound by Britomart in Spenser's *Faerie Queene* (Bk iii). He is the typification of unrestrained amorous passion.

**Busiris.** A mythical king of Egypt who, in order to avert a famine, used to sacrifice to the gods all strangers who set foot on his shores. Hercules was seized by him; and would have fallen a victim, but he broke his chain, and slew the inhospitable king.

Milton, following Sir Walter Raleigh, who, in his *History of the World*, says he was 'the first oppressor of the Israelites', gives the name to the Pharaoh who was drowned in the Red Sea.

> Vex'd the Red Sea coast, whose waves o'er-threw
> Busiris and his Memphian chivalry.
> *Paradise Lost*, i, 306

**Buskin.** Tragedy. The Greek tragic actors used to wear a sandal some two or three inches thick, to elevate their stature. To this sole was attached a very elegant buskin, and the whole was called *cothurnus*. *Cp.* Sock.

> Or what (though rare) of later age
> Ennobled hath the buskined stage.
> Milton, *Il Penseroso*, 79

**Buss.** To kiss. The word is obsolete; it is probably onomatopoeic in origin, but *cp.* Lat. *basium*, Ital. *bacio*, Sp. *beso*, and Fr. *baiser*.

> Yon towers, whose wanton tops do buss the clouds,
> Must kiss their own feet.
> Shakespeare, *Troilus and Cressida*, 4, 5

**Bust.** A frolic; a drunken debauch. The word is a vulgarization of *burst* (*q.v.*).

***Busted.*** Done for; exploded.

***Bust me.*** A mild oath, like 'blow me' (*q.v.*).

***To go on the bust.*** To go on the spree; to paint the town red.

**Buster.** Anything of large or unusual size or capacity; a 'whacking great lie'.

***To come a buster.*** To come a cropper; to meet with a serious set-back or fall.

**Butcher.** A title given to many soldiers and others noted for their bloodthirstiness. Achmed Pasha was called *djezzar* (the butcher), and is said to have whipped off the heads of his seven wives. He is famous for his defence of Acre against Napoleon I.

John, ninth lord Clifford (d.1461), also called *The Black*, was known as 'the Butcher'.

***The Bloody Butcher.*** The Duke of Cumberland (1721–65), second son of George II. So called from his barbarities in suppressing the rebellion of the young Pretender.

***The Royalist Butcher.*** Blaise de Montluc (1502–77), a Marshal of France, distinguished for his cruelties to the Protestants in the reign of Charles IX.

**Butter.** Soft soap, soft solder (pron. *saw-der*), 'wiping down' with winning words. *Punch* expressively calls it 'the milk of human kindness churned into butter'. (A.S. *butere*, Lat. *butyrum*, Gr. *boutyron*, i.e. *bouturos*, cow-cheese, as distinguished from goat- or ewe-butter.)

***Buttered ale.*** A beverage made of ale or beer mixed with butter, sugar, and cinnamon.

***He knows on which side his bread is buttered.*** He knows his own interest.

***He looks as if butter would not melt in his mouth.*** He looks like a dolt. He looks quite harmless and expressly made to be played upon. Yet beware, and 'touch not a cat but a glove'.

> She smiles and languishes, you'd think that butter would not melt in her mouth.
> Thackeray, *Pendennis*, lx

***He that has good store of butter may lay it thick on his bread. Cui multum est piperis, etiam oleribus immiscet***; he that has plenty of pepper can season his cabbage well.

***Soft*** or ***fair words butter no parsnips.*** Saying 'Be thou fed'. will not feed a hungry man. Mere words will not find salt to our porridge, or butter to our parsnips.

> Fair words butter no cabbage.
> Wycherley, *Plain Dealer*, V, iii (1674)

> Fine words, says our homely old proverb, butter no parsnips. Lowell

***To butter one's bread on both sides.*** To be wastefully extravagant and luxurious; also, to run with the hare and hunt with the hounds, to gain advantages from two sides at once.

**Buttercups.** So called because they were once supposed to increase the butter of milk. No doubt those cows give the best milk that pasture in fields where buttercups abound, not because these flowers produce butter, but because they grow only on sound, dry, old pastures, which afford the best food. Miller, in his *Gardener's Dictionary*, says they were so called 'under the notion that the yellow colour of butter is owing to these plants'.

**Butter-fingers.** Said of a person who lets things fall out of his hand. His fingers are slippery, and things slip from them as if they were greased with butter. Often heard on the cricket field.

> I never was a butter-fingers, though a bad batter.
>
> H. Kingsley

**Butterfly.** A 'fair-weather' person. One who is in good form when all is bright and when every prospect pleases, but is 'done for' when the clouds gather. A light, flippant, objectless young person.

In the cab-trade the name used to be given to those drivers who took to the occupation only in summer-time, and at the best of the season.

> The feeling of the regular drivers against these 'butterflies' is very strong.
>
> *Nineteenth Century* (March, 1893, p. 177)

***Butterfly kiss.*** A kiss with one's eyelashes, that is, stroking the cheek with one's eyelashes.

**Butter-tooth.** *See* Buck-tooth.

**Button.** The two buttons on the back of a coat, in the fall of the back, are a survival of the buttons on the back of riding-coats and military frocks of the 18th century, occasionally used to button back the coat-tails.

A decoy in an auction-room is colloquially known as a *button*, because he 'buttons' or ties the unwary to bargains offered for sale. The button fastens or fixes what else would slip away.

***A boy in buttons.*** A page, whose jacket in front is remarkable for a display of small round buttons, as close as they can be inserted, from chin to waist.

> The titter of an electric bell brought a large fat buttons, with a stage effect of being dressed to look small.
>
> Howell, *Hazard of New Fortunes*, ch. vii

***Bachelor's buttons.*** *See* Bachelor.

***Dash my buttons.*** Here, 'buttons' means lot or destiny, and 'dash' is a euphemistic form of a stronger word.

***He has not all his buttons.*** He is half-silly; 'not all there'; he is 'a button short'.

***The buttons come off the foils.*** Figuratively, the courtesies of controversy are neglected. The button of a foil is the piece of cork fixed to the end to protect the point and prevent injury in fencing.

> Familiarity with controversy ... will have accustomed him to the misadventures which arise when, as sometimes will happen in the heat of fence, the buttons come off the foils.
>
> *Nineteenth Century* (June, 1891, p. 925)

***The button of the cap.*** The tip-top. Thus, in *Hamlet*, Guildenstern says: 'On fortune's cap we are not the very button' (2, 2), i.e. the most highly favoured. The button on the cap was a mark of honour. Thus, in Imperial China the first grade of literary honour was the privilege of adding a gold button to the cap, a custom adopted in several collegiate schools of England; and the several grades of mandarins are distinguished by a different coloured button on the top of their cap. *Cp.* Panjandrum.

***'Tis in his buttons.*** He is destined to obtain the prize; he is the accepted lover. It used to be common to hear boys count their buttons to know what trade they are to follow, whether they are to do a thing or not, and whether some favourite favours them.

> 'Tis in his buttons; he will carry 't.
>
> Shakespeare, *Merry Wives of Windsor*, 3, 2

***To have a soul above buttons.*** To be worthy, or, rather, to consider oneself worthy, of better things; to believe that one has abilities too good for one's present employment. This is explained by George Colman in *Sylvester Daggerwood* (1795): 'My father was an eminent button-maker ... but I had a soul above buttons ... and panted for a liberal profession'.

***To press the button.*** To set in motion, literally or figuratively, generally by simple means as the pressing of a button will start electrically driven machinery or apparatus.

> Mediation was ready to come into operation by any method that Germany thought possible if only Germany would 'press the button' in the interests of peace.
>
> Sir Edw. Grey to the Brit. Ambassador at Berlin. 29 July, 1914

***To take by the button.*** To buttonhole. *See below.*

**Buttonhole**. A flower or nosegay worn in the buttonhole of a coat.

***To buttonhole a person.*** To detain one in conversation; to apprehend, as, 'to take fortune by the button'. The allusion is to a custom, now discontinued, of holding a person by the button or buttonhole in conversation. The French have the same locution: *Serrer le bouton* (*à quel qu'un*).

He went about buttonholing and boring everyone. H. Kingsley, *Mathilde*

***To take one down a buttonhole.*** To take one down a peg; to lower one's conceit.

Better mind yerselves, or I'll take ye down a buttonhole lower.
Mrs Stowe, *Uncle Tom's Cabin*, iv

**Button's.** *See* Will's.

**Buy.** *See also* Bought.

***To buy in.*** To collect stock by purchase; to withhold the sale of something offered at auction, because the bidding has not reached the 'reserve price'. On the Stock Exchange *buying in* is the term used when, a seller having sold stock that he is unable to deliver, the buyer purchases the stock himself in the market and charges the extra cost, if any, to the original seller.

***To buy off.*** To give a person money to drop a claim, put an end to contention, or throw up a partnership.

***To buy out.*** To redeem or ransom.

Not being able to buy out his life ...
Dies ere the weary sun set.
Shakespeare, *Comedy of Errors*, 1, 2

***To buy over.*** To induce one by a bribe to renounce his claim; to gain over by bribery.

***To buy over a person's head.*** To outbid him.

***To buy up.*** To purchase stock to such an amount as to obtain a virtual monopoly, and thus command the market; to make a corner, as 'to buy up corn', etc.

**Buying a Pig in a Poke.** *See* Pig.

**Buzz, To.** Either, to empty the bottle to the last drop; or, when there is not enough left in it to allow of a full glass all round the party, to share it out equally. Perhaps a corruption of *bouse*. *See* Boozed.

***Buzz.*** A rumour, a whispered report.

Yes, that, on every dream,
Each buzz, each fancy ...
He may enguard his dotage.
Shakespeare, *King Lear*, 1, 4

**Buzzard.** In Dryden's *Hind and the Panther* is meant for Dr Burnet, whose figure was lusty.

***Buzzard called hawk by courtesy.*** It is a euphemism – a brevet rank – a complimentary title.

The noble Buzzard ever pleased me best;
Of small renown, 'tis true; for, not to lie
We call him but a hawk by courtesy.
Dryden, *Hind and Panther*, iii, 1221

***Between hawk and buzzard.*** Not quite a lady or gentleman, nor quite a servant. Applied to 'bear-leaders' (*q.v.*), governesses, and other grown-up persons who used to be allowed to come down to dessert, but not to the dinner-table.

**By-and-by** now means a little time hence, but when the Bible was translated it meant instantly. 'When persecution ariseth ... by-and-by he is offended' (Matt. 13:21); rendered in Mark 4:17, by the word 'immediately'. Our *presently* means in a little time hence, but in French *présentement* means now, directly. Thus in France we see, *These apartments to be let presently*, meaning *now*– a phrase which would in English signify by-and-by.

**Bycorne.** *See* Bicorn.

**Byerly Turk.** *See* Darley Arabian.

**Bygones.** *Let bygones be bygones.* Let old grievances be forgotten and never brought to mind.

**By-blow.** An illegitimate child.

I it is have been cheated all this while,
Abominably and irreparably – my name
Given to a cur-cast mongrel, a drab's brat,
A beggar's bye-blow.
Browning, *Ring and the Book*, iv, 612

**By-laws.** Local laws. From *by*, a borough. *See* Byrlaw. Properly, laws by a town council, and bearing only on the borough or company over which it has jurisdiction.

**Byrlaw.** A local law in the rural districts of Scotland. The inhabitants of a district used to make certain laws for their own observance, and appoint one of their neighbours, called the *Byrlaw-man*, to carry out the pains and penalties. *Byr* = a burgh, common in such names as *Derby*, the burgh on the Derwent; *Grimsby* (*q.v.*), Grims-town, etc., and is present in *by-law* (*q.v.*).

**By the by.** *En passant*, laterally connected with the main subject. 'By-play' is side or secondary play; 'by-roads and streets' are those which branch out of the main thoroughfare. The first 'by' means *passing from one to another*, as in the phrase 'Day by day'. Thus 'By the by' is passing from the main subject to a *by* or secondary one.

**By the way.** An introduction to an incidental remark thrown in, and tending the same way as the discourse itself.

**Byron.** ***The Polish Byron.*** Adam Mickiewicz (1798–1855).

***The Russian Byron.*** Alexander Sergeivitch Pushkin (1799–1837).

**Byrsa.** *See* Bursa.

**Byteluys.** The name given to the elder daughter of Martin, the Ape, in Caxton's version of *Reynard the Fox*.

**Byzantine.** Another name for the *bezant* (*q.v.*).

***Byzantine art*** (from Byzantium, the ancient name of Constantinople). That symbolical system which was developed by the early Greek or Byzantine artists out of the Christian symbolism. Its chief features are the circle, dome, and round arch; and its chief symbols the lily, cross, vesica, and nimbus. St Sophia, at Constantinople, and St Mark, at Venice, are excellent examples of Byzantine architecture and decoration, and the Roman Catholic Cathedral at Westminster is a development of the same.

***Byzantine Empire.*** The Eastern or Greek Empire, which lasted from the separation of the Eastern and Western Empires on the death of Theodosius in AD 395, till the capture of Constantinople by the Turks in 1453.

***Byzantine historians.*** Certain Greek historians who lived under the Eastern Empire between the 6th and 15th centuries. They may be divided into three groups: (1) Those whose works form together continuous and complete history of the Byzantine empire; (2) general chroniclers who wrote histories of the world from the oldest period; and (3) writers on Roman antiquities, statistics, and customs.

# C

**C.** The form of the letter is a rounding of the Gr. *gamma* (Γ), which was a modification of the Phoenician sign for *gimel*, a camel. It originally corresponded with Gr. *gamma*, as its place in the alphabet would lead one to suppose.

***C.*** The French *c*, when it is to be sounded like *s*, has a mark under it (*ç*) called a *cedilla* (*q.v.*).

There is more than one poem written of which every word begins with C. There is one by Hamconius, called '*Certamen catholicum cum Calvinistis*', and another by Henry Harder. *See* Alliteration.

**Ca' canny.** A Scots expression meaning 'go easily', 'don't exert yourself'. It is used in trade union slang, and the method of 'ca' canny' is adopted by workmen for the purpose of bringing pressure on the employers when, in the workmen's opinion, a strike would be hardly justifiable, expedient, or possible. *Ca'* is Scots *caw*, to drive or impel.

**Ça Ira** (it will go). The name, and refrain, of a popular patriotic song in France which became the *Carillon National* of the French Revolution (1790). It went to the tune of the *Carillon National*, which Marie Antoinette was forever strumming on her harpsichord.

***'Ça Ira'.*** The rallying cry was borrowed from Benjamin Franklin of America, who used to say, in reference to the American revolution, '*Ah! ah! ça ira, ça ira!*' ('twill be sure to do).

The refrain of the French revolutionary version was:

> Ah! ça ira, ça ira, ça ira,
> Les aristocrates à la lanterne.

**Caaba.** *See* Kaaba.

**Cab.** A contraction of *cabriolet*, a small, one-horse carriage, so called from Ital. *capriola*, a caper, the leap of a kid, from the lightness of the carriage when compared with the contemporary cumbersome vehicles. They were introduced in London about 1823.

**Cabal.** A junto (*q.v.*) or council of intriguers. One of the Ministries of Charles II was called a 'cabal' (1670), because the initial letters of its members formed the word: **C**lifford, **A**shley, **B**uckingham, **A**rlington, and **L**auderdale. This accident may have popularised the word, but it was in use in England many years before this, and is the Hebrew *qabbalah*. *See* Cabbala.

> These ministers were emphatically called the Cabal, and they soon made the appellation so infamous that it has never since ... been used except as a term of reproach.
>
> Macaulay, *England*, I, ii

**Cabala, Cabalist.** *See* Cabbala.

**Caballero.** A Spanish knight or gentleman; also a grave and stately dance, so called from the ballad to the music of which it was danced. The ballad begins –

> Esta noche le mataron al caballero.

**Cabbage.** An old slang term for odd bits of cloth, etc., left over after making up suits and so on, appropriated by working tailors as perquisites. Thus the Tailor in Randolph's *Hey for Honesty* (about 1633) says:

> O iron age! that, like the ostrich, makes me feed on my own goose ... This cross-legged infelicity, sharper than my needle, makes me eat my own cabbage. Act V, Sc. i

Hence, a tailor is sometimes nicknamed 'Cabbage', and *to cabbage* means to pilfer, to filch.

> Your tailor, instead of shreds, cabbages whole yards of cloth. Arbuthnot's *John Bull*

*Cabbage* is also a common schoolboy term for a literary crib, or for some petty theft; and a cheap and nasty cigar is humorously called a *cabbage*.

**Cabbala.** The oral traditions of the Jews, said to have been delivered by Moses to the rabbis and from them handed down through the centuries from father to son by word of mouth. In mediaeval times the term included the occult philosophy of the rabbis, and the *cabbala* and its guardians, the *cabbalists*, were feared as possessing secrets of magical power. The word is the Heb. *qabbalah*, accepted tradition.

**Cabbalist.** A Jewish doctor who professed the study of the Cabbala (*q.v.*). In the Middle Ages the cabbalists were chiefly occupied in concocting and deciphering charms, mystical anagrams, etc., by unintelligible combinations of certain letters, words, and numbers; in search for the philosopher's stone; in prognostications, attempted or pretended intercourse with the dead, and suchlike fantasies.

**Cabinet Ministers.** In British politics, a deliberative committee of the principal members of the Government, who are privileged to consult and advise the sovereign (originally in his private *cabinet*, or chamber), and who lead, and are responsible to, Parliament. The number of members has varied from a dozen to as many as twenty-two, but it always contains the chief officers of state, viz. the Prime Minister, the First Lord of the Treasury (these offices are often combined), the Lord High Chancellor, Lord President of the Council, Lord Privy Seal, Chancellor of the Exchequer, the First Lord of the Admiralty, the Secretaries for Home Affairs, Foreign Affairs, the Colonies, India, Scotland, War (usually, not always), and the Lord Lieutenant of Ireland or his Secretary, and the Presidents of the Board of Trade, the Board of Agriculture, and the Board of Education. Of the other Ministers the following are sometimes included in the Cabinet: the Chancellor of the Duchy of Lancaster, the Postmaster-General, the Secretary to the Air Ministry, and the Ministers of Health, Labour, and Shipping. During the latter years of the Great War the Cabinet was swollen by the inclusion of many additional Ministers, such as those of Munitions, Transport, Blockade, Pensions, and Reconstruction, the Director-General of National Service, the Food Controller, etc., as well as Ministers without portfolio.

**Cabiri.** The Phoenician name for the seven planets collectively; also mystic and minor divinities worshipped in Asia Minor, Greece, and the islands. (Phoen. *kabir*, powerful.)

**Cable's Length.** 100 fathoms; a tenth of a sea-mile – 607.56 feet.

**Cabochon** (Fr.). A polished but uncut precious stone; chiefly applied to garnets, sapphires, amethysts, and rubies.

**Cachet** (Fr.). A seal; hence, a distinguishing mark, a stamp of individuality.

***Lettres de cachet*** (letters sealed). Under the old French régime, warrants, sealed with the king's seal, which might be obtained for a consideration, and in which the name was frequently left blank. Sometimes the warrant was to set a prisoner at large, but it was more frequently for detention in the Bastille. During the administration of Cardinal Fleury (1726–43) 80,000 of these *cachets* are said to have been issued, the larger number being against the Jansenists. In the reigns of Louis XV and XVI fifty-nine were obtained against the one family of Mirabeau. This scandal was abolished January 15th, 1790.

**Cacodaemon.** An evil spirit (Gr. *kakos daimon*). Astrologers give this name to the Twelfth House of Heaven, from which only evil prognostics proceed.

> Hie thee to hell for shame, and leave the world,
> Thou cacodemon.
>
> Shakespeare, *Richard III*, 1, 3

**Cacoethes** (Gr.). A 'bad habit'.

> As soon as he came to town, the political *Cacoethes* began to break out upon him with greater violence, because it had been suppressed.
>
> Swift, *Life of Steele*

***Cacoethes loquendi.*** A passion for making speeches or for talking.

***Cacoethes scribendi.*** The love of rushing into print; a mania for authorship.

> Tenet insanabile multos
> Scribendi cacoethes. Juv. VII, 51
> The incurable itch for scribbling infects many.

**Cacus.** In *classical mythology*, a famous robber, represented as three-headed, and vomiting flames. He lived in Italy, and was strangled by Hercules. Sancho Panza says of the Lord Rinaldo and his friends, 'They are greater thieves than Cacus'. (*Don Quixote*.)

**Cad.** A low, vulgar fellow, a bounder; also, before the term fell into its present disrepute, an omnibus conductor. The word is, like the Scots *caddie* (*q.v.*), probably from cadet (*q.v.*).

**Caddice** or **Caddis.** Worsted galloon, crewel. So named from the O.Fr. *cadaz*, the coarsest part of silk; with which the Ir. *cadan*, cotton, may be remotely connected. *See also* Caddy.

> He hath ribands of all the colours i' the rainbow; … caddisses, cambrics, lawns.
>
> Shakespeare, *Winter's Tale*, 4, 3

***Caddice-garter.*** A servant, a man of mean rank. When garters were worn in sight, the cheaper variety was worn by small tradesmen, servants, etc. Prince Henry calls Poins a 'caddice-garter' (*1 Henry IV*, 2, 4).

> Dost hear,
> My honest caddis-garter?
>
> Glapthorne, *Wit in a Constable*, 1639

**Caddie.** This means now almost solely the boy or man who carries a golfer's clubs on the links (and, now and then, gives the tyro advice). It is another form of *cadet* (*q.v.*), and was formerly in common use in Scotland for errand boys, odd-job men, chairmen, etc.

> All Edinburgh men and boys know that when sedan-chairs were discontinued, the old cadies sank into ruinous poverty, and became synonymous with roughs. The word was brought to London by James Hannay, who frequently used it.
>
> M. Pringle

**Caddy.** A ghost, a bugbear; from *cad*, a word of uncertain origin which in the 17th century meant a familiar spirit. This has no connection (as has been suggested) with *caddis*, a grub, which is probably from *caddice* (*q.v.*), the allusion being to the similarity of the caddis-worm to the larva of the silk-worm.

*Caddy* in *tea-caddy* is a Malay word (*kãli*), and properly denotes a weight of 1 lb. 5 oz. 2 dr., that is used in China and the East Indies.

**Cade.** ***Jack Cade legislation***. Pressure from without. The allusion is to the insurrection of Jack Cade, an Irishman, who headed about 20,000 armed men, chiefly of Kent, 'to procure redress of grievances' (1450).

**Cadency, Marks of.** *See* Difference.

**Cader Idris.** *Cader* in Welsh is 'chair', and *Idris* is the name of one of the old Welsh giants. The legend is that anyone who passes the night sitting in this 'chair' will be either a poet or a madman.

**Cadet.** Younger branches of noble families are called cadets from Fr. *cadet*, formed on Provençal *capdet*, a diminutive of Lat. *caput*, a head, hence, little head, little chieftain. Their armorial shields bore the *mark of cadency* (Lat. *cadere*, to fall). *See* Difference.

*Cadet* is a student at the Royal Military Academy at Woolwich, the Royal Military College at Sandhurst, or in one of His Majesty's training ships. From these places they are sent (after passing certain examinations) into the army as ensigns or second lieutenants, and into the navy as midshipmen.

**Cadger.** A sponger; one who lays himself out to obtain drinks, 'unconsidered trifles', and so on, without paying for them or standing his share; a whining beggar. Originally an itinerant dealer in butter, eggs, etc., who visited remote farmhouses and made what extra he could by begging and wheedling. The word may be connected with *catch*, but this is not certain.

Every cadger thinks himself as good as an earl.
McDonald, *Malcolm*, ch. xlv

**Cadi.** Arabic for a town magistrate or inferior judge. *See* Alcade.

**Cadmean Letters.** The sixteen simple Greek letters said, in *Greek mythology*, to have been introduced by Cadmus (*q.v.*) from Phoenicia.

*Cadmean Victory*. A victory purchased with great loss. The allusion is to the armed men who sprang out of the ground from the teeth of the dragon sown by Cadmus (*q.v.*), who fell foul of each other, only five escaping death.

**Cadmus.** In *Greek mythology*, the son of Agenor, king of Phoenicia, and Telephassa; founder of Thebes (Boeotia) and the introducer of the alphabet into Greece. (*Cp.* Palamedes.) The name is Semitic for 'the man of the East'. Legend says that, having slain the dragon which guarded the fountain of Dirce, in Boeotia, he sowed its teeth, and a number of armed men sprang up surrounding Cadmus with intent to kill him. By the counsel of Minerva, he threw a precious stone among them, who, striving for it, killed one another.

**Cadogan.** A particular method of dressing the hair affected by young French ladies in the 18th century, so called from a popular portrait of the first Earl of Cadogan. The fashion was introduced at the court of Montbéliard by the Duchesse de Bourbon.

**Caduceus.** A white wand carried by Roman heralds when they went to treat for peace; the wand placed in the hands of Mercury, the herald of the gods, of which poets feign that he could therewith give sleep to whomsoever he chose; wherefore Milton styles it 'his opiate rod' in *Paradise Lost*, xi, 133. It is generally pictured with two serpents twined about it (a symbol thought to have originated in Egypt), and – with reference to the serpents of Aesculapius – it was adopted as the badge of the Royal Army Medical Corps.

So with his dread caduceus Hermës led
From the dark regions of the imprisoned dead;
Or drove in silent shoals the lingering train
To Night's dull shore and Pluto's dreary reign.
Darwin, *Loves of the Plants*, ii, 291

**Cadurci.** The tribe anciently inhabiting Aquitania. Cahors is the modern capital.

**Caedmon.** Cowherd of Whitby, the greatest poet of the Anglo-Saxons. He lived in the latter half of the 7th century, and, according to Bede, he was an ignorant man and knew nothing of poetry until one night, when sleeping in the byre, he was miraculously commanded by an angel to sing the Creation and the beginning of created things. In his metrical paraphrase of Genesis we find the germ of Milton's *Paradise Lost*; the portions relating to the fall of the angels are most striking.

**Caelia.** In Spenser's *Faerie Queene* (I, x) the mistress of the House of Holiness, and mother of Faith (Fidelia), Hope (Speranza), and Charity (Charissa). Una conducts the Red Cross Knight to this house, and he there learns the value of repentance. The name 'Caelia' means 'the heavenly one'.

**Caerite Franchise, The.** A form of franchise in a Roman praefecture which gave the right of self-government, but did not confer the privileges of a Roman citizen or entitle the holder to vote. This was a privilege first given to the inhabitants of Caere who, during the Gallic War, had assisted the Romans. Later, cities and citizens who had merited disfranchisement were degraded to the same position, and consequently the term became one of disgrace.

**Caerleon.** The Isca Silurum of the Romans; a town on the Usk, in Wales, about 3 miles N.E. of Newport. It is the traditional residence of King Arthur, where he lived in splendid state, surrounded by hundreds of knights, twelve of whom he selected as Knights of the Round Table.

**Caesar.** The cognomen of Caius Julius *Caesar* was assumed by all the male members of his dynasty as a part of the imperial dignity, and after them by the successive emperors. After the death of Hadrian (138) the title was assigned to those who had been nominated by the emperors as their successors and had been associated with them in ruling. The titles *Kaiser* and *Tsar* are both forms of *Caesar.*

> Thou art an emperor, Caesar, keisar, and Pheezar.
> Shakespeare, *Merry Wives of Windsor*, 1, 3
>
> No bending knees shall call thee Caesar now.
> Shakespeare, *3 Henry VI*, 3, 1

***Caesar's wife must be above suspicion.*** The name of Pompeia having been mixed up with an accusation against P. Clodius, Caesar divorced her; not because he believed her guilty, but because the wife of Caesar must not even be suspected of crime. (Suetonius: *Julius Caesar*, 74.)

**Caesarian Operation.** The extraction of a child from the womb by cutting the abdomen; so called because Julius Caesar was thus brought into the world.

**Caesarism.** The absolute rule of man over man, with the recognition of no law divine or human beyond that of the ruler's will.

**Caeteris paribus.** *See* Ceteris.

**Caf.** *See* Kaf.

**Caftan.** A garment worn in Turkey and other Eastern countries. It is a sort of under-tunic or vest tied by a girdle at the waist. *Cp.* Gaberdine.

> Picturesque merchants and their customers, no longer in the big trousers of Egypt, but [in] the long caftans and abas of Syria.
> B. Taylor, *Lands of the Saracen*, ch. ix

**Cage.** ***To whistle*** or ***sing in the cage.*** The cage is a jail, and to whistle in a cage is to turn King's evidence, or peach against a comrade.

**Cagliostro.** Count Alessandro di Cagliostro was the assumed name of the notorious Italian adventurer and impostor, Giuseppe Balsamo (1743–95), of Palermo. He played a prominent part in the affair of the Diamond Necklace (*q.v.*), and among his many frauds was the offer of everlasting youth to all who would pay him for his secret.

**Cagmag.** Offal, bad meat; also a tough old goose; food which none can relish.

**Cagots.** A sort of gypsy race living in the Middle Ages in Gascony and Bearne, supposed to be descendants of the Visigoths, and shunned as something loathsome. *Cp.* Caqueux, Colliberts. In modern French, a hypocrite or an ultra-devout person is called a *cagot.*

**Cain and Abel.** The Mohammedan tradition is this: Cain was born with a twin sister who was named Aclima, and Abel with a twin sister named Jumella. Adam wished Cain to marry Abel's twin sister, and Abel to marry Cain's. Cain would not consent to this arrangement, and Adam proposed to refer the question to God by means of a sacrifice. God rejected Cain's sacrifice to signify his disapproval of his marriage with Aclima, his twin sister, and Cain slew his brother in a fit of jealousy.

**Cain-coloured Beard.** Yellowish, or sandy red, symbolic of treason. In the ancient tapestries Cain and Judas are represented with yellow beards; but it is well to note that in the extract below the word, in some editions, is printed '*cane*-coloured'. *See* Yellow.

> He hath but a little wee face, with a little yellow beard, a Cain-coloured beard.
> Shakespeare, *Merry Wives of Windsor*, 1, 4

**Cainites.** An heretical sect of the 2nd century. They renounced the New Testament in favour of *The Gospel of Judas*, which justified the false disciple and the crucifixion of Jesus; and they maintained that heaven and earth were created by the evil principle, and that Cain with his descendants were the persecuted party.

**Caius College** (Cambridge). Elevated by Dr John Kay, or Keye (1510–73), of Norwich, into a college, from its previous status of a hall (Gonville), in 1558. It had been originally established by Edmund Gonville in 1348.

**Cake.** Obsolete slang for a fool, a poor thing. *Cp.* Half-Baked.

***Cakes and ale.*** A jolly good time. Life is not all cakes and ale. Life is not all beer and skittles – all pleasure.

***I wish my cake were dough again.*** I wish I had never married. Bellenden Ker says the proverb is a corruption of *Ei w'hissche my keke was d'how en* *geen*, which he says is tantamount to 'Something whispers within me – repentance; would that my marriage were set aside.'

***My cake is dough.*** All my swans are turned to geese. *Occisa est res mea. Mon affaire est manquée*; my project has failed.

***The Land of Cakes.*** Scotland, famous for its oatmeal cakes.

> Land o' cakes and brither Scots. Burns

***To go like hot cakes.*** To be a great success; to go 'like anything'.

***To take the cake.*** To carry off the prize. The reference is to the negro 'cake-walk', the prize for which was a cake. It consists of walking round the prize cake in pairs, and umpires decide which pair walk the most gracefully.

In ancient Greece a cake was the award of the toper who held out the longest; and in Ireland the best dancer in a dancing competition was rewarded, at one time, by a cake.

> A churn-dish stuck into the earth supported on its flat end a cake, which was to become the prize of the best dancer ... At length the competitors yielded their claims to a young man ... who, taking the cake, placed it gallantly in the lap of a pretty girl to whom ... he was about to be married.
> Bartlett and Coyne, *Scenery and Antiquities of Ireland*, vol. ii, p. 64

***You cannot eat your cake and have it too.*** You cannot spend your money and yet keep it. You cannot serve God and Mammon.

**Calabre.** Squirrel fur; perhaps so called because originally imported from Calabria. Ducange says: 'At Chichester the "priest vicars" and at St Paul's the "minor canons" wore a calabre amyce'; and Bale, in his *Image of Both Churches*, alludes to the 'fair rochets of Raines (*Rennes*), and costly grey amicës of calaber and cats' tails'.

> The Lord Mayor and those aldermen above the chair ought to have their coats furred with grey amis, and also with changeable taffeta; and those below the chair with calabre and with green taffeta. Hutton, *New View of London*

**Calainos.** The most ancient of Spanish ballads. Calainos the Moor asked a damsel to wife; she consented, on condition that he should bring her the heads of the three paladins of Charlemagne – Rinaldo, Roland, and Olivier. Calainos went to Paris and challenged the paladins. First Sir Baldwin, the youngest knight, accepted the challenge and was overthrown; then his uncle Roland went against the Moor and smote him.

**Calamanco.** A Low German word of uncertain origin denoting a glossy woollen fabric, sometimes striped or variegated. The word has been applied attributively to a cat, in which connection it means striped or tortoiseshell.

**Calandrino.** A typical simpleton frequently introduced in Boccaccio's *Decameron*; expressly made to be befooled and played upon.

**Calatrava, Order of.** A Spanish military Order of Knighthood founded by Sancho III of Castile in 1158 to commemorate the capture of the fortress of Calatrava from the Moors in 1147. The first knights were the keepers of the fortress; their badge is a red cross, fleury, and is worn on the left breast of a white mantle.

**Calauria.** *Pro Delo Calauria* (Ovid: *Metamorphoses*, vii, 384). Calauria was an island in the Sinus Saronicus which Latona gave to Neptune in exchange for Delos. A *quid pro quo* (*q.v.*).

**Calceolaria.** Little-shoe flowers; so called from their resemblance to fairy slippers. (Lat. *calceolus*.)

**Calceos mutavit.** He has changed his shoes, that is, has become a senator. Roman senators were distinguished by their shoes, which were sandalled across the instep and up the ankles.

**Calculate** is from the Lat. *calculi* (pebbles), used by the Romans for counters. In the abacus (*q.v.*), the round balls were called *calculi*. The Greeks voted by pebbles dropped into an urn – a method adopted both in ancient Egypt and Syria; counting these pebbles was 'calculating' the number of voters.

***I calculate.*** A peculiarity of expression common in the western states of North America. In the southern states the phrase is 'I reckon', in the middle states 'I expect', and in New England 'I guess'. All were imported from the Mother Country by early settlers.

> Your aunt sets two tables, I calculate; don't she?
> Susan Warner, *Queechy*, ch. xix

***The calculator.*** A number of mathematical geniuses have been awarded this title; among them are:

Alfragan, the Arabian astronomer. Died 830.

Jedediah Buxton (1705–72), of Elmton, in Derbyshire; a farm labourer of no education.

George Bidder and Zerah Colburn (1804–40), who exhibited publicly.

Inaudi exhibited 'his astounding powers of calculatin' ' at Paris in 1880, his additions and subtractions, contrary to the usual procedure, were from left to right.

> Buxton, being asked 'How many cubical eighths-of-an-inch there are in a body whose three sides are 23,145,786 yards, 5,642,732 yards, and

54,965 yards?' replied correctly without setting down a figure.

Colburn, being asked the square root of 106,929 and the cube root of 268,336,125, replied before the audience had set the figures down.

Price, *Parallel History*, vol. ii, p. 570

**Caleb.** In Dryden's satire of *Absalom and Achitophel*, is meant for Lord Grey of Wark (Northumberland), one of the adherents of the Duke of Monmouth.

And, therefore, in the name of dulness, be
The well-hung Balaam [Earl of Huntingdon] and old Caleb free.
Lines 512–13

**Caledonia.** Scotland; the ancient Roman name, now used only in poetry and in a few special connections, such as the *Caledonian Railway*, the *Caledonian Canal*, etc.

Not thus, in ancient days of Caledon,
Was thy voice mute amid the festal crowd.
Scott

O Caledonia, stern and wild,
Meet nurse for a poetic child.
Scott, *Lay of the Last Minstrel*

**Calembour** (Fr.). A pun, a jest. From Wigand von Theben, a priest of *Kahlenberg* in Lower Austria, who was introduced in *Eulenspiegel* (*q.v.*), and other German tales. He was noted for his jests, puns, and witticisms; and in the French translations appeared as the *Abbé de Calembourg*, or *Calembour*.

**Calendar.**

***The Julian Calendar.*** *See* Julian.

***The Gregorian Calendar.*** A modification of the Julian, introduced in 1582 by Pope Gregory XIII, and adopted in Great Britain in 1752. This is called 'the New Style'. *See* Gregorian Year.

***The Mohammedan Calendar,*** used in Mohammedan countries, dates from July 16th, 622, the day of the Hegira (*q.v.*). It consists of 12 lunar months of 29 days, 12 hours, 44 minutes each; consequently the Mohammedan year consists of only 354 or 355 days. A cycle is 30 years.

***The French Revolutionary Calendar,*** adopted on October 5th, 1793, retrospectively as from September 22nd, 1792, and in force in France till January 1st, 1806, consisted of 12 months of 30 days each, with 5 intercalary days, called Sansculotides (*q.v.*) at the end. It was devised by Gilbert Romme (1750–95), the names of the months having been given by the poet, Fabre d'Eglantine (1755–94).

***The Newgate Calendar.*** *See* Newgate.

**Calender.** The Persian *galandar*, a member of a begging order of dervishes, founded in the 13th century by Qalandar Yusuf al-Andalusi, a native of Spain, who, being dismissed from another order, founded one of his own, with the obligation on its members of perpetual wandering. This feature has made the calenders prominent in Eastern romance; the story of the Three Calenders in the *Arabian Nights* is well known.

**Calends.** The first day of the Roman month. Varro says the term originated in the practice of *calling together* or assembling the people on the first day of the month, when the pontifex informed them of the time of the new moon, the day of the nones, with the festivals and sacred days to be observed. The custom continued till A.U.C. 450, when the *fasti* or *calendar* was posted in public places. *See* Greek Calends.

**Calepin, A.** A dictionary. (Ital. *calepino*.) Ambrosio Calepino, of Calepio, in Italy, was the author of a famous Latin dictionary (1502), so that 'my Calepin' was used in earlier days as my Euclid, my Liddell and Scott, according to Cocker, etc., became common later. Generally called Calepin, but the subjoined quotation throws the accent on the *le*.

Whom do you prefer
For the best linguist? And I sillily
Said that I thought Calepine's Dictionary.
Donne, *Fourth Satire*

**Caleys.** The Stock Exchange term for Caledonian Railway Ordinary Stock. A contraction of Cale-donians.

**Calf.** Slang for a dolt, a 'mutton-head', a raw, inexperienced, childish fellow. *See also* Calves.

***The golden calf.*** *See* Golden (Phrases).

***There are many ways of dressing a calf s head.*** Many ways of saying or doing a foolish thing; a simpleton has many ways of showing his folly; or, generally, if one way won't do we must try another. The allusion is to the banquets of the Calves' Head Club (*q.v.*).

***To eat the calf in the cow's belly.*** To be over-ready to anticipate; to count one's chickens before they are hatched.

***To kill the fatted calf.*** To welcome with the best of everything. The phrase is taken from the parable of the prodigal son (Luke 15:30).

**Calf-love.** Youthful fancy as opposed to lasting attachment.

I thought it was a childish besotment you had for the man – a sort of calf-love …
*Rhoda Broughton*

**Calf-skin.** Fools and jesters used to wear a calf-skin coat buttoned down the back. In allusion to this custom, Faulconbridge says insolently to the Archduke of Austria, who had acted most basely to Richard Coeur-de-Lion:

> Thou wear a lion's hide! Doff it, for shame,
> And hang a calf-skin on those recreant limbs.
> Shakespeare, *King John*, 3, 1

**Caliban.** Rude, uncouth, unknown; as a Caliban style, a Caliban language. The allusion is to Shakespeare's Caliban (*The Tempest*), the deformed, half-human son of a devil and a witch, slave to Prospero. In this character it has been said that Shakespeare had not only invented a *new creation*, but also a *new language*.

> Satan had not the privilege, as Caliban, to use new phrases and diction unknown. Dr Bentley

> Coleridge says, 'In him [Caliban], as in some brute animals, this advance to the intellectual faculties, without the moral sense, is marked by the appearance of vice.'

**Calibre.** *A mind of no calibre*: of no capacity. *A mind of great calibre*: of large capacity. Calibre is the *bore* of a gun, and, figuratively, the bore or compass of one's intelligence.

**Caliburn.** Same as *Excalibur*, King Arthur's well-known sword.

> Onward Arthur paced, with hand
> On Caliburn's resistless brand.
> Scott, *Bridal of Triermain*

**Calico.** So called from Calicut, in Malabar, once the great emporium of Hindustan and, next to Goa, the chief port for trade with Europe.

**Calidore, Sir.** In Spenser's *Faerie Queene* (Bk vi) the type of *courtesy*) and the lover of 'fair Pastorella'. He is described as the most courteous of all knights, and is entitled the 'all-beloved'; he typifies Sir Philip Sidney or the Earl of Essex. His adventure is against the Blatant Beast, whom he muzzles, chains, and drags to Faërie Land.

> Sir Gawain was the Calidore of the Round Table.
> Southey

**Caligula.** Roman emperor (AD 37–41); so called because, when he was with the army as a boy, he wore a military sandal called a *caliga*, which had no upper leather, and was used only by the common soldiers.

> 'The word *caligae*, however,' continued the Baron ... 'means, in its primitive sense, sandals; and Caius Caesar ... received the cognomen of Caligula, a *caligis, sive caligis levioribus, quibus adolescentior non fuerat in exercitu Germanici patris sui*.'
> Scott, *Waverley*, xlviii

Caligula was a voluptuous brute whose cruelty and excesses amounted almost to madness. Hence Horace Walpole coined the word *Caligulism*. Speaking of Frederick, Prince of Wales, he says:

> Alas! it would be endless to tell you all his Caligulisms. *Letter to France*, 29 Nov., 1745

***Caligula's horse.*** Incitatus. It was made a priest and consul, had a manger of ivory, and drank wine from a golden goblet.

**Caliph** or *Calif.* A title given to the successors of Mahomet (Arab. *Khalifah*, a successor; *khalafa*, to succeed). Among the Saracens a caliph is one vested with supreme dignity. The caliphate of Bagdad reached its highest splendour under Haroun al-Raschid, in the 9th century. For the last 200 years the appellation has been swallowed up in the titles of *Shah*, *Sultan*, *Emir*, etc.; but it is still used of rulers of Mohammedan States in their capacity as successors of Mohammed.

**Calipolis.** *See* Callipolis.

**Calisto and Arcas.** Calisto was an Arcadian nymph metamorphosed into a she-bear by Jupiter. Her son Areas having met her in the chase, would have killed her, but Jupiter converted him into a he-bear, and placed them both in the heavens, where they are recognised as the Great and Little Bear.

**Calixtines.** A religious sect of Bohemians in the 15th century; so called from *Calix* (the chalice), which they insisted should be given to the laity in the sacrament of the Lord's Supper, as well as the bread or wafer. They were also called Utraquists (*q.v.*).

**Call.** A 'divine' summons or invitation, as 'a call to the ministry'.

***A call before the curtain.*** An invitation to an actor to appear before the curtain, and receive the applause of the audience.

***A call bird.*** A bird trained as a decoy.

***A call-boy.*** A boy employed in theatres to 'call' or summon actors, when it is time for them to make their appearance on the stage.

***Call day,*** or ***call night.*** The name given at the Inns of Court to the dates on which students are called to the Bar.

***A call of the House.*** An imperative summons sent to every Member of Parliament to attend. This is done when the sense of the whole House is required.

***A call on shareholders.*** A demand to pay the balance of money due for shares allotted in a company, or a part thereof.

***A call to the Bar.*** The admission of a law student to the privileges of a barrister. *See* Bar.

***A call to the pastorate.*** An invitation to a minister by the members of a Presbyterian or Nonconformist church to preside over a certain congregation.

***A call to the unconverted.*** An invitation accompanied with promises and threats, to induce the unconverted to receive the gospel. Richard Baxter wrote a book so entitled (1657).

***Payable at call.*** To be paid on demand.

***The call of Abraham.*** The invitation or command of God to Abraham, to leave his idolatrous country, under the promise of being made a great nation.

***The call of God.*** An invitation, exhortation, or warning, by the dispensations of Providence (Isa. 22:12); divine influence on the mind to do or avoid something (Heb. 3:1).

***To call.*** To invite: as, the trumpet calls.

> If honour calls, where'er she points the way,
> The sons of honour follow and obey.
>
> Churchill, *The Farewell*

***To call*** (a man) ***out.*** To challenge him; to appeal to a man's honour to come forth and fight a duel.

***To call God to witness.*** To declare solemnly that what one states is true.

***To call in question.*** To doubt the truth of a statement; to challenge the truth of a statement. '*In dubium vocare*'.

***To call over the coals.*** *See* Coals.

***To call to account.*** To demand an explanation; to reprove.

***To be called*** (or ***sent***) ***to one's account.*** To be removed by death. To be called to the judgment seat of God to give an account of one's deeds, whether they be good, or whether they be evil.

> Cut off even in the blossoms of my sin,
> Unhouseled, disappointed, unaneled;
> No reckoning made, but sent to my account
> With all my imperfections on my head;
> O horrible! O horrible! most horrible.
>
> Shakespeare, *Hamlet*, 1, 5

***To call to arms.*** To summon to prepare for battle. '*Ad arma vocare*'.

***To call to mind.*** To recollect, to remember.

**Caller Herrings.** Fresh herrings. The adjective is also applied in Scotland to fresh air, water, etc.

**Calligraphy.** The art of beautiful handwriting: often used of writing that is very minute and yet clear. Pater Bale, in the 16th century, wrote in the compass of a silver penny the Lord's Prayer, the Creed, the Ten Commandments, two Latin prayers, his own name, the day of the month and date of the year since the accession of Queen Elizabeth, and a motto. With a glass this writing could be read. By photography a sheet of the *Times* newspaper has been reduced to a smaller compass.

**Calling.** A vocation, trade, or profession. The allusion is to the calling of the apostles by Jesus Christ to follow Him. In the legal profession persons must still be called to the Bar before they can practise.

*Effectual calling.* An invitation to believe in Jesus, rendered effectual by the immediate operation of the Holy Ghost.

**Calliope** (Gr., *beautiful voice*). Chief of the nine Muses (*q.v.*); the muse of epic or heroic poetry, and of poetic inspiration and eloquence. Her emblems are a stylus and wax tablets.

**Callipolis.** The wife of the Moor in the *Battle of Alcazar* (1594) by George Peele. It is referred to by Pistol in *2 Henry IV*, 2, 4. Scott frequently uses her as the typical lady-love, sweetheart, or charmer. Sir Walter always spells the name *Callipolis*, but Peele *Calipolis*. The drunken Mike Lambourne says to Amy Robsart:

> Hark ye, most fair Callipolis, or most lovely countess of clouts, and divine duchess of dark corners. *Kenilworth*, ch. xxxiii

And the modest Roland Graeme calls the beautiful Catherine his 'most fair Callipolis' (*The Abbot*, ch. xi).

**Callippic Period.** An intended correction of the Metonic Cycle (*q.v.*) by Callippus, the Greek astronomer of the 4th century BC. To remedy the defect in the Metonic Cycle Callippus quadrupled the period of Meton, making his Cycle one of seventy-six years, and deducted a day at the end of it, by which means he calculated that the new and full moons would be brought round to the same day and hour. His calculation, however, is not absolutely accurate, as there is one whole day lost every 553 years.

**Callirrhoe.** The lady-love of Chaereas, in Chariton's Greek romance, entitled the *Loves of Choereas and Callirrhoë*, probably written in the 6th century AD.

**Calomel.** Hooper says:

> This name, which means 'beautiful black', was originally given to the Aethiop's mineral, or black sulphuret of mercury. It was afterwards applied in joke by Sir Theodore Mayerne to the chloride of mercury, in honour of a favourite negro servant whom he employed to prepare it. As calomel is a *white* powder, the name is merely a jocular misnomer. *Medical Dictionary*

**Calotte** (Fr.). ***Régime de la calotte***. Administration of government by ecclesiastics. The *calotte* is the small skull-cap worn over the tonsure.

***Régiment de la Calotte.*** A society of witty and satirical men in the reign of Louis XIV. When any public character made himself ridiculous, a calotte was sent to him to 'cover the bald or brainless part of his noddle'.

**Caloyers.** Monks in the Greek Church, who follow the rule of St Basil. They are divided into *cenobites*, who recite the offices from midnight to sunrise; *anchorites*, who live in hermitages; and *recluses*, who shut themselves up in caverns and live on alms. (Gr. καλὸς and γέρων, beautiful old man.)

**Calpe.** Gibraltar, one of the Pillars of Hercules, the other, the opposite promontory in Africa (mod. Jebel Musa, or Apes' Hill), being anciently called *Abyla*. According to one account, these two were originally one mountain, which Hercules tore asunder; but some say he piled up each mountain separately, and poured the sea between them.

Heaves up huge Abyla on Afric's sand,
Crowns with high Calpë Europe's salient strand,
Crests with opposing towers the splendid scene,
And pours from urns immense the sea between.

Darwin, *Economy of Vegetation*

**Calumet.** This name for the tobacco-pipe of the North American Indians, used as a symbol of peace and amity, is the Norman form of Fr. *chalumeau* (from Lat. *calamus*, a reed), and was given by the French-Canadians to certain plants used by the natives as pipe-stems, and hence to the pipe itself.

The calumet, or 'pipe of peace', is about two and a half feet long, the bowl is made of highly polished red marble, and the stem of a reed, which is decorated with eagles' quills, women's hair, and so on.

To present the calumet to a stranger is a mark of hospitality and goodwill; to refuse the offer is an act of hostile defiance.

Gilche Manito, the mighty,
Smoked the calumet, the Peace-Pipe
As a signal to the nations.

Longfellow, *Hiawatha*, i

**Calvary.** The Latin translation of the Gr. *golgotha* (*q.v.*), which is a transliteration of the Hebrew word for 'a skull'. The name given to the place of our Lord's crucifixion. Legend has it that the skull of Adam was preserved here, but the name is probably due to some real or fancied resemblance in the configuration of the ground to the shape of a skull.

The actual site of Calvary has not been determined, though there is strong evidence in favour of the traditional site, which is occupied by the Church of the Holy Sepulchre. Another position which has strong claims is an eminence above the grotto of Jeremiah, outside the present wall and not far from the Damascus Gate on the north side of Jerusalem.

***A Calvary.*** A representation of the successive scenes of the Passion of Christ in a series of pictures, etc., in a church. The shrine containing the representations.

***A Calvary cross.*** A Latin cross mounted on three steps (or grises).

***Calvary clover.*** A common trefoil, *Medicago echinus*, said to have sprung up in the track made by Pilate when he went to the cross to see his 'title affixed' (Jesus of Nazareth, king of the Jews). Each of the three leaves has a little carmine spot in the centre; in the daytime they form a sort of cross; and in the flowering season the plant bears a little yellow flower, like a 'crown of thorns'. Julian tells us that each of the three leaves had in his time a white cross in the centre, and that the centre cross lasts visible longer than the others.

**Calvert's Entire.** The 14th Foot, now called the Prince of Wales's Own (West Yorks. Regiment). Called from their colonel, Sir Harry Calvert (1806–26), and *entire*, because three entire battalions were kept up for the good of Sir Harry, when adjutant-general. The term is, of course, a play on Calvert's malt liquor.

**Calves.** The inhabitants of the Isle of Wight are so called from a tradition that a calf once got its head firmly wedged in a wooden pale, and, instead of breaking up the pale, the farm-man cut off the calf's head.

***His calves are gone to grass***. Said of a spindle-legged man. And another mocking taunt is, 'Veal will be dear, because there are no calves.'

**Calves' Head Club.** Instituted in ridicule of Charles I, and apparently first mentioned in a tract (given in the *Harleian Miscellany*) of 1703 by Benjamin Bridgwater, stating that it first met in 1693. It lasted till about 1735. The annual banquet was held on January 30th, and consisted of calves' heads dressed in sundry ways to represent Charles and his courtiers; a cod's head, to represent Charles, independent of his kingly office; a pike with little ones in its mouth, an emblem of tyranny; a boar's head with an apple in its mouth to represent the king preying on his subjects, etc. After the banquet, the *Icon Basilikë* was burnt, and the parting cup 'To those worthy patriots who killed the tyrant,' was drunk.

**Calvinism.** The five chief points of Calvinism are:

(1) Predestination, or particular election.

(2) Irresistible grace.

(3) Original sin, or the total depravity of the natural man, which renders it morally impossible to believe and turn to God of his own free will.

(4) Particular redemption.

(5) Final perseverance of the saints.

**Calydon.** In classical geography, a city in Aetolia, Greece, near the forest which was the scene of the legendary hunt of the Calydonian boar (*see* Boar). Also, in Arthurian legend, the name given to a forest in the northern portion of England.

**Calypso.** In *classical mythology*, the queen of the island Ogygia on which Ulysses was wrecked. She kept him there for seven years, and promised him perpetual youth and immortality if he would remain with her for ever. Ogygia is generally identified with Gozo, near Malta.

**Cam and Isis.** The universities of Cambridge and Oxford; so called from the rivers on which they stand.

> May you, my Cam and Isis, preach it long,
> 'The right divine of kings to govern wrong.'
>
> Pope, *Dunciad*, iv, 187

**Cama.** The god of young love in *Hindu mythology*. His wife is Rati (*voluptuousness*), and he is represented as riding on a sparrow, holding in his hand a bow of flowers and five arrows (i.e. the five senses).

> Over hills with peaky tops engrail'd,
> And many a tract of palm and rice,
> The throne of Indian Cama slowly sail'd
> A summer fann'd with spice.
>
> Tennyson, *The Palace of Art*

**Camaldolites.** A religious order of great rigidity of life, founded early in the 11th century in the vale of Camaldoli, Tuscany, by St Romuald, a Benedictine.

**Camarilla.** Spanish for a small chamber or cabinet; hence, a clique, a nest of intriguers, the confidants or private advisers of the sovereign.

**Camarina.** *Ne moveas Camarinam* (Don't meddle with Camarina). Camarina, a lake in Sicily, was a source of malaria to the inhabitants, who, when they consulted Apollo about draining it, received the reply, 'Do not disturb it.' Nevertheless, they drained it, and ere long the enemy marched over the bed of the lake and plundered the city. The proverb is applied to those who remove one evil, but thus give place to a greater – leave well alone. The application is very extensive, as: Don't kill the small birds, or you will be devoured by insects; one pest may be a safeguard against a greater one.

A similar Latin phrase is *Anagyrin movere*.

> When the laird of Ellangowan drove the gypsies from the neighbourhood, though they had been allowed to remain there undisturbed hitherto, Dominie Sampson warned him of the danger by quoting the proverb '*Ne moveas Camarinam.*'
>
> Scott, *Guy Mannering*, ch. vii

**Cambalo's Ring.** Cambalo was the second son of Cambuscan in Chaucer's unfinished *Squire's Tale*. He is introduced, as Cambel (*q.v.*), in Spenser's *Faërie Queene* (Bk iv). The ring, which was given him by his sister Canacë (*q.v.*), had the virtue of healing wounds.

> Well mote ye wonder, how that noble knight,
> After he had so often wounded been,
> Could stand on foot now to renew the fight ...
> All was through virtue of the ring he wore;
> The which, not only did not from him let
> One drop of blood to fall, but did restore
> His weakened powers, and dulled spirits whet.
>
> Spenser, *Faërie Queene*, IV, iii, 23–24

**Cambel.** The name given by Spenser in his sequel to Chaucer's *Squire's Tale* (*Faërie Queene*, Bk iv) to Cambalo, brother of Canacë (*q.v.*). He challenged every suitor to his sister's hand, and overthrew all except Triamond, who married her.

**Camber.** In British legend, the second son of Brute (*q.v.*). Wales fell to his portion; which is one way of accounting for its ancient name of Cambria.

**Cambria.** The ancient name of Wales, the land of the Cimbri or Cymry.

> Cambria's fatal day. — Gray, *Bard*

> The Cambrian mountains, like far clouds,
> That skirt the blue horizon, dusky rise.
>
> Thomson, *Spring*, 961–62

**Cambrian Series.** The earliest fossiliferous rocks in North Wales, consisting principally of marine sediments which were formed after the close of Archean times and before the Ordovician period. So named by Sedgwick (1836).

**Cambric.** A kind of very fine white linen cloth, so named from Cambrai (Flem. *Kameryk*), in Flanders, where for long it was the chief manufacture.

> He hath ribbons of all the colours of the rainbow; inkles, caddises, cambricks, and lawns.
>
> Shakespeare, *Winter's Tale*, 4, 3

**Cambridge Apostles, The.** A debating society founded at Cambridge by John Sterling in 1826, and remarkable for the talent of its undergraduate members and for the success to which they attained in after life. Among them may be mentioned besides Sterling himself, Frederick Denison Maurice, Richard Chenevix Trench, John Kemble, Spedding, Monckton Milnes, Tennyson, and A. H. Hallam.

***Cambridge colours*** (*boat crews*). *See* College Colours.

**Cambuscan.** In Chaucer's unfinished *Squire's Tale*, the King of Sarra, in Tartary, model of all royal virtues. His wife was Elfeta; his two sons, Algarsife (*q.v.*) and Cambalo; and his daughter, Canacë. On her birthday (October 15th) the King of Arabia and India sent Cambuscan a 'steed of brass, which, between sunrise and sunset, would carry its rider to any spot on the earth'. All that was required was to whisper the name of the place in the horse's ear, mount upon his back, and turn a pin set in his ear. When the rider had arrived at the place required, he had to turn another pin, and the horse instantly descended, and, with another screw of the pin, vanished till it was again required. Milton refers to the story in *Il Penseroso* –

> Him that left half-told
> The story of Cambuscan bold.

**Cambyses.** A pompous, ranting character in Preston's 'lamentable tragedy' of that name (1570).

> Give me a cap of sack, to make mine eyes look red; for I must speak in passion, and I will do it in King Cambyses' vein.
>
> Shakespeare, *1 Henry IV*, 2, 4

**Camden Society.** An historical society founded in 1838 for the publication of early historic and literary remains connected with English history, and so named in honour of William Camden (1551–1623), the antiquary. In 1897 it amalgamated with the Royal Historical Society, and its long series of publications was transferred to that body.

**Camel.** The name of Mahomet's favourite camel was Al Kaswa. The mosque at Koba covers the spot where it knelt when Mahomet fled from Mecca. Mahomet considered the kneeling of the camel as a sign sent by God, and remained at Koba in safety for four days. The swiftest of his camels was Al Adha, who is fabled to have performed the whole journey from Jerusalem to Mecca in four bounds, and, in consequence, to have had a place in heaven allotted him with Al Borak (*q.v.*), Balaam's ass, Tobit's dog, and the dog of the seven sleepers.

***To break the camel's back.*** To pile on one thing after another till at last the limit is reached and a catastrophe or break-down caused. The proverb is 'It is the last straw that breaks the camel's back'. *See* Straw.

***It is easier for a camel to go through the eye of a needle, than for a rich man to enter into the kingdom of God*** (*see* Eye). In the Koran we find a similar expression: 'The impious shall find the gates of heaven shut; nor shall he enter till a camel shall pass through the eye of a needle.' In the Rabbinical writings is a passage which goes to prove that the word *camel* should not be changed into *cable*, as Theophylact suggests: 'Perhaps thou art one of the Pampedithians, who can make an elephant pass through the eye of a needle.'

> It is as hard to come, as for a camel
> To thread the postern of a needle's eye.
>
> Shakespeare, *Richard II*, 5, 5

Some think to avoid a difficulty by rendering Matt. 19:24, 'It is easier for a *cable* to go through the eye of a needle ...', but the word is κάμηλον, and the whole force of the passage rests on the 'impossibility' of the thing, as it is distinctly stated in Mark 10:24. 'How hard is it for them that *trust* in [their] riches, ἐπὶ τοᾶς χρήμασιν ...' It is impossible by the virtue of *money* or by bribes to enter the kingdom of heaven.

**Camellia.** The technical name of a genus, and the popular name of the species of evergreen shrubs; so named by Linnaeus in honour of G. J. Kamel (Lat. *Camellus*), a Jesuit who introduced it to Europe from the Philippines about 1739.

**Camelot.** In British fable, the legendary spot where King Arthur held his court. It has been tentatively located at various places – in Somerset, near Winchester (*q.v.*), in Wales, and even in Scotland.

**Cameo.** A precious stone, such as the sardonyx, onyx, or agate, having two layers of different colours, which is carved in relief in such a way that the lower layer serves as background to the raised carving. One of the most famous cameos in the world is the *Ste Chapelle* cameo, an onyx containing the *apotheosis of Augustus*, and now in the Bibliothèque Nationale, Paris. The word *cameo* or *gamaheu*, as it used to be known, is Italian, but its etymology and original meaning is unknown.

Albertus Magnus makes mention of stones that contain natural representations of various objects; Paracelsus called such 'natural talismans'; Gaffaret, in his *Curiosités inouïes*, attributes to them magical powers; and Pliny tells us that the 'Agate of Pyrrhus' contained a representation of the nine Muses, with Apollo in the midst.

**Cameron Highlanders.** The 79th Regiment of Infantry, raised by Allan Cameron, of Errock, in 1793. Now called 'The Queen's Own Cameron Highlanders'.

**Cameronian Regiment.** The 26th Infantry, which had its origin in a body of Cameronians (*q.v.*), in the Revolution of 1688. Now the 1st Battalion of the Scottish Rifles; the 2nd Battalion is the old No. 90.

**Cameronians.** The strictest sect of Scotch Presbyterians, organised in 1680, by the Covenanter and field preacher, Richard Cameron, who was slain in battle at Aird's Moss in 1680. He objected to the alliance of Church and State, and seceded from the Kirk, but in 1690 his followers submitted to the General Assembly, and they became merged with the Covenanters.

**Camilla.** In Roman legend a virgin queen of the Volscians. Virgil (*Aeneid*, vii, 809) says she was so swift that she could run over a field of corn without bending a single blade, or make her way over the sea without even wetting her feet.

> Not so when swift Camilla scours the plain.
> Flies o'er the unbending corn and skims along the main.
> Pope, *Essay on Criticism*, 372

**Camillus.** A Roman general who died 395 BC. He was five times Dictator, was falsely accused of embezzlement, and went into voluntary exile; but when the Gauls besieged Rome, he returned and delivered his country.

> Camillus, only vengeful to his foes.
> Thomson, *Winter*

**Camisarde** or **Camisado.** A night attack; so called because the attacking party wore a *camise* or camisard (*see* Camisards) over their armour, both to conceal it, and that they might the better recognise each other in the dark.

**Camisards.** In French history, the Protestant insurgents of the Cevennes, who resisted the violence of the dragonnades, after the revocation of the edict of Nantes (1685), and so called from the white shirts (*camisards*) worn by the peasants. Their leader was Cavalier, afterwards Governor of Jersey.

**Camisole.** A loose jacket worn by women when dressed in *negligé*; an underbodice worn immediately beneath a thin blouse.

*Camisole de force.* A strait waistcoat. Frequently mentioned in accounts of capital punishments in France.

**Camlan, Battle of.** In Arthurian legend the battle which put an end to the Knights of the Round Table, and at which Arthur received his death wound from the hand of his nephew Modred, who was also slain. It took place about AD 537, but its site (traditionally placed in Cornwall) is as conjectural as that of Camelot (*q.v.*).

> Nor ever yet had Arthur fought a fight
> Like this last, dim, weird battle of the west.
> Tennyson,
> *Idylls of the King: the Passing of Arthur*, 93

**Cammock.** *As crooked as a cammock.* The cammock is a crooked staff, or a stick with a crook at the head, like a hockey stick or shinty club; also, a piece of timber bent for the knee of a ship. The word is probably of Gaulish origin; it is found in Middle English, and there are Gaelic, Welsh, Irish, and Manx variants.

> Though the cammock, the more it is bowed the better it serveth; yet the bow, the more it is bent and occupied the weaker it waxeth.
> Lyly, *Euphues*

**Camorra.** A lawless, secret society of Italy organised early in the 19th century. It claimed the right of settling disputes, etc., and was so named from the blouse (Ital. *camorra*) worn by its members, the *Camorrists*.

**Campania** (Lat., level country). The ancient geographical name for the district south-east of the Tiber, containing the towns of Cumae, Capua, Baiae, Puteoli, Herculaneum, Pompeii, etc.

> Disdainful of Campania's gentle plains.
> Thomson, *Summer*

**Campaspe.** A beautiful woman, the favourite concubine of Alexander the Great. Apelles, it is said, modelled his Venus Anadyomene from her.

> When Cupid and Campaspe played
> At Cards for kisses, Cupid paid.
> Lyly, *Song from 'Campaspe'*

**Campbells are coming, The.** This soul-stirring song was composed in 1715, when the Earl of Mar raised the standard for the Stuarts against George I. John Campbell was Commander-in-Chief of his Majesty's forces, and the rebellion was quashed. The song is connected with the Relief of Lucknow in 1857; a Scotch woman lying ill on the ground heard the pibroch, and exclaimed, 'Dinna ye hear it? Dinna ye hear it? The pipes o' Havelock sound' –

> The Campbells are coming, O-ho! O-ho!
> The Campbells are coming, O-ho!
> The Campbells are coming to bonnie Loch Leven,
> The Campbells are coming, O-ho!

**Campbellites.** Followers of John McLeod Campbell (1800–72), who taught the universality of the atonement, for which, in 1830, he was ejected by the General Assembly of the Church of Scotland.

In the United States the name is sometimes given to the *Disciples of Christ*, a body founded by Thomas and Alexander Campbell in Pennsylvania in 1809. They reject creeds, practise immersion and weekly communion, and uphold Christian union on the foundation of the Bible alone. They are also known as the *New Lights*.

**Campceiling.** A ceiling sloping on one side from the vertical wall towards a plane surface in the middle. A corruption of *cam* (twisted or bent) ceiling. (Halliwell gives *cam*, 'awry'.)

**Campeador.** The Cid (*q.v.*).

**Canace.** In Chaucer's *Squire's Tale*, a paragon of women, daughter of Cambuscan (*q.v.*), to whom the king of Arabia and India sent as a present a mirror and a ring. The mirror would tell the lady if any man on whom she set her heart would prove true or false, and the ring (which was to be worn on her thumb) would enable her to understand the language of birds and to converse with them. It would also give the wearer perfect knowledge of the medicinal properties of all roots. Chaucer never finished the tale, but probably he meant to marry Canacë to some knight who would be able to overthrow her two brothers, Cambalo and Algarsife, in the tournament.

Spenser, however, continued it in the *Faërie Queene* (Bk i), and here Canacë was courted by a crowd of suitors, but her brother Cambel (*see* Cambalo) gave out that anyone who pretended to her hand must encounter *him* in single combat and overthrow him. She ultimately married Triamond, son of the fairy Agapë.

**Canache.** One of Actaeon's dogs. (Gr. 'the clang of metal falling'.)

**Canada Balsam.** Made from the *Abies balsamea* and *Abies canadensis*, a native of Canada.

**Canaille** (Fr., a pack of dogs). The mob, the rabble; a contemptuous name for the populace generally.

**Canard** (Fr., a duck). A hoax, a ridiculously extravagant report. Littré says that the term comes from an old expression, *vendre un canard à moitié*, to half-sell a duck. As this is no sale at all it came to mean 'to take in', 'to make a fool of'. Another explanation is that a certain Cornelissen, to try the gullibility of the public, reported in the papers that he had twenty ducks, one of which he cut up and threw to the nineteen, who devoured it greedily. He then cut up another, then a third, and so on till the nineteenth was gobbled up by the survivor – a wonderful proof of duck voracity.

**Canary.** Slang for 'a guinea' or 'sovereign'. Gold coin is so called because, like a canary, it is yellow.

*Canary-bird.* A jail-bird who 'peaches'. *See under* Sing (*To sing in tribulation* and *To sing out*).

**Cancan.** A very free and easy dance accompanied by extravagant and often indecent postures, and performed in the public halls and casinos of Paris.

> They were going through a quadrille with all those supplementary gestures introduced by the great Rigolboche, a notorious *danseuse*, to whom the notorious cancan owes its origin.
>
> A. Egmont Hake, *Paris Originals*, 1878

**Cancel,** to blot out, is merely 'to make lattice-work'. This is done by making a cross over the part to be omitted. (Lat. *cancello*, to make trellis.)

**Cancer.** One of the twelve signs of the zodiac (the Crab). It appears when the sun has reached its highest northern limit, and begins to go backward towards the south; but, like a crab, the return is sideways (June 21st to July 23rd).

According to fable, Juno sent Cancer against Hercules when he combated the Hydra of Lerne. It bit the hero's foot, but Hercules killed the creature, and Juno took it up to heaven.

**Candaules.** King of Lydia about 710 to 668 BC. Legend relates that he exposed the charms of his wife to Gyges (*q.v.*), whereupon the queen compelled him to assassinate her husband, after which she married the murderer, who became king, and reigned twenty-eight years.

**Candidate** (Lat. *candidatus*, clothed in white). One who seeks or is proposed for some office, appointment, etc. Those who solicited the office of consul, quaestor, praetor, etc., among the Romans, arrayed themselves in a loose white robe. It was loose that they might show the people their scars, and white in sign of fidelity and humility.

**Candide.** The hero of Voltaire's philosophical novel, *Candide, ou l'Optimisme* (1759). All sorts of misfortunes are heaped upon him, and he bears them all with cynical indifference.

**Candle.** *Bell, Book, and Candle. See* Bell.

***Fine* (or *Gay*) *as the king's candle.*** '*Bariolé comme la chandelle des rois*', in allusion to an ancient custom of presenting on January 6th, a candle of various colours at the shrine of the three kings of Cologne. It is generally applied to a woman overdressed, especially with gay ribbons and flowers. 'Fine as fivepence'.

***He is not fit to hold the candle to him.*** He is very inferior. The allusion is to link-boys who held candles in theatres and other places of night amusement.

> Others say that Mr Handel
> To Bonocini can't hold a candle. Swift

***The game is not worth the candle.*** The effort is not worth making; the result will not pay for the trouble, even the cost of the candle that lights the players.

***To burn the candle at both ends.*** *See* Burn.

***To hold a candle to the devil.*** To aid or countenance that which is wrong. The allusion is to the Catholic practice of burning candles before the images of saints.

> There is a story told of an old woman who set one wax taper before the image of St Michael, and another before the Devil whom he was trampling under foot. Being reproved for paying such honour to Satan, she naively replied: 'Ye see, your honour, it is quite uncertain which place I shall go to at last, and sure you will not blame a poor woman for securing a friend in each.'

When Jessica (*Merchant of Venice*, 2, 6) says to Lorenzo: 'What, must I hold a candle to my shame?' she means, Must I call attention to this disguise, and blazon my folly abroad? not, Must I glory in my shame?

***To sell by the candle.*** A species of sale by auction. A pin is thrust through a candle about an inch from the top, and bidding goes on till the candle is burnt down to the pin, when the pin drops into the candlestick, and the last bidder is declared the purchaser.

> The Council thinks it meet to propose the way of selling by 'inch of candle', as being the most probable means to procure the true value of the goods. — Milton, *Letters*, etc.

***To vow a candle to the devil.*** To propitiate the devil by a bribe, as some seek to propitiate the saints in glory by a votive candle.

***What is the Latin for candle?*** *See* Tace.

**Candle-holder.** An abettor. The reference is to the practice of holding a candle in the Catholic Church for the reader, and in ordinary life to light a workman when he requires more light.

> I'll be a candle-holder and look on.
>
> Shakespeare, *Romeo and Juliet*, 1, 4

**Candles of the Night.** The stars are so called by Shakespeare (*Merchant of Venice*, 5, 1). Milton enlarged upon the idea:

> O thievish Night,
> Why shouldst thou, but for some felonious end,
> In thy dark lantern thus close up the stars
> That Nature hung in heaven, and filled their lamps
> With everlasting oil, to give due light
> To the misled and lonely traveller? — *Comus*, 200

**Candlemas Day.** February 2nd, the feast of the Purification of the Virgin Mary, when Christ was presented by her in the Temple; one of the quarter days in Scotland. In Roman Catholic churches all the candles which will be needed in the church during the year are consecrated on this day; they symbolise Jesus Christ, called 'the light of the world', and 'a light to lighten the Gentiles'. The Romans had a custom of burning candles to scare away evil spirits.

> If Candlemas Day be dry and fair,
> The half o' winter's come and mair;
> If Candlemas Day be wet and foul,
> The half o' winter was gane at Youl.
>
> *Scotch Proverb*

> The badger peeps out of his hole on Candlemas Day, and, if he finds snow, walks abroad; but if he sees the sun shining he draws back into his hole. — *German Proverb*

**Canens.** A nymph, wife of Picus, King of the Laurentes. When Circe had changed Picus into a bird, Canens lamented him so greatly that she pined away, till she became a *vox et praeterea nihil*. (Ovid, *Metamorphoses*, 14 fab. 9.)

**Canephorus** (pl. *canephori*). A sculptured figure of a youth or maiden bearing a basket on the head. In ancient Greece the canephori bore the sacred things necessary at the feasts of the gods.

**Canicular Days** (Lat. *canicula*, dim. of *canis*, a dog). The dog-days (*q.v.*).

***Canicular period.*** The ancient Egyptian cycle of 1461 years or 1460 Julian years (also called a *Sothic period*, *q.v.*), during which it was supposed that any given day had passed through all the seasons of the year.

***Canicular year.*** The ancient Egyptian year, computed from one heliacal rising of the Dog Star (*Sirius*) to the next.

**Canister.** Old pugilists' slang for the head, which is the 'canister' or coffer of man's brains. 'To mill his canister' is to break his head. A 'canister cap' is a hat or cap.

**Canker.** The brier or dog-rose.

> Put down Richard, that sweet lovely rose.
> And plant this thorn, this canker, Bolingbroke.
>
> Shakespeare, *1 Henry IV*, 1, 3

Also a caterpillar that destroys leaves, buds, etc.

> As killing as the canker to the rose.
>
> Milton, *Lycidas*

**Canmore.** *See* Great Head.

**Cannae.** The place where Hannibal defeated the Romans under Varro and L. Aemilius Paulus with great slaughter in 216 BC. Any fatal battle that is the turning point of a great general's prosperity may be called his Cannae. Thus Moscow was the Cannae of Napoleon.

**Cannel Coal.** A corruption of *candle coal*, so called from the bright flame, unmixed with smoke, which it yields in combustion.

**Cannibal.** A word applied to those who eat human flesh. It is the Sp. *Canibales*, a corruption of *Caribes*, i.e. the *Caribs*, inhabitants of the Antilles, some of whom, when discovered by Columbus, were man-eaters.

> The natives live in great fear of the canibals (i.e. Caribals, or people of Cariba). Columbus

**Cannon.** This term in billiards is a corruption of *carom*, which is short for Fr. *carambole*, the red ball (*caramboler*, to touch the red ball). A cannon is a stroke by which the player's ball touches one of the other balls in such a way as to glance off and strike the remaining ball.

**Canny.** *See* Ca' canny.

**Canoe.** Like *cannibal*, *canoe* is one of the very few words we get from native West Indian. This is a Haytian word, *canoa*, and was brought to Europe by the Spaniards. It originally meant a boat hollowed out of a tree-trunk.

***Paddle your own canoe.*** Mind your own business. The caution was given by President Lincoln, but it is an older saying and was used by Capt. Marryat (*Settlers in Canada*, ch. viii) in 1844. Sarah Bolton's poem in *Harper's Magazine* for May, 1854, popularised it:

> Voyage upon life's sea,
> To yourself be true,
> And, whate'er your lot may be,
> Paddle your own canoe.

**Canon.** From Lat. and Gr. *canon*, a carpenter's rule, a rule, hence a standard (as 'the canons of criticism'), a model, an ordinance, as in Shakespeare's –

> Or that the Everlasting had not fixed
> His canon 'gainst self-slaughter. *Hamlet*, 1, 2

***The canon.*** Canon law (*q.v.*).

> Self-love which is the most inhibited sin in the canon. Shakespeare, *All's Well*, 1, 1

Also, the body of the books in the Bible which are accepted by the Christian Church generally as genuine and inspired; the whole Bible from Genesis to Revelation, excluding the Apocrypha. Called also the *sacred canon* and the *Canonical Books*.

The Church dignitary known as a *Canon* is a capitular member of a cathedral or collegiate church, usually living in the precincts, and observing the statutable rule or canon of the body to which he is attached. The canons, with the dean at their head, constitute the governing body, or *chapter*, of the cathedral.

***Canon law.*** A collection of ecclesiastical laws which serve as the rule of church government. The professors or students of canon law are known as *canonists*.

> Doubt not, worthy senators! to vindicate the sacred honour and judgment of Moses your predecessor, from the shallow commenting of scholastics and canonists. Milton, *Doctrine of Divorce, Introd.*

**Canonical Dress.** The distinctive or appropriate costume worn by the clergy according to the direction of the canon. Bishops, deans, and archdeacons, for instance, wear canonical hats. This distinctive dress is sometimes called simply 'canonicals'; Macaulay speaks of 'an ecclesiastic in full canonicals'. The same name is given also to the special robes of other professions, and to special parts of such robes, such as the *pouch* on the gown of an M.D., originally designed for carrying drugs; the *coif* of a serjeant-at-law, designed for concealing the tonsure; the *lambskin* on a B.A. hood, in imitation of the *toga candida* of the Romans; the *tippet* on a barrister's gown, meant for a wallet to carry briefs in; and the proctors' and pro-proctors' *tippet*, for papers – a sort of sabretache.

***Canonical Epistles.*** The seven catholic epistles, i.e. one of James, two of Peter, three of John, and one of Jude. The epistles of Paul were addressed to specific churches or to individuals.

***Canonical hours.*** The times within which the sacred offices may be performed. In the Roman Catholic Church they are seven – viz. matins, prime, tierce, sext, nones, vespers, and compline. Prime, tierce, sext, and nones are the first, third, sixth, and ninth hours of the day, counting from six in the morning. Compline is a corruption of *completorium* (that which completes the services of the day). The reason why there are seven canonical hours is that David says, 'Seven times a day do I praise thee' (Ps. 119:164).

In England the phrase means the time of the day within which persons can be legally married in a church, i.e. from eight in the morning to three p.m.

***Canonical obedience.*** The obedience due by the inferior to the superior clergy. Thus bishops owe canonical obedience to the archbishop of the same province.

**Canonicals.** *See* Canonical Dress.

**Canonist.** *See* Canon Law.

**Canopic Vases.** Vases used by the Egyptian priests for holding the viscera of bodies embalmed, four being provided for each body. So called from Canopus, in Egypt, where they were first used.

**Canopus.** A seaport in ancient Egypt, 15 miles N.E. of Alexandria. Also the name of the bright star in the southern constellation *Argo navis*. Except for Sirius this is the brightest star in the heavens.

> We drank the Libyan sun to sleep, and lit
> Lamps which out-burn'd Canopus.
>
> Tennyson, *Dream of Fair Women*

**Canopy** properly means a *gnat curtain*. Herodotus tells us (ii, 95) that the fishermen of the Nile used to lift their nets on a pole, and form thereby a rude sort of tent under which they slept securely, as gnats will not pass through the meshes of a net. Subsequently the hangings of a bed were so called, and lastly the canopy borne over kings. (Gr. *konops*, a gnat.)

**Canossa.** Canossa, in the duchy of Modena, is where, in January, 1077, the Emperor, Henry IV, went to humble himself before Gregory VII (Hildebrand).

Hence, *To go to Canossa*, to eat humble pie; to submit oneself to a superior after having refused to do so.

**Cant.** A whining manner of speech; class phraseology, especially of a pseudo-religious nature (Lat. *canto*, to sing, whence 'chant'). It seems to have been first used of the whining manner of speech of beggars, who were known as 'the canting crew' (*q.v.*). In Harman's *Caveat, or Warning, for Common Cursetors, vulgarly called Vagabonds* (1567), we read:

> As far as I can learne or understand by the examination of a number of them, their languag – which they terme peddelars Frenche or Canting – began but within these xxx yeeres.

And one of the examples of 'canting' that he gives begins:

> Bene Lightmans to thy quarromes, in what tipken hast thou lypped in this darkemans, whether in a lybbege or in the strummel? (Good-morrow to thy body, in what house hast thou lain in all night, whether in a bed or in the straw?)

The term was in familiar use in the time of Ben Jonson, signifying 'professional slang', and 'to use professional slang'.

> The doctor here …
> When he discourses of dissection
> Of *vena cava* and of *vena porta* …
> What does he else but cant? Or if he run
> To his judicial astrology,
> And trowl the *trine*, the *quartile*, and the *sextile* …
> Does he not cant?
>
> Ben Jonson, *The Staple of News*, IV, iv (1625)

**Cantabrian Surge.** The Bay of Biscay. So called from the Cantabri who dwelt about the Biscayan shore. Suetonius tells us that a thunderbolt fell in the Cantabrian Lake (Spain) 'in which twelve axes were found'. (*Galba*, viii.)

> She her thundering army leads
> To Calpê [Gibraltar] … or the rough
> Cantabrian Surge.
>
> Akenside, *Hymn to the Naiades*

**Cantart.** The name given to one of the daughters of Chanticleer, the Cock, in Caxton's version of *Reynard the Fox*. Her sisters were Coppen and Crayant.

**Cantate Sunday.** Rogation Sunday, the fourth Sunday after Easter. So called from the first word of the introit of the mass: 'Sing to the Lord'. Similarly 'Laetare Sunday' (the fourth after Lent) is so called from the first word of the mass.

**Canteen** means properly a wine-cellar (Ital. *cantina*, a cellar). Then a refreshment house in a barrack for the use of the soldiers. Then a vessel for holding liquid refreshment, carried by soldiers on the march.

**Canter.** An easy gallop; originally called a *Canterbury pace* or *gallop*, from the ambling gait adopted by mounted pilgrims to the shrine of St Thomas à Becket at Canterbury.

***A preliminary canter.*** Something which precedes the real business in hand. The reference is to the 'trial trip' of horses before the race begins.

***To win in a canter.*** Easily; well ahead of all competitors.

**Canterbury. *Canterbury is the higher rack, but Winchester the better manger*.** Canterbury is the higher see in rank, but Winchester the one which produces the most money. This was the reply of William de Edendon, Bishop of Winchester, when offered the archbishopric of Canterbury (1366). Now Canterbury is £15,000 a year, and Winchester £6,500.

***Canterbury Tales.*** Chaucer supposed that he was in company with a party of pilgrims going to Canterbury to pay their devotions at the shrine of Thomas à Becket. The party assembled at an inn in Southwark, called the *Tabard*, and there agreed to tell one tale each, both in going and returning. He who told the best tale was to be treated with a supper on the homeward journey. The work is incomplete, and we have none of the tales told on the way home.

***A Canterbury Tale*.** A cock-and-bull story: a romance. So called from Chaucer's *Canterbury Tales*.

**Canting Crew.** Beggars, gypsies, thieves, and vagabonds, who use 'cant' (*q.v.*). In 1696 'E. B., Gent.', published the first English Slang Dictionary, with the title 'A New Dictionary of the Terms, Ancient and Modern, of the Canting Crew in its several Tribes'.

**Canucks.** The name given in the United States to Canadians generally, but in Canada itself to Canadians of French descent. The origin is uncertain, but it has been suggested that it is a corruption of *Connaught*, a name originally applied by the French Canadians to Irish immigrants.

**Canvas** means cloth made of hemp (Lat. *cannabis*, hemp). *To canvas a subject* is to strain it through a hemp strainer, to sift it; and to *canvass a borough* is to sift the votes.

**Canvas City, A.** A military encampment.

> The Grand Master assented, and they proceeded accordingly, ... avoiding the most inhabited parts of the canvas city.
>
> Scott, *The Talisman*, ch. x

In 1851, during the Australian gold rush, a town of tents, known as Canvas Town, rose into being on the St Kilda Road, Melbourne.

**Caora.** A river described by Elizabethan voyagers (*see* Hakluyt), on the banks of which dwelt a people whose heads grew beneath their shoulders. Their eyes were in their shoulders, and their mouths in the middle of their breasts. Raleigh, in his *Description of Guiana*, gives a similar account of a race of men. *Cp.* Blemmyes.

**Cap.** The word is used figuratively by Shakespeare for the top, the summit (of excellence, etc.); as in *They wear themselves in the cap of the time* (*All's Well*, 2, 1), i.e. 'They are the ornaments of the age'; *a very riband in the cap of youth* (*Hamlet*, 4, 7); *thou art the cap of all the fools alive* (*Timon*, 4, 3); *on fortune's cap we are not the very button* (*Hamlet*, 2, 2); etc.

***Black cap.*** *See* Black.

***Cap acquaintance.*** A bowing acquaintance. One just sufficiently known to touch one's cap to.

***Cap and bells.*** The insignia of a professional fool or jester.

***Cap and feather days.*** The time of childhood.

> Here I was got into the scenes of my cap and feather days.
>
> Cobbett

***Cap and gown.*** The full academical costume of a university student, tutor, or master, worn at lectures, examinations, and after 'hall' (dinner).

> Is it a cap and gown affair?
>
> C. Bede, *Verdant Green*

***Cap in hand.*** Submissively. To wait on a man cap in hand is to wait on him like a servant, ready to do his bidding.

***Cap money.*** Money collected in a cap or hat; hence an improvised collection.

***Cap of Liberty.*** When a slave was manumitted by the Romans, a small Phrygian cap, usually of red felt, called *pileus*, was placed on his head, he was termed *libertinus* (a freedman), and his name was registered in the city tribes. When Saturninus, in 100 BC, possessed himself of the Capitol, he hoisted a similar cap on the top of his spear, to indicate that all slaves who joined his standard should be free; Marius employed the same symbol against Sulla; and when Caesar was murdered, the conspirators marched forth in a body, with a cap elevated on a spear, in token of liberty.

In the French Revolution the cap of liberty (*bonnet rouge*) was adopted by the revolutionists as an emblem of their freedom from royal authority.

***Cap of Maintenance.*** A cap of dignity anciently belonging to the rank of duke; the fur cap of the Lord Mayor of London, worn on days of state; a cap carried before the British sovereigns at their coronation. The significance of *maintenance* here is not known, but the cap was an emblem of very high honour, for it was conferred by the Pope three times on Henry VII and once on Henry VIII. By certain old families also it is borne in the coat of arms, either as a charge or in place of the wreath.

***Cater cap.*** A square cap or mortar-board. (Fr. *quartier.*)

***College cap.*** A trencher like the caps worn at the English Universities by students and bachelors of art, doctors of divinity, etc.

***Fool's cap.*** A conical cap with feather and bells, such as licensed fools used to wear. For the paper so called, *see* Foolscap.

***Forked cap.*** A bishop's mitre.

***John Knox cap.*** An early form of the trencher, mortar-board, or college cap (*q.v.*), worn at the Scottish Universities.

> A cap of black silk velvet, after the John Knox fashion.
>
> *Edinburgh University Calendar*

***Monmouth cap.*** *See* Monmouth.

***Phrygian cap.*** Cap of liberty (*q.v.*).

***Scotch cap.*** A cloth cap worn in Scotland as part of the national dress.

***Square cap.*** A trencher or mortar-board, like the college cap (*q.v.*).

***Statute cap.*** A woollen cap ordered by a statute of Queen Elizabeth in 1571 to be worn on holidays by all citizens for the benefit of the woollen trade. To a similar end, persons were at one time obliged to be buried in flannel.

> Well, better wits have worn plain statute caps.
>
> Shakespeare, *Love's Labour's Lost*, 5, 2

***Trencher cap,*** or ***mortar-board.*** A cap with a square board, generally covered with black cloth, and a tassel, worn with academical dress; a college cap (*q.v.*).

***A feather in one's cap.*** An achievement to be proud of; something creditable.

***I cap to that.*** I assent to it. The allusion is to a custom among French judges. Those who assent to the opinion stated by any of the bench signify it by lifting their toque from their heads.

***I must put on my considering cap.*** I must think about the matter before I give a final answer. The allusion is to the official cap of a judge, formerly donned when passing any sentence, but now only when passing sentence of death.

***If the cap fits, wear it.*** If the remark applies to you, apply it yourself. Hats and caps differ very slightly in size and appearance, but everyone knows his own when he puts it on.

***Setting her cap at him.*** Trying to catch him for a sweetheart or a husband. In the days when ladies habitually wore caps they would naturally put on the most becoming, to attract the attention and admiration of the favoured gentleman.

***To cap.*** To take off, or touch, one's cap to, in token of respect; also to excel.

> Well, that caps the globe. C. Brontë, *Jane Eyre*

***To cap a story.*** To go one better; after a good story has been told to follow it up with a better one of the same kind.

***To cap verses.*** Having the metre fixed and the last letter of the previous line given, to add a line beginning with that letter, thus:

> The way was long, the wind was cold (D).
> Dogs with their tongues their wounds do heal (L).
> Like words congealed in northern air (R).
> Regions Caesar never knew (W).
> With all a poet's ecstasy (Y).
> You may deride my awkward pace, etc. etc.

There are parlour games of capping names, proverbs, etc. in the same way, as: Plato, Otway, Young, Goldsmith, etc., 'Rome was not built in a day,' 'Ye are the salt of the earth,' 'Hunger is the best sauce,' 'Example is better than precept,' 'Time and tide wait for no man,' etc.

***To gain the cap.*** To obtain a bow from another out of respect.

> Such gains the cap of him that makes them fine,
> But keeps his book uncrossed.
>
> Shakespeare, *Cymbeline*, 3, 3

***To pull caps.*** To quarrel like two women, who pull each other's caps. An obsolete phrase, used only of women. In a description of a rowdy party in 18th century Bath we read:

> At length they fairly proceeded to pulling caps, and everything seemed to presage a general battle ... they suddenly desisted, and gathered up their caps, ruffles, and handkerchiefs.
>
> Smollett, *Humphry Clinker*: Letter xix

***To send the cap round.*** To make a collection.

***Wearing the cap and bells.*** Said of a person who is the butt of the company, or one who excites laughter at his own expense. The reference is to licensed jesters formerly attached to noblemen's establishments. *See* Cap and Bells *above*. Their headgear was a cap with bells.

> One is bound to speak the truth ... whether he mounts the cap and bells or a shovel hat [like a bishop]. Thackeray

***Your cap is all on one side.*** The French have the phrase *Mettre son bonnet de travers*, meaning 'to be in an ill-humour'. M. Hilaire le Gai explains it thus: '*La plupart des tapageurs de profession portent ordinairement le chapeau sur l'oreille.*' Many workmen, when they are bothered, push their cap on one side of the head, generally over the right ear, because the right hand is occupied.

**Cap-a-pie.** From head to foot; usually with reference to arming or accoutring. From O.Fr. *cap a pie* (Mod.Fr. *de pied en cap*).

> Armed at all points exactly cap-a-pie.
>
> Shakespeare, *Hamlet*, 1, 2
>
> I am courtier, cap-a-pè.
>
> Shakespeare, *Winter's Tale*, 4, 3

**Cape. *Spirit of the Cape.*** *See* Adamastor.

***Cape of Storms.*** *See* Storms.

**Capel Court.** A lane adjacent to the Stock Exchange in London where dealers congregate to do business; hence used sometimes for the Stock Exchange itself. Hence also *Capel Courtier*, a humorous term for a professional stock-dealer. So called from Sir William Capel, Lord Mayor in 1504.

**Caper.** *The weather is so foul not even a Caper would venture out.* A Manx proverb. A Caper is a fisherman of *Cape* Clear in Ireland, who will venture out in almost any weather.

**Caper Merchant.** A dancing-master who cuts 'capers'.

**Capers.** ***To cut capers.*** To spring upwards in dancing, and rapidly interlace one foot with the other; figuratively, to act in an unusual manner with the object of attracting notice.

> The quietest fellows are forced to fight for their *status quo*, and sometimes to cut capers like the rest.
>
> Le Fanu, *The House in the Churchyard*, p. 143

*Caper* here is from Ital. *capra*, a she-goat, the allusion being to the erratic way in which goats will jump about.

***Cut your capers!*** Be off with you!

***I'll make him cut his capers,*** i.e. rue his conduct.

**Capet.** Hugh Capet, the founder of the Capetian dynasty of France, is said to have been so named from the *cappa*, or monk's hood, which he wore as lay abbot of St Martin de Tours. The Capetians reigned over France till 1328, when they were succeeded by the House of Valois; but *Capet* was considered the family name of the kings, hence, Louis XVI was arraigned before the National Convention under the name of Louis Capet.

**Capful of Wind.** Olaus Magnus tells us that Eric, King of Sweden, was so familiar with evil spirits that what way soever he turned his cap the wind would blow, and for this he was called *Windy Cap*. The Laplanders drove a profitable trade in selling winds, as have many ancient and primitive peoples; and even so late as 1814, Bessie Millie, of Pomona (Orkney), used to sell favourable winds to mariners for the small sum of sixpence.

**Capital.** Money or money's worth available for production.

> His capital is continually going from him [the merchant] in some shape and returning to him in another.
>
> Adam Smith, *Wealth of Nations*, Bk ii, ch. 1

***Active capital.*** Ready money or property readily convertible into it.

***Circulating capital.*** Wages, or raw material. This sort of capital is not available a second time for the same purpose.

***Fixed capital.*** Land, buildings, and machinery, which are only gradually consumed.

***To make capital out of.*** To turn to account: thus, in politics, one party is always ready to make political capital out of the errors of the other.

**Capitals.** ***To speak in capitals.*** To speak very emphatically; to emphasise certain words with great stress in speech, as in print words given in capitals are meant to be distinctive.

**Capitano, El Gran** (i.e. the Great Captain). The name given to the famous Spanish general Gonsalvo de Cordova (1453–1515), through whose efforts Granada and Castile were united.

**Capite Censi.** In ancient Rome, freemen without property; the lowest rank of citizens; so called because they were counted simply by *the poll*, as they possessed nothing taxable.

**Capitulary.** A collection of ordinances or laws, especially those of the Frankish kings. The laws were known as *capitulars* because they were passed by a chapter (*q.v.*).

**Capon.** Properly, a castrated cock; but the name has been given to various fish, perhaps originally in a humorous way by friars who wished to evade the Friday fast and so eased their consciences by changing the name of the fish, and calling a chicken *a fish out of the coop*. Thus we have –

***A Crail's capon.*** A dried haddock.

***A Glasgow capon.*** A salt herring.

***A Severn capon.*** A sole.

***A Yarmouth capon.*** A red herring.

*Capon* is also an obsolete term for a love-letter, after the Fr. *poulet*, which means not only a chicken but also a love-letter, or a sheet of fancy note-paper. Thus Henri IV, consulting with Sully about his marriage, says: 'My niece of Guise would please me best, though report says maliciously that she loves poulets in paper better than in a fricassee.'

> Boyet ... break up this capon [i.e., open this love-letter].
>
> Shakespeare, *Love's Labour's Lost*, 4, 1

**Capot** (Fr., a hood). *Faire capot*. To win all the tricks; to gain a complete victory. *Cp*. Domino.

**Capricorn.** Called by Thomson, in his *Winter*, 'the centaur archer'. Anciently, the winter solstice occurred on the entry of the sun into Capricorn, i.e. the Goat; but the stars, having advanced a whole sign to the east, the winter solstice now falls at the sun's entrance into Sagittarius (the centaur archer), so that the poet is strictly right, though we commonly retain the ancient classical manner of speaking. Capricorn is the tenth, or, strictly speaking, the eleventh, sign of the zodiac (December 21–January 20).

According to *classic mythology*, Capricorn was Pan, who, from fear of the great Typhon, changed himself into a goat, and was made by Jupiter one of the signs of the zodiac.

**Captain, the Great.** *See* Capitano, El Gran.

***A led captain.*** An obsequious person, who dances attendance on the master and mistress of a house, for which service he has a knife and fork at the dinner table.

**Captain Armstrong.** A name for a cheating jockey – one who pulls a horse with a *strong arm*, and so prevents him winning.

**Captain Cauf's Tail.** In Yorkshire, the commander-in-chief of the mummers who used to go round from house to house on Plough Monday (*q.v.*). He was most fantastically dressed, with a cockade and many coloured ribbons; and he always had a genuine calf's (cauf's) tail affixed behind.

**Captain Copperthorne's Crew.** All masters and no men.

**Captain Stiff.** ***To come Captain Stiff over one.*** To treat one with cold formality.

> I shouldn't quite come Captain Stiff over him.
>
> S. Warren, *Ten Thousand a Year*

**Capua.** ***Capua corrupted Hannibal.*** Luxury and self-indulgence will ruin anyone. Hannibal was everywhere victorious over the Romans till he took up his winter quarters at Capua, the most luxurious city of Italy. When he left Capua his star began to wane, and, ere long, Carthage was in ruins and himself an exile. Another form of the saying is –

***Capua was the Cannae of Hannibal*** (*see* Cannae). We have a modern adaptation of this proverb: 'Moscow was the Austerlitz of Napoleon.'

**Capuchin.** A friar of the Franciscan Order (*q.v.*) of the new rule of 1525; so called from their *capuce* or pointed cowl.

**Capulet.** A noble house in Verona, the rival of that of Montague; Juliet is of the former, and Romeo of the latter. Lady Capulet is the beau-ideal of a proud Italian matron of the 15th century (Shakespeare, *Romeo and Juliet*). The expression so familiar, 'the tomb of all the Capulets', is from Burke; he uses it in his *Reflections on the Revolution in France* (vol. iii, p. 349), and again in his *Letter to Matthew Smith*, where he says:

> I would rather sleep in the southern corner of a country churchyard than in the tomb of the Capulets.

**Caput Mortuum** (Lat. *dead head*). An alchemist's term, used to designate the residuum left after exhaustive distillation or sublimation; hence, anything from which all that rendered it valuable has been taken away. Thus, a learned scholar paralysed is a mere *caput mortuum* of his former self. The French Directory, towards its close, was a mere *caput mortuum* of a governing body.

**Caqueux.** A sort of gypsy race in Brittany, similar to the Cagots of Gascony, and Colliberts of Poitou.

**Carabas.** ***He is a Marquis of Carabas.*** An ultra-conservative nobleman, of unbounded pretensions and vanity, who would restore the slavish foolery of the reign of Louis XIV; one with Fortunatus's purse, which was never empty. The character is taken from Perrault's tale of *Puss in Boots*, where he is Puss's master.

> Prêtres que nous vengeons
> Levez la dîme et partageons;
> Et toi, peuple animal,
> Porte encor le bât féodal …
> Chapeau bas! Chapeau bas!
> Gloire au marquis de Carabas! *Béranger*, 1816

The Marquis of Carabas in Disraeli's *Vivian Grey* is intended for the Marquis of Clanricarde.

**Carabinier.** *See* Carbineer.

**Caracalla.** Aurelius Antoninus, Roman Emperor, 211–17, was so called because he adopted the Gaulish *caracalla* in preference to the Roman toga. It was a large, close-fitting, hooded mantle, reaching to the heels, and slit up before and behind to the waist. *Cp.* Curtmantle.

**Carack.** *See* Carrack.

**Caradoc.** A Knight of the Round Table, noted for being the husband of the only lady in the queen's train who could wear 'the mantle of matrimonial fidelity'. He appears (as Craddocke) in the old ballad *The Boy and the Mantle* (given in Percy's *Reliques*):

> Craddocke called forth his ladye,
> And bade her come in;
> Saith, Winne this mantle, ladye,
> With a little dinne.

Also, in *history*, the British chief whom the Romans called Caractacus (lived about AD 50).

**Caraites.** A religious sect among the Jews, which arose about AD 750, and rigidly adhered to the words and letters of Scripture, regardless of metaphor, etc., rejecting the rabbinical interpretations and the Cabbala. The word is derived from *Caraïm*, equivalent to *scripturarii* (textualists).

**Carat.** A measure of weight, about $^{1}/_{150}$th of an ounce, used for precious stones; also a proportional measure of $^{1}/_{24}$th used to describe the fineness of gold, thus, gold of 22 carats has 22 parts pure gold and 2 parts alloy. The name is the Arabic *qirat*, meaning the seed of the locust tree, the weight of which represented the Roman *siliqua*, which was 1/24th of the golden *solidus* of Constantine, which was 1/6th of an ounce. It is from these fractions that it has come about that a carat is a twenty-fourth part. *See* Gold.

**Carbineer** or ***Carabineer***. A soldier armed with a short, light rifle (called a *carbine*) such as is used by cavalry. The word is from Fr. *carabine*, which is either from *Calabrinus*, a Calabrian (in which case the word would originally mean a skirmisher or light horseman), or from late Lat. *chadabula*, a kind of ballista for hurling projectiles. The 6th Dragoon Guards in the British Army are known as *the Carabiniers*.

**Carbonado.** Grilled meat or fish. Strictly speaking, a carbonado is a piece of meat cut crosswise for the gridiron (Lat. *carbo*, a coal).

> If he do come in my way, so; if he do not – if I come in his willingly, let him make a carbonado of me.
>
> Shakespeare, *1 Henry IV*, 5, 3

**Carbonari** (singular, *carbonaro*). This name, assumed by a secret political society in Italy (organised 1808–14), means *charcoal burners*. Their place of muster they called a 'hut'; its inside, 'the place for selling charcoal'; and the outside, the 'forest'. Their political opponents they called 'wolves'. Their object was to convert the kingdom of Naples into a republic. *See* Charbonnerie.

**Carcanet.** A small chain of jewels for the neck. (Fr. *carcan*, a collar of gold.)

> Like captain jewels in a carcanet.
>
> Shakespeare, *Sonnets*

**Carcass.** The shell of a house before the floors are laid and walls plastered; the skeleton of a ship, a wreck, etc. The body of a dead animal, so called from Fr. *carcasse*, Lat. *carcosium*.

> The Goodwins, I think they call the place; a very dangerous flat and fatal, where the carcases of many a tall ship lie buried.
>
> Shakespeare, *Merchant of Venice*, 3, 1

The name was also given to an obsolete bomb or shell, having three fuse-holes, which were projected from mortars, etc. They did not burst like shells, but the flames, rushing from the three holes set on fire everything within range.

> Charlestown, … having been fired by a carcass from Copp's Hill, sent up dense columns of smoke. Lessing, *United States*

**Card.** Slang for a queer fellow, an eccentric, a 'character'.

> You're a shaky old card; and you can't be in love with this Lizzie.
>
> Dickens, *Our Mutual Friend*, Bk iii, ch. i

Perhaps suggested by the phrase, 'a sure card'. *See below*. We thus have such phrases as the following:

***A cool card.*** A person who coolly asks for something preposterous or outrageous. 'Cool' in this connection means coolly impudent. *Cp.* Cooling card *below*.

***A great card.*** A bigwig; the boss of the season: a person of note.

***A knowing card.*** A sharp fellow, next door to a sharper. The allusion is to cardsharpers and their tricks.

> Whose great aim it was to be considered a knowing card. Dickens, *Sketches, etc.*

***A loose card.*** A worthless fellow who lives on the loose.

> A loose card is a card of no value, and, consequently the properest to throw away.
>
> Hoyle, *Games, etc.*

***A queer card.*** An eccentric person, 'indifferent honest'; one who *may* be 'all right', but whose proceedings arouse mild suspicion and do not inspire confidence.

***A sure card.*** A person one can fully depend on; a person sure to command success. A project to be certainly depended on. As a winning card in one's hand.

> A clear conscience is a sure card.
>
> Lyly, *Euphues* (1579)

Other phrases are directly from card-games, or from the 'card' of a compass, i.e. the dial on which the points of the compass are displayed. The first named group gives us, among others, such phrases as:

***A cooling card.*** An obsolete expression for something that cools one's ardour, probably derived from some old game of cards. It is quite common in Elizabethan literature. In *Euphues* (1579) Lyly calls the letter to Philantus 'a cooling card for Philantus and all fond lovers', and says –

> The sick patient must keep a straight diet, the silly sheep a narrow fold, poor Philantus must believe Euphues, and all lovers (he only excepted) are cooled with a card of ten or rather fooled with a vain toy.

***A card of ten*** was evidently an important card; Shakespeare has:

> A vengeance on your crafty wither'd hide!
> Yet I have faced it with a card of ten.
>
> *Taming of the Shrew*, 2, 2

which means either to put a bold face on it, or to meet an attack with craft and subtlety.

***A leading card.*** The strongest point in one's argument, etc.; a star actor. In card-games a person leads from his strongest suit.

***He played his cards well.*** He acted judiciously and skilfully, like a whist-player who plays his hand with judgment.

***On the cards.*** Likely to happen, projected, and talked about as likely to occur. This phrase may have allusion to the programme or card of the races, but is more likely to derive from fortune-telling by cards.

***That's the card.*** The right thing; the ticket; probably to card-games – 'that is the right card to play' – but it may refer to tickets of admission, cards of the races, programmes, etc.

> 10s. is about the card.
>
> Mayhew, *London Labour, etc.*

***That was my trump card.*** My best chance, my last resort.

***The cards are in my hands.*** I hold the disposal of events which will secure success; I have the upper hand, the whip-end of the stick.

> The Vitelli busied at Arezzo; the Orsini irritating the French; the war of Naples imminent; – the cards are in my hands. *Caesar Borgia*, xxix

***To count on one's cards.*** To anticipate success under the circumstances; to rely on one's advantages.

***To go in with good cards.*** To have good patronage; to have excellent grounds for expecting success.

***To play one's best card.*** To do that which one hopes is most likely to secure victory.

***To throw up the cards.*** To give up as a bad job; to acknowledge you have no hope of success. In some games of cards, as poker, a player has the liberty of saying whether he will play or not, and if one's hand is hopelessly bad he throws in his cards and sits out till the next deal.

From the compass card we have the phrase: *To speak by the card*, to be careful with one's words; to be as deliberate, and have as much claim to be right, as a compass.

> Law ... is the card to guide the world by.
>
> Hooker, *Ecc. Pol.*, Pt ii, sec. 5
>
> We must speak by the card, or equivocation will undo us. Shakespeare, *Hamlet*, 5, 1

It is possible that this phrase has reference to written documents, such as agreements made between a merchant and the captain of a vessel. To speak by the card may be to speak according to the indentures or written instructions, but when Osric tells Hamlet (5, 2) that Laertes is 'the card and calendar of gentry' the card is a card of a compass, containing all its points. Laertes is the card of gentry, in whom may be seen all its points.

**Cards.** It is said that there never was a good hand at whist containing four clubs. Such a hand is called 'The Devil's Four-poster'.

In Spain, spades used to be *columbines*; clubs, *rabbits*; diamonds, *pinks*; and hearts, *roses*. The present name for spades is *espados* (swords); of clubs, *bastos* (cudgels); of diamonds, *dineros* (square pieces of money used for paying wages); of hearts, *copas* (chalices).

The French for spades is *pique* (pikemen or soldiers); for clubs, *trèfle* (clover, or husbandmen); of diamonds *carreaux* (building tiles, or flagstones); of hearts, *coeur*.

The English spades is the French form of a pike, and the Spanish name; the clubs is the French trefoil, and the Spanish name.

***Court cards.*** *See* Court.

**Cardinal.** The Lat. *cardo* means a hinge; its adjective, *cardinalis* (from which we get 'cardinal'), meant originally 'pertaining to a hinge', hence 'that on which something turns or depends', hence 'the principal, the chief'. Hence, in Christian Rome a 'cardinal church' (*ecclesia cardinalis*) was a principal or parish church as distinguished from an oratory attached to such, and the chief priest (*presbyter cardinalis*) was the 'cardinal', the body (or 'College') of cardinals forming the Council of the Pope, and electing the Pope from their own number. This did not become a stabilised regulation till after the third Lateran Council (1173), since when the College of Cardinals has consisted of six cardinal bishops, fifty cardinal priests, and fourteen cardinal deacons.

The cardinals' 'Red hat' was made part of the official vestments by Innocent IV (1245) 'in token of their being ready to lay down their life for the gospel'.

**Cardinal Humours.** An obsolete medical term for the four principal 'humours' of the body, viz. blood, phlegm, yellow bile, and black bile.

**Cardinal Numbers.** The natural, primitive numbers, which answer the question 'how many?' such as 1, 2, 3, etc. 1st, 2nd, 3rd, etc., are *ordinal* numbers.

**Cardinal Points of the Compass.** Due north, west, east, and south. So called because they are the points on which the intermediate ones, such as NE, NW, NNE, etc., hinge or hang. (Lat. *cardo*, a hinge.)

The poles, being the points upon which the earth turns, were called in Latin *cardines* (*cardo*, a hinge, *see* Cardinal *above*), and the *cardinal points* are those which lie in the direction of the poles and of the sunrise and sunset. Thus, also, the winds that blow due East, West, North, and South are known as the *Cardinal Winds*. It is probably from the fact that the cardinal points are *four* in number that the cardinal humours, virtues, etc., are also *four*.

**Cardinal Signs** (of the zodiac). The two equinoctial and the two solstitial signs, Aries and Libra, Cancer and Capricorn.

**Cardinal Virtues.** Justice, prudence, temperance, and fortitude, on which all other virtues hang or depend. A term of the Schoolmen, to distinguish the 'natural' virtues from the 'theological' virtues (faith, hope, and charity).

**Cardinal Winds.** *See* Cardinal Points.

**Carduel.** The name given in the Arthurian romances to Carlisle, where Merlin prepared the Round Table.

**Care-cloth.** The fine silk or linen cloth laid over the newly married in the Catholic Church, or held over them as a canopy.

**Care Killed the Cat.** It is said that 'a cat has nine lives', yet care would wear them all out.

> Hang sorrow! care'll kill a cat.
>
> Ben Jonson, *Every Man in his Humour*, I, iii

**Care Sunday.** The fifth Sunday in Lent. 'Care' here means trouble, suffering; and Care Sunday means Passion Sunday (as in Old High Ger. *Kar-fritag* is Good Friday).

Care Sunday is also known as *Carle*, or *Carling Sunday*. It was an old custom, especially in the north, to eat parched peas fried in butter on this day, and they were called *Carlings*.

**Careme.** Lent; a corruption of *quadragesima*.

**Caricatures** mean 'sketches overloaded'; hence, exaggerated drawings. (Ital. *caricatura*, from *caricarë*, to load or burden.)

**Carillons,** in France, are chimes or tunes played on bells; but in England the suites of bells that play the tunes. The word is the O.Fr. *quarignon*, from late Lat. *quatrinio*, a chime played on four bells; carillons were formerly rung on four bells; nowadays the number is usually eight, but the 'bob maximus' (*see* Bob) is rung on twelve.

**Carle Sunday; Carlings.** *See* Care Sunday.

**Carlovingians** or ***Carolingians***. So called from Carolus Magnus, or Charlemagne. They were descended from Frankish lords in Austria in the 7th century, and furnished the second royal dynasty in France (751–987), a dynasty of German Emperors (752–911), and of Italian kings (774–961).

**Carmagnole.** Originally the name of a kind of jacket worn in France in the 18th century, and introduced there from Carmagnola, in Piedmont, where it was the dress of the workmen. It was adopted by the Revolutionists, and the name thus came to be applied to them, to the soldiers of the first Republic, and to a song and a wild kind of dance that became immensely popular and was almost invariably used at the executions of 1792 and 1793. The first verse of the song is:

> Madame Veto avait promis
> De faire égorger tout Paris,
> Madame Veto avait promis
> De faire égorger tout Paris.
> Maisson coup a manqué
> Grace a nos canonnié:
> Dansons la carmagnole, Vive le son, vive le son,
> Dansons la carmagnole, Vive le son du canon.

The word was subsequently applied to other revolutionary songs, such as *Ça ira*, the *Marseillaise*, the *Chant du Depart*; also to the speeches in favour of the execution of Louis XVI, called by M. Barrière *des Carmagnoles*.

**Carmelites.** Mendicant friars, the first rule of whose Order is said to have been given by John, patriarch of Jerusalem, AD 400, and to have been formed from the records of the prophet Elijah's life on Mount Carmel. Also called White Friars, from their white cloaks. *See* Barefooted.

**Carminative.** A medicine given to relieve flatulence. The name is a relic of the mediaeval theory of humours; it is from Lat. *carminare*, to card wool, which, in Italian, also meant 'to make gross humours fine and thin'. The object of carminatives is to expel wind, and they were supposed to effect this by combing out the gross humours as one combs out (or cards) the knots in wool.

**Carmine.** The dye made from the kermes insect, whence also *crimson*, through the Ital. *cremisino*.

**Carnation.** Flesh-colour. (Lat. *caro, carnis*, flesh.)

**Carney.** To wheedle, to caress, to coax. An old dialect word of unknown origin.

**Carnival.** The season immediately preceding Lent, ending on Shrove Tuesday, a period in many Roman Catholic countries devoted to amusement; hence, revelry, riotous amusement. From the Lat. *caro, carnis*, flesh, *levare*, to remove, signifying the abstinence from meat during Lent. The earlier word, *carnilevamen*, was altered in Italian to *carnevale*, as though connected with *vale*, farewell – farewell to flesh.

**Carol** (from O.Fr. *carole*, which is probably from Lat. *choraula*, a dance). The earliest meaning of the word in English is a round dance, hence a song that accompanied the dance, hence a light and joyous hymn, a meaning which came to be applied specially to, and latterly almost confined to, such a hymn in honour of the Nativity and sung at Christmas time by wandering minstrels. The earliest extant English Christmas carol dates from the 13th century, and was originally written in Anglo-Saxon; a translation of the first verse is here given. The first printed collection of Christmas carols came from the press of Wynkyn de Worde in 1521; it included the Boar's Head Carol, which is still sung at Queen's College, Oxford. For another example, *see* Boar's Head.

Lordings, listen to our lay –
We have come from far away
To seek Christmas;
In this mansion we are told
He his yearly feast doth hold;
'Tis today!
May joy come from God above,
To all those who Christmas love.

**Carolingians.** *See* Carlovingians.

**Carolus.** A gold coin of the reign of Charles I. It was at first worth 20*s.* but afterwards 23*s.*

**Carotid Artery.** An artery on each side of the neck, supposed by the ancients to be the seat of drowsiness, brought on by an increased flow of blood through it to the head. (Gr. *caroticos*, inducing sleep.)

**Carouse.** To drink deeply, to make merry with drinking; hence a drinking bout. The word is the German *garaus*, meaning literally 'right out' or 'completely'; it was used specially of completely emptying a bumper to someone's health.

The word *rouse*, a bumper, as in Shakespeare's:

The king doth wake tonight, and takes his rouse.
Hamlet, 1, 4

probably arose from the similarity of sound between 'to drink carouse' and 'to drink a rouse'.

**Carpathian Wizard.** Proteus, who lived in the island of Carpathus (now Scarpanto), between Rhodes and Crete, who could transform himself into any shape he pleased. He is represented as carrying a sort of crook in his hand, because he was an ocean shepherd and had to manage a flock of sea-calves.

By the Carpathian wizard's book.
Milton, *Comus*, 872

**Carpe Diem.** Enjoy yourself while you have the opportunity. Seize the present day. '*Dum vivimus, vivamus.*'

Carpe diem, quam minimum credula postere.
Horace, *Odes*, I, xi, 8

Seize the present, trust tomorrow e'en as little as you may.
Connington

**Carpet. *The magic carpet.*** The carpet which, to all appearances, is worthless, but which, if anyone sat thereon, would transport him instantaneously to the place he wished to go, is one of the stock properties of Eastern wonder-tales and romance. It is sometimes termed *Prince Housain's carpet*, because of the popularity of the *Story of Prince Ahmed* in *The Arabian Nights*, where it supplies one of the principal incidents; but the chief magic carpet is that of King Solomon, which, according to the Mohammedan legend related in the Koran, was of green silk. His throne was placed on it when he travelled, and it was large enough for all his forces to stand upon, the men and women on his right hand, and the spirits on his left. When all were arranged in order, Solomon told the wind where he wished to go, and the carpet, with all its contents, rose in the air and alighted at the place indicated. In order to screen the party from the sun, the birds of the air with outspread wings formed a canopy over the whole party.

***To be on the carpet,*** or ***to be carpeted.*** To be reprimanded, to be 'called over the coals', to get a 'wigging'.

***To bring a question on the carpet;*** to bring it up for consideration: a translation of Fr. *sur le tapis* (on the tablecloth) – i.e. before the House, under consideration. The question has been laid on the table of the House, and is now under debate.

**Carpet-bagger.** The name given in the United States to the Northern political adventurers, who sought a career in the Southern States after the Civil War of 1865. Their only 'property qualification' was in the personal baggage they brought with them, and they were looked upon with great suspicion. In America members of Congress and the State legislatures almost invariably reside in the district which they represent.

**Carpet-bag Government.** A government of mere adventurers; one organised by 'carpet-baggers' (*q.v.*).

**Carpet Knight.** One dubbed at Court by favour, not having won his spurs by military service in the field. Perhaps because mayors, lawyers, and civilians generally are knighted as they kneel *on a carpet* before their sovereign in contradistinction to those knighthoods that used to be conferred on the actual field of battle; but more probably with allusion to the preference shown by non-martial knights for the carpeted drawing-room over the tented field.

> The subordinate commands fell to young patricians, carpet-knights, who went on campaigns with their families and slaves.
>
> Froude, *Caesar*, ch. iv, p. 91

**Carpocratians.** A sect of gnostics; so called from Carpocrates, who flourished in the middle of the 2nd century. They maintained that the world was made by angels – that only the soul of Christ ascended into heaven – and that the body will have no resurrection. Many of their tenets resembled those of the Basilidians (*q.v.*).

**Carrack.** A large merchant ship which, in Elizabethan times, carried the valuable cargoes from the Spice Islands and the Far East to Portugal, and could readily be fitted out as a man-of-war.

> 'And now hath Sathanas,' seith he, 'a tayl
> Brodder than of a carrik is the sayl.'
>
> Chaucer, *Somnour's Prologue*, 23

**Carriage.** This used to mean, that which is carried, luggage.

> And after those days we took up our carriages, and went up to Jerusalem. Acts 21:15

In Num. 4:24, where the text gives 'burdens', the marginal rendering is 'carriage', and the usage is not at all uncommon in the English of that date.

**Carriage Company.** Persons who go visiting in their private carriage.

> Seeing a great deal of carriage company.
>
> Thackeray

**Carronades.** A short gun of large calibre like a mortar, having no trunnions and so differing from howitzers, first made in 1779 at the Carron foundry, Scotland. Carronades are fastened to their carriages by a loop underneath, and were chiefly used on ships, to enable heavy shot to be thrown at close quarters.

**Carry.** ***Carry arms! Carry swords!*** Military commands directing that the rifle or drawn sword is to be held in a vertical position in the right hand and against the right shoulder.

***Carry coals.*** *See* Coals.

***To carry everything before one.*** To be beyond competition; to carry off all the prizes. Similarly, a high wind carries everything before it.

***To carry fire in one hand and water in the other.*** To say one thing and mean another; to flatter, to deceive; to lull suspicion in order the better to work mischief.

> Altera manu fert aquam, altera ignem,
> Altera manu fert lapideum, altera panem ostentat.
>
> Plautus
>
> In one hand he carried water, in the other fire; in one hand he bears a stone, in the other he shows a piece of bread.

***To carry one's point.*** To succeed in one's aim. Candidates in Rome were balloted for, and the votes were marked on a tablet by points. Hence, *omne punctum ferre* meant 'to be carried *nem. con.*', or to gain every vote; and 'to carry one's point' is to carry off the points at which one aimed.

***To carry out*** or ***through.*** To continue a project to its completion.

***To carry out one's bat.*** Said of a cricketer who is 'not out' at the close of the game. Hence, figuratively, to outlast one's opponents, to succeed in one's undertaking.

***Carry swords!*** *See* Carry Arms.

***To carry the day.*** To win the contest; to carry off the honours of the day.

***To carry weight.*** In horse racing, to equalise the weight of two or more riders by adding to the lighter ones, till both (or all) the riders are made of uniform weight.

> He carries weight! he rides a race!
> 'Tis for a thousand pounds.
>
> Cowper, *John Gilpin*

Also, to have influence.

**Cart.** ***To put the cart before the horse*** is to reverse the right order or allocation of things.

> *French*: Mettre la charrette avant les boeufs.
> *Latin*: Currus bovem trahit
> Praepostere.
> *Greek*: Hysteron proteron.
> *German*: Die pferde hinter den wagen spannen.
> *Italian*: Metter il carro inanzi ai buoi.

**Carte blanche** (Fr.). A paper with only the signature written on it, so that the person to whom it is given may write his terms knowing that they will be accepted. Literally, a blank paper. It was originally a military phrase, referring to capitulation at discretion; but it is now used entirely in a figurative sense, conferring absolute freedom of action on one to whom it is given.

**Carte de visite** (Fr.). A visiting card; a photographic likeness on a card, originally intended to be used as a visiting card. The idea was started in 1857 by the Duke of Parma, but it never 'caught on'.

**Cartesian Philosophy.** The philosophical system of René Descartes (1596–1650), a founder of modern philosophy. The basis of his system is *cogito ergo sum. See* Cogito. Thought must proceed from soul, and therefore man is not wholly material; that soul must be from some

Being not material, and that Being is God. As for physical phenomena, they must be the result of motion excited by God, and these motions he termed *vortices*.

**Carthaginem esse Delendam.** *See* Delenda est Carthago.

**Carthaginian Faith.** Treachery. *See* Punica Fides.

**Carthusians.** An order of monks, founded about 1086 by St Bruno, of Cologne, who, with six companions, retired to the solitude of La Grande Chartreuse, thirteen miles north-east of Grenoble, and there built his famous monastery. In 1902 the monks were evicted by order of the French government, and in the following year their buildings and property were sold. *See* Chartreuse.

**Cartoons.** Designs drawn on *cartone* (pasteboard), like those of Raffaelle, formerly at Hampton Court, but now at South Kensington. They were bought by Charles I, and are seven in number: 'The Miraculous Draught of Fishes', 'Feed my Lambs', 'The Beautiful Gate of the Temple', 'Death of Ananias', 'Elymas the Sorcerer', 'Paul at Lystra', and 'Paul on the Mars Hill'.

> They were designs for tapestries to be worked in Flanders.
>
> Julia B. de Forest, *Short History of Art*, p. 246

**Cartridge Paper.** A stout, rough paper, originally manufactured for cartridges. The word is a corruption of *cartouche*, from *carta* (paper).

**Carvel-built.** A term in shipbuilding applied to a vessel whose planks are set edge to edge and do not overlap. From *Caravella* (Ital.) a large sailing ship. *See Clinker-built.*

**Carvilia.** *See* Morgan le Fay.

**Caryatids.** Figures of women in Greek costume, used in architecture to support entablatures. Caryae, in Laconia, sided with the Persians at Thermopylae; in consequence of which the victorious Greeks destroyed the city, slew the men, and made the women slaves. Praxiteles, to perpetuate the disgrace, employed figures of these women, instead of columns. *Cp.* Atlantes, Canephorus.

**Casabianca, Louis.** Captain of the French man-of-war, *L'Orient*. At the battle of Aboukir, having first secured the safety of his crew, he blew up his ship, to prevent it falling into the hands of the English. His little son, Giacomo Jocante, refusing to leave him, perished with his father. Mrs Hemans made a ballad on the incident, which was also celebrated by the French poets Lebrun and Chénier.

**Case. *The case is altered.*** *See* Plowden.

***To case.*** To skin an animal; to deprive it of its 'case'. *See First catch your hare, s.v.* Catch.

**Case-hardened.** Impenetrable to all sense of honour or shame. The allusion is to iron toughened by carbonising the surface in contact with charcoal in a case or closed box.

**Cashier.** To dismiss an officer from the army, to discard from society. (Dut. *casseren*, Fr. *casser*, to break; Ital. *cassarë*, to blot out.)

> The ruling rogue, who dreads to be cashiered,
> Contrives, as he is hated, to be feared.
>
> Swift, *Epistle to Mr Gay*, 137

**Cashmere.** *See* Kerseymere.

**Casimere.** *See* Beefington.

**Casino.** Originally, a little *casa* or room near a theatre where persons might retire, after the play was over, for dancing or music.

**Casket Homer.** *See* Homer.

**Casket Letters, The.** Letters supposed to have been written between Mary Queen of Scots and Bothwell, at least one of which was held to prove the complicity of the Queen in the murder of her husband, Darnley. They were kept in a casket which fell into the hands of the Earl of Morton (1567); they were examined and used as evidence (though denounced as forgeries by the Queen – who was never allowed to see them), and they disappeared after the execution of the Regent, the Earl of Gowrie (1584), in whose custody they had last been. They have never been recovered, and their authenticity is still a matter of dispute.

**Cassandra.** A prophetess. In Greek legend the daughter of Priam and Hecuba, gifted with the power of prophecy; but Apollo, whose advances she had refused, brought it to pass that no one believed her predictions, although they were invariably correct. She appears in Shakespeare's *Troilus and Cressida*.

> A *Cassandra* of the Crew [gypsies], after having examined my lines very diligently told me, etc.
>
> *Spectator*, July 30th, 1711

**Cassation. *The Court of Cassation*,** in France, is the highest Court of Appeal, the Court which can *casser* (quash) the judgment of other Courts.

**Cassi.** Inhabitants of what is now the Cassio hundred, Hertfordshire, referred to by Caesar, in his *Commentaries*. The name can still be traced in Cassiobury Park, just outside Watford.

**Cassibelan.** Uncle to Cymbeline, mentioned in Shakespeare's play of that name. He is the historical Cassivellaunus, a British prince who ruled over the Catrivellauni (in Herts, Bucks, and Berks), about 50 BC, and was conquered by Caesar.

When Julius Caesar … was in this Britain
And conquer'd it, Cassibelan, thine uncle, … for him
And his succession granted Rome a tribute,
Yearly three thousand pounds; which by thee lately
Is left untender'd. *Cymbeline*, 3, 1

Shakespeare drew his particulars from Holinshed, where it is Guiderius, not Cymbeline, who refuses to pay the tribute.

**Cassiopeia.** In *Greek mythology*, the wife of Cepheus, King of Ethiopia, and mother of Andromeda (*q.v.*). In consequence of her boasting of the beauty of her daughter, she was sent to the heavens as the constellation Cassiopeia, the chief stars of which form the outline of a lady seated in a chair and holding up both arms in supplication.

That starred Ethiop queen that strove
To set her beauty's praise above
The sea-nymphs and their powers offended.
Milton, *Il Penseroso*

**Cassiterides.** The tin islands, generally supposed to be the Scilly Islands and Cornwall; but possibly the isles in Vigo Bay are meant. It is said that the Veneti procured tin from Cornwall, and carried it to these islands, keeping its source a profound secret. The Phoenicians were the chief customers of the Veneti.

**Cast. *A cast of the eye.*** A squint. One meaning of the word cast is to twist or warp. Thus, a fabric is said to 'cast' when it warps; and seamen speak of 'casting', or turning the head of a ship on the tack it is to sail. We also speak of a 'casting vote' (*q.v.*).

My goode bowe clene cast [twisted] on one side.
Ascham, *Toxophilus*

***Cast down.*** Dejected. (Lat. *dejectus.*)

***To cast a sheep's eye at one.*** *See* Sheep.

***To cast about.*** To deliberate, to consider, as, 'I am casting about me how I am to meet the expenses.' A sporting phrase. Dogs, when they have lost scent, 'cast for it', i.e. spread out and search in different directions to recover it.

***To cast accounts.*** To balance or keep accounts. *To cast up a line of figures* is to add them together and set down the sum they produce. To cast or throw the value of one figure into another till the whole number is totalled.

***To cast anchor.*** To throw out the anchor in order to bring the vessel to a standstill. (Lat. *anchoram jacere.*)

***To cast aside.*** To reject as worthless.

***To cast beyond the moon.*** To form wild conjectures. One of Heywood's proverbs. At one time the moon was supposed to influence the weather, to affect the ingathering of fruits, to rule the time of sowing, reaping, and slaying cattle, etc.

I talke of things impossible, and cast beyond the moon. Heywood

***To cast in one's lot.*** To share the good or bad fortune of another.

***To cast in one's teeth.*** To throw a reproof at one. The allusion is to knocking one's teeth out by stones.

All his faults observed,
Set in a note book, learned and conned by rote,
To cast into my teeth.
Shakespeare, *Julius Caesar*, 4, 3

***To cast pearls before swine.*** To give what is precious to those who are unable to understand its value: a biblical phrase (*see* Matt. 7:6). If pearls are cast to swine, the swine would only trample them under foot.

***Casting vote.*** The vote of the presiding officer when the votes of the assembly are equal. This final vote casts, turns, or determines the question.

**Castaly.** A fountain of Parnassus sacred to the Muses. Its waters had the power of inspiring with the gift of poetry those who drank of them.

What was the great Parnassus' self to Thee,
Mount Skiddaw? In his natural sovereignty
Our British Hill is nobler far; he shrouds
His double front among Atlantic clouds,
And pours forth streams more sweet than Castaly.
Wordsworth, *Miscellaneous Sonnets*, 5

**Caste** (Port. *casta*, race). One of the hereditary classes of society in India; hence any hereditary or exclusive class, or the class system generally. The four Hindu castes are *Brahmins* (the priestly order), *Shatriya* (soldiers and rulers), *Vaisya* (husbandmen and merchants), *Sudra* (agricultural labourers and mechanics). The first issued from the mouth of Brahma, the second from his arms, the third from his thighs, and the fourth from his feet. Below these come thirty-six inferior classes, to whom the Vedas are sealed, and who are held cursed in this world and without hope in the next.

***To lose caste.*** To lose position in society. To get degraded from one caste to an inferior one.

**Castle-builder.** One who entertains sanguine hopes. One who builds 'castles in the air' (*q.v.*).

**Castles in the Air.** Visionary projects, day-dreams, splendid imaginings which have no real existence. In fairy tales we often have these castles built at a word, and vanishing as soon, like that built for Aladdin by the Genius of the Lamp. These air-castles are called by the French *Châteaux d'Espagne* or *Châteaux en Asie. See* Châteaux.

**Castle of Bungay.** In Camden's *Britannia* (1607) the following lines are attributed to Lord Bigod of Bungay:

Were I in my Castle of Bungay
Vpon the riuer of Waueney,
I would ne care for the King of Cockney.

The events referred to belong to the reign of Stephen or Henry II. The French have a proverb: *Je ne voudrais pas être roi, si j'étais prévot de Bar-sur-Aube*, I should not care to be king if I were Provost of Bar-sur-Aube (the most lucrative and honourable of all the provostships of France). A similar idea is expressed in the words –

And often to our comfort we shall find,
The sharded beetle in a safer hold
Than is the full-winged eagle.

Shakespeare, *Cymbeline*, 3, 3

Almost to the same effect Pope says:

And more true joy Marcellus exiled feels,
Than Caesar with a senate at his heels.

*Essay on Man*, iv, 257

**Castle of Indolence.** In Thomson's poem of this name (1748) it is situated in the land of Drowsiness, where every sense is steeped in enervating delights. The owner was an enchanter, who deprived all who entered his domains of their energy and free will.

**Castle Terabil** (or 'Terrible') in Arthurian legends stood in Launceston. It had a steep keep environed with a triple wall. Sometimes called Dunheved Castle.

**Castor.** Slang for a hat. *Castor* is the Latin for a beaver, and beaver (*q.v.*) was a hat made of beaver's skin.

The last effort of decayed fortune is expended in smoothing its dilapidated castor. The hat is the *ultimum moriens* of 'respectability'.

O. W. Holmes, *Aut of Breakfast Table*, viii

**Castor and Pollux.** In *Roman mythology*, the twin sons of Jupiter and Leda. Jupiter is said to have visited Leda in the form of a swan; she produced two eggs, from one of which sprang Castor and Clytemnestra, and from the other Pollux and Helen. Castor and Pollux, also known as the Dioscuri (*q.v.*), had many adventures, were worshipped as gods, and were finally placed among the constellations.

Their name used to be given by sailors to the St Elmo's Fire or Corposant (*q.v.*). If only one flame showed itself, the Romans called it *Helen*, and said that it portended that the worst of the storm was yet to come; but two or more luminous flames they called *Castor and Pollux*, and said that they boded the termination of the storm.

**Casuist.** One who resolves *casus conscientiae* (cases of conscience); figuratively, a hair-splitter. M. le Fevre called casuistry 'the art of quibbling with God'.

**Casus belli** (Lat.). A ground for war; an occurrence warranting international hostilities.

M. Cambon asked me what we should say about the violation of the neutrality of Belgium. I said that was a much more important matter; we were considering what statement we should make in Parliament tomorrow – in effect, whether we should declare violation of Belgian neutrality to be a *casus belli*.

Sir Edw. Grey to the Brit. Ambassador at Paris, 2 Aug., 1914

**Cat.** Called a 'familiar', from the mediaeval superstition that Satan's favourite form was a black cat. Hence witches were said to have a cat as their familiar. The superstition may have arisen from the classical legend of Galinthias (*q.v.*), who was turned into a cat and became a priestess of Hecate.

In ancient Rome the cat was a symbol of liberty. The goddess of Liberty was represented as holding a cup in one hand, a broken sceptre in the other, and with a cat lying at her feet. No animal is so great an enemy to all constraint as a cat.

In Egypt the cat was sacred to Isis, or the moon. It was held in great veneration, and was worshipped with great ceremony as a symbol of the moon, not only because it is more active after sunset, but from the dilation and contraction of its pupil, symbolical of waxing and waning. The goddess Bast (*see* Bubastis), representative of the life-giving solar heat, was portrayed as having the head of a cat, probably because that animal likes to bask in the sun. Diodorus tells us that whoever killed a cat, even by accident, was by the Egyptians punished by death, and according to Egyptian tradition, Diana assumed the form of a cat, and thus excited the fury of the giants.

***Cat Proverbs and Sayings.***

***A cat has nine lives.*** A cat is more tenacious of life than many animals. It is a careful, sly and suspicious beast, and – in the wild state – is strong, hardy, and ferocious; also, after a fall, it generally lights upon its feet without injury, the foot and toes being well padded.

*Tyb.*: What wouldst thou have with me?
*Mer.*: Good king of cats, nothing but one of your nine lives.

Shakespeare, *Romeo and Juliet*, 3, 1

A cat has nine lives, and a woman has nine cats' lives. Fuller, *Gnomologia*

***A cat may look at a king.*** An impertinent remark by an inferior, meaning, 'I am as good as you'; or 'Are you too mighty to be spoken to or looked at?' 'You may wear stars and ribbons, and I may be dressed in hodden grey, but a man's a man for a' that.' There was a political pamphlet published with this title in 1652.

***All cats love fish but fear to wet their paws.*** An old adage, said of one who is anxious to obtain something of value but does not care to incur the necessary trouble or risk. It was to this saying that Shakespeare referred in *Macbeth*, 1, 7:

> Letting 'I dare not' wait upon 'I would',
> Like the poor cat i' the adage.

***Before the cat can lick her ear.*** Never; before the Greek kalends. No cat can lick her ear. *See* Never.

***Care killed the cat.*** *See* Care.

***Cat i' the adage.*** *See* All cats love fish *above*.

***To cat.*** *See* Sick as a cat *below*.

***To cat the anchor.*** To hang the anchor on the *cathead*, a piece of timber outside the ship to which the anchor is hung to keep it clear of the ship.

> The decks were all life and commotion; the sailors on the forecastle singing 'Ho! cheerly, men!' as they catted the anchor.
> H. Melville, *Omoo*, xxxvi, p. 191

***Cheshire cat.*** *See* To grin like a Cheshire cat *below*.

***Dick Whittington and his cat.*** *See* Whittington.

***Enough to make a cat speak.*** Said of something (usually good liquor) that will loosen one's tongue.

> Come on your ways; open your mouth; there is that which will give language to your cat, open your mouth!
> Shakespeare, *Tempest*, 2, 2

***Hang me in a bottle like a cat.*** (*Much Ado about Nothing*, 1, 1.) In olden times a cat was for sport enclosed in a bag or leather bottle, and hung to the branch of a tree as a mark for bowmen to shoot at. Percy mentions a variant of this 'sport' in his *Reliques of Ancient English Poetry* (1765).

> It is still a diversion in Scotland to hang up a cat in a small cask or firkin, half filled with soot; and then a parcel of clowns on horsebark try to beat out the *ends* of it, in order to show their dexterity in escaping before the contents fall upon them. Vol I. p. 155 (Edn of 1794)

***In the dark all cats are grey.*** All persons are undistinguished till they have made a name.

***It is raining cats and dogs.*** Very heavily.

> I know Sir John would go, though he was sure it would rain cats and dogs.
> Swift, *Polite Conversation*, ii

We sometimes say, 'It is raining pitchforks,' which is the French locution, '*Il tombe des hallebardes.*'

***Kilkenny cats.*** *See* To fight like Kilkenny cats *below*.

***Like a cat on hot bricks.*** Very uneasy; not at all 'at home' in the situation, whatever it may be. If a cat were put upon hot bricks it would naturally be in a great hurry to get off.

***Muffled cats catch no mice*** (Ital. *Catta guantata non piglia sorice*). Said of those who work in gloves for fear of soiling their fingers.

***Not room to swing a cat.*** Swinging cats as a mark for sportsmen was at one time a favourite amusement. There were several varieties of this diversion. *See* Hang me in a bottle *above*, and To fight like Kilkenny cats *below*. It is probable that the custom of tormenting cats by the ignorant arose from their supposed connection with witches.

> Mrs Crupp had indignantly assured him that there wasn't room to swing a cat there; but as Mr Dick justly observed to me, ... 'You know, Trotwood, I don't want to swing a cat. I never do swing a cat. Therefore what does that signify to *me*!' Dickens, *David Copperfield*, ch. xxxv

Smollet had previously used the phrase in *Humphry Clinker*, Lett. xxxvi; and it is quite possible that *cat* was originally *cot*, the phrase being a sailor's expression, and the allusion to a swung hammock or cot.

***See how the cat jumps.*** *See* 'which way the wind blows'; which of two alternatives is likely to be the successful one before you give any opinion of its merit or adhesion to it, either moral or otherwise. The allusion is either to the game called 'tip-cat', in which before you strike you must observe which way the 'cat' has jumped up, or to the cruel sport mentioned above. *See* Hang me in a bottle.

> He soon saw which way the cat did jump,
> And his company he offered plump.
> *The Dog's-meat Man* (*Universal Songster*, 1825)

***Sick as a cat.*** Cats are very subject to vomiting. Hence the vomit of a drunkard is called a 'cat', and one is said *to cat*, or *to shoot the cat* in discarding it.

***To bell the cat.*** *See* Bell.

***To fight like Kilkenny cats.*** To fight till both sides have lost their all; to fight with the utmost determination and pertinacity. The story is that during the Irish rebellion of 1798 Kilkenny was garrisoned by a troop of Hessian soldiers, who amused themselves by tying two cats together by their tails and throwing them across a clothes-line to fight. The authorities resolved to put a stop to the 'sport', but, on the officer on duty approaching, one of the troopers cut the two tails with a sword, and the cats made off. When the officer inquired the meaning of the bleeding tails, he was told that two cats had been fighting and had devoured each other all but the tails.

Whatever the true story, it is certain that the municipalities of Kilkenny and Irishtown contended so stoutly about their respective boundaries and rights to the end of the 17th century, that they mutually impoverished each other, leaving little else than 'two tails' behind.

***To grin like a Cheshire cat.*** An old simile, popularised by Lewis Carroll –

> 'Please would you tell me,' said Alice a little timidly, … 'why your cat grins like that?' 'It's a Cheshire cat,' said the Duchess, 'and that's why.' *Alice in Wonderland* (1865), ch. vi

The phrase has never been satisfactorily accounted for, but it has been said that cheese was formerly sold in Cheshire moulded like a cat that looked as though it was grinning. The humorous explanation is that the cats there know that Cheshire is a County Palatine (*q.v.*), and that the idea is so funny that they are perpetually amused at it! The phrase is applied to persons who show their teeth and gums when they laugh.

***To let the cat out of the bag.*** To disclose a secret. It was formerly a trick among country folk to substitute a cat for a sucking-pig, and bring it in a bag to market. If any greenhorn chose to buy a 'pig in a poke' without examination, all very well; but if he opened the sack, 'he let the cat out of the bag', and the trick was disclosed.

> She let the cat out of her bag of verse … she almost proposed to her hero in rhyme.
>
> Meredith, *The Egotist*, iii

***To live a cat and dog life.*** To be always snarling and quarrelling, as a cat and dog, whose aversion to each other is intense.

> There will be jealousies, and a cat-and-dog life over yonder worse than ever.
>
> Carlyle, *Frederick the Great*, vol. ii, bk iv

***To turn cat-in-pan.*** To turn traitor, to be a turncoat. The phrase seems to be the Fr. *tourner côte en peine* (to turn sides in trouble).

> When George in pudding-time came o'er
> And moderate men looked big, sir,
> I turned a cat-in-pan once more,
> And so became a Whig, sir. *Vicar of Bray*

> There is a cunning which we in England call the turning of the *cat in the pan*; which is, when that which a man says to another, he lays it as if another had said it to him.
>
> Bacon, *Essays: Of Cunning*

The origin of the term is unknown. Johnson in his *Dictionary* says:

> Imagined by some to be rightly written *Catipan*, as coming from *Catipania*. An unknown correspondent imagines, very naturally, that it is corrupted from *Cate in the pan*.

Neither suggestion is accepted by modern philologists.

***Touch not a cat but a glove.*** The punning motto of the Mackintosh clan, whose crest is 'a cat-a-mountain salient guardant proper', with for supporters 'two cats proper'. 'Glove' here, besides its obvious meaning, stands for a *glaive*, the old Scottish broadsword; thus, the motto bears the additional meaning, 'Don't meddle with the Mountain Cat (i.e. the Mackintosh Clan) without a broadsword.' An early meaning of 'but' was 'without' or 'except': for another example of this use, see the Prayer Book version of Ps. 19:3.

***What can you have of a cat but her skin?*** Said of something that is useless for any purpose but one. In former times the cat's fur was used for trimming cloaks and coats, but the flesh is no good for anything.

***When the cat's away the mice will play.*** Advantage will be taken of the absence of the person in authority. An old proverb, found in many languages. It is given in Ray's Collection.

**Cat and Fiddle.** This public-house sign has been said to be a corruption of *Caton le fidèle*, meaning Caton, who, at some unspecified time, is supposed to have been an English Governor of Calais. Authority for this explanation is lacking; and it seems unnecessary to go beyond the words themselves and their humorous suggestion. In Farringdon (Devon) is the sign of *La Chatte Fidèle*, in commemoration of a faithful cat, and it has been suggested that the name simply indicated that the game of *cat* (trap-ball) and a *fiddle* for dancing were provided for customers. It is worth mentioning that the *Dunciad* (i, 224) refers in contempt to Cibber as 'the *Bear* and Fiddle of the town'.

**Cat and Kittens.** A public-house sign, alluding to the range of pewter-pots of various sizes that were so called. Stealing these pots was termed 'cat and kitten sneaking'.

**Cat and Mouse Act.** *To play cat and mouse* with one is 'to have him on a string'; while he is in your power to pretend constantly to let him go, but not actually to do so. During the Suffragette disturbances in England an Act was passed with the object of rendering nugatory the tactics of imprisoned suffragettes who went on 'hunger-strike' with the intention of reducing themselves to such a state of ill-health that the authorities would be bound to release them or let them die. Under this Act such 'hunger-strikers' could be set at liberty, but were liable to re-arrest as soon as they were sufficiently recovered to undergo the remainder of their sentence. The Act was not particularly successful.

**Cat-call.** A kind of whistle used at theatres by the audience to express displeasure or impatience. A hideous noise like the *call* or *waul* of a *cat*.

> I was very much surprised with the great consort of cat-calls ... to see so many persons of quality of both sexes assembled together a kind of caterwauling. *Spectator*, No. 361

**Cat-eyed.** Able to see in the dark.

**Cat Ice.** Very thin, almost transparent ice from which the water that was underneath has receded; so slight as to be unable to bear a cat.

**Cat-lap.** A contemptuous name for tea, or other 'soft' drink such as a cat could swallow; a non-alcoholic liquor.

> A more accomplished old woman never drank cat-lap. Scott, *Redgauntlet*, ch. xii

**Cat o' mountain.** The wild-cat; also the leopard, or panther; hence a wild, savage sort of man.

**Cat-o'-nine-tails.** A whip with nine lashes, used for punishing offenders, briefly called *a cat*; probably so called because it can be said to 'scratch' the back as a cat might. Popular superstition says that it has *nine* tails because a flogging by a 'trinity of trinities' would be both more sacred and more efficacious. Lilburn was scourged, in 1637, with a whip having only three lashes, but there were twenty knots in each tail, and, as he received a lash every three paces between the Fleet and Old Palace Yard, Cook says that 60,000 stripes were inflicted. Titus Oates was scourged, in the reign of James II, with a cat having six lashes, and, between Newgate and Tyburn, received as many as 17,000 lashes. The cat-o'-nine-tails once used in the British army and navy is no longer employed there, but a modified form of it is still used in the punishment of civilian ruffians.

**Cat Stane.** The name given to certain monoliths in Scotland (there is one near Kirkliston, Linlithgow), so called from Celtic *cath*, a battle, because they mark the site of some battle. They are not Druidical stones.

**Cat's Cradle.** A game played with a piece of twine by two children. The guess that the name is a corruption of *cratch-cradle*, or the manger cradle in which the infant Saviour was laid (cratch is the Fr. *crèche*, a rack or manger), is unsupported by any evidence.

**Cat's eye.** A vitreous variety of quartz, found principally in Ceylon and Malabar, and, when cut *en cabochon*, used *as a precious stone*.

**Cat's Foot.** *To live under the cat's foot.* To be under petticoat government; to be henpecked. A mouse under the paw of a cat lives but by sufferance and at the cat's pleasure.

**Cat's Melody, The.** Squalling.

> The children were playing the cat's melody to keep their mother in countenance.
>
> W. B. Yeats, *Fairy Tales of the Irish Peasantry*, p. 238

**Cat's Paw.** *To be made a cat's paw of*, i.e. the tool of another, the medium of doing another's dirty work. The allusion is to the fable of the monkey who wanted to get some roasted chestnuts from the fire, and used the paw of his friend, the cat, for the purpose.

> I had no intention of becoming a cat's paw to draw European chestnuts out of the fire.
>
> Com. Rodgers

At sea, light air during a calm causing a ripple on the water, and indicating a storm, is called by sailors a *cat's paw*, and seamen affirm that the frolics of a cat indicate a gale.

**Cat's Sleep.** A light sleep, taken while sitting in a chair; a sham sleep, like that of a cat watching a mouse.

**Catacomb.** A subterranean gallery for the burial of the dead, especially those at Rome. The origin of the name is unknown, but it does not appear to have been used till about the 5th century of our era (though the catacombs themselves were in existence, and used for burial, long before), and then only in connection with one cemetery, that of St Sebastian, on the Appian Way. This was called the Coemeterium Catacumbas, or, shortly, *Catacumbas*, which name in course of time was applied equally to similar cemeteries. *Catacumbas* was probably, therefore, a place-name, denoting the site of this particular cemetery.

> The most awful idea connected with the catacombs is their interminable extent, and the possibility of going astray in the labyrinth of darkness. Hawthorne, *Marble Faun*, iii

**Cataian.** A native of Cathay or China; hence, a thief, liar, or scoundrel, because the Chinese had the reputation of being such.

> I will not believe such a Cataian, though the priest of the town commended him for a true man.
> Shakespeare, *Merry Wives*, 2, 1

**Catamaran.** A scraggy old woman, a vixen; so called by a play on the first syllable. It properly means a raft consisting of three logs lashed together with ropes; used on the coasts of Coromandel and Madras.

> No, you old catamaran, though you pretend you never read novels …
> Thackeray, *Lovel the Widower*, ch. i

**Cataphrygians.** A sect of Montanist heretics, which arose in the 2nd century; so called because it was in Phrygia that Montanus first expounded his errors to them.

**Catastrophe** (Gr. *kata*, downwards, *strephein*, to turn). A turning upside down. Originally used of the change which produces the *dénouement* of a drama, which is usually a 'turning upside down' of the beginning of the plot.

**Catch** ***Catch as catch can.*** Get by hook or crook all you can; a phrase from the child's game of this name, or from the method of wrestling so called, in which the wrestlers are allowed to get a grip anyhow or anywhere.

> All must catch that catch can.
> Johnson, *Rambler*, No. 197

***Catch me at it.*** Most certainly I shall never do what you say.

> 'Catch me going to London!' exclaimed Vixen.
> Miss Braddon, *Vixen*

***Catch weights.*** A term in racing, meaning without restrictions as to weight.

***First catch your hare.*** It is generally believed that 'Mrs Glasse', in the *Art of Cookery*, gave this direction; but the exact words are, 'Take your hare when it is cased, and make a pudding, … etc.' To 'case' means to take off the skin, as in *All's Well* 3, 6, 'We'll make you some sport with the fox ere we case him.' 'First catch your hare,' however, is a very old phrase, and in the 13th century Bracton (Bk iv, tit. i, ch. xxi, sec. 4) has these words:

> Vulgariter dicitur, quod primo oportet cervum capere, et postea, cum captus fuerit, illum excoriare (it is vulgarly said that you must first catch your deer, and then, when it is caught, skin it).

'Mrs Glasse' was the pen-name of Dr John Hill (1716–75), who published *The Art of Cookery made Plain and Easy* in 1747 as *By a Lady*: the pseudonym was added later.

***To be caught bending.*** To be caught at a disadvantage. If you catch a small boy bending over it is easy to smack him on that portion of his anatomy provided by nature for the purpose. From a popular song of about 1912, the refrain of which is:

> What ho! If I catch you bending!

***To be caught napping.*** To suffer some disadvantage while off one's guard. Pheasants, hares, and other animals are sometimes surprised 'napping'.

***To catch a crab.*** In rowing, to be struck with the handle of one's oar; to fall backwards. This occurs when the rower leaves his oar too long in the water before repeating the stroke.

***To catch a tartar.*** Said of the biter bit. Grose says an Irish soldier in the Imperial service, in a battle against the Turks, shouted to his comrade that he had caught a Tartar. 'Bring him along, then,' said his mate. 'But he won't come,' cried Paddy. 'Then come along yourself,' said his comrade. 'Arrah!' replied Paddy, 'I wish I could, but he won't let me.'

> We are like the man who boasted of having caught a Tartar when the fact was that the Tartar had caught him. *Cautions for the Times*

***To catch on.*** To make its way; to become popular. As in

> One can never tell what sort of song will catch on with the public, but the one that does is a little gold mine.

***To catch out.*** In cricket, is to catch the ball of a batsman, whereby the striker is ruled out, that is, must relinquish his bat. Hence, when one is convicted of telling a lie one is said to be 'caught out'.

***To catch the Speaker's eye.*** To find the eye of the Speaker fixed on you; to be observed by the Speaker. In the House of Commons the member on whom the eye of the Speaker is fixed has the privilege of addressing the House.

***To lie upon the catch.*** To lie in wait; to try to catch one tripping.

***You'll catch it.*** You'll get severely punished. Here 'it' stands for the undefined punishment, such as a whipping, a scolding, or other unpleasant consequence.

**Catch-club.** *A member of the Catch-club.* A bum-bailiff, a tipstaff, a constable. The pun is obvious.

**Catchpenny.** A worthless article puffed off to catch the pennies of those who are foolish enough to buy them.

**Catchpole.** A constable; a law officer whose business it was to apprehend criminals. This is nothing to do with a *pole* or staff, nor with *poll*, the head, but is mediaeval Lat., *chassipullus*, one who hunts or chases fowls (*pullus*, a fowl).

**Catchword.** A popular cry, a word or a phrase adopted by any party for political or other purposes. 'Three acres and a cow', 'Your food will cost you more', 'What did you do in the Great War, daddy?' 'Hang the Kaiser', are good examples.

In printing, the first word on a page which is printed at the foot of the preceding page is known as the *catchword*; for the last two hundred years its use has been gradually dying out; and it is now dead, except in books of an intentionally archaic format. The first book so printed was a *Tacitus*, by John de Spira, 1469.

Printers also use the same name for the main words in a dictionary; i.e. those at the start of each article, printed in bold type so as to catch the eye.

In theatrical parlance, the *cue*, i.e. the last word or so of an actor's speech, is called the *catchword*.

**Catechumen.** One taught by word of mouth (Gr. *katecheein*, to din into the ears). Those about to be baptised in the early Church were first taught by word of mouth, and then catechised on their religious faith and duties.

**Cater-cousin.** An intimate friend; a remote kinsman. The name is not connected with a supposed (but never possible) Fr. *quatre-cousin*, a fourth cousin; it probably has reference to persons being *catered* for together, or boarded together, who would naturally become more or less intimate: 'friends so familiar that they eat together' (*Nares*).

Violante up and down was voluble
In whatsoever pair of eyes would perk
From goody, gossip, cater-cousin, sib,
Curious to peep at the inside of things.
Browning, *Ring and the Book*, ii, 511

His master and he, saving your worship's reverence, are scarce cater-cousins.
Shakespeare, *Merchant of Venice*, 2, 2

**Catgut.** Cord of various thicknesses, made from the intestines of animals (usually sheep, and never cats), and used for strings of musical instruments. Why it should have been called *cat*-gut has never been satisfactorily explained, unless it is with some humorous allusion to the sound produced by them, which may resemble caterwauling, or that it is a corruption of *kitgut*, *kit* being an old word for a small fiddle. In support of this we have the following from Cartwright's *The Ordinary* (1634):

*Hearsay*. Do you not hear her guts already squeak
Like kit-strings?
*Slicer*. They must come to that within
This two or three years: by that time she'll be
True perfect cat. Act i, 2

Here's a tune indeed! pish.
I had rather hear one ballad sung i' the nose now
Than all these simpering tunes played upon cat's-guts
And sung by little kitlings.
Middleton, *Women Beware Women*, iii, 2

Shakespeare, however, definitely gives catgut its true origin:

Now, divine air! Now is his soul ravished! Is it not strange that sheep's guts should hale souls out of men's bodies? Well, a horn for my money, when all's done. *Much Ado*, 2, 3

***Catgut scraper.*** A fiddler.

**Cathari,** or **Catharists.** Novatian heretics. The name means 'the Pure', and it was assumed by, or applied to, many later sects, such as the Paulicians, Manicheans, Waldenses, and even the English Puritans.

**Catharine, St.** St Catharine was a virgin of royal descent in Alexandria, who publicly confessed the Christian faith at a sacrificial feast appointed by the Emperor Maximinus, for which confession she was put to death by torture by means of a wheel like that of a chaff-cutter. Hence

***Catharine wheel,*** a sort of firework; also, a turning head over heels on the hands. Boys in the street, etc., often do so to catch a penny or so from passers-by.

***Catharine-wheel republics.*** 'Republics,' says Mr Lowell, 'always in revolution while the powder lasts.'

***Catharine-wheel window.*** A wheel-window, sometimes called a rose-window, with radiating divisions.

***The Order of St Catharine.*** A Russian order founded for ladies of the nobility by Peter the Great after his naval victory of Aland in 1714, and so named in compliment to his wife, Catharine.

***To braid St Catharine's tresses.*** To live a virgin.

Thou art too fair to be left to braid St Catharine's tresses. Longfellow, *Evangeline*

**Catharists.** *See* Cathari.

**Cathay.** Marco Polo's name for a country in Eastern Asia, roughly identical with Northern China; from *Ki-tah*, the name of the ruling race in those parts in the 10th century.

> Better fifty years of Europe than a cycle of Cathay.
>
> Tennyson, *Locksley Hall*

**Cathead.** *See To cat the anchor, under* Cat proverbs and sayings.

**Cathedrals of the Old Foundation.** The ancient cathedrals that existed in England before Henry VIII founded and endowed new cathedrals out of the revenues of the dissolved monasteries. These latter are known as *Cathedrals of the New Foundation.*

**Catherine.** *See* Catharine.

**Catholic.** The word (Gr. *katholikos*, general, universal) means general, universal, comprehensive – a sense which is seen in such a sentence as Wordsworth's –

> Creed and test
> Vanish before the unreserved embrace
> Of catholic humanity.
>
> *Ecclesiastical Sonnets*, III, xxxvi

Hence, from the Church point of view, it distinguishes first the whole body of Christians as apart from 'Jews heretics, and infidels': secondly, a member of a Church which claims the Apostolic Succession and direct descent from the earliest body of Christians; and thirdly, a member of the Roman Catholic Church, i.e. the Western or Latin branch of the ancient Catholic (or *universal*) Church which was formed at the Great Schism beginning in the 9th century and ending in 1054, the Greek (or Orthodox) Church forming the other section. *See* Catholic Church.

Alphonso I, King of Asturias, 739–57, was surnamed *The Catholic* on account of his zeal in erecting and endowing monasteries and churches. *See* Catholic King.

**Catholic and Apostolic Church.** The name given to the followers of Edward Irving (1792–1834), and to the Church founded by him in 1829. Also called Irvingites.

**Catholic Church.** The entire body of Christians considered as a whole, as distinguished from the Churches and sects into which it has divided. When the Western Church broke off from the Eastern (*see* Catholic *above*), the Eastern called itself the Orthodox Church, and the Western adopted the term Catholic. At the Reformation the Western Church was called by the Reformers the Roman Catholic Church, and the Established Church of England was called the 'Protestant Church', the 'Reformed National Church', or the 'Anglo-Catholic Church'. Many members of the Anglican Church still consider and call themselves Catholics; and they are perfectly justified in so doing, for the Roman, though claiming to be the first in direct descent, is not the *only* Catholic Church.

**Catholic Epistles.** Those Epistles in the New Testament not addressed to any particular church or individual; the *general* epistles, viz. those of James, Peter, and Jude, and the first of John; 2 John is addressed to a 'lady', and 3 John to Gaius, and these are usually included.

**Catholic King,** or *His Most Catholic Majesty*. A title given by the Pope to Ferdinand, King of Aragon (1474–1516), for expelling the Moors from Spain. *Cp.* Religious.

**Catholic League.** A confederacy of Catholics formed in 1614 to counterbalance the Evangelic League (*q.v.*) of Bohemia. The two Leagues kept Germany in perpetual disturbance, and ultimately led to the Thirty Years' War (1618–48).

**Catholic Roll.** A document which English Roman Catholics were obliged to sign on taking their seats as Member of Parliament. It was abolished, and a single oath prescribed to all members by the 260, 30 Victoria, c. 19 (1896).

**Catholicon.** A panacea, a universal remedy.

> Meanwhile, permit me to recommend,
> At the matter admits of no delay,
> My wonderful catholicon.
>
> Longfellow, *The Golden Legend*, i

**Catholicos.** The head of the Assyrian Nestorians. Now called the Patriarch of Armenia.

**Catiline's Conspiracy.** Lucius Sergius Catilina, 64 BC, conspired with a large number of dissolute young nobles to plunder the Roman treasury, extirpate the senate, and fire the capitol. Cicero, who was consul, got full information of the plot, and delivered his *first* Oration against Catiline November 8th, 63, whereupon Catiline quitted Rome. Next day Cicero delivered his *second* Oration, and several of the conspirators were arrested. On December 4th Cicero made his *third* Oration, respecting what punishment should be accorded to the conspirators. And on December 5th, after his *fourth* Oration, sentence of death was passed. Catiline tried to escape into Gaul, but, being intercepted, he was slain fighting, 62 BC.

**Catius.** In Pope's *Moral Essays* (Epist. i), intended for Charles Dartiquinave (1664–1737), an epicure and humorist who became the royal Purveyor-general. He preferred 'a rogue with venison to a rogue without'.

**Catkins.** The inflorescence of hazel, birch, willow, and some other trees; so called from their resemblance to a cat's tail.

See the yellow catkins cover
All the slender willows over.
Mary Howitt, *Voice of Spring*

**Cat-lap.** *See under* Cat.

**Cato. *He is a Cato*.** A man of simple life, severe morals, self-denying habits, strict justice, brusque manners, blunt of speech, and of undoubted patriotism, like the Roman censor of that name (234–149 BC).

**Cato Street Conspiracy.** A scheme entertained by Arthur Thistlewood and other conspirators to overthrow the Government by assassinating the Cabinet Ministers (February, 1820). So called from Cato Street, Edgware Road, where their meetings were held.

**Catsup.** *See* Ketchup.

**Catum, Al** [*the strong*]. A bow which fell into the hands of Mahomet when the property of the Jews of Medina was confiscated. In the first battle the prophet drew it with such force that it snapped in two.

**Caucus.** An American word, first recorded as having been used in Boston about 1750, introduced into English political slang and popularised by Joseph Chamberlain about 1878. In America it means a meeting of some division, large or small, of a political or legislative body, for the purpose of agreeing upon a united course of action in the main assembly. In England it has a disparaging significance and is applied opprobriously to an inner committee or organisation which seeks to manage affairs behind the backs of its party, or to concert measures for carrying out their political wishes in private. The origin of the word is unknown, but it may be connected with the Algonquin word *cau-cau-as-u*, one who advises.

> In all these places is a severall commander, which they call *Werowance*, except the *Chickahamanians*, who are governed by the priests and their Assistants, or their Elders called *Cawcawwassoughes*.
>
> *Capt. John Smith's 'Travels in Virginia'*; *6th Voyage*, 1606

> This day the caucus club meets ... in the garret of Tom Dawes, the adjutant of the Boston regiment.
>
> John Adams, *Diary*, vol. ii, p. 164, February, 1763

**Caudine Forks.** A narrow pass in the mountains near Capua, now called the Valley of Arpaia. It was here that the Roman army, under the consuls T. Veturius Calvinus and Sp. Postumius, fell into the hands of the Samnites (321 BC), and were made to pass under the yoke.

> Hard as it was to abandon an enterprise so very dear to him ... he did not hesitate to take the more prudent course of passing under (*sic*) the Caudine Forks of the Monroe doctrine, and leave Maximilian and the French bondholders to their fate. *Standard*, Nov. 17th, 1866

**Caudle.** Any sloppy mess, especially that sweet mixture of gruel and wine or spirits given by nurses to recently confined women and their 'gossips' who call to see the baby during the first month. The word simply means something warm (Lat. *calidus*).

**Caudle Lecture.** A curtain lecture. The term is derived from a series of papers by Douglas Jerrold, which were published in *Punch* (1846). These papers represent Job Caudle as a patient sufferer of the lectures of his nagging wife after they had gone to bed and the curtains were drawn.

**Caught Napping.** *See under* Catch.

**Caul.** The membrane on the head of some newborn infants, supposed to be a charm against death by drowning.

To be born with a caul was with the Romans tantamount to our phrase, 'To be born with a silver spoon in one's mouth', meaning 'born to good luck'. M. Francisque-Michel, in his *Philologie-Comparée*, p. 83, 4, says: '*Calle, espêce de coiffure, est synonyme de coiffé,*' and quotes the proverb, '*Ste Migorce! nous sommes nées coiffées*' (*La Comédie des Proverbes*, ii, 4.)

**Cauld-lad, The,** of Hilton Hall. A house-spirit, who moved about the furniture during the night. Being resolved to banish him, the inmates left for him a green cloak and hood, before the kitchen-fire, which so delighted him that he never troubled the house any more; but sometimes he might be heard singing –

> Here's a cloak, and here's a hood,
> The cauld-lad of Hilton will do no more good.

**Cauline, Sir.** The hero of one of the ballads in Percy's *Reliques*. He lived in the palace of the King of Ireland, and 'used to serve the wine'. He fell in love with Christabelle, the king's daughter, who secretly plighted her troth to him, but the king discovered the lovers in a bower, and banished Sir Cauline. He, however, returned just in time to slay a 'Soldain' who was seeking her hand, but died of the wounds received in the combat; and the fair Christabelle died of grief, having 'burst her gentle hearte in twayne'.

**Caurus.** The Latin name for the west-north-west wind, Anglicised by Chaucer as Chorus.

… the sonne is hid whan the sterres ben clustred by a swifte winde highte Chorus.

Borethius, Bk i, Mett. iii

The ground by piercing Caurus seared.

Thomson, *Castle of Indolence*, ii, 78

**Causa causans.** The initiating cause; the primary cause.

***Causa causata.*** The cause which owes its existence to the *causa causans*; the secondary cause.

***Causa vera*** (*a*) The immediate predecessor of an effect; (*b*) a cause verifiable by independent evidence. (Mill.)

In theology God is the *causa causans*, and creation the *causa causata*. The presence of the sun above the horizon is the *causa vera* of daylight, and his withdrawal below the horizon is the *causa vera* of night.

**Cause, The.** A mission; the object or project.

***To make common cause.*** To work for the same object. Here 'cause' is the legal term, meaning *pro* or *con*, as it may be, the cause or side of the question advocated.

***Cause célèbre*** (Fr.). Any famous law case or trial.

**Causes.** *Aristotelian causes* are these four:

(1) The *Efficient Cause*. That which immediately produces the effect.

(2) The *Material Cause*. The matter on which (1) works.

(3) The *Formal Cause*. The Essence or 'Form' ( = group of attributes) introduced into the matter by the efficient cause.

(4) The *Final* or *Ultimate Cause*. The purpose or end for which the thing exists or the causal change takes place. But God is called the ultimate Final Cause, since, according to Aristotle, all things tend, so far as they can, to realise some Divine attribute.

God is also called *The First Cause*, or the Cause Causeless, beyond which even imagination cannot go.

**Causerie.** Gossip, small talk; in journalism a chatty kind of essay or article, a set of gossipy paragraphs. (Fr. *causer*, to chat.)

**Cautelous.** Cautious, cunning, treacherous. (Lat. *cautela*, from *cavere*, to beware.)

Caught with cautelous baits.

Shakespeare, *Coriolanus*, 4, 1

Swear priests and cowards and men cautelous.

*Julius Caesar*, 2, 1

**Cauther, Al.** The lake of Paradise, the waters of which are sweet as honey, cold as snow, and clear as crystal. He who once tastes thereof will never thirst again. (The Koran.)

**Caution Money.** A sum deposited before entering college, or an Inn of Court, etc., by way of security for good behaviour.

**Cavalier.** A horseman; whence a knight, a gentleman. (Lat. *caballus*, a horse.)

***Personages styled The Cavalier.***

Eon de Beaumont (1728–1810), French diplomat and secret agent; *Chevalier d'Eon*.

Charles Breydel (1677–1744), Flemish landscape painter.

Francesco Cairo (*Cavaliere del Cairo*) (1598–1674), Italian historical and portrait painter.

Jean le Clerc, *le chevalier* (1587–1633), French painter.

Giov. Battista Marini (1569–1625), Italian poet; *Il cavalier*.

Andrew Michael Ramsay (1686–1743), Scottish-French writer.

***Cavalier*** or ***Chevalier de St George.*** James Francis Edward Stuart, called 'the Pretender', or 'the Old Pretender' (1688–1765).

***The Young Cavalier*** or ***the Bonnie Chevalier.*** Edward, the 'Young Pretender' (1720–85).

**Cavaliere servente** (Ital.). A cavalier in attendance; especially a man who devotes himself to running about after a married woman; much the same as a *cicisbeo* (*q.v.*).

An English lady asked of an Italian,
What were the actual and official duties
Of the strange thing some women set a value on
Which hovers oft about some married beauties,
Call'd 'cavalier servente'? a Pygmalion
Whose statues warm (I fear, alas! too true 't is)
Beneath his art. The dame, press'd to disclose them
Said – 'Lady, I beseech you to *suppose them.*'

Byron, *Don Juan*, IX, ii

**Cavaliers.** Adherents of Charles I. Those of the opposing Parliament party were called Roundheads (*q.v.*).

**Cavall.** 'King Arthur's hound of deepest mouth'. (*Idylls of the King*; Enid.)

**Cave in.** Shut up! have done! *I'll cave in his head* (break it). *His fortune has caved in* (has failed). *The bank has caved in* (come to a smash). *The affair caved in* (fell through). Common American expressions.

In mining, after a shaft has been sunk the earth round the sides falls or *caves* in, unless properly boarded; and if the mine does not answer, no care is taken to prevent a caving in.

**Cave of Adullam.** *See* Adullamites.

**Caveat.** Lat., 'let him beware': a notice directing the recipient to refrain from some act pending the decision of the Court. Hence,

***To enter a caveat.*** To give legal notice that the opponent is not to proceed with the suit in hand until the party giving the notice has been heard; to give a warning or admonition.

***Caveat emptor.*** Lat., 'let the purchaser beware'; i.e. the buyer must keep his eyes open, for the bargain he agrees to is binding. The full legal maxim is:

> Caveat emptor, quia ignorare non de' uit quod jus alienum emit – Let a purchaser beware, for he ought not to be ignorant of the nature of the property which he is buying from another party.

**Cavel.** A parcel or allotment of land; originally, a lot (that is cast). From Dut. *kavel*, a lot, whence *kaveln*, to assign by lot.

**Caviare.** The roe of the sturgeon, pickled, salted, and prepared for use as a relish. Caviare is an acquired taste and, as a rule, it is not appreciated by people until they have got used to it; hence Shakespeare's *caviare to the general* (*Hamlet*, 2, 2), above the taste or comprehension of ordinary people.

> He [Cobbett] must, I think, be caviare to the Whigs.
> Hazlitt, *Table-talk*

**Cavo-rilievo.** 'Relief', cut below the original surface, the highest parts of the figure being on a level with the surface.

**Caxon.** A worn-out wig: also a big cauliflower wig, worn out or not. It has been suggested that the word is from the personal name Caxon.

> People scarce could decide on its phiz,
> Which looked wisest – the caxon or jowl.
> Peter Pindar, *The Portfolio*

**Cean.** ***The Cean poet.*** Simonides, of Ceos.

> The Cean and the Teian muse.
> Byron, *Don Juan* (*Song*; *The Isles of Greece*)

**Cecilia, St.** A Roman lady who underwent martyrdom in the 3rd century. She is the patron saint of the blind, being herself blind; she is also patroness or musicians, and 'inventor of the organ'.

> At length divine Cecilia came,
> Inventress of the vocal frame.
> Dryden, *Alexander's Feast*

According to tradition an angel fell in love with her for her musical skill, and used nightly to visit her. Her husband saw the heavenly visitant, who gave to both a crown of martyrdom which he brought from Paradise. Dryden and Pope have written odes in her honour, and both speak of her charming an angel by her musical powers:

> He [Timotheus] raised a mortal to the skies,
> She [Cecilia] brought an angel down.
> Dryden, *Alexander's Feast*

**Cecil's Fast.** A dinner off fish. William Cecil, Lord Burghley, chief minister to Queen Elizabeth for nearly forty years, introduced a Bill to enjoin the eating of fish on certain days in order to restore the fish trade.

**Cedilla.** The mark (ç) under a French sibilant c. This mark is the letter z, which was originally placed at the side of the c but afterwards beneath it. (Ital. *zediglia*, Lat. *zeticula*, a little z, diminutive of Gr. *zeta*.)

**Ceelict, St.** An English name of St Calixtus, who is commemorated on October 14th, the day of the Battle of Hastings.

Brown Willis tells us there was a tablet once in Battle parish church with these words:

> This place of war is Battle called, because in battle here.
> Quite conquered and o'erthrown the English nation were.
> This slaughter happened to them upon St Ceelict's day, etc.

**Celestial City.** Heaven is so called by John Bunyan in his *Pilgrim's Progress*.

**Celestial Empire.** China; a translation of the Chinese *Tien Chao*, literally 'heavenly dynasty', alluding to the belief that the old Emperors were in direct descent from the gods. Hence, the Chinese themselves are sometimes spoken of as *Celestials*.

**Celestians.** Another name for the Pelagians (*q.v.*), from Celestius, a disciple of Pelagius. St Jerome called him 'a blockhead swollen with Scotch pottage' – Scotch being, in this case, what we now call Irish.

**Celestines.** An order of reformed Benedictine monks, founded about 1254 by Pietro di Murrhone who, in 1294, became Pope as Celestine V.

**Celia.** A common poetical name for a lady or lady-love. Thus, Swift had an ode in which Strephon describes Celia's dressing-room.

> Five hours, and who can do it less in,
> By haughty Celia spent in dressing.

*See also* Caelia.

**Celt.** A piece of stone, ground artificially into a wedge-like shape, with a cutting edge. Used, before the employment of bronze and iron, for knives, hatchets, and chisels.

**Celtic.** Applied to the peoples and languages of the great branch of the Aryans which includes the Irish, Manx, Welsh, ancient Cornish, Breton, and Scotch Gaels. Anciently the term was applied by the Greeks and Romans to the peoples of Western Europe generally, but when Caesar wrote of the Celtae he referred to the people of middle Gaul only. The word *Celt* probably means a warrior; fable accounts for it by the story of Celtina, daughter of Britannus, who had a son by Hercules, named Celtus, who became the progenitor of the Celts.

**Cemetery** properly means a sleeping-place (Gr. *koimeterion*, a dormitory). The Persians call their cemeteries 'The Cities of the Silent'. The Greeks thought it unlucky to pronounce the name of Death.

**Cenci.** *See* Beautiful Parricide.

**Cenobites.** *See* Caenobites.

**Cenomanni.** The name given to the inhabitants of Norfolk, Suffolk, and Cambridge by Caesar in his *Commentaries*.

**Cenotaph** (Gr. *kenos*, empty, *taphos*, tomb). A sepulchral monument raised to the memory of a person buried elsewhere. By far the most noteworthy to all of British race is that in Whitehall, London, which was dedicated on the second anniversary of Armistice Day (November 11th, 1920) to those who fell in the Great War, 1914–18.

Among the noted cenotaphs of the ancients are those of –

Aeneas to Deipho bus (*Aeneid*, i, 6; v, 505).
Andromache to Hector (*Aeneid*, i, 3; v, 302).
Aristotle to Hermias and Eubulus (*Diogenes Laertius*).
The Athenians to the poet Euripides.
Callimachus to Sopolis, son of Dioclides (*Epigram of Callimachus*, 22)
Catullus to his brother (*Epigram of Catullus*, 103).
Dido to Sichaeus (*Justin*, xviii, 6).
The Romans to Drusus in Germany, and to Alexander Severus, the emperor, in Gaul (*Suetonius: Life of Claudius*; and the *Anthologia*).
Statius to his father (*The Sylvae of Statius*, v, Epicedium 3).
Xenocrates to Lysidices (*Anthologia*).

**Censorius et sapiens.** Cato Major (234–149 BC) was so called.

**Centaur.** Mythological beasts, half horse and half man, fabled to have dwelt in ancient Thessaly; a myth the origin of which is probably to be found in the expert horsemanship of the original inhabitants. *See* Ixion. The Thessalian centaurs were invited to a marriage feast, and, being intoxicated, behaved with great rudeness to the women. The Lapithae took the women's part, fell on the centaurs, and drove them out of the country.

Feasts that Thessalian centaurs never knew.
Thomson, *Autumn*

**Cento** (Lat. a patchwork). Poetry made up of lines borrowed from established authors. It was an art freely practised in the decadent period of Greece and Rome, and Ausonius, who has a nuptial idyll composed from verses selected from Virgil, composed rules governing their manufacture. Among well-known examples are the *Homerocentones*, the *Cento Virgilianus* by Proba Falconia (4th cent.), and the hymns made by Metellus out of the Odes of Horace. Of modern centos the following portion of a Shakespearean cento that appeared in *English*, November, 1919, may serve as an example:

Let fame that all hunt after in their lives
Among the buzzing pleasèd multitude
For present comfort and for future good,
Taint not thy mind: nor let thy soul contrive
With all the fierce endeavour of your wit
To woo a maid in way of marriage,
As it is common for the younger sort,
The lunatic, the lover, and the poet:
Thus bad begins, and worse remains behind.
I see a man's life is a tedious one,
For it appears, by manifest proceeding,
There's nothing serious in mortality.
Life's but a walking shadow, a poor player,
And one man in his time plays many parts,
As an unperfect actor on the stage.

**Centre Party.** In politics, the party occupying a place between two extremes: the *left centre* is the more radical wing, and the *right centre* the more conservative. In the French Revolution *the Centre* of the Legislative Assembly included the friends of order.

In the Fenian rebellion, 1866, the chief movers were called *Head Centres*, and their subordinates *Centres*.

**Centre of Gravity.** That point on which a body acted on by gravity is balanced in all positions.

**Centumviri** (Lat. *centum*, a hundred, *vir*, a man). A body of judges appointed by the praetor to decide common causes among the Romans; all matters pertaining to testaments, inheritances, etc., were in their hands.

**Centurion** (Lat. *centum*, a hundred). A Roman officer who had the command of 100 men. There were sixty centurions, of varying ranks, to a legion, the chief being the first centurion of the first maniple of the first cohort; his title was Primus pilus prior, or Primipilus. The centurion's emblem of office was a vine-staff.

**Cephalus and Procris.** Made familiar to us by an allusion in the *Midsummer Night's Dream*. Cephalus was husband of Procris, who, out of jealousy, deserted him. He went in search of her, and rested awhile under a tree. Procris, knowing of his whereabouts, crept through some bushes to ascertain if a rival was with him; and he, hearing the noise and thinking it to be made by some wild beast, hurled his javelin into the bushes and slew her. When the unhappy man discovered what he had done, he slew himself in anguish of spirit with the same javelin.

*Pyramus*: Not Shafalus to Procrus was so true.
*Thisbe*: As Shafalus to Procrus, I to you.
Shakespeare, *Midsummer Night's Dream*, 5, 1

**Cepheus.** A northern constellation; named from Cepheus, King of Ethiopia, husband of Cassiopeia and father of Andromeda.

**Cepola.** ***Devices of Cépola***. Quips of law are so called from Bartholomew Cépola whose law-quirks, teaching how to elude the most express law, and to perpetuate lawsuits *ad infinitum*, have been frequently reprinted – once in 8vo, in black letter, by John Petit, in 1503.

**Ceraunium.** Some precious stone, perhaps the onyx, jasper, or opal; so called by the ancients from a notion that it was a thunder-stone. (Gr. *keraunos*, thunderbolt.) Early mineralogists used the term ceraunite of a meteorite.

**Cerberus.** A grim, watchful keeper, house-porter, guardian, etc. Cerberus, according to *Roman mythology*, is the three-headed dog that keeps the entrance of the infernal regions. Hercules dragged the monster to earth, and then let him go again. Orpheus lulled Cerberus to sleep with his lyre; and the Sibyl who conducted Aeneas through the Inferno, also threw the dog into a profound sleep with a cake seasoned with poppies and honey. *See under* Sop.

The origin of the fable of Cerberus may be found in the custom of the ancient Egyptians of guarding graves with dogs.

**Cercopes.** According to *Greek fable*, a race of thievish gnomes who robbed Hercules in his sleep. *Cp.* Achemon. They were said to have been changed into monkeys for attempting to deceive Zeus.

**Cerdonians.** A sect of heretics, founded by Cerdon, a Syrian Gnostic of the 2nd century, who maintained most of the errors of the Manichees (*q.v.*).

**Ceremonious, The.** Pedro IV of Aragon (1336–87) was so surnamed.

**Ceremony** (Lat. *caerimonia*). By way of accounting for this word, which is probably connected with Sanskrit *karman*, a religious action, a rite, Livy tells that when the Romans fled before Brennus, one Albinus, who was carrying his wife and children in a cart to a place of safety, overtook at Janiculum the Vestal virgins bending under their load, took them up and conveyed them to Caerë, in Etruria. Here they remained, and continued to perform their sacred rites, which were consequently called 'Caere-monia'.

***Master of the Ceremonies***. A Court official, first appointed by James I, to superintend the reception of ambassadors and strangers of rank, and to prescribe the formalities to be observed in levees and other grand public functions. The title is now given to one whose duty it is to see that all goes smoothly at balls and suchlike social gatherings: frequently abbreviated to 'M.C'.

**Ceres.** The Roman name of *Mother Earth*, the protectress of agriculture and of all the fruits of the earth; later identified with the Greek Demeter.

Dark frowning heaths grow bright with Ceres' store. Thomson, *Castle of Indolence*, ii, 27

**Cerinthians.** Disciples of Cerinthus, a heresiarch of the 1st century. They were the earliest Gnostics of the Judaeo-Christian Church; they denied the divinity of Christ, but held that a certain virtue descended into Him at baptism, which filled Him with the Holy Ghost.

**Cess.** A tax, contracted from assessment ('sess'); as a 'church-cess'. In Ireland the word is used sometimes as a contraction of success, meaning luck, as 'bad cess to you!'

***Out of all cess.*** Beyond all estimation or valuation.

The poor jade is wrung in the withers out of all cess. Shakespeare, *1 Henry IV*, 2, 1

**C'est magnifique.** *C'est magnifique, mais ce n'est pas la guerre*. 'It is magnificent, but it is not war.' The criticism on the charge of the Light Brigade at Balaclava, made on the field at the time, by the French General Bosquet to Mr A. H. Layard.

**Cestui que vie.** This and the two following are old Anglo-French legal terms (*cestui* = he, or him). The person for whose life any lands or hereditaments may be held.

***Cestui que use***, the person to whose use anyone is infeoffed of lands or tenements.

***Cestui que trust***, the person for whose benefit a trust has been created.

**Cestus.** The girdle of Venus, made by her husband Vulcan: but when she wantoned with

Mars it fell off, and was left on the 'Acidalian mount'. It was of magical power to move to ardent love. By a poetical fiction all women of irresistible attraction are supposed to be wearers of Aphrodite's girdle, or the cestus. It is introduced by Spenser in the *Faërie Queene* as the girdle of Florimel (*q.v.*); it gave to those who could wear it 'the virtue of chaste love and wifehood true', but if any woman not chaste and faithful put it on, it 'loosed or tore asunder' (*Faërie Queene*, III, vii, 31).

**Chabouk.** A long whip, or the application of whips and rods; a Persian and Chinese punishment.

> Drag forward that fakir, and cut his robe into tatters on his back with your chabouks.
>
> Scott, *The Surgeon's Daughter*, ch. xiv

> If that monarch did not give the chabuk to Feramorz, there would be an end to all legitimate government in Bucharia.
>
> T. Moore, *Lalla Rookh*

**Chacun a son gout.** 'Everyone has (*a*) his taste'; or, 'Everyone to (*à*) his taste.' The former is French, the latter is English-French. The phrase is much more common with us than it is in France, where we meet with the phrases – *Chacun a sa chacunerie* (everyone has his idiosyncrasy), and *chacun a sa marotte* (everyone has his hobby). In Latin *sua cuique voluptas*, every man has his own pleasures, 'as the goodman said when he kissed his cow'.

**Chaff.** ***An old bird is not to be caught with chaff.*** An experienced man, or one with his wits about him, is not to be deluded by humbug. The reference is to throwing chaff instead of birdseed to allure birds. Hence, perhaps –

***You are chaffing me.*** Making fun of me. A singular custom used to exist in Notts and Leicestershire some half a century ago. When a husband ill-treated his wife, the villagers emptied a sack of chaff at his door, to intimate that 'thrashing was done within'.

**Chair, The.** The office of chief magistrate in a corporate town; the office of a professor, etc., as 'The chair of poetry, in Oxford, is now vacant.' The word is furthermore applied to the president of a committee or public meeting. Hence the chairman himself. When debaters call out 'Chair', they mean that the chairman is not properly supported, and his words not obeyed as they ought to be. Another form of the same expression is, 'Pray support the Chair'.

***Below the chair.*** Said of one who has not yet reached the presidential position, as of an alderman who has not yet served the mayoralty.

***Passed the chair.*** One who has served the chief office.

***To take the chair.*** To become the chairman or president of a public meeting. The chairman is placed in some conspicuous place, like the Speaker of the House of Commons, and his decision is absolutely final in all points of doubt. Usually the persons present nominate and elect their own chairman; but in some cases there is an *ex officio* chairman.

**Chair-days.** Days of rest, old age.

> I had long supposed that the chair-days, the beautiful name for those days of old age ... was of Shakespeare's own invention ... but this is a mistake ... the word is current in Lancashire still.
>
> Trench, *English Past and Present*, v

> In thy reverence and thy chair-days, thus
> To die in ruffian battle.
>
> Shakespeare, *2 Henry VI*, 5, 2

**Chair of St Peter.** The office of the Pope of Rome, founded by St Peter, the apostle; but *St Peter's Chair* means the Catholic festival held in commemoration of the two episcopates founded by the apostle, one at Rome, and the other at Antioch (January 18th and February 22nd).

**Chalcedony.** A precious stone, consisting of half-transparent quartz; supposed by Pliny to be so called from Chalcedon, in Asia Minor. Its chief varieties are agate, carnelian, cat's-eye, chrysoprase, onyx, and sard.

Albertus Magnus says:

> It dispels illusions and all vain imaginations. If hung about the neck as a charm, it is a defence against enemies, and keeps the body healthful and vigorous. Bk i, ch. ii

**Chalk.** ***Chalk it up.*** Put it to his credit.

As good-humoured sarcasm, *Chalk it up!* is tantamount to saying, 'What you have done so astonishes me that I must make some more or less permanent record of it.'

***I'll chalk out your path for you*** – i.e. lay it down or plan it out as a carpenter or shipbuilder plans out his work with a piece of chalk.

***I can walk a chalk as well as you.*** I am no more drunk than you are. The allusion is to the ordeal to which men suspected of drunkenness are subjected at police stations, etc. They are required to walk along a line chalked on the floor, without deviating to the right or left.

***I cannot make chalk of one and cheese of the other.*** I must treat both alike; I must show no favouritism.

***I know the difference between chalk and cheese.*** Between what is worthless and what is valuable, between a counterfeit and a real article. Of course, the resemblance of chalk to cheese has something to do with the saying, and the alliteration helps to popularise it.

> This Scotch scarecrow was no more to be compared to him than chalk was to cheese.
>
> Scott, *Woodstock*, xxiv

***They are no more like than chalk is like cheese.*** There may be a slight apparent resemblance, but there is no real likeness.

***The tapster is undone by chalk,*** i.e. credit. The allusion is to scoring up credit on a tally with chalk. This was common enough early in the 19th century, when milk scores, bread scores, as well as beer scores, were general.

**Chalks. *I beat him by long chalks.*** Thoroughly. In allusion to the ancient custom of making merit marks with chalk, before lead pencils were so common.

***Walk your chalks.*** Get you gone. Lodgings wanted for the royal retinue used to be taken arbitrarily by the marshal and sergeant-chamberlain, the inhabitants were sent to the right about, and the houses selected were notified by a chalk mark. When Mary de Medicis, in 1638, came to England, Sieur de Labat was employed to mark 'all sorts of houses commodious for her retinue in Colchester'. The same custom is referred to in the *Life and Acts of Sir William Wallace*, in Edinburgh. The phrase is 'Walk, you're chalked', corrupted into *Walk your chalks*.

At one time it was customary for a landlord to give the tenant notice to quit by chalking the door.

> The prisoner has cut his stick, and walked his chalk, and is off to London.
>
> C. Kingsley, *Two Years Ago*, i

**Challenge.** This meant originally an accusation or charge, and secondarily a claim, a defiance. It comes through French from the Lat. *calumnia*, a false accusation, and is thus etymologically the same word as 'calumny'.

***Challenging a jury.*** This may be to object to all the jurors from some informality in the way they have been 'arrayed' or empanelled, or to one or more of the jurors, from some real or supposed disqualification or bias of judgment. In the first case it is a *challenge to the array*, and this must be based on some default of the sheriff, or his officer who arrayed the panel.

If any member of the jury is thought not qualified to serve, or if he is supposed to be biased, he may be challenged. In capital cases a prisoner may challenge persons without assigning any reason, and in cases of treason as many as thirty-five.

**Cham** (*kam*). The sovereign prince of Tartary, now written 'khan'.

> Fetch you a hair off the great Cham's beard.
>
> Shakespeare, *Much Ado about Nothing*, 2, 1

***The great Cham of Literature.*** Dr Samuel Johnson (1709–84).

**Chambre Ardente** (Fr.) In French history, the name given to certain Courts of Justice held under the *ancien régime*, for trying exceptional cases, such as charges of heresy, poisoning, etc. They were usually held at night, and both then and when held in the daytime were lighted by torches. These courts were devised by Cardinal Lorraine. The first was held in the reign of François I, for trying heretics. Brinvilliers and her associates were tried in a darkened court in 1680.

The same name is given to the room or hall in which a lying in state takes place, because it is usually furnished with lighted candles.

**Chameleon. *You are a chameleon,*** i.e. very changeable – shifting according to the opinions of others, as the chameleon, to a very limited extent, can change its hue to that of contiguous objects.

> As the chameleon, who is known
> To have no colours of its own,
> But borrows from his neighbour's hue,
> His white or black, his green or blue. Prior

**Champ de Mai.** The political assemblies held annually in May by the Carolingian kings of France: they were sometimes little more than fairs and pageants for the amusement of the freedmen who came to offer homage to their lord, and pay their annual gifts, but were sometimes for business purposes, especially when the king wished to consult his warriors about some expedition.

Napoleon I gave the name to the assembly he called together on May 1st, 1815, when he proclaimed the result of the plebiscite ratifying the proclamation of the *Acte additionnel*.

**Champak.** An Indian magnolia (*Michelia Champaca*). The wood is sacred to Buddha, and the strongly scented golden flowers are worn in the black hair of Indian women.

> The Champak odours fall.
>
> Shelley, *Lines to Indian Air*

**Champerty** (Lat. *campi partitio*, division of the land). A bargain with some person who undertakes at his own cost to recover property on condition of receiving a share thereof if he succeeds.

Champerty is treated as a worse offence; for by this a stranger supplies money to carry on a suit, on condition of sharing in the land or other property.

Parsons, *Contracts* (vol. ii, pt ii, ch. 3, p. 264)

**Champion of England.** A person whose office it is to ride up Westminster Hall on a Coronation Day, and challenge anyone who disputes the right of succession. The office was established by William the Conqueror, and was given to Marmion and his male descendants, with the manor of 'broad Scrivelsby'. De Ludlow received the office and manor through the female line; and at the Coronation of Richard II Sir John Dymoke succeeded through the female line also. Since then the office has continued in the Dymoke family, but the actual riding and challenge has been discontinued since the coronation of Queen Victoria.

These Lincoln lands the Conqueror gave,
That England's glove they might convey
To knight renowned amongst the brave –
The baron bold of Fonteney.

An Anglo-Norman Ballad modernised

**Chance.** *See* Main Chance.

***To chance your arm,*** or ***your luck.*** To run a risk in the hope of 'bringing it off' and obtaining a profit or advantage of some sort.

**Chancel** means a lattice screen. In the Roman law courts the lawyers were cut off from the public by such a screen. (Lat. *cancellus.*)

***Chancel of a church.*** That part of a church which contains the altar, and the seats set apart for the choir. It is generally raised a step or more above the floor of the nave.

**Chancellor.** A petty officer (*cancellarius*) in the Roman law courts stationed at the chancel (*q.v.*) as usher of the court. In the Eastern Empire he was a secretary or notary, subsequently invested with judicial functions. The office was introduced into England by Edward the Confessor, and under the Norman kings the chancellor was made official secretary of all important legal documents. In France the chancellor was the royal notary, president of the councils, and keeper of the Great Seal.

**Chancellor, Dancing.** *See* Dancing.

**Chancellor of England.** The *Lord Chancellor*, or the *Lord High Chancellor*. The highest judicial functionary of the nation, who ranks above all peers, except princes of the blood and the Archbishop of Canterbury. He is 'Keeper of the Great Seal', is called 'Keeper of His (or Her) Majesty's Conscience', and presides on the Woolsack in the House of Lords, and in the Chancery Division of the Supreme Court.

**Chancellor of the Exchequer.** The minister of finance in the Cabinet; the highest financial official of State in the kingdom.

**Chancery.** The highest division of the High Court of Justice, comprising a court of common law and a court of equity; it is the highest Court in the Empire, excepting only the House of Lords.

***To get a man's head into chancery*** is to get it under your arm, where you can pummel it as long as you like, and he cannot get it free without great difficulty. The allusion is to the long and exhausting nature of a Chancery suit. If a man once gets his head there, the lawyers punish him to their hearts' content.

When I can perform my mile in eight minutes, or a little less, I feel as if I had old Time's head in chancery. Holmes, *Autocrat*, ch. vii

**Chaneph** (Heb., a hypocrite). In Rabelais' *Pantagruel* (IV, lxiii) the island of religious hypocrites, inhabited by sham saints, tellers of beads, mumblers of *ave marias*, and friars who lived by begging.

**Change.** ***Ringing the changes.*** Repeating the same thing in different ways. The allusion is to bell-ringing. For the sharper's meaning of the term, *see* Ringing.

To know how many changes can be rung on a peal, multiply the number of bells in the peal by the number of changes that can be rung on a peal consisting of one bell less, thus: 1 bell no change; 2 bells, 1 x 2 = 2 changes; 3 bells, 2 x 3 = 6 changes; 4 bells, 6 x 4 = 24 changes; 5 bells, 24 x 5 = 120 changes; 6 bells, 720 changes, etc.

***Take your change out of that.*** Said to a person who insults you when you give him a *quid pro quo*, and tell him to take out the change. It is an allusion to shopping transactions, where you *settle* the price of the article, and put the surplus or change in your pocket.

**Changeling.** A peevish, sickly child. The notion used to be that the fairies took a healthy child, and left in its place one of their starveling elves which never did kindly.

The king doth keep his revels here tonight:
Take heed the queen come not within his sight;
For Oberon is passing fell and wrath,
Because that she as her attendant hath
A lovely boy, stolen from an Indian king:
She never had so sweet a changeling.

Shakespeare, *Midsummer Night's Dream*, 2, 1

**Chant du Départ.** After the *Marseillaise*, the most celebrated song of the French Revolution. It was written by M. J. Chénier for a public festival, held June 11th, 1794, to commemorate the taking of the Bastille. The music is by Mehul. A mother, an old man, a child, a wife, a girl, and three warriors sing a verse in turn, and the sentiment of each is, 'We give up our claims on the men of France for the good of the Republic.' *Cp*. Carmagnole.

La republique nous appelle,
Sachons vaincre on sachons périr;
Un Français doit vivre pour elle,
Pour elle un Français doit mourir.
M. J. Chénier

**Chantage.** Blackmail; money accepted by low-class journals to prevent the publication of scandals, etc. *Chantage* is the common name in France for this form of subsidy; and the word has been used in the same way in England.

**Chanticleer.** The cock, in the tale of *Reynard the Fox*, and in Chaucer's *Nonne Prestes Tale*; also in Rostand's well-known play of this name produced in Paris in 1910. (Fr. *chanter-clair*, to sing *clairment*, i.e. distinctly.)

My lungs began to crow like chanticleer.
Shakespeare, *As You Like It*, 2, 7

**Chantrey Bequest.** To learn that one's picture has been *purchased by the Chantrey Bequest* is the ambition of all young artists. When Sir Francis Leggatt Chantrey, the sculptor, died in 1841 he left a sum yielding about £3,000 a year to the Royal Academy, of which the President was to receive £300, the secretary £50, and the remainder was to be devoted to the purchase for the nation of works of art executed in Great Britain.

**Chaonian Bird, The.** The dove. So called because it delivered the oracles of Chaonia (*Dodona*).

But the mild swallow none with toils infest,
And none the soft Chaonian bird molest.
Ovid, *Art of Love*, ii

**Chaonian Food.** Acorns. So called from the oak trees of Chaonia or Dodona. Some think *beech-mast* is meant, and tell us that the bells of the oracle were hung on beech trees, not on oaks.

**Chaos** (*kaos*). Confusion; that confused mass of elemental substances supposed to have existed before God reduced creation into order. The poet Hesiod is the first extant writer that speaks of it.

Light uncollected, through the chaos urged
Its infant way; nor order yet had drawn
His lovely train from out the dubious gloom.
Thomson, *Autumn*, 732, 4

**Chap.** A man, properly a merchant. A chap-man (O.E. *ceap-mann*) is a merchantman or tradesman, 'if you want to buy, I'm your chap'. A good chap-man or chap became in time a good fellow. Hence, *A good sort of chap, a clever chap*, etc.

An awkward *customer* is an analogous phrase.

**Chap-book.** A cheap little book containing tales, ballads, lives, etc., sold by chapmen.

**Chapeau bras.** A soft three-cornered flat silk hat which could be folded and carried under the arm (Fr. *chapeau*, hat, *bras*, arm). It was used in France with the court dress of the 18th century.

**Chapel.** Originally, a chest containing relics, or the shrine thereof, so called from the *capella* (little cloak or cope) of St Martin, which was preserved by the Frankish kings as a sacred relic. The place in which it was kept when not in the field was called the *chapelle*, and the keeper thereof the *chapelain*. Hence, the name came to be attached to a sanctuary, or a place of worship other than a parish or cathedral church; and is now used for a place subsidiary to the parish church, or a place of worship not connected with the State, as a Methodist Chapel, a Baptist Chapel, etc.

In printing-house parlance a *chapel* is an association of journeymen, compositors, machine-men, etc., who meet periodically to discuss matters of common interest connected with their work, to decide upon the course of action to be taken in cases of disputes or differences between themselves and their employers, etc. The chairman is known as the 'father of the chapel'. The term dates from the early days of printing, when presses were set up in the chapels attached to abbeys, as those of Caxton in Westminster Abbey. *Cp*. Monk, Friar.

**Chapel of Ease.** A place of worship for the use of parishioners residing at a distance from the parish church.

**Chaperon.** A married or elderly lady who attends a young unmarried lady in public places and acts as her guide, adviser, and, when necessary, protector. So called from the Spanish hood worn by duennas in former times.

***To chaperon***. To accompany a young unmarried lady *in loco parentis*, when she appears in public or in society.

**Chapter.** From Lat. *caput*, a head. The *chapter* of a cathedral, composed of the canons (*see* Canon) and presided over by the dean, is so called from the ancient practice of the canons and monks reading at their meetings a *capitulum* (*cp*. Capitulary) or chapter of their Rule or of

Scripture. *Ire ad capitulum* meant 'to go to the (reading of the) chapter', hence, to the meeting, hence to the body which composed the meeting.

***Chapter of accidents.*** Unforeseen events. *To trust to the chapter of accidents* is to trust that something unforeseen may turn up in your favour.

***Chapter of possibilities.*** A may-be in the course of events.

***Dean and Chapter.*** *See* Canon *and* Capitulary.

***To the end of the chapter.*** To the end of a proceeding. The allusion is obvious.

***To give chapter and verse.*** To give the exact authority of a statement, as the name of the author, the title of the book, the date, the chapter referred to, and any other particular which might render the reference easily discoverable.

**Character.** An oddity. One who has a distinctive peculiarity of manner: Sam Weller is a character, so is Pickwick.

***In character.*** In harmony with a person's actions, etc.

***Out of character.*** Not in harmony with a person's actions, writings, profession, age, or status in society.

**Chare Thursday.** Another form of *Shear* or *Shere Thursday*; the same as *Maundy Thursday* (*q.v.*).

**Charge, To.** To make an attack or onset in battle. 'To charge with bayonets' is to rush on the enemy with levelled bayonets.

***Curate in charge.*** A curate placed by a bishop in charge of a parish where there is no incumbent, or where the incumbent is suspended.

***To charge oneself with.*** To take upon oneself the onus of a given task.

***To give charge over.*** To set one in authority over.

> I gave my brother Hanani ... charge over Jerusalem. Neh. 7:2

***To give in charge.*** To hand over a person to the charge of a policeman.

***To have in charge.*** To have the care of something.

***To return to the charge.*** To renew the attack.

***To take in charge.*** To 'take up' a person given in charge; to take upon oneself the responsibility of something.

**Chargé d' Affaires.** The proxy of an ambassador, or the diplomatic agent where none higher has been appointed.

**Charicleia.** The lady-love of Theagenes in the exquisite erotic Greek romance called *The Loves of Theagenes and Charicleia*, by Heliodoros, Bishop of Tricca, in Thessaly, in the 4th century.

**Charing Cross.** The original 'Charing Cross' was erected in the centre of the ancient village of Charing, which stood midway between the cities of London and Westminster, by Edward I to commemorate his Queen, Eleanor, because it was there that her coffin was halted for the last time on its progress from Harby, Notts, where the Queen died, to Westminster, where she was buried. The village may have been called *Charing* from some now forgotten connection with the village of that name near Ashford, Kent, or – conceivably – from *la chère reine*, the Blessed Virgin, because it was the usual halting place for funeral processions on their way from London to the Abbey; in no case can it be from *la chère reine* of Edward I, as the name was connected with this site very many years before her time.

The present cross is a copy (made to scale) by E. M. Barry, R.A., of the original one that was demolished by the Puritans in 1647, and that stood on the south side of Trafalgar Square on the site now occupied by the equestrian statue of Charles I. It was erected in 1865 in the courtyard of Charing Cross Station.

**Chariot.** According to *Greek mythology*, the chariot was invented by Erichthonius to conceal his feet, which were those of a dragon.

> Seated in car, by him constructed first
> To hide his hideous feet.
> Rose, *Orlando Furioso*, xxxvii, 27

***Chariot of the gods.*** So the Greeks called Sierra Leone, in Africa, a ridge of mountains of great height. A sierra means a saw, and is applied to a ridge of peaked mountains.

> Her palmy forests, mingling with the skies,
> Leona's rugged steep behind us flies.
> Camoens, *Lusiad*, Bk v

***Chariots*** or ***Cars.*** That of

> Admetus was drawn by lions and wild boars.
> Bacchus by panthers.
> Ceres by winged dragons.
> Cybele by lions.
> Diana by stags.
> Juno by peacocks.
> Neptune by sea-horses.
> Pluto by black horses.
> The Sun by seven horses (the seven days of the week).
> Venus by doves.

**Charity.** ***Charity begins at home.*** 'Let them learn first to show piety at home' (1 Tim. 5:4 and 8).

***Cold as charity.*** Than which what's colder to him who gives and him who takes?

**Charivari.** The clatter made with pots and pans, whistling, bawling, hissing, and so on. Our concert of 'marrow-bones and cleavers'; the German *Katzenmusik*, got up to salute with ridicule unequal marriages. The name was taken as that of a satirical journal founded in Paris by Charles Philipon in 1832, and hence in 1841 the London *Punch* adopted as its sub-title *The London Charivari*.

**Charlatan.** The following 'etymology' is suitable to a book of Phrase and Fable. One Latan, a famous quack and tooth-drawer, used to go about Paris in a gorgeous car, in which he had a travelling dispensary. A man with a horn announced his approach, and the delighted sightseers used to cry out, '*Voila! le char de Latan.*' When Dr Brewer lived in Paris he often saw this gorgeous car; the horn-man had a drum also, and M. Latan, dressed in a long robe, wore sometimes a hat with feathers, sometimes a brass helmet, and sometimes a showy cap.

Probably 'Latan' was an assumed name, for 'charlatan' is undoubtedly the Italian *ciarlatano*, a babbler or quack.

**Charlemagne.** His nine wives were Himiltrude, a poor Frankish woman, who bore him several children; Desiderata, who was divorced; Hildegarde, Fastrade (daughter of Count Rodolph the Saxon), and Luitgarde the German, all three of whom died before him; Maltegarde; Gersuinde the Saxon; Regina; and Adalinda.

***Charlemagne's peers.*** *See* Paladins.

***Charlemagne's sword.*** La Joyeuse.

***Faire Charlemagne.*** (Fr.). To carry off one's winnings without giving the adversaries 'their revenge'; alluding to the fact that Charlemagne withdrew from the game of life without giving up any of the fruits of his victories. *See also* Turpin.

**Charles.** Like Jane (*q.v.*), this is an ill-omened name for rulers:

***England:*** Charles I was beheaded by his subjects.

Charles II lived long in exile.

Charles Edward, the Young Pretender, died in poverty and disgrace in France.

***France:*** Charles II, the Fat, reigned wretchedly, was deposed, and died a beggarly dependent on the stinting bounty of the Archbishop of Metz.

Charles III, the Simple, died a prisoner in the castle of Péronne.

Charles IV, the Fair, reigned six years, married thrice, but buried all his children except one daughter, who was forbidden by the Salic law to succeed to the crown.

Charles VI lived and died an idiot or madman.

Charles VII starved himself to death, partly through fear of being poisoned and partly because of a painful and incurable abscess in his mouth.

Charles VIII accidentally smashed his head against the lintel of a doorway in the Château Amboise, and died in agony, leaving no issue.

Charles IX died at the age of twenty-four, harrowed in conscience for the part he had taken in the 'Massacre of St Bartholomew'.

Charles X spent a quarter of a century in exile, and less than six years after he succeeded to the throne, fled for his life and died in exile.

Charles le Téméraire, of Burgundy, lost his life at Nancy, where he was utterly defeated by the Swiss.

***Naples:*** Charles I saw the French massacred in the 'Sicilian Vespers', and experienced only disasters.

Charles II, the Lame, was in captivity at his father's death.

Charles III, his grandson, was assassinated.

**Charles I.** When Bernini's bust of Charles I was brought home, the King was sitting in the garden of Chelsea Palace. He ordered the bust to be uncovered, and at the moment a hawk with a bird in its beak flew by, and a drop of blood fell on the throat of the bust. The bust was ultimately destroyed when the palace was burnt down.

**Charles and the Oak.** When Charles II fled from the Parliamentary army after the battle of Worcester, he took refuge in Boscobel House; but it being unsafe to remain there, he concealed himself in an oak (September 3rd, 1651). Dr Stukeley says that this tree 'stood just by a horse-track passing through the wood, and the king, with Colonel Carlos, climbed into it by means of the hen-roost ladder. The family reached them victuals with a nut-hook.' (*Itinerarium Curiosum*, iii. p. 57, 1724.)

**Charles's Wain.** An old popular name for the Great Bear (*see* Bear). The constellation forms the rough outline of a wheelbarrow or rustic wagon, and the 'Charles' stands for 'Charlemagne', probably owing to the similarity of the names *Arcturus* (*see* Arctic) and *Arturus* (Lat. for *Arthur*), and the confusion in the popular mind between the legendary cycles of romance connected with King Arthur and Charlemagne respectively.

**Charleys,** or ***Charlies***. The old night watch, before the police force was organised in 1829; perhaps from Charles I, under whom the police system in London was reorganised in 1640.

**Charon's Toll.** A coin, about equal to a penny, placed in the mouth or hand of the dead by the ancient Greeks to pay Charon (*see* Styx) for ferrying the spirit across the river Styx to the Elysian fields.

**Chartism.** The political system of the Chartists, a body consisting principally of working men who, in 1838, demanded the *People's Charter*, which included universal suffrage, annual parliaments, stipendiary members, vote by ballot, equal representation, and the abolition of the property qualification for members of Parliament. The Chartists disappeared as a party about 1849.

**Chartreuse.** A greenish or yellowish liqueur, made of brandy, and various aromatic herbs, formerly manufactured by the monks of the Grande Chartreuse (*see* Carthusian).

**Charybdis.** A whirlpool on the coast of Sicily. Scylla (*q.v.*) and Charybdis are employed to signify two equal dangers. Thus Horace says an author trying to avoid Scylla, drifts into Charybdis, i.e. seeking to avoid one fault, falls into another.

The Homeric account says that Charybdis dwelt under an immense fig tree on the rock, and that thrice every day he swallowed the waters of the sea and thrice threw them up again; but later legends have it that he stole the oxen of Hercules, was killed by lightning, and changed into the gulf.

> Thus when I shun Scylla, your father, I fall into
> Charybdis, your mother.
>
> Shakespeare, *Merchant of Venice*, 3, 5

**Chase.** A small, unenclosed deer-forest held, for the most part, by a private individual, and protected only by common law. Forests are *royal* prerogatives, protected by the 'Forest Laws'.

An iron frame used by printers for holding sufficient type for one side of a sheet, where it is held tight by quoins, or small wedges of wood, is also called a *chase*. Here the word is the French *châsse*, from Lat. *capsa*, a case: the other *chase* given above is O.Fr. *chacier*, from Lat. *captiare*, to *chase*, frequentative of *capere*, to take.

**Chasidim.** After the Babylonish captivity the Jews were divided into two groups – those who accepted and those who rejected the Persian innovation. The former were called *chasidim* (pietists), and the latter *zadikim* (the upright ones).

**Château.** French for castle, mansion, country seat, and hence, an estate in the country. It is in this sense that the word is applied to many brands of wines – they are named after the manor on which the grapes are grown: as *Château Lafitte*, *Château La Tour*, *Château Margaux*, *Château Yquem*, etc.

**Châteaux en Espagne.** A castle in the air (*q.v.*); something that exists only in the imagination; literally, 'a castle in Spain'. Fashionable adventurers in France used to impose on the credulous and get money and social advantages out of them by telling tales of their 'Castles in Spain', which, needless to say, they did not possess.

**Chatterbox.** A talkative person. The Germans have *Plaudertasche* (chatterbag). Shakespeare speaks of the clack-dish. 'His use was to put a ducat in her clack-dish' (*Measure for Measure*, 3, 2) – i.e. the box or dish used by beggars for collecting alms, which the holder clatters to attract attention. We find also chatter-basket in old writers, referring to the child's rattle.

**Chatterhouse.** ***To go through the chatterhouse***. A children's phrase for going between the legs of one or more boys, set apart like an inverted Λ, who strike, with their hands or caps, the victim as he creeps through. The pun between chatterhouse and charterhouse is obvious.

**Chatterpie.** A familiar name for the magpie; also used figuratively for a chatterbox (*q.v.*).

**Chaucer of Painting, The.** Albert Dürer of Nuremberg (1471–1528) has been so called. Also, 'the prince of artists'.

**Chauvinism.** Blind and pugnacious patriotism of an exaggerated kind; unreasoning jingoism. Nicholas Chauvin, a soldier of the French Republic and Empire, was madly devoted to Napoleon and his cause. He was introduced as a type of exaggerated bellicose patriotism into quite a number of plays (Scribe's *Le Soldat Laboreur*, Cogniard's *La Cocarde Tricolure*, 1831, Bayard and Dumanoir's *Les Aides de Camps*, Charet's *Conscrit Chauvin*, are some of them), and his name was quickly adopted on both sides of the Channel.

> [In the 18th century France] became cosmopolitan. The country which has since been the birthplace of Chauvinism put away national pride almost with passion.
>
> J. C. Morrison, *Gibbon*

**Chawbacon.** A contemptuous name for an uncouth rustic, supposed to eat no meat but bacon.

**Chawed up.** Done for, utterly discomfited, demolished. (*American.*)

**Che sara, sara.** What shall be, will be. The motto of the Russells (Bedford).

> What doctrine call ye this, *Che sera, sera*:
> What will be, shall be?
>
> Marlowe, *Dr Faustus*, I, 48

**Cheap as a Sardinian.** A Roman phrase referring to the great crowds of Sardinian prisoners brought to Rome by Tiberius Gracchus, and offered for sale at almost any price.

**Cheap Jack.** A travelling vendor of small wares, who is usually ready to 'cheapen' his goods, i.e. take less for them than the price he first named. Jack (*q.v.*) is a term applied to inferior persons, etc.

**Cheapside Bargain.** A weak pun, meaning that the article was bought cheap or under its market value. Cheapside, London, is on the south side of the *Cheap* (or *Chepe*), one of the principal market-places of Old London, so called from A.S. *ceapian*, to buy, *cypan*, to sell, *ceap*, a price or sale.

**Cheater.** Originally an *Escheator* or officer of the king's exchequer appointed to receive dues and taxes. The present use of the word shows how these officers were wont to fleece the people. *Cp.* Catchpole; also the New Testament word 'publicans', or collectors of the Roman tax in Judaea, etc.

**Checkmate.** A term in chess meaning to place your adversary's king in such a position that, had it been any other piece, it could not escape capture. Figuratively, 'to checkmate' means to foil or outwit another; 'checkmated', outmanoeuvred. The term is from the Arabic *shat mat*, the king is dead, the phrase having been introduced into Old Spanish and Portuguese as *xaque mate*.

**Checks.** ***To hand in one's checks***. *See* Hand.

**Cheek.** ***Cheek by jowl.*** In intimate confabulation; *tête-à-tête*. Cheek is the A.S. *ceace*, and jowl is from A.S. *ceafl*, jaw, which became in Mid.E. *chowl*, and was confused with Mid.E. *cholle*, from A.S. *ceolur*, throat.

> I'll go with thee, cheek by jowl.
>
> Shakespeare, *Midsummer Night's Dream*, 3, 2

***None of your cheek.*** None of your insolence. 'None of your jaw' means none of your nagging or word irritation.

We say a man is very *cheeky*, meaning that he is saucy and presumptuous.

***To cheek***, or ***to give cheek.*** To be insolent, to be saucy. 'You must cheek him well', i.e. confront him with fearless impudence; face him out.

***To have the cheek.*** To have the face or assurance. 'He hadn't the cheek to ask for more.'

> On account of his having so much cheek.
>
> Dickens, *Bleak House*

**Cheese.** Tusser in his *Fire Hundred Points of Good Husbandry* (1573) says that a cheese, to be perfect, should not be like (1) Gehazi, i.e. dead white, like a leper; (2) not like Lot's wife, all salt; (3) not like Argus, full of eyes; (4) not like Tom Piper, 'hoven and puffed', like the cheeks of a piper; (5) not like Crispin, leathery; (6) not like Lazarus, poor; (7) not like Esau, hairy; (8) not like Mary Magdalene, full of whey or maudlin; (9) not like the Gentiles, full of maggots or gentils; and (10) not like a bishop, made of burnt milk: this last is a reference to the old phrase, *the bishop hath put his foot in it. See* Bishop.

***A green cheese.*** An unripe cheese; also a cheese that is eaten fresh (like a cream cheese) and is not kept to mature.

***Bread and cheese.*** Food generally, but of a frugal nature. 'Come and take your bread and cheese with me this evening' – that is, come and have a light supper, anything that's going.

***Cheese it!*** Stop it! stow it! Also (in thieves' slang) clear off, make yourself scarce.

***Hard cheese.*** Hard lines; rotten luck. The phrase is sometimes altered, for the sake of variety or additional emphasis, to 'hard cheddar'.

***He is quite the cheese*** or ***just the cheese*** – i.e. quite the thing. Here 'cheese' is the Persian and Urdu *chiz* (or *cheez*), meaning 'thing'. The phrase is of Anglo-Indian origin; but it has been popularly treated as being connected with the Eng. *cheese*, and thus we get the slang varieties, *That's prime Stilton*, or *double Glo'ster* – i.e. slap bang up. Hence such phrases as:

***It is not the cheese.*** Not the right thing; said of something of rather dubious propriety or morals.

> Who ever heard of a young lady being married without something to be married *in*?
> Well, I've heard Nudity is not the cheese on public occasions!
>
> Chas Reade, *Hard Cash*, ii, 186

***The moon made of green cheese.*** *See* Moon.

***'Tis an old rat that won't eat cheese.*** It must be a wondrously toothless man that is inaccessible to flattery; he must be very old indeed who can abandon his favourite indulgence; only a very cunning rat knows that cheese is a mere bait.

**Cheesemongers.** An old popular name (before the Peninsular War) for the 1st Lifeguards; either because up to that time they had never served overseas, or (traditionally) because when the regiment was remodelled in 1788 certain commissions were refused on the ground that the ranks were composed of tradesmen instead of, as formerly, of gentlemen. It is said that at Waterloo the commanding officer, when leading the regiment to a charge, cried, 'Come on, you damned cheesemongers!' since when the name was accepted as a compliment rather than a reproach.

**Cheeseparer.** A skinflint; one who would pare or shave off very thinly the rind of his cheese so as to waste the smallest possible quantity. The tale is told of a man who chose his wife out of three sisters by the way they ate their cheese. One pared it – she (he said) was mean; one cut it off extravagantly thick – she was wasteful; the third sliced it off in a medium way, and there his choice fell.

**Cheese-toaster.** A sword; also called a 'toasting-fork', etc.

> Put up thy sword betime;
> Or I'll so maul you and your toasting-iron
> That you shall think the devil is come from hell.
>
> Shakespeare, *King John*, 4, 3

> The sight of the blade, which glistened by moonlight in his face, checked, in some sort, the ardour of his assailant, who desired he would lay aside his toaster, and take a bout with him at equal arms.
>
> Smollett, *Peregrine Pickle*, ch. xxiv

**Cheesewring, The Devil's.** A mass of eight stones, towering to the height of thirty-two feet, in the Valley of Rocks, Lynmouth, Devon, so called because it looks like a gigantic cheese-press. The Kilmarth Rocks, and part of Hugh Lloyd's Pulpit (*q.v.*), present somewhat similar piles of stone.

**Chef d'Oeuvre** (Fr., literally, a chief work). A masterpiece.

**Chemistry.** From the Arab. *kimia*. *See* Alchemy.

*Inorganic chemistry* is that branch of chemistry which treats of metallic and non-metallic substances and their compounds, as opposed to *organic chemistry*, which is devoted to the investigation of carbon and its compounds, i.e. animal and vegetable substances.

**Chemosh.** The national god of the Moabites; very little is known of his cult, but human beings were sacrificed to him in times of crisis.

> Next, Chemos, the obscene dread of Moab's sons,
> From Aroer to Nebo, and the wild
> Of southmost Abarim.
>
> Milton, *Paradise Lost*, i, 406–8

**Chequers.** A public-house sign. The arms of Fitzwarren, the head of which house, in the days of the Henrys, was invested with the power of licensing vintners and publicans, may have helped to popularise this sign, which indicated that the house was duly licensed; but it has been found on houses in Pompeii, and probably referred to some game, like draughts, which might be indulged in on the premises. Gayton, in his *Notes on Don Quixote* (p. 340), in speaking of our public-house signs, refers to our notices of 'billiards, kettle-noddy-boards, tables, truncks, shovel-boards, fox-and-geese, and the like'. Also, payment of doles, etc., used to be made at certain public-houses, and a chequer-board was provided for the purpose. In such cases the sign indicated the house where the parish authorities met for that and other purposes.

***Chequers***, the country seat of the Prime Minister of England for the time being, was presented to the nation for this purpose by Sir Arthur and Lady Lee (Lord and Lady Lee of Fareham) in 1917, and was first officially occupied by the then Prime Minister (Mr David Lloyd George) in January, 1921. It is a Tudor mansion, standing in a large and well wooded estate in the Chilterns, about three miles from Princes Risborough, Bucks.

**Cheronean.** ***The Cheronean Sage***. Plutarch, who was born at Chaeronea, in Boeotia (AD 46–120).

> This phrase, O Cheronean sage, is thine.
>
> Beattie, *Minstrel*

**Cherry.** ***Cherry-breeches*** or ***cherry-pickers***. Familiar names for the 11th Hussars. *See* Cherubims.

***Cherry fairs***. The old counterpart of the modern tea-gardens; cherry-orchards where sales of fruit were held, such gatherings frequently developing into boisterous scenes. From their temporary character they came to be used as typifications of the evanescence of life; thus Gower says of this world, 'Alle is but a cherye-fayre,' a phrase frequently met with.

> This life, my son, is but a chery-fayre.
>
> *MS Bodl.* 221 (quoted by Halliwell)

***Cherry trees and the Cuckoo***. The cherry tree is strangely mixed up with the cuckoo in many cuckoo stories, because of the tradition that the cuckoo must eat three good meals of cherries before he is allowed to cease singing.

> Cuckoo, cuckoo, cherry tree,
> Good bird, prithee, tell to me
> How many years I am to see.

The answer is gathered from the number of times the cuckoo repeats its cry.

***The whole tree* or *not a cherry on it.*** '*Aut Caesar aut nullus.*' All in all or none at all.

***To make two bites of a cherry.*** To divide something too small to be worth dividing; to take two spells over a piece of work that should be done in one.

**Cherubims.** The 11th Hussars are so called, through a rather vulgar pun. Their trousers are of a *cherry* colour.

**Cheshire Cat.** *To grin like a Cheshire cat. See* Cat.

**Chess.** 'The game of the kings'; the word *chess* being the modern English representative of Persian *shah* (*see* Checkmate), a king. This word in Arabic was pronounced *shag*, which gave rise to the late Lat. *scaccus*, whence the O.Fr. *eschec*, Mod.Fr. *échecs*, and E. *chess*. Derivatives in other languages are *scacco* (Ital.), *jaque* (Span.), *xaque* (Port.), *schach* (Ger.).

**Chestnut.** A stale joke. The term is said to have been popularised in America by a Boston actor named Warren, who, on a certain apposite occasion, quoted from *The Broken Sword*, a forgotten melodrama by William Dimond, which was first produced in 1816 at Covent Garden. Captain Xavier, a principal character, is forever repeating the same yarns, with variations. He was telling about one of his exploits connected with a cork tree, when Pablo corrects him, 'A chestnut tree, you mean, captain.' 'Bah! (replied the captain) I say a cork tree'. 'A chestnut tree,' insists Pablo. 'I must know better than you (said the captain); it was a cork tree, I say.' 'A chestnut (persisted Pablo). I have heard you tell the joke twenty-seven times, and I am sure it was a chestnut.'

**Chestnut Sunday.** A Sunday in spring, generally that immediately before or after Ascension Day, is so called in the London district, because about that time the chestnut avenue at Hampton Court bursts into bloom and invites the town-dweller for a Sunday by the river.

**Cheval** (Fr., a horse).

***Cheval de bataille*** (Fr., literally 'horse of battle'). One's strong argument; one's favourite subject.

***Cheval de frise.*** An apparatus consisting of a bar carrying rows of pointed stakes, set up so that the bar can revolve. It was used in warfare as a defence against enemy cavalry, and is so called because first employed by the Frisians – who had few or no horses – in the siege of Groningen, Friesland, in 1594. A somewhat similar engine had been used before, but was not called by the same name. In German it is 'a Spanish horseman' (*ein Spanischer Reiter*).

***Cheval glass.*** A large, swinging mirror, long enough to reflect the whole of the figure; so called from the 'horse', or framework, which supports it.

**Chevalier de St George.** *See* Cavalier.

**Chevalier d'Industrie.** A man who lives by his wits and calls himself a gentleman; an adventurer, swindler.

> Be cautiously upon your guard against the infinite number of fine-dressed and fine-spoken chevaliers d'industrie and avanturiers, which swarm at Paris.
>
> Chesterfield, *Letters to his Son*, cxc (April 26th, 1750)

**Cheveril.** *He has a cheveril conscience.* An accommodating one; one that will easily stretch like cheveril or kid leather.

> Oh, here's a wit of cheveril, that stretches from an inch narrow to an ell broad!
>
> Shakespeare, *Romeo and Juliet*, 2, 4

> Your soft cheveril conscience would receive,
> If you might please to stretch it.
>
> Shakespeare, *Henry VIII*, 2, 3

**Chevy Chase.** There had long been a rivalry between the families of Percy and Douglas, which showed itself by incessant raids into each other's territory. Percy of Northumberland one day vowed he would hunt for three days in the Scottish border, without condescending to ask leave of Earl Douglas. The Scotch warden said in his anger, 'Tell this vaunter he shall find one day more than sufficient.' The ballad called *Chevy Chase* mixes up this hunt with the battle of Otterburn, which, Dr Percy justly observes, was 'a very different event'.

> To louder strains he raised his voice, to tell
> What woful wars in 'Chevy Chase' befell,
> When Percy drove the deer with hound and horn,
> Wars to be wept by children yet unborn.
>
> Gay, *Pastoral*, VI

**Chian Painter, The.** *See* Apelles.

**Chiar-oscuro.** A style of painting to represent only two colours, now called 'black and white'; also the production of the effects of light and shade in drawings, paintings, etc.

> Chiar-oscuro ... is the art of representing light in shadow and shadow in light, so that the parts represented in shadow shall still have the clearness and warmth of those in light; and those in light, the depth and softness of those in shadow. *Chambers' Encyclopaedia*, ii, p. 171

**Chibiabos.** The musician in Longfellow's *Hiawatha*; the harmony of nature personified.

He teaches the birds to sing and the brooks to warble as they flow. 'All the many sounds of nature borrow sweetness from his singing.'

Very dear to Hiawatha
Was the gentle Chibiabos.
For his gentleness he loved him.
And the magic of his singing.

Longfellow, *Hiawatha*, vi

**Chibouque.** A smoking-pipe with a long tube, used in the East (Turkish).

**Chic.** A French word of uncertain origin meaning in France effective style in painting, the knack of producing effects easily, but in England the correct, fashionable or stylish thing. The word may be connected with German *schick*, skill, tact, but this is by no means certain.

**Chicane.** A term used in bridge for a hand containing no trumps. Its general meaning is the use of mean, petty subterfuge, especially legal dodges and quibbles. It is a French word which, before being used for sharp practice in lawsuits, meant a dispute in games, particularly mall, and originally the game of mall itself. It seems to be ultimately from Persian *chaugan*, the crooked stick used in polo.

**Chichivache.** A fabulous animal that lived only on good women, and was hence all skin and bone, because its food was so extremely scarce; the antitype to Bicorn (*q.v.*). Chaucer introduced the word into English from French; but in doing so he changed *chichifache* (thin or ugly face) into *chichivache* (lean or meagre-looking cow), and hence the animal was pictured as a kind of bovine monstrosity.

O noble wyves, ful of heigh prudence,
Let noon humilitie your tonges nayle:
No lat no clerk have cause or diligence
To write of you a story of such mervayle
As of Griseldes, pacient and kynde,
Lest Chichivache you swolwe in hir entraile.

Chaucer, *Envoy to the Clerk's Tale*

Lydgate wrote a poem entitled *Bycorne and Chichevache*.

**Chick-a-biddy.** A child's name for a young chicken, and a mother's word of endearment to her young child. 'Biddy' is merely the call of a child, bid-bid-bid-bid to a chicken.

Do you, sweet Rob? Do you truly, chickabiddy?

Dickens, *Dombey and Son*

**Chicken.** ***Children and chicken must always be pickin'.*** Are always hungry and ready to eat food.

***Curses like chickens come home to roost.*** *See* Curses.

***Don't count your chickens before they are hatched.*** Don't anticipate profits before they come. One of Aesop's fables describes a market woman saying she would get so much for her eggs, with the money she would buy a goose; the goose in time would bring her so much, with which she would buy a cow, and so on; but in her excitement she kicked over her basket and all her eggs were broken. 'Don't crow till you are out of the wood' has a similar meaning. *Cp.* Alnaschar's Dream.

***Mother Carey's chickens.*** *See* Mother Carey.

***She's no chicken.*** She's not so young as she used to be.

She may very well pass for forty-three
In the dusk with a light behind her!

Sir W. S. Gilbert, *Trial by Jury*

***Where the chicken got the axe.*** *See To get it in the neck*, under Neck.

***Chicken of St Nicholas.*** So the Piedmontese call our 'ladybird', the little red beetle with spots of black. The Russians know it as 'God's little cow', and the Germans, who say it is sent as a messenger of love, 'God's little horse'.

***Chicken-hearted.*** Cowardly. Young fowls are remarkably timid, and run to the wing of the hen upon the slightest cause of alarm.

**Chien.** *Entre chien et loup* (Fr., literally 'between dog and wolf'). Dusk, between daylight and lamplight; owl-light. Perhaps because it is at that time, before the dog is placed on guard, that the shepherd may expect the wolf to come prowling round the sheepfold. *Cp.* Inter canem.

The best time to talk of difficult things is *entre chien et loup*, as the Guernsey folk say.

Mrs Edwardes, *A Girton Girl*, ch. xivi

**Child,** at one time, meant a female infant, and was the correlative of boy.

Mercy on 's! A barne, a very pretty barne. A boy or a child, I wonder?

Shakespeare, *Winter's Tale*, 3, 3

**Child of God.** In the Anglican and Catholic Church, one who has been baptised; others consider the phrase to mean one converted by special grace and adopted into the holy family of God's Church.

In my baptism, wherein I was made a member of Christ, the child of God, and an inheritor of the Kingdom of Heaven. *Church Catechism*

**Childe.** In *Childe Harold*, *Childe Roland*, *Childe Tristram*, etc., 'Childe' is a title of honour, like the Spanish 'infante' and 'infanta'. In the times of chivalry, noble youths who were candidates for knighthood were, during their time of probation, called *infans*, *valets*, *damoysels*, *bacheliers*, and *childe*.

**Childe Harold.** Byron's poem depicts a man sated of the world, who roams from place to place to flee from himself. The 'childe' is, in fact, Lord Byron himself, who was only twenty-one when he began, and twenty-eight when he finished the poem. In canto i (1809), he visited Portugal and Spain; in canto ii (1810), Turkey in Europe; in canto iii (1816), Belgium and Switzerland; and in canto iv (1817), Venice, Rome, and Florence.

**Childermass.** The Old English name for the festival, or mass, of the Holy Innocents (December 28th).

**Children. *The children in the wood*.** The foundation of this ballad, which is told in Percy's *Reliques*, appears again in a crude melodrama of 1599 by Robert Farrington, entitled *Two Lamentable Tragedies: the one of the Murder of Maister Beech, a chandler in Thames Streete, the other of a young child murthered in a wood by two ruffins with the consent of his unkle.* It is not known which is the earlier, the play or the ballad. The story is, shortly, as follows – The master of Wayland Hall, Norfolk, left a little son and daughter to the care of his wife's brother; both were to have money, but if the children died first the uncle was to inherit. After twelve months the uncle hired two ruffians to murder the babes; one of the ruffians relented and killed his fellow, leaving the children in a wood; they died during the night, and 'Robin Redbreast' covered them over with leaves. All things went ill with the wicked uncle; his sons died, his barns were fired, his cattle died, and he himself perished in gaol. After seven years the ruffian was taken up for highway robbery, and confessed the whole affair.

> Then sad he sung 'The Children in the Wood'.
> (Ah! barbarous uncle, stained with infant blood!)
> How blackberries they plucked in deserts wild,
> And fearless at the glittering falchion smiled;
> Their little corpse the robin-redbreast found,
> And strewed with pious bill the leaves around.
>
> Gay, *Pastoral VI*

***Children.*** Three hundred and sixty-five at a birth. It is said that the Countess of Henneberg accused a beggar of adultery because she carried twins, whereupon the beggar prayed that the countess might carry as many children as there are days in the year. According to the legend, this happened on Good Friday, 1276. All the males were named John, and all the females Elizabeth. The countess was forty-two at the time.

**Chiliasts** (Gr. *chilias*, a thousand). Those who believe that Christ will return to this earth and reign a thousand years in the midst of His saints. Originally a Judaistic theory, it became a heresy in the early Christian Church, and though it was condemned by St Damasus, who was Pope from 366 to 384, it was not extirpated. Article xli of the English Church, as published in 1553, further condemned Chiliasm; this Article was omitted in 1562. *Millenarians* is another name for the Chiliasts.

**Chillingham Cattle.** A breed of cattle preserved in the park of the Earl of Tankerville, supposed to be the last remnant of the wild oxen of Britain.

**Chillon.** *Prisoner of Chillon.* François de Bonnivard (d. about 1570), a Genevan prelate and politician. Byron makes him one of six brothers, all of whom suffered for their opinions. The father and two sons died on the battlefield; one was burnt at the stake; three were incarcerated in the dungeon of Chillon, on the edge of the Lake of Geneva – of these, two died, and François, who had been imprisoned for 'republican principles' by the Duke-Bishop of Savoy, was set at liberty by 'the Bearnais'.

**Chilminar and Baalbec.** Two cities built, according to Eastern legend, by the Genii, acting under the orders of Jan ben Jan, who governed the world long before the time of Adam. Chilminar, or the 'Forty Pillars', is Persepolis. They were intended as lurking places for the Genii to hide in.

**Chilo.** One of the 'Seven Sages of Greece' (*q.v.*).

**Chiltern Hundreds.** There are three, viz. Stoke, Desborough, and Burnham, Bucks. At one time the Chilterns, between Bedford and Hertford, etc., were much frequented by robbers, so a steward was appointed by the Crown to put them down. The necessity has long since ceased, but the office remains; and, since 1740, when a Member of Parliament wishes to vacate his seat, one way of doing so is by applying for the stewardship of the Chiltern Hundreds; for no member of Parliament may resign his seat, but if he accepts an office of profit under the Crown he is obliged to be re-elected if he wishes to remain a member. The Stewardship of the Manor of Northstead (Yorks) is used in the same way. The gift of both is in the hands of the Chancellor of the Exchequer; it was refused to a member for Reading in 1842.

The Stewardships of Old Sarum (Sussex), East Hendred (Berks), Poynings (Sussex), Hempholwic (Yorks), were formerly used for the same purpose, as were (till 1838) the Escheatorships of Minister and Ulster.

**Chimaera** (Gr. *chimaira*, a she-goat). A fabulous monster of *Greek mythology*, described by Homer as a monster with a goat's body, a lion's head, and a dragon's tail. It was born in Lycia, and was slain by Bellerophon. Hence the term is used in English for an illusory fancy, a wild, incongruous scheme.

**Chime in with, To.** To be in harmony with, to accord with, to fall in with. The allusion is to chiming bells.

> This chimed in with Mr Dombey's own hope and belief. Dickens, *Dombey and Son*

**Chimney Money** or **Hearth Money.** A yearly tax of two shillings levied on every fireplace in England and Wales; first levied in 1663 and abolished in 1689.

**Chimneypot Hat.** The ordinary cylindrical black silk hat, also known as the top-hat or silk hat; it is more formal and dressy than the soft felt hats or stiff bowlers.

**China Clay.** A mineral, obtained largely from Cornwall, used by papermakers to obtain finish and consistency, also for coating art and chromo papers.

**Chinese Gordon.** General Gordon (killed at Khartoum in 1885), who in 1863 was placed in command of the Ever-Victorious Army (*q.v.*) and in the following year succeeded, after thirty-three engagements, in putting down the Taëping rebellion, which had broken out in 1851. For this service Gordon was rewarded by the Emperor with the yellow jacket and peacock's feather of a mandarin of the first class.

**Chingachgook.** The Indian chief in Fenimore Cooper's *Last of the Mohicans*, *Pathfinder*, *Deerslayer*, and *Pioneer*. Called in French *Le Gros Serpent*.

**Chink.** Money; so called because it chinks or jingles in the purse. It is now rather vulgar slang, but was formerly in good repute as a synonym of coin.

> Have chinks in thy purse.
> Tusser, *Five Hundred Points* (1573)

> I tell you, he that can lay hold of her
> Shall have the chinks.
> Shakespeare, *Romeo and Juliet*, 1, 5

**Chintz.** A plural word that has erroneously become singular. The Hindi *chint* (from Sanskrit *chitra*, variegated) was the name given in the 17th century to the painted and stained calico imported from the East; but as the plural (*chints*) was more common in commercial use than the singular it came to be taken for a singular, and was written *chince* or *chinse* and finally *chintz*.

**Chios.** ***The man of Chios.*** Homer, who lived at Chios, near the Aegean Sea. Seven cities claim to be his place of birth –

> Smyrna, Rhodos, Colophon, Salamis, Chios, Argos, Athenae. Varro

**Chip.** ***A carpenter is known by his chips.*** A man is known to be a carpenter by the chips in his workshop, so the profession or taste of other men may be known by their manners or mode of speech. There is a broadcloth slang as well as a corduroy slang; a military, naval, school, and university slang, etc.

***A chip of the old block.*** A son or child of the same stuff as his father. The chip is the same wood as the block. Burke applied the words to William Pitt.

***Brother Chip.*** Properly a brother carpenter, but in its extended meaning applied to anyone of the same vocation as ourselves.

The ship's carpenter is, at sea, commonly addressed as 'chips'.

***Saratoga chips.*** Potatoes sliced thin while raw, and fried crisp. Sometimes called chipped potatoes, or simply 'chips'.

***Such carpenters, such chips.*** As the workman, so his work will be.

**Chiron.** The centaur who taught Achilles and many other heroes music, medicine, and hunting. Jupiter placed him in heaven among the stars as Sagittarius (*the Archer*).

In the *Inferno* Dante gives the name to the keeper of the lake of boiling blood, in the seventh circle of hell.

**Chirping Cup.** A merry-making glass or cup of liquor. Wine that maketh glad the heart of man, or makes him sing for joy.

> A chirping cup is my matin song,
> And my vesper bell is my bowl; Ding dong!
> *A Friar of Orders Grey*

> For wine we follow Bacchus through the earth;
> Great God of breathless cups and chirping mirth,
> Keats, *Endymion*, iv, 235

**Chisel.** ***I chiselled him*** means, I cheated him, or cut him out of something.

**Chitty-faced.** Baby-faced, lean. Probably connected with O.Fr. *chichifache* or *chichiface* (*see* Chichivache), and not with *chit*. A child or sprout. Both *chit* and *chitty-faced* are terms of contempt.

> Father came and found me squabbling with you chitty-faced thing as he would have me marry, so he asked what was the matter ... I told 'n in

> plain terms, if I were minded to marry, I'd marry to please myself, not him. And for the young woman that he provided for me, I thought it more fitting for her to learn her sampler and make dirt-pies than to look after a husband. Congreve, *Love for Love*, iv, 13

**Chivalry.** The paladins of Charlemagne were all scattered by the battle of Roncesvalles.

The champions of Dietrich were all assassinated at the instigation of Chriemhild, the bride of Etzel, King of the Huns.

The Knights of the Round Table were all extirpated by the fatal battle of Camlan.

***The flower of chivalry.*** *See* Flower.

**Chivy.** To chase or race; also a chase in the school game of 'Prisoners' Base'. One boy 'sets a chivy' by leaving his base, when one of the opposite side chases him, and if he succeeds in touching him before he reaches 'home', the boy touched becomes a prisoner. The word is a variant spelling of *chevy*, from *Chevy Chase* (*q.v.*).

**Chivy** or **Chivvy.** Slang for the face. An example of 'rhyming slang' (*q.v.*). Here the full term to rhyme with *face* is *Chevy Chase*.

**Chloe.** The shepherdess beloved by Daphnis in the pastoral romance of Longus, entitled *Daphnis and Chloe*, and hence a generic name among romance writers and pastoral poets for a rustic maiden – not always of the artless variety.

In Pope's *Moral Essays* (ii) Chloe is intended for Lady Suffolk, mistress of George II. 'Content to dwell in decencies for ever'; and Prior uses the name for Mrs Centlivre.

**Chock-full.** Absolutely full; no room for any more. It is a very old expression in English, dating back at least to Chaucer's time, though, apparently, not used by him. It does not seem to have any etymological connection with *choke* (as though meaning 'full enough to choke one'); but this spelling – as well as *chuck* – has been in common use.

> Ayr was holding some grand market; streets and inn had been chokefull during the sunny hours.
> Carlyle, in Froude's *Jane W. Carlyle*, vol. i, letter lxxxvii

**Choice.** ***Choice spirit.*** A specially select or excellent person, a leader in some particular capacity. From Antony's speaking of Caesar and Brutus as –

> The choice and master spirit of this age.
> Shakespeare, *Julius Caesar*, 3, 1

***Choice spirit of the age.*** Figuratively used for a gallant of the day; one who delights to exaggerate the whims of fashion.

***Hobson's choice.*** *See* Hobson.

***Of two evils choose the less.*** The proverb is given in John Heywood's collection (1546), but it is a good deal earlier, and occurs in Chaucer's *Troilus and Criseyde* (ii, 470) as –

> Of harmes two, the lesse is for to chese.

Thomas à Kempis (*Imit. Christi*, iii, 12) has –

> De duobus malis minus est semper eligendum (Of two evils the less is always to be chosen).

which is an echo of Cicero's

> Ex malis eligere minima oportere (Of evil one should select the least). *De officiis*, iii, 1

**Choke.** ***May this piece of bread choke me, if what I say is not true.*** In ancient times a person accused of robbery had a piece of barley bread, over which mass had been said, given him. He put it in his mouth uttering these words, and if he could swallow it without being choked he was pronounced innocent. Tradition ascribes the death of Earl Godwin to choking with a piece of bread after this solemn appeal. *See* Corsned.

**Choke-pear.** An argument to which there is no answer. A piece of iron in the shape of a pear, which was forced into the mouth, was an old instrument of torture. On turning a key, a number of springs thrust forth points of iron in all directions, so that the 'choke-pear' could not be removed except by means of the key.

**Choker.** Formerly a broad neckcloth, worn in full dress, and by waiters and clergymen; now a high, stiff collar. Of course, the verb *to choke* has supplied the word.

**Chop.** The various modern uses of *chop* represent two or three different words. *To chop*, meaning to cut a piece off with a sudden blow, is a variant spelling of *chap*, a cleft in the skin, and *to chap*, to open in long slits or cracks. From this we get:

***Chops of the Channel.*** The short broken motion of the waves, experienced in crossing the English Channel; also the place where such motion occurs. In this use, however, the word may be *chops*, the jaw (*see below*), because the Chops of the Channel is an old and well understood term for the entrance to the Channel from the Atlantic.

***Chop house.*** An eating-house where chops and steaks (i.e. pieces of meat – ribs – cut off and cooked separately) are served.

> I dine at the *Chop-House* three days a week, where the – good company wonders they never see you of late.
> Steele, *Spectator*, No. 308 (22 Feb., 1712)

In the three following phrases *chop* comes from the same root as *chap* in *chapman* (*q.v.*), and signifies to barter, exchange, or sell.

***To chop and change.*** To barter by rule of thumb; to fluctuate, to vary continuously; to exchange, as boys 'chop' one article for another.

***To chop logic.*** To bandy words; to altercate. Bacon says, 'Let not the council chop with the judge.'

How now, how now, chop logic! What is this?
'Proud', and 'I thank you', and 'I thank you not',
And yet 'not proud'.
Shakespeare, *Romeo and Juliet*, 3, 5

***The wind chops about.*** Shifts from point to point suddenly. Hence, *choppy*, said of a variable wind, and of the rough sea produced by such; and *to chop round* –

How the House of Lords and House of Commons chopped round.
Thackeray, *The Four Georges* (George I)

***Chop***, the face, and *chops*, the jaws or mouth, is a variant spelling of *chap* (as in *Bath chap*, the lower part of a pig's face, cured), which is the same word as the first mentioned, meaning a cleft, crack, or slit. From this come

***Chop-fallen***, or ***chap-fallen.*** Crestfallen; down in the mouth.

***Down in the chops.*** Down in the mouth; in a melancholy state; with the mouth drawn down.

***To lick one's chops.*** To relish in anticipation, either literally or metaphorically.

Finally, in the slang phrase *first chop*, the word is the Hindi *chhap*, a print or stamp, used in India and China by English residents for an official seal, also for a passport or permit; and a Chinese custom-house is known as a chop-house.

**Chopine** (Span. *chapin*). A high-heeled shoe. The Venetian ladies used to wear 'high-heeled shoes like stilts'. Hamlet says of the actress, 'Your ladyship is nearer to heaven, than when I last saw you, by the altitude of a chopine' (2, 2). *Cp.* Pantofles.

**Chopsticks.** The two thin sticks of wood or ivory that the Chinese use to eat with. They attain marvellous dexterity in the use of these implements, and the word is a rendering of Chin. *k'wâi-tsze*, meaning 'the quick ones'. In pidgin English (*q.v.*) *chop* means 'quick'.

**Choragus.** The leader of the chorus in the ancient Athenian drama.

At Oxford University the title is given to the assistant of the Professor of Music, but formerly to the officer who superintended the practice of music. *See* Coryphaeus.

**Choreutae.** A sect of heretics, who, among other errors, persisted in keeping the Sunday a fast.

**Choriambic Metre.** Horace gives us a great variety, but the main feature in all is the prevalence of the choriambus (— ⏑ ⏑ —). Specimen translations of two of these metres are subjoined:

(1) Horace, 1 *Odes*, viii.

— ⏑ ⏑ — | ⏑ — —
— ⏑ | — — | — ⏑ ⏑ — | — ⏑ ⏑ — | ⏑ — —

Lydia, why on Stanley
By the great gods, tell me, I pray, ruinous love you centre?
Once he was strong and manly,
Never seen now, patient of toil Mars' sunny camp to enter.
E. C. B.

(2) The other specimen is 1 *Odes*, xii.

— — | — ⏑ ⏑ — | ⏑ —
— — | — ⏑ ⏑ — | — ⏑ ⏑ — | ⏑ —

When you, with an approving smile,
Praise those delicate arms, Lydy, of Telephus,
Ah me! how you stir up my bile!
Heart-sick that for a boy you should forsake me thus.
E. C. B.

**Chouans.** French insurgents of the Royalist party during the Revolution. Jean Cottereau was their leader, nicknamed *Chouan* (a corruption of Fr. *chat-huant*, a screech-owl), because he was accustomed to warn his companions of danger by imitating the screech of an owl. Cottereau was followed by George Cadoudal. *See also* Companions of Jehu: Vendée.

**Choughs Protected.** *See* Birds.

**Chouse.** To cheat out of something. Gifford in 1814 made the conjecture that the word is from Turk. *chiaus*, a messenger or herald, because the interpreter of the Turkish embassy in England in 1609 defrauded his government of £4,000, and the notoriety of the swindle caused the word *chiaus* or *chouse* to be adopted. This is ingenious, but by no means certain; and no confirmation of the story of the swindling Turk (which first appeared in Chetwood's *Memoirs of Ben Jonson*, 1756) has so far been obtainable.

He is no chiaus.
Ben Jonson, *Alchemist*, i, 1 (1610)

**Chriem-hild.** *See* Kriemhild.

**Chrisom** or **Chrism** signifies properly 'the white cloth set by the minister at baptism on the head of the newly anointed with chrism' – a composition of oil and balm (Gr. *chrisma*, anointing, unction). In the Form of Private Baptism is this direction: 'Then the minister shall put the white vesture, commonly called the chrisome, upon the child.' The child thus baptised is called a *chrisom* or *chrisom child.* If it dies within the month, it is shrouded in the vesture; and hence, in the bills of mortality, even to 1726, infants that died within the month were termed chrisoms.

> A' made a finer end and went away an it had been any chrisom child.
>
> Shakespeare, *Henry V*, 2, 3

**Chriss-cross,** or **Christ-cross, Row.** The alphabet in a hornbook, which had a cross like the Maltese cross (✠) at the beginning and end.

> *Sir Ralph.* I wonder, wench, how I thy name might know.
> *Mall.* Why, you may find it, sir, in th' Christcross row.
> *Sir Ralph.* Be my schoolmistress, teach me how to spell it.
> *Mall.* No, faith, I care not greatly, if I tell it;
> My name is Mary Barnes.
>
> Porter: *Two Angry Women of Abington*, V, i (1599)

The word appears as *Christ-cross*, *crisscross*, etc., and Shakespeare shortened it to *cross-row*:

> He hearkens after prophecies and dreams;
> And from the cross-row plucks the letter G,
> And says a wizard told him that by G
> His issue disinherited should be.
>
> *Richard III*, 1, 1

As the Maltese cross was also sometimes used in place of XII to mark that hour on clocks the word has occasionally been used for noon:

> The feskewe of the Diall is upon the Chriss-crosse of Noone.
>
> *The Puritan Widow*, IV, ii (Anon., 1607)

**Christ-cross row.** *See* Chriss-cross.

**Christendom.** All Christian countries generally; formerly it also meant the state or condition of being a Christian. Thus, in Shakespeare's *King John*, the young prince says:

> By my christendom!
> So I were out of prison and kept sheep,
> I should be merry as the day is long. Act 4, sc. 1

**Christian.** A follower of Christ. So called first at Antioch (Acts 11:26). Also, the hero of Bunyan's allegory, *The Pilgrim's Progress.* He flees from the 'City of Destruction', and journeys to the 'Celestial City'. He starts with a heavy burden on his back, but it falls off when he stands at the foot of the cross.

***Most Christian Doctor.*** John Charlier de Gerson (1363–1429).

***Most Christian King.*** The style of the King of France since 1469, when it was conferred on Louis XI by Pope Paul II. Previously to that the title had been given in the 8th century to Pepin le Bref by Pope Stephen III (714–68), and again in the 9th century to Charles le Chauve.

> And thou, O Gaul, with gaudy trophies plumed,
> 'Most Christian king', Alas! in vain assumed.
>
> Camoens, *Lusiad*, bk vii

*Cp.* Religious.

**Christian Traditions.** There are Christian traditions of one kind and another connected with all the following animals and plants; particulars of them will be found under the respective names – Aspen, Ass, Calvary Clover, Crossbill, Dove, Elder, Haddock, John Dory, Judas tree, Passion-flower, Pig, Pigeon, Pike, Robin, Roodselken, Stork, Swallow.

*See also* Flowers with traditions: Thirteen.

**Christiana** (ch = k). The wife of Christian in Pt ii of Bunyan's *Pilgrim's Progress*, who started with her children and Mercy from the 'City of Destruction' long after her husband. She was placed under the guidance of Mr Great-Heart, and went, therefore, in 'silver slippers' along the thorny road.

**Christmas.** The rhyming slang (*q.v.*) for a railway guard. The missing word is 'card' – 'Christmas card'.

**Christmas Box.** A small gratuity given on Boxing Day (the day after Christmas Day) to those who render small services which are not directly paid for. Boxes placed in churches for casual offerings used to be opened on Christmas Day, and the contents, called the 'dole of the Christmas box', or the 'box money', were distributed next day by the priests.

Apprentices used, also, to carry a box round to their masters' customers for small gratuities. The custom in this form has been gradually dying out, but it is still usual for tradesmen's boys, messengers, crossing-sweepers, and others to look for a 'tip' on Boxing Day from those to whom their services have been rendered during the year.

**Christmas Carols.** *See* Carol.

**Christmas Day.** December 25th. In England, from the 7th to as late as the 13th century, the year was reckoned from Christmas Day; but in the 12th century the Anglican Church began the year on March 25th, a practice which was adopted by civilians at the beginning of the 14th century, and which remained in force till the reformation of the calendar in 1752. Thus, the civil, ecclesiastical, and legal year, which was used in all public documents, began on Christmas Day till the end of the 13th century, but the *historical* year had, for a very long time before then, begun on January 1st.

**Christmas Decorations.** The great feast of Saturn was held in December, when the people decorated the temples with such green things as they could find. The Christian custom is the same transferred to Him who was born in Bethlehem on Christmas Day. The holly or holy tree is called Christ's-thorn in Germany and Scandinavia, from its use in church decorations and its putting forth its berries about Christmas time. The early Christians gave an emblematic turn to the custom, referring to the 'righteous branch', and justifying the custom from Isaiah 60:13 – 'The glory of Lebanon shall come unto thee; the fir tree, the pine tree, and the box together, to beautify the place of my sanctuary.'

**Christmas Trees.** The modern English custom of having decorated and present-bearing Christmas trees comes from Germany, where it is probably a direct descendant of Yggdrasil (*q.v.*) of *Norse mythology*.

The ancient Egyptians, at the winter solstice, used a palm branch containing twelve leaves or shoots to symbolise the 'completion of the year'.

**Christolytes.** A Christian sect of the 6th century, which maintained that when Christ descended into hell, He left His soul and body there, and rose only with His heavenly nature.

**Christopher, St.** Legend relates that St Christopher was a giant who one day carried a child over a brook, and said, 'Chylde, thou hast put me in grete peryll. I might bere no greater burden.' To which the child answered, 'Marvel thou nothing, for thou hast borne all the world upon thee, and its sins likewise.' This is an allegory: Christopher means *Christ-bearer*; the *child* was Christ, and the *river* was the river of death.

**Chronicle Small Beer, To.** To note down events of no importance whatsoever.

> She was a wight, if ever such wight were ...
> To suckle fools and chronicle small beer.
>
> Shakespeare, *Othello*, 2, 1

**Chronon-hoton-thologos.** A burlesque pomposo, King of Queerummania, in Henry Carey's farce of the same name – 'the most tragical tragedy ever tragedised' – (1734). The name is used for any bombastic person who delivers an inflated address. *See* Aldiborontephoscophonio.

**Chrysaor** (ch = k). In Spenser's *Faërie Queene*, Sir Artegal's sword, 'that all other swords excelled' (V, i, 9). It typified justice (V, xii, 40).

**Chrysippus.** *Nisi Chrysippus fuisset, Porticus non esset.* Chrysippus of Soli was a disciple of Zeno the Stoic and Cleanthes, his successor. He did for the Stoics what St Paul did for Christianity – that is, he explained the system, showed by plausible reasoning its truth, and how it was based on a solid foundation. Stoicism was founded by Zeno; but if Chrysippus had not advocated it, it would never have taken root.

**Chrysomallus.** *See* Golden Fleece.

**Chuck Full.** A corruption of *chock full* (*q.v.*).

**Chukwa.** The tortoise at the South Pole on which, according to Hindu legend, the earth rests.

**Chum.** A crony, a familiar companion, properly a bedfellow. The word first appeared in the 17th century; its origin has not been ascertained, and the conjecture that it is a corruption either of *chamber-mate* or *comrade* has nothing to recommend it.

*To chum in with.* To be on very intimate and friendly terms with.

**Church.** This is the A.S. *circe*, or *cirice*, which comes through W.Ger. *kirika*, from Gr. *kuriakon*, a church, the neuter of the adjective *kuriakos*, meaning of, or belonging to, the Lord.

***High, Low,* and *Broad Church.*** Dr South says, 'The High Church are those who think highly of the Church and lowly of themselves; the Low Church, those who think lowly of the Church and highly of themselves,' which is about as sensible a differentiation as that of the bishop's butler who, when warned that there would be six clergymen to dinner, asked his master whether they were High or Low. 'That's a strange question,' said his lordship; 'why do you ask?' 'Well, my lord,' was the answer, 'it's like this: if they are 'Igh I knows there will be a lot of drinking and not much eating; and if they're Low, it'll be all eating and very little drinking; so I makes my preparations according!'

The *High Church* party in the Church of England is distinguished by its maintenance of sacerdotal claims, by the very great and preponderating efficacy with which it endows the sacraments, and by the apparent importance which it attaches to ritual and outward forms and ceremonies; the *Broad Church* party interprets formularies and dogmas in a liberal sense, and holds that the Church is broad enough for all religious parties, their own views of religion being chiefly of a moral nature, and their doctrinal views rounded and elastic; and the *Low Church* party comprises the Evangelicals, who hold opinions giving a low place to episcopal or priestly authority and claims, also to the inherent efficacy of the sacraments, and to matters of ecclesiastical organisation.

***The Anglican Church.*** In pre-Reformation days that part of the Catholic Church situated in England, but since the Reformation the English branch of the Protestant Church which, since 1532, has been known as the 'Established Church of England', because established by Act of Parliament. It disavows the authority of the Pope, and rejects certain dogmas and rules of the Roman Church.

***The Catholic Church.*** *See* Catholic. The Western Church called itself so when it separated from the Eastern Church. It is also called the Roman Catholic Church, to distinguish it from the Anglican Church or Anglican Catholic Church, a branch of the Western Church.

***The Established Church.*** The State Church, the Church officially recognised and adopted by any country. In England it is Episcopalian (*see* Anglican Church *above*), in Scotland Presbyterian, and in Wales, since the disestablishment of the Church of England in Wales by Act of Parliament in 1920, there is no Established Church.

***Church-ale.*** The word 'ale' is used in such composite words as *bride-ale*, *clerk-ale*, *church-ale*, *lamb-ale*, *Midsummer-ale*, *Scot-ale*, *Whitsun-ale*, etc., for revel or feast, ale being the chief liquor given. We talk now in the same way on giving 'a tea', and at the 'Varsity 'Will you wine with me after hall?' means, 'Will you come to my rooms for dessert – wine, fruit, and cigars, with coffee to follow?'

> The multitude call Church-ale Sunday their revelying day, which day is spent in bulbeatings, bearbeating, … dicying, … and drunkenness.
>
> W. Kethe (1570)

***The Church Invisible.*** Those who are known to God alone as His sons and daughters by adoption and grace. *See* Church Visible.

> There is … a Church visible and a Church invisible; the latter consists of those spiritual persons who fulfil the notion of the Ideal Church – the former is the Church as it exists in any particular age, embracing within it all who profess Christianity.
>
> F. W. Robertson, *Sermons* (series IV, ii)

***The Church Militant.*** The Church as consisting of the whole body of believers, who are said to be 'waging the war of faith' against 'the world, the flesh, and the devil'. It is therefore militant, or in warfare.

***Church scot.*** A tribute paid on St Martin's Day (November 11th) in support of the clergy in Anglo-Saxon times. It was originally paid in corn, but later other goods in kind, or money, was taken.

***The Church Triumphant.*** Those who are dead and gone to their rest. Having fought the fight and triumphed, they belong to the Church triumphant in heaven.

***The Church Visible.*** All ostensible Christians; all who profess to be Christians; all who have been baptised and admitted into Church Communion. *Cp.* Church Invisible.

***The Seven Churches of Asia.*** *See* Seven.

***To church a woman.*** To read the appointed service when a woman comes to church after a confinement to return thanks to God for her 'safe deliverance' and restored health.

***To go into the Church.*** To take holy orders, or become an 'ordained' clergyman.

**Churchwarden.** A long clay pipe, such as churchwardens used to smoke a century or so ago when they met together in the parish tavern, after they had made up their accounts in the vestry, or been elected to office at the Easter meeting.

> Thirty years have enabled these [briar-root pipesl to destroy short clays, ruin meerschaums, and even do much mischief to the venerable 'churchwarden'.
>
> *Notes and Queries*, April 25th, 1885, p. 323

**Churchyard Cough.** A consumptive cough indicating the near approach of death.

**Ci-devant** (Fr.). Former, of times gone by. As *Ci-devant governor* – i.e. once a governor, but no longer so. *Ci-devant philosophers* means philosophers of former days. In the time of the first French Republic the word was used as a noun, and meant a nobleman of the *ancien régime*.

> The appellation of mistress put her in mind of her ci-devant abigailship.
>
> Jane Porter, *Thaddeus of Warsaw*, ch. xxi

**Cicero.** The great Roman orator, philosopher, and statesman (106–43 BC), Marcus Tullius, said by Plutarch to have been called *Cicero* from Lat. *cicer* (a wart or vetch), because he had 'a flat excrescence on the tip of his nose'.

***La Bouche de Ciceron.*** Philippe Pot, prime minister of Louis XI (1428–94).

***The Cicero of France.*** Jean Baptiste Massillon (1663–1742), a noted pulpit orator.

***The Cicero of Germany,*** Johann III, elector of Brandenburg (1455–99).

***The Cicero of the British Senate.*** George Canning (1770–1827).

***The British Cicero.*** William Pitt, Earl of Chatham (1708–78).

***The Christian Cicero.*** Lucius Coelius Lactantius, a Christian father, who died about 330.

***The German Cicero.*** Johann Sturm, printer and scholar (1507–89).

**Cicerone.** A guide to point out objects of interest to strangers. So called from the great orator Cicero, in the same way as Paul was called by the men of Lystra 'Mercurius, because he was the chief speaker'. In a party of sightseers, the guide is 'the chief speaker'.

> Every glib and loquacious hireling who shows strangers about their pleasure-galleries, palaces and ruins is called [in Italy] a *cicerone* or a Cicero. Trench, *On the Study of Words*, iii

**Cicisbeo.** A dangler about women; the professed gallant of a married woman. *Cp.* **Cavaliere servente.** Also the knot of silk or ribbon which is attached to fans, walking-sticks, umbrellas, etc. *Cicisbeism*, the practice of dangling about women.

**Cicuta.** In Latin *cicuta* means the length of a reed up to the knot, such as the internodes, made into a panpipe. Hence Virgil (*Ecl.* ii, 36) describes a panpipe as '*septem compacta cicutis fistula*'. It is the hemlock, also called cow-bane, because cows not unfrequently eat it, and are sometimes killed by it. It is one of the most poisonous of plants, and it is said to have been the fatal draught given to Socrates.

> Sicut cicuta homini venenum est, sic cicutae vinum. Pliny, xiv, 7

> Quae poterant unquam satis expurgare cicutae. Horace, *2 Epist.* ii, 53

**Cid.** A corruption of *seyyid.* Arabic for *lord.* The title given to Roderigo or Ruy Diaz de Bivar (born about 1040, died 1099), also called El Campeador, the national hero of Spain and champion of Christianity against the Moors. His exploits, real and legendary, form the basis of many Spanish romances and chronicles, as well as Corneille's tragedy, *Le Cid* (1636).

***The Cid's horse.*** Babieca.

***The Cid's sword.*** Colada. The sword taken by him from King Bucar was called Tizona.

**Cid Hamet Benengeli.** The supposititious author upon whom Cervantes fathered *The Adventures of Don Quixote.*

> Of the two bad cassocks I am worth ... I would have given the latter of them as freely as even Cid Hamet offered his ... to have stood by. Sterne

**Cimmerian Darkness.** Homer (possibly from some story as to the Arctic night) supposes the Cimmerians to dwell in a land 'beyond the ocean-stream', where the sun never shone. (*Odys.*, xi, 14.)

> I carried am into waste wildernesse,
> Waste wildernes, amongst Cymerian shades,
> Where endles paines and hideous heavinesse,
> Is round about me heapt in darksome glades.
> Spenser, *Virgil's Gnat*

> In dark Cimmerian desert ever dwell.
> Milton, *L'Allegro*

The Cimmerians were known in post-Homeric times as an historical people on the shores of the Black Sea, whence the name *Crimea.*

**Cinchona** or *Quinine.* So named from the wife of the Contë del Chinchon, viceroy of Peru, who was cured of a tertian fever by its use, and who brought it to Europe in 1640. Linnaeus erroneously named it *Cin*chona for *Chin*chona. *See* **Peruvian Bark.**

**Cincinnatus.** A legendary Roman hero of about 500 to 430 BC, who, after having been consul years before, was taken from his plough to be Dictator. After he had conquered the Aequians and delivered his country from danger, he laid down his office and returned to his plough.

> And Cincinnatos, awful from the plough.
> Thomson, *Winter*, 512

***The Cincinnatus of the Americans,*** George Washington (1732–99).

> The Cincinnatos of the West. Byron

**Cinderella** (*little cinder girl*). Heroine of a fairy tale of very ancient, probably Eastern, origin, that was mentioned in German literature in the 16th century and was popularised by Perrault's *Contes de ma mère l'oye* (1697). Cinderella is drudge of the house, dirty with housework, while her elder sisters go to fine balls. At length a fairy enables her to go to the prince's ball; the prince falls in love with her, and she is discovered by means of a glass slipper which she drops, and which will fit no foot but her own.

The *glass* slipper is a mistranslation of *pantoufle en vair* (a fur, or sable, slipper), not *en verre.* Sable was worn only by kings and princes, so the fairy gave royal slippers to her favourite.

**Cinque Cento.** The Italian name for the *sixteenth* century (1501–1600), applied as an epithet to art and literature with much the same significance as *Renaissance* or *Elizabethan.* It was the revival of the classical or antique, but is generally understood as a derogatory term, implying debased or inferior art.

**Cinque Ports, The.** Originally the five seaports, Hastings, Sandwich, Dover, Romney, and Hythe, which were granted special privileges from the 13th to the 17th centuries, and even later, in consideration of their providing ships and men for the defence of the Channel. Subsequently Winchelsea and Rye were added.

**Cipher.** Dr Whewell's riddle is –

> A headless man had a letter (*o*) to write,
> He who read it (*naught*) had lost his sight;
> The dumb repeated it (*naught*) word for word,
> And deaf was the man who listened and heard (*naught*).

**Circe.** A sorceress in *Greek mythology*, who lived in the island of Aeaea. When Ulysses landed there, Circe turned his companions into swine, but Ulysses resisted this metamorphosis by virtue of a herb called *moly* (*q.v.*), given him by Mercury.

> Who knows not Circe,
> The daughter of the Sun, whose charmëd cup
> Whoever tasted lost his upright shape,
> And downward fell into a grovelling swine?
>
> Milton, *Comus*, 50–53

**Circle of Ulloa.** A white rainbow or luminous ring sometimes seen in Alpine regions opposite the sun in foggy weather. Named from Antonio de Ulloa (1716–95), a Spanish naval officer who founded the observatory at Cadiz and initiated many scientific enterprises.

**Circuit.** The journey made through the counties of Great Britain by the judges twice a year. There are six circuits in England, two in Wales, and three in Scotland. Those in England are called the South-Eastern, Midland, Northern, North-Eastern, Oxford, and Western Circuit; those of Wales, the North Wales and Chester, and the South Wales Division; and those of Scotland, the Southern, Western, and Northern.

**Circumbendibus, A.** *He took a circumbendibus*, i.e. he went round about and round about before coming to the point.

> Partaking of what scholars call the periphrastic and ambagitory, and the vulgar the circumbendibus. Scott, *Waverley*, ch. xxiv

**Circumcelliones.** *See* Agonistics.

**Circumlocution Office.** A term applied in ridicule by Dickens in *Little Dorrit* to our public offices, because each person tries to shuffle off every act to someone else; and before anything is done it has to pass through so many departments and so much time elapses that it is hardly worth having bothered about it.

> Whatever was required to be done, the Circumlocution Office was beforehand with all the public departments in the art of perceiving – How not to do it. Dickens, *Little Dorrit*, ch. x

**Cist** (Gr. *kiste*, Lat. *cista*). A chest or box. Generally used as a coffer for the remains of the dead. The Greek and Roman cist was a deep cylindrical basket made of wicker-work. The basket into which voters cast their tablets was called a 'cist'; but the mystic cist used in the rites of Ceres was latterly made of bronze. *Cp.* Kistvaen, Kist of Whistles.

**Cistercians.** A monastic order, founded at Cistercium or Citeaux by Robert, abbot of Molême, in Burgundy, in 1098, as a branch of the Benedictines; the monks are known also as *Bernardines*, owing to the patronage of St Bernard of Clairvaux about 1200. In 1664 the order was reformed on an excessively strict basis by Jean le Boutillier de Rance.

**Citadel** (Ital. *citadella*, a little city). In fortification, a small strong fort, constructed either within the place fortified, or at its most inaccessible spot, to give refuge for the garrison, that it may prolong the defence after the place has fallen, or hold out for the best terms of capitulation. Citadels generally command the interior of the place, and are useful, therefore, for overawing a population which might otherwise strive to shorten a siege.

**Citizen King, The.** Louis Philippe of France. So called because he was elected king by the citizens of Paris. (Born 1773, reigned 1830–48, died 1850.)

**City.** Strictly speaking, a *large* town with a corporation and cathedral; but any large town is so called in ordinary speech. In the Bible it means a town having walls and gates.

> The eldest son of the first man [Cain] builded a city (Gen. 4:17) – not, of course, a Nineveh or a Babylon, but still a city.
>
> Rawlinson, *Origin of Nations*, pt i, ch. i

***The City of a Hundred Towers.*** Pavia, in Italy; famous for its towers and steeples.

***The City College.*** Newgate. The wit belongs to the days when Newgate was used as a prison.

***The City of Bells.*** Strasburg.

> He was a Strasburgher, and in that city of bells had been a medical practitioner.
>
> Mayne Reid, *The Scalp Hunters*, ch. xxv

***The City of Brotherly Love.*** A somewhat ironical, but quite etymological, nickname of Philadelphia (Gr. *Philadelphia* means 'brotherly love').

***The City of David.*** Jerusalem. So called in compliment to King David (2 Sam. 5:7, 9).

***The City of Destruction.*** In Bunyan's *Pilgrim's Progress*, the world of the unconverted. Bunyan makes Christian flee from it and journey to the 'Celestial City', thereby showing the 'walk of a Christian' from conversion to death.

***The City of God.*** The Church, or whole body of believers; the kingdom of Christ, in contradistinction to the City of Destruction (*q.v.*). The phrase is that of St Augustine; one of his chief works bearing that title, *De Civitate Dei*.

***The City of Lanterns.*** A supposititious city in Lucian's *Verae Historiae*, situate somewhere beyond the zodiac. *Cp.* Lantern-Land.

***The City of Legions.*** Caerleon-on-Usk, where King Arthur held his court.

***The City of Lilies.*** Florence.

***The City of Magnificent Distances.*** Washington; famous for its wide avenues and splendid vistas.

***The City of Palaces.*** Agrippa, in the reign of Augustus, converted Rome from 'a city of brick huts to one of marble palaces'.

> Marmoream se relinquere quam latericiam accepisset. Suetonius, *Aug.* xxix

Calcutta is called the 'City of Palaces', and modern Paris well deserves the compliment.

***City of Refuge.*** Moses, at the command of God, set apart three cities on the east of Jordan, and Joshua added three others on the west, whither any person might flee for refuge who had killed a human creature inadvertently. The three on the east of Jordan were Bezer, Ramoth, and Golan; the three on the west were Hebron, Shechem, and Kedesh (Deut. 4:43; Josh. 20:1–8).

By Mohammedans, Medina, in Arabia, where Mahomet took refuge when driven by conspirators from Mecca, is known as 'the City of Refuge'. He entered it, not as a fugitive, but in triumph AD 622. Also called the *City of the Prophet*.

***The City of St Michael.*** Dumfries, of which city St Michael is the patron saint.

***The City of Saints.*** Montreal, in Canada, is so named because all the streets are named after saints. Salt Lake City, Utah, USA, also is known as the 'City of the Saints', from the Mormons who inhabit it.

***The Cities of the Plain.*** Sodom and Gomorrah.

> Abram dwelled in the land of Canaan, and Lot dwelled in the cities of the plain, and pitched his tent toward Sodom. Gen. 13:12

***The City of the Golden Gate.*** San Francisco. *See* Golden Gate.

***The City of the Prophet.*** Medina. *See* City of Refuge.

***The City of the Seven Hills.*** Rome, built on seven hills (*Urbs septacollis*). The hills are the Aventine, Caelian, Capitoline, Esquiline, Palatine, Quirinal, and Viminal.

The Aventine Hill was given to the people. It was deemed unlucky, because here Remus was slain. It was also called 'Collis Dianae', from the Temple of Diana which stood there.

The Caelian Hill was given to Caelius Vibenna, the Tuscan, who came to the help of the Romans in the Sabine war.

The Capitoline Hill or 'Mons Tarpeius', also called 'Mons Saturni', on which stood the great castle or capitol of Rome. It contained the Temple of Jupiter Capitolinus.

The Esquiline Hill was given by Augustus to Mecaenas, who built thereon a magnificent mansion.

The Palatine Hill was the largest of the seven. Here Romulus held his court, whence the word 'palace' (*palatium*).

The Quirinal Hill was where the Quires or Cures settled. It was also called 'Cabalious', from two marble statues of a horse, one of which was the work of Phidias, the other of Praxiteles.

The Viminal Hill was so called from the number of osiers (*vimines*) which grew there. It contained the Temple of Jupiter Viminalis.

***The City of the Sun.*** Baalbec, Rhodes, and Heliopolis, which had the sun for tutelary deity, were so called. It is also the name of a treatise on the Ideal Republic by the Dominican friar Campanella (1568–1639), similar to the *Republic* of Plato, *Utopia* of Sir Thomas More, and *Atlantis* of Bacon.

***The City of the Three Kings.*** Cologne; the reputed burial-place of the Magi (*q.v.*).

***The City of the Tribes.*** Galway; because it was anciently the home of the thirteen 'tribes' or chief families, who settled there in 1232 with Richard de Burgh.

***The City of the Violated Treaty.*** Limerick; because of the way in which the Pacification of Limerick (1691) was broken by England.

***The City of the Violet Crown.*** Athens is so called by Aristophanes (ἰοστέφανος – *see Equites*, 1323 and 1329; and *Acharnians*, 637). Macaulay refers to Athens as the 'violet-crowned city'. Ion (a violet) was a representative king of Athens, whose four sons gave names to the four Athenian classes; and Greece, in Asia Minor, was called Ionia. Athens was the city of 'Ion crowned its king' or 'of the Violet crowned'.

> Round the hills whose heights the first-born olive blossom brightened,
> Round the city brow-bound once with violets like a bride.

Up from under earth again a light that long since lightened
Breaks, whence all the world took comfort as all time takes pride. Swinburne, *Athens; an Ode*

**Civic Crown.** *See* Crown.

**Civil List.** The grant voted annually by Parliament to pay the personal expenses of the Sovereign, the household expenses, and the pensions awarded by Royal bounty; before the reign of William III it embraced all public expenditure, except that on the army and navy.

**Civil Magistrate.** A civic or municipal magistrate, as distinguished from ecclesiastical authority.

**Civil Service Estimates.** The annual Parliamentary grant to cover the expenses of the diplomatic services, the post office and telegraphs, education, the collection of the revenue, and other expenses neither pertaining to the Sovereign, the army, nor the navy.

**Civil War.** War between citizens (*civiles*). In English history the term is applied to the war between Charles I and his Parliament; but the War of the Roses was a civil war also. In America, the War of Secession (1861–65).

**Civus Romanus Sum.** 'I am a Roman citizen,' a plea which sufficed to arrest arbitrary condemnation, bonds, and scourging. Hence, when the centurion commanded Paul 'to be examined by scourging', he asked, 'Is it lawful for you to *scourge* a Roman citizen, and *uncondemned*?' (1) No Roman citizen could be condemned unheard; (2) by the Valerian Law he could not be bound; (3) by the Sempronian Law it was forbidden to *scourge* him, or to beat him with rods. *See also* Acts 16:37, etc.

**Clabber Napper's Hole.** Near Gravesend; said to be named after a freebooter; but more likely the Celtic *Caerber l'arber* (water-town lower camp).

**Clack Dish.** A dish or basin with a movable lid. Some two or three centuries ago beggars used to proclaim their want by clacking the lid of a wooden dish.

Can you think, I get my living by a bell and clack-dish ... How's that?
Why, begging, sir.
Middleton, *Family of Love* (1608)

**Clak-ho-haryah.** At Fort Vancouver the medium of intercourse with the natives used to be a mixture of Canadian-French, English, Indian, and Chinese. An Englishman went by the name of *Kint-shosh*, a corruption of King George; an American was called *Boston*; and the ordinary salutation was *clak-ho-haryah*. This, according to Isaac Taylor (*Words and Places*), is explained by the fact that the Indians, frequently hearing a trader named Clark addressed by his companions, 'Clark, how are you?' imagined this to be the usual English form of salutation.

**Clam.** A bivalve mollusc like an oyster, which burrows in sand or mud. In America especially they are esteemed as a delicacy. They are gathered only when the tide is out, hence the saying, 'Happy as a clam at high tide'. The word is also used as slang for the mouth, and for a stupid, close-mouthed person.

*Close as a clam.* Mean, close-fisted; from the difficulty with which a clam is made to open its shell and give up all it has worth having.

**Clan-na-Gael, The.** An Irish Fenian organisation founded in Philadelphia in 1881, and known in secret as the 'United Brotherhood'; its avowed object being to secure 'the complete and absolute independence of Ireland from Great Britain, and the complete severance of all political connection between the two countries, to be effected by unceasing preparation for armed insurrection in Ireland'.

**Clapboard.** From Ger. *klappholz* (*holz* = wood), meaning small pieces of split oak used by coopers for cask staves. In the United States a roofing board, made thin at one edge and overlapping the next one.

A little low and lonesome shed,
With a roof of clap-boards overhead.
Alice Cary, *Settlers' Christmas Eve*

In England the word was formerly used by coopers in the same way as in Germany, and also for wainscoting.

**Clapperclaw.** To jangle, to claw or scratch; to abuse, revile; originally meaning to claw with a clapper of some sort.

Now they are clapper-clawing one another; I'll go look on.
Shakespeare, *Troilus and Cressida*, 5, 4

**Clapper-dudgeons.** Abram-men (*q.v.*), beggars from birth. The *clapper* is the tongue of a bell, and in cant language the human tongue. *Dudgeon* is the hilt of a dagger: and perhaps the original meaning is one who knocks his *clap dish* (or Clack Dish, *q.v.*) with a dudgeon.

**Clap-trap.** Something introduced to win applause; something really worthless, but sure to take with the groundlings. A *trap* to catch applause.

**Claque.** A body of hired applauders at a theatre, etc.; said to have been originated or first systematised by a M. Sauton, who, in 1820, established in Paris an office to ensure the success of dramatic pieces. The manager ordered the required number of *claqueurs*, who were divided into *commissaires*, those who commit the pieces to memory and are noisy in pointing out its merits; *rieurs*, who laugh at the puns and jokes; *pleureurs*, chiefly women, who are to hold their pocket-handkerchiefs to their eyes at the moving parts; *chatouilleurs*, who are to keep the audience in good humour; and *bisseurs*, who are to cry 'bis' (encore).

*Claque* is also the French for an opera-hat, and Thackeray uses it with this sense:

> A gentleman in black with ringlets and a tuft stood gazing fiercely about him, with one hand in the arm-hole of his waistcoat and the other holding his claque. *Pendennis*, ch .xxv

**Claras.** The Stock Exchange term for Caledonian Railway Deferred Stock.

**Clare, Order of St.** A religious order of women, the second that St Francis instituted. It was founded in 1212, and took its name from its first abbess, Clara of Assisi. The nuns are called Minoresses and Poor Clares, or Nuns of the order of St Francis. *See* Franciscans.

**Clarenceux King-of-Arms.** The second in rank of the three English Kings-of-Arms (*q.v.*) attached to the Heralds' College (*q.v.*). His jurisdiction extends over the counties east, west, and south of the Trent. The name was taken in honour of the Duke of Clarence, third son of Edward III.

**Clarendon. *The Constitutions of Clarendon.*** Laws made by a general council of nobles and prelates, held at Clarendon, in Wiltshire, in 1164, to check the power of the Church, and restrain the prerogatives of ecclesiastics. These famous ordinances, sixteen in number, define the limits of the patronage and jurisdiction of the Pope in these realms.

***Clarendon type.*** A bold-faced, condensed type, such as that used for the 'catch-words' which head articles.

**Claret.** The English name for the red wines of Bordeaux, originally the yellowish or light red wines as distinguished from the white wines. The name – which is not used in France – is the O.Fr. *clairet*, diminutive of *clair*, from Lat. *clarus*, clear. Of course, the *colour* receives its name from the *wine*, not vice versa.

***Claret cup.*** A drink made of claret, brandy, lemon, borage, sugar, ice, and carbonated water.

***To broach one's claret,*** or ***to tap one's claret jug.*** To give one a bloody nose; blood is so called by pugilists from its claret colour, and 'tap' is meant for a pun – to broach and to knock.

**Claribel.** A character in Spenser's *Faërie Queene. See* Phaon.

**Classic Races.** The five chief horseraces in England, viz. the 2,000 and 1,000 guinea races for three-year-olds, run at Newmarket;. the Oaks for fillies only, three years old (£1,000); the Derby for colts and fillies three years old; and the St Leger for colts and fillies, those which have run in the Oaks or Derby being eligible.

**Classics.** The best authors. The Romans were divided by Servius into five classes. Any citizen who belonged to the highest class was called *classicus*, all the rest were said to be *infra classem* (unclassed). From this the best authors were termed *classici auctores* (classic authors), i.e. authors of the best or first class. The high esteem in which Greek and Latin were held at the revival of letters obtained for these authors the name of classic, emphatically; and when other first-rate works are intended some distinctive name is added, as the English, French, Spanish, etc., classics.

**Claude Lorraine** (i.e. of Lorraine). This incorrect form is generally used in English for the name of Claude Gelée (1600–82), the French landscape painter, born at Chamagne, in Lorraine.

**Clause Rolls.** *See* Close Rolls.

**Clavie.** *Burning of the Clavie* on New Year's Eve (old style) in the village of Burghead, on the southern shore of the Moray Firth. The clavie is a sort of bonfire made of casks split up. One of the casks is split into two parts of different sizes, and an important item of the ceremony is to join these parts together with a huge nail made for the purpose. Whence the name *clavus* (Lat.), a nail. Chambers, who in his *Book of Days* (vol. ii, p. 780) minutely describes the ceremony, suggests that it is a relic of Druid worship. The two unequal divisions of the cask probably symbolise the unequal parts of the old and new year.

**Clavileno.** In *Don Quixote* (II, iii, 4 and 5), the wooden horse on which the Don got astride in order to disenchant the Infanta Antonomasia and her husband, who were shut up in the tomb of Queen Maguncia, of Candaya. It was the very horse on which Peter of Provence carried off the fair Magalona; it was constructed by Merlin, and was governed by a wooden pin in the forehead. The word means *Wooden Peg. Cp.* Cambuscan.

**Claw.** The sharp, hooked nail of bird or beast, or the foot of an animal armed with claws. *To claw* is to lay one's hands upon things; to clutch, to tear or scratch as with claws; formerly it also meant to stroke, to tickle; hence to please, flatter, or praise. Thus *Claw me and I will claw thee*, means, 'praise me, and I will praise you', or, scratch my back, and I will do the same for you.

> Laugh when I am merry, and claw no man in his humour. Shakespeare, *Much Ado*, 1, 3

*Claw-backs.* Flatterers. Bishop Jewel speaks of 'the Pope's claw-backs'.

**Claymore.** The two-edged sword anciently used by Scottish Highlanders; from Gaelic *claidheamh* (a sword), and *mór* (great). *Cp.* Morglay.

> I've told thee how the Southrons fell
> Beneath the broad claymore.
> Aytoun, *Execution of Montrose*

**Clean.** Free from blame or fault.

> Create in me a clean heart, O God, and renew a right spirit within me. Psalm 51:10

Used adverbially, it means entirely, wholly; as, 'you have grown clean out of knowledge', i.e. wholly beyond recognition.

> 'E carried me away, to where a dooli lay,
> An' a bullet came an' drilled the beggar clean.
> 'E put me safe inside, An' just before 'e died,
> 'I 'ope you liked your drink,' sez Gunga Din.
> Kipling, *Gunga Din*

***A clean tongue.*** Not abusive, not profane, not foul.

***Cleanliness is next to godliness.*** An old saying, quoted by John Wesley (*Sermon* xcii, *On Dress*), Matthew Henry, and others. The origin is said to be found in the writings of Phinehas ben Yair, an ancient Hebrew rabbi.

***To clean down.*** To sweep down, to swill down.

***To clean out.*** To purify, to make tidy. Also, to win another's money till his pocket is quite empty; to impoverish one of everything. De Quincey says that Richard Bentley, after his lawsuit with Dr Colbatch, 'must have been pretty well cleaned out'.

***To clean up.*** To wash up, to put in order.

***To have clean hands.*** To be quite clear of some stated evil. Hence *to keep the hands clean*, not to be involved in wrong-doing; and 'clean-handed':

> Sort with thieves, if thus you feel –
> When folk clean-handed simply recognise
> Treasure whereof the mere right satisfies –
> But straight your fingers are on itch to steal!
> Browning, *Parleying with Francis Furini*

***To live a clean life.*** To live blameless and undefiled.

***To make a clean breast of it.*** To make a full and unreserved confession.

***To show a clean bill of health.*** *See* Bill.

***To show a clean pair of heels.*** To make one's escape by superior speed, to run away. Here 'clean' means free from obstruction.

***Clean and unclean animals.*** Among the ancient Jews (*see* Lev. 11) those animals which chew the cud and part the hoof were clean, and might be eaten. Hares and rabbits could not be eaten because (although they chew the cud) they do not part the hoof. Pigs and camels were unclean, because (although they part the hoof) they do not chew the cud. Birds of prey were accounted unclean. Fish with fins and scales were accounted fit food for man.

According to Pythagoras, who taught the doctrine of the transmigration of the soul, it was lawful for man to eat only those animals into which the human soul never entered, and those into which the human soul did enter were unclean or not fit for human food. This notion existed long before the time of Pythagoras, who learnt it in Egypt.

**Clear** (verb). ***To be quite cleared out.*** To have spent all one's money; to have not a farthing left. *Cleared out* means, my purse or pocket is cleared out of money.

***To clear an examination paper.*** To floor it, or answer every question set.

***To clear away.*** To remove, to melt away, to disappear.

***To clear for action.*** The same as 'to clear the decks'. *See below.*

***To clear off.*** To make oneself scarce, to remove oneself or something else; to take away.

***To clear out.*** To eject; to empty out, to make tidy.

***To clear out for Guam.*** A shipping phrase; used when a ship is bound for no specific place. In the height of the gold fever, ships carried passengers to Australia without making arrangements for return cargoes. They were, therefore, obliged to leave Melbourne in ballast, and to sail in search of homeward freights. The Custom House regulations required, however, that, on clearing outwards, some port should be named; and it became the habit of captains to name 'Guam' (a small island of the Ladrone group) as the hypothetical destination. Hence, the phrase meant to clear out for just anywhere.

***To clear the air.*** To remove the clouds, mists, and impurities; figuratively, to remove the misunderstandings or ambiguities of a situation, argument, etc.

***To clear the court.*** To remove all strangers, or persons not officially concerned in the suit.

***To clear the decks.*** To prepare for action by removing everything not required; playfully used of eating everything eatable on the dinner-table, etc.

***To clear the dishes.*** To empty them of their contents.

***To clear the land.*** A nautical phrase meaning to have good sea room.

***To clear the room.*** To remove from it every thing or person not required.

***To clear the table.*** To remove what has been placed on it.

***To clear up.*** To become fine after rain or cloudiness; to make manifest; to elucidate what was obscure; to tidy up.

**Clear** (the adjective). Used adverbially, *clear* has much the same force as the adverb *clean* (*q.v.*) – wholly, entirely; as, 'He is gone clear away,' 'Clear out of sight'.

***A clear day.*** An entire, complete day. 'The bonds must be left three clear days for examination,' means that they must be left for three days not counting the first or the last.

***A clear head.*** A mind that is capable of understanding things clearly.

***A clear statement.*** A straightforward and intelligible statement.

***A clear style*** (of writing). A lucid method of expressing one's thoughts.

***A clear voice.*** A voice of pure intonation, neither husky, mouthy, nor throaty.

***Clear grit.*** The right spirit, real pluck; also the genuine article, the real thing. Originally a piece of American slang.

In Canadian politics the name *Clear-grits* was given in the early 'eighties of last century to the Radicals.

**Clear-cole** (Fr. *claire colle*, clear glue or size). A mixture of size, alum, and whitening, for sizing walls. To cover over whatever might show through the coat of colour or paper to be put on it, also to make them stick or adhere more firmly.

**Clearing House.** The office or house where bankers do their 'clearing', that is, the exchanging of bills and cheques and the payment of balances, etc. Also, the house where the business of dividing among the different railway companies the proceeds of traffic passing over several lines for one covering payment is carried through. In London, the bankers' clearing house has been in Lombard Street since 1775. Each bank sends to it daily all the bills and cheques not drawn on its own firm; these are sorted and distributed to their respective houses, and the balance is settled by transfer tickets.

A 'clearing banker' is a banker who has the *entrée* of the clearing house.

> London has become the clearing-house of the whole world, the place where international debts are exchanged against each other. And something like 5,000 million pounds'-worth of checks and bills pass that clearing yearly.
>
> A. C. Perry, *Elements of Political Economy*, p. 363

**Cleave.** Two quite distinct words, the one meaning to *stick to*, and the other to *part from* or to *part asunder*. A man 'shall cleave to his wife' (Matt. 19:5). As one that 'cleaveth wood' (Ps. 141:7). The former is the A.S. *clifian*, to stick to, and the latter is *cleofan*, to split.

**Clement, St.** Patron saint of tanners, being himself a tanner. His day is November 23rd, and his symbol is an anchor, because he is said to have been martyred by being thrown into the sea with an anchor round his neck.

**Clench** and **Clinch.** The latter is a variant of the former, which is the M.E. *clenchen*, from A.S. (*be-*)*clencan*, to hold fast. In many uses the two words are practically synonymous, meaning to grasp firmly, to fasten firmly together by bending over the point of a nail, to make sure or firm; but *clench* is used in such phrases as 'he clenched his fists', 'he clenched his nerves bravely to endure the pain', 'to clench one's teeth'; while *clinch* is used in the more material senses, such as to turn the point of a nail in order to make it fast, and also in the phrase 'to clinch an argument'.

***That was a clincher.*** That argument was not to be gainsaid; that remark drove the matter home, and fixed it 'as a nail in a sure place'.

A lie is called a *clincher* from the tale about two swaggerers, one of whom said, 'I drove a nail right through the moon.' 'Yes,' said the other, 'I remember it well, for I went the other side and clinched it.' The French say, *Je lui ai bien rivé son clou* (I have clinched his nail for him).

**Cleombrotos.** A philosopher who so admired Plato's discourse on the immortality of the soul (in the *Phaedo*) that he jumped into the sea in order to exchange this life for a better. He was called *Ambraciota*, from *Ambracia*, in Epirus, the place of his birth.

He who to enjoy
Plato's elysium, leaped into the sea,
Cleombrotus. Milton, *Paradise Lost*, iii, 471–3

**Cleon.** In Browning's poem of this name the writer is supposed to be one of the poets alluded to by St Paul in Acts 17:28 ('As certain also of your own poets have said'). Cleon believes in Zeus under the attributes of the one God, but sees nothing in his belief to warrant the hope of immortality, which much disconcerts him. The poem is a protest against the inadequacy of the earthly life.

**Cleopatra** was introduced to Julius Caesar by Apollodorus in a bale of rich Syrian rugs. When the bale was unbound, there was discovered the fairest and wittiest girl of all the earth, and Caesar became her captive slave.

***Cleopatra and her pearl.*** It is said that Cleopatra made a banquet for Antony, the costliness of which excited his astonishment; and, when Antony expressed his surprise, Cleopatra took a pearl ear-drop, which she dissolved in a strong acid, and drank to the health of the Roman triumvir, saying, 'My draught to Antony shall far exceed it.' There are two difficulties in this anecdote – the first is that vinegar would not dissolve a pearl; and the next is, that any stronger acid would be wholly unfit to drink.

A similar story has been told of Sir Thomas Gresham. It is said that when Queen Elizabeth visited the Royal Exchange he pledged her health in a cup of wine in which a precious stone worth £15,000 had been crushed to atoms. Heywood refers to this in his play *If you know not me you know nobody* (1604):

Here fifteen thousand pounds at one clap goes
Instead of sugar; Gresham drinks the pearl
Unto his queen and mistress.

***Cleopatra's Needle.*** The obelisk so called, now in London on the Thames Embankment, was brought there in 1878 from Alexandria, whither it and its fellow (now in Central Park, New York) had been moved from Heliopolis by Augustus about 9 BC. It has no connection with Cleopatra, and it has carved on it hieroglyphics that tell of its erection by Thothmes III, a Pharaoh of the 18th dynasty who lived many centuries before her time.

***Cleopatra's nose.*** It was Blaise Pascal (d.1662) who said, 'If the nose of Cleopatra had been shorter, the whole face of the earth would have been changed' (*Pensées* viii, 29); the allusion, of course, being to the tremendous results brought about by her enslavement through her charm and beauty, first of Julius Caesar and then of Mark Antony.

**Clergy.** Ultimately from Gr. *kleros*, a lot or inheritance, with reference to Deut. 18:2 and Acts 1:17; thus, the men of God's lot or inheritance. In St Peter's first epistle (ch. v, 3) the Church is called 'God's heritage' or lot. In the Old Testament the tribe of Levi is called the 'lot or heritage of the Lord'.

***Benefit of clergy.*** *See* Benefit.

**Clerical Titles. *Clerk.*** As in ancient times the clergyman was about the only person who could write and read, the word *clerical*, as used in 'clerical error', came to signify an orthographical error. As the respondent in church was able to read, he received the name of *clerk*, and the assistants in writing, etc., are so termed in business. (Lat. *clericus*, a clergyman.)

***Curate.*** One who has the cure of souls. As the cure of the parish used to be virtually entrusted to the clerical stipendiary, the word *curate* was appropriated to this assistant.

***Parson.*** The same word as *person*. As Blackstone says, a parson is '*persona ecclesiae*, one that hath full rights of the parochial church'.

Though we write 'parson' differently, yet 'tis but 'person'; that is the individual person set apart for the service of such a church, and 'tis in Latin *persona*, and *personatus* is a parsonage. Indeed with the canon lawyers, *personatus* is any dignity or preferment in the church.

Selden, *Table-talk*

***Rector.*** One who has the parsonage and great tithes. The man who rules or guides the parish. (Lat., 'a ruler'.)

***Vicar.*** One who does the 'duty' of a parish for the person who receives the tithes. (Lat. *vicarius*, a deputy.) *Incumbents* and *Perpetual Curates* are now termed Vicars.

The French *curé* equals our vicar, and their *vicaire* our curate.

**Clerical Vestments. *White.*** Emblem of purity, worn on all feasts, saints' days, and sacramental occasions.

***Red.*** The colour of blood and of fire, worn on the days of martyrs, and on Whit Sunday, when the Holy Ghost came down like tongues of fire.

***Green.*** Worn only on days which are neither feasts nor fasts.

***Purple.*** The colour of mourning, worn on Advent Sundays, in Lent, and on Ember days.

***Black.*** Worn on Good Friday, and when masses are said for the dead.

**Clerimond.** Niece of the Green Knight (*q.v.*), bride of Valentine the brave, and sister of Ferragus the giant. (*Valentine and Orson.*)

**Clerk.** A scholar. Hence, *beau-clerc. See above*, Clerical Titles.

> All the clerks,
> I mean the learned ones, in Christian kingdoms.
> Have their free voices.
>
> Shakespeare, *Henry VIII*, 2, 2

***St Nicholas's Clerks.*** Old slang for thieves, highwaymen. St Nicholas was the patron saint of scholars.

> *Gadshill.* Sirrah, if they meet not with Saint Nicholas' clerks, I'll give thee this neck.
> *Chamberlain.* No, I'll none of it; I prithee, keep that for the hangman; for I know thou worship'st Saint Nicholas as truly as a man of falsehood may.
>
> Shakespeare, *1 Henry IV*, 2, 1

> I think there came prancing down the hill a couple of St Nicholas's clerks.
>
> Rowley, *Match at Midnight*, 1633

**Clerk-ale.** *See* Church-ale.

**Clerkenwell.** At the holy well in this district the parish clerks of London used to assemble yearly to play some sacred piece.

**Client.** In ancient Rome a *client* was a plebeian under the patronage of a patrician, who was therefore his *patron*. The client performed certain services, and the patron was obliged to protect his life and interests. The word in English means a person who employs the services of a legal adviser to protect his interests.

**Climacteric.** It was once believed by astrologers that the 7th and 9th years, with their multiples, especially the *odd* multiples (21, 27, 35, 45, 49, 63, and 81), were critical points in life; these were called the *Climacteric Years* and were presided over by Saturn, the malevolent planet. 63, which is produced by multiplying 7 and 9 together, was termed the *Grand Climacteric*, which few persons succeeded in outliving.

> There are two years, the seventh and the ninth, that commonly bring great changes in a man's life, and great dangers; wherefore 63, that contains both these numbers multiplied together, comes not without heaps of dangers.
>
> Levinus Lemnius

**Climax** means a *ladder* (Gr.), and is the rhetorical figure in which the sense rises gradually in a series of images, each exceeding its predecessor in force or dignity. Popularly, but erroneously, the word is used to denote the last step in the gradation, the point of highest development.

> In the very climax of his career ... he was stricken down.
>
> Chittenden, *Recollections of Lincoln*, ch. xiv

**Clinch, Clincher.** *See* Clench.

**Clinker-built,** said of a ship whose planks overlap each other, and are riveted together. The opposite to clinker-built is carvel-built (*q.v.*).

**Clio** was one of the nine Muses, the inventress of historical and heroic poetry.

Addison adopted the name as a pseudonym, perhaps because many of his papers in the *Spectator* are signed by one of the four letters in this word, probably the initial letters of Chelsea, London, Islington, Office. *Cp.* Notarikon.

**Clipper.** A fast-sailing ship; in Smyth's *Sailor's Word Book* (1867) said to be 'formerly chiefly applied to the sharp-built raking schooners of America, and latterly to Australian passenger-ships'. Hence:

***A clipping pace.*** Very fast.

> Leaving Bolus Head, we scudded on at a clipping pace, and the skiff yielded so much to the breeze that Bury said we must reef the mainsail.
>
> W. S. Trench, *Realities of Irish Life*, ch. x

***She's a clipper.*** Said of a stylish or beautiful woman – not necessarily of a 'fast' woman.

**Cliquot.** A nickname of Frederick William IV of Prussia; so called from his fondness for champagne (1795, 1840–61).

**Cloacina.** Goddess of sewers. (Lat. *cloaca*, a sewer.)

> Then Cloacina, goddess of the tide,
> Whose sable streams beneath the city glide,
> Indulged the modish flame: the town she roved,
> A mortal scavenger she saw, she loved.
>
> Gay, *Trivia*, ii

**Cloak and Sword Plays.** Swashbuckling plays, full of fighting and adventure. The name comes from the Spanish comedies of the 16th century dramatists, Lope de Vega and Calderon – the *Commedia de capa y espada*; but whereas with them it signified merely a drama of domestic intrigue and was named from the rank of the chief characters, in France – and, through French influence, in England – it was applied as above.

***Knight of the Cloak.*** Sir Walter Raleigh. So called from his throwing his cloak into a puddle for Queen Elizabeth to step on as she was about to enter her barge.

> 'Your lordship meaneth that Raleigh, the Devonshire youth,' said Varney, 'the Knight of the Cloak, as they call him at Court.'
>
> Scott, *Kenilworth*, ch. xvi

**Clock.** So church bells were once called. (Ger. *glocke*; Fr. *cloche*; Mediaeval Lat. *cloca*.)

***Clock.*** The tale about St Paul's clock striking thirteen is given in Walcott's *Memorials of Westminster*, and refers to John Hatfield, who died 1770, aged 102. He was a soldier in the reign of William III, and was brought before a court-martial for falling asleep on duty upon Windsor Terrace. In proof of his innocence he asserted that he heard St Paul's clock strike thirteen, which statement was confirmed by several witnesses.

**Clodhopper.** A rustic, a farmer's labourer, who hops or walks amongst the clods. The cavalry call the infantry 'clodhoppers' or 'footsloggers', because they have to walk instead of riding horse-back.

**Clog Almanac.** A primitive almanac or calendar, originally made of a four-square 'clog', or log of wood; the sharp edges were divided by notches into three months, every week being marked by a bigger notch. The faces contained the saints' days, the festivals, the phases of the moon, and so on, sometimes in Runic characters, whence the 'clog' was also called a 'Runic staff'. They are not uncommon, and specimens may be seen in the British Museum, the Bodleian, the Ashmolean, and other places at home and abroad.

**Cloister.** ***He retired into a cloister***, a monastery. Almost all monasteries have a cloister or covered walk, which generally occupied three sides of a quadrangle. Hence *cloistered*, confined, withdrawn from the world in the manner of a recluse:

> I cannot praise a fugitive, and cloistered virtue, unexercised and unbreathed, that never sallies out and sees her adversary, but slinks out of the race where that immortal garland is to be run for, not without dust and heat.
>
> Milton, *Areopagitica*

**Clootie.** *Auld Clootie.* Old Nick. The Scotch call a cloven hoof a *cloot*, so that Auld Clootie is Old Clovenfoot.

> And maybe, Tam, for a' my cants,
> My wicked rhymes an' drucken rants,
> I'll gie auld Cloven Clootie's haunts
> An unco slip yet,
> An' snugly sit, amang the saunts
> At Davie's hip yet!
>
> Burns, *Reply to a Trimming Epistle*

**Close Rolls.** Mandates, letters and writs of a private nature, addressed, in the Sovereign's name, to individuals, and folded or *closed* and sealed on the outside with the Great Seal.

> Close Rolls contain all such matters of record as were committed to close writs. These Rolls are preserved in the Tower.
>
> Jacob, *Law Dictionary*

***Patent Rolls*** (*q.v.*) are left *open*, with the seal hanging from the bottom.

**Close-time for Game.** *See* Sporting Seasons.

**Closh, Mynherr.** A Dutchman, or a Dutch Jack-tar. Closh is corrupt form of Claus, a contraction of Nicholas.

**Cloth, The.** The clergy; the clerical office; thus we say 'having respect for the cloth'.

**Clotho.** One of the Three Fates in *classic mythology*. She presided over birth, and drew from her distaff the thread of life; Atropos presided over death and cut the thread of life; and Lachesis spun the fate of life between birth and death. (Gr. *klotho*, to draw thread from a distaff.)

> A France slashed asunder with Clotho-scissors and civil war.
>
> Carlyle. (This is an erroneous allusion. It was Atropos who cut the thread.)

**Cloud.** A dark spot on the forehead of a horse between the eyes. A white spot is called a star, and an elongated star is a blaze. *See* Blaze.

> *Agrippa.* He [Antony] has a cloud on his face.
> *Enobarbus.* He were the worse for that were he a horse.
>
> Shakespeare, *Antony and Cleopatra*, 3, 2

***A clouded cane.*** A malacca cane clouded or mottled from age and use. These canes were very fashionable in the first quarter of nineteenth century and earlier.

> Sir Plume, of amber snuff-box justly vain,
> And the nice conduct of a clouded cane.
>
> Pope, *Rape of the Lock*, iv, 123

***Every cloud has a silver lining.*** There is some redeeming brightness in the darkest prospect; 'while there is life there is hope'.

> Though outwardly a gloomy shroud,
> The inner half of every cloud
> Is bright and shining:
> I therefore turn my clouds about,
> And always wear them inside out
> To show the lining.
>
> Ellen Thorneycroft Fowler, *The Wisdom of Folly*

***He is in the clouds.*** In dreamland; entertaining visionary notions; having no distinct idea about the matter in question.

***He is under a cloud.*** Under suspicion, in disrepute.

***The Battle above the Clouds.*** A name given to the Battle of Lookout Mountain, part of the Battle of Chattanooga fought during the American War of Secession on November 24th, 1863. The Federals under Grant defeated the Confederates, and part of the fight took place in a heavy mist on the mountains: hence the name.

***To blow a cloud.*** *See* Blow.

**Cloud, St.** Patron saint of nail-smiths, by a play upon the French word, *clou*, a nail.

**Cloven Foot.** *To show the cloven foot,* i.e. to show a knavish intention; a base motive. The allusion is to Satan, represented with the legs and feet of a goat; and, however he might disguise himself, he could never conceal his cloven feet. *See* Bag o' Nails, Clootie.

**Clover.** *He's in clover.* In luck, in prosperous circumstances, in a good situation. The allusion is to cattle feeding in clover fields.

**Club.** A society of persons who club together, or form themselves into a knot or lump. In this sense the word was originally applied to persons bound together by a vow (Ger. *gelübde*).

> [1190] was the era of chivalry, … for bodies of men uniting themselves by a sacred vow, *gelubde*, which word and thing have passed over to us in a singularly dwindled condition, 'club' we call it; and the vow … does not rank very high.
>
> Carlyle, *Frederick the Great*, vol. i. I, 111

**Club-bearer, The.** In *Greek mythology*, Periphetes, the robber of Argolis, is so called because he murdered his victims with an iron club.

**Club-land.** The West End of London round St James's, where the principal clubs are situated; the members of such clubs.

**Club-law.** The law of might or compulsion through fear of chastisement; 'might is right'; 'do it or get a hiding'.

**Club Parliament, The.** Another name for the Parliament of Bats. *See* Bats.

**Clue.** *I have not yet got the clue*; *to give a clue*, i.e. a hint. A clue is a ball of thread (A.S. *cleowen*). The only mode of finding the way out of the Cretan labyrinth was by a skein of thread, which, being followed, led the right way.

**Clumsy.** A Scandinavian word, meaning originally 'numbed with cold', and so 'awkward', 'unhandy'. Piers Plowman has 'thou clomsest for cold', and Wiclif has 'with clomsid handis' (Jer. 47:3).

**Cluricaune.** An elf in Irish folklore. He is of evil disposition and usually appears as a wrinkled old man. He has knowledge of hidden treasure and is the fairies' shoemaker. Another name for him is *Leprechaun* or *Lepracaun* (*q.v.*).

**Clydesdale Horses.** *See* Shire Horses.

**Clym of the Clough.** A noted archer and outlaw, supposed to have lived shortly before Robin Hood, who, with Adam Bell and William of Cloudesly, forms the subject of one of the ballads in Percy's *Reliques*, the three becoming as famous in the north of England as Robin Hood and Little John in the midland counties. Their place of resort was in Englewood Forest, near Carlisle. Clym of the Clough means Clement of the Cliff. He is mentioned in Ben Jonson's *Alchemist* (I, ii, 46).

**Clytie.** In *classical mythology*, an ocean nymph, in love with Apollo. Meeting with no return, she was changed into the heliotrope, or sunflower, which, traditionally, still turns to the sun, following him through his daily course.

> I will not have the mad Clytie
> Whose head is turn'd by the sun; …
> But I will woo the dainty rose,
> The queen of every one. Thos Hood, *Flowers*

**Cnidian Venus, The.** The exquisite statue of Venus by Praxiteles, formerly in her temple at Cnidus. It is known through the antique reproduction now in the Vatican.

**Co.** A contraction of *company*; as Smith and Co.

**Coach.** University slang for a private tutor; a pun on *getting on fast*. To get on fast you used to take a coach; you cannot get on fast without a private tutor – *ergo*, a private tutor is the coach to enable you to get on quickly.

> The books … are expensive, and often a further expense is entailed by the necessity of securing 'a coach'. Stedman, *Oxford*, ch. x

Hence, *to be coached* or *coached up*, to be prepared for an examination by a private tutor; *well coached up*, well crammed or taught.

***A slow coach.*** A dull, unprogressive person, somewhat fossilised.

> What a dull, old-fashioned chap thou be'st … but thou wert always a slow-coach.
>
> Mrs Gaskell, *Cibbis Marsh* (Era 2)

***To dine in the coach.*** In the captain's private room. The *coach* or *couch* of one of the old, large-sized men-of-war was a small apartment near the stern, the floor being formed of the aftmost part of the quarterdeck, and the roof by the poop.

***To drive a coach and four through an Act of Parliament.*** To find a way of infringing it or escaping its provisions without rendering oneself liable at law. It is said that a clever lawyer can always find for his clients some loophole of escape.

It is easy to drive a coach-and-four through wills, and settlements, and legal things.
H. R. Haggard

[Rice] was often heard to say … that he would drive a coach and six horses through the Act of Settlement.
Welwood

**Coal.** ***To blow the coals.*** To fan dissensions, to excite smouldering animosity into open hostility, as dull coals are blown into a blaze with a pair of bellows.

***To call,*** or ***haul, over the coals.*** To bring to task for shortcomings; to scold. At one time the Jews were 'bled' whenever the kings or barons wanted money; and one very common torture, if they resisted, was to haul them over the coals of a slow fire, to give them a 'roasting'. In Scott's *Ivanhoe*, Front-de-Boeuf threatens to haul Isaac over the coals.

Jamieson thinks the phrase refers to the ordeal by fire, a suggestion which is favoured by the French corresponding phrase, *mettre sur la sellette* (to put on the culprit's stool).

***To carry coals.*** To be put upon. 'Gregory, o' my word, we'll not carry coals' – i.e. submit to be 'put upon' (*Romeo and Juliet*, 1, 1). So in *Every Man out of his Humour*, 'Here comes one that will carry coals, *ergo*, will hold my dog'. The allusion is to the dirty, laborious occupation of coal-carriers, the most forlorn wretches being selected to carry coals to the kitchen, halls, etc.

***To carry coals to Newcastle.*** To do what is superfluous; to take something where it is already plentiful. Newcastle, of course, is a great coal port. The French say, '*Porter de leau à la rivière*' (to carry water to the river).

***To heap coals of fire on one's head.*** To melt down his animosity by deeds of kindness; to repay bad treatment with good.

If thine enemy be hungry, give him bread to eat; and if he be thirsty, give him water to drink; for thou shalt heap coals of fire upon his head.
Prov. 25:21, 22

***To post the coal,*** or ***cole.*** *See* Cole.

**Coal Brandy.** Burnt brandy. The ancient way to set brandy on fire was to drop in it a live or red-hot coal.

**Coaling,** in theatrical slang, means telling phrases and speeches, as, 'My part is full of "coaling lines"'. Possibly from *cole* (*q.v.*), money, such a part being a profitable one.

**Coalition Government.** A Government formed by various parties by a mutual surrender of principles; such as the Ministry of the Duke of Portland which included Lord North and Fox in 1783, and fell to pieces in a few months, and that of Lord Salisbury with the old Whig Party headed by Lord Hartington in 1886. The most famous Coalition in British history, however, is that formed in May, 1915, by Mr Asquith, when Mr Bonar Law with the Unionist and Conservative parties joined the Liberals – the whole being under Mr Asquith – for the better conduct of the Great War which had then been in progress for nearly 10 months. In spite of a General Election at the end of the War in 1918 and many changes of Government – Mr Lloyd George succeeded Mr Asquith as Premier in December, 1916 – the Coalition lasted till October, 1922.

**Coart.** The name of the Hare in the Old French version of *Reynard the Fox* (*q.v.*). *See* Coward: Cuwaert.

**Coast, To.** To free-wheel down a hill on a bicycle, etc.; to come down the hill without working the pedals, or – of motor-cycles and cars – with the engine cut off. The term was originally American or Canadian, an ice-covered slope down which one slides on a sledge being called a *coast*, and hence the action of sliding being termed *coasting*.

***Coasting lead.*** A sounding lead used in shallow water.

***Coasting trade.*** Trade between ports of the same country carried on by coasting vessels.

***Coasting waiter.*** An officer of Customs in the Port of London, whose duty it was to visit and make a return of coasting vessels which (from the nature of their cargo) were not required to report or make entry at the Custom House, but which were liable to the payment of certain small dues. The coasting waiter collected these, and searched the cargo for contraband goods. Like tide waiters, coasting waiters were abolished in the latter half of last century, and their duties have since been performed by the examining officer.

***The coast is clear.*** There is no likelihood of interference. None of the coastguards are about.

**Coat.** ***Cut your coat according to your cloth.*** Curtail your expenses to the amount of your income; live within your means. *Si non possis quod velis, velis id quod possis.*

***Near is my coat, but nearer is my skin.*** '*Tunica pallio propior est.*' '*Ego proximus mihi.*'

***To baste one's coat.*** To dust his jacket; to beat him.

***To wear the king's coat.*** To be a soldier.

***Turning one's coat for luck.*** It was an ancient superstition that this was a charm against evil spirits. *See* Turncoat.

> William found
> A means for our deliverance: 'Turn your cloaks',
> Quoth hee, 'for Pucke is busy in these oakes'.
>
> Bishop Corbett, *Iter Boreale*

**Coat of Arms.** Originally, a surcoat worn by knights over their armour, decorated with devices by which the wearer could be described and recognised; hence the heraldic device of a family. The practice of bearing on the armour or its covering some distinguishing mark is of very ancient date; but during the Crusades, when it seems to have been introduced into England, its rules and customs were codified, and 'heraldry' was brought almost to a science.

**Cob.** A short-legged, stout variety of horse, rather larger than a pony, from thirteen to nearly fifteen hands high. The word means big, stout. It also meant a tuft or head (from *cop*), hence eminent, large, powerful. The '*cob of the county*' is the great boss thereof. A *rich cob* is a plutocrat. Hence also a male, as a cob-swan.

Riding horses run between fifteen and sixteen hands in height, and carriage horses, between sixteen and seventeen hands.

**Cobalt.** From the Ger. *Kobold*, a gnome, the demon of mines. The metal was so called by miners partly because it was thought to be useless and partly because the arsenic and sulphur with which it was found in combination had bad effects both on their health and on the silver ores. Its presence was consequently attributed to the ill offices of the mine demon.

**Cobbler.** A drink made of wine (sherry), sugar, lemon, and ice. It is sipped up through a straw. *See* Cobbler's Punch.

> This wonderful invention, sir, ... is called cobbler – Sherry cobbler, when you name it long; cobbler when you name it short.
>
> Dickens, *Martin Chuzzlewit*, xvii

***A cobbler should stick to his last.*** Let no one presume to interfere in matters of which he is ignorant.

> Ne supra crepidam sutor judicaret.
>
> Pliny, xxv, x, 85

The tale goes that a cobbler detected a fault in the shoe-latchet of one of Apelles' paintings, and the artist rectified the fault. The cobbler next ventured to criticise the legs; but Apelles answered, 'Keep to your trade' – you understand about shoes, but not about anatomy.

***The Cobbler Poet.*** Hans Sachs of Nuremberg, prince of the master-singers of Germany (1494–1576).

***Cobbler's punch.*** Gin and water, with a little treacle and vinegar.

***Cobbler's toast.*** Schoolboys' bread and butter, toasted on the dry side and eaten hot.

**Coburg.** A corded or ribbed cotton cloth made in Coburg (Saxony), or in imitation thereof. Chiefly used for ladies' dresses.

**Cobweb.** The net spun by a spider to catch its prey. *Cob*, or *cop*, is an old word for a spider, so called from its round, stubby body; it is found in the A.S. *attorcoppa*, poisonous spider.

**Cock** (noun). In *classical mythology* the cock was dedicated to Apollo, the sun-god, because it gives notice of the rising of the sun. It was dedicated to Mercury, because it summons men to business by its crowing. And to Aesculapius, because 'early to bed and early to rise, makes a man healthy'.

According to Mohammedan legend the Prophet found in the first heaven a cock of such enormous size that its crest touched the second heaven. The crowing of this celestial bird arouses every living creature from sleep except man. The Moslem doctors say that Allah lends a willing ear to him who reads the Koran, to him who prays for pardon, and to the cock whose chant is divine melody. When this cock ceases to crow, the day of judgment will be at hand.

The Christian use of *a cock on church spires* is to warn men not to deny their Lord as Peter did, and to remind them that when he had done so the cock crew and he 'went out and wept bitterly'. Peter Le Neve affirms that a cock was the warlike ensign of the Goths, and therefore used in Gothic churches for ornament.

***A cock and bull story.*** A long, rambling, idle, or incredible yarn; a canard. There are various so-called explanations of the origin of the term, but the most likely is that it is connected with the old fables in which cocks, bulls, and other animals discoursed in human language on things in general. In Bentley's *Boyle Lecture* (1692) occurs the passage:

> That cocks and bulls might discourse, and hinds and panthers hold conferences about religion.

The 'hind and panther' allusion is an obvious reference to Dryden's poem (published five years before), and it is possible that the 'cocks and bulls' would have had some meaning that was as well known to contemporaries but has been long since forgotten. *See also* the closing chapter of Sterne's *Tristram Shandy*; the last words in the book are:

> L – d! said my mother, what is all this story about? – A cock and a bull, said *Yorick* – And one of the best of its kind, I ever heard.

The French equivalents are *faire un coq à l'âne* and *un conte de ma mère l'oie* (a mother goose tale), and it is worth noting that in Scotland a satire or lampoon and also a rambling, disconnected story used to be called a *cockalane*, direct from the Fr. *coq à l'âne*.

***A cock of hay*** or ***haycock.*** A small heap of hay thrown up temporarily. (Ger. *kocke*, a heap of hay; Norw. *kok*, a heap.)

***By cock and pie.*** We meet with *cock's bones, cock's wounds, cock's mother, cock's body, cock's passion*, etc., where we can have no doubt that the word is a minced oath, and stands for the sacred name which should never be taken in vain. The *Pie* is the table or rule in the old Roman offices, showing how to find out the service for each day (from Med. Lat. *pica*). The latter part of the oath is equivalent to 'the Mass book'.

> By cock and pie, sir, you shall not away tonight.
> Shakespeare, *2 Henry IV*, 5, 1

***Cock and Pie*** (as a public-house sign) is probably 'The Cock and Magpie'.

***Cock and Bottle.*** A public-house sign, probably meaning that draught and bottled ale may be had on the premises. If so, the word 'cock' would mean the tap.

***Cock of the North.*** George, fifth Duke of Gordon (1770–1836), who raised the Gordon Highlanders in 1795, is so called on a monument erected to his honour at Fochabers, in Aberdeenshire.

The brambling, or mountain finch, is also known by this name.

***Cock of the walk.*** The dominant bully or master spirit. The place where barndoor fowls are fed is *the walk*, and if there is more than one cock they will fight for the supremacy of this domain.

***Every cock crows on its own dunghill,*** or ***Ilka cock crows on its own midden.*** It is easy to brag of your deeds in your own castle when safe from danger and not likely to be put to the proof.

***Nourish a cock, but offer it not in sacrifice.*** This is the eighteenth Symbolic Saying in the Protreptics of Iamblichus. The cock was sacred to Minerva, and also to the sun and moon, and it would be impious to offer a sacrilegious offering to the gods. What is already consecrated to God cannot be employed in sacrifice.

***That cock won't fight.*** *See* Cock-fighting.

***The red cock will crow in his house.*** His house will be set on fire.

> 'We'll see if the red cock craw not in his bonnie barnyard ae morning.' 'What does she mean?' said Mannering ... 'Fire-raising,' answered the ... dominie. Scott, *Guy Mannering*, ch. iii

***To cry cock.*** To claim the victory; to assert oneself to be the superior. As a 'cock of the walk' (*q.v.*) is the chief or ruler of the whole walk, so to cry cock is to claim this cockship.

**Cock** (verb). In the following phrases, all of which connote assertiveness, obtrusiveness, or aggressiveness in some degree, the allusion is to gamecocks, whose strutting about, swaggering, and ostentatious pugnacity is proverbial.

***To cock the ears.*** To prick up the ears, or turn them as a horse does when he listens to a strange sound.

***To cock the nose*** or ***cock up the nose.*** To turn up the nose in contempt. *See* Cock your eye.

***To cock up your head, foot,*** etc. Lift up, turn up your head or foot.

***To cock your eye.*** To shut one eye and look with the other in a somewhat impertinent manner; to glance at questioningly. *Cp.* Cock-eye.

***To cock your hat.*** To set your hat more on one side of the head than on the other; to look knowing and pert. Soldiers cock their caps over the left side to 'look smart'. *Cp.* Cocked Hat.

**Cock-a-hoop.** Variously explained as being referable (*a*) to an old custom of taking the *cock* (i.e. the spigot) out of the barrel and setting it on the *hoop* thereof before commencing a regular drinking bout, and (*b*) to the Fr. *huppe*, a tufted crest, hence a specially feathered, and so specially lively or valuable, game-cock.

> And having routed a whole troop.
> With victory was cock-a-hoop.
> Butler, *Hudibras*, i, 3

***To sit cock-a-houp.*** Boastful, defiant, like a game-cock with his houpe or crest erect; eagerly expectant.

***Cock-boat.*** A small ship's boat; a very light or frail craft.

> That now no more we can the maine-land see,
> Have care, I pray, to guide the cock-bote well.
> Spenser, *Faërie Queene*, III, viii, 24

This 'cock-bote' had previously (III, vii, 27) been called a 'little bote' and a 'shallop'.

***Cokke*** or ***cocke,*** is an obsolete word for a small boat, and is probably connected with *cog*, an early kind of ship, from Scan. *kog*, *kogge*, a small vessel without a keel. Originally a wicker frame covered with leather or oil-cloth. The Welsh fishers used to carry them on their backs. *Cock* is here the M.E. *cog* or *cogge*, and O.Fr. *coque* or *cogue*, a kind of boat. *Cog* used to be used in English for a small boat, as by Chaucer:

This messagere adoun him gan to hye,
And fond Jasoun, and Ercules also,
That in a cogge to londe were y-go,
Hem to refresshen and to take the eyr.

*Legend of Good Women*, i, 1479

***Cock-crow.*** The Hebrews divided the night into four watches: (1) The 'beginning of the watches' or 'even' (Lam. 2:19); (2) 'The middle watch' or 'midnight' (Judges 7:19); (3) 'The cock-crowing'; (4) 'The morning watch' or 'dawning' (Exod. 14:24).

Ye know not when the master of the house cometh, at even, or at midnight, or at the cock-crowing, or in the morning. Mark 13:35

The Romans divided the day into sixteen parts, each one hour and a half, beginning at midnight. The third of these divisions (3 a.m.) they called *gallicinium*, the time when cocks begin to crow; the next was *conticinium*, when they ceased to crow; and fifth was *diluculum*, dawn.

If the Romans sounded the hour on a trumpet three times it would explain the diversity of the Gospels: 'Before the cock crow' (John 13:38, Luke 22:34, and Matt 26:34); but 'Before the cock crow *twice*' (Mark 14:30) – that is, before the trumpet has finished sounding.

*Apparitions vanish at cock crow.* This is a Christian superstition, the cock being the watch-bird placed on church spires, and therefore sacred.

The morning cock crew loud,
And at the sound it [the Ghost] shrunk in haste away,
And vanished from our sight.

Shakespeare, *Hamlet*, 1, 2

***Cock-eye.*** A squint. Cock-eyed, having a squint; cross-eyed. There seems to be no connection between this and the Irish and Gaelic *caog*, a squint; it may mean that such an eye has to be *cocked*, as the trigger of a gun is cocked, before it can do its work effectively; or it may be from the verb *to cock* (*q.v.*) in the sense of 'turning up' – as in *to cock the nose*.

**Cock-fighting** was introduced into Britain by the Romans. It was a favourite sport both with the Greeks and with the Romans.

***That beats cock-fighting.*** That is most improbable and extraordinary. The allusion is to the extravagant tales told of fighting-cocks.

He can only relieve his feelings by the ... frequent repetition, 'Well, that beats cock-fighting!'

Whyte-Melville

***That cock won't fight.*** That dodge won't answer; that tale won't wash. Of course, the allusion is to a bet being made on a favourite cock, which, when pitted, refuses to fight.

***To live like fighting-cocks.*** To live in luxury. Fighting-cocks used to be high fed in order to aggravate their pugnacity and increase their powers of endurance.

**Cock-horse.** *To ride a cock-horse.* To sit astride a person's foot or knee while he dances or tosses it up and down.

**Cock Lane Ghost.** A tale of terror without truth; an imaginary tale of horrors. In Cock Lane, Smithfield (1762), certain knockings were heard, which Mr Parsons, the owner, declared proceeded from the ghost of Fanny Kent, who died suddenly, and Parsons wished people to suppose that she had been murdered by her husband. All London was agog with this story; but it was found out that the knockings were produced by Parsons' daughter (a girl twelve years of age) rapping on a board which she took into her bed. Parsons was condemned to stand in the pillory. *Cp.* Stockwell Ghost.

**Cock Lorell's Bote.** A pamphlet published by Wynkyn de Worde about 1510, satirising contemporary lower middle class life and introducing all sorts of rogues and vagabonds in the guise of a crew which takes ship and sails through England. The tract was immensely popular, and Cock Lorell himself may have been an historical character. He figures in a song in Ben Jonson's *Gipsies Metamorphosed* (1621),

Cocklorell would needs have the devil his guest,
And bade him into the Peak to dinner,
Where never the frend had such a feast,
Provided him yet at the charge of a sinner;

and in Samuel Rowland's *Martin Mark-All* (1610) we are told that he was King of the Gypsies from 1501 to 1533, that he devised the twenty-five orders of vagabonds, and that he was 'the most notorious knave that ever lived'. His name was often used for a rogue or reprobate. *See* Lorel.

**Cock-pit.** The arena in which game-cocks were set to fight; also the name of a 17th century theatre built about 1618 on the site of a cock-pit in Drury Lane; and that of the after part of the orlop deck of an old man-of-war, formerly used as quarters for the junior officers and as a sick-bay in time of war.

> Captain Hardy, some fifty minutes after he had left the cock-pit, returned; and, again taking the hand of his dying friend and commander, congratulated him on having gained a complete victory. Southey, *Life of Nelson*, ch. ix

The judicial committee of the Privy Council was also so called, because the council-room is built on the old cock-pit of Whitehall palace.

> Great consultations at the cockpit about battles, duels, victories, and what not.
> *Poor Robin's Almanack*, 1730

***Cock-pit of Europe.*** Belgium has for long been so called because it has been the site of more European battles than any other country; Oudenarde, Ramillies, Fontenoy, Fleurus, Jemmapes, Ligny, Quatre Bras, Waterloo, were but the forerunners of the tremendous struggles that took place at the commencement of the Great War of 1914–18, when the Germans overran the country and took Liège, Namur, Louvain, Brussels, Antwerp, and fought the titanic battles at Ypres.

**Cock Sure.** As sure as a cock; meaning either 'with all the assurance (brazen-faced impudence) of a game-cock', or 'as sure as the cock is to crow in the morning', or even 'with the security and certainty of the action of a cock, or tap, in preventing the waste of liquor'.

Shakespeare employs the phrase in the sense of 'sure as the cock of a firelock'.

> We steal as in a castle, cock-sure.
> *I Henry IV*, 2, 1

And the phrase 'Sure as a gun' seems to favour the latter explanation.

**Cockade.** A badge worn on the head-dress of menservants of Royalty and of those holding His Majesty's commission, such as naval and military officers, diplomatists, lords-lieutenant, high sheriffs, etc. The English cockade is black and circular in shape with a projecting fan at the top, except for naval officers, for whom the shape is oval without the fan. This form of cockade was introduced from Hanover by George I; under Charles I the cockade had been scarlet, but Charles II changed it to white, and thus the *white cockade* became the badge of the Pretenders, William III adopting an orange cockade (as Prince of Orange). From Fr. *cocarde*, a plume, rosette, or bunch of ribbons, originally worn by Croatian soldiers serving in the French army, and used to fix the flaps of the hat in a cocked position.

The colours of the cockades of different countries are:

Austria: black and yellow.
Bavaria: light blue and white.
Belgium: black, yellow, and red.
France: the tricolour; formerly the royal colour – white.
Germany: black, white, and red.
Holland: orange.
Prussia: black and white.
Russia: green and white.
Spain: scarlet.

***To mount the cockade.*** To become a soldier.

**Cockaigne, Land of.** An imaginary land of idleness and luxury, famous in mediaeval story, and the subject of more than one poem, one of which, an early translation of a 13th century French work, is given in Ellis's *Specimens of Early English Poets*. In this 'the houses were made of barley sugar and cakes, the streets were paved with pastry, and the shops supplied goods for nothing'.

London has been so called (*see* Cockney), but Boileau applies the name to Paris.

Allied to the Ger. *kuchen*, a cake. Scotland is called the 'land of cakes'.

**Cockatrice.** A fabulous and heraldic monster with the wings of a fowl, tail of a dragon, and head of a cock. So called because it was said to be produced from a cock's egg hatched by a serpent. According to legend, the very look of this monster would cause instant death. In consequence of the *crest* with which the head is crowned, the creature is called a basilisk (*q.v.*). Isaiah says, 'The weaned child shall put his hand on the cockatrice' den' (11:8), to signify that the most obnoxious animal should not hurt the most feeble of God's creatures.

Figuratively, it means an insidious treacherous person bent on mischief.

> They will kill one another by the look, like cockatrices.
> Shakespeare, *Twelfth Night*, 3, 4

**Cocked Hat.** A hat with the brim turned, like that of a bishop, dean, etc. It is also applied to the *chapeau bras* (*q.v.*) and the military full-dress hat, pointed before and behind, and rising to a point at the crown, the *chapeau à cornes*. 'Cock' in this phrase means to turn; *cocked*, turned up.

*Knocked into a cocked hat.* In the game of ninepins, three pins were set up in the form of a triangle, and when all the pins except these three were knocked down, the set was technically said to be 'knocked into a cocked hat'. Hence, utterly out of all shape or plumb. A somewhat similar phrase is 'Knocked into the middle of next week'.

**Cocker.** *According to Cocker. All right, according to Cocker.* According to established rules, according to what is correct. Edward Cocker (1631–75) published an arithmetic which ran through sixty editions. The phrase, 'According to Cocker', was popularised by Murphy in his farce, *The Apprentice* (1756). *Cp.* Gunter.

**Cockle.** A bivalve mollusc, the shell of which was worn by pilgrims in their hats (*see* Cockle hats). The polished side of the shell was scratched with some rude drawing of the Virgin, the Crucifixion, or some other subject connected with the pilgrimage. Being blessed by the priest, they were considered amulets against spiritual foes, and might be used as drinking vessels.

***Cockle-boat.*** *See* Cock-boat.

***Cockle hat.*** A pilgrim's hat, especially the hat of a pilgrim to the shrine of St James of Compostella, in Spain: his symbol was really a scallop-shell, but the word *cockle* was more usually applied to it.

> And how shall I your true love know
> From many another one?
> Oh, by his cockle hat and staff,
> And by his sandal shoon.
>
> Old Ballad, *The Friar of Orders Grey*

***Hot cockles.*** *See* Hot.

***The Order of the Cockle.*** An order of knighthood created by St Louis in 1260, in memory of a disastrous expedition made by sea for the succour of Christians. Perrot says it scarcely survived its foundation.

***To cry cockles.*** To be hanged; from the gurgling noise made in strangulation.

***To warm the cockles of one's heart.*** Said of anything that pleases one immensely and gives one a gratifying sensation, such as a glass of really good port does. (Lat. *cochleae cordis*, the ventricles of the heart.)

**Cockney.** This is the M.E. *cokeney*, meaning 'a cock's egg' (*-ey* = A.S. *aeg*, an egg), i.e. a small egg with no yolk that is occasionally laid by hens; hence applied originally to a foolish, spoilt, cockered child:

> I made thee a wanton and thou hast made me a fool, I brought thee up like a cockney and thou hast handled me like a cock's-comb, I made more of thee than became a father and thou less of me than beseemed a child.
>
> Lyly, *Euphues* (1578)

From this the word came to signify a foolish or effeminate person; hence, by the country-dwellers – the majority of the population – it was applied to townsmen generally, and finally became restricted to its present meaning, one born within sound of Bow Bells, London; one possessing London peculiarities of speech, etc.; one who, hence, is – or is supposed to be – wholly ignorant of country sports, country life, farm animals, plants, and so on.

> As Frenchmen love to be bold, Flemings to be drunks, Welchmen to be called Britons, and Irishmen to be costermongers; so cockneys, especially she cockneys, love not aqua-vitae when 'tis good for them.
>
> Dekker Webster, *Westward Hoe*, II, ii (1607)

Shakespeare uses the word for a squeamish woman:

> Cry to it, nuncle as the cockney did to the eels, when she put them into the paste alive.
>
> *King Lear*, 2, 4

***The Cockney School.*** A nickname given by Lockhart (*see* quotation below) to the group of writers including Leigh Hunt, Hazlitt, Shelley, and Keats, most of whom were Londoners or lived in London. Lockhart was a strong partisan of the Lake School (*q.v.*) and had great animosity against writers with other aims or principles. Hunt he called 'the Cockney Homer', Hazlitt 'the Cockney Aristotle', and Haydon 'the Cockney Raphael'.

> If I may be permitted to have the honour of christening it, it may be henceforth referred to by the designation of the 'Cockney School'.
>
> Lockhart, *Blackwood's Magazine*, Oct., 1817

***The king of cockneys.*** A master of the revels chosen by students of Lincoln's Inn on Childermas Day (December 28th).

**Cock Robin.** Slang term for a printer in a small way of business.

***Cock robin shop.*** A small printing establishment.

**Cockshut,** or **Cockshut Time.** Twilight; the time when the *cockshut*, i.e. a large net employed to catch woodcocks, used to be spread. The net was so called from being used in a glade through which the woodcocks might *shoot* or dart.

> Let me never draw a sword again,
> Nor prosper in the twilight, cockshut light
> When I would fleece the wealthy passenger ...
> If I, the next time that I meet the slave,
> Cut not the nose from off the coward's face.
>
> *Arden of Feversham*, III, ii (1592)

*See also* Shakespeare's *Richard III*, 5, 3.

**Cockshy.** A free fling or 'shy' at something. The allusion is to the once popular Shrove-Tuesday sport of shying or casting stones or sticks at cocks. This sport is now superseded by pigeon-shooting, which is thought to be more aristocratic! but can hardly be deemed more humane.

**Cockswain.** *See* Coxswain.

**Cocktail.** An iced drink made of spirits mixed with bitters, sugar, and some aromatic flavouring. Champagne cocktail is champagne flavoured with Angostura bitters; soda cocktail is soda-water, sugar, and bitters.

> Did ye iver try a brandy cocktail, Cornel?
>
> Thackeray, *The Newcomes*, xiii

The origin of the term is unknown: the story given in the *New York World* (1891) to the effect that it is an Aztec word, and that 'the liquor was discovered by a Toltec noble, who sent it by the hand of his daughter Xochitl', to the king who promptly named it 'xoctl', whence 'cocktail' is a good specimen of the manufacture of popular etymologies.

**Cocky.** Bumptious, overbearing, conceited, and dogmatical; like a little bantam cock.

**Coconut.** ***Milk in the coconut.*** *See* Milk.

**Cocqcigrues.** *At the coming of the Cocqcigrues.* That good time coming, when every mystery shall be cleared up.

> 'That is one of the seven things,' said the fairy Bedonebyasyoudid, 'I am forbidden to tell till the coming of the Cocqcigrues.'
>
> C. Kingsley, *The Water Babies*, ch. vi

**Cocytus.** One of the five rivers of hell. The word means the 'river of lamentation'. The unburied were doomed to wander about its banks for 100 years. It flows into the river Acheron.

> Cocytus, named of lamentation loud
> Heard on the rueful stream.
>
> Milton, *Paradise Lost*, ii, 579

**Cod.** ***You can't cod me.*** You can't deceive me, or take a rise out of me. The word is probably an abbreviation of *codger* (*q.v.*).

**Codger.** A familiar and somewhat disrespectful term applied to an elderly man, generally one with some minor eccentricities. Originally a mean, stingy old chap: probably a variant of *cadger* (*q.v.*).

**Codille.** Triumph. A term in the game of ombre. When one of the two opponents of ombre has more tricks than ombre, he is said to have won codille, and takes all the stake that Ombre played for. Thus Belinda is said, in the *Rape of the Lock*, to have been 'between the jaws of ruin and Codille'. She wins with the 'king of hearts', and *she wins codille*.

**Codlin's your Friend, not Short.** (Dickens, *Old Curiosity Shop*, chap. xix.) Codlin had a shrewd suspicion that little Nell and her grandfather had absconded, and that a reward would be offered for their discovery. So he tried to bespeak the good will of the little girl in the hope of making something of it.

> None of the speakers has much to say in actual hostility to Lord Salisbury's speech, but they all harp upon the theory that Codlin is the friend, not Short.
>
> Newspaper paragraph, Oct. 13th, 1885

**Coehorns.** Small howitzers of about 4 2/3 inches calibre; so called from Baron van Coehorn, of Holland. They were in use in the early 18th century.

**Coenobites** or **Cenobites.** Monks who live in common, in contradistinction to hermits or anchorites. (Gr. *koinosbios.*)

**Coeur de Lion.** Richard I of England; so called from the prodigies of personal valour performed by him in the Holy Land. (1157, 1189–99.)

**Coffee.** The Turkish word is *qahwah*, which is pronounced *kahveh* and is applied to the infusion only, not to the plant or its berries.

It was an old custom in the Ardennes to take ten cups of coffee after dinner, and each cup had its special name. (1) Café, (2) Gloria, (3) Pousse Café, (4) Goutte, (5) Regoutte, (6) Surgoutte, (7) Rincette, (8) Re-rincette, (9) Sur-rincette, and (10) Coup de l'étrier.

Gloria is coffee with a small glass of brandy in lieu of milk; those following it have an ever-increasing quantity of alcohol; and the last is the 'stirrup cup'.

**Coffin.** A raised crust, like the lid of a basket. Hence Shakespeare speaks of a 'custard coffin' (*Taming of the Shrew*, 4, 3). (Gr. *kophinos*, a basket.)

> Of the paste a coffin will I rear.
>
> Shakespeare, *Titus Andronicus*, 5, 2

***To drive a nail into one's coffin.*** To do anything that would tend to cut short one's life; to put a spoke in one's wheel. Topers call a dram 'a nail in their coffin', in jocular allusion to the teetotal axiom.

> Care to our coffin adds a nail, no doubt;
> But every grin so merry draws one out.
>
> Peter Pindar, *Expostulatory Odes*, xv

**Coffin, Long Tom.** A sailor of noble daring, in *The Pilot*, by Fenimore Cooper.

**Cog.** A boat. *See* Cock-boat.

**Coggeshall.** ***A Coggeshall job.*** The saying is, that the Coggeshall folk wanted to divert the current of a stream, and fixed hurdles in the bed of it for the purpose. Another tale is that a mad dog bit a wheelbarrow, and the people, fearing it would go mad, chained it up in a shed. *Cp.* Gotham.

**Cogito, ergo sum.** The axiom formulated by Descartes (1596–1650) as the starting-place of his system of philosophy: it means 'I think, therefore I am.' Descartes, at the beginning, provisionally doubted everything, but he could not doubt the existence of the *ego*, for the mere fact that *I* doubt presupposes the existence of the *I*; in other words, the *doubt* could not exist without the *I*.

> He [Descartes] stopped at the famous formula, 'I think, therefore I am.' Yet a little consideration will show this formula to be full of snares and verbal entanglements. In the first place, the 'therefore' has no business there. The 'I am' is assumed in the 'I think', which is simply another way of saying 'I am thinking.' And, in the second place, 'I think' is not one simple proposition, but three distinct assertions rolled into one. The first of these is 'something called I exists'; the second is, 'something called thought exists'; and the third is, 'the thought is the result of the action of the I'.
>
> Now, it will be obvious to you, that the only one of these three propositions which can stand the Cartesian test of certainty is the second.
>
> Huxley, *Descartes' Discourse on Method*

**Coif.** Originally, a close-fitting cap; afterwards, the special head-dress worn by the old serjeants-at-law – hence sometimes called *Serjeants of the Coif.* It seems to have been a white hood, and its final representative was the white border to the wigs worn by Serjeants, the patch of black silk in the centre of the crown representing the cornered cap that was worn above it.

**Coiffé.** ***Il est né coiffé.*** He is born with a silver spoon in his mouth; born to fortune. *See* Caul.

> Quelques enfans viennent au monde avec une pellicule … que l'on appelle du nom de coeffe; et que l'on croit estre une marque de bonheur. Ce qui a donné lieu au proverbe françois …
>
> *Il est né coëffé. Traite des Superstitions*, 1679

**Coin.** ***Paid in his own coin.*** Tit for tat.

***To coin money.*** To make money with rapidity and ease.

> For the last four years … I literally coined money.
>
> F. Kemble, *Residence in Georgia*

**Coins.** *See* Angel, Bawbee, Carolus, Cross and pile, Crown, Dollar, Farthing, Florin, Groat, Guinea, Mancus, Penny, Pieces of Eight, Shilling, Sovereign, etc.

**Coke.** ***Coke upon Littleton.*** Eighteenth century slang for a mixture of tent and brandy. *Tent* was a deep red Spanish wine. Of course, 'Coke upon Littleton' is the lawyers' name for the reprint and translation of Littleton's *Tenures* (about 1465), published with a commentary by Sir Edward Coke, 1628–44.

***Go and eat coke.*** A vulgar exclamation of contempt or impatience.

***To cry coke.*** To cry peccavi; to ask for mercy.

**Colbronde** or **Colbrand.** The Danish giant slain by Guy of Warwick. By his death the land was delivered from Danish tribute.

> I am not Samson, nor Sir Guy, nor Colbrand,
> To mow 'em down before me.
>
> Shakespeare, *Henry VIII*, 5, 4

**Colcannon.** Potatoes and cabbage pounded together and then fried in butter (Irish). 'Col' is cole or cale, i.e. cabbage.

> About 1774 Isaac Sparks, the Irish comedian, founded in Long Acre a Colcannon Club.
>
> *The Athenaenum*, January 20th, 1875

**Cold-Bath Fields.** A district of Clerkenwell, London, so called from the baths established there, in 1697, for the cure of rheumatism, convulsions, and other nervous disorders.

The Fields were famous for the prison which was established there in the time of James I and not finally closed till 1886.

> As he went through Cold-Bath Fields he saw
> A solitary cell;
> And the Devil was pleased, for it gave him a hint
> For improving his prisons in Hell.
>
> Coleridge, *The Devil's Thoughts*

**Cold Blood.** ***Done in cold blood.*** (Fr. *sang froid.*) Not in the heat of temper; deliberately, and with premeditation. The allusion is to the ancient notion that the blood grew hot and cold, and this difference of temperature ruled the temper.

**Cold-blooded Animals.** As a rule, all invertebrate animals, and all fishes and reptiles, are cold-blooded, the temperature of their blood being about equal to the medium in which they live.

***Cold-blooded persons.*** Those not easily excited; those whose passions are not easily roused; those whose circulation is sluggish.

**Cold Chisel.** A steel chisel made in one piece and so tempered that it will cut cold metal when struck with a hammer.

**Cold Drawn Oil.** Oil that is extracted or expressed without the use of heat.

**Cold Pigeon.** A slang expression for a verbal message sent in place of a love-letter. This would be 'cold comfort' to the lover!

**Cold Shoulder.** *To show* or *give one the cold shoulder* is to assume a distant manner towards a person, to indicate that you wish to cut him. The reference is to a cold shoulder of mutton served to a stranger at dinner; there is not much of it, and even what is left is but moderate fare.

**Cold Steel.** *The persuasion of cold steel* is persuasion enforced at the point of the sword or bayonet.

**Cold Water Ordeal.** An ancient method of testing guilt or innocence. The accused, being tied under the arms, was thrown into a river. If he sank to the bottom he was held to be guiltless, and drawn up by the cord; but if he floated the water rejected him, because of his guilt.

**Cold Without.** An elliptical expression, meaning spirits mixed with *cold* water *without* sugar.

**Coldbrand.** *See* Colbronde.

**Coldstream Guards.** The second of the five regiments of Foot Guards. It was raised by General Monk in 1659–60, and in January, 1660, marched under him from Coldstream in Berwickshire with the object of bringing back Charles II to the throne.

**Cole.** An old canting term for money. *Cp.* Coaling.

> My lusty rustic, learn and be instructed. Cole is, in the language of the witty, money; the *ready*, the *rhino*.
>
> Shadwell, *Squire of Alsatia*, IV, xvi (1688)

***To post*** or ***tip the cole.*** To pay or put down the cash.

> If he don't tip the cole without more ado, give him a taste of the pump, that's all
>
> Harrison Ainsworth, *Jack Sheppard*

**Cole, King.** A legendary British king, described in the nursery rhyme as 'a merry old soul' fond of his pipe, fond of his glass, and fond of his 'fiddlers three'. Robert of Gloucester says he was father of St Helena (and consequently grandfather of the Emperor Constantine); and Colchester has been said to have been named after him, though it is more probable that the town is named from Lat. *colonia*.

**Colettines.** *See* Franciscans.

**Colin Clout.** A name which Spenser assumes in *The Shepherd's Calendar*, and in the pastoral entitled *Colin Clout's Come Home Again*, which represents his return from a visit to Sir Walter Raleigh, 'the Shepherd of the Ocean'. Skelton has previously (about 1520) used the name as the title of a satire directed against the abuses of the Church; he says:

> And if ye stande in doute
> Who brought this ryme aboute,
> My name is Colyn Cloute.

**Colin Tampon.** The nickname of a Swiss, as John Bull is of an Englishman, Brother Jonathan of a North American, and M. Crapaud of a Frenchman.

**Coliseum.** *See* Colosseum.

**Collar. *Against the collar.*** Somewhat fatiguing. When a horse travels uphill the collar distresses his neck, so foot travellers often find the last mile or so 'against the collar', or distressing.

***In collar.*** In harness. The allusion is to a horse's collar, which is put on when about to go to work.

***Out of collar.*** Out of work, out of a place.

***To collar.*** To seize (a person) by the collar; to prig; to appropriate without leave.

***To collar the cole.*** To prig the money. *See* Cole.

***To slip the collar.*** To escape from restraint; to draw back from a task begun.

***To work up to the collar.*** To work tooth and nail; not to shirk the work in hand. A horse that lets his collar lie loose on his neck without bearing on it does not draw the vehicle at all, but leaves another to do the real work.

> As regarded himself, the path lay plain. He must work up to the collar, hot and hard, leaving himself no time to feel the parts that were galled and wrung. Mrs Edwardes, *A Girton Girl*, ch. iv

**Collar-day.** A day on which the knights of the different orders when present at levees or other Court functions wear all their insignia and decorations, including the collar. There are about thirty-five collar-days in the year.

**Collar of Arsinoe,** or **Collar of Alphesibea,** given by her to her husband Alcmeon, was a fatal gift; so was the collar and veil of Eriphyle, wife of Amphiaraos.

**Collar of SS.** A decoration restricted to the Lord Chief Justices of the King's Bench, the Lord Chief Baron of the Exchequer, the Lord Mayor of London, the Kings-of-Arms, the Heralds, the Sergeant-at-Arms, and the Sergeant Trumpeter. It is composed of a series of golden S's joined together, and was originally the badge of the adherents of the House of Lancaster. *See* SS.

**Collectivism.** The opposite of Individualism (*q.v.*). A system in which the government would be the sole employer, the sole landlord, and the sole paymaster. Private property would be abolished, the land, mines, railways, etc., would be nationalised as the post office, telegraphs, telephones, etc., are now; everyone would be obliged to work for his living, and the State obliged to find the work.

**College.** The Lat. *collegium*, meaning colleagueship or partnership, hence a body of colleagues, a fraternity. In English the word has a very wide range, as, College of the Apostles, College of Physicians, College of Surgeons, Heralds' College, College of Justice, etc.; and on the Continent we have College of Foreign Affairs, College of War, College of Cardinals, etc.

In old slang a prison was known as a *college*, and the prisoners as *collegiates*. Newgate was 'New College', and *to take one's final at New College* was to be hanged. The King's Bench Prison was 'King's College', and so on.

**College Colours.**

**Cambridge Boat Crews**, light blue.
*Caius*, light blue and black.
*Catherine's*, blue and white.
*Christ's*, common blue.
*Clare*, black and golden yellow.
*Corpus*, cherry-colour and white.
*Downing*, chocolate.
*Emmanuel*, cherry-colour and dark blue.
*Jesus*, red and black.
*John's*, bright red and white.
*King's*, violet.
*Magdalene*, indigo and lavender.
*Pembroke*, claret and French grey.
*Peterhouse*, dark blue and white.
*Queens'*, green and white.
*Sidney Sussex*, red and blue.
*Trinity*, dark blue.
*Trinity Hall*, black and white.

**Oxford Boat Crews,** dark blue.
*Balliol*, pink, white, blue, white, pink.
*Brazenose*, black, and gold edges.
*Christ Church*, blue with red cardinal's hat.
*Corpus*, red with blue stripe.
*St Edmund Hall*, red, and yellow edges.
*Exeter*, black, and red edges.
*Jesus*, green, and white edges.
*John's*, yellow, black, red.
*Lincoln*, blue with mitre.
*Magdalen*, black and white.
*Merton*, blue, with white edges and red cross.
*New College*, three pink and two white stripes.
*Oriel*, blue and white.
*Pembroke*, pink, white, pink.
*Queen's*, red, white, blue, white, blue, white, red.
*Trinity*, blue, with double dragon's head, yellow and green, or blue with white edges.
*University*, blue, and yellow edges.
*Wadham*, light blue.
*Worcester*, blue, white, pink, white, blue.

**Trinity College, Dublin.**
*Boat Crews*, black and white.
*Football*, black and red.
*Hockey*, black and green.
*Cricket*, orange and green.

***College Colours*** (America) in football matches, boating, etc.
*Alleghany*, cadet blue and old gold.
*Amherst*, white and purple.
*Bates*, garnet.
*Boston University*, scarlet and white.
*Bowdoin*, white.
*Brown*, brown and white.
*Buchtel*, orange and blue.
*California (Berkeley)*, blue and gold.
*Colby*, silver grey.
*Columbia*, blue and white.
*Cornell*, cornelian and white.
*Dartmouth*, dark green.
*Dickinson*, red and white.
*Hamilton*, rose pink.
*Harvard*, crimson.
*Hobart*, orange and purple.
*Kenyon*, mauve.
*Lafayette*, white and maroon.
*Madison*, orange and maroon.
*Michigan*, blue and maize.
*New York University*, violet.
*Ohio University*, blue.
*Princeton*, orange and black.
*Rensselaer, Polytechnic*, cherry.
*Rochester*, blue and grey.
*Rutgers*, scarlet.
*Swarthmore*, garnet.
*Syracuse*, blue and pink.
*Trinity*, white and green.
*University of North Carolina*, white and blue.
*University of South Carolina*, red and blue.
*University of Pennsylvania*, blue and red.
*University of the South*, red and blue.
*University of Vermont*, old gold and green.
*University of Virginia*, cardinal and grey.
*Vassar*, pink and grey.
*Wesleyan*, cardinal and black.
*Williams*, royal purple.
*Wooster*, old gold.
*Yale*, blue.

**College Port.** The worst species of red wine that can be manufactured and palmed off upon young men at college.

**Colliberts.** A sort of gypsy race, similar to the *Cagots* of Gascony and the *Caqueux* of Brittany, who lived on boats in the rivers, chiefly in Poitou, now nearly extinct. In feudal times a collibert was a serf partly free, but bound to certain services. (Lat. *collibertus*, a fellow freedman.)

**Colluthians.** A religious sect which rose in the 4th century; so called from Colluthos of Alexandria, their founder.

**Colly, my Cow.** *Colly* is an old term of endearment for a cow, and properly refers only to a polled cow, one deprived of its horns. It is from

Scan. *Kolla*, a beast without horns (Icel. *kollr*, a shaven crown).

**Collyridians.** A sect of Arabian Christians, chiefly women, which first appeared in 373. They worshipped the Virgin Mary, and made offerings to her in a twisted cake (Gr. *kollura*).

**Collywobbles.** The gripes, or stomach-ache, usually accompanied with sundry rumblings in the stomach.

**Cologne.** ***The three kings of Cologne.*** The three Wise Men of the East, the Magi (*q.v.*), Gaspar, Melchior, and Balthazar, whose bones, according to mediaeval legend, were deposited in Cologne Cathedral.

**Colombier.** A standard size of drawing and plate papers measuring 23½ by 34½ inches. The name is derived from an ancient watermark of a dove (Fr. *colombe*), the emblem of the Holy Ghost.

**Colon.** One of the rabble leaders in *Hudibras* was Noel Perryan, or Ned Perry, an ostler, who loved bear-baiting, but was a very strait-laced Puritan of low morals.

**Colonnade, The.** *See* Cynic Tub.

**Colophon.** The end of a book; the statement containing information about the date, place, printer, and edition which, in the early days of printing, was given at the end of the book but which now appears on the title page. From Gr. *kolophon*, the top or summit, a word which, according to Strabo, is from Colophon, a city of Ionia, the inhabitants of which were such excellent horsemen that they would turn the scale of battle to the side on which they fought; hence *To add a colophon* means 'to supply the finishing stroke'.

> The volume was uninjured ... from title-page to celophon. Scott, *The Antiquary*

**Coloquintida, St.** Charles I was so called by the Levellers (*q.v.*), to whom he was as bitter as gall, or coloquintida (colocynth), the bitter-apple.

> The Levellers styled him [Charles I] an Ahab, and a Coloquintida, a man of blood, and the everlasting obstacle to peace and liberty.
>
> Howitt, *History of England*, ch. vi

**Colorado** (US America). The river (and hence the State) was so named by the Spanish explorers from its *coloured* (i.e. reddish) appearance.

**Colosseum.** The groat Flavian amphitheatre of ancient Rome, said to be so named from the colossal statue of Nero that stood close by in the Via Sacra. It was begun by Vespasian in AD 72, and for 400 years was the scene of the gladiatorial contests. The ruins remaining are still colossal and extensive, but quite two-thirds of the original building have been taken away at different times and used for building material.

Byron, adapting the exclamation of the 8th century pilgrims (and adopting a bad spelling), says:

> While stands the Coliseum, Rome shall stand;
> When falls the Coliseum, Rome shall fall;
> And when Rome falls – the world.
>
> *Childe Harold*, IV, cxlv

The name has since been applied to other amphitheatres and places of amusement. *Cp.* Palladium.

**Colossus** or **Colossos** (Lat. and Gr. for a gigantic statue). The Colossus of Rhodes, completed probably about 280 BC, was a representation of the sun-god, Helios, and commemorated the successful defence of Rhodes against Demetrius Poliorcetes in 304 BC. It was one of the Seven Wonders of the World; it stood 105 ft high, and is said to have been made from the warlike engines abandoned by Demetrius by the Rhodian sculptor Chares, a pupil of Lysippus. The story that it was built striding across the harbour and that ships could pass full sail, between its legs, rose in the 16th century, and has nothing to support it; neither Strabo nor Pliny makes mention of it, though both describe the statue minutely. Tickell out-herods Herod in the following lines:

> So, near proud Rhodes, across the raging flood,
> Stupendous form! the vast Colossus stood,
> While at one foot the thronging galleys ride,
> A whole hour's sail scarce reached the further side;
> Betwixt his brazen thighs, in loose array,
> Ten thousand streamers on the billows play.
>
> *On the Prospect of Peace*

> He doth bestride the narrow world
> Like a Colossus.
>
> Shakspeare, *Julius Caesar*, 1, 2

**Colour. Phrases.** ***A man of colour.*** A negro, or, more strictly speaking, one with negro blood.

> There are three great classes: (1) the pure whites, (2) the people of colour; (3) negroes and mulattoes. Edwards, *St Domingo*, i

***His coward lips did from their colour fly*** (Shakespeare, *Julius Caesar*, 1, 2). He was unable to speak. As cowards run away from their regimental colour, so Caesar's lips, when he was ill, ran away from their colour and turned pale.

***I should like to see the colour of your money.*** I should like to have some proof that you have any; I should like to receive payment.

***Off colour.*** Not up to the mark; run down; seedy; tainted.

***To change colour.*** To blush; especially to look awkward and perplexed when found out in some deceit or meanness.

***To colour up.*** To turn red in the face; to blush.

***To come off with flying colours.*** To be completely triumphant, to win 'hands down'. The allusion is to a victorious fleet sailing into port with all the flags flying at the mastheads.

***To come out in his true colours.*** To reveal one's proper character, divested of all that is meretricious.

***To describe (a matter) in very black colours.*** To see it with a jaundiced eye, and describe it accordingly; to describe it under the bias of strong prejudice.

***To desert one's colours.*** To become a turncoat; to turn tail. The allusion is to the military flag.

***To give colour*** or ***some plausible colour to the matter.*** To render it more plausible; to give it a more specious appearance.

***To paint in bright*** or ***lively colours.*** To see or describe things in *couleur de rose*.

***To put a false colour on a matter.*** To misinterpret it, or put a false construction on it.

***To sail under false colours.*** To act hypocritically; to try to attain one's object by appearing to be other than you are. The term is a nautical one, and refers to the practice of pirates approaching their unsuspecting prey with false colours at the mast.

***To see things in their true colours.*** To see them as they really are.

***Under colour of.*** Under pretence of; under the alleged authority of.

***Wearing his colours.*** Taking his part; being strongly attached to one. The idea is from livery.

> Jim could always count on every man, woman, and child, wherever he lived, wearing his colours, and backing him … through thick and thin.
>
> Boldrewood, *Robbery Under Arms*, ch. xiv

***With colours nailed to the mast.*** *À outrance*; to the bitter end. If the colours are nailed to the mast, they cannot be lowered to express submission.

> If they catch you at disadvantage, the mines for your life is the word; and so we fight them with our colours nailed to the mast.
>
> Scott, *The Pirate*, ch. xxi

***With the colours.*** Said of a soldier who is on the active strength of a regiment, as opposed to one in the reserve.

> The period … was raised from seven to nine years, *five* years being passed with the colours, and *four* in the reserve.
>
> *Edinburgh Review* (1886)

**Colours. Technical Terms. *Accidental colours.*** Those colours seen on a white ground after looking for some time at a bright object, such as the sun. The accidental colour of *red* is bluish green, of *orange* dark blue, of *violet* yellow, and the converse.

***Complementary colours.*** Colours which, in combination, produce white light.

> The colour transmitted is always complementary to the one reflected.
>
> Brewster, *Optics*, xii

***Fast colours.*** Colours which do not wash out in water.

***Fundamental colours.*** The seven colours of the spectrum: violet, indigo, blue, green, yellow, orange, and red.

***Primary,*** or ***simple colours.*** Colours which cannot be produced by mixing other colours. Those generally accepted as primary are red, yellow, and blue, but violet is sometimes substituted for the last named.

***Secondary colours.*** Those which result from the mixture of two or more primary colours, such as orange, green, and purple.

**College Colours.** *See* College.

**Colours, National.**

| | |
|---|---|
| Great Britain | *Red, white, and blue.* |
| Argentine | *Blue and white.* |
| Austria | *Red, white, and red.* |
| Belgium | *Black, yellow, and red.* |
| Bolivia | *Red, yellow, and green.* |
| Brazil | *Green and yellow.* |
| Bulgaria | *White, green, and red.* |
| Chili | *White, blue and red.* |
| China | *Yellow ochre.* |
| Colombia | *Yellow, blue, and red.* |
| Costa Rica | *Blue, white, red, white, and blue.* |
| Cuba | *Five horizontal stripes, blue and white.* |
| Denmark | *Red, with white cross.* |
| Ecuador | *Three horizontal stripes, yellow, blue, and red, the yellow being twice the width of the others.* |
| France | *Blue, white, and red, vertical stripes.* |
| Germany | *Black, red, and white* (Imperial); *Black, red and gold* (Republican). |
| Greece | *Nine horizontal stripes, blue and white.* |
| Guatemala | *Blue, white, and blue, vertical stripes.* |
| Hayti | *Blue and red.* |

| | |
|---|---|
| Honduras | *Blue, white, and blue, horizontal stripes.* |
| Irish Free State | *Orange, white and green.* |
| Italy | *Green, white, and red, vertical stripes.* |
| Japan | *White, with red disk in centre, from which spring sixteen red rays to edge.* |
| Liberia | *Eleven horizontal stripes, red and white.* |
| Luxemburg | *Red, white, and blue.* |
| Morocco | *Red.* |
| Mexico | *Green, white, and red, vertical stripes.* |
| Monaco | *Red and while, horizontal.* |
| Netherlands | *Red, white, and blue, horizontal stripes.* |
| Nicaragua | *Blue, white, and blue, horizontal stripes.* |
| Norway | *Red, with blue cross bordered with white.* |
| Panama | *Blue, white, red.* |
| Paraguay | *Red, white, blue, in horizontal stripes.* |
| Peru | *Red, white, and red, vertical stripes.* |
| Persia | *White, top edge green, bottom edge red.* |
| Portugal | *Red and green.* |
| Roumania | *Blue, yellow, and red, vertical stripes.* |
| Russia | *White, with blue St Andrew's cross.* |
| Salvador | *Nine horizontal stripes, blue and white.* |
| Serbia | *Red, blue, and white.* |
| Siam | *Red, with a white elephant.* |
| Sweden | *Blue, with yellow cross.* |
| Switzerland | *Red, with white cross.* |
| Turkey | *Green and red.* |
| Uruguay | *Nine horizontal stripes, blue and white.* |
| United States | *Stars on blue, white with red stripes.* |
| Venezuela | *Yellow, blue, and red, horizontal stripes.* |

**Colours: In symbolism, ecclesiastical use,** etc.

**Black:**

*In blazonry*, sable, signifying prudence, wisdom, and constancy; it is engraved by perpendicular and horizontal lines crossing each other at right angles.

*In art*, signifying evil, falsehood, and error.

*In Church decoration* it is used for Good Friday.

*As a mortuary colour*, signifying grief, despair, death. (In the Catholic Church violet may be substituted for black.)

*In metals* it is represented by lead.

*In precious stones* it is represented by the diamond.

*In planets* it stands for Saturn.

**Blue:**

Hope, love of divine works; (in dresses) divine contemplation, piety, sincerity.

*In blazonry*, azure, signifying chastity, loyalty, fidelity; it is engraved by horizontal lines.

*In art* (as an angel's robe) it signifies fidelity and faith; (as the robe of the Virgin Mary), modesty and (in the Catholic Church) humility and expiation.

*In Church decoration*, blue and green are used indifferently for ordinary Sundays, and blue for all weekdays after Trinity Sunday.

*As a mortuary colour* it signifies eternity (applied to Deity), immortality (applied to man).

*In metals* it is represented by tin.

*In precious stones* it is represented by sapphire.

*In planets* it stands for Jupiter.

**Pale Blue:**

Peace, Christian prudence, love of good works, a serene conscience.

**Green:**

Faith, gladness, immortality, the resurrection of the just; (in dresses) the gladness of the faithful.

*In blazonry*, vert, signifying love, joy, abundance; it is engraved from left to right.

*In art*, signifying hope, joy, youth, spring (among the Greeks and Moors it signifies victory).

*In Church decoration* it signifies God's bounty, mirth, gladness, the resurrection, and is used indifferently with blue for ordinary Sundays.

*In metals* it is represented by copper.

*In precious stones* it is represented by the emerald.

*In planets* it stands for Venus.

*As a railway signal* it means caution, go slowly.

**Pale Green:**

Baptism.

**Purple:**

Justice, royalty.

*In blazonry*, purpure, signifying temperance; it is engraved by lines slanting from right to left.

*In art*, signifying royalty.

*In metals* it is represented by quicksilver.

*In precious stones* it is represented by amethyst.

*In planets* it stands for Mercury.

**Red:**

Martyrdom for faith, charity; (in dresses) divine love. Innocent III says of martyrs and apostles, *'Hi et illi sunt flores rosarum et lilia convallium.'* (*De Sacr. alto Myst.*, i, 64.)

*In blazonry*, gules; blood-red is called sanguine. The former signifies magnanimity, and the latter, fortitude; it is engraved by perpendicular lines.

*In Church decoration* it is used for martyrs, for Ash Wednesday, for the last three days of Holy Week, and for Whit Sunday.

*In metals* it is represented by iron (the metal of war).

*In precious stones* it is represented by the ruby.

*In planets* it stands for Mars.

**White:**
*In blazonry*, argent; signifying purity, truth, innocence; in engravings *argent* is left blank.
*In art*, priests, Magi, and Druids are arrayed in white. Jesus after the resurrection should be draped in white.
*In Church decoration* it is used for festivals of our Lord, for Easter, and for all Saints except Martyrs.
*As a mortuary colour* it indicates hope.
*In metals* it is represented by silver.
*In precious stones* it is represented by the pearl.
*In planets* it stands for Diana or the Moon.

**Yellow:**
*In blazonry*, or; signifying faith, constancy, wisdom, glory; in engravings it is shown by dots.
*In modern art* or signifying jealousy, inconstancy, incontinence. In France the doors of traitors used to be daubed with yellow, and in some countries Jews were obliged to dress in yellow. In Spain the executioner is dressed in red and yellow.
*In Christian art* Judas is arrayed in yellow; but St Peter is also arrayed in golden yellow.
*In metals* it is represented by gold.
*In precious stones* it is represented by the topaz.
*In planets* it stands for Apollo or the Sun.

**Violet, Brown,** or **Grey**
are used in *Church decoration* for Advent and Lent; and in other symbolism *violet* usually stands for penitence, and *grey* for tribulation.

**Colours of University Boats,** etc. *See* College Colours.

**Colour-blindness.** In capacity of discerning one colour from another. The term was introduced by Sir David Brewster; formerly it was known as *Daltonism*, because it was first described by John Dalton, the scientist (who himself suffered from it), in 1794. It is of three sorts: (1) inability to discern any colours, so that everything is either black or white, shade or light; (2) inability to distinguish between primary colours, as red, blue, and yellow; or secondary colours, as green, purple, and orange; and (3) inability to distinguish between such composite colours as browns, greys, and neutral tints. Except in this one respect, the colour-blind may have excellent vision.

**Colour Sergeant.** The senior non-commissioned officer of a company of infantry. He used to have charge of the regimental colours in the field.

**Colporteur.** A hawker or pedlar; so called because he carries his basket or pack round his neck (Fr. *col*, neck, *porter*, to carry). The term is more especially applied to hawkers of religious books.

**Colt.** A person new to office; an awkward young fellow who needs 'breaking in'; specifically, in legal use, a barrister who attended a sergeant-at-law at his induction.

> I accompanied the newly made Chief Baron as his colt.
> Pollock

And in cricket, a professional during his first season in first-class cricket.

The word is used as an abbreviation for 'Colt's Revolver', patented by Col. Sam. Colt (USA) in 1835; and it is also an old nautical term for a piece of knotted rope 18 inches long for the special benefit of ship boys; a cat-o'-nine-tails.

> Look alive there, lads, or as sure as my name is Sam Weston I'll give the colt to the last man off the deck.
> J. Grant, *Dick Rodney*, ch. vii

***To colt.*** Obsolete slang for to befool, gull, cheat.

> *Harebrain*. We are fools, tame fools!
> *Bellamore*. Come, let's go seek him.
> He shall be hanged before he colt us so basely.
> Beaumont and Fletcher, *Wit Without Money*, III, ii

The verb is still used in provincial dialects for making a new-comer pay his footing.

**Colt-pixy.** A pixy, puck, or mischievous fairy. *To colt-pixy* is to take what belongs to the pixies, and is specially applied to the gleaning of apples after the crop has been gathered in.

**Colt's-tooth.** The love of youthful pleasure. Chaucer uses the word 'coltish' for skittish, and his Wife of Bath says:

> He was, I trowe, a twenty winter old,
> And I was fourty, if I shal seye sooth;
> But yet I hadde alwey a coltes tooth.
> *Prologue*, 602

Horses have colt's teeth at three years old, a period of their life when their passions are strongest.

> Well, said Lord Sands;
> Your colt's-tooth is not cast yet.
> Shakespeare, *Henry VIII*, 1, 3

> Her merry dancing-days are done;
> She has a colt's-tooth still, I warrant.
> King, *Orpheus and Eurydice*

**Columbine.** A stock character in old Italian comedy, where she first appeared about 1560, and thence transplanted to English pantomime. She was the daughter of Pantaloon (*q.v.*), and the sweetheart of Harlequin (*q.v.*), and, like him, was supposed to be invisible to mortal eyes. *Columbina* in Italian is a pet name for a lady-love, and means dove-like.

**Columbus of the Skies, The.** Sir William Herschel (1738–1822), discoverer of Uranus, was so called.

**Column. *The Column of Antoninus*.** Erected at Rome in AD 174, in memory of the Emperor Marcus Aurelius Antoninus. Like that of Trajan (*q.v.*), this column is covered externally with spiral bas-reliefs representing the wars carried on by the emperor. It is a Roman Doric column of marble on a square pedestal, and (omitting the statue) is 123 ft in height.

Sixtus V caused the original statue of this column to be supplanted by a figure of St Paul.

***The Column at Boulogne,*** or 'The Column of the Grand Army'; a marble Doric column, 176 ft high, surmounted by a bronze statue of Napoleon I, to commemorate the camp of Boulogne, formed 1804–5 with the intention of invading England.

***The Duke of York's Column,*** in London, at the top of the 'Waterloo Steps' leading from Waterloo Place into the Mall. Erected in 1830–3 in memory of Frederick, Duke of York, second son of George III, who died in 1827. It is of the Tuscan order, was designed by R. Wyatt, and is made of Aberdeen granite. It is 124 ft in height; it contains a winding staircase to the platform, and on the summit is a statue of the duke by Sir R. Westmacott.

***Columns,*** or ***Pillars, of Hercules.*** *See* Pillar.

***The Column of July.*** Erected in Paris in 1840, on the spot where the Bastille stood, to commemorate the revolution of July, 1830, when Charles X abdicated. It is a bronze Corinthian column, 13 ft in diameter and 154 ft in height, and is surmounted by a gilded statue of Liberty.

***London's Column.*** *See* Monument.

***The Nelson Column.*** In Trafalgar Square, London; was erected in 1843. The four lions, by Landseer, were added in 1867. It is a Corinthian column of Devonshire granite on a square base, copied from a column in the temple of Mars Ultor (the avenging god of war) at Rome; it stands 145 ft high, the statue surmounting it (by E. H. Baily, R.A.) being 17 ft high. The following reliefs in bronze are on the sides of the pedestal – (*North*) the battle of the Nile, where Nelson was wounded; (*south*) Nelson's death at the battle of Trafalgar; (*east*) the bombardment of Copenhagen; and (*west*) the battle of St Vincent.

***Column of the Place Vendôme.*** Paris, 1806–10; made of marble encased with bronze, and erected in honour of Napoleon I. The spiral outside represents in bas-relief the battles of Napoleon I, ending with Austerlitz in 1805. It is 142 ft in height and is an imitation of Trajan's Column. In 1871 the statue of Napoleon, which surmounted it, was hurled to the ground by the Communists, but in 1874 a statue of Liberty was substituted.

***Trajan's Column.*** At Rome; made of marble AD 114, by Apollodorus. It is a Roman Doric column of marble, 127½ ft in height, on a square pedestal, and has inside a spiral staircase of 185 steps lighted by 40 windows. It was surmounted by a statue of the Emperor Trajan, but Sixtus V supplanted the original statue by that of St Peter. The spiral outside represents in bas-reliefs the battles of the emperor.

**Coma Berenices.** *See* Berenice.

**Comazant.** Another name for Corposant (*q.v.*).

**Comb.** ***A crabtree comb.*** Slang for a cudgel. To smooth your hair with a crabtree comb, is to give the head a knock with a stick.

***Reynard's wonderful comb.*** This comb existed only in the brain of Master Fox. He said it was made of the Panthera's bone, the perfume of which was so fragrant that no one could resist following it; and the wearer of the comb was always cheerful and merry. (*Reynard the Fox.*)

***To comb one's head.*** To humiliate a person, or to give him a 'set down'.

> I'll carry you with me to my country box, and keep you out of harm's way, till I find you a wife who will comb your head for you.
>
> Bulwer-Lytton, *What will he do with it?*, iv, 16

***To comb out.*** To disentangle the hair, or remove foreign bodies from it, with a comb. During the Great War the term was given a slang use in connection with the English recruiting campaigns under the Military Service Acts. *A comb-out* was a thorough clearing out or clean sweep of men of military age in offices, works, etc., and getting them into the Army. Certain papers were constantly urging the authorities to *apply the comb* to the Government offices.

***To comb the cat.*** An old military and naval phrase for untangling the cords of a cat-o'-nine-tails by drawing it through the fingers.

***To comb your noddle with a three-legged stool*** (*Taming of the Shrew*, 1, 1) is to beat you about the head with a stool. Many stools, such as those used by milkmaids, are still made with three legs; and these handy weapons seem to have been used at one time pretty freely, especially by angry women.

***To cut one's comb.*** To take down a person's conceit. In allusion to the practice of cutting the combs of capons.

***To set up one's comb.*** To be cockish and vainglorious.

**Come and take them.** The reply of Leonidas, King of Sparta, to the messengers sent by Xerxes to Thermopylae. Xerxes said, 'Go, and tell those madmen to deliver up their arms.'

Leonidas replied, 'Go, and tell Xerxes to come and take them.'

**Come. *A come down.*** Loss of prestige or position.

> 'Now I'm your worship's washerwoman.' The dignitary coloured, and said that 'this was rather a come down'. Reade

***Can you come that?*** Can you equal it? Here, 'come' means to arrive at, to accomplish.

***Come February, Michaelmas, etc.*** A colloquialism for 'next February', etc.

> Come Lammas-eve at night shall she be fourteen.
> Shakespeare, *Romeo and Juliet*, 1, 3

***Come home.*** Return to your house; to touch one's feelings or interest.

> I doe now publish my Essayes; which, of all my other workes, have been most currant: for that, as it seems, they come home to men's businesse and bosomes.
> Bacon, *Epistle Dedicatory to the Essays*, 1625

***Come inside!*** A humorously scornful remark made to one who is talking nonsense or behaving in an idiotic manner. The allusion is to a picture in *Punch* showing a lunatic looking over the wall of an asylum at an angler fishing; and, when he hears that the latter has been there all day without getting a bite and proposes still to remain, the lunatic feelingly invites him to 'come inside' to the asylum.

***Come out.*** Said of a young lady after she has been introduced at Court, or has entered into society as a 'grown up' person. She 'comes out into society'.

***Don't try to come it over me.*** Don't try to boss me or order me about; don't set yourself in a position above me.

***Has he come it?*** Has he lent the money? Has he hearkened to your request? Has he come over to your side?

***If the worst come to the worst.*** *See* Worst.

***Marry come up!*** *See* Marry.

***To come a cropper.*** *See* Cropper.

***To come down a peg.*** *See* Peg.

***To come down handsome.*** To pay a good price, reward, subscription, etc.

***To come down upon one.*** To reproach, to punish severely, to make a peremptory demand.

***To come it strong.*** To lay it on thick; to exaggerate or overdo. *See* Draw it Mild.

***To come off.*** To occur, to take place, as 'my little holiday didn't come off after all'.

***To come off with honours.*** To proceed to the end successfully.

***To come over one.*** To wheedle one to do or give something; to cheat or overreach one; to conquer or get your own way.

***To come round.*** *See* Coming.

***To come short.*** Not to be sufficient. 'To come short of' means to miss or fail of attaining.

***To come the old soldier over one.*** To attempt to intimidate or bully one by an assumption of authority.

***To come the religious dodge.*** *See* Dodge.

***To come to.*** To amount to, to obtain possession. 'It will not come to much.'

***To come to blows.*** To start fighting.

***To come to grief, to hand.*** *See* Grief; Hand.

***To come to oneself.*** To regain consciousness after a fainting-fit, etc.

***To come to pass.*** To happen, to befall, to come about.

> What thou hast spoken is come to pass.
> Jer. 32:24
>
> It came to pass in those days that there went out a decree. Luke 2:1

***To come to stay.*** An American expression, used of something which possesses permanent qualities. 'Summer-time', for instance, being beneficial nearly all round, has 'come to stay'.

***To come to the hammer, the point, the scratch.*** *See* Hammer, Point, Scratch.

***To come under.*** To fall under; to be classed under.

***To come up smiling.*** To laugh at discomfiture or punishment; to emerge from disaster unruffled.

***To come up to.*** To equal, to obtain the same number of marks, to amount to the same quantity.

***To come upon the parish.*** To live in the workhouse; to be supported by the parish.

***To come Yorkshire over one.*** To bamboozle one, to overreach one. *See* Yorkshire.

***What's to come of it? What's to come of him?*** A contracted form of *become*. To *come of a good stock* is to be descended from a good family.

**Comedy** means a village song (Gr. *kome-ode*), referring to the village merry-makings, in which comic songs still take a conspicuous place. The Greeks had certain festal processions of great licentiousness, held in honour of Dionysos, in the suburbs of their cities, and termed *komoi* or village revels. On these occasions an ode was generally sung, and this ode was the foundation of Greek comedy. *Cp.* Tragedy.

***The Father of comedy.*** Aristophanes (about 450–380 BC), the Athenian dramatist.

**Comet Wine.** A term denoting wine of superior quality. A notion prevailed that the grapes of 'comet years', i.e. years in which remarkable comets appear, are better in flavour than those of other years.

> The old gentleman yet nurses some few bottles of the famous comet year (i.e. 1811), emphatically called comet wine. *The Times*

**Coming Round. *He is coming round.*** Recovering from sickness; recovering from a fit of the sulks; returning to friendship. Death is the end of life, and therefore recovering from 'sickness nigh unto death' is coming round the corner.

**Command Night.** In theatrical parlance, a night on which a certain play is performed by Royal command.

**Commandment. *The ten commandments.*** A common piece of slang in Elizabethan days for the ten fingers or nails.

> Could I come near your beauty with my nails
> I'd set my ten commandments in your face.
> Shakespeare, *2 Henry VI*, 1, 3

> As soon as you see the planets are out, in with you, and be busy with the ten commandments, under the sly.
> Longfellow, *Spanish Student*, III, v

***The eleventh commandment.*** An ironical expression, signifying either 'Don't tell tales out of school,' 'Nothing succeeds like success,' or 'Thou shalt not be found out.'

> After all, that Eleventh Commandment is the only one that is vitally important to keep in these days.
> B. H. Buxton, *Jennie of the Prince's*, iii, 314

**Comme il faut** (Fr.). As it should be; quite proper; quite according to etiquette or rule.

> It never can have been *comme il faut* in any age or nation for a man of note ... to be continually asking for money.
> Macaulay, *Trevelyan's Life*, vol. ii, ch. xiv

**Commendam. *A living in commendam*** is a living temporarily held by someone until an incumbent is appointed. The term was specially applied to a bishop who, when accepting the bishopric, had to give up all his preferments, but to whom such preferments were *commended* by the Crown till they could be properly transferred. This practice was abolished by Art of Parliament in 1836.

**Committee. *A committee of the whole house,*** in Parliamentary language, is when the Speaker leaves the chair and all the members form a committee, where anyone may speak once or more than once. In such cases the chair is occupied by the Chairman of Committees, elected with each new Parliament.

***A joint committee*** is a committee nominated partly by the House of Lords and partly by the House of Commons.

***A standing committee*** is a committee which continues to the end of the current session. To this committee are referred all questions which fall within the scope of their appointment.

**Commodore.** A corruption of 'commander' (Fr. *commandeur*; Dut. *kommandeur*). A naval officer ranking above a captain and below a rear-admiral, ranking with brigadier-generals in the army. By courtesy the title is given to the senior captain when two or more ships are in company; also to the president of a yacht club.

In the United States Navy the office has been abolished since 1899, but the title was retained as a retiring rank for captains.

**Common Pleas.** Civil actions at law brought by one subject against another – not by the Crown against a subject. The *Court of Common Pleas* was for the trial of civil (not capital) offences; in 1875 it was abolished, and in 1880 it was represented by the Common Pleas Division and merged in the King's Bench Division.

**Common Prayer. *The Book of Common Prayer.*** The book used by the Established Church of England in 'divine service'. Common, in this case, means *united*, or *general.*

> The first complete English Book of Common Prayer (known as the First Prayer-book of Edward VI) appeared in 1549; this was revised in 1552 and 1559; slight alterations were made at the Hampton Court Conference (1604), and it received its final form, except for some very minor changes after the Savoy Conference of 1662.

**Common Sense.** Natural intelligence; good, sound, practical sense; general sagacity. Formerly the expression denoted a supposed internal sense held to be common to all five senses, or one that acted as a bond or connecting medium for them.

**Commoner. *The Great Commoner.*** The elder William Pitt (1708–78), afterwards Earl of Chatham.

**Commons. *To put one on short commons.*** To stint him, to give him scanty meals. In the University of Cambridge the food provided for each student at breakfast is called his *commons*; hence food in general or meals.

***To come into commons.*** To enter a society in which the members have a common or general dinner table. To be removed from the society is to be *discommonsed*:

> He [Dryden] was in trouble [at Cambridge] on July 19th, 1652, when he was discommonsed and gated for a fortnight for disobedience and contumacy. Saintsbury, *Dryden*, ch. i

**Commonwealths, Ideal.** The most famous ideal, or imaginary, Commonwealths are those sketched by Plato in the *Republic* (from which all the others derive), by Cicero in his *De Republica*, by St Augustine in his *De Civitate Dei* (*The City of God*), by Dante in his *De Monarchia*, by Sir Thomas More in *Utopia* (1516), by Bacon in the *New Atlantis* (a fragment, 1616), by Campanella, a Dominican friar (about 1630), and Samuel Butler's *Erewhon* (1872).

To these some would add Johnson's *Rasselas* (1759), Lytton's *Coming Race* (1871), Bellamy's *Looking Backward* (1888), Wm Morris's *News from Nowhere* (1891), and some of Mr H. G. Wells's romances, such as *In the Days of the Comet* (1906) and *The World Set Free* (1914).

**Communist.** An advanced socialist; an adherent of communism.

> Communism means a self-supporting society distinguished by common labour, common property, and common means of intelligence and recreation.
> G. J. Holyoake in '*The Labour World*', No. 11, 1890

The difference between a communist and a socialist seems to be that the latter believes in payment according to work done and the former does not.

**Comnal.** The father of Fingal (*q.v.*).

**Companion Ladder.** The ladder leading from the poop to the main deck, also the staircase from the deck to a cabin.

**Companions of Jehu.** The *Chouans* (*q.v.*) were so called, from a fanciful analogy between their self-imposed task and that appointed to Jehu, on being set over the kingdom of Israel. Jehu was to cut off Ahab and Jezebel, with all their house, and all the priests of Baal. The Chouans were to cut off all who assassinated Louis XVI, and see that his brother (*Jehu*) was placed on the throne.

**Comparisons are Odorous.** So says Dogberry. (*Much Ado about Nothing*, 3, 5.)

> We own your verses are melodious,
> But then comparisons are odious.
> Swift, *Answer to Sheridan's 'Simile'*.

**Compass, Mariner's.** *See* Mariner's Compass.

**Complementary Colours.** *See* Colours.

**Compline.** The last of the seven canonical hours in the Roman Catholic Church, said about 8 or 9 p.m., and so called because it *completes* the series of the daily prayers or hours. From M.E. and O.Fr. *complie*, Lat. *completa* (hora).

In ecclesiastical Lat. *vesperinus*, from *vesper*, means evening service, and *completinus* seems to be formed on the same model.

**Complutensian Polyglot.** *See* Bible, specially named.

**Compos Mentis.** *See* Non compos mentis.

**Compostella.** The city in Spain where are preserved the relics of St James the Great; a corruption of *Giacomo-postolo* (James the Apostle). Its full name is Santiago (i.e. St James) de Compostella. *See* James, St.

*Compostella, Sacred chickens of. See* Adept.

**Compte rendu** (Fr.). The account already sent; the account of particulars delivered; a report of proceedings.

**Comrades.** Literally, those who sleep in the same *chamber* (*camera*). It is a Spanish military term derived from the custom of dividing soldiers into chambers, and the early form of the word in English is *camerade*.

**Comus.** In Milton's masque of this name, the god of sensual pleasure, son of Bacchus and Circe. The name is from the Gr. *komos*, carousal.

In the masque the elder brother is meant for Viscount Brackley, the younger brother is Mr Thomas Egerton, and the lady is Lady Alice Egerton, children of the Earl of Bridgewater, at whose castle in Ludlow it was first presented in 1634.

**Con amore** (Ital.). With heart and soul; as, 'He did it *con amore*' – i.e. lovingly, with delight, and therefore in good earnest.

**Con commodo** (Ital.). At a convenient rate. A musical term.

**Con spirito** (Ital.). With quickness and vivacity. A musical term.

**Conan.** The Thersites of *Fingal* (in Macpherson's *Ossian*); brave even to rashness.

***Blow for blow,*** or ***claw for claw, as Conan said.*** Conan made a vow never to take a blow without returning it; when he descended into the infernal regions, the arch fiend gave him a cuff, which Conan instantly returned, saying 'Claw for claw.'

> 'Blow for blow,' as Conan said to the devil.
> Scott, *Waverley*, ch. xxii

**Conceptionists.** *See* Franciscans.

**Concert Pitch.** The degree of sharpness or flatness adopted by musicians acting in concert, that all the instruments may be in accord. In England 'concert pitch' is usually slightly higher than the pitch at which instruments are generally tuned.

Hence the figurative use of the term: *to screw oneself up to concert pitch* is to make oneself absolutely ready, prepared for any emergency or anything one may have to do.

**Concerto** (Ital.). A composition in three movements intended to display the powers of some particular instrument, with orchestral accompaniments.

**Conchy.** *See* Conscientious Objector.

**Concierge** (Fr.). The door-porter of a public building, an hotel, or a house divided into flats, etc.

**Conciergerie** (Fr.). The office or room of a concierge, a porter's lodge; a state prison. During the Revolution it was the prison where the chief victims were confined prior to execution.

**Conclamatio.** Amongst the ancient Romans, the loud cry raised by those standing round a deathbed at the moment of death. It probably had its origin in the idea of calling back the departed spirit, and was similar to the Irish howl over the dead. 'One not howled over' (*corpus nondum conclamatum*) meant one at the point of death; and 'one howled for' was one given up for dead or really deceased. Hence the phrase *conclamatum est*, he is dead past all hope, he has been called and gives no sign. Virgil makes the palace ring with howls when Dido burnt herself to death.

> Lamentis, gemituque, et faemineo ululato,
> Texta fremunt. *Aeneid*, iv, 667

**Conclave.** Literally, a set of rooms, all of which can be opened by one key (Lat. *con clavis*). The word is applied to the little cells erected for the cardinals who meet to choose a new Pope; hence, the assembly of cardinals for this purpose; hence, any private assembly for discussion. Shakespeare used the word for the body of cardinals itself:

> And once more in my arms I bid him [Cardinal Campeius] welcome,
> And thank the holy conclave for their loves.
> *Henry VIII*, 2, 2

**Concordat.** An agreement made between a ruler and the Pope; as the Concordat of 1801 between Napoleon and Pius VII; the Concordat of 1516 between François I and Leo X to abolish the 'pragmatic sanction'; and the Germanic Concordat of 1448 between Frederick III and Nicholas V.

**Concrete Numbers.** *See* Abstract.

**Condottieri.** Leaders of mercenaries and military adventurers, particularly from about the 14th to 16th centuries. The most noted of these brigand chiefs in Italy were Guarnieri, Lando, Francesco of Carmagnola, and Francesco Sforza. The singular is Condottiere.

**Confederate States.** The eleven States which seceded from the Union in the American Civil War (1861–66) – viz. Georgia, North and South Carolina, Virginia, Tennessee, Alabama, Louisiana, Arkansas, Mississippi, Florida, Texas. They were all readmitted into the Union between 1866 and 1870.

**Confederation of the Rhine.** Sixteen German provinces in 1806 dissolved their connection with Germany, and allied themselves with France. It was dissolved in 1813.

**Confusion Worse Confounded.** Disorder made worse than before.

> With ruin upon ruin, rout on rout,
> Confusion worse confounded.
> Milton, *Paradise Lost*, ii, line 996

**Congé** (Fr., leave). 'To give a person his congé' is to dismiss him from your service. 'To take one's congé' is to give notice to friends of your departure. This is done by leaving a card at the friend's house with the letters PPC (*pour prendre congé*, to take leave) inscribed on the left-hand corner.

**Congé d'Elire** (Fr., leave to elect). A royal warrant given to the dean and chapter of a diocese to elect the person nominated by the Crown to their vacant see.

**Congleton Bears.** Men of Congleton. The tradition is that a Congleton parish clerk sold the church Bible to buy a bear, so that the townsmen could have some fun at bear-baiting.

**Congregationalists.** Those Protestant Dissenters who maintain that each congregation is an independent community, and has a right to make its own laws and choose its own minister. They derive from the Puritans and Independents of the time of Queen Elizabeth.

**Congreve Rockets.** A special kind of rocket invented in 1808 for use in war by Sir William Congreve (1772–1828). He was Controller of the Royal Laboratory at Woolwich.

**Congreves.** A predecessor of Lucifer matches, invented by Sir Wm Congreve (*see above*). The splints were first dipped in sulphur, and then tipped with chlorate of potash paste, in which gum was substituted for sugar, and there was added a small quantity of sulphide of antimony. The match was ignited by being drawn through a fold of sandpaper with pressure. *Cp.* Prometheans, Lucifers.

**Conjuring Cap.** ***I must put on my conjuring cap*** – i.e. your question requires deliberate thought, and I must reflect on it. Tradition says that Eric XIV, King of Sweden (1560–77), was a great believer in magic, and had an 'enchanted cap' by means of which he pretended to exercise power over the elements. When a storm arose, his subjects used to say 'The king has got on his conjuring cap'.

**Connecticut,** US America, is the Mohegan dialect *Quonaughicut*, meaning 'long tidal river'. In America the middle *c* is silent – *Conneticut.*

**Connubialis de Mulcibre fecit Apellem.** Love turned a blacksmith into a great artist. Said of Quentin Matsys, the blacksmith of Antwerp, who was in love with an artist's daughter. The father scorned the alliance, and said he should not be accepted unless he made himself a worthy artist. This Matsys did, and won his bride. The sentence may be seen on his monument outside Antwerp Cathedral.

**Conqueror.** *The Conqueror.*

Alexander the Great. *The conqueror of the world.* (356–23 BC.)

Alfonso I, of Portugal. (About 1109–1185).

Aurungzebe the Great. The most powerful of the Moguls. (1619, 1659–1707.)

James I of Aragon. (1206, 1213–76).

Mohammed II, Sultan of Turkey. (1430–81).

Othman or Osman I. Founder of the Turkish power. (1259, 1299–1326.)

Francisco Pizarro. *Conquistador.* So called because he conquered Peru. (1475–1541.)

William, Duke of Normandy. So called because he obtained England by conquest. (1027, 1066–87.)

**Conqueror's Nose.** A prominent straight nose, rising at the bridge. Charlemagne had such a nose, so had Henry the Fowler (Heinrich I of Germany); Rudolf I of Germany; Friedrich I of Hohenzollern, famous for reducing to order his unruly barons by blowing up their castles (1382–1440); our own 'Iron Duke'; Bismarck, the Iron Chancellor of Prussia, etc.

**Conquest, The.** The accession of William I to the crown of England (1066). So called because his right depended on his conquest of Harold, the reigning king.

**Conscience.** ***Conscience clause.*** A clause in an Act of Parliament to relieve persons with conscientious scruples from certain requirements in it. It generally has reference to religious matters, but it came into wider prominence in connection with the Compulsory Vaccination Act of 1898.

***Conscience Money.*** Money paid anonymously to Government by persons who have defrauded the revenue, or who have understated their income to the income-tax assessors. The sum is advertised in the *Gazette.*

***Court of Conscience.*** Established for the recovery of small debts in London and other trading places in the reign of Henry VIII. They were also called Courts of Requests, and are now superseded by county courts.

> Why should not Conscience have vacation,
> As well as other courts o' the nation?
>
> Butler, *Hudibras*, ii, 2

***Have you the conscience to*** [demand such a price]? Can your conscience allow you to [demand such a price]? Conscience is the secret monitor within man which accuses or excuses him, as he does what he thinks to be wrong or right.

***In all conscience.*** As, 'And enough too, in all conscience'. Meaning that the demand made is as much as conscience would tolerate without accusing the person of actual dishonesty; to the verge of that fine line which separates honesty from dishonesty.

***My conscience!*** An oath. I swear by my conscience.

***To make a matter of conscience of it.*** To treat it according to the dictates of conscience, to deal with it conscientiously.

***To speak one's conscience.*** To speak one's own mind, give one's own private thoughts or opinions.

> By my troth, I will speak my conscience of the
> king. Shakespeare, *Henry V*, 1, 4

**Conscientious Objector.** One who takes advantage of a *conscience clause* (*q.v.*), and so does not have to comply with some particular requirement of the law in question. The name used to be applied specially to those who would swear legally that they had a conscientious objection to vaccination; but during the English recruiting campaigns of the Great War it was given – usually with bitterness and contempt – to those who escaped, or attempted to escape, the duty imposed upon all fit men between certain ages of serving with the armed forces of the Crown by producing conscientious objections (on religious grounds) to fighting. These were also known as *Conchies* and *C.O'.s.*

**Conscript Fathers.** In Lat. *Patres Conscripti*. The Roman senate. Romulus instituted a senate consisting of a hundred elders, called *Patres* (Fathers). After the Sabines joined the State, another hundred were added. Tarquinius Priscus, the fifth king, added a third hundred, called *Patres Minorum Gentium*. When Tarquinius Superbus, the seventh and last king of Rome, was banished, several of the senate followed him, and the vacancies were filled up by Junius Brutus, the first consul. The new members were enrolled in the senatorial register, and called *Conscripti*; the entire body was then addressed as *Patres [et] Conscripti* or *Patres, Conscripti.*

**Consentes Dii.** The twelve chief Roman deities – Jupiter, Apollo, Mars, Neptune, Mercury, and Vulcan.

Juno, Vesta, Minerva, Ceres, Diana, and Venus.
Ennius puts them into two hexameter verses:
Juno, Vesta, Minerva, Ceres, Diana, Venus, Mars.
Mercurius, Jovi, Neptunus, Vulcanus, Apollo.
Called '*consentes*', says Varro,
Quia in consilium Jovis adhibebantur.

*De Lingua Latina*, vii, 28

**Consenting Stars.** Stars forming configurations for good or evil. In Judges 5:20, we read that 'the stars in their courses fought against Sisera', i.e. formed unlucky or malignant configurations.

... Scourge the bad revolting stars
That have consented unto Henry's death.

Shakespeare, *1 Henry VI*, 1, 1

**Conservative.** A medium Tory – one who wishes to preserve the union of Church and State, and not radically to alter the constitution. The word was first used in this sense in January, 1830, by J. Wilson Croker in the *Quarterly Review* – 'We have always been conscientiously attached to what is called the Tory, and which might with more propriety be called the Conservative, party' (p. 276).

Canning, ten years previously, had used the word in much the same way in a speech delivered at Liverpool in March, 1820.

**Consistory.** An ecclesiastical court. In the Church of Rome it is the assembly in council of the Pope and cardinals; in England it is a diocesan court, presided over by the chancellor of the diocese.

**Consolidated Fund.** In 1751 an Act was passed for consolidating the nine loans bearing different interests, into one common loan bearing an interest of three per cent. In 1889 this interest was reduced to two and three-quarter per cent.; and in 1903 to two and a half per cent. The fund is pledged for the payment of the interest of the national debt, the civil list, the salaries of the judges, ambassadors, and other high officials, etc.

**Consols.** A contraction of Consolidated Fund. *See above*.

**Constable** (Lat., *comes-stabuli*) means 'Master of the Horse'. *Cp*. Marshal. The *Constable of France* was the title of the principal officer of the household of the early Frankish kings, and from being the head groom of the stable he ultimately became commander-in-chief of the army, supreme judge of all military matters and matters pertaining to chivalry, etc. The office was abolished in 1627. The *Constable of England*, or *Lord High Constable*, was a similar official, but since 1521 the title has been granted only temporarily, for the purposes of Coronations.

***Drink the constable.*** *See* Morocco.

***To overrun*** or ***outrun the constable.*** To get into debt; to spend more than one's income; to talk about what you do not understand.

Quoth Hudibras, Friend Ralph, thou hast
Outrun the constable at last;
For thou hast fallen on a new
Dispute, as senseless as untrue.

Butler, *Hudibras*, i, 3

***Who's to pay the constable?*** Who is to pay the score? The constable arrests debtors, and, of course, represents the creditor; wherefore, to overrun the constable is to overrun your credit account. To pay the constable is to give him the money due, to prevent an arrest.

**Constantine, Donation of.** *See* Decretals.

**Constantine's Cross.** *See* Cross.

**Constituent Assembly.** The first of the national assemblies of the French Revolution; so called because its chief work was the drawing up of a new constitution for France. It sat from 1788 to 1791.

**Constitution.** The fundamental laws of a state; the way in which a state is organised or constituted – despotic, aristocratic, democratic, monarchic, oligarchic, etc.

***To give a nation a constitution.*** To give it fixed laws, and to limit the powers of the nominal ruler or head of the state, so that the people are not subject to arbitrary government or caprice. A despotism or autocracy is solely under the unrestricted will of the despot or autocrat.

***Constitutions of Clarendon.*** *See* Clarendon.

***Apostolic Constitutions.*** A doctrinal code relating to the Church, the duties of Christians, etc., contained in eight books of doubtful date, possibly as early as the 3rd century, but certainly later than the time of the Apostles, to whom at one time they were attributed.

**Consummatum est** (Lat.). It is finished: the last words of our Lord on the cross (John 19:30).

> *Meph.* O, what will I not do to obtain his soul?
> *Faust.* Consummatum est; this bill is ended,
> And Faustus hath bequeathed his soul to
> Lucifer. Marlowe, *Doctor Faustus*, v, 74

**Contango.** In Stock Exchange parlance, the sum paid by the purchaser of stock to the seller for the privilege of deferring the completion of the bargain till the next, or some future, settling day. At the outbreak of the Great War in 1914 this 'carrying over' was done away with. *Cp.* Backwardation.

**Contemplate.** To meditate or reflect upon; to consider attentively. The word takes us back to the ancient Roman augurs (*q.v.*), for the *templum* (whence our *temple*) was that part of the heavens which he wished to consult. Having mentally divided it into two parts from top to bottom, he watched to see what would occur; and this watching of the *templum* was called *contemplating*.

**Contempt of Court.** Refusing to conform to the rules of the law courts. *Consequential* contempt is that which tends to obstruct the business or lower the dignity of the court by indirection. *Direct* contempt is an open insult or resistance to the judge or others officially employed in the court.

**Contemptibles, The Old.** The original Expeditionary Force of 160,000 men that left England at the start of the Great War in August, 1914, to join the French and Belgians against Germany. The soldiers gave it themselves as a compliment, from an army order that was said to have been given at Aix on August 19th by the Kaiser to his generals.

> It is my royal and imperial command that you concentrate your energies for the immediate present upon one single purpose, and that is, that you address all your skill, and all the valour of my soldiers, to exterminate, first, the treacherous English, and to walk over General French's contemptible little army.

It is only fair to add that this 'order' is almost certainly apocryphal.

**Contenement.** A word used in Magna Charta, the exact meaning of which is not ascertainable, but which probably denotes the lands and chattels connected with a tenement; whatever befits the social position of a person, as the arms of a gentleman, the merchandise of a trader, the ploughs and wagons of a peasant, etc.

> In every case the contenement (a word expressive of chattels necessary to each man's station) was exempted from seizure.
> Hallam, *Middle Ages*, Pt ii, ch. viii

**Contentment is true Riches.** The wise saw of Democritus (about 460–357 BC), the laughing philosopher.

> Content is wealth, the riches of the mind;
> And happy he who can such riches find.
> Dryden, *Wife of Bath's Tale*

**Continence of a Scipio.** It is said that a beautiful princess fell into the hands of Scipio Africanus, and he refused to see her, 'lest he should be tempted to forget his principles'. Similar stories, whether fable or not, are told of many historical characters, including Cyrus (*see* Panthea), Anson and Alexander.

**Continental System.** A name given to Napoleon's plan for shutting out Great Britain from all commerce with the continent of Europe. He forbade under pain of war any nation of Europe to receive British exports, or to send imports to any of the British dominions. It began November 21st, 1806.

**Contingent.** The quota of troops furnished by each of several contracting powers, according to agreement. The word properly means something happening by chance; hence we call a fortuitous event a contingency.

**Contra** (Lat.). Against; generally in the phrase *pro and contra* or *pro and con* (*q.v.*). In bookkeeping a *contra* is an entry on the right-hand, or credit side, of the ledger. *See* Per Contra.

***Contra bonos mores*** (Lat.). Not in accordance with good manners; not *comme il faut* (*q.v.*).

***Contra jus gentium*** (Lat.). Against the law of nations; specially applied to usages in war which are contrary to the laws or customs of civilised peoples.

***Contra mundum*** (Lat.). Against the world at large. Used of an innovator or reformer who sets his opinion against that of everyone else, and specially connected with Athanasius in his vehement opposition to the Arians.

**Contretemps** (Fr.). A mischance, something inopportune. Literally, 'out of time'.

**Conventicle.** The word was applied originally by the early Christians to their meeting-places, but it was soon used contemptuously by their opponents, and it thus acquired a bad or derisive sense, such as a clandestine meeting with a sinister intention; a private meeting of monks to protest against the election of a proposed abbot, for instance, was called a conventicle. It now means a religious meeting, or meeting-place, of Dissenters, a chapel (*q.v.*).

*Conventicle Act.* An Act passed in 1664 declaring that a meeting of more than five persons held for religious worship and not in accordance with the Book of Common Prayer was a seditious assembly. It was repealed by the Toleration Act (1689).

**Convention Parliament, The.** Two Parliaments wore so called: one in 1660, because it was not held by the order of the king, but was convened by General Monk; and that convened on January 22nd, 1689, to confer the crown on William and Mary.

**Convey.** A polite term for *steal.* Thieves are, by a similar euphemism, called *conveyers.* (Lat. *conveho*, to carry away.)

> Convey, the wise it call, Steal! foh! a fico for the phrase.
>
> Shakespeare, *Merry Wives of Windsor*, 1, 3

> *Bolingbroke.* Go, some of you, convey him to the Tower.
>
> *Rich. II.* O, good! 'Convey'. Conveyers are ye all.
> That rise thus nimbly by a true king's fall.
>
> Shakespeare, *Richard II*, 4, 4

**Conway Cabal, The.** A faction organised by Gen. Thomas Conway, of the American Republican army, to supersede Washington and make Gen. Gates Commander-in-Chief. This was in 1777–8.

**Cooing and Billing,** like Philip and Mary on a shilling. The reference is to coins struck in 1555, in which Mary and her consort are placed face to face, and not cheek by jowl, the usual way.

> Still amorous, and fond, and billing,
> Like Philip and Mary on a shilling.
>
> *Hudibras*, Pt iii, 1

**Cook your Goose.** *See* Goose.

**Cooked.** *The books have been cooked.* The ledger and other trade books have been tampered with, in order to show a false balance.

**Cooking.** Terms belonging to cuisine applied to man under different circumstances:

Sometimes he is well *basted*; he *boils* with rage, is *baked* with heat, and *burns* with love or jealousy. Sometimes he is *buttered* and well buttered; he is often *cut up*, *devoured* with a flame, and *done brown.* We *dress his jacket* for him; sometimes he is *eaten up* with care; sometimes he is *fried.* We *cook his goose* for him, and sometimes he makes a goose of himself. We make a *hash* of him, and at times he makes a hash of something else. He gets into *hot water*, and sometimes into a *mess.* Is made into *mincemeat*, makes mincemeat of his money, and is often in a *pickle.* We are often asked to *toast* him, sometimes he gets well *roasted*, is sometimes *set on fire*, put into a *stew*, or is in a *stew* no one knows why.

A 'soft' is *half baked*, one severely handled is well *peppered*, to falsify accounts is to *cook* or *salt* them, wit is *Attic salt*, and an exaggerated statement must be taken *cum grano salis.*

A pert young person is a *sauce box*, a shy lover is a *spoon*, a rich father has to *fork out*, and is sometimes *dished* of his money.

***Connected with foods and drinks.***

A conceited man does not think small *beer* (or small potatoes) of himself, and one's mouth is called a *potato-trap.* A simpleton is a *cake*, a *gudgeon*, and a *pigeon.* Some are *cool as a cucumber*, others *hot as a quail.* A chubby child is a little *dumpling.* A woman may be a *duck*; a courtesan was called a *mutton* or *laced mutton*, and a large, coarse hand is a *mutton fist.* A greedy person is a *pig*, a fat one is a *sausage*, and a shy one, if not a sheep, is certainly *sheepish*; while a Lubin casts *sheep's eyes* at his ladylove. A coward is chicken-hearted, a fat person is *crummy*, and a cross one is *crusty*, while an aristocrat belongs to the *upper crust* of society. A Yeoman of the Guard is a *beef-eater*, a soldier a *red herring*, or a *lobster*, and a stingy, ill-tempered old man is a *crab.* A walking advertiser between two boards is a *sandwichman.* An alderman in his chain is a *turkey hung with sausages.* Two persons resembling each other are like as *two peas.* A chit is a mere *sprat*, a delicate maiden a *tit-bit*, and a colourless countenance is called a *whey-face.*

**Cool as a Cucumber.** Perfectly composed; not in the least angry or agitated.

**Cool Card; Cooling Card.** *See* Card.

**Cool Hundred, Thousand** (or any other sum). The whole of the sum named. Cool, in this case, is merely an emphatic; it may have originally had reference to the calmness and deliberation with which the sum was counted out and the total made up.

> He had lost a cool hundred, and would no longer play.
>
> Fielding, *Tom Jones*, VIII, xii

**Cool Tankard** or **Cool Cup.** A drink made of wine and water, with lemon, sugar, and borage; sometimes also slices of cucumber.

**Coon, A.** Short for *racoon*, a small North American animal, about the size of a fox, valued for its fur. The animal waa adopted as a badge by the old Whig party in the United States about 1840.

***A coon's age.*** Quite a long time; a 'month of Sundays' (US slang).

***A gone coon.*** A person in a terrible fix; one on the verge of ruin. The coon being hunted for its fur is a 'gone coon' when it is treed and so has no escape from its pursuers.

***To go the whole coon.*** An American equivalent of the English 'to go the whole hog'. *See* Hog.

**Cooper.** Half stout and half porter. The term arose from the old practice at breweries of allowing the coopers a daily portion of stout and porter. As they did not like to drink porter after stout, they mixed the two together.

**Coot.** ***A silly old coot. Stupid as a coot.*** The coot is a small waterfowl.

***Bald as a coot.*** The coot has a strong, straight, and somewhat conical bill, the base of which tends to push up the forehead, and there dilates, so as to form a remarkable bare patch.

**Cop.** To catch, lay hold of, capture. To 'get copped' is to get caught by the police, whence *cop* and *copper* (*q.v.*), a policeman. Perhaps connected with Lat. *capere*, to take, etc.

> 'I shall cut this tomorrow, ...' said the younger man. 'You'll be copped, then,' replied the other.
>
> T. Terrell, *Lady Delmar*

The word is used for catching almost anything, as punishment at school, or even an illness, fever, or cold:

> They thought I was sleepin', ye know,
> And they sed as I'd copped it o' Jim;
> Well, it come like a bit of a blow,
> For I watched by the deathbed of him.
>
> Sims, *Dagonel Ballads* (*The Last Letter*)

The East Anglian word to *cop* meaning to throw or toss (whence *cop-halfpenny*, a name for chuck-farthing) is not connected with this.

**Copernicanism.** The doctrine that the earth moves round the sun, in opposition to the doctrine that the sun moves round the earth; so called after Nicolas Copernicus (1473–1543), the Prussian astronomer. *Cp.* Ptolemaic system.

> Whereas it has come to the knowledge of the Holy Congregation that that false Pythagorean doctrine altogether opposed to Holy Scripture, on the mobility of the earth and the immobility of the sun, taught by Nicholas Copernicus ... This congregation has decreed that the said book of Copernicus be suspended until it be corrected.
>
> *Decree of the Holy Congregation of the Index*, 1616

**Copesmate.** Originally a person with whom one copes or contends; hence a colleague in office; hence a partner, companion.

> Mis-shapen Time, copesmate of ugly Night, ...
> Thou nursest all, and murderest all that are.
>
> Shakespeare, *Lucrece*, 925

**Cophetua.** An imaginary king of Africa, of great wealth, who 'disdained all womankind', and concerning whom a ballad is given in Percy's *Reliques*. One day he saw a beggar-girl from his window, and fell in love with her. He asked her name; it was Penelophon, called by Shakespeare Zenelophon (*Love's Labour's Lost*, 4, 1). They lived together long and happily, and at death were universally lamented.

> King Cophetua loved the beggar-maid.
>
> Shakespeare, *Romeo and Juliet*, 2, 1

**Coppen.** The name given to one of the daughters of Chanticleer, the Cock, in Caxton's version of *Reynard the Fox*. Her sisters were Cantart and Crayant.

**Copper.** Among the old alchemists copper was the symbol of Venus.

The name is given to the large vessel used for laundry purposes, cooking, etc., which was formerly made of copper but is now more usually of iron; also to pence, halfpence, farthings, cents, etc., although nowadays they are made of bronze; true copper coinage has not been minted in England since 1860.

In slang a *copper* is a policeman, i.e. one who 'cops', or catches, offenders. *See* Cop.

> There were cries of 'Coppers, Coppers!' In the yard, and then a violent struggle ... Whoever it was that was wanted had been evidently secured and dragged off to gaol.
>
> T. Terrell, *Lady Delmar*, 1

***Copper Captain.*** A 'Brummagem', or sham, captain; a man who 'swanks about' with the title but has no right to it. Michael Perez is so called in *Rule a Wife and have a Wife*, by Beaumont and Fletcher.

> To this copper-captain was confided the command of the troops. W. Irving

***Copper Nose.*** Oliver Cromwell; also called 'Ruby Nose', 'Nosey', and 'Nose Almighty', no doubt from some scorbutic tendency which showed itself in a big red nose.

***Copper-nosed Harry.*** Henry VIII. When Henry VIII had spent all the money left him by his miserly father, he minted an inferior silver coin, in which the copper alloy soon showed itself on the more prominent parts, especially the nose of the face; and hence the people soon called the king 'Old Copper-nose'.

**Copperheads.** Secret foes. Copperheads are poisonous snakes of North America (*Trigonocephalus contortrix*), which, unlike the rattlesnakes, give no warning of their attack. The name was applied by the early colonists to the Indians, then to the Dutch (*see* Washington Irving's *History of New York*), and, finally, in the Civil War to the pro-Southerners among the Northerners, the covert friends of the Confederates.

**Copronymus.** So Constantine V was surnamed (719, 741–75). 'Kopros' is the Greek for dung, and Constantine V was called Copronymus: '*Parce qu'il salit les fonts baptismaux lorsqu'on le baptisait.*'

**Copts.** The Jacobite Christians of Egypt, who have been since the Council of Chalcedon in 451 in possession of the patriarchal chair of Alexandria. The word is probably derived from Coptos, the metropolis of the Thebaid. These Christians conduct their worship in a dead language called 'Coptic' (language of the Copts).

> The Copts [or Egypt] circumcise, confess to their priests, and abstain from swine's flesh. They are Jacobites in their creed.
>
> S. Olin, *Travels in Egypt*, vol. i, ch. viii

**Copus.** University slang for a drink made of beer, wine, and spice heated together, and served in a 'loving-cup'. Variously accounted for as being dog-Latin for *cupellon Hippocratis* (a cup of hippocras), or short for *episcopus*, in which case it would be the same as the drink 'bishop' (*q.v.*).

**Copy.** A printer's term both for original MS, typescript, or printed matter that is to be set up in type.

***That's a mere copy of your countenance.*** Not your real wish or meaning, but merely one you choose to present to me.

**Copyhold Estate.** Land held by a tenant by virtue of a copy of the roll made by the steward of the manor from the court-roll kept in the manor-house.

> The villein took an oath of fealty to his lord for the cottage and land which he enjoyed from his bounty … These tenements were suffered to descend to their children … and thus the tenure of copyhold was established.
>
> Lingard, *England*, vol. ii, ch. i

**Copyright.** The exclusive right of multiplying for sale copies of works of literature, art, etc., or substantial parts thereof, allowed to the author or his assignees. The first copyright Act in England is that of 1709; modifications and additions to it were made at various times, and in 1842 a new Act was passed granting copyright for forty-two years after publication or until the expiration of seven years from the death of the author, which ever should be the longer.

This Act was superseded by the Copyright Act of 1911, under which the period of protection was extended to fifty years after the death of the author, irrespective of the date of publication of the book. This Act deals also with the copyright in photographs, engravings, architectural designs, musical compositions, gramophone records, etc.

> A copy of every copyright book has to be presented to the British Museum and, on application being made, to the Bodleian, the Cambridge University Library, the Advocates Library at Edinburgh, Trinity College, Dublin, and the National Library of Wales at Aberystwyth. Before the Act of 1842 Sion College, Glasgow, Aberdeen, and St Andrews Universities, and King's Inns, Dublin, also had compulsory presentation copies.

**Coq-à-l'âne** (Fr., a cock on an ass). A cock-and-bull story (*q.v.*); idle nonsense, as '*Il fait toujours des coq-à-l'âne*' – he is always doing silly things, or talking rubbish. The Scotch *cockalane* (*see* Cock and bull) is from this.

**Corah,** in Dryden's *Absalom and Achitophel* (*q.v.*), is meant for Titus Oates. North describes him as a short man, extremely ugly; if his mouth is taken for the centre, his chin, forehead, and cheek-bones would fall in the circumference. *See* Numb. 16.

> Sunk were his eyes, his voice was harsh and loud;
> Sure signs he neither choleric was, nor proud;
> His long chin proved his wit; his saint-like grace
> A church vermilion, and a Moses' face.
> His memory, miraculously great,
> Could plots, exceeding man's belief, repeat.
>
> Dryden, *Absalom and Achitophel*, i, 646

**Coral.** The Romans used to hang beads of red coral on the cradles and round the neck of infants, to 'preserve and fasten their teeth', and save them from 'the falling sickness'. It was considered by soothsayers as a charm against lightning, whirlwind, shipwreck, and fire. Paracelsus says it should be worn round the neck of children as a preservative 'against fits, sorcery, charms, and poison', and Norse legend says that it is fashioned beneath the waves by Marmendill. The *bells* on an infant's coral are a Roman Catholic addition, the object being to frighten away evil spirits by their jingle.

> Coral is good to be hanged about the neck of children … to preserve them from the falling sickness. It has also some special sympathy with nature, for the best coral … will turn pale and wan if the party that wears it be sick, and it comes to its former colour again as they recover.

> Sir Hugh Platt, *Jewel-House of Art and Nature* (1594)

**Coram judice** (Lat.). Under consideration; still before the judge.

**Corbant.** The rook, in the tale of *Reynard the Fox* (*q.v.*). Lat. *corvus*; Fr. *corbeau*.

**Corceca.** The typification of blindness of heart (Lat. *cor*, heart, *caecus*, blind) in Spenser's *Faërie Queene* (I, iii). She is a blind old woman, mother of Abessa (Superstition).

**Cordelia.** The youngest of Lear's three daughters, and the only one that loved him. She appears in Holinshed's *Chronicle* (whence Shakespeare drew most of his facts) as 'Cordeilla', as 'Cordell' in the *Mirour for Magistrates* (1555) and as 'Cordella' in the older play of *Leir* (1594). The form 'Cordelia' seems to appear for the first time in Spenser's *Faërie Queene* (ii, 10). *See* Lear, King.

***Cordelia's gift.*** A 'voice ever soft, gentle, and low; an excellent thing in woman'. Shakespeare, *King Lear*, 5, 3.

> It is her voice that he hears prevailing over the those [*sic*] of the rest of the company, ... for she has not Cordelia's gift.
>
> Miss Broughton, *Dr Cupid*

**Cordelier**, i.e. 'cord-wearer'. A Franciscan friar of the strict rule, an Observantin. *See* Franciscans. In the Middle Ages they distinguished themselves in philosophy and theology. Duns Scotus was one of their most distinguished members. The tale is that in the reign of St Louis these Minorites repulsed an army of infidels, and the king asked who those *gens de cordelies* (corded people) were. From this they received their appellation.

In the French Revolution the name *Club des Cordeliers* was given to a political club, because it held its meetings in an old convent of Cordeliers. The Cordeliers were the rivals of the Jacobins, and numbered among its members Paré (the president), Danton, Marat, Camille Desmoulins, Hébert, Chaumette, Dufournoy de Villiers, Fabre d'Eglantine, and others. They were far in advance of the Jacobins, and were the first to demand the abolition of the monarchy and the establishment of a commonwealth. The leaders were put to death between March 24th and April 5th, 1794.

> This club was nicknamed 'The Pandemonium', and Danton was called the 'Archfiend'. When Bailly, the mayor, locked them out of their hall in 1791, they met in the Tennis Court (Paris), and changed their name into the 'Society of the Rights of Man'; but they are best known by their original appellation.

***Il ne faut pas parler Latin devant les Cordeliers.*** Don't talk Latin before the Cordeliers, i.e. the Franciscans. A common French proverb, meaning that one should be careful what one says on a subject before those who are masters of it.

**Cordon** (Fr.). A ribbon or cord; especially the ribbon of an order of chivalry: also, a line of sentries or military posts enclosing some position; hence, an encircling line.

***Cordon bleu.*** A knight of the ancient order of the *St Esprit* (Holy Ghost); so called because the decoration is suspended on a blue ribbon. It was at one time the highest order in the kingdom of France.

The title is also given, as a facetious compliment, to a good cook; and to a member of the 'Blue Ribbon Army' (*q.v.*), i.e. a teetotaller.

***Cordon noir.*** A knight of the Order of St Michael, distinguished by a black ribbon.

***Cordon rouge.*** A chevalier of the Order of *St Louis*, the decoration being suspended on a red ribbon.

***Cordon sanitaire.*** A line of watchers posted round an infectious district to keep it isolated and prevent the spread of the disease; a sanitary cordon.

***Un grand cordon.*** A member of the French *Légion d'Honneur*. The cross is attached to a *grand* (broad) ribbon.

***Un repas de cordon bleu.*** A well cooked and well appointed dinner. The commandeur de Souvé, Comte d'Olonne, and some others, who were *cordons bleus* (i.e. knights of St Esprit), met together as a sort of club, and were noted for their excellent dinners. Hence, when anyone had dined well he said, '*Bien, c'est un vrai repas de cordon bleu.*'

**Corduroy.** A corded fabric, originally made of silk, and worn by the kings of France in the chase (Fr. *corde du roy*). It is now a coarse, thick ribbed cotton stuff, worn chiefly by labourers, gamekeepers, etc.

***Corduroys.*** Trousers made of corduroy.

***Corduroy road.*** A term applied to roads in the backwoods and swamps of the United States, Canada, etc., formed of tree trunks sawn in two longitudinally, and laid transversely. Such a road presents a ribbed appearance, like corduroy.

> Look well to your seat, 'tis like taking an airing
> On a corduroy road, and that out of repairing.
>
> Lowell, *Fable for Critics*

**Cordwainer.** Not a twister of cord, but a worker in leather. Our word is the Fr. *cordouannier* (a maker or worker of *cordouan*); the former a corruption of *Cordovanier* (a worker in Cordovan leather).

**Corflambo.** A giant personifying sensual passion in Spenser's *Faërie Queene* (iv, 8).

**Corineus.** A mythical hero in the suite of Brute, who conquered the giant Goëmagot (Gogmagog), for which achievement the whole western horn of England was allotted him. He called it Corinea, and the people Corineans, from his own name. *See* Bellerus.

In meed of these great conquests by them got,
Corineus had that province utmost west
To him assynëd for his worthy lot,
Which of his name and memorable gest,
He callëd Cornwall.

Spenser, *Faërie Queene*, ii,10

**Corinth.** ***Corinth's Pedagogue.*** Dionysius the younger, on being banished a second time from Syracuse, went to Corinth and became schoolmaster. He is called Dionysius the *tyrant*. Hence Lord Byron says of Napoleon:

Corinth's pedagogue hath now
Transferred his by-word to thy brow.

*Ode to Napoleon*

***Non cuivis homini contingit adire Corinthum.*** A tag from Horace (Ep. I, xvii), quoted of some difficult attainment that can be achieved only by good fortune or great wealth. Professor Corrington translates it:

You know the proverb, 'Corinth town is fair,
But 'tis not every man that can get there.'

Gellius, in his *Noctes Atticae*, i, 8, says that Horace refers to Laïs (*q.v.*), who sold her favours at so high a price that not everyone could afford to purchase them; but Horace says, 'To please princes is no little praise, for it falls not to every man's lot to go to Corinth.' That is, it is as hard to please princes as it is to get to Corinth, perhaps because of the expense, and perhaps because it is situated between two seas, and hence called Bimaris Corinthus.

***There is but one road that leads to Corinth.*** There is only one right way of doing anything. The Bible tells us that the way of evil is broad, because of its many tracks; but the way of life is narrow, because it has only one single footpath.

All other ways are wrong, all other guides are false. Hence my difficulty! – the number and variety of the ways. For you know, 'There is but one road that leads to Corinth.'

Pater, *Marius the Epicurean*, ch. 24

**Corinthian.** A licentious libertine; also a gentleman sportsman who rides his own horses on the turf, or sails his own yacht. The immorality of Corinth was proverbial both in Greece and Rome. The sporting rake in Pierce Egan's *Life in London* (1821) was known as 'Corinthian Tom', and in Shakespeare's day a 'Corinthian' was the 'fast man' of the period. *Cp.* Ephesian.

I am no proud Jack, like Falstaff; but a Corinthian, a lad of mettle, a good boy. *1 Henry IV*, 2, 4

***Corinthian brass.*** An alloy made of a variety of metals (said to be gold, silver, and copper) melted at the conflagration of Corinth in 146 BC, when the city was burnt to the ground by the consul Mummius. Vases and other ornaments, made by the Romans of this metal, were of greater value than if they had been silver or gold.

The Höng-hee vases (1426) of China were made of a similar alloy when the Imperial palace was burnt to the ground. They are priceless.

I think it may be of Corinthian brass,
Which was a mixture of all metals, but
The brazen uppermost.

Byron, *Don Juan*, vi, 56

**Corinthian Order.** The most richly decorated of the five orders of Greek architecture. The shaft is fluted, and the capital is bell-shaped and adorned with acanthus leaves. *See* Acanthus.

**Corked.** ***This wine is corked***–i.e. tastes of the cork.

**Corker.** ***That's a corker.*** That's a whopping great fib! Perhaps the allusion is to something that quite closes the discussion, settles the matter, 'corks' it up.

**Corking-pins.** Pins of the largest size, at one time used by ladies to keep curls on the forehead fixed and in trim. They used to be called *calkin* (pronounced *cawkin*) pins, but it is not known why.

**Cormoran.** The Cornish giant who, in the nursery tale, fell into a pit dug by Jack the Giantkiller. For this doughty achievement Jack received a belt from King Arthur, with this inscription –

This is the valiant Cornish man
That slew the giant Cormoran.

*Jack the Giant-killer*

**Corn.** ***There's corn in Egypt.*** There is abundance; there is a plentiful supply. Of course, the reference is to the Bible story of Joseph in Egypt.

***To tread on one's corns.*** To irritate one's prejudices; to annoy another by disregard to his pet opinions or habits.

***Up corn, down horn.*** An old saying suggesting that when corn is high or dear, beef is down or cheap, because persons have less money to spend on meat. It is hardly applicable to modern times – especially since the Great War.

**Corn-Law Rhymer.** Ebenezer Elliot (1781–1849), who wrote philippics against the corn laws.

> Is not the corn-law rhymer already a king?
>
> Carlyle

**Cornage.** A rent in feudal times fixed with relation to the number of horned cattle in the tenant's possession. In Littleton's *Tenures* (1574) it was mistakenly said to be 'a kind of tenure in grand serjeanty', the service being to blow a horn when an invasion of the Scots was imminent. Until the true meaning of the term was given in the Oxford Dictionary this was the explanation always given.

**Corneille du boulevard.** Guilbert de Pixérécourt (1773–1844), the French dramatist, was so named, because he was as outstanding in his own way as was Pierre Corneille (1606–84) in a greater. He was also surnamed *le Shakespeare du boulevard*.

**Corner.** The condition of the market with respect to a commodity which has been largely brought up, in order to create a virtual monopoly and enhance its market price; as a corner in pork, etc. The idea is that the goods are piled and hidden in a corner out of sight.

> The price of bread rose like a rocket, and speculators wished to corner what little wheat there was. *New York Weekly Times* (June 13, 1894)

***Driven into a corner.*** Placed where there is no escape; driven from all subterfuges and excuses.

***To make a corner.*** To combine in order to control the price of a given article, and thus secure enormous profits.

**Corner-stone.** A large stone laid at the base of a building to strengthen the two walls forming a right angle; in ancient buildings they were sometimes as much as 20 feet long and 8 feet thick. In figurative use, Christ is called (Eph. 2:20) the chief corner-stone because He united the Jews and Gentiles into one family; and daughters are called corner-stones (Ps. 154:12) because, as wives and mothers, they unite together two families.

> Why should we make an ambiguous word the corner-stone of moral philosophy?
>
> Jowett, *Plato*, iv, 30

**Cornet.** ***The terrible cornet of horse.*** A nickname of the elder Pitt (1708–78). He obtained a cornetcy in Lord Cobham's Horse in 1731.

**Cornish.** ***Cornish hug.*** A hug to overthrow you. The Cornish men were famous wrestlers, and tried to throttle their antagonist with a particular grip or embrace called the Cornish hug.

> The Cornish are Masters of the Art of Wrestling ... Their Hugg is a cunning close with their fellow-combatant; the fruits whereof is his fair fall, or foil at the least. It is figuratively appliable to the deceitful dealing of such who secretly design their overthrow, whom they openly embrace.
>
> Fuller, *Worthies* (1661)

***Cornish language.*** This member of the Brythonic branch of the Celtic languages became virtually extinct nearly 200 years ago. Doll Pentreath, the last person who could speak it, died, at the age of ninety-one, in 1777.

***Cornish names.***

> By Tre, Pol, and Pen.
> You shall know the Cornishmen.

Thus, *Tre* (a town) gives Trefry, Tregengon, Tregony, Tregothnan, Trelawy, Tremayne, Trevannion, Treveddoe, Trewithen, etc.

***Pol*** (a head) gives Polkerris Point, Polperro, Polwheel, etc.

***Pen*** (a top) gives Penkevil, Penrice, Penrose, Pentire, etc.

***The Cornish Wonder.*** John Opie (1761–1807), of Cornwall, the painter. It was 'Peter Pindar' (Dr Wolcot) who gave him this name.

**Cornstalks.** In Australia, especially in New South Wales, youths of colonial birth are so called; perhaps because they are often taller and more slender than their parents.

**Cornubian Shore.** Cornwall, famous for its tin mines.

> ... from the bleak Cornubian shore
> Dispense the mineral treasure, which of old
> Sidonian pilots sought.
>
> Akenside, *Hymn to the Naiads*

**Cornu-copia.** *See* Amalthaea's Horn.

**Cornwall.** The county is probably named from Celtic *corn*, *cornu*, a horn, with reference to configuration of the promontory. For the legendary explanation of the name, *see* Corineus.

**Coronach.** Lamentation for the dead, as anciently practised in Ireland and Celtic Scotland. (Gael. *comh rànach*, crying together.) Pennant says it was called by the Irish *hululoo*.

**Coronation Chair.** *See* Scone.

**Coroner.** Properly, the crown officer (Lat. *corona*, crown). In Saxon times it was his duty to collect the Crown revenues; next, to take charge of Crown pleas; but at present his duties are almost entirely confined to searching into cases of sudden or suspicious death. The coroner also holds inquiries, or inquests, on treasure trove. *Crowner* was formerly a vulgar way of pronouncing the word, hence Shakespeare's –

But is this law?
Ay, marry, is't; crowner's quest law.

*Hamlet*, 5, 1

**Coronet.** A crown inferior to the royal crown. A *duke's* coronet is adorned with strawberry leaves above the band; that of a *marquis* with strawberry leaves alternating with pearls; that of an *earl* has pearls elevated on stalks, alternating with leaves above the band; that of a *viscount* has a string of pearls above the band, but no leaves; that of a *baron* has only six pearls.

**Coronis.** Daughter of a King of Phocis, changed by Athena into a crow to enable her to escape from Neptune. There was another Coronis, mother of Aesculapius by Apollo, who slew her for infidelity.

**Corporal Violet.** *See* Violet.

**Corporation.** A large paunch. A *municipal corporation* is a body of men elected for the local government of a city or town, consisting of the mayor, aldermen, and councillors, all of whom (especially the first two) are supposed to be fat and prosperous and to have large capacity for food.

**Corposant.** The St Elmo's Fire (*q.v.*) or 'Castor and Pollux' of the Romans; the ball of fire which is sometimes seen playing round the masts of ships in a storm. So called from Span. *corpo santo*, holy body. Sometimes known as *comazant*.

**Corps Diplomatique** (Fr.). A diplomatic body; the foreign representatives at a Court collectively.

**Corpse Candle.** The *ignis fatuus* is so called by the Welsh because it was supposed to forebode death, and to show the road that the corpse would take. The large candle used at lich wakes – i.e. at the watching of a corpse before interment – had the same name.

**Corpus** (Lat., a body). The whole body or substance; especially the complete collection of writings on one subject or by one person, as the *Corpus poetarum Latinorum*, the *Corpus historicum medii aevi*, etc.

Bound up inseparably with the whole *corpus* of Christian Tradition.

Mozley, *Lectures on Miracles*

Also, short for Corpus Christi College.

***Corpus Christi.*** A festival of the Church, kept on the Thursday after Trinity Sunday, in honour of the Eucharist. It was instituted by Urban IV in 1264, and was the regular time for the performance of religious dramas by the trade guilds. In England many of the Corpus Christi plays of York, Coventry, and Chester are still extant.

***Corpus Christi College*** at Cambridge was founded in 1352, and the College of the same name at Oxford in 1516.

***Corpus delicti*** (Lat.). The material thing in respect to which a crime has been committed; thus a murdered body or a portion of the stolen property would be a 'corpus delicti'.

He knew he was guilty, ... he had taken the money that did not belong to him ... and had not repaid it; there was the absolute *corpus delicti* in court, in the shape of a deficiency of some thousands of pounds.

Trollope, *The Three Clerks*, ch. xl

**Corpuscular Philosophy.** The theory promulgated by Robert Boyle which sought to account for all natural phenomena by the position and motion of corpuscles. *Cp.* Atomic Philosophy.

**Corrector.** *See* Alexander the Corrector.

**Corroboree.** The name of a dance indulged in by Australian aborigines on festal or warlike occasions; hence any hilarious or slightly riotous assembly. The word belongs to the extinct language formerly used by the natives of Port Jackson, New South Wales.

**Corrouge.** The sword of Sir Otuel in mediaeval romance.

**Corrupticolae.** A sect of Monophysite heretics of the 6th century, who maintained that the body of Christ was *corruptible*. They were followers of a certain Severius, and so were also called *Severians*.

**Corruption of Blood.** Loss of title and entailed estates in consequence of treason, by which a man's *blood* is *attainted* and his issue suffers.

**Corsair** means properly 'one who gives chase'. Applied to the pirates of the northern coast of Africa. (Ital. *corso*, a chase; Fr. *corsaire*; Lat. *cursus*.)

**Corsned.** The piece of bread 'consecrated for exorcism', formerly given (in one form of the Old English 'ordeal') to a person to swallow as a test of his guilt (A.S. *cor*, choice, trial, *snaed*, piece). The words of 'consecration' were: 'May this morsel cause convulsions and find no passage if the accused is guilty, but turn to wholesome nourishment if he is innocent.' *See* Choke.

**Cortes.** The Spanish or Portuguese parliament. The word means 'court officers'.

**Cortina** (Lat., cauldron). The tripod of Apollo, which was in the form of a cauldron; hence, any tripod used for religious purposes in the worship of the ancient Romans.

**Corvinus.** Matthias I, King of Hungary, 1458–90, younger son of Janos Hunyady, was so called from the raven (Lat. *corvus*) on his shield.

Marcus Valerius is also said to have been so called because, in a single combat with a gigantic Gaul during the Gallic war, a raven flew into the Gaul's face and so harassed him that he could neither defend himself nor attack his adversary.

**Corybantes.** The Phrygian priests of Cybele, whose worship was celebrated with orgiastic dances and loud, wild music. Hence, a wild, unrestrained dancer is sometimes called a *corybant*; and Prof. Huxley (1890) even referred to the members of the Salvation Army as being 'militant missionaries of a somewhat corybantic Christianity'.

> Why speak of Roman pomps? ... a deeper dread
> Scattered on all sides by the hideous jars
> Of Corybantian cymbals, while the head
> Of Cybelè was seen, sublimely turreted!
>
> Wordsworth, *Processions*

**Corycian Cave.** A cave on Mount Parnassus; so called from the nymph Corycia. The Muses are sometimes in poetry called Corycides or the Corycian Nymphs.

> The immortal Muse
> To your calm habitations, to the cave
> Corycian ... will guide his footsteps.
>
> Akenside, *Hymn to the Naiads*

**Corydon.** A conventional name for a rustic, a shepherd; a brainless, love-sick spoony; from the shepherd in Virgil's *Eclogue* VII, and in Theocritus.

**Coryphaeus.** The leader and speaker of the chorus in Greek dramas; hence, figuratively, the leader generally, the most active member of a board, company, expedition, etc. At Oxford University the assistant of the Choragus (*q.v.*) is called the Coryphaeus.

> In the year 1626, Dr William Heather, desirous to ensure the study and practice of music at Oxford in future ages, established the offices of Professor, Choragus, and Coryphaeus, and endowed them with modest stipends.
>
> *Grove's Dictionary of Music*

***The Coryphaeus of German literature.*** Goethe, 'prince of German poets' (1749–1832).

***The Coryphaeus of Grammarians.*** Aristarchus of Samothrace (2nd century BC), a prince of grammarians and critics.

***The Coryphaeus of Learning.*** Richard Porson (1759–1808), the great English classical scholar.

**Coryphée.** A ballet-dancer; strictly speaking, the leader of the ballet: from Coryphaeus (*q.v.*).

**Cosmopolite** (Gr. *cosmospolites*). A citizen of the world. One who has no partiality to any one country as his abiding place; one who looks on the whole world with 'an equal eye'.

**Coss, Rule of.** An old name for algebra (also called the *Cossic Art*); from Ital. *regola di cosa*, *cosa* being an unknown quantity, or a 'thing'. *See* Whetstone of Witte.

**Cosset.** A pet; especially a pet lamb brought up in the house. Hence, *to cosset*, to make a pet of, to fondle, caress. Probably from A.S. *cot-saeta*, a dweller in a cottage.

**Costard.** A large, ribbed apple, and, metaphorically, a man's head. *Cp.* Costermonger.

> Take him over the costard with the hilts of thy sword.
>
> Shakespeare, *Richard III*, 1, 4

Shakespeare gives the name to a clown in *Love's Labour's Lost*, who apes the court wit of the period, but misapplies and miscalls like Mrs Malaprop or Dogberry.

**Costermonger.** A seller of eatables about the streets, properly an apple-seller; from *costard* (*q.v.*), and *monger*, a trader; A.S. *mangian*, to trade; a word still retained in iron-monger, cheese-monger, fish-monger, etc.

> Her father was an Irish costar-monger.
>
> Jonson, *The Alchemist*, iv, 1

**Cote-hardi.** A tight-fitting tunic buttoned down the front.

> He was clothed in a cote-hardi upon the gyse of Almayne [i.e. in the German fashion].
>
> Geoffroi de la Tour Landry

**Coterie.** A French word originally signifying something like our 'guild', a society where each paid his *quota*, but now applied to an exclusive set or clique, especially one composed of persons of similar tastes, aims, prejudices, etc.

> All coteries ... it seems to me, have a tendency to change truth into affectation
>
> E. C. Gaskell, *Charlotte Brontë*, vol. ii, ch. xi

**Cotillon.** Originally a brisk dance by four or eight persons, in which the ladies held up their gowns and showed their under-petticoats (Fr. *cotillon*, a petticoat). Later the dance became a very elaborate one with many added figures; but it is very rarely seen in modern ball-rooms.

**Cotswold.** ***You are as long a-coming as Cotswold barley.*** Cotswold, in Gloucestershire, is a very cold, bleak place on the wolds, exposed to the winds, and very backward in vegetation, but yet it yields a good late supply of barley.

***Cotswold lion.*** An ironical name for a sheep, for which Cotswold hills are famous.

Then will he look as fierce as a Cotssold lion.
Udall, *Roister Doister*, IV, vi (*c.*1566)

**Cotta,** in Pope's *Moral Essays* (Epistle 2). John Holles, fourth Earl of Clare, who married Margaret, daughter of Henry Cavendish, Duke of Newcastle, and was created Duke of Newcastle in 1694 and died 1711.

**Cottage Countess, The.** Sarah Hoggins, of Shropshire, daughter of a small farmer, who, in 1791, married Henry Cecil, ninth Marquis of Exeter and Lord of Burleigh. The bridegroom was at the time living under the name of John Jones, separated from his wife, who eloped with a clergyman, and subsequently obtained a divorce and an Act of Parliament to legitimatise the children of his second wife. Sarah Hoggins was seventeen at the time of her marriage, and 'John Jones' was thirty. They were married by licence in the parish church of Bolas. Tennyson's poem, *The Lord of Burleigh*, is founded on this episode.

**Cotton.** ***A cotton king.*** A rich Manchester cotton manufacturer, a regular king in wealth, style of living, equipage, number of employees, etc.

***To cotton to a person.*** To cling to one or take a fancy to a person. To stick to a person as cotton sticks to our clothes.

**Cottonian Library.** The library founded by the noted antiquary, Sir Robert Bruce Cotton (1571–1631), now in the British Museum. It is especially rich in original documents; in 1707 the collection was purchased by the nation; but, before it could be housed in the British Museum on the founding of that institution in 1753, it suffered considerable damage through fire (1731).

**Cottonopolis.** Manchester, the great centre of cotton manufactures.

**Cottys.** One of the three Hundred-handed giants, son of Uranus (Heaven) and Gaea (Earth). His two brothers were Briareus and Gyges. *See* Hundred-handed.

**Cotytto.** The Thracian goddess of immodesty, worshipped at Athens with licentious rites. *See* Baptes.

Hail! goddess of nocturnal sport,
Dark-veiled Cotytto.
Milton, Comus, 129, 130

Where are they, Cotytto or Venus,
Astarte or Ashtaroth, where?
Swinburne, *Dolores*

**Coucy.** Enguerrand III, Sire de Coucy, chief of the league formed during the minority of Louis IX (about 1227) against the mother of the king, won fame by his arrogant motto:

Roi je ne suis,
Ni Prince, ni comte, aussi,
Je suis Le Sire de Coucy

**Couleur de rose** (Fr., rose-coloured). Highly coloured; too favourably considered; overdrawn with romantic embellishments, like objects viewed through glass tinted with rose pink.

**Coulin.** A British giant mentioned by Spenser (*Faërie Queene*, II, x, 11); he was pursued by Debon (*q.v.*) till he came to a chasm, and, after leaping it, he slipped on the opposite side, fell back, and was killed.

**Council, Privy, Oecumenical, etc.** *See these words.*

**Counsel.** ***Keep your own counsel.*** Don't talk about what you intend to do. Keep your plans to yourself.

Now, mind what I tell you, and keep your own counsel.
Boldrewood, *Robbery Under Arms*, ch. vi

**Count.** A title of honour, used on the Continent and equivalent to English *earl* (A.S. *corl*, a warrior), of which *countess* is still the feminine and the title of the wife or widow of an earl. *Count* is from Lat. *comilem*, accusative of *comes*, a companion, which was a military title, as *Comes Littoris Saxonici*, Count of the Saxon Shore, the Roman general responsible for the south-eastern coasts of Britain.

**Count, To.** From O.Fr. *conter*, Lat. *computare* (*putare*, to think), to compute, to reckon.

***To count kin with one.*** A Scotch expression meaning to compare one's pedigree with that of another.

***Count not your chickens …*** *See* Chickens.

***To count out the House.*** To declare the House of Commons adjourned because there are not forty members present. The Speaker has his attention called to the fact, and if he finds that this is so, he declares the sitting over.

***To count upon.*** To rely with confidence on someone or something; to reckon on.

***To count without your host.*** *See* Reckon.

**Countenance, To.** To sanction; to support. Approval or disapproval is shown by the countenance. The Scripture speaks of 'the light of God's countenance', i.e. the smile of approbation; and to 'hide His face' (or countenance) is to manifest displeasure.

General Grant, neither at this time nor at any other, gave the least countenance to the efforts …
Nicolay and Hay, *Abraham Lincoln*, vol. ix, ch. ii

***To keep in countenance.*** To encourage, or prevent one losing his countenance or feeling dismayed.

***To keep one's countenance.*** To refrain from smiling or expressing one's thoughts by the face.

***Out of countenance.*** Ashamed, confounded. With the countenance fallen or cast down.

***To put one out of countenance*** is to make one ashamed or disconcerted. To 'discountenance' is to set your face against something done or propounded.

**Counter-caster.** One who keeps accounts, or casts up accounts by counters. Thus, at the opening of *Othello*, Iago in contempt calls Cassio 'a great arithmetician', and 'this counter-caster'; and in *The Winter's Tale*, the Clown says: 'Fifteen hundred shorn; what comes the wool to? I cannot do't without counters' (4, 3).

**Countercheck Quarrelsome.** Sir, how dare you utter such a falsehood? Sir, you know that it is not true. This, in Touchstone's classification (Shakespeare's *As You Like It*, 5, 4), is the third remove from the lie direct; or rather, the lie direct in the third degree.

> The Reproof Valiant, the Countercheck Quarrelsome, the Lie Circumstantial, and the Lie Direct, are not clearly defined by Touchstone. *That* is not true; how *dare* you utter such a falsehood; *if* you say so, you are a liar; you lie, or are a liar, seem to fit the four degrees.

**Counter-jumper.** A contemptuous epithet for a draper's assistant, who may be supposed to have to jump over the counter to go from one part of the shop to another.

**Counterpane.** A corruption of *counterpoint*, from the Lat. *culcita puncta*, a stitched quilt. This, in French, became *courte-pointe*, corrupted into *contre-pointe*, *counterpoint*, where point is pronounced 'poyn', corrupted into 'pane'.

**Countess.** *See* Count: Cottage Countess.

**Country.** ***Black Country.*** *See* Black.

***Country dance.*** A corruption of the Fr. *contre danse*; i.e. a dance where the partners face each other, as in Sir Roger de Coverley.

***Father of his country.*** *See* Father.

***To appeal,*** or ***go, to the country.*** To dissolve Parliament in order to ascertain the wish of the country by a new election of representatives.

**County.** A shire; originally the district ruled by a count. The name is also officially applied to *county boroughs*, i.e. towns with more than 50,000 inhabitants which, under the Local Government Act of 1888, rank as administrative counties. For various names of divisions of Counties, *see* Hundred.

***County family.*** A family belonging to the nobility or gentry with an ancestral seat in the county.

***County palatine.*** Properly, the dominion of an earl palatine (*see* Palatinate), a county over which the count had royal privileges. Cheshire and Lancashire are the only Counties Palatine in England now; but formerly Durham, Pembroke, Hexhamshire, and the Isle of Ely had this rank.

**Coup** (Fr.). Properly a blow or stroke, but used both in French and English in a large number of ways, as for a clap of thunder, a draught of liquids, a piece of play in a game (a move in chess, etc.), a stroke of policy or of luck, a trick, etc.

***A good coup.*** A good hit or haul.

***Coup d'essai.*** A trial-piece; a piece of work serving for practice.

> This work seems ... to be a respectable *coup d'essai*, written with some thought.
>
> J. W. Croker, *Essays; French Revolution*

***Coup d'état.*** A state stroke, and the term is applied to one of those bold measures taken by Government to prevent a supposed or actual danger; as when a large body of men are arrested suddenly for fear they should overturn the Government.

The famous *coup d'état*, by which Louis Napoleon became possessed of absolute power, took place on December 2nd, 1851.

***Coup de grâce.*** The finishing stroke; the stroke of mercy. When a criminal was tortured by the wheel or otherwise, the executioner gave him a *coup de grâce*, or blow on the head or breast, to put him out of his misery.

> This punishment [being broken on the wheel] consists in the executioner, with a bar of iron, breaking the shoulder-bones, arms, thigh-bones, and legs – taking alternate sides. The punishment is concluded by a blow across the breast, called the *coup de grâce*, or blow of mercy, became it removes the sufferer from his agony.
>
> Scott, *The Betrothed*; note to ch. xxx

***Coup de main.*** A sudden stroke, a stratagem whereby something is effected suddenly; a *coup*.

> It appears more like a line of march than a body intended for a *coup de main*, as there are with it bullocks and baggage of different kinds.
>
> Wellington, *Dispatches*, vol. i, p. 25

***Coup d'oeil.*** A view, glance, prospect; the effect of things at the first glance; literally 'a stroke of the eye'.

***Coup de pied de l'âne.*** Literally, a kick from the ass's foot; figuratively, a blow given to a vanquished or fallen man; a cowardly blow; an insult offered to one who has not the power of returning or avenging it. The allusion is to the fable of the sick lion kicked by the ass.

***Coup de soleil.*** A sunstroke, any malady produced by exposure to the sun.

***Coup de théâtre.*** An unforeseen or unexpected turn in a drama producing a sensational effect; a piece of claptrap, something planned for effect. Burke throwing down the dagger in the House of Commons (*see* Dagger scene) intended a *coup de théâtre*.

***Coup manqué.*** A false stroke, a miss, a failure.

> Shoot dead, or don't aim at all; but never make a *coup manqué*. Ouida, *Under Two Flags*, ch. xx

**Coupon.** In commercial phraseology, a coupon is a certificate of interest which is to be cut off (Fr. *couper*) from a bond and presented for payment. It bears on its face the date and amount of interest to be paid.

During the Great War the word was widely used in connection with the arrangements made during the shortage of food, coals, etc., as these necessaries could not be obtained without the production of a detachable portion (*coupon*) of one's permit.

In political phraseology *the coupon* was the official recognition given by Mr Lloyd George and Mr Bonar Law to parliamentary candidates who proclaimed their allegiance to the coalition programme at the General Election of December, 1918. Hence, *couponeer* a politician who accepted the 'coupon'.

**Courage of One's Opinion.** To have the courage of one's opinion means to utter, maintain, and act according to one's opinion, be the consequences what they may. The French use the same locution. Martyrs may be said to have had the courage of their opinions.

**Course. *Another course would have done it.*** A little more would have effected our purpose. It is said that the peasants of a Yorkshire village tried to wall in a cuckoo in order to enjoy an eternal spring. They built a wall round the bird, and the cuckoo just skimmed over it. 'Ah!' said one of the peasants, 'another carse would 'a' done it.'

> There is a school of moralists who, connecting sundry short-comings ... with changes in manners, endeavour to persuade us that only 'another carse' is wanted to wall in the cuckoo.
> *Nineteenth Century*, December, 1892, p. 920

***In course; in the course of nature.*** In the due and proper time or order, etc.; in the ordinary procedure of nature.

***Of course.*** Naturally; as would be expected. A *matter of course* is something that belongs to ordinary procedure, or that is customary.

***To hold,*** or ***keep on the course.*** To go straight; to do one's duty in that course [path] of life in which we are placed. The allusion is to racing horses.

> We are not the only horses that can't be kept on the courses – with a good turn of speed too.
> Boldrewood, *Robbery Under Arms*, ch. xv

**Court.** From Lat. *cohors*, *cohortem*, originally a coop or sheepfold. It was on the Latium hills that the ancient Latins raised their *cors* or *cohors*, small enclosures with hurdles for sheep, etc. Subsequently, as many men as could be cooped or folded together were called a *cohort*. The cattle-yard being the nucleus of the farm, became the centre of a lot of farm cottages, then of a hamlet, town, fortified place, and lastly of a royal residence.

***Court cards.*** A corruption of *coat card*, so called because these cards bear the representation of a clothed or *coated* figure, and not because the king, queen, and knave may be considered to belong to a Court.

> The Vikings, mere pirates from the *viks* or creeks of Scandinavia, have, by the same [metamorphic] process, been raised to the dignity of kings; just as *coat-cards* – the king, and queen, and knave in their gorgeous gowns – were exalted into *court cards*.
> Max Müller, *Chips from a German Workshop*, III, p. 301

The king of clubs originally represented the arms of the Pope; of spades, the King of France; of diamonds, the King of Spain; and of hearts, the King of England. The French kings in cards are called David (spades), Alexander (clubs), Caesar (diamonds), and Charles (hearts) – representing the Jewish, Greek, Roman, and Frankish empires. The queens or dames are Argine – i.e. Juno (hearts), Judith (clubs), Rachel (diamonds), and Pallas (spades) – representing royalty, fortitude, piety, and wisdom. They were likenesses of Marie d'Anjou, the queen of Charles VII; Isabeau, the queen-mother; Agnes Sorel, the king's mistress; and Joan d'Arc, the dame of spades, or war.

***Court Circular.*** The information concerning the movements and doings of Royalty and the Court generally, supplied to the newspapers by the Court Newsman. He gives reports of levees, drawing-rooms, state balls, royal concerts, meetings of the cabinet ministers, deputations to ministers, and so on. George III, in 1803, introduced the custom to prevent misstatements on these subjects.

***Court cupboard.*** A movable buffet to hold flagons, cans, cups, and beakers.

> Away with the joint-stools, remove the court-cupboard, look to the plate.
>
> Shakespeare, *Romeo and Juliet*, 1, 5

***Court fools.*** *See* Fools.

***Court holy water.*** An obsolete Elizabethan term for fair speeches, which look like promises of favour, but end in nothing.

> O nuncle, court holy-water in a dry house is better than this rain-water out o' door.
>
> Shakespeare, *King Lear*, 3, 2

In Florio's Italian Dictionary (1598) *Mantellizzare* is translated by 'to flatter or fawne upon, to court one with faire words or give court holy-water'.

***Court-leet.*** *See* Leet.

***Court plaster.*** The plaster of which the court ladies made their patches. These patches, worn on the face, were cut into all sorts of fanciful shapes, some even patching their faces with a coach and four, a ship in full sail, a chateau, etc. This ridiculous fashion was in vogue in the reign of Charles I; and in Queen Anne's time was employed as a political badge. *See* Patches.

> Your black patches you wear variously,
> Some cut like stars, some in half-moons, some lozenges.
>
> Beaumont and Fletcher, *Elder Brother*, iii, 2

***Court of Arches.*** *See* Arches.

***Court of love.*** A judicial court for deciding affairs of the heart, established in Provence during the palmy days of the Troubadours. The following is a case submitted to their judgment: A lady listened to one admirer, squeezed the hand of another, and touched with her toe the foot of a third. Query: Which of these three was the favoured suitor?

***Court of Pie-powder.*** *See* Pie-poudre.

***Court of Session.*** The supreme civil tribunal in Scotland. It dates from 1532, and represents the united powers of the Session of James I of Scotland, the Daily Council of James IV, and the Lords Auditors of Parliament. Since 1830 it has consisted of an Inner and an Outer House; the total number of judges is thirteen, including the Lord President (or Lord Justice General) and the Lord Justice Clerk.

***They are but in the Court of the Gentiles.*** They are not wholly God's people; they are not the elect, but have only a smattering of the truth. The 'Court of the Israelites' in the Jewish temple was for Jewish men; the 'Court of the Women' was for Jewish women; the 'Court of the Gentiles' was for those who were not Jews.

> Oh, Cuddie, they are but in the Court of the Gentiles, and will ne'er win farther ben, I doubt.
>
> Scott, *Old Mortality*, ch. viii

***Out of court.*** Not worth consideration; wholly to be discarded, as 'such and such an hypothesis is wholly out of court, and has been proved to be untenable'. 'No true bill'.

**Courtepy.** *See* Pea-jacket.

**Courtesy.** Civility, politeness. It was at the courts of princes and great feudatories that minstrels and pages practised the refinements of the age in which they lived. The word originally meant the manners of the court.

***Courtesy titles.*** Titles assumed or granted by social custom, but not of any legal value. The courtesy title of the eldest son of a duke is *marquis*; of a marquis is *earl*; of an earl is *viscount*. Younger sons of peers are by courtesy called *lord* or *honourable*, and the daughters are *lady* or *honourable*. These titles do not give the holders the right to sit in the House of Lords.

**Courtois.** The name given to the Hound in Caxton's version of *Reynard the Fox*.

**Cousin.** Blackstone says that Henry IV, being related or allied to every earl in the kingdom, artfully and constantly acknowledged the connection in all public acts. The usage has descended to his successors, and in royal writs and commissions an *earl* is still styled 'Our right trusty and well-beloved cousin', a *marquis* 'Our right trusty and entirely-beloved cousin', and a *duke* 'Our right trusty and right-entirely-beloved cousin'.

The word is also used by sovereigns in addressing one another formally; and in Italy it is a very high honour to be nominated by the king a 'Cousin of the King'.

***Cousin Betsy,*** or ***Betty.*** A half-witted person, a 'Bess of Bedlam' (*q.v.*).

> [None] can say Foster's wronged him of a penny, or gave short measure to a child or a cousin Betsy.
>
> Mrs Gaskell

***Cousin-german.*** The children of brothers and sisters, first cousins; kinsfolk. (Lat. *germanus*, a brother, one of the same stock.)

> There is three cozen-germans that has cozened all the hosts of Reading, of Maidenhead, of Colebrook, of horses and money.
>
> Shakespeare, *Merry Wives of Windsor*, 4, 5

***Cousin Jack.*** So Cornishmen are called in the western counties, and in the colonies where they are working as miners.

***Cousin Michael.*** The Germans are so called. *Michel*, in Old German, means 'gross'; Cousin Michael is meant to indicate a slow, heavy, unrefined, coarse-feeding people.

**Coûte que coûte** (Fr.). Cost what it may, at any price, be the consequences what they may.

> All the mother was in arms to secure her daughter's happiness, *coûte que coûte*.
>
> Chas Reade, *Hard Cash*

**Couvade.** The name given by anthropologists to the custom prevalent among some primitive races by which the father of a newly born infant makes a pretence of going through the same experiences as the mother, lies up for a time, abstains from certain foods, etc., as though he, too, were physically affected by the birth (from Fr. *couver*, to hatch). The custom has been observed by travellers in Guiana and other parts of South America, among some African tribes, in parts of China, Borneo, etc., and it was noted by the ancients as occurring in Corsica and among the Celtiberians.

**Cove.** An individual; as a *flash cove* (a swell), a *rum cove* (a man whose position and character is not quite obvious), a *gentry cove* (a gentleman), a *downy cove* (a very knowing individual), etc. The word is old thieves' cant; it appears (as *cofe*) in Harman's *Caveat* (1567).

**Covenanters.** A term applied, during the civil wars, to the Scotch Presbyterians, who, in 1643, united by 'solemn league and covenant' (*see under* Solemn) to resist the encroachments of Charles I on religious liberty.

**Covent Garden.** A corruption of *Convent* Garden; the garden and burial ground attached to the convent of Westminster, and turned into a fruit and flower market in the reign of Charles II. At the dissolution of the monasteries the site was granted to the Duke of Somerset; on his attainder in 1552 it passed to the Earl of Bedford, to whose descendants it belonged till 1914, when it was sold by the 11th Duke of Bedford.

**Coventry. *Coventry Mysteries.*** Miracle plays supposed to have been acted at Corpus Christi (*q.v.*) at Coventry till 1591. They were published in 1841 for the Shakespeare Society; but, though called *Ludus Coventriae* by Sir Robert Bruce Cotton's librarian in the time of James I, it is doubtful whether they had any special connection with the town.

***Parliaments held at Coventry.*** Two parliaments have been held in this city, one in 1404, styled *Parliamentum Indoctorum*; and the other in 1459, called *Parliamentum Diabolicum.*

***To send one to Coventry.*** To take no notice of him; to make him feel that he is in disgrace by having no dealings with him. *Cp.* Boycott. It is said that the citizens of Coventry had at one time so great a dislike to soldiers that a woman seen speaking to one was instantly tabooed; hence, when a soldier was sent to Coventry he was cut off from all social intercourse.

Hutton, in his *History of Birmingham*, gives a different version. He says that Coventry was a stronghold of the parliamentary party in the civil wars, and that troublesome and refractory royalist prisoners were sent there for safe custody.

**Cover. *To break cover.*** To start from the covert or temporary lair. The usual earth-holes of a fox being blocked the night before a hunt, the creature makes some gorse-bush or other cover its temporary resting-place, and as soon as it quits it the hunt begins.

**Coverdale's Bible** *See* Bible, the English.

**Coverley.** *Sir Roger de Coverley.* A member of an hypothetical club in the *Spectator*, 'who lived in Soho Square when he was in town'. Sir Roger is the type of an English squire in the reign of Queen Anne. He figures in thirty papers of the *Spectator.*

> Who can be insensible to his unpretending virtues and amiable weaknesses; his modesty, generosity, hospitality, and eccentric whims; the respect for his neighbours, and the affection of his domestics? Hazlitt

The well-known country dance was known by this name (or, rather, as *Roger of Coverly*) many years before Addison's time.

**Cow.** The cow that nourished Ymir with four streams of milk was called Audhumla (*q.v.*).

***Always behind, like a cow's tail.*** A proverbial saying of ancient date. *Cp. Tanquam coda vituli* (Petronius).

***Curst cows have curt horns.*** Angry men cannot do all the mischief they wish. Curst means 'angry' or 'fierce', and curt is 'short', as curt-mantle, curt-hose. The Latin proverb is, *Dat Deus immiti cornua curta bovi.*

> You are called plain Kate,
> And bonny Kate, and sometimes Kate the curst.
>
> Shakespeare, *Taming of the Shrew*, 2, 1

***Stick to the cow.*** Boswell, one night sitting in the pit of Covent Garden theatre with his friend

Dr Blair, gave an extempore imitation of a cow, which the house applauded. He then ventured another imitation, but failed, whereupon the doctor advised him in future to 'stick to the cow'.

***The cow knows not the worth of her tail till she loses it***, and is troubled with flies, which her tail brushed off.

> What we have we prize not to the worth
> Whiles we enjoy it; but being lack'd and lost,
> Why, then we rack the value.
>
> Shakespeare, *Much Ado about Nothing*, 4, 1

***The tune the old cow died of.*** *See* Tune.

***The whiter the cow, the surer is it to go to the altar.*** The richer the prey, the more likely is it to be seized.

> The system of impropriations grew so rapidly that, in the course of three centuries, more than a third part of all the benefices in England became such, and those the richest, for the whiter the cow, the surer was it to go to the altar.
>
> Blunt, *Reformation in England*, p. 63

**Cow-lick.** A tuft of hair on the forehead that cannot be made to lie in the same direction as the rest of the hair.

> This term must have been adopted from a comparison with that part of a … cow's hide where the hairs, having different directions, meet and form a projecting ridge, supposed to be occasioned by the animals licking themselves.
>
> Brockett, *Glossary of North Country Words*

**Coward.** Ultimately from Lat. *cauda*, a tail, the allusion seems to be either from an animal 'turning tail' when frightened, or from its cowering with its tail between its legs. In the French version of *Reynard the Fox* the Hare (*see* Cuwaert) is called *Coart*, which may refer either to his timidity or to the conspicuousness of his tail (O.Fr. *coe*) as it runs away.

A beast *cowarded*, in *heraldry*, is one drawn with its tail between its legs.

**Cowl.** ' 'Tis not the cowl (or hood) that makes the monk.' *See* Hood.

**Cowper Justice.** Cupar Justice (*q.v.*).

**Cowper-Temple Clause.** Clause 14 of the Education Act of 1870 (so called from its author), which regulated religious teaching in public elementary schools. It enacted that 'in any school provided by a School Board, no religious catechism or religious formulary which is distinctive of any particular denomination, shall be taught'. When the County Councils, under the Education Act of 1902, took over the old Board Schools, religious instruction in these (the 'provided' schools) still had to be undenominational, but in the 'non-provided' schools the managers, though in receipt of grants from public funds, were allowed to determine the character of the religious instruction given.

**Coxcomb.** An empty-headed, vain person. The ancient licensed jesters were so called because they wore a cock's comb in their caps.

> Coxcombs, an ever empty race,
> Are trumpets of their own disgrace.
>
> Gay, *Fables*, xix

**Coxswain.** The helmsman of a boat; originally the *swain* or *servant* of a *cock* (*see* Cock-boat). The old spelling of the word was *Cockswain*.

**Coyne and Livery.** An old Irish term for food and entertainment for soldiers, and forage for their horses, formerly exacted from private persons by Irish chiefs when on the march. *Coyne* is Irish *coinnemh*, billeting, or one billeted.

**Coystril.** A term of reproach, meaning a low fellow, a knave, a varlet.

> He's a coward and a coystril that will not drink to my niece. Shakespeare, *Twelfth Night*, 1, 3

It is a variant of obsolete *custrel*, an attendant on a knight, which seems to be connected with O.Fr. *coustillier*, a soldier armed with a *coustille*, i.e. a two-edged dagger. Every soldier in the life-guards of Henry VIII was attended by a man called a *coystrel* or *coystril*.

**Cozen.** To cheat. This is the same word as *cousin*; the Fr. *cousiner* means 'to sponge on' as well as 'to call cousin'; and in England a person who *cozened* another was one who went and stayed at his house and lived on him just because they were 'cousins'. *See* Shakespeare's *Merry Wives*, 4, 2 and 5, 5.

**Crab.** An ill-tempered fellow; sour as a crab-apple.

***To catch a crab.*** *See* Catch.

**Crack.** First-rate, excellent, quite at the top of its class; something that is 'cracked up' (*see below*), as a crack regiment, a crack hand of cards, a first-rate player, etc. Formerly the word was used substantively for a lively young fellow, a wag:

> Indeed, la! 'tis a noble child; a crack, madam.
>
> Shakespeare, *Coriolanus*, 1, 3

***A gude crack.*** In Scottish dialect, a good chat or conversation, also a good talker.

> Wi' merry sangs, an' friendly cracks,
> I wat they did na weary;
> And unco tales, an' funnie jokes –
> Their sports were cheap an' cheery.
>
> Burns, *Halloween*

> To be a gude crack … was essential to the trade of a 'puir body' of the more esteemed class.
>
> Scott, *Antiquary* (Introduction)

***Crack-brained.*** Eccentric; slightly mad.

***Cracked pipkins are discovered by their sound.*** Ignorance is betrayed by speech.

They bid you talk – my honest song
Bids you for ever hold your tongue;
Silence with some is wisdom most profound –
Cracked pipkins are discovered by the sound.
Peter Pindar, *Lord B. and his Motions*

***In a crack.*** Instantly. In a snap of the fingers, in the time taken by a crack or shot.

Do pray undo the bolt a little faster –
They're on the stair just now, and in a crack
Will all be here. Byron, *Don Juan*, I, cxxxvii

***To crack a bottle.*** To drink one. The allusion is to drunken frolics, when the bottles and glasses were broken during the bout. Miss Oldbuck says, in reference to the same custom, 'We never were glass-breakers in this house, Mr Lovel' (*Antiquary*); meaning they were not bottle-crackers, not given to drunken orgies. *See* Crush.

Dear Tom, this brown jug that now foams with mild ale,
From which I now drink to sweet Nan of the Vale,
Was once Toby Filpot's, a thirsty old soul
As e'er cracked a bottle, or fathomed a bowl.
O'Keefe, *Poor Soldier*

***To crack a crib.*** To break into a house as a thief. *See* Crib. Hence, *cracksman*, a burglar.

***To crack up.*** To praise highly, to eulogise.

We find them cracking up the country they belong to, no matter how absurd may be the boast.
Jas. Payn, *By Proxy*, ch. i

**Cracker.** In America a biscuit, especially a thin brittle biscuit that easily cracks, is called a *cracker*; in England the word is used for a small firework (called 'fire-cracker' in America), and for the ornamented 'bon-bon', in use at Christmas time and at children's parties, that goes off with a crack when pulled.

**Cracksman.** A burglar. *See* To crack a crib *above*.

**Cradle-holding.** A name given to land held by Borough-English (*q.v.*).

**Craft.** Skill, ability, trade (A.S. *craft*). A *craftsman* is a mechanic. A *handicraft* is manual skill, i.e. mechanical skill; *leechcraft* is skill in medicine (A.S., *loece*, a physician); and before *crafty* adopted its bad sense it meant merely skilful, ingenious.

***Small craft.*** Such vessels as schooners, sloops, cutters, and so on. A shipbuilder was at one time the prince of craftsmen, and his vessels were work of craft emphatically.

**Cram.** To tell what is not true. A *crammer*, an untruth. The allusion is to stuffing a person with useless rubbish.

**Crambe bis cocta** (Lat.). literally, 'cabbage boiled twice'; figuratively, a well-worn subject, a subject talked out. Juvenal says, '*Occidit miseros crambe repetita magistros*' (vii, 155), alluding to the Greek proverb, '*Dis krambe thanatos.*' *See* Crambo *below*.

There was a disadvantage in treading this Border district, for it had been already ransacked by the author himself, as well as by others; and, unless presented under a new light, was likely to afford ground to the objection of *Crambe bis cocta*. Scott, *The Monastery* (Introduction)

**Crambo.** A game which consists in someone setting a line which another is to rhyme to, but no one word of the first line must occur in the second. So called in allusion to the tag from Juvenal given in the preceding entry, which has been translated:

Like warmed-up cabbage served at each repast
The repetition kills the wretch at last.

*Dumb crambo* is a similar game, but there the words are expressed in pantomime or dumb show. Thus if 'cat' is the given word, the pantomimists would act Bat, Fat, Hat, Mat, Pat, Rat, Sat, etc., till the chosen word is guessed.

**Cramp-ring.** A ring that was consecrated by the king on Good Friday and was supposed to protect the wearer against cramp, 'falling sickness', etc.

Because Coshawk goes in a shag-ruff band, with a face sticking up in't which shows like an agate set in a cramp-ring, he thinks I'm in love with him.
Middleton, *The Roaring Girl*, IV, ii (1611)

The superstitious use of cramp-rings, as a preservative against fits, is not entirely abandoned; instances occur where nine young men of a parish each subscribe a crooked sixpence, to be moulded into a ring for a young woman afflicted with this malady.
Rokewode, *The Hundred of Thingoe* (*Suffolk*), Introd. (1838)

***To scour the cramp-ring.*** To be put into fetters; to be imprisoned. The allusion is obvious.

There's no muckle hazard o' scouring the cramp-ring. Scott, *Guy Mannering*, ch. xxiii

**Crank.** In Elizabethan thieves' slang, an Abram man (*q.v.*); so called from Ger. *krank* (sickly). Nowadays a *crank* is a person with a mental twist, an eccentric person, and the name is obviously an extension of the mechanical term.

**Cranmer's Bible.** *See* Bible, the English.

**Crannock.** An Irish measure which, in the days of Edward II, contained either eight or sixteen pecks. *Curnock* is another form of the word: this was a dry measure of varying capacity, but usually 3 bushels for wheat, 4 bushels for corn, and from 10 to 15 bushels for coal, lime, etc.

**Crapaud** or **Johnny Crapaud.** A Frenchman; according to Guillim's *Display of Heraldry* (1611), so called from a device of the ancient kings of France, 'three toads (Fr. *crapauds*) erect, saltant'. *See* Fleur-de-lis.

***Les anciens crapauds prenderont Sara*.** One of the cryptic 'prophecies' of Nostradamus (1503–66). Sara is *Aras* reversed, and when the French under Louis XIV took Aras from the Spaniards, this verse was remembered.

**Crape. *A saint in crape is twice a saint in lawn*.** (Pope, *Ep. to Cobham*, 136) Crape (a sort of bombazine, or alpaca) is the stuff of which cheap clerical gowns used to be made, and here means one of the lower clergy; 'lawn' refers to the lawn sleeves of a bishop, and here means a prelate. A good curate is all very well, but the same goodness in a bishop is exalted as something noteworthy.

**Cratur. *A drop of the cratur*.** *See* Creature.

**Cravat.** This neckcloth, worn by men, was introduced into France in the 17th century by Croatian soldiers, and was called from their national name, Cravate (O.Slav. *khruvat*). The Croats guarded the Turkish frontiers of Austria, and when France organised a regiment on the model of the Croats, their linen neckcloths were imitated, and the regiment was called 'The Royal Cravat'.

***The Bonny Cravat*.** An old public-house sign at Woodchurch, Kent; a corruption of *La bonne corvette*. Woodchurch was noted for smuggling, and the 'Bonnie Cravat' was a smuggler's hostelry.

***To wear a hempen cravat*.** To be hanged.

**Craven.** In M.E. *crauant*, the word is the O.Fr. *cravant*, pres. part. of *craver* or *crever*, to burst or break, hence to be overcome. The '-en' is a mistake for '*-ant*'; it makes the word look like a past participle instead of what it really is, a present.

When controversies were decided by an appeal to battle, the combatants fought with batons, and if the accused could either kill his adversary or maintain the fight till sundown he was acquitted. If he wished to call off, he cried out 'Craven!' and was held infamous.

**Crawlers.** *See* Growlers.

**Crawley. *Crooked as Crawley*** or ***Crawley brook***, a river in Bedfordshire. That part called the brook, which runs into the Ouse, is so crooked that a boat would have to go eighty miles in order to make a progress direct of eighteen. (Fuller, *Worthies*.)

**Crayant.** The name given to one of the daughters of Chanticleer, the Cock, in Caxton's version of *Reynard the Fox*. Her sisters were Coppen and Cantart.

**Creaking Doors Hang the Longest.** Delicate persons often outlive the more robust. Those who have some personal affliction, like the gout, often live longer than those who have no such taint.

**Creature.** Whisky or other spirits A contracted form of 'Creature-comfort'.

> When he chanced to have taken an overdose of the creature.
>
> Sir W. Scott, *Guy Mannering*, ch. xliv

***A drop of the creature*.** A little whisky. The Irish call it 'a drop of the cratur'.

***Creature-comforts*.** Food and other things necessary for the comfort of the body. Man being supposed to consist of body and soul, the body is the creature, but the soul is the 'vital spark of heavenly flame'.

> Mr Squeers had been seeking in creature-comforts [brandy and water] temporary forgetfulness of his unpleasant situation.
>
> Dickens, *Nicholas Nickleby*

**Credat Judaeus** or **Credat Judaeus Apella** (Horace, *Sat.* I, v, 100). Tell that to the marines; that may do for Apella, but I don't believe a word of it. Who Apella was, nobody knows, but Cicero mentions a person of this name in *Ad Atticum* (12, *ep.* 19).

**Credence Table.** The table near the altar on which the bread and wine are deposited before they are consecrated. In former times food was placed on a credence table to be tasted previously to its being set before the guests. This was done to assure the guests that the meat was not poisoned. (Ital. *credenza*, a shelf or buffet.)

**Crédit Foncier.** A French mortgage-loan society, licensed to borrow money for city and other improvements connected with estates, their security being the local rates. *Foncier* means 'landed', as *impôt foncier* (land tax), *bien foncier* (landed property), and so on.

**Crédit Mobilier.** A French loan society on personal estate, licensed to take part in trading enterprises, such as railways, and to carry on the business of stock-jobbers. The word *mobilier* means personal property, general stock, as *bien mobilier* (personal chattels), *mobilier vif et mort* (live and dead stock).

**Credo. *Credo quia impossibile*** (Lat.), I believe it because it is impossible. A paradox ascribed to St Augustine, but founded on a passage in Tertullian's *De Carne Christi*, IV:

Credibile est, quia ineptum est ... certum est, quia impossibile.

**Crême de la Crême** (Fr.). Literally, 'cream of the cream'; used figuratively for the very choicest part of something which itself is very choice.

**Cremona.** A violin of the greatest excellence; so called from Cremona, in Lombardy, where in the 17th and early 18th centuries lived violin makers of world-wide notoriety, such as Andrea Amati and Antonio his son, Antonius Stradivarius his pupil, and Giuseppe Guarnerius the pupil of Stradivarius. Cremona has long since lost its reputation.

In silvis viva silui; canora jam mortua cano.
*A motto on a Cremona*

Speechless, alive, I heard the feathered throng;
Now, being dead, I emulate their song. E. C. B

The organ-stop known as the *cremona* is so called from Ger. *krummhorn*, crooked horn. It is a reed stop of 8-foot tone.

***The Caledonian Cremona.*** *See* Fiddle, the Scotch.

**Creole.** A descendant of white people born in Mexico, South America, and the West Indies. (Span. *criadillo*, diminutive of *criado*, bred, brought up, native to the locality.) *Cp.* Mulatto.

***The Creole State.*** Louisiana.

**Crepidam.** *Ne supra crepidam sutor judicaret.* A cobbler should stick to his last. *See* Cobbler.

**Crescent.** Tradition says that 'Philip, the father of Alexander, meeting with great difficulties in the siege of Byzantium, set the workmen to undermine the walls, but a crescent moon discovered the design, which miscarried; consequently the Byzantines erected a statue to Diana, and the crescent became the symbol of the state'.

Another legend is that Othman, the Sultan, saw in a vision a crescent moon, which kept increasing till its horns extended from east to west, and he adopted the crescent of his dream for his standard, adding the motto, '*Donec repleat orbem.*'

**Crescent City, The.** New Orleans, in Louisiana, US.

**Crescit.** ***Crescit occulto velut arbor oevo*** (Horace, *Carmen* I, xii, 45), it grows as a tree grows with unnoticed growth. Sainte Beuve applied this line to the Catholic Church.

***Crescit sub pondere virtus,*** virtue thrives best in adversity. The allusion is to the palm tree, which grows better when pressed by an incumbent weight.

**Cresselle.** A wooden rattle used formerly in the Catholic Church during Passion Week, instead of bells, to give notice of Divine worship. Supposed to represent the rattling in the throat of Christ while hanging on the cross.

**Cresset.** A beacon light. The original cresset was an open metal cup at the top of a pole, the cup being filled with burning grease or oil. Hence the name; from O.Fr. *craisse* (Mod. Fr. *graisse*), grease.

**Cressida.** Daughter of Calchas, a Grecian priest, beloved by Troilus (*q.v.*). They vowed eternal fidelity to each other, and as pledges of their vow Troilus gave the maiden a sleeve, and Cressid gave the Trojan prince a glove. Scarce had the vow been made when an exchange of prisoners was agreed to. Diomed gave up three Trojan princes, and was to receive Cressid in lieu thereof. Cressid vowed to remain constant, and Troilus swore to rescue her. She was led off to the Grecian's tent, and soon gave all her affections to Diomed – nay, even bade him wear the sleeve that Troilus had given her in token of his love.

As false
As air, as water, wind or sandy earth,
As fox to lamb, as wolf to heifer's calf,
Pard to tho hind, or step-dame to her son;
'Yea', let them say, to stick the heart of falsehood,
'As false as Cressid'.
Shakespeare, *Troilus and Cressida*. 3, 2

**Cresswell, Madame.** A woman of infamous character who bequeathed £10 for a funeral sermon, in which nothing ill should be said of her. The Duke of Buckingham wrote the sermon, which was as follows: 'All I shall say of her is this – she was born w*ell*, she married *well*, lived *well* and died *well*; for she was born at Shad-well, married to Cress-well, lived at Clerken-well, and died in Bridewell'.

**Crestfallen.** Dispirited. The allusion is to fighting cocks, whose crest falls in defeat and rises rigid and of a deep red colour in victory.

Shall I seem crest-fallen in my father's sight?
Shakespeare, *Richard II*, 1, 1

**Crete.** ***Hound of Crete.*** A bloodhound.

*Coupe le gorge*, that's the word. I thee defy again,
O hound of Crete.
Shakespeare, *Henry V*, 2,1

***The Infamy of Crete.*** The Minotaur (*q.v.*).

There lay stretched
The infamy of Crete, detested brood
Of the feigned heifer.
Dante, *Hell*, xii (Cary's translation)

**Cretinism.** Mental imbecility accompanied by goitre. So called from the Crétins of the Alps. The word is a corruption of Christian (*Chrétien*), because, being baptised, and only idiots, they were 'washed from original sin', and incapable of actual sin. Similarly, idiots are called *innocents*. (Fr. *crétin*.)

**Crewel Garters.** Garters made of worsted or yarn.

> Ha! ha! look, he wears cruel garters.
> Shakespeare, *King Lear*, 2, 4

The resemblance in sound between *crewel* and *cruel* formerly gave rise to many puns, e.g. –

> Wearing of silk, why art thou so cruel?
> *Woman's a Weathercock* (1612)

**Crib.** Thieves' slang for a house or dwelling, as 'Stocking Crib' (a hosier's shop), 'Thimble Crib' (a silversmith's); also slang for a petty theft, and for a translation from Latin, Greek, etc., surreptitiously used by schoolboys in doing their lessons. *To crib* is to pilfer or purloin, and to copy someone else's work without acknowledging it, to plagiarise.

The word originally denoted a manger with bars; hence its application to a child's cot.

***To crack a crib.*** *See* Crack.

**Cricket.** The earliest mention of the game appears to be the reference in the Guild Merchant Book of Guildford, dated 1598, when John Denwick of Guldeford, being then about fifty-nine years of age, deposed that he had known a certain parcel of land 'for the space of Fyfty years and more', and that 'hee and several of his fellowes did runne and play there at Creckett and other plaies' when he was a scholar at the Guildford Free School. This would take the game back to the end of Henry VIII's reign, and it was certainly a Wykehamist game in the days of Elizabeth.

In 1700 two stumps were used 24 inches apart and 12 inches high, with long bails atop. A middle stump was added by the Hambledon Club in 1775, and the height of the stumps was raised to 22 inches, the present height. The length of run is 22 yards.

The first cricket club was the Hambledon, which practically came to an end in 1791, but existed in name till 1825.

The word *cricket* is probably from A.S. *cric*, *cryec*, a staff, and is thus connected with *crutch*.

***Merry as a cricket.*** *See* Grig.

**Crikey.** An exclamation; a mild oath; originally a euphemistic modification of *Christ*.

**Crillon.** *Where wert thou, Crillon?* Crillon, surnamed *the Brave*, in his old age went to church, and listened intently to the story of the Crucifixion. In the middle of the narrative he grew excited, and, unable to contain himself, cried out, '*Où étais-tu, Crillon?*' (What were you about, Crillon, to allow of such things as these?)

Crillon (1541–1615) was one of the greatest captains of the 16th century. He fought at the battle of Ivry (1590), and was entitled by Henri IV '*le brave des braves*'.

> Henri IV, after the battle of Argives (1589), wrote to Crillon: '*Prend-toi, brave Crillon, nous avons vaincu à Arques, et tu n'y étais pas.*' This letter has become proverbial.

**Crimen laesae Majestatis** (Lat.). High treason. *See* Lèse majesté.

**Crimp.** A decoy; especially one of those riverside pests who purport to supply ships with sailors, but who are in league with public-houses and low-class lodging-houses, into which they decoy the sailors and relieve them of their money under one pretence or another.

**Cripple.** Slang for a battered or bent sixpence; so called because it is hard to make it go.

**Cripplegate.** This district in the City of London was so called before the Conquest from the number of cripples who resorted thither to beg, because of the parish church of St Giles (*q.v.*), the patron of cripples (*Stow*). Churches dedicated to this saint are common in the suburbs of large towns, as St Giles of Norwich, Cambridge, Salisbury, etc.

**Crishna.** *See* Krishna.

**Crisis** properly means the 'ability to judge'. Hippocrates said that all diseases had their periods, when the humours of the body ebbed and flowed like the tide of the sea. These tidal days he called *critical days*, and the tide itself a *crisis*, because it was on these days the physician could determine whether the disorder was taking a good or a bad turn. The seventh and all its multiples were critical days of a favourable character. (Gr. *krinein*, to decide or determine.)

**Crispin.** A shoemaker. St Crispin was a shoemaker, and was therefore chosen for the patron saint of the craft. It is said that two brothers, Crispin and Crispian, born in Rome, went to Soissons, in France (AD 303), to propagate the Christian religion, and maintained themselves wholly by making and mending shoes. Probably the tale is fabulous, for *crepis* is Greek for a shoe, Latin *crepid-a*, and St Crepis or Crepid became Crepin and Crespin.

***St Crispin's Day.*** October 25th, the day of the battle of Agincourt. Shakespeare makes Crispin Crispian one person, and not two brothers. Hence Henry V says to his soldiers –

And Crispin Crispian shall ne'er go by ...
But we in it shall be remembered.

*Henry V*, 4, 3

***St Crispin's holiday.*** Every Monday, with those who begin the working week on Tuesday; a no-work day with shoemakers.

***St Crispin's lance.*** A shoemaker's awl.

**Criss-cross row.** *See* Chriss-cross.

**Criterion.** A standard to judge by. (Gr. *krinein*, to judge.)

**Critic.** A judge; an arbiter. (Gr. *krinein*, to judge, to determine.)

A captious, malignant critic is called a Zoilus (*q.v.*).

'And what of this new book the whole world makes such a rout about?' 'Oh, it is out of all plumb, my lord; quite an irregular thing! not one of the angles at the four corners is a right angle. I had my rule and compasses in my pocket.' 'Excellent critic!'

'And for the epic poem your lordship bade me look at, upon taking the length, breadth, height, and depth of it, and trying them at home upon an exact scale of Bossu's [Bossut's], 'tis out, my lord, in every one of its dimensions.' 'Admirable connoisseur!'

Sterne, *Tristram Shandy*, vol. iii, ch. xii

The abbé Charles Bossut (1730–1814) was a noted mathematician and geometer.

***Prince of critics.*** Aristarchus, of Byzantium, who compiled the rhapsodies of Homer. (2nd cent. BC.)

***Stop-watch critics.***

'And how did Garrick speak the soliloquy last night?' 'Oh, against all rule, my lord, most ungrammatically. Betwixt the substantive and the adjective, which should agree together in number, case, and gender, he made a breach, thus – stopping as if the point wanted settling; and betwixt the nominative case, which, your lordship knows, should govern the verb, he suspended his voice in the epilogue a dozen times, three seconds and three-fifths by a stop-watch, my lord, each time.' 'Admirable grammarian! But in suspending his voice was the sense suspended likewise? Did no expression of attitude or countenance fill up the chasm? Was the eye silent? Did you narrowly look?' 'I looked only at the stopwatch, my lord.' 'Excellent observer!'

Sterne, *Tristram Shandy*, vol. ill, ch. xii

**Croaker.** A raven, so called from its croak; one who takes a desponding view of things. Goldsmith, in his *Good-natured Man*, has a character so named.

**Croakumshire.** Northumberland is so called from the peculiar croaking of the natives in speaking. This is especially observable in Newcastle and Morpeth, where the people are said to be born with a burr in their throats, which prevents their giving effect to the letter *r*.

**Crocodile.** A symbol of deity among the Egyptians, because, says Plutarch, it is the only aquatic animal which has its eyes covered with a thin transparent membrane, by reason of which it sees and is not seen, as God sees all, Himself not being seen. To this he subsequently adds another reason, saying, 'The Egyptians worship God symbolically in the crocodile, that being the only animal without a tongue, like the Divine Logos, which standeth not in need of speech.' (*De Iside et Osiride*, vol. ii, p. 381.)

Achilles Tatius says, 'The number of its teeth equals the number of days in a year.' Another tradition is, that during the seven days held sacred to Apis, the crocodile will harm no one.

***Crocodile's tears.*** Hypocritical tears. The tale is that crocodiles moan and sigh like a person in deep distress, to allure travellers to the spot, and even shed tears over their prey while in the act of devouring it.

As the mournful crocodile
With sorrow snares relenting passengers.

Shakespeare, *2 Henry VI*, 3, 1

**Crocum in Ciliciam ferre.** To carry coals to Newcastle. *See* Coal. As Cilicia abounds with saffron, to send it there would be needless and extravagant excess. For a similar phrase, *see* Alcinoo.

**Croesus. *Rich as Croesus*.** Croesus, King of Lydia (ruled 560–546 BC), was so rich and powerful that all the wise men of Greece were drawn to his court, and his name became proverbial for wealth.

**Cromlech.** A megalithic monument of prehistoric times, consisting of a large flat stone resting on two or more others, like a table (Welsh *crom*, bent; *llech*, a flat stone). They are probably the uncovered remains of sepulchral chambers or cairns.

Weyland Smith's cave (Berkshire), Trevethy Stone (Cornwall), Kit's Coty House (Kent), are examples, and there are others at Plas Newydd (Anglesey) and in Cornwall; not a few are found in Ireland, as the 'killing-stone' in Louth. In Brittany, where they are known as *dolmens* (*q.v.*), Denmark, Germany, and some other parts of Europe, cromlechs are to be found.

**Cromwell's Bible.** *See* Bible, the English.

**Crone.** From Old North Fr. *carone*, a worn-out horse, which gives in Mod. Fr. *carogne*, a contemptuous word for a woman. It is from Lat. *caro*, flesh, and is so connected with *carrion*. *Crone* was also applied to an old ewe, and in this case is direct from Mid. Dutch, *kronie*, *karonie*, an old sheep, which has the same origin as *carone*.

> Take up the bastard; take 't up, I say; give 't to thy crone. Shakespeare, *Winter's Tale*, 2, 3

**Cronian Sea.** The north polar sea; so called from Cronos. Pliny says, '*A Thule unius diei navigatione mare* concretum, *a nonnullis* cronium *appellatur*.' (*Nat. Hist*., iv, 16.)

> As when two polar winds blowing adverse
> Upon the Cronian sea.
> Milton, *Paradise Lost*, x, 290

**Cronos** or **Cronus.** *See* Kronos.

**Crony.** A familiar friend. *An old crony* is an intimate of times gone by. The word was originally (17th cent.) University slang, and seems to have no connection with *crone* (*q.v.*); it may be from Gr. *kronios*, long-lasting (*kronos*, time), meaning a long-lasting friend.

**Crook.** ***By hook or crook.*** *See* Hook.

***There is a crook in the lot of every one.*** There is vexation bound up in every person's lot of life, a skeleton in the cupboard of every house. A crook in a stick is a bend, a part where the stick does not run straight, hence a 'shepherd's crook'. When lots were drawn by bits of stick, it was desirable to get sticks which were smooth and straight; but one without a crook, knot, or some other defect is rare. Thomas Boston (1676–1732) published a sermon entitled *The Crook in the Lot*.

**Crooked as Crawley.** *See* Crawley.

**Crop Up** (or) **Out.** To rise out of, to appear at the surface. A mining term. Strata which rise to the surface are said to *crop out*. We also say, such and such a subject *crops up* from time to time – i.e. rises to the surface; such and such a thing *crops out* of what you were saying – i.e. is *apropos* thereof.

**Cropper.** ***He came a cropper.*** He fell head over heels. *To get a cropper*. To get a bad fall. 'Neck and crop' means altogether, and to 'come a cropper' is to come to the ground neck and crop.

**Croquemitaine.** A hobgoblin, an evil sprite or ugly monster, used by French nurses to frighten their charges into good behaviour. In 1863 M. L'Epine published a romance with this title, telling the story of a god-daughter of Charlemagne whom he called 'Mitaine'. It was translated by Tom Hood (the Younger).

**Crore.** In India, a hundred lacs of rupees. *See* Lac.

**Crosier** (from late Lat. *crocia*; connected with our *crook*; confused with Fr. *croisier* from *crois*, Lat. *crux*, *crucis*, a cross). The pastoral staff of an abbot or bishop, and sometimes (but incorrectly) applied to an archbishop's staff, which terminates in a floriated cross, while a bishop's crosier has a curved, bracken-like head.

> A bishop turns his staff *outwards*, to denote his wider authority; an abbot (whose staff is the same as a bishop's) carries it turned *inwards*, to show that his jurisdiction is limited to his own inmates. When walking with a bishop an abbot covers his staff with a veil hanging from the knob, to show that his authority is veiled in the presence of his superior.

**Cross.** The cross is not solely a Christian symbol, originating with the crucifixion of the Redeemer. In Carthage it was used for ornamental purposes; runic crosses were set up by the Scandinavians as boundary marks, and were erected over the graves of kings and heroes; Cicero tells us (*De Divinatione*, ii, 27, and 80, 81) that the augur's staff with which they marked out the heaven was a cross; the Egyptians employed the same as a sacred symbol, and two buns marked with the cross were discovered at Herculaneum. It was a sacred symbol among the Aztecs long before the landing of Cortes; in Cozumel it was an object of worship; in Tabasco it symbolised the god of rain; and in Palinque it is sculptured on the walls with a child held up adoring it.

> The cross is not only a Christian symbol, it was also a Mexican symbol. It was one of the emblems of Quetzalcoatl, as lord of the four cardinal points, and the four winds that blow therefrom.
> Fiske, *Discovery of America*, vol. ii, ch. viii

The cross of the crucifixion is legendarily said to have been made of four sorts of wood (palm, cedar, olive, and cypress), to signify the four quarters of the globe.

> Ligna crucis palma, cedrus, cupressus, oliva.

In his *Monasteries of the Levant* (1849) Curzon gives the legend that Solomon cut down a cedar and buried it on the spot where the pool of Bethesda stood later. A few days before the crucifixion, this cedar floated to the surface of the pool, and was employed as the upright of the Saviour's cross.

It is said that Constantine, on his march to Rome, saw a luminous cross in the sky, in the shape and with the motto *In hoc vinces*, by this [sign] conquer. In the night before the battle of Saxa Rubra (312) a vision appeared to the Emperor in his sleep, commanding him to inscribe the cross and the motto on the shields of his soldiers. He obeyed the voice of the vision, and prevailed. The monogram is ΧΡιστος (Christ). *See* Gibbon's *Decline and Fall*, ch. xx.

This may be called a standing legend; for, besides St Andrew's cross, and the Dannebrog (*q.v.*), there is the story concerning Don Alonzo before the battle of Ourique in 1139, when the figure of a cross appeared in the eastern sky; Christ, suspended on it, promised the Christian king a complete victory, and the Moors were totally routed. This legend is commemorated by Alonzo's device, in a field argent five escutcheons azure, in the form of a cross, each escutcheon being charged with five bezants, in memory of the five wounds of Christ. *See* Labarum.

***The Invention of the Cross.*** A church festival held on May 3rd, in commemoration of the discovery (Lat. *invenire*, to discover) of the Cross (326) by St Helena (*q.v.*). At her direction, after a long and difficult search in the neighbourhood of the Holy Sepulchre (which had been over-built with heathen temples), the remains of the three buried crosses were found. These were applied to a sick woman, and that which effected her cure was declared to be the True Cross. The Empress had this enclosed in a silver shrine (after having carried a large piece to Rome), and deposited in a church that was built on the spot for the purpose.

In heraldry, as many as 285 varieties of cross have been recognised, but the twelve in ordinary use, and from which the others are derived, are: (1) The ordinary cross; (2) the cross humetté, or couped; (3) the cross urdé, or pointed; (4) the cross potent; (5) the cross crosslet; (6) the cross botonné, or treflé; (7) the cross moline; (8) the cross potence; (9) the cross fleury; (10) the cross paté; (11) the Maltese cross (or eight-pointed cross); (12) the cross cleché and fitché.

As a mystic symbol the number of crosses may be reduced to four:

***The Greek cross*** (+), found on Assyrian tablets, Egyptian and Persian monuments, and on Etruscan pottery.

***The crux decussata*** (X), generally called St Andrew's cross. Quite common in ancient sculpture.

***The Latin cross*** (†), or *crux immissa*. This symbol is found on coins, monuments, and medals long before the Christian era.

***The tau cross*** (T), or *crux commissa*. Very ancient indeed, and supposed to be a phallic emblem.

The tau cross with a handle (☥) or *crux ansata*, is common to several Egyptian deities, as Isis, Osiris, etc.; and is the emblem of immortality and life generally. The circle signifies the eternal preserver of the world, and the T is the monogram of Thoth, the Egyptian Mercury, meaning wisdom.

**Phrases:**

***As cross as a bear with a sore head, as the tongs, as two sticks.*** Common phrases used of one who is very vexed, peevish, or cross. The allusions are obvious.

***Everyone must bear his own cross.*** His own burden or troubles. The allusion is to the law that the person condemned to be crucified was to carry his cross to the place of execution.

***Hot cross buns.*** *See* Buns.

***On the cross.*** Not 'on the square', not straightforward. To get anything 'on the cross' is to get it unfairly or dishonestly. To *go* or *get on the cross* is to drift into bad ways, not to act honestly or not to go straight.

It's hard lines to think a fellow must grow up and get on the cross in spite of himself, and come to the gallow's foot at last, whether he likes it or not.

Boldrewood, *Robbery Under Arms*, ch. viii

***The judgement of the cross.*** An ordeal instituted in the reign of Charlemagne. The plaintiff and defendant were required to cross their arms upon their breast, and he who could hold out the longest gained the suit.

***To cross it off*** or ***out.*** To cancel it by running your pen across it. To cancel (*q.v.*) means to mark it with lattice lines, to make crosses all over it.

***To cross swords.*** To fight a duel; metaphorically, to meet someone in argument or debate.

***To cross the hand.*** Fortune-tellers of the gypsy race always bid their dupe to 'cross their hand with a bit of silver'. This, they say, is for luck. Of course, the sign of the cross warded off witches and all other evil spirits, and, as fortune-telling belongs to the black arts, the palm is signed with a cross to keep off the wiles of the devil. 'You need fear no evil, though I am a fortune-teller, if by the sign of the cross you exorcise the evil spirit.'

***To cross the line*** – i.e. the equator. To pass to the other side of the equator. It is still the custom on board ship to indulge in sports, merrymaking, and horseplay when crossing the line, and those who are doing it for the first time are usually subjected to humorous indignities. *Cv.* Ambassador.

**Cross and Ball.** The orb of royalty is a sphere or ball surmounted by a cross, an emblem of empire introduced in representations of our Saviour. The cross stands *above* the ball, to signify that the spiritual power is above the temporal.

**Cross and Pile.** The obverse and reverse sides of a coin, head and tail; hence, money generally, pitch and toss, etc. *Pile* is French for the reverse of a coin, and the other side for centuries was marked with a cross.

> A man may now justifiably throw up cross and pile for his opinions.
>
> Locke, *Human Understanding*

> Marriage is worse than cross I win, pile you lose.
>
> Shadwell, *Epsom Wells*

***I have neither cross nor pile.*** Not a penny in the world. The French phrase is, '*N'avoir ni croix ni pile.*'

> Whacum had neither cross nor pile.
>
> Butler, *Hudibras*, pt ii, 3

**Cross-bench.** Seats set at right angles to the rest of the seats in the House of Commons and the House of Lords, and intended for those members who are independent of any recognised party. Hence, *cross-bencher*, an independent, and the *cross-bench mind*, an unbiased or neutral mind.

**Crossbill.** The red plumage and the curious bill (the horny sheaths of which cross each other obliquely) of this bird are accounted for by a mediaeval fable which says that these distinctive marks were bestowed on the bird by the Saviour at the Crucifixion, as a reward for its having attempted to pull the nails from the Cross with its beak. Schwenckfeld in 1603 (*Theriotropheum Silesiae*) gave the fable in the Latin verses of Johannes Major; but it would be better known to English readers through Longfellow's translation ('The Legend of the Crossbill') from the German of Julius Mosen.

**Cross-biting.** Cheating; properly, cheating one who has been trying to cheat you – biting in return. Hence, *cross-biter* a swindler. *Laurence Crossbiter* is the name given to one of the rogues in *Cock Lorell's Bole* (*q.v.*).

**Cross-bones.** *See* Skull and crossbones.

**Cross-grained.** Patchy, ill-tempered, self-willed. Wood must be worked with the grain; when the grain crosses we get a knot or curling, which is hard to work uniform.

**Cross-legged Knights.** Crusaders were generally represented on their tombs with crossed legs.

> Sometimes the figure on the tomb of a knight has his legs crossed at the ankles, this meant that the knight went *one* crusade. If the legs are crossed at the knees, he went *twice*; if at the thighs he went *three times*.
>
> Ditchfield, *Our Villages*, 1889

***To dine with the cross-legged knights.*** *See* Dine.

**Cross-patch.** A disagreeable, ill-tempered person, male or female. Patch (*q.v.*) is an old name for a fool, and with the meaning 'fellow' it is common enough in Shakespeare, as a 'scurvy patch', a 'soldier's patch', 'What patch is made our porter?' 'a crew of patches', etc.

> Cross-patch, draw the latch,
> Sit by the fire and spin;
> Take a cup, and drink it up,
> Then call your neighbours in.
>
> Old Nursery Rhyme

**Cross questions.** ***Cross questions and crooked answers***. A parlour game which consists in giving ludicrous or irrelevant answers to simple questions. Hence, the phrase is used of one who is 'hedging', or trying by his answers to conceal the truth when he is being questioned.

**Cross-roads.** All (except suicides) who were excluded from holy rites were piously buried at the foot of the cross erected on the public road, as the place next in sanctity to consecrated ground. Suicides were ignominiously buried on the highway, generally at a crossing, with a stake driven through their body.

> Our orthodox coroner doubtless will find it a felo-de-se,
> And the stake and the cross-road, fool, if you will, does it matter to me?
>
> Tennyson, *Despair*

**Cross-row.** Short for Chriss-cross-row.

**Crotona's Sage.** Pythagoras. So called because at Crotona he established his chief school of philosophy (about 530 BC). Such success followed his teaching that the whole aspect of the town became more moral and decorous in a marvellously short time.

**Crouchmas.** An old name for the festival of the Invention of the Cross (May 3rd), also for Rogation Sunday and Rogation week. 'Crouch' is an old word for cross, especially in its religious signification; from Lat. *crux*.

> From bull-cow fast,
> Till Crouchmas be past.
>
> Tusser, *May Remembrances*

**Croud.** *See* Crowd.

**Crow.** A crow symbolises contention, discord, strife.

***As the crow flies.*** The shortest route between two given places. The crow flies straight to its destination. *Cp.* Bee-line.

***Jim Crow.*** *See* Jim.

***I must pluck a crow with you; I have a crow to pick with you.*** I am displeased with you, and must call you to account. I have a small complaint to make against you. In Howell's proverbs (1659) we find the following, 'I have a *goose* to pluck with you,' used in the same sense.

> If a crow help us in, sirrah, well pluck a crow together. Shakespeare, *Comedy of Errors*, 3, 1
>
> If not, resolve before we go,
> That you and I must pull a crow.
> Butler, *Hudibras*, pt ii, 2

***To crow over one.*** To exult over a vanquished or abased person. The allusion is to cocks, who always crow when they have gained a victory.

**Crowd, Croud,** or **Crouth.** An ancient Celtic species of fiddle with from three to six strings (Welsh *crwth*). Hence *crowder*, a player on a *crowd*. The last noted player on this instrument was John Morgan, who died 1720.

> Harke how the minstrels gin to shrill aloud
> Their merry musick that resounds from far
> The pipe, the tabor, and the trembling croud,
> That well agree withouten breach or jar.
> Spenser, *Epithalamion*
>
> I never heard the olde song of *Percy and Duglas*, that I found not my heart mooved more then with a trumpet: and yet is it sung but by some blinde Crouder, with no rougher voyce, then rude stile. Sidney, *Apologie for Poetrie*

**Crowdero.** In Butler's poem, one of the rabble leaders encountered by Hudibras at a bear-baiting. The original was one Jackson or Jephson, a milliner, of the New Exchange, Strand. He lost a leg in the Civil War, and fiddled on a crowd (*q.v.*) from alehouse to alehouse for his daily bread.

**Crown.** In heraldry, nine crowns are recognised: The oriental, the triumphal or imperial, the diadem, the obsidional crown, the civic, the crown vallery, the mural crown, the naval, and the crown celestial.

Among the Romans of the Republic and Empire crowns of various patterns formed marks of distinction for different services; the principal ones were:

- *The blockade crown* (*corona obsidionalis*), presented to the general who liberated a beleaguered army. This was made of grass and wild flowers gathered from the spot.
- *A camp crown* (*corona castrenses*) was given to him who first forced his way into the enemy's camp. It was made of gold, and decorated with palisades.
- *A civic crown* to one who saved a *civis* or Roman citizen in battle. It was of oak leaves, and bore the inscription, H.O.C.S. – i.e. *hostem occidit, civem servavit* (*a foe he slew, a citizen saved*).
- *A mural crown* was given to that man who first scaled the wall of a besieged town. It was made of gold and decorated with battlements.
- *A naval crown*, of gold, decorated with the beaks of ships, was given to him who won a naval victory.
- *An olive crown* was given to those who distinguished themselves in battle in some way not specially mentioned
- *An ovation crown* (*corona ovatio*) was by the Romans given to a general in the case of lesser victory. It was made of myrtle.
- *A triumphal crown* was by the Romans given to the general who obtained a triumph. It was made of laurel or bay leaves. Sometimes a massive gold crown was given to a victorious general. *See* Laurel.

***The iron crown of Lombardy*** is the crown of the ancient Longobardic kings. It was used at the coronation of Agilulph, King of Lombardy, in 591, and among others that have since been crowned with it are Charlemagne, as King of Italy (774), Henry of Luxemburg (the Emperor Henry VII), as King of Lombardy (1311), Frederick IV (1452), Charles V (1530), and in 1805 Napoleon put it on his head with his own hands.

In 1866, at the conclusion of peace, it was given up by Austria to Italy and was replaced in the cathedral at Monza, where Charlemagne had been crowned, and whence it had been taken in 1859. The crown is so called from a narrow band of iron about three-eighths of an inch broad, and one-tenth of an inch in thickness, within it, said to be beaten out of one of the nails used at the Crucifixion. According to tradition, the nail was given to Constantine by his mother, St Helena, who discovered the cross. The outer circlet is of beaten gold, and set with precious stones.

The *crown*, in English coinage, is a five-shilling piece, and is so named from the French *denier à la couronne*, a gold coin issued by Philip of Valois (1339) bearing a large crown on the obverse. The English crown was a gold coin of about 43½ grs till the end of Elizabeth's reign, except for a silver crown which was issued in the last coinage of Henry VIII and one other of Edward VI.

In the paper trade, *crown* is a standard size of printing paper measuring 15 by 20 inches; so called from an ancient watermark.

**Crown Office, The.** A department of the Central Office of the Supreme Court. It consists of the King's Coroner and Attorney, who is also Master, two Assistant Masters, a Chief Clerk, and some minor officials.

**Crown of the East.** Antioch, capital of Syria, which consisted of four walled cities, encompassed by a common rampart, that 'enrounded them like a coronet'.

**Crowner.** An old pronunciation of 'coroner' (*q.v.*), perhaps with the suggestion that he is an officer of the Crown.

> The crowner hath sat on her, and finds it Christian burial. Shakespeare, *Hamlet*, 5, 1

**Crow's Nest.** The 'look out' – generally a barrel fixed to the masthead – of an old-fashioned whaling-ship.

**Crozier.** *See* Crosier.

**Crucial.** ***A crucial test.*** A very severe and undeniable one. The allusion is to a fancy of Lord Bacon's, who said that two different diseases or sciences might run parallel for a time, but would ultimately cross each other: thus, the plague might for a time resemble other diseases, but when the *bubo* or boil appeared, the plague would assume its specific character. Hence the phrases *instantia crucis* (a crucial or unmistakable symptom), a crucial experiment, example, question, etc. *Cp.* Crux.

**Cruel, The.** Pedro, King of Castile (1334, 1350–69).

***Cruel garters.*** *See* Crewel.

**Crummy.** In obsolete slang, expressive of something desirable, as *that's crummy*, that's jolly good; also meaning plump, well developed, as *she's a crummy woman*, a fine, handsome woman. Among soldiers, however, the word has always meant lousy, infested with lice, and, owing to the Great War, this is now the only meaning attached to the word.

**Crump.** '*Don't you wish you may get it, Mrs Crump?*' Grose says Mrs Crump, a farmer's wife, was invited to dine with Lady Coventry, who was very deaf. Mrs Crump wanted some beer, but, awed by the purple and plush, said, in a half-whisper, 'I wish I had some beer, now.' Mr Flunkey, conscious that his mistress could not hear, replied in the same *aside*, 'Don't you wish you may get it?' At this the farmer's wife rose from table and helped herself. Lady Coventry, of course, demanded the reason, and the anecdote soon became a standing joke.

**Crumpet.** *See* Muffins.

**Crusades.** Wars undertaken in late mediaeval times by Christians against the Turks and Saracens for the recovery of the Holy Land and, nominally at least, for the honour of the cross. Each nation had its special colour, which, says Matthew Paris (i, 446), was *red* for France; *white* for England; *green* for Flanders; for Italy it was blue or *azure*; for Spain, *gules*; for Scotland, *a St Andrew's cross*; for the Knights Templars, *red on white*.

***The seven principal Crusades.***

(1) 1096–1100. Preached up by Peter the Hermit. Led by Godfrey of Bouillon, who took Jerusalem and founded a Christian kingdom in Palestine, himself becoming King of Jerusalem.

(2) 1147–49. At the instigation of St Bernard. Led by Louis VII and the Emperor Conrad. It was a failure.

(3) 1189–93. Led by Richard *Lionheart*, Frederick Barbarossa, and Philip Augustus. It did not succeed in recapturing Jerusalem, which the Mohammedans had taken in 1187.

(4) 1202–04. Led by Baldwin of Flanders and the Doge of Venice. It established a Latin Empire at Constantinople.

(5) 1228–29. Led by Frederick II. Palestine was ceded to Frederick, who was crowned king of Jerusalem.

(6) 1248–54 and (7) 1268–70. Unsuccessful expeditions undertaken by St Louis, Louis IX of France.

The so-called 'Children's Crusade', in which thousands of young people were lost by disease, shipwreck, and as captives and slaves, took place in 1212.

**Crush.** ***To crush a bottle*** – i.e. drink one. Milton has *crush the sweet poison* (*Comus*, 47). The idea is that of crushing the grapes. Shakespeare has also *burst* a bottle in the same sense (Induction of *Taming of the Shrew*). *See* Crack.

> Come and crush a cup of wine.
> Shakespeare, *Romeo and Juliet*, 1, 2

***To crush a fly on a wheel.*** Another form of 'to break a butterfly on a wheel'. *See under* Break.

**Crush-room.** A room at a theatre, opera house, etc., where the audience can collect and talk during intervals, wait for their carriages, and so on. When in use it is generally very crowded – the 'crush' is too great for the 'room'.

**Crusoe.** A solitary man; the only inhabitant of a place. The tale of Defoe, which describes Robinson Crusoe as cast on a desert island, is well known.

> Whence creeping forth, to Duty's call he yields
> And strolls the Crusoe of the lonely fields.
> Bloomfield, *Farmer's Boy*

**Crust.** *The upper crust* (of society). The aristocracy; the upper ten-thousand. The phrase was first used in *Sam Slick*. The upper crust was at one time the part of the loaf placed before the most honoured guests. Thus, in Wynkyn de

Worde's *Boke of Keruinge* (carving) we have these directions: 'Then take a lofe in your lyfte hande, and pare ye lofe rounde about; then cut the ouer-cruste to your souerayne ...'

**Crusted Port.** When port is first bottled its fermentation is not complete; in time it precipitates argol on the sides of the bottle, where it forms a crust. Crusted port, therefore, is port which has completed its fermentation.

The 'crust' is composed of argol, tartrate of lime, and colouring matter, thus making the wine more ethereal in quality and lighter in colour.

**Crusty.** Ill-tempered, apt to take offence; cross, peevish. In Shakespeare's play Achilles addresses the bitter Thersites with:

> How now, thou core of envy!
> Thou crusty batch of nature, what's the news?
>
> *Troilus and Cressida*, 5, 1

**Crutched Friars** is the Lat. *cruciati* (crossed) – i.e. having a cross embroidered on their dress. They were a minor order of friars, and first appeared in England in 1244.

**Crux.** A knotty point, a difficulty. *Instantia crucis* means a crucial test (*q.v.*), or the point where two similar diseases *crossed* and showed a special feature. It does not refer to the cross, an instrument of punishment; but to the crossing of two lines, called also a *node* or knot; hence a trouble or difficulty. *Quae te mala crux agitat?* (Plautus); What evil cross distresses you? – i.e. what difficulty, what trouble are you under?

***Crux ansata.*** The tau cross with a loop or handle at the top. *See* Cross.

***Crux commissa.*** *See* Cross.

***Crux decussata.*** A St Andrew's cross. *See* Cross.

***Crux immissa.*** *See* Cross.

***Crux pectoralis.*** The cross which bishops of the Church of Rome suspend over their breast.

**Cry.** For names of the distinctive cries of animals, *see* Animals.

***A far cry.*** A long way; a very considerable distance; used both of space and of time, as, 'it is a far cry from David to Disraeli', but they both were Jews, and had certain features in common; 'it's a far cry from Clapham to Kamschatka'. Sir Walter Scott several times uses the phrase, 'It's a far cry to Lochow (Lochawe)', and he tells us that this was

> A proverbial expression among the Campbells, meaning that their ancient hereditary dominions lay beyond the reach of an invading enemy.
>
> *Legend of Montrose*, ch. xii

***Great cry and little wool.*** A proverbial saying expressive of contempt or derision for one who promises great things but never fulfils the promises.

Originally the proverb ran, 'Great cry and little wool, as the Devil said when he sheared the hogs'; and it appears in this form in the ancient mystery of *David and Abigail*, in which Nabal is represented as shearing his sheep, and the Devil imitates the act by 'shearing a hog'.

> Thou wilt at best but suck a bull,
> Or shear swine, all cry and no wool.
>
> Butler, *Hudibras*, I, i, 851

***Hue and cry.*** *See* Hue.

***In full cry.*** In full pursuit. A phrase from hunting, with allusion to a yelping pack of hounds in chase.

***It's no good crying over spilt milk.*** It's useless bewailing the past – much better get busy and do something to repair it, if possible.

***To cry aim.*** *See* Aim.

***To cry cave.*** To give warning (Lat. *cave*, beware); used by schoolboys out of bounds, etc., when a master comes in sight.

***To cry havoc.*** *See* Havoc.

***To cry off.*** To get out of a bargain; to refuse to carry out one's promise.

***To cry quits.*** *See* Quit.

***To cry stinking fish.*** To belittle one's own endeavours, offerings, etc. 'To cry' here is to offer for sale by shouting one's wares in the street.

***To cry up.*** To praise loudly and publicly.

***To cry wolf.*** *See* Wolf.

**Crystalline.** ***The Crystalline sphere.*** According to Ptolemy, the ninth orb, identified by some with 'the waters which were above the firmament' (Gen. 1:7); it was placed between the 'primum mobile' and the firmament or sphere of the fixed stars and was held to have a shivering movement that interfered with the regular motion of the stars.

> They pass the planets seven, and pass the fixed
> And that crystalline sphere, whose balance weighs
> The trepidation talked.
>
> Milton, *Paradise Lost*, iii, 481

**Cub.** An ill-mannered lout. The cub of a bear is said to have no shape until its dam has licked it into form.

> A bear's a savage beast, of all
> Most ugly and unnatural;
> Whelped without form until the dam
> Has licked it into shape and frame.
>
> Butler, *Hudibras*, i, 3

**Cuba.** The Roman deity who kept guard over infants in their cribs and sent them to sleep. Lat. *cubo*, to lie down in bed.

**Cucking-stool.** A kind of chair formerly used for ducking scolds, disorderly women, dishonest apprentices, etc., in a pond. 'Cucking' is from the old verb *cuck*, to void excrement, and the stool used was often a close-stool.

> Now, if one cucking-stool was for each scold,
> Some towns, I fear, would not their numbers hold. *Poor Robin* (1746)

**Cuckold.** The husband of an adulterous wife; so called from *cuckoo*, the chief characteristic of this bird being to deposit its eggs in other birds' nests. Johnson says 'it was usual to alarm a husband at the approach of an adulterer by calling out "Cuckoo", which by mistake was applied in time to the person warned'. Greene calls the cuckoo 'the cuckold's quirister' (*Quip for an Upstart Courtier*, 1592), and the Romans used to call an adulterer a 'cuckoo', as '*Te cuculum uxor ex lustris rapit*' (Plautus, *Asinaria*, v, 3). *Cp.* Actaeon; Horn; *and see quotation under* Lady's Smock.

***Cuckold's Point.*** A spot on the riverside near Deptford. So called from a tradition that King John made there successful love to a labourer's wife.

**Cuckoo.** There are many old folk rhymes about this bird; one says:

> In April the cuckoo shows his bill;
> In May he sings all day;
> In June he alters his tune;
> In July away he'll fly;
> In August go he must.

Other sayings are:

> Turn your money when you hear the cuckoo, and you'll have money in your purse till he come again.

And –

> The cuckoo sings from St Tiburtius' Day (April 14th) to St John's Day (June 24th).

***Cuckoo oats and woodcock hay make a farmer run away.*** If the spring is so backward that oats cannot be sown till the cuckoo is heard (i.e. April), or if the autumn is so wet that the aftermath of hay cannot be got in till woodcock shooting (middle of November), the farmer must be a great sufferer.

***Cuckoo-spit.*** A frothy exudation deposited on plants by certain insects, especially the frog-hopper (*Aphrophora spumaris*), for the purpose of protecting the larvae. So called from an erroneous popular notion that the froth was spat out by cuckoos.

> It must be likewise understood with some restriction what hath been affirmed by *Isidore*, and yet delivered by many, that Cicades are bred out of Cuccow spittle or Woodsear; that is, that spumous, frothy dew or exudation, or both, found upon Plants, especially about the joints of Lavender and Rosemary, observable with us about the latter end of May.
> Sir Thos Browne, *Pseud. Epidemica*, v, 3

***Don't be a cuckoo!*** Don't be a silly ass; don't go and make a fool of yourself.

***To wall in the cuckoo.*** *See* Course.

**Cuculus.** ***Cuculus non facit monachum***, 'tis not the hood that makes the monk. *See* Hood.

**Cucumber-time.** The dull season in the tailoring trade. The Germans call it *Die saure gurken zeit* (pickled gherkin time). Hence the expression *Tailors are vegetarians*, because they live on 'cucumber' when without work, and on 'cabbage' (*q.v.*) when in full employ.

**Cudgel.** ***To cudgel one's brains.*** To make a painful effort to remember or understand something. The idea is from taking a stick to beat a dull boy under the notion that dullness is the result of temper or inattention.

> Cudgel thy brains no more about it; for your dull ass will not mend his pace with beating.
> Shakespeare, *Hamlet*, 5, 1

***To take up the cudgels.*** To maintain an argument or position. To fight, as with a cudgel, for one's own way.

> For some reason he did not feel as hot to take up the cudgels for Almira with his mother.
> M. E. Wilkins, *A Modern Dragon*

**Cue.** The tail of a sentence (Fr. *queue*), the catchword which indicates when another actor is to speak; a hint; the state of a person's temper, as 'So-and-so is in a good *or* bad cue.'

> When my cue comes, call me, and I will answer.
> Shakespeare, *Midsummer Night's Dream*, 4, 1

***To give the cue.*** To give the hint.

**Cuerpo.** *See* Querpo.

**Cuffy.** A negro; both a generic word and proper name; possibly from the English slang term 'cove' (*q.v.*).

> Sambo and Cuffey expand under every sky.
> Mrs Beecher Stowe, *Uncle Tom's Cabin*

**Cui bono?** Who is benefited thereby? To whom is it a gain? A common, but quite erroneous, meaning attached to the words is, What good will it do? For what good purpose? It was the question of the Roman judge L. Cassius Pedanius. *See* Cicero, *Rosc. Am.*, xxx, 84.

> Cato, that great and grave philosopher, did commonly demand, when any new project was propounded unto him, *cui bono*, what good will ensue in case the same is effected?
>
> Fuller, *Worthies* (The Design, i.)

**Cul de Sac** (Fr.). A blind alley, or alley blocked up at one end like a sack. Figuratively, an argument, etc., that leads to nothing.

**Culdees.** An ancient religious order in Ireland and Scotland from about the 8th to the 13th centuries. So called from the Old Irish *céle dé*, servant of God. The culdees were originally hermits or anchorites, but were later gathered into communities and were, finally, little more than secular canons.

**Cullinan Diamond.** The largest diamond ever known. It was discovered in 1905 at the Premier Mine in South Africa, and when found weighed 3,025¾ carats (about 1 lb 6 oz), as against the 186 1/16 carats of the famous Koh-i-Nûr (*q.v.*) in its uncut state. It was purchased by the South African Government for £150,000 and presented to Edward VII, and now forms part of the Crown Jewels, its estimated value being over £1,000,000. It was cut into a number of stones, of which the two largest weigh over 516 and 300 carats respectively. It was named from the manager of the mine at the time of its discovery.

**Cully.** A fop, a fool, a dupe. Perhaps a contracted form of *cullion*, a despicable creature (Ital. *coglione*). Shakespeare uses the word two or three times, as 'Away, base cullions!' (*2 Henry VI*, 1, 3), and again in *Taming of the Shrew*, 4, 2 – 'And makes a god of such a cullion'. *Cp.* Gull.

> You base cullion, you.
>
> Ben Jonson, *Every Man in his Humour*, iii, 2

**Culross Girdles.** The thin plate of iron used in Scotland for the manufacture of oaten cakes is called a 'girdle', for which Culross was long celebrated.

> Locks and bars, plough-graith and harrow-teeth! and why not grates and fireprongs, and Culross girdles?
>
> Scott, *Fair Maid of Perth*, ch. ii

**Culver.** A dove or pigeon; from A.S. *culfre*, which is probably an English word and unconnected with Lat. *columba*. Hence culver-house, a dove-cote.

> On liquid wing,
> The sounding culver shoots.
>
> Thomson, *Spring*, 452

**Culverin.** A long, slender piece of artillery employed in the 16th century to carry balls to a great distance. Queen Elizabeth's 'Pocket Pistol' in Dover Castle is a culverin. So called from Lat. *colubrinus* (Fr. *coulevrine*), snake-like.

> As three great Culverings for battrie bent,
> And levelled all against one certaine place,
> Doe all att once their thunders rage forth rent,
> That makes the walls to stagger with astonishment.
>
> Spenser, *Faërie Queene*, V, x, 34

**Culverkeys.** An old popular name for various plants, such as the bluebell, columbine, squill, etc., the flowers of which have some resemblance to a bunch of keys (O.E. *culfre*, a dove).

**Cum grano salis** (Lat.). With a grain of salt; there is some truth in the statement, but we must use great caution in accepting it.

**Cummer.** A gudewife, old woman. A variety of *gammer* which is a corruption of *grandmother*, as *gaffer* is of *grandfather*. It occurs scores of times in Scott's novels.

**Cunctator** (Lat., *the delayer*). Quintus Fabius Maximus (d.203 BC), the Roman general who baffled Hannibal by avoiding direct engagements, and wearing him out by marches, countermarches, and skirmishes from a distance. This was the policy by which Duguesclin forced the English to abandon their French possessions in the reign of Charles V. *Cp.* Fabian.

**Cuneiform Letters.** Letters like wedges (Lat. *cuneus*, a wedge). They form the writing of ancient Persia, Babylonia, Assyria, etc., and, dating from about 3800 BC to the early years of the Christian era, are the most ancient specimens of writing known to us. Cuneiform inscriptions first attracted interest in Europe in the early 17th century, but no deciphering was successful until 1802 (by Grotefend, of Hanover).

**Cunobelin.** A semi-mythical British king of the Silures, who is supposed to have lived about AD 75 and to have been the father of Caractacus. His name is preserved, in modified form, in Cymbeline, and in 'Cunobelin's gold-mines', the local name for the dene-holes in the chalk beds of Little Thurrock, Essex, which were traditionally used by Cunobelin for hiding.

**Cunstance.** A model of resignation, daughter of the Emperor of Rome. The Sultan of Syria, in order to marry her, turned Christian, whereupon his mother murdered him, and turned Cunstance adrift on a raft. The raft stranded on a rock near Northumberland, Cunstance was rescued, and eventually, after having been falsely accused of murder and proved innocent, was married to King Ella. She presented him with a son (Maurice), but during his absence Ella's mother, angry with Cunstance for introducing Christianity, put her on a raft with her baby.

They were rescued by a senator and taken to Rome, whither Ella, having put his mother to death, went on pilgrimage to atone for his crime. Here he fell in with his wife and son. Maurice succeeded his grandfather as Emperor of Rome, and at the death of Ella, Cunstance returned to her native land. (Chaucer, *The Man of Lawes Tale.*)

**Cup.** A mixture of strong ale with sugar, spice, and a lemon, properly served up hot in a silver cup. Sometimes a roasted orange takes the place of a lemon. If wine is added, the cup is called *bishop* (*q.v.*); if brandy is added, the beverage is called *cardinal.*

***He was in his cups.*** Intoxicated. *Inter pocula, inter vina.* (Horace, 3 *Odes*, vi, 20.)

***Let this cup pass from me.*** Let this trouble or affliction be taken away, that I may not be compelled to undergo it; this cup is 'full of the wine of God's fury', let me not be compelled to drink it. The allusion is to the Jewish practice of assigning to guests a certain portion of wine – as, indeed, was the custom in England at the close of the 18th century and the first quarter of the 19th.

***My cup runs over.*** My blessings overflow. Here cup signifies portion or blessing.

> My cup runneth over ... goodness and mercy shall follow me all the days of my life.
>
> Ps. 23:5, 6

***The cup of vows.*** In Scandinavia it was anciently customary at feasts to drink from cups of mead, and vow to perform some great deed worthy of the song of a skald. There were four cups: one to Odin, for victory; one to Frey, for a good year; one to Niörd, for peace; and one to Bragi, for celebration of the dead in poetry.

***There's many a slip 'twixt the cup and the lip.*** *See* Ancaeus.

***We must drink the cup.*** We must bear the burden awarded to us, the sorrow which falls to our lot. The allusion is to the words of our Lord in the garden of Gethsemane (Matt. 26:39; also 20:22); Christ *tasted* death for every man (Heb. 2:9). One way of putting criminals to death in ancient times was by poison; Socrates had hemlock to drink.

**Cupar.** ***He that will to Cupar maun to Cupar.*** A Scottish proverbial saying, meaning, he that will have his own way, must have it even to his injury. The reference is to the Cistercian monastery, founded here by Malcolm IV.

**Cupar Justice.** Same as 'Jedburgh Justice', hang first and try afterwards. It is sometimes called 'Cowper law', and it had its rise from a baron-baile in Coupar-Angus, before heritable jurisdictions were abolished. Abingdon Law is a similar phrase. It is said that Major-General Brown, of Abingdon, in the Commonwealth, first hanged his prisoners and then tried them. *See* Jedwood Justice, Lydford Law.

**Cupboard Love.** Love from interested motives. The allusion is to the love of children to some indulgent person who gives them something nice from her cupboard.

> Cupboard love is seldom true. *Poor Robin*

**Cupid.** The god of love in *Roman mythology* (Lat. *cupido*, desire, passion), identified with the Greek Eros; son of Mercury and Venus. He is usually represented as a beautiful winged boy, blindfolded, and carrying a bow and arrows, and one legend says that he wets with blood the grindstone on which he sharpens his arrows.

> Ferus et Cupido,
> Semper ardentes acuens sagittas.
>
> Horace, 2 *Odes*, viii, 14, 15

Well known statues of this little god are 'Cupid Sleeping', in Albano (Rome); 'Cupid playing with a Swan', in the Capitol; 'Cupid mounted on a Tiger' (Negroni); and 'Cupid stringing his Bow', in the Louvre (Paris). Raphael's painting of Cupid is in the Farnesina (Rome).

***Cupid and Psyche.*** An exquisite episode in the *Golden Ass* (*q.v.*) of Apuleius. It is an allegory representing the progress of the soul to perfection. William Morris retells the story in his *Earthly Paradise* (*May*). *See* Psyche.

***Cupid's golden arrow.*** Virtuous love.

***Cupid's leaden arrow,*** sensual passion.

> Deque sagittifera promsit duo tela pharetra
> Diversorum operum; fugat hoc, facit illud amorem.
> Quod facit auratum est et cuspide fulget acuta, –
> Quod fugat obtusum est, et habet sub arundine plumbum.
>
> Ovid, *Apollo and Daphne*

> I swear to thee by Cupid's strongest bow;
> By his best arrow with the golden head ...
> By that which knitteth souls and prospers love.
>
> Shakespeare, *Midsummer Night's Dream*

**Cupidon, Le Jeune.** Count d'Orsay (1798–1852) was so called by Byron. The Count's father was styled *Le Beau d'Orsay.*

**Cur.** A mongrel or worthless dog; hence, a fawning, mean-spirited fellow. The word is from Scandinavian *kurra*, to snarl, to grumble, and is first used in England with 'dog' – *kur-dogge*, a growling or snarling dog.

> Like a wylde Bull, that being at a bay
> Is bayted of a mastiffe, and a hound,
> And a curre-dog.
>
> Spenser, *Faërie Queene*, VI, v, 19

What would you have, you curs,
That like nor peace nor war?
Shakespeare, *Coriolanus*, 1, 1

**Curan.** *See* Argentile.

**Curate.** *See* Clerical Titles.

**Curé de Meudon** – i.e. Rabelais (*c*.1495–1553), who was first a monk, then a leech, then prebend of St Maur, and lastly curé of Meudon.

**Curetes.** A mythical people of Crete, to whom the infant Zeus was entrusted by his mother Rhea. By clashing their shields they drowned the cries of the infant, to prevent its father (Cronos) from finding the place where the babe was hid.

**Curfew Bell.** A bell that announces the time at which lights and fires are to be extinguished (Fr. *couvre-feu*, put out the fire); especially the bell rung in the reigns of William I and II at sunset in summer and at 8 o'clock in winter for this purpose.

The curfew tolls the knell of parting day.
Gray, *Elegy*

**Curmudgeon.** A grasping, miserly churl. Concerning this word Johnson says in his dictionary: 'It is a vitious manner of pronouncing *coeur mechant*, Fr., an unknown correspondent', meaning that this suggestion was supplied by some correspondent unknown; by a ridiculous blunder, Ash (1775) copied it into his dictionary as 'from Fr. *coeur*, unknown, *mechant* correspondent'! The actual etymology of the word has not been traced.

**Curnock.** *See* Crannock.

**Currant.** A corruption of *Corinth*, whence they were imported. Originally called 'raisins of Corauntz', *Corauntz* being Anglo-French for Corinth.

**Current.** ***The drift of the current*** is the rate per hour at which the current runs.

***The setting of the current*** is that point of the compass towards which the waters of the current run.

**Currente calamo** (Lat.). Offhand; without premeditation; written off at once, without making a rough copy first.

**Curry Favour.** A corruption of the M.E. *to curry favel*, to rub down Favel: *Favel* (or *Fauvel*) being the name of the horse in the 14th century French satire *Roman de Fauvel*, which was a kind of counterpart to the more famous romance, *Reynard the Fox*. Fauvel, the fallow-coloured horse, takes the place of Reynard, and symbolises cunning or duplicity; hence, to curry, or stroke down, Favel, was to enlist the services of duplicity, and so, to seek to obtain by insincere flattery or officious courtesy.

**Curse.** ***Curses, like chickens, come home to roost.*** Curses fall on the head of the curser, as chickens which stray during the day return to their roost at night.

***Cursing by bell, book, and candle.*** *See* Bell.

***Not worth a curse. I don't care a curse*** (or ***cuss***). Here 'curse' is the O.E. *creese* or *cerse*, Mod.E. *cress*, i.e. something quite valueless. Similarly, the Lat. *nihil* (*nihilum*) is *ne hilum*, not (worth) the black eye of a bean. Other phrases are 'not a straw', 'not a pin', 'not a rap', 'not a bit', 'not a jot', 'not a pin's point', 'not a button'.

Wisdom and witt nowe is not worthe a kerse.
William Langland, *Piers Plowman*

***The curse of Cain.*** One who is always on the move and has no abiding place is said to be 'cursed with the curse of Cain'. The allusion is to God's judgment on Cain after he had slain his brother Abel:

And now art thou cursed from the earth, … a fugitive and a vagabond shalt thou be in the earth. Gen. 4:11–12

***The curse of Scotland.*** The nine of diamonds. The origin of the term has never been decided, but it seems to be first recorded in the early 18th century, for in Houston's *Memoirs* (1715–47) we are told that Lord Justice-Clerk Ormistone

became universally hated in Scotland, where they called him the Curse of Scotland; and when the ladies were at cards playing the Nine of Diamonds (commonly called the Curse of Scotland) they called it the Justice Clerk.

The most plausible suggestion would seem to be that it refers to the arms of Dalrymple, Earl of Stair – viz. or, on a saltire azure, nine lozenges of the first. The earl was justly held in abhorrence for the massacre of Glencoe, and he was also detested in Scotland for his share in bringing about the Union with England in 1707.

Other attempts at accounting for the nickname are: (1) The nine of diamonds in the game of *Pope Joan* is called the Pope, the Antichrist of the Scottish reformers. (2) In the game of *comette*, introduced by Queen Mary, it is the great winning card, and the game was the curse of Scotland because it was the ruin of many families. (3) The word 'curse' is a corruption of *cross*, and the nine of diamonds is so arranged as to form a St Andrew's Cross; but as there is no evidence that the St Andrew's Cross was ever looked upon in Scotland as a curse, and as also the nine of hearts would do as well, this explanation must be abandoned. (4) Some say it was the card on which the 'Butcher Duke' wrote his cruel order after the Battle of Culloden; but this took place in 1746, which would seem to make it too late for the reference given above.

> Grose says of the nine of diamonds: 'Diamonds ... imply royalty ... and every ninth King of Scotland has been observed for many ages to be a tyrant and a curse to the country.' – *Tour Thro' Scotland*, 1789.
>
> It is a pity that Grose does not give the names of these kings.

***Curst cows have curl horns.*** *See* Cow.

**Curtain.** ***Curtain lecture.*** The nagging of a wife after she and her husband are in bed. *See* Caudle Lecture.

> Besides what endless brawls by wives are bred,
> The curtain lecture makes a mournful bed.
>
> Dryden

***Curtain raiser.*** *See* Lever de rideau.

***To ring down the curtain.*** To bring a matter to an end. A theatrical term. When the play is over, the bell rings and the curtain comes down.

The last words of Rabelais are said to have been, 'Ring down the curtain, the farce is played out.'

**Curtal Friar.** *Curtal* was originally applied to horses – a 'curtal horse' was one with its tail docked; hence the adjective came to be used for things in general that were cut down or shortened, and a 'curtal friar' was one who wore a short cloak. In later use (especially by Scott) it acquired a vaguely derisory or belittling significance.

> Some do call me the curtal Friar of Fountain Dale; others again call me in jest the Abbot of Fountain Abbey, others still again call me simply Friar Tuck.
>
> Howard Pyle, *The Merry Adventures of Robin Hood*, ii, p. 141

**Curtana.** The sword of mercy borne before the English kings at their coronation; it has no point and is hence *shortened* (O.Fr. *curt*, Lat. *curtus*). It is called the sword of Edward the Confessor, which, having no point, was the emblem of mercy. The royal sword of England was so called to the reign of Henry III.

> But when Curtana will not do the deed
> You lay the pointless clergy-weapon by,
> And to the laws, your sword of justice fly.
>
> Dryden, *Hind and Panther*, Pt ii, 419

**Curthose.** Robert II, Duke of Normandy (1087–1134); eldest son of William the Conqueror. He was also called 'Short thigh', as in Drayton's *The Tragicall Legend of Robert, Duke of Normandy, surnamed Shortthigh* (1596).

**Curtmantle.** Henry II. He introduced the Anjou mantle, which was shorter than the robe worn by his predecessors. (1133, 1154–89.) *Cp.* Caracalla.

**Curule Chair.** The chair of state among the ancient Romans; an elaborate kind of camp-stool inlaid with ivory, etc. As dictators, consuls, praetors, censors, and the chief ediles occupied such a chair, they were termed *curule* magistrates or *curules*. The word is connected either with *currus*, a chariot – perhaps because the chair was originally intended for use in a chariot – or with *curvus*, through the shape of its legs.

**Cushcow Lady.** A Yorkshire name for the ladybird (*q.v.*).

**Cushion.** ***Beside the cushion.*** Beside the question; not to the point; not pertinent to the matter in hand. Judge Jeffreys used the phrase, but it is a good deal older than his time.

***Cushion dance.*** A lively dance in which kissing while kneeling on a cushion was a prominent feature; popular in early Stuart times.

> In our court in Queen Elizabeth's time, gravity and state was kept up; in King James's time things were pretty well; but in King Charles's time there has been nothing but Trench-more and the cushion dance, *omnium gatherum*, tolly polly, *hoyte cum toyte*.
>
> Selden's *'Table Talk'* (*King of England*)

The dance survived in rural districts until comparatively recent times, and is probably still practised. John Clare (d.1864), the peasant poet of Northamptonshire, mentions it in his *May-Day Ballad*:

> And then comes the *cushion*, the girls they all shriek,
> And fly to the door from the old fiddler's squeak;
> But the doors they are fastened, so all must kneel down,
> And take the rude kiss from th' unmannerly clown.

***To miss the cushion.*** To make a mistake; to miss the mark.

**Cussedness.** Perversity; malice prepense; an evil temper. In this sense the word seems to have been originally an Americanism; the M.E. word *cursydnesse* meant sheer wickedness.

**Custard Coffin.** *See* Coffin.

**Customer.** Slang for a man or a fellow in a general way; usually with some qualification, as, *an ugly customer*, *a rum customer*, a person better left alone, as he is likely to show fight if interfered with. *Cp.* Card.

**Custos Rotulorum** (*keeper of the rolls*). The chief civil officer or principal justice of the peace of a county, to whose custody are committed the records or rolls of the sessions.

**Cut. *Cut and come again.*** Take a cut from the joint, and come for another if you like; a colloquial expression for 'there's plenty of it, have as much as you like'. It is used by Swift in *Polite Conversation*, ii.

***Cut and dry.*** Already prepared. 'He had a speech all cut and dry.' The allusion is to timber, cut, dry, and fit for use.

> Sets of phrases, cut and dry,
> Evermore thy tongue supply.
>
> Swift, *Betty the Grizette*

***Cut and run.*** Be off as quickly as possible. A sea phrase, meaning cut your cable and run before the wind.

***Cut neither nails nor hair at sea.*** Petronius says:

> Non licere cuiquam mortalium in nave neque ungues neque capillos deponere, nisi cum pelago ventus irascitur.

The cuttings of the nails and hair were votive offerings to Proserpine, and it would excite the jealousy of Neptune to make offerings to another in his own special kingdom.

***The cut of his jib.*** The contour or expression of his face. A sailor's phrase. The cut of a jib or foresail of a ship indicates her character, hence a sailor says of a suspicious vessel, he 'does not like the cut of her jib'.

***Cut off with a shilling.*** Disinherited. Blackstone tells us that the Romans set aside those testaments which passed by the natural heirs unnoticed; but if any legacy was left, no matter how small, it proved the testator's intention. English law has no such provision, but the notion at one time prevailed that the name of the heir should appear in the will; and if he was bequeathed 'a shilling', that the testator had not forgotten him, but disinherited him intentionally.

***Cut your coat according to your cloth.*** *See* Coat.

***Cut your wisdom teeth.*** *See* Wisdom tooth.

***Diamond cut diamond.*** *See* Diamond.

***He has cut his eye teeth.*** *See* Eye teeth.

***He'll cut up well.*** He is rich, and his property will cut into good slices.

***His life was cut short.*** He died prematurely. The allusion is to Atropos, one of the three Parcae, cutting the thread of life spun by her sister Clotho.

***I must cut my stick***–i.e. leave. The Irish usually cut a shillelah before they start on an expedition. *Punch* gives the following witty derivation: 'Pilgrims on leaving the Holy Land used to cut a palm-stick, to prove that they had really been to the Holy Sepulchre. So brother Francis would say to brother Paul, "Where is brother Benedict?" "Oh (says Paul), he has cut his stick!"–i.e. he is on his way home.'

***To cut.*** To renounce acquaintance. There are four sorts of cut–

(1) The *cut direct* is to stare an acquaintance in the face and pretend not to know him.

(2) The *cut indirect*, to look another way, and pretend not to see him.

(3) The *cut sublime*, to admire the top of some tall edifice or the clouds of heaven till the person cut has passed by.

(4) The *cut infernal*, to stoop and adjust your boots till the party has gone past.

***To cut a dash.*** To make a show; to get one's self looked at and talked about for a showy or striking appearance. 'Dashing' means *striking*–i.e. showy, as a 'dashing fellow' a 'dashing equipage'.

***To cut blocks with a razor.*** To do something astounding by insignificant means; to do something more eccentric than inexpedient; to 'make pin-cushions of sunbeams' (Swift). The tale is that Accius Navius, a Roman augur, opposed king Tarquin the Elder, who wished to double the number of senators. Tarquin sneered at his pretensions of augury, and asked if he could do what was then in his thoughts. 'Undoubtedly,' replied Navius; and Tarquin with a laugh said, 'Why, I was thinking whether I could cut through this whetstone with a razor.' 'Cut boldly,' cried Navius, and the whetstone was cleft in two. This story forms the subject of one of the *Bon Gaultier Ballads*, and Goldsmith refers to it in his *Retaliation*–

> In short, 'twas his [Burke's] fate, unemployed or in place, sir,
> To eat mutton cold, and cut blocks with a razor.

***To cut capers.*** *See* Capers.

***To cut one's comb.*** *See* Comb.

***To cut short*** is to shorten. 'Cut short all intermission' (*Macbeth*, 4, 3).

***To cut it short*** (*cp.* Audley) means to bring to an end what you are doing or saying.

***To cut the ground from under one,*** or ***from under his feet.*** To leave an adversary no ground to stand on, by disproving all his arguments.

***To cut the knot.*** To break through an obstacle. The reference is to the Gordian knot (*q.v.*) shown to Alexander, with the assurance that whoever loosed it would be made ruler of all Asia; whereupon the Macedonian cut it in two with his sword, and claimed to have fulfilled the prophecy.

***To cut the painter.*** *See* Painter.

***To cut up rough.*** To be disagreeable or quarrelsome about anything.

***Cut out.*** Left in the lurch; superseded. In cards, when there are too many for a game (say whist), it is customary for the players to cut out after a rubber, in order that another player may have a turn. This is done by the players cutting the cards on the table, and the lowest turn-up gives place to the new hand.

***He is cut out for a sailor.*** His natural propensities are suited for the vocation. The allusion is to cutting out cloth, etc., for specific purposes.

**Cuthbert.** A name given in contempt during the Great War to fit and healthy men of military age who, particularly in Government offices, were not 'combed out' to go into the Army; also, of course, to one who actually avoided military service. It was coined by 'Poy', the cartoonist of the *Evening News*, who represented these civilians as frightened-looking rabbits.

***St Cuthbert's beads.*** *See* Bead.

***St Cuthbert's duck.*** The eider duck; so called because it breeds in the Farne Islands, St Cuthbert's headquarters, and figures in the legends of the saint.

***St Cuthbert's Stone,*** and ***Well.*** A granite rock in Cumberland, and a spring of water close by.

**Cutler's Poetry.** Mere jingles or rhymes. Knives had, at one time, a distich inscribed on the blade by means of aqua fortis.

> Whose posy was
> For all the world like cutler's poetry
> Upon a knife.
>
> Shakespeare, *Merchant of Venice*, 5, 1

**Cutpurse.** Now called 'pickpocket'. The two words are of historical value. When purses were worn suspended from a girdle, thieves cut the string by which the purse was attached; but when pockets were adopted, and purses were no longer hung on the girdle, the thief was no longer a cutpurse, but became a pickpocket.

> To have an open ear, a quick eye, and a nimble hand, is necessary for a cutpurse.
>
> Shakespeare, *Winter's Tale*, 4, 3

***Moll Cutpurse.*** The familiar name of Mary Frith (about 1585–1660), a woman of masculine vigour, who not unfrequently assumed man's attire. She was a notorious thief and once attacked General Fairfax on Hounslow Heath, for which she was sent to Newgate. She escaped by bribery, and died at last of dropsy in the seventy-fifth year of her age. Middleton and Dekker's play *The Roaring Girl* (1611) is founded on her doings.

**Cutter's Law.** Not to see a fellow want while we have cash in our purse. Cutter's law means the law of purse-cutters, robbers, brigands, and highwaymen.

> I must put you in cash with some of your old uncle's broad-pieces. This is cutter's law; we must not see a pretty fellow want, if we have cash ourselves. Scott, *Old Mortality*, ch. ix

**Cuttle.** Captain Cuttle. An eccentric, kind-hearted sailor in Dickens's *Dombey and Son*; simple as a child, credulous of every tale, and generous as the sun. He is immortalised by the motto of *Notes and Queries*, 'When found make a note of.'

> Unfortunately, I neglected Captain Cuttle's advice, and am now unable to fnd it.
>
> W. H. Husk, *Notes and Queries*

**Cutty.** Scotch for short, as *cutty pipe*, a short clay pipe, *cutty spoons*, *cutty sark*, a short-tailed shirt, a *cutty*, a stumpy girl or woman, *cutty gun*, a popgun.

**Cutty Stool.** A small stool on which offenders were placed in the Scotch church when they were about to receive a public rebuke. *Cp.* Stool of Repentance.

**Cuwaert.** The name of the Hare in the old German version of *Reynard the Fox* (*q.v.*). In Caxton's translation he is called *Kywert*, and in the French version *Coart*. *See* Coward.

**Cwt** is C. *centum*, wt *weight*, meaning hundredweight. *Cp.* Dwt.

**Cyanean Rocks, The.** The Symplegades, two movable rocks at the entrance of the Euxine, i.e. where the Bosporus and Black Sea meet. They were said to close together when a vessel attempted to sail between them, and thus crush it to pieces. Cyanean means *blue-coloured*, and Symplegades means *dashers together*.

> Here are those hard rocks of trap, of a greenish-blue, coloured with copper, and hence called the Cyanean. Olivier

**Cycle.** A period or series of events or numbers which recur everlastingly in precisely the same order.

***Cycle of the moon,*** called 'Meton's Cycle', from Meton, who discovered it, is a period of nineteen years, at the expiration of which time the phases of the moon repeat themselves on the same days as they did nineteen years previously. *See* Callipic Period.

***Cycle of the sun.*** A period of twenty-eight years, at the expiration of which time the Sunday letters recur and proceed in the same order as they did twenty-eight years previously. In other words, the days of the month fall again on the same days of the week.

***The Platonic cycle*** or ***great year***. That space of time which, according to ancient astronomers, elapses before all the stars and constellations return to their former positions in respect to the equinoxes. Tycho Brahë calculated this period at 25,816 years, and Riccioli at 25,920.

> Cut out more work than can be done
> In Plato's year, but finish none.
>
> Butler, *Hudibras*, iii, 1

**Cyclic Poets.** Epic poets who, on the death of Homer, caught the contagion of his poems, and wrote continuations, illustrations, or additions thereto. These poets wrote between 800 and 550 BC, and were called *cyclic* because they confined themselves to the cycle of the Trojan war. The chief were Agias, Arctinos, Eugamon, Lesches and Strasinos.

> Besides the Homeric poems, the Greeks of this age possessed those of the poets named *Cyclic*, as they sang a traditional cycle of events …
>
> Keightley, *Greece*, Pt i, ch. xiv

**Cyclopean Masonry.** The old Pelasgic ruins of Greece, Asia Minor, and Italy, such as the Gallery of Tiryns, the Gate of Lions at Mycenae, the Treasury of Athens, and the Tombs of Phoroneus and Danaos. They are composed of huge blocks fitted together without mortar, with marvellous nicety, and are fabled to be the work of the Cyclops (*q.v.*). The term is also applied to similar structures in many parts of the world.

**Cyclops** (Gr., 'circular-eye'). One of a group of giants that, according to legend, inhabited Thrace. They had only one eye, and that in the centre of their forehead, and their work was to forge iron for Vulcan. They were probably Pelasgians, who worked in quarries, and attached a lantern to their forehead to give them light under ground. *Cp.* Arimaspians.

> Roused with the sound, the mighty family
> Of one-eyed brothers hasten to the shore,
> And gather round the bellowing Polypheme.
>
> Addison, *Milton Imitated*

**Cygnus.** *See* Phaeton's Bird.

**Cyllaros.** According to Virgil, the celebrated horse of Pollux (*Geor.*, iii, 90), but, according to Ovid, Castor's steed (*Met.*, xii, 408).

> He, O Castor, was a courser worthy thee.
> Coal-black his colour, but like jet it shone;
> His legs and flowing tail were white alone.
>
> Dryden, *Ovid's Metamorphoses*, xii

**Cyllenius.** Mercury. So called from Mount Cyllene, in Peloponnesus, where he was born.

**Cymbeline.** *See* Cassibelan, Cunobelin, Imogen.

**Cymochles.** In Spenser's *Faërie Queene* (II, iv, v, vi, and viii), a man of prodigious might, brother of Pyrochles, son of Acratas and Despite, and husband of Acrasia, the enchantress. He sets out to encounter Sir Guyon, but is ferried over the idle lake by Phaedria and forgets himself; he is slain by King Arthur (ca. viii).

**Cymodoce.** A sea nymph and companion of Venus in Virgil's *Georgics* (iv, 338) and *Aeneid* (v, 826). In Spenser's *Faërie Queene* (III, iv and IV, xii), she is a daughter of Nereus and mother of Marinell by Dumarin. She frees Florimel from the power of Proteus. The word means 'wave-receiving'.

***The Garden of Cymodoce.*** Sark, one of the Channel Islands. It is the title of a poem by Swinburne in his *Songs of the Springtides*.

**Cynaegiros.** It is said that when the Persians were pushing off from shore after the battle of Marathon, Cynaegiros, the brother of Aeschylos, the poet, seized one of their ships with his right hand, which was instantly lopped off; he then grasped it with his left, which was cut off also; lastly, he seized hold of it with his teeth and lost his head. *Cp.* Benbow.

**Cynic.** A snarling, churlish person. The ancient school of Greek philosophers known as the *Cynics* was founded by Antisthenes, a pupil of Socrates, and made famous by his pupil, Diogenes. They were ostentatiously contemptuous of ease, luxury, or wealth, and were given their name because Antisthenes held his school in the Gymnasium, *Cynosarges* (white dog), so called because a white dog once carried away part of a victim which Diomeos was there offering to Hercules. The effigy over Diogenes' pillar was a dog, with this inscription:

> 'Say, dog, I pray, what guard you in that tomb?'
> 'A dog.' – 'His name?' – 'Diogenes.' – 'From far?'
> 'Sinope.' – 'What! who made a tub his home?'
> 'The same; now dead, amongst the stars a star.'
>
> E.C.B.

**Cynic Tub, The.** The tub from which Diogenes lectured. Similarly we speak of the 'Porch' (*q.v.*), meaning Stoic philosophy; the 'Garden' (*q.v.*) Epicurean philosophy; the 'Academy' (*q.v.*), Platonic philosophy; and the 'Colonnade', meaning Aristotelian philosophy.

> [They] fetch their doctrines from the Cynic tub.
> Milton, *Comus*, line 708

**Cynosure.** The Pole star; hence, the observed of all observers. Greek for *dog's tail*, and applied to the constellation called *Ursa Minor*. As seamen guide their ships by the north star, and observe it well, the word 'cynosure' is used for whatever attracts attention, as 'The cynosure of neighbouring eyes' (*Milton*), especially for guidance in some doubtful matter.

**Cynthia.** The moon: a surname of Artemis or Diana. The Roman Diana, who represented the moon, was called Cynthia from Mount Cynthus in Delos, where she was born.

> And from embattled clouds emerging slow,
> Cynthia came riding on her silver car.
> Beattie, *Minstrel*

Pope, speaking of the inconstant character of woman, 'matter too soft a lasting mark to bear', says –

> Come, then, the colours and the ground prepare!
> Dip in the rainbow, trick her off in air;
> Choose a firm cloud, before it fall, and in it
> Catch, ere she change, the Cynthia of the minute.
> *Epistle*, ii, 17–20

By Elizabethan poets – Spenser, Phineas Fletcher, Raleigh, Ben Jonson, and others – the name was one of the many that was applied to Queen Elizabeth.

**Cypress.** A funeral tree; dedicated by the Romans to Pluto, because when once cut it never grows again. It is said that its wood was formerly employed for making coffins; hence Shakespeare's 'In sad cypress let me be laid' (*Twelfth Night*, 2, 4).

> Cypresse garlands are of great account at funeralls amongst the gentiler sort, but rosemary and bayes are used by the commons both at funeralls and weddings. They are plants which fade not a good while after they are gathered … and intimate that the remembrance of the present solemnity might not dye presently.
> Coles, *Introduction to the Knowledge of Plants*

**Cyprian.** Cyprus was formerly famous for the worship of Venus; hence the adjective has been applied to lewd or profligate persons and prostitutes.

> A Night Charge at Bow Street Office; with other matters worth knowing, respecting the unfortunate Cyprian, the feeling Coachman, and the generous Magistrate.
> Pierce Egan, *Life in London*, Bk ii, ch. ii (Chapter-heading).

***Cyprian brass*,** or ***aes Cyprium***, copper. Pliny (Bk xxxiv, c, ii) says, '*in Cypro enim prima aeris inventio fuit*'.

# D

**D.** This letter is the outline of a rude archway or door. It is called in Phoenician and Hebrew *daleth* (a door) and in Gr. *delta* (*q.v.*). In Egyptian hieroglyphics it is a man's hand.

**D.** or **d.** indicating a penny or pence, is the initial of the Lat. *denarius* (*q.v.*).

As a Roman numeral D stands for 500, and represents the second half of CIƆ, the ancient Etruscan sign for one thousand. D with a dash over it (D̄) is 5,000.

**D.O.M.** An abbreviation of the Lat. *Deo Optimo Maximo* (to God the best, the greatest), or *Datur omnibus mori* (it is allotted to all to die).

**D.T'.s.** A contraction of *delirium tremens.*

> They get a look, after a touch of D.T. which nothing else that I know of can give them.
>
> Indian Tale

**Da Capo (D.C.).** (*Ital.*) A musical term meaning, from the beginning – that is, finish with a repetition of the first strain.

**Dab.** Clever, skilled; as 'a dab-hand at it'. The origin is unknown, but it has been suggested that it is a contraction of the Lat. *adeptus*, an adept. 'Dabster' is another form.

> An Eton stripling, training for the law,
> A dunce at learning, but a dab at taw [marbles].
>
> Anon., *Logic, or, The Biter Bit*

**Dab, Din,** etc.

> Hab Dab and David Din
> Ding the deil o'er Dabson's Linn.

'Hab Dab' (Halbert Dobson) and 'David Din' (David Dun) were Cameronians who lived in a cave near 'Dabson's Linn', a waterfall near the head of Moffat Water.

> Here, legend relates, they encountered the devil in the form of a pack of dried hides, and after fighting him for sometime, they 'dinged' him into the waterfall.

**Dabbat** (*Dãbbatu 'larz*). In *Mohammedan mythology* the monster (literally 'reptile of the earth') that shall arise at the last day and cry that mankind have not believed in the Divine revelations.

> She will be 60 cubits high; will have the head of a bull, the eyes of a hog, the ears of an elephant, the horns of a stag, the neck of an ostrich, the breast of a lion, the colour of a tiger, the back of a cat, the tail of a ram, the legs of a camel, and the voice of an ass. She will appear three times in several places, will demonstrate the vanity of all religions except Islam, and will speak Arabic.

By some she is identified with the Beast of the Apocalypse. (Rev. 19:19; 20:10.)

**Dactyls.** Mythic beings connected with the worship of Cybele, in Crete, to whom is ascribed the discovery of iron. Their number was originally three – the Smelter, the Hammer, and the Anvil; but was afterwards increased to five males and five females, whence their name Dactyls or Fingers.

**Dad** or **Daddy.** A child's word (common to many languages) for 'father'. Used also for the person who acts as father at a wedding, for a stage-manager, for the superintendent of a casual ward, and in similar ways.

In Scott's *Fortunes of Nigel*, Steenie, Duke of Buckingham, calls King James 'My dear dad and gossip'.

**Daddy Long-legs.** A crane-fly; applied also to the long-legged spiders called 'harvestmen'.

**Daedalus.** A Greek who formed the Cretan labyrinth, and made for himself wings, by means of which he flew from Crete across the Archipelago. He is said to have invented the saw, the axe, the gimlet, etc., and his name is perpetuated in our *daedal*, skilful, fertile of invention, *daedalian*, labyrinthine or ingenious, etc. *Cp.* Icarus.

**Daffodil.** Legend says that the daffodil, or 'Lent Lily', was once white; but Persephone, who had wreathed her head with them and fallen asleep, was captured by Pluto, at whose touch the white flowers turned to a golden yellow. Ever since the flower has been planted on graves. Theophilus and Pliny tell us that they grow on the banks of Acheron and that the spirits of the dead delight in the flower, called by them the Asphodel. In England it used to be called the Affodil. (French, *asphodile*; Lat., *asphodelus*; Gr. *asphodelos.*)

> Flour of daffodil is a cure for madness.
>
> *Med. MS. Lincoln Cathedral*, f. 282

**Dagger** or **Long Cross** (†), used for reference to a note after the asterisk (*), is a Roman Catholic character, originally employed in church books, prayers of exorcism, at benedictions, and so on, to remind the priest where to make the sign of the cross. This sign is sometimes called an obelisk – that is, 'a spit'. (Gr., *obelos*, a spit.)

***Dagger***, in the arms of the City of London, commemorates Sir William Walworth's dagger, with which he slew Wat Tyler in 1381. Before this time the cognisance of the City was the sword of St Paul.

Brave Walworth, knight, lord mayor, that slew
  Rebellious Tyler in his alarmes;
The king, therefore, did give him in lieu
  The dagger to the city armes.
*Fourth year of Richard II* (1381). Fishmongers' Hall

***Dagger ale.*** The ale of the *Dagger*, a low-class gambling-house in Holborn, famous in Elizabethan times for its strong drink, furmety, and meat-pies. There was another tavern of the same name in Cheapside.

My lawyer's clerk I lighted on last night
In Holborn, at the *Dagger*.
Ben Jonson, *The Alchemist*, i, 1

***Dagger-scene in the House of Commons.*** Edmund Burke, during the French Revolution, tried a bit of bunkum by throwing down a dagger on the floor of the House, exclaiming as he did so: 'There's French fraternity for you! Such is the weapon which French Jacobins would plunge into the heart of our beloved king.' Sheridan spoilt the dramatic effect, and set the House in a roar by his remark: 'The gentleman, I see, has brought his knife with him, but where is his fork?' *Cp.* Coup de Théâtre.

***At daggers drawn.*** At great enmity, as if with daggers drawn and ready to rush on each other.

***To speak or look daggers.*** To speak or look so as to wound the sensibilities.

I will speak daggers to her; but will use none.
Shakespeare, *Hamlet*, 3, 2

**Daggle-tail** or **Draggle-tail.** A slovenly woman, the bottom of whose dress trails in the dirt. *Dag* (of uncertain origin) means loose ends, mire or dirt; whence *dag-locks*, the soiled locks of a sheep's fleece, and *dag-wool*, refuse wool.

**Dagobert. *King Dagobert and St Eloi*.** There is a French song very popular with this title. St Eloi tells the king his coat has a hole in it, and the king replies, '*C'est vrai, le tien est bon; prête-le moi*' 'Next the saint complains of the king's stockings, and Dagobert makes the same answer. Then of his wig and cloak, to which the same answer is returned. After seventeen complaints St Eloi said, 'My king, death is at hand, and it is time to confess,' when the king replied, 'Why can't you confess, and die instead of me?'

**Dagon.** A god of the Philistines, supposed – from very uncertain etymological and mythological indications – to have been symbolised as half woman and half fish.

Dagon his name: sea-monster, upward man
And downward fish; yet had his temple high
Rear'd in Azotus, dreaded through the coast
Of Palestine, in Gath and Ascalon,
And Accaron and Gaza's frontier bounds.
Milton, *Paradise Lost*, i, 462

**Dagonet, Sir.** The fool of King Arthur in the Arthurian legends; he was knighted by the king himself.

I remember at Mile End Green, when I lay at Clement's Inn, I was then Sir Dagonet in Arthur's show.
*2 Henry IV*, 3, 2 (Justice Shallow)

'Dagonet' was the pen-name of the late Mr G. R. Sims in the *Referee*.

**Daguerreotype.** A photographic process. So named from M. Daguerre, who greatly improved on the earlier efforts of himself and Nicéphore Nièpce in 1839.

**Dahak.** The Satan of Persia. According to *Persian mythology*, the ages of the world are divided into periods of 1,000 years. When the cycle of 'chiliasms' (1,000-year periods) is complete, the reign of Ormuzd will begin, and men will be all good and all happy; but this event will be preceded by the loosing of Dahak, who will break his chain and fall upon the world, and bring on man the most dreadful calamities. Two prophets will appear to cheer the oppressed, and announce the advent of Ormuzd.

**Dahlia.** This plant, bearing strikingly beautiful flowers, was discovered in Mexico by Humboldt in 1789; he sent specimens to Europe, and in 1791 it was named in honour of Dr Andrew Dahl, the Swedish botanist and pupil of Linnaeus. It was cultivated in France in 1802, and two years later in England.

**Daibutsu.** The great bronze Buddha at Kamakura, formerly the capital of Nippon (Japan). It is in a sitting posture, and is 50 ft high and 97 ft in circumference; the face is 8 ft long and the thumbs a yard round.

Above the old songs turned to ashes and pain,
Under which Death enshrouds the idols and trees
  with mist of sigh,
(Where are Kamakura's rising days and life of
  old?)
With heart heightened to hush, the Daibutsu for
  ever sits.
Yone Noguchi

**Daïkoku.** One of the seven gods of Good Fortune in the Japanese pantheon; he is invoked specially by artisans. He sits on a ball of rice, holding a magic mallet, each stroke of which confers wealth, and is usually accompanied by a rat. He is one of the most popular of the Japanese gods.

**Dairy.** From M. Eng. *dey* (A.S. *daege*), a maid-servant, the *-ry* denoting the place where her work was carried on, as in *bakery*. Chaucer spells the word *deyeyre*.

> The dey or farm-woman entered with her pitchers, to deliver the milk for the family.
>
> Scott, *Fair Maid of Perth*, ch. xxxii

**Dais.** The raised floor at the head of a dining-room, designed for the high, or principal, table, but originally the high table itself; from late Lat. *discus*, a table. The word was also used (as it still is in French) for a canopy, especially the canopy over the high table. Hence, *Sous le dais*, in the midst of grandeur.

**Daisies.** Rhyming-slang (*q.v.*) for boots, the full word being 'daisy-roots'.

**Daisy.** Ophelia gives the queen a daisy to signify 'that her light and fickle love ought not to expect constancy in her husband'. So the daisy is explained by Greene to mean a *Quip for an upstart courtier*.

The word is *Day's eye* (A.S. *daeges eage*), and the flower is so called because it closes its pinky lashes and goes to sleep when the sun sets, but in the morning expands its petals to the light. *Cp.* Violet.

> That well by reason men calle it male,
> The daisie, or else the eie of daie.
>
> Chaucer, *Legend of Good Women* (*Prol.*)

***Daisy-cutter.*** In cricket, a ball that is bowled all along the ground.

***Daisy-roots.*** Legend says that these, like dwarf-elder berries, stunt the growth, a superstition which probably arose from the notion that everything had the property of bestowing its own speciality on others. *Cp.* Fern seed.

> She robbed dwarf-elders of their fragrant fruit
> And fed him early with the daisy root,
> Whence through his veins the powerful juices ran,
> And formed the beauteous *miniature* of man.
>
> Tickell, *Kensington Gardens*

**Dak-bungalow.** *See* Bungalow.

**Dalai-Lama.** *See* Lama.

**Daldah.** Mahomet's favourite white mule.

**Dalkey, King of.** A burlesque officer, like the Mayor of Garratt (*q.v.*). Dalkey is a small island in St George's Channel, near Kingstown, a little to the south of Dublin Bay.

**Dalmatica** or **Dalmatic.** A robe, open in front, reaching to the knees, worn by Catholic bishops and deacons over the *alb* or *stole* when the Eucharist is administered. It is in imitation of the regal vest of Dalmatia, and was imported into Rome by the Emperor Commodus. Deacons have broader sleeves than sub-deacons, to indicate their duty to larger generosity; for a similar reason the sleeves of a bishop are larger than those of a priest. The two stripes before and behind are to show that the wearer should exercise his charity to all.

A similar robe is worn by kings at coronations and other great solemnities, to remind them of their duty of bountifulness to the poor.

**Daltonism.** *See* Colour-blindness.

**Dam.** The female parent of animals such as the horse, sheep, etc.; the counterpart of 'sire'; when used of human beings the word has always a very opprobrious significance. It is another form of *dame*. *See* The Devil and his Dam.

***Dam.*** An ancient Indian copper coin, of which 96 are supposed to go to the English penny. The expression *Not worth a damn* (*see* Damn) has been wrongly said to be a perversion of *Not worth a dam*, meaning this coin.

**Damage. *What's the damage?*** What have I to pay? How much is the bill? The allusion is to the law assessing damages to the plaintiff.

**Damasceening.** Producing upon steel a blue tinge and ornamental figures, sometimes inlaid with gold and silver, as in Damascus blades; so called from Damascus, which was celebrated in the Middle Ages for this class of ornamental art.

**Damask.** A figured linen fabric, so called from Damascus, where it was originally manufactured.

**Damayanti.** *See* Nala.

**Dame du Lac.** The Lady of the Lake (*q.v.*) of Arthurian romance, Vivien.

**Damiens' Bed of Steel.** Robert François Damiens, in 1757, attempted the life of Louis XV. As a punishment, and to strike terror into the hearts of all regicides, he was brutally tortured; he was chained to an iron bed that was heated, his right hand was burned in a slow fire, his flesh was torn with pincers and the wounds dressed with molten lead, boiling wax, oil, and resin, and he was ultimately torn to pieces by wild horses.

> The uplifted axe, the agonising wheel,
> Luke's iron crown, and Damiens' bed of steel.
>
> Goldsmith, *The Traveller* (1768)

**Damn. *Not worth a damn.*** Worthless; not even worth cursing at. The derivation of the phrase from the Indian coin, a *dam* (*q.v.*) has no foundation in fact. Goldsmith, in the *Citizen of the World*, uses the expression, 'Not that I care three damns.' Another vague imprecation, said to have been commonly used by the great Duke of Wellington, is *Not a twopenny damn*.

***To damn with faint praise.*** To praise with such a voice and in such measured terms as to show plainly secret disapproval.

> Damn with faint praise, assent with civil leer,
> And, without sneering, teach the rest to sneer.
> Pope, *Epistle to Arbuthnot*

**Damocles' Sword.** Evil foreboded or dreaded. Damocles, a sycophant of Dionysius the Elder, of Syracuse, was invited by the tyrant to try the felicity he so much envied. Accepting, he was set down to a sumptuous banquet, but overhead was a sword suspended by a hair. Damocles was afraid to stir, and the banquet was a tantalising torment to him. (Cicero.)

> These fears hang like Damocles' sword over every feast, and make enjoyment impossible.
> *Chambers's Encyclopaedia*

**Damon.** The name of a goatherd in Virgil's *Eclogues*, and hence used by pastoral poets for rustic swains.

**Damon and Pythias.** A type of inseparable friends. They were Syracusans of the first half of the 4th century BC: Pythias being condemned to death by Dionysius the tyrant, obtained leave to go home to arrange his affairs after Damon had agreed to take his place and be executed should Pythias not return. Pythias being delayed, Damon was led to execution, but his friend arrived just in time to save him. Dionysius was so struck with this honourable friendship that he pardoned both of them.

> Spenser fables that in the temple of Venus, Hercules and Hylas, Jonathan and David, Theseus and Pirithous, Pylades and Orestes, Titus and Gesippus,
> Damon and Pythias whom death could not sever:
> All these and all that ever had been tyde
> In bands of friendship, there did live for ever.
> *Faërie Queene*, IV, x, 27

**Damper** (*A*). A snap before dinner, which damps or takes off the edge of appetite; also a wet-blanket influence, a rebuff which damps one's courage.

Also a thin cake of flour and water baked in hot ashes. The mute of a stringed instrument is also a 'damper'.

**Damsel.** From the old French *damoisele*, the feminine form of *damoisel*, a squire; this is from Med. Lat. *domicellus*, a contracted form of *dominicellus*, the diminutive of *dominus*, lord. (Cf. Donzel.) In mediaeval France the *domicellus* or *damoiseau* was the son of a king, prince, knight, or lord before he entered the order of knighthood; the king's bodyguards were called his *damoiseaux* or *damsels*. Froissart styles Richard II *le jeune damoisel Richart*, and Louis VII (*Le Jeune*) was called the *royal damsel*.

**Damson.** Originally called the *Damascene plum*, from *Damascus*, it having been imported from Syria.

**Dan.** A title of honour meaning *Sir* or *Master* (Lat. *dominus*, *cp*. Span. *don*), common with the old poets, as Dan Phoebus, Dan Cupid, Dan Neptune, Dan Chaucer, etc. (*Cp*. Dom.)

> Dan Chaucer, well of English undefiled,
> On Fame's eternal beadroll worthy to be filed.
> Spenser, *Faërie Queene*, IV, ii, 32

***From Dan to Beersheba.*** From one end of the kingdom to the other; all over the world; everywhere. The phrase is Scriptural, Dan being the most northern and Beersheba the most southern city of the Holy Land. We have a similar expression, 'From Land's End to John o' Groats'.

**Danace.** An ancient Persian coin, worth rather more than the Greek *obolus* (*q.v.*), and sometimes, among the Greeks, placed in the mouth of the dead to pay their passage across the ferry of the Lower World.

**Danaë.** An Argive princess, daughter of Acrisius, King of Argos. He, told that his daughter's son would put him to death, resolved that Danae should never marry, and accordingly locked her up in an inaccessible tower. Zeus foiled the king by changing himself into a shower of gold, under which guise he readily found access to the fair prisoner, and she thus became the mother of Perseus.

**Danaides.** The fifty daughters of Danaus, King of Argos. They married the fifty sons of Aegyptus, and all but Hypermnestra, wife of Lynceus, at the command of their father murdered their husbands on their wedding night. They were punished in Hades by having to draw water everlastingly in sieves from a deep well.

Their names are given as follows:

| | |
|---|---|
| Actaea | wife of Periphas. |
| Adianta | Daiphron. |
| Adyta | Menalces. |
| Agave | Lycos. |
| Amymone | Encelados. |
| Anaxibia | Archelaos. |
| Antodica | Clytos. |
| Asteria | Choetos. |
| Autholea | Cisseus. |
| Autoinate | Architelos. |
| Autonoe | Eurylochos. |
| Brycea | Chthonios. |
| Callidice | Pandion. |
| Celeno | Hyxobios. |
| Chrysippe | Chrysippos. |

| | |
|---|---|
| Chrysothemis | Asteris. |
| Cleodara | Lixos. |
| Cleopatra | Agenor. |
| Clio | Asterias. |
| Critomedia | Antipaphos. |
| Damone | Amyntor. |
| Dioxipne | Aegyptos. |
| Electra | Peristhenes. |
| Erato | Bromios. |
| Eupheno | Hyperbios. |
| Eurydice | Dryas. |
| Evippe | Imbros. |
| Glauca | Alcis. |
| Glaucippa | Potamon. |
| Gorga | Hyppothooa. |
| Gorgophon | Proteus. |
| Helcita | Cassos. |
| Hippodamia | Ister. |
| Hippodica | Idras. |
| Hippomeduse | Alcmenon. |
| Hyperippa | Hippocoristes. |
| Hypermnestra | Lynceus. |
| Iphimedusa | Euchenor. |
| Mnestra | Egios. |
| Ocypete | Lampos. |
| Oime | Arbelos. |
| Pharte | Eurydamas. |
| Pilarga | Idmon. |
| Pirene | Agaptolemos. |
| Podarca | Oeneus. |
| Rhoda | Hippyoltos. |
| Rhodia | Chalcedon. |
| Sthenela | Sthenelos. |
| Stygna | Polyctor. |
| Theane | Phanthes. |

**Dance. *I'll lead you a pretty dance.*** I'll bother or put you to trouble. The French say, *Donner le bal à quelqu'un*. The reference is to the complicated dances of former times, when all followed the leader.

***St Vitus's dance.*** *See* Vitus.

***To dance and pay the piper.*** To work hard to amuse and to have to bear all the expense and take all the trouble oneself as well. The allusion is to Matt. 11:17:

> We have piped unto you, and ye have not danced.

***To dance attendance.*** To wait obsequiously, to be at the beck and call of another. The allusion is to the ancient custom of weddings, where the bride on the wedding-night had to dance with every guest, and play the amiable, though greatly tired and annoyed.

> Then must the poore bryde kepe foote with a dauncer, and refuse none, how scabbed, foule, droncken, rude, and shameless soever he be.
>
> Christen, *State of Matrimony*,1543

> I had thought
> They had parted so much honesty among them
> (At least, good manners) as not thus to suffer
> A man of his place, and so near our favour,
> To dance attendance on their lordships' pleasures.
>
> Shakespeare, *Henry VIII*, 5, 2

***To dance upon nothing.*** To be hanged.

**Dance of Death.** An allegorical representation of Death leading all sorts and conditions of men in a dance to the grave, originating in Germany in the 14th century as a kind of morality play, quickly becoming popular in France and England, and surviving later principally by means of pictorial art. There is a series of woodcuts, said to be by Hans Holbein (1538), representing Death dancing after all sorts of persons, beginning with Adam and Eve. He is beside the judge on his bench, the priest in the pulpit, the nun in her cell, the doctor in his study, the bride and the beggar, the king and the infant; but is 'swallowed up at last'.

> On the north side of Old St Paul's was a cloister, on the walls of which was painted, at the cost of John Carpenter, town clerk of London (15th century), a 'Dance of Death', or 'Death leading all the estate, with speeches of Death, and answers', by John Lydgate. The Death-Dance in the Dominican Convent of Basle was retouched by Holbein.
>
> Other well-known examples are those in the churchyard of the Monastery of the Innocents at Paris (1434), at Minden (traditionally dated 1383), one at a convent at Basle, said to have been painted by order of the prelates at the Council of Basle about 1432 and finally destroyed in 1805, and one in the Marienkirche at Lübeck.

**Dances, National.** When Handel was asked to point out the peculiar taste of the different nations of Europe in dancing, he ascribed the *minuet* to the French, the *saraband* to the Spaniard, the *arietta* to the Italian, and the *hornpipe* and the *morris-dance* to the English. To these might be added the *reel* to the Scots, and the *jig* to the Irish.

> *Religious and other dances*:
>
> *Astronomical dances*, invented by the Egyptians, designed (like our orreries) to represent the movements of the heavenly bodies.
>
> *The Bacchic dances* were of three sorts: grave (like our minuet), gay (like our gavotte), and mixed (like our minuet and gavotte combined).
>
> *The dance Champêtre*, invented by Pan, quick and lively. The dancers (in the open air) wore wreaths of oak and garlands of flowers.
>
> *Children's dances*, in Lacedemonia, in honour of

Diana. The children were nude; and their movements were grave, modest, and graceful.

*Corybantic dances*, in honour of Bacchus, accompanied with timbrels, fifes, flutes, and a tumultuous noise produced by the clashing of swords and spears against brazen bucklers.

*Funereal dances*, in Athens, slow, solemn dances in which the priests took part. The performers wore long white robes, and carried cypress slips in their hands.

*Hymeneal donces* were lively and joyous. The dancers being crowned with flowers.

*Jewish dances*. David danced in certain religious processions (2 Sam. 6:14). The people sang and danced before the golden calf (Exod. 32:19). And in the book of Psalms (150:4) we read, 'Praise Him with the timbrel and dance'. Miriam, the sister of Moses, after the passage of the Red Sea, was followed by all the women with timbrels and dances (Exod. 15:20).

*Of the Lapithae*, invented by Pirithous. These were exhibited after some famous victory, and were designed to imitate the combats of the Centaurs and Lapithae. These dances were both difficult and dangerous.

*May-day dances* at Rome. At daybreak lads and lasses went out to gather 'May' and other flowers for themselves and their elders; and the day was spent in dances and festivities.

*Military dances*. The oldest of all dances executed with swords, javelins, and bucklers. Said to be invented by Minerva to celebrate the victory of the gods over the Titans.

*Nuptial dances*. A Roman pantomimic performance resembling the dances of our harlequin and columbine.

*Pyrrhic dance*. *See* Pyrrhic.

*Salic dances*, instituted by Numa Pompilius in honour of Mars. They were executed by twelve priests selected from the highest of the nobility, and the dances were performed in the temple while sacrifices were being made and hymns sung to the god.

The Dancing Dervishes celebrate their religious rites with dances, which consist chiefly of spinning round and round a little allotted space, not in couples, but each one alone.

In ancient times the Gauls, the Germans, the Spaniards, and the English too had their sacred dances. In fact, in all religious ceremonies the dance was, and in many religions still is, an essential part of divine worship.

**Dancing Chancellor, The.** Sir Christopher Hatton (1540–91) was so called, because he first attracted Queen Elizabeth's notice by his graceful dancing in a masque at Court. He was Lord High Chancellor from 1587 till his death.

His bushy beard, and shoestrings green,  
His high-crowned hat and satin doublet,  
Moved the stout heart of England's queen,  
Though Pope and Spaniard could not trouble it.

Gray, *A Long Story*

**Dancing-water.** A magic elixir, common to many fairy-tales, which beautifies ladies, makes them young again, and enriches them. In the Countess d'Aulnoy's tale it fell in a cascade in the Burning Forest, and could only be reached by an underground passage. Prince Chery fetched a bottle of it for his beloved Fair-star, but was aided by a dove.

**Dandelion.** The leaves of the plant have jagged, tooth-like edges; hence its name, which is a form of the M.E. *dent de lyoun*, from Fr. *dent de lion*, lion tooth. Its Lat. name is *Taraxacum dens leonis*.

**Dander.** ***Is your dander up or riz?*** Is your anger excited? Are you in a rage? This is generally considered to be an Americanism, but it is of uncertain origin, and as a synonym for *anger* has been a common dialect word in several English counties. In the present sense it is more likely that it is one of the words (like *waffle*, and *hook* for a point of land) imported into America by the early Dutch colonists, from *donder*, thunder: the Dutch *op donderen* is to burst into a sudden rage.

He was as spunky as thunder, and when a  
Quaker gets his dander up, it's like a Northwester.

Seba Smith, *Letters of Major Jack Downing* (1830)

Other suggestions are that it is from *dandruff*, this being humorously substituted for the hair itself; that it is a figurative use of *dander*, the old name in the West Indies of America for a ferment used in the preparation of molasses; and that it is a euphemism for *damned anger*.

**Dandie Dinmont.** A jovial, true-hearted storefarmer, in Sir Walter Scott's *Guy Mannering*. Also a hardy, hairy short-legged terrier.

From this dog descended Davidson of Hyndlee's  
breed, the original Dandie-Dinmont.

T. Brown, *Our Dogs*, p. 104

**Dandiprat.** A small coin issued in the reign of Henry VII, value three halfpence. The term was also applied to a dwarf and a page – perhaps much as we now speak of a 'little twopenny-ha'penny fellow'; and in his translation of Virgil's *Aeneid*, Bk i (1582) Stanyhurst calls Cupid a 'dandiprat'.

**Dando.** One who frequents hotels, restaurants, and such places, satisfies his appetite, and decamps without payment. From Dando, hero of many popular songs in the early 19th century, who was famous for this.

**Dandy.** A coxcomb; a fop. The term seems to have originated in Scotland in the late 18th century, and may be merely the name *Andrew*, or a corruption of *dandiprat* (*q.v.*) or of the earlier *Jack-a-dandy*.

In paper-making the *dandy*, or *dauby-roller*, is the cylinder of wire gauze which comes into contact with paper while on the machine in a wet and elementary stage. It impresses the watermark, and also the ribs in 'laid' papers.

**Dane's Skin.** A freckled skin. Red hair and a freckled skin are the traditional characteristics of Danish blood.

**Dannebrog** or **Danebrog.** The national flag of Denmark (*brog* is Old Danish for cloth). The tradition is that Waldemar II of Denmark saw in the heavens a fiery cross which betokened his victory over the Esthonians (1219). This story is very similar to that of Constantine (*see* under Cross) and of St Andrew's Cross (*see* Andrew).

***The order of Danebrog.*** The second of the Danish orders of knighthood; instituted in 1219 by Waldemar II, restored by Christian V in 1671, and several times modified since.

**Dannocks.** Hedging-gloves. The word is said to be a corruption of *Doornick*, the Flemish name of Tournay, where they may have been originally manufactured. *Cp*. Dornick.

**Dansker.** A Dane. Denmark used to be called Danskë. Hence Polonius says to Reynaldo, 'Enquire me first what Danskers are in Paris'. (*Hamlet*, 2, 1)

**Dante and Beatrice.** Beatrice Portinari, who was only eight years old when the poet first saw her. His abiding love for her was chaste as snow and pure as it was tender. Beatrice married a nobleman, named Simone de Bardi, and died young, in 1290. Dante married Gemma, of the powerful house of Donati. In the *Divina Commedia* the poet is conducted first by Virgil (who represents human reason) through hell and purgatory; then by the spirit of Beatrice (who represents the wisdom of faith); and finally by St Bernard (who represents the wisdom from on high).

**Dantesque.** Dante-like – that is, a minute life-like representation of horrors, whether by words, as in the poet, or in visible form, as in Doré's illustrations of the *Inferno*.

**Daphnaida.** An elegy by Spenser (1591) on Douglas Howard Gorges, the only daughter of Lord Bindon. In general design and several details it is indebted to Chaucer's *Boke of the Duchesse*.

**Daphne.** Daughter of a river-god, loved by Apollo. She fled from the amorous god, and escaped by being changed into a laurel, thenceforth the favourite tree of the sun-god.

> Nay, lady, sit. If I but wave this wand,
> Your nerves are all chain'd up in alabaster,
> And you a statue, or, as Daphne was,
> Root-bound, that fled Apollo.
>
> Milton, *Comus*, 678

**Daphnis.** In *Greek mythology*, a Sicilian shepherd who invented pastoral poetry. He was a son of Mercury and a Sicilian nymph, was protected by Diana, and was taught by Pan and the Muses.

***Daphnis.*** The lover of Chloe (*q.v.*) in the Greek pastoral romance of Longus, in the 4th century. Daphnis was the model of Allan Ramsay's *Gentle Shepherd*, and the tale is the basis of St Pierre's *Paul and Virginia*.

**Dapple.** The name of Sancho Panza's donkey in *Don Quixote*. The word is probably connected with Icel. *depill*, a spot, and means blotched, speckled in patches. A *dapple-grey* horse is one of a light grey shaded with a deeper hue; a *dapple-bay* is a light bay spotted with bay of a deeper colour.

**Darbies.** Handcuffs. Probably so-called from a personal name, but not connected with 'Darby and Joan', as the use occurs many years before the first appearance of this loving couple.

> Hark ye! Jem Clink will fetch you the darbies.
>
> Scott, *Peveril of the Peak*

***Johnny Darbies***, policemen, is a perversion of the French *gensdarmes*, in conjunction with the above.

**Darby and Joan.** The type of loving, old-fashioned, virtuous couples. The names belong to a ballad written by Henry Woodfall, and the characters are said to be John Darby, of Bartholomew Close, who died 1730, and his wife, 'As chaste as a picture cut in alabaster. You might sooner move a Scythian rock than shoot fire into her bosom.' Woodfall served his apprenticeship to John Darby; but another account localises the couple in the West Riding of Yorkshire.

The French equivalent is *C'est St Roch et son chien*.

**Darbyites.** A name sometimes given to the Plymouth Brethren (*q.v.*), from John Nelson Darby (1800–82), one of the founders.

**Daric.** An ancient Persian gold coin, probably so called from *dara*, a king (*see* Darius), much in the same way as our *sovereign*, but perhaps from Assyrian *dariku*, weight. Its value is put at about 23*s*. It bears on one side the head of the king, and on the other a chariot drawn by mules. There was also a silver daric, worth one twentieth of the gold.

**Darius.** A Greek form of Persian *dara*, a king, or of Sanskrit *darj*, the maintainer. Gushtasp or Kishtasp assumed the title on ascending the throne in 521 BC, and is generally known as Darius the Great.

Legend relates that seven Persian princes agreed that he should be king whose horse neighed first; and the horse of Darius was the first to neigh.

It is said that Darius III (Codomannus), the last king of Persia, who was conquered by Alexander the Great (331 BC), when Alexander succeeded to the throne, sent to him for the tribute of golden eggs, but the Macedonian answered, 'The bird which laid them is flown to the other world, where Darius must seek them.' The Persian king then sent him a bat and ball, in ridicule of his youth; but Alexander told the messengers, with the bat he would beat the ball of power from their master's hand. Lastly, Darius sent him a bitter melon as emblem of the grief in store for him; but the Macedonian declared that he would make the Shah eat his own fruit.

**Dark.** ***A dark horse.*** A racing term for a horse of good pretensions, but of which nothing is positively known by the general public. Its merits are kept dark from betters and bookmakers.

> At last a liberal candidate has entered the field at Croydon. The Conservatives have kept their candidate back, as a dark horse.
>
> Newspaper paragraph, January, 1886

***A leap in the dark.*** A step the consequences of which cannot be foreseen. Thomas Hobbes is reported to have said on his death-bed, 'Now am I about to take my last voyage – a great leap in the dark.' Rabelais, in his last moments, said, 'I am going to the Great Perhaps,' and Lord Derby, in 1868, applied the words to the Reform Bill.

***The Dark Ages.*** The earlier centuries of the Middle Ages (*q.v.*); roughly, the era between the death of Charlemagne and the close of the Carlovingian dynasty; so called because of the intellectual darkness characteristic of the period.

***The dark Continent.*** Africa; concerning which the world was so long 'in the dark', and which, also, is the land of dark races.

***The darkest hour is that before the dawn.*** When Fortune's wheel is lowest, it must turn up again. When things have come to their worst, they must mend. In Lat., *Post nubila, Phoebus.*

***To keep dark.*** To lie perdu: to lurk in concealment.

> We'd get away to some of the far-out stations … where we could keep in the dark.
>
> Boldrewood, *Robbery Under Arms*, xvi

***To keep it dark.*** To keep it a dead secret; to refuse to enlighten anyone about the matter.

**Darken.** *To darken one's door.* To cross one's threshold: almost entirely used only in a threatening way, as 'Don't you dare to darken my door again!'

**Darky.** A negro.

**Darley Arabian.** About 1700 a Mr Darley, of Yorkshire, imported into England from Aleppo three thoroughbred Arabian stallions which became the founders of the line of thoroughbreds in England. *Darley Arabian* the sire of *Flying Childers*, and great-great-grandsire of *Eclipse*, was one; the others were *Byerby Turk* and *Godolphin Barb*. From the first comes the Herod breed, and from the second the Matchem.

**Darnex.** *See* Dornick.

**Dart.** *See* Abaris.

**Darwinian Theory.** Charles Darwin published in 1859 a work entitled *Origin of Species*, to prove that the numerous species now existing on the earth sprang originally from one or at most a few primal forms; and that the present diversity is due to special development and natural selection. Those plants and creatures which are best suited to the conditions of their existence survive and become fruitful; certain organs called into play by peculiar conditions of life grow with their growth, and strengthen with their strength, till they become so much a part and parcel of their frames as to be transmitted to their offspring. The conditions of life being very diverse, cause a great diversity of organic development, and, of course, every such diversity which has become radical is the parent of a new species. In recent times the Darwinian theory has undergone very considerable modification.

**Dash.** *One* dash under a word in MS means that the part so marked must be printed in italics; *two* dashes means small capitals; *three* dashes, large capitals.

***Cut a dash.*** *See* Cut.

***Dash my wig, buttons,*** etc. Dash is a euphemism for 'damn', and the words *wig*, *buttons*, etc., are relics of a fashion at one time adopted in comedies and by 'mashers' of swearing without using profane language.

**Dasim.** One of the sons of Eblis (*q.v.*).

**Date.** ***Not quite up to date.*** Not in the latest fashion, behind the times; said also of books somewhat in arrears of the most recent information.

**Date-palm.** *See* Phoenix dactylifera.

**Daughter.** ***The daughter of Peneus.*** The bay tree was so called because it grew in greatest perfection on the banks of the River Peneus.

***The daughter of the horseleech.*** One very exigeant; one for ever sponging on another. Prov. 30:15.

> Such and many suchlike were the morning attendants of the Duke of Buckingham – all genuine descendants of the daughter of the horseleech, whose cry is 'Give, give.'
>
> Scott, *Peveril of the Peak*, ch. xxvii

***The scavenger's daughter.*** *See* Scavenger.

**Dauphin.** The heir of the French crown under the Valois and Bourbon dynasties. Guy VIII, Count of Vienne, was the first so styled, because he wore *a dolphin* as his cognisance. The title descended in the family till 1349, when Humbert III ceded his seigneurie, the Dauphiné, to Philippe VI (de Valois), one condition being that the heir of France assumed the title of *le dauphin*. The first French prince so called was Jean, who succeeded Philippe; and the last was the Duc d'Angoulême, son of Charles X, who renounced the title in 1830.

***Grand Dauphin.*** Louis, Due de Bourgogne (1661–1711), eldest son of Louis XIV, for whose use was published the Latin classic entitled *Ad Usum Delphini*.

***Second* or *Little Dauphin.*** Louis, son of the Grand Dauphin (1682–1712).

**Davenport Brothers, The.** Two impostors from America who professed that spirits untied them when bound with cords, and that they played all sorts of instruments in a dark cabinet. The imposition was exposed in 1865.

**David.** In Dryden's *Absalom and Achitophel* (*q.v.*), represents Charles II.

> Once more the godlike David was restored
> And willing nations knew their lawful lord.

***St David.*** The patron saint of Wales (d.544): legend relates that he was son of Xantus, Prince of Ceretícu, now called Cardiganshire; he was brought up a priest, became an ascetic in the Isle of Wight, preached to the Britons, confuted Pelagius, and was preferred to the see of Caerleon or Menevia (i.e. *main aw*, narrow water or frith). Here the saint had received his early education, and when Dyvrig, the archbishop, resigned his see to him, St David removed the archiepiscopal residence to Menevia, which was henceforth called St David's. *Cp.* Taffy.

**David and Jonathan.** A type of inseparable friends. Similar examples of friendship were Pylades and Orestes (*q.v.*); Damon and Pythias (*q.v.*); etc.

> I am distressed for thee, my brother Jonathan. Very pleasant hast thou been to me. Thy love to me was wonderful, passing the love of women.
>
> 2 Sam.1:26

**Davideis.** An epic poem in four books by Abraham Cowley (1656) describing the troubles of King David.

> There is another sacred poem so called, by Thomas Elwood (1712).

**Davidians, Davists.** *See* Familists.

**Davus.** ***Davus sum, non Oedipus.*** I, Davus, am a plain, simple fellow, and no solver of riddles, like Oedipus. The words are from Terence's *Andria*, i, 2, 23, and are often quoted by one who has been set a difficult question. 'Ask me another! *Davus sum, non Oedipus!*'

> I tell the tale as it was told, nor dare to Venture a solution: 'Davus sum!'
>
> Byron, *Don Juan*, XIII, xiii

***Non te credas Davum ludere.*** Don't imagine you are deluding Davus. 'Do you see any white in my eye?' I am not such a fool as you think me to be.

**Davy.** ***I'll take my davy of it.*** I'll take my 'affidavit' it is true.

**Davy Jones.** A sailor's name for the supposed evil spirit of the sea.

*He's gone to Davy Jones's locker.* The nautical way of saying that a messmate is dead and has been buried at sea. It has been conjectured that Jones is a corruption of Jonah the prophet who was thrown into the sea.

> This same Davy Jones, according to the mythology of sailors, is the fiend that presides over all the evil spirits of the deep, and is seen in various shapes … warning the devoted wretch of death and woe.
>
> Smollett, *Peregrine Pickle*, xiii

**Davy's Sow.** ***Drunk as Davy's sow.*** Grose says: One David Lloyd, a Welshman, who kept an alehouse at Hereford, had a sow with six legs, which was an object of great curiosity. One day David's wife, having indulged too freely, lay down in the sty to sleep, and a company coming to see the sow, David led them to the sty, saying, as usual, 'There is a sow for you! Did you ever see the like?' One of the visitors replied, 'Well, it is the drunkenest sow I ever beheld.' Whence the woman was ever after called 'Davy's sow'. (*Classical Dictionary of the Vulgar Tongue*).

**Dawson, Bully.** A noted London sharper, who swaggered and led a most abandoned life about Blackfriars, in the reign of Charles II.

> Bully Dawson kicked by half the town, and half the town kicked by Bully Dawson.
>
> Charles Lamb

***Jemmy Dawson.*** The hero of a pathetic ballad by Shenstone, given in Percy's *Reliques*. Captain James Dawson joined the 'Young Chevalier', and was one of the Manchester rebels who was hanged, drawn, and quartered on Kennington Common in 1746. A lady of gentle blood was in love with the gallant young rebel, and died of a broken heart after witnessing his execution.

> Young Dawson was a gallant youth,
> A brighter never trod the plain;
> And well he lov'd one charming maid.
> And dearly was he lov'd again.

**Day.** When it begins. (1) With *sunset*: The Jews in their 'sacred year', and the Church – hence the eve of feast-days; the ancient Britons '*non dierum numerum, ut nos, sed noctium computant*', says Tacitus – hence 'se'n-night' and 'fort'night'; the Athenians, Chinese, Mahometans, etc., Italians, Austrians, and Bohemians. (2) With *sunrise*: The Babylonians, Syrians, Persians, and modern Greeks. (3) With *noon*: The ancient Egyptians and modern astronomers. (4) With *midnight*: The English, French, Dutch, Germans, Spanish, Portuguese, Americans, etc.

***A day after the fair.*** Too late; the fair you came to see is over.

***Day in, day out.*** All day long and every day.

> Sewing as she did, day in, day out.
>
> W. E. Wilkins, *The Honest Soul*

***Every dog has its day.*** *See* Dog.

***I have had my day.*** My prime of life is over; I have been a *man of light and leading, but am now 'out of the swim'*.

> Old Joe, sir ... was a bit of a favourite ... once; but he has had his day. Dickens

***I have lost a day.*** The exclamation (*Perdidi diem*) of Titus, the Roman emperor, when on one occasion he could call to mind nothing done during the past day for the benefit of his subjects.

***Today a man, tomorrow a mouse.*** In Fr., '*Aujourd'hui roi, demain rien.*' Fortune is so fickle that one day we may be at the top of the wheel, and the next day at the bottom.

***To lose the day.*** To lose the battle; to be defeated. *To win* (or *gain*) *the day* is to be victorious; to win the battle, the prize, or any competition.

**Day of the Barricades, Dupes.** *See these words.*

**Day-dream.** A dream of the imagination when the eyes are awake.

**Daylight.** Toast-masters used to cry out, 'Gentlemen, no daylights nor heeltaps.' This meant that the wineglass was to be full to the brim so that light could not be seen between the edge of the glass and the top of the wine; and that every drop of it must be drunk. *See* Heeltap.

**Daylights.** Pugilists' slang for the eyes.

***To darken one's daylights.*** To give one such a blow on the eyes as to prevent seeing.

**Daysman.** An umpire, judge, or intercessor. The obsolete verb *today* meant to appoint a day for the hearing of a suit, hence to judge between; and the man who *dayed* was the *daysman*. The word is used in Job 9:33; also by Spenser and others.

> If neighbours were at variance, they ran not straight to law;
> Daysmen took up the matter, and cost them not a straw.
>
> Anon. *New Custom*, I, ii (Morality Play: temp. Edw. VI)

**Dayspring.** The dawn: the commencement of the Messiah's reign.

> The dayspring from on high hath visited us.
>
> Luke 1:78

**Daystar.** The morning star. Hence the emblem of hope or better prospects.

> Again o'er the vine-covered regions of France,
> See the day-star of Liberty rise. Wilson, *Noctes*

**De bonne grâce** (Fr.) Willingly; with good grace.

**De die in diem** (Lat.). From day to day continuously, till the business is completed.

> The Ministry have elected to go on *de die in diem*.
>
> Newspaper paragraph

**De facto** (Lat.). Actually, in reality; in opposition to *de jure*, lawfully or rightfully. Thus John was *de facto* king, but Arthur was so *de jure*. A legal axiom says: '*De jure Judices, de facto Juratores, respondent*'; Judges look to the law, juries to the facts.

**De haut en bas** (Fr.). From head to foot; superciliously.

> She used to treat him a little *de haut en bas*.
>
> C. Reade

**De jure.** *See* De facto.

**De lunatico inquirendo** (Lat.). A writ issued to enquire into the state of a person's mind, whether it is sound or not. If not of sound mind, the person is said to be *non compos* (*q.v.*), and is committed to proper guardians.

**De mortuis nil nisi bonum** (Lat.). Of the dead speak kindly or not at all. 'Speak not evil of the dead' was one of the maxims of Chilo (*q.v.*).

**De nihilo nihil fit** (Lat.). You cannot make anything out of nothing.

**De novo** (Lat.). Afresh; over again from the beginning.

**De Profundis** (Lat.). Out of the deep; hence, an extremely bitter cry of wretchedness. Ps. 130 is so called from the first two words in the Latin version. It forms part of the Roman Catholic burial service.

**De rigueur** (Fr.). According to strict etiquette; quite *comme il faut*, in the height of fashion.

**De trop** (Fr.). Supererogatory, more than enough; also 'one too many'; when a person's presence is not wished for, that person is *de trop*.

***Rien de trop***, let nothing be in excess. Preserve in all things the golden mean.

**Dead.** ***Dead as a door-nail.*** The door-nail is either one of the heavy-headed nails with which large outer doors used to be studded, or the knob on which the knocker strikes. As this is frequently knocked on the head, it cannot be supposed to have much life left in it. The expression is found in *Piers Plowman*.

> Come thou and thy five men, and if I do not leave you all as dead as a door-nail, I pray God I may never eat grass more.
>
> Shakespeare, *2 Henry VI*, 4, 10 (Jack Cade.)

Other well-known similes are 'Dead as a shotten herring', 'as the nail in a coffin', 'as mutton', and Chaucer's 'as stoon (stone)'.

***Let the dead bury the dead.*** Let bygones be bygones. Don't rake up old and dead grievances.

> Let me entreat you to let the dead bury the dead, to cast behind you every recollection of bygone evils, and to cherish, to love, to sustain one another through all the vicissitudes of human affairs in the times that are to come.
>
> Gladstone, Home Rule Bill (February 13th, 1893)

***The wind is dead against us.*** Directly opposed to our direction. Instead of making the ship more lively, its tendency is quite the contrary.

***Dead drunk.*** So intoxicated as to be wholly powerless.

> Pythagoras has finely observed that a man is not to be considered dead drunk till he lies on the floor and stretches out his arms and legs to prevent his going lower. S. Warren

***Dead-eye.*** A block of wood with three holes through it, for the lanyards of rigging to reeve through, without sheaves, and with a groove round it for an iron strap. (Dana, *Seaman's Manual*, p. 92.) An old name for them is 'dead men's eyes'.

***Dead hand.*** One who is a 'dead hand' at anything can do it every time without fail. *See also* Hand, Dead Man's; Mortmain.

> First-rate work it was, too; he was always a dead hand at splitting.
>
> Boldrewood, *Robbery Under Arms*, xv

***Dead-heads.*** Those admitted to theatres, etc., without payment; they are 'dead' so far as the box-office receipts are concerned. The term is also applied to persons who receive something of value for which the taxpayer has to pay.

In nautical language, an obstruction floating so low in the water that only a small part of it is visible.

***Dead heat.*** A race in which two (or more) leading competitors reach the goal at the same time, thus making it necessary to run the race over again. *See* Heat.

***Dead horse.*** *Flogging the dead horse, See* Flogging.

***Working for a dead horse.*** Working for wages already paid.

***Dead languages.*** Languages no longer spoken; such as Greek, Latin, and Sanskrit.

***Dead letter.*** A law no longer acted upon. Also a letter which cannot be delivered by the postal authorities because the address is incorrect, or the person addressed cannot be found.

***Dead-letter Office.*** *See* Blind Department, *and* Dead Letter *above*.

***Dead lift.*** *I am at a dead lift.* In a strait or difficulty where I greatly need help; a hopeless exigency. A dead lift is the lifting of a dead or inactive body, which must be done by sheer force.

***Dead lights.*** Strong wooden shutters to close the cabin windows of a ship; they deaden or kill the daylight.

***To ship the dead lights.*** To fasten the shutter over the cabin window to keep out the sea when a gale is expected.

***Dead lock.*** A lock which has no spring catch. Metaphorically, a state of things so entangled, that there seems to be no practical solution.

> Things are at a dead-lock.

***Dead men.*** Empty bottles.

***Down among the dead men let me lie.*** Let me get so intoxicated as to slip from my chair, and lie under the table with the empty bottles. The expression is a witticism on the word *spirit*.

Spirit means life, and also alcohol; when the spirit is out the man is dead, and when the spirit is out of the bottle it also is dead.

***Dead men's shoes.*** *See* Shoe.

***Dead reckoning.*** A calculation of the ship's place without any observation of the heavenly bodies. An approximation made by consulting the log, compass, chronometer, the direction, wind, and so on. Such a calculation may suffice for many practical purposes, but must not be fully relied on.

***Dead ropes.*** Those which are fixed or do not run on blocks; so called because they have no activity or life in them.

***Dead Sea.*** The salt lake in Palestine, in the ancient Vale of Siddim; so called by the Romans (*Mare Mortuum*), also *Lacus Asphaltites*. The water is limpid, and of a bluish-green colour; no fish, crustacean, or mollusc can live in it, it supports no life other than microbes and a few very low organisms. It is about 46 miles long by 10 miles broad; its surface is about 1,300 ft below sea level, and it attains a depth of nearly 1,300 ft. The percentage of salt in the ocean generally is about three or four, but of the Dead Sea it is twenty-six or more.

***Dead Sea fruit.*** *See* Apples of Sodom.

***Dead set.*** *To be at a dead set*. To be set fast, so as not to be able to move. The allusion is to machinery.

***To make a dead set upon someone.*** To attack him resolutely, to set upon him; or, figuratively, to make a decided determination to bring matters to a crisis, the allusion being to dogs, bulls, etc., set on each other to fight.

***Dead weight.*** The weight of something without life; a burden that does nothing towards easing its own weight; a person who encumbers us and renders no assistance. *Cp*. Dead lift.

***Dead wind.*** A wind directly opposed to a ship's course; a wind dead ahead.

***Dead works.*** A theologian's term (from Heb. 9:14) denoting such works as do not earn salvation, or even assist in obtaining it.

**Deaf.** ***Deaf as an adder.*** 'The deaf adder stoppeth her ears, and will not hearken to the voice of the charmer, charm he never so wisely' (Ps. 58:4, 5). In the East, if a viper entered the house, the charmer was sent for, who enticed the serpent and put it into a bag. According to tradition, the viper tried to stop its ears when the charmer uttered his incantation, by applying one ear to the ground and twisting its tail into the other.

In the United States deaf adder is one of the names of the copperhead (*q.v.*).

***Deaf as a post.*** Quite deaf; or so inattentive as not to hear what is said. One might as well speak to a gatepost or log of wood.

***Deaf as a white cat.*** It is said that white cats are deaf and stupid.

***None so deaf as those who won't hear.*** The French have the same locution:

> *Il n'y a de pire sourd que celui qui ne veut pas entendre.*

**Deal.** From A.S. doel, a share, a portion; hence 'a tenth deal of flour' (Exod. 29:40).

***To deal the cards.*** To give each his dole or portion.

**Dean.** (Lat. *decanus*, one set over ten). The ecclesiastical dignitary who presides over the chapter (*q.v.*) of a cathedral or collegiate church, this having formerly consisted of *ten* canons (*q.v.*). In ecclesiastical use there are also deans not having chapters (such as the heads of Chapels Royal), and the Bishop of London is *ex officio* Dean of the Province of Canterbury. *Rural deans* are subsidiary officers of archdeacons.

The title 'Dean' is also borne by certain resident Fellows at English Universities who have special functions; and, in Scotland, to the President of the Faculty of Advocates (*Dean of Faculty*), and to certain magistrates (*Dean of Guild*).

*Dean of the Arches.* The judge presiding over the Court of Arches. *See* Arches.

**Dear.** ***Dear bought and far brought***, or **felt.** A gentle reproof for some extravagant purchase of luxury.

***My dearest foe.*** My most hated enemy. As 'my dearest friend' is one with whom I am on the greatest terms of friendship, so 'my dearest foe' is one with whom I am on the greatest terms of enmity.

> Would I had met my dearest foe in heaven,
> Or ever I had seen that day, Horatio.
>
> Shakespeare, *Hamlet*, 1, 2

***Oh, dear me!*** A very common exclamation; there is no foundation for the suggestion that it is a corruption of the Ital. *O Dio mio!* (Oh, my God!); it is more likely to have originated as a euphemism for the English '*Oh, damn me!*'

**Death.** Milton makes Death keeper, with Sin, of Hell-gate.

> The other shape
> (If shape it might be called that shape had none
> Distinguishable in member, joint or limb;

Or substance might be called that shadow seemed;)
The likeness of a kingly crown had on.

Milton, *Paradise Lost*, ii, 666–673

***Angel of Death.*** *See* Azrael.

***At death's door.*** On the point of death; very dangerously ill.

***Black Death.*** *See* Black.

***In at the death.*** Present when the fox was caught and killed; hence, present at the climax, or the final act, of an exciting event.

***Till death us do part.*** *See* Depart.

**Death from Strange Causes.**

***Aeschylus.*** was killed by the fall of a tortoise on his bald head from the claws of an eagle in the air. *Valerius Maximus*, ix, 12, and Pliny, *History*, vii, 7.

***Agathocles,*** tyrant of Sicily, was killed by a toothpick at the age of ninety-five.

***Anacreon*** was choked by a grape-stone. Pliny, *History*, vii, 7.

***Bacon*** died of a cold contracted when stuffing a fowl with snow to see whether by this means it would 'keep'.

***Burton*** (of the *Anatomy of Melancholy*) died on the very day that he himself had astrologically predicted.

***Chalchas,*** the soothsayer, died of laughter at the thought of having outlived the predicted hour of his death.

***Charles VIII,*** of France, conducting his queen into a tennis-court, struck his head against the lintel, and it caused his death.

***Fabius,*** the Roman praetor, was choked by a single goat-hair in the milk which he was drinking. Pliny, *History*, vii, 7.

***Frederick Lewis,*** Prince of Wales, son of George II, died from the blow of a cricket-ball.

***Gabrielle*** (*La belle*), the mistress of Henri IV, died from eating an orange.

***Lepidus (Quintus Aemilius)***, going out of his house, struck his great toe against the threshold and expired.

***Louis VI*** met with his death from a pig running under his horse and causing it to stumble.

***Otway,*** the poet, in a starving condition, had a guinea given him, out of which he bought a loaf of bread, and died while swallowing the first mouthful.

***Philomenes*** died of laughter at seeing an ass eating the figs provided for his own dessert. (Valerius Maximus.)

***George, Duke of Clarence,*** brother of Edward IV, was drowned in a butt of malmsey. *See* Malmsey.

***Saufeius (Appius)*** was choked to death supping up the white of an under-boiled egg. Pliny, *History*, vii, 33.

***William III*** died from his horse stumbling over a mole-hill.

***Zeuxis,*** the great painter, died of laughter at sight of a hag which he had just depicted.

**Death in the Pot.** During a dearth in Gilgal, there was made for the sons of the prophets a pottage of wild herbs, some of which were poisonous. When the sons of the prophets tasted the pottage, they cried out, 'There is death in the pot.' Then Elisha put into it some meal, and its poisonous qualities were counteracted (2 Kings 4:40).

**Death under Shield.** Death in battle.

> Her imagination had been familiarised with wild and bloody events ... and had been trained up to consider an honourable 'death under shield' (as that in a field of battle was termed) a desirable termination to the life of a warrior.
>
> Scott, *The Betrothed*, ch. vi

**Death-bell.** A tinkling in the ears, supposed by the Scotch peasantry to announce the death of a friend.

> O lady, 'tis dark, an' I heard the death-bell,
> An' I darena gae yonder for gowd nor fee.
>
> James Hogg, *Mountain Bard*

**Death-meal.** A funeral banquet.

> Death-meals, as they were termed, were spread in honour of the deceased.
>
> Scott, *The Betrothed*, ch. vii

**Death-watch.** Any species of Anobium, a genus of wood-boring beetles, that make a clicking sound, once supposed to presage death.

**Death's Head.** Bawds and procuresses used to wear a ring bearing the impression of a death's head in the time of Queen Elizabeth. Allusions not uncommon in plays of the period.

> Sell some of thy cloaths to buy thee a death's head, and put upon thy middle finger: your least considering bawd does so much.
>
> Massinger, *The Old Law*, iv, 1

**Deaths-man.** An executioner; a person who kills another brutally but lawfully.

> Great Hector's deaths-man.
>
> Heywood, *Iron Age*

**Debatable Land.** A tract of land between the Esk and Sark, claimed by both England and Scotland, and for a long time the subject of dispute. It was the haunt of thieves and vagabonds.

**Debon.** *See* Devonshire.

**Debonair** (*Le Débonnaire*). Louis I of France (778, 814–40), also called *The Pious*, son and successor of Charlemagne; a man of courteous manners, cheerful temper, but effeminate and deficient in moral energy.

**Debt of Nature.** *To pay the debt of Nature.* To die. Life is a loan, not a gift, and the debt is paid off by death.

> The slender debt to Nature's quickly paid.
>
> Quarles, *Emblems*

**Decameron.** The collection of 100 tales by Boccaccio (1353) represented as having been told in ten days (Gr. *deka*, ten, *hemera*, day) during the plague at Florence in 1348. The storytellers were also ten (seven ladies and three gentlemen), and they each told a tale on each day.

**December** (Lat., *the tenth month*). So it was when the year began in March with the vernal equinox; but since January and February have been inserted before it, the term is etymologically incorrect.

> The old Dutch name was *Winter-maand* (winter-month); the old Saxon, *Mid-winter-monath* (mid-winter-month); whereas June was *Mid-sumor-monath*. Christian Saxons called December *Se ura geóla* (the anti-yule). In the French Republican calendar it was called *Frimaire* (hoar-frost month, from November 22nd to December 20th).

*The Man of December.* Napoleon III (1808–73). He was made President of the French Republic December 11th, 1848; made his *coup d'état* December 2nd, 1851; and became Emperor December 2nd, 1852.

**Decide.** Literally, 'to cut out' (Lat. *caedere*, to cut). Several things being set before a person, he eliminates all but one, which he selects as his choice. A *decided man* is one who quickly eliminates every idea but the one he intends to adhere to.

**Decimo-sexto.** An obsolete expression for a little, insignificant person. The term comes from the book-trade: *sexto-decimo* (16 mo) is a book in which each sheet is folded to a sixteenth of its size, giving 32 pages; hence it is a small book. *Cp.* Duodecimo.

> How now! my dancing braggart in decimo-sexto!
> Charm your skipping tongue.
>
> Ben Jonson, *Cynthia's Revels*, I, i

**Deck.** A pack of cards, or that part of the pack which is left after the hands have been dealt.

> But whilst he thought to steal the single 'ten',
> The 'king' was slyly fingered from the deck.
>
> Shakepeare, *3 Henry VI*, 5, 1

***Clear the decks*** – i.e. get out of the way; your room is better than your company; I am going to be busy. A sea term. Decks are cleared before action.

***To sweep the deck.*** To clear off all the stakes. *See above*.

***To deck*** is to decorate or adorn. (Dut. *dekken*, to cover; perhaps connected with A.S. *theccan*, to thatch.)

> I thought thy bride-bed to have decked, sweet maid.
> And not have strewed thy grave.
>
> Shakespeare, *Hamlet*, 5, 1

**Decking Churches.** Isaiah (60:13) Says: 'The glory of Lebanon shall come unto thee, the fir tree, the pine tree, and the box together, to beautify the place of my sanctuary.' The 'glory of Lebanon' is the cedar tree. These are not the evergreens mainly used in church decorations, though they are all common in England. *Cp.* Holly.

**Deckle Edge.** The feathery edge occurring round the borders of a sheet of handmade or mould-made paper, due to the *deckle* or frame of the mould. It can be imitated in machine-made papers.

**Décolleté.** ***Nothing even décolleté should be uttered before ladies*** – i.e. bearing the least semblance to a *double entendre*. Décolleté is the French for a 'dress cut low about the bosom'.

**Decoration Day.** May 30th; set apart in the United States for decorating the graves of those who fell in the War of Secession (1861–5).

**Decoy Duck.** A bait or lure; a duck taught to allure others into a net, and employed for this purpose.

**Decree nisi.** *See* Nisi.

**Decretals.** The name given by ecclesiastical historians to the second part of the canon law, which contains the decrees and decisions of the early popes on disputed points.

The *False or Forged Decretals* were designed to support the claim of the popes to temporal as well as spiritual authority, and purport to be the decisions of some thirty popes of the first three centuries. The *Isidorian Decretals*, which form part of them, were compiled in the 9th century, and assigned to Isidore of Seville, who died in 636. They comprise nearly a hundred letters written in the names of the early popes, as Clement and Anacletus, as well as letters from their supposed correspondents and acts of fictitious councils.

The 9th century forgery known as the *Donation of Constantine* is also among the False Decretals. This purports to relate how Constantine the Great, when he retired to the Bosporus in 330, conferred all his rights, honours, and property as Emperor of the West on the Pope of Rome and his successors. It is said, also, to have been confirmed by Charlemagne.

**Decuman Gate.** In Roman antiquities, the principal entrance to a camp, situated on the side farthest from the enemy, and so called because it was guarded by the 10th cohort of each legion (*decimus*, tenth).

**Dedalian.** *See* Daedalus.

**Dee, Dr.** John Dee (1527–1608) was a famous astrologer; he was patronised by Queen Elizabeth, and was a man of vast knowledge, whose library, museum, and mathematical instruments were valued at £2,000. On one occasion the populace broke into his house and destroyed the greater part of his valuable collection, under the notion that Dee held intercourse with the devil. He ultimately died a pauper, at the advanced age of eighty-one, and was buried at Mortlake. He professed to be able to raise the dead, and had a magic mirror, a piece of solid pink-tinted glass about the size of an orange, in which persons were told they could see their friends in distant lands and how they were occupied. It was afterwards in Horace Walpole's collection at Strawberry Hill, and is now in the British Museum.

**Dee Mills.** *If you had the rent of Dee Mills, you would spend it all* (Cheshire proverb). Dee Mills, Cheshire, used to yield a very large annual rent.

> There was a jolly miller
> Lived on the river Dee;
> He worked and sung from morn to night –
> No lark so blithe as he;
> And this the burden of his song
> For ever used to be –
> 'I care for nobody, no, not I,
> If nobody cares for me'.
>
> Bickerstaff, *Love in a Village* (1762)

**Deer.** Supposed by poets to shed tears. The drops, however, which fall from their eyes are not tears, but an oily secretion from the so-called tear-pits.

> A poor, sequestered stag …
> Did come to languish … and the big round tears
> Coursed one another down his innocent nose
> In piteous chase.
>
> shakespeare, *As You Like It*, 2, 2

***Small deer.*** Any small animal; and used metaphorically for any collection of trifles or trifling matters.

> But mice and rats, and such small deer,
> Have been Tom's food for seven long year.
>
> Shakespeare, *Lear*, 3, 4

**Deerslayer.** The first of the Leatherstocking Novels (*q.v.*) by Fenimore Cooper, and one of the names given to the hero Natty Bumpo. He is typical of the hardy pioneers who pushed into the Far West, honourable, truthful, and brave as a lion.

**Deev.** *See* Div.

**Default.** ***Judgment by default*** is when the defendant does not appear in court on the day appointed. The judge gives sentence in favour of the plaintiff, not because the plaintiff is right, but from the default of the defendant.

**Defeat.** 'What though the field be lost? all is not lost.' (Milton, *Paradise Lost*, i, line 105–6)

'All is lost but honour' (*Tout est perdu fors l'honneur*). A saying founded on a letter written by François I to his mother after the Battle of Pavia in 1525.

> Madame, pour vous faire savoir comment se porte le ressort de mon infortune, de toutes choses ne m'est demouré que l'honneur et la vie qui est saulve …
>
> Madam, [I write] to let you know what chance there is of retrieving my misfortune, in which all that is left me is my honour, and my life which is safe …

**Defender of the Faith.** A title (Lat. *fidei defensor*) given by Pope Leo X to Henry VIII of England, in 1521, for a Latin treatise *On the Seven Sacraments.* Many previous kings, and even subjects, had been termed 'defenders of the Catholic faith', defenders of the Church', and so on, but no one had borne it as a title. The sovereign of Spain is entitled *Catholic*, and of France *Most Christian.*

> God bless the king! I mean the 'faith's defender!'
> God bless – no harm in blessing – the Pretender.
> But who Pretender is, or who is king –
> God bless us all! that's quite another thing.
>
> John Byrom (1692–1763)

Richard II, in a writ to the sheriffs, uses these words: '*Ecclesia cujus nos defensor sumus*,' and Henry VII, in the Black Book, was styled 'Defender of the Faith'.

**Deficient.** A *deficient* number is one of which the sum of all its divisors is less than itself, as 10, the divisors of which are 1, 2, 5 = 8, which is less than 10.

**Deficit, Madame.** Marie Antoinette; so called because she was always demanding money of her ministers, and never had any. According to the Revolutionary song:

La Boulangère a des écus,
Qui ne lui content guère.

*See* Baker.

**Degrees, Songs of.** Another name for the Gradual Psalms (*q.v.*).

**Dei Gratia** (Lat.). By the grace of God. Introduced into English charters in 1106; as much as to say, '*Dei non hominum gratia*', by divine right and not man's appointment. It appears as 'D.G'. on English coins. *Cp.* Graceless Florin.

From the time of Offa, King of Mercia (AD 780), we find occasionally the same or some similar assumption as, *Dei dono*, *Christo donante*, etc.

From about 676 to 1170 the Archbishop of Canterbury and some other ecclesiastical dignitaries used the same style; the Archbishop is now *divina providentia*.

**Dei Judicium** (Lat.). The judgment of God; so the judgment by ordeals was called, because it was taken as certain that God would deal rightly with the appellants.

**Deiphobus.** One of the sons of Priam, and, next to Hector, the bravest and boldest of all the Trojans. On the death of his brother Paris, he married Helen; but Helen betrayed him to her first husband, Menelaus, who slew him. He appears in the *Iliad* and *Aeneid*, and also in Shakespeare's *Troilus and Cressida*.

**Deidamia.** When Achilles (*q.v.*) was concealed in the island of Scyrus dressed as a woman he met this daughter of Lycomedes, and she became by him the mother of Pyrrhus or Neoptolemus.

**Deist.** *See* Theist.

**Deities.** The more important deities of *classical*, *Teutonic*, and *Scandinavian mythology* are given as entries in this work; the present list is only intended to include collective names and the gods of a few special localities, functions, etc.

*Air*: Ariel; Elves. *See* Elf.
*Caves* or *Caverns*: Hill-people, Pixies.
*Corn*: Ceres (Gr., Demeter).
*Domestic Life*: Vesta.
*Eloquence*: Mercury (Gr., Hermes).
*Evening*: Vesper.
*Fates, The*: Three in number (Gr.Parcae, Moirae, Keres; Scand., Norns).
*Fire*: Vulcan (Gr., Hephaistos), Vesta, Mulciber.
*Fairies*: (*q.v.*).
*Furies, The*: Three in number (Gr., Eumenides, Erinnyes).
*Gardens*: Priapus; Vertumnus with his wife Pomona.
*Graces, The*: Three in number (Gr., Charities).
*Hades*: Pluto, with his wife Proserpine (Gr., Aides and Persephone).
*Hills*: Pixies; Trolls. There are also Wood Trolls and Water Trolls.
*Home Spirits* (*q.v.*): Penates, Lares.
*Hunting*: Diana (Gr., Artemis).
*Justice*: Themis, Astraea, Nemesis.
*Love*: Cupid (Gr., Eros).
*Marriage*: Hymen.
*Medicine*: Aesculapius.
*Mines*: Trolls; Pixies.
*Morning*: Aurora (Gr., Eos).
*Mountains*: Oreads, from the Gr., ὄρος, a mountain; Trolls.
*Ocean*: Oceanides. *See* Sea, *below*.
*Poetry* and *Music*: Apollo, the nine Muses (*q.v.*).
*Rainbow*: Iris.
*Riches*: Plutus, Shakespeare speaks of 'Plutus' mine' (*Julius Caesar*, 4, 3).
*Rivers and Streams*: Fluviales (Gr., Potameides: Naiads; Nymphs).
*Sea, The*: Neptune (Gr., Poseidon), his son Triton, Nixies, Mermaids, Nereids.
*Shepherds* and their *Flocks*: Pan, the Satyrs.
*Springs*, *Lakes*, *Brooks*, etc.: Nereides or Naiads. *See* Rivers, *above*.
*Time*: Saturn (Gr., Chronos).
*Trees*: *See* Woods, *below*.
*War*: Mars (Gr., Ares), Bellona, Thor.
*Water-nymphs*: Naiads, Undine.
*Winds*: Aeolus.
*Wine*: Bacchus (Gr., Dionysos).
*Wisdom*: Minerva (Gr., Pallas, Athene, or Pallas-Athene).
*Woods*: Dryads (A Hamadryad presides over some particular tree), Wood-Trolls.
*Youth*: Hebe.

**Deianira.** Wife of Hercules, and the inadvertent cause of his death. Nessus (*q.v.*) told her that anyone to whom she gave a shirt steeped in his blood, would love her with undying love; she gave it to her husband, and it caused him such agony that he burnt himself to death on a funeral pile. Deianira killed herself for grief.

**Déjeuner à la Fourchette** (Fr.). Breakfast with forks; a cold collation; a breakfast in the middle of the day, with meat and wine; a lunch.

> The two gentlemen were consulting as to the best means of being useful to Mrs Becky, while she was finishing her interrupted *déjeuner à la fourchette*. Thackeray, *Vanity Fair*, ch. lxv

**Delaware.** The name of a State river, and bay in the United States; so called from Thomas West, Baron De la Warr (d.1618), first Governor of Virginia, in 1611.

**Delectable Mountains.** In Bunyan's *Pilgrim's Progress*, a range of mountains from which the 'Celestial City' may be seen. They are in Immanuel's land, and are covered with sheep, for which Immanuel had died.

**Delenda est Carthago,** Lat. 'Carthage must be destroyed.' The words with which Cato the Elder concluded every speech in the Senate when Carthage was such a menace to the power of Rome. They are now proverbial, and mean, 'That which stands in the way of our greatness must be removed at all hazards.'

**Delft,** or more correctly *Delf.* A common sort of pottery made at Delft in Holland. The town was noted from the 16th to the 18th centuries for its very excellent pottery; but since that time it has lost its reputation and manufactured only the cheaper kinds.

**Delia,** of Pope's line, 'Slander or poison dread from Delia's rage' (*Sat.* and *Ep.*, i, 81), was Lady Deloraine, who married W. Windam of Carsham, and died 1744. The person said to have been poisoned was Miss Mackenzie.

***Delia is not better known to our yard-dog.*** The person is so intimate and well known that the yard-dog will not bark at his approach. The line is from Virgil (*Eclogues*, iii, 67).

**Delias.** The Delian ship (i.e. the ship of Delos) that Theseus made and on which he went to Crete when he slew the Minotaur. In memory of this it was sent every fourth year with a solemn deputation to the Delian Apollo. During the festival, which lasted thirty days, no Athenian could be put to death, and as Socrates was condemned during this period his death was deferred till the return of the sacred vessel. The ship had been so often repaired that not a stick of the original vessel remained at that time.

**Delight. *The delight of mankind.*** So Titus, the Roman emperor, was entitled (40, 79–81).

**Delirium.** From the Lat. *lira* (the ridge left by the plough), hence the verb *de-lirare*, to make an irregular ridge in ploughing. *Delirus* was one who couldn't plough a straight furrow, hence a crazy, doting person, one whose mind wandered from the subject in hand: and *delirium* is the state of such a person. *Cp.* Prevarication.

***Delirium tremens.*** *See* D.T.

**Della Cruscans** or ***Della Cruscan School.*** A school of poetry started by some young Englishmen at Florence in the latter part of the 18th century. Their silly, sentimental affectations, which appeared in the *World* and the *Oracle*, created for a time quite a furore, but were mercilessly gibbeted in the *Baviad* and *Maeviad* of Gifford (1794 and 1795). The clique took its name from the famous Accademia della Crusca (literally, Academy of Chaff) which was founded in Florence in 1582 with the object of purifying the Italian language – sifting away its 'chaff' – and which (in 1611) published an important dictionary.

**Delos.** A floating island, according to *Greek legend*, ultimately made fast to the bottom of the sea by Poseidon. Apollo having become possessor of it by exchange, made it his favourite retreat. It is the smallest of the Cyclades.

**Delphi** or ***Delphos.*** A town of Phocis, at the foot of Mount Parnassus (the modern Kastri), famous for a temple of Apollo and for an oracle which was silenced only in the 4th century AD by Theodosius, and was celebrated in every age and country.

Delphi was looked upon by the ancients as the 'navel of the earth', and in the temple was kept a white stone bound with a red ribbon, to represent the navel and umbilical cord.

In the *Winter's Tale* (the same play in which he gives Bohemia a sea-coast) Shakespeare makes Delphos an island.

**Delphin Classics.** A set of Latin classics edited in France by thirty-nine scholars, under the superintendence of Montausier, Bossuet, and Huet, for the use of the Dauphin (Lat. *in usum Delphini*), i.e. the son of Louis XIV, called the *Grand Dauphin.* They were first published in 1674, and their chief value consists in their verbal indexes or concordances.

**Delta.** A tract of alluvial land enclosed by the mouth of a river. The name, from the Greek letter Δ, *delta*, was originally given to the area of the mouths of the Nile, which was of triangular shape: it has since been applied to similar formations, such as the deltas of the Danube, Rhine, Ganges, Indus, Mississippi, etc.

**Deluge.** *See* After me the deluge.

**Démarche** (Fr.). A step, measure, proceeding; especially one of a serious nature.

> The sudden, brusque, and peremptory character of the Austrian *démarche* makes it almost inevitable that in a very short time both Russia and Austria will have mobilised against each other.
>
> Sir Edw. Grey to the British Ambassador at Petrograd, 25 July, 1914

**Demerit** has reversed its original meaning (Lat. *demerere*, to merit, to deserve). The *de-* was originally intensive, as in 'de-mand', 'describe', 'de-claim', etc., but in mediaeval Latin it came to be regarded as privative, and in English the word hence had both a good and a bad sense, of which the latter is now the only one remaining.

My demerits [deserts]
May speak unbonneted.
Shakespeare, *Othello*, 1, 2

**Demesne.** *See* Manor.

**Demeter.** One of the great Olympian deities of ancient Greece, identified with the Roman Ceres (*q.v.*). She was the goddess of fruits, crops, and vegetation generally, and the protectress of marriage. Persephone (Proserpine) was her daughter.

**Demijohn.** A glass vessel with a large body and small neck, enclosed in wickerwork like a Florence flask, and containing more than a bottle. The word is from the Fr. *dame-jeanne*, 'Madam Jane', which has been thought to be a corruption of *Damaghan*, a town in Persia. There is, however, no support for this; it is more likely that the word is simply a popular name – 'Dame Jane' – like 'Bellarmine' (*q.v.*), but it is possible that it is from the Lat. *de mediana*, of middle size, or even *dimidium*, half.

**Demi-monde.** Female society only half acknowledged, as *le beau monde* is Society. The term was first used by Dumas *fils*, and has been sometimes incorrectly applied to mere fashionable courtesans.

[Dumas'] *demi-monde* is the link between good and bad society … the world of compromised women, a social limbo, the inmates of which … are perpetually struggling to emerge into the paradise of honourable and respectable ladies.
*Fraser's Magazine*, 1885

**Demi-rep.** A woman whose character has been blown upon, one 'whom everybody knows to be what nobody calls her' (Fielding). A contraction of *demi-reputation*.

**Demiurge.** In the language of the Platonists, that mysterious agent which made the world and all that it contains. The Logos or Word spoken of by St John, in the first chapter of his gospel, is the Demiurgus of Platonising Christians. In the Gnostic systems, Jehovah (as an eon or emanation of the Supreme Being) is the Demiurge. *See* Marcionites.

The power is not that of an absolute cause, but only a world-maker, a demiurge; and this does not answer to the human idea of deity.
Winchell, *Science and Religen*, ch. x

In some of the ancient Greek states the chief magistrate was called the *demiurgus*.

**Democracy.** A form of Government in which the sovereign power is in the hands of the people, and exercised by them directly or indirectly: also, a State so governed, and the body of the people, especially the non-privileged classes. (Gr. *demos-kratia*, the rule of the people.)

**Democritus.** The laughing philosopher of Abdera (lived about 460–357 BC). He should rather be termed the *deriding* philosopher, because he derided or laughed at people's folly or vanity. It is said that he put out his eyes that he might think more deeply.

Democritus, dear droll, revisit earth,
And with our follies glut thy heightened mirth.
Prior

***Democritus Junior.*** Robert Burton (1577–1640), author of *The Anatomy of Melancholy*.

**Demodocos.** A minstrel who, according to Homer (*Od.* viii), sang the amours of Mars and Venus in the court of Alcinous while Ulysses was a guest there.

**Demogorgon.** A terrible deity, whose very name was capable of producing the most horrible effects. He is first mentioned by the 4th century Christian writer, Lactantius, who, in so doing is believed to have broken the spell of a mystery, for *Demogorgon* is supposed to be identical with the infernal Power of the ancients, the very mention of whose name brought death and disaster, to whom reference is made by Lucan and others:

Must I call your master to my aid,
At whose dread name the trembling furies quake,
Hell stands abashed, and earth's foundations shake?
Rowe, *Lucan's Pharsalia*, vi

Hence Milton speaks of 'the dreaded name of Demogorgon' (*Paradise Lost*, ii, 965). According to Ariosto Demogorgon was a king of the elves and fays who lived on the Himalayas, and once in five years summoned all his subjects before him to give an account of their stewardship. Spenser (*Faërie Queene*, iv, ii, 47) says that he dwells in the deep abyss with the three fatal sisters.

**Demons, Prince of.** Asmodeus (*q.v.*), also called 'The Demon of Matrimonial Unhappiness'.

**Demos, King.** The electorate; the proletariat. Not the mob, but those who choose and elect our senators, and are therefore the virtual rulers of the nation.

**Demurrage.** An allowance made to the master or owners of a ship by the freighters for detaining her in port longer than the time agreed upon. (Lat., *demorari*, to delay.)

The extra days beyond the lay days … are called days of demurrage.
Kent, *Commentaries*, vol.iii, pt v, lecture xlvii, p.159

**Demy.** A size of paper between royal and crown, measuring 17½ by 22½ in. in printing papers, and 15½ by 20 in. in writing papers. It is from Fr. *demi* (half), probably meaning 'half imperial'.

***A Demy*** of Magdalen College, Oxford, is a foundation scholar, whose allowance or 'commons' was originally *half* that of a Fellow.

**Den. *God ye good den!*** An abbreviated form of the old salutation 'God give you *good even*(ing).'

> *Nurse*. God ye good-morrow, gentlemen.
> *Mer*. God ye good den, gentlewoman.
> Shakespeare, *Romeo and Juliet*, 2, 4

**Denarius.** A Roman silver coin equal in value to ten ases (*deni-ases*), or about 8½*d*. The word was used in France and England for the inferior coins, whether silver or copper, and for ready money generally. The initial '*d*'. for penny (*£ s. d.*) is from *denarius*.

> The denarius ... shown to our Lord ... was the tribute-money payable by the Jews to the Roman emperor, and must not be confounded with the tribute paid to the Temple.
> Madden, *Jewish Coinage*, ch. xi

***Denarius Dei*** (Lat. God's penny). An earnest of a bargain, which was given to the church or poor.

***Denarii St Petri,*** Peter's pence (q.v.).

**Denizen.** A person who lives *in* a country as opposed to foreigners who live *outside* (Lat. *de-intus*, from within, through O. Fr. *deinzein*). In English law the word means a made citizen – i.e. an alien who has been naturalised by letters patent.

> A denizen is a kind of middle state, between an alien and a natural-born subject, and partakes of both. Blackstone, *Commentaries*, Bk i, ch. x

**Denmark.** According to the *Roman de Rose*, Denmark means the country of Danaos, who settled here with a colony after the siege of Troy, as Brutus is said by the same sort of name-legend to have settled in Britain. Saxo-Germanicus, with equal absurdity, makes Dan, the son of Humble, the first king, to account for the name of the country.

**Denys, St.** The apostle to the Gauls and patron saint of France. He is said to have been beheaded at Paris in 272, and, according to tradition, carried his head, after martyrdom, for six miles in his hands and laid it on the spot where stands the cathedral bearing his name. The tale may have taken its rise from an ancient painting of the incident, in which the artist placed the head between the martyr's hands so that the trunk might be recognised.

***Montjoie Saint Denys!*** *See* Montjoie.

**Deo gratias** (Lat.). Thanks to God. *Cp.* Dei gratia.

**Deo juvante** (Lat.). With God's help; God willing.

**Deo, non fortuna** (Lat.). From God, not from mere luck; (I attribute it) to God and not to blind chance.

**Deo volente** (Lat.). God being willing; by God's will; usually contracted into D.V.

**Deoch-an-doruis.** *See* Doch-an-doroch.

**Deodand.** Literally, something 'given to God' (Lat. *deo-dandum*). In English law, a personal chattel which had been the cause of the death of a person which (till the custom was abolished in 1846) was forfeited and sold for some pious use. For instance, when a man met with his death through injuries inflicted by the fall of a ladder, the toss of a bull, or the kick of a horse, the cause of death was sold, and the proceeds given to the Church. The custom originated in the idea that as the person was sent to his account without the sacrament of extreme unction, the money could serve to pay for masses for his repose.

**Depart.** Literally, to part thoroughly; to separate effectually. The marriage service in the old prayer books had 'till death us depart', which has been corrupted into 'till death us do part'.

> 'Depart' is sound English for 'part asunder', which was altered to 'do part' in 1661, at the pressing request of the Puritans, who knew as little of the history of their national language as they did of that of their national Church.
> J. H. Blunt, *Annotated Book of Common Prayer*

**Department.** France is divided into departments, as Great Britain and Ireland are divided into counties or shires. From 1768 it was divided into *governments*, of which thirty-two were *grand* and eight *petit*. In 1790, by a decree of the Constituent Assembly, it was mapped out *de novo* into eighty-three departments. In 1804 the number of departments was increased to 107, and in 1812 to 130. In 1815 the territory was reduced to eighty-six departments, and continued so till 1860, when Savoy and Nice were added. The present number is eighty-seven, including Corsica but not the provinces of Alsace and Lorraine.

**Deputations. *The year of deputations*.** In Mohammedan history, the ninth year of the Hegira (*q.v.*), i.e. AD 631–2 when the tribes in large numbers submitted to Mahomet and sent deputations of peace.

**Derby Stakes.** Started by Edward Stanley, the twelfth Earl of Derby, in 1780, the year after his establishment of the Oaks stakes (*q.v.*).

***Derby Day*** is the day when the Derby stakes are run for, during the great Epsom Summer Meeting; it is usually either the Wednesday before or the second Wednesday after Whit Sunday. The Derby, known as the 'Blue Ribbon of the Turf', is for colts and fillies of three years old only; consequently, no horse can win it twice. The name of the race is pronounced *Dar*by, that of the town and county *Dur*by. *See* Classic Races.

**Dernier ressort** (Fr.). A last resort; a final court from which there is no appeal, hence a last resource.

**Derrick.** A temporary crane to remove goods from the hold of a vessel, etc.; so called from Derrick, the Tyburn hangman early in the 17th century. The name was first given to the gibbet; hence, from the similarity in shape, to the crane.

> He rides circuit with the devil, and Derrick must be his host, and Tyborne the inn at which he will light. Dekker, *Bellman of London* (1608)

**Derwentwater.** ***Lord Derwentwater's lights***. A local name for the Aurora borealis; James, Earl of Derwentwater, was beheaded for rebellion February 24th, 1716, and it is said that the northern lights were unusually brilliant that night.

**Desmas.** *See* Dysmas.

**Despair.** ***The Giant Despair***, in Bunyan's *Pilgrim's Progress*, lived in 'Doubting Castle'.

**Dessert** means simply the cloth removed (Fr. *desservir*, to clear the table); and dessert is that which comes after the cloth is removed.

**Destruction.** ***Prince of Destruction***. Tamerlane or Timour the Tartar (1333, 1370–1405), the terror of the East. He was conqueror of Persia and a great part of India, and was threatening China when he died.

**Desultory.** Those who rode two or more horses in the circus of Rome, and used to leap from one to the other, were called *desultores* (*de*, and *saltire*, to leap); hence *desultor* came in Latin to mean one inconstant, or who went from one thing to another; and desultory means after the manner of a desultor.

**Deucalion's Flood.** The Deluge, of *Greek legend*. Deucalion was son of Prometheus and Clymene, and was king of Phthia, in Thessaly. When Zeus sent the deluge Deucalion built a ship, and he and his wife, Pyrrha, were the only mortals saved. The ship at last rested on Mount Parnassus, and Deucalion was told by the oracle at Themis that to restore the human race he must cast the bones of his mother behind him. His interpretation of this was the stones of his mother Earth, so the two cast these as directed and those thrown by Deucalion became men, and those thrown by his wife became women. For the interchange between λαὸς (people), and λᾶας (a stone); *see* Pindar, *Olympic Games*, ix, 66.

**Deuce.** The two, in games with cards, dice, etc. (Fr. *deux*). The three is called 'Tray' (Fr. *trois*; Lat. *tres*).

> A gentleman being punched by a butcher's tray, exclaimed, 'Deuce take the tray.' 'Well,' said the boy, 'I don't know how the deuceis to take the tray'. *Jest Book*

The secondary sense of *deuce*, as in 'deuce take the tray', above, is probably from this; for the *deuce* was a most unlucky throw or draw, and hence came to be used in imprecations, such as 'the deuce to him', may bad luck attend him.

***Deuce-ace.*** A throw of two dice, one showing *one* spot and the other showing *two*; hence, exceptionally bad luck.

In other phrases *Deuce* seems to be a euphemism for Devil.

***Deuce take you.*** Get away! you annoy me.

***It played the deuce with me.*** It made me very ill; it disagreed with me; it almost ruined me.

***The deuce is in you.*** You are a very demon.

***What the deuce is the matter?*** What in the world is amiss?

**Deus.** ***Deus ex machina***. The intervention of some unlikely event, in order to extricate one from difficulties; such as, in a novel, a forced incident, like the arrival of a rich uncle from the Indies to help a young couple in their pecuniary embarrassments. Literally, it means 'a god (let down upon the stage) from the machine', the 'machine' being part of the furniture of the stage in an ancient Greek theatre.

**Devil.** Represented with a cloven foot, because by the Rabbinical writers he is called *seirizzim* (a goat). As the goat is a type of uncleanness, the prince of unclean spirits is aptly represented under this emblem.

In legal parlance a *devil* is a leader's assistant (also a barrister) who gets up the facts of a brief, with the laws bearing on it, and summarises the case for the pleader.

***The Attorney-General's devils*** are the Counsel of the Treasury, who not unfrequently get promoted to the bench.

***A printer's devil.*** A printer's message boy; formerly, the boy who took the printed sheets from the tympan of the press. Moxon says (1683): 'They do commonly so black and bedaub themselves that the workmen do jocosely call them devils.' The black slave employed by Aldo

Manuzio, Venetian printer, was thought to be an imp. Hence the following proclamation:

> I, Aldo Manuzio, printer to the Doge, have this day made public exposure of the printer's devil. All who think he is not flesh and blood may come and pinch him.
>
> *Proclamation of Aldo Manuzio*, 1490

In his *Divina Commedia* Dante gives the following names to the various devils:

| | |
|---|---|
| *Alichino.* | The allurer. |
| *Barbariccia.* | The malicious. |
| *Calcobrina.* | The grace-scorner. |
| *Caynazzo.* | The snarler. |
| *Ciriato Sannuto.* | The tusked boar. |
| *Dragnignazzo.* | The fell dragon. |
| *Farfarello.* | The scandalmonger. |
| *Grafficane.* | The doggish. |
| *Libicocco.* | The ill-tempered. |
| *Rubicante.* | The red with rage. |
| *Scarmiglione.* | The baneful. |

**Devil.** *Proverbial Phrases.*

***As the devil loves holy water.*** That is, not at all. Catholics teach that holy water drives away the devil. The Latin proverb is, '*Sicut sus amaricinum amat*' (as swine love marjoram). Lucretius, vi, 974, says, '*amaricinum fugitat sus*'.

***Beating the devil's tattoo.*** Tapping on the table with one's finger a wearisome number of times, or on the floor with one's foot; repeating any rhythmical mechanical sound with annoying pertinacity.

***Between the devil and the deep sea.*** Between Scylla and Charybdis; between two evils, each equally hazardous. The allusion seems to be to the herd of swine and the devils called Legion.

> In the matter of passing from one part of the vessel to another when she was rolling, we were indeed between the devil and the deep sea.
>
> *Nineteenth Century*, April, 1891, p. 664

***Cheating the devil.*** Mincing an oath; doing evil for gain, and giving part of the profits to the Church, etc. In a literal sense, cheating the devil is by no means unusual in monkish traditions. Thus the 'Devil's Bridge', over the Fall of the Reuss, in the canton of the Uri, Switzerland, is a single arch over a cataract. It is said that Satan knocked down several bridges, but promised the abbot, Giraldus of Einsiedel, to let this one stand, provided he would give him the first living thing that crossed it. The abbot agreed, and threw across it a loaf of bread, which a hungry dog ran after, and 'the rocks re-echoed with peals of laughter to see the devil thus defeated'. (Longfellow, *Golden Legend*, v.)

Rabelais says that a farmer once bargained with the devil for each to have on alternate years what grew under and over the soil. The canny farmer sowed carrots and turnips when it was his turn to have the undersoil share, and wheat and barley the year following. (*Pantagruel*, Bk iv, ch. xlvi.)

***Give the devil his due.*** Give even a bad man or one hated like the devil the credit he deserves.

> *Poins.* Jack, how agrees the devil and thee about thy soul, that thou soldest him on Good Friday last, for a cup of Madeira and a cold capon's leg?
>
> *Prince.* Sir John stands to his word, the devil shall have his bargain; for he was never yet a breaker of proverbs; he will give the devil his due.
>
> Shakespeare, *1 Henry IV*, 1, 2

***Gone to the devil.*** To ruin. The *Devil and St Dunstan* was the sign of a public-house, No. 2 Fleet Street, at one time much frequented by lawyers; but the phrase dates at least from the 15th century Mystery Plays, in which the devil, or the vice, played a prominent part.

***He needs a long spoon who sups with the devil.*** *See* Spoon.

***Here's the very devil to pay.*** Here's a pretty kettle of fish. I'm in a pretty mess; this is confusion worse confounded. *Cp.* The Devil to pay *below.*

***Needs must when the devil drives.*** If I must, I must. The French say: '*Il faut marcher quand le diable est aux trousses*'; and the Italians: '*Bisogna andare, quando il diavolo è nella coda.*'

> He must needs go that the Devil drives.
>
> Shakespeare, *All's Well that Ends Well*, 1, 3

***Pull devil, pull baker.*** Lie, cheat, and wrangle away, for one is as bad as the other. Sometimes 'parson' is substituted for 'baker', but the origin of neither is known.

> Like Punch and the Deevil rugging about the Baker at the fair.
>
> Scott, *Old Mortality*, ch. xxxviii

***Talk of the devil and he's sure to appear.*** Said of a person who has been the subject of conversation, and who unexpectedly makes his appearance. An older proverb still is: 'Talk of the Dule and he'll put out his horns'; but the modern euphemism is: 'Talk of an angel and you'll hear the fluttering of its wings.'

> Forthwith the devil did appear,
> For name him, and he's always near.
>
> Prior, *Hans Carvel*

***Tell the truth and shame the devil.*** A very old saying, of obvious meaning.

> *Glendower.* I can teach thee, cousin, to command the devil

*Hotspur*. And I can teach thee, coz, to shame the devil.
By telling truth: tell truth and shame the devil.
Shakespeare, *1 Henry IV*, 3, 1

***The devil among the tailors.*** Said when a regular rumpus is in progress; it is also the name of a game in which a top (the 'devil') is spun among a number of wooden men ('tailors') and knocks down as many as possible.

The first-mentioned use of the phrase is said to have originated through a row at a benefit performance about 1830 to the actor Wm Dowton. The piece was a burlesque called *The Tailors: a Tragedy for Warm Weather*, and a large number of tailors caused a riot outside the theatre (the Haymarket) as they considered it insulting to the trade.

***The devil and all.*** Everything, especially everything bad.

***The devil and his dam.*** The devil and something even worse; the idea perhaps being that a really bad woman can be worse than the worst of men, if she sets her mind to it.

Dam (*q.v.*) here may mean either *mother* (the usual meaning), or *wife*. Quotations may be adduced in support of either of these interpretations, and it is to be noted that frequently (*cp. Paradise Lost*, ii) there is no differentiation. Also, Rabbinical tradition relates that Lilith was the wife of Adam, but was such a vixen that Adam could not live with her, and she became the devil's dam. We also read that Belphegor 'came to earth to seek him out a dam'.

In many mythologies the devil is typified by an animal; the Irish and others call him a *black cat*; the Jews speak of him as a *dragon* (which idea is carried out in our George and the Dragon); the Japanese call him a species of *fox*; others say he is a *goat*, a *camel*, etc., and Dante associates him with *dragons*, *swine*, and *dogs*. In all which cases dam for mother is not inappropriate.

***The devil catch the hindmost.*** A phrase from late mediaeval magic; it was said that the devil had a school at Toledo, or at Salamanca, where the students, when they had made a certain progress in their studies, were obliged to run through a subterranean hall, and the last man was seized by the devil and became his imp.

***The devil in Dublin City.*** The Scandinavian form of Dublin was *Divelina*, and the Latin *Dublinia*. 'Dublin' is the Gael. *dhu linn*, the black pool. Devlin, in Co. Mayo, is the same word and preserves the Scandinavian form.

Is just as true's the deil's in hell
Or Dublin city. Burns, *Death and Dr Hornbrook*

***The devil is not so black as he is painted.*** Said in extenuation or mitigation, especially when it seems that exaggerated censure has been given. Every black has its white, as well as every sweet its sour.

***The devil looking over Lincoln.*** Said of a vitriolic critic or a backbiter. Fuller, in his *Worthies* (under *Oxford*), says the phrase may allude either to the 'stone picture of the Devil which doth [1661] or lately did overlook Lincoln Colledge', or to a grotesque sculpture at Lincoln Cathedral. The phrase occurs as early as 1562 (Heywood's *Proverbs*).

The famous devil that used to overlook Lincoln College, in Oxford, was taken down (Wednesday, September 15th, 1731), having about two years since [previously] lost his head in a storm. *Gentleman's Magazine*, 1831, p. 402

***The devil rides on a fiddlestick.*** Much ado about nothing. Beaumont and Fletcher, Shakespeare, and others, use the phrase. 'Fiddlesticks!' as an exclamation, means rubbish! nonsense! When the prince and his merry companions are at the *Boar's Head*, first Bardolph rushes in to warn them that the sheriff's officers are at hand, and anon enters the hostess to put her guests on their guard. But the prince says:

Heigh, heigh! the devil rides upon a fiddlestick; what's the matter?
Shakespeare, *1 Henry* IV, 2, 4

The following is perhaps a reminiscence of the old phrase:

The Devil, that old stager ... who leads
Downward, perhaps, but fiddles all the way.
Browning, *Red Cotton Night-cap Country*, ii

***The devil's advocate.*** *See* Advocate.

***The devil's daughter's portion.*** The saying is:

Deal, Dover, and Harwich,
The devil gave with his daughter in marriage,

because of the scandalous impositions practised in these seaports on sailors and occasional visitors.

***The devil's door.*** A small door in the north wall of some old churches, which used to be opened at baptisms and communions to 'let the devil out'. The north used to be known as 'the devil's side', where Satan and his legion lurked to catch the unwary.

***The devil sick would be a monk.***

When the Devil was sick, the devil a monk would be;
When the Devil got well, the devil a monk was he.

Said of those persons who in times of sickness

or danger make pious resolutions, but forget them when danger is past and health recovered. The lines are found as an interpolation in Urquhart and Motteux's translation of Rabelais (Bk iv, ch. xxiv). A correct translation of what Rabelais actually wrote is:

> 'There's a rare rogue for you,' said Eusthenes', 'there's a rogue, a rogue and a half. This makes good the Lombard's proverb, "Passato el Pericolo, gabbato el Santo" ' [when the danger is passed, the Saint is mocked].

***The devil to pay and no pitch hot.*** The 'devil' is a seam between the garboard-strake and the keel, and to 'pay' is to cover with pitch (O.Fr. *payer*, to pitch, whence Fr. *poix*; *see* Pay). In former times, when vessels were often careened for repairs, it was difficult to calk and pay this seam before the tide turned. Hence the locution, the ship is careened, the devil is exposed, but there is no pitch hot ready, and the tide will turn before the work can be done.

***To hold a candle to the devil.*** *See* Candle.

***To kindle a fire for the devil.*** To offer sacrifice, to do what is really sinful, under the delusion that you are doing God service.

***To lead one the devil's own dance.*** To give him any amount of trouble; to lead him right astray.

***To play the very devil with something.*** To muddle and mar it in such a way as to spoil it utterly.

***To pull the devil by the tail.*** To struggle constantly against adversity.

***To say the devil's paternoster.*** To grumble; to rail at providence.

***To whip the devil round the stump.*** An American phrase meaning to enjoy the fruits of evil-doing without having to suffer the penalty; to dodge a difficulty dishonestly but successfully.

***When the devil is blind.*** Never. Referring to the utter absence of all disloyalty and evil.

> Ay, Tib, that will be [i.e. all will be true and loyal] when the de'il is blind; and his e'en's no sair yet.
> Scott, *Guy Mannering*, ch. xxii

***Why should the devil have all the good tunes?*** A saying originating with Charles Wesley about 1740, when he utilised the music of the popular songs of the day to get his hymns sung and known.

**Devil.** *In Topographical Nomenclature.*

***Devil's Arrows.*** Three remarkable 'Druid' stones near Boroughbridge, Yorks, like *Harold's Stones*; they probably mark some ancient boundary.

***Devil's Bridge.*** There is a village in Cardiganshire of this name, so called because of its double bridge across a gorge of the river Mynach. The lower bridge dates from the 11th century, and is locally known as the Monks' Bridge, because it was built by, and for the use of, the monasteries in the neighbourhood; the upper bridge dates from 1735. *See also Cheating the Devil, in phrases above.*

***The Devil's Cheesewring.*** *See* Cheesewring.

***Devil's Coits.*** *See* Hackell's coit.

***The Devil's Current.*** Part of the current of the Bosporus is so called, from its great rapidity.

***Devil's Den.*** A cromlech in a valley, near Marlborough. It now consists of two large uprights and an impost. The third upright has fallen.

***The Devil's Dyke.*** A ravine in the South Downs, Brighton. The legend is, that St Cuthman, walking on the downs, plumed himself on having Christianised the surrounding country, and having built a nunnery where the dyke-house now stands. Presently the devil appeared and told him all his labour was vain, for he would swamp the whole country before morning. St Cuthman went to the nunnery and told the abbess to keep the sisters in prayer till after midnight, and then illuminate the windows. The devil came at sunset with mattock and spade, and began cutting a dyke into the sea, but was seized with rheumatic pains all over the body. He flung down his mattock and spade, and the cocks, mistaking the illuminated windows for sunrise, began to crow; whereupon the devil fled in alarm, leaving his work not half done.

The same name is given to a prehistoric earthwork in Cambridgeshire, stretching across Newmarket Heath from Rech to Cowledge.

***The Devil's Frying-pan.*** A Cornish tin-mine worked by the Romans.

***The Devil's Hole.*** A name of the Peak Cavern, in Derbyshire.

***The Devil's Nostrils.*** Two vast caverns separated by a huge pillar of natural rock in the mainland of the Zetland Islands. *See The Pirate*, ch. xxii.

***The Devil's Punch Bowl.*** A deep coombe on the S.W. side of Hindhead Hill, two miles N. of Haslemere, in Surrey. A similar dell in Mangerton Mountain, near Killarney, has the same name.

***The Devil's Throat.*** Cromer Bay. So called from its danger to navigation.

***The Devil's Tower.*** A great rectangular granite obelisk, over 600 feet in height, in the Black Hills, Dakota, USA.

**Devil.** *In Personal Nomenclature.*

***Devil Dick.*** A nickname of Richard Porson (1759–1808), the great English Greek scholar.

***Robert the Devil.*** *See* Robert Le Diable.

***The French Devil.*** Jean Bart (1651–1702), an intrepid French sailor, born at Dunkirk.

***The devil's missionary.*** A nickname given to Voltaire (1694–1778), and very likely to others.

***Son of the devil.*** Ezzelino (1194–1259), the noted Ghibelline leader and Governor of Vicenza; so called for his infamous cruelties.

> Fierce Ezelin, that most inhuman lord,
> Who shall be deemed by men the child of hell.
> Rose, *Orlando Furioso*, iii, 32

***The White Devil of Wallachia.*** Scanderberg, or George Castriota (1403–68), was so called by the Turks.

**Devil.** *In Common Terms and Names. See also* Phrases *above*.

***Devil and bag o' nails.*** *See* Bag o' Nails.

***Devil dodger.*** A sly hypocrite; a ranting preacher.

***Devil may care.*** Wildly reckless; also a reckless fellow.

***Devil on two sticks.*** The English name of Le Sage's novel *Le diable boiteux* (1707), in which Asmodeus (*q.v.*) plays an important part. It was dramatised by Foote in 1768. As slang the term is applied to a crusty old cripple. *See also* Diabolo.

***Devil's apple.*** The mandrake; also the thorn apple.

***Devil's bedpost.*** In card games, the four of clubs. *Cp.* Devil's four-poster *below*.

***Devil's Bible.*** *See* Devil's books *below*.

***Devil's bird.*** A Scots name for the yellow bunting; from its note, *deil*.

***Devil's bones.*** Dice, which are made of bones and lead to ruin.

***Devil's books***, or ***Devil's picture-book.*** Playing cards. A Presbyterian phrase, used in reproof of the term King's Books, applied to a pack of cards, from the Fr. *livre des quatre rois* (the book of the four kings). Also called the *Devil's Bible*.

***Devil's candle.*** So the Arabs call the mandrake, from its shining appearance at night.

> Those hellish fires that light
> The mandrake's charnel leaves at night.
> T. Moore, *Fire Worshippers*

***Devil's candlestick.*** The common stinkhorn fungus, *Phallus impudicus*; also called the *devil's horn* and the *devil's stinkpot*.

***Devil's coach-horse.*** A large rove-beetle, *Goerius olens*.

***Devil's coach-wheel.*** The corn crowfoot.

***Devil's daughter.*** A shrew. *Cp.* Devil's daughter's portion *in Phrases above*.

***Devil's dozen.*** Thirteen; twelve, and one over for the devil. *Cp.* Baker's Dozen.

***Devil's dust.*** The flock made from old rags torn up by a machine called the 'devil'; also the shoddy made from this.

> Does it beseem thee to weave cloth of devil's dust instead of pure wool? Carlyle (1840)

***Devil's fingers.*** The starfish; also belemnites.

***Devil's four-poster.*** A hand at whist with four clubs. It is said that such a hand is never a winning one. *Cp.* Devil's bedpost *above*.

***Devil's horn.*** *See* Devil's candlestick *above*.

***Devil's livery.*** Black and yellow. Black for death, yellow for quarantine.

***Devil's luck.*** Astounding good luck. Persons always lucky were thought at one time to have compounded with the devil.

> You won't have to pay his annuity very long; you have the Devil's luck in bargains, always.
> Dickens

***Devil's mass.*** Swearing at everybody and everything.

> Whin a bad egg is shut av the army he says the devil's mass ... an' manes svearin' at ivrything, from the commandher-in-chief down to the room-corpril. *Soldiers Three*, p. 95

***The Devil's Own.*** The 88th Foot, the Connaught Rangers. So called by General Picton from their bravery in the Peninsular War, 1809–14. Also the Inns of Court Territorials, which are chiefly recruited from among lawyers.

***The Devil's Parliament.*** The parliament which met at Coventry in 1459 and impeached the Yorkist leaders.

***The Devil's Paternoster.*** *See* To say the ... *in Phrases above*.

***Devil's snuff-box.*** A puff-ball; a fungus full of dust; one of the genus Lycoperdon.

**Devonshire.** English legend accounts for the name (which is really from that of the ancient Celtic inhabitants, the Damnonii) by saying that it is from Debon, one of the heroes who came with Brute from Troy. When Brutus allotted out the island, this portion became *Debon's share* (*shire!*).

> In mede of these great conquests by them got
> Corineus had that province utmost west.
> And Debon's share was that is Devonshire.
> Spenser, *Faërie Queene*, II, x, 12

***The Devonshire Poet.*** O. Jones, a journeyman wool-comber, who lived at the close of the 18th century. Other Devonshire poets are John Gay (1685–1732) of Barnstaple and Edward Capern (1819–94), called 'The rural Postman of Bideford'.

**Dew-beaters.** The feet; shoes to resist the wet.

> Hold out your dew-beaters till I take off the darbies [iron shoes or fetters].
>
> Scott, *Peveril of the Peak*

**Dexterity.** *Right-handed* skill. Lat. *dexter*, the right hand. *Cp.* Awkward, Sinister.

**Dey.** The title of the Mohammedan governors of Algiers, Tripoli and Tunis; originally applied to the commander of Janissaries at Algiers who (1710) became ruler. From Turk *dai*, maternal uncle.

**Dhuldul.** *See* Horse.

**Dhu'l Fakar.** *See* Fakar.

**Diable, Le.** Olivier Le Dain, the tool of Louis XI, and once the king's barber. So called because he was as much feared as the devil himself and even more disliked. He was hanged in 1484, after the death of the king.

**Diabolo.** An old game that was revived about 1907, in which the players have each two sticks connected with a cord on which they spin, and pass from one to the other, a reel-shaped top. It used to be called the 'devil on two sticks', the top being the 'devil'.

**Dialectics.** Logic in general; the art of disputation; the investigation of truth by analysis; that strictly logical discussion which leads to reliable results. Gr., *dialegein*, to speak thoroughly.

Kant used the word to signify the critical analysis of knowledge based on science, and Hegel for the philosophic process of reconciling the contradictions of experience in a higher synthesis.

The following questions from John of Salisbury are fair specimens of the dialectics of the Schoolmen (*q.v.*):

> When a person buys a whole cloak, does the cowl belong to his purchase?
>
> When a hog is driven to market with a rope round its neck, does the man or the rope take him?

**Diamond.** A corruption of *adamant* (*q.v.*). So called because the diamond, which cuts other substances, can be cut or polished with no substance but itself (Gr. *a damao*, what cannot be subdued).

In Spenser's *Faërie Queene* (Bk iv), Diamond is one of the three sons of Agapë. He was slain by Cambalo. *Cp.* Triamond.

***A diamond of the first water.*** A specially fine diamond, one of the greatest value for its size. The colour or lustre of a diamond is called its 'water'. Hence, figuratively, a man of the first water is a man of the highest merit.

***A rough diamond.*** An uncultivated genius; a person of excellent parts, but without society manners.

> As for Warrington, that rough diamond had not had the polish of a dancing-master, and he did not know how to waltz. Thackeray

***Black diamonds.*** *See* Black.

***Diamond cut diamond.*** Cunning outwitting cunning; a hard bargain over-reached. A diamond is so hard that it can only be ground by diamond dust, or by rubbing one against another.

***Diamond hammer.*** A pick for 'whetting' millstones. It is provided with several sharp-pointed teeth to give a uniform roughness to the surface of the stone. Also a steel pick with diamond-shaped point at each extremity to recut grooves in stone.

***The diamond jousts.*** Jousts instituted by King Arthur, 'who by that name had named them, since a diamond was the prize'. The story, as embroidered by Tennyson in his *Lancelot and Elaine* from Malory (Bk xviii, chs 9–20) is that Arthur found nine diamonds from the crown of a slain knight and offered them as the prize of nine jousts in successive years. Lancelot had won them all, but when he laid them before the queen, Guinevere, in a fit of jealousy – the result of believing false rumours about Lancelot and Elaine – flung them into the river a moment before the corpse of Elaine passed in the barge.

***The Diamond Necklace.*** The famous 'Diamond Necklace Affair' of French history (1783–5) centres round Marie Antoinette. Cardinal de Rohan, a profligate churchman, entertained a passion for the queen; and an adventuress, the Countess de Lamotte, partly by means of the queen's signatures, which were almost certainly forged, induced him to purchase for the queen, for about £85,000, a diamond necklace, originally made for Mme Dubarry. The cardinal handed the necklace to the countess, who sold it to an English jeweller and kept the money. When the time of payment arrived Boehmer, the jeweller, sent his bill in to the queen, who denied all knowledge of the matter. A nine months' trial ensued which created immense scandal.

***Diamond Pitt.*** Thomas Pitt (1653–1726), owner of the famous Pitt Diamond (*q.v.*), and grandfather of the Earl of Chatham, was so known.

***The Diamond Sculls.*** An annual sculling match taking place at the Henley Royal Regatta, and first rowed in 1844. The prize is a pair of crossed silver sculls not quite a foot in length, surmounted by an imitation wreath of laurel, and having a pendant of diamonds. It passes from winner to winner; but each winner receives a silver cup as a souvenir.

**Diana.** An ancient Italian and Roman divinity, later identified with the Olympian goddess Artemis, who was daughter of Zeus and Leto, and twin-sister of Apollo. She was the goddess of the moon and of hunting, protectress of women, and – in earlier times at least – the great mother goddess or Nature goddess. *Cp.* Selene. The temple of Diana at Ephesus, built by Dinochares, was set on fire by Herostratos, for the sake of perpetuating his name. The Ionians decreed that anyone who mentioned his name should be put to death, but this very decree gave it immortality. The temple was discovered in 1872 by Mr Wood.

***Diana of Ephesus.*** This statue, a cone surmounted by a bust covered with breasts, we are told, fell from heaven. If so, it was an aerolite; but Minucius (2nd cent. AD), who says he saw it, describes it as a wooden statue, and Pliny, a contemporary, tells us it was made of ebony. Probably the real 'image' was a meteorite, and in the course of time a wooden one was substituted.

The palladium of Troy, the most ancient image of Athena at Athens, the statues of Artemis at Tauris and Cybele at Pessinus, the sacred shield of the Romans, and the shrine of our Lady of Loretto, are examples of objects of religious veneration which were said to have been sent from heaven.

***Great is Diana of the Ephesians.*** A phrase sometimes used to signify that self-interest blinds the eyes, from the story told in Acts 19:24–28 of Demetrius, the Ephesian silversmith who made shrines for the temple of Diana.

***The Tree of Diana.*** *See* Philosopher's Tree.

**Dian's Worshippers.** Midnight revellers. So called because they return home by moonlight, and so, figuratively, put themselves under the protection of Diana (*q.v.*).

**Diapason.** The word is Greek (short for *dia pason chordon*, through all the chords) and means an harmonious combination of notes; hence harmony itself. Dryden says –

From harmony, from heavenly harmony
  The universal frame began;
From harmony to harmony
  Thro' all the compass of the notes it ran,
  The diapason closing full in man.
*Song for St Cecilia's Day*

According to the Pythagorean system, the world is a piece of harmony and man the full chord. *Cp.* Microcosm.

**Diaper.** A sort of variegated white cloth, so called from Gr. *dia*, through, *aspros*, white, white in places. The name is not connected with *Ypres*, nor with *jasper*.

**Diatessaron.** *See* Tatianists.

**Diavolo, Fra.** Michele Pozza, an insurgent of Calabria (1760–1806), round whom Scribe wrote a libretto for Auber's comic opera (1830).

**Dibs.** Money. *Cp.* Tips, gifts to schoolboys.

The knuckle-bones of sheep used for gambling purposes are called dibbs; and Locke speaks of stones used for the same game, which he calls *dib-stones*.

**Dicers' Oaths.** ***False as dicers' oaths.*** Worthless or untrustworthy, as when a gambler swears never to touch dice again. (Shakespeare, *Hamlet*, 3, 4.)

**Dick.** Richard; from *Ric*, short for the Anglo-Norman *Ricard*; the diminutive 'Dicky' is also common.

Jockey of Norfolk [Lord Howard], be not too bold,
For Dickon [*or* Dicky], thy master, is bought and sold.
Shakespeare, *Richard III*, 5, 3
(Dickon is Richard III)

*That happened in the reign of Queen Dick* – i.e. never; there never was a Queen Richard.

Richard Cromwell (1626–1712), son of the Protector whom, for a few months, he succeeded, was sometimes scornfully referred to as 'King Dick', and there were many popular sayings introducing the Crown as 'Dick's hatband'. Among them are:

*Dick's hatband was made of sand.* His regal honours were 'a rope of sand'.

*As queer as Dick's hatband.* Few things have been more ridiculous than the exaltation and abdication of the Protector's son.

*As tight at Dick's hatband.* The crown was too tight for him to wear with safety.

**Dickens.** *Dickens*, in *What the dickens*, is probably a euphemism for the devil, or Old *Nick*, and is nothing to do with Charles Dickens. *See* Boz. Mrs Page says:

I cannot tell what the dickens his name is.
Shakespeare, *Merry Wives of Windsor*, 3, 2

**Dickey.** In George II's time, a flannel petticoat.

A hundred instances I soon could pick ye –
 Without a cap we view the fair,
 The bosom heaving alto bare,
The hips ashamed, forsooth, to wear a dicky.

Peter Pindar, *Lord Auckland's Triumph*

It was afterwards applied to what were called false shirts – i.e. a starched shirt front worn over a flannel shirt or a dirty one; also to any other article of dress pretending to be what it isn't; and to leather aprons, children's bibs, the rumble behind a carriage, etc.

**Dicky.** A donkey; especially in East Anglia, where it was anciently called a Dick-ass or Dicky-ass. It is a term of endearment, as we call a pet bird a *dicky-bird*. The ass is called Dicky (little Richard), Cuddy (little Cuthbert), Neddy (little Edward), Jack-ass, Moke or Mike, etc.

**Dicky Sam.** A native-born inhabitant of Liverpool, as Tim Bobbin is a native of Lancashire.

**Didactic Poetry.** Poetry which uses the beauties of expression, imagination, sentiment, etc., for teaching some moral lesson, as Pope's *Essay on Man*, or the principles of some art or science, as Virgil's *Georgics*, Garth's *Dispensary*, or Darwin's *Botanic Garden*. (Gr. *didasko*, I teach.)

**Diddle.** To cheat in a small way, as 'I diddled him out of ...' Edgar Allan Poe wrote an essay on 'Diddling Considered as one of the Exact Sciences'.

A certain portion of the human race
Has certainly a taste for being diddled.

Hood, *A Black Job*

***Jeremy Diddler.*** An adept at raising money on false pretences. From Kenny's farce called *Raising the Wind*.

**Diderick.** *See* Dietrich.

**Dido.** The name given by Virgil to Elissa, founder and queen of Carthage. She fell in love with Aeneas, driven by a storm to her shores, who, after abiding awhile at Carthage, was compelled by Mercury to leave the hospitable queen. Elissa, in grief, burnt herself to death on a funeral pile. (*Aeneid*, i, 494–iii, 650). Dido is really the Phoenician name of Astarte (Artemis), goddess of the moon and protectress of the citadel of Carthage.

It was Porson who said he could rhyme on any subject; and being asked to rhyme upon the three Latin gerunds, which, in the old Eton Latin grammar, are called *-di*, *-do*, *-dum*, gave this couplet:

When Dido found Aeneas would not come,
She mourned in silence, and was Di-do dum(b).

**Die. *The die is cast.*** The step is taken, and I cannot draw back. So said Julius Caesar when he crossed the Rubicon – *jacta alea esto*, let the die be cast!

I have set my life upon the cast,
And I will stand the hazard of the die.

Shakespeare, *Richard III*, 5, 4

***Never say die.*** Never despair; never give up.

***Whom the gods love die young.*** This is from Menander – *Hon hoi theoi philousin apothneskei neos*. Demosthenes has a similar apophthegm. Plautus has the line, *Quem Di diligunt adolescens moritur* (*Bacch*. IV, vii, 18). *See* Byron: *Don Juan*, canto iv, 12.

**Die-hards.** In political phraseology *Die-hards* are the crusted members of any party (particularly the Tories who opposed any reform of the House of Lords, and the Unionists who refused to budge an inch in the direction of Irish Home Rule) who stick to their long-held theories through thick and thin, regardless of the changes that time or a newly awakened conscience may bring; those who would rather 'die in the last ditch' than admit the possibility of their having been shortsighted.

In military circles, the 57th Foot (West Middlesex Regiment). Their colonel (Inglis) at Albuera (1811), addressing his men, said: 'Die hard, my lads; die hard!' And they did die hard, for their banner was pierced with thirty bullets. Only one officer out of twenty-four survived, and only 168 men out of 584.

**Diego, San.** A modification of Santiago (St James), champion of the red cross, and patron saint of Spain.

**Dies.** *Dies Alliensis. See* Alliensis.

***Dies Irae*** (Lat., Day of Wrath). A famous mediaeval hymn on the last judgment, probably the composition of Thomas of Celano, a native of Abruzzi, who died in 1255. It is derived from the Vulgate version of Joel 2:31, and used by Catholics in the Mass for the Dead and on All Souls' Day. Scott has introduced the opening into his *Lay of the Last Minstrel*.

Dies irae, dies illa
Solvet saeclum in favilla,
Teste David cum Sibylla.
On that day, that wrathful day,
David and the Sibyl say,
Heaven and earth shall melt away. E. C. B.

***Dies non*** (Lat., a 'not' day). A non-business day. A law phrase, meaning a day when the courts do not sit and legal business is not transacted, as Sundays; the Purification, in Hilary term; the

Ascension, in Easter term; St John the Baptist, in Trinity term; and All Saints, with All Souls, in Michaelmas term. A contracted form of '*Dies non juridicus*', a non-judicial day.

**Dietrich of Bern.** The name given by the German minnesingers to Theodoric the Great (454–526), king of the Ostrogoths (Bern = Verona). He appears in many Middle High German poems, especially the *Nibelungenlied*, where he is one of the liegemen of King Etzel.

**Dieu.** *Dieu et mon droit* (God and my right). The parole of Richard I at the battle of Gisors (1198), meaning that he was no vassal of France, but owed his royalty to God alone. The French were signally beaten, but the battle-word does not seem to have been adopted as the royal motto of England till the time of Henry VI.

**Difference.** When Ophelia is distributing flowers (*Hamlet*, 4, 5) and says: 'You must wear your rue with a difference,' she is using the word in the heraldic sense and means 'you must wear it as though it were marked in such a way as will slightly change the usual meaning of the plant', which was a symbol of repentance ('herb of grace'); or, on the assumption that she was offering the flower to the Queen, Ophelia may have implied that they were both to wear rue: the one as the affianced of Hamlet, eldest son of the late king; the other as the wife of Claudius his brother, and the cadet branch.

In *heraldry*, *differences* or *marks of cadency* indicate the various branches of a family.

The eldest son, during the lifetime of his father, bears a *label*, i.e. a bar or fillet, having three pendants broader at the bottom than at the top.

The second son bears a *crescent*.

The third, a *mullet* (i.e. a star with five points).

The fourth, a *martlet*.

The fifth, an *annulet*.

The sixth, a *fleur-de-lis*.

The seventh, a *rose*.

The eighth, a *cross-moline*.

The ninth, a *double quatre foil*.

**Digest.** A compendium or summary arranged under convenient headings and titles, especially (and originally) the extracts from the body of Roman law compiled by Tribonian and sixteen assistants by order of Justinian, and arranged in 50 books (AD 533). *Cp.* Pandects.

**Diggings.** Lodgings, rooms, apartments. A word imported from California and its gold diggings.

> My friend here wants to take diggings; and as you were complaining that you would get someone to go halves with you, I thought I had better bring you together.
>
> Sir Arthur Conan Doyle, *A Study in Scarlet*, ch.1

**Digits.** The first nine numerals; so called from the habit of counting as far as ten on the fingers. (Lat. *digitus*, a finger.)

In astronomy, the word signifies the twelfth part of the diameter of the sun or moon; it is used principally in expressing the magnitude of an eclipse. Hence the title of F. W. Bain's book *A Digit of the Moon* (1899), which is a Hindu love story translated from the *Sansára-ságara-manthanam*.

**Dignus Vindice Nodus** (Lat.). Literally, a knot (or difficulty) worthy to be untied; hence a knotty point worthy to be made a civil action. The person who brought a civil action was called in Roman law *vindex*, and the action *vindicatio*. If a rightful possessor was the matter of dispute, the question became a *lis vindiciarum*; it was referred to the praetor, and a knotty point so referred was a '*dignus vindice nodus*'.

**Dii Penates** (Lat.). Household gods; now used colloquially for articles about the house that are specially prized. *Cp.* Lares.

**Dilemma.** *The horns of a dilemma.* A difficulty of such a nature that whatever way you attack it you encounter an equal amount of disagreeables. Macbeth, after the murder of Duncan, was 'on the horns of a dilemma'. If he allowed Banquo to live, he had reason to believe that Banquo would supplant him; if, on the other hand, he resolved to keep the crown for which 'he had 'filed his hands', he must 'step further in blood', and cut Banquo off.

'Lemma' means an assumption, a thing taken for granted (Gr. *lambanein*, to take). 'Dilemma' is a double lemma, a two-edged sword, or a bull which will toss you whichever horn you lay hold of, called by the Schoolmen *argumentum cornutum*.

> A young rhetorician said to an old sophist, 'Teach me to plead, and I will pay you when I gain a cause.' He never had a cause till his old tutor master sued for payment; and he argued, 'If I gain the cause I shall not pay you, because the judge will say I am not to pay; and if I lose my cause I shall not be required to pay, according to the terms of our agreement.' To this the master replied, 'Not so; if you gain your cause you must pay me according to the terms of our agreement; and if you lose your cause the judge will condemn you to pay me.'

**Dilettantë** (Ital.; pl. *dilettanti*). An amateur of the fine arts, in opposition to a professor; frequently applied to a trifling pretender to knowledge of some art or science.

These gentlemen are to be judged, not as dilettanti, but as professors. *Athenaeum*

**Diligence.** A four-wheeled stagecoach, drawn by four or more horses. Common in France before the introduction of railroads. The word is the same as the noun from *diligent*, which formerly meant speed, dispatch, as in Shakespeare's 'If your diligence be not speedy I shall be there before you' (*King Lear*, 1, 5).

**Dilly.** A stage-coach, as in the *Derby Dilly*, The word is, of course, an abbreviation of the above.

**Dismas.** *See* Dysmas.

**Dimensions.** *See* Fourth Dimension.

**Dimetae.** The ancient inhabitants of Carmarthenshire, Pembrokeshire, and Cardiganshire.

**Dimissory.** *A letter dimissory* is a letter from the bishop of one diocese to some other bishop, giving leave for the bearer to be ordained by him. Lat. *di-mittere*, to send away.

**Dimity.** Stout cotton cloth woven with raised patterns. It has been said to be so called from Damietta, in Egypt, but is really from the Gr. *dimitos* (double-thread). *Cp.* Samite.

**Din.** *To din it in one's ears. See* Ding.

**Dine, To.** ***To dine out.*** Properly, to dine away from home; but in slang use, to go without a dinner.

***To dine with Democritus.*** To be cheated out of one's dinner. Democritus was the derider, or philosopher, who laughed at men's folly.

***To dine with Duke Humphrey; to dine with Sir Thomas Gresham.*** To go dinnerless. *See* Humphrey.

***To dine with Mahomet.*** To die, and dine in paradise.

***To dine with the cross-legged knights.*** That is, to have no dinner at all. *Cp.* 'to dine with Duke Humphrey'. The knights referred to are the stone effigies of the Temple Church, where, at one time, lawyers met their clients. A host of vagabonds used to loiter about the church all day, in the hope of being hired as witnesses.

**Ding, To.** To strike. Now obsolete or only dialectical, it is the M.E. *dingen*, which is probably in origin Norse and connected with Icel. *dengjan*, to hammer.

The butcher's axe, like great Achilles' bat,
Dngs deadly downe ten-thousand-thousand flat.
Taylor, *Works* (1630)

***To ding it in one's ears.*** To repeat a subject over and over again; to teach by repetition. This phrase should properly be *To din*, etc.; but *din* has here become confused with the above.

**Ding-dong.** ***They went at it ding-dong.*** They fought in good earnest. *Ding-dong* is an onomatopoeic word, reproducing the sound of a bell; and here the suggestion is that the blows fell regularly and unfalteringly, like the hammer-strokes of a bell.

**Dinmont.** *See* Sheep.

***Dandie Dinmont.*** *See* Dandie.

**Dinos.** *See* Horse.

**Dint.** *By dint of war; by dint of argument; by dint of hard work.* Dint means a blow or striking (A.S. *dynt*); whence perseverance, power exerted, force; it also means the indentation made by a blow.

**Diocletian.** The name given to the king in the Italian version of *The Seven Wise Masters* (*q.v.*). His son was Erastus. The actual Diocletian (245–313), the Roman Emperor, was noted for his fierce persecution of the Christians, 303.

**Diogenes.** A noted Greek cynic philosopher (about 412–323 BC), who, according to Seneca, lived in a tub.

The whole world was not half so wide
To Alexander, when he cried
Because he had but one to subdue,
As was a paltry narrow tub to
Diogenes. Butler, *Hudibras*, i, 3

Diogenes was the surname of Romanus IV, Emperor of the East, 1067–71.

**Diomedes** or **Diomed.** In *Greek legend*, a hero of the siege of Troy, King of Aetolia, brave and obedient to authority. He survived the siege, but on his return home found his wife living in adultery, and saved his life by living an exile in Italy. His horses were Dinos and Lampon. *See* Horse.

***Diomedean swop.*** An exchange in which all the benefit is on one side. The expression is founded on an incident related by Homer in the *Iliad*. Glaucus recognises Diomed on the battlefield, and the friends change armour:

For Diomed's brass arms, of mean device,
For which nine oxen paid (a vulgar price),
He gave his own, of gold divinely wrought,
An hundred beeves the shining purchase bought.
Pope, *Iliad*, vi

**Dione.** A Titaness; daughter of Oceanus and Tethys, and mother by Jupiter of Venus. The name has been applied to Venus herself, and Julius Caesar, who claimed descent from her, was hence sometimes called *Dionaeus Caesar*.

So young Dione, nursed beneath the waves,
And rocked by Nereids in their coral caves …
Lisped her sweet tones, and tried her tender smiles. Darwin, *Economy of Vegetation*, ii

**Dionysia.** *See* Bacchanalia.

**Dionysius.** *See* Corinth's Pedagogue.

**Dionysus.** The Greek name of Bacchus (*q.v.*).

**Diophantine Analysis.** Finding commensurate values of squares, cubes, triangles, etc.; or the sum of a given number of squares which is itself a square; or a certain number of squares, etc., which are in arithmetical progression; so named from Diophantus, a celebrated Alexandrian mathematician of the 4th century AD.

> The following examples will give some idea of the theory:
> 1. To find two whole numbers, the *sum* of whose squares is a square;
> 2. To find three square numbers which are in arithmetical progression;
> 3. To find a number from which two given squares being severally subtracted, each of the remainders is a square.

**Dioscuri.** Castor and Pollux (*q.v.*). Gr. *Dios kouros*, sons of Zeus.

***The horses of the Dioscuri.*** Cyllaros and Harpagos. *See* Horse.

**Dip.** A cheap and common kind of candle, made by dipping into melted tallow the cotton which forms the wick.

***A farthing dip***, like *a rush*, is a synonym for something that is almost valueless.

**Diphthera** (Gr.). A piece of prepared hide or leather; specifically, the skin of the goat Amalthea, on which Jove wrote the destiny of man. *Diphtheria* is an infectious disease of the throat; so called from its tendency to form a false membrane.

**Diploma** (Gr.). Literally, something folded. Diplomas used to be written on parchment, folded, and sealed. The word is applied to licences given to graduates to assume a degree, to clergymen, to physicians, etc.; and also to the credentials of an ambassador, etc., authorising him to represent his Government; whence *diplomacy*, the negotiations, privileges, tact, etc., of a *diplomatist*.

**Diplomatics.** The name formerly (and sometimes still) given to the science of palaeography – that is, deciphering and investigating old charters, diplomas, titles, etc. Papebröch, the Bollandist, originated the study in 1675; but Mabillon, another Bollandist, reduced it to a science in his *De re Diplomatica*, 1681. Toustain and Tassin further developed it in their treatise entitled *Nouveau Traité de Diplomatique*, 1750–60.

**Diptych** (Gr. *diptuchos*, folded in two). A register folded into two leaves, opening like a book. The Romans kept in a book of this sort the names of their magistrates, and Catholics employed the word for the registers in which were written the names of those who were to be specially commemorated when oblations were made for the dead. The name is also given to altar pieces and other paintings that fold together in the middle on a hinge.

> The Greeks executed small works of great elegance, as may be seen in the diptychs, or ivory covers to consular records, or sacred volumes used in the church service.
>
> T. Flaxman, *Lectures on Sculpture*, iii, p. 98

**Dircaean Swan.** Pindar; so called from Dirce, a fountain in the neighbourhood of Thebes, the poet's birthplace (518–442 BC). The fountain is named from Dirce, who was put to death by the sons of Antiope for her brutal treatment of their mother, and was changed into the spring by Bacchus.

**Direct Action.** A method of attaining, or attempting to attain, political ends by non-political means (such as striking or withdrawing labour). If, for instance, any vital section of the community, such as the railwaymen or miners, desired nationalisation and came out on strike with a view to intimidating the nation into giving it after the nation, speaking through its elected representatives in Parliament, had refused it, that would be a case of direct action.

**Direct Tax.** One collected *directly* from the owner of property subject to the tax, as the income-tax. *Indirect taxes* are taxes upon marketable commodities, such as tea and sugar, the tax on which is added to the article, and is thus paid by the purchaser indirectly.

**Directory, The.** In French history, the constitution of 1795, when the executive was vested in five 'Directors', one of whom retired every year. After a sickly existence of four years, it came to an end at Napoleon's *coup d'état* of 18 Brumaire (November 9th), 1799.

**Dirleton.** ***Doubting with Dirleton, and resolving those doubts with Stewart.*** Doubting and answering those doubts, but doubting still. It is a Scottish phrase; and the allusion is to the *Doubts and Questions in the Law* (1698), by Sir John Nisbet of Dirleton, the Lord President, and Sir James Stewart's *Dirleton's Doubts and Questions ... Resolved and Answered* (1715). Of the former work Lord Chancellor Hardwicke remarked, 'His *Doubts* are better than most people's *certainties*.'

**Dirt.** Palmerston's definition was 'matter in the wrong place'. This is not strictly true: a diamond or sovereign lost on a road is matter in a wrong place, but is not dirt.

> If dirt were trumps what a capital hand you would hold! Charles Lamb to Martin Burney

***Dirt cheap.*** Very low-priced.

***Throw plenty of dirt and some will be sure to stick.*** Scandal always leaves a trail behind; find plenty of fault, and some of it will be believed. In Lat., *Fortiter calumniari, aliquid ad-haerebit*.

***To eat dirt.*** To put up with insults and mortification.

**Dirty.** ***The Dirty Half-Hundred.*** The 50th Foot (The Queen's Own), so called because during a Peninsular War battle the men wiped their faces with their black cuffs.

***The Dirty Shirts.*** The 101st Foot (2nd Munster Fusiliers), which fought at Delhi in their shirt-sleeves (1857).

**Dis.** The Roman name of the Greek Pluto (*q.v.*).

> Proserpine gathering flowers,
> Herself a fairer flower, by gloomy Dis
> Was gathered. Milton, *Paradise Lost*, iv, 270

**Disastrous Peace, The** (*La Paix Malheureuse*). A name given to the Treaty of Câteau Cambrésis (1559), which followed the battle of Gravelines. It was signed by France, Spain, and England, and by it France ceded the Low Countries to Spain, and Savoy, Corsica, and 200 forts to Italy. But she retained Calais.

**Discalced.** *See* Barefooted.

**Discharge Bible, The.** *See* Bible, Specially named.

**Disciples of Christ.** *See* Campbellites.

**Discipline, A.** A scourge used by Catholics for penitential purposes.

> Before the cross and altar a lamp was still burning, ... and on the floor lay a small discipline or penitential scourge of small cord and wire, the lashes of which were stained with recent blood.
> Scott, *The Talisman*, ch. iv

This is a transferred sense of one of the ecclesiastical uses of the word – the mortification of the flesh by penance.

**Discord.** Literally, severance of hearts (Lat. *discorda*). It is the opposite of *concord*, the coming together of hearts. In music, it means disagreement of sounds, as when a note is followed by another which is disagreeable to a musical ear.

***The apple of discord.*** *See* Apple.

**Discount.** *At a discount.* Not in demand; little valued; less esteemed than formerly; below par. (Lat. *dis-computare*, to depreciate.)

**Dish-clout.** ***To make a napkin out of one's dishclout.*** An old phrase meaning to marry one's cook, or contract some such misalliance.

**Dished.** *I was dished out of it.* Cheated out of it; or rather, someone else contrived to obtain it. When one is *dished* he is completely done for, and the allusion is to food which, when it is quite *done*, is *dished*. Hence, 'dishing the Whigs'.

> Where's Brummel? Dished! Byron, *Don Juan*

**Dismal Science, The.** *See* Science.

**Dismas, St.** *See* Dysmas.

**Disney Professor.** The Professor of Archaeology at Cambridge. This chair was founded in 1851 by John Disney (1779–1857), who also bequeathed his collection of marbles to the University.

**Dispensation** (Lat. *dispensatio*, from *dis-* and *pendere*, to weigh). The system which God chooses to *dispense* or establish between Himself and man. The dispensation of *Adam* was that between Adam and God; the dispensation of *Abraham*, and that of *Moses*, were those imparted to these holy men; the *Gospel* dispensation is that explained in the Gospels.

*A dispensation from the Pope.* Permission to *dispense* with something enjoined; a licence to do what is forbidden, or to omit what is commanded by the law of the Church, as distinct from the moral law.

**Distaff.** The staff from which the flax was drawn in spinning; hence, figuratively, woman's work, and a woman herself, the allusion being to the old custom of women, who spun from morning tonight. *Cp.* Spinster.

> I blush that we should owe our lives to such
> A king of distaffs! Byron, *Sardanapalus*, II, i

***St Distaff's Day.*** January 7th. So called because the Christmas festival terminated on Twelfth Day, and on the day following the women returned to their distaffs or daily occupations. It is also called *Rock Day*, 'rock' being an old name for the distaff.

> Give St Distaff all the right,
> Then give Christmas sport good-night,
> And next morrow everyone
> To his own vocatiön. (1657)
>
> What! shall a woman with a rock drive thee away?
> Fye on thee, traitor! *Digby Mysteries*

***The distaff side.*** The female side of a family; a branch descended from the female side.

***To have tow on the distaff.*** To have work in hand. Froissart says: '*Il aura en bref temps autres estoupes en sa quenouille.*'

He haddë more tow on his distaf
Than Gerveys knew.
Chaucer, *Miller's Tale*, 588

**Distemper.** An undue mixture (Lat. *distemperare*, to mix amiss). In medicine a distemper arises from the redundancy of certain secretions or morbid humours. The distemper in dogs is an undue quantity of secretions manifested by a running from the eyes and nose.

*Distemper,* the paint, is so called because, instead of being mixed with oil, it is mixed with a vehicle (as yolk of eggs or glue) that is soluble in water.

**Distrait** (Fr.). Absent-minded; also, an absent-minded person.

My friend Will Honeycomb is one of those sort of men who are very often absent in Conversation, and what the French call a *reveur* and a *distrait*.
*Spectator* (Budgell), May 29th, 1711

**Dithyrambic** (Gr., *dithyrambos*, a choric hymn). Dithyrambic poetry was originally a wild, impetuous kind of Dorian lyric in honour of Bacchus, traditionally ascribed to the invention of Arion of Lesbos (about 620 BC), who has hence been called *the father of dithyrambic poetry*.

**Dittany.** This plant (*Origanum dictamnus*), so named from Dicte in Crete, where it grew in profusion, was anciently credited with many medicinal virtues, especially in enabling arrows to be drawn from wounds and curing such wounds. In Tasso's *Jerusalem Delivered* (Bk ix) Godfrey is healed in this way.

Stags and hinds, when deeply wounded with darts, arrows, and bolts, if they do but meet the herb called dittany, which is common in Candia, and eat a little of it, presently the shafts come out, and all is well again; even as kind Venus cured her beloved by-blow Aeneas.
Rabelais (Urquhart andMotteux), Bk iv, ch. lxii

**Ditto** (Ital. *detto*, said; from Lat. *dictum*). That which has been said before; the same or a similar thing. The word is often, in writing, contracted to *do*.

***A suit of dittoes.*** Coat, waistcoat, and trousers all alike, or all ditto (the same).

***To say ditto.*** To endorse somebody else's expressed opinion.

**Div** or **Deev.** The generic name of certain malignant demons of *Persian mythology*, ferocious and gigantic spirits under the sovereignty of Eblis.

At Lahore, in the Mogul's palace, are pictures of Dews and Dives with long horns, staring eyes, shaggy hair, great fangs, ugly paws, long tails, and such horrible deformity, that I wonder the poor women are not frightened.
William Finch, *Purchas' Pilgrims*, vol. i

**Divan** (Tur. and Pers.). Primarily, a collection of sheets; hence, a collection of poems, a register (and the registrar) of accounts, the office where accounts are kept, a council or tribunal, a long seat or bench covered with cushions, a court of justice, and a custom house (whence *douane*). The word, in its ramifications and extensions, is somewhat like our *board* (*q.v.*); in England its chief meanings are a comfortable lounge seat, and a public smoking saloon or coffee-room.

**Dives.** The name popularly given to the rich man (Lat. *dives*) in our Lord's parable of the Rich Man and Lazarus: it is taken direct from the Vulgate.

Lazar and Dives liveden diversely,
And diverse guerdon hadden they ther-by.
Chaucer, *Somnour's Tale*, 169

**Divede.** When the members in the House of Commons interrupt a speaker by crying out *divide*, they mean, bring the debate to an end and put the motion to the vote – i.e. let the ayes divide from the noes, one going into one lobby, and the others into another.

**Divide and Govern** (Lat. *divide et impera*). A maxim of Machiavelli (1469–1527) meaning that if you divide a nation into parties, or set your enemies at loggerheads, you can have your own way. Coke, in his *Institutes* (pt iv, cap. i) speaks of the maxim as 'that exploded adage'.

Every city or house divided against itself shall not stand. Matt. 12:25

**Divination.** There are numerous species of divination referred to in the Bible. The following are the most notable, and to most of these there are many other allusions in the Bible beside those indicated.

Judicial Astrology (Dan. 2:2).
Witchcraft (1 Sam. 28).
Enchantment (2 Kings 21:6).
Casting Lots (Josh. 18:6).
By Necromancy (1 Sam. 28:12).
By Rhabdomancy or rods (Hos. 4:12).
By Teraphim or household idols (Gen. 31; 1 Sam. 15:23, R.V.).
By Hepatoscopy or inspecting the liver of animals (Ezek. 21:21, 26).
By Dreams and their Interpretations (Gen. 37:10).
Divination by fire, air, and water; thunder, lightning, and meteors; etc.
The *Urim and Thummin* was a prophetic breastplate worn by the High Priest.
(Consult: Gen. 37:5–11; 11, 12; 1 Sam. 28:12; 2 Chron. 33:6; Prov. 16:33; Ezek. 21:21; Hos. 3:4, 5, etc.)

**Divine, The.** As a *Personal Surname*.

Theophrastus, the name of the Greek philosopher (390–287 BC), means 'the Divine Speaker', an epithet bestowed on him by Aristotle, on account of which he changed his name from Tyrtamus.

Hypatia (*c.*370–415), who presided over the Neoplatonic School at Alexandria, was known as 'the Divine Pagan'.

Jean de Ruysbroek (*see* Ecstatic Doctor) was also called 'the Divine Doctor'.

A name given to Michael Angelo (1475–1564) was 'the Divine Madman'.

Ariosto (1474–1533), Italian poet, Raphael (1483–1520), the painter, Luis de Morales (1509–86), a Spanish religious painter, and Ferdinand de Herrera (1534–67), the Spanish lyric poet, were all known as 'the Divine'.

***The Divine Plant.*** Vervain. *See* Herba Sacra.

***The divine right of kings.*** The notion that kings reign by direct ordinance of God, quite apart from the will of the people. This phrase was much used in the 17th century on account of the pretensions of the Stuart kings; and the idea arose from the Old Testament, where kings are called 'God's anointed', because they were God's vicars on earth, when the Jews changed their theocracy for a monarchy.

> The right divine of kings to govern wrong.
>
> Pope, *Dunciad*, iv, 188

**Divining Rod.** A forked branch of hazel, suspended by the two prongs between the balls of the thumbs. The inclination of the rod, when controlled by a specially and somewhat mystically qualified person, called a *diviner*, is said to indicate by its movements the presence of water-springs, precious metal, oil, etc.

> Divining, or *dowsing* (*see* Dowse), as it is also called, has been the subject of numerous scientific investigations, and while these have shown that the claims of diviners can in many cases be substantiated, there is still no satisfactory scientific explanation of the phenomena. This method of discovering hidden treasure naturally lends itself to the exploitation of the fraudulent and the 'gulling' of the credulous.

**Division.** The sign ÷ for division was brought into use by John Pell (1611–85), the noted Cambridge mathematician who became Professor of Mathematics at Amsterdam in 1643.

**Divus** (Lat. a god; godlike). After the Augustan period this was conferred as an epithet on deceased Roman emperors, more with the idea of canonising them, of proclaiming them to be 'of blessed memory', than with that of enrolling them among the divinities. Thus, *Divus Augustus* means 'Augustus of blessed memory', not 'Divine Augustus'.

> The new cult of the 'divi imperatores' spread throughout the Empire, and became a force which helped to weld together the populations and to secure their loyalty to the ruling power. The cult gave a new semblance of dignity to the Senate. At the end of every reign it sat in judgment and decided whether the dead emperor was to be enrolled among the 'divi' or whether his memory was to be reckoned accursed ('damnatio memoriae').
>
> J. S. Reid (in *A Companion to Latin Studies*, 1910, ch. vi)

**Dixie Land.** Nigger land, i.e. the Southern States of the United States. It has been said to have got its name from 'Mason and *Dixon's* Line' (*q.v.*), which formed the boundary between the slave-holding and the 'free' States; but the explanation given below is more likely to be correct, for negroes would scarcely have sung such songs as 'I wish I were in Dixie' with such fervour and unanimity when they were already there – especially as they had little reason to love the cotton-growing districts to which the word refers. But it should be mentioned that 'Dixie' was also – to some negro minds – synonymous with 'Heaven'.

> When slavery existed in New York, one Dixie owned a large tract of land on Manhattan Island, and a large number of slaves. The increase of the slaves and of the abolition sentiment caused an emigration of the slaves to more thorough and secure slave sections, and the negroes who were thus sent off (many being born there) naturally looked back to their old houses, where they had lived in clover, with feelings of regret, as they could not imagine any place like Dixie's. Hence it became synonymous with an ideal locality combining ease, comfort, and material happiness of every description.
>
> *Charlestown Courier*, June 11th, 1885

*Dixie*, the soldier's name for a large cooking kettle, is the Hindi *degshi*, a pot, vessel.

**Dizzy.** A nickname of Benjamin Disraeli (Lord Beaconsfield) (1805–81).

**Djinn.** *See* Jinn.

**Djinnestan.** The realm of the jinns or genii of Oriental mythology.

**Do** (in *Music*). *See* Doh.

**Do.** A contraction of *ditto* (*q.v.*).

**Do.** A verb and auxiliary that is almost as useful in English as *faire* in French, and that forms part of countless phrases and lends itself to almost countless uses. Its chief modern significations are:

(Transitive) To put, as in *To put to death*; to bestow, cause to befall, etc., as *It did him no harm, To do a good turn*; to perform, perpetrate, execute, etc., as *To do one's work, Thou shalt do no murder, What will he do with it? All is done and finished.*

(Intransitive) To exert actively, to act in some way, as *Let us do or die, I have done with you, How do you do? I'm doing very well, thank you, That will do.*

(Causal and Auxiliary) Used instead of a verb just used, as *He plays as well as you do.* Periphrastically as an auxiliary of the Pres. and Past Indicative and the Imperative, used for the sake of emphasis, euphony, or clarity, also in negative and interrogative sentences: *I* do *wish you would let me alone, Not a word did he say, Billiards and drinking do make the money fly, Do you like jazzing? I do not care for it. Do tell me where you've been! Don't stop!*

***A do.*** A regular swindle, a fraud.

***Do as you would be done by.*** Behave to others as you would have them behave to you.

***To do away with.*** To abolish, put an end to, destroy entirely.

***To do for.*** To act for or manage for. *A man ought to do well for his children*; a landlady *does for* her lodgers. Also, to ruin, destroy, wear out. *I'll do for him*, I'll ruin him utterly, or even, I'll kill him; *taken in and done for*, cheated and fleeced; *this watch is about done for*, it's nearly worn out.

***To do it on one's head.*** Said of doing something with consummate ease; a rather scornful expression. 'I bet you couldn't walk a mile in seven minutes'; 'Pooh! I could do it on my head!'

***To do on.*** *See* Don.

***To do one, to do one down,*** or ***brown, to do one out of something.*** To cheat him, or trick him out of something; to get the better of him.

***To do one proud.*** To flatter him; to treat him in an exceptionally lavish and hospitable way.

***To do oneself proud,*** or ***well.*** To give oneself a treat.

***To do the grand, amiable,*** etc. To act (usually with some ostentation) in the manner indicated by the adjective.

***To do up.*** To repair, put in order. 'This chair wants doing up,' i.e. renovating. Also, to make tidy, to put up or fasten a parcel, and to wear out, tire. 'I'm quite done up,' I'm worn out, exhausted. *Cp.* Dup.

***To do without so-and-so.*** To deny oneself it, to manage without it.

***To have to do with.*** To have dealings or intercourse with, to have relation to. 'That has nothing to do with the case.'

***Well to do.*** In good circumstances, well off, well provided for.

**Dobbin.** A steady old horse, a child's horse. *Dobby*, a silly old man, also a house-elf similar to a brownie. All these are one and the same word, an adaptation of *Robin*, diminutive of *Robert*.

> Sober Dobbin lifts his clumsy heel.
>
> Bloomfield, *Farmer's Boy* (Winter)

The dobbies lived in the house, were very thin and shaggy, very kind to servants and children, and did many a little service when people had their hands full.

> The Dobby's walk was within the inhabited domains of the Hall.
>
> Scott, *Peveril of the Peak*, ch. x

**Dobby.** *See* Dobbin.

**Docetes.** An early Gnostic heretical sect, which maintained that Jesus Christ was divine only, and that His visible form, the crucifixion, the resurrection, etc., were merely illusions. (The word is Greek, and means *phantomists.*)

**Doch-an-doroch** (Gaelic). A Scottish term (now frequent under various spellings and pronunciations in the south) for a stirrup-cup; a final drink before saying 'Good-night' and going home. Variants are *doch-an-doris, deoch-an-doruis*, etc. *Cp.* Forfar.

**Doctor.** A name given to various adulterated or falsified articles because they are 'doctored', i.e. treated in some way that strengthens them or otherwise makes them capable of being passed off as something better than they actually are. Thus a mixture of milk, water, nutmeg, and rum is called *Doctor*; the two former ingredients being 'doctored' by the two latter.

Brown sherry is so called by licensed victuallers because it is concocted from a thin wine with the addition of unfermented juice and some spirituous liquor.

In nautical slang the ship's cook is known as 'the doctor', because he is supposed to 'doctor' the food; and a seventh son used to be so dubbed from the popular superstition that he was endowed with power to cure agues, the king's evil, and other diseases.

***Doctored dice.*** Loaded dice; dice which are so 'doctored' as to make them turn up winning numbers; also called simply *doctors*.

> 'The whole antechamber is full, my lord – knights and squires, doctors and dicers.'

'The dicers with their doctors in their pockets,
I presume'.
Scott, *Peveril of the Peak*, ch. xxviii

***I do not like thee, Dr Fell.***

I do not like thee, Dr Fell.
The reason why I cannot tell;
But this I know, I know full well,
I do not like thee, Dr Fell.

These well-known lines are by the 'facetious' Tom Brown (1663–1704), and the person referred to was Dr Fell, Dean of Christchurch (1625–86), who expelled him, but said he would remit the sentence if he translated the thirty-third Epigram of Martial:

Non amo te, Zabidi, nec possum dicere quare;
Hoc tantum possum dicere non amo te.

The above is the translation, which is said to have been given impromptu.

***The three best doctors are Dr Quiet, Dr Diet, and Dr Merryman.***

Si tibi deficiant medici, medici tibi fiant
Haec tria; Mens-laeta, Requies, Moderata-Diaeta.

***To doctor the accounts.*** To falsify them. They are *ill* (so far as you are concerned) and you falsify them to make them look *better*. The allusion is to drugging wine, beer, etc., and to adulteration generally.

***To doctor the wine.*** To drug it, or strengthen it with brandy; to make weak wine stronger, and 'sick' wine more palatable. The fermentation of cheap wines is increased by fermentable sugar. As such wines fail in aroma, connoisseurs smell at their wine.

***To have a cat doctored.*** A colloquialism for having a young tom-cat 'cut', or castrated.

***To put the doctor on a man.*** To cheat him. The allusion to 'doctored dice' is obvious.

***Who shall decide when doctors disagree?*** When authorities differ, the question *sub judice* must be left undecided. (Pope, *Moral Essays*, ep. iii, line 1.)

**Dr Faustus.** *See* Faust.

**Dr Fell.** *See above.*

**Doctor Mirabilis.** Roger Bacon (1214–92).

**Doctor My-Book.** Dr John Abernethy (1764–1831), so called because he used to say to his patients, 'Read *my book*' – on *Surgical Observations*.

**Dr Rezio** or *Pedro Rezio of Aguero*. The doctor of Barataria, who forbade Sancho Panza to taste any of the meats set before him. Roasted partridge was forbidden by Hippocrates; podrida was the most pernicious food in the world; rabbits are a sharp-haired diet; veal is prejudicial to health; but the governor might eat a 'few wafers, and a thin slice or two of quince'. (*Don Quixote*, II, iii, 10.)

**Doctors' Commons.** A locality near St Paul's, where the ecclesiastical courts were formerly held, wills preserved, and marriage licences granted, and where was held the common table of the Association of Doctors of Civil Law in London (dissolved 1858). To 'common' (*q.v.*) means to dine together; and the doctors had to dine there four days in each term. The actual building was demolished in 1867.

**Doctors of the Church.** Certain early Christian Fathers, especially four in the Greek (or Eastern) Church and four in the Latin (or Western) Church.

***(a) Eastern Church.*** St Athanasius of Alexandria (331), who defended the divinity of Christ against the Arians; St Basil the Great of Caesarea (379) and his co-worker St Gregory of Nazianzum (376); and the eloquent St John Chrysostom (398), Archbishop of Constantinople.

***(b) Western Church.*** St Jerome (420), translator of the Vulgate; St Ambrose (397), Bishop of Milan; St Augustine (430), Bishop of Hippo; and St Gregory the Great (604), the pope who sent St Augustine to England.

**Doddypoll.** A blockhead, a silly ass. *Poll*, of course, is the head; and *doddy* is the modern *dotty*, silly, from the verb *to dote*, to be foolish or silly. There is an Elizabethan romantic comedy (about 1595) called *The Wisdom of Doctor Doddypoll*, thought by some to be by George Peele.

***As wise as Dr Doddypoll.*** Not wise at all; a dunce.

**Dodge.** An artful device to evade, deceive, or bilk someone. The etymology is uncertain, but the word may be connected with Ger. *ducken* (earlier, *docken*), to dodge or duck.

***The tidy dodge.*** To dress up a disreputable family clean and tidy so as to excite sympathy, and make passers-by suppose they have by misfortune fallen from a respectable state in society.

***To come the religious dodge.*** To ask or seek some favour under pretence of a religious motive; to trade on religion.

**Dodger.** A 'knowing fellow'. One who knows all the tricks and ways of London life, and profits by such knowledge.

***The Artful Dodger.*** The sobriquet of John Dawkins, a young thief, up to every artifice and a perfect adept in villainy, in Dickens's *Oliver Twist*.

**Dodman.** A snail; the word is still in use in Norfolk. Fairfax, in his *Bulk and Selvedge* (1674), speaks of 'a snayl or dodman'.

> Doddiman, doddiman, put out your horn,
> Here comes a thief to steal your corn.
>
> Norfolk rhyme

*Hodmandod* is another variation of the same word.

**Dodona.** A famous oracle in the village of Dodona in Epiros, and the most ancient of Greece. It was dedicated to Zeus, and the oracles were delivered from the tops of oak and other trees, the rustling of the wind in the branches being interpreted by the priests. Also, brazen vessels and plates were suspended from the branches, and those, being struck together when the wind blew, gave various sounds from which responses were concocted. Hence the Greek phrase *Kalkos Dodones* (brass of Dodona), meaning a babbler, or one who talks an infinite deal of nothing.

***The black pigeons of Dodona.*** *See under* Pigeon.

**Dodson and Fogg.** The names of these lawyers, employed by the plaintiff in the famous case of 'Bardell *v.* Pickwick' (Dickens' *Pickwick*), are frequently used as a synonym for unscrupulous and dishonest solicitors.

**Doe. *John Doe and Richard Roe*.** Any plaintiff and defendant in an action of ejectment. They were sham names used at one time to save certain 'niceties of law'; but the clumsy device was abolished in 1852. Any mere imaginary persons, or men of straw. The names 'John o' Noakes' and 'Tom Styles' are similarly used.

**Doeg.** In Dryden's *Absalom and Achitophel* (*q.v.*), is meant for Elkanah Settle, a poet who wrote satires upon Dryden, but was no match for his great rival. Doeg was Saul's herdsman, who had charge of his mules and asses (1 Sam. 21:7; 22:18).

> Doëg, though without knowing how or why,
> Made still a blundering kind of melody …
> Let him rail on; let his invective Muse
> Have four-and-twenty letters to abuse,
> Which if he jumbles to one line of sense,
> Indict him of a capital offence.
>
> *Absalom and Achitophel*, Pt ii

**Doff** is do-off, as 'Doff your hat.' So *Don* is do-on, as 'Don your clothes.' *Dup* is do-up, as 'Dup the door' (*q.v.*).

> Doff thy harness, youth …
> And tempt not yet the brushes of the war.
>
> Shakespeare, *Troilus and Cressida*, 5, 3

**Dog.** This article is subdivided into five parts:

1. Dogs in Phrases and Colloquialisms.
2. Dogs of note in the Classics and in legend.
3. Dogs famous in History, Literature, Fiction, etc.
4. Dogs in Symbolism and Metaphor.
5. Dog – or dog's – in combination.

(1) *In Phrases and Colloquialisms*

***A black dog has walked over him.*** Said of a sullen person. Horace tells us that the sight of a black dog with its pups was an unlucky omen, and the devil has been frequently symbolised by a black dog.

***A cat and dog life.*** *See* Cat (To live a, etc.).

***A dead dog.*** Something utterly worthless. A Biblical phrase (*see* 1 Sam. 24:14, 'After whom is the king of Israel come out? After a dead dog?'). *Cp. also* Is thy servant, etc., *below*. There is no expression in the Bible of the fidelity, love, and watchful care of the dog.

***A dirty dog.*** One morally filthy; one who talks and acts nastily. In the East the dog is still held in abhorrence, as the scavenger of the streets. 'Him that dieth in the city shall the dogs eat' (1 Kings 14:11). The French say, *Crotté comme un barbet* (muddy or dirty as a poodle), whose hair, being very long, becomes filthy with mud and dirt if not tended.

***A dog in a doublet.*** A bold, resolute fellow. In Germany and Flanders the strong dogs employed for hunting the wild boar were dressed in a kind of buff doublet buttoned to their bodies. Rubens and Sneyders have represented several in their pictures. A false friend is called *a dog in one's doublet*.

***A dog in the manger.*** A churlish fellow, who will not use what is wanted by another, nor yet let the other have it to use. The allusion is to the well known fable of a dog that fixed his place in a manger, and would not allow an ox to come near the hay.

***A living dog is better than a dead lion.*** The meanest thing with life in it is better than the noblest without. The saying is from Eccles. 9:4. The Italians say 'A live ass is worth more than a dead doctor.'

***A dog's age.*** A very long time.

***A surly dog.*** A human being of a surly temper. *Dog* is often used for 'chap' or 'fellow': thus we have *a gay dog*, a man who is always out and about on pleasure, and *a sad dog*, which means much the same, but carries with it a touch of reproof.

***A well-bred dog hunts by nature.*** Breeding 'tells'. The French proverb is '*Bon chien chasse de race*.'

***Barking dogs seldom bite.*** *See* Bark.

***Between dog and wolf.*** The hour of dusk. *See* Chien.

***Brag's a good dog, etc.*** *See* Brag.

***Dog don't eat dog.*** A similar phrase to 'There's honour among thieves.' United we stand, divided we fall; *ecclesia ecclesiam non decimat.*

***Dogs howl at death.*** A widespread superstition.

In the rabbinical book it saith
The dogs howl when, with icy breath,
Great Sammaël, the angel of death,
Takes thro' the town his flight.

Longfellow, *Golden Legend*, iii

Nor would I now be well, mother, again if that could be.
For my desire is but to pass to Him that died for me.
I did not hear the dog howl, mother, or the death-watch beat.
There came a sweeter token when the night and morning meet.

Tennyson, *The May Queen*; *Conclusion*

***Every dog has his day.*** You may crow over me today, but my turn will come by and by. In Latin *Hodie mihi, eras tibi*, 'I died today, your turn will come in time.' '*Nunc mihi, nunc tibi, benigna*' (*fortuna*), fortune visits every man once; she favours me now, but she will favour you in your turn.

Thus every dog at last will have his day –
He who this morning smiled, at night may sorrow;
The grub today's a butterfly tomorrow.

Peter Pindar, *Odes of Condolence*

***Give a dog a bad name and hang him.*** If you want to do anyone a wrong, throw dirt on him or rail against him. When once a person's reputation has been besmirched he has a hard fight to 'make good', and, often, might as well be hanged as try to rehabilitate himself.

***He has not a dog to lick a dish.*** He has quite cleared out. He has taken away everything.

***He who has a mind to beat his dog will easily find a stick.*** If you want to abuse a person, you will easily find something to blame. Dean Swift says, 'If you want to throw a stone, every lane will furnish one.'

'Where there's a will there's a way.' In Latin, '*Qui vult caedere canem facile invenit fustem.*'

***Hungry dogs will eat dirty pudding.*** Those really hungry are not particular about what they eat, and are by no means dainty. The proverb is given by Heywood (1546). 'To the hungry soul every bitter thing is sweet' (Prov. 27:7). 'When bread is wanting oaten cakes are excellent.'

When Darius in his flight from Greece drank from a ditch defiled with dead carcasses, he declared he had never drunk so pleasantly before.

Scott uses the saying with a slight variation:

'All nonsense and pride,' said the laird. 'Scornful dogs will eat dirty puddings.'

*Redgauntlet*, ch. xi

***I am his Highness' dog at Kew; Pray tell me, sir, whose dog are you?*** Frederick Prince of Wales had a dog given him by Alexander Pope, and these words are said to have been engraved on his collar. They are still sometimes quoted with reference to an overbearing, bumptious person.

***Is thy servant a dog, that he should do this thing?*** Said in contempt when one is asked to do something derogatory or beneath one. The phrase is (slightly altered) from 2 Kings 8:13.

Sydney Smith, when asked if it was true that he was about to sit to Landseer, the animal painter, for his portrait replied. 'What! is thy servant *a dog* that he should do this thing?'

***It was the story of the dog and the shadow.*** A case of one who gives up the substance for its shadow, of one who throws good money after bad, of one who gives *certa pro incertis*. The allusion is to the well known fable of the dog who dropped his bone into the stream because he opened his mouth to seize the reflection of it.

***Lazy as Lawrence's***, or ***Ludlam's, dog.*** *See* Lazy.

***Let sleeping dogs lie; don't wake a sleeping dog.*** Let well alone; if some contemplated course of action is likely to cause trouble or land you in difficulties you had better avoid it.

It is nought good a sleping hound to wake,
Nor yeve a wight a cause to devyne.

Chaucer, *Troilus and Criseyde*, 3, 764

***Love me love my dog.*** If you love me you must put up with my faults, my little ways, or (sometimes) my friends. A rather selfish maxim! The French say '*Qui aime Bertrand aime son chien.*'

***Not to have a word to throw at a dog.*** Said of one who is sullen or sulky.

*Cel.* Why, cousin! why, Rosalind! Cupid have mercy! Not a word?
*Ros.* Not one to throw at a dog.

Shakespeare, *As You Like It*, 1, 3

***Old dogs will not learn new tricks.*** People in old age do not readily conform to new ways.

***St Roch and his dog.*** Emblematic of inseparable companions; like 'a man and his shadow'. One is never seen without the other. *See* Roch, St.

***Sick as a dog.*** Very sick. We also say 'Sick as a cat'. *See* Cat. The Bible speaks of dogs returning to their vomit (Prov. 26:11; 2 Pet. 2:22).

***The dogs of war.*** The horrors of war, especially famine, sword, and fire.

And Caesar's spirit, ranging for revenge,
With Até by his side, come hot from hell.
Shall in these confines, with a monarch's voice,
Cry 'Havoc', and let slip the dogs of war.

Shakespeare, *Julius Caesar*, 3,1

***The hair of the dog that bit you.*** 'The same again'. When a man has had a debauch, he is advised to take next morning 'a hair of the same dog', i.e. a glass (or two) of the tipple that caused the trouble, in allusion to an ancient notion that the burnt hair of a dog is an antidote to its bite. *Similia similibus curantur.*

***The more I see of men the more I love dogs.*** A very misanthropic saying, the meaning of which is obvious. It is probably French in origin – *Plus je vois les hommnes, plus j'admire les chiens.*

***There are more ways of killing a dog than by hanging.*** There is more than one way of achieving your object. The proverb is found in Ray's *Collection* (1742).

***Throw it to the dogs.*** Throw it away, it is useless and worthless.

Throw physic to the dogs! I'll none of it.

Shakespeare, *Macbeth*, 5, 3

***To blush like a dog***, or ***like a blue*** or ***black dog.*** Not to blush at all. Dogs, of course, do not blush – at least, not visibly!

***To call off the dogs.*** To desist from some pursuit or enquiry; to break up a disagreeable conversation. In the chase, if the dogs are on the wrong track, the huntsman calls them off.

***To die like a dog.*** To have a shameful, or a miserable, end.

***To go to the dogs.*** To go to utter ruin, morally or materially; to become impoverished.

***To help a lame dog over a stile.*** To give assistance to one in distress; to hold out a helping hand; to encourage.

Do the work that's nearest,
  Though it's dull at whiles,
Helping, when we meet them,
  Lame dogs over stiles.

Chas Kingslsy, *The Invitation*

***To lead the life of a dog.*** To live a wretched life, or a life of debauchery.

***To put on the dog.*** To behave in a conceited or bumptious manner.

***To rain cats and dogs.*** *See* Cat (*It is raining, etc.*).

***To wake a sleeping dog.*** *See* Let sleeping dogs lie, *above*.

***Try it on the dog!*** A jocular phrase used of medicine that is expected to be unpalatable, or of food that is suspected of being not quite fit for human consumption.

***What! keep a dog and bark myself!*** Must I keep servants and myself do their work?

***You can never scare a dog away from a greasy hide.*** It is difficult to free oneself from bad habits. The line is from Horace's *Satires* (ii, v, 83): *Canis a corio nunquam absterrebitur uncto.*

*(2) Dogs of Note in the Classics and in Legend.*

***Actaeon's fifty dogs.*** Alce (*strength*), Amarynthos (*from Amarythia, in Euboea*), Asbolos (*soot-colour*), Banos, Boreas, Canache (*ringwood*), Chediaetros, Cisseta, Coran (*cropped, crop-eared*), Cyllo (*halt*), Cyllopotes (*zigzag runner*), Cyprios (*the Cyprian*), Draco (*the dragon*), Dromas (*the courser*), Dromios (*seize-'em*), Echnobas, Eudromos (*good-runner*), Harpale (*voracious*), Harpiea (*tear-'em*), Ichnobate (*track-follower*), Labros (*furious*), Lacaena (*lioness*), Lachne (*glossy-coated*), Lacon (*Spartan*), Ladon (*from Ladon, in Arcadia*), Laelaps (*hurricane*), Lampos (*shining-one*), Leucos (*grey*), Lycisca, Lyncea, Machimos (*boxer*), Melampe (*black*), Melanchete (*black-coat*), Melanea (*black*), Menelea, Molossos (*from Molossos*), Napa (*begotten by a wolf*), Nebrophonos (*fawn-killer*), Ocydroma (*swift-runner*), Oresitrophos (*mountain-bred*), Oribasos (*mountain-ranger*), Pachytos (*thick-skinned*), Pamphagos (*ravenous*), Poemenis (*leader*), Pterelas (*winged*), Stricta (*spot*), Theridamas (*beast-tamer* or *subduer*), Theron (*savage-faced*), Thoös (*swift*), Uranis (*heavenly-one*).

***Geryon's dogs.*** Gargittios and Orthos. The latter was the brother of Cerberus, but had one head less. Hercules killed both these monsters.

***Icarius's dog.*** Maera (*the glistener*). *See* Icarius.

***Orion's dogs.*** Arctophonos (*bear-killer*), and Ptoophagos (the *glutton* of *Ptoon*, in Boeotia).

***Procris's dog.*** Laelaps. *See* Procris.

***Ulysses' dog.*** Argos; he recognised his master after his return from Troy, and died of joy.

***Aubry's dog***, or ***the dog of Montargis.*** Aubry of Montdidier was murdered, in 1371, in the forest of Bondy. His dog, Dragon, excited suspicion of Richard of Macaire by always snarling and flying at his throat whenever he appeared. Richard was condemned to a judicial combat with the dog, was killed, and, in his dying moments, confessed the crime.

> No doubt Diogenes is there, and no doubt Mr Toots has reason to observe him; for he comes straightway at Mr Toots's legs, and tumbles over himself in the desperation with which he makes at him, like a very dog of Montargis. ('Diogenes' was the dog given by Mr Toots to Florence Dombey.)
>
> Dickens, *Dombey and Son*

***Cuchullain's hound.*** Luath (*q.v.*).

***Fingal's dog.*** Bran (*q.v.*).

***King Arthur's favourite hound.*** Cavall.

***Llewellyn's greyhound.*** Beth Gelert (*q.v.*).

***Mauthe dog.*** (*See* Mauthe.)

***Montargis, dog of.*** Aubry's dog. (*See above*). A picture of the combat was for many years preserved in the Castle of Montargis.

***Roderick the Goth's dog.*** Theron.

***Seven Sleepers, Dog of the.*** Katmir who, according to Mohammedan tradition, was admitted to heaven. He accompanied the seven noble youths who fell asleep for 309 years to the cavern in which they were walled up, and remained standing for the whole time, neither moving, eating, drinking, nor sleeping.

***Tristran's dog.*** Hodain, or Leon.

*(3) Dogs Famous in History, Literature, Fiction, etc.*

***Boatswain.*** Byron's favourite dog; the poet wrote an epitaph on him and he was buried in the garden of Newstead Abbey.

***Bounce.*** Alexander Pope's dog.

***Boy.*** Prince Rupert's dog; he was killed at the battle of Marston Moor.

***Brutus.*** Landseer's greyhound; jocularly called 'The Invader of the Larder'.

***Bull's-eye.*** Bill Sykes's cur in Dickens's *Oliver Twist*.

***Dash.*** Charles Lamb's dog.

***Diamond.*** The little dog belonging to Sir Isaac Newton. One winter's morning he upset a candle on his master's desk, by which papers containing minutes of many years' experiments were destroyed. On perceiving this terrible catastrophe Newton exclaimed: 'Oh, Diamond, Diamond, thou little knowest the mischief thou hast done!' and at once set to work to repair the loss.

***Diogenes.*** A dog in Dickens's *Dombey and Son*. It was given by Mr Toots to Florence Dombey. *See quotation under* Aubry's dog, *above*.

***Flush.*** Mrs Browning's little spaniel, a present from Miss Mitford.

> Other dogs in thymy dew
> Tracked the hares and followed through
> Sunny moor or meadow;
> This dog only, crept and crept
> Next a languid cheek that slept
> Sharing in the shadow.
>
> Mrs Browning, *To Flush, my Dog*

***Geist.*** One of Matthew Arnold's dachshounds. He wrote the poem *Geist's Grave* in memory of him.

***Giallo.*** Walter Savage Landor's dog.

***Hamlet.*** A black greyhound belonging to Sir Walter Scott.

***Jip*** or ***Gypsy.*** Dora's pet dog in Dickens's *David Copperfield*.

***Kaiser.*** Another of Matthew Arnold's dachshounds. (*See* Geist *above*.) In his poem, *Kaiser Dead*, the poet mentions also Toss, Rover and Max.

***Lufra.*** The hound of Douglas, in Scott's *Lady of the Lake*.

***Maida.*** Sir Walter Scott's favourite deerhound.

***Mathe.*** Richard II's greyhound. It deserted the king and attached itself to Bolingbroke.

***Merrylegs.*** Signor Jupe's performing dog in Dickens's *Hard Times*.

***Toby.*** Punch's famous dog.

*(4) In Symbolism and Metaphor.*

***Dogs,*** in mediaeval art, symbolise fidelity. A dog is represented as lying at the feet of St Bernard, St Benignus, and St Wendelin; as licking the wounds of St Roch; as carrying a lighted torch in representations of St Dominic.

*In monuments* the dog is placed at the feet of women to symbolise affection and fidelity, as a *lion* is placed at the feet of men to signify courage and magnanimity. Many of the Crusaders are represented with their feet on a dog, to show that they followed the standard of the Lord as faithfully as a dog follows the footsteps of his master.

***Lovell the Dog.***

> The Rat, the Cat, and Lovell the Dog
> Rule all England under the Hog.

*See* Rat.

***The dog.*** Diogenes (412–323 BC). When Alexander went to see him the young King of Macedonia introduced himself with these words: 'I am Alexander, surnamed the Great,' to which the philosopher replied: 'And I am Diogenes, surnamed the Dog.' The Athenians raised to his memory a pillar of Parian marble, surmounted by a dog. (*See* Cynic.)

***The Dog of God.*** So the Laplanders call the bear which 'has the strength of ten men and the wit of twelve'.

***The Thracian dog.*** Zoïlus (4th cent. BC), the carping critic of ancient Greece.

> Like curs, our critics haunt the poet's feast,
> And feed on scraps refused by every guest;
> From the old Thracian dog they learned the way
> To snarl in want, and grumble o'er their prey.
>
> Pitt, *To Mr Spence*

*(5) In combination.*

*Dog-*, or *dog's-*, in combinations is used (besides in its literal sense as in *dog-biscuit*, *dog-collar*) for

(*a*) denoting the male of certain animals, as *dog-ape*, *dog-fox*, *dog-otter*.

(*b*) denoting inferior plants, or those which are worthless as food for man, as dog-brier, dog-cabbage, dog-leek, dog-lichen, dog-mercury, dog-parsley, dog-violets (which have no perfume), dog-wheat. *Cp.* Dog-grass, Dog-rose *below*.

(*c*) expressing spuriousness or some mongrel quality, as *dog's-logic*, *dog-Latin* (*q.v.*).

***Dog-cheap.*** Extremely cheap; 'dirt-cheap'.

***Dog-days.*** Days of great heat. The term comes from the Romans, who called the six or eight hottest weeks of the summer *caniculares dies.* According to their theory, the dog-star or Sirius, rising with the sun, added to its heat, and the dog-days (about July 3rd to August 11th) bore the combined heat of the dog-star and the sun. *See* Dog-star.

***Dog-fall.*** A fall in wrestling, when the two combatants touch the ground together.

***Dog-grass.*** Couch grass (*Triticum repens*), which is eaten by dogs when they have lost their appetite; it acts as an emetic and purgative.

***Dog-head.*** The part of a gun which bites or holds the flint.

***Dog-Latin.*** Pretended or mongrel Latin. An excellent example is Stevens' definition of a kitchen:

> As the law classically expresses it, a kitchen is 'camera necessaria pro usus cookare; cum saucepannis, stewpannis, scullero, dressero, coalholo stovis, smoak-jacko; pro roastandum, boilandum, fryandum et plum-pudding mixandum ...' *A Law Report* (*Daniel* v *Dishclout*)

***Dog-rose.*** The common wild rose (*Rosa canina*, Pliny's *cynorrodon*), so called because it was supposed by the ancient Greeks to cure the bite of mad dogs.

***Dog-sleep.*** A pretended sleep; also a light, easily broken sleep. Dogs seem to sleep with 'one eye open'.

***Dog-star.*** Sirius, the brightest star in the firmament, whose influence was anciently supposed to cause great heat, pestilence, etc. *See* Dog-days.

***Dog-vane.*** A nautical term for a small vane placed on the weather gunwale to show the direction of the wind. Sailors also apply it to a cockade.

***Dog-watch.*** The two short watches on board ship, one from four to six, and the other from six to eight in the evening, introduced to prevent the same men always keeping watch at the same time. *See* Watch.

***Dog-whipper.*** A beadle who used to keep dogs from the precincts of a church. Even so late as 1856 Mr John Pickard was appointed 'dog-whipper' in Exeter Cathedral, 'in the room of Mr Charles Reynolds, deceased'.

***Dog-whipping Day.*** October 18th (St Luke's Day). It is said that a dog once swallowed the consecrated wafer in York Minster on this day.

**Doggo.** *To lie doggo.* To get into hiding and remain there; to keep oneself secluded.

***Dog-goned.*** An American euphemism for the oath 'God-damned'.

> But when that choir got up to sing,
> I couldn't catch a word;
> They sung the moat doggonedest thing
> A body ever heard!
>
> Will Carleton, *Farm Ballad*

*See also* Dogs, Dog's, *below*.

**Dogaressa.** The wife of a doge (*q.v.*).

**Dogberry.** An ignorant, self-satisfied, overbearing, but good-natured night-constable in Shakespeare's *Much Ado About Nothing*; hence, an officious and ignorant Jack in office.

**Doge** (Lat. *dux*, a duke or leader). The chief magistrate in Venice while it was a Republic. The first doge was Paolo Anafesto (Paoluccio), 697, and the last, Luigi Manin (1789). *See* Bride of the Sea.

> For six hundred years ... her [Venice's] government was an elective monarchy, her ... doge possessing, in early times at least, as much independent authority as any other European sovereign.
>
> Ruskin, *Stones of Venice*, vol. I, ch. i

The chief magistrate of Genoa was called a doge from 1339 (Simon Boccanegra) down to 1797, when the government was abolished by the French.

**Dogget.** ***Dogget's coat and badge.*** The prize given in a rowing match for Thames watermen, which takes place, under the auspices of the Fish-mongers' Company, on or about August 1st every year. So called from Thomas Dogget (d.1721), an actor of Drury Lane, who signalised the accession of George I by instituting the race. It is from the 'Swan' at London Bridge to the 'Swan' at Chelsea. The 'coat' is an orange-coloured livery jacket.

**Dogmatic School.** *See* Empirics.

**Dogs.** A familiar name for the 17th Lancers (Duke of Cambridge's Own). The crest of this famous cavalry regiment is a Death's Head and Cross-bones, OR GLORY, whence the acrostic Death **O**r **G**lory Boy**S**.

In Stock Exchange phraseology, *dogs* means Newfoundland Telegraph shares, so called in allusion to Newfoundland dogs.

**Dogs'-ears.** The corners of leaves crumpled and folded down.

***Dogs'-eared.*** Leaves so crumpled and turned up. The ears of many dogs turn down and seem quite limp.

**Dogs'-meat.** Food unfit for consumption by human beings.

***Dogs'-meat and cats'-meat.*** Food cheap and nasty.

**Dog's-nose.** Gin and beer.

> 'Dog's-nose, which is, I believe, a mixture of gin and beer.'
> 'So it is,' said an old lady. *Pickwick Papers*

**Dogs, Isle of.** *See* Isle.

**Doh,** or **Do.** The first or tonic note of the solfeggio system of music.

***Doh, re, mi, fa, sol, la*** (Ital.); ***ut, re, mi, fa, sol, la*** (Fr.). The latter are borrowed from a hymn by Paulus Piaconus, addressed to St John, which Guido of Arezzo, in the 11th century, used in teaching singing:

> *Ut* queant lauds, *Re*-sonare fibris,
> *Mi*-ra gestorum *Fa*-mulituorum,
> *Sol*-ve pollutis *La*-biis reatum. *Sancte Joannes*
> *Ut*-tered be thy wondrous story,
> *Re*-prehensive though I be,
> *Me* make mindful of thy glory,
> *Fa*-mous son of Zacharee;
> *Sol*-ace to my spirit bring,
> *La*-bouring thy praise to sing. E. C. B.

*See* Aretinian Syllables.

**Doily.** A small cloth used to cover dessert plates, or a mat or napkin on which to stand plates, glasses, bottles, etc. In the 17th century the word was an adjective denoting a cheap woollen material; thus Dryden speaks of 'doyley petticoats', and Steele, in No. 102 of the *Tatler*, speaks of his 'doiley suit'. The Doyleys, from which the stuff was named, were linen-drapers at the east corner of Upper Wellington Street, Strand, from the late 17th century to 1850.

**Doings.** One of the convenient, noncommittal expressions (originally an Americanism) that sprang into general use during the Great War. At table 'Pass the doings' would be a request for the pickles, sauce, or some such 'extra', or 'There's doings today' would refer to pudding. But 'What are the doings like in the front line?' might be either a question about the food supplied or about the general conditions.

**Doit.** An old Dutch coin, worth about half a farthing; hence, any coin of very small value. In England the doit was prohibited by 3 Henry V c.1.

> When they will not give doit to relieve a lame beggar, they will lay out ten to see a dead Indian.
> Shakespeare, *The Tempest*, 2, 2

**Dokkalfar.** *See* Liosalfar.

**Dolce far niente** (Ital.). Delightful idleness. Pliny has '*Jucundum tamen nihil agere*' (*Ep.* viii, 9).

**Dolcinists.** *See* Dulcinists.

**Doldrums, The.** A condition of depression, slackness, or inactivity; hence applied by sailors to a region where ships are likely to be becalmed, especially that part of the ocean near the equator noted for calms, squalls, and baffling winds, between the N.E. and S.E. trade winds.

> But from the bluff-head, where I watched today,
> I saw her in the doldrums.
> Byron, *The Island*, canto ii, stanza 21

***In the doldrums.*** In the dumps.

**Dole** (Lat. *dolor*, grief, sorrow). Lamentation.

> What if …
> He now be dealing dole among his foes,
> And over heaps of slaughtered walk his way?
> Milton, *Samson Agonistes*, 1529

***To make dole.*** To lament, to mourn.

> Yonder they lie; the poor old man, their father, making such pitiful dole over them that all the beholders take this part with weeping.
> Shakespeare, *As You Like It*, 1, 2

**Dole** (A.S. *dal*, a portion, *doel*, deal). A portion allotted; a charitable gift, alms. Now used of a gratuity paid by Government to the unemployed, old age pensioners, etc.

> Heaven has in store a precious dole.
> Keble, *Christian Year* (4th Sunday after Trinity)

***Happy man be his dole.*** May his share or lot be that of a happy or fortunate man.

> Your father and my uncle have made motions: if it be my luck, so; if not, happy man be his dole!
> Shakespeare, *Merry Wives*, 3, 4

**Dollar.** The sign $, is probably a modification of the figure **8** as it appeared on the old Spanish 'pieces of eight', which were of the same value as the dollar.

The word is a variant of *thaler* (Low Ger. *dahler*; Dan. *daler*), and means 'a valley', our *dale*. The counts of Schlick, at the close of the 15th century, extracted from the mines at *Joachim's thal* (Joachim's valley) silver which they coined into ounce-pieces. These pieces, called *Joachim's thalers*, gained such high repute that they became a standard coin. Other coins being made like them were called *thalers* only. The American dollar equals 100 cents, in English money (nominally) 4*s*. 1½*d*.

**Dolly Shop.** A marine store where rags and refuse are bought and sold; so called from the black doll suspended over it as a sign to denote the sale of Indian silks and muslins. Dolly shops are, in reality, no better than unlicensed pawn-shops.

**Dolmen.** The name given in France to cromlechs (*q.v.*), particularly those of Brittany (Breton *tol*, a table, *men*, stone). They are often called by the rural population devils' tables, fairies' tables, and so on.

> The Indian dolmens ... may be said to be identical with those of Western Europe.
> Lubbock, *Prehistoric Times*, ch. v

***The Constantine Dolmen***, Cornwall, is 33 ft long, 14½ deep, and 18½ across. It is calculated to weigh 750 tons, and is poised on the points of two natural rocks.

**Dolopathos.** *See* Seven Wise Masters.

**Dolphin.** *Cp.* Dauphin. The dolphin is noted for its changes of colour when taken out of the water.

> Parting day
> Dies like the dolphin, whom each pang imbues
> With a new colour as it gasps away,
> The last still loveliest.
> Byron, *Childe Harold*, iv, 29

In mediaeval art, it symbolises social love.

**Dom** (Lat. *dominus*). A title applied in the Middle Ages to the Pope, and at a somewhat later period to other Church dignitaries. It is now restricted to priests and choir monks among the Benedictines, and to some few other monastic orders. The Sp. *don*, Port. *dom*, and M.E. *dan* (as in *Dan Chaucer*) are the same word.

**Domdaniel.** A fabled abode of evil spirits, gnomes, and enchanters, 'under the roots of the ocean' off Tunis, or elsewhere. It first appears in Chaves and Cazotte's *Continuation of the Arabian Nights* (1788–93), was introduced by Southey into his *Thalaba*, and used by Carlyle as synonymous with a den of iniquity. The word is Lat. *domus*, house or home, *Danielis*, of Daniel, the latter being taken as a magician.

**Domesday Book.** The book containing a record of the census or survey of England, giving the ownership, extent, value, etc., of all the different holdings, undertaken by order of William the Conqueror in 1086. It is in Latin, is written on vellum, and consists of two volumes, one a large folio of 382 pages, and the other a quarto of 450 pages. It was formerly kept in the Exchequer, under three different locks and keys, but is now in the Public Record Office. Northumberland, Cumberland, Westmorland, and Durham are not included, though parts of Westmorland and Cumberland are taken.

The value of all estates is given, firstly, as in the time of the Confessor; secondly, when bestowed by the Conqueror; and, thirdly, at the time of the survey. It is also called *The King's Book*, and *The Winchester Roll* because it was kept there. Printed in facsimile in 1783 and 1816.

The book was so called from A.S. *doom*, judgment, because every case of dispute was decided by an appeal to these registers. *Cp.* Exon Domesday.

**Dominations.** *See* Dominions.

**Dominic, St.** (1170–1221), who preached with great vehemence against the Albigenses, was called by the Pope 'Inquisitor-General', and was canonised by Gregory IX. He is represented with a sparrow at his side, and a dog carrying in its mouth a burning torch. The devil, it is said, appeared to the saint in the form of a sparrow, and the dog refers to the story that his mother, during her pregnancy, dreamt that she had given birth to a dog, spotted with black and white spots, which lighted the world with a burning torch.

**Dominica de brandonibus.** *See* Brandon.

**Dominical Letters.** The letters which denote the Sundays or *dies dominica*. The first seven letters of the alphabet are employed; if January 1st is a Sunday the dominical letter for the year will be A, if the 2nd is a Sunday it will be B, if the 3rd, C, and so on. In leap years there are two dominical letters, one for the period up to February 29th, and the other for the rest of the year.

**Dominicans.** An order of preaching friars, instituted by St Dominic in 1215, and introduced into England (at Oxford) in 1221. They were formerly called in England *Black Friars*, from their black dress, and in France *Jacobins*, because their mother-establishment in Paris was in the Rue St Jacques.

**Dominie Sampson.** A village schoolmaster and scholar in Scott's *Guy Mannering*; poor as a church mouse and modest as a girl. He cites Latin like a *porcus literarum*, and exclaims 'Prodigious!'

**Dominions.** The sixth of the nine orders in the mediaeval hierarchy of the angels. *See* Angel. They are symbolised in art by an ensign, and are also known as 'Dominations'.

**Domino** (Ital.). Originally a hooded cloak worn by canons; hence a disguise worn at masquerades consisting of a hooded garment, then the hood only, and finally the half mask covering an inch or two above and below the eyes, worn as a disguise.

The name came to be applied to the game probably through a custom of calling *faire domino* when winning with the last piece – much as the French still say *faire capot* (*capot* also means 'hood'); in the Navy and Army the last lash of a flogging is known as *the domino*.

**Don** is do-on, as 'Don your bonnet.' *See* Doff, Dup.

Then up he rose, and donned his clothes,
And dupp'd the chamber door.
Shakespeare, *Hamlet*, 4, 5

**Don.** A man of mark, an aristocrat. At the universities the masters, fellows, and noblemen are termed *dons*. The word is the Spanish form of Lat. *dominus*. *Cp*. Dan, Dom.

**Don Giovanni.** *See* Don Juan.

**Don Juan.** Don Juan Tenorio, the hero of a large number of plays and poems, as well as of Mozart's opera, *Don Giovanni*, and round whom numerous legends have collected, was the son of a leading family of Seville in the 14th century, and killed the commandant of Ulloa after seducing his daughter. To put an end to his debaucheries the Franciscan monks enticed him to their monastery and killed him, telling the people that he had been carried off to hell by the statue of the commandant, which was in the grounds.

His name has passed into a synonym for a rake, roué or aristocratic libertine, and in Mozart's opera (1787) Don Giovanni's valet, Leporello, says his master had 'in Italy 700 mistresses, in Germany 800, in Turkey and France 91, in Spain 1,003'. His dissolute life was dramatised by Gabriel Tellez in the 17th century, by Molière, Corneille, Shadwell, Grabbe (German), Dumas, and others, and in the 20th century by George Bernard Shaw (*Man and Superman*, 1903), Bataille, and Rostand.

In Byron's well-known poem (1819–24), when Juan was sixteen years old he got into trouble with Donna Julia, and was sent by his mother, then a widow, on his travels. His adventures in the Isles of Greece, at the Russian Court, in England, etc., form the story of the poem, which, though it extends to sixteen cantos and nearly 16,000 lines, is incomplete.

**Don Quixote.** The hero of the great romance of that name by the Spaniard, Cervantes, published at Madrid, Pt i, 1605, Pt ii, 1615. He is a gaunt country gentleman of La Mancha, gentle and dignified, affectionate and simple-minded, but so crazed by reading books of knight-errantry that he believes himself called upon to redress the wrongs of the whole world, and actually goes forth to avenge the oppressed and run a tilt with their oppressors. Hence, a *Quixotic* man, or a *Don Quixote*, is a dreamy, unpractical, but essentially good, man – one with a 'bee in his bonnet'.

**Donation of Constantine.** *See* Decretals.

**Donation of Pepin, The.** When Pepin conquered Ataulf (755) the exarchate of Ravenna fell into his hands. Pepin gave it, with the surrounding country and the Republic of Rome, to the Pope (Stephen II), and thus founded the Papal States and the whole fabric of the temporal power of the Popes.

Victor Emmanuel, King of Italy, dispossessed the Pope in 1870, and added the Papal States to the united kingdom of Italy.

**Donatists.** Followers of Donatus, a Numidian bishop of the 4th century who, on puritanical grounds, opposed Cecilianus. Their chief dogma is that the outward church is nothing, 'for the letter killeth, it is the spirit that giveth life'. St Augustine of Hippo vigorously combated their heresies.

**Doncaster.** The 'City on the river Don'. Celt. *Don*, that which spreads. Sigebert, monk of Gemblours, in 1100, derived the name from *Thong-ceaster*, the 'castle of the thong', and says that Hengist and Horsa purchased of the British king as much land as he could encompass with a leather thong, which they cut into strips, and so encompassed the land occupied by the city.

This is the old tale of Dido and the hide, and so is the Russian Yakutsks. *See* Bursa.

**Dondasch.** A giant of Eastern fable, contemporary with Seth, to whose service he was attached. He needed no weapons, as he could destroy anything by the mere force of his arms.

**Done Brown.** *See* Brown.

**Done for; Done up.** *See* Do.

**Donegild.** The wicked mother of Ella, King of Northumberland, in Chaucer's *Man of Lawes Tale*. *See* Cunstance.

**Donkey.** An ass. The word is of comparatively recent origin, being first recorded about 1782 (*Hickey's Memoirs*, ii, 276), and seems at first to have rhymed with 'monkey'. It is a diminutive, and may be connected with *dun*, in reference to its tint. 'Dun', in 'Dun in the mire' (*q.v.*), was a familiar name for a horse, and the 'donkey' is a smaller, or more diminutive beast of burden. For the tradition concerning the 'cross' on the donkey's back, *see* Ass.

***Not for donkey's years.*** Not for a long time, not for ever so long. The allusion turns on the pun – *donkey's ears*, which are notoriously long.

***The donkey means one thing and the driver another.*** Different people see from different standpoints, their own interest in every case directing their judgment. The allusion is to a fable in Phaedrus, where a donkey-driver exhorts his donkey to flee, as the enemy is at hand. The donkey asks if the enemy will load him with double pack-saddles. 'No,' says the man. 'Then,' replies the donkey, 'what care I whether you are my master or someone else?'

***To ride the black donkey.*** To be pigheaded, obstinate like a donkey. Black is added, not so much to designate the colour, as to express what is bad.

***Two more, and up goes the donkey.*** An old cry at fairs, the showman having promised the credulous rustics that as soon as enough pennies are collected his donkey will balance himself on the top of the pole or ladder, as the case may be. Needless to say, it is always a matter of 'two more pennies', and the trick is never performed. The phrase is used of a braggart whose actions do not come up to his pretensions.

***Who ate the donkey?*** An expression of contempt. It is said that when the French were fleeing from Spain after Vittoria, some stragglers entered a village, demanded rations, and were served with a donkey. Next day they were assaulted, and jeered at with the shout, 'Who ate the donkey?'

***Who stole the donkey?*** An old gibe against policemen. When the force was first established a donkey was stolen, but the police failed to discover the thief, and this gave rise to the laugh against them. The correct answer is 'The man with the white hat', because white hats were made of the skins of donkeys, many of which were stolen and sold to hatters.

**Donkey Engine, Pump,** etc. Small auxiliary engines or machines for doing subsidiary work.

**Donnybrook Fair.** This fair, held in August from the time of King John, till 1855, was noted for its bacchanalian orgies and light-hearted rioting. Hence it is proverbial for a disorderly gathering or a regular rumpus. The village was a mile and a half south-east of Dublin, and is now one of its suburbs.

**Dony.** Florimel's dwarf. (Spenser, *Faërie Queene*, III, v, V, ii.)

**Donzel.** A squire or young man of good birth not yet knighted. This is an anglicised form of Ital. *doncello*, from late Lat. *domicellus*. *See* Damsel.

> He is esquire to a knight-errant, donzel to the damsel.
> Butler, *Characters*

**Doolin of Mayence.** The hero of a French *chanson de geste* of the 14th century, and of a 15th century prose romance. He was the father of Ogier the Dane (*q.v.*).

***Doolin's sword.*** Merveilleuse (wonderful).

**Doom** (A. S. *dom*). The original meaning was law, or judgment, that which is set up, as a statute: hence, *the crack of doom*, the signal for the final judgmnt. The book of judgments compiled by King Alfred was known as the *domboc*.

**Doomsday Book.** *See* Domesday.

**Doomsday Sedgwick.** William Sedgwick, a fanatical prophet and preacher during the Commonwealth. He pretended to have had it revealed to him in a vision that doomsday was at hand; and, going to the house of Sir Francis Russell, in Cambridgeshire, he called upon a party of gentlemen playing at bowls to leave off and prepare for the approaching dissolution.

**Door.** The Anglo-Saxon *dor* (fem. *duru*). The word in many other languages is similar; thus, Dan. *dor*, Icel. *dyrr*, Gr. *thura*, Lat. *fores*, Ger. *thüre*.

***Dead as a door-nail.*** *See* Dead.

***Door-money.*** Payment taken at the doors for admission to an entertainment, etc.

***He laid the charge at my door.*** He accused me of doing it.

***Indoors.*** Inside the house; also used attributively, as, *an indoor servant*.

***Next door to it.*** Within an ace of it (*see* Ace); very like it; next-door neighbour to it.

***Out of doors.*** Outside the house; in the open air.

***Sin lieth at the door*** (Gen. 4:7). The blame of sin attaches to the wrongdoer, and he must take the consequences.

***The door must be either shut or open.*** It must be one way or the other; there is no alternative. From De Brueys and de Palaprat's comedy, *Le Grondeur* (produced 1691): the master scolds his servant for leaving the door open. The servant says that he was scolded the last time for shutting it, and adds: 'Do you wish it shut?' – 'No.' – 'Do you wish it open?' – 'No.' – 'Why,' says the man, 'it must be either shut or open.'

***To make the door.*** To make it fast by shutting and bolting it.

> Why at this time the doors are made against you.
> Shakespeare, *Comedy of Errors*, 3, 1

> Make the door upon a woman's wit, and it will out at the casement. *As You Like It*, 4, 1

**Door-opener, The.** So Crates, the Theban, was called, because every morning he used to go round Athens and rebuke the people for their late rising.

**Dope.** Properly, some thick or semi-fluid liquid used for food or as a lubricant (Dut. *doopen*, to dip). During the Great War the name was applied to a varnish used for aeroplane wings, the odour of which in some cases had a stupefying effect upon the workers. Hence it came to be used for noxious drugs, such as cocaine; and confirmed drug-takers have since been called *dope-fiends*. *Dope* is also used, figuratively, for flattery, or words that are intended to lead one into a false sense of security, power, etc.

**Dor.** *To dor the dotterel. See* Dotterel.

**Dora.** The popular name of the Defence of the Realm Act, 1914, under which many hundreds of regulations temporarily curbing the liberty of the subject were made. It passed into common speech in 1914 after having been used in the Law Courts by Mr Justice Scrutton.

**Dorado, El.** *See* El Dorado.

**Dorcas Society.** A woman's circle for making clothing for the poor. So called from Dorcas, in Acts 9:39, who made 'coats and garments' for widows.

**Dorchester.** *As big as a Dorchester butt.* Very corpulent. Of Toby Filpot it is said:

> His breath-doors of life on a sudden were shut,
> And he died full as big as a Dorchester butt.
> O'Keefe, *Poor Soldier*

**Dorian, Doric.** Pertaining to Doris, one of the divisions of ancient Greece, or to its inhabitants, a simple, pastoral people.

***Dorian Mode.*** In musical antiquities, a simple, solemn form of music, the first of the authentic Church modes.

***Doric dialect.*** The dialect spoken by the natives of Doris, in Greece. It was broad and hard. Hence, any broad dialect like that of rustics. Our own Bloomfield and Robert Burns are examples of British Doric.

***Doric order.*** The oldest, strongest, and simplest of the Grecian orders of architecture. The Greek Doric is simpler than the Roman imitation. The former stands on the pavement without fillet or other ornament, and the flutes are not scalloped. The Roman column is placed on a plinth, has fillets, and the flutings, both top and bottom, are scalloped.

***The Doric Land.*** Greece, Doris being a part of Greece.

> Through all the bounds
> Of Doric land. Milton, *Paradise Lost*, Bk i, 519

***The Doric reed.*** Pastoral poetry. Everything Doric was very plain, but cheerful, chaste, and solid.

> The Doric reed once more
> Well pleased, I tune. Thomson, *Autumn*, 3

**Dorigen.** The heroine of Chaucer's *Franklin's Tale*, which was taken from Boccaccio's *Decameron* (X, v), the original being in the Hindu *Vetála Panchavinsati*. She was married to Arviragus, but was greatly beloved by Aurelius, to whom she had been long known. Aurelius tried to win her, but Dorigen would not listen to him till the rocks round the coast of Britain were removed 'and there n'is no stone yseen'. Aurelius, by the aid of a magician, caused them all to disappear, and claimed his reward. Dorigen was very sad, but her husband insisted that she should keep her word, and she went to meet Aurelius, who, when he saw her grief and heard what Arviragus had counselled, said he would rather die than injure so true a wife and noble a gentleman.

**Dorinda,** in the verses of the Earl of Dorset, is Catherine Sedley, Countess of Dorchester, mistress of James II.

**Doris.** *See* Nereids.

**Dormer Window.** The window of an attic standing out from the slope of the roof; properly, the window of a bedroom. (O.Fr. *dormeor*, a dormitory.)

Thatched were the roofs, with dormer windows.
Longfellow, *Evangeline*, pt i, st. 1

**Dormy.** A golfing term of uncertain origin (perhaps connected with Fr. *dormir*, to sleep), which is applied to a player who is as many holes ahead of his opponent as there are holes left to play in the round. Thus, if when there are still three holes left Jones is three ahead of Brown, Jones is said to be 'dormy three'.

**Dornick.** Stout figured linen for tablecloths, etc.; so called from Doornik, the Flemish name of Tournay, where it was originally made. *Cp.* Dannocks. The word is spelt in many ways, e.g. Dornock, Darnex.

I have got ... a fair Darnex carpet of my own
Laid cross for the more state.
Fletcher, *The Noble Gentleman*, V, i

**Dorothea, St.** A martyr under Diocletian about 303. She is represented with a rose-branch in her hand, a wreath of roses on her head, and roses with fruit by her side; sometimes with an angel carrying a basket with three apples and three roses. The legend is that Theophilus, the judge's secretary, scoffingly said to her, as she was going to execution, 'Send me some fruit and roses, Dorothea, when you get to Paradise.' Immediately after her execution, while Theophilus was at dinner with a party of companions, a young angel brought to him a basket of apples and roses, saying, 'From Dorothea in Paradise', and vanished. Theophilus, of course, was a convert from that moment. The story forms the basis of Massinger's tragedy, *The Virgin Martyr* (1620).

**Dorset.** Once the seat of a British tribe, calling themselves *Dwr-trigs* (dwellers by the water). The Romans colonised the settlement, and Latinised *Dwr-trigs* into *Duro-trigës*. Lastly came the Saxons, and translated the original words into their own tongue, *dor-saetta*, *saetta* being a seat or settlement.

**Dositheans.** A religious sect which sprang up in the 1st century; so called because they believed that their founder Dositheus, a Samaritan magician contemporary with the apostles, had a divine mission.

**Doss.** Slang for a sleep; also for a bed or a place where one sleeps – a *doss-house*, *dossing-ken*. The word dates from the 18th century, and is probably connected with the old *dorse*, a back (Lat. *dorsum*, Fr. *dos*). Hence also *dosser*, one who sleeps in a common lodging-house.

**Dotheboys Hall.** A school in Dickens's *Nicholas Nickleby* where boys were taken in and done for by Mr Wackford Squeers, a puffing, ignorant, overbearing brute, who starved them and taught them nothing.

It is said that Squeers was a caricature of a Mr Shaw, a Yorkshire schoolmaster; but Mr Shaw was a kind-hearted man, whose boys were well fed, happy, and not ill taught. Like Squeers he had only one eye, and one daughter. The ruthless exposure of this kind of 'school' led to the closing or reformation of many of them.

**Dot.** *See* I.

***Dot and go one.*** An infant just beginning to toddle; one who limps in walking; a person who has one leg longer than the other.

***To dot one's i's.*** *See* I.

**Dotterel.** A doting old fool; an old man easily cajoled. So called from the bird, a species of plover, which is easily approached and caught.

***To dor the dotterel.*** Dor is an obsolete word meaning to trick or cheat. Whence the phrase means to cheat the simpleton.

**Douai Bible.** *See* Bible, the English. The English college at Douai was founded by William Allen (afterwards cardinal) in 1568. The Douai Bible translates such words as *repentance* by the word *penance*, etc., and the whole contains notes by Roman Catholic divines.

**Double** (Lat. *duplus*, twofold). One's double is one's *alter ego* (*q.v.*). The word is applied to such pairs as the Corsican brothers, the Dromio brothers, and the brothers Antipholus.

***A double first.*** In the first class both of the classical and mathematical final examinations, Oxford; or of the classical and mathematical triposes, Cambridge.

***At the double.*** Running; in double quick time. *See* Double Time.

***Double dealing.*** Professing one thing and doing another inconsistent with that promise.

[She] was quite above all double-dealing. She had no mental reservation. Maria Edgeworth

***Double Dutch.*** Gibberish, jargon, of a foreign tongue not understood by the hearer. Dutch is a synonym for foreign; and double implies something excessive, in a twofold degree.

***Double-edged.*** Able to cut either way; used metaphorically of an argument which makes both for and against the person employing it, or which has a double meaning.

'Your Delphic sword,' the panther then replied,
'Is double-edged and cuts on either side.'
Dryden, *Hind and Panther*, pt iii, 191

***Double entendre*** (Eng.-Fr. for *Un mot à double entente*, or à *deux ententes*). Words which secretly express a rude or coarse covert meaning, generally of an indelicate character. *Entendre* is the infinitive mood of the French verb, and is never used as a noun.

***Double or quits.*** The winner stakes his stake, and the loser promises to pay twice the stake if he loses again; but if he wins the second throw his loss is cancelled and no money passes.

***Double time.*** A military phrase, applied to orderly running on the march, etc. It is a quick march, the rate of progress (officially 165 steps of 33 in., i.e. 453¾ ft., to the minute) being *double* that of the ordinary walking pace. *See* To double up *below*.

***Double-tongued.*** Making contrary declarations on the same subject at different times; deceitful; insincere.

> Be grave, not double-tongued. 1 Tim. 3:8

***Double X.*** *See* X.

***Double-headed Eagle.*** *See* Eagle.

***To double a cape.*** Said of a ship that sails round or to the other side of a cape; its course is, as it were, bent back on itself.

> What capes he doubled, and what continent,
> The gulfs and straits that strangely he had past.
> Dryden, *Ideas*, stanza 1

Meredith uses the expression metaphorically in connexion with the relationships of man and woman:

> She [Diana] is fresher when speaking of the war of the sexes. For one sentence out of many, though we find it to be but the clever literary clothing of a common accusation: – '*Men may have rounded Seraglio Point: they have not yet doubled Cape Turk.*'
> Meredith, *Diana of the Crossways*, ch. i

***To double a part.*** Said of an actor playing two parts in the same piece.

***To double and twist.*** To prevaricate, act evasively, try by tortuous means to extricate oneself from a dilemma or difficulty. The phrase is taken from coursing – a hare 'doubles and twists' in the endeavour to escape from the hounds. In weaving, 'to double and twist' is to add one thread to another and twist them together.

***To double up.*** To fold together. 'To double up the fist' is to fold the fingers together so as to make the hand into a fist. 'To double a person up' is to strike him in the wind, so as to make him double up with pain.

In military phraseology, 'Double up there!' is an order to hurry, to 'get a move on', run. *See* Double Time *above*.

***To work double tides.*** To work extra hard, with all one's might.

**Doubting Castle.** The castle of the giant Despair, in which Christian and Hopeful were incarcerated, but from which they escaped by means of the key called 'Promise'. (Bunyan, *Pilgrim's Progress*.)

**Douceur** (Fr.). A gratuity for service rendered or promised; a tip.

**Douglas.** The Scottish family name is from the river Douglas in Lanarkshire, which is the Celtic *dhu glaise*, black stream, a name in use also in Ireland, the Isle of Man, etc., and in Lancashire corrupted to *Diggles*. Legend explains it by inventing an unknown knight who came to the assistance of some Scottish king. After the battle the king asked who was the 'Du-glass' chieftain, his deliverer, and received for answer *Sholto Duglass*, which is said to be good Gaelic for 'Behold the dark-grey man you enquired for.'

> 'I will not yield him an inch of way, had he in his body the soul of every Douglas that has lived since the time of the Dark Gray Man.'
> Scott, *The Abbot*, ch. xxviii

***Black Douglas.*** Sir William Douglas, lord of Nithsdale, who died about 1392. It was of this Douglas that Scott said:

> The name of this indefatigable chief has become so formidable, that women used, in the northern counties, to still their froward children by threatening them with the Black Douglas.
> *History of Scotland*, ch. xi

The 'Black Douglas' introduced by Scott in *Castle Dangerous* is James, eighth Lord Douglas, who lived about 100 years earlier, and twice took Douglas Castle from the English by stratagem.

***The Douglas Tragedy.*** A ballad in Scott's *Border Minstrelsy*, telling how Lord William steals away Lady Margaret Douglas and is pursued by her father and two brothers. A fight ensues; the father and his two sons are sore wounded; Lord William, also wounded, creeps to his mother's house and there dies; and the lady dies next morning.

**Douse the Glim.** Put out the candle; also, by extension, to blind a man. Among sailors 'to douse a sail' means to lower it in haste.

> 'And so you would turn honest Captain Goffe agrazing, would ye,' said an old weather-beaten pirate who had but one eye; 'what though he … made my eye dowse the glim … he is an honest man.' Scott, *The Pirate*, ch. xxxiii

***A douse in the chops.*** A heavy blow in the face.

> My fellow-sarvant Umphry Klinker bid him be sivil, and he gave the young man a douse in the chops; but l'fachins, Mr Klinker wa'n't long in his debt – with a good oaken sapling he dusted his doublet.
>
> Smollett, *Humphry Clinker*, Lett. xxxiv

**Dout.** A contraction of *do-out*, as don is of *do-on*, doff of *do-off*, and dup of *do-up*. In some southern counties they still say *dout the candle* and *dout the fire*, and call extinguishers *douters*.

> The dram of eale
> Doth all the noble substance dout.
>
> Shakespeare, *Hamlet*, 1, 4

**Dove.** The name means 'the diver-bird'; perhaps from its habit of ducking the head. So also Lat. *columba* is the Gr. *kolumbis* (a diver).

In Christian art the dove symbolises the Holy Ghost, and the seven rays proceeding from it the seven gifts of the Holy Ghost. It also symbolises the soul, and as such is sometimes represented coming out of the mouth of saints at death.

A dove bearing a ring is an attribute of St Agnes; St David is shown with a dove on his shoulder; St Dunstan and St Gregory the Great with one at the ear; St Enurchus with one on his head; and St Remigius with the dove bringing him holy chrism.

The clergy of the Church of England are allegorised as doves in Dryden's *Hind and Panther*, part iii, 947, 998–1002.

> A sort of doves were housed too near the hall ...
> [i.e. the private chapel at Whitehall]
> Our pampered pigeons, with malignant eyes.
> Beheld these inmates [the Roman Catholic clergy]
> Tho' hard their fare, at evening and at morn,
> A cruse of water and an ear of corn,
> Yet still they grudged that modicum.

*Doves' dung.* In 2 Kings 6:25, we are told that during the siege of Samaria 'there was a great famine ... and ... an ass's head was sold for fourscore pieces of silver, and the fourth part of a cab of dove's dung for five pieces of silver'. 'Ass's head' and 'dove's dung' are both undoubtedly incorrect, the true rendering probably being 'a homer of lentils' and 'pods of the carob (or locust) tree', the Hebrew for which expressions could easily be misread for the Hebrew for the others. Locust pods are still commonly sold in the East for food, and it is thought that they are the 'husks' referred to in the parable of the Prodigal Son.

**Dover.** In the professional slang of English cooks a *resurrection pie* or any *réchauffé* is called a *dover* (do over again).

***A jack of Dover.*** *See* Jack.

***When Dover and Calais meet.*** Never.

***Merry Dun of Dover.*** *See* Merry.

**Dovers.** The Stock Exchange term for South-Eastern railway shares. The line runs to Dover. *Cp.* Claras.

**Dovercourt.** A confused gabble; a babel. According to legend, Dovercourt church, in Essex, once possessed a cross that spoke; and Foxe says the crowd to the church was so great 'that no man could shut the door'. But Dovercourt also seems to have been noted for its scolds and chattering women.

> And now the rood of Dovercot did speak,
> Confirming his opinions to be true.
>
> *Grim, the Collier of Croydon* (1600)

> When bells ring round and in their order be,
> They do denote how neighbours should agree;
> But when they clam, the harsh sound spoils the sport
> And 'tis like women keeping Dovercourt.
>
> Lines in the Belfry of St Peter's, Shaftesbury

**Dovetail.** Metaphorically, to fit on or fit in nicely; to correspond. In carpentry it means the fitting one board into another by a tenon in the shape of a dove's tail, or wedge reversed.

**Dowlas, Mr.** A generic name for a linendraper, who sells dowlas, a coarse linen cloth, so called from Daoulas, in Brittany, where it was manufactured.

> *Mrs Quickly*. I bought you a dozen of shirts to your back.
>
> *Falstaff*. Dowlas, filthy dowlas: I have given them away to bakers' wives, and they have made bolters of them.
>
> *Quick*. Now, as I am true woman, holland of eight shillings an ell.
>
> Shakespeare, *1 Henry IV*, 3, 3

**Down.** ***Don't hit a man when he's down.*** When your opponent is defeated don't give him a further drubbing. A common phrase, used both directly and metaphorically.

***Down and out.*** Said of one who has not only come right down in the world but has, apparently, not the slightest chance of getting up again.

***Down at heel.*** *See* Heel.

***Down in the dumps.*** *See* Dumps.

***Down in the mouth.*** Out of spirits; disheartened. When persons are very sad and low spirited, the corners of the mouth are drawn down. *Down in the jib* is a nautical phrase of the same meaning.

***Down on his luck.*** In ill luck; short of cash and credit.

> 'I guess, stranger, you'll find me an ex-president down on his luck.'
>
> A. Egmont Hake, *Paris Originals* (Professors of Languages)

***Down on the nail.*** *See* Nail.

***Down with (so-and-so)!*** Away with! A cry of rage and exasperation, like the Fr. *à bos*. It is used humorously by topers who are emptying their glasses as quickly as they can be filled: 'Down with the drink!'

***He is very much run down.*** Very out of sorts; in need of a thorough rest and overhauling, like a clock that has *run down* and does not go properly when it is wound up.

***I am going down town.*** To the business part of the town. We say 'I am going up to town' when we mean out of the country into the chief city.

***I was down on him in a minute.*** I pounced on him directly; I detected his trick immediately. The allusion is to birds of prey.

***That suits me down to the ground.*** *See* Ground.

***The down train.*** The train away from London or the local centre, in contradistinction to *the up train*, which goes to it. We also have *the down platform*, etc.

***To down tools.*** To lay one's tools aside and come out on strike. The verb is popularly used of others beside manual workers; striking waiters, for instance, are said to have 'downed dishes', and waitresses would, of course, 'down caps and aprons'.

***To have a down on.*** To have a grudge or spite against.

***To run a man down.*** *See* Run.

***Ups and downs.*** The twists and turns of fortune; one's successes and reverses.

> Fraudulent transactions have their downs as well as their ups.
>
> Dickens, *Martin Chuzzlewit*, ch. xvi

**Downfall.** A heavy shower of rain; a loss of social position, collapse.

**Down-hearted.** Without spirit; the heart prostrated.

***Are we down-hearted?*** A popular cry, especially during the Great War, but of some years' earlier origin. The invariable answer was a vociferous shout of 'NO!'

**Downing College.** A college at Cambridge, founded by the will of Sir George Downing (a grandson of the Sir George of Downing Street, *q.v.*), who died in 1749. The college was chartered in 1800, after much litigation. He also founded the chair occupied by the *Downing Professor*, the Professor of the Laws of England at Cambridge.

**Downing Street.** A name often given to the heads of the British Government collectively, from No. 10, Downing Street (Westminster), the official town residence of the Prime Minister, where the meetings of the Cabinet are usually held. The street was named in honour of Sir George Downing (d.1684), a noted Parliamentarian and ambassador, who served under both Cromwell and Charles II.

**Downright.** Thoroughly, from top to bottom, throughout; 'downright honest', 'downright mad'; outspoken; utter, as a 'downright shame'.

***Downright Dunstable.*** *See* Dunstable.

**Downtrodden.** Despised, as one trodden under foot.

> I will lift
> The down-trod Mortimer as high i' the air
> As this ungrateful king.
>
> Shakespeare, *1 Henry IV*, 1, 3

**Downy.** ***Gone to the downy,*** gone to bed; bed being stuffed with down.

***A downy cove.*** A knowing fellow, *up to*, or, as formerly, *down to* every dodge.

Downy here means wide-awake, knowing; and in Vaux's *Flash Dictionary* (1812) *down* is given as a synonym for 'awake':

> When the party you are about to rob sees or suspects your intention, it is then said that *the cove is down*.

**Dowsabell.** A common name for a sweetheart, especially an unsophisticated country girl, in poems of Elizabethan times. It is the Fr. *douce et belle*, sweet and beautiful.

> It were not good … to cast away as pretty a dowsabell as any could chance to see in a summer's day. *The London Prodigal*, IV, i (1605)

Drayton has a poem, *The Ballad of Dowsabell.*

**Dowse** (*see also* Douse). To search for water, etc., with a divining-rod (*q.v.*), which is also called a *dowsing-rod*, and the practitioners of the art *dowsers*. The origin of the term is disputed, but as the art was introduced from Germany (in the 16th cent.) it may be connected with Ger. *deuten*, to declare or interpret.

**Doxy.** A tramp's cant word for his unmarried 'wife'; hence, a mistress or paramour. In the West of England babies are called *doxies*.

**Doyley.** *See* Doily.

**Dozen.** Twelve: the word is all that is left (in English) of the Latin *duodecim*, twelve, the *-en* representing the Latin suffix -ena. A *long dozen* is thirteen. *See* Baker's Dozen.

***To talk nineteen to the dozen.*** To talk at a tremendous rate, or with excessive vehemence.

**D.P.** or **Dom. Proc.** The House of Lords (Lat. *Domus Procerum*).

**Drachenfels** (Ger. Dragon-rock). So called from the legend that it was the home of the dragon slain by Siegfried, the hero of the Nibelungenlied.

> The castled crag of Drachenfels
> Frowns o'er the wide and winding Rhine,
> Whose breast of waters broadly swells
> Between the banks which bear the vine.
>
> Byron, *Childe Harold*, iii, 55

**Draconian Code.** One very severe. Draco was an Athenian law-maker of the 7th cent. BC, and the first to produce a written code of laws for Athens. As nearly every violation of his laws was a capital offence, Demades the orator said 'that Draco's code was written in blood'.

**Draft.** ***A draft on Aldgate pump.*** *See* Aldgate.

**Drag in, To.** To introduce a subject or remark inappropriately or abruptly. *Cp.* A Propos de Bottes; Neck and Crop.

***But why drag in Velasquez?*** It is said that the artist, Whistler, in the middle of a flood of compliments was told that he was the greatest painter since Velasquez, and that his reply was the gentle expostulation 'But why drag in Velasquez?' thereby suggesting that the remark would have been truer without the qualification. It is still sometimes quoted – either seriously or with the object of showing up someone's lack of modesty.

**Draggle-tail.** *See* Daggle-tail.

**Dragoman** (pl. *Dragomans*). A cicerone; a guide or interpreter to foreigners. (Arab. *targuman*, an interpreter; whence *targum*.)

> My dragoman had me completely in his power, and I resolved to become independent of all interpreters.
>
> Baker, *Albert Nyanza*, ch. i, p. 3

**Dragon.** The Greek word *drakon* comes from a verb meaning 'to see', to 'look at', and more remotely 'to watch' and 'to flash'.

A dragon is a fabulous winged crocodile, usually represented as of large size, with a serpent's tail; whence the words serpent and dragon are sometimes interchangeable. The word was used in the Middle Ages as the symbol of sin in general and paganism in particular, the metaphor being derived from Rev. 12:9, where Satan is termed 'the great dragon' and Ps. 91:13, where it is said that the saints 'shall trample the dragon under their feet'. Hence, in Christian art the dragon symbolises Satan or sin, as when represented at the feet of Christ and the Virgin Mary; and St John the Evangelist is sometimes represented holding a chalice, from which a dragon is issuing.

Among the many saints who are usually pictured with dragons may be mentioned St Michael, St George, St Margaret, Pope Sylvester, St Samson (Archbishop of Dol), St Donatus, St Clement of Metz; St Romain of Rouen, who destroyed the huge dragon, La Gargouille, which ravaged the Seine; St Philip the Apostle, who killed another at Hierapolis, in Phrygia; St Martha, who slew the terrible dragon, Tarasque, at Aix-la-Chapelle; St Florent, who killed a dragon which haunted the Loire; St Cado, St Maudet, and St Pol, who did similar feats in Brittany; and St Keyne of Cornwall.

In *classical legend* the idea of *watching* is retained in the story of the dragon who guards the golden apples in the garden of the Hesperides; and a duenna is poetically called a dragon:

> In England the garden of beauty is kept
> By a dragon of prudery placed within call.
>
> T. Moore, *Irish Melodies*, No. 2

Among the ancient Britons and Welsh the dragon was the national symbol on the war standard; hence the term, Pendragon (*q.v.*) for the *dux bellorum*, or leader in war (*pen* = head or chief).

***A flying dragon.*** A meteor.

***The Chinese dragon.*** In China, a five-clawed dragon is introduced into pictures and embroidered on state dresses as an amulet.

***The Dragon of Wantley.*** *See* Wantley.

***To sow dragons' teeth.*** To foment contentions; to stir up strife or war; especially to do something that is intended to put an end to strife but which brings it about later. The Philistines 'sowed dragons' teeth' when they took Samson, bound him, and put out his eyes; the ancient Britons did the same when they massacred the Danes on St Bryce's Day, as also did the modern Germans when they robbed France of Alsace Lorraine.

The reference is to the classical story of Cadmus, who slew the dragon that guarded the well of Ares and sowed some of its teeth, from which sprang up the men called Spartans, who all killed each other except five, who became the ancestors of the Thebans. Those teeth which Cadmus did not sow came to the possession of Aeetes, King of Colchis; and one of the tasks he enjoined on Jason was to sow them and slay the armed warriors that rose therefrom.

**Dragon's Hill.** A site in Berkshire where one

legend has it that St George killed the dragon. A bare place is shown on the hill, where nothing will grow, and there the blood of the dragon ran out.

In Saxon annals we are told that Cerdic, founder of the West Saxon kingdom, slew there Naud (or Natanleod, the people's refuge), the pendragon, with 5,000 men.

**Dragonades.** A series of religious persecutions by Louis XIV, prior to the revocation of the Edict of Nantes, which drove many thousand Protestants out of France. Their object was to root out 'heresy'; if the heretics would not recant they were left to the tender mercies of *dragoons* (hence the name), who were billeted on them and were given a free hand to treat them in any way they liked.

**Dragoons.** So called because they used to be armed with *dragons*, i.e. short muskets, which spouted out fire like the fabulous beast so named. The earliest of these muskets had the head of a dragon wrought on the muzzle.

**Drake.** The male of the duck. The word is of uncertain origin; it does not appear in Anglo-Saxon, and is first found in Middle English. It may be connected with Old High German *enterrich*, from *anut*, duck; the second element perhaps representing Old Norse *reki*, a king, in which case 'drake' would mean the 'duck-king'.

**Drama.** ***Father of Danish drama.*** Ludwig von Holberg (1684–1754).

***Father of French drama.*** Etienne Jodelle (1532–73).

***Father of Greek drama.*** Thespis (6th cent. BC).

***Father of Modern German drama.*** Andreas Griphius (1616–64).

***Father of Spanish drama.*** Lopë de Vega (1562–1635).

**Dramatic Unities.** The three dramatic unities, viz. the rules governing the so called 'classical' dramas, are founded on Renaissance misconceptions of passages in Aristotle's *Poetics*, and are hence sometimes – though very incorrectly – styled the *Aristotelean Unities*. They are, that in dramas there should be (1) Unity of Action, (2) Unity of Time, and (3) Unity of Place. Aristotle lays stress on (1), meaning that an organic unity, or a logical connection between the successive incidents, is necessary; but (2) was deduced by Castelvetro (1505–71), the 16th century Italian scholar and critic, from the passage in the *Poetics* where Aristotle, in comparing Epic Poetry and Tragedy, says that the former has no limits in time but the latter

> endeavours, as far as possible, to confine itself to a single revolution of the sun, or but slightly to exceed this limit

a passage which was merely an incidental reference to a contemporary custom and was never intended as the enunciation of an inviolable law of the drama. Having thus arrived at the Unity of Time, (3) the Unity of Place followed almost perforce, though there is not even a hint of it in Aristotle.

The theory of the Three Unities was formulated in Italy nearly a century before it was taken up in France (Cintio, Robortelli, Maggi, and Scaliger being the principal exponents), where it became, after much argument, the corner-stone of the literary drama. The principle had little success in England – despite the later championship of Dryden (see his *Essay on Dramatic Poesy*), Addison (as exemplified in his *Cato*), and others – and its first modern offspring was *La Sophoniste* (1629) by Mairet, though it was not till Corneille's triumph with *Le Cid* (1636) that the convention of the Three Unities can be said to have been finally adopted. It is almost unnecessary to add that Shakespeare, and every great dramatist not bound by a self-imposed tradition, was with Aristotle in holding that so long as the Unity of Action is observed the others do not matter. Ben Jonson's *The Alchemist* (1610) is, perhaps, the best example of the small class of English plays in which the Unities of Place and Time have been purposely adhered to.

**Dramatis Personae.** The characters of a drama, novel, or (by extension), of actual transaction.

**Drapier's Letters.** A series of letters written by Dean Swift to the people of Ireland and published in 1724, advising them not to take the copper money coined by William Wood. The patent had been granted to him by George I through the influence of the Duchess of Kendal, the king's mistress, and Wood and the Duchess were to share the profits (40 per cent.). These letters, which were signed 'M. B. Drapier', crushed the infamous job and the patent was cancelled.

**Drat 'em.** A variant of *Od rot 'em!* 'Od' (*q.v.*) being a minced form of 'God', and the vowel showing the same modification as in 'Gad!' or 'Gadzooks!'

**Draupnir.** Odin's magic ring, from which every ninth night dropped eight rings equal in size and beauty to itself. It was fashioned by the dwarfs.

**Draw. *A drawn game, battle, etc.*** One in which the result is in doubt, neither side having achieved success: perhaps so called from a battle in which the troops on both sides are *drawn off*, neither side claiming the victory.

***A good draw.*** A first-rate attraction – 'Performing elephants are always "a good draw" at circuses.' The noun also may mean a drawn game, or the result of drawing lots, etc.

***Draw it mild!*** Don't exaggerate! don't make your remarks (or actions, as the case may be) stronger than necessary. The allusion is to beer; just as we talk of remarks being highly flavoured, of strong language, of spicy words.

***Hanged, drawn, and quartered.*** Strictly speaking, the phrase should read *Drawn, hanged, and quartered*; for the allusion is to the sentence formerly passed on those convicted of high treason, which was that they should be *drawn* to the place of execution on a hurdle or at a horse's tail instead of being carried or allowed to walk, then hanged, and then quartered.

Later, drawing, or disembowelling, the criminal was added to the punishment after the hanging and before the quartering, and it was sometimes supposed that the 'drawn' in the phrase referred to this process instead of to the earlier one. Thus the sentence on Sir William Wallace was that he should be drawn (*detrahatur*) from the Palace of Westminster to the Tower, then hanged (*suspendatur*), then disembowelled or drawn (*devaletur*), then beheaded and quartered (*decolletur et decapitetur*).

> Lord Ellenborough used to say to those condemned, 'You are drawn on hurdles to the place of execution, where you are to be hanged, but *not* till you are dead; for, while still living, your body is to be taken down, your bowels torn out and burnt before your face; your head is then cut off, and your body divided into four quarters.' *Gentleman's Magazine*, 1803

***To draw a bead on somebody.*** To take aim at him with a rifle or revolver. The 'bead' referred to is part of the sighting apparatus.

***To draw a badger.*** *See* Badger.

***To draw a furrow.*** To plough or draw a plough through a field so as to make a furrow.

***To draw a person out.*** To entice a person to speak on any subject, to obtain information, or with the intention of ridiculing him.

***To draw amiss.*** To take the wrong direction. A hunting term, *to draw* meaning to follow scent.

***To draw blank.*** To meet with failure in one's pursuit. The allusion is to sportsmen 'drawing' a covert and finding no game. *To draw a blank* refers to having no luck in a lottery, sweepstake, etc.

***To draw the cork.*** To give one a bloody nose. *Cp.* Claret.

***To draw the King's (or Queen's) picture.*** To coin false money.

***To draw the nail.*** To release oneself from a vow. It was a custom in Cheshire when people agreed to do something, or to abstain from something, say drinking beer, they registered the vow by driving a nail into a tree, swearing to keep their vow as long as it remained there. If they wished to retract, the nail was withdrawn and the vow thereby was cancelled.

***To draw rein.*** To pull up short, to check one's course.

***To draw the line.*** To set a definite limit beyond which one refuses to go; to impose a restriction on one's behaviour from fear of going too far. 'He was utterly unprincipled, but he drew the line at blackmail,' i.e. he would stop short at blackmail, he would not blackmail anyone.

***To draw a bow at a venture; to draw the long bow.*** *See* Bow.

**Drawback.** Something to set against the profits or advantages of a concern. In commerce, it is duty charged on goods paid back again when the goods are exported.

> It is only on goods into which dutiable commodities have entered in large proportion and obvious ways that drawbacks are allowed.
> H. George, *Protection or Free Trade?* ch. ix

**Drawcansir.** A burlesque tyrant in Buckingham's *Rehearsal* (1671); hence, a blustering braggart. The character was a caricature of Dryden's Almanzor (*Conquest of Granada*). Drawcansir's opening speech (he has only three) is:

> He that dares drink, and for that drink dares die,
> And, knowing this, dares yet drink on, am I.
> *Rehearsal*, iv, 1

which parodies Almanzor's:

> He who dares love, and for that love must die,
> And, knowing this, dares yet love on, am I.
> *II Conquest of Granada*, IV, iii

*Cp.* Bayes, Bobadil.

**Drawing-room.** A room to which ladies *withdraw* or retire after dinner. Also a levee where ladies are presented to the sovereign.

**Drawlatch.** An old name for a robber, a housebreaker; i.e. one who entered by drawing up the latch with the string provided for the purpose and stole all he could carry away with him.

**Dreadnought.** The name given to a large battleship (17,900 tons) in the British Navy, built in 1906, and hence to the class of which it was the earliest. The name was an old one in the navy, and had been in use in Queen Elizabeth's time.

The Seamen's Hospital at Greenwich (founded in 1821) is often spoken of as the Dreadnought Hospital, because it was originally housed in the Thames on an old man-of-war of this name. It was drawn ashore in 1870.

**Dreamer.** *The Immortal Dreamer.* John Bunyan (1628–88).

**Dreams, The Gates of.** There are two, viz. that of ivory and that of horn. Dreams which delude pass through the Ivory Gate, those which come true pass through the Gate of Horn.

> That children dream not the first half-year; that men dream not in some countries, with many more, are unto me sick men's dreams; dreams out of the ivory gate, and visions before midnight.
> Sir Thos Browne, *On Dreams*

This fancy depends upon two puns: ivory in Greek is *elephas*, and the verb *elephairo* means 'to cheat with empty hopes'; the Greek for horn is *keras*, and the verb *karanoo* means 'to accomplish'.

Anchises dismisses Aeneas through the ivory gate, on quitting the infernal regions, to indicate the unreality of his vision.

> Sunt geminae somni portae: quarum altera fertur
> Cornea, qua veris facilis datur exitus umbris;
> Altera candenti perfecta nitens elephanto;
> Sed falsa ad coelium mittunt insomnia manes.
> Virgil, *Aeneid*, vi, 894–97

**Dreng.** An ancient Northumbrian term (from Danish) for a free tenant who held his land by a tenure dating from before the Conquest. It occurs in Domesday Book.

**Dress.** ***A dressing down.*** Usually, a thorough good talking to, a lashing with the tongue; but used also of a physical drubbing; a 'hiding'. To dress a horse down is to curry it, rub it, and comb it. To dress ore is to break it up, crush it, and powder it in the stamping mill.

***To dress one's jacket for him.*** The same as 'To dust, etc'. *See* Dust.

**Dreyfusard, Dreyfusite.** An advocate of the innocence of Capt. Alfred Dreyfus, an officer of the French artillery of Jewish descent, who was convicted in 1894 on a charge of having betrayed military secrets, degraded and sent to Devil's Island. In 1899 the first trial was annulled. He was brought back to France, retried, and again condemned, but shortly afterwards pardoned, though it was not until 1914 that he was finally and completely rehabilitated.

**Drink.** ***Drink-money.*** A 'tip'; a small gratuity to be spent on drinking the health of the giver; a *pourboire* (Fr., for drink).

***Drinking horns.*** In the East drinking cups made of rhinoceros horn used to be specially valued, as they were supposed to sweat if they contained any poison. In the North those made of narwhal tusk were considered the best, for they were held to counteract any poisonous effects.

***Drinking of healths.*** *See* Gabbara; Health.

***It is meat and drink to me.*** It is something that is almost essential to my well-being or happiness; something very much to be desired.

> It is meat and drink to me to see a clown.
> Shakespeare, *As You Like It*, 5, 1

***One must drink as one brews.*** One must take the consequences of his actions; 'as one makes his bed so must he lie in it'.

> I am grieved it should be said he is my brother, and take these courses: well, as he brews, so shall he drink.
> Jonson, *Every Man in his Humour*, ii, 1

***The big drink.*** An American expression for any large stretch of water, such as the Atlantic (*cp.* Herring-pond) or the Mississippi.

***Those who drink beer will think beer.*** A saying attributed to Warburton, Bishop of Gloucester (1698–1779). Some non-teetotaller parodied it with 'And those that drink water will think water' – suggesting that whatever might be said of the thoughts of a beer-drinker those of a teetotaller had very little strength in them.

***To drink at Freeman's Quay.*** To get one's drink at someone else's expense. It is said that at one time all porters and carmen calling at Freeman's Quay, near London Bridge, had a pot of beer given them gratis, but the explanation is scarcely necessary and probably untrue.

***To drink deep.*** To drink heavily, to excess, or habitually. Shakespeare uses the expression metaphorically:

> *Cant.* If it pass against us,
> We lose the better half of our possession; ...
> And to the coffers of the king beside,
> A thousand pounds by the year. Thus runs the bill.
> *Ely.* This would drink deep
> *Cant.* 'Twould drink the cup and all.
> *Henry V*, 1, 1

***To drink like a fish.*** To drink abundantly or excessively. Many fish swim with their mouths open, thus appearing to be continually drinking. The expression is found in Beaumont and Fletcher.

***To drink the cup of sorrow, etc.*** *See* Cup.

***To drink the waters.*** To take medicinal waters, especially at a spa.

> Annandale, when he learned that his two accomplices had turned approvers, retired to Bath, and pretended to drink the waters.
>
> Macaulay, *History of England*, ch. xvi

**Drive.** ***He is driving pigs,*** or ***driving pigs to market.*** Said of one who is snoring, because the grunt of a pig resembles the snore of a sleeper.

***To drive a good bargain.*** To exact more than is quite equable.

> Heaven would no bargain for its blessings drive.
>
> Dryden, *Astraea Redux*, i, 137

***To drive a quill.*** *See* Quilldrivers.

***To drive a roaring trade.*** To do a brisk business. The allusion is to a coachman who drives so fast that his horses pant and *roar* for breath.

***To drive the swine through the hanks of yarn.*** To spoil what has been painfully done; to squander thrift. In Scotland, the yarn wrought in the winter (called *the gude-wife's thrift*) is laid down by the burn-side to bleach, and is thus exposed to damage from passing animals, such as a herd of pigs, which may stray over them and do a vast amount of harm.

***To let drive.*** To attack; to fall foul of. A Gallicism. '*Se laisser aller à* ...' – i.e. to go without restraint.

> Thou knowest my old ward; here I [Falstaff] lay, and thus I bore my point. Four rogues in buckram let drive at me.
>
> Shakespeare, *1 Henry IV*, 2, 4

***What are you driving at?*** What do you want to prove? What do you want me to infer?

***Who drives fat oxen should himself be fat.*** Henry Brooke, in his *Gustavus Vasa* (1739), says: 'Who rules o'er free-men should himself be free'; Dr Johnson parodied the line – and the sentiment, with which he did not agree – with the above (Boswell, 1784).

**Driver of Europe** (*Le Cocher de l'Europe*). So the Empress of Russia used to call the Duc de Choiseul (1719–85), minister of Louis XV, because he had spies all over Europe, and thus ruled its political cabals.

**Droit d'Aubaine.** *Aubain* (Fr.) means 'alien', and *droit d'aubaine* the 'right over an alien's property'. In France the king was entitled, at the death of foreign residents (except Swiss and Scots), to all their movable estates, a right that was not finally abolished till 1819.

> Had I died that night of an indigestion, the whole world could not have suspended the effects of the *droits d'aubaine*: my shirts and black pair of breeches, portmanteau and all, must have gone to the king of France.
>
> Sterne, *Sentimental Journey* (Intro.)

**Dromio.** *The brothers Dromio.* Two brothers exactly alike, who served two brothers exactly alike, and the mistakes of masters and men form the fun of Shakespeare's *Comedy of Errors*, based on the *Menaechmi* of Plautus.

**Drone.** The male of the bee, which does no work but lives on the labours of the worker-bees; hence, a sluggard, an idle person who lives on the work or means of another.

The three lower pipes of a bagpipe are called the drones, because they produce an unchanging, monotonous bass humming like that of a bee.

**Drop.** ***A drop in one's eye.*** Not exactly intoxicated, but having had quite enough.

> We are na foul we're nae that fou,
> But just a drappie in our e'e!
>
> Burns, *Willie Brew'd a Peck o' Maut*

***A drop in the ocean.*** An infinitesimal quantity; something that scarcely counts or matters in comparison with the whole.

***A drop of the cratur.*** *See* Creature.

***A dropping fire.*** An irregular fusillade from small-arms, machine guns, etc.

***Drop serene.*** An old name for amaurosis, a disease of the optic nerve, causing blindness, without affecting the appearance of the eye. It was at one time thought that it was caused by a transparent, watery humour distilling on the nerve. The name is the English form of the Lat. *gutta serena*.

> So thick a drop serene hath quenched these orbs.
>
> Milton, *Paradise Lost*, iii, 25

***Prince Rupert's drops.*** *See* Rupert.

***To drop across.*** To encounter accidentally or casually.

> I happened to drop across Jones when I was out: it was quite a surprise.

***To drop an acquaintance.*** To allow the acquaintanceship to lapse by quietly ceasing to visit him, reply to his letters, etc.; to give him up.

***To drop in.*** To make a casual call, not invited; to pay an informal visit.

***To drop off.*** 'Friends drop off', fall away gradually. 'To drop off to sleep', to fall asleep (especially in weariness or sickness).

***To take a drop.*** A euphemism for taking what the drinker chooses to call by that term. It may be anything from a sip to a Dutchman's draught (*q.v.*).

***To take a drop too much.*** To be intoxicated. If it is the 'last straw which breaks the camel's back', it is the drop too much which produces intoxication.

***To take one's drops.*** To drink spirits in private.

**Drown. *Drowning men catch at straws.*** Persons in desperate circumstances cling in hope to trifles wholly inadequate to rescue or even help them.

***To drown the miller.*** *See* Miller.

**Drows.** *See* Trows.

**Drug.** *See* Dope. *A drug in the market.* Something not called for, which no one will buy. Anything with which a trader is overstocked and cannot dispose of in the ordinary way of business is said to be 'a drug in the market', probably because its movements are so very sluggish, as are those of a person who has been drugged.

**Druid.** A member of the ancient Gaulish and British order of priests, teachers of religion, magicians, or sorcerers. The word is the Lat. *druidae* or *druides* (always plural), which was borrowed from the Old Irish *drui* and Gaelic *draoi.* The druidic cult presents many difficulties, and practically our only literary sources of knowledge of it are Pliny and the Commentaries of Caesar, whence we learn that the rites of the Druids were conducted in oak-groves and that they regarded the oak and the mistletoe with peculiar veneration; that they studied the stars and nature generally; that they believed in the transmigration of souls, and dealt in 'magic'. Their distinguishing badge was a serpent's egg (*see below*), to which very powerful properties were credited. The order seems to have been highly organised, and according to Strabo every chief had his druid, and every chief druid was allowed a guard of thirty men.

In Butler's *Hudibras* (III, i) there is an allusion to the

> Money by the Druids borrowed,
> In t'other world to be restoréd.

This refers to a legend recorded by one Patricius (? St Patrick) to the effect that the Druids were wont to borrow money to be repaid in the life to come. His words are, '*Druidae pecuniam mutuo accipiebant in posteriore vita reddituri.*'

On account of the inferred connection between the Druids and the bards the name is still kept in use by the Welsh Eisteddfodds, and it is with this sense that Collins employed it in his eulogy on Thomson:

> In yonder grave a Druid lies.

***United Ancient Order of Druids.*** A secret benefit society founded in London in 1781. It now has lodges, or 'groves' as they are called, in many parts of the world.

***The Druids' egg.*** This wonderful egg was hatched by the joint labour of several serpents, and was buoyed into the air by their hissing. The person who caught it had to ride off at full speed, to avoid being stung to death; but the possessor was sure to prevail in every contest, and to be courted by those in power. Pliny says he had seen one of them, and that it was about as large as a moderate-sized apple.

**Druj.** *See* Ahriman.

**Drum.** A popular name in the 18th century – and later – for a crowded evening party, so called from its noise with, perhaps, a side allusion to the tea-*kettle* and *kettle*-drums.

> This is a riotous assembly of fashionable people, of both sexes, at a private house, consisting of some hundreds, not unaptly stiled a drum, from the noise and emptiness of the entertainment.
> Smollett, *Advice, a Satire* (1746)

***John*** (or ***Jack***) ***Drum's entertainment.*** Turning an unwelcome guest out of doors.

> O! for the love of laughter, let him fetch his drum; he says he has a stratagem for 't. When your lordship sees the bottom of his success in 't, and to what metal this counterfeit lump of ore will be melted, if you give him not John Drum's entertainment, your inclining cannot be removed.
> Shakespeare, *All's Well*, 3, 6

Marston wrote a comedy with the title *Jack Drum's Entertainment* (1600), in which he is supposed to have satirised Ben Jonson.

***Drum ecclesiastic.*** The pulpit cushion, often vigorously thumped by what are termed 'rousing preachers'.

> When Gospel trumpeter, surrounded
> With long-eared rout, to battle sounded;
> And pulpit, drum ecclesiastic,
> Was beat with fist instead of a stick.
> Butler, *Hudibras*, I, i

***Drum-head court-martial.*** One held in haste; like a court-martial summoned on the field round the big drum to deal summarily with an offender.

**Drummers.** An Americanism for commercial travellers, their vocation being to collect customers as a recruiting officer 'drums up' recruits.

**Drummond Light.** The limelight. So named from the inventor, Captain Thomas Drummond, R.E., about 1825.

> Wisdom thinks, and makes a solar *Drummond Light* of a point of dull lime.
> Geikie, *Entering on Life*, p. 211

**Drumsticks.** Legs, especially very thin ones, or the leg of a cooked fowl.

**Drunk.** ***Drunk as a fiddler.*** The reference is to the fiddler at wakes, fairs, and on board ship, who used to be paid in liquor for playing to the dancers.

***Drunk as a lord.*** Before the great temperance movement set in, in the latter half of the 19th century, those who could afford to drink thought it quite *comme il faut* to drink two, three, or even more bottles of port wine for dinner, and few dinners ended without placing the guests under the table in a hopeless state of intoxication; hence the expression.

***Drunk as Chloe.*** Chloe was the cobbler's wife of Linden Grove, to whom Prior, the poet, was attached. She was notorious for her drinking habits.

***Drunk as David's sow.*** *See* Davy's Sow.

Chaucer has *drunk as a mouse*, Wilson (1553) *drunk as a rat*, Massinger *drunk as a beggar*; other common similes are *drunk as a tinker*, and *drunk as a boiled owl*, or 'as an owl'.

**Drunkard's cloak.** A tub with holes for the arms to pass through, used in the 17th century for drunkards and scolds by way of punishment.

**Drunken Parliament, The.** The Parliament assembled at Edinburgh, January 1st, 1661, of which Burnet says the members 'were almost perpetually drunk'.

**Drunkenness.** It was an ancient notion that men in their cups exhibited the vicious qualities of beasts. Nash, in his *Pierce Penilesse* (1592), describes seven degrees of drunkenness – (1) the *Apedrunk*, who leaps and sings; (2) the *Lion-drunk*, who is quarrelsome; (3) the *Swine-drunk*, who is sleepy and puking; (4) the *Sheep-drunk*, wise in his own conceit, but unable to speak; (5) the *Martin-drunk*, who drinks himself sober again – Martin was the name of a kind of monkey; (6) the *Goat-drunk*, who is lascivious; and (7) the *Fox-drunk*, who is crafty, like a Dutchman in his cups. Barclay in his *Ship of Fools* (1508) had a similar list:

> Some sowe dronke, swaloynge mete without measure
> Some mawdelayne dronke, mournynge lowdly and hye ...
> Some are Ape dronke full of laughter and of teyes.

*Cp.* Maudlin.

**Drury Lane.** This famous London street (and, consequently, the theatre) is named from Drury House, built in the time of Henry VIII by Sir William Drury. It stood on a site about in the middle of the present Aldwych. The theatre is the fourth of the name, the first having been opened in 1663.

**Druses.** A people and sect of Syria, living about the mountains of Lebanon and Anti-Libanus. Their faith is a mixture of the Pentateuch, the Gospel, the Koran, and Sufism. They offer up their devotions both in mosques and churches, worship the images of saints, and yet observe the fast of Ramadan. Their name is probably from that of their first apostle, Ismail Darazi, or Durzi (11th century AD).

**Dry.** Thirsty. Hence to drink is to 'wet your whistle' (i.e. throat); and malt liquor is called 'heavy wet'.

***Dry goods.*** Merchandise such as cloth, stuffs, silks, laces, and drapery in general, as opposed to groceries.

***Dry lodgings.*** An old expression for sleeping accommodation without board. Gentlemen who took their meals at clubs lived in 'dry lodgings'.

> Dry Lodginge of seven weeks, £0 4*s*. 1*d*.
>
> Scott, *Old Mortality* ( Intr. Rob. Patterson *deb*. to Margaret Chrystale)

***Dry nurse.*** When a superior officer does not know his duty, and is instructed in it by an inferior officer, he is said to be dry nursed. The inferior nurses the superior, as a dry nurse rears an infant.

***Dry shave.*** A shave without soaping the face; to scrape the face with a piece of iron hoop; to scratch the face; to box it and bruise it.

> The fellow will get a dry shave.
>
> Peter Pindar, *Great Cry and Little Wool*, Ep. 1
>
> I'll shave her, like a punished soldier, dry.
>
> Peter Pindar, *The Lousiad*, canto ii

***Dry wine.*** Opposed to sweet or fruity wine. In sweet wine some of the sugar is not yet decomposed; in *dry* wine all the sugar has been converted into alcohol. In the same way we speak of a *dry biscuit* as opposed to a sweet biscuit.

**Dryad.** In *classical mythology*, a tree-nymph (Gr. *drus*, a tree) who was supposed to live in the trees and die when the trees died. Eurydice, the wife of Orpheus the poet, was a dryad. Also called *hamadryads* (Gr. *hama*, with).

**Dryasdust.** The name given by Scott to the fictitious 'reverend Doctor', a learned pundit, to whom he addressed the prefaces, etc., of many of his novels: hence, a heavy, plodding author, very prosy, very dull, and very learned; an antiquary.

> The Prussian Dryasdust, otherwise an honest fellow, and not afraid of labour, excels all other

Dryasdusts yet known … He writes big books wanting in almost every quality; and does not even give an *Index* to them. Carlyle

**Dualism.** A system of philosophy which refers all things that exist to two ultimate principles, such as Descartes' Thought (*res cogitans*) and Extension (*res extensa*), or – in the theological sense – good and evil. In modern philosophy it is opposed to monism (*q.v.*), and insists that the creator and creation, mind and body, are distinct entities.

**Dub** (A.S. *dubbian*). To make a knight by giving him *a blow* (probably from O.Fr. *aduber*, or *adober*, to strike), the idea being that the box on the ear received by the neophyte in the ancient ceremony of knighting was the last he would receive, as he would henceforth be free to maintain his own honour. The present ceremony is to tap the shoulder with a sword.

**Dub Up.** Pay down the money; 'fork out!' Another form of *dup* (*q.v.*), do up.

**Dubglas.** According to the *Historia Brittonum* by Nennius (about AD 800), the second, third, fourth, and fifth of King Arthur's twelve great battles were fought on this river. Nennius places it in Linnuis (i.e. Lindsey, Lincolnshire); but, as is the case in all Arthurian topography, its probable site is matter for conjecture.

**Dublin.** ***True as the De'il is in Dublin city.*** *See* Devil.

**Ducat.** A piece of money first coined in 1140 by Roger II of Sicily as Duke of the duchy (*ducato*) of Apulia. This was a silver coin. In 1284 the Venetians struck a gold coin with the legend *Sit tibi, Christe, datus, quem tu regis, iste ducatus* (may this duchy which you rule be devoted to you, O Christ), and through this the name, already in use, gained wider currency. The ducat mentioned by Shakespeare in *The Merchant of Venice* is the Spanish coin, valued at about 6*s*. 8*d*.

**Duchess.** The wife or widow of a duke; in slang use contracted to *dutch*, and applied to the elderly wife of a coster, as in the song 'My old dutch'.

**Duck.** A contraction of duck's egg (*see below*) or, 0, in cricket.

***A lame duck.*** A stock-jobber or dealer who will not, or cannot, pay his losses. He has to 'waddle out of the alley like a lame duck'.

'I don't like the looks of Mr Sedley's affairs … He's been dabbling on his own account I fear … and unless I see Amelia's ten thousand down you don't marry her. I'll have no lame duck's daughter in my family.'

Thackeray, *Vanity Fair*, ch. xiii

***Duck Lane.*** Duck Lane (now Duke Street, leading from Little Britain to Long Lane, in the City of London), in Queen Anne's time was famous for its second-hand bookstalls; it was the Charing Cross Road of the period.

Scotists and Thomists now in peace remain
Amidst their kindred cobwebs in Duck Lane.

Pope, *Essay on Criticism*

***Duck's egg.*** In cricket a score of 0 – i.e. no score at all; the cipher on the sheet resembling an egg. *To break one's duck's egg*, or *one's duck*, is, of course, to make one run or more.

***Ducks and Drakes.*** The ricocheting or rebounding of a stone thrown from the hand to skim along the surface of a pond or river. *To play ducks and drakes with one's money* is to throw it away carelessly and just on amusement, or for the sake of watching it go and making a splash.

What figured slates are best to make
On watery surface duck and drake.

Butler, *Hudibras*, ii, 3

Mr Locke Harper found out, a month after his marriage, that somebody had made ducks and drakes of his wife's money.

Dinah M. Craik, *Agatha's Husband*, ch. xxiii

***Like a dying duck in a thunderstorm.*** Quite chop-fallen, very woebegone.

***Duck'sfoot Lane.*** A lane in the City of London leading from Laurence Pountney Hill to Upper Thames Street. It has been suggested that the name is a corruption of *Duke's Foot Lane*, i.e. the footpath of the Dukes of Suffolk, whose manor house was there; but in the 17th century it was known as *Duxfield Lane*, and later as *Ducksfield* and *Duxford Lane*.

**Dud.** Something or somebody that is useless or a failure. The word became very common during the Great War, when it was applied to shells that did not explode, inefficient officers, unworkable pieces of mechanism, etc. Its origin is not known. Dut. *dood* means dead, but no connection between this and *dud* has been traced.

**Dude.** A masher. One who renders himself conspicuous by affectation of dress, manners, and speech. The word was invented in America about 1883, and soon became popular in London.

I should just as soon expect to see Mercutio smoke a cigarette, as to find him ambling about the stage with the mincing manners of a dude.

Jefferson, *Century Magazine*, January, 1890

**Dudgeon.** The handle of a dagger, at one time made of boxwood root, called 'dudgeon-wood'; a dagger with such a handle. Shakespeare says,

> I see thee still;
> And on thy blade and dudgeon gouts of blood,
> Which was not so before.
>
> Shakespeare, *Macbeth*, 2, 1

As a dagger with a wooden handle was considered very inferior to one with ivory or inlaid handle, *dudgeon* came to be used as a contemptuous expression, signifying poor sort of stuff, trash; but there does not seem to be any connection between this word and the *dudgeon* which implies resentment or angry feelings.

**Dudman and Ramhead.** *When Dudman and Ramhead meet.* Never. Dudman and Ramhead (now spelt Ramehead) are two forelands on the Cornish coast, about twenty miles asunder. *See* Never.

> Make yourself scarce! depart! vanish! or we'll have you summoned before the mayor of Halgaver, and that before Dudman and Ramhead meet.
>
> Scott, *Kenilworth*, iv

**Duds.** A word in use for five hundred years at least, signifying clothes of some sort; formerly coarse cloaks, but in modern use slang for any clothes, usually with a disparaging implication. Its origin is unknown.

A *dudder* or *dudsman* is a scarecrow, or man of straw dressed in cast off garments to frighten birds; also a pedlar who deals in articles of clothing and materials.

**Duende.** A Spanish goblin or house-spirit. Calderon has a comedy called *La Dama Duenda*.

**Duenna.** The female of the Spanish *don* (*q.v.*); strictly, the chief lady in waiting on the Queen of Spain, but, in common parlance, a lady who is half companion and half governess, in charge of the younger female members of a Spanish or Portuguese family; hence, in England, a chaperon – especially one who takes her duties very seriously.

> There is no duenna so rigidly prudent and inexorably decorous as a superannuated coquette.
>
> W. Irving, *Sketch-Book* (*Spectre Bridegroom*)

**Duergar.** A Norse name for the dwarfs of *Scandinavian mythology*; they dwell in rocks and hills, and are noted for their strength, subtlety, magical powers, and skill in metallurgy. According to the *Gylfaginning* they owe their origin to the maggots in the flesh of the first giant, Ymir (*q.v.*).

**Duessa** (*Double-mind* or *Falsehood*). In Spenser's *Faërie Queene* (Bk I) the 'scarlet woman', typifying the Roman Catholic Church, and (Bk V) Mary Queen of Scots. She was the daughter of Deceit and Shame, and assumed divers disguises to beguile the Red Cross Knight. In Bk I she is stripped of her gorgeous disguise, is found to be a hideous hag, and flees into the wilderness for concealment.

**Duffer.** A stupid, foolish, incompetent person, one of slow wit; the origin of the word is not clear, but *duff* is old thieves' slang for 'to fake', and as a counterfeit coin was called a *duffer* the name may have been transferred to persons who, similarly, were 'no good'.

**Duke** (Lat. *dux*, leader). The title belonging to the highest rank of nobility in England. It is of comparatively recent introduction, for the Norman kings, who were Dukes of Normandy, apparently did not care to raise anybody in England to this rank. The first English dukedom to be created was that bestowed by Edward III on his eldest son, the Black Prince, in 1338, when he was raised from Earl of Cornwall to Duke of Cornwall. The title is very rarely conferred; and since 1874 (Duke of Westminster) it has been conferred only on the Earl of Fife, who was created Duke of Fife on his marriage with Princess Louise (July 27th, 1889). On his death in 1912 his daughter, Princess Arthur of Connaught, became Duchess of Fife in her own right, by special remainder.

***Duke Combe.*** William Combe (1741–1820), author of *The Tours of Dr Syntax*, etc., was so called, because of the splendour of his dress, the profusion of his table, and the magnificence of his deportment, in the days of his prosperity. Having spent all his money he turned author, but passed the last fifteen years of his life in the King's Bench.

***Duke Humphrey.*** *See* Humphrey.

***The Duke of Exeter's daughter.*** A rack in the Tower of London, so called from a minister of Henry VI, who sought to introduce its use into England (1447).

> I was the lad that would not confess one word ... though they threatened to make me hug the Duke of Exeter's daughter.
>
> Scott, *Fortunes of Nigel*, xxv

***The Great Duke.*** The Duke of Wellington (1769–1852), also called 'the Iron Duke', a name later given to a famous battleship (1913).

***To meet one in the Duke's Walk.*** To fight a duel. Duke's Walk, near Holyrood Palace, was the favourite promenade of the Duke of York, afterwards James II, during his residence in Scotland; and it became the common rendezvous for settling 'affairs of honour', as the fields behind the present British Museum were in England.

> If a gentleman shall ask me the same question, I shall regard the incivility as equivalent to an invitation to meet him in the Duke's Walk.
>
> Scott, *Bride of Lammermoor*, ch. xxxiv

**Dukeries.** A district in Nottinghamshire, so called from the number of ducal residences in the vicinity, including Welbeck Abbey (Duke of Portland), Clumber (Duke of Newcastle), Thoresby (Earl Manvers), etc.

**Dulcarnon.** The horns of a dilemma (or *Syllogismum cornutum*); at my wits' end; a puzzling question. From an Arabic word meaning 'the possessor of two horns'. The 47th proposition of the First Book of Euclid is called the Dulcarnon, as the 5th is the Pon Asinorum, because the two squares which contain the right angle roughly represent horns. Chaucer uses the word in *Troylus and Cryseyde*, Bk iii, 931, 933.

***To be in Dulcarnon.*** To be in a quandary, or on the horns of a dilemma.

***To send one to Dulcarnon.*** To daze with puzzles.

**Dulce Domum.** A school holiday song: the words mean – *not*, as often supposed, 'sweet home', but – 'the sweet (sound of the word) "home" '. The song originated at Winchester, and is said to have been written by a boy who was confined for misconduct during the Whitsun holidays, 'as report says, tied to a pillar'. On the evening preceding the Whitsun holidays, the master, scholars, and choristers still walk in procession round the pillar, chanting the six stanzas of the song. The music is by John Reading (d.1692), who also composed the Adeste Fideles (*q.v.*).

> Dolce domum resonemus.
> Let us make the sweet song of home to resound.

**Dulce est Desipere in Loco.** It is delightful to play the fool occasionally; it is nice to throw aside one's dignity and relax at the proper time (Horace, *4 Odes*, xii, 28).

**Dulce et Decorum est pro Patria Mori.** It is sweet and becoming to die on our country's behalf, or to die for one's country (Horace, *3 Odes*, ii, 13).

**Dulcimer.** In Dan. 3:5, etc., this word is used to translate a Hebrew word rendered in Greek by *symphonia*, which was applied to a kind of bagpipe. In modern use a dulcimer is a hollow triangular chest strung with wires of varying lengths, which are struck with a little rod held in each hand.

**Dulcinea.** A lady-love. Taken from Don Quixote's *amie du coeur*. Her real name was Aldonza Lorenzo, but the knight dubbed her Dulcinea del Toboso.

> I must ever have some Dulcinea in my head – it harmonises the soul. Sterne
>
> 'Sir,' said Don Quixote, 'she is not a descendant of the ancient Caii, Curtii, and Scipios of Rome; nor of the modern Colonas and Orsini; nor of the Rebillas and Villanovas of Valencia; neither is she a descendant of the Palafoxes, Newcas, Rocabertis, Corellas, Lunas, Alagones, Ureas, Fozes, and Gurreas of Aragon: neither does the Lady Dulcinea descend from the Cerdas, Man-riquez, Mendozas, and Guzmans of Castile; nor from the Alencastros, Pallas, and Menezës of Portugal; but she derives her origin from a family of Toboso, near Mancha.' (Bk ii, ch. v.)

Sancho Panza says she was 'a stout-built sturdy wench, who could pitch the bar as well as any young fellow in the parish'.

**Dulcinists.** Heretics who followed the teaching of Dulcin, or Dolcinus, who led the heretical sect of Apostolicals after the execution of Sagarelli in 1300. He taught that God reigned from the beginning to the coming of Messiah; and that Christ reigned from His ascension to the 14th century, when He gave up His dominion to the Holy Ghost. Dulcin was burnt by order of Clement IV (1307). There is a reference to Dulcin in Dante's *Inferno* (xxviii, 55).

**Dulia.** *See* Latria.

**Dull as Ditch-water.** Uninteresting; a very common simile, ditch-water is stagnant and has no go in it.

**Dullness.** *King of dullness.* So Pope calls Colley Cibber (1671–1757), poet laureate after Eusden.

> 'God save king Cibber!' mounts in every note
> So when Jove's block descended from on high
> Loud thunder to the bottom shook the bog,
> And the hoarse nation croaked, 'God save king Log.' Pope, *Dunciad*, Bk i

**Dum-dum.** A half-covered steel-cased bullet which expands on striking anything and so produces a very terrible wound; so called from Dum-dum, near Calcutta, the former headquarters of the Bengal artillery and of the ammunition factory where they were first made. The use of dum-dum bullets is prohibited in warfare by practically every civilised nation.

**Dum sola** (Law Lat.). While single or unmarried.

**Dum spiro, spero** (Lat.). Literally, while I breathe, I hope; while there's life, there's hope. It is the motto of Viscount Dillon.

**Dum vivimus vivamus** (Lat.). While we live, let us enjoy life. The motto adopted by Dr Doddridge (1702–51), who translated and expanded it into the subjoined epigram:

'Live, while you live,' the epicure would say,
'And seize the pleasures of the present day.'
'Live, while you live,' the sacred preacher cries,
'And give to God each moment as it flies'.
Lord, in *my* views let each united be;
I live in pleasure, when I live to thee.

**Dumb-bell.** Originally, an apparatus for developing the muscles similar to that which sets church bells in motion. It consists of a flywheel with a weight attached, and the gymnast is carried by it up and down to bring his muscles into play. The present dumb-bell, which answers a similar purpose, has been given the same name.

***The dumb-bell Nebula.*** Nebula in the constellation Vulpecula, so called from its apparent shape.

**Dumb-cow.** An Anglo-Indian colloquialism for to brow-beat; to cow.

**Dumb Crambo.** *See* Crambo.

**Dumb Ox, The.** St Thomas Aquinas (1224–74), known afterwards as 'the Angelic Doctor' or 'Angel of the Schools'. Albertus Magnus, the tutor of the 'dumb ox', said of him: 'The dumb ox will one day fill the world with his lowing.'

**Dumb waiter.** A piece of dining-room furniture, fitted with shelves, to hold glasses, dishes, and plate. So called because it answers all the purposes of a waiter, and is not possessed of a tongue.

**Dummy.** In bridge or in three-handed whist the exposed hand is called dummy. Double-dummy bridge is bridge played by only two players but with the usual four hands.

**Dummies.** Empty bottles or drawers in a druggist's shop; wooden heads in a hairdresser's shop; lay figures in a tailor's shop; 'walkers-on' on the stage; bound volumes of blank paper to show the size, etc., of some forthcoming book; etc. etc. These all are dumb, actually or figuratively.

**Dump.** A name for various 'dumpy' objects of little value, such as leaden disks, and small coins such as one that was current in Australia in the early 19th century and was made by cutting a portion out of a Spanish dollar. Hence, *not worth a dump*. The word is probably a back formation from *dumpy*, short and thick.

Death saw two players playing cards,
But the game was not worth a dump.

Hood, *Death's Ramble*, stanza 14

**Dumps.** ***To be in*** or ***down in the dumps***. Out of spirits; in the 'sullens'. An absurd etymological fable derives it from Dumops (!), King of Egypt, who built a pyramid and died of melancholy. Gay's Third Pastoral is *Wednesday, or the Dumps*.

Why, how now, daughter Katharine? in your dumps?

Shakespeare, *Taming of the Shrew*, 2, 1

In Elizabethan times the name was given to any plaintive tune, and also to a slow and mournful sort of dance.

They would have handled me a new way;
The devil's dump had been danced then.

Beaumont and Fletcher, *The Pilgrim*, V, iv

**Dun.** One who importunes for payment of a bill. The tradition is that it refers to Joe Dun, a bailiff of Lincoln in the reign of Henry VII. The *British Apollo* (1708) said he was so active and dexterous in collecting bad debts that when anyone became 'slow to pay' the neighbours used to say to the creditors, 'Dun him' (send Dun after him).

An Universitie dunne ... is an inferior creditor of some ten shillings or downewards, contracted for horse hire, or perchance drinke, too weake to be put in suite.

Earle, *Microcosmographia* (1628)

***Squire Dun.*** The hangman between Richard Brandin and Jack Ketch.

And presently a halter got,
Made of the best strong hempen teer;
And, ere a cat could lick his ear,
Had tied him up with as much art
As Dunn himself could do for 's heart.

Cotton, *Virgil Travestied*, Bk iv

**Dun Cow.** The savage beast slain by Guy Warwick (*q.v.*). A huge tusk, probably that of an elephant, is still shown at Harwich Castle as one of the horns of the dun cow.

The fable is that it belonged to a giant, and was kept on Mitchell (Middle) Fold, Shropshire. Its milk was inexhaustible; but one day an old woman who had filled her pail, wanted to fill her sieve also. This so enraged the cow that she broke loose from the fold and wandered to Dunsmore heath, where she was slain.

**Dun in the Mire.** ***To draw Dun out of the mire.*** To lend a helping hand to one in distress; to assist when things are at a standstill. The allusion is to an Old English game, in which a log of wood, called Dun (a name formerly given to a cart-horse), is supposed to have fallen into the mire, and the players are to pull it out. Each does all he can to obstruct the others, and as often as possible the log is made to fall on someone's toes. Constant allusion is made to this game.

Sires, what? Dun is in the mire.
Chaucer, *Prologue to Maunciples Tale*

If thou art dun, we'll draw thee from the mire
Shakespeare, *Romeo and Juliet*, 1, 4

Well done, my masters lend 's your hands;
Draw Dun out of the ditch.
Draw, pull, helpe all. So, so; well done.
T. Drue, *Duchesse of Suffolke* (1624)

**Dunce.** A dolt; a stupid person. The word is taken from *Duns* Scotus (about 1265–1308), so called from his birthplace, Dunse, in Scotland, the learned schoolman and great supporter of the immaculate conception. His followers were called Dunsers or Scotists (*q.v.*). Tyndal says, when they saw that their hair-splitting divinity was giving way to modern theology, 'the old barking curs raged in every pulpit' against the classics and new notions, so that the name indicated an opponent to progress, to learning, and hence a dunce.

He knew what's what, and that's as high
As metaphysic wit can fly …
A second Thomas, or at once
To name them all, another Dunse.
Butler, *Hudibras*, i, 1

Duns Scotus was buried at Cologne; his epitaph reads:

Scotia me genuit, Anglia me suscepit,
Gallia me docuit, Colonia me tenet.

***The Parliament of Dunces.*** Convened by Henry IV at Coventry, in 1404, and so called because all lawyers were excluded from it. Also known as the Lawless, and Unlearned, Parliament.

**Dunciad.** The dunce-epic, a satire by Alexander Pope, first published in 1728 with Theobald figuring as the Poet Laureate of the realm of Dullness, but republished with an added fourth part in 1741 with Colley Cibber in that rôle. His installation is celebrated by games, the most important being the proposal to read, without sleeping, two voluminous works – one in verse and the other in prose; as everyone falls asleep, the games come to an end. The Laureate is later taken to the temple of Dullness, and is lulled to sleep on the lap of the goddess; and, during his slumber, sees in a vision the past, present, and future triumphs of the empire. Finally, the goddess, having destroyed order and science, establishes her kingdom on a firm basis, gives directions to her several agents to prevent thought and keep people to foolish and trifling pursuits, and Night and Chaos are restored, and the poem ends.

**Dunderhead.** A blockhead, or, rather, a muddle-headed person. The history of the word is obscure; *dunder* may be connected with the Scottish *donnered*, or merely be modelled on *blunder*. It appears in early 17th century works.

**Dundreary, Lord.** The impersonation of a good-natured, indolent, blundering, empty-headed swell, from the chief character in Tom Taylor's *Our American Cousin* (1858). E. A. Sothern created the character by the genius of his acting and the large additions he made to the original text. *Cp.* Brother Sam.

**Dunedin.** *See* Edinburgh.

**Dunghill!** Coward! Villain! This is a cockpit phrase; all cocks, except gamecocks, being called dunghills.

Out, dunghill! dar'st thou brave a nobleman?
Shakespeare, *King John*, 4, 3

That is, Dare you, a dunghill cock, brave a thoroughbred gamecock?

***Every cock crows on its own dunghill.*** *See* Cock.

**Dunheved Castle.** *See* Castle Terabil.

**Dunkers.** *See* Tunkers.

**Dunmow.** *To eat Dunmow bacon.* To live in conjugal amity, without even wishing the marriage knot to be less firmly tied. The allusion is to a custom said to have been instituted by Juga, a noble lady, in 1111, and restored by Robert de Fitzwalter in 1244; which was, that

> any person from any part of England going to Dunmow, in Essex, and humbly kneeling on two stones at the church door, may claim a gammon of bacon, if he can swear that for twelve months and a day he has never had a house-hold brawl or wished himself unmarried.

Between 1244 and 1772 eight claimants were admitted to eat the flitch. Their names merit immortality:

1445. Richard Wright, labourer, Bauburgh, near Norwich.
1467. Steven Samuel, of Little Ayston, Essex.
1510. Thomas Ley, fuller, Coggeshall, Essex.
1701. William and Jane Parsley, butcher, Much Easton, Essex. Same year, John and Ann Reynolds, Hatfield Regis.
1751. Thomas Shakeshaft, woolcomber, Weathersfield, Essex.
1763. *Names not recorded.*
1772. John and Susan Gilder, Tarling, Essex.

Allusions to the custom are very frequent in 17th and 18th century literature; and in the last years of the 19th century it was revived. Later it was removed to Ilford. The oath administered is in doggerel, somewhat as follows:

You shall swear, by the custom of our confession,
That you never made any nuptial transgression

Since you were married man and wife,
By household brawls or contentious strife;
Or, since the parish clerk said '*Amen*',
Wished yourselves unmarried again;
Or, in a twelvemonth and a day,
Repented not in thought anyway.
If to these terms, without all fear,
Of your own accord you will freely swear,
A gammon of bacon you shall receive,
And bear it hence with our good leave.
For this is our custom at Dunmow well known –
The sport is ours, but the bacon your own.

**Duns Scotus.** *See* Dunce.

**Dunscore.** ***The saut lairds o' Dunscore.*** Gentlefolk who have a name but no money. The tale is that the 'puir wee lairds of Dunscore' (a parish near Dumfries) clubbed together to buy a stone of salt, which was doled out to the subscribers in small spoonfuls, that no one should get more than his due quota.

**Dunstable.** Bailey, as if he actually believed it, gives the etymology of this word *Duns'stable*; adding Duns or 'Dunus was a robber in the reign of Henry I, who made it dangerous for travellers to pass that way.' It is Celtic *dun*, a hill-fortress, and *staple*, an emporium or market (from late Lat. or O.Fr.).

***Downright Dunstable.*** Very blunt, plain speaking, straightforward; like the Dunstable road (a part of the Roman Watling Street), which runs very evenly from London and has many long, straight stretches.

If this is not plain speaking, there is no such place as downright Dunstable.

Scott, *Redgauntlet*, ch. xvii

***Plain as the road to Dunstable.*** As Shakespeare says, 'Plain as way to parish church'. *See above*; but there may be some play on the word *dunce*.

**Dunstan, St.** (d.988). Archbishop of Canterbury (961), and patron saint of goldsmiths, being himself a noted worker in gold. He is represented in pontifical robes, and carrying a pair of pincers in his right hand, the latter referring to the legend that on one occasion at Glastonbury (his birthplace) he seized the devil by the nose with a pair of red-hot tongs and refused to release him till he promised never to tempt him again. *See also* Horseshoes.

The name *St Dunstan's* is now intimately associated with work for the blind, on account of the institution founded during the Great War, and for many years run by Sir Arthur Pearson (himself blind), at St Dunstan's House, Regent's Park, for the welfare and training of blinded soldiers and later of blind civilians.

**Duodecimo.** A book whose sheets are folded into twelve leaves each (Lat. *duodecim*, twelve), often called 'twelvemo', from the contraction 12mo. The book is naturally a small one, hence the expression is sometimes applied to other things of small size, such as a dwarf. *Cp.* Decimo-sexto.

**Duomo.** Italian for a cathedral; literally 'house', i.e. 'house of God'. Our *dome* is the same word.

The supreme executive of Florence suspended Savonarola from preaching in the Duomo.

Symonds, *Renaissance in Italy*

**Dup** is *do up*. Thus Ophelia says in one of her snatches, he 'dupped the chamber door', i.e. did up or pushed up the latch, in order to open the door, that he might 'let in the maid' (*Hamlet*, 4, 1).

Iche weene the porters are drunk. Will they not dup the gate today.

Edwards, *Damon and Pythias* (1571)

**Dupes, Day of the.** In French history, November 11th, 1630, when Marie de Medicis and Gaston, Duc d'Orléans extorted from Louis XIII a promise that he would dismiss his Minister, the Cardinal Richelieu. The cardinal went in all speed to Versailles, the king repented, and Richelieu became more powerful than ever. Marie de Medicis and Gaston, the 'dupes', had to pay dearly for their short triumph.

**Durandana** or ***Durindana***. Orlando's sword, given him by his cousin Malagigi. It once belonged to Hector, was made by the fairies, and could cleave the Pyrenees at a blow.

Nor plaited shield, nor tempered casque defends,
Where Durindana's trenchant edge descends.

Hoole, *Orlando Furioso*, Bk v

**Durante** (Lat.). During.

***Durante bene placito.*** During good pleasure.

***Durante minore aetate.*** During minority.

***Durante viduitate.*** During widowhood.

***Durante vita.*** For life.

**Durden, Dame.** A generic term for a good, old-fashioned housewife. In the old song she kept five serving girls to carry the milking pails, and five serving men to use the spade and flail; and of course the five men loved the five maids.

'Twas Moll and Bet, and Doll and Kate, and Dorothy Draggletail;
And John and Dick, and Joe and Jack, and Humphrey with his flail.

Anon.

**Duresley.** ***You are a man of Duresley***, i.e. a great liar and cheat. Duresley (or Dursley) is a market town in Gloucestershire, formerly famous for its broadcloth manufactory. *See* Fuller's *Worthies*.

**Dust.** Slang for money; probably in allusion to the moralist's contention that money is worthless.

***Down with the dust!*** Out with the money; dub up! The expression is at least three hundred years old, and it is said that Swift once took for the text of a charity sermon, 'He who giveth to the poor, lendeth to the Lord.' Having thrice repeated his text, he added: 'Now, brethren, if you like the security, *down with your dust*.' That ended his sermon!

***I'll dust your jacket for you.*** Give you a good beating; also used with *doublet*, *trousers*, etc., in place of jacket. *See* quotation from Smollett, *under* Douse in the Chops. The allusion is to dusting carpets, etc., by beating them with a stick.

***To bite the dust.*** *See* Bite.

***To kiss*** or ***lick the dust.*** *See* Kiss.

***To raise a dust, to kick up a dust.*** To make a commotion or disturbance.

***To shake the dust from one's feet.*** To show extreme dislike of a place, and to leave it with the firm intention of never returning. The allusion is to the Eastern custom.

> And whosoever shall not receive you or hear your words, when ye depart out of that house or city, shake off the dust of your feet. Matt. 10:14
>
> But the Jews ... raised persecution against Paul and Barnabas, and expelled them out of their coasts. But they shook off the dust of their feet against them, and came on to Iconium.
> Acts 13:50, 51

***To throw dust in one's eyes.*** To mislead. The allusion is to 'the swiftest runner in a sandy race, who to make his fellowes follow aloofe, casteth dust with his heeles into their envious eyes' (Cotgrave, 1611).

The Mohammedans had a practice of casting dust into the air for the sake of confounding the enemies of the faith. This was done by the Prophet on two or three occasions, as in the battle of Honein; and the Koran refers to it when it says: 'Neither didst thou, O Mahomet, cast dust into their eyes; but it was God who confounded them.'

**Dustman.** ***The dustman has arrived***, or 'The sandman is about.' It is bedtime, for the children rub their eyes, as if dust or sand was in them.

**Dusty.** *Well, it is none so dusty*, or *Not so dusty*. I don't call it bad; rather smart. Here *dusty* means mean, soiled, worthless.

**Dustyfoot.** *See* Piepowder Court.

**Dutch.** The word, properly meaning 'Hollandish', is the M.Dut. *Dutsch* or Ger. *Deutsch*, and formerly denoted the people of Germany or Teutons generally. In colloquial English use the adjective has a belittling or derisive application, sometimes meaning little more than 'foreign' or 'un-English', and sometimes with reference to the drinking habits of the 17th century Dutchman. *See* Dutch courage, concert, gold, *etc.*, *below*.

***Dutch auction.*** An auction in which the auctioneer offers the goods at gradually decreasing prices, the first bidder to accept being the purchaser; the reverse process to that of an ordinary auction.

***Dutch comfort.*** 'Tis a comfort it was no worse. The comfort derivable from the consideration that how bad soever the evil which has befallen you, a worse is at least conceivable.

***Dutch concert.*** A great noise and uproar, like that made by a party of intoxicated Dutchmen, some singing, others quarrelling, speechifying, wrangling, and so on.

***Dutch courage.*** The courage excited by drink; pot valour.

> The Dutch their wine, and all their brandy lose,
> Disarmed of that from which their courage grows;
> While the glad English, to relieve their toil,
> In healths to their great leader drink the spoil.
> Waller, *Instructions to a Painter for a Picture of the Victory over the Dutch, June 3, 1665*

***Dutch gleek.*** Tippling. Gleek (*q.v.*) is a game, and the phrase implies that the game loved by Dutchmen is drinking.

> Nor could be partaker of any of the good cheer except it were the liquid part of it, which they call 'Dutch Gleek'.
> Gayton, *Pleasant Notes upon Don Quixote* (1654)

***Dutch gold.*** Deutsche or German gold. An alloy of copper and zinc, invented by Prince Rupert of Bavaria.

***Dutch nightingales.*** Frogs. Similarly, Cambridgeshire nightingales; Liège nightingales, etc.

***Dutch uncle. I will talk to you like a Dutch uncle.*** Will reprove you smartly. For 'uncle' *cp.* Horace, *3 Od.* xii, 3, '*Metuentes patruae verbera linguae*' (dreading the castigations of an uncle's tongue), and *2 Sat.* iii, 88, '*Ne sis patruus mihi*' ('don't come the uncle over me').

***My old Dutch.*** Here the word is a contraction of *duchess* (*q.v.*), and is nothing to do with Holland or Germany.

***The Dutch have taken Holland.*** A quiz when anyone tells what is well known as a piece of wonderful news. Similar to *Queen Bess* (or *Queen Anne*) *is dead*.

**Dutchman.** ***I'm a Dutchman if I do.*** A strong refusal. During the rivalry between England and Holland, the word Dutch was synonymous with all that was false and hateful, and when a man said, 'I would rather be a Dutchman than do what you ask me,' he used the strongest terms of refusal that words could express.

***If not, I'm a Dutchman,*** means, I will do it, or I will call myself a Dutchman.

***The flying Dutchman.*** *See* Flying.

***Well, I'm a Dutchman!*** An exclamation of strong incredulity.

**Duty** means what is due or owing, a debt which should be paid. Thus obedience is the debt of citizens to rulers for protection, and service is the debt of persons employed for wages received.

> Strictly considered, all duty is owed originally to God only; but ... duties to God may be distributed ... into duties towards self, towards manhood, and towards God.
>
> Gregory, *Christian Ethics*, I, i

***England expects that every man will do his duty.*** Nelson's signal to his fleet just before the battle of Trafalgar (1805).

**Duumvirs** (Lat. *Duumvir*, one of the two men). Certain Roman officials who were appointed in pairs, like our London sheriffs; originally, those who had charge of the Sibylline books. Later, *duumviri* were appointed as magistrates, as naval directors, directors of public works, etc.

**Dwarf.** Dwarfs have figured in the legends and mythology of nearly every race, and Pliny gives particulars of whole races of them, possibly following travellers' reports of African pigmies. Among the Teutonic and Scandinavian peoples dwarfs held an important place in mythology. They generally dwelt in rocks, caves, and recesses of the earth, were the guardians of its mineral wealth and precious stones, and were very skilful in the working of these. They had their own king, as a rule were not inimical to man, but could, on occasion, be intensely vindictive and mischievous.

In England diminutive persons – dwarfs – were popular down to the 18th century as court favourites or household pets; and in later times they have frequently been exhibited as curiosities at circuses, etc.

**Dwt.** D-wt, i.e. *denarius-weight* (penny-weight). *Cp.* Cwt.

**Dymphna.** The tutelar saint of the insane. She is said to have been the daughter of an Irish prince of the 7th century, and was murdered at Gheel, in Belgium, by her own father, because she resisted his incestuous passion. Gheel has long been a centre for the treatment of the mentally afflicted.

**Dynamite Saturday.** January 24th, 1885, when great damage was done to the Houses of Parliament and the Tower of London by Fenian attacks with dynamite.

**Dysmas.** The traditional name of the Penitent Thief, who suffered with Christ at the Crucifixion. His relics are claimed by Bologna, and in some calendars he is commemorated on March 25th. In the apocryphal Gospel of Nicodemus he is called *Dimas* (and elsewhere *Titus*), and the Impenitent Thief *Gestas.*

**Dyvour.** The old name in Scotland for a bankrupt. From the 17th century till 1836 *dyvours* were by law compelled to wear an upper garment, half yellow and half brown, with parti-coloured cap and hose.

**Dyzemas Day.** Tithe day. (Por. *dizimas*, tithes; Law Lat. *decimae.*)

# E

**E.** This letter is the representative of the hieroglyphic fretwork, ☐ and of the Phoenician and Hebrew sign for a window, called in Hebrew *he*.

In *Logic*, E denotes a universal negative proposition, and is thus the opposite of A (*q.v.*).

The following legend is sometimes seen engraved under the two tables of the Ten Commandments in churches –

PRSVR Y PRFCT MN
VR. KP THS PRCPTS TN
The vowel E
Supplies the key.

**E.G.,** e.g. (Lat. *exempli gratia*). By way of example; for instance.

**E Pluribus Unum** (Lat.). One unity composed of many parts. The motto of the United States of America; taken from *Moretum* (line 103), a Latin poem attributed to Virgil.

**Eagle. *Thy youth is renewed like the eagle's*** (Ps. 103:5). This refers to the ancient superstition that every ten years the eagle soars into the 'fiery region', and plunges thence into the sea, where, moulting its feathers, it acquires new life. *Cp.* Phoenix.

She saw where he upstarted brave
Out of the well …
As eagle fresh out of the ocean wave,
Where he hath lefte his plumes all hory gray,
And decks himself with fethers youthly gay.
Spenser, *Faërie Queene*, I, xi, 34

As a public-house sign the eagle was originally a compliment to Queen Mary, whose badge it was. She put it on the dexter side of the shield, and the sun on the sinister – a conjugal compliment which gave great offence to her subjects.

***The Golden Eagle*** and the ***Spread Eagle*** are commemorative of the crusades; they were the devices of the emperors of the East, and formerly figured as the ensigns of the ancient kings of Babylon and Persia, of the Ptolemies and Seleucides. The Romans adopted the eagle in conjunction with other devices, but Marius made it the ensign of the legion, and confined the other devices to the cohorts. The French under the Empire assumed the same device.

The Romans used to let an eagle fly from the funeral pile of a deceased emperor. Dryden alludes to this custom in his stanzas on Oliver Cromwell after his funeral, when he says, 'Officious haste did let too soon the sacred eagle fly.'

In Christian art, the eagle is emblematic of St John the Evangelist, because, like that bird, he looked on 'the sun of glory'.

St Augustine, St Gregory the Great, and St Prisca are also often shown with an eagle. In *heraldry*, it signifies fortitude.

***The eagle doesn't hawk at flies.*** *See* Aquila.

**As a Personal Appellation.**

***The Eagle.*** Gaudenzio Ferrari (1481–1549), the Milanese painter.

***The Eagle of the doctors of France.*** Pierre d'Ailly (1350–1420), French cardinal and astrologer, who calculated the horoscope of our Lord, and maintained that the stars foretold the deluge.

***The Eagle of Brittany.*** Bertrand Duguesclin (1320–80), Constable of France.

***The Eagle of Divines.*** St Thomas Aquinas (1225–74).

***The Eagle of Meaux.*** Jacques Bénigne Bossuet (1627–1704), Bishop of Meaux, the grandest and most sublime of the pulpit orators of France.

***The Eagle of the North.*** Count Axel Oxenstierna (1583–1654), the Swedish statesman, was so called.

***The two-headed eagle.*** The German eagle has its head turned to our left hand, and the Roman eagle to our right hand. When Charlemagne was made 'Kaiser of the Holy Roman Empire', he joined the two heads together, one looking east and the other west; consequently, the late Austrian Empire, as the direct successor of the Holy Roman Empire, included the *Double-headed Eagle* in its coat of arms.

In Russia it was Ivan Vasilievitch who first assumed the two-headed eagle, when, in 1472, he married Sophia, daughter of Thomas Palaeologus, and niece of Constantine XIV, the last Emperor of Byzantium. The two heads symbolise the Eastern or Byzantine Empire and the Western or Roman Empire.

***Grand Eagle.*** A size of drawing paper, 28¾ by 42 in.; so called from a watermark first met with in 1314.

**Eagle-stones.** *See* Aetites.

**Ear** (A.S. *eáre*). *If your ears burn someone is talking of you.* This is a very old superstition; Pliny says, 'When our ears do glow and tingle, some do talk of us in our absence.' Shakespeare, in *Much Ado About Nothing* (3, 1), make Beatrice say, when Ursula and Hero had been talking of her,

'What fire is in mine ears?' Sir Thomas Browne ascribes the conceit to guardian angels, who touch the right ear if the talk is favourable and the left if otherwise. This is done to cheer or warn.

One ear tingles; some there be
That are snarling now at me.
Herrick, *Hesperides*

***About one's ears.*** Causing trouble. The allusion is to a hornet's nest buzzing about one's head; thus, to bring the house about one's ears is to set the whole family against him.

***Bow down thine ear.*** Condescend to hear or listen (Ps. 31:2).

***By ear.*** To sing or play *by ear* means to sing or play without knowledge of musical notes, depending on the ear only.

***Dionysius's Ear.*** A bell-shaped chamber connected by an underground passage with the king's palace. Its object was to enable the tyrant of Syracuse to overhear what was passing in the prison.

***Give ear to.*** Listen to; give attention to.

***I am all ear.*** All attention.

I was all ear,
And took in strains that might create a soul
Under the ribs of death. Milton, *Comus*, 574

***I'll send you off with a flea in your ear.*** *See* Flea.

***In at one ear, and out at the other.*** Forgotten as soon as heard.

the sermoun ... of Dame Resoun ...
It toke no sojour in myn hede.
For alle yede out at oon er
That in at that other she did lere.
*Romaunt of the Rose*, 5148 (*c.*1400)

***Lend me your ears.*** Pay attention to what I am about to say.

Friends, Romans, countrymen, lend me your ears;
I come to bury Caesar, not to praise him.
Shakespeare, *Julius Caesar*, 3, 2

***Little pitchers have large ears.*** *See* Pitcher.

***Mine ears hast thou bored.*** Thou hast accepted me as thy bond-slave for life. If a Hebrew servant declined to go free after six years' service, the master was to bore his ear with an awl, in token of his voluntary servitude (Exod. 21:6).

***No ear.*** A bad ear for music; 'ear-blind' or 'sound-blind'.

***Over head and ears.*** Wholly, desperately; said of being in love, debt, trouble, etc.

***To be willing to give one's ears.*** To be prepared to make a considerable sacrifice. The allusion is to the old practice of cutting off the ears of those who refused to disown offensive opinions.

***To come to the ears of.*** To come to someone's knowledge, especially by hearsay.

***To get the wrong sow by the ear.*** *See* Sow.

***To fall together by the ears.*** *See* Fall.

***To have itching ears.*** To enjoy scandalmongering, hearing news or current gossip. (2 Tim. 4:3.)

***To prick up one' ears.*** To listen attentively to something not expected, as horses prick up their ears at a sudden sound.

Like unbacked colts, they pricked their ears.
Shakespeare, *Tempest*, 4, 1

***To set people together by the ears.*** To create ill-will among them; to set them quarrelling and, metaphorically, pulling each other's ears, as dogs do when fighting.

When civil dudgeon first grew high,
And men fell out, they knew not why;
When hard words, jealousies, and fears,
Set folks together by the ears.
Butler, *Hudibras* (opening lines)

***To tickle the ears.*** To gratify the ear either by pleasing sounds or flattering words.

***To turn a deaf ear.*** To refuse to listen; to refuse to accede to a request.

***Walls have ears.*** *See* Wall.

***Within earshot.*** Within hearing. The allusion is obvious.

***You cannot make a silk purse out of a sow's ear.*** *See* Silk.

**Ear-finger.** The little finger, which is thrust into the ear if anything tickles it.

**Ear-marked.** Marked so as to be recognised; figuratively, marked or set aside for some special purpose. The allusion is to setting owner's marks on the ears of cattle and sheep.

The late president [Balmaceda] took on board a large quantity of silver, which had been ear-marked for a particular purpose.
Newspaper paragraph, Sept. 4, 1891

**Ears to Ear Bible, The.** *See* Bible, specially named.

**Earing.** Ploughing. (A.S. *erian*, to plough; *cp.* Lat. *aro.*)

And yet there are five years, in the which there shall neither be earing nor harvest. Gen. 45: 6

If the first heir of my invention prove deformed, I shall be sorry it had so noble a godfather, and never after ear so barren a land, for fear it yield me still so bad a harvest.
Shakespeare, *Dedication to 'Venus and Adonis'*

**Earl** (A.S. *eorl*, a man of position, in opposition to *ceorl*, a churl or freeman of the lowest rank; *cp.* Dan. *jarl*). The third in dignity in the British peerage, ranking next below Marquess (*q.v.*). In

Anglo-Saxon times, it was a title of the highest dignity and eminence, and was even applied to sovereign princes. Earl Godwin was a ruler of enormous power, as also were the earls created by the Norman kings. *Cp.* Viscount. William the Conqueror tried to introduce the word Count, but did not succeed, although the wife of an earl is still called a *countess.*

> The sheriff is called in Latin vice-comés, as being the deputy of the earl or comés, to whom the custody of the shire is said to have been committed. Blackstone, *Commentaries*, I, ix

***Earl Marshal.*** A high officer of state who presides over the College of Arms, grants armorial bearings, and is responsible for the arrangement of State ceremonials, processions, etc. Since 1483 the office has been hereditary in the line of the Dukes of Norfolk.

***Earl of Mar's Grey Breeks.*** The 21st Foot (the Royal Scots Fusiliers) are so called because they wore *grey breeches* when the Earl of Mar was their colonel (1678–86).

**Earthquakes.** According to *Indian mythology*, the world rests on the head of a great elephant, and when, for the sake of rest, the huge monster refreshes itself by moving its head, an earthquake is produced. The elephant is called 'Muha-pudma'.

> Having penetrated to the south, they saw the great elephant 'Muha-pudma', equal to a huge mountain, sustaining the earth with its head.
> *The Ramayana* (section xxxiii)

The lamas say that the earth is placed on the back of a gigantic frog, and when the frog stretches its limbs or moves its head, it shakes the earth. Other Eastern mythologists place the earth on the back of a tortoise.

Greek and Roman mythologists ascribe earthquakes to the restlessness of the giants which Jupiter buried under high mountains. Thus Virgil (*Aeneid*, iii, 578) ascribes the eruption of Etna to the giant Enceladus.

**Earwig.** A.S. *ear-wicga*, ear-beetle; so called from the erroneous notion that these insects are apt to get into our ears, and so penetrate the brain.

Metaphorically, one who whispers all the news and scandal going, in order to curry favour; a flatterer.

> Court earwigs banish from your ears.
> *Political Ballads* (1688)

**Ease.** From O.Fr. *eise*, Mod.Fr. *aise*.

***At ease.*** Without pain or anxiety.

***Chapel of ease.*** *See* Chapel.

***Ease her!*** A command given on a steamer to reduce speed. The next order is generally 'Back her!' and then 'Stop her!'

***Ill at ease.*** Uneasy, not comfortable, anxious.

***Stand at ease!*** A command given to soldiers to rest for a time. 'The gentlemen stood at ease' means stood in an informal manner.

***To ease one of his money*** or ***purse.*** To steal it.

**East.** The custom of *turning to the east* when the creed is repeated is to express the belief that Christ is the Dayspring and Sun of Righteousness. The altar is placed at the east end of the church to remind us of Christ, the Dayspring and Resurrection; and persons are buried with their feet to the East to signify that they died in the hope of the Resurrection.

The ancient Greeks always buried their dead with the face *upwards*, looking towards heaven; and the feet turned to the east or the rising sun, to indicate that the deceased was on his way to Elysium, and not to the region of night or the inferno. (Diogenes Laertius, *Life of Solon*, in Greek.)

**East-ender.** *See under* End.

**East Indies.** ***He came safe from the East Indies, and was drowned in the Thames.*** He encountered many dangers of great magnitude, but was at last killed where he thought himself secure.

***To send to the East Indies for Kentish pippins.*** To go round about to accomplish a very simple thing. To crush a fly on a wheel. To send to the Postmaster-General for a postage stamp.

**Easter.** The name was adopted for the Christian Paschal festival from A.S. *eastre*, a heathen festival held at the vernal equinox in honour of the Teutonic goddess of dawn, called by Bede *Eostre* (cognate with Lat. *aurora* and Sanskrit *ushas*, dawn). On the introduction of Christianity it was natural for the name of the heathen festival to be transferred to the Christian, the two falling about the same time.

Easter Sunday is the first Sunday after the Paschal full moon, i.e. the full moon that occurs on the day of the vernal equinox (March 21st) or on any of the next 28 days. Consequently, Easter Sunday cannot be earlier than March 22nd, or later than April 25th. This was fixed by the Council of Nice, AD 325.

It was formerly a common belief that the sun danced on Easter Day.

> But oh, she dances such a way,
> No sun upon an Easter day
> Is half so fine a sight.
> Sir John Suckling, *Ballad upon a Wedding*

Sir Thomas Browne combats the superstition:

> We shall not, I hope, disparage the Resurrection of our Redeemer, if we say the Sun doth not dance on Easter day. And though we would willingly assent unto any sympathetical exultation, yet cannot conceive therein any more than a Tropical expression.
>
> *Pseudodoxia Epidemica*, V, xxii

**Easter Eggs,** or **Pasch eggs,** are symbolical of creation, or the re-creation of spring. The practice of presenting them at Easter came into England from Germany in the 19th century. It may be a relic of Eastern religion and bear allusion to the mundane egg (*see* Egg), for which Ormuzd and Ahriman were to contend till the consummation of all things; but it is more likely connected with the old Romish rule that forbad the eating of eggs during Lent, but allowed them again at Easter. *See* Egg Feast.

> Bless, Lord, we beseech thee, this Thy creature of eggs, that it may become a wholesome sustenance to Thy faithful servants, eating it in thankfulness to Thee, on account of the resurrection of our Lord. Pope Paul V, *Ritual*

**Easterlings.** An old name (first used in the 16th century) for any foreigner coming to England from the East; but specially applied to the merchants from the Hanse towns of northern Germany.

**Eat.** To eat together was, in the East, a sure pledge of protection. A man once prostrated himself before a Persian grandee and implored protection from the rabble. The nobleman gave him the remainder of a peach which he was eating, and when the incensed multitude arrived, and declared that the man had slain the only son of the nobleman, the heart-broken father replied, 'We have eaten together; go in peace,' and would not allow the murderer to be punished.

***Let us eat, drink, and be merry, for tomorrow we die.*** *See* Is. 22:13. A traditional saying of the Egyptians who, at their banquets, exhibited a skeleton to the guests to remind them of the brevity of human life.

***To eat a man's salt.*** *See* Salt.

***To eat coke, humble pie, the leek.*** *See these words.*

***To eat its head off.*** Said of an animal (usually a horse) that eats more than he is worth, or whose work does not pay for the cost of keeping. A horse which stands in the stable unemployed 'eats its head off'.

***To eat one out of house and home.*** To eat so much that one will have to part with house and home in order to pay for it. It is the complaint of hostess Quickly to the Lord Chief Justice when he asks for 'what sum' she had arrested Sir John Falstaff. She explains the phrase by 'he hath put all my substance into that fat belly of his'. (Shakespeare, *2 Henry IV*, 2, 1.)

***To eat one's heart out.*** To fret or worry unreasonably; to allow one grief or one vexation to predominate over the mind, tincture all one's ideas, and absorb all other emotions.

***To eat one's terms.*** To be studying for the bar. Students are required to dine in the Hall of the Inns of Court at least three times in each of the twelve terms before they are 'called' to the bar.

***To eat one's words.*** To retract in a humiliating manner; to unsay what you have said; to eat your own lick, swallow your own spittle. The phrase is Biblical in origin. *See* Jer. 15:16.

***To eat well.*** To have a good appetite. But 'It eats well' means that what is eaten is agreeable or flavorous. To 'eat badly' is to eat without appetite or too little.

**Eau de Cologne.** A perfumed spirit, originally prepared at Cologne. The most famous maker was Jean Maria Farina.

**Eau de vie** (Fr. water of life). Brandy. A translation of the Latin *aqua vitae* (*q.v.*). This is a curious perversion of the Spanish *acqua di vite* (water or juice of the vine), rendered by the monks into *aqua vitae* instead of *aqua vitis*, and confounding the juice of the grape with the alchemists' elixir of life. The same error is perpetuated in the Italian *acqua vite*.

**Eavesdropper.** One who listens stealthily to conversation. The derivation of the term is not usually understood. The owners of private estates in Saxon times were not allowed to cultivate to the extremity of their possessions, but were obliged to leave a space for eaves. This space was called the *yfes-drype* (eaves-drip). An eavesdropper is one who places himself in the eaves-drip to overhear what is said in the adjacent house or field.

> Under our tents I'll play the eavesdropper,
> To hear if any mean to shrink from me.
>
> Shakespeare, *Richard III*, 5, 3

**Ebionites.** An heretical sect of the 1st and 2nd centuries, who denied the Divinity of Jesus Christ and his birth of a Virgin, and held that he was merely an inspired messenger. The name is from Heb. *ebyon*, poor, probably in allusion to some claim that they were 'the poor in spirit'.

> At the end of the second century the Ebionites were treated as heretics, and a pretended leader (Eblion) was invented by Tertullian to explain the name. Renan, *Life of Jesus*, ch. xi

**Eblis.** A jinn of *Arabian mythology*, the ruler of the evil genii, or fallen angels. Before his fall he was called Azazel (*q.v.*). When Adam was created, God commanded all the angels to worship him; but Eblis replied, 'Me thou hast created of smokeless fire, and shall I reverence a creature made of dust?' God was very angry at this insolent answer, and turned the disobedient angel into a Sheytân (devil), and he became the father of devils.

Another Mohammedan tradition has it that before life was breathed into Adam all the angels came to look at the shape of clay, among them Eblis, who, knowing that God intended man to be his superior, vowed never to acknowledge him as such and kicked the figure till it rang.

> When he said unto the angels, 'Worship Adam,' all worshipped him except Eblis. *Al Koran*, ii

Eblis had five sons, viz. (1) *Tír*, author of fatal accidents; (2) *Awar*, the demon of lubricity; (3) *Dásim*, author of discord; (4) *Sût*, father of lies; and (5) *Zalambûr*, author of mercantile dishonesty.

**Ebony.** ***God's image done in ebony.*** Negroes. Thomas Fuller gave birth to this expression.

**Ecce homo** (Lat., Behold the man). The name given to many paintings of our Lord crowned with thorns and bound with ropes, as He was shown to the people by Pilate, who said to them, '*Eccë homo!*' (John 19:5), especially those by Correggio, Titian, Guido, Van Dyck, Rembrandt, Poussin, and Albert Durer. In 1865 Sir John Seeley published a survey of the life and work of Christ with the title 'Ecce Homo'.

**Ecce signum.** See it, in proof. Behold the proof.

> I am eight times thrust through the doublet, four through the hose; my buckler cut through and through; my sword hacked like a handsaw – ecce signum! Shakespeare, *1 Henry IV*, 2, 4

**Eccentric.** Deviating from the centre (Lat. *ex centrum*); hence irregular, not according to rule. Originally applied to those planets which apparently wander round the earth, like comets, the earth not being in the centre of their orbit.

**Ecclesiastes.** One of the books in the Old Testament, arranged next to Proverbs, formerly ascribed to Solomon, because it says (verse 1), 'The words of the Preacher, the son of David, king in Jerusalem', but now generally assigned to an unnamed author of the 3rd century BC, writing after Malachi but before the time of the Maccabees. The Hebrew name is *Koheleth*, which means 'the Preacher'.

**Ecclesiastical.** *The father of ecclesiastical history*, Eusebius of Caesarea (about 264–340).

**Ecclesiasticus.** One of the books of the Old Testament Apocrypha, traditionally (and probably correctly) ascribed to a Palestinian sage named Ben Sirah, or Jesus, the Son of Sirach. In the Talmud it is quoted as *Ben Sira*, and in the Septuagint its name is *The Wisdom of Jesus, the Son of Sirach*. It was probably written early in the 2nd century BC. It was given its present name by early Greek Christians because, in their opinion, it was the chief of the apocryphal books, designated by them *Ecclesiastici Libri* (books to be read in churches), to distinguish them from the canonical Scriptures.

**Echidna** (*E-kid-na*). A monster of *classical mythology*, half woman, half serpent. She was mother of the Chimaera, the many-headed dog Orthos, the hundred-headed dragon of the Hesperides, the Colchian dragon, the Sphinx, Cerberos, Scylla, the Gorgons, the Lernaean hydra, the vulture that gnawed away the liver of Prometheus, and the Nemean lion.

Spenser makes her the mother of the Blatant Beast (*q.v.*):

> Echidna is a Monster direfull dred,
> Whom Gods doe hate, and heavens abhor to see;
> So hideous is her shape, so huge her hed,
> That even the hellish fiends affrighted bee
> At sight thereof, and from her presence flee;
> Yet did her face and former parts professe
> A faire young Mayden full of comely glee;
> But all her hinder parts did plaine expresse
> A monstrous Dragon, full of fearefull uglinesse.
> *Faërie Queene*, VI, vi, 10

**Echo.** The Romans say that Echo was a nymph in love with Narcissus, but her love not being returned, she pined away till only her voice remained.

> Sweet Echo, sweetest nymph, that liv'st unseen
> Within thy airy shell,
> By slow Meander's margent green …
> Canst thou not tell me of a gentle pair
> That likest thy Narcissus are?
> Milton, *Comus*, 230

***To applaud to the echo.*** To applaud vigorously – so loudly as to produce an echo.

***You echo my ideas.*** You merely say what I say; haying no ideas of your own you copy mine.

**Eckhardt.** *A faithful Eckhardt, who warneth everyone.* Eckhardt, in German legends, appears on the evening of Maundy Thursday to warn all persons to go home, that they may not be injured by the headless bodies and two-legged horses which traverse the streets on that night.

**Eclectics.** The name given to those who do not attach themselves to any special school (especially philosophers and painters), but pick and choose from various systems, selecting and harmonising those doctrines, methods, etc., which suit them (Gr. *ek-legein*, to choose, select). Certain Greek philosophers of the 1st and 2nd centuries BC were styled Eclectics; and there is the Eclectic school of painters, i.e. the Italians of the 17th century who followed the great masters, an Eclectic school of modern philosophy, founded by Victor Cousin, the Eclectic school of architecture, and so on.

**Eclipses** were considered by the ancient Greeks and Romans as bad omens. Nicias, the Athenian general, was so terrified by an eclipse of the moon, that he durst not defend himself from the Syracusans; in consequence of which his whole army was cut to pieces, and he himself was put to death.

The Romans would never hold a public assembly during an eclipse. Some of their poets feign that an eclipse of the moon is because she is gone on a visit to Endymion.

A very general notion was and still is among barbarians that the sun or moon has been devoured by some monster and hence the custom of beating drums and kettles to scare away the monster. The Chinese, Laps, Persians, and some others call the evil beast a dragon. The East Indians say it is a black griffin.

The notion of the ancient Mexicans was that eclipses were caused by sun and moon quarrels, in which one or other was beaten black and blue.

**Eclogue** (Gr., a selection). The word was originally used for Virgil's *Bucolics*, because they were *selected* poems; as they were all pastoral dialogues it came to denote such poems, and hence an *Eclogue* is now a pastoral or rustic dialogue in verse.

**Economy.** Literally, 'household management' (Lat. *aeconomia*, from Gr. *oikos*, house, *nemein*, to deal out). As we generally try to prevent extravagant waste and make the most of our means in our own homes, so the careful expenditure of money and of time, and also organisation and administration of affairs generally, are also called *economy*.

There are many British proverbs and sayings teaching the value of economy:

'No alchemy like frugality'; 'ever save, ever have'; 'a pin a day is a groat a year'; 'take care of the pence, and the pounds will take care of themselves'; 'many a mickle makes a muckle'; 'frae saving, comes having'; 'a penny saved is a penny gained'; 'little and often fills the purse'; and there is Mr Micawber's wise saying:

> Annual income twenty pounds, annual expenditure nineteen nineteen six, result happiness. Annual income twenty pounds, annual expenditure twenty pounds ought and six, result misery. Dickens, *David Copperfield*, ch. xii

***The Christian economy.*** The religious system based on the teachings of Jesus Christ as recorded in the New Testament.

***The economy of nature.*** The laws of nature, whereby the greatest amount of good is obtained; or the laws by which the affairs of nature are regulated and disposed; the system and interior management of the animal and vegetable kingdoms, etc.

> Animal ... economy, according to which animal affairs are regulated and disposed.
> Shaftesbury, *Characteristics*

***The Mosaic economy.*** The religious system revealed by God to Moses and set forth in the Old Testament.

***Political economy.*** Science of the production, distribution, and management of wealth, especially as dealing with the principles whereby the revenues and resources of a nation are made the most of. The question of Free Trade, for instance, is a problem in political economy: articles are cheaper, and therefore the buying value of money is increased; but, on the other hand, competition is increased, and therefore wages are lowered.

**Ecstasy** (Gr. *ek*, out, *stasis*, a standing). Literally, a condition in which one stands out of one's mind, loses one's wits, or is 'beside oneself'. St Paul refers to this when he says he was caught up to the third heaven and heard unutterable words, 'whether in the body, or out of the body, I cannot tell' (2 Cor. 12:2–4). St John also says he was 'in the spirit' – i.e. in an ecstasy – when he saw the apocalyptic vision (Rev. 1:10). The belief that the soul left the body at times was very general in former ages, and there was a class of diviners among the ancient Greeks called *Ecstatici*, who used to lie in trances, and when they came to themselves gave strange accounts of what they had seen while they were 'out of the body'.

**Ecstatic Doctor, The.** Jean de Ruysbroeck, the mystic (1294–1381).

**Ecstatici, The.** *See* Ecstasy.

**Ector, Sir.** The foster-father or King Arthur.

> The child was delivered unto Merlin, and he bare it forth unto Sir Ector, and made a holy man to christen him, and named him Arthur; and so Sir Ector's wife nourished him with her own pap. Malory, *Le Morte d'Arthur*, I, iii

**Edda.** This name – which may be from *Edda*, the great-grandmother in the Old Norse poem *Rigsthul*, or from the old Norse *odhr*, poetry, is given to two separate works or collections, viz. *The Elder* or *Poetic Edda*, and *The Younger Edda*, or *Prose Edda of Snorri*. The first-named was discovered in 1643 by an Icelandic bishop, and consists of mythological poems dating from the 9th century, and supposed to have been collected in the 13th century. They are of unknown authorship, but were erroneously attributed to Saemund Sigfusson (d.1133), and this has hence sometimes been called *Saemund's Edda*. The *Younger Edda* is a work in prose and verse by Snorri Sturluson (d.1242), and forms a guide to poets and poetry. It consists of the *Gylfaginning* (an epitome of Scandinavian mythology), the *Skaldskaparmal* (a glossary of poetical expressions, etc.), the *Hattatal* (a list of metres, with examples of all known forms of verse, with a preface, history of the origin of poetry, lists of poets, etc.).

**Eden.** Paradise, the country and garden in which Adam and Eve were placed by God (Gen. 2:15). The word means *delight, pleasure*.

**Eden Hall.** ***The luck of Eden Hall.*** An enamelled drinking-glass, made probably in Venice in the 10th century, in the possession of the Musgrave family at Eden Hall, Cumberland, and traditionally supposed to be endowed with fortune-bringing properties. The tale is that the butler once went to draw water from St Cuthbert's Well in the garden, when the fairies left this glass by the well while they danced, and that he ran off with it. Longfellow translated a German ballad on the subject. The superstition is –

> If that glass either break or fall,
> Farewell the luck of Eden Hall.

**Edge** (A.S. *ecg*). ***It is dangerous to play with edged tools.*** It is dangerous to tamper with mischief or anything that may bring you into trouble.

***Not to put too fine an edge upon it.*** Not to mince the matter; to speak plainly.

> He is, not to put too fine an edge upon it, a thorough scoundrel. Lowell

***To be on edge.*** To be very eager or impatient.

***To edge away.*** To move away very gradually, as a ship moves from the edge of the shore.

***To edge on.*** *See* Egg on.

***To fall by the edge of the sword.*** By a cut from the sword; to be slain in battle.

***To set one's teeth on edge.*** To give one the horrors; to induce a tingling or grating sensation in one's teeth, as from acids or harsh noises.

> In those days they shall say no more, the fathers have eaten a sour grape, and the children's teeth are set on edge. Jer. 31:29

> I had rather hear a brazen canstick turned,
> Or a dry wheel grate on the axle tree;
> And that would set my teeth nothing on edge.
> Nothing so much as mincing poetry.
> Shakespeare, *1 Henry IV*, 3, 1

**Edge-bone.** *See* Aitch-bone.

**Edgewise.** ***One cannot get in a word edgewise.*** The conversation is so engrossed by others that there is no getting in a word.

**Ediles.** *See* Aediles.

**Edinburgh.** Edwin's burgh; the fort built by Edwin, king of Northumbria (616–33). Dunedin (Gaelic *dun*, a fortress) and Edina are poetical forms.

**Edyrn.** Son of Nudd; called the 'Sparrowhawk', in Tennyson's *Marriage of Geraint* (*Idylls of the King*), which was founded on the story of *Geraint, Son of Erbin*, in Lady Charlotte Guest's translation of the *Mabinogion*. He ousted Yniol from his earldom, and tried to win Enid, the earl's daughter, but was overthrown by Geraint and sent to the court of King Arthur, where his whole nature was completely changed, and 'subdued to that gentleness which, when it weds with manhood, makes a man'.

**Eel.** ***A salt eel.*** A rope's end, used for scourging. At one time eelskins were used for whips.

> With my salt eele, went down in the parler, and there got my boy and did beat him.
> *Pepys' Diary* (April 24th)

***Eel-skins.*** Old-fashioned slang for extra tight trousers, or tightly fitting frocks.

***Holding the eel of science by the tail.*** To have a smattering of the subject, the kind which slips from the memory as an eel would wriggle out of one's fingers if held by the tail.

***To get used to it, as a skinned eel.*** It may be unpleasant at first, but habit will get the better of such annoyance.

> It ain't always pleasant to turn out for morning chapel, is it, Gig-lamps? But it's just like the eels with their skinning: it goes against the grain at first, but you soon get used to it.
> Cuthbert Bede, *Verdant Green*, ch. vii

***To skin an eel by the tail.*** To do things the wrong way.

**Effendi.** A Turkish title, about equal to the English 'Mr' or 'Esq.' but always following the name. It is given to emirs, men of learning, the high priests of mosques, etc.

**Effigy.** ***To burn*** or ***hang one in effigy.*** To burn or hang the representation of a person, instead of the person himself, in order to show popular hatred, dislike, or contempt. The custom comes from France, where the public executioner used to hang the effigy of the criminal when the criminal himself could not be found.

**Égalité.** Philippe, Duc d'Orléans (b.1747, guillotined 1793), father of Louis-Philippe, King of the French, assumed the name when he renounced his title and voted for the death of the king. The motto of the revolutionary party, with which he sided, was 'Liberty, fraternity, and equality (*égalité*)'.

**Egeria.** The nymph who instructed Numa in his wise legislation; hence, a counsellor, adviser.

> It is in these moments that we gaze upon the moon. It is in these moments that Nature becomes our Egeria. Lord Beaconsfield, *Vivian Grey*, III, vi

**Egg.** *See also* Shell.

***A bad egg.*** A bad speculation; a man whose promises are pie-crust, a 'bad lot'; a person or thing that does not come up to expectations.

***A duck's egg.*** *See* Duck.

***Don't put all your eggs in one basket.*** Don't venture all you have in one speculation; don't put all your property in one bank. The allusion is obvious.

***Easter eggs.*** *See* Easter; Egg Feast.

***From the egg to the apples.*** *See* Ab ovo.

***Golden eggs.*** Great profits. *See* Goose.

> I doubt the bird is flown that laid the golden eggs.
> Scott, *The Antiquary*

***I got eggs for my money.*** I gave valuable money, and received such worthless things as eggs. When Wolsey accused the Earl of Kildare for not taking Desmond prisoner, the Earl replied, 'He is no more to blame than his brother Ossory, who (notwithstanding his high promises) is glad to take eggs for his money,' i.e. is willing to be imposed on. (Campion, *History of Ireland*, 1633.)

***I have eggs on the spit.*** I am very busy, and cannot attend to anything else. The reference is to roasting eggs on a spit. They were first boiled, then the yolk was taken out, braided up with spices, and put back again; the eggs were then drawn on a 'spit', and roasted. As this required both dispatch and constant attention, the person in charge could not leave them.

> I forgot to tell you, I write short journals now; I have eggs on the spit. Swift

***Like as two eggs.*** Exactly alike.

> They say we are almost as like as eggs.
> Shakespeare, *Winter's Tale*, 1, 2

***Show him an egg, and instantly the whole air is full of feathers.*** Said of a very sanguine man, because he is 'counting his chickens before they are hatched'.

***Sure as eggs is eggs.*** Professor de Morgan suggested that this is a corruption of the logician's formula, '*x* is *x*'.

***Teach your grandmother to suck eggs.*** Attempting to teach your elders and superiors. The French say, 'The goslings want to drive the geese to pasture' (*Les oisons veulent mener les oies paître*).

***The mundane egg.*** The Phoenicians, Egyptians, Hindus, Japanese, and many other ancient nations maintained that the world was egg-shaped, and was hatched from an egg made by the Creator; and in some mythologies a bird is represented as laying the mundane egg on the primordial waters.

Anciently this idea was attributed to Orpheus, hence the 'mundane egg' is also called the *Orphic egg*.

> The opinion of the oval figure of the earth is ascrib'd to Orpheus and his disciples; and the doctrine of the mundane egg is so peculiarly his, that 'tis called by Proclus the Orphick egg.
> Burnet, *The Sacred Theory of the Earth* (1684)

***There is reason in roasting eggs.*** Even the most trivial thing has a reason for being done in one way rather than in some other. When wood fires were usual, it was more common to roast eggs than to boil them, and some care was required to prevent their being 'ill-roasted, all on one side', as Touchstone says (*As You Like It*, 3, 2).

> One likes the pheasant's wing, and one the leg;
> The vulgar boil, the learnëd roast an egg.
> Pope, *Epistles*, ii

***To crush in the egg.*** To nip in the bud; to ruin some scheme before it has been fairly started.

***To egg on.*** To incite, to urge on. Here *egg* is simply another form of *edge* – to edge on, i.e. to drive one nearer and nearer to the edge until the plunge is taken.

***To tread upon eggs.*** To walk gingerly, as if walking over eggs, which are easily broken.

***Will you take eggs for your money?*** 'Will you allow yourself to be imposed upon? Will you take kicks for halfpence?' This saying was in vogue when eggs were plentiful as blackberries.

> My honest friend, will you take eggs for money?
> Shakespeare, *Winter's Tale*, 1, 2

**Egg Feast,** or **Egg Saturday.** In Oxford the Saturday preceding Shrove Tuesday used to be so called because, as the eating of eggs was forbidden during Lent, the scholars took leave of them on that day. They were allowed again at Easter, hence the coloured 'Easter egg'.

**Egg-flip, Egg-hot, Egg-nog.** Drinks composed of warm spiced ale, with sugar, spirit, and eggs; or eggs beaten up with wine, sweetened and flavoured, etc.

**Egg Saturday.** *See* Egg Feast.

**Egg-trot,** or **Egg-wife's trot.** A cautious, jog-trot pace, like that of a housewife riding to market with eggs in her panniers.

**Egil.** Brother of Wieland, the Vulcan of *Northern mythology*. Egil was a great archer, and in the Saga of Thidrik there is a tale told of him the exact counterpart of the famous story about William Tell and the apple. *See* Tell.

**Eglantine.** In the romance of Valentine and Orson, daughter of King Pepin, and bride of her cousin Valentine. She soon died.

***Madame Eglantine.*** The prioress in Chaucer's *Canterbury Tales*. Good-natured, wholly ignorant of the world, vain of her courtly manners, and noted for her partiality to lapdogs, her delicate oath, 'by seint Eloy', her 'entuning the service swetely in her nose', and her speaking French 'after the scole of Stratford atte Bowe'.

**Ego** (Lat. 'I'). In various philosophical systems *ego* is used of the conscious thinking subject and *non-ego* of the object. The term *ego* was introduced into philosophy by Descartes, who employed it to denote the whole man, body and mind. Fichte later used the term *the absolute ego*, meaning thereby

> the non-individual being, neither subject nor object, which posits the world of individual egos and non-egos.

**Egoism.** The theory in Ethics which places man's *summum bonum* in self. The correlative of altruism, or the theory which places our own greatest happiness in making others happy. *Egoism* is selfishness pure, altruism is selfish benevolence. Hence *egoist*, one who upholds and practises this theory.

> To say that each individual shall reap the benefits brought to him by his own powers ... is to enunciate egoism as an ultimate principle of conduct.
> Spencer, *Data of Ethics*, p. 189

**Egotism.** The too frequent use of the word I; the habit of talking about oneself, or of parading one's own doings. *Egotist*, one addicted to egotism.

**Egypt,** in Dryden's satire of *Absalom and Achitophel*, means France.

> Egypt and Tyrus [Holland] intercept your trade,
> And Jebusites [Papists] your sacred rites invade.
> Pt i, 705–6

**Egyptian Days.** Unlucky days, days on which no business should be undertaken. The Egyptian astrologers named two in each month, but the last Monday in April, the second Monday of August, and the third Monday of December seem to have been specially baneful.

> For there ben xxliii Egypcyan dayes it folowyth that god sente mo wreches upon the Egypcyens than ten.
> Trevisa, *Trans. of 'De Proprietatibus Rerum' by Bartholomaeus Anglicus* (1398)

**Eider-down.** The down of the eider duck. This duck is common in Greenland, Iceland, and the Islands north and west of Scotland. It is about the size of a goose, and gives its name, which is old Norse, to the river Eider in Schleswig-Holstein.

**Eikon Basilike** (Gr. royal likeness). A book originally published in 1649 (?1648) as by Charles I, purporting to set forth the private meditations, prayers, thoughts on the political situation, etc., of the king during and before his imprisonment. Its authorship was claimed by John Gauden at the time of the Restoration (when he was seeking to obtain a bishopric, and was made Bishop of Worcester), but who was the actual author is still an open question.

> ... an incomparable picture of a stedfast prince, who acknowledges his weakness yet asserts the purity of his motives, the truth of his political and religious principles, the supremacy of his conscience. Such a dramatic presentment would not be above the ability of Gauden: and it is quite possible that he had before him, when he wrote, actual meditations, prayers and memoranda of the king, which perished when they had been copied and had found their place in the masterly mosaic.
> W. H. Hutton, in *Camb. Hist. of Eng. Lit*, vol. VII, ch, vi (1911)

**Eisell.** An old name for vinegar (acetic acid); through old Fr. from late Lat. *acetillum*, diminutive of *acetum*. Hamlet asks Laertes, *Woul't drink up eisell* – to show your love to the dead Ophelia? In the *Troy Book* of Lydgate we have the line 'Of *bitter* eysell and of eager (sour) wine'. And in Shakespeare's sonnets:

> I will drink
> Potions ef eysell, 'gainst my strong infection;
> No bitterness that I will bitter think,
> Nor double penance to correct correction
> Sonnet cxi

**Eisteddfod.** The meetings of the Welsh bards and others now held annually for the encouragement of Welsh literature and music. (Welsh, 'a sessions', from *eistedd*, to sit.)

**Ejusdem Farinae** (Lat.). Of the same kidney; *ejusdem generis*, of the same sort. The two phrases, indeed, mean the same thing.

**El Dorado** (Sp. the gilded). Originally, the name given to the supposed king of Manoa, the fabulous city of enormous wealth localised by the early explorers on the Amazon. He was said to be covered with oil and then powdered with gold-dust, an operation performed from time to time so that he was permanently, and literally, gilded. Many expeditions, both from Spain and England (two of which were led by Sir Walter Raleigh) tried to discover this king, and the name was later transferred to his supposed territory. Hence any extraordinarily rich region, or vast accumulation of gold, precious stones, or similar wealth.

> I do believe it is some jest; though faith!
> 'Tis mocking us somewhat too solemnly.
> I think his son has married the Infanta,
> Or found a mine of gold in El Dorado.
>
> Shelley, *The Cenci*, I, iii

> Pen began to fancy Eldorado was opening to him, and that his fortune was made from that day.
>
> Thackeray, *Pendennis*, vol. II, ch. iii

**Elagabalus.** A Syro-Phoenician sun-god, worshipped in Rome and represented under the form of a huge conical stone. The Roman emperor, originally Varius Avitus Bassanius (AD 205–22), son of a cousin of Caracalla but put forward as a son of Caracalla himself, was so called because in childhood he had been a priest of Elagabalus (or Heliogabalus). Of all the Roman emperors none exceeded him in debauchery: reigned about four years (AD 218–222), and was put to death by the praetorians. It is told of him that he invited the principal men of Rome to a banquet, and watched while they were being killed by being smothered in a shower of roses.

**Elaine.** The 'lily maid of Astotat' (*q.v.*), who in Tennyson's *Lancelot and Elaine* (*Idylls of the King*), in which he follows Malory (Bk xviii, ch. 9–20), loved Sir Lancelot 'with that love which was her doom'. Sir Lancelot's love was bestowed on the queen, and Elaine, realising the hopelessness of her situation, died. By her request her dead body was placed on a barge; a lily was in her right hand, and a letter avowing her love and showing the innocence of Lancelot in the left. An old servitor rowed, and when the barge stopped at the palace staith, King Arthur ordered the body to be brought in. The letter being read, Arthur directed that the maiden should be buried like a queen, with her sad story blazoned on her tomb. *See* Diamond jousts.

**Elberich.** The most famous dwarf of German romance. *See* Alberich.

**Elbow.** *See* Ell.

***A knight of the elbow.*** A gambler.

***At one's elbow.*** Close at hand.

***Elbow grease.*** Hard manual labour, especially rubbing and scrubbing. A humorous expression that was in use at least three hundred years ago. We say '*Elbow grease* is the best furniture oil.'

***Elbow room.*** Sufficient space for the work in hand.

***Out at elbows.*** Shabbily dressed, 'down at heel'; metaphorically, hackneyed, stale; thus, a play which has been acted too often is 'out at elbows', like a coat which is no longer presentable.

***To elbow one's way in.*** To push one's way through a crowd; to get a place by hook or crook.

***To elbow out; to be elbowed out.*** To supersede; to be ousted by a rival.

***To lift the elbow.*** To drink; usually said of a person who habitually takes rather more than is wise.

***Up to one's elbow.*** Very busy, full of work. Work piled up to one's elbows.

**Elden Hole.** ***Elden Hole needs filling.*** A reproof given to great braggarts. Elden Hole is a deep chasm in the Derbyshire Peak, long (though, of course, erroneously) reputed to be bottomless. *See* Scott's *Peveril of the Peak*, ch. iii.

**Elder Brethren.** *See* Trinity House.

**Elder tree.** A tree of evil associations in popular legend, and, according to mediaeval fable, that on which Judas Iscariot hanged himself, the mushroom-like excrescences on the bark still being known as *Judas's* (*or Jew's*) *ears. See also* Fig tree: Judas tree.

Sir John Maundeville, speaking (1364) of the Pool of Siloe, says, 'Fast by is the elder tree on which Judas hanged himself … when he sold and betrayed our Lord.' Shakespeare, in *Love's Labour's Lost*, 5, 2, says, 'Judas was hanged on an elder.'

> Judas he japed
> With Jewen silver,
> And sithen on an eller
> Hanged hymselve.
>
> *Vision of Piers Plowman*, Passus I

**Eleanor Crosses.** The crosses erected by Edward I to commemorate his queen, Eleanor, whose body was brought from Nottinghamshire to Westminster for burial. At each of the following places, where the body rested, a cross was set up: Lincoln, Newark, Grantham, Leicester, Stamford, Geddington, Northampton, Stony Stratford, Woburn, Dunstable, St Albans, Waltham, West Cheap (Cheapside) and Westminster. *See* Charing Cross.

**Eleatic Philosophy.** Founded by Xenophanes of Elea (about 530 BC), who in opposition to the current Greek system founded on polytheism and anthropomorphism, taught the unity and unchangeableness of the Divine. Through Parmenides and Zeno in the 5th century the school exercised great influence on Plato.

> The Homeric representations of the gods roused a protest on the part of the founder of the Eleatics, Xenophanes of Colophon, who says that 'Homer and Hesiod have imputed to the gods all that is blame and shame for men.'
>
> Sir John Sandys, *A History of Classical Scholarship*, vol. i, ch. ii

**Elecampane.** A composite plant (*Inula helenium*), the candied roots of which (like ginger) are used as a sweetmeat, and which was formerly fabled to have magical properties, such as curing wounds, conferring immortality, etc. Pliny tells us it sprang from Helen's tears.

> Here, take this essence of elecampane;
> Rise up, Sir George, and fight again.
>
> *Miracle Play of St George*

**Elector.** A prince who had a vote in the election of the Emperor of the Holy Roman Empire. In 1806 Napoleon broke up the old Empire, and the College of Electors was dissolved.

***The Great Elector.*** Frederick William of Brandenburg (1620–88).

**Electra.** One of the Pleiades (*q.v.*), wife of Dardanus. She is known as 'the Lost Pleiad', for it is said that she disappeared a little before the Trojan war, that she might be saved the mortification of seeing the ruin of her beloved city. She showed herself occasionally to mortal eye, but always in the guise of a comet. *See Od.*, v and *Il.*, xviii.

**Electricity** (Gr. *elektron*, amber). Thales (600 BC) observed that amber when rubbed attracted light substances, and this observation followed out has led to the present science of electricity.

> Bright amber shines on his electric throne.
>
> Darwin, *Economy of Nature*, i, 2

**Elegant Extracts.** The 85th Foot, remodelled in 1813 after the numerous court-martials which then occurred. The officers of the regiment were removed, and officers drafted from other regiments were substituted in their places. The 85th is now called the 'Second Battalion of the Shropshire Light Infantry'. The first battalion is the old 23rd.

At Cambridge, in the good old times, men who were too good to be plucked and not good enough for the poll, but who were yet allowed to pass, were nicknamed the *Elegant Extracts*. There was a similar limbo in the honour list, called the Gulf (*q.v.*), in allusion to the 'great gulf fixed'.

**Elegiacs.** Verse consisting of alternate hexameters (*q.v.*) and pentameters (*q.v.*), so called because it was the metre in which the elegies of the Greeks and Romans were usually written. In Latin it was commonly used by Ovid, Catullus, Tibullus, and others; the following is a good specimen of English elegiacs:

> Man with inviolate caverns, impregnable holds in his nature,
> Depths no storm can pierce, pierced with a shaft of the sun:
> Man that is galled with his confines, and burdened yet more with his vastness,
> Born too great for his ends, never at peace with his goal.
>
> Sir Wm Watson, *Hymn to the Sea* (1899)

**Elements.** In modern scientific parlance an *element* is a substance which resists analysis or splitting up into different substances; but in ancient and mediaeval philosophy it was one of the simple substances of which all things were held to be composed. Aristotle, following Empedocles of Sicily (*c.*450 BC ), taught that there were four, viz. fire, air, water, and earth; but later a fifth, the *quinta essentia*, or *quintessence*, which was supposed to be common to the four and to unify them, was added.

> Does not our life consist of the four elements?
>
> Shakespeare, *Twelfth Night*, 2, 3

> This theory of the five elements was the first chemical theory that had any force in it. We do not acknowledge the elements as such now; but we must be careful not to scorn them. *Our* elements may quite well become the joke of a future day.
>
> Edmunds and Hoblyn, *The Story of the Five Elements*, ch. i (1911)

***In one's element.*** In one's usual surroundings, within one's ordinary range of activity. The allusion is to the natural abode of any animals, as the air to birds, water to fish.

> Ferguson was in his element ... with the malevolent activity and dexterity of an evil spirit, he ran from outlaw to outlaw, chattered in every ear, and stirred up in every bosom savage animosities and wild desires.
>
> Macaulay, *History of England*, ch. v

***The elements.*** Atmospheric powers; the winds, storms, etc.

> Rumble thy bellyful! Spit, fire! spout, rain!
> Nor rain, wind, thunder, fire, are my daughters:
> I tax not you, you elements, with unkindness;
> I never gave you kingdom, call'd you children,
> You owe me no subscription: then, let fall
> Your horrible pleasure.
>
> Shakespeare, *King Lear*, 3, 2

**Elephant.** A symbol of temperance, eternity, and sovereignty.

***The Order of the Elephant*** is a Danish military order of knighthood, traditionally said to have been founded in 1189 in memory of a Danish soldier who slew one. Historically it dates from 1462; it was reconstituted in 1693, and is limited to princes of the blood and thirty knights. The badge is a white elephant carrying a tower and with a Hindu driver seated on its neck.

The elephant which, according to *Hindu mythology*, supports the world is called 'Muhapudma', and the tortoise which supports the elephant is called 'Chukwa'.

***King of the White Elephant.*** The proudest title borne by the old kings of Ava and Siam. In Ava the white elephant bore the title of 'lord', and had a minister of high rank to superintend his household. *Cp.* Fo-hi.

***Only an elephant can bear an elephant's load.*** An Indian proverb: Only a great man can do the work of a great man; also, the burden is more than I can bear; it is a load fit for an elephant.

***The land of the White Elephant.*** Siam.

***To have a white elephant to keep.*** To have an expensive and unprofitable dignity to support, or some possession the expense or responsibility of which is more than it is worth. The allusion is to the story of a King of Siam who used to make a present of a white elephant to courtiers whom he wished to ruin.

***Elephant Paper.*** A large-sized drawing-paper measuring 20 inches by 23. *Double Elephant* is a standard size of plate and drawing papers measuring 26¾ by 40 inches or printing paper 27 by 40 inches. *Long Elephant* is a term employed for paper hangings, 12 yards long, usually 22 inches wide. The name is probably from an ancient watermark.

**Elephant and Castle.** A public-house sign at Newington, said to derive its name from the skeleton of an elephant dug up near Battle Bridge in 1714. A flint-headed spear lay by the remains, whence it is conjectured that the creature was killed by the British in a fight with the Romans. Usually this public-house sign is intended to represent an elephant with a howdah. *Cp.* Pig and Tinderbox.

**Eleusinian Mysteries.** The religious rites in honour of Demeter or Ceres, performed originally at Eleusis, Attica, but later at Athens as part of the state religion. There were *Greater* and *Lesser Eleusinia*, the former being celebrated between harvest and seedtime and the latter in early spring. Little is known about the details, but the rites included sea bathing, processions, religious dramas, etc., and the initiated attained thereby a happy life beyond the grave.

**Eleven.** This is the A.S. *endlesfon*, from a Teutonic *ainlif*, the *ain-* representing 'one', and the suffix being cognate with the Lithuanian *-lika* (and probably with Lat. *linquere*, to leave, *liqui*, left) in *wenolika*, eleven, the meaning being that there is still one left to be counted after counting ten (the fingers of the two hands).

***At the eleventh hour.*** Just in time; from the parable in Matt. 20.

***The Eleven Thousand Virgins.*** *See* Ursula.

**Elf.** Originally a dwarfish being of *Teutonic mythology*, possessed of magical powers which it used either for the benefit or to the detriment of mankind. Later the name was restricted to a malignant kind of imp, and later still to those airy creatures that dance on the grass in the full moon, have fair golden hair, sweet musical voices, magic harps, etc.

Spenser relates (*Faërie Queene*, II, x, 70):

> How first Prometheus did create
> A man, of many partes from beasts derived ...
> That man so made he called Elfe, to weet
> Quick, the first authour of all Elfin kind.

He found a maid in the garden of Adonis, whom he called 'Fay', of 'whom all Fayres spring':

> Of these a mighty people shortly grew,
> And puissant kings, which all the world warrayd,
> And to themselves all nations did subdue.

Spenser's remark that *elf* means 'quick' is, of course, an invention; as also is the amusing one (mentioned with disapproval by Johnson, *s.v.* Goblin) that *Elf* and *Goblin* are derived from 'Guelf and Ghibelline'; the word is A.S. *oelf*, from Icel. *alfr*, and Teut. *alp*, a nightmare.

***Elf-arrows.*** Arrow-heads of the neolithic period are so called. At one time they were supposed to be shot by elves at people and cattle out of malice or revenge.

> There every herd by sad experience knows
> How, winged with fate, their elf-shot arrows fly,
> When the sick ewe her summer food forgoes,
> Or stretched on earth the heart-smit heifers lie.
> Collins, *Popular Superstitions*

***Elf-fire.*** The ignis-fatuus; also popularly called Will o' the Wisp, Jack o' lanthorn, Peg-a-lantern, or Kit o' the canstick (candlestick).

***Elf-locks.*** Tangled hair. It used to be said that one of the favourite amusements of Queen Mab was to tie people's hair in knots. When Edgar impersonates a madman, 'he elfs all his hair in knots'. (*Lear*, 2, 3.)

> This is that very Mab
> That plats the manes of horses in the night,
> And bakes the elf-locks in foul sluttish hairs.
> Shakespeare, *Romeo and Juliet*, 1, 4

***Elf-marked.*** Those born with a natural defect, according to the ancient Scottish superstition, are marked by the elves for mischief. Queen Margaret called Richard III:

> Thou elvish-marked, abortive, rooting hog!
> Shakespeare, *Richard III*, 1, 3

***Elf-shot.*** Afflicted with some unknown disease which was supposed to have been caused by an elf-arrow. The rinderpest would, in the Middle Ages, have been ascribed to elf-arrows (*q.v.*).

**Elgin Marbles.** A collection of ancient Greek bas-reliefs and statues made by Lord Elgin, and sent to England in 1812. They are chiefly fragments of the Parthenon at Athens. They were purchased by the Government for £35,000, and placed in the British Museum (1816).

**Elia.** A *nom de plume* adopted by Charles Lamb. (*Essays of Elia*.)

> The adoption of this signature was purely accidental. Lamb's first contribution to the *London Magazine* was a description of the old South-Sea House, where he had passed a few months' novitiate as a clerk … and remembering the name of a gay light-hearted foreigner, who fluttered there at the time, substituted his name for his own. Talfourd

**Eliab.** In Dryden's *Absalom and Achitophel*. (*q.v.*), is meant for Henry Bennet, Earl of Arlington. Eliab was one of the chiefs of the Gadites who joined David at Ziklag. (1 Chron. 12:9.)

> Hard the task to do Eliab right:
> Long with the royal wanderer [Charles II] he roved.
> And firm in all the turns of fortune proved.
> *Absalom and Achitophel*, Pt ii, 986

**Elidure.** A legendary king of Britain, who, according to some accounts, was advanced to the throne in place of his elder brother, Arthgallo (or Artegal), supposed by him to be dead. Arthgallo, after a long exile, returned to his country, and Elidure resigned to him the throne. Wordsworth has a poem on the subject (*Artegal and Elidure*); and Milton (*History of Britain*, Bk i) says that Elidure had 'a mind so noble, and so moderate, as is almost incredible to have been ever found'.

**Eligius, St.** *See* Eloy, St.

**Elijah's Melons.** Certain stones on Mount Carmel are so called.

> The story is that the owner of the land refused to supply the wants of the prophet, and consequently his melons were transformed into stones. Stanley, *Sinai and Palestine*

**Eliott's Tailors.** The 15th (King's) Hussars. In 1759 Lieutenant-Colonel Eliott enlisted a large number of tailors on strike into a cavalry regiment modelled after the Prussian hussars. This regiment so highly distinguished themselves, that George III granted them the honour of being called 'the King's'.

**Elissa.** Step-sister of Medina and Perissa, and mistress of Hudibras in Spenser's *Faërie Queene* (II, ii). She typifies moral deficiency and moroseness; she

> evermore did seeme
> As discontent for want of merth or meat;
> No solace could her Paramour intreat
> Her once to show, ne court nor dalliance,
> But with bent lowring browes, as she would threat,
> She scould, and frownd with froward countenance,
> Unworthy of faire ladies comely governance.
> *Faërie Queene*, II, ii, 35

By Virgil, Ovid, etc., Dido, Queen of Carthage, was sometimes called 'Elissa'.

**Elivagar.** In *Scandinavian mythology*, a cold venomous stream which issued from Niflheim, in the abyss called the Ginnunga Gap, and hardened into layer upon layer of ice. *See* Hvelgelmir.

**Elixir of Life.** The supposed potion of the alchemists that would prolong life indefinitely. It was imagined sometimes as a dry drug, sometimes as a fluid. *Elixir* (Arabic, a powder for sprinkling on wounds) also meant among alchemists the philosopher's stone, the tincture for transmuting metals, etc., and the name is now given to any sovereign remedy for disease – especially one of a 'quack' character.

**Elizabeth.** The name is originally Hebrew and means 'the oath of God', i.e. the oath in memory of the covenant made with Abraham. Among its large number of variants are: Eliza, Elsie, Elsabin (Scandinavian), Elspeth, Lizzy, Elisabet, Elisabetta, Elisavetta, Elise, Isabel, Isabeau, Isa, Lescinska (Russian), Betty, Betsy, Bettina, Bess, Bessy, Beth, etc.

***St Elizabeth of Hungary.*** Patron saint of queens, being herself a queen. She died in 1231 at the age of 24, and her day is November 19th. For the story of the conversion of flowers into bread, *see* Melon.

**Elizabethan.** After the style of things in the reign of Queen Elizabeth (1558–1603). Elizabethan architecture is a mixture of Gothic and Italian, prevalent in the reigns of Elizabeth and James I, and when referring to literature *Elizabethan* is generally held to include the writers of the time of James I; while by *Elizabethan Drama* is meant the drama of the period from the accession of Queen Elizabeth until the closing of the theatres in 1642.

**Ell.** An old measure of length which, like *foot*, was taken from a part of the body, viz. the forearm. The word (A.S. *eln*) is from a Teutonic word *alina*, the forearm to the tip of the middle finger, which also gives *elbow* (*q.v.*) and is cognate with Lat. *ulna*. The ell was of various lengths. The English ell was 45 inches, the Scotch ell only 37 inches, while the Flemish ell was three-quarters of a yard, and a French ell a yard and a half.

***Give him an inch, and he'll take an ell.*** Give him a little licence, and he will take great liberties, or make great encroachments.

***The King's Ell-wand.*** The group of stars called 'Orion's Belt'.

> The King's Ellwand, now foolishly termed the 'Belt of Orion'. Hogg, *Tales*

**Ella,** or **Alla.** King of Northumberland, who married Cunstance (*q.v.*), in Chaucer's *Man of Lawes Tale.*

**Ellyllon.** The name given by the ancient Welsh bards to the souls of the Druids, which, being too good for hell, and not good enough for heaven, wander upon earth till the judgment day, whenthey will be admitted to a higher state of being.

**Elmo.** *See* St Elmo.

**Elohim.** The plural form of the Heb. *eloah*, God, sometimes used to denote heathen gods collectively (Chemosh, Dagon, Baal, etc.), but more frequently used as a singular denoting one god, or God Himself. In 1 Sam. 28:13, where the witch of Endor tells Saul 'I saw gods (Heb. *elohim*) ascending out of the earth', this is an exceptional use of the word, and would seem to imply spirits of the departed, rather than gods. *See next article.*

**Elohistic and Jehovistic Scriptures.** *Elohim* and *Jehovah* (*Jahveh* or *Yahvé*) are two of the most usual of the many names given by the ancient Hebrews to the Deity, and the fact that they are both used with interchangeable senses in the Pentateuch gave rise to the theory, widely held by Hebraists and biblical critics, that these books were written at two widely different periods; the Elohistic paragraphs, being more simple, more primitive, more narrative, and more pastoral, being held to be the older; while the later Jehovistic paragraphs, which indicate a knowledge of geography and history, seem to exalt the priestly office, and are altogether of a more elaborate character, were subsequently enwoven with these. This theory was originally stated by Jean Astruc, the French scholar, in his *Conjectures sur les mémoires originaux, dont il paroit que Moyse s'est servi pour composer le livre de la Genèse* (1753), a book which formed the starting-point of all modern criticism of the Pentateuch.

**Eloi, St,** or **St Eligius.** Patron saint of artists and smiths. He was a famous worker in gold and silver, and was made Bishop of Noyon in the reign of Dagobert (6th century). His day is December 1st.

**Eloquent.** ***The old man eloquent*** Isocrates (436–338 BC), the Greek orator. When he heard that Grecian liberty was extinguished by the battle of Chaeronea, he died of grief.

> That dishonest victory
> At Chaeronea, fatal to liberty,
> Killed with report that old man eloquent.
> Milton, *Sonnets* (*To Lady Margaret Ley*)

***The eloquent doctor.*** Peter Aureolus (14th century), Archbishop of Aix, a schoolman.

**Elvidnir.** The hall of the goddess Hel (*q.v.*).

**Elysium.** The abode of the blessed in *Greek mythology*; hence *the Elysian Fields*, the Paradise or Happy Land of the Greek poets. *Elysian* means happy, delightful.

> O'er which were shadowy cast Elysian gleams.
> Thomson, *Castle of Indolence*, i, 44

> Would take the prisoned soul,
> And lap it in Elysium.
> Milton, *Comus*, 261–2

**Elzevir.** An edition of a classic author, published and printed by the family of Elzevir over the period from 1583 to about 1710. Some Elzevirs are highly prized by book collectors; they were long held to be immaculate, but the Virgil, one of the masterpieces, is certainly incorrect in some places.

**Em.** The unit of measure in printing. The standard is a pica em, and the width of a line is measured by the number of m's laid on their sides thus – ⩦ ⩦ ⩦ – that would equal the measure required. This dictionary is in double columns; each column equals 11½ pica ems in width, and one em is allowed for the space between. A system was introduced some years ago from the USA the unit of which is a 'point' equal to one-seventy-second of an inch, all letters, spaces, rules, etc., are multiples of this 'point', and the system is known as the 'point system'. Pica is 12 point. The point system is gradually superseding the older method.

**Embargo.** *To lay an embargo on him* or *it* is to impose certain conditions before you give your consent. It is from a Spanish word meaning an order issued by authority to prevent ships leaving port for a fixed period.

**Embarras de Richesse** (Fr.). A perplexing amount of wealth, or too great an abundance of anything; more matter than can conveniently be employed. The phrase was used as the title of a play by the Abbé d'Allainval (1753).

**Ember Days.** The Wednesday, Friday, and Saturday of the four *Ember Weeks*, which were fixed by the Council of Placentia (1095), as those containing the first Sunday in Lent, Whit Sunday, Holy Cross Day (September 14th), and St Lucia's Day (December 13th). The name is the M.E. *ymber*, from A.S. *ymbren* (i.e. *ymb*, about, *ryne*, running), a period or revolution.

**Ember Goose.** The northern diver or loon; called in Norway *imbre*, because it appears on the coast about the time of the Ember days in Advent. The German name of the bird is *Adventsvogel*.

**Emblem.** A symbolical figure: a picture with a hidden meaning which is 'cast into' (Gr. *em*, in, *ballein*, to cast) the visible device. Thus, a *balance* is an emblem of justice, *white* of purity, a *sceptre* of sovereignty.

Some of the most common and simple emblems of the Christian Church are:

***A chalice.*** The eucharist.

***The circle inscribed in an equilateral triangle.*** To denote the co-equality and co-eternity of the Trinity.

***A cross.*** The Christian's life and conflict; the death of Christ for man's redemption.

***A crown.*** The reward of the perseverance of the saints.

***A dove.*** The Holy Ghost.

***A hand from the clouds.*** To denote God the Father.

***A lamb, fish, pelican,*** etc. etc. The Lord Jesus Christ.

***A phoenix.*** The resurrection.

**Emblematical Poems.** Poems consisting of lines of different lengths so that when printed or written the outline of the poem on the page can be made to represent the object of the verse. Thus, George Herbert in the *Temple* prints a poem on the *Altar* that is shaped like an altar, and one on *Easter Wings* like wings. Puttenham in his *Arte of English Poesie* (1589) gives a chapter on this form of word-torture (which he calls 'Proportion in Figure'), giving examples of eggs, crosses, pillars, pyramids, etc., and it was gibbeted by Ben Jonson, Dryden, Addison, and others.

> As for altars and pyramids in poetry, he has outdone all men that way; for he has made a gridiron and a frying-pan in verse, that besides the likeness in shape, the very tone and sound of the words did perfectly represent the noise that is made by these utensils.
>
> Samuel Butler, *Character of a Small Poet*

**Emelye.** The sister-in-law of 'Duke Theseus', beloved by the two knights, Palamon and Arcyte, the former of whom had her to wife. It is of this lady the poet says, 'Up roos the sun, and up roos Emelye' (v. 1415).

> This passeth yeer by yeer, and day and day,
> Til it fil ones, in a morwe of May,
> That Emelye, that fairer was to sene
> Than is the lilie upon his stalke grene,
> And fressher than the May with floures newe.
> Er it were day, as was hir wone to do,
> She was arisen, and al redy dight;
> For May wol have no slogardye a-night.
>
> Chaucer, *Canterbury Tales*, *The Knighte's Tale*, 175

**Emerald.** According to Eastern tradition, if a serpent fixes its eyes upon an emerald it becomes blind (Ahmed ben Abdalaziz, *Treatise on Jewels*). Other properties were also given to it, and in *The Lover's Complaint* (usually printed as though by Shakespeare) the author speaks of:

> The deep-green emerald, in whose fresh regard
> Weak sights their sickly radiance do amend.

***The Emerald Isle.*** Ireland. This term was first used by Dr Drennan (1754–1820), in the poem called *Erin*. Of course, it refers to the bright green verdure of the island.

> Nor one feeling of vengeance presume to defile
> The cause or the men of the Emerald Isle.
>
> E. J. Drennan, *Erin*

**Emergency.** ***A sudden emergency*** is something which starts suddenly into view, or which rises suddenly out of the current of events. (Lat. *e-mergo*, to rise out of 'the water'.)

***Emergency man.*** One engaged for some special service.

***Emergency ration.*** A ration of food served out to soldiers on active service to be used only in a great emergency, when ordinary rations are unobtainable. As they are enclosed in a sealed metal case they are known also as *iron rations*; so *to be on iron rations* is a metaphor for being at one's last resource.

**Emeute** (Fr.). A seditious rising or small riot. Literally, a moving-out (Lat. *e-moveo*).

**Emilie.** The 'divine Emilie', to whom Voltaire wrote verses, was the Marquise du Châtelet, with whom he lived at Cirey for some ten years, between 1735 and 1749.

**Emmet** contracted into *Ant*: thus, *Em't*, *ent*, *ant* (A.S., *oemete*).

> A bracelet made of emmets' eyes.
>
> Drayton, *Court of Fairies*

**Emne.** An early variant of the adjective *even*, as in *your emne Christen*, i.e. your even or fellow Christian. Shakespeare (*Hamlet*, 5, 1) makes the Clown speak of 'your even Christian'.

**Emolument.** Literally, that which is ground out (Lat. emolere); originally perhaps the profit accruing to the miller, or the toll on what was ground. *Cp.* Grist to the Mill.

**Empedocles.** A Greek philosopher, poet, and statesman (about 500–430 BC), a disciple of Pythagoras. According to Lucian, he cast himself into the crater of Etna, that persons might suppose he was returned to the gods; but Etna threw out his sandal, and destroyed the illusion. (Horace, *Ars Poetica*, 404.)

> He who, to be deemed
> A god, leaped fondly into Aetna flames,
> Empedocles. Milton, *Paradise Lost*, iii, 471

Matthew Arnold published (1853) a classical drama with the title *Empedocles on Etna*.

**Emperor.** A standard size of drawing paper measuring 48 by 72 inches. This is the largest sheet made by hand.

***Emperor, not for myself, but for my people.*** The maxim of Hadrian, the Roman emperor (117–138).

***The Emperor of Believers.*** Omar I (581–644), father-in-law of Mahomet, and second caliph of the Mussulmans.

**Empire City, The.** New York, the great commercial city of the United States; and New York State, on account of its leading position in wealth, population, etc., is called the *Empire State*.

**Empirics.** An ancient Greek school of medicine founded by Serapion of Alexandria, who contended that it is not necessary to obtain a knowledge of the nature and functions of the body in order to treat diseases, but that experience is the surest and best guide (Gr. *empeiros*, experienced, from *peira*, trial). They were opposed to the Dogmatic School founded by Hippocrates, which made certain dogmas or theoretical principles the basis of practice. Hence any quack or pretender to medical skill is called an *empiric*.

> We must not
> So stain our judgment, or corrupt our hope,
> To prostitute our past-cure malady
> To empirics.
>
> Shakespeare, *All's Well That Ends Well*, 2, 1

**Employé** (Fr.). One employed by another, such as clerks, shopmen, servants, etc. Employée, a female employé. The word is now often written employee, which form is used for either sex.

**Empty Champagne Bottles.** Fellow commoners (*q.v.*) at Cambridge used to be so called, their academical dress being a gaudy purple and silver gown, resembling the silver foil round the neck of a champagne bottle. Very few of these wealthy magnates took honours.

**Empyrean.** According to Ptolemy, there are five heavens, the last of which is pure elemental fire and the seat of deity; this fifth heaven is called the empyrean (Gr. *empuros*, fiery); hence, in *Christian angelology*, the abode of God and the angels. *See* Heaven.

> Now had the Almighty Father from above.
> From the pure empyrean where He sits
> High throned above all height, bent down his eye.
>
> Milton, *Paradise Lost*, iii, 56

**En bloc** (Fr.). The whole lot together; *en masse*.

**En evidence** (Fr.). To the fore.

> Mr — has been much *en evidence* of late in the lobby; but as he has no seat, his chance of being in the ministry is very problematical.
>
> Newspaper paragraph

**En garçon** (Fr.). As a bachelor. 'To take me *en garçon*', without ceremony, as a bachelor fares in ordinary life.

**En grande toilette; en grande tenue** (Fr.). In full dress; popularly, in the height of fashion.

**En masse** (Fr.). The whole lot just as it stands; the whole.

**En papillotes** (Fr.). In a state of undress; literally, in curl-papers. Cutlets with frills on them are *en papillotes*.

**En famille** (Fr.). In the privacy of one's own home. 'Living *en famille*' is keeping oneself pretty much to oneself, not going out or paying calls to any great extent.

**En passant** (Fr.). By the way. A remark made *en passant* is one dropped in, almost an aside.

**En pension** (Fr.). *Pension* is payment for board and lodging; hence, a boarding-house. 'To live *en pension*' is to live at a boarding-house or at an hotel, etc., for a charge that includes board and lodging.

**En rapport** (Fr.). In harmony with; in sympathetic lines with.

**En route**. On the way; on the road or journey.

**Enceladus.** The most powerful of the hundred-armed giants, sons of Tartarus and Ge, who conspired against Zeus (Jupiter). The king of gods and men cast him down at Phlegra, in Macedonia, and threw Mount Etna over him. The poets say that the flames of the volcano arise from the breath of this giant.

> So fierce Enceladus in Phlegra stood.
>
> Hoole, *Jerusalem Delivered*

> I tell you, younglings, not Encelados,
> With all his threat'ning band of Typhon's brood,
> Shall seize this prey out of his father's hands.
>
> Shakespeare, *Titus Andronicus*, 4, 2

**Encomium.** From a Greek word meaning a eulogy or panegyric in honour of a victor in the Bacchic games; hence, praise, eulogy, especially of a formal nature. The encomium was sung in the procession which marched from *komi* to *kome*, i. e. village to village.

**Encore.** A good example of 'English French' (*q.v.*); our use of this word is unknown to the French, who say *bis* (twice) if they wish a thing to be repeated. *Encore un tasse* is 'another cup', *encore une fois* 'still once more'.

**Encratites.** A Gnostic and ascetical sect of the 2nd century, which condemned marriage, forbade eating flesh or drinking wine, and rejected all the luxuries and comforts of life as 'things sinful'. Saturninus and Marcion were the first leaders, and the sect was carried on by one, Tatian, in the 3rd century, who must not be confounded with Tatian the philosopher, a disciple of Justin Martyr, who lived in the 2nd century. The name is Greek, and signifies 'the self-disciplined' or 'continent'.

**Encroach.** Literally, to put on a hook, to 'hook', a little here and a little there. (Fr. *en croc*, on a hook.)

**End. *A rope's end.*** A short length of rope bound at the end with thread, and used for punishing the refractory.

***A shoemaker's end.*** A length of thread pointed with a bristle, and used by shoemakers.

***At a loose end.*** *See* Loose.

***At my wits' end.*** At a standstill how to proceed farther; at a non-plus.

***East End.*** *See* West End *below*.

***End it or mend it.*** Said when an *impasse* or a crisis is reached, when things are unbearable and something simply must be done.

***He is no end of a fellow.*** A capital chap; a most agreeable companion; perhaps an 'all round' man, who, naturally, has 'no end'.

***Odds and ends.*** Fragments, remnants, odd ends of miscellaneous articles; bits and pieces of trifling value.

***On end.*** Erect; also, in succession, without a break, as 'he'll go on talking for days on end'.

***One's latter end.*** The close of one's life.

> So the Lord blessed the latter end of Job more than his beginning. Job 42:12

***At the latter end,*** towards the close.

> At the latter end of a dinner.
>
> Shakespeare, *All's Well*, etc., 2, 5

***The end justifies the means.*** A casuistical motto, implying that it doesn't matter what steps you take to effect your purpose, or what suffering you cause to others, so long as the purpose is a good and desirable one in itself; that you may (if, indeed, such a thing is possible) 'do evil that good may come'.

> The End must justifie the means:
> He only Sins who Ill intends:
> Since therefore 'tis to Combat Evil;
> 'Tis lawful to employ the Devil.
>
> Prior, *Hans Carvel*

***The ends of the earth.*** The remotest parts of the earth, the regions farthest from civilisation.

***To be one's end.*** The cause or agent of his death.

> This apoplexie will be his end.
>
> Shakespeare, *2 Henry IV*, 4, 4

***To begin at the wrong end.*** To attempt to do something unmethodically. The allusion may be to thread wound on a card or bobbin; if anyone attempts to unwind it at the wrong end, he will entangle the thread and be unable to unwind it.

***To burn the candle at both ends.*** *See* Burn.

***To come to the end of one's tether.*** *See* Tether.

***To go off the deep end.*** To get unnecessarily excited; to run mildly amok for a while. Non-swimmers who go off the deep end at a swimming bath are 'out of their depth' at once and flounder about aimlessly and excitedly without doing any good.

***To have it at my finger's end.*** *See* Finger.

***To make two*** or ***both ends meet.*** To make one's income cover expenses; to keep out of debt. The allusion is to the effort needed in joining the ends of a tight belt or strap. The French say *joindre les deux bouts*.

***To put an end to.*** To terminate or cause to terminate.

***To the bitter end.*** *See* Bitter.

***West End, East End.*** The quarter or part of a town west or east of the central part. In London, and many other large towns, the West End is the fashionable quarter and the East End the part where the working-class population lives; hence *West-end style* means the style of the moneyed classes, and *an East-ender* is a rough, poorly dressed member of the proletariat.

**End of the World, The.** According to rabbinical legend, the world is to last six thousand years. The reasons assigned are (1) because the name *Yahweh* contains six letters; (2) because the Hebrew letter *m* occurs six times in the book of Genesis; (3) because the patriarch Enoch, who was taken to heaven without dying, was the sixth generation from Adam (Seth, Enos, Cainan, Mahalaleel, Jared, Enoch); (4) because God created the world in six days; (5) because six contains three binaries – the first 2000 years were for the law of nature, the next 2000 years the written law, and the last 2000 the law of grace.

> Seven would suit this fancy quite as well: there are seven days in a week; Jehovah contains seven letters; and Enoch was the seventh generation of the race of man; and the first two binaries were not equal periods.

**End-irons.** Two movable iron cheeks or plates, still used in cooking-stoves to enlarge or contract the grate at pleasure. The term explains itself, but must not be mistaken for *andirons* or 'dogs'.

**End Paper.** The blank fly-leaves of a book.

**End-stopped.** A term used in prosody denoting that the sense of the line to which it is applied is completed with the line and does not run over to the next; the opposite of *enjambment*. In the following lines the first is an example of enjambment, and the second is end-stopped:

> Awake, my St John, leave all meaner things
> To low ambition, and the pride of kings.
>
> Pope, *Essay on Man*, i, 1

**Endemic.** Pertaining to a locality. An endemic disease is one common to a particular district, from which it shows no tendency to spread. Thus intermittent fevers are endemic in marshy places.

**Endorse.** ***I endorse that statement.*** I accept it; I fully accord with it. The allusion is to the commercial practice of writing your name on the back of a bill of exchange or promissory note if you choose to make yourself responsible for it. (Lat., *in-dorsum*, on the back.)

**Endymion.** In *Greek mythology*, a beautiful youth, sometimes said to be a king and sometimes a shepherd, who, as he slept on Mount Latmus, so moved the cold heart of Selene, the Moon goddess, that she came down and kissed him and lay at his side. He woke to find her gone, but the dreams which she gave him were so strong and enthralling that he begged Zeus to give him immortality and allow him to sleep perpetually on Mount Latmus. Other accounts say that Selene herself bound him by enchantment so that she might come and kiss him whenever she liked. Keats used the story as the framework of his long allegory, *Endymion* (1817), and it forms the basis of Lyly's comedy, *Endimion, the Man in the Moone* (1585).

> The moon sleeps with Endymion,
> And would not be awaked.
>
> Shakespeare, *Merchant of Venice*, 5, 1

**Enemy.** ***How goes the enemy?*** or ***What says the enemy?*** What o'clock is it? Time is the enemy of man, especially of those who are behind time.

**Enfant Terrible** (Fr.). Literally, a terrible child. A precocious child; one who says or does awkward things at inconvenient times and 'gives his elders away'. The phrase is used also of young members of assemblies – such as the House of Commons – who have the knack of making themselves a regular nuisance.

**Enfilade** (Fr.) means literally to spin out; to put thread in (a needle), as *enfiler une aiguille*; to string beads by putting them on a thread, as *en filer des perles*. Bullets being compared to thread, we get the meaning to fire them through opposing ranks as thread through a needle; hence, to scour or rake with shot from the flank.

**England.** The name, of course, comes from the *Angles* (land of the Angles), who migrated from the east of the Elbe to Schleswig (between the

Jutes and the Saxons), and passed over in great numbers to Britain during the 5th century, but Verstegan (1605) quaintly says that Egbert was 'chiefly moved' to call his kingdom England 'in respect of Pope Gregory's changing the name of *Engelisce* into *Angellyke*'. And this 'may have moved our kings upon their best gold coins to set the image of an angel'. (*Restitution of Decayed Intelligence in Antiquities concerning ... the English Nation*, p. 147.)

**England's Darling.** A name given to Hereward the Wake (fl. 1070), the patriot who held the Isle of Ely against William the Conqueror. After a blockade of three months, Hereward and some of his followers escaped.

**Englander.** A name applied, now only humorously or somewhat contemptuously, by foreigners to Englishmen.

***Little Englander.*** One who would rather see England small, contented, and as self contained as possible than have her the head of a worldwide Empire, the possession of which might be a source of trouble and danger to her; the opposite to an Imperialist. The term came into prominence at the time of the South African War of 1899–1902.

**English.** The language of the people of England; also the people themselves. *Middle English* is the language as used from about 1150 to 1500; *Old English*, also called somewhat incorrectly *Anglo-Saxon*, is that in use before 1150.

In typography, *English* is a large size of type, two points (i.e. one-thirty-sixth of an inch) larger than pica and four points smaller than great primer.

***Borough English.*** *See* Borough.

***English French.*** A kind of perversity seems to pervade many of the words which we have borrowed from the French. Thus, our *curate* is the Fr. *vicaire*, and our *vicar* the Fr. *curé*.

*Encore* (Fr. *bis*).

Epergne (Fr. *surtout*); Surtout (Fr. *pardessus*).

Screw (Fr. *vis*), whereas the French *écrou* we call a *nut*; and our *vice* is *étau* in French.

Some still say *à l'outrànce* (Fr. *à outrance*).

We say *double entendre*, the French *à deux ententes*.

***Plain English.*** Plain, unmistakable terms. To tell a person *in plain English* what you think of him is to give him your very candid opinion without any beating about the bush.

***The King's*** (or ***Queen's***) ***English.*** English as it should be spoken; pure, grammatical, or 'correct' English. The term is found in Shakespeare (*Merry Wives*, 1, 4), but it is older, and was evidently common.

> These fine English clerkes wil saih thei speake in their mother tonge, if a manne should charge them for counterfeityng the Kinges Englishe.
>
> Wilson, *Arte of Rhetoricke* (1553)

***Queene's English*** occurs in Nash's *Strange Newes of the Intercepting Certaine Letters* (1593), and 'thou clipst the Kinge's English' in Dekker's *Satiromastix* (1602). Dean Alford's book *A Plea for the Queen's English* (1864) may have helped to popularise the phrase.

**Englishman.** The national nickname of an Englishman is 'John Bull' (*q.v.*). The old French nickname for an Englishman was 'Goddam'.

***An Englishman's house is his castle.*** Because so long as a man shuts himself up in his own house, no bailiff can break through the door to arrest him or seize his goods. In the third of his *Institutes* Sir Edward Coke (d.1634) says:

> A man's house is his castle, *et domus sua cuique tutissimum refugium.*

And, again, in his report on Semayne's case:

> The house of everyone is to him as his castle and fortress, as well for his defence against injury and violence as for his repose.

**Enid.** Only child of Yniol, and wife of Geraint, in Tennyson's *Marriage of Geraint* and *Geraint and Enid* (*Idylls of the King*). The stories are from the Welsh *Mabinogion*.

**Enjambment.** *See* End-stopped.

**Enlightened Doctor, The.** Raymond Lully of Palma (about 1234–1315), a Spaniard, and one of the most distinguished of the 13th century scholastic philosophers.

**Enniskillens.** The 6th Dragoons; instituted 1689, on account of their brave defence of the town of Enniskillen, in favour of William III.

This cavalry regiment must not be confounded with the Inniskillings or Old 27th Foot, now called the '1st battalion of the Royal Inniskilling Fusiliers', which is a foot regiment.

**Ennius.** The earliest of the great epic poets of Rome (about 239–169 BC), and chief founder of Latin literature.

***The English Ennius.*** Layamon (fl. about 1200), who made a late AngloSaxon paraphrase of Wace's *Roman de Brut*, has been so called, but the title is usually given to Chaucer.

> If Langland may be regarded in some respects as the Naevius of English poetry, Chaucer is certainly its Ennius ... inasmuch as he was the

first to impose on the early incivility of the English tongue the rules of harmony and proportion.

W. J. Courthope, *History of English Poetry*, vol .I, ch. vii

***The French Ennius.*** Guillaume de Lorris (about 1235–65), author of the *Romance of the Rose*. Sometimes Jehan de Meung (about 1260–1318), who wrote a continuation of the romance, is so called.

***The Spanish Ennius.*** Juan de Mena (d.1456), born at Cordova.

**Enough!** Enough! Stop now, you have said all that is needful; short for 'enough said!' which is often contracted to ' 'nuff said!'

***Enough is as good as a feast.*** A sufficiency is as good for the purpose as an excess.

**Enow.** The representative of the inflexional plural of the A.S. adjective *genogh* (mod. *enough*), and still called by Johnson in his Dictionary (1755) 'the plural of enough'. It was used for numbers reckoned by tale, as: There are chairs enow, nails enow, men enow, etc.; but now *enough* does duty for both words, and *enow* is archaic.

**Ensconce.** To hide; to put under cover. Literally, to place in a *sconce*, or fort. (Ger. *schanze*, a fort; Dan. *skandse*; Swed. *skans*; Lat. *abscondo*, to hide.)

**Ensigns.**

***America.*** The Stars and Stripes.

***The British Navy.*** The Union Jack (*q.v.*). The *white* ensign (Royal Navy) is the banner of St George with the Jack cantoned in the first quarter; the *red* ensign is that of the merchant service; the *blue*, that of the Navy reserve.

**Entail.** An estate in which the rights of the owner are *cut down* (Fr. *tailler*, to cut) by his being deprived of the power of alienating them and so barring the rights of his issue.

***To cut off the entail*** is to put an end to the limitation of an inheritance to a particular line or class of heirs.

**Entelechy** (Gr. *telos*, perfection). Aristotle's term for the complete realisation or full expression of a function or potentiality; the result of the union of Matter (*potentiality*) and Form (*reality*); e.g. the soul, considered as an end that is attained, is the Entelechy of the body.

> You can never get at the final entelechy which differentiates Shelley and Shakespeare from the average versifier, Cluvienus and myself from Pater or from Browne. Saintsbury, *Hist. of English Prose Rhythm*, Preface (1912)

In Rabelais' *Pantagruel* (Bk V, ch. xix), *intelechy* is the name given to the kingdom of the Lady Quintessence. The argument on the name, whether it is *entelechy* (perfecting and coming into actuality) or *endelechy* (duration) reflects the fierce disputes that took place among the mediaeval schoolmen on these two words.

**Entente cordiale** (Fr.). A cordial understanding between nations; not quite amounting to an alliance, but something more than a *rapprochement*. The term is not new, but is now usually applied to the *entente* between England and France that was arranged largely by the personal endeavours of Edward VII in 1906.

> If Guizot remains in office Normanby must be recalled, as the only chance of a renewal of the entente cordiale.
>
> *Greville's Diary*, p. 189 (1847)

**Enthusiast.** Literally, one who is possessed or inspired by a God (Gr. *en theos*). *Inspired* is very similar, being the Lat. *in spirare*, to breathe in (the god-like essence).

**Entire.** Ale, in contradistinction to 'cooper', which is half ale and half porter. As Calvert's entire, etc.

**Entre nous** (Fr.). Between you and me; in confidence.

> As for Pa, what d'ye think? – Mind it's all *entrenous*
> But you know, love, I never keep secrets from you–
> Why, he's writing a book!
>
> Moore, *The Fudge Family in Paris*, I

**Entrée.** ***To have the entrée.*** To be eligible for invitations to State balls and concerts.

**Entremets** (Fr.). Sweet foods or kickshaws served at table between the main dishes, courses, or removes; literally, things put between. *Entrées* are meat dishes of a minor kind.

**Eolian Harp.** *See* Aeolian.

**Eolithic Age, The.** The name given by palaeontologists to the earliest part of the Stone Age (Gr. *eos*, dawn, *lithos*, a stone), which is characterised by the rudest stone implements. These *eoliths* are found abundantly in parts of the North Downs, but many archaeologists refuse to accept them as the work of man.

**Eolus.** *See* Aeolus.

**Eon.** *See* Aeon.

**Epact** (Gr. *epagein*, to intercalate). The excess of the solar over the lunar year, the former consisting of 365 days, and the latter of 354, or eleven days fewer. The epact of any year is the number of days from the last new moon of the old year to the 1st of the following January.

**Ephebi.** Youths between the age of eighteen and twenty were so called at Athens. During this period they were trained to military duties, were maintained at the public cost, and wore a uniform. In later times entrance into this class became voluntary, and by the 2nd century BC courses in literature, rhetoric, and philosophy had replaced the military duties and instruction.

**Ephesian.** A jolly companion; a roysterer. The origin of the term is unknown. *Cp.* Corinthian, which Shakespeare used in much the same way.

> It is thine host, thine Ephesian, calls.
>
> Shakespeare, *Merry Wives of Windsor*, 4, 5

***Diana of the Ephesians.*** *See* Diana.

***The Ephesian poet.*** Hipponax, born at Ephesus in the 6th century BC

**Ephialtes.** A giant, brother of Otus (*q.v.*), who was deprived of his right eye by Apollo, and of his right eye by Hercules. The Greek word is from a verb meaning 'to leap upon' and it used to be given to the supposed demon which caused nightmares.

> [We refer unto sober examination] what natural effects can reasonably be expected, when to prevent the Ephialtes or night-Mare we hang up an hollow stone in our stables, when for amulets against Agues we use the chips of Gallows and places of execution.
>
> Sir Thos Browne, *Pseudodoxia Epidemica*, V, xxiii

> The night-hag, whom the learned call Ephialtes.
>
> Scott, *The Antiquary*, ch. x

**Ephors.** Spartan magistrates, five in number, annually elected from the ruling caste. They exercised control even over the kings and senate.

**Epic.** A poem of dramatic character dealing by means of narration with the history, real or fictitious, of some notable action or series of actions carried out under heroic or supernatural guidance. Epic poetry may be divided into two main classes: (*a*) the popular or national epic, including such works as the Greek *Iliad* and *Odyssey*, the Sanscrit *Mahabharata*, and the Teutonic *Niebelungenlied*; and (*b*) the literary or artificial epic, of which the *Aeneid*, Ariosto's *Orlando Furioso*, Tasso's *Gerusalemme Liberata*, and Milton's *Paradise Lost* are examples.

***Father of Epic Poetry.*** Homer.

**Epicurus.** The Greek philosopher (about 340–270 BC) who founded the Epicurean school. His axiom was that 'happiness or enjoyment is the *summum bonum* of life'. His disciples corrupted his doctrine into 'Good living is the object we should all seek', or, according to the drinking song, 'Who leads a good life is sure to live well'.

> Blest be the day, I 'scaped the wrangling crew,
> From Pyrrho's maze and Epicurus sty.
>
> Beattie, *Minstrel*

Hence, *epicure*, one devoted to sensual pleasures, especially those of the table; *epicurean*, pertaining to good eating and drinking, etc.

> Epicurean cooks
> Sharpen with cloyless sauce his appetite.
>
> Shakespeare, *Antony and Cleopatra*, 2, 1

**Epigoni.** *See* Thebes (*The Seven against Thebes*).

**Epimenides.** A Cretan poet and philosopher of the 7th century BC who, according to Pliny (*Natural History*), fell asleep in a cave when a boy, and did not wake for fifty-seven years, when he found himself endowed with miraculous wisdom. *Cp.* Rip Van Winkle.

> Like Epimenides, I have been sleeping in a cave: and, waking, see those whom I left children are bearded men.
>
> Lord Lytton

**Epiphany** (Gr. *epiphaneia*, an appearance, manifestation). The time of appearance, meaning the period when the star appeared to the wise men of the East. January 6th is the Feast of the Epiphany in commemoration of this.

**Episode** (Gr. coming in besides – i.e. adventitious). Originally, the parts in dialogue which were interpolated between the choric songs in Greek tragedy; hence, an adventitious tale introduced into the main story that can be naturally connected with the framework but which has not necessarily anything to do with it.

In music, an intermediate passage in a fugue, whereby the subject is for a time suspended.

> In ordinary fugues ... It is usual to allow a certain number of bars to intervene from time to time, after which the subject is resumed. The intervening bars ... are called Episodes.
>
> Ouseley, *Counterpoint*, xxii

**Epoch** (Gr. a stoppage, pause). A definite point of time; also the period that dates from such, the sequence of events that spring from it. The word is used with much the same sense as 'era'; we speak both of the 'Epoch' and the 'Era' of the Reformation, for instance.

> The incarnation of Christ is the greatest moral epoch in the universe of God.
>
> Stevens, *Parables Unfolded* (*The Lost Sheep*, p. 104)

**Epode** (Gr. *epodos*, from *adein*, to sing). In ancient Greek lyric poetry, the part after the strophe and antistrophe; in the epode the chorus returned to their places and remained stationary.

***Father of Choral Epode.*** Stesichoros of Sicily (632–552 BC).

**Eppur si muove!** (Ital. and yet it – i.e. the earthdoes move). The phrase said by a fable that dates only from 1757 to have been uttered in an undertone by Galileo immediately after his recantation of belief in the Copernican theory of astronomy and the motion of the earth, which was made before the Inquisition in 1633. There is very little doubt that it is wholly apochryphal.

**Epsom Races.** Horse races originally instituted by Charles I, and held on Epsom Downs for four days in May. The second day (Wednesday) is 'Derby day' (*q.v.*), and on the fourth the 'Oaks' (*q.v.*) is run.

There are other races held at Epsom besides the great four-day races – for instance, the City and Suburban and the Great Metropolitan (both handicap races).

**Epsom Salts.** Magnesium sulphate; used medicinally as a purgative, etc., and so called because it was originally (18th cent.) obtained by the evaporation of the water of a mineral spring in the vicinity of Epsom, Surrey.

**Equality.** The sign of equality in mathematics, two little parallel lines (=), was invented by Robert Recorde, who died 1558.

> As he said, nothing is more equal than parallel lines.

**Equation of Time.** The difference between mean and apparent time – i.e. the difference between the time as shown by a perfect clock and that indicated by a sundial. The greatest difference is at the beginning of November, when the sun is somewhat more than sixteen minutes slow. There are days in December, April, June, and September when the sun and the clocks agree.

**Eques Auratus.** An ancient Roman knight called *auratus* because he was allowed to gild his armour.

**Equipage.** To *equip* means to arm or furnish, and *equipage* is the furniture of a military man or body of troops. Hence *camp equipage* (all things necessary for an encampment); *field equipage* (all things necessary for the field of battle); *tea equipage* (a complete tea-service); a *prince's equipage*, and so on. Nowadays the word is often used for one's carriage and horses.

**Era.** A series of years beginning from some epoch or starting-point, as:

| | BC |
|---|---|
| The Era of the Greek Olympiads. | 776 |
| The Era of the Foundation of Rome | 753 |
| The Era of Nabonassar | 747 |
| The Era of Alexander the Great | 324 |
| The Era of the Seleucidae | 312 |
| The Era of Julian Era | 45 |

***The Mundane Era,*** or the supposed number of years between the Creation and the Nativity:

| | |
|---|---|
| According to the modern Greek Calendar | 7,388 |
| According to Josephus | 7,282 |
| According to Scaliger | 5,829 |
| According to the ancient Greek Church | 5,508 |
| According to Professor Hales | 5,411 |
| According to L'art de Vérifier les Dates | 4,968 |
| According to Archbishop Ussher | 4,004 |
| According to Calmet | 4,000 |
| According to the Jews | 3,760 |

***Other Eras:***

The Era of Abraham starts from Oct. 1, 2016 BC
The Era of Actium starts from Jan. 1 30 BC
The Era of American Independence, July 4, AD 1776
The Era of Armenia, July 9, AD 552
The Era of Augustas, 27 BC
The Era of Diocletian, Aug. 29, AD 284
The Era of Tyre, Oct. 19, 125 BC
The Era of the Chinese, 2697 BC
The Era of the French Republic, Sept. 22, AD 1792
The Era of the Hegira, July 16, AD 622
(The flight of Mahomet from Mecca.)
The Era of the Maccabees, 166 BC
The Era of Yezdegird (Persian), June 16, AD 632

The Christian Era begins from the birth of Christ.

**Erastians.** The followers of Thomas Lieber (1524–83), a German heretic who wrote a work on excommunication in which he advocated the imposition of restrictions on ecclesiastical jurisdiction. His name was Grecised into *Erastus* (i.e. the lovely, or beloved). *Erastianism*, i.e. state supremacy or interference in ecclesiastical affairs, is named from him. The Church of England is sometimes called 'Erastian', because the State controls its ritual and temporalities, and the sovereign, as the 'head' of it, appoints bishops and other dignitaries.

**Erastus.** *See* Diocletian.

**Erato.** One of the nine Muses (*q.v.*); the muse of erotic poetry; usually represented holding or playing a lyre.

**Erebus.** In *Greek mythology*, the son of Chaos and brother of Night; hence darkness personified. His name was given to the gloomy cavern underground through which the Shades had to walk in their passage to Hades.

> Not Erebus itself were dim enough
> To hide thee. Shakespeare, *Julius Caesar*, 2, 1

**Eretrian.** *The Eretrian bull,* Menedemos of Eretria, in Euboea; a Greek philosopher of about 350–270 BC, who founded the Eretrian school, a branch of the Socratic.

**Erewhon.** The name of the ideal commonwealth in Samuel Butler's philosophical novel of the same name (1872). It is, of course, an anagram on 'Nowhere'. *Cp.* Commonwealth, Ideal.

**Erigena.** John Scotus, called 'Scotus the Wise', who died about 890. He must not be confounded with Duns Scotus (*see* Dunce), who lived some four centuries after him.

**Erigone.** *See* Icarius.

**Erin.** Ireland (*q.v.*).

***Erin go bragh!*** Ireland for ever. *See* Mavournin.

**Erinyes.** In *Greek mythology*, daughters of Ge (Earth), avengers of wrong; the Furies. *See* Eumenides.

**Erix.** A giant mentioned by Rabelais. *See* Gemmagog.

**Erl-king.** In *German legend*, a malevolent goblin who haunts forests and lures people, especially children, to destruction. Goethe has a poem on him.

**Ermeline, Dame.** Reynard's wife, in the tale of *Reynard the Fox*.

**Ermine Street.** One of the most ancient roads in Britain; originally running from Colchester by way of Godmanchester and Lincoln to York, but later connected by the Romans with London, in the south, and the Wall of Hadrian in the north. The origin of the name is obscure, but it is not Roman. It may be connected with Old Teutonic *irmin*, mighty, large. The most important of the other so-called 'Roman roads' in Britain are *Watling Street*, *Icknield Street*, and the *Fosse* (*qq.v.*).

**Eros.** The Greek god of love, the youngest of all the gods; equivalent to the Roman Cupid (*q.v.*).

**Erostratus.** The Ephesian who set fire to the temple of Diana on the day that Alexander the Great happened to be born (356 BC). This he did to make his name immortal; and, in order to defeat his object, the Ephesians forbade his name ever to be mentioned.

**Erra-Pater.** The supposititious author of an almanack published about 1535 as *The Pronostycacion for ever of Erra Pater: a Jewe born in Jewery, a Doctour in Astronomye and Physycke*. It is a collection of astrological tables, rules of health, etc., and is arranged for use in any year.

> [He] had got him a suit of durance, that would last longer than one of Erra Pater's almanacks, or a cunstable's browne bill.
>
> Nash, *Nashe's Lenten Stuffe* (1599)

The almanacks were frequently reprinted, and nearly a hundred years later Butler says of William Lilly, the almanack-maker and astrologer:

> In mathematics he was greater
> Than Tycho Brahe or Erra Pater.
>
> *Hudibras,* 1, 1

**Erse.** The native language of the West Highlanders of Scotland, who are of Irish origin. The word, which is now nearly obsolete, is a variant of *Irish,* and was applied by the Scotch Lowlanders to the Highland dialect of Gaelic. In the 18th century Scotch was often called Erse, without distinction of Highland and Lowland; and Irish was spoken of as Irish Gaelic.

**Erswynd.** The name given to the wife of the Wolf (Isegrim) in Caxton's version of *Reynard the Fox*.

**Erudite.** *Most erudite of the Romans.* Marcus Terentius Varro (116–27 BC), a man of vast and varied erudition in almost every department of literature.

**Erythynus.** *Have no doings with the Erythynus,* i.e. 'don't trust a braggart'. This is the thirty-third symbol of the *Protreptics* of Iamblichus. The Erythynus is mentioned by Pliny (ix, 77) as a red fish with a white belly, and Pythagoras used it as a symbol of a braggadocio, who fable says is white-livered.

**Escorial,** or **Escurial.** The ancient palace of the Spanish sovereigns, containing also a monastery, church, and mausoleum, about twenty-seven miles north-west of Madrid. It is one of the most superb structures in Europe, and is built among rocks, as the name signifies. It was erected in 1563–84 as the result of a vow to St Laurence (hence the 'gridiron' shape of its plan) made by Philip II at the battle of St Quentin, 1557.

**Escuage** (O.Fr. *escu*, Lat. *scutum*, a shield). A feudal term meaning 'shield service', i.e. the obligation which bound a vassal to serve his lord in the field for forty days in the year at his own private charge.

**Esculapius.** *See* Aesculapius.

**Escutcheon of Pretence.** In heraldry, the small shield of a wife, either heiress or co-heiress, placed in the centre of her husband's shield.

**Esop.** *See* Aesop.

**Esoteric** (Gr.). Those within, as opposed to *exoteric,* those without. The term originated with Pythagoras, who stood behind a curtain when he gave his lectures. Those who were allowed to attend the lectures, but not to see his face, he called his *exoteric disciples*; but those who were allowed to enter the veil, his *esoteric.*

Aristotle adopted the same terms; those who attended his evening lectures, which were of a popular character, he called his *exoterics*; and those who attended his more abstruse morning lectures, his *esoterics.*

***Esoteric Buddhism.*** *See* Theosophy.

**Esplandian.** Son of Amadis and Oriana, and hero of Montalvo's continuation of *Amadis of Gaul* (*q.v.*).

**Esprit de corps** (Fr.). The spirit of pride in the society with which you are associated, and regard for its traditions and institutions. A military term – every soldier will stand up for his own corps.

**Esprit follet** (Fr.). A bogle which delights in misleading and tormenting mortals.

**Esquire** (Lat. *scutiger,* a shieldbearer). One who carried the *escu* or shield of a knight.

In 1893 (January 26th) C. H. Athill, Esq., Richmond Herald, wrote as follows from the Heralds' College:

> The following persons are legally 'Esquires': The sons of peers, the sons of baronets, the sons of knights, the eldest sons of the younger sons of peers, and their eldest sons in perpetuity, the eldest son of the eldest son of a knight, and his eldest son in perpetuity, the kings of arms, the heralds of arms, officers of the Army or Navy of the rank of captain and upwards, sheriffs of counties for life, J.P'.s of counties whilst in commission, Serjeants-at-law. Queen's [King's] counsel, serjeants-at-arms, Companions of the Orders of Knighthood, certain principal officers in the Royal household, deputy lieutenants, commissioners of the Court of Bankruptcy, masters of the Supreme Court, those whom the Sovereign, in any commission or warrant, styles esquire, and any person who, in virtue of his office, takes precedence of esquires.

To these doctors of law, barristers, physicians and graduates of the universities not in holy orders are often added; but the general use of the suffix by those who are not, strictly speaking, entitled to it, has robbed it of all distinction. It is never used in America, and rarely in the overseas parts of the Empire.

**Essays.** Lord Bacon's essays were the first in English that bore the name.

> To write just treatises requireth leisure in the writer and leisure in the reader ... which is the cause which hath made me choose to write certain brief notes ... which I have called essays. The word is late, but the thing is ancient.
>
> Suppressed Dedication to Prince Henry

**Essenes.** A puritanical and mystical sect of Jews, originating about the 2nd century BC, whose doctrines are supposed by some to have influenced those of our Saviour. They were communists who abjured every sort of fleshly indulgence, ate no animal food, drank only water, and whose only sacrifices to God were the fruits of the earth. They kept the Sabbath extremely strictly, always dressed in white, devoted themselves to contemplative studies, and held the Scriptures in great reverence, but interpreted them allegorically.

**Essex Lions.** Calves, for which the county is famous.

***Valiant as an Essex lion.*** Said ironically of a timid person. *Cp.* Cotswold.

**Estate** (O.Fr. *estat,* Lat. *status* from *stare,* to stand). *Estates of the realm.* The powers that have the administration of affairs in their hands, that on which the realm stands. The three estates of our own realm are the Lords Spiritual, the Lords Temporal, and the Commons; popularly speaking, the public press is termed the 'fourth estate' (*q.v.*). It is a great mistake to call the three estates of England the Sovereign, the Lords, and the Commons.

> Herod ... made a supper to his ... chief estates. Mark 6:21
>
> The king and the three estates of the realm assembled in parliament.
>
> Collect for Nov. 5

**Est-il-possible.** A nickname of Prince George of Denmark (1653–1708), the consort of Queen Anne. The story goes that when he was told of the abdication of his father-in-law, James II, all he did was to exclaim, 'Est-il possible?' and when told, further, of the several noblemen who had fallen away from him, 'Est-il possible?' exhausted his indignation.

**Estmere, King.** Hero of one of the ballads given in Percy's *Reliques.* He was a King of England who requested permission to pay suit to the daughter of King Adland. He was answered that Bremor, King of Spain, had already proposed to her and been rejected; but when the lady was introduced to the English king she accepted him. King Estmere started home to prepare for the wedding, but had not proceeded a mile when the King of Spain returned to press his suit, and threatened vengeance if it were not accepted. Estmere was requested to return, and, with his brother, rode into the hall of King Adland in the guise of harpers, when Bremor bade them leave their steeds in the stable. A quarrel ensued, in which the 'sowdan' was slain, and the two brothers put the retainers to flight.

**Estotiland.** An imaginary tract of land near the Arctic Circle in North America, said to have been discovered by John Scalvë, a Pole. It is mentioned, and shown, in Peter Heylin's *Microcosmos* (1622).

> The snow
> From cold Estotiland.
>
> Milton, *Paradise Lost*, x, 685

**Estramaçon** (Fr.). A blow or cut with a sword, hence also 'estramaçonner'. Scott uses the word in the sense of a feint or pretended cut. Sir Jeffrey Hudson, the dwarf, says:

> I tripped a hasty morris … upon the dining-table, now offering my sword [to the Duke of Buckingham], and now recovering it, I made … a sort of estramaçon at his nose, the dexterity of which consists in coming mightily near to the object without touching it.
>
> *Peveril of the Peak*, ch. xxxiv

**Estrich.** The old name for the ostrich (*q.v.*).

**Estrildis.** In Geoffrey of Monmouth's *History*, the daughter of a German king, and handmaid to the mythical King Humber. When Humber was drowned in the river that bears his name, Locrine fell in love with Estrildis, and would have married her, had he not been betrothed already to Guendoloena; but he had by her a daughter named Sabrina, and after his death Guendoloena threw both mother and child into the Severn.

**Eternal, The.** God.

***The Eternal City.*** Rome. The epithet occurs in Ovid, Tibullus, etc., and in many official documents of the Empire; also Virgil (Aeneid, i, 79) makes Jupiter tell Venus he would give to the Romans *imperium sine fine* (an eternal empire).

***The eternal fitness of things.*** The congruity between an action and the agent.

> Can any man have a higher notion of the rule of right, and the eternal fitness of things?
>
> Fielding, *Tom Jones*, Bk iv, ch. iv

***The eternal tables.*** In *Mohammedan legend*, a white pearl extending from east to west, and from heaven to earth, on which God has recorded every event, past, present, and to come.

**Etesian Wind.** A Mediterranean wind which rises annually (Gr. *etos*, a year) about the dog-days, and blows forty days together in the same direction. It is gentle and mild.

> Deem not, good Porteus, that in this my song
> I mean to harrow up thy humble mind.
> And stay that voice in London known so long;
> For balm and softness, an Etesian wind.
>
> Peter Pindar, *Nil Admiraro*

**Ethnic Plot.** The name Dryden gave in his *Absalom and Achitophel* (*q.v.*) to the Popish plot (*q.v.*). Charles II is called David, the royalists the Jews, and the Papists Gentiles or Ethnoi, whence the name.

> Saw with disdain an Ethnic plot begun.
> 'Gainst form and order they their power employ.
> Nothing to build, and all things to destroy.
>
> Pt i, 518, 532–3

**Ethnophrones** (Gr. *ethnos-phren*, heathen-minded). A sect of heretics of the 7th century, who combined such pagan practices as divination, augury, astrology, etc., with Christianity.

**Ethon.** The eagle or vulture that gnawed the liver of Prometheus.

**Etiquette.** The usages of polite society. The word means a ticket or card, and refers to the ancient custom of delivering a card of directions and regulations to be observed by all those who attended court. *That's the ticket* is still slang for 'that's correct' (behaviour, etc.). In French the word originally meant a soldier's billet.

> Etiquette … had its original application to those ceremonial and formal observances practised at Court.
>
> … The term came afterwards … to signify certain formal methods used in the transactions between Sovereign States.
>
> Burke, *Works*, vol. viii, p. 329

**Etna.** Virgil (*Aeneid*, iii, 578, etc.) ascribes its eruption to the restlessness of Enceladus, a hundred-headed giant, who lies buried under the mountain, where also the Greek and Latin poets placed the forges of Vulcan and the smithy of the Cyclops.

**Étrenne.** *See* Strenia.

**Ettrick Shepherd.** James Hogg (1770–1835), the Scotch poet, who was born in the forest of Ettrick, Selkirkshire.

**Etzel.** The name given in German heroic legend to Attila (d. AD 453), King of the Huns, a monarch ruling over three kingdoms and more than thirty principalities. In the Nibelungenlied he is made very insignificant, and sees his liegemen, and even his son and heir, struck down without any effort to save them, or avenge their destruction. Here he marries Kriemhild, the widow of Siegfried, called Gudrun in the *Elder Edda,* where Attila figures as *Atli.*

**Eucharist** (Gr. *eucharistos*, grateful). Literally, a thank-offering. Our Lord said, 'Do this in remembrance of me' – i.e. out of gratitude to me. *Cp.* Impanation.

**Eucrates.** *More shifts than Eucrates.* Eucrates, the miller, was one of the archons of Athens, noted for his shifts and excuses for neglecting the duties of the office.

**Eudoxians.** Heretics, whose founder was Eudoxius, patriarch of Antioch in the 4th century. They maintained that the Son had a will independent of the Father, and that sometimes their wills were at variance.

**Eugenius.** The friend and counsellor of Yorick in Sterne's *Tristram Shandy* is intended for John Hall Stevenson (1718–85), author of *Crazy Tales*, and a relative of Sterne.

**Eugubine Tables.** Seven bronze tables found near Gubbio (*Eugubium*) in Italy, in 1444. Of the inscriptions, five are Umbrian and Etruscan, and two are Latin.

> The Umbrian, the tongue of north-eastern Italy, is yet more fully represented to us by the Eugubine tablets ... supposed to be as old as the third and fourth centuries before our era.
>
> W. D. Whitney, *Study of Languages,* vi, p. 220

**Eulalie, St.** Eulalon (i.e. 'the sweetly-spoken') is one of the names of Apollo; but there is a virgin martyr called Eulalie, born at Barcelona. When she was only twelve the persecution of Diocletian broke out, and she, in the presence of the Roman judge, cast down the idols he had set up. She was martyred February 12th, 304, and is the patron saint of Barcelona and of sailors.

Longfellow calls Evangeline the 'Sunshine of St Eulalie'.

**Eulen-spiegel** (i.e. 'Owl-glass'), **Tyll.** A 14th-century villager of Brunswick round whom clustered a large number of popular tales of all sorts of mischievous pranks, first printed in 1515. The work has been attributed (probably erroneously) to Thomas Murner (1475–1530); it was translated into many languages and rapidly achieved wide popularity.

**Eumaeus.** The slave and swineherd of Ulysses; hence, a swineherd.

> This second Eumaeus strode hastily down the forest glade, driving before him ... the whole herd of his inharmonious charge. Scott

**Eumenides** (Gr. the good-tempered ones). A name given by the Greeks to the Furies, as it would have been ominous and bad policy to call them by their right name, *Erinyes* (*q.v.*).

**Eumnestes** (i.e. Memory). An old man 'of infinite remembrance' in Spenser's *Faërie Queene* (II, ix), the counsellor of Alma in the House of Temperance. He kept a little boy named Anamnestes (i.e. the Reminder) to fetch books from the shelves.

**Eunomians.** Heretics, the disciples of Eunomius, Bishop of Cyzicum in the 4th century. They maintained that the Father was of a different nature from the Son, and that the Son did not in reality unite Himself to human nature.

**Eupatridae.** The land-owning aristocracy of ancient Attica. These lords of creation were set aside by the time of Pericles, and a democratic form of government established.

**Euphemisms.** Words or phrases substituted, to soften down offensive expressions. Pope refers to the use of euphemisms in his lines.

> To rest the cushion and soft dean invite,
> Who never mentioned hell to ears polite.
>
> *Moral Essays*, epist. iv, 49

'His Satanic majesty'; 'light-fingered gentry'; 'a gentleman on his travels' (*one transported*); 'she has met with an accident' (*has had a child before marriage*); 'not quite correct' (*a falsehood*); 'an obliquity of vision' (*a squint*) are common examples.

**Eureka** (Gr., more correctly *Heureka,* I have found it). An exclamation of delight at having made a discovery; originally that of Archimedes, the Syracusan philosopher, when he discovered how to test the purity of Hiero's crown. The tale is, that Hiero delivered a certain weight of gold to a smith to be made into a votive crown, but, suspecting that the gold had been alloyed with an inferior metal, asked Archimedes to test it. The philosopher did not know how to proceed, but in stepping into his bath, which was quite full, observed that some of the water ran over. It immediately struck him that a body must remove its own bulk of water when it is immersed; silver is lighter than gold, therefore a pound-weight of silver will be more bulky than a pound-weight of gold, and would consequently remove more water. In this way he found that the crown was deficient in gold; and Vitruvius says:

> When the idea flashed across his mind, the philosopher jumped out of the bath exclaiming, 'Heureka! heureka!' and, without waiting to dress himself, ran home to try the experiment.

'Eureka!' is the motto of California, in allusion to the gold discovered there.

**Eurus.** The east wind; connected with Gr. *eos* and Lat. *aurora,* the dawn.

> While southern gales or western oceans roll,
> And Eurus steals his ice-winds from the pole.
> Darwin, *Economy of Vegetation,* canto vi

**Eurydice.** In *Greek mythology* the wife of Orpheus, killed by a serpent on her wedding night. Orpheus went down to the infernal regions to seek her, and was promised she should return on condition that he looked not back till she had reached the upper world. When the poet got to the confines of his journey, he turned his head to see if Eurydice were following, and she was instantly caught back again into Hades.

> Restore, restore Eurydice to life;
> Oh, take the husband or return the wife.
> Pope, *Ode on St Cecilia's Day*

**Eustathians.** The followers of Eustathius, Bishop of Sebaste, in Armenia, who was deposed by the council of Gangra in 380.

**Euterpe.** One of the nine Muses (*q.v.*); the inventor of the double flute; the muse of Dionysiac music; patroness of joy and pleasure, and of flute-players.

**Eutychians.** Heretics of the 5th century, violently opposed to the Nestorians. They maintained that Jesus Christ was entirely God previous to the incarnation, and entirely man during His sojourn on earth, and were thus the forerunners of the Monophysites (*q.v.*). The founder was Eutyches, an abbot of Constantinople, excommunicated in 448.

**Euxine Sea.** The Greek name for the Black Sea (*q.v.*), meaning the 'hospitable'. It was originally called by that people *Axeinos,* inhospitable, on account of its stormy character and rocky shores; but this name was changed euphemistically, as it was never thought wise to give a derogatory (even though true) name to any force of nature. *Cp.* Erinyes and Eumenides.

**Evangelic Doctor, The.** John Wyclif (1320–84), 'the morning star of the Reformation'.

**Evangeline.** The heroine of Longfellow's poem of that name. The subject of the tale is the expulsion of the inhabitants of Acadia (*Nova Scotia*) from their homes by order of George II.

**Evangelists.** The four Evangelists, Matthew, Mark, Luke, and John, are usually represented in art as follows:

***Matthew.*** With a pen in his hand, and a scroll before him, looking over his left shoulder at an angel. This Gospel was the first, and the angel represents the Being who dictated it.

***Mark.*** Seated writing, and by his side a couchant winged lion. Mark begins his gospel with the sojourn of Jesus in the wilderness, amidst wild beasts, and the temptation of Satan, 'the roaring lion'.

***Luke.*** With a pen, looking in deep thought over a scroll, and near him a cow or ox chewing the cud. The latter part refers to the eclectic character of St Luke's Gospel. He is also frequently shown as painting a picture, from the tradition that he painted a portrait of the Virgin.

***John.*** A young man of great delicacy, with an eagle in the background to denote sublimity.

The more ancient symbols were – for Matthew, *a man's face*; for Mark, *a lion*; for Luke, *an ox*; and for John, *a flying eagle*; in allusion to the four living creatures before the throne of God, described in the Book of Revelation: 'The first … was like a lion, and the second … like a calf, and the third … had a face as a man, and the fourth … was like a flying eagle' (4:7).

Another explanation is that Matthew is symbolised by a *man*, because he begins his gospel with the humanity of Jesus, as a descendant of David; Mark by a *lion*, because he begins his gospel with the scenes of John the Baptist and Jesus in the Wilderness; Luke by a *calf*, because he begins his gospel with the priest sacrificing in the temple; and John by an *eagle*, because he soars high, and begins his gospel with the divinity of the Logos. The four symbols are those of Ezekiel's cherubim.

Irenaeus says: 'The lion signifies the royalty of Christ; the calf His sacerdotal office; the man's face His incarnation; and the eagle the grace of the Holy Ghost.'

**Evans, William.** The giant porter (d.1632) of Charles I, who carried about in his pocket Sir Jeffrey Hudson, the king's dwarf. He was nearly eight feet high. Fuller speaks of him in his *Worthies*, and Scott introduces him in *Peveril of the Peak*.

> As tall a man as is in London, always excepting the king's porter, Master Evans, that carried you about in his pocket, Sir Geoffrey, as all the world has heard tell. Ch. xxxiii

**Events.** ***At all events.*** In any case; be the issue what it may; *utcumque ceciderit.*

***In the event.*** 'In the event of his being elected', means *in case*, or provided he is elected; if the result is that he is elected.

**Ever and Anon.** From time to time. *See* Anon.

**Ever-Sworded, The.** The 29th Regiment of Foot, now called the 'Worcestershire Regiment'. In 1746 a part of this regiment, then at St John's Island, was surprised by the French and massacred, when a command was issued that henceforth every officer, even at meals, should wear his sword. In 1842–59 the regiment was in the East Indies, and the order was relaxed, requiring only the captain and subaltern of the day to dine with their swords on.

**Ever-Victorious Army, The.** A force of Chinese, officered by Europeans and Americans, raised in 1861, and placed under the charge of Gordon. *See* Chinese Gordon. By 1864 it had stamped out the Taëping rebellion, which had broken out in 1851.

**Evidence, In.** Before the eyes of the people; to the front; actually present (Lat.). Evidence, meaning testimony in proof of something, has a large number of varieties, as –

*Circumstantial evidence.* That based on corroborative incidents.

*Demonstrative evidence.* That which can be proved without leaving a doubt.

*Direct evidence.* That of an eye-witness.

*External evidence.* That derived from history or tradition.

*Internal evidence.* That derived from conformity with what is known.

*Material evidence.* That which is essential in order to carry proof.

*Moral evidence.* That which accords with general experience.

*Presumptive evidence.* That which is highly probable.

*Prima facie evidence.* That which seems likely, unless it can be explained away.

*King's evidence.* That of an accessory against his accomplices, under the promise of pardon.

*Secondary evidence.* Such as is produced when primary evidence is not to be obtained.

*Self evidence.* That derived from the senses; manifest and indubitable.

**Evil Communications.** *Evil communications corrupt good manners.* The words are usually attributed to St Paul (1 Cor. 15:33); but he was evidently quoting Menander's saying, 'It must be that evil communications corrupt good dispositions.' Similar proverbs are, 'He who touches pitch must expect to be defiled' (from Eccles. 13:1); 'One scabbed sheep will infect a whole flock.'

> One sickly sheep infects the flock
> And poisons all the rest.
>
> Dr Watts, *Against Evil Company*

**Evil Eye.** It was anciently believed that the eyes of some persons darted noxious rays on objects which they glared upon. The first morning glance of such eyes was certain destruction to man or beast. Virgil speaks of an evil eye making cattle lean.

> Nescio quis teneros oculus mini fascinat agnos.
>
> *Ecl.* iii, 103

A *mascot* (*q.v.*) is the opposite of one with an evil eye.

**Evil May Day.** The name given to the serious rioting made on May 1st, 1517, by the London apprentices, who fell on the French residents. The riot was put down with difficulty, Sir Thomas More and the Earls of Shrewsbury and Surrey being among those who assisted.

> While thes rufflying continued syr Richard Cholmeley, knight, Lieutenaunt of the Towre, no great frende to the citie, in a frantyke fury losed certayn peces of ordinaunce, and shot into the citie, whiche did litle harme, howbeit his good wyl apered. *Hall's Chronicle*

Two hundred and seventy-eight of the rioters were arrested, of whom fifteen were hanged, drawn, and quartered. The insurrection forms the basis of the anonymous Elizabethan play, *Sir Thomas More.*

**Evil Principle.** *See* Ahriman.

**Evils.** *Of two evils, choose the least. See* Choice.

**Ewe-lamb.** A single possession greatly prized; in allusion to the story told in 2 Sam. 12:1–14.

**Ex** (Lat.). From, out of, after, or by reason of; it forms part of many adverbial phrases, of which those in common use in English are given below. As a prefix *ex,* when joined to the name of some office or dignity denotes a former holder of that office, or the holder immediately before the present holder. *An ex-president* is some former holder of the office; *the ex-president* is the same as 'the late president', the one just before the present one.

***Ex cathedra.*** With authority. The Pope, speaking *ex cathedra,* is said to speak with an infallible voice – to speak as the successor and representative of St Peter, and in his pontifical character. The words mean 'from the chair' – i.e. the throne of the pontiff – and are applied to all dicta uttered by authority, and ironically to self-sufficient, dogmatic assertions.

***Ex hypothesi.*** According to what is supposed or assumed; in consequence of assumption made.

***Ex libris.*** Laterally, 'from the (collection of) books'. The phrase is written in the books or printed on the bookplate, and is followed by the name of the owner in the genitive. Hence, a bookplate is often called an *ex libris.*

***Ex luce lucellum.*** A gain or small profit out of light. It was originally said of the old window-tax, and when Lowe, in 1871, proposed to tax lucifer matches, he suggested that the boxes should be labelled *Ex luce lucellum.*

> Lucifer aggrediens ex luce haurire lucellum
> Incidit in tenebras; lex nova fumus erat.

***Ex nihilo nihil fit.*** *See* De nihilo.

***Ex officio.*** By virtue of office. As, the Lord Mayor for the time being shall be *ex officio* one of the trustees.

***Ex parte.*** Proceeding only from one of the parties; hence, prejudiced. An *ex-parte* statement is a one-sided or partial statement, a statement made by one side without modification from the other.

***Ex pede Herculem.*** From this sample you can judge of the whole. Plutarch says that Pythagoras calculated the height of Hercules by comparing the length of various stadia in Greece. A stadium was 600 feet in length, but Hercules' stadium at Olympia was much longer; therefore, said the philosopher, the foot of Hercules was proportionately longer than an ordinary foot; and as the foot bears a certain ratio to the height, so the height of Hercules can be easily ascertained. *Ex ungue leonem*, a lion (may be drawn) from its claw, is a similar phrase.

***Ex post facto.*** From what is done afterwards; retrospective. An *ex post facto* law is a law made to meet and punish a crime after the offence has been committed.

***Ex professo.*** Avowedly; expressly.

> I have never written *ex professo* on the subject.
> Gladstone, *Nineteenth Century*, Nov., 1885

***Ex proprio motu.*** Of his (or its) own accord; voluntarily.

***Ex uno omnes.*** From the instance deduced you may infer the nature of the rest. A general inference from a particular example; if one oak bears acorns, all oaks will.

**Exaltation.** In old astrology, a planet was said to be in its 'exaltation' when it was in that sign of the zodiac in which it was supposed to exercise its strongest influence. Thus the exaltation of Venus is in Pisces, and her 'dejection' in Virgo.

> And thus, god woot, Mercurie is desolate
> In Pisces, wher Venus is exaltat.
> Chaucer, *Wife of Bath's Prologue*, 703

***Exaltation of the Cross.*** A feast held in the Roman Catholic Church on September 14th, originally in commemoration of the vision that appeared to Constantine (*see* Cross), but afterwards connected with the victory over the Persians in 627, when Heraclius recovered and restored to Calvary the cross that had been carried away by Khosroes the Persian.

**Excalibur.** The name of Arthur's sword (O.Fr. *Escalibor*), called by Geoffrey of Monmouth *Caliburn,* and in the *Mabinogion Caledvwlch.* There was a sword called *Caladbolg* famous in Irish legend, which is thought to have meant 'hard-belly', i.e. capable of consuming anything; this and the name *Excalibur* are probably connected.

By virtue of being the one knight who could pull Excalibur from a stone in which it had been magically fixed (from which has been put together another so-called derivation of the name, viz. Lat. *ex cal* [*ce*] *liber* [*are*], to free from the stone) Arthur was acclaimed as 'the right born king of all England'. After his last battle, when the king lay sore wounded, it was returned at his command by Sir Bedivere to the Lady of the Lake. *See* Malory, Bk xxi, ch. v, and Tennyson's *Passing of Arthur* (*Idylls of the King*).

> No sword on earth, were it the Excalibar of King Arthur, can cut that which opposes no steady resistance to the blow.
> Scott, *Talisman*, ch. xxvii

**Excellency, His.** A title given to colonial and provincial governors, ambassadors, and some other high officials.

**Excelsior** (Lat. higher). Aim at higher things still. It is the motto of the United States, and has been made popular by Longfellow's poem so named.

**Exception.** ***Exceptions prove the rule.*** They prove there is a rule, or there could be no exceptions; the very fact of exceptions proves there must be a rule.

> Exceptio probat regulam. Columella

***To take exception.*** To feel offended; to find fault with.

> Her manner was so ... respectful, that I could not take exception to this reproof. Farjeon

**Exchequer.** ***Court of Exchequer.*** In the subdivision of the court in the reign of Edward I, the Exchequer acquired a separate and independent position. Its special duty was to order the revenues of the Crown and recover the king's debts. It was called the *Scaccarium*, from Lat. *scaccum*, a chess-board, because a chequered cloth was used on the table of the court. Foss, in his *Lives of the Judges* (1848–57), says:

> All round the table was a standing ledge four fingers broad, covered with a cloth bought in the Easter Term, and this cloth was 'black rowed with strekes about a span', like a

chessboard. On the spaces of this cloth counters were arranged, marked for checking computations.

**Excise.** Literally, a piece cut off (Lat. *excido*). It is a toll or duty levied on articles of home consumption – a slice cut off from these things for the national purse.

> Taxes on commodities are either on production within the country, or on importation into it, or on conveyance or sale within it; and are classed respectively as excise, customs, or tolls.
> Mill, *Political Economy*, Bk v, ch. iii, p. 562

**Exclusion.** ***Bill of Exclusion***. A bill to exclude the Duke of York (afterwards James II) from the throne, on account of his being a Papist. Passed by the Commons, but rejected by the Lords, in 1679, it was revived in 1681 but never became law, partly because Charles II dissolved Parliament and refused to call another, and partly because of a fear in the country that the Bill was being used as a means of handing the Crown to Monmouth.

**Excommunication.** (1) The *greater* is exclusion of an individual from the seven sacraments, from every legitimate act, and from all intercourse with the faithful. (2) The *lesser* excommunication is sequestration from the services of the Church only. *See* Bell, Book, and Candle.

> The person excommunicated: *Os, orare, vale, communio, mensa negatur* (The person excommunicated is to be boycotted by the faithful in *os* (conversation), *orare* (prayer), *communio* (communion), *mensa*(board).
> Professor T. P. Gury, *Romish Moral Theology* (3rd ed., 1862)

The practice of excommunication was no doubt derived from the Jewish practice at the time of Christ, which entailed exclusion from religious and social intercourse (*cp.* Luke 6:22): the fact that this was a final step, following two gentler admonitions, led to the erroneous idea that there were three grades of excommunication among the Jews. *Cp.* Interdict.

**Excruciate.** To give one as much pain as crucifying him would do. (Lat. *ex crux,* where *ex* is intensive.)

**Exeat** (Lat. he may go out). Permission granted by a bishop to a priest to leave his diocese. In the universities, permission to a student to be absent during the period stated.

**Execrate.** To many Roman laws this tag was appended, 'If anyone breaks this law, *sacer esto*,' i.e. let his body, his family, and his goods be consecrated to the gods. When a man was declared *sacer,* anyone might kill him with impunity.

> If anyone hurt a tribune in word or deed, he was held accursed [*sacer*], and his goods were confiscated.
> Livy, iii, 55

**Exempli gratia** (Lat.). For the sake of example: abbreviated to 'e.g'. when used as the introduction to an example.

**Exequatur.** An official recognition of a person in the character of consul or commercial agent, authorising him to exercise his power; formerly, the authoritative recognition of a papal bull by a bishop, sovereign, etc. The word is Latin, and means, 'he may exercise' (the function to which he has been appointed).

**Exeter.** *See also* Exter.

***The Duke of Exeter's daughter.*** *See* Duke.

***The Exeter Book.*** A MS collection of Anglo-Saxon poetry presented about 1060 by Bishop Leofric to Exeter Cathedral, and still preserved in the library there. It includes poems and 'riddles' by Cynewulf (8th century), the legends of St Guthlac and St Juliana, 'Widsith', 'The Wanderer', 'The Complaint of Deor', etc.

The *Exon* or *Exeter Domesday* (*q.v.*) is also sometimes called the 'Exeter Book'.

**Exhibition.** A scholarship, i.e. a fixed sum spread over a definite period given by a school or university, etc., as a result of an examination for the purpose of assisting in defraying the cost of education. The word was formerly used for maintenance generally, pecuniary support, an allowance of meat and drink.

> They have founded six exhibitions of £15 each per annum, to continue for two years and a half.
> Taylor, *The University of Dublin*, ch. v

**Exit** (Lat. he goes out). A stage direction showing when an actor is to leave the stage; hence, the departure of an actor from the stage and departure generally, especially from life; also a door, passage, or way out.

> All the world's a stage,
> And all the men and women merely players:
> They have their exits and their entrances.
> Shakespeare, *As You Like It*, 2, 7

**Exodus** (Gr. *ex odos,* a journey out). The second book of the Old Testament, which relates the departure of the Israelites from Egypt under the guidance of Moses; hence, a going out generally, especially a transference of population on a considerable scale, as *the exodus from Ireland*, meaning the departure of the Irish in large numbers for America; and the *exodus of the Acadians* – i.e. the expulsion of these colonists from Nova Scotia in the reign of George II.

**Exon.** One of the four officers in command of the Yeomen of the Guard; the acting officer who resides at the court; an exempt. The word is an Anglicised pronunciation of the Fr. *exempt*, this having been the title of a junior officer (next below an ensign) in the Life Guards.

***Exon*** (short for Lat. *Exoniensis*, of *Exonia*, i.e. Exeter) is the signature of the Bishop of Exeter.

***Exon Domesday.*** A magnificent MS on 532 folio vellum leaves, for long preserved among the muniments at Exeter Cathedral, containing the survey of Wilts, Dorset, Somerset, Devon, and Cornwall. In 1816 it was published by Sir Henry Ellis as a Supplement to Domesday Book (*q.v.*).

**Exoteric.** *See* Esoteric.

**Expectation Week.** Between the Ascension and Whit Sunday, when the apostles continued praying 'in earnest expectation of the Comforter'.

**Experimental Philosophy.** Science founded on experiments or data, in contradistinction to moral and mathematical sciences; also called *natural philosophy*.

**Experimentum crucis** (Lat.). A decisive experiment. *See* Crucial.

**Experto crede** (Lat.). Believe one who has had experience in the matter. The phrase is used to add significance or weight to a warning.

**Exposé** (Fr.). A formal exposition; also, an inconvenient exposure of something which should have been kept out of sight. Thus we say a man *made a dreadful exposé* – i.e. told or did something which should have been kept concealed.

**Expression. *A geographical expression*.** A term applied to a tract of country the individual nationality of whose population has been lost or never acquired. Thus, from the time of its final partition until its reconstitution after the Great War, 'Poland' was a mere geographical expression.

**Exquisite.** Literally, one sought out (Lat. *ex, quaere*); a coxcomb, a dandy, one who thinks himself superlatively well dressed, and of most unexceptionable deportment.

> Exquisites are out of place in the pulpit; they should be set up in a tailor's window.
>
> Spurgeon, *Lectures to my Students*, viii

**Exter.** *That's Exter, as the old woman said when she saw Kerton.* A Devonshire saying, meaning, I thought my work was done, but I find much still remains before it is completed. 'Exter' is the popular pronunciation of Exeter, and 'Kerton' is Crediton. The tradition is that the woman in question was going for the first time to Exeter, and seeing the grand old church of Kerton (Crediton), supposed it to be Exeter Cathedral. 'That's Exter,' she said, 'and my journey is over'; but alas! she had still eight miles to walk.

**Extravagants,** or ***Extravagantes constitutiones.*** The papal constitutions of John XXII, and some few of his successors, supplemental to the 'Corpus Juris Canonici'. So called because they were not ranged in order with the other papal constitutions, but were left 'out-wanderers' (Lat. *extra,* on the outside, *vagari,* to wander) from the general code.

**Extreme Unction.** One of the seven sacraments of the Catholic Church, founded on James 5:14, 'Is any sick among you? let him call for the elders of the Church; and let them pray over him, anointing him with oil in the name of the Lord.'

**Extremes Meet.** A proverbial saying used of one who has 'boxed the compass' – as, for instance, a rabid socialist who becomes a steady-going Cabinet Minister.

***To go to extremes.*** To take final steps, have recourse to desperate measures.

**Eye. *A sheet in the wind's eye.*** An early stage of intoxication; not drunk, but 'getting on'.

***A sight for sore eyes.*** A proverbial expression used of something that is very welcome, pleasant, and unexpected.

***Do you see any green in my eye?*** Do I look credulous and easy to be bamboozled? Do I look like a greenhorn?

***Eyes to the blind.*** A staff; perhaps in allusion to that given to Tiresias (*q.v.*) by Athena, to serve him for the eyes of which she had deprived him.

***In my mind's eye.*** In my perceptive thought. The eye sees in two ways: (1) from without; and (2) from within. When we look at anything without, the object is reflected on the retina as on a mirror; but in deep contemplation the inward thought 'informs the eye'. It was thus Macbeth saw the dagger; and Hamlet tells Horatio that he saw his deceased father 'in his mind's eye'.

***In the wind's eye.*** Directly opposed to the wind.

***In the twinkling of an eye.*** Immediately, very soon; 'in a brace of shakes'. *Cp.* Bed-post.

***Mind your eye.*** Be careful or vigilant; keep a sharp look out; keep your eyes open to guard against mischief. Schoolboy wit, *Mens tuus ego.*

> 'Perhaps it may be so' (says I); 'but mind your eye, and take care you don't put your foot in it.'
>
> Haliburton

***My eye!*** or ***Oh, my eye!*** an exclamation of astonishment. *See* All my Eye.

***One-eyed.*** An expression of contempt; as, 'I've never been in such a one-eyed town,' i.e. such a poverty-stricken, mean, or unpleasing town.

***One-eyed peoples.*** *See* Arimaspians, Cyclops.

***One-eyed steak.*** Humorous slang for a kipper.

***One might see that with half an eye.*** Easily; at a mere glance.

***The eye of a needle.*** The words of Christ in Matt. 19:24:

> It is easier for a camel to go through the eye of a needle, than for a rich man to enter into the kingdom of God

enshrine a proverbial saying, and there is no need to suppose that by 'the eye of a needle' was intended the small arched entrance through the wall of a city, nor is there any evidence that such a gateway had any such name in Biblical time. *See* Camel. A similar Eastern proverb occurs at Matt. 23:24:

> Ye blind guides, which strain at a gnat and swallow a camel;

and 'In Media a camel can dance on a bushel,' meaning that there all things are possible, is another ancient Eastern saying.

***The Eye of Greece.*** Athens.

> Athens, the eye of Greece, mother of arts.
>
> Milton, *Paradise Regained*, iv, 240

***The Eye of the Baltic.*** Gottland, in the Baltic.

***The eye of the storm.*** An opening between the storm clouds. *Cp.* Bull's Eye.

***The king's eyes.*** His chief officers. An Eastern expression.

> One of the seven
> Who in God's presence, nearest to the throne
> Stand ready at command, and are his eyes
> That run thro' all the heavens, or down to earth
> Bear his swift errands.
>
> Milton, *Paradise Lost*, iii, 652

***To cast sheep's eyes at one.*** *See* Sheep.

***To cry one's eyes out.*** To cry immoderately or excessively.

***To get one's eye in.*** To become proficient at shooting, billiards, golf, bowls, etc.

***To give the glad eye.*** Usually said of a girl who shows by her look or glance that the attentions of the man to whom it is directed would not be unwelcome; an extension of 'to make eyes at'; to tip the wink.

***To have,*** or ***keep, an eye on.*** To keep strict watch on the person or thing referred to.

***To have an eye to.*** To keep constantly in view; to act from motives of policy. *See* Main Chance.

***To keep one's eyes skinned.*** To be particularly watchful.

***To make eyes at one.*** To look amorously or lovingly at another.

***To make someone open his eyes.*** To surprise him very much, and make him stare with wonder or admiration.

***To pipe your eye.*** *See* Pipe.

***To see eye to eye.*** To be of precisely the same opinion; to think both alike.

***Up to the eyes.*** Wholly, completely; as *up to the eyes in work*, very fully occupied, *mortgaged up to the eyes*, to the last penny obtainable.

**Eyelashes.** *To hang on by one's eyelashes.* To be just able to maintain one's position; hence, to be in difficulties.

**Eye-opener.** Something that furnishes enlightenment, or food for astonishment; also, a strong, mixed drink, especially a morning pick-me-up.

**Eye-service.** Unwilling service; the kind that is only done when under the eye of one's master.

> Servants, be obedient to them that are your masters ... not with eye service, as men pleasers; but as the servants of Christ. Eph. 6:5, 6

**Eye-sore.** Something that is offensive or painful to the sight; an annoyance, an object of disgust.

**Eye-teeth.** The canine teeth; so called because their fangs extend upwards nearly to the orbits of the eyes.

***He has cut his eye-teeth.*** *See* Teeth.

***To draw one's eye-teeth.*** To take the conceit out of a person; to fleece one without mercy; to make one suffer loss without *seeing* the manoeuvre by which it was effected.

> I guess these Yanks will get their eye-teeth drawn if they don't look sharp.
>
> W. Hepworth Dixon, *New America*, vol. i

**Eye-wash.** Flattery; soft sawder; fulsome adulation given for the purpose of blinding one to the real state of affairs.

**Eyre.** *Justices in Eyre.* The ancient itinerant judges who, from about 1100 to 1285, used to ride on circuit from county to county holding courts. *Eyre* is from late Lat. *iterare*, to journey, Lat. *iter*, a journey.

# F

**F.** The first letter in the runic futhorc (*q.v.*), but the sixth in the Phoenician and Latin alphabets, and their derivatives. The Egyptian hieroglyph represented a horned asp, and the Phoenician and Semitic character a peg.

***Double F*** (*Ff* or *ff*) as an initial in a few personal names, as *Ffoulkes*, *ffrench*, etc., is a mistaken use in *print* of the mediaeval or Old English capital F (𝔉) as it appears *written* in engrossed leases, etc. In script the old capital *F* looked very much like two small f's entwined, and it so appears in all old documents, and in many modern legal ones, not only in the case of personal names but of all words beginning with a capital *F*, as France (*Ffrance*), Flodden Field (*Fflodden ffield*), etc. There is thus no more reason for the *Ffoulkeses* and *ffaringtons* to perpetuate this absurd mistake than there would be for the Fishers or Frasers to adopt it.

***F is written on his face.*** The letter F used to be branded near the nose, on the left cheek of felons, on their being admitted to 'benefit of clergy'. The same was used for brawling in church. The custom was not abolished by law till 1822.

**F Sharp.** Slang for a flea; F, the initial letter, and sharp because of the bite. *Cp.* B Flats.

**F. E. R. T.** *See* Annunciation, Order of the.

**F. O. B.** Free on board; meaning that the shipper, from the time of shipment, is free from all risk.

**F's.** *The three f's.* Fixed tenure, Fair rent, Free sale. The platform of the Irish League in 1880.

**Fabian Society.** An association of socialists founded in January, 1884, by a small group of middle-class 'intellectuals', which included George Bernard Shaw and Sidney Webb, among others. As announced in its prospectus, it

> aims at 'the reorganisation of society by the emancipation of land and industrial capital from individual and class ownership, and the vesting of them in the community for the general benefit' ... and at 'the transfer to the community of the administration of such industrial capital as can conveniently be managed socially'.

The name is derived from Quintus Fabius (275–203 BC), surnamed 'Cunctator' (*q.v.*), the Roman general, who won his way against Hannibal by wariness, not by violence, by caution, not by defiance.

> It must be evident that the Fabian Society has a really gigantic task before it, the difficulties of which will not be lightened when the working classes come to understand that *small* ownership ... and small savings ... are just as strongly condemned by Collectivists as large estates and colossal fortunes.
>
> *Nineteenth Century*, November, 1892

> Fabian tactics lie in stealing inches, not in grasping leagues. *Liberal Review*, May 19th, 1894

**Fabius.** *See* Cunctator, *and* Fabian, *above.*

***The American Fabius.*** Washington (1732–99), whose military policy was similar to that of Fabius. He wearied out the English troops by harassing them, without coming to a pitched battle. Duguesclin pursued the same policy in France, by the advice of Charles V, whereby all the conquests of Edward and the Black Prince were retrieved.

***Fabius of the French.*** Anne, Duc de Montmorency, grand constable of France; so called from his success in almost annihilating the imperial army which had invaded Provence, by laying the country waste and prolonging the campaign (1493–1567).

**Fables.** *See* Aesop; Lokman; Pilpay. La Fontaine (1621–95) has been called the French Aesop, and John Gay (1685–1732) the English.

**Fabliaux.** The metrical tales, for the most part comic and satirical, and intended primarily for recitation of the Trouvères, or early poets north of the Loire, in the twelfth and thirteenth centuries. The word is used very widely, for it includes not only such tales as *Reynard the Fox*, but all sorts of familiar incidents of knavery and intrigue, legends, family traditions, and caricatures, especially of women.

**Fabricius.** A Roman hero (died about 270 BC), representative of incorruptibility and honesty. The ancient writers tell of the frugal way in which he lived on his farm, how he refused the rich presents offered him by the Samnite ambassadors, and how at death he left no portion for his daughters, whom the senate provided for.

> Fabricius, scorner of all-conquering gold.
>
> Thomson, *Seasons* (*Winter*)

**Fabulinus.** The god, mentioned by Varro, who taught Roman children to utter their first word (*fabulor*, to speak). It was Vagitanus (*q.v.*) who taught them to utter their first cry.

**Face.** A colloquialism for cheek, impudence, self-confidence, etc., as, 'He has face enough for anything,' i.e. cheek or assurance enough. The use is quite an old one:

> I admire thy impudence; I could never have had the face to have wheedled the poor knight so.
>
> Etherege, *She Would if She Could*, I, i (1668)

***A brazen face.*** A bold, defiant look. *See* Brazen-faced, *and cp.* Brass.

***A wry face.*** The features drawn awry, expressive of distaste.

***Face to face.*** In the immediate presence of each other; two or more persons facing each other. To accuse another 'face to face' means not 'behind his back' or in his absence, but while present.

***On the face of it.*** To all appearance; in the literal sense of the words.

***That puts a new face on the matter.*** Said when fresh evidence has been produced, or something has happened which sets the case in a new light and makes it look different.

***To draw a long face.*** To look dissatisfied or sorrowful, in which case the mouth is drawn down at the corners, the eyes are dejected, and the face has an elongated appearance.

***To face down.*** To withstand with boldness and effrontery.

***To face it out.*** To persist in an assertion which is not true. To maintain without changing colour or hanging the head.

***To face the music.*** To stand up boldly and meet some emergency without faltering.

***To fly in the face of.*** To oppose violently and unreasonably: to set at defiance rashly.

***To have two faces,*** or ***to keep two faces under one hood.*** To be double-faced; to pretend to be very religious, and yet live an evil life.

> We never troubled the Church … We knew we were doing what we ought not to do, and scorned to look pious, and keep two faces under one hood.
>
> Boldrewood, *Robbery Under Arms*, ch. ii

***To look a person in the face,*** or ***full in the face.*** To meet with a steady gaze; implying lack of fear, or, sometimes, a spirit of defiance.

***To make faces.*** To make grimaces with the face.

***To put a bold,*** or ***a good face on the matter.*** To make the best of a bad matter; to bear up under something disagreeable.

***To save one's face.*** Narrowly to avoid almost inevitable disgrace, disaster, or discomfiture.

***To set one's face against something.*** To oppose it; to resist its being done. The expression of the face shows the inclination of a person's mind.

***To shut the door in one's face.*** To put an end to the negotiations, or whatever is in hand; to take the final step.

**Faced.** With a facing, lining of the cuffs, etc.; used of an inferior article bearing the surface of a superior one, as when cotton-velvet has a silk surface.

***Bare-faced.*** *See* Barefaced.

***Shame-faced.*** Having shame expressed in the face. *Cp.* Shamefast.

**Face-card** or **Faced-card.** A court card, a card with a face on it.

**Facile princeps.** By far the best; admittedly first.

> Goethe, the greatest literary critic that ever lived, was more comprehensive and universally tolerant; but De Quincey was *facile princeps*, to the extent of his touch, among the English critics of his generation.
>
> D. Masson, *De Quincey*, ch. xii

**Facilis decensus Averno.** *See* Avernus.

**Facings.** *To put one through his facings.* To examine; to ascertain if what appears on the surface is superficial only.

> The Greek books were again had out, and Grace … was put through her facings. A. Trollope

**Façon de parler.** Idiomatic or usual form of speech; especially some form of words which, taken literally, might be interpreted in an offensive sense, but which is not intended to be so.

**Faction.** The Romans divided the combatants in the circus into classes, called *factions*, each class being distinguished by its special colour, like the crews of a boat-race. The four original factions were the leek-green (*prasina*), the sea-blue (*veneta*), the white (*alba*), and the rose-red (*rosea*). Two other factions were added by Domitian, the colours being golden yellow (*aurata*) and purple. As these combatants strove against each other, and entertained a strong *esprit de corps*, the word was easily applied to political partisans.

**Factotum** (Lat. *facere totum*, to do everything required). One who does for his employer all sorts of services. Sometimes called a *Johannes Factotum.* Formerly the term meant a busybody, or much the same as our 'Jack-of-all-trades', and it is in this sense that Greene used it in his famous reference to Shakespeare:

> There is an upstart Crow beautified with our feathers, that with his *Tygers heart wrapt in a Players hide*, supposes he is as well able to bumbast out a blanke verse as the best of you: but being an absolute *Johannes fac totum*, is in his owne conceit the onely Shake-scene in a countrie. *Greene's Groatsworth of Wit* (1592)

**Fad, A.** A hobby, a temporary fancy, a whim. Perhaps a contraction of faddle in 'fiddle-faddle'.

> Among the fads that Charley had taken up for a time ... was that of collecting old prints.
>
> Eggleston, *Faith Doctor*, ch. iii

**Fadda.** Mahomet's white mule.

**Fadge.** Probably a Scandinavian word, connected with *faga*, to suit. To suit or fit together, as, *It won't fadge*; *we cannot fadge together*; *he does not fadge with me.*

> How will this fadge?
>
> Shakespeare, *Twelfth Night*, 2, 2

The word is also old slang for a farthing.

**Fadha, Al.** Mahomet's silver cuirass, confiscated from the Jews on their expulsion from Medina.

**Fadladeen.** The great Nazir, or chamberlain of Aurungzebë's harem, in Moore's *Lalla Rookh.* The criticisms of this self-conceited courtier upon the tales are very racy and full of humour; and his crestfallen conceit when he finds out that the poet was the Prince in disguise is well conceived.

> He was a judge of everything – from the pencilling of a Circassian's eyelids to the deepest questions of science and literature; from the mixture of a conserve of roseleaves to the composition of an epic poem ... all the cooks and poets of Delhi stood in awe of him. T. Moore

**Faërie.** The land of the fays or faeries. The chief fay realms are Avalon, an island somewhere in the ocean; Oberon's dominions, situate 'in wilderness among the holtis hairy'; and a realm somewhere in the middle of the earth, where was Pari Banou's palace.

> For learnëd Colin [Spenser] lays his pipes to gage,
> And is to Faëry gone a pilgrimage.
>
> Drayton, *Eclogue*, iii

**Faërie Queene, The.** An allegorical romance of chivalry by Edmund Spenser, originally intended to have been in 12 books, each of which was to have portrayed one of the 12 moral virtues. Only six books of twelve cantos each, and part of a seventh, were written (I to III published in 1590, IV to VI in 1596, and the remaining fragments in 1611). It details the adventures of various knights, who personify different virtues, and belong to the court of Gloriana, the Faerie Queene, who sometimes typifies Queen Elizabeth.

The first book contains the legend of the Red Cross Knight (*the spirit of the Church of England*), and the victory of Holiness over Error.

The second book is the legend of Sir Guyon (*Temperance, or the golden mean*).

The third book is the legend of Britomartis (*Chastity, or love without lust*).

The fourth book tells the story of Cambel and Triamond (*Fidelity*).

The fifth book gives the legend of Artegal (*Justice*).

The sixth book, the legend of Sir Calidore (*Courtesy*).

The fragments of the seventh book – viz. cantos 6 and 7, and two stanzas of canto 3 – have for subject *Mutability*.

The plan of the *Faërie Queene* is borrowed from the *Orlando Furioso*, but the creative power of Spenser is more original, and his imagery more striking, than Ariosto's. Thomson says of him:

> [He] like a copious river, poured his song
> O'er all the mazes of enchanted ground.
>
> *The Seasons* (*Summer*), 1574–5

**Fag.** Modern slang for a cigarette. It is said to be short for 'fag-end' (*q.v.*), and the story is that it arose through street-boys asking passing cigarette-smokers to 'chuck us the *fag*, guvnor', meaning the *end*, which is dried, mixed with others, and then made into new cigarettes or smoked in a pipe.

In public schools a fag is a small boy who waits upon a bigger one. Possibly, in this sense, a contracted form of *factotum* (*q.v.*).

***It's too much fag.*** Too much trouble, too much needless exertion.

***Quite fagged out.*** Wearied with hard work; tired out.

**Fag-end.** Originally the selvedge or coarse end of a piece of cloth; hence, the remaining part of anything; as 'the fag-end of a leg of mutton', 'the fag-end of the century', or 'the fag-end of a session', which means the last few days before dissolution.

> I never yet saw a great House so neatly kept ... The Kitchen and Gutters and other Offices of noise and drudgery are at the fag-end; there's a Back-gate for the Beggars and the meaner sort of Swains to come in at.
>
> *Howell's Familiar Letters* (20 May, 1619)

> The old Kidderminster carpet ... burnt into holes with the fag-ends of cigars.
>
> Cuthbert Bede, *Verdant Green*, ch. iv

**Faggot.** A bundle of sticks; hence, other things made of ingredients bundled together, as a cheap kind of sausage or cake made of the 'insides' of pigs, with thyme, scraps of pork, sage, onions, and other herbs, fried together in grease. The origin of the word is unknown.

In mediaeval times heretics were often burned at the stake with faggots, hence an embroidered representation of a faggot was worn on the arm by those who had recanted their 'heretical' opinions. It was designed to show what they merited, but had narrowly escaped.

***Faggot votes.*** Votes obtained by the nominal transfer of property to a person whose income was not otherwise sufficient to qualify him for being a voter.

The 'faggot' was a bundle of property divided into small lots for the purpose stated above.

> Lord Lonsdale had conveyed to him a certain property, on which he was to vote in that borough, as, what was familiarly called a faggot vote.
> Sir F. Burdett, *Parl. Debates*, 1817

***Il y a fagots et fagots.*** There are divers sorts of faggots; every alike is not the same. The expression is in Molière's *Le Médecin malgré lui* (I, vi), where Sganarelle wants to show that his faggots are better than those of other persons: 'Ay, but those faggots are not so good as my faggots.'

***Sentir les fagots.*** To be heretical; to smack of the faggots. In allusion to the custom of burning heretics with blazing faggots. *See above.*

**Fahfah.** One of the rivers of Paradise in *Mohammedan mythology*.

**Faience.** Majolica. So called from Faenza, where, in 1299, it was first manufactured. It is termed majolica because the first specimens the Italians saw came from Majorca. In France it now means a fine ware not equal to porcelain.

**Faineant. *Les Rois Fainéants*** (the 'nonchalant' or 'do-nothing' kings). Clovis II (d.656) and his ten Merovingian successors on the French throne. The line came to an end in 751, when Pepin the Short usurped the crown. Louis V (last of the Carlovingian dynasty, d.987) received the same name.

> I am, you know, a complete *Roy Fainéant*, and never once interfered with my *Maire du Palais* in her proceedings.
> Scott, *Peveril of the Peak*, ch. xv

**Faint. *Faint heart ne'er won fair lady*.** An old proverb, with obvious meaning. It occurs in Phineas Fletcher's *Britain's Ida* (ca. v, st. 1), 1628, but is probably a good deal older.

> And let us mind, faint heart ne'er wan
> A lady fair;
> Wha does the utmost that he can,
> Will whiles do mair.
> Burns, *Epistle to Dr Blacklock*

**Fair. As Personal Epithet.**

Edwy, or Eadwig, King of Wessex (938–58).

Charles IV, King of France, *le Bel* (1294, 1322–8).

Philippe IV of France, *le Bel* (1268, 1285–1314).

***Fair Geraldine.*** *See* Geraldine.

***The Fair-haired.*** Harold I, King of Norway (reigned 872–930).

***Fair Maid of Anjou.*** Lady Edith Plantagenet (fl. 1200), who married David, Prince Royal of Scotland.

***Fair Maid of Brittany.*** Eleanor (d.1241), granddaughter of Henry II, and, after the death of Arthur (1203), the rightful sovereign of England. Her uncle, the usurper King John, imprisoned her in Bristol Castle, where she died. Her father, Geoffrey, John's elder brother, was Count of Brittany.

***Fair Maid of Kent.*** Joan (1328–85), Countess of Salisbury, wife of the Black Prince, and only daughter of Edmond Plantagenet, Earl of Kent. She had been twice married ere she gave her hand to the prince.

***Fair Maid of Norway.*** Margaret (1283–90), daughter of Eric II of Norway, and granddaughter of Alexander III of Scotland. Being recognised by the states of Scotland as successor to the throne, she set out for her kingdom, but died at sea from sea-sickness.

***Fair Maid of Perth.*** Katie Glover, the most beautiful young woman of Perth. Heroine of Scott's novel of the same name, she is supposed to have lived in the early 15th century, but is not a definite historical character, though her house is still shown at Perth.

***Fair Rosamond.*** *See* Rosamond.

**Phrases, etc.**

***A day after the fair.*** Too late for the fun; wise after the event. Here *fair* is (through French) from Lat. *feria*, a holiday, and is quite unconnected with the adjective *fair*, which is the A.S. *faeger*.

***A fair field and no favour.*** Every opportunity being given.

***By fair means.*** Straightforwardly; without deception or compulsion.

***Fair and soft goes far in a day.*** Courtesy and moderation will help one to effect a good deal of his purpose.

***Fair and square.*** Honestly, justly, with straightforwardness.

***Fair fall you.*** Good befall you.

***Fair game.*** A worthy subject of banter; one who exposes himself to ridicule and may be fairly made a butt of.

***Fair play is a jewel.*** As a jewel is an ornament of beauty and value, so fair play is an honourable thing and a 'jewel in the crown' of the player.

***Fair Trade.*** An old euphemism for smuggling.

> Neither Dirk Hatteraick nor any of his sailors, all well known men in the fair trade, were again seen upon that coast.
>
> Scott, *Guy Mannering*, ch. x

In politics the phrase signifies reciprocity of protection or free trade; that is, free trade to those nations that grant free trade to us, and *vice versa*.

***Fair words butter no parsnips.*** *See* Butter.

***In a fair way.*** On the right tack. The 'fair way' is the proper track through a channel, the clear run from hole to hole on a golf-course, etc.

***The fair sex.*** Women generally; the phrase was modelled on the French *le beau sexe*.

***To bid fair.*** To give good promise; to indicate future success or excellence as 'he bids fair to be a good —'.

**Fairy.** The names of the principal fairies and of groups of similar sprites known to fable and legend are given throughout the Dictionary.

> *See* Afreet, Ariel, Banshee, Bogy, Brownie, Bug, Cauld lad, Deev, Duende, Duergar, Elf, Esprit Follet, Fata, Genius, Gnome, Goblin, Hobgoblin, Jinn, Kelpie, Kobold, Leprechaun, Lutin, Mab, Monaciello, Naiad, Nix, Oberon, Oread, Ouph, Peri, Pigwiggin, Pixy, Puck, Robin Goodfellow, Stromkarl, Sylph, Troll, Undine, White Ladies.

According to some popular legends fairies are the dispossessed spirits which once inhabited human bodies, but are not yet meet to dwell with the 'saints in light'.

> All those airy shapes you now behold
> Were human bodies once, and clothed with earthly mould;
> Our souls, not yet prepared for upper light,
> Till doomsday wander in the shades of night.
>
> Dryden, *The Flower and the Leaf*

Fairies of nursery mythology wear a red conical cap; a mantle of green cloth, inlaid with wild flowers; green pantaloons, buttoned with bobs of silk; and silver shoon. Some accounts add that they carry quivers of adder-slough, and bows made of the ribs of a man buried where 'three lairds' lands meet'; that their arrows are made of bog-reed, tipped with white flints, and dipped in the dew of hemlock; and that they ride on steeds whose hoofs would not 'dash the dew from the cup of a harebell'.

> Fairies small Two foot tall,
> With caps red On their head
> Dance a round On the ground.
>
> Jasper Fisher, *Song from Fuimus Troes* (1633)

***Fairy darts.*** Flint arrow-heads. *See* Elf arrows.

***Fairy loaves*** or ***stones.*** Fossil sea-urchins, said to be made by the fairies.

***Fairy money.*** Found money. Said to be placed by some good fairy at the spot where it was picked up. 'Fairy money' is apt to be transformed into leaves.

***Fairy of the mine.*** A malevolent gnome (*q.v.*) supposed to live in mines, busying itself with cutting ore, turning the windlass, etc., but effecting nothing.

> No goblin, or swart fairy of the mine,
> Hath hurtful power o'er true virginity.
>
> Milton, *Comus*, 447

***Fairy rings.*** Circles of rank or withered grass, often seen in lawns, meadows, and grass-plots, and popularly supposed to be produced by fairies dancing on the spot. In sober truth, these rings are simply an agaric or fungus below the surface, which has seeded circularly, as many plants do. Where the ring is *brown* and almost *bare*, the 'spawn' has enveloped the roots and thus prevented their absorbing moisture; but where the grass is rank the 'spawn' itself has died, and served as manure to the young grass.

> You demi-puppets, that
> By moonshine do the green-sour ringlets make,
> Whereof the ewe not bites.
>
> Shakespeare, *Tempest*, 5, 1

***Fairy sparks.*** The phosphoric light from decaying wood, fish, and other substances. Thought at one time to be lights prepared for the fairies at their revels.

**Fait accompli** (Fr.). A scheme which has been already carried out; often used in the sense of stealing a march on some other party.

> I pointed out to Herr von Jagow that this *fait accompli* of the violation of the Belgian frontier rendered, as he would readily understand, the situation exceedingly grave, and I asked him whether there was not still time to draw back and avoid possible consequences, which both he and I would deplore. He replied that, for the reasons he had given me, it was now impossible for them to draw back.
>
> Sir Edward Goschen, British Ambassador in Berlin, to Sir Edward Grey, London, 8 Aug., 1914

**Faith.** ***Act of faith.*** *See* Auto da Fé.

***Defender of the Faith.*** *See* Defender.

***In good faith. 'Bona fide;' 'de bonne foi;'*** with no ulterior motive.

***To pin one's faith to.*** *See* Pin.

**Faithful,** in Bunyan's *Pilgrim's Progress*, is seized at Vanity Fair, burnt to death, and taken to heaven in a chariot of fire. A Puritan used to be called *Brother Faithful.* The active disciples of any cult are called *the faithful.*

***Commander of the Faithful.*** The Caliph is so called by Mohammedans.

***Father of the faithful.*** Abraham (Rom. 4; Gal. 3:6–9).

***Most Faithful King, The.*** The appellation by which the kings of Portugal used to be addressed by the Vatican. *Cp.* Religious.

**Faithists.** A mystico-spiritualistic sect founded about 1900 by Francis Theodore Alfred Davies, who later seceded and founded the Kosmon Church on similar lines. Their Bible is known as 'Oahspe' (*q.v.*), and among their beliefs are –

> That man being a trinity of Body, Spirit, Soul, he should unfold within his being the gifts of the Spirit, such as clairvoyance, clairaudience, psychometry, healing, prophecy, speaking with tongues, seership, inspiration, trance-speaking, protection, etc.

Their principal localities were Streatham and Balham in London, and Southend-on-Sea.

**Fakâr, Dhu'l.** The scimitar of Mahomet, which fell to his share when the spoil was divided after the battle of Bekr. It means 'The Trenchant'.

**Fake.** A fraud or swindle, as 'this antique table is a fake', i.e. it is not antique at all; also verb, as 'to fake antiques', 'to fake the accounts', i.e. to 'cook' them, falsify them. The word is old thieves' slang from Dutch or German, and was originally *feague. Feaguing* a horse was making it look younger or stronger than it really is for purposes of sale. *Cp.* To bishop.

**Fakir.** Properly, a Mohammedan religious beggar or mendicant. They wear coarse black or brown dresses, and a black turban over which a red handkerchief is tied, and perform menial offices connected with burials, the cleaning of mosques, and so on.

**Falcon** and **Falconet.** Pieces of light artillery of the 16th century, the names of which are borrowed from hawks. *Cp.* Saker.

***Falcon gentle.*** A goshawk.

***Falcon peregrine.*** *See* Peregrine.

**Fald-stool** (Old High Ger. *faldan*, to fold). A portable folding chair used by a bishop in a church other than his own cathedral; a small desk at which the Litany is sung or said; also the place at the south side of the altar at which sovereigns kneel at their coronation.

**Falernian.** A choice Italian wine, much esteemed by the ancient Romans, and so called because it was made of grapes from Falernus. There were three sorts – the rough, the sweet, and the dry.

> When Horace wrote his noble verse,
> His brilliant, glowing line,
> He must have gone to bed the worse
> For good Falernian wine.
> No poet yet could praise the rose
> In verse that so serenely flows
> Unless he dipped his Roman nose
> In good Falernian wine.
> Theodore Maynard, 'A Tankard of Ale' (1920)

**Fall.** (Noun)

In music, a sinking of tone, a cadence.

> That strain again! it had a dying fall:
> O! it came o'er my ear like the sweet sound
> That breathes upon a bank of violets,
> Stealing and giving odour.
> Shakespeare, *Twelfth Night*, 1, 1

> The strains decay,
> And melt away,
> In a dying, dying fall. Pope, *St Cecilia's Day*

***In the fall.*** In the autumn, at the fall of the leaf. Though now commonly classed as an Americanism the term was formerly in good use in England, and is found in the works of Drayton, Middleton, Raleigh, and other Elizabethans. In England it is now, except in provincial use, practically obsolete.

> What crowds of patients the town doctor kills,
> Or how, last fall, he raised the weekly bills.
> Dryden, *Juvenal*

***The Fall of man.*** The degeneracy of the human race in consequence of the disobedience of Adam. Adam fell, or ceased to stand his ground, under temptation.

***The fall of the drop,*** in theatrical parlance, means the fall of the drop-curtain at the end of the act or play.

***To ride for a fall.*** *See* Ride.

***To try a fall.*** To wrestle, when each tries to 'fall' or throw the other.

> I am given, sir ... to understand that your younger brother, Orlando, hath a disposition to come in disguised against me to try a fall.
> *As You Like It*, 1, 1

*See also* Falling-bands.

**Fall.** (Verb)

***To fall away.*** To lose flesh; to degenerate; to quit a party, as 'his adherents fell away one by one'.

***To fall back upon.*** To have recourse to.

***To fall flat.*** To lie prostrate or procumbent; to fail to interest, as 'the last act fell flat'.

***To fall foul of one.*** To make an assault on someone; to quarrel with, or run up against someone. A sea term. A rope is said to be *foul* when it is entangled; and one ship *falls foul* of another when it runs against her and prevents her free progress.

***To fall from.*** To violate, as 'to fall from his word'; to tumble or slip off, as 'to fall from a horse'; to abandon or go away from, as 'to fall from grace', to relapse into sin.

***To fall in.*** To take one's place with others; to concur with, as 'he fell in with my views' – that is, his views or ideas fell into the lot of my views or ideas. *Cp.* Fall Out.

***To fall in love with.*** To become enamoured of.

***To fall in with.*** To meet accidentally; to come across. This is a Latin phrase, *in aliquam casu incidere.*

***To fall into a snare.*** To stumble accidentally into a snare. This is a Latin phrase, *insidias incidere.* Similarly, to fall into disgrace is the Latin *in offensionem cadire.*

***To fall out.*** To quarrel; also, to happen. *Cp.* Fall In.

> Three children sliding on the ice
> Upon a summer's day:
> As it fell out they all fell in,
> The rest they ran away.
>
> Porson, *Mother Goose*

> See ye fall not out by the way. Gen. 45:24

In military parlance, to leave the ranks; hence, to take one's departure, to desert some cause.

***To fall short of.*** To be deficient of a supply. This is the Lat. *excido*, to fail. To fall short of the mark is a figure taken from archery, quoits, etc., where the missile falls to the ground before reaching the mark.

***To fall sick.*** To be unwell. A Latin phrase, *In morbum incidere. Cp.* Falling Sickness.

***To fall through.*** To fail of being carried out or accomplished.

***To fall to.*** To begin (eating, fighting, etc.).

> They sat down ... and without waiting ... fell to like commoners after grace.
>
> Kane, *Arctic Explorations*, vol. i, ch. xxx, p. 419

***To fall to the ground.*** To fail from lack of support; to become of no account. 'In view of what has happened my proposals fall to the ground,' i.e. are rendered useless.

***To fall together by the ears.*** To fight and scratch each other; to contend in strife. 'To *fall* together by the ears' is *inter se certare*; but 'to *set* together by the ears' is *discordium concitare. See* Ear.

***To fall under.*** To incur, as, 'to be under the reproach of carelessness'; to be submitted to, as, 'to fall under consideration', a Latinism, *In deliberationem cadere.*

***To fall upon.*** To attack, as 'to fall upon the rear', a Latin phrase, *ultimis incidere*; to throw oneself on, as, 'he fell on his sword', *manu sua cadere*; to happen on, as, 'On what day does Easter fall?'

***To fall upon one's feet.*** To escape a threatened injury; to light upon one's feet.

**Falling-bands.** Neck-bands which fall on the breast. They were common in the 17th century, when they were also called falls.

> Under that fayre ruffe so sprucely set
> Appeares a fall, a falling-band forsooth!
>
> Marston, *Scourge of Villainie, III* (1599)

**Falling Sickness.** Epilepsy, in which the patient falls suddenly to the ground. Shakespeare plays on the term:

> And honest Casca, we have the falling-sickness.
> *Brutus.* – He hath the falling-sickness.
> *Cassius.* – No, Caesar hath it not: but you, and I.
>
> Shakespeare, *Julius Caesar*, 1, 2

**Falling Stars.** Meteors. Mohammedans believe them to be firebrands flung by good angels against evil spirits when they approach too near the gates of heaven.

**Fal-lals.** Knick-knacks, trifling fripperies, ornaments of small value.

> Our god-child passed in review all her gowns, fichus, tags, bobbins, laces, silk stockings, and fallals. Thackeray, *Vanity Fair*, ch. vi

**Fallow.** *Fallow land* is land ploughed and harrowed but left unsown. The word is A.S. *foelging*, connected with *foelga*, harrows for breaking crops, and is nothing to do with the *fallow* of *fallow deer.* This means 'reddish yellow', and is the A.S. *fealu*, which is related to Dut. *vaal*, Ger. *fahl*, and Lat. *palidus*, pale.

**False. *False colours.*** *See* Colour.

***False quantity.*** A term used in prosody to denote the incorrect use of a long for a short vowel or syllable, or *vice versa.*

***The rule of false.*** A method of solving certain mathematical problems generally done by equations. Suppose the question is this: 'What number is that whose half exceeds its third by 12?' Assume any number you like as the supposed answer – say 96. Then, by the question, 96 ÷ 2 = 96 + 3 ÷ 12, or 48 = 32 + 12, i.e. 54, but 48 does not equal 54, the latter is 16 too much.

Well, now state by rule of proporthus, 16:12: :96 to the answer, which is 72, the number required.

**Falstaff.** A fat, sensual, boastful, and mendacious knight; full of wit and humour; he was the boon companion of Henry, Prince of Wales. (*1* and *2 Henry IV*, and *Merry Wives of Windsor*.) Hence, *Falstaffian*, possessing Falstaff's characteristics, or resembling his 'ragged regiment'.

**Falutin.** *See* High falutin.

**Fame.** ***Temple of Fame***. A Pantheon (*q.v.*) where monuments to the famous dead of a nation are erected and the memories honoured, especially that at Paris. Hence, *he will have a niche in the Temple of Fame*, he has done something that will cause his people to honour him and keep his memory green.

> The temple of fame is the shortest passage to riches and preferment.
>
> *Letters of Junius*, Letter lix

**Familiar,** or ***Familiar Spirit*** (Lat. *famulus*, a servant). A spirit slave, sometimes in human form, sometimes appearing as a cat, dog, raven, or other dumb creature, petted by a 'witch', and supposed to be her demon in disguise.

> Away with him! he has a familiar under his tongue.
>
> Shakespeare, *2 Henry VI*, 4, 7

**Familiarity.** ***Familiarity breeds contempt***. The proverb appears in English at least as early as the mid-16th century (Udall), and was well known in Latin.

**Familists.** Members of the 'Family of Love', a fanatical sect founded by David George, or Joriszoon, of Delft, who separated from the Anabaptists about 1535, and who were also known as Davists, or Davidians. They maintained that all men are of one family, and should love each other as brothers and sisters, and that complete obedience was due to all rulers, how tyrannical soever they might be.

**Fan.** ***I could brain him with his lady's fan*** (*1 Henry IV*, 2, 3) – i.e. knock his brains out with something whose weight and strength is very trifling, because his brains are to all intents and purposes negligible.

> Wer't not better
> Your head were broken with the handle of a fan,
> Or your nose bored with a silver bodkin?
>
> Fletcher, *Wit at Several Weapons*, v, i

**Fanatic.** Literally one who is possessed of the enthusiasm or madness of the temple, i.e. engendered by over-indulgence in religious observances (Lat. *fanum*, a temple – the Eng. *fane*). Among the Romans there were certain persons who attended the temples and fell into strange fits, in which they were credited with being able to see the spirits of the past and to foretell the events of the future.

> Earth's fanatics make
> Too frequently heaven's saints.
>
> Mrs Browning, *Aurora Leigh*, ii, 448

The word is also used adjectivally:

> Faith, fanatic faith, once wedded fast
> To some dear falsehood hugs it to the last
>
> Moore, *Lallah Rookh* (*The Veiled Prophet*)

**Fancy.** Love – i.e. the passion of the *fantasy* or imagination.

> Tell me where is fancy bred,
> Or in the heart or in the head.
>
> Shakespeare, *Merchant of Venice*, 3, 9

***The fancy***. Those who fancy, i.e. have a fondness for some particular sport or amusement; used specially with reference to pugilism and, attributively, to those who breed dogs, pigeons (dog-fancier, pigeon-fancier), etc.

**Fancy-free.** Not in love.

> In maiden meditation fancy-free.
>
> Shakespeare, *Midsummer Night's Dream*, 2, 2

**Fancy-man.** A *cavaliere servente* (*q.v.*) or *cicisbeo* (*q.v.*); one selected by a married lady to escort her to theatres, etc., to ride about with her, and to amuse her. The man she 'fancies' or likes. The term is more usual in the lower circles of society than in the upper.

**Fancy-sick.** Love-sick.

> All fancy-sick she is, and pale of cheer.
>
> Shakespeare, *Midsummer Night's Dream*, 3, 2

**Fanesii.** Pliny's name for a Scandinavian tribe whose ears were so long that they would cover their whole body.

**Fanfaron.** A swaggering bully; a cowardly boaster who blows his own trumpet. Scott uses the word for finery, especially for the gold lace worn by military men. Fr. *fanfare*, a flourish of trumpets.

> 'Marry, hang thee, with thy fanfarona about thy neck!' said the falconer.
>
> Scott, *The Abbot*, cxvii

Hence, *Fanfaronade*, swaggering; vain boasting; ostentatious display.

> The bishop copied this proceeding from the fanfaronade of M. Boufflers. Swift

**Fangled.** *See* New Fangled.

**Fanny, Lord.** A nickname given by Pope to Lord Hervey (1696–1743) for his effeminate and foppish manners. He painted his face, and was as pretty in his ways as a boarding-school miss. *See* Sporus.

> The lines are weak, another's pleased to say,
> Lord Fanny spins a thousand such a day.
>
> Pope, *Satires of Horace*, i

**Fantigue.** A fussy anxiety; that restless, nervous commotion which persons have who are overwrought. To get in a fantigue over something, to get thoroughly excited, hysterical, or out of humour about it.

**Fantoccini** [*fanto-cheny*]. A dramatic performance by puppets. (Ital. *fantoccio*, a puppet.)

**Fantom.** An old spelling of Phantom (*q.v.*).

**Far.**

***A far cry.*** *See* Cry.

***Far and away.*** Beyond comparison; *nullus proximus aut secundus*; as, 'far and away the best'; some person or thing beyond all rivalry.

***Far and wide.*** To a good distance in every direction. 'To spread the news far and wide', to blazon it everywhere.

***Far-fetched.*** Not closely connected; as, 'a far-fetched simile', a 'far-fetched allusion'. Also, obtained from a foreign or distant country, *quod rarum est, carum est.*

> The passion for long, involved sentences ... and far-fetched conceits ... passed away, and a clearer and less ornate style became popular.
>
> Lecky, *English in the Eighteenth Century*, vol. i, ch. 1

***Far from it.*** Not in the least; by no means; quite the contrary. If the answer to 'was he sober at the time?' is 'Far from it', the implication is that he was in a considerably advanced state of intoxication.

***Far gone.*** Deeply affected: as, 'far gone in love'.

**Far niente.** (*See* Dolce.)

**Farce.** A grotesque and exaggerated kind of comedy, full of ludicrous incidents and expressions. The word is the Old French *farce*, stuffing (from Lat. *farcire*, to stuff), hence an interlude stuffed into or inserted in the main piece, such interludes always being of a racy, exaggerated comic character.

> Farce is that in poetry which grotesque is in a picture. The persons and action of a farce are all unnatural, and the manners false, that is, inconsisting with the characters of mankind.
>
> Dryden, *Parallel of Poetry and Painting*

The following couplet was written by Garrick or Sir John Hill, M.D. (d.1775), who wrote farces as well as prescribed medicines:

> For physic and farces his equal there scarce is,
> His farces are physic, his physic a farce is.

**Farcy** or **Farcin.** A disease in horses, which consists of a swelling of the ganglions and lymphatic vessels and shows itself in little knots; very like glanders. The name is, like *farce* (above) from Lat. *farcire*, to stuff.

**Fardle** or **Fardel.** A variant of obsolete *furdle* (from which comes *furl*, to furl a sail), meaning to roll up; hence, that which is rolled up, i.e. a bundle or package.

> Who would fardels bear,
> To grunt and sweat under a weary life?
>
> Shakespeare, *Hamlet*, 3, 1
>
> Like a pedlar she went up and down:
> For she had got a pretty handsome pack,
> Which she had fardled neatly at her back.
>
> Drayton, *The Muse's Elysium*, vii

**Fare.** (A.S. *faran*, to go, to travel; connected with Lat. *portare*, to carry.) The noun formerly denoted a journey for which a sum was paid; but now the sum itself, and, by extension, the person who pays it.

**Farewell.** Goodbye; adieu. It was originally addressed to one about to start on a journey, expressing the wish that the *fare* (*see above*) would be a good one. Byron in his *Lines* to his wife plays on the phrase:

> Fare thee well! and if for ever,
> Still for ever, fare *thee well.*

***He cannot fare well but he must cry out roast meat.*** Said of one who blazons his good fortune on the house-top. *Sorex suo perit indicio.* Terence has the same idea: *Egomet meo indicio miser, quasi sorex, hodie perii* (*Eunuchus*, v, 7, 23).

**Farinae.** *See* Ejusdem Farinae.

**Farleu.** A duty of 6*d.* paid to the lord of the manor of West Slapton, in Devonshire, instead of his best beast; a form of heriot (*q.v.*).

**Farmer George.** George III; so called from his farmer-like manners, taste, dress, and amusements. (1738, 1760–1820.)

> A better farmer ne'er brushed dew from lawn.
>
> Byron, *Vision of Judgment*

**Farnese.** A noted Italian family, celebrated in the 16th and 17th centuries as soldiers and patrons of the arts. Its fortunes were laid by Alessandro Farnese, who was Pope as Paul III (1534–49), and who created the Duchy of Parma for his son, Pietro Luigi (1545).

***The Farnese Bull.*** A colossal group attributed to Apollonius and Tauriscus of Tralles, in Asia Minor. They belonged to the Rhodian school, and lived about 300 BC. The group represents

Dirce bound to the horns of a bull by Zethus and Amphion, for ill-using their mother. It was discovered in the Baths of Caracalla in 1546, and placed in the Farnese palace, in Rome. It is now at the Museo Nazionale, Naples.

***The Farnese Hercules.*** Glykon's copy (Early Empire period) of the famous statue of Lysippus, the Greek sculptor in the time of Alexander the Great. It represents the hero leaning on his club, with one hand on his back, as if he had just got possession of the apple of the Hesperides. It is now at the Museo Nazionale, Naples.

**Farrago.** *A farrago of nonsense.* A confused heap of nonsense. *Farrago* (Lat.) is properly a mixture of *far* (meal) with other ingredients for the use of cattle.

> Anquetil was derided … for having suffered a farrago of nonsense to be palmed off upon him by his Parsi teachers as the works of the sage Zoroaster.
>
> Whitney, *Oriental Studies* (Avesta), ch. vi

**Farringdon Ward** (London). Named from William de Farndon (or Farendon), goldsmith, who in 1281 bought the Aldermanry from John le Fevre. It was divided into two wards, Farndone Within and Farndone Without, in 1394.

**Farthing.** A fourth part. Penny pieces used to be divided into four parts thus, ⊕. One of these quarters was a *feorthing* or fourth part, and the name was applied to other coins beside the penny. Thus, we read in the *Grayfriar's Chronicle* –

> This yere the kynge made a newe quyne, as the nobylle, half-nobylle, and ferdyng-nobylle.

***I don't care for it a brass farthing.*** James II debased all the coinage, and issued, amongst other worthless coins, brass pence, halfpence, and farthings.

**Farthingale.** A sort of crinoline petticoat. The word is the O.Fr. *verdugale*, which is a corruption of Span. *verdugado*, green rods, referring to the twigs or switches of which the framework was made before whalebone was used for the purpose. The old derivation from Fr. *vertugarde*, 'guard for modesty', is amusing, but otherwise quite valueless.

**Fascinate.** Literally, to cast a spell by means of the eye (Lat. *fascinum*, a spell). The allusion is to the ancient notion of bewitching by the power of the eye. *Cp.* Evil Eye.

> None of the affections have been noted to fascinate and bewitch, but love and envy.
>
> Bacon, *Essays; Of Envy*

**Fash.** ***Dinna fash yoursel'!*** Don't get excited; don't get into a fatigue about it. The word is looked on as Scotch, but it is the Lat. *fastidium* (*fastus*, arrogance) through Provençal *fastigar* and O.Fr. *fascher* (Mod. Fr. *fâcher*).

**Fashion.** ***In a fashion*** or ***after a fashion***. 'In a sort of a way'; as, 'he spoke French in a fashion' (i.e. very badly) – 'French of Stratford atte Bowe'.

**Fast.** The adjective is used figuratively of a person of either sex who is addicted to pleasure and dissipation; a young man or woman who lives too fast – 'goes the pace' at such a rate that he (or she) is soon worn out.

***To play fast and loose.*** To run with the hare and hold with the hounds; to blow both hot and cold; to say one thing and do another. The allusion is probably to an old cheating game that used to be practised at fairs. A belt was folded, and the player was asked to prick it with a skewer, so as to pin it *fast* to the table; having so done, the adversary took the two ends, and *loosed* it or drew it away, showing that it had not been pierced at all.

> He forced his neck into a noose,<br>
> To show his play at fast and loose;<br>
> And when he chanced t'escape, mistook,<br>
> For art and subtlety, his luck.
>
> Butler, *Hudibras*, iii, 2

**Fasti.** Working days; when, in Rome, the law-courts were open. Holy days (*dies non*), when the law-courts were not open, were, by the Romans, called *ne-fasti.*

The *Fasti* were listed in calendars, and the registers of events occurring during the year of office of a pair of consuls was called *fasti consulares*; hence, any chronological list of events or office-holders became known as *fasti*, and hence such titles as *Fasti Academaei Mariscallanae Aberdonenses*, selections from the records of the Marischal College, Aberdeen.

**Fat.** ***A bit of fat.*** An unexpected stroke of luck; also, the best part of anything, especially, among actors, a good part in a play. In printers' slang *fat* is composition that does not entail a lot of setting, and hence can be done quickly.

***Fat-head.*** A silly fool, a dolt.

***The fat is in the fire.*** Something has been let out inadvertently which will cause a 'regular flare up'; it's all over, all's up with it. The allusion is to frying; if the grease is spilt into the fire, the coals smoke and blaze so as to spoil the food.

***The Fat:***

Alfonzo II of Portugal (1212–23).

Charles II of France, *le Gros* (832, 884–8).

Louis VI of France, *le Gros* (1078, 1108–37).

**Fata** (Ital., a fairy). Female supernatural beings introduced in Italian mediaeval romance, usually under the sway of Demogorgon (*q.v.*). In *Orlando Innamorato* we meet with the 'Fata Morgana' (*see* Morgan le Fay); in Bojardo, with the 'Fata Silvanella', and others.

***Fata Morgana.*** A sort of mirage in which objects are reflected in the sea, and sometimes on a kind of aerial screen high above it, occasionally seen in the neighbourhood of the Straits of Messina, so named from Morgan le Fay (*q.v.*) who was fabled by the Norman settlers in England to dwell in Calabria.

**Fatal Gifts.** *See* Cadmus, Collor of Arsinoe, Harmonia, Necklace, the Fatal, Nessus, Nibelungen Hoard, Opal Tolosa, etc.

**Fate. *The cruel fates*.** The Greeks and Romans supposed there were three *Parcae* or Fates, who arbitrarily controlled the birth, life, and death of every man. They were Clotho (who held the distaff), Lachesis (who spun the thread of life), and Atropos (who cut it off when life was ended), and are called 'cruel' because they pay no regard to the wishes of anyone. (Gr. *klotho*, to draw thread from a distaff; Lachesis from *lagchano*, to assign by lot; and *Atropos* = inflexible.)

**Father.** The name is given as a title to Catholic priests, especially confessors, superiors of convents, religious teachers, etc.; also to the senior member of a body or profession, as the *Father of the House of Commons*, the *Father of the Bench*, and to the originator or first leader of some movement, school, etc., as the *Father of Comedy* (Aristophanes), the *Father of English Song* (Caedmon). In ancient Rome the title was given to the senators (*cp.* Patrician, Conscript Fathers), and in ecclesiastical history to the early church writers and doctors. *See* Fathers *below*.

***To father a thing on one.*** To impute it to him; to assert that he was the originator of it.

***Father Mathew, Neptune, Prout,*** etc. *See these names.*

***Father of his Country.*** Cicero was so entitled by the Roman senate. They offered the same title to Marius, but he refused to accept it.

Several of the Caesars were so called – Julius, after quelling the insurrection of Spain: Augustus, etc.

Cosimo de' Medici (1389–1464).

George Washington, the first President of the United States (1732–99).

Andrea Doria (1468–1560). Inscribed on the base of his statue by his countrymen of Genoa.

Andronicus Palaeologus II assumed the title (about 1260–1332).

*Cp. also* 1 Chron. 4:14.

***Father of the Chapel.*** *See* Chapel.

***Father of Letters.*** François I of France (1494, 1515–47).

Lorenzo de' Medici, *the Magnificent* (1448–92).

***Father of the People.*** Louis XII of France (1462, 1498–1515). Henri IV was also termed 'the father and friend of the people' (1553, 1589–1610).

Christian III of Denmark (1502, 1534–59).

***Father of Waters.*** The Irrawaddy, in Burmah, and the Mississippi, in North America. The Nile is so called by Dr Johnson in his *Rasselas*.

The epithet *Father* is not uncommonly applied to rivers, especially those on which cities are built. The river is the father of the city, or the reason why the site was selected by the first settlers.

Say, Father Thames, for thou hast seen
  Full many a sprightly race
Disporting on thy margent green,
  The paths of pleasure trace.

Gray, *Distant Prospect of Eton College*

O Tiber, Father Tiber,
To whom the Romans pray.

Macaulay, *Lay of Horatius*

***Father Thoughtful.*** Nicholas Catinat (1637–1712), a marshal of France; so called by his soldiers for his cautious and thoughtful policy.

**Fathers of the Church.** The early advocates of Christianity, who may be thus classified:

(1) Five *apostolic fathers*, who were contemporary with the apostles – viz. Clement of Rome, Barnabas, Hermas, Ignatius, and Polycarp.

(2) The *primitive fathers*. Those advocates of Christianity who lived in the first three centuries. They were the five apostolic fathers (*q.v.*). together with the nine following: Justin, Theophilus of Antioch, Irenaeus, Clement of Alexandria, Cyprian of Carthage, Origen, Gregory Thaumaturgus, Dionysius of Alexandria, and Tertullian.

(3) The *fathers of the Greek Church* of the 4th and 5th centuries, viz. Eusebius, Athanasius, Basil the Great, Gregory Nazianzenus, Gregory of Nyssa, Cyril of Jerusalem, Chrysostom. Epiphanius, Cyril of Alexandria, and Ephraim, deacon of Edessa.

(4) The *fathers of the Latin Church*, of about the same period, viz. Lactantius, Hilary, Ambrose of Milan, Jerome, and St Augustine of Hippo.

***The last of the fathers.*** St Bernard (1091–1153). The schoolmen who followed treated their subjects systematically.

**Fatima.** The last of Bluebeard's wives. *See* Bluebeard. She was saved from death by the timely arrival of her brother with a party of friends. Mahomet's favourite daughter was called Fatima.

**Fatted Calf.** *See* Calf.

**Fault.** In geology, the break or displacement of a stratum of rock.

***At fault.*** Not on the right track. Hounds are at fault when the fox has jumped upon a wall, crossed a river, cut through a flock of sheep, or doubled like a hare, because the scent, i.e. the track, is broken.

***For fault of a better*** (Shakespeare, *Merry Wives*, 1, 4). In default of a better; no one (or nothing) better being available.

> I am the youngest of that name, for fault of a worse. Shakespeare, *Romeo and Juliet*, 2, 4

***In fault.*** To blame.

> Is Antony or we in fault for this?
>
> Shakespeare, *Antony and Cleopatra*, 3, 13

***No one is without his faults.*** No one is perfect. *Vitiis nemo sine nascitur.*

***To a fault.*** In excess; as, kind to a fault. Excess of every good is more or less evil.

***To find fault.*** To blame; to express disapprobation.

**Fauna.** The animals of a country at any given geological or modern period. The term was first used by Linnaeus in the title of his *Fauna Suecica* (1746), a companion volume to his *Flora Suecica* of the preceding year, and is the name of a Roman rural goddess, sister of Faunus.

> Nor less the place of curious plant he knows –
> He both his Flora and his Fauna shows.
>
> Crabbe, *Borough*

**Faust.** The hero of Marlowe's *Tragical History of Dr Faustus* (about 1589) and Goethe's *Faust* (1790–1833) is founded on Dr Johann Faust, or Faustus, a scoundrelly magician and astrologer, who was born in Wurtemberg and died about 1538. Many tales previously ascribed to other astrologers crystallised about him, he became the popular ideal 'of one who sought to sound the depths of this world's knowledge and enjoyment without help from God', and in 1587 he appeared for the first time as the central figure in a book (published at Frankfort-on-Main), which immediately became popular and was soon translated into English, French, and other languages. Marlowe

> Treated the legend as a poet, bringing out with all his power the central thought – man in the pride of knowledge turning from God. The voices of his good and evil angel in the ear of Faustus, the one bidding him repent and hope, the other bidding him despair, were devised by Marlowe himself for the better painting of a soul within the toils of Satan.
>
> Morley, *English Writers*, vol. ix, p. 255

The basis of the legend is that, in return for twenty-four years of further life during which he is to have every pleasure and all knowledge at his command, Faust sells his soul to the devil, and the climax is reached when, at the close of the period, the devil claims him for his own. Mephistopheles (*q.v.*) is his evil angel, and the supplier of all his desires.

Faustus is, says J. A. Symonds,

> A parable of the impotent yearnings of the Middle Ages – its passionate aspiration, its conscience-stricken desire, its fettered curiosity amid the cramping limits of imperfect knowledge, and irrational dogmatism. The indestructible beauty of Greek art, whereof Helen was the emblem, became, through the discovery of classic poetry and sculpture, the possession of the modern world. Mediaevalism took this Helen to wife, and their offspring, the Euphorion of Goethe's drama, is the spirit of the modern world.
>
> *Renaissance in Italy*, vol. II, p. 54

***The Devil and Dr Faustus.*** This story concerns Johann Fust, or Faustus (d. about 1467), one of the pioneers of printing, and is in no way connected with the Faust legend (*see above*). Fust was one of the earliest printers of Bibles, and is said to have passed off a large number as manuscripts for sixty crowns apiece, the usual price being five hundred crowns. The uniformity of the books, their rapid supply, and their unusual cheapness excited astonishment. Information was laid against him for magic, the brilliant red ink with which his copies were adorned was declared to be his blood; he was charged with dealings with the devil, and condemned to be burnt alive. To save himself, he revealed his secret to the Paris Parlement, and his invention became the admiration of the world.

**Faux pas** (Fr.). A 'false step'; a breach of manners or moral conduct.

The fact is, his Lordship, who hadn't it seems,
Form'd the slightest idea, not ev'n in his dreams,
That the pair had been wedded according to law,
Conceived that his daughter had made a *faux pas*.
Barham (Ingoldsby), *Some Account of a New Play*

**Favonius.** The Latin name for the zephyr or west wind. It means the wind *favourable* to vegetation.

If to the torrid Zone her way she bend,
Her the coole breathing of *Favonius* lend,
Thither command the birds to bring their quires,
That Zone is temprate.
Habbington, *Castara, To the Spring* (1634)

**Favour.** Ribbons made into a bow are called *favours* from being bestowed by ladies on the successful champions of tournaments. (*Cp.* True-Lovers' Knot.)

Here, Fluellen; wear thou this favour for me, and stick it in thy cap.
Shakespeare, *Henry V*, 4, 7

***To curry favour.*** *See* Curry.

**Favourites.** False curls on the temples; a curl of hair on the temples plastered with some cosmetic; whiskers made to meet the mouth.

Yet tell me, sire, don't you as nice appear
With your false calves, bardash, and fav'rites here?
Mrs Centlivre, *The Platonic Lady, Epilogue* (1721)

**Fax et focus.** *See* Fons.

**Fay.** *See* Fairy.

*Morgan le Fay*. *See* Morgan.

**Fearless** (Fr., *Sans peur*). Jean, Duke of Burgundy (1371–1419). *Cp.* Bayard.

**Feast of Reason.** Conversation on and discussion of learned and congenial subjects.

There St John mingles with my friendly bowl
The feast of reason and the flow of soul.
Pope, *Imitations of Horace*, ii, 1

**Feasts.** Anniversary days of joy. They are either immovable or movable. *The chief immovable feasts* in the Christian calendar are the four quarter-days – viz. the Annunciation or Lady Day (March 25th), the Nativity of John the Baptist (June 24th), Michaelmas Day (September 29th), and Christmas Day (December 25th). Others are the Circumcision (January 1st), Epiphany (January 6th), All Saints' (November 1st), All Souls' (November 2nd), and the several Apostles' days.

***The movable feasts*** depend upon Easter Sunday. They are –

Palm Sunday. The Sunday next before Easter Sunday.

Good Friday. The Friday next before Easter Sunday.

Ash Wednesday. The first day of Lent.

Sexagesima Sunday. Sixty days before Easter Sunday.

Ascension Day or Holy Thursday. Fortieth day after Easter Sunday.

Pentecost or Whit Sunday. The seventh Sunday after Easter Sunday.

Trinity Sunday. The Sunday next after Pentecost.

**Feather.** ***A broken feather in one's wing.*** A scandal connected with one.

If an angel were to walk about, Mrs Sam Hurst would never rest till she had found out where he came from; and perhaps whether he had a broken feather in his wing.
Mrs Oliphant, *Phoebe*

***A feather in your cap.*** An honour to you. The allusion is to the very general custom in Asia and among the American Indians of adding a feather to the headgear for every enemy slain. The ancient Lycians, and many others had a similar custom, and it is still usual for the sportsman who kills the first woodcock to pluck out a feather and stick it in his cap.

The custom, in one form or another, seems to be almost universal; in Hungary, at one time, none might wear a feather but he who had slain a Turk, and it will be remembered that when Gordon quelled the Taïping rebellion he was honoured by the Chinese Government with the 'yellow jacket and peacock's feather'.

***Birds of a feather flock together.*** *See* Bird.

***Fine feathers make fine birds.*** Said sarcastically of an overdressed person who does not live up to his (or her) clothes; or, still more metaphorically, of one whose expressed opinions do not coincide with his mode of life.

***In full feather.*** Flush of money. In allusion to birds not on the moult.

***In grand feather.*** Dressed 'to the nines'; also, in perfect health, thoroughly fit.

***In high feather.*** In exuberant spirits, joyous. When birds are moulting they mope about, but as soon as they regain their feathers their spirits revive.

***Of that feather.*** *See* Birds of a Feather.

***Prince of Wales's feathers.*** *See* Prince of Wales.

***Tarred and feathered.*** *See* Tar.

***Tickled with a feather.*** Easily moved to laughter. 'Pleased with a rattle, tickled with a straw' (Pope, *Essay on Man*), is more usual. *Rire de la moindre bagatelle.*

Also perturbed by trifles, worried by little annoyances.

From day to day some silly things
  Upset you altogether;
There's nought so soon convulsion brings
  As tickling with a feather.

Sims, *Ballads of Babylon* (Little Worries)

***To cut a feather.*** A ship going fast is said to cut a feather, in allusion to the ripple which she throws off from her bows. Metaphorically, 'to cut a dash'.

Jack could never cut a feather.

Scott, *The Pirate*, xxxiv

***To feather an oar.*** To turn the blade parallel with the surface of the water as the hands are moved forward for a fresh stroke. (The Greek *pteron* means both 'an oar' and 'a feather'; and the verb *pteroo*, to 'furnish with oars' or 'with feathers'.) The oar throws off the water in a feathery spray.

He feathered his oars with such skill and dexterity. *Jolly Young Waterman*

***To feather one's nest well.*** To acquire lots of money by work and economising, lucky speculation, marrying a rich woman, or anyhow; sometimes with the implication that the acquirer has not been too scrupulous. The allusion is to birds, which line their nests with feathers to make them soft and warm.

***To show the white feather.*** *See* White.

***To smooth one's ruffled feathers.*** To recover one's equanimity after an insult, etc.

**Featherweight.** Something of extreme lightness in comparison with others of its kind; as a jockey of 6 st., the lightest weight allowed in a handicap; or a boxer of 9 stone or under. In the paper trade the name is given to very light antique, laid or wove book papers. They are manufactured mainly from esparto, and are very loosely woven.

**Feature** (Lat. *facere*, to make) formerly meant the 'make' or general appearance of anything. Spenser speaks of God's 'secret understanding of our feature' – i.e. make or structure. It now means principally that part which is most conspicuous or important. Thus we speak of the chief feature of a painting, a garden, a book, etc.; and in the jargon of the picture-theatres – most of it, including the present example, introduced from America – a moving picture is said *to feature* such and such a popular favourite or incident, i.e. to present him, her, or it, on the screen.

**February.** The month of purification amongst the ancient Romans. (Lat. *februo*, to purify by sacrifice.)

Candlemas Day (*q.v.*), February 2nd, is the feast of the Purification of the Virgin Mary. It is said, if the weather is fine and frosty at the close of January and beginning of February, we may look for more winter to come than we have seen up to that time.

Si sol splendescat Maria Purificante,
Major erit glacies post festum quam fuit ante.

Sir T. Browne, *Vulgar Errors*

The Dutch used to term the month *Spokkelmaand* (vegetation-month); the ancient Saxons, *Sprote-cál* (from the sprouting of pot-wort or kele); they changed it subsequently to *Solmonath* (from the returning sun). In the French Republican calendar it was called *Pluviôse* train-month, January 20th to February 20th).

*See also* Fill-dyke.

**Fecit** (Lat., *he did it*). A word inscribed after the name of an artist, sculptor, etc., as David *fecit*, Goujon *fecit*; i.e. David painted it, Goujon sculptured it, etc.

**Federal States.** The name given in the American War of Secession (1861–65) to those northern states which combined to resist the eleven southern or Confederate states (*q.v.*).

**Fee.** This is an Anglo-French word, from Old High Ger. *fehu*, wages, money, property, cattle, and is connected with the A.S. *feoh*, cattle, goods, money. So in Lat. *pecunia*, money, from *pecus*, cattle. Capital is *capita*, heads (of cattle), and chattels is a mere variant.

***At a pin's fee.*** *See* Pin.

***Fee-farm.*** A tenure by which an estate is held in fee-simple without any other services from the tenant beyond a perpetual fixed rent. Fee-farm-rent is rent paid on lands let to *farm*, and not let in recompense of service at a greatly reduced value.

***Fee-penny.*** A fine for money overdue; an earnest or pledge for a bargain. Sir Thomas Gresham often wrote for money 'in order to save the fee-penny'.

***Fee simple.*** An estate free from condition or limitation, such as that of inheritance by any particular class of heirs. If restricted by conditions, it is called a 'Conditional Fee'.

***Fee tail, A.*** An estate limited to a person and his lawful heirs; an entailed estate.

***To hold in fee.*** To hold as one's lawful and absolute possession.

Once did She hold the gorgeous east in fee;
And was the safeguard of the west.

Wordsworth, *The Venetian Republic*

**Feeble.** ***Most forcible Feeble.*** Feeble is a 'woman's tailor', brought to Sir John Falstaff as a recruit (Shakespeare, *2 Henry IV*, 3, 2). He tells Sir John 'he will do his good will', and the knight replies, 'Well said, courageous Feeble! Thou wilt be as valiant as the wrathful dove, or most magnanimous mouse ... most forcible Feeble.' The phrase is sometimes applied to a writer whose language is very 'loud', but whose ideas are very jejune.

**Feed of Corn.** A quartern of oats, the quantity given to a horse on a journey when the ostler is told to give him a feed.

**Feet.** *See* Foot.

**Fehmgericht.** *See* Vehmgericht.

**Felixmarte.** The hero of *Felixmarie of Hyrcania*, a Spanish romance of chivalry by Melchior de Orteza Caballero de Ubeda (1566). The curate in *Don Quixote* condemned this work to the flames.

**Fell, Dr.** *See* Doctor Fell.

**Fellow Commoner.** A wealthy or married undergraduate of Cambridge, who pays extra to 'common' (i.e. dine) at the fellows' table. In Oxford, these demi-dons are termed *Gentlemen Commoners.*

In 'varsity slang these names were both given to empty bottles, the suggestion being that such students are, as a class, empty-headed.

**Felo de se.** The act of a suicide when he commits self-murder; also, the self-murderer himself. Murder is felony, and a man who murders himself commits this felony – *felo de se.*

> A *felo-de-se*, therefore, is he that deliberately puts an end to his own existence.
>
> Blackstone, *Commentaries*, Bk iv, ch. xiv

**Feme-covert.** A married woman, i.e. a woman who is under the *cover*, authority, or protection of her husband. The word is the Anglo-French and Old French form of Mod. Fr. *femme couverte*, and *couverte* is still used in fortification, etc., with the sense 'protected'.

**Feme-sole.** A single woman. *Feme-sole merchant.* A woman, married or single, who carries on a trade on her own account.

**Femme de Chambre** (Fr.). A chambermaid.

**Femynye.** A mediaeval designation for the kingdom of the Amazons. Gower terms Penthesilea 'queen of Feminee'.

> He [Theseus] conquered al the regne of Femynye.
> That whylom was y-claped Scithia;
> And weddede the quene Ipolita.
>
> Chaucer, *Knightes Tale*, 8

**Fen Nightingale.** A frog, which sings at night in the fens, as nightingales sing in the groves.

**Fence.** ***Fence Month,*** or ***Season.*** The fawning time of deer, i.e. from about fifteen days before Midsummer to fifteen days after it. Also the close season for fishing, etc.

***To sit on the fence.*** To dilly-dally, suspending judgment; to hedge. The characteristic attitude of 'Mr Facing-Both-Ways'.

**Fenchurch Street** (London). Probably so called from the *faenum* (hay) that used to be sold at Gracechurch Market. In the 14th century it was known as *Fancherch Street*, and all the evidence there is goes to show that the district was never low-lying or fenny.

**Fencibles.** A kind of militia raised for home service in 1759, again in 1778–9, and again in 1794, when a force of 15,000 was raised. It was disbanded in 1802. The word is short for *defensible.*

**Fenians.** An Anti-British secret association of disaffected Irishmen, formed simultaneously in Ireland by James Stephens and in New York by John O'Mahony in 1857, with the object of overthrowing the domination of England in Ireland, and making Ireland a republic. The word is from the Old Irish *Fene*, a name of the ancient Irish, confused with *Fianna*, the semi-mythological warriors who defended Ireland in the time of Finn. Scott, in his fictitious translation from Ossian in *The Antiquary* (ch. xxx), uses the term in place of Macpherson's 'Fingalians', i.e. the Norse followers of Fionnghal (Fingal): 'Do you compare your psalms to the tales of the bare-armed Fenians?' These ancient Fenians are represented as warriors of superhuman size, strength, and courage, and became the nucleus of a large cycle of legends.

The modern Fenian Brotherhood quickly spread in the United States, and invasions of Canada were attempted. The Association made many insurrectionary attempts (including dynamite outrages at Clerkenwell, 1865, and at the Tower of London and Houses of Parliament, 1885), but did nothing that could further their aims. Their leaders were termed 'head centres', and their subordinates 'centres'. *Cp.* Clan-na-Gael: Sinn Fein.

**Fennel.** Fennel was anciently supposed to be an inflammatory herb, thus 'to eat conger and fennel' (two hot things together) was provocative to libertinism. Hence Falstaff's remark about Poins:

He plays at quoits well, and eats conger and fennel, and drinks off candles' ends for flap-dragons, and rides the wild mare with the boys.
Shakespeare, *2 Henry IV*, 2, 4

It was also emblematical of flattery, and may have been included among the herbs distributed by Ophelia (*Hamlet*, 4, 5) for this reason.

Fenel is for flaterers,
An evil thing it is sure:
But I have alwaies meant truely,
With constant heart most pure.
*A Nosegay alwaies Sweet* (*in 'A Handful of Pleasan Delights'*, 1584)

Uppon a banke, bordring by, grew women's weedes Fenell. I meane for flatterers, fit generally for that sexe.
Greene, *A Quip for an Upstart Courtier* (1592)

The herb was also credited with being able to clear the sight, and was said to be the favourite food of serpents, with the juice of which they restore their sight when dim.

Above the lowly plants it towers
The fennel with its yellow flowers,
And in an earlier age than ours
Was gifted with the wondrous powers
Lost vision to restore.
Longfellow, *Goblet of Life*

**Fenrir** or **Fenris.** In *Scandinavian mythology* the wolf of Loki (*q.v.*). typifying, perhaps, the goading of a guilty conscience. He was the brother of Hel (*q.v.*), and when he gaped one jaw touched earth and the other heaven. In the *Ragnarok* he swallows the sun and conquers Odin; but being conquered by Vidar, he was cast into Niflheim, where Loki was confined.

**Ferae Naturae** (Lat., of savage nature). The legal term for animals living in a wild state, as distinguished from those which are domesticated.

Women are not comprised in our Laws of Friendship: they are *Ferae Naturae.*
Dryden, *The Mock Astrologer*, iv

**Ferguson.** *It's all very fine, Ferguson, but you don't lodge here.* A popular saying about the middle of last century. There is more than one account of its origin. One refers it to a young Scot of the name who got intoxicated at Epsom races and found it impossible to prevail on any hotel-keeper to take him in; another has it that Ferguson was a companion of the notorious Marquis of Waterford. In one of their sprees they got separated; the marquis went to bed at the house of his uncle, the Archbishop of Armagh, Charles Street, St James's Square; a thundering knock came at the door; and the marquis threw up the window and said: 'It is all very fine, Ferguson, but you don't lodge here,' only to find that the knocker was his uncle, the Archbishop! *See Notes and Queries*, January 16th, 1886, p. 46.

**Fern Seed.** ***We have the receipt of fern seed, we walk invisible*** (*1 Henry IV*, 4, 4). The seed of certain species of fern is so small as to be invisible to the naked eye, and hence the plant was believed to confer invisibility on those who carried it about their person. It was at one time believed that plants have the power of imparting their own speciality to their wearer. Thus, the yellow celandine was said to cure jaundice; wood-sorrel, which has a heart-shaped leaf, to cheer the heart; liverwort to be good for the liver, and so on.

Why did you think that you had Gygës' ring,
Or the herb that gives invisibility?

Beaumont and Fletcher, *Fair Maid of the Inn*, i, 1

The seeds of fern, which, by prolific heat
Cheered and unfolded, form a plant so great,
Are less a thousand times than what the eye
Can unassisted by the tube descry.
Blackmore, *Creation*

**Ferney.** ***The Patriarch*** or ***Philosopher of Ferney.*** Voltaire (1694–1778); so called because for the last twenty years of his life he lived at Ferney, a small sequestered village near Geneva, from which obscure retreat he poured forth his invectives against the French Government, the Church, nobles, nuns, priests, and indeed all classes.

**Ferohers.** The guardian angels of ancient *Persian mythology*. They are countless in number, and their chief tasks are for the well-being of man. The winged circular symbol, supposed to represent either them or the sun-god, and found on many Mesopotamian monuments, is also known as the *Feroher.*

**Ferracute** (i.e. *sharp iron*). A giant in Turpin's *Chronicle of Charlemagne*. He had the strength of forty men, and was thirty-six feet high. Though no lance could pierce his hide, Orlando slew him by divine interposition. *Cp.* Ferrau.

**Ferragus.** The giant of Portugal in *Valentine and Orson* (*q.v.*). He took Bellisant under his care after she had been divorced by the Emperor of Constantinople. The great 'Brazen Head' (*q.v.*), that told those who consulted it whatever they required to know, was kept in his castle. *Cp.* Ferrau.

**Ferrara.** *See* Andrea Ferrara.

**Ferrara Bible, The.** *See* Bible, Specially named.

**Ferrau** (in *Orlando Furioso*). Ferraute, Ferracute, or Ferragus, a Saracen, son of Lanfusa. He dropped his helmet in the river, and vowed he would never wear another till he had won that worn by Orlando. Orlando slew him with a wound in the navel, his only vulnerable part.

**Ferrex and Porrex.** Two sons of Gorboduc, a mythical British king, who divided his kingdom between them. Porrex drove his brother from Britain, and when Ferrex returned with an army he was slain, but Porrex was shortly after put to death by his mother. The story is told in Geoffrey of Monmouth's *Historia Regum Britanniae*, and it forms the basis of the first regular English tragedy, *Gorboduc*, or *Ferrex and Porrex*, written by Thomas Norton and Thomas Sackville, Lord Buckhurst, and acted in 1561.

**Fert.** *See* Annunciation, Order of the.

**Ferumbras.** *See* Fierabras.

**Fescennine Verses.** Lampoons; so called from Fescennia in Tuscany, where performers at merry-makings used to extemporise scurrilous jests of a personal nature to amuse the audience.

**Fesse** (Lat. *fascia*, a band). In *heraldry* is a band drawn horizontally across the shield, of which it occupies one-third. It represents the girdle worn by knights.

**Fetch.** A wraith – the disembodied ghost of a living person; hence *fetch-light*, or *fetch-candle*, a light appearing at night and supposed to foretell the death of someone.

> Fetches ... most commonly appear to distant friends and relations, at the very instant preceding the death of those they represent.
>
> Brand, *Popular Antiquities* (Death Omens)

**Fetches.** Excuses, tricks, artifices.

> Deny to speak with me? They are sick? they are weary?
> They have travelled all the night? Mere fetches.
>
> Shakespeare, *King Lear*, 2, 4

**Fetish.** The name given by the early Portuguese travellers to amulets and other objects supposed to have supernatural powers, used by the natives on the Guinea Coast; from Port, *feitço*, sorcery, charm (Lat. *factitius*, artificial). Hence, an idol, an object of unreasoning devotion. The word is frequently used metaphorically, as in Lowell's

> Public opinion, the fetish even of the nineteenth century. *Among My Books*

**Fetter Lane.** Probably the lane of the *faitours* (Anglo-Fr.), i.e. vagabonds, idlers. In the 14th century it was called *Faytureslane*, *Faitereslane*, *Faytoreslane*, *Faiturlane*, etc. In view of these spellings it is unlikely that it was named from the fewterers (the keepers of greyhounds), as has been suggested.

**Fettle,** as a verb, means *to repair*; *to smooth*; as a noun it means condition, state of health, as *in good fettle*. It is probably from the A.S. *fetch*, a girdle, with allusion to girding oneself up.

*Fettled ale.* Ale warmed and spiced, mulled. It is a dialectal use, principally North Country.

**Feu de joie** (Fr.). A running fire of guns on an occasion of rejoicing.

**Feud,** meaning 'revengeful hostility', is the A.S. *faehth* (hatred); but feud, a 'fief', is mediaeval Lat. *feudum*, and is connected with *fee* (*q.v.*).

**Feudal System, The.** A system founded on the tenure of feuds or fiefs, given in compensation for military service to the lord of the tenants. It was introduced into England by William the Conqueror, who made himself owner of the whole country and allowed the nobles to hold it from him by payment of homage and military and other service. The nobles in turn had vassals bound to them by similar obligations.

**Feuillants.** A reformed Cistercian order instituted by Jean de la Barrière in 1586. So called from the convent of Feuillans, in Languedoc, where they were established in 1577.

***The club of the Feuillants***, in the French Revolution, was composed of moderate Jacobins. So called because the convent of the Feuillants, near the Tuileries, was their original club-room (1791–2).

**Feuilleton** (Fr., from *feuille*, a leaf). The part of French newspapers devoted to tales, light literature, etc.; hence, in England a serial story in a newspaper, or the 'magazine page' which contains light articles, tit-bits, and so on.

**Fever-lurdan.** An old name for laziness or idleness when considered as a disease. Lurdan means a blockhead. (O. Fr. *lourdin*, Fr. *lourd*, heavy, dull, thick-headed.) Other dialect names for it are *fever-lurgan* and *fever-lurk*.

> Fever-lurk,
> Neither play nor work.

**Fey.** When a person suddenly changes his wonted manner of life, as when a miser becomes liberal, or a churl good-humoured, he is said to be *fey*, and near the point of death. The word is the A.S. *faege* (on the point of death, or doomed to die), but is now almost solely a Scotticism.

> She must be fey (said Triptolemus), and in that case has not long to live.
>
> Scott, *The Pirate*, ch. v

**Fezon.** Daughter of Savary, Duke of Aquitaine, demanded in marriage by a pagan, called the *Green Knight*; but Orson, having overthrown the pagan, was accepted by the lady instead. (*Valentine and Orson.*)

**Fi Fa.** *See* Fieri facias.

**Fiacre.** A French cab or hackney coach. So called from the hotel de St Fiacre, Paris, where the first station of these coaches was established by M. Sauvage, about 1650.

Legend has it that St Fiacre was the son of an Irish king, born in 600, who settled in France and built a monastery at Breuil. His day is August 30th.

**Fiars. *Striking the fiars*.** Taking the average price of corn. *Fiars* are the legal prices of grain as fixed by the sheriff of a county for the current year. It is a Scottish term, from M.E. and O.Fr. *feor*, Lat. *forum*, a market.

**Fiasco.** A failure, a mull. In Italy they cry *Olà, olà, fiasco!* to an unpopular singer.

The Italian *fiasco* means a flask, and it is uncertain how it became, in Venetian slang, to mean a failure. In this sense it seems to be under a hundred years old; the following is one of the (improbable) stories told to account for it:

> There was once a clever harlequin of Florence named Dominico Biancolelli, noted for his comic harangues. He was wont to improvise upon whatever article he held in his hand. One night he appeared holding a flask (*fiasco*); but failing to extract any humour whatsoever from his subject, he said, 'It is thy fault, fiasco,' and dashed the flask on the ground. After that a failure was commonly called in Florence a 'fiasco'.

**Fiat** (Lat. let it be done). *I give my fiat to that proposal.* I consent to it. A fiat in law is an order of the court directing that something stated be done.

***Fiat experimentum in corpore vili.*** *See* Corpus vile.

***Fiat justitia ruat caelum.*** *See* Piso's Justice.

**Fib.** An attendant on Queen Mab in Drayton's *Nymphidia*. Fib, meaning a falsehood, is the Latin *fabula, a fable.*

**Fico.** *See* Fig.

> Fico for the phrase.
> Shakespeare, *Merry Wives of Windsor*, 1, 3

> I see contempt marching forth, giving me the fico with his thombe in his mouth.
> *Wit's Miserie* (1596)

**Fiddle** (A.S. *fithele*; perhaps connected with mediaeval Lat. *vitula* or *vidula*, whence *violin*). In Stock Exchange slang a *fiddle* is one-sixteenth of a pound – 1*s.* 3*d.*

***Fit as a fiddle.*** In fine condition, perfect trim or order.

***He was first fiddle.*** Chief man, the most distinguished of the company.

***To play second fiddle.*** To take a subordinate part. The allusion is to the leader of concerts, who leads with a fiddle.

***The Scotch fiddle*** or ***Caledonian Cremona.*** The itch. As fiddlers scratch with a bow the strings of a fiddle, so persons suffering from skin-irritation keep scratching the part irritated.

***To fiddle about.*** To trifle, fritter away one's time, mess about, play at doing things instead of doing them. To fiddle with one's fingers is to move them about as a fiddler moves his fingers up and down the fiddle-strings.

> Mere trifling, or unprofitable fiddling about nothing. Barrow, *Sermons*, vol. i, sermon 7

**Fiddle-de-dee!** An exclamation signifying what you say is nonsense or moonshine.

> One, whom we see not, is; and one, who is not, we see;
> Fiddle, we know, is diddle; and diddle, we take it, is dee.
> Swinburne, *The Higher Pantheism in a Nutshell* (*a parody on Tennyson*)

**Fiddle-faddle. *It is all fiddle-faddle*.** Rubbishy nonsense; talk not worth attention. A ricochet word, of which we have a vast number, as 'flim-flam', 'helter-skelter', 'wishy-washy', etc.

> Pitiful fool that I was to stand fiddle-faddling in that way. Clough, *Amours de Voyage*, iv, 3

**Fiddler.** Slang for a sixpence; also for a farthing.

***Drunk as a fiddler.*** *See* Drunk.

***Fiddler's fare*** or ***pay.*** Meat, drink, and money.

***Fiddler's Green.*** The land of the leal or 'Dixie Land' of sailors; where there is perpetual mirth, a fiddle that never ceases to untiring dancers, plenty of grog, and unlimited tobacco.

***Fiddler's money.*** A silver penny. The fee given to a fiddler at a wake by each dancer.

***Fiddler's news.*** Stale news carried about by wandering fiddlers.

***Oliver's fiddler.*** Sir Roger L'Estrange (1616–1704). So called because he, at one time, was playing a fiddle or viol with others in the house of John Hingston when Cromwell was one of the guests.

**Fiddlesticks!** An exclamation signifying what

you say is not worth attention; much the same as *fiddle-de-dee* (*q.v.*).

***The devil rides on a fiddlestick.*** *See* Devil (Phrases).

**Fidei Defensor.** *See* Defender of the Faith.

**Fides Carbonarii.** Blind faith, faith of a child. A carbonaro (*see* Carbonari) being asked what he believed, replied: 'What the Church believes'; and, being asked again what the Church believes, made answer: 'What I believe.'

**Fie!** An exclamation indicating that what is reproved is dirty or indecent. It is an old word, and is found in Middle English, Old French, Latin, and many other languages; and it seems to be an instinctive sound uttered on experiencing a disagreeable smell.

> No word ne wryteth he
> Of thilke wikke ensample of Canacee,
> That lovede hir owne brother sinfully;
> Of swiche cursed stories I sey 'fy'.
>
> Chaucer, *Man of Lawes Prologue*, 77

**Field.** In *huntsman's* language, the field means all the riders.

In *heraldry*, it means the entire surface of the shield.

In *military* language, it means the place where a battle is fought, or is about to be fought; the battle itself, or the campaign.

In *sportsmen's* language it means all the horses of any one race. *To bet against the field* means to back a particular horse against all the rest entered for the race. *To keep back the field*, is to keep back the riders.

***In the field.*** A competitor for a prize. A term in horse-racing, as, 'So-and-so was in the field'. Also in war, as, 'the French were in the field already'.

***Master of the field.*** The winner; the conqueror in a battle.

***To take the field.*** To make the opening moves in a campaign; to move the army preparatory to battle.

***To win the field.*** To win the battle.

***Field-day.*** A day of particular excitement or importance. Thus, a clergyman jocosely calls a 'kept festival' his field-day. A military term, meaning a day when troops have manoeuvres or field practice.

***Field Marshal.*** A general officer of the highest rank in the British Army. The title was first used in 1736, and is conferred on generals who have rendered conspicuous services, and members of royal families. In 1920 there were 12 Field Marshals, including the Duke of Connaught, the Emperor of Japan, and Marshal Foch.

***Field officer.*** Any officer between captain and general, such as a major or a lieutenant-colonel.

***Field pieces.*** Small cannon carried into the field with an army.

***Field works.*** Works thrown up by an army besieging or defending a fortress, or in strengthening its position.

> Earth-forts, and especially field works, will hereafter play an important part in wars.
>
> W. T. Sherman, *Memoirs*, vol. ii, ch. xxiv (1875)

***Field of Blood.*** Aceldama (*q.v.*).

***Field of force.*** A term used in physics to denote the range within which a force, such as magnetism, is effective.

***Field of the Cloth of Gold.*** The plain, near Guisnes, where Henry VIII had his interview with François I in 1520; so called from the splendour and magnificence displayed there on the occasion.

***Field of vision*** or ***view.*** The space in a telescope, microscope, etc., within which the object is visible. If the object is not distinctly visible, it must be *brought into the field* by adjustment.

***Field of the Forty Footsteps.*** At the back of the British Museum, once called Southampton Fields, near the extreme north-east of the present Upper Montagu Street. The tradition is that at the time of the Duke of Monmouth's rebellion two brothers fought each other here till both were killed, and for many years forty impressions of their feet remained on the field, and no grass would grow there. The scene was built upon about 1800.

**Fierabras, Sir.** One of Charlemagne's paladins, and a leading figure in many of the romances. He was the son of Balan (*q.v.*), King of Spain, and for height of stature, breadth of shoulder, and hardness of muscle he never had an equal. He possessed all Babylon to the Red Sea; was seigneur of Russia, Lord of Cologne, master of Jerusalem, and even of the Holy Sepulchre. He carried away the crown of thorns, and the balsam which embalmed the body of our Lord, one drop of which would cure any sickness, or heal any wound in a moment. One of his chief exploits was to slay the 'fearful huge giant that guarded the bridge Mantible', famous for its thirty arches of black marble. His pride was laid low by Olivier, he became a Christian, was accepted by Charlemagne as a paladin, and ended his days in the odour of sanctity, 'meek as a lamb and humble as a chidden slave'. Sir Fierabras, or Ferumbras, figures in several mediaeval romances, and is allegorised as Sin overcome by the Cross. *See* Balan.

**Fieri facias** (Lat. cause it to be done). A judicial writ for one who has recovered damages in the courts, commanding the sheriff to see the judgment of the court duly carried out. It is often abbreviated to *fi fa*. The term was punningly used in Elizabethan times in connexion with red noses and men with 'fiery faces' through drink.

**Fiery Cross, The.** A signal anciently sent round the Scottish clans in the Highlands summoning them to assemble for battle. It was symbolical of fire and sword, and consisted of a cross the ends of which had been burnt and then dipped in the blood of some animal slain for the purpose – a relic of Gaelic rites. *See* Scott's *Lady of the Lake*, canto iii, for an account of it.

**Fifteen, The.** The Jacobite rebellion of 1715, when James Edward Stuart, 'the Old Pretender', with the Earl of Mar, made a half-hearted and unsuccessful attempt to gain the throne.

**Fifteen decisive Battles.** The battles given by Sir Edward Creasy in his book (1852) as having been 'decisive', i.e. as having effected some great and permanent political change, are:

1. Marathon (Sep., 490 BC), when Miltiades, with 10,000 Greeks, defeated 100,000 Persians under Datis and Artaphernes.
2. Syracuse (Sep., 413 BC), when the Athenians under Nicias and Demosthenes were defeated with a loss of 40,000 killed and wounded, and their entire fleet.
3. Arbela (Oct., 331 BC), when Alexander the Great overthrew Darius Codomanus for the third time.
4. Metaurus (207 BC), when the consuls Livius and Nero cut to pieces Hasdrubal's army, sent to reinforce Hannibal.
5. The Teutoberg Forest, where Arminius and the Gauls utterly overthrew the Romans under Varus, and thus established the independence of Gaul (AD 9).
6. Chalons (AD 451), when Aetius and Theodoric utterly defeated Attila, and saved Europe from devastation.
7. Tours (Oct., AD 732), when Charles Martel overthrew the Saracens under Abderahmen, and thus freed Europe from the Moslem yoke.
8. Hastings (Oct., 1066), when William of Normandy slew Harold II, and obtained the crown of England.
9. Orleans in 1429, when Joan of Arc secured the independence of France.
10. The defeat of the Spanish Armada in 1588, which destroyed the hopes of Spain and the Pope respecting England.
11. Blenheim (13 Aug., 1704), when Marlborough and Prince Eugene defeated Tallard, and thus prevented Louis XIV from carrying out his schemes.
12. Pultowa (July, 1709), when Peter the Great utterly defeated Charles XII of Sweden, and thus established the Muscovite power.
13. Saratoga (Oct., 1777), when General Gates defeated the British under General Burgoyne, and thus secured for the United States the alliance of France.
14. Valmy (Sep., 1792), when the French Marshal Kellermann defeated the Duke of Brunswick, and thus established for a time the French republic.
15. Waterloo (18 June, 1815), when Napoleon was defeated by the Duke of Wellington, and Europe was restored to its normal condition.

**Fifth-Monarchy Men.** A sect of English fanatics of about 1554 to 1560, who maintained that Jesus Christ was about to come a second time to the earth, and establish the fifth universal monarchy. The four preceding monarchies were the Assyrian, the Persian, the Macedonian, and the Roman. In politics, the Fifth-Monarchy Men were zealous reformers and levellers.

**Fig.** Most phrases that include the word *fig* have reference to the fruit as being an object of trifling value; but in *In full fig*, meaning 'in full dress', *figged out*, 'dressed up', etc., the word is a variant of *feague* (*see* Fake). *To fig up a horse* is to make it lively and spirited by artificial means; *to fig oneself out* is to dress oneself up 'regardless'.

> The speaker sits at one end all in full fig, with a clerk at the table below.
>
> Trollope, *West Indies*, ch. ix

***I don't care a fig for you; not worth a fig.*** Anything at all. Here fig is either an example of something comparatively worthless or the Spanish *fico* (*q.v.*) – adopted as English by the Elizabethans – a gesture of contempt made by thrusting the thumb between the first and second fingers, much as we say, 'I don't care that for you', snapping the fingers at the same time. *See* Thumb (*To bite one's thumb*).

> A fig for Peter. Shakespeare, *2 Henry VI*, 2, 9
>
> The figo for thy friendship.
>
> Shakespeare, *Henry V*, 3, 6

***I shan't buy my Attic figs in future, but grow them.*** Said by way of warning to one who is building castles in the air – 'don't count your chickens before they are hatched'. Xerxes boasted that he was going to conquer Attica, where the figs grew, and add it to his own empire; but he met defeat at Salamis, and 'never loosed his sandal till he reached Abdera'.

***In the name of the Prophet, Figs!*** A burlesque of the solemn language employed in eastern countries in the common business of life. The line occurs in the imitation of Dr Johnson's pompous style, in *Rejected Addresses*, by James and Horace Smith.

***Mercury fig.*** *See* Mercury.

**Fig Sunday.** An old provincial name for Palm Sunday. Figs used to be eaten on that day in commemoration of the blasting of the barren fig tree by our Lord (*see* Mark 11) which took place on the day following the triumphant entry into Jerusalem. Some say, however, that the practice arose from the Bible story of Zaccheus, who climbed up into a fig tree to see Jesus.

Many festivals still have their special foods; as, the goose for Michaelmas, pancakes for Shrove Tuesday, salt cod for Ash Wednesday, etc.

**Fig tree.** It is said that Judas hanged himself on a fig tree. *See* Elder tree,

> Quaeret aliquis qua ex arbore Judas se suspenderit? Arbor ficus fuisse dicitur. — Barradius

**Figaro.** A type of cunning dexterity, and intrigue. The character is in the *Barbier de Séville* (1775) and *Mariage de Figaro* (1784), by Beaumarchais. In the former he is a barber, and in the latter a valet; but in both he outwits everyone. There are several operas founded on these dramas, as Mozart's *Nozze di Figaro*, Paisiello's *Il Barbiere di Siviglia*, and Rossini's *Il Barbiere di Siviglia*.

**Figged out.** *See* Fig.

**Fight. *He that fights and runs away May live to fight another day*** (*Hudibras*, Pt iii, c. 3). An old saw found in many languages. Demosthenes, being reproached for fleeing from Philip of Macedon at Chaeronea, replied, 'A man that runs away may fight again.'

> He that fights and runs away
> May live to fight another day;
> But he that is in battle slain
> Can never rise to fight again.
>
> These well-known lines are often given as a quotation from Sir John Mennes, *Musarum Delictae* (1646), where, however, they do not occur.

***The Fighting Fifth.*** The 5th Foot, now the 'Northumberland Fusiliers'. This sobriquet was given to the regiment during the Peninsular War; it was also known as the 'Old and Bold Fifth', and 'the Duke of Wellington's Body-guard'.

***The Fighting Prelate.*** Henry Spencer, Bishop of Norwich, who greatly distinguished himself in the rebellion of Wat Tyler. He met the rebels in the field, with the temporal sword, then absolved them, and sent them to the gibbet.

> The Bishop of Norwich, the famous 'fighting prelate', had led an army into Flanders. — Lord Campbell

Nowadays any clergyman who distinguishes himself pugilistically usually becomes famous as *the fighting parson.*

***To fight for one's own hand.*** To uphold one's own cause, to struggle for one's own interest.

***To fight shy of.*** To avoid; to resist being brought into contest or conflict.

***To fight the tiger.*** An Americanism for gambling.

> After seeing 'fighting the tiger', as gaming is styled in the United States, I have arrived at the conclusion that gaming is more fairly carried on in the Monte Carlo casino than in any American gaming-house.
>
> *The Nineteenth Century*, Feb., 1890, p. 249

***To fight with gloves on.*** To spar without showing animosity, like boxers, with boxing gloves. Disputants fight with gloves on so long as they preserve all the outward amenities of debate, and conceal their hostility to each other by courtesy and forbearance.

***To live like fighting cocks.*** *See* Cock.

**Figure.** From Lat. *fingere*, to shape or fashion; not etymologically connected with Eng. *finger*, though the primitive method of calculating was doubtless by means of the fingers. For Roman figures, etc., *see* Numerals.

***A figure of fun.*** A droll appearance, whether from untidiness, quaintness, or other peculiarity. 'A pretty figure' is a rather stronger expression. They are chiefly applied to young children.

**Figure-head.** A figure on the head or projecting cutwater of a ship, which has ornamental value but is of no practical use; hence a nominal leader (often a titled person) who has no real authority but whose social or other position inspires confidence.

***To cut a figure.*** To make an imposing appearance through dress, equipage, and bearing. *To cut a sorry* or *a pretty figure* is the reverse.

***To make a figure.*** To make a name or reputation, to be a notability, as 'he makes no figure at court'.

***What's the figure?*** How much am I to pay? what 'figure' or sum does my debt amount to?

**Filch.** ***To steal or purloin.*** A piece of 16th-century thieves' slang of uncertain origin. *File* (*q.v.*) was used in much the same sense, but there is no evidence of etymological connection.

A *filch* or *filchman* was a staff with a hook at the end, for plucking clothes from hedges, articles from shop windows, etc.

> With cunning hast thou filched my daughter's heart.
>
> Shakespeare, *Midsummer Night's Dream*, 1, 2

**File.** Old slang for a rapscallion or worthless person; also for a pickpocket and to pick pockets. The origin of neither use is known. *Cp.* Filch.

***In single file.*** Single line; one behind another. (Fr. *file*, a row.)

***Rank and file.*** Soldiers and non-commissioned officers as apart from commissioned officers; hence, the followers in or private members of a movement as apart from its leaders. *Rank* refers to men standing abreast, *file* to men standing behind each other.

> It was only on the faith of some grand expedition that the credulous rank and file of the Brotherhood subscribed their dollars. *The Times*

**Filia Dolorosa.** The Duchesse d'Angoulême (1778–1851), daughter of Louis XVI. *See* Antigone, the Modern.

**Filibuster.** A piratical adventurer, a buccaneer (*q.v.*). The word is through Span. *filibustero* from Dut. *vrijbuiter*, a freebooter.

**Filioque Controversy.** An argument that long disturbed the Eastern and Western Churches, and the difference of opinion concerning which still forms one of the principal barriers to their fusion. The point was: Did the Holy Ghost proceed from the Father *and* the Son (*Filio-que*) or from the Father only? The Western Church maintains the former, and the Eastern the latter dogma. The *filio-que* was recognised by the Council of Toledo, 589.

> The gist of the argument is this: If the Son is one with the Father, whatever proceeds from the Father must proceed from the Son also. This is technically called 'The Procession of the Holy Ghost'.

**Fill-dyke.** The month of February, when the rain and melted snow fills the ditches to overflowing.

> February fill-dyke, be it black or be it white (wet or snowy);
> But if it be white it's better to like. Old Proverb

**Filomena.** Longfellow called Florence Nightingale (1820–1910) *St Filomena*, not only because Filomena resembles the Latin word for a nightingale, but also because this saint, in Sabatelli's picture, is represented as hovering over a group of sick and maimed, healed by her intercession.

> A Lady with a Lamp shall stand
> In the great history of the land,
> A noble type of good
> Heroic womanhood.
> Nor even shall be wanting here
> The palm, the lily, and the spear,
> The symbols that of yore
> Saint Filomena bore.
>
> Longfellow, *Santa Filomena*

**Filter** (Lat. *feltrum*, felt; *filtrum*, a strainer). Literally, to run through felt, as jelly is strained through flannel. The Romans strained the juice of their grapes through felt into the wine-vat, after which it was put into the casks.

**Filumena, St.** A saint unknown till 1802, when a grave was discovered in the Catacomb of St Priscilla on the Salarian Way (leading from Rome to Ancona), with this inscription on tiles: '*lumena paxte cymfi*', which, being rearranged, makes *Pax tecum Filumena*. Filumena was at once accepted as a saint, and so many wonders were worked by 'her' that she has been called *La Thaumaturge du Dixneuvième Siècle*. She is commemorated on August 10th.

**Fin.** *See* Flipper.

**Fin de siècle** (Fr., end of the century). Pertaining to or characteristic of the end of the 19th century; hence, ultra modern, quite up to date. Although the end of the 19th century is long past the phrase is still used in the latter sense.

**Finality John.** Earl Russell, who maintained that the Reform Bill of 1832 was a *finality*, yet in 1854, 1860, and 1866 brought forth other Reform Bills.

**Finance.** Old French, meaning an ending, especially the settlement of a debt, or the winding up of a dispute by the payment of ransom. Hence, revenue derived from fines or subsidies and, in the plural, available money resources. Thus we say, 'My finances are exhausted', meaning I have no more funds or available money.

***Financial year.*** The annual period for which accounts are made up.

**Finch Lane** (London). So called from the Finks, or Finkes, the 13th-century owners of the land. Robert Finke built the church of St Bennet Fink in the lane. It was removed in 1842 for the Royal Exchange, and the monuments taken to the church of St Peter le Poer, Old Broad Street.

**Find.** ***Findings keepings!*** An exclamation made when one has accidentally found something that does not belong to him, and implying that it is now the finder's property. This old saying is, of course, very faulty law, and acting upon it may lead one into serious trouble!

***You know what you leave behind, but not what you will find.*** And this it is that 'makes us rather bear the ills we have, than fly to others that we know not of'.

**Findon Haddock.** *See* Finnan.

**Fine.** ***Fine as fivepence.*** An old alliterative saying meaning splendidly dressed or turned out.

***Fine feathers make fine birds.*** *See* Feathers.

***In fine.*** To sum up; to come to a conclusion; in short.

***One of these fine days.*** Some time or other; at some indefinite (and often problematical) date in the future.

***The fine arts.*** Those arts which chiefly depend on a delicate or fine imagination, as music, painting, poetry and sculpture, as opposed to the *useful arts*, i.e. those which are practised for their utility and not for their own sake, as the arts of weaving, metalworking, and so on.

**Fingal.** The great Gaelic semi-mythological hero (*cp.* Fenian), father of Ossian (*q.v.*), who was purported by Macpherson to have been the original author of the long epic poem *Fingal* (1762), which narrates the hero's adventures. *See* Scott, *The Antiquary*, ch. xxii. He was the son of Comnal, an enormous giant, who could place his feet on two mountains, and then stoop and drink from a stream in the valley between.

***Fingal's cave.*** The basaltic cavern on Staffa, fabled to have been a home of Fingal.

**Finger** (A.S. *finger*). The old names for the fingers are:

A.S. *thuma*, the thumb.

*Towcher* (the finger that touches), *foreman*, or *pointer*. This was called by the Anglo-Saxons the *scite-finger*, i.e the shooting finger, and is now commonly known as the index finger, because it is the one used in pointing.

*Long-man* or *long finger*.

*Lech-man* or *ring-finger*. The former means 'medical finger', and the latter is a Roman expression, '*digitus annularis*'. Called by the Anglo-Saxons the *gold-finger*. This finger between the long and little finger was used by the Romans as a ring-finger, from the belief that a nerve ran through it to the heart. Hence the Greeks and Romans used to call it the *medical* finger, and used it for stirring mixtures, under the notion that nothing noxious could touch it without its giving instant warning to the heart. It is still a general notion in parts of England that it is bad to rub on salve or scratch the skin with any but the ring finger.

> At last he put on her medical finger a pretty, handsome gold ring, whereinto was enchased a precious toadstone of Beausse.
>
> Rabelais, *Pantagruel*, iii, 17

*Little-man* or *little finger*. Called by the Anglo-Saxons the *eár-finger*, because it can, from its diminutive size, be most easily introduced into the orifice of the ear.

The fingers each had their special significance in alchemy, and Ben Jonson says –

> The thumb, in chiromancy, we give to Venus;
> The fore-finger to Jove; the midst to Saturn;
> The ring to Sol; the least to Mercury.
>
> *Alchemist*, i, 2

***Blessing with the fingers.*** *See* Blessing.

**Phrases.**

***Cry, baby, cry; put your finger in your eye,*** etc. This nursery rhyme seems to be referred to by Shakespeare in his *Comedy of Errors*, 2, 2:

> No longer will I be fool.
> To put the finger in the eye and weep.

***Fingers and toes.*** The farrier's name for anbury, or ambury, i.e. a spongy wart on horses and oxen.

***Fingers were made before forks.*** Our natural gifts or advantages are of more value to us than our artificial ones. The saying is used (especially at meal times) when one wants to convey that ceremony is unnecessary.

> This Vulcan was a smith, they tell us,
> That first invented tongs and bellows;
> For breath and fingers did their works
> (We'd fingers long before we'd forks).
>
> King, *Art of Love*

***Finished to the finger-nail.*** Complete and perfect in every detail, to all the extremities. The allusion is obvious.

***His fingers are all thumbs.*** Said of a person awkward in the use of his hands.

***Lifting the little finger.*** Tippling. In holding a tankard or glass, most persons stick out or lift up the little finger.

***Light-fingered gentry.*** 'Priggers', pickpockets, thieves.

***My little finger told me that.*** The same as 'A little bird told me that' (*see* Bird), meaning, I know it, though you did not expect it. The former expression is from Molière's *Malade Imaginaire*.

By the pricking of my thumbs,
Something wicked this way comes.
Shakespeare, *Macbeth*, 4, 1

The popular belief was that an itching or tingling foretold some change or other.

***To be finger and glove with another.*** To be most intimate. The more usual expression is *to be hand in glove with.*

***To burn one's fingers.*** *See* Burn.

***To have a finger in the pie.*** To assist or mix oneself officiously in any matter. Said usually in contempt, or censoriously.

***To have it at one's fingers' ends.*** To be quite familiar with it and able to do it readily. The Latin proverb is *Scire tanquam ungues digitosque suos*, to know it as well as one's fingers and nails. The allusion is obvious; the Latin tag is referred to by Shakespeare in *Love's Labour's Lost*, 5, 1:

*Costard*: Go to; thou hast it ad dunghill, at the fingers' ends, as they say.
*Holofernes*: O, I smell false Latin: dunghill for unguem.

***To lay,*** or ***put, one's finger upon.*** To point out precisely the meaning, cause, etc.; to detect with complete accuracy.

***To twist someone round one's little finger.*** To do just what one likes with him, to be master of his actions.

***With a wet finger.*** Easily, directly. The allusion is to spinning, in which the spinner constantly wetted the forefinger with the mouth.

*Flores*: Canst thou bring me thither?
*Peasant*: With a wet finger.
*Wisdom of Dr Dodipoll* (about 1596)

I can bring myself round with a wet finger.
Scott, *Redgauntlet*, ch. xxiii (and in many other places).

**Finger-print.** An impression taken in ink of the whorls of lines on the finger. In no two persons are they alike, and they never change through the entire life of any individual; hence, they are of very great value as a means of identifying criminals. In 1892 Galton published a book drawing attention to this.

**Fingle-fangle.** A ricochet word from *fangle* (*see* New Fangled) meaning a fanciful trifle. It was fairly common in the 17th century, but is not heard nowadays, except as an archaism.

**Finnan Haddocks.** Haddocks smoked with green wood; so called from a place-name, either Findhorn in Elgin, or Findon in Kincardineshire, both fishing villages, where haddocks are cured. *See* Scott, *The Antiquary*, xxvi.

**Finny Tribe.** Fish; because of their fins. Locutions such as this were very common with the 18th century poets, who thought it distinctly *infra dig.* to call a spade a spade, or a fish a fish!

**Finsbury** (London). A corruption of *Fens*-bury. The nature of the land in early times is further attested by the names of *Moor*-gate and *Moor*-fields near by.

**Fion.** Another form of the name *Finn*, or *Fingal* (*q.v.*).

**Fionnuala.** The daughter of Lir in old Irish legend, who was transformed into a swan, and condemned to wander over the lakes and rivers of Ireland till the introduction of Christianity into that island. Moore has a poem on the subject in his *Irish Melodies.*

**Firapeel.** The name given to the Leopard in Caxton's version of *Reynard the Fox.*

**Firbolgs.** *See* Milesians.

**Fir-cone.** This forms the tip of the thyrsus (*q.v.*) of Bacchus because the juice of the fir tree (*turpentine*) used to be mixed by the Greeks with new wine to make it keep.

**Fir tree.** Atys was metamorphosed into a fir tree by Cybele, as he was about to lay violent hands on himself. (Ovid, *Metamorphoses*, x, 2.)

**Fire.** (A.S., *fyr*; Gr., *pur.*)

***A burnt child dreads the fire.*** *See* Burn.

***Between two fires.*** Subjected to attack, criticism, etc., from both sides at once.

***Coals of fire.*** *See* Coals.

***Fire away!*** Say on; say what you have to say. The allusion to firing a gun; as, You are primed up to the muzzle with something you want to say; fire away and discharge your thoughts.

'Foster, I have something I want you and Miss Caryl to understand.' 'Fire away!' exclaimed Foster. Watson, *The Web of a Spider*, ch. xv

***Greek fire.*** *See* Greek.

***I have myself passed through the fire; I have smelt the smell of fire.*** I have had experience in trouble, and am all the better for it. The allusion is to the refining of gold, which is passed through the fire and so purged of all its dross.

***I will go through fire and water to serve you***; i.e. through any difficulties or any test. The reference is the ordeals of fire and water which were common methods of trial in Anglo-Saxon times.

***If you will enjoy the fire you must put up with the smoke.*** You must take the sour with the sweet, you can't make omelettes without breaking eggs, every convenience has its inconvenience.

***Letters of fire and sword.*** Formerly in Scotland if a criminal refused to answer his citation, it was accounted treason, and 'letters of fire and sword' were sent to the sheriff, authorising him to use either or both these instruments to apprehend the contumacious party.

***More fire in the bed-straw.*** More mischief brewing. A relic of the times when straw was used for beds.

***No fire without smoke.*** No good without its mixture of evil.

***No smoke without fire.*** To every scandal there is some foundation.

***St Antony's Fire, St Elmo's Fire, St Helen's Fire, etc.*** See these names.

***The fat is in the fire.*** *See* Fat.

***The Great Fire of London*** (1666) broke out at Master Farryner's, the king's baker, in Pudding Lane, and after three nights and three days was arrested at Pie Corner. St Paul's Cathedral, eighty-nine other churches, 13,200 houses were burnt down, and 373 acres within the walls and 64 acres without were devastated. In the City itself only 75 acres 3 roods remained unconsumed.

***To fire,*** or ***to fire out.*** To discharge someone from one's employment suddenly and unexpectedly, as

> The office-boy was caught pinching the petty cash so was fired without notice.

This use was originally an Americanism, and seems to be an allusion to the discharge of a bullet from a firearm.

***To fire up.*** To become indignantly angry; to flare up, get unduly and suddenly excited.

***To set the Thames on fire.*** *See* Thames.

***We do not fire first, gentlemen.*** According to tradition this very chivalrous reply was made to Lord Charles Hay (in command of the Guards) at the opening of the battle of Fontenoy (1745) by the French Marquis d'Auteroche after the former had advanced from the British lines and invited the French commander to bid his men to fire. The story is told by the historian Espagnac as well as by Voltaire, but it is almost certainly *ben trovato*, and is not borne out by the description of the battle written a few days after the encounter by Lord Charles to his father, the Marquis of Tweeddale. *See* Carlyle's *Frederick the Great*, bk xv, ch. 8.

***Where there is smoke there is fire.*** Every effect is the result of some cause.

**Fire-brand.** An incendiary; one who incites to rebellion; like a blazing brand which sets on fire all it touches.

> Our fire-brand brother, Paris, burns us all.
> Shakespeare, *Troilus and Cressida*, 2, 2

**Fire-cross.** *See* Fiery Cross.

**Fire-drake** or **Fire-dragon.** A fiery serpent, and ignis-fatuus of large proportions, superstitiously believed to be a flying dragon keeping guard over hid treasures.

> There is a fellow somewhat near the door, he should be a brazier by his face, for, o' my conscience, twenty of the dog-days now reign in 's nose … That fire-drake did I hit three times on the head.
> Shakespeare, *Henry VIII*, 5, 3

**Fire-eaters.** Persons ready to quarrel for anything. The allusion is to the jugglers who 'eat' flaming tow, pour melted lead down their throats, and hold red-hot metal between their teeth. Richardson, in the 17th century – Signora Josephine Girardelli (the original Salamander), in the early part of the 19th century – and Chaubert, a Frenchman, of the present century, were the most noted of these exhibitors.

**Fire-new.** Spick and span new (*q.v.*).

> You should have accosted her; and with some excellent jests fire-new from the mint.
> Shakespeare, *Twelfth Night*, 3, 2

**Fire-ship.** A ship filled with combustibles sent against enemy vessels in order to set them on fire.

**Fire-worship.** Said to have been introduced into Persia by Phoedima, widow of Smerdis, and wife of Hystaspes (521–485 BC). It is not the sun that is worshipped, but God, who is supposed to reside in it; at the same time the Fire Worshippers reverence the sun as the throne of deity. *Cp.* Parsees.

**First.** ***A diamond of the first water.*** *See* Diamond.

***At first hand.*** By one's own knowledge or personal observation.

***First-chop.*** *See* Chop.

***First floor.*** In England the first floor is the story next above the ground-floor, or entrance floor; but in America it is the ground floor itself.

***First foot,*** or ***first footer.*** The first visitor at a house after midnight on New Year's Eve. In

Scotland and the North of England the custom of 'first-footing' is still very popular.

***First-fruits.*** The first profitable results of labour. In husbandry, the first corn that is cut at harvest, which, by the ancient Hebrews, was offered to Jehovah. We also use the word figuratively, as, the first-fruits of sin, the first-fruits of repentance.

***First nighter.*** One who makes a practice of attending the opening performance of plays.

***The First Gentleman of Europe.*** A nickname given to George IV, who certainly was first in rank.

> *He* the first gentleman of Europe! There is no stronger satire on the proud English society of that day than that they admired George. No, thank God, we can tell of better gentlemen.
>
> Thackeray, *The Four Georges; George IV*

***The First Grenadier of France.*** A title given by Napoleon to Latour d'Auvergne (1743–1800).

***The first stroke is half the battle.*** 'Well begun is half done.' 'A good lather is half the shave.'

**Fish.** The fish was used as a symbol of Christ by the early Christians because the letters of its Greek name – Ichthus (*q.v.*) – formed a monogram of the words Jesus. Christ, Son of God, Saviour.

Ivory and mother-o'-pearl counters used in card games, some of which are more or less fish-shaped, are so called, not from their shape, but from Fr. *fiche*, a peg, a card-counter. *La fiche de consolation* (a little piece of comfort or consolation) is the name given in some games to the points allowed for the rubber.

***A fish out of water.*** Said of a person who is out of his usual environment and so feels awkward and in the way; also of one who is without his usual occupation and is restless in consequence.

***A loose fish.*** A man of loose or dissolute habits. *Fish* as applied to a human being usually carries with it a mildly derogatory implication.

***A pretty kettle of fish.*** *See* Kettle.

***A queer fish.*** An eccentric person.

***All is fish that comes to my net.*** I turn everything to some use; I am willing to deal in anything out of which I can make a profit.

> Al is fishe that cometh to the net.
>
> G. Gascoigne, *The Steele Glas* (1576)

***He eats no fish.*** An Elizabethan way of saying that he is an honest man and one to be trusted, because he is not a papist. Roman Catholics were naturally opposed to the Government, and Protestants, to show their loyalty, refused to adopt their ritual custom of eating fish on Fridays.

> I do profess ... to serve him truly ... and to eat no fish.
>
> Shakespeare, *King Lear*, 1, 4

***I have other fish to fry.*** I am busy and cannot attend to anything else just now; I have more important matters on hand.

***Neither fish, flesh, nor fowl***; or ***neither fish, flesh, nor good red herring.*** Suitable to no class of people; fit for neither one thing nor another. Not fish (food for the monk), not flesh (food for the people generally), nor yet red herring (food for paupers).

***The best fish swim near the bottom.*** What is most valuable commercially is not to be found on the surface of the earth, nor is anything else really worth having to be obtained without trouble.

***There's as good fish in the sea as ever came out of it.*** Don't be disheartened if you've lost the chance of something good; you'll get another. 'It's not the only pebble on the beach.'

***To cry stinking fish.*** *See* Cry.

***To drink like a fish.*** *See* Drink.

***To feed the fishes.*** To be drowned; also, to be sea-sick.

***To fish for compliments.*** To try to obtain praise by one's manner or by putting leading questions.

***To fish in troubled waters.*** To scramble for personal advantage in times of rebellion, war, etc.; to try to make national calamity a means to personal profit.

***To fish the anchor.*** A nautical term meaning to draw up the flukes to the bulwarks after the anchor has been 'catted'.

***You must not make fish of one and flesh of the other.*** You must treat both alike. Fish is an inferior sort of animal food to flesh. The alliteration has much to do with the phrase.

**Fisherman, King.** In the legends of the Holy Grail (*q.v.*), the uncle of Perceval, and dweller in the Castle of the Grail, where the holy vessel is enshrined. In the *High History of the Holy Grail* Perceval visits King Fisherman, beholds the Grail three times, and is served from it; but he omits to ask what the miraculous food was and in consequence there

> came to pass so sore mischance in Greater Britain that all the lands and all the islands fell thereby into much sorrow.

King Fisherman was son of Alain li Gros and

Yglais, and brother of Pelles, King of the Lower Folk, and the King of Castle Mortal. The elucidation of the *High History of the Holy Grail* makes the legend an allegorisation of contemporary ecclesiastical history, with special reference to the Albigensian Crusade. King Fisherman is the Pope (the wearer of 'the Fisherman's Ring'); Yglais is, of course, Mother Church (Fr. *église*); Alain li Gros is Alain de l'Isle (*Doctor Universalis*), the King of the Lower Folk is the Abbot of Câteaux, the King of Castle Mortal is the Emperor, and Perceval is St Dominic.

***The Fisherman's Ring.*** The ring traditionally said to have belonged to St Peter, and still worn by the Pope on certain high ceremonial occasions.

**Fish Day** (Fr. *jour maigre*). A day when persons in the Roman Catholic Church are forbidden to eat meat without ecclesiastical permission.

**Fish-wife.** A woman who hawks fish about the streets.

Fish-wives are renowned for their powers of vituperation; hence the term is applied to any blatant, scolding woman.

**Fisk** (in *Hudibras*) was Nicholas Fisk, a physician and astrologer, who used to say that a physician never deserved his bread till he had no teeth to eat it. In his old age he was almost a beggar.

**Fitz** (Norman). Son of; as Fitz-Herbert, Fitz-William, Fitz-Peter, etc. It is sometimes assumed by illegitimate or morganatic children of royalties, as Fitz-Clarence, Fitz-roy, etc.

**Fitzwilliam Museum** (Cambridge University). So called from the 7th and last Viscount Fitzwilliam, who, in 1816, left £100,000, with books, paintings, etc., to form the nucleus of a museum for the benefit of the university. The present building was commenced in 1837.

**Five.** The pentad, one of the mystic numbers, being the sum of 2 + 3, the first *even* and first *odd* compound. Unity is God alone, i.e. without creation. Two is diversity, and three (being 1 + 2) is the compound of unity and diversity, or the two principles in operation since creation, and representing all the powers of nature.

***Bunch of fives.*** Pugilistic slang for the fist.

***The Five Boroughs.*** In English history, the Danish confederation of Derby, Lincoln, Leicester, Stamford, and Nottingham in the 9th and 10th centuries.

***The Five Members.*** Pym, Hampden, Haselrig, Strode, and Holles; the five members of the Long Parliament whom Charles I attempted to arrest in 1642.

***The Five-mile Act.*** An Act passed in 1665 (repealed in 1689) prohibiting ministers who had refused to subscribe to the Act of Uniformity from coming within five miles of any corporate town or the place of their old ministry.

***The Five-minute Clause.*** A provision sometimes inserted in deeds of separation, whereby it is stipulated that the deed is null and void if the husband and wife remain together five minutes after the separation is enjoined.

***The Five Nations.*** A description applied by Kipling to the British Empire – the Old Country, with Canada, Australia, South Africa, and India.

In American history the term refers to the five confederated Indian tribes inhabiting the present State of New York, viz. the Mohawks, Oneidas, Onondagas, Cayugas, and Senecas. Known also as the *Iroquois Confederacy*.

***The Five Points.*** *See* Calvinism.

***The five wits.*** Common sense, imagination, fantasy, estimation, and memory. Common sense is the outcome of the five senses; imagination is the 'wit' of the mind; fantasy is imagination united with judgment; estimation estimates the absolute, such as time, space, locality, and so on; and memory is the 'wit' of recalling past events.

> Four of his five wits went halting off.
>
> Shakespeare, *Much Ado*, 1, 1

> These are the five witts removyng inwardly:
> First, 'Common witte', and then 'Ymagination',
> 'Fantasy', and 'Estimation' truely,
> And 'Memory'.
>
> Stephen Hawes, *The Passe-tyme of Plesure* (1515)

Also used to mean the five senses.

> Alone and warming her five wits
> The white owl in the belfry sits.
>
> Tennyson

**Fiver.** A five-pound note. A 'tenner' is a ten-pound note.

**Fix.** *In a fix.* In an awkward predicament.

**Fixed Air.** An old name of carbonic acid gas, given to it by Dr Black (1754) because it existed in carbonate of magnesia in a fixed state.

**Fixed Oils.** The true oils; i.e. those which are not changed by heating or distillation, and which harden on exposure to the air, thus differing from *essential oils*. The glycarides, such as linseed and walnut oils, are examples.

**Fixed Stars.** Stars whose relative position to other stars is always the same, as distinguished from planets, which shift their relative positions.

**Flaccus.** Horace (65–8 BC), the Roman poet, whose full name was Quintus Horatius Flaccus.

**Flag.** For the colours of national flags *see* Colours, National.

On the *railways*, a *white* flag denotes that the line is clear and the driver can go ahead, the *red* is the danger signal and means 'no advance', and the *green* signifies 'go slow'.

> White is all right; Red is all wrong;
> Green is go cautiously bowling along.
>
> *Mnemonic Rhyme for Signalmen*

***A black flag*** is the emblem of piracy or of no quarter. *See* Black.

***A red flag.*** To display a red flag is to defy or dare to battle. Red is the signal of 'danger ahead', the emblem of blood and of revolution. A red flag is therefore commonly used by rebels and revolutionists, and *The Red Flag* is the battle song of advanced socialists and English 'Bolshies'.

***A white flag*** is the flag of truce or surrender, hence *to hang out the white flag* is to sue for quarter, to give in.

***A yellow flag*** signals contagious disease on board ship, and all vessels in quarantine or having contagious disease aboard are obliged to fly it.

***The flag's down.*** Indicative of distress. When the face is pale the 'flag is down'. Alluding to the ancient custom of taking down the flag of theatres during Lent, when the theatres were closed.

> 'Tis Lent in your cheeks, the flag's down.
>
> *Dodsley's Old Plays*, vol. v, p. 314 (*Mad World*)

***The flag of distress.*** A flag hoisted at the masthead in reverse position to signal that trouble of some sort is on board. In slang use the phrase denotes a card at one's window announcing 'lodgings' or 'board and lodgings'. The allusion is evident.

***To get one's flag.*** To become an admiral. *Cp.* Flag-Officer.

> I do not believe that the bullet is cast that is to deprive you of life, Jack; you'll get your flag, as I hope to get mine.
>
> Kingston, *The Three Admirals*, xiii

***To hang the flag half-mast high*** is in token of mourning or distress.

***To lower one's flag.*** To eat humble pie; to eat the leek; to confess oneself in the wrong; to eat one's own words.

***To strike the flag.*** To lower it or pull it down upon the cap. The phrase is used of an admiral relinquishing his command afloat; the action is also a token of respect, or submission, surrender.

***Trade follows the flag.*** *See* Follow.

**Flag Lieutenant.** An admiral's aide-de-camp.

**Flag-officer.** An admiral (*q.v.*), vice-admiral, or rear-admiral. These officers alone are privileged to carry a flag denoting rank. Admirals carry their flag at the main, vice-admirals at the fore, and rear-admirals at the mizen.

**Flag-ship.** A ship carrying a flag-officer (*q.v.*).

**Flagellants.** A sect of enthusiasts in the middle of the 13th century, who went in procession about the streets inflicting on themselves daily scourgings or flagellations, in order to merit thereby the favour of God. They were put down soon after their appearance, but revived at the time of the Black Death (*q.v.*) in the 14th century. Also called 'Brothers of the Cross'.

**Flagellum Dei** (Lat. *the scourge of God*). Attila was so called. *See* Scourge of God.

**Flam.** Flattery for an object; blarney; humbug.

> They told me what a fine thing it was to be an Englishman, and about liberty and property ... I find it was a flam.
>
> Godwin, *Caleb Williams*, vol. ii, ch. v

**Flamboyant Architecture.** A florid style which prevailed in France in the 15th and 16th centuries. So called from its flame-like tracery. The flamboyant architects of the decline, says Ruskin, were

> nothing but skilful masons, with more or less love of the picturesque, and redundance of undisciplined imagination, flaming itself away in wild and rich traceries, and crowded bosses of grotesque figure sculpture.

**Flame.** A sweetheart. 'An old flame', a quondam sweetheart. In Latin, *flamma* is used for *love*, and so is *feu* in French. *Ardeo*, to burn like fire, is also applied to the passion of love; hence, Virgil (*Ecl.* ii, 1), *Corydon ardebat Alexin*; and Horace (*Epod.* xiv, 9), *Arsit Anacreon Bathyllo*.

**Flaming.** Superb, captivating, ostentatious. The Fr. *flambant*, originally applied to those persons who dressed themselves in rich dresses 'flaming' with gold and silver thread.

***Flaming swords.*** Swords with a wavy or *flamboyant* edge, used now only for state purposes. The Dukes of Burgundy carried swords of this sort, and they were worn in our country till the accession of William III.

**Flaminian Way.** The great northern road of ancient Italy, constructed by C. Flaminius in 220 BC. It led from the Flaminian gate of Rome to Ariminium (Rimini).

**Flanders' Babies.** Cheap wooden jointed dolls common in the early 19th century.

**Flanders' Mare, The.** So Henry VIII called Anne of Cleves, his fourth wife whom he married in January, 1540, and divorced in July of the same year. She died at Chelsea in 1557.

**Flaneur** (Fr.). A lounger, gossiper. From *flaner*, to saunter about.

**Flap-dragons.** An old name for our 'snap-dragon', i.e. raisins soaked in spirit, lighted, and floating in a bowl of spirituous liquor. Gallants used to drink flap-dragons to the health of their mistresses, and would frequently have lighted candle-ends floating in the liquor to heighten the effect. Hence:

> He drinks off candles' ends for flap-dragons.
>
> Shakespeare, *2 Henry IV*, 2, 4

**Flapper.** A colloquialism for a young girl, a girl not yet 'out'; often any unmarried girl of presentable manners and appearance from about sixteen upwards. A young wild duck is called a flapper, but the girl probably gets her name from the large bow frequently tied to her hair, which flaps about as she moves.

**Flare-up.** A sudden outburst of anger; a rumpus or row. Also a banquet or jovial treat, with reference to the dazzle and splendour displayed.

**Flash.** Showy, smart, 'swagger'; as a *flash wedding*, a *flash hotel*, etc.

Also counterfeit, sham, fraudulent. *Flash notes* are forged notes; a *flash man* is a thief or the companion of thieves.

***A mere flash in the pan.*** All sound and fury, signifying nothing; like the attempt to discharge a gun that ends with a flash in the lock-pan, the gun itself 'hanging fire'.

**Flat.** One who is not sharp; also a self-contained suite of rooms on one floor.

***Flat as a flounder.*** I knocked him down flat as a flounder. A flounder is one of the flat-fish.

***Flat as a pancake.*** Quite flat. A pancake is a thin flat cake, fried in a pan.

***Flat race.*** A race on the 'flat' or level ground without obstacles, as opposed to a steeplechase, or 'over the sticks'.

***He is a regular flat-fish.*** A dull, stupid fellow, not up to anything. The play is upon *flat* (stupid), and such fish as plaice, dabs, and soles.

***The sharps and the flats.*** The rooks and the pigeons, cheats and their victims.

**Flatterer.** Vitellius (15–69), Roman Emperor for a short while in 69. He was a sycophant of Nero's, and his name became a synonym for a flatterer (Tacitus, *Ann.*, vi, 32).

***When flatterers meet, the devil goes to dinner.*** Flattery is so pernicious, so fills the heart with pride and conceit, so perverts the judgment and disturbs the balance of the mind, that Satan himself could do no greater mischief, so he goes to dinner and leaves the leaven of wickedness to operate its own mischief.

> Porteus, there is a proverb thou shouldst read:
> 'When flatterers meet, the devil goes to dinner.'
>
> Peter Pindar, *Nil Admirari*

**Flay a Fox, To.** To vomit.

> At the time of the paroxysm he used to flay a fox by way of antidote.
>
> Rabelais, *Pantagruel*, iv, 44

**Flea.** ***A flea's jump.*** It has been estimated that if a man, in proportion to his weight, could jump as high as a flea, he could clear St Paul's Cathedral with ease.

Aristophanes, in the *Clouds*, says that Socrates and Chaerephon tried to measure how many times its own length a flea jumped. They took in wax the size of a flea's foot; then, on the principle of *ex pede Herculem*, calculated the length of its body. Having found this, and measured the distance of the flea's jump from the hand of Socrates to Chaerephon, the knotty problem was resolved by simple multiplication.

***A mere flea-bite.*** A thing of no moment. Disraeli spoke of the national debt as a mere flea-bite; and it undoubtedly *was*, compared with what it has been since the Great War!

***Great fleas have little fleas.*** No matter what our station in life, we all have some 'hangers on'.

> Hobbes clearly proves that every creature
> Lives in a state of war by nature;
> So naturalists observe a flea
> Has smaller fleas that on him prey,
> And these have smaller still to bite 'em,
> And so proceed *ad infinitum.*
>
> Swift, *Poetry; a Rhapsody*

Another version, quoted by Augustus de Morgan in his *Budget of Paradoxes* (1872), runs:

> Great fleas have little fleas upon their backs to bite 'em,
> And little fleas have lesser fleas, and so *ad infinitum.*
> And the great fleas themselves in turn have greater fleas to go on,
> While these again have greater still, and greater still, and so on.

***Sent off with a flea in his ear.*** Peremptorily. A dog which has a flea in the ear is very restless, and runs off in terror and distress.

The phrase is quite an old one, and dates from at least the 15th century in English, and earlier in French. It is found in Heywood's *Proverbs*, Nash's *Pierce Penilesse*, Skoggin's *Jests*, etc.

> Ferardo ... whispering Philantus in the ear (who stood as though he had a flea in his ear), desired him to keep silence. Lyly, *Euphues* (1578)

Here the phrase implies that vexatious news has been heard; and in Deloney's *Gentle Craft* (1597) we have a similar instance, where a servant goes away shaking his head 'like one that hath a flea in his eare'.

**Flecknoe, Richard.** An Irish priest who printed a host of poems, letters, and travels, and died about 1678. As a poet, his name, like the names of Maevius and Bavius among the Romans, is proverbial for vileness. Dryden says he –

> Reigned without dispute
> Through all the realms of nonsense absolute.
> Dryden, *MacFlecknoe*

**Fleeced.** Cheated of one's money; sheared like a sheep.

**Fleet Book Evidence.** No evidence at all. The books of the Old Fleet prison are not admissible as evidence to prove a marriage.

**Fleet Marriages.** Clandestine marriages, at one time performed without banns or licence by needy chaplains, in Fleet Prison, London. As many as thirty marriages a day were sometimes celebrated in this disgraceful manner; and Malcolm tells us that 2,954 were registered in the four months ending with February 12th, 1705. Suppressed and declared null and void in 1774. *The Chaplain of the Fleet*, by Besant and Rice, contains a good account of the evils connected with Fleet marriages. *Cp. Liberties of the Fleet, under* Liberty.

**Fleet Street** (London). Now synonymous with journalism and newspaperdom, Fleet Street was a famous thoroughfare centuries before the first newspaper was published there at the close of the 18th century. It takes its name from the old Fleet River, which ran from Hampstead through Hockley-in-the-Hole to Saffron Hill, near where it joined the Hole Bourne (whence *Holborn*), flowing on with it under what is now Farringdon Street and New Bridge Street to fall into the Thames at Blackfriars. It was navigable for coal-boats, etc., as far as Holborn Bridge (near the present Viaduct), but latterly became so foul that in 1764 it was arched over, and it is now used as a sewer.

From the earliest times Fleet Street has been celebrated for its taverns; it used to stretch from Ludgate, at the corner of Old Bailey, to the Savoy, and there was a bridge (the Fleet Bridge) across the river at the modern Ludgate Circus.

**Flemish Account.** A sum less than that expected. In Antwerp accounts were kept in *livres*, *sols*, and *pence*; but the *livre* or pound was only 12*s*.; hence, an account of 100 livres Flemish was worth £60 only, instead of £100, to the English creditor.

**Flemish School.** A school of painting established by the brothers Van Eyck, in the 15th century. The chief *early* masters were Memling, Weyden, Matsys, and Mabuse. Of the *second* period, Rubens and Vandyck, Snyders, and the younger Teniers.

**Flesh and Blood.** Human nature.

> Bone and Skin, two millers thin,
> Would starve us all, or near it;
> But be it known to Skin and Bone
> That Flesh and Blood can't bear it.
> John Byrom, *Epigram on Two Monopolists*

**Flesh-pots. *Sighing for the flesh-pots of Egypt.*** Hankering for good things no longer at your command. The children of Israel said they wished they had died 'when they sat by the flesh-pots of Egypt' (Exod. 16:3) rather than embark on their long sojourn in the wilderness.

**Fleshed. *He fleshed his sword.*** Used it for the first time. *Men fleshed in cruelty* – i.e. initiated or used to it. A sportsman's expression. A sportsman allows a young dog or hawk to have the first game it catches for its own eating, thus at the same time rewarding it and encouraging its taste for blood. This 'flesh' is the first it has tasted, and fleshing its tooth thus gives the creature a craving for similar food.

> The wild dog
> Shall flesh his tooth on every innocent.
> Shakespeare, *2 Henry IV*, 4, 5

**Fleshly School, The.** In the *Contemporary Review* for October, 1871, Robert Buchanan published a violent attack on the poetry and literary methods of Swinburne, Rossetti, Morris, O'Shaughnessy, John Payne, and one or two others under the heading *The Fleshly School of Poetry*, and over the signature 'Thomas Maitland'. The incident created a big literary sensation; Buchanan at first denied the authorship but was soon obliged to admit it, and some years later was reconciled to Rossetti, his chief victim. Swinburne's very trenchant reply is to be found in his *Under the Microscope* (1872).

**Fleta.** An anonymous treatise on the common law of England, written in the 13th century by an unknown author while a prisoner in the Fleet.

**Fleur-de-lis, -lys,** or **-luce** (Fr. lily-flower). The name of several varieties of iris, and also of the heraldic lily, which is here shown and which was borne as a charge on the old French royal coat-of-arms.

In the reign of Louis VII (1137–80) the national standard was thickly charged with flowers. In 1365 the number was reduced by Charles VI to *three* (the mystical church number). Guillim, in his *Display of Heraldrie*, 1611, says the device is 'Three toads erect, saltant'; in allusion to which Nostradamus, in the 16th century, calls Frenchmen *crapauds*. The *fleur-de-lis* was chosen by Flavio Gioja to mark the north point of the compass, out of compliment to the King of Naples, who was of French descent. Gioja was an early 14th century Italian navigator to whom has been (incorrectly) ascribed the invention of the mariner's compass (*q.v.*).

**Flibbertigibbet.** One of the five fiends that possessed 'poor Tom' in *King Lear*. Shakespeare got the name from Harsnet's *Declaration of Egregious Popish Impostures* (1603), where we are told of forty fiends which the Jesuits cast out, and among the number was 'Fliberdigibet', a name which had previously been used by Latimer and others for a mischievous gossip. Shakespeare says he 'is the fiend of mopping and mowing, who possesses chambermaids and waiting women' (*Lear*, 4); and, again, that he 'begins at curfew and walks till the first cock', where he seems to identify him with the will o' the wisp, giving men pins and needles, squint eyes, harelips, and so on (*Lear*, 3, 4). Elsewhere the name is apparently a synonym for Puck. *Cp.* Obdicut.

**Flies.** *See* Fly.

**Fling.** ***I must have a fling at***... Throw a stone at something. To attack with words, especially sarcastically. To make a haphazard venture. Allusion is to hurling stones from slings.

***To fling oneself at someone's head.*** Said of a woman who makes desperate love to a man, angling obviously to catch him for a husband.

> 'Coxcomb?' said Lance; 'why, 'twas but last night the whole family saw her ... fling herself at my head.' Scott, *Peveril of the Peak*, ch. vii

***To have his fling.*** To live on the loose for a time; to sow his wild oats. The Scots have a proverb:

> Let him tak' his fling and find oot his ain wecht (weight)

meaning, give him a free hand and he'll soon find his level.

**Flint.** ***To skin a flint.*** *See* Skin.

**Flipper.** *Tip us your flipper.* Give me your hand. A flipper is the paddle of a turtle. 'Fin' is used in the same way – *tip us your fin.*

**Flirt.** A coquette. The word is from the verb flirt, as, 'to flirt a fan', i.e. to open it, or wave it, with a sharp, sudden motion. The fan being used for coquetting, those who coquetted were called 'flirts'. In Dr Johnson's day a *flirt*, according to his *Dictionary*, was 'a pert hussey'; and he gives an account of one in No. 84 of *The Rambler*, which, in some few particulars, resembles the modern article.

**Flittermouse.** A bat (*cp.* Ger. *fledermaus*). An earlier name was *flinder mouse*.

> Then came ... the flyndermows and the wezel and ther cam moo than xx whiche wolde not have comen yf the foxe had loste the feeld.
>
> Caxton, *Reynard the Fox*, xii

**Floaters** (Stock Exchange term). Exchequer bills and other unfunded stock. A new issue of capital, a new loan or company is said to be *floated* when it is placed on the market.

**Floating Academy.** The hulks; a convict ship.

**Flogged by deputy.** *See* Whipping Boy.

**Flogging a dead horse.** *See* Horse.

**Floor.** ***I floored him.*** Knocked him down on the floor; hence figuratively, to overcome, beat, or surpass. Thus, we say at an examination, 'I floored that paper', i.e. answered every question on it; 'I floored that problem' – did it perfectly, or made myself master of it. Similarly, *That was a floorer*, that blow knocked him to the floor; or *that paper or question was a floorer*, meaning it was too hard to be mastered.

**Flora.** Flowers generally; all the vegetable productions of a country or of a geological period, as *the flora of England*, *the flora of the coal period*. *Cp.* Fauna. Flora was the Roman goddess of flowers.

> Another Flora there, of bolder hues,
> And richer sweets beyond our garden's pride.
>
> Thomson, *Summer*

***Metropolis of flora.*** Aranjuez, in Spain, is so called, from its many beautiful gardens.

**Flora's Dial.** A fanciful or imaginary dial supposed to be formed by flowers which open or close at stated hours.

I. Dial of flowers which open at approximately the time given –

(*a*) The first twelve hours.

A.M.

1. (*Scandinavian Sowthistle closes.*)
2. Yellow Goat's-beard.
3. Common Ox-tongue.
4. Hawkweed: Late-flowering Dandelion; and Wild Succory.
5. White Water-lily: Naked-stalked Poppy; and Smooth Sowthistle.
6. Shrubby Hawkweed and Spotted Cat's-ears.
7. White Water-lily; Garden Lettuce; and African Marigold.
8. Scarlet Pimpernel; Mouse-ear Hawkweed; and Proliferous Pink.
9. Field Marigold.
10. Red Sandwort.
11. Star of Bethlehem.

Noon. Ice Plant.

(*b*) The second twelve hours.

P.M.

1. Common Purslane.
2. (*Purple Sandwort closes.*)
3. (*Dandelion closes.*)
4. (*White Spiderwort closes.*)
5. Julap.
6. Dark Crane's-bill.
7. (*Naked-stalked Poppy closes.*)
8. (*Orange Day-lily closes.*)
9. Cactus Opuntia.
10. Purple Bindweed.
11. Night-blooming Catch-fly.

Midnight. (*Late-flowering Dandelion closes.*)

II. Dial of flowers that close at the approximate hours –

(*a*) The first twelve hours.

A.M.

1. Scandinavian Sowthistle.
2. (*Yellow Goat's-beard opens.*)
3. (*Common Ox-tongue opens.*)
4. (*Wild Succory opens.*)
5. (*Several Sowthistles open.*)
6. (*Spotted Cat's-ear opens.*)
7. Night-flowering Catch-fly.
8. Evening Primrose.
9. Purple Bindweed.
10. Yellow Goat's-beard.
11. Bethlehem Star (*la dame d'onze heures*).

Noon. Field Sowthistle.

(*b*) The second twelve hours.

P.M.

1. Red or Proliferous Pink.
2. Purple Sandwort.
3. Dandelion or Field Marigold.
4. White Spadewort and Field Bindwort.
5. Common Cat's-ears.
6. White Water-lily.
7. Naked-stalked Poppy.
8. Orange Day-lily and Wild Succory.
9. Convolvulus Linnaeus and Chickweed.
10. Common Nipple-wort.
11. Smooth Sowthistle.

Midnight. Creeping Mallow and Late Dandelion.

**Florentine Diamond.** One of the large and famous diamonds in the world, weighing 133 carats. It formed part of the Austrian Crown Jewels, and previously belonged to Charles, Duke of Burgundy. Tradition relates that it was picked up by a peasant and sold for half a crown.

**Florian, St.** Patron saint of Poland; he was martyred by being drowned in the Enns, near Lorch, about 230. He is also the patron of mercers, having been himself of the same craft.

**Floriani.** A sect of heretics of the second century, a branch of the Valentinians led by Florinus, a priest at Rome. They maintained that God is the author of evil, and taught the Gnostic doctrine of two principles.

**Florid Architecture.** The later stages of the pointed style in England (about 1480–1537), often called the Tudor, remarkable for its florid character or profusion of ornament.

**Florida.** In 1512 Ponce de Leon sailed from France to the West in search of 'the Fountain of Youth'. He first saw land on Easter Day, which was then popularly called in Spain *pascua florida*, flowery Easter, and on that account called the new possession 'Florida'.

**Florimel.** A character in Spenser's *Faërie Queene* typifying the complete charm of womanhood. She was fair and chaste; her love for Marinell was not returned until after much tribulation and her seizure by Proteus and imprisonment in a submarine cell. She was the possessor of the Cestus (*q.v.*) of Venus, the prize of a tournament in which Sir Salgrane and several others took part, which could be worn only by the chaste, and when the False Florimel (who had been made out of wax by a witch to simulate the true one) tried to put it on she melted away.

> St Amand had long since in bitterness repented of a transient infatuation, had long since distinguished the true Florimel from the false.
>
> Lytton, *Pilgrims of the Rhine*, iii

**Florin.** An English silver coin representing 2*s*., or the tenth of a sovereign, first issued in 1849. Camden informs us that Edward III issued gold florins worth 6*s*., in 1337. The word is generally supposed to be derived from Florence; but as the coin had a lily on one side, probably it is connected with the Lat. *flos*, a flower. *Cp.* Graceless Florin.

**Florisando.** One of the knights in the Spanish version of *Amadis of Gaul* (*q.v.*), whose exploits and adventures are recounted in the 6th and following books.

**Florisel of Nicea.** A knight whose exploits and adventures form a supplemental part of the Spanish version of *Amadis of Gaul* (*q.v.*).

**Florismart.** One of Charlemagne's paladins, and the bosom friend of Roland.

**Florizel.** George IV, when Prince of Wales, corresponded under this name with Mrs Robinson, the actress, generally known as Perdita, that being the character in which she first attracted the prince's attention. The names, of course, come from Shakespeare's *Winter's Tale*. Florizel was a Prince of Bohemia, and our royal George was certainly a Bohemian Prince.

In Beaconsfield's *Emdymion* (1880) *Prince Florizel* is meant for Napoleon III.

**Flotsam and Jetsam.** Wreckage found in the sea or on the shore. 'Flotsam', goods found *floating* on the sea; 'jetsam', things thrown out of a ship to lighten it. (O.Fr. *floter*, to float: Fr. *jeter*, to throw out.) *Cp.* Lagan.

**Flower of Chivalry.** A name given to several knights of spotless reputation, e.g. –

Sir William Douglas, Knight of Liddesdale (slain 1353).

Bayard (*le chevalier sans peur et sans reproche*) (1475?–1524).

Sir Philip Sidney (1554–86).

**Flower of Kings** (Lat. *Flos regum*). King Arthur was so called by John of Exeter, who was Bishop of Winchester, and died 1268.

**Flowers and Trees.**

(1) Dedicated to heathen gods:

The Cornel cherry tree to Apollo.

| | |
|---|---|
| Cypress | Pluto. |
| Dittany | The Moon. |
| Laurel | Apollo. |
| Lily | Juno. |
| Maidenhair | Pluto. |
| Myrtle | Venus. |
| Narcissus | Ceres. |
| Oak | Jupiter. |
| Olive | Minerva. |
| Poppy | Ceres. |
| Vine | Bacchus. |

(2) Dedicated to saints:

| | | |
|---|---|---|
| Canterbury Bells | to | St Augustine of England. |
| Crocus | | St Valentine. |
| Crown Imperial | | Edward the Confessor. |
| Daisy | | St Margaret. |
| Herb Christophe | | St Christopher. |
| Lady's-smock | | The Virgin Mary. |
| Rose | | Mary Magdalene. |
| St John's-wort | | St John. |
| St Barnaby's Thistle | | St Barnabas. |

(3) National emblems:

| | | |
|---|---|---|
| Leek | emblem of | Wales. |
| Lily (*Fleur-de-lys*) | | France. |
| (*Giglio bianco*) | | Florence. |
| white | | the Ghibelline badge. |
| red | | badge of the Guelphs. |
| Linden | | Prussia. |
| Mignonette | | Saxony. |
| Pomegranate | | Spain. |
| Rose | | England. |
| red, Lancastrians; white, | | Yorkists. |
| Shamrock | | Ireland. |
| Thistle | | Scotland. |
| Violet | | Athens and Napoleon. |
| Sugar Maple | | Canada. |

(4) Symbols:

| | | |
|---|---|---|
| Boxis | a symbol of | the resurrection. |
| Cedars | | the faithful. |
| Corn-ears | | the Holy Communion. |
| Dates | | the faithful. |
| Grapes | | this is my blood. |
| Holly | | the resurrection. |
| Ivy | | the resurrection. |
| Lily | | purity. |
| Olive | | peace. |
| Orange-blossom | | virginity. |
| Palm | | victory. |
| Rose | | incorruption. |
| Vine | | Christ our Life. |
| Yew | | death. |

N.B. – The laurel, oak, olive, myrtle, rosemary, cypress, and amaranth are all funereal plants.

**Flowers in Christian Traditions.** Many plants and flowers, such as the aspen, elder, passion-flower, etc., play their part in Christian tradition. *See the names, also* Christian Traditions.

The following are said to owe their stained blossoms to the blood which trickled from the cross:

The *red anemone*; the *arum*; the *purple orchis*; the crimson-spotted leaves of the *roodselken* (a French tradition); the spotted *persicaria*, snake-weed.

**Flowery Kingdom, The.** China; a translation of the Chinese *Hwa-kwo*.

**Flowing Philosophers.** A name sometimes given to the followers of Heraclitus, one of whose fundamental tenets was that all things are in a constant flux of becoming and perishing.

**Fluellen.** A Welsh captain and great pedant in Shakespeare's *Henry V*, who, amongst other learned quiddities, attempted to draw a parallel between Henry V and Alexander the Great; but when he had said that one was born at Monmouth and the other at Macedon, both beginning with the same letter, and that there was a river in both cities, he had exhausted his parallelisms.

> His parallel is, in all essential circumstances, as incorrect as that which Fluellen drew between Macedon and Monmouth. Lord Macaulay

**Fluke.** A lucky chance, a stroke or action that accidentally meets with success, as in billiards when one plays for one thing and gets another. Hence an advantage gained by luck more than by skill or judgment.

**Flummery.** Flattering nonsense, palaver. In Wales it is a food made of oatmeal steeped in water and kept till it has become sour. In Cheshire and Lancashire it is the prepared skin of oatmeal mixed with honey, ale, or milk; pap; blanc-mange. (Welsh, *llymry*, wash-brew, from *llym*, sour or sharp.)

> You came … with your red coats and flashing buttons … and her head got turned with your flummery.
>
> W. G. Simms, *The Partizans*, ch. xxix (1835)

**Flummux, To.** To bamboozle; to deceive; to be in a quandary. 'I am regularly flummuxed' – i.e. perplexed. It is probably the Old English provincial word *flummocks*, to maul or mangle, or *flummock*, bewilderment, also untidiness or an untidy person.

> For the privates, the sergeants, and 'spectors,
> She flummuxed them all to a coon.
>
> G. R. Sims, *Moll Jarvis*; *Dagonet Ballads* (1879)

The mark ⊙ set on a street, gatepost, house, etc., as a warning to fellow-vagabonds not to go near, for fear of being given in charge, is known among the fraternity as a *flummux*.

**Flunkey.** A male livery servant, a footman, lackey. The word usually has a contemptuous implication and suggests snobbery and toadyism; hence *flunkeydom*, *flunkeyish*, etc., pertaining to toadies. Probably a Scottish form of *flanker*, i.e. one who runs at the side (of carriages, etc.). *Cp.* Fr. *flanquer*, to run at the side of.

**Flush.** In cards, a whole hand of one suit, as a 'flush of clubs', a 'flush of hearts', etc.

***Flush of money.*** Full of money. Similarly *a flush of water* means a sudden and full flow of water (Lat. *flux-us*).

**Flute. *The Magic Flute***, an opera by Mozart (*Die Zauberflöte*). The 'flute' was bestowed by the powers of darkness, and had the power of inspiring love. Unless purified the love was only lust, but, being purified by the Powers of Light, it subserved the holiest purposes. Tamino and Pamina are guided by it through all worldly dangers to the knowledge of Divine Truth.

**Flutter the Dovecotes, To.** To disturb the equanimity of a society. The phrase occurs in *Coriolanus* (5, 6).

> The important movement in favour of a general school of law flattered the dovecotes of the Inns of Court.
>
> *Nineteenth Century* (Nov. 1892, p. 779)

**Fly** (plural *flys*). A hackney coach, a cab. A contraction of *Fly-by-night*, as sedan chairs on wheels used to be called in the regency. These 'Fly-by-nights', patronised greatly by George, Prince of Wales, and his boon companions, during their wild night pranks at Brighton, were invented 1809 by John Butcher, a carpenter of Jew Street.

> In the morning we took a fly, an English term for an exceedingly sluggish vehicle, and drove up to the Minister's.
>
> Hawthorne, *Our Old House* (*Pilgrimage to Old Boston*, p. 171)

**Fly.** An insect (plural *flies*). For the theatrical use, *see* Flyman.

It is said that no fly was ever seen in Solomon's temple; and according to *Mohammedan legend*, all flies shall perish except one, and that is the bee-fly.

***The god* or *lord of flies.*** In the temple of Actium the Greeks used annually to sacrifice an ox to Zeus, who, in this capacity, was surnamed Apomyios, the averter of flies. Pliny tells us that at Rome sacrifice was offered to flies in the temple of Hercules Victor, and the Syrians offered sacrifice to the same tiny tormentors. *See* Achor, Beelzebub.

*Phrases.*

***Flies in amber.*** *See* Amber.

***He's a fly customer.*** A 'knowing card', a person who is very wide-awake, 'up to snuff'.

***No flying without wings.*** Nothing can be done without the proper means.

> Sine pennis volare haud facile est. Plautus

***On the fly.*** On the spree.

***The eagle doesn't hawk at flies.*** *See* Aquila.

***The fly in the ointment.*** The trifling cause that spoils everything; a biblical phrase.

> Dead flies cause the ointment of the apothecary to send forth a stinking savour; so doth a little folly him that is in reputation for wisdom and honour. Eccles. 10:1

***The fly on the coach-wheel.*** One who fancies himself of mighty importance, but who is in reality of none at all. The allusion is to Aesop's fable of a fly sitting on a chariot-wheel and saying, 'See what a dust I make!' *See also* La Fontaine's *Fables*, vii, 9.

***There are no flies on him.*** He's all right; he's very alert; you needn't be afraid of trusting him, he won't let you down.

***To come off with flying colours.*** *See* Colours.

***To crush a fly on a wheel.*** To make a mountain of a mole-hill; in allusion to the absurdity of taking a wheel used for torturing criminals and heretics for killing a fly, which one might destroy with a flapper.

***To fly a kite.*** *See* Kite.

***To fly in one's face.*** To get into a passion with a person; to insult; as a hawk, when irritated, flies in the face of its master.

***To fly in the face of danger.*** To run in a foolhardy manner into danger, as a hen flies in the face of a dog or cat.

***To fly in the face of providence.*** To act rashly, and throw away good opportunities; to court danger.

***To fly out at.*** To burst or break into a passion. The Latin, *involo in* ...

> Poor choleric Sir Brian would fly out at his coachman, his butler, or his gamekeeper, and use language ... which ... from any other master would have brought about a prompt resignation. *Good Words*, 1887

***To rise to the fly.*** To be taken in by a hoax, as a fish rises to the angler's fly and is caught.

> He [the professor] rose to the fly with a charming simplicity.
>
> Grant Allen, *The Mysterious Occurrence in Piccadilly*, Pt ii

**Fly-boy.** The boy in a printing-office who lifts the printed sheets off the press; so called because he catches the sheets as they fly from the tympan immediately the frisket is opened.

**Fly-by-night.** One who defrauds his creditors by decamping at night-time; also the early name of a sedan-chair, and later a horsed vehicle (hence Fly, a cab) designed in 1809 for speed.

**Fly-flat.** A racing man's term for a punter who thinks he knows all the ins and outs of the turf, but doesn't.

**Flying Dutchman.** A legendary spectral ship, supposed to be seen in stormy weather off the Cape of Good Hope, and considered ominous of ill-luck. Scott, in his note to *Rokeby*, ii, 11, says she was originally a vessel laden with precious metal, but a horrible murder having been committed aboard, the plague broke out among the crew, and no port would allow the vessel to enter. The ill-fated ship still wanders about like a ghost, doomed to be sea-tossed, but never more to enjoy rest. Captain Marryat's novel *The Phantom Ship* (1839) tells of Philip Vanderdecken's successful but disastrous search for his father, the captain of the *Flying Dutchman*.

> Then, 'mid the war of sea and sky,
> Top and top-gallant hoisted high,
> Full-spread and crowded every sail,
> The Demon-frigate braves the gale.
> And well the doomed spectators know
> The harbinger of wreck and woe.
>
> Scott, *Rokeby*, ii, 11

**Flyman.** In theatrical language, the scene-shifter, or the man in the 'flies', i.e. the gallery over the proscenium where the curtains, scenery, etc. are controlled.

***The flyman's plot.*** The list of all the articles required by the flyman in the play produced.

**Fo'c'sle.** *See* Forecastle.

**Fogy** or **Fogey.** ***An old fogy.*** Originally an old military pensioner of Edinburgh Castle, whose chief occupation was to fire the guns, or assist in quelling street riots; now, a man of advanced years and somewhat antiquated ideas. A disrespectful but good-humoured description.

> What has the world come to [said Thackeray] ... when two broken-nosed old fogies like you and me sit talking about love to each other.
>
> Trollope, *W. M. Thackeray*, ch. 1

**Fo-hi.** A hero of ancient Chinese legend. His mother, Moyë, was walking one day along a river bank when she became suddenly encircled by a rainbow, and at the end of twelve years gave birth to Fo-hi. During gestation she dreamed that she was pregnant with a white elephant: hence, according to some accounts, the honours paid to this beast throughout the East. *See* Elephant.

**Foil.** That which sets off something to advantage. The allusion is to the metallic leaf used by jewellers to set off precious stones. (Fr. *feuille*; Lat. *folium*; Gr. *phullon*, a leaf.)

> I'll be your foil, Laertes. In mine ignorance
> Your skill shall, like a star i' the darkest night,
> Stick fiery off indeed.
>
> Shakespeare, *Hamlet*, 5, 2

***He foiled me.*** He outwitted me.

> If I be foiled, there is but one ashamed who never was gracious.
>
> Shakespeare, *As You Like It*, 1, 2

***To run a foil.*** To puzzle; to lead astray. The track of game is called its *foil*; and an animal hunted will sometimes run back over the same foil in order to mislead its pursuers.

**Folio.** Properly, a ream or sheet in its standard size; but when used of books it denotes a book whose sheets have been folded once only, so that each sheet makes two leaves; hence, a book of large size. Demy folio = $11\frac{1}{4} \times 17\frac{1}{2}$ in., crown folio – 10 x 15 in., and so forth. It is from the Ital. *un libro in foglio*, through the Fr. *infolio*.

***Folio so-and-so***, in mercantile books means page so-and-so, and sometimes the two pages which lie exposed at the same time, one containing the credit and the other the debit of one and the same account. So called because ledgers, etc. are made in folio.

Printers call a page of MS or printed matter a *folio* regardless of size.

In conveyances, MSS, typewritten documents, etc. seventy-two words and in Parliamentary proceedings ninety words, make a *folio*.

**Folkland.** *See* Bockland.

**Folk-lore.** The study or knowledge of the superstitions, mythology, legends, customs, traditions, sayings, etc., of a people. The word was coined by W. J. Thoms, the editor of the *Athenaeum*, in 1846. A 'folklorist' is one who is more or less acquainted with these matters.

**Folk-mote** (*folk meeting*). A word used in England before the Conquest for what we now call a county or even a parish meeting.

**Follow.** ***Follow-my-leader.*** A parlour game in which each player must exactly imitate the actions of the leader or pay a forfeit.

***Follow your nose***, go straight on. *He followed his nose* – he went on and on without any discretion or thought of consequences.

***He who follows truth too closely will have dirt kicked in his face.*** Be not too strict to pry into abuse, for *Odium veritas parit*; *Summum jus suprema est injuria*.

***To follow suit.*** To do as the person before you has done. A phrase from card-playing.

***Trade follows the flag.*** The bigger your empire the greater will be your commercial opportunities, and consequently your trade. An imperialistic saying which contains, perhaps, rather more than half a truth.

**Follower.** A male sweetheart, particularly among servant-girls. Mistresses say to female servants, 'I allow no followers' – i.e. I do not allow men to come into my house to see you.

> The pretty near servant-maids had their choice of desirable followers.
>
> E. C. Gaskell, *Cranford*, ch. iii

**Folly.** A fantastic or foolishly extravagant country seat, built for amusement or vainglory. *Fisher's Folly*, a large and beautiful house in Bishopsgate, with pleasure-gardens, bowling-green, and hothouses, built by Jasper Fisher, one of the six clerks of Chancery and a Justice of the Peace, is an historical example. Queen Elizabeth lodged there; in 1620 it was acquired by the Earl of Devonshire, and its site is now occupied by Devonshire Square.

> Kirby's castle, and Fisher's folly,
> Spinola's pleasure, and Megse's glory.
>
> Stow, *Survey* (1603)

**Fond.** *A foolish, fond parent*. Here fond does not mean affectionate, but silly, from the obsolete *fon*, to act the fool, to become foolish (connected with our *fun*). Chaucer uses the word *fonne* for a simpleton (*Reeve's Tale*, 169); Shakespeare has 'fond desire', 'fond wretch', 'fond madwoman', etc., also the well known:

> Pray, do not mock me:
> I am a very foolish fond old man,
> Fourscore and upward, not an hour more or less;
> And, to deal plainly,
> I fear I am not in my perfect mind.
>
> *King Lear*, 4, 7

**Fons et Origo** (Lat.). The primary cause. *Fax et focus*, the instigator, as Juno was the *fax et focus* of the Trojan war.

**Font** or **Fount.** A complete set of type of the same body and face, with all the points, accents, figures, fractions, signs, etc., that ordinarily occur in printed books and papers. A complete fount (which, of course, includes *italics*) comprises 275 separate pieces of type, not including the special characters needed in almanacs, astronomical and medical works, etc. The word is French, *fonte*, from *fondre* (to melt or cast). *Cp*. Type; Letter.

***Greek inscription round baptismal font.*** *See* Palindrome.

***Taken to the font.*** Baptised. The font is the vessel employed for baptism. (Lat. *fons*, *fontem*, a fount.)

**Fontarabia.** Now called Fuenterrabia (in Lat., *Fons rapidus*), near the Gulf of Gascony. Here, according to legend, Charlemagne and all his chivalry fell by the sword of the Saracens. The French romancers say that the rear of the king's army being cut to pieces, Charlemagne returned and revenged their death by a complete victory.

When Charlemagne with all his peerage fell
By Fontarabia. Milton, *Paradise Lost*, i, 587

**Food.** ***Food for powder.*** Soldiers; especially raw recruits levied in times of war.

*Prince*: Tell me, Jack, whose fellows are these that come after?
*Fal*: Mine, Hal, mine.
*Prince*: I did never see such pitiful rascals.
*Fal*: Tut, tut; good enough to toss; food for powder, food for powder; they'll fill a pit as well as better: tush, man, mortal men, mortal men.
Shakespeare, *Henry IV*, 4, 2

***The food of the gods.*** *See* Ambrosia, Nectar.

***To become food for the worms***, or ***for the fishes.*** To be dead and buried, or to be drowned.

**Fool.** We have many old phrases in which this word plays the chief part; among those which need no explanation are: *A fool and his money are soon parted*; *Fortune favours fools*; *To fool about*; *There's no fool like an old fool*; etc. Others that may be mentioned are:

***A fool's bolt is soon shot*** (*Henry V*, 3, 7). Simpletons cannot wait for the fit and proper time, but waste their resources in random endeavours. The allusion is to bowmen in battle; the good soldier shot with a purpose, but the foolish soldier at random. *Cp*. Prov. 29:11.

***A fool's Paradise.*** To be in a fool's paradise is to be in a state of contentment or happiness that rests only on unreal, fanciful foundations; to believe and behave as though one were in better circumstances than one is. *Cp*. Limbus Fatuorum.

***As the fool thinks, so the bell clinks*** (Lat. *Quod valde volumus facile credimus*). A foolish person believes what he desires.

***Every man hath a fool in his sleeve.*** No one is always wise; there is something of the fool about everyone.

***Every man is a fool or his own physician at forty.*** Said by Plutarch (*Treatise on the Preservation of Health*) to have been a saying of Tiberius. It implies that by the age of 40 a man ought to have learnt enough about his own constitution to be able to keep himself in health.

***The Feast of Fools.*** A kind of Saturnalia, popular in the Middle Ages. Its chief object was to honour the ass on which our Lord made His triumphant entry into Jerusalem. This blasphemous mummery was held on the Feast of the Circumcision (Jan. 1). The office of the day was chanted in travesty, then a procession was formed and all sorts of foolery was indulged in. An ass was an essential feature, and from time to time the whole procession imitated braying, especially in the place of 'Amen'.

***The wisest fool in Christendom.*** James I was so called by Henri IV of France, who learnt the phrase of Sully.

***To be a fool for one's pains.*** To have worked ineffectively; to have had no reward for one's labours.

***To be a fool to.*** Not to come up to; to be very inferior to; as, 'bagatelle is a fool to billiards'.

***To fool about*** or ***around.*** To play the fool; to hang around in an aimless way.

***To fool away one's time, money, etc.*** To squander it, fritter it away.

***To make a fool of one.*** To impose on him, mislead him.

***Young men think old men fools, old men know young men are.*** An old saying quoted by Camden in his *Remains* (1605, p. 228) as by a certain Dr Metcalfe. It occurs also in Chapman's *All Fools*, v, ii (acted 1599).

**Court Fools.** From mediaeval times till the 17th century licensed fools or jesters were commonly kept at court, and frequently in the retinue of wealthy nobles. Thus we are told that the regent Morton had a fool, Patrick Bonny; Holbein painted Sir Thomas More's jester, Patison, in his picture of the chancellor; and as late as 1728 Swift wrote an epitaph on Dickie Pearce, the fool of the Earl of Suffolk, who died at the age of 63 and is buried in Berkeley Churchyard, Gloucestershire. Dagonet, the fool of King Arthur, is also remembered.

Among the most celebrated court fools are:

Rayère, of Henry I; Scogan, of Edward IV; Thomas Killigrew, called 'King Charles' jester' (1611–82); Archie Armstrong (d.1672), and Thomas Derrie, jesters in the court of James I.

James Geddes, to Mary Queen of Scots; his predecessor was Jenny Colquhoun.

Patch, the court fool of Elizabeth, wife of Henry VII.

Will Somers (d.1560), Henry VIII's jester, and Patche, presented to that monarch by

Cardinal Wolsey; and Robert Grene, jester in the court of Queen Elizabeth.

The fools of Charles V of France were Mitton and Thévenin de St Léger; Haincelin Coq belonged to Charles VI, and Guillaume Louel to Charles VII. Triboulet was the jester of Louis XII and François I (1487–1536); Brusquet, of whom Brantôme says 'he never had his equal in repartee', of Henri II; Sibilot and Chicot, of Henri III and IV; and l'Angély, of Louis XIII.

In *chess* the French name for the 'bishop' is *fou* (i.e. fool), and they used to represent it in a fool's dress; hence, Regnier says: *Les fous sont aux échecs les plus proches des Rois* (14 *Sat.*). *Fou* is said to be a corruption of an eastern word for an elephant (*see* Thomas Hyde's *De Ludis Orientalium*, i, 4,1689), and on old boards the places occupied by our 'bishops' were occupied by elephants.

The guild 'fools' of mediaeval times played an important part in the spread of literature and education. They formed a branch of the Troubadour organisation – a force which permeated Europe.

> 'The Jongleurs', says Mr T. E. Rowbotham, 'acted, if we may so express it, the same part which is played by publishers at the present day. The expression is not ours, but Petrarch's, who, in alluding to the functions of the jongleur in one of his letters to Boccaccio, explicitly introduces this comparison. He deduces their similarity to publishers, and compares the parallel condition of a work when it had been recited by a jongleur to admiring crowds and when it had been issued in print or manuscript by a publisher and sold to admiring purchasers.'

**Foolscap.** A standard size of printing paper measuring 13½ x 17 in. and of writing paper measuring 13¼ x 16½ in. The name is derived from an ancient watermark, of which the first known specimen occurs in 1540.

**Foot.** The foot as a measure of length (=12 in., ⅓ of a yard, or ·3047075 of a metre) is common to practically all nations and periods, and has never varied much more than does the length of men's feet, from which the name was taken.

In prosody, the term denotes a division in verse which consists of a certain number of syllables (or pauses) one of which is stressed. Here the term, which comes from Greece, refers to beating time with the foot.

***At one's feet.*** 'To cast oneself at someone's feet' is to be entirely submissive to him, to throw oneself on his mercy.

***Best foot foremost.*** Use all possible dispatch. To 'set on foot' is to set agoing. If you have various powers of motion, set your best foremost.

> Nay, but make haste; the better foot before.
>
> Shakespeare, *King John*, 4, 2

***Enter a house right foot foremost*** (Petronius). It is unlucky to enter a house or to leave one's chamber left foot foremost. Augustus was very superstitious on this point. Pythagoras taught that it is necessary to put the shoe on the right foot first. Iamblichus tells us this symbolised that man's first duty is reverence to the gods.

***First foot.*** *See* First.

***How are your poor feet?*** An old street-cry said to have originated at the Great Exhibition of London in 1862. Tramping about the grounds broke down all but trained athletes.

***I have not yet got my foot in.*** I am not yet familiar and easy with the work. The allusion is to the preliminary exercises in Roman foot-races. While the signal was waited for, the candidates made essays of jumping, running, and posturing, to excite a suitable warmth and make their limbs supple. This was 'getting their foot in' for the race. *Cp.* Hand.

***I have the measure*** or ***length of his foot.*** I know the exact calibre of his mind. The allusion is to the Pythagorean measurement of Hercules by the length of his foot. *See* Ex pede.

***To foot it.*** To walk the distance instead of riding it; also to dance.

> Lo how finely the graces can it foote to the Instrument.
>
> They dauncen deftly, and singen soote in their meriment.
>
> Spenser, *Shepherd's Calendar*, April

***To foot the bill.*** To pay it; to promise to pay the account by signing one's name at the foot of the bill.

***To have one's foot on another's neck.*** To have him at your mercy; to tyrannise over, or domineer over him completely. *See* Josh. 10:24.

> See, your foot is on our necks,
>
> We vanquish'd, you the Victor of your will.
>
> What would you more?
>
> Tennyson, *The Princess*, 165

***To light on one's feet.*** To escape a threatened danger. It is said that cats thrown from a height always light on their feet.

***To measure another's foot by your own last.*** To apply your personal standards to the conduct or actions of another; to judge people by yourself.

***To put down your foot on*** (a matter). Peremptorily to forbid it.

***To set a man on his feet.*** To start him off in business, etc., especially after he has 'come a cropper'.

***To show the cloven foot.*** To betray an evil intention. The devil is represented with a cloven foot.

***To trample under foot.*** To oppress, or outrage; to treat with the greatest contempt and discourtesy.

***With one foot in the grave.*** In a dying state.

***You have put your foot in it nicely.*** You have got yourself into a pretty mess. When porridge is burnt or meat over-roasted, we say, 'The bishop hath put his foot in.' *See* Bishop.

**Foot-breadth** or **Quern-biter.** The sword of Thoralf Skolinson the Strong, a companion of Hako I of Norway. *See* Swords.

**Footing.** ***He is on good footing with the world.*** He stands well with the world. This is a French phrase. *Être sur un grand pied dans le monde.* 'Grand pied' means 'large foot', and the allusion is to the time of Henry VIII, when the rank of a man was designated by the size of his shoe – the higher the rank the larger the shoe. The proverb would be more correctly rendered, 'He has a large foot in society'.

***To pay your footing.*** To give money for drink when you first enter on a trade. Entry money for being allowed to put your foot in the premises occupied by fellow-craftsmen. *Cp.* Garnish.

**Footlights.** *To appear before the footlights.* On the stage, where a row of lights is placed in front along the floor to lighten it up.

**Footmen.** *See* Running Footmen.

**Footnotes.** Notes placed at the bottom of a page.

> A trifling sum of misery
> Now added to the foot of thy account. Dryden

**Foot-pound.** The unit of result in estimating *work done* by machinery. Thus, if we take 1 lb as the unit of weight and 1 ft as the unit of distance, a foot-pound would be 1 lb weight raised 1 ft.

**Fop's Alley.** An old name for a promenade in a theatre, especially the central passage between the stalls, right and left, in the opera-house.

**Forbears.** Ancestors, predecessors – i.e. those born before the present generation.

> My name is Graeme, so please you, – Roland Graeme, whose forbears were designated of Heathergill, in the Debateable Land.
> Sir W. Scott, *The Abbot*, ch. xviii

**Forbidden Fruit, The.** Figuratively, unlawful indulgence. According to Mohammedan tradition the forbidden fruit partaken of by Eve and Adam was the banana or Indian fig, because fig-leaves were employed to cover the disobedient pair when they felt shame as the result of sin.

**Forcible Feeble.** *See* Feeble.

**Fore.** ***To the fore.*** In the front rank; eminent.

***To come to the fore.*** To stand out prominently; to distinguish oneself; to stand forth.

**Fore-and-Aft.** All over the ship; lengthwise, in opposition to 'athwartships' or across the line of the keel.

> A slight spar-deck fore-and-aft. Sir W. Raleigh

**Forecastle** (usually printed – and pronounced – fo'c'sle). So called because anciently this part of a vessel was raised and protected like a castle, so that it could command the enemy's deck. Dana's *Seaman's Manual* defines it as:

> That part of the upper deck forward of the foremast … In merchant ships, the forward part of the vessel under the deck, where the sailors live.

**Foreclose.** To put an end to. A legal term, meaning to close before the time specified; e.g. suppose I held the mortgage of a man called A, and A fails to fulfil his part of the agreement, I can insist upon the mortgage being cancelled, foreclosing thus our agreement.

**Forefathers' Day.** *See* Pilgrim Fathers.

**Fore-shortened.** Not viewed laterally, but more or less obliquely. Thus a man's leg lying on the ground, with the sole of the foot nearer the artist than the rest of the body, would be fore-shortened.

> He forbids the fore-shortenings, because they make the parts appear little. Dryden

**Forfar.** ***Do as the cow o' Forfar did, tak' a stannin' drink.*** A cow, in passing a door in Forfar, where a tub of ale had been placed to cool, drank the whole of it. The owner of the ale prosecuted the owner of the cow, but a learned bailie, in giving his decision, said, 'As the ale was drunk by the cow while standing at the door, it must be considered *doch-an-doroch* (stirrup-cup), to make a charge for which would be to outrage Scotch hospitality.' (Scott, *Waverley.*)

**Forget-me-nots of the Angels.** The stars are so called by Longfellow:

> Silently, one by one, in the infinite meadows of heaven,
> Blossom the lovely stars, the forget-me-nots of the angels. *Evangeline*

**Fork.** Old thieves' slang for a finger; hence *to fork out*, to produce and hand over, to pay up.

***A forked cap.*** A bishop's mitre; so called by John Skelton (early 16th cent.). It is cleft or forked.

***Fingers were made before forks.*** *See* Fingers.

***The forks.*** The gallows (Lat. *furca*). Cicero (*de Divinitate*, i, 26) says, *Ferens furcam ductus est*, often quoted in proof that criminals condemned to the cross were obliged to carry their own cross to the place of execution. But the ordinary meaning of *furca* is a kind of yoke to which the hands of criminals were fastened. The punishment was of three degrees of severity; (1) The *furca ignominiosa*; (2) the *furca paenalis*; and (3) the *furca capitalis*. The first was for slight offences, and consisted in carrying the *furca* on the shoulders, more or less weighted. The second consisted in carrying the *furca* and being scourged. The third was being scourged to death. The word *furcifer* meant what we call a gallows-bird or vile follow.

***The Caudine Forks.*** *See* Caudine.

**Forlorn Hope.** This phrase is the Dutch *verloren hoop*, the lost squad or troop, and is due to a misunderstanding, as the words are not connected with our *forlorn* or *hope*. The French equivalent is *enfants perdus*, the lost ones. The *forlorn hope* was originally a picked body of men sent in front to begin an attack; thus Cromwell says, 'Our *forlorn* of horse marched within a mile of the enemy', i.e. our horse picket sent forward to reconnoitre approached within a mile of the enemy's camp. It is now usually applied to a body of men specially selected for some desperate or very dangerous enterprise.

**Forma pauperis** (Lat. Plea of poverty). *To sue in forma pauperis*. When a person has just cause of a suit, but is so poor that he cannot raise the money necessary to enter it, the judge will assign him lawyers and counsel without the usual fees.

**Fortiter in re** (Lat.). Firmness in doing what is to be done; an unflinching resolution to persevere to the end. *See* Suaviter in modo.

**Fortunate Islands.** An ancient name for the Canary Islands; also, for any imaginary lands set in distant seas, like the 'Islands of the Blest', where every prospect pleases and man could live happy ever after.

> Their place of birth alone is mute
> To sounds that echo farther west
> Than your sire's Islands of the Blest.
>
> Byron, *The Isles of Greece* (*Don Juan*, iii)

**Fortunatus.** A hero of mediaeval legend (from Eastern sources) who possessed an inexhaustible purse, a wishing cap, etc. He appears in a German *Volksbuch* of 1509, Hans Sachs dramatised the story in 1553, and at Christmas, 1590, Dekker's *Pleasant Comedy of Old Fortunatus* was played before Queen Elizabeth.

***You have found Fortunatus' purse.*** Are in luck's way.

**Fortune.** ***Fortune favours the brave***. The expression is found in Terence – *Fortes fortuna adjuvat* (*Phormio*, i, 4); also in Virgil – *Audentes fortuna juvat* (*Aen*. x, 284), and many other classic writers.

**Forty.** A number of frequent occurrence in Scripture, and hence formerly treated as, in a manner, sacrosanct. Moses was forty days in the mount; Elijah was forty days fed by ravens; the rain of the flood fell forty days, and another forty days expired before Noah opened the window of the ark; forty days was the period of embalming; Nineveh had forty days to repent; our Lord fasted forty days; He was seen forty days after His resurrection, etc.

St Swithin betokens forty days' rain or dry weather; a quarantine extends to forty days; forty days, in the Old English law, was the limit for the payment of the fine for manslaughter; the privilege of sanctuary was for forty days; the widow was allowed to remain in her husband's house for forty days after his decease; a knight enjoined forty days' service of his tenant; a stranger, at the expiration of forty days, was compelled to be enrolled in some tithing; Members of Parliament were protected from arrest forty days after the prorogation of the House, and forty days before the House was convened; a new-made burgess had to forfeit forty pence unless he built a house within forty days, etc., etc.

The ancient physicians ascribe many strange changes to the period of forty; the alchemists looked on forty days as the charmed period when the philosopher's stone and elixir of life were to appear.

***Fool or physician at forty.*** *See* Fool.

***Forty stripes save one.*** The Jews were forbidden by the Mosaic law to inflict more than forty stripes on an offender, and for fear of breaking the law they stopped short of the number. If the scourge contained three lashes, thirteen strokes would equal 'forty save one'.

The Thirty-nine Articles of the Anglican Church used sometimes to be called 'the forty stripes save one' by irreverent young theological students.

## Fourteen

***Forty winks.*** A short nap.

***The Forty Immortals*** (or simply *the Forty*). The members of the French Academy, who number forty; sometimes applied also to the members of the English Royal Academy.

***The hungry 'Forties.*** The period just before and about the middle of the 19th century, when, largely owing to the high import duties on corn, bread and food generally was very dear.

***The roaring forties.*** The Atlantic Ocean between 40° and 50° north latitude; well known for its rough and stormy character.

**Forty-five.** 'The Forty-five' is the name given to the rebellion in favour of the Young Pretender (*q.v.*), of 1745.

'Number 45' is the celebrated number of Wilkes' *North Briton* (April 23rd, 1763), in which Cabinet Ministers were accused of putting a lie into the king's mouth.

**Forty-two Line Bible, The.** *See* Bible, Specially named.

**Forwards, Marshal.** Blücher (1742–1819) was called *Marschall Vorwärts*, from his constant exhortation to his soldiers in the campaigns preceding the great battle of Waterloo. *Vorwärts!* always *Vorwärts!*

**Fosse, The,** or **Fosse-way.** One of the four principal highways made by the Romans in England. It leads from Bath through Cirencester and Leicester and Lincoln, and had a fosse or ditch on each side of it. *Cp.* Ermine Street.

**Fou.** A Scotticism for drunk. It is, of course, a variant of *full.*

The clachan yill had made me canty.*
I was na fou, but just had plenty.
Burns, *Death and Dr Hornbook*

*The village ale had made me jolly.

**Foul-weather Jack.** Commodore Byron (1723–86), said to have been as notorious for foul weather as Queen Victoria was for fine.

**Fount of type.** *See* Font; Letter; Type. The *fount* is a set of type of one face and size, and is the Fr. *fonte*, from *fondre*, to melt, cast, or *found*. A maker of type is a 'type-*founder*'.

**Fountain of Youth.** In popular folk-tales, a fountain supposed to possess the power of restoring youth. Expeditions were fitted out in search of it, and at one time it was supposed to be in one of the Bahama Islands.

**Four Kings.** *The History of the Four Kings* (*Livre des Quatre Rois*). A pack of cards. In a French pack the four kings are Charlemagne, David, Alexander, and Caesar, representatives of the Franco-German, Jewish or Christian, Macedonian, and Roman monarchies.

**Four Letters, The.** *See* Tetragrammaton.

**Four Masters.** *The Annals of the Four Masters* is the name usually given to a collection of old Irish chronicles published in 1632–6 as Annals of the Kingdom of Ireland. The Four Masters (authors or compilers) were Michael O'Clery (1575–1643), Conaire his brother, his cousin Cucoigcriche O'Clery (d.1664), with Fearfeasa O'Mulconry.

**Four Sons of Aymon.** *See* Aymon.

**Fourierism.** A communistic system, so called from François Marie Charles Fourier (1772–1837), of Besançon. All the world was to be grouped into 'phalansteries', consisting each of 400 families or 1,800 individuals, who were to live in a common edifice, furnished with workshops, studios, and all sources of amusement. The several groups were at the same time to be associated together under a unitary government like the cantons of Switzerland or the United States. Only one language was to be admitted; all profits were to go to the common purse; talent and industry were to be rewarded; and no one was to be suffered to remain indigent, or without the enjoyment of certain luxuries and public amusement.

**Fourteen,** in its connection with Henri IV and Louis XIV. The following are curious and strange coincidences:

**Henri IV:**

14 letters in the name Henri-de-Bourbon. He was the 14th king of France and Navarre on the extinction of the family of Navarre. He was born on Dec. 14, 1553, the sum of which year amounts to 14; he was assassinated on May 14, 1610; and lived 4 times 14 years, 14 weeks, and 4 times 14 days.

14 May, 1552, was born Marguerite de Valois, his first wife.

14 May, 1588, the Parisians rose in revolt against him because he was a 'heretic'.

14 March, 1590, he won the great battle of Ivry.

14 May, 1590, was organised a grand ecclesiastical and military demonstration against him, which drove him from the faubourgs of Paris.

14 Nov., 1590, the Sixteen took an oath to die rather than submit to a 'heretic' king.

It was Gregory XIV who issued a Bull excluding Henri from the throne.

14 Nov., 1592, the Paris parlement registered the papal Bull.

14 Dec., 1599, the Duke of Savoy was reconciled to Henri IV.

14 Sept., 1606, was baptised the dauphin (afterwards Louis XIII) son of Henri IV.

14 May, 1610, Henry was assassinated by Ravaillac. For the dates see *Histoire de France,* by Bordier and Churton (1859).

**Louis XIV:**

14th of the name. He mounted the throne 1643, the sum of which figures equals 14. He died 1715, the sum of which figures also equals 14. He reigned 77 years, the sum of which two figures equals 14. He was born 1638, died 1715, which added together equals 3353, the sum of which figures comes to 14.

**Fourteen Hundred.** The cry raised on the Stock Exchange to give notice that a stranger has entered the 'House'. The term is said to have been in use in Defoe's time, and to have originated at a time when for a considerable period the number of members had remained stationary at 1399.

**Fourth Dimension, The.** The three dimensions of space universally recognised by mathematicians are length, breadth, and thickness. A line has only one dimension, length; a surface has two, length and breadth; a solid, and space generally, three, length, breadth, and thickness. The so called 'fourth dimension' is an extension hypothecated by mathematicians with the object of explaining equations of the fourth degree in analytical geometry, and adopted by many psychical investigators to explain certain apparently supernormal phenomena that are otherwise inexplicable. Its relationship to the three dimensions is assumed to be analogous to that borne by any one of these to the other two, i.e. it is a property that is to volume what volume is to area.

**Fourth Estate of the Realm.** The daily Press. The most powerful of all, the others (*see* Estates) being the Lords Spiritual, the Lords Temporal, and the Commons. Burke, referring to the Reporters' Gallery, is credited with having said, 'Yonder sits the Fourth Estate, more important than them all,' but it does not appear in his published works.

**Fourth of July.** *See* Independence Day.

**Fowler, The.** Henry I (876–936), son of Otto, Duke of Saxony, and King of Germany from 919 to 936, was, according to an 11th century tradition, so called because when the deputies announced to him his election to the throne, they found him fowling with a hawk on his fist.

**Fox.** As a name for the Old English broadsword *fox* probably refers to a maker's mark of a dog, wolf, or fox. *See Notes and Queries*, May 2nd, 1891, p. 356: 'The swords were manufactured by Julian del Rei of Toledo, whose trade-mark was a little dog, mistaken for a fox.'

The old Passau swordsmith's stamp of a running wolf known in Spain as the Perillo (or dog) gives numerous occasions for jokes.

Viscount Dillon, *Shakespeare's England*, I, iv, § 2

O signieur Dew, thou diest on point of fox,
Except, O signieur, thou do give to me
Egregious ransom. Shakespeare, *Henry V*, 4, 4

I had a sword, ay, the flower of Smithfield for a sword, a right fox i' faith.

Porter, *Two Angry Women of Abington* (1599)

***To fox.*** To steal or cheat; also to keep an eye on somebody without seeming so to do. A dog, a fox, and a weasel sleep, as they say, 'with one eye open'; and a child who is pretending to be asleep but isn't is said to be 'foxing'.

**Phrases.**

***A fox's sleep.*** A sleep with one eye on the *qui vive*. Assumed indifference to what is going on. *See above*.

***A wise fox will never rob his neighbour's hen-roost.*** It would soon be found out, so he goes farther from home where he is not known.

***Every fox must pay his skin to the furrier.*** The crafty shall be taken in their own wiliness.

***I gave him a flap with a fox-tail.*** I cajoled him; made a fool of him. The fox-tail was one of the badges of the motley, and to flap with a fox-tail is to treat one like a fool.

***Reynard the Fox.*** *See* Reynard.

***The fox and the grapes.*** 'It's a case of the fox and the grapes' is said of one who wants something badly but cannot obtain it, and so tries to create the impression that he doesn't want it at all. The allusion is to one of Aesop's fables. *See* Grapes.

***The Old Fox.*** Marshal Soult (1769–1851) was so nicknamed, from his strategic talents and fertility of resources.

***To flay the fox.*** *See* Flay.

***To set a fox to keep the geese*** (Lat. *Ovem lupo committere*). Said of one who entrusts his money to sharpers.

**Foxed.** A print or page of a book stained with reddish brown marks is said to be 'foxed'. Of course, the stain is so called because of its colour.

**Fox-fire.** The phosphoric light, without heat, which plays round decaying matter. It is the Fr. *faux*, or 'false fire'.

**Foxglove.** The flower is named from the animal and the glove. The reason for the second half is obvious from the finger-stall appearance of the flower, but it is not known how the fox came to be associated with it. Although it is called by the Welsh *Fairy's glove* and by the Irish *The Fairy Woman's Thimble*, there is no evidence that the flower is so named because it was thought to be the glove of the 'good *folks*' or fairies.

**Fox trot.** A modern ball-room dance of negro origin (like the 'bunny-hug', 'turkey-trot', etc.) introduced from America. A horse's *fox-trot* is the short steps it takes when changing from a trot to a walk.

**Foxy.** Strong-smelling, cunning, or red-haired; like a fox.

**Fra Diavolo.** Auber's opera of this name (1830) is founded on the exploits of Michele Pozza (1760–1806), a celebrated brigand and renegade monk, who evaded pursuit for many years amidst the mountains of Calabria.

**Fradubio** (*the Doubter*). In Spenser's *Faërie Queene* (I, ii, 28 ff.), the lover of Fraelissa (Frailty). Duessa (*q.v.*) turned his mistress into a tree and bewitched him into loving her; but when he accidentally discovered the foul deformities of the hag, and showed by his manner that he had done so, she turned him into a tree also.

**France.** *See* Frank.

**Francesca da Rimini.** Daughter of Guido da Polenta, Lord of Ravenna. Her story is told in Dante's *Inferno* (canto v). She was married to Giovanni Malatesta, Lord of Rimini, but her guilty love for his younger brother, Paolo, was discovered, and both were put to death by him about 1289. Leigh Hunt has a poem, and Silvio Pellico a tragedy, on the subject.

**Franceschini, Guido.** *See* Ring and the Book.

**Franciscans.** A religious order consisting of friars, novices, and lay brothers founded by St Francis of Assisi in 1206 and confirmed by Innocent III in 1210. By their rules they are bound to poverty, but the *Conventual Franciscans* (which branched off in 1230 and wear a black habit instead of grey) are allowed to possess revenues. They established themselves in England (Canterbury) in 1224, and other branches are the *Observantins* (friars of the Regular Observance) established in 1419 by St Bernardine of Sienna; these wear a black habit also, with a rope girdle, the latter giving them their alternative name, *Cordeliers*; the *Barefooted Franciscans*, or friars of the Stricter Observance, wearing grey, and established in 1555 by St Peter of Alcantara; the *Recollects* (grey), a reformed order established by John of Guadeloupe in 1500; and the *Capuchins* (grey), established in 1525 by Matthew Baschi of Urbino.

The Franciscans are known as *Minors* or *Minorites* in token of their humility, and as the *Greyfriars* from the original colour of their habit.

The *Order of Franciscan Nuns* was founded in 1212 by St Clare; they are hence known as the *Clares* or *Poor Clares*; also *Minoresses*. Various reformations have taken place in the Order, giving rise to the *Coleltines*, *Grey Sisters*, *Capuchin Nuns*, *Sisters of the Annunciation*, *Conceptionists*, and the *Urbanists*, the last named observing a modified rule and being permitted to hold property.

**Frangipani.** A perfume made of spices, orris-root, musk, etc. Mutio Frangipani, the famous Italian botanist, visited the West Indies in 1493. The sailors perceived a delicious fragrance as they neared Antigua, and Mutio told them it proceeded from tho *Plumeria rubra*. The plant was re-named Frangipani, and the distilled essence received the same name.

***Frangipani pudding*.** Pudding made of broken bread (Lat. *frangere*, to break; *panis*, bread).

**Frank.** One belonging to the Teutonic nations that conquered Gaul in the 6th century (whence the name *France*). By the Turks, Arabs, etc., of the Levant the name is given to any of the inhabitants of the western parts of Europe, as the English, Germans, Spaniards, French, etc.

**Frank-pledge.** The system by which, in Anglo-Saxon times, the freemen in a tithing were pledged for each other's good behaviour. Hallam says every ten men in a village were answerable for each other, and if one of them committed an offence the other nine were bound to make reparation, or to see that it was made.

**Frankelin's Tale** (Chaucer). *See* Dorigen.

**Frankenstein.** The young student in Mrs Shelley's romance of that name (1818). He made a soulless monster out of corpses from church-yards and dissecting-rooms, and endued it with life by galvanism. The tale shows how the creature longed for sympathy, but was shunned by everyone. It was only animal life, a parody on the creature man, powerful for evil, and the instrument of dreadful retribution on the student who usurped the prerogative of the Creator.

Mrs Shelley gave no name to the monster, and therefore he is not infrequently called 'Frankenstein' when alluded to. This, of course, is an error.

I believe it would be impossible to control the Frankenstein we should have ourselves created.
Lord Avebury (speech, 1886)

**Frater.** The refectory or dining-room of a monastery, where the brothers (Lat. *fratres*) met together for meals. Also called the *fratry*.

In old vagabonds' slang a *frater* was much the same as an Abram-man (*q.v.*).

A Frater goeth wyth a Lisence to beg for some Spittlehouse or Hospital. Their pray is comonly upon poore women as they go and come to the markets.
Awdeley, *Fraternity of Vacabondes* (1575)

**Frateretto.** A fiend mentioned by Edgar in *King Lear*; this is another of the names that Shakespeare obtained from Harsnet's *Declaration. See* Flibbertigibbet.

Frateretto calls me, and tells me Nero is an angler in the lake of darkness. Pray, innocent, and beware of the foul fiend. Act 3, 6

**Fraticellians** (*Little Brethren*). A sect of renegade and licentious monks which appeared about the close of the 13th century and threw off all subjection to the Pope, whom they denounced as an apostate. They had wholly disappeared by the 15th century.

**Frea.** *See* Freyja.

**Free.** ***A free and easy***. A social gathering where persons meet together without formality to chat and smoke. *In a free and easy way*; with an entire absence of ceremony.

***A free fight.*** A fight in which all and sundry engage, rules being disregarded; a regular scrimmage.

***Free on board.*** Said of goods delivered on board ship, or into the conveyance, at the seller's expense; generally contracted to F.O.B.

***I'm free to confess.*** There's nothing to prevent me admitting …; I'm willing to confess – usually with the implication that I'm not particularly keen on doing so.

***To have a free hand.*** *See* Hand.

***To make free with.*** To take liberties with; to treat whatever it is as one's own.

**Free Bench** (*francus bancus*). A legal term denoting a widow's right to a copyhold in certain English manors. It is not a dower or gift, but a free right independent of the will of the husband. Called *bench* because, upon acceding to the estate, she becomes a tenant of the manor, and entitled to sit on the *bench* at manorial courts.

**Free Coup** (in Scotland) means a piece of waste land where rubbish may be deposited free of charge; also the right of doing so.

**Free Lance.** *See* Lance.

**Free Spirit.** *Brethren of the Free Spirit.* Antinomian heretics of the 13th to 15th centuries in Italy, France, and Germany. They claimed 'freedom of spirit', and based their claims on Rom. 8:2–14, 'The law of the Spirit hath made me free from the law of sin and death.'

**Free Trade.** International trade that is free from 'protection', i.e. unrestricted by customs duties, tariffs, etc.

***The Apostle of Free Trade***. Richard Cobden (1804–65), who established the Anti-Corn Law League in 1838.

**Freebooter.** A pirate, an adventurer who makes his living by plundering; literally, one who obtains his booty free (Dut. *vrij*, free, *buit*, booty).

His forces consisted mostly of base people and free booters. Bacon

**Freehold.** An estate held in fee-simple or fee-tail; one on which no duty or service is owing to any lord but the sovereign. *Cp.* Copyhold.

**Freeman, Mrs.** The name assumed by the Duchess of Marlborough in her correspondence with Queen Anne. The queen called herself Mrs Morley.

**Freeman of Bucks.** A cuckold. The allusion is to the buck's horn. *See* Horns.

**Freeman's Quay.** ***Drinking at Freeman's Quay***. *See* Drinking.

**Freemasons.** It is only in the realm of Fable, not even in that of Tradition, that modern Freemasonry can be traced to Hiram of Tyre and the Temple of Solomon; the modern secret fraternity had its origin in England in the 17th century, and its connection with masons – the workers in stone – arises from the fact that the founders adopted many of the practices of the old masonic guilds as being most suitable to their purpose. These mediaeval guilds consisted of workmen who, by the nature of their calling, had to move from place to place; and their secret passwords, ritual, etc., were adopted so that when on their travels they could prove without difficulty that they were actually 'Free and Accepted Masons', and so obtain the comradeship of their brother masons as well as get employment. In each district where cathedrals and churches were being built 'lodges' were created, much as a branch of a trade union would be today, and these had their masters, wardens, and other officials.

The 'Free' is short for 'Free men'; accepted masons were free of their guild.

***The Lady Freemason.*** Women are not admitted into freemasonry, but the story goes that a lady was initiated in the early 18th century. She was the Hon. Elizabeth St Leger, daughter of Lord Doneraile, who hid herself in an empty clock-case when the lodge was held in her father's house, and witnessed the proceedings. She was discovered, and compelled to submit to initiation as a member of the craft. The story is fairly well authenticated.

**Freethinker.** One who will not allow his reason to be biased by revelation or ecclesiastical canons, as deists and atheists.

> There is no Necessity that every Squire in *Great Britain* should know what the Word Freethinker stands for; but it were much to be wished, that they who value themselves upon that conceited Title were a little better instructed in what it ought to stand for.
>
> Steele, *Spectator*, No. 234 (Nov. 28th, 1711)

**Freezing-point.** The temperature at which a liquid becomes solid; if mentioned without qualification 32° Fahrenheit (0° Centigrade), the freezing-point of water, is meant. For other liquids the name is added as the freezing-point of milk, sulphuric ether, quicksilver, and so on. In Centigrade and Réaumur's instruments zero marks the freezing-point.

**Freischütz** (the free-shooter). A legendary German archer in league with the devil, who gave him seven balls, six of which were to hit infallibly whatever the marksman aimed at, and the seventh was to be directed as the devil wished. F. Kind wrote the libretto, and Weber set to music, the opera based on the legend, called *Der Freischütz* (1820).

**Freki and Geri.** The two wolves of Odin.

**French Cream.** Brandy; from the custom (which came from France) of taking a cup of coffee with brandy in it instead of cream after dinner.

**French Leave.** *To take French leave.* To take without asking leave or giving any equivalent; also, to leave a party, house, or neighbourhood without bidding good-bye to anyone; to slip away unnoticed. This kind of back-handed compliment to our neighbours used to be very common (*cp.* 'French gout' for venereal disease), and many objectionable things or practices have been called 'French'.

It is only fair to say that the French have returned the courtesy in many ways. The equivalent of 'to take French leave' is *S'en aller* (or *filer*) *à l'anglaise*; in the 16th century a creditor used to be called *un Anglais*, a term used by Clement Marot; and even till recently, when a man excused himself from entering a café or theatre because he had no money, he would say: '*Non, non! je suis Anglé*' (I am cleared out).

**French of Stratford at Bow.** French as spoken by an Englishman who has only learnt it at a school at home.

> And Frensh, she [the nun] spak ful faire and fetisly.
> After the scole of Stratford atte Bowe,
> For Frensh of Paris was to hir unknowe.
>
> Chaucer, *Canterbury Tales, Prologue*, 124

**Frenchman.** The nickname of a Frenchman is 'Crapaud' (*q.v.*), 'Jean', 'Mossoo', 'Robert Macaire' (*q.v.*); but of a Parisian 'Grenouille' (*frog*).

***French Canadian,*** 'Jean Baptiste'.

***French peasantry,*** 'Jacques Bonhomme'.

***Done like a Frenchman, turn and turn again*** (*1 Henry VI*, 3, 4). The French were frequently ridiculed as a fickle, wavering nation. Dr Johnson says he once read a treatise the object of which was to show that a weathercock is a satire on the word *Gallus* (a Gaul or cock).

**Freshman.** A 'varsity name for an undergraduate in his first term, one who is 'not yet salted'. It was anciently a custom in the different colleges to play practical jokes on the new-comers. One of the most common was to assemble them in a room and make them deliver a speech. Those who acquitted themselves well had a cup of caudle; those who passed muster had a caudle with salt water; the rest had the salt water only. *Cp.* Bejan.

**Freyja.** In *Scandinavian mythology* the sister of Freyr and wife of Odin, who deserted her because she loved finery better than her husband (*see* Brisingamen). She is the fairest of the goddesses, goddess of love and also of the dead. She presides over marriages, and, besides being the Venus, may be called the Juno of Asgard. One account says that she flies through the air with the wings of a falcon, another that she rides in a chariot drawn by two cats. She is also known as *Frea*, *Frija*, *Frigg*, *Frige*, etc., and it is from her that our *Friday* is named.

**Freyr.** Son of Njörd (*q.v.*), originally one of the Vanir, but received among the Aesir after the war between the two. He was the Scandinavian god of fertility and peace, the dispenser of rain, and the patron god of Sweden and Iceland. His wife was Gerdr (*q.v.*), and among his treasures were

*Blodighofi* (Bloody-hoof), his horse, a golden helmet with the crest of a wild-boar *Gullinbursti* (i.e. with gold bristles), and the magic ship *Skithblathnir*, which could be folded up like a tent.

**Friar** (Lat. *frater*, a brother). A monk, especially one belonging to one of the four great mendicant orders, i.e. Franciscans, Dominicans, Augustinians, and Carmelites. *See these names.*

***Curial Friar.*** *See* Curtal.

In printer's slang a *friar* is a part of the sheet which has failed to receive the ink properly, and is therefore paler than the rest. As Caxton set up his press in Westminster Abbey, it is but natural that monks and friars should give foundation to some of the printer's slang. *Cp.* Monk.

**Friar Bungay.** A famous necromancer of the 15th century, whose story is much overlaid with legend. It is said that he 'raised mists and vapours which befriended Edward IV at the battle of Barnet'. In the old prose romance, *The Famous History of Friar Bacon*, and in Greene's *Honourable History of Friar Bacon and Friar Bungay* (acted 1591), he appears as the assistant to Roger Bacon (d.1292), and he is introduced into Lytton's *Last of the Barons*.

> [Friar Bungay is] the personification of the charlatan of science in the 15th century.
>
> Lytton, *The Last of the Barons*

**Friar Gerund.** A satirical romance by José Isla (1703–81) ridiculing the contemporary pulpit oratory of Spain; it is full of quips and cranks, tricks, and startling monstrosities.

**Friar John.** A prominent character in Rabelais' *Gargantua and Pantagruel*, a tall, lean, wide-mouthed, long-nosed friar of Seville, who dispatched his matins with wonderful celerity, and ran through his vigils quicker than any of his fraternity. He swore lustily and was a Trojan to fight:

> a right monk if ever there was any, since the monking world monked a monkery (I, xxvii).

In the original he is called 'Friar John *des Entommeures*': Urquhart mistakenly translated this as 'of the Funnels'; 'of the Trenchermen' is the best equivalent (*entamer*, to broach, to carve, with reference to a hearty appetite). *Entonnoirs* are 'funnels '; and as this word has been used as slang for the throat perhaps that accounts for the mistake.

**Friar Rush.** A legendary house-spirit who originated as a kind of ultra-mischievous and evil-dispositioned Robin Goodfellow in mediaeval German folk-tales (*Bruder Rausch*, i.e. intoxication, which shows us at once that Friar Rush was the spirit of inebriety). His particular duty was to lead monks and friars into wickedness and keep them in it. A prose *History of Friar Rush* appeared in English as early as 1568, and in 1601 Henslowe records a comedy (now lost), *Friar Rush and the Proud Woman of Antwerp*, by Day and Houghton.

**Friar Tuck.** Chaplain and steward of Robin Hood. Introduced by Scott in *Ivanhoe*. He is a pudgy, paunchy, humorous, self-indulgent, and combative clerical Falstaff. His costume consisted of a russet habit of the Franciscan order, a red corded girdle with gold tassel, red stockings, and a wallet. The name was probably given because his dress was *tucked* by a girdle at the waist; thus Chaucer says, 'Tucked he was, as is a frere about'.

> In this our spacious isle I think there is not one
> But he hath heard some talk of Hood and Little John;
> Of Tuck, the merry friar, which many a sermon made
> In praise of Robin Hood, his outlaws, and their trade.
>
> Drayton, *Polyolbion*, xxvi, 311–16

**Friar's Heel.** The outstanding upright stone at Stonehenge, formerly supposed by some to stand in the central axis of the avenue, is so called. Geoffrey of Monmouth says the devil bought the stones of an old woman in Ireland, wrapped them up in a wyth, and brought them to Salisbury Plain. Just before he got to Mount Ambre the wyth broke, and one of the stones fell into the Avon, the rest were carried to the plain. After the fiend had fixed them in the ground, he cried out, 'No man will ever find out how these stones came here'. A friar replied, 'That's more than thee canst tell', whereupon the foul fiend threw one of the stones at him and struck him on the heel. The stone stuck in the ground and remains so to the present hour.

**Friar's Lanthorn.** One of the many names given to the Will o' the Wisp, confused by Scott with Friar Rush (*q.v.*), whom Sir Walter seems to have considered as 'Friar with the Rush (light)':

> Better we had through mire and bush
> Been lanthorn-led by Friar Rush. *Marmion*
>
> She was pinched, and pulled, she said:
> And he by Friar's lantern led.
>
> Milton, *L'Allegro*, 103

**Friars Major** (*Fratres majores*). The Dominicans.

**Friars Minor** (*Fratres minores*). The Franciscans.

**Friar's Tale.** In the *Canterbury Tales* a tale throwing discredit on Summoners. Chaucer obtained it from the Latin collection, *Promptuarium Exemplorum*. It tells how a rascally 'sumpnour' met the devil disguised as a yeoman, swore eternal friendship, and agreed to share whatever they might get. They met a carter in difficulties, crying 'The devil take it, both horse and cart and hay!' and when the sumpnour urged his companion to do so the devil refused, as it was clear that the wish was not intended, literally. Later the sumpnour declared he would squeeze twelve pence out of a poor old woman for a sin that she had never committed; she pleaded poverty and implored mercy, and finally, her entreaties being in vain, consigned him to the devil. The seeming yeoman questioned her, and finding that she was completely in earnest, seized the sumpnour and carried him off. A similar story is told in Ireland of a farmer's wife at Crombogue. *See* Kennedy's *Legendary Fictions of the Irish Celts*, p. 147, 1866.

**Friday.** The sixth day of the week was the *dies Veneris* in ancient Rome, i.e. the day dedicated to Venus. The northern nations adopted the Roman system of nomenclature, and the sixth day was dedicated to their nearest equivalent to Venus, who was Frigg or Freyja (*q.v.*); hence the name *Friday* (A.S. *frige-daeg*). In France the Latin name was kept, and Friday is *Vendredi*.

Friday was regarded by the Norsemen as the luckiest day of the week: among Christians generally it has been regarded as the unluckiest, because it was the day of our Lord's crucifixion, and is accordingly a fast-day in the Catholic Church. Mohammedans (among whom Friday is the Sabbath) say that Adam was created on a Friday, and legend has it that it was on a Friday that Adam and Eve ate the forbidden fruit, and on a Friday that they died. Among the Buddhists and Brahmins it is also held to be unlucky; and the old Romans called it *nefastus*, from the utter overthrow of their army at Gallia Narbonensis. In England the proverb is that 'a Friday moon brings foul weather', but it is not, apparently, unlucky to be born on this day, for, according to the old rhyme, 'Friday's child is loving and giving'.

***Black Friday.*** *See* Black.

***Good Friday.*** *See* Good.

***He who laughs on Friday will weep on Sunday.*** Sorrow follows in the wake of joy. The line is taken from Racine's comedy, *Les Plaideurs*.

***Long Friday.*** Good Friday was so called by the Saxons, probably because of the long fasts and offices used on that day.

***Man Friday.*** The young savage found by Robinson Crusoe on a Friday, and kept as his servant and companion on the desert island; hence, a faithful and willing attendant, ready to turn his hand to anything.

***Never cut your nails on a Friday.*** 'Cut them on Friday you cut them for sorrow.' *See* Nail-paring.

**Friday Street** (London). So called, according to Stow, because it was the street of fishmongers who served Friday markets. The name is found in many towns and even villages.

**Friend.** A Quaker (*q.v.*), i.e. a member of the Society of Friends; also, one's second in a duel, as 'Name your friend', 'Captain B. acted as his friend'. In the law courts counsel refer to each other as 'my learned friend', though they may be entire strangers, just as in the House of Commons one member speaks of another as 'my honourable friend'.

***A friend at court.*** Properly, a friend in a court of law who watches the trial and tells the judge if he can discover an error (*see* Amicus curiae). The term is generally applied to a friend who is in a position to help one by influencing those in power.

***A friend in need is a friend indeed.*** The Latin saying (from Ennius) is, *Amicus certus in re incerta cernitur*, a sure friend is made known when (one is) in difficulty.

***A friendly suit,*** or ***action.*** An action at law brought, not with the object of obtaining a conviction or damages, but to discover the law on some debatable point, to get a legal and authoritative decision putting some fact on record.

***Better kinde frend than fremd kinde.*** This is the motto of the Waterton family, and it means 'better kind friend (i.e. neighbour) than a kinsman who dwells in foreign parts' (*cp.* Prov. 27:10, 'Better is a neighbour that is near, than a brother far off'). *Fremd* is an Old English word (from Old Teutonic) meaning foreign, strange, outlandish. Scott has a variant of the motto in *Quentin Durward* (ch. vi), 'Better kind fremit than fremit kindred', better a kind stranger than strange kinsmen.

***The Friend of Man.*** The name given ironically to the Marquis de Mirabeau (1715–89), father of Mirabeau, the French revolutionary orator. His great work was *L'Ami des Hommes*, hence the nickname.

***The soldier's friend.*** An official appointed by the authorities at the various pension boards to assist soldiers in making out and presenting their claims to pensions, etc.

**Friendship.** The classical examples of lasting friendship between man and man are Achilles and Patroclus, Pylades and Orestes, Damon and Pythias, and Nisus and Euryalus. *See these names.* To these should be added David and Jonathan (from the Bible). The two kings of Brentford and Tweedledum and Tweedledee come, perhaps, in a rather different category!

**Frigg,** or **Frigga.** *See* Freyja.

**Frills.** An Americanism for 'airs and graces'; as, *to put on frills*, to give oneself airs.

**Fringe.** The fringes on the garments of the Jewish priests were accounted sacred, and were touched by the common people as a charm. Hence the desire of the woman who had the issue of blood to touch the fringe of our Lord's garment. (Matt. 9:20–22.)

**Frippery.** Rubbish of a tawdry character; worthless finery; foolish levity. A *friperer* or *fripperer* was one who dealt in old clothes (*cp.* Fr. *friperie*, old clothes, cast-off furniture, etc.).

> Old clothes, cast dresses, tattered rags,
> Whose works are e'en the frippery of wit.
>
> Ben Jonson, *Epig.* I, lvi

Also, a shop where odds and ends, old clothes, and so on are dealt in. Hence Shakespeare's:

> We know what belongs to a frippery.
>
> *Tempest*, 4, 1

**Frith.** *By frith and fell.* By wold and wild, wood and common. *Frith* means ground covered with scrub or underwood; *fell* is connected with the German *fels* (rock), and means barren or stony places, a common.

**Frithiof.** A hero of Icelandic myth who married Ingëborg, daughter of a petty king of Norway, and widow of Hring, to whose dominions he succeeded. His adventures are recorded in the saga which bears his name, and which was written about the close of the 13th century. The name signifies 'the peacemaker'.

**Fritz.** Frederick the Great of Prussia (1712, 1740–86) was known as *Old Fritz*.

**Frog.** A frog and mouse agreed to settle by single combat their claims to a marsh; but, while they fought, a kite carried them both off. (Aesop, *Fables*, clxviii.)

> Old Aesop's fable, where he told
> What fate on to the mouse and frog befel.
>
> Cary, *Dante*, cxxiii

In Ovid's *Metamorphoses* (vi, 4) we are told that the Lycian shepherds were changed into frogs for mocking Latona.

> As when those hinds that were transformed to frogs
> Railed at Latona's twin-born progeny.
>
> Milton, *Sonnet*, vii

Frenchmen, properly *Parisians*, have been nicknamed Frogs or Froggies (*grenouilles*) from their ancient heraldic device (*see* Fleur-de-lis), which was three frogs or three toads. *Qu'en disent les grenouilles?* What do the frogs (people of Paris) say? – was in 1791 a common court phrase at Versailles. There was a point in the pleasantry when Paris was a quagmire, called *Lutetia* (mudland). *See* Crapaud.

***Frog's march.*** Carrying an obstreperous prisoner, face downwards, by his four limbs.

***It may be fun to you, but it is death to the frogs.*** A caution, telling one that one's sport should not be at the expense of other people's happiness. The allusion is to Aesop's fable of a boy stoning frogs for his amusement.

***Nic Frog.*** The Dutchman in Arbuthnot's *History of John Bull* (1712). Frogs are called 'Dutch nightingales'.

**Fronde.** A political party during the ministry of Cardinal Mazarin, in the minority of Louis XIV (1648–53). Its members, who were opposed to the court party, were called *Frondeurs* from *fronde*, a sling, they being likened to boys who sling stones about the streets and scamper away the moment anyone in authority approaches.

> It was already true that the French government was a despotism … and as speeches and lampoons were launched by persons who tried to hide after they had shot their dart, someone compared them to children with a sling (*fronde*), who let fly a stone and run away.
>
> C. M. Yonge, *History of France*, ch. viii

**Frost Saints.** *See* Ice Saints.

**Frozen Music.** Architecture. So called by F. Schlegel in his *Philosophie der Kunst*.

**Frozen Words.** Everyone knows the incident of the 'frozen horn' related by Munchausen, and Pantagruel and his companions, on the confines of the Frozen Sea, heard the uproar of a battle, which had been frozen the preceding winter, released by a thaw (Rabelais, Bk iv, ch. 56). The joke appears to have been well known to the ancient Greeks, for Antiphanes applies it to the discourses of Plato: 'As the cold of certain cities is so intense that it freezes the very words we utter, which remain congealed till the heat of summer thaws them, so the mind of youth is so thoughtless that the wisdom of Plato lies there frozen, as it were, till it is thawed by the ripened judgment of mature age' (Plutarch's *Morals*).

> The moment their backs were turned, little Jacob thawed, and renewed his crying from the point where Quilp had frozen him.
>
> Dickens, *Old Curiosity Shop*

> Truth in person doth appear
> Like words congealed in northern air.
>
> Butler, *Hudibras,* Pt i, 1, lines 147–8

**Frying-pan.** *Out of the frying-pan into the fire.* In trying to extricate yourself from one evil, you fell into a greater. The Greeks used to say, 'Out of the smoke into the flame' and the French say, '*Tombre de la poële dans la braise.*'

**Fub.** To hoax, impose upon, swindle. 'You are trying to fub me off with a cock-and-bull story.' Connected with Ger. *foppen*, to hoax. *Fob* is another form of the same word.

**Fudge.** A word of contempt bestowed on one who says what is absurd or untrue. A favourite expression of Mr Burchell in the *Vicar of Wakefield*.

In America a certain confection of toffee, or candy, etc., is known as *fudge*.

***Fudge-box.*** An attachment on newspaper printing machines to allow of late news being added on the machine while running. This news appears in the 'Stop-press' column, which is, consequently, called the *fudge-box*. In this sense the word is another form of *fadge* (*q.v.*).

***The Fudge Family in Paris.*** A series of metrical epistles by Thomas Moore (1818), purporting to be written by a family on a visit to Paris.

**Fuel.** *Adding fuel to fire.* Saying or doing something to increase the anger of a person already angry. The French say, 'pouring oil on fire'.

**Fuggers.** A noted family of German merchant-bankers, famous in the 15th and 16th centuries and proverbial for their great wealth. 'Rich as a Fugger' is common in Elizabethan dramatists. Charles V introduced some of the family into Spain, where they superintended the mines.

> I am neither an Indian merchant, nor yet a Fugger, but a poor boy like yourself.
>
> Guzman de Alfarache (1599)

**Fugleman.** Originally a leader of a wing (Ger. *flugel*, wing) or file; now applied to a soldier who stands in front of men at drill to show them what to do.

**Fulhams,** or **Fullams.** An Elizabethan name for loaded dice. Dice made with a cavity were called gourds; those made to throw the high numbers were high fullams or gourds, and those made to throw the low numbers were low fullams or gourds.

> For gourd and fullam holds
> And 'high' and 'low' beguile the rich and poor.
>
> Shakespeare, *Merry Wives of Windsor*, 1, 3

> Have their fulhams at command,
> Brought up to do their feats at hand.
>
> Butler, *Upon Gaming*

The name may be from Fulham, which was notorious as the resort of 'crooks'; or it may be a corruption of *full'um*, meaning a die that was 'full', or high.

**Full.** ***Full dress.*** The dress worn on occasions of ceremony; court dress, uniform, academicals, evening dress, etc., as the case may be. A *full-dress debate* is one for which preparation and arrangements have been made, as opposed to one arising casually.

***Full moon,*** or ***the full of the moon.*** The period when the whole disk of the moon is illuminated and it presents a perfect orb to the earth.

***Full of beans.*** *See* Bean.

***Full up.*** Quite full, occupied to its utmost capacity. Said also of one who is drunk. *Cp.* Fou.

***In full cry.*** Said of hounds that have caught the scent, and give tongue in chorus; hence, hurrying in full pursuit.

***In full fig.*** *See* Fig.

***In full swing.*** Fully at work; very busy; in full operation.

**Fulrompe.** The name given to the son of Martin the Ape in Caxton's version of *Reynard the Fox*.

**Fum,** or **Fung-hwang.** The phoenix (*q.v.*) of Chinese legend, one of the four symbolical animals presiding over the destinies of China. It originated from fire, was born in the Hill of the Sun's Halo, and has its body inscribed with the five cardinal virtues. One account says it has the forepart of a goose, the hindquarters of a stag, the neck of a snake, the tail of a fish, the forehead of a fowl, the down of a duck, the marks of a dragon, the back of a tortoise, the face of a swallow, the beak of a cock, is about six cubits high, and perches only on the woo-tung tree. It is this curious creature that is embroidered on the dresses of certain mandarins.

**Fum the Fourth.** George IV.

> And where is Fum the Fourth, our royal bird.
>
> Byron, *Don Juan,* xi, 78

**Fumage.** Another name for Hearth-money or Chimney-money (*q.v.*) (Lat. *fumus*, smoke).

**Fume.** ***In a fume***. In ill temper, especially from impatience.

**Fun.** ***To make fun of.*** To make a butt of; to ridicule; to play pranks on one.

***Like fun.*** Thoroughly, energetically, with delight.

> On'y look at the dimmercrats, see what they've done.
> Jest simply by stickin' together like fun.
> Lowell, *Biglow Papers* (First series, iv, st. 5)

**Fund.** ***The Funds,*** or ***The Public Funds***. Money lent at interest to Government on Government security; the national stock, which is the *foundation* of its operations.

***The sinking fund.*** Money set aside by the Government for paying off a part of the national debt. This money is 'sunk', or withdrawn from circulation, for the bonds purchased by it are destroyed.

***To be out of funds,*** out of money.

**Funeral.** Late Lat. *funeralis*, adj. from *funus*, a burial. *Funus* is connected with *fumus* (Sanskrit *dhû-mas*), smoke, and the word seems to have referred to the ancient practice of disposing of the dead by cremation. Funerals among the Romans took place at night by torchlight, that magistrates and priests might not be made ceremonially unclean by seeing a corpse, and so be prevented from performing their sacred duties.

Most of our funeral customs are derived from the Romans; as dressing in black, walking in procession, carrying insignia on the bier, the presence of mutes, raising a mound over the grave, called *tumulus* (whence our *tomb*), etc. In Roman funerals, too, the undertaker, attended by lictors dressed in black, marched with the corpse, and, as master of the ceremonies, assigned to each follower his proper place in the procession. The Greeks crowned the dead body with flowers, and placed flowers on the tomb also; and the Romans decked the funeral couch with leaves and flowers, and spread flowers, wreaths, and fillets on the tomb of friends.

Public games were held both in Greece and Rome in honour of departed heroes. Examples of this custom are numerous: as the games instituted by Hercules at the death of Pelops, those held by Achilles in honour of Patroclus (*Iliad*, Bk xxiii), those held by Aeneas in honour of his father Anchises (*Aeneid*, Bk v), etc.; and the custom of giving a feast at funerals came to us from the Romans, who not only feasted the friends of the deceased, but also distributed meat to the persons employed.

> Thrift, thrift, Horatio! the funeral baked meats
> Did coldly furnish forth the marriage tables.
> Shakespeare, *Hamlet*, 1, 2

**Fung-hwang.** *See* Fum.

**Funk.** *To be in a funk,* or *a blue funk,* may be the Walloon '*In de fonk zün*', literally to 'be in the smoke'. Colloquially to be in a state of trepidation from uncertainty or apprehension of evil. It first appeared in England at Oxford in the first half of the 18th century.

**Funny Bone.** A pun on the word *humerus*, the Latin (and hence scientific) name for the upper bone of the arm. It is the inner condyle of this, or, to speak untechnically, the knob, or *enlarged end* of the bone terminating where the ulnar nerve is exposed at the elbow. A knock on this bone at the elbow produces a painful sensation.

**Furbelow.** A corruption of *falbala*, a word in French, Italian, and Spanish to signify a sort of flounce.

> Flounced and furbelowed from head to foot.
> Addison

**Furcam et Flagellum** (Lat. gallows and whip). The meanest of all servile tenures, the bondman being at the lord's mercy, both life and limb. *Cp.* Forks.

**Furies, The.** The Roman name (*Furiae*) for the Greek Erinyes (*q.v.*), said by Hesiod to have been the daughters of Ge (the earth) and to have sprung from the blood of Uranus, and by other accounts to be daughters of night and darkness. They were three in number, Tisiphone (the Avenger of blood), Alecto (Implacable), and Megaera (Disputatious).

***The Furies of the Guillotine***. Another name for the *tricoteuses* (*q.v.*).

**Furor.** In Spenser's *Faërie Queene* (Bk ii) the personification of mad anger. He was son of Occasion, an old hag, and Sir Guyon bound him 'with a hundred iron chains and a hundred knots'.

**Fusberta.** Rinaldo's sword is so called in *Orlando Furioso*.

> This awful sword was as dear to him as Durindana or Fusberta to their respective masters.
> Sir W. Scott

**Fusiliers.** Foot-soldiers that used to be armed with a fusil or light musket. The word is now a misnomer, as the regiments so called carry rifles like those of the rest of the infantry. Similarly the name *Grenadier* survives, though the *grenade* has long since ceased to be the weapon of these soldiers.

**Fustian.** A coarse twilled cotton cloth with a velvety pile, probably so called from Fustat, a suburb of Cairo.

It is chiefly used now in its figurative sense meaning inflated or pompous talk, claptrap, bombast (*q.v.*), pretentious words.

Discourse fustian with one's own shadow.

Shakespeare, *Othello*, 2, 3

Some scurry quaint collection of fustian phrases, and uplandish words.

Heywood, *Faire Maide of the Exchange*, ii, 2

We have numerous phrases derived from materials of dress applied to speech, as bombast, shoddy, silken, etc. The mother of Artaxerxes said: 'Those who address kings must use silken words.' In French, *faire patte de velour* means to draw in one's claws, to soften with velvet words in order to seduce or win over.

**Futhorc.** The ancient Runic alphabet of the Anglo-Saxons and other Teutons; so called, on the same principle as the ABC, from its first six letters, viz., *f*, *u*, *th*, *o*, *r*, *k*.

**Fylfot.** A mystic sign or emblem, known also as the *swastika* and *gammadion*, and in heraldry as the *cross cramponee*, used (especially in Byzantine architecture and among the North American Indians) as an ornament, and as of religious import. It has been found at Hissarlik, on ancient Etruscan tombs, Celtic monuments, Buddhist inscriptions, Greek coins, etc., and has been thought to have represented the power of the sun, of the four winds, of lightning, and so on. Its shape is that of a right-angled cross, the arms of which are of equal length, with an additional piece at the extremity of each, fixed at a right-angle, each addition being of the same length and in the same direction. It is used nowadays in jewellery as an emblem of luck.

卐

The name *fylfot* was adopted by antiquaries from a MS of the 15th century, and is probably *fill foot*, signifying a device to fill the foot of a stained window.

# G

**G.** This letter is a modification of the Latin C (which was a rounding of the Greek *gamma*, Γ); till the 3rd century BC the *g* and *k* sounds were represented by the same letter, C. In the Hebrew and old Phoenician alphabets G is the outline of a camel's head and neck. Heb., *gimel*, a camel.

**G.C.B.** *See* Bath.

**G.O.M.** The initial letters of 'Grand Old Man', a nickname of honour given to Gladstone in his later years. Lord Rosebery first used the expression (26th April, 1882).

**Gab.** ***The gift of the gab*** or ***gob.*** Fluency of speech, also the gift of boasting, connected with *gabble*, and perhaps with *gab*, the mouth.

> There was a man named Job
> Lived in the land of Uz,
> He had a good gift of the gob,
> The same thing happen us.
>
> Book of Job, humorously ascribed to Zachary Boyd (d.1653)
>
> Thou art one of the knights of France, who hold it for glee and pastime to gab, as they term it, of exploits that are beyond human power.
>
> Scott, *Talisman*, ch. ii

**Gabbara.** The giant who, according to Rabelais, was 'the first inventor of the drinking of healths'. *See* Gemmagog.

**Gabble Ratchet.** *See* Gabriel's Hounds.

**Gabelle.** A tax; especially in French history a tax on salt. All the salt made in France had to be brought to the royal warehouses, and was there sold at a price fixed by the Government. The iniquity was that some provinces had to pay twice as much as others. Edward III jokingly called this monopoly 'King Philippe's *Salic* law'. It was abolished in 1789, together with the *corvée* (forced labour on the roads).

**Gaberdine.** A long, coarse cloak or gown, especially as worn in the Middle Ages by Jews and almsmen.

> You call me misbeliever, cut-throat dog,
> And spit upon my Jewish gabardine.
>
> Shakespeare, *Merchant of Venice*, 1, 3

The word is the Spanish *gabardina*, a frock worn by pilgrims; it may be of Eastern origin and connected with *caftan* (*q.v.*), or it may be connected with Ger. *wallfahrt*, a pilgrimage.

**Gaberlunzie.** A mendicant; or, more strictly speaking, one of the king's bedesmen, who were licensed beggars. The name has also been given to the wallet carried by a *gaberlunzie-man*. Its derivation is unknown.

**Gabriel** (i.e. ***man of God***). One of the archangels of *Hebrew mythology*, sometimes regarded as the angel of death, the prince of fire and thunder, but more frequently as one of the Deity's chief messengers, and traditionally said to be the only angel that can speak Syriac and Chaldee. The Mohammedans call him the chief of the four favoured angels, and the spirit of truth. In mediaeval romance he is the second of the seven spirits that stand before the throne of God (*Jerusalem Delivered*, bk i),and Milton makes him chief of the angelic guards placed over Paradise.

> Betwixt these rocky pillars Gabriel sat,
> Chief of the angelic guards. *Paradise Lost*, iv, 549

Longfellow, in his *Golden Legend*, makes him the angel of the moon, and says he brings to man the gift of hope.

> I am the angel of the moon ...
> Nearest the earth, it is my ray
> That best illumines the midnight way,
> I bring the gift of *hope*. *The Miracle Play*, iii

In the *Talmud* he appears as the destroyer of the hosts of Sennacherib, as the man who showed Joseph the way (Gen. 37:15), and as one of the angels who buried Moses (Deut. 34:6).

It was Gabriel who (we are told in the Koran) took Mahomet to heaven on Al-borak (*q.v.*), and revealed to him his 'prophetic lore'. In the Old Testament Gabriel is said to have explained to Daniel certain visions; in the New Testament he announced to Zacharias the future birth of John the Baptist, and appeared to Mary, the mother of Jesus. (Luke 1:26, etc.)

***Gabriel's horse.*** Haïzum.

***Gabriel's hounds,*** called also *Gabble Ratchet*. Wild geese. The noise of bean-geese in flight is like that of a pack of hounds in full cry. The legend is that they are the souls of unbaptised children wandering through the air till the Day of Judgment.

**Gabrielle.** La Belle Gabrielle (1571–99). Daughter of Antoine d'Estrées, grand-master of artillery, and governor of the Ile de France. Henri IV, towards the close of 1590, happened to sojourn for a night at the Château de Coeuvres, and fell in love with her. To throw a flimsy veil over his intrigue, he married her to Liancourt-Damerval, created her Duchess de Beaufort, and took her to live with him at court.

Charmante Gabrielle,
 Percé de mille dards,
Quand la gloire m'appelle
 A la suite de Mars. *Henri IV*

**Gad.** ***Gadding from place to place.*** Wandering from pillar to post without any profitable purpose.

Give water no passage, neither a wicked woman liberty to gad abroad. Eccles. 25:25

***By gad!*** An expletive; a euphemistic way of outwardly avoiding taking the name of God in vain. *Egad!* is another form.

***Gad-about.*** A person who spends day after day in frivolous visits, gadding from house to house.

**Gad-fly.** Not the *roving* but the *goading* fly (A.S. *gad*, a goad).

**Gadget.** An expressive word common among sailors, and introduced into general use during the Great War, popularised, apparently, by the Royal Air Force, where it was used for almost any little tool or appliance that was useful or by using which a job was made easier. Now applied to small accessories of all sorts. *Gadge* is an early Scots form of *gauge*, but there is no trace of any connection between this and *gadget*.

**Gadshill.** About 3 miles N.W. of Rochester. Famous for the attack of Sir John Falstaff and three of his knavish companions on a party of four travellers, whom they robbed of their purses (Shakespeare, *I Henry IV*, 2, 4), and also as a home of Charles Dickens, who died there in 1870.

Gadshill is also the name of one of the thievish companions of Sir John Falstaff.

**Gad-steel.** Flemish steel. So called because it is wrought in *gads*, or small bars (A.S. *gad*, a small bar; Icel., *gaddr*, a spike).

I will go get a leaf of brass,
And with a gad of steel will write these words.
Shakespeare, *Titus Andronicus*, 4, 1

**Gaels.** A contraction of *Gaid-heals* (Old Irish *Goidel*), said to mean 'hidden rovers'. The inhabitants of Scotland who maintained their ground in the Highlands against the Celts.

**Gaff.** Slang for humbug; also for a cheap public entertainment or a low-class music-hall.

***Crooked as a gaff.*** Here *gaff* is an iron hook at the end of a short pole, used for landing salmon, etc., or the metal spur of fighting-cocks. (Span. and Port. *gafa*, a boat-hook.)

***To blow the gaff.*** *See* Blow.

**Gaffer.** A rustic and respectful form of address to an old man, as 'Gaffer Grey', 'Good-day, gaffer'; a corruption of 'grandfather'. *Cp.* Gammer.

If I had but a thousand a year, Gaffer Green,
If I had but a thousand a year.
*Gaffer Green and Robin Rough*

**Gag.** In theatrical parlance, an interpolation. When Hamlet directs the players to say no more 'than is set down' (iii, 2) he cautions them against indulgence in gags.

***To apply the gag.*** Said of applying the closure in the House of Commons. Here *gag* is something forced into the mouth to prevent speech.

**Gai Saber.** *See* Gay Science, The.

**Gain's Alley.** *See* Hangman's Gains.

**Gala Day.** A festive day; a day when people put on their best attire. (Ital. *gala*, finery.)

**Galactic Circle.** The great circle passing centrally along the Galaxy, or Milky Way. It is to sidereal astronomy what the ecliptic is to planetary astronomy.

**Galahad, Sir.** In the Arthurian legends the purest and noblest knight of the Round Table. He is a late addition and was invented by Walter Map in his *Quest of the San Graal.* He was the son of Lancelot and Elaine: at the institution of the Round Table one seat (the *Siege Perilous*) was left unoccupied, and could be occupied only by the knight who could succeed in the Quest, all others who attempted it being swallowed by the earth. When Sir Galahad sat there it was discovered that it had been left for him. *See* Malory's *Morte d'Arthur*, Tennyson's *Idylls of the King* (*The Holy Grail*), etc.

There Galaad sat, with manly grace,
Yet maiden meekness in his face.
Sir W. Scott, *Bridal of Triermain*, ii, 13

**Galatea.** A sea-nymph, beloved by Polypheme, but herself in love with Acis. Acis was crushed under a huge rock by the jealous giant, and Galatea threw herself into the sea, where she joined her sister nymphs. Carlo Maratti (1625–1713) depicted Galatea in the sea and Polypheme sitting on a rock. Handel has an opera entitled *Acis and Galatea*. The Galatea beloved by Pygmalion (*q.v.*) was a different person altogether.

**Galathe.** Hector's horse.

There is a thousand Hectors in the field;
Now here he fights on Galathe his horse,
And there lacks work.
Shakespeare, *Troilus and Cressida*, 5, 5

**Galaxy, The.** The 'Milky Way'. A long white luminous track of stars which seems to encompass the heavens like a girdle. According to classic fable, it is the path to the palace of Zeus or Jupiter. (Gr. *gala*, *galaktos*, milk.)

Through all her courts
The vacant city slept; the busy winds,
That keep no certain intervals of rest,
Moved not; meanwhile the galaxy displayed
Her fires, that like mysterious pulses beat,
Aloft – momentous but uneasy bliss!
Wordsworth, *Vandracour and Julia*, 94

***A galaxy of beauty***. A cluster or coterie of handsome women.

**Gale.** A heavy wind. The three degrees are a *fresh* gale, a *strong* gale, and a *heavy* or *whole* gale.

**Galehault.** *See* Gemmagog.

**Galen.** A very famous Greek physician and philosopher of the 2nd century AD. For centuries he was the supreme authority in medicine. Hence, *Galenist*, a follower of Galen's medical theories; *Galenical*, a simple, vegetable medicine.

***Galen says 'Nay' and Hippocrates 'Yea'.*** The doctors disagree, and who is to decide? Hippocrates – a native of Cos, born 460 BC – was the most celebrated physician of antiquity.

**Galeotti, Martius.** Louis XI's Italian astrologer.

'Can thy pretended skill ascertain the hour of thine own death?'
'Only by referring to the fate of another,' said Galeotti.
'I understand not thine answer', said Louis.
'Know then, O king,' said Martius, 'that this only I can tell with certainty concerning mine own death, that it shall take place exactly twenty-four hours before your majesty's.'
Scott, *Quentin Durward*, ch. xxix

Thrasullus, the soothsayer to Tiberius, made the same diplomatic answer to the same question, and in each case it of course had the effect of making the ruler protect the life of the prophet.

**Galerana,** according to Ariosto (*Orlando Furioso*, Bk xxi), was wife of Charlemagne.

**Galère. *Que diable allait-il faire dans cette galère?*** What business had he to be in that galley? This is from Molière's comedy of *Les Fourberies de Scapin*. Scapin wants to bamboozle Géronte out of his money, and tells him that his master (Géronte's son) is detained prisoner on a Turkish galley, where he went out of curiosity. He adds, that unless the old man will ransom him, he will be taken to Algiers as a slave. Géronte replies to all that Scapin urges, 'What business had he to go on board the galley?' The retort is given to those who beg money to help them out of difficulties which they have brought on themselves. 'I grant you are in trouble, but what right had you to go on the galley?'

***Vogue la galère.*** *See* Vogue.

**Galiana.** A Moorish princess, whose father, King Gadalfe of Toledo, according to Spanish tradition, built for her a palace on the Tagus so splendid that the phrase 'a palace of Galiana' became proverbial in Spain.

**Galimatias.** Nonsense; unmeaning gibberish. The word first appeared in France in the 16th century, but its origin is unknown; perhaps it is connected with *gallimaufry* (*q.v.*). In his translation of Rabelais Urquhart heads ch. ii of Bk I a 'Galimatias of Extravagant Conceits found in an Ancient Monument'.

**Gall.** Bile; the very bitter fluid secreted by the liver; hence used figuratively as a symbol for anything of extreme bitterness.

***Gall and wormwood.*** Extremely disagreeable and annoying.

And I said, My strength and my hope is perished from the Lord: Remembering my affliction and my misery, the wormwood and the gall.
Lam. 3:18,19

***The gall of bitterness.*** The bitterest grief; extreme affliction. The ancients taught that grief and joy were subject to the gall as affection was to the heart, knowledge to the kidneys, and the gall of bitterness means the bitter centre of bitterness, as the heart of heart means the innermost recesses of the heart or affections. In the *Acts* it is used to signify 'the sinfulness of sin', which leads to the bitterest grief.

I perceive thou art in the gall of bitterness, and in the bond of iniquity. Acts 8:23

***The gall of pigeons.*** The story goes that pigeons have no gall, because the dove sent from the ark by Noah burst its gall out of grief, and none of the pigeon family has had a gall ever since.

For sin' the Flood of Noah
The dow she had nae ga'.
Jamieson, *Popular Ballads* (*Lord of Rorlin's Daughter*)

**Gallery. *To play to the gallery.*** To work for popularity. As an actor who sacrifices his author for popular applause, or a stump political orator 'orates' to catch votes.

The instant we begin to think about success and the effect of our work – to play with one eye on the gallery – we lose power, and touch, aud everything else.
Rudyard Kipling, *The Light that Failed*

*See under* Play, 'Playing to the gods'.

**Galley Halfpence.** Silver coin brought over by merchants ('galley-men') from Genoa, who used the Galley Wharf, Thames Street. These halfpence were larger than our own, and their use was forbidden in England early in the 15th century.

**Gallia.** France; the Latin name for Gaul.

> Impending hangs o'er Gallia's humbled coast.
> Thomson, *Summer*

***Gallia Braccata*** (*trousered Gaul*). Gallia Narbonensis was so called from the 'braccae', or trousers, which the natives wore in common with the Scythians and Persians.

***Gallia Comata.*** That part of Gaul which belonged to the Roman emperor, and was governed by legates (*legati*), was so called from the long hair (*coma*) worn by the inhabitants flowing over their shoulders.

**Gallicism.** A phrase or sentence constructed after the French idiom; as, 'When you *shall have returned* home you will find a letter on your table.' Government documents are especially guilty of this fault. In Matt. 15:32, is a Gallicism: 'I have compassion on the multitude, because *they continue* with me now three days, and have nothing to eat.' *Cp*. Mark 8:2.

**Galligantus.** One of the giants of nursery-lore slain by Jack the Giant Killer. Arrayed in his cap, which rendered him invisible, he went to the castle and read the inscription: 'Whoever can this trumpet blow, will cause the giant's overthrow.' He seized the trumpet, blew a loud blast, the castle fell down, Jack slew the giant, and was married soon after to a duke's daughter, whom he found there and rescued.

**Galligaskins.** A loose, wide kind of breeches worn by men in the 16th and 17th centuries.

> My galligaskins, that have long withstood
> The winter's fury and encroaching frosts …
> A horrid chasm disclos'd, with orifice
> Wide, discontinuous.
> J. Philips, *The Splendid Shilling* (1703)

> The taylor of Bisiter, he has but one eye;
> He cannot cut a pair of green galagaskins, if he were to try.
> Aubrey MS

The word is a corruption of Fr. *garguesque*, which was the Ital. *grechesca*, Greekish, referring to a Greek article of clothing.

**Gallimaufry.** A medley; any confused jumble of things; but strictly speaking, a hotch-potch made up of all the scraps of the larder. (Fr. *galimafrée*, the origin of which is unknown, though it is probably related to *galimatias*).

> He woos both high and low, both rich and poor,
> Both young and old, one with another, Ford;
> He loves the galimaufry [all sorts].
> Shakespeare, *Merry Wives*, 2, 1

**Galloglass.** An armed servitor (or foot-soldier) of an ancient Irish chief. O.Ir. and Gael. *gall*, a stranger, *óglách*, a warrior.

> The Galloglass are pycked and scelected men of great and mightie bodies, crewel without compassion.
> John Dymmok, *Treatise of Ireland* (1600)

**Galloway.** A horse less than fifteen hands high, of the breed which originally came from Galloway in Scotland.

> Thrust him downstairs! Know we not Galloway nags?
> Shakespeare, *2 Henry IV*, 2, 4

> The knights and esquires are well mounted on large bay horses, the common people on little Galloways.
> S. Lanier, *Boy's Froissart*, Bk i, ch. xiv

**Galore.** One of our words from Old Irish *go leor*, to a sufficiency; hence, in abundance, and abundance itself.

> For his Poll he had trinkets and gold galore,
> Besides of prize-money quite a store.
> *Jack Robinson* (*A Sailor's Song*)

**Galosh.** It is said that Henry VI wore half-boots laced at the side, and about the same time was introduced the shoe or clog called the 'galage' or 'gologe', meaning simply a covering; to which is attributed the origin of our word *galosh*. This cannot be correct, as Chaucer, who died twenty years before Henry VI was born, uses the word. The word comes to us from the Span. *galocha* (wooden shoes); Ger. *galosche*; Fr. *galoche*, which is probably from Gr. *kalopous*, a shoemaker's last.

> Ne werë worthy unbocle his galoche.
> Chaucer, *Squire's Tale*, 555

**Galvanism.** The branch of science dealing with electricity produced by chemical action, especially that of acids on metals; so called from Louis Galvani (1737–98), of Bologna, who noticed that some dead frogs which happened to be placed near an electric machine in motion exhibited signs of vitality. He subsequently discovered that similar convulsive effects were produced when the copper hooks on which the frogs were strung were suspended on the iron hook of the larder. Experiments soon led to the discovery of this important science.

***Galvanised iron.*** Sheet iron coated with zinc to protect it from rust, is so called because the zinc was originally deposited by means of galvanism. Nowadays the iron is simply immersed in molten zinc.

**Galway Jury.** An enlightened, independent jury. The expression has its birth in certain trials held in Ireland in 1635 upon the right of the king to the counties of Ireland. Leitrim, Roscommon, Sligo and Mayo gave judgment in favour of the Crown, but Galway opposed it; whereupon the sheriff was fined £1,000, and each of the jurors £4,000.

**Gama, Vasco da.** One of the greatest of the early Portuguese navigators (d.1524), was the first European to double the Cape of Good Hope. He is the hero of Camoëns' *Lusiad* (1572), where he is represented as sagacious, intrepid, tender hearted, pious, fond of his country, and holding his temper in full command. He is also the hero of Meyerbeer's posthumous opera *L'Africaine* (1865).

> Gama, captain of the venturous band,
> Of bold emprise, and born for high command,
> Whose martial fires, with prudence close allied,
> Ensured the smiles of fortune on his side.
>
> Camoëns, *Lusiad,* Bk i

**Gamaheu.** *See* Cameo.

**Gamboge.** So called from Cambodia or Camboja, whence it was first brought.

**Game.** Certain wild animals and birds, legally protected, preserved, and pursued for sport, such as hares, pheasants, partridges, grouse, heath-game, etc. *See* Sporting Season.

***Are you game for a spree?*** Are you inclined to join in a bit of fun? The allusion is to game-cocks, which never show the white feather, but are always ready for a fight.

***The game is not worth the candle.*** *See* Candle.

***The game is up.*** The scheme, endeavour, etc., has come to nothing; everything has failed.

***The game's afoot.*** The hare has started; the enterprise has begun.

> I see you stand like greyhounds in the slips,
> Straining upon the start. The game's afoot!
> Follow your spirit! Shakespeare, *Henry V*, 3, 1

***He's a game 'un!*** He's got some pluck; he's 'a plucked 'un'. Another allusion to game-cocks.

***He's at his little games again,*** or ***at the same old game.*** He's at his old tricks; he's gone back to his old habits or practices.

***To die game.*** To maintain a resolute attitude to the last. A phrase from cock-fighting.

***To have the game in one's hands.*** To have such an advantage that success is assured; to hold the winning cards.

***To play a waiting game.*** To bide one's time, knowing that that is the best way of winning; to adopt Fabian tactics (*q.v.*).

***To play the game.*** To act in a straightforward, honourable manner; to keep to the rules.

***Two can play at that game.*** If you claw me I can claw you; if you throw stones at me I can do the same to you; 'those who live in glass houses shouldn't throw stones'.

***You are making game of me.*** You are bamboozling me, 'pulling my leg', holding me up to ridicule.

**Game-leg.** A bad or lame leg. The term seems to be a shortened form of *gammy leg*, in which case it would be connected with Old French *gambi*, bent, crooked, from *gambe* (Mod. Fr: *jambe*), a leg.

**Gamelyn, The Tale of.** A Middle-English metrical romance, found among the Chaucer MSS and supposed to have been intended by him to form the basis of one of the unwritten *Canterbury Tales*. Gamelyn is a younger son to whom a large share of property had been bequeathed by the father. He is kept in servitude and tyrannically used by his elder brother until he is old enough effectually to rebel. After many adventures, during which he becomes a leader of outlaws in the woods, he comes to his own again with the help of the king, and justice is meted out to the elder brother and those who aided him. Thomas Lodge made the story into a novel – *Rosalynde, or Euphues' Golden Legacie* (1590) – and from this Shakespeare drew a large part of his *As You Like It*. The defeat of the wrestler, the loyalty of Adam Spencer, the outlaws, the free life of the greenwood are common to the *Tale* and the play; and, as has been said, 'the *Tale of Gamelyn* is *As You Like It* without Rosalind or Celia'.

**Gammadion.** The *fylfot* (*q.v.*), or swastika, so called because it resembles four Greek capital gammas (Γ) set at right angles.

**Gammer.** A rustic term for an old woman; a corruption of *grandmother*, with an intermediate form 'granmer'. *Cp.* Gaffer.

**Gammer Gurton's Needle.** The earliest English comedy with the exception of *Ralph Roister Doister*; acted at Christ's College, Cambridge, in 1552, and printed in 1575. It was published as 'By Mr S. Mr of Art', who remained unidentified until Isaac Reed in 1782 announced that he was Bishop Still. This, however, is very improbable, and the authorship is now definitely assigned to William Stevenson, who was a Fellow of Christ's College at the time of the first performance and who is known from the bursar's books to have written a play. The comedy is coarse and vigorous; it closes with the painful but farcical discovery of Gammer Gurton's missing needle in the seat of Hodge's breeches.

**Gammon.** Stuff to impose upon one's credulity; chaff; humbug. It was originally thieves' slang, and is connected with *game*, as in 'You are making game of me.'

*Gammon*, the buttock or thigh of a hog salted and cured, is the Fr. *jambon*, O. Fr. *gambon*, from *gambe*, the leg.

**Gammy.** *See* Game-leg.

**Gamp.** Sarah Gamp is a disreputable monthly nurse in Dickens's *Martin Chuzzlewit*, famous for her bulky umbrella and perpetual reference to Mrs Harris, a purely imaginary person, whose opinions always confirmed her own.

> Mrs Harris, I says to her, if I could afford to lay out all my fellow creeturs for nothink, I would gladly do it. Such is the love I bear 'em.

Hence, 'a regular Gamp' is a low-class, drink-sodden, uncertificated maternity nurse, a class now, happily, practically extinct in England; and an umbrella, especially a large, badly rolled cotton one, is called a 'gamp'.

**Gamut.** Originally, the first or lowest note in Guido of Arezzo's scale, corresponding to G on the lowest line of the modern bass stave; later, the whole series of notes recognised by musicians; hence, the whole range or compass – 'this spectrum is to the eye what the gamut is to the ear' (Tyndall).

It is *gamma ut*; *gamma* (the third letter of the Greek alphabet) was used by Guido to mark the first or lowest note in the mediaeval scale; and *ut* is the first word in the mnemonic stanza, *Ut queant laxis resonare fibris*, etc. (*see* Doh), containing the names of the hexachord. *Gamma ut*, or *G ut*. was added to the scale in the 11th century.

> Now therefore issued forth the spotted pack,
> With tails high mounted, ears hung low, and throats
> With a whole gamut fill'd of heavenly notes,
> For which, alas! my destiny severe,
> Though ears she gave me two, gave me no ear.
>
> Cowper, *The Needless Alarm*

**Gander.** ***Gander-cleugh.*** Folly cliff; that mysterious land where anyone who makes a 'goose of himself' takes up his temporary residence. The hypothetical Jedediah Cleishbotham, who edited the *Tales of My Landlord*, lived there, as Scott assures us.

***Gander-month.*** Those four weeks when the 'monthly nurse' rules the house with despotic sway, and the master is made a goose of.

***Gander-mooner.*** An old name for a man who went about with other women during the 'gander-month', while his wife was lying in after a confinement.

***What's sauce for the goose is sauce for the gander.*** Both must be treated exactly alike. Apple sauce is just as good for one as the other.

**Ganelon.** A type of black-hearted treachery, figuring in Dante's *Inferno* and grouped by Chaucer (*Nun's Priest's Tale*, 407) with Judas Iscariot and 'Greek Sinon, that broghtest Troye al outrely to sorwe'. He was Count of Mayence, one of Charlemagne's paladins. Jealousy of Roland made him a traitor; and in order to destroy his rival, he planned with Marsillus, the Moorish king, the attack of Roncesvalles.

> Have you not held me at such a distance from your counsels, as if I were the most faithless spy since the days of Ganelon?
>
> Scott, *The Abbot*, ch. xxiv

**Ganesha.** The god of wisdom in *Hindu mythology*, lord of the Ganas, or lesser deities. He was the son of Siva, is propitiated at the commencement of important work, at the beginning of sacred writings, etc.

> Camdeo bright and Ganesa sublime
> Shall bless with joy their own propitious clime.
>
> Campbell, *Pleasures of Hope*, i

**Gang Agley, To** (Scot.). To go wrong. The verb *to glee*, or *gley*, means to look asquint, sideways.

> The best-laid schemes of mice and men
> Gang aft agley. Burns, *To a Mouse*

**Gang-day.** The day when boys *gang* round the parish to beat its bounds. *See* Bounds.

**Gangway.** Originally, the boarded way (hence sometimes called the *gang-board*, gang, an alley) in the old galleys made for the rowers to pass from stem to stern, and where the mast was laid when it was unshipped; now, the board with cleats or bars of wood and a railing at each side by which passengers walk into or out of a ship.

> As we were putting off the boat they laid hold of the gangboard and unhooked it off the boat's stern. Cook, *Second Voyage*, Bk iii, ch. iv

***Below the gangway.*** In the House of Commons, on the farther side of the passage-way between the seats which separate the Ministry from the rest of the Members. To sit 'below the gangway' is to sit amongst the general members, and not among the Ministers or ex-Ministers and leaders of the Opposition.

**Ganges, The.** So named from *ganga* or *gunga*, a river; as in *Kishenganga*, the black river; *Neelganga*, the blue river; *Naraingunga*, the river of Naranyana or Vishnu, etc. The Ganges is the *Borra Ganga*, or great river.

> Those who through the curse, have fallen from heaven, having performed ablution in this

> stream, become free from sin; cleansed from sin by this water, and restored to happiness, they shall enter heaven and return again to the gods. *The Ramayana* (section xxxv).

**Ganymede.** In *Greek mythology*, the cup-bearer of Zeus, successor to Hebe, and the type of youthful male beauty. Originally a Trojan youth, he was taken up to Olympus and made immortal. Hence, a cup-bearer generally.

> Nature waits upon thee still,
> And thy verdant cup does fill;
> 'Tis fill'd wherever thou dost tread
> Nature's self's thy Ganymede.
> Cowley, *The Grasshopper* (*Anacreontics*)

**Gape.** ***Looking for gape-seed.*** Gaping about and doing nothing. A corruption of 'Looking agapesing'; *gapesing* (still used in Norfolk) is staring about with one's mouth open.

***Seeking a gape's nest*** (Devon). A *gape's nest* is a sight which one stares at with wide-open mouth. *Cp.* Mare's Nest.

**Garagantua.** A misspelling of Gargantua (*q.v.*), originated by Pope in his edition of Shakespeare (*As You Like It*, 3, 2).

**Garcias.** ***The soul of Pedro Garcias.*** Money. The story is that two scholars of Salamanca discovered a tombstone with this inscription: 'Here lies the soul of the licentiate Pedro Garcias'; and on searching found a purse with a hundred golden ducats. (*Gil Blas*, Preface.)

**Gardarike.** So Russia is called in the Eddas.

**Garden.** ***Garden City.*** A name given to Norwich, and to Chicago; also, as a generic name, to model suburbs and townships that have been planned with a special view to the provision of plenty of gardens, open spaces, and wide roads.

***The Garden*** or ***Garden Sect.*** The disciples of Epicurus, who taught in his own private garden.

> Epicurus in his garden was languid; the birds of the air have more enjoyment of their food.
> *Ecce Homo*

***The Garden of Eden.*** *See* Eden. The name as applied to Mesopotamia, with its vast sandy deserts, is nowadays somewhat ironical; but it is traditionally supposed to be its 'original site'.

***Garden of England.*** Kent and Worcestershire are both so called.

***Garden of Europe.*** Italy.

***Garden of France.*** Amboise, in the department of Indre-et-Loire; also Touraine.

***Garden of India.*** Oude.

***Garden of Ireland.*** Carlow.

***Garden of Italy.*** The island of Sicily.

***Garden of South Wales.*** The southern division of Glamorganshire.

***Garden of Switzerland.*** Thurgau.

***Garden of Spain.*** Andalusia.

***Garden of the Hesperides.*** *See* Hesperides.

***Garden of the Sun.*** The East Indian (or Malayan) Archipelago.

***Garden of the West.*** Illinois; Kansas ('the Garden State') is also so called.

***Garden of the World.*** The region of the Mississippi.

**Gardener.** ***Get on, gardener!*** Get on, you slow and clumsy coachman. The allusion is to a man who is both gardener and coachman.

***Gardener.*** Adam is so called.

> Thou, old Adam's likeness,
> Get to dress this garden.
> Shakespeare, *Richard II*, 3, 4

> From yon blue sky above us bent.
> The grand old gardener and his wife
> Smile at the claims of long descent.
> Lady Clara Vere de Vere

**Gardyloo.** *See* Jordeloo.

**Gargamelle.** In Rabelais' satire, daughter of the king of the Parpaillons (*butterflies*), wife of Grangousier, and mother of Gargantua (*q.v.*). On the day that she gave birth to him she ate sixteen quarters, two bushels, three pecks, and a pipkin of *dirt*, the mere remains left in the tripe which she had for supper; for, as the proverb says –

> Scrape tripe as clean as e'er you can,
> A tithe of filth will still remain.

She is said to be meant either for Anne of Brittany, or Catherine de Foix, Queen of Navarre.

**Gargantua.** A giant of mediaeval (perhaps Celtic) legend famous for his enormous appetite (Sp. *garganta*, gullet), adopted by Rabelais in his great satire (1532), and made the father of Pantagruel. One of his exploits was to swallow five pilgrims with their staves and all in a salad. He is the subject of a number of chap-books, and became proverbial as a voracious and insatiable guzzler.

> You must borrow me Gargantua's mouth first [before I can utter so long a word]; 'tis a word too great for any mouth of this age's size.
> Shakespeare, *As You Like It*, 3, 2

In some cases Rabelais seems to have been satirising Francis I under this name.

> According to Rabelais Gargantua was son of Grangousier and Gargamelle. Immediately he was born he cried out lustily 'Drink, drink!' whereupon his royal father exclaimed, '*Que grand*

*tu as!* which, being the first words he uttered after the birth of the child, were accepted as its name. It needed 17,913 cows to supply the babe with milk. When he went to Paris to finish his education he rode on a mare as big as six elephants, and took the bells of Notre Dame to hang on his mare's neck as jingles. After being fired at on his way home he combed his hair with a comb 900 feet long, when at every 'rake' seven bullets fell. Many other stories are told of him, and it was in honour of his great victory over Picrochole at the rock Clermond that he founded and endowed the Abbey of Theleme.

***Gargantua's mare.*** Attempts have been made to identify all the persons, incidents, and even many of the animals mentioned by Rabelais with historical characters, and Gargantua's 'great mare' has been held to stand for Mme d'Estampes and to depict the wilfulness and extravagance of court mistresses. Motteux, Rabelais' earliest English translator, who looks upon the romance as a satire on the Reform party, merely says, 'It is some lady.' Rabelais says –

> 'She was as big as six elephants, and had her feet cloven into fingers. She was of a burnt-sorrel hue, with a little mixture of dapple-grey; but, above all, she had a terrible tail, for it was every whit as great as the steeple pillar of St Mark.' When the beast got to Orléans, and the wasps assaulted her, she switched about her tail so furiously that she knocked down all the trees that grew in the vicinity, and Gargantua, delighted, exclaimed. '*Je trouve beau ce!*' wherefore the locality has been called 'Beauce' ever since.

***Gargantua's shepherds,*** according to Motteux, mean Lutheran preachers; but those who look upon the romance as a political satire think the Crown ministers and advisers are intended.

***Gargantua's thirst.*** Motteux says the 'great thirst' of Gargantua, and 'mighty drought' at Pantagruel's birth, refer to the withholding of the cup from the laity, and the clamour raised by the Reform party for the wine as well as the bread in the eucharist.

***Gargantuan.*** Enormous, inordinate, great beyond all limits. It needed 900 ells of Châtellerault linen to make the body of his shirt, and 200 more for the gussets; for his shoes 406 ells of blue and crimson velvet were required, and 1,100 cow-hides for the soles. He could play 207 different games, picked his teeth with an elephant's tusk, and did everything in the same 'large way'.

***A Gargantuan course of studies.*** A course including all languages, as well ancient as modern, all the sciences, all the -ologies and -onomies, with calisthenics, athletic sports, etc. etc. etc. Gargantua wrote to his son Pantagruel, commanding him to learn Greek, Latin, Chaldaic, Arabic; all history, geometry, arithmetic, and music; astronomy and natural philosophy, so that –

> There be not a river in all the world thou dost not know the name of, and nature of all its fishes; all the fowls of the air; all the several kinds of shrubs and herbs; all the metals hid in the bowels of the earth; with all gems and precious stones. I would furthermore have thee study the Talmudists and Cabalists, and get a perfect knowledge of man. In brief, I would have thee a bottomless pit of all knowledge. *Pantagruel*, Bk ii, 8

**Gargouille.** The great dragon that lived in the Seine, ravaged Rouen, and was slain by St Romanus, Bishop of Rouen, in the 7th century.

**Gargoyle.** A spout for rain-water in Gothic architecture, projecting from the wall so that the water falls clear, and usually carved into some fantastic shape, such as a dragon's head, through which the water flows. So named from Fr. *gargouille*, the throat, gullet.

**Garlic.** The old superstition that garlic can destroy the magnetic power of the loadstone has the sanction of Pliny, Solinus, Ptolemy, Plutarch, Albertus, Mathiolus, Rueus, Rulandus, Renodaeus, Langius, and others. Sir Thomas Browne places it among *Vulgar Errors* (Bk ii, ch. 3).

> Martin Rulandus saith that Onions and Garlick … hinder the attractive power [of the magnet] and rob it of its virtue of drawing iron, to which Renodaeus agrees; but this is all lies.
>
> W. Salmon, *The Complete English Physician*, ch. xxv (1693)

**Garnish.** In old prioson slang, the entrance money, to be spent in drink, demanded by jailbirds of new-corners. *Garnish* means emblelisment, extra decoration to dress, etc.; hence, it was applied by prisoners to fetters, and the garnish-money given for the 'honour' of wearing them. The custom become obsolete with the reform of prisons.

***Garratt. The Mayor of Garratt.*** Garratt is near Earlsfield, Wimbledon; the first 'mayor' was elected in 1778. He was really merely the chairman of an association of villagers formed to put a stop to encroachments on the common, and as his election coincided with a general election, the society made it a law that a new 'mayor' should be chosen at every general election. The addresses of these mayors, written by Garrick, Wilkes, and others, are satires on the corruption of electors and political squibs. The first Mayor of Garratt was 'Sir' John Harper, a retailer of brickdust; and the last was 'Sir' Harry Dimsdale, muffin-seller, in 1796. Foote has a farce entitled *The Mayor of Garratt*.

**Garraway's.** A noted coffee-house in Change Alley, Cornhill, which existed for over 200 years and was founded by Thomas Garway, a tobacconist and coffee merchant in the 16th century. Here the promoters of the South Sea Bubble met, sales were held periodically, and tea was introduced to England in 1657, selling for from 16*s*. to 50*s*. a pound.

**Garrotte** (Span. *garrote*, a stick). A Spanish method of execution by fastening a cord round the neck of the criminal and twisting it with a *stick* till strangulation ensued. In 1851 General Lopez was garrotted for attempting to gain possession of Cuba; and about that time the term was first applied to the practice of London thieves and roughs who strangled their victim while an accomplice rifled his pockets.

**Garter.** ***The Most Noble Order of the Garter.*** The highest order of knighthood in Great Britain and in the world, traditionally instituted by King Edward III about 1348, re-constituted in 1805 and 1831. The popular legend is that Joan, Countess of Salisbury, accidentally slipped her garter at a court ball. It was picked up by the king, who gallantly diverted the attention of the guests from the lady by binding the blue band round his own knee, saying as he did so, '*Honi soit qui mal y pense*' (*q.v.*). The order is limited to the Sovereign, the Prince of Wales, and other members of the Royal Family, with twenty-five Knights, and such foreign royalties as may be admitted by statute. Queen Mary and Queen Alexandra are Ladies of the Garter; and until, in 1912, Viscount Grey (then Sir Edward Grey) was admitted to the order, no commoner for centuries had been able to put 'K.G'. after his name.

Wearing the garters of a pretty maiden either on the hat or knee was a common custom with our forefathers. Brides usually wore on their legs a host of gay ribbons, to be distributed after the marriage ceremony amongst the bridegroom's friends; and the piper at the wedding dance never failed to tie a piece of the bride's garter round his pipe.

***Magic garters.*** In the old romances, etc., garters made of the strips of a young hare's skin saturated with motherwort. Those who wore them excelled in speed.

> Were it not for my magic garters …
> I should not continue the business long.
>
> Longfellow, *The Golden Legend*

***Prick the garter.*** An old swindling game, better known as 'Fast and loose'. *See under* Fast.

**Garvies.** Sprats; perhaps so called from Inchgarvie, the island in the Frith of Forth that supports the central pier of the Forth Bridge.

**Gasconade.** Absurd boasting, vainglorious braggadocio. It is said that a Gascon being asked what he thought of the Louvre in Paris, replied, 'Pretty well; it reminds me of the back part of my father's stables.' The vainglory of this answer is the more palpable when it is borne in mind that the Gascons were proverbially poor. The *Dictionary of the French Academy* gives the following specimen: 'A Gascon, in proof of his ancient nobility, asserted that they used in his father's house no other fuel than the bâtons of the family marshals.'

**Gaston.** Lord of Claros, one of Charlemagne's paladins.

**Gat-tooth.** Chaucer's 'Wife of Bath' was *gat-toothed* (*see Prol.* to *Cant. Tales*, 468, and *Wife of Bath's Prol.*, 603); this probably means that her teeth were set wide apart, with *gats*, i.e. openings or gaps between them; but some editors have thought it is *goat-toothed* (A.S. *gat*), i.e. lascivious, like a goat.

**Gate Money.** Money paid at the door or gate for admission to an enclosure where some entertainment or contest, etc., is to take place.

**Gate of Italy.** A narrow gorge between two mountain ridges in the valley of the Adige, in the vicinity of Trent and Roveredo.

**Gate of Tears.** The passage into the Red Sea. So called by the Arabs (*Bab-el-Mandeb*) from the number of shipwrecks that took place there.

> Like some ill-destined bark that steers
> In silence through the Gate of Tears.
>
> T. Moore, *Fire Worshippers*

**Gates of Dreams.** *See* Dreams.

**Gath.** In Dryden's *Absalom and Achitophel* (*q.v.*), means Brussels, where Charles II long resided while in exile.

> Had thus old David [Charles II] …
> Not dared, when fortune called him, to be king,
> At Gath an exile he might still remain.

***Tell it not in Gath.*** Don't let your enemies hear it. Gath was famous as being the birthplace of the giant Goliath.

> Tell it not in Gath, publish it not in the streets of Askelon: lest the daughters of the Philistines rejoice, lest the daughters of the uncircumcised triumph. 2 Sam. 1:20

**Gather.** ***He is gathered to his fathers.*** He is dead. A phrase from the Bible: 'All that generation were gathered unto their fathers' (Judges 2:10).

**Gauche** (Fr. *the left hand*). Awkward (*q.v.*). *See also* Adroit.

***Gaucherie.*** Things not *comme il faut*; behaviour not according to the received forms of society; awkward and untoward ways.

**Gaudy-day** (Lat. *gaudium*, joy). A holiday, a feast-day; especially an annual celebration of some event, such as the foundation of a college.

**Gaul.** In classical geography, the country inhabited by the Gauls, hence, in modern use, France. *Cisalpine Gaul* lay south and east of the Alps, in what is now northern Italy. *Transalpine Gaul* was north and north-west of the Alps, and included Narbonensis, Aquitania, Lugdunensis, and Belgica. It was inhabited by Franks, Germans, Burgundians, etc., and Celts, as well as Gauls.

> Insulting Gaul has roused the world to war.
> Thomson, *Autumn*
>
> Shall haughty Gaul invasion threat? Burns

**Gaunt.** ***John of Gaunt*** (1340–99), third son of Edward III; so called from Ghent, in Flanders, the place of his birth.

**Gauntlet.** ***To run the gauntlet.*** To be attacked on all sides, to be severely criticised. The word came into English at the time of the Thirty Years' War as *gantlope*, meaning the passage between two files of soldiers, and is the Swedish *gata*, a way, passage (*cp.* Gat-tooth *above*), and *lopp* (connected with our *leap*), a course. The reference is to a punishment formerly common among soldiers and sailors; the company or crew, provided with rope ends, were drawn up in two rows facing each other, and the delinquent had to run between them, while every man dealt him as severe a chastisement as he could.

***To throw down the gauntlet.*** To challenge. The custom in the Middle Ages, when one knight challenged another, was for the challenger to throw his gauntlet on the ground, and if the challenge was accepted the person to whom it was thrown picked it up.

**Gautama.** The family name of Buddha (*q.v.*). His personal name was Siddhattha, his father's name Suddhodana, and his mother's Maya. *Buddha* means 'The Enlightened', 'The One Who Knows', and he assumed this title at about the age of 36, when, after seven years of seclusion and spiritual struggle, he believed himself to have attained to perfect truth.

**Gauvaine.** Gawain (*q.v.*).

**Gavelkind.** A tenure of Saxon origin, still in force in some parts of Kent and formerly in Wales, Northumberland, and elsewhere, whereby land and property of persons dying intestate descended from the father to all his sons in equal proportions, or to the daughters in the absence of sons. The youngest had the homestead, and the eldest the horse and arms. The word is the A.S. *gafol*, tribute, tax (*cp.* Gabelle), and *kind*, nature, species.

> Coke (*1 Institutes*, 140 *a*) says the word is *gif eal cyn* (give all the kin).

**Gawain.** One of the most famous of the Arthurian knights, nephew of King Arthur, and probably the original hero of the Grail quest. He appears in the Welsh *Triads* and the *Mabinogion* as Gwalchmei, and in the Arthurian cycle is the centre of many episodes and poems. He is first represented as the flower of chivalrous knighthood, but later writers (including Malory) degraded him, probably on account of his connection with the Grail and to leave the literary field clear for Percival, until Tennyson, in *The Passing of Arthur*, makes Sir Bedivere brand him as 'light in life and light in death'. The Middle English poem (about 1360), *Sir Gawain and the Green Knight*, is a weird romance telling how Gawain beheads the Green Knight in single combat after having promised to meet him for a return stroke twelve months later at the Green Chapel. On the appointed day Gawain is there, and so is the Green Knight: Gawain's honour is, by arrangement, severely but successfully tested by the wife of the knight, and as he has proved himself true he escapes unharmed.

**Gay.** ***A gay deceiver,*** A Lothario (*q.v.*); a libertine.

> I immediately quitted the precincts of the castle, and posted myself on the high road, where the gay deceiver was sure to be intercepted on his return.
>
> Le Sage, *Gil Blas,* vii, i, 3 (Smollett's translation, 1749)

***The Gay Science.*** A translation of *gai saber*, the old Provençal name for the art of poetry. E. S. Dallas used it (1866) as the title for a treatise on Criticism. In explanation he says:

> Why the Gay Science, however? The lighthearted minstrels of Provence insisted on the joyfulness of their art ... Neither need anyone be repelled if this doctrine of pleasure strike the key-note, and suggest the title of the present work, in which an attempt will be made to show that a science of criticism is possible, and that it must of necessity

be the science of the laws of pleasure, the joy science, the Gay Science. *Preface*

A guild formed at Toulouse in 1323 with the object of keeping in existence the dying Provençal language and culture was called the *Gai Saber*. Its full title was 'The Very Gay Company of the Seven Troubadours of Toulouse'.

**Gaze.** ***To stand at gaze.*** To stand in doubt what to do. A term in forestry. When a stag first hears the hounds it stands dazed, looking all round, and in doubt what to do. Heralds call a stag which is represented full-faced, a 'stag at gaze'.

As the poor frighted deer, that stands at gaze.
Wildly determining which way to fly.
Shakespeare, *Rape of Lucrece*, 1149

***Gaze-hound.*** *See* Lyme-hound.

**Gazette.** A newspaper. The first newspapers were issued in Venice by the Government, and came out in manuscript once a month, during the war of 1563 between the Venetians and Turks. The intelligence was read publicly in certain places, and the fee for hearing it read was one *gazetta* (a Venetian coin, somewhat less than a farthing in value).

The first official English newspaper, called *The Oxford Gazette*, was published in 1642, at Oxford, where the Court was held. On the removal of the Court to London, the name was changed to *The London Gazette*. The name was revived in 1665, during the Great Fire. Now the official *Gazette*, published every Tuesday and Friday, contains announcements of pensions, promotions, bankruptcies, dissolutions of partnerships, etc. (*See* Newspapers.)

**Gazetted.** Posted in the *London Gazette* as having received some official appointment, been declared bankrupt, etc.

**Gazetteer.** A geographical and topographical index or dictionary; so called because the name of one of the earliest in English (L. Eachard's, 1693) was *The Gazetteer's or Newsman's Interpreter*, i.e. it was intended for the use of journalists, those who wrote for the *Gazettes.*

**Gear.** In machinery, the wheels, chains, belts, etc., that communicate motion to the working parts are called the gear or *gearing* (Sax. *gearwa*, clothing).

***In good gear.*** To be in good working order.

***Out of gear.*** Not in working condition, when the 'gearing' does not act properly; out of health.

**Gee-up!** and **Gee-whoa!** Interjections addressed to horses meaning respectively 'Go ahead!' and 'Stop!' From them came the childish 'gee-gee', a horse, a term adopted by sporting men and others, as in 'Backing the gee-gees'.

**Geese.** *See* Goose.

**Gehenna** (Heb., *g* hard). The place of eternal torment. Strictly speaking, it means simply the Valley of Hinnom (*Ge-Hinnom*), where sacrifices to Baal and Moloch were offered (Jer. 19:6, etc.), and where refuse of all sorts was subsequently cast, for the consumption of which fires were kept constantly burning.

And made his grove
The pleasant valley of Hinnom, Tophet thence
And black Gehenna called, the type of hell.
Milton, *Paradise Lost*, Bk i, 403

**Gelert.** Llewellyn's dog. *See* Beth Gelert.

**Gemara** (Aramaic, complement). The second part of the Talmud (*q.v.*), consisting of annotations, discussions, and amplifications of the *Mishna*, which is the first part. The *Mishna* is the interpretation of the written law, the *Gemara* the interpretation of the *Mishna*. There is the Babylonian *Gemara* and the Jerusalem *Gemara*. The former, which is the more complete, is by the academies of Babylon, and was completed about AD 500; the latter by those of Palestine, completed towards the close of the 4th or during the 5th century AD.

Scribes and Pharisees ... set little value on the study of the Law itself, but much on that of the commentaries of the rabbis, now embodied in the *Mishna* and *Gemara.*
Geikie, *Life of Christ*, vol. ii, ch. xxxvi

**Gemmagog.** According to Rabelais (Bk ii, ch. i), son of the giant Oromedon, and inventor of the Poulan shoes – i.e. shoes with a spur behind, and turned-up toes fastened to the knees. These shoes were forbidden by Charles V of France in 1365, but the fashion revived again.

The same authority says giants were great inventors: Erix invented tricks of thimble-rigging; Gabara, drinking healths; Hapmouche, drying and smoking neats' tongues; Morgan, 'who was the first in this World who played at Dice with Spectacles'; Galehault, the inventor of flagons; etc. etc. They were all direct ancestors of Gargantua and Pantagruel.

**Gems.** *See* Jewels.

**Gendarmes.** 'Men at arms', the armed police of France. The term was first applied to those who marched in the train of knights; subsequently to the cavalry; in the time of Louis XIV to a body of horse charged with the preservation of order; after the revolution to a military police chosen from old soldiers of good character; and now to the ordinary police.

**General Funk.** A panic.

> The influence of 'General Funk' was, at one time, far too prevalent among both the colonists and the younger soldiers.
>
> Montague, *Campaigning in South Africa*, ch. vi (1880)

**General Issue.** The plea of 'Not guilty' to a criminal charge; 'Never indebted' to a charge of debt; the issue formed by a general denial of the plaintiff's charge.

**Generalissimo.** The supreme commander, especially of a force drawn from two or more nations, or of a combined military and naval force. Called *Tagus* among the ancient Thessalians, *Brennus* among the ancient Gauls, *Pendragon* among the ancient Welsh or Celts.

**Generous.** ***Generous as Hatim.*** An Arabian expression. Hatim was a Bedouin chief famous for his warlike deeds and boundless generosity. His son was contemporary with Mahomet.

> Let Zál and Rustum blaster as they will,
> Or Hátim call to Supper – heed not you.
>
> Fitzgerald, *Rubáiyát of Omar Khayyám*, x

**Generic Names.** *See* Biddy.

**Geneva.** *See* Gin.

***The Geneva Bible.*** *See* Bible, the English.

***The Geneva Bull.*** A nickname given to Stephen Marshall (d.1655), a Presbyterian divine, and one of the authors of *Smectymnuus* (*q.v.*), because he was a disciple of John Calvin, of Geneva, and when preaching he roared like a 'bull of Bashan'.

***Geneva courage.*** Pot valour; the braggadocio which is the effect of having drunk too much gin (*q.v.*), or *geneva*. *Cp.* Dutch Courage. The word *Geneva*, punning on Calvinism and gin, is frequent in old allusions to drink. Thus Scott has:

> 'You have been reading Geneva print this morning already.' 'I have been reading the Litany,' said John, shaking his head, with a look of drunken gravity. *Old Mortality*, ch. xi

***Geneva Cross.*** *See* Red Cross.

***Geneva doctrines.*** Calvinism. Calvin, in 1541, was invited to take up his residence in Geneva as the public teacher of theology. From this period Geneva was for many years the centre of education for the Protestant youths of Europe.

**Geneviève, St.** (422–512). The sainted patroness of the city of Paris. Her day is January 3rd, and she is represented in art with the keys of Paris at her girdle, a devil blowing out her candle, and an angel relighting it, or as restoring sight to her blind mother, or guarding her father's sheep. She was born at Nanterre, and was influential in averting a threatened attack on Paris by Attila, the Hun.

**Genius** (pl. **Genii**). In *Roman mythology* the tutelary spirits that attended one from his cradle to his grave, and that governed his fortunes, determined his character, and so on. The Eastern genii were the Jinn (*q.v.*), entirely different from the Roman, not guardian or attendant spirits, but fallen angels, dwelling in Djinnistan, under the dominion of Eblis; the Roman were very similar to the guardian angels spoken of in Matt. 18:10; and in this sense Mephistopheles is spoken of as the *evil genius* (the 'familiar') of Faust. The Romans maintained that two genii attended every man from birth to death – one good and the other evil. Good luck was brought about by the agency of 'his good genius', and ill luck by that of his 'evil genius'.

The *genius loci* was the tutelary deity of a place.

> In the midst of this wreck … sat a large black cat. which, to a superstitious eye, might have presented the *genius loci*, the tutelar demon of the apartment. Scott, *The Antiquary*, ch. iii

The word is from the Lat. *gignere*, to beget (Gr. *gignesthai*, to be born), from the notion that birth and life were due to these *dii genitales.* Hence it is used for birth-wit or innate talent; hence propensity, nature, inner man. *Cras genium mero curabis* ('Tomorrow you shall indulge your inner man with wine'), Horace, *3 Odes*, xvii, 14. *Indulgere genio* (to give loose to one's propensity), Persius, v. 151. *Defrauda re genium suum* (to stint one's appetite, to deny oneself), Terence, *Phormio*, i, 1.

**Genovefa.** The heroine of an old German folktale (very like folk-tales from all parts of the world) which relates that she was the wife of a Count Palatine Siegfried, of Brabant, in the time of Charles Martel. Being suspected of infidelity, she was driven into the forest of Ardennes, where she gave birth to a son, who was nourished by a white doe. In time, Siegfried discovered his error, and restored his wife and child to their home. The name is another form of Geneviève.

**Genre Painter.** A painter of domestic, rural, or village scenes, such as *A Village Wedding*, *The Young Recruit*, *Blind Man's Buff*, *The Village Politician*, etc. Wilkie, Ostade, Gerard, Dow, etc., belonged to this class. In the drama, Victor Hugo introduced the genre system in lieu of the stilted, unnatural style of Louis XIV's era.

> We call those 'genre' canvases, whereon are painted idyls of the fireside, the roadside, and the farm; pictures of real life.
>
> E. C. Stedman, *Poets of America*, ch. iv

**Gens** (Lat. pl. *gentes*). A clan or sept in ancient Rome; a number of families deriving from a common ancestor, having the same name, religion, etc.

***Gens braccata*** (Lat.). Trousered people. The Romans wore no trousers ('breeches') like the Gauls, Scythians, and Persians. *Cp.* Gallia Braccata.

***Gens togata.*** *See* Toga.

**Gentle.** Belonging to a family (*gens, see above*) of position; well born; having the manners of genteel persons.

> We must be gentle, now we are gentlemen.
>
> Shakespeare, *Winter's Tale*, v, 2

The word is from Lat. *gentilis*, of the same family or *gens*, through O. Fr. *gentil*, high-born.

***The gentle craft.*** Shoe-making; so called from St Crispin, who is said to have been a Roman citizen of high birth who was converted to Christianity, left his native city on account of persecution, became a shoemaker at Soissons, and was martyred about 285.

> As I am a true shoemaker and a gentleman of the gentle craft, buy spurs yourselves, and I'll find ye boots these seven years.
>
> Dekker, *The Shoemaker's Holiday, or a Pleasant Comedy of the Gentle Craft*, I, i (1599)

Angling is also sometimes known as 'the gentle craft' – perhaps because there is nothing that can be called rough about its practice, perhaps with a punning allusion to the *gentles* or maggots sometimes used as bait.

***The Gentle Shepherd.*** A nickname given to George Grenville, the statesman (1712–70), by Pitt, afterwards Earl of Chatham. Grenville, in the course of one of his speeches, addressed the House interrogatively: 'Tell me where? tell me where?' Pitt hummed a line of a song then very popular, 'Gentle shepherd, tell me where?' The House burst into laughter; and the name stuck to Grenville. The line is from a song by Samuel Howard (1710–82), a writer of many popular lyrics.

**Gentleman** (formed on the model of Fr. *gentilhomme*). Properly, a man entitled to bear arms but not of the nobility; hence, one of gentle birth, of some position in society, and with the manners, bearing and behaviour appropriate to one in such a position: a man of 'family' (Lat. *gens, see above*).

> Be it spoken (with all reverent reservation of duty) the King who hath power to make Esquires, Knights, Baronets, Barons, Viscounts, Earls, Marquesses, and Dukes, *cannot make a Gentleman*, for Gentilitie is a matter of race, and of blood, and of descent, from Gentile and noble parents and anncestors, which no Kings can give to any, but to such as they beget.
>
> Edmond Howes, *B.L. Chronicle*, ch. xi (*Gent. Mag.*, vol. lxxxi, p. 124)

> To be a gentleman is to be one all the world over, and in every relation and grade of society. It is a high calling, to which a man must first be born and then devote himself for life.
>
> R. L. Stevenson, *The Amateur Emigrant*

Juliana Berners, in her 15th century *Book of Blazoning*, has a curious use of the word:

> Of the offspring of the gentilman Jafeth came Habraham, Moyses, Aron, and the profettys: and also the kyng of the right lyne of Mary, of whom that gentilman Jhesus was borne very god and man: after his manhode kyng of the londe of Judea of Jues, gentilman by is modre Mary prynce of Cote armure.

In the *York Mysteries* also (about 1440) we read, 'Ther schall a gentilman, Jesu, unjustely be judged.'

***A gentleman at large.*** A man of means, who does not have to work for his living, and is free to come and go as he pleases. Formerly the term denoted a gentleman attached to the court but having no special duties.

***A gentleman of fortune.*** A pirate, an adventurer (a euphemistic phrase).

***A gentleman of the four outs.*** A vulgar upstart, with-*out* manners, with-*out* wit, with-*out* money, and with-*out* credit. There are variants of the phrase, and sometimes the *outs* are increased to five:

> Out of money, and out of clothes,
> Out at the heels, and out at the toes,
> Out of credit – but, don't forget,
> Never *out of* but aye *in* debt!

***A gentleman's gentleman.*** A man-servant, especially a valet.

> *Fag.*: My master shall know this – and if *he* don't call him out *I* will.
>
> *Lucy*: Ha! ha! ha! You gentlemen's gentlemen are so hasty!
>
> Sheridan, *The Rivals*, II, ii

***A nation of gentlemen.*** So George IV called the Scots when, in 1822, he visited their country and was received with great expressions of loyalty.

***Gentleman Commoner.*** *See* Fellow Commoner.

***Gentleman Pensioner.*** *See* Gentlemen at Arms, below.

***Gentleman-ranker.*** A 'broken gentleman', i.e. one who has lost his social position and means, who enlists in the Army as a private soldier, often in the hope of getting a commission.

We're poor little lambs who've lost our way,
Baa! Baa! Baa!
We're little black sheep who've gone astray,
Baa – aa – aa!
Gentlemen-rankers out on the spree,
Dammed from here to Eternity,
God ha' mercy on such as we.
Baa!Yah! Bah! Kipling, *Gentlemen-Rankers*

***Gentleman Usher.*** A court official belonging to one of four classes, viz.: (1) *Gentlemen Ushers of the Privy Chamber*; these are in closest association with the Sovereign, wait on him at chapel, and conduct him in the absence of the Lord Chamberlain. (2) *Gentlemen Ushers Daily Waiters*, who are headed by Black Rod (*q.v.*) and officiate monthly by turns in the Presence Chamber. (3) *Gentlemen Ushers Quarterly Waiters*, who act as deputies for the preceding in their absence. (4) The *Gentleman Usher to the Robes*, who replaces the Groom of the Stole (*q.v.*), an office which was allowed to lapse at the accession of Queen Victoria, the *Mistress of the Robes* taking his place.

***Gentlemen at Arms, the Honourable Corps of.*** The Bodyguard of the Sovereign (formerly called *Gentlemen Pensioners*), acting in conjunction with the Yeomen of the Guard (*q.v.*). It consists of 40 retired officers of the Regular Army and Marines, and has a Lieutenant, Standard Bearer, and Clerk of the Cheque.

***The gentleman in black velvet.*** It was in these words that the 18th-century Jacobites used to toast the mole that made the molehill that caused William III's horse to stumble and so brought about his death.

The little gentleman in black velvet who did such service in 1702. Scott, *Waverley*, ch. xi

***The gentleman in brown.*** A 'Norfolk Howard', bed-bug.

***The old gentleman.*** The devil; Old Nick. Also a special card in a prepared pack, used for tricks or cheating.

***To put a churl upon a gentleman.*** To drink beer just after drinking wine.

**Geomancy** (Gr. *ge*, the earth; *manteia*, prophecy). Divining by the earth. Diviners in the 16th century made deductions from the patterns made by earth thrown into the air and allowed to fall on some flat surface, and drew on the earth their magic circles, figures, lines, etc.

**George, St.** The patron saint of England since about the time of the institution of the Order of the Garter (*c.*1348), when he was 'adopted' by Edward III. He is commemorated on April 23rd, a day further rendered sacred to English-speaking peoples as being the reputed birthday and the death-day of Shakespeare (1561–1616).

St George had been popular in England from the time of the early Crusades, for he was said to have come to the assistance of the Crusaders at Antioch (1089), and many of the Normans (under Robert, son of William the Conqueror) then took him as their patron.

St George was probably a Cappadocian who suffered martyrdom under Diocletian in 303. There are various versions of his *Acta*, one saying that he was a tribune and that he was asked to come and subdue a dragon that infested a pond at Silene, Libya, and fed on the dwellers in the neighbourhood. St George came, rescued a princess (Sabra) whom the dragon was about to make its prey, and slew the monster after he had wounded it and the princess had led it home in triumph by her girdle.

That St George is an historical character is beyond all reasonable doubt; but the somewhat hesitating assertion of Gibbon (*Decline and Fall*, ch. xxiii) that the patron saint of England was George of Cappadocia, the turbulent Arian Bishop of Alexandria, who was torn to pieces by the populace in 360 and revered as a saint by the opponents of Athanasius, has been fully disproved by the Jesuit Papebroch, Milner, and others.

The legend of St George and the dragon is simply an allegorical expression of the triumph of the Christian hero over evil, which St John the Divine beheld under the image of a dragon. Similarly, St Michael, St Margaret, St Silvester, and St Martha are all depicted as slaying dragons; the Saviour and the Virgin as treading them under their feet; St John the Evangelist as charming a winged dragon from a poisoned chalice given him to drink; and Bunyan avails himself of the same figure when he makes Christian prevail against Apolyon.

The legend forms the subject of an old ballad given in Percy's *Reliques*, in which St George was the son of Lord Albert of Coventry. His mother died in giving him birth, and the newborn babe was stolen away by the weird lady of the woods, who brought him up to deeds of arms. His body had three marks: a dragon on the breast, a garter round one of the legs, and a blood-red cross on the arm. When he grew to manhood he first fought against the Saracens, and then went to Silene (*see above*), where he rescued the Princess Sabra and slew the dragon.

St George naturally wished to wed the princess, but the king of Morocco and the king of Egypt, unwilling that Sabra should marry a Christian, sent him to Persia, and directed the 'sophy' to kill him. He was accordingly thrust into a dungeon, but making good his escape, carried off Sabra to England, where she became his wife, and they lived happily at Coventry together till their death.

The similarity of the 'rescue' portion of this story to those of Perseus and Andromeda, and Hesione, daughter of Laodemon, will be noticed.

***St George he was for England, St Denis was for France.*** This refers to the war-cries of the two nations – that of England was 'St George!' that of France, 'Montjoye St Denis!'

> Our ancient word of courage, fair 'St George',
> Inspire us with the spleen of fiery dragons.
>
> Shakespeare, *Richard III*, 5, 3

***St George's Cross.*** Red on a white field.

***When St George goes on horseback St Yves goes on foot.*** In times of war it was supposed that lawyers have nothing to do. St George is the patron of soldiers, and St Yves, or Yvo, an early French judge and lawyer noted for his incorruptibility and just decrees (d.1303, canonised 1347) of lawyers.

**George-a-Green.** ***As good as George-a-Green.*** Resolute-minded; one who will do his duty come what may. George-a-Green was the mythical *Pinder* (Pinner or Pindar) or pound-keeper of Wakefield, who resisted Robin Hood, Will Scarlett, and Little John single-handed when they attempted to commit a trespass in Wakefield.

> Were ye bold as George-a-Green,
> I shall make bold to turn again.
>
> Butler, *Hudibras*

Robert Greene wrote a comedy (published 1599) called *George-a-Greene, or the Pinner of Wakefield.*

**Geraint.** In *Arthurian legend*, a tributary prince of Devon, and one of the knights of the Round Table. In the *Mabinogion* story he is the son of Erbin, as he is in the French original, Chrestien de Troyes' *Eric et Enide*, from which Tennyson drew his *Geraint and Enid* in the *Idylls of the King*. In the latter, Geraint, overhearing part of Enid's words, fancied she was faithless to him and treated her for a time very harshly; but Enid nursed him so carefully when he was wounded that he saw his error, 'nor did he doubt her more, but rested in her fealty, till he crowned a happy life with a fair death'.

**Geraldine.** ***The Fair Geraldine.*** Lady Elizabeth Fitzgerald (d.1589) is so called in the Earl of Surrey's poems. She was the youngest daughter of the Earl of Kildare.

**Geranium.** The Turks say this was a common mallow changed by the touch of Mahomet's garment.

The word is Gr. *geranos*, a crane; and the wild plant is called 'Crane's Bill', from the resemblance of the fruit to the bill of a crane.

**Gerda,** or **Gerdhr.** In *Scandinavian mythology* (the *Skírnismál*), a young giantess, wife of Frey, and daughter of the frost giant Gymer. She is so beautiful that the brightness of her naked arms illumines both air and sea. According to the myth, Frey (the god of fruitfulness) married Gerda (the frozen earth), and she became the mother of children.

**German** or **Germane.** Pertaining to, nearly related to, as *cousins-german* (first cousins), *german to the subject* (bearing on or pertinent to the subject). This word has no connection with the *German* nation, but is Lat. *germanus*, of the same germ or stock.

> Those that are germane to him, though removed fifty times, shall all come under the hangman.
>
> Shakespeare, *Winter's Tale*, 4, 3

**German Comb.** The four fingers and thumb. The Germans were the last nation to adopt periwigs; and while the French were never seen without a comb in one hand, the Germans adjusted their hair by running their fingers through it.

> He apparelled himself according to the season, and afterwards combed his head with an Alman comb.
>
> Rabelais, Bk i, 21

**German Silver.** A silvery-looking alloy of copper, zinc, and nickel. It was first made in Europe at Hildburghausen, in Germany, in the early 19th century, but had been used by the Chinese time out of mind.

**Germany.** The English name for the German *Deutschland* (Fr. *Allemagne*) is the Lat. *Germania*, the source of which is not certain; it is thought to be the form given by the Romans to the Celtic or Gaulish name for the Teutons; in which case it may be connected either with Celt, *gair*, neighbour, *gavim*, war-cry, or *ger*, spear.

Geoffrey of Monmouth, recording popular eponymic legends, says that Ebrancus, a mythological descendant of Brute (*q.v.*) and founder of York (*Eboracum*), had twenty sons and thirty daughters. All the sons, except the eldest, settled in Germany, which was therefore called the land of the *germans* or brothers. Spenser, speaking of 'Ebranck', says:

An happy man in his first days he was,
And happy father of fair progeny;
For all so many weeks as the year has
So many children he did multiply!
Of which were twenty sons, which did apply
Their minds to praise and chivalrous desire.
Those germans did subdue all Germany,
Of whom it hight. *Faërie Queene*, II, x, 22

**Gerrymander.** So to divide a county or nation into representative districts as to give one special political party undue advantage over others. The word is derived from Elbridge Gerry, who adopted the scheme in Massachusetts when he was governor. Gilbert Stuart, the artist, looking at the map of the new distribution, with a little invention converted it into a salamander. 'No, no!' said Russell, when shown it, 'not a Salamander, Stuart, call it a Gerry-mander.'

Hence, to hocus-pocus statistics, election results, etc., so as to make them appear to give other than their true result, or so as to affect the balance.

**Gertrude, St.** An abbess (d.664), aunt of Charles Martel's father, Pepin. She founded hospices for pilgrims, and so is a patron saint of travellers, and is said to harbour souls on the first night of their three days' journey to heaven. She is also the protectress against rats and mice, and is sometimes represented as surrounded by them, or with them running about her distaff as she spins.

**Geryon.** In *Greek mythology*, a monster with three bodies and three heads, whose oxen ate human flesh, and were guarded by Orthros, a two-headed dog. Hercules slew both Geryon and the dog.

**Geryoneo.** In Spenser's *Faërie Queene* (V, xi) a giant with three bodies typifying Philip II of Spain (master of three kingdoms), the Spanish rule in the Netherlands, or sometimes the Inquisition. He was the son of Geryon.

**Gessler, Hermann.** The tyrannical Austrian governor of the three Forest Cantons of Switzerland who figures in the Tell legend. *See* Tell, William.

**Gesta Romanorum.** A pseudo-devotional compilation of popular tales in Latin (many from Oriental sources), each with an arbitrary 'moral' attached for the use of preachers, assigned – in its collected form – to about the end of the 14th century. The name, meaning 'The Acts of the Romans', is merely fanciful. It was first printed at Utrecht about 1472, and the earliest English edition is that of Wynkyn de Worde about 1510, but long before this the people had, through the pulpit, come to know it, and many English poets, from Chaucer to William Morris, have laid it under contribution. Shakespeare drew the plot of *Pericles* from the *Gesta Romanorum*, as well as the incident of the three caskets in the *Merchant of Venice*.

**Gestas.** The traditional name of the impenitent thief. *See* Dysmas.

**Get.** With its past and past participle *got*, one of the hardest worked words in the English language: the following example shows some of its uses – and abuses:

> I got on horseback within ten minutes after I got your letter. When I got to Canterbury I got a chaise for town; but I got wet through, and have got such a cold that I shall not get rid of in a hurry. I got to the Treasury about noon, but first of all got shaved and dressed. I soon got into the secret of getting a memorial before the Board, but I could not get an answer then; however, I got intelligence from a messenger that I should get one next morning. As soon as I got back to my inn, I got my supper, and then got to bed. When I got up next morning, I got my breakfast, and, having got dressed, I got out in time to get an answer to my memorial. As soon as I got it, I got into a chaise, and got back to Canterbury by three, and got home for tea. I have got nothing for you, and so adieu.
>
> Dr Withers

For phrases such as *To get out of bed the wrong side*, *To get the mitten*, *To get the wind up*, etc., *see* the main word in the phrase.

***How are you getting on?*** How do things fare with you? How are you prospering?

***To get at.*** To tamper with, bribe, influence to a wrong end; specially used in horse-racing. *See also Who are you getting at?* below.

***To get down to it.*** To set about your work or whatever it is you have in hand in downright earnest.

***To get it hot,*** or ***in the neck.*** To receive a thorough dressing down, beating, punishment, etc.

***To get off.*** To escape; also (of a girl) to become engaged to be married, or to make a promiscuous acquaintanceship with a man – to be 'picked up'. One girl will say to another, 'It's no good walking about the pier with a face like that, old thing; you'll never get off!' meaning that no young man will come along and take her to listen to the band and feed her on chocolates unless she looks a bit more pleasant.

***To get there.*** To succeed; to 'arrive'; attain one's object.

***To get under.*** To fail; to come down in the world. 'Get on or get under' – there's no alternative; if you don't do your best with your eyes on success you'll fail utterly and become the 'under-dog'.

***To get up.*** To rise from one's bed. To learn, as 'I must get up my Euclid.' To organise and arrange, as 'We will get up a bazaar.'

***To get well on,*** or ***well oiled.*** To become intoxicated. *Getting well on* is a very different thing from *getting on well*!

***Who are you getting at?*** Who are you trying to take a rise out of? Whose leg are you trying to pull? A question usually asked sarcastically by the intended butt.

***Your get-up was excellent.*** Your style of dress exactly suited the part you professed to enact. In the same way, *She was got up regardless*, her dress was splendid; money was no object when obtaining it – it was bought 'regardless of expense'.

**Gethsemane.** The *Orchis maculata*, supposed in legendary story to be spotted by the blood of Christ.

**Gewgaw.** A showy trifle. The word may be an imitation of Fr. *jou-jou*, a baby word for a toy (*jouer*, to play), or it may be from *givegove*, a M.E. reduplication of *give*. Double names of this kind for something paltry or insignificant are very common; e.g. *flip-flap*, *ping-pong*, *hurly-burly*, etc.

**Ghebers.** *See* Guebres.

**Ghibellines.** The imperial and aristocratic faction in Italy in the Middle Ages, opposed to the Guelphs (*see* Guelphs and Ghibellines). The name was the war-cry of the followers of the Emperor Conrad at the battle of Weinsberg (1140), and is the Italian form of Ger. *Waiblingen*, an estate in Wurtemberg then belonging to the Emperor's family, the House of Hohenstaufen. *See* Goblin.

**Ghost.** ***To give up the ghost.*** To die. The idea is that life is independent of the body, and is due to the habitation of the ghost or spirit in the material body. At death the ghost or spirit leaves this tabernacle of clay, and either returns to God or abides in the region of spirits till the general resurrection. Thus in Eccles. 12:7, it is said: 'Then shall the dust return to the earth as it was: and the spirit shall return unto God who gave it.'

> Man dieth, and wasteth away: yea, man giveth up the ghost, and where is he? Job 14:10

***The ghost of a chance.*** The least likelihood. 'He has not the ghost of a chance of being elected', not the shadow of a probability.

***The ghost walks.*** Theatrical slang for salaries are about to be paid; when there's no money in the treasury actors say 'the ghost won't walk this time'. The allusion is to *Hamlet* 1, 1, where Horatio asks the ghost if it 'walks' because

> Thou hast uphoarded in thy life
> Extorted treasure in the womb of earth.

**Ghost-word.** A term invented by Skeat (*Philol. Soc. Transactions*, 1886) to denote words that have no real existence but are due to the blunders of scribes, printers, or editors, etc.

> Like ghosts we may seem to see them, or may fancy that they exist; but they have no real entity. We cannot grasp them. When we would do so, they disappear.

*Acre-fight* and *slughorn* (*qq.v.*) are examples.

Intrusive letters that have no etymological right in a word but have been inserted through false analogy with words similarly pronounced (like the *gh* in *sprightly* or the *h* in *aghast*) are sometimes called *ghost-letters*.

**Giall.** The Styx of *Scandinavian mythology*, the river on the frontiers of Nifelheim, or hell. Over it the doomed pass on a golden bridge guarded by the maiden Mothguthr.

**Giallarhorn.** Heimdall's horn, the blast of which turned the world from its course, let loose the powers of evil, and thereby started the war against the Aesir. (*Scandinavian mythology*.)

**Gian ben Gian.** In Arabic legend, a king of the Jinn and founder of the Pyramids. He was overthrown by Azazael or Lucifer.

**Giants,** i.e. persons well above the average height and size, are by no means uncommon as 'sports' or 'freaks of nature'; but the widespread belief in pre-existing races or individual instances of giants among primitive peoples is due partly to the ingrained idea that the present generation is invariably a degeneration – 'There were giants in the earth in those days' (Gen. 6:4) – and partly to the existence from remote antiquity of cyclopaean buildings, gigantic sarcophagi, etc., and to the discovery from time to time in pre-scientific days of the bones of extinct monsters which were taken to be those of men. Among instances of the latter may be mentioned the following:

> A skeleton discovered at Lucerne in 1577 19 ft in height. Dr Plater is our authority for this measurement.

'Teutobochus', whose remains were discovered near the Rhone in 1613. They occupied a tomb 30 ft long. The bones of another gigantic skeleton were exposed by the action of the Rhone in 1456. If this was a human skeleton, the height of the living man must have been 30 ft.

Pliny records that an earthquake in Crete exposed the bones of a giant 46 cubits (i.e. roughly 75 ft) in height; he called this the skeleton of Orion, others held it to be that of Otus.

Antaeus is said by Plutarch to have been 60 cubits (about 90 ft) in height. He furthermore adds that the grave of the giant was opened by Serbonius.

The 'monster Polypheme'. It is said that his skeleton was discovered at Trapani, in Sicily, in the 14th century. If this skeleton was that of a man, he must have been 300 ft in height.

**Giants of the Bible.**

Anak. The eponymous progenitor of the Anakim (*see below*). The Hebrew spies said they were mere grasshoppers in comparison with these giants. (Josh. 15:14; Judges 1:20; and Numb. 13:33.)

Goliath of Gath (1 Sam. 17, etc.). His height is given as 6 cubits and a span; the cubit varied and might be anything from about 18 in. to 21 in., and a span was about 9 in.; this would give Goliath a height of between 9ft 9 in. and 11ft 3in.

Og, King of Bashan (Josh. 12:4, Deut. 3:8, 4:47, etc.), was 'of the remnant of the Rephaim'. According to tradition, he lived 3,000 years and walked beside the Ark during the Flood. One of his bones formed a bridge over a river. His bed (Deut. 3:11) was 9 cubits by 4 cubits.

The Anakim and Rephaim were tribes of reputed giants inhabiting the territory on both sides of the Jordan before the coming of the Israelites. The Nephilim, the offspring of the sons of God and the daughters of men (Gen. 6:4), a mythological race of semi-divine heroes, were also giants.

**Giants of Mythology, Legend and Romance.**

The giants of *Greek mythology* were, for the most part, sons of Tartarus and Ge. When they attempted to storm heaven, they were hurled to earth by the aid of Hercules, and buried under Mount Etna. Those of *Scandinavian mythology* were evil genii, dwelling in Jötunheim (*giantland*), who had terrible and superhuman powers, could appear and disappear, reduce and extend their stature at will, etc.

Many of the names here mentioned will be found at their appropriate places throughout the Dictionary, where *see* for further particulars.

Acamas. One of the Cyclops. (*Greek.*)

Adamastor.

Aegaeon, the hundred-handed. A Titan. (*Greek.*)

Agrios. One of the Titans. He was killed by the Parcae. (*Greek.*)

Alcion or Alcyoneus. Jupiter sent Hercules against him for stealing some of the Sun's oxen. But Hercules could not do anything, for immediately the giant touched the earth he received fresh strength (*cp. below*, Antaeus). At length Pallas carried him beyond the moon. His seven daughters were metamorphosed into halcyons. (*Argonautic Expedition*, i, 6.)

Algebar. Orion is so called by the Arabs.

Alifanfaron.

Aloeos. Son of Poseidon Canace. Each of his two sons was 27 cubits high. (*Greek.*)

Amerant. A cruel giant slain by Guy of Warwick (Percy, *Reliques.*)

Antaeus. (*Greek.*)

Arges. One of the Cyclops. (*Greek.*)

Ascapart.

Atlas.

Balan.

Bellerus. (*British legend.*)

Blunderbore. (*Nursery story.*)

Briareus. (*See below.*)

Brobdingnag. (Swift's *Gulliver's Travels.*)

Brontes. One of the Cyclops.

Burlond. (In the *Romance of Sir Tryamour.*)

Cacus.

Caligorant. An Egyptian giant. (Ariosto's *Orlando Furioso.*)

Caraculiambo. The giant that Don Quixote intended should kneel at the feet of Dulcinea.

Carus. (In the *Seven Champions.*)

Chalbroth. The stem of all the giant race. (Rabelais: *Pantagruel.*)

Christopher, St.

Coeos. Son of Heaven and Earth. He married Phoebe, and was the father of Latona. (*Greek.*)

Colebronde. (*British: Guy of Warwick.*)

Corflambo. (Spenser's *Faërie Queene.*)

Cormoran. (*British legend.*)

Cormorant. A giant discomfited by Bruin. (Spenser's *Faërie Queene*, vi, 4.)

Cottys. (*Greek.*)

Coulin.

Cyclops, The.

Dondasch. (*Eastern fable.*)

Enceladus. (*Greek.*)

Ephialtes. (*Greek.*)

Erix. (Rabelais.)

Eurytus. One of the giants that made war with the gods. Bacchus killed him with his thyrsus. (*Greek.*)

Ferragus. (*Valentine and Orson, etc.*)

Fierabras. (*Medieval romance.*)

Fingan, Finn, or Fion. (*Gaelic.*)

Gabbara. The inventor of drinking healths. (Rabelais.)

Galapas. A giant slain by King Arthur. (Malory.)

Galligantus.

Gargantua. (Rabelais.)

Garian. (In the *Seven Champions.*)

Gemmagog. (Rabelais.)

Geryoneo. (Spenser's *Faërie Queene*.)
Godmer. (*British*.)
Goemagot. (*British*.)
Gogmagog. King of the giant race of Albion; slain by Corineus.
Grangousier. Father of Gargantua. (Rabelais.)
Grantorto. (Spenser's *Faërie Queene*.)
Grumbo. (*Nursery story*.)
Guy of Warwick.
Gyges. One of the Titans. (*Greek*.)
Hapmouche. (Rabelais.)
Hippolytus. One of the giants who made war on the gods. He was killed by Hermes. (*Greek*.)
Irus.
Jotun. A giant of Jötunheim or Giant-land. (*Scandinavian*.)
Kottos. One of the Titans. He had a hundred hands. *Cp.* Aegeon, Briareus.
Malambruno. (Mentioned in *Don Quixote*, Pt II, Bk iii. ch. 45.)
Maugys. (*Mediaeval romance*.)
Mugello. (In the Charlemagne cycle.)
Orgoglio. (Spenser.)
Orion. (*Greek*.)
Otus. (*Greek*.)
Pantagruel. (Rabelais.)
Phidon. (In the *Seven Champions*.)
Polybotes. (*Greek*.)
Polyphemus. (*Greek*.)
Porphyrion. (*Greek*.)
Pyracmon. One of the Cyclops. (*Greek*.)
Raphsarus. (In the *Seven Champions*.)
Ritho. The giant who commanded King Arthur to send him his beard to complete the lining of a robe.
Skrymir. Lord of Jötunheim, the land of the giants in *Scandinavian myth*.
Steropes. One of the Cyclops. (*Greek*.)
Thaon. One of the giants who made war with the gods. He was killed by the Parcae. (*Greek*.)
Titans, The. (*Greek*.)
Tityos. (*Greek*.)
Typhoeus. (*Greek*.)
Typhon. (*Greek*.)
Yohak. The giant guardian of the caves of Babylon.
(Southey, *Thalaba*, Bk v.)

### Giants of Later Tradition.

Andronicus II was 10 ft in height. He was grandson of Alexius Comnenus. Nicetas asserts that he had seen him.

Charlemagne was nearly 8 ft in height, and was so strong he could squeeze together three horse-shoes with his hands.

Eleazer was 7 cubits (nearly 11 ft). Vitellus sent this giant to Rome; he is mentioned by Josephus. Goliath was 6 cubits and a span.

Gabara, the Arabian giant, was 9 ft 9 in. This Arabian giant is mentioned by Pliny, who says he was the tallest man seen in the days of Claudius.

Hardrada (*Harold*) was nearly 8 ft in height ('5 ells of Norway'), and was called 'the Norway giant'.

Maximinus I was 8 ft 6 in. in height. Roman emperor from about 235 to 238.

Osen (*Heinrich*) was 7 ft 6 in. in height at the age of 27, and weighed above 37 st. He was born in Norway.

Porus was 5 cubits in height (about 7½ft). He was an Indian king who fought against Alexander the Great near the Hydaspes. (Quintus Curtius, *De rebus gestis Alexandri Magni*.)

Josephus speaks of a Jew 10 ft 2 in.

Becanus asserts that he had seen a man nearly 10 ft high, and a woman fully 10 ft.

Gasper Bauhin speaks of a Swiss 8 ft in height.

Del Rio tells us he himself saw a Piedmontese in 1572 more than 9 ft in height.

A Mr Warren (in *Notes and Queries*. August 14th, 1875) tells us that his father knew a lady 9 ft in height, and adds 'her head touched the ceiling of a good-sized room'.

Vanderbrook says he saw at Congo a black man 9 ft high.

A giant was exhibited at Rouen in the early part of the 18th century 17 ft 10 in. (!) in height.

Gorapus, the surgeon, tells us of a Swedish giantess, who, at the age of 9, was over 10 ft in height.

Turner, the naturalist, tells us he *saw* in Brazil a giant 12 ft in height.

M. Thevet published, in 1575, an account of a South American giant, the skeleton of which he measured. It was 11 ft 5 in.

### Giants of Modern Times

(*more or less authenticated*).

Bamford (*Edward*) was 7 ft 4 in. He died in 1768, and was buried in St Dunstan's churchyard.

Bates (*Captain*) was 7 ft 11½ in. He was a native of Kentucky, and was exhibited in London in 1871. His wife, Anne Hannen Swan, a native of Nova Scotia, was also 7 ft 11½ in.

Blacker (*Henry*) was 7 ft 4 in. and most symmetrical. He was born at Cuckfield, in Sussex, in 1724, and was called 'The British Giant'.

Bradley (*William*) was 7 ft 9 in. in height. He was born in 1787, and died 1820. His birth is duly registered in the parish church of Market Weighton, in Yorkshire, and his right hand is preserved in the museum of the College of Surgeons.

Brice (*M. J.*) exhibited under the name of Anak, was 7 ft 8 in. in height at the age of 26. He was born in 1840 at Ramonchamp, in the Vosges, and visited England 1862–5. His arms had a stretch of 95½ in.

Brusted (*Von*) was 8 ft in height. This Norwegian giant was exhibited in London in 1880.

Busby (*John*) was 7 ft 9 in. in height, and his

brother was about the same. They were natives of Darfield, in Yorkshire.

Chang, the Chinese giant, was 8 ft 2 in. in height. He was exhibited in London in 1865–66, and again in 1880.

Cotter (*Patrick*) was 8 ft 7½ in. in height. This Irish giant died at Clifton, Bristol, in 1802. A cast of his hand is preserved in the museum of the College of Surgeons.

Daniel, the porter of Oliver Cromwell, was a man of gigantic stature.

Eleizegue (*Joachim*). Was 7 ft 10 in. in height. He was a Spaniard, and exhibited in the Cosmorama Regent Street, London, in the mid-19th century.

Evans (*William*) was 8 ft at death. He was a porter of Charles I, and died in 1632.

Frank (*Big*). Was 7 ft 8 in. in height. He was Francis Sheridan, an Irishman, and died in 1870.

Frenz (*Louis*) was 7 ft 4 in. in height. He was called 'the French giant', and his left hand is preserved in the museum of the College of Surgeons.

Gilly was 8 ft This Swedish giant was exhibited in the early part of the 10th century.

Gordon (*Alice*) was 7 ft in height. She was a native of Essex, and died in 1737, at the age of 19.

Hale (*Robert*) was 7 ft 6 in. in height. He was born at Somerton, in Norfolk, and was called 'the Norfolk giant' (1820–62).

Holmes (*Benjamin*) was 7 ft 6 in. in height. He was a Northumberland man, and was made sword-bearer of the Corporation of Worcester. He died in 1892.

Louishkin. A Russian giant of 8 ft 5 in.; drum-major of the Imperial Guards.

McDonald (*James*) was 7 ft 6 in. in height. Born in Cork, Ireland, and died in 1760.

McDonald (*Samuel*) was 6 ft 10 in. in height. This Scotchman was usually called 'Big Sam'. He was the Prince of Wales's footman, and died in 1802.

Magrath (*Cornelius*) was 7 ft 10 in. in height at the age of 16. He was an orphan reared by Bishop Berkeley, and died at the age of 20 (1740–60).

Mellon (*Edmund*) was 7 ft 6 in. in height at the age of 19. He was born at Port Leicester, in Ireland (1665–84).

Middleton (*John*) was 9 ft 3 in. in height. (*Cp.* Gabara, *above*.) 'His hand was 17 inches long and 8½ broad.' He was born at Hale, Lancashire, in the reign of James I. (Dr Plott, *Natural History of Staffordshire*, p. 295.)

Miller (*Maximilian Christopher*) was 8 ft in height. His hand measured 12 in., and his forefinger was 9 in. long. This Saxon giant died in London at the age of 60 (1674–1734).

Murphy was 8 ft 10 in. in height. An Irish giant of the late 18th century. He died at Marseilles.

O'Brien, or Charles Byrne, was 8 ft 4 in. in height. The skeleton of this Irish giant is preserved in the College of Surgeons. He died in Cockspur Street, London (1761–83).

O'Brien (*Patrick*) was 8 ft 7 in. in height. He died August 3, 1804, aged 39.

Riechart (*J. N.*) was 8 ft 4 in. in height. He was a native of Friedberg, and both his father and mother were of gigantic stature.

Salmeron (*Martin*) was 7 ft 4 in. in height. He was called 'The Mexican Giant'.

Sam (*Big*). *See* McDonald.

Sheridan. *See* Frank.

Swan (*Anne Hannen*). *See* **Bates**.

Toller (*James*) was 8 ft at the age of 24. He died in February, 1819.

In the museum of Trinity College, Dublin, is a human skeleton 8 ft 6 in. in height.

Thomas Hall, of Willingham, was 3 ft 9 in. at the age of 3.

**Giants, Battle of the.** A name given to the Battle of Marignano (1515), when Francis I of France defeated with heavy loss the Swiss mercenaries of the Italians.

**Giant's Causeway.** A formation of prismatic basaltic columns, projecting into the sea about 8 miles E.N.E. of Portrush, co. Antrim, on the north coast of Ireland. It is fabled to be the commencement of a road to be constructed by the giants across the channel, reaching from Ireland to Scotland.

**Giants' Dance, The.** Stonehenge, which Geoffrey of Monmouth says was removed from Killaraus, a mountain in Ireland, by the magical skill of Merlin.

> If you [Aurelius] are desirous to honour the burying-place of these men [who routed Hengist] with an everlasting monument, send for the Giants' Dance, which is in Killaraus, a mountain in Ireland.
>
> Geoffrey of Monmouth, *British History*, Bk viii, ch. 10

**Giant's Leap, The.** A name popularly given in many mountainous districts to two prominent rocks separated from each other by a wide chasm or open stretch of country across which some giant is fabled to have leapt while being pursued and so to have baffled his followers. Thomas Boreman, in his *Gigantick History* (1741), says that the legend of one is that Corineus, in his encounter with Goemagog, or Gogmagog, slung him on his shoulders, carried him to the top of a neighbouring cliff, and heaved him into the sea. Ever since then the cliff has been known as 'The Giant's Leap'.

**Giants' Ring, The.** A prehistoric circular mound near Milltown, Co. Down, Ireland. It is 580 ft in diameter, and has a cromlech in the centre.

**Giants' War with Zeus, The.** The War of the Giants and the War of the Titans should be kept distinct. The latter was *after* Zeus became god of heaven and earth, the former was *before* that time. Kronos, a Titan, had been exalted by his brothers to the supremacy, but Zeus dethroned him, after ten years' contest, and hurled the Titans into hell. The other war was a revolt by the giants against Zeus, which was readily put down by the help of the other gods and the aid of Hercules.

**Giaour.** Among Mohammedans, one who is not an adherent of their faith, especially a Christian; generally used with a contemptuous or insulting implication. The word is a variant of Guebre (*q.v.*).

> The city won for Allah from the Giaour,
> The Giaour from Othman's race again may wrest. Byron, *Childe Harold*, c. ii, st. 77

**Gib Cat.** A tom-cat. The male cat used to be called Gilbert. Tibert or Tybalt (*q.v.*) is the French form of Gilbert, and hence Chaucer, or whoever it was that translated that part of the *Romance of the Rose*, renders 'Thibert le Cas' by 'Gibbe, our Cat' (line 6204). Generally used of a castrated cat.

> I am as melancholy as a gib cat or a lugged bear.
> Shakespeare, *1 Henry IV*, 1, 2

**Gibberish.** Unmeaning talk; words without meaning; formerly, the lingo of rogues and gypsies. Johnson says in his *Dictionary* –

> As it was anciently written *gebrish* it is probably derived from the chymical cant [i.e., the mystical language of the alchemists], and originally implied the jargon of *Gebir* and his tribe.

But there is no evidence that the word ever was written *gebrish*, and it is much more likely to be a natural formation from *gibber* (though the latter was not, apparently, in use till later than *gibberish*), which is a variant of *jabber*.

Geber, the Arabian, was by far the greatest alchemist of the 11th century, and wrote several treatises in mystical jargon. Friar Bacon, in 1282, furnishes a specimen of this gibberish. He is giving the prescription for making gunpowder, and says –

> Sed tamen salis-petrae
> LURU MONE CAP URBE
> Et sulphuris.

The second line is merely an anagram of *Carbonum pulvere* (pulverised charcoal).

**Gibbet.** ***To gibbet the bread*** (Lincolnshire). When bread turns out ropy and is supposed to be bewitched, the good dame runs a stick through it and hangs it in the cupboard. It is gibbeted *in terrorem* to other batches.

**Gibeonite.** A slave's slave, a workman's labourer, a farmer's under-strapper, or Jack-of-all-work. The Gibeonites were made 'hewers of wood and drawers of water' to the Israelites (Josh. 9:27).

> And Giles must trudge, whoever gives command,
> A Gibeonite, that serves them all by turn.
> Bloomfield, *Farmer's Boy*

**Gibraltar.** The 'Calpe' and 'Pillars of Hercules' of the ancients. The modern name is a corruption of *Gebel-al-Tarik*, the Hill of Tarik, Tarik being a Saracen leader who, under the orders of Mousa, landed at Calpe in 710, utterly defeated Roderick, the Gothic King of Spain, and built a castle on the rock.

**Giff Gaff.** Give and take; good turn for good turn.

> I have pledged my word for your safety, and you must give me yours to be private in the matter giff gaff, you know. Scott, *Redgauntlet*, ch. xii

**Gift-horse.** ***Don't look a gift-horse in the mouth.*** When a present is made, do not enquire too minutely into its intrinsic value.

Latin: *Noli equi dentes inspicere donati. Si quis det mannos ne quaere in dentibus annos.* (*Monkish.*)

Italian: *A cavallao daio non guardar in bocca.*

French: *À cheval donné il ne faut pas regarder aux dents.*

Spanish: *A cavall dato no le mirem el diénte.*

**Gig-lamps.** Slang for spectacles, especially large round ones; the reason is obvious.

**Gigman.** A quite respectable person (in contempt); hence *gigmanity*, smug respectability, a word invented by Carlyle. A witness in the trial of John Thurtell (1823) said, 'I always thought him [Thurtell] a respectable man.' And being asked by the judge what he meant, replied, 'He [Thurtell] kept a gig.'

> A princess of the blood, yet whose father had sold his inexpressibles … in a word, Gigmanity disgigged. Carlyle, *Diamond Necklace*, ch. v

**Giggle.** ***Have you found a giggle's nest?*** A question asked in Norfolk when anyone laughs immoderately and senselessly. The meaning is obvious – have you found the place where inane laughs, or giggles, are made? *Cp.* Gape's nest.

**Giglet.** Formerly a light, wanton woman, the word is still in common use in the West of England for a giddy, romping, tomboy girl; and in Salop a flighty person is called a 'giggle'.

If this be
The recompense of striving to preserve
A wanton gigglet honest, very shortly
'Twill make all mankind panders.
Massinger, *The Fatal Dowry*, III, i (1619)

**Gilbertines.** An English religious order founded in the 12th century by St Gilbert of Sempringham. The monks observed the rule of the Augustinians and the nuns that of the Benedictines.

**Gilded Chamber, The.** A familiar name for the House of Lords.

**Gilderoy.** A famous cattle-stealer and highwayman of Perthshire, who is said to have robbed Cardinal Richelieu in the presence of the king, picked Oliver Cromwell's pocket, and hanged a judge. He was hanged in 1636; he was noted for his handsome person, and his real name was Patrick Macgregor. There are ballads on him in Percy's *Reliques*, Ritson's collection, etc., and a modern one by Campbell.

***To be hung higher than Gilderoy's kite*** is to be punished more severely than the very worst criminal. The greater the crime, the higher the gallows, was at one time a practical legal axiom. Haman, it will be remembered, was hanged on a very high gallows. The gallows of Montrose was 30 feet high. The ballad says:

Of Gilderoy sae fraid they were
They bound him mickle strong,
Tull Edenburrow they led him thair
And on a gallows hong;
They hong him high aboon the rest,
He was so trim a boy ...

**Giles.** A mildly humorous generic name for a farmer; the 'farmer's boy' in Bloomfield's poem was so called.

**Giles, St.** Patron saint of cripples. The tradition is that Childeric, king of France, accidentally wounded the hermit in the knee when hunting; and the hermit, that he might the better mortify the flesh, refusing to be cured, remained a cripple for life.

His day is September 1st, and his symbol a hind, in allusion to the 'heaven directed hind' which went daily to his cave near the mouth of the Rhone to give him milk. He is sometimes represented as an old man with an arrow in his knee and a hind by his side.

Churches dedicated to St Giles were usually situated in the outskirts of a city, and originally without the walls, cripples and beggars not being permitted to pass the gates. *See* Cripplegate.

**Giles of Antwerp.** Giles Coignet, the Flemish painter (1530–1600).

**Gills.** Humorous slang for the mouth.

***Blue about the gills.*** Down in the mouth; depressed looking.

***Rosy,*** or ***red about the gills.*** Flushed with liquor; getting 'well on'.

***White in the gills.*** Showing unmistakable signs of fear or terror – sometimes of sickness.

**Gillie.** A Gaelic word for a Highland manservant or attendant, especially one who waits on a sportsman fishing or hunting.

***Gillies' Hill.*** In the battle of Bannockburn (1314) King Robert Bruce ordered all the gillies, drivers of carts, and camp followers to go behind a height. These, when the battle seemed to favour the Scots, desirous of sharing in the plunder, rushed from their concealment with such arms as they could lay hands on; and the English, thinking them to be a new army, fled in panic. The height was ever after called The Gillies' Hill.

***Gillie-wet-foot.*** A barefooted Highland lad.

These gillie-wet-foots, as they were called, were destined to beat the bushes.
Scott, *Waverley*, ch. xiii

**Gillyflower.** Not the *July-flower*, but Fr. *giroflée*, from *girofle* (a clove), called by Chaucer 'gylofre'. The common stock, the wallflower, the rocket, the clove pink, and several other plants are so called. (Gr. *karuophullon*; Lat. *caryophyllum.*)

The fairest flowers o' the season
Are our carnations and streaked gillyflowers.
Shakespeare, *Winter's Tale*, 4, 2

**Gilpin, John**, of Cowper's famous ballad (1782) is a caricature of a Mr Beyer, an eminent linendraper at the end of Paternoster Row, where it joins Cheapside. He died 1791, at the age of 98. It was Lady Austin who told the adventure to our domestic poet, to divert him from his melancholy. The marriage adventure of Commodore Trunnion in *Peregrine Pickle* is very similar to the wedding-day adventure of John Gilpin.

John Gilpin was a citizen
Of credit and renown;
A trainband captain eke was he
Of famous London town.

**Gilt-edge Investments.** A phrase introduced in the last quarter of the 19th century to denote securities of the most reliable character, such as Consols and other Government and Colonial stock, first mortgages, debentures, and shares in first-rate companies, etc.

**Giltspur Street** (West Smithfield). The route taken by the gilt-spurs, or knights, on their way to Smithfield, where tournaments were held.

**Gimlet Eye.** A squint-eye; strictly, 'an eye that wanders obliquely', jocosely called a 'piercer'.

**Gimmer.** A jointed hinge; in Somersetshire, *gimmace.* These words, as also *gimmal*, are variants of *gemel*, a ring formed of two rings twisted together, from Lat. *gemellus*, the diminutive of *geminus*, a twin.

Their poor jades
Lob down their heads, dropping the hides and hips ...
And in their pale dull mouths the gimmal bit
Lies foul with chew'd grass, still and motionless.
Shakespeare, *Henry V*, 4, 2

**Gin.** A contraction of *Geneva*, the older name of the spirit, from Fr. *genièvre* (O.Fr. *genèvre*), juniper, the berries of which were at one time used to flavour the extract of malt in the manufacture of gin.

***Gin-sling.*** A drink made of gin, soda-water, lemon and sugar. 'Sling' has been said to be a corruption of *Collins*, the name of a waiter (period unknown) at Simmer's Hotel (now defunct), London, who is supposed to have invented it. But the term has been traced in America as far back as 1788, and it is more probable that it originated there as 'sling', in the sense of something that one *slings* down one's throat without a second thought. *Cp.* John Collins.

Rum, whiskey, brandy, gin, stinkibus, bitters, toddy, grog, slings and fifty other liquors all come under the denomination of spirits.
*Maryland Journal*, May 21, 1788

**Ginevra.** The young Italian bride who hid in a trunk with a spring-lock. The lid fell upon her, and she was not discovered till the body had become a skeleton. (Rogers, *Italy*.)

Be the cause what it might, from his offer she shrunk,
And Ginevra-like, shut herself up in a trunk.
Lowell

**Gingerbread.** Brummagem wares, showy but worthless. The allusion is to the gingerbread cakes fashioned like men, animals, etc., and profusely decorated with gold leaf or Dutch leaf, which looked like gold, commonly sold at fairs up to the middle of the 19th century.

***To take the gilt off the gingerbread.*** To destroy the illusion; to appropriate all the fun or profit and leave the *caput mortuum* behind.

**Gingerly.** Cautiously, with hesitating, mincing, or faltering steps. The word is over 400 years old in English; it is nothing to do with ginger, but is probably from O.Fr. *gensour*, comparative of *gent*, delicate, dainty.

They spend their goods ... upon their dansing minions, that mins it ful gingerlie, God wot, tripping like gotes, that an egge would not brek under their feet.
Stubbes, *Anatomy of Abuses*, II, i (1583)

Gingerly, as if treading upon eggs, Cuddie began to ascend the well-known pass.
Scott, *Old Mortality*, ch. xxv

**Gingham.** A playful equivalent of umbrella; properly, a cotton or linen fabric usually dyed in stripes; so called from a Malay word *ginggang* (that came to us through Dutch), meaning striped. Littré's derivation of *gingham* from *Guingamp*, in Brittany, has nothing to support it.

**Ginnunga Gap.** The abyss between Niflheim (the region of fog) and Muspelheim (the region of heat). It existed before either land or sea, heaven or earth as a chaotic whirlpool. (*Scandinavian mythology*.)

**Giovanni, Don.** *See* Don Juan.

**Gipsy.** A member of a dark-skinned nomadic race which first appeared in England about the beginning of the 16th century, and, as they were thought to have come from Egypt, were named *Egyptians*, which soon became corrupted to *Gypcians*, and so to its present form. They call themselves *Romany* (from Gypsy *rom*, a man, husband), which is also the name of their language – a debased Hindi dialect with large additions of words from Persian, Armenian, and many European languages.

The name of the largest group of European gypsies is *Atzigan*; this, in Turkey and Greece, became *Tshingian*, in the Balkans and Roumania *Tsigan*, in Hungary *Czigany*, in Germany *Zigeuner*, in Italy *Zingari*, in Portugal *Cigano*, and in Spain *Gitano*. The original name is said to mean 'dark man'. *See also* Bohemian.

There is a legend that the gypsies are waifs and strays on the earth, because they refused to shelter the Virgin and her child in their flight to Egypt.

**Gipsy, The.** Antony de Solario the Italian painter and illuminator, *Il Zingaro* (about 1382–1455).

**Giralda.** The name given to the great square tower of the cathedral at Seville (formerly a Moorish minaret), which is surmounted by a statue of St Faith, so pivoted as to turn with the wind. *Giralda* is a Spanish word, and means a weather-vane.

**Gird.** ***To gird up the loins.*** To prepare for hard work or a journey. The Jews wore a girdle only when at work or on a journey. Even to the present day, Eastern people, who wear loose dresses, gird them about the loins.

> The loose tunic was an inconvenient walking dress; therefore, when persons went from home, they tied a girdle round it. (2 Kings, 4:2; 9:1; Is. 5:27; Jer. 1:17; John 21: 7; Acts 12:8)

***To gird with the sword.*** To raise to a peerage. It was the Saxon method of investiture to an earldom, continued after the Conquest. Thus, Richard I 'girded with the sword' Hugh de Pudsey, the aged Bishop of Durham, making (as he said) 'a young earl of an old prelate'.

**Girdle.** ***A good name is better than a golden girdle.*** A good reputation is better than money. It used to be customary to carry money in the belt, or in a purse suspended from it, and a girdle of gold meant a 'purse of gold'. The French proverb, *Bonne renommée vaut mieux que ceinture dorée*, refers rather to the custom of wearing girdles of gold tissue, forbidden, in 1420, to women of bad character.

***Children under the girdle.*** Not yet born.

***He has a large mouth but small girdle.*** Great expenses but small means.

***He has undone her girdle.*** Taken her for his wife. The Roman bride wore a chaplet of flowers on her head, and a girdle of sheep's wool about her waist. A part of the marriage ceremony was for the bridegroom to loose this.

***If he be angry, he knows how to turn his girdle*** (*Much Ado about Nothing*, 5, 1). He knows how to prepare himself to fight. Before wrestlers engaged in combat, they turned the buckle of their girdle behind them. Thus, Sir Ralph Winwood writes to Mr Secretary Cecil:

> I said, 'What I spake was not to make him angry.' He replied, 'If I were angry, I might turn the buckle of my girdle behind me.' Dec. 17, 1602

***The girdle of Venus.*** *See* Cestus.

***To put a girdle round the earth.*** To travel or go round it. Puck says, 'I'll put a girdle round about the earth in forty minutes.' (*Midsummer Night's Dream*, 2, 2.)

**Girl.** This word is not present in Anglo-Saxon, but appears in Middle English (13th cent.), and its etymology has given rise to a host of guesses. It was formerly applicable to a child of either sex (a boy was sometimes distinguished as a 'knave girl'), and is nowadays applied to an unmarried woman of almost any age. It is probably a diminutive of some lost word cognate with Pomeranian *goer* and old Low German *gör*, a child. It appears nearly 70 times in Shakespeare, but only twice in the Authorised Version (Joel 3:3; Zech. 8:5).

> Bailey suggests Lat. *garrula*, a chatterbox.
> Minshew ventures for the Italian *girella*, a weathercock.
> Skinner goes in for A.S. *ceorl*, a churl.
> Junius thought it was from Welsh *herlodes*, and Dr Hickes from Icelandic *karlinna*, a woman.

**Girondists,** or **The Gironde.** The moderate republicans in the first French Revolution (1791–93). So called from the department of Gironde, which chose for the Legislative Assembly five men who greatly distinguished themselves for their oratory, and formed a political party. They were subsequently joined by Brissot (and were hence sometimes called the *Brissotins*), Condorcet, and the adherents of Roland.

**Gis.** A corruption of Jesus or J. H. S. Ophelia says, 'By Gis and by St Charity' (*Hamlet*, 4, 5).

**Gitano.** *See* Gipsy.

**Give.** For phrases such as *Give the devil his due*, *Give a dog a bad name and hang him*, *To give one beans*, etc., *see* the principal noun.

***A given name.*** A baptismal name, that we call a Christian name, is so called in America.

***To give and take.*** To be fair; in intercourse with others to practise forbearance and consideration. In horse-racing a *give and take plate* is a prize for a race in which the runners which exceed a standard height carry more, and those that come short of it less, than the standard weight.

***To give away.*** To hand the bride in marriage to the bridegroom, to act the part of the bride's father. Also, to let out a secret, inadvertently or on purpose; to betray an accomplice.

***To give in.*** To confess oneself beaten, to yield.

***To give it anyone, to give it him hot.*** To scold or thrash a person. As 'I gave it him right and left.' 'I'll give it you when I catch you.'

***To give oneself away.*** To betray oneself by some thoughtless action or remark; to damage one's own cause by carelessly letting something out.

***To give out.*** To make public. Also, to come to an end, to become exhausted; as 'My strength', or 'My money, has quite given out.'

***To give what for.*** To administer a good licking; to chastise soundly.

***To give way.*** To break down; to yield.

**Gizzard.** The strong, muscular second stomach of birds, where the food is ground, attributed humorously to man in some phrases.

***Don't fret your gizzard.*** Don't be so anxious; don't worry yourself.

***That stuck in his gizzard.*** Annoyed him, was more than he could stomach, or digest.

**Gjallarhorn.** *See* Giallarhorn.

**Glacis.** The sloping bank on the outer edge of the *covered way* in old fortifications.

**Glad.** ***To give the glad eye.*** *See* Eye.

***Glad rags.*** Evening dress; a common Americanism.

**Gladsheim.** A territory in the old Norse heaven where was situated Valhalla (*q.v.*) and twelve seats besides the throne of Alfader. The name means 'the world of gladness'.

**Gladstone.** A leather bag of various sizes, all convenient to be carried, is so called from the famous statesman (1809–98). His name was also given to cheap claret, because, in 1860, when Chancellor of the Exchequer, he reduced the duty on French wines.

**Glaeston's Sow.** *See* Glastonbury.

**Glamorgan.** Geoffrey of Monmouth says that Cundah and Morgan, the sons of Gonorill and Regan, usurped the crown at the death of Cordeilla. The former resolved to reign alone, chased Morgan into Wales, and slew him at the foot of a hill, hence called Gla-Morgan or Glyn-Morgan, valley of Morgan. (*See* Spenser, *Faërie Queene* II, x, 33.) The name is really Welsh for 'the district by the side of the sea' (*gwlad*, district, *mor*, the sea, *gant*, side).

**Glasgow, Arms of.** *See* Kentigern, St.

**Glasgow Magistrate.** A salt herring; so called because when George IV visited Glasgow some wag placed a salt herring on the iron guard of the carriage of a well-known magistrate who formed one of the deputation to receive him.

**Glass Breaker.** A wine-bibber. In the early part of the 19th century it was by no means unusual with topers to break off the stand of their wine glass, so that they might not be able to set it down, but were compelled to drink it clean off, without heel-taps.

> Troth, ye're nae glass-breaker; and neither am I, unless it be a screed wi' the neighbours, or when I'm on a ramble.
>
> Scott, *Guy Mannering*, ch. xlv

**Glass Houses. *Those who live in glass houses should not throw stones*.** Those who are open to criticism should be very careful how they criticise others. An old proverb found in varying forms from the time of Chaucer at least (*Troylus and Cresseide*, Bk ii). *Cp. also* Matt. 7:1–4.

**Glass Slipper** (of Cinderella). *See* Cinderella.

**Glasse, Mrs Hannah.** A name immortalised by the reputed saying in a cookery book, 'First catch your hare' (*which see under* Catch). It was a pseudonym of Dr John Hill (1716–75).

**Glassite.** A Sandemanian (*q.v.*).

**Glastonbury.** An ancient town in Somerset, dating from Roman times, and famous in the Arthurian and Grail cycles as the place to which Joseph of Arimathea came and as the burial place of King Arthur (*see* Avalon). It was here that Joseph planted his staff – the famous *Glastonbury Thorn* – which took root and burst into leaf every Christmas Eve. This name is now given to a variety of Crataegus, or hawthorn, which flowers about old Christmas Day, and is fabled to have sprung from Joseph's staff.

Selden, in his *Illustrations of Drayton*, says King Arthur's tomb was 'betwixt two pillars', and he adds –

> Henry II gave command to Henry de Blois, the abbot, to make great search for the body, which was found in a wooden coffin some sixteen foote deepe; and afterwards was found a stone on whose lower side was fixt a leaden cross with the name inscribed.

The authority of Selden no doubt is very great, but it is too great a tax on our credulity to credit this statement.

The name, A.S. *Glaestingaburh*, means 'the city of the Glaestings'. Its origin, says Professor Freeman,

> lurks in a grotesque shape, in that legend of Glaesting and his sow, a manifestly English legend, which either William of Malmesbury himself or some interpolator at Glastonbury has strangely thrust into the midst of the British legends. Glaesting's lost sow leads him by a long journey to an apple tree by the old church; pleased with the land, he takes his family, the Glaestingas, to dwell there.
>
> *English Towns*, p. 95

**Glauber Salts.** A strong purgative, so called from Johann Rudolph Glauber (1604–68), a German alchemist who discovered it in 1658 in his search for the philosopher's stone. It is sodium sulphate, crystallised below 34° C.

**Glaucus.** The name of a number of heroes in classical legend, including: (1) A fisherman of Boeotia, who became a sea-god endowed with the gift of prophecy and who instructed Apollo in the art of soothsaying. Milton alludes to him in *Comus*

(l. 895), and Spenser mentions him in the *Faërie Queene* (IV, xi, 13):

And Glaucus, that wise soothsayer understood

and Keats gives his name to the old magician whom Endymion met in Neptune's hall beneath the sea (*Endymion*, Bk iii). *See also* Scylla.

(2) A son of Sisyphus who would not allow his horses to breed; the goddess of Love so infuriated them that they killed him. Hence, the name is given to one who is so overfond of horses that he is ruined by them.

(3) A commander of the Lycians in the War of Troy (*Iliad*, Bk vi) who was connected by ties of ancient family friendship with his enemy, Diomed. When they met in battle they not only refrained from fighting but exchanged arms in token of amity. As the armour of the Lycian was of gold, and that of the Greek of brass, it was like bartering precious stones for French paste. Hence the phrase *A Glaucus swap*, of which the story of Moses, in Goldsmith's *Vicar of Wakefield*, and his bargain with the spectacle-seller is a good example.

**Glazier.** ***Is your father a glazier?*** Does he make windows, for you stand in my light and expect me to see through you?

**Gleek** (Ger. *gleich*, like). An old card-game, the object being to get three cards all alike, as three aces, three kings, etc. *Four* cards all alike, as four aces, four kings, etc., is known as *mournival.*

A mournival of aces, gleek of knaves,
Just nine a-piece. Albumazar, iii, 5

Poole in his *English Parnassus* (about 1650) called the four elements *Nature's first mournival.*

Gleek is played by three persons. The twos and threes are thrown out of the pack; twelve cards are then dealt to each player, and eight are left for stock, which is offered in rotation to the players for purchase. The trumps are called Tiddy, Tumbler, Tib, Tom, and Towser. Mention of it is of frequent occurrence in 16th and early 17th century literature.

**Gleipnir** (Old Norse, *the fetter*). In Scandinavian legend, the chain by which the wolf Fenrir was bound. It was extremely light, and made of the noise made by the footfalls of a cat, the roots of the mountains, the sinews of bears, the breath of fishes, the beards of women, and the spittle of birds. When the chain breaks, the wolf will be free and the end of the world will be at hand.

**Glencoe.** ***The massacre of Glencoe.*** The treacherous massacre of the Macdonalds of Glencoe on February 13th, 1692. Pardon had been offered to all Jacobites who submitted on or before December 31st, 1691. Mac-Ian, chief of the Macdonalds of Glencoe, delayed till the last minute, and, on account of the state of the roads, did not make his submission before January 6th. The Master of Stair (Sir John Dalrymple) obtained the king's permission 'to extirpate the set of thieves'. Accordingly, on February 1st, 120 soldiers, led by a Captain Campbell, marched to Glencoe, told the clan they were come as friends, and lived peaceably among them for twelve days; but on the morning of the 13th, the glenmen, to the number of thirty-eight, were scandalously murdered, their huts set on fire, and their flocks and herds driven off as plunder. Campbell and Scott have written poems, and Talfourd a play on the subject.

**Glendoveer.** The name given by Southey in his *Curse of Kehama* to a kind of sylph, the most lovely of the good spirits. The name is Sanskrit *ganharva* through the Fr. *grandouver.*

I am a blessèd Glendoveer,
'Tis mine to speak and yours to hear.
*Rejected Addresses* (Imitations of Southey)

**Glim.** *See* Douse the Glim.

**Gloria.** A cup of coffee with brandy in it instead of milk; also, a mixture of silk and wool used for covering umbrellas, etc.

**Gloria in Excelsis.** The doxology, 'Glory be to the Father', etc., so called because it begins with the words sung by the angels at Bethlehem. The first verse is said to be by St Basil, and the latter portion is ascribed to Telesphorus, AD 139. During the Arian controversy it ran thus: 'Glory be *to* the Father *by* the Son, and *in* the Holy Ghost'.

**Gloriana.** (Queen Elizabeth considered as a sovereign.) Spenser's name in his *Faërie Queene* for the typification of Queen Elizabeth. She held an annual feast for twelve days, during which time adventurers appeared before her to undertake whatever task she chose to impose upon them. On one occasion twelve knights presented themselves before her, and their exploits form the scheme of Spenser's allegory. The poet intended to give a separate book to each knight, but only six and a half books remain.

**Glorious John.** John Dryden, the poet (1631–1701).

**Glorious First of June.** June 1st, 1794, when Lord Howe, who commanded the Channel fleet, gained a decisive victory over the French.

**Glorious Uncertainty of the Law, The,** 1756. The toast of Mr Wilbraham at a dinner given to the judges and counsel in Serjeants Hall. This dinner was given soon after Lord Mansfield had overruled several ancient legal decisions and had introduced many innovations in the practice.

**Glory, Hand of.** In folk lore, a dead man's hand, preferably one cut from the body of a man who has been hanged (*see* Dead Man's Hand *under* Hand), supposed to possess certain magical properties.

> De hand of glory is hand cut off from a dead man as have been hanged for murther, and dried very nice in de shmoke of juniper wood.
>
> Scott, *The Antiquary* (Dousterwivel)

**Glory-hole.** A small room, cupboard, etc., where all sorts of rubbish and odds and ends are heaped.

**Glory be to the Father.** *See* Gloria in Excelsis.

**Gloucester.** The Celtic name of the town was *Caer Glou* (bright city); the Romans Latinised this to *Glevum colonia*; the Saxons restored the old *Glou*, and added *ceaster*, to signify it had been a Roman camp. Geoffrey of Monmouth says, when Arviragus married Genuissa, daughter of Claudius Caesar, he induced the emperor to build a city on the spot where the nuptials were solemnised; this city was called *Caer-Clau*'. 'Some', continues the same 'philologist', 'derive the name from the Duke Gloius, a son of Claudius, born in Britain on the very spot.'

**Glove.** In the days of chivalry it was customary for knights to wear a lady's glove in their helmets, and to defend it with their life.

> One ware on his headpiece his ladies sleve, and another bare on hys helme the glove of his dearlynge. Hall, *Chronicle*, *Henry IV*

On ceremonial occasions gloves are not worn in the presence of royalty, because one is to stand unarmed, with the helmet off the head and gauntlets off the hands, to show that there is no hostile intention.

Gloves used to be worn by the clergy to indicate that their hands are clean and not open to bribes; and in an assize without a criminal, the sheriff presents the judge with a pair of white gloves. Anciently, judges were not allowed to wear gloves on the bench; so to give a judge a pair of gloves symbolised that he need not take his seat.

***A round with gloves.*** A friendly contest; a fight with gloves.

> Will you point out how this is going to be a genteel round with gloves?
>
> Watson, *The Web of the Spider*, ch. ix

***Glove money.*** A bribe, a perquisite: so called from the ancient custom of presenting a pair of gloves to a person who undertook a cause for you. Mrs Croaker presented Sir Thomas More, the Lord Chancellor, with a pair of gloves lined with forty pounds in 'angels', as a 'token'. Sir Thomas kept the gloves, but returned the lining.

***Hand and glove.*** Sworn friends; on most intimate terms; close companions, like glove and hand.

> And prate and preach about what others prove,
> As if the world and they were hand and glove.
>
> Cowper, *Table Talk*, 172

***He bit his glove.*** He resolved on mortal revenge. On the 'Border', to bite the glove was considered a pledge of deadly vengeance.

> Stern Rutherford right little said,
> But bit his glove and shook his head.
>
> Scott, *Lay of the Last Minstrel*

***Here I throw down my glove.*** I challenge you. In allusion to an ancient custom of a challenger throwing his glove or gauntlet at the feet of the person challenged, and bidding him to pick it up. *To take up the glove* means to accept the challenge.

> I will throw my glove to Death itself, that there's no maculation in thy heart.
>
> Skakespeare, *Troilus and Cressida*, 4, 4

***Right as my glove.*** The phrase, says Scott, comes from the custom of pledging a glove as the signal of irrefragable faith. (*The Antiquary*.)

***You owe me a pair of gloves.*** A small present. The gift of a pair of gloves was at one time a perquisite of those who performed small services, such as pleading your cause, arbitrating your quarrel, or showing you some favour which could not be charged for, and often it was lined with glove money (*q.v.*). Relics of this ancient custom still survive here and there in the presentation of gloves to those attending weddings and funerals.

There also existed at one time the claim of a pair of gloves by a lady who chose to salute a gentleman caught napping in her company. In *The Fair Maid of Perth*, by Scott, Catherine steals from her chamber on St Valentine's morn, and, catching Henry Smith asleep, gives him a kiss. The glover says to him:

> Come into the booth with me, my son, and I will furnish thee with a fitting theme. Thou knowest the maiden who ventures to kiss a sleeping man wins of him a pair of gloves. Ch. v

Henry later offers the gloves, and Catherine accepts them.

**Glubdubdrib.** The land of sorcerers and magicians visited by Gulliver in his *Travels*. (*Swift*.)

**Gluckists.** A foolish rivalry excited in Paris (1774–80) between the admirers of Gluck and those of Piccinni (*see* Piccinnists) – the former a German musical composer, and the latter an Italian. Marie Antoinette was a Gluckist, and consequently Young France favoured the rival claimant. In the streets, coffee-houses, private houses, and even schools, the merits of Gluck and Piccinni were canvassed; and all Paris was ranged on one side or the other. This was, in fact, a contention between the relative merits of the German and Italian school of music.

**Glum.** A Norse hero (*Nials Saga*). He had a sword and cloak given him by his grandfather, which brought good luck to their possessors; but he gave the sword to Asgrim and the cloak to Gizur the White, after which everything went wrong with him. Old and blind, he retained his cunning long after he had lost his luck.

**Glumdalclitch.** A girl, nine years old, and only forty feet high, who had charge of Gulliver in Brobdingnag. (Swift, *Gulliver's Travels*.)

> Soon as Glumdalclitch missed her pleasing care,
> She wept, she blubbered, and she tore her hair.
> Pope

**Glutton, The.** Vitellius, the Roman emperor (15–69), reigned from January 4th to December 22nd, AD 69, was so called. *See* Apicius.

**Gnomes.** According to the Rosicrucian system, a misshapen elemental spirit, dwelling in the bowels of the earth, and guarding the mines and quarries. The word seems to have been first used (perhaps invented) by Paracelsus, and to be Gr. *ge-nomos*, earth-dweller. *Cp.* Salamander.

> The four elements are inhabited by spirits called sylphs, gnomes, nymphs, and salamanders. The gnomes or demons of the earth, delight in mischief.
> Pope, *Pref. Letter to the Rape of the Lock*

**Gnostics.** The *knowers*, opposed to *believers*, various sects in the first six centuries of the Christian era, which tried to accommodate Christianity to the speculations of Pythagoras, Plato, and other Greek and Oriental philosophers. They taught that knowledge, rather than mere faith, is the true key of salvation. In the Gnostic creed Christ is esteemed merely as an eon or divine attribute personified, like Mind, Truth, Logos, Church, etc., the whole of which eons made up this divine pleroma or fullness. St Paul, in several of his epistles, speaks of this 'Fullness (pleroma) of God'. (Gr. *Gnosticos*; *cp.* Agnostic.)

**Go. *A go.*** A fix, a scrape; as in *here's a go* or *here's a pretty go* – here's a mess or awkward state of affairs. Also a share or portion; as *I'd like another go of cheese*; or a tot, as *a go of gin*.

***A go-between.*** One who acts as an intermediary; one who interposes between two parties.

***All the go.*** All the fashion, quite in vogue. Drapers will tell you that certain goods 'go off well'. They are in great demand, all the mode.

> Her *carte* is hung in the West-end shops,
> With her name in full on the white below;
> And all day long there's a big crowd stops
> To look at the lady who's 'all the go'.
> Sims, *Ballads of Babylon* ('Beauty and the Beast')

***A regular goer.*** One who goes the pace; a 'hot lot'; a fast young man or woman.

***Go as you please.*** Not bound by any rules; do as you like; unceremonious.

***Go it, you cripples!*** Fight on, you simpletons; scold away, you silly or quarrelsome ones. An ironical form of encouragement.

***Go to!*** A curtailed oath. 'Go to the devil!' or some such phrase.

> *Cassius*: I [am] abler than yourself
> To make conditions.
> *Brutus*: Go to! You are not, Cassius.
> Shakespeare, *Julius Caesar*, 4, 3

> Go to Banff, and bottle skate.
> Go to Bath, and get your head shaved.
> Go to Bungay, and get your breeches mended.
> Go to Hexham. A kind of Alsatia or sanctuary in the reign of Henry VIII.
> Go to Jericho. (*See* Jericho.)
> Go to Putney; and many similar phrases humorously expressing contempt.

***Go-to-meeting clothes, behaviour, etc.*** One's best.

***I'll go through fire and water to serve you.*** *See* Fire.

***I've gone and done it!*** or ***I've been and gone and done it!*** There! I've done the very thing I oughtn't to have done! I've put my foot in it properly!

***It is no go.*** It is not workable. *Ça ira* in the French Revolution (it will go) is a similar phrase.

***That goes for nothing.*** It doesn't count; it doesn't matter one way or the other.

***That goes without saying.*** The French say: *Cela va sans dire*. That is a self-evident fact; well understood or indisputable.

***To give one the go-by.*** To pass without notice, to leave in the lurch.

***To go ahead.*** To prosper, make rapid progress towards ultimate success.

***To go back on one's word.*** To fail to keep one's promise.

***To go barmy, by the board, the whole hog, to the wall, with the stream,*** etc. In these and many similar phrases *see under* the principal word.

***To go for a man.*** To attack him, either physically or in argument, etc.

***To go farther and fare worse.*** To take more pains and trouble and yet find oneself in a worse position.

***To go hard with one.*** To prove a troublesome matter. 'It will go hard with me before I give up the attempt', i.e. I won't give it up until I have tried every means to success, no matter how difficult, dangerous, or painful it may be.

***To go in for.*** To follow as a pursuit or occupation; as 'he goes in for golf' or 'engineering'.

***To go it.*** To be fast, extravagant, headstrong in one's behaviour and habits. *To go it blind* is to act without stopping to deliberate. In poker, if a player chooses to 'go it blind', he doubles the *ante* before looking at his cards.

***To go off one's head, one's nut, onion, rocker,*** etc. Completely to lose control of oneself; to go mad, either temporarily or permanently; to go out of one's mind.

***To go on all fours.*** *See* All Fours.

***To go to the wall.*** *See* Wall.

***To go under.*** To become ruined; to fail utterly, lose caste, become one of the 'submerged tenth'.

Also to pass as, to be known as; as 'He goes under the name of "Mr Taylor", but we all know he is really "Herr Schneider" '.

**Goat.** From very early times the *goat* has been connected with the idea of sin (*cp.* Scapegoat) and associated with devil-lore. It is an old superstition in England and Scotland that a goat is never seen during the whole of a twenty-four hours, because once every day it pays a visit to the devil to have its beard combed. Formerly the devil himself was frequently depicted as a goat; and the animal is also a type of lust and lechery.

***Don't play the giddy goat!*** Don't make a ridiculous fool of yourself; keep yourself within bounds. A goat frolicking about is a very absurd sight.

***The Goat and Compasses.*** A tavern sign dating from the time of the Commonwealth; a corruption of 'God encompasses (us)'.

Some say it is the carpenters' arms – three goats and a chevron, the chevron being mistaken for a pair of compasses.

***To get one's goat.*** An Americanism for annoying one, making him wild, 'getting his rag out'; as, 'It gets my goat right and proper to see a man knocking his wife about.'

***To separate the sheep from the goats.*** To divide the worthy from the unworthy, part the good from the evil. A Biblical phrase, the allusion being to Matt. 25:32, 33:

> And before him shall be gathered all nations; and he shall separate them one from another, as a shepherd divideth his sheep from the goats.
>
> And he shall set the sheep on his right hand, but the goats on the left.

**Goatsucker** or **Goat-owl.** A name popularly given to the nightjar, from the ancient and very widespread belief that this bird sucks the udders of goats. In Greek, Latin, French, German, Spanish, and some other languages its name has the same signification.

**Gobbler.** A turkey-cock is so called from its cry.

**Gobelin Tapestry.** So called from the Gobelins, a French family of dyers founded by Jean Gobelin (d.1476); their tapestry works were taken over by Louis XVI as a royal establishment about 1670, and are still in the Faubourg St Marcel, Paris.

**Goblin.** A familiar demon, dwelling, according to popular belief, in private houses and chinks of trees; and in many parts miners attribute those strange noises heard in mines to them. The word is the Fr. *gobelin*, probably a diminutive of the surname *Gobel*, but perhaps connected with Gr. *kobalos*, an impudent rogue, a mischievous sprite, or with the Ger. *kobold* (*q.v.*). As a specimen of forced etymology, it may be mentioned that Johnson, in his *Dictionary*, records that:

> this word some derive from the *Gibellines*, a faction in Italy; so that *elfe* and *goblin* is *Guelph* and *Gibelline,* because the children of either party were terrified by their nurses with the name of the other (!)

**God.** A word common, in slightly varying forms, to all Teutonic languages, probably from a Sanskrit root, *ghu* – to worship; it is in no way connected with *good.*

It was Hiero, tyrant of Syracuse, who asked Simonides the poet, 'What is God?' Simonides asked to have a day to consider the question. Next day he desired two more days for reflection, then four, and so on. Hiero, greatly astonished, asked the reason, and Simonides made answer, 'The longer I think on the subject, the farther I seem from making it out.'

It was Voltaire who said, '*Si Dieu n'existait pas, il faudrait l'inventer.*'

***Gods of Classical Mythology.*** *See also* Deities (*and the individual names*).

*Greek and Roman* gods were divided into *Dii Majores* and *Dii Minores*, the greater and the lesser. The Dii Majores were twelve in number:

| Latin. | Greek. |
|---|---|
| Jupiter (*King*) | Zeus. |
| Apollo (*the sun*) | Apollon. |
| Mars (*war*) | Ares. |
| Mercury (*messenger*) | Hermes. |
| Neptune (*ocean*) | Poseidon. |
| Vulcan (*smith*) | Hephaistos. |
| Juno (*Queen*) | Hera. |
| Ceres (*tillage*) | Demeter. |
| Diana (*moon, hunting*) | Artemis. |
| Minerva (*wisdom*) | Athena. |
| Venus (*love and beauty*) | Aphrodite. |
| Vesta (*home-life*) | Hestia. |

Their blood was *ichor*, their food was *ambrosia*, their drink *nectar*.

*Four other deities are often referred to*:

| | |
|---|---|
| Bacchus (*wine*) | Dionysos. |
| Cupid (*the lad Love*) | Eros. |
| Pluto (*of the Inferno*) | Pluton. |
| Saturn (*time*) | Kronos. |

Of these, Proserpine (Latin) and Persephone (*Greek*) was the wife of Pluto, Cybele was the wife of Saturn, and Rhea of Kronos.

In Hesiod's time the number of gods was thirty thousand, and that none might be omitted the Greeks observed a Feast of the Unknown Gods.

> Some thirty thousand gods on earth we find
> Subjects of Zeus, and guardians of mankind.
>
> *Hesiod*, i, 250

***A god from the machine.*** *See* Deus ex Machina.

***Among the gods.*** In the uppermost gallery of a theatre, just below the ceiling, which was frequently embellished with a representation of a mythological heaven. The French call this celestial region *paradis*.

***Full of the god.*** Inspired, maenadic. (Lat. *Dei plenus.*)

***God bless the Duke of Argyle.*** *See* Argyle.

***God helps those who help themselves.*** In French, *Aide-toi, le ciel t'aidera.* (*La Fontaine*, vi, 18.) Regnier (*Sat*. xiii) had previously said *Aidez-vous seulement et Dieu vous aidera*; and among the *Fragments* of Euripides is:

> Bestir yourself, and then call on the gods,
> For heaven assists the man that laboureth.
>
> No. 435

***God made the country, and man made the town.*** Cowper in *The Task* (The Sofa 749). *Cp.* Cowley's 'God the first garden made, and the first city Cain' (*On Gardens*). Varro says in *De Re Rustica, Divina Natura dedit agros; ars humana aedificavit urbes.*

***God save the king.*** *See* National Anthem.

***God sides with the strongest.*** Fortune favours the strong. Napoleon I said, *Le bon Dieu est toujours du côté des gros bataillons*, God is always on the side of the big battalions, but the phrase is far older than his day. Tacitus (*Hist*. iv, 17) has *Deos fortioribus adesse*, the gods are on the side of the strongest; the Comte de Bussy, writing to the Count of Limoges, used it in 1677, as also did Voltaire in his Epistle *à M. le Riche*, February 6th, 1770. *Cp. also* Gibbon:

> The winds and the waves are always on the side of the ablest navigators.
>
> *Decline and Fall*, ch. lxviii

***God tempers the wind to the shorn lamb.*** The phrase comes from Sterne's *Sentimental Journey* (1782), *Maria*; but it was not original with Sterne, for *Dieu mesure le froid à la brebis tondue* appears in Henri Estienne's *Les Prèmices* (1594), and 'To a close-shorn sheep God gives wind by measure' in Herbert's *Jacula Prudentum* (1640). It may be noticed that though Sterne's version is more poetical, he did not improve the sense in substituting *lamb* for *sheep*; for lambs never are shorn!

***Man proposes, God disposes.*** An old proverb found in Hebrew, Greek, Latin, etc. In Prov. 16:9, it is rendered:

> A man's heart deviseth his way; but the Lord directeth his steps;

and Publius Syrus (No. 216) has:

> Homo semper aliud, Fortuna aliud cogitat
> (Man has one thing in view, Fate has another).

*Cp. also* Thomas à Kempis's *Imitatio* (I, xix):

> Homo instituit ille quidem, sed Deus decernit; and Dis aliter visum (the gods have willed otherwise). Virgil, *Aeneid*, ii, 428

***Whom God would destroy He first makes mad.*** A translation of the Latin version (*Quos Deus vult perdere, prius dementat*) of one of the *Fragments* of Euripides. *Cp. also Stultum facit fortuna quem vult perdere* (Publius Syrus, No. 612). He whom Fortuna would ruin he robs of his wits.

> For those whom God to ruin has designed,
> He fits for fate, and first destroys their mind.
>
> Dryden, *Hind and the Panther*, iii, 1093

***Whom the gods love die young.*** The Lat. *Quem Di diligunt, adolescens moritur* (Plautus: *Bacchides*, IV, vii, 18). Byron says:

> Heaven gives its favourites early death.
>
> *Childe Harold*, iv, 102

And again:

'Whom the gods love die young', was said of yore,
And many deaths do they escape by this;
The death of friends, and that which slays even more –
The death of friendship, love, youth, all that is,
Except mere breath; and since the silent shore
Awaits at last even those who longest miss
The old archer's shafts, perhaps the early grave
Which men weep over may be meant to save.

*Don Juan*, iv, 12

**God's Acre.** A churchyard or cemetery.

I like that ancient Saxon phrase, which calls
The burial ground God's Acre. Longfellow

**Godchild.** One for whom a person stands sponsor in baptism. A godson or a goddaughter.

**Goddam** or **Godon.** A name given by the French to the English at least as early as the 15th century, on account of the favourite oath of the English soldiers which was looked upon almost as a shibboleth. Joan of Arc is reported to have used the word on a number of occasions in contemptuous reference to her enemies; and in comparatively recent times it has appeared in farces, humorous papers, etc., as an equivalent for *un Anglais*.

**Godfather.** ***To stand godfather.*** To pay the reckoning, godfathers being generally chosen for the sake of the present they are expected to make the child at the christening or in their wills.

**Godiva, Lady.** Patroness of Coventry. In 1040, Leofric, Earl of Mercia and Lord of Coventry, imposed certain exactions on his tenants, which his lady besought him to remove; he said he would do so if she would ride naked through the town. Lady Godiva took him at his word, and the Earl faithfully kept his promise.

The legend is recorded by 'Matthew of Westminster' (early 14th cent.); and an addition of the time of Charles II asserts that everyone kept indoors at the time, but a certain tailor peeped through his window to see the lady pass and was struck blind in consequence. He has ever since been called 'Peeping Tom of Coventry'. The incident of Lady Godiva's ride is still annually commemorated at Coventry by a procession in which 'Lady Godiva' plays a leading part.

The privilege of cutting wood in the Herduoles, by the parishioners of St Briavel's Castle, in Gloucestershire, is said to have been granted by the Earl of Hereford (a former Lord of the Forest of Dean) on the same terms as those accepted by Lady Godiva.

**Godless Florin.** *See* Graceless Florin.

**Godmer.** A British giant, son of Albion, slain by Canutus, one of the companions of Brute.

Those three monstrous stones ...
Which that huge son of hideous Albion.
Great Godmer, threw in fierce contention
At bold Canutus: but of him was slain.

Spenser, *Faërie Queene*, II, x, 11

**Godolphin Barb.** *See* Darley Arabian.

**Goël.** The name among the ancient Jews for one who redeemed back to the family property that a member of it had sold; as this was usually done by the next of kin, on whom also devolved the duty of the avenger of blood, the name was later applied specially to the avenger of blood.

**Goemot** or **Goëmagot.** Names given in Geoffrey of Monmouth's *Chronicles* (I, xvi), Spenser's *Faërie Queene* (II, x, 10), etc., to Gogmagog (*q.v.*), the giant who dominated over the western horn of England. He was slain by Corineus, one of the companions of Brute.

**Gog** and **Magog.** In *British legend*, the sole survivors of a monstrous brood, the offspring of the thirty-three infamous daughters of the Emperor Diocletian, who murdered their husbands; and, being set adrift in a ship, reached Albion, where they fell in with a number of demons. Their descendants, a race of giants, were extirpated by Brute and his companions, with the exception of Gog and Magog, who were brought in chains to London and were made to do duty as porters at the royal palace, on the site of our Guildhall, where their effigies have been at least since the reign of Henry V. The old giants were destroyed in the Great Fire, and the present ones, fourteen feet high, were carved in 1708 by Richard Saunders. Formerly wickerwork models were carried in the Lord Mayors' Shows.

Children used to be told (as a very mild joke) that when these giants hear St Paul's clock strike twelve, they descend from their pedestals and go into the Hall for dinner.

In the Bible Magog is spoken of as a son of Japhet (Gen 10:2), in the *Revelation* Gog and Magog symbolise all future enemies of the kingdom of God, and in *Ezekiel* Gog is a prince of Magog, a terrible ruler of a country in the north, probably Scythia or Armenia. By rabbinical writers of the 7th century AD Gog was identified with Antichrist.

**Gogmagog Hill.** The higher of two hills, some three miles south-east of Cambridge. The legend is that Gogmagog fell in love with the nymph Granta, but the dainty lady would have nothing to say to the huge giant, and he was metamorphosed into the hill. (Drayton, *Polyolbion*, xxi)

**Golconda.** An ancient kingdom and city in India (west of Hyderabad), famous and powerful up to the early 17th century. The name is emblematic of great wealth, particularly of diamonds; but there never were diamond mines in Golconda, they were merely cut and polished there.

**Gold.** By the ancient alchemists, gold represented the sun, and silver the moon. In heraldic engravings gold (always called 'or') is represented by dots.

In Great Britain every article in gold is compared with a given standard of pure gold, which is supposed to be divided into twenty-four parts called *carats* (*q.v.*); gold equal to the standard is said to be twenty-four carats fine. Manufactured articles are never made of pure gold, but the quantity of alloy used has to be stated. Sovereigns (and most wedding rings) contain two parts of alloy to every twenty-two of gold, and are said to be twenty-two carats fine. Thus, 20 lb troy of standard gold are coined into 934 sovereigns and 1 half-sovereign; 1 oz troy is therefore worth £3 17*s.* 10½*d.* (£46 14*s.* 6*d.* per lb), and 1 oz of pure gold, on the same basis, £4 4*s.* 11½*d.* Since the Great War the market price of gold has, however, exceeded these figures. The best gold watch-cases contain six parts of silver or copper to eighteen of gold, and are therefore eighteen carats fine; cheaper gold articles may contain nine, twelve, or even fifteen parts of alloy.

***All he touches turns to gold.*** All his ventures succeed; he is invariably fortunate. The allusion is to the legend of Midas (*q.v.*).

***All that glisters is not gold*** (Shakespeare, *Merchant of Venice*, 2, 7). Don't be deceived by appearances.

All thing which that schineth as the gold
Nis not gold as that I have herd it told.

Chaucer, *Canon's Yeoman's Tale*, 243

Not all that tempts your wand'ring eyes
And heedless hearts, is lawful prize;
Nor all, that glisters, gold.

Gray, *Ode on Death of a Favourite Cat*

***Healing gold.*** Gold given to a king for 'healing' the king's evil, which was done by a touch.

***He has got the gold of Tolosa.*** His ill gains will never prosper. Caepio, the Roman consul, in his march to Gallia Narbonensis, desecrated the temple of the Celtic Apollo at Tolosa (Toulouse), and stole from it all the gold and silver vessels and treasure belonging to the Cimbrian Druids. This, in turn, was stolen from him while it was being taken to Massilia (Marseilles); and when he encountered the Cimbrians both he and Maximus, his brother-consul, were defeated, and 112,000 of their men were left upon the field (106 BC).

***Mannheim gold.*** A sort of pinchbeck, made of copper, zinc, and tin, used for cheap jewellery and invented at Mannheim, Germany.

***The gold of the Nibelungen.*** *See* Nibelungen Hoard.

***The Gold Purse of Spain.*** Andalusia is so called because it is the most fertile portion of Spain.

**Golden.** *In personal appellations.*

Jean Dorat (1510–88), one of the Pleiad poets of France, was so called ('Auratus') by a pun on his name.

***Golden Ball.*** Edward Hughes Ball, a dandy in the days of the Regency (fl. 1820–30). He married a Spanish dancer.

***The Golden-mouthed.*** St Chrysostom (d.407), a father of the Greek Church, was so called for his great eloquence.

***The Golden Stream.*** St John Damascene (d.756), author of *Dogmatic Theology*.

***The Golden-tongued*** (Gr. *Chrysologos*). St Peter, Bishop of Ravenna (d. about 449), was so called.

**Phrases**

***A good name is better than a golden girdle.*** *See* Girdle.

***The golden bowl is broken.*** Death has taken place. A biblical allusion:

Or ever the silver cord be loosed, or the golden bowl be broken, or the pitcher be broken at the fountain, or the wheel broken at the cistern; then shall the dust return to the earth as it was; and the spirit shall return unto God who gave it.

Eccles. 12:6, 7

***The golden section of a line.*** Its division into two such parts that the rectangle contained by the smaller segment and the whole line equals the square on the larger segment. (Euclid, ii, 11.)

***The three golden balls.*** *See* Balls.

***To keep the golden mean.*** To practise moderation in all things. The wise saw of Cleobulos, King of Rhodes (about 630–559 BC).

Distant alike from each, to neither lean,
But ever keep the happy Golden Mean.

Rowe, *The Golden Verses*

***To worship the golden calf,*** i.e. money. The reference is to the golden calf made by Aaron when Moses was absent on Mount Sinai (Exod. 32). Local tradition has it that Aaron's golden calf is buried in Rook's Hill, Lavant, near Chichester!

**Golden Age.** An age in the history of peoples of real or (more often) imaginary happiness, when everything was as it should be, or when the nation was at its summit of power, glory, and reputation; the best age, as the golden age of innocence, the golden age of literature. Ancient chronologers divided the time between Creation and the birth of Christ into ages; Hesiod describes five. *See* Age.

The 'Golden Ages' of the various nations are usually given as follows:

*Ancient Nations* –

Assyria. From the reign of Esarhaddon, third son of Sennacherib, to the fall of Nineveh (about 700 to 600 BC).

Chaldaeo-Babylonian Empire. From the reign of Nabopolassar to that of Belshazzar (about 606–538 BC).

China. The reign of Tae-tsong (618–626), and the era of the Tâng dynasty (626–684).

Egypt. The reigns of Sethos I and Rameses II (about 1350–1273 BC), the XIXth Dynasty.

Media. The reign of Cyaxares (about 634–594 BC).

Persia. From the reign of Khosru, or Chosroes, I, to that of Khosru II (about AD 531–628).

*Modern Nations* –

England. The reign of Elizabeth (1558–1603).

France. Part of the reigns of Louis XIV and XV (1640–1740).

Germany. The reign of Charles V (1519–58).

Portugal. From John I to the close of Sebastian's reign (1383–1578).

Prussia. The reign of Frederick the Great (1740–86).

Russia. The reign of Peter the Great (1672–1725).

Spain. The reign of Ferdinand and Isabella, when the crowns of Castile and Aragon were united (1474–1516).

Sweden. From Gustavus Vasa to the close of the reign of Gustavus Adolphus (1523–1632).

**Golden Apples.** *See* Apple of Discord; Atalanta's Race; Hesperides.

**Golden Ass, The.** A satirical romance by Apuleius, written in the 2nd century, and called the *golden* because of its excellency. It tells the adventures of Lucian, a young man who, being accidentally metamorphosed into an ass while sojourning in Thessaly, fell into the hands of robbers, eunuchs, magistrates, and so on, by whom he was ill-treated; but ultimately he recovered his human form. Boccaccio borrowed largely from it, as also did Le Sage (for *Gil Blas*), and others; and it contains the story of Cupid and Psyche – the latest born of the myths.

**Golden Bull, The.** An edict by the Emperor Charles IV, issued at the Diet of Nuremberg in 1356, for the purpose of fixing how the German emperors were to be elected. It was sealed with a golden *bulla*. *See* Bull.

**Golden Fleece, The.** The old Greek story is that Ino persuaded her husband, Athamas, that his son Phryxus was the cause of a famine which desolated the land. Phryxus was thereupon ordered to be sacrificed, but, being apprised of this, he made his escape over sea on the winged ram, Chrysomallus, which had a golden fleece. When he arrived at Colchis, he sacrificed the ram to Zeus, and gave the fleece to King Aeetes, who hung it on a sacred oak. It later formed the quest of Jason's celebrated Argonautic expedition, and was stolen by him. *See* Argo: Jason.

**Golden Fleece, The Order of the** (Fr. *l'ordre de la toison d'or*). An order of knighthood common to Spain and Austria, instituted in 1429 for the protection of the Church by Philip the Good, Duke of Burgundy, on his marriage with the Infanta Isabella of Portugal. In 1477, when the Habsburgs acquired the Burgundian dominions (including the Netherlands), the office of Grand Master passed to them; in 1558, on the death of Charles V, it went to Spain, but was re-claimed by Austria in 1714, after the cession to them of the Spanish Netherlands. Hence the independent existence of the order in both Spain and Austria. Its badge is a golden sheepskin with head and feet attached, and its motto *Pretium laborum non vile*. The selection of the fleece as a badge is perhaps best explained by the fact that the manufacture of wool had long been the staple industry of the Netherlands.

Australia has been called 'The Land of the Golden Fleece', because of the quantity of wool produced there.

**Golden Gate, The.** The name given by Sir Francis Drake to the strait connecting San Francisco Bay with the Pacific. San Francisco is hence called *The City of the Golden Gate*.

**Golden Horn, The.** The inlet of the Bosporus on which Constantinople is situated. So called from its curved shape and great beauty.

**Golden Legend, The.** (Lat. *Legenda aurea*.) A collection of so-called lives of the saints made by Jaques de Voragine in the 13th century; valuable for the picture it gives of mediaeval manners, customs, and thought. Jortin says that the 'lives' were written by young students of religious houses to exercise their talents by accommodating the narratives of heathen writers to Christian saints.

Longfellow has a dramatic poem entitled *The Golden Legend* (1851). It is based on a story by Hartmann von der Aue, a German minnesinger of the 12th century.

**Golden Number.** The number of the year in the Metonic Cycle (*q.v.*). As this consists of nineteen years it may be any number from 1 to 19, and in the ancient Roman and Alexandria calendars this number was marked in gold, hence the name. The rule for finding the golden number is:

> Add one to the number of years and divide by nineteen; the quotient gives the number of cycles since 1 BC and the remainder the golden number, 19 being the golden number when there is no remainder.

It is used in determining the Epact and the date of Easter.

**Golden Ointment.** Eye salve. In allusion to the ancient practice of rubbing 'stynas of the eye' with a gold ring to cure them.

> 'I have a sty here, Chilax.'
> 'I have no gold to cure it.'
> Beaumont and Fletcher, *Mad Lover*, v, i

**Golden Rose.** A cluster of roses and rosebuds growing on one thorny stem, all of the purest gold and chiselled with exquisite workmanship, bestowed by the Pope each year on the royal lady whose zeal for the Church has most shown itself by pious deeds or pious intentions. It is blessed on the fourth Sunday in Lent, and the Pope, at every benediction, inserts among its petals a few particles of amber and musk.

**Golden Rule, The.** 'Do as you would be done by.'

> Whatsoever ye would that men should do to you, do ye even so to them: for this is the law and the prophets. Matt. 7:12

**Golden Shower** or **Shower of gold.** A bribe, money. The allusion is to the classic tale of Zeus and Danae. *See* Danae.

**Golden State, The.** California; so called from its gold 'diggings'.

**Golden Town, The.** So Mainz or Mayence was called in Carlovingian times.

**Golden Valley, The.** The eastern portion of Limerick is so called, from its great natural fertility.

**Golden Verses.** Some Greek verses attributed to the school of Pythagoras (by some to Epicarmos, and by others to Empedocles), and so called because they contain in condensed form all the morals – the 'gold' – of the older epics. They may be translated as follows:

> Ne'er suffer sleep thine eyes to close
> Before thy mind hath run
> O'er every act, and thought, and word,
> From dawn to set of sun;
> For wrong take shame, but grateful feel
> If just thy course hath been:
> Such effort day by day renewed
> Will ward thy soul from sin. E. C. B.

**Golden Wedding.** The fiftieth anniversary of one's wedding, husband and wife being both alive.

**Goldy.** The pet name given by Dr Johnson to Oliver Goldsmith (1728–74). Garrick said of him, 'He wrote like an angel and talked like poor Poll.'

**Golgotha.** The place outside Jerusalem where Christ was crucified. The word is Aramaic and means 'a skull', and according to Jerome and others the place was so called from a tradition that Adam's skull had been found there. The more likely reason is that it designated a bare hill or rising ground, having some fancied resemblance to a bald skull.

> Golgotha seems not entirely unconnected with the hill of Gareb, and the locality of Goath, mentioned in Jer. 31:39, on the north-west of the city. I am inclined to fix the place where Jesus was crucified ... on the mounds which command the valley of Hinnom, above Birket-Mamila. Renan, *Life of Jesus*, ch. xxv

**Golgotha,** at the University church, Cambridge, was the gallery in which the 'heads of the houses' sat; so called because it was the place of skulls or heads. It has been more wittily than truly said that Golgotha was the place of empty skulls.

**Goliath.** The Philistine giant, slain by the stripling David with a small stone hurled from a sling. (1 Sam. 17:23–54)

**Golosh.** *See* Galosh.

**Gomarists.** Opponents of Arminius (*see* Arminians). So called from Francis Gomar, their leader (1563–1641).

**Gombeen Man.** A village usurer; a money-lender. The word is of Irish extraction.

> They suppose that the tenants can have no other supply of capital than from the gombeen man.
> Egmont Hake, *Free Trade in Capital*

**Gombo.** Pidgin French, or French as it is spoken by the coloured population of Louisiana, the French West Indies, Bourbon, and Mauritius.

> Creole is almost pure French, not much more mispronounced than in some parts of France;

> but Gombe is a mere phonetic burlesque of French, interlarded with African words, and other words which are neither African nor French, but probably belong to the aboriginal language of the various countries to which the slaves were brought from Africa.
>
> E. Wakefield, in *The Nineteenth Century*, October, 1891

**Gondola.** A long, narrow Venetian boat.

> Venice, in her purple prime ... when the famous law was passed making all gondolas black, that the nobles should not squander fortunes upon them. Curtis, *Potiphar Papers*, i, p. 31

Disraeli (*Lothair*, ch. xxvii) called the hansom cab 'the gondola of London', but more than forty years earlier (1827) a satire had appeared in *Mayfair* containing the lines:

> Their beauty half her glory veils
> In cabs, those gondolas on wheels.

**Gone Coon.** *See* Coon.

**Gone to the Devil.** *See* Devil.

**Goneril.** One of Lear's three daughters. Having received her moiety of Lear's kingdom, the unnatural daughter first abridged the old man's retinue, then gave him to understand that his company was troublesome. In Holinshed she appears as 'Gonorilla'. *Cp.* Cordelia.

**Gonfalon** or **Gonfanon.** An ensign or standard. A *gonfalonier* was a magistrate in certain of the old Italian republics that had a gonfalon

> Ten thousand thousand ensigns high advanced,
> Standards and gonfalons, 'twixt van and rear
> Stream in the air, and for distinction serve
> Of hierarchies, of orders, and degrees.
>
> Milton, *Paradise Lost*, v, 589

**Gonin.** ***C'est un Maître Gonin***. He is a sly dog. Maître Gonin was a famous French clown in the 16th century. *Un tour de Maître Gonin* means a cunning or scurvy trick. *Cp.* Aliboron.

**Gonnella's Horse.** Gonnella, the domestic jester of the Duke of Ferrara, rode on a horse all skin and bone. The jests of Gonnella are in print.

> His horse was as lean as Gonnella's, which (as the Duke said) 'Osso atque pellis totus erat' (Plautus). Cervantes, *Don Quixote*

**Gonsalez.** Fernan Gonsalez, the hero of many Spanish ballads, lived in the 10th century. His life was twice saved by his wife Sancha, daughter of Garcias, King of Navarre.

**Gonville and Caius.** *See* Caius.

**Good.** *The Good*. Among the many who earned – or were given – this appellation are:

Alfonso VIII (or IX) of Leon, 'The Noble and Good' (1158–1214).

Haco I, King of Norway (about 920–960).

Jean II of France, *le Bon* (1319, 1350–64).

Jean III, Duke of Brittany (1286, 1312–41).

Philip the Good, Duke of Burgundy (1396, 1419–67).

Réné, called *The Good King Réne*, Duke of Anjou, Count of Provence, Duke of Lorraine, and King of Sicily (1409–80).

The Prince Consort, *Albert the Good* (1819–61), husband of Queen Victoria.

**Goodbye.** A contraction of *God be with you.* Similar to the French adieu, which is *à Dieu* (I commend you to God).

**Good-cheap.** A Middle English phrase, meaning a good bargain (A.S. *ceap*, a bargain); the French *bon marché*.

> The sack that thou hast drunk me would have bought me lights as good cheap at the dearest chandler's in Europe.
>
> Shakespeare, *1 Henry IV*, 3, 3

**Good Duke Humphrey.** Humphrey, Duke of Gloucester (1391–1447), youngest son of Henry IV, said to have been murdered by Suffolk and Cardinal Beaufort (Shakespeare, *2 Henry VI*, 3, 2); so called because of his devotion to the Church.

**Good Friday.** The Friday preceding Easter Day, held as the anniversary of the Crucifixion. 'Good' here means *holy*; Christmas, as well as Shrove Tuesday, used to be called 'the good tide'.

***Born on Good Friday.*** According to old superstition, those born on Christmas Day or Good Friday have the power of seeing and commanding spirits.

**Good Parliament, The.** Edward I's Parliament of 1376; so called because of the severity with which it pursued the unpopular party of the Duke of Lancaster.

**Good Regent.** James Stewart, Earl of Moray (d.1570), a natural son of James V and half-brother of Mary Queen of Scots. He was appointed Regent of Scotland after the imprisonment of Queen Mary.

**Good Samaritan.** *See* Samaritan.

**Good Time.** ***There is a good time coming***. This has been for a long, long time a familiar saying in Scotland, and is introduced by Scott in his *Rob Roy*. Charles Mackay wrote a song so called:

> There's a good time coming, boys,
> A good time coming:
> We may not live to see the day,
> But earth shall glisten in the ray
> Of the good time coming.

Cannon-balls may aid the truth,
But thought's a weapon stronger;
We'll win our battle by its aid –
*Wait a little longer.*

This was written in 1846!

**Good and All, For.** Not tentatively, not in pretence, nor yet temporarily, but *bona fide*, and altogether.

The good woman never died after this, till she came to die for good and all.

L'Estrange, *Fables*

**Good for Anything.** Ripe for any sort of work.

After a man has had a year or two at this sort of work he is good … for anything.

Boldrewood, *Robbery Under Arms*, ch. xi

***Not good for anything.*** Utterly worthless; used up or worn down.

**Goodfellow.** *See* Robin Goodfellow.

**Goodman.** A husband or master. In Matt. 24:43, 'If the goodman of the house had known in what watch the thief would come, he would have watched.'

There's nae luck about the house
When our gudeman's awa. Mickle

***Goodman of Ballengeich.*** The assumed name of James V of Scotland when he made his disguised visits through the country districts around Edinburgh and Stirling, after the fashion of Haroun-al-Raschid, Louis XI, etc.

***Goodman's Croft.*** The name given in Scotland to a strip of ground or corner of a field left untilled, in the belief that unless some such place were left, the spirit of evil would damage the crop. Here Goodman is a propitiatory euphemism for the devil.

Scotchmen still living remember the corner of a field being left for the goodman's croft.

Tylor, *Primitive Culture*, ii, 370

**Goods.** ***I carry all my goods with me*** **(*Omnia mea mecum porto*)**. Said by Bias, one of the seven sages, when Priene was besieged and the inhabitants were preparing for flight.

***That fellow's the goods.*** He's all right, just the man for the job; there are no flies on him. In this and the next phrase the use of 'goods' is an Americanism.

***To deliver the goods.*** Said of one who fulfils his promises or who comes up to expectations. 'Yes,' says an employer to an applicant for a post, 'your references are all right and I like the look of you; but *can you deliver the goods*?'

**Goodwin Sands.** It is said that these dangerous sandbanks, stretching about 10 miles N.E. and S.W. some 5½ miles off the Kentish coast, consisted at one time of about 4,000 acres of low land (Lomea, the *Infera Insula* of the Romans) fenced from the sea by a wall, and belonging to Earl Godwin. William the Conqueror bestowed them on the abbey of St Augustine, Canterbury, and the abbot allowed the sea-wall to fall into a dilapidated state, so that the sea broke through in 1100 and inundated the whole. *See* Tenterden Steeple.

**Goodwood Races.** So called from the park in which they are held. They begin the last Tuesday of July, and last four days, the chief being Thursday, called the 'Cup Day'. These races, being held in a private park, the property of the Duke of Richmond, are very select.

**Goody.** A depreciative, meaning weakly, moral and religious. In French, *bon homme* is used in a similar way.

No doubt, if a Caesar or a Napoleon comes before some man of weak will … especially if he be a goody man, [he] will quail.

J. Cook, *Conscience*, lecture iv, p. 49

The word is also a rustic variant of *goodwife*, the mistress of a household (*cp.* Goodman), and is sometimes used as a title, like 'Gammer' (*q.v.*), as 'Goody Blake', 'Goody Dobson'.

***Goody-goody.*** Affectedly, or even hypocritically, pious, but with no strength of mind or independence of spirit.

***Goody Two-shoes.*** This nursery tale first appeared in 1765. It was written for Newbery, as it is said, by Oliver Goldsmith.

**Goose.** A foolish or ignorant person is called a *goose* because of the alleged stupidity of this bird; a tailor's smoothing-iron is so called because its handle resembles the neck of a goose. Note that the plural of the iron is *gooses*, not *geese*.

Come in, tailor; here you may roast your goose.

Shakespeare, *Macbeth*, 2, 3

***All his swans are turned to geese.*** All his expectations end in nothing; all his boasting ends in smoke. Like a person who fancies he sees a swan on a river, but finds it to be only a goose.

***Every man thinks his own geese swans.*** Everyone is prejudiced by self-love. Every crow thinks its own nestling the fairest. Every child is beautiful in its mother's eyes. *See* Aesop's fable, *The Eagle and the Owl.*

***Geese save the capitol.*** The tradition is that when the Gauls invaded Rome a detachment in single file clambered up the hill of the capitol so silently that the foremost man reached the top without being challenged; but while he was striding over the rampart, some sacred geese, disturbed by the noise began to cackle, and awoke the garrison. Marcus Manlius rushed to the wall and hurled the fellow over the precipice. To commemorate this event, the Romans carried a golden goose in procession to the capitol every year (390 BC).

> Those consecrated geese in orders,
> That to the capitol were warders,
> And being then upon patrol,
> With noise alone beat off the Gaul.
>
> Butler, *Hudibras*, ii, 3

***The Goose Bible.*** *See* Bible, specially named.

***Goose fair.*** A fair formerly held in many English towns about the time of Michaelmas (*q.v.*), when geese were plentiful. That still held at Nottingham was the most important.

***Goose month.*** The lying-in month for women. *Cp.* Gander month.

***The goose step.*** A step formerly *de rigueur* in the Prussian army for ceremonial purposes, 'marching past', and so on; at each pace the thigh had to be brought to a right-angle with the erect body. It was supposed to look extremely dignified when carried out by a well drilled body of men, but it was unmercifully ridiculed by the Allies during the Great War.

Also, balancing on one foot and moving the other back and forwards; a preliminary exercise for recruits.

***He can't say Bo! to a goose.*** *See* Bo.

***He killed the goose to get the eggs.*** He grasped at what was more than his due, and lost an excellent customer. The Greek fable says a countryman had a goose that laid golden eggs; thinking to make himself rich, he killed the goose to get the whole stock of eggs at once, but lost everything.

***He steals a goose, and gives the giblets in alms.*** He amasses wealth by overreaching, and salves his conscience by giving small sums in charity.

***I'll cook your goose for you.*** I'll pay you out. It is said that Eric, King of Sweden, coming to a certain town with very few soldiers, the enemy, in mockery, hung out a goose for him to shoot at. Finding, however, that the king meant business, and that it would be no laughing matter for them, they sent heralds to ask him what he wanted. 'To cook your goose for you,' he facetiously replied.

***Michaelmas goose.*** *See* Michaelmas.

***Mother Goose.*** Famous as giving the name to *Mother Goose's Nursery Rhymes*, which first seems to have been used in *Songs for the Nursery: or Mother Goose's Melodies for Children*, published by T. Fleet in Boston, Mass., in 1719. The story goes that Fleet married Elizabeth Goose, whose mother used to sing the rhymes to her grandson: but this explanation of the name is discounted by the fact that Perrault's *Contes de ma mère l'oye* ('Tales of my Mother Goose') had appeared in 1697.

***The Goose and Gridiron.*** A public-house sign, properly the coat of arms of the Company of Musicians – viz. a *swan* with expanded wings, within a *double tressure* [the gridiron], counter, flory, argent. Perverted into a goose striking the bars of a gridiron with its foot; also called 'The Swan and Harp'.

In the United States the name is humorously applied to the national coat-of-arms – the American eagle with a gridiron-like shield on its breast.

***The old woman is plucking her goose.*** A children's way of saying 'it is snowing'.

***The older the goose the harder to pluck.*** Old men are unwilling to part with their money.

***The Royal Game of Goose.*** The game referred to by Goldsmith (*Deserted Village*, 232) as being present in the ale-house –

> The pictures placed for ornament and use,
> The twelve good rules, the royal game of goose –

was a game of compartments through which the player progressed according to the cast of the dice. At certain divisions a goose was depicted, and if the player fell into one of these he doubled the number of his last throw and moved forward accordingly.

The 'twelve good rules' was a broadside showing a rough cut of the execution of Charles I with the following 'rules' printed below:

> 1. Urge no healths; 2. Profane no divine ordinances; 3. Touch no state matters; 4. Reveal no secrets; 5. Pick no quarrels; 6. Make no comparisons; 7. Maintain no ill opinions; 8. Keep no bad company; 9. Encourage no vice; 10. Make no long meals; 11. Repeat no grievances; 12. Lay no wagers.

These were said to have been 'found in the study of King Charles the First, of Blessed Memory', and in the 18th century were frequently framed and displayed in taverns.

***To get the goose.*** To get hissed on the stage.

***To shoe the goose.*** To fritter away one's time on unnecessary work; to mess about, trifle.

***Tuning goose.*** The entertainment given in Yorkshire when the corn at harvest was all safely stacked.

***Wayz Goose.*** *See* Wayz.

***What's sauce for the goose is sauce for the gander.*** *See* Gander.

**Gooseberry.** Slang for a chaperon (*see* To play gooseberry *below*); also called a *gooseberry-picker*.

***Gooseberry fool.*** A dish made of gooseberries scalded and pounded with cream. Probably so called because, as a food, it is only a 'trifle', a foolish thing.

***He played up old gooseberry with me.*** He took great liberties with my property, and greatly abused it; in fact, he played the very deuce with me and my belongings.

***The big gooseberry season.*** The dull time in journalism, when Parliament is not sitting, the Law Courts are up, and 'nobody' is in town, when the old-fashioned editor will publish accounts of giant gooseberries, sea-serpents, vegetable marrows, sweet peas, just to fill up: the 'silly season'.

***To play gooseberry.*** To act as chaperon: to go about with two lovers for appearance's sake. The person 'who plays propriety' is expected to hear, see, and say nothing. Perhaps so called because one performing this duty would turn to anything convenient, such as gooseberry-picking, to give the young people a chance.

**Goosebridge.** ***Go to Goosebridge.*** 'Rule a wife and have a wife.' Boccaccio (ix, 9) tells us that a man who had married a shrew asked Solomon what he should do to make her more submissive: and the wise king answered, 'Go to Goosebridge.' Returning home, deeply perplexed, he came to a bridge which a muleteer was trying to induce a mule to cross. The beast resisted, but the stronger will of his master at length prevailed. The man asked the name of the bridge, and was told it was 'Goosebridge'.

**Gordian Knot.** A great difficulty. Gordius, a peasant, being chosen king of Phrygia, dedicated his wagon to Jupiter, and fastened the yoke to a beam with a rope of bark so ingeniously that no one could untie it. Alexander was told that 'whoever undid the knot would reign over the whole East'. 'Well then,' said the conqueror, 'it is thus I perform the task,' and, so saying, he cut the knot in twain with his sword.

***To cut the Gordian knot*** is to get out of a difficult or awkward position by one decisive step, to solve a problem by a single brilliant stroke.

> Such praise the Macedonian got
> For having rudely cut the Gordian knot.
>
> Waller, *To the King*

> Turn him to any cause of policy,
> The Gordian knot of it he will unloose,
> Familiar as his garter.
>
> Shakespeare, *Henry V*, 1, 1

**Gordon Riots.** Riots in 1780, headed by Lord George Gordon, to compel the House of Commons to repeal the bill passed in 1778 for the relief of Roman Catholics. Gordon was of unsound mind, and he died in 1793, a proselyte to Judaism. Dickens has given a very vivid description of the Gordon riots in *Barnaby Rudge*.

**Gorgon.** Anything unusually hideous, particularly a hideous or terrifying woman. In classical mythology there were three Gorgons, with serpents on their heads instead of hair; Medusa was the chief, and the only one that was mortal; but so hideous was her face that whoever set eyes on it was instantly turned into stone. She was slain by Perseus, and her head placed on the shield of Minerva.

> What was that snaky-headed Gorgon shield
> That wise Minerva wore, unconquered virgin,
> Wherewith she freezed her foes to congealed
> stone?
> But rigid looks of chaste austerity,
> And noble grace, that dashed brute violence
> With sudden adoration and blank awe.
>
> Milton, *Comus*, 58

**Gorham Controversy.** This arose out of the refusal (1848) of the bishop of Exeter to institute the Rev. Cornelius Gorham to the vicarage of Brampford Speke, 'because he held unsound views on the doctrine of baptism'. After two years' controversy, the Privy Council decided in favour of Mr Gorham on the ground that differences of opinion on points left open were always thought consistent with subscription to the Articles, and that opinions similar to those of Gorham had been held by many eminent prelates and divines.

**Gorlois.** In Arthurian legend, Duke of Cornwall and husband of Igraine (*q.v.*). On the night that he was slain, through the enchantments of Merlin, Uther Pendragon came to Igraine in the likeness of Gorlois and made her the mother of King Arthur. Before the child was born Uther Pendragon married her.

**Gorramooloch.** A mysterious sea-monster, well known to the coast dwellers of Connemara, Mayo, and Donegal. Whether it is mammal, reptile, or fish is not known, but it has large wing-like fins, and is said to leap from the water to a height of fifty feet and more and catch the sea-birds on which it feeds.

**Gospel.** A panacea; a scheme to bring about some promised reform; a beau ideal. Of course the theological word is the A.S. *godspell*, i.e. 'good tidings', a translation of the Gr. *evangelion*, the good story.

> Mr Carnegie's gospel is the very thing for the transition period from social heathendom to social Christianity.
>
> *Nineteenth Century* (March, 1891, p. 380)

***Gospel according to ...*** The chief teaching of [so-and-so]. 'The Gospel according to Mammon' is the making and collecting of money. 'The Gospel according to Sir Pertinax Mac Sycophant', is bowing and cringing to those who are in a position to lend you a helping hand.

***The Gospel of Wealth.*** The hypothesis that wealth is the great end and aim of man, the one thing needful.

> The Gospel of Wealth advocates leaving free the operation of laws of accumulation.
>
> Carnegie, *Advantages of Poverty*

**Gospeller.** The priest who reads the Gospel in the Communion Service; also a follower of Wyclif, called the 'Gospel Doctor'; anyone who believes that the New Testament has in part, at least, superseded the Old.

***Hot Gospellers.*** A nickname applied to the Puritans after the Restoration.

**Gossamer.** According to legend, this delicate thread is the ravelling of the Virgin Mary's winding-sheet, which fell to earth on her ascension to heaven. It is said to be *God's seam*, i.e. God's thread. Actually, the name is from M.E. *gossomer*, literally *goose-summer*, or St Martin's summer (early November), when geese are eaten and gossamer is prevalent.

**Gossip.** A tattler; a sponsor at baptism, a corruption of *God-sibb*, a kinsman in the Lord. (A.S. *sibb*, relationship, whence *sibman*, kinsman; *he is our sib*, is still used.)

> Here, Andrew, carry this to my gossip, jolly father Boniface, the monk of St Martin's.
>
> Scott, *Quentin Durward*

> 'Tis not a maid, for she hath had gossip [sponsors for her child]; yet 'tis a maid, for she is her master's servant, and serves for wages.
>
> Shakespeare, *Two Gentlemen of Verona*, 3, 1

**Gotch.** A large stone jug with a handle (Norfolk). *Fetch the gotch, mor* – i.e. fetch the great water-jug, lassie.

> A gotch of milk I've been to fill.
>
> Bloomfield, *Richard and Kate*

**Goth.** One of an ancient tribe of Teutons which swept down upon and devastated large portions of southern Europe in the 3rd to 5th centuries, establishing kingdoms in Italy, southern France, and Spain. They were looked on by the civilised Romans as merely destroying barbarians; hence the name came to be applied to any rude, uncultured, destructive people.

> The Goths were divided by the Dnieper into East Goths (Ostrogoths), and West Goths (Visigoths), and were the most cultured of the German peoples.
>
> Baring-Gould, *Story of Germany*, p. 37

***The last of the Goths.*** *See* Roderick.

**Gotham.** *Wise Men of Gotham* – fools, wiseacres. The village of Gotham, in Nottinghamshire, was for centuries proverbial for the folly of its inhabitants, and many tales have been fathered on them, one of which is their joining hands round a thorn-bush to shut in a cuckoo. *Cp.* Coggeshall.

It is said that King John intended to make a progress through this town with the view of purchasing a castle and grounds. The townsmen had no desire to be saddled with this expense, and therefore when the royal messengers appeared, wherever they went they saw the people occupied in some idiotic pursuit. The king being told of it, abandoned his intention, and the 'wise men' of the village cunningly remarked, 'We ween there are more fools pass through Gotham than remain in it.'

A collection of popular tales of stupidity was published in the reign of Henry VIII as *Merie Tales of the Mad Men of Gotam, gathered together by A. B. of Phisike, Doctour.* This 'A. B.' has been supposed to be Andrew Boorde (d.1549).

N.B. Most nations have fixed upon some locality as their limbus of fools; thus we have Phrygia as the fools' home of Asia Minor, Abdera of the Thracians, Boeotia of the Greeks, Nazareth of the ancient Jews, Swabia of the modern Germans, and so on.

**Gothamites.** American cockneys. New York is satirically called Gotham.

> Such things as would strike ... a stranger in our beloved Gotham, and places to which our regular Gothamites are wont to repair.
>
> *Fraser's Magazine*, *Sketches of American Society*

**Gothic Architecture.** A style prevalent in Western Europe from the 12th to the 16th centuries, characterised by the pointed arch, clustered columns, etc. The name has nothing to do with the Goths, but was bestowed in contempt by the architects of the Renaissance period on mediaeval architecture, which they termed clumsy, fit only for barbarians or Goths.

> St Louis ... built the Ste Chapelle of Paris, ... the most precious piece of Gothic in Northern Europe. Ruskin, *Fors Clavigera*, vol. i

**Gouk** or **Gowk.** The cuckoo (from Icel. *gaukr*); hence, a fool, a simpleton.

***Hunting the gowk*** is making one an April fool. *See* April.

A *gowk storm* is a storm consisting of several days of tempestuous weather, believed by the peasantry to take place periodically about the beginning of April, at the time that the gowk or cuckoo visits this country; it is also, curiously enough, a storm that is short and sharp, a 'storm in a tea-cup'.

> That being done, he hoped that this was but a gowk-storm.
> Sir G. Mackenzie, *Memoirs*, p. 70

**Gourd.** 'Doctored' dice with a secret cavity were called *gourds. See* Fulhams.

***Jonah's gourd***. This plant (*see* Jonah 4:6–10), the Heb. *kikayõn*, was probably the Palma Christi, called in Egypt *kiki.* Niebuhr speaks of a specimen which he himself saw near a rivulet, which in October 'rose eight feet in five months' time'. And Volney says, 'Wherever plants have water the rapidity of their growth is prodigious. In Cairo,' he adds, 'there is a species of gourd which in twenty-four hours will send out shoots four inches long.' (*Travels*, vol. i, p. 71.)

**Gourmand** and **Gourmet** (Fr.). The *gourmand* is one whose chief pleasure is eating; but a *gourmet* is a connoisseur of food and wines. The *gourmand* regards quantity more than quality, the *gourmet* quality more than quantity. *See* Apicius.

> In former times [in France] *gourmand* meant a judge of eating, and *gourmet* a judge of wine ... Gourmet is now universally understood to refer to eating, and not to drinking.
> Hamerton, *French and English*, Pt v, ch. iv

***The gourmand's prayer***. 'O Philoxenos, Philoxenos, why were you not Prometheus?' Prometheus was the mythological creator of man, and Philoxenos was a great epicure, whose great and constant wish was to have the neck of a crane, that he might enjoy the taste of his food longer before it was swallowed into his stomach. (Aristotle, *Ethics*, iii, 10.)

**Gout.** The disease is so called from the Fr. *goutte*, a drop, because it was once thought to proceed from a 'drop of acrid matter in the joints'.

**Goutte de Sang.** The Adonis flower or pheasant's eye, said to be stained by the blood of Adonis, who was gored by a boar.

> O fleur si chère à Cytherée
> Ta corolle fut, en naissance
> Du sang d'Adonis colorée.

**Goven.** *St Goven's Bell. See* Inchcape.

**Gowan.** A Scotch word for various field flowers, especially the common daisy, sometimes called the *ewe-gowan*, apparently from the ewe, as being frequent in pastures fed on by sheep.

> Some bit waefu' love story, enough to mak the pinks an' the ewe-gowans blush to the very lip.
> *Brownie of Bodsbeck*, i, 215

**Gowk.** *See* Gouk.

**Gown.** ***Gown and town row***. In university towns, a scrimmage between the students of different colleges and the townsmen. These feuds go back at least to the reign of King John, when 3,000 students left Oxford for Reading, owing to a quarrel with the men of the town.

**Gownsman.** A student at one of the universities; so called because he wears an academical gown.

**Graal.** *See* Grail.

**Grab.** To clutch or seize. *I grabbed it*; *he grabbed him*, i.e. the bailiff caught him.

***Land grabber***. A common expression in Ireland during the last two decades of the 19th century, to signify one who takes the farm or land of an evicted tenant. The corresponding phrase in the 18th century was *Land Pirate.*

**Grace.** A courtesy-title used in addressing or speaking of dukes, duchesses, and archbishops. 'His Grace the Duke of Devonshire', 'My Lord Archbishop, may it please Your Grace', etc.

***Act of grace.*** A pardon: a general pardon granted by Act of Parliament, especially that of 1690, when William III pardoned political offenders, and that of 1784, when the estates forfeited for high treason in connection with 'the '45' were restored.

***Grace before*** (or ***after***) ***meat.*** A short prayer asking a blessing on, or giving thanks for, one's food. Here the word (which used to be plural) is a relic of the old phrase *to do graces* or *to give graces*, meaning to render thanks (Fr. *rendre grâces*, Lat. *gratias agere*), as in Chaucer's

> They weren right glad and joyeful, and answereden ful mekely and benignely, yeldinge graces and thankinges to hir lord Melibee.
> *Tale of Melibeus*, §71

***Grace card*** or ***Grace's card.*** The six of hearts is so called in Kilkenny. At the Revolution in 1688, one of the family of Grace, of Courtstown, in Ireland, equipped at his own expense a regiment of foot and troop of horse, in the service of King James. William of Orange promised him high honours if he would join the new party, but the indignant baron wrote on a card, 'Tell your master I despise his offer.' The card was the six of hearts, and hence the name.

***Grace cup.*** *See* Loving Cup.

***Grace Days,*** or ***Days of Grace.*** The three days over and above the time stated in a commercial bill. Thus, if a bill is drawn on June 20th, and is payable in one month, it is due on July 20th, but three 'days of grace' are added, bringing the date to July 23rd.

***The three Graces.*** In classical mythology, the goddesses who bestowed beauty and charm and were themselves the embodiment of both. They were the sisters Aglaia, Thalia, and Euphrosyne.

> They are the daughters of sky-ruling Jove,
> By him begot of faire Eurynome, ...
> The first of them hight mylde Euphrosyne,
> Next faire Aglaia, last Thalia merry;
> Sweete Goddesses all three, which me in mirth do cherry. Spenser, *Faërie Queene*, VI, x, 22

Andrea Appiani (1754–1817), the Italian fresco artist, was known as *the Painter of the Graces.*

***Time of grace.*** *See* Sporting Seasons.

***To get into one's good graces.*** To insinuate oneself into the favour of.

> Having continued to get into the good graces of the buxom widow. Dickens, *Pickwick*, ch. xiv

***With a good grace.*** Willingly; without hesitation.

***Year of Grace.*** The year of our Lord, Anno Domini. In University language it is the year allowed to a Fellow who has been given a College living, at the end of which he must resign either his fellowship or the living.

**Gracechurch Street** (London). The earliest known form in which the name occurs (1284) is *Garscherchestrate*; the *Gars* is A.S. *gaers*, grass, hay, herb, and the name denotes the street of the church built by the hay or herb market. Stow speaks of a herb market in this locality. *Cp.* Fenchurch.

**Graceless** or **Godless Florin.** The first issue of the English florin (1849), called 'Graceless' because the letters DG ('by God's grace') were omitted, and 'Godless' because of the omission of FD ('Defender of the Faith').

It happened that Richard Lalor Sheil, the master of the Mint at the time, was a Catholic, and the suspicion was aroused that the omission was made on religious grounds. The florins were called in and re-cast, and Mr Sheil left the Mint the following year.

**Gracioso.** The interlocutor in the Spanish *drame romantique.* He thrusts himself forward on all occasions, ever and anon directing his gibes to the audience.

**Gradanaites.** Another name for the Barsanians (*q.v.*).

**Gradely.** A north of England term meaning thoroughly; regularly; as *Behave yourself gradely. A gradely fine day.* The word is from Scand. *graith*, ready, prompt.

> Sammy'll fettle him graidely.
> Mrs H. Burnett, *That Lass o' Lowrie's*, ch. ii

**Gradgrind, Thomas.** A character in Dickens's *Hard Times*, typical of a man who measures everything with rule and compass, allows nothing for the weakness of human nature, and deals with men and women as a mathematician with his figures. He shows that *summum jus* is *suprema injuria.*

**Gradual.** An antiphon sung between the Epistle and the Gospel, as the deacon ascends the *steps* (late Lat. *graduales*) of the altar. Also, a book containing the musical portions of the service at mass – the *graduals*, *introits*, *kyries*, *gloria in excelsis*, *credo*, etc.

***The Gradual Psalms.*** Ps. 120 to 134 inclusive; probably so called because they were sung when the ascent to the inner court was made by the priests. In our Authorised Version they are called *Songs of Degrees*, and in the Revised Version *Songs of Ascents. Cp.* Hallel.

**Graemes, The.** A clan of freebooters who inhabited the Debatable Land (*q.v.*), and were transported to Ireland at the beginning of the 17th century.

**Grahame's Dyke.** A popular name for the remains of the old Roman wall between the friths of Clyde and Forth, the Wall of Antoninus.

> This wall defended the Britons for a time but the Scots and Picts assembled themselves in great numbers, and climbed over it ... A man named Grahame is said to have been the first soldier who got over, and the common people still call the remains of the wall 'Grahame's Dike'.
> Scott, *Tales of a Grandfather*

**Graiae.** *See* Phorcos.

**Grail, the Holy.** The cup or chalice traditionally used by Christ at the Last Supper, and the centre round which a huge *corpus* of mediaeval legend, romance, and allegory revolves.

According to one account, Joseph of Arimathaea preserved the Grail, and received into it some of the blood of the Saviour at the Crucifixion. He brought it to England, but it disappeared. According to others, it was brought by angels from heaven and entrusted to a body of knights who guarded it on top of a mountain, and when approached by anyone of not perfect purity it disappeared from sight, and its quest became the source of most of the adventures of the Knights of the Round Table. *But see also* Perceforest.

The mass of literature concerning the Grail cycle, both ancient and modern, is enormous; the chief sources of the principal groups of legends are: the *Peredur* (Welsh, given in the *Mabinogion*), which is the most archaic form of the Quest story; Wolfram's *Parzifal* (about 1210), the best example of the story as transformed by ecclesiastical influence; the 13th century French *Percival le Gallois* (founded on earlier English and Celtic legends which had no connection with the Grail), showing Percival in his later rôle as an ascetic hero (translated by Dr Sebastian Evans, 1893, as *The High History of the Holy Grail*); and the *Quête du St Graal*, which, in its English dress, forms Bks 13–18 of Malory's *Morte d'Arthur. See* Fisherman, King; Galahad; Percival.

It was the French poet, Robert le Boron (fl. about 1215), who, in his *Joseph d'Arimathie* or *Le Saint Graal*, first definitely attached the history of the Grail to the Arthurian cycle.

The framework of Tennyson's *Holy Grail* (1869, *Idylls of the King*), in which the poet expressed his 'strong feeling as to the Reality of the Unseen', is taken from Malory.

**Grain.** ***A knave in grain.*** A thoroughgoing knave, a knave all through. An old phrase which comes from dyeing. The brilliant crimson dye obtained from the kermes and cochineal insects used to be thought to come from some seed, or grain; it was of a very durable and lasting nature, dyed the thing completely and finally, through and through. Hence also the word *engrained*, as in 'an engrained (i.e. ineradicable) habit'.

How the red roses flush up in her cheeks,
And the pure snow with goodly vermeil stain
Like crimson dyed in grain!

Spenser, *Epithalamion*, 226

'Tis ingrain, sir; 'twill endure wind and weather.

Shakespeare, *Twelfth Night*, 1, 5

***To go against the grain.*** Against one's inclination. The allusion is to wood, which cannot be easily planed the wrong way of the grain.

Your minds,
Pre-occupied with what you rather must do
Than what you should, made you against the grain
To voice him consul.

Shakespeare, *Coriolanus*, 2, 3

***With a grain of salt.*** *See* Salt.

**Gramercy.** Thank you much; from O.Fr. *grant*, great, *merci*, reward, the full meaning of the exclamation being 'May God reward you greatly'. When Gobbo says to Bassanio, 'God bless your worship!' he replies, 'Gramercy. Wouldst thou aught with me?' (*Merchant of Venice*, 2, 2.)

**Grammar.** ***Caesar is not above the grammarians.*** Suetonius tells us (*De Grammaticis*, 22) that Tiberius was rebuked by a grammarian for some verbal slip, and upon a courtier remarking that if the word was not good Latin it would be in future, now that it had received imperial recognition, he was rebuked with the words *Tu enim Caesar civitatem dare potes hominibus, verbis non potes* (Caesar, you can grant citizenship to men, but not to words). Hence the saying, *Caesar non supra grammaticos.*

But when a later Emperor, the German, Sigismund I, stumbled into a wrong gender at the Council of Constance (1414), no such limitation would be admitted; he replied, *Ego sum Imperator Romanorum, et supra grammaticam* (I am the Roman Emperor, and am above grammar!).

***The Scourge of Grammar.*** So Pope, in the *Dunciad* (iii, 149), called Giles Jacob (1686–1744), a very minor poet, who, in his *Register of the Poets*, made an unprovoked attack on Pope's friend, Gay.

**Grammarians.** ***Prince of Grammarians.*** Apollonius of Alexandria (2nd cent. BC), so called by Priscian.

**Grand, Le.**

***Le Grand Bâtard.*** Antoine de Bourgogne (d.1504), a natural son of Philip the Good, famous for his deeds of prowess.

***Le Grand Corneille.*** Pierre Corneille, the French dramatist (1606–84).

***Le Grand Dauphin.*** Louis, son of Louis XIV (1661–1711).

***La Grand Mademoiselle.*** The Duchesse de Montpensier (1627–93), daughter of Gaston, Duc d'Orleans, and cousin of Louis XIV.

***Le Grand Monarque.*** Louis XIV, King of France (1638, 1643–1715).

***Le Grand Pan.*** Voltaire (1694–1778).

***Monsieur le Grand.*** The Grand Equerry of France in the reign of Louis XIV, etc.

**Grand Alliance.** Signed May 12th, 1689, between Germany and the States General, subsequently also by England, Spain and Savoy, to prevent the union of France and Spain.

**Grand Guignol.** *See* Guignol.

**Grand Lama.** *See* Lama.

**Grandee.** In Spain, a nobleman of the highest rank, who has the privilege of remaining covered in the king's presence.

**Grandison Cromwell.** The nickname given by Mirabeau to Lafayette (1757–1834), implying that he had all the ambition of a Cromwell, but wanted to appear before men as a Sir Charles Grandison – Richardson's hero, the union of a Christian and a gentleman, called by Scott 'the faultless monster that the world ne'er saw'.

**Grange.** Properly the *granum* (granary) or farm of a monastery, where the corn was kept in store. In Lincolnshire and the northern counties the name is applied to any lone farm, and houses attached to monasteries where rent was paid in grain were also called granges.

> Till thou return the Court I will exchange
> For some poor cottage, or some country grange.
>
> Drayton, *Lady Geraldine to Earl of Surrey*

Tennyson's poem, *Mariana*, was suggested by the line in Shakespeare's *Measure for Measure* (3, 1):

> There, at the moated grange resides this dejected Mariana.
> The broken sheds look'd sad and strange:
> Unlifted was the clinking latch;
> Weeded and worn the ancient thatch
> Upon the lonely moated grange.
>
> Tennyson, *Mariana*

**Grangerise.** To 'extra-illustrate' a book; to supplement it by the addition of illustrations, portraits, autograph letters, caricatures, prints, broadsheets, biographical sketches, anecdotes, scandals, press notices, parallel passages, and any other sort of matter directly or indirectly bearing on the subject. So called from James Granger (1723–76) who, in 1769, started the craze by publishing a *Biographical History of England* with blank pages for the insertion of extra illustrations, etc.

**Grangousier.** In Rabelais' satire, *Gargantua and Pantagruel*, a king of Utopia, who married, in 'the vigour of his old age', Gargamelle, daughter of the king of the Parpaillons, and became the father of Gargantua (*q.v*). Some say he is meant for Louis XII, but Motteux thinks the 'academy figure' of this old Priam was John d'Albret, King of Navarre.

**Grani.** In old Norse hero legends was the grey charger of Siegfried (Sigurd), whose swiftness exceeded that of the winds. Gunnar borrowed him from Siegfried and fruitlessly attempted to ride him through the flames to rescue Brunhild, but as soon as Siegfried himself mounted Grani recognised his master's spur and dashed through the fire.

**Granite City, The.** Aberdeen.

**Granite Redoubt.** The grenadiers of the Consular Guard were so called at the battle of Marengo in 1800, because when the French had given way they formed into a square, stood like stone against the Austrians, and stopped all further advance.

**Granite State, The.** New Hampshire is so called, because the mountainous parts are chiefly granite.

**Grantorto** (great wrong). In Spenser's *Faërie Queene* (V, xi, xii) a giant who withheld the inheritance of Irena (*Ireland*). He typifies Spain as the instigator of rebellion, and was slain by Sir Artegal.

**Grapes.** ***The grapes are sour.*** You disparage it because it is beyond your reach. The allusion is to Aesop's well-known fable of the fox, which tried in vain to get at some grapes, but when he found they were beyond his reach went away saying, 'I see they are sour.'

> There, economy was always 'elegant', and money-spending always 'vulgar' and ostentatious – a sort of sour grapeism, which made us very peaceful and satisfied.
>
> Mrs Gaskell, *Cranford*, ch. i

**Grape-sugar.** Another name for glucose (dextrose), a fermentable sugar, less sweet than cane-sugar, and obtained from dried grapes and other fruits as well as being made chemically. It is used in the manufacture of jams, beer, etc.

**Grass.** ***Gone to grass.*** Dead. The allusion is to the grass which grows over the dead. To be knocked down in a pugilistic encounter is to 'go to grass'; to have the sack is also to 'go to grass', the allusion being to a horse which is sent to grass when unfit for work.

***Not to let the grass grow under one's feet.*** To be very active and energetic.

> Captain Cuttle held on at a great pace, and allowed no grass to grow under his feet.
>
> Dickens, *Dombey and Son*

***A grass hand*** is a compositor who fills a temporary vacancy; hence *to grass*, to take only temporary jobs as a compositor.

***Grass widow.*** Formerly, an unmarried woman who has had a child; but now, a wife temporarily parted from her husband; also, by extension, a divorced woman.

The word has nothing to do with *grace* widow (a widow by courtesy), and the modern use seems to have originated among Anglo-Indians about the middle of last century, from the practice of European husbands sending their wives, during the hot season, to the hills – where grass is plentiful – while they worked in the sweltering plains below. Another suggestion is that the phrase arose in America, during the gold mania in California. A man would not unfrequently put his wife and children to board with some family while he went to the 'diggins'. This he called 'putting his wife to grass', as a horse is put to grass when not wanted or unfit for work.

**Grasshopper,** as the sign of a grocer, is the crest of Sir Thomas Gresham, the merchant grocer. The Royal Exchange, founded by him, used to be profusely decorated with grasshoppers, and the brass one on the eastern part of the present building escaped the fires of 1666 and 1838.

There is a tale that Sir Thomas was a foundling, and that a woman, attracted by the chirping of a grasshopper, discovered the outcast and brought him up. Except as a tale, this solution of the combination is worthless. *Gres* = grass (A.S. *graes*), and no doubt grasshopper is an heraldic rebus on the name.

**Grattan's Parliament.** The free Irish Parliament established in Dublin in 1782, when Grattan obtained the repeal of Poynings' Law (*q.v.*). It lasted till the coming into force of the Act of Union, January 1st, 1801.

**Grave.** Solemn, sedate, and serious in look and manner. This is Lat. *gravis*, heavy, grave; but 'grave', a place of interment, is A.S. *graef*, a pit; *graf-an*, to dig.

***Close as the grave.*** Very secret indeed.

***It's enough to make him turn in his grave.*** Said when something happens to which the deceased person referred to would very strongly object.

***Someone is walking over my grave.*** An exclamation made when one is seized with an involuntary convulsive shuddering.

***To carry away the meat from the grave.*** *See* Meat.

***With one foot in the grave.*** At the very verge of death. The expression was used by Julian, who said he would 'learn something even if he had one foot in the grave'. The parallel Greek phrase is, 'With one foot in the ferryboat', meaning Charon's.

**Gravelled. *I'm regularly gravelled.*** Nonplussed, like a ship run aground and unable to move.

> When you were gravelled for lack of matter.
>
> Shakespeare, *As You like It*, 4, 1

**Gray.** *See* Grey.

**Gray's Inn** (London) was the inn or mansion of the Lords de Grey, and the property belonged to them from at least as early as 1307 to 1505. It was let to students of law in the 14th century, and is still one of the four Inns of Court (*q.v.*).

**Grease.** Slang for money, especially that given as a bribe; 'palm-oil'.

***A hart of grease.*** *See* Hart.

***Like greased lightning.*** Very quick indeed. In America the faster express trains used to be called 'lightning expresses', and when they wanted to go further in describing them they said they were '*greased* lightning'.

***To grease one's palm*** or ***fist.*** To give a bribe.

> Grease my fist with a tester or two, and ye shall find it in your pennyworths.
>
> Quarles, *The Virgin Widow*, iv, 1, p. 40

> S. You must oyl it first
> C. I understand you –
> Greaze him i' the fist.
>
> Cartwright, *Ordinary* (1651)

***To grease the wheels.*** To make things run smoothly, pass off without a hitch; usually by the application of a little 'grease', i.e. money.

**Greaser.** The American name for a Mexican or Spanish American, generally in contempt.

**Great, The.**

Abbas I, Shah of Persia. (1557, 1585–1628.)
Albertus Magnus, the schoolman. (d.1280.)
Alexander, of Macedon. (356 BC, 340–323.)
Alfonso III, King of Asturias and Leon. (848, 866–912.)
Alfred, of England. (849, 871–901.)
St Basil, Bishop of Caesarea. (4th cent.)
Canute, of England and Denmark. (995, 1014–35.)
Casimir III, of Poland. (1309, 1333–70.)
Charles, King of the Franks and Emperor of the Romans, called *Charlemagne*. (742, 764–814.)
Charles III. Duke of Lorraine. (1543–1608.)
Charles Emmanuel I, Duke of Savoy. (1562–1630.)
Clovis, King of the Franks. (466–511.)
Condé. *See* Louis II, *below*.
Constantine I, Emperor of Rome. (272, 306–337.)
Cyrus, founder of the Persian Empire. (d.529 BC.)

Darius, King of Persia. (d.485 BC.)
Douglas (*Archibald, the great Earl of Angus,* also called *Bell-the-Cat* [*q.v.*].)
Ferdinand I, of Castile and Leon. (Reigned 1034–65.)
Frederick William, Elector of Brandenburg, surnamed *The Great Elector.* (1620–88.)
Frederick II, of Prussia. (1712, 1740–86.)
Gregory I, Pope. (544, 590–604.)
Gustavus Adolphus, of Sweden. (1594, 1611–32.)
Henri IV, of France. (1553, 1589–1610.)
Herod I, King of Judea. (73–3 BC.)
John I, of Portugal. (1357, 1385–1433.)
Justinian I, Emperor of the East. (483, 527–565.)
Leo I, Pope. (440–461.)
Leo I, Emperor of the East. (457–474.)
Leopold I, of Germany. (1640–1705.)
Lewis I, of Hungary. (1326, 1342–83.)
Louis II, de Bourbon, Prince of Condé, Duc d'Enghien (1621–86), always known as *The Great Condé.*
Louis XIV, called *Le Grand Monarque.* (1638, 1643–1714.)
Mahomet II, Sultan of the Turks. (1430, 1451–81.)
Maximilian, Duke of Bavaria, victor of Prague. (1573–1651.)
Cosmo di' Medici, first Grand Duke of Tuscany. (1519, 1537–74.)
Gonzales Pedro de Mendoza, *great Cardinal of Spain,* statesman and scholar. (1428–95.)
Nicholas I, Pope (was Pope from 858–867).
Otho I, Emperor of the Romans. (912, 936–973.)
Peter I, of Russia. (1672, 1689–1725.)
Pierre III, of Aragon. (1239, 1276–85.)
Sancho III, King of Navarre. (About 965–1035.)
Sapor III, King of Persia. (d.380.)
Sforza (*Giacomo*), the Italian general. (1369–1424.)
Sigismund II, King of Poland. (1467, 1506–48.)
Theodoric, King of the Ostrogoths. (454, 475–526.)
Theodosius I, Emperor. (346, 378–395.)
Matteo Visconti, Lord of Milan. (1252, 1295–1323.)
Vladimir, Grand Duke of Russia. (973–1015.)
Waldemar I, of Denmark. (1131, 1157–82.)

***Great Bear, The.*** *See* Bear.

***Great Bible, The.*** *See* Bible, The English.

***Great Bullet-head.*** George Cadoudal (1771–1804), leader of the *Chouans*, born at Brech, in Morbihan.

***Great Captain.*** *See* Capitano, El Gran.

***Great Cham of Literature.*** So Smollett calls Dr Johnson (1709–84).

***Great Commoner, The.*** William Pitt (1750–1806).

***Great Dauphin, The.*** *See* Grand.

***Great Elector, The.*** Frederick William, Elector of Brandenburg (1620, 1640–88).

***Great Go.*** At the universities, a familiar term for the final examination for the BA degree; at Oxford usually shorted to *Greats. Cp.* Little Go.

> Since I have been reading ... for my greats, I have had to go into all sorts of deep books.
>
> Grant Allen, *The Backslider,* Pt iii

***Great Harry, The.*** A man-of-war built by Henry VII, the first of any size constructed in England. It was burnt in 1553. *See* Henry Grâce de Dieu.

***Great Head.*** Malcolm III, of Scotland; also called *Canmore*, which means the same thing. (Reigned 1057–93.)

***Great Mogul.*** The title of the chief of the Mogul Empire (*q.v.*).

***Great Scott*** or ***Scot!*** An exclamation of surprise, wonder, admiration, indignation, etc. It seems to have originated in America about the late '60's of last century, perhaps in memory of Gen. Winfield Scott (d.1866), an unsuccessful candidate for the Presidency in 1852, perhaps as a euphemism for *Great God* (like *by gosh* for *by God*, etc.), the initial letter of the Ger. *Gott* being changed into *Sc.*

In England the expression is sometimes humorously extended to 'Great Scotland Yard!'

***Great Unknown, The.*** Sir Walter Scott, who published *Waverley* (1814), and the subsequent novels as 'by the author of Waverley', anonymously. It was not till 1827 that he admitted the authorship, though it was pretty well known.

***Great Unwashed, The.*** The artisan class. Burke first used the compound, but Sir Walter Scott popularised it.

**Grebenski Cossacks.** So called from the word *greben* (a comb). This title was conferred upon them by Czar Ivan I, because, in his campaign against the Tartars of the Caucasus, they scaled a mountain fortified with sharp spurs, sloping down from its summit, and projecting horizontally, like a comb.

**Grecian.** *See* Blue-coat School.

**Grecian Bend, The.** An affectation in walking assumed by English ladies in 1875. The silliness spread to America and other countries which affect passing oddities of fashion.

**Grecian Coffee-house,** in Devereux Court, the oldest in London, was originally opened by Pasqua, a Greek slave, brought to England in 1652 by Daniel Edwards, a Turkey merchant. This Greek was the first to teach the method of roasting coffee and to introduce the drink into the island.

**Grecian Stairs.** A corruption of *grecing stairs.* The word *grecings* or *greesings* (steps) survives in the architectural word *grees*, and in *de-grees.* There is still on the hill at Lincoln a flight of stone steps called '*Grecian stairs*'.

> And whanne poul cam to the grees it bifel that he was borun of knyhtis for strengthe of the peple (*A.V.*, and when he came upon the stairs, so it was, that he was borne of the soldiers for the violence of the people).
>
> Wyclif, *The Dedis of Apostles*, xxi (Acts 21:38)

> Let me speak like yourself and lay a sentence,
> Which as a grise or step, may help these lovers
> Into your favour. Shakespeare, *Othello*, 1, 3

**Greegrees.** The name given on the West Coast of Africa to amulets, charms, fetishes, etc.

***A gree-gree man.*** One who sells these.

**Greek. *A merry Greek.*** *See* Grig.

***All Greek to me.*** Quite unintelligible; an unknown tongue or language. Casca says, 'For mine own part, it was all Greek to me.' (Shakespeare, *Julius Caesar*, 1, 2)

***Last of the Greeks.*** Philopoemen, of Megalopolis, whose great object was to infuse into the Achaeans a military spirit, and establish their independence (252–183 BC).

***To play the Greek.*** To indulge in one's cups. The Greeks have always been considered a luxurious race, fond of creature comforts. Thus Cicero, in his oration against 'Verres', says: '*Discumbitur; fit sermo inter eos et invitatio, ut Graeco more biberetur: hospes hortatur, poscunt majoribus poculis; celebratur omnium sermone laetitiaque convivium.*' The law in Greek banquets was *E pithi e apithi* (Quaff, or be off!) (Cut in, or cut off!). In *Troilus and Cressida* (1, 2) Shakespeare makes Pandarus, bantering Helen for her love to Troilus, say, 'I think Helen loves him better than Paris'; to which Cressida, whose wit is to parry and pervert, replies, 'Then she's a merry Greek indeed,' insinuating that she was a 'woman of pleasure'. *See* Grig.

***When Greek meets Greek, then is the tug of war.*** When two men or armies of undoubted courage fight, the contest will be very severe. The line is slightly altered from a 17th-century play, and the reference is to the obstinate resistance of the Greek cities to Philip and Alexander, the Macedonian kings.

> When Greeks joined Greeks, then was the tug of war. Nathaniel Lee, *The Rival Queens*, IV, ii

**Greek Calends.** Never. To defer anything to the Greek Calends is to defer it *sine die.* There were no calends in the Greek months. *See* Never.

> Will you speak of your paltry prose doings in my presence, whose great historical poem, in twenty books, with notes in proportion has been postponed 'ad Graecas Kalendas'?
>
> Scott, *The Betrothed* (Intro.)

**Greek Church, The Orthodox.** The Eastern Church, the separation of which from the Western (Latin, or Roman) began in the 9th century and was completed in 1054, called 'Orthodox' because it adheres to the *Orthodoxa confessio Orientalis Ecclesiae.* It includes the Church subject to the patriarch of Constantinople, the Church in the kingdom of Greece, and the Russo-Greek Church, the latter being governed by the Holy Synod.

The Greek Church dissents from the doctrine that the Holy Ghost proceeds from the Father and the Son (*Filioque*), rejects the Papal claim to supremacy and the celibacy of the clergy, and administers the eucharist in both kinds to the laity; but the two churches agree in their belief of seven sacraments, transubstantiation, the adoration of the Host, confession, absolution, penance, prayers for the dead, etc.

**Greek Cross.** Same shape as St George's cross (✚). The Latin cross has the upright one-third longer than the cross-beam (✝).

St George's Cross is seen on our banners, where the crosses of St Andrew and St Patrick are combined with it. *See* Union Jack.

**Greek Fire.** A combustible composition used for setting fire to an enemy's ships, fortifications, etc., of nitre, sulphur, and naphtha. Tow steeped in the mixture was hurled in a blazing state through tubes, or tied to arrows. The invention is ascribed to Callinicos, of Heliopolis, AD 668, and it was first used by the Greeks at Constantinople.

**Greek Gift.** A treacherous gift. The reference is to the Wooden Horse of Troy (*q.v.*), or to Virgil's *Timeo Danaos et dona ferentes* (*Aeneid*, ii, 49), 'I fear the Greeks, even when they offer gifts.'

**Greek Trust.** No trust at all. '*Graeca fides*' was with the Romans no faith at all.

**Green.** Young, fresh, as *green cheese*, cream cheese, which is eaten fresh; *a green old age*, an old age in which the faculties are not impaired and the spirits are still youthful; *green goose*, a young or midsummer goose.

> If you would fat green geese, shut them up when they are about a month old.
>
> Mortimer, *Husbandry*

Immature in age or judgment, inexperienced, young.

My salad days
When I was green in judgment!
Shakespeare, *Antony and Cleopatra*, 1, 5

The text is old, the orator too green.
Shakespeare, *Venus and Adonis*, 806

Simple, raw, easily imposed upon; the characteristic greenhorn (*q.v.*).

'He is so jolly green,' said Charley.
Dickens, *Oliver Twist*, ch. ix

For its symbolism, etc., *see* Colours.

***Do you see any green in my eye?*** *See* Eye.

***If they do these things in the green tree, what shall be done in the dry?*** (Luke 23:31). If they start like this, how will they finish? Or, as Pope says (*Moral Essays*, *Ep. I*), 'Just as the twig is bent, the tree's inclined.'

***To give a girl a green gown.*** A 16th century phrase for romping with a girl in the fields or rolling her on the grass so that her dress is stained green; hence, sometimes, to go beyond the bounds of innocent amusement.

There's not a budding Boye, or Girle, this day,
But is got up, and gone to bring in May ...
Many a green-gown has been given;
Many a kisse, both odd and even.
Herrick, *Corinna's Going a-Maying*

***To look through green glasses.*** To feel jealous of one; to be envious of another's success. *Cp.* Green-eyed Monster *below*.

***The Board of Green Cloth.*** *See* Board.

***The moon made of green cheese.*** *See* Moon.

***The wearing of the green.*** An Irish patriotic and revolutionary song, dating from 1798. Green (*cp.* Emerald Isle) was the emblematic colour adopted by Irish Nationalists.

They're hanging men and women for the wearing of the green.

***Gentlemen of the Green Baize Road.*** Whist players. 'Gentlemen of the Green Cloth Road', billiard players. (*See Bleak House*, ch. xxvi, par. 1.) Probably the idea of sharpers is included, as 'Gentlemen of the Road' means highwaymen.

***Green Dragoons.*** The old 13th Dragoons (whose regimental facings were green). Now called the 13th Hussars, and the regimental facings have been white since 1861.

***Green hands.*** A nautical phrase for inferior sailors. *See* Able-bodied Seaman, *and cp.* Greenhorn *below*.

***The Green Horse.*** The 5th Dragoon Guards; because they have *green* for their regimental facings.

***The Green Howards.*** The 19th Foot, named from the Hon. Charles Howard, colonel from 1738 to 1748. Green was the colour of their regimental facings, now white, and the regiment is called 'The Princess of Wales' Own'.

***The Green Isle.*** Ireland. *See* Emerald Isle.

***The Green Knight.*** In the old romance, *Valentine and Orson*, a Pagan who demanded Fezon in marriage but, overcome by Orson, resigned his claim.

***Gawain and the Green Knight.*** *See* Gawain.

***Green Linnets.*** The 39th Foot, so called from the colour of their facings. Now the Dorsetshire, and the facings are white.

***Green Man.*** This common public-house sign probably represents either a Jack-in-the-Green (*q.v.*), or a gamekeeper, who used at one time to be dressed in green.

But the 'Green Man' shall I pass by unsung,
Which mine own James upon his sign-post hung?
His sign, his image – for he once was seen
A squire's attendant, clad in keeper's green.
Crabbe, *Borough*

The public-house sign, *The Green Man and Still*, is probably from the arms of the Distillers' Company, the supporters of which were two Indians, which, by the sign-painters, were depicted as clad in green boughs like a 'green man' or Jack-in-the-Green.

On a golf course the green-man is the club servant who is responsible for the putting greens.

***Green Ribbon Day*** in Ireland is March 17th, St Patrick's Day, when the shamrock and green ribbon are worn as the national badge.

***Green room.*** The common waiting-room beyond the stage at a theatre for the performers; so called because at one time the walls were coloured green to relieve the eyes affected by the glare of the stage lights.

***Green wax.*** In old legal practice an estreat formerly delivered to the sheriff by the Exchequer for levy. It was under the seal of the court, which was impressed upon green wax.

**Greenbacks.** A legal tender note in the United States, first issued in 1862, during the Civil War, as a war-revenue measure; so called because the back is printed in green. In 1878, the amount of greenbacks for permanent circulation was fixed at 346,681,016 dollars; in rough numbers, about 70 millions sterling.

**Green-eyed Monster, The.** So Shakespeare called jealousy:

*Iago*. O! beware, my lord, of jealousy;
It is the green-ey'd monster which doth mock
The meat it feeds on. *Othello*, 3, 3

A greenish complexion was formerly held to be indicative of jealousy; and as cats, lions, tigers, and all the green-eyed tribe 'mock the meat they feed on', so jealousy mocks its victim by loving and loathing it at the same time.

**Greener.** A slang term for a foreigner who commences to learn either tailoring or shoe-making on his arrival in England.

**Greengage.** A variety of plum introduced into England from France (with others) by Sir William Gage of Norfolk, about 1725, and named in honour of him. Called by the French 'Reine Claude', out of compliment to the daughter of Anne de Bretagne and Louis XII, generally called *la bonne reine* (1499–1524).

**Greenhorn.** A novice at any trade, profession, sport, etc., a simpleton, a youngster. *Cp.* Green Hand; Greener.

**Greenlander.** A native of Greenland, which was originally so called (*Grönland*) by the Norsemen in the 10th century with the idea that if only they gave the country a good name it would induce settlers to go there! Facetiously applied to a greenhorn.

**Greensleeves.** A very popular ballad in Elizabethan days, first published in 1581, given *in extenso* in Clement Robinson's *Handefull of Pleasant Delites* (1584), and twice mentioned by Shakespeare (*Merry Wives*, 2, 1, and 5, 5). It tells of an inconstant ladylove (Lady Greensleeves) and was sung to the older tune of 'Christmas comes but once a year'. The first verse and the refrain are:

Alas my love, ye do me wrong,
To cast me off discurteously:
And I have loved you so long,
Delighting in your companie.
Greensleeves was all my joy,
Greensleeves was my delight:
Greensleeves was my hart of gold,
And who by Ladie Greensleeves.

The tune was also used as a popular dance, and as late as 1717 it was still remembered:

If while the Mind was in her Leg,
The Dance affected nimble Peg;
Old Madge, bewitch'd at Sixty-one,
Calls for *Green Sleeves* and *Jumping Joan*.

Matt. Prior, *Alma*, ca. ii

**Greenwich.** So named by Danish settlers; it means 'the green place on the bay' (*wich*, *vig*), or place situated on the coast or near the mouth of a river; as Sandwich, Lerwick, Schleswig.

***Greenwich barbers.*** Retailers of sand; so called because the inhabitants of Greenwich used to 'shave the pits' in the neighbourhood to supply London with sand.

***Greenwich stars.*** The stars used by astronomers for the lunar computations in the nautical ephemeris.

***Greenwich time.*** Mean time for the meridian of Greenwich, i.e. the system of time in which noon occurs at the moment of passage of the mean sun over the meridian of Greenwich. It is the standard time adopted by astronomers; it is in legal use throughout Great Britain, Ireland, France, Belgium, Spain, Portugal, the Faröe Islands, Gibraltar, Algeria, St Thomas and Princes Isles, the Ivory Coast, Dahomey, and Morocco; and from it all civilised nations compute their time.

**Gregorian Calendar.** *See* Calendar.

**Gregorian Chant.** Plain-song; a mediaeval system of church music, so called because it was introduced into the service by Gregory the Great (600).

**Gregorian Epoch.** The epoch or day on which the Gregorian calendar commenced – March, 1582.

**Gregorian Telescope.** The first form of the reflecting telescope, invented by James Gregory, professor of mathematics at St Andrews (1663).

**Gregorian Tree.** The gallows; so named from Gregory Brandon and his son, Robert (who was popularly known as 'Young Gregory'), hangmen from the time of James I to 1649. Sir William Segar, Garter Knight of Arms, granted a coat of arms to Gregory Brandon. *See* Hangmen.

This trembles under the black rod, and he
Doth fear his fate from the Gregorian tree.

*Mercutius Pragmaticus* (1641)

**Gregorian Year.** The civil year, according to the correction introduced by Pope Gregory XIII in 1582. *See* Calendar. The equinox which occurred on March 25th, in the time of Julius Caesar, fell on March 11th in the year 1582. This was because the Julian calculation of 365¼ days to a year was 11 min. 10 sec. too much. Gregory suppressed ten days, so as to make the equinox fall on March 21st, as it did at the Council of Nice, and, by some simple arrangements, prevented the recurrence in future of a similar error.

The New Style, as it was called, was adopted in England in 1752, when Wednesday, September 2nd, was followed by Thursday, September 14th.

This has given rise to a double computation, as Lady Day, March 25th, Old Lady Day, April 6th; Midsummer Day, June 24th, Old Midsummer Day, July 6th; Michaelmas Day, September 29th, Old Michaelmas Day, October 11th; Christmas Day, December 25th, Old Christmas Day, January 6th.

**Gregories.** Hangmen. *See* Gregorian Tree.

**Gregory.** A feast held on St Gregory's Day (March 12th), especially in Ireland but formerly common to all Europe.

**Grenadier.** Originally a soldier whose duty in battle was to throw grenades, i.e. explosive shells, weighing from two to six pounds, thrown by the hand. There were some four or five tall, picked men, chosen for this purpose from each company; later each regiment had a special company of them; and when, in the 18th century, the use of grenades was discontinued (not to be revived till the Great War), the name was retained for the company composed of the tallest and finest men. In the British Army it now survives only in the *Grenadier Guards*, the First regiment of Foot Guards (3 battalions), noted for their height, fine physique, traditions, and discipline.

**Grendel.** The mythical, half-human monster in *Beowulf* (*q.v.*), who nightly raided the king's hall and slew the sleepers; he was slain by Beowulf.

**Gresham, Sir Thomas.** *See* Cleopatra and the Pearl; Grasshopper.

***To dine with Sir Thomas Gresham.*** *See* Dine.

**Greta Hall.** ***The poet of Greta Hall.*** Southey, who lived at Greta Hall, in the Vale of Keswick (1774–1843).

**Grethel, Gammer.** The hypothetical narrator of the *Nursery Tales* edited by the brothers Grimm.

**Gretna Green Marriages.** Runaway matches. In Scotland, all that is required of contracting parties is a mutual declaration before witnesses of their willingness to marry, so that elopers reaching Gretna, a hamlet near the village of Springfield, Dumfriesshire, 8 miles NW of Carlisle, and just across the border, could (up to 1856) get legally married without either licence, banns, or priest. The declaration was generally made to a blacksmith.

Crabbe has a metrical tale called *Gretna Green*, and a 'Gretna Green marriage' has formed the motive, or an incident, of countless romances, stories, and ballads.

**Grève.** ***Place de Grève.*** The Tyburn of old Paris, where for centuries public executions took place. The present Hôtel de Ville occupies part of the site, and what is left of the *Place* is now called the *Place de l'Hôtel de Ville*. The word *grève* means the strand of a river or the shore of the sea, and the *Place* is on the bank of the Seine.

> Who has e'er been to Paris must needs know the Grève,
> The fatal retreat of th' unfortunate brave,
> Where honour and justice most oddly contribute
> To ease Hero's pains by a halter or gibbet.
>
> Prior, *The Thief and the Cordelier*

**Grey Cloak.** A City of London alderman who has passed the chair; so called because his official robe is furred with grey amis.

**Grey Friars.** Franciscans (*q.v.*). Black Friars are Dominicans, and White Friars Carmelites.

**Grey Goose Feather,** or **Wing.** 'The grey goose wing was the death of him' – the arrow which is winged with grey goose feathers.

**Grey Mare.** *See* Mare.

**Grey Sisters.** *See* Franciscans.

**Grey Washer by the Ford, The.** An Irish wraith which seems to be washing clothes in a river, but when the 'doomed man' approaches she holds up what she seemed to be washing, and it is the phantom of himself with his death wounds from which he is about to suffer. (Hon. Emily Lawless, *Essex in Ireland*, p. 245–6)

**Greybacks.** A facetious name given by soldiers to lice – which are also called the 'Scots Greys', in allusion to the regiment and the supposed partiality of these pests for Scotsmen.

**Greybeard.** An old man – generally a doddering old fellow; also an earthen pot for holding spirits; a large stone jar. *Cp.* Bellarmine.

> We will give a cup of distilled waters … unto the next pilgrim that comes over; and ye may keep for the purpose the grunds of the last greybeard.
>
> Scott, *Monastery*, ch. ix

**Greyhound.** Juliana Berners, in the *Boke of St Albans* (1486) gives the following as 'the propreteïs of a goode Grehound':

> A greyhounde shoulde be heded like a snake, And necked like a Drake; Foted like a Kat, Tayled like a Rat; Syded like a Teme, Chyned like a Beme.

'Syded like a teme' probably means both sides alike, a plough-team being meant.

***Greyhound.*** The Greyhound as a public-house sign is in honour of Henry VII, whose badge it was; it is still the badge (in silver) of the King's Messengers.

**Greys.** ***The Scots Greys.*** The 2nd (Royal North British) Dragoons, so called because they are mounted on grey horses. *Cp.* Greybacks.

**Gridiron.** Emblematic of St Lawrence, because in his martyrdom he was broiled to death on a gridiron. In allusion thereto the church of St Lawrence Jewry in the City of London has a gilt gridiron for a vane. The gridiron is also an attribute of St Faith, who was martyred like St Lawrence; and St Vincent, who was partially roasted on a gridiron covered with spikes, AD 258. *See* Escorial.

**Grief.** ***To come to grief.*** To meet with disaster; to be ruined; to fail in business. As lots of money is the fullness of joy, so the want of it is the grief of griefs.

**Griffin.** A mythical monster, also called *Griffon*, *Gryphon*, etc., fabled to be the offspring of the lion and eagle. Its legs and all from the shoulder to the head are like an eagle, the rest of the body is that of a lion. This creature was sacred to the sun, and kept guard over hidden treasures. *See* Arimaspians.

> [The Griffin is] an Emblem of valour and magnanimity, as being compounded of the Eagle and lion, the noblest Animals in their kinds; and so is it appliable unto Princes, Presidents, Generals, and all heroick Commanders; and so is it also born in the Coat-arms of many noble Families of *Europe*.
>
> Sir Thos Browne, *Pseudodoxia Epidemica*, III, xi

Among Anglo-Indians a newcomer, a greenhorn (*q.v.*) is called a *griffin*; and the residue of a contract feast, taken away by the contractor, half the buyer's and half the seller's, is known in the trade as *griffins*.

**Grig.** ***Merry as a grig.*** A grig is a cricket, or grasshopper; but it is by no means certain that the animal is referred to in this phrase (which is at least as old as the mid-sixteenth century); for *grig* here may be a corruption of *Greek*, 'merry as a Greek', which dates from about the same time. Shakespeare has: 'Then she's a merry Greek'; and again, 'Cressid 'mongst the merry Greeks' (*Troilus and Cressida*, 1, 2; 4, 4); and among the Romans *Graecari* signified 'to play the reveller'.

**Grim.** The giant in Bunyan's *Pilgrim's Progress* (pt ii), who tried to stop pilgrims on their way to the Celestial City, but was slain by Mr Greatheart. *See also* Grimsby: Grim's Dyke.

**Grimalkin.** An old she-cat, especially a wicked- or eerie-looking one: from *grey* and *Malkin* (*q.v.*). Shakespeare makes the Witch in *Macbeth* say, 'I come, Graymalkin.' The cat was supposed to be a witch and was the companion of witches.

**Grimbert.** The name given to the Badger in Caxton's version of *Reynard the Fox*. His wife was Slopecade.

**Grimm's Law.** The law of the permutation of consonants in the principal Aryan languages, first formulated by Jacob L. Grimm, the German philologist, in 1822. Thus, what is *p* in Greek, Latin, or Sanskrit, becomes *f* in Gothic, and *b* or *f* in the Old High German; what is *t* in Greek, Latin, or Sanskrit becomes *th* in Gothic, and *d* in Old High German; etc. Thus changing *p* into *f*, and *t* into *th*, 'pater' becomes 'father'.

**Grimsby** (Lincolnshire). Founded, according to the old legend, by Grim, the fisherman who saved the life of Havelok (*q.v.*), son of the king of Denmark. Grim was laden with gifts by the royal parent, and returned to Lincolnshire, where he built the town whose ancient seal still contains the names of 'Gryme' and 'Habloc'.

**Grim's Dyke.** The name given to the great fortified fosse which formerly enclosed Salisbury and Silchester, and was probably built in prehistoric times by the first invaders from the Continent as a protection against the aborigines.

**Grin.** ***To grin like a Cheshire cat.*** *See* Cat.

***You must grin and bear it.*** Resistance is hopeless; you may make up a face, if you like, but you cannot help yourself.

**Grind.** To work up for an examination; to grind up the subjects set, and to grind into the memory the necessary 'cram'.

***To grind one down.*** To reduce the price asked; to lower wages. A knife, etc., is gradually reduced by grinding.

***To take a grind.*** To take a constitutional walk; to cram into the smallest space the greatest amount of physical exercise. This is the physical grind. The literary grind is a turn at hard study.

**Grinders.** The double teeth which grind the food put into the mouth. The Preacher speaks of old age as the time when 'the grinders cease because they are few' (Eccles. 12:3).

***To take a grinder.*** To insult another by applying the left thumb to the nose and revolving the right hand round it, as if working a hand-organ or coffee-mill; done when someone has tried to practise on your credulity, or to impose upon your good faith.

**Grise** or **Grize.** *See* Grecian Stairs.

**Grisilda** or **Griselda.** The model of enduring patience and obedience, often spoken of as 'Patient Grisel'. She was the heroine of the last tale in Boccaccio's *Decameron*, obtained by him from an old French story, *Parement des Femmes*, translated from Boccaccio by Petrarch, and thence used by Chaucer for his *Clerk's Tale* in the *Canterbury Tales*.

The synopsis of the story is:

> The Marquis of Saluzzo, having been prevailed upon by his subjects to marry, in order to please himself in the affair, made choice of a country-man's daughter [viz. Griselda], by whom he had two children, which he pretended to put to death. Afterwards, feigning that he was weary of her, and had taken another, he had his own daughter brought home, as if he had espoused her, whilst his wife was sent away destitute. At length, being convinced of her patience, he brought her home again, presenting her children, now grown up, and ever afterwards loved and honoured her as his lady.

The trials to which the flinty-hearted marquis subjected his innocent wife are almost as unbelievable as the fortitude with which she is credited to have borne them, and perhaps it is just as well that, as Chaucer says in his own 'Envoy' to the *Clerk's Tale*:

> Grisilde is dead, and eke her pacience.
> And both at once buried in Italie.

**Grist. *All grist that comes to my mill.*** All is appropriated that comes to me; all is made use of that comes in my way. Grist is all that quantity of corn which is to be ground at one time. *See* Emolument.

***To bring grist to the mill.*** To bring profitable business or gain; to furnish supplies.

**Grit.** *See* Clear Grit, *s.v.* Clear.

**Grizel.** A variant – like *Grissel* – of *Griselda* (*q.v.*). Octavia, wife of Mark Antony and sister of Augustus Caesar, is called the 'patient Grizel' of Roman story.

> For patience she will prove a second Grissel.
> Shakespeare, *Taming of the Shrew*, 2, 1

**Groaning Chair.** A rustic name for a chair in which a woman sits after her confinement to receive congratulations. Similarly 'groaning cake' and 'groaning cheese' (called in some dialects *kenno*, because its making was kept a secret) are the cake and cheese which used to be provided in 'Goose month' (*q.v.*), and 'groaning malt' was a strong ale brewed for the occasion.

> For a nurse, the child to dandle,
> Sugar, soap, spiced pots and candle,
> A groaning chair and eke a cradle.
> *Poor Robin's Almanack*, 1676

> Meg Merrilles descended to the kitchen to secure her share of the groaning malt.
> Scott, *Guy Mannering*, ch. iii

**Groat.** A silver fourpence. The Dutch had a coin called a *groot* (i.e. *great*, with reference to its thickness), hence the fourpenny-piece of Edward III was the *groat* or *great* silver penny. The modern fourpenny-piece – never officially, but often popularly, called a *groat* – was issued from 1836 to 1856, the issue of the true groat having ceased in 1662.

> He that spends a groat a day idly, spends idly above six pounds a year.
> Franklin, *Necessary Hints*

***You half-faced groat.*** A 16th century colloquialism for 'You worthless fellow'. The debased groats issued in the reign of Henry VIII had the king's head in profile, but those in the reign of Henry VII had the king's head with the full face. *See King John*, 1, 1.

> Thou half-faced groat! You thick-cheeked chitty-face!
> Munday, *The Downfal of Robert, Earle of Huntingdon* (1598)

**Groats.** Husked oat or wheat, fragments rather larger than grits (A.S. *grut*, coarse meal).

***Blood without groats is nothing.*** Family without fortune is worthless. The allusion is perhaps to black pudding, which consists chiefly of blood and groats formed into a sausage.

**Grog.** Any spirits, but especially rum, diluted with water. Admiral Vernon, who was nicknamed *Old Grog* by his sailors because he walked the deck in rough weather in a *grogram cloak*, was the first to dilute the rum on board ship, hence the name. *Sixwater grog* is one part rum to six parts of water.

***Grog-blossoms.*** Blotches or pimples on the face produced by over-indulgence in drink.

**Grogram.** A coarse kind of taffeta made of silk and mohair or silk and wool, stiffened with gum. A corruption of the Fr. *gros-grain.*

> Gossips in grief and grograms clad.
> Praed, *The Troubadour*, c. i, st. 5

***The blood of the Grograms.*** *See* Blood.

**Grommet.** *See* Grummet.

**Groom of the Stole.** *See* Stole.

**Gross.** The French word *gros*, big, bulky, corpulent, coarse, which in English has developed many meanings not present in French. Thus, a *gross* is twelve dozen; a *great gross*, twelve gross; *gross weight* is the entire weight without deductions; *gross average* is the general average. A *villein in gross* was a villein the entire property of his master, and not attached to the land; a *common in gross* is one which is entirely personal property, and does not belong to the manor. *Cp.* Advowson in gross.

**Grotesque.** Literally, in 'Grotto style'. The chambers of ancient buildings revealed in mediaeval times in Rome were called *grottoes*, and as the walls of these were frequently decorated with fanciful ornaments and *outré* designs, the word *grotesqué* (*grotesco*) came to be applied to similar ornamentation.

**Grotto.** ***Pray remember the grotto.*** This cry is still occasionally raised by small children in the street who collect old shells, bits of coloured stone or pottery, with leaves, flowers, and so on, build a little 'grotto', and kneel beside it with their caps ready for pennies. The custom should be restricted to July 25th (St James's Day), for it is – though few of the little beggars can be expected to know it – a relic of the old shell grottoes which were erected with an image of the saint for the behoof of those who could not afford the pilgrimage necessary to pay a visit on that day to the shrine of St James of Compostella. The keeper of the grotto is supposed to remind the passer-by to remember it is St James's Day, and not to forget their offering to the saint.

**Ground.** ***Ground floor.*** The story level with the ground outside; or, in a basement-house, the floor above the basement.

***Ground swell.*** A long, deep rolling or swell of the sea, caused by a recent or distant storm, or by an earthquake.

***It would suit me down to the ground.*** Wholly and entirely.

***To break ground.*** To be the first to commence a project, etc.; to take the first step in an undertaking.

***To gain ground.*** To make progress; to be improving one's position or prospects of success.

***To have the ground cut from under one's feet.*** To see what one has relied on for support suddenly removed.

***To hold one's ground.*** To maintain one's authority; popularity, etc.; not to budge from one's position.

***To lose ground.*** To become less popular or less successful; to drift away from the object aimed at.

***To shift one's ground.*** To try a different plan; to change one's argument or the basis of one's reasoning.

***To stand one's ground.*** Not to yield or give way; to stick to one's colours: to have the courage of one's opinion.

**Groundlings.** The *canaille*; those who occupied the cheapest portion of an Elizabethan theatre, i.e. the pit, which was the bare ground in front of the stage, without any seats. The actor who today 'plays to the gallery' in Elizabethan times

> Split the ears of the groundlings.
>
> Shakespeare, *Hamlet*, 3, 2

**Growlers.** The old four-wheeled cabs were called 'growlers' from the surly and discontented manners of their drivers, and 'crawlers' from their slow pace.

> Taken as whole, the average drivers of hansom cab ... are smart, intelligent men, sober, honest, and hardworking ... They have little ... in common with the obtrusive, surly besotted drivers of the 'growlers' and 'crawlers'.
>
> *Nineteenth Century*, March, 1893, p .473

**Grub Street.** The former name of a London street in the ward of Cripplegate Without, which, says Johnson, was

> Much inhabited by writers of small histories, dictionaries, and temporary poems; whence any mean production is called *grubstreet*.

The word is used allusively for needy authors, literary hacks, and their work.

In 1830 the name was changed to Milton Street – *not* from the poet, though he lived in the neighbourhood for years and was buried at St Giles's, Cripplegate – but in honour of the carpenter and builder who was ground landlord at the time. The street leads north out of Fore Street, Moorfields, to Chiswell Street.

**Gruel.** ***To give him his gruel.*** To give him severe punishment; properly, to kill him. The allusion is to the practice in 16th century France of giving poisoned possets – an art brought to perfection by Catherine de Medicis and her Italian advisers.

**Grumbo.** A giant in the nursery tale of *Tom Thumb* (*q.v.*). A raven dropped Tom at the giant's castle; he crept up Grumbo's sleeve, and the giant shook him into the sea, where a fish swallowed him. The fish, having been caught and brought to Arthur's table, was the means of introducing Tom to the British king, by whom he was knighted.

**Grummet.** The cabin-boy on board ship; the youth whose duty it is to take in the topsails, or top the yard for furling the sails or slinging the yards. The name is also given to a ring of rope made by laying a single strand, and to a powder-wad.

**Grundy.** ***What will Mrs. Grundy say?*** What will our very proper and strait-laced neighbours say? The phrase is from Tom Morton's *Speed the Plough* (1798). In the first scene Mrs Ashfield shows herself very jealous of neighbour Grundy, and farmer Ashfield says to her: 'Be quiet, wull ye? Always ding, dinging Dame Grundy into my ears. What will Mrs Grundy zay? What will Mrs Grundy think? ...'

They eat, and drink, and scheme, and plod,
They go to church on Sunday;
And many are afraid of God,
And more of Mrs Grundy.
Locker Lampson, *London Lyrics*

**Gruyère.** A town in Switzerland which gives its name to a kind of cheese made there.

**Gryll.** ***Let Gryll be Gryll****, and have his hoggish mind* (Spenser, *Faërie Queene*, II, xii, 87). Don't attempt to wash a blackamoor white; the leopard will never change his spots. Gryll is the Gr. *grullos*, a hog. When Sir Guyon disenchanted the forms in the Bower of Bliss (*q.v.*) some were exceedingly angry, and Gryll, who had been metamorphosed by Acrasia into a hog, abused him most roundly.

**Gryphon.** *See* Griffin.

**Guadiana.** According to the old legend the Spanish river was so called from the Squire of Durandartë of this name. Mourning the fall of his master at Roncesvalles, he was turned into the river. *See Don Quixote*, ii, 23. Actually, it is Arabic *wadi*, a river, and *Anas*, its classical name (*Strabo*).

**Guard.** ***To be off one's guard.*** To be careless or heedless.

***To put one on his guard.*** To 'give him the tip', show him where the danger lies.

A *guardroom* is the place where military offenders are detained; and a *guardship* is a ship stationed in a port or harbour for its defence.

**Guards of the Pole.** *See* Bear, the Great.

**Guarinos.** One of Charlemagne's paladins, taken captive at Roncesvalles. Refusing to become a Moslem, he was cast into a dungeon, where he lay for seven years. A joust was then held, and Guarinos was allowed to try his hand at a target. He knelt before the Moor, stabbed him to the heart, and then vaulted on his grey horse Trebozond, and escaped to France.

**Gubbings.** The wild and savage inhabitants in the neighbourhood of Brent Tor, Devon, who, according to Fuller in his *Worthies* (1661) –

> lived in holes, like swine; had all things in common; and multiplied without marriage. Their language was vulgar Devonian ... They lived by pilfering sheep; were fleet as horses; held together like bees; and revenged every wrong. One of the society was always elected chief, and called *King of the Gubbings.*

**Gudgeon.** ***Gaping for gudgeons.*** Looking out for things extremely improbable. As a gudgeon is a bait for fish, it means a *lie*, a *deception.*

***To swallow a gudgeon.*** To be bamboozled with a most palpable lie, as silly fish are caught by gudgeons. (Fr. *goujon*, whence the phrase *avaler le goujon*, to swallow the bait, to die.)

Make fools believe in their foreseeing
Of things before they are in being;
To swallow gudgeons ere they're catched.
And count their chickens ere they're hatched.
Butler, *Hudibras*, ii, 3

**Gudrun.** The heroine of the great popular German epic poem, *Gûdrûn*, or *Kûdrûn*, written about 1210, and founded on a passage in the prose Edda (*q.v.*). She was the daughter of Hetel, king of Ireland, and was betrothed to Herwig of Seeland, but Hartmut, the King of Norway, carried her off captive. As she would not marry him he put her to all sorts of menial work, such as washing the dirty linen. Thirteen years later her brother and lover appeared on the scene with an army; they laid waste the country, razed the castle, released the prisoners, carried Hartmut off captive, and Gudrun and Herwig were married – to live happy ever after. Gudrun is the German type of wifely loyalty and love.

**Gudule** or **Gudila, St.** Patron saint of Brussels, daughter of Count Witger, died 712. She is represented with a lantern, from a tradition that she was one day going to the church of St Morgelle with a lantern, which went out, but the holy virgin lighted it again with her prayers.

**Guebres** or **Ghebers.** Followers of the ancient Persian religion, reformed by Zoroaster; fire worshippers; Parsees. The name, which was bestowed upon them by their Arabian conquerors, is now applied to fire-worshippers generally.

**Guelder Rose.** The *Rose de Gueldre*, i.e. of the ancient province of Guelder or Guelderland, in Holland.

**Guelphs and Ghibellines.** Two great parties whose conflicts made so much of the history of Italy and Germany in the 12th, 13th, and 14th centuries. The Guelphs were the papal and popular party in Italy; their name is the Italian form of *Welfe*, as 'Ghibelline' is that of *Waiblingen*, and the origin of these two words is this: At the battle of Weinsburg, in Suabia (1140), Conrad, Duke of Franconia, rallied his followers with the war-cry *Hie Waiblingen* (his family estate), while Henry the Lion, Duke of Saxony, used the cry of *Hie Welfë* (the family name). The Ghibellines supported in Italy the side of the German emperors; the Guelphs opposed it, and supported the cause of the Pope.

The reigning dynasty in Great Britain, the royal House of Windsor, is, through the ducal House of Brunswick, descended from the Guelphs.

**Guendoloena.** According to Geoffrey of Monmouth, daughter of Corineus and wife of Locrine, son of Brute, the legendary king of Britain. She was divorced, and Locrine married Estrildis, by whom he already had a daughter named Sabrina. Guendoloena, greatly indignant, got together a large army, and near the river Stour a battle was fought, in which Locrine was slain. Guendoloena now assumed the government, and one of her first acts was to throw both Estrildis and Sabrina into the river Severn.

**Guenever.** *See* Guinever.

**Guerilla War.** A petty war carried on by bodies of irregular troops acting independently of each other. From Span, *guerilla*, diminutive of *guerra*, war. The word is applied to the armed bands of peasants, and to individuals, who carry on irregular war on their own account, especially at such time as their government is contending with invading armies.

**Guerinists.** An early 17th century sect of French Illuminati (*q.v.*), founded by Peter Guérin. They were Antinomians, and claimed a special revelation of the Way to Perfection.

**Guerino Meschino** [*the Wretched*]. An Italian romance, half chivalric and half allegoric, first printed in Padua in 1473. Guerino was the son of Millon, King of Albania. On the day of his birth his father was dethroned, and the child was rescued by a Greek slave, and called Meschino. When he grew up he fell in love with the Princess Elizena, sister of the Greek Emperor, at Constantinople.

**Guernsey Lily.** *See* Misnomers.

**Guess.** The modern American use of the verb, meaning to think, to suppose, to be pretty sure (as in 'I guess I'll have some pie, but I'll be ill after it, I guess'), was good colloquial English before America was colonised. Shakespeare has:

*Bed*: Ascend, brave Talbot; we will follow thee.
*Tal*: Not all together: better far, I guess,
That we do make our entrance several ways.
*1 Henry VI*, 2, 1

and Spenser:

But now is time, I gesse, homeward to go.
*Shepherd's Calendar*, June, 117

**Gueux, Les.** The league of Flemish nobles organised in 1565 to resist the introduction of the Spanish Inquisition into the Netherlands by Philip II of Spain. The word means 'ragamuffins' or 'beggars'; and the origin of its application is said to be that when the Duchess of Parma made inquiry about them of Count Berlaymont, he told her they were 'the scum and offscouring of the people' (*les gueux*). The party took the name in defiance, and dressed like beggars, substituting a fox's tail for a feather, etc.

**Guiderius.** The elder son of Cymbeline (*q.v.*), a legendary king of Britain during the reign of Augustus Caesar. In Shakespeare's *Cymbeline* Guiderius and his brother Arviragus were stolen in infancy by Belarius, a banished nobleman, out of revenge, and were brought up by him in a cave. When the Romans invaded Britain the two young men so distinguished themselves that they were introduced to the king, and Belarius related their history. Geoffrey of Monmouth says that Guiderius succeeded his father, and was slain by Hamo.

**Guides.** The military name for men formed into companies for reconnoitring purposes; especially a regiment of cavalry and infantry in the Punjab Frontier Force of the Anglo-Indian army, originally raised by Sir Henry Lawrence about 1840.

In the French army the Guides were created in 1744 as a small company, but the number was gradually increased, and they relinquished their special duties, till in Napoleon's time they formed a personal bodyguard of 10,000 strong.

Napoleon III made the corps a part of the Imperial Guard.

**Guido,** surnamed *the Savage* (in *Orlando Furioso*), son of Constantia and Amon, therefore younger brother of Rinaldo. He was also Astolpho's kinsman. Being wrecked on the coast of the Amazons, he was doomed to fight their ten male champions. He slew them all, and was then compelled to marry ten of the Amazons. He made his escape with Aleria, his favourite wife, and joined the army of Charlemagne.

**Guido Franceschini.** The nobleman in Browning's *Ring and the Book* who tried to repair his fortune by marrying Pompilia, the putative child of Pietro and Violante. *See* Ring and the Book.

**Guignol.** The principal character in a popular French puppet-show (very like our 'Punch and Judy') dating from the 18th century. As the performance comprised *macabre* and gruesome incidents the name came to be attached to short plays of this nature; hence *Grand Guignol*, a series of such plays, or the theatre in which they are performed, in Paris and other places, as London.

**Guildhall.** Properly, the meeting-place of a trade guild, i.e. an association of persons exercising the same trade or craft, formed for the protection and promotion of their common interests. In London the guilds became of importance in the 14th century, and as it came about that the Corporation was formed almost entirely from among their members their Hall was used as the Town Hall or headquarters of the Corporation, as it still is today. Here are the Court of Common Council, the Court of Aldermen, the Chamberlain's Court, the police court presided over by an alderman, the Corporation Art Gallery, Museum, etc.

The ancient guilds are today represented by the Livery Companies (*q.v.*).

**Guillemites.** *See* William of Maleval, St.

**Guillotine.** So named from Joseph Ignace Guillotin (1738–1814), a French physician, who proposed its adoption to prevent unnecessary pain.

It was introduced April 25th, 1792, and is still used in France. A previous instrument invented by Antoine Louis (1723–92), a French surgeon, was called a Louisette. The Maiden (*q.v.*) was a similar instrument.

In English Parliamentary phraseology the terms 'guillotine', 'to guillotine', 'to apply the guillotine', signify the curtailment of a debate by fixing beforehand when the vote on the various parts of a Bill must be taken.

**Guinea.** A gold coin current in England from 1663 to 1817, originally made of gold from Guinea in West Africa and intended for use in the Guinea trade. The earliest issues bore a small elephant beneath the head of the king. The nominal value was originally 20*s.*; from 1717 it was legal tender for 21*s.*, but its actual value varied, and in 1695, owing to the bad condition of silver coin, was as high as 30*s.*

It is still the custom for professional fees, subscriptions, the price of racehorses, pictures, and other luxuries, to be paid in guineas, though there is no such coin current. *See* Spade Guinea.

**Guinea-dropper.** A cheat. The term is about equal to thimble-rig, and alludes to an ancient cheating dodge of dropping counterfeit guineas.

> Who now the guinea-dropper's bait regards,
> Tricked by the sharper's dice or juggler's cards?
>
> Gay, *Trivia*, iii, 249

**Guinea Fowl.** So called because it was brought to us from the coast of Guinea, where it is very common.

> Notwithstanding their harsh cry ... I like the Guinea-fowl. They are excellent layers, and enormous devourers of insects.
>
> D. G. Mitchell, *My Farm of Edgewood*, ch. iii

**Guinea-hen.** An Elizabethan synonym for a prostitute.

> Ere ... I would drown myself for the love of a Guinea-hen, I would change my humanity with a baboon.
>
> Shakespeare, *Othello*, 1, 3

**Guineapig.** A term used in financial circles for a purely 'ornamental' director of a public company, generally a man of title or social position who allows his name to be used in return for his fees – which formerly amounted to a guinea and a lunch each time he attended a board meeting.

Also, a midshipman; for as a guineapig is neither a pig nor a native of Guinea, so a middy is neither a sailor nor an officer.

> He had a letter from the captain of the *Indiaman*, offering you a berth on board as guineapig, or midshipman.
>
> Captain Marryat, *Poor Jack*, ch. xxxi

A special juryman who is paid a guinea a case; a military officer assigned to some special duty, for which he receives a guinea a day, etc., are sometimes so called; as is also a clergyman without cure, who takes occasional duty for a guinea a sermon.

**Guinever** (Geoffrey of Monmouth's *Guanhumara*, the Welsh *Gwenhwyvar*, meaning 'the white ghost'). In the Arthurian legends, the wife of King Arthur. Geoffrey of Monmouth says she was descended from a family of Romans, was brought up by Duke Cador of Cornwall, and surpassed in beauty all the women of the island. According to Malory she was the daughter of Leodegrance, king of the land of Cameliard. She entertained a guilty passion for Sir Launcelot of the Lake, one of the knights of the Round Table, but during the absence of King Arthur in his expedition against Leo, king of the Romans, she was seduced by Modred, her husband's nephew, who had usurped the kingdom. Arthur hastened back, Guinever fled, and a desperate battle was fought, in which Modred was slain and Arthur mortally wounded. Guinever took the veil at Almesbury, where later she died. She was buried at Glastonbury, and has left her name as a synonym for a beautiful, faithless, but repentant wife.

**Guise's Motto.** '*À chacun son tour*', on the standards of the Duc de Guise, who put himself at the head of the Catholic League in the 16th century, meant, 'My turn will come.'

**Gule.** ***The Gule of August.*** August 1st, Lammas Day, a quarter day in Scotland, and half quarter day in England. The word is probably the Welsh *gwyl* (Lat. *vigilia*), a festival.

'Gula Augusti' initium mensis Augusti. Le Gule d'August, in statuo Edw. III, a 31 c. 14 *averagium aestivale fieri debet inter Hokedai et gulam Augusti.* Ducange, *Glossarium Manuale*, vol. iii, p. 866

**Gules.** The heraldic term for red, the most honourable colour, signifying valour, justice, and veneration, and hence given to kings and princes. In engraving it is shown by perpendicular parallel lines. French; from mediaeval Latin *gulae*, ermine dyed red.

With man's blood paint the ground, gules, gules.
Shakespeare, *Timon of Athens*, 4, 3

And threw warm gules on Madeline's fair breast.
Keats, *Eve of St Agnes*

**Gulf.** A man that goes in for honours at the Universities who is not good enough to be classed and yet has shown sufficient merit to pass. When the list is made out a line is drawn after the classes, and the few names put below are in the 'gulf', and those so honoured are 'gulfed'. In the good old times these men were not qualified to stand for the classical tripos.

The ranks of our curatehood are supplied by youths whom, at the very best, merciful examiners have raised from the very gates of 'pluck' to the comparative paradise of the 'Gulf'. *Saturday Review*

***A great gulf fixed.*** An impassable separation. The allusion is to the parable of Dives and Lazarus (Luke 16:26).

**Gulf Stream.** The great, warm ocean current which flows out of the Gulf of Mexico (whence its name) and, passing by the eastern coasts of the United States, is, near the banks of Newfoundland, deflected across the Atlantic to modify the climate of Western Europe as far north as Spitzbergen and Nova Zembla. It washes the shores of the British Isles.

The amount of heat transferred by the Gulf Stream from equatorial regions into the North Atlantic ... amounts to no less than one-fifth part of the entire heat possessed by the North Atlantic. T. Croll, *Climate and Time*, ch. i

**Gulistan** (Pers. *the garden of roses*). The famous recueil of moral sentences by Sadi (about 1190–1291), the most celebrated of Persian poets, except, perhaps, Omar Khayyám. It consists of sections on kings, dervishes, contentment, love, youth, old age, social duties, etc., with many stories and philosophical sayings.

**Gull.** A well-known Elizabethan synonym for one who is easily duped, especially a scion of the upper classes (*cp.* Bejan). Dekker wrote his *Gull's Hornbook* (1609) as a kind of guide to the behaviour of contemporary gallants.

**Gulliver, Lemuel.** The hero of the famous *Travels into Several Remote Nations of the World, by Lemuel Gulliver, first a Surgeon, and then a Captain of several ships*, i.e. to Lilliput, Brobdingnag, Laputa, and the Houyhnhnms, written by Jonathan Swift (1726).

*Gulliver's Travels*, frequently looked upon as a mere children's book, is in reality a biting social and political satire.

Whether we read it, as children do, for the story, or as historians, for the political allusions, or as men of the world, for the satire and philosophy, we have to acknowledge that it is one of the wonderful and unique books of the world's literature.
Edmund Gosse, *History of English Literature*

**Gunpowder Plot.** The project of a few Roman Catholics to destroy James I with the Lords and Commons assembled in the Houses of Parliament, on November 5th, 1605. It was to be done by means of gunpowder when the king went in person to open Parliament. Robert Catesby originated the plot, and Guy Fawkes undertook to fire the gunpowder. The plot was betrayed, and Guy Fawkes was arrested the night before it was to have been put into execution.

**Gunter's Chain,** for land surveying, is so named from Edmund Gunter (1581–1626), the great mathematician and professor of Astronomy at Gresham College, 1619–26. It is sixty-six feet long, and divided into one hundred links. As ten square chains make an acre, it follows that an acre contains 100,000 square links.

***Gunter's scale*** is a two-foot rule having scales of chords, tangents, etc., and logarithmic lines, engraved on it; it is used in surveying and navigation for the mechanical solving of problems.

**Gurgoyle.** *See* Gargoyle.

**Gurme.** The Celtic Cerberus. While the world lasts it is fastened at the mouth of a vast cave; but at the end of the world it will be let loose, when it will attack Tyr, the war-god, and kill him.

**Gutenberg's Bible.** *See* Bible, Specially named.

**Guthlac, St,** of Crowland, Lincolnshire, is represented in Christian art as a hermit punishing demons with a scourge, or consoled by angels while demons torment him. He was a member of the royal family of Mercia in the 7th century.

**Guthrum.** ***Silver of Guthrum's Lane.*** Fine silver was at one time so called, because the chief gold and silver smiths of London resided there in the 13th and 14th centuries. The street, which is now called *Gutter Lane*, and runs from

Cheapside into Gresham Street, was originally *Gudrun's* or *Goderun's Lane*. The hall of the Goldsmiths' Company is still in the same locality.

**Gutter. *All goes down Gutter Lane.*** He spends everything on his stomach. The play is between Gutter Lane, London (*see* Guthrum), and Lat. *guttur* (the throat), preserved in our word *guttural* (a throat letter).

***Gutter children, guttersnipes.*** Street Arabs.

***Out of the gutter.*** Of low birth; of the street-Arab class; one of the submerged.

**Guy of Warwick.** An English hero of legend and romance, whose exploits were first written down by some Anglo-Norman poet of the 12th century and were, by the 14th century, accepted as quite authentic history.

To obtain Phelis (Felice) as his wife he undertook many knightly deeds. He rescued the daughter of the Emperor of Germany, and went to fight against the Saracens, slaying the doughty Coldran, Elmaye King of Tyre, and the soldan himself. Then he returned and wedded Phelis; but in forty days went back to the Holy Land, where he slew the giant Amarant, and many others. He again returned to England, and slew at Winchester Colbrand, the Danish giant, in single combat, thus redeeming England from Danish tribute. At Windsor he destroyed a boar of 'passing might and strength'; on Dunsmore Heath he slew the 'Dun-cow of Dunsmore, a monstrous wyld and cruell beast'; and in Northumberland a dragon 'black as any cole'. Having achieved all this, he became a hermit near Warwick. Daily he went 'incog.' to his own castle and begged bread of his wife Phelis; but on his death-bed he sent her a ring, by which she recognised her lord, and went to close his dying eyes.

> I am not Sampson, nor Sir Guy, nor Colbrand, to mow them down before me.
>
> Shakespeare, *Henry VIII*, 5, 5

**Guy's Hospital.** Founded in 1722 by Thomas Guy (*c.*1645–1724), bookseller, miser, and philanthropist. He amassed an immense fortune in 1720 by speculations in the South Sea Stock, and gave £238,292 to found and endow the hospital.

**Gwynn, Nell** (1652–87). An actress, and one of the mistresses of Charles II. She was a great favourite with the public, and her eldest son by the King, Charles Beauclerk (b.1670), was the founder of the ducal house of St Albans. Scott mentions her in *Peveril of the Peak*; in ch. xi he speaks of 'the smart humour, Mrs Nelly'; and in ch. xl Lord Chaffinch says of 'Mrs Nelly, wit she has; let her keep herself warm with it in worse company, for the cant of strollers is not language for a prince's chamber.'

**Gyges.** A king of Lydia of the 7th century BC, who founded a new dynasty, warred against Asurbanipal of Assyria, and is memorable in legend for his ring and his prodigious wealth.

According to Plato, Gyges descended into a chasm of the earth, where he found a brazen horse; opening the sides of the animal, he found the carcass of a man, from whose finger he drew off a brazen ring which rendered him invisible.

It was by the aid of the ring that he obtained possession of the wife of Candaules (*q.v.*) and, through her, of his kingdom.

**Gymnosophists.** A sect of ancient Hindu philosophers who went about with naked feet and almost without clothing. They lived in woods, subsisted on roots, and never married. They believed in the transmigration of souls. Strabo divides them into Brahmins and Samans. (Gr. *gumnos*, naked; *sophistes*, sages.)

**Gyp.** The name at Cambridge (and at Durham) for a college servant, who acts as valet to two or more undergraduates, the counterpart of the Oxford *scout*. He differs from a bedmaker, inasmuch as he does not make beds: but he runs on errands, waits at table, wakes men for morning chapel, brushes their clothes, and so on. The word is probably from *gippo*, a 17th-century term for a scullion.

**Gypsy.** *See* Gipsy.

**Gyromancy.** A kind of divination performed by walking round in a circle or ring until one fell from dizziness, and so was in a fit state to see visions, talk gibberish, etc.

**Gytrash.** A north-of-England spirit, which, in the form of horse, mule, or large dog, haunts solitary ways, and sometimes comes upon belated travellers.

> I remembered certain of Bessie's tales, wherein figured a ... spirit called a Gytrash.
>
> Charlotte Brontë, *Jane Eyre*, xii

**H.** The form of our capital H is through the Roman and Greek directly from the Phoenician (Semitic) letter *Heth* or *Kheth*, which, having two cross-bars instead of one, represented a fence. The corresponding Egyptian hieroglyph was a sieve, and the Anglo-Saxon rune is called *haegel*, hail.

**HMS.** His *or* Her Majesty's service *or* ship, as HMS *Wellington*.

**Habeas Corpus.** The 'Habeas Corpus Act' was passed in 1679, and defined a provision of similar character in Magna Charta, to which also it added certain details. Its chief purpose was to prohibit any judge, under severe penalties, from refusing to issue to a prisoner a Writ of Habeas Corpus by which the jailer was obliged to produce the prisoner in court in person and to certify the cause of imprisonment, thus preventing people being imprisoned on mere suspicion, and making it illegal for one to be left in prison an indefinite time without trial.

It further provides that every accused person shall have the question of his guilt decided by a jury of twelve, and not by a Government agent or nominee; that no prisoner can be tried a second time on the same charge; that every prisoner may insist on being examined within twenty days of his arrest, and tried at the next session; and that no one may be sent to prison beyond the seas, either within or without the British dominions.

*Habeas Corpus* means 'You are to produce the body.'

The Habeas Corpus Act has been suspended in times of political and social disturbance, and its provisions have been more than once amended and extended. During the Great War it was not in force so far as certain offences against the Crown or its military and naval forces were concerned.

A Habeas Corpus Act was passed in Ireland in 1782, and in Scotland its place is taken by the *Wrongous Imprisonment Act* of 1701.

**Haberdasher.** The word is probably connected with A.Fr. *hapertas*, a word of unknown origin denoting some kind of fabric; but Prof. Weckley makes what he calls the 'dubious' conjecture that it is from O.Fr. *avoir* (*aveir*), goods, property (as in *avoirdupois*), and Fr. and Provençal *ais*, a shop-board. An older, and perhaps more dubious, suggestion is that it is from the German equivalent of our old 'What d'ye lack?' – *Habt ihr das?* Have you that?

To match this saint there was another,
As busy and perverse a brother,
An haberdasher of small wares
In politics and state affairs.

Butler, *Hudibras*, iii, 2

**Habit is second nature.** The wise saw of Diogenes, the cynic (412–323 BC).

Shakespeare: 'Use almost can change the stamp of nature' (*Hamlet*, 3, 4).

French: *L'habitude est une seconde nature.*

Latin: *Usus est optimus magister.*

**Habsburg** is a contraction of *Habichts-burg* (Hawk's Tower); so called from the castle on the right bank of the Aar, built in the 11th century by Werner, Bishop of Strasburg, whose nephew (Werner II) was the first to assume the title of 'Count of Habsburg'. His great-grandson, Albrecht II, assumed the title of 'Landgraf of Sundgau'. His grandson, Albrecht IV, in the 13th century, laid the foundation of the greatness of the House, the original male line of which became extinct on the death of Charles VI in 1740. The late imperial family of Austria were the Habsburg-Lorraines, springing from the marriage of Maria Theresa, daughter of Charles VI, with Francis I, Duke of Lorraine, in 1736.

**Hack.** Short for *hackney* (*q.v.*), a horse let out for hire; hence, one whose services are for hire, especially a literary drudge, compiler, furbisher-up of better men's work. Goldsmith, who well knew from his own experience what the life was, wrote an 'Epitaph' on one:

Here lies poor Ned Purdon, from misery freed,
Who long was a bookseller's hack;
He led such a damnable life in this world, –
I don't think he'll wish to come back.

**Hackell's Colt.** A vast stone near Stanton Drew, Somersetshire; so called from a tradition that it was a *coit* thrown by Sir John Hautville. In Wiltshire three huge stones near Kennet are called the *Devil's coits*.

**Hackney.** Originally (14th cent.) the name given to a class of medium-sized horses, distinguishing them from war-horses. They were used for ordinary riding, and later the name was applied to a horse let out for hire – whence *hackney carriage* and *hackney writer* or *hack* (*q.v.*), a drudge whose pen is for hire.

The knights are well horsed, and the common people and others on litell *hakeneys* and geldynges.
Froissart

The word is the name of the northern suburb of London, in the fields round which the horses to be sold at the great horse fairs at Smithfield used to be turned to grass. Part of the road leading from Hackney to Smithfield is still called 'Mare Street' – a reminder of the time when strings of horses for sale used to traverse it.

**Haddock.** According to tradition, it was a haddock in whose mouth St Peter found the piece of money, the *stater* or shekel (Matt. 27:17), and the two marks on the fish's neck are said to be impressions of the finger and thumb of the apostle. It is a pretty story, but haddocks cannot live in the fresh water of the Lake of Gennesaret. *Cp.* John Dory.

O superstitious dainty, Peter's fish,
How com'st thou here to make so goodly dish?
Metellus, *Dialogues* (1693)

**Hades.** In Homer, the name of the god (Pluto) who reigns over the dead; but in later classical mythology the abode of the departed spirits, a place of gloom but not necessarily like the Christian *Hell*, a place of punishment and torture. As the state or abode of the dead it corresponds to the Hebrew *Sheol*, a word which, in the authorised version, has frequently been translated by the misleading *Hell*. Hence *Hades* is sometimes vulgarly used as a euphemism for *Hell*.

The word is usually derived from Gr. *a*, privative, and *idein*, to see, i.e. the unseen: but this derivation is not at all certain. *Cp.* Inferno.

**Hadith** (Ar., *a saying* or *tradition*). The traditions about the prophet Mahomet's sayings and doings. This compilation, which was made in the 10th century by the Moslem jurists Moshin and Bokhari, forms a supplement to the Koran as the Talmud to the Jewish Scriptures. Like the Jewish *Gemara*, the Hadith was not allowed originally to be committed to writing, but the danger of the traditions being perverted or forgotten led to their being placed on record.

**Hadj.** The pilgrimage to the Kaaba (temple of Mecca), which every Mohammedan feels bound to make once at least before death. Those who neglect to do so 'might as well die Jews or Christians'. These pilgrimages take place in the twelfth month of each year, Zu 'll Hajjia, roughly corresponding to our August.

**Hadji.** A Mohammedan who has made the *Hadj* or pilgrimage to the Prophet's tomb at Mecca. Every Hadji is entitled to wear a green turban.

**Haemony.** The name invented by Milton (*Comus*, 638) for a mythical plant which is of 'sovereign use 'gainst all enchantments, mildew, blast, or damp, or ghastly Furies' apparition'. The reference is probably to *Haemonia*, an old name for Thessaly, a country specially endowed with mystical associations by the ancient Greeks, but Coleridge rather fancifully says the word is *haema-oinos* (blood-wine), and refers to the blood of Jesus Christ, which destroys all evil. The leaf, says Milton, 'had prickles on it' but 'it bore a bright golden flower'. With this explanation the *prickles* become the crown of thorns, the *flower* the fruits of salvation.

**Hafiz.** The great Persian poet (fl. 14th cent.), and one of the greatest poets of the world. His *ghazels* (i.e. songs, odes) tell of love and wine, nightingales, flowers, the instability of all things human, of Allah and the Prophet, etc.; and his tomb at Shiraz is still the resort of pilgrims. The name *Hafiz* is Arabic for 'one who knows the Koran and Hadith (*q.v.*) by heart'.

**Hag.** A witch or sorceress; originally, an evil spirit, demon, harpy. (A.S. *haegtesse*, a witch or hag.)

How now, you secret, black, and midnight hags?
Shakespeare, *Macbeth*, 4, 1

***Hag-knots.*** Tangles in the manes of horses, etc., supposed to be used by witches for stirrups. The term is common in the New Forest. Seamen use the word *hag's-teeth* to express those parts of a matting, etc., which spoil its general uniformity.

**Hagarenes.** An old name for the Saracens, Arabs, or the Moors, who were supposed to be descendants of Hagar, Abraham's bondwoman.

San Diego ... hath often been seen conquering ... the Hagarene squadrons.
Cervantes, *Don Quixote*, Pt ii, Bk iv, 6

**Hagen.** In the *Nibelungenlied* and the old Norse sagas (where he is called Hogni), a Burgundian knight, liegeman to the king, Gunther (*q.v.*), in some accounts his brother and in others a distant kinsman. According to the best known of the legends Hagen, to avenge Siegfried's supposed bad treatment of Brunhild, Gunther's wife, treacherously slew Siegfried by stabbing him between the shoulders, his only vulnerable point. He then deposited the dead body at the door of the chamber of Kriemhild, Siegfried's wife, leading her to suppose that he had been murdered by assassins. She, however, knew that Hagen was her enemy, and when she sent to Worms for the 'Nibelung Hoard', Hagen seized it, and buried it secretly somewhere beneath the

Rhine, intending himself to enjoy it. Kriemhild, with a view of vengeance, married Etzel (i.e. Attila), king of the Huns, and after the lapse of seven years invited the king of Burgundy, with Hagen and many others, to the court of her husband. A terrible broil was stirred up in the banquet hall, which ended in the slaughter of all the Burgundians but two (Gunther and Hagen), who were taken prisoner and given to Kriemhild, who cut off both their heads. *See* Kriemhild. There are other versions of the story, many of them quite contradictory, and the rough and treacherous Hagen appears in many legends. His person is thus described in the great German epic:

> Well-grown and well-compacted was that redoubted guest;
> Long were his legs and sinewy, and deep and broad his chest;
> His hair, that once was sable, with grey was dashed of late;
> Most terrible his visage, and lordly was his gait.
>
> *Nibelungenlied*, st. 1789

**Haggadah.** The portion of the Midrash (*q.v.*) which contains rabbinical interpretations of the historical and legendary, ethical, parabolic, and speculative parts of the Hebrew Scriptures: the portion devoted to law, practice, and doctrine is called the *Halachah*. They were commenced in the 2nd century AD and completed by the 11th.

**Ha-ha.** A ditch or sunk fence serving the purpose of a hedge without breaking the prospect.

**Haidee.** In Byron's *Don Juan* (ii–iv) the beautiful Greek girl who found Don Juan when he was cast ashore and restored him to animation. 'Her hair was auburn, and her eyes were black as death.' Her mother, a Moor, was dead, and her father, Lambro, a rich Greek pirate, was living on one of the Cyclades. She and Juan fell in love with each other during the absence of Lambro from the island. On his return Juan was sent from the island; Haidee went mad and, after a lingering illness, died.

**Hail.** Health, an exclamation of welcome, like the Lat. *salve*. It is from the Icel. *heill*, hale, healthy, and represents the A.S. greeting *wes hāl* (may you) be in whole (or good) health. *Hail*, the frozen rain, is A.S. *hagol*.

> All hail, Macbeth! Hail to thee, thane of Glamis.
>
> Shakespeare, *Macbeth*, 1, 3

***Hail fellow well met.*** One on easy, familiar terms; an intimate acquaintance.

> Hail fellow well met, all dirty and wet;
> Find out, if you can, who's master, who's man.
>
> Swift, *My Lady's Lamentation*

***To hail a ship* or *an omnibus*.** To call to those on board.

**Hair.** One single tuft is left on the shaven crown of a Mussulman, for Mahomet to grasp hold of when drawing the deceased to Paradise.

> And each scalp had a single long tuft of hair.
>
> Byron, *Siege of Corinth*

The scalp-lock of the North American Indians, left on the otherwise bald head, is for a conquering enemy to seize when he tears off the scalp.

The ancients believed that till a lock of hair is devoted to Proserpine, she refuses to release the soul from the dying body. When Dido mounted the funeral pile, she lingered in suffering till Juno sent Iris to cut off a lock of her hair; Thanatos did the same for Alcestis, when she gave her life for her husband; and in all sacrifices a forelock was first cut off from the head of the victim as an offering to the black queen.

> 'Hunc ego Diti
> Sacrum jussa fero, teque isto corpore solvo.'
> Sic ait, et dextra crinem secat ...
> ... atque in ventos vita recessit.
>
> Virgil, *Aeneid*, iv, 702–5

It was an old idea that a person with red hair could not be trusted, from the tradition that Judas had red hair.

> *Rosalind*. His very hair is of the dissembling colour.
> *Celia*. Somewhat browner than Judas's.
>
> Shakespeare, *As You Like It*, 3, 4

A man with black hair but a red beard was the worst of all. The old rhyme says:

> A red beard and a black head,
> Catch him with a good trick and take him dead.

*See also* Red-haired Persons.

Byron says, in *The Prisoner of Chillon* –

> My hair is grey, but not with years,
> Nor grew it white
> In a single night,
> As men's have grown from sudden fears.

and it is a well authenticated fact that this can take, and has taken, place. It is told that Ludovico Sforza became grey in a single night; Charles I, also, while he was on his trial; and Marie Antoinette grew grey from grief during her imprisonment.

**Phrases.**

***Against the hair.*** Against the grain, contrary to its nature.

> If you should fight, you go against the hair of your professions.
>
> Shakespeare, *Merry Wives of Windsor*, 2, 3

***Both of a hair.*** As like as two peas, or hairs; also, similar in disposition, taste, or trade, etc.

***Hair by hair you will pull out the horse's tail.*** Slow and sure wins the race.

> Little drops of water, little grains of sand,
> Make the mighty ocean and the pleasant land.
>
> Julia A. Carney

Plutarch says that Sertorius, in order to teach his soldiers that perseverance and wit are better than brute force, had two horses brought before them, and set two men to pull out their tails. One of the men, a burly Hercules, tugged and tugged, but all to no purpose; the other was a sharp, weazen-faced tailor, who plucked one hair at a time, amidst roars of laughter, and soon left the stump quite bare.

***Keep your hair on!*** Vulgar slang for Don't lose your temper, old bean! don't get so excited! *Wool* is sometimes substituted for *hair* in this phrase.

***The hair of the dog that bit you.*** *See* Dog.

***To a hair*** or ***To the turn of a hair.*** To a nicety.

***To comb one's hair the wrong way.*** To cross or vex one by running counter to one's prejudices, opinions, or habits.

***To make one's hair stand on end.*** To terrify him suddenly, give him a good fright. A terrified cat will contract its skin till the hairs seem to be bristling from the body at right angles; and Dr Andrews, of Beresford Chapel, Walworth, who attended Probert under sentence of death, says: 'When the executioner put the cords on his wrists, his hair, though long and lanky, of a weak iron-grey, rose gradually and stood perfectly upright, and so remained for some time, and then fell gradually down again.'

> Fear came upon me and trembling, ... [and] the hair of my flesh stood up. Job 4:14, 15

***To split hairs.*** To argue over petty points, make fine, cavilling distinctions, quibble over trifles.

***To tear one's hair.*** To show signs of extreme anguish, grief, or vexation.

***Without turning a hair.*** Without indicating any sign of fatigue or distress. The phrase is from the stable; for when horses sweat they show it by a roughening of the hair.

**Hair-brained.** *See* Hare-brained.

**Hair-breadth 'scape.** A very narrow escape from some danger or evil. In measurement the forty-eighth part of an inch is called a 'hair-breadth'.

> Wherein I spake of most disastrous chances
> Of moving accidents by flood and field.
> Of hair-breadth 'scapes i' th' imminent deadly breach.
>
> Shakespeare, *Othello*, 1, 3

**Hair-raising.** Terrifying; the idea being that of making one's hair stand on end. Plays and stories with very eerie or frightening plots are called *hair-raisers.*

**Hair-splitting.** Cavilling about very minute differences. *See* To split hairs *above*.

> Nothing is more fatal to eloquence than attention to fine hair-splitting distinctions.
>
> Mathews, *Oratory and Orators*, ch. ii

**Hair Stane.** A hoar-stone (*q.v.*) is so called in Scotland.

**Hajar al-Aswad.** The famous black stone in the north-east corner of the Kaaba; it is an irregular oval, about 7 in. in breadth, and is surrounded with a circle of gold. The legend is that when Abraham wished to build the Kaaba, the stones came to him of their own accord, and the patriarch commanded all the faithful to kiss this one.

The stone is probably an aerolite, and it was worshipped long before Mahomet's day, for in the 2nd century AD. Maximus Tyrius spoke of the Arabians paying homage to it, and Persian legend states that it was an emblem of Saturn.

Ibn Abbas reports that the Prophet said that when it came from Paradise it was whiter than milk, and that it had become black through the sins of the millions that had kissed it. On the Day of the Resurrection it is to have two eyes, by which it will recognise all those who have kissed it, and a tongue with which it will bear witness to Allah.

**Hake.** ***We lose in hake, but gain in herring.*** Lose one way, but gain in another. Herring are persecuted by the hake, which are therefore driven away from a herring fishery.

**Halachah.** The division of the Midrash (*q.v.*) that deals with the interpretation of the law, points of doctrine, etc. *See* Haggadah; *and cp.* Gemara, Mishna.

> The halachah ... had even greater authority than the Scriptures of the Old Testament, since it explained and applied them.
>
> Edersheim, *Life of Jesus the Messiah*, vol. i, bk i, ch. i

**Halcyon Days.** A time of happiness and prosperity. Halcyon is the Greek for a kingfisher, compounded of *hals* (the sea) and *kuo* (to brood on). The ancient Sicilians believed that the kingfisher laid its eggs and incubated for fourteen days, before the winter solstice, on the surface of the sea, during which time the waves of the sea were always unruffled.

> Amidst our arms as quiet you shall be
> As halcyon brooding on a winter's sea.
>
> Dryden

> The peaceful king fishers are met together
> About the deck and prophesie calm weather.
>
> Wild, *Iter Boreale*

**Half.** ***Half and half.*** A mixture of two liquors, especially porter and ale, in equal quantities. A *half-and-half* sort of person is an insincere one – one who 'blows hot and cold' – and to do a thing in a *half-and-half* way is to do it badly, only half do it.

***Half done, as Elgin was burnt.*** In the wars between James II of Scotland and the Douglases in 1452, the Earl of Huntly burnt one-half of the town of Elgin, being the side which belonged to the Douglases, but left the other side standing because it belonged to his own family (Scott, *Tales of a Grandfather*, xxi).

***Half is more than the whole.*** This is what Hesiod said to his brother Perseus, when he wished him to settle a dispute without going to law. He meant 'half of the estate without the expense of law will be better than the whole after the lawyers have had their pickings'. The remark, however, has a very wide signification. Thus an *embarras de richesse* is far less profitable than a sufficiency. A large estate to one who cannot manage it is impoverishing. A man of small income will be poorer with a large house and garden to keep up than if he lived in a smaller tenement. Increase of wealth, if expenditure is more in proportion, tendeth to poverty.

> Unhappy they to whom God has not revealed,
> By a strong light which must their sense control,
> That half a great estate's more than the whole.
>
> Cowley, *Essays in Verse and Prose*, iv

***Half-seas over.*** Midway between one condition and another; now usually applied to a person getting on for drunk.

> I am half-seas o'er to death. Dryden
>
> I have just left the Right Worshipful and his Myrmidons about a Sneaker of Five Gallons. The whole Magistracy was pretty well disguised before I gave 'em the Slip. Our Friend the Alderman was half Seas over.
>
> *Spectator*, No. 616 (Nov. 5th, 1714)

***Half the battle.*** *See* Battle.

***He is only half-baked.*** He is soft, a noodle. *See* Baked.

***My better half.*** *See* Better.

***Not half. Not half bad*** means 'not at all bad'; pretty good, indeed; better than I had expected; but *Not half!* (or *Not 'arf!* as it is usually printed) has a more ironical meaning, and means something like '*Rather! I should think so!*' 'Bill punished Joe in that 'ere fight, wot?' 'Not 'arf he didn't' – the reply is intended to convey that Joe's 'punishment' was *very* severe.

***To do a thing by halves.*** To do it in a slapdash manner, very imperfectly.

***To go halves.*** To share something equally with another.

***Too clever by half.*** Far too sharp or cunning.

**Half-deck.** The quarters of the second mate, carpenters, coopers, boatswain, and all secondary officers. *Quarter-deck*, the quarters of the captain and superior officers. In a gun-decked ship *half-deck* is below the *spar-deck*, and extends from the mainmast to the cabin bulkheads.

**Half-mast high.** The position of a flag flying from the middle of the flagstaff in token of respect to a dead person.

**Halfpenny.** ***I am come back again, like a bad ha'penny.*** Like something unwanted. A facetious way of saying 'More free than welcome'. As a bad ha'penny is returned to its owner, so have I returned to you, and you cannot get rid of me.

**Half-timer.** One engaged in some occupation for only half the usual time; especially a child attending school for half time and working the rest of the day. Half-timers were done away with by the Education Act of 1918.

**Half-tone block.** A typographic printing-block for illustrations, produced by photographing on to a prepared plate through a screen or grating which breaks up the picture of the object to be reproduced into small dots of varying intensity, thus giving the lights and shades, or *tones*.

**Half-world.** *See* Demi-monde.

**Halgaver.** ***Summoned before the mayor of Halgaver.*** The mayor of Halgaver is an imaginary person, and the threat is given to those who have committed no offence against the laws, but are simply untidy and slovenly. Halgaver is a moor in Cornwall, near Bodmin, famous for an annual carnival held there in the middle of July. Charles II was so pleased with the diversions when he passed through the place on his way to Scilly that he became a member of the 'self-constituted' corporation. The mayor of Garratt (*q.v.*) is a similar 'magnate'.

**Halifax.** One explanation of the name is that it is *halig fax*, holy hair. According to Camden the town was formerly called Horton, and the story is that a clerk there who had been jilted cut off his quondam sweetheart's head and hung it in a yew tree. The head was reverenced as a holy relic, and in time it rotted away, leaving little filaments beneath the bark like fine threads. These were regarded as the *fax* or hair (A.S. *feax*) of the murdered maiden.

Another account has it that the name means *holy face*, from an image of John the Baptist's head that was kept in a hermitage there.

Halifax, Nova Scotia, was so called by the Hon. Edward Cornwallis, the governor, in compliment to his patron, the Earl of Halifax (1749).

***Halifax Law.*** By this (law), whoever committed theft in the liberty of Halifax was to be executed on the Halifax gibbet, a kind of guillotine.

> At Hallifax the law so sharpe doth deale,
> That whoso more than thirteen pence doth steale,
> They have a jyn that wondrous quick and well
> Sends thieves all headless into heaven or hell.
>
> Taylor (the Water Poet), *Works*, ii (1630)

***Hull, Hell, and Halifax.*** *See* Hull.

**Hall Mark.** The mark stamped by the Goldsmiths' Company and Government Assay Offices on gold or silver articles after they have been assayed: a *leopard's head* for London (Goldsmith's Hall); an *anchor* for Birmingham; *a sword between three wheat sheaves* for Chester; *a castle with three towers* for Exeter; *five lions on a cross* for York; a *crown* for Sheffield; *three castles* for Newcastle-on-Tyne; a *castle* for Edinburgh; a *tree and a salmon with a ring in its mouth* for Glasgow; a figure of *Hibernia* for Dublin, etc.

Besides the hall mark there is the *standard* mark, which for England is a *lion passant*; for Edinburgh a *thistle*; for Glasgow a *lion rampant*; and for Ireland a *crowned harp* for 22 carat gold, a *plume of three feathers* for 20 carat, and a *unicorn's head* for 18 carat. If the article stamped contains less pure metal than the standard coin of the realm, the number of carats is marked on it.

Besides the hall mark, the standard mark, and the carat-figure, there is the date-mark, which consists of a single letter of the alphabet. In London only twenty letters are used, beginning with A, omitting J, and ending with U; but most of the other Assay Offices use the alphabet to Z, some including both I and J. As soon as one series is ended a new one is started from A in a type that has not previously been used at that office – Roman, Italic, Old English, capitals, or small letters, etc. – so, given the *letter* and the *place-mark*, the date of manufacture can be ascertained on referring to a table.

Lastly, the head of the reigning sovereign is stamped on those gold or silver objects on which duty has been paid.

**Hall of Odin.** The rocks, such as Halleberg and Hunneberg, from which the Hyperboreans, when tired of life, used to cast themselves into the sea; so called because they were the vestibule of the Scandinavian Elysium.

**Hall' Sunday.** The Sunday preceding Shrove Tuesday; the next day is called Hall' Monday or Hall' Night. The Tuesday is also called Pancake Day, and the day preceding Callop Monday, from the special foods popularly prepared for those days. All three were days of merrymaking. Hall' is a contraction of *Hallow*, meaning holy or festal.

**Hallel.** A Jewish hymn of praise sung at the four great festivals, consisting of Ps. 113 to 118 both included. Ps. 136 was called the Great Hallel. And sometimes the Songs of Degrees (*see* Gradual Psalms) sung standing on the fifteen steps of the inner court seem to be so called (i.e. 120 to 137 both included).

> Along this [path] Jesus advanced, preceded and followed by multitudes with loud cries of rejoicing, as at the Feast of Tabernacles, when the Great Hallel was daily sung in their processions. Gelkie, *Life of Christ*, vol. ii, ch. 55

In the following quotation the Songs of Degrees are called the Great Hallel.

> Eldad would gladly have joined in praying the Great Hallel, as they call the series of Psalms from the 120 to the 137, after which it was customary to send round the [paschal] cup a fifth time, but midnight was already too near.
>
> *Eldad the Pilgrim*, ch. ix

**Hallelujah** is the Heb. *halelu-Jah*, 'Praise ye Jehovah'.

***Hallelujah Lass.*** A name given, with a humorously contemptuous import, to female members of the Salvation Army in the early days of that movement.

***Hallelujah Victory.*** A victory said to have been gained by some newly baptised Britons over the Picts and Scots near Mold, Flintshire in 429. They were led by Germanus, Bishop of Auxerre, and commenced the battle with loud shouts of 'Hallelujah!'

**Hallowe'en.** October 31st, which in the old Celtic calendar was the last day of the old year, its night being the time when all the witches and warlocks were abroad and held their wicked revels. On the introduction of Christianity it was taken over as the Eve of All Hallows, or All Saints, and – especially in Scotland and the north of England – it is still devoted to all sorts of games in which the old superstitions can be traced. *See* Burns's poem *Hallowe'en*.

**Hallucinations** (Lat. *hallucinari*, for *alucinari*, to wander in mind). The mind informing the senses, instead of the senses informing the mind. There can be no doubt that the senses may be excited by the mind (from within, as well as from without). Macbeth saw the dagger of his imagination as distinctly as the dagger which he held in his hand; Malebranche declared that he heard the voice of God; Descartes thought he was followed by an invisible person, telling him to pursue his search for truth; Goethe says that, on one occasion, he met an exact counterpart of himself; Scott was fully persuaded that he had seen the ghost of the deceased Byron. All such hallucinations (due to mental disturbances) are of such stuff as dreams are made of.

**Halo.** In Christian art the same as a nimbus (*q.v.*). The luminous circle round the sun or moon caused by the refraction of light through a mist is also called a halo. The word is from Gr. *halos*, originally a circular threshing-floor.

**Hamadryads.** *See* Dryad.

**Hameh.** In *Arabian mythology*, a bird formed from the blood near the brains of a murdered man. This bird cries '*Iskoo'nee!*' (Give me drink!), meaning drink of the murderer's blood; and this it cries incessantly till the death is avenged, when it flies away.

**Hamel.** The name given to the Cow in Caxton's version of *Reynard the Fox*.

**Hamet.** *See* Cid Hamet.

**Hamiltonian System.** A method of teaching foreign languages by interlinear translations, suggested by James Hamilton (1769–1831).

**Hamlet. *It's Hamlet without the Prince*.** Said when the person who was to have taken the principal place at some function is absent. The allusion, of course, is to Shakespeare's *Tragedie of Hamlet, Prince of Denmark*, which would lose all its meaning if the part of the Prince were omitted.

The play is based on a crude story told by the 13th century Saxo Grammaticus (a Danish chronicler) in his *Historia Danica* (first printed 1514), which found a place in Pierre de Belleforest's *Histoires Tragiques* (1570), a French miscellany of translated legend and romance. This formed the groundwork of the lost pre-Shakespearean play – the so-called *Ur-Hamlet* (Ger. *Ur*, original) – which Shakespeare with his magic wand transformed into the greatest dramatic masterpiece of the modern – and, probably, any – world.

**Hammer.** In Personal Appellatives.

Pierre d'Ailly (1350–1425), *Le Marteau* (= hammer) *des Hérétiques*, president of the council that condemned John Huss.

St Augustine (354–430) is called by Hakewell 'that renowned pillar of truth and hammer of heresies'.

John Faber (1478–1541), the German controversialist, was surnamed *Malleus Hereticorum*, from the title of one of his works.

St Hilary, Bishop of Poitiers (d.368), was known as 'The Hammer of the Arians'.

Charles Martel (*q.v.*).

Edward I (1239–1307), 'Longshanks', was called 'The Hammer of the Scots'. On his tomb in Westminster Abbey is the inscription '*Edwardus longus Scotorum Malleus hic est*'.

The second name of Judas *Maccabeus*, the son of Mattathias the Hasmonean, is thought by some to denote that he was a 'Hammer' or 'Hammerer', because *Makkébeth* is Hebrew for a certain kind of hammer.

**Phrases.**

***Gone to the hammer.*** Applied to goods sent to a sale by auction; the auctioneer giving a rap with a small hammer when a lot is sold, to intimate that there is an end to the bidding, hence *to sell under the hammer*.

***They live hammer and tongs.*** Are always quarrelling. They beat each other like hammers, and are as 'cross as the tongs'.

> Both parties went at it hammer and tongs; and hit one another anywhere and with anything.
>
> James Payn

***To be hammered.*** A Stock Exchange term, used of one who is in the 'House' officially declared a defaulter. This is done by the 'Head Waiter', who goes into the rostrum and, before making the announcement, attracts the attention of the members present by striking the desk with a hammer.

***To hammer away at anything.*** To go at it doggedly; to persevere.

**Hammercloth.** The cloth that covers the driver's seat, or 'box', in an old-fashioned coach, but not so called because in this box a hammer, nails, bolts, etc., used to be carried, as the name occurs more than a century before the seat was used for this purpose. The name may have arisen because *hammering* played a part in the preparation of the cloth; or it may be connected with Dan. *hammel*, a swingle-bar, or with *hammock*, the seat which the cloth covers being formed of straps or webbing stretched between two crutches like a sailor's hammock.

**Hampton Court Conference.** A conference held at Hampton Court in January, 1604, to settle the disputes between the Church party and the Puritans. It lasted three days. Its chief result was a few slight alterations in the Book of Common Prayer, but it is here that the first suggestion was made for the official retranslation of the Bible which resulted in the 'Authorised Version' of 1611.

**Hanafites.** One of the four sects of Sunnites (*q.v.*).

**Hanaper.** ***Hanap*** was the mediaeval name for a goblet or wine-cup, and the *hanaper* (connected with *hamper*) was the wickerwork case that surrounded it. Hence the name was given to any round wicker basket and especially to one in which documents that had passed the Great Seal were kept in the Court of Chancery. The office where the Chancellor carried on his business – the Exchequer, or a branch thereof – thus came to be known as the *Hanaper*, and its officials as Comptrollers, Clerks, etc., of the Hanaper. In England these were abolished in 1842, but in Ireland the official title of the Permanent Secretary to the Chancery Division and to the Lord Chancellor is still 'Clerk of the Crown and Hanaper'.

> He had, indeed, four silver hanaps of his own, which had been left him by his grandmother.
>
> Scott, *Quentin Durward*, ch. iv

**Hanbalites.** One of the four sects of Sunnites (*q.v.*).

**Hand.** A symbol of fortitude in Egypt, of fidelity in Rome. Two hands symbolise concord; by a closed hand Zeno represented dialectics, and by an open hand eloquence.

In early art the Deity was frequently represented by a hand extended from the clouds; sometimes the hand was open, with rays issuing from the fingers, but generally it was in the act of benediction, i.e. with two fingers raised.

In card-games the word is used for the game itself, for an individual player (as 'a good *hand* at whist') or the cards held by him.

> A saint in heaven would grieve to see such 'hand'
> Cut up by one who will not understand.
>
> Crabbe, *Borough*

Also for style of workmanship, handwriting, etc. ('he writes a good *hand*').

Operatives at a factory are called *hands*, much as we speak of so many 'head of cattle'; and as a measure of length a hand = four inches. Horses are measured up the fore leg to the shoulder, and are called 14, 15, 16 (as it may be), hands high.

***Dead man's hand.*** It is said that carrying a dead man's hand will produce a dead sleep. *See* Glory, Hand of. Another superstition is that a lighted candle placed in the hand of a dead man gives no light to anyone but him who carries the hand. Hence burglars, even to the present day in some parts of Ireland, employ this method of concealment. *Cp.* Dead Hand.

***The Red Hand,*** or ***Bloody Hand,*** in coat armour is the device of Ulster (*see* Red Hand of Ulster), and is carried as a charge on the coats of arms of English and Irish baronets (*not* on those of Scotland or Nova Scotia). The privilege arose thus – James I in 1611 created two hundred baronets on payment of £1,000 each to provide means for the settlement of Ulster, and from this connection with Ulster they were awarded the badge of the 'open red hand', up to that time borne by the O'Neills.

The 'bloody hand' is also borne privately by a few families; its presence is generally connected with some traditional tale of blood, and in some cases the badge was never to be expunged till the bearer had passed, by way of penance, seven years in a cave, without companion, without shaving, and without uttering a single word.

In Aston church, near Birmingham, is a coat of arms of the Holts, the 'bloody hand' of which is thus accounted for:

> Sir Thomas Holt, some two hundred years ago, murdered his cook in a cellar with a spit, and, when pardoned for the offence the king enjoined him, by way of penalty, to wear ever after a 'bloody hand' in his family coat.

In the church of Stoke d'Abernon, Surrey, there is a red hand upon a monument, the legend of which is that:

> A gentleman shooting with a friend was so mortified at meeting with no game that he swore he would shoot the first live thing he met. A miller was the victim of this rash vow, and the 'bloody hand' was placed in his family coat to keep up a perpetual memorial of the crime.

Similar legends are told of the red hand in Wateringbury church, Kent; of the red hand on a table in the hall of Church-Gresly, in Derbyshire; and of others. *Cp.* Bloody Hand.

**Phrases.**

***A bird in the hand.*** *See* Bird.

***An empty hand is no lure for a hawk.*** You must not expect to receive anything without giving a return.

***A note of hand.*** A promise to pay made in writing and duly signed.

***An old hand at it.*** One who is experienced at it.

***A poor hand.*** An unskilful one. 'He is but a poor hand at it', i.e. he is not skilful at the work.

***All hands.*** The nautical term for the whole of the crew.

***It is believed on all hands.*** It is generally (or universally) believed.

***At first*** or ***second hand.*** As the original (*first*) purchaser, owner, hearer, etc., or (*second*) as one deriving, learning, etc., through another party.

***At hand.*** Conveniently near. 'Near at hand', quite close by. In French, *À la main.*

***By hand.*** Without the aid of machinery or an intermediate agent. A letter 'sent by hand' is one delivered by a personal messenger, not sent through the post. A child 'brought up by hand' is one reared on the bottle instead of being breast-fed.

***By the hand of God. Accidit divinitus.*** *See* Act of God.

***Cap in hand.*** Suppliantly, humbly; as, 'To come cap in hand'. *See* Cap.

***From hand to hand.*** From one person to another.

***Hand in hand.*** In friendly fashion: unitedly.

> Now we maun totter down, John,
> But hand in hand we'll go.
>
> Burns, *John Anderson, my John*

***Hand over hand.*** To go or to come up hand over hand, is to travel with great rapidity, as climbing a rope or a ladder, or as one vessel overtakes another. Sailors in hauling a rope put one hand over the other alternately as fast as they can. In French, *Main sur main.*

***Hands up!*** The order given by the captors to soldiers, 'gunmen', etc., when taken prisoner. The hands are to be held stretched high above the head to preclude any possibility of resistance or the use of revolvers, etc.

***He is my right hand.*** My principal assistant, my best and most trustworthy man. In France, *C'est mon bras droit.*

***In hand.*** Under control, in possession; also, under progress.

> Keep him well in hand.
> I have some in hand, and more in expectation.
> I have a new book or picture in hand.

***In one's own hands.*** In one's sole control, ownership, management, responsibility, etc.

***Kings have long hands.*** *See* King.

***Laying on of hands.*** *See* To lay hands on, *below.*

***Many hands make light work.*** An old proverb (given in Ray's *Collection*, 1742) enshrining the wisdom of a fair division of labour. Of course, it does not always hold as, on occasion, 'too many cooks spoil the broth'. The Romans had a similar saying, *Multorum manibus grande levatur onus*, by the hands of many a great work is lightened.

***Off hand.*** At once, summarily, without stopping to take thought.

***Off one's hands.*** No longer under one's responsibilities; able to maintain oneself. If something – or somebody – is left *on one's hands* one has to take entire responsibility.

***On the other hand.*** A phrase used in the presentation of a case meaning 'from *that* point of view', as opposed to the point of view already mentioned.

***Out of hand.*** At once; done with, over.

> We will proclaim you out of hand.
>
> Shakespeare, *3 Henry VI*, 4, 7
>
> And, were these inward wars once out of hand,
> We would, dear lords, unto the Holy Land.
>
> Shakespeare, *2 Henry IV*, 3, 1

Also with the meaning 'beyond control'; as, 'these children are quite out of hand'.

***The hand that rocks the cradle rules the world.*** The destinies of a nation are in the hands of the mothers, who have the upbringing of the future citizens and rulers. The line is from the poem 'What Rules the World?' by the American poet, William Ross Wallace (1819–81):

> They say that man is mighty,
> He governs land and sea,
> He wields a mighty sceptre
> O'er lesser powers that be;
> But a mightier power and stronger
> Man from his throne has hurled.
> And the hand that rocks the cradle
> Is the hand that rules the world.

***They are hand and glove.*** Inseparable companions, of like tastes and like affections. They fit each other like hand and glove.

***To ask*** or ***give the hand of so-and-so.*** To ask or give her hand in marriage.

***To bear a hand.*** To come and help. *Come on, lads, bear a hand!* means, bend to your work immediately.

***To change hands.*** To pass from a possessor to someone else.

***To come to hand.*** To be received; to come under one's notice. 'Your letter came to hand yesterday.'

***To come to one's hand.*** It is easy to do.

***To get one's hand in.*** To become familiar with the work in hand.

***To get the upper hand.*** To obtain the mastery.

***To give one's hand upon something.*** To take one's oath on it; to pledge one's honour to keep the promise.

***To hand down to posterity.*** To leave for future generations.

***To hand in one's checks.*** To die. An American phrase derived from poker and such games, where *checks* is American for counters. When one handed them in one had finished, was 'cleaned out'. Also, *to pass in*, or *cash*, *one's checks*.

***To hand round.*** To pass from one person to another in a regular series.

***To hand a sail.*** To take it in, to furl it. A nautical phrase.

***To have a free hand.*** To be able to do as one thinks best without referring the matter to one's superiors; to be quite uncontrolled by outside influences.

***To have a hand in the matter.*** To have a finger in the pie. In French, '*Mettre la main à quelque chose.*'

***My hands are full.*** I am fully occupied; I have as much work to do as I can manage. The plural of 'handful' is 'handfuls', *not* 'handsful'.

***To kiss hands.*** *See* Kiss.

***To lay hands on.*** To apprehend; to lay hold of.

> Lay hands on the villain.
>
> Shakespeare, *Taming of the Shrew*, 5, 1

In ecclesiastical use the *laying on of hands*, or *imposition of hands* is the laying on, or the touch, as in signing the cross, of a bishop's hands in ordination or confirmation.

Among the Romans a hand laid on the head of a person indicated the right of property. Thus if a person laid claim to a slave, he laid his hand upon him in the presence of the praetor (*Aulus Gellius*, xx, 19).

***To lend a hand.*** To help; to give assistance.

***To live from hand to mouth.*** To live without any provision for the morrow.

***To play for one's own hand.*** To look after Number One; to act entirely for one's own advantage.

***To play into someone's hands.*** Unwittingly or carelessly to act so that the other party gets the best of it; to do just what will help him and not advance your own cause.

***To serve someone hand and foot.*** To be at his beck and call; to be his slave.

***To shake hands.*** To salute by giving a hand received into your own a shake; to bid adieu.

> Fortune and Antony part here; even here
> Do we shake hands.
>
> Shakespeare, *Antony and Cleopatra*, 4, 10

The custom of shaking hands in confirmation of a bargain has been common to all nations and all ages. In feudal times the vassal put his hands in the hands of his overlord on taking the oath of fidelity and homage.

***To strike hands.*** To make a contract, to become surety for another. *See* Prov. 7:1, 17:18, and 22:26.

***To take a hand.*** To play a part, especially in a game of cards, etc.

***To take in hand.*** To undertake to do something; to take the charge of.

***To take something off one's hands.*** To relieve one of something troublesome, as 'Will no one take this [task] off my hands?'

***To wash one's hands of a thing.*** To have nothing to do with it after having been concerned in the matter; to abandon it entirely. The allusion is to Pilate's washing his hands at the trial of Jesus.

> When Pilate saw that he could prevail nothing, but that rather a tumult was made, he took water, and washed his hands before the multitude, saying, I am innocent of the blood of this just person; see ye to it. Matt. 27:24

***To win hands down.*** To be victor without the slightest difficulty. The allusion is to horse-racing; if the jockey wins with his hands down it shows that he had not had to worry himself – he had a 'walk-over'.

***With a heavy hand.*** Oppressively; without sparing. 'To rule with a heavy hand' is to rule without mercy.

> It is a damned and a bloody work;
> The graceless action of a heavy hand,
> If that it be the work of any hand.
>
> Shakespeare, *King John*, 4, 3

***With a high hand.*** *See* High.

***With clean hands.*** *See* Clean.

**Hand Gallop.** A slow and easy gallop, in which the horse is kept well in hand.

**Hand of Glory.** *See* Glory, Hand of, *and* Dead Man's Hand *above*.

**Hand Paper.** A particular sort of paper well known in the Record Office, and so called from its water-mark, which goes back to the 15th century.

**Handfasting.** A 'marriage on approval', formerly in vogue on the border. A fair was at one time held in Dumfriesshire, at which a young man was allowed to pick out a female companion to live with him. They lived together for twelve months, and if they both liked the arrangement were man and wife. This was called *hand-fasting* or *hand-fastening*.

This sort of contract was common among the Romans and Jews, and is not unusual in the East even now.

> 'Knowest thou not that rite, holy man?' said Avenel ...; 'then I will tell thee. We bordermen ... take our wives for a year and a day; that space gone by, each may choose another mate, or, at their pleasure, [they] may call the priest to marry them for life, and this we call handfasting.' Scott, *The Monastery*, ch. xxv

**Handicap.** A game at cards not unlike loo, but with this difference – the winner of one trick has to put in a double stake, the winner of two tricks a triple stake, and so on. Thus: if six persons are playing, and the general stake is 1*s*., and A gains three tricks, he gains 6*s*., and has to 'hand i' the cap' or pool 3*s*. for the next deal. Suppose A gains two tricks and B one, then A gains 4*s*. and B 2*s*., and A has to stake 3*s*. and B 2*s*. for the next deal.

> To the 'Mitre Tavern' in Wood Street, a house of the greatest note in London. Here some of us fell to handicap, a sport I never knew before, which was very good.
>
> Pepys, Sept. 18th, 1680

***Handicap,*** in racing, is the adjudging of various weights to horses differing in age, power, or speed, in order to place them all, as far as possible, on an equality. If two unequal players challenge each other at chess, the superior gives up a piece, and this is his handicap. So called from the custom of drawing lots out of a hat or cap.

***The Winner's Handicap.*** The winning horses of previous races being pitted together are first handicapped according to their respective merits: the horse that has won three races has to carry a greater weight than the horse that has won only two, and this latter more than its competitor who is winner of a single race only.

**Handirons.** *See* Andirons.

**Handkerchief.** ***To throw the handkerchief.*** In some children's games to throw or drop the handkerchief to a child is to signify that he or she is to run after the child who does it: the phrase is hence used allusively of the person who is next to follow: thus, the chairman at a meeting will (quite figuratively, of course) 'throw the handkerchief' (make the sign) to the man who is to make the next speech.

***With handkerchief in one hand and sword in the other.*** Pretending to be sorry at a calamity, but prepared to make capital out of it.

> Maria Theresa stands with the handkerchief in one hand, weeping for the woes of Poland, but with the sword in the other hand, ready to cut Poland in sections, and take her share.
>
> Carlyle, *The Diamond Necklace*, ch. iv

**Handle.** ***A handle to one's name.*** Some title, as 'lord', 'sir', 'doctor'. The French say *M. sans queue*, a man without a tail (handle to his name).

***To give a handle to ...*** To give grounds for suspicion; as, 'He certainly gave a handle to the rumour'.

> He gave a handle to his enemies, and threw stumbling-blocks in the way of his friends.
>
> Hazlitt, *Spirit of the Age* (James Macintosh)

**Handsel** (A.S. *handselen*, delivery into the hand). A gift for luck; earnest-money; the first money received in a day. Hence *Handsel Monday*, the first Monday of the year, when little gifts used to be given before our Boxing Day (*q.v.*) took its place. To 'handsel a sword' is to use it for the first time; to 'handsel a coat', to wear it for the first time, etc.

**Handsome.** ***Handsome is as handsome does.*** It is one's *actions* that count, not merely one's appearance or promises. The proverb is in Ray's *Collection* (1742), and is also given by Goldsmith in *The Vicar of Wakefield* (ch. i).

> When our neighbours would say: 'Well, upon my word, Mrs Primrose, you have the finest children in the whole country.' 'Ay, neighbour,' she would answer, 'they are as heaven made them – handsome enough if they be good enough; for handsome is that handsome does.' And then she would bid the girls hold up their heads, who, to conceal nothing, were certainly very handsome.

***To do the handsome towards one, to act handsomely.*** To be liberal, generous.

**Handwriting on the Wall.** An announcement of some coming calamity, or the imminent fulfilment of some doom. The allusion is to the handwriting on Belshazzar's palace wall announcing the loss of his kingdom (Dan. 5:5–31).

**Hang.** ***Hang it all! I'll be hanged!*** Exclamations of astonishment or annoyance; mild imprecations.

***Hanged, drawn, and quartered.*** *See* Drawn.

***Hanging and wiving go by destiny.*** 'If a man is doomed to be hanged, he will never be drowned.' And 'marriages are made in heaven', we are told.

The proverb is given in Heywood's *Collection* (1546) as 'Wedding's destiny and hanging likewise'; and Shakespeare has:

The ancient saying is no heresy –
Hanging and wiving goes by destiny.
*Merchant of Venice*, 2, 9

If matrimony and hanging go
By dest'ny, why not whipping too?
Butler, *Hudibras*, Pt ii, canto i, 839–44

***To get the hang of a thing.*** To understand the drift or connection; to acquire the knack.

***To hang about.*** To loaf, loiter. In America to *hang around* is more usual.

***To hang back.*** To hesitate to proceed.

***To hang by a thread.*** To be in a very precarious position. The allusion is to the sword of Damocles (*q.v.*).

***To hang fire.*** To fail in an expected result. The allusion is to a gun or pistol which fails to go off.

***To hang in the bell ropes.*** To have one's marriage postponed after the banns have been published at church; the bells 'hang fire'.

***To hang on.*** To cling to; to persevere; to be dependent on.

***To hang on by the eyelids*** is to maintain one's position only with the greatest difficulty or by the slightest of holds.

***Where do you hang out?*** Where are you living or lodging? The allusion being to the custom, now almost entirely restricted to public-houses, of hanging before one's shop a sign indicating the nature of the business carried on within.

'I say, old boy, where do you hang out?' Mr Pickwick replied that he was at present suspended at the George and Vulture.
Dickens, *Pickwick Papers*, ch. xxx

**Hangdog Look.** A guilty, shamefaced look.

**Hanger.** A short sword or dagger that hung from the girdle; also the girdle itself. The word is probably not connected with Pers. *khandjar*, a dagger.

Men's swords in hangers hang fast by their side.
J. Taylor (1630)

**Hanging Gardens of Babylon.** A square garden (according to Diodorus Siculus), 400 ft each way, rising in a series of terraces from the river in the northern part of Babylon, and provided with earth to a sufficient depth to accommodate trees of a great size. These famous gardens were one of the Seven Wonders of the World, and according to tradition were constructed by Nebuchadnezzar to gratify his wife Amytis, who felt weary of the flat plains of Babylon, and longed for something to remind her of her native Median hills.

**Hangman's Gains,** and **Gain's Alley** (London), in the liberty of St Katherine. Strype says it is a corruption of 'Hammes and Guynes', so called because refugees from those places were allowed to lodge there in the reign of Queen Mary after the loss of Calais. These narrow streets were demolished at the building of St Katherine's Dock, 1827.

**Hangmen** and **Executioners.**

The best known to history are:

Bull, the earliest hangman whose name survives (about 1593).
Jock Sutherland.
Derrick, who cut off the head of Essex in 1601.
Gregory Brandon (about 1648), and Robert Brandon, his son, who executed Charles I. These were known as 'the two Gregories' (*see* Gregorian Tree).
Squire Dun, mentioned in *Hudibras* (Pt iii, c. 2).
Jack Ketch (1678) executed Lord Russell and the Duke of Monmouth.
Rose, the butcher (1686).
Edward Dennis (1780), introduced in Dickens's *Barnaby Rudge*.
Thomas Cheshire, nicknamed 'Old Cheese'.
John Calcraft; Marwood; Berry; etc.
Of French executioners, the most celebrated are Capeluche, headsman of Paris during the terrible days of the Armagnacs and Burgundians; and the two brothers Sanson, who were executioners during the first French Revolution.

The fee given to the executioner at Tyburn used to be 13½*d*., with 1½*d*. for the rope.

For half of thirteen-pence ha'penny wages
I would have cleared all the town cages,
And you should have been rid of all the stages
I and my gallows groan.
*The Hangman's Last Will and Testament* (*Rump Songe*)

Noblemen who were to be beheaded were expected to give the executioner from £7 to £10 for cutting off their head; and it is still the case that any peer who comes to the halter can claim the privilege of being suspended by a silken rope.

**Hankey Pankey.** Jugglery; fraud.

**Hansard.** The printed official report of the proceedings and debates in the British Houses of Parliament, so called from Luke Hansard (1752–1828), who commenced the *Journal of the House of Commons* in 1774.

**Hanse Towns.** The maritime cities of Germany, which belonged to the Hanseatic League (*q.v.*).

The Hanse towns of Lubeck Bremen, and Hamburg are commonwealths even now (1877).
Freeman, *General Sketch*, ch. x, p. 174

**Hanseatic League.** The confederacy, first established in 1239, between certain cities of Northern Germany for their mutual prosperity and protection. The diet which used to be held every three years was called the *Hansa* (Old High German for *Association*), and the members of it *Hansards*. The league in its prosperity comprised 85 towns; it declined rapidly in the Thirty Years' War; in 1669 only six cities were represented; and the last three members of the league (Hamburg, Lubeck, and Bremen) joined the German Customs Union in 1889.

**Hansel; Hansel Monday.** *See* Handsel.

**Hansom.** A light two-wheeled cab, very popular in London before the introduction of taxicabs early in this century, in which the driver sat behind and above the body of the vehicle, and communicated with the passenger through a trap-door in the roof. Invented by Aloysius Hansom (1803–82), an architect of Birmingham.

**Hapmouche.** The giant fly-catcher, mentioned by Rabelais, who invented the art of drying and smoking neats' tongues. *See* Gemmagog.

**Happy.** ***Happy as a clam.*** *See* Clam.

***Happy dispatch.*** *See* Hara-kiri.

***Happy family.*** The name given in travelling menageries to a collection of all sorts of animals of different and antagonistic habits living together peaceably.

***Happy-go-lucky.*** Thoughtless, indifferent, carefree.

***Happy is the nation that has no history.*** The old proverb says in other words what Gibbon remarked in the *Decline and Fall*, ch. iii:

> History is, indeed, little more than the register of the crimes, follies, and misfortunes of mankind.

Montesquieu said much the same:

> Heureux les peuples dont l'histoire est ennuyeux.

***The Happy Valley.*** The home of the Prince of Abyssinia in Johnson's tale of *Rasselas* (1759). It is placed in the kingdom of Amhara, and was inaccessible except in one spot through a cave in a rock. It was a Garden of Peace, completely isolated from the world, and replete with every luxury; but life there was so monotonous that the philosopher, Imlac, and the Prince, Rasselas, were glad to escape.

**Hapsburg.** *See* Habsburg.

**Har.** According to the *Gylfaginning*, one of the later sagas, Har, Jafuhar, and Thridhi (i.e. the High One, the Equally High One, and the Third) are the Scandinavian Trinity, 'The Mysterious Three' who sit on three thrones above the Rainbow. The next in order are the Aesir (*q.v.*), of which Odin, the chief, lives in Asgard, on the heavenly hills between Earth and the Rainbow; and the third order is the Vanir (*see* Van). This appearance of a Trinity in the Scandinavian theogeny is possibly due to Christian influence.

**Hara.** In *Hindu mythology*, one of the names of Siva (*q.v.*).

**Hara-kiri** (Jap. *hara*, the belly, *kiri* to cut). A method of suicide by disembowelling practised by Japanese military officials, daimios, etc., when in serious disgrace or liable to be sentenced to death. The first recorded instance of *hara-kiri*, or *Happy Dispatch*, as it is also called, is that of Tametomo, brother of Sutoku, an ex-Emperor in the 12th century, after a defeat at which most of his followers were slain.

**Harapha.** The name given by Milton in *Samson Agonistes* (ll. 1068, 1079) to a giant of Gath, who went to mock Samson in prison, but durst not venture within his reach. Milton seems to have got the name from the Hebrew word *Raphah* (pl. *Rephaim*, *see* Giants of the Bible), which, in 2 Sam. 21:18, is translated 'giant'.

**Harbinger.** One who looks out for lodgings, etc.; a courier; hence, a forerunner, a messenger. (O.H.Ger. *hari*, an army, *bergan*, to lodge.)

> I'll be myself the harbinger, and make joyful
> The hearing of my wife with your approach.
>
> Shakespeare, *Macbeth*, 1, 4

**Hard.** ***Hard and fast.*** Strict, unalterable. A 'hard and fast rule' is one that must be rigidly adhered to and cannot be relaxed for anyone. Originally a nautical phrase, used of a ship run aground.

***Hard by.*** Near. *Hard* here means close, pressed close together; hence firm or solid, in close proximity to.

> Hard by a sheltering wood.
>
> David Mallet, *Edwin and Emma*

***Hard cash.*** Money; especially actual money – as opposed to cheques or promises – 'down on the nail'; formerly coin as distinguished from banknotes.

***Hard hit.*** Seriously damaged by monetary losses; as 'He was hard hit in the slump after the war'; also, badly smitten with love.

***Hard labour.*** Enforced labour often added to the punishment of criminals receiving a sentence of six months or over. It used to consist largely of working the treadmill, stone-breaking, oakum-picking, etc.

***Hard lines.*** Hard terms; 'rather rough treatment'; exacting. *Lines* here means 'one's lot in life', as, 'The lines are fallen unto me in pleasant places; yea, I have a goodly heritage' (Ps. 16:6), i.e. my lot is excellent.

> That was hard lines upon me, after I had given up everything. G. Eliot

***Hard of hearing.*** Unable to hear properly; rather deaf.

***Hard up.*** Short of money. Originally a nautical phrase; when a vessel was hard put to it by stress of weather the order *Hard up the helm!* was given, and the tiller was put up as far as possible to windward so as to turn the ship's head away from the wind. So, when a man is 'hard up' he has to weather the storm as best he may.

***To go hard with.*** To fare ill with; usually followed by *but*, implying 'unless so-and-so happens'.

> *Speed.*: Nay, that I can deny by a circumstance.
> *Pro.*: It shall go hard but I'll prove it by another.
> Shakespeare, *Two Gentlemen of Verona*, 1, 1

**Hardouin.** Jean Hardouin (1646–1729), the learned Jesuit, chronologer, and numismatist, and librarian to Louis le Grand, was so sceptical that he doubted the truth of all received history, denied the authenticity of the *Aeneid* of Virgil, the *Odes* of Horace, etc., placed little faith in deductions drawn from medals and coins, regarded all councils before that of Trent as chimerical, etc., thus he became typical of the doubting philosopher.

> Even Père Hardouin would not enter his protest against such a collection. Dr A. Clarke, *Essay*

**Hardshell.** A term used in American politics for an 'out-and-outer', one prepared, and anxious, to 'go the whole hog'. It was originally applied to a very strict and rigid sect of Baptists, their somewhat weaker brethren being known as *Softshells*.

**Hardy.** Brave or daring, hence the phrase, *hardi comme un lion*.

Among those who have been surnamed 'The Hardy' are:

William Douglas, defender of Berwick (d.1302);

Philippe III of France (1245, 1270–85); and

Philippe II, Duke of Burgundy (1342, 1363–82).

**Hare.** It is unlucky for a hare to cross your path, because witches were said to transform themselves into hares.

> A witch is a kind of hare
> And marks the weather
> As the hare doth.
> Ben Jonson, *Sad Shepherd*, ii, 2

In the North, until comparatively recently, if a fisherman on his way to the boats chanced to meet a woman, parson, or hare, he turned back, being convinced that he would have no luck that day.

> The superstitious is fond in observation, servile in feare ... This man dares not stirre forth till his breast be crossed, and his face sprinkled: if but an hare crosse him the way, he returnes.
> Bp Hall, *Characters* (1608)

According to mediaeval 'science', the hare was a most melancholy beast, and ate wild succory in the hope of curing itself; its flesh, of course, was supposed to generate melancholy in any who partook of it.

> *Fal.*: 'Sblood, I am as melancholy as a gib cat, or a lugged bear.
> *Prince*: Or an old lion, or a lover's lute.
> *Fal.*: Yea, or the drone of a Lincolnshire bagpipe.
> *Prince*: What sayest thou to a hare, or the melancholy of Moor-ditch?
> Shakespeare, *1 Henry IV*, 1, 2

Another superstition was that hares are sexless, or that they change their sex every year.

> Snakes that cast their coats for new,
> Cameleons that alter hue,
> Hares that yearly sexes change.
> Fletcher, *Faithful Shepherd*, iii, 1

And among the Hindus the hare is sacred to the moon because, as they affirm, the outline of a hare is distinctly visible in the full disk.

***The Order of the Hare.*** An order of twelve knights traditionally said to have been created by Edward III in France, on an occasion when he thought that a great shouting raised by the French army heralded the onset of battle, but found afterwards it was on account of a hare running between the two armies.

***The quaking hare,*** in Dryden's *Hind and Panther*, means the Quakers.

> Among the timorous kind, the quaking hare
> Professed neutrality, but would not swear.
> Pt i, 37, 38

**Phrases.**

***First catch your hare.*** *See* Catch.

***Mad as a March hare.*** Hares are unusually shy and wild in March, which is their rutting season.

Erasmus says 'Mad as a marsh hare', and adds, 'hares are wilder in marshes from the absence of hedges and cover'.

***The hare and the tortoise.*** Everyone knows the fable of the race between the hare and the tortoise, won by the latter; and the moral, 'Slow and steady wins the race.' The French equivalent is *Pas à pas le boeuf prend le lièvre*.

***To hold with the hare and run with the hounds.*** To play a double and deceitful game, to be a traitor in the camp. To run with the hounds as if intent to catch the hare, all the while being the secret friend of poor Wat. In the American war these double-dealers were called Copperheads (*q.v.*).

***To kiss the hare's foot.*** To be too late for anything, to be a day after the fair. The hare has gone by, and left its footprint for you to salute. A similar phrase is *To kiss the post*.

**Hare-brained.** Mad as a March hare, giddy, foolhardy.

> Let's leave this town; for they [the English] are
> hair-brained slaves,
> And hunger will enforce them to be more eager.
> Shakespeare, *1 Henry VI*, 1, 2

**Harefoot.** The surname given to Harold I, youngest son of Canute (1035–40).

**Hare-lip.** A cleft lip; so called from its resemblance to the upper lip of a hare. It was fabled to be caused at birth by an elf or malicious fairy.

> This is the foul fiend Flibbertigibbet. He begins at curfew, and walks till the first cock. He ... squints the eye and makes the hare-lip.
> Shakespeare, *King Lear*, 3, 4

**Hare-stone.** Another form of *Hoar-stone* (*q.v.*).

**Harem.** The name given by Mohammedans to those apartments which are appropriated exclusively to the female members of a family. The word is Arab. *haram*, from *harama*, be prohibited.

**Harikiri.** *See* Hara-kiri.

**Harleian.** Robert Harley, Earl of Oxford (1661–1724) and his son Edward were great collectors of manuscripts, scarce tracts, etc. Their library was purchased by the nation in 1753 and deposited in the British Museum, and the *Harleian MSS* are amongst its most valuable literary and historical possessions. The *Harleian Miscellany* (10 vols, first published 1744–6) contains reprints of nearly 700 tracts, etc., mostly of the 16th and 17th centuries; and since 1870 the Harleian Society has published over 100 volumes of Registers, Visitations, and Pedigrees.

**Hark Back, To.** To return to the subject – *revenons à nos moutons*. A call to the dogs in fox-hunting, when they have overrun the scent, 'Hark [dogs] come back'; so 'Hark for'ards!' 'Hark away!' etc.

**Harlequin.** In the British pantomime, a sprite supposed to be invisible to all eyes but those of his faithful Columbine (*q.v.*). His office is to dance through the world and frustrate all the knavish tricks of the Clown, who is supposed to be in love with Columbine. He derives from *Arlecchino*, a stock character of Italian comedy (like Pantaloon and Scaramouch), whose name was in origin probably that of a sprite or hobgoblin. One of the demons in Dante is named 'Alichino', and another devil of mediaeval demonology was 'Hennequin'.

Our Christmas pantomime or harlequinade is essentially a British entertainment, first introduced by Mr Weaver, a dancing-master of Shrewsbury, in 1702.

> What Momus was of old to Jove
> The same a harlequin is now.
> The former was buffoon above,
> The latter is a Punch below.
> Swift, *The Puppet Show*

The prince of Harlequins was John Rich (1681–1761).

***Harlequin.*** So Charles Quint (1500–58) was called by François I of France.

**Harlot.** 'Popular' etymology used to trace this word to Arlotta, mother of William the Conqueror, but it is O.Fr. *herlot* and Ital. *arlotto*, a base fellow, vagabond, and was formerly applied to males as well as females. Hence Chaucer speaks of 'a sturdy harlot ... that was her hostes man'.

> He was gentil harlot, and a kinde;
> A bettre felaw shulde man no wher finde.
> Chaucer, *Canterbury Tales*, prol. 649

> The harlot king is quite beyond mine arm.
> Shakespeare, *Winter's Tale*, 2, 3

The earliest sense of the word may have been 'camp-follower', and if so it represents O.H.Ger. *hari*, war, and *lotter* (A.S. *loddere*), a beggar, wastrel.

**Harm. *Harm set, harm get.*** Those who lay traps for others get caught themselves. Haman was hanged on his own gallows. Our Lord says, 'They that take the sword shall perish with the sword' (Matt. 26:52).

**Harmattan.** A wind which blows periodically from the interior parts of Africa towards the Atlantic. It prevails in December, January, and February, and is generally accompanied with fog, but is so dry as to wither vegetation and cause human skin to peel off.

**Harmonia. *Harmonia's Necklace.*** An unlucky possession, something that brings evil to all who possess it. Harmonia was the daughter of Mars and Venus. On her marriage with King Cadmus, she received a necklace which proved fatal to all who possessed it. *Cp.* Fatal Gifts.

On the same occasion Vulcan, to avenge the infidelity of her mother, made the bride a present of a robe dyed in all sorts of crimes, which infused wickedness and impiety into all her offspring. *Cp.* Nessus. Both Harmonia and Cadmus, after having suffered many misfortunes, and seen their children a sorrow to them, were changed into serpents.

Medea, in a fit of jealousy, sent Creusa a wedding robe, which burnt her to death.

**Harmonious Blacksmith, The.** A well-known air written by Handel, or, rather, based by him on an earlier air. The grave of the blacksmith, the ringing of whose hammer set Handel to work on it, is still to be seen in the little churchyard at Whitchurch – where Handel was organist – near Edgware, Middlesex.

**Harness.** ***Out of harness.*** Not in practice, retired. A horse out of harness is one not at work.

***To die in harness.*** To continue in one's work or occupation till death. The allusion is to soldiers in armour or harness.

> At least we'll die with harness on our back.
>
> Shakespeare, *Macbeth*, 5, 5

***Harness cask.*** A large cask or tub with a rim cover, containing a supply of salt meat for immediate use. Nautical term.

***Harness Prize.*** A prize founded at Cambridge in memory of William Harness (d.1869), editor of a Life of Shakespeare, of the Plays of Massinger and Ford, etc., for the best essay connected with Shakespearean literature. Awarded every third year.

**Haro.** ***To cry out haro to anyone.*** To denounce his misdeeds, to follow him with hue and cry. 'Ha rou' was the ancient Norman hue and cry, and the exclamation made by those who wanted assistance, their person or property being in danger.

In the Channel Isles, *Haro!* said to have been originally *Ha! ho! à l'aide, mon prince!* is a protest still in vogue when one's property is endangered, and is still a form of legal appeal. It is supposed to be an appeal to Rollo, King of Normandy.

**Haroot** and **Maroot.** Angels in mediaeval angelology, who, in consequence of their want of compassion to man, were susceptible of human passions, and were sent upon earth to be tempted. They were kings of Babel, and teachers of magic and the black arts.

**Haroun al Raschid.** Calif of Bagdad, of the Abbasside line (763–809). His adventures and stories connected with him form a large part of the *Arabian Nights' Entertainments* (*q.v.*).

**Harp.** The cognisance of Ireland. According to tradition, one of the early kings of Ireland was named David, and this king took the *harp* of the Psalmist as his badge. But King John, to distinguish his Irish coins from the English, had them marked with a triangle, either in allusion to St Patrick's explanation of the Trinity, or to signify that he was king of England, Ireland, and France, and the harp may have originated from this. Henry VIII was the first to adopt it as the Irish device, and James I to place it in the third quarter of the royal achievement of Great Britain.

***To harp for ever on the same string.*** To be for ever teasing one about the same subject. There is a Latin proverb, *Eandem cantilenam recinere.*

> Still harping on my daughter.
>
> Shakespeare, *Hamlet*, 2, 1

**Harpagon.** A miser; from the miser of that name in Molière's *L'Avare* (1668).

**Harpocrates.** The Greek form of the Egyptian Heru-P-Khart (Horus the Child), who is figured as a youth, and, as he has one finger pointing to his mouth, was adopted by them as the god of silence.

> I assured my mistress she might make herself perfectly easy on that score [his mentioning a certain matter to anyone], for I was the Harpocrates of trusty valets. *Gil Blas*, iv, 2

**Harpy.** In classical mythology, a winged monster with the head and breasts of a woman, very fierce, starved-looking, and loathsome, living in an atmosphere of filth and stench, and contaminating everything which they came near. Homer mentions but *one* harpy. Hesiod gives *two*, and later writers *three*. Their names, Ocypeta (*rapid*), Celeno (*blackness*), and Aello (*storm*), indicate that these monsters were personifications of whirlwinds and storms.

***He is a regular harpy.*** One who wants to appropriate everything; one who sponges on another without mercy.

> I will … do you any embassage … rather than hold three words conference with this harpy.
>
> Shakespeare, *Much Ado*, 2, 1

**Harridan.** A haggard old beldame. So called from the Fr. *haridelle*, a worn-out jade of a horse.

**Harrier.** A dog for hare-hunting, whence the name.

**Harrington.** A farthing. So called from Lord Harrington, to whom James I granted a patent (1613) for making them of brass. 'Drunken Barnaby' says –

Thence to Harrington be it spoken,
For name-sake I gave a token
To a beggar that did crave it.
*Drunken Barnaby's Journal*

I will not bate a Harrington of the sum.
Ben Jonson, *The Devil is an Ass*, ii, 1

**Harris. *Mrs Harris.*** The fictitious crony of Sarah Gamp, to whom the latter referred for the corroboration of all her statements, and whom she made the bank on which she might draw to any extent for self-praise. Betsy Prig said, 'Bother Mrs Harris; I don't believe there's no sich a person!' and she was quite right (Dickens, *Martin Chuzzlewit*).

Not Mrs Harris in the immortal narrative was more quoted and more mythical. *Lord Lytton*

**Harry. *By the Lord Harry.*** A mild imprecation, the person referred to being the devil. *See below.*

By the Lord Harry, he says true.
Congreve, *Old Bachelor*, II, i

***Old Harry.*** A familiar name for the devil; Old Scratch. Probably from the personal name (*cp. Old Nick*), but perhaps with some allusion to the word *harry*, meaning to plunder, harass, lay waste, from which comes the old *harrow*, as in the title of the 14th century *estrif*, or miracle-play, *The Harrowing of Hell.*

***To play Old Harry.*** To play the devil; to ruin, or seriously damage.

**Hart.** In Christian art, the emblem of solitude and purity of life. It was the attribute of St Hubert, St Julian, and St Eustace. It was also the type of piety and religious aspiration (Ps. 42:1). *Cp.* Hind.

***Hart of grease.*** A hunter's phrase for a fat venison; a stag full of the pasture, called by Jaques 'a fat and greasy citizen' (*As You Like It*, 1, 1).

It is a hart of grease, too, in full season, with three inches of fat on the brisket.
Scott, *The Monastery*, ch. xvii

***Hart royal.*** A male red deer, when the crown of the antler has made its appearance, and the creature has been hunted by a king.

***The White Hart,*** or ***Hind,*** with a golden chain, in public-house signs, is the badge of Richard II, which was worn by his adherents. It was adopted from his mother, Joan of Kent, whose cognisance it was.

**Hartnet.** The daughter of Rukenaw (the ape's wife) in *Reynard the Fox* (*q.v.*). The word in old German means *hard* or *strong strife*.

**Harum Scarum.** Giddy, hare-brained; or a person so constituted. From the old *hare* (*cp.* Harry) to harass, and *scare*; perhaps with the additional allusion to the 'madness of a March *hare*'.

Who's there? I s'pose young harum-scarum.
*Cambridge Facetiae: Collegian and Porter.*

**Haruspex** (pl. *haruspices*). Officials among the Etruscans and ancient Romans who interpreted the will of the gods by inspecting the entrails of animals offered in sacrifice (O.Lat. *haruga*, a victim; *specio*, I inspect). Cato said, 'I wonder how one haruspex can keep from laughing when he sees another.'

**Harvard University.** The oldest University in the United States, situated at Cambridge, Mass. and founded in 1636 by the general court of the colony in Massachusetts Bay. In 1638 its name was given to it in honour of John Harvard (1607–38), who had left to it his library and half his estate.

**Harvest Moon.** The full moon nearest the autumnal equinox, which rises for several days nearly at sunset, and at about the same time.

**Hash.** A mess, a muddle; as, 'a pretty hash he made of it'.

***I'll soon settle his hash for him.*** I will soon smash him up; ruin his schemes; 'cook his goose'; 'put my finger in his pie'; 'make mincemeat of him'. Our slang is full of such phrases. *See* Cooking.

About earls as goes mad in their castles,
And females what settles their hash.
Sims, *Dagonet Ballads* (*Polly*)

**Hassan-Ben-Sabah.** The Old Man of the Mountain, founder of the sect of the Assassins (*q.v.*).

**Hassock.** A footstool, properly one made of coarse grass (A.S. *hassuc*), or sedge (Welsh *hesg*).

Hassocks should be gotten in the fens, and laid at the foot of the said bank ... where need required. Dugdale, *Imbanking*, p. 322

**Hat.** How Lord Kingsale acquired the right of wearing his hat in the royal presence is this: King John and Philippe II of France agreed to settle a dispute respecting the duchy of Normandy by single combat. John de Courcy, Earl of Ulster, was the English champion, and no sooner put in his appearance than the French champion put spurs to his horse and fled. The king asked the earl what reward should be given him, and he replied, 'Titles and lands I want not, of these I have enough; but in remembrance of this day I beg the boon, for myself and successors, to remain covered in the presence of your highness and all future sovereigns of the realm.'

Lord Forester claims the same right, which is said to have been granted to his ancestor, John Forester, of Watling Street, Salop, by Henry VIII.

The privilege was at one time more extensive; Motley informs us that all the Spanish grandees had the privilege of being covered in the presence of the reigning monarch; and to this day, in England, any peer of the realm has the right to sit in a court of justice with his hat on.

***A cockle hat.*** A pilgrim's hat. So called from the custom of putting cockle-shells upon their hats, to indicate their intention or performance of a pilgrimage.

How should I your true love know
  From another one?
By his cockle-hat and staff.
  And his sandal shoon.
Old Ballad, quoted in Hamlet, iv, 5

***A white hat.*** A white hat used to be emblematical of radical proclivities, because the Radical reformer, 'Orator' Hunt (d.1835) used to wear one during the Wellington and Peel administration.

Street arabs used to accost a person wearing a white hat with the question, 'Who stole the donkey?' and a companion used to answer, 'Him wi' the white hat on'.

***Knocked into a cocked hat.*** *See* Cocked.

***Never wear a brown hat in Friesland.*** When at Rome do as Rome does. In Friesland (a province of the Netherlands) the inhabitants used to cover the head first with a knitted cap, a high silk skull-cap, a metal turban, and over all a huge flaunting bonnet. A traveller once passed through the province with a common brown wide-awake, and was hustled by the workmen, jeered at by the women, pelted by the boys, and sneered at by the magnates as a regular guy.

***Pass round the hat.*** Gather subscriptions into a hat.

***To eat one's hat.*** Indicative of strong emphasis. 'I'd eat my hat first' = 'I'd be hanged first'.

'If I knew as little of life as that, I'd eat my hat and swallow the buckle whole,' said the clerical gentleman. Dickens, *Pickwick*, ch. xlii

***To hang up one's hat in a house.*** To make oneself at home; to become master of a house. Visitors, making a call, carry their hats in their hands.

***You are only fit to wear a steeple-crowned hat.*** To be burnt as a heretic. The victims of the Inquisition were always decorated with such a headgear.

**Hat-trick.** Taking three wickets at cricket with three successive balls. A bowler who did this used to be entitled to a new hat at the expense of his club.

**Hats and Caps.** Two political factions of Sweden in the 18th century, the former favourable to France, and the latter to Russia. Carlyle says the latter were called caps, meaning nightcaps, because they were averse to action and war; but the fact is that the French partisans wore a French *chapeau* as their badge, and the Russian partisans wore a Russian cap.

**Hatches.** ***Put on the hatches.*** Figuratively, shut the door. (A.S. *haece*, a gate; *cp. haca*, a bar or bolt.)

***Under hatches.*** Very depressed; down in the world; also, dead and buried. The hatches of a ship are the coverings over the hatchways (or openings in the deck of a vessel) to allow of cargo, etc., being easily discharged.

For though his body's under hatches
  His soul has gone aloft.
Chas Dibdin, *Tom Bowling*

These lines are inscribed on Dibdin's tombstone at St Martin's in the Fields.

**Hatchet.** ***To bury the hatchet.*** *See* Bury.

***To throw the hatchet.*** To exaggerate heavily, tell falsehoods. In allusion to an ancient game where hatchets were thrown at a mark, like quoits. It means the same as drawing the longbow (*q.v.*).

**Hatef** (= *the deadly*). One of Mahomet's swords, confiscated from the Jews when they were exiled from Medina.

**Hater.** ***I love a good hater.*** I like a man to be with me or against me, either to be hot or cold. Dr Johnson called Bathurst the physician a 'good hater', because he hated a fool, and he hated a rogue, and he hated a Whig; 'he', said the Doctor, 'was a very good hater.'

**Hatrenette.** The name given to the younger daughter of Martin, the Ape, in Caxton's version of *Reynard the Fox*.

**Hattemists.** A Dutch sect of the 17th century, so called from Pontin von Hattem, of Zeeland, a Lutheran pastor who was deposed for heresy and his admiration of Spinoza. They denied the expiatory sacrifice of Christ, and the doctrine of original sin, and held other Antinomian tenets.

**Hatto.** A 10th century archbishop of Mainz, a noted statesman and councillor of Otho the Great, proverbial for his perfidy, who, according to tradition (preserved in the *Magdeburg Centuries*), was devoured by mice. The story says that in 970 there was a great famine in Germany, and Hatto, that there might be better store for the rich, assembled the poor in a barn, and burnt them to death, saying: 'They are like mice, only good to devour the corn.' By and by an army of mice came against the archbishop, who, to escape the plague, removed to a tower on the Rhine, but hither came the mouse-army by hundreds and thousands, and ate him up. The tower is still called Mouse-tower (*q.v.*).

And in at the windows and in at the door,
And through the walls by thousands they pour,
And down through the ceiling, and up through the floor
From the right and the left, from behind and before,
From within and without, from above and below,
And all at once to the bishop they go.
They have whetted their teeth against the stones,
And now they are picking the bishop's bones;
They gnawed the flesh from every limb,
For they were sent to do judgment on him.

Southey, *Bishop Hatto*

Many similar legends, or versions of the same legend, are told of the mediaeval Rhineland.

Count Graaf raised a tower in the midst of the Rhine, and if any boat attempted to evade payment of toll, the warders shot the crew with crossbows. One year a famine prevailed, and the count made a corner in wheat and 'profiteered' grossly; but an army of rats, pressed by hunger, invaded his tower, and falling on the old baron, worried him to death and then devoured him.

Widerolf, bishop of Strasburg (in 997), was devoured by mice because he suppressed the convent of Seltzen, on the Rhine.

Bishop Adolf of Cologne was devoured by mice or rats in 1112.

Freiherr von Güttingen collected the poor in a great barn, and burnt them to death; and being invaded by rats and mice, ran to his castle of Güttingen. The vermin, however, pursued him and ate him clean to the bones, after which his castle sank to the bottom of the lake, 'where it may still be seen'.

A similar tale is recorded in the chronicles of William of Mulsburg, Bk ii; and *cp*. Pied Piper.

**Hatton Garden** (London). Now the English headquarters of the diamond trade, is so named from Queen Elizabeth's favourite, Sir Christopher Hatton (*see* Dancing Chancellor), whose mansion and grounds formerly occupied the site.

**Haussmannisation.** The pulling down of buildings, districts, etc., and the construction on the site of new streets and cities, as Baron Haussmann (1809–91) remodelled Paris. By 1868 he had saddled Paris with a debt of about £35,000,000, and two years later was dismissed from his office of Prefect of the Seine.

**Haute Claire.** The sword of Oliver, Charlemagne's favourite paladin.

**Hautville Coit.** A huge stone, said to weigh about 30 tons, at the top of a hill at Stanton Drew, Somerset. The tradition is that this 'coit' was thrown there as the clearing of his spade by the giant, Sir John Hautville, from Mary's Knolle Hill, about a mile off, the place of his abode.

**Havelok the Dane.** A hero of mediaeval romance. He was the orphan son of Birkabegn, king of Denmark, was exposed at sea through the treachery of his guardians, and the raft drifted to the coast of Lincolnshire. Here a fisherman named Grim found the young prince, and brought him up as his own son. In time it so happened that an English princess stood in the way of certain ambitious nobles, who resolved to degrade her by uniting her to a peasant, and selected the young foundling for the purpose; but Havelok, having learnt the story of his birth, obtained the aid of an army of Danes to recover his wife's possessions. In due time he became king of Denmark and part of England; Grim was suitably rewarded, and with the money founded the town of Grimsby (*q.v.*).

**Haver-cakes.** Oaten cakes (Scand. *hafre*; Ger. *hafer*, oats).

**Havering** (Essex). Popular etymology accounts for the name with a legend that says that while Edward the Confessor was dwelling in this locality, an old pilgrim asked alms, and the king replied: 'I have no money, but I *have a ring*,' and, drawing it from his forefinger, gave it to the beggar. Some time after the old man handed it to some other pilgrims, and said: 'Give this to your king, and say within six months he shall die.' The request was complied with, and the prediction fulfilled.

**Haversack.** Strictly speaking, a bag to carry oats in. *See* Haver-cakes. It now means a soldier's ration-bag slung from the shoulder; a gunner's leather-case for carrying charges.

**Havock.** An old military command to massacre without quarter. This cry was forbidden in the ninth year of Richard II on pain of death. In a 14th century tract entitled *The Office of the Constable and Mareschall in the Tyme of Werre* (contained in the Black Book of the Admiralty), one of the chapters is, 'The peyne of hym that crieth havock, and of them that followeth him *quis inventus fuerit qui clamorem inceperit qui vocatur havok*.

Cry Havock, and let slip the dogs of war.

Shakespeare, *Julius Caesar*, 3, 1

**Havre, Le.** A contraction of *Le havre* (the haven, harbour) *de notre Dame de grâce*.

**Hawcubites.** Street bullies in the reign of Queen Anne. It was their delight to molest and ill-treat the old watchmen, women, children, and feeble old men who chanced to be in the streets after sunset. The succession of these London pests after the Restoration was: The Muns, the Tityre Tus, the Hectors, the Scourers, the Nickers, then the Hawcubites (1711–14), and then the Mohocks – most dreaded of all.

From Mohock and from Hawcubite,
  Good Lord deliver me,
Who wander through the streets at nighte,
  Committing cruelty.
They slash our sons with bloody knives,
  And on our daughters fall;
And, if they murder not our wives,
  We have good luck withal.

**Hawk.**

(1) Different parts of a hawk:

*Arms.* The legs from the thigh to the foot.
*Beak.* The upper and crooked part of the bill.
*Beams.* The long feathers of the wings.
*Clap.* The nether part of the bill.
*Feathers summed and unsummed.* Feathers full *or* not full grown.
*Flags.* The next to the principals.
*Glut.* The slimy substance in the pannel.
*Gorge.* The crow or crop.
*Haglurs.* The spots on the feathers.
*Mails.* The breast feathers.
*Nares.* The two little holes on the top of the beak.
*Pannel.* The pipe next to the fundament.
*Pendent feathers.* Those behind the toes.
*Petty singles.* The toes.
*Pounces.* The claws.
*Principal feathers.* The two longest.
*Sails.* The wings.
*Sear* or *sere.* The yellow part under the eyes.
*Train.* The tail.

(2) Different sorts of hawk:

*Gerfalcon.* A Gerfalcon (esp. the Tercel, or male) is for a king.
*Falcon* or *Tercel gentle.* For a prince.
*Falcon of the rock.* For a duke.
*Falcon peregrine.* For an earl.
*Bastard hawk.* For a baron.
*Sacre* and a *Sacret.* For a knight.
*Lanare* and *Lanret.* For a squire.
*Merlin.* For a lady.
*Hoby.* For a young man.
*Goshawk.* For a yeoman.
*Tercel.* For a poor man.
*Sparrow-hawk.* For a priest
*Musket.* For a holy-water clerk.
*Kesterel.* For a knave or servant.

Dame Juliana Berners

The 'Sore-hawk' is a hawk of the first year; so called from the French, *sor* or *saure*, brownish-yellow.

(3) The dress of a hawk:

*Bewits.* The leathers with the hawk-bells, buttoned to the bird's legs.
*Creanse.* A packthread or thin twine fastened to the leash in disciplining a hawk.
*Hood.* A cover for the head, to keep the hawk in the dark. A *rufter hood* is a wide one, open behind. *To unstrike the hood* is to draw the strings that the hood may be in readiness to be pulled off.
*Jesses.* The little straps by which the leash is fastened to the legs.
*Leash.* The leather thong for holding the hawk.

(4) Terms used in falconry:

*Casting.* Something given to a hawk to cleanse her gorge.
*Cawking.* Treading.
*Cowering.* When young hawks, in obedience to their elders, quiver and shake their wings.
*Crabbing.* Fighting with each other when they stand too near.
*Hack.* The place where a hawk's meat is laid.
*Imping.* Repairing a hawk's wing by engrafting a new feather.
*Inke* or *Ink.* The breast and neck of a bird that a hawk preys on.
*Intermewing.* The time of changing the coat.
*Lure.* A figure of a fowl made of leather and feathers.
*Make.* An old staunch hawk that sets an example to young ones.
*Mantling.* Stretching first one wing and then the other over the legs.
*Mew.* The place where hawks sit when moulting.
*Muting.* The dung of hawks.
*Pelf* or *pill.* What a hawk leaves of her prey.
*Pelt.* The dead body of a fowl killed by a hawk.
*Perch.* The resting-place of a hawk when off the falconer's wrist.
*Plumage.* Small feathers given to a hawk to make her cast.
*Quarry.* The fowl or game that a hawk flies at.
*Rangle.* Gravel given to a hawk to bring down her stomach.
*Sharp set.* Hungry.
*Tiring.* Giving a hawk a leg or wing of a fowl to pull at.

The peregrine when full grown is called a *blue-hawk*.

The hawk was the symbol of Ra or Horus, the sun-god of the Egyptians.

*See* Birds (protected by superstitions).

***I know a hawk from a handsaw*** (*Hamlet*, 2, 2). Handsaw is probably a corruption of *hernshaw* (a heron). I know a hawk from a heron, the bird of prey from the game flown at; I know one thing from another.

***Neither hawk nor buzzard.*** Of doubtful social position – too good for the kitchen, and not good enough for the family; not hawks to be fondled and petted – the 'tasselled gentlemen' of the days of falconry – nor yet buzzards – a dull kind of falcon synonymous with dunce or plebeian. 'Neither flesh, fowl, nor good red herring.'

**Hawker's News** or **'Piper's News'**. News known to all the world. *Un secret de polichinelle.*

**Hawkeye.** One of the names of Natty Bumpo. *See* Leatherstocking.

**Hawse-hole.** ***He has crept through the hawse-hole,*** or ***He has come in at the hawse-hole.*** That is, he entered the service in the lowest grade; he rose from the ranks. A naval phrase. The hawse-hole of a ship is that through which the cable of the anchor runs.

**Hawthorn.** The symbol of 'Good Hope' in the Language of Flowers, because it shows the winter is over and spring is at hand. The Athenian girls used to crown themselves with hawthorn flowers at weddings, and the marriage-torch was made of hawthorn. The Romans considered it a charm against sorcery, and placed leaves of it on the cradles of newborn infants.

The hawthorn was chosen by Henry VII for his device, because the crown of Richard III was discovered in a hawthorn bush at Bosworth.

**Hay, Hagh,** or **Haugh.** An enclosed estate; rich pasture-land, especially a royal park; as Bilhagh (*Billa-haugh*), Beskwood- or Bestwood-hay, Lindeby-hay, Welley-hay or Wel-hay. These were 'special reserves' of game for royalty alone.

***A bottle of hay.*** *See* Bottle.

***Between hay and grass.*** Too late for one and too soon for the other.

***Neither hay nor grass.*** That hobbledehoy state when a youth is neither boy nor man.

***Make hay while the sun shines.*** Strike while the iron is hot; take time by the forelock; one today is worth two tomorrows.

**Haysugge.** *See* Isaac.

**Hazazel.** The scapegoat. *See* Azazel.

**He Bible, The.** *See* Bible, Specially named.

**Head.** Cattle are counted by the *head*; labourers by *hands*, as 'How many hands do you employ?'; soldiers by their *arms*, as 'So many rifles, bayonets', etc.; guests at dinner by the *cover*, as 'Covers for ten', etc.

Human beings are, in some circumstances, counted as 'heads', as, for instance, in contracting for meals the caterer will take the job at so much 'a head' – i.e. for each person.

***Better be the head of an ass than the tail of a horse.*** Better be foremost amongst commoners than the lowest of the aristocracy; better be the head of the yeomanry than the tail of the gentry. 'Better to reign in hell than serve in heav'n' (Milton, *Paradise Lost*, I, 263).

***Get your head shaved.*** You are a dotard. Go and get your head shaved like other lunatics. *See* Bath.

> Thou thinkst that monarchs never can act ill,
> Get thy head shaved, poor fool, or think so still.
>
> Peter Pindar, *Ode Upon Ode*

***Head and shoulders.*** A phrase of sundry shades of meaning. Thus 'head and shoulders taller' means considerably taller; 'to turn one out head and shoulders' means to drive one out forcibly and without ceremony.

***Heads I win, tails you lose.*** A common 'catch' for the unwary; for in tossing up a coin with such an arrangement, the person who *makes* the bargain must of necessity win, and the person who accepts it must inevitably lose.

***Heads or tails.*** Guess whether the coin tossed up will come down with head-side uppermost or not. The side not bearing the head has various devices, which are all included in the word tail, meaning opposite to the head. The ancient Romans used to play this game, but said, 'Heads or ships.'

> Cum pueri denarios in sublime jactantes 'capita aut navia', lusu teste vetustatis exclamant.
>
> *Macroblus Saturnalia*, i, 7

***He has quite turned her head.*** He has so completely enchanted her that she is unable to take a reasonable view of the situation.

***He has a head on his shoulders.*** He is up to snuff; he is a clever fellow, with brains in his head.

***He has quite lost his head.*** He is in a quandary or quite confused.

***I can make neither head nor tail of it.*** I cannot understand it at all. A gambling phrase.

***Off one's head.*** Deranged; delirious; extremely excited. Here 'head' means intelligence, understanding, etc. His intelligence or understanding has deserted him.

***Over head and ears.*** *See* Ear.

***To bundle one out head and heels. Sans cérémonie***, altogether. There was a custom, at one time far too frequent in cottages, for a whole family to sleep together in one bed head to heels or *pednam'ené*, as it was termed in Cornwall; to bundle the whole lot out of bed was to turn them out head and heels.

***To come to a head.*** To ripen, to reach a crisis. The allusion is to the ripening, or coming to a head, of a suppurating boil or ulcer.

***To eat his head off.*** To cost more in food than one is worth; to do little or no work. The phrase comes from the stable.

***To give one his head.*** To allow him complete freedom, let him go just as he pleases. Another 'horsy' phrase.

***To head off.*** To intercept; get ahead of and force to turn back.

***To hit the nail on the head.*** To guess aright; to do the right thing. The allusion is obvious. The French say, *Vous avez frappé au but* (You have hit the mark); the Italians have the phrase, *Havete dato in brocca* (You have hit the pitcher), alluding to a game where a pitcher stood in the place of Aunt Sally (*q.v.*). The Lat. *Rem acu tetigisti* (You have touched the thing with a needle), refers to the custom of probing sores.

***To keep one's head above water.*** To avoid bankruptcy. The allusion is to swimming; so long as one's head is above water one's life remains, but bad swimmers find it hard to keep their heads above water.

***To lose one's head.*** To become confused and muddle-headed.

***To make head,*** or ***headway.*** To get on, to struggle effectually against something.

***To take it into one's head.*** To conceive a notion.

**Heady.** Wilful; also, affecting the head, as 'The wine or beer is heady.'

**Health. *Drinking healths*.** This custom, of immemorial antiquity, is said by William of Malmesbury to have taken its rise from the death of young King Edward the Martyr (979), who was traitorously stabbed in the back while drinking a cup of wine presented to him by his mother Elfrida. According to Rabelais the giant, Gabbara, was 'the first inventor of the drinking of healths'. He was an ancestor of Gargantua.

It was well known to the ancients; thus, when Theramenes was condemned by the Thirty Tyrants to drink hemlock, he said: '*Hoc pulcro Critiae*' – the man who condemned him to death. In drinking healths we hold our hands up towards the person toasted and say, 'Your health …' The Greeks handed the cup to the person toasted and said, 'This to thee', *Graeci in epulis poculum alicui tradituri, eum nominare solent*. Our holding out the wineglass is a relic of this Greek custom.

The Romans had a curious fashion of drinking the health of their lady-loves, and that was to drink a bumper to each letter of her name. Hudibras satirises this custom, which he calls 'spelling names with beer-glasses' (ii, 1). In Plautus, we read of a man drinking to his mistress with these words: *Bene vos, bene nos, bene te, bene me, bene nostrum etiam Stephanium* (Here's to you, here's to us *all*, here's to thee, here's to me, here's to our dear — ). (*Stich*. v, 4) Persius (v, 1, 20) has a similar verse: *Bene mihi, bene vobis, bene amicae nostrae* (Here's to myself, here's to you, and here's to I shan't say who). Martial, Ovid, Horace, etc., refer to the same custom.

The Saxons were great health-drinkers, and Geoffrey of Monmouth (Bk vi, 12) says that Hengist invited King Vortigern to a banquet to see his new levies. After the meats were removed, Rowena, the beautiful daughter of Hengist, entered with a golden cup full of wine, and, making obeisance, said, *Lauerd king, wacht heil*' (Lord King, your health). The king then drank and replied, *Drinc heil* (Here's to you). *See* Nipperkin; Wassail.

**Heap. *Struck all of a heap*.** Struck with astonishment. *Être ahuri*. The idea is that of confusion, having the wits bundled together in a heap.

**Hearse.** Originally a framework shaped like an ancient harrow (O.Fr. *herce*, a harrow), holding candles and placed over a bier or coffin. These frames at a later period were covered with a canopy, and lastly were mounted on wheels and became the modern carriage for the dead.

**Heart.** In Christian art the *heart* is an attribute of St Theresa. *The flaming heart* is the symbol of charity, and an attribute of St Augustine, denoting the fervency of his devotion. The heart of the Saviour is frequently so represented.

***The Bleeding Heart.*** *See* Bleeding.

**Phrases, Proverbs, etc.**

***A heart to heart talk.*** A confidential talk in private; generally one in which good advice is offered, or a warning or reprimand given.

***After my own heart.*** Just what I like; in accordance with my wish; the heart being the supposed seat of the affections.

***Be of good heart.*** Cheer up. In Latin, *Fac, bono animo sis*; the heart being the seat of moral courage.

***From the bottom of one's heart.*** Fervently; with absolute sincerity.

***His heart is in the right place.*** He is kind and sympathetic in spite, perhaps, of appearances. He is perfectly well disposed.

***His heart sank into his boots.*** In Latin, *Cor illi in genua decidit*. In French, *Avoir la peur au ventre*. The last two phrases are very expressive: Fear makes the knees shake, and it gives one a stomach ache; but the English phrase suggests that his heart or spirits sank as low as possible short of absolutely deserting him.

***His heart was in his mouth.*** That choky feeling in the throat which arises from fear, conscious guilt, shyness, etc.: a little more and he'd lose his heart, or courage, altogether.

> The young lover tried to look at his ease ... but his heart was in his mouth.
>
> Miss Thackeray, *Mrs Dymond*, p. 136

***In one's heart of heart.*** In the farthest, innermost, most secure recesses of one's heart.

> Give me that man
> That is not passion's slave, and I will wear him
> In my heart's core, ay, in my heart of heart.
>
> Shakespeare, *Hamlet*, 2, 2

The phrase is too often heard as 'heart of *hearts*', the idea probably being that *if* one had a number of hearts the principal, governing one is that referred to; but this, as will be seen from Shakespeare's very clear reference to the 'heart's core', involves a fundamental misunderstanding. *Cp.* also:

> Even the very middle of my heart
> Is warmed. *Cymbeline*, 2, 6

***Out of heart.*** Despondent; without sanguine hope. Lat. *Animum despondere*. Fr. *Perdre courage*.

***Set your heart at rest.*** Be quite easy about the matter. In French, *Mettez votre coeur à l'aise*. The heart is the supposed organ of the sensibilities (including the affections, etc.).

***Take heart.*** Be of good courage. Moral courage at one time was supposed to reside in the heart, physical courage in the stomach, wisdom in the head, affection in the reins or kidneys, melancholy in the bile, spirit in the blood, etc. In French, *prendre courage*.

***To break one's heart.*** To waste away or die of disappointment. 'Broken-hearted', hopelessly distressed. In French, *Cela me fend le coeur*. It is not impossible, physiologically, to die 'of a broken heart'; but it never happens through grief.

***To eat one's heart out.*** To brood over some trouble to such an extent that one wears oneself out with the worry of it; to suffer from hopeless disappointment in expectations.

***To have at heart.*** To cherish as a great hope or desire; to be earnestly set on.

***To learn by heart.*** *See* Learn.

***To lose one's heart to.*** To fall in love with somebody 'head over ears'.

***To take heart of grace.*** To pluck up courage; not to be disheartened or down-hearted when all seems to be going against one. This expression may be based on the promise, 'My grace is sufficient for thee' (2 Cor. 12:9); by this grace St Paul says, 'When I am weak then am I strong'. Take grace into your heart, rely on God's grace for strength, with grace in your heart your feeble knees will be strengthened.

On the other hand, it may merely be in punning reference to *Hart of Grease* (*q.v.*).

***To set one's heart upon.*** Earnestly to desire it. *Je l'aime de tout mon coeur*; the heart being the supposed seat of the affections.

***To take to heart.*** To feel deeply pained at something which has occurred. In Latin, *Percussit mihi animum; iniquo animo ferre*. In French, *Prendre une affaire à coeur*.

***To wear one's heart upon one's sleeve.*** To expose one's secret intentions to general notice; the reference being to the custom of tying your lady's favour to your sleeve, and thus exposing the secret of the heart. Iago says:

> When my outward action doth demonstrate
> The native act and figure of my heart
> In compliment extern, 'tis not long after
> But I will wear my heart upon my sleeve
> For daws to peck at: I am not what I am.
>
> Shakespeare, *Othello*, 1, 6

***With all my heart***, or ***with my whole heart and soul.*** With all the energy and enthusiasm of which I am capable. In French, *S'y porter de tout son coeur*. Mark 12:33 says, 'Love [God] with all thy heart [affection], all thy soul [or glow of spiritual life].'

***With heart and hand.*** With enthusiastic energy.

**Heartbreaker.** A flirt. Also a particular kind of curl; called in French *accroche-coeur*. A loose ringlet worn over the shoulders, or a curl over the temples.

**Heartrending.** Very pathetic. *Qui déchire le coeur*: the heart as the seat of the affections.

**Heartwhole.** Not in love; the affections not given to another.

I in love? ... I give you my word I am heart whole
Scott, *Redgauntlet* (letter 13)

**Heart of Midlothian.** The old jail, the Tolbooth of Edinburgh, taken down in 1817. Sir Walter Scott has a novel so called.

**Heartsease.** The *viola tricolor*. It has a host of fancy names; as, the 'Butterfly flower', 'Kiss me quick', a 'Kiss behind the garden gate', 'Love in idleness' (*q.v.*), 'Pansy', 'Three faces under one hood', the 'Variegated violet', 'Herba Trinitatis', etc.

**Hearth Money.** *See* Chimney Money.

**Heat.** One course in a race; that part of a race run as an 'instalment' of the main event. One, two, or more heats make a race. A *dead heat* is a heat in which two or more competitors are tied for the first place.

Feigned Zeal, you saw, set out with speedier pace,
But the last heat Plain Dealing won the race.
Dryden, *Albion and Albanius; Epilogue*

**Heathen.** Literally, a dweller on a heath, i.e. some remote part where Christian doctrines would not penetrate till long after they had been accepted in towns. The word may have been influenced by Gr. *ethnos*, a nation, the Gentiles, i.e. persons other than Christians or Jews.

**Heaven** (A.S. *heofon*). The word properly denotes the abode of the Deity and His angels – 'heaven is My throne' (Is. 66:1, and Matt. 5:34) – but it is also used in the Bible and elsewhere for the air, the upper heights as 'the fowls of heaven', 'the dew of heaven', 'the clouds of heaven'; 'the cities are walled up to heaven' (Deut. 1:28); and a tower whose top should 'reach unto heaven' (Gen. 11:4); the starry firmament, as, 'Let there be lights in the firmament of heaven' (Gen. 1:14).

In the Ptolemaic system (*q.v.*) the heavens were the successive spheres of space enclosing the central earth at different distances and revolving round it at different speeds. The first seven were those of the so-called Planets, viz. the Moon, Mercury, Venus, the Sun, Mars, Jupiter, and Saturn; the eighth was the firmament of heaven containing all the fixed stars; the ninth was the crystalline sphere, invented by Hipparchus (2nd cent. BC), to account for the precession of the equinoxes. These were known as *The Nine Heavens* (*see* Nine Spheres); the tenth – added much later – was the primum mobile.

Sometimes she deemed that Mars had from above
Left his fifth heaven, the powers of men to prove.
Hoole, *Orlando Furioso*, Bk xiii

**The Seven Heavens** (of the Mohammedans).

***The first heaven*** is of pure silver, and here the stars, each with its angel warder, are hung out like lamps on golden chains. It is the abode of Adam and Eve.

***The second heaven*** is of pure gold and is the domain of John the Baptist and Jesus.

***The third heaven*** is of pearl, and is allotted to Joseph. Here Azrael, the angel of death, is stationed, and is for ever writing in a large book or blotting words out. The former are the names of persons born, the latter those of the newly dead.

***The fourth heaven*** is of white gold, and is Enoch's. Here dwells the Angel of Tears, whose height is '500 days' journey', and he sheds ceaseless tears for the sins of man.

***The fifth heaven*** is of silver and is Aaron's. Here dwells the Avenging Angel, who presides over elemental fire.

***The sixth heaven*** is composed of ruby and garnet, and is presided over by Moses. Here dwells the Guardian Angel of heaven and earth, half-snow and half-fire.

***The seventh heaven*** is formed of divine light beyond the power of tongue to describe, and is ruled by Abraham. Each inhabitant is bigger than the whole earth, and has 70,000 heads, each head 70,000 mouths, each mouth 70,000 tongues and each tongue speaks 70,000 languages, all for ever employed in chanting the praises of the Most High.

***To be in the seventh heaven.*** Supremely happy. The Cabbalists maintained that there are seven heavens, each rising in happiness above the other, the seventh being the abode of God and the highest class of angels. *See also* Paradise.

**Heavies, The.** The heavy cavalry, especially the Dragoon Guards, which consists of men of greater build and height than Lancers and Hussars. *Cp.* Light Troops. Also guns of large calibre and great weight, as opposed to light artillery.

**Heavy Man.** In theatrical parlance, an actor who plays foil to the hero, such as the king in *Hamlet*; Iago is another 'heavy man's' part as foil to Othello.

**Heavy-armed Artillery.** The garrison artillery. The 'light-armed artillery' are Royal Horse Artillery.

**Hebe.** Goddess of youth, and cupbearer to the celestial gods. She had the power of restoring the aged to youth and beauty (*Greek mythology*).

Wreathed smiles
Such as hang on Hebe's cheek,
And love to live in dimple sleek.
Milton, *L'Allegro*

**Hebron.** In Dryden's *Absalom and Achitophel* (*q.v.*), in the first part stands for Holland, but in the second part for Scotland. Hebronite, a native of Holland or Scotland.

**Hecate.** One of the Titans of *Greek mythology*, and the only one that retained her power under the rule of Zeus. She was the daughter of Perses and Asteria, and became a deity of the lower world after taking part in the search for Proserpine. She taught witchcraft and sorcery, and was a goddess of the dead, and as she combined the attributes of, and became identified with, Selene, Artemis, and Persephone, she was represented as a triple goddess and was sometimes described as having three heads – one of a horse, one of a dog, and one of a lion. Her offerings consisted of dogs, honey, and black lambs, which were sacrificed to her at cross-roads. Shakespeare refers to the triple character of this goddess:

And we fairies that do run
By the triple Hecate's team.
*Midsummer Night's Dream*, 5, 2

**Hecatomb.** In Greek antiquities, a sacrifice consisting of a hundred head of oxen (*hekaton*, a hundred); hence, a large number. Keats speaks of 'hecatombs of vows', Shelley of 'hecatombs of broken hearts', etc.

It is said that Pythagoras, who, we know, would never take life, offered up 100 oxen to the gods when he discovered that the square of the hypothenuse of a right-angled-triangle equals both the squares of the other two sides. This is the 47th of Bk i of 'Euclid', called the Dulcarnon (*q.v.*).

**Hector.** Eldest son of Priam, the noblest and most magnanimous of all the Trojan chieftains in Homer's *Iliad*. After holding out for ten years, he was slain by Achilles, who lashed him to his chariot, and dragged the dead body in triumph thrice round the walls of Troy. The *Iliad* concludes with the funeral obsequies of Hector and Patroclus.

In modern times his name has somewhat deteriorated, for it is used today for a swaggering bully, and 'to hector' means to browbeat, bully, bluster.

How often have I told you that English women are not to be treated like Circassian slaves. We have the protection of the world; we are to be won by gentle means only, and not to be hectored, and bullied, and beat into compliance.
Fielding, *Tom Jones*, X, viii

***The Hector of Germany.*** Joachim II, Elector of Brandenburg (1514–71).

***You wear Hector's cloak.*** You are paid in your own coin for trying to deceive another. When Thomas Percy, Earl of Northumberland, in 1569, was routed, he hid himself in the house of Hector Armstrong, of Harlaw. This villain betrayed him for the reward offered, but never after did anything go well with him; he went down, down, down, till at last he died a beggar on the roadside.

**Hecuba.** Second wife of Priam, and mother of nineteen children, including Hector. When Troy was taken by the Greeks she fell to the lot of Ulysses. She was afterwards metamorphosed into a dog, and threw herself into the sea. Her story has furnished a host of Greek tragedies.

I have heard my grandsire say full oft,
Extremity of griefs would make men mad;
And I have read that Hecuba of Troy
Ran mad through sorrow.
Shakespeare, *Titus Andronicus*, 4, 1

**Hedge.** ***To hedge***, in betting, is to protect oneself against loss by cross bets. As a hedge is a defence, so cross betting is hedging.

He [Godolphin] began to think ... that he had betted too deep ... and that it was time to hedge.
Macaulay, *England*, vol. iv, ch. xvii

The word is used attributively for persons of low origin, vagabonds who ply their trade in the open, under – or between – the hedges, etc.; hence for many low and mean things, as *hedge-priest*, a poor or vagabond parson; *hedge-writer*, a Grub Street author; *hedge-marriage*, a clandestine one, etc.; *hedge-born swain*, a person of mean, or illegitimate, birth (*1 Henry VI*, 4, 1); *hedge-school*, a school kept in the open air, at one time common in Ireland; etc.

**Hedonism.** The doctrine of Aristippus, that pleasure or happiness is the chief good and chief end of man (Gr. *hedone*, pleasure).

**Heel.** ***Achilles' heel.*** *See* Achilles.

***Down***, or ***out at heels.*** In a sad plight, in decayed circumstances, like a beggar whose stockings are worn out at the heels.

A good man's fortune may grow out at heels.
Shakespeare, *King Lear*, 2, 2

***To cool*** or ***kick one's heels.*** To be kept waiting a long time, especially after an appointment has been given one.

***To lay by the heels.*** To render powerless. The allusion is to the stocks, in which vagrants and other petty offenders were confined by the ankles.

***To lift up the heel against.*** To spurn, physically or figuratively; to treat with contumely or contempt: to oppose, to become an enemy. As an unruly horse kicks the master who trusts and feeds him.

> Yea, mine own familiar friend, in whom I trusted, which did eat of my bread, hath lifted his heel against me. Ps. 12:9

***To show a light*** or ***fair pair of heels.*** To abscond, run away and get clear.

> Two of them saw me when I went out of doors, and chased me, but I showed them a fair pair of heels. Scott, *Peveril of the Peak*, ch. xxiv

***To take to one's heels.*** To run off.

**Heel-tap. *Bumpers all round, and no heel-taps*.** The bumpers are to be drained to the bottom of the glass.

**Heep, Uriah.** An abject toady, malignant as he is base; always boasting of his *'umble* birth, *'umble* position, *'umble* abode, and *'umble* calling. (Dickens, *David Copperfield.*)

**Hegemony. *The hegemony of nations*.** The leadership. (Gr. *hegemonia*, from *ago*, to lead.)

**Hegira** (Arab. *hejira*, the departure). The epoch of the flight of Mahomet from Mecca to Medina when he was expelled by the magistrates, July 15th, 622. The Mohammedan calender starts from this event.

**Heimdall.** One of the gods of *Scandinavian mythology*, son of the nine virgins, daughters of Aegir, and in many attributes identical with Tíw. He is called the *white god with the golden teeth*, and, as the watchman or sentinel of Asgard (*q.v.*), dwelt on the edge of heaven, guarded the bridge Bifrost (the rainbow), and possessed a mighty horn whose blast could be heard throughout the universe. He could see for a hundred miles by day or night, slept less than a bird, and heard the grass grow, and even the wool on a lamb's back. At the end of the world he is to wake the gods with his horn.

**Heimskringla.** An important collection of sixteen sagas containing an account of the history of Norway – sketched through the medium of biography – and a compendium of ancient Scandinavian mythology and poetry. It is probably by Snorri Sturluson (d.1241). *See* Edda.

**Heir-apparent.** The actual heir who will succeed if he outlive the present holder of the crown, estate, etc., as distinguished from the *heir-presumptive*, whose succession may be broken by the birth of someone nearer akin to the holder. Thus, in the time of Queen Victoria, the Princess Royal was heir-presumptive till the Prince of Wales, afterwards Edward VII, was born. At the death of his predecessor the heir-apparent becomes *heir-at-law*.

**Hel.** The name in late *Scandinavian mythology* of the queen of the dead; also of her place of abode, which was the home of the spirits of those who had died in their beds as distinguished from Valhalla, the abode of heroes slain in battle. She dwelt beneath the roots of the sacred ash (*Yggdrasil*), and was the daughter of Loki.

> Down the yawning steep he rode
> That led to Hela's drear abode
> Gray, *Descent of Odin*

**Hel Keplein.** A mantle of invisibility belonging to the dwarf Laurin (*q.v.*).

**Heldenbuch** (Ger. *Book of Heroes*). The name given to the collection of songs, sagas, etc., recounting the traditions and myths of Dietrich of Bern. Much of it is ascribed to Wolfram von Eschenbach, and it was edited by O. Janicke and others in 1866.

**Helen.** The type of female beauty, more especially in those who have reached womanhood. Daughter of Zeus and Leda, and wife of Menelaos, king of Sparta. She eloped with Paris, and thus brought about the siege and destruction of Troy.

> For which men all the life they here enjoy
> Still fight, as for the Helens of their Troy.
> Lord Brooke, *Treatie of Humane Learning*
>
> She moves a goddess and she looks a queen.
> Pope, *Homer's Iliad*, iii

***St Helen's fire.*** The St Elmo's Fire, or Corpozant (*q.v.*), occasionally on the masts of ships, etc. If the flame is single, foul weather is said to be at hand; but if two or more flames appear, the weather will improve. *See* Castor and Pollux.

**Helena.** The type of a lovely woman, patient and hopeful, strong in feeling, and sustained through trials by her enduring and heroic faith. (Shakespeare, *All's Well that Ends Well.*)

**Helena, St.** Mother of Constantine the Great. She is represented in royal robes, wearing an imperial crown, because she was empress. Sometimes she carries in her hand a model of the Holy Sepulchre, an edifice raised by her in the East;

sometimes she bears a large cross, typical of her alleged discovery (*see* Invention of the Cross, *under* Cross); sometimes she also bears the three nails by which the Saviour was affixed to the cross. She died about 328, and is commemorated on August 18th.

**Helenus.** The prophet, the only son of Priam that survived the fall of Troy. He fell to the share of Pyrrhus when the captives were awarded; and because he saved the life of the young Grecian was allowed to marry Andromache, his brother Hector's widow. (Virgil, *Aeneid.*)

**Helicon.** The home of the Muses, a part of the Parnassus, a mountain range in Greece. It contained the fountains of Aganippe and Hippocrene, connected by 'Helicon's harmonious stream'. The name is used allusively of poetic inspiration.

> From Helicon's harmonious springs
> A thousand rills their mazy progress take:
> The laughing flowers, that round them blow
> Drink life and fragrance as they flow.
>
> Gray, *The Progress of Poesy*

**Heliopolis,** the City of the Sun, a Greek form of (1) Baalbek, in Syria; and (2) of An, in ancient Egypt, noted for its temple of Actis, which may be the Beth Shemesh, or Temple of the Sun, referred to in Jer. 43:13.

**Helios.** The Greek sun-god, who rode to his palace in Colchis every night in a golden boat furnished with wings. He is called Hyperion by Homer, and, in later times, Apollo.

**Heliotrope.** Apollo loved Clytie (*q.v.*), but forsook her for her sister Leucothoe. On discovering this, Clytie pined away; and Apollo changed her at death to a flower, which, always turning towards the sun, is called heliotrope. (Gr. 'turn-to-sun'.)

The bloodstone, a greenish quartz with veins and spots of red, used to be called 'heliotrope', the story being that if thrown into a bucket of water it turned the rays of the sun to blood-colour. This stone also had the power of rendering its bearer invisible.

> No hope had they of crevice where to hide,
> Or heliotrope to charm them out of view
>
> Dante, *Inferno*, xxiv

> The other stone is heliotrope, which renders those who have it invisible.
>
> Boccaccio, *The Decameron*, Novel iii, Eighth day

**Hell.** This word occurs twenty-one times in the Authorised Version of the New Testament. In eight instances the Greek word is *Hades*; in twelve instances it is *Gehenna*; and in one it is *Tartarus* (*all of which see*).

Hades: Matt. 11:23*, 16:18*; Luke. 16:23*; Acts 2:31*; Rev. 1:18*, 6:8*, 20:13*, 14*.

Gehenna: Matt. 5:22, 29, 30, 10:28, 18:9, 23:15, 33; Mark 9:43, 45, 47; Luke 12:5; James 3:6.

Tartarus: 2 Pet. 2:4.

In the Revised Version the word is used only thirteen times, and those verses in which it is rendered by *Hades* are distinguished by an asterisk in the list above.

According to the Koran, Hell has seven portals leading into seven divisions (*Surah* xv, 44); nothing is said in the text as to how these are apportioned, but later Mohammedan commentators have allotted them as follows:

(1) Jahannam, for wicked Mohammedans, all of whom will be sooner or later taken to paradise;
(2) The Flamer (*Lathà*), for Christians;
(3) The Smasher (*Hutamah*), for Jews;
(4) The Blazer (*Sàir*), for Sabians;
(5) The Scorcher (*Sakar*), for Magians;
(6) The Burner (*Jahim*), for idolaters; and
(7) The Abyss (*Hawiyah*), for hypocrites.

The Hell, or *Arka*, of the Jewish Cabalists is divided into seven lodges, one under another (*Joseph ben Abraham Gikatilla*) –

| | | | Presiding Angel* |
|---|---|---|---|
| (1) Gehennom | The heat 60 times that of fire. (Here it 'snows fire'.) | Absalom and Israelites who break the law | Kushiel |
| (2) The Gates of Death | 60 times hotter than No. 1 | Doeg | Lahatiel |
| (3) The Shadow of Death | 60 times hotter than No. 2 | Korah | Shaftiel |
| (4) The Pit of Corruption | 60 times hotter than No. 3 | Jeroboam | Maccathiel |
| (5) The Mire of Clay | 60 times hotter than No. 4 | Ahab | Chutriel |
| (6) Abaddon | 60 times hotter than No. 5 | Micah | Pasiel |
| (7) Sheol | 60 times hotter than No. 6 or over two and three quarter billion (2,799,360,000.000) times hotter than fire | Elisha, son of Abuya, Sabbath-breakers, idolaters, and uncircumcised | Dalkiel |

*All these presidents are under Duma, the Angel of Silence, who keeps the three keys of the three gates of hell.

True Buddhism admits of no Hell, properly so called (*cp.* Nirvana), but certain of the more superstitious acknowledge as many as 136 places of punishment after death, where the dead are sent according to their degree of demerit.

Classic authors tell us that the Inferno is encompassed by five rivers: Acheron, Cocytus, Styx, Phlegethon, and Lethe. Acheron, from the Gr. *achos-reo*, grief-flowing; Cocytus, from the Gr. *kokuo*, to weep, supposed to be a flood of tears; Styx, from the Gr. *stugeo*, to loathe; Phlegethon, from the Gr. *phlego*, to burn; and Lethe, from the Gr. *lethe*, oblivion.

> Five hateful rivers round Inferno run,
> Grief comes the first, and then the Flood of tears,
> Next loathsome Styx, then liquid Flame appears.
> Lethe comes last, or blank oblivion. *E. C. B.*

*Cp.* Inferno.

**Phrases.**

***Go to hell!*** A very emphatic way of saying 'Off with you!' 'Clear out!' 'Go to the devil!'

***Hell and chancery are always open.*** There's not much to choose between lawyers and the devil. An old saying, given in Fuller's *Collection* (1732).

***Hell, Hull, and Halifax.*** *See* Hull.

***Hell is paved with good intentions.*** This occurs as a saying of Dr Johnson (Boswell's *Life*, ann. 1775), but it is a good deal older than his day. It is given by George Herbert (1633) as 'Hell is full of good meanings and wishes.'

> It has been more wittily than charitably said that hell is paved with good intentions; they have their place in heaven also.
>
> Southey, *Colloquies*, v

***It was hell broken loose.*** Said of a frightful state of anarchy or disorder; an awful 'rumpus'.

> Why, here you have the awfulest of crimes
> For nothing! Hell broke loose on a butterfly!
> A dragon born of rose-dew and the moon!
>
> Browning, *Ring and the Book*, iv, 1601

***The road to hell is easy.*** *Facilis descensus Averno. See* Avernus.

***The Vicar of Hell.*** *See* Vicar.

***To give one hell.*** To make things very hot for him; to give him a good rowing, or a severe castigation.

***To Hell or Connaught.*** This phrase, usually attributed to Cromwell, and common to the whole of Ireland, rose thus: during the Commonwealth all the native Irish were dispossessed of their lands in the other three provinces and ordered to settle in Connaught, under pain of death.

***To lead apes in hell.*** *See* Ape.

***To play hell and tommy.*** To raise Cain, to kick up the deuce of a row; thoroughly to upset things.

***To ride hell for leather.*** To ride with the utmost speed, 'all out'.

***To work, play,*** etc., ***like hell.*** To do it feverishly, or with all the power at one's disposal.

**Hell Broth.** A magical mixture prepared for evil purpose. The witches in *Macbeth* made it. *See* act 4, 1.

**Hell Gate.** A dangerous passage between Great Barn Island and Long Island, North America. The Dutch settlers of New York called it Hoell-gat (whirling-gut), corrupted into Hell Gate. Flood Rock, its most dangerous reef, has been blown up.

**Hell Gates,** according to Milton, are ninefold – three of brass, three of iron, and three of adamant; the keepers are Sin and Death. *See Paradise Lost*, Bk ii, 643–76.

**Hellenes.** 'This word had in Palestine three several meanings: Sometimes it designated the pagans; sometimes the Jews, speaking Greek, and dwelling among the pagans; and sometimes proselytes of the gate, that is, men of pagan origin converted to Judaism, but not circumcised' (John 7:35, 12:20; Acts 14:1, 17:4, 18:4, 21:28). (Renan: *Life of Jesus*, xiv.)

The Greeks were called *Hellenes*, from Hellen, son of Deucalion and Pyrrha, their legendary ancestor; the name has descended to the modern Greeks, and their ruler is not 'King of Greece', but 'King of the Hellenes'. The ancient Greeks called their country 'Hellas'; it was the Romans who applied to it the name 'Graecia', which, among the inhabitants themselves, referred only to Epirus.

> The first and truest Hellas, the mother-land of all Hellenes, was the land which we call Greece, with the islands round about it. There alone the whole land was Greek, and none but Hellenes lived in it.
>
> Freeman, *General Sketch*, ch. ii

***Hellenic.*** The common dialect of the Greek writers after the age of Alexander. It was based on the Attic.

***Hellenistic.*** The dialect of the Greek language used by the Jews. It was full of Oriental idioms and metaphors.

***Hellenists.*** Those Jews who used the Greek or Hellenic language.

**Hellespont.** The 'sea of Helle'; so called because Helle, the sister of Phryxus, was drowned there.

She was fleeing with her brother through the air to Colchis on the golden ram to escape from Ino, her mother-in-law, who most cruelly oppressed her, but turning giddy, she fell into the sea. It is the ancient name of the Dardanelles.

**Helmet.** Those of Saragossa were most in repute in the days of chivalry.

***Close helmet.*** The complete headpiece, having in front two movable parts, which could be lifted up or let down at pleasure.

*Visor.* One of the movable parts; it was to look through.

*Bever*, or *drinking-piece.* One of the movable parts, which was lifted up when the wearer ate or drank. It comes from the Italian verb *bevere* (to drink).

*Morion.* A low iron cap, worn only by infantry.

***Mahomet's helmet.*** Mahomet wore a double helmet; the exterior one was called *al mawashah* (the wreathed garland).

***The helmet of Perseus*** rendered the wearer invisible. This was the 'helmet of Hades', which, with the winged sandals and magic wallet, he took from certain nymphs who held them in possession; but after he had slain Medusa he restored them again, and presented the Gorgon's head to Athena (Minerva), who placed it in the middle of her aegis.

> The pointed helmet in the bas-reliefs from the earliest palace of Nimroud appears to have been the most ancient … Several were discovered in the ruins. They were iron, and the rings which ornamented the lower part … were inlaid with copper.
>
> Layard, *Nineveh and its Remains*, vol. ii, Pt ii, ch. iv

In heraldry, the helmet, resting on the chief of the shield, and bearing the crest, indicates rank.

- *Gold*, with six bars, or with the visor raised (in full face), for royalty;
- *Steel, with gold bars,* varying in number (in profile), for a nobleman;
- *Steel, without bars, and with visor open* (in profile), for a knight or baronet;
- *Steel, with visor closed* (in profile), for a squire or gentleman.

**Helon,** in Dryden's *Absalom and Achitophel* (*q.v.*), is meant for the Earl of Feversham.

**Helot.** A slave in ancient Sparta; hence, a slave or serf. The Spartans used to make a helot drunk as an object-lesson to the youths of the evils of intemperance. Dr Johnson said of one of his old acquaintances:

> He is a man of good principles; and there would be no danger that a young gentleman should catch his manner; for it is so very bad, that it must be avoided. In that respect he would be like the drunken Helot.
>
> *Boswell's 'Life'*, ann. 1779

**Helter-skelter.** Higgledy-piggledy; in hurry and confusion. A jingling expression, more or less imitating the clatter of swiftly moving feet; post-haste, as Shakespeare uses the expression (*2 Henry IV*, 5, 3):

> Sir John I am thy Pistol and thy friend,
> And helter-skelter have I rode to thee,
> And tidings do I bring.

**Helve. *To throw the helve after the hatchet.*** To be reckless, to throw away what remains because your losses have been so great. The allusion is to the fable of the wood-cutter who lost the head of his axe in a river and threw the handle in after it.

**Helvetia.** Switzerland. So called from the Helvetii, a powerful Celtic people who dwelt thereabouts.

> See from the ashes of Helvetia's pile
> The whitened skull of old Servetus smile.
>
> Holmes

**Hemp. *When hempe is spun England is done.*** Lord Bacon says he heard the prophecy when he was a child, and he interpreted it thus: Hempe is composed of the initial letters of *H*enry, *E*dward, *M*ary, *P*hilip, and *E*lizabeth. At the close of the last reign 'England was done', for the sovereign no longer styled himself 'King of England', but 'King of Great Britain and Ireland'. *See* Notarikon.

***Hempen caudle, collar,*** etc. A hangman's rope.

> Ye shall have a hempen caudle then, and the help of a hatchet. Shakespeare, *2 Henry VI*, 4, 7

***Hempen fever.*** Death on the gallows, the rope being made of hemp.

***Hempen widow.*** The widow of a man who has been hanged.

> Of a hempen widow the kid forlorn.
>
> Ainsworth, *Jack Sheppard*

**Hemus** or **Haemus.** A chain of mountains in Thrace. According to mythology, Haemos, son of Boreas, was changed into a mountain for aspiring to divine honours.

**Hen. *A grey hen.*** A stone bottle for holding liquor. Large and small pewter pots mixed together are called 'hen and chickens'.

> A dirty leather wallet lay near the sleeper … also a grey-hen which had contained some sort of strong liquor.
>
> Miss Robinson, *Whitefriars*, ch. viii

***A whistling maid and crowing hen is neither fit for God nor men.*** A whistling maid means a witch, who whistles like the Lapland witches to call up the winds; they were supposed to be in league with the devil. The crowing of a hen was supposed to forebode a death. The usual interpretation is that masculine qualities in females are undesirable.

***As fussy as a hen with one chick.*** Over-anxious about small matters; over-particular and fussy. A hen with one chick is for ever clucking it, and never leaves it in independence a single moment.

***Hen and chickens.*** In Christian art this device is emblematical of God's providence. *See* Matt. 23:37. *See also* Grey hen *above*.

***Hen-pecked.*** A man who tamely submits to the snubs and snarls of his wife is said to be 'hen-pecked'.

**Henchman.** A faithful follower. Originally a squire or attendant, especially one who looked after the horses (A.S. *hengest*, horse, and *man*).

> I do but beg a little changeling boy
> To be my henchman.
>
> Shakespeare, *Midsummer Night's Dream*, 2, 1

**Hengist** and **Horsa.** The semi-legendary leaders of the Jutes, who landed in England at Ebbsfleet, Kent, in 449. Horsa is said to have been slain at the battle of Aylesford, about 455, and Hengist to have ruled in Kent till his death in 488. Ger. *hengst* (a stallion), and Horsa is connected with our word horse. If the names of the two brothers, probably they were given them from the devices borne on their arms.

**Henricans** or **Henricians.** A religious sect; so called from Henricus, its founder, an Italian monk, who, in the 12th century, undertook to reform the vices of the clergy. He rejected infant baptism, festivals, and ceremonies. Henricus was imprisoned by Pope Eugenius III in 1148.

**Henry Grâce de Dieu.** The largest ship built by Henry VIII. It carried 72 guns, 700 men, and was 1,000 tons burthen. *See* Great Harry.

**Hephaestos.** The Greek Vulcan.

**Heptameron, The.** A collection of Italian and mediaeval stories, many of them of a somewhat licentious nature, written by – or at any rate ascribed to – Marguerite of Angoulême, Queen of Navarre (1492–1549), and published posthumously in 1558. They were supposed to have been related in seven days, hence the title (Gr. *hepta*, seven, *hemera*, day; *cp*. Decameron; Hexameron).

**Heptarchae** (Gr., seven governments). The *Saxon Heptarchy* was the division of England into seven parts, each of which had a separate ruler: as Kent, Sussex, Wessex, Essex, East Anglia, Mercia, and Northumbria. It flourished in various periods from the 6th to the 9th centuries under a Bretwalda (*q.v.*), but seldom consisted of exactly seven members, and the names and divisions were constantly changing.

**Hera.** The Greek Juno, the wife of Zeus. (The word means 'chosen one', *haireo*.)

**Heracleidae.** The descendants of Heracles (Lat. *Hercules*).

**Heraldry.** The herald (O.Fr. *heralt*, *heraut*) was an officer whose duty it was to proclaim war or peace, carry challenges to battle, and messages between sovereigns, etc.; nowadays war or peace is still proclaimed by the heralds, but their chief duty as court functionaries is to superintend state ceremonies such as coronations, installations, etc., and also to grant arms, trace genealogies, attend to matters of precedence, honours, etc.

The English *College of Arms*, or *Heralds' College*, was established by Richard III. It consists of three kings of arms, six heralds, and four pursuivants, under the Earl Marshal, which office is hereditary in the line of the Duke of Norfolk.

***The three kings of arms*** are Garter (*blue*), Clarenceux, and Norroy (*purple*).

***The six heralds*** are styled Somerset, Richmond, Lancaster, Windsor, Chester, and York.

***The four pursuivants*** are Rouge Dragon, Blue Mantle, Portcullis, and Rouge Croix.

***Garter King of arms*** is so called from his special duty to attend at the solemnities of election, investiture, and installation of Knights of the Garter; he is Principal King of Arms for all England.

***Clarenceux King of arms.*** So called from the Duke of Clarence, brother of Edward IV. His jurisdiction extends over England south of the Trent.

***Norroy King of arms*** has similar jurisdiction to Clarenceux, only on the north side of the Trent.

The 'Bath King of Arms' is not a member of the Heralds' College, and is concerned only with the Order of the Bath.

The Scottish and Irish officers of Arms are, unlike those of England, directly under the Government, and are not connected with the Earl Marshal or Garter.

In *Scotland* the heraldic college consists of *Lyon King of arms*, three heralds (*Albany*, *Ross*, and *Rothesay*), and three pursuivants (*Carrick*, *March*, and *Unicorn*).

In *Ireland* it consists of *Ulster King of arms*, two heralds (*Dublin* and *Cork*), and one pursuivant (*Athlone*).

In *Blazonry*, the *coat of arms* represents the knight himself from whom the bearer is descended.

The *shield* represents his body, and the *helmet* his head.

The *flourish* is his mantle.

The *motto* is the ground or moral pretension on which he stands.

The *supporters* are the pages, designated by the emblems of bears, lions, and so on.

There are nine *points* on the *shield* or *escutcheon*, distinguished by the first nine letters of the alphabet – three at top, A, B, C; three down the middle, D, E, F; and three at the bottom, G, H, I. The first three are *chiefs*; the middle three are the *collar point*, *fess point*, and *nombril* or *navel point*; the bottom three are the *base* points.

The *colours*, or *tinctures*, used in heraldry are:

*Or*, gold.
*Argent*, silver.
*Gules*, red.
*Azure*, blue.
*Sable*, black.
*Vert*, green.
*Purpure*, purple.

Besides these there are the different furs, as *ermine, vair*, and their arrangements as *erminois*, *erminites*, *pean*, *potent*, *verry*, etc.

In blazoning the arms of royalties the old heralds frequently used the names of the planets for the tinctures, and in noblemen's arms the names of precious stones, the equivalents being:

*Sol* – topaz – *or*.
*Luna* - pearl – *argent*.
*Saturn* – diamond – *sable*.
*Mars* – ruby – *gules*.
*Jupiter* – sapphire – *azure*.
*Venus* – emerald – *vert*.
*Mercury* – amethyst – *purpure*.

The heraldic terms denoting the positions of beasts shown in coats of arms, as crests, etc., are:

*Couchant*, lying down (emblematic of sovereignty).

*Counter-passant*, moving in opposite directions.

*Coward* or *Coué*, with tail hanging between the legs.

*Dormant*, sleeping.

*Gardant*, full-faced.

*Hauriant*, standing on its tail (of fishes).

*Issuant*, rising from the top or bottom of an ordinary.

*Lodged*, reposing (of stags, etc.).

*Naiant*. Swimming (of fishes).

*Nascent*, rising out of the middle of an ordinary.

*Passant*, walking, the face in profile (emblematic of resolution).

*Passant gardant*, walking, with full face (emblematic of resolution and prudence).

*Passant regardant*, walking and looking behind.

*Rampant*, rearing, with face in profile (emblematic of magnanimity).

*Rampant gardant*, erect on the hind legs; full face (emblematic of prudence).

*Rampant regardant*, erect on the hind legs; side face looking behind (emblematic of circumspection).

*Regardant*, looking back (emblematic of circumspection).

*Salient*, springing (emblematic of valour).

*Sejant*, seated (emblematic of counsel).

*Statant*, standing still.

*Trippant*. Running (of stags, etc.).

*Volant*. Flying.

**Herb of Grace.** Rue is so called probably because (owing to its extreme bitterness) it is the symbol of repentance.

> Here did she fall a tear; here in this place,
> I'll set a bank of rue, sour herb of grace;
> Rue, even for ruth, here shortly shall be seen,
> In the remembrance of a weeping queen.
>
> Shakespeare, *Richard II*, 3, 4

Jeremy Taylor, quoting from the *Flagellum Daemonum*, a form of exorcism by Father Jerome Mengus (used in exorcising Martha Brosser in 1599), says:

> First, they are to try the devil by holy water, incense, sulphur, rue, which from thence, as we suppose came to be called 'herb of grace', – and especially St John's wort, which therefore they call 'devil's flight', with which if they cannot cast the devil out, yet they may do good to the patient.
>
> *A Disuasive from Popery*, I, ii, 9 (1664)

Roman Catholics still sprinkle holy water with a bunch of rue. It was for centuries supposed to prevent contagion.

**Herb Trinity.** The popular name for the pansy (*q.v.*), *Viola tricolor*; also called 'Three-faces-under-a-hood'; the markings of the pansy account for both names. *Cp*. Heartsease.

**Herba Sacra.** The 'divine weed', vervain, said by the old Romans to cure the bites of all rabid animals, to arrest the progress of venom, to cure the plague, to avert sorcery and witchcraft, to reconcile enemies, etc. So highly esteemed was it that feasts called *Verbenalia* were annually held in its honour. Heralds wore a wreath of vervain when they declared war; and the Druids held vervain in similar veneration.

Lift your boughs of vervain blue,
Dipt in cold September dew;
And dash the moisture, chaste and clear,
O'er the ground, and through the air.
Now the place is purged and pure.
W. Mason, *Caractacus* (1759)

**Hercules.** A hero of ancient Greek myth, who was possessed of superhuman physical strength and vigour. He is represented as brawny, muscular, short-necked, and of huge proportions. The Pythian told him if he would serve Eurystheus for twelve years he should become immortal: accordingly he bound himself to the Argive king, who imposed upon him twelve tasks of great difficulty and danger:

(1) To slay the Nemean lion.

(2) To kill the Lernean hydra.

(3) To catch and retain the Arcadian stag.

(4) To destroy the Erymanthian boar.

(5) To cleanse the stables of King Augeas.

(6) To destroy the cannibal birds of the Lake Stymphalis.

(7) To take captive the Cretan bull.

(8) To catch the horses of the Thracian Diomedes.

(9) To get possession of the girdle of Hippolyte, Queen of the Amazons.

(10) To take captive the oxen of the monster Geryon.

(11) To get possession of the apples of the Hesperides.

(12) To bring up from the infernal regions the three-headed dog Cerberos.

The Nemean *lion* first he killed, then Lerne's *hydra* slew;
The Arcadian *stag* and monster *boar* before Eurystheus drew;
Cleansed Augeas' *stalls*, and made the *birds* from Lake Stymphalis flee;
The Cretan *bull*, and Thracian *mares*, first seized and then set free;
Took prize the Amazonian *belt*, brought Geryon's *kine* from Gades;
Fetched *apples* from the Hesperides and Cerberos from Hades. *E. C. B.*

After death Hercules took his place in the heavens as a constellation, and is still to be seen between Lyra and Corona Borealis.

***The Attic Hercules.*** Theseus, who went about like Hercules, destroying robbers and achieving wondrous exploits.

***The Farnese Hercules.*** A celebrated statue, copied by Glykon from an original by Lysippus, and now in the Farnese Palace at Rome. It exhibits the hero, exhausted by toil, leaning upon his club; his left hand rests upon his back, and grasps one of the apples of the Hesperides. A copy stands in the gardens of the Tuileries, Paris. *See* Thomson's *Liberty*, Bk iv.

**Hercules' Choice.** Immortality the reward of toil in preference to pleasure. Xenophon tells us when Hercules was a youth he was accosted by Virtue and Pleasure, and asked to choose between them. Pleasure promised him all carnal delights, but Virtue promised immortality. Hercules gave his hand to the latter, and, after a life of toil, was received amongst the gods.

**Hercules' Horse.** Arion, given him by Adrastos. It had the power of speech, and its feet on the right side were those of a man.

**Hercules' Labour** or **The Labour of an Hercules.** Very great toil. Hercules was appointed by Eurystheus to perform twelve labours requiring enormous strength or dexterity.

It was more than the labour of an Hercules could effect to make any tolerable way through your town. Cumberland, *The West Indian*

**Hercules' Pillars.** *See* Pillars.

**Hercules Secundus.** Commodus, the Roman Emperor (180–92), gave himself this title. Dissipated and inordinately cruel, he claimed divine honours and caused himself to be worshipped as Hercules. It is said that he killed 100 lions in the amphitheatre, and that he slew over a thousand defenceless gladiators.

**Herculean Knot.** A snaky complication on the rod or caduceus of Mercury, adopted by the Grecian brides as the fastening of their woollen girdles, which only the bridegroom was allowed to untie. As he did so he invoked Juno to render his marriage as fruitful as that of Hercules, whose numerous wives all had families, amongst them being the fifty daughters of Thestius, each of whom conceived in one night. *See* Knot.

**Herefordshire Kindness.** A good turn rendered for a good turn received. Latin proverbs, *Fricantem refrica*; *Manus manum lavat.* Fuller says the people of Herefordshire 'drink back to him who drinks to them'.

**Heretic.** From a Greek word meaning 'one who chooses', hence *heresy* means simply 'a choice'. A heretic is one who chooses his own creed instead of adopting one set forth by authority.

The principal heretical sects of the first six centuries were:

First Century: The *Simonians* (from Simon Magus), *Cerinthians* (Cerinthus), *Ebionites* (Ebion), and *Nicolaitans* (Nicholas, deacon of Antioch).

Second Century: The *Basilidians* (Basilides), *Carpocratians* (Carpocrates), *Valentinians* (Valentinus), *Gnostics* (Knowing Ones), *Nazarenes*, *Millenarians*, *Cainites* (Cain), *Sethians* (Seth), *Quartodecimans* (who kept Easter on the fourteenth day of the first month), *Cerdonians* (Cerdon), *Marcionites* (Marcion), *Montanists* (Montanus), *Alogians* (who denied the 'Word'), *Artotyrites* (*q.v.*), and *Angelics* (who worshipped angels).

*Tatianists* belong to the 3rd or 4th century. The Tatian of the 2nd century was a Platonic philosopher who wrote *Discourses* in good Greek; Tatian the heretic lived in the 3rd or 4th century, and wrote very bad Greek. The two men were widely different in every respect, and the authority of the heretic for 'four gospels' is of no worth.

Third Century: The *Patri-passians*, *Arabaci*, *Aquarians*, *Novatians*, *Origenists* (followers of Origen), *Melchisedechians* (who believed Melchisedec was the Messiah), *Sabellians* (from Sabellius), and *Manicheans* (followers of Mani).

Fourth Century: The *Arians* (from Arius), *Colluthians* (Colluthus), *Macedonians*, *Agnetae*, *Apollinarians* (Apollinaris), *Timotheans* (Timothy, the apostle), *Collyridians* (who offered *cakes* to the Virgin Mary), *Seleucians* (Seleucius), *Priscillians* (Priscillian), *Anthropomorphites* (who ascribed to God a human form), *Jovinianists* (Jovinian), *Messalians*, and *Bonosians* (Bonosus).

Fifth Century: The *Pelagians* (Pelagius), *Nestorians* (Nestorius), *Eutychians* (Eutychus), *Theo-paschites* (who said all the three persons of the Trinity suffered on the cross).

Sixth Century: The *Predestinarians*, *Incorruptibilists* (who maintained that the body of Christ was incorruptible), the new *Agnoetae* (who maintained that Christ did not know when the day of judgment would take place), and the *Monothelites* (who maintained that Christ had but one will).

**Heriot.** The ancient right of the lord of a manor to the best beast or chattel of a deceased copyhold tenant. The word is compounded of the Sax. *here* (army), *geatwe* (equipments), because originally it was military furniture, such as armour, arms, and horses paid to the lord of the fee.

**Hermae.** *See* Hermes.

**Hermaphrodite.** A human body having both sexes; a vehicle combining the structure of a wagon and cart; a flower containing both the male and female organs of reproduction. The word is derived from the fable of Hermaphroditus, son of Hermes and Aphrodite. The nymph Salmacis became enamoured of him, and prayed that she might be so closely united that 'the twain might become one flesh'. Her prayer being heard, the nymph and boy became one body. (Ovid, *Metamorphoses*, iv, 347.)

Though hermaphroditism in human beings to the extent of the combination in one person of certain characteristics of the two sexes is not unknown, a *true* hermaphrodite is very rare indeed, and the so-called examples are almost invariably merely cases of the malformation of the reproductive organs.

The Jewish Talmud contains several references to hermaphrodites; they are recognised in English law, and an old French law allowed them great latitude. The ancient Athenians commanded that they should be put to death. The Hindus and Chinese enact that every hermaphrodite should choose one sex and keep to it. According to fable, all persons who bathed in the fountain Salmacis, in Caria, became hermaphrodites.

> Some think by comparing Gen. 1:27, with Gen. 2:20–4, that Adam at first combined in himself both sexes.

**Hermensul** or **Ermensul.** A Saxon idol, worshipped in Westphalia and broken up by Charlemagne, who converted its temple into a Christian church. It stood on a column, holding a standard in one hand and a balance in the other. On its breast was the figure of a bear, and on its shield a lion. Probably it was a war-god.

**Hermes.** The Greek Mercury, whose busts, known as *Hermae*, were affixed to stone pillars and set up as boundary marks at street corners, and so on. The Romans used them also for garden decorations.

Among alchemists Hermes was the usual name for quicksilver or mercury (*q.v.*).

> So when we see the liquid metal fall
> Which chemists by the name of Hermes call.
>
> Hoole, *Ariosto*, Bk viii

*See also* Milton's *Paradise Lost*, iii, 603.

**Hermetic Art** or **Philosophy.** The art or science of alchemy; so called from Hermes Trismegistus (the Thrice Greatest Hermes), the name given by the Neo-Platonists to the Egyptian god Thoth, its hypothetical founder.

***Hermetic books.*** Forty-two books fabled to have been written from the dictation of Hermes Trismegistus (*see above*), dealing with the life and thought of ancient Egypt. Iamblichus gives their number as 20,000, but Manetho raises it to 36,525. They state that the world was made out of fluid; that the soul is the union of light and life; that nothing is destructible; that the soul transmigrates; and that suffering is the result of motion. A French translation of some of them was made by Ménard in 1866.

***Hermetic powder.*** A sympathetic powder, supposed to possess a healing influence from a distance; so called by mediaeval philosophers out of compliment to Hermes Trismegistus. (Sir Kenelm Digby, *Discourse Concerning the Cure of Wounds by the Sympathetic Powder*, 1644.)

> By his side a pouch he wore
> Replete with strange hermetic powder,
> That wounds nine miles point-blank would solder.
> Butler, *Hudibras*, i, 2

***Hermetically sealed.*** Closed securely. Thus we say, 'My lips are hermetically sealed', meaning so as not to utter a word of what has been imparted; from sealing a vessel *hermetically*, i.e. as a chemist, a disciple of Hermes Trismegistus, would, by heating the neck of the vessel till it is soft, and then twisting it till the aperture is closed up.

**Hermit. *Peter the Hermit*** (1050–1115). Preacher of the first crusade, which he led as far as Asia Minor.

**Hermite. *Tristem*** or ***Tristan l'Hermite*** (1405–93). Provost-marshal of Louis XI. He was infamous for his cruelty, and was the main instrument in carrying into effect the nefarious schemes of his wily master, who used to call him his gossip. Scott introduces him in *Anne of Geierstein* and *Quentin Durward*.

**Hermodr.** The son of Odin who journeyed to Hel and made the unsuccessful attempt to recall Balder to the Upper World. It is he who, with Bragi, receives and welcomes to Valhalla all heroes who fall in battle. (*Scandinavian mythology*.)

**Herne the Hunter.** *See* Wild Huntsman.

**Hero. *No man is a hero to his valet*.** An old – but not always true – saying. Plutarch has the idea both in his *De Iside* and *Regum et Imperatorum Apothegmata* –

> My personal servant does not think so much of these things as I do.

And Montaigne in his *Essays* (Bk iii, ch. ii) amplifies the idea –

> Tel a esté miraculeux au monde, auquel sa femme et son valet n'ont rien veu seulement de remarquable; peu d'hommes ont esté admirez par leur domestiques. (Such an one has been, as it were, miraculous in the world in whom his wife and valet have seen nothing even remarkable; few men have been admired by their servants.)

*Cp.* the Latin saying frequently quoted by Bacon, *Verior fama e domesticis emanat* (Truer fame comes from one's servants), and Matt. 13:57 –

> A prophet is not without honour save in ... his own house.

> In short, he was a perfect cavaliero
> And to his very valet seemed a hero.
> Byron, *Beppo*, xxxiii

**Hero and Leander.** The old Greek tale is that Hero, a priestess of Venus, fell in love with Leander, who swam across the Hellespont every night to visit her. One night he was drowned, and heart-broken Hero drowned herself in the same sea. The story is told in one of the poems of Musaeus, and in Marlowe and Chapman's *Hero and Leander*.

Lord Byron and Lieutenant Ekenhead repeated the experiment of Leander and accomplished it in 1 hour 10 minutes. The distance, allowing for drifting, would be about four miles. In *Don Juan* Byron says of his hero:

> A better swimmer you could scarce see ever.
> He could, perhaps, have pass'd the Hellespont,
> As once (a feat on which ourselves we prided)
> Leander, Mr Ekenhead, and I did.
> *Canto*, II, cv

**Heroic Age.** That age of a nation which comes between the purely mythical period and the historic. This is the age when the sons of the gods were said to take unto themselves the daughters of men, and the offspring partake of the twofold character.

**Heroic Medicines.** Those which either kill or cure.

**Heroic Size** in sculpture denotes a stature superior to ordinary life, but not colossal.

**Heroic Verse.** That verse in which epic poetry is generally written. In Greek and Latin it is *hexameter* verse, in English it is ten-syllable iambic verse, either in rhymes or not; in Italian it is the *ottava rima*. So called because it is employed to celebrate heroic exploits.

**Herod. *To out-herod Herod*.** To outdo in wickedness, violence, or rant, the worst of tyrants. Herod, who destroyed the babes of Bethlehem (Matt. 2:16), was made (in the ancient mysteries) a ranting, roaring tyrant; the extravagance of his rant being the measure of his bloody-mindedness. *Cp.* Pilate.

> Oh, it offends me to the soul to hear a robustious, periwig-pated fellow tear a passion to tatters, to very rags, to split the ears of the groundings ... it out-herods Herod.
>
> Shakespeare, *Hamlet*, 3, 2

**Herostratus.** *See* Erostratus.

**Herring.** ***Dead as a shotten herring.*** The shotten herring is one that has shot off or ejected its seed, and hence is worthless.

> Go thy ways, old Jack; die when thou wilt. If manhood, good manhood, be not forgot upon the face of the earth, then am I a shotten herring. There live not three good men unhanged in England, and one of them is fat and grows old.
>
> Shakespeare, *1 Henry IV*, 2, 4

***Drawing a red herring across the path.*** Trying to divert attention from the main question by some side issue. A red herring (i.e. one dried, smoked, and salted) drawn across a fox's path destroys the scent and sets the dogs at fault.

***Neither barrel the better herring.*** Much of a muchness; not a pin to choose between you; six of one and half a dozen of the other. The herrings of both barrels are so much alike that there is no choice whatever.

> Two feloes being like flagicious, and neither barell better herring, accused either other, the kyng Philippus ... sitting in iudgement vpon them ... condemned both the one and the other with banishmente.
>
> Erasmus, *Apophthegmes*

***Neither fish, flesh, nor good red herring.*** Something insipid and not good eating. Neither one thing nor another.

***The Battle of the Herrings.*** A sortie made during the Hundred Years War (February 12th, 1429) by the men of Orléans, during the siege of their city, to intercept a supply of food being brought by the English under Sir John Fastolf to the besiegers. The English repulsed the onset, using barrels of herrings, which were among the supplies, as a defence; hence the name.

***The king of the herrings.*** The *Chimaera*, or sea-ape, a cartilaginous fish which accompanies a shoal of herrings in their migrations.

**Herring-bone** (in building). Courses of stone laid angularly, thus: Also applied to strutting placed between thin joists to increase their strength.

Also a peculiar stitch in needlework, chiefly used in working flannel.

**Herring-pond, The.** A name humorously given to various dividing seas, especially to the Atlantic, which separates America from the British Isles. The English Channel, the North Sea, and the seas between Australasia and the United Kingdom are also so called.

> He'll plague you now he's come over the herring-pond. Scott, *Guy Mannering*, ch. xxxiv

**Hertha.** *See* Nerthus.

**Hesione.** Daughter of Laomedon, King of Troy, and sister to Priam. Her father exposed her to a sea-monster in order to appease the wrath of Apollo and Poseidon, but she was rescued by Hercules, who made the stipulation that he should receive a certain reward. Laomedon did not keep his promise, so Hercules slew him, took Troy, and gave Hesione to Telamon, by whom she became the mother of Teucer. The refusal of the Greeks to give her up to Priam is given as one of the causes of the Trojan War.

**Hesperia** (Gr., western). Italy was so called by the Greeks, because it was to them the 'Western Land'; and afterwards the Romans, for a similar reason, transferred the name to Spain.

**Hesperides.** Three sisters who guarded the golden apples which Hera received as a marriage gift. They were assisted by the dragon Ladon. Hercules, as the last of his 'twelve labours', slew the dragon and carried some of the apples to Eurystheus.

Many poets call the place where these golden apples grew the 'garden of the Hesperides'. Shakespeare (*Love's Labour's Lost*, 4, 3) speaks of 'climbing trees in the Hesperides'. (*See Comus*, lines 402–6.)

> Show thee the tree, leafed with refined gold,
> Whereon the fearful dragon held his seat.
> That watched the garden called Hesperides.
>
> Robert Greene, *Friar Bacon and Friar Bungay* (1589)

**Hesperus.** The evening star, because it sets in the west. *See* Hesperia.

> Ere twice in murk and occidental damp
> Moist Hesperus hath quenched his sleepy lamp.
>
> Shakespeare, *All's Well that Ends Well*, 2, 1

**Hesychasts.** The 'Quietists' of the East in the 14th century. They placed perfection in contemplation. (Gr. *hesuchia*, quiet.) (*See* Gibbon's *Decline and Fall*, lxiii.) Milton well expresses their belief in his *Comus*:

> Till oft converse with heavenly habitants
> Begin to cast a beam on the outward shape,
> And turns it by degrees to the soul's essence
> Till all be made immortal. (470–4.)

**Hetman.** A general or commander-in-chief. (Ger. *hauptmann*, chief man.) The chief of the

Cossacks of the Don used to be so called. He was elected by the people, and the mode of choice was thus: The voters threw their fur caps at the candidate they voted for, and he who had the largest number of caps at his feet was the successful candidate. The last elected Hetman was Count Platoff (1812–14).

> After the peace, all Europe hailed their hetman, Platoff, as the hero of the war.
>
> J. S. Mosby, *War Reminiscences*, ch. xi

**Hexameron.** Six days taken as one continuous period; especially the six days of the Creation.

> 'Every winged fowl' was produced on the fourth day of the Hexameron.
>
> W. E. Gladstone, *Nineteenth Century*, January, 1866

**Hexameter.** The metre in which the Greek and Latin epics were written, and which has been more or less imitated in English in such poems as Longfellow's *Evangeline*, Clough's *Bothie*, Kingsley's *Andromeda* (probably the best), etc.

The line consists, says Professor Saintsbury (*Manual of English Prosody*, iv, 1):

> Of six feet, dactyls or spondees at choice for the first four, but normally always a dactyl in the fifth and always a spondee in the sixth – the latter foot being by special licence sometimes allowed in the fifth also (in which case the line is called spondaic), but never a dactyl in the sixth. To this metre, and to the attempts to imitate it in English, the term should be strictly confined, and never applied to the Alexandrine or iambic trimeter.

Verse consisting of alternate hexameters and pentameters (*q.v.*) is known as elegiac (*q.v.*). Coleridge illustrates this in his:

> In the hexameter rises the fountain's silvery column;
> In the pentameter aye falling in melody back.

The Authorised Version of the Bible furnishes a number of examples of 'accidental' hexameter lines; the following are well known:

> How art thou fallen from Heaven, O Lucifer son of the Morning.
>
> Why do the heathen rage and the people imagine a vain thing?
>
> God is gone up with a shout, the Lord with the sound of the trumpet.

**Hexapla** (Gr., sixfold). The collection of Old Testament texts collated by Origen (3rd cent. AD), and containing in parallel columns the Hebrew text in Hebrew and in Greek characters, the Septuagint (with emendations), and the versions of Aquila, Theodotion, and Symmachus.

**Hiawatha.** The Iroquois name of a hero of miraculous birth who came (under a variety of names) among the North American Indian tribes to bring peace and goodwill to man. In Longfellow's poem (1855) he is an Ojibway, son of Mudjekeewis (the west wind) and Wenonah. His mother died in his infancy, and Hiawatha was brought up by his grandmother, Nokomis, daughter of the Moon. He represents the progress of civilisation among the American Indians. He first wrestled with Mondamin (Indian maize), whom he subdued, and gave to man bread-corn. He then taught man navigation; then he subdued the Mishe-Nahma or sturgeon, and told the people to 'bring all their pots and kettles and make oil for winter'. His next adventure was against Megissogwon, the magician, 'who sent the fiery fever on man; sent the white fog from the fen-lands; sent disease and death among us'; he slew the terrible monster, and taught man the science of medicine. He next married 'Laughing Water', setting the people an example to follow. Lastly, he taught the people picture-writing. When the white man landed and taught the Indians the faith of Jesus, Hiawatha exhorted them to receive the words of wisdom, to reverence the missionaries who had come so far to see them, and departed 'to the kingdom of Ponemah, the land of the Hereafter'.

***Hiawatha's mittens.*** 'Magic mittens made of deer-skin; when upon his hands he wore them, he could smite the rocks asunder.'

***Hiawatha's moccasins.*** Enchanted shoes made of deer-skin. 'When he bound them round his ankles, at each stride a mile he measured.'

**Hibernia.** The Latin name for Ireland, and hence still used in poetry. It is a variant of the old Celtic *Erin*.

> While in Hibernia's fields the labouring swain,
> Shall pass the plough o'er skulls of warriors slain.
>
> Hughes, *House of Nassau*

**Hic Jacets.** Tombstones, so called from the first two words of their inscriptions; 'Here lies …'

> By the cold *Hic Jacets* of the dead.
>
> Tennyson, *Idylls of the King* (*Vivien*)

**Hickathrift, Tom.** A hero of nursery rhyme, fabled to have been a poor labourer in the time of the Conquest, of such enormous strength that, armed with an axletree and cartwheel only, he killed a giant who dwelt in a marsh at Tilney, Norfolk. He was knighted and made governor of Thanet.

**Hickory.** ***Old Hickory.*** General Andrew Jackson (1767–1845), President of the United States, 1829–37. He was first called 'Tough', from his great powers of endurance, then 'Tough as hickory', and lastly, 'Old Hickory'.

**Hidalgo.** The title in Spain of the lower nobility. The word is from Lat. *filius de aliquo*, son of someone, or, as we should say, the son of a 'somebody'. In Portuguese it is *Fidalgo*.

**Hide of Land.** The term applied in Anglo-Saxon times to a portion of land that was sufficient to support a family; usually from 60 to 100 acres, but no fixed number. A hide of good arable land was smaller than a hide of inferior quality.

**Higgledy-piggledy.** In great confusion; at sixes and sevens; perhaps with reference to a higgler or pedlar whose stores are all huddled together. *Higgledy* would then mean after the fashion of a higgler's basket; *piggledy* is a ricochet word suggested by this.

**High-born.** Of aristocratic birth; *D'une haute naissance*; *Summo loco natus*.

> A wind blew out of a cloud, chilling
> My beautiful Annabel Lee.
> So that her high-born kinsman came
> And bore her away from me
>
> E. A. Poe, *Annabel Lee*

**High-brow.** A superior person; especially one who, in his own estimation at least, is intellectually superior; one who takes an academic view of things. The epithet came from the USA.

**High Church.** *See* Church.

**High Days.** Festivals. *On high days and holidays.* Here 'high' = grand or great; as, *un grand jour*.

**High falutin** or **Hifaluten.** An Americanism for oratorical bombast, affected pomposity, tall talk. The word is perhaps a variant of *high-flown*.

> The genius of hifaluten, as the Americans call it ... has received many mortal wounds lately from the hands of satirists ... A quizzical Jenkins lately described the dress of a New York belle by stating that 'she wore an exquisite hyphaluten on her head, while her train was composed of transparent fol-de-rol, and her petticoat of crambambuli flounced with Brussels three-ply of a No. 1'.
>
> Hingston, *Introduction to Josh Billings*

***None of your high falutin airs with me.*** Don't come it; I don't want any of your swell ways.

**High Hand.** ***With a high hand.*** Arrogantly. To carry things with a high hand in French would be: *Faire une chose haut la main*.

**High Heels** and **Low Heels.** The names of two factions in Swift's tale of Lilliput (*Gulliver's Travels*), satirising the High and Low Church parties.

**High Places,** in Scripture language, means elevated spots where sacrifices were offered. Idolatrous worship was much carried on in high places. Some were evidently artificial mounds, for the faithful are frequently ordered to remove or destroy them. Hezekiah removed the high places (2 Kings 18:4), so did Asa (2 Chron. 14:3), Jehoshaphat (2 Chron. 17:6), Josiah, and others. On the other hand, Jehoram and Ahaz made high, places for idolatrous worship. *Cp.* Hills.

**High Seas.** All the sea which is not the property of a particular country. The sea three miles out from the coast belongs to the country, and is called 'territorial waters'. High seas, like highways, means for the public use. In both cases the word *high* means 'chief', 'principal'. (Lat. *altum*, 'the main sea'; *altus*, 'high'.)

**High Tea.** A meal served about the usual teatime which includes, besides tea, fish, cold meats, pastry, etc.

> A well understood 'high tea' should have cold roast beef at the top of the table, a cold Yorkshire pie at the bottom, a mighty ham in the middle. The side dishes will comprise soused mackerel, pickled salmon (in due season), sausages and potatoes, etc., etc. Rivers of tea, coffee, and ale, with dry and buttered toast, sally-lunns, scones, muffins and crumpets, jams and marmalade.
>
> *Daily Telegraph*, May 9th, 1893

**High Words.** Angry words.

**Highgate.** A North London suburb, so called from a gate set up there about 400 years ago to receive tolls for the bishop of London, when the old miry road from Gray's Inn Lane to Barnet was turned through the bishop's park. The village being perched on a hill explains the first part of the name.

***Sworn at Highgate.*** A custom anciently prevailed at the public-houses in Highgate to administer a ludicrous oath to all travellers who stopped there. The party was sworn on a pair of horns fastened to a stick –

(1) Never to kiss the maid when he can kiss the mistress.

(2) Never to eat brown bread when he can get white.

(3) Never to drink small beer when he can get strong – unless he prefers it.

There is still a club at Highgate which makes an annual event of swearing in neophytes on the horns.

**Highland Bail.** Fists and cuffs; to escape the constable by knocking him down with the aid of a companion.

> The mute eloquence of the miller and smith, which was vested in their clenched fists, was prepared to give highland bail for their arbiter (Edie Ochiltree).
>
> Scott, *The Antiquary*, ch. xxix

**Highland Mary.** The most shadowy of Robert Burns's sweethearts, but the one to whom he addressed some of his finest poetry, including 'My Highland Lassie, O', 'Highland Mary' ('Ye banks and braes and streams around the castle o' Montgomery'), 'Thou Ling'ring Star', and – perhaps – 'Will ye go to the Indies, my Mary?'

She is said to have been a daughter of Archibald Campbell, a Clyde sailor, and to have died young about 1784 or 1786. Nothing authentic is known of her, and there is little or no reliance to be placed in the few indications that Burns gave, either in his poems or in his letters to Mrs Dunlop.

> Seriously examined, her cult – for cult it is – is found an absurdity: but persons of repute have taken the craze, so that it is useful to remark that the Mary Campbell of tradition is a figment of the General Brain, for whose essential features not so much as the faintest outline is to be found in the confusion of amorous plaints and cries of repentance or remorse, which is all that we have to enlighten us from Burns ... The one thing in it worth acknowledging and perfectly plain is that the Highland Mary of the Mariolater is but a 'devout imagination'.
>
> *Henley and Henderson's Edition of Burns's 'Poems'*, vol. iii, p. 309

**Highlanders of Attica.** The operative class, who had their dwellings on the hills (*Diacrii*).

**Highlands.** The Scottish Highlands include all the country on the northern side of a line drawn from the Moray Firth to the river Clyde, or (which is about the same thing) from Nairn to Glasgow.

**Highness.** A title of honour (used with a possessive pronoun) given to royalties and a few others of very exalted rank. In England the title *Royal Highness* was formerly given to the Sovereign, his consort, his sons and daughters, brothers and sisters, paternal uncles and aunts, grandsons and granddaughters being the children of sons, and great-grandchildren being the children of an eldest son of any Prince of Wales; but by the proclamation of June 17th, 1917 (when the style, the House of Windsor, was adopted), the title *Royal Highness* was confined in future to children of the Sovereign and to grandchildren in the male line.

James I was the first King of England to be styled 'Your Royal Highness'; Oliver Cromwell and his wife were both called 'Your Highness'; as are some of the Indian princes today.

***Serene Highness*** was a title of many of the members of the former German Imperial, Royal, and Ducal Houses.

**Hilary Term,** in the Law Courts, begins on the day after Plough Monday (*q.v.*) and ends the Wednesday before Easter. It is so called in honour of St Hilary, whose day is January 13.

**Hildebrand.** The Nestor of German romance. His story is told in the *Hildebrandslied*, an Old High German poem, and he also appears in the *Nibelunglied*, *Dietrich von Bern*, etc. Like Maugis among the heroes of Charlemagne, he was a magician as well as champion.

***Hildebrand.*** Pope Gregory VII (1013, 1073–85).

***A Hildebrand.*** One resembling Gregory VII, noted for subjugating the power of the German emperors; and specially detested by the early reformers for his ultra-pontifical views.

**Hildesheim.** Legend relates that a monk of Hildesheim, an old city of Hanover, doubting how with God a thousand years could be as one day, listened to the singing of a bird in a wood, as he thought for three minutes, but found the time had been three hundred years. Longfellow introduced this tale in his *Golden Legend*, calling the monk Felix.

**Hill Folk.** So Scott calls the Cameronian Scotch Covenanters, who met clandestinely among the hills. Sometimes the Covenanters generally are so called.

A class of beings in Scandinavian tradition between the elves and the human race were known as 'hill folk' or 'hill people'. They were supposed to dwell in caves and small hills, and to be bent on receiving the benefits of man's redemption.

**Hill Tribes.** The barbarous tribes dwelling in remote parts of the Deccan or plateau of Central India.

**Hills.** Prayers were offered on the tops of high hills, and temples built on 'high places', from the notion that the gods could better hear prayers on such places, as they were nearer heaven. It will be remembered that Balak (Num. 23:24) took Balaam to the top of Peor and other high places when Balaam wished to consult God. We often read of 'idols on every high hill' (Ezek. 6:13). *Cp.* High Places.

***Old as the hills.*** Very old indeed.

**Himiltrude.** One of the wives of Charlemagne (*q.v.*). She surpassed all other women in nobleness of mien.

**Hinc illae lacrymae** (Lat., 'hence those tears'. Terence, *Andria*, I, i, 99). This was the real offence; this was the true secret of the annoyance; this, *entre nous*, was the real source of the vexation.

> *Lady Loadstone*: He keeps off all her suitors, keeps the portion.
> Still in his hands; and will not part withal,
> On any terms.
> *Palate.*: *Hine illae lachrymae*:
> Thence flows the cause of the main grievance.
> Ben Jonson, *Magnetic Lady*, I, i

**Hind.** Emblematic of St Giles, because 'a heaven-directed hind went daily to give him milk in the desert, near the mouth of the Rhone'. *Cp.* Hart.

***The hind of Sertorius.*** Sertorius was invited by the Lusitanians to defend them against the Romans. He had a tame white hind, which he taught to follow him, and from which he pretended to receive the instructions of Diana. By this artifice, says Plutarch, he imposed on the superstition of the people.

> He feigned a demon (in a hind concealed)
> To him the counsels of the gods revealed.
> Camoens, *Lusiad*, i

***The milk-white hind,*** in Dryden's *Hind and the Panther*, means the Roman Catholic Church, milk-white because 'infallible'. The panther, full of the spots of error, is the Church of England.

> Without unspotted, innocent within,
> She feared no danger, for she knew no sin.
> Part I, 3, 4

**Hindustan.** India; properly, the country watered by the river Indus, i.e. the country known by the ancients as 'India'. From Pers. *hindu*, water, *stan*, district or region. The suffix is common in the East, as Afghanistan, Beloochistan, Gulistan (the district of roses), Kafiristan (the country of the unbelievers), etc.

**Hindustan Regiment.** The old 76th; so called because it first distinguished itself in Hindustan. It is also called the *Seven and Sixpennies*, from its number. Now the 2nd battalion of the West Riding, the 1st being the old No. 33rd.

**Hinny.** *See* Mule.

**Hinzelmann.** The most famous house-spirit or kobold of German legend. He lived four years in the old castle of Hudemühlen, where he had a room set apart for him. At the end of the fourth year (1588) he went away of his own accord, and never again returned.

**Hip.** ***To have one on the hip.*** To have the mastery over him in a struggle; to 'catch him bending'.

'Now, infidel, I have thee on the hip' (*Merchant of Venice*); and again, 'I'll have our Michael Cassio on the hip' (*Othello*). The term is derived from wrestlers, who seize the adversary by the hip and throw him.

> In fine he doth apply one speciall drift,
> Which was to get the pagan on the hip,
> And having caught him right, he doth him lift
> By nimble sleight, and in such wise doth trip,
> That down he threw him.
> Sir J. Harington, *Orlando Furioso*, XLVI, cxvii, 4

***To smite hip and thigh.*** To slay with great carnage. A Biblical phrase.

> And he smote them hip and thigh with great slaughter.
> Judges 15:8

**Hip! Hip! Hurrah!** The old-fanciful explanation of the origin of this cry is that *hip* is a notarikon (*q.v.*), composed of the initials of *Hierosolyma est Perdita*, and that when the German knights headed a Jew-hunt in the Middle Ages, they ran shouting 'Hip! Hip!' as much as to say 'Jerusalem is destroyed.'

***Hurrah*** (*q.v.*) was derived from Sclavonic *hu-raj* (to Paradise), so that *Hip! hip! hurrah!* would mean 'Jerusalem is lost to the infidel, and we are on the road to Paradise.' These etymons may be taken for what they are worth!

**Hipped.** Melancholy, low-spirited, suffering from a 'fit of the blues'. *The hip* was formerly a common expression for morbid depression (now superseded by *the pip*); it is an abbreviation of *hypochondria*.

**Hipper-switches.** A dialect name for coarse willow withes. A *hipper* is a coarse osier used in basket-making, and an osier field is a *hipperholm*. A suburb of Halifax, Yorks, is called Hipperholme-with-Brighouse.

**Hippo.** ***Bishop of Hippo.*** A title by which St Augustine (354–430) is sometimes designated. Hippo was a town in Numidia, N. Africa, near the modern Bona. It was destroyed by the Vandals in 430.

**Hippocampus.** (Gr. *hippos*, horse; *kampos*, sea monster.) A seahorse, having the head and forequarters resembling those of a horse, with the tail and hindquarters of a fish or dolphin. It was the steed of Neptune (*q.v.*).

**Hippocras.** A cordial of the late Middle Ages and down to Jacobean times made of Lisbon and Canary wines, bruised spices, and sugar; so called from being passed through *Hippocrates' sleeve* (*q.v.*).

When these [i.e. other wines] have had their course which nature yeeldeth, sundrie sorts of artificial stuffe as ypocras and wormewood wine, must in like maner succeed in their turnes.

*Harrison's Description of England*, II, vi (1577)

Hippocrates in the Middle Ages was called 'Ypocras' or 'Hippocras'. Thus:

Well knew he the old Esculapius,
And Deiscorides, and eek Rufus,
Old Ypocras, Haly, and Galien.

Chaucer, *Canterbury Tales* (*Prologue*, 431)

**Hippocratean School.** The 'Dogmatic' school of medicine, founded by Hippocrates (d.357 BC). *See* Empirics.

**Hippocrates' Sleeve.** A woollen bag of a square piece of flannel, having the opposite corners joined, so as to make it triangular. Used by chemists for straining syrups, decoctions, etc., and anciently by vintners, whence the name of Hippocras (*q.v.*).

**Hippocrene** (Gr. *hippos*, horse; krene, fountain). The fountain of the Muses on Mount Helicon, produced by a stroke of the hoof of Pegasus; hence poetic inspiration.

O for a beaker full of the warm South.
Full of the true, the blushful Hippocrene,
With beaded bubbles winking at the brim
And purple-stained mouth;
That I might drink, and leave the world unseen.

Keats, *Ode to a Nightingale*

**Hippodamia.** *See* Briseis.

**Hippogriff** (Gr. *hippos*, a horse; *gryphos*, a griffin). The winged horse, whose father was a griffin and mother a filly. A symbol of love (Ariosto, *Orlando Furioso*, iv, 18, 19).

So saying, he caught him up, and without wing
Of hippogrif, bore through the air sublime,
Over the wilderness and o'er the plain.

Milton, *Paradise Regained*, iv, 541–3

**Hippolyta.** Queen of the Amazons, and daughter of Mars. Shakespeare has introduced the character in his *Midsummer Night's Dream*, where he betroths her to Theseus, Duke of Athens. In classic fable it is her sister Antiope who married Theseus, although some writers justify Shakespeare's account. Hippolyta was famous for a girdle given her by her father, and it was one of the twelve labours of Hercules to possess himself of this prize.

**Hippolytus.** Son of Theseus, King of Athens. He was dragged to death by wild horses, and restored to life by Esculapius.

**Hippomenes.** The name given in Boeotian legend to the Greek prince, who ran a race with Atalanta (*q.v.*) for her hand in marriage. He had three golden apples, which he dropped one by one, and which the lady stopped to pick up. By this delay she lost the race.

**Hiren.** A strumpet. She was a character in Greene's lost play (about 1594), *The Turkish Mahomet and Hyren the Fair Greek*, and is frequently referred to by Elizabethan dramatists. *See* Shakespeare's *2 Henry IV*, 2, 4, Dekker's *Satiromastix*, IV, iii, Massinger's *Old Law*, IV, i, Chapman's *Eastward Hoe*, II, i, etc. The name is a corruption of the Greek 'Irene'.

**Hispania.** Spain. So called from the Phoenician word *Sapan*, or *Span*, the skin of the marten (or perhaps rabbit), which was procured from Spain in great quantities.

**History.** ***The Father of History.*** Herodotus, the Greek historian (5th cent. BC). So called by Cicero.

***The Father of Ecclesiastical History.*** Eusebius of Caesarea (about 264–340).

***Father of French History.*** André Duchesne (1584–1640).

***Father of Historic Painting.*** Polygnotus of Thaos (fl. 463–435 BC).

***Happy is the nation that has no history.*** *See* Happy.

**Histrionic,** pertaining to the drama or to theatrical matters, is from the Lat. *histrio*, a stage-player. *History* is quite another word, being the Greek *historia*, *histor*, a judge, allied to *histamai*, to know.

**Hit.** ***A great hit.*** A piece of good luck. From the game *hit and miss*, or the game of backgammon, where 'two hits equal a gammon'.

***To hit it off.*** To describe a thing tersely and epigrammatically; to make a sketch truthfully and quickly.

***To hit it off together.*** To agree together, or suit each other.

***To hit the nail on the head.*** *See* Head.

***To make a hit.*** To meet with great approval; to succeed unexpectedly in an adventure or speculation.

**Hitch.** ***Hitch your wagon to a star.*** Aim high; don't be content with low aspirations. The phrase is from Emerson's essay *Civilisation*. Young expressed much the same idea in his *Night Thoughts* (viii):

Too low they build who build beneath the stars.

***There is some hitch.*** Some impediment. A horse is said to have a hitch in his gait when he is lame.

***To hitch.*** To get on smoothly; to fit in consistently; also, to harness: as, 'You and I hitch on well together'; 'These two accounts do not hitch in with each other.' A lame horse goes about jumping, and to jump together is to be in accord. So the two meanings apparently contradictory hitch together. Compare *prevent*, meaning to aid and to resist.

**Hoarstone.** A stone marking out the boundary of an estate, properly an old, grey, lichen-covered stone. They are also called 'Hour-stones' and (in Scotland) 'Hare Stanes', and have been erroneously taken for Druidical remains.

**Hob and nob.** *See* Hob-nob.

**Hobbema. *The English Hobbema.*** John Crome (1768–1821), 'Old Crome', of Norwich, whose last words were, 'O Hobbema, Hobbema, how I do love thee!' Meindert Hobbema (1638–1709) was a Dutch landscape painter.

***The Scotch Hobbema.*** Patrick Nasmyth (born at Edinburgh, 1787, died 1831), the landscape painter, was so called.

**Hobbididance.** The prince of dumbness, and one of the five fiends that possessed 'poor Tom'. (Shakespeare, *King Lear*, 4, 1.) The name came from Harsnet's *Declaration. Sec* Flibbertigibbet.

**Hobbinol.** The shepherd in Spenser's *Shepherd's Calendar* who sings in praise of Eliza, queen of shepherds (Queen Elizabeth). He typifies Spenser's friend and correspondent Gabriel Harvey (d.1630), the poet and writer.

**Hobbism.** The principles of Thomas Hobbes (1588–1679), author of *Leviathan* (1651). He taught that religion is a mere engine of state, and that man acts wholly on a consideration of self; even his benevolent acts spring from the pleasure he experiences in doing acts of kindness.

**Hobbledehoy.** A raw, awkward young fellow, neither a man nor a boy, but 'betwixt and between'. The word is generally taken as being connected with *hobble*, in reference to an awkward, clumsy gait; but this is hardly borne out by the early forms of the word, which include such spellings as *hobbard de hoy*, *habber de hoy*, *hobet a hoy*, etc. The first syllable is probably *hob*, a clown, as seen in *Hobbididance*, *Hobbinol*, etc., and is connected with *Robert* or *Robin*, as in *Robin Goodfellow*. There is very little etymological support for the theory that would connect the word with the *hobby* hawk.

> The first seven yeeres bring up as a childe,
> The next to learning, for waxing too wilde.
> The next keepe under sir hobbard de hoy,
> The next a man, no longer a boy.
>
> Tusser, *Hundred Good Points* (1573)

**Hobblers** or **Hovellers.** An old name for longshoremen – especially on the Kentish coast – who acted as pilots although they were not licensed, and got their living by rendering casual assistance to vessels in distress, plundering wrecks, warning smugglers, etc.

The word was also applied to seafaring men whose duties were to reconnoitre, carry intelligence, harass stragglers, act as spies, intercept convoys, pursue fugitives, etc.

> Hobblers were another description of cavalry more lightly armed, and taken from the class of men rated at 15 pounds and upwards.
>
> Lingard, *History of England*, vol. iv, ch. ii

**Hobby.** A favourite pursuit; a personal pastime that interests or amuses one.

There are two words *hobby*, and they are apt to be confused. The earlier, meaning a medium-sized horse, is the M.E. *hobyn* (*cp. Dobbin* as a name for a horse), the later, a small species of falcon, is the O.F. *hobé* or *hobet*, from Lat. *hobetus*, a falcon. It is from the first that our 'hobby', a pursuit, comes. It is through *hobby-horse*, a light frame of wickerwork, appropriately draped, in which someone performed ridiculous gambols in the old morris dances, and later applied to a child's plaything consisting of a stick with a horse's head on one end. *To ride a hobby-horse* was, thus, to play an infantile game of which one soon tired; and the transition is shown in a sentence in one of Wesley's sermons (No. lxxxiii):

> Everyone has (to use the cant term of the day) his hobby-horse! Something that pleases the great boy for a few hours (1790).

**Hobgoblin.** An impish, ugly, and mischievous sprite, particularly Puck or Robin Goodfellow (*q.v.*). The word is a variant of *Rob-Goblin* – i.e. the goblin Robin, just as Hodge is the nickname of Roger.

> Those that Hobgoblin call you, and sweet Puck,
> You do their work, and they shall have good luck.
>
> Shakespeare, *Midsummer Night's Dream*, 2, 1

**Hob-nob.** A corruption of *hab nab*, meaning 'have or not have', hence hit or miss, at random; and, secondarily, give or take, whence also an open defiance.

> The citizens in their rage shot habbe or nabbe [hit or miss] at random.
>
> Holinshed, *History of Ireland*

He writes of the weather hab nab and as the toy takes him, chequers the year with foul and fair.
*Quack Astrologer* (1673)

He is a devil in private brawls … hob nob is his word, give 't or take 't.
Shakespeare, *Twelfth Night*, 3, 4

Not of Jack Straw, with his rebellious crew,
That set king, realm and laws at hab or nab [defiance].
Sir J. Harington, *Epigram*, iv

***To hobnob*** or ***hob and nob together.*** To be on intimate terms of good-fellowship, hold close and friendly conversation with, etc.; especially to drink together as cronies – probably with the meaning of 'give and take'. *See above.*

'Have another glass!' 'With you Hob and nob,' returned the sergeant. 'The top of mine to the foot of yours – the foot of yours to the top of mine – Ring once, ring twice – the best tune on the Musical Glasses! Your health.'
Dickens, *Great Expectations*, ch. v

Drink to Fortune, drink to Chance,
While we keep a little breath!
Drink to heavy Ignorance!
Hob-and-nob with brother Death!
Tennyson, *The Vision of Sin*

**Hob's Pound.** Difficulties, great embarrassment. *To be in Hob's pound* is to be in the pound of a *hob* or *hoberd* – i.e. a fool or ne'er-do-well – paying for one's folly.

**Hobson's Choice.** This or none; 'take it or leave it'. Tobias Hobson was a carrier and innkeeper at Cambridge in the 17th century, who erected the handsome conduit there, and settled 'seven lays' of pasture ground towards its maintenance. 'He kept a stable of forty good cattle, always ready and fit for travelling; but when a man came for a horse he was led into the stable, where there was great choice, but he obliged him to take the horse which stood nearest to the stable door; so that every customer was alike well served, according to his chance, and every horse ridden with the same justice.' (*Spectator*, No. 509.)

Milton wrote two quibbling epitaphs upon this eccentric character.

**Hock.** So called from Hockheim, on the Maine, where the best is supposed to be made. It used to be called hoccamore.

Restored the fainting high and mighty
With brandy, wine, and aqua-vitae;
And made 'em stoutly overcome
With Bacrack, Hoccamore, and Mum.
Butler, *Hudibras*, III, iii, 297

**Hock Cart.** The last cartload of harvest; probably connected with *hockey*. *See* **Hockey Cake**.

The harvest swains and wenches bound,
For joy, to see the hock cart crowned.
Herrick, *Hesperides*, p. 114

**Hock-day** or **Hock Tuesday.** The second Tuesday after Easter Day, long held as a festival in England; it was the time for paying church dues, and landlords received an annual tribute called *Hock-money*, for allowing their tenants and serfs to commemorate it (*see Kenilworth*, ch. xxxix). Its origin is unknown; but the old idea that it commemorates the massacre of the Danes in 1002 does not seem to be tenable, as this took place in November.

Hoke Monday was for the men and Hock Tuesday for the women. On both days the men and women alternately, with great merryment, obstructed the public road with ropes, and pulled passengers to them, from whom they exacted money to be laid out in pious uses.
Brand, *Antiquities*, vol. i, p. 187

**Hockey.** A game in which each player has a hooked stick or bandy with which to strike the ball. Hockey is simply the diminutive of *hook*.

**Hockey Cake.** The cake given out to the harvesters when the hock cart (*q.v.*) reached home. *Hockey* is the old name in the eastern counties for the harvest-home feast.

**Hockley-i'-the-Hole.** Public gardens near Clerkenwell Green, famous in Restoration times for bear- and bull-baiting, dog- and cock-fights, etc., and for its butchers. Pope called Colley Cibber –

This mess, tossed up of Hockley-hole and White's;
Where dukes and butchers join to wreathe my crown,
At once the bear and fiddle of the town.
*Dunciad*, I, 222

**Hocus Pocus.** The words formerly uttered by conjurers when performing a trick; hence the trick or deception itself, also the juggler himself.

O Pope, had I thy satire's darts
To gie the rascals their deserts,
I'd rip their rotten, hollow hearts
An' tell aloud
Their jigglin, hocus-pocus arts
To cheat the crowd!
Burn, *To the Rev. J. M'Math*

The phrase dates from the early 17th century, and is the opening of a ridiculous string of mock Latin used by some well-known performer (*Hocus pocus, toutus talontus, vade celerita jubes*), the first two words of which may have been intended as a parody of *Hoc est corpus*, occurring in the Roman Communion Service, while the whole was reeled off merely to occupy the attention of the audience.

Our word *hoax* is probably a contraction of *hocus pocus*, which also supplies the verb *to hocus*, to cheat, bamboozle, tamper with.

**Hodge.** A familiar and slightly contemptuous name for a farm labourer or peasant; an abbreviated form of Roger, as Hob is of Robert or Robin.

> Barrin' the wet, Hodge 'ud ha' been a-harrowin'
> o' white peasen i' the outfield.
>
> Tennyson, *Queen Mary*, IV, iii

**Hodge-podge.** A medley, a mixed dish of 'bits and pieces all cooked together'. The word is a corruption of *hotch-pot* (*q.v.*).

**Höder.** Balder's twin brother; the God of Darkness in *Scandinavian mythology*; the blind god who killed Balder, at the instigation of Loki, with an arrow made of mistletoe. Höder typifies night, as Balder typifies day.

> And Balder's pile of the glowing sun
> A symbol true blazed forth;
> But soon its splendour sinketh down
> When Höder rules the earth.
>
> *Frithiof-Saga*, *Balder's Bale-Fire*

**Hodmandod.** *See* Dodman.

**Hoenir** or **Hönir.** One of the minor gods of the Scandinavian pantheon. He travelled with Odin and Loki, and his special province seems to have been the punishment of injustice.

**Hog.** Properly a male swine, castrated, and – as it is raised solely for slaughter – killed young. The origin of the word is not certain, but it may originally have referred to age more than to any specific animal. Thus, boars of the second year, sheep between the time of their being weaned and shorn, colts, and bullocks a year old, were all called *hogs* or *hoggets*, which name was specially applied to a sheep after its first shearing, a 'hogget-fleece' being the first shearing. A boar three years old is a 'hog-steer'.

In slang use a *hog* is a gluttonous, greedy, or unmannered person, and motorists who, caring nothing for the rights or convenience of other travellers, drive in a selfish and reckless manner wanting the whole road to themselves are called *road-hogs*.

Formerly, any small silver coin, a shilling or sixpence, or (in America) a ten-cent piece, was contemptuously styled a *hog*. *See also* Isthmus of Suez.

**Phrases.**

***Hog in armour.*** A person of awkward manners dressed so fine that he cannot move easily; perhaps a corruption of '*Hodge* in armour'. *See* Hodge.

***Hog-shearing.*** Much ado about nothing. 'It's great cry and little wool, as the Devil said when he sheared his hogs.' *See* Cry.

***To go the whole hog.*** To do the thing completely and thoroughly, without compromise or reservation; to go the whole way. Hence the expression *whole-hogger*, one who will see the thing through to the bitter end, and 'damn the consequences'. At the time of Mr Joseph Chamberlain's great agitation on behalf of Protection (1903, *et sqq.*) those who advocated a complete tariff of protective duties regardless of possible 'reciprocity' were called the *whole-hoggers*.

***To drive one's hogs to market.*** To snore very loudly.

***To hear as a hog in harvest.*** In at one ear and out at the other; hear without paying attention. Giles Firmin says, 'If you call hogs out of the harvest stubble, they will just lift up their heads to listen, and fall to their shack again.' (*Real Christian*, 1670.)

***You have brought your hogs to a fine market.*** You have made a pretty kettle of fish; said in derision when one's projects turn out ill.

**Hogs-Norton.** A village in Oxfordshire, now called Hook Norton. *I think you were born at Hogs-Norton.* A reproof to an ill-mannered person.

> I think thou wast born at Hoggs-Norton where
> piggs play upon the organs.
>
> Howell, *English Proverbs* (1660)

**Hogen Mogen.** Holland or the Netherlands; so called from *Hoogë en Mogendë* (high and mighty), the Dutch style of addressing the States-General.

> But I have sent him for a token
> To your low country Hogen-Mogen.
>
> Butler, *Hudibras*, III, i, 1440

**Hogmanay.** The name given in Scotland to the last day of the year, also to an entertainment or present given on that day. It is from the French, and probably represents the O.Fr. *aiguillanneuf*, which has been (somewhat doubtfully) explained as standing for *au guy l'an neuf*, '(good luck) to the mistletoe of the new year'.

It is still the custom in parts of Scotland for persons to go from door to door on New Year's Eve asking in rude rhymes for cakes or money; and in Galloway the chief features are 'taking the cream off the water', wonderful luck being attached to a draught thereof; and 'the first foot' (*q.v.*) or giving something to drink to the first person who enters the house.

**Hogni.** *See* Hagen.

**Hogshead.** A large cask containing approximately 52½ gallons; also, the measure of this, apart from the cask. The word dates from the 14th century and is composed of *hog* and *head*, and not of *ox* and *hide*, or of any of the other fancy etymologies that have been proposed. The reason for the name is obscure; but *cp.* the name of a Low German measure for beer, *bullenkop*, bull's head.

**Hoi Polloi** (Gr. 'the many'). The common herd, the masses, the majority.

> If by the people yon understand the multitude, the *hoi polloi*, 'tis no matter what they think; they are sometimes in the right, sometimes in the wrong; their judgment is a mere lottery.
>
> Dryden, *Essay on Dramatic Poesy* (1668)

At the Universities the poll-men, i.e. those who take a degree without honours, are colloquially known as the *hoi polloi*.

**Hoity-toity.** A reduplicated word (like *harum-scarum*, *mingle-mangle*, *hugger-mugger*, etc.), probably formed from the obsolete verb *hoit*, to romp about noisily. It is used as an adjective, meaning 'stuck up', haughty, or petulant; as a noun, meaning a good romp or frolic; and as an interjection expressing disapproval or contempt of one's airs, assumptions, etc.

> 'I do not speak on your account, Mrs Honour' [said Mrs Western's maid], 'for you are a civilised young woman; and when you have seen a little more of the world, I should not be ashamed to walk with you in St James's Park.' 'Hoity toity!' cries Honour, 'Madam is in her airs, I protest.'
>
> Fielding, *Tom Jones*, Bk vii, ch. viii

*See also* the quotation from Selden given under Cushion Dance, where *hoyte-cum-toyte* is used of rowdy behaviour.

**Holborn.** This London name, originally that of the northern portion of the Fleet stream, is not a corruption of Old Bourne, as Stow asserts, but of Holeburne, the *burne* or stream in the *hole* or hollow. It is spelt Holeburne in *Domesday Book*, i, 127a; and in documents connected with the nunnery of St Mary, Clerkenwell (during the reign of Richard II).

***To ride backwards up Holborn Hill.*** To go to be hanged. The way to Tyburn from Newgate was up Holborn Hill, and criminals used to sit or stand with their backs to the horse when drawn to the place of execution.

> I shall live to see you ride up Holborn Hill.
>
> Congreve, *Love for Love*

**Hold.** ***Hold hard!*** Stop; go easy; keep a firm hold, seat, or footing, as there is danger else of being overthrown. A caution given when a sudden change of *vis inertiae* is about to occur.

***Hold off!*** Keep at a distance. In Fr. *Tenez-vous à distance!*

***Hold the fort!*** Maintain your position at all costs. Immortalised as a phrase from its use by General Sherman, who signalled it to General Corse from the top of Kenesaw in 1864 during the American Civil War.

***To cry hold.*** To give the order to stop; in the old tournaments, when the umpires wished to stop the contest they cried out 'Hold!'

> Lay on Macduff,
> And damn'd be him that first cries, 'Hold, enough!'
>
> Shakespeare, *Macbeth*, 5, 8

***To hold the candle to one, a candle to the devil.*** *See* Candle.

***To hold forth.*** To speak in public; to harangue; to declaim. An author holds forth certain opinions or ideas in his book, i.e. exhibits them or holds them out to view. A speaker does the same in an oratorical display.

***To hold good.*** To be valid, or applicable. We say 'such and such a proverb is very true, but it does not hold good in every case', i.e. it does not always apply.

***To hold in.*** To restrain. The allusion is to horses reined up tightly.

***To hold in esteem.*** To regard with esteem.

***To hold on one's way.*** To proceed steadily; to go on without taking notice of interruptions or being delayed.

***To hold one guilty.*** To adjudge or regard as guilty. The Fr. *tenir*.

***To hold one in hand*** or ***in play.*** To divert one's attention, or amuse in order to get some advantage.

***To hold one's own.*** To maintain one's own opinion, position, way, etc. Maintain means to hold with the hand (Lat. *manus teneo*).

***To hold one's tongue.*** To keep silence. In Coverdale's Bible (1535), where the Authorised Version has 'But Jesus held his peace' (Matt. 26:63) the reading is 'Jesus helde his tonge.'

***To hold out.*** To endure, persist; not to succumb.

***To hold over.*** To keep back, retain in reserve, defer.

***To hold up.*** To stop, as a highwayman does, with the object of robbing. In the good old times coaches were 'held up'; nowadays a few armed desperadoes can 'hold up' a railway train.

***To hold water.*** To bear close inspection; to endure a trial; generally used negatively, as 'That statement of yours won't hold water', i.e. it will prove false as soon as it is examined. A vessel that will hold water is safe and sound.

**Holdfast.** A means by which something is clamped to another; a support.

***Brag is a good dog, but Holdfast is a better.*** *See* Brag.

**Hole. *A better 'ole.*** Any situation that is preferable to that occupied at present. The phrase came into being during the Great War, and the allusion is to an incident – pictured by Captain Bairnsfather – in which a soldier 'taking cover' in a shell-hole objects to leaving it until a 'better 'ole' is provided.

***In a hole.*** In an awkward predicament; in a difficulty or a position from which it is not easy to extricate oneself.

***It is a hole and corner business.*** There's something 'fishy' about it – it's underhand, secret for a bad or shady purpose.

***To make a hole in anything.*** To consume a considerable portion of it – as, 'A weekend at Brighton makes a hole in a five-pound note.'

***To pick holes in.*** To find fault with; properly, to *cause* some depreciation and then complain of it. The older phrase was *to pick a hole in one's coat*.

And shall such mob as thou, not worth a groat,
Dare pick a hole in such a great man's coat?
Peter Pindar, *Epistle to John Nichols*

Hear Land o' cakes and brither Scots,
Frae Maidenkirk to Johnny Groat's.
If there's a hole in a' your coats
I rede you tent it;
A chiel's amang yon taking notes,
And, faith, he'll prent it.
Burns, *On the late Capt. Grose*

**Holger Danske.** The national hero of Denmark. *See* Ogier the Dane.

**Holiday. *Give the boys a holiday.*** This custom of marking some specially noteworthy event is of great antiquity; it is said that Anaxagoras, on his death-bed, being asked what honour should be conferred upon him, replied, 'Give the boys a holiday.'

***Holiday speeches.*** Fine or well turned speeches or phrases; complimentary speeches. We have also 'holiday manners', 'holiday clothes', meaning the best we have.

Aye, aye, sir. I know your worship loves no holiday speeches. Scott, *Redgauntlet*, ch. iii

With many holiday and lady terms
He questioned me.
Shakespeare, *1 Henry IV*, 1, 3

**Holland.** The country gets its name from the well wooded (*holt*, wood) land around Dordrecht, to which it was originally applied; the district in South Lincolnshire is called 'Holland' from *holl* (*adj.*), lying in a hollow, i.e. low-lying land.

***Holland,*** the cloth, is so called because it was originally manufactured in, and imported from, Holland; its full name was *holland cloth. Hollands*, or properly *Hollands gin*, is the Dut. *Hollandsch genever*.

**Hollow. *I beat him hollow.*** Completely, thoroughly. *Hollow* is, perhaps, here a corruption of *wholly*.

**Holly.** The custom of decking the interiors of churches and houses with holly at Christmas-time is of great antiquity, and was probably employed by the early Christians at Rome in imitation of its use by the Romans in the great festival of the Saturnalia, which occurred at the same season of the year.

**Hollyhock** is the A.S. *holihoc*, the *holy mallow*, i.e. the marsh-mallow. It is a mistake to derive the second syllable from *oak*.

**Holy Alliance.** A league formed by Russia, Austria, and Prussia in 1815 to regulate the affairs of Europe after the fall of Napoleon 'by the principles of Christian charity' – meaning that every endeavour would be made to stabilise the existing dynasties and to resist all change. It lasted until 1830, and was joined by all the European sovereigns except those of England and Turkey, and the Pope.

**Holy City.** That city which the religious consider most especially connected with their religious faith, thus:

*Allahabad* is the Holy City of the Mohammedans of India.
*Benares* of the Hindus.
*Cuzco* of the ancient Incas.
*Fez* of the Western Arabs.
*Jerusalem* of the Jews and Christians.
*Kairwan*, near Tunis. It contains the Okbar Mosque in which is the tomb of the prophet's barber.
*Mecca* and *Medina* of the Mohammedans.
*Moscow* and *Kief* of the Russians, the latter being the cradle of Christianity in Russia.

**Holy Coat.** *See* Tréves.

**Holy Cross** (or **Holy Rood**) **Day.** September 14th, the day of the Feast of the Exaltation of the Cross, called by the Anglo-Saxons 'Rood-mass-day', and kept in honour of the exposition of a portion of the true Cross in the basilica erected at Jerusalem by the Empress Helene, *c*.326. Another event connected with it is the recovery of the piece of the Cross, which had been stolen from Jerusalem in 614 by Chosroes, King of Persia, by Heraclius in 629.

It was on this day that the Jews in Rome used to be compelled to go to church, and listen to a sermon – a custom done away with about 1840 by Pope Gregory XVI. *See* Browning's *Holy Cross Day* in *Dramatic Romances* (1855).

**Holy Family.** The infant Saviour and his attendants, as Joseph, Mary, Elizabeth, Anne, the mother of Mary, and John the Baptist. All the five figures are not always introduced in pictures of the 'Holy Family'.

**Holy Ghost, The.** The third Person of the Trinity, the Divine Spirit; represented in art as a dove.

The seven gifts of the Holy Ghost are: (1) counsel, (2) the fear of the Lord, (3) fortitude, (4) piety, (5) understanding, (6) wisdom, and (7) knowledge.

***The Order of the Holy Ghost.*** A French order of knighthood (*Ordre du Saint-Esprit*), instituted by Henri III in 1578 to replace the Order of St Michael. It was limited to 100 knights, and has not been revived since the revolution of 1830.

***The Procession of the Holy Ghost.*** *See* Filioque.

***The Sin against the Holy Ghost.*** Refusal to believe in the witness and revelation of Jesus Christ, or in His Godhead. As the Son reveals the Father to mankind so the Holy Ghost reveals the grace and meritorious atonement and promises of Christ to the heart of the believer. The Holy Ghost is the Comforter who, 'when he is come … will reprove the world of sin … because they believe not on Me' (John 16:7–9).

**Holy Isle.** Lindisfarne, in the North Sea, about eight miles from Berwick-upon-Tweed. It was once the see of the famous St Cuthbert, but is now in the diocese of Durham. The ruins of the old cathedral are still visible.

Ireland was called the Holy Island on account of its numerous saints.

Guernsey was so called in the 10th century in consequence of the great number of monks residing there.

**Holy Land, The.**

(1) Christians call *Palestine* the Holy Land, because it was the site of Christ's birth, ministry, and death.

(2) Mohammedans call *Mecca* the Holy Land, because Mahomet was born there.

(3) The Chinese Buddhists call *India* the Holy Land, because it was the native land of Sakya-muni, the Buddha (*q.v.*).

(4) The Greek considered *Elis* as Holy Land, from the temple of Olympian Zeus and the sacred festival held there every four years.

**Holy League, The.** A combination formed by Pope Julius II in 1511 with Venice, Maximilian of Germany, Ferdinand III of Spain, and various Italian princes, to drive the French out of Italy.

Other leagues have been called by the same name, particularly that formed in the reign of Henri III of France (1576), under the auspices of Henri de Guise, 'for the defence of the Holy Catholic Church against the encroachments of the reformers', i.e. for annihilating the Huguenots.

**Holy Maid of Kent, The.** Elizabeth Barton, who incited the Roman Catholics to resist the Reformation, and imagined that she acted under direct inspiration. Having denounced the doom and speedy death of Henry VIII for his marriage with Anne Boleyn, she was hanged at Tyburn in 1534. Sir Walter Scott (*Abbot*, xiii) calls her 'The Nun of Kent'.

**Holy Office, The.** *See* Inquisition.

**Holy of Holies.** The innermost apartment of the Jewish temple, in which the ark of the covenant was kept, and into which only the high priest was allowed to enter, and that but once a year – the Day of Atonement. Hence, a private apartment, a *sanctum sanctorum* (*q.v.*).

**Holy Orders.** *See* Orders.

**Holy Places.** Places in which the chief events of our Saviour's life occurred, such as the sepulchre, Gethsemane, the supper-room, the Church of the Ascension, the tomb of the Virgin, and so on.

> In 1852 … a dispute between Greek and Latin religions as to the custody of the holy places at Jerusalem, followed by the diplomatic rivalries of their respective patrons, Russia and France, produced a crisis.
>
> Morley, *Life of Gladstone*, Bk iv, ch. iii

**Holy Roman Empire, The.** The name given to the often very nebulous confederation of Central European States that subsisted, either in fact or in theory, from AD 800, when Charlemagne was crowned Emperor of the West, until the abdication of Francis II (Francis I of Austria) in 1806. It was first called 'Holy' by Barbarossa, in allusion both to its reputed divine appointment, and to the interdependence of Empire and Church; it comprised the German-speaking peoples of Central Europe, and was ruled by an elected Emperor, who claimed to be the representative of the ancient Roman Emperors.

The name has been sometimes brought forward as an excellent instance of contradiction in terms, the confederation not properly being entitled to either of the three epithets – 'Holy', 'Roman', or 'Empire'.

**Holy Rood Day.** *See* Holy Cross Day.

**Holy Thursday.** Ascension Day (*q.v.*), i.e. the Thursday but one before Whitsun, is what is generally meant by this among Anglicans; but by Roman Catholics and others Maundy Thursday (*q.v.*), i.e. the Thursday before Good Friday, is sometimes called 'Holy Thursday'. *See also* In Coena Domini.

**Holy Saturday.** *See* Holy Week.

**Holy War.** A war in which religious fanaticism plays, or purports to play, a considerable part. The Crusades, the Thirty Years' War, the wars against the Albigenses, etc., were so called.

**Holy Water.** Water blessed by a priest or bishop for holy uses, and used to sprinkle over the people before High Mass, etc.

***As the devil loves holy water.*** Not at all.

***Holy water sprinkler.*** A military club of mediaeval times, set with spikes. So called facetiously because it makes the blood to flow as water sprinkled by an aspergillum.

**Holy Week.** Passion Week (*q.v.*), the last week in Lent. It begins on Palm Sunday; the fourth day is called 'Spy Wednesday'; the fifth is 'Maundy Thursday'; the sixth is 'Good Friday'; and the last 'Holy Saturday' or the 'Great Sabbath'.

> Holy Week has been called *Hebdomada Muta* (Silent Week); *Hebdomada Inofficiosa* (Vacant Week); *Hebdomada Penitentialis*; *Hebdomada Indulgentiae*; *Hebdomada Luctuosa*; *Hebdomada Nigra*; and *Hebdomada Ultima*.

**Holy Writ.** The Bible.

> Trifles light as air
> Are to the jealous confirmations strong
> As proofs of holy writ.
>
> Shakespeare, *Othello*, 3, 3

**Holywell Street.** An old London street that used to run parallel with the Strand, from St Dunstan's Church to St Clement Danes, and was thrown into the Strand itself by the improvements that took place in that quarter in the closing years of the last century, and that resulted in the formation of Kingsway and Aldwych. It was commonly known as 'Booksellers' Row', from the large number of second-hand booksellers who had their shops there. (This name has since been transferred to Charing Cross Road, to which many of the booksellers migrated.)

Fitzstephens, in his description of London in the reign of Henry II, speaks of 'the excellent springs at a small distance from the city', whose waters are most sweet, salubrious, and clear, and whose runnels murmur over the shining stones. Among these are Holywell, Clerkenwell, and St Clement's well.

**Home. *At home.*** At one's own house and prepared to receive visitors. An *at home* is a more or less informal reception for which arrangements have been made. *To be at home to somebody* is to be ready and willing to receive him; *to be at home with a subject* is to be familiar with it, quite conversant with it.

***Home, sweet home.*** This popular English song first appears in the opera *Clari, the Maid of Milan* (Covent Garden, 1823). The words are by John Howard Payne (an American), and the music by Sir Henry Bishop, who professed to have founded it on a Sicilian air.

***Not at home.*** A familiar locution for 'not prepared to receive visitors' – or the one who is applying for admission; it does not necessarily mean 'away from home'.

> An old story, sometimes attributed to Swift, is that once when Scipio Nasica called on the poet Ennius, the servant said, 'Ennius is not at home,' but Nasica could see him plainly in the house. A few days later Ennius returned the visit, and Nasica called out, 'Not at home.' Ennius instantly recognised the voice, and remonstrated. 'You are a nice fellow' (said Nasica); 'why, I believed your slave, and you won't believe me.'

***One's long home.*** The grave.

> Man goeth to his long home, and the mourners go about the streets. Eccles. 12:5

***To come home to one.*** To reach one's heart; to become thoroughly understood or realised.

> I doe now publish my Essayes; which, of all my other workes, have been most Currant: For that, as it seems they come home, to Mens Businesse, and Bosomes.
>
> Bacon, *Epistle Dedicatorie to the 'Essayes'* (1625)

***To make oneself at home.*** To dispense with ceremony in another person's house, to act as though one were at home.

***Who goes home?*** When the House of Commons breaks up at night the door-keeper asks this question of the members. In bygone days all members going in the direction of the Speaker's residence went in a body to see him safe home. The question is still asked, but is a mere relic of antiquity.

**Homer.** The name given to the entirely unknown poet – or group of poets perhaps – to whom is assigned the authorship of the *Iliad* (*q.v.*) and the *Odyssey* (*q.v.*), the greatest monuments of ancient or modern epic poetry. It is much doubted whether any such person ever existed, but the name (which means 'one who puts together') rests on very ancient tradition, and the date at which the poems are thought to have received their final shape is conjecturally put at anywhere between the 12th and the 9th century BC.

> No doubt was ever entertained by the ancients respecting the personality of Homer. Pindar, Aristotle, Plato, and others, all assumed this fact; nor did they even doubt that the *Iliad* and *Odyssey* were the work of one mind.
>
> R. W. Browne, *Historical Classical Literature*, Bk i, ch. iv

Homer's birthplace is quite unknown. The old rhyme, founded on an epigram preserved by Aulus Gellius, says:

> Seven cities warred for Homer being dead,
> Who living had no roof to shroud his head.
>
> Heywood, *Hierarchie of the Blessed Angels* (1635)

the 'seven cities' being Smyrna, Rhodes, Colophon, Salamis, Chios, Argos, and Athens. *See* Scio's.

Among the many names and epithets that have been bestowed on him are Melesigenes (*q.v.*); the Man of Chios (*see* Chios); the Blind Old Man; and Maeonides (*q.v.*). He is spoken of as *Maeonius senex*, and his poems as *Maeoniae chartae* or *Maeonia carmina*.

Milton has been called *the English Homer*, Ossian *the Gaelic Homer*, Plato *the Homer of philosophers*; Byron called Fielding *the prose Homer of human nature*; and Dryden (*Essay on Dramatic Poesy*) says:

> Shakespeare was the Homer, or father of our dramatic poets; Jonson was the Virgil, the pattern of elaborate writing; I admire him but I love Shakespeare.

***The Casket Homer.*** An edition corrected by Aristotle, which Alexander the Great always carried about with him, and laid under his pillow at night with his sword. After the battle of Arbela, a golden casket richly studded with gems was found in the tent of Darius; and Alexander being asked to what purpose it should be assigned, replied, 'There is but one thing in the world worthy of so costly a depository,' saying which he placed therein his edition of Homer.

***Homer a cure for the ague.*** *See* Ague.

***Homer sometimes nods.*** Even the best of us is liable to make mistakes. The line is from Horace's *De Arte Poetica* (359):

> Quandoque bonus dormitat Homerus!
> Verum operi longo fas es obrepere somnum.
> (Sometimes good Homer himself even nods; but in so long a work it is allowable if there should be a drowsy interval or so.)

**Homoeopathy** (Gr. *homoios pathos*, like disease). The plan of curing a disease by minute doses of a medicine which would in healthy persons produce the disease. The principle of vaccination is a sort of homoeopathy, producing in a healthy person a mitigated form of the disease guarded against. The theory was first formulated and practised by Samuel Hahnemann (1755–1843), a German physician.

> Tut, man! one fire burns out another's burning!
> One pain is lessened by another's anguish …
> Take thou some new infection to the eye,
> And the rank poison of the old will die.
>
> Shakespeare, *Romeo and Juliet*, 1, 2

**Honey.** An expression of endearment (with allusion to sweetness), formerly common in England, but now more usually connected with the American negro.

> Him thinketh verraily that he may see
> Noë's flood come walwing as the see
> To drenchen Alisoun, his hony dere
>
> Chaucer, *Miller's Tale*, 429

**Honeydew**. A sweet substance found on the leaves of lime trees and some other plants. Bees and ants are fond of it. It is probably the excretion of the aphis, and gets its popular name from its great sweetness coupled with its dew-like appearance.

> Some framed faire lookes, glancing like evening lights,
> Others sweet words, dropping like honny dew.
>
> Spenser, *Faërie Queene*, II, v, 33

**Honeymoon.** The month when all is sweetness, the first after marriage, especially that part of it spent away from home. The name originally did not include the idea of 'month' at all, but had reference to the ever-changing character of the moon.

Of all the lunar things that change
The one that shows most fickle and strange,
And takes the most eccentric range,
Is the moon – so called – of honey!

Thos Hood, *Miss Kilmansegg* (*Her Honeymoon*)

**Honeysuckle.** *See* Misnomers.

**Hong Merchants.** Those Chinese merchants who, under licence from the government of China, held the monopoly of trade with Europeans till 1842, when the restriction was abolished by the Treaty of Nanking. The Chinese applied the word *hong* to the foreign factories situated at Canton.

**Honi. *Honi soit qui mal y pense*.** The translation of this old French motto of the Crown of England and of the Most Noble Order of the Garter (*see* Garter) as usually given is 'Evil be [to him] who thinks evil of this', the reference being to the old tradition that Edward III at a court ball picked up the blue garter of the beautiful Countess of Salisbury, which had accidentally fallen off, and bound it round his own knee, using these words, and adding, 'I will bring it about that the proudest noble in the realm shall think it an honour to wear this band.' The incident, so the story goes, determined him to abandon his plan of forming an order of the Round Table, and he formed instead the order of the Garter.

Another account, however, says that it was Edward's own Queen who dropped her garter, that it was adopted by the soldiers going to the war in France as the badge, and that the 'it' (*y*) of the motto referred, not to the garter itself, but to the military expedition that it symbolised – 'Accursed be he who thinks ill of it.'

**Honorificabilitudinitatibus.** A made up word on the Lat. *honorificabilitudo*, honourableness, which frequently occurs in Elizabethan plays as an instance of sesquipedalian pomposity, etc.

Thou art not so long by the head as honorificabilitudinitatibus.

Shakespeare, *Love's Labour's Lost*, 5, 1

Physitions deafen our ears with the honorificabilitudinitatibus of their heavenly Panachoea, their soveraigne Guiacum.

*Nashe's* '*Lenten Stuffe*' (1599)

*See* Long Words.

**Honour.** In feudal law, a superior seigniory, on which other lordships or manors depended by the performance of customary services. At bridge, whist, etc., the *honours* are the four highest trump cards – ace, king, queen, and knave.

***An affair of honour.*** A dispute to be settled by a duel. Duels were generally provoked by offences against the arbitrary rules of etiquette, courtesy, or feeling, called the laws 'of honour'; and, as these offences were not recognisable in the law courts, they were settled by private combat.

***Crushed by his honours.*** The allusion is to the legend of the Roman damsel, Tarpeia, who agreed to open the gates of Rome to King Tatius, provided his soldiers would give her the ornaments which they wore on their arms. As they entered they threw their shields on her and crushed her, saying as they did so, 'These are the ornaments worn by Sabines on their arms.'

Draco, the Athenian legislator, was crushed to death in the theatre of Aegina, by the number of caps and cloaks showered on him by the audience, as a mark of their high appreciation of his merits. A similar story is told of the mad Emperor, Elagabalus (*q.v.*), who smothered the leading citizens of Rome with roses.

***Debts of honour.*** Debts contracted by betting or gambling, so called because these debts cannot be enforced as such by law.

***Honours of war.*** The privilege allowed to an enemy, on capitulation, of being permitted to retain their offensive arms. This is the highest honour a victor can pay a vanquished foe. Sometimes the troops so treated are allowed to march with all their arms, drums beating, and colours flying.

***Laws of honour.*** Certain arbitrary rules which the fashionable world tacitly admits; they wholly regard deportment, and have nothing to do with moral offences. Breaches of this code are punished by expulsion or suspension from society, 'sending to Coventry' (*q.v.*).

***Legion of Honour.*** *See* Legion.

***Point of honour.*** An obligation which is binding because its violation would offend some conscientious scruple or notion of self-respect.

***Word of honour.*** A gage which cannot be violated without placing the breaker of it beyond the pale of respectability and good society.

**Honourable.** *See* Right Honourable.

**Hood. *'Tis not the hood* (or *cowl*) *that makes the monk*** (Lat. *Cucullus non facit monachum*). We must not be deceived by appearances, or take for granted that things and persons are what they seem to be.

Signior Lucio, did not you say you knew that Friar Lodowick to be a dishonest person?

*Lucio: Cucullus non facit monachum*: honest in nothing, but in his clothes; and one that hath spoke most villainous speeches of the duke.

Shakespeare, *Measure for Measure*, 5, 1

> They should be good men; their affairs are righteous
> But all hoods make not monks.
>
> Shakespeare, *Henry VIII*, 3, 1

The origin of the phrase is probably to be found in these lines from St Anselm's *Carmen de Contemptu Mundi* (11th cent.):

> Non tonsura facit monachum, non horrida vestis;
> Sed virtus animi, perpetuusque rigor.

The following are the chief academic hoods forming part of the official robes of the holders of various degrees at the Universities:

*Black* silk *without* lining: B.D. Cambridge, Oxford, Dublin.

Black stuff, with broad white fur trimming: B.A. or LL.B. Cambridge.

Black corded silk, with narrow white fur trimming: B.A. Oxford.

Black silk: With white silk lining, M.A. Cambridge; with dark red silk lining, M.A. Oxford; with dark blue silk lining, Dublin; with russet-brown lining, M.A. London.

*Blue* silk, with white fur trimming, B.C.L. Oxford.

*Brown* (silk or stuff), edged with russet-brown, B.A. London.

Scarlet cloth: Lined with crimson silk, D.C.L. Oxford; with pink silk, D.C.L. Dublin; D.D. Cambridge; with black silk, D.D. Oxford; lined with light cherry-coloured silk, LL.D. Cambridge.

Scarlet cashmere hood: Lined with silk, D.D. Dublin; with white silk, D.C.L. Durham.

Violet hoods are St Andrew's.

The higher the degree the longer the hood; a bachelor's hood only reaches to the knees, but a doctor's to the heels.

**Hood, Robin.** *See* Robin Hood.

**Hoodlum** (American slang). A rough hooligan. The word was originally confined to the particular variety native to San Francisco.

**Hoodman Blind.** Now called 'Blind-man's Buff'.

> What devil was't
> That thus hath cozened you at hoodman blind?
>
> Shakespeare, *Hamlet*, 3, 4

**Hook. *Above your hook.*** Beyond your comprehension; beyond your mark. The allusion is perhaps to hat-pegs placed in rows, the higher rows being beyond the reach of small statures.

***By hook or crook.*** Either rightfully or wrongfully; somehow; one way or another.

There is more than one attempted explanation of the phrase; but it is most likely that it has reference to some of the tools carried by thieves, such as the vagabonds who stole clothes hanging on the line, small objects from open windows, etc., by means of a hook or a crook. The following quotation from Spenser would seem to point to some such origin:

> Thereafter all that mucky pelfe he tooke,
> The spoil of peoples evill gotten good,
> The which her sire had scrap't by hooke and crooke.
>
> *Faërie Queene*, V, ii, 27

On the other hand, it is recorded that formerly the poor of a manor were allowed to go into the forests with a *hook* and *crook* to get wood. What they could not reach they might pull down with their crook.

> Dymnure Wood was ever open and common to the ... inhabitants of Bodmin ... to bear away upon their backs a burden of lop, crop, hook, crook, and bag wood. *Bodmin Register* (1525)

The French equivalent is *De bric et de broc*.

***He is off the hooks.*** Done for, laid on the shelf, superseded, dead. The bent pieces of iron on which the hinges of a gate rest and turn are called *hooks*: if a gate is off the hooks it is in a bad way, and cannot readily be opened and shut.

***Hook it! Take your hook! Sling your hook!*** Be off! Be off about your business!

***On one's own hook.*** On one's own responsibility or account. An angler's phrase.

***With a hook at the end.*** 'My assent is given with a hook at the end' means that it is given with a very decided 'mental reservation'. In some parts it is still the custom for a witness when he swears falsely to crook his finger into a sort of hook, and this is supposed sufficient to annul the perjury. It is a crooked oath, an oath 'with a hook at the end'. *Cp.* Over the Left, *under* Left.

**Hookey Walker.** *See* Walker.

**Hooligan.** A violent young rough. The term originated in the last years of the 19th century from the name of one of this class. From it is derived the substantive *hooliganism*.

> The original *Hooligans* were a spirited Irish family of that name whose proceedings enlivened the drab monotony of life in Southwark towards the end of the 19th century. The word is younger than the Australian *larrikin*, of doubtful origin, but older than Fr. *apache*.
>
> Ernest Weekley, *Romance of Words* (1912)

**Hooped Pots.** Drinking pots at one time were marked with bands, or hoops, set at equal distances, so that when two or more drank from the same tankard no one should take more than his share. Jack Cade promises his followers that 'seven halfpenny loaves shall be sold for a penny; the three-hooped pot shall have ten hoops; and I will make it felony to drink small beer'. (Shakespeare, *2 Henry VI*, 4, 2.)

> I beleeve hoopes in quart pots were invented to that ende, that every man should take his hoope, and no more.
>
> Nash, *Pierce Pennilesse* (1592)

**Hop.** ***To hop the twig.*** Usually, to die; but sometimes to run away from one's creditors, as a bird eludes a fowler, 'hopping from spray to spray'.

There are numerous phrases to express the cessation of life; for example, 'to kick the bucket'; 'to lay down one's knife and fork'; 'to peg out' (from cribbage); 'to be snuffed out' (like a candle); 'to throw up the sponge'; to fall asleep'; 'to enter Charon's boat'; 'to join the majority'; and 'to give up the ghost'.

**Hop-o'-my-Thumb.** A pigmy or midget. The name has been given to several dwarfs, as well as being commonly used as a generic term. Tom Thumb in the well known nursery tale is quite another character. He was the son of peasants, knighted by King Arthur, and killed by a spider.

> You Stump-o'-the-Gutter, you Hop-o'-my-Thumb,
> Your husband must from Liiliput come.
>
> Kane O'Hara, *Midas*
>
> Plaine friend, Hop-o'-my-Thumb, know you who we are? *Taming of a Shrew* (Anon. 1594)

**Hope.** *See* Pandora's Box.

Thomas Campbell (1777–1844) was known as *The Bard of Hope*, on account of his poem, 'The Pleasures of Hope' (1799).

**Hopkinsians.** A sect of Independent Calvinists who followed the teaching of Samuel Hopkins (1721–1803), a minister at Newport, Rhode Island, whose *System of Divinity* was published shortly before his death. They held most of the Calvinistic doctrines, but entirely rejected the doctrines of imputed sin and imputed righteousness. The speciality of the system is that true holiness consists in disinterested benevolence, and that all sin is *selfishness*. The sect as such no longer exists, but the tenets held by it are by no means extinct.

**Horace.** The Roman lyric poet, born 65 BC, died 8 BC.

***Horace of England.*** George, Duke of Buckingham, preposterously declared Cowley to be the Pindar, Horace, and Virgil of England. Ben Jonson was nicknamed Horace by Dekker in the so-called 'War of the Theatres'.

***Horace of France.*** Jean Macrinus or Salmon (1490–1557); and Pierre Jean de Beranger (1780–1857), also called the *French Burns*.

***Horace of Spain.*** The brothers Lupercio (1559–1613) and Bartolme (1562–1631) Argensola.

**Horn.** ***Astolpho's horn.*** Logistilla gave Astolpho at parting a horn that had the virtue to appal and put to flight the boldest knight or most savage beast. (Ariosto, *Orlando Furioso*, Bk viii.)

***Cape Horn.*** So named by Schouten, a Dutch mariner, who first doubled it (1616). He was a native of Hoorn, in north Holland, and named the cape after his native place.

***The Horn gate.*** *See* Dreams, Gates of.

***Horn of fidelity.*** Morgan la Fay sent a horn to King Arthur, which had the following 'virtue': No lady could drink out of it who was not 'to her husband true'; all others who attempted to drink were sure to spill what it contained. This horn was carried to King Mark, and 'his queene with a hundred ladies more' tried the experiment, but only four managed to 'drinke cleane'. Ariosto's *enchanted cup* possessed a similar spell.

***Horn of plenty.*** Amalthea's horn (*q.v.*), the cornucopia, an emblem of plenty.

Ceres is drawn with a ram's horn in her left arm, filled with fruits and flowers; sometimes they are being poured on the earth, and sometimes they are piled high in the horn as in a basket. Diodorus (iii, 68) says the horn is one from the head of the goat by which Jupiter was suckled.

***King Horn.*** *See under* King.

***Moses' Horns.*** *See* Moses.

**Phrases.**

***Horn with horn*** or ***horn under horn.*** The promiscuous feeding of bulls and cows, or, in fact, all horned beasts that are allowed to run together on the same common.

***My horn hath He exalted*** (1 Sam. 2:10; Ps. 89:24, etc.). He has given me the victory, increased my sway. Thus, *Lift not up your horn on high* (Ps. 75:5) means, do not behave scornfully, maliciously, or arrogantly. In these passages 'horn' symbolises power, and its exaltation signifies victory or deliverance. In Daniel's vision (Dan. 7) the 'fourth beast, dreadful and terrible, and strong exceedingly', had ten horns, symbolical of its great might.

> Now, from Heaven-sanctioned victory, Peace is sprung;
> In this firm hour Salvation lifts her horn.
> Wordsworth, *Poems to National Independence*, xliv

***The horns of a dilemma.*** *See* Dilemma.

***To come*** (or ***be squeezed***) ***out at the little end of the horn.*** To come off badly in some affair; get the worst of it; fail conspicuously.

***To draw in one's horns.*** To retract, or mitigate, a pronounced opinion; to restrain pride. In French, *Rentrer les cornes*. The allusion is to the snail.

***To put to the horn.*** To denounce as a rebel, or pronounce a person an outlaw, for not answering to a summons. In Scotland the messenger-at-arms used to go to the Cross of Edinburgh and give three blasts with a horn before he proclaimed judgment of outlawry.

***To the horns of the altar. Usque ad aras amicus***. Your friend even to the horns of the altar – i.e. through thick and thin. In swearing, the ancient Romans held the horns of the altar, and one who did so in testimony of friendship could not break his oath without calling on himself the vengeance of the angry gods.

The altar in Solomon's temple had a projection at each of the four corners called 'horns'; these were regarded as specially sacred, and probably typified the great might of God (*cp. above*).

> Upon Thine altar's horn of gold
> Help me to lay my trembling hold.
> Keble, *Christian Year; 1st Sun. aft. Easter*

***To wear the horns.*** To be a cuckold. This old term is possibly connected with the chase. In the rutting season one stag selects several females, who constitute his harem, till another stag contests the prize with him. If beaten he is without associates till he finds a stag feebler than himself, who is made to submit to similar terms. As stags are horned, and have their mates taken from them by their fellows, the application is palpable.

Another explanation (*see* N.E.D.) is that it is due

> to the practice formerly prevalent of planting or engrafting the spurs of a castrated cock on the root of the excised comb, where they grew and became horns, sometimes of several inches long.

In support of this it is noteworthy that *hahnrei*, the German equivalent for *cuckold*, originally signified a capon.

***To show one's horns.*** To let one's evil intentions appear. The allusion, like that in 'to show the cloven hoof', is to the Devil – 'Old Hornie'.

***To take the bull by the horns.*** *See* Bull.

**Horn-book.** A thin board of oak about nine inches long and five or six wide, on which was printed the alphabet, the nine digits, and sometimes the Lord's Prayer, the Creed, and the Angelic Salutation. Horn-books were in use in elementary schools for the poor when books were scarce and expensive, and survived well into the 18th century. They had a handle, and were covered in front with a sheet of thin horn; the back was often ornamented with a rude sketch of St George and the Dragon. *See* Chriss-cross Row.

> Thee will I sing, in comely wainscot bound,
> And golden verge inclosing thee around;
> The faithful horn before, from age to age
> Preserving thy invulnerable page;
> Behind, thy patron saint in armour shines,
> With sword and lance to guard the sacred lines.
> Tickell, *The Horn Book*

> Their books of stature small they took in hand
> Which with pellucid horn secured are,
> To save from finger wet the letters fair.
> Shenstone, *Schoolmistress*

***Death and Doctor Hornbook.*** In this biting satire by Robert Burns 'Doctor Hornbook' stands for John Wilson the apothecary, whom the poet met at the Tarbolton Masonic Lodge.

**Horner, Little Jack.** *See* Jack.

**Hornet. *To poke your head into a hornet's nest. To bring a hornet's nest about your ears.*** To get into trouble by meddling. The bear is very fond of honey, and often gets stung by poking its snout by mistake into a hornet's nest in search of its favourite dainty.

**Hornie. *Auld Hornie*.** The devil, so called in Scotland. The allusion is to the horns with which Satan is generally represented.

> O thou! whatever title suits thee,
> Auld Hornie, Satan, Nick, or Clootie.
> Burns, *Address to to the Deil*

**Hornpipe.** The dance is so called because it used to be danced to the *pib-corn* or *hornpipe*, an instrument consisting of a pipe each end of which was made of horn. Johnson in his *Dictionary* mistakenly said that it was 'danced commonly to *a horn*'.

**Horoscope.** The scheme of the twelve houses by which astrologers tell your fortune. *See* Houses, Astrological. The word (Greek) means the 'hour-scrutinised', because it is the disposition of the heavens at the exact hour of birth which is examined.

> Is it too late then, Evelyn Hope?
> What, your soul was pure and true,
> The good stars met in your horoscope.
> Made you of spirit, fire, and dew.
> Browning, *Evelyn Hope*

**Hors de combat** (Fr., out of battle). Incapable of taking any further part in the fight.

> He (i.e., Cobbett) levels his antagonists, he lays his friends low, and puts his own party *hors de combat.* Hazlitt, *Table Talk*

**Hors d'oeuvre** (Fr., outside the work). A relish served at the beginning of a dinner as a whet to the appetite, not as an integral part of the food. In French the expression is also used in architecture for an outbuilding or outwork, and as a literary term for a digression or interpolated episode.

**Horse.**

**In Phrase and Proverb.**

***A dark horse.*** A horse whose merits as a racer are not known to the general public; hence, a person who keeps his true capabilities to himself till he can produce them to the best advantage.

***A nod is as good as a wink to a blind horse.*** Said of one who is determined not to take a hint, or to see a point; also used with the contrary meaning, viz. 'I twig your meaning, though you speak darkly of what you purpose; but mum's the word.'

***A one-horse show.*** *See* One.

***As strong as a horse.*** Very strong. *Horse* is often used with intensive effect; as, *to work*, or *to eat*, *like a horse*.

***Don't look a gift-horse in the mouth.*** *See* Gift-horse.

***Flogging the dead horse.*** Trying to revive interest in a subject out of date. Bright said that Earl Russell's Reform Bill (1867) was a 'dead horse', and every attempt to create any enthusiasm in its favour was like 'flogging the dead horse'.

***Horse and foot.*** The cavalry and infantry; hence all one's forces; with all one's might.

> Cook's son, duke's son, son of a belted earl,
> Forty thousand horse and foot going to Table Bay!
> Rudyard Kipling, *The Absent Minded Beggar* (1899)

***I will win the horse or lose the saddle.*** Neck or nothing; double or quits. The story is that a man made the bet of a horse that another could not say the Lord's Prayer without a wandering thought. The bet was accepted, but before halfway through the person who accepted the bet looked up and said, 'By the by, do you mean the saddle also?'

***One man may steal a horse, while another may not look over the hedge.*** Some people are specially privileged, and can take liberties, or commit crimes, etc., with impunity, while others get punished for very trivial offences. An old proverb; given by Heywood (1546).

***Riding the wooden horse.*** Being strapped to a wooden contrivance shaped something like a horse's back, and soundly flogged. A military punishment now discontinued.

***The grey mare is the better horse.*** *See* Mare.

***They cannot draw*** (or ***set***) ***horses together.*** They cannot agree together. The French say, *Nos chiens ne chassent pas ensemble*.

***'Tis a Trojan horse.*** A deception, a concealed danger. *See* Wooden Horse of Troy.

***'Tis a good horse that never stumbles.*** Everyone has his faults; Homer sometimes nods. *See* Homer.

***To back the wrong horse.*** To make an error in judgment, and suffer for it. A phrase from the Turf. Speaking in the House of Lords (January 19th, 1897), Lord Salisbury said:

> I consider that both parties have been mistaken in their policy toward the Turkish Empire; they staked their money on the wrong horse at the time of the Crimean War.

***To be on one's high horse, to ride the high horse.*** To be overbearing and arrogant; to give oneself airs.

***To ride on the horse with ten toes.*** To walk; to ride on Shanks's mare (*q.v.*).

***To set the cart before the horse.*** *See* Cart.

***When the horse is stolen, lock the stable door.*** Said in derision when obvious precautions are taken *after* a loss or disaster. The French say, *Après la mort, le médecin*. Somewhat similar is, 'After beef, mustard'.

***Working on the dead horse.*** Doing work which has been already paid for. Such work is a dead horse, because you can get no more out of it.

***You can take a horse to the water but you cannot make him drink.*** There is always *some* point at which it is impossible to get an obstinate man to proceed farther in the desired direction – charm you never so wisely. The proverb is an old one, and is found in Heywood (1846).

**In Fable and Story.**

According to classical mythology, Poseidon (Neptune) created the horse; and, according to Virgil, the first person that drove a four-in-hand was Erichthonius:

Primus Erichthonius currus et quatuor ausus
Jungere equos. *Georg*. iii, 113

***A horse wins a kingdom.*** It is said that on the death of Smerdis (522 BC), the several competitors for the throne of Persia agreed that he should be king whose horse neighed first when they met on the day following. The groom of Darius showed his horse a mare on the place appointed, and immediately it arrived at the spot on the following day the horse began to neigh, and won the crown for its master.

*Directions for riding and driving.*
Up a hill hurry not,
Down a hill flurry not,
On level ground spare him not.
On a Milestone near Richmond, Yorks

***Flesh-eating horses.*** The horses of Diomed, tyrant of Thrace (not Diomede, son of Tydeus); he fed his horses on the strangers who visited his kingdom. Hercules vanquished the tyrant, and gave the carcass to the horses to eat.

Like to the Thracian tyrant who, they say,
Unto his horses gave his guests for meat,
Till he himself was made their greedy prey.
And torn in pieces by Alcides great.
Spenser, *Faërie Queene*, V, viii, 31

***O'Donohue's white horses.*** Waves which come on a windy day, crested with foam. The hero reappears every seventh year on May-day, and is seen gliding, to sweet but unearthly music, over the lakes of Killarney, on his favourite white horse. He is preceded by groups of fairies, who fling spring flowers in his path.

Moore has a poem on the subject in his *Irish Melodies*; it refers to a tradition that a young and beautiful girl became enamoured of O'Donohue, the visionary chieftain, and threw herself into the lake that he might carry her off for his bride.

***The brazen horse.*** *See* Cambuscan.

***The Trojan horse.*** *See* Wooden Horse of Troy.

***Horse-chestnut.*** In his *Herball* (1597) Gerarde tells us that the tree is so called –

For that the people of the East countries do with the fruit thereof cure their horses of the cough … and such like diseases.

Another explanation is that when a slip is cut off obliquely close to a joint, it presents a miniature of a horse's hock and foot, shoe and nails. (*Cp.* Horse-vetch.) But the use of *horse-* attributively to denote something that is inferior, coarse, or unrefined, is quite common.

***Horse-faced.*** Having a long, coarse face.

***Horse Latitudes.*** A region of calms between 30° and 35° North; perhaps so called because sailing-ships carrying horses to America or the West Indies were often obliged to lighten the vessel by casting them overboard when calm-bound in these latitudes, or because this neighbourhood was found to be specially fatal to horses.

***Horse-laugh.*** A coarse, vulgar laugh.

He plays rough pranks … and has a big horse-laugh in him when there is a fop to be roasted.
Carlyle, *Frederick the Great*, vol. i, Bk iv, ch. ii

***Horse-leech.*** A type of insatiable voracity; founded on the blood-sucking habits of the worm, and the well-known passage in the Bible:

The horseleach hath two daughters, crying Give, give. Prov. 30:15

Marbeck, the commentator, in 1581, explains the 'two daughters' –

that is, two forks in her tongue, which he heere calleth her two daughters, whereby she sucketh the bloud, and is never saciate.

Insatiably he sucks
And clings, and pulls – a horse-leech, whose deep maw
The plethoric King Swellfoot could not fill.
Shelley, *Oedipus Tyrannus*, I, i

***Horse Marines. Go and tell that to the horse marines!*** Said in derision to the teller of some unbelievable yarn or specially 'tall' story.

Tell that to the marines, the sailors won't believe it. Scott, *Redgauntlet*, ch. xiii

Of course, there is no such force; the Royal Marines are confined to artillery and infantry, and do not include cavalry. To belong to the 'Horse Marines' means to be an awkward lubberly recruit. *Cp.* Marine.

***Horse-milliner.*** One who makes up and supplies decorations for horses; hence a horse-soldier more fit for the toilet than the battlefield. The expression was used by Chatterton in his *Excelent Balade of Charitie* (Rowley Poems), and Scott revived it.

One comes in foreign trashery
Of tinkling chain and spur
A walking haberdashery
Of feathers, lace, and fur:
In Rowley's antiquated phrase,
Horse milliner of modern days.
*Bridal of Triermain*, ii, 3

***Horse-play.*** Rough play.

***Horse-power.*** The standard theoretical unit of rate of work, equal to the raising of 33,000 lb one foot high in one minute. This was fixed by Watt, who, when experimenting to find some settled way of indicating the power exerted by his steam-engine, found that a strong dray horse working at a gin for eight hours a day averaged

22,000 foot-pounds per minute. He increased this by 50 per cent., and this, ever since, has been 1 horsepower.

To obtain the indicated horse-power of a steam-engine the following is the formula:

$$\frac{P \times A \times L \times 2R}{33{,}000}$$

P, pressure (in lb) per sq. inch on the piston.
A, area (in inches) of the piston.
L, length (in feet) of the stroke.
R, number of revolutions per minute.

To obtain the actual or effective horse-power from 10 to 20 per cent. (according to the class of engine) has to be deducted from the result, to allow for the power required to drive the engine itself.

***Horseshoes. It is lucky to pick up a horseshoe.*** This is from the old notion that a horseshoe nailed to the house door was a protection against witches. Lord Nelson had one nailed to the mast of the ship *Victory*.

> The legend is that the devil one day asked St Dunstan, who was noted for his skill in shoeing horses, to shoe his 'single hoof'. Dunstan, knowing who his customer was, tied him tightly to the wall and proceeded with his job, but purposely put the devil to so much pain that he roared for mercy. Dunstan at last consented to release his captive on condition that he would never enter a place where he saw a horseshoe displayed.

> Straws laid across my path retard;
> The horseshoes nailed, each threshold's guard.
> Gay, *Fable* xxiii, Pt 1

In 1251 Walter le Brun, farrier, in the Strand, London, was to have a piece of land in the parish of St Clements, to place there a forge, for which he was to pay the parish six horseshoes, which rent was paid to the Exchequer every year, and is still rendered to the Exchequer by the Lord Mayor and citizens of London, to whom subsequently the piece of ground was granted.

> In the reign of King Edward I Walter Marescullus paid at the *crucem lapideam* six horse-shoes with nails, for a certain building which he held of the king *in capite* opposite the stone cross. Blount, *Ancient Tenures*

***Horse-vetch.*** The vetch which has pods shaped like a horseshoe; sometimes called the 'horse-shoe vetch'. *Cp.* Horse Chestnut.

**Horsy Man, A.** One who affects the manners and style of a jockey or horse-dealer.

**Hortus Siccus** (Lat., a dry garden). A collection of plants dried and arranged in a book.

**Horus.** One of the major gods of the ancient Egyptians, a blending of Horus the Elder, the sun-god (corresponding to the Greek Apollo), and Horus the Child (*see* Harpocrates), the son of Osiris and Isis. He was represented in hieroglyphics by a hawk, which bird was sacred to him, or as a hawk-headed man; and his emblem was the winged sun-disk. In many of the myths he is hardly distinguishable from Ra.

**Hospital** (Lat. *hospitale*, *hospitium*, from *hospes*, a guest). Originally a hospice, or hostel for the reception of pilgrims, the word came to be applied to a charitable institution for the aged and infirm (as in *Greenwich Hospital*, *Chelsea Hospital*), to similar institutions for the education of the young (as in *Christ's Hospital*), and so, finally, to its present usual sense, a place where the sick and wounded are cared for, and where medical students gain their experience in the treatment of disease, etc. The words *hostel* and *hotel* are 'doublets' of *hospital*. Another common variation is *hospice*.

**Hospitallers.** First applied to those whose duty it was to provide *hospitiem* (lodging and entertainment) for pilgrims. The most noted institution of the kind was at Jerusalem, which gave its name to an order called the Knights Hospitallers, or the Knights of St John at Jerusalem; afterwards they were styled the Knights of Rhodes, and then Knights of Malta (*q.v.*), Rhodes and Malta being conferred on them at different times.

> The first crusade ... led to the establishment of the Christian kingdom of Jerusalem, in 1099. The chief strength of the kingdom lay in the two orders of military monks – the Templars and the Hospitallers or Knights of St John.
> Freeman, *General Sketch*, ch. xi

The present *Order of the Hospital of St John of Jerusalem in England* (with headquarters at St John's Gate, Clerkenwell) is not connected with the ancient Order. It received a Royal Charter of Incorporation in 1888, and a supplemental charter (empowering the Grand Prior to establish Priories in any part of the British Dominions) in 1907, and it exists for the purpose of carrying on ambulance and other charitable work.

**Host.** The consecrated bread of the Eucharist is so called in the Latin Church because it is regarded as a real victim consisting of flesh, blood, and spirit, offered up in sacrifice; so called from *hostia*, the Latin word for a sheep when offered up in sacrifice (a larger animal was *victima*). At the Benediction it is exposed for adoration or carried in procession in a transparent vessel called a 'monstrance'.

***The elevation of the Host.*** The celebrant lifting up the consecrated wafers above his head, that the people may see the paten and adore 'the Host' while his back is turned to the congregation.

***Host.*** An army, a multitude. At the breaking up of the Roman Empire the first duty of every subject was to follow his lord into the field, and the proclamation was *bannire in hostem* (to order out against the foe), which soon came to signify 'to order out for military service', and *hostem facere* came to mean 'to perform military service'. *Hostis* (military service) next came to mean the *army* that went against the foe, whence this word *host. Host*, one who entertains guests, is from Lat. *hospes*, a guest.

***To reckon without your host.*** To reckon from your own standpoint only. Guests who calculate their expenses at an hotel will often leave out certain items which the landlord adds in.

> Found in few minutes, to his cost,
> He did but count without his host.
>
> Butler, *Hudibras*, I, iii, 22

**Hostler** or **Ostler,** nowadays the man who looks after the horses of travellers at an inn, was originally the innkeeper, *hostelier*, keeper of an hostelry, himself. The so-called derivation of *ostler* from *oat-stealer* is merely a joke.

**Hot. *He* (*or she*)*'s a hot'un,*** or ***a hot member.*** Said of a person who is a bit of a rake – usually in a tone approaching awe or admiration. Also used intensively, as 'a hot 'un at billiards', i.e. an accomplished player.

***Hot air.*** Empty talk, boasting, threats, etc.; bombast. Hence, a *hot-air merchant*, one whose 'vaporisings' are 'full of sound and fury, signifying nothing'; a declamatory windbag.

***Hot cockles.*** A Christmas game. One blindfolded knelt down, and being struck had to guess who gave the blow.

> Thus poets passing time away,
> Like children at hot-cockles play. (1653)

***Hot cross buns.*** *See* Bun.

***Hot-foot.*** With speed; fast.

> And the Blackfoot who courted each foeman's approach,
> Faith, 'tis hot-foot he'd fly from the stout Father Roach.
>
> Lover

'Blackfoot' (*q.v.*) was the name of an Irish faction, similar to the Terry Alts in the early part of the 19th century.

***Hot stuff.*** 'So-and-so's hot stuff'; he's a hot 'un (*see above*); also said of almost anything that is admirable in its own way: 'Carpentier's boxing is hot stuff.'

***I'll make the place too hot to hold him.*** I'll 'show him up', or otherwise make this so unpleasant and disagreeable for him that he will not be able to stand it.

***I'll give it him hot and strong.*** I'll rate him most soundly and severely. Liquor very hot and strong takes one's breath away, and is apt to choke one. Similarly, *to get it hot*, to get severe punishment.

***To blow hot and cold.*** *See* Blow.

***To get into hot water.*** To get into difficulties, or in a state of trouble and anxiety. There may be an allusion to the old Anglo-Saxon ordeals here.

**Hotch-pot.** This word is used with the same significance as *hotch-potch* (*q.v.*), but it also has a legal use, which descends from Norman times in England, and is, apparently, the earlier. It meant the amalgamating of landed property that had belonged to a person dying intestate for the purpose of dividing the whole between the heirs in equal, or legal, shares.

It was also applied to such cases as the following:

Suppose a father has advanced money to one child, at his death this child receives such sum as, added to the loan, will make his share equal to that of the other members of the family. If not content, he must bring into *hotch-pot* the money that was advanced, and the whole is then divided amongst all the children according to the terms of the will.

**Hotch-potch** (Fr. *hochepot*; *hocher*, to shake together, and *pot*). A hodge-podge (*q.v.*); a mixed dish; a confused mixture or jumble; a thick broth containing meat and vegetables.

> A sort of soup, or broth, or brew,
> Or hotchpotch of all sorts of fishes.
>
> Thackeray, *Ballad of Bouillabaisse*

**Hotspur.** A fiery person who has no control over his temper. Harry Percy (d.1403), son of the first Earl of Northumberland (*see* Shakespeare, *1 Henry IV*), was so called. Lord Derby (d.1879), the Prime Minister, was sometimes called the '*Hotspur of debate*'. Lytton, in *New Timon*, calls him 'frank, haughty, bold, the Rupert of debate'.

**Hound. *To hound a person*** is to persecute him, or rather to set on persons to annoy him, as hounds are let from the slips at a hare or stag.

***You hound!*** An expression of the utmost contempt; you dirty cad! you cur!

**Hour. *A bad quarter of an hour.*** *See* Quart d'heure.

***At the eleventh hour.*** Just in time not to be too late; only just in time to obtain some benefit. The allusion is to the parable of labourers hired for the vineyard (Matt. 20).

***My hour is not yet come.*** The time for action has not yet arrived; properly, the hour of my death is not yet fully come. The allusion is to the belief that the hour of one's death is preordained.

> When Jesus knew that his hour was come.
> John 13:1

***In an evil hour.*** Acting under an unfortunate impulse. In astrology we have our lucky and unlucky hours.

***In the small hours of the morning.*** One, two, and three, after midnight.

***To keep good hours.*** To return home early every night; to go to bed betimes. Also, to be punctual in attending to one's work.

**Houri.** The black-eyed damsels of the Mohammedan Paradise, possessed of perpetual youth and beauty, whose virginity is renewable at pleasure; hence, in English use, any dark-eyed and attractive beauty.

Every believer will have seventy-two of these *houris* in Paradise, and, according to the Koran, his intercourse with them will be fruitful or otherwise, according to his wish. If an offspring is desired, it will grow to full estate in an hour.

**House. *A house of call.*** Some house, frequently a public-house, that one makes a point of visiting or using regularly; a house where workers in a particular trade meet when out of employment, and where they may be engaged.

***A house of correction.*** A jail governed by a keeper. Originally it was a place where vagrants were made to work, and small offenders were kept in ward for the correction of their offences.

***House to house.*** Performed at every house, one after another; as, 'a house-to-house canvass'.

***Like a house afire.*** Very rapidly. 'He is getting on like a house afire' means he is getting on excellently.

***The House.*** The workhouse; also a familiar name for Christ Church, Oxford, the London Stock Exchange, the House of Commons, etc.

***The House of ...*** denotes a royal or noble family with its ancestors and branches, as the *House of Windsor* (the British Royal Family), the *House of Stuart*, the *House of Brunswick*, etc.; also a commercial establishment or firm as the *House of Tellson*, the banking firm in Dickens's *Tale of Two Cities*, the *House of Cassell*, the publishers, etc.

***The House of God.*** Not solely a church, or a temple made with hands, but any place sanctified by God's presence. Thus, Jacob in the wilderness, where he saw the ladder set up leading from earth to heaven, said, 'This is none other but the house of God, and this is the gate of heaven' (Gen. 28:17).

***The House that Jack built.*** There are numerous similar glomerations. For example, the Hebrew parable of *The Two Zuzim*. The summation runs thus:

10. This is Yavah who vanquished
9. Death which killed
8. The butcher which slew
7. The ox which drank
6. The water which quenched
5. The fire which burnt
4. The stick which beat
3. The dog which worried
2. The cat which killed
1. The kid which my father bought for two zuzim.

(A zuzim was about a farthing.)

***To bring down the house.*** *See* Bring.

***To cry*** or ***proclaim from the housetop.*** To announce something in the most public manner possible. Jewish houses had flat paved roofs. Here the ancient Jews used to assemble for gossip; here, too, not infrequently, they slept; and here some of their festivals were held. From the housetops the rising of the sun was proclaimed, and public announcements were made.

> That which ye have spoken [whispered] in the ear ... shall be proclaimed upon the housetops.
> Luke 12:3

***To eat one out of house and home.*** *See* Eat.

***To keep house.*** To maintain an establishment. 'To go into housekeeping' is to start a private establishment.

***To keep a good house.*** To supply a bountiful table.

***To keep open house.*** To give free entertainment to all who choose to come.

***To throw the house out of the windows.*** To throw all things into confusion from exuberance of spirit.

**House-bote.** A term in old law denoting the amount of wood that a tenant is allowed to take from the land for repairs to the dwelling and for fuel. *Bote* is A.S. profit, compensation. *See* Boot.

**House-flag.** The distinguishing flag of a company of shipowners or of a single shipowner, as, for instance, that of the Cunard Company.

**House-leek.** Grown formerly on house-roofs, from the notion that it warded off lightning, fever, and evil spirits. Charlemagne made an edict that every one of his subjects should have house-leek, or 'Jove's beard', as it is also called, on his roof. The words are, *Et habet quisque supra domum suum Jovis barbam.*

> If the herb house-leek or syngreen do grow on the housetop, the same house is never stricken with lightning or thunder.
>
> Thomas Hill, *Natural and Arts. Conclusion* (16th cent.)

**Houses, Astrological.** In judicial astrology the whole heaven is divided into twelve portions by means of great circles crossing the north and south points of the horizon, through which the heavenly bodies pass every twenty-four hours. Each of these divisions is called a *house*; and in casting a horoscope (*q.v.*) the whole is divided into two parts (beginning from the east), six above and six below the horizon. The eastern ones are called the *ascendant*, because they are about to rise; the other six are the *descendant*, because they have already passed the zenith. The twelve houses each have their special functions – (1) the house of life; (2) fortune and riches; (3) brethren; (4) parents and relatives; (5) children; (6) health; (7) marriage; (8) death; (9) religion; (10) dignities; (11) friends and benefactors; (12) enemies.

Three houses were assigned to each of the four ages of the person whose horoscope was to be cast, and his lot in life was governed by the ascendancy or descendancy of these at the various periods, and by the stars which ruled in the particular 'houses'.

**Household, The.** Specifically, the immediate members of the Royal Family, with their retinue, court officials, servants, and attendants.

> [Lowther] had become a courtier; he had two good places, one in the Treasury, the other in the Household.
>
> Macaulay, *Hist. of England*, ch. xviii

***Household gods.*** The Lares and Penates (*q.v.*), who presided over the dwellings and domestic concerns of the ancient Romans; hence, in modern use, the valued possessions of home, all those things that go to endear it to one.

> Bearing a nation with all its household gods into exile. Longfellow, *Evangeline*

***Household Troops.*** Those troops whose special duty it is to attend the sovereign and guard the metropolis. They consist of the 1st and 2nd Life Guards, the Royal Horse Guards, and the five regiments of Foot Guards, the Grenadiers, Coldstreams, Scots, Irish, and Welsh Guards.

**Housel.** To give the Sacrament to (A.S. *husel*; connected with Goth. *hunsly*, sacrifice). *Cp.* Unhouselled.

> Children were christened, and men houseled and assoyled through all the land, except such as were in the bill of excommunication by name expressed. Holinshed, *Chronicle*

**Houssain.** Brother of Prince Ahmed in one of the *Arabian Nights* stories. He possessed a piece of carpet or tapestry of such wonderful power that anyone had only to sit upon it, and it would transport him in a moment to any place to which he desired to go.

> If Prince Houssain's flying tapestry or Astolpho's hippogriff had been shown, he would have judged them by the ordinary rules, and preferred a well-hung chariot.
>
> Sir Walter Scott

**Houyhnhnms** (*whinms*, or *whinhims*). A race of horses endowed with reason and all the finer characteristics of man, introduced with caustically satirical effect by Swift in his *Gulliver's Travels*. The name was the author's invention, coined in imitation of the 'whinny' of a horse.

> Nay, would kind Jove my organ so dispose
> To hymn harmonious Houyhnhnms through the nose
> I'd call thee Houhnhnm, that high-sounding name;
> Thy children's noses all should twang the same.
>
> Pope, *Mary Gulliver to Capt. Lemuel Gulliver; an Epistle*

**Howard. *All the blood of all the Howards.*** All the nobility of our best aristocracy. The ducal house of Norfolk, the family name of which is *Howard*, stands at the head of the English peerage, and is interwoven in all our history.

> What could ennoble sots, or slaves, or cowards?
> Alas! not all the blood of all the Howards.
>
> Pope, *Essay on Man*, iv, 216

It has been said that 'Howard is from hog-ward', and that the original Howards were so called from their avocation, which was to tend the pigs; but this is by no means certain. *Hogward* gives the surnames *Hoggard*, *Hoggart*, and *Hogarth*; 'Howard' is more likely to be a form of *Hayward*, originally the village official who guarded cattle grazing on the common and saw that they did not stray on to the ground where was grown the grass for the winter's hay.

The name 'Howard' does not appear in the Norfolk pedigree till the 15th century, when one of the co-heiresses of the 5th Duke of Norfolk of the old line – a Mowbray – married Sir Robert Howard. Their son, Sir John, was made 1st Duke of the present line in 1483. *See* Norfolk-Howards.

***The female Howard.*** Mrs Elizabeth Fry (1780–1845), the Quaker philanthropist and worker in prisons; so called in allusion to John Howard (1726–90), who is celebrated for his exertions on behalf of prison reform and for the successes which attended his efforts. He visited prisons not only in the United Kingdom and Ireland, but all over the Continent, and in 1777 published *The State of Prisons in England and Wales*, etc.

The radiant path that Howard trod to Heaven.
Bloomfield, *Farmer's Boy; Autumn*

**Howdie** or **Howdy.** The Scottish word for a midwife.

When skirlin weanies see the light,
Thou maks the gossips clatter bright,
How fumbling cuifs their dearies slight;
Wae worth the name!
Nae howdie gets a social night.
Or plack frae them.
Burns, *Scotch Drink*

**Howleglass.** An old form of *Owlglass. See* Eulenspiegel.

**Hrimfaxi.** *See* Horse.

**Hub.** The nave of a wheel; a boss. The Americans call Boston, Massachusetts, 'The hub of the solar system'; i.e. the centre round which everything revolves and is dependent.

Boston State-house is the hub of the solar system.
Holmes, *Autocrat of the Breakfast Table*, ch. vi, p. 143.

Calcutta swaggers as if it were the hub of the universe. *Daily News*, 1886

***Up to the hub.*** Fully, entirely, as far as possible. If a cart sinks in the mud up to the hub, it can sink no lower; if a man is thrust through with a sword up to the hub, the entire sword has passed through him; and if a quoit strikes the hub, it is not possible to do better.

I shouldn't commune with nobody that didn't believe in election up to the hub.
Mrs Stowe, *Dred*, vol. i, p. 311

**Hubal.** An idol of the pre-Mohammedan Arabs, brought from Bulka, in Syria, by Amir Ibn-Lohei, who asserted that it would procure rain when wanted. It was the statue of a man in red agate; one hand being lost, a golden one was supplied. He held in his hand seven arrows without feathers, such as the Arabians use in divination. It was destroyed in the eighth year of 'the Flight'.

**Hubert, St.** Patron saint of huntsmen (d.727). He was the son of Bertrand, Duc d'Acquitaine, and cousin of King Pepin. Hubert was so fond of the chase that he neglected his religious duties for his favourite amusement, till one day a stag bearing a crucifix menaced him with eternal perdition unless he reformed. Upon this he entered the cloister, became in time Bishop of Liège, and the apostle of Ardennes and Brabant. Those who were descended of his race were supposed to possess the power of curing the bite of mad dogs.

In art he is represented as a bishop with a miniature stag resting on the book in his hand, or as a huntsman kneeling to the miraculous crucifix borne by the stag.

**Hudibras.** A satirical poem in three parts and nine cantos (published 1663–78) by Samuel Butler, so named from its hero, who is said to be a caricature of Sir Samuel Luke, a patron of Butler. The *Grub Street Journal* (1731) maintains it was Colonel Rolle, of Devonshire, with whom the poet lodged for some time, and adds that the name is derived from Hugh de Bras, the patron saint of the county. He represents the Presbyterian party, and his squire the Independents.

'Tis sung there is a valiant Mameluke,
In foreign land ycleped [*Sir Samuel Luke*].
Butler, *Hudibras*, i, 1

There are two characters of this name in Spenser's *Faërie Queene*: (1) the lover of Elissa (II, ii), typifying rashness, and (2) a legendary king of Britain (II, x, 25).

**Hudibrastic Verse.** A doggerel eight-syllable rhyming verse, after the style of Butler's *Hudibras*.

**Hudson, Sir Jeffrey** (1619–82). The famous dwarf, at one time page to Queen Henrietta Maria. When he was thirty years old he was 18 in. high, but he later reached 3 ft 6 in. or 3 ft 9 in. He was a captain of horse in the Civil War; and afterwards was captured by pirates and sold as a slave in Barbary, but managed to escape. Scott introduced him in his *Peveril of the Peak*, ch. xxxiv; Vandyke immortalised him by his brush; and his clothes are said to be preserved in Sir Hans Sloane's museum.

**Hue and Cry.** The old legal name for the official outcry made when calling for assistance in the pursuit of a criminal escaping from justice (O.Fr.

*huer*, to shout). Persons failing to respond when the 'hue and cry' was raised were liable to penalties; hence, a clamour or outcry, a cry of alarm.

> But now by this, with noyse of late uprore,
> The hue and cry was raysed all about.
>
> Spenser, *Faërie Queene*, VI, xi, 46

**Hug.** ***To hug the shore.*** In the case of a ship, to keep as close to the shore as is compatible with the vessel's safety, when at sea.

***To hug the wind.*** To keep a ship close hauled.

**Hugger-mugger.** One of a large class of reduplicated words (*cp. namby-pamby*, *skimble-skamble*, *flip-flap*, etc.) of uncertain origin, but probably an extension of *hug*. Clandestinely, secretly; also, in an untidy, disorderly manner.

The king in *Hamlet* says of Polonius: 'We have done but greenly in hugger-mugger to inter him' – i.e. to smuggle him into the grave clandestinely and without ceremony.

North, in his *Plutarch*, says: 'Antonius thought that his body should be honourably buried, and not in hugger-mugger' (clandestinely).

Ralph says:

> While I, in hugger-mugger hid,
> Have noted all they said and did.
>
> Butler, *Hudibras*, iii, 3

In modern speech we say – *He lives in a hugger-mugger sort of way*; *the rooms were all hugger-mugger* (disorderly).

**Hugh of Lincoln.** It is said that the Jews in 1255 stole a boy of 8 years old named Hugh, whom they tortured for ten days and then crucified or drowned in a well. Eighteen of the richest Jews of Lincoln were hanged for taking part in this affair, and more would have been put to death had it not been for the intercession of the Franciscans; the boy was buried in state. This is the subject of *The Prioress's Tale* of Chaucer, and it is given in *Alphonsus of Lincoln* (1459), etc. In Rymer's *Foedera* are several documents relating to this event. *Cp.* William of Norwich.

**Huginn and Muninn.** In *Scandinavian mythology*, the two ravens that sit on the shoulders of Odin; they typify *thought* and *memory*.

> Perhaps the nursery saying, 'A little bird told me that', is a corruption of Hugo and Munin, and so we have the old Northern superstition lingering about us without our being aware of it.
>
> Julia Goddard, *Joyce Dormer's Story*, ii, 11

**Huguenot.** The French Protestants (Calvinists) of the 16th and 17th centuries. The name was first applied to the revolutionaries of Geneva by the adherents of the Duke of Savoy, about 1560, and is probably an adaptation of the Ger. *eidgenossen*, confederates.

Philippe de Mornay (1549–1623), the great supporter of the French Protestants, was nicknamed 'the Huguenot Pope'.

**Huitzilopochtli.** *See* Mexitl.

**Hulda.** The old German goddess of marriage and fecundity, who sent bridegrooms to maidens and children to the married. The name means 'the Benignant', and is a euphemistic appellation.

***Hulda is making her bed.*** It snows.

**Hulking.** ***A great hulking fellow.*** A great overgrown one. A hulk is a large, unwieldy ship, or the body of a superannuated one, that looks very clumsy as it lies ashore. Shakespeare says – referring to Falstaff:

> Harry Monmouth's brawn, the hulk Sir John
> Is prisoner to your son. *2 Henry IV*, 1, 1

**Hull.** An old beggars' and vagabonds' 'prayer', quoted by Taylor, the Water Poet (early 17th cent.), was:

> From Hull, Hell, and Halifax,
> Good Lord, deliver us.

'Hell' was probably the least feared as being farthest from them; Hull was to be avoided because it was so well governed that beggars had little chance of getting anything without doing hard labour for it; and Halifax, because anyone caught stealing cloth in that town was beheaded without intermediate proceedings.

**Hullabaloo.** Uproar. The word is fairly modern (middle of the 17th cent.); it is of uncertain origin, but is probably a reduplicated word formed on *holloa!* or *hullo! Cp.* Hurly-burly.

**Hulsean Lectures.** Instituted by the Rev. John Hulse, of Cheshire, in 1777. Some four or six sermons on Christian evidences are preached annually at Great St Mary's, Cambridge, by the *Hulsean Lecturer*, who, till 1860, was entitled the *Christian Advocate*. Hulse, who died in 1790, also bequeathed estates to the University as an endowment for a Hulsean Professor of Divinity, and for certain Hulsean prizes.

**Hum and haw, To.** To hesitate to give a positive plain answer; to hesitate in making a speech. To introduce *hum* and *haw* between words which ought to follow each other freely.

**Huma.** A fabulous Oriental bird which never alights, but is always on the wing. It is said that every head which it overshadows will wear a crown. The bird suspended over the throne of

Tippoo Sahib at Seringapatam represented this poetical fancy.

In the first chapter of the *Autocrat of the Breakfast Table* a certain popular lecturer is made to describe himself, in allusion to his many wanderings, to this bird: 'Yes, I am like the Huma, the bird that never lights; being always in the cars, as the Huma is always on the wing.'

**Humanitarians.** A name that used to be given to certain Arian heretics who believed that Jesus Christ was only man. The disciples of St Simon were so called also, because they maintained the perfectibility of human nature without the aid of grace.

Nowadays the term is usually applied (often with slightly contemptuous import) to philanthropists whose object is the welfare of humanity at large.

**Humanities** or **Humanity Studies.** Grammar, rhetoric, and poetry, with Greek and Latin (*literae humaniores*); in contradistinction to divinity (*literae divinae*).

> The humanities ... is used to designate those studies which are considered the most specially adapted for training ... true humanity in every man.
>
> Trench, *Study of Words*, Lect. iii

A degree, L.H.D., Litterarum Humaniorum Doctor (Doctor of Humane Letters), is given at some of the American Universities.

**Humber.** The legendary king of the Huns, who are fabled to have invaded Britain about 1000 BC; he was defeated in a great battle by Locrine, and his body was cast into the river Abus, which was forthwith renamed the Humber. (*Geoffrey of Monmouth.*)

> Their chieftain Humber namëd was aright
> Unto the mighty streame him to betake,
> Where he an end of battell and of life did make.
>
> Spenser, *Faërie Queene*, II, x, 16

**Humble Bee.** A corruption of the Ger. *hummel bee*, the buzzing bee. Sometimes called the Dumble-dor. Also Bumble-bee, from its booming drone.

**Humble Cow.** A cow without horns.

> 'That', said John with a broad grin, 'was Grizzel chasing the humble cow out of the close.'
>
> Scott, *Guy Mannering*, ch. ix

**Humble Pie.** ***To eat humble pie***. To come down from a position you have assumed; to be obliged to take 'a lower room'. Here 'humble' is a pun on *umble*, the umbels being the heart, liver, and entrails of the deer, the huntsman's perquisites. When the lord and his household dined the venison pasty was served on the dais, but the *umbles* were made into a pie for the huntsman and his fellows, who took the lower seats.

**Humbug.** A hoax or imposition; also (as verb) to hoax, cajole, impose upon. The word is of unknown origin, but was new in the middle of the 18th century, and the Earl of Orrery, writing in the *Connoisseur* in 1754, called it a –

> New-coined expression, which is only to be found in the nonsensical vocabulary and sounds absurd and disagreeable whenever it is pronounced.

**Humming Ale.** Strong liquor that froths well, and causes a humming in the head of the drinker.

> Let us fortify our stomachs with a slice or two of hung beef, and a horn or so of humming stingo.
>
> Pierce Egan, *Tom and Jerry*, ch. vii

**Hummums.** The hotel of this name in Covent Garden is on the site of an old bathing establishment founded here about 1631; so called from the Pers. *humoun* (a sweating or Turkish bath).

**Humour.** As *good humour*, *ill* or *bad humour*, etc. According to an ancient theory, there are four principal humours in the body: phlegm, blood, choler, and black bile. As any one of these predominates it determines the temper of the mind and body; hence the expressions sanguine, choleric, phlegmatic, and melancholic humours. A just balance made a good compound called 'good humour'; a preponderance of any one of the four made a bad compound called an ill or evil humour. *See* Ben Jonson's *Every Man Out of His Humour* (*Prologue*).

**Humpback, The.** Geronimo Amelunghi, *Il Gobodi Pisa*, an Italian burlesque poet of the mid-16th century.

Andrea Solario, the Italian painter, *Del Gobbo* (1470–1527).

**Humphrey.** ***To dine with Duke Humphrey***. To have no dinner to go to. Humphrey, Duke of Gloucester, son of Henry IV, the 'Good Duke Humphrey' (*see under* Good), was renowned for his hospitality. At death it was reported that a monument would be erected to him in St Paul's, but his body was interred at St Albans. The tomb of Sir John Beauchamp (d.1358), on the south side of the nave of old St Paul's, was popularly supposed to be that of the Duke; and when the promenaders left for dinner, the poor stay-behinds who had no dinner to go to, or who feared to leave the precincts of the cathedral because, once outside, they could be arrested for debt, used to say to the gay sparks who asked if they were going, that they would 'dine with Duke Humphrey' that day.

The expression used to be very common; and a similar one was *To sup with Sir Thomas Gresham*, the Exchange built by Sir Thomas being a common lounge.

Though little coin thy purseless pocket line,
Yet with great company thou art taken up;
For often with Duke Humphrey thou dost dine,
And often with Sir Thomas Gresham sup.

Hayman, *Quodlibet* (*Epigram on a Loafer*), 1628

**Humpty Dumpty.** A little deformed dwarf, 'humpy' and 'dumpy'. There used to be a drink of this name, composed of ale boiled with brandy; and it is also applied – in allusion to the old nursery rhyme – to an egg, and to anything that is, or may be, irretrievably shattered.

**Hundred.** An English county division dating from pre-Conquest times, and supposed to be so called either because it comprised exactly one hundred hides of land, or one hundred families, who were grouped together for civil and military purposes, these families being collectively responsible to the authorities in cases of crime within the 'hundred'.

Northumberland, Cumberland, Westmorland, and Durham were divided into 'wards' (*q.v.*).

Yorkshire, Lincolnshire, and Notts, into 'wapentakes' (*q.v.*). Yorkshire has also a special division, called 'ridings' (*q.v.*).

Kent was divided into five 'lathes' (*q.v.*), with subordinate hundreds.

Sussex into six 'rapes' (*q.v.*), with subordinate hundreds.

***Great,*** or ***long hundred.*** Six score, a hundred and twenty.

***Hero of the hundred fights.*** Conn, a legendary Irish king, was so called by O'Gnive, the bard of O'Niel: 'Conn, of the hundred fights, sleeps in his grass-grown tomb.' The epithet has also been applied to Nelson, Wellington, and other famous commanders.

***Hundreds and thousands.*** A name given by sweetstuff-sellers to almost any very tiny comfits.

***It will be all the same a hundred years hence.*** An exclamation of despair – it doesn't much matter *what* happens. It is an old saying, and occurs in Ray's *Collection*, 1742. A similar one is:

A thousand pounds and a bottle of hay
Is all one thing at Doom's-day. Ray

***Not a hundred miles off.*** An indirect way of saying in this very neighbourhood, or very spot. The phrase is employed when it would be indiscreet or dangerous to refer more directly to the person or place hinted at.

***The Chiltern Hundreds.*** *See* Chiltern.

***The Hundred Days.*** The days between March 20th, 1815, when Napoleon reached the Tuileries, after his escape from Elba, and June 28th, the date of the second restoration of Louis XVIII. These hundred days were noted for five things:

The additional Act to the constitutions of the empire, April 22;
The Coalition;
The Champ de Mai, June 1;
The battle of Waterloo, June 18;
The second abdication of Napoleon in favour of his son, June 22.

Napoleon left Elba February 26th; landed near Cannes March 1st, entered Paris March 20th, and signed his abdication June 22nd.

The address of the Count de Chambord, the prefect, begins: 'A hundred days, sire, have elapsed since the fatal moment when your Majesty was forced to quit your capital in the midst of tears.' This is the origin of the phrase.

***The Hundred-eyed.*** Argus, in Greek and Latin fable. Juno appointed him guardian of Io (the cow), but Jupiter caused him to be put to death; whereupon Juno transplanted his eyes into the tail of her peacock.

***The Hundred-handed.*** Three of the sons of Uranus, viz. Aegaeon or Briareus, Kottos, and Gyges or Gyes. After the war between Zeus and the Titans, when the latter were overcome and hurled into Tartarus, the Hundred-handed ones were set to keep watch and ward over them.

Sometimes Cerberus (*q.v.*) is so called, because from his three necks sprang writhing snakes instead of hair.

***The Hundred Years War.*** The long series of wars between France and England, beginning in the reign of Edward III, 1337, and ending in that of Henry VI, 1453.

The first battle was a naval action off Sluys, and the last the fight at Castillon. It originated in English claims to the French crown, and resulted in the English being expelled from the whole of France, except Calais.

**Hungary Water.** Made of rosemary flowers and spirit, said to be so called because the receipt was given by a hermit to a Queen of Hungary.

**Hungr** (*hunger*). The dish out of which the Scandinavian goddess Hel (*q.v.*) was wont to feed.

**Hungry.** ***Hungry dogs will eat dirty puddings.*** *See* Dog.

There are many common similes expressive of hunger, among which are – hungry as a hawk, a hunter, a church mouse (*cp.* Poor), a dog. James Thomson (*Seasons: Winter*) has 'Hungry as the grave', and Oliver Wendell Holmes 'Hungry as the chap that said a turkey was too much for one, not enough for two'.

***The Hungry Forties.*** A term applied to the period prior to the repeal of the Corn Laws by Sir Robert Peel in 1846, when, owing to the high price of food, distress was very common among the working population.

**Hunks. *An old hunks*.** A screw, a hard, selfish, mean fellow. The term appears in late Elizabethan times when it was a name commonly given to performing bears – and probably has its origin in some unknown person of cross (*cp.* 'Cross as a bear') or miserly character.

**Hunt. *Like Hunt's dog, he would neither go to church nor stay at home*.** A Shropshire saying. The story is that one Hunt, a labouring man, kept a mastiff, which, on being shut up while his master went to church, howled and barked so as to disturb the whole congregation; whereupon Hunt thought he would take him to church the next Sunday, but the dog positively refused to enter. The proverb is applied to a self-willed person, who will neither be led nor driven.

**Hunter. *Mr and Mrs Leo Hunter*.** Persons who hunt up the celebrities, or 'lions', to grace their parties and bring them renown and reputation. They appeared (in print) originally in Dickens's *Pickwick Papers*.

**Hunting. *He who hunts two hares leaves one and loses the other*.** No one can do well or properly two things at once, he 'falls between two stools'. 'No man can serve two masters.'

> Like a man to double business bound,
> I stand in pause where I shall first begin
> And both neglect. Shakespeare, *Hamlet*, 3, 3

**Huntindon.** Literally, 'the hunter's hill'. It was called by the Saxons *Huntantun*, and in Doomsday *Hunter's dune*, and appears to have derived its name from its situation in a country which was anciently an extensive forest well suited for purposes of the chase.

**Huntingdonians.** Members of 'the Countess of Huntingdon's Connection', a sect of Calvinistic Methodists founded in 1748 by Selina, widow of the ninth Earl of Huntingdon, and George Whitefield, who had become her chaplain after his separation from the Wesleys.

**Huon de Bordeaux.** The hero of a mediaeval French *chanson de geste* of that name, a late prose version of which was translated into English by Lord Berners in the time of Henry VIII.

Huon wished to go from Syria to Babylon, and learnt that the shortest and best way was through a wood sixteen leagues long, and full of fairies; that few could go that way because King Oberon was sure to encounter them. Whoever spoke to him was lost for ever, and if a traveller refused to answer him, he raised a most horrible storm of wind and rain, and made the forest seem one great river. Huon proceeded on his way, and finally addressed Oberon, who told him the history of his birth. They became great friends, and when Oberon went to Paradise he left Huon his successor as lord and king of Mommur. He married Esclairmond, and was crowned 'King of all Faerie'.

**Hurdy-gurdy.** A stringed musical instrument, like a rude guitar, the 'music' of which is produced by the friction of a rosined wheel on the strings, which are 'stopped' by means of keys. It was the forerunner of the modern barrel-organ or piano-organ of the streets.

**Hurlo-Thrumbo.** A ridiculous burlesque, which in 1729–30 had an extraordinary run at the Haymarket theatre. So great was its popularity that a club called 'The Hurlo-Thrumbo Society' was formed. The author was Samuel Johnson (1691–1773), a half-mad dancing master, who put this motto on the title-page when the burlesque was printed:

> Ye sons of fire, read my *Hurlo-Thrumbo*,
> Turn it betwixt your finger and your thumbo,
> And being quite undone, be quite struck dumbo.

**Hurly-burly.** Uproar, tumult, especially of battle. A reduplication of *hurly*. *Cp.* Hullabaloo.

> Now day began to break, and the army to fall again into good order, and all the hurly-burly to cease. *North's Plutarch, Antonius* (1579)

> When the hurly-burly's done,
> When the battle's lost and won.
> The Witches, in *Macbeth*, 1, 1

In the *Garden of Eloquence* (1577) the word is given as a specimen of onomatopoeia.

**Hurrah.** A later (17th cent.) form of the earlier *huzza*, an imitative sound expressing joy, enthusiasm, pleasure at victory, etc. The word may be connected with the Low Ger. *hurra*, in which case it was probably introduced by soldiers about the time of the Thirty Years' War.

The Norman battle-cry was 'Ha Rollo!' or 'Ha Rou!'

The Saxon cry of 'Out! Out, Holy Crosse!' rose high above the Norman sound of 'Ha Rou! Ha Rou, Notre Dame!'

Lord Lytton, *Harold*, Bk xii, ch. 8

**Hurricane.** An 18th century term for a large private party or rout; so called from its hurry, bustle, and noise. *Cp.* Drum.

The word is West Indian, and was introduced through Spanish; it means a very violent storm of wind.

**Hurry.** An imitative word, probably connected with *hurl* (as in *hurly-burly*), which first appears in Shakespeare:

She spied the hunted boar,<br>
Whose frothy mouth ...<br>
A second fear through all her sinews spread,<br>
Which madly hurries her she knows not whither.

*Venus and Adonis*, 904

***Don't hurry, Hopkins.*** A satirical reproof to those who are not prompt in their payments. It is said that one Hopkins, of Kentucky, gave a creditor a promissory note on which was this memorandum, 'The said Hopkins is not to be hurried in paying the above.'

**Hurry-skurry.** Another ricochet word with which our language abounds. It means a confused haste, or rather, haste without waiting for the due ordering of things; pell-mell.

**Husband.** The word is Anglo-Saxon, from *hus*, house, and Old Norse *bondi*, a freeholder or yeoman, from *bua*, to dwell; hence the word is literally a house-owner in his capacity as head of the household, and so came to be applied to a man joined to a woman in marriage, who was, naturally, the head of his household. When Sir John Paston, writing to his mother in 1475, said –

I purpose to leeffe alle heer, and come home to you and be your hosbonde and balyff

he was merely proposing to come and manage her household for her. We use the word in the same sense in such phrases as *To husband one's resources.*

Tusser was in error when he derived the word from 'houseband', as in the following distich:

The name of the husband, what is it to say?<br>
Of wife and of *house*-hold the *band* and the stay.

*Five Hundred Points of Good Husbandry*

**Husbands' Boat.** The name that used to be given to the boat which left London on Saturday, and took to Margate those fathers of families who were spending the holidays in that neighbourhood during the summer months.

I shall never forget the evening when we went down to the jetty to see the husbands' boat come in.

*The Mistletoe Bough*

**Hush-money.** Money given as a bribe for silence or 'hushing' a matter up.

**Hushai.** In Dryden's *Absalom and Achitophel* (*q.v.*) is Laurence Hyde, Earl of Rochester (1641–1711). Hushai was David's friend, who opposed the counsels of Ahithophel, and caused the plot of Absalom to miscarry; so Rochester defeated the schemes of Shaftesbury, and brought to naught the rebellion of the Duke of Monmouth.

**Hussar.** An Hungarian word (*huszar*), which is ultimately from the same Greek word that gives us our *corsair*. It was applied in the time of Matthias Corvinus – Hunyadi – (mid-15th cent.), to a body of light horsemen, and was hence adopted in various European armies to denote light cavalry.

**Hussites.** Followers of John Huss, the Bohemian reformer, in the 15th century. *Cp.* Bethlemenites.

**Hussy.** Nowadays a word of contempt, implying an ill-behaved girl, a 'jade' or 'minx', this is no other than the honourable appellation *housewife* (pron. 'hussif'). Just as *wench* has come down in the world, and *woman* seems to be coming down, so *hussy* has been degraded.

**Hustings.** An Anglo-Saxon word, meaning originally the immediate council of the king, from *hus*, house (i.e. the royal house), and *thing*, assembly; the *hus-thing* was the assembly of the house as apart from the *thing*, the general assembly of the people. London has still its *Court of Hustings*, which is held by the Lord Mayor, Sheriffs, Recorder and Aldermen to consider gifts offered to the City, and which was formerly the supreme court (common pleas, probate, etc.) of the City. The hustings of elections were, previous to the Ballot Act of 1872, the platforms from which candidates made their election addresses, etc.; hence *to be beaten at the hustings* means to lose at an election.

**Hutchinsonians.** Followers of Anne Hutchinson (d.1643), an antinomian reformer of New England, who retired to Rhode Island, and with fifteen of her children was murdered by the Indians.

**Hutin.** ***Louis le Hutin***. Louis X (1289, 1314–16) was so nicknamed. It means 'the quarreller', 'the stubborn or headstrong one', and it is uncertain why the name was given to this insignificant king of France.

**Hutkin.** A word in some dialects for a cover for a sore finger, made by cutting off the finger of an old glove; called also a *hut*, *hutch*, and *hutchkin*.

**Huzza!** An exclamation of joy or applause; the forerunner of *Hurrah!* (*q.v.*). The word has no etymology, being merely an extension of an involuntary vocable, such as *Chut!* or *Pshaw!*

**Hvergelmir.** A fountain in Niflheim, whence issue the twelve poisonous rivers (*Elivagar*), which generatece, snow, wind, and rain. (*Scandinavian mythology*.)

**Hyacinth.** According to Grecian fable, the son of Anyclas, a Spartan king. The lad was beloved by Apollo and Zephyr, and as he preferred the sun-god, Zephyr drove Apollo's quoit at his head, and killed him. The blood became a flower, and the petals are inscribed with the signature A I, meaning woe. (Virgil, *Eclogues*, iii, 106.)

**Hyades** (Gr. *huein*, to rain). Seven nymphs placed among the stars, in the constellation Taurus, which threaten rain when they rise with the sun. The fable is that they wept the death of their brother Hyas so bitterly that Zeus, out of compassion, took them to heaven.

> The seaman sees the Hyades
> Gather an army of Cimmerian clouds ...
> All-fearful folds his sails, and sounds the main.
> Lifting his prayers to the heavens for aid
> Against the terror of the winds and waves.
>
> Marlowe, *1 Tamburlaine*, III, ii

**Hydra.** A monster of the Lernean marshes, in Argolis. It had nine heads, and it was one of the twelve labours of Hercules to kill it. As soon as he struck off one of its heads, two shot up in its place; hence *hydra-headed* applied to a difficulty which goes on increasing as it is combated.

***Hydra-headed multitude.*** The rabble, which not only is many-headed numerically, but seems to grow more numerous the more it is attacked and resisted.

**Hyena.** Held in veneration by the ancient Egyptians. It is fabled that a certain stone, called the 'hyaenia', is found in the eye of the creature, and Pliny asserts (*Nat. Hist.*, xxxvii, 60) that when placed under the tongue it imparts the gift of prophecy.

> The skilful Lapidarists of Germany affirm that this beast hath a stone in his eye (or rather his head) called Hyaena or Hyaenius.
>
> Topsell, *Four-footed Beasts* (1607)

**Hygeia.** Goddess of health in *Greek mythology*, and the daughter of Aesculapius (*q.v.*). Her symbol was a serpent drinking from a cup in her hand.

**Hyksos** (*Shepherd Kings*). A line of six or more foreign rulers over Egypt, who reigned for about 250 years between the XIIth and XVIIIth Dynasties, i.e. somewhere about 2000 BC. It is uncertain whence they came, who they were, what they did, or whither they went; they left little in the way of records or monuments, and practically all that is known of them is the (historically speaking) very unsatisfactory notice gleaned by Josephus from Manetho.

> The exact nationality of the Hyksos is still a matter of dispute. All we know for certainty is that they came from Asia, and they brought with them in their train vast numbers of Semites.
>
> Sayce, *Races of the Old Testament* (1891)

**Hylas.** A boy beloved by Hercules, carried off by the nymphs while drawing water from a fountain in Mysia.

**Hyleg.** That planet, or point of the sky, which, according to astrologers, dominates at man's birth, and influences his whole life. The word is probably Persian.

**Hymen.** Properly, a marriage song of the ancient Greeks; later personified as the god of marriage, represented as a youth carrying a torch and veil – a more mature Eros, or Cupid.

**Hymettus.** A mountain in Attica, famous for its honey. *Cp.* Hybla.

> There, flowery hill, Hymettus, with the sound
> Of bees' industrious murmur, oft invites
> To studious musing.
>
> Milton, *Paradise Regained*, IV, 247

**Hymir.** In *Scandinavian mythology*, a giant with a frosty beard who personifies the inhospitable sea. He owned the kettle in which the gods brewed their ale, and it was he who took Thor in his boat when that god went to kill the Midgard serpent, and robbed him of his prey.

**Hymnus Eucharisticus.** *See* Eucharist.

**Hyperbole.** The rhetorical figure of speech which consists of exaggeration or extravagance in statement for the purpose of giving effect but not intended to be taken *au pied de la lettre* – e.g. 'the waves were mountains high'.

> Hyperboles are of two kinds; either such as are employed in description, or such as are suggested by the warmth of passion.
>
> Lindley Murray, *English Grammar*, 1, p. 510

**Hyperboreans.** A happy people of early Greek legend, who were supposed to dwell on the other side of the spot where the North Wind had its birth, and therefore to enjoy perpetual warmth and sunshine. They were said to be the oldest of the human race, the most virtuous, and the most happy; to dwell for some thousand years under a cloudless sky, in fields yielding double harvests, and in the enjoyment of perpetual spring.

Later fable held that they had not an atmosphere like our own, but one consisting wholly of feathers. Both Herodotus and Pliny mention this fiction, which they say was suggested by the quantity of snow observed to fall in those regions. (Herodotus, iv, 31.)

**Hyperion.** In *Greek mythology*, one of the Titans, son of Uranus and Ge, and father of Helios, Selene, and Eos (the Sun, Moon, and Dawn). The name is sometimes given by poets to the sun itself, but not by Keats in his wonderful 'poetical fragment' of this name (1820).

**Hypermnestra.** Wife of Lynceus, and the only one of the fifty daughters of Danaos who did not murder her husband on their bridal night. *See* Danaides.

**Hypnotism.** The art of producing trance-sleep, or the state of being hypnotised. Dr James Braid of Manchester gave it this name (1843), after first having called it *neuro-hypnotism*, an inducing to sleep of the nerves (Gr.).

> The method, discovered by Mr Braid, of producing this state ... appropriately designated ... hypnotism, consists in the maintenance of a fixed gaze for several minutes ... on a bright object placed somewhat above [the line of sight], at so short a distance [as to produce pain].
>
> Carpenter, *Principles of Mental Physiology*, ii, i

**Hypochondria** (Gr. *hypo*, *chondros*, under the cartilage – i.e. the spaces on each side of the epigastric region). A morbid depression of spirits for which there is no known or defined cause, so called because it was supposed to be caused by some derangement in these parts, which were held to be the seat of melancholy.

**Hypocrite.** ***Prince of hypocrites.*** Tiberius Caesar (42 BC, AD 14 to 37) was so called because he affected a great regard for decency, but indulged in the most detestable lust and cruelty.

Abdallah Ibn Obba and his partisans were called *The Hypocrites* by Mahomet, because they feigned to be friends, but were in reality foes.

***Hypocrites' Isle.*** *See* Chaneph.

**Hypodorian Mode.** *See* Aeolian.

**Hypostatic Union.** The union of the three Persons in the Trinity; also the union of the Divine and Human in Christ. The *hypostasis* (Gr. *hypo*, under, *stasis*, standing, hence foundation, essence) is the personal existence as distinguished both from *nature* and *substance*.

> We do not find, indeed, that the hypostatic pre-existence of Christ was an article of their creed [i.e. of the Nazarenes].
>
> Fisher, *Supernatural Origin of Christianity*, essay v, p. 319

**Hyson.** One of the varieties of Chinese green tea; so called from *hei-ch'un*, bright spring. *Young hyson*, a still better variety, is *Yü-ch'ien*, before the rains, meaning that the leaf is picked before the commencement of the rainy season.

**Hyssop.** David says (Ps. 51:7): 'Purge me with hyssop, and I shall be clean.' The reference is to the custom of ceremonially sprinkling the unclean with a bunch of hyssop dipped in water, in which had been mixed the ashes of a red heifer. This was done as they left the Court of the Gentiles to enter the Court of the Women (Numb. 19:17).

**Hysteron Proteron** (Gr., 'hinder former'). An inversion, putting 'the cart before the horse'; the figure of speech in rhetoric in which, usually for the sake of emphasis, the word that should come last is placed first, or the second of two consecutive propositions is stated first.

# I

**I.** The ninth letter of the alphabet, also of the futhorc (*q.v.*), representing the Greek *iota* and Semitic *yod*. The written (and printed) *i* and *j* were for long interchangeable; it was only in the 19th century that in dictionaries, etc., they were treated as separate letters (in Johnson's *Dictionary*, for instance, *iambic* comes between *jamb* and *jangle*), and hence in many series – such as the signatures of sheets in a book, hall-marks on plate, etc. – either I or J is omitted. *Cp.* U.

The dot on the small *i* is not originally part of the letter, but was introduced about the 11th century as a diacritic in cases where two *i*'s came together (e.g. *filii*) to distinguish between these and *u*.

***To dot one's i's.*** To be meticulous – particular about things of apparently no consequence.

***To dot the i's and cross the t's.*** To clinch an argument; to perfect some piece of work by putting the last finishing touches to it.

**I.H.S.** – i.e. the Greek ΙΗΣ, meaning ΙΗΣους (Jesus), the long e (H) being mistaken for a capital H, and the dash perverted into a cross. The letters being thus obtained, St Bernardine of Siena, in 1347, applied them to *Jesus Hominum Salvator* (Jesus, the Saviour of men), another application being *In hac salus* (safety in this, i.e. the Cross).

**IOU,** i.e. 'I owe you'. The memorandum of a debt given by the borrower to the lender. It requires no stamp unless it specifies a day of payment, when it becomes a *bill*, and must be stamped.

**I.R.A.** The Irish Republican Army, which opposed the Crown forces, R.I.C., 'Black and Tans', etc., in the rebellion that preceded the grant of dominion status in 1921.

**I.R.B.** Irish Republican Brotherhood, the Fenians of the eighteen-sixties, etc.

**Iambic.** An *iamb*, or *iambus*, is a metrical foot consisting of a short syllable followed by a long one, as *away*, *deduce*, or an unaccented followed by an accented, as *be gone! Iambic* verse is verse based on iambs, as, for instance, the Alexandrine measure, which consists of six iambuses:

> I think the thoughts you think; and if I have the knack
> Of fitting thoughts to words, you peradventure lack,
> Envy me not the chance, yourselves more fortunate!
>
> Browning, *Fifine at the Fair*, lxxvi

***Father of Iambic verse,*** Archilochos of Paros (fl. *c.*700 BC).

**Ianthe,** to whom Lord Byron dedicated his *Childe Harold*, was Lady Charlotte Harley, born 1801, and only eleven years old at the time. He borrowed it from Landor, who had thus 'etherealised' the middle name of his early sweetheart Sophia *Jane* Swift, who became the Countess de Molande and died in Paris in 1851. Landor wrote many poems in her praise. Shelley gave the name to his infant daughter.

**Iapetos.** Son of Uranus and Ge, father of Atlas, Prometheus, Epimetheus, and Menoetius, and ancestor of the human race, hence called *genus Iapeti*, the progeny of Iapetus (classical mythology).

**Iberia,** Spain; the country of the Iberus, the ancient name of the river Ebro.

***Iberia's Pilot.*** Christopher Columbus (1446?-1507).

> Launched with Iberia's pilot from the steep,
> To worlds unknown, and isles beyond the deep.
>
> Campbell, *The Pleasures of Hope*, ii

**Ibid.** A contraction of Lat. *ibidem*, in the same place.

**Ibis.** A sacred bird of the ancient Egyptians, specially connected with the god Thoth, who in the guise of an Ibis escaped the pursuit of Typhon. Its white plumage symbolised the light of the sun, and its black neck the shadow of the moon, its body a heart, and its legs a triangle. It was said that it drank only the purest of water, and that the bird was so fond of Egypt that it would pine to death if transported elsewhere. The practical reason for the protection of the Ibis – for it was a crime to kill it – was that it devours crocodiles' eggs, serpents and all sorts of noxious reptiles and insects. *Cp.* Ichneumon.

**Iblis.** *See* Eblis.

**Ibraham.** The Abraham of the Koran.

**Icarius.** In Greek legend an Athenian who was taught the cultivation of the vine by Dionysus (Bacchus). He was slain by some peasants who had become intoxicated with wine he had given them, and who thought they had been poisoned. They buried the body under a tree; his daughter Erigone, searching for her father, was directed to the spot by the howling of his dog Maera, and when she discovered the body she hanged herself for grief. Icarius became the constellation *Boötes*, Erigone the constellation *Virgo*, and Maera the star *Procyon*, which rises in July, a little before the dog-star.

**Icarus.** Son of Daedalus (*q.v.*). He flew with his father from Crete; but the sun melted the wax with which his wings were fastened on, and he fell into the sea, hence called the Icarian.

> *Glo.*: Why, what a peevish fool was that of Crete;
> That taught his son the office of a fowl!
> And yet, for all his wings, the fool was drown'd.
> *K. Hen.*: I, Daedalus; my poor boy, Icarus;
> Thy father, Minos, that denied our course;
> The sun, that sear'd the wings of my sweet boy
> Thy brother Edward, and thyself the sea,
> Whose envious gulf did swallow up his life.
>
> Shakespeare, *3 Henry VI*, 5, 6

**Ice. *A sword of ice-brook temper.*** Of the very best quality. The Spaniards used to plunge their swords and other weapons, while hot from the forge, into the brook Salo [Xalon], near Bilbilis, in Celtiberia, to harden them. The water of this brook is very cold.

> It is a sword of Spain, the ice-brook temper
>
> Shakespeare, *Othello*, 5, 2

***Ice Saints*** or ***Frost Saints.*** Those saints whose days fall in what is called 'the black-thorn winter' – that is, the second week in May (between 11 and 14). Some give only three days, but whether 11, 12, 13 or 12, 13, 14 is not agreed. May 11th is the day of St Mamertus, May 12th of St Pancras, May 13th of St Servatius, and May 14th of St Boniface.

***The ice-blink.*** The name given by mariners to a luminous appearance of the sky, caused by the reflection of light from ice. If the sky is dark or brown, the navigator may be sure that there is water; if it is white, rosy, or orange-coloured, he may be certain there is ice. The former is called a 'water sky', the latter an 'ice sky'.

The Danish name for the great ice-cliffs of Greenland is 'The Ice-blink':

> O'er rocks, seas, islands, promontories spread
> The Ice-Blink rears its undulated head
>
> Montgomery, *Greenland*, iii, 63

***To break the ice.*** To broach a disagreeable subject; to open the way, take the first step, make the plunge. In allusion to breaking ice for bathing.

> [We] An' if you break the ice, and do this feat ...
> Will not so graceless be, to be ingrate.
>
> Shakespeare, *Taming of the Shrew*, 1, 2

***To skate over thin ice.*** To take unnecessary risks, especially in conversation or argument; to touch on dangerous subjects very lightly.

**Iceberg.** A mass of ice, broken from a glacier which ends in the sea and floated about the ocean by the currents. The magnitude of some icebergs is considerable. One seen off the Cape of Good Hope was two miles in circumference, and a hundred and fifty feet high. For every cubic foot above water there must be at least eight feet below; their weight must, therefore, be enormous, and the danger to shipping – witness the *Titanic* disaster of April, 1912 – is very great.

**Iceland Dogs.** Shaggy, white dogs, once great favourites with ladies as lap-dogs. Shakespeare mentions them in *Henry V*, where he makes Pistol call Nym in contempt a 'prick-eared cur of Iceland'.

> Iceland dogges curled and rough all over, which, by reason of the length of their heire make showe neither of face nor of body.
>
> Fleming, *Of English Dogges* (1576)

**Iceni.** *See* Warrior Queen.

**Ich Dien.** According to a Welsh tradition, Edward I promised to provide Wales with a prince 'who could speak no word of English', and when his second son Edward (afterwards Edward II) was born at Carnarvon he presented him to the assembly, saying in Welsh *Eich dyn* (behold the man).

The more general belief is that it was the motto of John, King of Bohemia, slain by the Black Prince at Cressy in 1346, and that the Black Prince assumed it – together with the king's cognisance, the plume of three ostrich feathers – out of modesty, to indicate that 'he served under the king his father'.

**Ichabod.** A son of Phinehas, born just after the death of his father and grandfather (1 Sam. 4:21). The name (Heb. I-kabhoth) means 'where is the glory?' It is usually popularly translated by 'the glory has departed'.

**Ichneumon.** A weasel-like animal (also called 'Pharaoh's rat') found in Egypt and venerated by the ancient Egyptians because, like the ibis (*q.v.*), it feeds on serpents, mice, and other vermin, and is especially fond of crocodiles' eggs. According to legend, it steals into the mouths of crocodiles when they gape, and eats out their bowels. The name is Greek, and means 'one who tracks, or traces out'.

**Ichor.** In *classical mythology*, the colourless blood of the gods. (Gr., juice.)

> [St Peter] patter'd with his keys at a great rate,
> And sweated through his apostolic skin:
> Of course his perspiration was but ichor,
> Or some such other spiritual liquor.
>
> Byron, *Vision of Judgment*, xxv

**Ichtnus.** Greek for 'fish', which in primitive times was used as a symbol of Christ because the word is formed of the initial letters of *I*esous, *CH*ristos, *TH*eou, *U*ios, *S*oter, Jesus Christ, Son of God, Saviour. This notarica is found on many seals, rings, urns, and tombstones belonging to the early times of Christianity, and was supposed to be a 'charm' of mystical efficacy.

**Icknield Street,** or **Way.** One of the principal of the old 'Roman' roads in Britain. It crossed the country from Norfolk to Cornwall, and large parts of it date from pre-Roman times.

> Its name of the Icknield Way connects this road with the Iceni, whom the Romans found settled in our Norfolk and Suffolk, and points back to days in which this tribe stood supreme in south east Britain.
>
> J. R. Green, *Making of England*, ch. iii

**Icon Basilike.** *See* Eikon.

**Iconoclasts** (Gr., 'image breakers'). Reformers who rose in the Eastern Church in the 8th century, and were specially opposed to the employment of pictures, statues, emblems, and all visible representations of sacred objects. The crusade against these things began in 726 with the Emperor Leo III (the Isaurian), and continued for one hundred and twenty years under Constantine Copronymus, Leo the Armenian, Theophilus, and other Byzantine Emperors, who are known as the *Iconoclast Emperors*.

> The eighth century, the age of the Iconoclasts, had not been favourable to literature.
>
> Isaac Taylor, *The Alphabet*, vol. ii, ch. viii

**Idaean Mother.** Cybele, who had a temple on Mount Ida, in Asia Minor.

**Ideal Republics.** *See* Commonwealths.

**Idealism.** ***Subjective idealism,*** taught by Fichte (1762–1814), supposes the object (say a tree) and the image of it on the mind is all one. Or rather, that there is no object outside the mental idea.

***Objective idealism,*** taught by Schelling (1775–1854), supposes that the tree and the image thereof on the mind are distinct from each other.

***Absolute idealism,*** taught by Hegel (1770–1831), supposes there is no such thing as phenomena; that mind, through the senses, creates its own world. In fact, that there is no real, but all is mere ideal.

***Personal Idealism,*** as expounded by William James (1842–1910), lays special emphasis on the authority of the will and the initiative of the self in experience, as opposed to the tendency of Absolute Idealism to minimise the working of the individual soul.

**Idealists.** They may be divided into two distinct sections –

(1) Those who follow Plato, who taught that before creation there existed certain types or ideal models, of which *ideas* created objects are the visible images. Malebranche, Kant, Schelling, Hegel, etc., were of this school.

(2) Those who maintain that all phenomena are only subjective – that is, mental cognisances only within ourselves, and what we see and what we hear are only brain impressions. Of this school were Berkeley, Hume, Fichte, and many others.

**Ides.** In the Roman calendar the 15th of March, May, July, and October, and the 13th of all the other months; always eight days after the Nones.

***Beware the Ides of March.*** Said as a warning of impending and certain danger. The allusion is the warning received by Julius Caesar before his assassination:

> Furthermore, there was a certain soothsayer that had given Caesar warning long time afore, to take heed of the day of the Ides of March (which is the fifteenth of the month), for on that day he should be in great danger. That day being come, Caesar going into the Senate-house and speaking merrily unto the soothsayer, told him, 'The Ides of March be come': 'So be they,' softly answered the soothsayer, 'but yet are they not past.'
>
> Plutarch, *Julius Caesar* (North's trans.).

*See also* Shakespeare's *Julius Caesar*, 1, 2; 3, 1, etc.

**Idiot.** Originally – in Greece – a private person, one not engaged in any public office, hence an uneducated, ignorant person. Hence Jeremy Taylor says, 'Humility is a duty in great ones, as well as in idiots' (private persons). The Greeks have the expressions, 'a priest or an idiot' (layman), 'a poet or an idiot' (prose-writer). In 1 Cor. 14:16, where the Authorised Version has 'how shall he who occupieth the place of the unlearned say Amen …?' Wyclif's version reads '… who fillith the place of an idyot, how schal he seie amen …?'

**Idle Bible, The.** *See* Bible, specially named.

**Idle Lake.** The lake on which Phaedria or Wantonness cruised in her 'small Gondelay' (gondola). It led to Wandering Island. (Spenser, *Faërie Queene*, II, vi.)

**Idol Shepherd.** This phrase, from Zech. 11:17, 'Woe to the idol shepherd that leaveth his flock,' is often met with in 17th-century controversial writings. 'Idol' here means self-seeking, counterfeit, pseudo; the Revised Version has 'worthless'. A similar use is in Browne's *Answer to Cartwright* (1585), 'What remaineth but an Idol or counterfet crist?' *See* Idle Bible *under* Bible, specially named.

**Idomeneus.** King of Crete, an ally of the Greeks at Troy. After the city was burnt he made a vow to sacrifice whatever he first encountered, if the gods granted him a safe return to his kingdom. It was his own son that he first met; he offered him up to fulfil his vow, but a plague followed, and the king was banished from Crete as a murderer. (*Iliad.*) *Cp.* Iphigenia.

**Iduna** or **Idun.** In *Scandinavian mythology*, daughter of the dwarf Svald, and wife of Bragi. She was guardian of the golden apples which the gods tasted as often as they wished to renew their youth, and seems to personify the year between March and September, when the sun is north of the equator. Her apples indicate fruits generally. Loki carries her off to Giant-Land, when the Sun descends below the equator, and steals her apples. Iduna makes her escape in the form of a sparrow when the Sun again, in March, rises above the equator; and both gods and men rejoice in her return.

**Ifreet.** *See* Afreet.

**Igerna.** *See* Igraine.

**Ignaro.** Foster-father of Orgoglio in Spenser's *Faërie Queene* (I, viii). Whatever question Arthur asked, the old dotard answered, 'He could not tell.' *Cp.* Non mi ricordo. Spenser says this old man walks one way and looks another, because ignorance is always 'wrong-headed'.

**Ignatius, St.** According to tradition, St Ignatius was the little child whom our Saviour set in the midst of His disciples for their example. He was a convert of St John the Evangelist, was consecrated Bishop of Antioch by St Peter, and is said to have been thrown to the beasts in the amphitheatre by Trajan, about 107. He is commemorated on February 1st, and is represented in art accompanied by lions, or chained and exposed to them, in allusion to his martyrdom.

***Father Ignatius.*** The Rev. Joseph Leycester Lyne (d.1908), for some time head of the English Benedictines at the Norwich Protestant monastery, afterwards at Llanthony.

The Hon. and Revd Geo. Spencer (1799–1864), formerly a clergyman of the Church of England, who joined the Roman communion, and became Superior of the order of Passionists, was also known as 'Father Ignatius'.

***St Ignatius Loyola.*** *See* Loyola.

**Ignis Fatuus.** The 'Will o' the wisp' or 'Friar's lanthorn' (*q.v.*), a flame-like phosphorescence flitting over marshy ground (due to the spontaneous combustion of gases from decaying vegetable matter), and deluding people who attempt to follow it: hence, any delusive aim or object, or some Utopian scheme that is utterly impracticable. The name means 'a foolish fire'; it is also called 'Jack o' Lantern', 'Spunkie', 'Walking Fire', and 'Fair Maid of Ireland'.

> When thou rannest up Gadshill in the night to catch my horse, if I did not think thou hadst been an *ignis fatuus* or a ball of wildfire, there's no purchase in money.
>
> Shakespeare, *1 Henry IV*, 3, 3

According to a Russian superstition, these wandering fires are the spirits of still-born children which flit between heaven and the Inferno.

**Ignoramus.** One who ignores the knowledge of something; one really unacquainted with it. It is an ancient law term. The grand jury used to write *Ignoramus* on the back of indictments 'not found' or not to be sent into court. Hence *ignore*. The present custom is to write 'No true bill'.

***To ignore a bill*** is to write on it *ignoramus*.

> 'Ignoramus' is the word properly used by the Grand Enquest ... and written upon the bill.
>
> Cowell

**Ignorantines.** A name given to the Brothers of Charity, or Brethren of Saint Jean-de-Dieu, an order of Augustinian mendicants founded in 1495 in Portugal by John of Monte Major (d.1550), to minister to the sick poor, and introduced into France by Marie de Medici.

It was also given, later, to a religious association founded by the Abbé de la Salle in 1724 in France, for educating gratuitously the children of the poor.

**Igraine, Igerna,** or **Igerne.** Wife of Gorlois (*q.v.*), Duke of Tintagel, in Cornwall, and mother of King Arthur. His father, Uther Pendragon, married Igraine thirteen days after her husband was slain.

**Ihram.** The ceremonial garb of Mohammedan pilgrims to Mecca; also, the ceremony of assuming it.

> We prepared to perform the ceremony of *Al-Ihram* (assuming the pilgrim garb) ... we donned the attire, which is nothing but two new cotton cloths each six feet long by three and a

half broad, white with narrow red stripes and fringes ... One of these sheets, technically armed the *Rid* i, is thrown over the back, and exposing the arm and shoulder, is knotted at the right side in the style of *Wishah*. The *Izar* is wrapped round the loins from waist to knee, and, knotted or tucked in at the middle, supports itself.

Burton, *Pilgrimage to Al-Madinah and Mecca*, xxvi

**Iliad** (Gr. *Ilias*, gen. *Iliad-os*, the land of Ilium). The tale of the siege of Troy, or Ilium, an epic poem for centuries attributed to Homer (*q.v.*), in twenty-four books. Menelaus, King of Sparta, received as his guest Paris, a son of Priam, King of Troy, who ran away with Helen, wife of Menelaus. Menelaus induced the Greeks to lay siege to Troy to avenge the perfidy, and the siege lasted ten years. The poem begins in the tenth year with a quarrel between Agamemnon, King of Mycenae and commander-in-chief of the allied Greeks, and Achilles, the hero who had retired from the army in ill temper. The Trojans now prevail, and Achilles sends his friend Patroclus to oppose them, but Patroclus is slain. Achilles, in a desperate rage, rushes into the battle, and slays Hector, the commander of the Trojan army. The poem ends with the funeral rites of Hector.

***An Iliad of woes.*** A number of evils falling one after another; there is scarce a calamity in the whole catalogue of human ills that finds not mention in the *Iliad*.

Demosthenes used the phrase (*Ilias kakon*), and it was adopted by Cicero (*Ilias malorum*) in his *Ad Atticum*, viii, 11.

It opens another Iliad of woes to Europe.

Burke, *On a Regicide Peace*, ii

***The Iliad in a nutshell.*** *See* Nutshell.

***The French Iliad.*** The *Romance of the Rose* (*see under* Rose) has been so called. Similarly, the *Nibelungenlied* (*q.v.*). and the *Lusiad* (*q.v.*). have been called respectively the *German* and *Portuguese Iliad*.

**Ilk** (A.S. *ilca*, the same). Only used – correctly – in the phrase *of that ilk*, when the surname of the person spoken of is the same as the name of his estate; *Bethune of that ilk* means 'Bethune of Bethune'. It is a mistake to use the phrase 'All that ilk' to signify all of that name or family.

**Ill May-day.** *See* Evil May-day.

**Ill-starred.** Unlucky; fated to be unfortunate. Othello says of Desdemona, 'O ill-starred wench!' Of course, the allusion is to the astrological dogma that the stars influence the fortunes of mankind.

Where'er that ill-starred home may lie.

Moore, *Fire Worshippers*

**Illinois.** Originally the name of a confederacy of North American Indian tribes who were allied to the French. *Illini* means 'man', and the French substituted their plural termination *-ois* for the Indian *-uk*.

**Illuminated Doctor.** Raymond Lully (1254–1315), the Spanish scholastic philosopher; also Johann Tauler (1294–1361), the German mystic.

**Illuminati.** The baptised were at one time so called, because a lighted candle was given them to hold as a symbol that they were illuminated by the Holy Ghost.

The name has been given to, or adopted by, several sects and secret societies professing to have superior enlightenment, especially to a republican society of deists, founded by Adam Weishaupt at Ingoldstadt in Bavaria, 1776, having for its object the establishment of a religion consistent with 'sound reason'.

Among others to whom the name has been applied are the Hesychasts (*q.v.*); the Alombrados, a Spanish sect founded about 1575 by the Carmelite, Catherine de Jesus, and John of Willelpando, the members of which rejected the sacraments; the French Guerinists (*q.v.*); and the Rosicrucians (*q.v.*).

**Illuminator, The.** The surname given to St Gregory of Armenia (257–331), the apostle of Christianity among the Armenians.

**Illustrious, The.**

Albert V, Duke and second Emperor of Austria (1398–1439).

Nicomedes II of Bithynia (d.89 BC).

Ptolemy V, King of Egypt, *Epiphanes* (210, 205–181 BC).

Jam-shid (Jam the *Illustrious*), nephew of Tah Omurs, fifth king of the Paisdadian dynasty of Persia (about 840–800 BC).

Kien-lông, fourth of the Manchu dynasty of China (1709–99).

**Image-breakers, The.** *See* Iconoclasts.

**Imaum** or **Imam.** A member of the priestly body of the Mohammedans. He recites the prayers and leads the devotions of the congregation. The sultan as 'head of the Moslems' is an Imaum, and the title is also given to the Prince of Muscat and to the heads of the four orthodox Moslem sects. The word means *teacher* or *guide*. *Cp.* Ulema.

**Imaus.** The Himalaya. Heylin in his *Cosmography* (1657), Bk iii, p. 640, says it is the great mountain range –

> which beginning neare the shores of the Northern Ocean runneth directly towards the South; dividing the Greater Asia into East and West, and crossing Mount Taurus in right angles.

The word means *snow* hills (*hima*, snow).

> The huge incumbrance of horrific woods
> From Asian Taurus, from Imaus stretched
> Athwart the roving Tartar's sullen bounds.
> Thomson, *Autumn*

**Imbecile.** One mentally weak. The original meaning was probably one who leans 'on a stick' (Lat. *imbecillis*, from *inbacillum*).

**Imbrocata** (Ital.). An old fencing term for a thrust over the arm.

> If your enemie bee cunning and skilfull, never stand about giving any foine or imbrocata, but this thrust or stoccata alone, neither it also [never attempt] unlesse you be sure to hit him.
> Saviolo, *Practise of the Duello* (1595)

**Imbroglio** (Ital.). A complicated plot; a misunderstanding between nations and persons of a complicated nature.

**Immaculate Conception.** This dogma, that the Virgin Mary was conceived without original sin, was first broached by St Bernard, was stoutly maintained by Duns Scotus and his disciples, but was not received by the Roman Catholic Church as an article of faith till 1854. It was proclaimed by Pius IX in these words:

> That the most blessed Virgin Mary, in the first moment of her conception, by a special grace and privilege of Almighty God, in virtue of the merits of Christ, was preserved immaculate from all stain of original sin.

**Immolate.** To sacrifice; literally, 'put meal on one' (Lat. *immolare*, to sprinkle with meal). The reference is to the ancient Roman custom of sprinkling wine and fragments of the sacred cake (*mola salsa*) on the head of a victim to be offered in sacrifice.

**Immortal.** ***The Immortal.*** Yông-Tching (1723–36), third of the Manchu dynasty of China, assumed the title.

***The Immortal Tinker.*** John Bunyan (1628–88), a tinker by trade.

***The Immortals.*** The forty members of the French Academy; also the name given to a body of 10,000 foot-soldiers, which constituted the bodyguard of the ancient Persian kings, and to other highly trained troops.

In the British Army the 76th Foot were called 'The Immortals', because so many were wounded, but not killed, in India (1788–1806). This regiment, with the old 33rd, now form the two battalions of the West Riding regiment.

**Imp.** A graft (A.S. *impian*), a shoot; hence offspring, and a child. In hawking, 'to imp a feather' was to engraft or add a new feather for a broken one. The needles employed for the purpose were called 'imping needles'.

The noun 'imp' child, did not formerly connote mischievousness or tricksiness as it now does; Cromwell, writing to Henry VIII, speaks of 'that noble imp your son'.

> Let us pray for ... the king's most excellent majesty and for ... his beloved son Edward, our prince, that most angelic imp. *Pathway to Prayer*

Milton calls the serpent 'fittest imp of fraud' (*Paradise Lost*, ix, 89).

**Impanation.** The dogma of Luther that the body and soul of Christ are infused into the eucharistic elements after consecration; and that the bread and wine are united with the body and soul of Christ in much the same way as the body and soul of man are united. The word means *putting into the bread.*

**Impar congressus Achilli.** No match for Achilles; the combatants were not equally matched. Said of Troilus (Virgil, *Aeneid*, i, 475).

**Imperial.** A tuft of hair on the chin, all the rest of the beard and all the whiskers being shaved off. So called from the Emperor Napoleon III, who set the fashion.

A standard size of printing paper measuring between 22 X 30 in. and 22 X 32 in. Also of writing paper measuring 22 X 30 in.

In Russia there used to be current a gold coin, value 15 roubles, called an 'imperial'.

**Imperium in Imperio** (Lat.). An empire within an empire; a government independent of the general authorised government.

**Impertinence.** In legal phraseology, a matter introduced into an affidavit, etc., not pertinent to the case.

**Imponderables** (Lat., things without weight). Heat, light, electricity, and magnetism were, it was at one time supposed, the phenomena of imponderable substances; that of heat was called *caloric*. This theory is now exploded, but the term is still sometimes applied to the hypothetical ether.

**Imposition.** A task given in schools, etc., as a punishment. Of course, the word is taken from the verb *impose*, as the task is imposed. In the sense of a *deception* it means to 'put a trick on a person', hence, the expressions 'to put on one', 'to lay it on thick', etc.

***Imposition of hands.*** The bishop laying his hand on persons confirmed or ordained (Acts 6, 8, 19). *See* To lay hands on *under* Hand.

**Impossibilities** (phrases).

Gathering grapes from thistles.
Fetching water in a sieve.
Washing a blackamoor white.
Catching wind in cabbage nets.
Flaying eels by the tail.
Making cheese of chalk.
Squaring the circle.
Turning base metal into gold.
Making a silk purse of a sow's ear.
(And hundreds more.)

**Imprimatur.** A mark of approval; properly, official licence to print a book, especially a licence from the Roman Catholic Church, or – where censorship exists – from the official censor. The word is the 3rd sing. pres. subj. of Lat. *imprimere*, 'let it be printed'.

> What advantage is it to be a man, over it is to be a boy at school, if we have only escaped the ferula, to come under the fescue of an Imprimatur? If serious and elaborate writings, as if they were no more than the theme of a grammar-lad under his pedagogue, must not be uttered without the cursory eyes of a temporising and extemporising licenser? Milton, *Areopagitica*

**Impropriation.** Profits of ecclesiastical property in the hands of a layman, who is called the *impropriator*. *Appropriation* is the term used when the profits of a benefice are in the hands of a college or spiritual corporation.

**In Coena Domini** (Lat., At the Lord's Supper). The papal bull published annually on Maundy Thursday (the Feast of the Lord's Supper) from the 14th century to 1770, fulminating curses and excommunications against all heretics and against all temporal powers and others who wronged the Church by taxing the clergy, levying on ecclesiastical lands, appealing to a general council, etc. It was added to and altered from time to time, and its ecclesiastical, as apart from its political, anathemas are included in the *Apostolicae Sedis*, issued by Pius IX in 1869.

**In commendam** (Lat., in trust). The holding of church preferment for a time, on the recommendation of the Crown, till a suitable person can be provided. Thus a benefice-holder who has become a bishop and is allowed to hold his living for a time is said to hold it *in commendam*.

**In esse.** In actual existence (Lat. *esse*, to be), as opposed to *in posse*, in potentiality. Thus a living child is 'in esse', but before birth is only 'in posse'.

**In extenso** (Lat.). At full length, word for word, without abridgment.

**In extremis** (Lat.). At the very point of death; *in articulo mortis*.

**In fieri.** In the course of accomplishment; on the way (Lat. *fieri*, to become, to be done, made, etc.).

**In flagrante delicto.** Red-handed; in the very fact (Lat., while the offence is flagrant).

**In forma pauperis** (Lat.). In the character of a pauper. For many centuries in England persons without money or the means of obtaining it have been allowed to sue in the courts *in forma pauperis*, when the fees are remitted and the suitor is supplied gratis with the necessary legal advice, counsel, etc.

**In gremio legis** (Lat.). Under the protection of (literally, at the breast of) the law.

**In limine** (Lat.). At the outset, at the threshold.

**In loco parentis** (Lat.). In the position of being in a parent's place.

**In medias res** (Lat.). In the middle of the subject. In novels and epic poetry, the author generally begins *in medias res*, and explains the preceding events as the tale unfolds. In history, on the other hand, the author begins *ab ovo* (*q.v.*).

**In memoriam** (Lat.). In memory of.

**In nubibus** (Lat.). In the clouds; not in actual existence; in contemplation.

**In partibus** (Lat.). A 'bishop *in partibus*' is a bishop in any country, Christian or otherwise, whose title is from some old see which has fallen away from the Catholic faith. The full phrase is *in partibus infidelium*, in the regions of infidels, and the title is generally conferred on a Church dignitary without an actual see. The custom is confined to the Roman Catholic Church.

**In petto** (Ital.). Held in reserve, kept back, something done privately, and not announced to the general public. (Lat. *in pectore*, in the breast).

***Cardinals in petto.*** Cardinals about to be elected, but not yet publicly announced. Their names are *in pectore* (of the Pope).

**In posse.** *See* In esse.

**In propria persona** (Lat.). Personally, and not by deputy or agents.

**In re** (Lat.). In the matter of; on the subject of; as *In re* Jones *v.* Robinson. But *in rem*, against the property or thing referred to.

**In situ** (Lat.). In its original place.

> I at first mistook it for a rock *in situ*, and took out my compass to observe the direction of its cleavage. Darwin, *Voyage in the Beagle*, ix

**In statu quo** or *In statu quo ante* (Lat.). In the condition things were before the change took place. Thus, two nations arming for war may agree to lay down arms on condition that all things be restored to the same state as they were before they took up arms.

**In terrorem** (Lat.). As a warning, to deter others by terrifying them.

> 'He should be tried', said a fourth, 'for conspiring his own death, and hanged *in terrorem*.'
> Scott, *Peveril of the Peak*, ch. xlii

**In toto** (Lat.). Entirely, altogether.

**In vacuo** (Lat.). In a vacuum – i.e. in a space from which, nominally altogether, and really almost, all the air has been taken away.

**In vino veritas** (Lat.). *See* Vino.

**In-and-In.** A game for three, played with four dice, once extremely common, and frequently alluded to. 'In' is a throw of doubles, 'in-and-in' a throw of double doubles, which sweeps the board.

> I have seen … three persons sit down at twelve-penny In and In, and each draw forty shillings a-piece. *Nicker Nicked* (1668: *Harl. Misc.*, II)

**Ins and Outs of the Matter, The.** All the details, both direct and indirect.

> If you want to know the ins and outs of the Yankees … I know all their points, shape, make, and breed. Haliburton

Sometimes the 'Ins' means those in office, and the 'Outs' those out of office, or in Opposition.

**Inaugurate.** To instal into some office with appropriate ceremonies, to open or introduce formally. From Lat. *inaugurare*, which meant first to take omens from the flight of birds by augury (*q.v.*), and then to consecrate or instal after taking such omens.

**Inbread.** *See* Baker's Dozen.

**Inca.** A king or royal prince of the ancient Peruvians. The empire of the Incas was founded by Manco Capac about the middle of the 13th century.

> The Inca was a war-chief, elected by the Council to carry out its decision.
> Brinton, *The American Race* (*South American Tribes*), pt i, ch. ii, p. 211

**Inchcape Rock.** A rocky reef (also known as the Bell Rock) about 12 miles from Arbroath in the North Sea (Inch or Innis means *island*). It is dangerous for navigators, and therefore the abbot of Arbroath, or 'Aberbrothok', fixed a bell on a float, which gave notice to sailors of its whereabouts. Southey's ballad tells how Ralph the Rover, a sea pirate, cut the bell from the float, and was wrecked on his return home on the very rock.

> A similar tale is told of St Goven's bell, in Pembrokeshire. In the chapel was a silver bell, which was stolen one summer evening by pirates, but no sooner had the boat put to sea than it was wrecked. The silver bell was carried by sea-nymphs to the brink of a well, and whenever the stone of that well is struck the bell is heard to moan.

**Incog.** i.e. **Incognito** (Ital.). Under an assumed name or title. When a royal person travels, and does not wish to be treated with royal ceremony, he assumes some inferior title for the nonce, and travels *incog*.

**Incorruptible, The.** Robespierre. *See* Sea-green.

**Incubus.** A nightmare, anything that weighs heavily on the mind. In mediaeval times it denoted an evil spirit who was at one time supposed to consort with women in their sleep. (Lat. *incubo*, nightmare, from *incubare*, to lie on.)

> Merlin was the son of no mortal father, but of an Incubus; one of a class of beings not absolutely wicked, but far from good, who inhabit the regions of the air.
> Bullfinch, *Age of Chivalry*, pt i, ch. iii

**Indenture.** A written contract, especially one between an apprentice and his master; so called because the two documents had their edges indented in such a manner that they would fit precisely into each other.

**Independence Day.** July 4th, which is kept as a national holiday in the United States of America, because the declaration by the American States, declaring the colonies free and independent and absolved from all allegiance to Great Britain, was signed on that day (1776).

**Index.** The 'Roman Index' includes the *Index Librorum Prohibitorum* and the *Index Expurgatorius*. The former contains a list of such books as are absolutely forbidden to be read by Catholics. The latter contains such books as are forbidden till certain parts are omitted or amended. Rules for the guidance of the compilers were formulated by the Council of Trent (1563), and the first *Index* was published under Pius IV in 1561. The lists are made out by a board of cardinals (*Congregation of the Index*). Besides the Protestant Bibles, and the works of such heretics as Arius and Calvin, we find in the lists the following well-known names:

Of *English authors*: Addison, Bacon, Chaucer, Gibbon, Goldsmith, Hallam, Andrew Lang, Locke, J. S. Mill, Milton, Robertson, Whately, etc., and even some children's tales.

Of *French authors*: Arnauld, Calvin, Descartes, Fénelon, l'Abbé Fleury, Loisy, Malebranche, Montaigne, Voltaire, etc.

Of *Italian authors*: Dante, Guicciardini, Sismondi, etc.

Of *German authors*: Kant, Luther, etc.

**India Paper.** A creamy-coloured printing-paper originally made in China and Japan from vegetable fibre, and used for taking off the finest proofs of engraved plates; hence *India proof*, the proof of an engraving on India paper, before lettering.

The *India paper* (or *Oxford India paper*) used for printing Bibles and high-class 'thin paper' and 'pocket' editions, is a very thin, tough, and opaque imitation of this.

**Indian. *American Indians*.** When Columbus landed on one of the Bahamas he thought that he had reached India, and in this belief gave the natives the name of Indians. Nowadays, in order to avoid ambiguity, the American Indians are known by ethnologists as *Amerinds*.

India is so named from Indus (the river), in Sanskrit *Sindhu*, in Persic *Hindu* (the water). *Hindustan* is the *stan* or 'country' of the river *Hindus*.

**Indian Drug** or **Weed, The.** Tobacco. Here the reference is, of course, to the *West Indies*.

> His breath compounded of strong English beere,
> And th' Indian drug, would suffer none come neere.
> Taylor, the Water Poet (1630)

**Indian File.** One after the other, singly. The American Indians, when they go on an expedition, march one by one. The one behind carefully steps in the footprints of the one before, and the last man of the file is supposed to obliterate the footprints. Thus, neither the track nor the number of invaders can be traced.

**Indian Summer.** The autumnal summer, occurring as a rule in the early part of October. It is often the finest and mildest part of the whole year, especially in North America.

> The gilding of the Indian summer mellowed the pastures far and wide. The russet woods stood ripe to be stript, but were yet full of leaf. The purple of heath-bloom, faded but not withered, tinged the hills ... Fieldhead gardens bore the seal of gentle decay; ... its time of flowers and even of fruit was over.
> C. Brontë, *Shirley*, ch. xxvii

**Individualists.** Individualists hold that as little as possible should be done for its subjects by the State, as much as possible being left to free individual initiative.

Socialism (*q.v.*) tends to treat the individual as merely a part of the State, holding his possessions (if any) simply by its permission, while Individualism regards the State as a collection of separate units, with rights of life and property independently, which the State does not confer but merely guarantees.

Extreme individualists hold that all government is an evil, though it may be a necessary evil, and the 'anarchists' profess the extremest form of the creed.

> Individualism rests on the principle that a man shall be his own master.
> Draper, *Conflict between Religion and Science*, ch. xi

**Induction** (Lat., the act of leading in). When a clergyman is inducted to a living he is led to the church door, and the ring which forms the handle is placed in his hand. The door being opened, he is next led into the church, and the fact is announced to the parish by tolling the bell.

**Indulgence.** In the Roman Catholic Church, the entire or partial remission of punishment due to sin either in this world or in purgatory. The Church is regarded as the bank of the infinite merits of Christ, and gives such indulgences like cheques on a bank. In the Middle Ages indulgences were of high commercial value, and it was the sale of them that first roused the ire of Luther and prepared the way for the Reformation.

***The Declaration of Indulgence.*** The proclamation of James II in 1687 which annulled religious tests and the penal laws against Roman Catholics and Dissenters. The refusal of certain ecclesiastics to read this in their churches led to the Trial of the Seven Bishops.

**Ineffable.** *See* Affable.

**Inertia.** That want of power in matter to change its state either from rest to motion, or from motion to rest. Kepler calls it *Vis inertiae*. (*Ars* in Latin is the Gr. *arete*, power or inherent force; *In-ars* is the absence of this power.)

**Infallibility.** The doctrine that the Pope, when speaking *ex cathedra* (*q.v.*) on a question of Catholic doctrine or morals, is free from error arose in the Middle Ages in connection with the pseudo-Isidorian decretals, but did not become an accepted dogma of the Church until the Vatican Council of 1870. The promulgation of the dogma, which, after having been agreed to by the Council (many members dissenting or abstaining from voting), was publicly read by Pius IX at St Peter's, includes the words:

> We teach and define that it is a dogma divinely revealed, that the Roman pontiff, when he speaks *ex cathedra* – that is, when in discharge of the office of pastor and doctor of all Christians, by virtue of his supreme apostolic authority, he defines a doctrine regarding faith or morals to be held by the universal church, by the divine assistance promised to him in blessed Peter (Luke 22:32) – is possessed of that infallibility with which the divine Redeemer willed that his Church should be endowed for defining doctrine regarding faith or morals.

**Infamous.** Applied to one of ill fame (Lat. *in*, negative, *fama*, fame, report, from *fari*, to speak).

**Infant.** Literally, one who is unable to speak (Lat. *infans*, ultimately from *in*, negative, and *fari*, to speak. *Cp.* Infamous *above*). Used as a synonym of 'childe', as in *Childe Harold* (*q.v.*), meaning a knight or youth of gentle birth, the word was once of common occurrence. Thus, as in the following passage, Spenser frequently refers to Prince Arthur in this way:

> The Infant harkened wisely to her tale,
> And wondered much at Cupid's judg'ment wise.
>
> *Faërie Queene*, VI, viii, 25

**Infanta.** Any princess of the blood royal, except an heiress of the crown, is so called in Spain and, formerly, in Portugal.

**Infante.** All the sons of the sovereigns of Spain bear this title, as, formerly, did those of Portugal, except the crown prince, who is called in Spain the Prince of Asturias.

**Infantry.** Foot soldiers. This is the same word as *infant* (*q.v.*); it is the Italian *infanteria*, a foot soldier, from *infanta*, a youth; hence, one who is too inexperienced to serve in the cavalry.

**Infernal Column.** So the corps of Latour d'Auvergne (1743–1800) – 'the First Grenadier of France' – was called, from its terrible charges with the bayonet.

The same name – *Colonnes infernales* – was given, because of their brutality, to the twelve bodies of republican troops which 'pacified' La Vendée in 1793, under General Thurreau.

**Inferno.** We have Dante's notion of the infernal regions in his *Inferno*; Homer's in the *Odyssey*, Bk xi; Virgil's in the *Aeneid*, Bk vi; Spenser's in the *Faërie Queene*, Bk ii, canto 7; Ariosto's in *Orlando Furioso*, Bk xvii; Tasso's in *Jerusalem Delivered*, Bk iv.; Milton's in *Paradise Lost*; Fenelon's in *Télémaque*, Bk xviii; and Beckford's in his romance of *Vathek*. *See* Hell: Hades.

**Infra Dig.** Not in accordance with one's position and character. Short for Lat. *infra dignitatem*, beneath (one's) dignity.

**Infralapsarian.** The same as a Sublapsarian (*q.v.*).

**Ingoldsby.** The pseudonym of the Rev. Richard Harris Barham (1788–1845), as author of the *Ingoldsby Legends*, which appeared in Bentley's *Miscellany* and the *New Monthly Magazine*, and later (1840 and 1847) in book form.

**Ingrain Colours.** *See* Knave in Grain *under* Grain.

**Injunction.** A writ forbidding a person to encroach on another's privileges; as, to sell a book which is only a colourable copy of another author's book; or to infringe a patent; or to perform a play based on a novel without permission of the novelist; or to publish a book the rights of which are reserved. Injunctions are of two sorts – temporary and perpetual. The first is limited 'till the coming on of the defendant's answer'; the latter is based on the merits of the case, and is of perpetual force.

**Ink.** From Lat. *encaustum* (Gr. *enkaustos*, burnt in), the name given to the purple fluid used by the Roman emperors for writing with.

***Inkhorn terms*.** A common term in Elizabethan times for pedantic expressions which smell of the lamp. The *inkhorn* was the receptacle for ink which pedants and pedagogues wore fastened to the clothing.

> I know them that thinke rhetorique to stand wholie upon darke wordes, and hee that can catch an ynke horne terme by the taile, him they coumpt to be a fine Englishman.
>
> Wilson, *Arte of Rhetorique* (1553)

Shakespeare uses the phrase, an 'Inkhorn mate' (*1 Henry VI*, 3, 1).

***Ink-slinger*.** A contemptuous name for a writer, especially for a journalist.

**Inkle and Yarico.** The hero and heroine of the drama of that name (1787) by George Colman the younger. The story is from the *Spectator*, No. 11. Inkle is a young Englishman who is lost in the Spanish main; he falls in love with Yarico, an Indian maiden, who lives with him as his wife; but no sooner does he find a vessel to take him to Barbados than he sells her for a slave.

**Inn.** The word is Anglo-Saxon, and meant originally an ordinary dwelling-house, residence, or lodging. Hence Clifford's Inn, once the mansion of De Clifford; Lincoln's Inn, the abode of the Earls of Lincoln; Gray's Inn, that of the Lords Gray, etc.

Now, whenas Phoebus, with his fiery waine,
Unto his inne began to draw apace.
Spenser, *Faërie Queene*, VI, iii, 29

**Inns of Court.** The four voluntary societies which have the exclusive right of calling to the English Bar. They are all in London, and are the Inner Temple, the Middle Temple, Lincoln's Inn, and Gray's Inn. Each is governed by a board of benchers. *See* Bar: Bencher.

**Innings.** ***He has had a long*, or *a good innings*.** A good long run of luck. An *innings* in cricket is for the time that the eleven or an individual is having its turn batting at the wicket and is not out scouting in the field.

**Innocent, An.** An idiot or born fool was formerly so called. *Cp.* Benet.

Although he be in body deformed, in minde foolish, an innocent borne, a begger by misfortune, yet doth he deserve a better than thy selfe. Lyly, *Euphues* (1579)

***The Feast of the Holy Innocents.*** The 28th December, to commemorate Herod's massacre of the children of Bethlehem under two years old, with the design of cutting off the infant Jesus (Matt. 2:16).

***The massacre of the innocents.*** The name facetiously given in parliamentary circles (with an allusion to the above) to Bills that are left over at the end of a session for lack of time to deal with them.

**Innuendo.** An implied or covert hint of blame, a suggestion that one dare not make openly, so it is made indirectly, as by a nod; originally a law term, meaning the person nodded to or indirectly referred to (Lat., *innuo*, to nod to).

**Ino.** *See* Leucothea.

**Inoculation.** Originally, the horticultural practice of grafting a *bud* (Lat. *oculus*) *in*to an inferior plant, in order to produce flowers or fruits of better quality; hence, introducing into the body infectious matter which produces a mild form of the disease against which this treatment is counted on to render one immune.

**Inogene.** Spenser's name for the wife of Brute, the Trojan, a legendary king of Britain.

Thus Brute this realme unto his rule subdewd,
And raigned long in great felicity,
Loved of his friends, and of his foes eschewd,
He left three sons, his famous progeny,
Born of fayre Inogene of Italy.
Spenser, *Faërie Queene*, ii, 10

The chronicles call her *Ignoge*, and say that she was 'of Greece'.

**Inquisition.** A court instituted to enquire into offences against the Roman Catholic religion, and fully established by Gregory IX in 1235. Torture, as a means of extracting recantations or evidence, was first authorised by Innocent IV in 1252, and those found guilty were handed over to the secular arm to be dealt with according to the secular laws of the land. The Inquisition was only once introduced into England (viz., at the trials of the Templars, who were suppressed in 1308); it was most active in southern Europe, particularly in Spain, where it flourished from 1237 to 1820. It was suppressed in France in 1772.

**Insane Root, The.** A plant which is not positively identified, but which was probably henbane or hemlock, supposed to bereave anyone who took it of his senses. Banquo says of the witches:

Were such things here as we do speak about?
Or have we eaten on the insane root
That takes the reason prisoner?
Shakespeare, *Macbeth*, 1, 3

There were many plants to which similar properties were, rightly or wrongly, attributed, such as the mandrake, belladonna (deadly nightshade), poppy, etc.; and *cp.* Moly.

**Inscription** (*on coins*). *See* Legend.

**Inspired Idiot, The.** Oliver Goldsmith (1728–74) was so called by Walpole.

**Institutes.** A digest of the elements of a subject, especially of law. The most celebrated is the *Institutes of Justinian*, completed in AD 533 at the order of the Emperor. It was based on the earlier *Institutes of Gaius*, and was intended as an introduction to the Pandects (*q.v.*). Other *Institutes* are those of Florentius, Callistratus, Paulus, Ulpian, and Marcian.

**Instructions to the Committee.** A means empowering a Committee of the House of Commons to do what it would not otherwise be empowered to do.

An 'Instruction' must be supplementary and auxiliary to the Bill under consideration.
It must fall within the general scope and framework of the Bill in question.
It must not form the substance of a distinct measure.

**Insubri.** Ancient name for that part of Lombardy which now includes Milan, Como, Pavia, Lodi, Novara, and Vercelli. Its inhabitants were the *Insubres.*

**Insult.** Literally, to leap on (the prostrate body of a foe); hence, to treat with contumely (Lat. *insultare*, *saltus*, a leap). Terence says, *Insultare fores calcibus* (*Eunuchus*, ii, 2, 54). It will be remembered that the priests of Baal, to show their indignation against their gods, 'leaped upon the altar which they had made' (1 Kings 18:26). *Cp.* Desultory.

**Intaglio** (Ital.). A design cut in a gem, like a crest or initials in a stamp. The design does not stand out in relief, as in a cameo (*q.v.*), but is hollowed in.

**Intentions.** ***The road to hell is paved with good intentions.*** *See* Hell.

**Inter alia** (Lat.). Among other things or matters.

**Inter canem et lupum** (Lat.). Between two difficulties or dangers equally formidable. Between Scylla and Charybdis. Literally, 'between dog and wolf'. *See* Chien.

**Inter nos** (Lat.). Confidentially, between ourselves; in French, *entre nous.*

**Intercalary** (Lat. *inter*, between, *calare*, to proclaim solemnly). An intercalary day is a day foisted in between two others, as February 29th in leap year; so called because, among the Romans, this was a subject for solemn proclamation. *Cp.* Calends.

> It was the custom with Greeks to add, or, as it was termed, intercalate, a month every other year.
>
> Priestley, *On History*, xiv

**Interdict.** In the Roman Catholic Church an *Interdict* is a sentence of excommunication directed against a place and/or its inhabitants; if the place only is under the interdict the sacraments cannot be administered there, burials with religious ceremonies are prohibited, and all church communion is in abeyance. The most remarkable instances are:

586. The Bishop of Bayeux laid an interdict on all the churches of Rouen, in consequence of the murder of the Bishop Prétextat.

1081. Poland was laid under an interdict by Gregory VII, because Boleslas II had murdered Stanislaus at the altar.

1180. Scotland was put under a similar ban by Pope Alexander III.

1200. France was interdicted by Innocent III, because Philippe Auguste refused to marry Ingelburge, who had been betrothed to him.

1209. England was under similar sentence for six years (Innocent III), in the reign of King John.

In France, Robert *the Pious*, Philippe I, Louis VII, Philippe *Auguste*, Philippe IV, and Napoleon I, have all been subjected to the Papal thunder. In England, Henry II and John. Victor Emmanuel of Italy was excommunicated by Pius IX for despoiling the Papacy of a large portion of its temporal dominions.

**Interest** (Lat. *interesse*, to be a concern to). The *interest* of money is the sum which a borrower agrees to pay a lender for its use. *Simple interest* is interest on the principal, or money lent, only; *compound interest* is interest on the principal plus the interest as it accrues: this latter used to be called *usury*.

***To take an interest*** in anything is to make it a concern of yours, something which may affect your pleasure or well-being.

***In an interesting condition.*** Said of a woman who is expecting to become a mother. The phrase was in use in the 18th century.

**Interim of Augsburg.** *See* Augsburg.

**Interlard** (Fr.). Originally to 'lard' meat, i.e. to put strips of fat between layers of lean meat; hence, metaphorically, to mix irrelevant matter with the solid part of a discourse. Thus we say, 'To interlard with oaths', to 'interlard with compliments', etc.

> They interlard their native drinks with choice
> Of strongest brandy.
>
> Philips, *Cider* ii

**Interloper.** One who 'runs' between traders and upsets their business by interfering with their actual or supposed rights. The word came into English through the Dutch trade in the 16th century, and the *lope* is a dialect form of *leap* confused with Dut. *loopen*, to run (as in *elope*).

**Interpellation.** The equivalent in the French Chamber to 'moving the adjournment' in our House of Commons. It is an interruption to the order of the day by asking a Minister some question of importance the subject of which would come under his department. From Lat. *interpellare*, to interrupt by speaking, literally, to drive between.

**Interpolate.** To insert spurious matter in a book or document; to gag. Literally, to polish or furbish up (Lat. *polire*, to polish).

**Interpreter, Mr.** The Holy Spirit personified, in Bunyan's *Pilgrim's Progress.* He is lord of a house a little way beyond the Wicket Gate. Here Christian was kindly entertained and shown many wonderful sights of an allegorical character. Christiana and her party also stopped here later.

**Interrex** (Lat.). A person appointed to hold the office of king during a temporary vacancy.

**Intoxication.** Properly speaking, poisoning. The word is derived from the Greek *toxicon*, poison used for putting on the tips of arrows, *toxon* being the Greek for a bow and arrow.

**Intrigue.** From the Latin *trieae*, *trifles*, perplexities, whence the verb *intrico*, to entangle (connected with Greek *thrix*, a hair). We have recently re-introduced (from France) the transitive verb, as 'Mr So-and-so is a very intriguing author,' 'A London public that is intrigued by cinema stars'; but in the 17th and 18th centuries this use was not at all rare.

**Invalide** (Fr.). A four-sou piece, so called because it was debased to the value of three sous and a half.

> Tien, prens cet invalide, à ma santé va boire.
>
> *Deux Arlequins* (1691)

***Hôtel des Invalides.*** The great institution founded by Louis XIV at Paris in 1670 for disabled and superannuated soldiers. Besides Napoleon's tomb, in the Church of the Invalides, it contains large numbers of military trophies, statues, paintings, etc., and a museum of artillery and mediaeval and renaissance armour.

**Invention of the Cross.** *See* Cross.

**Inventors.** A curious instance of the *sin* of invention is mentioned in the *Bridge of Allan Reporter*, February, 1803:

> It is told of Mr Ferguson's grandfather, that he invented a pair of fanners for cleaning grain, and for this proof of superior ingenuity he was summoned before the Kirk Session, and reproved for trying to place the handiwork of man above the time-honoured practice of cleaning the grain on windy days, when the current was blowing briskly through the open doors of the barn.

It is extraordinary how many inventors have been 'hoist with their own petard'; the following list – in which some entries will no doubt be found that belong to the realm of fable – is by no means complete:

*Bastille.* Hugues Aubriot, Provost of Paris, who built the Bastille, was the first person confined therein. The charge against him was heresy.

*Brazen Bull.* Perillos of Athens made a brazen bull for Phalaris, Tyrant of Agrigentum, intended for the execution of criminals, who were shut up in the bull, fires being lighted below the belly. Phalaris admired the invention, and tested it on Perillos himself, who was the first person baked to death in the horrible monster.

*Cannon.* The Earl of Salisbury was the first to use cannon, and was the first Englishman killed by a cannon ball.

*Catherine Wheel.* The inventor of St Catherine's Wheel, a diabolical machine consisting of four wheels turning different ways, and each wheel armed with saws, knives, and teeth, was killed by his own machine; for when St Catherine was bound on the wheel, she fell off, and the machine flew to pieces. One of the pieces struck the inventor, and other pieces struck several of the men employed to work it, all of whom were killed. (*Metaphrastes.*)

*Eddystone.* Henry Winstanley erected the first Eddystone lighthouse. It was a wooden polygon, 100 feet high, on a stone base; but it was washed away by a storm in 1703, and the architect himself perished in his own edifice.

*Gallows* and *Gibbet.* We are told in the book of *Esther* that Haman devised a gallows 50 cubits high on which to hang Mordecai, by way of commencing the extirpation of the Jews; but the favourite of Ahasuerus was himself hanged thereon. We have a repetition of this incident in the case of Enguerrand de Marigni, Minister of Finance to Philippe the Fair, who was hung on the gibbet which he had caused to be erected at Montfaucon for the execution of certain felons; and four of his successors in office underwent the same fate.

*Guillotine.* J. B. V. Guillotin, M.D., of Lyons, was guillotined, but it is an error to credit him with the invention of the instrument. The inventor was Dr Joseph Agnace Guillotin.

*Iron Cage.* The Bishop of Verdun, who invented the Iron Cages, too small to allow the person confined in them to stand upright or lie at full length, was the first to be shut up in one; and Cardinal La Balue, who recommended them to Louis XI, was himself confined in one for ten years.

*Iron Shroud.* Ludovico Sforza, who invented the Iron Shroud, was the first to suffer death by this horrible torture.

*Maiden.* The Regent Morton of Scotland, who invented the Maiden (*q.v.*), was the first to be beheaded thereby.

*Ostracism.* Clisthenes introduced the custom of Ostracism (*q.v.*), and was the first to be banished thereby.

The *Perriere* was a piece of mediaeval artillery for throwing stones of 3,000 lb in weight; and the inventor fell a victim to his own invention by the accidental discharge of a perriere against a wall.

*Porta a Faenza*. Filippo Strozzi counselled the Duke Alessandro de Medici to construct the Porta a Faenza to intimidate the Florentines, and here he was himself murdered.

*Sanctuary*. Utropius induced the Emperor Arcadius to abolish the benefit of sanctuary; but a few days afterwards he committed some offence and fled for safety to the nearest church. St Chrysostom told him he had fallen into his own net, and he was put to death. (*Life of St Chrysostom*.)

*Turret-ship*. Cowper Coles, inventor of the turret-ship, perished in the *Captain* off Finisterre September 7th, 1870.

*Witch-finding*. Matthew Hopkins, the witch-finder, was himself tried by his own tests, and put to death as a wizard.

**Investiture.** The ceremonial clothing (Lat. *vestire*, to clothe) or investing of an official, dignitary, sovereign, etc., with the special robes or insignia of his office. Thus, a pair of gloves is given to a Freemason in France; a cap is given to a graduate; a crown, etc., to a sovereign, etc.; and a crosier and ring are placed in the hands of a church dignitary on his induction into office.

In the 11th and 12th centuries the kings of Europe and the pope were perpetually at variance about the right of investiture; the question was, did the right of appointing to vacant bishoprics and other ecclesiastical dignities belong to the spiritual or to the temporal power, the pope or the king? The Emperor Henry V relinquished his claim in 1111, but his action was not followed by the other European sovereigns.

**Invincible Doctor.** William of Occam (d.1347), or Ockham (a village in Surrey), the scholastic philosopher. He was also called *Doctor Singularis*, and *Princeps Nominalium*, for he was the reviver of nominalism.

**Invincibles, The Irish.** A Fenian secret society founded in Dublin in 1881 with the object of doing away with the English 'tyranny' and killing the 'tyrants'. Members of this society were responsible for the Phoenix Park murders in 1882.

**Invisibility,** according to fable, might be obtained in a multitude of ways. For example:

*Alberich's cloak*, 'Tarnkappe', which Siegfried got possession of, rendered him invisible. (*Nibelungenlied*.)

A *chamelon* carried in the breast would render a person invisible, as would a *capon stone* ('Alectoria'), if carried on the person.

A *dead hand*. It was believed that a candle placed in a dead man's hand gives no light to any but those who use it. *See* Hand.

The *helmet* of Perseus and the helmet that Pluto gave to the Cyclops (*Orci Galea*) both rendered the wearers invisible.

*Jack the Giant-killer* had a cloak of invisibility as well as a cap of knowledge.

*Otnit's ring*. The ring of Otnit, King of Lombardy, according to the *Heldenbuch*, possessed a similar charm.

*Reynard's wonderful ring* had three colours, one of which (green) caused the wearer to become invisible. (*Reynard the Fox, q.v.*).

*See also* Fern Seed; Gyges' Ring; Heliotrope.

The Druids were supposed to possess the power of making themselves invisible by producing a magic mist; and this spell, the *faeth fiadha*, appears in the stories of St Patrick and other early British saints.

**Invulnerability.** There are many fabulous instances of this having been acquired. According to ancient Greek legend, a dip in the river Styx rendered Achilles invulnerable, and Medea rendered Jason, with whom she had fallen in love, proof against wounds and fire by anointing him with the Promethean unguent.

Siegfried was rendered invulnerable by anointing his body with dragon's blood. (*Nibelungenlied*.)

**Ionian Mode.** A species of mediaeval church music in the key of C major, in imitation of the ancient Greek mode so called. It was the last of the 'authentic' church modes, and corresponded to the modern major diatonic scale. *Cp.* Gregorian.

**Ionic Architecture.** So called from Ionia, where it took its rise. The capitals are decorated with volutes, and the cornice with dentils. The shaft is fluted; the entablature either plain or embellished.

> The people of Ionia formed their order of architecture on the model of a young woman dressed in her hair, and of an easy, elegant shape; whereas the Doric had been formed on the model of a robust, strong man. Vitruvius

**Ionic School.** The school of philosophy that arose in Ionia in the 6th century BC, and which formed the starting-point of the whole of Greek philosophy. It included Thales, Anaximander, Anaximenes, Heraclitus, and Anaxagoras; and the great advance they made was the recognition that matter, motion, and physical causation were themselves manifestations of the Absolute Reality. They also tried to show that all created things spring from one universal physical cause; Thales said it was water, Anaximenes thought it was air, Anaxagoras that it was atoms, Heraclitus maintained that it was fire or caloric, while Anaximander insisted that the elements of all things are eternal, for *ex nihilo nihil fit*.

**Iormungandr.** *See* Jormungandr.

**Iota.** *See* I; Jot.

**Iphicles' Oxen.** ***Quid hoc ad Iphicli boves?*** What has that to do with the subject in hand? What has that to do with Hecuba? So in *L'Avocat* the judge had to pull up the shepherd every minute with the question, *Mais, mon ami, revenons à nos moutons*.

Neleus promised to give his daughter in marriage to Bias if he would bring him the oxen of Iphicles, which were guarded by a very fierce dog. Melampus was caught in the act of stealing them and was cast into prison. He afterwards told Astyocha, wife of Iphicles, how to become the mother of children (by steeping iron-rust in wine for ten days and then drinking it), and, as the treatment was effective (she became the mother of eight sons), Iphicles gave him the coveted herd, and his brother married the daughter of Neleus. (Odyssey, xi; Iliad, xiii, 23; Apollodoros, i, 9; Pausanias, iv, 36.)

When Tressilian wanted Dominie Holiday to tell him of a smith who could shoe his horse the pedagogue kept starting from the point, and Tressilian says to him:

> Permit me to ask, in your own learned phrase, *Quid hoc ad Iphycli boves*, what has that to do with my poor nag? Sir W. Scott, *Kenilworth*, ch. ix

**Iphigenia.** In classic legend, the daughter of Agamemnon and Clytemnestra. One account says that her father, having offended Artemis by killing her favourite stag, vowed to sacrifice to the angry goddess the most beautiful thing that came into his possession in the next twelve months; this was an infant daughter. The father deferred the sacrifice till the fleet of the combined Greeks that was proceeding to Troy reached Aulis and Iphigenia had grown to womanhood. Then Calchas told him that the fleet would be wind-bound till he had fulfilled his vow; accordingly the king prepared to sacrifice his daughter, but Artemis at the last moment snatched her from the altar and carried her to heaven, substituting a hind in her place. Euripides, Aeschylus, and Sophocles all wrote tragedies on Iphigenia.

The similarity of this legend to the Scripture stories of Jephthah's vow, and Abraham's offering of his son Isaac, is noticeable. *Cp.* Idomeneus.

**Ipse dixit** (Lat., he himself said so). A mere assertion, wholly unsupported. 'It is his *ipse dixit*', implies that there is no guarantee that what he says is so.

**Ipso facto** (Lat., by the very fact). Irrespective of all external considerations of right or wrong; absolutely. It sometimes means the act itself carries the consequences (as excommunication without the actual sentence being pronounced).

> By burning the Pope's bull, Luther *ipso facto* [by the very deed itself] denied the Pope's supremacy.
> Heresy carries excommunication *ipso facto*.

**Ipswich.** A corruption of *Gypeswick*, the town on the river 'Gyppen', now called the Orwell.

**Irak.** The name given at different times to varying portions of Mesopotamia (*q.v.*), Babylonia, and the surrounding country. It is now the official name of that portion of the country ruled by the king of Irak under British suzerainty.

**Iram.** An enchanted garden of old Persian legend, planted by the mythological king Shaddád, and for centuries sunk deep in the sands of Arabia. *See* Jamshid.

**Iran.** The empire of Persia; originally, the land of the Aryans (*q.v.*).

> Avenge the shame
> His race hath brought on Iran's name.
> Thomas Moore, *Fire Worshippers*

**Ireland.** Called by the natives 'Erin', i.e. *Eri-innis*, or *Iar-innis* (west island).

By the Welsh 'Yver-den' (west valley).

By Apuleius 'Hibernia', which is *Iernia*, a corruption of *Iar-inni-a*.

By Juvenal (ii, 260) 'Juverna' or 'Juberna', the same as *Ierna* or *Iernia*.

By Claudian 'Ouernia', the same.

By moderns 'Ireland', which is *Iar-en-land* (land of the west).

***The fair maid of Ireland.*** Ignis fatuus (*q.v.*).

> He had read in former times of a Going Fire, called 'Ignis Fatuus', the fire of destiny; by some, 'Will with the Wisp', or 'Jack with the Lantern'; and likewise, by some simple country people, 'The Fair Maid of Ireland', which used to lead wandering travellers out of their way.
> *The Seven Champions of Christendom*, i, 7

***The three great saints of Ireland.*** St Patrick, St Columba, and St Bridget.

***Ireland scholarships.*** Four scholarships of £30 a year in the University of Oxford, founded by Dr John Ireland, Dean of Westminster, in 1825, for Latin and Greek. They are tenable for four years. He also founded an 'Exegetical Professorship' of £800 a year.

**Irena.** In Spenser's *Faërie Queene* (Bk v), the personification of Ireland whose inheritance was withheld by the tyrant Grantorto (*q.v.*). Sir Artegal (*Justice*) is sent by the Faërie Queene to succour the distressed lady, and, Grantorto being slain, she is restored to her throne and reigns in peace.

**Iris.** Goddess of the rainbow, or the rainbow itself. In *classic mythology* she is called the messenger of the gods when they intended *discord*, and the rainbow is the bridge or road let down from heaven for her accommodation. When the gods meant *peace* they sent Mercury.

> I'll have an Iris that shall find thee out
> Shakespeare, *2 Henry VI*, 3, 2

Besides being poetically applied to the rainbow the name, in English, is given to the coloured membrane surrounding the pupil of the eye, and to a genus of plants (Iridaceae) having large, bright-coloured flowers and tuberous roots.

**Irish Stew.** *See* Stew.

**Iron.** ***If you have too many irons in the fire, some will burn.*** If you have more affairs in hand than you can properly attend to, some of them will be neglected and turn out badly. Both these locutions refer to the heaters or 'irons' employed in laundries.

***In irons.*** In fetters.

***Iron rations.*** Bully beef; tinned meat. Also emergency rations (*q.v.*).

***Pig iron.*** *See under* Pig.

***Strike while the iron is hot.*** Don't miss a good opportunity; seize time by the forelock; make hay while the sun shines.

***The Iron Age.*** The age of cruelty and hard-heartedness. When Hubert tells Prince Arthur he must burn his eyes out, the young prince replies, 'Ah, none but in this iron age would do it'. (Shakespeare, *King John*, 4, 1.)

The era between the death of Charlemagne and the close of the Carlovingian dynasty is sometimes so called from its almost ceaseless wars. It is sometimes called the *leaden* age for its worthlessness, and the *dark* age for its barrenness of learned men. *See also* Age.

***The Iron Cross.*** A Prussian military decoration (an iron Maltese cross, edged with silver and bearing the initials 'F.W.', i.e. Friedrich Wilhelm, and date 1871), formerly awarded for valour in the field.

***The Iron Crown of Lombardy.*** *See* Crown.

***The Iron Duke.*** The Duke of Wellington (1769–1852) was so called from his iron will.

***The iron entered into his soul.*** The anguish or annoyance is felt most keenly. The phrase arose in a mistranslation from the Hebrew of Psalm 105:18, which appeared in the Vulgate and was copied in some of the earlier English translations, but corrected in the Authorised Version. The Hebrew says 'his person entered into the iron' (i.e. he was laid in irons); but Coverdale and some others – following the Vulgate – have 'They hurte his fete in the stockes, the yron pearsed his herte'.

> I saw the iron enter into his soul, and felt what sort of pain it was that ariseth from hope deferred.
> Sterne, *Sentimental Journey*

***The iron horse.*** The railway locomotive.

***The Iron Maiden of Nuremberg.*** A mediaeval instrument of torture used in Germany for 'heretics', traitors, parricides, etc. It was a box big enough to admit a man, with folding-doors, the whole studded with sharp iron spikes. When the doors were pressed to these spikes were forced into the body of the victim, who was left there to die in horrible torture.

***The man in the iron mask.*** *See* Mask.

***Shooting-iron.*** Slang for a small firearm, especially a pistol or revolver.

***To rule with a rod of iron.*** To rule tyrannically.

**Iron-arm.** François de la Noue (1531–91), the Huguenot soldier, *Bras de Fer*, was so called. Fierabras (*q.v.*) is another form of the same.

**Iron-hand** or the **Iron-handed.** Goetz von Berlichingen (about 1480–1562), a German baron, who lost his right hand and had one made of iron to supply its place. Some accounts say that it was lost at the siege of Landshut, others that it was struck off in consequence of his having disregarded a law prohibiting duels.

**Iron-tooth.** Frederick II, Elector of Brandenburg (1440–70).

**Ironside.** Edmund II (about 989–1016), King of the West Saxons from April to November, 1016, was so called, from his iron armour.

***Nestor Ironside.*** Sir Richard Steele assumed the name in *The Guardian*.

**Ironsides.** The soldiers that served under Cromwell were so called, especially after the battle of Marston Moor, where they displayed an iron resolution. The name had first been applied only to a special regiment of stalwarts.

**Irony.** A dissembling (Gr. *eiron*, a dissembler, *eironeia*); hence, subtle sarcasm, language having a meaning different from the ostensible one and which will be understood correctly by the initiated. *Socratic irony* is an assumption of ignorance, as a means of leading on and eventually confuting an opponent.

***The irony of fate.*** A strange fatality which has brought about something quite the reverse of what might have been expected.

> By the irony of fate the Ten Hours Bill was carried in the very session when Lord Ashley, having changed his views on the Corn Laws, felt it his duty to resign his seat in Parliament.
>
> *The Leisure Hour*, 1887

**Iroquois.** The name given by the French (from one of their war-cries) to the five (now six) confederate tribes of North American Indians, viz. the Mohawks, Oneidas, Onondagas, Cayugas, Senecas, and sixth the Tuscaroras, added in 1712, forming 'The Six Nations of the Iroquois Confederacy'.

**Irrefragable Doctor.** Alexander Hales (d.1245), an English Franciscan, author of *Summa Theologiae*, and founder of the scholastic theology.

**Irresistible.** Alexander the Great went to consult the Delphic oracle before he started on his expedition against Persia. He chanced, however, to arrive on a day when no responses were made. Nothing daunted, he went in search of the Pythia, and when she refused to attend, took her to the temple by force. 'Son,' said the priestess, 'thou art irresistible.' 'Enough,' cried Alexander; 'I accept your words as my response.'

**Irritable Genus** or the '*Genus irritabile*' (Horace, *Epistles*, ii, 2, 102). Poets, and authors generally.

> It [publishers'] is a wrathful trade, and the irritable genus comprehends the bookselling as well as the book-writing species.
>
> Scott, *The Monastery* (Introd).

**Irus.** The beggar of gigantic stature, who kept watch over the suitors of Penelope. His real name was Arneos, but the suitors nicknamed him Irus because he carried their messages for them. Ulysses, on his return, felled him to the ground with a single blow, and flung his corpse out of doors.

***Poorer than Irus.*** A Greek proverb, adopted by the Romans and the French, alluding to the beggar referred to above.

**Irvingites.** Members of the Catholic Apostolic Church, founded by the Rev. Edward Irving in 1829; they believed in the gift of tongues.

**Isaac.** A hedge-sparrow; a dialect form of *haysugge*, or *haysuck*, an obsolete name for the bird (used by Chaucer). The name meant a *sucker* (small thing) that lived in a *hay* or hedge; a corruption of Chaucer's word, *heisuagge*.

**Isabelle.** The *colour* so called is the yellow of soiled calico. A yellow-dun horse is, in France, *un cheval isabelle*. To account for this word it is said that Isabel of Austria, daughter of Philip II, at the siege of Ostend vowed not to change her linen till the place was taken. As the siege lasted three years, we may well suppose that it was somewhat soiled by three years' wear; but as the siege was not over till 1604 and the word appears in an extant list of Queen Elizabeth's clothes of July, 1600 ('one rounde gowne of Isabella-colour satten'), this fable must be given up.

Another story attaches it to Isabella of Castile, who, we are told, made a vow to the Virgin not to change her linen till Granada fell into her hands; this siege also lasted longer than ladies are wont to wear their body-linen, and as it took place about the middle of the 15th century this *may* be the origin.

**Isaf.** A pre-Mohammedan Arabian idol in the form of a man, brought from Syria, and placed in Es-Safa, near the temple of Mecca. The story is that Isaf was a man converted into stone for impiety, and that Mahomet suffered it to remain as a warning to his disciples.

**Isenbras** or **Isumbras, Sir.** A hero of mediaeval romance (including, as usual, visits to the Holy Land and the slaughter of thousands of 'Saracens'), first proud and presumptuous, when he was visited by all sorts of punishments; afterwards, penitent and humble, his afflictions were turned into blessings. It was in this latter stage that he one day carried on his horse two children of a poor woodman across a ford.

**Isengrin** or **Isgrim**, the wolf, afterwards created Earl of Pitwood, in the beast-epic of *Reynard the Fox*. Isengrin typifies the barons, and Reynard the church; and the gist of the tale is to show how Reynard bamboozles his uncle Wolf. (Ger. *Isegrimm*, a wolf, a surly fellow).

**Iseult.** *See* Ysolde.

**Ishban,** in *Absalom and Achitophel*, is Sir Robert Clayton, who'd 'e'en turn loyal to be made a peer' (Pt ii).

**Ishbosheth,** in Dryden's *Absalom and Achitophel*, is meant for Richard Cromwell. His father, Oliver, is Saul. At the death of Saul, Ishbosheth was acknowledged king by a party, and reigned two years, when he was assassinated. (Part i, 57, 58.)

They who, when Saul was dead, without a blow,
Made foolish Ishbosheth the crown forego.

The actual Ishbosheth (= man of shame) was the son of Saul, who was proclaimed King of Israel at his father's death (*see* 2 Sam. 4), and was almost immediately superseded by David.

**Ishtar.** The Babylonian goddess of love and war (Gr. *Astarte*), corresponding with the Phoenician Ashtoreth (*q.v.*), except that while the latter was identified with the moon Ishtar was more frequently identified with the planet Venus. She was the wife of Bel.

**Isiac Tablet** (i.e. tablet of Isis). A spurious Egyptian monument sold by a soldier to Cardinal Bembo in 1527, and preserved at Turin. It is of copper, and on it are represented most of the Egyptian deities in the mysteries of Isis. It was said to have been found at the siege of Rome in 1525.

**Isidorian Decretals.** *See* Decretals.

**Isinglass.** A corruption of the Dutch *huyzenblas*, a sturgeon's bladder (Ger. *hausen*, sturgeon): it is prepared from the bladders and sounds of sturgeon, and was introduced from Holland in the 16th century.

**Isis.** The principal goddess of ancient Egypt, sister and wife of Osiris, and mother of Horus. She was identified with the moon (Osiris being a sun-god), and the cow was sacred to her, its horns representing the crescent moon which, in Egypt, appears lying on its back.

Her chief temples were at Amydos, Busiris, and Philae; she is represented as a queen, her head being surmounted by horns and the solar disk or by the double crown. Proclus mentions a statue of her which bore the inscription –

I am that which is, has been, and shall be. My veil no one has lifted. The fruit I bore was the Sun –

hence *to lift the veil of Isis* is to pierce to the heart of a great mystery.

She was identified with Io, Aphrodite, and others by the Greeks; with Selene, Ceres, Venus, Juno, etc., by the Romans; and the Phoenicians confused her with Ashtoreth. Her worship as a nature goddess was very popular among the later Greeks and with the Romans of republican times. Milton, in *Paradise Lost* (I, 478), places her among the fallen angels.

**Isis, River.** *See* Thames.

**Islam.** The Mohammedan religion, the whole body of Mohammedans, the true Mohammedan faith. The Moslems say every child is born in Islam, and would continue in the true faith if not led astray. The word means *resignation* or *submission to the will of God.*

Islam consists of five duties:

(1) Bearing witness that there is but one God.
(2) Reciting daily prayers.
(3) Giving the appointed and legal alms.
(4) Observing the Ramazan (a month's fast).
(5) Making a pilgrimage to Mecca at least once in a lifetime.

**Islands of the Blest.** *See* Fortunate Islands.

**Isle of Dogs.** A peninsula on the left bank of the Thames between the Limehouse and Blackwall reaches, opposite Greenwich. It is said to be so called because it was here that Edward III kept his greyhounds; but another explanation is that it is a corruption of *Isle of Ducks*, from the number of wild fowl anciently inhabiting the marshes.

**Ismene.** In Greek legend, daughter of Oedipus and Jocasta. Antigone was buried alive by the order of King Creon, for burying her brother Polynices, slain in combat by his brother Eteocles. Ismene declared that she had aided her sister, and requested to be allowed to share the same punishment.

**Isocrates. *The French Isocrates*.** Esprit Fléchier (1632–1710), Bishop of Nismes, specially famous for his funeral orations. Isocrates himself (d.338 BC) was one of the great orators of Athens and was distinguished as a teacher of eloquence.

**Israel,** in Dryden's *Absalom and Achitophel* (*q.v.*), stands for England.

**Israelites.** A small sect of religious enthusiasts who claim that, while the Jews follow the Law and the Christians the Gospel, they adhere to and acknowledge both. They are vegetarians and – as they abstain so far as possible from taking life of any sort – ardent pacifists: also, they never cut their hair or shave.

**Israfil.** The angel of music of the Mohammedans. He possesses the most melodious voice of all God's creatures, and is to sound the Resurrection Trump which will ravish the ears of the saints in paradise. Israfil, Gabriel, and Michael were the three angels that, according to the Koran, warned Abraham of Sodom's destruction.

In Heaven a spirit doth dwell
Whose heart-strings are a lute;
None sing so wildly well
As the angel Israfel,

And the giddy Stars (so legends tell),
Ceasing their hymns, attend the spell
Of his voice, all mute. E. A. Poe, *Israfel*

**Issachar,** in Dryden's satire of *Absalom and Achitophel* (*q.v.*), means Thomas Thynne (1648–82), of Longleat, known as 'Tom of Ten Thousand'. He was a friend of the Duke of Monmouth, and was married to Lady Elizabeth Percy, widow of the Earl of Ogle; before the match was consummated he was murdered by ruffians hired by Count Königsmark, another of the lady's suitors, and she, within three months, married the Duke of Somerset.

***Issachar's ears.*** Ass's ears. The allusion is to Gen. 49:14: 'Issachar is a strong ass couching down between two burdens.'

Is't possible that you, whose ears
Are of the tribe of Issachar's ...
Should yet be deaf against a noise
So roaring as the public voice?
S. Butler, *Hudibras to Sidrophel*

**Issue.** The point of law in debate or in question. 'At issue', under dispute.

***To join issue.*** To take opposite views of a question, or opposite sides in a suit.

***To join issues.*** To leave a suit to the decision of the court because the parties interested cannot agree.

**Istar.** *See* Ishtar.

**Isthmian Games.** Games consisting of chariot races, running, wrestling, boxing, etc., held by the ancient Greeks in the Isthmus of Corinth every alternate spring, the first and third of each Olympiad. Epsom races, and other big sporting events, have been called our 'Isthmian games' in allusion to these.

**Isthmus of Suez.** The covered bridge of St John's College, Cambridge, is so called, because it connects the college with the grounds on the other side of the river. 'Suez' here is a pun on the Lat. *sus* (a hog), the Johnians being nicknamed *hogs* in University slang.

**Isumbras.** *See* Isenbras.

**It. *I'm it!*** I'm a person of some importance; I'm at the top of the tree (in a particular line). When used with the proper emphasis a lot of irony can be conveyed by this little word.

***In for it.*** About 'to catch it'; on the point of being in trouble.

You are in for it, I can tell you. I would not stand in your shoes for something.

In such phrases as this, and as *to come it strong*, *to rough it*, etc., *it* is the indefinite object of the transitive or intransitive verb.

**Italic.** Pertaining to Italy, especially ancient Italy and the parts other than Rome.

***Italic type*** or ***italics*** (the type in which the letters, instead of being erect – as in Roman – slope from left to right, *thus*) was first used by Aldo Manuzio in printing the Aldine classics. It was called by him 'Cursive' (a running hand; Lat. *curro*, to run). Virgil was the first author printed in this type (1501). Francesco of Bologna cast it.

***The words italicised*** in the Bible have no corresponding words in the original. The translators supplied these words to render the sense of the passage more full and clear.

***Italic School of Philosophy.*** The Pythagorean (6th cent. BC), so called because Pythagoras taught in Italy.

***Italic version.*** An early Latin version of the Bible, prepared from the Septuagint. It preceded the Vulgate, or the version by St Jerome.

**Itch, To.** Properly, to have an irritation of the skin which gives one a desire to scratch the part affected; hence, figuratively, to feel a constant teasing desire for something. The figure of speech enters into many phrases; as, *to itch* or *to have an itch for gold*, to have a longing desire for wealth; *an itching palm* means the same:

Let me tell you, Cassius, you yourself
Are much condemned to have an itching palm
Shakespeare, *Julius Caesar*, 4, 3

Similarly, *to have itching ears*, is to be very desirous for news or novelty:

The time will come when they will not endure the sound doctrine; but, having itching ears, will heap to themselves teachers after their own lusts. 2 Tim. 4:3 (R.V.)

And *My fingers itch to be at him* means, 'I am longing to give him a sound thrashing.'

It was formerly a popular idea that the itching of various parts foretold various occurrences; for instance, if your right palm itched you were going to receive money, the itching of the left eye betokened grief, and of the right pleasure:

My right eye itches now, so I shall see
My love. Theocritus, 1, 37

Itching of the lips of course foretold that they were shortly to kiss or be kissed; of the nose, that strangers were at hand:

We shall ha' guests today
... My nose itcheth so.
Dekker, *Honest Whore*

And of the thumb, that evil approaches

By the pricking of my thumbs.
Something evil this way comes.
Shakespeare, *Macbeth*, 4, 1

**Ithacensian Suitors, The.** The suitors of Penelope (*q.v.*).

All the ladies, each and each.
Like the Ithacensian suitors in old time,
Stared with great eyes, and laughed with alien lips.
Tennyson, *The Princess*, iv

**Ithuriel.** The angel who, with Zephon (*q.v.*), was, in Milton's *Paradise Lost*, commissioned by Gabriel to search for Satan, after he had effected his entrance into Paradise. The name is Rabbinical, and means 'the discovery of God'.

Ithuriel and Zephon, with winged speed
Search through this garden; leave unsearched no nook.
*Paradise Lost*, Bk iv, 788

He was armed with a spear, the slightest touch of which exposed deceit. Hence, when Satan squatted like a toad 'close to the ear of Eve', Ithuriel made him resume his proper form:

Him [i.e. Satan], thus intent Ithuriel with his spear
Touched lightly; for no falsehood can endure
Touch of celestial temper, but returns
Of force to its own likeness.
*Paradise Lost*, iv, 810

The acute pen of Lord Hailes, which, like Ithuriel's spear, conjured so many shadows from Scottish history, dismissed among the rest those of Banquo and Fleance.
Sir W. Scott

**Itinerary.** The account of a route followed by a traveller. The Itinerary of Antoninus marks out all the main roads of the Roman Empire, and the stations of the Roman army. The Itinerary of Peutinger (*Tabula Peutingeriana*) is also an invaluable document of ancient geography, executed AD 393, in the reign of Theodosius the Great, and hence called sometimes the *Theodosian Table*.

**Its.** One of the words by the use of which Chatterton betrayed his forgeries. He wrote in a poem purporting to be the work of a 15th century priest, 'Life and its goods I scorn', but the word was not in use till more than two centuries later than his supposed time, it (*hit*) and *his* being the possessive case.

For love and devocioun towards god also hath *it* infancie and it hath *it* comyng forewarde in groweth of age.
Udal's Erasmus, *Luke*, vii (1548)

Learning hath *his* infancy, when it is but beginning and almost childish; then *his* youth … then *his* strength of yeares … and lastly, *his* old age.
Bacon, *Essays; of Vicissitude of Things* (1625)

*Its* does not occur in any play of Shakespeare published in his lifetime, but there is one instance in the First Folio of 1623 (*Measure for Measure*, 1, 2), as well as nine instances of *it's*. Nor does *its* occur in the Authorised Version of the Bible (1611), the one instance of it in modern editions (Lev. 25:5) having been substituted for *it* in the Bible printed for Hills and Field in 1660.

**Ivan.** The Russian form of John, called *Juan* in Spain, *Giovanni* in Italian.

***Ivan the Terrible.*** Ivan IV of Russia (1530, 1533–84), infamous for his cruelties, but a man of great energy. He first adopted the title of Tsar.

**Ivanhoe.** Sir Walter Scott took the name of his hero from the village of Ivanhoe, or Ivinghoe, in Bucks, a line in an old rhymed proverb – 'Tring, Wing, and Ivanhoe' – having attracted his attention.

**Ivanovitch.** The national impersonation of the Russians as a people, as *John Bull* is of the English, *Brother Jonathan* of the Americans, *Jean Crapaud* of the French, and *Cousin Michael* of the Germans.

**Ivories.** Teeth; also dice, billiard balls, dominoes, etc.

***To show one's ivories.*** To display one's teeth.

***To wash one's ivories.*** To rinse the mouth; to drink.

**Ivory Gate.** *See* Dreams, Gates of.

**Ivory shoulder.** *See* Pelops.

**Ivy** (A.S., *ifig*). Dedicated to Bacchus from the notion that it is a preventive of drunkenness. But whether the Dionysian ivy is the same plant as that which we call *ivy* is doubtful, as it was famous for its golden berries, and was termed *chryso-carpos*. An ivy wreath was the prize of the Isthmian games, till it was superseded by a pine garland.

In Christian symbolism *ivy* typifies the everlasting life, from its remaining continually green.

***Like an owl in an ivy-bush.*** *See* Owl.

**Ivy Lane.** In the time of Henry III this street out of Paternoster Row was called *Alsies Lane*, probably from the name of a local landowner; this became *Alfies* Lane, which was further corrupted to *Yviese*, and so *Yvi*, or *Ivy* Lane.

**Ixion.** In Greek legend, a king of the Lapithae who was bound to a revolving wheel of fire in the Infernal regions, either for his impious presumption in trying to imitate the thunder of heaven, or for boasting of the favours supposed to have been conferred on him by Hera, Zeus having sent a cloud to him in the form of Hera, and the cloud having become by him the mother of the Centaurs (*q.v.*).

# J

**J.** The tenth letter of the alphabet; a modern letter, only differentiated from I (*q.v.*), the consonantal functions of which it took, in the 17th century, and not completely separated till the 19th. There is no roman J or j in the 1611 Authorised Version of the Bible. In the Roman system of numeration it was (and in medical prescriptions still is) used in place of i as the final figure in a series – iij, vij, etc., for our iii, vii.

**Jaafer.** At the battle of Muta (629), when the Mohammedans for the first time fought, and defeated, the Christians, Jaafer carried the sacred banner of the Prophet. One hand being lopped off, he held it with the other; the other being struck off, he embraced it with his two stumps; his head being cleft in twain, he flung himself on the banner staff, and the banner was detained thus till Abdallah seized it and handed it to Khaled. A similar tale is told of Cynaegiros (*q.v.*).

**Jachin and Boaz.** The two great bronze pillars set up by Solomon at the entrance of his Temple – *Jachin* being the right-hand (southern) pillar, and the name probably expressing permanence, immovability, and *Boaz* being the left-hand (northern) pillar typifying the Lord of all strength. *See* 1 Kings 7:21; Ezek. 40:49.

> The props of such proud seminaries fall,
> The Jachin and the Boaz of them all.
>
> Cowper, *Tirocinium*, 499

**Jack.** A personal name, probably a diminutive of *John*, but confused with the French diminutive of *Jacob*, viz. *Jacques* (*q.v.*).

The name has a place in a number of common English phrases (which are given first below), and is used in a large number of transferred senses, which – except when they have already been given among the phrases – are here grouped under one or other of the following headings:

(i) As applied to men, usually in a contemptuous sense.

(ii) Indicative of *quasi*-personality.

(iii) Applied to machinery and contrivances taking the place of a workman or servant.

(iv) Applied to inferior articles.

(v) In names of animals, usually denoting the male sex or smallness, and of plants of inferior kind.

(vi) 'Jack' in history, legend, story, etc.

**Phrases.**

***A good Jack makes a good Jill.*** A good husband makes a good wife, a good master makes a good servant. Jack, a generic name for man, husband, or master; and Jill for a woman.

***A Jack of all trades is master of none.*** One who can turn his hand to anything is not usually an expert in any one branch. *Jack of all trades* is a contemptuous expression – he is a sciolist.

***Before you can say Jack Robinson.*** Immediately. Grose says that the saying had its birth from a very volatile gentleman of that name, who used to pay flying visits to his neighbours, and was no sooner announced than he was off again; Halliwell says (*Archaic Dictionary*, 1846):

> The following lines from 'an old play' are elsewhere given as the original phrase –
> A warke it ys as easie to be done
> As tys to saye *Jacke! robys on.*

But the 'old play' has never been identified, and both these accounts are palpably *ben trovato.* The phrase was in use in the 18th century, and is to be found in Fanny Burney's *Evelina* (1778), II, xxxvii.

***Every Jack shall have his Jill.*** Every man may find a wife if he likes; or rather, every country rustic shall find a lass to be his mate.

> Jack shall have his Jill,
> Nought shall go ill;
> The man shall have his mare again, and all shall be well.
>
> Shakespeare, *Midsummer Night's Dream*, 3, 2

***Every man Jack of them.*** All without exception, even the most insignificant. Shakespeare uses the word in the same sense in *Cymbeline*, 2, 1 – 'Every Jack-slave hath his bellyful of fighting.'

***Jack Drum's Entertainment.*** *See* Drum.

***Jack's as good as his master.*** An old proverb (like 'When Adam delv'd and Eve span'; *see* Adam) indicating the equality of man. It was the wise Agur (*see* Proverbs, 30:22) who placed 'a servant when he reigneth' as the first of the four things that the earth cannot bear.

***Jack will never be a gentleman.*** A mere parvenu will never be like a well-bred gentleman but will always betray his origin.

> The world is grown so bad
> That wrens make prey where eagles dare not perch!

> Since every Jack became a gentleman
> There's many a gentle person made a Jack.
> Shakespeare, *Richard III*, 1, 3

***To be upon their jacks.*** To have the advantage over one. The reference is to the jack, or jerkin, a coat of mail quilted with stout leather.

***To jack up one's job.*** To abandon it, throw it up. Probably a corruption of *chuck up*. Similarly, *to be quite jacked up* is to be done for, ruined, finished.

***To make one's jack.*** To be successful. The allusion is to the jack in games, such as bowls.

***To play the Jack.*** To play the rogue, the knave, or the 'giddy goat'. To deceive or lead astray like Jack-o'-lantern, or *ignis fatuus*.

> – your fairy, which you say, is a harmless fairy, has done little better than played the Jack with us.
> Shakespeare, *Tempest*, 4, 1

(i) *Applied to Men* (*usually in contempt*).

***Cheap Jack.*** *See* Cheap.

***Cousin Jack.*** *See* Cousin.

***Jack Adams.*** A fool.

***Jack-a-dandy.*** A term of endearment for a smart, bright little fellow; a 'Jemmy Jessamy'.

> Smart she is, and handy, O!
> Sweet as sugar-candy, O! …
> And I'm her Jack-a-dandy, O!

***Jack-a-dandy*** is also rhyming-slang for brandy.

***Jack-a-dreams.*** *See* John-a-dreams.

***Jack-a-Lent.*** A kind of Aunt Sally which was thrown at in Lent; hence, a puppet, a sheepish booby. Shakespeare says: 'You little Jack-a-Lent, have you been true to us?' (*Merry Wives*, 3, 3).

> Thou, that when last thou wert put out of service,
> Travell'dst to Hampstead Heath on an Ash Wednesday
> Where thou didst stand six weeks the Jack of Lent,
> For boys to hurl, three throws a penny, at thee,
> To make thee a purse.
> Ben Jonson, *Tale of a Tub*, IV, iii

***Jack among the maids.*** A favourite with the ladies; a ladies' man.

***Jackanapes.*** A pert, vulgar, apish little fellow; a prig. The word first appears as a derisive nickname for William de la Pole, Duke of Suffolk (murdered in 1450), whose badge was the clog and chain of a tame ape. *Jackanapes* must, however, have been in use before it became a nickname, and it is uncertain whether the *-napes* is connected originally with *ape* or with *Naples*, *Jackanapes* being a *Jack* (monkey) of (imported from) *Naples*, just as *fustian-a-napes* was fustian from Naples. There is an early 15th-century record of monkeys being sent to England from Italy; and by the 16th century, at all events, *Jackanapes* was in use as a proper name for a tame ape. *See also* Jack-a-Napes *below*.

> I will teach a scurvy jackanape priest to meddle or make.
> Shakespeare, *Merry Wives of Windsor*, 1, 4

***Jackass.*** An unmitigated fool.

***Jack-at-a-pinch.*** One who lends a hand in an emergency; a clergyman, for instance, who has no cure, but officiates for a fee in any church where his assistance is required.

***Jack Brag.*** *See* Brag.

***Jackdaw.*** A prating nuisance.

***Jack-in-office.*** A conceited official or upstart, who presumes on his appointment to give himself airs.

***Jack-in-the-green.*** A youth or boy who moves about concealed by a wicker framework covered with leaves and boughs as part of the chimney-sweeps' revels on May Day. An old English custom now dead or dying.

***Jack Ketch.*** A hangman. *See sect.* vi *below*.

***Jack of all trades.*** *See* Phrases *above*.

***Jack of both sides.*** One who tries to favour two antagonistic parties, either from fear or for profit.

***Jack out of office.*** One no longer in office; one dismissed from his employment.

> I am left out; for me nothing remains,
> But long I will not be Jack-out-of-office.
> Shakespeare, *1 Henry VI*, 1, 1

***Jack Pudding.*** A buffoon, a mountebank; perhaps originally one who performed tricks, such as swallowing a certain number of yards of black pudding.

***Jack-sauce.*** An insolent sauce-box, 'the worst Jack of the pack'. Fluellen says one who challenges another and refuses to fight is a 'Jack-sauce' (*Henry V*, 4, 7).

***Jack-snip.*** A botching tailor.

***Jack Sprat.*** A dwarf; as if sprats were dwarf mackerels. Children, by a similar metaphor, are called small fry.

***Jack Tar.*** A common sailor, whose hands and clothes are tarred by the ship tackling.

(ii) *In Quasi-Personal Uses.*

***Jack-a-lantern***, or ***Jack-o'-lantern.*** A will o' the wisp. *See* Ignis Fatuus.

***Jack Drum.*** *See* Drum.

***Jack Frost.*** The personification of frost or frosty weather.

***Jack-in-the-box.*** A toy consisting of a box out of which, when the lid is raised, a figure springs.

***Jack in the cellar.*** Old slang for an unborn child: a translation of the Dutch expression for the same *Hans in kelder*.

***Jack of cards.*** The knave or boy of the king and queen of the same suit.

***Jack o' the bowl.*** The brownie or house spirit of Switzerland; so called from the custom of placing for him every night on the roof of the cowhouse a bowl of fresh sweet cream. The contents are sure to disappear before morning.

***Jackey.*** A monkey. *Cp.* Jackanapes *above*.

***Yellow jack.*** The yellow fever.

(iii) *Applied to Machinery* and contrivances taking the place of a workman or servant.

A very large number of appliances and parts of appliances are called by this name; such as the *jack*, *bottlejack*, or *roastingjack*, used for turning the meat when roasting before an open fire; the *jack* used for lifting heavy weights; the rough stool or wooden horse used for sawing timber on; etc. Other instances of this use are:

***Boot-jack.*** An instrument for drawing off boots, which used to be done by inferior servants.

***Jack-block.*** A block attached to the topgallant-tie of a ship.

***Jack-in-the-basket.*** The cap or basket on the top of a pole to indicate the place of a sandbank at sea, etc.

***Jack-o'-the clock*** or ***clock-house.*** The figure which, in some old public clocks, comes out to strike the hours on the bell.

> Strike like Jack o' the clock-house, never but in season. Wm Strode, *Floating Island* (1655)

> *King Richard*: Well, but what's o'clock?
> *Buckingham*: Upon the stroke of ten.
> *K.R.*: Well, let it strike.
> *B.*: Why let it strike?
> *K.R.*: Because that, like a jack, thou keep'st the stroke
> Betwixt thy begging and my meditation.
> Shakespeare, *Richard III*, 4, 2

***Jack-roll.*** The cylinder round which the rope of a well coils.

***Jack-screw.*** A large screw rotating in a threaded socket, used for lifting heavy weights.

***Lifting-jack.*** A machine for lifting the axle tree of a carriage when the wheels are cleaned.

***Smoke-jack.*** An apparatus in a chimney-flue for turning a spit. It is made to revolve by the upward current of smoke and air.

(iv) *Applied to inferior articles* which bear the same relation to the thing imitated as 'Jack' does to a 'gentleman' (*see* Phrases *above*), as to the small flag carried at the bow in ships (*cp.* Union Jack); a small drinking vessel made of waxed leather, the large one being called a *black-jack* (*q.v.*):

> Body of me, I am dry still; give me the Jack, boy.
> Beaumont and Fletcher, *Bloody Brother*, 2, 2

Also to an inferior kind of armour consisting of a leather surcoat worn over the hauberk, from the 14th to the 17th century. It was formed by overlapping pieces of steel fastened by one edge upon canvas, coated over with cloth or velvet, and was worn by the peasantry of the English borders in their skirmishes with moss-troopers, etc. North, in his translation of Plutarch (1579; *Life of Crassus*), applies the word to the armour of the Parthians:

> For himself [i.e., Crassus] and his men with weak and light staves, brake upon them that were armed with curaces of steel, or stiff leather jacks.

And the 'jack' at bowls is so called because it is very small in comparison with the bowls themselves.

***A Jack*** and ***a half-jack.*** Counters resembling a sovereign and a half-sovereign; used at gaming-tables.

***Jack boots.*** Cumbrous boots of thick leather worn by fishermen, cavalrymen, etc.

***Jack of Dover.*** Some unidentified eatable mentioned by Chaucer in the *Cook's Prologue*. 'Our host', addressing the cook, says:

> Now telle on, Roger, loke that it be good;
> For many a pastee hastow laten blood,
> And many a Jakke of Dover hastow sold
> That hath been twyes hoot and twyes cold.

Professor Skeat says that this is 'probably a pie that had been cooked more than once'; another suggestion is that it means some sea-fish (*cp.* John Dory); while another is that it is the heel-taps of bottles of wine collected into a *jack*, and, by being served to customers, made to 'do over' (*Dover*) again!

***Jack plane, Jack saw.*** A plane or saw to do the rough work before the finer instruments are used.

***Jack rafter.*** A rafter in a hipped roof, shorter than a full-sized one.

**Jack rib.** An inferior rib in an arch, being shorter than the rest.

**Jack timbers.** Timbers in a building shorter than the rest.

**Jack towel.** A coarse, long towel hung on a roller, for servants' use.

(v) *Applied to animals and plants:* usually with reference to the male sex, smallness, or inferiority.

**Jackass, Jack-baker** (a kind of owl), **Jack** or **dog fox, Jack hare, Jack hern, Jack rat, Jack shark, Jack snipe**: a young pike is called a *Jack*, so also were the male birds used in falconry.

**Jack-in-the-hedge, Jack-go-to-bed-at-noon, Jack-jump-about,** and **Jack-in-the-bush,** are names of various common wild flowers.

**Jack-curlew.** The whimbrel, a small species of curlew.

**Jack-in-a-bottle.** The long-tailed tit-mouse, or bottle-tit; so called from the shape of its nest.

**Jack-rabbit.** A large prairie-hare of North America; shortened from *Jackass-rabbit*, a name given to it on account of its very long ears and legs.

(vi) *In History, story, etc.*

**Jack Amend-All.** One of the nicknames given to Jack Cade (killed 1450), the leader of 'Cade's Rebellion'. He promised to remedy all abuses.

**Jack-a-Napes.** The nickname of William de la Pole, Duke of Suffolk, who was beheaded at sea (off Dover), possibly at the instigation of the Duke of York (1450). The name was given to him on account of his device, the clog and chain of an ape, which was also the cause of another of his names – 'Ape-clogge'. *See also* Jackanapes *in sect.* i *above.*

**Jack and the Beanstalk.** A nursery tale found among all sorts of races from Icelanders to Zulus. As we know it, it is of Teutonic origin: the 'beanstalk' is the ash, Yggdrasil, of the *Eddas*; the giant is All-Father, whose three treasures are a harp – i.e. the wind, bags full of treasures – i.e. the rain, and the red hen which laid golden eggs – that is, the genial sun. 'Jack' typifies Man, who avails himself of these treasures and becomes rich.

**Jack and Jill.** The well known nursery rhyme is a relic of a Norse myth, accounting for the dark patches in the moon: the two children are said to have been kidnapped by the moon while drawing water, and they are still to be seen with the bucket hanging from a pole resting on their shoulders.

An otherwise unknown comedy *Jack and Jill* is mentioned in the Revels Accounts as having been played at court in 1567–8. *Jill*, or *Gill*, is an abbreviation of *Gillian*, for *Juliana*.

**Jack the Giant-killer.** The hero of this old nursery tale owed much of his success to his four marvellous possessions – an invisible coat, a cap of wisdom, shoes of swiftness, and a resistless sword. When he put on his coat no eye could see him; when he had his shoes on no one could overtake him; his sword would cut through everything; and when his cap was on he knew everything he required to know. The story is given by Walter Map (and later by Geoffrey of Monmouth), who obtained it in the early 13th century from a French chronicle.

**Jack Horner.** The usually accepted explanation of the old nursery rhyme 'Little Jack Horner' is that Jack was steward to the Abbot of Glastonbury at the time of the Dissolution of the Monasteries, and that he, by a subterfuge, became possessed of the deeds of the Manor of Mells, which is in the neighbourhood and which is still owned by his descendants of the same name. Some say that these deeds with others were sent to Henry VIII concealed, for safety, in a pasty; that 'Jack Horner' was the bearer; and that on the way he lifted the crust and extracted this 'plum'.

**Jack Ketch.** A hangman and executioner, notorious for his barbarity, who was appointed about 1663 and died in 1686. He was the executioner of William, Lord Russell, for his share in the Rye House Plot (1683) and of Monmouth (1685). In 1686 he was turned out of office for insulting one of the sheriffs, and was succeeded by a butcher named Rose. Rose, however, was himself hanged within four months, whereupon Ketch was reinstated. As early as 1678 his name had appeared in a ballad, and by 1702 it was associated with the Punch and Judy puppet-play, which had recently been introduced from Italy.

> Ketch the executioner, a wretch who had butchered many brave and noble victims, and whose name has, during a century and a half, been vulgarly given to all who have succeeded him in his odious office.
>
> Macaulay, *Hist. of England*, vol. i, ch. v

**Jack of Newbury.** John Winchcombe (d.1520), a wealthy clothier in the reign of Henry VIII. He was the hero of many chap-books, and is said to have kept 100 looms in his own house at Newbury, while legend relates that he equipped at his own expense 100 to 200 of his men to aid the king against the Scots in Flodden Field.

***Jack the Ripper.*** An unknown person who committed a series of murders in the East End of London on prostitutes in 1888–89. He gave himself the name, and the mystery surrounding his crimes made it very widely known.

The first murder was April 2nd, 1888; the next was August 7th; the third was August 31st; the fourth was September 8th; the fifth was September 30th, when two women were murdered; the sixth was November 9th; the seventh was December 20th, in a builder's yard; the eighth was July 17th, 1889, at Whitechapel; the ninth was September 17th.

***Jack Straw.*** The name (or nickname) of one of the leaders in the Peasants' Revolt of 1381. There is an allusion to him in Chaucer's *Nun's Prologue* (1386), and the name soon came to signify a man of straw, a worthless sort of person.

It shall be but the weight of a strawe, or the weight of Jack Strawe more.
Thos Nash, *Nashe's Lenten Staffe* (1598)

**Jackal.** A toady. One who does the dirty work of another. It was once thought that the jackals hunted in troops to provide the lion with prey, hence they were called the 'lion's providers'. No doubt the lion will at times avail himself of the jackal's assistance by appropriating prey started by these 'hunters', but it would be folly to suppose that the jackal acted on the principle of *vos non vobis. See* Lion's Provider.

**Jacket.** Diminutive of *jack*, a surcoat (whence the armour, *see* Jack, sect. iv).

The skin of a potato is called its 'jacket'. Potatoes brought to table unpeeled are said to be 'with their jackets on'.

*To dust one's jacket,* or *to give one a good jacketing. See* Dust.

**Jacksonian Professor.** The professor of natural and experimental philosophy at Cambridge. The professorship was founded in 1782 by the Rev. Richard Jackson, a fellow of Trinity.

**Jacob's Ladder.** The ladder seen by the patriarch Jacob in a vision (Gen. 28:12). *Jacob* is, on this account, a cant name for a ladder, and steep and high flights of steps going up cliffs, etc., are often called *Jacob's ladders*, as is a flaw in a stocking where only the woof threads are left, the warp threads giving a ladder-like appearance. There is a garden flower also so called.

**Jacob's Staff.** A pilgrim's staff; from the Apostle James (Lat. *Jacobus*), who is usually represented with a staff and scallop shell.

As he had travelled many a summer's day
Through boiling sands of Arabie and Ynd;
And in his hand a Jacob's staff to stay
His weary limbs upon.
Spenser, *Faërie Queene*, Bk i, canto vi, 32–35

Also the name of an obsolete instrument for taking heights and distances.

Reach then a soaring quill, that I may write
As with a Jacob's staff to take her height.
Cleveland, *The Hecatomb to his Mistress*

***Jacob's stone.*** The Coronation Stone (*see* Scone) is sometimes so called, because of the legend that it was on this stone that Jacob's head rested when he had the vision of the angels ascending and descending the ladder (Gen. 28:11).

**Jacobins.** The Dominicans were so called in France from the 'Rue St Jacques', Paris, where they first established themselves in 1219; and the French Revolutionary club (known as the 'Society of Friends of the Constitution' when founded at Versailles in 1789) took the name because, on their removal to Paris, they met in the hall of an ex-convent of Jacobins, in the Rue St Honoré.

**Jacobites.** The partisans of James II (Lat. *Jacobus*) and the exiled members of his house, after William III had superseded him.

***Jacobites.*** An Oriental sect of Monophysites, so called from Jacobus Baradaeus, Bishop of Edessa, in Syria, in the 6th century. The Jacobite Church comprises three Patriarchates, viz., those of Alexandria, Antioch, and Armenia.

**Jacobus.** The unofficial name of a gold coin of the value of from 20*s*. to 24*s*., struck in the reign of James I.

**Jacquard Loom.** So called from Jos. Marie Jacquard (1752–1834), of Lyons, its inventor. It is a machine for weaving figures upon silks and muslins.

**Jacquerie, La.** An insurrection of the peasantry of France in 1358, excited by the oppressions of the privileged classes and Charles the Bad of Navarre, while King Jean II was a prisoner in England; so called from *Jacques*, or *Jacques Bonhomme*, the generic name (like our 'Hodge') given to the French peasantry. They banded together, fortified themselves and declared war to the death against every gentleman in France, but in six weeks some 12,000 of the insurgents were cut down, and the rebellion suppressed with the greatest determination.

**Jacques** (*Fr.*). A generic name for the poor artisan class in France (*see* Jacquerie, La, *above*), so called from the *jaque*, a rough kind of waistcoat, sleeved, and coming almost to the knees, that they used to wear.

> Jacques, il me faut troubler ton somme;
> Dans le village, un gros huissier
> Rude et court, suivi du messier:
> C'est pour l'impôt, las! mon pauvre homme,
> Lève-toi, Jacques, lève-toi,
> Voici venir l'huissier du roi.
>
> Béranger (1831)

***Jacques Bonhomme.*** *See* Jacquerie, La.

**Jactitation of Marriage.** A false assertion by a person of being married to another. This is actionable. *Jactitation* means literally 'a throwing out', and here means 'to utter', i.e. 'to throw out publicly'. The term comes from the old Canon Law.

**Jade.** The fact that in mediaeval times this ornamental stone was supposed, if applied to the side, to act as a preservative against colic is enshrined in its name, for *jade* is from the Spanish *piedra de ijada*, stone of the side; and its other name, *nephrite*, is from Gr. *nephros*, kidney. Among the North American Indians it is still worn as an amulet against the bite of venomous snakes, and to cure the gravel, epilepsy, etc.

**Jade.** A worthless horse. An old woman (used in contempt). A young woman (not necessarily contemptuous).

**Jagganath.** *See* Juggernaut.

**Jahannam.** A name of the Mohammedan hell (*q.v.*) or of the first of its seven divisions. The word is the same as the Hebrew *Gehenna* (*q.v.*).

**Jam.** Used in a slang way for something really nice, especially if unexpected; something delightful, tip-top.

> There must have been a charming climate in Paradise and [the] connubial bliss [there] … was real jam. Sam Slick, *Human Nature*

***Money for jam.*** Money (or money's worth) for nothing; an unexpected bit of luck.

**Jambres.** *See* Jannes.

**Jambuscha.** Adam's preceptor, according to the pre-Adamites. Sometimes called Boan, and Zagtith.

**James.** A sovereign; a jacobus (*q.v.*); also called a 'jimmy'. *Half a jimmy* is half a sovereign.

**James, St.** The Apostle St James the Great is the patron saint of Spain. Legend states that after his death in Palestine his body was placed in a boat with sails set, and that next day it reached the Spanish coast; at Padron, near Compostella, they used to show a huge stone as the veritable boat. According to another legend, it was the *relics* of St James that were miraculously conveyed to Spain in a ship of marble from Jerusalem, where he was bishop. A knight saw the ship sailing into port, his horse took fright, and plunged with its rider into the sea. The knight saved himself by 'boarding the marble vessel', but his clothes were found to be entirely covered with scallop shells.

The saint's body was discovered in 840 by divine revelation to Bishop Theodomirus, and a church was built at Compostella for its shrine.

St James is commemorated on July 25th, and is represented in art sometimes with the sword by which he was beheaded, and sometimes attired as a pilgrim, with his cloak covered with shells.

***St James the Less.*** His attribute is a fuller's club, in allusion to the instrument by which he was put to death after having been precipitated from the summit of the temple at Jerusalem in AD 62. He is commemorated on May 1st. *Less* means the shorter of stature.

***The Court of St James's.*** The British court, to which foreign ambassadors are officially accredited. King George V holds drawing-rooms and levées in St James's Palace, Pall Mall; but Queen Anne, the four Georges, and William IV resided in this palace.

**Jamshid.** In Persian legend, the fourth king of the Pishdadian Dynasty, i.e. the earliest, who is fabled to have reigned for 700 years and to have had the Deevs, or Genii, as his slaves. He possessed a seven-ringed golden cup, typical of the seven heavens, the seven planets, the seven seas, etc., which was full of the elixir of life; it was hidden by the genii and was said to have been discovered while digging the foundations of Persepolis.

> I know too where the genii hid
> The jewelled cup of their king Jamshid,
> With life's elixir sparkling high.
>
> Thomas Moore, *Paradise and the Peri*

> Iram indeed is gone with all his rose,
> And Jamshyd's Sev'n-ring'd Cup where no one knows.
>
> FitzGerald, *Rubaiyat of Omar Khayyám*

**Jane.** A small Genoese silver coin; so called from Fr. *Gênes*, Genoa.

> Because I could not give her many a Jane.
>
> Spenser, *Faërie Queene*, III, vii, 58

**Janissaries** or **Janizaries** (Turk. *yeni-tscheri*, new corps). A celebrated militia of the Ottoman Empire, raised by Orchan in 1326, originally, and for some centuries, compulsorily recruited from the Christian subjects of the Sultan. It was blessed by Hadji Bektash, a saint, who cut off a sleeve of his fur mantle and gave it to the captain. The captain put the sleeve on his head, and from this circumstance arose the fur cap worn by these foot-guards. In 1826, having become too formidable to the state, they were abolished after a massacre in which many thousands of the Janissaries perished.

**Jannes** and **Jambres.** The names under which St Paul (2 Tim. 3:8) referred to the two magicians of Pharaoh who imitated some of the miracles of Moses (Exod. 7). The names are not mentioned in the Old Testament, but they appear in the Targums and other rabbinical writings, where tradition has it that they were sons of Balaam, and that they perished either in the crossing of the Red Sea, or in the tumult after the worship of the golden calf.

**Jansenists.** A sect of Christians, who held the doctrines of Cornelius Jansen, Bishop of Ypres, in West Flanders. Jansen professed to have formulated the teaching of Augustine, AD 1640, which resembled Calvinism in many respects. He taught the doctrines of 'irresistible grace', 'original sin', and the 'utter helplessness of the natural man to turn to God'. Louis XIV took part against them, and they were put down by Pope Clement XI, in 1705, in the famous bull Unigenitus (*q.v.*).

**Januarius, St.** The patron saint of Naples, a bishop of Benevento who was martyred during the Diocletian persecution, 304. He is commemorated on September 19th, and his head and two vials of his blood are preserved in the cathedral at Naples. This congealed blood is said to bubble and liquefy three times a year, on the Saturday before the first Sunday in May, September 19th, and December 16th; also whenever the head is brought near to the vials.

**January.** The month dedicated by the Romans to Janus (*q.v.*), who presided over the entrance to the year and, having two faces, could look back to the year past and forward on the current year.

> The Dutch used to call this month *Lauw-maand* (frosty-month); the Saxons, *Wulf-monath*, because wolves were very troublesome then from the great scarcity of food. After the introduction of Christianity, the name was changed to *Se aeftera geóla* (the after-yule); it was also called *Forma monath* (first month). In the French Republican calendar it was called *Nivôse* (snow-month, December 20th to January 20th).

***January and May. It's a case of January and May.*** Said when an old man marries a charming young lady. The allusion is to the Merchant's Tale in Chaucer's *Canterbury Tales*, in which May, a lovely girl, married January, a Lombard baron sixty years of age.

**Janus.** The ancient Roman deity who kept the gate of heaven; hence the guardian of gates and doors. He was represented with two faces, one in front and one behind, and the doors of his temple in Rome were thrown open in times of war and closed in times of peace. The name is used allusively both with reference to the double-facedness and to war. Thus, Milton says of the Cherubim:

> Four faces each
> Had, like a double Janus. *Paradise Lost*, xi, 129

And Tennyson –

> State-policy and church-policy are conjoint,
> But Janus-faces looking diverse ways.
> *Queen Mary*, III, ii

While Dante says of the Roman eagle that it –

> composed the world to such a peace,
> That of his temple Janus barr'd the door.
> *Paradiso*, vi, 83 (Cary's tr).

**Japanese Vellum.** An extremely costly hand-beaten Japanese paper manufactured from the inner bark of the mulberry tree.

**Japhetic.** An adjective sometimes applied to the Aryan family.

> The Indo-European family of languages as known by various designations. Some style it *Japhetic*, as if it appertained to the descendants of the patriarch Japheth [son of Noah]; as the *Semitic* tongues [appertain] to the descendants of Shem.
> Whitney, *Languages, etc.*, lect. v

**Japon.** The trade name of a British-made substitute for Japanese vellum (*q.v.*), which is so close an imitation of the genuine article that it has been mistaken for it by the Japanese importers.

**Jarkman.** Sixteenth-century slang for an Abram-man (*q.v.*), especially one who was able to forge passes, licences, etc. *Jark* was rogues' cant for a seal, whence also a licence of the Bethlehem Hospital to beg.

**Jarnac. *Coup de Jarnac*.** A treacherous and unexpected attack; so called from Guy Chabot, Sieur de Jarnac, who, in a duel with La Châteigneraie, on July 10th, 1547, in the presence of Henri II, first 'hamstrung' his opponent and then, when he was helpless, slew him.

**Jarndyce *v.* Jarndyce.** An interminable Chancery suit in Dickens's *Bleak House*. The character of Jarndyce is that of a kind-hearted, easy fellow, who is half ashamed that his left hand should know what his right hand gives.

**Jarvey.** Old slang for a hackney-coach driver; from the personal name *Jarvis*, with a possible allusion to St Gervaise, whose symbol in art is a whip.

> I pity them ere Jarvies a sitting on their boxes all night and waiting for the nobs what is dancing.
>
> Disraeli, *Sybil*, V, vii (1845)

**Jason.** The hero of Greek legend who led the Argonauts (*q.v.*) in the quest for the Golden Fleece. He was the son of Aeson, king of Iolcus, was brought up by the centaur, Chiron, and when he demanded his kingdom from his half-brother, Pelias, who had deprived him of it, he was told he could have it in return for the Golden Fleece. Jason thereupon gathered together the chief heroes of Greece and set sail in the *Argo*. After many tests and trials he, through the help of Medea (*q.v.*), was successful. He married Medea, but later deserted her, and, according to one account, he killed himself with grief, according to another was crushed to death by the keel of his old ship, *Argo*, while resting beneath it.

**Jaundice** (Fr. *jaune*, yellow). *A jaundiced eye.* A prejudiced eye which sees 'faults that are not'. It was a popular belief that to the eye of a person who had the jaundice everything looked of a yellow tinge.

> All seems infected that th' infected spy,
> As all seems yellow to the jaundiced eye.
>
> Pope, *Essay on Criticism*, ii, 359

**Javan.** In the Bible the collective name of the Greeks (Is. 66:19, and Ezek. 27:13, and elsewhere), who were supposed to be descended from Javan, the son of Japheth (Gen. 10:2).

**Jaw.** Words of complaint; wrangling, abuse, jabber. *To jaw*, to annoy with words, to jabber, wrangle, or abuse.

***A break-jaw word; a jaw-breaker.*** A very long word, or one hard to pronounce.

***Hold your jaw.*** Hold your tongue or jabber.

***Pi jaw.*** A contemptuous term for pious talk, or for an ostentatiously pious or goody-goody person.

***What are you jawing about?*** What are you jabbering or wrangling about?

**Jay.** Old slang for a frivolous person, a wanton.

> This jay of Italy … hath betrayed him.
>
> Shakespeare, *Cymbeline*, 3, 4

In its modern sense of a simpleton, a plunger, one who spends his money recklessly, the word is said to be simply the letter J, the initial letter of one Juggins, a man who, in 1887, made a fool of himself by losses on the turf.

**Jazey.** A wig; a corruption of Jersey, and so called because they used to be made of Jersey flax and fine wool.

**Jazz.** A voluptuous dance of negro origin, accompanied by a wild, irregular kind of music, which has been spoken of as –

> that synchronising supersyncopation that, originating in New Orleans, has aggravated the feet and fingers of America into a shimmying, tickle-toeing, snapping delirium and now [i.e., 1919] is upsetting the swaying equilibrium of the European dance.

The dance, and the music, emerged from the negro shanties of New Orleans in 1915, and in March, 1916, Bert Kelly's 'Jazz Band' (the first to be so called) was engaged by the Boosters' Club, of Chicago, scored an immediate success, and started the thing on its conquering career.

The origin of the name is uncertain. One account is that it is an adaptation of the name of one *Razz*, who was a band conductor in New Orleans about 1904; another that it has long been a common word to the negro and on the Barbary coast, and means simply 'to mess 'em up and slap it on thick', and another that it was the spontaneous production of a brain-wave on the part of the above-mentioned Mr Bert Kelly.

**Je maintiendrai** (Fr., I will maintain). The motto of the House of Nassau. When William III came to England he retained the motto, but added to it, 'I will maintain *the liberties of England and the Protestant religion.*'

**Je ne sais quoi** (Fr., I know not what). An indescribable something; as 'There was a *je ne sais quoi* about him which made us dislike him at first sight.'

**Jeames.** A flunkey. The *Morning Post* used sometimes to be so called, because of its never failing solicitude for the flunkey-employing classes and its flunkey-like attitude towards them.

Thackeray wrote *Jeames's Diary* (published in *Punch*), of which Jeames de la Pluche – a 'super' flunkey – was the hero.

**Jean Crapaud.** A Frenchman. *See* Crapaud.

**Jebusites.** In Dryden's *Absalom and Achitophel* (*q.v.*), the Roman Catholics. England was Roman Catholic before the Reformation, and Jerusalem was called Jebus before the time of David.

> Succeeding times did equal folly call,
> Believing nothing, or believing all.
> The Egyptian rites the Jebusites embraced,
> When gods were recommended by their taste.
>
> Pt i, 117–23

**Jedwood Justice.** Putting an obnoxious person to death first, and trying him afterwards. This sort of justice was dealt to moss-troopers. Same as *Jedburgh justice*, *Jeddart justice*. We have also 'Cupar justice' and 'Abingdon law'.

> Jedwood justice – hang in haste and try at leisure.
> Scott, *Fair Maid of Perth*, ch. xxxii

**Jehennam.** *See* Jahannam.

**Jehovah.** *See* To take God's name in vain, *under* Name.

**Jehovistic.** *See* Elohistic.

**Jehu.** A coachman, especially one who drives at a rattling pace.

> The watchman told, saying, ... The driving is like the driving of Jehu the son of Nimshi; for he driveth furiously. 2 Kings 9:20

**Jekyll.** ***Dr Jekyll and Mr Hyde.*** The two phases of one man, 'the law of his members warring against the law of his mind'. Jekyll is the 'would do good', Hyde is 'the evil that is present'. The phrase comes from R. L. Stevenson's *The Strange Case of Dr Jekyll and Mr Hyde*, first published in 1886.

**Jellyby, Mrs.** The type of the enthusiastic, unthinking philanthropist who forgets that charity should begin at home. She figures in Dickens's *Bleak House*, and would do anything for the poor fan-makers and flower-girls of Borrioboolah Gha, but she shamefully neglects her own children and would bundle into the street a poor beggar dying of starvation on her step.

**Jemmy** (the diminutive or pet form of *James*). Slang for quite a number of different things, as a burglar's crow-bar, usually made in sections that can be screwed together; a sheep's head, boiled or baked, said to be so called from the tradition that James IV of Scotland breakfasted on a sheep's head just before the battle of Flodden Field (September 9th, 1513); also, a greatcoat; and – as an adjective – spruce, dandified. *See* Jemmy Jessamy.

> She presently returned with a pot of porter and a dish of sheep's heads; which gave occasion to several pleasant witticisms on the part of Mr Sikes, founded upon the singular coincidence of jemmies, being a cant name, common to them, and also to an ingenious instrument much used in his profession.
> Dickens, *Oliver Twist*, ch. xx

**Jemmy Dawson.** *See* Dawson.

**Jemmy Jessamy.** A Jack-a-dandy; a lady's fondling, 'sweet as sugar-candy'.

> This was very different language to that she had been in the habit of hearing from her Jemmy Jessamy adorers.
> Thackeray, *Barry Lyndon*, ch. xiii

**Jemmy O'Goblin.** Slang for a sovereign. *Cp.* James.

**Jenny Wren.** The sweetheart of Robin Redbreast in the old nursery rhyme.

> Robin promised Jenny, if she would be his wife, she should 'feed on cherry-pie and drink currant-wine'; and he says:
> 'I'll dress you like a goldfinch,
> Or any peacock gay;
> So, dearest Jen, if you'll be mine
> Let us appoint the day.'

Jenny replies:

> 'Cherry-pie is very nice,
> And so is currant wine;
> But I must wear my plain brown gown
> And never go too fine.'

**Jeofail.** The old legal term for an error, omission, or oversight in proceedings at law. The word is the Anglo-Fr. *jeo fail*, O.Fr. *je faille*, I am at fault. There were several statutes of Jeofail for the remedy of slips or mistakes.

**Jeopardy.** Hazard, danger. It was originally a term in chess, and signified an even game, hence an uncertain chance, something hazardous. The word is Fr. *jeu*, game, *parti*, divided.

**Jereed.** A wooden javelin used by the Turks and Persians in various sports and exercises.

> Away, away for life he rides:
> Swift as the hurl'd on high jerreed
> Springs to the touch his startled steed.
> Byron, *The Giaour*

**Jeremiad.** A pitiful tale, a tale of woe to produce compassion; so called from the 'Lamentations' of the prophet Jeremiah.

**Jeremiah.** ***The British Jeremiah.*** Gibbon so calls Gildas (fl. 6th cent.), author of *Lamentations over the Destruction of Britain*.

**Jericho.** Used in a number of phrases for the sake of giving verbal definition to some altogether indefinite place. The reason for fixing on this particular town is possibly to be found in 2 Sam. 10:5, and 1 Chron. 19:5.

> And the king said, Tarry at Jericho until your beards be grown.

***Go to Jericho with you.*** A euphemistic turn of phrase for 'Go and hang yourself', or something more offensive still.

***Gone to Jericho.*** No one knows where.

***I wish you were at Jericho.*** Anywhere out of my way.

**Jerked Beef.** 'Jerked' is here a corruption of Peruv. *charqui*, meat cut into strips and dried in the sun.

**Jerkin.** A short coat or jacket, formerly made of leather; a close waistcoat.

> A plague of opinion, one may wear it on both sides, like a leather jerkin.
>
> Shakespeare, *Troilus and Cressida*, 3, 3

**Jeroboam.** A very large wine bottle or flagon, so called in allusion to the 'mighty man of valour' who 'made Israel to sin' (1 Kings 11:28, 14:16). Its capacity is not very definite; some say it is from ten to twelve quarts, but the more usual allowance is eight. A *magnum* = 2 quart bottles; a *tappit hen* = 2 magnums; a *jeroboam* = 2 tappit hens; and a *rehoboam* = 2 jeroboams or 16 quart bottles. *See these names*, and *cp.* Jorum.

> Some 'jeroboams' of very old rum went at 65*s.* each; several 'tappit-hens' of rum fetched 34*s.*; and some 'magnums', 17*s.* each.
>
> *Truth*, 31st March, 1887

**Jerome, St.** A father of the Western Church, and translator of the Vulgate (*q.v.*). He was born about 340, and died at Bethlehem in 420. He is generally represented as an aged man in a cardinal's dress, writing or studying, with a lion seated beside him.

**Jeronimo.** The chief character in the *Spanish Tragedy* by Thomas Kyd (acted about 1590). On finding his application to the king ill-timed, he says to himself, 'Go by, Jeronimo,' which tickled the fancy of the audience so that it became for a time a street jest, and was introduced into many contemporary plays, as in Shakespeare's *Taming of the Shrew* (*Induction*), Jonson's *Every Man in his Humour* (1, v), Dekker's *Shoemaker's Holiday* (II, i), etc.

**Jerry-built.** Unsubstantial. A 'jerry-builder' is a speculative builder who runs up cheap, unsubstantial houses, using materials of the commonest kind. The name is probably in some way connected with *Jeremiah*.

**Jerry Diddler.** *See* Diddle.

**Jerry-shop,** or **Tom and Jerry Shop.** A low-class beerhouse. Probably the *Tom and Jerry* was a public-house sign when Pierce Egan's *Life in London* (1821), in which these are leading characters, was popular.

**Jerrymander.** *See* Gerrymander.

**Jerry Twitcher.** *See* Twitcher.

**Jersey** is Caesar's-ey – i.e. Caesar's island, so called in honour of Julius Caesar.

**Jerusalem.** Julian the Apostate, the Roman Emperor (d.363), with the intention of pleasing the Jews and humbling the Christians, said that he would rebuild the temple and city, but was mortally wounded before the foundation was laid, and his work set at naught by 'an earthquake, a whirlwind, or a fiery eruption' (*see* Gibbon's *Decline and Fall*, ch. xxiii).

Much has been made of this by early Christian writers, who dwell on the prohibition and curse pronounced against those who should attempt to rebuild the city, and the fate of Julian is pointed out as an example of Divine wrath.

> Well pleased they look for Sion's coming state,
> Nor think of Julian's boast and Julian's fate.
>
> Crabbe, *Borough*

***Jerusalem,*** in Dryden's *Absalom and Achitophel* (*q.v.*), means London (Pt i, v. 86, etc).

***The New Jerusalem.*** The paradise of Christians in allusion to Rev. 21.

**Jerusalem Artichoke.** *Jerusalem* is here a corruption of Ital. *Girasolë*. Girasole is the sunflower, which this vegetable resembles both in leaf and stem.

**Jerusalem Chamber.** The Chapterhouse of Westminster Abbey. Henry IV died there, March 20th, 1413.

> It hath been prophesied to me many years,
> I should not die but in Jerusalem.
>
> Shakespeare, *2 Henry IV*, 4, 5

Pope Silvester II was told the same thing, and he died as he was saying Mass in a church so called (Bacon, *Tusculum*).

The Lower House of Convocation now meets in the Jerusalem Chamber.

**Jerusalem Cross.** A cross potent. *See* Potent.

**Jerusalem Delivered.** An Italian epic poem in twenty books, by Torquato Tasso (1544–95). It was published in 1581, and was translated into English by Edward Fairfax in 1600.

> The crusaders, encamped on the plains of Tortosa, chose Godfrey for their chief, and Alandine, King of Jerusalem, made preparations of defence. The overtures of Argantes to Godfrey being declined, he declared war in the name of the king of Egypt. The Christian army having reached Jerusalem, the king of Damascus sent Armida to beguile the Christians; she told an artful tale by which she drew off several of the most puissant. It was found that Jerusalem could never be taken without the aid of Rinaldo; but Rinaldo had withdrawn from the army, because Godfrey had cited him to answer for the death of Girnando, slain in a duel. Godfrey, being

informed that the hero was dallying with Armida in the enchanted island, sent to invite him back to the army; he returned, and Jerusalem was taken in a night attack. As for Armida, after setting fire to her palace, she fled into Egypt, and offered to marry any knight who slew Rinaldo; but when she found the Christian army was successful she fled from the field. The love of Rinaldo returned; he pursued her and she relented. The poem concludes with the triumphant entry of the Christian army into the Holy City, and their devotions at the tomb of the Redeemer. The two chief episodes are the loves of Olindo and Sophronia, and of Tancred and Corinda.

**Jess** (through Fr. from Lat. *jactus*, a cast, throw). A short strap of leather tied about the legs of a hawk to hold it on the fist. Hence, metaphorically, a bond of affection, etc.

> If I prove her haggard,
> Though that her jesses were my dear heart-strings,
> I'd whistle her off. Shakespeare, *Othello*, 3, 3

**Jessamy Bride.** The 'fancy name' given by Goldsmith to Mary Horneck when he fell in love with her in 1769. *Cp.* Jemmy Jessamy.

**Jesse,** or **Jesse Tree.** A genealogical tree, usually represented as a vine or as a large brass candlestick with many branches, tracing the ancestry of Christ, called a 'rod out of the stem of Jesse' (Is. 11:1). Jesse is himself sometimes represented in a recumbent position with the vine rising out of his loins; hence a stained-glass window representing him thus with a tree shooting from him containing the pedigree of Jesus is called a *Jesse window*.

**Jesters.** *See* Court Fools, *under* Fools.

**Jesuit.** The popular name of members of the 'Society of Jesus', founded by Ignatius Loyola in 1533, who, when asked what name he would give his order, replied, 'We are a little battalion of Jesus.' The order was founded to combat the Reformation and to propagate the faith among the heathen, but through its discipline, organisation, and methods of secrecy, it soon acquired such political power that it came into conflict with both the civil and religious authorities; it was driven from France in 1594, from England in 1579, from Venice in 1607, from Spain in 1767, from Naples in 1768; in 1773 it was suppressed by Pope Clement XIV, but it was revived in 1814.

Owing to the casuistical principles maintained by many of its leaders and attributed to the order as a whole the name *Jesuit* has acquired a very opprobrious signification both in Protestant and Roman Catholic countries, and a *Jesuit*, or *Jesuitical person* means (secondarily) a deceiver, prevaricator, one who 'lies like truth', or palters with us in a double sense, that 'keeps the word of promise to our ear, and breaks it to our hope'.

***Jesuit's bark.*** *See* Peruvian.

**Jesus Paper.** Paper of large size (about 28½ in. by 21½) chiefly used for engravings. Originally it was stamped with the initials IHS.

**Jet.** So called from the River Gages, in Lycia, Asia Minor, on the banks of which it was collected by the ancients. It was originally called *gagates*, corrupted into *gagat*, *jet*.

**Jetsam** or **Jetson.** Goods cast into the sea to lighten a ship (Fr. *jeter*, to cast out). *See* Flotsam: Ligan.

**Jettator** (Ital. *jettatura*). One with an evil eye, who always brings ill-luck. The opposite of the mascotte (*q.v.*), who with a 'good eye' always brings good fortune.

> Their glance, if you meet it, is the jettatura, or evil-eye. Mrs Gaskell, *An Accursed Race*

**Jeu d'esprit** (Fr.). A witticism.

**Jeu de mot** (Fr.). A pun; a play on some word or phrase.

**Jeunesse dorée** (Fr.). The 'gilded youth' of a nation; that is, the rich and fashionable young unmarried men.

> There were three of the *jeunesse dorée*, and, as such, were pretty well known to the ladies who promenade the grand circle.
> T. Terrel, *Lady Delmar*, ix

**Jew.** In Dryden's *Absalom and Achitophel* (*q.v.*) the *Jews* stand for those English who were loyal to Charles II, called David.

> The Jews, a headstrong, moody, murmuring race,
> God's pampered people, whom, debauched with ease,
> No king could govern, nor no god could please.
> Pt i, 45

***Jews born with tails.*** *See* Tailed Men.

***Rich as a Jew.*** This expression arose in the Middle Ages, when Jews were almost the only money-lenders, and were certainly the most wealthy of the people. There are still many Jews of great wealth.

***Jew's-harp.*** It is not known how or why this very simple musical instrument got its name (known from the 16th cent.); it has no special connection with the Jews, and is not a bit like a harp or a trumpet. It was called by Bacon *jeu-trompe*, by Beaumont and Fletcher, *jew-trump*, and in Hakluyt's *Voyages* (1595), *jew's-harp*.

***Jew's Ear.*** A fungus that grows on the Judas-tree (*q.v.*); its name is due to a mistranslation of its Latin name, *Auricula Judae*, i.e. Judas's ear.

***Jew's Myrtle.*** Butcher's broom is so called, from the popular notion that it formed the crown of thorns placed by the Jews on the Saviour's head.

***Worth a Jew's-eye.*** According to fable, this expression arose from the custom of torturing Jews to extort money from them. The expedient of King John is well known: he demanded 10,000 marks of a rich Jew of Bristol; the Hebrew resisted, but the tyrant ordered that one of his teeth should be tugged out every day till the money was forthcoming. In seven days the sufferer gave in, and John jestingly observed, 'A Jew's eye may be a quick ransom, but Jew's teeth give the richer harvest.'

Launcelot, in the *Merchant of Venice*, 2, 5, puns upon this phrase when he says to Jessica:

> There will come a Christian by
> Will be worth a Jewess' eye.

**Jewels** have (or had) in the popular belief special significations in various ways. For instance, each month was supposed to be under the influence of some precious stone –

| | | |
|---|---|---|
| *January* | Garnet | *Constancy.* |
| *February* | Amethyst | *Sincerity.* |
| *March* | Bloodstone | *Courage.* |
| *April* | Diamond | *Innocence.* |
| *May* | Emerald | *Success in love.* |
| *June* | Agate | *Health and long life.* |
| *July* | Cornelian | *Content.* |
| *August* | Sardonyx | *Conjugal fidelity.* |
| *September* | Chrysolite | *Antidote to madness.* |
| *October* | Opal | *Hope.* |
| *November* | Topaz | *Fidelity.* |
| *December* | Turquoise | *Prosperity.* |

The signs of the zodiac were represented by –

| | | | |
|---|---|---|---|
| *Aries* | Ruby. | *Libra* | Jacinth. |
| *Taurus* | Topaz. | *Scorpio* | Agate. |
| *Gemini* | Carbuncle. | *Sagittarius* | Amethyst. |
| *Cancer* | Emerald. | *Capricornus* | Beryl. |
| *Leo* | Sapphire. | *Aquarius* | Onyx. |
| *Virgo* | Diamond. | *Pisces* | Jasper. |

And among heralds and astrologists jewels represented special tinctures or planets, as the topaz 'or' (*gold*), and *Sol*, the sun; the pearl or crystal, 'argent' (*silver*), and the moon; the ruby, 'gules' (*red*), and the planet Mars; the sapphire, 'azure' (*blue*), and Jupiter; the diamond, 'sable' (*black*), and Saturn; the emerald, 'vert' (*green*), and Venus; the amethyst 'purpure' (*purple*), and Mercury.

***These are my jewels!*** *See* Treasures.

**Jezebel.** ***A painted Jezebel.*** A flaunting woman of bold spirit but loose morals; so called from Jezebel, wife of Ahab, King of Israel (*see* 2 Kings, 9:31).

> Mrs Jenkins was all bespattered with dirt as well as insulted with the opprobrious name of 'painted Jezebel'.
>
> Smollett, *Humphry Clinker* (18 June)

**Jezreelites.** A small sect, with headquarters at Gillingham, Kent, believing that Christ redeemed only *souls*, and that the *body* is saved by belief in the Law. It was founded in 1876 by James White (1840–85), who had been a private in the Army, and took the name James Jershom Jezreel. They are also called the 'New and Later House of Israel', and their object is to be numbered among the 144,000 (*see* Rev. 7:4) who at the Last Judgment will be endowed with immortal bodies. 'Prince Jezreel' was succeeded by his wife 'Queen Esther' (formerly Clarissa Rogers); she died in 1888, and Edward Rogers (d.1907) took the leadership; at his death Michael Keyfor Mills (d.1922), who was born in Detroit, was 'converted' in 1888, and settled in Gillingham, succeeded him as 'Prince Michael'.

**Jib.** A triangular sail borne in front of the foremast. It has the bowsprit for a base in small vessels, and the jib-boom in larger ones, and exerts an important effect, when the wind is abeam, in throwing the ship's head to leeward.

The *jib-boom* is an extension of the bowsprit by the addition of a spar projecting beyond it. Sometimes the boom is further extended by another spar called the *flying jib-boom*. The *jib-topsail* is a light sail flying from the extreme forward end of the flying jib-boom, and set about half-way between the mast and the boom.

***The cut of his jib.*** A sailor's phrase, meaning the expression of a person's face. Sailors recognise vessels at sea by the cut of the jibs, and in certain dialects the *jib* means the lower lip. Thus, *to hang the jib* is to look ill-tempered, or annoyed.

***To jib.*** To start aside, to back out; a 'jibbing horse' is one that is easily startled; 'my mother never bred a jibber' means, I'm not the man to back out of it or to refuse to undertake it. It is probably from the sea-term, to *gybe*, i.e. to change tacks by bearing away before the wind.

**Jiffy.** ***In a jiffy.*** In a minute; in a brace of shakes; before you can say 'Jack Robinson'. The origin of the word is unknown, but it is met with as early as the late 18th century.

**Jig,** from *gigue*. A short piece of music much in vogue in olden times, of a very lively character, either six-eight or twelve-eight time, and used for dance-tunes. It consists of two parts, each of eight bars. Also the dance itself.

> You jig, you amble, and you lisp.
>
> Shakespeare, *Hamlet*, 3, 1

**Jill.** A generic name for a lass, a sweetheart. *See* Jack and Jill *under* Jack, *sect*. vi.

> Every Jack has got his Jill (i.e. Ilka laddie has his lassie).
>
> Burns

**Jilt.** To throw one's sweetheart over after having promised to get married. *See* Basket – *To give the basket*.

**Jim Crow.** A popular nigger song and dance of last century; introduced by T. D. Rice, the original 'nigger minstrel', at Washington in 1835, and brought to the Adelphi, London, in the following year. A renegade or turncoat was called a 'Jim Crow', from the burden of the song, *Wheel about and turn about*.

**Jingo.** A word from the unmeaning jargon of the 17th-century conjurers (*cp*. Hocus-pocus), probably substituted for *God*, in the same way as *Gosh*, *Golly*, etc., are. In Motteux's translation of Rabelais (1694), where the original reads *par Dieu* (Bk iv, lvi), the English rendering is 'By jingo'; but there is a possibility that the word is Basque *Jinko* or *Jainko*, God, and was introduced by sailors.

> Hey, Jingo! What the de'il's the matter?
> Do mermaids swim in Dartford water?
>
> Swift, *Actaeon or The Original Horn Fair*

The modern meaning of the word, a blustering so-called 'patriot' who is itching to go to war on the slightest provocation – a *Chauvinist* in France – is from a music-hall song by G. W. Hunt, which was popular in 1878 when the country was supposed to be on the verge of intervening in the Russo-Turkish War on behalf of the Turks:

> We don't want to fight; but, by Jingo, if we do,
> We've got the ships, we've got the men, and got the money too.

The Russophobes became known as the *Jingoes*, and such policy has been labelled *Jingoism* ever since.

**Jinks.** ***He is at high jinks***. The present use of the phrase expresses the idea of pranks, fun, and jollity.

> The froliesome company had begun to practise the ancient and now forgotten pastime of *High Jinks*. The game was played in several different ways. Most frequently the dice were thrown by the company, and those upon whom the lot fell were obliged to assume and maintain for a time a certain fictitious character, or to repeat a certain number of fescennine verses in a particular order. If they departed from the characters assigned ... they incurred forfeits, which were compounded for by swallowing an additional bumper.
>
> Scott, *Guy Mannering*, xxxvi

**Jinn.** Demons of *Arabian mythology*, according to fable created from fire two thousand years before Adam was made of earth, and said to be governed by a race of kings named Suleyman, one of whom 'built the pyramids'. Their chief abode is the mountain Kâf, and they assume the forms of serpents, dogs, cats, monsters, or even human beings, and become invisible at pleasure. The evil jinn are hideously ugly, but the good are exquisitely beautiful. The word is a plural; its singular is *jinnee*.

**Jinnistan.** The Fairy Land of the Arabs (*see above*), the chief province of which is *The Country of Delight*, and the capital *The City of Jewels*.

**Joachim, St.** The father of the Virgin Mary. Generally represented as an old man carrying in a basket two turtledoves, in allusion to the offering made for the purification of his daughter. His wife was St Anne.

**Joan, Pope.** A supposed female 'pope' between Leo IV and Benedict III in the 9th century. She is said to have been born in England and educated at Cologne, passing under the name of Joannes Anglicus. Blondel, a Calvinist, wrote a book in 1640 to prove that no such person ever occupied the papal chair; but at least a hundred and fifty authors between the 13th and 17th centuries repeat the tale as an historic fact. Dillinger critically examined the question in 1868, but the entire mythicality of the legend had long been recognised.

**Job** (*ō* long). The personification of poverty and patience, in allusion to the patriarch whose history is given in the Bible.

> I am as poor as Job, my lord, but not so patient.
>
> Shakespeare, *2 Henry IV*, 1, 2

In the Koran Job's wife is said to have been either Rahmeh, daughter of Ephraim, son of Joseph, or Makhir, daughter of Manasses; and the tradition is recorded that Job, at the command of God, struck the earth with his foot from the dunghill where he lay, and instantly there welled up a spring of water with which his wife washed his sores, and they were miraculously healed.

***Job's comforter.*** One who means to sympathise with you in your grief, but says that you brought it on yourself; thus in reality adding weight to your sorrow.

***Job's post.*** A bringer of bad news.

***Job's pound.*** Bridewell; prison.

**Job** (*o* short). A piece of chance work; a public work or office not for the public benefit, but for the profit of the person employed; a sudden blow or 'dig' into one; a 'jab'; also, among printers, all kinds of work not included in the term 'book-work' or newspapers.

***A bad job.*** An unsuccessful work; one that brings loss instead of profit; a bad speculation.

***A job lot.*** A lot of miscellaneous goods to be sold a bargain.

***A ministerial job.*** Sheridan says – 'Whenever any emolument, profit, salary, or honour is conferred on any person not deserving it – that is a job; if from private friendship, personal attachment, or any view except the interest of the public, anyone is appointed to any public office ... that is a job.'

> No cheek is known to blush, or heart to throb,
> Save when they lose a question or a job,
>
> Pope, *Essay on Criticism*, i, 104

***To do the job for one.*** To kill him.

**Jobation.** A scolding; so called from the patriarch Job.

> Jobation ... means a long, dreary homily, and has reference to the tedious rebukes inflicted on the patriarch Job by his too obliging friends.
>
> G. A. Sala (*Echoes*), Sept. 6th, 1884

**Jobber.** One who does small jobs; one who buys from merchants to sell to retailers; a middle-man. A 'stock-jobber' is a member of the Stock Exchange who acts as an intermediary between buying and selling stockbrokers – who are also members. The relationship between the *jobber* and the *broker* is much the same as that between the wholesaler and the retailer in trade.

**Jockey.** Properly, 'a little Jack' (*q.v.*). So in Scotch, 'Ilka Jeanie has her Jockie.'

***All fellows. Jockey and the laird*** (man and master). (*Scotch proverb.*)

***To jockey.*** To deceive in trade; to cheat; to indulge in sharp practice.

**Jockey of Norfolk.** Sir John Howard (d.1485), the first Howard to be Duke of Norfolk, and a firm adherent of Richard III. On the night before the battle of Bosworth, where he was slain, he found in his tent the warning couplet:

> Jockey of Norfolk, be not too bold.
> For Dickon, thy master, is bought and sold

**Joe Miller.** *See* Miller.

**Joey.** A groat; so called from Joseph Hume, MP, who, about 1835, strongly recommended the coinage for the sake of paying short cab-fares, etc.

In Australia a young kangaroo is called a *joey*.

**Jog.** ***Jog away; jog off; jog on.*** Get away; be off; keep moving. Shakespeare uses the word *shog* in the same sense – as, 'Will you shog off?' (*Henry V*, 2, 1); and again in the same play, 'Shall we shog?' (2, 3). Beaumont and Fletcher use the same expression in *The Coxcomb* – 'Come, prithee, let us shog off.' In the *Morte d'Arthur* we have another variety – 'He shokkes in sharpely' (rushes in). The words are connected with *shock*, and *shake*.

> Jog on a little faster, pri'thee,
> I'll take a nap and then be wi' thee.
>
> R. Lloyd, *The Hare and the Tortoise*

***Give his memory a jog.*** Remind him of something that has slipped his memory.

***Jog-trot.*** A slow but regular pace.

**Joggis** or **Jogges.** *See* Jougs.

**John.** The English form of Lat. and Gr. *Johannes*, from Heb. *Jochanan*, meaning 'God is gracious.' The feminine form, *Johanna*, or *Joanna*, is nearer the original. The French equivalent of 'John' is *Jean* (formerly *Jehan*), the Italian *Giovanni*, Russian *Ivan*, Gaelic *Ian*, German *Johann* or *Johannes*, which is contracted to *Jan*, *Jahn*, and *Hans*.

For many centuries John has been one of the most popular of masculine names in England – probably because it is that of St John the Evangelist, St John the Baptist and many other saints.

There have been 23 Popes of this name, nearly all of whom were bad, unfortunate, or mere nonentities; England has had one King John (also unfortunate), and her last Prince of the name died in boyhood (1919). The most famous 'Johns' of history are probably *John of Gaunt* (1340–99), the fourth son of Edward III, and *Don John of Austria* (1547–78), illegitimate son of the Emperor Charles V, celebrated as a military leader, for his naval victory over the Turks at Lepanto (1571), and as Governor of the Netherlands.

The principal Saints of the name are:

***St John the Evangelist*** or ***the Divine.*** His day is December 27th, and he is usually represented bearing a chalice from which a serpent issues, in allusion to his driving the poison from a cup presented to him to drink. Tradition says that he took the Virgin Mary to Ephesus after the

Crucifixion, that in the persecution of Domitian (96) he was plunged into a cauldron of boiling oil, and was afterwards banished to the isle of Patmos (where he is said to have written the Book of Revelation), but shortly returned to Ephesus, where he died.

***St John the Baptist.*** Patron saint of missionaries, because he was sent 'to prepare the way of the Lord'. His day is June 24th, and he is represented in a coat of sheepskins (in allusion to his life in the desert), either holding a rude wooden cross, with a pennon bearing the words, *Ecce Agnus Dei*, or with a book on which a lamb is seated; or holding in his right hand a lamb surrounded by a halo, and bearing a cross on the right foot.

***St John of Beverley.*** Bishop of Hexham, and later of York (d.721), his name formed the war-cry of the English in the border warfare of the Middle Ages. It was he who ordained the Venerable Bede. He is commemorated on May 7th.

***St John Chrysostom,*** who was bishop of Constantinople from 398 till he was deposed by the Arians in 403. Four years later he was slain by his enemies in Pontus. His day is January 27th.

***St John of the Cross.*** A Carmelite and founder (1568) of the Discalced Carmelites. He died in 1591, shortly after his order had been suppressed, and was canonised in 1726. His day is November 24th.

***St John Damascene.*** One of the Fathers of the Eastern Church. He was born at Damascus, opposed the Iconoclasts (*q.v.*), and died about 770. He is commemorated on May 6th.

***St John of Nepumuk.*** A Bohemian priest of the 14th century, who was drowned by order of the brutal Wenceslaus IV, partly because he tried to restrain the licentiousness of the king, partly because he refused to reveal to him the confessions of the queen. *Nepumuk*, or *Nepomuk* is the French *né*, born, and Pomuk, the village of his birth. His day is May 16th.

**John-a-Dreams.** A stupid, dreamy fellow, always in a brown study and half asleep.

> Yet I,
> A dull and muddy-mettled rascal, peak,
> Like John-a-dreams, unpregnant of my cause,
> And can say nothing.
>
> Shakespeare, *Hamlet*, 2, 2

**John-a-Droynes.** An Elizabethan term for a country bumpkin. There is a foolish character in Whetstone's *Promos and Cassandra* (1578), who, being seized by informers, stands dazed, and suffers himself to be quietly cheated out of his money. In *Superbiae Flagellum*, by John Taylor, the Water Poet (1621), we read of 'Jack and Jill, and John a Drones his issue', the meaning evidently being 'the rag, tag, and bobtail'.

**John Anderson, my Jo.** Burns's well-known poem is founded on an 18th century song (unfit for print in these – or any – days) which, in its turn, was a parody of a mid-16th century anti-Roman Catholic song in ridicule of the Sacraments of the Church. The whole is given in the *Percy Folio MS*. The first verse is:

> John Anderson, my Jo, com in as ye gae by.
> And ye sall get a Sheip's held weel baken in a pye;
> Weel baken in a pye, and the haggis in a pat:
> John Anderson, my Jo, cum in and ye's get that.

**John-a-Nokes and John-a-Stiles.** Names formerly given, instead of the very impersonal 'A and B', to fictitious persons in an imaginary action at law: hence either name may stand for 'just anybody'. *Cp.* Doe.

> Poets gyve names to men they write of, which argueth a conceite of an actuall truth, and so, not being true, prooves a falshood. And doth the Lawyer lye then, when under the names of *John a stile* and *John a noakes*, hee puts his case?
>
> Sir Philip Sidney, *An Apologie for Poetrie* (1595)

**John Audley.** *See* Audley.

**John Barleycorn.** *See* Barleycorn.

**John Bull.** The national nickname for an Englishman, represented as a bluff, kindhearted, bull-headed farmer. The character is from Dr Arbuthnot's satire *The History of John Bull*, which was originally published in 1712 as *Law is a Bottomless Pit*. 'John Bull' is the Englishman, the Frenchman is termed *Lewis Baboon*, the Dutchman *Nicholas Frog*, etc.

> One would think, in personifying itself, a nation would ... picture something grand, heroic, and imposing, but it is characteristic of the peculiar humour of the English, and of their love for what is blunt, comic, and familiar, that they have embodied their national oddities in the figure of a sturdy, corpulent old fellow ... with red waistcoat, leather breeches, and a stout oaken cudgel ... [whom they call] John Bull.
>
> Washington Irving

In the early years of last century there was a scurrilous journal of this name, and in the early years of this (1906) the name was adopted for a weekly edited by Mr Horatio Bottomley. Owing to the fact that it forms a convenient vent for all sorts of real and imaginary grievances one often hears the phrase Why not write to *John Bull* about it? ironically addressed to a 'grouser'.

> Before editing *John Bull*, Mr Bottomley was interested in journalism.
> Kennedy Jones, *Fleet Street and Downing Street* (1920), p. 54, *note*

**John Chinaman.** Either a Chinaman or the Chinese as a people.

**John Collins.** A drink consisting of gin, soda water, lemon, and ice. *See* Gin-sling.

**John Company.** The old 'Honourable East India Company'. It is said that 'John' is a perversion of 'Hon.'; no doubt *Hon.*, like *Hans*, may be equal to *John*, but probably 'John Company' is allied to the familiar 'John Bull'. The Company was abolished in 1857, in consequence of the Indian Mutiny.

> In old times 'John Company' employed four thousand men in its warehouses.
> *Old and New London*, ii, 185

**John Doe.** *See* Doe.

**John Dory.** A golden yellow fish, the *Zeus faber*, common in the Mediterranean and round the south-western coasts of England. Its name was *dory* (Fr. *dorée*, golden) long before the *John* was added; this was probably a humorous amplification – from the name of some real or imaginary person – with, perhaps, a side allusion to Fr. *jaune*, yellow.

There is a tradition that it was from this fish (*but see* Haddock) that St Peter took the stater. Hence it is called in French *le poisson de St Pierre*, and in Gascon, the *golden* or *sacred cock*, meaning St Peter's cock. Like the haddock, it has an oval black spot on each side, said to be the finger-marks of St Peter, when he held the fish to extract the coin.

**John Drum's Entertainment.** *See* Drum.

**John in the Wad.** Another name for the will-o'-the-wisp. *See* Ignis Fatuus.

**John Long.** ***To wait for John Long, the carrier.*** To wait a long time; to wait for John, who keeps us a long time.

**John o' Groat's.** The story is that John o' Groat (or Jan Groot) came with his two brothers from Holland in the reign of James IV of Scotland, and purchased lands on the extreme north-eastern coast of Scotland. In lime the o'Groats increased, and there came to be eight families of the name. They met regularly once a year in the house built by the founder, but on one occasion a question of precedency arose, and John o' Groat promised them the next time they came he would contrive to satisfy them all. Accordingly he built an eight-sided room, with a door in each side, and placed an octagonal table therein. This building went ever after with the name of *John o' Groat's House*; its site is the Berubium of Ptolemy, in the vicinity of Duncansby Head.

> Hear, land o' cakes and brither Scots,
> Frae Maidenkirk to Johnny Groat's …
> A chield's amang you takin' no es,
> And, faith, he'll prent it.
> Burns, *Captain Grose*

***From John o' Groat's to the Land's End.*** From Dan to Beersheba, from one end of Great Britain to the other.

**John Roberts.** Obsolete slang for a very large tankard, supposed to hold enough drink for any ordinary drinker to last through Saturday and Sunday. This measure was introduced into Wales in 1886 to compensate topers for the Sunday closing, and derived its name from John Roberts, MP, author of the Sunday Closing Act.

**John Thomas.** A generic name for a flunkey; or footman with large calves and bushy whiskers.

**John Tamson's Man.** A henpecked husband; one ordered here, there, and everywhere. Tamson – i.e. spiritless, a *Tame-son.*

> 'The deil's in the wife!' said Cuddle. 'D'ye think I am to be John Tamson's man and maistered by a woman a' the days o' my life?'
> Scott, *Old Mortality*, ch. xxxix

**John with the Leaden Sword.** John of Lancaster, Duke of Bedford (d.1435), third son of Henry IV, who acted as regent in France from 1422 to 1429, was so called by Earl Douglas.

**John, King, and the Abbot of Canterbury.** The story, as told in Percy's *Reliques*, is that John, being jealous of the state kept by the abbot, declared he should be put to death unless within three weeks he answered three questions that were set him. A shepherd undertook the task, so with crozier, mitre, rochet, and cope, he presented himself before the king. 'What am I worth?' was the first question. 'Well,' was the reply, 'the Saviour was sold for thirty pence, and your majesty is a penny worse than He.' The king laughed, and demanded what he had to say to the next question, How long would it take him to ride round the world? and the man replied, 'If you rise with the sun and ride with the sun, you will get round the world in a day.' Again the king was satisfied, and demanded that the respondent should tell him what he was thinking. 'You are thinking,' said the shepherd, 'that I am the abbot of Canterbury, but I am only a poor shepherd who am come to ask your majesty's pardon for him and me.' The king was so pleased with the jest that he would have made the shepherd abbot of Canterbury; but the man pleaded that he could neither write nor read, whereupon the king dismissed him, and gave him a pension of four nobles a week.

***Mess-John*** or ***Mass-John.*** A priest.

***Poor John.*** *See* Poor.

***Prester John.*** *See* Prester.

**Johnnies.** The short name on the Stock Exchange for the shares of the Johannesburg Consolidated Investment Co., Ltd.

A 'nut', i.e. a superfine, dandified youth, was known as a *Johnny* in the latter part of last century, and in the early part the word seems to have been applied indiscriminately to the British bourgeois. Byron, February 23rd, 1824, writes to Murray his publisher respecting an earthquake:

> If you had but seen the *English Johnnies*, who had never been out of a cockney workshop before … [running away …].

**Johnny-cake.** An American name for a cake made of maize-meal, formerly much esteemed as a delicacy. It is said to be a corruption of *journey*-cake.

> The real name is Journey cake: that is, cake made in haste for a journey. *Johnny Cake!* We might as well call it Tommy or Pelatiah cake!
>
> *Philadelphia Public Ledger* (22 May, 1836)

**Johnny Raw.** A nervous novice, a 'Verdant Green'; a newly enlisted soldier; an adult apprentice in the ship trade.

> The impulse given to ship-building by the continental war, induced employers to take persons as apprentices who had already passed their majority. This class of men-apprentices, generally from remote towns, were called 'Johnny Raws' by the fraternity.
>
> C. Thomson, *Autobiography*, p. 73

**Joint. *Out of joint.*** Disordered, disorganised. If the body is out of joint it cannot move easily, and so is it with the body corporate.

> The time is out of joint; O cursed spite,
> That ever I was born to set it right!
>
> Shakespeare, *Hamlet*, 1, 5

**Jolly.** A sailor's nickname for a marine, a militiaman being a *tame jolly*.

> To stand and be still to the Birken'ead drill is a damn tough bullet to chew,
> An' they done it, the Jollies, – 'Er Majesty's Jollies – soldier an' sailor too!
>
> Kipling, *Soldier an' Sailor Too*

The noun is also slang for a man who bids at auctions with no intention of buying, but merely to force up the price.

As an adjective and adverb, *jolly* frequently has an intensive, approving, or ironical effect:

> All was jolly quiet at Ephesus before St Paul came thither. John Trapp, *Commentary* (1656)
>
> 'Tis likely you'll prove a jolly surly groom.
>
> Shakespeare, *Taming of the Shrew*, 3, 2
>
> It's a jolly shame, it is! – He's a jolly good chap!
>
> *Modern*

***A jolly dog.*** A *bon vivant*: a jovial fellow.

***The jolly god.*** Bacchus. The Bible speaks of wine which 'maketh glad the heart of man'.

***A jolly good fellow.*** A very social and popular person. When toasts are drunk 'with musical honours' the chorus usually is –

> For he's a jolly good fellow [three times].
> And so say all of us,
> With a hip, hip, hip, hooray!

***The Jolly Roger.*** *See* Roger.

**Jolly-boat.** A small boat usually hoisted at the stern of a ship. *Jolly* here is probably connected with the Danish *jolle*, Dut. *jol*, and our *yawl*.

**Jonas,** in Dryden's *Absalom and Achitophel* (*q.v.*), is a punning name for Sir William *Jones*, Attorney-General, who conducted the prosecution of the Popish Plot (June 25th, 1674).

> Not bull-faced Jonas, who could statutes draw
> To mean rebellion and make treason law.
>
> *Absalom and Achitophel*, Pt i, 520

**Jonathan, Brother.** *See* Brother.

**Jonathan's.** A noted coffee-house in Change Alley, described in the *Tatler* as the general mart of stock-jobbers.

> Yesterday the brokers and others … came to a resolution that [the new building] instead of being called 'New Jonathan's', should be called 'The Stock Exchange' … The brokers then collected sixpence each, and christened the house with punch. Newspaper par. (July 15, 1773)

**Jonathan's Arrows.** They were shot to give warning, and not to hurt (1 Sam. 20:36).

> If the husband would reprove his wife … his words; like Jonathan's arrows, should be shot, not to hurt, but only to give warning.
>
> Le Fanu, *The House in the Churchyard*, ch. xcix

**Jones, Davy.** *See* Davy.

**Jordan.** A name anciently given to a pot used by alchemists and doctors, then transferred (as a vulgarism) to a chamber-pot. The word is thought to have been originally *Jordan-bottle*, i.e. a bottle in which pilgrims and crusaders brought back water from the River Jordan.

> Why, they will allow us ne'er a jordan, and then we leak in the chimney; and your chamber-lie breeds fleas like a loach.
>
> Shakespeare, *1 Henry IV*, 2, 1

***Jordan almond.*** Here *Jordan* has nothing to do with the river (*cp.* Jerusalem Artichoke), but is a corruption of Fr. *jardin*, garden. The Jordan almond is a fine variety which comes chiefly from Malaga.

***Jordan passed.*** Death over. The Jordan separated the wilderness [of the world] from the Promised Land, and thus came to be regarded almost as the Christian 'Styx' (*q.v.*).

> If I still hold closely to Him,
> What hath He at last?
> Sorrow vanquished, labour ended,
> Jordan passed.
>
> John Mason Neale, *Stephen the Sabaite*

**Jordeloo.** Notice given to passengers when dirty water was thrown from the chamber windows into the street; a corruption of Fr. *Gare de l'eau.*

> At ten o'clock at night the whole cargo is flung out of a back window that looks into some street or lane, and the maid calls 'Gardy loo' to the passengers. Smollett, *Humphry Clinker*

> The lass had made the Gardy loo out of the wrong window. Scott, *Heart of Midlothian*, xxvii

**Jormungandr** or **Midgardsormen** (i.e. earth's monster). The great serpent of *Scandinavian mythology*, brother of Hela and Fenrir (*q.v.*), and son of Loki, the spirit of evil. It lay at the root of the celestial ash till All-Fader cast it into the ocean; it then grew so large that in time it encompassed the whole world, and was for ever biting its own tail.

**Jorum.** A large drinking-bowl, intended specially for punch. The name is thought to be connected with King *Joram* (*cp.* Jeroboam), who 'brought with him vessels of silver, and vessels of gold, and vessels of brass' (2 Sam. 8:10).

**Josaphat.** An Indian prince converted by the hermit Barlaam. *See* Barlaam and Josaphat.

**Joseph.** One not to be seduced from his continency by the severest temptation is sometimes so called. The reference is to Joseph in Potiphar's house (Gen. 39). *Cp.* Bellerophon.

A great-coat used to be known by the same name, in allusion to Joseph, who left his garment, or upper coat, behind him.

> Mrs Buby herself made her appearance; her venerable person, endued with what was then called a joseph, an ample garment, which had once been green, but now, betwixt stains and patches, had become like the vesture of the patriarch whose name it bore – a garment of divers colours. Scott, *The Pirate*, ch. xi

***Joseph, St.*** Husband of the Virgin Mary, and the reputed father of Jesus. He is the patron saint of carpenters, because he was of that craft.

In art Joseph is represented as an aged man with a budding staff in his hand. His day is March 19th.

***Joseph of Arimathea.*** The rich Jew, probably a member of the Sanhedrin, who believed in Christ but feared to confess it, and, after the Crucifixion, begged the body of the Saviour and deposited it in his own tomb (*see* Matt. 27:57–60, Mark 15:42). Legend relates that he was imprisoned for 42 years, during which time he was kept alive miraculously by the Holy Grail (*see* Grail), and that on his release by Vespasian, about AD 63, he brought the Grail and the spear with which Longinus wounded the crucified Saviour, to Britain, and there founded the abbey of Glastonbury (*q.v.*), whence he commenced the conversion of Britain.

The origin of these legends is to be found in a group of apocryphal writings of which the *Evangelium Nicodemi* is the chief; these were worked upon at Glastonbury between the 8th and 11th centuries, were further embellished by Robert de Borron in the 13th, the latter version (by way of Walter Map) being woven by Malory into his *Morte d'Arthur.*

**Joss.** An idol or house-god of the Chinese; every family has its joss. A temple is called a *joss-house*, and a *joss-stick* is a stick of scented wood which is burnt as incense in a joss-house.

**Jot.** A very little, the least quantity possible. The iöta [ι] (*see* I) is the smallest letter of the Greek alphabet, called the Lacedemonian letter.

> Heven and erthe shal soner passe away then one iote of goddis worde shal passe unfulfilled.
>
> Geo. Joy, *An Apology to W. Tindale* (1535)

> This bond doth give thee here no jot of blood.
>
> Shakespeare, *Merchant of Venice*, 4, 1

**Jotham,** in Dryden's *Absalom and Achitophel* (*q.v.*), means Saville, Marquis of Halifax. The original Jotham (*see* Judges 9:7) uttered the parable of *The Trees Choosing a King* when the men of Shechem made Abimelech king.

**Jotunheim.** Giant land. The home or region of the Scandinavian giants or *Jötunn.*

**Jougs.** The Scottish pillory, or, more properly, an iron ring or collar fastened by a short chain to a wall, and used as a pillory. Jamieson says, 'They punish delinquents, making them stand in "jogges", as they call their pillories.' The word is really the same as *yoke* (Lat. *jugum*), and *jug* (*q.v.*), thieves' cant for a prison, is probably connected with it.

Staune ane wholl Sabothe daye in ye joggis.
Glen, *History of Dumbarton*

**Jourdain, Monsieur.** The type of the bourgeois placed by wealth in the ranks of gentlemen, who makes himself ridiculous by his endeavours to acquire their accomplishments. The character is from Molière's comedy *Le Bourgeois Gentilhomme* (1670).

**Journal** (O.Fr., from Lat. *diurnalis*, diurnal, *dies*, a day).

Applied to newspapers, the word strictly means a daily paper; but the extension of the term to weekly and other periodicals is sanctioned by custom. Thus *Pitman's Journal* is a weekly and the *Hibbert Journal* a quarterly.

**Journey-weight.** The weight of certain parcels of gold and silver in the mint. A *journey of gold* is fifteen pounds troy, which is coined into 701 sovereigns, or double that number of half-sovereigns. A *journey of silver* is sixty pounds troy, which, before the alteration in the silver coinage (1920), was coined into 3,960 shillings. So called because this weight of coin was at one time esteemed a day's mintage (Fr. *journée*).

**Jove.** Another name of Jupiter (*q.v.*), the later being *Jovis pater*, father Jove. The Titans made war against Jove, and tried to dethrone him.

Not stronger were of old the giant crew,
Who sought to pull high Jove from regal state.
Thomson, *Castle of Indolence*, canto 1

Milton, in *Paradise Lost*, makes Jove one of the fallen angels (i, 512).

**Jovial.** Merry and sociable, like those born under the planet Jupiter, which astrologers considered the happiest of the natal stars.

Our jovial star reigned at his birth.
Shakespeare, *Cymbeline*, 5, 4

**Joy.** ***The seven joys of the Virgin***. *See* Mary.

**Joyeuse.** A name given to more than one sword famous in romance, but especially to Charlemagne's, which bore the inscription *Decem praeceptorum custos Carolus*, and was buried with him.

**Joyeuse Garde** or **Garde-Joyeuse.** The estate given by King Arthur to Sir Launcelot of the Lake for defending the Queen's honour against Sir Mador. It is supposed to have been at Berwick-on-Tweed, but the Arthurian topography is all very indefinite.

**Juan Fernandez.** *See* Robinson Crusoe.

**Jubilee.** In Jewish history the year of *jubilee* was every fiftieth year, which was held sacred in commemoration of the deliverance from Egypt. In this year the fields were allowed to lie fallow, land that had passed out of the possession of those to whom it originally belonged was restored to them, and all who had been obliged to let themselves out for hire were released from bondage. The year of jubilee was proclaimed with trumpets of ram's horn, and takes its name from *jobil*, a ram's horn. (*See* Lev. 25:11–34, 39–54; and 27:16–24).

Hence any fiftieth anniversary, especially one kept with great rejoicings, is called a *Jubilee*, and the name has been applied to other outbursts of joy or seasons of festivity, such as the *Shakespeare Jubilee*, which was held at Stratford-on-Avon in September, 1769, and the *Protestant Jubilee*, celebrated in Germany in 1617 at the centenary of the Reformation.

King George III held a *Jubilee* on October 25th, 1809, that being the day before he *commenced* the fiftieth year of his reign; and Queen Victoria celebrated hers on June 21st, 1887, two days after she had *completed* her fiftieth year on the throne. Ten years later Queen Victoria kept her *Diamond Jubilee* as a thanksgiving for sixty years of queenhood, and a reign the length of which exceeded that of any of her predecessors. The only other English monarchs to have *Jubilees* were Henry III (who reigned for 56 years and 6 weeks), and Edward III (51 years and nearly 5 months).

In the Catholic Church Pope Boniface VIII instituted a *Jubilee* in 1300 for the purpose of granting indulgences, and ordered it to be observed every hundred years. Clement VI reduced the interval to fifty years, Urban IV to thirty, Sixtus IV to twenty-five; but now a *Jubilee* is ordained at irregular intervals, and very rarely for a whole year. There was one in 1900.

**Judas,** in Dryden's *Absalom and Achitophel* (*q.v.*), was meant for Mr Furgueson, a Nonconformist. He was ejected in 1662 from his living of Godmersham, Kent, took part in political intrigues, and joined the Duke of Monmouth, whom he afterwards betrayed.

***Judas Kiss.*** A deceitful act of courtesy. Judas betrayed his Master with a kiss (Matt. 26:49).

So Judas kissed his Master,
And cried, 'All hail!' whenas he meant *all harm*.
Shakespeare, *3 Henry VI*, 5, 7

***Judas Slits*** or ***Holes.*** The peepholes in a prison door, through which the guard looks into the cell to see if all is right; when not in use, the holes are covered up.

It was the faint click made by the cover of the 'Judas' as it falls back into the place over the slit where the eyes have been.

*The Century, Russian Political Prisons*, February, 1888, p. 524

***Judas Tree.*** A leguminous tree of southern Europe (*Cercis siliquastrum*) which flowers before the leaves appear, so called because of a Greek tradition that it was upon one of these trees that Judas Iscariot hanged himself. But *see* Elder tree, which is also sometimes called by the same name. *See also* Marsiglio.

***Judas-coloured Hair.*** Fiery red. In the Middle Ages Judas Iscariot was represented with red hair and beard, as also was Cain.

His very hair is of the dissembling colour, something browner than Judas's.

Shakespeare, *As You Like It*, 2, 4

**Jude, St.** Represented in art with a club or staff, and a carpenter's square, in allusion to his trade. His day is October 28th.

**Judge's Black Cap.** *See* Black Cap.

**Judges' Robes.** In the criminal courts, where the judges represent the sovereign, they appear in full court dress, and wear a scarlet robe; but in nisi prius courts the judge sits merely to balance the law between civilians, and therefore appears in his judicial undress, or violet gown.

**Judica.** The fifth Sunday after Lent, i.e. Passion Sunday, so called from the first word of the service for the day, *Judiça me, Domine* (Judge me, O Lord; Ps. 43).

**Judicium Crucis.** A form of ordeal which consisted in stretching out the arms before a cross, till one party could hold out no longer, and lost his cause. It is said that a bishop of Paris and abbot of St Denis appealed to this judgment in a dispute they had about the patronage of a monastery; each of the disputants selected a man to represent him, and the man selected by the bishop gave in, so that the award was given in favour of the abbot.

**Jug** or **Stone Jug.** A prison. It is curious that Gr. *keramos*, potter's earth and anything made with it, as a jug, also meant a prison or dungeon. *See* Jougs.

***Jugged hare.*** Hare stewed in a jug or jar.

***To be jugged.*** To be put in prison.

**Juggernaut** or **Jagganath.** A Hindu god, 'Lord of the World', having his temple at Puri, in Orissa. The legend, as told in the *Ayeen-Akbery*, is that a learned Brahman was sent to look out a site for a temple. The Brahman wandered about for many days, and then saw a crow dive into the water, and having washed, made obeisance to the element. This was selected as the site of the temple. While the temple was a-building the king, Indica Dhumna, had a prophetic dream, telling him that the true form of Vishnu should be revealed to him in the morning. When the king went to see the temple he beheld a log of wood in the water, and this log he accepted as the realisation of his dream, enshrining it in the temple.

Jagganath is regarded as the remover of sin. His image is on view three days in the year: the first day is the Bathing Festival, when the god is washed; he is then supposed to have a cold for ten days, at the end of which he is again brought out and taken in his car to the nearest temple; a week later the car is pulled back amid the rejoicings of the multitude at his recovery. It was on the final day that fanatical devotees used to throw themselves to be crushed beneath the wheels of the enormous, decorated machine, in the idea that they would thus obtain immediate admission to Paradise. Hence the phrase *the car of Juggernaut* is used of customs, institutions, etc., beneath which people are ruthlessly and unnecessarily crushed.

Reason shall no longer blindly bow
To the vile pagod things, that o'er her brow,
Like him of Jaghernaut drive trampling now.

Thos Moore, *Fudge Family in Paris*

**Juggler** (Lat. *joculator*, a player). In the Middle Ages, jugglers accompanied the minstrels and troubadours, and added to their musical talents sleight of hand, antics, and feats of prowess, to amuse the company assembled. In time the music was dropped as the least attractive, and tricks became the staple of wandering performers.

**Juggs.** *See* Jougs.

**Julian, St.** Patron saint of travellers and of hospitality, looked upon in the Middle Ages as the epicure of saints. Thus, after telling us that the Frankleyn was 'Epicurus owne sone', Chaucer says:

An householdere, and that a greet was he;
Seint Julian he was in his contree.

*Canterbury Tales, Prologue*, 339

In art he is represented as accompanied by a stag in allusion to his early career as a hunter; and either receiving the poor and afflicted, or ferrying travellers across a river.

**Julian.** Pertaining to Julius Caesar (100–44 BC), particularly with reference to the Calendar (i.e. the 'Old Style') instituted by him in 46 BC (the *Julian Year* consisting of 365¼ days), which was in general use in Western Europe till it was corrected by Gregory XIII in 1582, in England till 1752, and still in use in Russia. To allow for the odd quarter day Caesar ordained that every fourth year should contain 366 days, the additional day being introduced after the 6th of the calends of March, i.e. February 24th. Caesar also divided the months into the number of days they at present contain, and July (*q.v.*). is named in his honour.

**Julienne Soup.** Clear meat soup, containing chopped vegetables, especially carrots; said to be so called after Julien, a French cook of Boston.

**Julium Sidus.** The comet which appeared at the death of Julius Caesar, and which in court flattery was called the apotheosis of the murdered man.

**July.** The seventh month, named by Mark Antony, in honour of Julius Caesar, who was born in it. It was previously called *Quintilis*, as it was the fifth month of the Roman year; its Anglo-Saxon name was *litha se aefterra* (lithe, mild).

> The old Dutch name for it was *Hooy-maand* (hay-month); the old Saxon, *Maed-monath* (because the cattle were turned into the meadows to feed), and *Lida aeftevr* (the second mild or genial month). In the French Republican calendar it was called Messidor (harvest-month, June 19th to July 18th).

Until the late 18th century, July was accented on the first syllable; why the change took place no one seems to know.

> Her lips were red; and one was thin,
> Compar'd to that was next her chin
> (Some bee had stung it newly):
> But, Dick, her eyes so guard her face,
> I durst no more upon them gaze
> Than on the sun in July.
> Suckling, Ballad Upon a Wedding (1646)

And even as late as 1798 Wordsworth wrote:

> In March, December, and in July,
> 'Tis all the same with Harry Gill;
> The neighbours tell, and tell you truly,
> His teeth they chatter, chatter still.
> Goody Blake and Harry Gill

**Jumala.** The supreme god of the ancient Finns and Lapps. The word is sometimes used by the Scandinavian poets for the Almighty.

> On a lonely cliff
> An ancient shrine he found, of Jumala the seat,
> For many a year gone by closed up and desolate.
> Freithiof-Saga, The Reconciliation

**Jump.** To fit or unite with like a graft; as, our inventions meet and jump in one. Hence the adverb exactly, precisely.

> Good advice is easily followed when it jumps with our own … inclinations.
> Lockhart, Sir Walter Scot, ch. x

***To jump a claim.*** An expression from the miners' camps, meaning to seize somebody else's 'claim', i.e. his diggings, in his absence and work it oneself; or, to take his mine by force; hence, to annex property by stealing a march on the owner.

***To jump at an offer.*** To accept eagerly.

***To jump over the broomstick.*** To marry in an informal way. A 'brom' is the bit of a bridle; to 'jump the brom' is to skip over the marriage restraint, and 'broomstick' is a mere corruption.

> A Romish wedding is surely better than jumping over a broomstick. G. A. Sala

***Jumper.*** Nowadays the name is given to almost any kind of knitted outer body-garment worn by women, but formerly it meant a very rough, loose jacket or outer shirt made of canvas or other coarse material and worn principally by bargees, longshoremen, porters, etc. It is from the obsolete jump, a short coat worn by men two hundred years ago, connected with Fr. jupe, and jupon, a petticoat.

***Counter-jumper.*** *See* Counter.

**Jumpers.** Another name for the Shakers (*q.v.*), or some similar sect, especially some Welsh Methodists of the mid-18th century.

**June.** The sixth month, named from the Roman *Junius* gens. Ovid says, *Junius a juvenum nomine dictus* (*Fasti*, v, 78).

> The old Dutch name was *Zomer-maand* (summer-month); the old Saxon, *Sere-monath* (dry-month), and *Lida-aerra* (joy time). In the French Republican calendar the month was called *Prairial* (meadow-month, May 20th to June 18th).

***June marriages lucky.*** 'Good to the man and happy to the maid'. This is an old Roman superstition. The festival of Juno moneta was held on the calends of June, and Juno was the great guardian of the female sex from birth to death.

**Junius.** ***The Letters of Junius*** are a series of anonymous letters, the authorship of which has never been finally settled, which appeared in the London *Public Advertiser* from November 21st, 1768, to January 21st, 1772, and were directed against Sir William Draper, the Duke of Grafton, and the Ministers generally. The author himself said, 'I am the sole depositary of my secret, and it shall die with me'; they were probably by Sir Philip Francis (1740–1818). Mr Pitt told Lord

Aberdeen that he knew who wrote them, and that it was not Francis; and Edmund Burke, his brother William, Earl Temple, Charles Lloyd, and John Roberts (clerks at the Treasury), John Wilkes, Dr Butler, Bishop of Hereford, Lord George Sackville, and even Gibbon are among those to whom they have been credited. The following extract from Letter LXVII, addressed to the Duke of Grafton, may be taken as a specimen of the literary and vitriolic excellence of the *Letters of Junius*:

> The unhappy baronet [Sir Jas Lowther] has no friends even among those who resemble him. You, my Lord, are not yet reduced to so deplorable a state of dereliction. Every villain in the kingdom is your friend: and, in compliment to such amity, I think you should suffer your dismal countenance to clear up. Besides, my Lord, I am a little anxious for the consistency of your character. You violate your own rules of decorum, when you do not insult the man whom you have betrayed.

**Junk.** Salt meat supplied to vessels for long voyages (*cp.* Harness Cask), so called because it is hard and tough as old rope-ends, which may have got the name *junk* from the rush-like shore plant, *Juncus maritimus*. Junk is often called 'salt horse'.

**Junker.** A young German noble (*jung*, young, *herr*, sir), a member of the reactionary, aristocratic party in the old Empire, principally remembered for their bullying and overbearing methods and their narrow-minddedness.

> You know his pretensions. He gives himself the airs of a demi-god walking the pavement – civilians and their wives swept into the gutter; they have no right to stand in the way of the great Prussian Junker ... You know the type of motorist, the terror of the roads, with a 60-h.p. car. He thinks the roads are made for him, and anybody who impedes the action of his car by a single mile is knocked down. The Prussian Junker is the road hog of Europe. Small nationalities in his way hurled to the roadside. bleeding and broken; women and children crushed under the wheels of his cruel car; Britain ordered out of his road. All I can say is this. If the old British spirit is alive in British hearts that bully will be torn from his seat.
>
> Lloyd George, Speech, Sept. 19th, 1914

**Junket.** Curded cream with spice, etc.; any dainty. So called because it was originally made in a rush basket (Ital. *giuncata*, from Lat. *juncus*, a rush).

> You know there wants no junkets at the feast.
>
> Shakespeare, *Taming of the Shrew*, 2, 2

***Junketing.*** Feasting, merrymaking.

> But great is song
> Used to great ends ... for song
> Is duer unto freedom, force and growth
> Of spirit than to junketing and love.
>
> Tennyson, *Princess*, Pt iv

**Juno.** The 'venerable ox-eyed' wife of Jupiter, and queen of heaven, of *Roman mythology*. She is identified with the Greek Hera, was the special protectress of marriage and of woman, and was represented as a war goddess.

***Junonian bird.*** The peacock, dedicated to the goddess-queen.

**Junta.** In Spain a council or legislative assembly other than the Cortes (*q.v.*), which may be summoned either for the whole country, for one of its separate parts, or for some special object only. The most famous is that called together by Napoleon in 1808.

> I had also audience of the King, to whom I deliver'd two Memorials since, in His Majesty's name of *Great Britain*, that a particular Junta of some of the Council of State and War might be appointed to determine the business.
>
> *Howell's Letters*, Bk i, sect. iii, 10 (Madrid, Jan. 5th, 1622)

**Junto.** In English history, the name given to a faction that included Wharton, Russell, Lord-Keeper Somers, Charles Montague, and several other men of mark, who ruled the Whigs in the reign of William III for nearly twenty years, and exercised a very great influence over the nation. The word is a corruption of *junta* (*q.v.*).

**Jupiter.** The supreme deity of *Roman mythology*, corresponding to the Greek Zeus (*see* Jove), son of Cronos, or Saturn (whom he dethroned) and Rhea. He was the special protector of Rome, and as Jupiter Capitolinus – his temple being on the Capitoline Hill – presided over the Roman games. He determined the course of all human affairs and made known the future to man through signs in the heavens, the flight of birds (*see* Augury), etc.

As Jupiter was lord of heaven and prince of light, *white* was the colour sacred to him; hence, among the mediaeval alchemists *Jupiter* designated tin. In heraldry Jupiter stands for *azure*, the blue of the heavens.

His statue by Phidias (taken to Constantinople by Theodosius I and there destroyed by fire in AD 475) was one of the Seven Wonders of the World.

***Jupiter Scapin.*** A nickname of Napoleon Bonaparte, given him by the Abbé de Pradt. Scapin is a valet famous for his knavish tricks, in Molière's comedy of *Les Fourberies de Scapin*.

***Jupiter tonans*** (the thundering Jupiter). A complimentary nickname given to the London *Times* in the days of its greatness, i.e. about the middle of the 19th century.

***Jupiter's beard.*** House leek. Supposed to be a charm against evil spirits and lightning. Hence grown at one time very generally on the thatch of houses.

**Jurassic Rocks.** The group of limestone rocks embracing the strata between the top of the Rhaetic Beds and the base of the Purbeckian Rocks, thus including the Lias and Oolites. So named from the Swiss *Jura*, where they are typically developed.

**Jury Mast.** A temporary mast, a spar used for the nonce when the mast has been carried away. The origin of the term is unknown; it has been in use for certainly over three hundred years, and was probably a bit of sailor's wit.

'Jury' has been humorously tacked on to other nouns, giving to the word a makeshift or temporary significance, e.g. *Jury-leg*, a wooden leg:

> I took the leg off with my saw ... seared the stump ... and made a jury leg that he shambles about with as well as ever he did.
>
> Scott, *The Pirate*, ch. xxxiv

**Jus civile** (Lat.). Civil law.

**Jus divinum** (Lat.). Divine law.

**Jus et norma loquendi.** The right method of speaking and pronouncing established by the custom of each particular nation.

> Multa renascentur quae jam cecidere, cadentque
> Quae nunc sunt in honore vocabula, si volet usus,
> Quem penes arbitrium est, et jus, et norma loquendi.
> Horace, *Ars Poetica*, 70
>
> Yes, words long faded may again revive;
> And words may fade now blooming and alive,
> If usage wills it so, to whom belongs
> The rule and law, the government of tongues.
> (Conington's translation)

**Jus gentium** (Lat.). International law.

**Jus mariti** (Lat.). The right of the husband to the wife's property.

**Jusquauboutiste.** One who is prepared to see a thing through to the finish. The word was coined during the Great War from Fr. *jusqu'au bout*, up to the end.

**Just, The.** Among rulers and others who have been given this surname are:

Aristides, the Athenian (d.468 BC).

Baharam, styled *Shah Endeb*, fifth of the Sassanidiae (276–96).

Casimir II, King of Poland (1117, 1177–94).

Ferdinand I, King of Aragon (1373, 1412–16).

Haroun al-Raschid. The most renowned of the Abbasside califs, and the hero of several of the *Arabian Nights* stories (765, 786–808).

James II, King of Aragon (1261–1327).

Khosru or Chosroes I of Persia (531–79), called by the Arabs *Molk al Adel* (the Just King).

Pedro I of Portugal (1320, 1357–67).

**Juste milieu** (Fr.). The golden mean.

> The Church of England is the *juste milieu*.
>
> Lady Bloomfield, *Reminiscences*, II, p. 18 (1883)

**Justice.** *See* Jedwood Justice.

***Justices in Eyre.*** *See* Eyre.

***Poetic justice.*** That ideal justice which poets exercise in making the good happy, and the bad unsuccessful in their evil schemes.

**Juvenal** (Lat., from *juvenis*). A youth; common in Shakespeare, thus:

> The juvenal, the prince your master, whose chin is not yet fledged.
> *2 Henry IV*, 1, 2

**Juveniles.** In theatrical parlance, those actors who play young men's parts; in journalistic and book-trade slang, periodicals or books intended for the young.

**K.** The eleventh letter of the alphabet, representing the Greek *kappa*, and Hebrew *kaph*. The Egyptian hieroglyphic for *k* was a bowl. The Romans, after the C was given the K sound, gave up the use of the letter, except in abbreviated forms of a few words from Greek; thus, false accusers were branded on the forehead with a K (*kalumnia*), and the Carians, Cretans, and Cilicians were known as *the three bad K's*.

*K* is the recognised abbreviation of *Knight* in a large number of Orders (but the abbreviation of 'Knight' *per se* is *Kt*).

The chief of these in England are:

| | | |
|---|---|---|
| *K.B.E.* | Knight Commander of the British Empire. | |
| *K.C.B.* | | Bath. |
| *K.C.I.E.* | | Indian Empire. |
| *K.C.M.G.* | | St Michael and St George. |
| *K.C.S I.* | | Star of India. |
| *K.C.V.O.* | | Victorian Order |
| *K.G.* | Knight of the Garter. | |
| *K.P.* | | St Patrick (Irish). |
| *K.T.* | | the Thistle (Scotch). |

**K. K. K.** The initials branded by the Ku Klux Klan (*q.v.*) on their victims.

**K. of K.** A familiar way of referring to Earl *K*itchener of *K*hartoum (1850–1916).

**Ka Me, Ka Thee.** You scratch my back and I'll scratch yours; one good turn deserves another; do me a service, and I will give you a helping hand when you require one. It is an old proverb, and appears in Heywood's collection (1546).

> Ka me, ka thee, is a proverb all over the world.
>
> Scott, *Kenilworth*, ch. v

**Kaaba** (Arabic, *kabah*, a square house). A shrine of Mecca, said to have been built by Ishmael and Abraham on the spot where Adam first worshipped after his expulsion from Paradise, and where, after being a wanderer on the face of the earth for two hundred years, he received pardon. In the north-east corner is the famous 'black stone' (*see* Hajar al-Aswad).

**Kaf, Mount.** The huge mountain in the middle of which, according to Mohammedan myth, the earth is sunk, as a night light is placed in a cup. Its foundation is the emerald *Sakhrat*, the reflection of which gives the azure hue to the sky.

**Kaffir** (Arabic, *Kafir*, an infidel). A name formerly given to Hottentots who rejected the Moslem faith, also to the natives of *Kafiristan* ('the country of the infidels'), in northern Afghanistan; but now restricted to the Bantu races of South Africa, especially the Xosa tribe.

***Kaffirs, Kaffir market*.** The Stock Exchange names for shares in South African mines, and for the market in which they are dealt.

**Kailyard School.** A school of writers, who took their subjects from Scottish humble life; it flourished in the 'nineties of last century, and included such writers as Ian Maclaren, J. J. Bell, S. R. Crockett, and (Sir) J. M. Barrie. The name is due to the motto – 'There grows a bonnie brier bush in our kailyard' – used by Ian Maclaren for his *Beside the Bonnie Brier Bush* (1894).

**Kaiser.** The German form of *Caesar*; the title formerly used by the head of the Holy Roman Empire, and by the German Emperor and the Emperor of Austria. It was Diocletian who (about 284) ordained that *Caesar* should be the title of the Emperor of the West, and it is thence that the modern *Kaiser* takes its rise.

**Kalevala.** The national epic of the Finns, compiled from popular songs and oral tradition by the Swedish philologist, Elias Lönnrott (1802–84), who published his first edition of 12,000 verses in 1835, and a second, containing some 22,900 verses, in 1849.

The hero is a great magician, Wainarnoinen, and a large part of the action turns on Sampo, an object that gives one all his wishes.

The epic is influenced by, but by no means dependent upon, *Teutonic* and *Scandinavian mythology*, and, to a less extent, by Christianity. It is written in unrhymed alliterative trochaic verse, and is the prototype, both in form and content, of Longfellow's *Hiawatha*.

**Kali.** The Hindu goddess after whom Calcutta receives its name, Kali-ghat, the steps of Kali, i.e. those by which her worshippers descended from the bank to the waters of the Ganges. She was the wife of Siva (*q.v.*), was the acme of bloodthirstiness, many human sacrifices being made to her, and it was to her that the Thugs sacrificed their victims. Her idol is black, besmeared with blood; she has red eyes, four arms with blood-stained hands, matted hair, huge fang-like teeth, and a protruding tongue that drips with blood.

She wears a necklace of skulls, earrings of corpses, and is girdled with serpents.

**Kaliyuga.** The last of the four Hindu periods contained in the great Yuga (*q.v.*).

**Kalki.** *See* Avatar.

**Kalmar.** ***The Union of Kalmar.*** A treaty made on July 12th, 1397, uniting the kingdoms of Norway, Sweden and Denmark. This union lasted till it was dissolved by Gustavus Vasa in 1523.

**Kalmucks** – i.e. *Khalmuiku* (apostates) from Buddhism. A race of nomadic Mongols, extending from western China to the valley of the Volga, and adhering to a debased form of Buddhism.

**Kalpa.** A day and night of Brahma, a period of 4,320,000,000 solar-sidereal years; the whole duration of time from the creation to the destruction of the world. Some say there are an infinity of Kalpas, others limit the number to thirty.

**Kalpa-Tarou.** A tree in *Indian mythology* from which might be gathered whatever a person desired – 'the tree of the imagination'.

**Kalyb.** The 'Lady of the Woods', who stole St George from his nurse, brought him up as her own child, and endowed him with gifts. St George enclosed her in a rock, where she was torn to pieces by spirits (*Seven Champions of Christendom*, Pt i).

**Kam.** Crooked; a Celtic word. *Clean kam*, perverted into *kim kam*, means wholly awry, clean from the purpose.

> This is clean kam – merely awry.
>
> Shakespeare, *Coriolanus*, 3, 1

**Kama.** The Hindu god of love. *See* Cama.

**Kami.** A god or divinity in *Shinto*, the native religion of Japan; also the title given to daimios and governors, about equal to our 'lord'.

**Kamsin.** A simoom or hot, dry, southerly wind, which prevails in Egypt and the deserts of Africa from about the middle of March to the first week in May.

> I have two dromedaries here, fleeter than the Kamsin.
>
> Disraeli, *Tancred*, Bk iv, ch. iv

**Kansa.** *See* Krishna.

**Karaites.** *See* Caraites.

**Karma** (Sans., action, fate). In Buddhist philosophy, the name given to the results of action, especially the cumulative results of a person's deeds in one stage of his existence as controlling his destiny in the next.

Among Theosophists the word has a rather wider meaning, viz. the unbroken sequence of cause and effect; each effect being, in its turn, the cause of a subsequent effect. It is a Sanskrit word, meaning 'action' or 'sequence'.

> The laws which determine the physical attribution, condition of life, intellectual capacities, and so forth, of the new body, to which the Ego is drawn by affinities ... are ... in Buddhism [called] Karma.
>
> *Nineteenth Century*, June, 1893, p. 1025

**Karmathians.** A Mohammedan sect which rose in Irak in the 9th century. Its founder was Karmat, a labourer who professed to be a prophet; they were communistic pantheists and rejected the forms and ceremonies of the Koran, which they regarded as a purely allegorical work.

**Karoon.** The Arabic form of *Korah* (Numb. 16), who, according to the commentators of the Koran, was the most wealthy and most beautiful of all the Israelites. It is said that he built a large palace, which he overlaid with gold, and that the doors of his palace were solid gold. He was the Croesus of the Mohammedans, and guarded his wealth in a labyrinth.

**Karttikeya.** The Hindu Mars, and god of war. He is said to have been born without a mother and to have been fostered by the Pleiades or *Krittikas*, whence he is sometimes called 'the son of Krittikas'. He is shown riding on a peacock, with a bow in one hand and an arrow in the other, and is known also as *Skanda* and *Kumara*.

**Kaswa, Al.** Mahomet's favourite camel, which fell on its knees in adoration when the prophet delivered the last clause of the Koran to the assembled multitude at Mecca. This is one of the dumb creatures admitted into the Moslem paradise.

**Katerfelto.** A generic name for a quack or charlatan. Gustavus Katerfelto was a celebrated quack who became famous during the influenza epidemic of 1782, when he exhibited in London his solar microscope and created immense excitement by showing the infusoria of muddy water. The doctor used to aver that he was the greatest philosopher since the time of Sir Isaac Newton. He was a tall man, dressed in a long, black gown and square cap, and died in 1799.

> Katerfelto with his hair on end,
> At his own wonders wondering for his bread.
>
> Cowper, *Task*, *The Winter Evening* (1782)

**Kathay.** China. *See* Cathay.

**Katmir.** *See* Ketmir.

**Kay, Sir.** In Arthurian romance, son of Sir Ector and foster-brother of King Arthur, who made him his seneschal. He is represented as a rude and boastful knight, the first to attempt an achievement, but very rarely successful.

**Kayward.** *See* Kywert.

**Kebla-Noma.** The pocket compass carried by Mussulmans to direct them which way to turn when they pray. *See below.*

**Keblah.** The point towards which Mohammedans turn when they worship, i.e. the Kaaba (*q.v.*) at Mecca; also the niche or slab (called the *mihrab*) on the interior wall of a mosque indicating this direction.

> The prophet had wavered between Mecca and Jerusalem as the Keblah of prayer for his disciples. Milman, *Latin Christianity*, VII, vi

**Kedar's Tents.** This world. Kedar was a son of Ishmael (Gen. 25:15), and was the ancestor of an important tribe of nomadic Arabs. The phrase means houses in the wilderness of this world, and comes from Ps. 120:5: 'Woe is me, that I sojourn in Mesech, that I dwell in the tents of Kedar.' Seton Merriman's novel *In Kedar's Tents* (1897) tells the adventures of a wandering, exiled Irishman who joins the anti-Carlist forces in Spain.

> Ah me! ah me! that I
> In Kedar's tents here stay;
> No place like that on high;
> Lord, thither guide my way. Crossman

**Kedgeree** (Hindi, *khichri*). In India a stew of rice, vegetables, eggs, butter, etc.; but in England a dish of re-cooked fish with boiled rice, eggs, sauce, etc., is so called.

**Keel-hauling** or **-haling.** Metaphorically, a long, troublesome, and vexatious examination or repetition of annoyances from one in authority. The term comes from a practice that was formerly common in the Dutch and many other navies of tying delinquents to a yardarm with weights on their feet, and dragging them by a rope under the keel of a ship, in at one side and out at the other. The result was often fatal.

**Keelson** or **Kelson.** A beam running lengthwise above the keel of a ship, and bolted to the middle of the floor-frames, in order to stiffen the vessel. The termination *son* is probably Swedish *svin*, and Norwegian *svill*, a sill.

**Keening.** A weird lamentation for the dead, common in Galway. The coffin is carried to the burying place, and while it is carried three times round, the mourners go to the graves of their nearest kinsfolk and 'keen'. The word is Ir. *caoine*, from *caoinim*, to weep.

**Keep.** One's *keep* is the amount that it takes to maintain one; heard in such phrases as *You're not worth your keep*. The *keep* of a mediaeval castle was the main tower or stronghold, the donjon.

***Keep your breath to cool your porridge.*** Look after your own affairs, and do not put your spoke in another person's wheel. Husband your strength to keep your own state safe and well, and do not waste it on matters in which you have really no concern. Don't scold or rail at me, but look at home.

***Keep your hair on!*** *See* Hair.

***Keep your own counsel.*** *See* Counsel.

***Keep your powder dry.*** Keep prepared for action; keep your courage up. The phrase comes from a story told of Oliver Cromwell. During his campaign in Ireland he concluded an address to his troops, who were about to cross a river before attacking, with the words – 'Put your trust in God; but be sure to keep your powder dry.'

***To keep at arm's length.*** To prevent another from being too familiar.

***To keep body and soul together.*** *See* Body.

***To keep company with.*** To associate with one of the other sex with a view of marriage, to 'walk out with'. The phrase is almost confined to domestic servants and persons of a similar status.

***To keep down.*** To prevent another from rising to an independent position; to keep in subjection; also to keep expenses low.

***To keep good hours.*** *See* Hour.

***To keep house, open house,*** etc. *See* House.

***To keep in.*** To repress, to restrain; also, to confine boys in the classroom after school hours as a punishment.

***To keep in with.*** To continue to maintain friendly relations with.

***To keep it dark.*** *See* Dark.

***To keep one's countenance.*** *See* Countenance.

***To keep one's terms.*** To reside in college, attend the Inns of Court, etc., during the recognised term times.

***To keep the pot a-boiling.*** *See* Pot.

***To keep touch.*** *See* Touch.

***To keep up.*** To continue, as, 'to keep up a discussion'; to maintain, as, 'to keep up one's courage', 'to keep up appearances'; to continue *pari passu*, as 'Keep up with the rest.'

**Kehama.** The Hindu rajah in Southey's epic, *The Curse of Kehama* (1810), who obtains and sports with supernatural powers.

**Kelpie** or **Kelpy.** A spirit of the waters in the form of a horse, in Scottish fairy lore. It was supposed to take a delight in the drowning of travellers, but also occasionally helped millers by keeping the mill-wheel going at night.

> Every lake has its Kelpie or Water-horse, often seen by the shepherd sitting upon the brow of a rock, dashing along the surface of the deep, or browsing upon the pasture on its verge.
> Graham, *Sketches of Perthshire*

**Kelso Convoy.** An old Scottish expression; see extract below.

> It's no expected your honour suld leave the land; it's just a Kelso convoy, a step and a half ower the door stane. Scott, *The Antiquary*, ch. xxx

**Kendal Green.** Green cloth for foresters; so called from Kendal, Westmorland, famous at one time for this manufacture. Kendal green was the livery of Robin Hood and his followers. In Rymer's *Faedera* (ii, 83) is a letter of protection, dated 1331, and granted by Edward III to John Kempe of Flanders, who established cloth-weaving in the borough. Lincoln was also famous at one time for dyeing green.

> How couldst thou know these men in Kendal green when it was so dark thou couldst not see thy hand? Shakespeare, *1 Henry IV*, 2, 4

**Kenelm, St.** An English saint, son of Kenwulf, King of Wessex in the early 9th century. He was only seven years old when, by his sister's order, he was murdered at Clente-in-Cowbage, Gloucestershire. The murder, says Roger of Wendover, was miraculously notified at Rome by a white dove, which alighted on the altar of St Peter's, bearing in its beak a scroll with these words:

> In Clent cow pasture, under a thorn,
> Of head bereft, lies Kenelm king-born.

St Kenelm's 'day' is July 17th.

**Kenna.** *See* Kensington Garden.

**Kenne.** A stone that by mediaeval naturalists was fabled to be formed in the eye of the stag. It was used as an antidote to poison. *Cp.* Hyena.

**Kennel.** A dog's shelter; from Lat. *canis* (a dog), Ital. *canile*; but *kennel*, a gutter, is, like *channel* and *canal*, from Lat. *canalis*, a pipe (our *cane*) through which water was conveyed.

**Kenno.** The dialect name of a large rich cheese, made by the women of the family with a great affectation of secrecy for the refreshment of the gossips who were in the house at the birth of a child. After all had eaten their fill what was left was divided among the gossips and taken home. The Kenno is supposed to be a relic of the secret rites of the *Bona Dea.*

**Kensington Garden.** A mock-heroic poem by Thomas Tickell (published 1722) peopling Kensington Gardens, which a few years before had been laid out, with fairies. The gardens were the royal domain of Oberon, and the hero is Albion, son of 'Albion's royal blood', who was stolen thence by a fairy named Milkah. He later fell in love with Kenna, daughter of Oberon, and after many adventures and a war caused by Oberon's opposition they were married and 'lived happy ever after'.

**Kent** (Lat. *Cantium*), the territory of the Kantii or Cantii; Old British, *Kant*, a corner or headland. In the reign of Queen Elizabeth Kent was so notorious for highway robbery that the word signified a 'nest of thieves'.

> Some bookes are arrogant and impudent;
> So are most thieves in Christendome and Kent.
> Taylor, the Water Poet (1630)

'Kent' and 'Christendom' have been verbally associated from very early times, partly, no doubt, because of the alliteration, partly, perhaps, because it was to Kent that St Augustine first brought Christianity.

***A man of Kent.*** One born east of the Medway. These men went out with green boughs to meet the Conqueror, and obtained in consequence a confirmation of their ancient privileges from the new king. They call themselves the *invicti.*

***A Kentish man.*** A resident of West Kent.

***The Fair Maid of Kent.*** *See* Fair.

***The Holy Maid of Kent.*** *See* Holy.

**Kent Cap.** A standard size of brown paper measuring 22 by 18 in.

**Kent's Cavern,** or **Hole.** A large cave in the limestone rock near Torquay, Devon. Many palaeolithic flints and other implements, as well as animal remains, have been discovered there.

**Kentigern, St.** The patron saint of Glasgow, born of royal parents about 510. He is said to have founded the cathedral at Glasgow, where he died in 601. He is represented with his episcopal cross in one hand, and in the other a salmon and a ring, in allusion to the well-known legend:

> Queen Langoureth had been false to her husband, King Roderich, and had given her lover a ring. The king, aware of the fact, stole upon the knight in sleep, abstracted the ring, threw it into

the Clyde, and then asked the queen for it. The queen, in alarm, applied to St Kentigern, who after praying, went to the Clyde, caught a salmon with the ring in its mouth, handed it to the queen and was thus the means of restoring peace to the royal couple, and of reforming the repentant queen.

The Glasgow arms include the salmon with the ring in its mouth, and also an oak tree, a bell hanging on one of the branches, a bird at the top of the tree:

The tree that never grew,
The bird that never flew,
The fish that never swam,
The bell that never rang.

The oak and bell are in allusion to the story that St Kentigern hung a bell upon an oak to summon the wild natives to worship.

St Kentigern is also known as 'St Mungo', for *Mungho* (i.e. dearest) was the name by which St Servan, his first preceptor, called him. His day is January 13th.

**Kentish Fire.** Rapturous applause, or three times three and one more. The expression originated with the protracted cheers given in Kent to the No-Popery orators in 1828–9. Lord Winchilsea, who proposed the health of the Earl of Roden on August 15th, 1834, said: 'Let it be given with the "Kentish Fire".'

**Kentishmen's Tails.** *See* Tails.

**Kepler's Laws.** Astronomical laws first enunciated by Johann Kepler (1571–1630). They formed the basis of Newton's work, and are the starting-point of modern astronomy: They are:

(1) That the orbit of a planet is an ellipse, the sun being in one of the foci.

(2) That every planet so moves that the line drawn from it to the sun describes equal areas in equal times.

(3) That the squares of the times of the planetary revolutions are as the cubes of their mean distances from the sun.

**Kernel.** ***The kernel of a matter;*** its gist, true import; the core or central part or it. The word is the A.S. *cyrnel*, diminutive of *corn.*

**Kersey.** A coarse cloth, usually ribbed, and woven from long wool; said to be so named from Kersey, in Suffolk, where it was originally made. Shakespeare uses the word figuratively ('russet yeas and honest kersey noes', *Love's Labour's Lost*, 5, 2), with the meaning plain or homely.

**Kerseymere.** A corruption of Casimir, a man's name. A twilled fine woollen cloth of a particular make, formerly called *cassimere*, a variation of *cashmere*, its present name being due to confusion with *kersey* (*see above*). *Cashmere*, a fine woollen material, is so called because it is made from hair of the goats of Kashmir, a native state to the north of British India.

**Kerton.** *See* Exter.

**Kestrel.** A hawk of a base breed, hence a worthless felllow.

No thought of honour ever did assay
His baser brest; but in his kestrell kynd
A pleasant veine of glory he did find ...
Spenser, *Faërie Queene*, II, iii, 4

**Ketch.** *See* Jack Ketch, under Jack, vi.

**Ketchup.** A sauce made from mushrooms, tomatoes, etc., which originally, with its name, came from the Far East.

Soy comes in Tubbs from Jappan, and the best ketchup from Tonquin; yet good of both sorts are made and sold very cheap in China.
Lockyer, *Trade with India* (1711)

The word is from Chinese, through Malay, *kechap.*

**Ketmir** or **Katmir.** The dog of the Seven Sleepers (*q.v.*), called in the Mohammedan version 'Al Rakhim'.

**Kettle.** Thieves' slang for a watch; a *tin kettle* is a silver watch and a *red kettle* a gold one.

***A kettle of fish.*** An old Border name for a kind of *fête champêtre*, or picnic by the river-side in which newly caught salmon is the chief dish. Having thickened some water with salt to the consistency of brine, the salmon is put therein and boiled; and when fit for eating, the company partake in gypsy fashion. The discomfort of this sort of picnic probably gave rise to the phrase 'A pretty kettle of fish', meaning an awkward state of affairs, a mess, a muddle.

The whole company go to the waterside today to eat a kettle of fish. Scott, *St Ronan's Wel.*, xii

The surgeon ... was now come to acquaint Mr Tow-wouse that his guest was in such extreme danger of his life, that he scarce saw any hopes of his recovery. 'Here's a pretty kettle of fish,' cries Mrs Tow-wouse, 'you have brought upon us! We are like to have a funeral at our own expense.' Fielding, *Joseph Andrews*, I, xii

**Kettledrum.** A drum made of a thin hemispherical shell of brass or copper with a parchment top.

Also, an obsolete name for an afternoon tea-party, so called because it was on a somewhat smaller scale than the regular 'drum' (*q.v.*), and also in playful allusion to the presence of the tea *kettle.*

**Kevin, St.** An Irish saint of the 6th century, of whom legend relates that, like St Senanus, he retired to an island where he vowed no woman should ever land. Kathleen tracked him to his retirement, but the saint hurled her from a rock, and her ghost never left the place while he lived. A rock at Glendalough (Wicklow) is shown as the bed of St Kevin. Moore has a poem on this tradition (*Irish Melodies*, iv).

**Kex.** The dry, hollow stem of umbelliferous plants, like the hemlock. Tennyson says in *The Princess*, 'Though the rough kex break the starred mosaic'. Nothing breaks a pavement like the growth of grass or lichen through it.

**Key.** Metaphorically, that which explains or solves some difficulty, problem, etc., as *the key to a cipher*, the means of interpreting it, *the key to a 'roman à clef'*, the list showing whom the fictional characters represent in actual life. Also, a place which commands a large area of land or sea, as Gibraltar is the *key of the Mediterranean*, and, in the Peninsular War, Ciudad Rodrigo (taken by Wellington, 1812) was known as the *key of Spain.*

In music the lowest note of a scale is the *keynote*, and gives its name to the scale, or *key*, itself: hence the figurative phrases *in key*, *out of key*, in or out of harmony with.

**Phrases.**

***St Peter's keys.*** The cross-keys on the papal arms symbolising the power of the keys (*see below*).

***The Gold Key.*** The office of Groom of the Stole (*see* Stole), the holder of which had a golden key as his emblem.

***The key shall be upon his shoulder.*** He shall have the dominion, shall be in authority, have the keeping of something. It is said of Eliakim that God would lay upon his shoulder the key of the house of David (Is. 22:22). The chamberlain of the court used to bear a key as his insignia, and on public occasions the steward slung his key over his shoulder, as our mace-bearers carry their mace.

***The king's keys.*** An old legal phrase for the crowbars, hammers, etc., used to force an entrance so that a warrant could be executed.

> The door, framed to withstand attacks from excisemen, constables, and other personages, considered to use the king's key ... set his efforts at defiance. Scott, *Redgauntlet*, ch. xix

***The power of the keys.*** The supreme ecclesiastical authority vested in the pope as successor of St Peter. The phrase is derived from St Matt. 16:19:

> And I will give unto thee the keys of the kingdom of heaven: and whatsoever thou shalt bind on earth shall be bound in heaven: and whatsoever thou shalt loose on earth shall be loosed in heaven.

***To have the key of the street.*** To be locked out of doors; to be turned out of one's home.

***To put the key under the door.*** To shut up the house and go away.

**The Key in Fable.**

Keys of stables and cowhouses have not infrequently, even at the present day, a stone with a hole through it and a piece of horn attached to the handle. This is a relic of an ancient superstition. The *halig*, or holy stone, was looked upon as a talisman which kept off the fiendish Mara (nightmare); and the horn was supposed to ensure the protection of the god Pan.

***Key and Bible.*** Formerly employed as a method of divination. The Bible is opened either at Ruth, ch. i, or at Psalm 51, and a door-key is placed inside the Bible, so that the handle projects beyond the book. The Bible is then tied with a piece of string and held by the fourth fingers of the accuser and defendant, who must repeat the words touched by the wards of the key. The key was then supposed to turn towards the guilty person, and the Bible fall to the ground.

***The Cross Keys*** as a public-house sign has an ecclesiastical origin (*see* St Peter's keys, *above*). St Peter is always represented in art with two keys in his hand; they are consequently the insignia of the papacy, and are borne saltire-wise, one of gold and the other of silver. They also form the arms of the Archbishop of York; the Bishop of Winchester bears two keys and sword in saltire, and the bishops of St Asaph, Gloucester, Exeter, and Peterborough bear two keys in saltire. The *cross-keys* are also the emblem of St Servatius, St Hippolytus, St Geneviève, St Petronilla, St Osyth, St Martha, and St Germanus of Paris.

**Key-cold.** Deadly cold, lifeless. A key, on account of its coldness, is still sometimes employed to stop bleeding at the nose.

> Poor key-cold figure of a holy king!
> Pale ashes of the house of Lancaster!
> Thou bloodless remnant of that royal blood
> Shakespeare, *Richard III*, 1, 2

**Keys, The House of.** The representative branch of the Legislature, or *Tynwald*, of the Isle of Man, which consists of two branches, viz. the Governor and Council, and this House. Since 1866 the twenty-four members of the House of Keys have been popularly elected every seven years; previous to that date the House was self-elected, vacancies being filled by the House presenting to the governor 'two of the eldest and worthiest men of the isle', one of which the governor nominated.

The governor and his council consists of the governor, the bishop, the attorney-general, two deemsters (or judges), the clerk of the rolls, the water bailiff, the archdeacon, and the vicar-general.

**Keystone.** ***The Keystone State.*** Pennsylvania; so called from its position and importance.

**Keyne, St.** A Celtic saint, daughter of Brychan, King of Brecknock in the 5th century. Concerning her well, near Liskeard, Cornwall, it is said that if a bridegroom drinks therefrom before his bride, he will be master of his house; but if the bride gets the first draught, the grey mare will be the better horse. Southey has a ballad on this tradition; the man left his wife at the porch and ran to the well to get the first draught; but when he returned his wife told him his labour had been in vain, for she had 'taken a bottle to church'.

**Khaki.** A Hindu word, meaning *dusty*, or *dust-coloured*, from *khak*, dust. Khaki was first used by British troops at the time of the Indian Mutiny, when it was adopted as the uniform for an irregular corps of Guides, raised at Meerut, hence called the *Khaki Risala* (*Risala* = squadron). In 1882 the War Office discussed the question of adopting it as the general active service uniform, but, though certain regiments wore it then, and in the Omdurman campaign in Egypt sixteen years later, on the North-West Frontier, etc., this was not done until the Boer War of 1809–1902.

The local magistrate, R. H. Wallace Dunlop, who raised the troops referred to above, published (1858) *Service with the Khakee Ressalah, or Meerut Volunteer Horse*, 1857–8.

**Khamsin.** *See* Kamsin.

**Khedive.** The title by which, from 1867 to 1914, the ruler of Egypt, as viceroy of the Sultan of Turkey, was known. The word is Turkish (from Persian) and means a prince, or viceroy.

In 1914 Egypt was a semi-independent tributary state of Turkey, occupied by British troops. The then Khedive, Abbas II, joined the Central Powers, and was promptly deposed, a British Protectorate being declared. The title then disappeared, and the new ruler, Hussein Kamil, became *Sultan* of Egypt.

**Kiblah.** *See* Keblah.

**Kick.** Slang for a sixpence, but only in compounds. 'Two-and-a-kick' = two shillings and sixpence.

***He's not got a kick left in him.*** He's done for, 'down and out'. The phrase is from pugilism.

***More kicks than ha'pence.*** More abuse than profit. Galled 'monkey's allowance' in allusion to monkeys led about to collect ha'pence by exhibiting 'their parts'. The poor brutes get the kicks if they do their parts in an unsatisfactory manner, but the master gets the ha'pence collected.

***Quite the kick.*** Quite a dandy. The Italians call a dandy a *chic*. The French *chic* means knack, as *avoir le chic*, to have the knack of doing a thing smartly.

> I cocked my hat and twirled my stick,
> And the girls they called me quite the kick.
>
> George Colman the Younger

***To get the kick out.*** To be summarily dismissed; given the sack or 'the Order of the Boot'.

***To kick one's heels.*** *See* Heel.

***To kick against the pricks.*** To protest when all the odds are against one; to struggle against overwhelming opposition. *See* Acts 9:5, and 26:14, where the reference is to an ox kicking when goaded, or a horse when pricked with the rowels of a spur. *Cp.* also 1 Sam. 2:29 – 'Wherefore kick ye at my sacrifice and at mine offering', why do you protest against them?

***To kick over the traces.*** Not to follow the leader, but to act independently; as a horse refusing to run in harness kicks over the traces.

> If the new member shows any inclination to kick over the traces, he will not be their member long. Newspaper paragraph

***To kick the beam.*** To be of light weight; to be of inferior consequence. When one pan of a pair of scales is lighter than the other, it flies upwards and 'kicks the beam' of the scales.

***To kick the bucket.*** *See* Bucket.

***To kick up a dust, a row,*** etc. To create a disturbance. 'A pretty kick up' is a great disturbance. The phrase 'to kick up the dust' explains the other phrases.

**Kickshaws.** Made dishes, odds and ends, and dainty trifle of small value. Formerly written 'kickshose'. (Fr. *quelque chose*.)

> Some pigeons, Davy, a couple of short-legged hens, joint of mutton, and any pretty little tiny kickshaws.
>
> Shakespeare, *2 Henry IV*, 5, 1

**Kicksy-wicksy.** Full of whims and fancies, uncertain; hence, figuratively, a wife. Taylor, the water poet, calls it *kicksie-winsie*, but Shakespeare spells it *kicky-wicky*.

He wears his honour in a box unseen
That hugs his kicky-wicky here at home,
Spending his manly marrow in her arms,
Which should sustain the bound and high curvet
Of Mars's fiery steed.

*All's Well that Ends Well*, 2, 3

**Kid.** A faggot or bundle of firewood. *To kid* is to bind up faggots. In the parish register of Kneelsal church there is the following item: 'Leading kids to church, 2*s.* 6*d.*', that is, carting faggots to church.

***Kid.*** A young child; in allusion to kid, the young of the goat, a very playful and frisky little animal.

The verb *to kid*, to make a fool of, and the noun *kid* in such phrases as 'I'll give you a hiding, and no kid about it', probably comes from this.

**Kidney.** Temperament, disposition; stamp.

***Men of another kidney*** or ***of the same kidney.*** The *reins* or *kidneys* were even by the Jews supposed to be the seat of the affections.

**Kildare's Holy Fane.** Famous for the 'Fire of St Bridget', which was inextinguishable, because the nuns never allowed it to go out. Every twentieth night St Bridget was fabled to return to tend the fire. Part of the chapel still remains, and is called 'The Firehouse'.

**Kilkenny Cats.** *See* Cat.

**Kill.** The slaying of some animal, generally a bullock, tied up by hunters in a jungle, to allure some wild beast to the spot preparatory to a hunting party being arranged.

A shikarie brought us the welcome tidings of a tiger-kill only a mile and a half from the camp. The next day there was no hunt, as the ground round the panther-kill was too unfavourable to permit of any hunting.

*Nineteenth Century*, August, 1886

***To kill two birds with one stone.*** *See* Bird.

**Killed by Kindness.** It is said that Draco, the Athenian legislator, met with his death from his popularity, being smothered in the theatre of Aegina by the number of caps and cloaks showered on him by the spectators (590 BC). Thomas Heywood wrote a play called *A Woman Killed with Kindness* (1603).

**Killing.** Irresistible, overpowering, fascinating, or bewitching; so as to compel admiration and notice.

Those eyes were made so killing.

Pope, *Rape of the Lock*, v, 64

***A killing pace.*** Too hot or strong to last; exceptionally great; exhausting.

***Killing no murder.*** A pamphlet published in Holland and sent over to England in 1657 advising the assassination of Oliver Cromwell. It purported to be by one William Allen, a Jesuit, and has constantly been attributed to Silas Titus (later made a colonel and Groom of the Bedchamber by Charles II), but it was actually by Col. Sexby, a Leveller, who had gone over to the Royalists, and who, in 1656, narrowly failed in an attempt to murder Cromwell.

The texts on the title-page are:

And all the People of the Land rejoiced: and the City was quiet, after that they had slain Athaliah with the Sword. 2 Chron. 23:21

Now after the Time that Amaziah did turn away from following the Lord, they made a conspiracy against him in Jerusalem, and he fled to Lachish; but they sent to Lachish after him, and slew him there. 2 Chron. 25:27

**Kin, Kind.**

*King*: But now, my cousin Hamlet, and my son –
*Ham.*: A little more than kin, and less than kind.

Shakespeare, *Hamlet*, 1, 2

***Kin*** or ***kinsman*** is a relative by marriage or blood more distant than father and son.

***Kind*** means of the same sort of genus, as mankind or man-genus.

Hamlet says he is more than *kin* to Claudius (as he was stepson), but still he is not of the same *kind*, the same class. He is not a bird of the same feather as the king.

**Kindhart.** A jocular name for a tooth-drawer in the time of Queen Elizabeth. Kindhart, the dentist, is mentioned by Rowland in his *Letting of Humours-Blood in the Bead-vaine* (1600); and in Rowley's *New Wonder*.

Mistake me not, Kindhart ...
He calls you tooth-drawer. Act i, 1

The dedication in Chettle's *Kind-heartes Dreame* (which contains a reference to Shakespeare and was published in 1592) begins:

Gentlemen and good-fellowes, (whose kindnes having christened mee with the name of kind-heart, bindes me in all kind course I can to deserve the continuance of your love) let it not seeme strange (I beseech ye) that he that all dayes of his life hath beene famous for drawing teeth, should now in drooping age hazard contemptible infamie by drawing himselfe into print.

**King.** The A.S. *cyning*, from *cyn*, a nation or people, and the suffix *-ing*, meaning 'of', as 'son of', 'chief of', etc. In Anglo-Saxon times the king was elected by the Witenagemot, and was therefore the *choice of the nation.*

**Phrases.**

***A cat may look at a king.*** *See* Cat.

***A king's bad bargain.*** Said of a soldier (or sailor) who turns out a malingerer or to be of no use; in allusion to the shilling formerly given by the recruiting sergeant to a soldier on enlistment.

***A king of shreds and patches.*** In the old mysteries Vice used to be dressed as a mimic king in a particoloured suit (Shakespeare, *Hamlet*, 3, 4). The phrase has been applied to hacks who compile books for publishers but supply no originality of thought or matter.

***A king should die standing.*** *See* Dying Sayings: *Louis XVIII.*

***King Cotton.*** Cotton, the staple of the southern States of America, and one of the chief articles of manufacture in England. The expression was first used by James H. Hammond in the United States Senate in 1858.

***King James's Bible.*** *See* Bible, the English.

***King Log and King Stork.*** *See* Log.

***King of Misrule.*** In mediaeval and Tudor times, the director of the Christmas-time horseplay and festivities, called also the *Abbot*, or *Lord*, *of Misrule*, and in Scotland the *Master of Unreason.* At Oxford and Cambridge one of the Masters of Arts superintended both the Christmas and Candlemas sports, for which he was allowed a fee of 40*s*. A similar 'lord' was appointed by the lord mayor of London, the sheriffs, and the chief nobility. Stubbs tells us that these mock dignitaries had from twenty to sixty officers under them, and were furnished with hobby-horses, dragons, and musicians. They first went to church with such a confused noise that no one could hear his own voice. Polydore Vergil says of the Feast of Misrule that it was 'derived from the Roman Saturnalia', held in December for five days (17th to 22nd). The Feast of Misrule lasted twelve days.

> If we compare our Bacchanalian Christmases and New Year-tides with these Saturnalia and Feasts of Janus, we shall finde such near affinitye between them … that wee must needs conclude the one to be the very ape or issue of the other.
>
> Prynne, *Histrio-Mastix* (1632)

***King of the Bean.*** *See* Bean-king.

***King of Yvetot.*** *See* Yvetot.

***King Pétaud.*** *See* Pétaud.

***Kings are above grammar.*** *See* Grammar.

***Kings have long hands.*** Do not quarrel with a king, as his power and authority reach to the end of his dominions. The Latin proverb is, *An nescis longas regibus esse manus* (Ovid, *Heroides*, 17, 166), and the German, *Mit grossen Herren es ist nicht gut Kirschen zu essen*, 'It is not good to eat cherries with great men, as they throw the stones in your eyes'.

> There's such divinity doth hedge a king,
> That treason can but peep to what it would.
>
> Shakespeare, King in *Hamlet*, 4, 5

***King's evidence.*** *See* Evidence.

***Like a king.*** When Porus, the Indian prince, was taken prisoner, Alexander asked him how he expected to be treated. 'Like a king,' he replied; and Alexander made him his friend.

***Pray aid of the king.*** When someone, under the belief that he has a right to the land, claims rent of the king's tenants, they appeal to the sovereign, or 'pray aid of the king'.

***The books of the four kings.*** A pack of cards.

> After supper were brought in the books of the four kings.
>
> Rabelais, *Gargantua and Pantagruel*, i, 22

***The king of beasts.*** The lion.

***The King of Spain's trumpeter.*** A donkey. A pun on the word *don*, a Spanish magnate.

***The King of Terrors.*** Death.

***The king of the forest.*** The oak, which not only braves the storm, but fosters the growth of tender parasites under its arms.

***The king's cheese goes half in paring.*** A king's income is half consumed by the numerous calls on his purse.

***The King's English.*** *See* English.

***The King's Oak.*** The oak under which Henry VIII sat, in Epping Forest, while Anne (Boleyn) was being executed.

***The King's picture.*** Money; so called because coin is stamped with 'the image' of the reigning sovereign.

***The Three Kings of Cologne.*** The Magi (*q.v.*).

***In Personal Names, Nicknames, Placenames, etc.***

***King Franconi.*** Joachim Murat (1767–1815) was so called because of his resemblance to the mountebank Franconi.

***King of Kings.*** In the Prayer Book the term, of course, refers to the Deity, but it has been assumed by many Eastern rulers, especially

Artaxerxes, first Sassanid king of Persia (about 226–240).

***King of the King.*** Cardinal Richelieu (1585–1642) was so called, because of the way in which he ruled Louis XIII of France.

***The Factory King.*** Richard Oastler, of Bradford (1789–1861), the successful advocate of the Ten Hours Bill.

***The King of Bath.*** *See* Bath.

***The King of the Beggars.*** *See* Beggars.

***The King of the Border.*** A nickname of Adam Scott of Tushielaw (executed 1529), a famous border outlaw and chief.

***The King of Dunces.*** In his first version of the *Dunciad* (1712), Pope gave this place of honour to Lewis Theobald; but in the edition of 1742 Colley Cibber was put to reign in his stead.

***The King of Men.*** A title given both to Zeus and Agamemnon.

***The King of Painters.*** A title assumed by Parrhasius, the painter, a contemporary of Zeuxis (400 BC). Plutarch says he wore a purple robe and a golden crown.

***The King of Preachers.*** Louis Bourdaloue (1632–1704), the eloquent French Jesuit.

***The King of Rome.*** A *title* conferred by Napoleon I on his son, the Duke of Reichstadt (1811–32), on the day of his birth. Also called *L'Aiglon* by Edmond Rostand in his famous play.

***The King of Waters.*** The river Amazon, in South America.

***The King of the World.*** The title (in Hindi *Shah Jehan*) assumed by Khorrum Shah, third son of Selim Jehan Ghir, and fifth of the Mogul emperors of Delhi (reigned 1628–58).

***The King over the water.*** The Young Pretender, or Chevalier Charles Edward Stuart (1720–88).

> My father so far compromised his loyalty as to announce merely 'The king', as his first toast after dinner, instead of the emphatic 'King George' ... Our guest made a motion with his glass, so as to pass it over the water-decanter which stood beside him, and added, 'Over the water'.
> Scott, *Redgauntlet*, letter v

***King's Cave.*** Opposite to Campbelton; so called because it was here that King Robert Bruce and his retinue lodged when they landed on the mainland from the Isle of Arran.

***King's Crag.*** Fife, in Scotland. Called 'king' because Alexander III of Scotland was killed there (1286).

> As he was riding in the dusk of the evening along the sea-coast of Fife, betwixt Burnt-island and King-horn, he approached too near the brink of the precipice, and his horse, starting or stumbling, he was thrown over the rock and killed on the spot ... The people of the country still point out the very spot where it happened, and which is called 'The King's Crag'.
> Scott, *Tales of a Grandfather*, vi

***King's Cross.*** Up to the accession of George IV this London locality was called 'Battle Bridge' and had an infamous notoriety. The name was changed in 1821, when the neighbourhood was being developed by speculative builders.

***King's Lynn (Lynn Regis).*** The town in Norfolk has been so called since the time of the dissolution of the monasteries, when certain Church property fell into the hands of King Henry VIII. Previously its name was *Lynn Episcopi* (Bishop's Lynn). *Lynn* is Celtic for a deep pool.

**King Horn.** The hero of a French metrical romance of the 13th century, and the original of our *Horne Childe*, generally called *The Geste of Kyng Horn.* The nominal author is a certain *Mestre Thomas.*

Horn's father, Murry, King of Suddene, is killed by invading Saracens, and Horn is set adrift in a boat. He lands at Westernesse, is welcomed by the king, and falls in love with the king's daughter, Rymenhild. This causes his banishment, but after seven years, filled with the usual adventures, he returns just in time to save Rymenhild from a forced marriage and to marry her himself. Horn then leaves to recover his father's kingdom, and having done so comes back for his wife, arriving just in time to save her from a traitorous friend. Horn then takes Rymenhild to his own country, where they reign as king and queen.

**Kingly Titles.** *See* Rulers, Titles of.

**King-maker, The.** Richard Neville, Earl of Warwick (1420–71); so called because, when he sided with Henry VI, Henry was king, but when he sided with Edward IV, Henry was deposed and Edward crowned. He was killed at the battle of Barnet.

***King of Arms.*** *See* Heraldry (*College of Arms*).

**King's** [or **Queen's**] **Bench.** The Supreme Court of Common Law; so called because at one time the sovereign presided in this court, and the court followed the sovereign when he moved from one place to another. Originally called the *Aula Regia*, it is now a division of the High Court of Judicature.

**King's** [or **Queen's**] **Counsel.** A barrister who has 'taken silk' and has precedence over the other barristers, the juniors; he is technically a Counsel to the Crown, and is appointed to this rank by the Lord Chancellor.

**King's Evil.** Scrofula; so called from a notion which prevailed from the reign of Edward the Confessor to that of Queen Anne that it could be cured by the royal touch. The Jacobites considered that the power did not descend to William III and Anne because the 'divine' hereditary right was not fully possessed by them, but the office remained in our Prayer-Book till 1719. Prince Charles Edward, when he claimed to be Prince of Wales, touched a female child for the disease in 1745; but the last person touched in England was Dr Johnson, in 1712, when only thirty months old, by Queen Anne. The practice was introduced by Henry VII of presenting the person 'touched' with a small gold or silver coin, called a touchpiece. The one presented to Dr Johnson has St George and the Dragon on one side and a ship on the other; the legend of the former is *Soli deo gloria*, and of the latter *Anna D: G.M.BR.F:ET.H.REG.* (Anne, by the Grace of God, of Great Britain, France, and Ireland Queen).

We are told that Charles II touched 92,107 persons. The smallest number in one year was 2,983, in 1669; and the largest number was in 1684, when many were trampled to death. (*See* Macaulay's *History of England*, ch. xiv.) John Brown, a royal surgeon, had to superintend the ceremony.

*Cp. Macbeth*, 4, 3:

*Malcolm*: Comes the king forth, I pray you?
*Doctor*: Ay, sir; there are a crew of wretched souls
That stay his cure; their malady convinces
The great assay of art; but, at his touch
Such sanctity hath heaven given his hand,
They presently amend.

The French kings laid claim to the same divine power from the time of Clovis, AD 481, and on Easter Sunday, 1686, Louis XIV touched 1,600 persons, using these words: *Le roy te touche, Dieu te guerisse.*

**Kings, Days fatal to.** Much foolish superstition has been circulated respecting certain days supposed to be 'fatal' to the crowned heads of Great Britain. The following notes will help the reader to discriminate truth from fiction:

Of our thirty-seven sovereigns who have died since 1066 *Sunday* has been the last day of the reign of seven, *Tuesday* and *Thursday* that of six each, *Monday* and *Friday* of five, and *Wednesday* and *Saturday* of four.

*Sunday*: Henry I, Edward III, Henry VI, James I, William III, Anne, George I.

*Monday*: Stephen, Richard II, Henry IV, Henry V, Richard III.

*Tuesday*: Richard I, Edward II, Charles I, James II, William IV, Victoria.

*Wednesday*: John, Henry III, Edward IV, Edward V.

*Thursday*: William I, William II, Henry II, Edward VI, Mary I, Elizabeth.

*Friday*: Edward I, Henry VIII, Charles II, Mary II, Edward VII.

*Saturday*: Henry VII, George II, George III, George IV.

**Kingdom Come.** Death, the grave, execution, the next world.

And forty pounds be theirs, a pretty sum,
For sending such a rogue to kingdom come.
Peter Pindar, *Subjects for Painters*

**Kingsale.** The premier baron of Ireland, Lord Kingsale, is one of the two British subjects who claim the right of wearing a hat in the presence of royalty. *See* Hat.

**Kingston Bridge.** A card bent so that when the pack is cut it is cut at this card.

**Kingston-on-Thames.** Named *King's stone* from a large square block of stone near the town hall, on which the early Anglo-Saxon monarchs knelt when they were appointed to the kingly office: Edward the Elder, Athelstan, Edmund, Ethelred, Edred, Edwy, and Edward the Martyr received on this stone the royal unction. The stone is now enclosed.

**Kingstown** (Ireland), formerly called Dunleary. The name was changed in 1821 out of compliment to George IV, who visited Ireland that year, and left Dunleary harbour for his return home on September 5th.

**Kinless Loons.** The judges whom Cromwell sent into Scotland were so termed, because they had no relations in the country and so were free from temptation to nepotism. They tried the accused solely on the merits of the case.

**Kiosk.** A Turkish summer-house or pavilion supported by pillars which were usually covered with vines or flowering creepers and often enclosed a fountain. In England and western Europe the name is given to bandstands, pavilions for the sale of refreshments, etc., and to small enclosed stalls for the sale of newspapers in the street.

**Kirk of Skulls.** Gamrie Church, in Banffshire; so called because the skulls and other bones of the Norsemen who fell in the neighbouring field, the *Bloody Pots*, were built into its walls.

**Kirke-grim.** The nix or sprite of Norse folk-tale who keeps order in churches and punishes those employed to keep them tidy if they fail in their duty.

**Kirke's Lambs.** The Queen's Royal West Surrey Regiment. Called 'Kirke' from Piercy Kirke, their colonel, 1682–91; and 'Lambs' from their badge, the *Paschal Lamb*, the crest of the house of Braganza, in compliment to Queen Catharine, to whom they were a guard of honour in her progress to London.

**Kirkrapine.** The 'robber of churches' in Spenser's *Faërie Queene* (I, iii, 16–22), the lover of Abessa (Superstition), and the typification of the plundering of the Church by the wealthy clergy. While Una was in the hut of Corcēca, Kirkrapine forced his way in and was torn to pieces by her lion, i.e. the Reformation.

> He was to weet a stout and sturdie thiefe,
> Wont to robbe Churches of their ornaments,
> And poore mens boxes of their due reliefe,
> Which given was to them of good intents.
>
> *Faërie Queene*, I, iii, 17

**Kismet.** Fate, destiny; or the fulfilment of destiny; from Turk. *qismat*, portion, lot (*qasama*, to divide).

> A noise is in the mountains, in the mountains, and I know.
> The voice that shook our palaces – four hundred years ago:
> It is he that saith not 'Kismet'; it is he that knows not fate;
> It is Richard, it is Raymond, it is Godfrey in the gate!
>
> G. K. Chesterton, *Lepanto*

**Kiss.** A very ancient and widely spread mode of salutation, frequently mentioned in the Bible, both as an expression of reverence and adoration and as a greeting or farewell between friends. Esau embraced Jacob, 'fell on his neck and kissed him' (Gen. 33:4), the repentant woman kissed the feet of Christ (Luke 7:45), and the disciples from Ephesus 'fell on Paul's neck and kissed him' (Acts 20:37). But kissing between the sexes was unknown among the ancient Hebrews, and while the cheek, forehead, beard, hands, and feet might be kissed the lips might not, the passage in the Bible (Prov. 24:26, *see* marginal note in Revised Version) that seems to contradict this being a mistranslation. 'Kiss the Son, lest He be angry' (Ps. 2:12), means worship the Son of God. This is the only reference in the Bible to the Kiss of Homage.

The old custom of 'kissing the bride' comes from the Salisbury rubric concerning the Pax (*q.v.*).

In billiards (and also bowls) a *kiss* is a very slight touch of one moving ball on another, especially a second touch, accidental or designed; and the name also used to be given to a little drop of sealing-wax accidentally let fall beside the seal.

***Kiss-behind-the-garden-gate.*** A country name for a pansy; perhaps a practical way of saying *Pensez de moi* ('think of me'), which is the flower's significance in 'flower language'.

***Kiss the place to make it well.*** Said to be a relic of the custom of sucking poison from wounds. St Martin of Tours, when he was at Paris, observed at the city gates a leper full of sores; and, going up to him, he kissed the sores, whereupon the leper was instantly made whole (Sulpicius Severus: *Dialogues*). Similar stories are told of St Mayeul, and quite a number of saints.

> Who ran to help me, when I fell,
> And would some pretty story tell,
> Or kiss the place to make it well?
> My Mother.
>
> Ann Taylor, *My Mother*

***Kissing the Pope's toe.*** Matthew of Westminster says it was customary formerly to kiss the hand of his Holiness; but that a certain woman, in the 8th century, not only kissed the Pope's hand, but 'squeezed it'. The Church magnate, seeing the danger to which he was exposed, cut off his hand, and was compelled in future to offer his foot, a custom which has continued to the present hour.

***To kiss the book.*** To kiss the Bible, or the New Testament, after taking an oath; the kiss of confirmation or promise to act in accordance with the words of the oath and a public Acknowledgement that you adore and fear to offend, by breaking your oath, the God whose book you reverence.

> In the English Courts, the Houses of Parliament, etc., non-Christians and others who have scruples against making a parade of their religion (or lack of it) in this way are now permitted to affirm without going through this ceremony. Mr Bradlaugh refused to take an oath, and after some years of contention the law was altered.

***To kiss*** or ***lick the dust.*** To be completely overwhelmed or humiliated; to be slain. In Ps. 72:9, it is said, 'his enemies shall lick the dust'.

***To kiss hands.*** To kiss the hand of the sovereign either on accepting or retiring from office.

Kissing the hand of, or one's own hand to, an idol was a usual form of adoration; if the statue was low enough the devotees kissed its hand; if not, kissed their own hands and waved them to the image. God said he had in Israel seven thousand persons who had not bowed unto Baal, 'every mouth which hath not kissed him' (1 Kings 19:18).

> Many ... whom the fame of this excellent vision had gathered thither, confounded by that matchless beauty, could but kiss the finger-tips of their right hands at sight of her, as in adoration to the goddess Venus herself.
>
> Pater, *Marius the Epicurean*, ch. v

***To kiss the gunner's daughter.*** *See* Gunner.

***To kiss the hare's foot.*** *See* Hare.

***To kiss the rod.*** *See* Rod.

**Kissing-comfit.** The candied root of the Sea Holly (*eryngium maritimum*) prepared as a lozenge, to perfume the breath.

**Kissing-crust.** The crust where the lower lump of bread kisses the upper. In French, *baisure de pain.*

**Kist-vaen.** Welsh for a rude stone sepulchre or mausoleum, like a chest with a flat stone for a cover.

> At length they reached a grassy mound, on the top of which was placed one of those receptacles for the dead of the ancient British chiefs of distinction, called Kist-vaen, which are composed of upright fragments of granite, so placed as to form a stone coffin.
>
> Scott, *The Betrothed*, ch. xxix

**Kist of Whistles.** A church-organ (Scotch). *Kist* is the same word as *cist* (*q.v.*), a chest.

**Kit.** From Dut. *kitte*, a wooden receptacle made of hooped staves; hence that which contains the necessaries, tools, etc., of a workman; and hence the articles themselves collectively.

***A soldier's kit.*** His outfit.

***The whole kit of them.*** The whole lot.

**Kit.** A small three-stringed fiddle, formerly used by dancing masters. The word is from the obsolete *gitterne* (Fr. *quitterne*), a sort of guitar.

**Kit-cat Club.** A club formed about the beginning of the 18th century by the leading Whigs of the day, and held in the house of Christopher Catt, a pastrycook of Shire Lane, which used to run north from Temple Bar to Carey Street (its site is now covered by the Law Courts). Christopher Catt's mutton pies, which were eaten at the club, were also called *kit-cats*, and in the *Spectator* (No. IX) we are told that it was from these the club got its name.

> Steele, Addison, Congreve, Garth, Vanbrugh, Manwaring, Stepney, Walpole, and Pulteney were of it; so was Lord Dorset and the present Duke. Manwaring ... was the ruling man in all conversation ... Lord Stanhope and the Earl of Essex were also members ... Each member gave his [picture].
>
> Pope to Spence

Sir Godfrey Kneller painted forty-two portraits of the club members for Jacob Tonson, the secretary, whose villa was at Barn Elms, and where latterly the club was held. In order to accommodate the paintings to the height of the club-room, he was obliged to make them three-quarter lengths (28 in. by 36 in.), hence a three-quarter portrait is still called a *kit-cat*.

**Kitchen.** An old term, still used in some parts of rural Scotland, for a relish eaten with bread, as cheese, bacon, dried fish, etc.

> A hungry heart wad scarce seek better kitchen to a barley scone.
>
> Scott, *The Pirate*, ch. xi

**Kitchen-middens.** Prehistoric mounds (referred to the Neolithic Age) composed of sea-shells, bones, kitchen refuse, rude stone implements, and other relics of early man. They were first noticed on the coast of Denmark, but have since been found in the British Isles, North America, etc.

**Kite.** In lawyers' slang, a junior counsel who is allotted at an assize court to advocate the cause of a prisoner who is without other defence.

In Stock Exchange slang, a worthless bill.

***To fly the kite.*** To 'raise the wind' by questionable methods, such as by sending begging letters to persons of charitable reputation or by means of worthless bills. *See above.*

**Klepts** (Gr. robbers). The name given to those Greeks who, after the conquest of their country by the Turks in the 15th century, refused to submit and maintained their independence in the mountains. They degenerated – especially after the War of Independence (1821–8) – into brigands, hence the word is often used for a lawless bandit or brigand.

**Knave** (A.S. *cnafa*, Gr. *knabe*). Originally merely a boy or male-child, then a male servant or one in low condition, and finally – its present sense – an unprincipled and dishonourable rascal.

> The tyme is come, a knave-child she ber:
> Mauricius at the font-stoon they him calle.
>
> Chaucer, *Man of Lawe's Tale*, 722
>
> And sche bare a knave child that was to reulynge alle folkis in an yrun gherde (*Auth. Ver.* And she brought forth a man child, who was to rule all nations with a rod of iron).
>
> Wyclif's Bible, Rev.12:5

In cards the *knave* (or *jack*), the lowest court card of each suit, is the common soldier or servant of the royalties.

***He lived like a knave, and died like a fool.*** Said by Warburton of Henry Rich, first Earl of Holland (1590–1649), the turncoat. He went to the scaffold dressed in white satin, trimmed with silver.

***Knave of hearts.*** A flirt.

***Knave of Sologne.*** More knave than fool. The French say, *Un niais de Sologne*. Sologne is a part of the departments of Loiret et Loire-et-Cher.

**Knee. *Knee tribute.*** Adoration or reverence, by prostration or bending the knee. *Cp.* Lip-service.

> Coming to receive from us
> Knee-tribute yet unpaid, prostration vile.
>
> Milton, *Paradise Lost*, 5, 782

***Weak-kneed.*** Irresolute, not thorough: as, *a weak-kneed Christian*, a Laodicean, neither hot nor cold.

**Kneph.** Another name of the Egyptian god Amen-Ra (*q.v.*).

**Knickerbockers,** or **Knickers.** Loose-fitting breeches, gathered in at the knee, and worn by boys, cyclists, sportsmen, tourists, etc., and by women as an undergarment. So named from George Cruikshank's illustrations of *Knickerbocker's History of New York*, a burlesque published in 1809 by Washington Irving, where the Dutch worthies are drawn with very loose knee-breeches. The name *Knickerbacker* is found among the old Dutch inhabitants of New York a century and more earlier; it probably signified a *baker* of *knickers*, i.e. clay marbles.

**Knife.** The emblem of St Agatha, St Albert, and St Christiana.

***The flaying knife*** is the emblem of St Bartholomew, because he was flayed.

***He is a capital knife-and-fork,*** a good trencherman.

> He did due honour to the repast; he ate and drank, and proved a capital knife-and-fork even at the risk of dying the same night of an indigestion.
>
> Gaboriau, *Promise of Marriage*, vi

***The knife of academic knots.*** Chrysippus, so called because he was the keenest disputant of his age (280–207 BC).

***War to the knife.*** Deadly strife.

**Knife** = sword or dagger.

> That my keen knife see not the wound it makes.
>
> Shakespeare, *Macbeth*, 1, 5

**Knifeboard.** The long, back-to-back benches that used to run longitudinally down the middle of the roof of the old horse omnibuses. In the 'nineties of last century the present transverse 'garden seats' gradually took their place.

**Knight** (A.S. *cniht*). Originally meaning merely a boy or servant, the word came to denote a man of gentle birth who, after serving at court or in the retinue of some lord as a page and esquire, was admitted with appropriate ceremonies to an honourable degree of military rank and given the right to bear arms.

The Knight, or *Knight Bachelor*, of today is a commoner who is the possessor of a personal and non-hereditary dignity conferred by the sovereign, carrying with it the prefix 'Sir' and a place in the Table of Precedence next above County Court Judges and next below Knight Commanders of the Order of the British Empire. The wife of a Knight is usually entitled 'Lady' or 'Dame', but this, as in the case of Baronets, is a matter of courtesy only, not of right.

There are nine *Orders of Knighthood* in the British Empire, viz. (in the following order of precedence) the Garter, the Thistle, St Patrick, the Bath, the Star of India, St Michael and St George, the Indian Empire, the Royal Victorian Order, and the British Empire. After these come the Knights Bachelor, who are members of no Order and who do not constitute an order. *Bachelor* here is Fr. *bas chevalier*, signifying 'lower than the Knight of an order'.

The word *knight* is used in various slang or jocular phrases denoting a member of some trade or profession, follower of some calling or occupation, etc. Thus we have *Knight of the blade*, a roystering bully, *Knight of the cleaver*, a butcher, *Knight of the cue*, a billiard player, *Knight of the needle*, a tailor, *Knight of the pestle*, a druggist, *Knight of the road*, a footpad, *Knight of the spigot*, a tapster, *Knight of the wheel*, a cyclist, etc. etc.

***Cross-legged Knights.*** *See* Cross-legged.

***Knight Bachelor.*** *See* Knight, *above*.

***Knight Banneret.*** *See* Banneret.

***Knight Baronet.*** The title originally given to Baronets (*q.v.*) when the degree was instituted by James I in 1611.

***Knight errant.*** A mediaeval knight, especially a hero of those long romances so mercilessly satirised by Cervantes in *Don Quixote*, who wandered about the world in quest of adventure and in search of opportunities of rescuing damsels in distress and performing other chivalrous deeds.

It seemed unto him [Don Quixote] very requisite and behooveful ... that he himself should become a knight-errant, and go throughout the world, with his horse and armour, to seek adventures, and practise in person all that he had read was used by knights of yore; revenging all kinds of injuries, and offering himself to occasions and dangers, which, being once happily achieved, might gain him eternal renown.

Cervantes, *Don Quixote* (Shelton's tr. 1612)

**Knight Marshal.** *See* Marhsalsea.

**Knight of Grace.** A member of the lower order of the Knights of Malta. *See* Malta.

**Knight of industry.** Slang for a sharper; one who lives on his wits.

**Knight of the post.** A man who had stood in the pillory or had been flogged at the whipping-post was so called; hence, one who haunted the purlieus of the courts, ready to be hired for a bribe to give false witness, go bail for a debtor for pay, etc.

'A knight of the post,' quoth he, 'for so I am termed; a fellow that will sweare you anything for twelve pence.'

Nash, *Pierce Penilesse* (1592)

These perjured knaves be commonly old knightes of the post, that are foisted off from being taken for bale at the king's bench, or other places, and seeing for open perjuries they are refused there, they take that course of life.

Greene, *Second Part of Conycatching* (1591)

**The Knight of the Rueful Countenance.** Don Quixote (*q.v.*).

**Knight of the Shire.** The old name for one of the two gentlemen of the rank of knight who represented a county or shire in the English Parliament; a member elected by a county, in contradistinction to a borough member.

**Knight of the square flag.** A knight banneret, in allusion to cutting off the points of his pennon when he was raised to this rank on the battlefield.

**The Knight of the Swan.** Lohengrin (*q.v.*).

**Knight service.** The tenure of land, under the feudal system, on the condition of rendering military service to the Crown.

**Knight's fee.** The amount of land for which, under the feudal system, the services of a knight were due to the Crown. There was no fixed unit, some were larger than others; William the Conqueror created 60,000 such fees when he came to England, and in his time all who had £20 a year in lands or income were compelled to be knights.

**Knights of Columbus.** A fraternal and benevolent association of Roman Catholic men in America, founded at New Haven, Conn., in 1882. During the Great War it did for the American troops in Europe much the same kind of work as our Young Men's Christian Association did for the British and Allied Armies.

**Knights of Labour.** A secret organisation of workmen in the United States, founded at Philadelphia in 1869. Its objects are to regulate wages, the degree of skill to be exacted from workmen, the length of a day's work, and to control strikes. This league enjoins when a strike is to be made, and when workmen of the union may resume work.

**Knights of the Round Table.** *See* Round Table.

**Knights of Windsor.** A small order of knights, originally founded by Edward III in 1349 as the 'Poor Knights of the Order of the Garter'. It was at first formed of 26 veterans, but since the time of Charles I the numbers have been fixed at thirteen for the Royal Foundation and five for the Lower, with a superior officer as Governor. The members are retired meritorious military officers who are the reverse of well off. They are granted apartments at Windsor Castle and pensions ranging from £50 to £130 a year. They must be in residence for at least nine months in the year, must attend St George's Chapel on saints' days, and occasionally act as guards of honour. Their present uniform was assigned by William IV, who made their title the 'Military Knights of Windsor'; and their early connection with the Order of the Garter is still retained in many ways, as, for instance, every K.G. on appointment has to give a sum of money for distribution among them, and the Sovereign appoints members in his capacity as head of the Order of the Garter.

**Knights Templar.** *See* Templar.

**Knightenguild.** The Guild of thirteen 'cnihts' (probably youthful scions of noble houses attached to the court) to which King Edgar, or, according to other accounts, Canute, gave that easternmost portion of the City of London now called *Portsoken Ward*, on the following conditions: (1) Each knight was to be victorious in three combats – one on the earth, and one under, and one in the water; and (2) each was, on a given day, to run with spears against all comers in East Smithfield. William the Conqueror confirmed the same unto the heirs of these knights, whose descendants, in 1125, gave all the property and their rights to the newly founded Priory of Holy Trinity.

**Knightrider Street.** This old City of London street is so called, says Stow, 'of Knights well armed and mounted at the Tower Royall, ryding from thence through that street west to Creede Lane, and so out at Ludgate'. Leigh Hunt says the name originated in a sign or some reference to the Heralds' College in the vicinity.

**Knipperdollings.** A sect of 16th century German anabaptists, so called from their leader, Bernard Knipperdolling, who was active about 1530–35, and was one of the leaders of the insurrection of Münster.

**Knock, To.** Slang for to create a great impression, to be irresistible; as in Albert Chevalier's song, 'Knocked 'em in the Old Kent Road' (1892), i.e. astonished the inhabitants, filled them with admiration.

***To knock about*** or ***around.*** To wander about town 'seeing life' and enjoying oneself.

***A knock-about act.*** A music-hall term for a noisy, boisterous act in which (usually) a couple of red-nosed comedians indulge in violent horseplay.

***Knock-kneed.*** With the knees turned inwards so that they knock together in walking.

***To be knocked into a cocked hat,*** or ***into the middle of next week.*** To be thoroughly beaten. *See* Cocked.

***To get the knock*** (or ***the nasty knock***). To have a blow (actual or figurative) that finishes one off. It can be applied to one who has gone bankrupt, a competitor in some race who is utterly exhausted, a man who has had a lot too much to drink, etc.

***To knock out of time.*** To settle one's hash for him, double him up. The phrase is from pugilism, and refers to disabling an opponent so that he is unable to respond when the referee calls 'Time'.

***To knock spots off someone*** or ***something.*** To beat him soundly, get the better of it, do the job thoroughly. The allusion is probably to pistol-shooting at a cardboard target, when a good shot will 'knock spots off' the bull.

***To knock the bottom*** or ***the stuffing out of anything.*** To confound, bring to naught, especially to show that some argument or theory is invalid and 'won't hold water'.

***To knock under.*** To acknowledge oneself defeated, in argument or otherwise, to knuckle under. Perhaps from the old custom of a disputant who gets the worst of it tapping the under side of the table to signify the same, or from the habit, in hard-drinking days, of subsiding under the table as they succumb.

> He that flinches his Glass, and to Drink is not able,
> Let him quarrel no more, but knock under the table. *Gentleman's Journal*, March, 1691–2

***Knock-out.*** Primarily, a disabling blow, especially (in pugilism) one out of guard on the point of the chin, which puts the receiver to sleep and so finishes the fight. Hence, a complete surprise that comes on one all of a sudden, as 'it's a fair knock-out!' also a champion in any walk of life, a man (or woman) who goes the pace or does surprising things – 'He's a regular knock-out!'

In the auction room a *knock-out* is a sale at which a gang combine to keep the prices artificially low, so that they obtain the goods and afterwards sell them among themselves, dividing the profits. The gang, and its individual members, are also called a *knock-out*.

**Knockers.** Goblins, or kobolds (*q.v.*), who dwell in mines, and indicate rich veins of ore by their presence. In Cardiganshire and elsewhere miners attribute the strange noises so frequently heard in mines to these spirits.

**Knot.** (Lat. *nodus*, Fr. *noeud*, Dan. *knude*, Dut. *knot*, A.S. *cnotta*, allied to *knit.*)

***He has tied a knot with his tongue he cannot untie with his teeth.*** He has got married. He has tied the marriage-knot (*q.v.*) by saying, 'I take thee for my wedded wife', etc, but it is not to be untied so easily.

***Gordian knot.*** *See* Gordian.

***Knots of May.*** *See* Nut.

***The ship went six or seven knots an hour.*** This means that the rate of progress was six or seven nautical miles per hour, but a *knot* does *not* equal a nautical mile. The log-line is divided into lengths by knots, and is run out while a sand-glass runs for either 28 or 30 seconds. In the Navy the 28-second line is used, and in this case the *knot* measures 47 ft 3 in.; the mercantile marine employ the 30-second line, and their *knot* is 50 ft 8 in., the same proportion of a nautical mile as half a minute is of an hour. Note is taken of the number of knots run out in half a minute, and this gives the rate per hour.

***True lovers' knot.*** Sir Thomas Browne thinks the knot owes its origin to the *nodus Herculanus*, a snaky complication in the caduceus or rod of Mercury, in which form the woollen girdle of the Greek brides was fastened (*Pseudodoxia Epidemica*, V, xxii).

***To seek for a knot in a rush.*** Seeking for something that does not exist. Not a very wise phrase, seeing there are *jointed* rushes, probably not known when the proverb was first current. The *Juncus acutiflorus*, the *Juncus lampocarpus*, the *Juncus obtusiflorus*, and the *Juncus polycephalus*, are all jointed rushes.

**Knout** (Russ. *knut'*, probably connected with *knot*). A long, hard leather thong or a knotted bunch of thongs formerly used in Russia for corporal punishment on prisoners; hence, a symbolification of supremely autocratic rule.

**Know Thyself.** The admonition of the oracle of Apollo at Delphi; also attributed (by Diogeneus Laertius, i, 40) to Thales, also to Solon the Athenian lawgiver, Pythagoras, and others.

**Know-Nothings.** A secret political society in the United States, also called the 'American party'. It arose in 1853, and its members replied to every question about their society, 'I know nothing about it.' Their object was to accomplish the repeal of the naturalisation laws, and of the law which excluded all but natives from holding office. It split on the slavery question and died out soon after 1856.

> Its chief principle was that no one who had not been 21 years in the United States should have any part in the government.

**Knowledge-box.** Slang for the head, as being the 'box' of the brain, the seat of all knowledge.

**Knuckle-duster.** A metal instrument, originally used by desperadoes in America, which is fitted to the fist, and may be readily used in offence or defence. It was used in England against the infamous attacks of Spring-heel Jack.

> In fighting, a horrible contrivance is sometimes used, called in savage irony *knuckle-dusters*, an iron instrument contrived to cover the knuckles so as to protect them from injury when striking a blow, adding force at the same time, and with knobs or points projecting, so as to disfigure and mutilate the person struck.
>
> Schele de Vere, *Americanisms*, ch. vi

**Knuckle. *To knuckle under.*** To acknowledge oneself beaten, to sue for pardon; in allusion to the old custom of striking the under side of a table with the knuckles when defeated in an argument. *Cp.* To knock under.

***To knuckle down to it.*** To work away at it, heart and soul; to do one's best.

**Knut.** *See* Nut.

**Kobold.** A house-spirit in German superstition; similar to our Robin Goodfellow, and the Scotch brownie. Also a gnome who works in the mines and forests.

**Kochlani.** Arabian horses of royal stock, of which genealogies have been preserved for more than 2,000 years. It is said that they are the offspring of Solomon's stud. (*Niebuhr.*)

**Koheleth.** *See* Ecclesiastes.

**Koh-i-Nûr** (Pers. mountain of light). A large diamond which, since 1849, has been among the British Crown Jewels. It is said to have been known 2,000 years ago, but its authentic history starts in 1304, when it was wrested by the Sultan, Al-eddin, from the Rajah of Malwa. From his line it passed in 1526 to Humaiun, the son of Sultan Baber, and thence to Aurungzebe (d.1707), the Mogul Emperor, who used it for the eye of a peacock in his famous peacock throne at Delhi. In 1739 it passed into the hands of Nadir Shah, who called it the Koh-i-nûr. It next went to the monarchs of Afghanistan, and when Shah Sujah was depossessed he gave it to Runjit Singh, of the Punjab, as the price of his assistance towards the recovery of the throne of Cabul. After his death (1839) it was kept in the treasury at Lahore, and when the Punjab was annexed to the British Crown in 1849 it was, by stipulation, presented to Queen Victoria. At this time it weighed $186\frac{1}{16}$ carats, but after its acquisition it was cut down to $106\frac{1}{16}$ carats. There is a tradition that it always brings ill luck to its possessor.

**Kohl** or **Kohol.** Finely powdered antimony, used by women in Persia and the East to blacken the inside of their eyelids.

> And others mix the Kohol's jetty dye
> To give that long, dark languish to the eye.
>
> Thomas Moore, *Lalla Rookh*, Pt i

**Konx Ompax.** The words of dismissal in the Eleusinian Mysteries. *Konx* is the sound made by a pebble as it falls into the voting urn; *ompax* is a compound of two words meaning *like* or *resembling*, and the Latin *pax* (Ital. *basta*) an exclamation of dismissal, signifying that the proceedings have come to an end.

**Koppa.** An ancient Greek letter, disused as a letter in classical Greek, but retained as the sign for the numeral 90.

**Korâh.** *See* Asaph.

**Korân,** or, with the article, *Al Korân.* The bible or sacred book of the Mohammedans, containing the religious, social, civil, commercial, military, and legal code of Islam. It is rather remarkable that we call our Bible the *writing* (Scripture), and the Arabs call theirs the *recitation* or *reading*, which is the meaning of the name. The Koran, which contains 114 chapters, or *Surahs*, is said to have been communicated to the prophet at Mecca and Medina by the angel Gabriel, with the sound of bells. It is written in Arabic and was compiled from Mohammed's own lips.

**Korrigans.** Nine fays of Breton folklore, who can predict future events, assume any shape they like, move quick as thought from place to place, and cure diseases or wounds. They are not more than two feet high, have long flowing hair, which they are fond of combing, dress only with a white veil, are excellent singers, and their favourite haunt is beside some fountain. They flee at the sound of a bell or benediction, and their breath is most deadly.

**Kosher.** A Hebrew word denoting that which is permitted by or fulfils the requirements of the law; applied usually to food – especially to meat which has been slaughtered and prepared in the prescribed manner. *Cp.* Treffa.

**Kosmon Church.** A secession from the Faithists (*q.v.*). The name – a shocking example of the misuse of Greek – was given it in the belief that the doctrines held were suitable for all the world (Gr. *kosmos*, the world).

**Koumiss** or ***Kumiss*** (Tartar, *kumiz*). Fermented mare's milk used as a beverage by the Tartar tribes of Central Asia. A slightly alcoholic drink of a similar kind is made with great ceremony in Siberia. It consists of sour cow's milk, sugar, and yeast.

> Kumiss is still prepared from mare's milk by the Calmucks and Nogais, who, during the process of making it, keep the milk in constant agitation.
>
> Rawlinson, Herodotus, vol. iii, bk iv, p. 2

**Kraken.** A sea-monster of vast size, supposed to have been seen off the coast of Norway and on the North American coasts, and probably founded on a hurried observation of one of the gigantic squids or cuttlefish. It was first described (1752) by Pontoppidan in his *History of Norway*. Pliny speaks of a sea-monster in the Straits of Gibraltar, which blocked the entrance of ships.

> Below the thunders of the upper deep;
> Far, far beneath in the abysmal sea,
> His ancient, dreamless, uninvaded sleep
> The Kraken sleepeth.
>
> Tennyson, *The Kraken* (1830)

The shoal called the Shambles at the entrance of Portland Roads was very dangerous before the breakwater was constructed. According to local legend, at the bottom of the gigantic shaft are the wrecks of ships seized and sunk by the huge spider *Kraken*, called also the *fish-mountain*.

**Kralitz Bible, The.** *See* Bible, specially named.

**Kratim.** The dog of the Seven Sleepers. More correctly called Katmir or Ketmir (*q.v.*).

**Kremlin, The.** A gigantic pile of buildings in Moscow of every style of architecture: Arabesque, Gothic, Greek, Italian, Chinese, etc., enclosed by battlemented and many-towered walls 1½ miles in circuit. It contains palaces and cathedrals, churches, convents, museums and barracks, arcades and shops, the great bell, and, before the Revolution, the Russian treasury, government offices, the ancient palace of the patriarch, a throne-room, etc. It was built by two Italians, Marco and Pietro Antonio, for Ivan III in 1485 to 1495, but the Great Palace, as well as many other buildings, dates only from the middle of the 19th century, previous palaces, etc., having been destroyed at various times. There had been previously a wooden fortress on the spot.

> Towers of every form, round, square, and with pointed roofs, belfries, donjons, turrets, spires, sentry-boxes fixed on minarets, steeples of every height, style, and colour; palaces, domes, watch-towers, walls embattlemented and pierced with loop-holes, ramparts, fortifications of every description, chiosks by the side of cathedrals; monuments of pride and caprice, voluptuousness, glory, and piety.
>
> De Custine, *Russia*, ch. xxii

The name is from Russ. *kreml*, a citadel, and other towns beside Moscow possess kremlins, but none on this scale.

**Kreutzer Sonata, The.** This work by Beethoven (1803), for the piano and violin, is so called because it was dedicated to the French violinist and composer Rodolphe Kreutzer (1766–1831).

**Kreuzer.** A small copper coin in Southern Germany and Austria, formerly of silver and marked with a cross (Ger. *kreuz*, Lat. *crux*). It is worth (nominally) one-third of a penny.

**Krishna** (*the black one*). One of the greatest of the Hindu deities, the god of fire, lightning, storms, the heavens, and the sun, usually regarded as the eighth avatar (*q.v.*) of Vishnu. One story relates that Kansa, demon-king of Mathura, having committed great ravages, Brahma prayed to Vishnu to relieve the world of its distress; whereupon Vishnu plucked off two hairs, one white and the other black, and promised they should revenge the wrongs of the demon-king. The black hair became Krishna.

Another myth says that Krishna was the son of Vasudeva and Devaki, and when he was born among the Yadavas at Mathura, between Delhi and Agra, his uncle, King Kansa, who had been warned by heaven that this nephew was to slay him, sought to kill Krishna, who was, however, smuggled away. He was brought up by shepherds, and later killed his uncle and became King of the Yadavas in his stead. He was the Apollo of India and the idol of women. His story is told in the Bhagavadghita and Bhagavatapurana.

**Krita.** The first of the four Hindu periods contained in the great Yuga (*q.v.*).

**Kronos** or **Cronus.** One of the Titans of *Greek mythology*, son of Uranus and Ge, father (by Rhea) of Hestia, Demeter, Hera, Hades, Poseidon, and Zeus. He dethroned his father as ruler of the world, and was in turn dethroned by his son, Zeus. By the Romans he was identified with Saturn (*q.v.*).

**Ku-Klux-Klan.** A secret society in the Southern States of America, directed principally against the negroes, which arose about 1866. Its murders and terrorism grew so formidable that in 1871 an Act of Congress was passed suppressing it: but, though for a time its activities were driven under ground, it was still very much alive fifty years later.

> The Ku-Klux-Klan, a secret society active in the Southern States, has of late committed a great number of crimes on the plea of upholding the supremacy of the white race. In particular it has spread terror in large areas of Texas. A favourite device is to abduct and tar and feather persons who come under displeasure, or brand them with the initials K.K.K. Many murders are also laid to the charge of the society. *The Times*, Oct. 5, 1921

**Kudos** (Gr.). Praise, glory; used in English slang for credit.

**Kufic.** Ancient Arabic letters; so called from Kufa, a town in the pashalic of Bagdad, noted for expert copyists of the ancient Arabic MSS.

***Kufic coins.*** Mohammedan coins with Kufic or ancient Arabic characters. The first were struck in the eighteenth year of the Hegira (AD 638).

**Kultur.** The German imperial system of intellectual, moral, aesthetic, economic, and political progress, which is characterised by the subordination of the individual to the State – of the subject to the Emperor – and through the power of which it was hoped, by Germany, that 'kultur' would be imposed on the rest of the world.

It does not mean the same as our *culture*, which is translated by *bildung*.

**Kumara** (*the youthful*). A name, or, rather, epithet, of the Hindu war-god Karttikeya (*q.v.*).

**Kumiss.** *See* Koumiss.

**Kurma.** *See* Avatar.

**Kursaal** (Ger. *kur*, cure, *saal*, room). A public room or building for the use of visitors, especially at German watering places and health resorts.

**Kuru.** A noted legendary hero of India, the contests of whose descendants form the subject of two Indian epics. He was a prince of the lunar race, reigning over the country round Delhi.

**Kvasir.** *See* Odhroerir.

**Kyanise.** To apply corrosive sublimate to timber in order to prevent dry rot; so called from J. H. Kyan (d.1830), the inventor of the process, which was patented in 1832.

**Kyle.** The central district of Ayrshire.

> Kyle for a man, Carrick for a coo [cow],
> Cunningham for butter, Galloway for woo' [wool].

Kyle, a strong corn-growing soil; Carrick, a wild hilly portion, only fit for feeding cattle; and Cunningham, a rich dairy land.

**Kyrie Eleison** (Gr., 'Lord have mercy'). The short petition used in the liturgies of the Eastern and Western Churches, as a response at the beginning of the Roman Mass and in the Anglican Communion Service. Also, the musical setting for this.

**Kyrle Society, The.** Founded 1877, for decorating the walls of hospitals, schoolrooms, mission-rooms, cottages, etc.; for the cultivation of small open spaces, window gardening, the love of flowers, etc.; and improving the artistic taste of the poorer classes. It was named in memory of John Kyrle (1637–1724), Pope's 'Man of Ross'. *See* Ross.

**Kywert** or **Kayward.** The name given to the Hare in Caxton's version of *Reynard the Fox*. *See* Coward.

# L

**L.** This letter, the twelfth of the alphabet, in Phoenician and Hebrew represents an ox-goad, *lamed*, and in the Egyptian hieroglyphic a lioness.

**L,** for a pound sterling, is the Lat. *libra*, a pound. In the Roman notation it stands for 50, and with a line drawn above the letter, for 50,000.

**LL.D.** Doctor of Laws – i.e. both civil and canon. The double L is the plural, as in MSS, the plural of MS (manuscript), pp., pages, etc.

**L.S.** Lat. *locus sigilli*, that is, the place for the seal.

**L. S. D.** Lat. *libra* (a pound); *solidus* (a shilling); and *denarius* (a penny); introduced by the Lombard merchants, from whom also we have *Cr.* (creditor), *Dr* (debtor), *bankrupt*, *do* or *ditto*, etc.

**La Belle Sauvage.** The site on the north side of Ludgate Hill now occupied by the House of Cassell, but famous from at least the 15th century for the inn that stood there, for the dramatic performances that took place in its courtyard in the 16th and early 17th centuries, and as the starting-place for coaches to the eastern counties in the 18th century, and until the advent of railways.

In view of the use to which La Belle Sauvage is now put it is somewhat remarkable that as early as 1579 it should have been famous for the good literature that was produced there: Stephen Gosson, in his *Schoole of Abuse*, a diatribe against the low tastes of the age, goes out of his way to compliment the dramas played in this yard:

> And as some of the players are farre from abuse: so some of their Playes are without rebuke: which are as easily remembered as quickly reckoned. The twoo prose Bookes plaied at the Belsavage, where you shall finde never a worde without wit, a line without pith, never a letter placed in vaine.
>
> Stephen Gosson, *The Schoole of Abuse* (1579)

The origin of the name is uncertain, but the legend which has connected it with Pocahontas (who died in 1617) is absurd. As early as 1530 it appears as 'The belle Savage', and in 1555 as '"la Bell Savage" otherwise "le Bell Savoy"'. The inn would seem to have been originally called 'The Bell', or 'The Bell on the Hoop' (the latter was common as part of inn names) and, at some early date, to have been owned by one 'Savage'; for, in a deed enrolled in the Close Rolls of 1453 John Frensh confirms to his mother Joan Frensh

> all that tenement or inn with its appurtenances called Savagesynn, alias vocat 'le Belle on the Hope', in the parish of St Bridget in Fleet Street.

(Fleet Street at that time extended up Ludgate Hill to the Old Bailey.) It is not known when the names of the owner and of the inn amalgamated, but it must have been, as shown above, not later than 1530.

> They now returned to their inn, the famous Bell Savage. Scott, *Kenilworth*, ch. xiii

**La Mancha, the Knight of.** Don Quixote de la Mancha, the hero of Cervantes' romance *Don Quixote*. La Mancha, an old province of Spain, is now a part of Ciudad Real.

**La-di-da.** A yea-nay sort of fellow, with no backbone; an affected fop with a drawl in his voice. Also used adjectivally, as 'in a la-di-da' sort of way.

> I wish that French brother of his, the Parisian la-de-da, was more like him, more of an American.
>
> A. G. Gunter, *Baron Montez*, III, viii (1893)

**Labadists.** A religious sect of the 17th century, so called from Jean Labadie, of Bourg-en-Guienne (1610–74), who left the Jesuits and became a Protestant in 1650. They were Christian communists who sought reform of morals more than reform of doctrine, and, believing that all days were holy, they rejected the observance of fasts, feasts, and holy days. The sect fell to pieces in the middle of the 18th century.

**Labarum.** The standard borne before the Roman emperors. It consisted of a gilded spear, with an eagle on the top, while from a cross-staff hung a splendid purple streamer, with a gold fringe, adorned with precious stones. Constantine substituted a crown for the eagle, and inscribed in the midst the mysterious monogram. *See* Cross.

**Labe, Queen.** The Circe of the Arabians, who, by her enchantments, transformed men into horses and other brute beasts. She is introduced into the *Arabian Nights' Entertainments*, where Beder, Prince of Persia, marries her, defeats her plots against him, and turns her into a mare. Being restored to her proper shape by her mother, she turns Beder into an owl; but the prince ultimately regains his own proper form.

**Labourer.** ***The labourer is worthy of his hire.*** In Latin: *Digna canis pabulo*. 'The dog must be bad indeed that is not worth a bone.' Hence the Mosaic law, 'Thou shalt not muzzle the ox that treadeth out the corn.'

***The Statute of Labourers.*** An attempt made in 1349 to fix the rate of wages at which labourers should be compelled to work. It followed the

'Black Death', and decreed that the men must work for their former employers, and at the old wages.

**Labyrinth.** A Greek word of unknown (but probably Egyptian) origin, denoting a mass of buildings or garden walks, so complicated as to puzzle strangers to extricate themselves; a maze. The maze at Hampton Court, formed of high hedges, is a labyrinth on a small scale. The chief labyrinths of antiquity are:

(1) The Egyptian, by Petesuchis or Tithoes, near the Lake Moeris. It had 3,000 apartments, half of which were underground. (1800 BC.)

Pliny, xxxvi, 13; and Pomponius Mela, i, 9

(2) The Cretan, by Daedalus, for imprisoning the Minotaur. The only means of finding a way out of it was by help of a skein of thread. (*See* Virgil, *Aeneid*, v.)

(3) The Cretan conduit, which had 1,000 branches or turnings.

(4) The Lemnian, by the architects Smilis, Rholus, and Theodorus. It had 150 columns, so nicely adjusted that a child could turn them. Vestiges of this labyrinth were still in existence in the time of Pliny.

(5) The labyrinth of Clusium, made by Lars Porsena, King of Etruria, for his tomb.

(6) The Samian, by Theodorus (540 BC). Referred to by Pliny; by Herodotus, ii, 145; by Strabo, x; and by Diodorus Siculus, i.

(7) The labyrinth at Woodstock, built by Henry II to protect the Fair Rosamund.

**Lac of Rupees.** One hundred thousand rupees. The nominal value of the Indian rupee is 2*s*., and at this rate of exchange a lac of rupees = £10,000. Its value varies, however, according to the market value of silver. The rupee has been as low is 1*s*. 1*d*. At the time of writing it is worth 1*s*. 5½*d*., a lac, therefore, = £7,291 13*s*. 4*d*. One hundred lacs (i.e. ten million rupees) is a *crore*.

**Lace.** ***I'll lace your jacket for you,*** beat you, flog you severely. Perhaps a play on the word *lash*.

***Laced Mutton.*** *See* Mutton.

***Tea*** or ***coffee laced with spirits,*** a cup of tea or coffee qualified with brandy or whisky.

> Deacon Bearcliff ... had his pipe and his teacup, the latter being laced with a little spirits.
>
> Scott, *Guy Mannering*, ch. xi
>
> Dandie ... partook of a cup of tea with Mrs Allan, just laced with two teaspoonfuls of cogniac.
>
> Ditto, ch. lii

**Lacedaemonian Letter.** The Greek ι (*iota*), the smallest of the letters. *See* Jot.

**Lacedaemonians, The.** An old nickname of the Duke of Cornwall's Light Infantry; because in 1777 their colonel made a long harangue, under heavy fire, on Spartan discipline and the military system of the Lacedaemonians. *Cp.* Red Feathers.

**Lachesis.** The Fate who spins life's thread, working into the woof the events destined to occur. *See* Fate.

**Lackadaisical.** Affected, pensive, sentimental, artificially tender. The word is an extension of the old *lacka-daisy*, which, in its turn, is an extended form of *lackaday!* or *alackaday!* an exclamation of regret, sorrow, or grief.

**Laconic.** Pertaining to Laconia or Sparta; hence very concise and pithy, for the Spartans were noted for their brusque and sententious speech. When Philip of Macedon wrote to the Spartan magistrates, 'If I enter Laconia, I will level Lacedaemon to the ground,' the ephors sent back the single word, 'If'. Caesar's dispatch *Veni, vidi, vici* (*q.v.*) and Sir Charles Napier's apocryphal 'Peccavi' (*q.v.*) are well-known examples of laconisms; as is *Punch*'s 'Advice to those about to Marry – Don't!'

**Ladas.** Alexander's messenger, noted for his swiftness of foot, mentioned by Catullus, Martial, and others. Lord Rosebery's horse *Ladas* won the Derby in 1894.

**Ladon.** The name of the dragon which guarded the apples of the Hesperides (*q.v.*), also of one of the dogs of Actaeon.

**Ladrones.** The island of thieves; so called, in 1519, by Magellan, on account of the thievish habits of the aborigines.

**Lady.** Literally 'the bread-maker', as *lord* (*q.v.*) is 'the bread-guarder'. A.S. *hloefdige*, from *hláf*, loaf, and a supposed noun *dige*, a kneader, connected with Gothic *deigan*, to knead. The original meaning was simply the female head of the family, the 'housewife', a use which is still seen in the phrase (now a vulgarism) 'your good lady', for 'your wife'.

***Ladybird, Lady fly,*** or ***Lady cow.*** The small red coleopterous insect of the genus *Coccinella* with black spots, called also Bishop Barnaby (*q.v.*), and, in Yorkshire, the Cushcow Lady.

***Lady Bountiful.*** The benevolent lady of a village. The character is from Farquhar's *Beaux' Stratagem* (1707).

***Lady Chapel.*** The small chapel east of the altar, or behind the screen of the high altar; dedicated to the Virgin Mary.

***Lady Day.*** March 25th, to commemorate the Annunciation of Our Lady, the Virgin Mary. It used to be called 'St Mary's Day in Lent' to distinguish it from other festivals in honour of the Virgin, which were also, properly speaking, 'Lady Days'. There is a tradition that Adam was created on this day.

***Lady-killer.*** A male flirt; a great favourite with the ladies or one who devotes himself to their conquest.

***Lady Margaret Professor.*** The holder of the Chair of Divinity, founded in 1502, at Cambridge by Lady Margaret Beaufort, the mother of Henry VII, who also founded Christ's (1505) and St John's Colleges (1508).

***The Lady of England.*** The Empress Maud, or Matilda, daughter of Henry I of England, and wife of the Emperor Henry V of Germany. The title of *Domina Anglorum* was conferred upon her by the Council of Winchester, April 7th, 1141. (Rymer, *Faedera*, i.)

Charlotte M. Tucker (d.1893), a writer for children, used the signature 'A.L.O.E.', meaning 'A Lady of England'.

***The Lady of the Lake.*** In the Arthurian legends, Vivien, the mistress of Merlin. She lived in the midst of an imaginary lake which apparently prevented access, surrounded by knights and damsels. *See* Lancelot.

In Scott's poem of this name (1810) the lady is Ellen Douglas, who lived with her father near Loch Katrine.

***The Lady of the Lamp.*** A name given by wounded soldiers to Florence Nightingale (1820–1910) because in contemporary prints she went the rounds of the hospital wards in the Crimea carrying a lighted lamp. *See* Filomena.

***Our Lady of Mercy.*** A Spanish order of knighthood, instituted in 1218 by James I of Aragon, for the deliverance of Christian captives amongst the Moors. Within the first six years, as many as 400 captives were rescued by these knights.

***Lady of pleasure,*** or ***of easy virtue.*** Slang for a prostitute.

***Our Lady of the Rock.*** A miraculous image of the Virgin found by the wayside between Salamanca and Ciudad Rodrigo in 1409.

***The Lady of Shallott.*** *See* Shallott.

***Our Lady of the Snows.*** A fanciful name, given by Kipling in *The Five Nations* (1903) to Canada.

***Lady's Mantle.*** *See* Alchemilla.

***Lady's Smock.*** A common name for the Cuckoo-flower or garden cress (*Cardamine pratensis*); also sometimes applied to the convolvulus, Canterbury bells, and other flowers.

> When daisies pied and violets blue
> And lady-smocks all silver-white
> And cuckoo-buds of yellow hue
> Do paint the meadows with delight,
> The cuckoo then, on every tree,
> Mocks married men: for thus sings he,
> Cuckoo;
> Cuckoo, cuckoo: O, word of fear,
> Unpleasing to a married ear!
>
> Shakespeare, *Love's Labour's Lost*, 5, 2

So-called because the flowers are supposed to resemble linen exposed to whiten on the grass.

***The Ladies' Mile.*** Rotten Row, the part of Hyde Park most frequented by ladies on horse-back.

***Ladies' Plate.*** Formerly, a horse-race in which the riders were women.

> On the Monday succeeding St Wilfred's Sunday, there were for many years at Roper's Common [a race] called the Lady's Plate, of £15 value, for horses, etc., ridden by women.
>
> *Sporting Magazine,* vol xx, New Series, p. 287

***Naked Lady.*** *See* Naked.

**Laelaps.** In *classical mythology*, the powerful dog given by Diana to Procris, who gave it to Cephalus (*q.v.*). While pursuing a wild boar it was metamorphosed into a stone. The name, which was originally that of one of Actaeon's fifty dogs, means 'the hurricane'.

**Laestrygones.** *See* Lestrigons.

**Laetare Sunday** (i.e. Rejoice Sunday, *Lat.*). The fourth Sunday in Lent, so called from the first word of the Introit, which is from Is. 66:10, '*Rejoice* ye with Jerusalem, and be glad with her all ye that love her.' It is on this day that the Pope blesses the Golden Rose.

**Lagado.** In Swift's *Gulliver's Travels*, the capital of Balnibarbi, celebrated for its grand academy of projectors, where the scholars spend their time in such useful projects as making pincushions from softened rocks, extracting sunbeams from cucumbers, and converting ice into gunpowder.

**Lagan,** or **Ligan.** Goods thrown overboard, but marked by a buoy in order to be found again. An Anglo-Fr. word, probably connected with Icel. *lagnir*, a sea-net.

**Laid.** The term used in the paper trade of the ribbed appearance in papers, due to manufacture on a mould or by a dandy on which the wires are *laid* side by side instead of being *wove* transversely.

**Laïs.** The name of two celebrated Greek courtezans; the earlier was the most beautiful woman of Corinth, and lived at the time of the Peloponnesian War. The beauty of Laïs the Second so excited the jealousy of the Thessalonian women that they pricked her to death with their bodkins. She was the contemporary and rival of Phryne and sat to Apelles as a model. Demosthenes tells us that Laïs sold her favours for 10,000 (Attic) drachmae (about £300), and adds *tanti non ema paenitere*. (Horace, *I Epis.* xvii, 1:36.)

**Laissez faire** (Fr., let us alone). The principle of allowing things to look after themselves, especially the policy of non-interference by Government in commercial affairs. The phrase comes from the motto of the mid-18th century 'Physiocratic' school of French economists, *Laissez faire, laissez passer* (let us alone, let us have free circulation for our goods), who wished to have all customs duties abolished and thus anticipated the later Free-traders.

**Lake Dwellings.** Prehistoric human dwellings on certain lakes in Switzerland, Ireland, etc., built on piles at their shallow edges. They are mentioned by Herodotus, but the remains found in various examples show that they date from times very much earlier than his.

**Lake School, The.** The name applied in derision by the *Edinburgh Review* to Wordsworth, Coleridge, and Southey, who resided in the Lake District of Cumberland and Westmorland, and sought inspiration in the simplicity of nature, and to the poets who followed them.

Charles Lamb, Lloyd, and 'Christopher North' are sometimes placed among the 'Lake Poets' or 'Lakers'.

**Lakin.** ***By'r lakin.*** An oath, meaning 'By our Ladykin', or Little Lady, where little does not refer to size, but is equivalent to *dear*.

> By'r lakin, a parlous [perilous] fear.
>
> Shakespeare, *Midsummer Night's Dream*, 3, 1

**Laksmi** or **Lakshmi.** One of the consorts of the Hindu god Vishnu, and mother of Kama (*q.v.*). She is goddess of beauty, wealth, and pleasure, and the Ramayana describes her as springing, like Venus, from the foam of the sea.

**Lalla Rookh** (*tulip cheek*). In Thomas Moore's poem of that name (1817), the supposed daughter of Aurungzebe, Emperor of Delhi, betrothed to Aliris, Sultan of Lesser Bucharia. On her journey from Delhi to the valley of Cashmere, she is entertained by the young Persian poet Feramorz, who relates the four tales of the romance, and with whom she falls in love.

**Lama.** The Tibetan word *blama* (*b* silent) for a Buddhist priest or monk. The *Grand Lama* or *Dalai Lama* (the Sacred Lama) was, under the more or less nominal suzerainty of China, the ruler of Tibet, but he fled to India in 1910 before the Chinese troops, was deposed, and Tibet has since been in an unsettled state. The *Teshu*, or *Tashi, Lama* is the chief lama of Mongolia. The religion of both Mongolia and Tibet is called *Lamaism* and is a corrupt form of Buddhism. The priests are housed in great monasteries known as *lamasseries*.

**Lamb.** In Christian art, an emblem of the Redeemer, in allusion to John 1:29, 'Behold the Lamb of God, which taketh away the sin of the world.'

It is also the attribute of St Agnes, St Genevieve, St Catherine, and St Regina. John the Baptist either carries a lamb or is accompanied by one. It is also introduced symbolically to represent any of the 'types' of Christ; as Abraham, Moses, and so on.

The word is used ironically to denote a rough or bully, especially in the plural for a gang of such. In Limehouse, for instance, a party of street terrorists would call themselves 'the Limehouse Lambs'.

***Lamb-ale.*** The 'ale', or merry-making formerly given by the farmer when his lambing was over. *Cp.* Church-ale.

***Lamb's wool.*** A beverage consisting of the juice of apples roasted with spiced ale.

> The pulpe of the roasted apples, in number foure or five … mixed in a wine quart of faire water, laboured together untill it come to be as apples, and ale, which we call lambes wool.
>
> *Johnson's Gerard*, p. 1460

***The Vegetable, Tartarian,*** or ***Scythian Lamb.*** The woolly rootstalk of a polypodiaceous fern (*Dicksonia barometz*), found in the Far East, and supposed in mediaeval times to be a kind of hybrid animal and vegetable. The down is used in India for stanching wounds.

> And there groweth a maner of Fruyt, as thoughe it weren Gowrdes; and when thei ben rype, men kutten hem a to, and men fynden with inne a lytylle Best, in Flessche, in Bon and Blode, as though it were a lytylle Lomb, withouten Wolle. And men eten bothe the Frut and the Best; and that is a gret Marveylle.
>
> *Travels of Sir John Mandeville, Kt* (Mid-14th cent.)

**Lamb's Conduit Street** (London). Stow says, 'One William Lamb, citizen and clothworker, born at Sutton Valence, Kent, did found near unto Oldbourne a faire conduit and standard;

from this conduit, water clear as crystal was conveyed in pipes to a conduit on Snow Hill' (March 26th, 1577). The conduit was taken down in 1746.

**Lambert's Day, St.** September 17th. St Lambert, a native of Maestricht, lived in the 7th century.

> Be ready, as your lives shall answer it,
> At Coventry, upon St Lambert's day.
>
> Shakespeare, *Richard II*, 1, 1

**Lame Duck.** *See* Duck.

**Lame King.** A Grecian oracle had told Sparta, to 'Beware of a lame king'. Agesilaus was lame, and during his reign Sparta lost her supremacy.

**Lamerock, Sir.** In Arthurian romance one of the Knights of the Round Table, son of Sir Pellinore, and brother of Sir Percival. He had an amour with his own aunt, the wife of King Lot.

**Lamia.** A female phantom, whose name was used by the Greeks and Romans as a bugbear to children. She was a Libyan queen beloved by Jupiter, but robbed of her offspring by the jealous Juno; and in consequence she vowed vengeance against all children, whom she delighted to entice and devour.

> ... a troop of nice wantons, fair women, that like to Lamiae had faces like angels, eies like stars, brestes like the golden front in the Hesperides, but from the middle downwards their shapes like serpents.
>
> Greene, *A Quip for an Upstart Courtier* (1592)

Witches in the Middle Ages were called *Lamiae*, and Keats's poem *Lamia* (1820), which relates how a bride when recognised returned to her original serpent form, represents one of the many superstitions connected with the race. Keats's story came (through Burton) from Philostratus' *De Vita Apollonii*, Bk iv. In Burton's rendering, the sage Apollonius, on the wedding night –

> found her out to be a serpent, a lamia ... When she saw herself descried, she wept, and desired Apollonius to be silent, but he would not be moved, and thereupon she, plate, house, and all that was in it, vanished in an instant; many thousands took notice of this fact, for it was done in the midst of Greece.
>
> *Anatomy of Melancholy*, Pt iii, sect. ii, memb. i, subsect. i

**Lammas Day.** August 1st; one of the regular quarter days in Scotland, and in England the day on which, in Anglo-Saxon times, the first-fruits were offered. So called from A.S. *hlāfmaesse*, the loaf-mass.

***At latter Lammas.*** A humorous way of saying 'Never'.

**Lamourette's Kiss.** A term used in France (*baiser Lamourette*) to denote an insincere or ephemeral reconciliation. On July 7th, 1792, the Abbé Lamourette induced the different factions of the Legislative Assembly to lay aside their differences, but the reconciliation was unsound and very short-lived.

**Lamp. *The Lamp of Heaven.*** The moon. Milton calls the stars 'lamps'.

> Why shouldst thou ...
> In thy dark lantern thus close up the stars,
> That Nature hung in heaven, and filled their lamps
> With everlasting oil, to give due light
> To the misled and lonely traveller?
>
> *Comus*, 200–204

***The Lamp of Phoebus.*** The sun. Phoebus is the mythological personification of the sun.

***The Lamp of the Law.*** Irnerius the Italian jurist was so called. He was the first to lecture on the Pandects of Justinian after their discovery at Amalfi in 1137.

***Sepulchral lamps.*** The Romans are said to have preserved lamps in some of their sepulchres for centuries, and many legends are told of their never-dying combustion. In the papacy of Paul III (1534–40) one was found in the tomb of Tullia (Cicero's daughter), which had been shut up for 1,550 years, and at the dissolution of the monasteries a lamp was found which is said to have been burning 1,200 years. Two are preserved in Leyden museum.

***It smells of the lamp.*** Said of a literary composition that bears manifest signs of midnight study; one that is over-laboured. In Lat. *olet lucernam*. Plautus (*Paenulus*, I, ii. 119) has *Et oleum et operam perdidi*, I have lost both my time and my trouble (literally, my oil and my labour).

**Lampadion.** The received name of a lively, petulant courtesan, in the later Greek comedy.

**Lampoon.** A sarcastic or scurrilous personal satire, so called from Fr. *lampons*, let us drink, which formed part of the refrain of a 17th century French drinking song. Sir Walter Scott says –

> These personal and scandalous libels, carried to excess in the reign of Charles II, acquired the name of lampoons from the burden sung to them: 'Lampone, lampone, camerada lampone' – Guzzler, guzzler, my fellow guzzler.

**Lampos and Phaeton.** The two steeds of Aurora. One of Actaeon's dogs was also called Lampos.

**Lampreel.** The name given to the Cony, or Rabbit, in Caxton's version of *Reynard the Fox*. Also called *Laprel* (Fr. *lapin*, a rabbit).

**Lancasterian.** Of or pertaining to Joseph Lancaster (1778–1838), an educational reformer who introduced the monitorial system into schools.

**Lancastrian.** An adherent of the Lancastrian line of kings, or one of these kings (Henry IV, V, VI), who were descended from John of Gaunt, Duke of Lancaster (d.1399), third son of Edward III, as opposed to the *Yorkists*, who sprang from Edmund, Duke of York, Edward III's fourth son. The Lancastrian badge was the red rose and the Yorkist the white.

**Lance.** An attribute in Christian art of St Matthew and St Thomas, the apostles; also of St Longinus, St George, St Adalbert, St Barbara, St Michael, and several others.

*Astolpho* had a lance of gold that with enchanted force dismounted everyone it touched. (*Orlando Furioso*, Bk ix.)

***A free lance.*** One who acts on his own judgment, and not from party motives; a journalist who is not definitely attached to, or on the salaried staff of, any one paper.

The reference is to the Free Companies of the Middle Ages, called in Italy *condottieri*, and in France *compagnies grandes*, which were free and willing to sell themselves to any master and any cause, good or bad.

***Lance-corporal.*** A private soldier acting as a corporal, usually as a first step to being promoted to that rank. Similarly, a *lance-sergeant* is a corporal who performs the duties of a sergeant on probation.

***Lance-knight.*** An old term for a foot-soldier; a corruption of *lansquenet* or *lancequenet*, a German foot-soldier.

**Lancelot du Lac.** One of the earliest romances of the Round Table (1494).

Sir Lancelot was the son of King Ban of Brittany, but was stolen in infancy by Vivienne, the Lady of the Lake (*q.v.*); she plunged with the babe into the lake (whence the cognomen of *du Lac*), and when her *protégé* was grown into man's estate, presented him to King Arthur. Sir Lancelot went in search of the Grail (*q.v.*), and twice caught sight of it. Though always represented in the Arthurian romances as the model of chivalry, bravery, and fidelity, Sir Lancelot was the adulterous lover of Guinevere, wife of King Arthur, his friend, and it was through this love that the war, which resulted in the disruption of the Round Table and the death of Arthur, took place.

Elaine (*q.v.*), 'the lily maid of Astolat', fell in love with Lancelot; the love was not returned, and she died. By another Elaine, daughter of King Pelles, he (through a stratagem) unwittingly became the father of Sir Galahad. At the close of his life the repentant knight became a hermit, and died in the odour of sanctity.

In the Scottish metrical romance, which was founded on the French *roman* about the end of the 15th century, Galiot, a neighbouring king, invades Arthur's territory, and captures the castle of Lady Melyhalt among others. Sir Lancelot goes to chastise Galiot, sees Queen Guinevere and falls in love with her. Sir Gawayne is wounded in the war, and the romance ends when Sir Lancelot is taken prisoner.

**Lancers.** The dance so called, an amplified kind of quadrille, was introduced by Laborde from Paris in 1836. It is in imitation of military evolutions in which men used lances.

**Land. *The Land of Beulah*** (Is. 62:4). In *The Pilgrim's Progress* it is that land of heavenly joy where the pilgrims tarry till they are summoned to enter the Celestial City; the Paradise before the resurrection.

***The Land of Cakes.*** *See* Cake.

***The Land of Nod.*** To go to the land of Nod is to go to bed. There are many similar puns, and more in French than in English. Of course, the reference is to Gen. 4:16, 'Cain went … and dwelt in the land of Nod,' which seems to mean 'the land of wandering' rather than any definite locality.

***The Land o' the Leal.*** The land of the faithful or blessed; a Scotticism for a hypothetical land of happiness, loyalty, and virtue, hence heaven, as in Lady Nairn's song –

I'm wearin' awa'
To the land o' the leal.

Gladstone, in one of his Midlothian campaigns, once amused the natives by using the phrase as a complimentary synonym for Scotland itself.

***The Land of Promise,*** or ***the Promised Land.*** Canaan, which God promised to give to Abraham for his obedience. *See* Ex. 12:25, Deut. 9:28, etc.

***The Land of Steady Habits.*** A name given to the State of Connecticut, which was the original stronghold of Presbyterianism in America and the home of the notorious Blue Laws (*q.v.*).

***See how the land lies.*** See what we have to do; see in what state the land is that we have to travel over. Joshua sent spies (2:1) 'to view the land' before he attempted to pass the Jordan.

Put your blankets down there, boys, and turn in.
You'll see how the land lies in the morning.
Boldrewood, *Robbery Under Arms,* ch. xi

**Land-damn.** A term of uncertain meaning and origin used (possibly inadvertently) by Shakespeare and, apparently, by no one else – though it has been stated, on insufficient authority, to be in dialectal use today.

You are abus'd, and by some putter-on
That will be damn'd for't; would I knew the villain,
I would land-damn him. *Winter's Tale*, 2, 1

**Land-hunger.** A craving for the ownership of land; also the state in which the progress of a community is retarded because it has not sufficient land with which to support itself.

**Land League.** An association of Irish extremists formed in Ireland in 1879 to agitate for the reduction, or annihilation, of rent, introduction of peasant proprietorship, and the settlement of the land question generally.

**Land-loupers,** vagrants. *Louper* is from the Dutch *looper*, to run. Persons who fly the country for crime or debt. Louper, loper, loafer, and luffer are varieties of the German *läufer*, a vagrant, a runner.

**Land-lubber.** An awkward or inexpert sailor on board ship.

**Land-slide.** Used metaphorically of a crushing defeat at the polls, or of a complete reversal of the votes; as at the General Election of 1906, when a Unionist majority of 68 in the House of Commons gave place to a Liberal majority of 273, or, including the Nationalists, of 356.

**Landau.** A four-wheeled carriage, the top of which may be thrown back; first made at Landau, in Bavaria, in the 18th century.

**Landeyda.** The ancient standard of Denmark, which bore Odin's raven as an emblem. *See under* Raven.

**Landscape.** A country scene, or a picture representing this. The word comes from Dutch *scape* being connected with our *shape*, and the A.S. *scap-an*, to shape, to give a form to. The old word in English was *Landskip*.

***Father of landscape gardening.*** André Lenôtre (1613–1700).

**Lane. *'Tis a long lane that has no turning.*** Every calamity has an ending. The darkest day, stop till tomorrow, will have passed away.

Hope peeps from a cloud on our squad,
Whose beams have been long in deep mourning;
'Tis a lane, let me tell you, my lad,
Very long that has never a turning.
Peter Pindar, *Great Cry and Little Wool,* epist. 1

**Lang Syne** (*Scotch*, long since). In the olden time, in days gone by.

There was muckle fighting about the place langsyne. Scott, *Guy Mannering*, ch. xi

The song called *Auld Lang Syne*, usually attributed to Robert Burns, is really a new version by him of a very much older song: in Watson's Collection (1711) it is attributed to Francis Sempill (d.1682), but it is probably even earlier. Burns says in a letter to Thomson, 'It is the old song of the olden times, which has never been in print … I took it down from an old man's singing,' and in another letter, 'Light be the turf on the heaven-inspired poet who composed this glorious fragment.'

**Langbourn Ward.** One of the wards in the City of London, originally (12th cent.) called the 'Ward of Lange-borde', and later the 'Lombard Street Ward'. It took its name from Lombard Street, which intersects it, the *-bourn* being a 13th century corruption and leading Stow into the mistake that there was originally a stream named the *Lang Bourne* running down Fenchurch Street and Lombard Street to the Thames.

**Langstaff, Launcelot.** The pseudonym under which *Salmagundi* was published (1807), the authors being Washington Irving, William Irving and J. K. Paulding.

**Language.** Slang for swear-words, i.e. 'bad language'. *Not so much of your language, there!* means 'Don't swear such a lot.'

***Language was given to men to conceal their thoughts.*** *See* Speech.

***The three primitive languages.*** The Persians say that Arabic, Persian, and Turkish are three primitive languages. Legend has it that the serpent that seduced Eve spoke Arabic, the most suasive language in the world; that Adam and Eve spoke Persian, the most poetic of all languages; and that the angel Gabriel spoke Turkish, the most menacing.

**Langue d'oc; langue d'oïl.** The former is the old Provençal language, spoken on the south of the River Loire; the latter, Northern French, spoken in the Middle Ages on the north of that river, the original of modern French. So called because our 'yes' was in Provençal *oc* and in the northern speech *oïl* (*oui*).

**Lansquenet.** *See* Lance-knight.

**Lantedo.** *See* Adelantado.

**Lantern.** In Christian art, the attribute of St Gudule and St Hugh.

***À la lanterne!*** Hang him to the lamp-post! a cry and custom introduced into Paris during the French revolution.

***Lantern jaws.*** Cheeks so thin and hollow that one may almost see daylight through them, as light shows through the horn of a lantern.

> A husband poor, care-bitten, sorrow-sunk,
> Little, long-nosed, bush-bearded, lantern-jawed,
> Forty-six years old.
>
> Browning, *Ring and the Book*, iv, 717

***The feast of lanterns.*** A popular Chinese festival, celebrated at the first full moon of each year. Tradition says that the daughter of a famous mandarin one evening fell into a lake. The father and his neighbours went with lanterns to look for her, and happily she was rescued. In commemoration thereof a festival was ordained, and it grew in time to be the celebrated 'feast of lanterns'.

***Lantern Land.*** The land of literary charlatans, pedantic graduates in arts, doctors, professors, prelates, and so on ridiculed as 'Lanterns' by Rabelais (with a side allusion to the divines assembled in conference at the Council of Trent) in his *Pantagruel*, v, 33. *Cp.* City of Lanterns.

**Laocoon.** A son of Priam and priest of Apollo of Troy, famous for the tragic fate of himself and his two sons, who were crushed to death by serpents while he was sacrificing to Poseidon, in consequence of his having offended Apollo. The group representing these three in their death agony, now in the Vatican, was discovered in 1506, on the Esquiline Hill (Rome). It is a single block of marble, and is attributed to Agesandrus, Athenodorus, and Polydorus of the School of Rhodes in the 2nd century BC. It has been restored.

Lessing called his treatise on the limits of poetry and the plastic arts (1766) *Laocoon* because he uses the famous group as the peg on which to hang his dissertation.

> Since I have, as it were, set out from the Laocoon, and several times return to it, I have wished to give it a share also in the title. Preface

**Laodamia.** The wife of Protesilaus, who was slain before Troy. She begged to be allowed to converse with her dead husband for only three hours, and her request was granted; when the respite was over, she voluntarily accompanied the dead hero to the shades. Wordsworth has a poem on the subject (1815).

**Laodicean.** One indifferent to religion, caring little or nothing about the matter, like the Christians of that church, mentioned in the book of Revelation (3:14–18).

**Lapithae.** A people of Thessaly, noted in *Greek legend* for their defeat of the Centaurs at the marriage-feast of Hippodamia, when the latter were driven out of Pelion. The contest was represented on the Parthenon, the Theseum at Athens, the Temple of Apollo at Basso, and on numberless vases.

**Laprel.** *See* Lampreel.

**Lapsus Linguae.** (*Lat.*) A slip of the tongue, a mistake in uttering a word, an imprudent word inadvertently spoken.

> We have also adopted the Latin phrases *lapsus calami* (a slip of the pen), and *lapsus memoriae* (a slip of the memory).

**Laputa.** The flying island inhabited by scientific quacks, and visited by Gulliver in his 'travels' (Swift). These dreamy philosophers were so absorbed in their speculations that they employed attendants called 'flappers', to flap them on the mouth and ears with a blown bladder when their attention was to be called off from 'high things' to vulgar mundane matters.

> Realising in a manner the dreams of Laputa, and endeavouring to extract sunbeams from cucumbers. De Quincey

**Lapwing.** Shakespeare refers to two peculiarities of this bird: (1) to allure persons from its nest, it flies away and cries loudest when farthest from its nest; and (2) the young birds run from their shells with part thereof still sticking to their heads.

> Far from her nest the lapwing cries away.
>
> *Comedy of Errors*, 4, 2
>
> This lapwing runs away with the shell on his head. *Hamlet*, 5, 2

The first peculiarity, referred to in Ray's *Proverbs*, as well as by other dramatists and also by Shakespeare himself in other passages, made the lapwing a symbol of insincerity; and the second that of a forward person, one who is scarcely hatched.

> *Giov.*: If I live,
> I'll charge the French foe in the very front
> Of all my troops, the foremost man.
> *Fran. de Med.*: What! What!
> *Giov.*: And will not bid my soldiers up, and follow,
> But bid them follow me.
> *Brach*: Forward lapwing!
> He flies with the shell on's head.
>
> Webster, *The White Devil*, II,i

**Laquedem, Isaac.** The name given in Flanders, in the 14th century, to the Wandering Jew (*q.v.*).

**Lar.** *See* Lares.

**Larboard.** *See* Starboard.

**Larder.** A place for keeping bacon (Lat. *laridum*), from O.Fr. *lardier* or *lardoir*, a storeroom for bacon. This shows that swine were the chief animals salted and preserved in olden times.

***The Douglas Larder.*** The English garrison and all its provisions in Douglas Castle, Lanark, seized by 'the Good' Lord James Douglas, in 1307.

> He caused all the barrels containing flour, meat, wheat, and malt to be knocked in pieces, and their contents mixed on the floor; then he staved the great hogsheads of wine and ale, and mixed the liquor with the stores; and last of all, he killed the prisoners, and flung the dead bodies among this disgusting heap, which his men called, in derision of the English, 'The Douglas Larder'.
>
> Scott, *Tales of a Grandfather*, ix

***Robin Hood's Larder.*** *See* Oaks.

***Wallace's Larder*** is very similar to Douglas's. It consisted of the dead bodies of the garrison of Ardrossan, in Ayrshire, cast into the dungeon keep. The castle was surprised by Wallace in the reign of Edward I.

**Lares and Penates.** Used as a collective expression for home, and for those personal belongings that make home homely and individual to one. In ancient Rome the *lares* (sing. *lar*) were the household gods, usually deified ancestors or heroes; the *penates* were also guardian deities of the household (and the State), but were more in the nature of personifications of the natural powers, their duty being to bring wealth and plenty rather than to protect and ward off danger. The *Lar familiaris* was the spirit of the founder of the house, which never left it, but accompanied his descendants in all their changes.

**Large.** A vulgarism for excess, as *That's all very fine and large*, that's a trifle steep, 'coming it a bit thick', etc.; *To talk large*, to brag, 'swank' in conversation, talk big; *a large order*, an exaggerated claim or statement, a difficult undertaking.

***To sail large.*** A nautical phrase for to sail with the wind not straight astern, but 'abaft the beam'.

***Set at large.*** At liberty. It is a French phrase; *prendre le large* is to stand out at sea, or occupy the main ocean, so as to be free to move. Similarly, to be set at large is to be placed free in the wide world.

**Lark.** A spree or frolic. The word is a modern adaptation (about 1800) of the dialectal *lake*, sport, from M.E. *laik*, play, and A.S. *lác*, contest. *Skylark*, as in *skylarking* about, etc., is a still more modern extension. Hood plays on the two words – for the name of the bird, the old *laverock*, A.S. *lāferce*, is in no way connected with this – in his well-known lines:

> So, Pallas, take thine owl away
> And let us have a lark instead!

***When the sky falls we shall catch larks.*** *See* Sky.

**Larrikin.** An Australian term for a street rough. It arose about 1870, and is probably a corruption of *Larry* (short for *Lawrence*), just as *hooligan* (*q.v.*) is from a personal name.

**Larvae.** A name among the ancient Romans for malignant spirits and ghosts. The *larva* or ghost of Caligula was often seen (according to Suetonius) in his palace.

> [Fear] sometimes representeth strange apparitions, as their fathers and grandfathers ghosts, risen out of their graves, and in their winding-sheets: and to others it sometimes sheweth Larves, Hobgoblins, Robbin-good-fellowes, and such other Bug-beares and Chimeraes.
>
> *Florio's Montaigne*, I, xvii

**Lascar.** An East Indian sailor employed on European vessels. The natives of the East Indies call camp-followers *lascars*. (Hindu *lash-kar*, a soldier.)

**Last Man, The.** Charles I was so called by the Parliamentarians, meaning that he would be the last king of Great Britain. His son, Charles II, was called *The Son of the Last Man.*

**Last of the Barons, The.** Another name given to Warwick, the King-maker (*q.v.*).

**Last of the Fathers, The.** St Bernard (1091–1153), Abbot of Clairvaux.

**Last of the Goths, The.** Roderick, who was the last of the kings of the Visigoths in Spain, and died in 711. Southey has a tale in blank verse on him.

**Last of the Greeks, The.** The general, Philopoemen of Arcadia (253–183 BC).

**Last of the Knights, The.** The Emperor Maximilian I (1459–1519).

**Last of the Romans.** A title, or sobriquet, given to a number of historical characters, among whom are –

Marcus Junius Brutus (85–42 BC), one of the murderers of Caesar.

Caius Cassius Longinus (d.42 BC), so called by Brutus.

Stilicho, the Roman general under Theodosius.

Aetius, the general who defended the Gauls against the Franks and other barbarians, and defeated Attila near Châlons in 451. So called by Procopius.

François Joseph Terasse Desbillons (1711–89), a French Jesuit; so called from the elegance and purity of his Latin.

Pope called Congreve *Ultimus Romanorum*, and the same title was conferred on Dr Johnson, Horace Walpole, and C. J. Fox.

**Last of the Saxons, The.** King Harold (1022–66), who was defeated and slain at the Battle of Hastings.

**Last of the Tribunes, The.** Cola di Rienzi (1314–54), who led the Roman people against the barons.

**Last of the Troubadours, The.** Jacques Jasmin, of Gascony (1798–1864).

**Last Words.** *See* Dying Sayings.

**Lateran.** The ancient palace of the Laterani, which was appropriated by Nero and later given by the Emperor Constantine to the popes. Fable derives the name from *lateo*, to hide, and *rana*, a frog, and accounts for it by saying that Nero once vomited a frog covered with blood, which he believed to be his own progeny, and had it hidden in a vault. The palace built on its site was called the 'Lateran', or the palace of the *hidden frog*.

***Lateran Council.*** One of the five oecumenical councils held in the Lateran Church at Rome. They are (1) 1123; held under Calixtus II; it confirmed the Concordat of Worms; (2) 1139, when Innocent II condemned Anacletus II and Arnold of Brescia; (3) 1179, under Alexander III; it was concerned with the election of popes; (4) 1215, when Innocent III condemned the Albigenses; and (5) 1512–17, under Julius II and Leo X, when the Canons of the Council of Pisa were abrogated.

The locality in Rome so called contains the Lateran palace, the Piazza, and the Basilica of St John Lateran. The Basilica is the Pope's cathedral church. The palace (once a residence of the popes) is now a museum.

***St John Lateran*** is called the *Mother and Head of all Churches*. It occupies part of the site of the palace, which escheated to the Crown through treason, and was given to the Church by the Emperor Constantine. From the balcony of this church the Pope blesses the people of the whole world.

**Lathe.** An old division of a county, containing a number of hundreds. The term is now confined to Kent, which is divided into five *lathes*. In Sussex similar county divisions are called *rapes*.

Spenser, in his *Description of Ireland* (1596), uses *lathe* or *lath* for the division of a hundred:

> If all that tything failed, then all that lath was charged for that tything; and if the lath failed, then all that hundred was demanded for them [i.e. turbulent fellows], and if the hundred, then the shire.

**Latin.** The language spoken by the ancient inhabitants of Latium, in Italy, and by the ancient Romans. Alba Longa was head of the Latin League, and, as Rome was a colony of Alba Longa, it is plain to see how the Roman tongue was Latin.

The tale is that the name *Latium* is from *lateo*, to lie hid, and was so called because Saturn lay hid there, when he was driven out of heaven by the gods.

According to Roman tradition the Latini were the aborigines, and Romulus and Remus were descended from Lavinia, daughter of their king, Latinus (*q.v.*).

The earliest specimen of the Latin language known is an inscription of the 5th century BC, or even earlier, found in the Forum in 1899 on a pyramidal stone. This, unfortunately, was broken and the upper half missing; as the lines were written alternately from the bottom upwards and the top downwards, the meaning of the inscription cannot be ascertained.

The fragment of a hymn of the Arval Brethren, formerly thought to be very ancient, dates only from the early part of the 3rd cent. AD. The *hymn* itself, of which this is a corrupt form, is of very great antiquity, but the tablet is comparatively modern. It was discovered in 1778 in the grove of the *Dea Dia*, five miles from Rome on the Via Campana.

***Classical Latin.*** The Latin of the best authors of the Golden or Augustan Age (about 75 BC to AD 145), as Livy, Tacitus, and Cicero (prose), Horace, Virgil, and Ovid (poets).

***Dog Latin.*** *See* Dog-Latin.

***Late Latin.*** The period which followed the Augustan Age, to about AD 600; it includes the Church Fathers.

***Low Latin.*** Mediaeval Latin, mainly early French, Italian, Spanish, and so on.

***Middle,*** or ***Mediaeval, Latin.*** Latin from the 6th to the 16th century AD, both inclusive. In this Latin, prepositions frequently supply the cases of nouns.

***Thieves' Latin.*** Cant or jargon employed as a secret language by rogues and vagabonds.

***The Latin Church.*** The Western Church, in contradistinction to the Greek or Eastern Church.

***The Latin cross.*** Formed thus: †. The Greek cross has four equal arms, thus: +.

***The Latin races.*** The peoples the basis of whose language is Latin; i.e. the Italians, Spanish, Portuguese, and French.

**Latinus.** Legendary king of the Latini, the ancient inhabitants of Latium. *See* Latin. According to Virgil, he opposed Aeneas on his first landing, but subsequently formed an alliance with him, and gave him his daughter, Lavinia, in marriage. Turnus, King of the Rutuli, declared that Lavinia had been betrothed to him; the issue was decided by single combat, and Aeneas being victor, obtained Lavinia for his wife and became by her the ancestor of Romulus, the mythical founder of Rome.

The name Latinus is given to one of the Italian heroes in Tasso's *Jerusalem Delivered*; he and his five sons were all slain in battle by the Soldan Solyman in a single hour.

**Latitudinarians.** A Church of England party in the time of Charles II, opposed both to the High Church party and to the Puritans. The term is now applied to those persons who attach little importance to dogma and what are called orthodox doctrines.

**Latium.** *See* Latin.

**Latona.** The Roman name of the Greek Leto, mother by Jupiter of Apollo and Diana. Milton, in one of his sonnets, refers to the legend that when she knelt by a fountain in Delos with her infants in arms to quench her thirst, some Lycian clowns insulted her and were turned into frogs.

> As when those hinds that were transformed to frogs
> Railed at Latona's twin-born progeny,
> Which after held the sun and moon in fee.

**Latria and Dulia.** Greek words adopted by the Roman Catholics; the former to express that supreme reverence and adoration which is offered to God alone; and the latter, that secondary reverence and adoration which is offered to saints. *Latria* is from the Greek suffix *-latreia*, worship, as in our ido*latry*; *dulia* is the reverence of a *doulos* or slave.

**Latter-day Saints.** *See* Mormonism.

**Lattice.** *See* Red Lattice.

**Laugh.** ***He laughs best that laughs last.*** A game's not finished till it's won – so don't start crowing too early! In Ray's *Collection* (1742) is 'Better the last smile than the first laughter', and the French have the proverb *Il rit bien qui rit le dernier*.

***It's no laughing matter.*** It's really serious; it's no subject for merriment.

***Laugh and grow fat.*** An old saw, expressive of the wisdom of keeping a cheerful mind. One of the works of Taylor, the Water Poet, has the title *Laugh and be Fat* (about 1625), and in Trapp's *Commentaries* (1617), on 2 Thess. 3:11, he says, 'Whose whole life is to eat and drink ... and laugh themselves fat'.

***To have the laugh of one.*** To be able to make merry at another's expense, generally to that other's surprise and confusion.

***To laugh in one's sleeve.*** *See* Sleeve.

***To laugh on the wrong,*** or ***the other, side of one's mouth.*** To be made to feel vexation and annoyance after mirth or satisfaction; to be bitterly disappointed; to cry.

> Thou laughest there; by and by thou wilt laugh on the wrong side of thy face.
> Carlyle, *The Diamond Necklace,* ch. iii

***To laugh out of court.*** To cover with ridicule and so treat as not worth considering.

***To laugh to scorn.*** To treat with the utmost contempt.

> All they that see me laugh me to scorn; they shoot out the lip, they shake the head. Ps. 22:7

**Laughing Philosopher.** Democritus of Abdera (5th cent. BC), who viewed with supreme contempt the feeble powers of man. *Cp.* Weeping Philosopher.

**Laughing-stock.** A butt for jokes.

**Launcelot.** *See* Lancelot.

**Launfal, Sir.** One of the Knights of the Round Table. His story is told in a metrical romance written by Thomas Chestre in the reign of Henry VI.

He was steward to King Arthur, and fell in love with Tryamour, who gave him an unfailing purse, telling him that if he ever wished to see her all he had to do was to retire into a private room, and she would instantly be with him. Sir Launfal excited much attention at court by his great wealth; but having told Gwennere, daughter of Ryon, King of Ireland, who solicited his love, that she was not worthy to kiss the feet of his ladylove, the queen accused him, as Potiphar's wife did Joseph, of insulting her. Thereupon Arthur told him that, unless he made good his word by producing this paragon of women, he should be burned alive. On the day appointed Tryamour arrived; Launfal was justified; he was set at liberty and accompanied his mistress to the isle of Oleron, and no man ever saw him more.

**Laura.** The lady of this name immortalised by Petrarch is generally held to have been Laure de Noves, who was born at Avignon in 1308, was married in 1325 to Hugues de Sede, and died of the plague in 1348, the mother of eleven children. It was Petrarch's first sight of her, in the church of St Clara Avignon, on April 6th, 1327 (exactly 21 years before her death) that, he says, made him a poet.

**Lauras** (Gr. *laura*), an alley. An aggregation of separate cells under the control of a superior. In monasteries the monks live under one roof; in lauras they live each in his own cell apart; but on certain occasions they assemble and meet together, sometimes for a meal, and sometimes for a religious service.

**Laureate, Poet.** *See* Poet Laureate.

**Laurel.** The Greeks gave a wreath of laurels to the victor in the Pythian games, but the victor in the Olympic games had a wreath of wild olives, in the Nemean games a wreath of green parsley, and in the Isthmian games a wreath of dry parsley or green pine-leaves.

The ancients believed that laurel communicated the spirit of prophecy and poetry. Hence the custom of crowning the pythoness and poets, and of putting laurel leaves under one's pillow to acquire inspiration. Another superstition was that the bay laurel was antagonistic to the stroke of lightning; but Sir Thomas Browne, in his *Vulgar Errors*, tells us that Vicomereatus proves from personal knowledge that this is by no means true.

*Laurel*, in modern times, is a symbol of victory and peace, and of excellence in literature and the arts. St Gudule, in Christian art, carries a laurel crown.

**Laurin.** The dwarf-king in the German folk-legend *Laurin*, or *Der Kleine Rosengarten*. He possesses a magic ring, girdle, and cap, and is attacked in his rose-garden, which no one may enter on pain of death, by Dietrich of Bern. The poem belongs to the late 13th century, and is attributed to Heinrich von Offerdingen.

**Lavaine, Sir.** A knight of Arthurian romance, brother of Elaine, the 'lily maid of Astolat'. In Tennyson's *Elaine* (*Idylls of the King*) he accompanied Sir Lancelot when he went, *incognito*, to tilt for the ninth diamond. He is described as young, brave, and a true knight.

**Lavender.** The earliest form of the word is Med. Lat. *livendula*, and it is probably, like our *livid*, from *livere*, to make bluish; as, however, the plant has for centuries been used by laundresses for scenting linen, and in connection with the bath, later forms of the word are associated with *lavare*, to wash. The modern botanical name is *Lavandula*. It is a token of affection.

> He from his lass him lavender hath sent,
> Showing his love, and doth requital crave.
>
> Drayton, *Eclogue*

***Laid up in lavender.*** Taken great care of, laid away, as things are put in lavender to keep off moths. Persons who are in hiding, and even articles that are pawned, are said to be *in lavender*.

> The poore gentleman paies so deere for the lavender it is laid up in, that if it lies long at the broker's house he seems to buy his apparel twice.
>
> Greene, *A Quip for an Upstart Courtier* (1592)

**Lavinia.** Daughter of Latinus (*q.v.*), betrothed to Turnus, King of the Rutuli. When Aeneas landed in Italy, Latinus made an alliance with the Trojan hero, and promised to give him Lavinia to wife. This brought on a war between Turnus and Aeneas, which was decided by single combat, in which Aeneas was victor. (Virgil, *Aeneid*, vi.)

Shakespeare gives the name to the daughter of Titus Andronicus in the play of that name.

**Lavolta** (Ital., the turn). A lively dance, in which was a good deal of jumping or capering, whence its name. Troilus says, 'I cannot sing, nor heel the high lavolt' (*Troilus and Cressida*, 4, 4). It originated in the 16th century in Provence or Italy, and is thus described:

> A lofty jumping or a leaping round,
> Where arm in arm two dancers are entwined,
> And whirl themselves with strict embracements bound,
> And still their feet an anapest do sound.
>
> Sir John Davies, *The Orchestra* (1594)

**Law. *In-laws.*** A humorous way of referring to one's relations by marriage – mother-in-law, sisters-in-law, etc. *In-law* is short for *in Canon law*, the reference being to the degrees of affinity within which marriage is prohibited.

***Law-calf.*** A bookseller's term for a special kind of binding in plain sheep or calf used largely for law-books.

> Gentlemen who had no briefs to show carried under their arms goodly octaves, with a red label behind, and that underdone-pie-crust-coloured cover, which is technically known as 'law calf'.
>
> Dickens, *Pickwick Papers*, ch. xxxiv

***Law Latin.*** The debased Latin used in legal documents. *Cp.* Dog Latin.

***Law Lords.*** Members of the House of Lords who are qualified to deal with the judicial business of the

House, i.e. the Lord High Chancellor, the Lord Chief Justice, the Master of the Rolls, the Lords of Appeal in Ordinary (who are, as a rule, holders of life peerages only), and such peers as are holding or have held high judicial office.

***Possession is nine points of the law.*** *See* Nine.

***Quips of the law.*** *See* Cepola.

***The laws of the Medes and Persians.*** Unalterable laws.

> Now, O king ... sign the writing, that it be not changed, according to the law of the Medes and Persians which altereth not. Dan. 6:8

***The Man of Lawes Tale*** in Chaucer's *Canterbury Tales* (*see* Cunstance) is borrowed, with numerous interpolations, from the fabulous Anglo-French Chronicle by Nicholas Trivet, an English Dominican of the first half of the 14th century. Similar stories are found in Gower and in the metrical romance, *Emare*. The treason of the knight who murders Hermengilde resembles an incident in the French *Roman de la Violette*, the English metrical romance of *Le bone Florence of Rome* (in Ritson), and a tale in the *Gesta Romanorum*, c. 69.

***To give one law.*** A sporting term 'law', meaning the chance of saving oneself. Thus a hare or a stag is allowed 'law' – i.e. a certain start before any hound is permitted to attack it; and a tradesman allowed 'law' is one to whom time is given to 'find his legs'.

***To have the law of one.*** To take legal proceedings against him.

***To lay down the law.*** To speak in a dictatorial manner; to give directions or order in an offensive and high-handed way.

***To take the law into one's own hands.*** To try to secure satisfaction by force; to punish, reward, etc., entirely on one's own responsibility without obtaining the necessary authority.

**Law's Bubble.** *See* Mississippi Bubble.

**Lawing** (*Scots*). A tavern reckoning: from older Scots *lauch*, connected with old Norse *lag*, market-price.

> Landlady, count the lawin,
> The day is near the dawin;
> Ye're a blind drunk, boys,
> And I'm but jolly fou. Burns, *Song*

**Lawless Parliament, The.** Another name for the Unlearned Parliament (*q.v.*).

**Lawn.** Fine, thin cambric, used for the rochets of Anglican bishops, ladies' handkerchiefs, etc. So called from *Laon* (O.Fr. *Lan*), a town in the Aisne department of France, which used to be famous for its linen factories.

***Man of lawn.*** A bishop.

**Lawn-market.** The old place for executions in Edinburgh; hence, *to go up the Lawn-market*, in Scotch parlance, means to go to be hanged.

> Up the Lawn-market, down the West Bow,
> Up the lang ladder, down the short low.
> Schoolboy Rhyme (Scotland)

> They [the stolen clothes] may serve him to gang up the Lawn-market in, the scoundrel.
> Scott, *Guy Mannering*, ch. xxxii

**Lawrence, St.** The patron saint of curriers, who was broiled to death on a gridiron. He was deacon to Sextus I and was charged with the care of the poor, the orphans, and the widows. In the persecution of Valerian (258), being summoned to deliver up the treasures of the church, he produced the poor, etc., under his charge, and said to the praetor, 'These are the church's treasures.' He is generally represented as holding a gridiron, and is commemorated on August 10th.

The phrase *Lazy as Lawrence* is said to take its origin from the story that when being roasted over a slow fire he asked to be turned, 'for', said he, 'that side is quite done'. This expression of Christian fortitude was interpreted by his torturers as evidence of the height of laziness, the martyr being too indolent even to wriggle.

***St Lawrence's tears*** or ***The fiery tears of St Lawrence.*** *See* Shooting Stars.

**Lawyers' Bags.** Some red, some blue. In the Common Law, *red* bags are reserved for K.C.'s; but a stuff-gownsman may carry one 'if presented with it by a silk'. Only *red* bags may be taken into Common Law Courts, *blue* must be carried no farther than the robing-room. In Chancery Courts the etiquette is not so strict.

**Lay.** Pertaining to the people, or laity (Lat. *laicus*) as distinguished from the clergy. Thus, a *lay brother* is one who, though not in holy orders, is received into a monastery and is bound by its vows.

A *layman* is, properly speaking, anyone not in holy orders; but the term is also used by professional men – especially doctors and lawyers – to denote one not of their particular profession.

**Lay** (the verb). ***To lay about one.*** To strike out lustily on all sides.

> He'll lay about him today.
> Shakespeare, *Troilus and Cressida*, 1, 2

***To lay out.*** (*a*) To disburse.

(*b*) To display goods; place in convenient order what is required for wear.

(*c*) To prepare a corpse for the coffin, by placing the limbs in order, and dressing the body in its grave-clothes.

***To lay to one's charge.*** To attribute an offence to a person.

> And he [Stephen] kneeled down, and cried with a loud voice, Lord lay not this sin to their charge. Acts, 7:60. The phrase occurs again in the Bible, e.g. Deut. 21:8; Rom. 8:33, etc.

**Lay Figures.** Wooden figures with free joints, used by artists chiefly for the study of drapery. The word was earlier *layman*, from Dut. *leeman*, a contraction of *ledenman*, i.e. *led* (now *lid*), a joint, and *man*, man. Horace Walpole uses *layman* (1762), but *lay figure* had taken its place by the end of the 18th century.

**Layman.** *See* Lay Figure.

**Lazar House** or **Lazaretto.** A house for lazars, or poor persons affected with contagious diseases. So called from the beggar Lazarus (*q.v.*).

**Lazarillo de Tormes.** A comic romance, something in the *Gil Blas* style, the object being to satirise all classes of society. Lazarillo, a light, jovial, audacious manservant, sees his masters in their undress, and exposes their foibles. It was by Diego Hurtado de Mendoza, general and statesman of Spain, and was published in 1553.

**Lazarites.** A body of missionaries founded by St Vincent de Paul under order of Pope Urban VIII in 1632, and so termed from the priory of St Lazare, at Paris, which was their headquarters till 1792.

**Lazarone** (Ital.). The mob. Originally applied to Neapolitan vagrants who lived in the streets and idled about begging, now and then doing odd jobs. So called from the hospital of St Lazarus, which served as a refuge for the destitute of Naples. Every year they elected a chief, called the *Capo Lazzaro*. Masaniello, in 1647, with these vagabonds accomplished a revolution, and in 1798 Michele Sforza, at the head of the Lazzaroni, successfully resisted Championnet, the French general.

**Lazarus.** Any poor beggar; so called from the Lazarus of the parable, who was laid daily at the rich man's gate (Luke 16).

**Lazy. *Lazy as Ludlam's dog, which leaned his head against the wall to bark.*** Fable has it that Ludlam was a sorceress who lived in a cave near Farnham, Surrey. Her dog was so lazy that when the rustics came to consult her it would hardly condescend to give notice of their approach, even with the ghost of a bark. (Ray: *Proverbs.*)

***Lazy as Lawrence's dog*** is a similar old saying. *Lawrence* and *laziness* have for long been connected, probably owing to the alliteration, but possibly in allusion to the story told of St Lawrence (*q.v.*) at his martyrdom. One of Miss Edgeworth's tales, in the *Parents' Assistant*, is called *Lazy Lawrence*.

***Lazy-bones.*** A lazy fellow, a regular idler. The expression is some hundreds of years old.

> Go tell the Labourers, that the lazie bones
> That will not worke, must seeke the beggars gaines.
> Nicholas Breton, *Pasquil's Madcap* (1600)

***Lazy man's load.*** One too heavy to be carried; so called because lazy people, to save themselves the trouble of coming a second time, are apt to overload themselves.

**Lazzaroni.** *See* Lazarone.

**L'État c'est Moi** (Fr., I am the State). The reply traditionally ascribed to Louis XIV when the President of the Parlement of Paris offered objections 'in the interests of the State' to the king's fiscal demands. This was in 1655, when Louis was only 17 years of age; on this principle he acted with tolerable consistency throughout his long reign.

**Le Roi le Veut** (Fr., The king wills it). The form of royal assent made by the clerk of the old French Parlement to Bills submitted to the Crown. The dissent is expressed by *Le roi s'avisera* (the king will give it his consideration).

**Leach.** *See* Leech.

**Lead** (the metal) was, by the ancient alchemists, called Saturn.

***Swinging the lead.*** Army slang for concocting a plausible yarn out of which one hopes to derive some personal benefit. Soldiers 'swing the lead' when they make up a story about illness at home when they want to obtain leave, for instance, or when they give exaggerated accounts of their position in civil life with the idea of impressing their comrades.

The *lead*, or *blacklead*, of a *lead pencil* contains no lead at all, but is composed of plumbago or graphite, an almost pure carbon with a touch of iron. It was so named in the 16th century, when it was thought to be or to contain the metal.

***To strike lead.*** To make a good hit.

> That, after the failure of the king, he should 'strike lead' in his own house seemed … an inevitable law. Bret Harte, *Fool of Five Forks*

**Lead** (the verb; A.S. *laed-an*).

***To lead apes in hell.*** *See* Ape.

***To lead by the nose.*** *See* Nose.

***To lead one a pretty dance.*** *See* Dance.

**Leadenhall Market, Street,** etc. (City of London). So named from the ancient manor of the Nevilles, on the site of which the Leadenhall district is built. The name (La Ledenehalle) appears as early as 1296, and in a grant of 1315, when it was in the possession of Dame Margaret de Nevill, it is called 'la sale de plum (i.e. *Salle de plomb*, hall of lead) suz Cornhulle'. The origin of the name is unknown, but it may be that the mansion was roofed with lead, a notable thing in those days.

**Leader** or **leading article.** A newspaper article in large type, by the editor or one of the editorial staff. So called because it takes the lead or chief place in the summary of current topics, or because it is meant to lead public opinion. A short editorial article is called a *leaderette*.

The leading counsel in a case, the senior counsel on a circuit, the first fiddle of an orchestra, the first cornet of a military band, etc., is also called the *leader*.

**Leading.** ***Leading case.*** A lawsuit that forms a precedent in deciding others of a similar kind.

***Leading lady*** or ***man.*** The actress or actor who takes the chief role in a play.

***Leading note*** (***music***). The sharp seventh of the diatonic scale, which *leads* to the octave, only half a tone higher.

***Leading question.*** A question so worded as to suggest an answer. 'Was he dressed in a black coat?' leads to the answer 'Yes.' In cross-examining a witness, leading questions are permitted, because the chief object of a cross-examination is to obtain contradictions.

***Men of light and leading.*** Men capable of illuminating the way and guiding the steps of others. The phrase is Burke's:

> The men of England, the men, I mean, of light and leading in England … would be ashamed … to protest any religion in name, which, by their proceedings, they appear to contemn.
>
> *Reflections on the Revolution in France*

But he seems to have derived it from Milton, who, in his *Address to the Parliament*, prefixed to his notes on the *Judgment of Martin Bucer Concerning Divorce*, says:

> I owe no light, or leading received from any man in the discovery of this truth, what time I first undertook it in 'the Doctrine and Discipline of Divorce'.

Disraeli was rather fond of the phrase: he used it in *Sybil* – 'A public man of light and leading' (Bk v, ch. i) – as well as in speeches.

***To be in leading-strings*** is to be under the control of another. Leading-strings are those strings used for holding up infants just learning to walk.

**Leaf.** Before the invention of paper one of the substances employed for writing upon was the leaves of certain plants. The reverse and obverse pages of a book are still called leaves; and the double page of a ledger is termed a 'folio', from *folium*, a leaf. *Cp.* the derivation of *paper* itself, from *papyrus*, and *book*, from *boc*, a beech tree. There are many ancient MSS written on palm or other leaves still extant.

***To take a leaf out of my book.*** To imitate me; to do as I do. The allusion is to literary plagiarisms.

***To turn over a new leaf.*** To amend one's ways. The French equivalent is: *Je lui ferai chanter une autre chanson*. But in English 'To make a person sing another tune' means to make him eat his words, or change his note for one he will not like so well.

**League.** ***The Holy League.*** Several leagues are so denominated. The three following are the most important: 1511, by Pope Julius II; Ferdinand the Catholic, Henry VIII, the Venetians, and the Swiss against Louis XII; and that of 1576, founded at Peronne for the maintenance of the Catholic Faith and the exclusion of Protestant princes from the throne of France. This league was organised by the Guises to keep Henri IV from the throne.

***The League of Nations.*** A league, having headquarters at Geneva, formed after the close of the Great War of 1914–18, largely through the exertions of Mr Woodrow Wilson, President of the United States 1913–21, whose action was, however, repudiated by the United States, with the result that this nation is not a participator in the League.

With this exception the original members were the signatories of the Treaty of Peace at Versailles (June 28th, 1919), on behalf of the Allies, with certain other States (later entrants being here marked with an asterisk), viz.:

| | |
|---|---|
| *Albania. | China. |
| *Austria. | *Colombia. |
| Belgium. | *Costa Rica. |
| Bolivia. | Cuba. |
| Brazil. | Czecho Slovakia. |
| The British Empire. | *Denmark. |
| *Chile. | *Esthonia. |
| *Finland. | Panama. |

| | |
|---|---|
| France. | *Paraguay. |
| Greece. | *Persia. |
| Guatemala.. | Peru. |
| Haiti. | Poland. |
| Honduras | Portugal. |
| Italy. | Rumania. |
| Japan. | Salvador. |
| *Latvia. | Siam. |
| Liberia. | *Spain. |
| *Lithuania. | *Sweden. |
| *Luxemburg. | *Switzerland. |
| *Netherlands. | Uruguay. |
| *Nicaragua. | *Venezuela. |
| *Norway. | Yugo-Slavia. |

The territorial integrity and existing political independence of all members is guaranteed by the League, and in cases of dispute between members arbitration, with a time limit, is agreed upon. The League is founded on a Covenant and a Charter of XXVI Articles, the High Contracting Parties agreeing to the Covenant in order to promote International Co-operation and to achieve International Peace and Security, by the acceptance of obligations not to resort to War –

by the prescription of open, just, and honourable relations between Nations:

by the firm establishment of the understandings of International Law as the actual rule of conduct among Governments: and

by the maintenance of justice and a scrupulous regard for all Treaty Obligations in the dealings of Organised Peoples with one another.

The Council of the League consists of the representatives of the British Empire, France, Italy, and Japan, with four others elected from among the remaining members.

**Leak.** ***To leak out.*** To come clandestinely to public knowledge. As a liquid leaks out of an unsound vessel, so the secret oozes out unawares.

***To spring a leak.*** Said of ships, etc., that open or crack so as to admit the water.

**Leal.** Anglo-Fr. and O.Fr. *leel*, our loyal; trusty, law-abiding; now practically confined to Scotland.

***Land of the leal.*** *See* Land.

**Leander.** *See* Hero and Leander.

**Leaning Tower.** The one at Pisa, in Italy, the campanile of the cathedral, is 181 ft high, 57½ ft in diameter at the base, and leans about 14 ft. It was begun in 1174, and the sinking commenced during construction. At Caerphilly, in Glamorganshire, there is a tower which leans 11 ft in 80.

> The Leaning Tower of Pisa continues to stand because the vertical line drawn through its centre of gravity passes within its base.
>
> Ganot, *Physics*

**Leap Year.** A year of 366 days, a *bissextile* year (*q.v.*); i.e. in the Julian and Gregorian calendars any year whose date is exactly divisible by four except those which are divisible by 100 but not by 400. Thus 1900 (though exactly divisible by 4) was not a leap year, but 2000 will be.

In ordinary years the day of the month which falls on Monday this year will fall on Tuesday next year, and Wednesday the year after; but the fourth year will leap over Thursday to Friday. This is because a day is added to February, the reason being that the astronomical year (i.e. the time that it takes the earth to go round the sun) is approximately 365¼ days (365·2422), the difference between ·25 and ·2422 being righted by the loss of the three days in 400 years.

It is an old saying that during leap year *the ladies may propose, and, if not accepted, claim a silk gown.* Fable has it that the custom was originated by St Patrick, who was once told by St Bridget that a mutiny had broken out in her nunnery, the ladies claiming the right of 'popping the question', which seems a particularly strange thing for *nuns* to do. However, St Patrick said he would concede them the right every seventh year, when St Bridget threw her arms round his neck, and exclaimed, 'Arrah, Pathrick, jewel, I daurn't go back to the girls wid such a proposal. Make it one year in four.' St Patrick replied, 'Bridget, acushla, squeeze me that way agin, an' I'll give ye leap year, the longest of the lot.' St Bridget, upon this, popped the question to St Patrick himself, who, of course, could not marry; so he patched up the difficulty as best he could with a kiss and a silk gown.

An Act of the Scottish Parliament, passed in the year 1228, is said to have been unearthed which runs:

> Ordonit that during ye reign of her maist blessed maiestie, Margaret, ilka maiden ladee, of baith high and lowe estait, shall hae libertie to speak ye man she likes. Gif he refuses to tak hir to bee his wyf, he shale be mulct in the sum of ane hundridty pundes, or less, as his estait may bee, except and alwais gif he can make it appeare that he is betrothit to anither woman, then he schal be free.

The year 1228 was, of course, a leap year; but there was no 'blessed maiestie, Margaret', at the time, for Alexander II (married to Joanna, daughter of the English King John) reigned over Scotland from 1214 to 1249.

**Lear, King.** A legendary king of Britain, who in

his old age divided his kingdom between Goneril and Regan, two of his daughters, who professed great love for him. These two daughters drove the old man mad by their unnatural conduct, while the third, Cordelia (*q.v.*), who had been left portionless, succoured the old man and came with an army to dethrone her two sisters, but was captured and slain in prison. King Lear died over her body. (Shakespeare, *King Lear*.)

Camden tells a similar story of Ina, King of the West Saxons (*see Remains*, p. 306, 1674). The story of King Lear is given in the *Gesta Romanorum* (of a Roman emperor), in the old romance of *Perceforest*, and by Geoffrey of Monmouth in his *Chronicles*, whence Holinshed, Shakespeare's immediate source, transcribed it. Spenser introduced the same story into his *Faërie Queene* (II, x). *See* Lir.

**Learn.** ***To learn a person a thing,*** or ***to do something*** is now a provincialism, but was formerly quite good English. Thus, in the Prayer Book version of the Psalms we have 'Lead me forth in thy truth and learn me', and 'such as are gentle them shall he learn his way' (25:4, 8); and other examples of this use of *learn* as an active verb will be found at Ps.119:66 and 132:13.

> The red plague rid you
> For learning me your language.
>
> Shakespeare, *Tempest*, 1, 2

***To learn by heart.*** The heart is the seat of understanding; thus the Scripture speaks of men 'wise in heart'; and 'slow of heart' means dull of understanding. To learn by *heart* is to learn and understand, but we commonly employ the phrase as a synonym for committing to memory; to learn by *rote* is to learn so as to be able to repeat.

**Learned.** Coloman, king of Hungary (1095–1114), was called *The Learned*. *Cp.* Beauclerc.

***The learned Blacksmith.*** Elihu Burritt (1811–79), the linguist, who was at one time a blacksmith.

***The learned Painter.*** Charles Lebrun (1619–90), so called from the great accuracy of his costumes.

***The learned Tailor.*** Henry Wild, of Norwich (1684–1734), who mastered, while he worked at his trade, the Greek, Latin, Hebrew, Chaldaic, Syriac, Persian, and Arabic languages.

**Least Said the soonest Mended.** Explanations and apologies are quite useless, and only make bad worse.

**Leather.** ***Nothing like leather.*** My interest is the best nostrum. The story is that a town in danger of a siege called together a council of the chief inhabitants to know what defence they recommended. A mason suggested a strong wall, a shipbuilder advised 'wooden walls', and when others had spoken, a currier arose and said, 'There's nothing like leather.'

> Another version is, 'Nothing like leather to administer a thrashing.'

***It is all leather or prunella.*** Nothing of any moment, all rubbish; through a misunderstanding of the lines by Pope, who was drawing a distinction between the work of a cobbler and that of a parson.

> Worth makes the man, and want of it the fellow;
> The rest is all but leather or prunella.
>
> Pope, *Essay on Man*

Prunella is a worsted stuff, formerly used for clergymen's gowns, etc., and for the uppers of ladies' boots, and is probably so called because it was the colour of a *prune*.

**Leathering.** ***To give one a leathering.*** To beat him with a leather belt; hence, to give him a regular drubbing.

**Leatherstocking Novels.** The novels by Fenimore Cooper dealing with 'the wild West' in which Natty Bumpo, nicknamed *Leatherstocking* and *Hawkeye*, is a leading character. They are *The Pioneers* (1823), *The Last of the Mohicans* (1826), *The Prairie* (1826), *The Pathfinder* (1840), and *The Deerslayer* (1841). 'Leatherstocking' was a hardy backwoodsman, a type of the race who pushed into the Far West of North America as pioneers.

> [In the novels] there is little historical background, but the vivid descriptions of wood, lake, and prairie, and of the daily life of Indian and huntsman, give the finest picture extant of natural scenes and human conditions that have long passed away.
>
> Dr Baker, *Guide to the Best Fiction*

**Leave in the Lurch.** *See* Lurch.

**Leave out in the Cold, To.** To slight, to take little or no interest in a person; to pass by unnoticed. The allusion is to a person calling at a house with a friend and the friend not being asked to come in.

**Leave some for Manners.** In *Ecclesiasticus* it is written:

> Leave off first for manners' sake; and be not unsatiable, lest thou offend. 31:17

**Leaves without Figs.** Show of promise without fulfilment. Words without deeds. Keeping the promise to the ear and breaking it to the sense. Of course, the allusion is to the barren fig tree referred to in Luke 13.

**Leda.** In *Greek mythology*, the mother by Zeus (who is fabled to have come to her in the shape of a swan) of two eggs, from one of which came Castor and Clytemnestra, and from the other Pollux and Helen. The subject of Leda and the Swan has been a favourite with artists. Paul Veronese, Correggio, and Michael Angelo have all left paintings of it.

**Leda Bible, The.** *See* Bible, specially named.

**Lee.** In nautical language, the side or quarter opposite to that against which the wind blows; the sheltered side, the side away from the windward or weather side. From A.S. *hlēo, hlēow*, a covering or shelter.

***Lee shore.*** The shore under the lee of a ship, or that towards which the wind blows.

***Lee side.*** *See* Leeward.

***Lee tide.*** A tide running in the same direction as the wind blows; if in the opposite direction it is called *a tide under the lee*.

***Take care of the lee hatch.*** A warning to the helmsman to beware lest the ship goes to the leeward of her course – i.e. the part towards which the wind blows.

***To lay a ship by the lee.*** An obsolete phrase for to heave to; i.e. to arrange the sails of a ship flat against the masts and shrouds so that the wind strikes the vessel broadside and thus causes her to make little or no headway.

***Under the lee of the land.*** Under the shelter of the cliffs which break the force of the winds.

***Under the lee of a ship.*** On the side opposite to the wind, so that the ship shelters or wards it off.

**Leech.** One skilled in medicine or 'leech-craft'; the word, which is now obsolete, is the A.S. *laece*, one who relieves pain, from *lacnian*, to heal. The blood-sucking worm, the *leech*, gets its name probably from the same word, *the healer*.

> And straightway sent, with carefull diligence,
> To fetch a leach the which had great insight
> In that disease. Spenser, *Faërie Queene*, I, x, 23

***Leech-finger.*** *See* Medicinal Finger.

**Leeds.** The Stock Exchange term for Lancashire and Yorkshire Railway Ordinary Stock.

**Leek.** The national emblem of Wales. The story is that St David, patron saint of the Welsh, on one occasion caused his countrymen under King Cadwallader to distinguish themselves from their Saxon foes by wearing a leek in their caps.

Shakespeare makes out that the Welsh wore leeks at the battle of Poitiers, for Fluellen says:

> If your majesties is remembered of it, the Welshmen did good service in a garden where leeks did grow, wearing leeks in their Monmouth caps, which, your majesty know, to this hour is an honourable badge of the service; and I do believe your majesty takes no scorn to wear the leek upon St Tavy's Day. *Henry V*, 4, 7

***To eat the leek.*** To be compelled to eat your own words, or retract what you have said. Fluellen (in Shakespeare's *Henry V*) is taunted by Pistol for wearing a leek in his hat. 'Hence,' says Pistol, 'I am qualmish at the smell of leek.' Fluellen replies, 'I beseech you … at my desire … to eat this leek.' The ancient answers, 'Not for Cadwallader and all his goats.' Then the peppery Welshman beats him, nor desists till Pistol has swallowed the entire abhorrence.

**Lees.** ***There are lees to every wine.*** The best things have some defect. A French proverb.

> Doubt is the lees of thought.
> Boker, *Doubt*, etc., i, 11

***Settling on the lees.*** Making the best of a bad job; settling down on what is left, after having squandered the main part of one's fortune.

**Leet** or **Court-leet.** A manor court for petty offences, held once a year; the day on which it was held. The word is probably connected with A.S. *lathe* (*q.v.*), a division of a county.

> Who has a breast so pure,
> But some uncleanly apprehensions
> Keep leets and law-days and in session sit
> With meditations lawful?
> Shakespeare, *Othello*, 3, 3

**Leeward.** Toward the lee (*q.v.*), or that part towards which the wind blows; *windward* is in the opposite direction, viz., in the teeth of the wind. *See* A-weather: Lee.

**Left.** The *left* side of anything is frequently considered to be unlucky, of bad omen (*cp.* Augury; Sinister), the *right* the reverse.

In politics the *left* is the opposition, the party which, in a legislative assembly, sits on the left of the Speaker or President. The *left wing* of a party is composed of its extremists, the 'irreconcilables'.

***A left-handed compliment.*** A compliment which insinuates a reproach.

***A left-handed marriage.*** A morganatic marriage (*q.v.*), in which the husband gave his *left* hand to the bride instead of the right, when saying, 'I take thee for my wedded wife.'

***A left-handed oath.*** An oath not intended to be binding.

***Over the left.*** A way of expressing disbelief,

incredulity, or a negative. The allusion is, perhaps, to morganatic marriages (*q.v.*). When a woman so married claimed to be a wedded wife, she could be told that such was the case 'over the left'.

**Leg.** In many phrases, e.g. 'to find one's legs', 'to put one's best leg foremost', *leg* is interchangeable with *foot* (*q.v.*).

***Leg and leg.*** Equal, or nearly so, in a race, game, etc. *Cp.* Neck and neck.

***On his legs.*** Mr So-and-So is on his legs, has risen to make a speech.

***On its last legs.*** Moribund; obsolete; ready to fall out of cognisance.

***Show a leg, there!*** Jump out of bed and be sharp about it! A phrase from the Navy.

***To give a leg up.*** To render timely assistance, 'to help a lame dog over a stile'. Originally from horsemanship – to help one into the saddle.

***To have good sea legs.*** To be a good sailor; to be able to stand the motion of the ship without getting sea sick.

***To make a leg.*** To make a bow, especially an old-fashioned obeisance, drawing one leg backward.

> The pursuivant smiled at their simplicitye,
> And making many leggs, tooke their reward.
>
> *The King and Miller of Mansfield*

***To set on his legs.*** So to provide for one that he is able to earn his living without further help.

***To stand on one's own legs.*** To be independent, to be earning one's own living. Of course, the allusion is to being nursed, and standing 'alone'.

***Without a leg to stand on.*** Divested of all support; tottering, on the brink of ruin; with no chance of success.

**Leg-bail.** A runaway. *To give leg-bail*, to cut and run.

**Leg Bye.** In cricket, a run scored from a ball which has glanced off any part of a batsman's person except his hand.

**Leg of Mutton School, The.** So Eckhart called those authors who lauded their patrons in prose or verse, under the hope of gaining a commission, a living, or, at the very least, a dinner for their pains.

**Legal tender.** Money which, by the law of the particular country, a creditor is bound to accept in discharge of a debt. In England the tender of gold, Treasury notes, and Bank of England notes is legal up to any amount, with the one exception that a creditor of the Bank of England cannot be compelled to receive his money in Bank of England notes. Silver is not legal tender for sums over forty shillings, nor bronze for sums over one shilling.

**Legem Pone.** Old slang for money paid down on the nail, ready money; from the opening words of the first of the psalms appointed to be read on the twenty-fifth morning of the month – *Legem pone mihi, Domine, viam justificationum tuarum* (Teach me, O Lord, the way of thy statutes, Ps. 119:33). March 25th is the first pay-day of the year, and thus the phrase became associated with cash down.

> Use *legem pone* to pay at thy day,
> But use not *oremus* for often delay.
>
> Tusser, *Good Husbandry* (1557)

*Oremus* (let us pray) is in frequent use in the Roman Catholic liturgy. Its application to a debtor who is suing for further time is obvious.

**Legend.** Literally and originally, 'something to be read' (Lat. *legenda*, from *legere*, to read); hence the narratives of the lives of saints and martyrs were so termed from their being read, especially at matins, and after dinner in the refectories. Exaggeration and a love for the wonderful so predominated in these readings, that the word came to signify a traditional story, especially one popularly regarded as true, a fable, a myth.

> A *myth* is a pure and absolute imagination; a *legend* has a basis of fact, but amplifies, abridges, or modifies that basis at pleasure.
>
> Rawlinson, *Historic Evidences*, lecture i, p. 231, note 2

In *Numismatics* the legend is the inscription impressed in letters on a coin or medal. Formerly the words on the obverse only (i.e. round the head of the sovereign) were called the *legend*, the words on the reverse being the inscription; but this distinction is no longer recognised by numismatics.

**Legenda Aurea.** *See* Golden Legend.

**Leger.** *See* St Leger.

**Legion.** ***My name is Legion: for we are many*** (Mark 5:9). A proverbial expression somewhat similar to hydra-headed. Thus, in bad times we say of the unemployed, 'Their name is Legion'; so also of diseases arising from want of cleanliness, the evils of ignorance, and so on.

***The Thundering Legion.*** *See* Thundering.

**Legion of Honour.** An order of distinction and reward instituted by Napoleon in 1802, for either military or civil merit.

It was, at the outset, limited to 15 *cohortes*, each

composed of 7 *grands officiers*, 20 *commandants*, 30 *officiers*, and 350 *légionnaires*, making in all 6,105 members; but it was reorganised by Louis XVIII in 1814, and again by Napoleon III in 1852, and now comprises 80 *grands croix*, 200 *grands officiers*, 1,000 *commandeurs*, 4,000 *officiers*, with *chevaliers* to whose creation there is no fixed limit.

The order holds considerable property, out of which it distributes pensions to members and maintains schools for their daughters.

**Leglen-girth.** ***To cast a leglen-girth.*** To have made a *faux pas*, particularly by having an illegitimate child; to have one's reputation blown upon. *Leglen* is Scottish for a milk-pail, and a *leglen-girth* is its lowest hoop.

**Leicester.** The town gets its name from Lat. *Legionis castra*, the camp of the legion, it having been the headquarters of a legion during the Roman occupation of Britain. *Caerleon*, in Wales, *Leon*, Spain, and *Ledjûn*, in Palestine, owe their names to the same cause.

***Leicester Square*** (London). So called from the family mansion of the Sydneys, Earls of Leicester, which stood on the north-east side in the 17th century.

**Lely** (*Sir Peter*), the painter, was the son of Vander Vaas or Faes, of Westphalia, whose house had a lily for its sign. Both father and son went by the nickname of Le-lys (the Lily), a sobriquet which Peter afterwards adopted as his cognomen.

**Lemnian Earth.** A kind of bole, or clayey earth, of a reddish or yellowish grey colour, found in the island of Lemnos, said to cure the bites of serpents and other wounds. It was made into cakes, and was called *terra sigillata*, because these were sealed by a priest before being vended.

**Lemnos.** The island where Vulcan fell when Jupiter flung him out of heaven. One myth connected with Lemnos tells how the women of the island, in revenge for their ill-treatment, murdered all the men. The Argonauts (*q.v.*) found the place an 'Adamless Eden'; they were received with great favour by the women, and as a result of their few months' stay the island was repopulated: the queen, Hypsipyle, became the mother of twins by Jason.

**Lemon.** ***Lemon, Salts of.*** *See* Misnomers.

***Lemon sole.*** The name of the flat-fish has nothing to do with the fruit but is from *limande*, a dab or flat-fish. This may be connected with O. Fr. *limande*, a flat board, but may also be from Lat. *limus*, mud, the fish being essentially a bottom fish.

***The answer's a lemon.*** A senseless and ridiculous repartee; used as a form of reply to some particularly silly or unanswerable conundrum. If it means anything it means much the same as, *Ask me another!* or *Go and boil your head!*

**Lemster Ore.** Fine wool, of which Leominster carpets are made.

> A bank of moss,
> Spongy and swelling, and far more
> Soft, than the finest Lemster ore.
>
> Herrick, *Oberon's Palace*

**Lemures.** The name given by the Romans to the spirits of the dead, especially spectres which wandered about at night-time to terrify the living. *Cp.* Larvae. (Ovid, *Fasti*, v.)

> The lars and lemures moan with midnight plaint.
>
> Milton, *Ode on the Nativity*

**Lemuria.** The name given to a lost land that is supposed to have connected Madagascar with India and Sumatra in prehistoric times. *See* W. Scott Elliott's *The Lost Lemuria* (1904). *Cp.* Atlantis.

**Lens** (Lat., a lentil or bean). Glasses used in optical instruments are so called because the double convex one, which may be termed the perfect lens, is of a bean shape.

**Lent** (A.S. *lencten*). *Lenctentid* (spring tide) was the Saxon name for March, because in this month there is a manifest lengthening of the days. As the chief part of the great fast, from Ash Wednesday to Easter, falls in March, this period received the name of the *Lencten-faesten*, or Lent.

The fast of thirty-six days was introduced in the 4th century. Felix III (483–492) added four days in 487, to make it correspond with our Lord's fast in the wilderness.

***Galeazzo's Lent.*** A form of torture devised by Galeazzo Visconti, Duke of Milan, 1395–1402, calculated to prolong the unfortunate victim's life for forty days.

***Lent lily.*** The daffodil, which blooms in Lent.

**Lenten.** Frugal, stinted, as food in Lent. Shakespeare has 'lenten entertainment' (*Hamlet*, 2, 2); 'a lenten answer' (*Twelfth Night*, 1, 5); 'a lenten pye' (*Romeo and Juliet*, 2, 4).

> And with a lenten salad cooled her blood.
>
> Dryden, *Hind and Panther*, iii, 27

**Leodogrance,** of Camiliard, the father of Guinevere, wife of King Arthur.

**Leonard, St.** A Frank at the court of Clovis in the 6th century. He founded the monastery of Noblac, and is the patron saint of prisoners, Clovis having given him permission to release all whom he visited. He is usually represented as a deacon, and holding chains or broken fetters in his hand.

**Leonidas of Modern Greece.** Marco Bozzaris, who with 1,200 men put to rout 4,000 Turco-Albanians, at Kerpenisi, but was killed in the attack (1823). He was buried at Missolonghi.

**Leonine.** Lion-like; also, relating to one of the popes named *Leo*, as *the Leonine City*, the part of Rome surrounding the Vatican, which was fortified by Leo IV in the 9th century.

***Leonine contract.*** A one-sided agreement; so called in allusion to the fable of *The Lion and his Fellow-Hunters*. *Cp.* Glaucus Swop, *under* Glaucus.

***Leonine Verses.*** Latin hexameters, or alternate hexameters and pentameters, rhyming at the middle and end of each respective line. These fancies were common in the 12th century, and are said to have been popularised by and so called from Leoninus, a canon of the Church of St Victor, in Paris; but there are many such lines in the classic poets, particularly Ovid. In English verse, any metre which rhymes middle and end may be called a Leonine verse. One of the most noted specimens of the true Leonine tells of a Jew who fell into a pit on Saturday and refused to be helped out because it was his Sabbath. His comrade, being a Christian, refused to aid him the day following, because it was Sunday:

> Tende manus, *Salomon*, ego te de stercore *collam*.
> Sabbata nostra *colo*, de stercore surgere *nolo*.
> Sabbata nostra *quidem* Salomon celebrabis *ibidem*.
> 'Help for you out of this mire; here give me your hand, Hezekiah.'
> 'No! 'tis the Sabbath, a time labour's accounted a crime.
> If on the morrow you've leisure, your aid I'll accept with much pleasure.'
> 'That will be my Sabbath, so, here I will leave you and go.' E.C.B.

**Leopard.** So called because it was thought in mediaeval times to be a cross between the lion (*leo*), or lioness, and the *pard*, which was the name given to a panther that had no white specks on it.

References to the impossibility of a leopard changing its spots are frequent; the allusion is to Jeremiah 13:23.

> Lions make leopards tame.
> Yea; but not change his spots.
> Shakespeare, *Richard II*, 1, 1

In Christian art the leopard represents that beast spoken of in Revelation 13:1–8, with seven heads and ten horns; six of the heads bear a nimbus, but the seventh, being 'wounded to death', lost its power, and consequently is bare.

> And the beast which I saw was like unto a leopard, and his feet were as the feet of a bear, and his mouth as the mouth of a lion. Rev. 13:2

In heraldry the leopard is supposed to typify warriors who have performed some bold enterprise with force, courage, promptitude, and activity. The lions in the royal coat of arms of England were formerly called and depicted as leopards, the idea being that no lion would permit another to remain on the same field.

> Talbot bidding his men
> 'renew the fight,
> Or tear the lions out of England's coat'
> Shakespeare, *1 Henry VI*, 1, 5
> has Elizabethan words in his mouth, for the 'lion passant gardant' of the Tudor heralds was a 'leopard' for the mediaeval kings and their followers.
> Oswald Barron, in *Shakespeare's England*, vol. ii, p. 90

***The Knight of the Couching Leopard.*** Sir Kenneth, or rather the Earl of Huntingdon, Prince Royal of Scotland, who followed, *incognito*, Richard I to the Crusade, and is the chief character of Scott's *Talisman*.

**Leopolita Bible.** *See* Bible, specially named.

**Leprachaun.** The fairy shoemaker of Ireland; so called because he is always seen working at a single shoe (*leith*, half, *brog*, a shoe or brogue). Another of his peculiarities is that he has a purse that never contains more than a single shilling.

> Do you not catch the tiny clamour,
> Busy click of an elfin hammer,
> Voice of the Leprachaun singing shrill,
> As he merrily plies his trade?
> W. B. Yeats, *Fairy and Folk Tales*

He is also called lubrican, cluricaune (*q.v.*), etc. In Dekker and Middleton's *Honest Whore* (Pt II, III, i), Hippolito speaks of Bryan, the Irish footman, as 'your Irish lubrican'.

**Lerna.** ***A Lerna of ills*** (***malorum Lerna***). A very great evil. Lake Lerna is where Hercules destroyed the hydra which did incalculable evil to Argos.

> Spain was a Lerna of ills to all Europe while it aspired to universal monarchy.
> P. Motteux, *Preface to Rabelais*

**Lesbian.** Pertaining to Lesbos, one of the islands of the Greek Archipelago, or to Sappho, the famous poetess of Lesbos, and to the practices attributed to her.

**_The Lesbian Poets._** Terpander, Alcaeus, Arion, and Sappho, all of Lesbos.

**_The Lesbian rule._** A flexible rule used by ancient Greek masons for measuring curved mouldings, etc.; hence, figuratively, a pliant and accommodating principle or rule of conduct.

**Lèse Majesté.** High treason, a crime against the sovereign (Lat. *laesa majestas*, hurt or violated majesty). In pre-war Germany, the last Kaiser, William II, had such exaggerated ideas of himself and his office that it was not difficult for a German subject to be guilty of this crime without being in the least aware of it.

**Lessian Diet.** Great abstinence; so called from Leonard Lessius (d.1623), a physician who prescribed very stringent rules for diet. *Cp.* Banting.

**Lestrigons.** A fabulous race of cannibal giants who lived in Sicily. Ulysses (*Odyss.* x) sent two of his men to request that he might land, but the king of the place ate one for dinner and the other fled. The Lestrigons assembled on the coast and threw stones against Ulysses and his crew; they fled with all speed, but many men were lost. *Cp.* Polyphemus.

**Let,** to permit, is the A.S. *laet-an*, to suffer or permit; but *let*, to hinder, now obsolete or archaic, is the verb *lett-an*.

> Oftentimes I purposed to come unto you, but was let hitherto. Rom. 1:18
>
> Yf any man had rathere bestowe thys tyme upon hys owne occupatyon ... he is not letted nor prohibited. More, *Utopia*, II, iv

**Lethe.** In *Greek mythology*, one of the rivers of Hades, which the souls of all the dead are obliged to taste, that they may forget everything said and done when alive. (Gr. *letho*, *latheo*, *lanthano*, to cause persons not to know.)

> Here, in a dusky vale where Lethe rolls
> Old Bavius sits, to dip poetic souls,
> And blunt the sense. Pope, *Dunciad*, iii, 23

**Lethean dew.** Dreamy forgetfulness; a brown study.

> The soul with tender luxury you [Muses] fill,
> And o'er the senses Lethean dews distill.
> Falconer, *The Shipwreck*, iii, 4

**Letter.** The name of a character used to represent a sound, and of a missive or written message, are, through O.Fr. *lettre*, both from Lat. *littera*, a letter of the alphabet, the plural of which (*litterae*) denoted an epistle. The plural, with the meaning literature, learning, erudition (as in *man of letters*, *republic of letters*, etc.), dates in English from at least the time of King Alfred, and is seen in Cicero's *otium literatum*, lettered ease.

The number of letters in the English alphabet is 26, but in a fount of type 206 characters are required; these are made up of Roman lower-case (i.e. small letters), capitals, and small capitals; included are the diphthongs (Æ, ae, etc.) and ligatures (ff, fi, fl, ffi, ffl), the remaining characters being the accented letters, i.e. those with the grave (\`), acute (´), circumflex (ˆ), diaeresis (¨), or tilde (˜), and the 'cedilla c (ç)'. To these characters must be added the figures, fractions, points (, !, etc.), brackets, reference marks (*, §, etc.), and commercial and mathematical signs (£, %, +, etc.) in common use. *Cp.* Typographical Signs; Font.

The proportionate use of the letters of the alphabet is given as follows:

| | | | | | | | |
|---|---|---|---|---|---|---|---|
| E | 1,000 | H | 540 | F | 236 | K | 88 |
| T | 770 | R | 528 | W | 190 | J | 55 |
| A | 728 | D | 392 | Y | 184 | Q | 50 |
| I | 704 | L | 360 | P | 168 | X | 46 |
| S | 680 | U | 296 | G | 168 | Z | 22 |
| O | 672 | C | 280 | B | 158 | | |
| N | 670 | M | 272 | V | 120 | | |

Consonants, 5,977. Vowels, 3,400.

Another 'fount-scheme' gives a rather different order, viz. e, t, a, o, i, n, s, r, h, d, l, u, c, m, f, w, y, p, g, b, v, k, j, q, x, fi, ff, fl, z, ffi, ffl. 'e' accounts for 7·83 per cent. of the fount, 'z' for 0·17, and the first twelve characters here given for 50 per cent. of the whole. The least wanted character is the italic capital *Ç*, of which it has been calculated that only five are necessary for a million type.

As initials the order of frequency is very different, the proportion being:

| | | | | | | | |
|---|---|---|---|---|---|---|---|
| S | 1,194 | M | 439 | W | 272 | Q | 58 |
| C | 937 | F | 388 | G | 266 | K | 47 |
| P | 804 | I | 377 | U | 228 | Y | 23 |
| A | 574 | E | 340 | O | 206 | Z | 18 |
| T | 571 | H | 308 | V | 172 | X | 4 |
| D | 505 | L | 298 | N | 153 | | |
| B | 463 | R | 291 | J | 69 | | |

*See also* Type; Font.

**Letter-Gae.** A jocular Scottish name (after Allan Ramsay, 1715) for the precentor of a kirk, he who leads off the singing, and *lets go*.

> There were no sae mony hairs on the warlock's face as there's on Letter-gae's ain at this moment.
> Scott, *Guy Mannering*, ch. xi

**Letter-lock.** A lock that cannot be opened unless letters on exterior movable rings are arranged in a certain order.

> A strange lock that opens with A M E N.
> Beaumont and Fletcher, *Noble Gentleman*

**Letter of Bellerophon.** *See* Bellerophon.

**Letter of Credit.** A letter written by a merchant or banker to another, requesting him to credit the bearer with certain sums of money. *Circular Notes* are letters of credit carried by gentlemen when they travel.

**Letter of Licence.** An instrument in writing made by a creditor, allowing a debtor longer time for the payment of his debt.

**Letter of Marque.** A commission authorising a privateer to make reprisals on a hostile nation till satisfaction for injury has been duly made. *Marque* is from Provençal *marcar*, Med. Lat. *marcare*, to seize as a pledge.

**Letter of Safe Conduct.** A writ under the Great Seal, guaranteeing safety to and fro to the person named in the passport.

**Letter of Slains.** In old Scottish law a petition to the Crown from the relatives of a murdered person, declaring that they have received satisfaction (*assythment*), and asking pardon for the murderer.

> You are aware the blood-wit was made up … by assythment, and that I have since expedited letters of slains.
> Scott, *Waverley*, xlviii

**Letter of Uriah.** *See* Uriah.

**Letters Missive.** An order from the Lord Chancellor to a peer to put in an appearance to a bill filed in chancery.

**Letters of Administration.** The legal instrument granted by the Probate Court to a person appointed administrator to one who has died intestate.

**Letters of Horning.** In Scottish history, signed orders putting rebels to the horn. *See* Horn.

**Letters of Junias.** *See* Junius.

**Letters Patent,** or **Overt.** *See* Patent.

**Lettres de Cachet.** *See* Cachet.

**Leucadia** or **Leucas.** One of the Ionian Islands, now known as Santa Maura. Here is the promontory from which Sappho threw herself into the sea when she found her love for Phaon was in vain.

> Haste, Sappho, haste, from high Leucadia throw
> Thy wretched weight, nor dread the deeps below!
> There injured lovers, leaping from above,
> Their flames extinguish, and forget to love.
> Pope, *Sappho to Phaon*

**Leucippus.** Founder of the Atomistic School of Greek philosophy (about 500 BC).

**Leucothea (*The White Goddess*).** So Ino, the mortal daughter of Cadmus and wife of Athamas, was called after she became a sea goddess. Athamas in a fit of madness slew one of her sons; she threw herself into the sea with the other, imploring assistance of the gods, who deified both of them. Her son, Melicertes, then renamed Palaemon, was called by the Romans Portunus, or Portumnus, and became the protecting genius of harbours.

> By Leucothea's lovely hands,
> And her son who rules the strands!
> Milton, *Comus*, 896–7

**Levant.** ***He has levanted*** – i.e. made off, decamped. A *levanter* is an absconder, especially one who makes a bet, and runs away without paying his bet if he loses. From Span. *levantar el campo*, or *la casa*, to break up the camp or house.

**Levant and Couchant.** Applied in legal phraseology to cattle which have strayed into another's field, and have been there long enough to lie down and sleep. The owner of the field can demand compensation for such intrusion. (Lat. *levantes et cubantes*, rising up and going to bed.)

**Levant and Ponent Winds.** The east wind is the Levant, and the west wind the Ponent. The former is from Lat. *levare*, to raise (sunrise), and the latter from *ponere*, to set (sunset).

> Forth rush the Levant and the Ponent winds.
> Milton, *Paradise Lost*, x, 704

> Levant, the region, strictly speaking, means the eastern shore of the Mediterranean; but is often applied to the whole East.

**Levée** (Fr., lit., a rising, i.e. from bed). An official reception of men only by the sovereign or his representative, held usually in the afternoon.

It was customary for the queens of France to receive at the hour of their *levée* – i.e. while making their toilet – the visits of certain noblemen. The court physicians, messengers from the king, the queen's secretary, and some few others demanded admission as a right, so ten or more persons were often in the dressing-room while the queen was making her toilet and sipping her coffee.

***Levée en masse*** (Fr.). A patriotic rising of a whole nation to defend their country.

**Level.** ***Level-headed.*** Shrewd, business-like, characterised by common sense; said of one who 'has his head screwed on the right way'.

***To do one's level best.*** To exert oneself to the utmost. This term, and that above, were originally American slang, and come from the gold-diggings of California.

***To find one's own level.*** Said of a person who, after making an unsuccessful start, arrives at the position in society, business, etc., to which his gifts or attainments entitle him.

***To level up,*** or ***down.*** To bring whatever is being spoken of – as the state of some class of society, the standard of wages, and so on – up or down to the level of some similar thing.

> Your levellers wish to level *down* as far as themselves; but they cannot bear levelling *up* to themselves.
>
> Dr Johnson, *Remark to Boswell*, 1763

**Levellers.** In English history, a body of ultra-Republicans in the time of Charles I and the Commonwealth, who wanted all men to be placed on a level, particularly with respect to their eligibility to office. John Lilburne was one of the leaders of the sect, which was active from 1647 to 1649, when it was suppressed by Cromwell's troops.

In Irish history the name was given to the 18th century agrarian agitators, afterwards called Whiteboys (*q.v.*). Their first offences were levelling the hedges of enclosed commons; but their programme developed into a demand for the general redress of all agrarian grievances.

**Lever de Rideau** (Fr., curtain-raiser). A short sketch performed on the stage before 'drawing up the curtain' on the real business.

**Leviathan.** The name (Hebrew for 'that which gathers itself together in folds', *Cp.* Is. 27:1) given in the Bible to a mythic sea-serpent, though in Job 40:1, it is possible that the reference is to the crocodile. *Cp.* Behemoth.

The name is applied to a ship of great size –

> Like leviathans afloat
> Lay their bulwarks on the brine.
>
> Campbell, *Battle of the Baltic*

from the reference in Ps. 104:25, 26 –

> This great and wide sea, wherein are things creeping innumerable, both small and great beasts. There go the ships: there is that leviathan, whom thou hast made to play therein.

But this is a mistranslation of the Hebrew, the correct rendering being – according to Dr Cheyne –

> ... There dragons move along; (yea), Leviathan whom thou didst appoint ruler therein.

Hobbes took the name as the title for his treatise on 'the Matter, Forme, and Power of a Commonwealth Ecclesiasticall and Civil' (1651), and applied it to the Commonwealth as a political organism. He says:

> I have set forth the nature of man, (whose Pride and other Passions have compelled him to submit himselfe to Government;) together with the great power of his Governour whom I compared to *Leviathan,* taking that comparison out of the two last verses of the one and fortieth of *Job*; where God having set forth the great power of *Leviathan*, calleth him King of the Proud.
>
> *Leviathan*, Pt ii, ch. xxviii

***The Leviathan of Literature.*** Dr Johnson (1709–84).

**Levites.** In Dryden's *Absalom and Achitophel* (*q.v.*), means the Dissenting clergy who were expelled by the Act of Conformity.

**Lewis Baboon.** Louis XIV of France is so called in Arbuthnot's *History of John Bull.* Of course, there is a play upon the word Bourbon.

**Lex non scripta** (Lat., unwritten law). The common law, as distinguished from the statute or written law. Common law does not derive its force from being recorded, and though its several provisions have been compiled and printed, the compilations are not statutes, but simply remembrancers.

**Lex talionis** (Lat.). The law of retaliation; tit for tat.

**Leyden jar.** A glass vessel partly coated, inside and out, with lead foil, and used to accumulate electricity; invented by Vanleigh, of Leyden, Holland, in 1745.

**Lia-fail.** The Irish name of the Coronation Stone, or Stone of Destiny, of the ancient Irish kings. *See* Scone; Tanist Stone.

**Liakura.** The modern name of Mount Parnassus (*q.v.*).

> But where is he that hath beheld
> The peak of Liakura unveiled.
>
> Byron, *The Giaour*

**Liar. *I'm a bit of a liar myself!*** A satirical phrase, originating in America, addressed to one who is manifestly 'drawing the long bow' or 'playing Munchausen'.

***Liars should have good memories.*** This old proverb, which is found in many languages and was quoted by St Jerome in the 4th century, has been traced to Quintillian's *Mendacem memorem esse oportet.* 'It is fitting that a liar should be a man of good memory' (*Institutes*, IV, ii, 91). It occurs in Taverner's translation of Erasmus's *Proverbs* (1539) –

> A lyer ought not to be forgetfull.

And Montaigne says (*Essayes*, I, ix):

> It is not without reason, men say, that *he who hath not a good and readie memorie, should never meddle with telling of lies, and feare to become a liar.*

**Libeaus Desconus.** *See* Lybius.

**Libel** (Lat. *libellus*, a little book). A writing of a defamatory nature, one which contains malicious statements ridiculing someone or calculated to bring him into disrepute, etc.; a lampoon, a satire. Originally a plaintiff's statement of his case, which usually 'defames' the defendant, was called a 'libel', for it made a 'little book'.

***The greater the truth, the greater the libel***, a dictum of Lord Ellenborough (about 1789), who amplified it by the explanation – 'if the language used were true, the person would suffer more than if it were false'.

For, oh 'twas nuts to the Father of Lies
(As this wily fiend is nam'd in the Bible)
To find it settled by laws so wise,
That the greater the truth, the worse the libel
Thos Moore, *A Case of Libel*

Burns, in some lines written at Stirling, attributes the saying to the Earl of Mansfield –

Dost not know that old Mansfield, who writes like the Bible,
Says: 'The more 'tis a truth, sir, the more 'tis a libel?'

**Liber Albus** (Lat., the white book). A compilation of the laws and customs of the City of London, made in 1419, by John Carpenter, town clerk.

**Liber Niger. *The Black Book of the Exchequer***, compiled by Gervase of Tilbury, in the reign of Henry II. It is a roll of the military tenants.

**Liberal.** A political term introduced in the early 19th century from Spain and France (where it denoted 'advanced' or revolutionary politicians), and employed in 1815 by Byron, Leigh Hunt, and others as the title of a periodical representing their views in politics, religion, and literature. It was originally bestowed upon the advanced Whigs as a term of reproach, but when the moderate Whigs formed a coalition with the Tories and the advanced Whigs with the Radicals, it was adopted by the latter party; it came into general use about 1831, when the Reform Bill, in Lord Grey's Ministry, gave it prominence.

Influenced in a great degree by the philosophy and the politics of the Continent, they [the Whigs] endeavoured to substitute cosmopolitan for national principles, and they baptised the new scheme of politics with the plausible name of 'Liberalism'. Disraeli, June 24, 1872

***Liberal Unionists***. Those Liberals who united, in 1886, with Lord Salisbury and the Conservative party to oppose Home Rule for Ireland. Lord Hartington, afterwards Duke of Devonshire, and Mr Joseph Chamberlain were the chief of those who seceded.

**Liberator, The.** The Peruvians so call Simon Bolivar (1783–1830), who established the independence of Peru. Daniel O'Connell (1775–1847) was also so called, because he led the agitation which resulted in the repeal of the Penal Laws and the Emancipation of the Irish Roman Catholics.

***Liberator of the World***. So Benjamin Franklin (1706–90) has been called.

**Libertarians.** *See* Agent.

**Libertine.** A debauchee, a dissolute person; one who puts no restraint on his personal indulgence.

A libertine, in earlier use, was a speculative free-thinker in matters of religion and in the theory of morals ... but [it has come] to signify a profligate.
Trench, *On the Study of Words*, lecture iii

In the New Testament the word is used to mean a freedman (Lat. *Libertinus*).

Then there arose certain of the synagogue, which is called the synagogue of the Libertines, ... disputing with Stephen. Acts 6:9

There was a sect of heretics in Holland, led, about 1525, by Quintin, a factor, and Copin. They maintained that nothing is sinful but to those who think it sinful, and that perfect innocence is to live without doubt.

**Liberty** means 'to do what one likes'. (Lat. *liber*, free.)

*Civil Liberty*. The liberty of a subject to conduct his own affairs as he thinks proper, provided he neither infringes on the equal liberty of others, nor offends against the good morals or laws under which he is living.

*Moral Liberty*. Such freedom as is essential to render a person responsible for what he does, or what he omits to do.

*Natural Liberty*. Unrestricted freedom to exercise all natural functions in their proper places; the state of being subject only to the laws of nature.

*Political Liberty*. The freedom of a nation from any unjust abridgment of its rights and independence; the right to participate in political elections and civil offices, and to have a voice in the administration of the laws under which one lives.

*Religious Liberty*. Freedom in religious opinions, and in both private and public worship, provided such freedom in no wise interferes with the equal liberty of others.

***The liberty of the press.*** The right to publish what one pleases, subject only to penalty if the publication is mischievous, hurtful, or libellous to the state or individuals.

***Cap of Liberty.*** *See* Cap.

***Liberty Enlightening the World.*** The colossal statue standing on Bedloe's (or Liberty) Island, at the entrance of New York Harbour, presented to the American people by France in commemoration of the centenary of the American Declaration of Independence, and inaugurated in 1886. It is of bronze, 155 ft in height (standing on a pedestal 135 ft high), and represents a woman, draped, and holding a lighted torch in her upraised hand. It is the work of the Alsatian sculptor, Auguste Bartholdi (1834–1904).

The statue of Liberty, placed over the entrance of the Palais Royal, Paris, was modelled from Mme Tallien.

***The liberties of the Fleet.*** The district immediately surrounding the Fleet, the old debtors' prison in the City of London, in which prisoners were sometimes allowed to reside, and beyond which they were not allowed to go. They included the north side of Ludgate Hill and the Old Bailey to Fleet Lane, down the lane to the market, and on the east side along by the prison wall to the foot of Ludgate Hill.

The word *liberty* was also used to denote the areas belonging to the City of London, but lying immediately without the City walls which, in course of time, were attached to the nearest ward within the walls, and to the surroundings of the Tower of London. *See* Tower Liberty.

**Libitina.** The goddess who, in ancient Italy, presided over funerals. She was identified by the Romans with Prosperpina, and her name was frequently used as a synonym for death itself.

We shift, and bedeck, and bedrape us,
Thou art noble and nude and antique;
Libitina thy mother, Priapus
Thy father, a Tuscan and Greek.

Swinburne, *Dolores*, st. vii

**Libra** (Lat., the balance). The seventh sign of the Zodiac (and the name of one of the ancient constellations), which the sun enters about September 22 and leaves about October 22. At this time the day and night being weighed would be found equal.

**Library.** Before the invention of paper the thin rind between the solid wood and the outside bark of certain trees was used for writing on; this was in Lat. called *liber*, which came in time to signify also a 'book'. Hence our *library*, the place for books; *librarian*, the keeper of books; and the French *livre*, a book.

Some interesting facts concerning books and libraries will be found in Disraeli's *Curiosities of Literature.*

***A circulating library.*** A library from which the books may be borrowed and taken by readers to their homes under certain restrictions.

***A living*** or ***walking library.*** Longinus (213–273), the philosopher and rhetorician, was so called.

**Libya.** Africa, or all the north of Africa between Egypt and the Atlantic Ocean. It was the Greek name for Africa in general. The Romans used the word sometimes as synonymous with Africa, and sometimes for the fringe containing Carthage.

**Lich.** A dead body (A.S. *lic*; Ger. *leiche*).

***Lich-fowls.*** Birds that feed on carrion, as night-ravens, etc.

***Lich-gate.*** The shed or covered place at the entrance of churchyards, intended to afford shelter to the coffin and mourners, while they wait for the clergyman to conduct the *cortège* into the church.

***Lich-owl.*** The screech-owl, superstitiously supposed to foretell death.

***Lich-wake*** or ***Lyke-wake.*** The funeral feast or the waking of a corpse, i.e. watching it all night.

Then, if thy Lords their purpose urge,
Take our defiance loud and high:
Our slogan is their lyke-wake dirge,
Our moat the grave where they shall lie.

Scott, *Lay of the Last Minstrel*, IV, xxvi

In a pastoral written by Aelfric in 998 for Wilfsige, Bishop of Sherborne, the attendance of the clergy at lyke-wakes is forbidden.

Scott gives a specimen of the old 'Lyke-wake Dirge' in his *Border Minstrelsy*.

***Lich-way.*** The path by which a funeral is conveyed to church, which not unfrequently deviates from the ordinary road. It was long supposed that wherever a dead body passed became a public thoroughfare.

**Lich-field.** ***The field of the dead*** (*see* Lich, *above*). The town in Staffordshire is said to be so called in memory of a massacre of the Christians during the persecution of Diocletian (about 304). Lichfield in Hampshire commemorates a similar slaughter, or a forgotten battlefield, as also in all probability does Leckhampstead, in Buckinghamshire.

**Lick.** ***I licked him.*** I flogged or beat him. A *licking* is a thrashing, a good hiding, or – in games – a defeat, as *I gave him a good licking at billiards.*

***It licks me.*** Slang for 'I don't understand it at all,' 'I can't make it out'.

***To go at a great lick.*** To run, ride, etc., at great speed; to put on a spurt.

***To lick into shape.*** To make presentable; to give a good appearance, decent manners, etc., to. In allusion to the tradition that the cubs of bears are cast shapeless, and remain so till the dam has licked them into proper form. *See* Bear.

> So watchful Bruin forms, with plastic care,
> Each growing lump, and brings it to a bear.
> Pope, *Dunciad,* i, 101

***To lick one's lips.*** To give evident signs of the enjoyment of anticipation.

***To lick one's shoes.*** To be humble or abjectly servile towards one. *Cp.* Lickspittle.

***To lick the dust*** or ***the ground.*** *See* To kiss the dust *under* Kiss.

**Lickpenny.** Something or someone that makes the money go – that 'licks up' the pennies. Lydgate (about 1425) wrote a humorous poem called *London Lyckpenny* in which (anticipating the Scotsman of the 'bang went saxpence' story) he shows that life in London makes the money fly.

> Law is a lick-penny, Mr Tyrrel.
> Scott, *St Ronan's Well,* xxviii

**Lickspittle.** A servile toady.

> His heart too great, though fortune little,
> To lick a rascal statesman's spittle. Swift
>
> It is only in England that literary men are invariably lickspittles.
> Borrow, *Lavengro,* III, 319

**Lictors.** Binders (Lat. *ligo*, to bind or tie). These Roman officers were so called because they bound the hands and feet of criminals before they executed the sentence of the law.

> The lictors at that word, tall yeomen all and strong,
> Each with his axe and sheaf of twigs, went down into the throng. Macaulay, *Virginia*

**Lie.** A falsehood (A.S. *lyge*, from *lēogan*, to lie).

***A lie hath no feet.*** Because it cannot stand alone. In fact, a lie wants twenty others to support it, and even then is in constant danger of tripping. *Cp.* Liar (*Liars should have good memories*).

***A white lie.*** A conventional lie, such as telling a caller that Mrs A or Mrs B is not at home, meaning not 'at home' to that particular caller.

> It is said that Dean Swift called on a friend, and was told by Jeames that 'master is not at home'. The friend called on the dean, and Swift, opening the window, shouted, 'Not at home'. When the friend expostulated, Swift said, 'I believed your footman when he said his master was not at home; surely you can believe the master himself when he tells you he is not at home.'

***Lying for the whetstone.*** *See* Whetstone.

***The Father of lies.*** Satan (John 8:44).

***The greatest lie.*** In Heywood's *Four P's*, an interlude of about 1543, a Palmer, a Pardoner, a Poticary, and a Pedlar disputed as to which could tell the greatest lie. The Palmer said he had never seen a woman out of patience; whereupon the other three P's threw up the sponge, saying such a falsehood could not possibly be outdone.

***The lie circumstantial, direct, etc.*** *See* Countercheck.

***To give one the lie.*** To accuse him to his face of telling a falsehood.

***To give the lie to.*** To show that such and such a statement is false; to belie.

**Lie** (A.S. *licgan*, to 'bide or rest).

> Lie heavy on him, earth, for he
> Laid many a heavy load on thee.

This is part of Dr Evans's epitaph on Sir John Vanbrugh (1664–1726), the dramatist, herald, and architect. The 'heavy loads' referred to were Blenheim, Greenwich Hospital (which he finished), Castle Howard in Yorkshire, and other massive buildings.

***To lie at the catch.*** In Bunyan's *Pilgrim's Progress* Talkative says to Faithful, 'You lie at the catch, I perceive.' To which Faithful replies, 'No, not I; I am only for setting things right.' *To lie at* or *on the catch* is to lie in wait or to lay a trap to catch one.

***To lie in state.*** Said of a corpse of a royal or distinguished person that is displayed to the general public.

***To lie low.*** To conceal oneself or one's intentions.

> All this while Brer Rabbit lay low.
> Joel Chandler Harris, *Uncle Remus*

***To lie over.*** To be deferred; as, this question must lie over till next sessions.

***To lie to.*** To stop the progress of a vessel at sea by reducing the sails and counterbracing the yards; hence, to cease from doing something.

> We now ran plump into a fog, and were obliged to lie to.
> Lord Dufferin, *Letters from High Latitudes*

***To lie to one's work.*** To work energetically.

***To lie with one's fathers.*** To be buried in one's native place.

> I will lie with my fathers, and thou shalt carry me out of Egypt. Gen. 47:30

***To lie up.*** To refrain from work, especially on account of ill health; to rest.

**Liege.** The word means one bound, a bondsman (O.Fr. *lige*, connected with O.H. Ger. *ledig*, free);

hence, vassals were called *liege-men* – i.e. men bound to serve their lord, or *liege lord.*

> Unarmed and bareheaded, on his knees, and with his hands placed between those of his lord, he [the military tenant] repeated these words: 'Hear, my lord, I have become your liegeman of life and limb, and earthly worship; and faith and truth I will bear to you to live and die.'
>
> Lingard, *History of England,* vol. ii, ch. i

**Lien.** A bond. (Lat. *ligamen*, from *ligare*, to bind). Legally, a bond on goods for a debt; a right to retain goods in a creditor's hands till he has satisfied a legal claim for debt.

**Lieutenant** (pronounce *lef-ten-unt*) is the Latin *locum-tenens*, through the French. A *Lieutenant-Colonel* is the colonel's deputy. *The Lord-Lieutenant* of Ireland represents the Crown in that country.

**Life** (A.S. *lif*). ***Drawn from life.*** Drawn or described from some existing person or object.

***For life.*** As long as life continues.

***For the life of me.*** True as I am alive. Even if my life depended on it. A strong asseveration, originally 'under pain of losing my life'.

> Nor could I, for the life of me, see how the creation of the world had anything to do with what I was talking about.
>
> Goldsmith, *Vicar of Wakefield*

***Large as life.*** Of the same size as the object represented.

***On my life.*** I will answer for it by my life.

***People of high life.*** The upper ten, the *haut monde.*

***To bear a charmed life.*** To escape accidents in a marvellous manner.

***To know life.*** To be well versed in the niceties of social intercourse, good breeding, manners, etc.; to be up to all the dodges by which one may be imposed upon.

***To see life.*** To 'knock about' town, where life may be seen at its fullest; to move in smart or fast society.

***To the life.*** In exact imitation. 'Done to the life'.

**Life Guards.** The two senior cavalry regiments of the Household Troops (*q.v.*), the members of which are all not less than six feet high; hence, a fine, tall, manly fellow is called 'a regular Life Guardsman'.

**Life Policy.** An assurance to be paid after the death of the person.

**Life Preserver.** A buoyant jacket, belt, or other appliance, to support the human body in water; also a loaded staff or knuckle-duster for self-defence.

**Lift.** ***To have one at a lift*** is to have one in your power. When a wrestler has his antagonist in his hands and lifts him from the ground, he has him 'at a lift', or in his power.

> 'Sirra,' says he, 'I have you at a lift.
> Now you are come unto your latest shift.'
>
> Percy, *Reliques*, *Guy and Amarant*

**Lifter.** A thief. We still call one who plunders shops a 'shop-lifter'.

> Is he so young a man, and so old a lifter?
>
> Shakespeare, *Troilus and Cressida*, 1, 2

**Lifting.** In Scotland, the raising of the coffin on to the shoulders of the bearers. Certain ceremonies preceded the funeral.

> When at the funeral of an ordinary husbandman, one o'clock was named as the hour for 'lifting', the party began to assemble two hours previously.
>
> Saladin, *Agnostic Journal*, Jan. 14, 1893, p. 27

At the first service were offered meat and ale; at the second, shortbread and whisky; at the third, seed-cake and wine; at the fourth, currant-bun and rum; at the last, sugar-biscuits and brandy.

***Lifting the little finger.*** *See* Finger.

**Ligan.** *See* Lagan.

**Light.** The A.S. of this word in both senses, i.e. illumination and smallness of weight, is *lēoht*, but in the former sense it is connected with Ger. *licht*, Lat. *lux*, and Gr. *leukos* (white), and in the latter with Ger. *leicht*, Gr. *elachus* (not heavy), and Sansk. *laghu.* The verb *to light*, to dismount, to settle after flight, is A.S. *lihtan*, from the last mentioned *lēoht*, originally meaning to lighten, or relieve of a burden.

***According to his lights.*** According to his information or knowledge of the matter; or, according to the capacity he has for forming opinions on it.

***Ancient lights.*** A sign put up on a building to show that the owner thereof has a right to the light coming from adjacent property, and consequently, no building may be erected there without his consent, if it would interfere with his light.

***Before the lights.*** In theatrical parlance, on the stage, i.e. before the foot-lights.

***Light comedian.*** One who takes humorous, but not *low*, parts. Orlando, in *As You Like It*, might be taken for a 'light comedian'; Tony Lumpkin (*She Stoops to Conquer*), and Paul Pry (in Poole's comedy of that name, 1825) are parts for a 'low comedian'.

***Light and leading.*** *See* Leading.

***Light-fingered.*** *See* Finger.

***Light gains make a heavy purse.*** Small profits and a quick return, is the best way of gaining wealth.

***Light literature.*** Reading matter intended for entertainment; books, etc. that are the reverse of 'ponderous'.

***Light o' love.*** An inconstant or loose-principled woman; a harlot.

***Light troops.*** Light cavalry, meaning i.e. lancers and hussars, who are neither such large men as the 'Heavies', nor yet so heavily equipped.

***The light of one's countenance.*** The bright smile of approbation and love.

> Lift up the light of Thy countenance on us.
>
> Ps. 4:6

***The light of the age.*** Maimonides or Rabbi Moses ben Maimon, of Cordova (1135–1204).

***The light of the harem.*** The Sultana Nourmahal in Moore's *Lalla Rookh*, afterwards called *Nourjehan* (Light of the World). She was the bride of Selim.

***To bring to light.*** To discover and expose.

> The duke yet would have dark deeds darkly answered; he would never bring them to light; would he were returned!
>
> Shakespeare, *Measure for Measure*, 3, 2

***To light upon.*** To discover by accident; to come across by a lucky chance. Thus, Dr Johnson wrote to Mrs Thrale (Oct. 16th, 1799), 'How did you light on your specifick for the tooth-ach?'

***To make light of.*** To treat as of no importance; to take little notice of.

> Behold, I have prepared my dinner: my oxen and my fatlings are killed, and all things are ready; come unto the marriage.
>
> But they made light of it, and went their ways, one to his farm, another to his merchandise.
>
> Matt. 22:4, 5

***To put out one's light.*** To kill him, 'send him into the outer darkness'. Othello says, 'Put out the light and then put out the light.'

***To stand in one's own light.*** To act in such a way as to hinder advancement.

***To throw*** or ***shed light upon.*** To elucidate, to explain.

**Lighthouse.** *See* Pharos.

**Lightning.** Hamilcar (d.228 BC), the Carthaginian general, was called 'Barca', the Phoenician for 'lightning' (Heb. *Barak*), both on account of the rapidity of his march and for the severity of his attacks.

*Chain lightning.* Two or more flashes of lightning repeated without intermission.

*Forked lightning.* Zig-zag lightning.

*Globular lightning.* A meteoric ball [of fire], which sometimes falls on the earth and flies off with an explosion.

**Lightning Conductor.** A metal rod raised above a building with one end in the earth, to carry off the lightning and prevent its injuring the building.

**Lightning Preservers.** The most approved classical preservatives against lightning were the eagle, the sea-calf, and the laurel. Jupiter chose the first, Augustus Caesar the second, and Tiberius the third (*Columella*, x; Sueton. in *Vit. Aug.*, xc; ditto in *Vit. Tib.*, lxix). *Cp.* House-leek.

Bodies scathed and persons struck dead by lightning were said to be incorruptible; and anyone so distinguished was held by the ancients in great honour. (J. C. Bullenger, *De Terrae Motu*, etc., v, 11.)

**Lightning Rod.** *See* Lightning Conductor.

**Liguorians.** A congregation of missionary priests called also Redemptorists, founded in 1732, by St Alphonsus Liguori, and confirmed by Benedict XIV in 1759. Their object is the religious instruction of the people and the assisting of poor and neglected parishes.

**Liguria.** The ancient name of a part of Cisalpine Gaul, including the modern Genoa, Piedmont, some of Savoy, etc. In 1797 Napoleon founded a 'Ligurian Republic', with Genoa as its capital, and embracing also Venetia and a part of Sardinia. It was annexed to France in 1805.

***The Ligurian Sage.*** Aulus Persius Flaccus (AD 34–62), born at Volaterrae, in Etruria, famous for his *Satires*.

**Lilburne.** *If no one else were alive, John would quarrel with Lilburne.* John Lilburne (d.1657) was a contentious Leveller (*q.v.*) in the Commonwealth; so rancorous against rank that he could never satisfy himself that any two persons were exactly on the same level.

> Is John departed? and is Lilburne gone?
> Farewell to both – to Lilburne and to John.
> Yet, being gone, take this advice from me.
> Let them not both in one grave buried be.
> Here lay ye John, lay Lilburne thereabout;
> For if they both should meet, they would fall out.
>
> Epigrammatic Epitaph

**Lilith.** A Semitic (in origin probably Babylonian) demon supposed to haunt wildernesses in stormy weather, and to be specially dangerous to children and pregnant women. She is referred to in Is. 34:14, as the 'screech-owl' (Revised

Version, 'night monster', and in margin 'Lilith'); and the Talmudists give the name to a wife that Adam is fabled to have had before Eve, who, refusing to submit to him, left Paradise for a region of the air, and still haunts the night. Superstitious Jews put in the chamber occupied by their wife four coins inscribed with the names of Adam and Eve and the words 'Avaunt thee, Lilith!' Goethe introduced her in his *Faust*, and Rossetti in his *Eden Bower* adapted the Adamitic story, making the Serpent the instrument of Lilith's vengeance. *See* The Devil and his Dam *under* Devil, and *Cp.* Lamia.

> It was Lilith, the wife of Adam ...
> Not a drop of her blood was human,
> But she was made like a soft sweet woman.
>
> D. G. Rossetti, *Eden Bower*

**Lilli-Burlero Bullen-a-lah.** Said to have been the watchword of the Irish Roman Catholics in their massacres of the Protestants in 1641, the words were adopted as the refrain of a piece of political doggerel satirising James II (written by Lord Wharton), which contributed not a little to the success of the great revolution of 1688. Burnet says, 'It made an impression on the (king's) army that cannot be imagined ... The whole army, and at last the people, both in city and country, were singing it perpetually ... never had so slight a thing so great an effect.'

The song is referred to in Sterne's *Tristram Shandy*, ch. ii, and is given in Percy's *Reliqes* (series ii, Bk 3). Chappell attributes the air to Henry Purcell.

**Lilliput.** The country of pigmies ('Lilliputians') to whom Gulliver was a giant. (Swift, *Gulliver's Travels*).

**Lily, The.** There is a tradition that the lily sprang from the repentant tears of Eve as she went forth from Paradise.

In Christian art, the lily is an emblem of chastity, innocence, and purity. In pictures of the Annunciation, Gabriel is sometimes represented as carrying a lily-branch, while a vase containing a lily stands before the Virgin, who is kneeling in prayer. St Joseph holds a lily-branch in his hand, indicating that his wife Mary was a virgin.

***Lily of France.*** The device of Clovis was three black toads (*see* Crapaud); but the story goes that an aged hermit of Joye-en-valle saw a miraculous light stream one night into his cell, and an angel appeared to him holding an azure shield of wonderful beauty, emblazoned with three gold lilies that shone like stars, which the hermit was commanded to give to Queen Clotilde; she gave it to her royal husband, whose arms were everywhere victorious, and the device was thereupon adopted as the emblem of France. (*See Les Petits Bollandistes*, vol. vi, p. 426.) Tasso, in his *Jerusalem Delivered*, terms the French *Gigli d'oro* (golden lilies). It is said the people were commonly called *Liliarts*, and the kingdom *Lilium* in the time of Philippe le Bel, Charles VIII, and Louis XII. *See* Fleur-de-lys.

> Now by the lips of those ye love, fair gentleman of France,
> Charge for the golden lilies – upon them with the lance!
>
> Macaulay, *The Battle of Ivry*

> The burghers of Ghent were bound by solemn oath not to make war upon the lilies.
>
> Millington, *Heraldry*, i

Florence is 'The City of Lilies'.

By 'the lily in the field' in Matt. 6:28, which is said to surpass Solomon in all his glory, is meant simply the wild lily, probably a species of iris. Our 'lily of the valley' – with which this is sometimes confused – is one of the genus *Convallaria*, a very different plant.

**Lily Maid of Astolat.** *See* Elaine.

**Limb.** Slang for a mischievous rascal, a young imp; it is short for the older *Limb of the devil*, where the word implies 'agent' or 'scion'. Dryden called Fletcher 'a limb of Shakespeare'.

***Limb of the law.*** A clerk articled to a lawyer, a sheriff's officer, a policeman, or other legal assistant. Just as the *limbs* of the body do what the *head* directs, so these obey the commands of the *head* of the office.

**Limbo.** A humorous name (from *limbus*) given to prison and to some place where things are stowed, too good to destroy but not good enough to use. *Cp.* Al Araf.

**Limbus** (Lat. border, fringe, edge). The borders of hell; the portion assigned by the Schoolmen to those departed spirits to whom the benefits of redemption did not apply through no fault of their own.

***Limbus Fatuorum.*** The Paradise of Fools. As fools or idiots are not responsible for their works, the old Schoolmen held that they are not punished in purgatory and cannot be received into heaven, so they go to a special 'Paradise of Fools'.

> Then might you see
> Cowls, hoods, and habits, with their wearers tossed
> And fluttered into rags; then relics, beads,
> Indulgences, dispenses, pardons, bulls,
> The sport of winds. All these, upwhirled aloft,
> Into a Limbo large and broad, since called
> The Paradise of Fools.
>
> Milton, *Paradise Lost*, iii, 489

*Cp.* Fool's Paradise *under* Fool.

***Limbus of the Moon.*** *See* Moon.

***Limbus patrum.*** The half-way house between earth and heaven, where the patriarchs and prophets who died before the death of the Redeemer await the Last Day; when they will be received into heaven. Some hold that this is the 'hell' into which Christ descended after He gave up the ghost on the cross.

Shakespeare uses *limbo patrum* for 'quod', jail, confinement.

> I have some of them in limbo patrum, and there they are like to dance these three days.
> *Henry VIII*, 5, 4

***Limbus Puerorum.*** The Child's Paradise, for children who die before they are baptised or are responsible for their actions.

**Limehouse.** Violent and vitriolic abuse of one's political opponents: so called out of compliment to an oratorical display by Mr Lloyd George at Limehouse, London, on July 30th, 1909, when he poured forth scorn and abuse on dukes, landlords, financial magnates, etc., many of whom, in the course of later events, became his best friends. Hence, *Limehousing*, indulging in such abuse.

**Limerick.** A nonsense verse in the metre, popularised by Edward Lear in his *Book of Nonsense* (1846), of which the following is an example:

> There was a young lady of Wilts,
> Who walked up to Scotland on stilts;
> When they said it was shocking
> To show so much stocking,
> She answered, 'Then what about kilts?'

The name was not given till much later, and comes from the chorus, 'We'll all come up, come up to Limerick', which was interposed after each verse as it was improvised and sung by a convivial party.

**Limp.** A word formed of the initials of Louis (XIV), James (II), his wife Mary of Modena, and the Prince (of Wales), and used as a Jacobite toast in the time of William III. *Cp.* Notarikon.

**Limpet.** A term applied in sarcasm after the Great War to those holders of well paid Government posts which had been created primarily for war purposes, who 'stuck to them like grim death' though the necessity for their continuance was not generally apparent.

**Lincoln.** A hybrid Celtic and Latin name, *Lindumcolonia*, *Lindum*, the name of the old British town, meaning 'the hill fort on the pool'.

***The devil looking over Lincoln.*** *See* Devil.

***Lincoln green.*** Lincoln, at one time, was noted for its light green, as was Coventry for its blue, and Yorkshire for its grey cloth. *Cp.* Kendal Green.

> Swains in shepherds' gray, and girls in Lincoln green.
> Drayton, *Polyolbion*, xxv, 262

**Lincoln College** (Oxford). Founded by Richard Fleming, Bishop of Lincoln, in 1427, and completed by Thomas Rotherham, Bishop of Lincoln (afterwards Archbishop of York and Lord Chancellor), in 1479.

**Lincoln's Inn.** One of the four Inns of Court (*q.v.*), in London. Henry Lacy, Earl of Lincoln, built a mansion here in the 14th century on ground which had belonged to the Black Friars, but was granted to him by Edward I. A Bishop of Chichester, in the reign of Henry VII, granted leases here to certain students of law.

**Lindabrides.** A heroine in *The Mirror of Knighthood*, whose name at one time was a synonym for a kept mistress, in which sense it was used by Scott, *Kenilworth* and *Woodstock*.

**Linden.** The German name (largely used in England) for lime trees. *Unter den Linden* ('under the limes') is the name of the principal street in Berlin, where are situated the University, the Academy, many palaces, the statue of Frederick the Great, etc.; it is about 1,100 yds. in length.

Baucis (*see* Philemon) was converted into a linden tree.

**Lindor.** One of the conventional names given by the classical poets to a rustic swain, a lover *en bergère*.

> Do not, for heaven's sake, bring down Corydon and Lindor upon us.
> Sir Walter Scott

**Line. *All along the line.*** In every particular, as in such phrases as –

> The accuracy of the statement is contested all along the line by persons on the spot.

***Crossing the line.*** Sailing across the Equator. Advantage is usually taken of this for all sorts of sports aboard ship, especially for playing such tricks as 'Ambassador' (*q.v.*) on those who are crossing for the first time.

***The line.*** In the British Army all regular infantry regiments except the Foot Guards, the Rifle Brigade, and the Marines.

***Line of battle.*** The order of troops drawn up so as to present a battle-front. There were three lines – the van, the main body, and the rear. A fleet drawn up in *line of battle* is so arranged that the ships are ahead and astern of each other at stated distances. *To break the enemy's line* is to derange his order of battle, and so put him to confusion.

**_Line of beauty._** According to Hogarth, a curve thus ⁀; but the line which may be beautiful for one object would be hideous in another. What would Hogarth have said to a nose or mouth which followed his line of beauty?

**_Line of direction._** The line in which a body moves, a force acts, or motion is communicated. In order that a body may stand without falling, a line let down from the centre of gravity must fall within the base on which the object stands. Thus the leaning tower of Pisa does not fall, because this rule is preserved.

**_Line of life._** In palmistry, the crease in the left hand beginning above the web of the thumb, and running towards or up to the wrist.

> The nearer it approaches the wrist the longer will be the life, according to palm-lorists. If long and deeply marked, it indicates long life with very little trouble; if crossed or cut with other marks, it indicates sickness.

**_Line upon line._** Admonition or instruction repeated little by little (a line at a time).

> Line upon line, line upon line, here a little and there a little. Is. 28:10

**_Line of operations._** *See* Base of Operations.

**_Hard lines._** Hard luck, a hard lot. Here *lines* means an allotment measured out.

**_No day without its line._** A saying attributed by Pliny to the Greek artist Apelles (*nulla dies sine linea*), who said he never passed a day without doing at least one line, and to this steady industry owed his great success. The words were adopted as his motto by the industrious novelist Anthony Trollope.

**_On the line._** Said of a picture that at the Royal Academy is hung in a position that is kept only for the best exhibits.

**_The lines have fallen to me in pleasant places_** (Ps. 16:6). The part allotted to me and measured off by a measuring line. The allusion is to drawing a line to mark out the lot of each tribe, hence line became the synonym of lot, and lot means position or destiny.

**_The thin red line._** British infantrymen in action. The old 93rd Highlanders were so described at the battle of Balaclava by W. H. Russell, because they did not take the trouble to form into a square; their regimental magazine is named *The Thin Red Line*.

**_To read between the lines._** To discern the secret meaning. One method of cryptography is to write so that the hidden message is revealed only when alternate lines are read. Thus lines 2, 4, 6 of the following cryptogram would convey the warning to Lord Monteagle of the Gunpowder Plot.

> My lord, having just returned from Paris,
> (2) stay away from the house tonight
> and give me the pleasure of your company,
> (4) for God and man have concurred to punish
> those who pay not regard to their health,
> and
> (6) the wickedness of the time
> adds greatly to its wear and tear.

**_What line are you in?_** What trade or profession are you of? Commercial travellers use the word frequently to signify the sort of goods which they have to dispose of; as, one travels 'in the hardware line', another 'in the drapery line', or 'grocery line', etc.

**Lingo.** Talk, language, especially some peculiar or technical phraseology; from *lingua*, tongue.

**Lingua Franca.** A species of Italian mixed with French, Greek, Arabic, etc., spoken on the coasts of the Mediterranean. Also, any jumble of different languages.

> A clear and solemn voice ... pronounced the words in the sonorous tone of the readers of the mosque, and in the lingua Franca, mutually understood by Christians and Saracens.
> Scott, *The Talisman,* ch. xiii

**Lining of the Pocket.** Money.

> My money is spent: Can I be content
> With pockets deprived of their lining?
> *The Lady's Decoy, or Man Midwife's Defence,* 1738, p. 4

When the great court tailor wished to obtain the patronage of Beau Brummel, he made him a present of a dress-coat lined with bank-notes. Brummel wrote a letter of thanks, stating that he quite approved of the coat, and he especially admired the lining.

**Linnaean System.** The artificial classification adopted by the great Swedish naturalist Linnaeus (d.1778), who arranged his three kingdoms of animals, vegetables, and minerals into classes, orders, genera, species, and varieties, according to certain characteristics.

**Linne, The Heir of.** The hero of an old ballad, given in Percy's *Reliques*, which tells how he wasted his substance in riotous living, and, having spent all, sold his estates to John o' the Scales, his steward, reserving only a 'poor and lonesome lodge in a lonely glen'. When no one would lend or give him money, he retired to the lodge, where was dangling a rope with a running noose. He put it round his neck and sprang aloft, but he fell to the ground, and when he came to espied two chests of beaten gold, and a third full of white money, over which was written –

> Once more, my sonne, I sette thee clere.
> Amend thy life and follies past;
> For but thou amend thee of thy life,
> That rope must be thy end at last.

The heir of Linne now returned to his old hall, where he was refused the loan of forty pence by his quondam steward; one of the guests told John o' the Scales he ought to have lent it, as he had bought the estate cheap enough. 'Cheap call you it?' exclaimed John; 'why, he shall have it back for 100 marks less.' 'Done,' said the heir of Linne, and thus recovered his estates.

**Lion. *As an Agnomen***

***Alp Arslan,*** son of Togrul Beg, the Perso-Turkish monarch (reigned 1063–72) was surnamed *The Valiant Lion.*

***Ali Pasha,*** called *The Lion of Janina*, overthrown in 1822 by Ibrahim Pasha. (1741, 1788–1822.)

***Arioch*** (fifth of the dynasty of Ninu, the Assyrian), called Arioch Ellasar – i.e. Arioch Melech al Asser, *the Lion King of Assyria.* (1927–1897 BC.)

***Damelowiez,*** Prince of Haliez, who founded Lemberg (*Lion City*) in 1259.

***Gustavus Adolphus,*** called *The Lion of the North.* (1594, 1611–32.)

***Hamza,*** called *The Lion of God and of His Prophet.* So Gabriel told Mahomet his uncle was enregistered in heaven.

***Henry,*** Duke of Bavaria and Saxony, was called *The Lion* for his daring courage. (1129–95.)

***Louis VIII*** of France was called *The Lion* because he was born under the sign Leo. (1187, 1223–26.)

***Richard I.*** Coeur de Lion (*Lion's heart*), so called for his bravery. (1157, 1189–99.)

***William*** of Scotland, so called because he chose a red lion *rampant* for his cognisance. (Reigned 1165–1214.)

*See* Lion of God *below.*

***As an Emblem***

A lion is emblem of the tribe of Judah; Christ is called 'the lion of the tribe of Judah'.

> Judah is a lion's whelp: ... he couched as a lion, and as an old lion; who shall rouse him up?
>
> Gen. 49:9

***The lion an emblem of the resurrection.*** According to tradition, the lion's whelp is born dead, and remains so for three days, when the father breathes on it and it receives life. Another tradition is that the lion is the only animal of the cat tribe born with its eyes open, and it is said that it sleeps with its eyes open. This is not a fact, but undoubtedly it sleeps watchfully and lightly.

St Mark the Evangelist is symbolised by a *lion* because he begins his gospel with the scenes of St John the Baptist and Christ in the wilderness. *See* Evangelists.

***In Story and Legend***

***Cybele*** is represented as riding in a chariot drawn by two tame lions.

***Pracriti,*** the goddess of nature among the Hindus, is represented in a similar manner.

***Hippomenes*** and ***Atalanta*** (fond lovers) were metamorphosed into lions by Cybele.

***Hercules*** is said to have worn over his shoulders the hide of the Nemean lion (*see* Nemean), and the personification of Terror is also arrayed in a lion's hide.

The story of Androcles and the lion (*see* Androcles) has many parallels, the most famous of which are those related of St Jerome and St Gerasimus:

While St Jerome was lecturing one day, a lion entered the schoolroom, and lifted up one of its paws. All the disciples fled; but Jerome, seeing that the paw was wounded, drew out of it a thorn and dressed the wound. The lion, out of gratitude, showed a wish to stay with its benefactor. Hence the saint is represented as accompanied by a lion.

St Gerasimus, says the story, saw, on the banks of the Jordan, a lion coming to him, limping on three feet. When it reached the saint, it held up to him the right paw, from which Gerasimus extracted a large thorn. The grateful beast attached itself to the saint, and followed him about as a dog.

Half a score of such tales are told by the Bollandists in the *Acta Sanctorum*; and in more recent times a similar one was told of Sir George Davis, an English consul at Florence at the beginning of the 19th century. One day he went to see the lions of the great Duke of Tuscany. There was one which the keepers could not tame; but no sooner did Sir George appear than it manifested every symptom of joy. Sir George entered its cage, when the lion leaped on his shoulder, licked his face, wagged its tail, and fawned on him like a dog. Sir George told the great duke that he had brought up the creature; but as it grew older it became dangerous, and he sold it to a Barbary captive. The duke said that he had bought it of the very same man, and the mystery was solved.

***Sir Iwain de Galles,*** a hero of romance, was attended by a lion, which, in gratitude to the knight who had delivered it from a serpent with which it had been engaged in deadly combat, ever after became his faithful servant, approaching the knight with tears, and rising on his hind-feet like a dog.

***Sir Geoffrey de Latour*** was aided by a lion against the Saracens; but the faithful brute was drowned in attempting to follow the vessel in which the knight had embarked on his departure from the Holy Land.

***Phrases***

***The lion will not touch the true prince*** (*1 Henry IV*, 2, 4). This is an old superstition, and has been given a Christian significance, the 'true prince' being the Messiah, who is called 'the lion of the tribe of Judah'. It is applied to any prince of blood royal, supposed at one time to be hedged around with a sort of divinity.

> Fetch the Numidian lion I brought over;
> If she be sprung from royal blood, the lion
> He'll do you reverence, else …
> He'll tear her all to pieces.
>
> Fletcher, *The Mad Lover*, iv, v

***In Heraldry***

Ever since 1164, when it was adopted as a device by Philip I, Duke of Flanders, the lion has figured largely and in an amazing variety of positions as an heraldic emblem, and, as a consequence, in public-house signs. The earliest and most important attitude of the heraldic lion is *rampant* (the device of Scotland), but it is also shown as *passant*, *passant gardant* (as in the shield of England), *salient*, *sejant*, etc., and even *dormant*. *For these terms see* Heraldry.

***The lions in the arms of England.*** They are three lions passant gardant, i.e. walking and showing the full face. The first was that of Rollo, Duke of Normandy, and the second represented the country of Maine, which was added to Normandy. These were the two lions borne by William the Conqueror and his descendants. Henry II added a third lion to represent the Duchy of Aquitaine, which came to him through his wife Eleanor. Any lion not rampant is called a *lion leopardé*, and the French heralds call the lion passant a *leopard*; accordingly Napoleon said to his soldiers, 'Let us drive these leopards (the English) into the sea.'

Since 1603 the royal arms have been supported as now by (dexter) the English lion and (sinister) the Scottish unicorn (*see* Unicorn); but prior to the accession of James I the sinister supporter was a family badge. Edward III, with whom supporters began, had a lion and eagle; Henry IV, an antelope and swan; Henry V, a lion and antelope; Edward IV, a lion and bull; Richard III, a lion and boar; Henry VII, a lion and dragon; Elizabeth, Mary, and Henry VIII, a lion and greyhound.

***The lion in the arms of Scotland*** is derived from the arms of the ancient Earls of Northumberland and Huntingdon, from whom some of the Scotch monarchs were descended. The *tressure* is referred to the reign of Achaius (d. about 819), who made a league with Charlemagne, 'who did augment his arms with a double trace formed with Floure-de-lyces, signifying thereby that the lion henceforth should be defended by the ayde of Frenchemen'. (Holinshed, *Chronicles.*)

Sir Walter Scott says the lion rampant in the arms of Scotland was first assumed by William of Scotland, and has been continued ever since.

> William, King of Scotland, having chosen for his armorial bearing a Red Lion *rampant*, acquired the name of William the Lion; and this rampant lion still constitutes the arms of Scotland; and the president of the heraldic court … is called Lord Lion King-at-Arms.
>
> *Tales of Grandfather*, iv

***A lion at the feet of crusaders or martyrs,*** in effigy, signifies that they died for their magnanimity.

***The Lion of St Mark,*** or ***of Venice.*** A winged lion sejant, holding an open book with the inscription *Pax tibi, Marce, Evangelista Meus.* A sword-point rises above the book on the dexter side, and the whole is encircled by an aureola.

Among other distinctive lions that appear in blazonry and on the signs of inns, etc., may be mentioned:

***Blue,*** the badge of the Earl of Mortimer, also of Denmark.

***Crowned,*** the badge of Henry VIII.

***Golden,*** the badge of Henry I, and also of Percy, Duke of Northumberland.

***Rampant,*** with the tail between its legs and turned over its back, the badge of Edward IV as Earl of March.

***Red,*** of Scotland; also the badge of John of Gaunt, Duke of Lancaster, who assumed this badge as a token of his claim to the throne of Castile.

***Sleeping,*** the device of Richard I.

***Statant gardant*** (i.e. standing and showing a full face), the device of the Duke of Norfolk.

***White***, the device of the Dukes of Norfolk; also of the Earl of Surrey, Earl of Mortimer, and the Fitz-Hammonds.

> For who, in field or foray slack,
> Saw the blanche lion e'er fall back? [Duke of Norfolk]
> Scott, *Lay of the Last Minstrel*

**Lion of God.** Ali-Ben-Abou-Thaleb (602–61), the son-in-law of Mahomet, was so called because of his zeal and his great courage. His mother called him at birth *Al Haïdara*, 'the Rugged Lion'.

**Lion-hunter.** One who hunts up a celebrity to adorn or give prestige to a party. Mrs Leo Hunter, in *Pickwick*, is a good satire on the name and character of a lion-hunter.

**Lion of St Mark.** *See under* Lion, *heraldry.*

**Lion Sermon, The.** Preached in St Katharine Cree Church, Leadenhall Street, London, in October, to commemorate 'the wonderful escape' of Sir John Gayre, about 250 years ago, from a lion which he met with on being shipwrecked on the coast of Africa. Sir John was Lord Mayor in 1647.

> Sir John Gayre bequeathed £200 for the relief of the poor on condition that a commemorative sermon was preached annually at St Katharine Cree. It is said that Sir John was on his knees in prayer when the lion came up, smelt about him, prowled round and round him, and then stalked off.

**Lions.** The lions of a place are sights worth seeing, or the celebrities; so called from the ancient custom of showing strangers, as chief of London sights, the lions at the Tower. The Tower menagerie was abolished in 1834.

**Lion's Head.** In fountains the water is often made to issue from the mouth of a lion. This is a very ancient custom. The Egyptians thus symbolised the inundation of the Nile, which happens when the sun is in Leo (July 28th to August 23rd), and the Greeks and Romans adopted the device for their fountains.

**Lion's Mouth.** ***To place one's head in the lion's mouth.*** To expose oneself needlessly and foolhardily to danger.

**Lion's Provider.** A jackal; a foil to another man's wit, a humble friend who plays into your hand to show you to best advantage. The jackal (*q.v.*) feeds on the lion's leavings, and is said to yell to advise the lion that they have roused up his prey, serving the lion in much the same way as a dog serves a sportsman.

> ... the poor jackals are less foul,
> As being the brave lion's keen providers,
> Than human insects catering for spiders.
> Byron, *Don Juan,* ix, 27

**Lion's Share.** The larger part: all or nearly all. In *Aesop's Fables*, several beasts joined the lion in a hunt; but, when the spoil was divided, the lion claimed one quarter in right of his prerogative, one for his superior courage, one for his dam and cubs, 'and as for the fourth, let who will dispute it with me'. Awed by his frown, the other beasts yielded and silently withdrew. *Cp.* Montgomery.

**Lionise a Person, To,** is either to show him the *lions*, or chief objects of attraction, or to make a lion of him, by fêting him and making a fuss about him.

**Liosalfar.** The light elves of *Scandinavian mythology*, mentioned in the *Gylfaginning* as being brighter than the sun, and contrasted with the *dokkalfar*, or dark elves, who are blacker than pitch. They dwell in Alfheim.

**Lip.** ***Lip homage*** or ***service.*** Verbal devotion. Honouring with the lips while the heart takes no part nor lot in the matter. *See* Matt. 15:8; Is. 29:13.

***To bite one's lip.*** To express vexation and annoyance, or to suppress some unwanted emotion as laughter or anger.

***To carry a stiff upper lip.*** To be self-reliant: to bear oneself courageously in face of difficulties or danger.

***To curl the lip.*** To express contempt or disgust with the mouth.

***To hang the lip.*** To drop the under lip in sullenness or contempt. Thus in Shakespeare's *Troilus and Cressida* (3, 1) Helen explains why her brother Troilus is not abroad by saying, 'He hangs the lip at something.'

> A foolish hanging of thy nether lip.
> Shakespeare, *1 Henry IV*, 2, 4

***To shoot out the lip.*** To show scorn.

> All they that see me laugh me to scorn. They shoot out the lip; they shake the head ... Ps. 22:7

**Lir, King.** The earliest known original of the King in Shakespeare's tragedy *King Lear*, an ocean god of early Irish and British legend. He figures in the romance *The Fate of the Children of Lir* as the father of Fionnuala (*q.v.*). On the death of Fingula, the mother of his daughter, he married the wicked Aoife, who, through spite, transformed the children of Lir into swans, doomed to float on the water till they heard the first mass-bell ring. Moyle versified this legend:

> Silent, O Moyle, be the roar of thy water,
> Break not, ye breezes, your chain of repose,
> While murmuring mournfully, Lir's lovely daughter
> Tells to the night-stars the tale of her woes.
> *Irish Melodies*, No. ii, 9

Lir was fabled to be a descendant of Brutus, and appears in early Welsh chronicles as *Lear*, or *Leyr* (the founder of Leicester), whence – through Geoffrey of Monmouth, by whose time other legends had crystallised round him – Shakespeare obtained the framework of his plot.

**Lisbon.** Camoëns, in the *Lusiad*, derives the name from *Ulyssippo* (Ulysses' polis or city), and says that it was founded by Ulysses; but it is in fact the old Phoenician *Olisippo*, the walled town. The root *Hippo* appears as the name of more than one ancient African city, also in Orippo, Lacippo, and other Spanish towns.

**Lismahago.** A proud but poor, and very conceited, Scotch captain, in Smollett's *Humphry Clinker*. Fond of disputation, jealous of honour, and brimful of national pride, he marries Miss Tabitha Bramble.

**Lisuarte of Greece.** One of the knights whose adventures and exploits are recounted in the latter part of the Spanish version of *Amadis of Gaul*. This part was added by Juan Diaz.

**Lit de Justice.** Properly the seat occupied by the French king when he attended the deliberations of his *parlement*; hence, the session itself, any arbitrary edict. As the members derived their power from the king, when the king was present their power returned to the fountain-head, and the king was arbitrary. What he then proposed could not be controverted, and, of course, had the force of law. The last *lit de justice* was held by Louis XVI in 1787.

**Little.** ***Little by little.*** Gradually; a little at a time.

***Many a little makes a mickle.*** The real Scotch proverb is: 'A wheen o' mickles mak's a muckle,' where mickle means *little*, and muckle *much*; but the Anglo-Saxon *micel* or *mycel* means 'much', so that, if the Scotch proverb is accepted, we must give a forced meaning to the word 'mickle'.

**Little Britain.** The name given in the old romances to Armorica, now Brittany; also called Benwic.

The street in the City of London of this name was first so called in the time of Queen Elizabeth; previously it was known as *Britten* or *Brettone Street*, and is said to have been so called because the Dukes of Brittany had had a mansion on this site. The old name of the northern part of Little Britain was *Duke Street*.

**Little Corporal, The.** Napoleon Bonaparte. So called after the battle of Lodi, in 1796, from his low stature, youthful age, and amazing courage. He was barely 5 ft 2 in. in height.

**Little-endians.** In Swift's *Gulliver's Travels* (*Voyage to Lilliput*) the faction which insisted on interpreting the vital direction contained in the 54th chapter of the Blundecral: 'All true believers break their eggs at the convenient end', as meaning the *little end*, and waged a destructive war against those who adopted the alternative (*cp.* Big-endians). The godfather of the emperor happened to cut his finger while breaking his egg at the big end, and published a decree commanding all his subjects to break them in future at the small end. This led to a terrible war, and to the publication of many hundreds of large treatises; and today the terms are still used in connection with hostilities or arguments arising out of trifling differences of opinion, etc., especially in matters of doctrine. In Swift's satire the Big-endians typify the Catholics, and the Little-endians the Protestants.

**Little Englanders.** An opprobrious name which became popular about the time of the last Boer War for those who refused to 'think imperially', upheld the doctrine that the English should concern themselves with England only, and were opposed to any extension of the Empire.

**Little Gentleman in Velvet.** 'The little gentleman in velvet', i.e. the mole, was a favourite Jacobite toast in the reign of Queen Anne. The reference was to the mole that raised the molehill against which the horse of William III stumbled at Hampton Court. By this accident the king broke his collar-bone, a severe illness ensued, and he died early in 1702.

**Little-go.** A preliminary examination of a general nature which all undergraduates must pass (unless excused on account of having passed certain other exams) before proceeding to take any examination for a degree. The *Little-go* is almost invariably taken in or before the first term. There is no examination at Oxford corresponding with this, but *Smalls* (*cp.* Mods) is much on its level.

**Little Jack Horner.** *See* Jack (vi).

**Little John.** A semi-legendary character in the Robin Hood cycle, a big stalwart fellow, first named John Little (or John Nailor), who encountered Robin Hood, and gave him a sound thrashing, after which he was rechristened, and Robin stood godfather. He is introduced by Scott in *The Talisman*.

> 'This infant was called John Little,' quoth he;
> 'Which name shall be changed anon.
> The words we'll transpose, so wherever he goes,
> His name shall be called Little John.'
>
> Ritson, *Robin Hood*, xxi

**Little Mary.** *See* Mary.

**Little Masters.** A name applied to certain designers who worked for engravers, etc., in the 16th and 17th centuries, because their designs were on a small scale, fit for copper or wood. The most famous are Jost Amman, Hans Burgmair (who made drawings in wood illustrative of the triumph of the Emperor Maximilian), Albert Altdorfer, and Henrich Aldegraver. Albert Durer and Lucas van Leyden made the art renowned and popular.

**Little Paris.** Brussels and Milan used to be so called, from their gaiety and resemblance in miniature to the French capital.

**Little Parliament, The.** Another name for the Barebones Parliament (*q.v.*).

**Little Pedlington.** The stock name for a village of quackery and cant, humbug, egotism, and narrow-mindedness. It comes from a farce by John Poole.

**Little Red Ridinghood.** This nursery tale is, with slight alterations, common to Sweden, Germany, and France. It comes to us from the French *Le Petit Chaperon Rouge*, in Charles Perrault's *Contes des Temps*, and was probably derived from Italy. The *finale*, which tells of the arrival of a huntsman who slits open the wolf and restores little Red Ridinghood and her grandmother to life, is a German addition.

**Liturgy.** The Greek word from which this comes means *public service*, or *worship of the gods*, and the arranging of the dancing and singing on public festivals, the equipping and manning of ships, etc. In the Church of England it means the religious forms prescribed in the Book of Common Prayer.

**Liver.** The liver was anciently supposed to be the seat of love; hence, when Longaville reads the verses, Biron says, in an aside, 'This is the liver-vein, which makes flesh a deity' (Shakespeare, *Love's Labour's Lost*, 4, 3), and in *The Merry Wives of Windsor* (2, 1) Pistol speaks of Falstaff as loving Ford's wife 'with liver burning hot'.

Another superstition concerning this organ was that the liver of a coward contained no blood; hence such expressions as *white-livered*, *lily-livered*, and Sir Toby's remark in *Twelfth Night* (2, 2):

> For Andrew, if he were opened, and you find so much blood in his liver as will clog the foot of a flea, I'll eat the rest of the anatomy.

In the auspices taken by the Greeks and Romans before battle, if the liver of the animals sacrificed was healthy and blood-red, the omen was favourable; but if pale, it augured defeat.

**Liverpool.** There have been many guesses at the origin of this place-name (which was first recorded about 1190, as *Leverpol*), the most probable deriving it from Welsh *Llyr-pwl*, the sea-pool, though both the Norse *hlithar polir*, the pool of the slape, and Eng. *lither* (stagnant) *pool* have something to recommend them. In *Past and Present* (Bk ii, ch. v) Carlyle played on the latter etymology:

> The Creek of the Mersey … is a *Lither*-pool, a lazy or sullen pool, no monstrous pitchy City.

It was in the 17th century that antiquarians invented the *liver*, a supposed mythic bird, to account for the name. They evolved it from the bird in the arms of the city, which was intended for an heraldic representation to the eagle of St John the Evangelist.

A native of Liverpool is called a *Liverpudlian* or a *Dicky Sam*.

**Livery.** What is delivered. The clothes of a manservant delivered to him by his master. The stables to which your horse is delivered for keep. Splendid dresses were formerly given to all the members of royal households; barons and knights gave uniforms to their retainers, and even a duke's son, serving as a page, was clothed in the *livery* of the prince he served.

> What livery is we know well enough; it is the allowance of horse-meate to keepe horses at livery; the which word, I guess, is derived of delivering forth their nightly food.
>
> *Spenser on Ireland*

The colours of the livery of men-servants should be those of the field and principal charge of the armorial shield; hence the royal livery is scarlet trimmed with gold.

**Livery Companies.** The modern representatives in the City of London of the old City Guilds (*see* Guildhall), so called because they formerly wore distinctive costumes, or *liveries* (*see above*) for special occasions. The names of the companies are not, today, any guide to the profession or occupation of the 'liverymen' (except, perhaps, in a few cases, such as the Stationers'), but they show the origin of the company, and many of the present members are descendants of prominent men in the particular business.

The twelve 'great' companies, in order of civic precedence, with the date of their formation or incorporation, are:

| | |
|---|---|
| Mercers (1293). | Merchant Taylors (1326). |
| Grocers (1345). | Haberdashers (1448). |
| Drapers (1364). | Salters (1394). |
| Fishmongers (1433). | Ironmongers (1463). |
| Goldsmiths (1327). | Vintners (1437). |
| Skinners (1319). | Clothworkers (1527). |

The Grocers' were originally known as the *Pepperers*, and the Haberdashers' the *Hurrers*. Samuel Pepys was Master (1677) of the Clothworkers', which was a 16th-century incorporation of the Shearmen and Fullers' Guild.

The first twelve of the lesser livery companies, in order of civic precedence, are:

| | |
|---|---|
| Dyers. | Barbers. |
| Tallowchandlers. | Brewers. |
| Cutlers. | Armourers & Braziers. |
| Leathersellers. | Bakers. |
| Girdlers. | Pewterers. |
| Waxchandlers. | Butchers. |

There are about 90 City companies of old standing, nearly all of which contribute largely from their funds to charities (especially in the matter of education), and about 40 of which have their own 'Halls' in the City.

**Liverymen.** The freemen of the London livery companies are so called because they were entitled to wear the livery of their respective companies.

**Livy of France, The.** Juan de Mariana (1537–1624).

**Livy of Portugal, The.** João de Barros, the best of the Portuguese historians (1496–1570).

**Lizard.** Supposed, at one time, to be venomous, and hence a 'lizard's leg' was an ingredient of the witch's cauldron in *Macbeth*.

> Poison be their drink! …
> Their chiefest prospect murdering basilisks!
> Their softest touch as smart as lizard's stings!
> Shakespeare, *2 Henry VI*, 3, 2

***Lizard Point*** (Cornwall). Gaelic, 'the point of the high (*ard*) fort (*lis*)'. *Ard* appears in a large number of place names – *Ardrossan* (the little high point), *Ardwick* (the high town), the *Ardennes* (high valleys), etc., and *Lis*, in *Lismore*, *Liskeard*, *Ballylesson* (the town of the little fort), etc.

**Lloyd's.** An association of underwriters, merchants, shipowners, brokers, etc., principally dealing with ocean-borne commerce, marine insurance, and the publication of shipping intelligence. So called because the society was founded (1689) in Tower Street, and moved (1691) to a coffee-house kept in Lombard Street by one Edward Lloyd. In 1774 the offices, or *Lloyd's Rooms*, were removed to the Royal Exchange; in 1928 to Leadenhall Street.

***Lloyd's books.*** Two enormous ledger-like volumes, placed on desks at the entrance (right and left) of Lloyd's Rooms. They give the principal arrivals, and all losses by wrecks, fire, or other accidents at sea. The entries are written in a fine, bold Roman hand, legible to all.

***Lloyd's List.*** A periodical, in which the shipping news received at Lloyd's Rooms is published. It has been issued regularly from 1726; since 1800 as a daily.

***Lloyd's Register.*** A register of ships, British and foreign, published yearly.

**Loaf.** In sacred art a loaf held in the hand is an attribute of St Philip the Apostle, St Osyth, St Joanna, St Nicholas, St Godfrey, and of many other saints noted for their charity to the poor.

***Half a loaf is better than no bread.*** An old saying; if you can't get all you want, try to be content with what you do get. Heywood (1546) says:

> Throw no gift at the giver's head;
> Better is half a loaf than no bread.

***Never turn a loaf in the presence of a Menteith.*** An old Scottish saying. It was Sir John Stewart de Menteith who betrayed Wallace to the English. When he turned a loaf set on the table, his guests were to rush upon the patriot and secure him. (Scott, *Tales of a Grandfather*, vii.)

***With an eye to the loaves and fishes.*** With a view to the material benefits to be derived. The allusion is to the Gospel story of the crowd following Christ, not for the spiritual doctrines He taught, but for the loaves and fishes distributed by Him amongst them.

> Jesus answered them and said, Verily, verily, I say unto you, Ye seek Me, not because ye saw the miracles, but because ye did eat of the loaves, and were filled. John 6:26

**Loafer.** One who idles away his time, or saunters about as though he had all his life to do it in; a lazy 'do-nothing'. The word was originally American slang (about 1830), and was probably German – either a mispronunciation of *lover*, or from *laufen*, to run, go, move.

> John, the eldest son, adopted the ancient and honourable profession of a loafer. To lie idle in the sun, in front of some small grogshop, to attend horse-races, cock-fights, and gander-pullings … were pleasures to him.
> Mrs Beecher Stowe, *Dred* (1856), ch. viii

**Loathly Lady.** A stock character of the old romances who is so hideous that everyone is deterred from marrying her. When, however, she at last finds a husband her ugliness – the effect of enchantment – disappears, and she becomes a model of beauty. Her story – a very common one, in which sometimes the enchanted beauty has to assume the shape of a serpent or some hideous monster – is the feminine counterpart of that of 'Beauty and the Beast' (*q.v.*).

**Lob.** Old thieves' slang for a till. Hence *lob-sneak*, one who robs the till; *lob-crawling*, on the prowl to rob tills.

**Lob's Pound.** Old slang for prison, the stocks, or any other place of confinement.

**Lobby.** A vestibule or corridor, usually giving access to several apartments, from Med. Lat. *lobia*, a word used in the monasteries for the passages (connected with *lodge*). In the Houses of Parliament the name is given to the corridors ('Division Lobbies') to which members of the Commons go to vote, and also to the large ante-room to which the public are admitted. The latter gives us the verb *to lobby*, to solicit the vote of a member or to seek to influence members, and the noun *lobbyist*, one who does this.

***The Bill will cross the lobbies.*** Be sent from the House of Commons to the House of Lords.

**Loblolly.** A sailors' term for spoon-victuals, pap, water-gruel, and so on.

***Loblolly boy.*** A surgeon's mate in the Navy, a lad not yet out of his spoon-meat.

> Loblolly-boy is a person on board a man-of-war who attends the surgeon and his mates, but knows as much about the business of a seaman as the author of this poem.
>
> *The Patent* (1776)

**Lobsters.** Soldiers used to be popularly called lobsters, because they were 'turned red' when enlisted into the service. But the term was originally applied to a troop of horse soldiers in the Great Rebellion, clad in armour which covered them as a shell.

> Sir William Waller received from London (in 1643) a fresh regiment of 500 horse, under the command of Sir Arthur Haslerig, which were so prodigiously armed that they were called by the king's party 'the regiment of lobsters', because of their bright iron shells with which they were covered, being perfect cuirassiers, and were the first seen so armed on either side.
>
> Clarendon, *History of the Rebellion*, iii, 91

***Died for want of lobster sauce.*** Sometimes said of one who dies or suffers severely because of some trifling disappointment, pique, or wounded vanity. At the grand feast given by the great Condé to Louis XIV, at Chantilly, Vatel, the *chef*, was told that the lobsters intended for sauce had not arrived, whereupon he retired to his private room, and, leaning on his sword, ran it through his body, unable to survive such a dire disappointment.

**Lochiel.** The title of the head of the clan Cameron.

> And Cameron, in the shock of steel,
> Die like the offspring of Lochiel.
>
> Scott, *The Field of Waterloo*

The hero of Campbell's poem, *Lochiel's Warning* (1802), is Donald Cameron, known as *The Gentle Lochiel.* He was one of the Young Pretender's staunchest adherents, and escaped to France with him after Culloden (1746). He took service in the French army, but died two years later.

**Lochinvar,** being in love with a lady at Netherby Hall, persuaded her to dance one last dance. She was condemned to marry a 'laggard in love and a dastard in war', but her young chevalier swung her into his saddle and made off with her, before the 'bridegroom' and his servants could recover from their astonishment. (Scott, *Marmion.*)

**Lock, Stock, and Barrel.** The whole of anything. The lock, stock, and barrel of a gun is the complete instrument.

> The property of the Church of England, lock, stock, and barrel, is claimed by the Liberationists.
>
> Newspaper paragraph, 1885

**Lockhart.** Legend has it that when the good Lord James, on his way to the Holy Land with the heart of King Robert Bruce, was slain in Spain fighting against the Moors, Sir Simon Locard, of Lee, was commissioned to carry back to Scotland the heart, which was interred in Melrose Abbey. In consequence thereof he changed his name to Lock-heart, and adopted the device of *a heart within a fetterlock*, with this motto: '*Corda serrata pando*' (Locked hearts I open).

> For this reason men changed Sir Simon's name from Lockhard to Lockheart, and all who are descended from Sir Simon are called Lockhart to this day. Scott, *Tales of a Grandfather*, xi

**Lockman.** In the Isle of Man, the under-sheriff or Coroner's officer. The name used to be given in Scotland to the public executioner.

**Locksley.** So Robin Hood is sometimes called, from the village in which he was born; in Scott's *Ivanhoe* he adopted this name at the tournament (*see* ch. xiii).

**Locksley Hall.** Tennyson's poem of this name (1842) deals with an imaginary place and an imaginary hero. The Lord of Locksley Hall fell in love with his cousin Amy; she marries a rich clown, and he, indignant at this, declares he will wed a savage; he changes his mind, however, and decides, 'Better fifty years of Europe than a cycle of Cathay.'

In 1886 Tennyson published *Locksley Hall Sixty Years After*, another dramatic poem.

> The method in the old *Locksley Hall* and the new is the same. In each the maker is outside his work, and in each we have to deal with it as strictly 'impersonal'.
>
> W. E. Gladstone, *Nineteenth Century*, Jan., 1887

**Locksmith's Daughter.** A key.

**Locofocos.** A trade-name coined in America as that of a self-igniting cigar (patented in New York, 1834), but quickly transferred to lucifer matches, and then to the extreme Radicals, or Equal Rights faction, in America, because, at a meeting in Tammany Hall (1835), when the chairman left his seat, and the lights were suddenly extinguished, with the hope of breaking up the turbulent assembly, those in favour of extreme measures drew from their pockets their *locofocos*, re-lighted the gas, and got their way.

> When friction matches were first invented they were called 'Lucifer' in compliment to his Satanic highness; but in course of time the *locus in quo*, where he is supposed to dwell, was substituted in place of his name, and hence they were given the name *loco-foco*, the place of fire.
>
> Shields, *Life of Prentiss* (1884)

**Locrine.** Father of Sabrina, and eldest son of the mythical Brutus, King of ancient Britain. On the death of his father he became king of Loegria. (Geoffrey, *Brit. Hist.*, ii, 5.)

> Virgin daughter of Locrine,
> Sprung from old Anchises' line.
>
> Milton, *Comus*, 942–3

An anonymous tragedy, based on Holinshed and Geoffrey of Monmouth, was published under this name in 1595. As the words 'Newly set foorth, overseene and corrected, By *W. S.*' appear on the title-page, it was at one time ascribed to Shakespeare. It has also been ascribed to Marlowe, Greene, and Peele – the weight of evidence being rather in favour of the last named.

**Locum tenens** (Lat.). One (especially a doctor) acting temporarily for another.

**Locus delicti.** The place where a crime was committed.

**Locus in quo** (Lat.). The place in question, the spot mentioned.

**Locus poenitentiae** (Lat). Place for repentance – that is, the licence of drawing back from a bargain, which can be done before any act has been committed to confirm it. In the interview between Esau and his father Isaac, St Paul says that the former 'found no place for repentance, though he sought it carefully with tears' (Heb. 12:17) – i.e. no means whereby Isaac could break his bargain with Jacob.

**Locus sigilli** (Lat.). The place where the seal is to be set; usually abbreviated in documents to 'L.S.'

**Locus standi** (Lat.). Recognised position, acknowledged right or claim, especially in courts of law. We say such-and-such a one has no *locus standi* in society.

**Locusta.** One who murders those she professes to nurse, or those whom it is her duty to take care of. The original Locusta lived in the early days of the Roman empire, poisoned Claudius and Britannicus, and attempted to destroy Nero; but, being found out, she was put to death.

**Lode.** Originally a ditch that guides or leads water into a river or sewer, from A.S. *lād*, way, course (connected with *to lead*); hence, in mines, the vein that leads or guides to ore.

**Lodestar.** The North Star or Pole Star; the *leading-star* by which mariners are guided (*see* Lode).

> Your eyes are lodestars.
>
> Shakespeare, *Midsummer Night's Dream*, 1, 1

**Lodestone, Loadstone.** The magnet or stone that guides (*see above*).

**Lodona.** The Lodden, an affluent of the Thames in Windsor Forest. Pope, in *Windsor Forest*, says it was a nymph, fond of the chase, like Diana. It chanced one day that Pan saw her, and tried to catch her; but Lodona fled from him, imploring Cynthia to save her from her persecutor. No sooner had she spoken than she became 'a silver stream which ever keeps its virgin coolness'.

**Loegria** or **Logres.** England is so called by Geoffrey of Monmouth, from Locrine (*q.v.*).

> His [Brute's] three sons divide the land by consent:
> Locrine had the middle part, Loëgra.
>
> Milton, *History of England*, Bk i
>
> Thus Cambria to her right, what would herself restore,
> And rather than to lose Loegria, looks for more.
>
> Drayton, *Polyolbion*, iv

**Log.** An instrument for measuring the velocity of a ship in motion. In its simplest form it is a flat piece of wood, some six inches in radius, in the shape of a quadrant, and made so that it will float perpendicularly. To this is fastened the log-line, knotted at intervals. *See* Knot.

***A King Log.*** A *roi fainéant*, a king who rules in peace and quietness, but never makes his power felt. In allusion to the fable of the frogs asking for a king. Jupiter first threw them down a log of wood, but they grumbled at so spiritless a king. He then sent them a stork, which devoured them eagerly.

**Log-book.** On board ship, the journal in which the 'logs' are entered by the chief mate. It contains also all general transactions pertaining to the ship and its crew, such as the strength and course of the winds, the conduct and misconduct of the men, and, in short, everything worthy of note.

**Log-rolling.** The combination of different interests, on the principle of 'Claw me, I'll claw you'. Applied in politics to the 'give and take' principle, by which one party will further certain interests of another in return for assistance given in passing their own measures, and in literary circles to mutual admiration criticism. One friend praises the literary work of another with the implied understanding of receiving from him in return as much as he gives. The mutual admirers are called 'log-rollers', and the allusion (originally American) is to neighbours who assist a new settler to roll away the logs of his 'clearing'.

**Loganberry.** A cross between the raspberry and blackberry; so called from Judge Logan, of California, who was the first to cultivate it (end of 19th century).

**Logan Stones.** Rocking stones; large masses of stone so delicately poised by nature that they will rock to and fro at a touch. There are many logan stones in Cornwall, Derbyshire, Yorkshire, and Wales, and some well known specimens in Scotland and Ireland; they were formerly used in connection with Druidical rites. When the Logan Rock (about 70 tons) at Land's End was displaced by a naval lieutenant (1824), he was ordered to replace it, which he did at a cost of some £2,000.

> Pliny tells us of a rock near Harpasa which might be moved with a finger.
>
> Ptolemy says the Gygonian rock might be stirred with a stalk of asphodel.
>
> Half a mile from St David's is a Logan stone, mounted on divers other stones, which may be shaken with one finger.
>
> At Golcar Hill (Yorkshire) is one which has lost its property from being hacked by workmen who wanted to find out its secret.
>
> In Pembrokeshire is a rocking stone, rendered immovable by the soldiers of Cromwell, who held it to be an encouragement to superstition.
>
> The stone called Menamber in Sithney (Cornwall) was also rendered immovable by the soldiers, under the same notion.

**Loggerheads. *Fall to loggerheads;*** to squabbling and fisticuffs. The word is used by Shakespeare. *Logger* was the name given to the heavy wooden clog fastened to the legs of grazing horses to prevent them straying.

**Logistilla.** The good fairy in *Orlando Furioso*, sister of Alcina the sorceress. She teaches Ruggiero to manage the hippogriff, and gives Astolpho magic book and horn.

**Logres, Logria.** *See* Loegria.

**Logris.** Same as Locrine (*q.v.*).

**Lohengrin.** A son of Percival, in *German legend*; attached to the Grail Cycle, and Knight of the Swan. He appears at the close of Wolfram von Eschenbach's *Parzival* (about 1210), and in other German romances, where he is the deliverer of Elsa, Princess of Brabant, who has been dispossessed by Tetramund and Ortrud. He arrives at Antwerp in a skiff drawn by a swan, champions Elsa, and becomes her husband on the sole condition that she shall not ask his name or lineage. She is prevailed upon to do so on the marriage-night, and he, by his vows to the Grail, is obliged to disclose his identity, but at the same time disappears. The swan returns for him, and he goes; but not before retransforming the swan into Elsa's brother Gottfried, who, by the wiles of the sorceress Ortrud, had been obliged to assume that form. Wagner has an opera on the subject, composed (words and music) in 1847.

**Loins. *Gird up your loins.*** Brace yourself for vigorous action, or energetic endurance. The Jews wore loose garments, which they girded about their loins when they travelled or worked.

> Gird up the loins of your mind. 1 Pet. 1:13

***My little finger shall be thicker than my father's loins*** (1 Kings 12:10). My lightest tax shall be heavier than the most oppressive tax of my predecessor. The arrogant answer of Rehoboam to the deputation which waited on him to entreat an alleviation of 'the yoke' laid on them by Solomon. The reply caused the revolt of all the tribes, except those of Judah and Benjamin.

**Loki.** The god of strife and spirit of evil in *Norse mythology*, son of the giant Firbauti and Laufey, or Nal, the friend of the enemy of the gods, and father of the Midgard Serpent (Jormungandr), Fenrir, and Hel. It was he who artfully contrived the death of Balder (*q.v.*). He was finally chained to a rock with ten chains, and – according to one legend – will so continue till the Twilight of the Gods appears, when he will break his bonds; the heavens will disappear, the earth be swallowed up by the sea, fire shall consume the elements, and even Odin, with all his kindred deities, shall perish. Another story has it that he was freed at Ragnarok, and that he and Heimdall fought till both were slain.

**Lokmân.** A fabulous personage, the supposed author of a collection of Arabic fables. The name is founded on *Lugman*, the title of the 31st Surah of the Koran, in which occur the words 'We gave to Lugman wisdom'. Like Aesop, he is said to have been a slave, noted for his ugliness.

**Lollards.** The early German reformers and the followers of Wyclif were so called. An ingenious derivation is given by Bailey, who suggests the Latin word *lolium* (darnel), because these reformers were deemed 'tares in God's wheat-field', but the name is from Mid. Dut. *lollaerd*, a mutterer, one who mumbles over prayers and hymns.

Gregory XI, in one of his bulls against Wyclif, urged the clergy to extirpate this *lolium.*

**Lombard.** A banker or moneylender, so called because the first bankers were from Lombardy, and set up in Lombard Street (London), in the Middle Ages.

> I am an honester man than Will. Coppersmith, for all his great credit among the Lombards.
>
> Steele, *The Tatler*, No. lvii

The business of lending money on pawns was carried on in England by Italian merchants or bankers as early as the reign of Richard I. By the time of Edward I, a messuage was confirmed to these traders where Lombard Street now stands; they exercised a monopoly in pawnbroking till the reign of Queen Elizabeth, but the trade was first recognised in law by James I. *Lombard* is a contraction of Longobards, the name of the ancient inhabitants of that part of Italy. Among the richest of the Lombard merchant princes was the celebrated Medici family, from whose armorial bearings the insignia of three golden balls has been derived.

***All Lombard Street to a China orange.*** An old saying, implying very long odds. Lombard Street, London, is the centre of great banking and mercantile transactions. To stake the wealth of London against a common orange is to stake what is of untold value against a mere trifle.

> 'It is Lombard Street to a China orange,' quoth Uncle Jack. Bulwer Lytton, *The Caxtons*

**London.** The origin of the name is uncertain, but it first appears in Tacitus (Lib. XIV, ch. xxxiii, AD 61):

> At Suetonius mira constantia medios inter hostes Londinium perrexit, cognomento quidem coloniae non insigne, sed copia negotiatorum et commeatum maxime celebre.

Stow, following Geoffrey of Monmouth, says that it was originally called Troynovant (*q.v.*), and that Caesar's 'cittie of the Trinobantes' meant London. By later Latin writers it was frequently called 'Londinium Augusta'.

The first syllable may represent Welsh *lli*, water, and the second be the Celtic *dun*, a hill-fort – the fort on the water; *lon-* may equally well be Celtic *lon*, a marsh, or *llwyn*, a grove, while another authority says that it is Welsh *llong*, a ship – the City of Ships.

Francis Crossley derives the name from *Luan-dun* (Celtic), City of the Moon, and tradition says there was once a temple of Diana (the Moon) where St Paul's now stands; but he says that Greenwich (*q.v.*) is *Grianwich* (City of the Sun), also Celtic. It would fill a page to give a list of guesses made at the derivation of the word London.

**London Bridge.** There was a bridge over the Thames in the 10th century. There was a new one of wood in 1014. The stone bridge (1176–1209) was by Peter of Colechurch. New London Bridge, constructed of granite, was begun in 1824, and finished in seven years. It was designed by Sir John Rennie, and cost £1,458,000. Till 1750 London Bridge was the only bridge crossing the Thames in London.

***London Bridge was built upon wool-packs.*** An old saying commemorating the fact that in the reign of Henry II the new stone bridge over the Thames was paid for by a tax on wool.

**London Stone.** The ancient Roman stone now fixed for security in the wall of St Swithin's church, facing Cannon Street station, and guarded by an iron grille. It has two inscriptions, one in Latin and one in English. The latter runs thus:

> London stone. Commonly believed to be a Roman work, long placed about xxxv feet hence towards the south-west, and afterwards built into the wall of this church, was, for more careful protection and transmission to future ages, better secured by the churchwardens in the year of OUR LORD MDCCCLXIX.

It is supposed to have been the central milliarium (*milestone*) of Roman London, similar to that in the Forum of Rome, from which the high roads radiated and were measured.

**Long.** For *Long chalks*, *dozen*, *home*, *odds*, etc., *see* these words.

***So long*.** Goodbye, till we meet again.

**Long-headed.** Clever, sharp-witted. Those who believe in the shape and bumps of the head think that a long head indicates shrewdness.

**Long Meg of Westminster.** A noted virago in the reign of Henry VIII, round whose exploits a comedy (since lost) was performed in London in 1594.

> *Lord Proudly*: What d'ye this afternoon?
> *Lord Feesimple*: Faith, I have a great mind to see *Long Meg* and *The Ship* at the Fortune.
> Field, *Amends for Ladies*, II, i (1618)

Her name has been given to several articles of unusual size. Thus, the large blue-black marble in the south cloister of Westminster Abbey, over the grave of Gervasius de Blois, is called 'Long Meg of Westminster'. Fuller says the term is applied to things 'of hop-pole height, wanting breadth proportionable thereunto', and refers to a great gun in the Tower so called, taken to Westminster in troublous times; and in the *Edinburgh Antiquarian Magazine* (September, 1769) we read of Peter Branan, aged 104, who was 6 ft 6 in. high, and was commonly called *Long Meg of Westminster*, *Cp.* Meg.

***Long Meg and her daughters.*** In the neighbourhood of Penrith, Cumberland, is a circle of 67 (Camden says 77) stones, some of them 10 ft high, ranged in a circle. Some seventeen paces off, on the south side, is a single stone, 15 ft high, called *Long Meg*, the shorter ones being called *her daughters*.

> This, and the Robrick stones in Oxfordshire, are supposed to have been erected at the investiture of some Danish kings, like the Kingstoler in Denmark and the Moresteen in Sweden.
> Camden, *Britannia*

**Long Parliament.** The parliament that sat 12 years and 5 months, from November 2nd, 1640, to April 20th, 1653, when it was dissolved by Cromwell. A fragment of it, called 'The Rump' (*q.v.*), continued till the Restoration, in 1660.

**Long-Sword (*Longue épée*).** The surname of William, the first Duke of Normandy (d.943). He was the great-great-grandfather of William the Conqueror, and so a direct ancestor of our reigning House. The name was also given to William, third Earl of Salisbury (d.1226), a natural son of Henry II and (probably) the Fair Rosamund.

**Long Tail. *Cut and long tail.*** One and another, all of every description. The phrase had its origin in the practice of cutting the tails of certain dogs and horses, and leaving others in their natural state, so that cut and long tail horses or dogs included all the species. Master Slender says he will maintain Anne Page like a gentlewoman. 'Ah!' says he –

> That I will, come cut and long tail under the degree of a squire [i.e. as well as any man can who is not a squire].
> Shakespeare, *Merry Wives of Windsor*, 3, 4

***How about the long-tailed beggar?*** A reproof given to one who is drawing the longbow too freely. The tale is that a boy who had been a short voyage pretended on his return to have forgotten everything belonging to his home, and asked his mother what she called that 'long-tailed beggar', meaning the cat.

**Long Words.** 'Honorificabilitudinitatibus' (*q.v.*) has often been called the longest word in the English language; 'quadradimensionality' is almost as long, and 'antidisestablishmentarianism' beats it by one letter.

While there is some limit to the coining of polysyllabic words by the conglomeration of prefixes, combining forms, and suffixes (e.g. 'deanthropomorphisation', 'inanthropomorphisability'), there is little to the length to which chemists will go in the nomenclature of compounds, and none at all to that indulged in by facetious romancers like Rabelais, the author of *Croquemitaine*. The chemists furnish us with such concatenations (for they are scarcely *words*) as 'nitrophenylenediamine', and 'tetramethyldiamidobenzhydrols'; but the worst in this sort are far surpassed by the nonsense words found in Urquhart and Motteux's translation of Rabelais. The following come from a single chapter (Bk IV, ch. xv):

> He was grown quite esperru-quanchurelubelouzerireliced down to his very heel …
>
> … not satisfied with thus poaching, blacking and blueing, and morrambouzevezengozequoquemorgasacbaquevezinemaffreloding my poor eyes …
>
> What Mr Manhound, was it not enough thus to have morcrocastebezasteverestegrigeligoscopapopondrillated us all in our upper members with your botched mittens, but you must also apply such morderegripippitabirofreluchamburelurecaquelurintimpaniments on our shinbones with the hard tops and extremities of your cobbled shoes

In the 'spoof' catalogue of the books in the library of St Victor (Bk ii. ch. vii) is one with the title 'Antipericatametanaparbeugedamphicribrationes Toordicantium'.

Sesquipedalian place-names in Britain include Drimtaidhvrickhillichattan, in the Isle of Mull, Argyleshire, and the famous village in Anglesea, Llanfairpwllgwyngyllgogerychwyrndrobwllll-andyssiliogogogoch. In the postal directory the first twenty letters only are given as a sufficient address for practical purposes, but the full name contains 59 letters. The meaning is, 'The church of St Mary in a hollow of white hazel, near to the rapid whirlpool, and to St Tisilio church, near to a red cave'.

The longest English surname is said to be Featherstonehaugh; but this is easily surpassed in Greece and Eastern Europe, and it is said that in 1867 there was an employee in the Finance Department at Madrid named Juan Nepomuceno de Burionagonatotorecagageazcoecha.

The longest English monosyllables are probably 'stretched' and 'screeched'.

The German language lends itself to very extensive agglomerations of syllables, but the following official title of a North Bohemian officia 'Lebensmittelzuschlusseinstellungskommissionsvorsitzenderstellvertreter', i.e. Deputy-President of the Food-Rationing-Winding-up-Commission – would be hard to beat.

**Longboat.** Formerly the largest boat carried by a sailing ship, built so as to take a great weight. A longboat is often from 30 to 40 feet long, having a beam from ·29 to ·25 of its length. It has a heavy flat floor, and is carvel-built.

**Longbow.** ***To draw the longbow***. *See* Bow.

**Longchamps.** The racecourse at the end of the Bois de Boulogne, Paris. An abbey formerly stood there, and it has long been celebrated for the promenade of smartly dressed Parisians which takes place on the Wednesday, Thursday, and Friday of Passion Week.

The custom dates from the time when all who could do so went to the abbey to hear the Ténèbres sung in Passion Week; and it survives as an excellent opportunity to display the latest spring fashions.

**Longevity.** The oldest man of modern times was Thomas Carn, if we may rely on the parish register of St Leonard's, Shoreditch, where it is recorded that he died in the reign of Queen Elizabeth, aged 207. He was born in 1381, in the reign of Richard II, lived in the reigns of ten sovereigns, and died in 1588. Old Jenkins was only 160 when he died, and remembered going (when he was a boy of twelve) with a load of arrows, to be used in the battle of Flodden Field. Parr died at the age of 152. William Wakley (according to the register of St Andrew's Church, Shifnal, Salop) was at least 124 when he died. He was baptised at Idsal 1590, and buried at Adbaston, November 28th, 1714, and he lived in the reigns of eight sovereigns. Mary Yates, of Lizard Common, Shifnal, married her third husband at the age of 92, and died in 1776, at the age of 127.

**Longinus**, or **Longius.** The traditional name of the Roman soldier who smote our Lord with his spear at the Crucifixion. In the romance of King Arthur, this spear was brought by Joseph of Arimathea to Listenise, when he visited King Pellam, 'who was nigh of Joseph's kin'. Sir Balim the Savage, being in want of a weapon, seized this spear, with which he wounded King Pellam. 'Three whole countries were destroyed' by that one stroke, and Sir Balim saw 'the people thereof lying dead on all sides'.

**Longo Intervallo.** ***Proximus sed longo intervallo***. Next (it is true), but at what a vast distance! Generally quoted *Longo intervallo*.

**Longshoremen.** *See* Alongshoremen.

**Look.** To look *black*, *blue*, *daggers*, a *gift-horse*, etc., *see* these words.

***Look before you leap.*** Consider well before you act. *Melius est cavere semper, quam patiri semel.*

And look before you ere you leap,
For, as you sow, you're like to reap.
Butler, *Hudibras*, canto ii, Pt ii, 502

***To look one way and row another. Olera spectant, lardum tollunt***. To aim apparently at one thing, but really to be seeking something quite different.

***To look through blue glasses*** or ***coloured spectacles.*** To regard actions in a wrong light; to view things distorted by prejudice.

**Lookers-on.** ***Lookers on see most of the game***. Of course, if they know anything about the game; for their attention is not occupied by trying to win, and they are able to watch both sides at once. An old form of the proverb is: *The man on the dyke always hurls well*; he can see the faults of the hurlers and criticise them.

**Looking Back.** *It is unlucky to look back.* The superstition arose from the fate of Lot's wife, who looked back towards Sodom and was turned to a pillar of salt (Gen. 19:26).

**Looking-glass.** ***It is unlucky to break a looking-glass***. The nature of the ill-luck varies; thus, if a maiden, she will never marry; if a married woman, it betokens a death, etc. This superstition arose from the use made of mirrors in former times by magicians. If in their operations the mirror used was broken, the magician was obliged to give over his operation, and the unlucky enquirer could receive no answer.

**Loony.** A simpleton; a 'natural'. Corruption of *lunatic.*

**Loophole.** A way of escape, an evasion. The word was first used in fortification (late 16th cent.), and was probably imported from Holland, *loop* representing Dut. *luipen*, to watch or peer (*gluip*, a narrow opening).

**Looping the Loop.** The airman's term for the evolution which consists of describing a perpendicular circle in the air with his machine; at the top of the circle, or 'loop', the airman and the areoplane are, of course, upside down. The term comes from a kind of switchback that used to be popular at fairs, etc., in which a rapidly moving car or bicycle performed a similar evolution on a perpendicular circular track.

**Loose.** Figuratively – of lax morals; dissolute, dissipated.

> Drummond ... was a loose and profane man: but a sense of honour which his two kinsmen wanted restrained him from a public apostasy.
>
> Macaulay, *Hist. of Eng.*, ch.vi

***A loose fish.*** *See* Fish.

***At a loose end.*** Without employment, or uncertain what to do next.

***Having a tile loose.*** *See* Tile.

***On the loose.*** Dissolute (which is *dis-solutus*). *Living on the loose* is leading a dissolute life.

***To play fast and loose.*** *See* Fast.

**Loose-coat Field.** The battle near Empingham (Rutland) in 1470. So called because the rebels under Sir Robert Welles, being attacked by the Yorkists, threw off their coats that they might flee the faster.

> Cast off their country's coats to haste their speed away;
> Which 'Loose-coat Field' is called e'en to this day.
>
> Drayton, *Polyolbion*, xxii

**Loose-strife.** The name of this plant is an instance of erroneous translation. The Greeks called it *lusimachion*, from the personal name *Lusimachos*, and this was treated as though it were *lusi-*, from *luein*, to loose, and *mache*, strife. Pliny refers the name to one of Alexander's generals, said to have discovered its virtues, but the mistake obtained such currency that the author of *Flora Domestica* tells us that the Romans put these flowers under the yokes of oxen to keep them from quarrelling with each other; for (says he) the plant keeps off flies and gnats and thus relieves horses and oxen from a great source of irritation. Similarly in Fletcher's *Faithful Shepherdess* (II, ii), we read –

> Yellow Lysimachus, to give sweet rest,
> To the faint shepherd, killing, where it comes,
> All busy gnats, and every fly that hums.

**Lope.** *See* Slope.

**Lorbrulgrud.** The capital of Brobdingnag, in Swift's *Gulliver's Travels.* The word is humorously said to mean 'Pride of the Universe'.

**Lord.** A nobleman, a peer of the realm; formerly (and in some connections still), a ruler, a master, the holder of a manor; also, one's husband, as in Tennyson's –

> You hold the woman is the better man:
> A rampant heresy, such as if it spread
> Would make all women kick against their lords.
>
> *Princess*, iv, 410

The word is a contraction of A.S. *hlāford*, *hlāf*, loaf, and modern *ward*, i.e. the *bread-guardian*, or *-keeper*, the head of the household (*cp.* Lady); all members of the *House of Lords* are *Lords* (the Archbishops and Bishops being *Lords Spiritual*, and the lay peers *Lords Temporal*); and the word is given as a courtesy title as a prefix to the Christian and surname of the younger sons of dukes and marquises, and to the eldest sons of viscounts and earls when the fathers hold subordinate titles as barons, and as a title of honour to certain official personages, as the Lord Chief Justice and other Judges, the Lord Mayor, Lord Advocate, Lord Rector, etc. A baron is called by his title of peerage (either a surname or territorial designation), prefixed by the title 'Lord', as 'Lord Dawson', 'Lord Islington', and it may also be substituted in other than strictly ceremonial use for 'Marquis', 'Earl', or 'Viscount', the *of* being dropped, as 'Lord Salisbury' (for 'the Marquis of Salisbury'), 'Lord Derby' ('The Earl of Derby'), etc.; this cannot be done in the case of dukes.

***Drunk as a lord.*** *See* Drunk.

***In the Year of our Lord.*** *See* Anno Domini.

***Lord Harry.*** *See* Harry.

***Lord Mayor.*** *See* Alderman.

***Lord Mayor's Day,*** November 9th. So called because the Lord Mayor of London enters office on that day, and inaugurates his official dignity with a procession through the City to the Royal Courts of Justice, followed by a grand banquet at the Guildhall.

***Lord of the Ascendant.*** *See* Ascendant.

***Lord of Creation.*** Man.

> Replenish the earth, and subdue it: and have dominion over the fish of the sea, and over the fowl of the air, and over every living thing that moveth upon the earth ... Behold, I have given you every herb bearing seed ... and every tree ...
>
> Gen. 1:28, 29

***Lord of the Isles.*** Donald of Islay, who in 1346 reduced the Hebrides under his sway. The title had been borne by others for centuries before, and is now borne by the Prince of Wales. One of Scott's metrical romances is so called.

***Lord of Misrule.*** *See* King of Misrule.

***Lords and ladies.*** The popular name of the wild arum, *Arum maculatum.*

> Lords and ladies
> By the water –
> Pale their faces,
> Slender throated,
> Decked with laces,
> Greenly coated.
> Fairest maid is
> Arum's daughter.
>
> Lady Lindsay, *A String of Beads*

***My Lord.*** The correct form to use in addressing Judges of the Supreme Court (usually slurred to 'M'Lud'), also the respectful form of address to bishops, noblemen under the rank of a Duke, Lord Mayors, Lord Provosts, and the Lord Advocate.

***The Lord knows who, what, where, etc.*** Flippant expressions used to denote one's own entire ignorance of the matter.

> Great families of yesterday we show,
> And lords, whose parents were the Lord knows who.
>
> Defoe, *The True-Born Englishman*, 374

> Ask where's the north? At York, 'tis on the Tweed;
> In Scotland, at the Orcades; and there,
> At Greenland, Zembla, or the Lord knows where.
>
> Pope, *Essay on Man*, ii, 217

***The Lord's Day.*** Sunday.

***To live like a lord.*** To 'do oneself well', to fare luxuriously, live like a fighting-cock (*q.v.*).

***To lord it,*** or ***lord it over.*** To play the lord; to rule tyranically, to domineer.

> Yon grey towers that still
> Rise up as if to lord it over air.
>
> Wordsworth, *The Punishment of Death*, Sonn. i

***When our Lord falls in our Lady's lap.*** When Easter Sunday falls on the same date as Lady Day (March 25th). This is said to bode ill for England. In the 19th century the combination occurred only twice (1883 and 1894); in the 20th its sole occurrence is in 1951.

**Lorel.** A worthless person; a rogue or blackguard. The word is from *loren*, the past part, of the old verb *leese*, to lose, and is chiefly remembered through 'Cock Lorell'. *See* Cock Lorell's Bote.

> Here I set before the good Reader the leud, lousey language of these lewtering Luskes and lasy Lorrels, wherewith they bye and sell the common people as they pas through the countrey. Whych language they terme Peddelar's Frenche.
>
> *Harman's Caveat* (1567)

**Loretto.** ***The house of Loretto.*** The Santa Casa, the reputed house of the Virgin Mary at Nazareth. It was 'miraculously' translated to Fiume in Dalmatia in 1291, thence to Recanati in 1294, and finally to a plot of land belonging to a certain Lady *Lauretta*, situated in Italy, 3 m. from the Adriatic, and about 14 SSE from Ancona, round which the town of Loretto sprang up. The chapel contains bas-reliefs showing incidents in the life of the Virgin, and a rough image which is traditionally held to have been carved by St Luke.

> Our house may have travelled through the air, like the house of Loretto, for aught I care.
>
> Goldsmith, *The Good-natured Man*, iv, 1

There is a Loretto in Styria – Mariazel (*Mary in the Cell*), so called from the miracle-working image of the Virgin, made of ebony, and very ugly; another in Bavaria (*Altötting*), near the river Inn, where there is a shrine of the Black Virgin; and one in Switzerland, at Einsiedeln, a village containing the shrine of the 'Black Lady of Switzerland', a church of black marble with an image of ebony.

**Loss.** ***To be at a loss.*** To be unable to decide. To be puzzled or embarrassed. As: 'I am at a loss for the proper word.' *Je m'y perds*, or *Je suis bien embarrassé de dire.*

**Lothair.** A novel by Benjamin Disraeli (Lord Beaconsfield), pub. 1870. The characters are supposed to represent the following persons:

The Oxford Professor, Goldwin Smith.
Grandison, Cardinals Manning and Wiseman.
Lothair, Marquis of Bute.
Catesby, Monseigneur Capel.
The Duke and Duchess, the Duke and Duchess of Abercorn.
The Bishop, Bishop Wilberforce.
Corisande, one of the Ladies Hamilton.

**Lothario.** ***A gay Lothario.*** A gay libertine, a seducer of women, a debauchee. The character is from Rowe's tragedy *The Fair Penitent* (1703), which is founded on Massinger's *Fatal Dowry*, though Rowe probably got the *name* from Davenant's *Cruel Brother* (1630), where is a similar character with the same name.

Is this that haughty, gallant, gay Lothario?
*Fair Penitent*, v, 1

**Lothian** (Scotland). So named, according to tradition, from King Lot, or Lothus, Llew, the second son of Arthur, also called Lothus. He was the father of Modred, leader of the rebellious army that fought at Camlan, AD 537.

**Lotus.** A name given to many plants, e.g. by the Egyptians to various species of water-lily, by the Hindus and Chinese to the Nelumbo (a water-bean, *Nymphaeaceae speciosum*), their 'sacred lotus', and by the Greeks to *Zizyphus Lotus*, a north African shrub of the natural order Rhamneae, the fruit of which was used for food.

According to Mahomet a lotus tree stands in the seventh heaven, on the right hand of the throne of God, and the Egyptians pictured God sitting on a lotus above the watery mud. Jamblichus says the leaves and fruit of the lotus tree being *round* represent 'the motion of intellect'; its towering up through mud symbolises the eminency of divine intellect over matter; and the Deity sitting on it implies His intellectual sovereignty. (*Myster. Egypt.*, sec. 7, cap. ii, p. 151.)

The classic myth is that *Lotis*, a daughter of Neptune, fleeing from Priapus was changed into a tree, which was called *Lotus* after her, while another story goes that *Dryope* of Oechalia was one day carrying her infant son, when she plucked a lotus flower for his amusement, and was instantaneously transformed into a lotus.

**Lotus-eaters** or **Lotophagi,** in Homeric legend, are a people who ate of the lotus tree (thought to be intended for *Zizyphus Lotus*, *see above*), the effect of which was to make them forget their friends and homes, and to lose all desire of returning to their native country, their only wish being to live in idleness in Lotus-land (*Odyssey*, xi). Hence, a *lotus-eater* is one living in ease and luxury. *See* Tennyson's poem on this subject.

**Louis, St.** (Louis IX of France, 1215, 1226–70), is usually represented as holding the Saviour's crown of thorns and the cross; sometimes, however, he is pictured with a pilgrim's staff, and sometimes with the standard of the cross, the allusion in all cases being to his crusades.

**Louisette.** *See* Guillotine.

**Louisiana,** USA. So named in compliment to Louis XIV of France. Originally applied to the French possessions in the Mississippi Valley.

The *Louisiana Purchase* was the acquirement by the US Government in 1803 of New Orleans and a vast tract of territory extending westward from the Mississippi to the Rockies, and northward from the Gulf of Mexico to the Canadian border, from the French under Napoleon (then First Consul) for the sum of $15,000,000.

**Louver** or **Louvre.** The tower or turret of mediaeval buildings, originally designed for a sort of chimney to let out the smoke by means of *louvre boards*, i.e. narrow sloping and overlapping boards which, while allowing smoke to emerge, prevented the entrance of rain. *Louvre* is the old Fr. *lover* or *lovier*, probably from Old High Ger. *lauba*, whence our *lodge*.

**Louvre.** The former royal palace of the French kings in Paris.

Dagobert is said to have built here a hunting-seat, but the present magnificent pile of buildings was begun by Francis I in 1541. Since the French Revolution the greater part of the Louvre has been used for the national museum and art gallery.

He'll make your Paris Louvre shake for it.
Shakespeare, *Henry V*, 2, 4

**Love.** The word is connected with Sanskrit *lubh*, to desire (Lat. *lubet*, it pleases), and was *lufu* in A.S.

***A labour of love.*** Work undertaken for the love of the thing, without regard to pay.

***Love and lordship never like fellowship.*** Neither lovers nor princes can brook a rival.

***Love in a cottage.*** A marriage for love without sufficient means to maintain one's social status. 'When poverty comes in at the door, love flies out of the window.'

Love in a hut, with water and a crust,
Is – Love, forgive us! – cinders, ashes, dust;
Love in a palace is, perhaps, at last
More grievous torment than a hermit's fast.
Keats, *Lamia*, Pt ii

***Love me, love my dog.*** If you love anyone, you will like all that belongs to him. St Bernard quotes this proverb in Latin, *Qui me amat, amat et canem meam*; French, *Qui aime Bertrand, aime son chien.*

***Love's Girdle.*** *See* Cestus.

***Not for love* or *money.*** Unobtainable, either for payment or for entreaties.

***The Abode of Love.*** *See* Agapemone.

***The family of love.*** Certain fanatics in the 16th century, holding tenets not unlike those of the Anabaptists. They were founded by David Joris (or George), a Dutchman (1501–65), and in England formed a sect of the Puritans in the reign of Queen Elizabeth. They are also known as the 'Familists'.

***The god of love.*** Generally meaning either Eros (Gr.) or Cupid (*Roman mythology*). Among the Scandinavians Freyja was the goddess of sexual love, and among the Hindus Kama more or less takes the place of Eros.

***There is no love lost between so and so.*** Because the persons referred to have no love for each other; what does not exist cannot be lost. Formerly the phrase was used in exactly the opposite sense – it was *all* love between them, and none of it went a-missing. In the old ballad *The Babes in the Wood* we have –

> No love between these two was lost
> Each was to other kind.

***To play for love.*** To play without stakes, for nothing. In tennis *love* in scoring signifies nothing, i.e. no score.

***Love-lock.*** A small curl worn by women, plastered to the temples; sometimes called a *beau* or *bow* catcher. A man's 'love-lock' is called a *bell-rope* – i.e. a rope to pull the *belles* after them. At the latter end of the 16th century the love-lock was a long lock of hair hanging in front of the shoulders, curled and decorated with bows and ribbons.

***Love-powders*** or ***Potions*** were drugs to excite lust. Once these love-charms were generally believed in; thus, Brabantio accuses Othello of having bewitched Desdemona with 'drugs to waken motion'; and Lady Grey was accused of having bewitched Edward IV 'by strange potions and amorous charms' (Fabian, p. 495).

**Love-in-Idleness.** One of the numerous names of the pansy or heartsease (*q.v.*). Fable has it that it was originally white, but was changed to purple by Cupid.

> Yet marked I where the bolt of Cupid fell,
> It fell upon a little Western flower.
> Before, milk-white, now purple with love's wound;
> The maidens call it Love-in-idleness.
> Shakespeare, *Midsummer Night's Dream*, 2, 1

**Love's Labour's Lost.** The exact form of the title of this, probably the first of Shakespeare's plays (1588), cannot be ascertained, but that we give is the generally accepted form, the first 's' denoting the possessive, and the second the contraction of 'is'. On the title-page of the first quarto it is given as 'A Pleasant Conceited Comedie called, Loves labors lost', with no apostrophes; the running head-line of this edition, however, is 'Love's Labour's Lost', while the title given to the play in the first folio (1623) is 'Loves Labour's Lost'. Other variants are Meres's 'Love labors lost' and Robert Tofle's 'Loves Labour Lost' (both 1598), Sir Walter Cope's 'Loves Labore lost' (1604), Drummond of Hawthornden's 'Loves Labors Lost' (1606), and Dryden's 'Love's labour lost' (1672).

**Lovel, the Dog.** *See* Rat, Cat, etc.

**Lovelace.** The principal male character of Richardson's novel *Clarissa Harlowe* (1748). He is a selfish voluptuary, a man of fashion, whose sole ambition is to seduce young women, and he is – like Lothario (*q.v.*) – often taken as the type of a libertine. Crabbe calls him 'rich, proud, and crafty; handsome, brave, and gay'.

**Lover's Leap.** A name given (often with some legend attached) to precipitous rocks in many parts. *Cp.* Leucadia.

**Loving** or **Grace Cup.** A large cup passed round from guest to guest at formal banquets, especially at College, Court, and in the City of London. Miss Strickland says that Margaret Atheling, wife of Malcolm Canmore, in order to induce the Scots to remain for grace, devised the grace cup, which was filled with the choicest wine, and of which each guest was allowed to drink *ad libitum* after grace had been said. (*Historic Sketches.*)

On the introduction of Christianity, the custom of wassailing was not abolished, but it assumed a religious aspect. The monks called the wassail bowl the *poculum caritatis* (loving cup), a term still retained in the London companies, but in the universities the term *Grace Cup* is more general.

> At the Lord Mayor's or City companies' banquets the loving-cup is a silver bowl with two handles, a napkin being tied to one of them. Two persons stand up, one to drink and the other to defend the drinker. Having taken his draught, the first wipes the cup with the napkin, and passes it to his 'defender', when the next person rises to defend the new drinker, and so on to the end.

**Low.** ***To lay low*** is transitive, and means to overthrow or to kill; *to lie low* is intransitive, and means to be abased, or dead, and (in slang use) to bide one's time, to do nothing at the moment.

***In low water.*** Financially embarrassed; or, in a bad state of health. The phrase comes from seafaring men; *cp.* 'stranded', 'left high and dry'.

**Low-bell.** A bell formerly used in night-fowling. The birds were first roused from their slumber by its tinkling, and then dazzled by a *low* (Sc. for 'a blaze' or 'flame') so as to be easily caught. The word *low-bell* was, however, in earlier use for any small bell, such as a sheep-bell, without any connection with lights or fowling.

> The sound of the low-bell makes the birds lie close, so that they dare not stir whilst you are pitching the net: for the sound thereof is dreadful to them: but the sight of the fire, much more terrible, makes them fly up, so that they become instantly entangled in the net.
>
> *British Sportsman* (1792)

**Low Church.** The *Times* defines a Low Churchman as one 'who loves a Jew and hates the Pope'. We now call a Calvinistic episcopalian one of the Low Church because he holds 'church rituals' and the dogma of 'apostolic succession' in lower esteem than personal grace and faith in the 'blood of the atonement'.

**Low Sunday.** The Sunday next after Easter.

> The popular English name of Low Sunday has probably arisen from the contrast between the joys of Easter and the first return to ordinary Sunday services. On this Sunday, or sometimes on the fourth Sunday after Easter, it was the custom, in primitive days, for those who had been baptised the year before to keep an anniversary of their baptism, which was called the Annotine Easter, although the actual anniversary of the previous Easter might fall on another day.
>
> *Blunt's Annotated Book of Common Prayer*

**Lower Case.** The printer's name for the small letters (minuscules) of a fount of type, as opposed to the capitals; these are, in a type-setter's 'case', on a *lower* level than the others.

**Lower Empire.** The later Roman, especially the Western Empire, from about the foundation of the Eastern Empire in 364 to the fall of Constantinople in 1453.

**Lower House, The.** The second of any two legislative chambers; in England, the House of Commons.

**Lower your sail, To.** To salute; to confess yourself submissive or conquered; to humble oneself. A nautical phrase.

**Lowndean Professor.** The professor of astronomy and geometry at Cambridge; so called from Thomas Lowndes (d.1748) who bequeathed funds for the founding of the chair.

**Loyal.** Only one regiment of all the British army is so called, and that is the Loyal North Lancashire, in two battalions, No. 47 and No. 81. It was so called in 1793, and probably had some allusion to the French revolutionists.

**Loyola, St Ignatius** (1491–1556). Founder of the Society of Jesus (the order of Jesuits), is depicted in art with the sacred monogram IHS on his breast, or as contemplating it, surrounded by glory in the skies, in allusion to his claim that he had a miraculous knowledge of the mystery of the Trinity vouchsafed to him. He was a son of the Spanish ducal house of Loyola, and after being severely wounded at the siege of Pampeluna (1521) left the army and dedicated himself to the service of the Virgin. His Order of the Society of Jesus (*see* Jesuits), which he projected in 1534, was confirmed by Paul III in 1540.

**Luath.** The name of Burns's favourite dog, and that which he gave to the poor man's dog representing the peasantry in his poem *The Twa Dogs.* Burns got the name from Macpherson's *Ossian*, where it is borne by Cuchullin's dog.

> A ploughman's collie,
> A rhyming, ranting, raving billie,
> Wha for his friend and comrade had him,
> And in his freaks had Luath ca'd him
> After some dog in Highland sang
> Was made lang syne – Lord knows how lang.
>
> Burns, *The Twa Dogs*

**Lubber's Hole.** A seaman's name for the vacant space between the head of a lower mast and the edge of the top, because timid boys, or 'lubbers', get through it to the top, to avoid the danger and difficulties of the 'futtock shrouds'. Hence, some means for, or method of, wriggling through one's difficulties.

**Lubberkin** or **Lubrican.** *See* Leprachaun.

**Lucasian Professor.** A professor of mathematics at Cambridge. The professorship was endowed by a bequest from Henry Lucas (d.1663), MP for the University.

**Lucasta,** to whom Richard Lovelace sang (1649), was Lucy Sacheverell, called by him *lux casta*, i.e. Chaste Lucy.

**Luce.** The full-grown pike (*Esox lucius*), from Gr. *lukos*, a wolf, meaning the wolf of fishes.

Shakespeare plays upon the words *luce* and *louse* (*Merry Wives*, 1, 1) at the expense of Justice Shallow, who stands for his old enemy, Sir Thomas Lucy. According to Ferne's *Blazon of Gentry* (1586) the arms of the Lucy family were

'Gules, three lucies hariant, argent', but Dugdale (*Warwickshire*, 1656) gives a representation of a quartering of the Lucy arms where the 'dozen white luces' are shown.

> They may give the dozen white luces in their coat.
> Shakespeare, *Merry Wives*, 1, 1

*Luce* was also formerly used as a contraction of *fleur-de-lys* (*q.v.*). The French messenger says to the Regent Bedford –

> Cropped are the flower de luces in your arms;
> Of England's coat one-half is cut away.
> Shakespeare, *1 Henry VI*, 1, 1

Referring of course to the loss of France.

**Lucian.** The chief character in the *Golden Ass* of Apuleius (2nd cent. AD), a work which is in part an imitation of the *Metamorphoses* by Lucian, the Greek satirist who lived about 120 to 200. In the *Golden Ass* Lucian, changed into an ass, is the personification of the follies and vices of the age.

**Lucifer.** Venus, as the morning star. When she *follows* the sun and is an evening star, she is called *Hesperus*.

Isaiah applied the epithet 'Day-star' to the king of Babylon who proudly boasted that he would ascend to the heavens and make himself equal to God, but who was fated to be cast down to the uttermost recesses of the pit. This epithet was translated into 'Lucifer' –

> Take up this proverb against the king of Babylon, and say, ... How art thou fallen, from heaven, O Lucifer, son of the morning! Is. 14:4, 12

By St Jerome and other Fathers the name was applied to Satan. Hence poets feign that Satan, before he was driven out of heaven for his pride, was called Lucifer, and Milton, in *Paradise Lost*, gives this name to the demon of 'Sinful Pride', and hence, too, the phrase *Proud as Lucifer*.

**Lucifer-match,** or **Lucifer.** The name given by the inventor to one of the earliest forms (about 1832) of matches tipped with a combustible substance and ignited by friction, an improvement on the Congreves and Prometheans (*qq.v.*); hence, any match igniting by friction.

**Lucifera.** In Spenser's *Faërie Queene* (I, iv) the typification of pride (*see* Lucifer), luxury, and worldliness, and chief of the Seven Deadly Sins. She lived in a splendid place, only its foundation was of sand; the door stood always open, and she gave welcome to every comer. Her carriage was drawn by six different animals – viz. an ass, swine, goat, camel, wolf, and lion, on each of which rode one of the Sins, Satan himself being coachman. While here the Red Cross Knight was attacked by Sansjoy, who would have been slain if Duessa had not rescued him.

**Luciferians.** A sect of the 4th century, who refused to hold any communion with the Arians, who had renounced their 'errors' and been readmitted into the Church. So called from Lucifer, Bishop of Cagliari, in Sardinia, their leader.

**Lucinian.** The young prince, son of Dolopathos, the Sicilian monarch entrusted to the care of Virgil, the philosopher. *See* Seven Wise Masters.

**Lucius.** One of the mythical kings of Britain, placed as the great-great-grandson of Cymbeline (*q.v.*), and fabled as the first Christian king. He is supposed to have died about 192. *See* Pudens.

**Luck.** Accidental good fortune. (Dut., *luk*: Ger. *glück*, verb *glücken*, to succeed, to prosper.)

***Down on one's luck.*** Short of cash and credit.

***He has the luck of the devil,*** or ***the devil's own luck.*** He is extraordinarily lucky; everything he touches turns to gold.

***Give a man luck and throw him into the sea.*** Meaning that his luck will save him even in the greatest extremity. Jonah and Arion were cast into the sea, but were carried safely to land, the one by a whale and the other by a dolphin.

***Luck*** or ***lucky penny.*** A trifle returned to a purchaser for good luck; also a penny with a hole in it, supposed to ensure good luck.

***Not in luck's way.*** Not unexpectedly promoted, enriched, or otherwise benefited.

***The Luck of Eden Hall.*** *See* Eden Hall.

***There's luck in odd numbers.*** *See* Odd.

**Lucky.** In Scotland a term of familiar but respectful endearment for any elderly woman; often used of the landlady of an ale-house.

***A lucky dip***, or ***bag.*** A tub or other receptacle in which are placed a number of articles covered with bran or the like. Much in request at bazaars and so on, where the visitors pay so much for a 'dip' and take what they get.

***A lucky stone.*** A stone with a natural hole through it. *Cp.* Luck Penny.

***The lucky bone.*** The small bone of a sheep's head; prized by beggars and tramps, as it is supposed to bring luck for the whole day on which it is received.

***To cut one's lucky*** (thieves' slang). To decamp or make off quickly: to 'cut one's stick' (*q.v.*). As *luck* means chance, the phrase may signify, 'I must give up my chance and be off.'

***To strike lucky.*** *See* Strike.

**Lucullus sups with Lucullus.** Said of a glutton who gormandises alone. Lucullus was a rich Roman soldier, noted for his magnificence and self-indulgence. Sometimes above £1,700 was expended on a single meal, and Horace tells us he had 5,000 rich purple robes in his house. On one occasion a very superb supper was prepared, and when asked who were to be his guests the 'rich fool' replied, 'Lucullus will sup tonight with Lucullus' (110–57 BC).

**Lucus a non lucendo.** An etymological contradiction; a phrase used of etymologists who accounted for words by deriving them from their opposites. It means literally 'a grove (called *lucus*) from not being lucent' (*lux*, light, *luceo*, to shine). It was the Roman grammarian Honoratus Maurus Servius (fl. end of 4th cent. AD) who provided this famous etymology. In the same way *ludus*, a school, may be said to come from *ludere*, to play, and our word *linen*, from *lining*, because it is used for linings.

> One Tryphiodorus ... composed an Epick Poem ... of four and twenty books, having entirely banished the letter *A* from his first Book, which was called *Alpha* (as *Lucus a non Lucendo*) because there was not an *Alpha* in it.
>
> Addison, *Spectator*, No. 59

**Lucy, St.** Patron saint for those afflicted in the eyes. She is supposed to have lived in Syracuse and to have suffered martyrdom there about 303. One legend relates that a nobleman wanted to marry her for the beauty of her eyes; so she tore them out and gave them to him, saying, 'Now let me live to God.' Hence she is represented in art carrying a palm branch and a platter with two eyes on it. Her day is December 13th.

**Lud.** A mythical king of Britain, stated by the old chroniclers to have been the eighth in succession from Brute and to have died in 862 BC. He was the father of Bladud, founder of Bath. This King Lud must either have started as a deity or have been early euhemerised, for temples to him existed both on the Severn and the Thames (*see* Ludgate Hill); but the King Lud whom Geoffrey of Monmouth supposes to have founded London was a king of the Trinobantes, a brother of Cassivelaunus, and is dated about 66 BC.

***General Lud.*** *See* Luddites.

**Lud's Town.** London; so called from King Lud. *See above.*

> And on the gates of Lud's town set your heads.
>
> Shakespeare, *Cymbeline*, 4, 2

**Luddites.** Discontented workmen who, from 1811 to 1816, went about the manufacturing districts (especially Nottingham) breaking machines, under the impression that machinery threw men out of work. So called from Ned Lud, of Leicestershire, an imbecile who was much hounded by boys. One day he chased a set of tormentors into a house, and broke two stocking-frames, whence the leader of these rioters was called *General Lud.*

> In the winter of 1811 the terrible pressure of this transition from handicraft to machinery was seen in the Luddite, or machine-breaking, riots which broke out over the northern and midland counties; and which were only suppressed by military force.
>
> J. R. Green, *Short History*, x, § iv

**Ludgate.** One of the gates in the old City walls of London standing (till 1760) on Ludgate Hill, a few yards above the Old Bailey. It was probably on the site of a gate in the later Roman wall, but its first mention (as *Lutgata*) occurs in the early 12th century. Suggestions have been made that the true origin of the name is to be found in *Floodgate* (or *Fleetgate*, *cp. Fleet Street*, which at one time extended to Ludgate), or in A.S. *leode*, people, nation (*cp.* the *Porto del populi* of Rome).

> Ludgate was used as a free prison in 1373, but soon lost that privilege. A romantic story is told of Sir Stephen Forster, who was lord mayor in 1454. He had been a prisoner at Ludgate, and begged at the gate, where he was seen by a rich widow, who bought his liberty, took him into her service, and afterwards married him. To commemorate this Sir Stephen enlarged the prison accommodation, and added a chapel. The old gate was taken down and rebuilt in 1586. The new-built gate was destroyed in the Great Fire of London, and the next gate (used also as a prison for debtors) was pulled down in 1760.

Stow says:

> King Lud, repairing the city, called it after his name *Lud's town*: the strong gate which he built in the west part he likewise named Lud-gate. In the year 1260 the gate was beautified with images of Lud and other kings. Those images, in the reign of Edward VI, had their heads smitten off ... Queen Mary did set new heads upon their old bodies again. The twenty-eighth of Queen Elizabeth the gate was newly and beautifully built, with images of Lud and others, as before.
> *Survey of London*

> [Lud] Built that gate of which his name is hight,
> By which he lies entombëd solemnly.
>
> Spenser, *Faërie Queene*, ii, x, 46

**Ludlum.** *See* Lazy.

**Luez.** *See* Luz.

**Luff.** The weather-gauge; the part of a vessel towards the wind. (Dut. *loef*, a weather-gauge.)

***Luff!*** Put the tiller on the lee-side. This is done to make the ship sail nearer the wind.

A ship is said to *spring her luff* when she yields to the helm by sailing nearer the wind.

**Lufra.** Douglas's dog, 'the fleetest hound in all the North' (Scott's *Lady of the Lake*, v, 25).

**Luggnagg.** In *Gulliver's Travels*, an island where people live for ever. Swift shows the evil of such a destiny, unless accompanied with eternal youth. *See* Struldbrugs.

**Luke, St.** Patron saint of painters and physicians. Tradition says he painted a portrait of the Virgin Mary. Col. 4:14 states that he was a physician, but of course the word may have been used in a metaphorical sense. His day is October 18th.

In art he is usually represented with an ox lying near him, and often with painting materials. Sometimes he is pictured as painting the Virgin and infant Saviour. Metaphrastus mentions his skill in painting, and John of Damascus speaks of his portrait of the Virgin (*cp.* Loretto). Many pictures still extant are attributed to St Luke; but the artist was probably St Luke, the Greek hermit; for certainly these meagre Byzantine productions were not the works of the evangelist.

***St Luke's Club*** or ***The Virtuosis.*** An artists' club, established in England by Vandyke about 1638, and held at the Rose Tavern, Fleet Street. There was an academy of St Luke founded by the Paris artists in 1391; one at Rome, founded in 1593, but based on the 'Compagnia di San Luca' of Florence, founded in 1345; a similar one was established at Sienna in 1355.

***St Luke's Summer.*** The latter end of autumn, called by the French *l'été de S. Martin*.

> In such St Luke's short summer lived these men,
> Nearing the goal of threescore years and ten.
>
> Morris, *Earthly Paradise* (March)

***As light as St Luke's bird.*** Not light at all, but quite the contrary. St Luke is generally represented writing, while behind him is an ox, symbolical of sacrifice, St John, the Evangelist with whom he was generally represented, being accompanied by an eagle. The suggestion of the ox is that St Luke begins his gospel with the priest sacrificing in the Temple.

**Luke's Iron Crown.** A symbolification of political tyranny.

> The lifted axe, the agonising wheel,
> Luke's iron crown, and Damien's bed of steel,
> To men remote from power but rarely known,
> Leave reason, faith, and conscience all our own.
>
> Goldsmith, *The Traveller*, 435

George and Luke Dosa headed an unsuccessful revolt in Hungary in the early part of the 16th century. *George* underwent the torture of the red-hot iron crown, as a punishment for allowing himself to be proclaimed king; Goldsmith slips in attributing the incident to *Luke*.

**Lumber.** Formerly a pawnbroker's shop (from *Lombard*, *q.v.*). Thus Lady Murray (*Lives of the Baillies*, 1749) writes: 'They put all the little plate they had in the lumber, which is pawning it, till the ships came home.'

**Lumine Sicco, In** (Lat. in a dry light). Disinterestedly; as a dry question to be resolved without regard to other matters.

> If physiological considerations have any meaning, it will be always impossible for women to view the subject [of women's suffrage] *in lumine sicco*.
>
> *Nineteenth Century*, April, 1886

**Lump.** ***If you don't like it, you may lump it.*** Whether you like to do it or not, no matter; it must be done.

**Lumpkin, Tony** (Goldsmith's *She Stoops to Conquer*). A sheepish, mischievous, idle, cunning lout, 'with the vices of a man and the follies of a boy'; fond of low company, but giving himself the airs of the young squire.

**Luna.** An ancient seaport of Genoa, whence the marble quarried in the neighbourhood is called 'marmo lunense'. (*Orlando Furioso*.)

**Lunar Month.** From new moon to new moon, i.e. the time taken by the moon to revolve round the earth, about 29½ days. Popularly, the lunar month is 28 days. In the Jewish and Mohammedan calendars, the lunar month commences at sunset of the day when the new moon is first seen after sunset, and varies in length, being sometimes 29 and sometimes 30 days.

**Lunar Year.** Twelve lunar months, i.e. about 354⅓ days.

**Lunatics.** Literally, moon-struck persons. The Romans believed that the mind was affected by the moon, and that 'lunatics' were more and more frenzied as the moon increased to its full.

> The various mental derangements ... which have been attributed to the influence of the moon, have given to this day the name *lunatics* to persons suffering from serious mental disorders.
>
> Crozier, *Popular Errors*, ch. iv

**Lunch, Luncheon.** *unch* was originally a variant of *lump*, meaning a piece or slice of bread, etc. In Percyvall's Spanish–English Dictionary (1591) the translation of *louja de tocino* is given 'a lump of bacon'. The *-eon* is a later extension, perhaps representing *-ing* ('Noonings and intermealiary Lunchings', Brome's *Mad Couple*, about 1650), but affected by the suffix of *nuncheon*.

**Lungs of London.** The parks and open spaces. In a debate, June 30th, 1808, respecting encroachments upon Hyde Park, Windham said it was one of the 'lungs of London'.

**Lunsford.**

> Make children with your tones to run for't,
> As bad as Bloodybones or Lunsford.
>
> Butler, *Hudibras*, iii, 2

Sir Thomas Lunsford was governor of the Tower; a man of most vindictive temper, and the dread of everyone.

**Lupercal, The.** In ancient Rome, an annual festival held on the spot where Romulus and Remus were suckled by the wolf (*lupus*), on February 15th, in honour of Lupercus, the Lycaean Pan (so called because he protected the flocks from wolves). It was on one of these occasions that Antony thrice offered Julius Caesar the crown, and Caesar refused, saying, 'Jupiter alone is king of Rome.'

> You all did see that on the Lupercal,
> I thrice presented him a kingly crown,
> Which he did thrice refuse.
>
> Shakespeare, *Julius Caesar*, 3, 2

**Lupus in fabula** (Lat., the wolf in the story). A remark made when someone who is being discussed unexpectedly walks in; equivalent to 'Talk of the devil he's sure to appear'. In the quotation below the allusion is to the well-known fable of *The Wolf and the Lamb*.

> '*Lupus in fabula*,' answered the abbot, scornfully. 'The wolf accused the sheep of muddying the stream, when he drank in it above her.'
>
> Scott, *The Monastery*, last chapter

**Lurch. *To leave in the lurch*.** To leave a person in a difficulty. In cribbage one is *left in the lurch* when his adversary has run out his score of sixty-one holes before he himself has turned the corner (or pegged his thirty-first) hole. In some old card-games it is a *slam*, that is, when one side wins the entire game before the other has scored a point.

**Lush.** Beer and other intoxicating drinks. The word is something over 130 years old, and is of uncertain origin. Up to about 1895 there was a convivial society of actors called 'The City of Lushington', which met in the Harp Tavern, Russell Street, and claimed to have been in existence for 150 years. *Lush* may have come from the name of this club, though it is just as likely that the club took its name from the *lush* – for which it was famous.

**Lusiad, The.** The Portuguese national epic, written by Camoëns, and published in 1572. It relates the stories of illustrious actions of the *Lusians*, or Portuguese, of all ages, but deals principally with the exploits of Vasco da Gama and his comrades in their 'discovery of India'. Gama sailed three times to India – (1) with four vessels, in 1497, returning to Lisbon in two years and two months; (2) in 1502, with twenty ships, when he was attacked by the Zamorin or king of Calicut, whom he defeated, and returned to Lisbon the year following; and (3) when John III appointed him viceroy of India. He established his government at Cochin, where he died in 1525. It is the *first* of these voyages which is the groundwork of the epic; but its wealth of episode, the constant introduction of mythological 'machinery', and the intervention of Bacchus, Venus, and other deities, make it far more than a mere chronicle of a voyage.

**Lusitania.** Ancient name for Portugal. *See* Lusus.

**Lustral.** Properly, pertaining to the *Lustrum* (*q.v.*); hence, purificatory, as *lustral water*, the water used in Christian as well as many pagan rites for aspersing worshippers. In Rome the priest used a small olive or laurel branch for sprinkling infants and the people.

**Lustrum.** In ancient Rome the purificatory sacrifice made by the censors for the people once in five years, after the census had been taken (from *luere*, to wash, to purify); hence, a period of five years.

> Posterity will ask …
> Some fifty or a hundred lustrums hence,
> What was a monitor in George's days?
>
> Cowper, *The Task*, ii, 577

**Lusus.** Pliny (iii, 1) tells us that Lusus was the companion of Bacchus in his travels, and settled a colony in Portugal; whence the country was termed *Lusitania*, and the inhabitants *Lusians*, or *the sons of Lusus*.

**Lusus Naturae** (Lat.). A freak of nature; as a man with six toes, a sheep with two heads, or a stone shaped like some well known object, etc.

**Lutestring.** A glossy silk fabric; the French *lustrine* (from *lustre*).

***Speaking in lutestring.*** Flash, highly polished oratory. The expression was used more than once by Junius. Shakespeare has 'taffeta phrases and silken terms precise'. We call inflated speech 'fustian' (*q.v.*) or 'bombast' (*q.v.*); say a man talks *stuff*; term a book or speech made up of other men's brains, *shoddy* (*q.v.*); sailors call telling a story 'spinning a yarn', etc. etc.

**Lutetia** (Lat. *lutum*, mud). The ancient name of Paris, which, in Roman times, was merely a collection of mud hovels. Caesar called it *Lutetia Parisiorum* (the mud-town of the Parisii), which gives the present name *Paris.*

**Lutin.** A goblin in the folklore of Normandy; similar to the house-spirits of Germany. The name was formerly *netun*, and is said to come from the Roman sea-god *Neptune*. When the *lutin* assumes the form of a horse ready equipped it is called *Le Cheval Bayard.*

***To lutin.*** To twist hair into elf-locks. These mischievous urchins are said to tangle the mane of a horse or head of a child so that the hair must be cut off.

**Luz** or **Luez.** The indestructible bone; the nucleus of the resurrection body of Rabbinical legend.

> The learnèd rabbins of the Jews
> Write there's a bone which they call luez …
>
> Butler, *Hudibras,* iii, 2

> 'How doth a man revive again in the world to come?' asked Hadrian; and Joshua Ben Hananiah made answer, 'From luz in the back-bone.' He then went on to demonstrate this to him; He took the bone luz, and put it into water, but the water had no action on it; he put it in the fire, but the fire consumed it not; he placed it in a mill, but could not grind it; and laid it on an anvil, but the hammer crushed it not.
>
> Lightfoot

**LXX.** *See* Septuagint.

**Lybius, Sir.** A very young knight in the metrical romance *Libeaus Desconus* (*The Fair Unknown*), of the early 14th century, who undertook to rescue the lady of Sinadone. After overcoming various knights, giants, and enchanters, he entered her palace, but the whole edifice fell to pieces about his ears, and a horrible serpent coiled round his neck and kissed him. The spell being broken, the serpent turned into the lady of Sinadone, who forthwith married her rescuer.

**Lycanthropy.** The insanity afflicting a person who imagines himself to be some kind of animal and exhibits the tastes, voice, etc., of that animal; formerly the name given by the ancients to those who imagined themselves to be wolves (Gr. *lukos*, wolf, *anthropos*, man). The *werewolf* (*q.v.*) has sometimes been called a *lycanthrope*; and *lycanthropy* was sometimes applied to the form of witchcraft by which witches transformed themselves into wolves.

**Lycaon.** In *classical mythology*, a king of Arcadia, who, desirous of testing the divine knowledge of Jove, served up human flesh on his table; for which the god changed him into a wolf. His daughter, Callisto, was changed into the constellation the Bear, whence this is sometimes called *Lycaonis Arctos.*

**Lycidas.** The name under which Milton celebrates the untimely death of Edward King, Fellow of Christ College, Cambridge, who was drowned in his passage from Chester to Ireland, August 10th, 1637. He was the son of Sir John King, Secretary for Ireland.

**Lycisca** (*half-wolf, half-dog*). One of the dogs of Actaeon; a common term in Latin poetry for a shepherd's dog (*see* Virgil's *Eclogue* iii, 18).

**Lycopodium.** A genus of perennial plants comprising the club-mosses, so called from their fanciful resemblance to a wolf's foot (Gr. *lukos*, wolf, *pous, podos*, foot); the powder from the spore-cases of some of these is used in surgery as an absorbent and also – as it is highly inflammable – for stage-lightning.

**Lyddite.** A high-explosive composed mainly of picric acid; so called from *Lydd*, in Kent, where are situated the artillery ranges on which it was first tested in 1888.

**Lydford Law.** Punish first and try afterwards. Lydford, in the county of Devon, was a fortified town, where were held the courts of the Duchy of Cornwall. Offenders against the stannary laws were confined before trial in a dungeon so loathsome and dreary that the prisoners frequently died before they could be brought to trial: *Cp.* Cupar Justice.

**Lydia.** The ancient name of a district in the middle of Asia Minor which was an important centre of early civilisation and exerted much influence on Greece. Gyges (716 BC) was one of its most famous rulers, and the Empire flourished until its overthrow by the Persians under Cyrus (546 BC).

In Ariosto's *Orlando Furioso* the name is given to a daughter of the King of Lydia, who was sought in marriage by Alcestes, a Thracian knight; his suit was refused, but eventually Lydia set him all sorts of dangerous tasks to 'prove the ardour of his love', finally inducing him to kill all his allies, and when she had thus cut off the claws of this lovesick lion she mocked him. Alcestes pined and died, and Lydia was doomed to endless torment in hell, where she told Astolpho her story.

**Lydian Poet, The.** Alcman of Lydia (fl. 670 BC).

**Lying for the whetstone.** *See* Whetstone.

**Lyke-wake.** *See* Lich-wake (Lich).

**Lyme-**, or **Lyam-hound.** The bloodhound, so called from Lyme, or Lyam, the leash (Lat. *ligare*, to tie). By mediaeval huntsmen the lyme-hound was used for tracking down the wounded buck, and the *gaze-hound* for killing it.

> Thou art the lyme-hound, I am the gaze-hound ... Thou hast deep sagacity and unrelenting purpose, a steady, long-breathed malignity of nature, that surpasses mine. But then, I am the bolder, the more ready, both at action and expedient ... I say ... shall we hunt in couples?
> Scott, *Kenilworth*, ch. iv

**Lynceus.** One of the Argonauts (*q.v.*). He was so sharp-sighted that he could see through the earth, and distinguish objects nine miles off.

> That Lynceus may be matched with Gautard's sight. Hall, *Satires*, iv, 1
>
> Non possis oculo quantum contendere Lynceus.
> Horace, *1 Epistle*, i, 28

**Lynch Law.** Mob-law, law administered by private persons. The origin of the term is unknown; old editions of Webster's *Dictionary* referred it to James Lynch, a farmer of Piedmont, Virginia, saying that, as Piedmont was seven miles from any law court, the neighbours, in 1686, selected him to pass sentence on offenders for the nonce. Other conjectures father the phrase on a certain James Lynch Fitz-Stephen, said to have been warden of Galway in 1526, and to have passed sentence of death on his own son for murder; on Charles Lynch, a Virginian justice of the peace who was indemnified in 1782 for having imprisoned political opponents on his own responsibility, and on Lynche's Creek, South Carolina, where, in 1786, a body of men known as *Regulators* used to meet and try cases themselves because the regular administration of justice in those parts was lacking.

The term is first recorded in 1817, and is certainly American in origin, though there is an old northern English dialect word *linch*, meaning to beat or maltreat.

**Lynchnobians.** In Rabelais (V, xxxiii) certain studious and honest people living in 'Lantern-land'. The word means students who live by candlelight, and under it Rabelais satirised the learned pundits of the day. The word was used by Seneca (*Ep.* 122, §16) –

> [Sp. Papinius] nihil consumebat nisi noctem; itaque credo dicentibus illum quibusdam avarum et sordidum: vos, inquit, illum et lychnobium dicetis.

**Lynx.** The animal proverbial for its piercing eyesight is a fabulous beast, half dog and half panther, but not like either in character. The cat-like animal now called a lynx is not remarkable for keen-sightedness. The word is probably related to Gr. *lussein*, to see. *Cp.* Lynceus.

> Oh, I must needs o' the sudden prove a lynx
> And look the heart, that stone-wall, through and through
> Such an eye, God's may be – not yours nor mine.
> Browning, *The Ring and the Book*, xi, 917

**Lyon King-of-Arms.** The chief heraldic officer for Scotland; so called from the *lion rampant* in the Scottish regal escutcheon. *See* Heraldry, *also* Lion.

**Lyonnesse.** 'That sweet land of Lyonnesse' – a tract of land fabled to stretch between the Land's End and the Scilly Isles, now submerged full 'forty fathoms under water'. Arthur came from this mythical country.

> Faery damsels met in forest wide
> By knights of Logres, or of Lyones,
> Lancelot, or Pelleas, or Pellenore.
> Milton, *Paradise Regained*, ii, 359

**Lyre.** That of Terpander and Olympus had only three strings; the Scythian lyre had five; that of Simonides had eight; and that of Timotheus had twelve. It was played either with the fingers or with a plectrum. The lyre is called by poets a 'shell', because the cords of the lyre used by Orpheus, Amphion, and Apollo were stretched on the shell of a tortoise. Hercules used boxwood.

*Amphion* built Thebes with the music of his lyre, for the very stones moved of their own accord into walls and houses.

*Arion* charmed the dolphins by the music of his lyre, and when the bard was thrown overboard one of them carried him safely to Taenarus.

*Hercules* was taught music by Linus. One day, being reproved, the strong man broke the head of his master with his own lyre.

*Orpheus* charmed savage beasts, and even the infernal gods, with the music of his lyre, or – as some have it, lute.

# M

**M.** The thirteenth letter of the English alphabet (the twelfth of the ancient Roman, and twentieth of the *futhorc*), *M* in the Phoenician character represented the wavy appearance of water, and is called in Hebrew *mem* (water). The Egyptian hieroglyphic represented the owl. In English *M* is always sounded, except in words from Greek, in which it is followed by *n*, as *mnemonics*, *Mnason* (Acts 21:16).

In Roman numerals *M* stands for 1,000 (Lat. *mille*) – MDCCCCXXII = one thousand, nine hundred and twenty-two.

Persons convicted of manslaughter, and admitted to the benefit of clergy, used to be branded with an *M*. It was burnt on the brawn of the left thumb.

*What is your name? N or M.* (Church Catechism.) *See* N.

**M,** to represent the human face. Add two dots for the eyes, thus, ·M. These dots being equal to O's, we get OMO (*homo*) Latin for man.

> Who reads the name,
> For *man* upon his forehead, there the M
> Had traced most plainly.
>
> Dante, *Purgatory*, xxiii

**M'.** The first letter of certain Celtic surnames (*M'Cabe, M'Ian, M'Mahon*, etc.) represents *Mac*, and should be so pronounced.

**M.B. Waistcoat.** A clerical cassock waistcoat was so called (about 1830) when first introduced by the High Church party. M. B. means 'mark of the beast'.

> He smiled at the folly which stigmatised an 'M.B. waistcoat'. Mrs Oliphant, *Phoebe Juno*, ii 3

**M.P.** Member of Parliament, but in slang use, Member of the Police.

**MS** (pl. MSS). Manuscript; applied to literary works either in handwriting or typescript. (Lat. *manuscriptum*, that which is written by the hand.)

**Mab** (perhaps the Welsh *mab*, a baby). The 'fairies' midwife' – i.e. employed by the fairies as midwife to deliver man's brain of dreams. Thus when Romeo says, 'I dreamed a dream tonight', Mercutio replies, 'Oh, then, I see Queen Mab hath been with you.' Scott follows in the same track: 'I have a friend who is peculiarly favoured with the visits of Queen Mab', meaning with dreams (*The Antiquary*). When Mab is called 'queen', it does not mean sovereign, for Titania as wife of King Oberon was Queen of Faery, but simply female. A.S. *quén* or *cwén* (modern *quean*) meant neither more nor less than *woman*; so 'elf-queen', and the Danish *ellequinde*, mean *female elf*, and not 'queen of the elves'.

Excellent descriptions of Mab are given by Shakespeare (*Romeo and Juliet*, 1, 4), by Ben Jonson, by Herrick, and by Drayton in *Nymphidea*.

**Macaber** (or **Macabre**), **the Dance.** *See* Dance of Death.

**Macadamise.** A method of road-making introduced about 1820 by John L. Macadam (1756–1836), consisting of layers of broken stones of nearly uniform size, each layer being separately crushed into position by traffic, or (later) by a heavy roller.

**Macaire, Robert.** The typical villain of French comedy; from the play of this name (a sequel to *L'Auberge des Adrets*) by Frédéric Lemaître and Benjamin Antier (1834): Macaire is –

> le type de la perversité, de l'impudence, de la friponnerie audacieuse, le héros fanfaron du vol et de l'assassinat.

'Macaire' was the name of the murderer of Aubrey de Montdidier in the old French legend; he was brought to justice by the sagacity of Aubrey's dog, the Dog of Montargis. *See* Dog.

**Macaroni.** A coxcomb (Ital. *un maccheróne*, *see* next entry). The word is derived from the Macaroni Club, instituted in London about 1760 by a set of flashy men who had travelled in Italy, and introduced at Almack's subscription table the new-fashioned Italian food, *macaroni*. The Macaronies were the most exquisite fops that ever disgraced the name of man; vicious, insolent, fond of gambling, drinking, and duelling, they were (about 1773) the curse of Vauxhall Gardens.

An American regiment raised in Maryland during the War of Independence was called The Macaronies from its showy uniform.

**Macaronic Latin.** Dog Latin (*q.v.*), modern words with Latin endings, or a mixture of Latin and some modern language. From the Italian *macheroni* (macaroni), originally a medley or mixture of coarse meal, eggs, and cheese. The law pleadings of G. Steevens, as *Daniel* v. *Dishclout* and *Bullum* v. *Boatum*, are excellent examples.

**Macaronic Verse.** Verses in which foreign words are ludicrously distorted and jumbled together, as in Porson's lines on the threatened invasion of England by Napoleon or J. A. Morgan's 'translation' of Canning's *The Elderly Gentleman*, the first two verses of which are –

Prope ripam fluvii solus
A senex silently sat
Super capitum ecce his wig
Et wig super, ecce his hat.

Blew Zephyrus alte, acerbus,
Dum elderly gentleman sat;
Et a capite took up quite torve
Et in rivum projecit his hat.

It seems to have been originated by Odaxius of Padua (born *c.*1450), but was popularised by his pupil, Teofilo Folengo (Merlinus Coccaius), a Mantuan monk of noble family, who published a book entitled *Liber Macaronicorum*, a poetical rhapsody made up of words of different languages, and treating of 'pleasant matters' in a comical style (1520).

In England a somewhat similar kind of verse was practised rather earlier. Skelton's *Phyllyp Sparowe* (1512), which contains a good deal of it, begins –

Pla ce bo,
Who is there, who?
*Di le xi*,
Dame Margery.

and Dunbar's *Testament of Andrew Kennedy* (1508) –

I will na priestis for me sing,
Dies illa, Dies irae,
Na yet na bellis for me ring,
Sicut semper solet fieri –

though not true macaronic, is a near approach.

A. Cunningham in 1801 published *Delectus Macaronicorum Carminum*, a history of macaronic poetry.

**Macbeth.** The story of Shakespeare's tragedy (written 1605–6, acted certainly in 1610 and probably four years earlier, and first printed in the First Folio, 1623) is taken from Holinshed, who copied it from the *History of Scotland*, by Hector Boece (1527).

> History states that Macbeth slew Duncan at Bothgowan, near Elgin, in 1039, and not, as Shakespeare says, at his castle of Inverness; the attack was made because Duncan had usurped the throne, to which Macbeth had the better claim. As a king Macbeth proved a very just and equitable prince, but the partisans of Malcolm got head, and succeeded in deposing Macbeth, who was slain in 1056, at Lumphanan. He was thane of Cromarty [Glamis] and afterwards of Moray [Cawdor].
>
> Lardner, *Cabinet Cyclopaedia*

Ambition is the dominant trait in the character of Lady Macbeth, and to gain her ends she hesitates at nothing. Her masterful mind sways the weaker Macbeth to 'the mood of what she liked or loathed'. She is a Medea, or Catherine de' Medici, or Caesar Borgia in female form.

> The real name of Lady Macbeth was Graoch, and instead of being urged to the murder of Duncan through ambition, she was goaded by deadly injuries. She was, in fact, the granddaughter of Kenneth IV, killed in 1003, fighting against Malcolm II.
>
> Lardner, *Cabinet Cyclopaedia*, vol. i, 17

**Maccabaeus.** The surname given to Judas (the central figure in the struggle for Jewish independence, about 170–160 BC), third son of Mattathias, the Hasmonaean, and hence to his family or clan. It has generally been supposed that the name is connected with Heb. *Makké-beth*, hammer (Judas being the *Hammerer* of the Syrians just as Charles *Martel* was of the Saracens), but this view is open to many weighty objections, and the origin of the name is wholly obscure.

**Maccabees, The.** The family of Jewish heroes, descended from Mattathias the Hasmonaean (*see above*) and his five sons, John, Simon, Judas, Eleazar, and Jonathan, which delivered its race from the persecutions of the Syrian king Antiochus Epiphanes (175–164 BC), and established a line of priest-kings which lasted till supplanted by Herod in 40 BC. Their exploits are told in the two *Books of the Maccabees*, the last books in the Apocrypha.

**Macdonald.** ***Lord Macdonald's breed.*** Parasites. It is said that a Lord Macdonald (son of the Lord of the Isles) once made a raid on the mainland. He and his followers, with other plunder, fell on the clothes of the enemy, and stripping off their own rags, donned the smartest and best they could lay hands on, with the result of being overrun with parasites.

**Macduff.** The thane of Fife in Shakespeare's *Macbeth* (*q.v.*). His castle of Kennoway was surprised by Macbeth, and his wife and babes 'savagely slaughtered'. Macduff vowed vengeance and joined the army of Siward, to dethrone the tyrant. On reaching the royal castle of Dunsinane they fought, and Macbeth was slain.

> History states that Macbeth was defeated at Dunsinane, but escaped from the battle and was slain at Lumphanan in 1056.
>
> Lardner, *Cabinet Cyclopaedia*, i, p. 17

**Mace.** Originally a club armed with iron, and used in war; now a staff of office pertaining to certain dignitaries, as the Speaker of the House of Commons, Lord Mayors and Mayors, etc. Both sword and mace are symbols of dignity, suited to the times when men went about in armour, and sovereigns needed champions to vindicate their rights.

**Macedon is not worthy of thee,** is what Philip said to his son Alexander, after his achievement with the horse Bucephalus, which he subdued to his will, though only eighteen years of age.

Edward III, after the battle of Crecy, in which the Black Prince behaved very valiantly, exclaimed, 'My brave boy, go on as you have begun, and you will be worthy of England's crown.'

**Macedonian Madman, The.** *See* Madman.

**Macedonians.** A religious sect, so named from Macedonius, an Arian patriarch of Constantinople, in the 4th century. They denied the divinity of the Holy Ghost, and that the essence of the Son is the same in kind with that of the Father.

**MacFarlane's Geese.** The proverb is that 'MacFarlane's geese like their play better than their meat'. The wild geese of Inch-Tavoe (Loch Lomond) used to be called *MacFarlane's Geese* because the MacFarlanes had a house on the island, and it is said that they never returned after the destruction of that house. One day James VI visited the chieftain, and was highly amused by the gambols of the geese, but the one served at table was so tough that the king exclaimed, 'MacFarlane's geese like their play better than their meat'.

**MacFlecknoe,** in Dryden's famous satire (1682), is Thomas Shadwell (1640–92), poet laureate in succession to his attacker (1688) when Dryden, having become Roman Catholic, refused to take the oath.

The original *Flecknoe* (Richard, d. about 1678) was an Irish Roman Catholic priest, doggerel sonneteer, and playwright. Shadwell, according to Dryden, was his double.

The rest to some slight meaning make pretence,
But Shadwell never deviates into sense.

*MacFlecknoe*, 19

**MacGirdie's Mare,** used by degrees to eat less and less, but just as he had reduced her to a straw a day the poor beast died. This is an old Greek joke, which is well known to schoolboys who have been taught the *Analecta Minora*. (*See Waverley*, p. 54.)

**Macgregor.** The motto of the MacGregors is, 'E'en do and spair nocht', said to have been given them in the 12th century by a king of Scotland. While the king was hunting he was attacked by a wild boar, when Sir Malcolm requested permission to encounter the creature. 'E'en do,' said the king, 'and spair nocht.' Whereupon the strong baronet tore up an oak sapling and dispatched the enraged animal. For this defence the king gave Sir Malcolm permission to use the said motto, and, in place of a Scotch fir, to adopt for crest *an oak tree eradicate, proper*.

Another motto of the MacGregors is *Sriogal mo dhream*, i.e. 'Royal is my tribe'.

The MacGregors furnish the only instance of a race being forbidden to bear its family name. It was proscribed by James VI owing to the treachery of the family, who then took the name of Murray. Charles II restored them to their estates and name in 1661, but under William and Mary the law of proscription again came into force, and it was not till 1822 that Sir John Murray, as he then was, obtained by royal licence the right to resume the ancient name of his family, MacGregor.

***Rob Roy MacGregor***. *See* Rob Roy.

**Macheath, Captain.** A highwayman, hero of *The Beggar's Opera*, by Gay. A fine, gay, bold-faced and dissolute ruffian, game to the very last.

**Machiavelli, Niccolo** (1469–1527). The celebrated Florentine statesman, and author of *Il Principe*, an exposition of unscrupulous statecraft, whose name has long been used as an epithet or synonym for an intriguer or for an unscrupulous politician, while political cunning and overreaching by diplomacy and intrigue are known as *Machiavellianism* or *Machiavellism*. The general trend of *Il Principe* ('The Prince', 1573) is to show that rulers may resort to any treachery and artifice to uphold their arbitrary power, and whatever dishonourable acts princes may indulge in are fully set off by the insubordination of their subjects.

***The Imperial Machiavelli***. Tiberius, the Roman emperor (42 BC to AD 37). His political axiom was – 'He who knows not how to dissemble knows not how to reign.' It was also the axiom of Louis XI of France.

**Mackerel Sky.** A sky dappled with detached rounded masses of white cloud, something like the markings of a mackerel.

***To throw a sprat to catch a mackerel***. *See* Sprat.

**Mackintosh.** Cloth waterproofed with caoutchouc, by a process patented by Charles Mackintosh in 1823; also, a coat or cloak made of this.

**Mackworth's Inn.** *See* Barnard's Inn.

**Macmillanites.** A religious sect of Scotland, who in 1743 seceded from the Cameronians because they wished to adhere more strictly to the principles of the Reformation in Scotland; so named from John Macmillan, their leader. They called themselves the 'Reformed Presbytery'.

**Macon.** A poetical and romance name of Mecca, the birthplace of Mahomet; hence, a name of the Prophet himself.

> Praised (quoth he) be Macon whom we serve.
>
> Fairfax, *Tasso*, xii, 10

**MacPherson.** Fable has it that during the reign of David I of Scotland, a younger brother of the chief of the powerful clan Chattan became abbot of Kingussie. His elder brother died childless, and the chieftainship devolved on the abbot. He procured the needful dispensation from the Pope, married the daughter of the thane of Calder, and a swarm of little 'Kingussies' was the result. The good people of Inverness-shire called them the *Mac-phersons*, i.e. the sons of the parson.

**Macreons.** The island of the Macreons in Rabelais (Bk IV, ch. xxv), has been taken by some commentators – rather unconvincingly – to be intended for Great Britain. The word is Greek, and means *long-lived*. Rabelais describes a terrible storm at sea (possibly a typification of the persecutions of the Reformers), in which Pantagruel and his fleet were tempest-tossed, but contrived to enter one of the harbours of this island, which was so called because no one was put to death there for his religious opinions. It was full of antique ruins, which may be taken as a symbol of decayed popery and ancient superstitions.

**Macrocosm** (Gr. the *great world*), in opposition to the microcosm, the *little world*. The ancients looked upon the universe as a living creature, and the followers of Paracelsus considered man a miniature representation of the universe. The one was termed the Macrocosm, the other the Microcosm (*q.v.*).

**Mad. *Mad as a hatter.*** The probable origin of this phrase is 'Mad as an *adder*' (A.S. *naeddre*, A.S. *atter* being 'poison'), but evidence is wanting. It was popularised by Lewis Carroll (*Alice in Wonderland*, 1865), but was well known earlier, and was used by Thackeray (*Pendennis*, ch. x) in 1849

***Mad as a March hare.*** *See* Hare.

***The Mad Cavalier.*** Prince Rupert (1619–82), noted for his rash courage and impatience of control. He was a grandson of James I, through his mother, Elizabeth, and was famous as a cavalry leader on the Royalist side during the English Civil War.

***The Mad Parliament.*** The Parliament which assembled at Oxford in 1258, and broke out into open rebellion against Henry III. It confirmed the Magna Charta, the king was declared deposed, and the government was vested in the hands of twenty-four councillors, with Simon de Montfort at their head.

***The Mad Poet.*** Nathaniel Lee (about 1653–92), who was confined for four years in Bedlam, and wrote some of his best poetry there.

**Madame.** So the wife of Philippe, Duc d'Orléans, was styled in the reign of Louis XIV; other ladies were only Madame This or That.

***Madame la Duchesse.*** Wife of Henri-Jules de Bourbon, eldest son of Prince de Condé.

***Madame la Princesse.*** Wife of the Prince de Condé, and natural daughter of Louis XIV. *See* Monsieur.

**Mademoiselle.** The daughter of Philippe, Duc de Chartres, grandson of Philippe, Duc d'Orléans, brother of Louis XIV.

***La Grande Mademoiselle.*** The Duchesse de Montpensier, cousin to Louis XIV, and daughter of Gaston, Duc d'Orléans.

**Madge.** A popular name for the barn owl.

> 'Sdeins, an I swallow this, I'll ne'er draw my sword in the sight of Fleet-street again while I live; I'll sit in a barn with madge-howlet, and catch mice first.
>
> Ben Jonson, *Every Man in his Humour*, II, i

**Madman. *Macedonia's Madman.*** Alexander the Great (356, 336–323 BC).

***The Brilliant Madman*** or ***Madman of the North.*** Charles XII of Sweden (1682, 1697–1718).

> Heroes are much the same, the point's agreed,
> From Macedonia's madman to the Swede.
>
> Pope, *Essay on Man*, iv

**Madness.** In Perthshire there are several wells and springs dedicated to St Fillan, which are still places of pilgrimage. These wells are held to be efficacious in cases of madness. Even in recent times lunatics have been bound to the holy stone at night, under the expectation that St Fillan would release them before dawn, and send them home in their right minds.

**Madoc.** A legendary Welsh prince, youngest son of Owain Gwyneth, king of North Wales, who died in 1169. According to tradition he sailed to

America, and established a colony on the southern branches of the Missouri. About the same time the Aztecs forsook Aztlan, under the guidance of Yuhidthiton, and founded the empire called Mexico, in honour of Mexitli, their tutelary god. Southey's poem, *Madoc* (1805), harmonises these two events.

**Madonna** (Ital. my lady). Specially applied to representations of the Virgin Mary.

**Mador, Sir.** In Arthurian legend, the Scottish knight slain in single combat by Sir Launcelot of the Lake in defence of the reputation of Queen Guinever.

**Maeander.** *See* Meander.

**Maecenas.** A patron of letters; so called from C. Cilnius Maecenas (d.8 BC), a Roman statesman in the reign of Augustus, who kept open house for all men of letters, and was the special friend and patron of Horace and Virgil. Nicholas Rowe so called the Earl of Halifax on his installation to the Order of the Garter (1714).

***The last English Maecenas.*** Samuel Rogers (1763–1855), poet and banker.

**Maelström** (Norw. whirling stream). A dangerous whirlpool off the coast of Norway, between the islands of Moskenaso and Varo (in the Lofoden Islands), where the water is pushed and jostled a good deal, and where, when the wind and tide are contrary, it is not safe for small boats to venture near. It was anciently thought that it was a subterranean abyss, penetrating the globe, and communicating with the Gulf of Bothnia.

The name is given to other whirlpools, and also, figuratively, to any turbulent or overwhelming situation.

**Maeonides**, or **The Maeonian Poet.** Homer (*q.v.*), either because he was the son of Maeon, or because he was born in Maeonia (Asia Minor).

**Maera.** The dog of Icarius (*q.v.*).

**Maeviad.** *See* Baviad.

**Maffick.** To celebrate an event, especially an occasion of national rejoicing, with wild and extravagant exuberance. From the uproarious scenes and unrestrained exultation that took place in London on the night of May 18th, 1900, when the news of the relief of Mafeking (besieged by the Boers since the previous November) became known.

**Mafia.** In Sicily, those who take part in active hostility to the law, viz. the greater part of the population. *Mafia* is often erroneously stated to denote an organised secret society.

**Mag.** A contraction of magpie. *What a mag you are!* You chatter like a magpie. What a jabberer! A prating person is called 'a mag'.

***Not a mag to bless myself with.*** Not a halfpenny.

**Maga.** A familiar name for *Blackwood's Magazine*.

**Magalona.** *See* Maguelone.

**Magazine.** A place for stores (Arab. *makhzan*, a storehouse). This meaning is still retained for military and some other purposes; but the word now commonly denotes a periodical publication containing contributions by various authors. How this came about is seen from the *Introduction* to the *Gentleman's Magazine* (1731) – the first to use the word in this way:

> This Consideration has induced several Gentlemen to promote a Monthly Collection to treasure up, as in a Magazine, the most remarkable Pieces on the Subjects abovemention'd.

**Magdalene.** An asylum for the reclaiming of prostitutes; so called from Mary Magdalene or Mary of Magdala, 'out of whom He had cast seven devils' (Mark 16:9).

**Magdeburg Centuries.** The first great work of Protestant divines on the history of the Christian Church. It was begun at Magdeburg by Matthias Flacius, in 1552, and published at Basle (13 volumes), 1560–74. As each century occupies a volume, the thirteen volumes complete the history to 1300.

**Magellan, Straits of.** So called after Fernao de Magelhaes (d.1521), the Portuguese navigator, who discovered them in 1520.

**Magenta.** A brilliant red aniline dye derived from coal-tar, named in commemoration of the battle of Magenta, when the Austrians were defeated by the French and Sardinians just before it was discovered, in 1859.

**Maggot.** There was an old idea that whimsical or crotchety persons had maggots in their brains –

> Are you not mad, my friend? What time o' th' moon is't?
> Have not you maggots in your brains?
>
> Fletcher, *Women Pleased*, III, iv (1620)

Hence we have the adjective *maggoty*, whimsical, full of fancies. Fanciful dance tunes used to be called *maggots*, as in *The Dancing Master* (1716) there are many such titles as 'Barker's maggots', 'Cary's maggots', 'Draper's maggots', etc., and in 1685 S. Wesley published a volume with the title *Maggots; or Poems on Several Subjects*.

***When the maggot bites***. When the fancy takes us. Swift, making fun of the notion, says that if the bite is hexagonal it produces poetry; if circular, eloquence; if conical, politics.

Instead of maggots the Scotch say, 'His head is full of bees'; the French, *Il a des rats dans la tête* (*cp.* our slang 'Rats in the garret'); and in Holland, 'He has a mouse's nest in his head'.

**Magi** (Lat.; pl. of *magus*). Literally 'wise men'; specifically, the Three Wise Men of the East who brought gifts to the infant Saviour. Tradition calls them Melchior, Gaspar, and Balthazar, three kings of the East. The first offered *gold*, the emblem of royalty; the second, *frankincense*, in token of divinity; and the third, *myrrh*, in prophetic allusion to the persecution unto death which awaited the 'Man of Sorrows'.

Melchior means 'king of light'.
Gaspar, or Caspar, means 'the white one'.
Balthazar means 'the lord of treasures'.

Mediaeval legend calls them the Three Kings of Cologne, and the Cathedral there claims their relics. They are commemorated on January 2nd, 3rd, and 4th, and particularly at the Feast of the Epiphany.

Among the ancient Medes and Persians the *Magi* were members of a priestly caste credited with great occult powers, and in Camoëns' *Lusiad* the term denotes the Indian Brahmins. Ammianus Marcellinus says that the Persian *magi* derived their knowledge from the Brahmins of India (i, 23), and Arianus expressly calls the Brahmins 'magi' (i, 7).

**Magic Rings, Wands, etc.** *See these words.*

**Magician.** ***The Great Magician*** or ***Wizard of the North***. Professor Wilson ('Christopher North') gave Sir Walter Scott the name, because of the wonderful fascination of his writings.

***Magician of the North***. The title assumed by Johann Georg Hamann (1730–88), a German philosopher and theologian.

**Magliabecchi, A.** A book-worm; from Antonio Magliabecchi (1633–1714), librarian to Cosmo III, Grand Duke of Tuscany. He never forgot what he had once read, and could turn at once to the exact page of any reference.

**Magna Charta.** The *Great Charter* of English liberty extorted from King John, 1215; called by Spelman –

> Augustissimum Anglicarum, liberta tum diploma et sacra anchora.

It contained (in its final form) 37 clauses, and is directed principally against abuses of the power of the Crown and to guaranteeing that no subject should be kept in prison without trial and judgment by his peers.

**Magnanimous, The.** Alfonso V of Aragon (1385, 1416–58).

Chosroes or Khosru, King of Persia, twenty-first of the Sassanides, surnamed *Noushirwan* (the Magnanimous) (531–579).

**Magnano.** One of the leaders of the rabble that attacked Hudibras (*Hudibras*, Pt i, 2) at a bear-baiting. The character is a satire on Simeon Wait, the tinker and Independent preacher who called Cromwell the 'archangel who did battle with the devil'.

**Magnet.** The loadstone; so called from *Magnesia*, in Lydia, where the ore was said to abound. Milton uses the adjective for the substantive in the line 'As the magnetic hardest iron draws' (*Paradise Regained*, ii, 168).

**Magnetic Mountain.** A mountain of mediaeval legend which drew out all the nails of any ship that approached within its influence. It is referred to in *Mandeville's Travels* and in many stories, such as the tale of the Third Calender and one of the voyages of Sinbad the Sailor in the *Arabian Nights*.

**Magnificat.** The hymn of the Virgin (Luke 1:46–55) beginning 'My soul doth magnify the Lord' (*Magnificat anima mea Dominum*), used as part of the daily service of the Church since the beginning of the sixth century, and at Evening Prayer in England for over 800 years.

***To correct Magnificat before one has learnt Te Deum***. To try to do that for which one has no qualifications; to criticise presumptuously.

***To sing the Magnificat at matins***. To do things at the wrong time, or out of place. The Magnificat belongs to vespers, not to matins.

**Magnificent, The.** Chosroes of Persia. *See* Magnanimous.

Lorenzo de Medici (1448–92), *Il Magnifico*, Duke of Florence.

Robert, Duke of Normandy, also called *Le Diable* (1028–35).

Soliman I, greatest of the Turkish sultans (1490, 1520–66).

**Magnifique ... Guerre.** *C'est magnifique, mais ce n'est pas la guerre*. Admirable, but not according to rule. The comment on the field of the French General Bosquet to Mr A. H. Layard on the charge of the Light Brigade at Balaclava. It has frequently been attributed to Marshal Canrobert.

> It is because the clergy, as a class, are animated by a high ideal ... that they, as a class, are incomparably better than they need be ... *C'est magnifique, mais ce n'est pas la guerre.*
>
> *Nineteenth Century*, April, 1866

**Magnolia.** A genus of North American flowering trees so called from Pierre Magnol (1638–1715), professor of botany at Montpellier.

**Magnum.** A large-sized bottle for wine, double the size of the ordinary bottle – holding two quarts or thereabouts. *Cp.* Jeroboam.

***Magnum bonum*** (Lat. 'great and good'). A name given to certain choice potatoes, and also plums. Burns, in the following extract, evidently meant by it a magnum (*see above*):

> And Welsh, who ne'er yet flinch'd his ground,
> High-wav'd his magnun-bonum round
> With Cyclopeian fury.
>
> *An Election Ballad: Dumfries Burghs*

***Magnum opus.*** The chief or most important of one's literary works.

> My magnum opus, the 'Life of Dr Johnson' ... is to be published on Monday, 16th May.
>
> Boswell, *Letter to Rev. W. Temple*, 1791

**Magophony** (Gr. *magosphonos*, the magi-slaughter). The massacre of the Magi by the Persians in 521 BC, a famous event in Persian history. Smerdis usurped the throne on the death of Cambyses; but seven Persians, conspiring together, slew Smerdis and his brother; whereupon the people put all the Magi to the sword, and elected Darius, son of Hystaspes, to the throne.

**Magpie.** Formerly 'maggot-pie', *maggot* representing *Margaret* (*cp. Robin* redbreast, *Tom*-tit, and the old *Phyllyp*-sparrow), and *pie* being the Lat. *pica*.

> Augurs and understood relations have
> (By magotpies, and choughs, and rooks) brought forth
> The secret'st man of blood.
>
> Shakespeare, *Macbeth*, 3, 4

The magpie has generally been regarded as an uncanny bird; in Sweden it is connected with witchcraft, in Devonshire if a peasant sees one he spits over his shoulder three times to avert ill luck, and in Scotland magpies flying near the windows of a house foretell the early death of one of its inmates.

The following rhyme about the number of magpies seen in the course of a walk is old and well-known:

> One's sorrow, two's mirth,
> Three's a wedding, four's a birth,
> Five's a christening, six a dearth,
> Seven's heaven, eight is hell,
> And nine's the devil his ane sel'.

In target-shooting the score made by a shot striking the outermost division but one is called a *magpie* because it was customarily signalled by a black and white flag; and formerly bishops were humorously or derisively called magpies because of their black and white vestments.

> Lawyers, as Vultures, had soared up and down;
> Prelates, like Magpies, in the Air had flown.
>
> *Howell's Letters, Lines to the Knowing Reader* (1645)

**Maguelone** or **Magalona.** Heroine of *The History of the Fair Magalona, Daughter of the King of Naples*, etc., an old French romance, mentioned by Cervantes in *Don Quixote*. *See* Peter of Provence.

**Magus.** *See* Simon Magus.

**Mah-abadean Dynasty.** The first dynasty of *Persian mythology*. Mah (*the great*) Abad and his wife were the only persons left on the earth after the great cycle, and from them the world was peopled. Azer Abad, the fourteenth and last of this dynasty, left the earth because 'all flesh had corrupted itself', and a period of anarchy ensued.

**Mahabharata.** One of the two great epic poems of ancient India (*cp.* Ramayana), about eight times as long as the *Iliad* and *Odyssey* together. Its main story is the war between descendants of Kuru and Pandu, but there are an immense number of episodes.

**Maha-pudma.** *See* Tortoise.

**Maharajah** (Sansk., 'great king'). The title of certain native rulers of India whose territories are very extensive. The wife of a Maharajah is a *Maharanee*.

**Mahâtma** (Sansk., 'great soul'). Max Muller tells us that –

> Mahâtma is a well known Sanskrit word applied to men who have retired from the world, who, by means of a long ascetic discipline, have subdued the passions of the flesh, and gained a reputation for sanctity and knowledge. That these men are able to perform most startling feats, and to suffer the most terrible tortures, is perfectly true.
>
> *Nineteenth Century*, May, 1893

By the Esoteric Buddhists the name is given to adepts of the highest order, a community of whom is supposed to exist in Tibet, and by Theosophists to one who has reached perfection spiritually, intellectually, and physically. As his knowledge is perfect he can produce effects which, to the ordinary man, appear miraculous.

**Mahdi** (Arab, 'the divinely directed one'). The expected Messiah of the Mohammedans; a title often assumed by leaders of insurrection in the Sudan, especially Mohammed Ahmed (1843–85) who led the rising of 1883, and who, say some, is not really dead, but sleeps in a cavern near Bagdad, and will return to life in the fullness of time to overthrow Dejal (anti-Christ). The Shiahs believe that the Mahdi has lived (some sects maintaining that he is in hiding), but the Sunnis hold that he is still to appear.

**Mahmut.** The name of the famous 'Turkish' spy (*q.v.*).

**Mahomet** or **Mohammed** (Arab., 'the praised one'). The titular name of the founder of Islam (*q.v.*), or Mohammedanism (born at Mecca about 570, died at Medina, 632), which was adopted by him about the time of the Hegira to apply to himself the Messianic prophecies in the Old Testament (Haggai 2:7, and elsewhere). His original name is given both as Kotham and Halabi.

***Angel of.*** When Mahomet was transported to heaven, he says: 'I saw there an angel, the most gigantic of all created beings. It had 70,000 heads, each had 70,000 faces, each face had 70,000 mouths, each mouth had 70,000 tongues, and each tongue spoke 70,000 languages; all were employed in singing God's praises.'

> This would make more than 31,000 trillion languages and nearly five billion mouths.

***Banner of.*** Sanjaksherif, kept in the Eyab mosque, at Constantinople.

***Bible of.*** The Koran.

***Bow.*** Catum.

***Camel (swiftest).*** Adha.

***Cave.*** The cave in which Gabriel appeared to Mahomet (610) was in the mountain of Hirâ, near Mecca.

***Coffin.*** Legend used to have it that Mahomet's coffin is suspended in mid-air at Medina without any support.

The story probably arose from the rough drawings sold to visitors.

> Sp'ritual men are too transcendent …
> To hang, like Mahomet, in the air,
> Or St Ignatius at his prayer,
> By pure geometry. Butler, *Hudibras*, III, ii, 602

***Cuirass.*** Fadha.

***Daughter (favourite).*** Fatima.

***Dove.*** Mahomet had a dove which he fed with wheat out of his ear. When it was hungry it used to light on the prophet's shoulder, and thrust its bill into his ear to find its meal. Mahomet thus induced the Arabs to believe that he was divinely inspired.

> Was Mahomet inspired with a dove?
> Shakespeare, *1 Henry VI*, i, 2

***Father.*** Abdallah, of the tribe of Koreish. He died a little before or a little after the birth of Mahomet.

***Father-in-law*** (father of Ayesha). Abu-Bekr. He succeeded Mahomet and was the first calif.

***Flight from Mecca*** (called the Hegira), AD 622 He retired to Medina.

***Grandfather*** (paternal). Abd-el-Mutallib, who adopted the orphan boy, but died in two years.

***Hegira.*** *See above, Flight.*

***Horse.*** Al Borak (*The Lightning*). It conveyed the prophet to the seventh heaven. *See* Borak.

***Miracles.*** Several are traditionally mentioned, but many of the True Believers hold that he performed no miracle. That of the moon is best known.

Habib the Wise asked Mahomet to prove his mission by cleaving the moon in two. Mahomet raised his hands towards heaven, and in a loud voice summoned the moon to do Habib's bidding. Accordingly, it descended to the top of the Kaaba (*q.v.*) made seven circuits, and, coming to the prophet, entered his right sleeve and came out of the left. It then entered the collar of his robe, and descended to the skirt, clove itself into two plaits, one of which appeared in the east of the skies and the other in the west; and the two parts ultimately reunited and resumed their usual form.

***Mother of.*** Amina, of the tribe of Koreish. She died when Mahomet was six years old.

***Mule.*** Fadda.

***Paradise of.*** The ten animals admitted to the Moslem's paradise are:

(1) The dog Kratim, which accompanied the Seven Sleepers.

(2) Balaam's ass, which spoke with the voice of a man to reprove the disobedient prophet.

(3) Solomon's ant, of which he said, 'Go to the ant, thou sluggard …'

(4) Jonah's whale.

(5) The ram caught in the thicket, and offered in sacrifice in lieu of Isaac.

(6) The calf of Abraham.

(7) The camel of Saleb.

(8) The cuckoo of Bilkis.

(9) The ox of Moses.

(10) Mahomet's horse, Borak.

***Standard.*** Bajura.

***Stepping-stone.*** The stone upon which the prophet placed his foot when he mounted Al Borak on his ascent to heaven. It rose as the beast rose, but Mahomet, putting his hand upon it, forbade it to follow him, whereupon it remained suspended in mid-air, where the True Believer, if he has faith enough, may still behold it.

***Swords.*** Dhu'l Fakar (*the trenchant*), Al Battar (*the beater*), Medham (*the keen*), and Hatef (*the deadly*).

***Successor.*** (*See above, Father-in-law.*)

***Tribe.*** On both sides, the Koreish.

***Uncle,*** who took charge of Mahomet at the death of his grandfather, Abu Tâlib.

***Wives.*** Ten in number, viz. (1) Kadija, a rich widow of the tribe of Koreish, who had been twice married already, and was forty years of age. For twenty-five years she was his only wife, but at her death he married nine others, all of whom survived him.

*The nine wives*. (1) Ayesha, daughter of Abu Bekr, only nine years old on her wedding-day. This was his youngest and favourite wife.

(2) Sauda, widow of Sokram, and nurse to his daughter Fatima.

(3) Hafsa, a widow twenty-eight years old, who also had a son. She was daughter of Omeya.

(4) Zeinab, wife of Zaid, but divorced in order that the prophet might take her to wife.

(5) Barra, wife of a young Arab and daughter of Al Hareth, chief of an Arab tribe. Both father and husband were slain in a battle with Mahomet. She was a captive.

(6) Rehana, daughter of Simeon, and a Jewish captive.

(7) Safiya, the espoused wife of Kenana. Kenana was put to death. Safiya outlived the prophet forty years.

(8) Omm Habiba – i.e. mother of Habiba; the widow of Abu Sofian.

(9) Maimuna, fifty-one years old, and a widow, who survived all his other wives.

Also ten or fifteen concubines, chief of whom was Mariyeh, mother of Ibrahim, the prophet's son, who died when fifteen months old.

> In order to justify his amours Mahomet added a new chapter to the Koran, which may be found in Gagnier's *Notes upon Abulfeda*, p. 151.

***Year of Deputations.*** AD 630, the 8th of the Hegira.

***If the mountain will not come to Mahomet, Mahomet must go to the mountain.*** When Mahomet introduced his system to the Arabs, they asked for miraculous proofs. He then ordered Mount Safa to come to him, and as it did not move, he said, 'God is merciful. Had it obeyed my words, it would have fallen on us to our destruction. I will therefore go to the mountain, and thank God that He has had mercy on a stiffnecked generation.' The phrase is often used of one who, not being able to get his own way, bows before the inevitable.

**Mahoun, Mahound.** Names of contempt for Mahomet, a Moslem, a Moor, particularly in romances of the Crusades. The name is sometimes used as a synonym for 'the Devil'.

> Ofttimes by Termagant and Mahound swore.
>
> Spenser, *Faërie Queene*, VI, vii, 47

> Mahound is in his paradise above the eastern star,
> (*Don John of Austria is going to the war.*) …
> And his voice through all the garden is a thunder sent to bring
> Black Azrael and Ariel and Ammon on the wing.
>
> G. K. Chesterton, *Lepanto*

**Mahu.** One of the fiends whose names Shakespeare got from Harsnett (*see* **Hobbididance**) and introduced into *King Lear*.

> Five fiends have been in poor Tom at once: of lust, as Obidicut; Hobbididance, prince of dumbness; Mahu, of stealing; Modo, of murder; Flibbertigibbet of mopping and mowing. (iv, 1.)

**Maid Marian.** A female character in the old May games and morris dances, in the former usually being Queen of the May. In the later Robin Hood ballads she became attached to the cycle as the outlaw's sweetheart, probably through the performance of Robin Hood plays at May-day festivities. The part of Maid Marian both in the games and the dance was frequently taken by a man dressed as a woman.

> [The Courtier] must, if the least spot of morphew come on his face, have his oyle of tartar, his *lac virginis,* his camphir dissolved in verjuice, to make the foole as faire, for sooth, as if he were to playe Maid Marian in a May-game or moris daunce.
>
> Green, *Quip for an Upstart Courtier* (1592)

**Maid of Athens,** immortalised by Byron, was Theresa Macri. Some twenty-four years after this poem was written she was in dire poverty, without a single vestige of beauty, and with a large family.

**Maid of Norway.** Margaret (1283–90), daughter of Eric II and Margaret of Norway. On the death of Alexander III of Scotland (1285), her maternal grandfather, she was acknowledged Queen of Scotland, and was betrothed to Edward, son of Edward I of England, but she died on her passage to Scotland.

**Maid of Orleans.** Joan of Arc (1412–31), who raised the siege of Orleans in 1429.

**Maid of Saragossa.** Augustina Zaragoza, distinguished for her heroism when Saragossa was besieged in 1808 and 1809, and celebrated by Byron in his *Childe Harold* (I, liv–lvi).

**Maiden.** A machine resembling the guillotine, used in Scotland in the 16th and 17th centuries for beheading criminals, and introduced there by the Regent Morton from Halifax, Yorkshire, for the purpose of beheading the laird of Pennycuick. It was also called 'the widow'.

***He who invented the maiden first hanselled it.*** Morton is erroneously said to have been the first to suffer by it. Thomas Scott, one of the murderers of Rizzio, was beheaded by it in 1566, fifteen years before the Regent's execution.

**Maiden Assize.** One in which there is no person to be brought to trial. We have also the expressions *maiden tree*, one never lopped; *maiden fortress*, one never taken; *maiden speech*, etc. In a maiden assize, the sheriff of the county presents the judge with a pair of white gloves. *Maiden* conveys the sense of unspotted, unpolluted, innocent; thus Hubert says to the king –

> This hand of mine
> Is yet a maiden and an innocent hand,
> Not painted with the crimson spots of blood.
> Shakespeare, *King John*, 4, 2

**Maiden King, The.** Malcolm IV of Scotland (1141, 1153–65).

> Malcolm … son of the brave and generous Prince Henry … was so kind and gentle in his disposition, that he was usually called Malcolm the Maiden. Scott, *Tales of a Grandfather*, iv

**Maiden** or **Virgin Queen.** Elizabeth, Queen of England, who never married. (1533, 1558–1603.)

**Maiden Town.** A town never taken by the enemy (*cp.* Maiden Assize *above*). Also, specifically, Edinburgh, from tradition that the maiden daughters of a Pictish king were sent there for protection during an intestine war.

**Mailed Fist, The.** Aggressive military might; from a phrase (*gepanzerte Faust*) made use of by William II of Germany when bidding adieu to Prince Henry of Prussia as he was starting on his tour to the Far East (December 16th, 1897):

> Should anyone essay to detract from our just rights or to injure us, then up and at him with your mailed fist.

**Mainbrace.** ***To splice the mainbrace.*** A nautical phrase for to serve out grog; hence to indulge freely in strong drink. Literally, the *mainbrace* is the rope by which the mainyard of a ship is set in position, and to *splice* it would be to join the two ends together again when broken.

**Main Chance, The.** Profit or money, probably from the game called hazard, in which the first throw of the dice is called the *main*, which must be between four and nine, the player then throwing his *chance*, which determines the main.

***To have an eye to the main chance.*** To keep in view the money or advantage to be made out of an enterprise.

**Maintenance** (Fr. *main*, *tenir*, to hold in the hand, maintain). Means of support or sustenance; in legal phraseology, officious intermeddling in litigation with which one has rightfully nothing whatever to do. *Cp.* Champerty. Actions for maintenance are rare, but damages can be recovered for this abuse of legal process.

***Cap of Maintenance.*** *See* Cap.

**Maitland Club.** A club of literary antiquaries, instituted at Glasgow in 1828. It published or reprinted a number of works of Scottish historical and literary interest.

**Maize.** American superstition had it that if a damsel finds a blood-red ear of maize, she will have a suitor before the year is over.

> Even the blood-red ear to Evangeline brought not her lover. Longfellow, *Evangeline*

**Majesty.** Henry VIII was the first English sovereign who was styled 'His Majesty', though it was not till the time of the Stuarts that this form of address had become stereotyped, and in the Dedication to James I prefixed to the Authorised Version of the Bible (1611) the King is addressed both in this way and as 'Your Highness'.

> The Lord of Heaven and earth blesse your Maiestie with many and happy dayes, that as his Heavenly hand hath enriched your Highnesse with many singular and extraordinary Graces, etc.

Henry IV was 'His Grace'; Henry VI, 'His Excellent Grace'; Edward IV, 'High and Mighty Prince'; Henry VII, 'His Grace' and 'His Highness'; Henry VIII, in the earlier part of his reign, was styled 'His Highness'. 'His Sacred Majesty' was a title assumed by subsequent sovereigns, but was afterwards changed to 'Most Excellent Majesty'. 'His Catholic Majesty' is the king of Spain, and 'His Most Christian Majesty' the former kings of France.

In heraldry, an eagle crowned and holding a sceptre is said to be 'an eagle in his majesty'.

**Majolica Ware.** A pottery originally made in the island of Majorca or Majolica. *See* Faience.

**Majority.** ***He has joined the majority.*** He is dead. Blair says, in his *Grave*, ''Tis long since Death had the majority.'

**Make.** In America this word is much more frequently used with the meaning put ready for use than it is with us; we have the phrase *to make the bed*, and Shakespeare has *make the door* (*see* Door), but in the States such phrases as *Have you made my room?* – i.e. put it tidy, are common. *To make good*, *to make one's pile*, *to make a place* (i.e. to arrive there), are among the many Americanisms in which this word is used. *To make a die of it*, to die, is another.

> Why, Tom, you don't mean to make a die of it?
> R. M. Bird, *Nick of the Woods* (1837)

***On the make.*** Looking after one's own personal advantage; intent on the 'main chance'.

***To make away with.*** To put or take out of the way, run off with; to squander; also to murder; *to make away with oneself* is to commit suicide.

***To make believe.*** To pretend; to play a game at; as, 'To make believe that one's asleep'.

> We will make believe that there are fairies in the world. Kingsley, *Water Babies*, ch. ii

*Make-believe* is also used as a noun –

> The public is quite ready to play at a game of make-believe; i.e. the public is quite ready to be fooled with its eyes open.

***To make bold.*** *See* Bold.

***To make for.*** To conduce; as, 'His actions make for peace'; also to move towards; hence, in slang use, to attack.

***To make free with.*** To take liberties with, use as one's own.

***To make good.*** To fulfil one's promises or to come up to expectations, to succeed.

> Whether or not the new woman Mayor would 'make good' was of real interest to the country at large.
> *Evening Post* (*New York*), Sept. 14th, 1911.

Also to replace, repair, or compensate for; as, 'My car was damaged through your carelessness, so now you'll have to make it good.'

***To make it up.*** To become reconciled after a quarrel.

***To make off.*** To run away, to abscond.

***What make you here?*** What do you want? What are you come here for? Formerly in good use, but now regarded as a vulgarism; *cp.* the French *Que faites-vous ici?*

> Now, sir, what make you here?
> Shakespeare, *As You Like it*, 1, 1
>
> 'Twas in Margate last July, I walk'd upon the pier,
> I saw a little vulgar boy – I said, 'What make you here?'
> *Ingoldsby Legends, Misadventures at Margate*

**Makeshift.** A temporary arrangement during an emergency.

**Make-up.** The materials used by an actor for painting his face and otherwise transforming his appearance to suit a character on the stage; the manner in which he is *made up*; hence, in colloquial use, the sum of one's characteristics, idiosyncrasies, etc. In *printing* the *make up* is the arrangement of the printed matter in columns, pages, etc.

**Make-weight.** A small addition as compensation or an 'extra', as a piece of meat, cheese, bread, etc., thrown into the scale to make the weight correct. Similarly, a supplement to one's wages by a grant or bonus is sometimes known as a *make-wage*.

**Malagigi.** *See* Maugis.

**Malagrowther, Malachi.** The signature of Sir Walter Scott to a series of letters contributed in 1826 to the *Edinburgh Weekly Journal* upon the lowest limitation of paper money to £5. They caused an immense sensation, similar to that produced by *Drapier's Letters* (*q.v.*), or Burke's *Reflections on the French Revolution*.

**Malakoff.** This fortification, which was carried by storm by the French, September 8th, 1855 (and consequently the ducal title), was named from a drunken Russian sailor who lived at Sebastopol, and, being dismissed the dockyards in which he had been employed, opened a liquor-shop on the hill outside the town. His old friends gathered round, other houses sprang up, and 'Malakoff', as it came to be called, was ultimately fortified.

**Malambruno.** A giant in Cervantes' *Don Quixote* (II, iii, 45); he enchanted Antonomasia and her husband, and Don Quixote achieved their disenchantment by mounting the wooden horse, Clavileno.

**Malaprop, Mrs.** The famous character in Sheridan's *The Rivals*. Noted for her blunders in the use of words (Fr. *mal à propos*). 'As headstrong as an *allegory* on the banks of the Nile' is one of her grotesque misapplications; and she has given us the word *malapropism* to denote such mistakes.

**Malbecco.** A 'cankered, crabbed earle' in Spenser's *Faërie Queene* (III, x) wealthy, very miserly, and the impersonation of self-inflicted torments. His young wife, Helenore, set fire to his house, and eloped with Sir Paridel, whereupon Malbecco cast himself from a rock, and his ghost was metamorphosed into Jealousy.

**Malbrouk** or **Marlbrough.** The old French song, '*Malbrouk s'en va-t-en guerre*' (Marlborough is off to the wars), is said to date from 1709, when the Duke of Marlborough was winning his battles in Flanders, but did not become popular till it was applied to Charles Churchill, 3rd Duke of Marlborough, at the time of his failure against Cherbourg (1758), and was further popularised by its becoming a favourite of Marie Antoinette about 1780, and by its being introduced by Beaumarchais into *Le Mariage de Figaro* (1784). The air, however (the same as our 'We won't go home till morning'), is of far older date, was well known in Egypt and the East, and is said to have been sung by the Crusaders. According to a tradition recorded by Châteaubriand, the air came from the Arabs, and the tale is a legend of Mambron, a crusader.

> Malbrouk s'en va-t-en guerre,
> Mironton, mironton, mirontaine;
> Malbrouk s'en va-t-en guerre,
> Nul sait quand reviendra.
> Il reviendra z'à pâques –
> Mironton, mironton, mirontaine …
> Ou à la Trinité.

**Male.** Applied in the vegetable kingdom to certain plants which were supposed to have some masculine property or appearance, as the *male fern* (*Nephrodium filix-mas*), the fronds of which cluster in a kind of crown; and to precious stones – particularly sapphires – that are remarkable for their depth or brilliance of colour.

> Saul shuddered; and sparkles 'gan dart
> From the jewels that woke in his turban, at once with a start,
> All its lordly male-sapphires, and rubies courageous at heart.
> Browning, *Saul*

**Malebolge.** The eighth circle of Dante's *Inferno* (Canto xviii), containing ten *bolgi* or pits. The name is used figuratively of any cesspool of filth or iniquity.

> In the Room of Arras Rouge
> Satan sits from Malebouge.
> Lewis Spence, *The Room of Arras Rouge* (*Songs Satanic*, etc., 1913)

**Malecasta.** The impersonation of lust in Spensers' *Faërie Queene*, III, i. She is mistress of Castle Joyous.

**Maleger.** The incarnation of evil passions in Spenser's *Faërie Queene*, II, xi. He was 'thin as a rake', and cold as a serpent, and attacks the Castle of Temperance with a rabble in twelve troops, typifying the seven deadly sins and the lusts of the five senses. Prince Arthur stabs him again and again, but it is like stabbing a shadow, and finally he calls to mind that every time the earl touches the earth his strength is renewed, so he squeezes all his breath out and tosses the body into a lake. *Cp.* Antaeus.

**Malengin.** The typification of guile in Spenser's *Faërie Queene*, V, ix. Being attacked by Sir Artegal and his iron man, he turned himself first into a fox, then to a bush, then to a bird, then to a hedgehog, then to a snake; but Talus was a match for all his deceits, and killed him.

**Malepardus.** Reynard's castle in the romance of *Reynard the Fox* (*q.v.*) is so called.

**Malesuada Fames** (Lat.). Hunger is a bad counsellor. From Virgil's *Aeneid*, vi, 276. The French say, '*Vilain affamé, demi enragé*.'

**Malikites.** One of the four sects of Sunnites (*q.v.*).

**Malkin.** An old diminutive of Matilda; formerly used as a generic term for a kitchen-wench or untidy slut; also for a cat (*see* Grimalkin), and for a scarecrow or grotesque puppet.

> All tongues speak of him …
> The kitchen malkin pins
> Her richest lochram 'bout her reechy neck,
> Clambering the walls to eye him.
> Shakespeare, *Coriolanus*, ii, 1

The name was also sometimes given to the Queen of the May (*see* Maid Marian):

> Put on the shape of order and humanity,
> Or you must marry Malkin, the May lady.
> Beaumont and Fletcher, *Monsieur Thomas*, II, ii

**Mall, The.** A broad promenade in St James's Park, London, so called because the game of *Pall-mall* (*q.v.*) used to be played there; the *mall* was the mallet with which the ball was struck.

> Noe persons shall after play carry their malls out of St James's Parke without leave of the said keeper. *Order Book of General Monk* (1662)

**Mallows. *Abstain from mallows*.** This is the thirty-eighth symbol in the Protreptics. Pythagoras tells us that mallow was the first messenger sent by the gods to earth to indicate to many that they sympathised with them and had pity on them. To make food of mallows would be to dishonour the gods. Mallows are cathartic.

**Malmesbury, the Philosopher of.** Thomas Hobbes (1588-1679), author of *Leviathan* (*q.v.*), from his birthplace.

**Malmsey Wine** is the wine of Malvasia, in the Morea, and is the same name as *Malvoisie*.

George, Duke of Clarence, was, according to tradition, drowned in a butt of malmsey in 1477–8, by order of his brother, Richard III. Holinshed says, 'finallie the duke was cast into the Tower, and therewith adjudged for a traitor, and privily drowned in a butt of malmesie, the eleventh of March, in the beginning of the seventeenth yeare of the kinge's reigne.'

> I have an abridgement of an English Chronicle, which drowns the Duke of Clarence in a rundlet of malmsey; the Duke might as soon be drowned in a thimble; but, perhaps, it is a whole tun in the Chronicle, for my book is but a pitome.
>
> *The Last Dying Words of Col. Pride* (*A Satirical Pamphlet*, 1680)

*See* Shakespeare's *Richard III*, 1, 4.

**Malt.** ***A malt worm.*** A toper, especially a well soaked beer-drinker.

> I am joined with no foot-landrakers, no long-staff sixpenny strikers, none of these mad mustachio-purple-hued malt worms; but with nobility and tranquillity. Shakespeare, *1 Henry IV*, 2, 1

***In meal or malt.*** *See* Meal.

***When the malt gets aboon the meal.*** When persons, after dinner, get more or less fuddled.

> When the malt begins to get aboon the meal, they'll begin to speak about government in kirk and state. Scott, *Old Mortality*, ch. iv

The famous *Sermon on Malt* is generally credited to the Puritan divine John Dod (about 1549–1645), rector of Fawsley, Northants, called *the Decalogist*, from his exposition of the Ten Commandments (1604).

**Malta, Knights of,** or *Hospitallers of St John of Jerusalem*. Some time after the first crusade (1042), some Neapolitan merchants built at Jerusalem a hospital for sick pilgrims and a church which they dedicated to St John; these they committed to the charge of certain knights, called *Hospitallers of St John*. In 1310 these Hospitallers, having developed into a military Order, took the island of Rhodes, and changed their title into *Knights of Rhodes*. In 1522 they were expelled by the Turks, and took up their residence in Malta, which was ruled by the Grand Master until the island was taken by the French in 1798. The Order is now extinct as a sovereign body, but maintains a lingering existence in Italy, Germany, France, etc., and. in Malta, where it still confers titles of 'Marquis' and 'Count'. *See* Hospitallers.

**Maltese Cross.** Made thus: ✠. Originally the badge of the Knights of Malta, formed of four barbed arrowheads with their points meeting in the centre. In modified and elaborated forms it is the badge of many well-known Orders, etc., as our Victoria Cross and Order of Merit, and the old Prussian Iron Cross.

**Malthusian Doctrine.** That population increases more than the means of increasing subsistence does, so that in time, if no check is put upon the increase of population, many must starve or all be ill fed. Promulgated by T. R. Malthus (1766–1835), especially in his *Essay on Population* (1798). Applied to individual nations, like Britain, it intimated that something must be done to check the increase of population, as all the land would not suffice to feed its inhabitants.

**Malum,** in Latin, means *an apple*; and *malus, mala, malum* means *evil*. Southey, in his *Commonplace Book*, quotes a witty etymon given by Nicolson and Burn, making the noun derived from the adjective, in allusion, possibly, to the apple eaten by Eve; and there is the schoolboy joke showing how *malo* repeated four times can be translated into a tolerable and fairly lengthy quatrain :

> *Malo*, I would rather be
> *Malo*, Up an apple tree
> *Malo*, Than a bad man
> *Malo*, In adversity.

***Malum in se*** (Lat.). What is of itself wrong, and would be so even if no law existed against its commission, as lying, murder, theft.

***Malum prohibitum*** (Lat.). What is wrong merely because it is forbidden, as eating a particular fruit was wrong in Adam and Eve, because they were commanded not to do so.

**Mamamouchi.** A 'spoof' Turkish title or dignity invented by Molière (*Bourgeois Gentilhomme*), which M. Jourdain is told has been conferred upon him by the Grand Signior. Hence, sometimes used in England of a mock honour or a fantastic piece of buffoonery. Better be a country gentleman in England than a foreign Mamamouchi.

**Mambrino.** A pagan king of old romance, introduced by Ariosto into *Orlando Furioso*. He had a helmet of pure gold which rendered the wearer invulnerable, and was taken possession of by Rinaldo. This is frequently referred to in *Don Quixote*, and we read that when the barber was caught in a shower and clapped his brazen basin on his head, Don Quixote insisted that this was the enchanted helmet of the Moorish king.

**Mamelukes** (Arab. *mamluc*, a slave). The slaves brought from the Caucasus to Egypt, and formed into a standing army, who, in 1254, raised one of their body to the supreme power. They reigned over Egypt till 1517, when they were overthrown by the Turkish Sultan, Selim

I, and the country, though nominally under a Turkish viceroy, was subsequently governed by twenty-four Mameluke beys. In 1811 the Pasha of Egypt, Mohammed Ali, by a wholesale massacre annihilated the Mamelukes.

**Mammet,** or **Maumet.** An idol; hence a puppet or doll (as in *Romeo and Juliet*, 3, 5, and *1 Henry IV*, 2, 3). The word is a corruption of *Mahomet*. Mohammedanism being the most prominent non-Christian religion with which Christendom was acquainted before the Reformation, it became a generic word to designate any false faith; even idolatry is called *mammetry*; and in a 14th century MS Bible (first edited by A. C. Paues, 1904) 1 John 5:21, reads –

> My smale children, kepe ye you from mawmetes and symulacris.

**Mammon.** The god of this world. The word in Syriac means riches, and it occurs in the Bible (Matt. 6:24, Luke 16:13): 'Ye cannot serve God and mammon'. Spenser (*Faërie Queene*, II, vii) and Milton (who identifies him with Vulcan or Mulciber, *Paradise Lost*, i, 738–51) both make Mammon the personification of the evils of wealth and miserliness.

> In the *Faërie Queene*, Mammon says if Sir Guyon will serve him he shall be the richest man in the world; but the knight says money has no charm for him. Mammon then takes him to his smithy, and tells him he may make what orders he likes, but Guyon declines to make any. The god then offers to give him Philotine to wife, but Guyon will not accept the honour. Lastly, he takes him to Proserpine's bower, and tells him to pluck the golden fruit, and rest on the silver stool; Sir Guyon again refuses, and after three days' sojourn in the infernal regions is led back to earth.

> Mammon led them on –
> Mammon, the least erected Spirit that fell
> From Heaven; for even in Heaven his looks and thoughts
> Were always downward bent, admiring more
> The riches of Heaven's pavement, trodden gold,
> Than aught divine or holy.
> Milton, *Paradise Lost*, 1, 678

***The Mammon of Unrighteousness.*** Money; *see* Luke 16:9.

***Sir Epicure Mammon.*** A worldly sensualist in Ben Jonson's *Alchemist*.

**Mammoth Cave.** In Edmonson county, Kentucky; the largest known in the world, discovered in 1809. It comprises a large number of chambers, with connecting passages said to total 150 miles, and covers an area of nearly 10 miles in diameter.

**Man.** Man in the Moon: Man of Blood, Brass, December, Sin, Straw, War, etc. *See these words.*

***Man about town.*** A fashionable idler.

***Man Friday.*** *See* Friday.

***Man-Mountain.*** *See* Quinbus Flestrin.

***Man of letters.*** An author, a literary scholar.

***Man of the World.*** One 'knowing' in worldcraft; no greenhorn. Charles Macklin brought out a comedy (1704), and Henry Mackenzie a novel (1773) with the title.

***Man of war.*** A warship in the navy of a government; though the name is masculine, always spoken of as 'she'. Formerly the term was used to denote a fighting man ('the Lord is a man of war', Ex. 15:3).

The name of the 'Man of War Rock', in the Scilly Islands, is a corruption of Cornish *men* (or *maen*) *an vawr*, meaning ' big rock'.

The popular name of the marine hydrozoan, *Physalia pelagica*, is the *Portuguese man of war*, or, simply, *man of war*.

***Man-of-war bird.*** The frigate-bird.

***Man proposes, but God disposes.*** So we read in the *Imitatio Christi* (*Homo proponit, sed Deus disponit*, I, xix, 2). Herbert (*Jacula Prudentum*) has nearly the same words; as also has Montluc: *L'homme propose et Dieu dispose* (*Comédie de Proverbes*, iii, 7).

***The Man in Black.*** A well-known character in Goldsmith's *Citizen of the World*; supposed to have been drawn from the author's father.

***The Man in the Iron Mask.*** *See* Mask.

***The Man of Destiny.*** Napoleon I (1761, 1804–14, d.1821). He looked on himself as an instrument in the hands of destiny.

> The Man of Destiny … had power for a time to bind kings with chains, and nobles with fetters of iron.
> Scott

G. B. Shaw used the epithet as the title of a play about Napoleon.

***The Man of Ross.*** *See* Ross.

***The New Man.*** The regenerated man. In Scripture phrase the unregenerated state is called *the old man*.

***The Threefold Man.*** According to Diogenes Laertius, the body was composed of (1) a mortal part; (2) a divine and ethereal part, called the *phren*; and (3) an aerial and vaporous part, called the *thumos*.

According to the Romans, man has a threefold soul, which at the dissolution of the body resolves itself into (1) the *Manes*; (2) the *Anima* or Spirit; (3) the *Umbra*. The Manes went either to Elysium or Tartarus; the Anima returned to the gods; but the Umbra hovered about the body as unwilling to quit it.

According to the Jews, man consists of body, soul, and spirit.

**Man, Isle of.** The origin of the name is doubtful, but it may be O.Celt. *man*, a place. The *Old English Chronicle* calls it *Mon ege* (Mona's Isle), Orderic (about 1100) *Insula Man*; while Caesar called it *Mona*, Pliny *Monapia*, and Ptolemy *Monarina*. To Bede the island was *Mevaniae Insulae*, and Nennius gives it its current Latin name as well as its native name – *Eubonia, id est Manau*. The Manx form is *Eilan Mhannin*.

**Manchester.** The name – which is given in Domesday Book as *Mamecestre*, and in the *Old English Chronicle* as *Mameceaster* – is of doubtful origin, but the *mam-* is probably Celtic *mam*, rounded, breast-like, in which case the word would be a Latin and Celtic hybrid denoting 'the camp by the round hill'. A native of Manchester is a *Mancunian*, from *Mancunium*, the mediaeval Latin name of the city.

***The Manchester Massacre.*** *See* Peterloo.

***The Manchester Poet.*** Charles Swain (1803–74).

***The Manchester School.*** The name given in derision by Disraeli to the Cobden-Bright group of Free Trade economists in 1848. Hence, Free Traders, and Free Trade principles generally.

**Manciple.** A purveyor of food, a steward, or clerk of the kitchen. Chaucer has a 'manciple' in his *Canterbury Tales*. (Lat. *manceps, mancipis*, a buyer, manager.)

**Mancus.** An Anglo-Saxon coin worth thirty pence. In the reign of Ethelbert, King of Kent, money accounts were kept in *pounds*, *mancuses*, *shillings*, and *pence*. Five pence = one shilling, Thirty pence = one mancus. Mancuses were in gold and silver also.

**Mandamus** (Lat., we command). A writ of King's Bench, commanding the person or corporation, etc., named to do what the writ directs. So called from the opening word.

**Mandarin** is not a Chinese word, but one given by the Portuguese colonists at Macao to the officials called by the natives *Kwan*. It is from Malay and Hindi *mantri*, counsellor, from Sansk. *mantra*, counsel (*man*, to think).

***The nine ranks of mandarins*** were distinguished by the button in their cap – 1, ruby; 2, coral; 3, sapphire; 4, an opaque blue stone; 5, crystal; 6, an opaque white shell; 7, wrought gold; 8, plain gold; and 9, silver.

> The whole body of Chinese mandarins consists of twenty-seven members. They are appointed for (1) imperial birth; (2) long service; (3) illustrious deeds; (4) knowledge; (5) ability; (6) zeal; (7) nobility; and (8) aristocratic birth. Gutzlay

The word is sometimes used derisively for over-pompous officials, as, 'The mandarins of our Foreign Office'.

**Mandate** (Lat. *mandatum*, *mandare*, to command). An authoritative charge or command; in law, a contract of bailment by which the mandatory undertakes to perform gratuitously a duty regarding property committed to him. After the Great War it was decided by the victorious Powers that the former extra-European colonies and possessions of Germany and Turkey should be governed under *mandate* by one or other of the Powers. Thus, the German colonies in West Africa and parts of the Turkish possessions in Palestine and Mesopotamia became *mandatory spheres* under Great Britain.

**Mandeville, Sir John.** *See* Maundrel.

**Mandrabul. *From gold to nothing, like Mandrabul's offering.*** The story is that Mandrabul, having found a goldmine, in Samos, offered to Juno a golden ram for the discovery; next year he gave a silver one, then a brazen one, and in the fourth year nothing. The proverb 'to bring a noble to ninepence, and ninepence to nothing' carries the same meaning.

**Mandrake.** The root of the mandrake, or mandragora, often divides in two, and presents a rude appearance of a man. In ancient times human figures were cut out of the root, and wonderful virtues ascribed to them, such as the production of fecundity in women (Gen. 30:14–16). It was also thought that mandrakes could not be uprooted without producing fatal effects, so a cord used to be fixed to the root, and round a dog's neck, and the dog being chased drew out the mandrake and died. Another fallacy was that a small dose made a person vain of his beauty, and a large one made him an idiot; and yet another that when the mandrake is uprooted it utters a scream, in explanation of which Thomas Newton, in his *Herball to the Bible*, says, 'It is supposed to be a creature having life, engendered under the earth of the seed of some dead person put to death for murder.'

> Shrieks like mandrakes, torn out of the earth.
>
> Shakespeare, *Romeo and Juliet*, 4, 3

***Mandrakes called love-apples.*** From the old notion that they excited amorous inclinations; hence Venus is called *Mandragoritis*, and the Emperor Julian, in his epistles, tells Calixenes that he drank its juice nightly as a love-potion.

***He has eaten mandrake.*** Said of a very indolent and sleepy man, from the narcotic and stupefying properties of the plant, well known to the ancients.

> Give me to drink mandragora ...
> That I might sleep out this great gap of time
> My Antony is away.
>
> Shakespeare, *Antony and Cleopatra*, 1, 5

**Manduce.** The personification (? or deification) of gluttony, mentioned by Plautus, Juvenal, etc., and adopted by Rabelais as the prime object of worship of the Gastrolaters, a people whose god was their belly.

> It is a monstrous ... figure, fit to frighten little children; its eyes are bigger than its belly, and its head larger than all the rest of its body, ... having a goodly pair of wide jaws, lined with two rows of teeth, which, by the magic of a small twine ... are made to clash, chatter, and rattle against the other, as the jaws of St Clement's dragon (called *graulli*) on St Mark's procession at Metz. *Pantagruel*, iv, 59

**Manes. *To appease his Manes*.** To do when a person is dead what would have pleased him or was due to him when alive. The spirit or ghost of the dead was by the Romans called his *Manes*, which never slept quietly in the grave so long as survivors left its wishes unfulfilled. February 19th was the day when all the living sacrificed to the shades of dead relations and friends – a kind of non-Christian All Souls' Day.

> *Manes* is probably from the old word *manis*, i.e. 'bonus', 'quod eos venerantes manes vocarent, ut Graeci *chrestous*'. (*See* Lucretius, iii, 52.)

**Manfred.** Count Manfred, the hero of Byron's dramatic poem of this name (1817), sold himself to the Prince of Darkness, was wholly without human sympathies, and lived in splendid solitude among the Alps. He once loved the Lady Astarte (*q.v.*), who died, but Manfred went to the hall of Arimanes to see her, and was told that he would die the following day. The next day the Spirit of his Destiny came to summon him; the proud count scornfully dismissed it, and died.

**Mani.** The moon, in *Scandinavian mythology*, the son of Mundilfoeri (*q.v.*), taken to heaven by the gods to drive the moon-car. He is followed by a wolf, which, when time shall be no more, will devour both Mani and his sister Sol.

**Mani, Manes,** or **Manichaeus.** The founder of Manichaeanism (*see below*), born in Persia probably about 216, prominent at the court of Sapor I (240–72), but crucified by the Magians in 277.

**Manichaeans** or **Manichees.** The followers of Mani (*see above*), who taught that the universe is controlled by two antagonistic powers, viz. light or goodness (identified with God), and darkness, chaos, or evil. The system was the old Babylonian nature-worship modified by Christian and Persian influences, and its own influence on the Christian religion was, even so late as the 13th century, deep and widespread. St Augustine was a member of the body for some nine years. One of Mani's claims was that though Christ had been sent into the world to restore it to light and banish the darkness His apostles had perverted his doctrine and he, Mani, was sent as the Paraclete to restore it. The headquarters of Manichaeanism were for many centuries at Babylon, and later at Samarkand. *Cp.* Cathari.

**Manitou.** The Great Spirit of the American Indians. The word is Algonkin, and means either the Great Good Spirit or the Great Evil Spirit.

**Manlian Orders.** Overstrained severity. Manlius Torquatus, the Roman consul, gave orders in the Latin war that no Roman, on pain of death, should engage in single combat; but one of the Latins provoked young Manlius by repeated insults, and Manlius slew him. When the young man took the spoils to his father, Torquatus ordered him to be put to death for disobedience.

**Manly,** in the *Plain Dealer*, by Wycherly. He is violent and uncouth, but presents an excellent contrast to the hypocritical Olivia (*q.v.*). *See* Alceste.

**Manna** (Ex. 16:15), popularly said to be a corrupt form of *man-hu* (What is this?). The marginal reading gives – 'When the children of Israel saw it [the small round thing like hoar-frost on the ground], they said to one another, What is this? for they wist not what it was.'

> And the house of Israel called the name thereof manna: and it was like coriander seed, white; and the taste of it was like wafers made with honey. (Verse 31.)

The word is more probably the Egyptian *mennu*, a waxy exudation of the tamarisk (*Tamarix gallica*).

***Manna of St Nicholas of Bari.*** The name given to a colourless and tasteless poison, sold by a notorious female poisoner of 16th-century Italy named Tofana, who confessed to having poisoned six hundred persons by its means.

**Manningtree** (Essex). Noted for its Whitsun fair, where an ox was roasted whole. Shakespeare makes Prince Henry call Falstaff 'a roasted Manningtree ox, with the pudding in his belly' (*1 Henry IV*, 2, 4).

> You shall have a slave eat more at a meale than ten of the guard; and drink more in two days than all Manningtree does at a Witsun-ale.

**Manoa.** The fabulous capital of El Dorado (*q.v.*), the houses of which city were said to be roofed with gold.

**Manon Lescaut.** A novel by the Abbé Prevost (1733). It is the history of a young man, the Chevalier des Grieux, possessed of many brilliant and some estimable qualities, but, being intoxicated by a fatal attachment to Manon, a girl who prefers luxury to faithful love, he is hurried into the violation of every rule of conduct.

**Manor.** *Demesne* (i.e. 'domain') land is that near the demesne or dwelling (*domus*) of the lord, and which he kept for his own use. *Manor* land was all that remained (*maneo*), and was let to tenants for money or service; originally, a barony held by a lord and subject to the jurisdiction of his court-baron.

> In some manors there was *common land* also, i.e. land belonging in common to two or more persons, to the whole village, or to certain natives of the village.

***Lord of the manor.*** The person of corporation in whom the rights of a manor are vested.

**Mansard Roof,** also called the *curb roof.* A roof in which the rafters, instead of forming a ʌ, are broken on each side into an elbow, the lower rafters being nearly vertical and the upper much inclined. It was devised by François Mansard (1598–1666), the French architect, to give height to attics.

**Mansfield.** ***The Miller of Mansfield.*** The old ballad (given in Percy's *Reliques*) tells how Henry II, having lost his way, met a miller, who took him home to his cottage. Next morning the courtiers tracked the king, and the miller discovered the rank of his guest, who, in merry mood, knighted his host as 'Sir John Cockle'. On St George's Day, Henry II invited the miller, his wife and son, to a royal banquet, and after being amused with their rustic ways, made Sir John 'overseer of Sherwood Forest, with a salary of £300 a year'.

**Mansion.** The Latin *mansio* (from *manere*, to remain, dwell) was simply a tent pitched on the march, hence sometimes a 'day's journey' (Pliny, xii, 14). Subsequently the word was applied to a roadside house for the accommodation of strangers (Suetonius, *Tit.* 10).

***Mansion House***, now the name of the official residence of a Lord Mayor, was formerly used of any important dwelling, especially the houses of lords of the manor and of high ecclesiastics.

**Mantalini, Madame.** A fashionable milliner in Dickens's *Nicholas Nickleby*, near Cavendish Square. Her husband, whose original name was 'Muntle', noted for his white teeth, minced oaths, and gorgeous morning gown, is an exquisite man-milliner, who lives on his wife's earnings, and ultimately goes to 'the demnition bow-wows'.

**Mantible.** A bridge mentioned in some of the mediaeval romances of thirty arches of black marble, guarded by 'a fearful huge giant', slain by Sir Fierabras.

**Mantle of Fidelity.** The old ballad 'The Boy and the Mantle', in Percy's *Reliques*, tells how a little boy showed King Arthur a curious mantle, 'which would become no wife that was not leal'. Queen Guinever tried it, but it changed from green to red, and red to black, and seemed rent into shreds. Sir Kay's lady tried it, but fared no better; others followed, but only Sir Cradock's wife could wear it. The theme is a very common one in old story, and was used by Spenser in the incident of Florimel's girdle.

**Mantuan Swan, Bard,** etc. Virgil, a native of Mantua, in Italy. Besides his great Latin epic, he wrote pastorals and Georgics.

> Ages elapsed ere Homer's lamp appeared,
> And ages ere the Mantuan Swan was heard.
>
> Cowper, *Table-Talk*, 557

**Manu.** *See* Menu.

**Manucodiata.** An old name for a bird of paradise; from Malay *manuqdewata*, the bird of the gods.

> Less pure the footless fowl of heaven, that never
> Rests upon earth, but on the wing for ever,
> Hovering o'er flowers, their fragrant food inhale.
> Drink the descending dew upon the way;
> And sleep aloft while floating on the gale.
>
> Southey, *Curse of Kehama*, xxi, 6

**Manufacturer.** *See* Surgeon.

**Manumit.** To set free; properly 'to send from one's hand' (*e manu mittere*). One of the Roman ways of freeing a slave was to take him before the chief magistrate and say, 'I wish this man to be free.' The lictor or master then turned the slave round in a circle, struck him with a rod across the cheek, and let him go.

**Manure** (Fr. *main-oeuvre*). Literally 'handwork', hence tillage by manual labour, hence the dressing applied to lands. Milton uses the word in its original sense in *Paradise Lost*, iv, 628:

> Yon flowery arbours, … with branches overgrown
> That mock our scant manuring.

And in xi, 28, says that the repentant tears of Adam brought forth better fruits than all the trees of Paradise that his hands 'manured' in the days of innocence.

**Many.** ***Many a mickle makes a muckle,*** or ***Many a little makes a mickle.*** Little and often fills the purse. *See* Little.

***Many men, many minds,*** i.e. as many opinions as there are persons to give them; an adaptation of Terence's *Quot homines tot sententiae* (*Phormio*, II, iv, 14).

***Too many for me*** or ***One too many for me.*** More than a match. *Il est trop fort pour moi.*

> The Irishman is cunning enough; but we shall be too many for him. Mrs Edgeworth

**Maori.** The aboriginal Polynesian inhabitants of New Zealand; a native word meaning *indigenous*.

**Mara.** The Satan of *Buddhist mythology*.

> The ten chief Sins came – Mara's mighty ones,
> Angels of evil.
> Sir Edwin Arnold, *Light of Asia*, VI, xix, 159

**Marabou.** A large stork or heron of western Africa, so called from Arab. *murabit*, a hermit, because among the Arabs these birds were held to be sacred. Its feathers are used by ladies for headgear, neck-wraps, etc.

**Marabouts.** A priestly order of Morocco (Arab. *murabit*, a hermit) which, in 1075, founded a dynasty and ruled over Morocco and part of Spain till it was put an end to by the Almohads in the 12th century.

**Marais, Le.** *See* Plain.

**Maranatha** (Syriac, *the Lord will come* – i.e. to execute judgment). A word which, with *Anathema* (*q.v.*), occurs in 1 Cor. 16:22, and has been erroneously taken as a form of anathematising among the Jews; hence, used for a terrible curse.

**Maravedi** or **Marvedie.** A very small Spanish copper coin, worth less than a farthing and long obsolete. There are frequent references to it in Elizabethan and 17th-century literature. In the 11th and 12th centuries there was a Portuguese gold coin of the same name, equivalent to about 14*s*.

> What a trifling, foolish girl you are, Edith, to send me by express a letter crammed with nonsense about books and gowns, and to slide the only thing I cared a marvedie about into the postscript. Scott, *Old Mortality*, ch. xi

**Marbles.** *See* Arundelian: Elgin.

**Marcella.** A fair shepherdess whose story forms an episode in *Don Quixote*.

**Marcellus.** This character in Dibdin's *Bibliomania* (1809–11) is meant for Edmund Malone (1741–1812), the well-known editor of Shakespeare.

**March.** The month is so called from 'Mars', the Roman war-god and patron deity.

> The old Dutch name for it was *Lent-maand* (lengthening-month), because the days sensibly lengthen; the old Saxon name was *Hrèth-monath* (rough month, from its boisterous winds); the name was subsequently changed to *Length-monath* (lengthening month); it was also called *Hlyd-monath* (boisterous month). In the French Republican calendar it was called *Ventose* (windy month, February 20th to March 20th).

***A bushel of March dust is worth a king's ransom.*** Because we want plenty of dry, windy weather in March to ensure good crops. The fine for murder used to be proportioned to the rank of the person killed. The lowest was £10, and the highest £60; the former was the ransom of a churl, and the latter of a king.

***He may be a rogue, but he's no fool on the march.*** Though his honesty may be in question he is a useful sort of person to have about.

***March borrows three days from April.*** *See* Borrowed Days.

***Mad as a March hare.*** *See* Hare.

***To steal a march on.*** *See* Steal.

**Marches.** The A.S. *mearc*, a mark, by way of Fr. *marche*, a frontier. The boundaries between England and Wales, and between England and Scotland, were called 'marches', and the word is the origin of our *marquis*, the lord of the march.

***Riding the marches*** – i.e. beating the bounds of the parish (Scotch). *See* Bounds, Beating the.

**Marching Watch.** The guard of civilians enrolled in London during the Middle Ages to keep order in the streets on the Vigils of St Peter and St John the Baptist during the festivities then held; used also of the festivities themselves. Henry VIII approved of the pageants, etc., and on one occasion, to encourage them, took his queen, Katherine of Aragon, to witness the proceedings at 'the King's Heade in Cheape'.

The custom fell into abeyance in 1527 on account of the sweating sickness, but was revived a few years later.

**Marchington** (Staffordshire). Famous for a crumbling short cake. Hence the saying that one of crusty temper is 'as short as Marchington wake-cake'.

**Marchioness, The.** The half-starved girl-of-all-work in Dickens's *Old Curiosity Shop*. As she has no name of her own Dick Swiveller gives her that of 'Sophronia Spynx', and eventually marries her.

**Marchpane.** The old name for the confection of almonds, sugar, etc., that we call *marzipan*, this being the German form of the original Ital. *marzapane*, and adopted by us in the 19th century in preference to our own well-established word, because we imported the stuff largely from Germany.

> *First Serv.*: Away with the joint-stools, remove the court-cupboard, look to the plate. Good thou, save me a piece of marchpane.
>
> Shakespeare, *Romeo and Juliet*, 1, 5

**Marcionites.** An ascetic Gnostic sect, founded by Marcion of Sinope in the 2nd century, and surviving till the 7th or even later. They believed in a good God, first revealed by Christ (whose incarnation and resurrection they rejected), in an evil God, i.e. the Devil, and in 'Demiurge', the name they gave to the imperfect God of the Jews.

**Marcley Hill.** Legend states that this hill in Herefordshire, on February 7th, 1571, at six o'clock in the evening, 'roused itself with a roar, and by seven next morning had moved 40 paces'. It kept on the move for three days, carrying all with it; it overthrew Kinnaston chapel, and diverted two high roads at least 200 yards from their former route. Twenty-six acres of land are said to have been moved 400 yards. (Speed, *Herefordshire*.)

**Marcos de Obregon.** The Spanish romance, *Relaciones de la Vida del Escudero Marcos de Obregon*, by Vincente Espinel (1618) was said by Voltaire (without sufficient reason) to be the groundwork of Le Sage's *Gil Blas*.

**Marcosians.** A small sect of Gnostics of the 2nd century, so called from the Egyptian Marcus. They are mentioned by Irenaeus, and were noted for their apocryphal books and religious fables.

**Mardi Gras** (Fr., 'fat Tuesday'). The last day of the Lent carnival in France, Shrove Tuesday, which is celebrated with all sorts of festivities. In Paris a fat ox used to be paraded through the principal streets, crowned with a fillet, and accompanied with mock priests and a band of tin instruments in imitation of a Roman sacrificial procession.

**Mare.** The Cromlech at Gorwell, Dorsetshire, is called the White Mare; the barrows near Hambleton, the Grey Mare.

***Away the mare.*** Off with the blue devils, good-bye to care. This mare is the incubus called the nightmare.

***To cry the mare*** (Herefordshire and Shropshire). In harvesting, when the ingathering is complete, a few blades of corn left for the purpose have their tops tied together. The reapers then place themselves at a certain distance, and fling their sickles at the 'mare'. He who succeeds in cutting the knot cries out 'I have her!' 'What have you?' 'A mare.' 'Whose is she?' The name of some farmer whose field has been reaped is here mentioned. 'Where will you send her?' The name of some farmer whose corn is not yet harvested is here given, and then all the reapers give a final shout.

***To win the mare or lose the halter.*** To play double or quits; all or nothing.

***The grey mare is the better horse.*** The woman is paramount; said of a wife who 'bosses' her husband. Macaulay says (*Hist. Eng.*, I, iii) – 'I suspect (the proverb) originated in the preference generally given to the grey mares of Flanders over the finest coach-horses of England'; but as the saying is recorded in England from earlier than the date of importation of Flemish horses this explanation is probably incorrect.

> As long as we have eyes, or hands, or breath,
> We'll look, or write, or talk you all to death,
> Yield, or she-Pegasus will gain her course.
> And the grey mare will prove the better horse.
>
> Prior, *Epilogue to Mrs Manley's 'Lucius'*

***The grey mare's tail.*** A cataract that is made by the stream which issues from Lochskene, in Scotland, so called from its appearance.

***The two-legged mare.*** The gallows.

***Shanks's mare.*** One's legs or shanks.

***Money will make the mare to go.*** You can do anything if only you have the money.

> 'Will you lend me your mare to go a mile?'
> ' No, she is lame leaping over a stile.'
> 'But if you will her to me spare,
> You shall have money for your mare.'
> 'Oh, ho! say you so?
> Money will make the mare to go.'
>
> *Old Glees and Catches*

***Whose mare's dead?*** What's the matter? Thus, in *2 Henry IV*, when Sir John Falstaff sees Mistress Quickly with the sheriff's officers, evidently in a state of great discomposure, he cries,

> How now? Whose mare's dead? What's the matter? Act 2:1

***To find a mare's nest*** is to make what you suppose to be a great discovery, but which turns out to be either no discovery at all or else all moonshine.

> Why does thou laugh?
> What mare's nest hast thou found?
> Beaumont and Fletcher, *Bonduca*, v, 2

In some parts of Scotland the expression is *a skate's nest*, and in Cornwall they say *You have found a wee's nest, and are laughing over the eggs.* In Devon, nonsense is called a *blind mare's nest.*

**Mare clausum** (Lat., a closed sea). A sea that is closed by a certain Power or Powers to the unrestricted trade of other nations, as, e.g. the Black Sea; the free and open sea is called *mare liberum.* Selden in 1635 published a treatise with the title *Mare Clausum.*

**Mareotic Luxury.** In ancient times the people living on the shores of Lake Moeris, the *Arva Mareotica* mentioned by Ovid (*Metamorphoses*, ix, 73), were famous for their voluptuous ease and idleness. Here were produced the white grapes from which was made the favourite beverage of Cleopatra, mentioned both by Horace (*Odes*, i, 37) and Virgil (*Georgics*, ii, 91).

**Marforio.** *See* Pasquinade.

**Margaret.** A country name for the magpie (*q.v.*); also for the daisy, or marguerite, so called from its pearly whiteness, *marguerite* being Old French for a pearl.

> The daise, a flour white and redde,
> In French called 'la belle Marguerite'.

***Lady Margaret Professor.*** A professor of divinity both at Oxford and Cambridge, the professorship being founded in 1502 by Lady Margaret Beaufort, mother of Henry VII, who also endowed Christ's and St John's College at Cambridge. These lectures are given for the 'voluntary theological examination', and treat upon the *Fathers*, the *Liturgy*, and the *priestly duties*. *Cp.* Norrisian.

**Margaret, St.** The chosen type of female innocence and meekness, represented as a young woman of great beauty, bearing the martyr's palm and crown, or with the dragon as an attribute. Sometimes she is delineated as coming from the dragon's mouth, for legend says that the monster swallowed her, but on making the sign of the cross he suffered her to quit his maw.

Another legend has it that Olybrius, governor of Antioch, captivated by her beauty, wanted to marry her, and, as she rejected him with scorn, threw her into a dungeon, where the devil came to her in the form of a dragon. Margaret held up the cross, and the dragon fled.

St Margaret is the patron saint of the ancient borough of Lynn Regis, and on the corporation seal she is represented as standing on a dragon and wounding it with the cross. The inscription is 'SVB . MARGARETA . TERITUR . DRACO . STAT . CRUCE. LAETA'. She is commemorated on July 20th.

**Margate.** This name does not mean 'the sea-gate' (Lat. *mare*, sea), but the road (A.S. *geat*) by the *mere* or lake, now drained. In the 13th century it appears both as *Meregate* and *Mergate.*

**Margin.** In many old books a commentary was printed in the margin (as in our Bible of the present day); hence the word was often used for a commentary itself, as in Shakespeare's –

> His face's own margent did quote such amazes.
> *Love's Labour's Lost*, 2, 1
>
> I knew you must be edified by the margent.
> *Hamlet*, 5, 2

And Lyly's –

> Beware my Comment, 'tis odds the margent shall bee as full as the text.
> *Pappe with a Hatchet* (1589)

**Margites.** The name – and hero – of an ancient Greek poem mentioned by Aristotle as the original of comedy. The word means 'the Booby', and was taken by Pope to be the name of some specially famous nincompoop.

> Margites was the name ... whom Antiquity recordeth to have been dunce the first.
> Pope, *Dunciad* (*Martinus Scriblerus*)

**Marguerite des Marguerites** (*the pearl of pearls*). So François called his sister, Marguerite de Valois (1492–1549), authoress of the *Heptameron.* She married twice: first, the Duc d'Alençon, and then Henri d'Albret, king of Navarre, and was the mother of Henry IV of France.

Sylvius de la Haye published (1547) a collection of her poems with the title *Marguerites de la marguerite des princesses*, etc.

**Margutte.** A giant in Pulci's *Morgante Maggiore*, ten feet high, who died of laughter on seeing a monkey pulling on his boots.

**Maria.** In Sterne's *Sentimental Journey*, a fair, quick-witted, amiable maiden, whose banns were forbidden by the curate who published them; in consequence of which she lost her reason, and used to sit by the roadside near Moulines, playing vesper hymns to the Virgin all day long.

**Marigold.** The plant *Calendula officinalis* and its bright yellow flower are so called in honour of the Virgin Mary.

> This riddle, Cuddy, if thou canst, explain …
> What flower is that which bears the Virgin's name,
> The richest metal added to the same?
>
> Gay, *Pastoral*

In 17th-century slang a marigold (or 'marygold') meant a sovereign, but now it denotes one million sterling.

***Marigold window.*** The same as a 'rose window' (*q.v.*).

**Marine.** ***The female Marine.*** Hannah Snell, of Worcester (born 1723), who (according to an untrustworthy tradition – *see Notes and Queries*, December 3rd, 1892) took part in the attack on Pondicherry. It is said that she ultimately opened a public-house in Wapping, but retained her male attire.

***Tell that to the Marines.*** *See* Horse Marines. In nautical parlance a greenhorn or a land-lubber afloat is often called 'a marine' in contempt; but Kipling and others speak highly of the Royal Marines. *See* Jolly.

Empty bottles were at one time called 'marines', because the Royal Marines were looked down upon by the regular seamen, who considered them useless. A marine officer was once dining at a mess-table, when the Duke of York said to the man in waiting, 'Here, take away these marines.' The officer demanded an explanation, when the duke replied, 'They have done their duty, and are prepared to do it again.'

**Mariner's Compass.** Traditionally claimed by the Chinese to have been in use as early as 2364 BC, but first recorded as being used for sea travel by a Chinese writer of about AD 800. It was introduced to Europe by Marco Polo, but it is probable that it was known – as the result of independent discovery – in the 12th century. *See* Fleur-de-lis.

**Marinism.** Excessive literary ornateness and affectation. So named from Giambattista Marini (1569–1625), the Neapolitan poet, famous for his whimsical comparisons, pompous and overwrought descriptions, and 'conceits'.

**Marino Faliero.** The forty-ninth doge of Venice, elected 1354. He joined a conspiracy to overthrow the republic, under the hope and promise of being made a king, but was betrayed by Bertram, one of the conspirators, and was beheaded on the 'Giant's Staircase', the place where the doges were wont to take the oath of fidelity. In Byron's tragedy of this name (1820) we are told that Michel Steno, having behaved indecently to women at a civic banquet, was kicked off the solajo by order of the doge. In revenge he wrote a scurrilous libel against the dogaressa; and the doge joined the conspiracy because he was furious with the Council of Forty for condemning the young patrician to only one month's imprisonment.

**Mariotte's Law.** At a given temperature, the volume of a gas is inversely as the pressure. So called from Edme Mariotte (d.1684), a noted French physicist.

**Marivaudage.** An imitation of the style of Marivaux (1688–1763), author of several comedies and novels. *Il tombe souvent dans une métaphysique alambiquée* (far-fetched, overstrained) *pour laquelle on a créé le nom de marivaudage.*

> Ce qui constitue le marivaudage, c'est une rechercher affectée dans le style, une grande subtilité dans les sentiments, et une grande complication d'intrigues.
>
> Bouillet, *Dict Universel*, etc.

**Marjoram.** ***As a pig loves marjoram.*** Not at all. 'How did you like so-and-so?' Ans.: 'Well, as a pig loves marjoram.' Lucretius tells us (vi, 974), *Amaricinum fugitat sus*, swine shun marjoram; but it is not at all certain that the Latin *amaricus* is identical with our *marjoram.*

**Mark.** ***A man of mark.*** A notable or famous man; one who has 'made his mark' (*q.v.*) in some walk of life.

***Beside the mark.*** Not to the point; a phrase from archery, in which the *mark* was the target.

***God bless*** or ***save the mark!*** An ejaculation of contempt or scorn. Hotspur, apologising to the king for not sending the prisoners according to command (Shakespeare, *I Henry IV*, 1, 3), says the messenger was a 'popinjay', who made him mad with his unmanly ways, and who talked 'like a waiting gentlewoman of guns, drums, and wounds (God save the mark!)'; and in *Othello* (1, 1) Iago says he was 'his Moorship's ancient; God bless the mark!' expressive of derision and contempt.

Sometimes the phrase is used to avert ill fortune or an evil omen, as in –

> To be ruled by my conscience, I should stay with the Jew my master, who, God bless the mark! is a kind of devil. *Merchant of Venice*, 2, 2

I saw the wound, I saw it with mine eyes (God
save the mark!) upon his manly breast.
*Romeo and Juliet*, 3, 2

And sometimes it refers simply to the perverted natural order of things, as 'travelling by *night* and resting (save the mark!) by day'.

Its origin is unknown, and there is no evidence in favour of the widely quoted assumption that it arose from archery. It seems to have been originally a formula used for averting evil omens, and was in early use by midwives at the delivery of a child with a 'birth-mark'.

***Mark time!*** Move the feet alternately as in marching, but without advancing or retreating from the spot.

***The mark of the beast.*** To set the 'mark of the beast' on an object or pursuit (such, for instance, as dancing, theatres, gambling, etc.) is to denounce it, to run it down as unorthodox. The allusion is to Rev. 16:2; 19:20

A certain kind of clerical waistcoat that used to be considered 'Popish' in the '60s and '70s of last century was known as the 'Mark of the Beast', or 'M.B' waistcoat (*q.v.*).

***To make one's mark.*** To distinguish oneself. To write one's name (or make one's mark) on the page of history.

In olden times persons who could not write 'made their mark' as they do now, but we find over and over again in ancient documents words such as these: 'This (grant) is signed with the sign of the cross for its greater assurance (or) greater inviolability', and after the sign follows the name of the donor.

***To toe the mark.*** To line up abreast of the others; so, to 'fall in' and do one's duty.

***Up to the mark.*** Generally used in the negative; as, 'Not quite up to the mark', not good enough, not up to the standard fixed by the assay office for gold and silver articles; not quite well.

**Mark Banco.** *See* Banco.

**Mark, King.** A king of Cornwall in the Arthurian romances, Sir Tristram's uncle. He lived at Tintagel, and is principally remembered for his treachery and cowardice, and as the husband of Isolde the Fair, who was passionately enamoured of his nephew, Tristram (*q.v.*).

**Mark, St,** in art, is represented as being in the prime of life; sometimes habited as a bishop, and, as the historian of the resurrection, accompanied by a winged lion. He holds in his right hand a pen, and in his left the Gospel. His day is April 25th.

***St Mark's Eve.*** An old custom in North-country villages is for people to sit in the church porch on this day (April 24th) from 11 at night to 1 in the morning for three years running, and the third time they will see the ghosts of those who are to die that year pass into the church.

' 'Tis now', replied the village belle,
'St Mark's mysterious eve …
The ghosts of all whom Death shall doom
Within the coming year
In pale procession walk the gloom,
Amid the silence drear.' J. Montgomery

*Poor Robin's Almanack* for 1770 refers to another superstition:

On St Mark's Eve, at twelve o'clock,
The fair maid will watch her smock,
To find her husband in the dark,
By praying unto good St Mark.

Keats has an unfinished poem on the subject, and he also refers to it in *Cap and Bells* (lvi):

Look in the Almanack – Moore never lies –
April the twenty-fourth, – this coming day
Now breathing its new bloom upon the skies,
Will end in St Mark's Eve; you must away,
For on that eve alone can you the maid convey.

**Market-penny.** A toll surreptitiously exacted by servants sent out to buy goods for their master; secret commission on goods obtained for an employer.

**Marks of Gold and Silver.** *See* Hall Mark.

**Marks in Printing.** *See* Typographical Signs.

**Marlborough. *Statutes of Marlborough*.** Laws passed in 1267 by a parliament held in Marlborough Castle. They reaffirmed in more formal fashion the Provisions of Westminster of a few years earlier.

**Marmion.** A romantic poem by Scott (pub. 1808), telling the story of Lord Marmion, an entirely fictional character, who is located in the Border Country in the time of Henry VIII and James IV of Scotland. He was slain at the battle of Flodden.

**Marmo Lunense.** *See* Luna.

**Maro.** Virgil (70–19 BC), whose full name was Publius Virgilius Maro; born on the banks of the river Mincio, at the village of Andes, near Mantua.

Sweet Maro's muse, sunk in inglorious rest,
Had silent slept amid the Mincian reeds.
Thomson, *Castle of Indolence*

**Marocco** or **Morocco.** The name of Banks's horse (*q.v.*).

**Maronites.** A tribe or sect of Syrian Christians, in a loose way united to the Roman Catholic Church but still retaining the Syrian liturgy and many of their peculiarities. They descend from a sect of Monothelites of the 8th century, and are so called from their chief seat, the monastery of Maron, on the slopes of Lebanon, which was named from Maron (Syriac, 'my lord', or 'master'), Patriarch of Antioch in the 6th century.

**Maroon.** To set a person on an inhospitable shore and leave him there (a practice common with pirates and buccaneers); a corruption of *Cimarron*, a word applied by Spaniards to anything unruly, whether man or beast. As a noun the word denotes runaway slaves or their descendants who live in the wilds of Dutch Guiana, Brazil, etc. Those of Jamaica are the offspring of runaways from the old plantations or from Cuba, to whom, in 1738, the British Government granted a tract of land, on which they built two towns.

***Maroon,*** the firework that explodes like a cannon going off, is so called from Fr. *marron*, a chestnut, probably with reference to the popping of chestnuts when being roasted.

**Marplot.** An officious person who defeats some design by gratuitous meddling. The name is given to a silly, cowardly, inquisitive Paul Pry, in *The Busybody* (1710), by Mrs Centlivre. Similarly we have Shakespeare's 'Sir Oliver *Mar-text*', the clergyman in *As You Like It*, and 'Sir Martin *Mar-All*', the hero of the Duke of Newcastle's comedy of that name, which was founded on Molierè's *L'Étourdi*.

**Marprelate Controversy.** The name given to the vituperative paper war of about 1589, in which the Puritan pamphleteers attacked the Church of England under the pseudonym 'Martin Marprelate'. Thomas Cooper, Bishop of Winchester, defended the Church, and the chief of the 'Martinists' were probably Udall, Throckmorton, Penry, and Barrow. Udall died in prison (1592); Penry and Barrow were executed in 1593. Some thirty pamphlets are known to have been published with this signature.

**Marque.** *See* Letter of.

**Marquess** or **Marquis** (O.Fr. *marchis*, warden of the marches). A title of nobility, in England ranking next below that of Duke (*q.v.*). It was first conferred on Richard II's favourite, Robert de Vere, Earl of Oxford, who was created Marquess of Dublin in 1385.

**Marriage Knot, The.** The bond of marriage effected by the legal marriage service. The Latin phrase is *nodus Herculeus*, and part of the marriage service was for the bridegroom to loosen (*solvere*) the bride's girdle, not to *tie* it. In the Hindu marriage ceremony the bridegroom hangs a ribbon on the bride's neck and ties it in a knot. Before the knot is tied the bride's father may refuse consent unless better terms are offered, but immediately the knot is tied the marriage is indissoluble. The Parsees bind the hands of the bridegroom with a sevenfold cord, seven being a sacred number. The ancient Carthaginians tied the thumbs of the betrothed with leather lace.

> Hamilcar desired to unite them immediately by an indissoluble betrothal. In Salambo's hands was a lance, which she offered to Narr Havas. Their thumbs were then tied together by a leather lace, and corn was thrown over their heads.
> Flaubert, *Salambo*, ch. xi

The practice of throwing rice (*see* Rice) is also Indian.

**Marriages. *Prohibited seasons for marriages in the Catholic Church.***

(1) Ab Adventu usque ad Epiphaniam (from Advent to Epiphany).

(2) A Septuagesima usque ad octavus Pasche inclusive (from Septuagesima to the Sunday after Easter).

(3) A secunda feria in Rogationibus usque ad primam dominicam post Pentacosten (from the second Rogation day to the first Sunday after Pentecost exclusive).

(*Liber Sacerdotalis ... Secundum Ritum Sanctae Romanae ei Apostolicae Ecclesiae*; 1537.)

**Marriages are Made in Heaven.** This does not mean that persons in heaven 'marry and are given in marriage', but that the partners joined in marriage on earth were foreordained to be so united. E. Hall (1499–1547) says, 'Consider the old proverbe to be true that saieth: Marriage is destinie.' *Cp.* 'Hanging and wiving, etc.', *under* Hang.

**Married Women** take their husband's surname. This was a Roman custom. Thus Julia, Octavia, etc., married to Pompey, Cicero, etc., would be called Julia of Pompey, Octavia of Cicero. Our married women are named in the same way, omitting 'of'.

**Marrow.** A Scots and North-country word (obsolete except in dialect) for a mate or companion, hence a husband or wife, and (of things) an article that makes a pair with another. The origin of the word is unknown.

> Busk ye, busk ye, my bonnie bonnie bride,
> Busk ye, busk ye, my winsome marrow.
> W. Hamilton, *The Braes of Yarrow* (1774)

> Wearin' a pair o' boots 'at wisna marrows!
> Barrie, *A Window in Thrums*, ch. xv

**Marrow-bones.** ***Down on your marrow-bones!*** Down on your knees! A humorous way of telling a person he had better beg pardon.

***The marrow-bone stage.*** Walking. The leg-bone is the marrow-bone of beef and mutton, and the play is on Marylebone (London), formerly pronounced 'Marrybun'.

**Marrow Controversy.** A memorable struggle in Scotland about 1719 to 1722, between Puritanism and Presbyterianisn; so called from Edward Fisher's *Marrow of Modern Divinity*, a book of ultra evangelical tendency (pub. 1644), which was condemned by the General Assembly in 1720.

Abelli, Bishop of Rhodes (d.1691), wrote the *Medulla Theologica*.

**Marrow-men.** The twelve ministers who signed the remonstrance to the General Assembly for condemning the evangelical doctrines of the 'Marrow' (*see above*); the chief were Thomas Boston and Ralph and Ebenezer Erskine.

**Marry!** An oath, meaning by Mary, the Virgin.

> Yea, marry! you say true.
>
> Foxe, *Book of Martyrs*

***Marry come up!*** An exclamation of disapproval, about equal to 'Draw it mild!' May Mary come up to my assistance, or to your discomfort!

> Marry come up, you saucy jade!

**Mar's Year.** The year 1715, noted for the rebellion of the Earl of Mar.

> Auld uncle John wha wedlock's joys
> Sin Mar's year did desire.
>
> Burns, *Halloween*, 27

**Mars.** The Roman god of war; identified in certain aspects with the Greek Ares. He was also the patron of husbandmen.

The planet of this name was so called from early times because of its reddish tinge, and under it, says the *Compost* of *Ptholomeus*, 'is borne theves and robbers ... nyght walkers and quarell pykers, bosters, mockers, and skoffers; and these men of Mars causeth warre, and murther, and batayle. They wyll be gladly smythes or workers of yron ... lyers, gret swerers ... He is red and angry ... a great walker, and a maker of swordes and knyves, and a sheder of mannes blode ... and good to be a barboure and a blode letter, and to drawe tethe.'

Among the alchemists Mars designated iron, and in Camoëns's *Lusiad* typifies divine fortitude. As Bacchus, the evil demon, is the guardian power of Mohammedanism, so Mars is the guardian of Christianity.

***The Mars of Portugal.*** Alfonso de Albuquerque, Viceroy of India (1452–1515).

**Marseillaise.** The grand song of the French revolution. Claude Joseph Rouget de Lisle (1760–1835), an artillery officer in garrison at Strasburg, composed both the words and the music (April 24th, 1792). On July 30th, 1792, the Marseillaise volunteers entered Paris singing the song; and the Parisians, enchanted with it, called it the *Hymne des Marseillais*.

**Marshal** (A.S. *mere*, mare, *scealc*, servant; O.Fr. *mareschal*). Originally one who tended horses, either as a groom or farrier; now the title of high officials about the Court, in the armed forces, etc. In the Army *Field-Marshal* (*q.v.*) is the highest rank; in the Royal Air Force Marshal of the Air, Air Chief Marshal, Air-Marshal, and Air Vice-Marshal, correspond to Field-Marshal, General, Lieutenant-General, and Major-General respectively.

***Marshal Vorwärts*** (Ger. forward). Blucher; so called for his persistence in attacking and pursuing the French during the campaign of 1813.

***Marshal of the Army of God, and of Holy Church.*** The Baron Robert Fitzwalter, appointed by his brother barons to lead their forces in 1215 to obtain from King John redress of grievances. Magna Charta was the result.

**Marshalsea Prison.** An old prison in Southwark, London (demolished in 1849), so called because it was formerly governed by a *Knight Marshal*, i.e. an official of the Royal Household who took cognisance of offences committed within the royal verge and who presided over the *Marshalsea Court* (amalgamated with the Queen's Bench in 1842). It was the Marshal of this prison who was beheaded by the rebels under Wat Tyler in 1381.

**Marsiglio** or **Marsilius.** The Saracen king in the Charlemagne romances, who plotted the attack upon Roland, under 'the tree on which Judas hanged himself'. With a force of 600,000 men he overthrew the paladin, but was afterwards defeated by Charlemagne, and hanged on the selfsame tree.

**Marsyas.** The Phrygian flute-player who challenged Apollo to a contest of skill, and, being beaten by the god, was flayed alive for his presumption. From his blood arose the river so called. The flute on which Marsyas played was one Athena had thrown away, and, being filled with the breath of the goddess, discoursed most excellent music. The interpretation of this fable is as follows: A contest long existed between the lutists and the flautists as to the superiority of their respective instruments. The Dorian mode, employed in the worship of Apollo, was performed on lutes; and the Phrygian mode, employed in the rites of Cybele, was executed by flutes, the reeds of which grew on the banks of the river Marsyas. As the Dorian mode was preferred by the Greeks, they said that Apollo beat the flute-player.

**Marteau des Heretiques.** Pierre d'Ailly, so called *l'Aigle de la France*. (1350–1420.)

**Martel.** The surname given to Charles, son of Pépin d'Héristal (about 690–791), probably because of his victory over the Saracens, who had invaded France under Abd-el-Rahman in 732. It is said that Charles 'knocked down the foe, and crushed them beneath his axe, as a *martel* or hammer crushes what it strikes'. Another suggestion is that he was so called because his patron saint (and the patron saint of Tours, near which he gained his great victory) was *St Martellus* (or *Martin*).

**Martello Towers.** Round towers about forty feet in height, of great strength, and situated on a coast or river-bank. Many of them were built on the south-eastern coasts of England about 1804, to repel the threatened Napoleonic invasion; and they took their name from *Mortella* (Corsica), where a tower from which these were designed had proved, in 1794, extremely difficult to capture.

**Mar-text.** *See* Marplot.

**Martha, St,** patron saint of good housewives, is represented in art in homely costume, bearing at her girdle a bunch of keys, and holding a ladle or pot of water in her hand. Like St Margaret, she is accompanied by a dragon bound, for she is said to have destroyed one that ravaged the neighbourhood of Marseilles, but she has not the palm and crown of martyrdom. She is commemorated on July 29th, and is patron of Tarascon.

**Martian Laws.** Laws traditionally said to have been compiled by Martia, wife of Guithelin, great-grandson of Mulmutius, who established in England the Mulmutine Laws (*q.v.*). Alfred translated both these codes into Saxon-English.

> Guynteline … whose queen, … to show her upright mind,
> To wise Malmutius' laws her Martian first did frame.
> Drayton, *Polyolbion*, viii

**Martin.** One of the swallow tribe; probably so called from the Christian name *Martin* (St Martin's bird is the *goose*), but possibly because it appears in England about March (the *Martian* month) and disappears about Martinmas.

In *Reynard the Fox* (*q.v.*) *Martin* is the Ape; Rukenaw was his wife, Fubrumpe his son, and Byteluys and Hattenette his two daughters; and in Dryden's *Hind and the Panther*, an allegory, *Martin* means the Lutheran party; so called by a pun on the name of Martin Luther.

**Martin, St.** The patron saint of innkeepers and drunkards, usually shown in art as a young mounted soldier dividing his cloak with a beggar. He was born of heathen parents but was converted in Rome, and became Bishop of Tours in 371, dying at Caudes forty years later. His day is November 11th, the day of the Roman *Vinalia*, or Feast of Bacchus; hence his purely accidental patronage (as above), and hence also the phrase *Martin drunk. See* Drunkenness.

The usual illustration of St Martin is in allusion to the legend that when he was a military tribune stationed at Amiens he once, in midwinter, divided his cloak with a naked beggar, who craved alms of him before the city gates. At night, the story says, Christ Himself appeared to the soldier, arrayed in this very garment.

***Martin drunk.*** Very intoxicated indeed; a drunken man 'sobered' by drinking more. *See* Drunkenness *and* St Martin, *above*. Baxter uses the name as a synonym of a drunkard:

> The language of Martin is there [in heaven] a stranger. *Saint's Rest*

***St Martin's bird.*** The goose, whose blood was shed 'sacrificially' on November 11th, in honour of that saint. *See below*.

***St Martin's beads, jewellery, lace, rings***, etc. Cheap, counterfeit articles. When the old collegiate church of St Martin's le Grand was demolished at the Dissolution of the Monasteries, hucksters established themselves on the site and carried on a considerable trade in artificial jewels, Brummagem ornaments, and cheap ware generally. Hence the use of the saint's name in this connection in Elizabethan and 17th-century writings.

> Certayne lyght braynes … wyll rather weare a Marten chayne, the pryce of viiid. then they woulde be unchayned.
> Becon, *Jewel of Joy* (*about* 1558)

> This kindnesse is but like Alchimy or Saint Martin's rings, that are faire to the eye, and have a rich outside, but if a man breake them asunder and looke into them (etc.).
> Fenner, *Compter's Commonwealth* (1618)

***St Martin's goose.*** November 11th, St Martin's

Day, was at one time the great goose feast of France. The legend is that St Martin was annoyed by a goose, which he ordered to be killed and served up for dinner. He died from the repast, and the goose was 'sacrificed' to him on each anniversary.

***St Martin of Bullions.*** The St Swithin of Scotland. His day is July 4th, and the saying is that if it rains then, rain may be expected for forty days.

> 'By St Martin of Bullion –'
> 'And what hast thou to do with St Martin?'
> 'Nay, little enough sir, unless when he sends such rainy days that we cannot fly a hawk.'
> Scott, *The Abbot*, xv

***St Martin's running footman.*** The devil, traditionally assigned to St Martin for such duties on a certain occasion.

> Who can tell but St Martin's running footman may still be hatching us some further mischief.
> Rabelais, *Pantagruel*, iv, 23

***St Martin's summer.*** *See* Summer.

**Martinet.** A strict disciplinarian; so called from the Marquis de Martinet, a young colonel in the reign of Louis XIV, who remodelled the infantry, and was slain at the siege of Doesbourg, in 1672 (Voltaire, *Louis XIV*, c. 10). The cat-o'-nine-tails, called a 'martinet', which was formerly used in French schools, probably has no connection with this word, but is an adaptation of the very much older *martinet*, a military engine used in mediaeval times for hurling large stones.

**Martinmas.** The feast of St Martin, November 11th. *His Martinmas will come, as it does to every hog* – i.e. all must die. November was the great slaughtering time of the Anglo-Saxons, when beeves, sheep, and hogs, whose food was exhausted, were killed and salted. Thus the proverb intimates that our day of death will come as surely as that of a hog at St Martin's-tide.

**Martyr** (Gr.), simply means a witness, but is applied to one who witnesses a good confession with his blood.

***The martyr king.*** Charles I of England, beheaded January 30th, 1649.

***Martyr to science.*** A title conferred on anyone who loses his health or life through his devotion to science; especially Claude Louis, Count Berthollet (1748–1822), who tested in his own person the effects of carbolic acid on the human frame, and died under the experiment.

**Marvedie.** *See* Maravedi.

**Marvellous. *The marvellous boy*.** Thomas Chatterton (1752–70), the poet, author of *Rowley Poems*.

> I thought of Chatterton, the marvellous boy,
> The sleepless soul, that perished in his pride.
> Wordsworth, *Resolution and Independence*

**Mary.** As *the Virgin*, she is represented in art with flowing hair, emblematical of her virginity.

As *Mater Dolorosa*, she is represented as somewhat elderly, clad in mourning, head draped, and weeping over the dead body of Christ.

As *Our Lady of Dolours*, she is represented as seated, her breast being pierced with seven swords, emblematic of her seven sorrows.

As *Our Lady of Mercy*, she is represented with arms extended, spreading out her mantle, and gathering sinners beneath it.

As *The glorified Madonna*, she is represented as bearing a crown and sceptre, or a ball and cross, in rich robes and surrounded by angels.

*Her seven joys.* The Annunciation, Visitation, Nativity, Adoration of the Magi, Presentation in the Temple, Finding Christ amongst the Doctors, and the Assumption.

*Her seven sorrows.* Simeon's Prophecy, the Flight into Egypt, Christ Missed, the Betrayal, the Crucifixion, the Taking Down from the Cross, and the Ascension, when she was left alone.

***Little Mary.*** A euphemism for the stomach; from the play of that name by Sir J. M. Barrie (1903).

***The four Marys.*** Mary Beaton (or *Bethune*), Mary Livingston (or *Leuson*), Mary Fleming (or *Flemyng*), and Mary Seaton (or *Seyton*); called the 'Queen's Marys', that is, the ladies of the same age as Mary, afterwards Queen of Scots, and her companions. Mary Carmichael was not one of the four, although introduced in the well-known ballad.

> Yestre'en the queen had four Marys,
> This night she'll hae but three:
> There was Mary Beaton, and Mary Seaton,
> Mary Carmichael, and me.

**Mary Anne** or **Marianne.** A slang name for the guillotine. *See below*.

**Mary Anne Associations.** Secret republican societies in France. The name was adopted by the Republican party because Ravaillac was instigated to assassinate Henri IV (1610) by reading the treatise *De Rege et Regio Institutione*, by *Mariana*.

> The Mary Annes, which are essentially republicans, are scattered about all the French provinces.
> Disraeli, *Lothair*

**Mary, Highland.** *See* Highland Mary.

**Mary Magdalene, St.** Patron saint of penitents, being herself the model penitent of Gospel history.

In art she is represented either as young and beautiful, with a profusion of hair, and holding a box of ointment, or as a penitent, in a sequestered place, reading before a cross or skull.

**Mary Queen of Scots.** Shakespeare being under the patronage of Queen Elizabeth, and knowing her jealousy, would not, of course, praise openly her rival queen; but in the *Midsummer Night's Dream* (2, 1) composed in 1592, five years after the execution of Mary, he wrote these exquisite lines:

Thou rememberest
Since once I sat upon a promontory,
And heard a *mermaid* on a *dolphin's* back
Uttering such dulcet and harmonious breath,
That the *rude sea* grew civil at her song;
And *certain stars* shot *madly from their spheres*,
To hear the sea-maid's music. Act 2:1

These have been conjectured to refer to the ill-fated queen.

*Mermaid* and *sea-maid*, Mary; on the *dolphin's* back, she married the *Dolphin* or *Dauphin* of France; *the rude sea grew civil*, the Scotch rebels; *certain stars*, the Earl of Northumberland, the Earl of Westmoreland, and the Duke of Norfolk; *shot madly from their spheres*, that is, revolted from Queen Elizabeth, bewitched by the *sea-maid's* sweetness.

***The Queen of Scots' pillar*** is a column in the Peak Cavern, Derbyshire, as clear as alabaster, and is so called because on one occasion, when going to throw herself on the mercy of Elizabeth, the Queen of Scots proceeded thus far, and then returned.

**Marybuds.** The flower of the marigold (*q.v.*). Like many other flowers, they open at daybreak and close at sunset.

And winking marybuds begin
To ope their golden eyes.
Shakespeare, *Cymbeline*, 2, 3

**Marygold.** *See* Marigold.

**Maryland** (USA) was so named in compliment to Henrietta Maria, Queen of Charles I. In the Latin charter it is called *Terra Mariae*.

**Marylebone** (London) is not a corruption of *Marie la bonne*, but 'Mary on the bourne', i.e. the Tyburn (*q.v.*), as Holborn is 'Old Bourne'.

**Masaniello.** A corruption of TomMASo ANIELLO, a Neapolitan fisherman, who led the revolt of July, 1647. The great grievance was heavy taxation, and the immediate cause of Masaniello's interference was the seizure of his property because his wife had smuggled flour. He obtained a large following, was elected chief of Naples, and for nine days ruled with absolute control; but then he was betrayed by his own people, shot, and his body flung into a ditch. Next day, however, it was reclaimed and interred with a pomp and ceremony never equalled in Naples.

Auber's opera *La Muette de Portici* (1828) takes the story for its groundwork.

**Mascot.** A person or thing that is supposed to bring good luck (*cp.* Jettator). The word is French slang (perhaps connected with Provençal *masco*, a sorcerer), and was popularised in England by Audran's opera, *La Mascotte*, 1880.

Ces envoyés du paradis,
Sont des Mascottes, mes amis,
Heureux celui que le ciel dote d'une Mascotte.
*La Mascotte*

I tell you she was a Mascotte of the first water.
Tippitywitchet, *Ludgate Monthly*, Nov., 1891

**Mashackering and Misguggling.** Mauling and disfiguring.

I humbly protest against mauling and disfiguring this work; against what the great Walter Scott would, I think, have called mashackering and misguggling, after the manner of Nicol Muschat (in *The Heart of Midlothian*), when he put an end to his wife.
W. E. Gladstone, *Nineteenth Century*, November, 1885

Donald had been misguggled by ane of these doctors about Paris.
Scott, *Waverley*, ch. xviii

**Masher.** An old-fashioned term for a 'nut' or dude (*q.v.*); an exquisite; a lardy-dardy swell who dresses aesthetically, behaves killingly, and thinks himself a Romeo. This sort of thing used to be called 'crushing' or killing, and, as mashing is crushing, the synonym was substituted about 1880. A lady-killer, a crusher, a masher, all mean the same thing.

**Mask, the Man in the Iron.** A mysterious individual held for over forty years as a State prisoner by Louis XIV at Pignerol and other prisons, ultimately dying in the Bastille, Nov. 19th, 1703, with his identity still undisclosed. His name was given as 'Marchiali' when he was buried; but despite the numerous conjectures and wide research that have been made, no one to this day knows for certain who he was. We can only say that the most probable name so far put forward is that of General du Bulonde, who, in

1691, raised the siege of Cuneo against the orders of Catinat. In 1891 Capt. Bazeriès published in *Le Temps* translations of some cipher dispatches, apparently showing that this is the solution; but if it is it can be only part of it, and Bulonde must have taken the place of some earlier masked prisoner, for *l'homme au masque de fer* was at Pignerol in 1666 and was transferred to the island of St Marguerite twenty years later – i.e. well before the siege of Cuneo.

Other persons who have been suggested with more or less probability are:

A twin brother of Louis XIV; or, perhaps, an elder brother, whose father is given both as Cardinal Mazarin and the Duke of Buckingham.

Louis, Duc de Vermandois, natural son of Louis XIV by De la Vallière, who was imprisoned for life because he gave the Dauphin a box on the ears.

Count Girolamo Mattioli, Minister to the Duke of Mantua. In 1678 he acted treacherously towards Louis in refusing to give up the fortress of Casale – the key of Italy – after signing a treaty promising to do so, and in consequence was lured on to French soil, captured, and imprisoned at Pignerol.

Among the less likely names that have been put forward are the Duke of Monmouth, Avedick (an Armenian patriarch), Fouquet (the disgraced Minister of Finance), the Duc de Beaufort (who disappeared at the siege of Candia in 1669), and Mattioli's secretary, Jean de Gonzague.

**Mason and Dixon's Line.** The southern boundary line which separated the free states of Pennsylvania from what were at one time the slave states of Maryland and Virginia. It lies in 39° 43' 26" north latitude, and was fixed by Charles Mason and Jeremiah Dixon, English astronomers and surveyors (1763–7).

**Mass. *High Mass*** or 'Grand Mass' is sung by choristers, and celebrated with the assistance of a deacon and sub-deacon.

***Low Mass*** (so called *quia submissa voce celebratur*) is read without singing; there is one between these two called the 'chanted mass', in which the service is chanted by the priest.

There are also a number of special masses, as the *mass of the Beatae*, *mass of the Holy Ghost*, *mass of the dead*, *of a saint*, *of security*, *dry mass*, *votive mass*, *holiday mass*, *Ambrosian mass*, *Gallic mass*, *mass of the presanctified* (for Good Friday), etc.

> Pope Celestinus ordained the *introit* and the *gloria in excelsis*.
> Pope Gregory the Great ordered the *kyrie eleison* to be repeated nine times, and introduced the prayer.
> Pope Gelasius ordained the Epistle and Gospel.
> Pope Damasus introduced the *Credo*.
> Pope Alexander put into the canon the following clause: '*Qui pridie quam pateretur*'.
> Pope Sextus introduced the *Sanctus*.
> Pope Innocent the *pax*.
> Pope Leo the *Orate Fratres*, and the words in the canon: '*Sanctum Sacrificium et immaculatam Hostiam*'.
> E. Kinesman, *Lives of the Saints*, p. 187 (1623)

**Massachusetts** (USA). So called from the tribe of Indians of that name. Its origin is not clear; one suggestion is that it means 'the Blue Mountains', and another that it is *massa*, great, *wadehuash*, mountain, *et*, near, i.e. near-the-great-mountain.

**Massacre of the Innocents.** The slaughter of the male children of Bethlehem 'from two years old and under', when Jesus was born (Matt. 2:16). This was done at the command of Herod the Great in order to cut off 'the babe' who was destined to become 'King of the Jews'.

In parliamentary phraseology, the phrase denotes the withdrawal at the close of a session of the bills which time has not rendered it possible to consider and pass.

**Mast. *To serve before the mast*.** To be one of the common sailors, whose quarters are in the forward part of the ship; hence, to be at the bottom rung of the ladder, or to be of humble birth. The half-deck is the sanctum of the second mate, and, in Greenland fishers, of the spikeoneer, harpooners, carpenters, coopers, boatswains, and all secondary officers.

> I myself come from before the mast.
> Scott, *The Antiquary*, ch. xx

**Master** (through O.Fr. *maistre*, or A.S. *maegester*, from Lat. *magister*).

***Little Masters.*** *See* Little.

***Master-at-arms.*** The first-class petty officer in the Navy who acts as head of the ship's police.

***Master Mason.*** A freemason who has attained the third degree.

***Master of sentences.*** *See* Sentences.

***Master of the Rolls.*** *See* Rolls.

***Old Masters.*** The great painters (especially of Italy and the Low Countries) who worked from the 13th century to about the end of the 16th, or a little later. Also their paintings.

**Mastic.** A kind of chewing-gum made of the resin of *Pistachio Lentiscus*, a tree of the Levant and other Eastern parts, formerly much used in medicine. It was said to promote appetite, and therefore only increased the misery of a hungry man.

Like the starved wretch that hungry mastic chews,
But cheats himself and fosters his disease.
West, *Triumphs of the Gout* (Lucian)

**Matador.** In Spanish bull-fights, the man who has to kill the bull (Lat. *mactare*, to kill).

In the game of ombre, *Spadille* (the ace of spades), *Manille* (the seven of trumps), and *Basto* (the ace of clubs) are called 'Matadors'.

Now move to war her sable Matadores …
Spadillo first, unconquerable lord,
Led off two captive trumps, and swept the board,
As many more Manillo forced to yield,
And marched a victor from the verdant field.
Him Basto followed …
Pope, *Rape of the Lock*, canto iii

In the game of dominoes of this name the double-blank and all the 'stones' that of themselves make seven (6–1, 5–2, and 4–3) are 'matadors', and can be played at any time.

**Matamore.** A poltroon, a swaggerer, a Bobadil (*q.v.*). It is composed of two Spanish words, *matar-Moros* (a slayer of Moors). *See* Moor-slayer.

Your followers … must bandy and brawl in my court … like so many Matamoros.
Scott, *Kenilworth*, ch. xvi

**Mate.** ***A man does not get his hands out of the tar by becoming second mate.*** A second mate is expected to put his hands into the tar bucket for tarring the rigging, like the men below him. The first mate is exempt from this dirty work.

**Maté.** Paraguay tea, made from the leaves of the Brazilian holly (*Ilex Paraguayensis*), is so called from the vessel in which it is infused. The vessels are generally hollow gourds.

**Materialism.** The doctrines of a *Materialist*, who maintains that there is nothing in the universe but matter, the mind is a phenomenon of matter, and that there is no ground for assuming a spiritual First Cause, as against the orthodox doctrine that the soul is distinct from the body, and is a portion of the Divine essence breathed into the body. Materialism is opposed to Idealism; in the ancient world its chief exponents were Epicurus and Lucretius, in modern times the 18th-century French philosophers, Helvétius, d'Holbach, and Lamettrie.

**Mathew, Father.** Theobald Mathew (1790–1856), called *The Apostle of Temperance*. He was an Irish priest, and in his native country the success of his work in behalf of total abstinence was almost miraculous.

O Father Mathew!
Whatever path you
In life pursue
God grant your Reverence
May brush off never hence
Our mountain dew!
*An Irishman to Father Mathew*, Walter Savage Landor

**Mathurin, St.** Patron saint in France of idiots and fools. He was a priest of the 3rd century, and was particularly popular in the Middle Ages. His day is November 1st.

***The malady of St Mathurin.*** Folly, stupidity. A French expression.

**Matriculate** means to enrol oneself in a society (Lat. *matricula*, a roll or register). The University is called our *alma mater* (propitious mother). The students are her *alumni* (foster-children), and become so by being enrolled in a register after certain forms and examinations.

**Matsya.** *See* Avatar.

**Matter-of-fact.** Unvarnished truth; prosaic, unimaginative, as a 'matter-of-fact swain'.

**Matterhorn.** The German name of the mountain in the Pennine Alps known to the French as *Mont Cervin* and to the Italians as *Monte Silvio*; so called from its peak (*horn*) and the scanty patches of green meadow (*matter*) which hang around its base. Above a glacier-line 11,000 feet high, it rises in an almost inaccessible obelisk of rock to a total elevation of 14,703 feet. It was first scaled in 1865 by Whymper, when four of his party lost their lives.

Figuratively any danger, desperate situation threatening destruction, or leap in the dark, as *the matrimonial Matterhorn*.

**Matthew, St.** Represented in art (1) as an evangelist – an old man with long beard – an angel generally standing near him dictating his Gospel; (2) As an apostle, in which capacity he bears a purse, in reference to his calling as a publican; sometimes he carries a spear, sometimes a carpenter's rule or square. His symbol is an angel, or a man's face (*see* Evangelists), and he is commemorated on September 21st.

Legend has it that St Matthew preached for 15 years in Judea after the Ascension, and then carried the Gospel to Ethiopia, where he was martyred.

***In the last of Matthew.*** At the last gasp, on one's last legs. This is a German expression, and arose thus: a Catholic priest said in his sermon that Protestantism was in the last of Matthew, and, being asked what he meant, replied, 'The last five words of the Gospel of St Matthew are these: "The end of this dispensation".' Of course, he quoted the Latin version; ours is less correctly translated 'the end of the *world*'.

**Matthew Parker's Bible: Matthew's Bible.** *See* Bible, the English.

**Maudlin.** Stupidly sentimental. *Maudlin drunk* is the drunkenness which is sentimental and inclined to tears. *Maudlin slip-slop* is sentimental chit-chat. The word is derived from Mary *Magdalen*, who is drawn by ancient painters with a lackadaisical face, and eyes swollen with weeping.

**Maugis,** or **Malagigi.** The Nestor of French romance, like Hildebrand in German legend. One of Charlemagne's paladins, a magician and champion, he was cousin to Rinaldo.

**Maugys.** A giant in the old metrical romance, *Libaeus Desconnus*. He keeps a bridge leading to a castle in which a beautiful lady is imprisoned. Sir Lybius, one of Arthur's knights, does battle with the giant; the contest lasts a whole summer's day, but terminates with the death of the giant and liberation of the lady.

**Maul of Monks, The.** Thomas Cromwell (1485–1540), visitor-general of English monasteries, many of which he summarily suppressed.

**Maumet, Maumetry.** *See* Mammet.

**Maunds, the Royal,** or **Maundy Money.** Gifts in money given by the sovereign on Maundy Thursday to the number of aged poor persons that corresponds with his age. It used to be distributed by the Lord High Almoner; but since 1883 the Clerk of the Almonry Office has been responsible for the distribution which takes place in Westminster Abbey, and for which special money (silver pennies, fourpenny pieces, etc.) is usually coined. The custom began in 1368, in the reign of Edward III, and is a relic of the 'washing of the feet' (*see* Maundy Thursday). James I distributed the doles personally.

> Entries of 'al maner of things yerly yevin by my lorde of his Maundy, and my laidis, and his lordshippis children'.
>
> *Household Book of the Earl of Northumberland*, 1512

**Maundrel.** A foolish, vapouring gossip. The Scots say, 'Haud your tongue, maundrel'. As a verb it means to babble, to prate, as in delirium, in sleep, or intoxication. The term is said to be from Sir John *Mandeville*, the fictitious name of a supposed 14th-century traveller in the Far East, the account of whose adventures (earliest MS, 1371) is full of idle gossip and most improbable events.

**Maundy Thursday.** The day before Good Friday is so called from the Latin *dies mandati* (the day of Christ's great mandate). After He had washed His disciples' feet, He said, 'A new commandment give I unto you, that ye love one another' (St John 13:34). In the monasteries it was the custom to wash the feet of as many poor people as there were monks, and for centuries in England the sovereign, as a token of humility, did the same. Mention is made in the Wardrobe Book of Edward I of money being given on Easter Eve to thirteen poor people whose feet the Queen had washed; the custom is said to have been kept up even as late as the time of James II, but for long now the distribution of money (*see* Maunds) is all that is left of it.

Spelman wrongly derives the word from *maund* (a basket), because on the day before the great fast good Catholics brought out their broken food in *maunds* to distribute to the poor. This custom in many places gave birth to a fair, as the Tombland Fair of Norwich, held on the plain before the Cathedral Close.

**Mauritania.** Morocco and Algiers, the land of the ancient Mauri or Moors. The kingdom of Mauretania was annexed to the Roman Empire in AD 42, and was finally disintegrated when overrun by the Vandals in 429.

**Mausoleum.** Originally the name of the tomb of Mausolus, King of Caria, to whom Artemisia (his wife) erected at Halicarnassus a splendid sepulchral monument 353 BC. Parts of this sepulchre, which was one of the Seven Wonders of the World, are now in the British Museum. The name is now applied to any sepulchral monument of great size or architectural quality.

The chief mausoleums are: that of Augustus; that of Hadrian, i.e. the castle of St Angelo, at Rome; that erected in France to Henry II by Catherine de' Medicis; that of St Peter the Martyr in the church of St Eustatius, by G. Balduccio in the 14th century; and that erected to the memory of Louis XVI.

**Mauthe Dog.** A ghostly black spaniel that for many years haunted Peel Castle, in the Isle of Man. It used to enter the guardroom as soon as candles were lighted, and leave it at daybreak. While this spectre dog was present the soldiers forbore all oaths and profane talk. One day a drunken trooper entered the guardhouse alone out of bravado, but lost his speech and died in three days. Scott refers to it in his *Lay of the Last Minstrel*, vi stanza, 26, and again in a long note to ch. xv of *Peveril of the Peak*.

**Mauther.** An old dialect word in East Anglia for a young girl; frequently altered to *Modder*, *Morther*, *Mor*, etc. Its etymology is obscure, but the word does not seem to be connected with *mother*.

> *Kastril* (*to his sister*): Away! you talk like a foolish mauther. Ben Jonson, *Alchemist*, IV, iv

> When once a giggling morther you,
> And I a red-faced chubby boy,
> Sly tricks you played me not a few,
> For mischief was your greatest joy.
> Bloomfield, *Richard and Kate*

***Well, Mor, where have you been this long while?*** and ***I s'y, Mor, come hither!*** are, in Norfolk, still common modes of addressing a young girl.

**Mauvais ton** (Fr.). Bad manners. Ill-breeding, vulgar ways.

**Mauvaise honte** (Fr.). Bad or silly shame. Bashfulness, sheepishness.

**Mauvaise plaisanterie** (Fr.). A rude or ill-mannered jest; a jest in bad taste.

**Mavournin.** Irish (*mo mhurnín*) for 'My darling'. Erin mavournin = Ireland, my darling; Erin go bragh = Ireland for ever!

> Land of my forefathers, Erin go bragh! ...
> Erin mavournin, Erin go bragh!
> Campbell, *Exile of Erin*

Sydney Smith's humorous remark was –

> *Erin go bragh!* A far better anthem would be, Erin go bread and cheese.
> *Fragment on the Irish Roman Catholic Church*

**Mawworm.** A hypocritical pretender to sanctity, a pious humbug. From the character of this name in Isaac Bickerstaffe's *The Hypocrite* (1769).

> The Scapin of Politics walks hand-in-hand with the Mawworm of Morality.
> Robt Buchanan, *The Coming Terror* (1891)

**Maximum** and **Minimum** (Lat.). The *greatest* and the *least* amount; as, the maximum profits or exports and the minimum profits or exports; the maximum and minimum price of corn during the year. The terms are also employed in mathematics, etc.; a *maximum and minimum thermometer* is one that indicates the highest and lowest temperatures during a specified period.

**May.** The Anglo-Saxons called this month *thrimilce*, because then cows can be milked three times a day; the present name is the Latin *Maius* (*mensis*), from *Maia*, the goddess of growth and increase, connected with *major*.

> The old Dutch name was *Blou-maand* (blossoming month). In the French Republican calendar the month was called *Floréal* (the time of flowers, April 20th to May 20th).

***Here we go gathering nuts of May.*** *See* Nuts.

***It's a case of January and May.*** *See* January.

***May unlucky for weddings.*** This is a Roman superstition, and is referred to by Ovid. In this month were held the festivals of *Bona Dea* (the goddess of chastity), and the feasts of the dead called *Lemuralia*.

> Nec viduae taedis eadem, nec virginis apta
> Tempora; quae nupsit, non diuturna fuit;
> Haec quoque de causa, si te proverbia tangunt,
> Mente malum Maio nubere vulgus ait.
> Ovid, *Fasti*, v, 496, etc.

***May meetings.*** The annual gatherings, usually held in London in May and June, of the religious and charitable societies, to hear the annual reports and appeals for continued or increased support, etc.

**May-day.** Polydore Virgil says that the Roman youths used to go into the fields and spend the calends of May in dancing and singing in honour of Flora, goddess of fruits and flowers. The English consecrated May-day to Robin Hood and the Maid Marian, because the favourite outlaw died on that day, and villagers used to set up Maypoles (*q.v.*), and spend the day in archery, morris dancing, and other amusements.

The old custom of singing the *Hymnus Eucharisticus* on the top of Wolsey's Tower, Oxford, as the clock strikes five on May Morning is still kept up by the choristers of Magdalen. This is a relic of the requiem mass that, before the Reformation, was sung at this spot and time for the repose of the soul of Henry VII. The opening lines of the hymn are:

> Te Deum Patrem colimus,
> Te laudibus prosequimur;
> Qui corpus cibo reficis,
> Coelesti mentem gratia.

***Evil May Day.*** *See* Evil.

**Maypole, Queen**, etc. Dancing roung the Maypole on May Day, 'going a-Maying', electing a May Queen, and lighting bonfires, are all remnants of the old nature-worship of our ancestors, and may be traced to the most ancient times. The chimneysweeps used to lead about a

Jack-i'-the-green, and the custom is not yet quite extinct, especially in country towns.

Any very tall, ungainly woman is sometimes called a 'Maypole', a term which was bestowed as a nickname on the Duchess of Kendal, one of George I's mistresses.

***The Maypole in the Strand.*** This ancient London landmark, referred to more than once by 18th-century writers, stood on a spot now occupied by St Mary-le-Strand, where formerly stood a cross. In place of this a Maypole was set up by John Clarges, the blacksmith, whose daughter Ann became the wife of Monk, Duke of Albemarle. It was taken down in 1713, and replaced by a new one erected opposite Somerset House. This had two gilt balls and a vane on its summit, and on holidays was decorated with flags and garlands. It was removed in 1718, and sent by Sir Isaac Newton to Wanstead Park to support the largest telescope in Europe.

> Captain Baily ... employed four hackney coaches, with drivers in liveries, to ply at the Maypole in the Strand, fixing his own rates, about the year 1634.
> Note 1, *The Tatler*, iv, p. 415

> Amid that area wide they took their stand,
> Where the tall maypole once o'erlooked the Strand,
> But now (so Anne and piety ordain)
> A church collects the saints of Drury Lane.
> Pope, *Dunciad* II, 217 (1728)

> What's not destroyed by Time's devouring hand?
> Where's Troy, and where's the Maypole in the Strand?
> J. Bramston (d.1744), *The Art of Politics*

**Mayduke Cherries.** So called from Médoc, a district of France, whence the cherries first came to us.

**Mayeux.** Since about 1830 the stock name in French plays for a vain and licentious hunchback, who always has a wide command of slang and wit.

**Mayflower.** The name of the ship that took the Pilgrim Fathers (*q.v.*) from Southampton to Massachusetts in 1620. It was only about 180 tons – which can be profitably compared with the 56,000 tons of the White Star liner *Majestic*, which now does much the same voyage. Some of the timbers of the old *Mayflower* are said to have been discovered as forming part of a barn at Jordans, Bucks.

**Mayonnaise.** A sauce made with pepper, salt, oil, vinegar, and the yolk of an egg beaten up together. The word is French; its origin is unknown, but it has been conjectured (Weekley, *Etym. Dict.*, 1921) that it was originally called *mahonnaise* in honour of the capture of Mahon, Minorca, by Richelieu in 1756. In English the colour *magenta* has a similar origin.

**Mayor.** The chief magistrate of a city, elected by the citizens, and holding office for twelve months.

> The chief magistrate of London is The Right Hon. the Lord Mayor, one of the Privy Council.
> Since 1389 the magistracy of York has been headed by a Lord Mayor, and the other English towns in which the chief magistrate is Lord Mayor are Birmingham, Liverpool, Manchester, Leeds, Sheffield, Bristol, Hull, Bradford and Newcastle-on-Tyne.

At the Conquest the sovereign appointed the chief magistrates of cities. That of London was called the Port-Reeve, but Henry II changed the word to the Norman *maire* (our mayor). John made the office annual; and Edward III (in 1354) conferred the title of 'The Right Hon. the Lord Mayor of London'.

The first Lord Mayor's Show was in 1458, when Sir John Norman went by water in state, to be sworn in at Westminster; and the cap and sword were given by Richard II to Sir William Walworth, for killing Wat Tyler.

***Mayor of Garratt.*** *See* Garratt.

***Mayor of the Bull-ring*** (Old Dublin). This official and his sheriffs were elected on May Day and St Peter's Eve 'to be captaine and gardian of the batchelers and the unwedded youth of the civitie'. For the year the 'Mayor' had authority to punish those who frequented houses of ill-fame. He was termed 'Mayor of the Bull-ring' because he conducted any bachelor who married during his term of office to an iron ring that used to hang in the market place and to which bulls were tied for baiting, and made him kiss it.

**Mayor of the Palace** (*Maire du Palais*). The superintendent of the king's household, and steward of the royal *leudes* (companies) of France, before the accession of the Carlovingian dynasty.

**Mazarine Bible, The.** *See* Bible, Specially named.

**Mazeppa, Ivan** (1644–1709). The hero of Byron's poem was born of a noble Polish family in Podolia, became a page in the court of John Casimir, King of Poland, but intrigued with Theresia, the young wife of a Podolian count, who had the young page lashed naked to a wild horse, and turned adrift. The horse dropped dead in the Ukraine, where Mazeppa was released and cared for by Cossacks. He became secretary to the hetman, and at his death was appointed his successor. Peter I created him Prince of the Ukraine, but in the wars with Sweden Mazeppa deserted to Charles XII and fought against Russia at Pultowa. After the loss of this battle, Mazeppa fled to Valentia, and then to Bender, where he committed suicide. Byron makes Mazeppa tell his tale to Charles after the battle of Pultowa.

**Mazer.** A large drinking vessel originally made of maple-wood, and so called from O.Fr. *masere*, O.H.Ger. *masar*, a knot in wood, maple wood.

> A mazer wrought of the maple ware.
>
> Spenser, *Calendar* (August)

> 'Bring hither', he said, 'the mazers four
> My noble fathers loved of yore.'
>
> Sir Walter Scott, *Lord of the Isles*

**Mazikeen** or **Shedeem.** A species of beings in *Jewish mythology* resembling the Arabian Jinn (*q.v.*), and said to be the agents of magic and enchantment. When Adam fell, says the Talmud, he was excommunicated for 130 years, during which time he begat demons and spectres, for, it is written 'Adam lived 130 years and (i.e. before he) begat children in his own image' (Gen. 5:3). (*Rabbi Jeremiah ben Eliezar.*)

> And the Mazikeen shall not come nigh thy tents.
>
> Ps. 91:5 (Chaldee version)

***Swells out like the Mazikeen ass.*** The allusion is to a Jewish tradition that a servant, whose duty it was to rouse the neighbourhood to midnight prayer, one night mounted a stray ass and neglected his duty. As he rode along the ass grew bigger and bigger, till at last it towered as high as the tallest edifice, where it left the man, and where next morning he was found.

**Meal.** ***In meal or in malt.*** Directly or indirectly; in one way or another. If much money passes through the hand, some profit will be sure to accrue either 'in meal or in malt', and a certain percentage of one or the other is the miller's perquisite.

> When other interests in the country (as the cotton trade, the iron trade, and the coal trade) had been depressed, the Government had not been called upon for assistance in meal and malt.
>
> Sir William Harcourt, *On Agricultural Depression*, 13th April, 1894

**Meal-tub Plot.** A pretended conspiracy against Protestants, fabricated by Thomas Dangerfield (d.1685) in 1679, so called because he said that the papers relating to it were concealed in a meal-tub in the house of Mrs Cellier, a Roman Catholic. She was tried for high treason and acquitted, while Dangerfield was convicted of libel, whipped, and pilloried.

**Mealy-mouthed** is the Greek *meli-muthos* (honey-speech), and means velvet-tongued, afraid of giving offence.

**Meander.** To wind, to saunter about at random; so called from the Maeander, a winding river of Phrygia. The term is also applied to an ornamental pattern of winding lines, used as a border on pottery, wall decorations, etc.

**Measure** (O.Fr. *mesure*, Lat. *mensura*, *metiri*, to measure). *Beyond measure*, or *out of all measure*. Beyond all reasonable degree; exceedingly, excessively.

> Thus out of measure sad.
>
> Shakespeare, *Much Ado about Nothing*, 1, 3

***To measure one's length on the ground.*** To fall flat on the ground; to be knocked down.

> If you will measure your lubber's length, tarry.
>
> Shakespeare, *King Lear*, 1, 4

***To measure other people's corn by one's own bushel.*** *See* Bushel.

***To measure strength.*** To wrestle together; to fight, to contest.

***To measure swords.*** To try whether or not one is strong enough or sufficiently equally matched to contend against another. The phrase is from duelling, in which the seconds measure the swords to see that both are of one length.

> So we measured swords and parted.
>
> Shakespeare, *As You Like It*, 5, 4

***To take the measure of one's foot.*** To ascertain how far a person will venture; to make a shrewd guess of another's character. The allusion is to '*Ex pede Herculem*'.

**Measure for Measure.** The plot of Shakespeare's play (acted 1604, first printed 1623) is founded on Whetstone's *Promos and Cassandra* (1582), which was taken from the 85th tale in Cinthio's *Hecatommithi* (1565). Promos is called by Shakespeare, 'Lord Angelo'; and Cassandra is 'Isabella'. Her brother, called by Shakespeare 'Claudio', is named Andrugio in the story.

**Meat, Bread.** These words tell a tale; for both can connote food in general. The Italians and Asiatics eat little animal food, and with them the word *bread* stands for food; so also with the poor, whose chief diet it is; but the English consume meat very plentifully, and this word, which simply means food, almost exclusively implies animal food. In the banquet given to Joseph's brethren, the viceroy commanded the servants 'to set on *bread*' (Gen. 43:31). In Ps. 104:27, it is said of fishes, creeping things and crocodiles, that God giveth them their *meat* in due season.

***To carry off meat from the graves.*** To be as poor as a church mouse; to be so poor as to descend to robbing the tombs of offerings. The

Greeks and Romans used to make feasts at certain seasons, when spirits were supposed to return to their graves, and the fragments were left on the tombs for the use of the ghosts. Hence the Latin proverb *Eleemosynam sepulcri patristui* (Alms on your father's grave).

**Medamothi.** The island at which the fleet of Pantagruel landed on the fourth day of their voyage, and where they bought many choice curiosities, such as the picture of a man's voice, an echo drawn to life, Plato's ideas, the atoms of Epicuros, a sample of Philomela's needlework, and other objects of vertu which could be obtained in no other portion of the globe (Rabelais, *Pantagruel*, iv, 3). The word is Greek, and has the same meaning as More's *Utopia* and Butler's *Erewhon*, i.e. 'Nowhere'.

**Médard, St.** The French 'St Swithin'; his day is June 8th.

> Quand il pleut à la Saint-Medard
> Il pleut quarante jours plus tard.

He was Bishop of Noyon and Tournai in the 6th century, and founded the Festival of the Rose at Salency, which is kept up to this day, the most virtuous girl in the parish receiving a crown of roses and a purse of money.

Legend says that a sudden shower once fell which wetted everyone to the skin except St Médard; he remained dry as a toast, for an eagle had spread his wings over him, and ever after he was termed *maître de la pluie*.

**Medea.** In Greek legend, a sorceress, daughter of Aetes, King of Colchis. She married Jason, the leader of the Argonauts, whom she aided to obtain the golden fleece, and was the mother of Medus, whom the Greeks regarded as the ancestor of the Medes. *See* Harmonia.

***Medea's kettle*** or ***cauldron.*** A means of restoring lost youth. Medea cut an old ram to pieces, threw the pieces into her cauldron, and a young lamb came forth. The daughters of Pelias thought to restore their father to youth in the same way; but Medea refused to utter the magic words, and the old man ceased to live.

> Get thee Medea's kettle and be boiled anew.
>
> Congreve, *Love for Love*, iv

**Medham** (Arab., the keen). One of Mahomet's swords, taken from the Jews when they were exiled from Medina.

**Mediaeval Ages.** *See* Middle Ages.

**Medicine.** From the Lat. *medicina*, which meant both the physician's art and his laboratory, and also a medicament. The alchemists applied the word to the philosopher's stone, and the elixir of life; hence Shakespeare's

> How much unlike art thou, Mark Antony!
> Yet, coming from him, that great medicine hath
> With his tinct gilded thee.
>
> *Antony and Cleopatra*, 1, 5

And the word was – and is – frequently used in a figurative sense, as –

> The miserable have no other medicine
> But only hope.
>
> *Measure for Measure*, 3, 1

Among the North American Indians *medicine* is a spell, charm, or fetish, and sometimes even Manitou (*q.v.*) himself, hence *Medicine-man*, a witch-doctor or magician.

> The medicine-man was the religious dignitary, his influence over the tribe being that of fear rather than of awe and spiritual dignity.
>
> Charles Morris, *The Aryan Race* (1888)

***The Father of Medicine.*** Aretaeus of Cappadocia, who lived at the close of the first and beginning of the second centuries, and Hippocrates of Cos (460–377 BC) are both so called.

***Medicinal days.*** In ancient practice the sixth, eighth, tenth, twelfth, sixteenth, eighteenth, etc., of a disease; so called because, according to Hippocrates, no 'crisis' (*q.v.*) occurs on these days, and medicine may be safely administered.

***Medicinal-finger.*** Also the *leech-finger* or *leech-man*. The finger next to the little finger, the ring finger; so called in mediaeval times because of the notion that it contained a vein that led direct to the heart.

**Medina.** In Spenser's *Faërie Queene* (II, ii) the typification of 'the golden mean' (Lat. *medium*). She was step-sister of Perissa (*excess*) and Elissa (*deficiency*), who could never agree upon any subject.

***Medina*** (Arab., city). The second holy city of the Mohammedans, called 'Yathrib' before Mahomet fled thither from Mecca, but afterwards Medinat-al-Nabi (the city of the prophet), whence its present name. In Spain there are four or five Medinas. *Medina-Sidonia* was so called by the Moors because it was believed to be on the site of the city Asidur, which was founded by Phoenicians from Sidon.

**Mediterranean.** The midland sea; the sea in the middle of the (Roman) earth (Lat. *medius*, middle, *terra*, land).

***The Key of the Mediterranean.*** The Rock of Gibraltar, which commands the entrance between Europe and Africa.

**Medusa.** The chief of the Gorgons (*q.v.*) of *Greek mythology*. Legend says that she was a beautiful maiden, specially famous for her hair; but that she violated the temple of Athene, who thereupon transformed her hair into serpents and made her face so terrible that all who looked on it were turned to stone. Perseus, assisted by Athene (who lent him her shield wherein he looked only on the *reflection* of Medusa during his attack), struck off her head, and by its means rescued Andromeda (*q.v.*) from the monster. Medusa was the mother by Poseidon of Chrysaor and Pegasus.

**Meerschaum** (Ger. sea-froth). This mineral (used for making tobacco-pipes), from having been found on the seashore in rounded white lumps, was ignorantly supposed to be sea-froth petrified; but it is a compound of silica, magnesia, lime, water, and carbonic acid. When first dug it lathers like soap, and is used as a soap by the Tartars.

**Meg.** Formerly slang for a guinea, but now signifying a halfpenny. *Cp.* Mag.

> No, no; Meggs are Guineas; Smelts are half-guineas.
>
> Shadwell, *Squire of Alsatia* I, i (1688)

***Mons Meg.*** A great 15th-century piece of artillery in the castle of Edinburgh, made at Mons, in Flanders. It was considered a palladium by the Scotch. *Cp.* Long Meg.

> Sent awa' our crown, and our sword, and our sceptre and Mons Meg to be keepit by thae English ... in the Tower of London [*N.B. – It was restored in* 1828].
>
> Scott, *Rob Roy*, ch. xxvii

***Roaring Meg.*** Formerly any large gun that made a great noise when let off was so called, as Mons Meg herself and a cannon given by the Fishmongers of London, and used in 1689. Burton says: 'Music is a roaring Meg against melancholy.'

> Drowning the noise of their consciences ... by ringing their greatest Bells, discharging their roaring-megs. Trapp, *Comment on Job* (1656)

**Megarian School.** A philosophical school, founded by Euclid, a native of Megara, and disciple of Socrates. It combined the ethical doctrines of Socrates with the metaphysic of the Eleatics (*q.v.*).

**Megarians.** The inhabitants of Megara and its territory, Megaris, Greece, proverbial for their stupidity; hence the proverb, 'Wise as a Megarian' – i.e. not wise at all; yet *see above*.

**Megrims.** A corruption of the Greek *hemicrania* (half the skull), through the French *migraine*. A neuralgic affection generally confined to one brow, or to one side of the forehead; whims, fancies.

**Meinie,** or **Meiny.** A company of attendants; a household: from O.Fr. *meyné*, *mesnie*, from Lat. *mansionem*, *mansio*, a house. Our word *menial* has much the same derivation and significance.

> With that the smiling Kriemhild forth stepped a little space.
> And Brunhild and her meiny greeted with gentle grace. Lettsom's *Nibelungenlied*, stanza 604

**Meistersingers.** Burgher poets of Germany, who attempted, in the 14th to 16th centuries, to revive the national minstrelsy of the *Minnesingers* (*q.v.*), which had fallen into decay. Hans Sachs, the cobbler (1494–1576), was the most celebrated.

***Die Meistersinger von Nürnberg.*** An opera by Wagner (1868) in which he satirised his critics.

**Mejnoun and Leilah.** A Persian love-tale, the *Romeo and Juliet* or *Pyramus and Thisbe* of Eastern romance.

**Mekhitarists.** An Armenian order of Roman Catholic monks who are principally concerned with the interests of Armenians and have published many of their ancient MSS. It was founded by Peter Mekhitar at Constantinople in 1701, and received papal confirmation in 1712. Its rule is similar to that of the Benedictines, and since 1717 its headquarters have been on the island of San Lazzaro, south of Venice.

**Melampod.** Black hellebore; so called from Melampus, a famous soothsayer and physician of Greek legend, who with it cured the daughters of Praetus of their melancholy (Virgil, *Georgics*, iii, 550).

> My seely sheep, like well below,
> They need not melampode;
> For they been hale enough I trow,
> And liken their abode. Spenser, *Eclogue*, vii

**Melancholy.** Lowness of spirits, supposed at one time to arise from a redundance of black bile (Gr. *melas chole*).

***Melancholy Jacques.*** So Jean Jacques Rousseau (1712–78) was called for his morbid sensibilities and unhappy spirit. The expression is from Shakespeare, *As You Like It*, 2, 1.

**Melanchthon** is merely the Greek for *Schwarzerde* (black earth), the real name of this reformer (1497–1560). Similarly, *Oecolampadius* is the Greek version of the German name *Hausschein*, and *Desiderius Erasmus* is one Latin and one Greek rendering of the name *Gheraerd Gheraerd.*

**Melanuros. *Abstain from the Melanurus*.** This is the sixth symbol in the *Protreptics*. Melan-uros means the 'black-tailed'. Pythagoras told his disciples to abstain from that which has a black tail, in other words, from such pleasures and pursuits as end in sorrow, or bring grief. The Melanuros is a Mediterranean fish of the perch family which, in Roman times, was sacred to the terrestrial gods.

**Melchisedecians.** Heretics of the early 3rd century who held that Melchisedec was not a man but a heavenly power, that he was the mediator between God and the angels whereas Christ was merely the mediator between God and man, and that therefore he was superior to Christ. Some believed him to be Christ Himself or the Holy Ghost.

**Meleager.** A hero of Greek legend, son of Oeneus of Calydon and Althaea, distinguished for throwing the javelin, for slaying the Calydonian boar, and as one of the Argonauts. It was declared by the fates that he would die as soon as a piece of wood then on the fire was burnt up; whereupon his mother snatched the log from the fire and extinguished it; but after Meleager had slain his maternal uncles, his mother threw the brand on the fire again, and Meleager died.

The death of Meleager was a favourite subject in ancient reliefs. The famous picture of Charles le Brun is in the Musée Imperiale of Paris.

**Melesigenes.** So Homer (*q.v.*) is sometimes called, because one tradition fixes his birthplace on the banks of the Meles, in Ionia.

> But higher sung
> Blind Melesigenes – then Homer called.
>
> Milton, *Paradise Regained*

**Meletians.** An heretical sect of the 4th and 5th centuries, followers of Meletius, Bishop of Lycopolis, Egypt, who is said to have sacrificed to idols in order to avoid the persecutions of Diocletian. Hence the name is sometimes applied to a trimmer in religion.

**Meliadus.** Father of Tristram in the Arthurian romances, and King of Lyonesse. He was drawn to a chase by the wiles of a fay who was in love with him, and from whose thraldom he was ultimately released by Merlin.

**Meliboeus** or **Melibe.** The central figure in Chaucer's prose *Tale of Meliboeus* (*Canterbury Tales*), which is a translation of a French rendering of Albertano da Brescia's Latin *Liber Consolationis et Concilii*. Meliboeus is a wealthy young man, married to Prudens. One day, when gone 'into the fields to play', enemies of his beat his wife and left his daughter for dead. Meliboeus resolved upon vengeance, but his wife persuaded him to call together his enemies, and he told them he forgave them 'to this effect and to this ende, that God of His endeles mercy wole at the tyme of oure deyinge forgive us oure giltes that we have trespased to Him in this wreeched world'.

**Meliboean Dye.** A rich purple. Meliboea, in Thessaly, was famous for the *ostrum*, a fish used in dyeing purple.

> A military vest of purple flowed,
> Lovelier than Meliboean.
>
> Milton, *Paradise Lost*, xi, 242

**Melicertes.** Son of Ino, a sea deity of Greek legend (*see* Leucothea). Athamas imagined his wife to be a lioness, and her two sons to be lion's cubs. In his frenzy he slew one of the boys, and drove the other (named Melicertes) with his mother into the sea. The mother became a sea goddess, and the boy the god of harbours.

**Melisande.** The same as Melusina (*q.v.*).

**Melisendra.** In romance, the supposed daughter of Marsilio and Charlemagne, married to his nephew Don Gwyferos. She was taken captive by the Moors, and confined seven years in a dungeon, when Gwyferos rescued her. See *Don Quixote* II, ii, 7, where the story is played as a puppet-show.

**Melissa.** The prophetess in *Orlando Furioso*, who lived in Merlin's cave. Bradamant gave her the enchanted ring to take to Rogero; so, assuming the form of Atlantes, she went to Alcina's island, and not only delivered Rogero, but disenchanted all the forms metamorphosed in the island. In Book xix she assumes the form of Rodomont, and persuades Agramant to break the league which was to settle the contest by single combat. A general battle ensues.

In Spenser's *Faërie Queene* (VI, xii) Melissa is Pastorella's handmaid.

**Mell Supper.** Harvest supper; in Scotland and the northern counties the last sheaf of corn cut is called the *mell*, and when the harvest is borne a woman carries a *mell-doll*, i.e. a straw image dressed up like a young girl, on top of a pole among the reapers.

**Mellifluous Doctor, The.** St Bernard (1091–1153), whose writings were called a 'river of Paradise'.

**Melodrama.** Properly (and in the early 19th cent.) a drama in which song and music were introduced (Gr. *melos*, song), an opera. These pieces were usually of a sensational character, and now – the musical portions having been gradually dropped – the word denotes a lurid, sensational play, with plenty of appeal to the emotions and invariably a happy ending in which the villain gets all he so richly deserves.

**Melon.** The Mohammedans say that the eating of a melon produces a thousand good works. There are certain stones on Mount Carmel called *Stone Melons*. The tradition is that Elijah saw a peasant carrying melons, and asked him for one. The man said they were not melons but stones, and Elijah instantly converted them into stones.

A like story is told of St Elizabeth of Hungary. She gave so bountifully to the poor as to cripple her own household. One day her husband met her with her lap full of something, and demanded of her what she was carrying. 'Only flowers, my Lord,' said Elizabeth, and to save the lie God converted the loaves into flowers.

**Melpomene.** The muse of tragedy.

> Up then Melpomene, thou mournfullest Muse of mine,
> Such cause of mourning never hadst afore.
>
> Spenser, *Shepherd's Calendar*, *November*

**Melusina,** or **Melisande.** The most famous of the *fées* of French romance, looked upon by the houses of Lusignan, Rohan, Luxembourg, and Sassenaye as their ancestor and founder. Having enclosed her father in a high mountain for offending her mother, she was condemned to become every Saturday a serpent from her waist downward. She married Raymond, Count of Lusignan, and made her husband vow never to visit her on a Saturday; but the count hid himself on one of the forbidden days, and saw his wife's transformation. Melusina was now obliged to quit her husband, and was destined to wander about as a spectre till the day of doom, though some say that the count immured her in the dungeon of his castle. *Cp.* Undine.

A sudden scream is called *un cri de Mélusine*, in allusion to the scream of despair uttered by Melusina when she was discovered by her husband; and in Poitou certain gingerbread cakes bearing the impress of a beautiful woman '*bien coiffée*', with a serpent's tail, made by confectioners for the May fair in the neighbourhood of Lusignan, are still called Mélusines.

**Melyhalt, Lady.** In the old romances, a powerful subject of King Arthur, whose domains Galiot invaded. She chose Galiot as her lover.

**Memento mori** (Lat., remember you must die). An emblem of mortality, such as a skull; something to put us in mind of the shortness and uncertainty of life.

> I make as good use of it [Bardolph's face] as many a man doth of a death's head or a memento mori.
>
> Shakespeare, *Henry IV*, 3, 3

**Memnon.** The Oriental or Ethiopian prince who, in the Trojan War, went to the assistance of his uncle Priam and was slain by Achilles. His mother Eos (the Dawn) was inconsolable for his death, and wept for him every morning.

The Greeks called the statue of Amenophis III, in Thebes, that of Memnon. When first struck by the rays of the rising sun it is said to have produced a sound like the snapping asunder of a cord. Poetically, when Eos kissed her son at daybreak, the hero acknowledged the salutation with a musical murmur.

> Memnon bending o'er his broken lyre.
>
> Darwin, *Economy of Vegetation*, i, 3

*Memnon's sister*, in *Il Penseroso*, is perhaps the Himera, mentioned by Dictys Cretensis; but Milton is supposed to have invented her, because it might be presumed that any sister of the black but comely Memnon would be likewise.

> Black, but such as in esteem
> Prince Memnon's sister might beseem.
>
> *Il Penseroso*, 18

The legend given by Dictys Cretensis (Bk vi) is that Himera, on hearing of her brother's death, set out to secure his remains, and encountered at Paphos a troop laden with booty, and carrying Memnon's ashes in an urn. Pallas, the leader of the troop, offered to give her either the urn or the booty, and she chose the urn.

Probably all that is meant is this: Black so delicate and beautiful that it might beseem a sister of Memnon the son of Aurora or the early day-dawn.

**Memorable.** ***The ever memorable.*** John Hales, of Eton (1584–1656), scholar and Arminian divine.

**Memory.** ***The Bard of Memory,*** Samuel Rogers (1763–1855), the banker-poet; author of *The Pleasures of Memory* (1792).

***Memory Woodfall,*** William Woodfall (1746–1803), brother of the Woodfall of *Junius*, and editor of the *Morning Chronicle*, would attend a debate, and, without notes, report it accurately next morning.

**Menah.** A large stone worshipped by certain tribes of Arabia between Mecca and Medina. Like most other Arabian idols it was demolished in the eighth year of 'the flight'. It is, in fact, a rude stone brought from Mecca, the sacred city, by pilgrims who wished to carry away with them some memento of their Holy Land.

**Menalcas.** Any shepherd or rustic. The name figures in the *Eclogues* of Virgil and the *Idyls* of Theocritus.

**Menamber.** A rocking-stone in the parish of Sithney (Cornwall) which at one time a little child could move. Cromwell's soldiers thought it fostered superstition, and rendered it immovable.

**Mendelism.** The theory of heredity promulgated by Gregor Johann Mendel (1822–84), the Austrian scientist and Abbot of Brünn, showing that the characters of the parents of cross-bred offspring reappear in certain proportions in successive generations according to definite laws. *Mendel's Law* was discovered by him in 1865 through experiments with peas.

**Mendicant Orders,** or **Begging Friars.** The orders of the Franciscans (*Grey Friars*), Augustines (*Black Friars*), Carmelites (*White Friars*), and Dominicans (*Preaching Friars*).

**Menechmians.** Persons exactly like each other; so called from the *Menaechmi* of Plautus, the basis of Shakespeare's *Comedy of Errors*, in which not only the two Dromios are exactly like each other, but Antipholus of Ephesus is the facsimile of his brother, Antipholus of Syracuse.

**Menecrates.** In ancient legend, a physician of Syracuse, of such unbounded vanity that he called himself Jupiter. Philip of Macedon invited him to a banquet, but served him with incense only.

> Such was Menecrates of little worth,
> Who Jove, the saviour, to be called presumed,
> To whom of incense Philip made a feast.
> Lord Brooke, *Inquisition upon Fame*, etc.

**Menelaus.** Son of Atreus, brother of Agamemnon, and husband of Helen, through whose desertion of him was brought about the Trojan War. He was the King of Sparta or of Lacedaemon.

**Menevia.** A form of the old name, *Mynyw*, of St David's (Wales). Its present name is from Dewi, or David, the founder of the episcopal see in the 6th century.

**Meng-tse.** The fourth of the sacred books of China; so called from the name of its author (d. about 290 BC), Latinised into Mencius. It was written in the 4th century BC. Confucius or Kung-fu-tse wrote the other three; viz. Ta-heo (*School of Adults*), Chong-yong (*The Golden Mean*), and Lun-yu (or *Book of Maxims*).

***Mother of Meng.*** A Chinese expression, meaning 'an admirable teacher'. Meng's father died soon after the birth of the sage, and he was brought up by his mother.

**Menippus,** the cynic, was born at Gadara, Syria, in the 3rd century BC. He was called by Lucian 'the greatest snarler and snapper of all the old dogs' (*cynics*).

Varro wrote the *Satyrae Menippeae*, and in imitation of it a political pamphlet, in verse and prose, designed to expose the perfidious intentions of Spain in regard to France, and the criminal ambition of the Guise family, was published in 1593 as *The Menippean Satire*. The authors were Pierre Leroy (d.1593), Pithou (1539–96), Passerat (1534–1602), and Rapin, the poet (1540–1608).

**Mennonites.** Followers of Simons Menno (1492–1559), a native of Friesland, who modified the fanatical views of the Anabaptists. The sect still survives, in the United States as well as in Holland and Germany.

**Menthu.** *See* Bakha.

**Mentor.** A guide, a wise and faithful counsellor; so called from Mentor, a friend of Ulysses, whose form Minerva assumed when she accompanied Telemachos in his search for his father.

**Menu** or **Manu.** In Hindu philosophy, one of a class of Demiurges of whom the first is identified with Brahma. Brahma divided himself into male and female, these produced *Viraj*, from whom sprang the first *Menu*, a kind of secondary creator. He gave rise to ten *Prajapatis* ('lords of all living'); from these came seven *Menus*, each presiding over a certain period, the seventh of these being *Menu Vaivasvata* ('the sun-born') who is now reigning and who is looked upon as the creator of the living races of beings. To him are ascribed the *Laws of Menu*, now called the *Manavadharmashastra*, a section of the Vedas containing a code of civil and religious law compiled by the Manavans.

**Meo periculo** (Lat. at my own risk). On my responsibility; I being bond.

> 'I will vouch for Edie Ochiltree, *meo periculo*,' said Oldbuck. Scott, *The Antiquary*, ch. xxxviii

**Mephibosheth,** in Dryden's *Absalom and Achitophel*, Pt ii (*q.v.*), is meant for Samuel Pordage (d.1691), a poetaster.

**Mephistopheles.** A manufactured name (possibly from three Greek words meaning 'not loving the light') of a devil or familiar spirit which first appears in the late mediaeval Faust legend; he is well known as the sneering, jeering, leering tempter in Goethe's *Faust*. He is mentioned by Shakespeare (*Merry Wives*, 1, 1) and Fletcher as *Mephostophilus*, and in Marlowe's *Faustus* as *Mephostopilis*.

**Mercator's Projection** is Mercator's chart or map for nautical purposes. The meridian lines are at right angles to the parallels of latitude. It is so called because it was devised by Gerhard Kremer (= merchant, pedlar) (1512–94), whose surname Latinised is *Mercator*.

**Merchant of Venice.** The interwoven stories of Shakespeare's comedy (written 1598, published 1600) are drawn from mediaeval legends the germs of which are found in the *Gesta Romanorum*. The tale of the bond is ch. xlviii, and that of the caskets is ch. xcix. Much of the plot is also given in the 14th century *Il Pecorone* of Ser Giovanni; but Shakespeare could not read Italian, there was no translation in his day, and it is more than doubtful whether he ever saw or was aware of it.

**Mercia.** One of the ancient Anglian kingdoms of the Heptarchy, founded soon after the middle of the 6th century. It flourished under Penda in the 7th century; in the 8th, under Ethelbald and Offa, it became overlord, but in 827 was incorporated with Wessex, to be revived again as an earldom until the Norman Conquest. It embraced a large part of the Midlands, stretching from the Humber to the Thames, and westward to the Welsh Marches.

**Merciless** (or **Unmerciful**) **Parliament, The** (from February 3rd to June 3rd, 1388). A junto of fourteen tools of Thomas, Duke of Gloucester, which assumed royal prerogatives, and attempted to depose Richard II.

**Mercilla.** *See* Soldan.

**Mercurial.** Light-hearted, gay, volatile; because such were supposed by the astrologers to be born under the planet Mercury.

***Mercurial finger.*** The little finger, which, if pointed denotes eloquence, if square sound judgment.

The thumb, in chiromancy, we give to Venus,
The forefinger to Jove, the midst to Saturn,
The ring to Sol, the least to Mercury.

Ben Jonson, *Alchemist*, i, 1

**Mercury.** The Roman equivalent of the Greek Hermes (*q.v.*), son of Maia and Jupiter, to whom he acted as messenger. He was the god of science and commerce, the patron of travellers and also of rogues, vagabonds, and thieves. Hence, the name of the god is used to denote both a messenger and a thief:

Delay leads impotent and snail-pac'd beggary:
Then fiery expedition be my wing,
Jove's Mercury, and herald for a king.

Shakespeare, *Richard III*, 4, 3

My father named me Autolycus; who being, as I am, littered under Mercury, was likewise a snapper-up of unconsidered trifles.

Shakespeare, *Winter's Tale*, 4, 2

Mercury is represented as a young man with winged hat and winged sandals (*talaria*), bearing the *caduceus* (*q.v.*), and sometimes a purse.

Posts with a marble head of Mercury on them used to be erected where two or more roads met, to point out the way. (Juvenal, viii, 53.)

In astrology, Mercury 'signifieth subtill men, ingenious, inconstant: rymers, poets, advocates, orators, phylosophers, arithmeticians, and busie fellowes', and the alchemists credited it with great powers and used it for a large number of purposes. *See* Ben Jonson's masque, *Mercury Vindicated*.

***Mercury fig*** (Lat. *Ficus ad Mercurium*). The first fig gathered off a fig tree was by the Romans devoted to Mercury. The proverbial saying was applied generally to all first fruits or first works.

***You cannot make a Mercury of every log.*** Pythagoras said: *Non ex quovis ligno Mercurius fit*. That is, 'Not every mind will answer equally well to be trained into a scholar.' The proper wood for a statue of Mercury was box – *vel quod hominis pultorem prae se ferat, vel quod materies sit omnium maxime aeterna*. (Erasmus.)

**Mercy.** The seven corporal works of mercy are:

(1) To tend the sick.
(2) To feed the hungry.
(3) To give drink to the thirsty.
(4) To clothe the naked.
(5) To house the homeless.
(6) To visit the fatherless and the afflicted.
(7) To bury the dead. Matt. 25:35–40

**Meridian.** Sometimes applied, especially in Scotland, to a noonday dram of spirits.

He received from the hand of the waiter the meridian, which was placed ready at the bar.

Scott, *Redgauntlet*, ch. i

**Merino Sheep.** A Spanish breed of sheep, very valuable for their wool. The word is the Latin *majorinus*, and may originally have indicated a specially large breed of sheep, or have been the official designation of the overseer of the pastures.

**Merlin.** The historical Merlin was a Welsh or British bard, born towards the close of the 5th century, to whom a number of poems have been very doubtfully attributed. He is said to have become bard to King Arthur, and to have lost his reason and perished on the banks of the river after a terrible battle between the Britons and their Romanised compatriots about 570.

His story has been mingled with that of the enchanter Merlin of the Arthurian romances, which, however, proceeds on different lines. This Prince of Enchanters was the son of a damsel seduced by a fiend, but was baptised by Blaise, and so rescued from the power of Satan. He became an adept in necromancy, but was beguiled by the enchantress Nimuë, who shut him up in a rock, and later Vivien, the Lady of the Lake, entangled him in a thornbush by means of spells, and there he still sleeps, though his voice may sometimes be heard.

He first appears in Nennius (as Ambrosius); Geoffrey of Monmouth wrote the *Vita Merlini* (about 1145); this was worked upon by Wace and Robert de Borron, and formed the basis of the English prose romance *Merlin*, and of most of the Merlin episodes in the Arthurian cycle. *See also* Spenser's *Faërie Queene* (III, iii), and Tennyson's *Idylls*.

> Now, though a Mechanist, whose skill
> Shames the degenerate grasp of modern science,
> Grave Merlin (and belike the more
> For practising occult and perilous lore)
> Was subject to a freakish will
> That sapped good thoughts, or scared them with defiance.
> Wordsworth, *The Egyptian Maid*

***The English Merlin.*** William Lilly (1602–81), the astrologer, who published two tracts under the name of 'Merlinus Anglicus' and was the most famous charlatan of his day.

**Merlin Chair.** An invalid's chair, which can be propelled by the hands of the occupant. So called from the inventor, J. J. Merlin (d.1803).

**Mermaid.** The popular stories of the mermaid, a fabulous marine creature half woman and half fish – allied to the Siren (*q.v.*) of classical mythology – probably arose from sailors' accounts of the dugong, a cetacean whose head has a rude approach to the human outline, and the mother while suckling her young holds it to her breast with one flipper, as a woman holds her infant in her arm. If disturbed she suddenly dives under water, and tosses up her fish-like tail.

In Elizabethan plays the term is often used for a courtesan. *See* Massinger's *Old Law*, iv, 1, Shakespeare's *Comedy of Errors*, 3, 2, etc.

***The Mermaid Tavern.*** The famous meeting-place (in Bread Street, Cheapside) of the wits, literary men, and men about town in the early 17th century. Among those who met there at a sort of early club were Ben Jonson, Sir Walter Raleigh, Beaumont, Fletcher, John Selden, and in all probability Shakespeare.

> What things have we seen
> Done at the Mermaid! Heard words that have been
> So nimble, and so full of subtile flame,
> As if that everyone from whence they came
> Had meant to put his whole wit in a jest.
> Beaumont, *Lines to Ben Jonson*

***Mermaid's glove.*** The largest of the British sponges (*Halichondria palmata*), so called because its branches resemble fingers.

***Mermaid's purses.*** The horny cases of the eggs of the ray, skate, or shark, frequently cast up by the waves on the sea-beach.

**Merope.** One of the Pleiades; dimmer than the rest, because, according to Greek legend, she married a mortal. She was the mother of Glaucus.

**Merops' Son.** One who thinks he can set the world to rights, but can't. Agitators, demagogues, and Bolsheviks, are sons of Merops. The allusion is to Phaeton, son of Merops, who thought himself able to drive the car of Phoebus, but, in the attempt, nearly set the world on fire.

**Merovingian Dynasty.** The dynasty of Merovius, a Latin form of *Merwig* (great warrior), who is said to have ruled over the Franks in the 5th century. The dynasty rose to power under Clovis (d.511), and gradually gave way before the Mayors of the Palace (*q.v.*), until in 751 the Merovingians were deposed by Pepin the Short, grandson of Pepin of Heristal.

**Merrie England.** *See* Merry.

**Merrow** (Irish, *muirrúghach*). A mermaid, believed by Irish fishermen to forebode a coming storm.

> It was rather annoying to Jack that, though living in a place where the merrows were as plenty as lobsters, he never could get a right view of one.
> W. B. Yeats, *Fairy and Folk Tales*, p. 63

> Merrows are of human shape above but from the waist like a fish. The females are attractive, but the males have green teeth, green hair, pig's eyes, and red noses. Fishermen dread to meet them.

**Merry.** The original meaning is *pleasing, delightful*; hence, *giving pleasure*; hence *mirthful, joyous*.

The old phrase *Merrie England* (*Merry London*, etc.) merely signified that these places were pleasant and delightful, not necessarily bubbling over with merriment; and so with *the merry month of May*.

> Thou Saint George shalt called bee,
> Saint George of mery England, the signe of victoree.
> Spenser, *Faërie Queene*, I, x, 61
>
> Thus all through merry Islington
> These gambols did he play.
> Cowper, *John Gilpin*

The phrase *merry men*, meaning the companions at arms of a knight or outlaw (especially Robin Hood), is really for *merry meinie*. *See* Meinie.

***Merry Andrew.*** A buffoon, jester, or attendant on a quack doctor at fairs. Said by Hearne (1735) – with no evidence – to derive from Andrew Borde (d.1549), physician to Henry VIII, who to his vast learning added great eccentricity. Prior has a poem on 'Merry Andrew'. Andrew is a common name in old plays for a manservant, as Abigail is for a waiting-woman.

***Merry as a cricket, grig.*** *See* Grig.

***Merry Dancers.*** The northern lights, so called from their undulatory motion. The French also call them *chèvres dansantes* (dancing goats).

***Merry Dun of Dover.*** In Scandinavian folktale, an enormous ship which knocked down Calais steeple in passing through the Straits of Dover, while the pennant swept a flock of sheep off Dover cliffs into the sea. The masts were so lofty that a boy who ascended them would grow grey before he could reach deck again.

***Merry Greek.*** *See* Grig.

***Merry Maidens.*** The ancient stone circle (of 19 stones) in St Buryan parish, 5 miles from Penzance, Cornwall. It is 76 ft in diameter. Also called *Rosemodris Circle*.

***Merry men.*** *See* Merry, *above*.

***Merry Men of Mey.*** An expanse of broken water which boils like a cauldron in the southern side of the Stroma channel, in the Pentland Firth.

***Merry Monarch.*** Charles II.

***Merry Monday.*** An old name for the day before Shrove Tuesday.

***Merrythought.*** The furcula or wishing-bone in the breast of a fowl; sometimes broken by two persons, and the one who holds the larger portion has his wish, as it is said.

***'Tis merry in hall, when beards wag all*** (*2 Henry IV*, 5, 3). It is a sure sign of mirth when the beards of the guests shake with laughter.

***To make merry.*** To be jovial, festive; *to make merry over*, to treat with amusement or ridicule, to make fun of.

**Merse.** The south-easterly part of Berwickshire was so called because it was the *merc*, *march*, or frontier of England and Scotland. It gives the second half of the title to the Earl of Wemyss and March.

**Merton College.** Founded by Walter de Merton (d.1277), Bishop of Rochester, and Lord High Chancellor in 1264. He was, through this foundation, the originator of the collegiate system still maintained in the older English Universities.

**Meru.** The 'Olympus' of the Hindus; a fabulous mountain in the centre of the world, 80,000 leagues high, the abode of Vishnu, and a perfect paradise.

**Merveilleuse** (Fr. marvellous). The sword of Doolin of Mayence (*q.v.*). It was so sharp that when placed edge downwards it would cut through a slab of wood without the use of force.

The term is also applied to the dress worn by the fops and ladies of the Directory period in France, who were noted for their extravagance and aping of classical Greek modes.

**Meschino.** *See* Guerino Meschino.

**Mesmerism.** So called from Friedrich Anton Mesmer (1733–1815), of Meersburg, Baden, who introduced his theory of 'animal magnetism' into Paris in 1778. It has long since fallen into disrepute.

**Mesopotamia** (Gr. the land between the rivers, i.e. the Euphrates and Tigris). The territory bounded by Kurdistan on the N. and N.E., the Persian Gulf on the S. and S.E., Persia on the E., and Syria and the Arabian Desert on the W. Since the Great War – as a consequence of which it was freed from Turkish rule and constituted a separate kingdom – its name has been changed to *Irak* (*q.v.*), or *Iraq*.

***The true 'Mesopotamia' ring.*** Something high-sounding and pleasing, but wholly past comprehension. The allusion is to the story of an old woman who told her pastor that she 'found great support in that blessed word *Mesopotamia*'.

**Mess.** The usual meaning today is a dirty, untidy state of things, a muddle, a difficulty (*to get into a mess*); but the word originally signified a portion of food (Lat. *missum*, *mittere*, to send; *cp.* Fr. *mets*, viands, Ital. *messo*, a course of a meal); thence it came to mean mixed food – especially for an animal – and so a confusion, medley, jumble.

Another meaning was, a small group of persons (usually four) who at banquets sat together and were served from the same dishes. This use gave rise not only to the army and navy *mess* (used also at the Inns of Court), but to the Elizabethans using it in place of 'four' or 'a group of four'. Thus, Lyly says, 'Foure makes a messe, and we have a messe of masters' (*Mother Bombie*, ii, 1), and Shakespeare calls the four sons of Henry his 'mess of sons' (*2 Henry VI*, 1, 4); and says (*Love's Labour's Lost*, 4, 3), 'You three fools lacked me ... to make up the mess.'

**Messalina.** Wife of the Emperor Claudius of Rome; she was executed by order of her husband in AD 48. Her name has become a byword for lasciviousness and incontinency. Catherine II of Russia (1729–96) has sometimes been called *The Modern Messalina*.

**Metals.** Metals used to be divided into two classes – *Noble*, and *Base*. The *Noble*, or *Perfect, Metals* were gold and silver, because they were the only two known that could not be changed or 'destroyed' by fire; the remainder were *Base*, or *Imperfect*.

*The seven metals in alchemy.*
Gold, Apollo or the sun.
Silver, Diana or the moon.
Quicksilver, Mercury.
Copper, Venus.
Iron, Mars.
Tin, Jupiter.
Lead, Saturn.

The only metals used in heraldry are *or* (gold) and *argent* (silver).

**Metamorphic Rocks.** Sedimentary or eruptive rocks whose original character has been more or less altered by changes beneath the surface of the earth. These include gneiss, mica-schist, clay-slate, marble, and the like, which have become more or less crystalline.

**Metaphysics** (Gr. after-physics, so called because the disciples of Aristotle held that matter or nature should be studied before mind). The science of metaphysics is the consideration of things in the abstract – that is, divested of their accidents, relations, and matter; the philosophy of being and knowing; the theoretical principles forming the basis of any particular science; the philosophy of mind.

**Metathesis.** A figure of speech in which letters or syllables are transposed, as 'You occupew my pie [py]', instead of 'You *occupy my pew*'; *daggletrail* for 'draggle-tail', etc.; the same as a Spoonerism (*q.v.*).

**Methodists.** A name given (1729) by a student of Christ Church to the brothers Wesley and their friends, who used to assemble on given evenings for religious conversation, because of the methodical way in which they observed their principles. The word was in use many centuries earlier for those (especially physicians) who attached great importance to method, and the name was at one time applied to the Jesuits, because they were the first to give systematic representations of the method of polemics. Gale (1678) speaks of a religious sect called 'the New Methodists' (*Court of the Gentiles*).

***Primitive Methodists.*** A secession from the Methodists, led by Hugh Bourne in 1810. They adopted this name because they reverted to the original methods of preaching of the Wesleys.

**Methuselah.** ***Old as Methuselah.*** Very old indeed, almost incredibly old. He is the oldest man mentioned in the Bible, where we are told (Gen. 5:27) that he died at the age of 969.

**Metonic Cycle, The.** A cycle of nineteen years, at the end of which period the new moons fall on the same days of the year; so-called because discovered by the Greek astronomer, Meton, 432 BC. In 330 a slight error in it was put right by Calippus, who, to allow for odd hours, laid down that at the end of four cycles (76 years) one day was to be omitted.

**Metropolitan.** A prelate who has suffragan bishops subject to him. The two metropolitans of England are the two archbishops, and the two of Ireland the archbishops of Armagh and Dublin. The word does not mean the prelate of the metropolis (Gr. *meter*, mother, *polis*, city) in a secular sense, but the prelate of a 'mother city' in an ecclesiastical sense – i.e. a city which is the mother or ruler of other cities. Thus, the Bishop of London is not a metropolitan, but the Archbishop of Canterbury is *metropolitanus et primus totius Angliae*, and the Archbishop of York *primus et metropolitanus Angliae*.

In the Greek Church a metropolitan ranks next below a patriarch and next above an archbishop.

**Meum and Tuum.** That which belongs to me and that which is another's. *Meum* is Latin for 'what is mine', and *tuum* is Latin for 'what is thine'. If a man is said not to know the difference between *meum* and *tuum*, it is a polite way of saying he is a thief.

***'Meum est propositum in taberna mori'*.** A famous drinking song usually credited to Walter Map, who died in 1210.

> Meum est propositum in taberna mori;
> Vinum sit oppositum morientis ori
> Ut dicant cum venerint angelorum chori:
> Deus sit propitius huic potatori (etc.).
>
> It is my intention to die in a tavern. May wine be placed to my dying lips, that when the choirs of angels shall come they may say, 'God be merciful to this drinker.'

**Mews.** Stables, but properly a cage for hawks when moulting (O.F. *mue*, Lat. *mutare*, to change). The word has acquired its present meaning because (in the 17th cent.) the royal stables were built upon the site (now occupied by the National Gallery) where formerly the king's hawks were kept; and the name was transferred from the establishment for hawks to that of horses.

**Mexitl,** or **Mextli.** The principal god of the ancient Mexicans (whence the name of their country), to whom enormous sacrifices, running into many thousands of human beings, were offered at a time. Also called *Huitzilopochtli*.

**Mezentius.** A legendary king of the Tyrrhenians, noted for his cruelties and impiety, who put his subjects to death by tying a living man to a dead one. He was driven from his throne by his subjects, and fled to Turnus, King of the Rutuli. When Aeneas arrived he fought with Mezentius, and slew both him and his son Lausus.

> He stretches out the arm of Mezentius, and fetters the dead to the living.
>
> C. Brontë, *Shirley*, ch. xxxi
>
> This is like Mezentius in Virgil ... Such critics are like dead coals; they may blacken, but cannot burn. Broom, *Preface to Poems*

**Mezzo relievo** (Ital.). Moderate relief; applied to figures which project more than those of *basso relievo* (*q.v.*), but less than those of *alto relievo* (*q.v.*).

**Mezzotint,** or **Mezzo tinto** (Ital., medium tint). A process of engraving in which a copper plate is uniformly roughened so as to print a deep black, lights and half-lights being then produced by scraping away the burr; also a print from this, which is usually a good imitation of an Indian-ink drawing.

**Micah Rood's Apples.** Apples with a spot of red in the heart. The story is that Micah Rood was a prosperous farmer at Franklin. In 1693 a pedlar with jewellery called at his house, and next day was found murdered under an apple tree in Rood's orchard. The crime was never brought home to the farmer, but next autumn all the apples of the fatal tree bore inside a red blood-spot, called 'Micah Rood's Curse', and the farmer died soon afterwards.

**Micawber.** An incurable optimist; from Dickens's Mr Wilkins Micawber (*David Copperfield*), a great speechifier and letter-writer, and projector of bubble schemes sure to lead to fortune, but always ending in grief. Notwithstanding his ill success, he never despaired, but felt certain that something would 'turn up' to make his fortune. Having failed in every adventure in the old country, he emigrated to Australia, where he became a magnate.

**Michael, St.** The great prince of all the angels and leader of the celestial armies.

> And there was war in heaven: Michael and his angels fought against the dragon; and the dragon fought and his angels, and prevailed not.
>
> Rev. 12:7, 8

> Go, Michael, of celestial armies prince,
> And thou, in military prowess next,
> Gabriel; lead forth to battle these my sons
> Invincible; lead forth my armèd Saints
> By thousands and by millions ranged for fight.
>
> Milton, *Paradise Lost*, vi, 44

His day ('St Michael and All Angels') is Sept. 29th (*see* Michaelmas), and in the Roman Church he is also commemorated on May 8th, in honour of his apparition in 492 to a herdsman of Monte Gargano. In the Middle Ages he was looked on as the presiding spirit of the planet Mercury, and bringer to man of the gift of prudence.

> The planet Mercury, whose place
> Is nearest to the sun in space,
> Is my allotted sphere;
> And with celestial ardour swift
> I bear upon my hands the gift
> Of heavenly *prudence* here.
>
> Longfellow, *Golden Legend*, *The Miracle Play*, iii

In art St Michael is depicted as a beautiful young man with severe countenance, winged, and either clad in white or armour, bearing a lance and shield, with which he combats a dragon. In the final judgment he is represented with scales, in which he weighs the souls of the risen dead.

***St Michael's chair.*** It is said that any woman who sits on St Michael's Chair, Cornwall, will rule the roost as long as she lives.

***Cousin Michael.*** *See* Michel.

***The Order of St Michael and St George.*** A British order of knighthood, instituted in 1818 (enlarged and extended on four occasions since), and conferred on natural-born British subjects who hold, or have held, high official rank in the Colonies, or as a reward for services in relation to the foreign affairs of the Empire. It is limited to one hundred Knights Grand Cross, three hundred Knights Commanders, and six hundred Companions; and its chapel is in St Paul's Cathedral.

**Michael Angelo.** The celebrated painter, born 1475, died 1564, full name, Michelangelo Buonarroti.

***The Michael-Angelo of battle-scenes.*** Michael-Angelo Cerquozzi (1600–60), a native of Rome, famous for his battle scenes and shipwrecks.

***Michel-Ange des Bamboches.*** Peter van Laar (1613–73), the Dutch painter.

***Michael-Angelo of Music.*** Christoph Willibald von Gluck (1714–87), the German musical composer.

***Michael-Angelo of Sculptors.*** Pierre Puget (1622–94), the French sculptor. Also Réné Michael Slodtz (1705–64).

**Michaelmas Day.** September 29th, the Festival of St Michael and All Angels (*see* Michael, *above*), one of the quarter-days when rents are due, and the day when magistrates are elected.

The custom of eating goose at Michaelmas (*see also* St Martin's Goose) is many centuries old, and probably arose solely because geese were plentiful and in good condition at this season, and we are told that tenants formerly presented their landlords with one to keep in their good graces. The popular story, however, is that Queen Elizabeth, on her way to Tilbury Fort on September 29th, 1588, dined at the seat of Sir Neville Umfreyville, and partook of goose, afterwards calling for a bumper of Burgundy, and giving as a toast, 'Death to the Spanish Armada!' Scarcely had she spoken when a messenger announced the destruction of the fleet by a storm. The queen demanded a second bumper, and said, 'Henceforth shall a goose commemorate this great victory.' This tale is marred by the awkward circumstances that the fleet was dispersed by the winds in July, and the thanksgiving sermon for the victory was preached at St Paul's on August 20th. Gascoigne, who died 1577, refers to the custom of goose-eating at Michaelmas as common:

> At Christmas a capon, at Michaelmas a goose,
> And somewhat else at New Yere's tide, for feare the lease flies loose.

**Michal.** In Dryden's *Absalom and Achitophel* (*q.v.*) is meant for Queen Catherine, wife of Charles II, who appears as David. Michal, of course, was David's wife (1 Sam. 18:20).

**Michel** or **Cousin Michael.** A German. The French call a fool who allows himself to be taken in by thimble-rigs and card tricks *mikel.* In Old French the word *mice* occurs, meaning a fool. *See* Michon.

**Miching Malicho.**

> *Oph.*: What means this, my lord?
> *Ham.*: Marry, this is Miching Malicho; it means mischief.
> *Oph.*: Belike this show imports the argument of the play. Shakespeare, *Hamlet*, 3, 2

The meaning of this phrase is not at all certain, but it is usually taken that *miching* is 'skulking' (*miche*, from O.Fr. *muchier*, *mucier*, to hide), and *malicho* is a form of Span. *malhecco*, a misdeed, mischief; hence skulking or sneaking mischief. The form we give is that of the First Folio; in the First Quarto the words appear as *myching Mallico*, and in the Second Quarto *munching Mallico*.

**Michon,** according to Cotgrave, is a 'block, dunce, dolt, jobbernol, dullard, loggerhead'. *Michon*, *mikel*, and *Cousin Michel*, all the Italian *miccio*, an ass.

**Mickle, Many a.** *See* Little, many a.

**Mickleton Jury.** A corruption of mickle-tourn (*magnus turnus*), i.e. the jury of court leets, which were visited at Easter and Michaelmas by the county sheriffs in their *tourns.* In Anglo-Saxon times the great council of the kings was known as the *Mickle-moot* (great assembly).

**Microcosm** (Gr. little world). So man is called by Paracelsus. The ancients considered the world (*see* Macrocosm) as a living being; the sun and moon being its *two eyes*, the earth its *body*, the ether its *intellect*, and the sky its *wings.* When man was looked on as the world in miniature, it was thought that the movements of the world and of man corresponded, and if one could be ascertained, the other could be easily inferred; hence arose the system of astrology, which professed to interpret the events of a man's life by the corresponding movements, etc., of the stars. *Cp.* Diapason.

**Midas.** A legendary king of Phrygia who requested of the gods that everything he touched might be turned to gold. His request was granted, but as his food became gold the moment he touched it, he prayed the gods to take their favour back. He was then ordered to bathe in the Pactolus, and the river ever after rolled over golden sands.

Another story told of him is, that when appointed to judge a musical contest between Apollo and Pan, he gave judgment in favour of the satyr; whereupon Apollo in contempt gave the king a pair of ass's ears. Midas hid them under his Phrygian cap; but his barber discovered them, and, not daring to mention the matter, dug a hole and relieved his mind by whispering in it 'Midas has ass'sears', then covering it up again. Budaeus gives a different version. He says that Midas kept spies to tell him everything that transpired throughout his kingdom, and the proverb 'kings have long arms' was changed to 'Midas has long ears'.

A parallel of this tale is told of Portzmach, king of a part of Brittany. He had all the barbers of his kingdom put to death, lest they should announce to the public that he had the ears of a horse. An intimate friend was found willing to shave him, after swearing profound secrecy; but not able to contain himself, he confided his secret to the sands of a river bank. The reeds of this river were used for pan-pipes and hautbois, which repeated the words 'Portzmach – King Portzmach has horse's ears'.

**Midden.** ***Better marry over the midden than over the moor.*** Better seek a wife among your neighbours whom you know than among strangers of whom you know nothing. The midden is the domestic rubbish heap.

***Ilka cock craws loodest on its ain midden.*** In English, 'Every cock crows loudest on his own dunghill.'

***Kitchen midden.*** *See* Kitchen.

**Middle Ages.** The period from about 476 (the fall of the Roman Empire) to 1453 (the capture of Constantinople by the Turks). It varies a little with almost every nation; in France it is usually dated from Clovis to Louis XI (481 to 1461); in England, from the Heptarchy to the accession of Henry VII (409 to 1485). The earlier part of this time (to about 1200) is usually referred to as the Dark Ages (*q.v.*).

**Middlesex.** The territory of the Middle Saxons – that is, between Essex, Sussex, and Wessex.

**Midgard.** In *Scandinavian mythology*, the abode of the first pair, from whom sprang the human race. It was made of the eyebrows of Ymer, and was joined to Asgard by the rainbow bridge called Bifrost.

Asgard is the abode of the celestials.
Utgard is the abode of the giants.
Midgard is between the two – better than Utgard, but inferior to Asgard.

**Midgardsormen.** *See* Jormungandr.

**Mid-Lent Sunday.** The fourth Sunday in Lent. It is called *dominica refectionis* (Refection Sunday), because the first lesson is the banquet given by Joseph to his brethren, and the gospel of the day is the miraculous feeding of the five thousand. It is the day on which simnel cakes (*q.v.*) are eaten, and it is also called Mothering Sunday (*q.v.*).

**Midnight Oil.** Late hours.

***Burning the midnight oil.*** Sitting up late, especially when engaged on literary work.

***Smells of the midnight oil.*** *See* It smells of the lamp *under* Lamp.

**Midrash.** The rabbinical investigation into and interpretation of the Old Testament writings, which began when the Temple at Jerusalem was destroyed and was committed to writing in a large number of commentaries between the 2nd and 11th centuries AD. The three ancient *Midrashim* (*Mechiltha*, *Sifre*, and *Sifra* – first half of the 2nd century) contain both the Halachah and the Haggadah (*q.v.*).

**Midsummer.** The week or so round about the summer solstice (June 21st). *Midsummer Day* is June 24th, St John the Baptist's Day, and one of the quarter days.

***Midsummer ale.*** Festivities which used to take place in rural districts at this season. Here *Ale* has the same extended meaning as in 'Church-ale' (*q.v.*).

***Midsummer madness.*** Olivia says to Malvolio, 'Why, this is very midsummer madness' (*Twelfth Night*, 3, 4). The reference is to the rabies of dogs, which was supposed to be brought on by midsummer heat. People who were a bit inclined to be mad used to be said *to have but a mile to midsummer*.

***Midsummer men.*** Orpine or Livelong, one of the Sedum tribe; so called because it used to be set in pots or shells on midsummer eve, and hung up in the house to tell damsels whether their sweethearts were true or not. If the leaves bent to the right, it was a sign of fidelity; if to the left, the 'true-love's heart was cold and faithless'.

**Midsummer Moon.** '*'Tis midsummer moon with you*'; you are stark mad. Madness was supposed to be affected by the moon, and to be aggravated by summer heat; so it naturally follows that the full moon at midsummer is the time when madness would be most outrageous.

What's this midsummer moon?
Is all the world gone a-madding?
Dryden, *Amphitryon*, iv, 1

**Midsummer Night's Dream.** Shakespeare's comedy (acted 1595, first printed 1600) is indebted to Chaucer's *Knight's Tale* for the Athenian setting, and to Ovid's *Metamorphoses* for the Pyramus and Thisbe interlude; but its airy grace and the ingenious interweaving of the four separate threads are all Shakespeare's own.

**Midwife** (A.S., *mid*, with; *wif*, woman). The nurse who is *with* the mother in her labour.

***Midwife of men's thoughts.*** So Socrates termed himself; and, as Mr Grote observes, 'No other man ever struck out of others so many sparks to set light to original thought.' Out of his intellectual school sprang Plato and the Dialectic system; Euclid and the Megaric; Aristippus and the Cyrenaic; Antisthenes and the Cynic; and his influence on the mind was never equalled by any teacher but One, of whom it was said, 'Never man spake like this man.'

**Mihrab.** *See* Keblah.

**Mikado** (Jap. *mi*, exalted; *kado*, gate or door). The title of the Emperor of Japan (*cp.* Shogun). The name is much like that of the Sultan of Turkey – the Sublime Porte.

**Mike.** ***To mike,*** or ***to do a mike.*** To idle away one's time, pretending to be waiting for a job, or just hanging about and avoiding one. The word may be from *miche*, to skulk (*see* Miching Malicho).

Shall the blessed sun of heaven prove a micher [truant loiterer]?
Shakespeare, *1 Henry IV*, 2, 4

**Milan.** A contraction of the ancient name of the town, *Mediolanum*, in the middle of the plain, i.e. the Plain of Lombardy. In the Middle Ages Milan was famous for its steel, used for making swords, chain armour, etc.

Canst thou take up a fallen link in my Milan hauberk? Scott, *Fair Maid of Perth*, ch. xi

***The edict of Milan.*** Proclaimed by Constantine, after the conquest of Italy (313), to secure to Christians the restitution of their civil and religious rights.

***The Milan Decree.*** A decree made by Napoleon, dated 'Milan, Dec. 27th, 1807', declaring 'the whole British Empire to be in a state of blockade, and forbidding all countries either from trading with Great Britain or from even using an article of British manufacture'.

This very absurd decree was killing the goose which laid the golden eggs, for England was the best customer of the very countries thus restricted from dealing with her.

**Milanion.** *See* Atalanta's Race.

**Mildendo.** The metropolis of Lilliput (in Swift's *Gulliver's Travels*), the wall of which was 2½ ft in height, and at least 11 in. thick. The city was an exact square; two main streets divided it into four quarters, and the emperor's palace, Belfaborac, was in its centre.

**Mile.** A measure of length; in the British Empire and the United States, 1,760 yds; so called from Lat. *mille*, a thousand, the Roman lineal measure being 1,000 paces, or about 1,680 yds. The old Irish and Scottish miles were a good deal longer than the standard English, that in Ireland (still in use in country parts) being 2,240 yds.

The *Nautical* or *Geographical Mile*, is supposed to be one minute of a great circle of the earth; but as the earth is not a true sphere the length of a minute is variable, so a mean length – 6,080 ft (2,026 yds 2 ft) – has been fixed by the British Admiralty. The Geographical Mile varies slightly with different nations, so there is a further *International Geographical Mile*, which is invariable at one-fifteenth of a degree of the earth's equator, equal to about 4·61 statute miles of 5,280 ft.

**Milesian Fables.** A Greek collection of witty but obscene short stories by Antonius Diogenes, and compiled by Aristides, of *Miletus* (2nd cent. BC), whence the name. They were translated into Latin by Sisenna about the time of the civil wars of Marius and Sylla, and were greedily read by the luxurious Sybarites, but are no longer extant. Similar stories, however, are still sometimes called *Milesian Tales*.

**Milesians.** Properly, the inhabitants of Miletus, but the name has been given to the ancient Irish because of the legend that two sons of Milesius, a fabulous king of Spain, conquered the country and repeopled it after exterminating the Firbolgs – the aborigines.

My family, by my father's side, are all the true ould Milesians, and related to the O'Flahertys, and O'Shaughnesses, and the M'Lauchlins, the O'Donnaghans, O'Callaghans, O'Geogaghans, and all the thick blood of the nation; and I myself am an O'Brallaghan, which is the ouldest of them all. Macklin, *Love à la Mode*

**Milk, To.** Slang for to get money out of somebody in an underhand way; also, to plunder one's creditors, and (in mining) to exhaust the veins of ore after selling the mine.

***A land of milk and honey.*** One abounding in all good things, or of extraordinary fertility. Joel 3:18 speaks of 'the mountains flowing with milk and honey'. Figuratively used to denote all the blessings of heaven.

> Jerusalem the golden,
> With milk and honey blest.

***Milk and water.*** Insipid, without energy or character; baby-pap (literature, etc.); also called *Milk for babes*.

***Milk teeth.*** The first, temporary, teeth of a child.

***The milk of human kindness.*** Sympathy, compassion. The phrase is from Shakespeare's *Macbeth*, 1, 4.

> These gentle historians, on the contrary, dip their pens in nothing but the milk of human kindness.
>
> Burke, *Letter to a Noble Lord* (1796)

***So that accounts for the milk in the coconut!*** Said when a sudden discovery of the reason for some action or state of things is made. *No milk in the coconut* means half daft, balmy, crazed; *coconut* here being a synonym for *head*.

***To cry over spilt milk.*** *See* Cry.

**Milksop.** An effeminate person; one without energy, one under petticoat government. The allusion is to young, helpless children, who are fed on pap.

**Milky Way.** A great circle of stars entirely surrounding the heavens, apparently so crowded together that they look to the naked eye like a 'way' or stream of faint 'milky' light. The *Galaxy* or *Via Lactea*.

> A broad and ample road, whose dust is gold
> And pavement stars, as stars to thee appear,
> Seen in the galaxy – that Milky Way,
> Thick, nightly, as a circling zone, thou seest
> Powdered with stars.
>
> Milton, *Paradise Lost*, vii, 577, etc.

**Mill.** To fight, or a fight. It is the same word as the mill that grinds flour (from Lat. *molere*, to grind). Grinding was anciently performed by pulverising with a stone or pounding with the hand. *To mill* is to beat with the fist, as persons used to beat corn with a stone.

***The mill cannot grind with water that is past.*** An old proverb, given in Herbert's *Collection* (1639). It implies both that one must not miss one's opportunities and that it is no good crying over spilt milk.

> And a proverb haunts my mind,
> As a spell in cast;
> 'The mill cannot grind
> With the water that is past.'
>
> Sarah Doudney, *Lesson of the Watermill*

***The mills of God grind slowly.*** Retribution may be delayed, but it is sure to overtake the wicked. The *Adagia* of Erasmus puts it, *Sero molunt deorum molae*, and the sentiment is to be found in many authors, ancient and modern.

> The mills of God grind slowly, yet they grind exceeding small;
> Though with patience He stands waiting, with exactness He grinds all.
>
> Longfellow, *Retribution*

**Millenarians.** *See* Chiliasts.

**Millenial Church.** *See* Shakers.

**Millennium.** A thousand years (Lat., *mille annus*). In Rev. 20:2, it is said that an angel bound Satan a thousand years, and in verse 4 we are told of certain martyrs who will come to life again, and 'reign with Christ a thousand years'. 'This', says St John, 'is the first resurrection'; and this is what is meant by the millennium.

**Miller. *A Joe Miller.*** A stale jest. A certain John Mottley compiled a book of facetiae in 1739, which he, without permission, entitled *Joe Miller's Jests*, from Joseph Miller (1684–1738), a popular comedian of the day who could neither read nor write. A stale jest is still called a 'Joe Miller', implying that it is stolen from Mottley's compilation.

> A man must serve his time to every trade
> Save censure – critics all are ready made,
> Take hackney'd jokes from Miller, got by rote,
> With just enough of learning to misquote ...
> Care not for feeling – pass your proper jest,
> And stand a critic, hated yet caress'd.
>
> Byron, *English Bards and Scotch Reviewers*

***More water glideth by the mill than wots the miller of*** (*Titus Andronicus*, 2, 1). Many things are done in a house which the master and mistress never dream of.

***To drown the miller.*** To put too much water into spirits, or tea. The idea is that the supply of water is so great that even the miller, who uses a water wheel, is drowned with it.

***To give one the miller.*** To engage one in conversation till enough people have gathered round to set upon the victim with stones, dirt, garbage, and all the arms which haste supplies a mob with (*see* Mill).

***Miller's thumb.*** A small freshwater fish four or five inches long, *Cottus gobio*, called the *Bullhead*, from its large head.

***To put the miller's eye out.*** To make broth or pudding so thin that even a miller's eye would be puzzled to find the flour.

Lumps of unleavened flour in bread are sometimes called *miller's eyes*.

**Milliner.** A corruption of *Milaner*; so called from Milan, in Italy, which at one time gave the law to Europe in all matters of taste, dress, and elegance.

Nowadays one nearly always means a woman when one speaks of a milliner, but it was not always so; Ben Jonson, in *Every Man in his Humour*, i, 3, speaks of a 'milliner's wife', and the French have still *une modiste* and *un modiste*.

***Man-milliner.*** An effeminate one, or one who busies himself over trifles.

> The Morning Herald sheds tears of joy over the fashionable virtues of the rising generation, and finds that we shall make better man-milliners, better lacqueys, and better courtiers than ever.
>
> Hazlitt, *Political Essays* (1814)

**Millstone. *Hard as the nether millstone.*** Unfeeling, obdurate. The lower or 'nether' of the two millstones is firmly fixed and very hard; the upper stone revolves round it on a shaft, and the corn, running down a tube inserted in the upper stone, is ground by the motion of the upper stone round the lower one.

***The millstones of Montisci.*** They produce flour of themselves, whence the proverb, 'Grace comes from God, but millstones from Montisci'. (Boccaccio, *Decameron*, day viii, novel 3).

***To look*** (or ***see***) ***through a millstone.*** To be wonderfully sharpsighted.

> Then ... since your eies are so sharp that you can not only looke through a milstone, but cleane through the minde ... Lyly, *Euphues*

***To weep millstones.*** Not weep at all.

> Bid Glos'ter think on this, and he will weep –
> Aye, millstones, as he lessoned us to weep.
>
> Shakespeare, *Richard III*, 1, 6

**Millwood, Sarah.** *See* Barnwell.

**Milo.** A celebrated Greek athlete of Crotona in the late 6th cent. BC. It is said that he carried through the stadium at Olympia a heifer four years old, and ate the whole of it afterwards. When old he attempted to tear in two an oak tree, but the parts closed upon his hands, and while held fast he was devoured by wolves. *See* Polydamus.

**Milton.** 'Milton', says Dryden, in the preface to his *Fables*, 'was the poetical son of Spenser ... Milton has acknowledged to me that Spenser was his original.'

***Milton of Germany.*** Friedrich G. Klopstock (1724–1803), author of *The Messiah*. Coleridge says he is 'a very German Milton indeed'.

**Mimir.** The Scandinavian god of wisdom, a water-demon, and one of the most celebrated of the giants. The Vanir, with whom he was left as a hostage, cut off his head. Odin embalmed it by his magic art, pronounced over it mystic runes, and ever after consulted it on critical occasions. Mimir dwelt under the roof of Yggdrasil (*q.v.*), where was Mimir's Well (*Mimisbrunnr*), in which all wisdom lay concealed, and from which Mimir drank with the horn Gjallar. Odin gave one of his eyes to be permitted to drink of its waters, and thereby became the wisest of the gods.

**Mimosa.** Niebuhr says the Mimosa 'droops its branches whenever anyone approaches it, seeming to salute those who retire under its shade'. The name reflects this notion, as the plant was thought to *mimic* the motions of animals, as does the Sensitive Plant.

**Mince Pies** at Christmas time are said to have been emblematical of the manger in which our Saviour was laid. The paste over the 'offering' was made in form of a *cratch* or *hay-rack*. Southey speaks of –

> Old bridges dangerously narrow, and angles in them like the corners of an English mince-pie, for the foot-passengers to take shelter in.
>
> *Esprinella's Letters*, III, 384 (1807)

***Mince pies.*** Rhyming slang for 'the eyes'.

**Mincemeat. *To make mincemeat of.*** Utterly to demolish; to shatter to pieces. Mincemeat is meat minced, i.e. cut up very fine.

**Mincing Lane** (London). Called in the 13th century *Menechinelane*, *Monechenelane*, etc., and in the time of Henry VIII *Mynchyn Lane*. The name is from A.S. *mynechenn*, a nun (fem. of *munuc*, monk), and the street is probably so called from the tenements held there by the nuns of St Helen's, in Bishopsgate Street.

**Mind. *Mind your own business; mind your eye***, etc. *See these words*.

***To have a mind for it.*** To desire to possess it; to wish for it. Mind = desire, intention, is by no means uncommon; 'I mind to tell him plainly what I think.' (2 *Henry VI*, 4, 1.) 'I shortly mind to leave you.' (2 *Henry VI*, 4, 1.)

**Minden Boys.** The 20th Foot, now the Lancashire Fusiliers; so called from their noted bravery at Minden, Prussia, Aug. 1st, 1759.

**Minerva.** The Roman goddess of wisdom and patroness of the arts and trades, fabled to have sprung, with a tremendous battle-cry, fully armed from the head of Jupiter. She is identified with the Greek Athene, and was one of the three chief deities, the others being Jupiter and Juno. She is represented as grave and majestic, clad in a helmet and with drapery over a coat of mail, and bearing the aegis on her breast. The most famous statue of this goddess was by Phidias, and was anciently one of the Seven Wonders of the World.

***Invita Minerva.*** Against the grain. Thus, Charles Kean acted comedy *invita Minerva*, his *forte* lying another way. Sir Philip Sidney attempted the Horatian metres in English verse *invita Minerva*. The phrase is from Horace's *Ars Poetica*, l. 385 – *Tu nihil invita dices faciesve Minerva* (Beware of attempting anything for which nature has not fitted you).

***The Minerva Press.*** A printing establishment in Leadenhall Street, London, famous in the late 18th century for its trashy, ultra-sentimental novels, which were characterised by complicated plots, and the labyrinths of difficulties into which the hero and heroine got involved before they could be married.

**Miniature.** Originally, a rubrication or a small painting in an illuminated MS, which was done with *minium* or red lead. Hence, the word came to express any small portrait or picture on vellum or ivory; but it is in no way connected with the Latin *minor* or *minimus*.

**Minims** (Lat. *Fratres Minimi*, least of the brethren). A term of self-abasement assumed by an order of monks founded by St Francis of Paula, in 1453; they went barefooted, and wore a coarse, black woollen stuff, fastened with a woollen girdle, which they never put off, day or night. The order of St Francis of Assisi had already engrossed the 'humble' title of *Fratres Minores* (inferior brothers). The superior of the minims is called *corrector*.

**Minister.** Literally, an inferior person, in opposition to *magister*, a superior. One is connected with the Latin *minus*, and the other with *magis*. Our Lord says, 'Whosoever will be great among you, let him be your minister', where the antithesis is well preserved; and Gibbon mentions –

> a multitude of cooks, and inferior ministers, employed in the service of the kitchens.
>
> *Decline and Fall*, ch. xxxi

The minister of a church is a man who *serves* the parish or congregation; and the minister of the Crown is the sovereign's or state's servant.

Florimond de Remond, speaking of Albert Babinot, one of the disciples of Calvin, says, 'He was a student of the Institutes, read at the hall of the Equity school in Poitiers, and was called *la Ministerie*.' Calvin, in allusion thereto, used to call him 'Mr Minister', whence not only Babinot but all the other clergy of the Calvinistic Church were called *ministers*.

**Minnehaha** (*Laughing-water*). The lovely daughter of the old arrow-maker of the Dacotahs, and wife of Hiawatha in Longfellow's poem. She died of famine.

**Minnesingers.** Minstrels. The lyric poets of 12th to 14th century Germany were so called, because the subject of their lyrics was *minne-sang* (love-ditty). The chief *minnesingers* were Heinrich von Ofterdingen, Wolfram von Eschenbach, Walther von der Vogelheide, and (the earliest) Heinrich von Veldeke. All of them were men of noble birth, and they were succeeded by the Meistersingers (*q.v.*).

**Minoan.** *See* Minos.

**Minories** (London). So called from the Abbey of the *Minoresses* of St Mary of the Order of St Clare which, till the Dissolution of the Monasteries, stood on the site. The street leads from Aldgate High Street to Tower Hill, and seems to have got this name about the end of the 16th century.

**Minorites,** or **Minors.** *See* Franciscans.

**Minos.** A legendary king and lawgiver of Crete, made at death supreme judge of the lower world, before whom all the dead appeared to give an account of their stewardship, and to receive the reward of their deeds. He was the husband of Pasiphae and the owner of the labyrinth constructed by Daedalus. From his name we have the adjective *Minoan*, pertaining to Crete: the *Minoan period* is the Cretan bronze age, roughly about 2500–1200 BC.

**Minotaur.** A mythical monster with the head of a bull and the body of a man, fabled to have been the offspring of Pasiphae and a bull that was sent to her by Poseidon. Minos (*q.v.*) kept it in his labyrinth and fed it on human flesh, 7 youths and 7 maidens being sent as tribute from Athens every year for the purpose. Theseus slew this monster.

**Minstrel.** Originally, one who had some official duty to perform (Lat. *ministerialis*), but quite early in the Middle Ages restricted to one whose duty it was to entertain his employer with music, story-telling, juggling, etc.; hence a travelling gleeman and entertainer, such, for instance, as the modern *nigger minstrels*.

**Mint.** The name of the herb is from Lat. *menth* (Gr. *mintha*), so called from Minthe, daughter of

Cocytus, and a favourite of Pluto. This nymph was metamorphosed by Pluto's wife (Proserpine) out of jealousy, into the herb called after her name. The fable means that mint is a capital medicine. Minthe was a favourite of Pluto, or death, that is, was sick and on the point of death; but was changed into the herb mint, that is, was cured thereby.

> Could Pluto's queen, with jealous fury storm
> And Minthe to a fragrant herb transform? Ovid

***The Mint,*** a place where money is coined, gets its name from A.S. *mynet*, representing Lat. *moneta*, money.

**Minute.** A minute of time (one-sixtieth part of an hour) is so called from the mediaeval Latin *pars minuta prima*, which, in the old system of sexagesimal fractions, denoted *one-sixtieth* part of the unit. In the same way, in Geometry, etc., a minute is *one-sixtieth* part of a degree.

A *minute* of a speech, meeting, etc., is a rough draft taken down in *minute* or small writing, to be afterwards *engrossed*, or written larger. It is from the Fr. *minute*.

***Minute gun.*** A signal of distress at sea, or a gun fired at the death of a distinguished individual; so called because a minute elapses between the discharges.

**Miolnir** (i.e. lightning). The magic hammer of Thor (*q.v.*). It was fashioned by the dwarfs, and Thor used it in peace to bless and in war to shatter. It would never miss whatever it was thrown at, always returned to the owner of its own accord, and became so small when not in use that it could be put into Thor's pocket.

**Miramolin.** The title in the Middle Ages of the Emperor of Morocco.

**Mirror.** ***Alasnam's mirror.*** The 'touchstone of virtue', showed if the lady beloved was chaste as well as beautiful. (*Arabian Nights; Prince Zeyn Alasnam.*)

***Cambuscan's mirror.*** Sent to Cambuscan by the King of Araby and Ind; it warned of the approach of ill fortune, and told if love was returned. (Chaucer, *Canterbury Tales*; *The Squire's Tale.*)

***Lao's mirror*** reflected the mind and its thoughts, as an ordinary mirror reflects the outward seeming. (Goldsmith, *Citizen of the World*, xlv.)

***Merlin's magic mirror,*** given by Merlin to King Ryence. It informed the king of treason, secret plots, and projected invasions. (Spenser, *Faërie Queene*, iii, 2.)

***Reynard's wonderful mirror.*** This mirror existed only in the brain of Master Fox; he told the queen lion that whoever looked in it could see what was done a mile off. The wood of the frame was not subject to decay, being made of the same block as King Crampart's magic horse. (*Reynard the Fox*, ch. xii.)

***Vulcan's mirror*** showed the past, the present, and the future. Sir John Davies tells us that Cupid gave it to Antinous, and Antinous gave it to Penelope, who saw therein 'the court of Queen Elizabeth'.

***The Mirror for Magistrates.*** A large collection of poems, published 1555–59, by William Baldwin, George Ferrers, and many others, with an 'Induction' (1563) by Thomas Sackville. It contained in metrical form biographical accounts of the Falls of Princes. It was much extended in four later editions up to 1587.

***The Mirror of Human Salvation.*** *See* Speculum, etc.

***The Mirror of Knighthood.*** One of the books in Don Quixote's library, a Spanish romance (*Cavallero del Febo*, 'The Knight of the Sun'), one of the Amadis group. It was at one time very popular.

> The barber, taking another book, said, 'This is the *Mirror of Knighthood*.' Pt 1, bk i, 6

Butler calls *Hudibras* 'the Mirror of Knighthood' (bk i, 15).

**Mirza** (Pers., royal prince). The term is used in two ways by the Persians; when *prefixed* to a surname it is simply a title of honour; but when *annexed* to the surname, it means a prince of the blood royal.

**Miscreant** means a false believer. (Fr., *mis-créance*.) A term first applied to the Mohammedans, who, in return, call Christians *infidels*, and associate with the word all that we mean by 'miscreants'.

**Mise** (O.Fr., expenses). Means an honorarium, especially that given by the people of Wales to a new Prince of Wales on his entrance upon his principality, or by the people of the county palatine of Chester on change of an Earl (*note*, the Prince of Wales is always Earl of Chester). At Chester a mise-book is kept, in which every town and village is rated to this honorarium.

Littleton (*Dict.*) says the usual sum is £500.

***Mise-en-scène*** (Fr., setting on stage). The stage setting of a play, including the scenery, properties, etc., and the general arrangement of the piece. Also used metaphorically.

**Misers.** The most renowned are:

*Baron Aguilar* or Ephraim Lopes Pereira d'Aguilar (1740–1802), born at Vienna and died at Islington, worth £200,000.

*Daniel Dancer* (1716–94). His sister lived with him, and was a similar character, but died before him, and he left his wealth to the widow of Sir Henry Tempest, who nursed him in his last illness.

*Sir Harvey Elwes*, who died worth £250,000, but never spent more than £110 a year. His sister-in-law inherited £100,000, but actually starved herself to death, and her son *John* (1714–89), M.P., an eminent brewer in Southwark, never bought any clothes, never suffered his shoes to be cleaned, and grudged every penny spent in food.

*Thomas Guy*, founder of Guy's Hospital (*q.v.*).

*William Jennings* (1701–97), a neighbour and friend of Elwes, died worth £200,000. *See* Harpagon.

**Misère** (Fr., misery, poverty). In solo whist and some other card games the declaration made when the caller undertakes to lose every trick.

**Miserere.** The fifty-first psalm is so called because its opening words are *Miserere mei Deus* (Have mercy upon me, O God. *See* Neck-verse.) One of the evening services of Lent is called *miserere*, because this penitential psalm is sung, after which a sermon is delivered. The under side of a folding seat in choir-stalls is called a *miserere*, or, more properly, a *misericord*; when turned up it forms a ledge-seat sufficient to rest the aged in a kneeling position.

**Misguggling.** *See* Mashackering.

**Mishna** (Heb., repetition or instruction). The collection of moral precepts, traditions, etc., forming the basis of the Talmud; the second or oral law (*see* Gemara). It is divided into six parts: (1) agriculture; (2) Sabbaths, fasts, and festivals; (3) marriage and divorce; (4) civil and penal laws; (5) sacrifices; (6) holy persons and things.

**Misnomers.** In English nomenclature we have many words and short phrases that can be called 'misnomers'; some of these have arisen through pure ignorance (and when once a useful word has been adopted and taken to our bosoms nothing – not even conviction of etymological errors – will eradicate it), some through confusion of ideas or the taking of one thing for another, and some through the changes that time brings about. *Catgut*, for instance, was in all probability, at one time made from the intestines of a *cat*, and now that sheep, horses, asses, etc., but never *cats*, are used for the purpose the name still remains.

A large number of these 'misnomers' will be found scattered throughout this book (*see especially* Cleopatra's Needle, German Silver, Honeydew, Humble Pie, Indians (American), Jerusalem Artichoke, Meerschaum, Mother of Pearl, Pompey's Pillar, Sand-blind, Slug-horn, Ventriloquism, Wolf's-bane, and Wormwood); and we give a few more below:

*Black beetles* are neither black nor beetles; their alternative name, *cockroach*, is not much better, for their connection with *cocks* or with *roaches* is still less obvious than with beetles!

*Blacklead* is plumbago or graphite, a form of carbon, and has no lead in its composition. *See under* Lead.

*Blind worms* are no more blind than *moles* are; they have very quick and brilliant eyes, though somewhat small.

*Brazilian grass* does not come from Brazil or even grow in Brazil, nor is it a grass. It consists of strips of a palm-leaf (*Chamaerops argentea*), and is chiefly imported from Cuba.

*Burgundy pitch* is not pitch, nor is it manufactured or exported from Burgundy. The best is a resinous substance prepared from common frankincense, and brought from Hamburg; but by far the larger quantity is a mixture of resin and palm oil.

*China*, as a name for porcelain, gives rise to the contradictory expressions British china, Sèvres china, Dresden china, Dutch china, Chelsea china, etc.; like wooden or iron milestones, brass shoe-horns, coppers for our bronze coinage, etc.

*Dutch clocks* are not of Dutch but German (*Deutsch*) manufacture.

*Elements.* Fire, air, earth, and water, still often called 'the four elements', are not elements at all.

*Forlorn hope* (*q.v.*) is not etymologically connected with *hope*, though the term is usually employed in connection with almost hopeless enterprises.

*Galvanised iron* is not galvanised. It is simply iron coated with zinc, and this is done by dipping the iron into molten zinc.

*Guernsey lily* (*Nerine* or *Imbrofia sarniensis*) is not a native of Guernsey but of Japan and South Africa. It was discovered by Kaempfer in Japan, and the ship which was bringing specimens of the new plant to Europe was wrecked on the coast of Guernsey; some of the bulbs that were washed ashore took root and germinated, hence the misnomer.

*Guinea-pigs* (*q.v.*) have no connection with the pig family, nor do they come from Guinea.

*Honeysuckle.* So named because of the old but entirely erroneous idea that bees extracted honey therefrom. The honeysuckle is useless to the bee.

*Indian ink* comes from China, not from India.

*Rice paper* is not made from rice, but from the pith of the Formosan plant, *Aralia papyrifera*, or hollow plant, so called because it is hollow when the pith has been pushed out.

*Running the gauntlet* (*see* Gauntlet) has nothing to do with gauntlets (gloves), though these may be used in the process.

*Salt of lemon* is in reality potassium acid oxalate, or potassium quadroxalate.

*Silver paper*, in which chocolates, etc., are sometimes wrapped, is not, of course, made from silver. It is usually composed of tin-foil.

*Slow-worm.* Not so called because it is *slow*; the first syllable is corrupted from slay, and it was called the *slay-worm* (= serpent) from the idea that this perfectly harmless creature was venomous.

*Titmouse.* Nothing to do with *mouse*, though the erroneous plural – *titmice* – has now probably 'come to stay'. The second syllable represents A.S. *māse*, used of several small birds. Tit is Scandinavian, and also implies 'small', as in *titbit*.

*Tonquin beans.* A geographical blunder, for they are the seeds, the *Dipteryx odorata*, from Tonka, in Guiana, not Tonquin, in Asia.

*Turkeys* do not come from Turkey, but North America, through Spain, or India. The French call them 'din-don', i.e. *d'Inde* or *coq d'Inde*, a term equally incorrect.

*Turkey rhubarb* neither grows in Turkey, nor is it imported from Turkey. It grows in the great mountain chain between Tartary and Siberia, and is a Russian monopoly.

*Turkish baths* are not of Turkish origin.

*Well-beloved.* Louis XV. A most inappropriate title for this most detestable and detested of all kings.

*Whalebone* (*q.v.*) is no bone at all, nor does it possess any properties of bone. It is a substance attached to the upper jaw of the whale, and serves to strain the water which the creature takes up in large mouthfuls.

**Misprision.** (Fr. *mépris*). Concealment, neglect of; in law, an offence bordering on a capital offence.

***Misprision of felony.*** Neglecting to reveal a felony when known.

***Misprision of treason.*** Neglecting to disclose or purposely concealing a treasonable design.

**Misrule, Feast of.** *See* King of Misrule.

**Miss, Mistress, Mrs** (masteress, lady-master). Miss used to be written Mis, and is the first syllable of Mistress; Mrs is the contraction of Mistress, called Mis'ess. Even in the reign of George II unmarried ladies used to be styled Mrs; as, Mrs Lepel, Mrs Bellenden, Mrs Blount, all unmarried ladies. (*See* Pope's *Letters*).

Early in Charles II's reign, Evelyn tells us that 'lewd women began to be styled Misse' nowadays, and certainly since Elizabethan times, a woman who lives with a man as his wife but without being so is termed his 'mistress'.

***Mistress Roper.*** The Marines, or any one of them; so called by the regular sailors, because they handle the ropes like girls, not being used to them.

***The mistress of the night.*** The tuberose is so called because it emits its strongest fragrance after sunset.

In the language of flowers, the tuberose signifies 'the pleasures of love'.

***The mistress of the world.*** Ancient Rome was so called, because all the known world gave it allegiance.

***To kiss the mistress.*** To make a good hit, to shoot right into the eye of the target; in bowls to graze another bowl with your own; the *Jack* used to be called the 'mistress', and when one ball just touches another it is said 'to kiss it'.

> Rub on, and kiss the mistress.
>
> Shakespeare, *Troilus and Cressida*, 3, 2

**Miss.** To fail to hit, or – in such phrases as *I miss you now you are gone* – to lack, to feel the want of.

***A miss is as good as a mile.*** A failure is a failure be it ever so little, and is no more be it ever so great; a narrow escape is an escape, and a more easy one is no more. An old form of the phrase was *An inch in a miss is as good as an ell.*

> He was very near being a poet – but a miss is as good as a mile, and he always fell short of the mark.
>
> Scott, *Journal*, 3 Dec., 1825

***The missing link.*** A popular term for the hypothetical being that is supposed, according to the theory of evolution, to bridge the gap between man and the anthropoid apes. Haeckel held it to be *Pithecanthropus erectus*; but scientists are not agreed, either on this or on the number of 'missing links' there may be. Professor Woodward, in a lecture on the Rhodesian skull discovered at Broken Hill in 1921, said –

> The Rhodesian man was one of the links in the chain of which many species would be found. It would be a long time before a connecting series of missing links would be discovered which would be convincing.

**Mississippi Bubble.** The French 'South Sea Scheme', and equally disastrous. It was projected by the Scots financier, John Law (1671–1729), and had for its object the payment of the National Debt of France, which amounted to 208 millions sterling, on being granted the exclusive trade of Louisiana, on the banks of the Mississippi. Inaugurated in 1717, it was taken up by the French Government, but in 1720 the 'bubble' burst, France was almost ruined, Law fled to Russia, and his estates were confiscated.

**Mistletoe** (A.S. *mistiltán; mistil* being both basil and mistletoe, and *tán*, a twig). The plant grows as a parasite on various trees, especially the apple tree, and was held in great veneration by the Druids when found on the oak. Shakespeare calls it 'the *baleful* mistletoe' (*Titus Andronicus*, 2, 3), perhaps in allusion to the Scandinavian legend that it was with an arrow made of mistletoe that Balder (*q.v.*) was slain, but probably with reference either to the popular but erroneous notion that mistletoe berries are poisonous, or to the connection of the plant with the human sacrifices of the Druids. It is in all probability for this latter reason that mistletoe is rigorously excluded from church decorations.

***Kissing under the mistletoe.*** An English Christmas-time custom, dating back at least to the early 17th century. The correct procedure, now rarely observed, is that as the young man kisses a girl under the mistletoe he should pluck a berry, and that when the last berry is gone there should be no more kissing.

***The Mistletoe Bough.*** This old song is about the daughter of a Lord Lovel who, on her wedding-day, was playing at hide and seek, and selected an old oak chest for her hiding-place. The chest closed with a spring lock, and many years after her skeleton was discovered. Rogers introduces the legend in his *Italy* (Pt i, 18) –

> The bride was Ginevra, only child of Orsini, 'an indulgent father'. The bridegroom was Francesco Doria, 'her playmate from her birth, and her first love'. The chest in which she was buried alive in her bridal dress was an heirloom, 'richly carved by Antony of Trent, with Scripture stories from the life of Christ'. It came from Venice, and had 'held the ducal robes of some old ancestor'. Francesco, weary of his life, flew to Venice, and 'flung his life away in battle with the Turk'. Orsini went mad, and spent the live-long day 'wandering as in quest of something, something he could not find'. Fifty years afterwards the chest was removed by strangers and the sketeton discovered.

A similar narrative is given by Collet in his *Relics of Literature*, and another is among the *Causes Célèbres*.

Marwell Old Hall, once the residence of the Seymour, and afterwards of the Dacre family, has a similar tradition attached to it, and (according to the *Post Office Directory*) 'the very chest became the property of the Rev. J. Haygarth, a rector of Upham'.

**Mistpoeffers.** *See* Barisal Guns.

**Mistral, The.** A violent north-west wind blowing down the Gulf of Lyons; felt particularly at Marseilles and the south-east of France.

**Mistress.** *See* Miss.

**Mithra** or **Mithras.** The god of light of the ancient Persians, one of their chief deities, and the ruler of the universe. Sometimes used as a synonym for the sun. The word means *friend*, and this deity is so called because he befriends man in this life, and protects him against evil spirits after death. He is represented as a young man with a Phrygian cap, a tunic, a mantle on his left shoulder, and plunging a sword into the neck of a bull (*see Thebais*, i). The Mithraic rites –

> have been maintained by a constant tradition, with their penances and tests of the courage of the candidate for admission, through the Secret Societies of the Middle Ages and the Rosicrucians, down to the modern faint reflex of the latter, the Freemasons.
>
> Knight, *Symbolical Language*

Sir Thomas More called the Supreme Being of his *Utopia* 'Mithra'.

**Mithridate.** A confection named from Mithridates IV, King of Pontus and Bithynia (d. about 63 BC), who is said to have made himself immune from poisons by the constant use of antidotes. It was supposed to be an antidote to poison, and contained seventy-two ingredients.

> What brave spirit could be content to sit in his shop … selling Mithridatum and dragon's water to infected houses?
>
> Beaumont and Fletcher, *Knight of the Burning Pestle* (1608)

**Mitre** (Gr. and Lat. *mitra*, a headband, turban). The episcopal mitre symbolises the cloven tongues of fire which descended on the apostles on the day of Pentecost (Acts 2:1–12). Dean Stanley tells us that the cleft represents the crease made when the mitre is folded and carried under the arm, like an opera hat.

***The Mitre Tavern.*** A place of resort in the time of Shakespeare; it was in Mitre Court, leading south of Cheapside, and was in existence from before 1475 till the Great Fire (1666), when it was destroyed and not rebuilt. There was another tavern of the same name in Fleet Street (*see* Barrey's *Ram Alley*, v, 1611).

**Mitten. *To give one the mitten*.** To reject a sweetheart; to jilt. Possibly with punning allusion to Lat. *mitto*, to send (about your business), whence dismissal; to get your dismissal.

> There is a young lady I have set my heart on, though whether she is going to give me hern, or give me the mitten I ain't quite satisfied.
>
> Sam Slick, *Human Nature*, p. 90

**Mittimus** (Lat., we send). A command in writing to a jailer, to keep the person named in safe custody. Also a writ for removing a record from one court to another, so called from the first word of the writ.

**Mitton. *The Chapter of Mitton*.** So the battle of Mitton was called, because so many priests took part therein. It was fought in 1319, and the Scots defeated the forces of the Archbishop of York.

> So many priests took part in the fight that the Scots called it the Chapter of Mitton – a meeting of the clergymen belonging to a cathedral, being called a chapter.
>
> Scott, *Tales of a Grandfather*, x

**Mizentop, maintop, foretop.** A 'top' is a platform fixed over the head of a lower mast, resting on the trestle trees, to spread the rigging of the topmast. The mizenmast is the aftermost mast of a ship; the foremast is in the forward part of a ship; the mainmast is between these two.

> He was put into the mizentop, and served three years in the West Indies; then he was transferred to the maintop, and served five years in the Mediterranean; and then he was made captain of the foretop, and served six years in the East Indies; and at last he was rated captain's coxswain in the *Druid* frigate.
>
> Capt. Marryat, *Poor Jack*, ch. i

**Mjólnir.** *See* Miolnir.

**Mnemosyne.** Goddess of memory and mother by Zeus of the nine Muses of *Greek mythology*. She was the daughter of Heaven and Earth (Uranus and Ge).

> To the Immortals every one
> A portion was assigned of all that is;
> But chief Mnemosyne did Maia's son
> Clothe in the light of his loud melodies.
>
> Shelley, *Homer's Hymn to Mercury*, lxxiii

**Moabite Stone, The.** An ancient *stele*, bearing the oldest extant Semitic inscription, now in the Louvre, Paris. The inscription, consisting of thirty-four lines in Hebrew-Phoenician characters, gives an account of the war of Mesha, King of Moab, who reigned about 850 BC, against Omri, Ahab, and other kings of Israel (*see* 2 Kings, 3). Mesha sacrificed his eldest son on the city wall in view of the invading Israelites. The stone was discovered by the Rev. F. Klein at Dibhan in 1868, and is 3 ft 10 in. high, 2 ft broad and 14½ in. thick. The Arabs resented its removal, and splintered it into fragments, but it has been restored.

**Moakkibat.** A class of angels, according to *Mohammedan mythology*, two of whom attend every child of Adam from the cradle to the grave. At sunset they fly up with the record of the deeds done since sunrise. Every good deed is entered ten times by the recording angel on the credit or right side of his ledger, but when an evil deed is reported the angel waits seven hours, 'if haply in that time the evil-doer may repent'. (The Koran.)

**Moat, Battle of the.** A battle between Mahomet and Abu Sofian (chief of the Koreishites) before Medina; so called because the prophet had a moat dug before the city to keep off the invaders, and in it much of the fighting took place.

**Mob.** A contraction of the Latin *mobile vulgus* (the fickle crowd). The term was first applied to the people by the members of the Green-ribbon Club, in the reign of Charles II. (*Northern Examiner*, p. 574.)

**Mob-cap.** A cap worn indoors by women and useful for concealing hair that is not yet 'done'. It was formerly called *mab-cap*, from the old verb *mab*, to dress untidily.

**Mock-beggar Hall** or **Manor.** A grand, ostentatious house, where no hospitality is afforded, neither is any charity given.

> No times observed, nor charitable lawes,
> The poor receive their answer from the dawes
> Who, in their cawing language, call it plaine
> *Mock-begger Manour*, for they come in vaine.
>
> Taylor, *The Water Cormorant* (1622)

**Mockery. *'It will be a delusion, a mockery, and a snare.'*** Thomas, Lord Denman, in his judgment on the case of The Queen *v.* O'Connell (1844).

**Modality,** in scholastic philosophy, means the *mode* in which anything exists. Kant divides our judgment into three modalities: (1) *Problematic*, touching possible events; (2) *Assertoric*, touching real events; (3) *Apodictic*, touching necessary events.

**Modo.** The fiend mentioned in *King Lear* (4, 1) as he who urges to murder; one of the five that possessed 'Poor Tom'. *See* Mahu.

**Modred.** One of the Knights of the Round Table in Arthurian romance, nephew and betrayer of King Arthur. He is represented as the treacherous knight. He revolted from the king, whose wife he seduced, was mortally wounded in the battle of Camlan, in Cornwall, and was buried in the island of Avalon.

In Tennyson's *Guinevere* (*Idylls of the King*) Sir Modred sows discord amongst the Knights of the Round Table, and tampered with the 'lords of the White Horse', the brood that Hengist left. When the king went to punish Sir Lancelot for his guilty relationship with the queen, he left Sir Modred in charge of the kingdom. Modred raised a revolt, and the king was slain in his attempt to quash it.

**Mods.** In Oxford a contracted form of moderations. The three necessary examinations in Oxford are the Smalls, the Mods, and the Greats. No one can take a class till he has passed the Mods.

> While I was reading for Mods I was not so unsettled in my mind.
>
> Grant Allen, *The Backslider*, Pt iii

**Modus operandi** (Lat.). The mode of operation; the way in which a thing is done or should be done.

**Modus vivendi** (Lat., way of living). A mutual arrangement whereby persons not at the time being on friendly terms can be induced to live together in harmony. The term may be applied to individuals, to societies, or to peoples.

**Mofussil** (East Indies). The subordinate divisions of a district; the rural districts as apart from the chief city or seat of government, which is called the *sudder*; provincial.

> To tell a man that fatal charges have been laid against him, and refuse him an opportunity for explanation, this is not even Mofussil justice.
>
> *The Times*

**Mogul.** ***The Mogul Empire.*** The Mohammedan-Tatar Empire in India which began in 1526 with Baber, great-grandson of Timur, or Tamerlane, and split up after the death of Aurungzebe in 1707, the power passing to the British and the Mahrattas. The Emperor was known as the *Great* or *Grand Mogul*; besides those mentioned, Akbar, Jahangir, and Shah Jehan are the most noteworthy.

***Mogul cards.*** The best quality playing-cards were so called because the wrapper, or the 'duty card' (cards are subject to excise duty) was decorated with a representation of the Great Mogul. Inferior cards were called 'Harrys', 'Highlanders', and 'Merry Andrews' for a similar reason.

**Mohair** (Probably the Arabic *mukhayyar*, goat's-hair cloth). It is the hair of the Angora goat, introduced into Spain by the Moors, and thence brought into Germany.

**Mohammed.** *See* Mahomet.

**Mohel.** The official at a Jewish synagogue who performs the operation in the rite of circumcision.

**Mohocks.** A class of ruffians who in the 18th century infested the streets of London. So called from the Indian Mohawks. One of their 'new inventions' was to roll persons down Snow Hill in a tub; another was to overturn coaches on rubbish-heaps. (*See* Gay, *Trivia*, iii.)

A vivid picture of the misdoings in the streets of London by these and other brawlers is given in *The Spectator*, No. 324.

> You sent your Mohocks next abroad,
> With razors armed, and knives;
> Who on night-walkers made inroad,
> And scared our maids and wives;
> They scared the watch, and windows broke …
>
> *Plot upon Plot* (about 1713)

**Molinism.** The system of grace and election taught by Louis Molina, the Spanish Jesuit (1535–1600).

> The Pope's great self–Innocent by name …
> 'Twas he who first bade leave those souls in peace,
> Those Jansenists, renicknamed Molinists, …
> 'Leave them alone,' bade he, 'those Molinists!
> Who may have other light than we perceive,
> Or why is it the whole world hates them thus?'
>
> Browning, *The Ring and the Book*, 1, 300–17

His doctrine was that grace is a free gift to all, but that the consent of the will must be present before that grace can be effective.

**Moll Cutpurse.** *See* Cutpurse.

**Moll Thomson's Mark.** ***Take away this bottle, it has Moll Thomson's mark on it.*** Moll Thomson is M.T. (*empty*).

**Molloch, May,** or **The Maid of the Hairy Arms.** An elf of folklore who mingles in ordinary sports, and will even direct the master of the house how to play dominoes or draughts. Like the White Lady of Avenel, May Molloch is a sort of banshee.

**Molly.** ***He's a regular Molly.*** Said of a man or big boy who interferes with women's work, such as kitchen business, dressmaking, personal decoration, and so on. *Cp.* Betty.

**Molly Coddle.** A pampered creature, afraid that the winds of heaven should visit him too roughly; a Molly (*q.v.*); not a valetudinarian, but ever fearing lest he should be so.

**Molly Maguires.** An Irish secret society organised in 1843. Stout, active young Irishmen, dressed up in women's clothes, blackened faces, and otherwise disguised, to surprise those employed to enforce the payment of rents. Their victims were ducked in bog-holes, and many were beaten most unmercifully.

A similar secret society in the mining districts of Pennsylvania was (about 1877) known by the same name.

> The judge who tried the murderer was elected by the Molly Maguires; the jurors who assisted him were themselves Molly Maguires. A score of Molly Maguires came forward to swear that the assassin was sixty miles from the spot on which he had been seen to fire at William Dunn … and the jurors returned a verdict of Not Guilty.
>
> W. Hepworth Dixon, *New America*, ii, 28

**Molly Mog.** This celebrated beauty was an innkeeper's daughter, at Oakingham, Berks. She was the toast of the gay sparks of the first half of the 18th century, and died unmarried in 1766, at the age of sixty-seven. Gay has a ballad on this *Fair Maid of the Inn*, in which the 'swain' alluded to is Mr Standen, of Arborfield, who died in 1730. It is said that Molly's sister Sally was the greater beauty. A portrait of Gay still hangs in the inn.

**Molmutius** or **Mulmutius.** *See* Mulmutine Laws.

**Moloch.** Any influence which demands from us the sacrifice of what we hold most dear. Thus, *war* is a Moloch, *king mob* is a Moloch, the *guillotine* was the Moloch of the French Revolution, etc. The allusion is to the god of the Ammonites, to whom children were 'made to pass through the fire' in sacrifice (*see* 2 Kings 23:10). Milton says he was worshipped in Rabba, in Argob, and Basan, to the stream of utmost Arnon. (*Paradise Lost*, i, 392–398.)

**Moly.** The mythical herb given, according to Homer, by Hermes to Ulysses as an antidote against the sorceries of Circe.

> Black was the root, but milky white the flower,
> Moly the name, to mortals hard to find.
>
> Pope's *Odyssey*, x, 365

> That moly
> That Hermes once to wise Ulysses gave.
>
> Milton, *Comus*, 655

The name is given to a number of plants, especially of the *Allium* (garlic) family, as the wild garlic, the Indian moly, the moly of Hungary, serpent's moly, the yellow moly, Spanish purple moly, Spanish silver-capped moly, and Dioscorides' moly.

They all flower in May, except 'the sweet moly of Montpelier', which blossoms in September.

**Momiers** (Fr., men of mummery). The French nickname for an evangelical party of Switzerland, somewhat resembling our Methodists. They arose in 1818, and made way both in Germany and France.

**Momus.** One who carps at everything. Momus, the sleepy god of the Greeks, son of Nox (Night), was always railing and carping.

> Momus, being asked to pass judgment on the relative mrits of Neptune, Vulcan, and Minerva, railed at them all. He said the horns of a bull ought to have been placed in the shoulders, where they would have been of much greater force; as for man, he said Jupiter ought to have made him with a window in his breast, whereby his real thoughts might be revealed.

Hence Byron's –

> Were Momus' lattice in our breasts …
>
> *Werner*, iii, 1

**Monaciello** (Ital., little monk). A sort of incubus in Neapolitan folklore, described as a thick little man, dressed in a monk's garment and broad-brimmed hat. Those who will follow when he beckons will be led to a spot where treasure is concealed. Sometimes, however, it is his pleasure to pull the bedclothes off, and sometimes to sit perched on a sleeper.

**Monarchians.** An heretical sect of the 3rd century, who maintained that God is one, immutable and primary. Their opponents turned upon them, and nicknamed them *Patripassians* (*q.v.*), saying that according to such a doctrine God the Father must have suffered on the cross. So called from Gr. *monos*, one; *arche*, rule, because of their claim that they possessed the one true rule in Christian belief.

**Monday.** The second day of the week; called by the Anglo-Saxons Mōnandaeg, i.e. the day of the Moon.

***That Monday feeling.*** Disinclination to return to work after the weekend break; or, in the case of clergymen, the feeling of lassitude that follows the labours of Sunday.

***To keep Saint Monday.*** A habit of too many British working men, who like to make Monday a day of rest to give them a chance of getting over the effects of the drink consumed on Saturday night and Sunday.

**Money.** Shortly after the Gallic invasion of Rome, in 344 BC, Lucius Furius (or according to other accounts, Camillus), built a temple to Juno Moneta (the *Monitress*) on the spot where the house of Manlius Capitolinus stood; and to this temple was attached the first Roman mint, as to the temple of Saturn was attached the *aerarium* (public treasury). Hence the 'ases' there coined were called *moneta*, and hence our word *money*.

Juno is represented on medals with instruments of coinage, as the hammer, anvil, pincers, and die. *See* Livy, vii, 28, and Cicero, *De Divinitate*, i, 15.

The oldest coin of Greece bore the impress of an ox. Hence a bribe for silence was said to be an 'ox on the tongue'. Subsequently each province had its own impress:

*Athens*, an owl (the bird of wisdom).
*Baeotia*, Bacchus (the vineyard of Greece).
*Delphos*, a dolphin.
*Macedonia*, a buckler (from its love of war).
*Rhodes*, the disc of the sun (the Colossus was an image to the sun).

Rome had a different impress for each coin:

For the *As*, the head of Janus on one side, and the prow of a ship on the reverse.
The *Semi-as*, the head of Jupiter and the letter S.
The *Sextants*, the head of Mercury, and two points to denote two ounces.
The *Triens*, the head of a woman (? Rome or Minerva) and three points to denote three ounces.
The *Quadrans*, the head of Hercules, and four points to denote four ounces.

***Money makes the mare to go.*** *See* Mare.

**Mongrel Parliament.** The Parliament that met at Oxford in 1681 and passed the Exclusion Bill.

**Monism.** The doctrine of the oneness of mind and matter, God and the universe. It ignores all that is supernatural, any dualism of mind and matter, God and creation; and there can be no opposition between God and the world, as unity cannot be in opposition to itself. Monism teaches that 'all are but parts of one stupendous whole, whose body nature is, and God the soul'; hence, whatever is, only conforms to the cosmical laws of the universal ALL.

Haeckel explained it thus in 1866: 'Monism (the correlative of Dualism) denotes a unitary conception, in opposition to a supernatural one. Mind can never exist without matter, nor matter without mind.' As God is the same 'yesterday, today, and for ever', creation must be the same, or God would not be unchangeable.

**Monitor.** So the Romans called the nursery teacher. The *Military Monitor* was an officer to tell young soldiers of the faults committed against the service. The *House Monitor* was a slave to call the family of a morning, etc.

A shallow-draught ironclad with a flat deck, sharp stern, and one or more movable turrets, is so called. They were first used in the American War of Secession, and were so named by the inventor, Captain Ericsson, because they were to be 'severe monitors' to the leaders of the Southern rebellion.

**Monk.** In printing, a black smear or blotch made by leaving too much ink on the part. Caxton set up his printing-press in the *scriptorium* of Westminster Abbey (*see* Chapel); and the association gave rise to the slang expressions *monk* and *friar* (*q.v.*) for black and white defects.

**Monk Lewis.** Matthew Gregory Lewis (1775–1818) is so called from his novel entitled *The Monk* (1795).

**Monkey.** Slang for £500 or (in America) $500; also for a mortgage (sometimes extended to *a monkey with a long tail*), and among sailors the vessel which contains the full allowance of grog for one mess. A child, especially an active, meddlesome one, is often called 'a little monkey' for obvious reasons.

***Monkey's allowance.*** More kicks than halfpence. The allusion is to the monkeys carried about for show; they pick up the halfpence, but carry them to the master, who keeps kicking or ill-treating the poor creatures to urge them to incessant tricks.

***Monkey board.*** In the old-fashioned horsed knifeboard omnibuses, the step on which the conductor stood, and on which he often skipped about like a monkey.

***Monkey jacket.*** A short coat worn by seamen; so called because it has 'no more tail than a monkey', or, more strictly speaking, an ape.

***Monkey puzzle.*** The Chilean pine, *Araucaria imbricata*, whose twisted and prickly branches puzzle even a monkey to climb.

***Monkey spoons.*** Spoons having on the handle a heart surmounted by a monkey, at one time given in Holland at marriages, christenings, and funerals. At weddings they were given to some immediate relative of the bride; at christenings and funerals to the officiating clergyman. Among the Dutch, drinking is called 'sucking the monkey', because the early morning appetiser of rum and salt was taken in a monkey spoon.

***Monkey tricks.*** Mischievous, ill-natured, or deceitful actions. *Don't get up to your monkey tricks with me*, i.e. You'd better not try to do me down or get the better of me.

***To get one's monkey up.*** To be riled or enraged; monkeys are extremely irritable and easily provoked.

***To monkey with*** or ***about.*** To tamper with or play mischievous tricks. *To monkey with the cards* is to try to arrange them so that the deal will not be fair; *to monkey with the milk* is to add water to it and then sell it as pure and unadulterated.

***To pay in monkey's money*** (*en monnaie de singe*) – in goods, in personal work, in mumbling and grimace. In Paris when a monkey passed the Petit Pont, if it was for sale four deniers' toll had to be paid; but if it belonged to a showman and was not for sale, it sufficed if the monkey went through his tricks.

> It was an original by Master Charles Charmois, principal painter to King Megistus, paid for in court fashion with monkey's money.
>
> Rabelais, *Gargantua and Pantagruel*, iv, 3

***To suck the monkey.*** Sailors' slang for surreptitiously sucking liquor from a cask through a straw (*see* Monkey, *above*); and when milk has been taken from a coconut, and rum has been substituted, 'sucking the monkey' is drinking this rum.

> What the vulgar call 'sucking the monkey'
> Has much less effect on a man when he's funky.
>
> *Ingoldsby Legends*, *The Black Mousquetaire*

**Monkir.** *See* Munkar.

**Monmouth.** The town at the mouth of the Monnow, surname of Henry V of England, who was born there.

***Monmouth cap.*** A soldier's cap.

> The soldiers that the Monmouth wear,
> On castles' tops their ensigns rear.
>
> The best caps were formerly made at Monmouth, where the cappers' chapel doth still remain. Fuller, *Worthies of Wales*, p. 50

***Monmouth Street*** (London) takes its name from the unfortunate son of Charles II, executed for rebellion in 1685. Later Dudley Street, St Giles, and now forming part of Shaftesbury Avenue close to Soho Square, where the Duke of Monmouth had his town house, it was formerly noted for its second-hand clothes shops; hence the expression *Monmouth Street finery* for tawdry, pretentious clothes.

> [At the Venetian carnival] you may put on whate'er
> You like by way of doublet, cape, or cloak,
> Such as in Monmouth-street, or in Rag Fair
> Would rig you out in seriousness or joke.
>
> Byron, *Beppo*, v

**Monophysites** (Gr. *monos phusis*, one nature). A religious sect in the Levant who maintained that Jesus Christ had only one nature, and that divine and human were combined in much the same way as the body and soul in man. They arose upon the condemnation of the Eutychian heresy at the Council of Chalcedon, 451, and are still represented by the Coptic, Armenian, Abyssinian, and Jacobite Churches.

**Monotheism** (Gr. *monos theos*, one God). The doctrine that there is but one God.

> The only large monotheism known to historic times is that of Mahomet.
>
> Gladstone, in *Contemporary Review*, June, 1876

**Monothelism** or **Monothelitism** (Gr. *monos-thelema*, one single will). The doctrine that, although Christ has two distinct natures, He had but *one will*, His human will being merged in the divine. The Monothelites arose within the Eastern Church in the early part of the 7th century.

**Monroe Doctrine.** The doctrine first promulgated by James Monroe (President of the United States, 1817–25) in 1823, to the effect that the American States are never to entangle themselves in the broils of the Old World, nor to suffer it to interfere in the affairs of the New; and they are to account any attempt on the part of the Old World to plant their systems of government in any part of North America not at the time in European occupation dangerous to American peace and safety. The capture of Manila and the cession of the Philippine Islands to the United States in 1898, and still more the part the States took in assisting to defeat the Germans on European soil, in arranging peace terms, and conferring on the apportionment of mandates, etc., all over the world, has abrogated a large part of this famous Doctrine.

**Mons Meg.** *See* Meg.

**Monsieur.** The eldest brother of the king of France was formerly so called, especially Philippe, Duc d'Orléans, brother to Louis XIV (1640–1701); other gentlemen were only Monsieur This or That.

***Monsieur de Paris.*** The public executioner or Jack Ketch of France.

> Riccardo de Albertes was a personal friend of all the 'Messieurs de Paris', who served the Republic. He attended all capital executions.
>
> Newspaper Paragraph, January 25th, 1893

***Monsieur le Grand.*** The Great Equerry of France.

***The Peace of Monsieur.*** The peace that the Huguenots, the Politiques, and the Duke d'Alençon ('Monsieur') obliged Henri III of France to sign in 1576. By it the Huguenots and the Duke gained great concessions.

**Monsoon** (Arab. *mausim*, time, season). A periodical wind; especially that which blows off S.W. Asia and the Indian Ocean from the south-west from April to October, and from the north-east during the rest of the year.

**Mont** (Fr., hill). The technical term in palmistry for the eminences at the roots of the fingers.

> That at the root of the
>
> *thumb* is the Mont de Mars.
> *index finger* is the Mont de Jupiter.
> *long finger* is the Mont de Saturne.
> *ring finger* is the Mont de Soleil.
> *little finger* is the Mont de Venus.
>
> The one between the thumb and index finger is called the Mont de Mercure and the one opposite the Mont de Lune.

**Mont de Piété.** A pawnshop in France; first instituted as *monti di pieta* (charity loans) under Leo X, at Rome, by charitable persons who wished to rescue the poor from usurious money-lenders. They advanced small sums of money on the security of pledges, at a rate of interest barely sufficient to cover the working expenses of the institution. Both the name and system were introduced into France and Spain. Public granaries for the sale of corn are called in Italian *Monti frumentarii*. 'Monte' means a public or state loan; hence also a 'bank'.

**Montagnards.** *See* Mountain, The.

**Montanists.** Heretics of the 2nd century; so called from Montanus, a Phrygian, who asserted that he had received from the Holy Ghost special knowledge that had not been vouchsafed to the apostles. They were extremely ascetic, believed in the speedy coming of the Second Advent, and quickly died out.

**Monteer Cap.** *See* Montero.

**Monteith.** A scalloped basin to cool and wash glasses in; a sort of punch-bowl, made of silver or pewter, with a movable rim scalloped at the top; so called, according to Anthony Wood, in 1683 from 'a fantastical Scot called "Monsieur Monteigh" who at that time or a little before wore the bottome of his cloake or coate so notched ◡◡◡◡'.

> New things produce new names, and thus Monteith
> Has by one vessel saved his name from death.
>
> King

**Montem.** A custom observed every three years till 1847 by the boys of Eton College, who proceeded on Whit Tuesday *ad montem* (to a mound called Salt Hill), near Slough, and exacted a gratuity called *salt money* from all who passed by. Sometimes as much as £1,000 was thus collected, and it was used to defray the expenses of the senior scholar at King's College, Cambridge.

**Montero** or **Monteer Cap.** So called from the headgear worn by the *monteros d'Espinoza* (mountaineers), who once formed the interior guard of the palace of the Spanish king. It had a spherical crown, and flaps that could be drawn over the ears. Scott tells us that Sir Jeffrey Hudson wore 'a large Montero hat', meaning a Spanish hat with a feather (*Peveril of the Peak*, ch. xxxv).

**Montesinos.** A knight in the old romances who retired to a cave near the castle of Rochafrida because he had received some cause of offence at the French court; Don Quixote made a special point of visiting it (Bk ii, ch. 23). Tradition ascribes the river Guadiana to this cave as its source, whence the river is sometimes called Montesinos.

**Montgomery.** A Norman name, not Welsh. The town was founded by a Norman named Baldwin, and was in Welsh called *Trefaldwyn*, 'house of Baldwin': in 1086 it was taken by Roger Montgomery, Earl of Shrewsbury, Count of the Marches to William the Conqueror, and it was given his name – which is a French place-name, the *Hill of Gomeric*.

***Montgomery's division, all on one side.*** This is a French proverb, and refers to the Free Companies of the 16th century, of which a Montgomery was a noted chief. The booty he took he kept himself.

**Month.** One of the twelve portions into which the year is divided. Anciently a new month started on the day of the new moon, or the day after; hence the name (A.S. *mōnath*), which is connected with *moon*. *See* Lunar Month; and, for the months themselves *see* their names throughout this Dictionary.

The old mnemonic for remembering the number of days in each month runs –

Thirty days hath September,
April, June, and November,
February eight-and-twenty all alone
And all the rest have thirty-one,
Unless that Leap Year doth combine
And give to February twenty-nine.

This, with slight variations, is to be found in Grafton's *Chronicles* (1590), the play *The Return from Parnassus* (1606), etc. In Harrison's *Description of England* (prefixed to Holinshed's *Chronicle*, 1577) is the Latin version:

Junius, Aprilis, Septémq; Novemq: tricenos,
Unum plus reliqui, Februs tenet octo vicenos,
At si bissextus fuerit superadditur unus.

***A month of Sundays.*** An indefinite long time; never. *See* Never.

Such another chance might never turn up in a month of Sundays.

Boldrewood, *Robbery Under Arms*, ch. xi

***A month's mind.*** Properly the Mass, or lesser funeral solemnities, that in pre-Reformation days was said for a deceased person on the day one month from his death. The term often occurs in old wills in connection with charities to be disbursed on that day.

Shakespeare uses the term figuratively for an irresistible longing (for something); a great desire –

I see you have a month's mind for them.

Shakespeare, *Two Gentlemen of Verona*, 1, 2

As also does Samuel Butler –

For if a trumpet sound or drum beat,
Who hath not a month's mind to combat?

*Hudibras*, I, ii, 111

And others; and it has been conjectured that here the allusions are to the *longings* of a pregnant woman, which start in the first month of pregnancy.

**Monthawi, Al** (Arab., the destroyer). One of Mahomet's lances, confiscated from the Jews when they were exiled from Medina.

**Montjoie St Denis.** The war-cry of the French. *Montjoie* is a corruption of *Mons Jovis*, as the little mounds were called which served as direction-posts in ancient times; hence it was applied to whatever showed or indicated the way, as the banner of St Denis, called the Oriflamme. The Burgundians had for their war-cry, 'Montjoie St André'; the dukes of Bourbon, 'Montjoie Notre Dame'; and the kings of England used to have 'Montjoie St George'.

*Montjoie* was also the cry of the French heralds in the tournaments, and the title of the French king of arms.

Where is Mountjoy the herald? speed him hence:
Let him greet England with our sharp defiance.

Shakespeare, *Henry V*, 3, 5

**Montserrat.** The Catalonians aver that this mountain was riven and shattered at the Crucifixion. Every rift is filled with evergreens. Similar legends exist with regard to many other mountains. (Lat., *mons serratus*, the mountain jagged like a saw.)

**Monumental City.** Baltimore, US, is so called because it abounds in monuments; witness the obelisk, the 104 churches, etc.

**Monument, The.** The fluted Roman-Doric column of Portland stone (202 ft high) built by Sir Christopher Wren to commemorate the Great Fire of London in 1666. It stands near the north end of London Bridge, about the spot where the fire started.

The old inscription (effaced in 1831) maintained that the fire had been caused –

by ye treachery and malice of ye popish factiö, in order to ye carrying on their horrid plott for extirpating the Protestant religion and old English liberty, and the introducing popery and slavery.

and it was this that made Pope refer to it as –

London's column, pointing at the skies
Like a tall bully, lifts the head, and lies.

*Moral Essays*, III, 339

**Monuments.** When looking at monuments and effigies, etc., in our churches, it may be useful to remember the following general rules.

*Saints* lie to the east of the altar, and are elevated above the ground; the higher the elevation, the greater the sanctity. Martyrs are much elevated.

*Holy men* not canonised lie on a level with the pavement.

*Founders of chapels*, etc., lie with their monument built into the wall.

Figures with their hands on their breasts, and chalices, represent *priests*.

Figures with crozier, mitre, and pontificals, represent *prelates*.

Figures with armour represent *knights*.

Figures with legs crossed represent either *crusaders* or *married men*, but those with a scallop shell are certainly *crusaders*.

Female figures with a mantle and large ring represent *nuns*.

In the age of chivalry the woman was placed on the man's right hand; but when chivalry declined she was placed on his left hand.

It may usually be taken that inscriptions in

Latin, cut in capitals, are of the first twelve centuries; those in Lombardic capitals and French, of the 13th; those in German text, of the 14th; while those in the English language and Roman characters are subsequent to the 14th century.

Tablets against the wall came in with the Reformation; and brasses are for the most part subsequent to the 13th century.

**Moon.** The word is probably connected with the Sanskrit root *me-*, to measure (because time was measured by it). It is common to all Teutonic languages (Goth, *mêna*, O.Frisian *môna*, O.Norm, *máne*, A.S. *móna*, etc.), and is almost invariably masculine. In the Edda the *son* of Mundilfoeri is Mani (moon), and *daughter* Sôl (sun); so it is still with the Lithuanians and Arabians, and so was it with the ancient Slavs, Mexicans, Hindus, etc., and the Germans to this day have *Frau Sonne* (Mrs Sun) and *Herr Mond* (Mr Moon).

The Moon is represented in five different phases: (1) new; (2) full; (3) crescent or decrescent; (4) half; and (5) gibbous, or more than half. In pictures of the Assumption of the Virgin, it is shown as a crescent under her feet; in the Crucifixion it is eclipsed, and placed on one side of the cross, the sun being on the other; in the Creation and Last Judgment it is also introduced by artists.

In *classical mythology* the moon was known as *Hecate* before she had risen and after she had set; as *Astarte* when crescent; as *Diana* or *Cynthia* (she who 'hunts the clouds') when in the open vault of heaven; as *Phōebe* when looked upon as the sister of the sun (i.e. *Phōebus*); and was personified as *Selene* or *Luna*, the lover of the sleeping *Endymion*, i.e. moonlight on the fields (*see these names*).

The moon is called *triform*, because it presents itself to us either *round*, or *waxing* with horns towards the east, or *waning* with horns towards the west.

One legend connected with the moon was that there was treasured everything wasted on earth, such as misspent time and wealth, broken vows, unanswered prayers, fruitless tears, abortive attempts, unfulfilled desires and intentions, etc. In Ariosto's *Orlando Furioso* Astolpho found on his visit to the Moon (Bk xviii and xxxiv, 70) that bribes were hung on gold and silver hooks; princes' favours were kept in bellows; wasted talent was kept in vases, each marked with the proper name, etc.; and in *The Rape of the Lock* (canto v) Pope tells us that when the Lock disappeared –

> Some thought it mounted to the lunar sphere,
> Since all things lost on earth are treasured there,
> There heroes' wits are kept in pond'rous vases,
> And beaux' in snuff-boxes and tweezer-cases.
> There broken vows and death-bed alms are found
> And lovers' hearts with ends of ribbon bound,
> The courtier's promises, and sick man's prayers,
> The smiles of harlots, and the tears of heirs
> Cages for gnats, and chains to yoke a flea,
> Dried butterflies, and tomes of casuistry.

Hence the phrase, *the limbus of the moon*.

***I know no more about it than the man in the moon.*** I know nothing at all about the matter.

***It's all moonshine.*** Bunkum; nonsense; it's a 'tale told by an idiot'. The light of the moon was formerly held to have very deleterious effects on mental stability. *See* Lunatic.

***Mahomet and the Moon.*** *See* Mahomet.

***Minions of the moon.*** Thieves who rob by night (*see 1 Henry IV*, 1, 2).

***Moon-calf.*** An inanimate, shapeless abortion formerly supposed to be produced prematurely by the cow owing to the malign influence of the moon.

> A false conception, called *mola*, i.e. moon-calf ...
> a lump of flesh without shape or life.
>
> Holland, *Pliny*, vii, 15

***Moon-drop.*** In Latin, *virus lunare*, a vaporous foam supposed in ancient times to be shed by the moon on certain herbs and other objects, when influenced by incantations.

> Upon the corner of the moon,
> There hangs a vaporous drop profound;
> I'll catch it ere it come to ground.
>
> Shakespeare, *Macbeth*, 3, 5

*Cp.* Lucan's *Pharsalia*, vi, 669, where Erichtho is introduced using it:

> Et virus large lunare ministrat.

***Moonlight flit.*** A clandestine removal of one's furniture during the night, to avoid paying one's rent or having the furniture seized in payment thereof.

***Moon-rakers.*** A nickname of people of Wiltshire. The absurd story offered to account for the name is that in the 'good old times' they were noted smugglers, and one night, seeing the coastguard on the watch, they sunk some smuggled whisky in the sea. When the coast was clear they employed rakes to recover their goods, when the coastguard reappeared and asked what they were doing. Pointing to the reflection of the moon in the water, they replied,

'We are trying to rake out that cream cheese yonder.'

***Moon's men.*** Thieves and highwaymen who ply their trade by night.

> The fortune of us that are but Moon's-men doth ebb and flow like the sea.
>
> Shakespeare, *1 Henry IV*, 1, 2

***Moonstone.*** A variety of feldspar, so called on account of the play of light which it exhibits. It contains bluish white spots, which, when held to the light, present a silvery play of colour not unlike that of the moon.

***Once in a blue moon.*** *See* Blue Moon.

***The cycle of the moon.*** *See* Cycle.

***The Island of the Moon.*** Madagascar is so named by the natives.

***The limbus of the moon.*** *See above.*

***The man in the moon.*** Some say it is a man leaning on a fork, on which he is carrying a bundle of sticks picked up on a Sunday. The origin of this fable is from Numb. 15:32-36. Some add a dog also; thus the prologue in *Midsummer Night's Dream* says, 'This man with lantern, dog, and bush of thorns, presenteth moonshine'; Chaucer says 'he stole the bush' (*Test. of Cresseide*). Another tradition says that the man is Cain, with his dog and thorn bush; the thorn bush being emblematical of the thorns and briars of the fall, and the dog being the 'foul fiend'. Some poets make out the 'man' to be Endymion, taken to the moon by Diana.

***The Mountains of the Moon*** means simply White Mountains. The Arabs call a white horse 'moon-coloured'.

***To aim*** or ***level at the moon.*** To be very ambitious; to aim in shooting at the moon.

***To cast beyond the moon.*** *See* Cast.

***To cry for the moon.*** To crave for what is wholly beyond one's reach. The allusion is to foolish children who want the moon for a plaything. The French say, 'He wants to take the moon between his teeth' (*Il veut prendre la lune avec le dents*), alluding to the old proverb about 'the moon', and a 'green cheese'.

***You have found an elephant in the moon*** – found a mare's nest. Sir Paul Neal, a conceited virtuoso of the 17th century, gave out that he had discovered 'an elephant in the moon'. It turned out that a mouse had crept into his telescope, which had been mistaken for an elephant in the moon. Samuel Butler has a satirical poem on the subject called *The Elephant in the Moon.*

***You would have me believe that the moon is made of green cheese*** – i.e. the most absurd thing imaginable.

> You may as soon persuade some Country Peasants, that the Moon is made of Green-Cheese (as we say) as that 'tis bigger than his Cart-wheel. Wilkins, *New World*, i (1638)

**Moor-slayer** or **Mata-moros.** A name given to St James, the patron saint of Spain, because, as the legends say, in encounters with the Moors he came on his white horse to the aid of the Christians.

**Moors.** In the Middle Ages, the Europeans called all Mohammedans *Moors*, in the same manner as the Eastern nations called all inhabitants of Europe *Franks*. Camoëns, in the *Lusiad* (Bk viii), gives the name to the Indians.

**Moot.** In Anglo-Saxon times, the assembly of freemen in a township, tithing, etc. *Cp.* Witenagemot. In legal circles the name is given to the students, debates on supposed cases which formerly took place on the halls of Inns of Court. The benchers and the barristers, as well as the students, took an active part.

Hence, *moot case* or *moot point*, a doubtful or unsettled question, a case that is open to debate.

**Mop.** A statute fair at which servants seek to be hired. Carters fasten to their hats a piece of whipcord; shepherds, a lock of wool; grooms, a piece of sponge; and others a broom, pail or *mop*, etc. When hired a cockade with streamers is mounted. The origin of the name – which was in use in the 17th century – is not certain, but is probably an allusion to the mops carried by domestics.

***Mop.*** One of Queen Mab's attendants.

***All mops and brooms.*** Intoxicated.

***Mops and mows.*** Grimaces; here *mop* is connected with the Dutch *mopken*, to pout.

**Moplahs.** Descendants of Arab traders who married Hindus on the Malabar coast, now numbering about a million and a half. They are fanatical Mohammedans, but have adopted many Hindu customs, and are rabid teetotallers and earnest proselytisers. Their chief priest is stationed at Tirurangadi, and their fanaticism makes them an easy tool in the hands of seditious agitators.

**Moral. *The moral Gower.*** John Gower (d.1408), the poet, is so called by Chaucer (*Troilus and Criseyde*, v, 1).

***Father of moral philosophy.*** Thomas Aquinas (1227–74).

**Moran's Collar.** In Irish folk-tale, the collar of Moran, the wise councillor of Feredach the Just, an early king of Ireland, before the Christian era, which strangled the wearer if he deviated from the strict rules of equity. Of course, the collar is an allegory of obvious meaning.

**Morat.** ***Morat and Marathon twin names shall stand*** (*Childe Harold*, III, 64). Morat, in Switzerland, is famous for the battle fought in 1476, in which the Swiss defeated Charles le Téméraire of Burgundy.

**Moratorium** (Lat. *morari*, to delay). A legal permission to defer for a stated time the payment of a bond, debt, or other obligation. This is done to enable the debtor to pull himself round by borrowing money, selling effects, or otherwise raising funds to satisfy obligations. The device was adopted in 1891 in South America during the panic caused by the Baring Brothers' default of some twenty millions sterling, and the word came into popular use during the Great War, and afterwards in connection with the inability of Germany to pay to date the stated amount due as reparations under the Treaty of Versailles.

> In Great Britain, on Aug. 6th, 1914, a moratorium was proclaimed giving the banks power to retain certain sums credited to them and putting off the payment of Bills of Exchange and other debts for a month; this was later extended to Oct. 4th, and a partial renewal to assist certain interests was allowed to Nov. 4th.

**Moravians.** A religious community tracing its origin from John Huss (*see* Bohemian Brethren), expelled by persecution from Bohemia and Moravia in the 17th century. They are often called *The United Brethren*.

**Morbleu!** A French oath, a euphemism for *Mort de Dieu* (death of God), similar to our old *'sdeath* (God's death). In the same way *parbleu* is a euphemism for *par Dieu* (by God). *Cp.* Ventre St Gris.

**More.** ***More or less.*** Approximately; in round numbers; as 'It is ten miles, more or less, from here to there', i.e. it's about ten miles.

***The more one has, the more he desires.*** In French, *Plus il en a, plus il en veut*. In Latin, *Quo plus habent, eo plus cupiunt*.

> My more having would be a source
> To make me hunger more.
>
> Shakespeare, *Macbeth*, 4, 3

***The more the merrier, the fewer the better cheer,*** or ***fare.*** The proverb is found in Ray's *Collection* (1742), and in Heywood's (1548).

***To be no more.*** To exist no longer; to be dead.

> Cassius is no more. Shakespeare, *Julius Caesar*

**More of More Hall.** *See* Wantley, Dragon of.

**Morgan.** The first 'who played at Dice with Spectacles' (*see* Gemmagog).

**Morgan le Fay.** The fairy sister of King Arthur; one of the principal characters in Arthurian romance and in Celtic legend generally; also known as *Morgaine* and (especially in *Orlando Furioso*) as *Morgana* (*see* Fata Morgana).

In the Arthurian legends it was Morgan le Fay who revealed to the King the intrigues of Lancelot and Guinevere. She gave him a cup containing a magic draught, and Arthur had no sooner drunk it than his eyes were opened to the perfidy of his wife and friend.

In *Orlando Furioso* she is represented as living at the bottom of a lake, and dispensing her treasures to whom she liked; and in *Orlando Innamorato* she first appears as 'Lady Fortune', but subsequently assumes her witch-like attributes. In Tasso her three daughters, Morganetta, Nivetta, and Carvilia, are introduced.

In the romance of *Ogier the Dane* Morgan le Fay receives Ogier in the Isle of Avalon when he is over one hundred years old, restores him to youth, and becomes his bride.

**Morganatic Marriage.** A marriage between a man of high (usually royal) rank and a woman of inferior station, by virtue of which she does not acquire the husband's rank and neither she nor the children of the marriage are entitled to inherit his title or possessions; often called a 'left-handed marriage' (*q.v.*) because the custom is for the man to pledge his troth with his left hand instead of the right. George William, Duke of Zell, married Eleanora d'Esmiers in this way, and the lady took the name and title of Lady of Harburg; her daughter was Sophia Dorothea, the wife of George I. An instance of a morganatic marriage in the British Royal Family is that of George, Duke of Cambridge (1819–1904), cousin of Queen Victoria and uncle of Queen Mary, who married morganatically in 1840. His children took the surname Fitz-George.

The word comes from the mediaeval Latin phrase *matrimonium ad morganaticam*, the last word representing the O.H.Ger. *morgangeba*, morning-gift; the meaning being that the children were entitled to nothing of the father's beyond his first, or 'morning' gift, i.e. the privilege of being born.

**Morgane, Morganetta.** *See* Morgan le Fay.

**Morgante Maggiore.** A serio-comic romance in verse, by Pulci, of Florence (1485). The characters had appeared previously in many of the old romances; Morgante is a ferocious giant, converted by Orlando (the real hero) to Christianity. After performing the most wonderful feats, he died at last from the bite of a crab.

Pulci was practically the inventor of this species of poetry, called by the French *bernesque*, from Berni, who greatly excelled in it.

**Morgiana.** The clever, faithful, female slave of Ali Baba, who pries into the forty jars, and discovers that every jar, but one, contains a man. She takes oil from the only one containing it, and, having made it boiling hot, pours enough into each jar to kill the thief concealed there. At last she kills the captain of the gang, and marries her master's son. (*Arabian Nights; Ali Baba and the Forty Thieves*).

**Morglay.** The sword of Sir Bevis of Hamtoun (*q.v.*); also a generic name for a sword. The word is really the same as 'Claymore' (*q.v.*).

> As to his further praise, how for that dangerous fight
> The great Armenian king made noble Bevis knight:
> And having raiséd pow'r, Damascus to invade,
> The General of his force this English hero made.
> Then, how fair Josian gave him Arundell his steed,
> And Morglay his good sword, in many a gallant deed
> Which manfully he tried.
>
> Drayton, *Polyolbion*, II, 327

> Carrying their morglays in their hands.
>
> Beaumont and Fletcher, *Honest Man's Fortune*, I, i

**Morgue.** A mortuary, a building, especially that in Paris, where the bodies of persons found dead are exposed to view so that people may come and identify them. The origin of the name is unknown; it does not seem to be connected in any way with *mors*, death, and is probably the same word as *morgue*, meaning of stately or haughty mien. It was formerly applied to prison vestibules, where new criminals were placed to be scrutinised, that the prison officials might become familiar with their faces and general appearance.

> On me conduit donc au petit chastelet, où du guichet estant passé dans la morgue, un homme gros, court, et carré, vint à moy.
>
> Assoucy, *La Prison de M. Dassouch* (1674), p. 35

> Morgue. Endroit où l'on tient quelque temps ceux que l'on écroue, afin que les guichetiers puissent les reconnaître ensuit.
>
> Fleming and Tibbins, vol ii, p. 688

**Morgue la Faye.** The form taken by the name Morgan le Fay (*q.v.*) in *Ogier the Dane*.

**Morisonianism.** The religious system of James Morison, the chief peculiarities being the doctrines of universal atonement, and the ability of man unaided to receive or reject the Gospel. James Morison, in 1841, separated from the 'United Secession', now merged into the 'United Presbyterian'. The Morisonians call themselves the 'Evangelical Union'.

**Morley, Mrs.** The name under which Queen Anne corresponded with 'Mrs Freeman' (the Duchess of Marlborough).

**Mormonism.** The religious and social system of the Mormons, or Latter-day Saints; largely connected in the minds of most people with the practice of polygamy, which became part of the Mormon code in 1852, was very widely indulged in, but is now a diminishing – if not vanished – quantity. Hence the phrase *a regular Mormon*, for a flighty person who cannot keep to one wife or sweetheart.

The fraternity takes its name from *The Book of Mormon*, or *Golden Bible*, which is pretended to have been written on golden plates by the angel Mormon, but was in reality abstracted from a romance (1811) by the Rev. Solomon Spaulding (1761–1816) by Joseph Smith (1805–44), and claimed by him as a direct revelation. Smith was born in Sharon, Windsor county, Vermont, and founded the denomination in 1830. He was cited thirty-nine times into courts of law, and was at last assassinated by a gang of ruffians while in prison at Carthage. His successor was Brigham Young (1801–77), a carpenter, who led the 'Saints', driven from home by force, to the valley of the Salt Lake, 1,500 miles distant, generally called Utah, but by the Mormons themselves *Deseret* (Bee-country), the New Jerusalem, where they have been settled, despite many disputes with the United States Government, since 1848.

The Mormons accept the Bible as well as the *Book of Mormon* as authoritative, though, naturally, they interpret it in their own way; they hold the doctrines of repentance and faith (putting a curious construction on the latter); and they believe in baptism, the Eucharist, the literal resurrection of the dead, and in the Second Coming, when Christ will have the seat of His power in Utah. Marriage may be either for time or for eternity; in the latter case consummation is unnecessary, for the man and the wife or wives he has taken in this way will spend the whole of the afterlife together; in the former case the rite is gone through solely that the community may be increased and multiplied. One good point among the Mormons is that every man, woman, and child capable of work has suitable work to do in the community, and has to do it.

**Morning.** The first glass of whisky drunk by Scotch fishermen in salutation to the dawn. One fisherman will say to another, 'Hae ye had your morning, Tam?'

> Having declined Mrs Flockhart's compliment of a 'morning', ... he made his adieus.
>
> Scott, *Waverley*, ch. xliv

**Morning Star of the Reformation.** John Wyclif (1324–84).

**Morocco.** Strong ale made from burnt malt, used in the annual feast at Levens Hall, Westmorland (the seat of Sir Alan Desmond Bagot), on the opening of Milnthorpe Fair. It is put into a large glass of unique form, and the person whose turn it is to drink is called the 'colt'. He has to 'drink the constable', i.e. stand on one leg and say 'Luck to Levens as long as Kent flows', then drain the glass or forfeit one shilling. *See also* Marocco.

***Morocco men*.** Men who, about the end of the 18th century, used to visit public-houses touting for illegal lottery insurances. Their rendezvous was a tavern in Oxford Market, on the Portland estate.

**Morpheus.** Ovid's name for the son of Sleep, and god of dreams; so called from Gr. *morphe*, form, because he gives these airy nothings their form and fashion. Hence the name of the narcotic, *morphine*, or *morphia*.

**Morrice, Gil** (or **Childe**). The hero of an old Scottish ballad, a natural son of an earl and the wife of Lord Barnard, and brought up 'in the gude grene wode'. Lord Barnard, thinking the Childe to be his wife's lover, slew him with a broadsword, and setting his head on a spear gave it to 'the meanest man in a' his train' to carry to the lady. When she saw it she said to the baron, 'Wi' that same spear, O pierce my heart, and put me out o' pain'; but the baron replied, 'Enouch of blood by me's bin spilt, sair, sair I rew the deid', adding –

> I'll ay lament for Gil Morice,
> As gin he were mine ain;
> I'll neir forget the dreiry day
> On which the youth was slain.
>
> *Percy's Reliques*, ser. iii, 1

Percy says this pathetic tale suggested to Home the plot of his tragedy, *Douglas*.

**Morris Dance.** A grotesque dance, popular in England in the 15th century and later, in which the dancers usually represented characters from the Robin Hood stories (*see* Maid Marian). It was brought from Spain in the reign of Edward III, and was originally a military dance of the Moors, or Moriscos – hence its name.

**Morse Code.** A system of sending messages by telegraph, heliograph, flags, etc., invented by S. F. B. Morse (1791–1872), an American artist. Each letter, figure, and punctuation mark is represented by dots, dashes, or a combination of them; thus dot, dash(. —) stands for *a*, dash, dot, dot, dot(— . . .) for *b*, a single dot for *e*, four dots and a dash(. . . . —) for 4, etc. In military signalling a short flash or a rapid dip of the flag corresponds with the dot, and a long or slow with the dash.

**Mortal. *A mortal sin*.** A 'deadly' sin, one which excludes from heaven; opposed to *venial*.

> Earth trembled from her entrails, ... some sad drops
> Wept at completing of the mortal Sin
> Original; while Adam took no thought.
>
> Milton, *Paradise Lost*, ix, 1003

In slang and colloquial speech the word is used to express something very great – as 'He's in a mortal funk', 'There was a mortal lot of people there', or as an emphatic expletive – 'You can do any mortal thing you like'.

**Mortar-board.** A college cap surmounted by a square 'board' covered with black cloth. The word is possibly connected with Fr. *mortier*, the cap worn by the ancient kings of France, and still used officially by the chief justice or president of the court of justice, but is more likely an allusion to the small square board on which a bricklayer carries his mortar – frequently balanced on his head.

**Morte d'Arthur, Le** (*see* Arthurian romances), was compiled by Sir Thomas Malory from French originals, and printed by Caxton in 1485. It contains –

*The Prophecies of Merlin.*
*The Quest of the St Graal.*
*The Romance of Sir Lancelot of the Lake.*
*The History of Sir Tristram*; etc., etc.

Tennyson has a *Morte d'Arthur* among his poems.

**Morther.** *See* Mauther.

**Mortimer.** Fable has it that this family name derives from an ancestor in crusading times, noted for his exploits on the shores of the Dead

Sea (*De Mortuo Mari*). Fact, however, is not so romantic. *De Mortemer* was one of William the Conqueror's knights and is mentioned in the Roll of Battle Abbey; he was tenant in chief of *Mortemer*, a township in Normandy.

**Mortmain** (O.Fr., Lat. *mortua manus*, dead hand). A term applied to land that was held inalienably by ecclesiastical or other corporations. In the 13th century it was common for persons to make over their land to the Church and then to receive it back as tenants, thus escaping their feudal obligations to the king. In 1279 the *Statute of Mortmain* prohibiting grants of land to the 'dead hand' of the Church was passed.

**Morton's Fork.** Archbishop Morton's plan for increasing the royal revenues, in the time of Henry VII, so arranged that nobody should escape. Those who were rich were forced to contribute on the ground that they could well afford it, those who lived without display on the ground that their economies must mean that they were saving money.

**Mortstone.** A rock of Morte Point, Devon.

***He may remove Mortstone.*** A Devonshire proverb, said incredulously of husbands who pretend to be masters of their wives. It also means, 'If you have done what you say, you can accomplish anything.'

**Morven.** Fingal's realm; probably Argyllshire and its neighbourhood.

**Moses. *The horns of Moses' face.*** Moses is conventionally represented with horns, owing to a blunder in translation. In Ex. 34:29, 30, where we are told that when Moses came down from Mount Sinai 'the skin of his face shone', the Hebrew for this *shining* may be translated either as 'sent forth *beams*' or 'sent forth *horns*'; and the Vulgate took the latter as correct, rendering the passage – *quod cornuta esset facies sua. Cp.* Hab. 3:4, 'His brightness was as the light; He had horns [*rays of light*] coming out of His hand.'

Michael Angelo followed the earlier painters in depicting Moses with horns.

***Moses' rod.*** The divining-rod (*q.v.*) is sometimes so called, after the rod with which Moses worked wonders before Pharaoh (Ex. 2:2–5).

**Moslem** or **Muslim.** A Mohammedan, the pres. part. of Arab. *aslama*, to be safe or at rest, whence Islam (*q.v.*). The Arabic plural *Moslemin* is sometimes used, but *Moslems* is more common.

**Mosstrooper.** A robber, a bandit; applied especially to the marauders who infested the borders of England and Scotland, who encamped on the *mosses* (A.S. *mos*, a bog).

**Mother.** Properly a female parent (Sansk. *mātr*, Gr. *mētēr*, Lat. *mater*, A.S. *mōdor*, Ger. *mutter*, Fr. *mère*, etc.); hence, figuratively, the source or origin of anything, the head or headquarters of a religious or other community, etc.

***Mother Ann, Bunch, Goose, Shipton,*** etc. *See* these names.

***Mother Carey's chickens.*** Stormy petrels. Mother Carey is *mata cara*, dear mother. The French call these birds *oiseaux de Notre Dame* or *aves Sanctae Mariae. See* Captain Marryat's *Poor Jack*, where the superstition is fully related.

***Mother Carey's Goose.*** The great black petrel or fulmar of the Pacific.

***Mother Carey is plucking her goose.*** It is snowing. *Cp.* Hulda. Sailors call falling snow *Mother Carey's chickens*.

***Mother Church.*** The Church considered as the central fact, the head, the last court of appeal in all matters pertaining to conscience or religion. St John Lateran, at Rome (*see* Lateran), is known as the Mother and Head of all Churches. Also, the principal or oldest church in a country or district; the cathedral of a diocese.

***Mother country.*** One's native country; or the country whence one's ancestors have come to settle. England is the *Mother country* of Australia, New Zealand, Canada, etc. The German term is *Fatherland*.

***Mother Earth.*** When Junius Brutus (after the death of Lucretia) formed one of the deputation to Delphi to ask the Oracle which of the three would succeed Tarquin, the response was, 'He who should first kiss his mother.' Junius instantly threw himself on the ground, exclaiming, 'Thus, then, I kiss thee, Mother Earth,' and he was elected consul.

***Mother-of-pearl.*** The inner iridescent layers of the shells of many bivalve molluscs, especially that of the pearl oyster.

***Mother-sick.*** Hysterical. Hysteria in women used to be known as 'the mother'.

> She [Lady Bountiful] cures rheumatisms, ruptures and broken shins in men; green-sickness, obstructions, and fits of the mother in women; the king's evil, … etc.
>
> Farquhar, *The Beaux Stratagem*, I, i

***Mother-wit.*** Native wit, a ready reply; the wit which 'our mother gave us'.

***Mothers' meeting.*** A meeting of working-class mothers held periodically in connection with some church or denomination, at which the women can get advice or religious instruction, drink tea, gossip, and sometimes do a little needle-work. Hence, applied in slang to any gossiping group of people – men, as well as women.

***The Mother of Believers.*** Among Mohammedans, Ay-e-shah, the second and favourite wife of Mahomet, who was called the 'Father of Believers'.

***The Mother of Cities*** (*Amu-al-Bulud*). Balkh is so called.

***Does your mother know you're out?*** A jeering remark, addressed to a presumptuous youth or to a silly simpleton.

***Oh, mother, look at Dick!*** Said in derision when someone is showing off, or doing something easy with the idea of being applauded for his skill.

***Tied to one's mother's apron-strings.*** *See* Apron.

**Mothering Sunday.** Mid-Lent Sunday, a great holiday, when the Pope blesses the golden rose, children go home to their mothers to feast on 'mothering cakes', and 'simnel cakes' (*q.v.*) are eaten. It is said that the day received its appellation from the ancient custom of visiting the 'mother church' on that day; but to school-children it always meant a holiday, when they went home to spend the day with their mother or parents.

**Motion.** ***The laws of motion,*** according to Galileo and Newton.

(1) If no force acts on a body in motion, it will continue to move uniformly in a straight line.

(2) If force acts on a body, it will produce a change of motion proportionate to the force, and in the same direction (as that in which the force acts).

(3) When one body exerts force on another, that *other* body reacts on it with equal force.

**Motley.** ***Men of motley.*** Licensed fools; so called because of their dress.

> Motley is the only wear.
>
> Shakespeare, *As You Like It*, 2, 7

**Motu proprio** (Lat.). Of one's own motion; of one's own accord.

**Mouchard** (Fr.). A spy, *qui fait comme les mouches, qui voient si bien sans en avoir l'air*. At the close of the 17th century, those *petits-maîtres* who frequented the Tuileries to see and be seen were called *mouchards* (flymen).

**Mountain.** ***Mountain ash.*** *See* Rowan tree.

***Mountain dew.*** Scotch whisky; formerly that from illicit stills hidden away in the mountains.

***If the mountain will not come to Mahomet,*** etc. *See* Mahomet.

***The mountain*** (*La Montagune*). The extreme democratic party in the French Revolution, the members of which were known as *Les Montagnards* because they seated themselves on the highest benches of the hall in which the National Convention met. Their leaders were Danton and Robespierre, Marat, St André, Legendre, Camille-Desmoulins, Carnot, St Just, and Collot d'Herbois, the men who introduced the 'Reign of Terror'. Extreme Radicals in France are still called *Montagnards.*

***The mountain in labour.*** A mighty effort made for a small effect. The allusion is to the celebrated line '*Parturiunt montes, nascetur ridiculus mus*' (*Ars Poetica*, 139), which Horace took from a Greek proverb preserved by Athenaeus.

> The story is that the Egyptian King Tachos sustained a long war against Artaxerxes Ochus, and sent to the Lacedemonians for aid. King Agesilaus went with a contingent, but when the Egyptians saw a little, ill-dressed lame man, they said: '*Parturiebat mons; formidabat Jupiter; ille vero murem peperit.*' ('The mountain laboured, Jupiter stood aghast, and a mouse ran out.') Agesilaus replied, 'You call me a mouse, but I will soon show you I am a lion.'

Creech translates Horace, 'The travailing mountain yields a silly mouse'; and Boileau, '*La montagne en travail enfante une souris.*'

***The Old Man of the Mountains*** (*Sheikh-al-Jebal*). Hassan ben Sabbah, the founder of the Assassins (*q.v.*), who made his stronghold in the mountain fastnesses of Lebanon. He died in 1124, and in 1256 his dynasty, and nearly all the Assassins, were exterminated by the Tartar prince, Hulaku.

***To make mountains of molehills.*** To make a difficulty of trifles. *Arcem ex cloaca facere*. The corresponding French proverb is, *Faire d'un mouche un éléphant*.

**Mountebank.** A vendor of quack medicines at fairs, etc., who attracts the crowd by doing juggling feats or other antics from the tail of a cart or other raised platform; hence, any charlatan or self-advertising pretender. The *bank* or bench was the counter on which shopkeepers displayed their goods, and street-vendors used to *mount* on their *bank* to patter to the public. The Italian word, from which ours comes, is *montambanco*, and the French *saltimbanque*.

**Mourning. *Black.*** To express the privation of light and joy, the midnight gloom of sorrow for the loss sustained. The colour of mourning in Europe; also in ancient Greece and the Roman Empire.

***Black and white striped.*** To express sorrow and hope. The mourning of the South Sea Islanders.

***Greyish brown.*** The colour of the earth, to which the dead return; used for mourning in Ethiopia.

***Pale brown.*** The colour of withered leaves. The mourning of Persia.

***Sky blue.*** To express the assured hope that the deceased has gone to heaven; used in Syria, Armenia, etc.

***Deep blue.*** The colour of mourning in Bokhara, also that of the Romans of the Republic.

***Purple and violet.*** To express royalty, 'kings and priests to God'. The colour of mourning for cardinals and the kings of France; in Turkey the colour is violet.

***White.*** Emblem of 'white-handed hope'. Used by the ladies of ancient Rome and Sparta, also in Spain till the end of the 15th century. Henry VIII wore white for Anne Boleyn.

***Yellow.*** The sear and yellow leaf. The colour of mourning in Egypt and in Burmah, where also it is the colour of the monastic order. In Brittany, widows' caps among the *paysannes* are yellow. Anne Boleyn wore yellow mourning for Catherine of Aragon. Some say yellow is in token of exaltation. *See also* Black Cap.

**Mournival.** *See* Gleek.

**Mouse.** The soul was often supposed in olden times to make its way at death through the mouth of man in the form of some animal, sometimes a pigeon, sometimes a mouse or rat. A red mouse indicated a pure soul; a black mouse, a soul blackened by pollution; a pigeon or dove, a saintly soul.

Exorcists used to drive out evil spirits from the human body, and Harsnet gives several instances of such expulsions in his *Popular Impositions* (1604).

***Mouse*** is slang for a black eye, and was formerly in common use as a term of endearment. Similar terms from animals are, *bird* or *birdie*, *pussy*, and *lamb*; but *cow* and, still more so, *bitch* are deadly insults. 'You little monkey' is an endearing reproof to a child. Dog and pig are used in a bad sense, as 'You dirty dog'; 'You filthy pig'. Brave as a lion, surly as a bear, crafty as a fox, proud as a peacock, fleet as a hare, and several phrases of a like character are in common use.

> 'God bless you, mouse,' the bridegroom said,
> And smakt her on the lips.
>
> Warner, *Albion's Eng.*, p. 17

***It's a bold mouse that nestles in the cat's ear.*** Said of one who is taking an unnecessary risk. An old proverb, given by Herbert (1639).

***Poor as a church mouse.*** *See* Poor.

***The mouse that hath but one hole is quickly taken.*** Have two strings to your bow. The proverb appears in Herbert's *Collection* (1639), and is found in many European languages. In Latin it was *Mus non uni fidit antro*, the mouse does not trust to one hole.

***When the cat's away the mice will play.*** *See* Cat.

**Mouse Tower, The.** A mediaeval watch-tower on the Rhine, near Bingen, so called because of the tradition that Archbishop Hatto (*q.v.*) was there devoured by mice. The tower, however, was built by Bishop Siegfried, two hundred years after the death of Hatto, as a toll-house for collecting the duties upon all goods which passed by. The German *maut* means 'toll', (mouse is *maus*), and the similarity of the words together with the great unpopularity of the toll on corn gave rise to the tradition.

**Mouth. *Down in the mouth.*** *See* Down.

***His mouth was made.*** He was trained or reduced to obedience, like a horse trained to the bit.

> At first, of course, the fireworker showed fight ... but in the end 'his mouth was made', his paces formed, and he became a very serviceable and willing animal.
>
> Le Fanu, *House in the Churchyard*, ch. xcix

***That makes my mouth water. Cela fait venir l'eau à la bouche.*** The fragrance of appetising food excites the salivary glands. The phrase means – that makes me long for or desire it.

***Hold your mouth!*** A rougher equivalent of 'hold your tongue!'; keep silent.

***To laugh on the wrong side of one's mouth.*** *See* Laugh.

***To mouth one's words.*** To talk affectedly or pompously; to declaim.

> He mouths a sentence as curs mouth a bone.
>
> Churchill, *The Rosciad*, 322

***To open one's mouth wide.*** To name too high a price.

**Moutons. *Revenons à nos moutons*** (Fr.). Literally 'Let us come back to our sheep', but always used to express 'let us return to our subject'. The phrase is taken from the 14th century French comedy *La Farce de Maître Pathelin*, or *l'Avocat Pathelin* (line 1282), in which a woollen-draper charges a shepherd with ill-treating his sheep. In telling his story he kept for ever running away from his subject; and to throw discredit on the defendant's attorney (Pathelin), accused him of stealing a piece of cloth. The judge had to pull him up every moment with, '*Mais, mon ami, revenons à nos moutons.*' The phrase is frequently quoted by Rabelais. *See* Patelin: Sans Souci, Enfans.

**Move. *Give me where to stand, and I will move the world.*** So said Archimedes of Syracuse; and the instrument he would have used is the lever.

***To move the adjournment of the House*** (i.e. the House of Commons). To bring forward a motion of adjournment, which can only be done in certain special circumstances. This is the only method by which the rules of the House allow a member to bring up, without notice, business which is not on the order paper.

**Mowis.** The bridegroom of snow, who, in American Indian tradition, wooed and won a beautiful bride; but when morning dawned, Mowis left the wigwam, and melted into the sunshine. The bride hunted for him night and day in the forests, but never saw him more.

**Mozaide.** The 'Moor', settled in Calicut, who befriended Vasco da Gama when he first landed in India.

**Much.** The miller's son in the Robin Hood stories. In the morris-dances he played the part of the Fool, and his great feat was to bang the head of the gaping spectators with a bladder of peas.

**Much Ado about Nothing.** Shakespeare's comedy, named from a proverbial saying of the time, and with only the slightest relevance to the plot, was probably written in 1599, and was published in 1600.

**Muckle. *Many a mickle makes a muckle*.** *See under* Little.

**Muff.** A person who is awkward at outdoor sports, or who is effeminate, dull, or stupid; probably so called as a sneering allusion to the use of muffs to keep one's hands warm. The term does not seem to be older than the early part of last century, but there is a Sir Henry Muff in Dudley's interlude, *The Rival Candidates* (1774), a stupid, blundering dolt, who is not only unsuccessful at the election, but finds that his daughter has engaged herself during his absence.

**Muffins and Crumpets.** Muffins is probably *pain-moufflet*, soft bread. Du Cange describes the *panis mofletus* as bread of a more delicate nature than ordinary, for the use of prebends, etc., and says it was made fresh every day. Crumpets is *crumple-ettes*, (cakes with) little crumples. *Crumpet* is also slang for the head – *I caught him one on the crumpet* – I gave him a blow on the head.

**Mufti.** An Arabic word meaning an official expounder of the Koran and Mohammedan law; but used in English to denote *civil*, as distinguished from *military* or official costume. Our meaning dates from the early 19th century, and probably arose from the resemblance that the flowered dressing-gown and tasselled smoking-cap worn by officers at that time when in the quarters off duty bore to the stage get-up of an Eastern mufti. The corresponding French term for our *to be in mufti* is *être en civil*, or *en bourgeois*, or – in army slang – *ête en pékin*.

**Mug-house.** An ale-house was so called in the 18th century. Some hundred persons assembled in a large tap-room to drink, sing, and spout. One of the number was made chairman. Ale was served to the guests in their own mugs, and the place where the mug was to stand was chalked on the table.

**Mugello.** The giant that, according to the romance, was slain by Averardo de Medici, a commander under Charlemagne. The tale is interesting, for it is said that the Medici took the three balls of his mace, now the pawnbrokers' sign (*see* Balls), for their device.

**Muggins.** Slang for a fool or simpleton – a *juggins* is the same thing; also for a pettifogging magnate, a village leader. Muggins is not uncommon as a surname, and it is as well to remember that those bearing it usually like to hear it pronounced *Mewgins*.

**Muggletonian.** A follower of one Lodovic Muggleton (1609–98), a journeyman tailor, who, about 1651, set up for a prophet. He was sentenced to stand in the pillory, and was fined £500. The members of the sect – which maintained a sort of existence till about 1865 – believed that their two founders, Muggleton and John Reeve, were the 'two witnesses' spoken of in Rev. 11:3.

**Mugwump.** An Algonquin word meaning a chief; in Eliot's Indian Bible the word 'centurion' in the Acts is rendered *mugwump*. It is now applied in the United States to independent members of the Republican party, those who refuse to follow the dictum of a caucus, and all political Pharisees whose party vote cannot be relied on.

> 'I suppose I am a political mugwump,' said the Englishman. 'Not yet,' replied Mr Reed. 'You will be when you have returned to your allegiance.'
>
> *The Liverpool Echo*, July 19th, 1886

**Muhajirun.** *See* Ansar.

**Mulatto** (Span., from *mulo*, a mule). The offspring of a negress by a white man; loosely applied to any half-breed. *Cp.* Creole.

**Mulciber.** A name of Vulcan (*q.v.*) among the Romans; it means *the softener*, because he softened metals.

> Round about him [Mammon] lay on every side
> Great heaps of gold that never could be spent:
> Of which some were rude ore, not purified
> Of Mulciber's devouring element.
>
> Spenser, *Faërie Queene*, II, vii, 5

**Mule.** The offspring of a male ass and a mare; hence, a hybrid between other animals (or plants), as a *mule canary*, a cross between a canary and a goldfinch. The offspring of a stallion and a she-ass is not, properly speaking, a mule, but a *hinny*.

Very stubborn or obstinate people are sometimes called *mules*, in allusion to the well-known characteristic of the beast; and the *spinning-mule* was so called because it was –

> a kind of mixture of machinery between the warp-machine of Mr Arkwright and the woof-machine or hand-jenny of Mr Hargrave.
>
> *Encyc. Britannica*, 1797

***To shoe one's mule.*** To appropriate moneys committed to one's trust.

> He had the keeping and disposall of the moneys, and yet shod not his own mule.
>
> *History of Francion* (1655)

**Mull.** ***To make a mull of a job*** is to fail to do it properly. It is either a contraction of *muddle*, or from the old verb *to mull*, to reduce to powder.

Among Anglo-Indians members of the service in the Madras Presidency are known as *Mulls*. Here the word stands for *mulligatawny*.

**Mulla.** ***The Bard of Mulla's silver stream.*** So Spenser was called by Shenstone, because at one time his home in Ireland was on the banks of the Mulla, or Awbeg, a tributary of the Blackwater.

**Mulmutine Laws.** The code of Dunvallo Mulmutius, the sixteenth legendary King of the Britons (about 400 BC), son of Cloten, King of Cornwall. It is said to have been translated by Gildas from British into Latin, and to have formed the basis of King Alfred's code, which obtained in England till the Conquest. (Holinshed, *History of England*, iii, 1.)

> Mulmutius made our laws,
> Who was the first of Britain which did put
> His brows within a golden crown, and called
> Himself a king. Shakespeare, *Cymbeline*, 3, 1

**Mulready Envelope.** An envelope resembling a half-sheet of letter-paper, when folded, having on the front an ornamental design much like the wrapper of a comic annual by William Mulready (1786–1863), the artist. When the penny postage envelopes were first introduced (1840), these were the stamped envelopes of the day; they remained in circulation for one year only.

> A set of those odd-looking envelope-things,
> Where Britannia (who seems to be crucified) flings
> To her right and her left, funny people with wings
> Amongst elephants, Quakers, and Catabaw kings. –
> And a taper and wax, and small Queen's-heads in packs,
> Which, when notes are too big you must stick on their backs. *Ingoldsby Legends*

**Multipliers.** So alchemists, who pretended to multiply gold and silver, were called. An Act was passed (2 Henry IV, c. 4) making the 'art of multiplication' felony. In the *Canterbury Tales*, the Canon's Yeoman (*see Prologue* to his *Tale*) says he was reduced to poverty by alchemy, adding: 'Lo, such advantage is't to multiply.'

**Multitude, Nouns of.** Dame Juliana Berners, in her *Booke of St Albans* (1486), says, in designating companies we must not use the names of multitudes promiscuously, and examples her remark thus:

> We say a *congregacyon* of people, a *hoost* of men, a *felyshyppynge* of yeomen, and a *bevy* of ladyes; we must speak of a *herde* of dere, swannys, cranys, or wrenys, a *sege* of herons or bytourys, a *muster* of pecockes, a *watche* of nyghtyngales, *fllyghte* of doves, a *claterynge* of choughes, a *pryde* of lyons, a *slewthe* of beeres, a *gagle* of geys, a *skulke* of foxes, a *sculle* of frerys, a *pontificalitye* of prestys and a *superfluyte* of nonnes. *Booke of St Albans* (1486)

She adds, that a strict regard to these niceties better distinguishes 'gentyl men from ungentylmen', than regard to the rules of grammar, or even to the moral law.

The following nouns of multitude and their uses should be noted:

*Batch* or *Caste* of bread.
*Bench* of bishops, magistrates, etc.
*Bevy* of roes, quails, larks, pheasants, ladies, etc.
*Board* of directors.
*Brood* of chickens, etc.
*Catch* of fish taken in nets, etc.
*Clump* of trees.
*Cluster* of grapes, nuts, stars, etc.
*Congregation* of people at church, etc.
*Covey* of game birds.
*Crew* of sailors.
*Drove* of horses, ponies, beasts, etc.
*Federation* of states, trade unions, etc.
*Fell* of hair.
*Fleet* of ships.
*Flight* of bees, birds, stairs, etc.
*Flock* of birds, sheep, geese, etc.
*Galaxy* of beauties.
*Gang* of slaves, prisoners, thieves, etc.
*Haul* of fish caught in a net.
*Herd* of bucks, deer, harts, seals, swine, etc.
*Hive* of bees.
*League* of Nations, Association Football clubs, etc.
*Legion* of 'foul fiends'.
*Litter* of pigs, whelps, etc.
*Mob* of roughs, wild cattle, etc.
*Multitude* of men. In law, more than ten.
*Muster* of peacocks.
*Mute* of hounds.
*Nest* of rabbits, ants, etc.; shelves, etc.
*Pack* of hounds, playing cards, grouse, etc.
*Panel* of jurymen.
*Pencil* of rays, etc.
*Posse* of sheriff's officers.
*Pride* of lions.
*Rabble* of men ill-bread and ill-clad.
*Rookery* of rooks and seals, &of unhealthy houses.
*Rouleau* of money.
*School* of whales, etc.
*Shoal* of mackerel, herring, etc.
*Shock* of hair, corn, etc.
*Skein* of ducks, thread, worsted.
*Skulke* of foxes.
*String* of horses.
*Stud* of mares.
*Swarm* of bees, locusts, etc.
*Take* of fish.
*Team* of oxen, horses, etc.
*Tribe* of goats.

**Multum in parvo** (Lat.). Much [information] condensed into few words or into a small compass.

**Mum.** A strong beer made in Brunswick; said to be so called from Christian Mumme, by whom it was first brewed in the late 15th century.

***Mum's the word.*** Keep what is told you a profound secret. *See* Mumchance.

> Seal up your lips, and give no words but – mum.
>
> Shakespeare, *2 Henry VI*, 1, 2

**Mumbo Jumbo.** The name given by Europeans (possibly from some lost native word) to a bogy or grotesque idol venerated by certain African tribes; hence, any object of blind and unreasoning worship.

Mungo Park in his *Travels in Africa* says that Mumbo Jumbo is not an idol, any more than the American *Lynch*, but merely one disguised to punish unruly wives. It not infrequently happens that a house which contains many wives becomes unbearable. In such a case, either the husband or an agent disguises himself as 'Mumbo Jumbo' and comes at dusk with a following, making the most hideous noises possible. When the women have been sufficiently scared, 'Mumbo' seizes the chief offender, ties her to a tree, and scourges her, amidst the derision of all present.

**Mumbudget.** An old exclamation meaning 'Silence, please'; perhaps from a children's game in which silence was occasionally necessary. *Cp.* Budget, Cry; *and* Mumchance, *below*.

> Have these bones rattled, and this head
> So often in thy quarrel bled?
> Nor did I ever winch or grudge it,
> For thy dear sake. Quoth she, Mumbudget.
>
> Butler, *Hudibras*, I, iii, 208

**Mumchance.** Silence. Mumchance was a game of chance with dice, in which silence was indispensable. *Mum* is connected with *mumble* (Ger. *mummeln*; Dan. *mumle*, to mumble). *Cp.* Mumbudget.

> And for 'mumchance', howe'er the *chance* may fall,
> You must be *mum* for fear of spoiling all.
>
> *Machiavell's Dogg*

**Mummer.** A contemptuous name for an actor; from the parties that formerly went from house to house at Christmas-time *mumming*, i.e. giving a performance of St George and the Dragon and the like, in dumb-show.

> Peel'd, patch'd, and piebald, linsey-woolsey brothers.
> Grave mummers! sleeveless some, and shirtless others.
>
> Pope, *Dunciad*, III, 115

**Mummy** is the Arabic *mum*, wax used for embalming; from the custom of anointing the body with wax and wrapping it in cerecloth.

***Mummy wheat.*** Wheat said to have been taken from ancient Egyptian tombs, which, when sown, fructifies. No seed, however, will preserve its vitality for centuries, and what is called *mummy* *wheat* is a species of corn commonly grown on the southern shores of the Mediterranean.

**Mumpers.** Beggars; from the old slang to *mump*, to cheat or to sponge on others, probably from Dutch *mompen*, to cheat. In Norwich, Christmas waits used to be called 'Mumpers'.

> A parcel of wretches hopping about by the assistance of their crutches, like so many Lincoln's Inn Fields mumpers, drawing into a body to attack the coach of some charitable lord. Ned Ward, *The London Spy*, Pt v

***Mumping day.*** St Thomas' Day, December 21st, is so called in some parts of the country, because on this day the poor used to go about begging, or, as it was called, 'a-gooding', that is, getting gifts to procure *good things* for Christmas.

In Lincolnshire the name used to be applied to Boxing Day (*q.v.*); in Warwickshire the term used was 'going a-corning', i.e. getting gifts of corn.

**Munchausen, Baron.** A traveller who meets with the most marvellous adventures, the hero of a collection of stories by Rudolf Erich Raspe, published in English in 1785. The incidents were compiled from various sources, including the adventures of an actual Hieronymus Karl Friedrich von Münchhausen (1720–97), a German officer in the Russian army, noted for his marvellous stories, Bebel's *Facetiae*, Castiglione's *Cortegiano*, Bildermann's *Utopia*, etc. The book is a satire either on Baron de Tott, or on Bruce, whose *Travels in Abyssinia* were looked upon as mythical when they first appeared.

**Mundane Egg.** *See* Egg.

**Mundilfoeri.** One of the giant race of *Scandinavian mythology*. He was the father of Mani and Sol (*moon* and *sun*).

**Mundungus.** Bad tobacco; originally offal, or refuse, from Span *mondongo,* black pudding.

In Sterne's *Sentimental Journey* (1768), the word is used as a name for Samuel Sharp, a surgeon, who published *Letters from Italy*; and Smollett, who published *Travels through France and Italy* (1766), 'one continual snarl', was called 'Smelfungus'.

**Munera** (Lat. *munero*, to present or bestow). In Spenser's *Faërie Queene* (V, ii), the typification of bribery. She was the daughter of Pollente, the Saracen, to whom he gave all the spoils he took from those who fell into his power. Talus, the iron page, of Sir Artegal, chopped off her golden hands and silver feet, and tossed her into the moat.

**Mungo, St.** An alternative name for St Kentigern (*q.v.*).

**Muninn.** One of Odin's two ravens. *See* Huginn.

**Munkar** and **Nakir.** Two black angels of *Mohammedan mythology* who interrogate the dead immediately after burial. The first two questions they ask are, 'Who is your Lord?' and 'Who is your prophet?' Their voices are like thunder, their aspects hideous; if the scrutiny is satisfactory the soul is gently drawn forth from the lips of the deceased, and the body is left to repose in peace; if not, the body is beaten about the head with clubs half iron and half flame, and the soul is wrenched forth by racking torments.

> Do you not see those spectres that are stirring the burning coals? They are Monkir and Nakir. Beckford, *Vathek*

**Murderer's Bible, The.** *See* Bible, specially named.

**Muscadins.** Parisian exquisites who aped those of London about the time of the French Revolution. They wore top-boots with thick soles, knee-breeches, a dress-coat with long tails, and a high stiff collar, and carried a thick cudgel called a *constitution*. It was thought 'John Bullish' to assume a huskiness of voice, a discourtesy of manners, and a swaggering vulgarity of speech and behaviour.

> Cockneys of London, Muscadins of Paris. Byron, *Don Juan*, viii, 124

**Muscular Christianity.** Healthy or strong-minded Christianity, which braces a man to fight the battle of life bravely and manfully. The term was applied to the teachings of Charles Kingsley – somewhat to his annoyance.

> It is a school of which Mr Kingsley is the ablest doctor; and its doctrine has been described fairly and cleverly as 'muscular Christianity'. *Edinburgh Review*, Jan., 1858

**Muses.** In *Greek mythology* the nine daughters of Zeus and Mnemosyne; originally goddesses of memory only, but later identified with individual arts and sciences. The paintings of Herculaneum show all nine in their respective attributes. They are:

*Calliope:* the chief of the Muses.
*Clio:* heroic exploits and history.
*Euterpe:* Dionysiac music and the double flute.
*Thalia:* gaiety, pastoral life, and comedy.
*Melpomene:* song, harmony, and tragedy.
*Terpsichore:* choral dance and soung.
*Erato:* the lyre and erotic poetry.
*Polyhymnia:* the inspired and stately hymn.
*Urania:* celestial phenomena, and astronomy.

*See* these names.

**Museum.** Literally, a home or seat of the Muses. The first building to have this name was the university erected at Alexandria by Ptolemy Soter about 300 BC.

**Mushroom.** Slang for an umbrella, on account of the similarity in shape; and as mushrooms are of very rapid growth, applied figuratively to almost anything that 'springs up in the night', as a new, quickly built suburb, an upstart family, and so on. In 1787 Bentham said – somewhat unjustly – 'Sheffield is an oak; Birmingham is a mushroom.'

***To mushroom.*** To expand into a mushroom shape; said especially of certain soft-nosed rifle-bullets used in big-game shooting.

**Music. *Father of modern music.*** Mozart (1756–91) has been so called.

***Father of Greek music.*** Terpander (fl. 676 BC).

***The prince of music.*** Giovanni Pierluigi da Palestrina (1524–94).

***Music hath charms, etc.*** The opening line of Congreve's *Mourning Bride*.

Music hath charms to soothe a savage breast,
To soften rocks, or bend a knotted oak.

The allusion is to Orpheus (*q.v.*), who –

With his lute made trees,
And the mountain tops that freeze,
Bow themselves when he did sing.
Shakespeare, *Henry VIII*, 3, 1

And the lines are among those most frequently misquoted in the whole of English poetry, the words 'a savage breast' being turned into 'the savage beast'. James Bramston, in his *Man of Taste* (1733), wittily substituted for the second line, 'And therefore proper at a sheriff's feast'.

***The music of the spheres.*** *See* Spheres.

***To face the music.*** *See* Face.

**Musical Notation.** *See* Doh.

**Musical Small-coal Man.** Thomas Britton (1654–1714), a coal-dealer of Clerkenwell, who established a musical club over his shop in which all the musical celebrities of the day took part.

**Musicians. *Father of musicians.*** Jubal, 'the father of all such as handle the harp and organ' (Gen. 4:21).

**Musits** or **Musets.** Gaps in a hedge; places through which a hare makes his way to escape the hounds.

The many musits through the which he goes
Are like a labyrinth to amaze his foes.
Shakespeare, *Venus and Adonis*

The passing of the hare through these gaps is termed *musing*. The word is from O.Fr. *muce*, a hiding-place.

**Muslim.** *See* Moslem.

**Muslin.** So called from Mosul, in Asia, where it was first manufactured (Fr. *mousseline*, Ital. *mussolino*).

**Mustard.** So called because originally *must*, new wine (Lat. *mustus*, fresh, new) was used in mixing the paste. Fable, however, alleges that the name arose because in 1382 Philip the Bold, Duke of Burgundy, granted to the town of Dijon, noted for its mustard, armorial bearings with the motto *Moult me tarde* [*Multum ardeo*, I ardently desire]. The arms and motto, engraved on the principal gate, were adopted as a trade-mark by the mustard merchants, and got shortened into Moult-tarde (to burn much).

***After meat, mustard.*** Expressive of the sentiment that something that would have been welcome a little earlier has arrived too late, I have now no longer need of it. *C'est de la moutarde après dîner*.

**Mutton** (Fr. *mouton*, a sheep). In old slang, a prostitute, frequently extended to *laced mutton*.

*Speed*: Ay, sir: I, a lost mutton, gave your letter to her, a laced mutton; and she, a laced mutton, gave me, a lost mutton, nothing for my labour.
Shakespeare, *Two Gentlemen of Verona*, 1, 1

The old lecher hath gotten holy mutton to him, a Nunne, my lord.
Greene, *Friar Bacon*

It was with this suggestion that Rochester wrote his mock epitaph on Charles II:

Here lies our mutton-eating king,
Whose word no man relies on;
He never *said* a foolish thing,
And never *did* a wise one.

***Come and eat your mutton with me.*** Come and dine with me.

***Dead as mutton.*** Absolutely dead.

***Mutton fist.*** A large, coarse, red fist.

***Muttons.*** A Stock Exchange term for the Turkish '65 loan, partly secured by the sheep-tax.

***To return to our muttons.*** To come back to the subject. *See* Moutons.

**Mutual Friends.** Can people have mutual friends? Strictly speaking *not*; but, especially since Dickens adopted the solecism in the title of his novel, *Our Mutual Friend* (1864), many people object to the correct term, *common friends. Mutual* implies reciprocity from one to the other (Lat. *mutare*, to change); the friendship between two friends should be mutual, but this mutuality cannot be extended to a third party.

*Edwin and Emma*

**Mynheer.** The Dutch equivalent for 'Mr'; hence, sometimes used for a Dutchman.

'Tis thus I spend my moments here,
And wish myself a Dutch mynheer.

Cowper, *To Lady Austin*

**Myrmidons of the Law.** Bailiffs, sheriffs' officers, and other law menials. Any rough fellow employed to annoy another is the employer's myrmidon.

The Myrmidons were a people of Thessaly who followed Achilles to the siege of Troy, and were distinguished for their savage brutality, rude behaviour, and thirst for rapine.

**Myrrha.** The mother of Adonis, in Greek legend. She is fabled to have had an unnatural love for her own father, and to have been changed into a myrtle tree.

**Myrrophores** (Gr., myrrh bearers). The three Marys who went to see the sepulchre, bearing myrrh and spices (*see* Mark 16:1). In Christian art they are represented as carrying vases of myrrh in their hands.

**Mysterium.** The letters of this word which, until the time of the Reformation, was engraved on the Pope's tiara, are said to make up the number 666 (*see* Number of the Beast). *See also* Rev. 17:5.

**Mystery.** In English two totally distinct words have been confused here; *mystery*, the archaic term for a handicraft, as in *the art and mystery of printing*, is the same as the French *métier* (trade, craft, profession), and is the M.E. *mistere*, from mediaeval Lat. *misterium, ministerium*, ministry.

***Mystery***, meaning something beyond human comprehension, is (through French) from the Lat. *mysterium* and Gr. *mustes*, from *muein*, to close the eyes or lips. It is from this sense that the old miracle-plays, mediaeval dramas in which the characters and story were drawn from sacred history, were called *Mysteries*, though, as they were frequently presented by members of some single guild, or *mystery* in the handicraft sense, even here the words were confused and opening made for many puns.

***The three greater mysteries.*** In ecclesiastical language, the Trinity, Original Sin, and the Incarnation.

# N

**N.** The fourteenth letter of our alphabet; represented in Egyptian hieroglyph by a water-line (~~). It was called *nun* (a fish) in Phoenician, whence the Greek *nu*.

**N,** a numeral. Gr. ν = 50, but, ν = 50,000. N (Lat.) = 90, or 900, but N̄ = 90,000, or 900,000.

**n.** The sign ~ (*tilde*) over an 'n' indicates that the letter is to be pronounced as though followed by a 'y', as *cañon* = *canyon*. It is used almost solely in words from Spanish.

**n-dimensional.** A mathematical term meaning, having an indefinite number of dimensions, as *n-dimensional space*. *Cp.* n*th*.

**n ephelkustic.** The Greek nu (ν) added for euphony to the end of a word that terminates with a vowel when the next word in the sentence begins with a vowel.

**N. H.** Bugs. The letters are the initials of Norfolk Howard (*q.v.*).

**N** or **M.** The answer given to the first question in the Church of England Catechism; and it means that here the person being catechised gives his or her *name* or *names*, Lat. *nomen vel nomina*. The abbreviation for the plural *nomina* was – as usual – the doubled initial (*cp.* 'LL.D.' for Doctor of Laws); and this, when printed (as it was in old Prayer Books) in black-letter and close together, 𝔑𝔑. came to be taken for 𝔐.

In the same way the *N.* in the marriage-service ('I *M.* take thee *N.* to my wedded wife') merely indicates that the *name* is to be spoken in each case; but the *M.* and *N.* in the publication of banns ('I publish the Banns of Marriage between *M.* of — and *N.* of —') stand for *maritus*, bridegroom, and *nupta*, bride.

**Nab.** Colloquial for to seize suddenly, without warning. (*Cp.* Norw. and Swed. *nappa*, Dan., *nappe*). Hence *nabman*, a sheriff's officer or police-constable.

> Old Dornton has sent the nabman after him at last.
>
> Scott, *Guy Mannering* (dramatised by Terry, ii, 3)

**Nabob.** Corruption of the Hindu *nawab*, plural of *naib*, a deputy-governor under the Mogul Empire. These men acquired great wealth and lived in splendour; hence, *Rich as a nabob* came to be applied in England to a merchant who had attained great wealth in the Indies, and returned to live in his native country.

**Nabonassar, Era of.** An era that was in use for centuries by the Chaldean astronomers, and was generally followed by Hipparchus and Ptolemy. It commenced at midday, Wed., Feb. 26th, 747 BC, the date of the accession of Nabonassar (d.733 BC), as King of Babylonia. The year consisted of 12 months of 30 days each, with 5 complementary days added at the end. As no intercalary day was allowed for, the first day of the year fell one day earlier every four years than the Julian year; consequently, to transpose a date from one era to another it is necessary to know the exact day and month of the Nabonassarian date, and to remember that 1460 Julian years are equal to 1461 Babylonian.

**Naboth's Vineyard.** The possession of another coveted by one able to possess himself of it. (1 Kings 21).

> The little Manor House property had always been a Naboth's vineyard to his father.
>
> *Good Words*, 1887

**Nabu.** *See* Nebo.

**Nadab,** in Dryden's *Absalom and Achitophel* (*q.v.*) is meant for Lord Howard of Escrick, a profligate who laid claim to great piety. Nadab offered incense with strange fire, and was slain by the Lord (Lev. 10:2); and Lord Howard, while imprisoned in the Tower, is said to have mixed the consecrated wafer with a compound of roasted apples and sugar, called lamb's-wool.

> And canting Nadab let oblivion damn,
> Who made new porridge of the paschal lamb
>
> *Absalom and Achitophel*, Pt i, 538–9

**Nadir.** An Arabic word, signifying that point in the heavens which is directly opposite to the zenith, i.e. directly under our feet; hence, figuratively, the lowest depths of degradation.

> The seventh century is the nadir of the human mind in Europe.
>
> Hallam, *Hist. Lit. in Midd. Ages*, I, i, 4

**Naevius.** *See* Accius Naevius.

**Nag, Nagging.** Constant fault-finding. (A.S. *gnag-an*, to gnaw, bite.) We call a slight but constant pain, like a toothache, a *nagging pain*.

**Nag's Head Consecration.** On the passing of the second Act of Uniformity in Queen Elizabeth's reign (1559), fourteen bishops vacated their sees, and all the other sees, except Llandaff, were at the time vacant. The question was how to obtain consecration so as to preserve the apostolic succession unbroken, as Llandaff refused to officiate at Parker's consecration. In this dilemma (the story runs) Scory, a deposed bishop, was sent for, and officiated at the Nag's Head tavern, in Cheapside, thus transmitting the succession.

Such is the tale; Strype refutes it, and so does Dr Hook. We are told that it was not the *consecration* which took place at the Nag's Head, but only that those who took part in it dined there subsequently; and, further, that Bishops Barlow, Scory, Coverdale, and Hodgkins, all officiated at the consecration.

**Naglfar.** The ship of the Scandinavian giants, in which they will embark on 'the last day' to give battle to the gods. It is made of the nails of the dead (Old Norse, *nagl*, and *fara*, to make), and is piloted by Hrymir.

**Naiads.** Nymphs of lakes, fountains, rivers, and streams in *classical mythology*.

> You nymphs, call'd Naiads, of the wand'ring brooks,
> With your sedg'd crowns, and ever-harmless looks,
> Leave your crisp channels, and on this green land
> Answer your summons: Juno does command.
>
> Shakespeare, *Tempest*, 4, 1

**Nail. *The nails with which our Lord was fastened to the cross*** were, in the Middle Ages, objects of great reverence. Sir John Maundeville says, 'He had two in his hondes, and two in his feet; and of on of theise the emperour of Canstantynoble made a brydille to his hors, to bere him in bataylle; and throghe vertue thereof he overcam his enemyes' (c. vii). Fifteen are shown as relics. *See* Iron Crown.

In ancient Rome a nail was driven into the wall of the temple of Jupiter every 13th September. This was originally done to tally the year, but subsequently it became a religious ceremony for warding off calamities and plagues from the city. Originally the nail was driven by the *praetor maximus*, subsequently by one of the consuls, and lastly by the dictator (*see* Livy, vii, 3).

***A nail*** was formerly a measure of weight of 8 lb. It was used for wool, hemp, beef, cheese, etc. It was also a measure of length, = 2¼ in.

> *Motto:* You shall have ... a dozen beards, to stuffe two dozen cushions.
> *Licio:* Then they be big ones.
> *Dello:* They be halfe a yard broad, and a nayle, three quarters long, and a foote thick.
>
> Lyly, *Midas*, V, ii (1589)

***For want of a nail.*** 'For want of a nail, the shoe is lost; for want of a shoe, the horse is lost; and for want of a horse, the rider is lost' (Herbert, *Jacula Prudentum*).

***Hard as nails.*** Stern, hard-hearted, unsympathetic; able to stand hard blows like nails. The phrase is used both with a physical and a figurative sense; a man in perfect training is 'as hard as nails', and bigotry, straitlacedness, rigid puritanical pharisaism, make people 'hard as nails'.

> I know I'm as hard as nails already; I don't want to get more so. Edna Lyall, *Donovan*, ch. xxiii

***Hung on the nail.*** Up the spout, put in pawn. The custom referred to is the old one of hanging each pawn on a nail, with a number attached, and giving the customer a duplicate thereof.

***I nailed him*** (or ***it***). I hooked him, I pinned him, meaning I secured him. Is. (22:23) says, 'I will fasten him as a nail in a sure place'.

***On the nail.*** At once; without hesitation; as, 'to pay down on the nail'.

In O'Keefe's *Recollections* we are told that in the centre of Limerick Exchange is a pillar with a circular plate of copper about 3 ft in diameter, called *The Nail*, on which the earnest of all Stock Exchange bargains has to be paid; there were four pillars called *Nails* and used for a similar purpose at Bristol; and at the Liverpool Exchange there was a plate of copper called *The Nail* on which bargains were settled. But the phrase cannot come from any such source, as it was common in England by the 16th century, long before Exchanges were in existence. *Cp.* Supernaculum.

***To drive a nail into one's coffin.*** *See* Coffin.

***To hit the nail on the head.*** To come to a right conclusion. In Latin, *Rem tenes.* The Germans have the exact phrase, *Den Nagel auf den kopf treffen.*

***To nail to the counter.*** To convict and expose as false or spurious; as, 'I nailed that lie to the counter at once.' From the custom of shopkeepers nailing false money that is passed to them to the counter as a warning to others that 'once bit's twice shy'.

***Tooth and nail.*** *See* Tooth.

***With colours nailed to the mast.*** *See* Colours.

***Nail-paring.*** Superstitious people are very particular as to the day on which they cut their nails. The old rhyme is:

> Cut them on Monday, you cut them for health;
> Cut them on Tuesday, you cut them for wealth;
> Cut them on Wednesday, you cut them for news;
> Cut them on Thursday a new pair of shoes;
> Cut them on Friday, you cut them for sorrow;
> Cut them on Saturday, you see your true love tomorrow;

Cut them on Sunday, your safety seek
The devil will have you the rest of the week.

Another rhyme conveys an even stronger warning on the danger of nail-cutting on a Sunday:

A man had better ne'er be born
As have his nails on a Sunday shorn.

**Nain Rouge** (Fr. red dwarf). A lutin or house spirit of Normandy, kind to fishermen. There is another called *Le petit homme rouge* (the little red man).

**Nairs** or **Nayres.** The aristocrats of Malabar; the noble and military caste. *See* Poleas.

**Naïveté** (Lat. *nativum*, native). Ingenuous simplicity; the artless innocence of one ignorant of the conventions of society. The term is also applied to poetry, painting, and sculpture.

**Naked.** A.S. *nacod*, a common Teutonic word, connected with Lat. *nudus*, nude. Destitute of covering; hence, figuratively, defenceless, exposed; without extraneous assistance, as *with the naked eye*, i.e. without a telescope or other optical aid.

***Naked boy,*** or ***lady.*** The meadow saffron (*Colchicum autumnale*); so called because, like the almond, peach, etc., the flowers come out before the leaves. It is poetically called 'the leafless orphan of the year', the flowers being orphaned or destitute of foliage.

The *Naked Boy Courts* and *Alleys*, of which there are more than one in the City of London, are named from the public-house sign, which is said to have been adopted in the 16th century because, owing to the constant changes in fashion, it was impossible to clothe the boy without his almost immediately becoming old-fashioned.

***The naked truth.*** The plain, unvarnished truth; truth without trimmings. The fable says that Truth and Falsehood went bathing; Falsehood came first out of the water, and dressed herself in Truth's garments. Truth, unwilling to take those of Falsehood, went naked.

**Nakir.** *See* Munkar.

**Nala.** In Hindu legend, a king of Nishadha, and husband of Damayanti, whose story is one of the best known in the *Mahabharata*. Damayanti, through enchantment, falls in love with Nala without ever having seen him; the gods want her for themselves, and employ the unsuspecting Nala as their advocate; she declares that none but Nala shall possess her, whereupon the four gods appear in Nala's shape and Damayanti is obliged to make her choice, which she does – correctly. Nala is then given many magic gifts by the gods; the wedding is celebrated; but later Nala loses his all by gambling, and becomes a wanderer, while Damayanti returns to her father's court. Many tribulations and adventures (in which magic performs a large part) befall the lovers before they are reunited.

**Namby-pamby.** Wishy-washy; insipid, weakly sentimental: said especially of authors. It was the nickname of *Ambrose* Philips (1671–1749), bestowed upon him by Harry Carey, the dramatist, for his verses addressed to Lord Carteret's children, and was adopted by Pope.

**Name.**

What's in a name? That which we call a rose,
By any other name would smell as sweet.
Shakespeare, *Romeo and Juliet*, 21, 2

***Give a dog a bad name.*** *See* Dog.

***Give it a name.*** Tell me what it is you would like, said when offering a reward, a drink, etc.

***In the name of.*** In reliance upon; or by the authority of.

***Their name liveth for evermore.*** These consolatory words, so often seen on memorials to those who fell in the Great War, are from the Apocrypha:

Their bodies are buried in peace; but their name liveth for evermore. Ecclus. 44:14

***To call a person names.*** To blackguard him by calling him nicknames, or hurling opprobrious epithets at him.

Sticks and stones
May break my bones,
But names can never hurt me. Old Rhyme

***To name the day.*** To fix the day of the wedding – which is a privilege belonging to the bride to be.

***To take God's name in vain.*** To use it profanely, thoughtlessly, or irreverently.

Thou shalt not take the name of the Lord thy God in vain. Exod. 20:7

Among all primitive peoples, and the ancient Hebrews were no exception, the *name* of a deity is regarded as his manifestation, and is treated with the greatest respect and veneration; and among savage tribes there is a widespread feeling of the danger of disclosing one's name, because this would enable an enemy by magic means to work one some deadly injury; the Greeks were particularly careful to disguise or reverse uncomplimentary names (*see* Erinnyes, Eumenides, Euxine).

The name Jehovah itself is an instance of the extreme sanctity with which the name of God was invested, for this is a disguised form of the name. This word jhvh, the sacred tetragrammaton (*q.v.*), was too sacred to use, so the scribes added the vowels of *Adonai*, thereby indicating that the reader was to say *Adonai* instead of jhvh. At the time of the Renaissance these vowels and consonants were taken for the sacred name itself, and hence *Jehovah* or *Yahwe*. *Cp.* The Seven Names of God, *under* Seven.

**Nancy, Miss.** An effeminate, foppish youth.

The celebrated actress, 'Mrs' Anne Oldfield (*see* Narcissa) was nicknamed 'Miss Nancy'.

**Nankeen.** So called from Nankin, in China. It is the natural yellow colour of Nankin cotton.

**Nanna.** Wife of Balder, *Scandinavian mythology*. When the blind god Hodur slew her husband, she threw herself upon his funeral pile and was burnt to death.

**Nantes.** *Edict of Nantes.* The decree of Henri IV of France, published from Nantes in 1598, securing freedom of religion to all Protestants. Louis XIV revoked it in 1685.

**Nap.** The doze or short sleep gets its name from A.S. *hnaeppian*, to sleep lightly; the surface of cloth is probably so called from Mid. Dutch *noppe*; and *Nap*, the card game, is so called in honour of Napoleon III.

***To catch one napping.*** *See* Catch.

***To go nap.*** To set oneself to make five tricks (all one can) in the game of Nap; hence, to risk all you have on some venture, to back it through thick and thin.

**Naphtha.** The Greek name for an inflammable, bituminous substance coming from the ground in certain districts; in the Medea legend it is the name of the drug used by the witch for anointing the wedding robe of Glauce, daughter of King Creon, whereby she was burnt to death on the morning of her marriage with Jason.

**Napier's Bones.** The little slips of bone or ivory on which were figures, invented by Baron Napier of Merchiston (1550–1617), for shortening the labour of trigonometrical calculations. By shifting these rods the result required is obtained.

**Napoleon III.** Few men have had so many nicknames.

Man of December, so called because his *coup d'état* was December 2nd, 1851, and he was made emperor December 2nd, 1852.

Man of Sedan, and, by a pun, *M. Sedantaire*. It was at Sedan he surrendered his sword to William I, King of Prussia (1870).

Man of Silence, from his great taciturnity.

Comte d'Arenenberg, the name and title he assumed when he escaped from the fortress of Ham.

Badinguet, the name of the mason who changed clothes with him when he escaped from Ham. The emperor's partisans were called *Badingueux*, those of the empress were *Montijoyeaux*.

Boustrapa is a compound of Bou[logne], Stra-[sbourg], and Pa[ris] the places of his noted escapades.

Rantipole = harum-scarum, half-fool and half-madman.

Verhuel. A patronymic, which cannot be here explained.

There are some curious numerical coincidences connected with Napoleon III and Eugénie. The last complete year of their reign was 1869. (In 1870 Napoleon was dethroned and exiled.)

Now, if to the year of coronation (1852), you add either the birth of Napoleon, or the birth of Eugénie, or the capitulation of Paris, or the date of marriage, the sum will always be 1869. For example:

| | | | |
|---|---|---|---|
| 1852 | Coronation. | 1852 | |
| 1 | | 1 | |
| 8 | Birth of | 8 | Birth of |
| 0 | Napoleon. | 2 | Eugénie. |
| 8 | | 6 | |
| 1869 | | 1869 | |

| | | | |
|---|---|---|---|
| 1852 | | 1852 | |
| 1 | | 1 | |
| 8 | Date of | 8 | Capitulation of |
| 5 | marriage. | 7 | Paris. |
| 3 | | 1 | |
| 1869 | | 1869 | |

And if to the year of *marriage* (1853) these dates are added, they will give 1870, the fatal year.

**Napoo.** Soldier slang (introduced during the Great War) for 'nothing doing' or for something that is no use. Such-and-such a proposal, or so-and-so is 'napoo' – i.e. not the slightest good. It represents the French phrase, *Il n'y en a plus*, there is no more of it.

**Nappy Ale.** Strong ale has been so called for many centuries, probably because it contains a *nap* or frothy head.

**Naraka.** The hell of *Hindu mythology*. It has twenty-eight divisions, in some of which the victims are mangled by ravens and owls; in others they are doomed to swallow cakes boiling hot, or walk over burning sands. Each division has its name; *Rurava* (fearful) is for liars and false witnesses; *Rodha* (obstruction) for those who plunder a town, kill a cow, or strangle a man; *Sûkara* (swine) for drunkards and stealers of gold; etc.

**Narcissa,** in the *Night Thoughts*, was Elizabeth Lee, Dr Young's step-daughter. In Night, iii, the poet says she was privately buried at Montpelier, because, being a Protestant, she was 'denied the charity that dogs enjoy'.

In Pope's *Moral Essays* 'Narcissa' stands for the celebrated actress, 'Mrs' Anne Oldfield (1683–1730). When she died her remains lay in state attended by two noblemen. She was buried in Westminster Abbey in a very fine Brussels lace head-dress, a holland shift, with a tucker and double-ruffles of the same lace, new kid gloves, etc.

> 'Odious! in woollen? 'Twould a saint provoke!'
> Were the last words that poor Narcissa spoke.
>
> Pope, *Moral Essays*, i, 246

*In woollen* is an allusion to a law enacted for the benefit of the wool-trade, that all shrouds were to be made of wool.

**Narcissus.** The son of Cephisus in *Greek mythology*; a beautiful youth saw his reflection in a fountain, and thought it the presiding nymph of the place. He tried to reach it, and jumped into the fountain, where he died. The nymphs came to take up the body that they might pay it funeral honours, but found only a flower, which they called by his name. (Ovid's *Metamorphoses*, iii, 346, etc.)

> Plutarch says the plant is called Narcissus from the Greek *narke* (numbness), and that it is properly *narcosis*, meaning the plant which produces numbness or palsy.

Echo fell in love with Narcissus.

> Sweet Echo, sweetest nymph that liv'st unseen …
> Canst thou not tell me of a gentle pair,
> That likest thy Narcissus are?
>
> Milton, *Comus*, 235

**Nardac.** The highest title of honour in the realm of Lilliput (Swift's *Gulliver's Travels*). Gulliver received this distinction for carrying off the whole fleet of the Blefuscudians.

**Narrowdale Noon.** To defer a matter *till Narrowdale noon* is to defer it indefinitely. Narrowdale is the local name for the narrowest part of Dovedale, Derbyshire, in which dwell a few cotters, who never see the sun all the winter, and when its beams first pierce the dale in the spring it is only for a few minutes in the afternoon.

**Naseby.** Fable has it that this town in Northamptonshire is so called because it was considered the *navel* (A.S. *nafela*) or centre of England, just as Delphi (*q.v.*) was considered 'the navel of the earth'. Fact, however, must destroy the illusion: the town's name in Domesday Book is *Navesberi*, showing that it was the *burgh* or dwelling of Hnaef, a Dane.

**Naso.** The 'surname' of Ovid (Publius Ovidius Naso, 43 BC–18 AD), the Roman poet, author of *Metamorphoses*. Naso means 'nose', hence Holofernes' pun; 'And why Naso, but for smelling out the odoriferous flowers of fancy.' (Shakespeare, *Love's Labour's Lost*, 4, 2.)

**Nasser.** The Arabian merchant whose fables were the delight of the Arabs. D'Herbelot tells us that when Mohammed read them the Old Testament stories they cried out with one voice that Nasser's tales were the best; upon which the Prophet gave his malediction on Nasser, and all who read him.

**Nastrond.** The worst place of torment in the ancient Scandinavian hell, where serpents incessantly pour forth venom from the high walls, and where the murderer and the perjured are doomed to live for ever. The word means, 'the strand of the dead', *nà*, a dead body, and *strond*, a strand.

**National Anthem.** It is said by some that both the words and music of 'God save the King', the British national anthem, were composed by Dr John Bull (d.1628), organist at Antwerp cathedral 1617–28, where the original MS is still preserved. Others attribute them to Henry Carey, author of *Sally in our Alley*. The words, 'Send him victorious', etc., look like a Jacobite song, and Sir John Sinclair tells us he saw that verse cut in an old glass tankard, the property of P. Murray Threipland, of Fingask Castle, whose predecessors were staunch Jacobites.

No doubt the words have often been altered. The air and opening words were probably suggested by the *Domine Salvum* of the Catholic Church. In 1605 the lines, 'Frustrate their knavish tricks', etc., were perhaps added in reference to the Gunpowder Plot; and in 1740 Henry Carey reset both words and music for the Mercers' Company on the birthday of George II.

The *National Anthems* or principal patriotic songs of the leading nations are:

Austria: In the old Empire, *Gott erhalte Franz den Kaiser, Unsern guten Kaiser Franz* (God protect Franz the Kaiser, our good Kaiser Franz); air by Haydn.

Belgium: The *Brabançonne* (*q.v.*).

Denmark: *The Song of the Danebrog* (*see* Danebrog); *Kong Christian stod ved hoïen Mast, Rög og Damp* (King Christian stood beside the lofty mast, In mist and smoke).

France: The *Marseillaise* (*q.v.*).

Germany: In the former German Empire, *Deutschland über alles* (Germany over all), and *Die Wacht am Rhein* (The watch – or guard – on the Rhine).

Holland: *Wien Neerlandsch bloed in de aders vloeit, Van vreemde smetten vrij* … (Let him in whose veins flows the blood of the Netherlands, free from an alien strain …)

Hungary: The Rakoczy March; *Tied vagyok, tied hazán! E siv e lélek!* (Thine, I am, thine, my fatherland, heart and soul!).

Italy: Mercantini's *Italy has awaked*; *Si scopron le tombe, si levano i morti* (The tombs are opened, the dead are rising).

Norway: *Ja, vi elsker det te Landet som det stiger frem* (Yes, we love our country, just as it is).

Russia: In the days of the Empire, *God protect the Tsar*; the air by Lwoff is sung in England to –

God the All-terrible King who ordainest,
Great winds thy clarion, lightning thy sword.

Sweden: du *gamla du friska, du fjellhöga Nord, Du tysta, Du glädjerika sköna!* (Thou ancient, free, and mountainous North! Thou silent, joyous, and beautiful North!)

Switzerland: *Rufst du, mein Vaterland. Sieh uns mit Herz und Hand, All dir geweiht!* (Thou call'st, my Fatherland! Behold us, heart and hand, all devoted to thee!)

The United States: *The Star-spangled Banner*. *See* Stars and Stripes.

In Wales the chief patriotic song is *March of the Men of Harlech*; in Scotland, *Scots wha hae wi' Wallace bled!* and in Ireland *The Wearing o' the Green*, *A Nation once Again*, or *Who Fears to Speak of 'Ninety-eight?*

**National Colours.** (*See* Colours.)

**National Convention.** The assembly of deputies which assumed the government of France on the overthrow of the throne in 1792. It succeeded the National Assembly (*cp.* Constituent Assembly).

**National Debt.** Money borrowed by a Government, on the security of the taxes, which are pledged to the lenders for the payment of interest. The portion of our National Debt which is converted into bonds or annuities is known as the *Funded debt*, and the portion that is repayable at a stated time or on demand as the *Floating debt*.

*The National Debt* in William III's reign was £15,730,439.

At the commencement of the American war, £128,583,635.

At the close thereof, £249,851,628.

At the close of the French war, £840,850,491.

The existence of National Debts is almost entirely due to wars, as the following figures will show in the case of the British Debt.

Just before the Revolution of 1688 it stood at £664,263; the Revolution added nearly £16,000,000; the Marlborough campaigns in Queen Anne's reign added nearly £38,000,000, the American War, in George III's, £121,000,000, and the Napoleonic Wars (1793–1816) over £600,000,000, bringing the total debt in 1816 to £900,436,000. At Queen Victoria's accession (1837) this had been reduced to £788,000,000; the Crimean War added £33,000,000, and thereafter reductions were made annually (with only five exceptions) till 1899, the year of the outbreak of the Boer War, when the Debt stood at £628,021,572. This war added over £160,000,000, but from 1904 to the outbreak of the Great War reductions were made annually (with one exception), so that in 1914 the Debt was £651,270,091. Since then the increases, directly or indirectly entirely attributable to the Great War, have been:

| | |
|---|---|
| 1914–15 | 457,546,985 |
| 1915–16 | 1,031,931,568 |
| 1916–17 | 1,870,697,264 |
| 1917–18 | 1,860,404,729 |
| 1918–19 | 1,563,098,792 |
| 1919–20 | 396,794,871 |
| | £7,180,474,209 |

bringing the British National Debt on March 31st, 1921, to the enormous total of £7,831,744,300.

In Germany the Funded Debt stood at 5,000,000,000 marks on April 1st, 1914; on May 31st, 1921, it had risen to 78,345,000,000 marks, and the Floating Debt to 199,134,000,000 marks.

**Nations, Battle of the.** A name given to the great battle of Leipzig in the Napoleonic wars (Oct. 16th–19th, 1813), when the French under Napoleon were defeated by the coalition armies, consisting of the Prussians, Russians, Austrians, and Swedes.

**Native** (Lat., *nativus*, produced by birth, natural). In feudal times, one born a serf. After the Conquest, the natives were the serfs of the Normans. Wat Tyler said to Richard II:

> The firste peticion was that he scholde make alle men fre thro Ynglonde and quiete, so that there scholde not be eny native man after that time.
>
> Higden, *Polychronicon*, viii, 457

Legally, a person is a native of the place of his parents' domicile, wherever he himself may have happened to be born.

Oysters raised in artificial beds are called *natives*, though they may be, and frequently are, imported. This is because artificially reared oysters are the best, and for centuries the best oysters were those actually taken from British waters. It is a case of the transference of a convenient name.

**Nativity, The.** Christmas Day, the day set apart in honour of the Nativity or Birth of Christ.

***The Cave of the Nativity.*** The tradition that the rock cave near Constantine's basilica, S. Maria a Praesepio, is the birthplace of the Saviour dates from the time of St Jerome (d.420), when Bethlehem had been a wood-covered wilderness since it was devastated by Hadrian three hundred years before. The chancel of the basilica was subsequently built over it. In the recess, a few feet above the ground is a stone slab with a star cut in it, to mark the supposed spot where Christ was born, and near it is a hollow scraped out of the rock, said to be the place where the Infant was laid.

***To cast a man's nativity.*** The astrologers' term for constructing a plan or map of the position, etc., of the twelve 'houses' which belong to him, and explaining the scheme.

**Natty Bumpo.** The central figure in the 'Leather Stocking' novels (*q.v.*). He appears as the Deerslayer, the Pathfinder, Hawk-eye (*Last of the Mohicans*), and the Trapper in the *Prairie*, in which he dies.

**Natural.** A born idiot; one on whom education can make no impression. As nature made him, so he remains.

***A natural child.*** One not born in lawful wedlock. The Romans called the children of concubines *naturales*, children according to nature, and not according to law.

> Cui pater est populus, pater est sibi nullus omnes;
> Cui pater est populus non habet ille patrem.
>
> Ovid

***Natural Philosophy.*** *See* Experimental.

**Nature.** *In a state of nature*. Nude or naked.

**Naught, Nought.** These are merely variants of the same word, *naught* representing A.S. *na whit* and *nought*, *no whit*. In most senses they are interchangeable; but nowadays *naught* is the more common form, except for the name of the cipher, which is usually *nought*.

*Naught* was formerly applied to things that were bad or worthless, as in 2 Kings 2:19, 'The water is naught and the ground barren', and it is with this sense that Jeremiah (24:2) speaks of 'naughty figs':

> One basket had very good figs, even like the figs that are first ripe ... The other basket had very naughty figs; which could not be eaten.

The Revised Version did away with the old 'naughty' and substituted 'bad'; and in the next verse, where the Authorised calls the figs 'evil', the Douai Version has:

> The good figges, exceeding good, and the naughtie figges, exceeding naught: which can not be eaten because they are naught.

**Nautical Mile.** *See* Mile.

**Navvy.** A contraction of navigator. One employed to make railways.

> Canals were thought of as lines of inland navigation, and a tavern built by the side of a canal was called a 'Navigation Inn'. Hence it happened that the men employed in excavating canals were called 'navigators', shortened into navvies.
>
> Spencer, *Principles of Sociology*, vol. i, appendix C, p. 834

**Nay-word.** Password. Slender, in *The Merry Wives of Windsor*, says:

> We have a nay-word how to know each other. I come to her in white and cry *Mum*, she cries *Budget*, and by that we know one another.
>
> Shakespeare

**Nayres.** *See* Nairs.

**Nazaraeans** or **Nazarenes.** A sect of Jewish Christians, who believed Christ to be the Messiah, that He was born of the Holy Ghost, and that He possessed a Divine nature, but who, nevertheless, conformed to the Mosaic rites and ceremonies.

**Nazarene.** A native of Nazareth; our Lord is so called (John 18:5, 7; Acts 24:5), though He was born in Bethlehem.

**Nazareth.** ***Can any good thing come out of Nazareth?*** (John 1:46). A general insinuation against any family or place of ill repute. Can any great man come from such an insignificant village as Nazareth?

**Nazarite.** One separated or set apart to the Lord by a vow. They refrained from strong drink, and allowed their hair to grow. (Heb. *nazar*, to separate. Numb. 6:1–21.)

**Ne plus ultra** (Lat., nothing further, i.e. perfection). The most perfect state to which a thing can be brought. We have *ne plus ultra* corkscrews, and a multitude of other things. *See* Plus ultra.

**Neaera.** Any sweetheart or ladylove. She is mentioned by Horace, Virgil, and Tibullus.

> To sport with Amaryllis in the shade,
> Or with the tangles of Neaera's hair
>
> Milton, *Lycidas*

**Near,** meaning *mean*, is rather a curious play on the word *close* (close-fisted). What is 'close by' is near.

**Near Side** and **Off Side.** Left side and right side. 'Near wheel' means that to the coachman's left hand: and 'near horse' (in a pair) means that to the left hand of the driver. In a four-in-hand the two horses on the left side of the coachman are the near wheeler and the near leader. Those on the right-hand side of the coachman are 'off' horses. This, which seems an anomaly, arose when the driver *walked* beside his team. The teamster always walks with his right arm nearest the horse, and therefore, in a pair of horses, the horse on the left side is nearer than the one on his right. Thus, 2 is the near wheeler and 1 the near leader, 4 is the off wheeler and 3 the off leader.

1↑3
2|4
Coachman.

**Nebo.** A god of the Babylonians (properly, *Nabu*) mentioned in Is. 46:1, and corresponding more or less with the classical Hermes. He was the patron of Borsippa, near Babylon, and was regarded as the inventor of the art of writing, as well as the god of wisdom and the herald of the gods. The name occurs in many Babylonian royal names (Nebuchadrezzar, Nebushasban [Jer. 39:13], Nebuzaradan [2 Kings. 25:8], etc.), but it is very doubtful whether it is present, as has been stated, in the place-name *Nebo*, or the personal name *Barnabas*.

**Nebuchadnezzar.** This name, which is now firmly fixed in English, is a mistake, for it is a misrendering in the Hebrew of Daniel (and consequently in English and other translations) of the Babylonian *Nabu-kudur-usur*, and should be *Nebuchadrezzar*, as indeed it is given in Jer. 21:2, etc. The French call him *Nabuchodonosor*, or *Nabuchodorosor*, which are nearer the Greek transliteration. The name means *Nebo protects the crown*. *See* Nebo.

Nebuchadnezzar was the greatest king of Assyria, and reigned for forty-three years (604–561 BC). He restored his country to its former prosperity and importance, practically rebuilt Babylon, restored the temple of Bel, erected a new palace, embanked the Euphrates, and probably built the celebrated Hanging Gardens. His name became the centre of many legends, and the story related by Daniel (4:29–33) that he was one day walking –

> in the palace of the kingdom of Babylon and said, 'Is not this great Babylon that I have built … by the might of my power, and for the honour of my majesty?' And 'the same hour … he was driven from men, and did eat grass as oxen, and his body was wet with the dew of heaven, till his hairs were grown like eagles' feathers, and his nails like birds' claws'

is an allusion to the suspension of his interest in public affairs, which lasted, as his inscription records, for four years.

**Necessitarians.** *See* Agent.

**Necessity.** ***Necessity knows no law.*** These were the words used by Dr von Bethmann-Hollweg, the German Imperial Chancellor, in the Reichstag on August 4th, 1914, as a justification for the German infringement of Belgian neutrality:

> Gentlemen, we are now in a state of necessity (*Notwehr*), and necessity (*Not*) knows no law. Our troops have occupied Luxemburg and perhaps have already entered Belgian territory.

To quote Milton –

> So spake the Fiend, and with necessity,
> The tyrant's plea, excused his devilish deeds.
>
> *Paradise Lost*, iv, 393

The phrase is, of course, not original. Cromwell used it in a speech to Parliament on September 12th, 1654, but to very different purpose:

> Necessity hath no law. Feigned necessities, imaginary necessities, are the greatest cozenage men can put upon the Providence of God, and make pretences to break known rules by.

It is common to most languages. Publilius Syrus has *Necessitas dat legem, non ipsa accipit* (Necessity gives the law, but does not herself accept it), and the Latin proverb *Necessitas non habet legem* appears in *Piers Plowman* (14th century) as 'Neede hath no lawe'.

***To make a virtue of necessity.*** To 'grin and bear it'; 'what can't be cured must be endured'.

> Thanne is it wisdom, as it thinketh me
> To maken vertu of necessitee.
>
> Chaucer, *Knighte's Tale*, 3041

> Are you content to be our general?
> To make a virtue of necessity

And live, as we do, in this wilderness?
Shakespeare, *Two Gentlemen of Verona*, 4, 1

Quintilian has *laudem virtutis necessitati damus*; St Jerome (epistle 54, section 6), *Fac de necessitate virtutem*. In the *Roman de la Rose*, line 14058, we find *S'il ne fait de necessite virtu*, and Boccaccio has *Si come savia fatta della necessita*.

**Neck.** Low slang for brazen impudence, colossal cheek.

***Neck and crop.*** Entirely. The crop is the gorge of a bird; a variant of the phrase is, *neck and heels*, as I bundled him out neck and heels. There was a punishment formerly in vogue which consisted in bringing the chin and knees of the culprit forcibly together, and then thrusting him into a cage.

***Neck and neck.*** Very near in merit; very close competitors. A phrase used in horse races, when two or more horse run each other very closely.

***Neck or nothing.*** Desperate. A racing phrase; to win by a neck or to be nowhere – i.e. not counted at all because unworthy of notice.

***Oh that the Roman people had but one neck!*** The words of Caligula, the Roman emperor. He wished that he could slay them all with one stroke.

***Stiff-necked.*** Obstinate and self-willed. In the *Psalms* we read: 'Speak not with a stiff neck' (75:5); and in Jer. 17:23, 'They obeyed not, but made their necks stiff'; and Isaiah (48:4) says: 'Thy neck is an iron sinew'. The allusion is to a wilful horse, ox, or ass, which will not answer to the reins.

***To break the neck of an enterprise.*** To begin it successfully, and overcome the first difficulties. Well begun is half done.

***To get it in the neck.*** To be completely defeated, thoroughly castigated, soundly rated, etc. The phrase is an Americanism, from the picturesque expression of one who has just been 'through it' – *I got it where the chicken got the axe* – which, of course, is 'in the neck'.

**Necklace.** A necklace of coral or white bryony beads used to be worn by children to aid their teething. Necklaces of hyoscyamus or henbane-root have been recommended for the same purpose.

***Diamond necklace.*** *See* Diamond.

***The fatal necklace.*** Cadmus received on his wedding-day the present of a necklace, which proved fatal to everyone who possessed it. Some say that Vulcan, and others that Europa, gave it to him. Harmonia's necklace (*q.v.*) was a similar fatal gift.

**Neck-verse.** The first verse of Ps. 51. *See* Miserere. 'Have mercy upon me, O God, according to Thy loving-kindness: according unto the multitude of Thy tender mercies blot out my transgressions.'

He [a treacherous Italian interpreter] by a fine cunny-catching corrupt translation, made us plainly to confesse, and cry Misserere, ere we had need of our necke-verse.
Nash, *The Unfortunate Traveller* (1594)

This verse was so called because it was the trial-verse of those who claimed Benefit of Clergy (*q.v.*), and if they could read it, the ordinary of Newgate said, '*Legit ut clericus*', and the prisoner *saved his neck*, being only burnt in the hand and set at liberty.

If a clerk had been taken
For stealing of bacon,
For burglary, murder, or rape.
If he could but rehearse
(Well prompt) his neck-verse,
He never could fail to escape.
*British Apollo* (1710)

**Necromancy.** Prophesying by calling up the dead, as the witch of Endor called up Samuel. (Gr. *nekros*, the dead; *manteia*, prophecy.)

**Nectar** (Gr.). The drink of the gods of *classical mythology*. Like their food, *Ambrosia*, it conferred immortality. Hence the name of the *nectarine*, so called because it is 'as sweet as nectar'.

The Koran tells us 'the righteous shall be given to drink pure wine sealed with musk'.

**Needfire.** Fire obtained by friction; formerly supposed to defeat sorcery, and cure diseases assigned to witchcraft, especially cattle diseases. In Henderson's *Agricultural Survey of Caithness* (1812) we are told that as late as 1785 –

when the stock of any considerable farmer was seized with the murrain, he would send for one of the charm doctors to superintend the raising of a need-fire.

**Needful, The.** Ready money, cash.

**Needham.** ***You are on the high-road to Needham*** – to ruin or poverty. The pun is on the *need*, but there is a Needham in Suffolk. *Cp.* Land of Nod.

**Needle.** ***Looking for a needle,*** etc. *See* Bottle.

***The eye of a needle.*** *See* Eye.

***To get the needle.*** To become thoroughly vexed, or even enraged, and to show it. A variant of the phrase is *to get the spike*.

***To hit the needle.*** Hit the right nail on the head, to make a perfect hit. A term in archery, equal to hitting the bull's-eye.

**Negative. *The answer is in the negative.*** The circumambulatory Parliamentary way of pronouncing the monosyllable *No*.

***Negative pregnant.*** *See* Pregnant.

**Negro Offspring.** White father and negro mother: *mulatto*.

White father and mulatto mother: *quadroon*.

White father and quadroon mother: *quitero*.

White father and quintero mother: *white*.

**Negus.** The drink – port or sherry, with hot water, sugar, and spices – is so called from a Colonel Francis Negus (d.1732), who first concocted it.

The supreme ruler of Abyssinia is entitled *the Negus*, from the native *n'gus*, meaning crowned.

**Nehushtan** (2 Kings 18:4). Bits of brass, worthless fragments. The name given by Hezekiah to the pieces of the brazen serpent after he had broken it (2 Kings 18:4).

> Such matters to the agitators are Nehushtan.
>
> *Nineteenth Century*, Dec., 1892, p. 998

**Neiges d'Antan, Les** (Fr.). A thing of the past. Literally, 'last year's snows', from the refrain of Villon's well-known *Ballade des Dames du Temps Jadis* –

> Prince, n'enquerez de semaine
> Où elles sont, ni de cet an,
> Que ce refrain ne vous remaine;
> Mais où sont les neiges d'antan!

> Where are the snows of yester-year?
> The whole has melted away like the *neiges d'antan*.
>
> *Nineteenth Century*, June, 1891, p. 893

**Nem. con.** Unanimously. A contraction of the Latin *nemine contradicente* (no one opposing).

**Nem. diss.** Without a dissentient voice. (Lat. *nemine dissentiente*.)

**Nemean.** Pertaining to Nemea, the ancient name of a valley in Argolis, Greece, about 10 m. S.W. of Corinth.

***The Nemean Games.*** One of the four great national festivals of Greece, celebrated at Nemea every alternate year, the second and fourth of each Olympiad. Legend states that they were instituted in memory of Archemorus, who died from the bite of a serpent as the expedition of the Seven against Thebes was passing through the valley.

The victor's reward was at first a crown of olive leaves, but subsequently a garland of ivy. Pindar has eleven odes in honour of victors.

***The Nemean Lion.*** A terrible lion which kept the people of the valley in constant alarm. The first of the twelve Labours of Hercules was to slay it; he could make no impression on the beast with his club, so he caught it in his arms and squeezed it to death. Hercules ever after wore the skin as a mantle.

> My fate cries out,
> And makes each petty artery in this body
> As hardy as the Nemean lion's nerve.
>
> Shakespeare, *Hamlet*, 1, 4

**Nemesis.** The Greek goddess who allotted to men their exact share of good, or bad fortune, and was responsible for seeing that everyone got his due and deserts; the personification of divine retribution. Hence, retributive justice generally, as *the Nemesis of nations*, the fate which, sooner or later, has overtaken every great nation of the ancient and modern world.

> And though circuitous and obscure
> The feet of Nemesis how sure!
>
> Sir William Watson, *Europe at the Play*

**Nemo Me Impune Lacessit** (Lat.). No one injures me with impunity. The motto of the Order of the Thistle (*q.v.*).

**Neolithic Age, The** (Gr. *neos*, new, *lithos*, a stone). The later Stone Age of Europe, the earlier being called the Palaeolithic (Gr. *palaios*, ancient). Stone implements of the Neolithic age are polished, more highly finished, and more various than those of the Palaeolithic, and are found in kitchen-middens and tombs, with the remains of recent and extinct animals, and sometimes with bronze implements. Neolithic man knew something of agriculture, kept domestic animals, used boats, and caught fish.

**Neoptolemus** or **Pyrrhus.** Son of Achilles; called *Pyrrhus* from his yellow hair, and *Neoptolemus* because he was a new soldier, or one that came late to the siege of Troy. According to Virgil, it was this youth who slew the aged Priam. On his return home he was murdered by Orestes, at Delphi.

**Nepenthe** or **Nepenthes** (Gr. *ne*, not, *penthos*, grief). An Egyptian drug mentioned in the *Odyssey* (iv, 228) that was fabled to drive away care and make persons forget their woes. Polydamna, wife of Thonis, king of Egypt, gave it to Helen, daughter of Jove and Leda.

> That nepenthes which the wife of Thone
> In Egypt gave the Jove-born Helena.
>
> Milton, *Comus*, 695–6

**Nephelo-coccygia** (Gr., cloud-cuckoo-land). A town in the clouds built by the cuckoos to cut off from the gods the incense offered by man, so as to compel them to come to terms. (Aristophanes, *The Birds*).

> Without flying to Nephelo-coccygia we can meet with sharpers and bullies. — Macaulay

**Nephew** (Fr. *neveu*, Lat. *nepos*). Both in Latin and in archaic English the word means a grandchild, or descendant. Hence, in the Authorised Version of 1 Tim. 5:4, we read – 'If a woman have children or nephews', but in the Revised 'grandchildren'. Propertius has it, *Me inter seros laudabit Roma nepotes* (posterity).

Niece (Lat. *neptis*) also means a granddaughter or female descendant. *See* Nepotism.

**Nepomuk.** *See* St John of Nepumuk, *under* John.

**Nepotism** (Lat. *nepos*, a nephew or kinsman). An unjustifiable elevation of one's own relations to places of wealth and trust at one's disposal.

**Neptune.** The Roman god of the sea, corresponding with the Greek Poseidon (*q.v.*), hence used allusively for the sea itself. Neptune is represented as an elderly man of stately mien, bearded, carrying a trident, and sometimes astride a dolphin or a horse. *See* Hippocampus.

> ... great Neptune with this threeforkt mace,
> That rules the Seas, and makes them rise or fall;
> His dewy lockes did drop with brine apace
> Under his Diademe imperiall.
>
> Spenser, *Faërie Queene*, IV, xi, 11

**Neptunian** or **Neptunist.** The name given to certain 18th-century geologists, who held the opinion of Werner (1750–1817), viz. that all the great rocks of the earth were once held in solution in water, and were deposited as sediment. The *Vulcanists* or *Plutonians* ascribed them to the agency of fire.

**Nereids.** The sea-nymphs of *Greek mythology*, the fifty daughters of Nereus and 'grey-eyed' Doris. The best known are Amphitrite, Thetis, and Galatea; Milton refers to another, Panope – in *Lycidas* (line 99) –

> The air was calm, and on the level brine
> Sleek Panope with all her sisters played.

And the names of all will be found in Spenser's *Faërie Queene*, Bk iv, c. xi, verses 48–57. Here are thirty-three of them –

> The Nereids all, who live among the caves.
> And valleys of the deep, Cymodecè,
> Agavè, blue-eyed Hallia and Nesaea,
> Speio and Thoë, Glaucè and Actaea,
> Iaira, Melitè and Amphinomè,
> Apseudès and Nemertès, Callianassa,
> Cymothoë, Thaleia, Limnorrhea,
> Clymenè, Ianeira and Ianassa,
> Doris and Panopè and Galatea,
> Dynamenè, Dexamenè and Maira,
> Ferusa, Doto, Proto, Callianeira,
> Amphithoë, Oreithuia and Amathea.
>
> Robt Bridges, *Eros and Psyche* (*March*)

*See also* Camoëns' *Lusiad* (Bk ii).

**Nereus.** A sea-god of *Greek mythology*, represented as a very old man. He was the father of the fifty Nereids (*q.v.*), and his special dominion was the Aegean Sea.

**Neri.** *See* Bianchi.

**Nero, A.** Any bloody-minded man, relentless tyrant, or evil-doer of extraordinary savagery; from the depraved and infamous Roman Emperor, C. Claudius Nero (AD 54–86), who set fire to Rome to see, it is said, 'what Troy would have looked like when it was in flames', and fiddled as he watched the conflagration.

**Nero of the North.** Christian II of Denmark (1480, 1534–58, 1559), also called 'The Cruel'. He massacred the Swedish nobility at Stockholm in 1520, and thus prepared the way for Gustavus Vasa and Swedish freedom.

**Nerthus** or **Hertha.** The name given by Tacitus to a German or Scandinavian goddess of fertility, or 'Mother Earth', who was worshipped on an island. She roughly corresponds with the classical Cybele; and is probably confused with the Scandinavian god *Njorthr or Niordhr* (*q.v.*), the protector of sailors and fishermen. *Nerthus* and *Njorthr* alike mean 'benefactor'.

> Before ever land was,
> Before ever the sea,
> Or soft hair of the grass,
> Or fair limbs of the tree,
> Or the flesh-coloured fruit of my branches,
> I was, and thy soul was in me.
>
> Swinburne, *Hertha*

**Nessus.** ***Shirt of Nessus.*** A source of misfortune from which there is no escape; a fatal present. The legend is that Hercules ordered Nessus (the centaur) to carry his wife Dejanira across a river. The centaur attempted to carry her off, and Hercules shot him with a poisoned arrow. Nessus, in revenge, gave Dejanira his tunic, deceitfully telling her that it would preserve her husband's love, and she gave it to her husband, who was devoured by the poison still remaining in it from his own arrow as soon as he put it on. He was at once taken with mortal pains; Dejanira hanged herself from remorse, and the hero threw himself on a funeral pile, and was borne away to Olympus by the gods. *Cp.* Harmonia's Robe.

> While to my limbs th' envenomed mantle clings,
> Drenched in the centaur's black, malignant gore.
>
> West, *Triumphs of the Gout* (Lucian)

**Nest-egg.** Money laid by. The allusion is to the custom of placing an egg in a hen's nest to induce her to lay her eggs there. If a person has saved a little money, it serves as an inducement to him to increase his store.

**Nestor.** King of Pylos, in Greece; the oldest and most experienced of the chieftains who went to the siege of Troy. Hence the name is frequently applied as an epithet to the oldest and wisest man of a class or company. Samuel Rogers, for instance, who lived to be 92, was called 'the Nestor of English poets'.

**Nestorians.** Followers of Nestorius, Patriarch of Constantinople, 428–431. He maintained that Christ had two distinct natures, and that Mary was the mother of His human nature, which was the mere shell or husk of the divine. They spread in India and the Far East, and remains of the Nestorian Christians, their inscriptions, etc. are still found in China, but the greater part of their churches were destroyed by Timur (Tamerlane) about 1400.

**Nethinim.** The temple servants of the ancient Hebrews (*see* Ezra. 7:7). They were originally slaves, but after the exile had a much more important position and formed part of the privileged *personnel* attached to the Temple. The word means *the appointed, the given to God.*

**Never.** There are numerous locutions to express this idea; as –

> At the coming of the Coqueligrues (Rabelais, *Pantagruel*).
> At the Latter Lammas.
> On the Greek Calends.
> In the reign of Queen Dick.
> On St Tib's Eve.
> In a month of five Sundays.
> When two Fridays or three Sundays come together.
> When Dover and Calais meet.
> When Dudman and Ramehead meet.
> When the world grows honest.
> When the Yellow River runs clear.

**Newcastle-on-Tyne** was so called (*Noef-Chastel-sur-Tine*, or *Novum Castellum*) from the castle built there by Robert, son of the Conqueror, in 1080, to defend the neighbourhood from the Scots. Previous names were, in Roman times, *Pons Aelii*, and, by the Anglo-Saxons, *Munechecaster* (Monks' castle).

**Newcastle-under-Lyme** was known as *Novum Oppidum* (Latin, New Town) till about 1200, when the new castle was built to supply the place of an older one which stood at Chesterton-under-Lime, about two miles distant.

***To carry coals to Newcastle.*** *See* Coal.

**Newfangled.** Applied to anything of a quite new or different fashion; a novelty. The older word was *new-fangle* –

> Men loven of propre kinde newfangelnesse
> As briddes doon that men in cages fede ...
> So newfangel ben they of hir mete,
> And loven novelryes of propre kinde.
>
> Chaucer, *Squire's Tale*, 602, 610

M.E. *fangel*, from A.S. *fang*, past part. of *fōn*, to take, meaning 'always ready to take, or grasp at, some new thing'.

**Newgate** (London). According to Stow this was first built in the city wall in the time of Henry I, but excavations have shown that there was a Roman gate here, about 31 ft in width. It may have fallen into disuse, and have been repaired by Henry I, the present name being given at the time.

***Newgate Gaol*** was originally merely a few cells over the gate; the first great prison here was built in 1422, and the last in 1770–83. For centuries it was the gaol for the City and for the County of Middlesex; it was demolished in 1902, and the Central Criminal Court (opened 1905) erected on its site.

From its prominence, *Newgate* came to be applied as a general name for gaols, and Nash, in his *Pierce Penilesse* (1592) says it is 'a common name for all prisons, as *homo* is a common name for a man or woman'.

***Newgate Calendar, The.*** A biographical record of the more notorious criminals confined at Newgate; begun in 1773 and continued at intervals for many years. In 1824–8 A. Knapp and Wm Baldwin published, in 4 vols, *The Newgate Calendar, comprising Memoirs of Notorious Characters*; and in 1886 C. Pelham published his *Chronicles of Crime, or the New Newgate Calendar* (2 vols). The term is often used as a comprehensive expression embracing crime of every sort.

> I also felt that I had committed every crime in the Newgate Calendar.
>
> Dickens, *Our Mutual Friend*, ch. xiv

***Newgate fashion.*** Two by two. Prisoners used to be conveyed to Newgate coupled together in twos.

> Must we all march?
> Yes, two and two, Newgate fashion.
>
> Shakespeare, *1 Henry IV*, 3, 3

***Newgate fringe.*** The hair worn under the chin, or between the chin and the neck. So called because it occupies the position of the rope when men are about to be hanged.

***Newgate knocker.*** A lock of hair twisted into a curl, worn by costermongers and persons of similar station. So called because it resembles a knocker, and the wearers were too often inmates of Newgate.

**Newland.** A bank-note used to be so called. *See* Abraham Newland.

**New Lights, The.** *See* Campbellites.

**News.** The letters N(orth) E(ast) W(est) S(outh) used to be prefixed to newspapers to show that they obtained information from the four quarters of the world, and the supposition that our word *news* is thence derived is at least ingenious; the old-fashioned way of spelling the word, *newes*, is alone fatal to the conceit. Fr. *nouvelles* is the real source.

News is conveyed by letter, word, or mouth
And comes to us from North, East, West and South.
*Will's Recreations*

The word is now nearly always construed as singular ('the news is very good this morning'), but it was formerly treated as a plural, and in the *Letters of Queen Victoria* the Queen, and most of her correspondents, followed that rule:

The news from Austria are very sad, and make one very anxious.
To the King of the Belgians, 20 Aug., 1861

**New Style.** The reformed or Gregorian Calendar, adopted in England in 1752. *See* Gregorian Year.

**Newtonian Philosophy.** The astronomical system that in the late 17th century displaced the Copernican (*see* Copernicanism), together with the theory of universal gravitation. So called after Sir Isaac Newton (1642–1727), who established the former and discovered the latter.

Nature and Nature's laws lay hid in night
God said, 'Let Newton be', and all was light.
Pope

**New World.** America; the Eastern Hemisphere is called the Old World.

**New Year's Day.** January 1st. The Romans began their year in March; hence *September*, *October*, *November*, *December* for the 7th, 8th, 9th, and 10th months. Since the introduction of the Christian era, Christmas Day, Lady Day, Easter Day, March 1st and March 25th have in turns been considered as New Year's Day; but at the reform of the calendar in the 16th century (*see* Calendar), January 1st was accepted by practically all Christian peoples.

In England the civil and legal year began on March 25th till after the alteration of the style, in 1752, when it was fixed, like the historic year, to January 1st. In Scotland the legal year was changed to January 1st as far back as 1600.

***New Year's gifts.*** The giving of presents at this time was a custom among both the Greeks and the Romans, the latter calling them *strenae*, whence the French term *étrenne* (a New Year's gift). Nonius Marcellus says that Tatius, King of the Sabines, was presented with some branches of trees cut from the forest sacred to the goddess Strenia (*strength*), on New Year's Day, and from this incident the custom arose.

Our forefathers used to bribe the magistrates with gifts on New Year's Day – a custom abolished by law in 1290, but even down to the reign of James II the monarchs received their *tokens*.

**Newt.** *See* Nickname.

**Nibelungenlied, The.** A Middle High German poem, the greatest monument of early German literature, founded on old Scandinavian legends contained in the *Volsunga Saga* and the *Edda*, and written in its present form by an anonymous South German of the early part of the 13th century.

Nibelung was a mythical king of a race of Scandinavian dwarfs dwelling in *Nibelheim* (i.e. 'the home of darkness, or mist'). These *Nibelungs*, or *Nibelungers*, were the possessors of the wonderful 'Hoard' of gold and precious stones guarded by the dwarf Alberich; and their name passed to later holders of the Hoard, Siegfried's following and the Burgundians being in turn called 'the Nibelungs'.

Siegfried, the hero of the first part of the poem, became possessed of the Hoard, and gave it to Kriemhild as her marriage portion. After his murder Kriemhild carried it to Worms, where it was seized by Hagen and Gunther. They buried it in the Rhine, intending later to enjoy it; but they were both slain for refusing to reveal its whereabouts, and the Hoard remains for ever in the keeping of the Rhine Maidens.

The first part of the *Nibelungenlied* relates the marriage of Gunther, King of Burgundy, with Brunhild; the marriage of Siegfried with Kriemhild, his murder by Hagen, the removal of the 'Nibelungen Hoard' to Burgundy, and its seizure and burial in the Rhine by Gunther and

Hagen. It contains nineteen lays, divided into 1,188 four-line stanzas. The second part tells of the marriage of the widow Kriemhild with King Etzel (Attila), the visit of the Burgundians to the court of the Hunnish king, and the death of all the principal characters, including Gunther, Hagen, and Kriemhild. This part contains twenty lays, divided into 1,271 four-line stanzas; and the whole, thirty-nine lays, 2,459 stanzas, or 9,836 lines. For further particulars about the legends and the principal characters, *see* the names mentioned above.

**Nic Frog.** *See* Frog.

**Nice.** ***The Council of Nice.*** The first oecumenical council of the Christian Church, held under Constantine the Great in 325 at Nice, or Nicaea, in Bithynia, Asia Minor, to condemn the Arian heresy, to affirm the consubstantiality of the Son of God, and to deal with points of discipline. The seventh oecumenical council was also held at Nice (787).

**Nicene Creed.** The Creed formulated at the great Council of Nice (325). It is used in the Holy Communion Service of the Church of England, and was first adopted in the Roman Church in 1014. In the Eastern Church it was first introduced in 471, and still forms part of the Baptism Service as well as of the Eucharist.

> The Nicene, or more correctly, the Niceno-Constantinopolitan Creed, from the solemn sanction thus given to it by the great Oecumenical Councils, stands in a position of greater authority than any other; and amid their longstanding divisions is a blessed bond of union between the three great branches of the one Catholic Church – the Eastern, the Roman, and the Anglican, of all whose Communion Offices it forms a part.
>
> J. H. Blunt, *Annotated Book of Common Prayer*

**Nicholas, St.** One of the most popular saints in Christendom, especially in the East. He is the patron saint of Russia, of Aberdeen, of parish clerks, of scholars (who used to be called *clerks*), of pawnbrokers (because of the three bags of gold – transformed to the three gold balls – that he gave to the daughters of a poor man to save them from earning their dowers in a disreputable way), of little boys (because he once restored to life three little boys who had been cut up and pickled in a salting-tub to serve for bacon), and is invoked by sailors (because he allayed a storm during a voyage to the Holy Land) and against fire. Finally, he is the original of Santa Claus (*q.v.*).

Little is known of his life, but he is said to have been Bishop of Myra (Lycia) in the early 4th century, and one story relates that he was present at the Council of Nice (325) and there buffeted Arius on the jaw. His day is December 6th, and he is represented in episcopal robes with either three purses of gold, three gold balls, or three small boys, in allusion to one of the above legends.

***Clerks*** or ***Knights of St Nicholas.*** *See* Clerk.

***St Nicholas's Bishop.*** *See* Boy Bishop.

**Nick.** Slang for to pilfer; and, in the 18th century, for to break windows by throwing coppers at them:

> His scattered pence the flying Nicker flings,
> And with the copper shower the casement rings.
>
> Gay, *Trivia*, iii

***He nicked it.*** Won, hit, accomplished it. A nick is a winning throw of dice in the old game of 'hazard'.

***In the nick of time.*** Just at the right moment. The allusion is to tallies marked with nicks or notches. *Cp.* Prick of Noon.

***Old Nick.*** The Devil. The term was in use in the 17th century, and is perhaps connected with the German *Nickel*, a goblin (*see* Nickel), or in some forgotten way with St Nicholas. Butler's derivation from Nicholas Machiavelli is, of course, poetical licence:

> Nick Machiavel had ne'er a trick
> (Though he gives name to our old Nick)
> But was below the least of these.
>
> *Hudibras*, iii, 1

***To nick the nick.*** To hit the exact moment. Tallies used to be called 'nicksticks'. Hence, to make a record of anything is 'to nick it down', as publicans nick a score on a tally.

**Nicka-Nan Night.** The night preceding Shrove Tuesday is so called in Cornwall, because boys play tricks and practical jokes on that night. On the following night they go round again from house to house singing –

> Nicka, nicka nan,
> Give me some pancake and then I'll be gone;
> But if you give me none
> I'll throw a great stone
> And down your doors shall come.

**Nickel.** The metal is so called from the German *kupfernickel*, the name given to the ore from which it was first obtained (1754) by Axel P. von Cronstedt. *Kupfer* means copper, and *Nickel* is the name of a mischievous goblin fabled to inhabit mines in Germany; the name was given to it because, although it was copper-coloured, no copper could be got from it, and so the *Nickel* was blamed.

**Nicker, or Nix.** In *Scandinavian folklore*, a water-wraith, or kelpie, inhabiting sea, lake, river, and waterfall. They are sometimes represented as half-child, half-horse, the hoofs being reversed, and sometimes as old men sitting on rocks wringing the water from their hair. The female nicker is a *nixy*. *Cp*. Nicor.

> Another tribe of water-fairies are the Nixes, who frequently assume the appearance of beautiful maidens. Dyer, *Folk-lore of Plants*, ch. vii

**Nickname.** Originally *an eke-name*, *eke* being an adverb meaning 'also', A.S. *ēac*, connected with *iecan*, to supply deficiencies in or to make up for. *A newt* in the same way was originally 'an eft' or 'an evt'; 'v' and 'u' being formerly interchangeable gave us 'neut', or 'newt'.

The 'eke' of a beehive is the piece added to the bottom to enlarge the hive.

**Nicknames.** *National Nicknames*:

For an *American* of the United States, 'Brother Jonathan'.

For a *Dutchman*, 'Nic Frog' and 'Mynheer Closh'.

For an *Englishman*, 'John Bull'.

For a *Frenchman*, 'Crapaud', Johnny or Jean, Robert Macaire.

For *French Canadians*, 'Jean Baptiste'.

For *French reformers*, 'Brissotins'.

For *French peasantry*, 'Jacques Bonhomme'.

For a *German*, 'Cousin Michael' or 'Michel'; Hun; Jerry; Fritz.

For an *Irishman*, 'Paddy'.

For an *Italian*, 'Antonio', or 'Tony'.

For a *Russian*, 'A bear'.

For a *Scot*, 'Sawney'.

For a *Spaniard* or *Portuguese*, 'Dago'.

For a *Swiss*, 'Colin Tampon'.

For a *Turk*, 'Infidel'.

**Nickneven.** A gigantic malignant hag of Scotch superstition. Dunbar has well described this spirit in his *Flyting of Dunbar and Kennedy*.

**Nicodemused into nothing.** To have one's prospects in life ruined by a silly name; according to the proverb, 'Give a dog a bad name and hang him.' It is from Sterne's *Tristram Shandy* (vol. i, 19):

> How many Caesars and Pompeys ... by mere inspiration of the names have been rendered worthy of them; and how many ... might have done ... well in the world ... had they not been Nicodemused into nothing.

**Nicolaitanes.** Certain apostate Christians of the 1st century, mentioned in Rev. 2 (6 and 15), and by Irenaeus, Tertullian, and other early Christian Fathers. The reason of the name is unknown, as indeed is everything about them except that they apparently had tried to lead the members of the Seven Churches of Asia astray.

**Nicor.** A variant of *nicker* (*q.v.*); specifically a sea-devil who eats sailors.

> My brother saw a nicor in the Northern sea. It was three fathoms long, with the body of a bison-bull, and the head of a cat, the beard of a man, and tusks an ell long, lying down on its breast. It was watching for the fishermen.
> Kingsley, *Hypatia*, ch. xii

**Nicotine.** So named from *Nicotiana*, the Latin name of the tobacco plant, given to it in honour of Jean Nicot, Lord of Villemain, who was French ambassador in Madrid and introduced the weed into France in 1560.

**Niddhöggr.** The monster serpent of *Scandinavian mythology*. He lies hid in the pit Hvergelmer, and for ever gnaws the roots of Yggdrasil (*q.v.*), and sucks the corpses of the dead.

**Niflheim** (i.e. mist-home). The region of endless cold and everlasting night of *Scandinavian mythology*, ruled over by Hela. It consisted of nine worlds, to which were consigned those who die of disease or old age; it existed 'from the beginning' in the North, and in its middle was the well Hvergelmir (*q.v.*), from which flowed the twelve rivers.

**Nightcap.** A glass of liquor before going to bed. Supposed to promote sleep.

> The nightcap is generally a little whisky left in the decanter. To do it honour it is taken neat. Then all get up and wish 'good-night'.
> Max O'Rell, *Friend MacDonald*, iii

**Nightingale.** The Greek legend is that Tereus, King of Thrace, fetched Philomela to visit his wife, Procne, who was her sister; but when he reached the 'solitudes of Heleas' he dishonoured her, and cut out her tongue that she might not reveal his conduct. Tereus told his wife that Philomela was dead, but Philomela made her story known by weaving it into a peplus, which she sent to Procne. Procne, in revenge, cut up her own son and served it to Tereus, and as soon as the king discovered it he pursued his wife, who fled to Philomela; whereupon the gods changed all three into birds; Tereus became the *hawk*, his wife the *swallow*, and Philomela the *nightingale*, which is still called Philomel (*lit.* lover of song) by the poets.

Youths and maidens most poetical ...
Full of meek sympathy must heave their sighs
O'er Philomela's pity-pleading strains.
Coleridge, *The Nightingale*

***The Swedish Nightingale.*** The great operatic singer, Jenny Lind (1821–86), afterwards Mme Goldschmidt. She was a native of Stockholm.

**Nightmare.** A sensation in sleep as if something heavy were sitting on one's breast; formerly supposed to be caused by a monster (*see* Incubus) who actually did this; it was not unfrequently called the *night-hag*, or the *riding of the witch*. The second syllable is the A.S. *mare* (old Norse *mara*), an incubus, and appears again in the French equivalent *cauchemar*, *lit.* 'the fiend that tramples'.

I do believe that the witch we call Mara has been dealing with you.
Scott, *The Betrothed*, ch. xv

***Nightmare of Europe, The.*** Napoleon Bonaparte was so called.

**Nihilism** (Lat. *nihil*, nothing). An extreme form of socialism, the prelude to Bolshevism (*see* Bolshevist), which took form in Russia in the 'fifties of last century, and was specially active in the 'seventies, and later, under Bakounin. It aimed at anarchy and the complete overthrow of law, order, and all existing institutions, with the idea of re-forming the world *de novo*. The following was the code of the Nihilists:

(1) Annihilate the idea of a God, or there can be no freedom.
(2) Annihilate the idea of right, which is only might.
(3) Annihilate civilisation, property, marriage, morality and justice.
(4) Let your own happiness be your only law.

The name was given to them by the novelist, Turgenieff.

**Nihilo. *Ex nihilo nihil fit*.** *See* Nothing.

**Nil admirari** (Lat.). To be stolidly indifferent. Neither to wonder at anything nor yet to admire anything. The tag is from Horace (*Ep*. I, vi, 1):

Nil admirari prope res est una, Numici,
Solaque, quae possit facere et servare beatum.
(Not to admire, Numicius, is the best –
The only way to make and keep men blest.)
Connington

**Nil desperandum.** Never say die; never give up in despair; another tag from Horace (*Carmen*, I, vii, 27):

Nil desperandum Teucro duce et auspice Teucro (There is naught to be despaired of when we are under Teucer's leadership and auspices).

**Nile.** The Egyptians used to say that the swelling of the Nile was caused by the tears of Isis. The feast of Isis was celebrated at the anniversary of the death of Osiris, when Isis was supposed to mourn for her husband.

***The hero of the Nile.*** Horatio, Lord Nelson (1758–1805).

**Nimbus** (Lat., a cloud). In Christian art a halo of light placed round the heads of eminent personages. There are three forms: (1) *Vesica piscis*, or fish form (*cp*. Ichthus), used in representations of Christ and occasionally of the Virgin Mary, extending round the whole figure; (2) a circular halo; (3) radiated like a star or sun. The enrichments are, (1) for our Lord, a cross; (2) for the Virgin, a circlet of stars; (3) for angels, a circlet of small rays, and an outer circle of quatrefoils; (4) the same for saints and martyrs, but with the name often inscribed round the circumference; (5) for the Deity the rays diverge in a triangular direction. Nimbi of a square form signify that the persons so represented were living when they were painted.

The nimbus was used by heathen nations long before painters introduced it into sacred pictures of saints, the Trinity, and the Virgin Mary. Proserpine was represented with a nimbus; the Roman emperors were also decorated in the same manner, because they were *divi*.

**Nimini-pimini.** Affected simplicity. Lady Emily, in General Burgoyne's *The Heiress*, III, ii (1786), tells Miss Alscrip the way to acquire the paphian 'Mimp' is to stand before a glass and keep pronouncing *nimini-pimini* – 'The lips cannot fail to take the right plie'.

The conceit was borrowed by Dickens in *Little Dorrit*, where Mrs General tells Amy Dorrit –

*Papa* gives a pretty form to the lips. *Papa*, *potatoes*, *poultry*, *prunes*, and *prism* are all very good words for the lips; especially *prunes* and *prism*.

The form miminy-piminy is also in use:

A miminy-piminy, *Je-ne-sais-quoi* young man. –
Sir W. S. Gilbert, *Patience*, II

**Nimrod.** Any daring or outstanding hunter; from the 'mighty hunter before the Lord' (Gen. 10:9), which the Targum says means a 'sinful hunting of the sons of men'. Pope says of him, he was 'a mighty hunter, and his prey was man' (*Windsor Forest*, 62); so also Milton interprets the phrase (*Paradise Lost*, xii, 24, etc.).

The legend is that the tomb of Nimrod still exists in Damascus, and that no dew ever falls upon it, even though all its surroundings are saturated.

**Nincompoop.** A poor thing of a man. Said to be a corruption of the Latin *non compos* (*mentis*), but of this there is no evidence. The last syllable is probably connected with Dut. *poep*, a fool.

**Nine.** Nine, five, and three are mystical numbers – the *diapason* (*q.v.*), *diapente*, and *diatrion* of the Greeks. Nine consists of a trinity of trinities. According to the Pythagoreans man is a full chord, or eight notes, and Deity comes next. Three, being the trinity, represents a perfect *unity*; twice three is the perfect *dual*; and thrice three is the perfect *plural*. This explains why nine is a mystical number.

From the earliest times the number nine has been regarded as of peculiar significance. Deucalion's ark, made by the advice of Prometheus, was tossed about for *nine* days, when it stranded on the top of Mount Parnassus. There were the *nine* Muses (*q.v.*), frequently referred to as merely 'the Nine' –

Descend, ye Nine! Descend and sing
The breathing instruments inspire.
Pope, *Ode on St Cecilia's Day*

There were *nine Gallicenae* or virgin priestesses of the ancient Gallic oracle; and Lars Porsena swore by the *nine* gods –

Lars Porsena of Clusium
By the nine gods he swore
That the great house of Tarquin
Should suffer wrong no more.
Macaulay, *Lays of Ancient Rome* (Horatius, i)

who were Juno, Minerva, and Tinia (*the three chief*), Vulcan, Mars, Saturn, Hercules, Summanus, and Vedius; while the *nine* of the Sabines were Hercules, Romulus, Esculapius, Bacchus, Aeneas, Vesta, Santa, Fortuna, and Fides.

Niobe's children lay *nine* days in their blood before they were buried; the Hydra had *nine* heads; at the *Lemuria*, held by the Romans on May 9th, 11th, and 13th, persons haunted threw black beans over their heads, pronouncing nine times the words: 'Avaunt, ye spectres, from this house!' and the exorcism was complete (*see* Ovid's *Fasti*).

There were *nine* rivers of hell, or, according to some accounts the Styx encompassed the infernal regions in *nine* circles; and Milton makes the gates of hell 'thrice three-fold; three folds are brass, three iron, three of adamantine rock'. They had nine folds, nine plates, and nine linings. (*Paradise Lost*, ii, 645.)

Vulcan, when kicked from Olympus, was *nine* days falling to the island of Lemnos; and when the fallen angels were cast out of heaven, Milton says '*Nine* days they fell' (*Paradise Lost*, vi, 871).

In the early Ptolemaic system of astronomy, before the Primum Mobile (*q.v.*) was added, there were *nine* spheres; hence Milton, in his *Arcades*, speaks of the 'celestial syrens' harmony that sit upon the *nine* enfolded spheres'. They were those of the Moon, Mercury, Venus, the Sun, Mars, Jupiter, Saturn, and the Firmament or that of the fixed stars, and the Crystalline Sphere. In *Scandinavian mythology* there were *nine* earths, Hel (*q.v.*) being the goddess of the ninth; there were *nine* worlds in Niflheim, and Odin's ring dropped eight other rings (*nine* rings of mystical import) every *ninth* night.

In folk-tale *nine* appears many times. The Abracadabra was worn *nine* days, and then flung into a river; in order to see the fairies one is directed to put '*nine* grains of wheat on a four-leaved clover'; *nine* knots are made on black wool as a charm for a sprained ankle; if a servant finds *nine* green peas in a peascod, she lays it on the lintel of the kitchen door, and the first man that enters in is to be her cavalier; to see *nine* magpies is most unlucky; a cat has *nine* lives (*see also* Cat o' Nine Tails); and the *nine* of Diamonds is known as the Curse of Scotland (*q.v.*).

The weird sisters in *Macbeth* sang, as they danced round the cauldron, 'Thrice to thine, and thrice to mine, and thrice again to make up *nine*'; and then declared 'the charm wound up'; and we drink a *Three-times-three* to those most highly honoured.

Leases used to be granted for 999 years, that is *three* times *three-three-three*. Even now they run for ninety-nine years, the dual of a trinity of trinities.

*See also* the *Nine Points of the Law*, in Phrases, *below*, and the Nine Worthies, under Worthies.

There are *nine* orders of angels (*see* Angels); in Heraldry there are *nine* marks of cadency and *nine* different crowns recognised: and among ecclesiastical architects there are *nine* crosses, viz., altar crosses, processional crosses, roods on lofts, reliquary crosses, consecration crosses, marking crosses, pectoral crosses, spire crosses, and crosses pendent over altars.

**Phrases.**

***A nine days' wonder.*** Something that causes a great sensation for a few days, and then passes into the limbo of things forgotten. An old proverb is: 'A wonder lasts nine days, and then the puppy's eyes are open', alluding to dogs which, like cats, are born blind. As much as to say, the eyes of the public are blind in astonishment for nine days, but then their eyes are open, and they see too much to wonder any longer.

> *King*: You'd think it strange if I should marry her.
> *Gloster*: That would be ten days' wonder, at the least.
> *King*: That's a day longer than a wonder lasts.
> Shakespeare, *3 Henry VI*, 3, 2

***Dressed up to the nines.*** To perfection from head to foot.

***Nine-tail bruiser.*** Prison slang for the cat-o'-nine-tails (*q.v.*).

***Nine tailors make a man.*** *See* Tailors.

***Nine times out of ten.*** Far times more often than not; in a great preponderance.

***Possession is nine points of the law.*** It is every advantage a person can have short of actual right. The 'nine points of the law' have been given as –

> (1) A good deal of money; (2) a good deal of patience; (3) a good cause; (4) a good lawyer; (5) a good counsel; (6) good witnesses; (7) a good jury; (8) a good judge; and (9) good luck.

***To look nine ways.*** To squint.

**Ninepence.** ***Nice as ninepence.*** A corruption of 'Nice as nine-pins'. In the game of nine-pins, the 'men' are set in three rows with the utmost exactitude or nicety.

***Nimble as ninepence.*** Silver ninepences were common till the year 1696, when all unmilled coin was called in. These ninepences were very *pliable* or 'nimble', and, being bent, were given as love tokens, the usual formula of presentation being *To my love, from my love*. There is an old proverb, *A nimble ninepence is better than a slow shilling*.

**Ninus.** Son of Belus, husband of Semiramis, and the reputed builder of Nineveh. It is at his tomb that the lovers meet in the Pyramus and Thisbe travesty:

> *Pyr.*: Wilt thou at Ninny's tomb meet me straight way?
> *This.*: 'Tide life, 'tide death, I come without delay.
> Shakespeare, *Midsummer Night's Dream*, 5, 1

**Niobe.** The personification of maternal sorrow. According to *Grecian fable*, Niobe, the daughter of Tantalus and wife of Amphion, King of Thebes, was the mother of twelve children, and taunted Latona because she had only two – Apollo and Diana. Latona commanded her children to avenge the insult, and they caused all the sons and daughters of Niobe to die. Niobe was inconsolable, wept herself to death, and was changed into a stone, from which ran water, 'Like Niobe, all tears' (*Hamlet*, 1, 2).

***The Niobe of nations.*** So Byron styles Rome, the 'lone mother of dead empires', with 'broken thrones and temples'; a 'chaos of ruins'; a 'desert where we steer stumbling o'er recollections'. (*Childe Harold*, iv, 79.)

**Niordhr** or **Njorthr.** The Scandinavian god of the sea, the protector of seafaring men, he who ruled the winds, calmed the seas, and warded off fire. He was one of the Aesir, and father, by his wife Skadhi (*q.v.*) of Frey and Freyja. His home was Noatun ('the place of ships'). The name means 'benefactor'; *cp.* Nerthus.

**Nip.** ***Nip of whisky; just a nip,*** etc. Short for 'nipperkin' (*q.v.*).

***Number Nip.*** Another name for Rübezahl (*q.v.*).

***To nip in the bud.*** To destroy before it has had time to develop; usually said of bad habits, tendency to sin, etc. Shakespeare has –

> The third day comes a frost, a killing frost;
> And, when he thinks, good easy man, full surely
> His greatness is a-ripening, *nips his root*.
> And then he falls, as I do. *Henry VIII*, 3, 2

**Nip-cheese** or **Nip-farthing.** A miser, who nips or pinches closely his cheese and farthings. Among sailors the purser is nicknamed 'Nipcheese'. (Dutch, *nypen*.)

**Nipper.** Slang for a small boy, especially an assistant to a navvy or a costermonger. Either because he 'nips' about, that is moves or steps smartly, or because he 'nips' articles that don't rightly belong to him, i.e. 'pinches' or appropriates them.

**Nipperkin.** A small wine and beer measure containing about half a pint, or a little under; now frequently called 'a nip'.

> His hawk-economy won't thank him for't
> Which stops his petty nipperkin of port.
> Peter Pindar, *Hair Powder*

The traditional Devon and Cornish song *The Barley Mow* starts with drinking the health out of the 'jolly brown bowl', and at each chorus increases the size of the receptacle until in the sixteenth and last we have –

> We'll drink it out of the ocean, my boys,
> Here's a health to the barley-mow!
> The ocean, the river, the well, the pipe, the hogshead, the half-hogshead, the anker, the half-anker, the gallon, the half-gallon, the pottle, the quart, the pint, the half a pint, the quarter-pint, the nipperkin, *and the* jolly brown bowl!

**Nirvana** (Sansk., a blowing out, or extinction). Annihilation, or rather the final deliverance of the soul from transmigration (*see* Buddhism).

**Nisi** (Lat. unless). In Law a 'rule *nisi*' is a rule *unless* cause be shown to the contrary.

***Decree nisi.*** A decree of divorce granted on the condition that it does not take effect until made *absolute*, which is done at the expiration of six months *unless* reasons why it should not have meantime come to light. Every decree of divorce is, in the first instance, a *decree nisi* – sometimes humorously called a 'decree *nas-ty*'.

***Nisi prius*** (unless previously). Originally a writ commanding a sheriff to empanel a jury which should be at the Court of Westminster on a certain day *unless* the judge of assize *previously* come to his county, as –

> 'We command you to come before our justices at Westminster on the morrow of All Souls', NISI PRIUS justiciarii domini regis ad assisas capiendas venerint – i.e. unless previously the justices of our lord the king come to hold their assizes at (the court of your own assize town).

The second Statute of Westminster (1285) instituted Judges of *nisi prius*, who were appointed to travel through the shires three times a year to hear civil causes; and such causes tried before Judges of Assize are still known as 'Causes of Nisi prius'.

**Nisroch.** The Assyrian god in whose temple Sennacherib was worshipping when he was slain (2 Kings 19:37). Nothing is known of the god, and the name is probably a corruption either of Asur or of Nusku, a god connected with Nebo (*q.v.*).

**Nitouche. *Faire la Sainte Nitouche*,** to pretend to great sanctity, to look as though butter would not melt in one's mouth. Sainte Nitouche is the name given in France to a hypocrite; it is a contraction of *n'y touche*.

> It is certainly difficult to believe hard things of a woman who looks like Ste Nitouche in profile.
> John Oliver Hobbes, *Some Emotions and a Moral*, ch. iii

**Nivetta.** *See* Morgan le Fay.

**Nix.** *See* Nicker. The word is also slang for 'nothing'. 'You can't get him to work for nix', i.e. without paying him. In this sense it is from Ger. *nichts*, nothing.

**Nizam.** A title of sovereignty in Hyderabad (India), contracted from *Nizam-ul-mulk* (regulator of the state), the style adopted by Asaf Jah, who obtained possession of the Deccan in 1713. The name *Caesar* was by the Romans used precisely in the same manner, and descended to modern times as *Kaiser*.

**Njorthr.** *See* Nerthus.

**No-Popery Riots.** Those of Edinburgh and Glasgow, February 5th, 1779. Those of London, occasioned by Lord George Gordon, in 1780.

**Noah's Ark.** A name given by sailors to a white band of cloud spanning the sky like a rainbow and in shape something like the hull of a ship. If east and west expect dry weather, if north and south expect wet.

***Noah's Wife.*** According to legend she was unwilling to go into the ark, and the quarrel between the patriarch and his wife forms a prominent feature of *Noah's Flood*, in the Chester and Townley Mysteries.

> Hastow nought herd, quod Nicholas, also
> The sorwe of Noë with his felawshipe
> Er that he mighte gete his wyf to shipe?
> Chaucer, *Miller's Tale*, 352

**Noakes, John o'.** *See* John-a-Nokes.

**Nob.** Slang for the head (probably from *knob*); also for a person of rank and position (contraction of *noble* or *nobility*). *Cp.* Snob.

**Nobel Prizes.** Prizes established by the will of Alfred Bernard Nobel (1833–96), the Swedish chemist and inventor of dynamite, etc., to encourage work in the cause of humanity. There are five prizes given annually, each of about £7,000, as follows: (1) for the most noteworthy work in *physics*, (2) in *chemistry*, (3) in *medicine* or *physiology*, (4) in *idealistic literature*, and (5) in the furtherance of universal peace. W. C. Röntgen, Mme Curie, A. Carrel, Rudyard Kipling, Maeterlinck, Hauptmann, Rabindranath Tagore, Romain Rolland, Elihu Root, and President Wilson are among those to whom the prizes have been awarded.

**Noble.** A former English gold coin, so called on account of the superior excellency of its gold. Nobles were originally disposed of as a reward for good news, or important service done; first minted by Edward III, they remained in use till the time of Henry VIII; their nominal value was 6*s*. 8*d*. to 10*s*.

***Noble.*** The Lion, the King of all the Beasts, in Caxton's edition of *Reynard the Fox* (*q.v.*).

***The Noble.*** Charles III of Navarre (1361–1425). Soliman *Tchelibi*, Turkish prince at Adrianople (d.1410).

***The Noble Science.*** The old epithet for fencing or boxing, now usually called 'The Noble Art of Self-Defence'.

> ... a bold defiance
> Shall meet him, were he of the noble science.
> Beaumont and Fletcher, *Knight of the Burning Pestle*, II, i

**Noblesse oblige** (Fr.). Noble birth imposes the obligation of high-minded principles and noble actions.

**Noctes Ambrosianae.** A series of papers on literary and topical subjects, in the form of dialogues, contributed to *Blackwood's Magazine*, 1822–35. They were written principally by Professor Wilson, 'Christopher North'.

> Lockhart was in the habit of taking walks with Wilson every morning, and of supping with Blackwood at Ambrose's, a small tavern in Edinburgh. One night Lockhart said, 'What a pity there has not been a shorthand writer here to take down all the good things that have been said!' and next day he produced a paper from memory, and called it *Noctes Ambrosianae*. That was the first of the series. The part ascribed to Hogg, the Ettrick Shepherd, is purely supposititious.

**Nod. *A nod is as good as a wink to a blind horse.*** *See under* Horse

***On the nod.*** On credit. *To get a thing on the nod* is to get it without paying for it at the time – and often without any definite intention of paying for it at all. The phrase is from the auction-room; one buys articles by a mere nod of the head to the clerk, and the formalities are attended to later.

***The Land of Nod.*** *See* Land.

**Noddy. *A Tom Noddy*** is a very foolish or half-witted person, 'a noodle'. The marine birds called noddies are so silly that anyone can go up to them and knock them down with a stick. It seems more than likely that the word is connected with *to nod* but it has been suggested that it was originally a pet form of *Nicodemus*.

**Noël.** In English (also written *Nowell*), a Christmas carol, or the shout of joy in a carol; in French, Christmas Day. The word is Provençal *nadal*, from Lat. *natalem*, natal.

> Nowells, nowells, nowells!
> Sing all we may,
> Because that Christ, the King,
> Was born this blessed day. Old Carol

**Nokes.** *See* John-a-Nokes.

**Nolens volens.** Whether willing or not. Two Latin participles meaning 'being unwilling (or) willing'. *Cp.* Willy-nilly.

**Noli me tangere** (Lat., touch me not). The words Christ used to Mary Magdalene after His resurrection (John 20:17), and given as a name to a plant of the genus *Impatiens*. The seed-vessels consist of one cell in five divisions, and when the seed is ripe each of these, on being touched, suddenly folds itself into a spiral form and leaps from the stalk. *See* Darwin's *Loves of the Plants*, ii, 3.

**Noll. *Old Noll.*** Oliver Cromwell was so called by the Royalists. Noll is a familiar form of *Oliver*.

**Nolle prosequi** (Lat., to be unwilling to prosecute). A petition from a plaintiff to stay a suit. *Cp.* Non pros.

**Nolo episcopari** (Lat., I am unwilling to be made a bishop). The formal reply supposed to be returned to the royal offer of a bishopric. Chamberlayne says (*Present State of England*, 1669) that in former times the person about to be elected modestly refused the office twice, and if he did so a third time his refusal was accepted.

**Nom. *Nom de guerre*** is French for a 'war name', but really means an assumed name. It was customary at one time for everyone who entered the French army to assume a name; this was especially the case in the times of chivalry, when knights were known by the device on their shields.

***Nom de plume.*** English-French for 'pen name', or pseudonym, the name assumed by a writer, cartoonist, etc., who does not choose to give his own to the public; as *Currer Bell* (Charlotte Brontë), *Fiona McLeod* (William Sharp), *Henry Seton Merriman* (Hugh Stowell Scott), etc. Occasionally, as in the case of *Voltaire* (François Marie Arouet) and *De Stendhal* (Marie Henri Beyle), the assumed name quite replaces the true name.

**Nominalists.** The schoolmen's name for one who – following William of Occam – denied the objective existence of abstract ideas; also, the name of a sect founded by Roscelin, Canon of Compiègne (1040–1120), who maintained that if the Father, Son, and Holy Ghost are *one God*, they cannot be three distinct *persons*, but must be simply three *names* of the same being; just as father, son, and husband are three distinct names of one and the same man under different conditions. Abélard, Hobbes, Locke, Bishop Berkeley, Condillac, and Dugald Stewart are noted Nominalists. *Cp.* Realists.

**Non.** The Latin negative, *not*; adopted in English, and very widely employed, as a prefix of negation, e.g. in *non-abstainer*, *nonconformist*, *non-existent*, *non-resident*, *nonsense*, *non-suit*, etc.

***Non amo te, Sabidi.*** *See* I do not like thee, Dr Fell, *under* Doctor.

***Non Angli sed angeli*** (Lat., Not Angles, but angels). Words attributed to Gregory the Great, then Abbot of St Andrea, about 578, when he saw some fair-haired English captives exposed for sale in the slave-market at Rome.

***Non assumpsit*** (Lat., he has not undertaken). The legal term for a plea denying promise or undertaking by the defendant.

***Non compos mentis*** (Lat., not of sound mind). Said of a lunatic, idiot, drunkard, or one who has lost memory and understanding by accident or disease.

> The prisoner not denying the fact, and persisting before the court that he looked upon it as a compliment, the jury brought him in *non compos mentis.* Addison, *Tatler*, 5 Dec., 1710

***Non dolet.*** *See* Arria.

***Non-ego.*** *See* Ego.

***Non est.*** A contraction of Lat. *Non est inventus* (not to be found). They are the words which the sheriff writes on a writ when the defendant is not to be found in his bailiwick.

***Non mi ricordo*** (Ital., I do not remember). A shuffling way of saying 'I don't choose to answer that question'. It was the usual answer of the Italian courier and other Italian witnesses when under examination at the trial of Queen Caroline, wife of George IV, in 1820.

***Non placet*** (Lat., it is unpleasing). The formula used, especially by the governing body of a University, for expressing a negative vote.

***Non pros.*** for Lat. *Non prosequi* (not to prosecute). The judgment of *Non pros.* is one for costs, when the plaintiff stays a suit.

***Non sequitur*** (Lat., it does not follow). A conclusion which does not follow from the premises stated; an inconsequent statement, such as Artemus Ward's –

> I met a man in Oregon who hadn't any teeth – not a tooth in his head – yet that man could play on the bass drum better than any man I ever met.

**Nonce.** The old phrase 'for *then once*' (i.e. 'for that time only') read as 'for *the nonce*'.

***Nonce-word.*** A temporary word that is coined for the occasion. *Birellism*, *couponeer*, *Limehouse*, *Puseyite*, and many others to be found throughout this Dictionary, are examples.

**Non-com.** A non-commissioned officer in the army.

**Nonconformists.** In England, members of Protestant bodies who do *not conform* to the doctrines of the Church of England (also called *Dissenters* and *Noncons*); especially the 2,000 clergymen who, in 1662, left the Church rather than submit to the conditions of the Act of Uniformity – i.e. 'unfeigned assent to all and everything contained in the Book of Common Prayer'.

**Nones.** In the ancient Roman calendar, the *ninth* (Lat. *nonus*) day before the Ides; in the Roman Catholic Church, the office for the *ninth* hour after sunrise, or 3 p.m.

> On March the 7th, June, July,
> October, too, the nones you spy;
> Except in these, those Nones appear
> On the 5th day of all the year.
> If to the Nones you add an 8
> Of every ide you'll find the date. E. C. B.

**Nonjurors.** Those clergymen who refused to take the oath of allegiance to the new government after the Revolution (1691). They were Archbishop Sancroft with eight bishops, and four hundred clergymen, all of whom were ejected from their livings. *Cp.* Seven Bishops, The.

**Nonplus** (Lat., no more). A quandary; a state of perplexity when 'no more' can be said on the subject. When a man is *nonplussed* or has *come to a nonplus* in an argument, it means that he is unable to deny or controvert what is advanced against him. *To nonplus* a person is to put him into such a fix.

**Norfolk-Howards.** Bugs. The two names are the 'highest' non-royal names in the country, for *Howard* is the family name of the Duke of *Norfolk*, the premier Duke and Earl, and the Hereditary Earl Marshal and Chief Butler of England. On June 26th, 1862, an advertisement (which may have been a 'spoof' one) appeared in *The Times* to the effect that –

> I, Norfolk Howard, heretofore called and known by the name of Joshua Bug, late of Epsom, in the county of Surrey, now of Wakefield, in the county of York, and landlord of the Swan Tavern, in the same county, do hereby give notice that on the 20th day of this present month … I did wholly abandon the use of the surname of Bug, and assumed, took, and used, and am determined … to be called and known by the name of Norfolk Howard only … duly enrolled by me in the High Court of Chancery.

**Norns, The.** The three giant goddesses who, in *Scandinavian mythology*, presided over the fates of both men and gods. Anciently there was only one Norn, *Urdhr* (i.e. the power of fate), but later two others were added, and the three became known as *Urdhr* (the Past), *Verdhandi* (the Present), and *Skuld* (the Future), who determine the fate of men by carving rune-staves and with them casting lots. They appeared at the cradle on the birth of a child, and dwelt at the root of Yggdrasil (*q.v.*) beside the well Urdar, from which they daily sprinkled Yggdrasil to preserve it from decay. The Three Weird Sisters in *Macbeth* are probably connected with the Norns; and *cp.* Fate.

**Norrisian Professor.** A Professor of Divinity in Cambridge University. This professorship was founded in 1760 by John Norris, of Whitton, Norfolk. The four divinity professors are Lady Margaret's, the Regius, the Norrisian, and the Hulsean.

**Norroy** (i.e. north roy, or king). The third king of arms is so called, because his office is on the north side of the river Trent; that of the south side is called Clarencieux (*q.v.*).

**North.** It is said that the poor have a great objection to being buried on the north side of a churchyard. They seem to think only evil-doers should be there interred. Probably the chief reason is the want of sun; but the old idea is that the east is *God's* side, where His throne is set; the west, *man's* side, the Galilee of the Gentiles; the south, the side of the '*spirits made just' and angels*, where the sun shines in his strength; and the north, the *devil's* side. *Cp.* The Devil's door, *under* Devil.

> As men die, so shall they arise; if in faith, in the Lord, towards the south … and shall arise in glory; if in unbelief … towards the north, then are they past all hope.
>
> Coverdale, *Praying for the Dead*

***He's too far north for me.*** Too canny, too cunning to be taken in; very hard in making a bargain. The inhabitants of Yorkshire are supposed to be very canny, especially in driving a bargain; and when you get to Aberdeen —!

**North-east Passage, The.** A way to India from Europe round the north extremity of Asia. It had been often attempted even in the 16th century. Hence Beaumont and Fletcher:

> That everlasting cassock, that has worn
> As many servants out as the North-east Passage
> Has consumed sailors. *The Woman's Prize*, ii, 2

**Northamptonshire Poet.** John Clare (1793–1864), son of a farmer at Helpstone.

**Northern.** ***The Northern Bear.*** Russia has been so called.

***The Northern Gate of the Sun.*** The sign of Cancer, or summer solstice; so called because it marks the northern tropic.

***The Northern Lights.*** The Aurora Borealis (*q.v.*).

> [The old King goes] up with music
> On cold starry nights,
> To sup with the Queen
> Of the gay Northern Lights.
>
> Allingham, *The Fairies*

***The Northern Wagoner.*** The genius presiding over the Great Bear, or Charles's Wain (*q.v.*), which contains seven large stars.

> By this the northern wagoner has set
> His sevenfold team behind the stedfast star [*the pole-star*]. Spenser, *Faërie Queene*, I, ii, 1

Dryden calls the Great Bear *the Northern Car*, and similarly the crown in Ariadne has been called *the Northern Crown*.

**Norway, Maid of.** *See* Maid.

**Nose.** ***A nose of wax.*** *See* Wax.

***As plain as the nose on your face.*** Extremely obvious, patent to all.

***Bleeding of the nose.*** According to some, a sign that one is in love. Grose says if it bleeds one drop only it forebodes sickness, if three drops the omen is still worse; but Melton, in his *Astrologaster*, says, 'If a man's nose bleeds one drop at the *left* nostril it is a sign of good luck, and *vice versa*.'

***Cleopatra's nose.*** *See* Cleopatra.

***Golden nose.*** Tycho Brahe (d.1601), the Danish astronomer. He lost his nose in a duel, so adopted a golden one, which he attached to his face by a cement which he carried about with him.

***Led by the nose.*** Is. 37:29, says, 'Because thy rage against Me … is come up into Mine ears, therefore will I put My hook in thy nose … and will turn thee back …' Horses, asses, etc., led by bit and bridle, are led by the nose. Hence Iago says of Othello, he was 'led by the nose as asses are' (1, 3). But buffaloes, camels, and bears are actually led by a ring inserted in their nostrils.

> Though authority be a stubborn bear, yet he is often led by the nose with gold.
>
> Shakespeare, *Winter's Tale*, 4, 4

***Nose tax.*** It is said that in the 9th century the Danes imposed a poll tax in Ireland, and that this was called the 'Nose Tax', because those who neglected to pay were punished by having their nose slit.

***To count noses.*** A horse-dealer counts horses by the *nose*, as cattle are counted by the *head*; hence, the expression is sometimes ironically used of numbering votes, as in the Division lobbies.

***To cut off your nose to spite your face,*** or ***to be revenged on your face.*** To act out of pique in such a way as to injure yourself; as to throw up a good situation in a fit of temper.

***To follow one's nose.*** To go straight ahead; to proceed without deviating from the path.

> Juan, following honour and his nose,
> Rush'd where the thickest fire announced most foes.
> Byron, *Don Juan*, VIII, xxxii

***To keep one's nose to the grindstone.*** To keep hard at work. Tools, such as scythes, chisels, etc., are constantly sharpened on a stone or with a grindstone.

> Be to the poor like on to whunstane.,
> And haud their noses to the grunstane.
> Burns, *Dedication to Gavin Hamilton*

***To pay through the nose.*** To pay an excessive price, or at an exorbitant rate. There may be some connection between this old phrase, 'rhino' (*q.v.*), slang for money, and Gr. *rhinos*, the nose; or there may be an allusion to nose-bleeding and being *bled* for money.

***To poke*** or ***thrust one's nose in.*** Officiously to intermeddle with other people's affairs; to intrude where one is not wanted.

***To put one's nose out of joint.*** To supplant a person in another's good graces; to upset one's plans; to humiliate a conceited person.

> Lesbia gave hereself the airs ... till Alice came and put her nose out of joint, for which she never forgave her.
> Hy Kingsley, *Geoffrey Hamlyn*, xxxiii

***To snap one's nose off.*** To speak snappishly. To *pull* (or *wring*) *the nose* is to affront by an act of indignity; to *snap one's nose* is to affront by speech. Snarling dogs snap at each other's noses.

***To take pepper in the nose.*** *See* Pepper.

***To turn up one's nose.*** To express contempt. When a person sneers he turns up the nose by curling the upper lip.

***To wipe one's nose.*** *See* Wipe.

***Under one's very nose.*** Right before one; in full view.

**Nose-bag.** A visitor to a house of refreshment who brings his own victuals and calls for a glass of water or lemonade. The reference is to carrying the feed of a horse in a nose-bag to save expense.

**Nosey.** Very inquisitive; given to overmuch poking of the nose into other people's business. One who does this is often called a *NoseyParker*.

The Duke of Wellington was familiarly called 'Nosey' by the soldiery. His 'commander's nose' was a very distinguishing feature of the Iron Duke. The nickname was also given to Oliver Cromwell. *See* Copper-nose.

**Nostradamus, Michel.** A French astrologer (1503–66) who published an annual 'Almanack' as well as the famous *Centuries* (1555) containing prophecies which, though the book suffered papal condemnation in 1781, still occasions controversy from time to time. His prophecies are couched in most ambiguous language, hence the saying *as good a prophet as Nostradamus* – i.e. so obscure that none can make out your meaning.

**Nostrum** (Lat., our own). It is applied to a quack medicine, the ingredients of which are supposed to be a secret of the compounders; also, figuratively, to any political or other scheme that savours of the charlatan.

**Notables.** An assembly of nobles or notable men, in French history, selected by the king to form a parliament. They were convened in 1626 by Richelieu, and not again till 1787 (a hundred and sixty years afterwards), when Louis XVI called them together with the view of relieving the nation of some of its pecuniary embarrassments. The last time they ever assembled was November 6th, 1788.

**Notarikon.** A cabalistic word (Gr. *notarikon*, Lat. *notarius*, a shorthand-writer) denoting the old Jewish art of using each letter in a word to form another word, of using the initials of the words in a sentence to form another word, etc., as *Cabal* itself (*q.v.*) was fabled to have been formed from Clifford, Ashley, Buckingham, Arlington, and Lauderdale, and as the term *Ichthus* (*q.v.*) was applied to the Saviour. Other instances will be found under a.e.i.o.u., Clio, Hempe, Limp, and Smectymnuus; *cp. also* Hip.

**Notch.** ***Out of all notch***. *See* Scotch.

**Nothing.** ***Mere nothings.*** Trifles; unimportant things or events.

> You shapeless nothing in a dish,
> You that are but almost a fish –
> Cowper, *The Poet, the Oyster*, etc.

***Next to nothing.*** A very little. As, 'It will cost next to nothing,' 'He eats next to nothing.'

***Nothin' doin'!*** A slang expression, generally implying that you are disappointed in your expectations.

***Nothing venture, nothing have.*** If you daren't throw a sprat you mustn't expect to catch a mackerel; don't be afraid of taking a risk now and then. A very old proverb.

***Out of nothing one can get nothing;*** the Latin *Ex nihilo nihil fit* – i.e. every effect must have a cause. It was the dictum by which Xenophanes, founder of the Eleatic School (*q.v.*), postulated the theory of the eternity of matter. Persius (*Satires*, iii, 84) has *De nihilo nihilum, in nihilum nil posse reverti*, From nothing nothing, and into nothing can nothing return.

We now use the phrase as equivalent to 'You cannot get blood from a stone', or expect good work from one who has no brains.

***That's nothing to you,*** or ***to do with you.*** It's none of *your* business.

***There's nothing for it but ...*** There's no alternative; take it or leave it.

***To come to nothing.*** To turn out a failure; to result in naught.

***To make nothing of.*** To fail to understand; not to succeed in some operation.

**Nothingarian.** A humorous name for one who has no religious beliefs of any kind; formed on the model of *Latitudinarian*, *Supralapsarian*, etc.

**Nourmahal** (Arab., The Light of the Harem). One of the ladies in the harem of the Caliph Haroun al-Raschid, afterwards called Nourjehan (Light of the World). The story of her love for Selim and how she regained his lost affections by means of a love-spell is told in Moore's *Lalla-Rookh*.

**Nous** (Gr., mind, intellect). Adopted in English and used more or less facetiously for intelligence, 'horse-sense'.

> This is the genuine head of many a house,
> And much divinity without a nous.
>
> Pope, *Dunciad*, iv, 244

***Nous*** was the Platonic term for mind, or the first cause, and the system of divinity here referred to is that which springs from blind nature.

**Nous avons changé tout cela** (Fr. we have changed all that). A facetious reproof to one who lays down the law upon everything, and talks contemptuously of old customs, old authors, old artists, and old everything. The phrase is taken from Molière's *Médecin Malgré Lui*, II, vi (1666):

> *Géronte*: Il n'y a qu' seule chose qui m'a choqué; c'est l'endroit du foie et du coeur. Il me semble que vous les placez autrement qu'ils ne sont; que le coeur est du côté gauche, et le foie du côté droit.
>
> *Sganarelle*: Oui; cela étoit autrefois ainsi; mais nous avons changé tout cela, et nous faisons maintenant la médecine d'une méthode toute nouvelle.
>
> *Géronte*: C'est ce que je ne savois pas, et je vous demande pardon de mon ignorance.

**Nova Scotia.** *See* Acadia.

**Novatians.** Followers of Novatianus, a presbyter of Rome in the 3rd century. They differed little from the orthodox Catholics, but maintained that the Church had no power to allow one who had lapsed to be readmitted. *Cp.* Cathari.

**November** (Lat. *novem*, nine). The ninth month in the ancient Roman calendar, when the year began in March, now the eleventh. The old Dutch name was *Slaght-maand* (slaughter-month, the time when the beasts were slain and salted down for winter use); the old Saxon, *Wind-monath* (wind-month, when the fishermen drew their boats ashore, and gave over fishing till the next spring); it was also called *Blot-monath* – the same as *Slaght-maand*. In the French Republican calendar it was called *Brumaire* (fog-month, October 22nd to November 21st).

**Nowell.** *See* Noël.

**Nowhere, Lands of.** *See* Medamothi.

**Noyades** (Fr. drownings). A means of execution adopted by Carrier at Nantes, in the French Revolution (1793–4). Prisoners to be 'removed' were first bound and then stowed in the hold of a vessel which had a movable bottom. This was sent to the middle of the Loire, the vessel was scuttled, and the victims drowned. Nero, at the suggestion of Anicetus, attempted to drown his mother in the same manner.

**n*th*,** or **n*th* plus one,** in University slang, means to the utmost degree. Thus, *Cut to the nth* means wholly unnoticed by a friend. The expression is taken from the index of a mathematical formula, where $n$ stands for any number, and $n + 1$, one more than any number. Hence, *n-dimensional*, having an indefinite number of dimensions, *n-tuple* (on the analogy of *quadruple*, *quintuple*, etc.), having an indefinite number of duplications.

**Nude.** Rabelais (iv. xxix) wittily says that a person without clothing is dressed in 'grey and cold' of a comical cut, being 'nothing before, nothing behind, and sleeves of the same'. King Shrovetide, monarch of Sneak Island, was so arrayed.

The nude statues of Paris are said to be draped in 'cerulean blue'.

**'Nuff said!** *See* Enough.

**Nulla linea.** *See* No day without its line *under* Line.

**Nulli secundus** (Lat. second to none). The motto of the Coldstream Guards, which regiment is hence sometimes spoken of as the *Nulli Secundus Club*.

**Numbers.** Pythagoras looked on numbers as influential principles; in his system –

1 was Unity, and represented Deity, which has no parts.
2 was Diversity, and therefore disorder; the principle of strife and all evil.
3 was Perfect Harmony, or the union of unity and diversity.
4 was Perfection; it is the first square (2 x 2 = 4).
5 was the prevailing number in Nature and Art.
6 was Justice.
7 was the climacteric number in all diseases; called the *Medical Number*. *See* Climacteric.

With the ancient Romans 2 was the most fatal of all the numbers; they dedicated the second month to Pluto, and the second day of the month to the Manes.

In old ecclesiastical symbolism the numbers from 1 to 13 were held to denote the following –

1 The Unity of God.
2 The hypostatic union of Christ, both God and man.
3 The Trinity.
4 The number of the Evangelists.
5 The wounds of the Redeemer: two in the hands, two in the feet, one in the side.
6 The creative week.
7 The gifts of the Holy Ghost (Rev. 1:12), and the seven times Christ spoke on the cross.
8 The number of beatitudes (Matt. 5:3–11).
9 The nine orders of angels.
10 The number of the Commandments.
11 The number of the Apostles who remained faithful.
12 The original college.
13 The final number after the conversion of Paul.

***Apocalyptic number,* 666.** *See* Number of the Beast *below*.

***Back number.*** A number of a paper or periodical issued previously to the current one; hence an out-of-date or old-fashioned person or thing.

***Cyclic number.*** A number the final digit of whose square is the same; 5 (25) and 6 (36) are examples.

***Golden number.*** *See* Golden.

***His days are numbered.*** They are drawing to a close; he is near death.

> God hath numbered thy kingdom, and finished it.
> Dan. 5:26

***Irrational number.*** A definite number not expressible in a definite number of digits, as the root of a number that cannot be exactly extracted.

***Medical number.*** In the Pythagorean system (*see above*), 7.

***Number Nip.*** The same as Rübezahl (*q.v.*).

***Number of the Beast, The.*** 666; a mystical number of unknown meaning but referring to some man mentioned by St John.

> Let him that hath understanding count the number of the beast; for it is the number of a man; and his number is Six hundred threescore and six.
> Rev. 13:18

Among the Cabalists every letter represented a number, and one's number was the sum of these equivalents to the letters in one's name. If, as is probable, the *Revelation* was written in Hebrew, the number would suit either Nero, Hadrian, or Trajan – all persecutors; if in Greek, it would fit Caligula or *Lateinos*, i.e. the Roman Empire; but almost any name in any language can be twisted into this number, and it has been applied to many persons assumed to have been Antichrist, as Apostates, Diocletian, Evanthas, Julian the Apostate, Luther, Mahomet, Paul V, Silvester II, Napoleon Bonaparte, Charles Bradlaugh, William II of Germany, and several others; as well as to certain phrases supposed to be descriptive of 'the Man of Sin', as Vicar-General of God, Kakos Odegos (bad guide), Abinu Kadescha Papa (our holy father the pope), e.g. –

M a o m e t i s
40, 1, 70, 40, 5, 300, 10, 200 = 666
L a t e i n o s
30, 1, 300, 5, 10, 50, 70, 200 = 666

The *Nile* is emblematic of the year.

N e i l o s
50, 5, 10, 30, 70, 200 = 365

One suggestion is that St John chose the number 666 because it just fell short of the holy number 7 in every particular; was straining at every point to get there, but never could. *See also* Mysterium.

***Odd numbers.*** *See* Odd.

***To consult the Book of Numbers.*** A facetious way of saying, 'to put it to the vote', 'to call for a division'.

***Your number's up.*** You are in a very serious position; you are just about to 'get the sack', or, in some cases, to die. A soldier's phrase; in the American army a soldier who has just been killed or has died is said to have 'lost his mess number'. An older phrase used in the British Navy was 'to lose the number of his mess'.

**Numerals.** All our numerals and ordinals up to a million (with one exception) are Anglo-Saxon. The one exception is *Second*, which is French. The Anglo-Saxon word was *other*, as First, Other, Third, etc., but as this was ambiguous the Fr. *seconde* was early adopted. Million is from Lat. *mille*, a thousand.

The primitive method of counting was by the fingers (*cp.* Digit); thus in the Roman system of numeration the first four were simply i, ii, iii, iiii; five was the outline of the hand simplified into a v; the next four figures were the two combined, thus, vi, vii, viii, viiii; and ten was a double v, thus, x. At a later period iiii and viiii were expressed by one less than five (i-v) and one less than ten (i-x); nineteen was ten-plus-nine (x + ix), etc. *See also* Arabic Figures.

**Nunc Dimittis.** The Song of Simeon (Luke 2:29), 'Lord, now lettest thou thy servant depart in peace', so called from the opening words of the Latin version, *Nunc dimittis servum tuum, Domine.*

Hence, *to receive one's Nunc dimittis*, to be given permission to go; *to sing one's Nunc dimittis*, to show great delight at departing.

The Canticle is sung in the Evening Service of the Church of England, and has been used at Compline or Vespers throughout the Church from the earliest times.

**Nuncheon.** Properly, 'the noontide draught'; M.E. *noneschenh* (*none*, noon, and *schench*, a cup or draught); hence, light refreshments between meals, lunch. The word *luncheon* has been affected by the older *nuncheon*. *Cp.* Bever.

> Laying by their swords and truncheons,
> They took their breakfasts, or their nuncheons.
>
> Butler, *Hudibras*, I, i, 345

**Nunky.** Slang for 'Uncle' (*q.v.*), especially as meaning a pawnbroker; or for 'uncle Sam' (*see* Sam).

***Nunky pays for all.*** The American Government (*see* Sam) has to 'stand the racket'.

**Nuremberg Eggs.** Watches. Watches were invented at Nuremberg about 1500, and were egg-shaped.

**Nurr and Spell.** *See* Knurr.

**Nursery.** A room set apart for the use of young children (Lat. *nutrire*, to nourish); hence, a garden for rearing plants (tended by a *nurseryman*).

In horse-racing, *Nurseries* are races for two-year-olds; and figuratively the word is used of any place or school of training for the professions, etc.

> Under William Rufus the Chancery became a nursery of clever and unscrupulous churchmen.
>
> Freeman, *The Norman Conquest*, V, 135

***Nursery cannons.*** In billiards, a series of cannons played so that the balls move as little as possible.

**Nut.** Slang for the head; perhaps so called from its resemblance to a nut.

> If we charged or broke or cut
> You could bet your bloomin' nut
> 'E'd be waiting fifty paces right flank rear.
>
> Kipling, *Gunga Din*

Also slang for a swell young man about town, a dude (in this sense frequently written – and pronounced – with an initial *k*, *knut*); from a music-hall song of the early 20th century, 'I'm Gilbert the Filbert, I'm one of the Nuts'.

***A hard nut to crack.*** A difficult question to answer; a hard problem to solve.

***He who would eat the nut must first crack the shell.*** The gods give nothing to man without great labour, or *Nil sine magno vita labore dedit mortalibus. Qui nucleum esse vult, frangit nucem* (Plautus). In French *Il faut casser le noyau pour en avoir l'amande*. It was Heraclides who said, 'Expect nothing without toil.'

***Here we go gathering nuts of May.*** This burden of the old children's game is a perversion of 'Here we go gathering *knots* of may', referring to the old custom of gathering knots of flowers on May-day, or, to use the ordinary phrase, 'to go a-maying'. Of course there are no nuts to be gathered in May.

***It is time to lay our nuts aside*** (Lat. *relinquere nuces*). To leave off our follies, to relinquish boyish pursuits. The allusion is to an old Roman marriage ceremony, in which the bridegroom, as he led his bride home, scattered nuts to the crowd, as if to symbolise to them that he gave up his boyish sports.

***Off one's nut.*** Crazy, daft.

> To go off their nuts about ladies,
> As dies for young fellars as fights.
>
> Sims, *Dagonet Ballads* (*Polly*)

***That's nuts to him.*** A great pleasure, a fine treat.

> To edge his way along the crowded paths of life, warning all human sympathy to keep its distance, was what the knowing ones call nuts to Scrooge. Dickens, *A Christmas Carol*, i

***To be dead nuts on.*** To be very much pleased with, highly gratified with.

> My aunt is awful nuts on Marcus Aurelius: I beg your pardon, you don't know the phrase; my aunt makes Marcus Aurelius her Bible.
>
> Wm Black, *Princess of Thule*, xi

**Nut-brown Maid, The.** An English ballad, dating (probably) from the late 15th century, first printed in *Arnolde's Chronicle* (Antwerp, 1502). It tells how the 'Not-browne Mayd' was wooed and won by a knight who gave out that he was a banished man. After describing the hardships she would have to undergo if she married him, and finding her love true to the test, he revealed himself to be an earl's son, with large hereditary estates in Westmorland.

Now, syth that ye have shewed to me
 The secret of your mynde,
I shall be playne to you agayne,
 Lyke as ye shall me fynde:
Syth it is so, that ye wyll go,
 I wolle not leve behynde;
Shall never be sayd, the not-browne mayd
 Was to her love unkynde:
Make you redy, for so am I,
 Allthough it were anone;
For, in my mynde, of all mankynde
 I love but you alone.

The ballad is given in Percy's *Reliques*, and forms the basis of Prior's *Henry and Emma*.

**Nutcrack Night.** All Hallows' Eve, when it is customary in some places to crack nuts in large quantities.

**Nutcrackers.** The East Kent Regiment, the old 3rd Foot: so called because at Albuera they opened and retreated, but in a few minutes came again into the field, cracked the heads of the Polish Lancers, and did most excellent service.

**Nutmeg State.** The nickname of Connecticut. The story is that the inhabitants at one time manufactured wooden nutmegs for export.

**Nutshell.** ***The 'Iliad' in a nutshell.*** Pliny (vii, 21) tells us that the *Iliad* was copied in so small a hand that the whole work could lie in a walnut shell; his authority is Cicero (*Apud Gellium*, ix, 421).

Whilst they (as Homer's *Iliad* in a nut)
A world of wonders in one closet shut.

On the Tradescants' Monument, Lambeth Churchyard

Huet, Bishop of Avranches (d.1721), proved by experiment that a parchment 27 by 21 centimetres would contain the entire *Iliad*, and that such a parchment would go into a common-sized nut; he wrote eighty verses of the *Iliad* (which contains in all 501,930 letters) on a single line of a page similar to this Dictionary. This would be 19,000 verses to the page, or 2,000 more than the *Iliad* contains.

In the Harleian MSS (530) is an account of Peter Bales, a clerk of the Court of Chancery about 1590, who wrote out the whole Bible so small that he inclosed it in a walnut shell of English growth. Lalanne describes, in his *Curiosités Bibliographiques*, an edition of Rochefoucault's *Maximes*, published by Didot in 1829, on pages one inch square, each page containing 26 lines, and each line 44 letters. Charles Toppan, of New York, engraved on a plate one-eighth of an inch square 12,000 letters; the *Iliad* would occupy 42 such plates engraved on both sides. George P. Marsh says, in his *Lectures*, he has seen the entire Koran in a parchment roll four inches wide and half an inch in diameter.

***To lie in a nutshell.*** To be explained in a few words; to be capable of easy solution.

# O

**O.** The fifteenth letter of our alphabet, the fourteenth of the ancient Roman, and the sixteenth of the Phoenician and Semitic – in which it was called 'the eye'. Its name in Anglo-Saxon was *oedel*, home.

> A headless man had a letter [o] to write,
> He who read it [*naught*] had lost his sight.
> The dumb repeated it [*naught*] word for word,
> And deaf was the man who listened and heard [*naught*].
> Dr Whewell

***Round as Giotto's O.*** Said of work that is perfect and complete, but done with little labour. The story is that the Pope, wishing for an artist to undertake some special decorations, sent to Giotto for a specimen of his work, and the artist in front of the messenger and with his unaided hand drew a circle with red paint. The messenger, in amazement, asked Giotto if that were all. Giotto replied, 'Send it, and we shall see if His Holiness understands the hint.'

> I saw ... that the practical teaching of the masters of Art was summed up by the O of Giotto.
> Ruskin, *Queen of the Air*, iii

***The Fifteen O's,*** or ***the O's of St Bridget.*** Fifteen meditations on the Passion, composed by St Bridget. Each begins with *O Jesu*, or a similar invocation.

***The Seven O's,*** or ***the O's of Advent.*** The seven Antiphons to the Magnificat formerly sung at evensong during the third and fourth weeks of Advent (December 16th to 23rd, omitting St Thomas's Day, December 21st). They commence with (1) *O Sapientia*, (2) *O Adonai*, (3) *O Radix Jesse*, (4) *O Clavis David*, (5) *O Oriens Splendor*, (6) *O Rex gentium*, and (7) *O Emmanuel*. They are sometimes called *The Christmas O's*.

**O'.** An Irish patronymic. (Gael. *ogha*, It. *oa*, a descendant.)

**O'.** in *tam-o'-shanter, what's o'clock? cat-o'-nine-tails*, etc., stands for *of*; but in such phrases as *He comes home late o' nights, I go to church o' Sundays*, it represents M.E. *on*.

**O. K.** Telegraphese (originally American slang) for 'all correct' (*orl korrect*).

**O. P. Riots.** When the new Covent Garden theatre was opened in 1809 the charges of admission were increased; but night after night for three months a throng crowded the pit, shouting 'O. P'. (*old prices*); much damage was done, and the manager was obliged at last to give way.

**O tempora! O mores!** (Lat., from Cicero's *Pro Rege Deiotaro*, xi, 31). Alas! how the times have changed for the worse! Alas! how the morals of the people are degenerated!

**O Yes! O Yes! O Yes!** *See* Oyez.

**Oaf.** A corruption of *ouph* (elf). A foolish lout or dolt is so called from the notion that idiots are changelings, left by the fairies in place of the stolen ones.

> This guiltless oaf his vacancy of sense
> Supplied, and amply too, by innocence.
> Byron, *Verses found in a Summer-house*

> Then ye returned to your trinkets; then ye contented your souls
> With the flannelled fools at the wicket, or the muddied oafs at the goals.
> Rudyard Kipling, *The Islanders*

**Oahspe.** The bible of the Faithists (*q.v.*), said to have been spiritually given to the American author, J. P. Newborough.

The Faithists account for the title by saying that 'O' is the sound of the waves on the beach, 'Ah' is the expression used by man when looking up to the heavens, and 'Spe' stands for the Spirit.

**Oak.** The oak was in ancient times sacred to the god of thunder because these trees are said to be more likely to be struck by lightning than any other. Among the Druids the oak was held in the greatest veneration.

***Royal Oak Day.*** *See* Oak-apple Day.

***To sport one's oak.*** To be 'not at home'. At the Universities the 'chambers' have two doors, the usual room-door and another, made of oak, outside it; when the 'oak' is shut or 'sported' it indicates either that the occupant of the room is out, or that he does not wish to be disturbed by visitors.

***When the ash is before the oak we are sure to have a soak.*** The tradition is, if the oak gets into leaf before the ash we may expect a fine and productive year; if the ash precedes the oak in foliage, we may anticipate a cold summer and unproductive autumn.

> In 1816, 1817, 1821, 1823, 1828, 1829, 1830, 1838, 1840, 1845, 1850, and 1859, the ash was in leaf a full month before the oak, and the autumns were unfavourable. In 1831, 1832, 1838, 1853, 1860, the two came into leaf about the same time, and the years were not remarkable either way; whereas in 1818, 1819,

1820, 1822, 1824, 1825, 1826, 1827, 1833, 1834, 1835, 1836, 1837, 1842, 1846, 1854, 1868, and 1869, the oak displayed its foliage several weeks before the ash, the summers were dry and warm, and the harvests abundant.

*Some Famous Oaks:*

The *Abbot's Oak*, near Woburn Abbey, is so called because the Woburn abbot was hanged on one of its branches, in 1537, by order of Henry VIII.

The *Bull Oak*, Wedgenock Park, was growing at the time of the Conquest.

*Cowthorpe Oak*, near Wetherby, in Yorkshire, will hold seventy persons in its hollow. It is said to be over 1,600 years old.

The *Ellerslie Oak*, near Paisley, is reported to have sheltered Sir William Wallace and 300 of his men.

*Fairlop Oak*, in Hainault Forest, was 36 ft in circumference a yard from the ground. It was blown down in 1820.

*Owen Glendower's Oak*, at Shelton, near Shrewsbury, was in full growth in 1403, for in this tree Owen Glendower witnessed the great battle between Henry IV and Henry Percy. Six or eight persons can stand in the hollow of its trunk. Its girth is 40¼ ft.

The *Major Oak*, Sherwood Forest, Edwinstowe, according to tradition, was a full-grown tree in the reign of King John. The hollow of the trunk will hold fifteen persons, but a new bark has considerably diminished the opening. Its girth is 37 or 38 ft, and the head covers a circumference of 240 ft.

The *Parliament Oak*, Clipston, in Sherwood Forest, is the tree under which Edward I, in 1282, held his parliament. He was hunting when a messenger came to tell him of the revolt of the Welsh. He hastily convened his nobles under the oak, and it was resolved to march at once against Llewellyn, who was slain. It was still standing in 1895, but was supported by props.

The *Oak of the Partisans*, in Parcy Forest, St Ouen, in the department of the Vosges, is 107 ft in height. At the beginning of this century it was 706 years old.

*Queen's Oak*, Huntingfield, Suffolk, is so named because near this tree Queen Elizabeth shot a buck.

The *Reformation Oak*, on Mousehold Heath, near Norwich, is where the rebel Ket held his court in 1549, and when the rebellion was stamped out nine of the ringleaders were hanged on this tree.

*Robin Hood's Larder* is an oak in Sherwood Forest. The tradition is that Robin Hood used its hollow trunk as a hiding-place for the deer he had slain. Late in the last century some schoolgirls boiled their kettle in it, and burnt down a large part of the tree, but every effort was made to preserve what remained.

*The Royal Oak. See* Oak-apple Day.

*Sir Philip Sydney's Oak*, near Penshurst, was planted at his birth in 1554, and was memorialised by Ben Jonson and Waller.

The *Swilcar Oak*, in Needwood Forest, Staffordshire, is between 600 and 700 years old.

*William the Conqueror's Oak*, in Windsor Great Park, is 38 feet in girth.

The *Winfarthing Oak* is said to have been 700 years old at the time of the Conquest.

**Oak-apple Day** (also called *Royal Oak Day*). May 29th, the birthday of Charles II, commanded by Act of Parliament in 1664 to be observed as a day of thanksgiving. A special service – expunged only in 1859 – was inserted in the Book of Common Prayer.

It was in the month of September that Charles concealed himself in an oak (the 'Royal Oak') at Boscobel. The battle of Worcester was fought on Wednesday, September 3rd, 1651, and Charles arrived at Whiteladies, about three-quarters of a mile from Boscobel House, early the next morning. He returned to England on his birthday, when the Royalists displayed a branch of oak in allusion to his hiding in this tree.

**Oaks, The.** One of the 'classic' horse-races; it is for three-year-old fillies, and is run at Epsom on the Friday after the Derby (*q.v.*). So called by the twelfth Earl of Derby, who established the race in 1779, from an estate of his near Epsom named 'The Oaks'.

**Oannes.** A Babylonian god having a fish's body and a human head and feet. In the daytime he lived with men to instruct them in the arts and sciences, but at night retired to the depths of the Persian Gulf. He has been identified with Ea of the cuneiform inscriptions.

**Oar.** ***To put your oar into my boat.*** To interfere with my affairs. 'Paddle your own canoe, and don't put your oar into my boat.'

***To rest on one's oars.*** To take an interval of rest after hard work. A boating phrase.

***To toss the oars.*** To raise them vertically, resting on the handles. It is a form of salute.

**Oasis** (Coptic, *ouahe*, from *ouih*, to dwell). A fertile spot in the midst of a desert country, especially in the desert of Africa where wells of water or small lakes are to be found and vegetation is pretty abundant. Hence a sudden cessation of pain, or a sudden pleasure in the midst of monotonous existence, is sometimes called 'a perfect oasis'.

**Oath.** *See* Swear.

**Oats.** ***He has sown his wild oats.*** He has left off his gay habits and is become steady. The reference is to the folly of sowing wild, i.e. bad, grain instead of good; but it is worth noting that in Denmark the thick vapours which rise just before the land bursts into vegetation are called *Lokkens havre* (Loki's wild oats), and when the fine weather succeeds, the Danes say, '*Loki has sown his wild oats.*'

**Obadiah.** A slang name for a Quaker.

**Obeahism.** The belief in and practice of obeah, i.e., a kind of sorcery or witchcraft prevalent in West Africa and formerly in the West Indies. *Obeah* is a native word, and signifies something put into the ground, to bring about sickness, death, or other disaster.

**Obelisk.** *See* Dagger.

**Obermann.** The impersonation of high moral worth without talent, and the tortures endured by the consciousness of this defect. From Senancour's psychological romance of this name (1804), in which Obermann, the hero, is a dreamer perpetually trying to escape from the actual.

**Oberon.** King of the Fairies, husband of Titania. Shakespeare introduces them in his *Midsummer Night's Dream*. The name is probably connected with Alberich (*q.v.*) the king of the elves.

He first appears in the mediaeval French romance, *Huon de Bordeaux*, where he is a son of Julius Caesar and Morgan le Fay. He was only three feet high, but of angelic face, and was lord and king of Mommur. At his birth the fairies bestowed their gifts – one was insight into men's thoughts, and another was the power of transporting himself to any place instantaneously; and in the fullness of time legions of angels conveyed his soul to Paradise.

**Obidicut.** The fiend of lust, and one of the five that possessed 'poor Tom'.

> Five fiends have been in poor Tom at once; of lust, as Obidicut; Hobbididance, prince of dumbness; Mahu, of stealing; Modo, of murder, and Flibbertigibbet, of mopping and mowing; who since possesses chambermaids and waiting-women.
>
> Shakespeare, *King Lear*, 5, 1

*Cp.* Flibbertigibbet.

**Obiism.** The same as Obeahism (*q.v.*).

**Obiter dictum** (Lat.). An incidental remark, an opinion expressed by a judge, but not judicially. An *obiter dictum* has no authority beyond that of deference to the wisdom, experience, and honesty of the person who utters it; but a judicial sentence is the verdict of a judge bound under oath to pronounce judgment only according to law and evidence.

**Object; Objective.** *See* Subject.

**Obolus.** An ancient Greek copper coin worth five lepta, or about a halfpenny. Also a silver coin of the Byzantine Empire, worth about three times as much. It is to this latter that the phrase 'Give an obolus to poor old Belisarius' (*see* Belisarius) refers.

**Observantins.** *See* Franciscans.

**Obstacle Race.** A race over – or under – obstacles such as gates, nets, sails laid on the ground, through hoops or tubs, etc.

**Obverse.** That side of a coin or medal which contains the principal device. Thus, the obverse of our coins is the side which contains the sovereign's head; the other side is the 'reverse'.

**Occam's Razor.** *Entia non sunt multiplicanda* (entities are not to be multiplied). With this axiom, which means that all unnecessary facts or constituents in the subject being analysed are to be eliminated, Occam dissected every question as with a razor.

William of Occam, the *Doctor Singularis et Invincibilis* (d.1347), was a scholastic philosopher, famous as the great advocate and reviver of nominalism (*q.v.*).

**Occasion.** A lame old hag in Spenser's *Faërie Queene* (II, iv), mother of Furor, and symbolical of the cause of anger. She was quite bald behind, but Sir Guyon seized her by the forelock, threw her to the ground, and ultimately vanquished her.

***To improve the occasion.*** To draw a moral lesson from some event which has occurred.

**Occult Sciences** (Lat. *occultus*, related to *celare*, to hide). Magic, alchemy, and astrology; so called because they were hidden mysteries.

**Oceana.** A philosophical treatise on the principles of government by James Harrington (1656). *See* Commonwealths, Ideal.

**Octavo.** A book in which each sheet of paper is folded into eight leaves (16 pages); contracted thus – 8vo. (Ital. *un' ottavo*, Fr. *in octavo*, Lat. *octo*, eight.) An octavo can be of almost any size, dependent entirely on the size of the sheets before folding. Each size has its own name; this Dictionary is a Demy octavo.

**October.** The eighth month of the ancient Roman calendar (Lat. *octo*, eight) when the year began in March; the tenth of ours. The old Dutch name was *Wyn-maand*; the Anglo-Saxon, *Winmonath* (wine-month, or the time of vintage); also *Teo-monath* (tenth-month), and *Winter-fylleth* (winter full-moon). In the French Republican calendar it was *Vendémiaire* (time of vintage, September 22nd to October 21st).

***A tankard of October.*** A tankard of the best and strongest ale, brewed in October.

> He was in high favour with Sir Geoffrey, not merely on account of his sound orthodoxy and deep learning, but [also for] his excellent skill in playing at bowls, and his facetious conversation over a pipe and tankard of October.
>
> Scott, *Peveril of the Peak*, ch. iv

**Od.** *See* Odyle.

**Odal.** *See* Udal.

**Odd Numbers.** *There's luck in odd numbers.* This is a very ancient fancy. According to the Pythagorean system, 'all nature is a harmony', man is a full chord; and all beyond is Deity, so that *nine* represents Deity. A major chord consists of a fundamental or tonic, its major third, and its just fifth. As the odd numbers are the fundamental notes of nature, the last being Deity, it will be easy to see how they came to be considered the great or lucky numbers. *Cp.* Diapason, Number.

> Good luck -lies in odd numbers ... They say, there is divinity in odd numbers, either in nativity, chance, or death.
>
> Shakespeare, *Merry Wives of Windsor*, 5, 1

The odd numbers 1, 3, 5, 7, 9 (*which see*) seem to play a far more important part than the even numbers. *One* is Deity, *three* the Trinity, *five* the chief division, *seven* is the sacred number, and *nine* is three times three, the great climacteric.

*Numero Deus impare gaudet* (the god delights in odd numbers – Virgil, *Eclogues*, viii, 75). Three indicates the 'beginning, middle, and end'. The Godhead has three persons; so in *classic mythology* Hecate had threefold power; Jove's symbol was a triple thunderbolt, Neptune's a sea-trident, Pluto's a three-headed dog; the Fates were three, the Furies three, the Graces three, the Horae three; the Muses three-times-three. There are seven notes, nine planets, nine orders of angels, seven days a week, thirteen lunar months, or 365 days a year, etc.; five senses, five fingers on the hand and toes on the foot, five vowels, five continents, etc.

**Odds.** ***At odds.*** At variance.

***By long odds.*** By a great difference; as, 'He is the best man by long odds.' In horse-racing, *odds* are the ratio by which the amount staked by one party to a bet exceeds that of the other; hence long odds indicates a big variance in this ratio.

***Odds and ends.*** *See* End.

***That makes no odds.*** No difference; never mind; that is no excuse. An application of the betting phrase.

**Od's,** used in oaths, as:

***Od's bodikins!*** or ***Odsbody!*** means 'God's body'.

***Od's pittikins!*** God's pity.

***Od's plessed will!*** (*Merry Wives of Windsor*, 1, 1.)

***Od rot 'em!*** *See* Drat.

***Od-zounds!*** God's wounds.

**Odhir.** The husband of Freyja, the Scandinavian goddess. He left her, and she searched for him through many lands, shedding tears which turned to drops of pure gold.

**Odhroerir.** The 'poet's mead' of the Scandinavian gods. It was made of Kvasir's blood mixed with honey, and all who partook of it became poets. Kvasir was the wisest of all men, and could answer any question put to him. He was fashioned out of the saliva spat into a jar by the Aesir and Vanir on their conclusion of peace, and was slain by the dwarfs Fjalar and Galar.

**Odin.** The Scandinavian name of the god called by the Anglo-Saxons Woden (*q.v.*).

***The vow of Odin.*** A matrimonial or other vow made before the 'Stone of Odin', in the Orkneys. This is an oval stone, with a hole in it large enough to admit a man's hand. Anyone who violated a vow made before this stone was held infamous.

**Odium theologicum** (Lat.). The bitter hatred of rival theologians. No wars so sanguinary as holy wars; no persecutions so relentless as religious persecutions; no hatred so bitter as theological hatred.

**Odor lucri** (Lat.). The sweets of gain; the delights of money-making.

> Every act of such a person is seasoned with the *odor lucri*. Scott, *The Betrothed* (Intro.)

**Odour.** ***In good odour; in bad odour.*** In favour, out of favour; in good repute, in bad repute.

***The odour of sanctity.*** In the Middle Ages it was held that a sweet and delightful odour was given off by the bodies of saintly persons at their death, and also when their bodies, if 'translated', were disinterred. Hence the phrase, *he died in the odour of sanctity*, i.e. he died a saint. The Swedenborgians say that when the celestial angels are present at a deathbed, what is then cadaverous excites a sensation of what is aromatic.

There is an 'odour of iniquity' as well as an 'odour of sanctity', and Shakespeare has a strong passage on the disodour of impiety. Antiochus and his wicked daughter were killed by lightning, and the poet says:

A fire from heaven came and shrivelled up
Their bodies, e'en to loathing; for they so stunk
That all those eyes adored them ere their fall
Scorned now their hand should give them burial.
*Pericles*, 2, 4

**Odrysium Carmen.** The poetry of Orpheus, a native of Thrace, called *Odrysia tellus*, because the Odryses were its chief inhabitants.

**Odyle.** The name formerly given to the hypothetical force which emanates from a medium to produce the phenomena connected with mesmerism, spirit-rapping, table-turning, and so on. Baron von Reichenbach (1788–1869) called it *Od force*, and taught that it pervaded all nature, especially heat, light, crystals, magnets, etc., and was developed in chemical action; and also that it streamed from the fingers of specially sensitive persons.

That od-force of German Reichenbach
Which still from female finger-tips burns blue.
Mrs Browning, *Aurora Leigh*, vii, 295

**Odyssey.** The epic poem of Homer which records the adventures of *Odysseus* (Ulysses) in his home-voyage from Troy. The word is an adjective formed out of the hero's name, and means the *things* or *adventures* of Ulysses.

**Oecumenical Councils.** Ecclesiastical councils whose findings are – or were – recognised as applying to the whole of the Christian world (Gr. *oikoumenikos*, the inhabited – *ge*, earth being understood), and the members of which were drawn from the whole Church. There are twenty-one recognised, nine Eastern and twelve Western.

The Nine Eastern: (1) Jerusalem; (2 and 8) Nice, 325, 787; (3, 6, 7, 9) Constantinople, 381, 553, 680, 869; (4) Ephesus, 431; (5) Chalcedon, 451.

The Twelve Western: (10, 11, 12, 13, 19) Lateran, 1123, 1139, 1179, 1215, 1517; (14, 15) Synod of Lyons, 1245, 1274; (16) Synod of Vienne, in Dauphiné, 1311; (17) Constance, 1414; (18) Basle, 1431–43; (20) Trent, 1545–63; (21) Vatican, 1869.

Of these, the Church of England recognises only six, viz.:

325 of *Nice*, against the Arians.
381 of *Constantinople*, against 'heretics'.
431 of *Ephesus*, against the Nestorians and Pelagians.
451 of *Chalcedon*, when Athanasius was restored.
553 of *Constantinople*, against Origen.
680 of *Constantinople*, against the Monothelites.

**Oedipus.** ***I am no Oedipus.*** I cannot guess what you mean. Odipus guessed the riddle of the Sphinx (*q.v.*), and saved Thebes from her ravages. *Cp.* Davus.

**Oeil de Boeuf** (Fr. 'bull's-eye'). A large reception room (*salle*) in the palace of Versailles, lighted by round, 'bull's-eye' windows. The ceiling, decorated by Van der Meulen, contained likenesses of the children of Louis XIV.

***Les Fastes de l'Oeil de Boeuf.*** The annals of the courtiers of the Grand Monarque; hence, anecdotes of courtiers generally.

**Off** (of; Lat. *ab*, from, away). The house is a *mile* off – i.e. is 'away' or 'from' us a mile. The word preceding off defines its scope. To be '*well* off' is to be away or on the way towards well-being; to be *badly* off is to be away or on the way to the bad.

The *off-side* of horses when in pairs is that to the *right* hand of the coachman (*cp.* Near); and a football umpire calls *Off-side!* and awards a penalty kick when a player has kicked the ball there being none of his opponents except the goal-keeper between himself and his opponent's goal – unless he himself has taken the ball there. The off-side rules vary, of course, with the different varieties of football.

An act of behaviour, a thing, a person, etc., is said to be *a bit off* when it is not quite up to the mark – it is a bit 'off colour' (*see* Colour); and a girl is said 'to get off' when she has become engaged to be married; sometimes, when this does not happen, the reason is that she has 'gone off', i.e. the years have not been kind to her.

**Offa's Dyke.** An entrenchment which runs from Beachley, near the mouth of the Wye, to Flintshire. If not actually the work of Offa, King of Mercia (about 757–96) it was repaired by him, and he availed himself of it as a line of demarcation between him and the Welsh, though it by no means tallied with his territory either in extent or position.

**Office, the Divine.** *See* Breviary.

**Office, the Holy.** The Inquisition (*q.v.*).

**Og,** King of Bashan, according to *Rabbinical mythology* was an antediluvian giant, saved from the flood by climbing on the roof of the ark. After the passage of the Red Sea, Moses first conquered Sihon, and then advanced against the giant Og (whose bedstead, made of iron, was above 15 ft long and nearly 7 ft broad, Deut. 3:11). The legend says that Og plucked up a mountain to hurl at the Israelites, but he got so entangled with his burden that Moses was able to kill him without much difficulty.

In Dryden's *Absalom and Achitophel* (*q.v.*), Og stands for Thomas Shadwell (*see* MacFlecknoe). He was very large and fat.

**Ogham.** The alphabet in use among the ancient Irish and British nations. There were twenty characters, each of which was composed of any number of thin strokes from one to five, which were arranged and grouped above, below, or across a horizontal line.

The word is connected with *Ogmios*, the name, according to Lucian, of a Gaulish god who presided over speech.

**Ogier the Dane.** One of the great heroes of mediaeval romance; a paladin of Charlemagne, and son of Geoffrey, King of Denmark, of which country (as Holger Danske) he is still the national hero. Fairies attended at his birth, and bestowed upon him divers gifts. Among these fairies was Morgan le Fay (*q.v.*), who when the knight was a hundred years old embarked him for Avalon, 'hard by the terrestrial paradise'. On reaching the island he entered the castle, where he found a horse sitting at a banquet-table. The horse, who had once been a mighty prince, conducted him to Morgan le Fay, who gave him a ring which removed all infirmities and restored him to ripe manhood, and a crown which made him forget his country and past life, and introduced him to King Arthur. Two hundred years rolled on, and France was invaded by the Paynims. Morgan le Fay now sent Ogier to defend '*le bon pays de France*'; and when he had routed the invaders she took him back to Avalon, where he remains until the time for him to reappear on this earth of ours has arrived. William Morris gives a rendering of the romance in his *Earthly Paradise* (*August*).

**Ogres** of nursery story are giants of very malignant disposition, who live on human flesh. The word was first used (and probably invented) by Perrault in his *Contes* (1697), and is thought to be made up from *Orcus*, a name of Pluto, the god of Hades.

**Ogygia.** *See* Calypso.

**Ogygian Deluge.** A flood of Greek legend, supposed to have taken place two hundred years before Deucalion's flood, when Ogyges was King of Boeotia.

> Varro tells us that the planet Venus underwent a great change in the reign of Ogyges. It changed its diameter, its colour, its figure, and its course.

**Oi Polloi,** properly *Hoi Polloi* (Gr.). The commonalty, the many. In University slang the 'poll men', or those who take degrees without 'honours'.

**Oil.** ***Oil of palms.*** *See* Palm-oil.

***To oil the knocker.*** To fee the porter. The expression is from Racine's *Les Plaideurs*; '*On n'entre point chez lui sans graisser le marteau*' ('No one enters *his* house without oiling the knocker').

***To pour oil on troubled waters.*** To soothe by gentle words; to bring about a state of calm after great anger or excitement, etc., by tact and diplomacy.

The allusion is to the well known fact that during a storm at sea the force of the waves striking against a ship is very much lessened by pouring out heavy oil. In Bede's *Ecclesiastical History* (735) it is said that St Aidan gave a young priest who was to convoy a maiden destined for the bride of King Oswin a cruse of oil to pour on the sea if the waves became stormy. A storm did arise, and the priest, pouring the oil on the waves, actually reduced them to a calm.

***To strike oil.*** To make a happy hit or valuable discovery. The phrase refers to hitting upon or discovering a bed of petroleum or mineral oil.

**Old.** Used in slang and colloquial talk as a term of endearment or friendship, as in *My dear old chap*, *my old man* (i.e. my husband); as a general disparagement, as in *Old cat*, *old fogy*, *old geezer*, *old stick-in-the-mud*; and as a common intensive, as in Shakespeare's 'Here will be an old abusing of God's patience and the king's English', and in the modern *Any old thing will do*, *We're having a high old time*.

For names such as Old Grog, Harry, Noll, Rowley, Scratch, Tom, etc., *see these words*.

***Old and Bold.*** The old 14th Foot, the Prince of Wales's Own (West Yorkshire Regiment).

**_Old Bags._** John Scott, Lord Chancellor Eldon (1751–1838); so called from his carrying home with him in different bags the cases still pending his judgment.

**_Old Bold._** The 1st Battalion Worcestershire Regiment, the old 29th Foot.

**_Old Bold Fifth._** The Northumberland Fusiliers; formerly the 5th Foot.

**_Old Bona Fide._** Louis XIV (1638, 1643–1715).

**_Old boots._** *See* Boots.

**_Old Cracow Bible._** *See* Bible, Specially named.

**_Old Dominion._** Virginia. Every Act of Parliament to the Declaration of Independence designated Virginia 'the Colony and Dominion of Virginia'. Captain John Smith, in his *History of Virginia* (1629), calls this 'colony and dominion' *Ould Virginia*, in contradistinction to *New England*, and other British settlements.

**_Old Dozen._** The Suffolk Regiment, formerly the 12th Foot.

**_Old Faith Men._** *See* Philippins.

**_Old Fogs._** The 87th Foot, the Royal Irish Fusiliers, so called from the war-cry '*Fag-an-Bealach*' (Clear the way), pronounced *Faug-a-bollagh*.

**_Old Glory._** The United States Flag. *See* Stars and Stripes.

**_Old King Cole._** *See* Cole.

**_Old Lady of Threadneedle Street._** *See* Threadneedle.

**_Old Man Eloquent._** Isocrates; so called by Milton. When he heard of the result of the battle of Chaeronea, which was fatal to Grecian liberty, he died of grief.

> That dishonest victory
> At Chaeronea, fatal to liberty,
> Killed with report that Old Man Eloquent.
>
> Milton, *Sonnets*

**_Old Man of the Mountain._** Hassan-ben-Sabah, the sheik Al Jebal, and founder of the sect called Assassins (*q.v.*).

**_Old Man of the Sea._** In the *Arabian Nights* story of *Sinbad the Sailor*, the Old Man of the Sea, hoisted on the shoulders of Sinbad, and clung there for many days and nights, much to the discomfort of Sinbad, who finally released himself by making the Old Man drunk. Hence, any burden, figurative or actual, of which it is impossible to free oneself without the greatest exertions is spoken of as *an Old Man of the Sea*.

**_Old Reeky._** *See* Auld Reekie.

**_Old Style – New Style._** Terms used in chronology; the *Old Style* being the Julian Calendar (*q.v.*), and the *New Style* the Gregorian (*q.v.*). *See also* Calendar.

**_Old World._** So Europe, Asia, and Africa are called when compared with North and South America (the New World).

**Oldbuck.** An antiquary; from the character of Jonathan Oldbuck, a whimsical virtuoso in Scott's *Antiquary*.

**Oldenburg Horn.** A horn long in the possession of the reigning princes of the House of Oldenburg, but now in the collection of the King of Denmark. According to tradition, Count Otto of Oldenburg, in 967, was offered drink in this silver-gilt horn by a 'wild woman', at the Osenborg. As he did not like the look of the liquor, he threw it away, and rode off with the horn.

**'Ole, a better.** *See* Hole.

**Olet lucernam** (Lat. proverb). It smells of the lamp. *See* Lamp.

**Oleum adde camino.** To pour oil on fire; to aggravate a wound under pretence of healing it (Horace, *Satires*, ii, 3, 321).

**Olewey.** The name given to the wife of Bellin, the Ram, in Caxton's version of *Reynard the Fox*.

**Oligarchy** (Gr. *oligos*, the few; *arche*, rule). A government in which the supreme power is vested in a small number of families or a few members of a class.

**Olio** (Span. *olla*, a stew, or the pot in which it is cooked, from Lat. *olla*, a pot). In Spain a mixture of meat, vegetables, spices, etc., boiled together and highly seasoned; hence, any hotchpotch of various ingredients, as a miscellaneous collection of verses, drawings, pieces of music, etc.

**Olivant.** The magic horn of Roland, Charlemagne's paladin. It could be heard for twenty miles.

**Olive.** In ancient Greece the olive was sacred to Pallas Athene, in allusion to the story (*see* Athens) that at the naming of Athens she presented it with an olive tree. It was the symbol of peace, and also an emblem of fecundity, brides wearing or carrying an olive garland as ours do a wreath of orange blossom. A crown of olive was the highest distinction of a citizen who had deserved well of his country, and was the highest prize in the Olympic Games.

**_To hold out the olive branch._** To make overtures for peace; in allusion to the olive being an ancient symbol of peace. In some of Numa's medals the king is represented holding an olive twig, indicative of a peaceful reign.

***Olive branches.*** A facetious term for children in relation to their parents: the allusion is to 'Thy wife shall be as a fruitful vine ... thy children like olive plants round about thy table' (Ps. 128:3).

> The wife and olive branches of one Mr Kenwigs.
> Dickens, *Nicholas Nickleby*, xiv

**Oliver.** Charlemagne's favourite paladin, who, with Roland, rode by his side. He was the son of Regnier, Duke of Genoa (another of the paladins), and brother of the beautiful Aude. His sword was called *Hauteclaire*, and his horse *Ferrant d'Espagne*.

***A Roland for an Oliver.*** *See* Roland.

**Olivetans.** Brethren of 'Our Lady of Mount Olivet', an offshoot of the Benedictines. The order was founded in 1313 by Bernard Tolomei, of Siena.

**Olla Podrida** (Span. putrid pot). Odds and ends, a mixture of scraps or *pot au feu*, into which every sort of eatable is thrown and stewed. *Cp.* Olio. Figuratively, the term means an incongruous mixture, a miscellaneous collection of any kind, a medley.

**Olympia.** The ancient name of a valley in Elis, Peloponnesus, so called because here were held the famous games in honour of the Olympian Zeus (*see below*). In the valley was built the Altis, an enclosure of about 500 ft by 600 ft, which contained, besides the temple of Zeus, the Heroeum, the Metroum, etc., the Stadium, with gymnasia, baths, etc. Hence, the name has been given to large buildings in which sporting events, spectacles, exhibitions, and so on can be presented under cover.

**Olympiad.** Among the ancient Greeks, a period of four years, being the interval between the celebrations of the Olympic Games (*q.v.*). The first Olympiad began in 776 BC, and the last (the 293rd) in AD 393.

**Olympian Zeus,** or **Jove.** A statue by Phidias, one of the 'Seven Wonders of the World'. Pausanias (vii, 2) says when the sculptor placed it in the temple at Olympia (433 BC), he prayed the god to indicate whether he was satisfied with it, and immediately a thunderbolt fell on the floor of the temple without doing the slightest harm.

It was a chryselephantine statue, i.e. made of ivory and gold, and though seated on a throne, was 60 ft in height. The left hand rested on a sceptre, and the right palm held a statue of Victory in solid gold. The robes were of gold, and so were the four lions which supported the footstool. The throne was of cedar, embellished with ebony, ivory, gold, and precious stones.

It was removed to Constantinople in the 5th century AD, and perished in the great fire of 475.

**Olympic Games.** The greatest of the four sacred festivals of the ancient Greeks, held at Olympia (*q.v.*) every fourth year, in the month of July. The festival commenced with sacrifices and included racing, wrestling, and all kinds of contests, ending on the fifth day with processions, sacrifices, and banquets to the victors – who were garlanded with olive leaves.

**Olympus.** The home of the gods of ancient Greece, where Zeus held his court, a mountain about 9,800 ft high on the confines of Macedonia and Thessaly. It is used for any pantheon, as 'Odin, Thor, Balder, and the rest of the Northern Olympus'.

**Om.** Among the Brahmans, the mystic equivalent for the name of the Deity; it has been adopted by modern occultists to denote absolute goodness and truth or the spiritual essence.

***Om mani padme hum*** ('Om, the jewel, is in the lotus: amen'). The mystic formula of the Tibetans and northern Buddhists used as a charm and for many religious purposes. They are the first words taught to a child and the last uttered on the death-bed of the pious. Tho lotus symbolises universal being, and the jewel the individuality of the utterer.

**Ombre.** A card-game, introduced into England from Spain in the 17th century, and very popular till it was supplanted by quadrille, about 1730. It was usually played by three persons, and the eights, nines, and tens of each suit were left out. Prior has an epigram on the game; he was playing with two ladies, and Fortune gave him 'success in every suit but hearts'. Pope immortalised the game in his *Rape of the Lock*.

**Omega.** The last letter of the Greek alphabet. *See* Alpha.

**Omelet.** ***You can't make omelets without breaking eggs***. Said by way of warning to one who is trying to 'get something for nothing' – to accomplish some desired object without being willing to take the necessary trouble or make the necessary sacrifice. The phrase is a translation of the French *On ne saurait faire une omelette sans casser des oeufs*.

**Omen.** Some phenomenon or unusual event taken as a prognostication either of good or evil; a prophetic sign or augury. The Latin word was adopted in the 16th century; its origin is unknown, but it is thought to be connected with *audire*, to hear. Some well known examples of accepting omens, apparently evil, as of good augury are:

Leotychides II, of Sparta, was told by his augurs that his projected expedition would fail, because a viper had got entangled in the handle of the city key. 'Not so,' he replied. 'The key caught the viper.'

When Julius Caesar landed at Adrumetum he happened to trip and fall on his face. This would have been considered a fatal omen by his army; but, with admirable presence of mind, he exclaimed, 'Thus I take possession of thee, O Africa!' Told of Scipio also.

When William the Conqueror leaped upon the English shore he fell on his face, and a great cry went forth that it was an ill-omen; but the duke exclaimed: 'I have taken seisin of this land with both my hands.'

**Omnibus** (dative pl. of Lat. *omnis*, all = for all). The name was first applied to the public vehicle in France in 1828. In the following year it was adopted by Shillibeer for the vehicles which he started on the Paddington Road, London. The plural is, of course, *omnibuses*, not *omnibi*; and the word is generally abbreviated to *bus*, without any initial apostrophe – just as *cabriolet* became *cab*, not *cab*'.

***Omnibus Bill.*** The Parliamentary term for a Bill embracing clauses that deal with a number of different subjects, as a Revenue Bill dealing with Customs, Taxes, Stamps, Excise, etc.

***Omnibus box.*** A box at a theatre for which the subscription is paid by several different parties, each of which has the right of using it.

***Omnibus train.*** An old name for a train that stops at all stations – a train *for all*, as apart from the specials and the expresses that ran between only a few stations.

**Omnium** (Lat. of all). The particulars *of all* the items, or the assignment *of all* the securities, of a government loan.

***Omnium gatherum.*** Dog Latin for a *gathering* or collection *of all* sorts of persons and things; a miscellaneous gathering together without regard to suitability or order.

**Omphale.** In Greek legend, the masculine but attractive Queen of Lydia, to whom Hercules was bound a slave for three years. He fell in love with her, and led an effeminate life spinning wool, while Omphale wore the lion's skin and was lady paramount.

**On dit** (Fr. they say). A rumour, a report, a bit of gossip; as, 'There is an *on dit* on Exchange that Germany will pay up its reparations.'

**One.** The word has a good many indefinite applications, as a person or thing of the kind implied or already mentioned (*I like those hats; I must buy one*), an unspecified person (*One doesn't do that sort of thing*), someone or something, anyone or anything. *There is One above* is a reference to the Deity; *the Evil One* is the Devil.

***By one and one.*** Singly, one at a time; entirely by oneself.

Though we whistled your love from her bed tonight, I trow she would not run,
For the sin ye do by two and two ye must pay for one by one!
Rudyard Kipling, *Tomlinson*

***He was one too many for me.*** He was a little bit too clever, he outwitted me.

***Number one.*** Oneself; hence, *to take care of number one*, to look after oneself, to seek one's own interest; to be selfish.

***One and all.*** Everybody individually and jointly. The phrase is the motto of Cornishmen.

***One-horse.*** Third-rate, petty, insignificant; as, *a one-horse show*, *a one-horse little town*, etc. The phrase is of American origin, and the allusion is to a person of little property who could only afford one horse instead of a pair for his cart.

***One in the eye, on the nose, in the bread-basket,*** etc. A blow on the spot indicated – the last being slang for the stomach.

***One of these days.*** At some unspecified time in the future, generally the rather remote and uncertain future.

***To go one better than he did.*** To do a little more, give a little more, promise a little more, etc., than he did. The phrase is from card-playing; at poker if one wishes to continue betting one has to 'go' at least 'one better', i.e. raise the stake.

**Oneida Community, The.** *See* Perfectionists.

**Onus** (Lat.). The burden, the responsibility; as, 'The whole *onus* must rest on your own shoulders.'

***Onus probandi*** (Lat. the burden of proving). The obligation of proving some proposition, accusation, etc.; as, 'The *onus probandi* rests with the accuser.'

**Onyx** is Greek for a finger-nail; so called because the colour of an onyx resembles that of the finger-nail.

**Opal** (Gr. *opallios*, probably from Sansk. *upala*, a gem). This semi-precious stone – a vitreous form of hydrous silica – is well known for its play of iridescent colours, and has long been considered to bring ill luck. Alphonso XII of Spain (1874–85) is said to have had one that seemed to be fatal. On his wedding-day he presented it in a ring to his wife, and her death occurred soon afterwards. Before the funeral he gave the ring to his sister, who died a few days later. The king then presented it to his sister-in-law, and she died within three months. Alphonso, astounded at these fatalities, resolved to wear the ring himself, and within a very short time he too was dead. The Queen Regent then suspended it from the neck of the Virgin of Almudena of Madrid.

> Not an opal
> Wrapped in a bay-leaf in my left fist.
> To charm their eyes with.
>
> Ben Jonson, *New Inn*, i, 6

**Open Question.** *See* Question.

**Open Secret.** *See* Secret de Polichinelle.

**Open Sesame.** *See* Sesame.

**Operations, Base of, Line of.** *See* Base.

**Opinicus.** A fabulous monster, composed of dragon, camel, and lion, used in heraldry. It forms the crest of the Barber Surgeons of London. The name seems to be a corruption of *Ophincus*, the classical name of the constellation, the serpent (Gr. *ophis*).

**Opium-eater.** Thomas De Quincey (1785–1859), author of *The Confessions of an English Opium-Eater* (1821).

**Opponency.** *See* Act and Opponency.

**Oppidan.** At Eton College, a student not on the foundation, but who boards in the town (Lat. *oppidum*, town).

**Optimë.** In Cambridge phraseology a graduate in the second or third division of the Mathematical Tripos, the former being *Senior Optimes* and the latter *Junior Optimes*. The term comes from the Latin phrase formerly used – *Optime disputasti* (You have disputed very well). The class above the Optimes is composed of Wranglers (*q.v.*).

**Optimism.** The doctrine that 'whatever is, is right', that everything which happens is for the best. It was originally set forth by Leibniz (1646-1716) from the postulate of the omnipotence of God, and is cleverly travestied by Voltaire in his *Candide, ou l'Optimisme* (1759) where Dr Pangloss continually harps on the maxim that 'all is for the best in this best of all possible worlds'.

**Opus** (Lat. a work). *See* Magnum Opus.

***Opus operantis.*** *Ex opere operato* is a phrase used by theologians to express the efficiency of acts irrespective of the intention of the agent or patient. *Ex opere operantis* implies the concurrence of intention on the part of the agent; it is the personal piety of the person who does the act, and not the act itself, that causes it to be an instrument of grace. Thus in the Eucharist, it is the faith of the recipient which makes it efficient for grace.

***Opus operatum.*** The thing done; the theologian's term for expressing the effect of sacraments irrespective of the disposition of the receivers of them. Thus, baptism is said by many to convey regeneration to an infant in arms.

**Oracle** (Lat. *oraculum*, from *orare*, to speak, to pray). The answer of a god or inspired priest to an inquiry respecting the future; the deity giving responses; the place where the deity could be consulted, etc.; hence, a person whose utterances are regarded as profoundly wise, an infallible, dogmatical person –

> I am Sir Oracle,
> And when I ope my lips let no dog bark.
>
> Shakespeare, *Merchant of Venice*, 1, 1

In ancient Greece oracles were extremely numerous, and very expensive to those who consulted them. The most famous were the –

Oracle of Apollo, at Delphi, the priestess of which was called the Pythoness; at Delos, and at Claros.

Oracle of Diana, at Colchis; of Esculapius, at Epidaurus, and another in Rome.

Oracle of Hercules, at Athens, and another at Gades.

Oracle of Jupiter, at Dodona (the most noted); another at Ammon, in Libya; another at Crete.

Oracle of Mars, in Thrace; Minerva, in Mycenae; Pan, in Arcadia.

Oracle of Triphonius, in Boeotia, where only men made the responses.

Oracle of Venus, at Paphos, another at Aphaca, and many others.

In most of the temples women, sitting on a tripod, made the responses, many of which were either ambiguous or so obscure as to be misleading; to this day, our word *oracular* is still used of obscure as well as of authoritative pronouncements.

The difficulty of 'making head or tail' of oracles is well illustrated by the following classic examples:

When Croesus consulted the Delphic oracle respecting a projected war, he received for answer, '*Croesus Halyn penetrans magnum, pervertet opum vim*' (When Croesus passes over the river Halys, he will overthrow the strength of an empire). Croesus supposed the oracle meant he would overthrow the enemy's empire, but it was his own that he destroyed.

Pyrrhus, being about to make war against Rome, was told by the oracle: '*Aio te, Aeacide, Romanos vincere posse*' (I say, Pyrrhus, that you the Romans can conquer), which may mean either *You, Pyrrhus, can overthrow the Romans,* or *Pyrrhus, the Romans can overthrow you.*

Another prince, consulting the oracle on a similar occasion, received for answer, '*Ibis redibis nunquam per bella peribis*' (You shall return never you shall perish by the war), the interpretation of which depends on the position of the comma; it may be *You shall return, you shall never perish in the war*, or *You shall return never, you shall perish in the war*, which latter was the fact.

Philip of Macedon sent to ask the oracle of Delphi if his Persian expedition would prove successful, and received for answer –

The ready victim crowned for death
Before the altar stands.

Philip took it for granted that the 'ready victim' was the King of Persia, but it was Philip himself.

When the Greeks sent to Delphi to know if they would succeed against the Persians, they were told –

Seed-time and harvest, weeping sires shall tell
How thousands fought at Salamis and fell.

But whether the Greeks or the Persians were to be 'the weeping sires', no indication was given, nor whether the thousands 'about to fall' were to be Greeks or Persian.

When Maxentius was about to encounter Constantine, he consulted the guardians of the Sibylline Books as to the date of the battle, and the prophetess told him, '*Illo die hostem Romanorum esse periturum*,' but whether Maxentius or Constantine was 'the enemy of the Roman people' the oracle left undecided.

In the Bible we have a similar equivoke: When Ahab, King of Israel, was about to wage war on the king of Syria, and asked Micaiah if Ramoth-Gilead would fall into his hands, the prophet replied, 'Go, for the Lord will deliver the city into the hands of the king' (1 Kings 22:15, 35).

***The Oracle of the Church.*** St Bernard of Clairvaux (1091–1153).

***The Oracle of the Holy Bottle.*** The oracle to which Rabelais (Bks iv and v) sent Panurge and a large party to obtain an answer to a question which had been put to sibyl and poet, monk and fool, philosopher and witch, judge and 'sort', viz. 'whether Panurge should marry or not?' The oracle was situated at Bacbuc (*q.v.*) 'near Cathay in Upper Egypt', and the story has been interpreted as a satire on the Church. The celibacy of the clergy was for long a moot point, and the 'Holy Bottle' or cup to the laity was one of the moving causes of the schisms from the Church. The crew setting sail for the Bottle refers to Anthony, Duke of Vendôme, afterwards king of Navarre, setting out in search of religious truth.

***The oracle of the sieve and shears.*** *See* Sieve.

***To work the oracle.*** To induce another to favour some plan or to join in some project, generally by manoeuvring behind the scenes. Also – in slang – to raise money.

They fetched a rattling price through Starlight's working the oracle with those swells.

Boldrewood, *Robbery Under Arms*, ch. xii

**Orange.** This distinctive epithet of the ultra Protestants of Northern Ireland and of Ulstermen generally, it is said, became attached to them because in 1795 two members of the famous 'Orange Lodge' of Freemasons (which had been revived in Belfast about 1780) were active in raising the Orange Lodges (*see below*), an armed force of Protestant volunteers – hence called 'Orange boys' – in defence of civil and religious liberty.

*The Orange Lodge* was named in honour of *William of Orange* (William III), the Protestant opposer of James II in the 'Glorious Revolution' of 1689, and the victor at the Battle of the Boyne (1690).

William III's territorial name came from Orange (anciently Arausio), a town on the Rhone 13 miles north of Avignon, and capital of the former principality of the same name, which dated from the 11th century. From 1373 to 1530 it belonged to the House of Châlons; through failure of male heirs it then fell through a sister of Philibert, the last prince of that House, to William the Silent, Prince of Nassau, who thereupon became Prince of Orange-Nassau, or simply 'of Orange'. His grandson, William II, married Mary, daughter of our Charles I, and they were the parents of William of Orange, our William III, husband of Mary, daughter of his uncle and enemy, James II.

The principality remained in the hands of the House of Orange-Nassau till 1702, and was finally annexed to France by the Treaty of Utrecht, 1713. The title 'Prince of Orange' is still borne by the heir-presumptive to the throne of Holland, which is occupied by the House of Nassau.

**Orange blossom.** The conventional decoration for the bride at a wedding, introduced as a custom into England from France about 1820. The *orange* is said to indicate the hope of fruitfulness, as few trees are more prolific, while the *white blossoms* are symbolical of innocence.

Hence the phrase, *to go gathering orange blossoms*, to look for a wife.

**Orange Lilies.** The nickname of the old 35th Foot, now the Royal Sussex, Regiment. Their facings were *orange* till 1832; and *lilies* represent the white plumes given in recognition of their gallantry at Quebec in 1759, when they routed the Royal Roussillon French Grenadiers.

**Orange Lodges** or **Clubs** are referred to in print as early as 1769. Thirty years later the Orangemen were a very powerful society, having a 'grand lodge' extending over the entire province of Ulster and through all the centres of Protestantism in Ireland. *See* Orange *above*.

**Orangemen.** A name given to the members of an Orange Lodge; originating in their respect for the memory of William III of the House of Orange. *See* Orange *above*.

**Orange Peel.** A nickname given to Sir Robert Peel when Chief Secretary for Ireland (1812–18), on account of his strong anti-Catholic proclivities.

**Orange-tawny.** The ancient colour appropriated to clerks and persons of inferior condition. It was also the colour worn by the Jews. Hence Bacon says, 'Usurers should have orange-tawny bonnets, because they do Judaise' (*Essay* xli). Bottom the weaver asked Quince what colour beard he was to wear for the character of Pyramus:

> I will discharge it in either your straw-colour beard, your orange-tawny beard, your purple-in-grain beard, or your French-crown-colour beard, your perfect yellow.
>
> *Midsummer Night's Dream*, I, 2

**Orator Henley.** The Rev. John Henley (1692–1756), who for about thirty years delivered lectures on theological, political, and literary subjects.

**Orator of the Human Race, The.** *See* Anacharsis Clootz.

**Orc.** A sea-monster fabled by Ariosto, Drayton, Sylvester, etc., to devour men and women. The name was sometimes used for the whale. Milton speaks of the Mount of Paradise being 'pushed by the hornéd flood':

> Down the great river to the opening Gulf,
> And there take root, an island salt and bare,
> The haunt of seals, and orcs, and sea-mews' clang.
>
> *Paradise Lost*, xi, 833

**Orchard** properly means a garden-yard. *Hortyard* was one of the old spellings, and in this form its connection with Lat. *hortus*, a garden, is clear.

> The hortyard entering [he] admires the fair
> And pleasant fruits. Sandys

**Orchid.** The Stock Exchange slang term for a titled member of the House, one with a handle to his name. The tale is that many years ago a young scion of the nobility was heard to remark to a friend, 'You know, when I'm in the House I feel like an orchid in a turnip-field!'

**Orcus.** A Latin name for Hades, the abode of the dead. Spenser speaks of a dragon whose mouth was –

> All set with iron teeth in ranges twain,
> That terrified his foes, and armed him,
> Appearing like the mouth of *Orcus* griesly grim.
>
> *Faërie Queene*, VI, xii, 26

**Ordeal** (A.S. *ordēl*, related to *adaelan*, to deal, allot, judge). The ancient Anglo-Saxon and Teutonic practice of referring disputed questions of criminality to supernatural decision, by subjecting the suspected person to physical tests by fire, boiling water, battle, etc.; hence, figuratively, an experience testing endurance, patience, courage, etc.

This method of 'trial' was based on the belief that God would defend the right, even by miracle if needful. All ordeals, except the ordeal of battle, were abolished in England by law in the early 13th century.

In *Ordeal of battle* the accused person was obliged to fight anyone who charged him with guilt. This ordeal was allowed only to persons of rank.

*Ordeal of fire* was also for persons of rank only. The accused had to hold in his hand a piece of red-hot iron, or to walk blindfold and barefoot among nine red-hot plough-shares laid at unequal distances. If he escaped uninjured he was accounted innocent, *aliter non*. This might be performed by deputy.

*Ordeal of hot water* was for the common people. The accused was required to plunge his arm up to the elbow in boiling water, and was pronounced guilty if the skin was injured in the experiment.

*Ordeal of cold water* was also for the common people. The accused, being bound, was tossed into a river; if he *sank* he was acquitted, but if he *floated* he was accounted guilty. This ordeal remained in use for the trial of witches to comparatively recent times.

In the *Ordeal of the bier* a person suspected of murder was required to touch the corpse; if guilty the 'blood of the dead body would start forth afresh'.

In that of the *cross* plaintiff and defendant had to stand with their arms crossed over their breasts, and he who could endure the longest won the suit. *See also* Judicium Crucis.

The *Ordeal of the Eucharist* was for priests. It was supposed that the elements would choke him, if taken by a guilty man.

In the *Ordeal of the Corsned* (*q.v.*) consecrated bread and cheese was similarly given. Godwin, Earl of Kent, is said to have been choked when, being accused of the murder of the king's brother, he submitted to this ordeal.

> In Ceylon, a man suspected of theft is required to bring what he holds dearest before a judge, and placing a heavy stone on the head of his substitute, says 'May this stone crush thee to death if I am guilty of this offence.'
>
> In Tartary, an ostiack sets a wild bear and a hatchet before the tribunal, saying, as he swallows a piece of bread, 'May the bear devour me, and the hatchet chop off my head, if I am guilty of the crime laid to my charge.'

**Order!** When members of the House of Commons and other debaters call out *Order!* they mean that the person speaking is in some way breaking the rule or *order* of the assembly, and has to be *called to order*.

***Architectural orders.*** *See* Architecture.

***Holy orders.*** A clergyman is said to be *in holy orders* because he belongs to one of the *orders* or ranks of the Church. In the Church of England these are three, viz., Deacon, Priest, and Bishop; in the Roman Catholic Church there is a fourth, that of Subdeacon.

In ecclesiastical use the term also denotes a fraternity of monks or friars (as the *Franciscan Order*), and also the Rule by which the fraternity is governed.

***The order of the day*** in parliamentary parlance, is applied to the prearranged agenda of 'Private Members' Bills'. On Friday these bills always stand after 'notices of motions'. *See* Question.

***To move for the Order of the Day*** is a proposal to set aside a government measure on a private members' day (Friday), and proceed to the agenda prearranged. If the motion is carried, the agenda must be proceeded with, unless a motion 'to adjourn' is carried.

**Ordinary.** In Law an ordinary is one who has an 'ordinary or regular jurisdiction' in his own right, and not by deputation. Thus a judge who has authority to take cognizance of causes in his own right is an ordinary. A bishop is an ordinary in his own diocese, because he has authority to take cognizance of ecclesiastical matters therein; an archbishop is the ordinary of his province, having authority in his own right to receive appeals therein from inferior jurisdictions. The chaplain of Newgate was also called the ordinary thereof.

A meal prepared at an inn at a fixed rate for all comers is called an 'ordinary'; hence, also, the inn itself:

> 'Tis almost dinner; I know they stay for you at the ordinary.
>
> Beaumont and Fletcher, *Scornful Lady*, iv, 1

And in Heraldry the 'ordinary' is a simple charge, such as the chief, pale, fesse, bend, bar, chevron, cross, or saltire.

**Oread** (pl. *Oreads* or *Oreades*). Nymphs of the mountains. (Gr. *oros*, a mountain.)

> The Ocean-nymphs and Hamadryades,
> Oreads and Naiads, with long weedy locks,
> Offered to do her bidding through the seas,
> Under the earth, and in the hollow rocks.
>
> Shelley, *Witch of Atlas*, xxii

**Orelia.** The steed of Don Roderick, the last of the Goths, noted for its speed and symmetry.

**Orellana.** The name formerly used for the river Amazon, so called from Francisco de Orellana, lieutenant of Pizarro, who was the first to explore it (about 1537–41).

**Oremus.** *See* Legem pone.

**Orestes.** *See* Pylades.

**Orfeo and Heurodis**. The tale of Orpheus and Eurydice (*q.v.*), with the Gothic machinery of elves or fairies.

**Orgies.** Drunken revels, riotous feasts; hence, figuratively, wild or licentious extravagance. So called from the Gr. *orgia*, the secret, nocturnal festivals in honour of Bacchus (*q.v.*).

**Orgoglio** (Ital. Arrogant Pride, or Man of Sin). In Spenser's *Faërie Queene* (I, vii, and viii), a hideous giant as tall as three men, son of Earth and Wind. Finding the Red Cross Knight at the fountain of Idleness, he beats him with a club and makes him his slave. Una, hearing of these mischances, tells King Arthur, who liberates the knight and slays the giant.

He typifies the tyrannical power of the Church of Rome; in slaying him Arthur first cut off his *left arm* – i.e. Bohemia was first cut off from the Church of Rome; then the giant's *right leg* – i.e. England, when Orgoglio fell to earth, and was easily dispatched.

**Oriana.** The beloved of Amadis of Gaul, who called himself Beltenebros when he retired to the Poor Rock. (*Amadis de Gaul*, ii, 6.)

The name is also given to the nurseling of a lioness, with whom Esplandian, son of Oriana and Amadis, fell in love, and for whom he underwent all his perils and exploits. She is represented as the fairest, gentlest, and most faithful of womankind.

Queen Elizabeth is sometimes called the 'peerless Oriana', especially in the madrigals entitled the *Triumphs of Oriana* (1601).

**Oriel College, Oxford.** The fifth in age of the Oxford Colleges, founded in 1326 by Edward II and his almoner, Adam de Brome, who was its first Provost. The name comes from a messuage in Oxford called *La Oriole*, which was granted to the College at its foundation, but the origin of this name is unknown.

*Oriel* in *oriel window*, is also obscure. The name originally denoted a gallery or balcony, then a gallery in a private chapel, then a small private apartment which had a window looking into the chapel. It may be connected with Late Lat. *autaeum*, a curtain (*aula*, hall), but this is by no means certain.

**Orientation.** The placing of the east window of a church due east (Lat. *oriens*), that is, so that the rising sun may at noon shine on the altar. Anciently, churches were built with their axes pointing to the rising sun on the saint's day; so that a church dedicated to St John was not parallel to one dedicated to St Peter, but in the building of modern churches the saint's day is not, as a rule, regarded.

Figuratively, orientation is the correct placing of one's ideas, mental processes, etc., in relation with themselves and with current thought – the ascertainment of one's ' bearings'.

**Oriflamme** (Fr. 'flame of gold'). The ancient banner of the kings of France, first used as a national banner in 1119. It was a crimson flag cut into three 'vandykes' to represent 'tongues of fire', with a silken tassel between each, and was carried on a gilt staff (*un glaive tout doré où est attaché une bannière vermeille*). This celebrated standard was the banner of St Denis; but when the Counts of Vexin became possessed of the abbey it passed into their hands. In 1082 Philippe I united Vexin to the crown, and the sacred Oriflamme fell to the king. It was carried to the field after the battle of Agincourt, in 1415. The romance writers say that 'mescreans' (infidels) were blinded by merely looking on it. In the *Roman de Garin* the Saracens cry, 'If we only set eyes on it we are all dead men'; and Froissart records that it was no sooner unfurled at Rosbecq than the fog cleared away from the French, leaving their enemies in misty darkness.

In the 15th century the Oriflamme was succeeded by the blue standard powdered with fleurs-de-lis, and the last heard of the original Oriflamme is a mention in the inventory of the Abbey of St Denis dated 1534.

**Origenists.** An early Christian sect who drew their opinions from the writings of Origen (d. about 254). They maintained Christ to be the Son of God only by adoption, believed in a literal, moral, and mystical interpretation of the Bible, and in the pre-existence of souls, and were not adherents of the doctrine of the eternity of future punishments.

**Original Sin.** *See* Sin.

**Orillo.** One of the magicians in Ariosto's *Orlando Furioso* (Bk viii). His life depended – literally – upon a single hair, but he was able, when his head was cut off, to put it on again. Astolpho encountered him, cut off his head, and fled with it. Orillo mounted and gave chase, but meanwhile Astolpho cut the hair from the head, and as soon as that was severed the head died, and the magician's body fell lifeless.

**Orinda the Matchless.** Mrs Katherine Philipps (1631–64), the poetess and letter-writer. She first adopted the signature 'Orinda' in her correspondence with Sir Charles Cotterell, and afterwards used it for general purposes. Her praises were sung by Cowley, Dryden, and others.

Dryden's lines –

> O double sacrilege on things divine,
> To rob the relic and deface the shrine;
> But thus Orinda died.
>
> *Elegy on Mrs Anne Killigrew*

refer to the fact that both ladies died of smallpox.

**Orion.** A giant hunter of *Greek mythology*, noted for his beauty. He was blinded by Oenopion, but Vulcan sent Cedalion to be his guide, and his sight was restored by exposing his eyeballs to the sun. Being slain by Diana, he was made one of the constellations, and is supposed to be attended with stormy weather. His wife was named Side, and his dogs Arctophonus and Ptoöphagus.

With fierce winds Orion armed
Hath vexed the Red-Sea coast.
Milton, *Paradise Lost*, I, 305

**Orkneys.** The name is probably connected with the old *orc* (*q.v.*), a whale, and either Gaelic *innis* or Norse *ey*, an island – 'the isles of whales'. For centuries the Orkneys were a jarldom of Norway or Denmark, and it was not till 1590 that the latter renounced its claim to sovereignty. They had passed to the Scottish crown in 1468 after having been in the possession of the Earls of Angus for nearly 250 years.

**Orlando.** The Italian form of 'Roland' (*q.v.*), one of the great heroes of mediaeval romance, and the most celebrated of Charlemagne's paladins. He appears under this name in the romances mentioned below, and in other works.

***Orlando Furioso*** (Orlando mad). An epic poem in 45 cantos, by Ariosto (published 1515–33). Orlando's madness is caused by the faithlessness of Angelica, but the main subject of the work is the siege of Paris by Agramant the Moor, when the Saracens were overthrown. In the pagan army were two heroes – Rodomont, called the Mars of Africa, and Rogero. The latter became a Christian convert. The poem ends with a combat between these two, and the overthrow of Rodomont.

The epic is full of anachronisms. We have Charlemagne and his paladins joined by King Edward of England, Richard Earl of Warwick, Henry Duke of Clarence, and the Dukes of York and Gloucester (Bk vi). Cannon are employed by Cymosco, King of Friza (Bk iv), and also in the siege of Paris (Bk vi). We have the Moors established in Spain, whereas they were not invited over by the Saracens for nearly 300 years after Charlemagne's death. In Bk xvii the late mediaeval Prester John (*q.v.*) appears, and in the last three books Constantine the Great, who died 337.

There are English translations by Sir John Harrington (1591), Hoole (1783), and W. S. Rose (1823–31).

About 1589 a play (printed 1594) by Robert Greene entitled *The History of Orlando Furioso* was produced. In this version Orlando marries Angelica.

***Orlando Innamorato*** (Orlando in love). A romance in verse by Boiardo telling the love of Roland (*q.v.*) and Angelica. Boiardo died in 1494, not having finished the work, and Ariosto wrote his *Orlando Furioso* (*see above*) as a sequel to it. In 1541 Berni turned it into burlesque.

**Ormandine.** The necromancer who by his magic arts threw St David for seven years into an enchanted sleep, from which he was redeemed by St George. (*The Seven Champions of Christendom*, i, 9.)

**Ormulum.** A long poem in Transition, or Early Middle, English, of which only a 'fragment' of some 10,000 lines is extant. It is so called from the author, Orm, or Ormin, an Augustinian canon –

This boc iss nemmed Ormulum
Forrthi that Orm itt wrohhte –

and in it the Gospel for each day is versified and elaborated with expositions out of Aelfric, Bede, and Augustine. It was written in the early 13th century.

**Ormuzd** or **Ahura Mazda.** The principle or angel of light and good, and creator of all things, according to the Magian system. He is in perpetual conflict with Ahriman (*q.v.*), but in the end will triumph. The Latin form of the name is *Oromasdes*.

And Oromaze, Joshua, and Mahomet,
Moses and Buddh, Zerdusht, and Brahm, and Foh,
A tumult of strange names, which never met
Before, as watchwords of a single woe
Arose.
Shelley, *Revolt of Islam*, X, xxxi

**Orosius.** A Latin writer of the early 5th century AD, whose *General History*, from the Creation to AD 417, is frequently referred to by historians and was translated into Anglo-Saxon by Alfred the Great. Orosius was a native of Tarragona, in Spain, and a friend of St Augustine's.

**Orpheus.** A Thracian poet of Greek legend (son of Apollo and Calliope), who could move even inanimate things by his music – a power that was also claimed for the Scandinavian Odin. When his wife Eurydice (*q.v.*) died he went into the infernal regions, and so charmed Pluto that she was released on the condition that Orpheus would not look back till they reached the earth. He was just about to place his foot on the earth when he turned round, and Eurydice vanished from him in an instant.

Orpheus' self may … hear
Such strains as would have won the ear
Of Pluto to have quite set free
His half-regained Eurydice.
Milton, *L'Allegro*, 145–50

The prolonged grief of Orpheus at his second loss so enraged the Thracian women that in one of their Bacchanalian orgies they tore him to pieces. The fragments of his body were collected by the Muses and buried at the foot of Mount Olympus, but his head had been thrown into the river Hebrus, whither it was carried into the sea, and so to Lesbos, where it was separately interred.

What could the Muse herself that Orpheus bore,
The Muse herself, for her enchanting son,
Whom universal nature did lament,
When, by the rout that made the hideous roar,
His gory visage down the stream was sent,
Down the swift Hebrus to the Lesbian shore?
Milton, *Lycidas*, 58

***Orpheus of Highwaymen.*** So Gay has been called on account of his *Beggar's Opera* (1728).

**Orphic.** Connected with Orpheus, the mysteries associated with his name, or the doctrines ascribed to him; similar to his music in magic power. Thus, Shelley says –

Language is a perpetual Orphic song,
Which rules with Daedal harmony a throng
Of thoughts and forms, which else senseless
and shapeless were.
*Prometheus Unbound*, IV, i, 415

***The Orphic egg.*** *See* Egg, the Mundane.

**Orrery.** A complicated piece of mechanism showing by means of clockwork the movements of the planets, etc., round the sun. It was invented about 1700 by George Graham, who sent his model to Rowley, an instrument maker, to make one for Prince Eugene. Rowley made a copy of it for Charles Boyle, third Earl of Orrery, in whose honour it was named. One of the best is Fulton's, in Kelvin Grove Museum, Glasgow.

**Orsin.** One of the leaders of the rabble that attacked Hudibras (*q.v.*) at a bear-baiting. He was 'famous for wise conduct and success in war'. Joshua Gosling, who kept the bears at 'Paris Garden', in Southwark, was the original of this character.

**Orson.** Twin brother of Valentine in the old romance, *Valentine and Orson* (*q.v.*). The twins were born in a wood near Orleans, and Orson (Fr. *ourson*, a little bear) was carried off by a bear, which suckled him with her cubs. When he grew up he was the terror of France, and was called the *Wild Man of the Forest*. He was reclaimed by Valentine, overthrew the Green Knight, and married Fezon, the daughter of Duke Savary of Aquitaine.

**Orthodox Church, The.** *See* Greek Church.

**Orthodox Sunday,** in the Eastern Church, is the First Sunday in Lent, to commemorate the restoration of images in 843.

In the Church of England, on the first day in Lent, 'Ash Wednesday', the clergy are directed to read 'the ... sentences of God's cursing against impenitent sinners'.

**Orts.** Crumbs; refuse. (Low Ger. *ort* – i.e. what is left after eating.)

***I shall not eat your orts*** – i.e. your leavings.

Let him have time a beggar's orts to crave.
Shakespeare, *Rape of Lucrece*, 985

**Ortus. *Ortus a quercu, non a salice.*** Latin for 'sprung from an oak, and not from a willow' – i.e. stubborn stuff; one that cannot bend to circumstances.

**Ortwin.** One of the heroes of the *Nibelungenlied* (*q.v.*); brother of Gudrun, and son of Hagen's daughter, Hilda.

**Orvietan** or **Venice Treacle,** once believed to be a sovereign remedy against poison, hence sometimes used of an antidote; so named from Orvieto, Italy, where it is said to have been first used.

With these drugs will I, this very day, compound
the true orvietan. Scott, *Kenilworth*, ch. xiii

**Os Sacrum**. *See* Luz. A triangular bone situate at the lower part of the vertebral column, of which it is a continuation. Some say that this bone was so called because it was in the part used in sacrifice, or the sacred part; Dr Nash says it is so called 'because it is much bigger than any of the vertebrae'; but the Jewish rabbins say the bone is called sacred because it resists decay, and will be the germ of the 'new body' at the resurrection. (*Hudibras*, pt iii, canto 2.)

**Osiris.** One of the chief gods of *Egyptian mythology*: judge of the dead, ruler of the kingdom of ghosts, the Creator, the god of the Nile, and the constant foe of his brother (or son), Set, the principle of evil. He was the husband of Isis (*q.v.*), and represents the setting sun (*cp.* Ra). He was slain, but came to life again and was revenged by Horus and Thoth.

The name means *Many-eyed.* Osiris was usually depicted as a mummy wearing the crown of Upper Egypt, but sometimes as an ox.

Nor is Osiris seen
In Memphian grove or green,
Trampling the unshowered grass with lowings
loud. Milton, *Christ's Nativity*, 213

**Osmand.** A necromancer in *The Seven Champions of Christendom*, i, 19, who by enchantment raised an army to resist the Christians. Six of the

Champions fell, whereupon St George restored them; Osmand tore out his hair, in which lay his magic power, bit his tongue in two, disembowelled himself, cut off his arms, and then died.

**Ossa.** *See* Pelion.

**Ossian (Oisin).** The legendary Gaelic bard and warrior of about the end of the 3rd century, son of Finn (Fingal), and reputed author of *Ossian's Poems*, published 1760–3, by James Macpherson, who professed that he had translated them from MSS collected in the Highlands. A great controversy as to the authenticity of the supposed originals was aroused; the question has not yet been finally settled, but it is generally agreed that Macpherson, while compiling from ancient sources, was the principal author of the poems as published. The poems are full of the Celtic glamour and charm, but are marred by rant and bombast.

**Ostend Manifesto.** A declaration made in 1857 by the Ministers of the United States in England, France, and Spain, 'that Cuba must belong to the United States'. Till 1898 the island belonged to Spain, when, as one of the results of the Spanish-American War, it was freed and was for four years under the military rule of the United States. In 1902 it was formed into an autonomous republic.

**Ostler.** *See* Hostler.

**Ostracism** (Gr. *ostrakon*, an earthen vessel). Black-balling, boycotting, expelling; exclusion from society or common privileges, etc. The word arose from the ancient Greek custom of banishing one whose power was a danger to the state, the voting for which was done by the people recording their votes on tiles or potsherds. The custom of ostracising is widespread. St Paul exhorts Christians to 'come out from' idolaters (2 Cor. 6:17); and the Jews ostracised the Samaritans. The French phrases, *Damner une boutique* and *Damner une ville*, convey the same idea; and the Catholic Church anathematises and interdicts.

**Ostrich.** At one time the ostrich was fabled, when hunted, to run a certain distance and then thrust its head into a bush, thinking, because it cannot see, that it cannot be seen (*cp.* Crocodiles); this supposed habit is the source of many allusions, e.g. –

> Whole nations, fooled by falsehood, fear, or pride,
> Their ostrich-heads in self-illusion hide.
>
> Moore, *Sceptic*

Another source of literary allusion to the bird is its habit of eating indigestible things like stones and metals to assist the functions of the gizzard –

> Ah, villain! thou wilt betray me, and get a thousand crowns of the king by carrying my head to him; but I'll make thee eat iron like an ostrich, and swallow my sword like a great pin, ere thou and I part.
>
> Shakespeare, *2 Henry VI*, 4, 10

Hence, *ostrich-stomachs*, stomachs that will digest anything.

***Ostrich eggs*** are often suspended in Eastern churches as symbols of God's watchful care. It used to be thought that the ostrich hatches her eggs by gazing on them, and if she suspends her gaze even for a minute or so, the eggs are addled. Furthermore, we are told that if an *egg* is bad the ostrich will break it; so will God deal with evil men.

> Oh! even with such a look as fables say
> The mother ostrich fixes on her eggs,
> Till that intense affection
> Kindle its light of life.
>
> Southey, *Thalaba*

**Ostrog Bible, The.** *See* Bible, specially named.

**Othello.** Shakespeare's tragedy (written and performed in 1604, first printed 1622) is founded on a tale in Cinthio's *Hecatommithi* (1565) – *Un Capitano More* (decad. iii, Nov. vii).

> Othello, a Moor, was commander of the Venetian army, and eloped with Desdemona. Brabantio accused him of necromancy, but Desdemona refuted the charge. The Moor, being then sent to drive the Turks from Cyprus, won a signal victory. On his return, Iago, Othello's 'ancient' (i.e. ensign or lieutenant), played upon his jealousy, and persuaded him that Desdemona had been false to him with Cassio. He therefore murdered her, and after learning how he had been duped by Iago, slew himself.

***Othello's occupation's gone*** (3, 3). A phrase sometimes used when one is 'laid on the shelf', no longer 'the observed of all observers'.

**Other Day, The.** Originally this meant 'the second day', either forward or backward, *other* being the Anglo-Saxon equivalent for *second*, as in Latin *unus*, *alter*, *tertius*; or *proximus*, *alter*, *tertius*. Starting from today, and going backwards, yesterday was the *proximus ab illo*; the day before yesterday was the *altera ab illo*, or the other day; and the day preceding that was *tertius ab illo*, or three days ago. Now the phrase is used to express 'a few days ago', 'not so long since'.

**Otium cum dignitate** (Lat. leisure with dignity). Retirement after a person has given up business and has saved enough to live upon in comfort. The words were taken as a motto by Cicero.

> *Otium cum dignitate* is to be had with £500 a year as well as with 5,000.
>
> Pope, *Letters* (Wks, vol. x, p. 110)

**Ottava Rima.** A stanza of eight ten-syllabled lines, rhyming *a b a b a b c c*, used by Keats in his *Isabella*, Byron in *Don Juan*, etc. It was originally Italian and was employed by Tasso (the lines were eleven-syllabled), Ariosto, and many others.

**Ottoman Empire.** The Turkish Empire, so called from Othman, or Osman, I, the founder about 1300 of the reigning dynasty. Our *ottoman*, a kind of sofa having some resemblance to an oriental couch, is, of course, the same word.

**Otus.** A giant of Greek fable, brother of Ephialtes (*q.v.*). Both grew 9 in. every month, and Pliny says that Otus was 46 cubits (about 66 ft) in height.

**Out. *Murder will out.*** The secret is bound to be revealed; 'be sure your sin will find you out'.

> O blisful god, that art so just and trewe!
> Lo, how that thou biwreyest mordre alway
> Mordre wol out, that see we day by day
>
> Chaucer, *Nun's Priest's Tale*, 232

***Out and out.*** Incomparably, by far, or beyond measure; as, 'He was out and out the best man.'

***Out and outer.*** Slang for a thorough-going fellow – either good or bad. A rascal may be 'a regular out and outer' (in which case there are few to exceed him in rascality), and so may a good, honest man.

***Out of it.*** Left on one side, not included.

***Outed.*** Expelled, ejected.

***To go all out.*** In sport, racing, etc., to do one's very best – to put out every effort to win.

***To have it out.*** To contest either physically or verbally with another to the utmost of one's ability; as, 'I mean to have it out with him one of these days'; 'I had it out with him' – i.e. 'I spoke my mind freely and without reserve.' The idea is that of letting loose pent up disapprobation.

**Ovation.** An enthusiastic display of popular favour, so called from the ancient Roman *ovatio* or minor triumph, in which the general after a bloodless victory or one over slaves entered the city on horseback or on foot, instead of in a chariot as in the greater triumph, and was crowned with myrtle instead of with gold.

**Over. *Half seas over.*** *See* Half.

***It's all over with him.*** He's finished, he can't go any farther, he's 'shot his bolt'. Said also of one who has been given up by the doctors.

***Over and over again.*** Very frequently. (In Lat., *Iterum iterumque*.)

**Overy.** The church of St Mary Overy, Southwark, was, according to Stow, founded by a ferry-woman named Mary Overy, who, long before the age of bridges, devoted her savings to this purpose. This, of course, is fable; the name is a contraction of *St Mary's over the river*.

**Owl,** the emblem of Athens, where owls abounded. As Athena (Minerva) and Athenae (Athens) are the same word, the owl was given to Minerva for her symbol also.

The Greeks had a proverb, *To send owls to Athens*, which meant the same as our *To carry coals to Newcastle*. *See also* Madge.

***I live too near a wood to be scared by an owl.*** I am too old to be frightened by a bogy; I am too old a stager to be frightened by such a person as you.

***Like an owl in an ivy-bush.*** Having a sapient, vacant look, as some persons have when in their cups; having a stupid vacant stare. Owls are proverbial for their judge-like solemnity; ivy is the favourite plant of Bacchus, and was supposed to be the favourite haunt of owls.

> Good ivy, say to us what birds hast thou?
> None but the owlet that cries 'How how!'
>
> Carol (time Henry VI)

Gray, in his *Elegy*, and numerous other poets bracket the two:

> From yonder ivy-mantled tower
> The moping owl doth to the moon complain.

***Owl light.*** Dusk; the gloaming, 'blind man's holiday'. Fr., *Entre chien et loup*.

***The owl was a baker's daughter.*** According to a Gloucestershire legend, our Saviour went into a baker's shop for something to eat. The mistress put a cake into the oven for Him, but her daughter said it was too large, and reduced it half. The dough, however, swelled to an enormous size, and the daughter cried out, 'Heugh! heugh! heugh!' and was transformed into an owl. Ophelia alludes to the tradition –

> Well, God 'ield you! They say the owl was a baker's daughter. Shakespeare, *Hamlet*, 4, 5

**Owlglass.** *See* Eulenspiegel.

**Ox.** One of the four figures which made up Ezekiel's cherub (i, 10). It is the emblem of the priesthood, and was assigned to St Luke (*q.v.*) as his symbol because he begins his gospel with the Jewish priest sacrificing in the Temple.

In early art the ox is usually given as the emblem of St Frideswide, St Leonard, St Sylvester, St Medard, St Julietta, and St Blandina.

***He has an ox on his tongue.*** *See under* Money.

***Ox-eye.*** A sailor's name for a cloudy speck which indicates the approach of a storm. When Elijah heard that a speck no bigger than a 'man's hand' might be seen in the sky, he told Ahab that a torrent of rain would overtake him before he could reach home (1 Kings 17:44, 45). Thomson alludes to this storm signal in his *Summer*.

***The black ox hath trod on your foot,*** or ***hath trampled on you*:** Misfortune has come to you or your house; sometimes, you are henpecked. A black ox was sacrificed to Pluto, the infernal god, as a white one was to Jupiter.

> Venus waxeth old; and then she was a pretie wench, when Juno was a yong wife; now crowes foote is on her eye, and the blacke oxe hath trod on her foot. Lyly, *Sapho and Phao*, IV, ii

***The dumb ox.*** St Thomas Aquinas (1227–74), so named by his fellow students at Cologne, on account of his dullness and taciturnity. Albertus said: 'We call him the dumb ox, but he will give one day such a bellow as shall be heard from one end of the world to the other.'

***To muzzle the ox that treadeth out the corn*** (Deut. 25:4). Not to pay for work done; to expect other persons will work for nothing. The labourer is worthy of his hire, and to withhold that hire is to muzzle the ox that treadeth out your corn.

***To play the giddy ox.*** To act the fool generally; to behave in an irresponsible or over-hilarious manner. There was an old phrase, *to make an ox of one*, meaning the same as the modern *to make a fool of one*; and in the *Merry Wives of Windsor* (5, 5) we have –

> *Fal.:* I do begin to perceive that I am made an ass.
> *Ford.:* Ay, and an ox too; both the proofs are extant.

**Oxford Blues.** The Royal Horse Guards were so called in 1690 because of their blue facings.

**Oxford Colours** (*boat-crews*). *See* College Colours.

**Oxford Frame.** A picture frame made so that the wooden sides cross each other at the corners and project an inch or two; much used for photographs of college groups and so on.

**Oxford Movement, The.** A High Church movement which originated at Oxford in 1833 under the leadership of Pusey, Newman (afterwards a Cardinal in the Roman Church), and Keble. It was strongly opposed to anything in the way of Latitudinarianism, and sought to bring back into the service of the Church much of the ritual, ornaments, etc., that had been dispensed with at the time of the Reformation. *See* Tracts for the Times.

**Oxgang.** An Anglo-Saxon land measure of no very definite quantity, but as much as an ox could *gang* over or cultivate. Also called a *bovate*. The Latin *jugum* was a similar term, which Varro defines '*Quod juncti boves uno die exarare possunt.*'

> Eight oxgangs made a carucate (*q.v.*). If an oxgang were as much as one ox could cultivate, its average would be about fifteen acres.

**Oyer and terminer.** An Anglo-French legal phrase meaning 'to hear and determine'. *Commissions* or *Writs of oyer and terminer* as issued to judges on circuit twice a year in every country directing them to hold courts for the trial of offences.

**Oyez! Oyez! Oyez!** (O. Fr., *hear ye!*). The call made by a public crier, court officer, etc., to attract attention when a proclamation is about to be read out. Sometimes written *O yes!*

**Oyster.** ***And did you ever see an oyster walk upstairs?*** A satirical query sometimes addressed to one who has been telling unbelievable yarns about his own experiences.

***Close as a Kentish oyster.*** Absolutely secret; hermetically sealed. Kentish oysters are proverbially good, and all good oysters are fast closed.

***Never eat an oyster unless there's an R in the month.*** Good advice; which limits the eating of oysters to the months from September to April inclusive. The legal close-time for oysters in England and Scotland, however, extends only from June 15th to Aug. 4th, thus freeing all May and parts of June and August.

***Who eats oysters on St James's Day will never want.*** St James's Day is the first day of the oyster season (August 5th), when oysters are an expensive luxury eaten only by the rich.

**Oz.** The abbreviation for an ounce is the 15th century contraction of Ital. *onza*. The 'z' here does not play the same part as that in 'viz.' (*q.v.*).

# P

**P.** The sixteenth letter in the English alphabet; called *pe*, 'mouth', by the Phoenicians and ancient Hebrews, and represented in Egyptian hieroglyph by a shutter.

In the 16th century Placentius, a Dominican monk, wrote a poem of 253 hexameter verses called *Pugna Porcorum*, every word of which begins with the letter *p*. It opens thus:

> Plaudite, Porcelli, porcorum pigra propago –

which may be translated –

> Praise Paul's prize pig's prolific progeny

***The Four P's.*** A 'merry interlude' by John Heywood, written about 1540. The four principal characters are 'a Palmer, a Pardoner, a Poticary (apothecary), and a Pedlar'.

***The five P's.*** William Oxberry (1784–1824) was so called, because he was Printer, Poet, Publisher, Publican, and Player.

**P.C.** The Roman *patres conscripti*. *See* Conscript Fathers.

**P., P.P., P.P.P.** (in music). P = piano, pp = pianissimo, and ppp = pianississimo. Sometimes pp means *più piano* (more softly).

So f = forte, ff = fortissimo, and fff = fortississimo.

**P.P.C.** *See* Congé.

**P.S.** (Lat., *post-scriptum*). Written afterwards – i.e. after the letter or book was finished.

**P's** and **Q's.** ***Mind your P's and Q's.*** Be very circumspect in your behaviour.

Several explanations have been suggested, but none seems to be wholly satisfactory. One is that it was an admonition to children learning the alphabet – and still more so to printers, apprentices sorting type – because of the similar appearance of these tailed letters; another that in old-time bar-parlours in the accounts that were scored up for beer 'P' stood for 'pints' and 'Q' for 'quarts', and of course the customer when settling up would find it necessary 'to mind his P's and Q's', or he would pay too much; and yet another – from France – is that in the reign of Louis XIV, when huge wigs were worn, and bows were made with great formality, two things were specially required: a 'step' with the feet, and a low bend of the body. In the latter the wig would be very apt to get deranged, and even to fall off. The caution, therefore, of the French dancing-master to his pupils was, 'Mind your P's (i.e. *pieds*, feet) and Q's (i.e. *queues*, wigs).'

**Pabulum Acherontis.** *See* Acheron.

**Pacific Ocean.** So named by Magellan in 1520, because there he enjoyed calm weather and a placid sea after the stormy and tempestuous passage of the adjoining straits.

***The Pacific.***

Amadeus VIII, Duke of Savoy (1383, 1391–1139; d.1451). He was Pope, as Felix V, from 1440 to 1449.

Frederick III, Emperor of Germany (1415, 1440–93).

Olaf III of Norway (1030–93).

**Pack.** ***Packing a jury.*** Selecting persons on a jury whose verdict may be relied on from proclivity, far more than on evidence.

***To pack up.*** Slang for to take one's departure; to have no more to do with the matter; also to die.

***To send one packing.*** To dismiss him summarily and without ceremony.

**Packstaff.** *See* Pikestaff.

**Pacolet.** A dwarf in the romance of *Valentine and Orson* (*q.v.*). He was in the service of Lady Clerimond, and had a winged horse which carried off Valentine, Orson, and Clerimond from the dungeon of Ferragus to King Pepin's palace, and afterwards bore Valentine to the palace of Alexander, Emperor of Constantinople, his father; hence, a very swift horse, that will carry the rider anywhere, is called a *horse of Pacolet* (Fr.).

> I fear neither shot nor arrow, nor any horse how swift soever he may be, not though he could outstrip the Pegasus of Perseus or of Pacolet, being assured that I can make good my escape.
>
> Rabelais, *Gargantua*, Bk ii, 24

**Pactolus.** ***The golden sands of the Pactolus.*** The Pactolus is a small river in Lydia, Asia Minor, long famous for its gold which, according to legend, was due to Midas (*q.v.*) having bathed there. Its gold was exhausted by the time of Augustus.

**Padding.** The padding of coats and gowns is the wool, etc., put in to make the figure of the wearer more shapely. Figuratively, stuff in books, speeches, etc., to spin them out.

**Paddington Fair.** A public execution. Tyburn, where executions formerly took place, is in the parish of Paddington. Public executions were abolished in England in 1868.

**Paddock.** ***Cold as a paddock.*** A paddock is a toad or frog; and we have the corresponding phrases 'cold as a toad', and 'cold as a frog'.

Here a little child I stand,
Heaving up my either hand;
Cold as Paddocks though they be,
Here I lift them up to Thee,
For a Benison to fall
On our meat and on us all.

Herrick, *Grace for a Child*

**Paddy, Paddywhack.** An Irishman; from Patrick (Ir. *Padraig*). In slang both terms are used for a loss of temper, a rage on a small scale; and the latter also denotes the gristle in roast meat.

**Padre.** The name given by soldiers and sailors to a chaplain. It is Spanish and Portuguese for 'father', and was adopted in the British Army in India from the natives, who had learned the term from the Portuguese.

**Padua** was long supposed by the Scottish to be the chief school of necromancy; hence Scott says of the Earl of Gowrie –

He learned the art that none may name
In Padua, far beyond the sea.

*Lay of the Last Minstrel*

**Paduasoy.** A silk stuff, the French *pou-* or *pout-de-soie*, introduced into England in the 17th century and for 150 years or so called *poudesoy* or *poodesoy*. The material had no connection with Padua, but there was a 'say' or serge manufactured there which was known as *Padua say*, and the name *Paduasoy* is due to confusion with this.

**Paean.** The name, according to Homer, of the physician to the gods. It was used in the phrase *Io Paean* as the invocation in the hymn to Apollo, and later in hymns of thanksgiving to other deities; hence *paean* has come to mean any song of praise or thanksgiving, any shout of triumph or exultation.

Io paeans let us sing,
To physicke's and to poesie's king.

Lyly, *Midas*, v, 3

**Pagan.** The long held idea that this word – which etymologically means a villager, a rustic (Lat. *paganus*) – acquired its present meaning because the Christian Church first established itself in the cities, the village dwellers continuing to be heathen, has been shown by recent research to be incorrect. The name arose from a Roman military colloquialism. *Paganus* (rustic) was the soldier's contemptuous name for a civilian or for an incompetent soldier, and when the early Christians called themselves *miles Christi* (soldiers of Christ) they adopted the soldier-slang, *paganus*, for those who were not 'soldiers of Christ'. *See* the last note but one to ch. xxi of Gibbon's *Decline and Fall*. *Cp.* Heathen.

**Pagoda.** A Buddhist temple or sacred tower in India, China, etc., especially a slender, storied tower built over the relics of a saint. The word is Portuguese, and was formed by them in the 16th century on some now unknown native word which may have been the Persian *but-kadah*, idol-house, or some form of *bhagavat*, holy, divine.

***Pagoda*** was also the name of a gold coin, value about 7*s*., formerly current in Southern India. Hence the phrase:

***To shake the pagoda tree.*** To make money readily in the Far East.

I have granted a pension of 400 pagodas *per annum* to the family of the late Reza Saheb.

Wellington's Dispatches, I, p. 31 (1799)

The amusing pursuit of 'shaking the pagoda-tree' once so popular in our Oriental possessions.

Theodore Hook, *Gilbert Gurney*, I, p. 45

**Paid.** *See* Pay.

**Paint.** ***To paint the lily.*** To indulge in hyperbolical praise, to exaggerate the beauties, good points, etc., of the subject to a very considerable extent.

To gild refined gold, to paint the lily,
To throw a perfume on the violet, …
Is wasteful and ridiculous excess

Shakespeare, *King John*, 4, 2

***To paint the lion.*** A sailor's term, meaning to strip a person naked and then smear the body all over with tar.

***To paint the town red.*** To have a high old time; to cause some disturbance in town by having a noisy spree – especially after one has been abroad for some long while.

**Painter.** The rope by which a ship's boat can be tied to the ship, a buoy, mooring-post, etc. The word is probably an extended sense of the 14th century *peyntour*, the rope which held the anchor to the ship's side (now called the *shank-painter*), which was from Fr. *pendre*, Lat. *pendere*, to hang.

***To cut the painter.*** To sever connection; to send one to the right about in double quick time. In the late 19th century the phrase was much used in reference to a possible severance between her Colonial Empire and Great Britain.

On the contrary, the idea of 'cutting the painter' is not popular.

E. Kinglake, *The Australian at Rome* (1891)

**Painting.** It is said that Apelles, being at a loss to delineate the foam of Alexander's horse, dashed his brush at the picture in despair, and did by accident what he could not accomplish by art.

This story is related of many other artists, and the incident is said actually to have occurred to Michael Angelo when painting the interior of the dome of St Peter's at Rome.

Many legends are told of pictures so painted that the objects depicted have been taken for the things themselves. It is said, for instance, that Apelles painted Alexander's horse so realistically that a living horse mistook it and began to neigh. Velasquez painted a Spanish admiral so true to life, that Philip IV mistook the painting for the man and reproved it severely for not being with the fleet. Zeuxis painted some grapes so well that birds flew at them to peck them. Quentin Matsys painted a fly on a man's leg so inimitably that Mandyn, the artist, tried to brush it off with his handkerchief. Parrhasios, of Ephesus, painted a curtain so well that Zeuxis was deceived by it, and told him to draw it aside that he might see the picture behind it; and Myron, the Greek sculptor, is said to have fashioned a cow so true to nature that a bull mistook it for a living animal.

**Pair Off.** When two members of Parliament, or two opposing electors, agree to absent themselves, and not to vote, so that one neutralises the vote of the other, they are said to *pair off*. In the House of Commons this is usually arranged by the Whips.

**Paix. *La Paix des Dames.*** The treaty concluded at Cambray, in 1529, between François I and Charles V of Germany; so called because it was brought about by Louise of Savoy (mother of the French king) and Margaret, the emperor's aunt.

**Pal.** A good friend, a mate, boon companion. It is a gipsy word meaning a brother or mate.

**Palace** originally meant a dwelling on the Palatine Hill (*see* Palatinate) of Rome, where Augustus and, later, Tiberius and Nero built their mansions. The word was hence transferred to other royal and imperial residences; then to similar buildings, such as *Blenheim Palace*, *Dalkeith Palace*, and to the official residence of a bishop; and finally to a glorified place of amusement as the *Crystal Palace*, the *People's Palace*, and – in irony – to a *Gin palace*.

In parts of Devonshire cellars for fish, storehouses cut in the rock, etc., are called *palaces* or *pallaces*; but this may be from the old word *palis*, a space enclosed by a palisade.

All that cellar and the chambers over the same, and the little pallace and landing-place adjoining the River Dart.

Lease granted by the Corporation of Totnes in 1703

**Paladin.** Properly, an officer of, or one connected with, the palace (*q.v.*), palatine (*q.v.*); usually confined in romance to the Twelve Peers of Charlemagne's court, and hence applied to any renowned hero or knight-errant.

The most noted of Charlemagne's paladins were Allory de l'Estoc; Astolfo; Basin de Genevois; Fierambras or Ferumbras; Florismart; Ganelon, the traitor; Geoffroy, Seigneur de Bordelois, and Geoffroy de Frises; Guerin, Duc de Lorraine; Guillaume de l'Estoc, brother of Allory; Guy de Bourgogne; Hoël, Comte de Nantes; Lambert, Prince de Bruxelles; Malagigi; Nami or Nayme de Bavière; Ogier the Dane; Oliver (*q.v.*); Otuël; Richard, Duc de Normandie; Rinaldo; Riol du Mans; Roland (*q.v.*), otherwise Orlando; Samson, Duc de Bourgogne; and Thiry or Thiery d'Ardaine. Of these, twelve at a time seemed to have formed a special bodyguard to the king.

Who bear the bows were knights in Arthur's reign,
Twelve they, and twelve the peers of Charlemain.

Dryden, *The Flower and the Leaf*

**Palaemon.** In Roman legend, a son of Ino (*see* Leucothea), and originally called Melicertes. Palaemon is the name given to him after he was made a sea-god, and as Portumnus he was the protecting god of harbours. The story is given in Spenser's *Faërie Queene* (IV, xi); in the same poet's *Colin Clout* his name is used for Thomas Churchyard, the poet.

**Palaeography.** *See* Diplomatics.

**Palaeolithic Age, The.** (Gr. *palaios*, old, *lithos*, a stone). The earlier of the two periods into which the Stone Age of Europe is divided (*cp.* Neolithic).

**Palamedes.** In Greek legend, one of the heroes who fought against Troy. He was the son of Nauplios and Clymene, and was the reputed inventor of lighthouses, scales and measures, the discus, dice, etc., and was said to have added four letters to the original alphabet of Cadmus. It was he who detected the assumed madness of Ulysses, in revenge for which the latter encompassed his death. The phrase, *he is quite a Palamedes*, meaning 'an ingenious person', is an allusion to this hero.

In Arthurian romance, *Sir Palamedes* is a Saracen knight who was overcome in single combat by Tristram. Both loved Isolde, the wife of King Mark; and after the lady was given up by the Saracen, Tristram converted him to the Christian faith, and stood his godfather at the font.

Tasso introduces a *Palamedes of Lombardy* in his *Jerusalem Delivered* (III, ii). He joined the crusaders with his brothers, Achilles and Sforza, and was shot by Clorinda with an arrow.

**Palamon and Arcite.** Two young Theban knights of romance whose story (borrowed from Boccaccio's *Le Teseide*) is told by Chaucer in his *Knight's Tale*, by Fletcher and (probably) Shakespeare in *The Two Noble Kinsmen* (1634) and elsewhere. Both were in love with Emilia, sister-in-law to the Duke of Athens, in whose hands they were prisoners. In time they obtained their liberty, and the Duke appointed a tournament, promising Emilia to the victor. Arcite prayed to Mars to grant him victory, Palamon prayed to Venus to grant him Emilia. Arcite won the victory, but, being thrown from his horse, died; and Palamon, though not the winner, won the prize for which he prayed and fought.

**Palatinate.** The province of a *palatine* who originally was an officer of the imperial palace at Rome (*cp.* Palace). This was on the *Palatine Hill*, which was so called from Pales, a pastoral deity, whose festival was celebrated on April 21st, the 'birthday of Rome', to commemorate the day when Romulus, the wolf-child, drew the first furrow at the foot of the hill, and thus laid the foundation of the 'Roma Quadrata', the most ancient part of the city.

In Germany *The Palatinate* was the name of a former very powerful and extensive state on the Rhine, and it is still that of the detached portion of Bavaria to the west of the Rhine bounded by Baden, Alsace, Rhenish Prussia and Hesse.

In England Cheshire and Lancashire are *palatine* counties. *See* County Palatine.

**Pale, The English.** The name given in the 15th century to that part of Ireland which had been colonised in the 12th century by Henry II, viz., the districts of Cork, Dublin, Drogheda Waterford, and Wexford. It was only in these districts the English law prevailed, hence the phrases, *Within the pale*, and *Outside the pale*. By the 16th century the English Pale had so much contracted that it embraced only the district about 20 miles round Dublin.

**Pales.** The Roman god of shepherds and their flocks. *See* Palatinate *above*.

**Palestine Soup.** A humorous name for soup made of Jerusalem artichokes (*q.v.*). This is a good example of blunder begetting blunder.

**Palimpsest** (Gr. *palin*, again, *psestos*, scraped). A parchment on which the original writing has been effaced and something else has been written. When parchment was scarce the scribes used to erase what was written on it and use it again. As sometimes they did not rub it out entirely, many works that would otherwise have been lost have been recovered. Thus Cicero's *De Republica*, which was partially erased to make room for a commentary of St Augustine on the Psalms, has been restored.

The word is also used figuratively; Central Asia, for instance, has been called a palimpsest, because there present barbarism overlies a bygone civilisation, and De Quincey (*Suspiria Profundis*) calls the human brain 'a mighty palimpsest'.

**Palindrome** (Gr. *palin dromo*, to run back again). A word or line which reads backwards and forwards alike, as *Madam*, also *Roma tibi subito motibus ibit amor*. They have also been called *Sotadics*, from their reputed inventor, Sotades, a scurrilous Greek poet of the 3rd century BC

Probably the longest palindrome in English is –
Dog as a devil deified
Deified lived as a god –

and others well known are Napoleon's reputed saying –

Able was I ere I saw Elba *and*
Lewd did I live, evil did I dwel.

The following Greek palindrome is very celebrated:

ΝΙΨΟΝΑΝΟΜΗΜΑΤΑΜΗΜΟΝΑΝΟΨΙΝ

i.e., wash my transgressions, not only my face. It appears as the legend round many fonts, notably that in the basilica of St Sophia, Constantinople, those at St Stephen d'Egres, Paris, and St Menin's Abbey, Orleans; and, in England, round the fonts of St Martin's, Ludgate Hill, St Mary's, Nottingham, at Dulwich College; and in churches at Worlingsworth (Suffolk), Harlow (Essex), Knapton (Norfolk), and Hadleigh (Suffolk).

**Palinode** (Gr. a singing again). A song or discourse recanting a previous one; such as that of Stesichorus to Helen after he had been struck blind for singing evil of her, or Horace's *Ode* (Bk I, xvi), which ends –

... nunc ego mitibus
Mutare quaero tristia, dum mihi
fias recantatis amica
obprobriis animumque reddas.

Watts has a palinode in which he retracts the praise bestowed upon Queen Anne. In the first part of her reign he wrote a laudatory poem to the queen, but he says that the latter part deluded his hopes and proved him a false prophet.

**Palinurus** (in English *Palinure*). Any pilot, especially a careless one; from the steersman of Aeneas (Virgil's *Aeneid*), who went to sleep at the helm and fell overboard and was drowned.

Lost was the nation's sense, nor could be found,
While the long solemn unison went round:
Wide and more wide, it spread o'er all the realm;
Even Palinurus nodded at the helm.

Pope, *Dunciad*, iv, 611

**Palissy Ware.** Dishes and similar articles of pottery covered with models of fish, reptiles, shells, flowers, leaves, etc., carefully coloured and enamelled in high relief; so called after Bernard Palissy (1510–89), the famous French potter and enameller.

**Pall.** The covering thrown over a coffin, is the Latin *pallium*, a square piece of cloth used by the Romans to throw over their shoulders, or to cover them in bed; hence a coverlet.

*Pall*, the long sweeping robe worn by sovereigns at their coronation, by the Pope, archbishops, etc., is the Roman *palla*, which was only worn by princes and women of honest fame. This differed greatly from the *pallium*, which was worn by freemen and slaves, soldiers, and philosophers.

Sometimes let gorgeous Tragedy
In sceptred pall come sweeping by.

Milton, *Il Penseroso*

***Pall-bearers.*** The custom of appointing men of mark for pall-bearers came to us from the Romans. Julius Caesar had magistrates for his pall-bearers; Augustus Caesar had senators; Germanicus had tribunes and centurions; Aemilis L. Paulus had the chief men of Macedonia who happened to be at Rome at that time; but the poor were carried on a plain bier on men's shoulders.

**Pall Mall.** This fine thoroughfare in the West End of London has been so called since the early 18th century because it is the place where formerly the game of Palle-malle (Ital. *palla*, ball, *maglia*, mallet) was played. When first built, about 1690, it was named Catherine Street, in honour of Catherine of Braganza. 'Pale malle', says Cotgrave –

is a game wherein a round boxball is struck with a mallet through a high arch of iron. He that can do this most frequently wins.

It was fashionable in the reign of Charles II, and the walk called the Mall in St James's Park was appropriated to it for the king and his court.

In town let me live then, in town let me die,
For in truth I can't relish the country, not I.
If one must have a villa in summer to dwell,
O, give me the sweet shady side of Pall Mall!

Chas Morris (*d.* 1832), *The Contrast*

**Palladium.** In classical story, the colossal wooden statue of Pallas in the citadel of Troy, which was said to have fallen from heaven, and on the preservation of which it was believed that the safety of the city depended. It was carried away by the Greeks, and the city burnt to the ground; and later it was said to have been taken to Rome.

Hence, the word is now figuratively applied to anything on which the safety of a people, etc. is supposed to depend, as the great stone of Scone (*q.v.*), now forming part of the British Coronation throne.

The liberty of the press is the palladium of all the civil, political, and religious rights of an English man. *Letters of Junius, Dedication*

*See also* Abaton: Ancile: Eden Hall.

The rare metallic element found associated with platinum and gold was named *palladium* by its discoverer, Wollaston (1803) from the newly discovered asteroid, *Pallas*; and the same name has been given to a place of amusement in London, apparently through the mistaken idea that the ancient Palladium, like the Colosseum (*q.v.*), was something akin to a circus.

**Pallas.** A name of Minerva (*q.v.*), sometimes called *Pallas Minerva*. According to fable, Pallas was one of the Titans, and was killed by Minerva, who flayed him, and used his skin for armour. More likely the word is either from *pallo*, to brandish, the compound implying 'Minerva who brandishes the spear', or simply *pallax*, virgin.

**Pallium.** The square woollen cloak worn by the men in ancient Greece, corresponding to the Roman *toga*. Hence the Romans called themselves *gens togata*, and the Greeks *gens palliata*.

At the present time the scarf-like vestment of white wool with red crosses, worn by the Pope and certain metropolitans and archbishops, is called the *pallium*.

**Palm.** The well known tropical and subtropical tree gets its name from the Latin *palma*, which was a transferred use of *palma*, the palm of the hand, applied to the tree because of the spread-hand or open fan-like appearance of the fronds. The English *palm* (of the hand) represents M.E. (and Fr.) *paume*.

The palm tree is said to grow faster for being weighed down. Hence it is the symbol of resolution overcoming calamity. It is believed by Orientals to have sprung from the residue of the clay of which Adam was formed.

***An itching palm.*** A hand ready to receive bribes. The old superstition is that if your palm itches you are going to receive money.

> Let me tell you, Cassius, you yourself
> Are much condemned to have an itching palm.
> Shakespeare, *Julius Caesar*, 4, 3

***Palm oil.*** Bribes, or rather money for bribes, fees, etc.

> In Ireland the machinery of a political movement will not work unless there is plenty of palm-oil to prevent friction.
> *Irish Seditions from 1792 to 1880*, p. 39

> The rich may escape with whole skins, but those without 'palm-oil' have scant mercy.
> *Nineteenth Century*, Aug., 1892, p. 312

***Palm Sunday.*** The Sunday next before Easter. So called in memory of Christ's triumphant entry into Jerusalem, when the multitude strewed the way with palm branches and leaves. (John 12.)

***Sad Palm Sunday.*** March 29th, 1463, the day of the battle of Towton, the most fatal of all the battles in the War of the Roses. It is said that over 37,000 Englishmen were slain.

> Whose banks received the blood of many thousand men,
> On 'Sad Palm Sunday' slain, that Towton field we call ...
> The bloodiest field betwixt the White Rose and the Red.
> Drayton, *Polyolbion*, xxviii

***Palmy days.*** Prosperous or happy days, as those were to a victorious gladiator when he went to receive the palm branch as the reward of his prowess.

***To bear the palm.*** To be the best. The allusion is to the Roman custom of giving the victorious gladiator a branch of the palm tree.

***To palm off.*** To pass off fraudulently. The allusion is to jugglers, who conceal in the palm of their hand what they pretend to dispose of in some other way.

> You may palm upon us new for old. Dryden

**Palmam qui meruit ferat** (Let him bear the palm who has deserved it) was Nelson's motto, and is that of the Royal Naval College. The line conies from Jortin's *Lusus Poetici* (1748), *Ad ventos*, stanza iv:

> Et nobis faciles parcite et hostibus,
> Concurrant pariter cum ratibus rates:
> Spectent numina ponti, et
> Palmam qui meruit, ferat.

**Palmer.** A pilgrim to the Holy Land who was privileged to carry a palm staff, and who spent all his days in visiting holy shrines, living on charity.

> His sandals were with travel tore,
> Staff, budget, bottle, scrip he wore;
> The faded palm-branch in his hand
> Showed pilgrim from the Holy Land.
> Scott, *Marmion*, 1, 27

At the dedication of palmers prayers and psalms were said over them as they lay prostrate before the altar; they were sprinkled with holy water, and received a consecrated palm branch.

**Palmerin.** The hero of a number of 16th century Spanish romances of chivalry, on the lines of *Amadis of Gaul*. The most famous are *Palmerin de Oliva*, and *Palmerin of England*. Southey published an abridged translation of the latter.

**Palmy.** *See* Palm.

**Paludament.** A distinctive mantle worn by a Roman general in the time of war. This was the 'scarlet robe' in which Christ was invested. (Matt. 27:28.)

> Immediately came 'sweeping by', in gorgeous paludaments, Paullus or Marius.
> De Quincey, *Confessions of an English Opium-eater*

> They flung on him an old scarlet paludamentum – some cast-off war-cloak with its purple laticlave from the Praetorian wardrobe.
> Farrar, *Life of Christ*, ch. lx

**Pam.** The knave of clubs in certain card-games, also the name of a card-game; short for *Pamphile*, French for the knave of clubs.

This word is sometimes given as an instance of Johnson's weakness in etymology. He says it is 'probably from *palm*, victory; as *trump* from *triumph*'.

**Pampas.** Treeless plains, some 2,000 miles long and from 300 to 500 broad, in South America. They cover an area of 750,000 square miles. It is the Spanish form of Peruvian *bamba*, meaning *flats* or *plains*.

**Pampero, The.** A dry, north-west wind that blows in the summer season from the Andes across the pampas to the sea-coast.

**Pamphlet.** A small unbound book of a few sheets stitched together, usually on some subject of merely temporary interest; so called from O.Fr. *Pamphilet*, the name of a 12th century erotic Latin poem which was very popular in the Middle Ages.

> This word has been the subject of much etymological guesswork. One 'authority' derived it from a supposed Pamphila, a Greek lady, whose chief work was said to be a commonplace book of anecdotes, epitomes, notes, etc.; Johnson suggested *par-un-filet* (held 'by a thread') – i.e. stitched, but not bound, while another 'derivation' is *paginae filatae* (pages tacked together).

**Pamphyle.** A sorceress who converted herself into an owl (*Apuleius*). There was another Pamphyle, the daughter of Apollo, who first taught women to embroider with silk.

> In one very remote village lives the sorceress Pamphyle, who turns her neighbours into various animals … Lucius, peeping … thro' a chink in the door, [saw] the old witch transform herself into an owl.
>
> Pater, *Marius the Epicurean*, ch. v

**Pan** (Gr. all, everything). The god of pastures, forests, flocks, and herds of *Greek mythology*; also the personification of deity displayed in creation and pervading all things. He is represented with the lower part of a goat, because of the asperity of the earth, and the upper part of a man, because ether is the 'hegemonic of the world'; his lustful nature symbolised the spermatic principle of the world; the leopard's skin that he wore indicated the immense variety of created things; and his character of 'blameless' symbolised that wisdom which governs the world.

> Universal Pan,
> Knit with the Graces and the Hours in dance,
> Led on the eternal spring.
>
> Milton, *Paradise Lost*, iv, 266

Legend has it that at the time of the Crucifixion, just when the veil of the Temple was rent in twain, a cry swept across the ocean in the hearing of many, 'Great Pan is Dead', and that at the same time the responses of the oracles ceased for ever. *See* Mrs Browning's poem of this name.

**Panacea** (Gr. all-healing). A universal cure. Panacea was the daughter of Aesculapius (god of medicine), and of course the medicine that cures is the daughter or child of the healing art.

In the Middle Ages the search for the panacea was one of the alchemists' self-imposed tasks; and fable tells of many panaceas, such as the Promethean unguent which rendered the body invulnerable, Aladdin's ring, the balsam of Fierabras (*q.v.*), and Prince Ahmed's apple (*see* Apple). *Cp. also* Achilles' Spear, Medea's Kettle, Reynard's Ring, etc.

**Pancake.** A thin, flat 'cake' made in a frying-pan. It was originally intended to be eaten after dinner to stay the stomachs of those who went to be shriven; hence, Shrove Tuesday (*q.v*), a special day for these, came to be called *Pancake Day*, and the Shrove-bell the *Pancake Bell*,

**Pancras, St.** One of the patron saints of children (*cp.* Nicholas), martyred in the Diocletian persecution (304) at Rome at the age of 13. His day is May 12th, and he is usually represented as a boy, with a sword in one hand and a palm-branch in the other.

The first church to be consecrated in England (by St Augustine, at Canterbury) was dedicated to St Pancras.

**Pandarus.** A Lycian leader and ally of the Trojans in Greek legend. Owing to his later connection with the story of Troilus and Cressida, he was taken over by the romance writers of the Middle Ages as a procurer. *See* Pander.

**Pandects of Justinian** (Gr. *pandektes*, all receiver or encloser). A compendium of Roman civil law made in the 6th century by the order of the Emperor Justinian. It comprises 50 books, and contains the decisions to which Justinian gave the force of law. The story that the copy now in the Laurentian Library at Florence was found at Amalfi (1137), and gave a spur to the study of civil law which changed the whole literary and legal aspect of Europe, is not now credited.

**Pandemonium** (Gr. all the demons). A wild, unrestrained uproar, a tumultuous assembly, a regular row. The word was first used by Milton as the name of the principal city in Hell. It was formed on the analogy of *Pantheon* (*q.v.*).

> The rest were all
> Far to the inland retired, about the walls
> Of Pandemonium city and proud seat
> Of Lucifer.
>
> *Paradise Lost*, x, 424 (*see also* i, 756)

**Pander.** ***To pander to one's vices*** is to act as an agent to them, and such an agent is termed a pander from *Pandarus*, who procures for Troilus (*q.v.*) the love and graces of Cressida. In *Much Ado about Nothing* it is said that Troilus was 'the first employer of pandars' (5, 2).

Let all pitiful goers-between be called to the world's end after my name, call them all 'Pandars'. Let all constant men be 'Troiluses', all false women be 'Cressids', and all brokers-between, 'Pandars'. Say, Amen.

Shakespeare, *Troilus and Cressida*, 3, 2

**Pandora's Box.** A present which seems valuable, but which is in reality a curse; like that of Midas (*q.v.*), who found his very food became gold, and so uneatable.

Prometheus made an image and stole fire from heaven to endow it with life. In revenge, Jupiter told Vulcan to make the first woman, who was named Pandora (i.e. the All-gifted), because each of the gods gave her some power which was to bring about the ruin of man. Jupiter gave her a box which she was to present to him who married her. Prometheus distrusted Jove and his gifts, but Epimetheus, his brother, married the beautiful Pandora, and – against advice – accepted the gift of the god. Immediately he opened the box all the evils that flesh is heir to flew forth, and have ever since continued to afflict the world. According to some accounts the last thing that flew out was Hope; but others say that Hope alone remained.

**Pangloss, Dr** (Gr. all tongues). The pedantic old tutor to the hero in Voltaire's *Candide, ou l'Optimisme* (1759). His great point was his incurable and misleading optimism; it did him no good and brought him all sorts of misfortune, but to the end he reiterated 'all is for the best in this best of all possible worlds'.

**Panhandle.** In the United States a narrow strip of territory belonging to one State which runs between two others, such as the Texas Panhandle, the Panhandle of Idaho, etc. West Virginia is known as *the Panhandle State.* The allusion is obvious.

**Panic.** The word comes from the god Pan (*q.v.*), because sounds heard by night in the mountains and valleys, which gave rise to sudden and groundless fear, were attributed to him. There are various legends accounting for the name; one is that on one occasion Bacchus, in his Indian expeditions, was opposed by an army far superior to his own, and Pan advised him to command all his men at dead of night to raise a simultaneous shout. This was rolled from mountain to mountain by innumerable echoes, and the Indians, thinking they were surrounded on all sides, took to sudden flight. *Cp.* Judges 7:18-21.

**Panjandrum.** ***The Grand Panjandrum***, 'with the little red button a-top'. *See* Button. A village boss, who imagines himself the 'Magnus Apollo' of his neighbours. The word occurs in Foote's farrago of nonsense which he composed to test old Macklin, who said he had brought his memory to such perfection that he could remember anything by reading it over once. There is more than one version of the test passage; the following is as well authenticated as any:

So she went into the garden to cut a cabbage-leaf to make an apple-pie, and at the same time a great she-bear came running up the street and popped its head into the shop. 'What! no soap?' So he died, and she – very imprudently – married the barber. And there were present the Picninnies, the Joblillies, the Garyulies, and the Grand Panjandrum, himself with the little red button a-top, and they all fell to playing the game of catch-as-catch-can till the gunpowder ran out at the heels of their boots.

It is said that Macklin was so indignant at this nonsense that he refused to repeat a word of it.

**Panope.** *See* Nereids.

**Pantables.** *See* Pantofles.

**Pantagruel.** The principal character in Rabelais' great satire *The History of Gargantua and Pantagruel* (the first part published in 1535, the last posthumously in 1564), King of the Dipsodes, son of Gargantua (*q.v.*), and by some identified with Henri II of France. He was the last of the giants, and Rabelais says he got his name from the Greek *Panta*, all, and Arab. *Gruel*, thirsty, because he was born during the drought which lasted thirty and six months, three weeks, four days, thirteen hours, and a little more, in that year of grace noted for having 'three Thursdays in one week'. He was covered with hair at birth, 'like a young bear', and was so strong that though he was chained in his cradle with four great iron chains, like those used in ships of the largest size, he stamped out the bottom, which was made of weavers' beams, and, when loosed by the servants, broke his bonds into five hundred thousand pieces with one blow of his infant fist. When he grew to manhood he knew all languages, all sciences, and all knowledge of every sort, out-Solomoning Solomon in wisdom. His immortal achievement was his voyage from Utopia in quest of the 'oracle of the Holy Bottle' (*q.v.*).

Wouldst thou not issue forth …
To see the third part in this earthy cell
Of the brave acts of good Pantagruel.

Rabelais, *To the Spirit of the Queen of Navarre*

**Pantagruelion.** The name given by Rabelais to hemp, of which the hangman's rope is made, 'because Pantagruel was the inventor of a certain use which it serves for, exceeding hateful to felons, unto whom it is more hurtful than strangle-weed to flax'.

> The figure and shape of the leaves are not much different from those of the ash tree or the agrimony, the herb itself being so like the Eupatorio that many herbalists have called it the 'Domestic Eupatorio', and the Eupatorio the 'Wild Pantagruelion'. *Pantagruel*, iii, 49

**Pantagruelism.** Coarse and boisterous buffoonery and humour, especially with a serious purpose – like that for which Pantagruel was famous.

> Pantagruelism, or, if you like, Rabelaism, did not, during the sixteenth century, make much progress beyond the limits of France.
> Thos Wright, *History of Caricature*, etc. (1865)

**Pantaloon.** The breeches, trousers, or under-drawers of various kinds (now often called *pants*) get their name from Pantaloon, a Venetian character in 16th century Italian comedy, a lean and foolish old man dressed in loose kind of trousers and slippers. His name is said to have come from San Pantaleone (a patron saint of physicians and very popular in Venice), and he was adopted by the later harlequinades and pantomimes as the butt of the clown's jokes.

> The sixth age shifts
> Into the lean and slipper'd pantaloon,
> With spectacles on nose and pouch on side,
> His youthful hose well sav'd, a world too wide
> For his shrunk shank; and his big manly voice,
> Turning again toward childish treble, pipes
> And whistles in his sound.
> Shakespeare, *As You Like It*, 2, 7

***Playing Pantaloon.*** Playing second fiddle; being the cat's-paw of another; servilely imitating.

**Pantechnicon** (Gr. belonging to all the arts). The name was originally coined for a bazaar for the sale of artistic work built about 1830 in Motcomb Street, Belgrave Square; as this was unsuccessful the building was converted into a warehouse for storing furniture, and the name retained. It is now often used in place of *pantechnicon van*, a furniture removing van.

**Panthea.** In classical history the wife of Abradatus, King of Susa. He joined the Assyrians against Cyrus, and she was taken captive. Cyrus refused to visit her, that he might not be tempted by her beauty, and Abradatus, charmed by this restraint, joined his party. Shortly after he was slain in battle, and Panthea put an end to her life, falling on the body of her husband.

**Pantheism.** The doctrine that God is everything and everything is God; a monistic theory elaborated by Spinoza, who, by his doctrine of the Infinite Substance, sought to overcome the opposition between mind and matter, body and soul.

**Pantheon.** A temple dedicated to all the gods (Gr. *pan.* all, *theos*, god); specifically, that erected at Rome by Agrippa, son-in-law to Augustus. It is circular, nearly 150 ft in diameter, and of the same total height; since the early 7th century, as Santa Maria Rotunda, it has been used as a Christian Church.

The Pantheon at Paris was originally the church of St Geneviève, built by Louis XV and finished 1790. The following year the Convention gave it its present name, and set it apart as the shrine of those Frenchmen whom their country wished to honour.

**Panther** (earlier **Panthera**). In mediaeval times this animal was supposed to be friendly to all beasts except the dragon, and to attract them by a peculiarly sweet odour it exhaled. Swinburne, in *Laus Veneris*, makes use of this tradition, but gives it a rather different significance:

> As one who hidden in deep sedge and reeds
> Smells the rare scent made where a panther feeds,
> And tracking ever slotwise the warm smell
> Is snapped upon by the warm mouth and bleeds,
> His head far down the hot sweet mouth of her –
> So one tracks love, whose breath is deadlier.

In the old *Physiologus* the panther was the type of Christ, but later, when the savage nature of the beast was more widely known, it became symbolical of evil and hypocritical flattery; hence Lyly's comparison (in *Euphues, the Anatomy of Wit*) of the beauty of women to

> a delicate bait with a deadly hook, a sweet panther with a devouring paunch, a sour poison in a silver pot.

The mediaeval idea is reflected in (or perhaps arose from) the name, which is probably of Oriental origin but was taken as from Gr. *panther*, all beasts.

In *Reynard the Fox* (*q.v.*) Reynard affirms that he sent the queen a comb made of panthera bone, 'more lustrous than the rainbow, more odoriferous than any perfume, a charm against every ill, and a universal panacea'.

***The Spotted Panther*** in Dryden's *Hind and Panther* (1687) typifies the Church of England, as being full of the spots of error; whereas the Church of Rome is faultless as the milk-white hind.

The panther, sure the noblest next the hind,
And fairest creature of the spotted kind;
Oh, could her inborn stains be washed away
She were too good to be a beast of prey. Pt i

**Pantile.** A roofing-tile curved transversely to an ogee shape. In the 18th century as Dissenters' chapels were – like cottages – frequently roofed with these, such meeting-houses were sometimes called *pantile-shops*, and the word was used in the sense of dissenting. Mrs Centlivre, in *A Gotham Election* (1715), contrasts the *pantile crew* with a good churchman.

The Parade at Tunbridge Wells, known as the *Pantiles*, was so called because the name was erroneously applied in the 18th century to such flat Dutch tiles as those with which it is paved.

**Pantisocracy** (Gr. all of equal power). The name given by Coleridge to the communistic, Utopian society that he, with Southey, George Burnett, and others intended (about 1794) to form on the banks of the Susquehannah River. The scheme never came to anything, owing chiefly to the absence of funds.

All are not moralists, like Southey, when
He prated to the world of 'Pantisocrasy'.
Byron, *Don Juan*, iii, 93

**Pantofles,** or **Pantables.** Slippers, especially loose ones like those worn by Orientals.

***To stand upon one's pantofles.*** To stand on one's dignity, get on the high horse. It was a common proverbial phrase from the 16th to the 18th century.

I note that for the most part they stand so on their pantofles that they be secure of perils, obstinate in their own opinions ... ready to shake off their old acquaintance without cause, and to condemn them without colour.
Lyly, *Euphues, the Anatomy of Wit* (1578)

Puttenham, in his *Arte of English Poesie* (1589), shows how the phrase probably arose. 'The actor', he says, 'did walk upon those high-corked shoes or pantofles, which now they call in Spain and Italy *Shoppini*.' *Cp*. Chopine.

**Pantomime,** according to etymology, should be *all* dumb show, but in modern practice it is partly dumb show and partly grotesque speaking. The principal characters are Harlequin (*q.v.*) and Columbine, who never speak, and the Clown and Pantaloon, who keep up a constant fire of fun.

**Panurge** (Gr. *pan*, all, *ergos*, worker, the 'all-doer', i.e. the rogue, he who will 'do anything or anyone'). The roguish companion of Pantagruel, and one of the principal characters in Rabelais' satire. He was a desperate rake, was always in debt, had a dodge for every scheme, knew everything and something more, was a boon companion of the mirthfullest temper and most licentious bias; but was timid of danger, and a desperate coward. The third, fourth, and fifth (last) books of the satire are taken up with the adventures of Panurge, and the rest in their endeavour to find by divination whether or not he should marry. Besides Pantagruel, Panurge consulted lots, dreams, a sibyl, a deaf and dumb man, the old poet Rominagrobis, the chiromancer Herr Trippa, the theologian, Hippothadée, the physician Rondibilis, the philosopher Trouillogan, the court fool Triboulet, and, lastly, the Oracle of the Holy Bottle; and to every one of the very obscure answers Panurge received, whether it seemed to point to 'Yes' or to 'No', he invariably found insuperable objections.

Some 'commentators' on Rabelais have identified Panurge with Calvin, others with Cardinal Lorraine; and this part of the satire seems to be an echo of the great Reformation controversy on the celibacy of the clergy.

The main idea in Panurge is the absence of morality in the wide Aristotelian sense, with the presence of almost all other good qualities.
Saintsbury, *Hist. of French Literature*

**Pap.** *He gives pap with a hatchet.* He does or says a kind thing in a very brusque and ungracious manner. One of the scurrilous tracts against Martin Marprelate (*see* Marprelate), published in 1589, was entitled *Pap with a Hatchet*.

**Paper.** So called from the *papyrus* the giant water reed from which the Egyptians manufactured a material for writing on.

***Not worth the paper it's written on.*** Said of an utterly worthless statement, promise, etc.

***Paper credit.*** Credit allowed on the score of bills, promissory notes, etc., that show that money is due to the borrower.

***Paper money*** or ***currency.*** Bank notes as opposed to coin, or bills used as currency. Sometimes postal orders and post office money-orders are included in the term; but as these are 'not negotiable' it is incorrect.

***Paper profits.*** Hypothetical profits shown on a company's prospectus, etc.

***The Paper King.*** John Law, the projector of the Mississippi Scheme (*q.v.*).

***To paper a house.*** In theatrical phraseology, to fill the theatre with 'deadheads', or non-paying spectators, admitted by paper orders.

***To send in*** (or ***to receive***) ***one's papers.*** To resign one's appointment, commission, etc., *or* to receive one's dismissal.

**Paphian.** Relating to Venus, or rather to Paphos, a city of Cyprus, where Venus was worshipped; a Cyprian; a prostitute.

**Papimany.** In Rabelais' satire (ix, xlv) the country of the Papimanes, i.e. those who are madly devoted to, or have a *mania* for, the Pope; hence, any priest-ridden country.

**Papyrus.** *See* Paper. The written scrolls of the ancient Egyptians are called *papyri*, because they were written on this.

**Par** (Lat., equal). Stock *at par* means that it is to be bought at the price it represents. Thus, £100 stock if quoted at £105 would be £5 *above par*; if at £95, it would be £5 *below par*. A person in low spirits or ill health is said to be 'below par'.

In journalism *a par* is a paragraph, a note of a few lines on a subject of topical interest.

**Paraclete.** The advocate; one *called to* aid or support another; from the Greek *para-kalein*, to call to. The word is used as a title of the Holy Ghost, the Comforter.

> O source of uncreated Light,
> The Father's promised Paraclete!
>
> Dryden, *Veni, Creator Spiritus*

**Paradise.** The Greeks borrowed this word from the Persians, among whom it denoted the enclosed and extensive parks and pleasure grounds of the Persian kings. The Septuagint translators adopted it for the garden of Eden, and in the New Testament and by early Christian writers it was applied to Heaven, the abode of the blessed dead.

> An old word, 'paradise', which the Hebrews had borrowed from the Persians, and which at first designated the 'parks of the Achaemenidae'.
>
> Renan, *Life of Jesus*, xi

***A fool's paradise.*** *See* Fool.

***Paradise and the Peri.*** *See* Peri.

***Paradise Lost.*** Milton's epic poem – the greatest epic in any modern language – was published in 12 books in 1667. It tells the story –

> Of Man's first disobedience and the fruit
> Of that forbidden tree whose mortal taste
> Brought death into the World, and all our woe
> With loss of Eden.

Satan rouses the panic-stricken host of fallen angels with tidings of a rumour current in Heaven of a new world about to be created. He calls a council to deliberate what should be done, and they agree to send him to search for this new world. Satan, passing the gulf between Hell and Heaven and the limbo of Vanity, enters the orb of the Sun (disguised as an angel), and, having obtained the information, goes to Paradise in the form of a cormorant. Seating himself on the Tree of Life, he overhears Adam and Eve talking about the prohibition made by God, and at once resolves upon the nature of his attack. Gabriel sends two angels to watch over the bower of Paradise, and Satan flees. Raphael is sent to warn Adam of his danger, and tells him the story of Satan's revolt and expulsion from Heaven, and why and how this world was made. After a time Satan returns to Paradise in the form of a mist, and, entering the serpent, induces Eve to eat of the forbidden fruit. Adam eats 'that he may perish with the woman whom he loved'. Satan returns to Hell to tell his triumph, and Michael is sent to lead the guilty pair out of the Garden.

Milton borrowed largely from the epic of Du Bartas (1544–90) entitled *The Week of Creation*, which was translated into almost every European language; and he was indebted to St Avitus (d.523), who wrote in Latin hexameters *The Creation*, *The Fall*, and *The Expulsion from Paradise*, for his description of Paradise (Bk i), of Satan (Bk ii), and other parts.

In 1671 *Paradise Regained* (in four books), written by Milton on the suggestion of his Quaker friend, Thomas Ellwood, was published. The subject is the Temptation. Eve, being tempted, fell, and lost Paradise; Jesus, being tempted, resisted, and regained Paradise.

***Paradise shoots.*** The lign aloe; said to be the only plant descended to us from the Garden of Eden. When Adam left Paradise he took a shoot of this tree, and from it the lign aloes have been propagated.

***The Earthly Paradise.*** In mediaeval times it was a popular belief that paradise, a land – or island – where everything was beautiful and restful, and where death and decay were unknown, still existed somewhere on earth and was to be found for the searching. It was usually located far away to the east; Cosmas (7th cent.) placed it beyond the ocean east of China, in 9th century maps it is shown in China itself, and the fictitious letter of Prester John to the Emperor Emmanuel Comnenus states that it was within three days' journey of his own territory – a 'fact' that is corroborated by Mandeville. The Hereford map (13th cent.) shows it as a circular island near India, from which it is separated not only by the sea, but also by a battlemented wall. *Cp.* Brandan, St.

The *Prologue* to William Morris's collection of narrative poems with this title (1868-71) tells how a party of adventurers left a Scandinavian port during a pestilence to search for the Earthly Paradise. After many misadventures the remnant of the band discovered it, were hospitably received, and regaled their hosts each month with versified renderings of old-world stories from classical and Scandinavian legend.

***The Paradise of Fools.*** *See* Limbus Fatuorum.

**Parallel. *None but himself can be his parallel.*** Wholly without a peer; *Quaeris Alcidae parem; nemo proximus nec secundus.* The line occurs in Lewis Theobald's *The Double Falsehood* (1727), iii, 1, a play which Theobald tried to palm off on the literary world as by Shakespeare. There are many similar sentences; for example:

Nemo est, nisi ipse.

Seneca, *Hercules Furens*, i, 84

And but herself admits no parallel.

Massinger, *Duke of Millaine*, iii, 4 (1662)

None but himself can parallel.

*Anagram on John Lilburn* (1658)

**Paraphernalia.** Literally, all that a woman can claim at the death of her husband beyond her jointure (Gr. *para*, beside, *pherne*, dowry). In the Roman law her paraphernalia included the furniture of her chamber, her wearing apparel, her jewels, etc. Hence personal attire, fittings generally, anything for show or decoration.

**Parashurama.** *See* Avatar.

**Parasite** (Gr. *para sitos*, eating at another's cost). A plant or animal that lives on another; hence a hanger-on, one who fawns and flatters for the sake of what he can get out of it – a 'sponger'.

**Parbleu!** *See* Morbleu!

**Parcae** (Lat. *pars*, a lot). The Fates (*see* Fate) – Clotho, Lachesis, and Atropos.

**Parchment.** So called from Pergamum (now Bergamo), in Mysia, Asia Minor, where it was used for the purpose of writing when Ptolemy prohibited the exportation of papyrus from Egypt.

**Pardon Bell.** The Angelus bell. So called because of the indulgence once given for reciting certain prayers forming the Angelus (*q.v.*).

**Pardoner's Tale,** in Chaucer's *Canterbury Tales*, is that of *Death and the Rioters*, which comes from an Oriental source through the Italian *Cento Novelle Antiche*.

Three rioters in a tavern agreed to hunt down Death and kill him. As they went their way they met an old man, who told them that he had just left him sitting under a tree in the lane close by. Off posted the three rioters, but when they came to the tree they found a great treasure, which they agreed to divide equally. They cast lots which was to carry it home, and the lot fell to the youngest, who was sent to the village to buy food and wine. While he was gone the two who were left agreed to kill him, and so increase their share; but the third bought poison to put into the wine, in order to kill his two *confrères*. On his return with his stores, the two set upon him and slew him, then sat down to drink and be merry together; but, the wine being poisoned, all the three rioters found Death under the tree as the old man had said.

***The Pardoner's mitten.*** Whoever put this mitten on would be sure to thrive in all things.

He that his hondë put in this metayn,
He shal have multiplying of his grayn,
Whan he hath sowen, be it whete or otes,
So that ye offre pans [pence] or ellës grootes.

Chaucer, *Prologue to The Pardoner's Tale*

**Pari passu.** At the same time; in equal degrees; two or more schemes carried on at once and driven forward with equal energy, are said to be carried on *pari passu*, which is Latin for *equal strides* or the equally measured pace of persons marching together.

The cooling effects of surrounding matter go on nearly *pari passu* with the heating.

Grove, *Correlation of Physical Forces*, p. 64

**Pariah.** A member of the lowest caste of Hindu in Southern India, from a native word meaning 'a drummer', because it was these who beat the drums at certain festivals.

Europeans often extend the term to those of no caste at all, hence it is applied to outcasts generally, the lowest of the low.

There was no worst
Of degradation spared Fifine; ordained from first
To last, in body and soul, for one life-long debauch,
The Pariah of the North, the European Nautch!

Browning, *Fifine at the Fair*, xxxi

**Parian Chronicle.** One of the Arundelian Marbles (*q.v.*), found in the island of Paros, and bearing an inscription which contains a chronological register of the chief events in the mythology and history of ancient Greece during a series of 1,318 years, beginning with the reign of Cecrops (about 1580 BC), and ending with the archonship of Diognetus (264 BC), of which nearly the last hundred years is now lost.

**Paridell.** A libertine in Spenser's *Faërie Queene* (III, viii, ix, x, IV, ii, v, ix, etc.) typifying the Earl of Westmoreland. Pope uses the name for a young gentleman that travels about and seeks adventure, because he is young, rich, and at leisure.

> Thee, too, my Paridel, she marked thee there,
> Stretched on the rack of a too-easy chair,
> And heard thy everlasting yawn confess
> The pains and penalties of idleness.
>
> *Dunciad*, iv, 341

**Paris.** In Greek legend, the son of Priam, King of Troy, and Hecuba; and through his abduction of Helen (*q.v.*) the cause of the siege of Troy. Before his birth Hecuba dreamed that she was to bring forth a firebrand, and, as this was interpreted to mean that the unborn child would bring destruction to his house, the infant Paris was exposed on Mount Ida. He was, however, brought up by a shepherd, and grew to perfection of beautiful manhood. When the golden Apple of Discord (*see under* Apple) was thrown on the table of the gods it was Paris who had to judge between the rival claims of Hera (Juno), Aphrodite (Venus), and Athene (Minerva); each goddess offered him bribes – the first power, the second the most beautiful of women, and the third martial glory. He awarded the Apple and the title of 'Fairest' to Aphrodite, who in return assisted him to carry off Helen, for whom he deserted his wife, Oenone, daughter of the river-god, Cebren. At Troy Paris earned the contempt of all by his cowardice, and he was fatally wounded with a poisoned arrow by Philoctetes at the taking of the city.

**Paris,** the capital of France. So called from the ancient Celtic tribe, the *Parisii*, whose capital – the modern *Paris* – was known to the Romans as *Lutetia Parisiorum*, the mud-town of the Parisii. *See* Lutetia. Rabelais gives a whimsical derivation of the name. He tells (I, xvii) how Gargantua played a disgusting practical joke on the Parisians who came to stare at him, and the men said it was a sport 'par ris' (to be laughed at); wherefore the city was called Par-'is.

The heraldic device of the city of Paris is a ship. As Sauval says, '*L'ile de la cité est faite comme un grand navire enfoncé dans la vase, et échoué au fil de l'eau vers le milieu de la Seine.*' This form of a ship struck the heraldic authorities, who, in the latter half of the Middle Ages, emblazoned it in the shield of the city.

***Monsieur de Paris.*** The public executioner of Paris.

***Plaster of Paris.*** Gypsum, especially calcined gypsum used for making statuary casts, keeping broken limbs rigid for setting, etc. It is found in large quantities in the quarries of Montmartre, near Paris.

**Paris-Garden.** A bear-garden; a noisy, disorderly place. In allusion to the famous bull- and bear-baiting gardens of that name at Bankside, Southwark, on the site of a house owned by Robert de Paris in the reign of Richard II. In 1594 the 'Swan Theatre' was erected here, and in 1613 this gave way to 'The Hope'.

> Do you take the court for a Paris-garden?
>
> Shakespeare, *Henry VIII*, 5, 3

**Parisian Wedding, The.** The massacre of St Bartholomew, which took place (Aug. 24th, 1572) during the festivities at the marriage of Henri of Navarre and Margaret of France.

> Charles IX, although it was not possible for him to recall to life the countless victims of the Parisian Wedding, was ready to explain those murders. Motey, *Dutch Republic*, iii, 9

**Parlement.** Under the old *régime* in France, the sovereign court of justice where councillors were allowed to plead, and where justice was administered in the king's name. The Paris Parlement received appeals from all inferior tribunals, but its own judgments were final. It took cognisance of all offences against the crown, the peers, the bishops, the corporations, and all high officers of state; and, though it had no legislative power, had to *register* the royal edicts before they could become law. The *Parlements* were abolished by the Constituent Assembly in 1790.

**Parliament.** From the French *Parlement* (*see above*), from *parler*, to speak, with the suffix *-ment*, denoting action, etc.

> My Lord Coke tells us *Parliament* is derived from 'parler le ment' (to speak one's mind). He might as honestly have taught us that *firmament* is 'firma mentis' (a farm for the mind), or 'fundament' the bottom of the mind.
>
> Rymer, *On Parliaments*

A number of English Parliaments have received special characteristic names, and the more important of these will be found in their alphabetical places. *See*, for instance, *under* Addled: Barebones: Bats: Convention: Devil's: Drunken: Dunces: Good: Grattan's: Long: Mad: Merciless: Mongrel: Pensioner: Rump: Useless: Wondermaking.

***Parliamentary train.*** A train which carries passengers at a minimum rate fixed by

Parliament. In 1845 this was fixed at a penny a mile, a rate which remained in force until it was raised by Act of Parliament during the Great War.

**Parlour.** Originally the reception room in a monastery, etc., where the inmates could see and speak to (Fr. *parler*) their friends.

***Parlour boarder.*** A pupil at a boarding-school who lives with the principal and receives extra care and attention. Hence, used of one in a privileged position.

***Parlour tricks.*** Accomplishments that are useful in company, at At Homes, etc., such as singing, witty conversation, and so on.

**Parlous.** A corrupt form of *perilous*, in slang = our modern use of 'awful', amazing, wondrous.

> Oh! 'tis a parlous lad.
> Shakespeare, *As You Like It*, 3, 2

**Parmenianists.** A name given to the Donatists (*q.v.*), from Parmenianus, Bishop of Carthage, the great antagonist of Augustine.

**Parmesan.** A cheese made at Parma, in Italy.

**Parnassus.** A mountain near Delphi, Greece, with two summits, one of which was consecrated to Apollo and the Muses, the other to Bacchus. It is said to have been anciently called *Larnassus*, because Deucalion's ark, *larnax*, stranded there after the flood. After the oracle of Delphi was built at its foot it received the name of Parnassus, which Peucerus says is a corruption of *Har Nahas* (hill of divination). The Turks call it *Liakura*.

Owing to its connection with the Muses, Parnassus came to be regarded as the seat of poetry and music, and we still use such phrases as *To climb Parnassus*, meaning 'to write poetry'.

> O, were I on Parnassus hill,
> Or had o' Helicon my fill,
> That I might catch poetic skill,
> To sing how dear I love thee! Burns, *Song*

***The Legislator*** or ***Solon of Parnassus***. Boileau (1636–1711) was so called by Voltaire, because of his *Art of Poetry*, a production unequalled in the whole range of didactic poetry.

**Parnassian School.** The name given to an important group of French poets flourishing from about 1850 to 1890, from a collection of their poems entitled *Parnasse contemporain* (1866). They were followers of De Musset, and include Leconte de Lisle, Baudelaire, François Coppée, and Sully-Prudhomme.

In England the group of poets following Rossetti and William Morris have sometimes been referred to as 'the Parnassians'.

**Parody.** ***Father of Parody.*** Hipponax of Ephesus (6th cent. BC). *Parody* means an ode which perverts the meaning of another ode. (Gr. *para ode*.)

**Parole** (Fr.). A verbal promise given by a soldier or prisoner of war, that he will not abuse his leave of absence; also, the watchword of the day.

**Parolles.** ***He was a mere Parolles.*** A pretender, a man of words, and a pedant. The allusion is to the faithless, bragging, slandering villain who dubs himself 'captain', pretends to knowledge which he has not, and to sentiments he never feels, in Shakespeare's *All's Well that Ends Well*.

> I know him a notorious liar,
> Think him a great way fool, solely a coward;
> Yet these fixed evils sit so fit on him
> That they take place ... Act 1, 1

**Parr.** ***Old Parr.*** Thomas Parr, the 'old, old, very old man', was said to have lived in the reigns of ten sovereigns, to have married a second wife when he was 120 years old, and to have had a child by her. He was a husbandman, born – by repute – in Salop in 1483, and died in 1635, aged 152 years. Mr Thoms, editor of *Notes and Queries*, examined the evidence in his *Records of Longevity*, and, though Parr certainly lived to a great age, found no confirmation for the generally accepted dates.

**Parrot-coal.** Cannel-coal is so called in Scotland and the North; perhaps because of the crackling or chattering noise it makes when burnt.

**Parsees.** Guebres or fire-worshippers (*q.v.*); descendants of Persians who fled to India during the Mohammedan persecutions of the 7th and 8th centuries, and still adhere to their Zoroastrian religion. *See also* Silence (*Towers of Silence*). The word means *People of Pars* – i.e. Persia.

**Parsifal.** *See* Percival.

**Parsley.** ***He has need now of nothing but a little parsley*** – i.e. he is dead. A Greek saying; the Greeks decked tombs with parsley, because it keeps green a long time.

**Parson.** *See* Clerical titles.

**Parson Adams.** A leading character in Fielding's *Joseph Andrews* (1742), often taken as the type of the simple-minded, hard-working, and learned country curate who is totally ignorant of 'the ways of the world'.

> As he never had any intention to deceive, so he never suspected such a design in others. He was generous, friendly, and brave to an excess; but simplicity was his characteristic; he did, no

more than Mr Colley Cibber, apprehend any such passions as malice and envy to exist in mankind. *Joseph Andrews*, ch. i

He was drawn from Fielding's friend, the Rev. William Young, who edited Ainsworth's *Latin Dictionary* (1752).

**Part.** A portion, piece, or fragment.

***For my part.*** As far as concerns me.

***For the most part.*** Generally, as a rule.

***In good part.*** Favourably.

***Part and parcel.*** An essential part, portion, or element.

'Well, Mr Squeers,' he said, welcoming that worthy with his accustomed smile, of which a sharp look and a thoughtful frown were part and parcel, 'how do *you* do?'

Dickens, *Nicholas Nickleby*

***Part of speech.*** A grammatical class of words of a particular character. The old rhyme by which children used to be taught the parts of speech is:

Three little words you often see
Are articles, *a*, *an*, and *the*.
A noun's the name of anything;
As *school* or *garden*, *hoop* or *swing*.
Adjectives tell the kind of noun;
As *great*, *small*, *pretty*, *white*, or *brown*.
Instead of nouns the pronouns stand;
*Her* head, *his* face, *our* arms, *your* hand.
Verbs tell of something being done;
To *read*, *count*, *sing*, *laugh*, *jump*, or *run*.
How things are done the adverbs tell;
As *slowly*, *quickly*, *ill*, or *well*.
Conjunctions join the words together;
As, men *and* women, wind *or* weather.
The preposition stands before
A noun, as *in* or *through* a door.
The interjection shows surprise;
As, *oh!* how pretty! *ah!* how wise!
The whole are called nine parts of speech,
Which reading, writing, speaking teach.

***Part up!*** Slang for 'hand over', as in 'If you don't soon part up with the money you owe me there'll be trouble.' An extension of the use is the old saying (Tusser, 1573) *A fool and his money are soon parted.*

***Till death do us part.*** *See* Depart.

***To play a part.*** To perform some duty or pursue some course of action; also, to act deceitfully. The phrase is from the stage, where an actor's *part* is the words or the character assigned to him.

All the world's a stage,
And all the men and women merely players.
They have their exits and their entrances;
And one man in his time plays many parts.

Shakespeare, *As You Like It*, 2, 7

Why is the Past belied with wicked art,
The Future made to play so false a part?

Wordsworth, *The Warning*, 140

***To take part.*** To assist; to participate.

But Lilla pleased me, for she took no part
In our dispute.

Tennyson, *The Princess; Conclusion*, 29

***To take the part of.*** To side with, to support the cause of.

***A man of parts.*** An accomplished man; one who is clever, talented, or of high intellectual ability.

Low in the world, because he scorns its arts.
A man of letters, manners, morals, parts;
Unpatronised, and therefore little known.

Cowper, *Tirocinium*, 672

**Partant pour la Syrie.** The favourite march of the French troops in the Second Empire. The words were by Count Alexander de Laborde (1810), and the music – attributed to Queen Hortense, mother of Napoleon III – was probably by the flautist Philippe Drouet. The ballad tells how young Dunois followed his lord to Syria, and prayed the Virgin 'that he might prove the bravest warrior, and love the fairest maiden'. Afterwards the count said to Dunois, 'To thee we owe the victory, and my daughter I give to thee.' Moral: *Amour à la plus belle; honneur au plus vaillant.*

**Parthenon.** The great temple at Athens to Athene *Parthenos* (i.e. the Virgin), many of the sculptured friezes and fragments of pediments of which are now in the British Museum among the Elgin Marbles (*q.v.*). The Temple was begun by the architect Ictinus about 450 BC, and the embellishment of it was mainly the work of Phidias, whose colossal chryselephantine statue of Athene was its chief treasure.

**Parthenope.** Naples; so called from Parthenope, the siren, who threw herself into the sea out of love for Ulysses, and was cast up on the bay of Naples.

**Parthenopean Republic.** The transitory Republic of Naples, established with the aid of the French in Jan., 1799, and overthrown by the Allies in the following June, when the Bourbons were restored.

**Particularists.** Those who hold the doctrine of *particular* election and redemption, i.e. the election and redemption of some, not all, of the human race.

**Parting.** ***Parting cup.*** *See* Stirrup Cup.

***The parting of the ways.*** Said of a critical moment when one has to choose between two different courses of action. The allusion, of course, is to a place at which a road branches off in different directions.

For the difficulties in which we find ourselves now, the parting of the ways was in 1853, when the Emperor Nicholas's proposals were rejected.
Lord Salisbury, Speech (19 Jan., 1897)

**Partington. *Dame Partington and her mop*.** A taunt against those who try to withstand progress. Sydney Smith, speaking on the Lords' rejection of the Reform Bill, October, 1831, compares them to Dame Partington with her mop, trying to push back the Atlantic. 'She was excellent,' he says, 'at a slop or puddle, but should never have meddled with a tempest.'

The story is that a Mrs Partington had a cottage on the shore at Sidmouth, Devon. In November, 1824, a heavy gale drove the waves into her house, and the old lady laboured with a mop to sop the water up.

B. P. Shillaber, the American humorist, published the *Life and Sayings of Mrs Partington* (1854), the old lady – like Mrs Malaprop – constantly misusing words.

**Partlet.** The hen in Chaucer's *Nun's Priest's Tale*, and in *Reynard the Fox* (*q.v.*). A partlet was a ruff worn in the 16th century by women, and the reference is to the frill-like feathers round the neck of certain hens.

In the barn the tenant cock
Close to partlet perched on high.
Cuningham

***Sister Partlet with her hooded head***, allegorises the cloistered community of nuns in Dryden's *Hind and Panther*, where the Roman Catholic clergy are likened to barnyard fowls.

**Partridge. *Always partridge!*** *See* Perdrix.

***St. Partridge's Day.*** September 1st, the first day of partridge shooting.

**Parturiunt montes. *Parturiunt montes, nascetur ridiculus mus*.** The mountain was in labour, etc. *See under* Mountain.

**Party.** Person or persons under consideration. 'This is the next party, your worship' – i.e. the next case to be examined. 'This is the party that stole the things' – the person or persons accused.

If an evil spirit trouble any, one must make a smoke... and the party shall be no more vexed.
Tobit 6:7

In slang and low speech *party* is often used as though it were synonymous with *person*, as – 'That fat old party in the corner'.

**Parvenu** (Fr., arrived). An upstart; one who has risen from the ranks. The word was made popular in France by Marivaux' *Paysan Parvenu* (1735).

The insolence of the successful *parvenu* is only the necessary continuance of the career of the needy struggler. Thackeray, *Pendennis*, II, xxi

**Parvis** (*Paravisus*, a Low Latin corruption of *paradisus*, a church close, especially the court in front of St Peter's at Rome in the Middle Ages). The 'place' or court before the main entrance of a cathedral. In the parvis of St Paul's lawyers used to meet for consultation, as brokers do in exchange. The word is now applied to the room above the church porch.

A segeant of lawe, war and wys,
That often haddé ben atté parvys.
Chaucer, *Canterbury Tales*

**Parsival.** *See* Percival.

**Pasch Eggs.** Easter eggs, given as an emblem of the resurrection. They are generally coloured, and if a name is written on it with grease, which does not absorb the colouring matter, the pasch egg appears with a name on it.

*Pasch* comes through Fr. *pasque* (Easter), from Hebrew *pasakh*, the Passover.

The day before Easter Sunday is called *Egg Saturday*.

**Pasha.** A Turkish title borne by governors of provinces and certain military and civil officers of high rank. There were three grades of pashas, which were distinguished by the number of horse-tails carried before them and planted in front of their tents. The highest rank were those of *three tails*; the grand vizier was always such a pasha, as also were commanding generals and admirals; generals of division, etc., were pashas of *two tails*; and generals of brigades, rear admirals and petty provincial governors were pashas of *one tail*.

**Pasht.** *See* Bubastis.

**Pasiphae.** In Greek legend, a daughter of the Sun and wife of Minos, King of Crete. She was the mother of Ariadne, and also (through intercourse with a white bull given by Poseidon to Minos) of the Minotaur (*q.v.*).

**Pasque Eggs.** *See* Pasch Eggs.

**Pasquinade.** A lampoon or political squib, having ridicule for its object; so called from Pasquino, an Italian tailor of the 15th century, noted for his caustic wit. Some time after his death, a mutilated statue was dug up, representing Ajax supporting Menelaus, or

Menelaus carrying the body of Patroclus, or else a gladiator, and was placed at the end of the Braschi Palace near the Piazza Navoni. As it was not clear what the statue represented, and as it stood opposite Pasquin's house, it came to be called 'Pasquin'. The Romans affixed their political, religious, and personal satires to it, hence the name. At the other end of Rome was an ancient statue of Mars, called *Marforio*, to which were affixed replies to the Pasquinades.

> Then the procession started, took the way
> From the New Prisons by the Pilgrim's Street
> The street of the Governo, Pasquin's Street,
> (Where was stuck up, 'mid other epigrams,
> A quatrain … but of all that, presently!)
>
> Browning, *The Ring and the Book*, xii, 137

**Pass.** ***A pass*** or ***A common pass***. At the Universities, an ordinary degree, without honours. A candidate getting this is called a *passman*.

**Passée** (Fr., past). Used in a pitying or derogatory sense of a woman who is getting on in years, is *past* her prime; also of anything that is out of date.

**Passelyon.** A young foundling brought up by Morgan le Fay whose amorous adventures are related in the old romance *Perceforest*, vol. iii.

**Passepartout** (Fr., pass everywhere). A master-key; also a simple kind of picture-frame in which the picture is placed between a sheet of card-board and a piece of glass, the whole being held together by strips of paper pasted over the edges.

**Passim** (Lat. here and there, in many places). A direction often found in annotated books which tells the reader that reference to the matter in hand will be found in many passages in the book mentioned.

> I'll prove that such the opinion of the critic is
> From Aristotle *passim*.
>
> Byron, *Don Juan*, III, cxi

**Passing Bell.** *See* Bell.

**Passion Flower.** A plant of the genus *Passiflora*, whose flowers bear a fancied resemblance to the instruments of the Passion. *Cp.* Pike's Head. It seems to have first got its name in mediaeval Spain.

> The *leaf* symbolises the spear.
> The five *anthers*, the five wounds.
> The *tendrils*, the cords or whips.
> The column of the *ovary*, the pillar of the cross.
> The *stamen*, the hammers.
> The three *styles*, the three nails.
> The *fleshy threads* within the flowers, the crown of thorns.
> The *calyx*, the glory or nimbus.
> The *white* tint, purity.
> The *blue* tint, heaven.
> It keeps open three days; symbolising the three years' ministry. (Matt. 12: 40.)

**Passion Sunday.** *See* Judica.

**Passionists.** Members of the very ascetic order, the Congregation of Discalced Clerks of tho Passion of our Lord, founded by St Paul of the Cross in 1728 at Monte Argentoro, an island off the coast of Tuscany, for the purpose of giving retreats and holding missions. The monks wear on the breast of their black cassocks a heart surmounted by a cross and the inscription *Jesu Christi Passio*, worked in white.

**Passover.** A Jewish festival to commemorate the deliverance of the Israelites, when the angel of death (that slew the first-born of the Egyptians) *passed over* their houses, and spared all who did as Moses commanded them. It is held from the 15th to the 22nd of the first month, Nisan, i.e. about April 13th to 20th.

**Passy-measure Pavin.** *See* Pavan.

**Paston Letters.** A series of letters (with wills, leases, and other documents) written by or to members of the Paston family in Norfolk between the years 1424 and 1509. They passed from the Earl of Yarmouth to Peter le Neve, antiquary; then to Mr Martin, of Palgrave, Suffolk; were then bought by Mr Worth, of Diss; and then passed to Sir John Fenn, who, in 1787, edited two volumes of them as *Original Letters written during the Reigns of Henry VI, Edward IV, and Richard III by various Persons of Rank*. In 1872–5 James Gairdener re-edited them in three volumes, and included some 500 additional letters besides a voluminous introduction and notes. The *Letters* are an invaluable source of information concerning the customs and business methods of the upper middle classes of 15th century England.

**Patavinity.** A provincial idiom in speech or writing; so called from Patavium (*Padua*), the birthplace of Livy, whose writings contain certain dialectical peculiarities. *Cp.* Patois.

**Patch.** A fool; so called originally from the nickname of Cardinal Wolsey's jester, Sexton, who got this nickname either from Ital. *pazzo*, a fool, or from the motley or patched dress worn by licensed fools.

> What a pied ninny's this! thou scurvy patch!
>
> Shakespeare, *The Tempest*, 3, 2

***Cross-patch.*** An ill-tempered person.

***Not a patch upon.*** Not to be compared with; as, 'His horse is not a patch upon mine', 'My patch is better than his garment'.

***To patch up a quarrel.*** To arrange the matter in a not very satisfactory way; a coat that has been torn and then 'patched up' is pretty sure to break out again; so is a quarrel.

**Patelin.** The artful cheat in the 14th century French comedy *L'Avocat Pathelin*. *Cp.* Moutons. The French say, *Savoir son Patelin* (to know how to bamboozle you). On one occasion he wanted William Josseaume to sell him cloth on credit, and artfully praised the father of the merchant, winding up with this *ne plus ultra*, 'He did sell on credit, or even lend to those who wished to borrow.'

**Patent** (through Fr. from Lat. *patentem*, lying open). Open to the perusal of anybody. A thing that is *patented* is protected by letters patent (*see below*).

***Letters patent.*** Documents from the sovereign or a crown officer conferring a title, right, privilege, etc., such as a title of nobility, or the exclusive right to make or sell for a given number of years some new invention. So called because they are written upon open sheets of parchment, with the seal of the sovereign or party by whom they were issued pendent at the bottom. Close letters are folded up and sealed on the outside.

***Patent Rolls.*** Letters patent collected together on parchment rolls. They extend from 1201, and each roll contains a year, though in some cases the roll is subdivided into two or more parts. Each sheet of parchment is numbered, and called a *membrane*; for example, the 8th sheet, say, of the 10th year of Henry III is cited thus: 'Pat. 10, Hen. III, m. 8'. If the document is on the back of the roll it is called dorso, and 'd' is added to the citation. *Cp.* Close Rolls.

**Paternoster** (Lat., Our Father). The Lord's Prayer; from the first two words in the Latin version. Every tenth bead of a rosary is so called, because at that bead the Lord's Prayer is repeated; and the name is also given to a certain kind of fishing tackle, in which hooks and weights to sink them are fixed alternately on the line, somewhat in rosary fashion.

***A paternoster-while.*** Quite a short time; the time it takes one to say a paternoster.

***To say the devil's paternoster.*** *See* Devil.

**Paternoster Row** (London) was probably so named from the rosary or paternoster makers. There is mention as early as 1374 of a Richard Russell, a 'paternosterer' who dwelt there, and we read of 'one Robert Nikke, a paternoster maker and citizen', in the reign of Henry IV. Another suggestion is that it was so called because funeral processions on their way to St Paul's began their *pater noster* at the beginning of the Row.

**Pathfinder.** One of the names of Natty Bumpo (*q.v.*) in Fenimore Cooper's Leatherstocking Novels (*q.v.*). It was given to the American Major-General John Charles Fremont (1813–90), who conducted four expeditions across the Rocky Mountains.

**Patient Grisel.** *See* Griselda.

**Patmos.** The island of the Sporades in the Aegean Sea (now called *Patmo* or *Patino*) to which St John retired – or was exiled (Rev. 1:9). Hence the name is used allusively for a place of banishment or solitude.

**Patois.** Dialectic peculiarity, provincialism in speech. *Cp.* Patavinity. It is a 13th-century French word of unknown origin.

**Patres Conscripti.** *See* Conscript Fathers.

**Patriarch** (Gr. *patria*, family, *archein*, to rule). The head of a tribe or family who rules by paternal right; applied specially (after Acts 7:8) to the twelve sons of Jacob, and to Abraham, Isaac, and Jacob and their forefathers. In one passage (Acts 2:29) David also is spoken of as a patriarch.

In the early Church 'Patriarch', first mentioned in the council of Chalcedon, but virtually existing from about the time of the council of Nice, was the title of the highest of Church officers. He ordained metropolitans, convened councils, received appeals, and was the chief bishop over several countries or provinces, as an archbishop is over several dioceses. It was also the title given by the popes to the archbishops of Lisbon and Venice, in order to make the patriarchal dignity appear distinct from and lower than the papal, and is that of the chief bishop of various Eastern sects, as the Jacobites, Armenians, and Maronites.

In the Orthodox Eastern Church the bishops of Constantinople, Alexandria, Antioch, and Jerusalem are patriarchs; and within a religious order the title is given to the founder, as St Benedict, St Francis, and St Dominic.

**Patrician.** Properly speaking, one of the *patres* (fathers) or senators of Rome (*see* Patres Conscripti), and their descendants. As they held for many years all the honours of the state, the word came to signify the magnates or nobility of a nation, the aristocrats.

**Patrick, St.** The apostle and patron saint of Ireland (commemorated on March 17th) was not an Irishman, but was born at what is now Dumbarton (about 373), his father, Calpurnius, a deacon and Roman official, having come from 'Bannavem Taberniae', which was probably near the mouth of the Severn. As a boy he was captured in a Pictish raid and sold as a slave in Ireland. He escaped to Gaul about 395, where he studied under St Martin at Tours before returning to Britain. There he had a supernatural call to preach to the heathen of Ireland, so he was consecrated and in 432 landed at Wicklow. He at first met with strong opposition, but, going north, he converted first the chiefs and people of Ulster, and later those of the rest of Ireland. He founded many churches, including the cathedral and monastery of Armagh, where he held two synods. He is said to have died at Armagh (about 464) and to have been buried either at Down or Saul – though one tradition gives Glastonbury as the place of his death and burial. Downpatrick cathedral claims his grave. The visitor used to be shown a spot where some of the mould had been removed, and was told that pilgrims took away a few grains as a charm, under the belief that the relic would insure good health, and help to atone for sin. If he went on to ask why there was no memorial or monument, he was informed that both Protestants and Catholics agreed to erect a suitable one, but could not agree upon the inscription or design. Whatever the Protestants erected in the day the Catholics pulled down at night, and *vice versa*. Tired of this toil of Penelope, the idea was abandoned. As a matter of fact, the supposed grave is now covered with a massive slab of granite, for which Irishmen of every religious persuasion subscribed.

St Patrick left his name to almost countless places in Great Britain and Ireland, and many legends are told of his miraculous powers – healing the blind, raising the dead, etc. Perhaps the best known tradition is that he cleared Ireland of its vermin.

> The story goes that one old serpent resisted him; but he overcame it by cunning. He made a box, and invited the serpent to enter it. The serpent objected, saying it was too small; but St Patrick insisted it was quite large enough to be comfortable. After a long contention, the serpent got in to prove it was too small, when St Patrick slammed down the lid, and threw the box into the sea.

In commemoration of this St Patrick is usually represented banishing the serpents; and with a shamrock leaf, in allusion to the tradition that when explaining the Trinity to the heathen priests on the hill of Tara he used this as a symbol.

***St Patrick's Cross.*** The same shape as St Andrew's Cross (✕), only different in colour, viz. red on a white field.

***St Patrick's Purgatory.*** A cave in a small island in Lough Derg (between Galway, Clare, and Tipperary). In the Middle Ages it was a favourite resort of pilgrims who believed that it was the entrance to an earthly purgatory. The legend is that Christ Himself revealed it to St Patrick and told him that whoever would spend a day and a night therein would witness the torments of hell and the joys of heaven. Henry of Saltrey tells how Sir Owain (*q.v.*) visited it, and Fortunatus, of the old legend, was also one of the adventurers. It was blocked up by order of the Pope on St Patrick's Day, 1497, but the interest in it long remained, and the Spanish dramatist Calderon (d.1681) has a play on the subject – *El Purgatorio de San Patricio*.

> Why should all your chimney-sweepers be Irishmen?
> Faith, that's soon answered, for St Patrick, you know, keeps purgatory; he makes the fire, and his countrymen could do nothing if they cannot sweep the chimneys.
>
> Dekker, *Honest Whore*, Pt II, I, i

***The Order of St Patrick.*** A British order of knighthood, instituted by George III in 1783 and revised in 1905, consisting of the Sovereign, the Lord Lieutenant (as Grand Master), and twenty-two knights. Its motto is *Quis Separabit?*

**Patrico.** Sixteenth century thieves' slang for hedge priests who for a fee married people under a hedge, as Abraham-men (*q.v.*).

**Patripassians.** The name given by their opponents to the Monarchians (*q.v.*), an early heretical sect which 'confounded the Persons', and according to whose theory God the Father must have experienced the Passion on the cross.

**Patroclus.** The gentle and amiable friend of Achilles, in Homer's *Iliad*. When Achilles refused to fight in order to annoy Agamemnon, he sent him in his own armour at the head of the Myrmidons to the battle, and he was slain by Hector.

**Patter.** To chatter, to clack, also the running talk of cheap Jacks, conjurers, etc., is from *Paternoster* (*q.v.*). The priest recited it in a low, rapid, mechanical way till he came to the words, 'and lead us not into temptation', which he spoke aloud, and the choir responded, 'but deliver us from evil'. In our Prayer Book, the priest is directed to say the whole prayer 'with a *loud* voice'.

**Patter,** the patter of little feet, of rain, etc., is not connected with the above. It is a frequentative of *pat*, to strike gently.

**Pattern.** From the same root as *patron* (Lat. *pater*, father). As a *patron* ought to be an example, so pattern has come to signify a model.

**Paul, St.** Patron saint of preachers and tentmakers (*see* Acts 18:3). Originally called Saul, his name, according to tradition, was changed in honour of Sergius Paulus, whom he converted (Acts 13:6–12).

His symbols are a sword and open book, the former the instrument of his martyrdom, and the latter indicative of the new law propagated by him as the apostle of the Gentiles. He is represented of short stature, with bald head and grey, bushy beard; and legend relates that when he was beheaded at Rome (AD 66), after having converted one of Nero's favourite concubines, milk instead of blood flowed from his veins. He is commemorated on June 30th.

***A Paul's man.*** A braggart; a captain out of service, with a long rapier; so called because the Walk down the centre of old St Paul's, London, was at one time the haunt of stale knights. These loungers were also known as *Paul's Walkers*. Jonson called Bobadil (*q.v.*) a Paul's man, and in his *Every Man out of his Humour* (1599) is a variety of scenes in the interior of St Paul's. Harrison Ainsworth also describes them in his *Old St Paul's*.

**Paul the Hermit, St.** The first of the Egyptian hermits. When 113 years old he was visited by St Antony, himself over 90, and when he died in 341 St Antony wrapped his body in the cloak given to him by St Athanasius, and his grave was dug by two lions. His day is Jan. 15th, and he is represented as an old man, clothed with palm-leaves, and seated under a palm tree, near which are a river and loaf of bread.

**Paul of the Cross, St.** Paul Francis Danei (1694–1775), founder of the Passionists (*q.v.*).

**Paul Pry.** *See* Pry.

**Paulianists.** A 3rd century sect of Unitarian heretics, so called from Paul of Samosata, a Patripassian who was Bishop of Antioch from 260 to 272, when he was deposed. He may be considered the father of the Socinians.

**Paulicians.** A religious sect of the Eastern Empire, an offshoot of the Manichaeans. It originated in the 7th century, and became extinct in the 13th. They were the followers of Constantino of Mananalis, and were called Paulicians because of the veneration in which they held the apostle Paul. They rejected the worship of the Virgin and of saints, denied the doctrine of transubstantiation, maintained that all matter is evil, and held that as Christ's body was purely ethereal he did not suffer.

**Pavan** or **Pavin.** A stately Spanish dance of the 16th and 17th centuries, said to be so called because in it the dancers stalked like peacocks (Lat. *pavones*), the gentlemen with their long robes of office, and the ladies with trains like peacocks' tails. The pavan, like the minuet, ended with a quick movement called the *galliard*, a sort of gavotte.

***Every pavan has its galliard.*** Every sage has his moments of folly. Every white must have its black, and every sweet its sour.

***Passy-measures pavin.*** A reeling dance or motion, like that of a drunken man, from side to side. The tipsy Sir Toby Belch says of 'Dick surgeon' –

> He's a rogue and a passy-measures pavin. I hate a drunken rogue.
>
> Shakespeare, *Twelfth Night*, 5, 1

The *passy-measure* was a slow dance, the Italian *passamezzo* (a middle pace or step). Also called a *cinque measure*, because it consisted of five measures – 'two singles and a double forward, with two singles side'.

**Pawnbroker's Sign, The.** *See* Balls, Mugello.

**Pawnee.** Anglo-Indian for water (Hind. *pani*, water).

***Brandy pawnee.*** Brandy and water.

**Pax** (Lat. peace). The 'kiss of peace', which is given in the Roman Church at High Mass. It is omitted on Maundy Thursday, from horror at the kiss of Judas.

Also a sacred utensil used when mass is celebrated by a high dignitary. It is sometimes a crucifix, sometimes a tablet, and sometimes a reliquary, and is handed round to be kissed as a symbolic substitute for the 'kiss of peace'.

The old custom of 'kissing the bride', which took place immediately before the Communion of the newly-married couple and still obtains in some churches, is derived from the Salisbury rubric concerning the Pax in the Missa Sponsalium:

> Tunc amoto pallio, surgant ambo sponsus et sponsa; et accipiat sponsus pacem a sacerdote, et ferat sponsae osculans eam et neminem alium, nec ipse, nec ipsa; sed statim diaconus vel clericus a presbytero pacem accipiens, ferat aliis sicut solitum est.

***Pax!*** The schoolboy's cry of truce.

***Pax Britannica.*** The peace imposed by British rule. The phrase is modelled on the Latin *Pax Romana*, the peace existing between the different members of the Roman Empire.

***Pax vobis*** (*cum*) (Peace be unto you). The formula used by a bishop instead of 'The Lord be with you', wherever this versicle occurs in Divine service. They are the words used by Christ to His Apostles on the first Easter morning.

**Pay,** to discharge a debt, is through O.Fr. *paier*, from Lat. *pax*, peace, by way of *pacare*, to appease. The nautical *pay*, to cover with hot tar for waterproofing, represents Lat. *picare*, from *pix*, pitch.

***Here's the devil to pay, and no pitch hot.*** *See* Devil.

***I'll pay him out.*** I'll be a match for him, I'll punish him.

> They with a foxe-tale him soundly did paye.
>
> *The King and Northerne Man* (1640)

***To pay off old scores.*** *See* Score.

***To pay with the roll of the drum.*** Not to pay at all. No soldier can be arrested for debt when on the march.

> How happy the soldier who lives on his pay,
> And spends half-a-crown out of sixpence a day;
> He cares not for justices, beadles, or bum,
> But pays all his debts with the roll of the drum.
>
> O'Keefe

***Who's to pay the piper?*** Who is to stand Sam? who is to pay the score? The phrase comes from the story of the Pied Piper (*q.v.*), who agreed to rid Hamelin city of rats and mice, and when he had done so was refused his pay.

From the corresponding French phrase, *payer les violons*, it would seem to mean who is to pay the fiddler or piper if we have a dance on the green.

***You can put paid to that.*** You can treat it as finished, it's all over, done with; it's a 'wash-out'. A phrase from the counting-house; when 'Paid' is put to an account it's finished with.

**Pea-jacket.** A rough overcoat worn by seamen, etc.; probably from the Dutch *pig* or *pije*, a coarse thick cloth or felt. The 'courtepy', the short (Fr. *court*) jacket worn by Chaucer's 'Clerk of Oxonford', is from the same word:

> Ful thredbar was his overest courtepy,
> For he had getten him yet no benefyce.
>
> *Canterbury Tales*, *Prologue*, 290

**Peace. *A Bill of Peace.*** A Bill intended to secure relief from perpetual litigation. It is brought by one who wishes to establish and perpetuate a right which he claims, but which, from its nature, is controversial.

***If you want peace, prepare for war.*** A translation of the Latin proverb, *Si vis pacem, para bellum*. It goes a step farther than the advice given by Polonius to his son (*Hamlet*, 1, 3), for you are told, whether you are 'in a quarrel' or not, always to bear yourself so that all possible opposers 'may beware of thee'.

***Peace at any price.*** Lord Palmerston sneered at the Quaker statesman, John Bright, as a 'peace-at-any-price man'; during the Great War *pacifist* was in vogue to express the same thing. *Cp.* Conchie.

> Though not a 'peace-at-any-price' man, I am not ashamed to say I am a peace-at-almost-any-price man.
>
> Lord Averbury, *The Use of Life*, xi (1894)

***Peace with honour.*** A phrase popularised by Beaconsfield on his return from the Congress of Berlin (1878), when he said:

> Lord Salisbury and myself have brought you back peace – but a peace I hope with honour, which may satisfy our Sovereign and tend to the welfare of the country.

It is, of course, much older than this. Shakespeare uses it more than once, e.g.:

> We have made peace
> With no less honour to the Antiates
> Than shame to the Romans. *Coriolanus*, 5, 5

And Pepys writes in his *Diary* on May 25th, 1663:

> With peace and honour I am willing to spare anything so as to keep all ends together.

***The King's peace.*** The general peace of law-abiding subjects; originally the protection secured by the king to those employed on his business.

> To kill an alien, a Jew, or an outlaw, who are all under the king's peace or protection, is as much murder as to kill the most regular born Englishmen.
>
> *Blackstone's Commentaries*, IV, xiv

***The kiss of peace.*** *See* Pax.

***The Perpetual Peace.*** The peace concluded June 24th, 1502, between England and Scotland, whereby Margaret, daughter of Henry VII, was betrothed to James IV; a few years afterwards the battle of Flodden Field was fought. The name has also been given to other treaties, as that between Austria and Switzerland in 1474, and between France and Switzerland in 1516.

***To keep the peace.*** To refrain from disturbing the public peace or doing anything that might result in strife or commotion. Wrongdoers are sometimes *bound over to keep the peace* for a certain time by a magistrate; a specified sum of money is deposited, and if the man commits a breach of the peace during that time he is not only arrested but his deposit is forfeit.

**Peace-makers, The.** The nickname of the Bedfordshire Regiment, because for many years they had no battles on their colours.

**Peach.** To inform, to 'split'; a contraction of *impeach.* The word is one of those that has degenerated to slang after being in perfectly good use.

**Peacock. *By the peacock!*** An obsolete oath which at one time was thought blasphemous. The fabled incorruptibility of the peacock's flesh caused the bird to be adopted as a type of the resurrection.

There is a story that when George III had partly recovered from one of his attacks of insanity his Ministers got him to read the King's Speech, and he ended every sentence with the word *peacock.* The Minister who drilled him said that *peacock* was an excellent word for ending a sentence, only kings should not let subjects hear it, but should whisper it softly. The result was a perfect success, and the pause at the close of each sentence had an excellent effect.

***The peacock's feather.*** An emblem of vainglory, and in some Eastern countries a mark of rank.

As a literary term the expression is used of a borrowed ornament of style spatchcocked into the composition; the allusion being to the fable of the jay who decked herself out in peacock's feathers, making herself an object of ridicule.

The peacock's tail is emblem of an Evil Eye, or an ever-vigilant traitor; hence the feathers are considered unlucky, and the superstitious will not have them in the house. The classical legend is that Argus (*see* **Argus-eyed**), who had 100 eyes, was changed into a peacock by Juno, the eyes forming the beautifully coloured disks in the tail.

**Peal. *To ring a peal*** is to ring 5,040 changes; any number of changes less than that is technically called a *touch* or *flourish*. Bells are first *raised*, and then *pealed.*

> This society rung … a true and complete peal of 5,040 grandsire triples in three hours and fourteen minutes.
>
> Inscription in Windsor Curfew Tower

**Pearls.** Dioscorides and Pliny mention the belief that pearls are formed by drops of rain falling into the oyster-shells while open; the raindrops thus received being hardened into pearls by some secretions of the animal.

Cardan says (*De Rerum Varietate*, vii, 34) that pearls are polished by being pecked and played with by doves.

> The liquid drops of tears that you have shed
> Shall come again, transform'd to orient pearl.
>
> Shakespeare, *Richard III*, 4, 4

> Pearls … are believed to be the result of an abnormal secretory process caused by an irritation of the mollusk consequent on the intrusion into the shell of some foreign body, as a grain of sand, an egg of the mollusk itself, or perhaps some cercarian parasite.
>
> G. F. King, *Gems. etc.*, ch. xii

Cleopatra (*q.v.*) and Sir Thomas Gresham are said to have dissolved pearls in wine by way of making an ostentatious display of wealth, and a similar act of vanity and folly is told by Horace (2 *Satire*, iii, 239). Clodius, son of Aesop the tragedian, drew a pearl of great value from his ear, melted it in vinegar, and drank to the health of Cecilia Metella. This story is referred to by Valerius Maximus, Macrobius, and Pliny. Horace says,

> Qui sanior, ac si
> Illud idem in rapidum flumen jaceretve cloacam?
> How say you? had the act been more insane
> To fling it in a river or a drain?
>
> Conington's tr.

***The Pearl Coast.*** So the early Spanish explorers named the Venezuelan coast from Cumana to Trinidad; the islands off this coast were called *the Pearl Islands.* This district was the site of large pearl-fisheries.

**Peasants' War, The.** The name given to the insurrections of the peasantry of southern Germany in the early 16th century, especially to that of 1524 in Swabia, Franconia, Saxony, and other German states, in consequence of the tyranny and oppression of the nobles, and which was ended by the battle of Frankenhausen (1525), when many thousands of the peasants were slain. In 1502 was the rebellion called the *Laced Shoe*, from its cognisance; in 1514, the

*League of Poor Conrad*; in 1523, the *Latin War*. *See* Bundschuh.

**Peascod.** ***Winter for shoeing, peascod for wooing.*** The allusion in the latter clause is to the custom of placing a peascod with nine peas in it on the door-lintel, under the notion that the first man who entered through the door would be the husband of the person who did so. Another custom is alluded to by Browne –

> The peascod greene oft with no little toyle
> Hee'd seeke for in the fattest, fertil'st soile,
> And rend it from the stalke to bring it to her
> And in her bosome for acceptance woo her.
>
> *Britannia's Pastora*

**Pec.** Old Eton slang for money. A contraction of the Latin *pecunia*.

**Peccavi.** ***To cry peccavi.*** To acknowledge oneself in the wrong. It is said that Sir Charles Napier, after the battle of Hyderabad, in 1843, used this word as a pun upon his victory – '*Peccavi*' (I have sinned, i.e. Sinde).

**Peck.** Some food. 'To have a peck', is to have something to eat.

***Peckish.*** Hungry, or desirous of something to eat. Of course 'peck' refers to fowls, etc., which peck their food.

> When shall I feel peckish again.
>
> Disraeli, *Sybil*, Bk vi, ch. iii

**Pecker.** ***Keep your pecker up.*** As the mouth is in the head, *pecker* (the mouth) means the head; and to 'keep your pecker up', means to keep your head up, or, more familiarly, 'keep your tail up'; 'never say die'.

**Peckham.** ***All holiday at Peckham.*** – i.e. no appetite, not peckish; a pun on the word peck, as going to Bedfordshire is a pun on the word bed.

***Going to Peckham.*** Going to dinner.

**Pecksniff.** A canting hypocrite, who speaks homilies of morality, does the most heartless things 'as a duty to society', and forgives wrong-doing in nobody but himself. (Dickens, *Martin Chuzzlewit*.)

**Pectoral Cross.** *See* Crux pectoralis.

**Peculiar.** A parish or church which was exempt from episcopal jurisdiction, as a royal chapel, etc. Peculiars were abolished in 1849.

***The Court of Peculiars.*** A branch of the Court of Arches which had jurisdiction over the 'peculiars' of the archbishop of Canterbury. *See above*.

***The Peculiar People.*** Properly, the Jews – the 'Chosen people'; but taken as a title by a sect founded in 1838, the chief characteristic of which is that its members refuse all medical aid and, as a consequence, are frequently in conflict with the authorities. They have a strong belief in the efficacy of prayer; they subscribe to no creed and have no recognised preachers or clergy.

**Peculium.** Private and individual property or possession. Originally applied to the property which the Roman slaves were allowed to acquire and over which their masters had no right or control.

**Pecuniary.** From *pecus*, cattle, especially sheep. Varo says that sheep were the ancient medium of barter and standard of value. Ancient coin was marked with the image of an ox or sheep.

**Pedagogue** (Gr. *pais*, boy, *agein*, to lead). A 'boy-leader', hence, a schoolmaster – now usually one who is pompous and pedantic. In ancient Greece the *pedagogos* was a slave whose duty it was to attend the boy whenever he left home.

**Pedlar** is not a tramp who goes on his feet, as if from the Lat. *pedes*, feet. The name is probably from the *ped*, a hamper without a lid in which are stored fish or other articles to hawk about the streets. In Norwich there is a place called the Ped-market, where women expose eggs, butter, cheese, etc., in open hampers.

***Pedlar's Acre*** (Lambeth). According to tradition, a pedlar of this parish left a sum of money, on condition that his picture, with a dog, should be preserved for ever in glass in one of the church windows. In the south window of the middle aisle, sure enough, such a picture exists; but probably it is a rebus on *Chapman*, the name of some benefactor. In Swaffham church there is a portrait of one John Chapman, a great benefactor, who is represented as a pedlar with his pack, and in that town a similar tradition exists.

***Pedlars' French.*** The jargon or cant of thieves, rogues, and vagabonds. 'French' was formerly widely used to denote anything or anyone that was foreign, and even Bracton uses the word 'Frenchman' as a synonym of foreigner.

> Instead of Pedlars' French, gives him plain language.
>
> Beaumont and Fletcher, *Faithful Friends*, i, 2

**Peeler.** Slang for a policeman; first applied to the Irish Constabulary founded when Sir Robert Peel was Chief Secretary (1812–18), and afterwards, when Peel as Home Secretary introduced the Metropolitan Police Act (1829), to the English policeman. *Cp.* Bobby. In the 16th century the word was applied to robbers, from *peel* (later *pill*), to plunder, strip of possessions, rob. Holinshed, in his *Scottish Chronicle* (1570), refers to Patrick Dunbar, who 'delivered the countrie of these peelers'. *Cp.* also Milton's *Paradise Regained*, iv, 136:

That people ... who, once just,
Frugal, and mild, and temperate, conquered well
But govern ill the nations under yoke,
Peeling their provinces, exhausted all
By lust and rapine.

**Peep-o'-Day Boys.** The Irish Protestant faction in Ulster of about 1786; they were precursors of the Orangemen (*q.v.*), and were active from the period mentioned; so called because they used to visit the houses of their Roman Catholic opponents (called *Defenders*) at 'peep of day' searching for arms or plunder.

**Peeping Tom of Coventry.** *See* Godiva, Lady.

**Peers of the Realm.** The five orders of Duke, Marquess, Earl, Viscount, and Baron (*see these names*). The word peer is the Latin *pares* (equals), and in feudal times all great vassals were held equal in rank.

***The Twelve Peers of Charlemagne.*** *See* Paladins.

**Peg.** ***A square peg in a round hole.*** One who is doing (or trying to do) a job for which he is not suited; e.g. a bishop refereeing a prize-fight.

***Come down a peg.*** Humiliated; lowered in dignity, tone, demands, etc.

Well, he has come down a peg or two, and he don't like it. Haggard

***I am a peg too low.*** I am low-spirited, moody; I want another draught to cheer me up. Our Saxon ancestors used tankards with pegs inserted at equal intervals, so that when two or more drank from the same bowl no one might exceed his fair proportion (*cp.* Pin – *In merry pin*). We are told that St Dunstan introduced the fashion to prevent brawling.

Come, old fellow, drink down to your peg!
But do not drink any farther, I beg.
Longfellow, *Golden Legend*, iv

***There are always more round pegs than round holes.*** Always more candidates for office than places to dispose of.

***To peg away at it.*** To stick at it persistently, in spite of difficulties and discouragement.

***To take one down a peg.*** To take the conceit out of a braggart or pretentious person. The allusion here is not to peg-tankards, but to a ship's colours, which used to be raised and lowered by pegs; the higher the colours are raised the greater the honour, and to take them down a peg would be to award less honour.

Trepanned your party with intrigue,
And took your grandees down a peg.
Butler, *Hudibras*, ii, 2

**Pegasus.** The winged horse on which Bellerophon (*q.v.*) rode against the Chimaera. When the Muses contended with the daughters of Pieros, Helicon rose heavenward with delight; but Pegasus gave it a kick, stopped its ascent, and brought out of the mountain the soul-inspiring waters of Hippocrene; hence, the name is used for the inspiration of poetry.

Then who so will with vertuous deeds assay
To mount to heaven, on Pegasus must ride,
And with sweete Poets verse be glorified.
Spenser, *Ruines of Time*, 425

Now, if my Pegasus should not be shod ill,
This poem will become a moral model.
Byron, *Don Juan*, V, ii

**Peine forte et dure.** A species of torture applied to contumacious felons who refused to plead; it usually took the form of pressing the accused to death by weights. The following persons were executed in this way: Juliana Quick, in 1442; Anthony Arrowsmith, in 1598; Walter Calverly, in 1605; Major Strangways, in 1657; and even in 1741 a person was pressed to death at the Cambridge assizes. Abolished 1772.

**Pelagians.** Heretical followers of the British monk Pelagius (a Latinised form of his native Welsh name, *Morgan*, the sea), who in the 4th and early 5th centuries was fiercely opposed by St Augustine, and was condemned by Pope Zosimus in 418. They denied the doctrine of original sin or the taint of Adam, and maintained that we have power of ourselves to receive or reject the Gospel.

**Pelf.** ***Filthy pelf.*** Money; usually with a contemptuous implication – as we speak of 'filthy lucre', or 'Who steals my purse steals *trash.*'

How blest the maid ...
Who knows not pomp, who heeds not pelf;
Whose heaviest sin it is to look
Askance upon her pretty Self
Reflected in some crystal brook.
Wordsworth, *The Three Cottage Girls*

The word is from O.Fr. *pelfre*, connected with our *pilfer*, and was originally used of stolen or pilfered goods, ill-gotten gains.

**Pelias.** The huge spear of Achilles, which none but the hero could wield; so called because it was cut from an ash growing on Mount Pelion (*q.v.*).

**Pelican.** In Christian art, a symbol of charity; also an emblem of Jesus Christ, by 'whose blood we are healed'. St Jerome gives the story of the pelican restoring its young ones destroyed by serpents, and his salvation by the blood of Christ; and the old popular fallacy that pelicans fed their young with their blood arose from the fact that when the parent bird is about to feed its brood, it macerates small fish in the large bag attached to its under bill, then pressing the bag against its breast, transfers the macerated food to the mouths of the young. The correct term for the heraldic representation of the bird in this act is *a pelican in her piety*, *piety* having the classical meaning of filial devotion.

The mediaeval *Bestiary* tells us that the pelican is very fond of its brood, but when the young ones begin to grow they rebel against the male bird and provoke his anger, so that he kills them; the mother returns to the nest in three days, sits on the dead birds, pours her blood over them, revives them, and they feed on the blood.

> Than sayd the Pellycane,
> When my byrdts be slayne
> With my bloude I them reuyue [revive]
> Scrypture doth record,
> The same dyd our Lord,
> And rose from deth to lyue.
>
> Skelton, *Armoury of Birds*

***The Pelican State***. Louisiana, USA, which has a pelican in its device.

**Pelides.** The patronymic of Achilles (*q.v.*), the son of Peleus.

> Like Pelides, bold beyond control,
> Homer raised high to heaven the loud impetuous song
>
> Beattie, *Minstrel*

**Pelion.** ***Heaping Pelion upon Ossa***. Adding difficulty to difficulty, embarrassment to embarrassment, etc. When the giants tried to scale heaven, they placed Mount Pelion upon Mount Ossa, two peaks in Thessaly, for a scaling ladder (*Odyssey*, xi, 315).

> I would have you call to mind the strength of the ancient giants, that undertook to lay the high mountain Pelion on the top of Ossa, and set among those the shady Olympus.
>
> Rabelais, IV, xxxviii

**Pell-mell.** Headlong; in reckless confusion. From the players of pall-mall (*q.v.*), who rushed heedlessly to strike the ball.

**Pellean Conqueror.** Alexander the Great, born at Pella, in Macedonia.

> Remember that Pellean conqueror.
>
> Milton, *Paradise Regained*, ii

**Pelleas, Sir.** One of the Knights of the Round Table, famed for his great strength. He is introduced into the *Faërie Queene* (VI, xii) as going after the 'blatant beast' when it breaks the chain with which it had been bound by Sir Calidore. *See also Tennyson's Pelleas and Ettare.*

**Pells.** ***Clerk of the Pells***. An officer of the Exchequer, whose duty it was to make entries on the *pells* or parchment rolls. Abolished in 1834.

**Pelmanism.** A system of mind and memory training originated by W. J. Ennever in the closing years of last century, and so called because it was an easy name to remember. Owing to its success, and its very extensive advertising, the verb *to pelmanise*, meaning to obtain good results by training the memory, was coined.

**Pelops.** Son of Tantalus, and father of Atreus and Thyestes. He was king of Pisa in Elis, and was cut to pieces and served as food to the gods. The Morea was called Peloponnesus, the 'island of Pelops', from this mythical king.

***The ivory shoulder of Pelops***. The distinguishing or distinctive mark of anyone. The tale is that Demeter ate the shoulder of Pelops when it was served up by Tantalus; when the gods put the body back into the cauldron to restore it to life, this portion was lacking, whereupon Demeter supplied one of ivory.

> Not Pelops' shoulder whiter than her hands.
>
> W. Browne, *Britannia's Pastorals*, ii, 3

**Pelorus.** Cape di Faro, a promontory of Sicily. (Virgil, *Aeneid*, iii, 6, 7.)

> As when the force
> Of subterranean wind transports a hill
> Torn from Pelorus.
>
> Milton, *Paradise Lost*, Bk 1, 232

**Pen.** An interesting word etymologically, for it is the Latin *penna*, a feather, both of which words are derived from the Sanskrit root *pet-*, to fly. *Pet-* gave Sansk. *patra* (feather); this became in Lat. *penna* (Eng. *pen*), and in O.Teut. *fethrō* (Ger. *feder*, Dut, *veder*, Eng. *feather*). Also, in O.Fr. *penne* meant both *feather* and *pen*, but in Mod.Fr. it is restricted to the long wing- and tail-feathers and to heraldic plumes on crests, while *pen* is *plume*. Thus, the French and English usage has been vice versa, English using *plume* in heraldry, French using *penne*, the English writing implement being named *pen*, and the French *plume*.

***Pen-name***. A pseudonym. *See* Nom de Guerre.

**Penates.** *See* Dii penates.

**Pencil.** Originally, a painter's brush, and still used of very fine paint-brushes, from Lat. *penicillum*, a paint-brush, diminutive of *peniculus*, a brush, which itself is a diminutive of *penis*, a tail. When the modern pencil came into use in the early 17th century it was known as a *dry pencil* or a *pencil of black lead*.

***Knight of the pencil.*** A bookmaker; a reporter; also anyone who makes his living by scribbling.

***Pencil of rays.*** All the rays that issue from one point or can be focused at one point; so called because a representation of them has a brush-like appearance.

**Pendente lite** (Lat.). Pending the trial; while the suit is going on.

**Pendragon.** A title conferred on several British chiefs in times of great danger, when they were invested with supreme power, especially (in the Arthurian legends) to Uther Pendragon, father of King Arthur. The word is Welsh *pen*, head, and *dragon* (the reference being to the war-chief's dragon standard); and it corresponded to the Roman *dux bellorum*.

A legend recorded by Geoffrey of Monmouth relates that when Aurelius, the British king, was poisoned by Ambron, during the invasion of Pascentius, son of Vortigern, there 'appeared a star at Winchester of wonderful magnitude and brightness, darting forth a ray, at the end of which was a globe of fire in form of a dragon, out of whose mouth issued forth two rays, one of which extended to Gaul and the other to Ireland'. Uther ordered two golden dragons to be made, one of which he presented to Winchester, and the other he carried with him as his royal standard, whence he received the title 'Pendragon'.

**Penelope.** The wife of Ulysses and mother of Telemachus in Homeric legend. She was a model of all the domestic virtues.

***The Web of Penelope.*** A work 'never ending, still beginning'; never done, but ever in hand. Penelope, according to Homer, was pestered by suitors at Ithaca while Ulysses was absent at the siege of Troy. To relieve herself of their importunities, she promised to make a choice of one as soon as she had finished weaving a shroud for her father-in-law. Every night she unravelled what she had done in the day, and so deferred making any choice till Ulysses returned and slew the suitors.

**Penelophon.** The name of the beggar-maid loved by King Cophetua (*q.v.*) as given in the old ballad (Percy's *Reliques*). Shakespeare called her 'Zenelophon'.

**Penelva.** A knight whose adventures and exploits form a supplemental part of the Spanish romance entitled *Amadis de Gaul* (*q.v.*).

**Penetralia** (Lat. the innermost parts). The private rooms of a house; the secrets of a family. Properly, the part of a Roman temple to which the priest alone had access, where the sacred images were housed, the responses of the oracles made, and the sacred mysteries performed. The Holy of Holies was the *penetralia* of the Jewish Temple.

**Peninsular War.** The war carried on, under the Duke of Wellington, against the French in Portugal and Spain, between 1808 and 1814. It was brought about through the French attack on Spain and Portugal, and, so far as England was concerned, was the most important of the Napoleonic Wars. It resulted in the French being driven from the Peninsula.

**Penitential Psalms.** The seven psalms expressive of contrition – viz. the vi, xxxii, xxxviii, li, cii, cxxx, cxliii. From time immemorial they have all been used at the Ash Wednesday services; the first three at Matins, the 51st at the Commination, and the last three at Evensong.

**Pennals.** So the freshmen of the Protestant universities of Germany were called in the 17th cent., from the *pennale* or pen-cases which they carried with them when they attended lectures.

Hence *pennalism*, rough and cruel bullying, the *pennals* being the 'fags' of the older students and subjected to all sorts of persecution.

**Pennant, Pennon.** The former – the long narrow streamer borne at the masthead of warships – is the nautical form of the latter, which was the name of the small pointed or swallow-tailed flag formerly borne on knights' spears, and still carried by lancer regiments on their lances and as their ensign. *Pennon* is from Lat. *penna*, a feather (*see* Pen), and *pennant* was formed on it through a confusion with *pendant* (Lat. *pendere*, to hang), because it *hangs* from the masthead. It is sometimes, but erroneously, taken as representing the 'whip' with which, according to the popular story, the English admiral was to defeat Van Tromp when he hoisted a broom to signify his intention of sweeping the ships of England off the seas.

**Penny** (A.S. *pening*). The English bronze coin worth one-twelfth of a shilling – often called a *copper*, because from 1797 to 1860 pennies were made of copper. From Anglo-Saxon times till the reign of Charles II pennies were of silver, and between that time and 1797 none were coined, though copper halfpence and farthings were. Silver pennies are still coined, but only in very small quantities and solely for use as Maundy Money (*q.v.*). The weight of a new penny is one-third of an ounce avoirdupois, and it is legal tender up to twelve pence.

The plural *pennies* is used of the number of coins, and *pence* of value; and the word is sometimes used to denote coins of low value of other nations, such as in Luke 20:24, where it stands for the Roman denarius.

***A pretty penny.*** A considerable sum of money, an unpleasantly large sum; as 'The Great War cost us a pretty penny.'

***A penny for your thoughts!*** Tell me what you are thinking about. Addressed humorously to one in a 'brown study'. The phrase occurs in Heywood's *Proverbs* (1546).

***A penny saved is a penny earned*** (or *gained*, etc.). An old adage intended to encourage thrift in the young.

***He has got his pennyworth.*** He has got good value for his money; sometimes said of one who has received a good drubbing.

***In for a penny in for a pound.*** I may as well 'be hung for a sheep as a lamb'. I've done wrong; I'm bound to be punished; and if I go a little farther in my wrong-doing the punishment will be little – if any – worse.

***My penny of observation*** (*Love's Labour's Lost*, 3, 1). My pennyworth of wit; my natural observation or mother-wit. Perhaps there is some pun on *penny* and *penetration*.

***No penny, no paternoster.*** No pay, no work; you'll get nothing for nothing. The allusion is to pre-Reformation days, when priests would not perform services without payment.

***Penny a-liner.*** The old name for a contributor to the newspapers who was not on the staff, because he used to be paid a penny a line. As it was to his interest to 'pad' as much as possible the word is still used in a contemptuous way for a second-rate writer or newspaper hack; but a man who does this work is now usually called a *linage-man*, a *space-man*, or simply a *free lance*.

***Penny-dreadful*** or ***-horrible.*** A cheap, trashy boys' book, full of crude horrors and highly coloured excitement. 'Shilling shocker' is a name for a similar article of higher price, but no higher literary value.

***A penny-father.*** A miser, a penurious person, who 'husbands' his pence.

> To nothing fitter can I thee compare
> Than to the son of some rich penny-father,
> Who having now brought on his end with care,
> Leaves to his son all he had heap'd together.
>
> Drayton: *Idea*, X, i

***Penny-fish.*** A name given to the John Dory (*q.v.*) because of the round spots on each side left by St Peter's fingers.

***Penny gaff.*** A concert or rude music-hall entertainment for which the entrance charge is one penny. *See* Gaff.

***Penny-leaf.*** A country name for the navelwort or wall pennywort (*Cotyledon umbilicus*), from its round leaves.

***Penny-pies.*** A name given to the above and also to the moneywort (*Sibthorpia europaea*).

***Penny readings.*** Parochial entertainments, consisting of readings, music, etc., for which one penny admission is charged.

***Penny weddings.*** Weddings formerly in vogue among the poor in Scotland and Wales at which each of the guests paid a small sum of money not exceeding a shilling. After defraying the expenses of the feast, the residue went to the newly married pair, to aid in furnishing their house.

> Vera true, vera true. We'll have a' to pay … a sort of penny-wedding it will prove, where all men contribute to the young folks' maintenance.
>
> Scott, *Fortunes of Nigel*, ch. xxvii

***Penny wise and pound foolish.*** Said of one who is in danger of 'spoiling the ship for a ha'porth of tar', like the man who lost his horse from his penny wisdom in saving the expense of shoeing it afresh when one of its shoes was loose; hence, one who is thrifty in small matters and careless over large ones is said to be *penny wise*.

***Take care of the pence and the pounds will take care of themselves.*** An excellent piece of advice, which Chesterfield records in his *Letters to his son* (Feb. 5th, 1750) as having been given by 'old Mr Lowndes, the famous Secretary of the Treasury, in the reigns of King William, Queen Anne, and George I'. Chesterfield adds –

> To this maxim, which he not only preached, but practised, his two grandsons, at this time, owe the very considerable fortunes that he left them.

The saying was cleverly parodied in the *Advice to a Poet*, which goes 'Take care of the *sense* and the *sounds* will take care of themselves.'

***Tenpenny nails.*** *See* Tenpenny.

***To turn an honest penny.*** To earn a little money by working for it.

**Pennyroyal.** The name of this herb (*Mentha pulegium*), a species of mint, is not connected with the coin, but is a corruption of *pulyole ryale*, from the Latin *pulegium*, thyme (so called from *pulex*, a flea, because it was supposed to be harmful to fleas), and Anglo-French *réal*, royal. The French call the herb *pouliot*, from *pou*, a louse.

**Pennyweight.** 24 grains, i.e. one-two-hundred-and-fortieth of a pound troy; so called because it was formerly the same proportion of the old 'Tower pound' (i.e. 22½ grains), which was the exact weight of a new silver penny.

***Pension.*** Etymologically, that which is *weighed out* (Lat. *pensionem*, payment, from *pendere*, to weigh, also to pay, because payment was originally weighed out. *Cp.* our *pound*, both a weight and a piece of money).

***Pension***, a boarding-house (to live *en pension*, i.e. as a boarder), though now pronounced and treated as though French, was, in the 17th century, ordinary English; this use arose because *pension* was the term for any regular payment made for services rendered, such as payment for board and lodging.

**Pensioner.** The counterpart at Cambridge of the Oxford commoner (*q.v.*), i.e. an undergraduate who pays for his own commons, etc., and is neither a sizar nor on the foundation of a college.

At the Inns of Court the *pensioner* is the officer who collects the periodical payments made by the members for the upkeep of the Inn.

***Gentlemen Pensioners.*** The old name for the members of the Honourable Corps of Gentlemen-at-arms, who form the nearest guard and principal military corps of the Household of the Sovereign. The Corps was instituted by Henry VIII in 1509, and consists of forty members, with a Lieutenant, Standard Bearer, and Clerk of the Cheque.

***The Pensioner*** (or ***Pensionary***) ***Parliament.*** That from May 8th, 1661, to Jan. 24th, 1679; convened by Charles II, and so called because of the many pensions it granted to adherents of the king.

**Pentacle.** A five-pointed star, or five-sided figure, used in sorcery as a talisman against witches, etc., and sometimes worn as a folded headdress of fine linen, as a defence against demons in the act of conjuration. It is also called the Wizard's Foot, and Solomon's Seal (*signum Salamonis*), and is supposed to typify the five senses, though, as it resolves itself into three triangles, its efficacy may spring from its being a triple symbol of the Trinity.

> And on her head, lest spirits should invade,
> A pentacle, for more assurance, laid.
>
> Rose, *Orlando Furioso*, iii, 21

> The Holy Pentacles numbered forty-four, of which seven were consecrated to each of the planets Saturn, Jupiter, Mars, and the Sun; five to both Venus and Mercury; and six to the Moon. The divers figures were enclosed in a double circle, containing the name of God in Hebrew, and other mystical words.

**Pentameter.** In prosody, a line of five feet, dactyls or spondees divided by a caesura into two parts of two and a half feet each – the line used in alternation with the hexameter (*q.v.*) in Latin elegiac verse. The name is sometimes wrongly applied to the English five-foot iambic line.

> In the hexameter rises the fountain's silvery column,
> In the pentameter aye falling in melody back.
>
> Coleridge, *Example of Elegiac Metre*

**Pentapolin.** In Cervantes' *Don Quixote* (I, iii, 4), the drover of a flock of sheep, whom Don Quixote conceived to be the Christian King of the Garamantians and surnamed the *Naked Arm*, because he always entered the field with his right arm bare.

**Pentapolis.** The name given in ancient history to a number of groups or confederations of five cities (Gr. *penta*, five, *polis*, city), especially the Dorian Pentapolis in Asia Minor – Cnidos, Cos, Lindos, Ialysos, and Camiros, and the five cities of Italy in the exarchate of Ravenna – Rimini, Pesaro, Fano, Sinigaglia, and Ancona – which were given by Pepin to the Pope.

**Pentateuch.** The first five books of the Old Testament, supposed to be written by Moses. (Gr. *penta*, five, *teuchos*, a tool, book.)

***The Samaritan Pentateuch.*** The Hebrew text as preserved by the Samaritans; it is said to date from 400 bc.

**Pentecost** (Gr., *pentecoste*, fiftieth). The festival held by the Jews on the fiftieth day after the second day of the Passover; our Whit Sunday, which commemorates the descent of the Holy Spirit on the Apostles on the Day of Pentecost (Acts 2).

**Penthesilea.** Queen of the Amazons who, in the post-Homeric legends, fought for Troy; she was slain by Achilles. Hence, any strong, commanding woman; Sir Toby Belch, in *Twelfth Night* (2, 3), calls Maria by this name.

**Peony.** So called, according to fable, from Paeon, the physician who cured the wounds received by the gods in the Trojan war. The seeds were, at one time, worn round the neck as a charm against the powers of darkness.

> About an Infants neck hang Peonie,
> It cures Alcydes cruell Maladie.
>
> *Sylvester's Du Barias*, I, iii, 712

**People's Charter.** *See* Chartism.

**People of God, The.** *See* Shakers.

**Pepper.** ***To pepper one well.*** To give one a good basting or thrashing.

***To take pepper i' the nose.*** To take offence. The French have a similar locution, *La moutarde lui monte au nez.*

> Take you pepper in the nose, you mar our sport.
>
> Middleton, *The Spanish Gipsy*, IV, iii

***When your daughter is stolen close Pepper Gate.*** Pepper Gate used to be on the east side of the city of Chester. It is said that the daughter of the mayor eloped, and the mayor ordered the gate to be closed up. 'Lock the stable-door when the steed is stolen.'

**Pepper-and-salt.** A light grey colour, especially applied to cloth for dresses.

**Peppercorn Rent.** A nominal rent. A pepper-berry is of no appreciable value, and given as rent is a simple acknowledgement that the tenement virtually belongs to the person by whom the peppercorn is given.

Cowper makes a figurative use of the custom –

> True. While they live, the courtly laureate pays
> His quit-rent ode, his pepper-corn of praise.
>
> *Table-talk*, 110

**Per contra** (Lat.). A commercial term for on the opposite side of the account. Used also of arguments, etc.

**Per saltum** (Lat. by a leap). A promotion or degree given without going over the ground usually prescribed. Thus, a clergyman on being made a bishop has the degree of D.D. given him *per saltum* – i.e. without taking the B.D. degree, and waiting the usual five years.

**Perceforest.** An early 14th century French prose romance (said to be the longest in existence), belonging to the Arthurian cycle, but mingling with it the Alexander romance. After Alexander's war in India he comes to England, of which he makes Perceforest, one of his knights, king. The romance tells how Perceforest established the Knights of the Franc Palais, how his grandson brings the Grail to England, and includes many popular tales, such as that of the Sleeping Beauty.

**Percival, Sir.** The Knight of the Round Table who, according to Malory's *Morte d'Arthur* (and Tennyson's *Idylls of the King*), finally won a sight of the Holy Grail (*q.v.*). He was the son of Sir Pellinore and brother of Sir Lamerocke, but in the earlier French romances – based probably on the Welsh *Mabinogi* and other Celtic originals – he has no connection with the Grail, but here (as in the English also) he sees the lance dripping blood, and the severed head surrounded by blood in a dish. The French version of the romance is by Chrêtien de Troies (12th cent.), which formed the basis of Sebastian Evans's *The High History of the Holy Graal* (1893). The German version, *Parsifal* or *Parzival*, was written some 50 years later by Wolfram von Eschenbach, and it is principally on this version that Wagner drew for his opera, *Parsifal* (1882).

**Percy.** When Malcolm III of Scotland invaded England, and reduced the castle of Alnwick, Robert de Mowbray brought to him the keys of the castle suspended on his lance; and, handing them from the wall, thrust his lance into the king's eye; from which circumstance, the tradition says, he received the name of 'Pierce-eye', which has ever since been borne by the Dukes of Northumberland.

> This is all a fable. The Percies are descended from a great Norman baron, who came over with William, and who took his name from his castle and estate in Normandy.
>
> Scott, *Tales of a Grandfather*, iv

**Perdita.** In Shakespeare's *Winter's Tale*, the daughter of Leontes and Hermione of Sicily. She was abandoned by order of her father, and put in a vessel which drifted to 'the sea-coast of Bohemia', where the infant was discovered by a shepherd, who brought her up as his own daughter. In time Florizel, the son and heir of the Bohemian king Polixenes, fell in love with the supposed shepherdess. The match was forbidden by Polixenes, and the young lovers fled to Sicily. Here the story is cleared up, and all ends happily in the restoration of the lost (Fr. *perdu*) Perdita to her parents, and her marriage with Florizel.

Mrs Robinson, the actress and mistress of George IV when Prince of Wales, was specially successful in the part of Perdita, and she assumed this name, the Prince being known as Florizel.

**Perdrix, toujours perdrix.** Too much of the same thing. Walpole tells us that the confessor of one of the French kings reproved him for conjugal infidelity, and was asked by the king what he liked best. 'Partridge', replied the priest, and the king ordered him to be served with partridge every day, till he quite loathed the sight of his favourite dish. After a time, the king visited him, and hoped he had been well served, when the confessor replied, *Mais oui, perdrix, toujours perdrix*. 'Ah! ah!' replied the amorous monarch, 'and one mistress is all very well, but not "*perdrix, toujours perdrix*".'

> Soup for dinner, soup for supper, and soup for breakfast again.
>
> Farquhar, *The Inconstant*, iv, 2

**Père la Chaise.** This great Parisian cemetery is on the site of a religious settlement founded by the Jesuits in 1626, and later enlarged by Louis XIV's confessor, Père la Chaise. After the Revolution, the grounds were laid out for their present purpose, and were first used in May, 1804.

**Peregrine Falcon.** A falcon of wide distribution, formerly held in great esteem for hawking, and so called (13th cent.) because taken when on their passage or *peregrination*, from the breeding place, instead of straight off the nest, as was the case with most other hawks (Lat. *peregrinus*, a foreigner, one coming from foreign parts).

Dame Juliana Berners in the *Book of St Albans* (*see* Hawk) tells us that the peregrine was for an earl. The hen is the *falcon* of falconers; the cock the *tercel*.

The word was formerly used as synonymous with *pilgrim*, and (adjectivally) for one travelling abroad.

**Perfect Number.** One of which the sum of all its divisors exactly measures itself, as 6, the divisors of which are 1, 2, 3 = 6. These are very scarce; indeed, from 1 to forty million there are only seven, viz. 6, 28, 496, 8128, 130816, 2096128, and 33550336.

**Perfectionists.** Members of a communistic sect founded by J. H. Noyes (1811–86) in Vermont about 1834, and removed by him and settled at Oneida, New York, 1847–8. Its chief features were that the community was held to be one family, mutual criticism and public opinion took the place of government, and wives were – theoretically, at least – held in common, till 1879, when, owing to opposition, this was abandoned. In 1881 the sect, which had prospered exceedingly through its thrift and industry, voluntarily dissolved and was reorganised as a joint-stock company.

**Perfume** means simply 'from smoke' (Lat. *per fumum*), the first perfumes having been obtained by the combustion of aromatic woods and gums. Their original use was in sacrifices, to counteract the offensive odours of the burning flesh.

**Perhaps.** ***I am going to seek a great perhaps.*** One of the last sayings of Rabelais. *See* Dying Sayings.

> Good heavens! And this is what you call the flower of life: and age, and darkness, and the grand Perhaps lying close in the rear of it.
>
> Carlyle, *Life in London*, xii

**Peri.** Originally, a beautiful but malevolent sprite of Persian myth, one of a class which was responsible for comets, eclipses, failure of crops, etc.; in later times applied to delicate, gentle, fairy-like beings, begotten by fallen spirits who direct with a wand the pure in mind the way to heaven. These lovely creatures, according to the Koran, are under the sovereignty of Eblis; and Mahomet was sent for their conversion, as well as for that of man.

> Like peris' wands, when pointing out the road
> For some pure spirit to the blest abode.
>
> Thomas Moore, *Lalla Rookh*, Pt i

The name is often applied to any beautiful, fascinating girl.

***Paradise and the Peri.*** The second tale in Moore's *Lalla Rookh*. The Peri laments her expulsion from heaven, and is told she will be readmitted if she will bring to the gate of heaven the 'gift most dear to the Almighty'. After a number of unavailing offerings she brought a guilty old man, who wept with repentance, and knelt to pray. The Peri offered the *Repentant Tear*, and the gates flew open.

**Pericles, Prince of Tyre.** According to Sir Sidney Lee, the greater portion of this play, which was ascribed to Shakespeare in all the Quartos (1st, 1608), but was not admitted to the collected works before the Third Folio (1664), was by George Wilkins, author of *The Miseries of Inforst Marriage* (1607), etc. The original story was the work of a late Greek romance writer and was extremely popular in mediaeval times. The hero was *Apollonius* of Tyre, and under this name the story occurs in the *Gesta Romanorum*, Gower's *Confessio Amantis* (Bk viii), and elsewhere.

**Perillo Swords.** *Perillo* (Span.) is a 'little stone' – the 'trade mark' on the swords made by Julian del Rey, a famous armourer of Toledo and Zaragoza. Perillo swords were made of the steel produced from the mines of Mondragon. The swords given by Catherine of Aragon to Henry VIII on their wedding-day were all *Perillo* blades.

Their usual inscription was, 'Draw me not without reason, sheathe me not without honour.'

**Perillos and the Brazen Bull.** *See under* Inventors.

**Perilous Castle.** The castle of 'the good' Lord Douglas was so called in the reign of Edward I, because Douglas destroyed several English garrisons stationed there, and vowed to be revenged on anyone who should dare to take possession of it. Scott calls it 'Castle Dangerous' (*see* Introduction of *Castle Dangerous*).

**Perion.** A fabulous king of Gaul, father of Amadis in the mediaeval romance, *Amadis of Gaul* (*q.v.*).

**Peripatetic School.** The school or system of philosophy founded by Aristotle, who used to walk about (Gr. *peri*, about, *patein*, to walk) as he taught his disciples in the covered walk of the Lyceum. This colonnade was called the *peripatos*.

**Perissa.** The typification of excessive exuberance of spirits in Spenser's *Faërie Queene* (II, ii). She was the mistress of Sansloy and a step-sister of Elissa (*q.v.*).

> In wine and meats she flowed above the bank,
> And in excess exceeded her own might;
> In sumptuous tire she joyed herself to prank,
> But of her love too lavish.
>
> *Faërie Queene*, II, ii, 36

**Periwig.** *See* Peruke.

**Periwinkle.** The plant gets its name from Lat. *pervinca*, which may mean either to conquer completely or to bind around, but *why* it should have received this name is unknown, though it may earlier have been applied to some climbing plant. In Italy it used *to be wreathed round* dead infants, and hence its Italian name, *fiore di morto*.

The sea-snail of this name was called in A.S. *pinewinkle*, the first syllable probably being cognate with Lat. *pina*, a mussel, and *winkle* from A.S. *wincel*, a corner, with reference to its much convoluted shell.

**Perk.** The derivation of the word is unknown, but as it is first met with (14th cent.) in connection with the popinjay (parrot) it may have something to do with *perch*, the parrot bearing itself on its perch in a *perky* or jaunty way; and in some instances (e.g. 'The eagle and the dove pearke not on one branch', Greene's *Perimedes*, and 'Caesar's crowe durst never cry *Ave* but when she was pearked on the Capitoll', Greene's *Pandosto*) it is not always easy to differentiate the two meanings.

***You begin to perk up a bit*** – i.e. to get a little fatter and more plump after an illness.

**Permian Strata.** The uppermost strata of the Palaeozoic series, consisting chiefly of red sandstone and magnesian limestone, which rest on the carboniferous strata; so called by Sir Roderick Murchison (1841) from Perm, in Russia, where they are most distinctly developed.

**Perpetual Motion.** The term applied to some theoretical force that will move a machine for ever of itself – a mirage which holds attractions for some minds much as did the search for the philosophers' stone, the elixir of life, and the fountain of perpetual youth in less enlightened times.

It is quite possible, theoretically, at least, to eliminate all friction, air resistance, and wear and tear, and if this were done a body to which motion had been given would, unless interfered with, retain it for ever; but *only on the condition that it were given no work to do*; once connect the ideal spinning top with a wheel or crank and the spin would inevitably come to an end.

**Persecutions, The Ten Great.** (1) Under Nero, AD 64; (2) Domitian, 95; (3) Trajan, 98; (4) Hadrian, 118; (5) Pertinax, 202, chiefly in Egypt; (6) Maximin, 236; (7) Decius, 249; (8) Valerian, 257; (9) Aurelian, 272; (10) Diocletian, 302.

> It would be well if these were the only religious persecutions; but, alas! those on the other side prove the truth of the Founder: 'I came not to send peace, but a sword' (Matt. 10:34). Witness the long persecutions of the Waldenses and Albigenses, the thirty years' war of Germany, the persecution of the Guises, the Bartholomew slaughter, the wars of Louis XIV on the revocation of the Edict of Nantes, the Dragonnades, and the wars against Holland. Witness the bitter persecutions stirred up by Luther, which spread to England and Scotland. No war so lasting, so relentless, so bloody as religious wars.

**Persepolis,** called by the Persians 'The Throne of Jam-sheid', by whom it was founded. Jam-sheid removed the seat of government from Balk to Istakhar. *See* Chilminar.

**Perseus.** In Greek legend, the hero son of Zeus and Danaë (*q.v.*). He and his mother were set adrift in a chest, but were rescued through the intervention of Zeus, and he was brought up by King Polydectes, who, wishing to marry his mother, got rid of him by giving him the almost hopeless task of obtaining the head of Medusa (*q.v.*). He, with the help of the gods, was successful, and with the head (which turned all that looked on it to stone) he rescued Andromeda (*q.v.*), and later metamorphosed Polydectes and his guests to stone.

Before his birth an oracle had foretold that Acrisius, Danaë's father, would be slain by Danaë's son; and this came to pass, for, while taking part in the games at Larissa, Perseus accidentally slew his grandfather with a discus.

**Person.** From Lat. *persona*, which meant originally a mask worn by actors (perhaps from *per sonare*, to sound through), and later was transferred to the character or personage represented by the actor (*cp.* our *dramatis personae*), and so to any human being in his definite character, at which stage the word was adopted in English through the O.Fr. *persone*.

***Confounding the Persons***. The heresy of Sabellius (*see* Sabellianism), who declared that Father, Son, and Holy Ghost were but three names, aspects, or manifestations of one God, the orthodox doctrine being that of the Athanasian Creed –

> We worship one God in Trinity, and Trinity in Unity; Neither confounding the Persons, nor dividing the Substance (*Neque confundentes personas, neque substantiam seperantes*).

*Person* here indicates the individual Unity of the Father, of the Son, and of the Holy Ghost, *Substance* indicates their Collective Unity; and 'dividing the Substance' is asserting that the essential qualities of the Trinity belong to either Person separately from, or in a different degree from, the other Persons. *Cp.* Trinity.

**Persona grata** (Lat.). An acceptable person; one liked.

> The Count [Münster] is not a *persona grata* at court, as the royal family did not relish the course he took in Hanoverian affairs in 1866.
>
> *Truth*, Oct. 22, 1885

**Perth** is Celtic for a bush. The county of Perth is the county of bushes.

***The Five Articles of Perth.*** Those passed in 1618 by order of James VI, enjoining the attitude of kneeling to receive the elements; the observance of Christmas, Good Friday, Easter, and Pentecost; the right of confirmation, etc. They were ratified August 4, 1621, called *Black Saturday*, and condemned in the General Assembly of Glasgow in 1638.

**Peru.** ***From China to Peru***. From one end of the world to the other; world-wide. Equivalent to the biblical 'from Dan to Beersheba'. The phrase comes from the opening of Johnson's *Vanity of Human Wishes* –

> Let observation with extensive view
> Survey mankind from China to Peru.
>
> Boileau (*Sat.* viii, 3) had previously written:
>
> De Paris au Pérou, du Japon jusqu'à Rome.

**Peruke** (Fr. *perruke*, the origin of which is unknown though the word has been conjecturally derived from Lat. *pilus*, hair). The wigs are first mentioned in the 16th century; in the next century they became very large, and the fashion began to wane in the reign of George III. *Periwig*, which has been further corrupted into *wig*, is a corrupt form of *peruke*.

**Peruvian Bark,** called also **Jesuit's Bark,** because it was introduced into Spain by the Jesuits. 'Quinine', from the same tree, is called by the Indians *quinquina*. *See* Cinchona.

**Petard.** ***Hoist with his own petard***. Beaten with his own weapons, caught in his own trap; involved in the danger intended for others, as were many designers of instruments of torture. *See list under* Inventors. The petard was a thick iron engine of war, filled with gunpowder, and fastened to gates, barricades, and so on, to blow them up. The danger was lest the engineer who fired the petard should be blown up in the explosion.

> Let it work;
> For 'tis the sport, to have the engineer
> Hoist with his own petard; and it shall go hard
> But I will delve one yard below their mines,
> And blow them at the moon.
>
> Shakespeare, *Hamlet*, 3, 4

**Pétaud.** ***'Tis the court of King Pétaud, where everyone is master***. There is no order or discipline at all. This is a French proverb. *Le roi Pétaud* (Lat. *peto*, I beg) was the title of the chief who was elected by the fraternity of beggars in mediaeval France, in whose court all were equal.

**Peter, St.** The patron saint of fishermen, being himself a fisherman; the 'Prince of the Apostles'. His day is June 29th, and he is usually represented as an old man, bald, but with a flowing beard, dressed in a white mantle and blue tunic, and holding in his hand a book or scroll. His peculiar symbols are the keys, and a sword.

Tradition tells that he confuted Simon Magus, who was at Nero's court as a magician, and that in 66 he was crucified with his head downwards at his own request, as he said he was not worthy to suffer the same death as our Lord.

***St Peter's fingers.*** The fingers of a thief. The allusion is to the fish caught by St Peter with a piece of money in its mouth. They say that a thief has a fish-hook on every finger.

***St Peter's fish.*** The John Dory (*q.v.*); also, the haddock.

***Great Peter.*** A bell in York Minster, weighing 10¾ tons, and hung in 1845.

***Lord Peter.*** The Pope in Swift's *Tale of a Tub.*

***To peter out.*** To come gradually to an end, to give out. The phrase came from the American mining camps of about '49, but its origin is not known.

***To rob Peter to pay Paul.*** *See* Rob.

**Peter-boat: Peterman.** A fishing-boat made to go either way, the stem and stern being alike. They are still in common use round the mouth of the Thames, and were so called from *Peterman*, a term up to the 17th century for a fisherman.

> I hope to live to see dog's meat made of the old usurer's flesh; ... his skin is too thick to make parchment, 'twould make good boots for a peterman to catch salmon in.
>
> Chapman, *Eastward Ho*, II, ii

**Peter** (or **Peter's**) **Pence.** An annual tribute of one penny, paid at the feast of St Peter to the see of Rome, collected, at first, from every family, but afterwards restricted to those 'who had the value of thirty pence in quick or live stock'. This tax was collected in England from about the middle of the 8th century till it was abolished by Henry VIII in 1534.

**Peter-see-me.** A favourite Spanish wine was so called in the 17th century. The name is a corruption of *Pedro Ximenes*, the name of a grower who introduced a special grape.

> Peter-see-me shall wash thy noul
> And malaga glasses fox thee;
> If, poet, thou toss not bowl for bowl
> Thou shalt not kiss a doxy.
>
> Middleton, *Spanish Gipsy*, III, 1

**Peter the Hermit.** *See* Hermit.

**Peterloo,** or the **Manchester Massacre.** The dispersal by the military on August 16th, 1819, of a large crowd of operatives who had assembled at St Peter's Field, Manchester, to hear 'Orator' Hunt speak in favour of Parliamentary Reform. The arrest of Hunt was ordered, but, as this was impossible and riot was feared, the magistrates gave the hussars orders to charge. Some six persons were killed in the charge, many were injured, and the arrest of Hunt (who was given two years' imprisonment) was effected.

The name, of course, was founded on *Waterloo*, then fresh in the popular mind.

**Petit-Maître** (Fr.). A fop; a lad who assumes the manners, dress, and affectations of a man. The term arose before the Revolution, when a great dignitary was styled a *grand-maître*, and a pretentious one a *petit-maître*.

**Petit Sergeanty.** *See* Sergeanty.

**Petitio principii.** A begging of the question, or assuming in the premises the question you undertake to prove. In mediaeval logic a principium was an essential, self-evident principle from which particular truths were deducible; the assumption of this principle was the *petitio*, i.e. begging, of it. It is the same as 'arguing in a circle'.

> Petitio Principii, as defined by Archbishop Whately, is the fallacy in which the premise either appears manifestly to be the same as the conclusion, or is actually proved from the conclusion, or is such as would naturally and properly so be proved.
>
> J. S. Mill, *System of Logic*, II, p. 389

**Petitioners and Abhorrers.** Two political parties in the reign of Charles II. When that monarch was first restored he used to grant everything he was asked for; but after a time this became a great evil, and Charles enjoined his loving subjects to discontinue their practice of 'petitioning'. Those who agreed with the king, and disapproved of petitioning, were called *Abhorrers*; those who were favourable to the objectionable practice were nicknamed *Petitioners*.

**Petrel.** *The stormy petrel.* A small sea-bird (*Procellaria pelagica*), so named, according to tradition, from the Ital. *Petrello*, little Peter, because during storms they seem to fly patting the water with each foot alternately as though walking on it, in allusion to St Peter, who walked on the Lake of Gennesareth. Sailors call them 'Mother Carey's chickens'. The term is used figuratively of one whose coming always portends trouble, one who can be calculated upon to 'raise Cain' wherever he goes or whatever he does.

**Petrobrusians.** A religious sect, founded about 1105 by Peter Bruys, or de Brueys, an eloquent but ignorant priest of Provence. His teaching was essentially anti-sacerdotal; he declaimed against churches, asserting that a stable was as good as a cathedral for worship, and a manger equal to an altar; he rejected infant baptism, and particularly objected to the worship of the Cross or the use of crucifixes, for, said he, the accursed tree should be held in horror by all Christians as the instrument of the torture and death of our Saviour.

**Petto.** ***In petto.*** In secrecy, in reserve (Ital., in the breast). The pope creates cardinals *in petto* – i.e. in his own mind – and keeps the appointment to himself till he thinks proper to announce it.

> Belgium, a department of France *in petto* – i.e. in the intention of the people.
>
> *The Herald*, 1837

**Petty Cury** (Cambridge) means 'The Street of Cooks', from Lat. *curare*, to cure or dress food. It is called *Parva Cokeria* in a deed dated 13 Edward III. Probably at one time it was part of the Market Hall.

**Peutingerian Map.** A map of the roads of the ancient Roman world, constructed in the time of Alexander Severus (AD 226), discovered in the early 16th century by Conrad Peutinger, of Augsburg.

**Pewter.** ***To scour the pewter.*** To do one's work.

> But if she neatly scour her pewter,
> Give her the money that is due t' her.
>
> King, *Orpheus and Eurydice*

**Pfister's Bible.** *See* Bible, Specially named.

**Phaedria.** The typification in Spenser's *Faërie Queene* (II, vi) of wantonness; she was handmaid to Acrasia the enchantress, and sailed about Idle Lake in a gondola. Seeing Sir Guyon she ferried him across the lake to the floating island, where Cymochles attacked him. Phaedria interposed, the combatants desisted, and the little wanton ferried the knight Temperance over the lake again.

**Phaeton.** In classical myth, the son of Phoebus (the Sun); he undertook to drive his father's chariot, but was upset and thereby caused Libya to be parched into barren sands, and all Africa to be more or less injured, the inhabitants blackened, and vegetation nearly destroyed, and would have set the world on fire had not Zeus transfixed him with a thunderbolt.

> Gallop apace, you fiery-footed steeds,
> Towards Phoebus' mansion; such a waggoner
> As Phaeton would whip you to the west,
> And bring in cloudy night immediately.
>
> Shakespeare, *Romeo and Juliet*, 3, 2

The name is given to a light, four-wheeled open carriage usually drawn by two horses.

***Phaeton's bird.*** The swan. Cygnus, son of Apollo, was the friend of Phaeton and lamented his fate so grievously that Apollo changed him into a swan, and placed him among the constellations.

**Phalanx.** The close order of battle in which the heavy-armed troops of a Grecian army were usually drawn up. Hence, any number of people distinguished for firmness and solidity of union.

**Phalaris.** ***The brazen bull of Phalaris.*** *See under* Inventors.

***The epistles of Phalaris.*** A series of 148 letters said to have been written by Phalaris, Tyrant of Agrigentum, Sicily, in the 6th century BC, and edited by Charles Boyle in 1695. Boyle maintained them to be genuine, but Richard Bentley, applying the then new methods of historical criticism, proved that they were forgeries of about the 7th or 8th centuries, AD. *See* Boyle Controversy.

**Phantom.** A spirit or apparition, an illusory appearance; from M.E. and O.Fr. *fantosme*, Gr. *phantasma* (*phanein*, to show).

***Phantom corn.*** The mere ghost of corn; corn that has as little body as a spectre.

***Phantom fellow.*** One who is under the ban of some hobgoblin; a half-witted person.

***Phantom flesh.*** Flesh that hangs loose and flabby; formerly supposed to be bewitched.

***The Phantom Ship.*** The 'Flying Dutchman' (*q.v.*).

**Phaon.** In Spenser's *Faërie Queene* (II, iv), a young man ill-treated by Furor, and rescued by Sir Guyon. He loved Claribel, but Philemon, his friend, persuaded him that Claribel was unfaithful, and, to prove his words, made him see what appeared to be Claribel holding an assignation with a groom. Rushing forth, Phaon met the true Claribel, whom he slew on the spot. When tried for the murder it came out that the groom was Philemon, and the supposed Claribel her maid. He poisoned Philemon, and would have murdered the maid, but she escaped, and while he pursued her he was attacked by Furor. This tale is designed to show the evil of intemperate revenge. In some editions of the poem *Phedon* is the name, not *Phaon*.

**Pharamond.** In the Arthurian romances, a Knight of the Round Table, who is said to have been the first king of France, and to have reigned in the early 5th century. He was the son of

Marcomir and father of Clodion.

La Calprenède's novel *Pharamond, ou l'Histoire de France*, was published in 1661.

**Pharaoh.** The title or generic appellation of the kings in ancient Egypt. The word originally meant 'the great house', and its later use arose much in the same way as, in modern times, 'the Holy See' for the Pope, or 'the Sublime Porte' for the Sultan of Turkey.

None of the Pharaohs mentioned in the Old Testament has been certainly identified, owing to the great obscurity of the references and the almost entire absence of reliable chronological data.

According to the Talmud, the name of Pharaoh's daughter who brought up Moses was *Bathia*.

In Dryden's satire *Absalom and Achitophel* (*q.v.*) 'Pharaoh' stands for Louis XIV of France.

> If Pharaoh's doubtful succour he [Charles II] should use,
> A foreign aid would more incense the Jews [English nation].

***Pharaoh's chicken***, or ***hen.*** The Egyptian vulture, so called from its frequent representation in Egyptian hieroglyphics.

***Pharaoh's corn.*** The grains of wheat sometimes found in mummy cases. *See* Mummy-wheat.

***Pharaoh's rat.*** *See* Ichneumon.

***Pharaoh's serpent.*** A chemical toy consisting of sulpho-cyanide of mercury, which fuses into a serpentine shape when lighted; so called in allusion to the magic serpents of Exod. 7:9–12.

**Pharisees** (Heb. *perusim*, from *perash*, to separate) means 'those who have been set apart', not as a sect but as a school of ascetics who attempted to regulate their lives by the letter of the Law. The opprobrious sense of the word was given it by their enemies, because the Pharisees came to look upon themselves as holier than other men, and refused to hold social intercourse with them. The Talmud mentions the following classes:

(1) The 'Dashers', or 'Bandy-legged' (*Nikfi*), who scarcely lifted their feet from the ground in walking, but 'dashed them against the stones', that people might think them absorbed in holy thought (Matt. 21:44).

(2) The 'Mortars', who wore a 'mortier', or cap, which would not allow them to see the passers-by, that their meditations might not be disturbed. Having eyes, they saw not (Mark 8:18).

(3) The 'Bleeders', who inserted thorns in the borders of their gaberdines to prick their legs in walking.

(4) The 'Cryers', or 'Inquirers', who went about crying out, 'Let me know my duty, and I will do it' (Matt 19:16–22).

(5) The 'Almsgivers', who had a trumpet sounded before them to summon the poor together (Matt. 6:2).

(6) The 'Stumblers', or 'Bloody-browed' (*Kizai*), who shut their eyes when they went abroad that they might see no women, being 'blind leaders of the blind' (Matt. 15:14). Our Lord calls them ' blind Pharisees', ' fools and blind'.

(7) The 'Immovables', who stood like statues for hours together, 'praying in the market places' (Matt. 6:5).

(8) The 'Pestle Pharisees' (*Medinkia*), who kept themselves bent double like the handle of a pestle.

(9) The 'Strong-shouldered' (*Shikmi*), who walked with their back bent as if carrying on their shoulders the whole burden of the law.

(10) The 'Dyed Pharisees', called by our Lord 'Whited Sepulchres', whose externals of devotion cloaked hypocrisy and moral uncleanliness. (*Talmud of Jerusalem*, *Berakoth*, ix; *Sota*, v, 7; *Talmud of Babylon. Sota*, 22 b.)

**Pharos.** A lighthouse; so called from the lighthouse – one of the Seven Wonders of the World – built by Ptolemy Philadelphus in the island of Pharos, off Alexandria, Egypt. It was 450 feet high, and, according to Josephus, could be seen at the distance of 42 miles. Part was blown down in 793.

> Let our girls flit,
> Till the storm die! but had you stood by us,
> The roar that breaks the Pharos from his base
> Had left us rock.
>
> Tennyson, *The Princess*, vi, 339

**Pharsalia.** An epic in Latin hexameters by Lucan. It tells of the civil war between Pompey and Caesar, and of the battle of Pharsalus (48 BC) in which Pompey, with 45,000 legionaries, 7,000 cavalry, and a large number of auxiliaries, was decisively defeated by Caesar, who had only 22,000 legionaries and 1,000 cavalry. Pompey's battle-cry was *Hercules invictus*; that of Caesar, *Venus victrix*.

**Pheasant.** The 'Phasian bird'; so called from Phasis, a river of Colchis, whence the bird is said to have spread westward.

**Phedon.** An alternative name of Phaon (*q.v.*).

**Phenomenon** (pl. phenomena) means simply what has appeared (Gr. *phainomai*, to appear). It is used in science to express the visible result of an experiment. In popular language it means a prodigy, and *phenomenal* (as 'a phenomenal success') is slang for prodigious.

> *Phenomenal*, soon, we hope, to perish, unregretted, is (at least indirectly, through the abuse of *phenomenon*) from Metaphysics; [such words are] at present, enjoying some vogue as slang, and come from regions that to most of us are overhead.
>
> H. W. and F. G. Fowler, *The King's English*, ch. i (1906)

**Phigalian Marbles.** A series of twenty-three sculptures in alto-relievo, discovered in 1812 at Phigalia, in Arcadia, forming part of the Elgin Marbles (*q.v.*), now in the British Museum. They represent the combat of the Centaurs and Lapithae, and that of the Greeks and Amazons.

**Philadelphists.** *See* Behmenists.

**Philandering.** Coquetting with a woman; paying court, and leading her to think you love her, but never declaring your preference. *Philander* literally means 'a lover of men' (Gr. *philos*, loving, *andros*, man), but as the word was made into a proper noun and used for a lover by Ariosto in *Orlando Furioso* (followed by Beaumont and Fletcher in *The Laws of Candy*), it obtained its present signification. In Norton and Sackville's *Gorboduc* (1561) Philander is the name of a staid old counsellor.

**Philemon and Baucis.** Poor cottagers of Phrygia (husband and wife), who, in Ovid's story (*Metamorphoses*, iii, 631), entertained Jupiter so hospitably that he promised to grant them whatever request they made. They asked that both might die together, and it was so. Philemon became an oak, Baucis a linden tree, and their branches intertwined at the top.

**Philip.** ***Philip, remember thou art mortal.*** A sentence repeated to the Macedonian king every time he gave an audience.

***Philip sober.*** When a woman who asked Philip of Macedon to do her justice was snubbed by the petulant monarch, she exclaimed, 'Philip, I shall appeal against this judgment.' 'Appeal!' thundered the enraged king, 'and to whom will you appeal?' 'To Philip sober,' was her reply.

***St Philip*** is usually represented bearing a large cross, or a basket containing loaves, in allusion to John 6:5–7. He is commemorated on May 1st.

**Philippic.** A severe scolding; a speech full of acrimonious invective. So called from the orations of Demosthenes against Philip of Macedon, to rouse the Athenians to resist his encroachments. The orations of Cicero against Antony are called 'Philippics'.

**Philippins** or **Philipoftschins.** A small Russian Manichaean sect, so called from the founder, Philip (about 1680), a monk who gained the title Pustos-Wiat (Saint of the Desert). They were called *Old Faith Men*, because they cling with tenacity to the old service books, old version of the Bible, old hymn book, old prayer book, and all customs previous to the reforms of Nekon, in the 17th century. About 1730 the Empress Anne sent commissioners to enquire into the state of their monasteries, but, rather than give any information, they burnt themselves alive within their own walls.

**Philisides.** Sir Philip Sidney (*Phili' Sid*). Spenser uses the word in the *Pastoral Aeglogue on the Death of Sir Philip* –

> Philisides is dead.

**Philistines.** The ill-behaved and ignorant; persons lacking in liberal culture or of low and materialistic ideas. This meaning of the word is due to Matthew Arnold, who adapted it from *Philister*, the term applied by students at the German universities to the townspeople, the 'outsiders'. This is said to have arisen at Jena, because, after a 'town and gown' row in 1689, which resulted in a number of deaths, the university preacher took for his text 'The Philistines be upon thee' (Judges 16).

> The people who believe most that our greatness and welfare are proved by our being very rich, and who most give their lives and thoughts to becoming rich, are just the very people whom we call the Philistines.
>
> M. Arnold, *Culture and Anarchy* (1869)

**Philoclea,** in Sidney's *Arcadia*, is Lady Penelope Devereux, with whom he was in love; the lady married another, and Sir Philip transferred his affections to Frances, eldest daughter of Sir Francis Walsingham.

**Philoctetes.** The most famous archer in the Trojan war, to whom Hercules, at death, gave his arrows. He joined the allied Greeks, with seven ships, but in the island of Lemnos, his foot being bitten by a serpent, ulcerated, and became so offensive that the Greeks left him behind. In the tenth year of the siege Ulysses commanded that he should be sent for, as an oracle had declared that Troy could not be taken without the arrows of Hercules. Philoctetes accordingly went to Troy, slew Paris, and Troy fell.

The *Philoctetes* of Sophocles is one of the most famous Greek tragedies.

**Philomel.** *See* Nightingale.

**Philosopher.** The sages of Greece used to be called *sophoi* (wise men), but Pythagoras thought the word too arrogant, and adopted the compound *philosophoi* (lover of wisdom), whence 'philosopher', one who courts or loves wisdom.

Marcus Aurelius (121–180) was surnamed *The Philosopher* by Justin Martyr, and the name was also conferred on Leo VI, Emperor of the East (d.911), and Porphyry, the Neo-platonic opponent of Christianity (d.305).

The leading philosophers and Schools of Philosophy in Ancient Greece were –

***Philosophers of the Academic sect.*** Plato, Speusippos, Xenocrates, Polemon, Crates, Crantor, Arcesilaos, Careades, Clitomachos, Philo, and Antiochos.

***Philosophers of the Cynic sect.*** Antisthenes, Diogenes of Sinope, Monimos, Onesicritos, Crates, Metrocles, Hipparchia, Menippos, and Menedemos of Lampsacos.

***Philosophers of the Cyrenaic sect.*** Aristippos, Hegesias, Anniceris, Theodoros, and Bion.

***Philosophers of the Eleac*** or ***Eretriac sect.*** Phaedo, Plisthenes, and Menedemos of Eretria.

***Philosophers of the Eleatic sect.*** Xenophanes, Parmenides, Melissos, Zeno of Tarsos, Leucippos, Democritos, Protagoras, and Anaxarchos.

***Philosophers of the Epicurean sect.*** Epicuros, and a host of disciples.

***Philosophers of the Heraclitan sect.*** Heraclitos; the names of his disciples are unknown.

***Philosophers of the Ionic sect.*** Anaximander, Anaximenes, Anaxagoras, and Archelaos.

***Philosophers of the Italic sect.*** Pythagoras, Empedocles, Epicharmos, Archytas, Alcmaeon, Hippasos, Philolaos, and Eudoxos.

***Philosophers of the Megaric sect.*** Euclid, Eubulides, Alexinos, Euphantos, Apollonios, Chronos, Diodoros, Ichthyas, Clinomachos, and Stilpo.

***Philosophers of the Peripatetic sect.*** Aristotle, Theophrastos, Straton, Lyco, Aristo, Critolaos, and Diodoros.

***Philosophers of the Sceptic sect.*** Pyrrho and Timon.

***Philosophers of the Socratic sect.*** Socrates, Xenophon, Aeschines, Crito, Simon, Glauco, Simmias, and Cebes.

***Philosophers of the Stoic sect.*** Zeno, Cleanthes, Chrysippos, Zeno the Less, Diogenes of Babylon, Antipater, Panaetios, Epictetus, Marcus Aurelius, and Posidonios.

**Philosopher's Egg.** A mediaeval preservative against poison and cure for the plague. The shell of a new egg was pricked, the white blown out, and the place filled with saffron or a yolk of an egg mixed with saffron.

**Philosophers' Stone.** The hypothetical substance which, according to the mediaeval alchemists, would convert all baser metals into gold. Its discovery was the prime object of all the alchemists; and to the wide and unremitting search that went on for it we are indebted for the birth of the science of Chemistry, as well as for many inventions. It was in searching for this treasure that Bötticher stumbled on the manufacture of Dresden porcelain; Roger Bacon on the composition of gunpowder; Geber on the properties of acids; Van Helmont on the nature of gas; and Dr Glauber on the 'salts' which bear his name.

In Ripley's treatise, *The Compound of Alchymy* (*temp.* Edward IV), we are told the twelve stages, or 'gates', in the transmutation of metals. These are: (1) Calcination; (2) Dissolution; (3) Separation; (4) Conjunction; (5) Putrefaction; (6) Congelation; (7) Cibation; (8) Sublimation; (9) Fermentation; (10) Exaltation; (11) Multiplication; and (12) Projection. Of these the last two were of much the greatest importance; the former consisted in the 'augmentation' of the elixir, the latter in the penetration and transfiguration of metals in fusion by casting the powder of the philosophers' stone upon them, which is then called the 'powder of projection'. According to one legend, Noah was commanded to hang up the true and genuine philosophers' stone in the ark, to give light to every living creature therein; while another relates that Deucalion (*q.v.*) had it in a bag over his shoulder, but threw it away and lost it.

**Philosopher's Tree,** or **Diana's Tree.** An amalgam of crystallised silver, obtained from mercury in a solution of silver; so called by the alchemists, with whom Diana stood for silver.

**Philotime** (Gr. lover of honour). In Spenser's *Faërie Queene* (II, vii), the daughter of Mammon (*q.v.*) and presiding Queen of Hell.

**Philoxenos of Leucadia.** The ancient Greek epicure of whom it is told that he wished he had the neck of a crane, that he might enjoy the taste of his food the longer (Aristotle, *Ethics*, iii, 10).

**Philter** (Gr. *philtron*, from *philein*, to love). A draught or charm to incite in another the passion of love. The Thessalian philters were the most renowned, but both the Greeks and Romans used these dangerous potions, which sometimes produced insanity. Lucretius is said to have been driven mad by a love-potion, and Caligula's death is attributed to some philters administered to him by his wife, Caesonia. Brabantio says to Othello –

> Thou hart practised on her [Desdemona] with foul charms,
> Abused her delicate youth with drugs or minerals
> That weaken motion.
>
> Shakespeare, *Othello*, 1, 1

**Phineus.** In Greek legend a blind king and prophet of Thrace, contemporary with the Argonauts. Whenever he wanted to eat, the Harpies came and took away or defiled his food.

> Blind Thamyris, and blind Moeonides,
> And Tiresias, and Phineus, prophets old
>
> Milton, *Paradise Lost*, iii, 34

**Phiz,** the face, is a contraction of physiognomy.

> Th' emphatic speaker dearly loves t' oppose,
> In contact inconvenient, nose to nose,
> As if the gnomon on his neighbour's phiz,
> Touch'd with a magnet, had attracted his.
>
> Cowper, *Conversation*, 269

**Phlegethon** (Gr. *phlego*, to burn). A river of liquid fire in Hades. It flowed into the river Acheron.

> Fierce Phlegethon,
> Whose waves of torrent fire inflame with rage.
>
> Milton, *Pardise Lost*, ii

**Phlegra.** The legendary site in Macedonia where the giant, led by Encelados, attacked the gods.

**Phlogiston** (Gr., burnt up). The name used by early chemists to denote the principle of inflammability that was supposed to be a necessary constituent of combustible material. It was introduced by the German chemist Georg Ernst Stahl, in 1702, and belief in the theory lasted for nearly a century.

**Phocensian Despair.** Desperation which terminates in victory. In the days of Philip, King of Macedon, the men of Phocis had to defend themselves single-handed against the united forces of all their neighbours, because they presumed to plough a sacred field belonging to Delphi. The Phocensians suggested that they should make a huge pile, and that all the women and children should join the men in one vast human sacrifice. The pile was made, and everything was ready, but the men of Phocis, before mounting the pile, rushed in desperation on the foe, and obtained a signal victory.

**Phoebe.** A Titaness of classical myth, daughter of Uranus and Ge; also a name of Diana as goddess of the moon.

**Phoebus** (Gr., the Shining One). An epithet of Apollo, god of the sun. In poetry the name is sometimes used of the sun itself, sometimes of Apollo as the leader of the Muses.

> The rays divine of vernal Phoebus shine.
>
> Thomson, *Spring*

> Blind Melesigenes, thence Homer called,
> Whose poem Phoebus challenged for his own.
>
> Milton, *Paradise Regained*, iv, 260

**Phoenix.** A fabulous Arabian bird, the only one of its kind, that is said to live a certain number of years, at the close of which it makes in Arabia a nest of spices, sings a melodious dirge, flaps its wings to set fire to the pile, burns itself to ashes, and comes forth with new life, to repeat the former one.

> The enchanted pile of that lonely bird,
> Who sings at the last his own death-lay,
> And in music and perfume dies away.
>
> Thomas Moore, *Paradise and the Peri*

It is to this bird that Shakespeare refers in *Cymbeline* (1, 7):

> If she be furnished with a mind so rare,
> She is alone the Arabian bird.

The phoenix was adopted as a sign over chemists' shops through the association of this fabulous bird with alchemy. Paracelsus wrote about it, and several of the alchemists employed it to symbolise their vocation.

***Phoenix dactylifera.*** The date-palm; so called because of the ancient idea that this tree, if burnt down or if it falls through old age, will rejuvenate itself and spring up fairer than ever. Shakespeare may be referring to it in *The Tempest* (3, 3):

> Now I will believe
> That there are unicorns; that in Arabia
> There is one tree, the phoenix throne; one phoenix
> At this hour reigning there.

***Phoenix period*** or ***cycle,*** generally supposed to be 500 years; Tacitus tells us it was 250 years; R. Stuart Poole that it was 1,460 Julian years, like the Sothic Cycle; and Lipsius that it was 1,500 years. Now, the phoenix is said to have appeared in Egypt five times: (1) in the reign of Sesostris; (2) in the reign of Amasis; (3) in the reign of

Ptolemy Philadelphus; (4) a year or two prior to the death of Tiberius; and (5) in AD 334, during the reign of Constantine. These dates being accepted, a Phoenix Cycle consists of 300 years; thus, Sesostris, 866 BC; Amasis, 566 BC; Ptolemy, 266 BC; Tiberius, AD 34; Constantine, AD 334. In corroboration of this suggestion it must be borne in mind that Jesus Christ, who died AD 34, is termed *the Phoenix* by monastic writers. Tacitus (*Annales*, vi, 28) mentions the first three of these appearances.

**Phoenix Park** (Dublin). A corruption of the Gaelic *Fionn-uisge*, the clear water, so called from a spring at one time resorted to as a chalybeate spa.

**Phooka** or **Pooka.** A hobgoblin of Irish folk lore, a spirit of most malignant disposition, who hurries people to their destruction. He sometimes comes in the form of an eagle, and sometimes in that of a horse, like the Scotch kelpie (*q.v.*).

> Irish superstition makes the phooka palpable to the touch. To its agency the peasantry usually ascribe accidental falls.
>
> T. C. Croker, *Fairy Legends and Traditions of the South of Ireland*, vol. i, p. 316

**Phorcos.** 'The old man of the sea' of *Greek mythology*. He was the father of the three Graiae, who were grey from their birth, and had but one eye – which was stolen by Perseus as one of the means through which he was to obtain the head of Medusa – and one tooth common to the three.

**Phrygians.** An early Christian sect, so called from Phrygia, where they abounded. They regarded Montanus as their prophet, and laid claim to the spirit of prophecy.

***Phrygian cap.*** The cap of liberty (*q.v.*).

***Phrygian mode.*** In music, the second of the 'authentic' ecclesiastical modes. It had its 'final' on E and its 'dominant' on C, and was derived from the ancient Greek mode of this name, which was warlike. It was used for hymns and anthems.

**Phryne.** A famous Athenian courtesan of the 4th century BC, who acquired so much wealth by her beauty that she offered to rebuild the walls of Thebes if she might put on them this inscription: 'Alexander destroyed them, but Phryne the hetaera rebuilt them.' It is recorded of her that when she was being tried on a capital charge her defender, who failed to move the judges by his eloquence, asked her to uncover her bosom. She did so, and the judges, struck by such astounding beauty, acquitted her on the spot.

She is said to have been the model for Praxiteles' Cnidian Venus, and also for Apelles' picture of Venus Rising from the Sea.

**Phylactery** (Gr. *phylacterion*, from *phylasso*, to watch). A charm or amulet worn by the ancient Jews on the wrist or forehead. It consisted of four slips of parchment, each bearing a text of Scripture, enclosed in two black leather cases. One case contained Exod. 13:1–10, 11–16; and the other case Deut. 6:4–9, 11:13–21. The idea arose from the command of Moses, 'Therefore shall ye lay up these my words in your heart ... and bind them for a sign upon your hand ... as frontlets between your eyes' (Deut. 11:18).

**Phynnodderee** (the Hairy-one). A Manx spirit, similar to the Scotch 'brownie', and German 'kobold'. He is said to have been a fairy who was outlawed because he absented himself without leave from Fairy-court on the great levee day of the Harvest Moon, to dance in the glen of Rushen with a pretty Manx maid whom he was courting.

**Physician** (Gr. *phusis*, nature).

***Every man a fool or a physician.*** *See* Fool.

***The Physician finger.*** The third. *See* Medicinal Finger.

***The Beloved Physician.*** St Luke (*q.v.*), so called by St Paul in Col. 4:14.

***The Prince of Physicians.*** Avicenna, the Arabian (980–1037).

**Piarists.** A secular order of the Roman Catholic Church, founded at Rome at the close of the 16th century by St Joseph of Calasanctius, for the better instruction and education of the middle and higher classes.

**Picador** (Span.). An agile horseman, who, in bull fights, is armed with a gilt spear (*pica dorada*), with which he pricks the bull to madden him for the combat. Hence, a skilful debater or one who excels at rapid repartee is sometimes called a picador.

**Picards.** An immoral sect of fanatics prevalent in Bohemia and the Vaudois in the early 15th century, said to be so called from Picard of Flanders, their founder, who called himself the New Adam, and tried to introduce the custom of living nude, like Adam in Paradise. They were suppressed by Ziska in 1421.

**Picaresque.** The term applied to the class of literature that deals sympathetically with the adventures of clever and amusing rogues (Span. *picaresco*, roguish, knavish). The earliest example of the picaresque novel is Mendoza's *Lazarillo de Tormes* (1554). Le Sage's *Gil Blas* (1715) is perhaps the best known. Nash's *Jack Wilton* (1594) is the earliest English example, and others are Defoe's *Moll Flanders* and *Colonel Jack*.

**Piccadilly.** This well-known London thoroughfare is named from a house that stood near the corner of Sackville Street and, in the early 17th century, was nicknamed *Pickadilly Hall*. One early account (1656) says the house was so called because it was the 'outmost or *skirt* house of the Suburbs that way'; another – of the same date – because it was built by one Higgins, a tailor, who made his fortune by selling 'piccadilles'.

The 'piccadille' was originally 'the round hem or the several divisions set together about the skirt of a Garment', and was so called because it was pierced (Sp. *picado*) or slashed; thence it came to be applied to the stiff collar that supported the ruff of 17th century gallants.

**Piccaninny,** or **Piccannin** (West Indian negro, from Sp. *pequeño*, small). A little negro child of the West Indies and southern USA; also, in South Africa, applied to small Kafir children, and sometimes to native children in Australia.

**Piccinists.** The followers in Paris and elsewhere of Niccolo Piccino (1728–1800), the Neapolitan opera composer, who, about 1774–80, raised a storm in the musical world by their quarrel with the followers of Gluck. *See* Gluckists. They contended that music is the alpha and omega of opera, and the dramatic part is of very minor importance.

**Pick-a-back.** On the back or shoulders, as a pack is carried. The term dates at least from the early 16th century, but its precise origin, and the force of the *pick-*, are unknown. Other forms of it are *a-pigga-back*, *piggy-back*, *pick-back*, etc.

**Pickle-herring.** The German term for a clown or buffoon, from a humorous character of that name in an early 17th-century play. It was adopted in England through Addison's mention in the *Spectator* (No. 47, 1711), where he wrongly attributes it to the Dutch.

> Their high State Tragedy … becomes a Pickle-herring-Farce to weep at, which is the worst kind of Farce. Carlyle, *Sarto Resartus*, I, ix

**Pickers and Stealers.** The hands.

> *Rosencrantz:* My lord, you once did love me.
> *Hamlet:* And do still, by these pickers and stealers. Shakespeare, *Hamlet*, 3, 3

In French *argot* hands are called *harpes*, which is a contracted form of *harpions*; and harpion is the Italian *arpione*, a hook used by thieves to pick linen, etc., from hedges. A *harpe d'un chien* means a dog's paw, and *Il mania très bien ses harpes* means he used his fingers very dexterously.

**Pickle.** ***A rod in pickle.*** One ready to chastise with at any moment; one 'preserved' for use.

***I'm in a pretty pickle.*** In a sorry plight, or state of disorder.

> How cam'st thou in this pickle?
> Shakespeare, *Tempest*, 5, 1

**Pickwickian.** ***In a Pickwickian tense.*** Said of words or epithets, usually of a derogatory or insulting kind, that, in the circumstances in which they are employed, are not to be taken as having quite the same force or implication as they naturally would have. The allusion is to the scene in ch. i of Dickens's *Pickwick Papers* when Mr Pickwick accused Mr Blotton of acting in 'a vile and calumnious manner', whereupon Mr Blotton retorted by calling Mr Pickwick 'a humbug'. It finally was made to appear that both had used the offensive words only in a Pickwickian sense, and that each had, in fact, the highest regard and esteem for the other.

> Lawyers and politicians daily abuse each other in a Pickwickian sense. Bowditch

**Picnic.** The word came into use in England about 1800 to denote a fashionable party, often but not always in the open air, at which each guest contributed towards the provisions. It is a translation of Fr. *pique-nique* (which had much the same meaning), the origin of which is uncertain.

**Picrochole** (Gr. *pikros*, bitter, *chole*, bile, choler). The choleric king of Lerné, in Rabelais (Bk i), defeated by Gargantua. He had a thirst for conquest and territorial aggrandisement, and has been supposed to stand for Charles V of Spain.

**Picts.** The ancient inhabitants of Scotland, of unknown race. They were gradually dispossessed after the coming of the Scots (Goidels) from northern Ireland, about AD 500, and after the union of the Pictish kingdom with that of the Scots under Kenneth MacAlpin (844) the remnant was driven to the far north-east. The name is probably not native, but was given them by the Romans because they tattooed their bodies (Lat. *picti*, painted).

***Picts' houses.*** Underground pre-historic dwellings found in the Orkneys and on the east coast of Scotland, and attributed to the Picts.

**Picture** (Lat. *pictura*, from *pictus*, past part. of *pingere*, to paint). A model, or beau-ideal, as, *He is the picture of health*; *A perfect picture of a house*.

***Picture Bible.*** A name given to the *Biblia pauperum* (*q.v.*).

***The pictures.*** A colloquial and convenient way of referring to a cinematograph entertainment; 'I'm going to the pictures tonight' is a shortened form of 'I'm going to see the moving pictures tonight'.

**Pidgin-English.** The semi-English jargon used by semi-Anglicised Chinamen, consisting principally of mispronounced English words with certain native grammatical constructions. For instance, the Chinese cannot pronounce *r*, so replace it with *l* – *te-le* for 'three', *solly* for 'sorry', etc. – and, in Chinese, between a numeral and its noun there is always inserted a word (called the 'classifier') and this, in Pidgin-English, is replaced by piece – e.g. *one piece knifee, two piece hingkichi* (handkerchiefs). *Pidgin* is a corruption of *business*.

**Piebald.** Parti-coloured (especially black and white like a magpie), usually of horses. The word is from *pie*, the magpie (*q.v.*), and *bald*, of which one of the meanings was 'streaked with white', as in the 'bald-faced stag'.

**Pieces of Eight.** The old Spanish silver *peso* (piastre) or dollar of 8 reals, equivalent to about 1*s*. 8*d*. It was marked with an 8, and was in use in the 17th and 18th centuries.

**Pied-à-terre** (Fr., foot on the ground). A temporary lodging, or a country residence; a footing.

> Mr Harding, however, did not allow himself to be talked over into giving up his own and only *pied-à-terre* in the High Street.
>
> Anthony Trollope, *Barchester Towers*

**Pied de la lettre, Au** (Fr., to the foot of the letter). Quite literally – close to the letter.

> A wild enthusiastic young fellow, whose opinions one must not take *au pied de la lettre*.
>
> Thackeray, *Pendennis*, I, xi

**Pied Piper of Hamelin.** The legend is that the town of Hameln (Westphalia) was infested with rats in 1284, that a mysterious Piper, clad in a parti-coloured suit, appeared in the town and offered to rid it of the vermin for a certain sum, that the townspeople accepted the offer, the Pied Piper fulfilled his contract, and that then the payment was withheld. On the following St John's Day he reappeared, and again played his pipe. This time all the children of the town, in place of the rats, followed him; he led them to a mountain cave where all disappeared save two – one blind, the other dumb, or lame: and one legend adds that the children did not perish in the mountain, but were led over it to Transylvania, where they formed a German colony.

> To blow the pipe his lips he wrinkled,
> And green and blue his sharp eyes twinkled, …
> And ere three notes his pipe had uttered …
> Out of the houses rats came tumbling –
> Great rats, small rats, lean rats, brawny rats,
> Brown rats, black rats, grey rats, tawny rats,
> And step by step they followed him dancing,
> Till they came to the river Weser. Browning

**Piepowder Court.** A court of justice formerly held at fairs, which had summary powers in cases of dispute between those buyers and sellers who were there temporarily. Literally, a 'wayfarer's court', *piepowder* being from Fr. *pied-poudreux*, dusty-footed (also, a vagabond). The duties of these old Courts of Piepowder are now performed at the Petty Sessions.

> Is this well, goody Joan, to interrupt my market in the midst, and call away my customers? Can you answer this at the pie-poudres?
>
> Ben Jonson, *Bartholomew Fair*, III, i

**Pierrot** (i.e. 'Little Peter'). A character originally in French pantomime, representing a man in growth and a child in mind and manners. He is generally the tallest and thinnest man that can be got, has his face and hair covered with white powder or flour, and wears a white gown with very long sleeves and a row of big buttons down the front.

**Piers Plowman.** *See* Vision of Piers Plowman.

**Pieta.** A representation of the Virgin Mary embracing the dead body of her Son. Filial or parental love was called *pietas* by the Romans.

**Pietists.** A 17th century sect of Lutherans who sought to introduce a more moral life and a more 'evangelical' spirit of doctrine into the reformed church. In Germany the word is about equal to our vulgar use of Methodist.

**Pig** (*see also* Hog). The pig was held sacred by the ancient Cretans because Jupiter was suckled by a sow; it was immolated in the mysteries of Eleusis; was sacrificed to Hercules, to Venus, and to the Lares by all those who sought relief from bodily ailments. The sow was sacrificed to Ceres 'because it taught men to turn up the earth'; and in Egypt it was slain at grand weddings on account of its fecundity.

In the forefeet of pigs is a very small hole, which may be seen when the hair has been carefully removed. The tradition is that the legion of devils entered by these apertures. There are also round it some six rings, the whole together not larger than a small spangle; they look as if burnt or branded into the skin, and the tradition is that they are the marks of the devil's claws when he entered the swine (Mark 5:11–15).

***A pig in a poke.*** A blind bargain. The French say *Acheter chat en poche*. The reference is to a common trick in days gone by of trying to palm off on a greenhorn a cat for a sucking-pig. If he opened the sack he 'let the cat out of the bag', and the trick was disclosed. The French *chat en poche* refers to the fact, while our proverb regards the trick. *Pocket* is diminutive of *poke*.

***A pig's whisper.*** A very short space of time; properly a grunt – which doesn't take long.

> You'll find yourself in bed in something less than a pig's whisper. Dickens, *Pickwick*, ch. xxxii

***Bartholomew pigs.*** *See* Bartholomew.

***He has brought his pigs to a pretty market.*** He has made a very bad bargain; he has managed his business in a very bad way. Pigs were for long a principal article of sale with rustics, and till recently the cottager looked to pay his rent by the sale of his pigs.

***Pig-a-back.*** *See* Pick-a-back.

***Pig-headed.*** Obstinate, contrary.

***Pig iron.*** Iron cast in oblong ingots now called *pigs* but formerly *sows*. *Sow* is now applied to the main channel in which the molten liquid runs, the smaller branches which diverge from it being called pigs, and it is the iron from these which is called *pig iron*.

***Pigs and whistles.*** Trifles.

***To go to pigs and whistles*** is to be ruined, to go to the deuce.

> I would be nane surprised to hear the morn that the Nebuchadnezzar was a' gane to pigs and whistles, and driven out with the divors bill to the barren pastures of bankruptcy.
>
> Galt, *The Entail*, I, ix

***Pigs in clover.*** People who have any amount of money but don't know how to behave themselves as gentlefolk. Also, a game consisting of a box divided into recesses into which one has to roll marbles by tilting the box.

***Please the pigs.*** 'I'll come on Tuesday – please the pigs'; i.e. if circumstances permit. *Deo volente*. The suggestions that this phrase was originally 'please the pyx' or 'please the pixies', are ingenious, but there is no evidence to back them.

***St Anthony's pig.*** *See* Anthony.

***The Pig and Tinderbox.*** An old colloquial name for the Elephant and Castle public-house; in allusion to its sign of a pig-like elephant surmounted by an erection intended to represent a castle but which might pass as a tinderbox.

***To drive one's pigs to market.*** *See* Hog.

***To drive pigs.*** To snore.

***To pig together.*** To share and share alike, especially in lodgings in a small way; formerly it meant to sleep two (or more) in the same bed.

***To stare like a stuck pig.*** With open mouth and staring eyes, as a pig that is being killed; in the utmost astonishment, mingled sometimes with fear.

***When the pigs fly.*** Never.

*See also* Sow.

**Pigeon.** Slang for a dupe, an easily gullible person, a gull (*q.v.*). To pigeon is to cheat or gull one of his money by almost self-evident hoaxes. Pigeons are very easily caught by snares, and in the sporting world sharps and flats are called 'rooks and pigeons'. Thackeray has a story entitled 'Captain Rook and Mr Pigeon'. In French argot a dupe is *pechon*, or *peschon de ruby*; where *pechon* or *peschon* is the Italian *piccione* (a pigeon), and *de ruby* is a pun on *dérobé* bamboozled.

***Flying the pigeons.*** Stealing coals from a cart or sack between the coal dealer's yard and the house of the customer.

***Flying the blue pigeon.*** *See* Blue-pigeon Flyer.

***Pigeon English.*** An incorrect form of 'Pidgin-English' (*q.v.*).

***Pigeon-hole.*** A small compartment for filing papers; hence, a matter that has been put on one side and forgotten is often said to have been *pigeonholed*. In pigeon-lockers a small hole is left for the pigeons to walk in and out.

***Pigeon-livered.*** Timid, easily frightened, like a pigeon. The bile rules the temper, and the liver the bile.

> It cannot be
> But I am pigeon-liver'd, and lack gall
> To make oppression bitter, or ere this
> I should have fatted all the region kites
> With this slave's offal.
>
> Shakespeare, *Hamlet*, 2, 2

***Pigeon pair.*** A boy and girl, twins. It was once supposed that pigeons always sit on two eggs which produce a male and a female, and these twin birds live together in love the rest of their lives.

***That's my pigeon*** (with the emphasis on *my*). That's *my* affair, and you had better leave it alone; that concerns me only.

***The black pigeons of Dodona.*** Two black pigeons, we are told, took their flight from Thebes, in Egypt; one flew to Libya, and the other to Dodona (*q.v.*). On the spot where the former alighted, the temple of Jupiter Ammon was erected; in the place where the other settled, the oracle of Jupiter was established, and there the responses were made by the black pigeons that inhabited the surrounding groves. This fable is probably based on a pun upon the word *peleiai*, which usually meant 'old women', but in the dialect of the Epirots signified pigeons or doves.

***To pluck a pigeon.*** To cheat a gullible person of his money; to fleece a greenhorn.

> 'Here comes a nice pigeon to pluck,' said one of the thieves. C. Reade

**Piggin.** *See* Pig-wife *below*.

**Pigmies.** *See* Pygmies.

**Pigskin.** A saddle, the best being made of pigskin. 'To throw a leg across a pigskin' is to mount a horse.

**Pigsney** or **Pigsnie.** A word of endearment formerly commonly used to a girl. It is simply 'pig's eye', the eye being one of one's most precious possessions, and the pig having a specially small one.

> Hir shoes were laced on hir legges hye;
> She was a prymerole, a pigges-nye
> For any lord to leggen in his bedde,
> Or yet for any good yeman to wedde.
> Chaucer, *Miller's Tale*, 81

**Pigtails.** The Chinese; so called because the Tartar tonsure and braided queue are very general.

In England the word first appeared (17th cent.) as the name of a tobacco that was twisted into a thin rope; and it was used of the plait of twisted hair worn by sailors till the early 19th century, as it still is of that worn by schoolgirls.

**Pig-wife.** A woman who sells crockery. A *piggin* was a small pail, especially a milk-pail; and a *pig* a small bowl, cup, or mug.

**Pigwiggen.** An elf in Drayton's *Nymphidia* (1627), in love with Queen Mab. He combats the jealous Oberon with great fury.

> Pigwiggen was this Fairy Knight,
> One wond'rous gracious in the sight
> Of fair Queen Mab, which day and night
> He amorously observed.

**Pi-jaw.** *See* Jaw.

**Pike.** The Germans have a tradition that when Christ was crucified all fishes dived under the waters in terror, except the pike, which, out of curiosity, lifted up its head and beheld the whole scene; hence the fancy that in a pike's head all the parts of the Crucifixion are represented, the cross, three nails, and a sword being distinctly recognisable. *Cp.* Passion-flower.

**Pikestaff.** ***Plain as a pikestaff.*** Quite obvious and unmistakable. The earlier form of the phrase (mid-16th cent.) was *plain as a packstaff*, i.e. the staff on which a pedlar carried his pack, which was worn plain and smooth.

> O Lord! what absurdities! as plain as any packstaff. Dryden, *Amphitryon*, III, i

**Pilate.** Tradition has it that Pontius Pilate's later life was so full of misfortune that, in Caligula's time, he committed suicide in Rome. His body was cast into the Tiber, but evil spirits disturbed the water so much that it was retrieved and taken to Vienne, where it was thrown into the Rhone, eventually coming to rest in the recesses of a lake on Mount Pilatus (*q.v.*) opposite Lucerne. Another legend states that the suicide occurred so that he might escape the sentence of death passed on him by Tiberius because of his having ordered the crucifixion of Christ; and yet another that both he and his wife became penitent, embraced Christianity, and died peaceably in the faith.

Tradition gives the name Claudia Procula, or Procla, to Pilate's wife, and by some she has been identified with the Claudia of 2 Tim. 4:21.

***Pilate voice.*** A loud, ranting voice. In the old mysteries all tyrants were made to speak in a rough, ranting manner. Thus Bottom the Weaver (*q.v.*), after a rant 'to show his quality', exclaims, 'That's 'Ercles' vein, a tyrant's vein'; and Hamlet describes a ranting actor as 'out-heroding Herod'.

> The Miller, that for-drunken was al pale …
> … in Pilates vois he gan to crye,
> And swoor by armes and by blood and bones,
> 'I can a noble tale for the nones
> With which I wol now quyte the Knightes tale.'
> Chaucer, *Miller's Prologue*, 12-19

**Pilatus, Mount.** In Switzerland. So called because during westerly winds it is covered with a white 'cap' of cloud (Lat. *pileatus*, covered with the *pileus*, or felt cap). The similarity of the name with that of Pilate (*q.v.*) gave rise to one of the legends mentioned above; another tradition has it that Pilate was banished to Gaul by Tiberius, wandered to this mount and threw himself into a black lake on its summit, and it is further stated that once a year Pilate appears on the mountain and that whoever sees the ghost will die before the year is out. In the 16th century a law was passed forbidding anyone to throw stones into the lake, for fear of bringing a tempest on the country.

**Pilgarlic** or **Pill'd Garlic.** A 16th-century term for a bald-headed man, especially one whose hair had fallen off through disease, and had left a head that was suggestive of a bit of peeled garlic. Stow says of one getting bald: 'He will soon be a peeled garlic like myself'; and the term was later used of any poor wretch avoided and forsaken by his fellows, and, in a humorous or self-pitying way, of oneself.

> After this [feast] we jogged off to bed for the night; but never a bit could poor pilgarlic sleep one wink, for the overlasting jingle of bells.
>
> Rabelais, *Pantagruel*, v, 7

**Pilgrim Fathers.** The 102 Puritans who, in 1620, went to North America in the *Mayflower* (*q.v.*). Most of them came from Lincolnshire; they sailed from Delft Haven in July, 1620, called at Southampton, and on September 6th left Plymouth. They landed in Massachusetts Bay December 22nd (still commemorated as *Forefathers' Day*), and formed the nucleus of the New England states.

**Pilgrimage.** The chief places in the West were Walsingham and Canterbury (England); Fourvières, Puy, and St Denis (France); Rome, Loretto, Genetsano, and Assisi (Italy); Compostella, Guadalupe, and Montserrat (Spain); Oetting, Zell, Cologne, Trier, and Einsiedeln (Germany).

***The Pilgrimage of Grace.*** The rising on behalf of the Catholics that broke out in Lincolnshire in the autumn of 1536. It quickly assumed large proportions, but was finally extinguished in March, 1537, by the Council of the North, over 70 of the rebels being executed. Robert Aske, the Archbishop of York, Lord Darcy, and the Percies were the principal leaders.

**Pill. *To gild the pill.*** To soften the blow; to make a disagreeable task less offensive, as pills used to be gilded (and are now sugar-coated) to make them more pleasant to the taste and sight.

**Pillar. *From pillar to post.*** Hither and thither; from one thing to another without any definite purpose; harassed and worried. The phrase was originally *from post to pillar*, and comes from the old tennis-courts in allusion to the banging about of the balls.

***Pillar Saints.*** *See* Stylites.

***The Pillars of Hercules.*** The opposite rocks at the entrance of the Mediterranean, one in Spain and the other in Africa. The tale is that they were bound together till Hercules tore them asunder in order to get to Gades (Cadiz). The ancients called them Calpe and Abyla; we call them Gibraltar and Mount Hacho, on which stands the fortress of Ceuta. Macrobius ascribes the feat of making the division to Sesostris (the Egyptian Hercules), Lucan follows the same tradition; and the Phoenicians are said to have set on the opposing rocks two large pyramidal columns to serve as seamarks, one dedicated to Hercules and the other to Astarte.

***I will follow you even to the pillars of Hercules.*** To the end of the world. The ancients supposed that these rocks marked the utmost limits of the habitable globe.

**Pillory.** Punishment by the pillory was not finally abolished in England till 1837, but since 1815 it had been in force only for perjury. In Delaware, USA, it was a legal punishment down to 1905, and it is still in use in China. In France it was abolished in 1848.

> The following eminent men have been put in the pillory for literary offences – Leighton, for tracts against Charles I; Lilburn, for circulating the tracts of Dr Bastwick; Bastwick, for attacking the Church of England; Wharton the publisher; Prynne, for a satire on the wife of Charles I; Daniel Defoe, for a pamphlet entitled *The Shortest Way with Dissenters*, etc.

**Pilot.** Through Fr. from Ital. *pilota*, formerly *pedota*, which is probably connected with Gr. *pedon*, a rudder.

***Pilot balloon.*** A small balloon sent up to try the wind; hence, figuratively, a feeler; a hint thrown out to ascertain public opinion on some point.

***Pilot fish.*** The small sea-fish, *Naucrates ductor*, so called because it is supposed to pilot the shark to its prey.

***The pilot that weathered the storm.*** William Pitt, son of the first Earl of Chatham. George Canning, in 1802, wrote a song so called in compliment to him, for his having steered us safely through the European storm stirred up by Napoleon.

**Pilpay** or **Bidpay.** The name given as that of the author of *Kalilah and Dimnah* (otherwise known as *The Fables of Pilpay*), which is the 8th century Arabic version of the Sanskrit *Panchatantra*. The word is not a true name, but means 'wise man' (Arab. *bidbah*), and was applied to the chief scholar at the court of an Indian prince.

**Pimlico** (London). At one time a district of public gardens much frequented on holidays. It received its name from Ben Pimlico, famous in the late 16th and early 17th centuries for his nut-brown ale, who had a tavern at Hoxton and, later, one in the neighbourhood of Chelsea.

> Have at thee, then, my merrie boyes, and beg for
> old Ben Pimlico's nut-brown ale.
>
> *Newes from Hogsdon* (1598)

**Pin.** The original *pin* (A.S. *pinn*, connected with *pinnacle*) was a small tapered peg of wood, horn, metal, etc., and it is quite a mistake to suppose that pins were invented in the reign of François I, and introduced into England by Catherine Howard, fifth wife of Henry VIII. In 1347, 200 years before the death of François, 12,000 pins were delivered from the royal wardrobe for the use of the Princess Joan.

***At a pin's fee.*** At an extremely low estimate; valueless.

> I do not set my life at a pin's fee.
>
> Shakespeare, *Hamlet*, 1, 4

***I don't care a pin,*** or ***a pin's point.*** In the least.

> [the Red-cross Knight] not a pin
> Does care for look of living creature's eye.
>
> Spenser, *Faërie Queene*, I, v, 4

***I do not pin my faith upon your sleeve.*** I am not going to take your *ipse dixit* for gospel. In feudal times badges were worn, and the partisans of a leader used to wear his badge, which was pinned on the sleeve. Sometimes these badges were changed for some reason, hence, people learned to be chary of judging by appearances, and would say – 'You wear the badge, but I do not intend to pin my faith on your sleeve.'

***In merry pin.*** In merry mood, in good spirits.

> The Callender, right glad to find
> His friend in merry pin,
> Return'd him not a single word,
> But to the house went in.
>
> Cowper, *John Gilpin*, st. 45

The origin of the term is not certain; it may be in reference to the *pin* or key of a stringed instrument by which it is kept to the right pitch, or it may be an allusion to the *pins* or pegs of peg-tankards (*see* Peg – *I am a peg too low*). By the rules of 'good fellowship' a drinker was supposed to stop drinking *only at a pin*, and if he went beyond it, was to drink to the next one. As it was hard to stop exactly at the pin, the effort gave rise to much mirth, and the drinker had generally to drain the tankard.

> No song, no laugh, no jovial din
> Of drinking wassail to the pin.
>
> Longfellow, *Golden Legend*

***Not worth a pin.*** Wholly worthless.

***Pin money.*** A lady's allowance of money for her own personal expenditure. At one time pins were a great expense to a woman, and in 14th and 15th century wills there are often special bequests for the express purpose of buying pins; when they became cheap and common the ladies spent their allowances on other fancies, but the term *pin money* remained in vogue.

> *Miss Hoyden:* Now, nurse, if he gives me two hundred a year to buy pins, what do you think he'll give me to buy fine petticoats?
>
> *Nurse:* Ah, my dearest, he deceives thee foully, and he's no better than a rogue for his pains! These Londoners have got a gibberage with 'em would confound a gipsy. That which they call pin-money is to buy their wives everything in the varsal world, down to their very shoe-ties.
>
> Vanbrugh, *The Relapse*, V, v (1697)

***Pins and needles.*** The tingling sensation that comes over a limb when it has been numbed, or 'asleep'.

***On pins and needles.*** 'On thorns', 'on edge'; in a state of fearful expectation or great uneasiness.

***Policy of pin pricks.*** A policy of petty annoyances. The term came into prominence during the strained relations between England and France in 1898, and is an Anglicisation of the very much older French phrase, *un coup d'épingle*.

***There's not a pin to choose between them.*** They're as like as two peas, practically no difference.

***To tirl at the pin.*** *See* Tirl.

***Weak on his pins.*** Weak in his legs, the legs being a man's 'pegs' or supporters.

***You could have heard a pin drop.*** Said of a state – especially a sudden state in the midst of din – of complete silence. Leigh Hunt speaks of 'a pin-drop silence' (*Rimini*, I, 144).

**Pinch.** ***A pinch for stale news.*** A schoolboy's punishment to one of his mates for telling as news what is well known.

***At a pinch.*** In an urgent case; if hard pressed. There are things that one cannot do in the ordinary way, but that one may manage 'at a pinch'.

***To be pinched for money.*** To be in financial straits, hard up. Hence, *to pinch and scrape*, or *to pinch it*, to economise.

***To pinch.*** Slang for to steal.

***Where the shoe pinches.*** *See* Shoe.

**Pinchbeck.** Brummagen gold; an alloy of copper (5 parts) and zinc (1 part); so called from Christopher Pinchbeck (d.1732), a manufacturer of cheap watches and imitation jewellery in Fleet Street. Hence used figuratively of anything spurious, of deceptive appearance, or low quality.

> Where in these pinchbeck days, can we hope to find the old agricultural virtue in all its purity?
>
> Trollope, *Framley Parsonage*

**Pindar (Pinder** or **Pinner) of Wakefield.** *See* George-a-Green. A *pinder* was one who impounded straying cattle and looked after the pound.

**Pindaric Verse.** Irregular verse; a poem of various metres, and of lofty style, in imitation of the odes of Pindar. *Alexander's Feast*, by Dryden, and *The Bard*, by Gray, are examples.

**Pine-bender, The.** *See* Sinis.

**Pine-tree State.** Maine, which has forests of these trees, and bears a pine tree on its coat of arms.

**Pink.** The flower is so called because the edges of the petals are *pinked* or notched. The verb *to pink* means to pierce or perforate, also to ornament dress material by punching holes in it so that the lining can be seen, scalloping the edges, etc. In the 17th century it was commonly used of stabbing an adversary, especially in a duel.

***In pink.*** In the scarlet coat of a fox-hunter. The colour is not pink, but no hunting man would call it anything else. *Cp.* Redcoats.

***In the pink.*** In a first-rate state of health; flourishing (*cp. next*).

***The pink of perfection.*** The flower or very acme of perfection. In the same way Shakespeare (*Romeo and Juliet*, 2, 4) has 'the pink of courtesy'.

**Piou-piou.** O.Fr. slang for an infantryman, now superseded by *poilu* (*q.v.*). Perhaps a corruption of *pion*, a pawn. Cotgrave, however, thought (1611) the French foot-soldiers were so called from their habit of pilfering chickens, whose cry is *piou piou*.

**Pious.** The Romans called a man who revered his father *pius*; hence Antoninus was called *Pius*, because he requested that his adoptive father (Hadrian) might be ranked among the gods. *Aeneas* was called *Pius* because he rescued his father from the burning city of Troy. The Italian word *pietà* (*q.v.*) has a similar meaning.

***The Pious.*** Ernest I, founder of the House of Gotha. (1601–74.)

Robert, son of Hugues Capet. (971, 996–1031.)

Louis I of France. *See* Debonair.

Eric IX of Sweden. (d.1161.)

Frederick III, Elector Palatine. (1575–76.)

**Pip.** The pips on cards and dice were not named from the seeds of fruit, for in this sense the word (earlier *peep*, origin obscure) dates from the 16th century, while the seeds were not so called till the beginning of the 19th. This is merely an abbreviated form of *pippin*, which denoted the seed long before it denoted apples raised from seed. *To be pipped* is to be blackballed or defeated, the black ball being the 'pip'.

***Pip emma.*** Soldier slang for PM. Originally telephonese, as on the phone 'twelve pip emma' cannot be misunderstood, whereas 'twelve PM' might be. In the same way *ack emma* stands for AM.

***To have*** or ***get the pip.*** To be thoroughly 'fed up', downhearted, and miserable. Probably connected with the blackballing term (*see above*).

***To get one's second pip.*** To be promoted from subaltern to full lieutenant. These army ranks are marked by 'pips' on the shoulder-straps.

**Pipe.** ***As you pipe, I must dance.*** I must accommodate myself to your wishes. 'He who pays the piper calls the tune.'

***Piping hot.*** Hot as water which pipes or sings; hence, new, only just out.

***Piping times of peace*** (Shakespeare, *Richard III*, 1, 1). Times when there was no thought of war and the pastoral pipe instead of the martial trumpet was heard on the village greens.

***Put that in your pipe and smoke it.*** Digest that, if you can. An expression used by one who has given an adversary a severe rebuke.

***The pipe of peace.*** *See* Calumet.

***To pipe one's eye.*** To snivel, weep.

***To put one's pipe out.*** To spoil his piping; to make him change his key or sing a different tune; to 'take his shine out'.

**Pipeclay.** Routine; fossilised military dogmas of no real worth, such as excessive attention to correctness in dress, drill, etc. (*Cp.* Red Tape.) Pipeclay was at one time largely used by soldiers for making their gloves, accoutrements, and clothes look clean and smart.

**Pipe Rolls** or **Great Rolls of the Pipe.** The series of Great Rolls of the Exchequer, beginning 2 Henry II, and continued to 1834, and probably so called either because of the cylindrical shape of the Rolls, or because they were kept in pipe-like cases. Bacon's account (*see below*) is, of course, fanciful. The Pipe Rolls form a magnificent series of documents, and contain complete accounts of the Crown revenues as rendered by the Sheriffs of the different counties. They are now in the Public Record Office, Chancery Lane.

***Office of the Clerk of the Pipe.*** A very ancient office in the Court of Exchequer, where leases of Crown lands, sheriffs' accounts, etc., were made out. It existed in the reign of Henry II, and was abolished in the reign of William IV. Bacon says, 'The office is so called because the whole receipt of the court is finally conveyed into it by means of divers small pipes or quills, as water into a cistern.'

**Piper. *Piper's news.*** Stale news; 'fiddler's news' (*q.v.*).

***The Pied Piper.*** *See* Pied.

***Tom Piper.*** So the piper is called in the morris dance.

Tom Piper referred to by Drayton seems to have been a sort of jongleur or *raconteur* of short tales.

> Tom Piper is gone out, and mirth bewailes,
> He never will come in to tell us tales.

***Who's to pay the piper?*** *See* Pay.

**Pippin.** *See* Pip.

**Pirie's Chair.** 'The lowest seat of hell'.

> In Pirie's chair you'll sit, I say,
> The lowest seat o' hell;
> If ye do not amend your ways,
> It's there that ye must dwell.
>
> *Child's English and Scottish Ballads, The Courteous Knight*

**Pirithous.** King of the Lapithae, in Greek legend: proverbial for his love of Theseus (*q.v.*).

**Pis-aller** (Fr. worst course). A makeshift; something for want of a better; a *dernier ressort*.

> She contented herself with a *pis-aller*, and gave her hand … in six months to the son of the baronet's steward. Scott, *Waverley*, ch. v

**Piso's Justice.** Verbally right, but morally wrong. Seneca tells us that Piso condemned a man on circumstantial evidence for murder; but when the suspect was at the place of execution, the man supposed to have been murdered appeared. The centurion sent the prisoner to Piso, and explained the case to him; whereupon Piso condemned all three to death, saying, *Fiat justitia* (Lat. let justice be done). The condemned man was executed because sentence of death had been passed upon him, the centurion because he had disobeyed orders, and the man supposed to have been murdered because he had been the cause of death to two innocent men, and *fiat justitia ruat caelum* (let justice be done though the heavens should fall).

**Pistol.** Formerly *pistolet*; so called from the old *pistolese*, a dagger or hanger for the manufacture of which Pistoia, in Tuscany, was famous.

***Pocket pistol.*** *See* Pocket.

***To fire one's pistol in the air.*** Purposely to refrain from injuring an adversary. The phrase is often used of argument, and refers to the old practice of duellers doing this when they wished to discharge a 'debt of honour' without incurring risks.

**Pit-a-pat. *My heart goes pit-a-pat.*** Throbs, palpitates. An echoic or a mere ricochet word, of which there are a great many in English – as 'fiddle-faddle', 'harum-scarum', 'ding-dong', etc.

> Anything like the sound of a rat
> Makes my heart go pit-a-pat.
>
> Browning, *Pied Piper of Hamelin*

**Pitch.** The black resinous substance gets its name from Lat. *pix*; the verb (to fling, settle, etc.) is the M.E. *pichen*, *pykken*.

***A pitched battle.*** One for which both sides have made deliberate preparations.

***Pitch and pay.*** Pay up at once. There is a suppressed pun in the phrase: 'to pay a ship' is to pitch it.

> The word is pitch and pay – trust none.
>
> Shakespeare, *Henry V*, 2, 3

***Pitch and toss.*** A game in which coins are pitched at a mark, the player getting nearest having the right to toss all the others' coins into the air and take those that come down with heads up. Hence, *to play pitch and toss* with one's money, prospects, etc.; to gamble recklessly, to play ducks and drakes.

> The bounding pinnace played a game
> Of dreary pitch and toss;
> A game that, on the good dry land,
> Is apt to bring a loss.
>
> Thos Hood, *The Sea Spell*

***To pitch into one.*** To assail him vigorously; to give it him hot.

***Touch pitch, and you will be defiled.*** 'The finger that touches rouge will be red.' 'Evil communications corrupt good manners.' 'A rotten apple injures its companions.' Shakespeare introduces the proverb in *Much Ado* (3, 3).

**Pitcher.** From Lat. *picarium* or *bicarium*; the word is a doublet of Beaker (*q.v.*).

***Little pitchers have long ears.*** Little folk or children hear what is said when you little think it. The ear of a pitcher is the handle, made somewhat in the shape of a man's ear.

***The pitcher went once too often to the well.*** The dodge was tried once too often, and utterly failed. The sentiment is proverbial in most European languages.

**Pithecanthrope.** The name given by Haeckel in 1868 to the hypothetical 'missing link' (*q.v.*); from Gr. *pithekos*, ape, and *anthropos*, man. Later, *Pithecanthropus* was the generic name given to the remains of the extinct man-like ape discovered in the Pliocene of Java in 1891.

**Pitris.** The spirits of the dead among the Hindus; the 'Manes'.

**Pitt Diamond.** A diamond of just under 137 carats found at the Parteal mines, India, and bought by Thomas Pitt (*see* Diamond Pitt) in 1702 from a thief for a sum (said to have been £20,400) far below its real value. Hence Pope's reference –

> Asleep and naked as an Indian lay,
> An honest factor stole a gem away.
>
> *Moral Essays*, Ep. iii, 361

Pitt sold the diamond in 1717 to the Regent Orleans (hence it is also called the 'Regent Diamond') for £135,000; it later adorned the sword-hilt of Napoleon, and is still in the possession of France. Its original weight, before cutting, was 410 carats, and its present value is probably well over half a million sterling.

**Pitt's Pictures.** 'Blind' windows used to be so called, because many windows were blocked up when William Pitt augmented the window tax in 1784, and again in 1797.

**Pittacus.** One of the 'Seven Sages' of Greece. His great sayings were: (1) 'Know the right time', and (2) ' 'Tis a sore thing to be eminent.'

**Pixie** or **Pixy.** A sprite or fairy of folklore, especially in Cornwall and Devon, where some hold them to be the spirits of infants who have died before baptism. The Pixy monarch has his court like Oberon, and sends his subjects on their several tasks. The word is probably Celtic, but its history is unknown.

**Place aux dames** (Fr.). Make way for the ladies; 'ladies first, if you please'.

**Placebo** (Lat. I shall please, *or* be acceptable). Vespers for the dead; because in the old church services this was the opening word of the first antiphon – *Placebo Domino in regione vivorum*, I will walk before the Lord in the land of the living (Ps. 116:9).

As sycophants and those who wanted to get something out of the relatives of the departed used to make a point of attending this service and singing the *Placebo* the phrase *to sing Placebo* came to mean 'to play the flatterer or sycophant'; and Chaucer (who in the *Merchant's Tale* gives this as a name to a parasite) has –

> Flatereres been the develes chapelleyns that singen evere *Placebo*.
>
> *Parson's Tale*, § 40

**Place-makers' Bible, The.** *See* Bible, Specially named.

**Plagiarist,** one who appropriates another's ideas, etc., in literature, music, and so on, means strictly one who kidnaps a slave (Lat. *plagiarius*). Martial applies the word to the kidnappers of other men's brains.

**Plain, The.** The Girondists were so called in the French Revolutionary National Convention, because they sat on the level floor or plain of the hall. After their overthrow this part of the House was called the *marais* or swamp, and included such members as were under the control of the Mountain (*q.v.*).

***It's all plain sailing.*** It's perfectly straightforward; there need be no hesitation about the course of action. A nautical phrase which should be written *plane*, not *plain*.

***Plane sailing*** is the art of determining a ship's position on the assumption that the earth is flat and she is sailing, therefore, on a plane, instead of a spherical, surface, which is a simple and easy method of computing distances.

**Plan of Campaign, The.** A scheme promulgated by the Nationalist MP for East Mayo, Mr John Dillon, in October, 1886. It provided that Irish tenants on an estate should band together, and decide what reduction of rent they should claim. If the landlord agreed, well and good; if not, the tenants were to pay into a campaign fund the amount offered, the money thus raised to be used in fighting the landlord if he went to law to recover his rents.

**Planets.** The heavenly bodies that revolve round the sun in approximately circular orbits; so called from Gr. (through Lat. and O.Fr.) *planasthai*, to wander, because, to the ancients, they appeared to wander about among the stars instead of having fixed places.

The *primary planets* are Mercury, Venus, the Earth, Mars, Jupiter, Saturn, and Neptune; these are known as the *major planets*, the asteroids between the orbits of Mars and Jupiter being the *minor planets*.

The *secondary planets* are the satellites, or moons, revolving round a primary.

Mercury and Venus are called *Inferior Planets* because their orbits are nearer to the sun than the Earth's; the remaining major planets are *Superior Planets*.

Only five of the planets were known to the ancients (the Earth, of course, not being reckoned), viz. Mercury, Venus, Mars, Jupiter, and Saturn: but to these were added the Sun and the Moon, making seven in all. Among the astrologers and alchemists

| | |
|---|---|
| The Sun (Apollo) represented | Gold. |
| The Moon (Diana) | Silver. |
| Mercury | Quicksilver. |
| Venus | Copper. |
| Mars | Iron. |
| Jupiter | Tin. |
| Saturn | Lead. |

In heraldry the arms of royal personages used to be blazoned by the names of planets (*see* Heraldry).

***Planet-struck.*** A blighted tree is said to be planet-struck. Epilepsy, paralysis, lunacy, etc., are attributed to the malignant aspects of the planets. Horses are said to be planet-struck when they seem stupefied, whether from want of food, colic, or stoppage.

> They with speed
> Their course through thickest constellations held,
> Spreading their bane; the blasted stars looked wan,
> And planets, planet-strook, real eclipse
> Then suffered. Milton, *Paradise Lost*, x, 410

***To be born under a lucky*** (or ***unlucky***) ***planet.*** According to astrology, some planet, at the birth of every individual, presides over his destiny. Some of the planets, like Jupiter, are lucky; and others, like Saturn, are unlucky. *See* Houses, Astrological.

**Plank, A.** Any one portion or principle of a political *platform* (*q.v.*).

***To walk the plank.*** To be put to the supreme test; also, to be about to die. Walking the plank was a mode of disposing of prisoners at sea, much in vogue among the South Sea pirates in the 17th century.

**Plantagenet,** from *planta genista* (broom-plant), the family cognisance first assumed by Geoffrey, Count of Anjou (d.1151), during a pilgrimage to the Holy Land, as a symbol of humility. By his wife Matilda, daughter of Henry I of England, he was father of Henry II, the founder of the House of Plantagenet.

***The House of Plantagenet.*** Henry II and the English kings descended in the direct male line from him, viz.:

| | |
|---|---|
| Henry II | Edward I |
| Richard I | Edward II |
| John | Edward III |
| Henry III | Richard II. |

They reigned from 1154 to 1399. *Cp.* Angevin.

**Plate.** In horse-racing, the gold or silver cup forming the prize; hence the race for such a prize.

***Selling plate.*** A race in which owners of starters have to agree beforehand that the winner shall be sold at a previously fixed price.

***Plates of meat.*** Rhyming slang for 'feet'; often abbreviated to *plates*.

**Platform.** The policy or declaration of the policy of a political party, that on which the party stands, each separate principle being called a *plank* of the platform.

In this sense the word is an Americanism dating from rather before the middle of last century; but in Elizabethan times and later it was used of a plan or scheme of Church government and of political action.

> Queen Elizabeth, in answer to the *Supplication* of the Puritans (offered to the Parliament in 1586), said she 'had examined the platform, and account it most prejudicial to the religion established, to her crown, her government, and her subjects'.

**Platonic.** Pertaining to or ascribed to Plato, the great Greek philosopher (d. about 347 BC) who taught a form of Idealism that attributed real Being to general concepts or Ideas and denied the existence of individual things, the world of *sense* being an illusion, the world of *thought* all.

***Platonic bodies.*** An old name for the five regular geometric solids described by Plato – viz. the tetrahedron, hexahedron, octahedron, dodecahedron, and icosahedron, all of which are bounded by like, equal, and regular planes.

***Platonic love.*** Spiritual love between persons of opposite sexes; the friendship of man and woman, without anything sexual about it. The phrase is founded on a passage towards the end of the *Symposium* in which Plato was extolling not the non-sexual love of a man for a woman, but the loving interest that Socrates took in young men – which was pure, and therefore noteworthy in the Greece of the period.

> I am convinced, and always was, that Platonic Love is Platonic nonsense.
>
> Richardson, *Pamela*, I, lxxviii

***The Platonic Year.*** The same as the Platonic Cycle. *See under* Cycle.

***Platonism*** is characterised by the doctrine of pre-existing eternal ideas, and teaches the immortality and pre-existence of the soul, the dependence of virtue upon discipline, and the trustworthiness of cognition.

**Plaudite** (Lat. 'applaud, ye!' – hence our word *plaudit*). The appeal for applause at the conclusion of Roman plays, especially the comedies of Terence; hence the end of a play.

> Here we may strike the *Plaudite* to our play; my lord Fool's gone; all our audience will forsake us.
>
> Chapman, *Monsieur D'Olive*, IV, ii

**Play.** 'This may be play to you, 'tis death to us.' The allusion is to Aesop's fable of the boys throwing stones at some frogs.

***As good as a play.*** Intensely amusing. It is said to have been the remark of Charles I when he attended the discussion of Lord Ross's 'Divorce Bill'.

***Played out.*** Out of date; no longer in vogue; exhausted.

***Playing to the 'gods'.*** Degrading one's vocation *ad captandum vulgus*. The 'gods' in theatrical phrase are the spectators in the uppermost gallery, the *ignobile vulgus*. The ceiling of Drury Lane Theatre – only just above the gallery – was at one time painted in imitation of the sky, with cupids and deities. In French this gallery is nicknamed *paradis*.

***To play the deuce.*** *See* Deuce.

**Pleader, Pleading.** *See* Special Pleading.

**Plebeians.** Common people; properly it means the free citizens of Rome, who were neither patricians nor clients. They were, however, free Landowners, and had their own 'gentës'.

**Plebiscite.** In Roman history, a law enacted by the 'comitia' or assembly of tribes; nowadays it means the direct vote of the whole body of citizens of a State on some definite question.

In France, the resolutions adopted in the Revolution by the voice of the people, and the general votes given during the Second Empire – such as the general vote to elect Napoleon III emperor of the French.

**Pledge.** To guarantee; to assign as security; hence, in drinking a toast, to give assurance of friendship by the act of drinking.

> Drink to me only with thine eyes,
> And I will pledge with mine.
>
> Ben Jonson

***To take the pledge.*** To bind oneself by a solemn undertaking to abstain from intoxicating liquors; the *pledge* being the guarantee or security – your pledged word.

**Pleiades.** The cluster of stars in the constellation Taurus, especially the seven larger ones out of the great number that compose the cluster; so called by the Greeks, possibly from *plein*, to sail, because they considered navigation safe at the return of the Pleiades, and never attempted it after those stars disappeared.

The *Pleiades* were the seven daughters of Atlas and Pleione. They were transformed into stars, one of which, Electra (*q.v.*), is invisible, some said out of shame, because she alone married a human being, while others held that she hides herself from grief for the destruction of the city and royal race of Troy. She is known as 'the lost Pleiad':

> One of those forms which flit by us, when we
> Are young, and fix our eyes on every face; ...
> Whose course and home we know not, nor shall know
> Like the lost Pleiad seen no more below.
>
> Byron, *Beppo*, xiv

The name *The Pleiad* has frequently been given to groups of seven specially illustrious persons, e.g.:

(1) The Seven Wise Men of Greece (*q.v.*), sometimes called the *Philosophical Pleiad*.

(2) *The Pleiad of Alexandria*. A group of seven contemporary poets in the 3rd century BC, viz. Callimachus, Apollonius of Rhodes, Aratus, Philiscus (called *Homer the Younger*), Lycophron, Nicander, and Theocritus.

(3) *Charlemagne's Pleiad*, the group of scholars with which the Emperor surrounded himself, viz. Charlemagne (who, in this circle, was known as 'David'), Alcuin ('Albinus'), Adelard ('Augustine'), Angilbert ('Homer'), Riculfe ('Damaetas'), Varnefrid, and Eginhard.

(4) *The French Pleiad* of the 16th century, who wrote poetry in the metres, style, etc., of the ancient Greeks and Romans. Of these, Ronsard was the leader, the others being Dorat, Du Bellay, Remi-Belleau, Jodelle, Baïf, and Ponthus de Thyard.

***The second French Pleiad.*** Seven contemporary poets in the reign of Louis XIII, very inferior to the 'first Pleiad'. They are Rapin, Commire, Larae, Santeuil, Ménage, Dupérier, and Petit.

**Plon-plon.** The sobriquet of Prince Napoleon Joseph Charles Bonaparte (1822–91), son of Jerome Bonaparte, an adaptation of *Craint-plon* (Fear-bullet), the nickname he earned in the Crimean War.

**Plotcock.** The old Scotch form of the Roman Pluto, by which Satan is meant. Chaucer calls Pluto the 'king of Faërie', and Dunbar names him 'Pluto the elrich incubus'.

**Plough.** Another name for 'Charles's Wain' or the 'Great Bear' (*q.v.*).

***Fond, Fool,*** or ***White Plough.*** The plough dragged about a village on Plough Monday. Called *white*, because the mummers who drag it about are dressed in white, gaudily trimmed with flowers and ribbons. Called *fond* or *fool*, because the procession is fond or foolish – not serious, or of a business character.

***Plough Monday.*** The first Monday after Twelfth Day is so called because it is the end of the Christmas holidays, and the day when men return to their plough or daily work. It was customary on this day for farm labourers to draw a plough from door to door of the parish, and solicit 'plough-money' to spend in a frolic. The queen of the banquet was called Bessy. *Cp.* Distaff.

***Speed the plough,*** or ***God speed the plough.*** A wish for success and prosperity in some undertaking. It is a very old phrase, and occurs as early as the 15th century in the song sung by the ploughmen on Plough Monday.

***To be ploughed.*** To be 'plucked' or 'turned down' at an examination; to fail to pass.

***To plough the sands.*** To engage in some altogether fruitless labour, to work with no chance of success.

***To plough with another's heifer.*** To adopt his methods, ideas, etc. A biblical phrase. When the men of Timnath gave Samson the answer to his riddle, he replied:

> If ye had not plowed with my heifer, ye had not found out my riddle. Judges 14:18

***To put one's hand to the plough.*** To undertake a task; to commence operations in earnest.

> And Jesus said unto him No man, having put his hand to the plough, and looking back, is fit for the kingdom of God. Luke 9:62

**Plover.** Another old synonym for a dupe or 'gull' (*q.v.*); also for a courtesan.

***To live like a plover.*** To live on nothing, to live on air. Plovers, however, live on small insects and worms, which they hunt for in newly ploughed fields.

**Plowden.** '*The case is altered*,' *quoth Plowden.* There is more than one story given by way of accounting for the origin of this old phrase – used by Jonson as the title of one of his comedies (1598). One of them says that Plowden was an unpopular priest, and, to get him into trouble, he was inveigled into attending mass performed by a layman. When impeached for so doing, the cunning priest asked the layman if it was he who officiated. 'Yes,' said the man. 'And are you a priest?' said Plowden. 'No,' said the man. 'Then,' said Plowden, turning to the tribunal, '*the case is altered*, for it is an axiom with the Church, "No priest, no mass".'

Another story fathers the phrase on Edmund Plowden (1518–85), the great lawyer. He was asked what legal remedy there was against some hogs that had trespassed on complainant's ground. 'There is very good remedy,' began Plowden, but when told that they were his own hogs, said, '*Nay, then, the case is altered.*'

**Pluck,** meaning courage, determination, was originally pugilistic slang of the late 18th century, and meant much the same as *heart.* A 'pug' who was lacking in pluck was a coward, he hadn't the heart for his job; the *pluck* of an animal is the heart, liver, and lungs, that can be removed by one pull or *pluck. Cp.* the expressions bold *heart*, lily-*livered*, a man of another *kidney*, *bowels* of mercy, a *rein* of fun, it raised his *bile*, etc.

A rejected candidate at an examination is said to be *plucked*, because formerly at the Universities, when degrees were conferred and the names were read out before presentation to the Vice-Chancellor, the proctor walked once up and down the room, and anyone who objected might signify his dissent by *plucking* the proctor's gown. This was occasionally done by tradesmen to whom the candidate was in debt.

***A plucked pigeon.*** One fleeced out of his money; one plucked by a rook or sharper.

> There were no smart fellows whom fortune had troubled, … no plucked pigeons or winged rooks, no disappointed speculators, no ruined miners.
> Scott, *Peveril of the Peak*, ch. xi

***He's a plucked 'un.*** He's a plucky chap; there's no frightening *him*.

***I'll pluck his goose for him.*** I'll cut his crest, lower his pride, make him eat humble pie. Comparing the person to a goose, the threat is to pluck off his feathers in which he prides himself.

**Plugson of Undershot.** Carlyle's typical commercial Radical in the middle of the 19th century, who found that no decent Tory would shake hands with him; but at the close of the century found free-competition company with latter-day Tories.

> There are two motive forces which may impel the Plugsons of Toryism ... the pressure is not great enough to ... overcome the *vis inertia* of Plugson and Co.
>
> *Nineteenth Century*, Dec., 1892, p. 878

**Plum.** Old slang for a very large sum of money (properly £100,000), or for its possession. Nowadays the figurative use of the word means the very best part of anything, the 'pick of the basket', a windfall, or one of the prizes of life, as 'The plums (i.e. the chief and highly paid positions) of the Civil Service should go by merit, not influence.'

**Plumes.** ***In borrowed plumes.*** Assumed merit; airs and graces not merited. The allusion is to the fable of the jackdaw who dressed up in peacock's feathers.

***To plume oneself on something.*** To be proud of it, conceited about it; to boast of it. A plume is a feather, and to plume oneself is to feather one's own conceit.

> Mrs Bute Crawley ... plumed herself upon her resolute manner of performing [what she thought right]. Thackeray, *Vanity Fair*

**Plump.** To give all one's votes to a single candidate, or to vote for only one when one has the right to vote for more. The earlier phrase was *to give a plumper*, or *to vote plump*.

**Plunger.** One who *plunges*, i.e. gambles recklessly, and goes on when he can't afford it in the hope that his luck will turn. The Marquis of Hastings was the first person so called by the turf. One night he played three games of draughts for £1,000 a game, and lost all three. He then cut a pack of cards for £500 a cut, and lost £5,000 in an hour and a half. He paid both debts before he left the room.

**Plus ultra.** The motto in the royal arms of Spain, It was once *Ne plus ultra* ('thus far and no farther'), in allusion to the pillars of Hercules, the *ne plus ultra* of the world; but after the discovery of America, and when Charles V inherited the crown of Aragon and Castile, with all the vast American possessions, he struck out *ne*, and assumed the words *plus ultra* for the national motto, the suggestion being that Spain *can* go farther.

**Pluto.** The ruler of the infernal regions in *Roman mythology*, son of Saturn, brother of Jupiter and Neptune, and husband of Proserpine (*q.v.*); hence, the grave, the place where the dead go to before they are admitted into Elysium or sent to Tartarus.

> Brothers, be of good cheer, this night we shall sup with Pluto.
>
> Leonidas to the three hundred Spartans before the battle of Thermopylae

> Th' infernal powers,<br>
> Covering your foe with cloud of deadly night,<br>
> Have borne him hence to Pluto's baleful bowers.
>
> Spenser, *Faërie Queene*, I, v, 14

**Plutocrat.** *See* Plutus.

**Plutonian** or **Plutonist.** *See* Vulcanist.

**Plutonic Rocks.** Granites, certain porphyries and other igneous unstratified crystalline rocks, supposed to have been formed at a great depth and pressure, as distinguished from the volcanic rocks, which were formed near the surface. So called by Lyell from *Pluto*, as the lord of elemental fire.

**Plutus.** In *Greek mythology*, the god of riches. Hence, *Rich as Plutus*, and *plutocrat*, one who exercises influence or possesses power through his wealth. The legend is that he was blinded by Zeus so that his gifts should be equally distributed and not go only to those who merited them.

**Plymouth Brethren.** A sect of Evangelical Christians that arose at Plymouth about 1830. They have no regular ministry, and look upon all Christians as their brethren, holding that national churches are too lax and dissenters too sectarian. Sometimes called 'Darbyites' (*q.v.*), from one of their founders.

**Pocahontas.** Daughter of Powhatan, an Indian chief of Virginia, born about 1595. She is said to have rescued Captain John Smith, when her father was on the point of killing him. She subsequently married John Rolfe, one of the settlers at Jamestown, was baptised under the name of Rebecca, and in 1616 was brought to England, where she became an object of curiosity and frequent allusion in contemporary literature. She died at Gravesend in 1617.

> I have known a princess, and a great one,<br>
> Come forth of a tavern –<br>
> Not go in, sir, though –

She must go in, if she came forth: the blessed
Pocahontas, as the historian calls her,
And great king's daughter of Virginia,
Hath been in womb of tavern.

Ben Jonson, *Staple of News*, II, i (1625)

**Pocket.** The word is used by airmen to denote a place where a sudden drop or acceleration is experienced, owing to a local variation in air-pressure.

***Pocket borough.*** A parliamentary borough where the influence of the magnate was so powerful as to be able to control the election of any candidate.

***Pocket judgment.*** A bond under the hand of a debtor, countersigned by the sovereign. It could be enforced without legal process, but for long has fallen into disuse.

***Pocket pistol.*** Colloquial for a flask carried in 'self-defence', because we may be unable to get a dram on the road.

***Queen Elizabeth's pocket pistol.*** A formidable piece of ordnance given to Queen Elizabeth by the Low Countries in recognition of her efforts to protect them in their reformed religion. It used to overlook the Channel from Dover cliffs, but in 1894 was removed to make room for a modern battery. It bore the following inscription (in Flemish):

Load me well and keep me clean,
And I'll carry a ball to Calais Green.

***Put your pride in your pocket.*** Lay it aside for the nonce.

***To be in,*** or ***out of pocket.*** To be a gainer *or* a loser by some transaction.

***To pocket an insult.*** To submit to an insult without showing annoyance.

***To put one's hand in one's pocket.*** To give money (generally to some charity).

**Pococurante** (Ital., *poco curante*, caring little). Insouciant, devil-may-care, easy-go-lucky. Hence, *pococurantism*, indifference to matters of importance but concern about trifles. Also used for one who in argument leaves the main gist and rides off on some minor and indifferent point.

**Podsnap.** A pompous, self-satisfied man in Dickens's *Our Mutual Friend*, the type of one who is extremely proud of the patronage of his rich acquaintances and is overburdened with stiff-starched etiquette and self-importance. Hence, *Podsnappery*.

> He always knew exactly what Providence meant. Interior and less respectable men might fall short of that mark, but Mr Podsnap was always up to it. And it was very remarkable (and must have been very comfortable) that what Providence meant was invariably what Mr Podsnap meant.
>
> *Our Mutual Friend*, Bk I, ch. ii

**Poet Laureate.** A court official, appointed by the Prime Minister, whose duty it is (or *was*) to compose odes in honour of the sovereign's birthday and in celebration of State occasions of importance, in return for £200 a year and a butt of sack.

The first Poet Laureate officially recognised as such was Ben Jonson, but in earlier times there had been an occasional *Versificator Regis*, and Chaucer, Skelton, Spenser, and Daniel were called 'Laureates' though not appointed to that office. The following is the complete list of Poets Laureate:

Ben Jonson, 1619–37.
Sir William Davenant, 1660–68.
John Dryden, 1670–88.
Thomas Shadwell, 1688–92.
Nahum Tate, 1692–1715.
Nicholas Rowe, 1715–18.
Laurence Eusden, 1718–30.
Colley Cibber, 1730–57.
William Whitehead, 1757–85.
Thomas Warton, 1785–90.
Henry James Pye, 1790–1813.
Robert Southey, 1813–43.
William Wordsworth, 1843–50.
Alfred Tennyson, 1850–92.
Alfred Austin, 1896–1913.
Robert Bridges, 1913–

The term arose from the ancient custom in the universities of presenting a laurel wreath to graduates in rhetoric and poetry. There were at one time 'doctors laureate', 'bachelors laureate', etc.; and in France authors of distinction are still at times 'crowned' by the Academy.

**Poeta nascitur non fit.** Poets are born, not made. *See* Born.

**Poets' Corner, The.** The southern end of the south transept of Westminster Abbey, first so called by Oliver Goldsmith because it contained the tomb of Chaucer. Addison had previously (*Spectator*, No. 26, 1711) alluded to it as the 'poetical Quarter', in which, he says –

> I found there were Poets who had no Monuments, and Monuments which had no Poets.

Besides Chaucer's tomb it contains that of Spenser, and either the tombs of or monuments to Drayton, Ben Jonson, Shakespeare (a statue), Milton (bust), Samuel Butler, Davenant, Cowley, Prior, Gay, Addison, Thomson, Goldsmith, Dryden, Dr Johnson, Sheridan,

Burns, Southey, Coleridge, Campbell, Macaulay, Longfellow, Dickens, Thackeray, Tennyson, and Browning.

The term *Poet's Corner* is also facetiously applied to the part of a newspaper in which poetical contributions are printed.

**Pogrom.** An organised massacre, especially those directed against the Jews in Russia in 1905 and later. The word is Russian, and means devastation (*gromit*, to thunder, to destroy unmercifully).

**Poilu.** The popular name for the French private soldier, equivalent to our 'Tommy Atkins'. It sprang into use during the Great War, and means literally 'hairy', but it had been used by Balzac as meaning 'brave'.

**Point.** Defined by Euclid as 'that which hath no parts'. Playfair defines it as 'that which has position but not magnitude', and Legendre says it 'is a limit terminating a line', which suggests that a point could not exist, even in imagination, without a line, and presupposes that we know what a *line* is. In regard to Euclid's definition, we say: *Ex nihilo nihil fit*.

***A point of honour.*** *See* Honour.

***A point-to-point race.*** A race, especially a steeplechase, direct from one point to another; a cross-country race.

***Armed at all points.*** Armed to the teeth; having no parts undefended.

> A figure like your Father,
> Arm'd at all points exactly, *Cap a Pe*,
> Appears before them.
>
> Shakespeare, *Hamlet*, 1, 2

***Come to the point!*** Speak out plainly what you want; don't beat about the bush, but avoid circumlocution and get to the gist of the matter.

***In point of fact.*** A stronger way of saying 'As a fact', or 'As a matter of fact'.

***Not to put too fine a point upon it.*** Not to be over delicate in stating it; the prelude to a blunt though truthful remark.

***To carry one's point.*** To attain the desired end; to get one's way.

***To dine on potatoes and point.*** To have potatoes without any relish or extras, a very meagre dinner indeed. When salt was dear and the cellar was empty parents used to tell their children to *point* their potato to the salt cellar, and eat it. This was potato and point, and the 'joke' lies in the allusion to a *point-steak*, which is the best portion.

***To give one points.*** To be able to accord him an advantage and yet beat him; to be considerably better than he.

***To make a point of doing something.*** To treat it as a matter of duty, or to make it a special object. The phrase is a translation of the older French *faire un point de*.

***To stand on points.*** On punctilios; delicacy of behaviour. In the following quotation Theseus puns on the phrase, the side allusion being that Quince in the delivery of his Prologue had taken no notice of the stops, or *points*:

> This fellow doth not stand upon points.
>
> Shakespeare, *Midsummer Night's Dream*, 5, 1

***To stretch a point.*** To exceed what is strictly right. There may be an allusion here to the tagged laces called *points*, formerly used in costume; to 'truss a point' was to tie the laces which held the breeches; to 'stretch a point' to stretch these laces, so as to adjust the dress to extra growth, or the temporary fullness of good feeding.

***To truss his points.*** To tie the points of hose. The points were the cords pointed with metal, like shoe-laces, attached to doublets and hose; being very numerous, some second person was required to 'truss' them or fasten them properly.

> I hear the gull [Sir Piercie] clamorous for someone to truss his points. He will find himself fortunate if he lights on anyone here who can do him the office of groom of the chamber. Scott, *The Monastery*, ch. xvi

**Point-blank.** Direct. A term in gunnery; when a cannon is so placed that the line of sight is parallel to the axis and horizontal, the discharge is point-blank, and was supposed to go direct, without curve, to an object within a certain distance. In French *point blanc* is the white mark or bull's-eye of a target, to hit which the ball or arrow must not deviate in the least from the exact path.

> Now art thou within point-blank of our jurisdiction regal.
>
> Shakespeare, *2 Henry VI*, 4, 7

**Point d'appui** (Fr.). A standpoint; a fulcrum; a position from which yon can operate; a pretext to conceal the real intention. Literally the point of support.

> The material which gives name to the dish is but the *point d'appui* for the literary cayenne and curry-powder, by which it is recommended to the palate of the reader. *The Athenaeum*

**Point de Judas** (Fr.). The number 13. The twelve apostles and our Lord made thirteen at the Last Supper.

**Point-devise** (Fr. the point devised, the desired object). Punctilious; minutely exact. Holofernes says, 'I abhor such insociable and *point de vise* companions, such rackers of orthography.'

> You are rather *point de vise* in your accoutrements.
> Shakespeare, *As You Like It*, 3, 2

**Poison.** It is said that poisons had no effect on Mithridates, King of Pontus. This was Mithridates VI (d.63 BC), called the Great, who succeeded his father at the age of eleven, and fortified his constitution by drinking antidotes to poisons which might at any moment be administered to him by persons about the court. *See* Mithridate.

**Poisson d'Avril** (Fr. April fish). The French equivalent for our 'April fool' (*q.v.*).

> The mackerel, says Oudin, is called the *poisson d'Avril, 'parce que les macquereaux se prennent et se mangent environ ce mois-la'*.

**Poke.** A bag, pouch, or sack – from which comes our *pocket*, a little poke. The word is rarely used nowadays, except in the phrase *To buy a pig in a poke* (*see* Pig). The word is not connected with the verb *to poke*.

***Poke bonnet.*** A long, straight, projecting bonnet, commonly worn by women in the early 19th century, and still worn by Salvation Army lasses and old-fashioned Quaker women. Why it was so called is not clear – probably because it projects or *pokes* out.

***To poke fun at one.*** To make one a laughing-stock.

> At table he was hospitable and jocose, always poking good-natured fun at Luke.
> E. Lynn Lynton, *Lizzie Lorton of Greyrigg*, ch. xii

**Poker.** Slang for a very stiff, formal, unbending sort of person; also for the 'squire Bedels who at Oxford and Cambridge carry a silver mace or *poker* before the Vice-Chancellor.

The reason why a *poker* is set leaning against the upper bars of a fire to draw it up is to make a cross to keep off Lob, the house spirit, who loves to lie before the fire, and, like Puck and Robin Goodfellow, enjoys mischief and practical jokes.

**Poker-work.** Ornamentation on wood, done by executing designs by means of the point of a hot poker or 'heater' of an Italian iron. By charring different parts more or less, various tints can be obtained.

**Poky.** Cramped, narrow, confined; as, *a poky corner*. Also poor and shabby.

> The ladies were in their pokiest old headgear.
> Thackeray, *The Newcomes*, ch. lvii

**Polack.** An inhabitant of Poland. The term is not used now, *Pole* having for long taken its place.

> So frowned he once, when, in an angry parle,
> He smote the sledded Polacks on the ice.
> Shakespeare, *Hamlet*, 1, 1

**Pole.** The stake, mast, measure (16½ ft), etc., gets its name from Lat. *palus*, a pale or stake; *pole* – the *North Pole*, *magnetic pole*, etc. – is from Gr. *polos*, an axis, pivot.

***Barber's pole.*** *See* Barber.

***The Poles are the vintagers in Normandy.*** The Norman vintage consists of apples beaten down by poles. The French say, *En Normandie l'on vendange avec la gaule*, where gaule is a play on the word Gaul, but really means a pole.

***Under bare poles.*** *See* Bare.

**Poleas.** The labouring classes of Malabar, as distinguished from the Nairs, the military and ruling caste.

**Polichinelle.** *See* Secret.

**Polish Off.** To finish out of hand. In allusion to articles polished.

***I'll polish him off in no time.*** I'll set him down, give him a drubbing.

***To polish off a meal.*** To eat it quickly, and not keep anyone waiting.

**Polixenes.** Father of Florizel and King of Bohemia in Shakespeare's *Winter's Tale* (*q.v.*).

**Poll** (of Teutonic origin), means the head; hence, the number of persons in a crowd ascertained by counting heads, hence the counting of voters at an election, and such phrases as *to go to the polls*, to stand for election, and *poll tax*, a tax levied on everybody.

The Cambridge term, *the Poll*, meaning students who obtain only a pass degree, i.e. a degree without honours, is probably from Gr. *hoi polloi*, the common herd. These students – *poll men*, are said to *go out in the poll*, and to take a *poll degree*.

**Pollente.** In Spenser's *Faërie Queene* (V, ii) the puissant Saracen, father of Munera, who took his station on 'Bridge Perilous', and attacked everyone who crossed it, bestowing the spoil upon his daughter. He was slain by Sir Artegal, and is supposed to typify Charles IX of France, notorious for the slaughter of Protestants on St Bartholomew's Eve.

**Pollux.** In *classical mythology* the twin brother of Castor (*q.v.*).

**Polly.** Mary. The change of M for P in pet names is by no means rare; e.g. –

*Margaret.* Maggie or Meggy, becomes Peggie, and Pegg or Peg.

*Martha.* Matty becomes Patty.

In the case of *Mary – Polly* we see another change by no means unusual – that of *r* into *l* or *ll*. Similarly, *Sarah* becomes Sally; *Dorothea*, Dora, becomes Dolly; *Harry*, Hal.

**Polonius.** A garrulous old courtier, in Shakespeare's *Hamlet*, typical of the pompous, sententious old man. He was father of Ophelia, and lord chamberlain to the king of Denmark.

**Polony.** A corruption of *Bologna* (*sausage*).

**Poltergeist.** A household spirit, well known to spiritualists, remarkable for throwing things about, plucking the bedclothes, making noises, etc. It is a German term – *polter*, noise, *geist*, spirit.

**Polt-foot.** A club-foot. Ben Jonson calls Vulcan, who was lame, the 'polt-footed philosopher'.

> Venus was content to take the blake Smith (i.e., blacksmith Vulcan) with his powlt foote.
>
> Lyly, *Euphues*

**Poltroon.** A coward; from Ital. *poltro*, a bed, because cowards are sluggards and feign themselves sick a-bed in times of war.

In falconry the name was given to a bird of prey, with the talons of the hind toes cut off to prevent its flying at game, probably owing to the old idea that the word was derived from Lat. *pollice truncus*, maimed in the thumb, because conscripts who had no stomach for the field used to disqualify themselves by cutting off their right thumb.

**Polybotes.** One of the giants who fought against the gods. The sea-god pursued him to Cos, and, tearing away part of the island, threw it on him and buried him beneath the mass.

**Polycletus.** A sculptor of Sicyon, of the late 5th century BC, who deduced a canon of the proportions of the several parts of the human body, and made a statue of a Persian bodyguard, which was admitted by all to be a model of the human form, and was called 'The Rule' (the standard).

**Polycrates,** Tyrant of Samos, was so fortunate in all things that Amasis, King of Egypt, advised him to chequer his pleasures by relinquishing something he greatly prized. Whereupon Polycrates threw into the sea a beautiful seal, the most valuable of his jewels. A few days afterwards a fine fish was sent him as a present, and in its belly was found the jewel. Amasis, alarmed at this good fortune, broke off his alliance, declaring that sooner or later this good fortune would fail; and not long afterwards Polycrates was shamefully put to death by Oroetes, who had invited him to his court.

> Richard, in surveying his guests, … had feelings not unlike those which lulled King Polycrates of old.
>
> G. Gissing, *Demos*, ch. xii

**Polydamas.** A Grecian athlete of immense size and strength. He killed a fierce lion without any weapon, stopped a chariot in full career, lifted a mad bull, and died at last in attempting to stop a falling rock. *Cp.* Milo.

**Polydore.** The name assumed by Guiderius, in Shakespeare's *Cymbeline*.

**Polyhymnia.** The Muse of lyric poetry, and inventor of the lyre. *See* Muses.

**Polyphemus.** One of the Cyclops, an enormous giant, with only one eye, and that in the middle of his forehead, who lived in Sicily. When Ulysses landed on the island, this monster made him and twelve of his crew captives; six of them he ate, and then Ulysses contrived to blind him, and escape with the rest of the crew (*cp.* Lestrigons). Polyphemus was in love with Galatea, a sea-nymph who had set her heart on the shepherd Acis; Polyphemus, in a fit of jealousy, crushed him beneath a rock.

**Poma Alcinoo dare.** *See* Alcinoo.

**Pomatum.** Another name for *pomade*, which was so called because it was originally made by macerating over-ripe apples (Fr. *pommes*) in grease.

> There is likewise made an ointment with the pulpe of Apples and Swines grease and Rose water, which is used to beautifie the face … called in shops *pomatum*, of the Apples whereof it is made.
>
> Gerarde, *Herbal*, III, xcv (1597)

**Pomfret Cakes.** *See* Pontefract.

**Pommard.** A red Burgundy wine, so called from a village of that name in the Côte d'Or, France. In France the word is sometimes colloquially used for cider (or beer), the pun being on *pomme*, apple.

**Pommel.** The pommel of a sword is the rounded knob terminating the hilt, so called on account of its apple-like shape (Fr. *pomme*, apple); and *to pommel one*, now to pound him with your fists, was originally to beat him with the pommel of your sword.

**Pomona.** The Roman goddess of fruits and fruit trees (Lat. *pomum*), hence fruit generally.

Bade the wide fabric unimpaired sustain
Pomona's store, and cheese, and golden grain.
Bloomfield, *Farmer's Boy*

**Pompadour,** as a colour, is claret purple, so called from Louis XV's mistress, the Marquise de Pompadour (1721–64). The 56th Foot is called the Pompadours, from the claret facings of their regimental uniforms. There is an old song supposed to be an elegy on John Broadwood, a Quaker, which introduces the word:

Sometimes he wore an old brown coat,
  Sometimes a pompadore,
Sometimes 'twas buttoned up behind,
  And sometimes down before.

**Pompey.** A generic name formerly used of a black footman, as *Abigail* used to be of a lady's maid. One of Hood's jocular book-titles was *Pompeii; or, Memoirs of a Black Footman, by Sir W. Gill.* (Sir W. Gell wrote a book on Pompeii.)

**Pompey's Pillar.** A Corinthian column of red granite, nearly 100 ft high, erected at Alexandria by Publius, Prefect of Egypt, in honour of Diocletian and to record the conquest of Alexandria in 296. It has about as much right to be called *Pompey's* pillar as the obelisk of Heliopolis, re-erected by Rameses II at Alexandria, has to be called *Cleopatra's Needle*.

**Pompilia.** The heroine of Browning's *The Ring and the Book*. She is brutally treated by her husband, Count Guido Franceschini, but makes her escape under the protection of the young priest, Caponsacchi. She subsequently gives birth to a son, and is stabbed to death by her husband.

**Pongo.** In the old romance *The Seven Champions of Christendom*, an amphibious monster of Sicily, a cross between a 'land-tiger and sea-shark'. He devoured five hundred Sicilians, leaving the island for twenty miles round without inhabitant, and was eventually slain by the three sons of St George. Early writers gave the name to the chimpanzee or gorilla.

**Ponocrates.** Gargantua's tutor, in Rabelais' *Pantagruel and Gargantua*.

**Pons Asinorum** (Lat. the asses' bridge). The fifth proposition, Bk i, of Euclid – the first difficult theorem, which dunces rarely get over for the first time without stumbling. It is anything but a 'bridge'; it is really *pedica asinorum*, the 'dolt's stumbling-block'.

**Pontefract** or **Pomfret Cakes.** Liquorice lozenges impressed with a castle; so called from being made at Pontefract. The name of the town is still frequently pronounced *pumfret*, representing the Anglo-Norman and Middle English spelling *Pontfret*. The place was called *Fractus Pons* by Orderic (1097) and *Pontefractus* by John of Hexham (about 1165), in allusion to the old Roman bridge over the Aire, broken down by William I in 1069, remains of which were still visible in the 16th century.

**Pontiff.** The term was formerly applied to any bishop, but now only to the Bishop of Rome – the Pope – i.e. the Sovereign Pontiff. It means literally one who has charge of the bridges, as these were in the particular care of the principal college of priests in ancient Rome, the head of which was the Pontifex Maximus (Lat. *pons, pontis*, a bridge).

Well has the name of Pontifex been given
Unto the church's head, as the chief builder
And architect of the invisible bridge
That leads from earth to heaven
Longfellow, *Golden Legend*, v

**Pontius Pilate's Body-guard.** The 1st Foot Regiment, now called the Royal Scots, the oldest regiment in the service. The fable is that when in the French service as *Le Régiment de Douglas* they had a dispute with the Picardy regiment about the antiquity of their respective corps. The Picardy officers declared they were on duty on the night of the Crucifixion, when the colonel of the 1st Foot replied, 'If we had been on guard, we should not have slept at our posts.'

**Pony.** Slang for £25; also (especially in the USA) for a translation crib, also for a small beer-glass holding a little under a gill.

In card-games the person on the right hand of the dealer, whose duty it is to collect the cards for the dealer, is called the *pony*, from Lat. *pone*, 'behind', being behind the dealer.

**Pooka.** *See* Phooka.

**Poor.** ***Poor as a church mouse.*** In a church there is no cupboard or pantry, where mice most do congregate.

***Poor as Job.*** The allusion is to Job being deprived by Satan of everything he possessed.

***Poor as Lazarus.*** This is the beggar Lazarus, full of sores, who was laid at the rich man's gate, and desired to be fed from the crumbs that fell from Dives' table (Luke 16:13–31).

***Poor Clares.*** *See* Franciscans.

***Poor Jack*** or ***John.*** Dried hake. We have 'john dory', a 'jack' (pike), a 'jack shark', etc., and *Jack* may here be a play on the word 'Hake', and John a substitute for Jack.

'Tis well thou art not fish; if thou hadst, thou hadst been poor-john.

Shakespeare, *Romeo and Juliet*, 1, 1

*Cp.* the jocular proof that an eel pie is a pigeon pie. An eel pie is a fish pie, a fish pie may be jack pie, a jack pie is a john pie, and a john pie is a pie john (pigeon).

***Poor man.*** The blade-bone of a shoulder of mutton is so called in Scotland. In some parts of England it is termed a 'poor knight of Windsor', because it holds the same relation to 'Sir Loin' as a Windsor knight does to a baronet. Scott (*Bride of Lammermoor*, ch. xix) tells of a laird who, being asked by an English landlord what he would have for dinner, produced the utmost consternation by saying, 'I think I could relish a morsel of a poor man.'

***Poor Richard.*** The assumed name of Benjamin Franklin in a series of almanacks from 1732 to 1757. They contained maxims and precepts on temperance, economy, cleanliness, chastity, and other homely virtues; and several ended with the words, 'as poor Richard says'.

***Poor Robin's Almanack.*** A farcical almanack, parodying those who seriously indulged in prophecy, published at intervals from 1664 to as late as 1828. The early issues have often been attributed to Herrick, but they were the work of one (or both) of the brothers Robert ('Robin') and William Winstanley. The original title was:

Poor Robin. An Almanack. After a New Fashion. Wherein the Reader may see (if he be not blinde) many remarkable things worthy of Observation. Containing a two-fold Kalendar, viz., the Julian or English; and the Roundheads or Fanaticks; several Saints' days, and Observations upon every Month. Written by Poor Robin, Knight of the Burnt-Island a well-wisher to the Mathematicks. Calculated for the Meridian of Limehouse, over against Cuckolds-haven; the Longitude and Latitude whereof is set down in the Foreheads of all jealous-pated Husbands.

As a specimen of the 'predictions', the following, for January, 1664, may be taken as an example:

Strong Beer and good Fires are as fit for this Season as a Halter for a Thiefe: and when every Man is pleas'd, then 'twill be a Merry World indeed ... This Month we may expect to hear of the Death of some Man, Woman, or Child, either in Kent or Christendom.

***There are none poor but those whom God hates.*** This does not mean that poverty is a punishment, but that the only poverty worthy of the name is poverty of God's grace. In this sense Dives may be the poor man, and Lazarus the beggar abounding in that 'blessing of the Lord which maketh rich'.

**Pope.** The word represents the A.S. *papa*, from ecclesiastical Latin, and Gr. *pappas*, the infantile word for *father* (*cp.* modern 'papa'); it is not connected with Lat. *popa*, which denoted an inferior Roman (pagan) priest who brought the victim to the altar and felled it with an axe. In the early Church the title was given to many bishops; Leo the Great (440–61) was the first to use it officially, and in the time of Gregory VII (1073–85) it was, by decree, specially reserved to the Bishop of Rome. *Cp.* Pontiff.

According to Platina, Sergius II (844–6) was the first pope who changed his name on ascending the papal chair. Some accounts have it that his name was Hogsmouth, others that it was 'Peter di Porca', and he changed it out of deference to St Peter, thinking it arrogant to style himself Peter II.

Gregory the Great (591) was the first pope to adopt the title *Servus Servorum Dei* (the Servant of the Servants of God). It is founded on Mark 10:44.

Fye upon all his jurisdiccions
And upon those whiche to hym are detters;
Fye upon his bulles breves and letters
Wherein he is named *Servus Servorum.*

*Rede Me and be nott Wrothe*, v, 13 (1528)

The title *Vicar of Christ*, or *Vicar of God*, was adopted by Innocent III, 1198. *See also* Tiara.

The election of Pius XI (1922) raised the number of Italian popes to 209. France claims second place with only 15, and Greece follows with 9; then come Germany with 7, Asia with 5, Africa and Spain each with 3, Dalmatia with 2, and Palestine, Thrace, Holland, Portugal, Candia, and England with 1 each. The last non-Italian pope was Adrian VI, who came from Utrecht, and reigned for less than a year in 1522.

***The Black Pope.*** The General of the Jesuits.

***The Pope of Geneva.*** A name given to Calvin (1509–64).

***The Pope's eye.*** The tender piece of meat (the lymphatic gland) surrounded by fat in the middle of a leg of mutton. The French call it *Judas's eye*, and the Germans *the priest's tit-bit*.

***The Pope's slave.*** So Cardinal Cajetan (d.1534) called the Church.

***The Red Pope.*** The Prefect of the Propaganda (*q.v.*).

***Pope Joan.*** A mythical female pope, fabled in the Middle Ages to have succeeded Leo IV (855). The vulgar tale is that Joan conceived a violent passion for the monk Folda and in order to get admission to him assumed the monastic habit. Being clever and popular, she was elected pope, but was discovered through giving birth to a child during her enthronisation. The whole story has long since been exploded.

The name was given to a once popular card-game played with an ordinary pack *minus* the eight of diamonds (called the 'Pope Joan'), and a circular revolving tray divided into eight compartments.

**Popefigland.** An island in Rabelais' satire (Bk iv, ch. 45), inhabited by the Gaillardets (Fr. gay people), rich and free, till, being shown the pope's image, they exclaimed, 'A fig for the pope!' whereupon the whole island was put to the sword, its name changed to Popefigland, and the people were called Popefigs.

**Popinjay.** An old name for a parrot (ultimately of Arabic origin; Gr. *papagos*), hence a conceited or empty-headed fop.

> I then, all smarting with my wounds being cold,
> To be so pestered with a popinjay,
> Answered neglectingly I know not what,
> He should or he should not.
>
> Shakespeare, *1 Henry IV*, 1, 3

***The Festival of the Popinjay.*** The first Sunday in May, when a figure of a popinjay, decked with parti-coloured feathers and suspended from a pole, served as a target for shooting practice. He whose ball or arrow brought down the bird by cutting the string by which it was hung, received the proud title of 'Captain Popinjay', or 'Captain of the Popinjay', for the rest of the day, and was escorted home in triumph. *See* Scott's *Old Mortality*, ch. ii.

**Popish Plot.** A fictitious plot implicating the Duke of York and others in high place, invented by Titus Oates (1678) who alleged that the Catholics were about to massacre the Protestants, burn London, and assassinate the king. Some thirty innocent persons were executed, and Oates obtained great wealth by revealing the supposed plot, but ultimately he was pilloried, whipped and imprisoned.

**Poplar.** The poplar was consecrated to Hercules, because he destroyed Kakos in a cavern of Mount Aventine, which was covered with poplars. In the moment of triumph the hero plucked a branch from one of the trees and bound it round his head. When he descended to the infernal regions, the heat caused a profuse perspiration which blanched the under surface of the leaves, while the smoke of the eternal flames blackened the upper surface. Hence the leaves of the poplar are dark on one side and white on the other.

The *white poplar* is fabled to have originally been the nymph Leuce, beloved by Pluto. He changed her into this at death.

**Poplin.** This silk and worsted material, now made chiefly in Ireland, gets its name from the old *papal* (Ital. *papalino*) city of Avignon, because up to the 17th century that was the chief seat of its manufacture.

**Porcelain,** from Ital. *porcellana*, 'a little pig', the name given by the early Portuguese traders, to cowrie-shells, the shape of which is not unlike a pig's back, and later to Chinese earthenware, which is white and glossy, like the inside of these shells.

**Porch, The.** A philosophic sect, generally called Stoics (Gr. *stoa*, a porch), because Zeno, the founder, gave his lectures in the public ambulatory, *Stoa paecile*, in the agora of Athens.

> The successors of Socrates formed societies which lasted several centuries: the Academy, the Porch, the Garden. Seeley, *Ecce Homo*

**Porcus. *The Latins call me 'porcus'.*** A sly reproof to anyone boasting, showing off, or trying to make himself appear greater than he is. The fable says that a wolf was going to devour a pig, when the pig observed that it was a Friday, when no good Catholic would eat meat. Going on together, the wolf said to the pig, 'They seem to call you by many names.' 'Yes,' said the pig, 'I am called swine, grunter, hog, and I know not what besides. The Latins call me *porcus*.' '*Porpus*, do they?' said the wolf. 'Well, porpoise is a fish, and we may eat fish on a Friday,' and devoured him without another word.

**Pork, Pig.** The former is Norman-French, the latter Saxon.

> Pork, I think, is good Norman-French and so, when the brute lives, and is in charge of a Saxon slave, she goes by her Saxon name; but becomes a Norman, and is called *pork*, when she is carried to the castle-hall. Scott, *Ivanhoe*

**Porphyrion.** One of the giants of *Greek mythology* who made war with the gods. He hurled the island of Delos against Zeus, who, with the aid of Hercules, overcame him.

**Porphyrogenitus.** A surname of the Byzantine Emperor, Constantine VII (911–59). It signifies 'born in the purple' (Gr. *porphuros*, purple, *gennetos*, born), and a son born to a sovereign after his accession is called a *porphyrogenito*. *Cp.* Purple.

**Porridge. *Everything tastes of porridge*.** However we may deceive ourselves, whatever castles in the air we may construct, the fact of home life will always intrude. Sir Walter Scott tells us of an insane man who thought the asylum his castle, the servants his own menials, the inmates his guests. 'Although,' said he, 'I am provided with a first-rate cook and proper assistants, and although my table is regularly furnished with every delicacy of the season, yet so depraved is my palate that everything I eat tastes of porridge.' His palate was less vitiated than his imagination.

***He has supped all his porridge.*** Eaten his last meal; he is dead.

***Keep your breath to cool your porridge.*** A rude remark made to one who is giving unwanted or unsought advice. It won't be taken any way, and the suggestion is that the adviser may want it himself some day.

> Well, Friar, spare your breath to cool your porridge; come, let us now talk with deliberation, fairly and softly.
>
> Rabelais, *Pantagruel*, etc., V, xxviii

***Not to earn salt to one's porridge.*** To earn practically nothing; to be a 'waster'.

**Port.** The origin of the nautical term, meaning the left-hand side of a ship when looking forward, is not certain; but it is probably from *port*, a harbour. The word has been in use for over three centuries, and in course of time took the place of the earlier *larboard* (*q.v.*) which was so easily confused with *starboard*. When the steering-gear was on the starboard (i.e. *steer-board*) side it was almost a necessity to enter port and tie up at the harbour with the larboard side towards the *port*, and this probably accounts for the name.

A vessel's *port-holes* are so called from Lat. *porta*, a door; the harbour is called a *port* from Lat. *portus*, a haven; the dark red wine gets its name *port* from *Oporto*, Portugal, whence it is exported; and *port*, the way of bearing oneself, etc. (Queen Elizabeth, says Speed, daunted the Ambassador of Poland 'with her stately port and majestical deporture') from Lat. *portare*, to carry.

***Any port in a storm.*** Said when one is in a difficulty and some not particularly good way out offers itself; a last resource.

**Port Royal.** A convent about 8 miles S.W. of Versailles which in the 17th century became the headquarters of the Jansenists (*q.v.*). The community was suppressed by Louis XIV in 1660, but later again sprang into prominence and was condemned by a bull of Clement XI in 1708. Two years later the convent, which had been removed to Paris about 1637, was razed to the ground.

**Porte, The Sublime.** The central office of the Ottoman Government in Constantinople; hence, the Government or the Empire itself. The term is French in origin, *sublime* signifying 'lofty' or 'high and mighty'. Constantinople has twelve gates, and near one of these is a building with a lofty gateway called 'Bab-i-humajun', in which is the official residence of the vizier, and the offices of all the chief ministers of state, whence all the imperial edicts are issued.

**Porteous Riot.** At Edinburgh in September, 1736. C. Porteous was captain of the city guard, and, at the execution of a smuggler named Wilson, ordered the guards to fire on the mob, which had become tumultuous; six persons were killed, and eleven wounded. Porteous was condemned to death, but reprieved; whereupon the mob burst into the jail where he was confined, and, dragging him to the Grassmarket (the usual place of execution), hanged him by torchlight on a barber's pole. Scott introduces the riot in his *Heart of Midlothian*.

**Portia.** A rich heiress and 'lady barrister' in Shakespeare's *Merchant of Venice* (*q.v.*), in love with Bassanio. Her name is often used allusively for a female advocate.

**Portland Vase.** A cinerary urn of transparent dark blue glass, coated with opaque white glass cut in cameo fashion, found in a tomb (supposed to be that of Alexander Severus) near Rome in the 17th century. In 1770 it was purchased from the Barberini Palace by Sir William Hamilton for 1,000 guineas, and came afterwards into the possession of the Duke of Portland, one of the trustees of the British Museum, who placed it in that institution for exhibition. In 1845 a lunatic named Lloyd dashed it to pieces, but it was so skilfully repaired that the damage is barely visible. It is ten inches high, and six in diameter at the broadest part.

**Portmanteau Word.** An artificial word made up of parts of others, and expressive of a combination denoted by those parts – such as *squarson*, a 'cross' between a *squire* and a *parson*.

Lewis Carroll invented the term in *Through the Looking-Glass*, ch. vi; *slithy*, he says, means *lithe* and slimy, *mimsy* is *flimsy* and *miserable*, etc. So called because there are two meanings 'packed up' in the one word.

**Portsoken Ward.** The most easterly of the City of London wards – the old *Knighten Guild* (*q.v.*) – lying outside the wall in the parish of St Botolph, Aldgate. Its name indicates the *soke* or franchise of the city (*not* of the gate). *Port* is an old name for any city, and occurs in *Portreeve*, the chief city officer.

**Poseidon.** The god of the sea in *Greek mythology*, the counterpart of the Roman Neptune (*q.v.*). He was the son of Cronos and Rhea, brother of Zeus and Pluto, and husband of Amphitrite. It was he who, with Apollo, built the walls of Troy, and as the Trojans refused to give him his reward he hated them and took part against them in the Trojan War. Earthquakes were attributed to him, and he was said to have created the first horse.

**Poser.** Formerly used of an examiner, one who *poses* (i.e. 'opposes') questions, especially a bishop's examining chaplain and the examiner at Eton for the King's College fellowship. Nowadays the word usually denotes a puzzling question or proposition.

**Posh.** Modern slang for smart, swagger, well-turned-out; as, 'You're looking very posh today', spruce and well groomed.

**Posse** (Lat. to be able). A body of men – especially constables – who are armed with legal authority.

***Posse Comitatus.*** The whole force of the county – that is, all the male members of a county over fifteen, who may be summoned by a sheriff to assist in preventing a riot, the rescue of prisoners, or other unlawful disorders. Clergymen, peers, and the infirm are exempt.

**Post.** ***Beaten on the post.*** Only just beaten; a racing term, the 'post' being the winning-post.

***By return of post.*** By the next mail in the opposite direction; originally the phrase referred to the messenger, or 'post' who brought the dispatch and would return with the answer.

***From pillar to post.*** *See* Pillar.

***Knight of the post.*** *See* Knight.

***Post-and-rail.*** Wooden fencing made of posts and rails. In Australia roughly made tea in which the stalks are floating is called *post-and-rail tea*.

***Post captain.*** A term used in the Navy from about 1730 to 1830 to distinguish an officer who held a captain's commission from one of inferior rank who was given the title by courtesy because he was in command of a small ship or was acting as captain, etc. A ship of under 20 guns was not entitled to a full – or post – captain.

***Post haste.*** With great speed or expedition. The allusion is to the old coaching days, when travelling by relays of horses, or with horses placed on the road to expedite the journey, was the rule in cases of urgency.

***Post paper.*** A standard size of paper measuring 15 x 19¼ in. in writing papers, and 15½ x 19¼ in. in printings; so called from an ancient watermark which has been supposed to represent a post-horn. This horn or bugle mark was, however, in use as early as 1314, long before anything in the nature of a postman or his horn existed. It is probably the famous horn of Roland (*q.v.*).

> The old original post [paper] with the stamp in the corner representing a post-boy riding for life, and twanging his horn.
>
> Mrs Gaskell, *Cranford*, ch. v

***Post term*** (Lat. *post terminum*, after the term). The legal expression for the return of a writ after the term, and for the fee that then is payable for its being filed.

***To be well posted in a subject.*** To be thoroughly acquainted with it, well informed. Originally an American colloquialism, probably from the counting-house, where ledgers are *posted*.

***To run your head against a post.*** To go to work heedlessly and stupidly, or as if you had no eyes.

**Post** (Lat., in compounds). *Post factum* (Lat.). After the act has been committed.

***Post hoc, ergo propter hoc*** (Lat.). After this, therefore *because of* this; expressive of the fallacy that a sequence of events is always the result of cause and effect. The swallows come to England in the spring, but do not bring the spring.

***Post meridian*** (Lat.). After noon; usually contracted to 'PM'.

> 'Twas post meridian half-past four,
> By signal I from Nancy parted.
>
> Dibdin, *Sea Songs*

***A post-mortem degree.*** In old University slang, a degree given to a candidate after having failed at the poll.

> He had not even the merit of being a plodding man and he finally took what used to be called a *post-mortem* degree. *My Rectors*, p. 63

**Post mortem** (Lat.), After death; as a post-mortem examination for the purpose of ascertaining the cause of death.

**Post obit** (Lat. *post obitum*, after the death, i.e. of the person named in the bond). An agreement to pay for a loan a larger sum of money, together with interest at death.

**Poste restante** (Fr., remaining post). A department at a post office to which letters may be addressed for callers, and where they will remain (with certain limits) until called for.

**Posteriori.** *See* A posteriori.

**Posy** properly means a copy of verses presented with a bouquet. It now means the verses without the flowers, as the 'posy of a ring', or the flowers without the verses, as a 'pretty posy'.

> He could make anything in poetry, from the posy of a ring to the chronicle of its most heroic wearer.
>
> Stedman, *Victorian Poets* (Landor), p. 47

**Pot. *A big pot.*** An important person, a personage; a leader of his class or group.

***A pot of money.*** A large amount of money; especially a large stake on a horse.

***A little pot is soon hot.*** A small person is quickly 'riled'. Grumio makes humorous use of the phrase in *The Taming of the Shrew* (4, 1).

***A watched pot never boils.*** Said as a mild reproof to one who is showing impatience; watching and anxiety won't hasten matters.

***Gone to pot.*** Ruined, gone to the bad. The allusion is to the pot into which bits of already cooked meat are cast prior to their making their last appearance as hash.

***The pot calls the kettle black.*** Said of a person who accuses another of faults similar to those committed by himself. The French say, 'The shovel mocks the poker' (*la pelle se moque du fourgon*).

***The pot of hospitality.*** The *pot au feu* which in Ireland used to be shared with anyone who dropped in at mealtimes, or required refreshment.

> And the 'pot of hospitality' was set to boil upon the fire, and there was much mirth and heartiness and entertainment.
>
> *Nineteenth Century*, Oct., 1891, p. 643

***To keep the pot a-boiling.*** To go on paying one's way and making enough to live on; also, to keep things going briskly, to see that the interest does not flag.

**Pot-boiler.** Anything done merely for the sake of the money it will bring in – because it will 'keep the pot a-boiling', i.e. help to provide the means of livelihood; applied specially to work of small merit by artists or literary men.

**Pot-hooks.** Nickname of the old 77th Foot (2nd Battalion, Middlesex Regiment), because the sevens of their badge resembled pot-hooks.

**Pot-hunter.** One who in athletic contests, etc., is keener on winning prizes (often silver cups, or *pots*) than on the sport; it is, of course, a term of reproach among sportsmen.

**Pot-luck. *Come and take pot-luck with me.*** Come and take a family dinner at my house; we'll all 'dip into the pot' and share anything that's going, *sans cérémonie*.

**Pot Valiant.** Made courageous by liquor.

**Pot-wallopers,** before the passing of the Reform Bill (1832), were those who claimed a vote as householders, because they had boiled their own pot at their own fireplace in the parish for six months. The earlier form was *pot-waller*, from A.S. *weallan*, to boil.

**Potato.** This very common vegetable (*Solanum tuberosum*) was introduced into Ireland (and thence into England) from America by Sir Walter Raleigh about 1584, but the name (from Haitian *batata*) properly belonged to another tuberous plant (*Batata edulis*, of the natural order *Convolvulaceae*), now known as the *sweet potato*, which was supposed to have aphrodisiac qualities. It is to this latter that Falstaff refers when he says 'Let the sky rain potatoes' (*Merry Wives*, 5, 5), and there are many allusions to it in contemporary literature.

***Potato-bogle.*** So the Scots call a scarecrow, the head of these bird-bogies being a big potato or turnip.

***To think small potatoes of it.*** To think very little of it, to account it of very slight worth, or importance. 'Coke is very small potatoes at the gasworks – you can have it for the asking.'

**Poteen** (Irish *poitin*, little pot). Whisky that is produced privately in an illicit still, and so escapes duty.

**Potent.** *Cross potent.* An heraldic cross, each limb of which has an additional cross-piece like the top of a T or the head of an old-fashioned crutch; so called from Fr. *potence*, a crutch. It is also known as a *Jerusalem cross*.

**Potiphar's Wife** is unnamed both in the Bible and the Koran. Some Arabian commentators have called her Rahil, others Zuleika, and it is this latter name that the 15th century Persian poet gives her in his *Yúsuf and Zulaikha.*

In C. J. Wells's poetic drama *Joseph and His Brethren* (1824), of which she is the heroine, she is named Phraxanor.

**Potpourri** (Fr.). A mixture of dried sweet-smelling flower-petals and herbs preserved in a vase. Also a hotchpotch or olla podrida. In music, a medley of favourite tunes strung together.

*Pourri* means rotting [flowers], and potpourri, strictly speaking, is the vase containing the sweet mixture.

**Pots.** Stock Exchange slang for the 'North Staffordshire Railway stock'. Of course, the allusion is to 'the potteries'.

**Pott.** A size of printing and writing paper (15½ in. x 12½ in.); so called from its original watermark, a pot, which really represented the Holy Grail.

**Poult.** A chicken, or the young of the turkey, guinea-fowl, etc. The word is a contraction of *pullet*, from late Lat. *pulla*, a hen, whence *poultry*, *poulterer*, etc.

**Poulter's Measure.** In prosody, a metre consisting of alternate Alexandrines and fourteeners, i.e. twelve-syllable and fourteen-syllable lines. The name was given to it by Gascoigne (1576) because, it is said, poulterers – then called *poulters* – used sometimes to give twelve to the dozen and sometimes fourteen. It was a common measure in early Elizabethan times; the following specimen is from a poem by Surrey:

Good ladies, ye that have your pleasures in exile,
Step in your foot, come take a place, and mourn with me a while;
And such as by their lords do set but little price
Let them sit still, it skills them not what chance come on the dice.

**Pound.** The unit of weight (Lat. *pondus*, weight); also cash to the value of twenty shillings sterling, because in the Carlovingian period the Roman pound (twelve ounces) of pure silver was coined into 240 silver pennies. The symbols £ and *lb* are for *libra*, the Latin for a pound.

***In for a penny, in for a pound.*** *See* Penny.

***Pound of flesh.*** The whole bargain, the exact terms of the agreement, the bond *literatim et verbatim.* The allusion is to Shylock, in *The Merchant of Venice*, who bargained with Antonio for a 'pound of flesh', but was foiled in his suit by Portia, who said the bond was expressly a pound of flesh, and therefore (1) the Jew must cut the exact quantity, neither more nor less than a just pound; and (2) in so doing he must not shed a drop of blood.

**Poverty. *When poverty comes in at the door, love flies out at the window.*** An old proverb, given in Ray's *Collection* (1742), and appearing in many languages. Keats says much the same in *Lamia* (Pt ii):

Love in a hut, with water and a crust,
Is – Love forgive us – cinders, ashes, dust.

**Powder. *I'll powder your jacket for you.*** A corruption of Fr. *poudrer*, to dust.

***Not worth powder and shot.*** Not worth the trouble; the thing shot won't pay the cost of the ammunition.

**Poynings' Law** or **Statute of Drogheda.** An Act of Parliament passed in Ireland in 1495 (10 Henry VII, ch. 22) at the summons of Sir Edward Poynings (d.1521), then Lord Deputy, providing that no Parliament could be called together in Ireland except under the Great Seal of England, that its Acts must be submitted to the English Privy Council before becoming law, and declaring all general statutes hitherto made in England to be in force in Ireland also. It was repealed in 1782.

**Praemonstratensian.** *See* Premonstratensian.

**Praemunire.** A writ charging a sheriff to summon one accused of an indictable offence committed over seas, authorised by the *Statute of Praemunire* (1392); so called from the words *praemunire facias*, thou cause to warn (so and so) that appear in the opening sentence. The Statute was soon used specially to prevent the purchase in Rome of excommunications, etc., and to stop the assertion or maintenance of papal jurisdiction in England and the denial of the ecclesiastical supremacy of the Crown. Offenders could be punished by outlawry, forfeiture of goods, and attachment.

**Pragmatic Sanction.** *Sanctio* in Latin means a 'decree or ordinance with a penalty attached', or, in other words, a 'penal statute'. *Pragmaticus* means 'relating to state affairs', so that Pragmatic Sanction is a penal statute bearing on some important question of state. The term was first applied by the Romans to those statutes which related to their provinces. The French applied the phrase to certain statutes which limited the jurisdiction of the Pope; but generally it is applied to an ordinance fixing the succession in a certain line.

***Pragmatic Sanction of St Louis,*** 1268, forbade the court of Rome to levy taxes or collect subscriptions in France without the express sanction of the king. It also gave plaintiffs in the ecclesiastical courts the right to appeal to the civil courts. The 'Constitutions of Clarendon' were to England what the 'Pragmatic Sanction' was to France.

***Pragmatic Sanction of Charles VII (of France),*** 1438, defining and limiting the power of the Pope in France. By this ordinance the authority of a general council was declared superior to the dictum of the Pope; the clergy were forbidden to appeal to Rome on any point affecting the secular condition of the nation; and the Roman pontiff was forbidden to appropriate a vacant benefice, or to appoint either bishop or parish priest.

***Pragmatic Sanction of 1713.*** Whereby the succession of the Austrian Empire was made hereditary in the female line, in order to transmit the orown to Maria Theresa, the daughter of Charles VI.

This is emphatically *the* Pragmatic Sanction, unless some qualification is added restricting the term to some other instrument.

***Pragmatic Sanction of Naples,*** 1759, whereby Carlos II of Spain ceded the succession to his third son in perpetuity.

**Pragmatism** (Gr. *pragma*, deed). The philosophical doctrine that the only test of the truth of human cognitions or philosophical principles is their practical results, i.e. their workableness. It does not admit 'absolute' truth, as all truths change their trueness as their practical utility increases or decreases. The word was introduced in this connection about 1875 by the American logician C. S. Peirce (1839–1914) and was popularised by William James, whose *Pragmatism* was published in 1907.

**Prajapatis.** *See* Menu.

**Prayer-wheel.** A device used by the Tibetan Buddhists as an aid or substitute for prayer, the use of which is said to be founded on a misinterpretation of the Buddha's instructions to his followers, that they should 'turn the wheel of the law' – i.e. preach Buddhism incessantly – we should say as a horse in a mill. It consists of a pasteboard cylinder inscribed with – or containing – the mystic formula *Om mani padme hum* (*q.v.*) and other prayers, and each revolution represents one repetition of the prayers.

**Pre-Adamites.** The name given by Isaac de la Peyrère (1655) to a race of men whom he supposed to have existed long before the days of Adam. He held that only the Jews are descended from Adam, and that the Gentiles derive from these 'Pre-Adamites'.

**Prebend** (O.Fr. from late Lat. *praebenda*, a grant, pension). The stipend given out of the revenues of the college or cathedral to a canon; he who enjoys the prebend is the *prebendary*, though he is sometimes wrongly called the *prebend*.

**Precarious** (Lat. *precarius*, obtained by prayer) is applied to what depends on our prayers or requests. A *precarious tenure* is one that depends solely on the will of the owner to concede to our prayer; hence uncertain, not to be depended on.

**Preceptor.** Among the Knights Templars a *preceptory* was a subordinate house or community (the larger being *commanderies*), and the *Preceptor* or *Knight Preceptor* was the superior of a preceptory, the *Grand Preceptor* being the head of all the preceptories in a province. The three of highest rank were the Grand Preceptors of Jerusalem, Tripolis, and Antioch.

**Précieuses Ridicules, Les.** A comedy by Molière (1659). The chief characters are Aminte and Polixène, who assume the airs of the Hôtel de Rambouillet (*q.v.*), a coterie of savants of both sexes in the 17th century. The members of this society were termed *précieuses* – i.e. 'persons of distinguished merit' – and the *précieuses ridicules* means a ridiculous apeing of their ways and manners.

> The affected dialogue of the *Précieuses*, as they were styled, who formed the coterie of the Hotel de Rambouillet, afforded Molière matter for his admirable comedy, *Les Précieuses Ridicules*.
>
> Scott, *The Monastery* (*Introd.*)

**Precious Stones.** The ancients divided precious stones into male and female. The darker stones were called the males, and the light ones were called the females. Male sapphires approach indigo in colour, but the female ones are sky-blue. Theophartus mentions the distinction.

> The tent shook, for mighty Saul shuddered; and sparkles 'gan dart
> From the jewels that woke in his turban, at once with a start,
> All its lordly male-sapphires, and rubies courageous at heart.
>
> Browning, *Saul*, viii

Each month, according to the Poles, is under the influence of a precious stone:

| | | |
|---|---|---|
| January | Garnet | *Constancy.* |
| February | Amethyst | *Sincerity.* |
| March | Bloodstone | *Courage.* |
| April | Diamond | *Innocence.* |
| May | Emerald | *Success in love.* |
| June | Agate | *Health and long life.* |
| July | Cornelian | *Content.* |
| August | Sardonyx | *Conjugal felicity.* |
| September | Chrysolite | *Antidote to madness.* |
| October | Opal | *Hope.* |
| November | Topaz | *Fidelity.* |
| December | Turquoise | *Prosperity.* |

*In relation to the signs of the Zodiac –*

| | |
|---|---|
| Aries | Ruby. |
| Taurus | Topaz. |
| Gemini | Carbuncle. |
| Cancer | Emerald. |
| Leo | Sapphire. |
| Virgo | Diamond. |
| Libra | Jacinth. |
| Scorpio | Agate. |
| Sagittarius | Amethyst. |
| Capricornus | Beryl. |
| Aquarius | Onyx. |
| Pisces | Jasper. |

*In relation to the planets –*

| | | |
|---|---|---|
| Saturn | Turquoise | *Lead.* |
| Jupiter | Cornelian | *Tin.* |
| Mara | Emerald | *Iron.* |
| Sun | Diamond | *Gold.* |
| Venus | Amethyst | *Copper.* |
| Moon | Crystal | *Silver.* |
| Mercury | Loadstone | *Quicksilver.* |

It was an idea of the ancients that precious stones were dewdrops condensed and hardened by the sun.

**Precocious** means ripened by the sun before it has attained its full growth (Lat. *prae*, before, *coquere*, to cook); hence, premature; development of mind or body beyond one's age.

> Many precocious trees, and such as have their spring in winter, may be found. Brown

**Prelate** (Lat. *prae latus*, carried before) means simply a man preferred, a man promoted to an ecclesiastical office which gives him jurisdiction over other clergymen. Cardinals, bishops, abbots, and archdeacons were at one time so called, but the term is restricted in the Protestant Church to bishops.

**Premier.** The *Prime* Minister, or *first* minister of the Crown, formerly (17th cent.) called the *Premier Minister*, from Fr. *Ministre premier*, first minister.

***Première,*** the feminine of Fr. *premier*, is used in English of the first performance of a play.

***Ce n'est que le premier pas qui coûte;*** it is only the first step that costs anything. Pythagoras used to say, 'The beginning is half the whole.'

> Incipe dimidium facti est coepisse. Ausonius
> Dimidium facti, qui coepit, habet.
> Horace, Ep., I, ii, 41
> Well begun is half done.

**Premillenarians.** *See* Second (*Second Adventists*).

**Premonstratensian** or ***Norbertine Order***. An order of Augustinians founded by St Norbert in 1120 in the diocese of Laon, France. A spot was pointed out to him in a vision, and he termed the spot *Pré Montré* or *Pratum Monstratum* (the meadow pointed out). The order possessed thirty-five monasteries in England – where they were known as the White canons of the rule of St Augustine – at the time of the Dissolution.

**Prepense.** ***Malice prepense***, malice designed or deliberate; 'malice aforethought' (Lat. *prae*, before, Fr. *penser*, to think).

**Preposterous** (Lat. *prae*, before, *posterus*, coming after). Literally, 'putting the cart before the horse'; hence, contrary to reason or common sense.

> Your misplacing and preposterous placing is not all one in behaviour of language, for the misplacing is alwaies intollerable, but the preposterous is a pardonable fault, and many times gives a pretie grace unto the speech. We call it by a common saying to *set the* carte before the horse.
>
> Puttenham, *Arte of English Poesie*, Bk iii, ch. xxii (1589)

**Pre-Raphaelite Brotherhood, The.** A group of artists formed in London in 1848, consisting originally of Holman Hunt, Millais, and Rossetti, having for its objects a closer study of nature than was practised by those bound by the academical dogmas, and the cultivation of the methods and spirit of the early Italian (the 'pre-Raphael') painters. The group was championed by Ruskin, but was attacked by many artists and critics, and after its second exhibition (1850) Rossetti gave up exhibiting, Millais resigned, and Holman Hunt's methods underwent a change. The term *Pre-Raphaelite* was later applied to work characterised by exaggerated attention to detail, and high finish or 'finnickiness'.

> ... a society which unfortunately, or rather unwisely, has given itself the name of 'Pre-Raphaelite'; unfortunately, because the principles on which its members are working are neither pre- nor post-Raphaelite, but everlasting. They are endeavouring to paint

with the highest possible degree of completion, what they see in nature, without reference to conventional or established rules; but by no means to imitate the style of any past epoch.

Ruskin, *Modern Painters*, pt ii, sect. vi, ch. iii, § 16, n.

**Presbyterian Church.** A Church governed by elders or presbyters (Gr. *presbuteros*, elder), and ministers, all of equal ecclesiastical rank; especially the United Presbyterian Church of Scotland, which was formed in 1847 by the union of the United Secession and Relief Churches, and which in 1900 united with the Free Church of Scotland.

**Presence.** *See* Real Presence.

**Presents.** ***Know all men by these presents*** – i.e. by the writings or documents now present. (Lat. *per presentes*, by the [writings] present.)

**Press-gang.** The name given to the bands of men who, up to about the end of the Napoleonic wars, used to go about the country impressing men into the army or navy, especially the latter.

**Prester John** (i.e. John the Presbyter). A fabulous Christian king and priest, supposed in mediaeval times to have reigned over a wonderful country somewhere in the heart of Asia in the 12th century. He figures in Ariosto (*Orlando Furioso*, Bks xvii–xix), and has furnished materials for a host of mediaeval legends.

I will fetch you a toothpicker now from the farthest inch of Asia; bring you the length of Prester John's foot; fetch you a hair off the great Cham's beard …

Shakespeare, *Much Ado about Nothing*, 2, 1

According to 'Sir John Mandeville' he was a lineal descendant of Ogier the Dane (*q.v.*), who penetrated into the north of India with fifteen of his barons, among whom he divided the land. John was made sovereign of Teneduc, and was called *Prester* because he converted the natives. Another tradition says he had seventy kings for his vassals, and was seen by his subjects only three times in a year. So firm was the belief in his existence that the Pope, Alexander III (d.1181), sent him letters by a special messenger. The messenger never returned.

The centuries go by, but Prester John endures for ever
With his music in the mountains and his magic on the sky. Alfred Noyes, *Forty Singing Seamen*

**Prestige.** This word has a strangely metamorphosed meaning. The Lat. *praestigiae* means juggling tricks, hence *prestidigitateur* (Fr.), one who juggles with his fingers. We use the word for that favourable impression which results from good antecedents. The history of the change is this: Juggling tricks were once considered a sort of enchantment; to enchant is to charm, and to charm is to win the heart.

**Presto.** The name frequently applied to himself by Swift in his *Journal to Stella*. According to his own account (*Journal*, August 1st, 1711) it was given him by the Duchess of Shrewsbury, an Italian:

The Duchess of Shrewsbury asked him, was not that Dr –, Dr –, and she could not say my name in English, but said Dr Presto, which is Italian for Swift.

**Preston and his Mastiffs.** ***To oppose Preston and his mastiffs*** is to be foolhardy, to resist what is irresistible. Christopher Preston established the Bear Garden at Hockley-in-the-Hole in the time of Charles II, and was killed in 1709 by one of his own bears.

… I'd as good oppose
Myself to Preston and his mastiffs loose.

Oldham, *III Satyr of Juvenal*

**Pretender.** ***The Old Pretender.*** James Francis Edward Stuart (1688–1766), son of James II.

***The Young Pretender.*** Charles Edward Stuart (1720–88), son of the 'Old Pretender'.

God bless the king, I mean the faith's defender
God bless – no harm in blessing – the Pretender.
Who that Pretender is, and who is king –
God bless us all! – that's quite another thing.

John Byrom

**Pretext.** A pretence. From the Latin *praetexta*, a dress embroidered in the front worn by Roman magistrates, priests, and children of the aristocracy between the age of thirteen and seventeen. The *praetextatae* were dramas in which actors personated those who wore the praetexta; hence persons who pretend to be what they are not.

**Prevarication.** The Latin word *varico* is to straddle, and *praevaricor*, to go zigzag or crooked. The verb, says Pliny, was first applied to men who ploughed crooked ridges, and afterwards to men who gave crooked answers in the law courts, or deviated from the straight line of truth. *Cp.* Delirium.

**Prevent.** Precede, anticipate. (Lat. *prae-venio*, to go before). And as what goes before us may hinder us, so prevent means to hinder or keep back.

My eyes prevent the night watches.

Ps. 119:148

Prevent us, O Lord, in all our doings.

*Common Prayer Book*

**Previous Question.** *See* Question.

**Priam.** King of Troy when that city was sacked by the Greeks, husband of Hecuba, and father of fifty children, the eldest of whom was Hector. When the gates of Troy were thrown open by the Greeks concealed in the wooden horse, Pyrrhus, the son of Achilles, slew the aged Priam.

**Priamond.** In Spenser's *Faërie Queene* (IV, ii) the elder brother of Diamond and Triamond, sons of Agape, a fairy. He was very daring, and fought on foot with battleaxe and spear. He was slain by Cambalo.

**Priapus.** In *Greek mythology*, the god of reproductive power and fertility (hence of gardens), and protector of shepherds, fishermen, and farmers. He was the son of Dionysus and Aphrodite, and in later times was regarded as the chief deity of lasciviousness and obscenity.

We shift, and bedeck, and bedrape us,
  Thou art noble and nude and antique,
Libitina thy mother, Priapus
  Thy father, a Tuscan and Greek.

Swinburne, *Dolores*, vii

**Prick.** Shakespeare has, ''Tis now the prick of noon' (*Romeo and Juliet*, 2, 4), in allusion to the mark on the dial – made by pricking or indenting with a sharp instrument – that indicated 12 o'clock.

The annual choosing of sheriffs used to be done by the king, who pricked the names on a list at haphazard. Sheriffs are still 'pricked' by the king, but the names are chosen beforehand.

***Prick-eared.*** So the Puritans and Roundheads were called, because they had their hair cut short and covered their heads with a black skull-cap drawn down tight, leaving the ears exposed.

***Pricklouse.*** An old contemptuous name for a tailor.

***Prick-song.*** Written music for singing, as distinguished from music learnt by ear. So called because the notes were originally pricked in on the parchment. The term has long been obsolete.

***Prick the garter.*** *See* Garter.

***The prick of conscience.*** Remorse tormenting reflection on one's misdeeds. In the 14th century Richard of Hampole wrote a devotional treatise with this title.

***To kick against the pricks.*** To strive against odds, especially against authority. *Prick*, here, is an ox-goad, and the allusion is to Acts 9:5 – 'It is hard for thee to kick against the pricks.'

***To prick up one's ears.*** To pay particular attention; to do one's best to follow what is going on. In allusion to the twitching of a horse's ears when its attention is suddenly attracted.

**Pride,** meaning ostentation, finery, or that which persons are proud of. Spenser talks of 'lofty trees yclad in summer's pride' (verdure). Pope, of a 'sword whose ivory sheath (was) inwrought with envious pride' (ornamentation); and in this sense the word is used by Jacques in that celebrated passage –

Why, who cries out on pride [dress]
That can therein tax any private party?
What woman in the city do I name
When that I say 'the city woman bears
The cost of princes on unworthy shoulders'?
... What is he of baser function
That says his bravery [finery] is not of my cost?

Shakespeare, *As You Like It*, 2, 7

***Fly pride, says the peacock,*** proverbial for pride (Shakespeare: *Comedy of Errors*, 4, 3). The pot calling the kettle black.

The heraldic peacock is said to be *in his pride* when depicted with the tail displayed and the wings drooping.

***The pride of the morning.*** That early mist or shower which promises a fine day. The morning is too proud to come out in her glory all at once – or the proud beauty being thwarted weeps and pouts awhile. Keble uses the phrase in a different sense when he says:

Pride of the dewy Morning,
  The swain's experienced eye
From thee takes timely warning,
  Nor trusts the gorgeous sky.

Keble, *25th Sunday after Trinity*

**Pride's Purge.** The Long Parliament, not proving itself willing to condemn Charles I, was *purged* of its unruly members by Colonel Pride, who entered the House with two regiments of soldiers (December 6th, 1648), imprisoned sixty members, drove one hundred and sixty out into the streets, and left only sixty – the 'Rump' (*q.v.*).

**Pridwen, Pridwin.** The name in the Welsh legends of King Arthur's shield, bearing on it a picture of the Virgin.

The temper of his sword, the tried 'Excaliber'
The bigness and the length of 'Rone', his noble spear
With 'Pridwin', his great shield, and what the proof could bear.

Drayton

**Prig.** An old cant word (probably a variant of Prick) for to filch or steal, also for a thief. In the *Winter's Tale* the clown calls Autolycus a 'prig that haunts wakes, fairs, and bear-baitings'.

Shadwell uses the term for a pert coxcomb, and nowadays it denotes a conceited, formal, or didactic person – one who tries to teach others how to comport themselves, etc., without having any right to do so.

*Shamwell:* Cheatly will help you to the ready; and thou shalt shine, and be as gay as any spruce prig that ever walked the street.

*Belford Senior:* Well, adad, you are pleasant men, and have the neatest sayings with you; 'ready', and 'spruce prig', and abundance of the prettiest witty words.

Shadwell, *The Squire of Alsatia*, I, i (1688)

**Prima Donna** (Ital. first lady). The principal female singer in an opera.

***Prima facie*** (Lat.). At first sight. A *prima facie* case is a case or statement which, without minute examination into its merits, seems plausible and correct.

It would be easy to make out a strong *prima facie* case, but I should advise the more cautious policy of *audi alteram partem*.

**Primary Colours.** *See* Colours.

**Prime** (Lat. *primus*, first). In the Catholic Church the first canonical hour of the day, beginning at 6 a.m. Milton terms sunrise 'that sweet hour of prime' (*Paradise Lost*, v, 170); and the word is used in a general way of the first beginnings of anything, especially of the world itself. *Cp*. Tennyson's 'dragons of the prime' (*In Memoriam*, lvi).

***Prime Minister.*** The first minister of the Crown; the Premier (*q.v.*).

***Prime Number.*** The Golden Number; also called simply 'the Prime'.

**Primed.** Full and ready to deliver a speech. We say of a man whose head is full of his subject, 'He is primed to the muzzle.' Also a euphemism for 'drunk'. Of course, the allusion is to firearms.

**Primer.** Originally the name of the Prayer-book used by laymen in pre-Reformation England; as this was used as a child's first reading-book – generally with the addition of the A B C, etc. – the name was transferred to such books, and so to elementary books on any subject.

***Great primer.*** A large-sized type rather smaller than eighteen-point, running 51 ems (*q.v.*) to the foot or four lines and a quarter to the inch. As This,

***Long primer.*** A smaller-sized type, 9½ point, As This ; 89 ems (*q.v.*) to a foot, or 7½ lines to the inch.

**Primero.** A very popular card-game for about a hundred years after 1530, in which the cards had three times their usual value, four were dealt to each player, the principal groups being flush, prime, and point. *Flush* was the same as in poker, *prime* was one card of each suit, and *point* was reckoned as in piquet.

I left him at primero with the Duke of Suffolk.

Shakespeare, *Henry VIII*, 1, 2

**Primrose.** A curious corruption of the French *primerole*, which is the name of the flower in M.E. This is from the late Lat. *primula*, and the *rose* (as though from *prima rosa*, the first, or earliest, rose) is due to a popular blunder.

**Primum mobile** (Lat. the first moving thing), in the Ptolemaic system of astronomy, was the ninth (later the tenth) sphere, supposed to revolve round the earth from east to west in twenty-four hours, carrying with it all the other spheres (*q.v.*). Milton refers to it as 'that first mov'd' (*Paradise Lost*, iii, 483), and Sir Thomas Browne (*Religio Medici*) uses the phrase, 'Beyond the first movable', meaning outside the material creation. According to Ptolemy the *primum mobile* was the boundary of creation, above which came the empyrean (*q.v.*), or seat of God.

The term is figuratively applied to any machine which communicates motion to others; and also to persons and ideas suggestive of complicated systems. Thus, Socrates may be called the *primum mobile* of the Dialectic, Megaric, Cyrenaic, and Cynic systems of philosophy.

**Primus** (Lat. first). The archbishop, or rather 'presiding bishop', of the Episcopal Church of Scotland. He is elected by the other six bishops, and presides in Convocation, or meetings relative to church matters.

***Primus inter pares***. The first among equals.

**Prince** (Lat. *princeps*, chief, leader). A royal title which, in England, is now limited to the sons of the sovereign and their sons. *Princess* is similarly limited to the sovereign's daughters and his sons' (but not daughters') daughters.

***Crown Prince.*** The title of the heir-apparent to the throne in some countries, as Sweden, Denmark, and Japan (formerly also in Germany).

***Prince Consort.*** A prince who is the husband of a reigning Queen, as Albert of Saxe-Coburg-Gotha, husband of Queen Victoria, and the husband of Wilhelmina, Queen of the Netherlands.

***Prince Imperial.*** The title of the heir-apparent in the French Empire of 1852–70.

***Prince of Asturias.*** The title of the heir-apparent to the Spanish throne.

***Prince of Piedmont.*** The Italian heir-apparent.

***Prince of the Church.*** A cardinal.

***Prince of Wales.*** *See* Wales.

***Prince Rupert's drops.*** *See* Rupert.

**Principalities.** Members of one of the nine orders of angels in mediaeval angelology. *See* Angel.

> In the assembly next upstood
> Nisroch, of Principalities the prime.
> Milton, *Paradise Lost*, vi, 447

**Printers' Bible, The.** *See* Bible, Specially named.

**Printers' Marks.**

? is $^{q}_{o}$ – that is, the first and last letters of *quaestio* (question).

! is $\frac{I}{o}$. *Io* in Latin is the interjection of joy.

§ is a Greek p (π), the initial letter of *paragraph*, but printers call it a section mark.

* is used by the Greek grammarians to arrest attention to something striking (*asterisk* or star).

† is used by the Greek grammarians to indicate something objectionable (*obelisk* or dagger).

**Printing.** *See* Em.

***Father of English printing.*** William Caxton (1422–91), who, at Westminster, set up the first printing-press in England, and in 1477 issued the first English printed book – *The Dictes and Sayings of the Philosophers.*

**Priori.** *See* A priori.

**Priscian's Head.** ***To break Priscian's head*** (in Latin, *Diminuere Prisciani caput*). To violate the rules of grammar. Priscian was a great grammarian of the early 6th century, whose name is almost synonymous with grammar.

> And held no sin so deeply red
> As that of breaking Priscian's head
> Butler, *Hudibras*, pt ii, 2

> *Sir Nathaniel*: Laus Deo, bone intelligo,
> *Holofernes*: Bone! – *bons* for *bene*: Priscian a little scratch'd; 'twill serve.
> Shakespeare, *Love's Labour's Lost*, 5, 1

**Priscillianists.** Followers of Priscillian, an heretical Spaniard, executed at Treves in 385. Their beliefs were a mixture of Christianity, Gnosticism, and Manichaeanism.

**Prisoner of Chillon, The.** *See* Chillon.

**Prithu.** The favourite hero of the Indian Purânas. Vena having been slain for his wickedness, and leaving no offspring, the saints rubbed his right arm, and the friction brought forth Prithu. Being told that the earth had suspended for a time its fertility, Prithu went forth to punish it, and the Earth, under the form of a cow, fled at his approach; but being unable to escape, promised that in future 'seed-time and harvest should never fail'.

**Privolvans.** The antagonists of the Subvolvans, in S. Butler's satirical poem called *The Elephant in the Moon.*

> These silly ranting Privolvans
> Have every summer their campaigns,
> And muster like the warlike sons
> Of Rawhead and of Bloodybones. V, 85, etc.

**Privy Council.** The council chosen by the sovereign originally to administer public affairs, but now never summoned to assemble as a whole except to proclaim the successor to the Crown on the death of the Sovereign. It usually includes Princes of the Blood, the two Primates, the Bishop of London, the great officers of State and of the Royal Household, the Lord Chancellor and Judges of the Courts of Equity, the Chief Justices of the Courts of Common Law, the Judge Advocate, some of the Puisne Judges, the Speaker of the House of Commons, the Lord Mayor of London, Ambassadors, Governors of Colonies, the Commander-in-Chief, and many politicians. The business of the Privy Council is now performed by Committees (of which the Cabinet is technically one), such as the Judicial Committee of the Privy Council; and the great departments of State – the Board of Trade, Local Government Board, Board of Education, etc., are, in theory, merely committees of the Privy Council. Privy Councillors are entitled to the prefix 'the Right Honourable', and rank next after Knights of the Garter, who may be commoners.

**Privy Seal.** The seal which the sovereign uses in proof of assent to a document, kept in the charge of a high officer of State known as the Lord Privy Seal. In matters of minor importance it is sufficient to pass the Privy Seal, but instruments of greater moment must have the Great Seal also.

**Pro and con.** (Lat.). For and against. 'Con.' is a contraction of *contra*. *The pros and cons* of a matter is all that can be said for or against it.

**Pro tanto** (Lat.). As an instalment, good enough as far as it goes, but not final; for what it is worth.

> I heard Mr Parnell accept the Bill of 1886 as a measure that would close the differences between the two countries; but since then he

stated that he had accepted it as a *pro tanto* measure ... It was a parliamentary bet, and he hoped to make future amendments on it.

Joseph Chamberlain, April 10th, 1893

**Pro tempore** (Lat.). Temporarily; for the time being, till something is permanently settled. Contracted into *pro tem.*

**Probate** (Lat. proved). The probate of a will is the official proving of it, and a copy certified by an officer whose duty it is to attest it. The original is retained in the court registry, and executors cannot act until probate has been obtained.

**Probole** (Gr.). Properly, a bony process or projection on the skull, but applied by certain early heretics to Jesus Christ on the ground that He was divine only because he was divinely begotten, in fact, He was a shoot of the divine stem. This heresy was combated by Irenaeus, but was subsequently revived by Montanus and Tertullian.

**Procès-verbal** (Fr.). A detailed and official statement of some fact; especially a written and authenticated statement of facts in support of a criminal charge.

**Procne.** *See* Nightingale.

**Procris.** ***Unerring as the dart of Procris.*** When Procris fled from Cephalus out of shame, Diana gave her a clog (Laelaps) that never failed to secure its prey, and a dart which not only never missed aim, but which always returned of its own accord to the shooter. *See* Cephalus.

**Procrustes' Bed.** Procrustes, in Greek legend, was a robber of Attica, who placed all who fell into his hands upon an iron bed. If they were longer than the bed he cut off the redundant part, if shorter he stretched them till they fitted it; he was slain by Theseus. Hence, any attempt to reduce men to one standard, one way of thinking, or one way of acting, is called placing them on Procrustes' bed.

Tyrant more cruel than Procrustes old,
Who to his iron-bed by torture fits
Their nobler parts, the souls of suffering wits.

Mallet, *Verbal Criticism*

**Procyon.** The Lesser Dog-star, *alpha* in *Canis Minoris.* It is the eighth brightest star in the heavens. *See* Icarius.

**Prodigal.** Festus says the Romans called victims wholly consumed by fire *prodigae hostiae* (victims prodigalised), and adds that those who waste their substance are therefore called prodigals. This derivation is, of course, incorrect. Prodigal is Lat. *pro-ago* or *prod-igo*, to drive forth, and persons who had spent all their patrimony were 'driven forth' to be sold as slaves to their creditors.

***The Prodigal.*** Albert VI, Duke of Austria (1418–63).

**Prodigious!** *See* Domine Sampson.

**Prodigy** (Lat. *prodigium*, a portent, prophetic sign). *The prodigy of France.* Guillaume Budé (1467–1540); so called by Erasmus.

***The Prodigy of Learning.*** Samuel Hahnemann (1755–1843), the German, was so called by J. Paul Richter.

**Profane** means literally before or outside the temple (Lat. *pro fanum*); hence *profanus* was applied to those persons who came to the temple and remaining outside and unattached, were not initiated.

**Profile** means shown by a thread (Ital. *profilo*; Lat. *filum*, a thread). A profile is an outline, but especially a view, or drawing or some other representation, of the human face outlined by the median line.

**Profound.** ***The Profound Doctor.*** Thomas Bradwardine, Richard Middleton, and other 14th century scholastic philosophers were given the title.

***Most Profound Doctor.*** Aegidius de Columna (d.1316), a Sicilian schoolman.

**Prog.** The verb was used in the 16th century for to poke about for anything, especially to forage for food; hence the noun is slang for food, but its origin is unknown. Burke says, 'You are the lion, and I have been endeavouring to prog for you.'

So saying, with a smile she left the rogue
To weave more lines of death, and plan for prog.

Dr Wolcot, *Spider and Fly*

**Progress.** ***To report progress***, in parliamentary language, is to conclude for the night the business of a bill, and defer the consideration of all subsequent items thereof till the day nominated by the Prime Minister; hence, to put off anything till a more convenient time.

**Projection.** ***Powder of projection.*** A form of the 'Philosopher Stone' (*q.v.*), which was supposed to have the virtue of changing baser metals into gold. A little of this powder, being cast into the molten metal, was to *project* from it pure gold.

**Proletariat.** The lowest class of the community, labourers and wage-earners who are destitute of property. In ancient Rome the *proletarii* contributed nothing to the state but his *proles*, i.e. offspring; they could hold no office, were ineligible for the army, and were useful only as breeders of the race.

**Prometheus** (Gr. Forethought). One of the Titans of Greek myth, son of Iapetus and the ocean-nymph Clymene, and famous as a benefactor to man. It is said that Zeus employed him to make men out of mud and water, and that then, in pity for their state, he stole fire from heaven and gave it to them. For this he was chained by Zeus to Mount Caucasus, where an eagle preyed on his liver all day, the liver being renewed at night. He was eventually released by Hercules, who slew the eagle. It was to counterbalance the gift of fire to mankind that Zeus sent Pandora (*q.v.*) to earth with her box of evils.

**Promethean.** Capable of producing fire; pertaining to Prometheus (*q.v.*). The earliest 'safety' matches, made in 1805 by Chancel, a French chemist, who tipped cedar splints with paste of chlorate of potash and sugar, were known as 'Prometheans'. They were dipped into a little bottle containing asbestos wetted with sulphuric acid, and burst into flame on being withdrawn.

***Promethean fire.*** The vital principle; the fire with which Prometheus quickened into life his clay images.

> I know not where is that Promethean heat
> That can thy light relume.
>
> Shakespeare, *Othello*, 5, 2

***The promethean unguent.*** Made from a herb on which some of the blood of Prometheus had fallen. Medea gave Jason some of it, and thus rendered his body proof against fire and warlike instruments.

**Promised Land** or **Land of Promise.** Canaan; so called because God promised Abraham, Isaac, and Jacob that their offspring should possess it.

**Proof.** A printed sheet to be examined and approved before it is finally printed. The *first*, or *foul*, proof is that which contains all the workman's errors; when these are corrected the impression next taken is called a *clean* proof and is submitted to the author; the final impression, which is corrected by the reader *ad unguem*, is termed the *press* proof.

***Proof Bible, The.*** *See* Bible, specially named.

***Proof prints.*** The first impressions of an engraving. *India proofs* are those taken off on India paper. *Proofs before lettering* are those taken off before any inscription is engraved on the plate. After the proofs the connoisseur's order of value is – (1) prints which have the letters only in outline; (2) those in which the letters are shaded with a black line; (3) those in which some slight ornament is introduced into the letters; (4) those in which the letters are filled up quite black.

***Proof spirit.*** A term applied to spirituous liquors in which .495 of the *weight* and .5727 of the *volume* is absolute alcohol, and the specific gravity is 0.91984. When the mixture has more alcohol than water it is called *over proof*, and when less it is termed *under proof*.

**Prooshan Blue.** A term of great endearment, when, after the battle of Waterloo, the Prussians were immensely popular in England. Sam Weller, in Dickens's *Pickwick Papers*, addresses his father as 'Vell, my Prooshan Blue'.

**Propaganda.** The Congregation, or College, of the Propaganda (*Congregatio de propaganda fide*) is a committee of cardinals established at Rome by Gregory XV, in 1622, for propagating throughout the world the Roman Catholic religion. Hence the term is applied to any scheme, association, etc., for making proselytes or influencing public opinion in political, social, and international, as well as in religious matters.

**Property Plot**, in theatrical language, means a list of all the 'properties' or articles which will be required in the play produced. Such as the bell, when Macbeth says, 'The bell invites me'; the knocking apparatus for the porter ('Heard you that knocking?'); tables, chairs, banquets, tankards, etc., etc. Everything stored in a theatre for general use on the stage is a 'prop', these are the manager's props: an actor's 'props' are the clothing and other articles which he provides for his own use.

**Prophet, The.** The special title of Mahomet. According to the Koran there have been 200,000 prophets but only six of them brought new laws or dispensations, viz. Adam, Noah, Abraham, Moses, Jesus, and Mahomet.

***The Great*** or ***Major Prophets.*** Isaiah, Jeremiah, Ezekiel, and Daniel; so called because their writings are more extensive than the prophecies of the other twelve.

***The Minor*** or ***Lesser Prophets.*** Hosea, Joel, Amos, Obadiah, Micah, Jonah, Nahum, Habakkuk, Zephaniah, Haggai, Zechariah, and Malachi, whose writings are less extensive than those of the four Great Prophets.

**Propositions,** in logic, are of four kinds, called A, E, I, O. 'A' is a universal affirmative, and 'E' a universal negative; 'I' a particular affirmative, and 'O' a particular negative.

Asserit A, negat E, verum generaliter ambo
Asserit I, negat O, sed particulariter ambo.
A asserts and E denies some *universal* proposition;
I asserts and O denies, but with *particular* precision.

**Props,** in theatrical slang, means properties (*see* Property Plot, *above*).

**Prorogue** (Lat. *pro-rogo*, to prolong). *The Parliament was prorogued.* Dismissed for the holidays, or suspended for a time. If dismissed entirely it is said to be 'dissolved'.

**Pro's.** Professionals, especially actors, and those who take money for playing cricket, football, billiards, etc., or are paid sportsmen.

**Proscenium.** The front part of the stage, between the drop-curtain and orchestra. (Gr. *proskenion*; Lat. *proscenium*.)

**Proscription.** A sort of hue and cry; so called because among the Romans the names of the persons *proscribed* were written out, and the tablets bearing their names were fixed up in the public forum, sometimes with the offer of a reward for those who should aid in bringing them before the court. If the proscribed did not answer the summons, their goods were confiscated and their persons outlawed. In this case the name was engraved on brass or marble, the offence stated, and the tablet placed conspicuously in the marketplace.

**Prose** means straightforward speaking or writing (Lat. *oratio prosa* – i.e. *pro-versa*), in opposition to foot-bound speaking or writing, *oratio vincta* (fettered speech – i.e. poetry).

It was Monsieur Jourdain, in Molière's *Le Bourgeois Gentilhomme*, who suddenly discovered that he had been talking prose for twenty years without knowing it.

'Really,' exclaimed Lady Ambrose, brightening, '*Il y a plus de vingt ans que je dis de la prose, sons que j'en susse rien.*' Aud so it seems that I have known history without suspecting it, just as Mons. Jourdain talked prose.

Mallock, *The New Republic*, Bk iii, ch. 2

**Proselytes.** From Gr. *proselutos*, one who has come to a place; hence, a convert, especially (in its original application) to Judaism. Among the Jews proselytes were of two kinds – viz. 'The proselyte of righteousness' and the 'stranger that is within thy gate' (*see* Hellenes). The former submitted to circumcision and conformed to the laws of Moses; the latter went no farther than to refrain from offering sacrifice to heathen gods, and from working on the Sabbath.

**Proserpina** or **Proserpine.** The Roman counterpart of the Greek goddess Persephone, queen of the infernal regions and wife of Pluto. As the personification of seasonal changes she passed six months of the year on Olympus, and six in Hades; while at Olympus she was beneficent, but in Hades was stern and terrible. Legend says that as she was amusing herself in the meadows of Sicily Pluto seized her and carried her off in his chariot to the infernal regions for his bride. In her terror she dropped some of the lilies she had been gathering, and they turned to daffodils.

O Proserpina,
For the flowers now, that frighted thou let'st fall
From Dis' waggon! daffodils,
That come before the swallow dares, and take
The winds of March with beauty.

Shakespeare, *Winter's Tale*, 4, 4

In later legend Proserpine was the goddess of sleep, and in the myth of *Cupid and Psyche*, by Apuleius, after Psyche had long wandered about searching for her lost Cupid, she is sent to Proserpine for 'the casket of divine beauty', which she was not to open till she came into the light of day. Just as she was about to step on earth Psyche thought how much more Cupid would love her if she were divinely beautiful; so she opened the casket and found it contained Sleep, which instantly filled all her limbs with drowsiness, and she slept as it were the sleep of death.

Thou art more than the day or the morrow, the seasons that laugh or that weep,
For these give joy and sorrow; but thou, Proserpina, sleep.

Swinburne, *Hymn to Proserpine*

**Prosperity Robinson.** Viscount Goderich, Earl of Ripon (1782–1859), Chancellor of the Exchequer in 1823, so called by Cobbett. In 1825 he boasted in the House of the prosperity of the nation, and his boast was not yet cold when the great financial crisis occurred.

**Prospero.** The rightful Duke of Milan in *The Tempest*, deposed by his brother. Drifted on a desert island, he practised magic, and raised a tempest in which his brother was shipwrecked. Ultimately Prospero *broke his wand*, and his daughter married the son of the King of Naples. *The Tempest* was the last play that Shakespeare wrote, and it is generally thought that Prospero is an allegorical picture of the dramatist bidding farewell to his work.

**Protarchontes.** *See* Barbeliots.

**Protean.** Having the aptitude to change its form: ready to assume different shapes. *See* Proteus.

**Protectionist.** One who advocates the imposition of import duties, to 'protect' home produce or manufactures.

**Protector, The.** William Marshall, Earl of Pembroke (d.1219), appointed Regent on the accession of Henry III (1216).

Humphrey, Duke of Gloucester (1391–1447), Protector of England during the minority of his nephew, Henry VI (1422–47).

Richard, Duke of Gloucester, afterwards Richard III. He took Edward V into his custody on the death of Edward IV (1483), and was named Protector of the Kingdom.

Edward Seymour, Duke of Somerset, Protector and Lord Treasurer in the reign of his nephew, Edward VI (1548).

***The Lord Protector of the Commonwealth.*** Oliver Cromwell (1653–58).

**Protestant.** A member of a Christian Church upholding the principles of the Reformation, or (loosely) of any Church not in communion with Rome. Originally, one of the party which adhered to Luther who, in 1529, 'protested' against the decree of Charles V of Germany, and appealed from the Diet of Spires to a general council.

***The Protestant Pope.*** Clement XIV. He ordered the suppression of the Jesuits (1773), and was one of the most enlightened men who ever sat in the chair of St Peter.

**Proteus.** In Greek legend, Neptune's herdsman, an old man and a prophet, famous for his power of assuming different shapes at will. Hence the phrase, *As many shapes as Proteus* – i.e. full of shifts, aliases, disguises, etc. and the adjective *protean*, readily taking on different aspects, ever-changing.

Proteus lived in a vast cave, and his custom was to tell over his herds of sea-calves at noon, and then to sleep. There was no way of catching him but by stealing upon him at this time and binding him; otherwise he would elude anyone by a rapid change in shape.

> The changeful Proteus, whose prophetic mind,
> The secret cause of Bacchus' rage divined,
> Attending, left the flocks, his scaly charge,
> To graze the bitter weedy foam at large.
>
> Camoëns, *Lusiad*, vi

**Protevangelium.** The *first* (Gr. *protos*) gospel, applied to an apocryphal gospel which had been attributed to St James the Less. The name is also given to the curse upon the serpent in Gen. 3:15:

> And I will put enmity between thee and the woman, and between thy seed and her seed; it shall bruise thy head, and thou shalt bruise his heel,

which has been regarded as the earliest utterance of the gospel.

**Prothalamion.** The term coined by Spenser (from Gr. *thalamos*, a bridal chamber) as a title for his 'Spousall Verse' (1596) in honour of the double marriage of Lady Elizabeth and Lady Katherine Somerset, daughters of the Earl of Worcester, to Henry Gilford and William Peter, Esquires. Hence, a song sung in honour of the bride and bridegroom before the wedding.

**Proto-martyr.** The first martyr (Gr. *protos*, first). Stephen the deacon is so called (Acts 5:7), and St Alban is known as the proto-martyr of Britain.

**Protocol.** The first rough draft or original copy of a dispatch, which is to form the basis of a treaty; from Gr. *proto-koleon*, a sheet glued to the front of a manuscript, or to the case containing it, and bearing an abstract of the contents and purport.

**Protoplasm** (Gr. *proto*, first, *plasma*, thing moulded). The physical basis of life; the material of which the cells from which all living organisms are developed is composed. It is a viscid, semi-fluid, semi-transparent substance composed of a highly unstable combination of oxygen, hydrogen, carbon, and nitrogen, capable of spontaneous movement, contraction, etc. It can best be seen in the simpler jellyfishes. Sarcode (Gr. *sarcos*, flesh) is an earlier name of the substance.

**Protozoa.** The lowest division of the animal kingdom, comprising the simplest animal forms, which consist of a single cell or a group of cells not differentiated into two or more tissues. The amoeba is a representative of the former class, the volvox of the latter.

**Proud, The.** Otho IV, Emperor of Germany (1175, 1209–18).

Tarquin II of Rome. *Superbus.* (Reigned 535–10, d.496 BC.)

***The proud Duke.*** Charles Seymour, Duke of Somerset. He would never suffer his children to sit in his presence, and would never speak to his servants except by signs (d.1748).

***Proud as Lucifer; proud as a peacock.***

**Province.** From Lat. *provincia*, the name given by the Romans to a territory brought under subjugation, possibly because previously conquered (*pro*, before, *vincere*, to conquer). It is now applied, in the plural, to districts in a country, usually at a distance from the metropolis, whence the special meaning of *provincial* – narrow, unpolished, rude – and to the territory under the ecclesiastical control of an archbishop or metropolitan.

The *Provincial of an Order* is the superior of all the monastic houses of that Order in a given province.

**Prudhomme.** The French colloquialism for a man of experience and great prudence, of estimable character and practical good sense. Your *Monsieur Prudhomme* is never a man of genius and originality.

**Prunella.** A dark, smooth, woollen stuff of which clergymen's and barristers' gowns used to be made; probably so termed from its colour – plum, or prune. It is still in use for gaiters and the uppers of boots.

***All leather and prunella.*** *See* Leather.

**Prussian Blue.** So called because it was discovered by a Prussian, viz. Diesbach, a colourman of Berlin, in 1704. It was sometimes called *Berlin* blue. It is hydrated ferric ferro-cyanide, and *prussic acid* (hydrocyanic acid) is made from it.

**Pry, Paul.** An idle, meddlesome fellow, who has no occupation of his own, and is always interfering with other folk's business. The term comes from the hero of John Poole's comedy, *Paul Pry* (1825).

**Psalms.** Seventy-three psalms are inscribed with David's name, twelve with that of Asaph the singer; eleven go under the name of the Sons of Korah, a family of singers; one (i.e. Ps. 90) is attributed to Moses. The whole compilation is divided into five books: Bk1, from 1 to 41; Bk 2, from 42 to 72; Bk 3, from 73 to 89; Bk 4, from 90 to 106; Bk 5, from 107 to 150.

The *Book of Psalms* – or much of its contents – was for centuries attributed to David (hence called *the sweet psalmist* of Israel), but it is very doubtful whether he wrote any of them, and it is certain that the majority belong to a later period. The tradition comes from the author of Chronicles, and in 2 Sam. 22 is a psalm attributed to David that is identical with Ps. 18. Also, the last verse of Ps. 72 ('the prayers of David the son of Jesse are ended') seems to suggest that he was the author up to that point.

*See* Gradual Psalms; Penitential Psalms, *etc.*

**Psaphon's Birds.** Puffers, flatterers. Psaphon, in order to attract the attention of the world, reared a multitude of birds, and having taught them to pronounce his name, let them fly.

> To what far region have his songs not flown,
> Like Psaphon's birds, speaking their master's name.
> Moore, *Rhymes on the Road*, iii

**Pschent.** The royal double crown of ancient Egypt, combining that of Upper Egypt – a high conical white cap terminating in a knob – with the red one of Lower Egypt, the latter being the outermost.

**Pseudonym.** *See* Nom de Plume.

**Psycarpax** (Gr., granary thief). Son of Troxartas, King of the Mice. The Frog-king offered to carry the young prince over a lake, but scarcely had he got midway when a water-hydra appeared, and King Frog, to save himself, dived under water. The mouse, being thus left on the surface, was drowned, and this catastrophe brought about the battle of the Frogs and Mice.

> The soul of great Psycarpax lives in me,
> Of great Troxartas' line.
> Parnell, *Battle of the Frogs and Mice*, i

**Psyche** (Gr., breath; hence, life, or soul itself). In 'the latest-born of the myths', *Cupid and Psyche*, an episode in the *Golden Ass* of Apuleius (2nd century AD), a beautiful maiden beloved by Cupid, who visited her every night, but left her at sunrise. Cupid bade her never seek to know who he was, but one night curiosity overcame her prudence; she lit the lamp to look at him, a drop of hot oil fell on his shoulder, and he awoke and fled. The abandoned Psyche then wandered far and wide in search of her lover; she became the slave of Venus, who imposed on her heartless tasks and treated her most cruelly; but ultimately she was united to Cupid, and became immortal.

**Ptolemaic System.** The system promulgated by Ptolemy, the celebrated astronomer of Alexandria in the 2nd century AD, to account for the apparent motion of the heavenly bodies. He taught that the earth is fixed in the centre of the universe, and the heavens revolve round it from east to west, carrying with them the sun, planets, and fixed stars, in their respective spheres (*q.v.*), which he imagined as solid coverings (like so many skins of an onion) each revolving at different velocities. This theory, with slight modifications, held the field till the time of Copernicus (16th cent.).

**Public** (Lat. *publicus*, earlier *poplicus* from *poplus*, later *populus*, the people). The people generally and collectively; the members generally of a state, nation, or community. Also, a colloquial contraction of 'public-house', frequently abbreviated still further to 'pub'.

We can laugh out loud when merry,
We can romp at kiss in the ring,
We can take our beer at a public,
We can loll on the grass and sing.
James ('B.V.') Thomson, *Sunday at Hampstead*, i, 9

The simple life I can't afford,
Besides, I do not like the grub –
I want a mash and sausage, 'scored' –
Will someone take me to a pub?
G. K. Chesterton, *Ballade of an Anti-Puritan*

**Publicans.** The name given in the New Testament to the provincial representatives (*publicani*, servants of the state) of the *Magister* or master tax-collector who resided at Rome. The taxes were farmed by a contractor called the *Manceps*, who divided the whole taxable area into convenient districts, each of which was under a *Magister*.

**Pucelle, La.** Fr. 'The Maid', i.e. of Orleans, Jeanne d'Arc (1410–31). Voltaire wrote a mock-heroic, satirical and in parts scurrilous, poem with this title.

**Puck.** A mischievous, tricksy sprite of popular folk-lore, also called Robin Goodfellow (*q.v.*), originally an evil demon, but transformed and popularised in his present form by Shakespeare (*Midsummer Night's Dream*), who shows him as a merry wanderer of the night, 'rough, knurly-limbed, faun-faced, and shock-pated, a very Shetlander among the gossamer-winged' fairies around him. The name seems to be connected with *Pooka*, or *Phooka* (*q.v.*).

**Pucka,** an Indian word in very common use, meaning substantial, real, permanent, hence *bona fide*. 'He is a commander, but not a pucka one' (i.e. only acting as such, *pro tempore*). 'The king reigns, but his ministers are the pucka rulers.' It is applied, especially by soldiers, to anything or anybody of outstanding excellence, as 'a pucka feed', 'a pucka jockey', 'a pucka billet', etc.

**Pudding-time.** A time when pudding is obtainable, hence a lucky or fortunate time; said of one who arrives just 'in the nick of time'.

But Mars ...
In pudding-time came to his aid.
Butler, *Hudibras*, i, 2

**Pudens.** A soldier in the Roman army, mentioned in 2 Tim. 4:21, in connection with Linus and Claudia. According to tradition, Claudia, the wife of Pudens, was a British lady; Linus, otherwise called Cyllen, was her brother; and Lucius 'the British king', the grandson of Linus. Tradition further adds that Lucius wrote to Eleutherus, Bishop of Rome, to send missionaries to Britain to convert the people.

**Puff.** An onomatopoeic word, suggestive of the sound made by puffing wind from the mouth. As applied to inflated or exaggerated praise, extravagantly worded advertisements, reviews, etc., it dates at least from the early 17th century, and the implication is that such commendation is really as worthless and transitory as a puff of wind.

In Sheridan's *The Critic* (1779) Puff, who, he himself says, is 'a practitioner in panegyric, or, to speak more plainly, a professor of the art of puffing' gives a catalogue of puffs:

> Yes, sir – puffing is of various sorts, the principal are, the puff direct, the puff preliminary, the puff collateral, the puff collusive and the puff oblique, or puff by implication. These all assume, as circumstances require, the various forms of letter to the editor, occasional anecdote, impartial critique, observation from correspondent, or advertisement from the party. *The Critie*, I, ii

***Puffed up.*** Conceited; elated with conceit or praise; filled with wind. A *puff* is a tartlet with a very light or puffy crust.

> That no one of you be puffed up one against another. 1 Cor. 4: 6

***Puff-ball.*** A fungus of the genus *Lycoperdon*, so called because it is ball-shaped and when it is ripe it bursts and the spores come out in a 'puff' of fine powder.

**Puisne Judges** means the younger-born judges. They are the judges of the High Court of Justice other than the Lord Chancellor, the Lord Chief Justice, the Master of the Rolls, and the Lord Chief Justice of the Common Pleas. The word is the same, etymologically, as *puny*. (Fr. *puisné*, subsequently born; Lat. *post natus*.)

**Pukka.** *See* Pucka.

**Pull.** ***A long pull, a strong pull, and a pull all together*** – i.e. a steady, energetic, and systematic co-operation. The reference may be either to a boat, where all the oarsmen pull together with a long and strong pull at the oars; or it may be to the act of hauling with a rope, when a simultaneous strong pull is indispensable.

***Pull devil pull baker.*** Let each one do the best for himself in his own line of business, but let not one man interfere in that of another.

> It's all fair pulling, 'pull devil, pull baker', someone has to get the worst of it. Now it's us [bushrangers], now it's them [the police] that gets ... rubbed out.
>
> Boldrewood, *Robbery under Arms*, ch. xxxvii

***The long pull.*** The extra quantity of beer supplied by a publican to his customer over and above the pint or half-pint ordered and paid for. Under the restrictions imposed during the Great War this was abolished by order, as it is a form of 'treating'.

***To have the pull of*** or ***over one.*** To have the advantage over him; to be able to dictate terms or make him do what you wish.

***To pull bacon.*** To spread the fingers out after having placed one's thumb on the nose.

***To pull one's weight.*** To do the very best one can, exert oneself to the utmost of one's ability. The phrase comes from rowing; an oarsman who does not put all his weight into the stroke tends to become a passenger.

***To pull oneself together.*** To 'buck up', rouse oneself to renewed activity.

***To pull someone's leg.*** To delude him in a humorous way, lead him astray by chaff, exaggeration, etc.

***To pull through.*** To get oneself well out of a difficulty – such as over a serious illness, through a stiff examination, etc.

***To pull through.*** To work in harmony with one end in view; to co-operate heartily.

**Pullman.** Properly a well fitted railway saloon or sleeping-car built at the Pullman Carriage Works, Illinois; so called from the designer, George M. Pullman (1831–97) of Chicago. The word is now applied to other luxurious railway saloons, and to motor-cars.

**Pummel.** *See* Pommel.

**Pump.** ***To pump one*** is to extract information out of him by artful questions; to draw from him all he knows as one draws water from a well by gradual pumping. Ben Jonson, in *A Tale of a Tub* (IV, iii) has 'I'll stand aside whilst thou pump'st out of him his business.'

**Pumpernickel.** The coarse rye-bread ('brown George') eaten by German peasants, especially in Westphalia. Thackeray applied the term as a satirical nickname to petty German princelings ('His Transparency, the Duke of Pumpernickel') who made a great show with the court officials and etiquette, but whose revenue was almost *nil*.

**Pun.** ***He who would make a pun would pick a pocket.*** Dr Johnson is generally credited with this silly dictum, but the correct version is – 'Any man who would make such an execrable pun would not scruple to pick my pocket', the remark addressed by the critic, John Dennis (1657–1734) to Purcell. *See* the *Public Advertiser*, Jan. 12th, 1779, and the *Gentleman's Magazine*, vol. ii, p. 324; also the note to Pope's *Dunciad*, bk i, l. 63.

> The 'execrable pun' was this: Purcell rang the bell for the *drawer* or waiter, but no one answered it. Purcell, tapping the table, asked Dennis 'why the table was like the tavern?' Ans. 'Because there is no drawer in it.'

**Puna Winds, The.** The prevailing winds for four months in the *Puna* (table-lands of Peru). They are most dry and parching winds and when they blow it is necessary to protect the face with a mask, from the heat by day and the intense cold of the night.

**Punch.** The name of this beverage, which was introduced into England from India in the early 17th century, has generally been held to derive from Hindustani *panch*, five, because it has five principal ingredients (viz., spirit, water, spice, sugar, and some acid fruit essence). There are, however, linguistic, and phonetic objections to accepting this derivation – as well as the fact that early recipes give anything from three to six principal ingredients, and there was no reason why it should have been named from five – and it is just as likely that it is merely a contraction by sailors engaged in the East Indian trade of *puncheon*, the large cask from which their grog was served.

**Punch, Mr.** The hero – and the story – of the popular puppet show, *Punch and Judy*, are of Italian origin, the name being a contraction of *Punchinello*. In the 18th century the suggestion was made that the name was from a popular and ugly low comedian named Puccio d'Aniello, but nothing definite is known of him, and the conjecture is probably an example of 'popular etymology'. Another suggestion is that the name is derived from that of Pontius Pilate in the old mystery plays.

The show first appeared in England a little before the accession of Queen Anne, and the story is attributed to Silvio Fiorillo, an Italian comedian of the 17th century. Punch, in a fit of jealousy, strangles his infant child, whereupon his wife, Judy, fetches a bludgeon with which she belabours him till he seizes another bludgeon, beats her to death, and flings the two bodies into the street. A passing police officer enters the house; Punch flees, but is arrested by an officer of the Inquisition and shut up in prison, whence he escapes by means of a golden key. The rest is an allegory, showing how the light-hearted Punch triumphs over (1) Ennui, in the shape of a dog, (2) Disease, in the disguise of a doctor, (3) Death, who is beaten to death, and (4) the Devil himself, who is outwitted.

The satirical humorous weekly paper, *Punch, or the London Charivari*, is, of course, named from 'Mr Punch'. It first appeared on July 17th, 1841.

***Pleased as Punch.*** Greatly delighted. Our old friend is always singing with self-satisfaction in his naughty ways, and his evident 'pleasure' is contagious to the beholders.

***Suffolk punch.*** A short, thick-set cart-horse. The term was formerly applied to any short fat man, and is probably the same word as above, though it may be connected with *puncheon*, the large cask.

> I did hear them call their fat child Punch, which pleased me mightily, that word having become a word of common use for everything that is thick and short.
>
> Pepys' Diary, 30 Apr., 1669

**Punctual.** No bigger than a point, exact to a point or moment. (Lat. *ad punctum*.) Hence the angel, describing this earth to Adam, calls it 'This opacous earth, this punctual spot' – i.e. a spot no bigger than a point (Milton: *Paradise Lost*, viii, 23).

**Punctuality. *Punctuality is the politeness of kings*** (*L'exactitude est la politesse des rois*). A favourite maxim of Louis XVIII, but attributed by Samuel Smiles to Louis XIV.

> 'Punctuality', said Louis XIV, 'is the politeness of kings.' It is also the duty of gentlemen, and the necessity of men of business.
>
> *Self-Help*, ch. ix

**Pundit.** An East Indian scholar, skilled in Sanskrit, and learned in law, divinity, and science. We use the word for a *porcus literarum*, one more stocked with book lore than deep erudition.

**Punic Apple.** A pomegranate; so called because it is the pomum or 'apple' belonging to the genus *Punica*.

**Punica fides.** Treachery, violation, of faith, the faith of the Carthaginians, Lat. *Punicus*, earlier *Poenicus*, meaning a Phoenician, hence applied to the Carthaginians, who were of Phoenician descent. The Carthaginians were accused by the Romans of breaking faith with them, a most extraordinary instance of the 'pot calling the kettle black'; for whatever infidelity they were guilty of, it could scarcely equal that of their accusers. *Cp.* Attic Faith.

> Our Punic faith
> Is infamous, and branded to a proverb.
>
> Addison, *Cato*, ii

**Pup.** Slang for a *pupil*, especially an undergraduate studying with a tutor.

As applied to the young of dogs, the word is an abbreviation of *puppy*, which represents Fr. *poupée*, a dressed doll, a plaything.

An empty-head, impertinent young fellow is frequently called *a young puppy*, hence Douglas Jerrold's epigram – more witty than true –

> Dogmatism is only puppyism come to maturity.

**Purbeck** (Dorsetshire). Noted for a marble used in ecclesiastical ornaments. Chichester cathedral has a row of columns of this limestone. The columns of the Temple church, London; the tomb of Queen Eleanor, in Westminster Abbey; and the throne of the archbishop in Canterbury cathedral, are other specimens.

**Pure, Simon.** *See* Simon Pure.

**Purgatory.** The doctrine of Purgatory, according to which the souls of the departed suffer for a time till they are *purged* of their sin, is of ancient standing, and was held in a modified form by the Jews, who believed that the soul of the deceased was allowed for twelve months after death to visit its body and the places or persons it especially loved. This intermediate state they called by various names, as 'the bosom of Abraham', 'the garden of Eden', 'upper Gehenna'. The Sabbath was always a free day, and prayer was supposed to benefit those in this intermediate state.

The outline of this doctrine was annexed by the early Fathers, and was considerably strengthened by certain passages in the New Testament, particularly Rev. 6:9–11, and 1 Pet. 3:18 and 19. The first decree on the subject was promulgated by the Council of Florence, in 1439; and in 1562 it was finally condemned by the Church of England, the XXIInd of the

'Articles of Religion' stating that –

> The Romish Doctrine concerning Purgatory ... is a fond thing vainly invented, and grounded upon no warranty of Scripture, but rather repugnant to the Word of God.

**Puritans.** Seceders from the Reformed Church in the time of Queen Elizabeth; so called because, wishing for a more radical purification of religion, they rejected all human traditions and interference in religious matters, acknowledging the sole authority of the 'pure Word of God', without 'note or comment'. Their motto was: 'The Bible, the whole Bible, and nothing but the Bible'. The English Puritans were sometimes by the Reformers called *Precisionists*, from their preciseness in matters called 'indifferent'. Andrew Fuller named them *Non-conformists*, because they refused to subscribe to the Act of Uniformity.

> The Puritan hated bearbaiting, not because it gave pain to the bear, but because it gave pleasure to the spectators. Indeed he generally contrived to enjoy the double pleasure of tormenting both spectators and bear.
>
> Macaulay, *History of England*, Bk i, ch. ii

**Purkinje's Figures.** In optics, figures produced by shadows of the retinal blood-vessels on a wall when a person entering a dark room with a candle moves it up and down obliquely, approximately on a level with the eyes. So named from the Bohemian physiologist, J. E. Purkinje (1787–1869).

**Purler.** A cropper, or heavy fall from one's horse in a steeplechase or in the hunting-field; also, a knockdown blow.

> Seraph's white horse cleared it, but falling with a mighty crash, gave him a purler on the opposite side. Ouida, *Under Two Flags*, ch. vi

**Purlieu.** The outlying parts of a place, the environs; originally the borders or outskirts of a forest, especially a part which was formerly part of the forest. So called from O.Fr. *pourallé*, a place free from the forest laws. Henry II, Richard I, and John made certain lands forest lands; Henry III allowed certain portions all round to be freed from the restrictions imposed on the royal forests, and the 'perambulation' by which this was effected was called *pourallée*, a going through. The *lieu* (as though for 'place') was an erroneous addition due to English pronunciation and spelling of the French word.

> In the purlieus of this forest stands
> A sheepcote fenced about with olive trees.
>
> Shakespeare, *As You Like It*, 4, 3

**Purple.** The colour of ecclesiastical mourning and penitence (hence worn during Lent); also that of the dress of emperors, kings, and cardinals; from the Lat. *purpura* which was formed on Gr. *porphyra*, meaning both the shell-fish which yielded Tyrian purple (a species of *Murex*), and the purplish marble, *porphyry*. It is one of the tinctures (*purpure*) used in heraldry, and in engravings is shown by lines running diagonally from sinister to dexter (i.e. from right to left as one looks at it). *See* Colours.

***Born in the purple.*** Said of the child of a king or emperor (*see* Porphyrogenitus), hence of anyone of exalted birth or 'born with a silver spoon in his mouth'. The expression comes from a Byzantine custom which ordained that the empress should be brought to bed in a chamber the walls of which were lined with porphyry, or purple.

***Purple patches.*** Highly coloured or brilliant passages in a literary work which is (generally speaking) otherwise undistinguished. The allusion is to Horace's *De Arte Poetica*, 1. 15:

> Inceptis gravibus plerumque et magna professis,
> Purpureus, late qui splendeat, unus et alter
> Adsuitur pannus.
>
> (Often to weighty enterprises and such as profess great objects, one or two purple patches are sewed on to make a fine display in the distance.)

**Pursuivants.** The lowest grade of the officers of arms composing the College of Arms, or Heralds' College, the others, under the Earl Marshal, being (1) the Kings of Arms, and (2) the Heralds.

England has four Pursuivants, viz. *Rouge Croix*, *Bluemantle*, *Rouge Dragon*, and *Portcullis*; Scotland has three, viz. *Carrick*, *March*, and *Unicorn*; and Ireland one, *Athlone*.

**Pursy.** Broken-winded, or in a bloated state in which the wind is short and difficult (Fr. *poussif*).

***A fat and pursy man.*** Shakespeare has 'pursy Insolence', the insolence of Jesurun, 'who waxed fat and kicked'. In *Hamlet* we have 'the fatness of these pursy times' – i.e. wanton or self-indulgent times.

**Purûravas and Urvasi.** An Indian myth similar to those of Cupid and Psyche and Apollo and Daphne. King Purûravas fell in love with Urvasi, a heavenly nymph, who consented to become his wife on certain conditions. These conditions being violated, Urvasi disappeared, and Purûravas, inconsolable, wandered everywhere to find her. Ultimately he succeeded, and they were indissolubly united.

**Puseyite.** A High Church follower of Dr E. B. Pusey (1800–82), Professor of Hebrew at Oxford, one of the leaders of the 'Oxford Movement', and a chief contributor to the *Tracts for the Times*. *See* Tractarians.

**Push.** Military slang for a strong concerted forward movement, a general attack; hence, by extension, for a body of troops engaged on an offensive; a gang, crowd, 'crush'.

***To give one the push.*** To give him his congé, give him the sack.

***To push off.*** To commence the game, the operations, etc. A phrase from boating – one starts by pushing the boat off from the bank. *Push off!* said imperatively, is equivalent to 'Get you gone!' 'Go to the devil!'

**Puss.** A conventional call-name for a cat; applied also (in the 17th cent. and since) to hares. Its origin is unknown, though it is present in many Teutonic languages. The derivation from Lat. *lepus*, a hare, Frenchified into *le pus*, is of course, only humorous.

***Puss in Boots.*** This nursery tale, *Le Chat Botté*, is from Straparola's *Nights* (1530), No. xi, where Constantine's cat procures his master a fine castle and the king's heiress. It was translated from the Italian into French in 1585, and appeared in Perrault's *Les contes de ma Mère l'Oie* (1697), through which medium it reached England. In the story the clever cat secures a fortune and a royal partner for his master, who passes off as the Marquis of Carabas, but is in reality a young miller without a penny in the world.

**Put.** A clown, a silly shallow-pate, a butt, one easily 'put upon'.

> Queer country puts extol Queen Bess's reign.
>
> Bramson

***Put and take.*** A game of chance played with a modification of the old 'tee-to-tum', one side of which is marked *Put* – signifying that the player pays – and another with *Take*. It was immensely popular for a few months about Christmastime, 1921.

**Pygmalion.** A sculptor and king of Cyprus in Greek legend, who, though he hated women, fell in love with his own ivory statue of Aphrodite. At his earnest prayer the goddess gave life to the statue and he married it.

> Few, like Pygmalion, doat on lifeless charms,
> Or care to clasp a statue in their arms.
>
> S. Jenyns, *Art of Dancing*, canto i

The story is told in Ovid's *Metamorphoses*, x, and appeared in English dress in John Marston's *Metamorphosis of Pygmalion's Image* (1598). Morris retold it in *The Earthly Paradise* (*August*), and W. S. Gilbert adapted it in his comedy of *Pygmalion and Galatea* (1871), in which the sculptor is a married man. His wife (Cynisca) was jealous of the animated statue (Galatea), which, after considerable trouble, voluntarily returned to its original state.

**Pygmies.** The name used by Homer and other classical writers for a supposed race of dwarfs said to dwell somewhere in Ethiopia; from Gr. *pugme*, the length of the arm from elbow to knuckles. Fable has it that every spring the cranes made war on them and devoured them; they used an axe to cut down corn-stalks; when Hercules went to the country they climbed up his goblet by ladders to drink from it, and while he was asleep two whole armies of them fell upon his right hand, and two upon his left and were rolled up by Hercules in his lion's skin. It is easy to see how Swift has availed himself of this Grecian legend in his *Gulliver's Travels*.

The term is now applied to certain dwarfish races of Central Africa (whose existence was first demonstrated late in the 19th century), Malaysia, etc.; also to small members of a class, as the *pygmy hippopotamus*.

**Pylades and Orestes.** Two friends in Homeric legend, whose names have become proverbial for friendship, like those of Damon and Pythias, David and Jonathan. Orestes was the son, and Pylades the nephew, of Agamemnon, after whose murder Orestes was put in the care of Pylades' father (Strophius), and the two became fast friends. Pylades assisted Orestes in obtaining vengeance on Aegisthus and Clytemnestra, and afterwards married Electra his friend's sister.

**Pylon.** Properly a monumental gateway (Gr. *pulon*), especially of an Egyptian temple; now usually applied to the obelisks that mark out the course in an aerodrome.

**Pyramid.** There are some 70 pyramids still remaining in Egypt, but those specially called *The* Pyramids are the three larger in the group of eight known as the *Pyramids of Gizeh*. Of these the largest, the *Great Pyramid*, is the tomb of Cheops, a king of the 4th Dynasty, about 4000 BC. It was 480 ft in height (now about 30 ft less), and the length of each base is 755 ft. The Second Pyramid, the tomb of Chephren (also 4th Dynasty) is slightly smaller (472 ft by 706 ft);

and the Third, the tomb of Menkaura, or Mycerinus (4th Dynasty, about 3630 BC), is much smaller (215 ft by 346 ft). Each contains entrances, with dipping passages leading to various sepulchral chambers.

**Pyramus.** A Babylonian youth in classic story (*see* Ovid's *Metamorphoses*, iv), the lover of Thisbe. Thisbe was to meet him at the white mulberry tree near the tomb of Ninus, but she, scared by a lion, fled and left her veil which the lion besmeared with blood. Pyramus, thinking his lady-love had been devoured, slew himself, and Thisbe coming up soon afterwards, stabbed herself also. The blood of the lovers stained the white fruit of the mulberry tree into its present colour. The 'tedious brief scene' and 'very tragical mirth' presented by the rustics in *A Midsummer Night's Dream* is a travesty of this legend.

**Pyrochles.** The personification in Spenser's *Faërie Queene* (II, iv) of fiery anger (Gr. *pur*, fire).

Behind his back he bore a brazen shield,
On which was drawen fair, in colours fit,
A flaming fire in midst of bloody field,
And round about the wreath this word was writ,
*Burnt I do burne.* *Faërie Queene*, II, iv, 38

In Sidney's *Arcadia* Pyrocles and Musidorus are heroes whose exploits before they reach Arcadia are related.

**Pyrodes,** son of Clias, was so called, according to Pliny (vii, 56), because he was the first to strike fire from flint. (Gr. *pur*, fire.)

**Pyrrha.** The wife of Deucalion (*q.v.*) in Greek legend. They were the sole survivors of the deluge sent by Zeus to destroy the whole human race, and repopulated the world by casting stones behind them.

Men themselves, the which at first were framed
Of earthly mould, and form'd of flesh and bone,
Are now transformed into hardest stone;
Such as behind their backs (so backward bred)
Were thrown by Pyrrha and Deucalion.
Spenser, *Faërie Queene*, V, *Introd.*, 2

**Pyrrhic Dance.** The famous war-dance of the Greeks; so called from its inventor, Pyrrichos, a Dorian. It was a quick dance, performed in full armour to the flute, and its name is still used for a metrical foot of two short, 'dancing' syllables. The *Romaika*, still danced in Greece, is a relic of the ancient Pyrrhic dance.

Ye have the Pyrrhic dance as yet:
Where is the Pyrrhic phalanx gone?
Byron, *The Isles of Greece*

**Pyrrhic Victory.** A ruinous victory. Pyrrhus, king of Epirus, after his victory over the Romans at Asculum (279 BC), when he lost the flower of his army, said to those sent to congratulate him, 'One more such victory and Pyrrhus is undone.'

**Pyrrhonism.** Scepticism, or philosophic doubt; so named from Pyrrho (4th cent. BC), the founder of the first Greek school of sceptical philosophy. Pyrrho maintained that nothing was capable of proof and admitted the reality of nothing but sensations.

Blessed be the day I 'scaped the wrangling crew
From Pyrrho's maze and Epicurus' sty.
Beattie, *Minstrel*

**Pythagoras.** The Greek philosopher and mathematician of the 6th century BC (born at Samos), to whom was attributed the enunciation of the doctrines of the transmigration of souls and of the harmony of the spheres, and also the proof of the 47th proposition in the 1st book of Euclid, which is hence called the *Pythagorean proposition*. He taught that the sun is a movable sphere, and that it, and the earth, and all the planets revolve round some central point which they called 'the fire'. He maintained that the soul has three vehicles: (1) the *ethereal*, which is luminous and celestial, in which the soul resides in a state of bliss in the stars; (2) the *luminous*, which suffers the punishment of sin after death; and (3) the *terrestrial*, which is the vehicle it occupies on this earth.

Pythagoras was noted for his manly beauty and long hair; and many legends are related of him, such as that he distinctly recollected previous existences of his own, having been (1) Aethalides, son of Mercury, (2) Euphorbus the Phrygian, son of Panthous, in which form he ran Patroclus through with a lance, leaving Hector to dispatch the hateful friend of Achilles, (3) Hermotimus, the prophet of Clazomenae: and (4) a fisherman. To prove his Phrygian existence he was taken to the temple of Hera, in Argos, and asked to point out the shield of the son of Panthous, which he did without hesitation.

Rosalind alludes to this theory (*As You Like It*, 3, 2) when she says:

I was never so be-rhymed since Pythagoras' time that I was an Irish rat, which I can hardly remember.

It is also elaborated in the scene between Feste and Malvolio in *Twelfth Night*, 4, 2:

*Clown*: What is the opinion of Pythagoras concerning wild fowl?
*Mal.*: That the soul of our grandam might haply inhabit a bird.

*Clown*: What thinkest thou of his opinion?
*Mal.*: I think nobly of the soul, and no way approve his opinion.

Other legends assert that one of his thighs was of gold, and that he showed it to Abaris, the Hyperborean priest, and exhibited it in the Olympic games; also that Abaris gave him a dart by which he could be carried through the air and with which he expelled pestilence, lulled storms, and performed other wonderful exploits.

It was also said that Pythagoras used to write on a looking-glass in blood and place it opposite the moon, when the inscription would appear reflected on the moon's disc; and that he tamed a savage Daunian bear by 'stroking it gently with his hand', subdued an eagle by the same means, and held absolute dominion over beasts and birds by 'the power of his voice' or 'influence of his touch'.

***The letter of Pythagoras.*** The Greek upsilon, Υ; so called because it was used by him as a symbol of the divergent paths of virtue and vice.

> They placed themselves in the order and figure of Y, the letter of Pythagoras, as cranes do in their flight. Rabelais, *Pantagruel*, iv, 33

***The Pythagorean Tables.*** *See* Table.

**Pythian Games.** The games held by the Greeks at Pytho, in Phocis, subsequently called Delphi. They took place every fourth year, the second of each Olympiad.

**Pythias.** *See* Damon.

**Python.** The monster serpent hatched from the mud of Deucalion's deluge, and slain near Delphi by Apollo.

# Q

**Q.** The seventeenth letter of the English alphabet, and nineteenth (*koph*) of the Phoenician and Hebrew, where, in numerical notation, it represented 90 (in late Roman, 500). In English *q* is invariably followed by *u* (except occasionally in transliteration of some Arabic words), and it never occurs at the end of a word.

***Q in a corner.*** An old children's game, perhaps the same as our 'Puss in the corner'; also something not seen at first, but subsequently brought to notice. The thong to which seals are attached in legal documents is in French called the *queue*; thus we have *lettres scellées sur simple queue* or *sur double queue*, according to whether they bear one or two seals. In documents where the seal is attached to the deed itself, the corner where the seal is placed is called the *queue*, and when the document is sworn to the finger is laid on the *queue*.

***In a merry Q*** (cue). Humour, temper; thus Shakespeare says, 'My cue is villainous melancholy' (*King Lear*, 1, 2).

***Old Q.*** William Douglas, third Earl of March, and fourth Duke of Queensberry (1724–1810), notorious for his dissolute life and escapades, especially on the turf.

***On the strict Q.T.*** With complete secrecy. 'Q.T.' stands for 'quiet'.

***To mind one's P's and Q's.*** *See* P.

**Q.E.D.** (Lat. *Quod erat demonstrandum*, which was to be demonstrated). Appended to the theorems of Euclid – Thus have we proved the proposition stated above, as we were required to do.

**Q.E.F.** (Lat. *Quod erat faciendum*, which was to be done). Appended to the problems of Euclid – Thus have we done the operation required.

**Q.P.** (Lat. *Quantum placet*). Used in prescriptions to signify that the quantity may be as little or much as you like. Thus, in a cup of tea we might say 'Milk and sugar *q.p.*'

**Q.S.** (Lat. *Quantum sufficit*, as much as suffices). Appended to prescriptions to denote that as much as is required may be used. Thus, after giving the drugs in minute proportions, the apothecary may be told to 'mix in liquorice, *q.s.*'

**Q.T.** See *On the strict Q.T.*, above.

**Q.V.** (Lat. *quantum vis*). As much as you like, or *quantum valeat*, as much as is proper.

***q.v.*** (Lat. *quod vide*). Which see.

**Quack** or **Quack Doctor;** once called *quack-salver*. A puffer of salves; an itinerant drug-vendor at fairs, who mounted his tailboard and 'quacked' forth the praises of his wares to the gaping rustics. Hence, a charlatan.

> Saltimbancoes, quacksalvers, and charlatans deceive them in lower degrees.
>
> Sir Thomas Browne, *Pseudodoxia Epidemica*, I, iii

**Quad.** The university contraction for *quadrangle*, the college grounds; hence, *to be in quad* is to be confined to your college grounds. *Cp.* Quod.

**Quadragesima Sunday.** The first Sunday in Lent; so called because it is, in round numbers, the fortieth day before Easter.

**Quadragesimals.** The farthings or payments formerly made in commutation of a personal visit to the mother-church on Mid-Lent Sunday: also called Whitsun farthings.

**Quadrilateral.** The four fortresses of Peschiera and Mantua on the Mincio, with Verona and Legnago on the Adige. Now demolished.

***The Prussian Quadrilateral.*** The old fortresses of Luxemburg, Coblentz, Sarrelouis, and Mayence.

**Quadrille.** An old card-game played by four persons with an ordinary pack of cards from which the eights, nines, and tens, have been withdrawn. It displaced ombre (*q.v.*) in popular favour about 1730, and was followed by whist.

The square dance of the same name was of French origin, and was introduced into England in 1813 by the Duke of Devonshire.

**Quadrillion.** In English numeration, a million raised to the fourth power, represented by 1 followed by 24 ciphers; in American and French numeration it stands for the fifth power of a thousand, i.e. 1 followed by 15 ciphers. *Cp.* Billion.

**Quadrivium.** The collective name given by the Schoolmen of the Middle Ages to the four 'liberal arts' (Lat. *quadri-* four, *via* way), viz., arithmetic, music, geometry, and astronomy. The quadrivium was the 'fourfold way' to knowledge; the *trivium* (*q.v.*) the 'threefold way' to eloquence; both together comprehended the seven arts or sciences enumerated in the following hexameter:

Lingua, Tropus, Ratio Numerus, Tonus, Angulus, Astra.

And in the two following:

*Gram.* loquitur, *Dia.* vera docet, *Rhet.* verba colorat, *Mus.* cadit, *Ar* numerat, *Geo.* ponderat, *Ast.* colit astra.

**Quadroon.** A person with one-fourth of black blood; the offspring of a mulatto woman by a white man. The mulatto is half-blooded, one parent being white and the other black.

**Quadruple Alliance.** An international alliance for offensive or defensive purposes of four powers, especially that of Britain, France, Austria, and Holland in 1718, to prevent Spain recovering her Italian possessions, and that of Britain, France, Spain, and Portugal in 1834 as a counter-move to the 'Holy Alliance' between Russia, Prussia, and Austria. Another is that of 1674, when Germany, Spain, Denmark, and Holland formed an alliance against France to resist the encroachments of Louis XIV.

**Quaestio vexata** (Lat.). A vexed, or open, question.

**Quail.** The bird was formerly supposed to be of an inordinately amorous disposition, hence its name was given to a courtesan.

> Here's Agamemnon, an honest fellow enough, and one that loves quails.
>
> Shakespeare, *Troilus and Cressida*, 5, 1

Agamemnon, being obliged to give up his mistress, took the mistress of Achilles to supply her place. This brought about a quarrel between the two, and Achilles refused to have anything more to do with the siege of Troy.

**Quakers.** A familiar name for members of the Society of Friends, an evangelical religious body having no definite creed and no regular ministry, founded by George Fox, 1648–50. It appears from the founder's *Journal* that they first obtained the appellation (1650) from the following circumstance – 'Justice Bennet, of Derby', says Fox, 'was the first to call us Quakers, because I bade him quake and tremble at the word of the Lord.'

> Quakers (that, like lanterns, bear
> Their light within them) will not swear.
>
> Butler, *Hudibras*, ii, 2

***The Quaker Poet.*** Bernard Barton (1784–1849).

**Quarantine** (Ital. *quaranta*, forty). The period, originally forty days, that a ship suspected of being infected with some contagious disorder is obliged to lie off port.

In law the term is also applied to the forty days during which a widow who is entitled to a dower may remain in the chief mansion-house of her deceased husband.

***To perform quarantine*** is to ride off port during the time of quarantine.

**Quarrel** (O.Fr. *quarel*, from late Lat. *quadrellus*, diminutive of *quadrus*, a square). A short, stout, square-headed bolt or arrow used in the crossbow; also, a square or diamond-shaped pane of glass for a window.

***Quarrel,*** to engage in contention, to fall out (from O.Fr. *querele*, Lat. *querela*, complaint, *queri*, to complain).

***To quarrel over the bishop's cope*** – over something which cannot possibly do you any good; over goat's wool. A newly appointed Bishop of Bruges entered the town in his cope, which he gave to the people; and the people, to part it among themselves, tore it to shreds, each taking a piece.

***To quarrel with your bread and butter.*** To act contrary to your best interest; to snarl at that which procures your living, like a spoilt child, who shows its ill-temper by throwing its bread and butter to the ground. To cut off your nose to be avenged on your face.

**Quarry.** An object of chase, especially the bird flown at in hawking or the animal pursued by hounds or hunters. Originally the word denoted the entrails, etc., of the deer which were placed on the animal's *skin* after it had been flayed, and given to the hounds as a reward. The word is the O.Fr. *cuirée*, skinned from *cuir* (Lat. *corium*), skin.

> Your castle is surprised; your wife and babes
> Savagely slaughter'd; to relate the manner,
> Were, on the quarry of these murder'd deer
> To add the death of you.
>
> Shakespeare, *Macbeth*, 4, 3

The place where marble, stone, etc., is dug out is called a *quarry*, from O.Fr. *quarriere*, Lat. *quadrare*, to square, because the stones were *squared* on the spot.

**Quart d'heure.** ***Un mauvais quart d'heure*** (Fr. a bad quarter of an hour), used of a short, disagreeable experience, such as a 'wigging' or 'hauling over the coals'; also of the time between the arrival of one's guests and the announcement 'dinner is served'.

**Quarter.** The fourth part of anything, as of a year or an hour, or any material thing.

In *weights* a *quarter* is 28 lb, i.e. a fourth of a hundredweight; as a measure of capacity for grain it is 8 bushels, which used to be one-fourth, but is now one-fifth of a load. In the *meat trade* a *quarter* of a beast is a fourth part, which includes one of the legs. A *quarter* in the United States coinage is the fourth part of a dollar; and in an heraldic shield the *quarters* are the divisions made by central lines drawn at right angles across the shield, the 1st and 4th quarters being in the *dexter chief* and *sinister base* (i.e. left-hand top and right-hand bottom when looking at it), and the 2nd and 3rd in the *sinister chief* and *dexter base*.

***To grant quarter.*** To spare the life of an enemy in your power. The origin of the phrase is not certain, but the old suggestion that it originated from an agreement anciently made between the Dutch and the Spaniards, that the ransom of a soldier should be the quarter of his pay, is not borne out. It is more likely due to the fact that the victor would have to provide his captive with temporary quarters.

**Quarter Days.** (1) *New Style* – Lady Day (March 25th), Midsummer Day (June 24th), Michaelmas Day (September 29th), and Christmas Day (December 25th).

(2) *Old Style* – Old Lady Day (April 6th), Old Midsummer Day (July 6th), Old Michaelmas Day (October 11th), and Old Christmas Day (January 6th).

*Quarter Days in Scotland* –

Candlemas Day (February 2nd), Whitsunday (May 15th), Lammas Day (August 1st), and Martinmas Day (November 11th).

**Quarterdeck.** The upper deck of a ship from the mainmast to the stern. In men-of-war it is used by officers only, and in liners is reserved for first-class passengers. Hence, *to behave as though one were on his own quarterdeck*, to behave as though he owned the place.

**Quartered.** *See* Drawn *under* Draw.

**Quartermaster.** In the army, the officer whose duty it is to attend to the *quarters* of the soldiers. He superintends the issue of stores, food and clothing.

In the navy, the petty officer who, besides other duties, has charge of the steering of the ship, the signals, stowage, etc.

**Quarters.** Residence or place of abode; as, *winter quarters*, the place where an army lodges during the winter months. We say 'this quarter of the town', meaning this district or part; the French speak of the *Quartier Latin* – i.e. the district or part of Paris where the medical schools, etc., are located; the Belgians speak of *quartiers à louer*, lodgings to let; and bachelors in England often say, 'Come to my quarters' – i.e. apartments.

> There shall no leavened bread be seen with thee, neither shall there be leaven seen ... in all thy quarters.
> Exod. 13:7

**Quarto.** A size of paper made by folding the sheet twice, giving *four* leaves, or eight pages; hence, a book composed of sheets folded thus. *Cp.* Folio, Octavo. The word is often written '4to.'

**Quartodecimans.** Members of an early Christian sect (principally in Asia Minor) who maintained that Easter should be celebrated on the day of the Jewish Passover, the 14th of Nizan, whether this fell on a Sunday or not. They were condemned in 325 by the Council of Nice.

**Quashee.** A generic name of a negro; from West African *Kwasi*, a name often given to a child born on a Sunday. *Cp.* Quassia.

**Quasi** (Lat. as if). Prefixed to denote that so-and-so is not the real thing, but may be almost accepted in its place; thus a

***Quasi contract*** is not a real contract, but something which has the force of one.

***Quasi historical.*** Apparently historical; more or less so, or pretending to be so and almost succeeding.

***Quasi tenant.*** The tenant of a house sublet.

**Quasimodo Sunday.** The first Sunday after Easter; so called because the 'Introit' of the day begins with these words: *Quasi modo geniti infantes* (1 Pet. 2:2). Also called 'Low Sunday' (*see* Quashee *above*) (*q.v.*).

**Quassia.** An American plant, or rather genus of plants, named after Quassi, a negro, who, in 1730, was the first to make its medicinal properties known.

> Linnaeus applied this name to a tree of Surinam in honour of a negro, Quassi ... who employed its bark as a remedy for fever; and enjoyed such a reputation among the natives as to be almost worshipped by some.
> Lindley and Moors, *Treatise of Botany*, Pt ii, p. 947

**Quatorzièmes.** *See* Thirteen.

**Queen.** A female reigning sovereign, or the consort of a king; from A.S. *cwen*, a woman (which also gives *quean*, a word still sometimes used slightingly or contemptuously of a woman), from an ancient Aryan root that gave the Old Teutonic stem *kwen-*, Zend *genā*, Gr. *gunē*, Slavonic *zená*, O.Ir. *ben*, etc., all meaning 'woman'. In the 4th century translation of the Bible by Ulfilas we meet with *gens* and *gino* ('wife' and 'woman'); and in the Scandinavian languages *karl* and *kone* still mean 'man' and 'wife'. *Cp.* King; *see* Mab.

**Queen Consort.** The wife of a reigning king.

**Queen Dowager.** The widow of a deceased king.

**Queen Mother.** The mother of a reigning sovereign; also, a queen who is a mother.

> If you hold it fit, after the play
> Let his queen mother all alone entreat him
> To show his griefs. Shakespeare, *Hamlet*, 3, 1

**Queen of the May.** *See* May.

**Queen Regnant.** A queen who holds the crown in her own right, in contradistinction to a *Queen Consort*.

**Queen's Bench; Queen's Counsel.** *See* King's.

**Queen's College** (Oxford), **Queens' College** (Cambridge). Note the position of the apostrophe in each case – an important matter. The Oxford college was founded (1340) by Robert de Eglesfield in honour of *one* queen, Philippa, consort of Edward III, to whom he was confessor. The Cambridge college numbers *two* Queens as its founders, viz. Margaret of Anjou, consort of Henry VI (1448), and Elizabeth Woodville, Edward IV's consort, who refounded the college in 1465.

**Queen's Day.** November 17th, the day of the accession of Queen Elizabeth, first publicly celebrated in 1570, and for over three centuries kept as a holiday in Government offices and at Westminster School.

November 17th at Merchant Taylors' School is a holiday also, now called Sir Thomas White's Founder's Day.

**Queen's ware.** Glazed Wedgwood earthenware of a creamy colour.

**Queen's weather.** A fine day for a fête; so called because Queen Victoria was, for the most part, fortunate in having fine weather when she appeared in public.

**The Queen of Glory.** An epithet of the Virgin Mary.

**The Queen of Hearts.** Elizabeth (1596–1662), daughter of James I, the unfortunate Queen of Bohemia, so called in the Low Countries from her amiable character and engaging manners, even in her lowest estate.

**The Queen of Heaven.** The Virgin Mary. In ancient times, among the Phoenicians, Astarte; Greeks, Hera; Romans, Juno; Hecate; the Egyptian Isis, etc., were also so called; but as a general title it applied to Diana, or the Moon, also called *Queen of the Night*, and *Queen of the Tides*. In Jer. 7:18, we read: 'The children gather wood, ... and the women knead dough to make cakes to the queen of heaven', i.e. the Moon.

**The Queen of Love.** Aphrodite, or Venus.

> Poor queen of love in thine own law forlorn
> To love a cheek that smiles at thee in scorn!
> Shakespeare, *Venus and Adonis*, 251

**The White Queen.** Mary Queen of Scots; so called because she dressed in *white* mourning for her French husband.

**The Queen's English.** *See* King's English.

**The Queen's Marys.** *See* Mary.

**The Queen's Pipe.** A name given in Queen Victoria's reign to a furnace at the Victoria Docks for destroying (by the Inland Revenue authorities) contraband and worthless tobacco, etc.

**Queen Anne.** Daughter of James II and Anne Hyde (b.1664). She reigned over Great Britain from 1702 to 1714, and her name is still used in certain colloquial phrases.

**Queen Anne is dead.** A slighting retort made to the teller of stale news.

**Queen Anne style.** The style in buildings, furniture, silver-ware, etc., characteristic of her period. Domestic architecture, for instance, was noted for many angles, gables, quaint features, and irregularity of windows.

**Queen Anne's Bounty.** A fund created out of the firstfruits and tenths which were part of the papal exactions before the Reformation. The *firstfruits* are the whole first year's profits of a clerical living, and the *tenths* are the tenth part annually of the profits of a living. Henry VIII annexed both these to the Crown, but Queen Anne formed them into a perpetual fund for the augmentation of poor livings and the building of parsonages. The sum equals about £14,000 a year.

**Queen Anne's fan.** Your thumb to your nose and your fingers spread.

**Queen Dick.** Richard Cromwell (d.1712), son of the Protector, Oliver, was sometimes so called.

**In the reign of Queen Dick.** *See* Dick.

**Queen Square Hermit.** Jeremy Bentham (1748–1832), who lived at No. 1 Queen Square, London. He was the father of the political economists called Utilitarians, whose maxim is, 'The greatest happiness of the greatest number'.

**Queenhithe** (London). The hithe or strand for lading and unlading barges and lighters in the City. Called 'queen' from being part of the dowry of Eleanor, Queen of Henry II.

**Queenstown** (Ireland), formerly called the Cove of Cork. The name was changed in 1850, out of compliment to Queen Victoria, when she visited Ireland with the Prince Consort, and created her eldest son Earl of Dublin.

**Queer.** Colloquial for out of sorts, not up to the mark, also slang for drunk; and thieves' cant for anything base and worthless, especially counterfeit money.

***A queer cove.*** An eccentric person, a rum customer; also *Queer card. See* Card.

***That has put me in Queer Street.*** That has posed or puzzled me; 'upset my apple-cart'.

***To live in Queer Street.*** To be of doubtful solvency. The punning suggestion has been made that the origin of the phrase is to be found in a *query* (?) with which a tradesman might mark the name of such a one in his ledger.

***To queer one's pitch.*** To forestall him; to render his efforts nugatory by underhand means.

**Querelle d'Allemand.** *See* Allemand.

**Quern-biter.** The sword of Haco I of Norway. A quern (A.S. *cweorn*) is a primitive hand-mill, made of two stones, for grinding corn.

> Quern-biter of Hacon the Good,
> Wherewithal at a stroke he hewed
> The millstone through and through.
>
> Longfellow, *Wayside Inn* (*Musician's Tale*, 12)

**Querno.** Camillo Querno, of Apulia, hearing that Leo X (1513–22) was a great patron of poets, went to Rome with a harp in his hand, and sang his *Alexias*, a poem containing 20,000 verses. He was introduced to the Pope as a buffoon, but was promoted to the laurel.

> Rome in her Capitol saw Querno sit,
> Throned on seven hills the Antichrist of wit.
>
> *Dunciad*, ii

**Querpo.** *In querpo*. In one's shirtsleeves; in undress (Span. *en cuerpo*, without a cloak).

> Boy, my cloak and rapier: it fits not a gentleman of my rank to walk the streets in querpo.
>
> Beaumont and Fletcher, *Love's Cure*, ii, 1

**Question.** When members of the House of Commons or other debaters call out *Question*, they mean that the person speaking is wandering away from the subject under consideration.

***A leading question.*** *See* Leading.

***An open question.*** A statement, proposal, doctrine, or supposed fact, respecting which private opinion is allowed, such, for instance, as the question in the Anglican Church, whether the Lord's Supper should be taken fasting (before breakfast), or whether it may be taken at noon, or in the evening. In the House of Commons every member may vote as he likes, regardless of party politics, on an open question.

***Out of the question.*** Not worth discussing, not to be thought of; quite foreign to the subject.

***Questions and commands.*** An old Christmas game, in which the 'commander' bids one of his subjects to answer a question which is asked. If he refuses, or fails to satisfy the commander, he must pay a forfeit or have his face smutted.

> While other young ladies in the house are dancing or playing at questions and commands, she [the devotee] reads aloud in her closet.
>
> *The Spectator*, No. 354 (Hotspur's Letter), April 16, 1712

***The previous question.*** The question whether the matter under debate shall be put to the vote or not. In Parliament, and debates generally, when one party wishes that a subject should be shelved it is customary to 'move the previous question'; if this is carried the original discussion comes to an end, for it has been decided that the matter shall not be put to the vote.

Moving the previous question, says Erskine May –

> is an ingenious method of avoiding a vote upon any question that has been proposed, but the technical phrase does little to elucidate its operation. When there is no debate, or after a debate is closed, the Speaker ordinarily puts the question as a matter of course, ... but by a motion for the previous question, this act may be intercepted and forbidden.
>
> *Parliamentary Practice*, p. 303 (9th edn)

A motion for 'the previous question' cannot be made on an amendment, nor in a select committee, nor yet in a committee of the whole house.

***To beg the question.*** *See* Beg.

***To pop the question.*** To propose or make an offer of marriage. As this important demand is supposed to be unexpected, the question is said to be 'popped'.

**Questionists.** In the examinations for degrees at Cambridge it was customary, at the beginning of the January term, to hold 'Acts', and the candidates for the Bachelor's degree were called 'Questionists'. They were examined by a moderator, and afterwards the fathers of other colleges 'questioned' them for three hours in Latin, and the dismissal uttered by the Regius Professor indicated what class you would be placed in, or that respondent was plucked, in which case the words were simply *Descendas domine*.

**Queubus.** ***The equinoctial of Queubus.*** This line has Utopia on one side and Medamothi (Gr. nowhere) on the other. It was discovered on the Greek Kalends (i.e. never) by Outis (Gr. nobody) after his escape from the giant's cave, and is ninety-one degrees from the poles.

> Thou wast in very gracious fooling last night, when thou spokest of Pigrogromitus, the Vapians passing the equinoctial of Queubus. 'Twas very good, i' faith
>
> Shakespeare, *Twelfth Night*, 2, 3

**Queue.** French for tail (*cp.* Q in a Corner), hence used of a pigtail, or long plait of hair, also for a line of people waiting their turn at a booking-office, theatre, shop, etc.

***To queue up.*** A term that came into prominence during the Great War, especially in connection with the food shortage, when hundreds of people had to wait for hours in long lines before they could obtain their 'rations' at the butcher's, grocer's, etc.

**Quey.** A female calf, a young heifer; from O.Scand. *kviga*, meaning the same thing.

***Quey calves are dear veal.*** An old proverb, somewhat analogous to 'killing the goose which lays the golden eggs'. Female calves should be kept and reared for cows.

**Qui s'excuse, s'accuse** (Fr.). He who excuses himself, or apologises, condemns himself.

**Qui vive?** (Fr.). Literally, *Who lives?* but used as a sentry's challenge and so equivalent to our *Who goes there?* which in French would be *Qui va là?*

***To be on the qui vive.*** On the alert; to be quick and sharp; to be on the tiptoe of expectation, like a sentinel. (*See above*.)

**Quia Emptores.** A statute passed in the reign of Edward I (1290), to insure the lord paramount his fees arising from escheats, marriages, etc. By it freemen were permitted to sell their lands on condition that the purchaser should hold from the chief lord, and it resulted in a great increase of landowners holding direct from the Crown. So called from its opening words.

**Quibble.** An evasion; a juggling with words; probably a frequentative of the older *quib*, from Lat. *quibus*, a word constantly occurring in legal documents and so associated with the 'quirks and quillets of the law'.

**Quick.** Living; hence animated, lively; hence fast, active, brisk (A.S. *cwic*, living, alive). Our expression, 'Look alive', means Be brisk.

***Quicksand*** is sand which shifts its place as if it were alive. *See* Quick.

***Quickset*** is living hawthorn set in a hedge, instead of dead wood, hurdles, and palings. *See* Quick.

***Quicksilver*** is *argentum vivum* (living silver), silver that moves about like a living thing. (A.S. *cwic seolfor*.)

> Swift as quicksilver
> It courses through the natural gates
> And alleys of the body.
>
> Shakespeare, *Hamlet*, 1, 5

***The quick and dead.*** The living and the dead.

**Quid.** Slang for a sovereign (or a pound note). It occurs in Shadwell's *Squire of Alsatia* (1688), but its origin is unknown. A suggested derivation may be mentioned. Quo = anything, and *Quid pro quo* means an equivalent generally. If now a person is offered anything on sale he might say, I have not a *quid* for your *quo*, an equivalent in cash.

> A working-man can't do much on three quid a week nowadays. Common modern saying

In *a quid of tobacco*, meaning a piece for chewing, *quid* is another form of *cud*.

**Quid-libet.** *See* Quodlibet.

**Quid pro quo** (Lat.). Tit for tat; a return given as good as that received; a Roland for an Oliver; an equivalent.

**Quid rides** (Lat. Why are you laughing?). It is said that Lundy Foot, a Dublin tobacconist, set up his carriage, and that Curran, when asked to furnish him with a motto, suggested this. The witticism is, however, attributed to H. Callender also, who, we are assured, supplied it to one Brandon, a London tobacconist.

'Rides' in English, one syllable; in Latin it is two.

**Quiddity.** The essence of a thing, or that which differentiates it from other things – 'the Correggiosity of Correggi', 'the Freeness of the Free'. Hence used of subtle, trifling distinctions, quibbles, or captious argumentation. Schoolmen say *Quid est?* (what is it?) and the reply is, the *Quid* is so and so, the *What* or the nature of the thing is as follows. The latter *quid* being formed into a barbarous Latin noun becomes *Quidditas*. Hence *Quid est?* (what is it?). Answer: *Talis est quidditas* (its essence is as follows).

> He knew …
> Where entity and quiddity
> (The ghosts of defunct bodies) fly.
>
> Butler, *Hudibras*, i, 1

**Quidnunc** (Lat. What now?). One who is curious to know everything that's going on, or pretends to know it; a self-important newsmonger and gossip. It is the name of the leading character in Murphy's farce *The Upholsterer*, or *What News?*

**Quietism.** A form of religious mysticism based on the doctrine that the essence of religion consists in the withdrawal of the soul from external objects, and in fixing it upon the contemplation of God; especially that taught by the Spanish mystic, Miguel Molinos (1640–96), who taught the direct relationship between the soul and God. His followers were termed Molinists, or *Quietists*. *See* Molinism.

**Quietus** (late Lat. *quietus est*, he is quit). The writ of discharge formerly granted to those barons and knights who personally attended the king on a foreign expedition, exempting them also from the claim of scutage or knight's fee. Subsequently the term was applied to the acquittance which a sheriff receives on settling his account at the Exchequer; and, later still, to any discharge, as of an account, or even of life itself.

> You had the trick in audit-time to be sick till I had signed your quietus.
>
> Webster, *Duchess of Malfi*, III, ii (1623)

> Who would fardels bear ...
> When he himself might his quietus make
> With a bare bodkin? Shakespeare, *Hamlet*, 3, 1

**Quill-drivers.** Writing clerks.

**Quillet.** An evasion. This may be an abbreviation of the old word *quillity* (formed on analogy with *quiddity*) meaning a quibble, or it may be from Lat. *quidlibet*, i.e. 'anything you choose'. A fanciful suggestion is that it came to England from the French law courts, where each separate allegation in the plaintiff's charge, and every distinct plea in the defendant's answer began with *qu'il est*; whence *quillet*, to signify a false charge, or an evasive answer.

> Oh, some authority how to proceed;
> Some tricks, some quillets, how to cheat the devil. Shakespeare, *Love's Labour's Lost*, 4, 3

**Quinapalus.** A kind of 'Mrs Grundy' or 'Mrs Harris' invented by Feste, the Clown in *Twelfth Night*, when he wished to give some saying the weight of authority. Hence sometimes 'dragged in' when one wishes to clench an argument by some supposed quotation.

> What says Quinapalus: 'Better a witty fool, than a foolish wit.' Shakespeare, *Twelfth Night*, 1, 5

**Quinbus Flestrin.** The man-mountain. So the Lilliputians called Gulliver (ch. ii). Gay has an ode to this giant.

> Bards of old of him told,
> When they said Atlas' head
> Propped the skies. Gay, *Lilliputian Ode*

**Quinine.** *See* Cinchona.

**Quinquagesima Sunday** (Lat. *fiftieth*). Shrove Sunday, or the first day of the week which contains Ash Wednesday. It is so called because in round numbers it is the fiftieth day before Easter.

**Quinsy.** This is a curious abbreviation. The Latin word is *quinanchia*, and the Greek *kunanché*, from *kuon anche*, dog strangulation, because persons suffering from quinsy throw open the mouth like dogs, especially mad dogs. It first appeared in English (14th cent.) as *qwinaci* and later forms were *quynnancy* and *squinancy*. *Squinancy-wort* is still a name given to the small woodruff (*Asperula cynanchica*), which was used as a cure for quinsy by the herbalists.

**Quintessence.** The fifth essence. The ancient Greeks said there are four elements or forms in which matter can exist – fire, air, water, and earth (*see* Elements); the Pythagoreans added a fifth, the fifth essence – quintessence – *ether*, more subtile and pure than fire, and possessed of an orbicular motion, which flew upwards at creation and formed the material basis of the stars. Hence the word stands for the essential principle or the most subtile extract of a body that can be procured. Horace speaks of 'kisses which Venus has imbued with the quintessence of her own nectar'.

> Swift to their several quarters hasted then
> The cumbrous elements – earth, flood, air, fire;
> But this ethereal quintessence of heaven
> Flew upward ... and turned to stars
> Numberless as thou seest.
>
> Milton, *Paradise Lost*, iii, 716

***Queen Quintessence***. The Queen of Entelechy (*q.v.*) in Rabelais' *Gargantua and Pantagruel* (Bk V, xix–xxv).

**Quintilians.** Members of a 2nd century heretical sect of Montanists, said to have been founded by one Quintilia, a prophetess. They made the Eucharist of bread and cheese, and allowed women to become priests and bishops.

**Quintillion.** In English, the fifth power of a million, 1 followed by 30 ciphers; in France and the United States the cube of a million, a million multiplied by a thousand four times over, 1 followed by 18 ciphers. *Cp.* Billion.

**Quip Modest, The.** Sir, it was done to please myself. Touchstone says (*As You Like It*, 5, 4): 'If I sent a person word that his beard was not well cut, and he replied he cut it to please himself,' he would answer with the quip modest, which is six removes from the lie direct; or, rather, the lie direct in the sixth degree.

**Quis custodiet custodes?** (Lat.) [The shepherds keep watch over the sheep], but who is there to keep watch over the shepherds? Said when one is not certain of the integrity of one whom one has placed in a position of trust.

**Quis separabit?** (Lat. Who shall separate us?) The motto adopted by the Most Illustrious Order of St Patrick when it was founded in 1783.

**Quit.** Discharged from an obligation, 'acquitted'.

> To John I owed great obligation;
> But John unhappily thought fit
> To publish it to all the nation –
> Now I and John are fairly quit. Prior

***Cry quits.*** When two boys quarrel, and one has had enough, he says, 'Cry quits', meaning, 'Let us leave off, and call it a drawn game.' So in an unequal distribution, he who has the largest share restores a portion and 'cries quits', meaning that he has made the distribution equal. Here quit means 'acquittal' or discharge.

***Double or quits.*** *See* Double.

***Quit rent.*** A rent formerly paid by a tenant whereby he was released from feudal service. The term is still used of the small annual sum paid by some freeholders and copyholders in lieu of services due from them.

**Quixote, Don.** *See* Don Quixote.

***The Quixote of the North.*** Charles XII of Sweden (1682, 1697–1718), also called *The Madman.*

**Quixotic.** Having foolish and unpractical ideas of honour, or schemes for the general good, like Don Quixote (*q.v.*).

**Quiz.** One who banters or chaffs another. The origin of the word – which appeared about 1780 – is unknown; but fable accounts for it by saying that a Mr Daly, manager of a Dublin theatre, laid a wager that he would introduce into the language within twenty-four hours a new word of no meaning. Accordingly, on every wall, or all places accessible, were chalked up the four mystic letters, and all Dublin was enquiring what they meant. The wager was won, and the word remains current in our language.

**Quo warranto.** A writ against a defendant (whether an individual or a corporation) who lays claim to something he has no right to; so named because the offender is called upon to show *quo warranto* (rem) *usurpavit* (by what right or authority he lays claim to the matter of dispute).

**Quoad hoc** (Lat.). To this extent, with respect to this.

**Quod.** Slang for prison. Probably the same word as *quad* (*q.v.*), which is a contraction of *quadrangle*, the enclosure in which prisoners are allowed to walk, and where whippings used to be inflicted. The word was in use in the 17th century.

> Flogged and whipped in quod.
> Hughes, *Town Brown's Schooldays*

**Quodlibet** (Lat. What you please). Originally a philosophical or theological question proposed for purposes of scholastic debate, hence a nice and knotty point, a subtlety. *Quidlibet* is a form of the same word.

**Quondam** (Lat.). Former. We say, *He is a quondam schoolfellow* – my former schoolfellow; *my quondam friend*, *the quondam chancellor*, etc.

> My quondam barber, but 'his lordship' now.
> Dryden

**Quorum** (Lat., of whom). The lowest number of members of a committee or board, etc., the presence *of whom* is necessary before business may be transacted; formerly, also, certain Justices of the Peace – hence known as Justices of the Quorum – chosen for their special ability, one or more of whom had to be on the Bench at trials before the others could act. Slender calls Justice Shallow justice of the peace and quorum. (*Merry Wives of Windsor*, 1, 1).

**Quos ego.** A threat of punishment for disobedience. The words, from Virgil's *Aeneid* (i, 135), were uttered by Neptune to the disobedient and rebellious winds, and are sometimes given as an example of aposiopesis, i.e. a stopping short for rhetorical effort, 'Whom I –', said Neptune, the 'will punish' being left to the imagination.

> Neptune had but to appear and utter a *quos ego* for these windbags to collapse, and become the most subservient of salaried public servants.
> *Truth*, January, 1886

**Quot. *Quot homines, tot sententiae*** (Lat.). As many minds as men; there are as many opinions as there are men to hold them. The phrase is from Terence's *Phormio* (II, iv, 14).

***Quot linguas calles, tot homines vales*** (Lat.). As many languages as you know, so many separate individuals you are worth. Attributed to Charles V.

**Quota** (Lat.). The allotted portion or share; the rate assigned to each. Thus we say, 'Every man is to pay his quota towards the feast.'

# R

**R.** The eighteenth letter of the English alphabet (seventeenth of the Roman) representing the twentieth of the Phoenician and Hebrew. In the ancient Roman numeration it stood for 80. In England it was formerly used as a branding mark for rogues, particularly kidnappers.

It has been called the 'snarling letter' or 'dog letter', because a dog in snarling utters a sound resembling r-r-r-r-r, r-r-r-r-r, etc. – sometimes preceded by a g.

> Irritata canis quod R R quam plurima dicat.
>
> Lucillus

In his *English Grammar made for the Benefit of all Strangers* Ben Jonson says –

> R is the dog's letter, and hurreth in the sound; the tongue striking the inner palate, with a trembling about the teeth.

And see the Nurse's remark about R in *Romeo and Juliet*, 2, 4.

℞ in prescriptions. The ornamental part of this letter is the symbol of Jupiter (♃), under whose special protection all medicines were placed. The letter itself (*Recipe*, take) and its flourish may be thus paraphrased: 'Under the good auspices of Jove, the patron of medicines, take the following drugs in the proportions set down.' It has been suggested that the symbol is for *Responsum Raphaelis*, from the assertion of Dr Napier and other physicians of the 17th century, that the angel Raphael imparted the virtues of drugs.

***The R months.*** *See under* Oyster.

***The three R's.*** Reading, writing, and arithmetic. The phrase is said to have been originated by Sir William Curtis (d.1829), who gave this as a toast.

> The House is aware that no payment is made except on the 'three R's'.
>
> Mr Cory, M.P: in House of Commons, Feb. 28th, 1867

**R. A. P.** Rupees, annas, and pies, in India; corresponding to our *£ s. d.*

**R. I. P.** *Requiescat in pace*. Latin for May he (or she) Rest in Peace; a symbol used on mourning cards, tombstones, etc.

**Ra.** The principal deity of ancient Egypt, one of the numerous forms of the sun-god, and the supposed ancestor of all the Pharaohs. He was the protector of men and vanquisher of evil; Nut, the sky, was his father, and it was said of him that every night he fought with the serpent, Apepi. He is usually represented as hawk-headed, and is crowned with the solar disk and uraeus. *See* Osiris.

**Rabelaisian.** Coarsely and boisterously satirical; grotesque, extravagant, and licentious in language; reminiscent in literary style of the great French satirist François Rabelais (1483–1553).

Dean Swift, Thomas Amory (d.1788, author of *John Buncle*), and Sterne have all been called 'the English Rabelais' – but the title is not very fitting; indeed, the title is a contradiction in terms; Rabelais was so essentially a Frenchman of the Renaissance that it is impossible to think of an English counterpart of any period.

> If we are to seek for an approximation of Aristophanic humour, we shall find it perhaps in Rabelais. Rabelais exhibits a similar disregard for decency, combining the same depth of purpose and largeness of insight with the same coarse fun.
>
> J. A. Symonds, *Studies of Greek Poets*

**Rabicano** or **Rabican.** Astolpho's horse in Ariosto's *Orlando Furioso* (Argalia's, in Boiardo's *Orlando Inamorato*, had the same name). Its sire was Wind, and its dam Fire. It fed on unearthly food.

**Raboin.** *See* Tailed Men.

**Rabsheka.** In Dryden's *Absalom and Achitophel* (*q.v.*), is meant for Sir Thomas Player. Rabshakeh was the officer sent by Sennacherib to summon the Jews to surrender, and he told them insolently that resistance was in vain (2 Kings, 18).

> Next him, let railing Rabsheka have place –
> So full of zeal, he has no need of grace. Pt 2

**Races.** The principal horse-races in England are run at Newmarket, Doncaster, Epsom, Goodwood, and Ascot (*see* Classic Races), but there are a large number of other courses where important meetings are held, and the greatest event in the world of steeple-chasing – the Grand National – is run at Aintree, near Liverpool.

There are seven annual race meetings at Newmarket: (1) The Craven; (2) first spring; (3) second spring; (4) July; (5) first October; (6) second October; (7) the Houghton.

At Doncaster races are held for two days about the middle of May, four days early in September, and two days toward the end of October.

The Epsom meeting (when the Derby, Oaks,

Coronation Cup, etc., are run) is held for four days in the first week of June.

Goodwood (four days) starts on the last Tuesday in July, and Ascot (four days) in the middle of June.

The following are the principal English horse-races, with distances and *venue*:

Alexandra Cup (Ascot), 2 m. 6 fur. 86 yd.
Ascot Cup, 2½ m.
Ascot Stakes, about 2 m.
Batthyany Plate (Lincoln), 5 fur.
Cambridgeshire Stakes (Newmarket), 9 fur.
Cesarewitch Stakes (Newmarket), 2¼ m.
Champagne Stakes (Doncaster), 5 fur. 152 yd.
Champion Stakes (Newmarket), 1 m. 6 fur.
Chester Cup, about 2¼ m.
Chesterfield Cup (Goodwood), 1 m. 2 fur.
City and Suburban H'cap (Epsom), about 1¼ m.
Criterion Stakes (Newmarket), 6 fur.
Derby Cup, 1 m. 6 fur.
The Derby (Epsom), 1½ m.
Dewhurst Plate (Newmarket), 7 fur.
Doncaster Cup, about 2 m.
Eclipse Stakes (Sandown), about 1¼ m.
Gold Cup (Ascot), 2½ m.
Gold Vase (Ascot), 2 m.
Goodwood Cup, 2 m. 5 fur.
Goodwood Plate, 2 m. 3 fur.
Grand Military Gold Cup (Sandown), 3 m.
Grand National Steeplechase (Aintree), 4 m. 856 yd.
Great Ebor H'cap (York), 1 m. 6 fur.
Great Metropolitan H'cap (Epsom), 2¼ m.
Great Yorkshire H'cap (Doncaster), 1 m. 6 fur. 632 yd.
Jubilee H'cap (Kempton), 1¼ m.
July Stakes (Newmarket), 5 fur. 142 yd.
Lincolnshire H'cap (Lincoln), 1 m.
Liverpool Autumn Cup, lm. 3 fur.
Liverpool Summer Cup, 1 m. 3 fur.
Manchester Cup, 1½ m.
Manchester November H'cap, 1½ m.
Middle Park Plate (Newmarket), 6 fur.
New Stakes (Ascot), 5 fur. 136 yd.
Northumberland Plate (Newcastle), 2 m.
The Oaks (Epsom), 1½ m.
The One Thousand Guineas (Newmarket), 1 m.
Portland Plate (Doncaster), 5 fur. 132 yd.
Princess of Wales's Stakes (Newmarket), 1½ m.
Royal Hunt Cup (Ascot), 7 fur. 166 yd.
St Leger (Doncaster), 1 m. 6 fur. 132 yd.
Stewards' Cup (Goodwood), 6 fur.
The Two Thousand Guineas (Newmarket), 1 m.

Many of the more important of these races will be found entered in their alphabetical places throughout this Dictionary.

**Rache.** A hound that hunts by scent (A.S. *raecc*, a hound, A.Nor. *brache*, Ger. *bracken*). They were later called 'running hounds' and then simply 'hounds', and were used in the Middle Ages for stag, wild boar, and buck hunting.

> And first I will begin with raches and their nature, and then greyhounds and their nature, and then alaunts and their nature, ... and then I shall devise and tell the sicknesses of hounds and their diseases.
>
> Edward, 2nd Duke of York, *The Master of Game*, *Prologue* (about 1410)

**Rack.** A flying scud, drifting clouds. (Icel. *rek*, drift; *recka*, to drive).

> The cloud-capped towers, the gorgeous palaces,
> The solemn temples, the great globe itself,
> Yea, all which it inherit, shall dissolve,
> And ... leave not a rack behind.
>
> Shakespeare, *Tempest*, 4, 1

The instrument of torture so called (connected with Ger. *recken*, to strain) was a frame in which a man was fastened and his arms and legs *stretched* till the body was lifted by the tension several inches from the floor. Not infrequently the limbs were forced thereby out of their sockets. Coke says that the rack was first introduced into the Tower by the Duke of Exeter, constable of the Tower, in 1447, whence it was called the 'Duke of Exeter's daughter'.

***Rack,*** the framework for putting plates and other things on; the grating for holding fodder, etc., is probably connected with this.

***Rack and ruin.*** Utter destitution. Here 'rack' is a variety of *wrack* and *wreck*.

> The worst of all University snobs are those unfortunates who go to rack and ruin from their desire to ape their betters.
>
> Thackeray, *Book of Snobs*, ch. xv

***To lie at rack and manger.*** To live without thought of the morrow, like cattle or horses whose food is placed before them without themselves taking thought; hence, to live at reckless expense.

> When Virtue was a country maide,
> And had no skill to set up trade.
> She came up with a carrier's jade,
> And lay at rack and manger.
>
> *Life of Robin Goodfellow* (1628)

***To rack one's brains.*** To strain them to find out or recollect something; to puzzle about something.

**Rack Rent.** The actual value or rent of a tenement, and not that modified form on which the rates and taxes are usually levied; an exorbitant rent, one which is 'racked' or stretched.

**Racket.** Noise or confusion. The word is probably imitative, like *crack*, *bang*, *splash*, etc.

***To stand the racket.*** To bear the expense; to put up with the consequences.

**Racy.** Having distinctive or characteristic piquancy. It was first applied to wine, and comes to us from the Spanish and Portuguese *raiz* (root), meaning having a radical or distinct flavour.

Rich, racy verse, in which we see
The soil from which they come, taste, smell, and see. Cowley

***Racy of the soil.*** Characteristic of the inhabitants, especially the dwellers in the country, workers on the land.

**Radcliffe Library.** A famous library at Oxford, founded with a bequest of £40,000 left for the purpose by Dr John Radcliffe (d.1714), and originally intended for a medical library.

**Radegonde** or **Radegund, St.** Wife of Clothaire, king of the Franks (558–61).

***St Radegonde's lifted stone.*** A stone 60 feet in circumference, placed on five supporting stones, said by the historians of Poitou to have been so arranged in 1478, to commemorate a great fair held on the spot in the October of that year. The country people insist that Queen Radegonde brought the impost stone on her head, and the five uprights in her apron, and arranged them all as they appear to this day.

**Radegone.** *See* Radigund.

**Radevore.** A kind of cloth, probably tapestry, known in the 14th century. It has been suggested (Skeat) that it was named from Vaur, in Languedoc, *ras* (Eng. *rash*, a smooth – *rased* – textile fabric) *de Vor*.

This woful lady ylern'd had in youthe
So that she worken and embrowden kouthe,
And weven in hire stole the radevore
As hyt of wommen had be y-woved yore.
Chaucer, *Legend of Good Women*, 2351

**Radical.** The term was first applied as a party name in 1818 to Henry Hunt, Major Cartwright, and others of the same clique, ultra-Liberals verging on republicanism, who wished to introduce *radical* reform, i.e. one that would go to the root (Lat. *radix, radic-is*) of the matter, in the electoral system, and not merely to disfranchise and enfranchise a borough or two. Bolingbroke, in his *Discourses on Parties* (1735), says, 'Such a remedy might have wrought a *radical cure* of the evil that threatens our constitution.'

The term is not now much used, the extremists among the Liberals tending to merge in the Labour Party.

**Radigund.** Queen of the Amazons in Spenser's *Faërie Queene* (V, iv, 33, etc.), reigning over

A goodly citty and a mighty one,
The which of her owne name she called Radegone.

Getting the better of Sir Artegal in a single combat, she compelled him to dress in 'woman's weeds', and to spin flax. Britomart went to the rescue, cut off the Amazon's head, and liberated her knight.

**Radit usque ad cutem** (Lat.). He shaved off all his hair (instead of only trimming it); said of a 'near' man who always wants his 'pound of flesh'.

**Rag.** A tatter, hence a remnant (as 'not a rag of decency', 'not a rag of evidence'), hence a vagabond or ragamuffin.

Lash hence these overweening rags of France.
Shakespeare, *Richard III*, 5, 3

The word was old cant for a farthing, and was also used generally to express scarcity – or absence – of money:

Money by me? Heart and good-will you might,
But surely, master, not a rag of money.
Shakespeare, *Comedy of Errors*, 4, 4

In university slang (and now in general slang) *a rag* is a boisterous jollification, usually intended to annoy someone in particular or as a general defiance of authority, in which practical jokes and horseplay have a large share. *To rag* a man is to torment him in a rough and noisy fashion.

***Glad rags.*** *See* Glad.

***Rag-tag and bob-tail.*** The rabble, the 'great unwashed'. The common expression in the 16th and 17th centuries was *the tag and rag*.

***The Rag.*** The Army and Navy Club. 'The rag', of course, is the flag.

'By the way, come and dine tonight at the Rag,' said the major.
*Truth*, *Queer Story*, April 1, 1886

***Rag water.*** Whisky (*thieves' jargon*).

**Ragamuffin.** A *muffin* is a poor thing of a creature, a 'regular muff'; so that a *ragamuffin* is a sorry creature in rags.

I have led my ragamuffins where they are peppered. Shakespeare, *I Henry IV*, 5, 3

**Ragged Robin.** A wildflower (*Lychnis floscuculi*). The word is used by Tennyson for a pretty damsel in ragged clothes.

The prince
Hath picked a ragged robin from the hedge.
Tennyson, *Idylls of the King; Enid*

**Raghu.** A legendary king of Oude, belonging to the dynasty of the Sun. The poem called the *Raghu-vansa*, in nineteen cantos, gives the history of these mythic kings.

**Ragman Roll.** The set of documents recording the names of the Scottish barons who paid homage to Edward I on his progress through Scotland in 1291, now in the Public Record Office. The name probably arose from the quantity of seals hanging from it, and it still survives in the 'vulgar tongue' as 'rigmarole' (*q.v.*).

**Ragnarok.** The Götterdammerung (*q.v.*), or Twilight of the Gods, in the old *Scandinavian mythology*. The day of doom, when the present world and all its inhabitants will be annihilated. Vidar of Vali will survive the conflagration, and reconstruct an imperishable universe.

> And, Frithiof, mayst thou sleep away
> Till Ragnarok, if such thy will.
>
> *Frithiof-Saga*, *Frithiof's Joy*

**Ragout.** A seasoned dish; stewed meat and vegetables highly seasoned. Fr. *ragoûter* (*re*, again, *goûter*, to taste) means to coax a sick person's appetite.

**Rahu.** The demon that, according to Hindu legend, causes eclipses. He one day quaffed some of the nectar of immortality, but was discovered by the Sun and Moon, who informed against him, and Vishnu cut off his head. As he had already taken some of the nectar into his mouth, the head was immortal, and he ever afterwards hunted the Sun and Moon, which he caught occasionally, causing eclipses.

**Rail.** ***To sit on the rail.*** To hedge or to reserve one's decision. A common American phrase, expressive of the same meaning as our ' to sit on the fence' (*q.v.*).

> If he said 'Yes', there was an end to any church support at once; if 'No', he might as well go home at once. So he tried to sit on the rail again.
> T. Terrell, *Lady Dalmar*, ch. i

**Railway King, The.** George Hudson (1800–71), chairman of the North Midland Company, and for a time the dictator of the railway speculations. In one day he cleared the large sum of £100,000. Sydney Smith gave him the name.

**Rain.** ***To rain cats and dogs.*** In *northern mythology* the cat is supposed to have great influence on the weather, and English sailors still say, ' The cat has a gale of wind in her tail,' when she is unusually frisky. Witches that rode upon the storms were said to assume the form of cats; and the stormy north-west wind is called the *cat's-nose* in the Harz district even at the present day.

The dog is a signal of *wind*, like the wolf, both which animals were attendants of Odin, the storm god. In old German pictures the wind is figured as the 'head of a dog or wolf', from which blasts issue.

So *cat* may be taken as a symbol of the down-pouring rain, and the *dog* of the strong gusts of wind accompanying a rainstorm.

**Rainbow.** The old fable has it that if one reaches the spot where a rainbow touches the earth and digs there one will be sure to find a pot of gold. Hence visionaries, wool-gatherers, day-dreamers, are sometimes called *rainbow chasers*, because of their habit of hoping for impossible things.

**Raining tree** or **Rain tree.** Old travellers to the Canaries frequently mentioned a linden tree from which sufficient water to supply all the men and beasts of the whole of the island of Fierro was said to fall. Of course, in certain states of the weather moisture will condense and collect on the broad leaves of many trees.

The *Tamia caspia* of the Eastern Peruvian Andes is known as the *rain tree*, as also is *Pithecolobium saman*, an ornamental tropical tree, one of the mimoseae and *Brunefelsia pubescens*, a tree whose flowers are odorous before rain.

**Rainy Day, A.** Evil times.

***Lay by something for a rainy day.*** Save something against evil times.

**Raison d'être** (Fr.). The reason for a thing's existence, its rational ground for being; as 'Once crime were abolished there would be no *raison d'être* for the police.'

**Rajah.** Sanskrit for king, cognate with Lat. *rex*. The title of an Indian king or prince, given later to tribal chiefs and comparatively minor dignitaries and rulers; also to Malayan and Japanese chiefs, as Rajah Brooke, of Sarawak. *Maha-rajah* means the 'great rajah'.

**Rake.** A libertine. A contraction of rakehell, used by Milton and others.

> And far away amid their rakehell bands
> They speed a lady left all succourless
>
> Francis Quarles

**Rakshas.** Evil spirits of Hindu legend, who guard the treasures of Kuvera, the god of riches. They haunt cemeteries and devour human beings; assume any shape at will, and their strength increases as the day declines. Some are hideously ugly, but others, especially the female spirit's, allure by their beauty.

**Rakush.** *See* Ruksh.

**Rally** is *re-alligo*, to bind together again. (French *rallier*). In Spenser it is spelt 're-allie' –

> Before they could new consels re-allie.
>
> *Faërie Queene*

> Yes, we'll rally round the flag, boys,
> We'll rally once again.
>
> G. F. Root, *Battle-cry of Freedom*

A *rally* in lawn-tennis, badminton, etc., is a rapid return of strokes. *To rally*, meaning to banter or chaff is not connected with this word, but from Fr. *railler*, to deride; our *raillery* is really the same word.

**Ralph** or **Ralpho.** The squire of Hudibras (*q.v.*). The model was Isaac Robinson, a zealous butcher in Moorfields, always contriving some queer art of church government. He represents the Independent party, and Hudibras the Presbyterian.

> He was himself under the tyranny of scruples as unreasonable as those of ... Ralpho. Macaulay

In England *Ralph* is usually rhymed with *safe*, in America with *Alf*; the rhyme with *half* is also allowable, but not common.

**Ralph Roister Doister.** The title of the earliest English comedy; so called from the chief character. Written by Nicholas Udall about 1533 for performance by the boys at Eton, where he was then headmaster.

**Ram.** Formerly, the usual prize at wrestling matches. Thus Chaucer says of his Miller, 'At wrastlynge he wolde "bere" awey the ram.' (*Canterbury Tales: Prologue*, 548.)

***The Ram feast.*** Formerly held on May morning at Holne, Dartmoor, when a ram was run down in the 'Ploy Field' and roasted whole, with its skin and fur, close by a granite pillar. At midday a scramble took place for a slice, which was supposed to bring luck to those who got it.

***The Ram and Teazle.*** A public-house sign, in compliment to the Clothiers' Company. The *ram* with the golden fleece is emblematical of wool, and the *teazle* is used for raising the nap of wool spun and woven into cloth.

***The ram of the Zodiac.*** This is the famous Chrysomallon, whose golden fleece was stolen by Jason in his Argonautic expedition. It was transposed to the stars, and made the first sign of the Zodiac.

> The Vernal signs the Ram begins;
> Then comes the Bull; in May the Twins;
> The Crab in June; next Leo shines;
> And Virgo ends the northern signs. E. C. B

**Rama.** The seventh incarnation of Vishnu (*see* Avatar). Rama performed many wonderful exploits, such as killing giants, demons, and other monsters. He won Sita to wife because he was able to bend the bow of Siva.

**Ramachandra.** *See* Avatar.

**Ramadan.** The ninth month of the Mohammedan year, and the Mussulman's Lent or Holy Month (also transliterated Ramazan).

> As the Moslem year is calculated on the system of twelve lunar months, Ramazan is liable at times to fall in the hot weather, when abstinence from drinking as well as from food is an extremely uncomfortable and inconvenient obligation. What wonder, then, that the end of the fast is awaited with feverish impatience?
>
> H. M. Batson, *Commentary on Fiizgerald's 'Omar'*, st. xc

**Rama-Yana** (i.e. the deeds of Rama). The history of Rama, the great epic poem of ancient India, ranking with the Mahabharata (*q.v.*), and almost with the *Iliad.* It is ascribed to the poet Valmiki, and, as now known, consists of 24,000 stanzas in seven books.

**Rambouillet, Hôtel de.** The house in Paris where, about 1615, the Marquise de Rambouillet, disgusted with the immoral and puerile tone of the time, founded the *salon* out of which grew the *Académie française.* Mme de Sévigné, Descartes, Richelieu, Bossuet, and La Rochefoucauld were among the members. They had a language of their own, calling common things by uncommon names, and so on; the women were known as *Les précieuses* and the men as *Esprits doux.* Preciosity, pedantry, and affectation led to the disruption of the coterie which, after having performed a good and lasting service, was finally demolished by the satire of Molière's *Les précieuses ridicules* (1659) and *Les femmes savantes* (1672).

**Ramiel.** The Rabbinical name of one of the fallen angels cast out of heaven; it means *one that exalts himself against God.*

> Nor stood unmindful Abdlel to annoy
> The atheist crew, but with redoubled blow
> Ariel, and Arioch, and the violence
> Of Ramiel scorch'd and blasted.
>
> Milton, *Paradise Lost*, vi, 369

**Raminagobris.** Rabelais (*Pantagruel* III, xxi) under this name satirises Guillaume Crétin, a poet in the reigns of Charles VIII, Louis XII, and François I.

In La Fontaine's fables the name is given to the great cat chosen as judge between the weasel and the rabbit.

**Rampage.** ***On the rampage.*** Acting in a violently excited or angry manner. The word was originally Scotch, and is probably connected with *ramp*, to storm and rage.

**Rampallion.** A term of contempt; probably a 'portmanteau word' of *ramp* and *rapscallion*; in Davenport's *A New Trick to Cheat the Devil* (1639) we have: 'And bold rampallion-like, swear and drink drunk.'

> Away, you scullion! you rampallion! you fustilarian! I'll tickle your catastrophe.
>
> Shakespeare, *2 Henry IV*, 2, 1

**Rampant.** The heraldic term for an animal, especially a lion, shown rearing up with the fore paws in the air; strictly, a *lion rampant* should stand on the sinister hind-leg, with both fore-legs elevated, the dexter above the sinister, and the head in profile.

**Ran** or **Rana.** In *Norse mythology*, goddess of the sea, and wife of Aegir (*q.v.*). Her name signifies robbery, and it was she who caught seafarers in her net and drew them down to her dwelling beneath the waves.

> 'May Rana keep them in the deep,
> As is her wont,
> And no one save them from the grave,'
> Cried Helgehont.
>
> *Frithiof-Saga*, *The Banishment*

**Randan.** ***On the randan.*** On the spree; having a high old time in town. There was a popular music-hall song in the 'nineties of last century in which the exploits of the 'randy dandy boys' out on the spree were related.

**Randem-Tandem.** Three horses driven tandem fashion. *See* Tandem.

**Ranee** or **Rani.** A Hindu queen; the feminine of Rajah (*q.v.*).

**Rank.** A row, a line (especially of soldiers); also high station, dignity, eminence, as –

> The rank is but the guinea's stamp,
> The man's the gowd, for a' that!
>
> Burns, *Is there for Honest Poverty?*

***Rank and fashion.*** People of high social standing; the 'Upper Ten'.

***Rank and file.*** *See* File.

***Risen from the ranks.*** Said of a commissioned officer in the army who has worked his way up from private soldier – from the ranks. Often called a *ranker*. Hence applied to a self-made man in any walk of life.

**Ransom.** In origin the same word as *redemption*, from Lat. *redemptionem*, through O.Fr. *rançon*, earlier *redempçon*.

***A king's ransom.*** A large sum of money.

**Rantipole.** A harum-scarum fellow, a madcap (Dut. *randten*, to be in a state of idiocy, and perhaps *poll*, a head or person). Napoleon III was called *Rantipole*, for his escapades at Strasbourg and Boulogne.

**Ranz des vaches.** Simple melodies played by the Swiss mountaineers on their Alp-horn when they drive their herds to pasture, or call them home. *Des vaches*, of course, is 'of the cows'; the meaning of *ranz* is not so certain, but it is thought to be a dialectal variation of *ranger*, the call being made *pour ranger des vaches*, to bring the cows home.

**Rap.** ***Not worth a rap.*** Worth nothing at all. The rap was a base halfpenny, intrinsically worth about half a farthing, circulated in Ireland in 1721, because small coin was so very scarce.

> Many counterfeits passed about under the name of raps.
>
> Swift, *Drapier's Letters*

**Rape.** One of the six divisions into which Sussex is divided; it is said that each has its own river, forest, and castle. *Herepp* is Norwegian for a parish district, and *rape* in Doomsday Book is used for a district under military jurisdiction, but connection between the two words is doubtful.

**Rape of the Lock.** Lord Petre, in a thoughtless moment of frolic gallantry, cut off a lock of Arabella Fermor's hair (*see* Belinda); and this liberty gave rise to the bitter feud between the two families, which Pope worked up into the best heroi-comic poem of the language. The first sketch was published in 1712 in two cantos, and the complete work, including the most happily conceived machinery of sylphs and gnomes, in five cantos in 1714. Pope, under the name of Esdras Barnevelt, apothecary, later pretended that the poem was a covert satire on Queen Anne and the Barrier Treaty.

> Say, what strange motive, goddess, could compel
> A well-bred lord to assault a gentle belle;
> O say, what stranger cause, yet unexplored,
> Could make a gentle belle reject a lord.
>
> Introduction to the Poem

**Raphael.** One of the principal angels of Jewish angelology. In the book of Tobit we are told how he travelled with Tobias into Media and back again, instructing him on the way how to marry Sara and to drive away the wicked spirit. Milton calls him the 'sociable spirit', and the 'affable archangel' (*Paradise Lost*, vii, 40), and it was he who was sent by God to advertise Adam of his danger.

Raphael, the sociable spirit, hath designed
To travel with Tobias, and secured
His marriage with the seven-times-wedded maid
*Paradise Lost*, v, 221–3

Longfellow makes him the angel of the Sun:

I am the angel of the Sun,
Whose flaming wheels began to run
When God Almighty's breath
Said to the darkness and the night,
'Let there be light,' and there was light, –
I bring the gift of faith.
*Golden Legend*, *The Miracle Play*, iii

Raphael is usually distinguished in art by a pilgrim's staff, or carrying a fish, in allusion to his aiding Tobias to capture the fish which performed the miraculous cure of his father's eyesight.

**Raphaelesque.** In the style of the great Italian painter Raphael (1483–1520), who was specially notable for his supreme excellence in the equable development of all the essential qualities of art – composition, expression, design, and colouring.

***Raphael's cartoons.*** *See* Cartoon.

**Rapparee.** A wild Irish plunderer; so called from his being armed with a *rapaire*, or half-pike.

**Rappee.** A coarse species of snuff, manufactured from dried tobacco by an instrument called in French a *râpe*, or rasp; so called because it is *râpé*, rasped.

**Rara avis** (Lat. a rare bird). A phenomenon; a prodigy; a something quite out of the common course. First applied by Juvenal to the black swan, which, since its discovery in Australia, is quite familiar to us, but was quite unknown before.

Rara avis in terris nigroque simillima cygno (a bird rarely seen on the earth, and very like a black swan) Juvenal, vi, 165

**Rare Ben.** The inscription on the tomb of Ben Jonson, the dramatist (1573–1637), in the Poets' Corner, Westminster Abbey, 'O rare Ben Jonson', was, says Aubrey, 'done at the charge of Jack Young [afterwards knighted], who, walking there when the grave was covering, gave the fellow eighteenpence to cut it'.

**Raree Show.** A peep-show; a show carried about in a box. In the 17th century, when this word appears in England, most of the travelling showmen were Savoyards, and this represents their attempt at English pronunciation.

**Rascal.** Originally a collective term for the rabble of an army, the commonalty, the mob, this word was early (14th cent.) adopted as a term of the chase, and for long almost exclusively denoted the lean, worthless deer of a herd. In the late 16th century it was retransferred to people, and so to its present meaning, a mean rogue, a scamp, a base fellow. Shakespeare says, 'Horns! the noblest deer hath them as huge as the rascal'; Palsgrave calls a starveling animal, like the lean kine of Pharaoh, 'a rascall refus beest' (1530). The French have *racaille* (riff-raff).

Come, you thin thing; come, you rascal.
Shakespeare, *2 Henry IV*, 5, 4

***Rascal counters.*** Pitiful *£ s. d.*, 'filthy lucre'. Brutus calls money paltry compared with friendship, etc.

When Marcus Brutus grows so covetous,
To lock such rascal counters from his friends
Be ready, gods, with all your thunderbolts,
Dash him to pieces.
Shakespeare, *Julius Caesar*, 4, 5

**Rasiel.** The angel who, according to the Talmud, was the tutor of Adam.

**Rasselas.** Prince of Abyssinia, in Dr Johnson's philosophical romance of that name (1759). He dwells in a secluded 'Happy Valley', shut off from all contact with the world or with evil, and his story points the moral of Omar – that it is best to 'take the Cash and let the Credit go'.

'Rasselas' is a mass of sense, and its moral precepts are certainly conveyed in striking and happy language. The mad astronomer who imagined that he possessed the regulation of the weather and the distribution of the seasons, is an original character in romance; and the happy valley in which Rasselas resides is sketched with poetical feeling. Young

**Rat.** The Egyptians and Phrygians deified rats. The people of Bassora and Cambay to the present time forbid their destruction. In Egypt the rat symbolised utter destruction, and also wise judgment, the latter because rats always choose the best bread.

Pliny tells us (VIII, lvii) that the Romans drew presages from these animals, and to see a *white* rat foreboded good fortune. The bucklers at Lanuvium being gnawed by rats presaged ill-fortune, and the battle of the Marses, fought soon after, confirmed this superstition. Prosperine's veil was embroidered with rats.

***As wet as,*** or ***like a drowned rat.*** Soaking wet; looking exceedingly dejected. Drowned rats certainly look deplorably wet, but so also do drowned mice, drowned cats, drowned dogs, etc.

***I smell a rat.*** I perceive there is something concealed which is mischievous. The allusion is to a cat *smelling* a rat, while unable to *see* it.

***Irish rats rhymed to death.*** It was once a prevalent opinion that rats in pasturages could be extirpated by anathematising them in rhyming verse or by metrical charms. This notion is frequently alluded to by ancient authors. Thus, Ben Jonson says: 'Rhyme them to death, as they do Irish rats' (*Poetaster*); Sir Philip Sidney says: 'Though I will not wish unto you … to be rimed to death, as is said to be done in Ireland' (*Defence of Poesie*); and Shakespeare makes Rosalind say: 'I was never so be-rhymed since … I was an Irish rat,' alluding to the Pythagorean doctrine of the transmigration of souls (*As You Like It*, 3, 2).

***Rats!*** An exclamation of incredulity, wonder, surprise, etc.

***To rat.*** To forsake a losing side for the stronger party, as rats are said to forsake unseaworthy ships. One who deserts his party, as a 'blackleg' during a strike, is sometimes called a rat.

> Averting …
> The cap of sorrow from their lips,
> And fly like rats from sinking ships.
>
> Swift, *Epistle to Mr Nugent*

***To take a rat by the tail.*** French colloquialism (*Prendre un rat par la queue*) for to cut a purse. The phrase dates back to the age of Louis XIII. Of course, a cutpurse would cut the purse at the string, or else he would spill the contents.

***Rat, Cat, and Dog.***

> The Rat, the Cat, and Lovell the Dog,
> Rule all England under the Hog.

The *Rat*, i.e. Rat-cliff; the *Cat*, i.e. Cat-esby; and *Lovel the Dog*, is Francis, Viscount Lovel, the king's 'spaniel'. The *Hog* or boar was the crest of Richard III. William Collingham, the author of this rhyme, was put to death for his pregnant wit.

**Rat-killer.** Apollo received this aristocratic soubriquet from the following incident: Crinis, one of his priests, having neglected his official duties, Apollo sent against him a swarm of rats; but the priest, seeing the invaders coming, repented and obtained forgiveness of the god, who annihilated the swarms which he had sent with his far-darting arrows.

**Ratatosk.** The squirrel that runs up and down Yggdrasil (*q.v.*), the tree of old Norse myth.

**Ratisbon, Interim of.** *See* Augsburg.

**Rattening.** Destroying or taking away a workman's tools, or otherwise incapacitating him from doing work, with the object of forcing him to join a trade union or to obey its rules. The term used to be common in Yorkshire, but is not heard much nowadays.

**Ravana.** A gigantic ten-faced demon of Hindu legend, who was fastened down between heaven and earth for 10,000 years by Siva's leg, for attempting to move the hill of heaven to Ceylon.

**Raven.** A bird of ill omen; fabled to forebode death and bring infection and bad luck generally. The former notion arises from their following an army under the expectation of finding dead bodies to *raven* on; the latter notion is a mere offshoot of the former, seeing pestilence kills as fast as the sword.

> The boding raven on her cottage sat,
> And with hoarse croakings warned us of our fate.
>
> Gay, *Pastorals*; *The Dirge*

> Like the sad-presaging raven that tolls
> The sick man's passport in her hollow beak,
> And, in the shadow of the silent night,
> Does shake contagion from her sable wing.
>
> Marlowe, *Jew of Malta* (1592)

Jovianus Pontanus relates two skirmishes between ravens and kites near Beneventum, which prognosticated a great battle, and Nicetas speaks of a skirmish between crows and ravens as presaging the irruption of the Scythians into Thrace. Cicero was forewarned of his death by the fluttering of ravens, and Macaulay relates the legend that a raven entered the chamber of the great orator the very day of his murder and pulled the clothes off his bed. Like many other birds, ravens indicate by their cries the approach of foul weather, but 'it is ful unleful to beleve that God sheweth His prevy counsayle to crowes, as Isidore sayth'.

> Of inspired birds ravens are accounted the most prophetical. Accordingly, in the language of that district, 'to have the foresight of a raven' is to this day a proverbial expression.
>
> Macaulay, *History of St Kilda*, p. 174

When a flock of ravens forsakes the woods we may look for famine and mortality, because 'ravens bear the characters of Saturn, the author of these calamities, and have a very early perception of the bad disposition of that planet'. *See* Athenian Oracle, Supplement, p. 476.

> As if the great god Jupiter had nothing else to doe but to dryve about jacke-dawes and ravens.
>
> Carneades

According to Roman legend ravens were once as white as swans and not inferior in size; but one day a raven told Apollo that Coronis, a Thessalian nymph whom he passionately loved, was faithless. The god shot the nymph with his dart; but, hating the tell-tale bird –

He blacked the raven o'er,
And bid him prate in his white plumes no more.
Addison, *Translation of Ovid*, Bk ii

In Christian art the raven is an emblem of God's Providence, in allusion to the ravens which fed Elijah. St Oswald holds in his hand a raven with a ring in its mouth; St Benedict has a raven at his feet; St Paul the Hermit is drawn with a raven bringing him a loaf of bread, etc.

***The fatal raven,*** consecrated to Odin, the Danish war god, was the emblem on the Danish standard, *Landeyda* (the desolation of the country), and was said to have been woven and embroidered in one noontide by the daughters of Regner Lodbrok, son of Sigurd, that dauntless warrior who chanted his death-song (the *Krakamal*) while being stung to death in a horrible pit filled with deadly serpents. If the Danish arms were destined to defeat, the raven hung his wings; if victory was to attend them, he stood erect and soaring, as if inviting the warriors to follow.

The Danish raven, lured by annual prey,
Hung o'er the land incessant.
Thomson, *Liberty*, Pt iv

***The two ravens that sit on the shoulders of Odin*** are called Huginn and Muninn (*Mind* and *Memory*).

**Ravenstone** (Ger. *rabenstein*). The old stone gibbet of Germany; so called from the ravens which are wont to perch on it.

Do you think
I'll honour you so much as save your throat
From the Ravenstone, by choking you myself?
Byron, *Werner*, ii, 2

**Raw. *Johnny Raw.*** A raw recruit; a 'new chum', greenhorn.

***To touch one on the raw.*** To mention something that makes a person wince, like touching a horse on a raw place in cleaning him.

**Rawhead and Bloody-Bones.** A bogy at one time the terror of children.

Servants awe children and keep them in subjection by telling them of Rawhead and Bloodybones. Locke

**Raymond** (in *Jerusalem Delivered*). Master of 4,000 infantry, Count of Toulouse, equal to Godfrey in the 'wisdom of cool debate' (Bk iii). This Nestor of the Crusaders slew Aladine, the king of Jerusalem, and planted the Christian standard upon the tower of David (Bk xx).

**Razee.** An old naval term for a ship of war cut down (or *razed*) to a smaller size, as a seventy-four reduced to a frigate.

**Razor. *To cut blocks with a razor.*** *See* Cut.

**Razzia.** An incursion made by the military into an enemy's country for the purpose of carrying off cattle or slaves, or for enforcing tribute. It is the French form of an Arabic word, and is usually employed in connection with Algerian and North African affairs.

**Razzle-dazzle.** A boisterous spree, a jollification in which – as a rule – alcohol plays a not unimportant part.

***On the razzle-dazzle.*** On the spree; on an hilarious drunken frolic.

**Re** (Lat.). Respecting; in reference to; as, '*re* Brown', in reference to the case of Brown.

**Reach** of a river. The part which lies between two points or bends: so called because it *reaches* from point to point.

When he drew near them he would turn from each,
And loudly whistle till he passed the Reach.
Crabbe, *Borough*

**Read. *To read between the lines.*** *See* Line.

***To read oneself in.*** Said of a clergyman on entering upon a new incumbency, because one of his first duties is to give a public reading of the Thirty-nine Articles in the church to which he has just been appointed, and to make the Declaration of Assent.

**Reader.** The designation of certain lecturers at many of the Universities, as the *Reader in Roman Law* (Durham), the *Reader in Phonetics* (London). In the Inns of Court, one who reads lectures in law. In printing, one who reads and corrects proof-sheets before publication. In a publisher's office, one who reads and reports on manuscripts submitted for publication.

**Ready.** An elliptical expression for ready money. Goldsmith says, *Aes in presenti perfectum format* ('Ready-money makes a man perfect'). (*Eton Latin Grammar.*)

Lord Strut was not very flush in the 'ready'.
Dr Arbuthnot

**Ready-to-Halt.** A pilgrim in Pt ii of Bunyan's *Pilgrim's Progress* who journeyed on crutches. He joined the party under the charge of Mr Great-heart, but 'when he was sent for' he threw away his crutches, and, lo! a chariot bore him into paradise.

**Real Presence.** The doctrine that Christ Himself is present in the bread and wine of the Eucharist after consecration. In the Church of England 'real' implies that –

The Body of Christ is given, taken, and eaten, in the Supper, only after an heavenly and spiritual manner. (Thirty-nine Articles; No. xxviii)

In the Roman Catholic and Lutheran Churches 'real' implies that the actual Body is present – in the former case by transubstantiation, and in the latter by consubstantiation.

**Ream** (ultimately from Arab, *rizmah*, a bundle).

A ream of paper, unless otherwise specified, contains 480 sheets; a 'perfect' ream for printing papers contains 516 sheets; a ream of envelope paper contains 504 sheets, and of news, 500 sheets.

An 'insides' ream contains 480 sheets all 'insides', i.e. 20 good or inside quires of 24 sheets; a 'mill' ream contains 480 sheets, and consists of 18 'good' or 'insides' quires of 24 sheets each, and 2 'outsides' quires of 24 sheets each.

**Rearmouse** or **Reremouse.** The bat (A.S., *hrere-mus*, probably the fluttering-mouse, from *hrere-an*, to move or flutter). Of course, the 'bat' is not a winged mouse.

**Reason.** ***It stands to reason.*** It is logically manifest; this is the Latin *constat* (*constare*, literally, to stand together).

***The Goddess of Reason.*** The central figure in a blasphemous mockery of Christianity that formed part of the orgies during the worst phase of the French Revolution. The rôle was taken by various young women of questionable repute, who, in turns, were enthroned and 'worshipped' in the cathedral of Notre Dame. Mlle Candeille, of the Opéra, was one of the earliest of these 'goddesses' (Nov. 10th, 1793); she wore a red Phrygian cap, a white frock, a blue mantle, and tricolour ribbons; her head was filleted with oak-leaves, and in her hand she carried the pike of Jupiter-Peuple. Others were Mme Momoro (wife of the printer), and the actresses Mlle Maillard and Mlle Aubray. The procession was attended by the municipal officers and national guards, while troops of ballet girls carried 'torches of truth'; and, incredible as it may seem, Gobet (Archbishop of Paris), and nearly all the clergy stripped themselves of their canonicals, and, wearing red nightcaps, joined in this blasphemous mockery. So did Julien of Toulouse, a Calvinistic minister.

> Mrs Momoro, it is admitted, made one of the best goddesses of Reason, though her teeth were a little defective.
>
> Carlyle, *French Revolution*, vol. iii, Bk v, 4

***The woman's reason.*** 'I think so just because I *do* think so' (*see Two Gentlemen of Verona*, 1, 2).

> First then a woman will, or won't, depend on't;
> If she will do't, she will, and there's an end on't.
>
> Aaron Hill, *Epilogue to 'Zara'*

**Rebecca's Camels Bible.** *See* Bible, specially named.

**Rebeccaites.** Welsh rioters in 1843, who, led by a man in woman's clothes, went about demolishing turnpike gates. The name was taken from Gen. 24:60. When Rebecca left her father's house, Laban and his family 'blessed her', and said, 'Let thy seed possess the gate of those that hate them.'

**Rebellion, the Great.** In English history, the struggle between Parliament (the people) and the Crown, which began in the reign of James I, broke into Civil War in 1642, and culminated in the execution of Charles I (Jan. 29th, 1649).

The revolts in favour of the Stuarts in 1715 and 1745 (*see* Fifteen; Forty-five) have also each been called *The Rebellion.*

**Rebus** (Lat., with things). A hieroglyphic riddle, *non verbis sed rebus.* The origin of the word has, somewhat doubtfully, been traced to the baso-chiens of Paris who, during the carnival, used to satirise the follies of the day in squibs called *De rebus quae geruntur* (on the current events), and, to avoid libel actions, employed hieroglyphics either wholly or in part.

In heraldry the name is given to punning devices on a coat of arms suggesting the name of the family to whom it belongs: as the broken spear on the shield of Nicholas *Breakspear* (Pope Adrian IV).

**Rechabites.** Members of a teetotal benefit society (the Independent Order of Rechabites), founded in 1835, and so named from Rechab, who enjoined his family to abstain from wine and to dwell in tents (Jer. 35:6, 7).

**Recipe, Receipt.** *Recipe* is Latin for take, and contracted into ℞ is used in doctors prescriptions. The dash through the R represents ♃, the symbol of Jupiter, and ℞ means *Recipe, deo volente.*

**Reckon.** ***I reckon.*** A peculiar phraseology common in the Southern States of America. Those in New England say, 'I guess.' (*Cp.* Calculate.)

***Day of reckoning.*** Settlement day; when one has to pay up one's account or fulfil one's obligation; also used of the Day of Judgment.

***Dead reckoning.*** *See under* Dead.

***Out of one's reckoning.*** Having made a mistake – in the date, in one's expectation, etc., or an error of judgment.

***To reckon without one's host.*** *See* Host.

**Recollects.** *See* Franciscans.

**Record.** That which is *recorded* (originally 'got by heart' – Lat. *cor, cordis*, heart); hence the modern meaning, the best performance or most striking event of its kind recorded, especially in such phrases as *to beat the record*, *to do it in record time*, etc.; also the engraved disk on which music that can be audibly transmitted by means of a gramophone is recorded.

***Court of Record.*** A court whose proceedings are officially recorded and can be produced as evidence.

**Recreant** is one who yields (from O.Fr. *recroire*, to yield in trial by combat); alluding to the judicial combats, when the person who wished to give in cried for mercy, and was held a coward and infamous.

**Rector.** *See* Clerical Titles.

**Red.** One of the *primary colours* (*q.v.*); in heraldry said to signify magnanimity and fortitude; in ecclesiastical use worn in honour of martyrs, and on Ash Wednesday and the remaining days of Holy Week and on Whit-Sunday; and in popular folklore the colour of magic.

> Red is the colour of magic in every country, and has been so from the very earliest times. The caps of fairies and musicians are well-nigh always red.
>
> Yeats, *Fairy and Folk Tales of the Irish Peasantry*, p. 61

Nowadays it is more often symbolical of anarchy and revolution – 'Red ruin, and the breaking up of laws' (Tennyson, *Guinevere*, 421). In the French Revolution the *Red Republicans* were those extremists who never hesitated to dye their hands in blood in order to accomplish their political object, and in Bolshevist Russia the *Reds*, with their *Red Army*, have played the same part. In Russia red is supposed to be the beautiful colour. *Kracá* is beauty; *kracnie* is red. This may account for its adoption by the Bolsheviki, but, in general, red is regarded as the colour of liberty. *See* Red flag *below*.

In the old ballads *red* was frequently applied to gold ('the gude red gowd'), and this use still survives in thieves' cant, a gold watch being a *red kettle*, and the chain a *red tackle*. One of the names given by the alchemists to the Philosophers' Stone (*q.v.*) was *the red tincture*, because, with its help, they hoped to transmute the base metals to gold.

***Admiral of the Red.*** *See* Admiral.

***Red Book.*** A directory relating to the court, the nobility, and the 'Upper Ten' generally. The *Royal Kalendar*, published from 1767 to 1893, was known by this name, as also Webster's *Royal Red Book*, a similar work, first issued in 1847.

The name is also given to other special works covered in red, as, e.g. the old Austro-Hungarian Empire, the official parliamentary papers of which corresponded to our 'Blue Books' (*q.v.*). A book which gave account of the court expenditure in France before the Revolution, and an English manuscript containing the names of those who held lands *per baroniam* in the reign of Henry II, etc.

***The Red Book of Hergest.*** A Welsh manuscript of the 14th century, containing the *Mabinogion* (*q.v.*), poems by Taliesin and Llywarch Hen, a history of the world from Adam to AD 1320, etc. It is now the property of Jesus College, Oxford.

***The Red Book of the Exchequer.*** *Liber ruber Scaccarii* in the Record Office. It was compiled in the reign of Henry III (1246), and contains the returns of the tenants *in capite* in 1166, who certify how many knights' fees they hold, and the names of those who hold or held them; also the only known fragment of the Pipe Roll of Henry II, copies of the important Inquisition returned into the exchequer in 13 John, and matter from the Pipe Rolls and other sources. It was printed in the Rolls Series (edited by Hubert Hall) in 1896.

***Red button.*** In the Chinese Empire a mandarin of the first class wore one of these as a badge of honour in his cap. *Cp.* Panjandrum.

> An interview was granted to the admiral [Elliot] by Kishen, the imperial commissioner, the third man in the empire, a mandarin of first class and red button.
>
> Howitt, *History of England*, 1841, p. 471

***Mother Red Cap.*** An old nurse 'at the Hungerford Stairs'. Dame Ursley, or Ursula, another nurse, says of her rival –

> She may do very well for skippers' wires, chandlers' daughters, and suchlike, but nobody shall wait on pretty Mistress Margaret … excepting and saving myself.
>
> Scott, *Fortunes of Nigel*

***Not a red cent.*** No money at all; 'stony-broke'. An Americanism; the cent used to be copper, but is now an alloy of copper, tin, and zinc.

***Red Comyn.*** Sir John Comyn of Badenoch, nephew of John Balliol, king of Scotland, so called from his ruddy complexion and red hair, to distinguish him from his kinsman 'Black

Comyn', who was swarthy and black-haired. He was stabbed by Robert Bruce (1306) in the church of the Minorites at Dumfries, and afterwards dispatched by Lindesay and Kirkpatrick.

***The Red Crescent.*** The Turkish equivalent of the Red Cross (*q.v.*), i.e. the military hospital service.

***Red Cross.*** The badge adopted by all civilised nations (except Mohammedans, who, in its place, use the *Red Crescent*), in accordance with the Geneva Convention of 1864, as that of military ambulance and hospital services, hospital ships, etc. It is a red Greek cross on a white ground, and is also called the *Geneva Cross.*

Hence the name of various national societies for the relief of the wounded and sick.

Also, the St George's Cross (*q.v.*), the basis of the Union Jack, and the old national emblem of England.

***The Red Cross Knight*** in Spenser's *Faërie Queene* (Bk I) is a personification of St George, the patron saint of England. He typifies Christian Holiness, and his adventures are an allegory of the Church of England. The Knight is sent by the Queen to destroy a dragon which was ravaging the kingdom of Una's father. With Una he is driven into Wandering Wood, where they encounter Error, and pass the night in Hypocrisy's cell. Here he is deluded by a false vision and, in consequence, abandons Una and goes with Duessa (False-faith) to the palace of Pride. He is persuaded by Duessa to drink of an enchanted fountain, becomes paralysed, and is taken captive by Orgoglio, whereupon Una seeks Arthur's help, and the prince goes to the rescue. He slays Orgoglio, and the Red Cross Knight is taken by Una to the house of Holiness to be healed. On leaving Holiness they journey onwards, and as they draw near the end of their quest, the dragon flies at the knight, who has to do battle with it for three whole days before he succeeds in slaying it. The Red Cross Knight and Una are then united in marriage.

***The Red Feathers.*** The Duke of Cornwall's Light Infantry. They cut to pieces General Wayne's brigade in the American War, and the Americans vowed to give them no quarter. So they mounted red feathers that no others might be subjected to this threat. They still wear red puggarees on Indian service. *See* Lacedaemonians.

***Red flag.*** The emblem of anarchy, Bolshevism, Communism, and red revolution and rebellion generally. English Communists have a 'battle hymn' with this title, which has been adopted also as that of anarchical and seditious journals. The red flag was used during the French Revolution as the symbol of insurrection and terrorism, and in the Roman Empire it signified war and a call to arms.

***Red-handed.*** In the very act; as though with red blood of murder still on his hand.

***The Red Hand of Ulster.*** *See* Ulster.

***Red-haired persons*** have for centuries had the reputation of being deceitful and unreliable – probably owing to the tradition that Judas Iscariot (*q.v.*) had red hair. The fat of a dead red-haired person used to be in request as an ingredient for poisons (*see* Middleton's *The Witch*, V, ii), and Chapman says that flattery, like the plague –

> Strikes into the brain of man,
> And rageth in his entrails when he can,
> Worse than the poison of a red-hair'd man.
>
> *Bussy d'Ambois*, iii, ii

The old rhyme says –

> With a red man rede thy rede;
> With a brown man break thy bread;
> At a pale man draw thy knife;
> From a black man keep thy wife.

*See also* Hair.

***The Red Hat.*** The cardinalate.

> David Beatoun was born of good family ... and was raised to a red hat by Pope Paul III.
>
> Prince, *Parallel History*, vol. ii, p.81

***Red herring.*** *See* Herring.

***Indian red.*** Red haematite (peroxide of iron), found abundantly in the Forest of Dean, Gloucestershire. It is of a deep, laky hue, used for flesh tints. *Persian red*, which is of a darker hue with a sparkling lustre, is imported from the island of Ormuz in the Persian Gulf.

The Romans obtained this pigment from the island of Elba. *Insulam exhaustis chalybum generosa metallis* (Ovid).

***Red Indians.*** The North-American Indians; so called because of their copper-coloured skin; also called *redskins* and *red men.* The Mormons regard them as a branch of the Hebrew race, who lost their priesthood, and with it their colour, intelligence, and physiognomy, through disobedience.

***A red-laced jacket.*** Military slang for a flogging.

***Red-lattice phrases.*** Pot-house talk. A red

lattice at the doors and windows was formerly the sign that an alehouse was duly licensed; see the page's quip on Bardolph in *2 Henry IV*, 2, 2 – "a calls me e'en now, my lord, through a red lattice, and I could discern no part of his face from the window.'

> I, I, I myself sometimes, leaving the fear of heaven on the left hand, ... am fain to shuffle, to hedge and to lurch; and yet you rogue, will ensconce your rags ... your red-lattice phrases ... under the shelter of your honour.
>
> Shakespeare, *Merry Wives of Windsor*, 2, 2

***The Red Laws.*** The civil code of ancient Rome. Juvenal says, *Per lege rubras majoram leges* (*Satires*, xiv, 193). The civil laws, being written in vermilion, were called *rubrica*, and *rubrica vetavit* means, It is forbidden by the civil laws.

> The praetor's laws were inscribed in *white* letters, as Quintilian informs us (xii, 3 '*praetores edicta sua in albo proponebant*') and imperial rescripts were written in purple.

***Red-letter day.*** A lucky day; a day to be recalled with delight. In almanacs, saints' days and holidays are printed in red ink, other days in black; and only these have special services in our Prayer Book.

> 'It's a great piece of luck, ma'am,' said Mrs Belfield, 'that you should happen to come here of a holiday! ... Why, you know, ma'am, today is a red-letter day!'
>
> Fanny Burney, *Cecilia*, X, vi

***To see the red light.*** To be aware of approaching disaster. Often said of one who's pretty sure his 'number is up', he's going to 'get the sack' or a serious reprimand. The phrase comes from the railway-line, where the red light signifies danger.

***Red man.*** A term of the old alchemists, used in conjunction with 'white woman' to express the affinity and interaction of chemicals. In the long list of terms that Surface scoffingly gives (Ben Jonson's *The Alchemist*, II, iii) 'your red man and your white woman' are mentioned.

The French say that a red man commands the elements, and wrecks off the coast of Brittany those whom he dooms to death. The legend affirms that he appeared to Napoleon and foretold his downfall.

*See also* Red Indians, *above*.

***To paint the town red.*** *See* Paint.

***Red rag.*** Old slang for the tongue. In French, *Le chiffon rouge*; and *balancer le chiffon rouge* means to prate.

> Discovering in his mouth a tongue,
> He must not his palaver balk;
> So keeps it running all day long,
> And fancies his red rag can talk.
>
> Peter Pindar, *Lord B. and his Motions*

Also in the phrase *Like a red rag to a bull*, anything that is calculated to excite rage.

***Red Sea.*** So called by the Romans (*Mare rubrum*) and by the Greeks, as a translation of the Semitic name, the reason for which is uncertain; also formerly called the 'Sedgy Sea', because of the seaweed which collects there.

***To see red.*** To give way to excessive passion or anger; to be violently moved, run amok.

***Red snow.*** Snow reddened by the presence of a minute alga, *Protococcus nivalis*, in large numbers. It is not at all uncommon in arctic and alpine regions, where its sanguine colour formerly caused it to be regarded as a portent of evil.

***Red tape.*** Official formality, or rigid adherence to rules and regulations, carried to excessive lengths; so called because lawyers and government officials tie their papers together with red tape. Charles Dickens is said to have introduced the expression; but it was the scorn continually poured upon this evil of officialdom by Carlyle that brought it into popular use.

During the Great War many attempts – some ill-advised – were made to get rid of 'red tape' in the great Government departments; and perhaps the worst feature of it is that, after all, it has its uses, and without it things are liable to go wrong and get into fearsome muddles. What is wanted is 'the happy mean' – and happy means are not always easily discoverable.

**Redan** (Fr. *redent*, notched or jagged like teeth). The simplest of fieldworks, and very quickly constructed. It consists of two faces at an angle formed thus, the angle, of salient, being towards the enemy.

**Redbreasts.** The old Bow Street 'runners', police officers combining the duties of informers, detectives, and general agents.

> The Bow Street runners ceased out of the land soon after the introduction of the new police. I remember them very well as standing about the door of the office in Bow Street. They had no other uniform than a blue dress-coat, brass buttons ... and a bright red cloth waistcoat ... The slang name for them was 'Redbreasts'.
>
> Dickens, *Letters*, vol. ii, p 178

**Redcoats.** British soldiers, from the colour of the uniform formerly universal in line regiments. Red is the colour of the royal livery;

and it is said that this colour – technically called 'pink' (*q.v.*) – was adopted by huntsmen because fox-hunting was declared a royal sport by Henry II.

**Redder.** One who tries to separate parties fighting, the adviser, the person who *redes* or interferes. Thus the proverb, 'The redder gets aye the warst lick of the fray.'

Those that in quarrels interpose
Must often wipe a bloody nose.
Gay, *Fables*, No. 34

Hence, a blow received by a peace-maker who interferes between two combatants is called a *redding-blow*, or *-stroke*.

Said I not to ye, 'Make not, meddle not'; beware of the redding-straik?
Scott, *Guy Mannering*, ch. xxvii

**Rede** (A.S. *raed*). Counsel, advice; also as verb. *To reck one's own rede.* To be governed by one's own better judgment.

Do not, as some ungracious pastors do,
Show me the steep and thorny way to heaven,
Whilst, like a puffed and reckless libertine,
Himself the primrose path of dalliance treads,
And recks not his own rede.
Shakespeare, *Hamlet*, 1, 3

**Reductio ad absurdum.** A proof of inference arising from the demonstration that every other hypothesis involves an absurdity. Thus, suppose I want to prove that the direct road from two given places is the shortest, I should say, 'It must either be the shortest or not the shortest. If *not* the shortest, then some other road is the direct road; but there cannot be two shortest roads, therefore the direct road must be the shortest.'

**Reduplicated** or **Ricochet Words.** There are probably some hundreds of these words, which usually have an intensifying force, in use in English. The following, from ancient and modern sources, will give some idea of their variety: chit-chat, click-clack, clitter-clatter, dilly-dally, ding-dong, drip-drop, fal-lal, flim-flam, fiddle-faddle, flip-flap, flip-flop, handy-pandy, harum-scarum, helter-skelter, heyve-keyve, higgledy-piggledy, hob-nob, hodge-podge, hoity-toity, hubble-bubble, hugger-mugger, hurly-burly, mingle-mangle, mish-mash, mixy-maxy, namby-pamby, niddy-noddy, niminy-piminy, nosy-posy, pell-mell, ping-pong, pit-pat, pitter-patter, pribbles and prabbles, randem-tandem, randy-dandy, razzle-dazzle, rift-raff, roly-poly, shilly-shally, slip-slop, slish-slosh, tick-tack, tip-top, tittle-tattle, wibble-wobble, wig-wag, wiggle-waggle, wish-wash, wishy-washy.

**Ree.** An interjection formerly used by teamsters when they wanted the horses to go to the right. 'Heck!' or 'Hey!' was used for the contrary direction.

Who with a hey and ree the beasts command.
*Micro Cynicon* (1599)

***Riddle me, riddle me ree.*** Expound my riddle rightly.

**Reed.** ***A broken*** or ***bruised reed.*** Something not to be trusted for support; a weak adherent. Egypt is called a broken reed, in which Hezekiah could not trust if the Assyrians made war on Jerusalem, 'which broken reed if a man leans on, it will go into his hand and pierce it' (*see* 2 Kings 18:21; Is.6:6).

Lean not on Earth, 'twill pierce thee to the heart;
A broken reed at best; but oft, a spear.
Young, *Night Thoughts*, ii

***A reed shaken by the wind.*** A person blown about by every wind of doctrine. John the Baptist (said Christ) was not a 'reed shaken by the wind', but from the very first had a firm belief in the Messiahship of the Son of Mary, and this conviction was not shaken by fear or favour. *See* Matt. 11:7.

**Reef.** *He must take in a reef or so.* He must reduce his expenses; he must retrench. A reef is that part of a sail which is between two rows of eyelet holes. The object of these eyelet holes is to reduce the sail reef by reef as it is required.

**Reekie, Auld.** A familiar name for Edinburgh. It is said that Durham of Largo, one of the old, patriarchal lairds, was in the habit of regulating the time of evening worship by the appearance of the smoke of Edinburgh. When it increased, in consequence of the good folk preparing supper, he would say, 'It is time noo, bairns, to tak the buike and gang to our beds, for yonder's auld Reekie, I see, putting on her night-cap.'

Yonder is auld Reekie. You may see the smoke hover over her at twenty miles' distance.
Scott, *The Abbot*, xvii

**Reel.** *Right off the reel.* Without intermission. A reel is a device for winding rope. A reel of cotton is a certain quantity wound on a bobbin.

We've been travelling best part of twenty-four hours right off the reel.
Boldrewood, *Robbery under Arms*, ch. xxxi

In the cinematograph world a *reel* is a convenient length of film for winding on one spool and showing at one performance; hence, a *five-reel story* is a long one – one 'to be continued in our next'.

The Scotch dance, *reel*, is from Gaelic *righil* or *ruithil*.

**Reeve's Tale, The.** One of the 'broadest' in Chaucer's *Canterbury Tales*, and fittingly placed in the mouth of one who is neither an ecclesiastic nor one of the 'gentles', but an upper servant. The tale occurs frequently in the jest- and story-books of the 16th and 17th centuries. Boccaccio has it in the *Decameron* (Day xi, nov. vi), but Chaucer probably took it from Jean de Bove's fabliau, *Gombert et des Deux Clercs*.

**Referendum.** The submission of a definite political question to the whole electorate for a direct decision by the general vote. This is not done in Great Britain, but is a general rule in Switzerland. After the Great War certain questions, as the apportionment of Schleswig-Holstein and other disputed areas, were submitted to a plebiscite, which is not quite the same thing as a referendum, but is the taking of a general vote as to future policy.

**Refresher.** An extra fee paid to a barrister in long cases in addition to his retaining fee, originally to remind him of the case entrusted to his charge.

**Regan.** The second of King Lear's unfilial daughters, in Shakespeare's tragedy – 'most barbarous, most degenerate'. She was married to the Duke of Cornwall.

**Regatta.** A boat-race, or organised series of boat-races; the name originally given to the races held between Venetian gondoliers, the Italian meaning 'strife' or 'contention'.

**Regent's Park** (London). This park, covering 472 acres, was originally attached to a palace of Queen Elizabeth, but at the beginning of the 17th century much of the land was let on long leases, which fell in early in the 19th century. It was laid out by the architect, John Nash (d.1835) for the Prince Regent (George IV), and named in honour of him.

**Regiomontanus.** The Latin equivalent of *Königsberger*, adopted as a patronymic by Johann Müller (1436–76), the German mathematician and astronomer, who was born at Königsberg and became Bishop of Ratisbon.

**Regium donum** (Lat.). An annual grant of public money to the Presbyterian, Independent, and Baptist ministers of Ireland. It began in 1672, and was commuted in 1869.

**Regius Professor.** One who holds in an English university a professorship founded by Henry VIII. Each of the five Regius Professors of Cambridge receives a royally-endowed stipend of about £40. In the universities of Scotland they are appointed by the Crown. The present stipend is about £400 or £500.

**Regulars.** All the British military forces serving in the army as a profession, as distinct from the *Auxiliary Forces*, viz. the Special Reserve (which takes the place of the old Militia), and the Territorial Force (i.e. Yeomanry and the old Volunteers).

**Rehoboam** (2 Chron. 13:7). A fanciful name sometimes given to a measure of claret, a double jeroboam (*q.v.*).

1 rehoboam = 2 jeroboams or 32 pints.
1 jeroboam = 2 tappet-hens or 16 pints.
1 tappet-hen = 2 magnums or 8 pints.
1 magnum = 2 quarts or 4 pints.

Charlotte Brontë – *why* is not known – applied the name to some sort of clerical hat.

> He [Mr Helstone] was short of stature [and wore] a rehoboam, or shovel hat, which he did not … remove. *Shirley*, ch. i

**Reimkennar, A.** A sorceress among the ancient Scandinavians, one who *kens*, or is skilled in, numbers. Norna of the Fitful Head (in Scott's *The Pirate*) was a Reimkennar, 'a controller of the elements'.

**Rein** (connected with *retain*, from Lat. *retinere*, to hold back). The strap attached to the bit, used in guiding horses. *To give the reins.* To let go unrestrained; to give licence.

***To take the reins.*** To assume the guidance or direction.

**Reinikin.** The name given to Reynard's youngest son in Caxton's version of *Reynard the Fox*. His brothers were Reynardin and Rossel.

**Reins** (Lat. *renes*). The kidneys, supposed by the Hebrews and others to be the seat of knowledge, pleasure, and pain. The Psalmist says (16:7), 'My reins instruct me in the night season', Solomon (Prov. 23:16), 'My reins shall rejoice when thy lips speak right things', and Jeremiah says (Lam. 3:13), God 'caused his arrows to enter into my reins', i.e. sent pain into my kidneys.

**Reldresal.** Principal secretary for private affairs in the court of Lilliput and great friend of Gulliver (Swift, *Gulliver's Travels*). When it was proposed to put the Man-Mountain to death for high treason, Reldresal moved that the 'traitor should have both his eyes put out, and be suffered to live that he might serve the nation'.

**Relics, Christian.** Among the relics which are officially shown in Rome, and publicly adored by the highest dignitaries of the Christian Church, with all the magnificence of ecclesiastical pomp and ritual, the following may be mentioned:

A bottle of the Virgin's milk.
The cradle and swaddling clothes of the infant Jesus.
The cross of the penitent thief.
The crown of thorns.
The finger of Thomas with which he touched the wound in the side of Jesus.
Hair of the Virgin Mary.
The handkerchief of St Veronica, on which the face of Jesus was miraculously pictured.
Hay of the Manger in which the infant Jesus was laid.
Heads of Peter, Paul, and Matthew.
The inscription set over the cross by the order of Pilate.
Nails used at the crucifixion.
Piece of the chemise of the Virgin Mary.
The silver money given to Judas by the Jewish priests, which he flung into the Temple, and was expended in buying the potters' field as a cemetery for strangers.
The table on which the soldiers cast lots for the coat of Jesus.

Brady (*Clavis Calendaria*, p. 240) mentions many others, some of which are actually impossibilities, as, for example, a rib of the *Verbum caro factum*, a vial of the sweat of St Michael when he contended with Satan, and some of the rays of the star which guided the wise men.

**Religious.** ***His Most Religious Majesty.*** The title by which the kings of England were formerly addressed by the Pope. It still survives in the Prayer Book, in the Prayer 'for the High Court of Parliament under our most religious and gracious King at this time assembled' (which was written, probably by Laud, in 1625), and in James I's Act for a Thanksgiving on the Fifth of November occurs the expression 'most great, learned, and religious king'.

In the Middle Ages, and later, the Popes did not use the names of the various sovereigns, but addressed them by special appellations: thus the king of France was always addressed by the Vatican as 'Most Christian'; the king of Austria as 'Most Apostolic'; the king of Spain as 'Most Catholic'; the king of Portugal as 'Most Faithful'; the king of England as 'Most Religious'.

**Rem acu.** You have hit the mark; you have hit the nail on the head. *Rem acu tetigisti* (Plautus, *Rudens*, v, ii, 19).

> '*Rem acu* once again,' said Sir Piercie.
>
> Scott, *The Monastery*, ch. xvi

**Remember!** The last injunction of Charles I, on the scaffold, to Bishop Juxon. It has been interpreted as meaning that Charles, who was at heart a Catholic, felt that his misfortunes were a divine visitation on him for retaining church property confiscated by Henry VIII, and made a vow that if God would restore him to the throne, he would restore this property to the Church. He was asking the Bishop to remember this vow, and to see that his son carried it out. Charles II, however, wanted all the money he could get, and the church lands were never restored.

**Remigius, St.** Remy (438–533), bishop and confessor, is represented as carrying a vessel of holy oil, or in the act of anointing therewith Clovis, who kneels before him. When Clovis presented himself for baptism, Remy said to him, 'Sigambrian, henceforward burn what thou hast worshipped, and worship what thou hast burned.'

**Remis atque velis,** or **Remis velisque** (Lat.). With oars and sails. Tooth and nail; with all dispatch.

> We were going *remis atque velis* into the interests of the Pretender, since a Scot had presented a Jacobite at court.
>
> Scott, *Redgauntlet* (conclusion)

**Remonstrants.** Another name for the Arminians (*q.v.*).

**Renaissance** (Fr., re-birth). The term applied, broadly, to the movement and period of transition between the mediaeval and modern worlds which, beginning with Petrarch and sequent Italian humanists in the 14th century, was immensely stimulated by the fall of Constantinople (1453), resulting in the dissemination of Greek scholarship and Byzantine art, the invention of printing (about the same time), and the discovery of America (1492). In England this revival first manifested itself in the early years of the 16th century, and affected principally literature and, later, architecture.

> All the Renaissance principles of art tended, as I have before often explained, to the setting Beauty above Truth, and seeking for it always at the expense of Truth. And the proper punishment of such pursuit – the punishment which all the laws of the universe rendered inevitable – was, that those who thus pursued beauty should wholly lose sight of beauty.
>
> Ruskin, *Modern Painters*, IV, xvi, § 12

**Renard.** ***Une queue de renard.*** A mockery. At one time a common practical joke was to fasten a fox's tail behind a person against whom a laugh was designed. Panurge (*q.v.*) never refrained from attaching a fox's tail or the ears of a leveret behind a Master of Arts or Doctor of Divinity, whenever he encountered them. (*Gargantua* ii, 16.) *See also* Reynard.

> C'est une petite vipère,
> Qui n'épargneroit pas son père,
> Et qui par nature ou par art
> Scait couper la queue au renard
>
> Beaucaire, *L'Embarras de la Foire*

**Renault of Montauban.** One of Charlemagne's knights and paladins. In the last chapter of *The Four Sons of Aymon*, Renault, as an act of penance, carries the hods of mortar for the building of St Peter's, at Cologne.

> Since I cannot improve our architecture, ... I am resolved to do like Renault of Montauban, and I will wait on the masons ... As it was not in my good luck to be cut out for one of them, I will live and die the admirer of their divine writings.
>
> Rabelais, *Pantagruel*, Bk v. Prol.

**Rendezvous.** The place to which you are to repair, a meeting, a place of muster or call. Also used as a verb. (Fr., *rendez*, betake; *vous*, yourself.)

> His house is a grand rendezvous of the *élite* of Paris.
>
> The Imperial Guard was ordered to rendezvous in the Champs de Mars.

**René, *Le bon Roi René*** (1408–80). Son of Louis II, Duc d'Anjou, Comte de Provence, father of Margaret of Anjou. The last minstrel monarch, just, joyous, and debonair; a friend to chase and tilt, but still more so to poetry and music. He gave in largesses to knights-errant and minstrels (so says Thiebault) more than he received in revenue.

> Studying to promote, as far as possible, the immediate mirth and good humour of his subjects ... he was never mentioned by them excepting as *Le bon Roi René*, a distinction ... due to him certainly by the qualities of his heart, if not by those of his head.
>
> Scott, *Anne of Geierstein*, ch. xxix

**Repenter Curls.** The long ringlets of a lady's hair. *Repentir* is the French for a penitentiary, and *les repenties* are the girls sent there for reformation. Mary Magdalen had such long hair that she wiped off her tears therewith from the feet of Jesus. Hence the association of long curls and reformed (*repenties*) prostitutes.

**Reply Churlish.** Sir, you are no judge; your opinion has no weight with me. Or, to use Touchstone's illustration (*As You Like It*, 5, 4), 'If a courtier tell me my beard is not well cut, and I disable his judgment, I give him the reply churlish, which is the fifth remove from the lie direct, or, rather, the lie direct in the fifth degree.'

**Reproof Valiant.** Sir, allow me to tell you that is not the truth. This is Touchstone's fourth remove from the lie direct, or, rather, the lie direct in the fourth degree (*see above*).

> The reproof valiant, the countercheck quarrelsome, the lie circumstantial, and the lie direct, are not clearly defined by Touchstone. The following, perhaps, will give the distinction required: *That* is not true; How *dare* you utter such a falsehood; *If* you said so, you are a liar; You are a liar, or you lie.

**Republic of Letters, The.** The world of literature; authors generally and their influence. Goldsmith, in *The Citizen of the World*, No. 20 (1760), says it 'is a very common expression among Europeans': it is found in Molières *Le Mariage Forcé*, Sc. vi (1664).

**Republican Queen.** Sophia Charlotte (1668–1705), wife of Frederick I of Prussia, was so nicknamed. Charlottenburg was named after this philosophical lady.

**Requests, Court of.** *See* Conscience, Court of.

**Reremouse.** *See* Rearmouse.

**Resolute. *The Resolute Doctor.*** John Baconthorp (d.1346), head of the Carmelites in England (1329–33) and commentator on Aristotle.

***The Most Resolute Doctor.*** Guillaume Durandus de St Pourçain, (d. about 1333), a French Dominican philosopher, bishop of Méaux (1326), and author of *Commentaires sur Pierre Lombard* (publ. 1508).

**Responsions.** *See* Smalls.

**Restorationists.** The followers of Origen's opinion that all persons, after a purgation proportioned to their demerits, will be restored to Divine favour and taken to Paradise.

**Resurrection Men.** Grave robbers, body-snatchers (*q.v.*). First applied to Burke and Hare, in 1829, who rifled graves to sell the bodies for dissection, and sometimes even murdered people for the same purpose.

> The body-snatchers, they have come,
> And made a snatch at me;
> 'Tis very hard them kind of men
> Won't let a body be.
> The cock it crows – I must be gone –
> My William, we must part:
> But I'll be yours in death although
> Sir Astley has my heart.
>
> Hood, *Mary's Ghost*

The reference is to Sir Astley Cooper (d.1841), the great surgeon and lecturer on anatomy.

**Retiarius** (Lat.). A gladiator who made use of a net (*rete*), which he threw over his adversary.

As in the thronged amphitheatre of old
The wary Retiarius trapped his foe.
Thomson, *Castle of Indolence*, canto ii

**Retort Courteous, The.** Sir, I am not of your opinion; I beg to differ from you; or, to use Touchstone's illustration (*As You Like It*, 5, 4), 'If I said his beard was not cut well, he was in the mind it was.' The lie seven times removed; or rather, the lie direct in the seventh degree.

**Returned Letter Office.** *See* Blind Department.

**Reveillé** (Fr. *réveiller*, to awake). The signal, by bugle or beat of drums notifying soldiers that it is time to rise, and informing the sentries that they may forbear from challenging.

**Revenons à nos moutons.** *See* Moutons.

**Reverend.** An archbishop is *the Most Reverend* (Father in God); a bishop, *the Right Reverend*; a dean, *the Very Reverend*; an archdeacon, *the Venerable*; all the rest of the clergy, *the Reverend*.

**Revised Version, The.** *See* Bible, the English.

**Revival of Letters, The.** A term applied to the Renaissance (*q.v.*) in so far as the movement reacted on literature. It really commenced earlier – at the close of the Dark Ages (*q.v.*) – but it received its chief impulse from the fall of Constantinople (1453) and the consequent dispersal over Europe of Greek MSS and Greek scholars.

**Revue.** A theatrical entertainment characterised by bright and witty songs and music, dancing, and constant change, with almost entire absence of plot and (hence the name) usually allusions to current topics.

*Revue* amuses by fun, by satire of passing events, by gorgeous spectacle which delights the child in all of us, by song and dance, by glimpses of drama, by the agility of man and the beauty of woman, above all by the rapid alternation of these elements; its crowning virtue is variety.
A. B. Walkley, in *The Times*, 22 Mar., 1922

**Reynard.** A fox. Caxton's form of the name in his translation (from the Dutch) of the *Roman de Renart* (*see* Reynard the Fox, *below*). *Renart* was the Old French form, from Ger. *Reginhart*, a personal name; the Dutch was *Reynaerd* or *Reynaert*.

Where prowling Reynard trod his nightly round.
Bloomfield, *Farmer's Boy*

***Reynard the Fox.*** A mediaeval beast-epic, satirising contemporary life and events in Germany, in which all the characters are animals. The chief of them, Reynard, typifies the church; his uncle, Isengrin the wolf, the baronial element; and Nobel the lion, the regal.

The germ of the story is found in Aesop's fable, *The Fox and the Lion*; this was built upon by more than one writer, but the *Roman* as we now know it is by a Fleming named *Willem*, of the early 13th century, of which a new and enlarged version was written about 1380 by an unknown author, Caxton having made his translation from a late 15th century Dutch version of this, which was probably by Herman Barkhusen.

***False Reynard.*** By this name Dryden describes the Unitarians in his *Hind and Panther*.

With greater guile
False Reynard fed on consecrated spoil;
The graceless beast by Athanasius first
Was chased from Nice, then by Socinus nursed.
Pt i, 51–54

***Reynard's globe of glass.*** Reynard, in *Reynard the Fox* (*see above*), said he had sent this invaluable treasure to her majesty the queen as a present; but it never came to hand, inasmuch as it had no existence except in the imagination of the fox. It was supposed to reveal what was being done – no matter how far off – and also to afford information on any subject that the person consulting it wished to know.

***Your gift was like the globe of glass of Master Reynard.*** *Vox et praeterea nihil.* A great promise, but no performance.

**Reynardine.** In *Reynard the Fox* the eldest son of Reynard. He assumed the names of Dr Pedanto and Crabron. His brothers were Rossel and Reinikin.

**Reynold of Montalbon.** *See* Renault.

**Rezio.** *See* Dr Rezio.

**Rhadamanthus.** One of the three judges of hell; Minos and Aeacus being the other two. (*Greek mythology*.)

**Rhampsinitos.** The Greek form of Rameses III, the richest of the Egyptian kings, who amassed seventy-seven millions sterling, which he secured in a treasury of stone, but by an artifice of the builder he was robbed every night.

Herodotus (Bk ii, ch. 121) tells us that two brothers were the architects of the treasury, and that they placed in the wall a removable stone, through which they crept every night to purloin the store. The king, after a time, noticed the diminution and set a trap to catch the thieves. One of the brothers was caught in the trap, but the other brother, to prevent detection, cut off his head and made good his escape.

The tale is almost identical with that of Trophonius, told by Pausanias.

**Rhapsody,** meant originally 'songs strung together' (Gr. *rapto*, to sew or string together; *ode*, a song). The term was applied to the books of the *Iliad* and *Odyssey*, of which bards collected together a number of fragments, enough to make a connected 'ballad', and sang them as our minstrels sang the deeds of famous heroes. Those bards who sang the *Iliad* wore a *red* robe, and those who sang the *Odyssey* a *blue* one. Pisistratus of Athens had all these fragments carefully compiled into their present form.

**Rheims-Douai Version, The.** *See* Douai Bible.

**Rhino.** Slang for money; the term was in use as early as the 17th century. *See under* Nose, *To pay through the nose.*

Some as I know,
Have parted with their ready rhino.
*The Seaman's Adieu* (1670)

**Rhodian Bully, The.** The Colossus of Rhodes (*q.v.*).

Yet fain wouldst thou the crouching world bestride,
Just like the Rhodian bully o'er the tide.
Peter Pindar, *The Lusiad*, canto 2

**Rhodian Law, The.** The earliest system of marine law known to history; compiled by the Rhodians about 900 BC.

**Rhopalic Verse.** Verse consisting of lines in which each successive word has more syllables than the one preceding it (Gr., *rhopalon*, a club, which is much thicker at one end than at the other).

| Rem | tibi | confeci, |
|---|---|---|
| Spes | deus | aeternae-est |
| Hope | ever | solaces |
| 1 | 2 | 3 |
| doctissime, | dulcisonorum | |
| stationis | conciliator | |
| miserable | individuals. | |
| 4 | 5 | |

**Rhyme.** ***Neither rhyme nor reason.*** Fit neither for amusement nor instruction. An author took his book to Sir Thomas More, chancellor in the reign of Henry VIII, and asked his opinion. Sir Thomas told the author to turn it into rhyme. He did so, and submitted it again to the lord chancellor. 'Ay! ay!' said the witty satirist, 'that will do, that will do. 'Tis rhyme now, but before it was neither rhyme nor reason'.

The lines on his pension, traditionally ascribed to Spenser, are well known:

I was promised on a time
To have reason for my rhyme;
From that time unto this season,
I received nor rhyme nor reason.

**Rhymer.** ***Thomas the Rhymer.*** A border poet and seer of the close of the 13th century, also called Thomas of Erceldoune and Thomas Learmont. He is the reputed author of a number of poems, including one on Tristran (which Scott believed to be genuine), and is fabled to have predicted the death of Alexander III of Scotland, the Battle of Bannockburn, the union of England and Scotland under James VI, etc. Of course he must not be confused with Thomas Rymer (d.1713), Historiographer Royal to William III. *See* True Thomas.

**Rhyming Slang.** A kind of slang, formerly even more popular than it is now with costers, etc., in which the word intended was replaced by one that rhymed with it, as 'Charley Prescott' for *waistcoat*, 'plates of meat' for *feet.* When the rhyme is a compound word the rhyming part is almost invariably dropped, leaving one who does not know the lingo somewhat in the dark. Thus Chivy (Chevy) Chase rhymes with 'face', by dropping 'chase' *chivy* remains, and becomes the accepted slang word. Similarly, daisies=*boots*, thus: daisy-roots will rhyme with 'boots', drop the rhyme and *daisy* remains. By the same process *sky* is slang for *pocket*, the compound word which gave birth to it being 'sky-rocket'. 'Christmas', a *railway guard*, as 'Ask the Christmas', is, of course, from 'Christmas-card'; and 'raspberry', *heart*, is 'raspberry-tart'.

Then came a knock at the Rory o' More [door]
Which made my raspberry beat.

Other examples are given under their proper heads.

**Rhyming to Death.** The Irish at one time believed that their children and cattle could be 'eybitten', that is, bewitched by an evil eye, and that the 'eybitter', or witch, could 'rime' them to death: *See* Rats.

**Ribbonism.** The principles, etc., of the Ribbon Society, a secret Roman Catholic association organised in Ireland about 1808. Its two main objects were (1) to secure fixity of tenure, called the tenant-right; and (2) to deter anyone from taking land from which a tenant has been ejected. The name arose from a ribbon worn as a badge in the buttonhole.

Plying a person secretly with threatening letters in order to drive him out of the neighbourhood, or to compel him to do something he objects to used to be known as the *Ribbon dodge*, because the Ribbon men sent such letters, often decorated with rude drawings of coffins, cross-bones, or daggers, to obnoxious neighbours.

**Ribston Pippin.** So called from Ribston, in Yorkshire, where the first pippins, introduced from Normandy about 1707, were planted. It is said that Sir Henry Goodricke planted three pips; two died, and from the third came all the Ribston apple trees in England.

**Rice.** The custom of throwing rice after a bride comes from India, rice being, with the Hindus, an emblem of fecundity. The bridegroom throws three handfuls over the bride, and the bride does the same over the bridegroom. With us the rice is thrown by neighbours and friends. *Cp.* Marriage Knot.

***Rice Christians.*** Converts to Christianity for worldly benefits, such as a supply of rice to Indians. Profession of Christianity born of lucre, not faith.

***Rice-paper.*** *See* Misnomers.

**Richard Roe.** *See* Doe.

**Richmond. *Another Richmond in the field.*** Said when another unexpected adversary turns up. The reference is to Shakespeare's *Richard III*, 5, 4, where the king, speaking of Henry of Richmond (afterwards Henry VII), says –

> I think there be six Richmonds in the field;
> Five have I slain today, instead of him.
> A horse! a horse! my kingdom for a horse!

**Rick Mould. *Fetching the rick mould*** is a 'flat-catching' trick played during the hay-harvest. The greenhorn is sent to borrow a rickmould, with strict injunction not to drop it. Something very heavy is put in a sack, and hoisted on the greenhorn's back; and when he has carried it carefully in the hot sun to the hayfield he gets well laughed at for his pains.

**Ricochet.** The skipping of a flung stone over water ('ducks and drakes'), the bound of a bullet or other projectile after striking; hence, applied to anything repeated over and over again, e.g. the fabulous bird that had only one note. Marshal Vauban (1633–1707) invented a *ricochet battery*, the application of which was ricochet firing.

**Riddle.** Josephus relates how Hiram, King of Tyre, and Solomon had once a contest in riddles, when Solomon won a large sum of money but he subsequently lost it to Abdemon, one of Hiram's subjects.

Plutarch states that Homer died of chagrin because he could not solve a certain riddle. *See* Sphinx.

***Riddle me riddle me ree.*** *See* Ree.

***A riddle of claret.*** Thirteen bottles, a magnum and twelve quarts; said to be so called because in certain old golf clubs magistrates invited to the celebration dinner presented the club with this amount, sending it in a *riddle* or sieve.

**Ride. *Riding the marches.*** *See* Bounds, Beating the.

***To ride abroad with St George, but at home with St Michael***; said of a henpecked braggart. St George is represented as riding on a war charger whither he listed; St Michael, on a dragon. Abroad a man rides, like St George, on a horse which he can control and govern; but at home he has 'a dragon' to manage, like St Michael.

***To ride and tie.*** Said of a couple of travellers who have only one horse between them. One rides on ahead and then ties the horse up and walks on, the other taking his turn on the horse when he has reached it.

***To ride for a fall.*** To proceed with one's business recklessly; usually, also desperately and regardless of consequences.

***To ride up Holborn Hill.*** *See* Holborn.

**Rider.** An addition to a manuscript, like a codicil to a will; an additional clause tacked to a bill in Parliament, *over-riding* the preceding matter when the two come into collision; hence, a corollary or obvious supplement, and, in Euclid, etc., a subsidiary problem.

**Ridiculous. *There is but one step from the sublime to the ridiculous.*** In his *Age of Reason* (1794), Pt ii, *note*, Tom Paine said, 'The sublime and the ridiculous are often so nearly related that it is difficult to class them separately. One step above the sublime makes the ridiculous, and one step above the ridiculous makes the sublime again.'

Napoleon, who was a great admirer of Tom Paine, used to say, 'Du sublime au ridicule il n'y a qu'un pas.'

**Riding.** The three administrative divisions of Yorkshire are so called because each forms the *third* part of the county, A.S. *thriding*; the initial *th-* of the old word being lost through amalgamation with the *east*, *west*, or *north*. The divisions of Tipperary are (and those of Lincolnshire formerly were) also called ridings.

Some others of the counties have special names for their parts, as the *laths* of Kent and *rapes* of Sussex.

**Ridotto** (Ital.). An assembly where the company is first entertained to music, and then joins in dancing. The word originally meant music reduced to a full score (Lat. *reductus*).

**Rien de trop.** *See* De trop.

**Riff-raff.** The offscouring of society, perhaps the 'refuse and sweepings'. *Raff* in Swedish means sweepings, but the old French term *rif et raf* meant one and all, whence the phrase *Il n'a laissé ni rif ni raf* (he has left nothing behind him). Gabriel Harvey (in *Pierce's Supererogation*, 1593) speaks of 'the riffe-raffe of the scribbling rascality'.

> I have neither ryff nor ruff [rag to cover me nor roof over my head]. *Coventry Myst.*, p. 224

**Rifle.** The firearm gets its name from the spiral grooves (Low Ger. *riffel*, Swed. *refla*) in the bore, which give the bullet a rotatory motion. The verb, *to rifle*, meaning to pillage or plunder, is connected with this through the O.Fr. *rifler*, to graze, scratch, strip, etc.

**Rift in the Lute.** A small defect which mars the general result.

> Unfaith in aught is want of faith in all
> It is the little rift within the lute
> That by-and-by will make the music mute,
> And ever widening slowly silence all.
> Tennyson, *Martin and Vivien*; *Vivien's Song*

**Rig.** There is more than one word in these three letters, but the etymology and division of them are alike uncertain. In the sense of dressing it was originally applied to a ship; a ship that is thoroughly furnished with spars, gear, tackle, and so on is *well rigged*, and its ropes and stays are its *rigging*. Hence, *a good rig out*, a first-rate outfit in clothes, equipment, etc.

The word also formerly was used of a strumpet, and a lewd woman was said to be *riggish*. Also, a hoax or dodge; hence a swindle, and the phrase *to rig the market*, to raise or lower prices by underhand methods so that one can make a profit.

***To run the rig.*** To have a bit of fun, or indulge in practical jokes.

> He little thought when he set out
> Of running such a rig. Cowper, *John Gilpin*

**Rigadoon.** A lively dance for two people, said to have been invented towards the close of the 17th century by a dancing-master of Marseilles named *Rigadou*.

> Isaac's Rigadoon shall live as long
> As Raphael's painting, or as Virgil's song.
> Jenyns, *Art of Dancing*, canto ii

**Rigdum Funnidos,** a character in Carey's burlesque of *Chrononhotonthologos* (1734).

The name of this character supplied the sobriquet given by Sir Walter Scott to John Ballantyne (1774–1821), his publisher, because he was full of fun.

> A quick, active, intrepid, little fellow … full of fun and merriment … all over quaintness and humorous mimicry, … a keen and skilful devotee of all manner of field-sports from fox-hunting to badger-baiting inclusive.
> Lockhart

**Right.** In politics the *Right* is the Conservative party, because in the continental chambers the Conservatives sit on the right-hand side of the Speaker, the Liberals, Radicals, and Labour on the left.

***It'll all come right in the end.*** The cry of the optimist when things are going wrong and he has good reason to fear the worst.

***In one's right mind.*** Sane; in a normal state after mental excitement. The phrase comes from Mark 5:15:

> And they … see him that was possessed with the devil, and had the legion, sitting, and clothed, and in his right mind.

***Miner's right.*** The Australian term for a licence to dig for gold – a formidable looking document, engrossed on parchment.

***Right as a trivet.*** Quite right; in an excellent state. The trivet was originally a three-legged stand – a tripod – and the allusion is to its always standing firmly on its three legs.

***Right foot foremost.*** It is still considered unlucky to enter a house, or even a room, on the left foot, and in ancient Rome a boy was stationed at the door of a mansion to caution visitors not to cross the threshold with their left foot, which would have been an ill omen.

***Right-hand man.*** An invaluable, or confidential, assistant; originally applied to the cavalryman at the right of the line, whose duties were of great responsibility.

***Right Honourable.*** A prefix to the title of earls, viscounts, barons, and the younger sons of dukes and marquesses. All privy councillors and some lord mayors and other civic dignitaries are also *Right Honourables*. The corresponding prefix for a marquess is *The Most Honourable*, and for a duke *His Grace*. Younger sons of earls, and all sons of viscounts and barons are *Honourables*, as are justices of the High Court, maids of honour, and certain Colonial and Indian ministers. Members of Parliament when in the House are usually addressed as 'My honourable friend', or 'the honourable member for So-and-so'.

***Righto!*** or ***Right ho!*** A colloquial form of cheerful assent; *right you are* is a similar exclamation.

***Right of way.*** The legal right to make use of a certain passage whether high road, by-road, or private road. Private right of way may be claimed by immemorial usage, special permission, or necessity; but a funeral *cortège* or bridal party having passed over a certain field does not give to the public the right of way, as many suppose.

***To do one right.*** To be perfectly fair to him, to do him justice.

> King Charles, and who'll do him right now?
>
> Browning, *Cavalier Tunes*

In Elizabethan literature the phrase is very common, and meant to answer when one's health had been drunk.

> *Falstaff* [*To* Silence, *who drinks a bumper*]: Why, now you have done me right.
>
> Shakespeare, *2 Henry IV*, 5, 3

***To send one to the right about.*** To clear him off, send him packing – generally 'with a flea in his ear'.

**Rights. *Declaration of Rights.*** An instrument submitted to William and Mary and accepted by them (February 13th, 1689), setting forth the fundamental principles of the constitution. The chief items are: The Crown cannot levy taxes without the consent of Parliament, nor keep a standing army in times of peace; the Members of Parliament are free to utter their thoughts, and a Parliament is to be convened every year; elections are to be free, trial by jury to be inviolate, the right of petition not to be interfered with, and the Sovereign should take the oath against Transubstantiation and not marry a Roman Catholic.

***To rights.*** In apple-pie order.

***To put things to rights.*** To put every article in its proper place.

**Rig-marie.** An old Scottish coin of low value. The word originated from one of the 'billon' coins struck in the reign of Queen Mary, which bore the words *Reg. Maria* as part of the legend.

> Billon is mixed metal for coinage, especially silver largely alloyed with copper.

**Rigmarole.** A rambling, disconnected account, an unending yarn.

> You never heard such a rigmarole ... He said he thought he was certain he had seen somebody by the rick and it was Tom Bakewell who was the only man he knew who had a grudge against Farmer Blaize and if the object had been a little bigger he would not mind swearing to Tom and would swear to him for he was dead certain it was Tom only what he saw looked smaller and it was pitch-dark at the time ... etc.
>
> Meredith, *Richard Feverel*, ch. xi

The word is said to be a popular corruption of *Ragman Roll* (*q.v.*); it is recorded from the early 18th century.

**Rigol.** A circle or diadem (Ital. *rigolo*, a little wheel).

> [Sleep] That from this golden rigol hath divorced
> So many English kings.
>
> Shakespeare, *2 Henry IV*, 4, 4

**Rig-veda.** *See* Veda.

**Rigwoodie.** Unyielding; stubborn. A *rigwiddie* is the band which crosses the back of a horse to hold up the shafts of a cart (*rig* = back, *withy* = twig).

> Withered beldams, auld and droll,
> Rigwoodie hags. Burns, *Tam O'Shanter*

**Rile.** A dialect word, common in Norfolk and other parts for stirring up water to make it muddy; hence, to excite or disturb, and hence the modern colloquial meaning, to vex, annoy, make angry. It comes from O.Fr. *roillier*, to roll or flow (of a stream).

**Rimfaxi.** *See* Hrimfaxi.

**Rimmon.** The Babylonian god who presided over storms. Milton identifies him with one of the fallen angels:

> Him followed Rimmon, whose delightful seat
> Was fair Damascus, on the fertile bank
> Of Abbana and Pharphar, lucid streams.
>
> *Paradise Lost*, Bk i, 467

***To bow the knee to Rimmon.*** To palter with one's conscience; to do that which one knows to be wrong so as to save one's face. The allusion is to Naaman obtaining Elisha's permission to worship the god when with his master (2 Kings, 5:18).

**Rinaldo.** One of the great heroes of mediaeval romance (also called Renault of Montauban, Regnault, etc.), a paladin of Charlemagne, cousin of Orlando (*q.v.*), and one of the four sons of Aymon. He was the owner of the famous horse Bayard, and is always painted with the characteristics of a borderer – valiant, ingenious, rapacious, and unscrupulous.

In Tasso's *Jerusalem Delivered* Rinaldo was the Achilles of the Christian army, despising gold and power but craving renown. He was the son of Bertoldo and Sophia, and nephew of Guelpho. At fifteen he joined the Crusaders as an adventurer, and having slain Gernando, was summoned by Godfrey to public trial, but went into voluntary exile.

In Ariosto's *Orlando Furioso* he appears as the son of the fourth Marquis d'Este, Lord of Mount Auban or Albano, eldest son of Amon or Aymon, nephew of Charlemagne, and Bradamant's brother. He was the rival of his cousin Orlando, but Angelica detested him. He was called 'Clarmont's leader', and brought an auxiliary force of English and Scots to Charlemagne, which 'Silence' conducted into Paris.

**Ring.** The noun (meaning a circlet) is the A.S. *hring*; the verb (to sound a bell, or as a bell) is from A.S. *hringan*, to clash, ring, connected with Lat. *clangere*, to clang.

Custom decrees that if a man or woman is willing to marry but is not engaged, a ring should be worn on the index finger of the left hand; if engaged, on the second finger; if married, on the third finger; but if there is no desire to marry, on the little finger.

A ring worn on the forefinger is supposed to indicate a haughty, bold, and overbearing spirit; on the long finger, prudence, dignity, and discretion; on the marriage finger, love and affection; on the little finger, a masterful spirit. *Cp.* Wedding Finger.

As the forefinger was held to be symbolical of the Holy Ghost, priests used to wear their ring on this in token of their spiritual office.

The use of a ring as the emblem of marriage is of very ancient date, and perhaps arose from the circumstance that the ring was the seal with which orders were 'signed' (Gen. 38:18; Esth. 3:10–12), so the woman who had the ring could issue commands as her husband, and was in every respect his representative. The delivery of a ring was a sign that the giver endowed the person who received it with all the power he himself possessed (Gen. 41:42).

> In the Roman espousals the man gave the woman a ring by way of pledge, and the woman put it on the third finger of her left hand, because it was believed that a nerve ran from that finger to the heart.
>
> Macrobius, *Sat.* vii, 15

Amongst the Romans, only senators, chief magistrates, and in later times knights, enjoyed the *jus annuli aurei*, the right to wear a ring of gold. The emperors conferred this upon whom they pleased, and Justinian extended the privilege to all Roman citizens.

***Rings Noted in Fable.***

***Agramant's ring.*** This enchanted ring was given by Agramant to the dwarf Brunello, from whom it was stolen by Bradamant and given to Melissa. It passed successively into the hands of Rogero and Angelica (who carried it in her mouth) (*Orlando Furioso*, Bk v).

***The ring of Amasis.*** A ring with the same story as that of Polycrates. *See below.*

***Corcud's ring.*** This magic ring was composed of six metals, and ensured the wearer success in any undertaking in which he chose to embark (*Chinese Tales*; *Corcud and his Four Sons*).

***The Doge's ring.*** The doge of Venice, on Ascension Day, used to throw a ring into the sea from the ship *Bucentaur* (*q.v.*), to denote that the Adriatic was subject to the republic of Venice as a wife is subject to her husband. *See* Doge.

***The ring of Edward the Confessor.*** It is said that Edward the Confessor was once asked for alms by an old man, and gave him his ring. In time some English pilgrims went to the Holy Land, and happened to meet the same old man, who told them he was John the Evangelist, and gave them the identical ring to take to 'Saint' Edward. It was preserved in Westminster Abbey.

***The ring of Gyges.*** *See* Gyges.

***The ring of Innocent.*** On May 29th, 1205, Innocent III sent John, King of England, four gold rings set with precious stones, and explained that the *rotundity* signifies *eternity* – remember we are passing through time into eternity; the *number* signifies the *four* virtues which make up constancy of mind – viz. justice, fortitude, prudence, and temperance; the *material* signifies 'wisdom from on high', which is as gold purified in the fire; the *green* emerald is emblem of 'faith', the *blue* sapphire of 'hope', the *red* garnet of 'charity', and the *bright* topaz of 'good works'. (Rymer, *Faedera*, vol. i, 139.)

***Dame Liones' ring,*** given by her to Sir Gareth during a tournament. It ensured the wearer from losing blood when wounded.

> 'This ring', said Dame Liones, 'increaseth my beauty … That which is green it turns red, and that which is red it turns green. That which is blue it turns white and that which is white it turns blue. Whoever beareth this ring can never lose blood, however wounded.'
>
> *History of Prince Arthur*, i, 146

***Luned's ring*** rendered the wearer invisible. Luned or Lynet gave it to Owain, one of King Arthur's knights.

> Take this ring, and put it on thy finger, with the stone inside thy hand, and close thy hand upon it. As long as thou concealest the stone the stone will conceal thee.
>
> *Mabinogion* (*Lady of the Fountain*)

***The Ring of the Nibelung.*** *See* Nibelung.

***The ring of Ogier*** (*q.v.*) was given him by Morgan le Fay. It removed all infirmities, and restored the aged to youth again.

***Otnit's ring of invisibility*** belonged to Otnit, King of Lombardy, and was given to him by the queen-mother when he went to gain the soldan's daughter in marriage. The stone had the virtue of directing the wearer the right road to take in travelling (*The Heldenbuch*).

***Polycrates' ring*** was flung into the sea to propitiate Nemesis, and was found again by the owner inside a fish. *Cp.* Kentigern.

***Reynard's wonderful ring.*** This ring, which existed only in the brain of Reynard, had a stone of three colours – red, white, and green. The *red* made the night as clear as the day; the *white* cured all manner of diseases; and the *green* rendered the wearer of the ring invincible (*Reynard the Fox*, ch. xii).

***Solomon's ring,*** among other wonderful things, sealed up the refractory Jinni in jars, and cast them into the Red Sea.

***The steel ring,*** made by Seidel-Beckit, enabled the wearer to read the secrets of another's heart (*Oriental Tales*; *The Four Talismans*).

***The talking ring*** was given by Tartaro, the Basque Cyclops, to a girl whom he wished to marry. Immediately she put it on, it kept incessantly saying 'You there, and I here'. In order to get rid of the nuisance, the girl cut off her finger, and threw it and the ring into a pond.

This Basque legend is given in Campbell's *Popular Tales of the West Highlands*, and in Grimm's *Tales* (*The Robber and his Sons*).

**Phrases.**

***A ring of bells.*** A set of bells (from three to twelve) for change ringing, tuned to the diatonic scale.

***It has the true ring*** – has intrinsic merit; bears the mark of real talent. A metaphor taken from the custom of judging genuine money by its 'ring' or sound.

***Ring off!*** Stop it! shut up! From the expression commonly used on the telephone when one has a wrong connection or it is desired that the conversation should cease.

***Ringing the changes.*** Properly, producing continual changes on a set of bells without repetition, *changes* being variations – according to certain rules – from the regular striking order.

Figuratively the phrase has two meanings: (1) to try every way of doing a thing, to 'run a thing to death', work it for all it's worth, etc., as in –

> I have likewise seen an Hymn in Hexameters to the Virgin *Mary* which filled a whole Book tho' it consisted but of the eight following Words:
>
> *Tot, tibi, sunt, Virgo, dotes, quot, sidera, Caelo*
>
> The Poet rung the changes upon these eight several Words and by that Means made his Verses almost as numerous as the Virtues and the Stars which they celebrated.
>
> Addison, *Spectator*, No. lx

(2) to swindle one over a transaction by bamboozling him in changing money. For example: A man goes to a tavern and asks for a drop of Scotch (8*d*.); he lays a ten-shilling note on the bar and receives nine shillings and fourpence in change. 'Oh!' says the man, 'give me the note back, I have such a lot of change.' He offers ten shillings in silver as he is handed the note, but just before the barmaid takes it he puts the lot together and says, 'There, let's have a quid instead of the note and silver.' This is done, and, of course, the barmaid loses ten shillings by the transaction.

***The Ring.*** Bookmakers or pugilists collectively, and the sports they represent; because the spectators at a prize-fight or race form a ring round the competitors. Specifically, *The Ring* is the hall for prize-fights in the Blackfriars Road.

***To lead the ring.*** *See* Ringleader.

***To make a ring.*** To combine in order to control the price of a given article. If the chief merchants of any article (say salt, flour, or sugar) combine, they can fix the selling price, and thus secure enormous profits.

***To make rings round one.*** To defeat him completely in some sport or competition, etc.; to outclass him easily.

***To ring an anchor.*** To haul it up so that its ring is at the hawse-hole or cathead.

***Ring posies*** or ***mottoes.***

(1) A E I (Greek for '*Always*').
(2) For ever and for aye.
(3) In thee, my choice, I do rejoice.
(4) Let love increase.
(5) May God above Increase our love.
(6) Not two but one Till life is gone.

(7) My heart and I, Until I die.
(8) When this you see, Then think of me.
(9) Love is heaven, and heaven is love.
(10) Wedlock, 'tis said, In heaven is made.

**Ring and the Book, The.** A long poem (20,934 lines), by Robert Browning, telling twelve times over, from different points of view, the story of a *cause célèbre* of Italian history (1698). Guido Franceschini, a Florentine nobleman of shattered fortune, marries Pompilia, an heiress, to repair his state. Pompilia is a supposititious child of Pietro, supplied by his wife, Violante, to prevent certain property going to an heir not his own. When the bride discovers the motive of the bridegroom, she reveals to him this fact, and the first trial occurs to settle the said property. The count treats his bride so brutally that she quits his roof under the protection of Caponsacchi, a young priest, and takes refuge in Rome. Guido follows and has them arrested; a trial ensues, a separation is permitted. Pompilia is sent to a convent and Caponsacchi is suspended for three years. Pompilia's health gives way, and as the birth of a child is expected, she is permitted to leave the convent and live with her putative parents. She pleads for a divorce, but, pending the suit, the child is born. The count, hearing thereof, murders Pietro, Violante, and Pompilia; but, being taken red-handed, is executed.

**Ringing Island.** One of the disguises under which the Church of Rome was satirised by Rabelais. It is an *island* because it is cut off from the world; and *ringing* because its bells are incessantly ringing: at matins, vespers, mass, sermon-time, noon, vigils, eves, and so on. It is entered only after four days' fasting, without which none in the Church enter holy orders.

**Ringleader.** The moving spirit, the chief, in some enterprise, especially one of a mutinous character; from the old phrase *to lead the ring*, the *ring* being a group of associated persons.

**Riot.** In Common Law there are five elements necessary to make a tumult, or disturbance of the peace, a riot, viz.:

(1) A number of persons, three at least; (2) common purpose; (3) execution or conception of the common purpose; (4) an intent to help one another by force if necessary against any person who may oppose them in the execution of their common purpose; (5) force or violence not merely used in demolishing, but displayed in such a manner as to alarm at least one person of reasonable firmness and courage.

If there are twelve persons or more present and they continue riotously and tumultuously together for one hour after the proclamation in the king's name ordering them to disperse has been read by a justice of the peace or other authorised person, the rioters are guilty of felony and can be punished by penal servitude for life (formerly it was a capital offence). This proclamation is popularly known as 'reading the Riot Act', for it is the opening section of the Riot Act of 1714 that is read on such occasions.

***To run riot.*** To act without restraint or control; to act in a very disorderly way. The phrase was originally used of hounds which had lost the scent.

**Rip.** ***He is a sad rip.*** A sad rake or debauchee; seems to be a perversion of *rep*, rep-robate, as in *demirep*.

> Some forlorn, worn-out old rips, broken-kneed and broken-winded.
>
> Du Maurier, *Peter Ibbetson*, Pt vi, p. 376

**Rip Van Winkle.** *See* Winkle.

**Riphaean Rocks.** A range of mountains in Scythia. Called by the Russians *Weliki Camenypoys* (great stone girdle).

**Ripon.** ***True as Ripon steel.*** Ripon used to be famous for its steel spurs, which were the best in the world. The spikes of a Ripon spur would strike through a shilling-piece without turning the point.

**Ripping.** Excellent, tip-top.

**Riquet with a Tuft.** One of Charles Perrault's fairy-tales (*Riquet à la Houppe*), borrowed from Straparola's *Nights*, and imitated by Madame Villeneuve in her *Beauty and the Beast*. Riquet is the acme of ugliness, but had the power of endowing her he loved best with wit and intelligence. He falls in love with a beautiful woman as stupid as Riquet is ugly, but possessing the power of endowing the person she loves best with beauty. The two marry and exchange gifts.

**Rise.** ***On the rise.*** Going up in price; becoming more valuable, especially of stocks and shares.

***To get a rise.*** Colloquial for to have an increase in salary.

***To take a rise out of one.*** To raise a laugh at his expense, to make him a butt. Hotten says this is a metaphor from fly-fishing; the fish *rise* to the fly, and are caught.

**Rising in the Air.** *See* Levitation.

**Ritschlianism.** The tenets held by the German theologian Albert Ritschl (1822–89) and his followers, viz. that metaphysics and philosophy had no bearing on theology and that Jesus Christ himself was the ground of knowledge of all parts of the theological system.

**Rivals.** Originally 'persons dwelling on opposite sides of a river' (Lat. *rivalis*, a riverman). Caelius says there was no more fruitful source of contention than river-right, both with beasts and men, not only for the benefit of its waters, but also because rivers are natural boundaries. Hence Ariosto compares Orlando and Agrican to 'two hinds quarrelling for the river-right' (xxiii, 83).

**Rivers.** *Miles in length.*

About 3,500, the Nile, the longest river in Africa, and almost the longest in the world.

About 2,400, the Volga, the longest river in Europe.

About 3,200, the Yang-tze-Kiang, the longest river in Asia.

About 3,900, the Lower Mississippi and the Missouri. The Mississippi itself, the longest river in North America, is 2,553 miles from mouth to source.

About 4,700, the Amazon, the longest river in South America and in the world.

About 228, the Thames, the longest river in Great Britain.

**Roach.** ***Sound as a roach***. An old saying; a translation of the French *Sain comme une gardon.*

**Road.** ***All roads lead to Rome.*** All efforts of thought converge in a common centre.

***Gentlemen of the road*** or ***knights of the road.*** Highwaymen. A first-class highwayman, like Dick Turpin, is a 'Colossus of Roads'.

In the mountain districts of North America a highwayman used to be called a *road agent*, and the term is still applied to bandits who hold up trains, motor-cars, etc.

> Road-agent is the name applied in the mountains to a ruffian who has given up honest work in the store, in the mine, in the ranch, for the perils and profits of the highway.
>
> W. Hepworth Dixon, *New America*, i, 14

***On the road.*** Progressing towards; as, *On the road to recovery;* said also of actors when 'on tour', and of commercial travellers.

***Road hog.*** *See* Hog.

***The rule of the road*** –

> The rule of the road is a paradox quite,
> In riding or driving along;
> If you go to the left you are sure to go right,
> If you go to the right you go wrong.

***To take to the road.*** To turn highwayman or become a tramp.

**Roads** or **Roadstead,** as 'Yarmouth Roads', a place where ships can safely *ride* at anchor. *Road*, A.S. *rād*, comes from *rīdan*, to ride.

**Roan.** A reddish-brown. This word used to be derived from Rouen, the town, because this was an Old French spelling of it (*un cheval rouen*); but there can be no connection, as the Italian was *rovano* or *roano*, and its etymology is unknown. Rouen may have given its name to *roan*, the soft sheepskin leather.

***Roan Barbary***. The famous charger of Richard II, which ate from his royal hand.

> Oh, how it yearned my heart when I beheld
> In London streets, that coronation day,
> When Bolingbroke rode on roan Barbary,
> That horse that thou so often hast bestrid,
> That horse that I so carefully have dressed.
>
> Shakespeare, *Richard II*, 5, 5

**Roarer.** A broken-winded horse is so called from the noise it makes in breathing.

**Roaring.** ***He drives a roaring trade.*** He does a great business; his employees are driven till all their wind is gone.

***Roaring boys.*** The riotous blades of Ben Jonson's time, whose delight it was to annoy quiet folk. At one time their pranks in London were carried to an alarming extent.

> And bid them think on Jones amidst this glee,
> In hope to get such roaring boys as he.
>
> *Legend of Captain Jones* (1659)

Dekker and Middleton wrote a play (1611) on Moll Cutpurse (*q.v.*) which they called *The Roaring Girl.*

***Roaring Meg.*** *See* Meg.

***The Roaring Forties.*** *See* Forty.

***The roaring game.*** So the Scots call the game of curling.

**Roast.** ***To roast a person*** is to banter him unmercifully; also, to give him a wigging, give him 'a hot time of it'. Shakespeare, in *Hamlet*, speaks of roasting 'in wrath and fire'.

***To rule the roast.*** To have the chief direction; to be paramount.

The phrase was common in the 15th century, and it is possible that *roast* was originally *roost*, the reference being to a cock, who decides which hen is to roost nearest to him; but it is unlikely; in Thomas Heywood's *History of Women* (about 1630) we read of 'her that ruled the roast in the kitchen'.

John, Duke of Burgoyne, ruled the rost, and governed both King Charles ... and his whole realme. Hall, *Union* (1548)

Ah, I do domineer, and rule the roast.
Chapman, *Gentleman Usher*, V, i (1606)

Geate you nowe up into your pulpittes like bragginge cocks on the rowst, flappe your winges and crowe out aloude.
Bp Jewell (d.1571)

**Rob.** ***To rob Peter to pay Paul.*** To take away from one person in order to give to another;or merely to shift a debt – to pay it off by incurring another one. Fable has it that the phrase alludes to the fact that on December 17th, 1550, the abbey church of St Peter, Westminster, was advanced to the dignity of a cathedral by letters patent; but ten years later it was joined to the diocese of London again, and many of its estates appropriated to the repairs of St Paul's Cathedral. But it was a common saying long before this date, and had been used by Wyclif about 1380:

How should God approve that you rob Peter, and give this robbery to Paul in the name of Christ?
*Select Works*, III, 174

The hint of the President, Viglius, to the Duke of Alva when he was seeking to impose ruinous taxation in the Netherlands (1569) was that –

it was not desirable to rob St Peter's altar in order to build one to St Paul.
Motley, *Dutch Republic*, III, v

**Rob Roy** (*Robert the Red*). A nickname given to Robert M'Gregor (1671–1734), a noted Scottish outlaw and freebooter, on account of his red hair. He assumed the name of Campbell about 1716, and was protected by the Duke of Argyle. He may be termed the Robin Hood of Scotland.

Rather beneath the middle size than above it, his limbs were formed upon the very strongest model that is consistent with agility ... Two points in his person interfered with the rules of symmetry; his shoulders were so broad ... as to give him the air of being too square in respect to his stature; and his arms, though round, sinewy, and strong, were so very long as to be rather a deformity. Scott, *Rob Roy*, ch. xxiii

**Robert.** The personal name is sometimes applied to the 'man in blue', the policeman. The allusion is to Sir Robert Peel – *cp.* Peeler, and Bobby.

Highwaymen and bandits are called *Robert's men* from *Robin Hood.*

***King Robert of Sicily.*** A metrical romance of the Trouveur, taken from the *Story of the Emperor Jovinian* in the *Gesta Romanorum*, and borrowed from the *Talmud.* It finds a place in the *Arabian Nights*, the Turkish *Tutinameh*, the Sanskrit *Panchatantra*, and has been *réchauffé* by Longfellow.

**Robert the Devil** or **Le Diable.** Robert, third Duke of Normandy (1028–35), father of William the Conqueror. He supported the English athelings against Canute, and made the pilgrimage to Jerusalem; many legends grew up around him, and he got his name for his daring and cruelty. The Norman tradition is that his wandering ghost will not be allowed to rest till the Day of Judgment. He is also called *Robert the Magnificent*.

Meyerbeer's opera *Roberto il Diavolo* (1831) is founded on this story. The duke is depicted as a libertine, and the opera shows the struggle in Robert between the virtue inherited from his mother, and the vice imparted by his father.

Robert François Damiens (1715–57), who attempted to assassinate Louis XV, was also called 'Robert le Diable'.

**Robespierre's Weavers.** The fish-women and other female rowdies who joined the Parisian Guard, and helped to line the avenues to the National Assembly in 1793, and clamour 'Down with the Girondists!'

**Robin.** *A round robin. See* Round.

**Robin Goodfellow.** A 'drudging fiend', and merry domestic fairy, famous for mischievous pranks and practical jokes; also known as 'Puck', the son of Oberon, and the fairies' jester. The story is that at night-time he will sometimes do little services for the family over which he presides. The Scots call this domestic spirit a *brownie*; the Germans, *kobold* or *Knecht Ruprecht*. The Scandinavians called it *Nissë God-dreng*.

Either I mistake your shape and making quite,
Or else you are that shrewd and knavish sprite
Called Robin Goodfellow ...
Those that Hob-goblin call you, and sweet Puck,
You do their work, and they shall have good luck.
Shakespeare, *Midsummer Night's Dream*, 2, 1

**Robin Gray, Auld.** Words by Lady Anne Lindsay, daughter of the Earl of Balcarres, and afterwards Lady Barnard, in 1772, written to an old Scotch tune called 'The bridegroom grat when the sun gaed down'. Auld Robin Gray was the herdsman of her father. When Lady Anne had written a part, she called her younger sister for advice. She said, 'I am writing a ballad of virtuous distress in humble life. I have oppressed my heroine with sundry troubles: for example, I have sent her Jamie to sea, broken her father's arm, made her mother sick, given her Auld Robin Gray for a lover, and want a fifth sorrow; can you help me to one?' 'Steal the cow, sister Anne,' said the little Elizabeth; so the cow was stolen awa', and the song completed.

Lady Anne later wrote a sequel in which Auld Robin Gray was good enough to die, whereupon Jeannie married Jamie.

**Robin Hood.** This traditionary outlaw and hero of English ballads is mentioned by the Scottish historian Fordun, who died about 1386, and also by Langland in the *Vision of Piers Plowman*, Bk v, 402 (*q.v.*), but which of these is the earlier is uncertain. It is doubtful whether he ever lived – the truth probably being that the stories associated with his name crystallised gradually round the personality of some popular local hero of the early 13th century – but the legends are that he was born in 1160 at Locksley, Notts, or, alternatively, that he was the outlawed Earl of Huntingdon, Robert Fitzooth, in disguise. Fitz- being omitted leaves Ooth, and converting *th* into *d* it became 'Ood'.

Another suggestion (Ten Brink) is that in the Robin Hood legends we have a late reminder of the old Scandinavian mythology of our ancestors. About the 12th century Woden was given the name 'Robin' (the Fr. form of *Ruprecht*, corresponding to *Henodperaht*), and the tales of outlawry may be a later form of the legend of the Wild Huntsman, connected with Woden.

According to Stow, he was an outlaw in the reign of Richard I (12th cent.). He entertained one hundred tall men, all good archers, with the spoil he took, but 'he suffered no woman to be oppressed, violated, or otherwise molested; poore men's goods he spared, abundantlie relieving them with that which by theft he got from abbeys and houses of rich carles'.

Robin Hood's companions in Sherwood Forest and Barnsdale, Yorks, were Little John, Friar Tuck, Will Scarlet, Allen-a-Dale, George-a-Greene and Maid Marian. According to one tradition, Robin Hood and Little John were two heroes defeated with Simon de Montfort at the battle of Evesham, in 1265. Fuller, in his *Worthies*, considers the outlaw an historical character, but Thierry says he simply represents the remnant of the old Saxon race, which lived in perpetual defiance of the Norman oppressors from the time of Hereward.

The traditions about Fulk FitzWarine, great-grandson of Warine of Metz, so greatly resemble those connected with 'Robin Hood', that some suppose them to be both one. FitzWarine quarrelled with John, and when John was king he banished Fulk, who became a bold forester.

The first published collection of ballads about the hero was the *Lytel Geste of Robin Hood*, printed by Wynkyn de Worde about 1490.

The stories about him formed the basis of early dramatic representations and were later amalgamated with the morris dances (*q.v.*) and May-day revels.

***A Robin Hood wind.*** A cold thaw-wind. Tradition runs that Robin Hood used to say he could bear any cold except that which a thaw-wind brought with it.

***Bow and arrow of Robin Hood.*** The traditional bow and arrow of Robin Hood are religiously preserved at Kirklees Hall, Yorkshire, the seat of Sir George Armytage; and the site of his grave is pointed out in the park.

***Death of Robin Hood.*** He was bled to death treacherously by a nun, instigated to the foul deed by his kinsman, the prior of Kirklees, Yorkshire, near Halifax. Introduced by Scott in *Ivanhoe*.

***Epitaph of Robin Hood.***

Hear, underneath this latil stean,
Laiz Robert earl of Huntington;
Nea arcir ver az hie sae geud,
An pipl kauld him Robin Heud.
Sich utlaz az he an hiz men
Vll England nivr si agen.

Obit. 24. *Kalend Dikembris*, 1247

Notwithstanding this epitaph other traditions assert that Robin Hood lived into the reign of Edward III, and died in 1325. One of the ballads relates how Robin Hood took service under Edward II.

***Many talk of Robin Hood who never shot with his bow.*** Many brag of deeds in which they took no part. Many talk of Robin Hood, and wish their hearers to suppose they took part in his adventures, but they never put a shaft to one of his bows; nor could they have bent it even if they had tried.

> They cry out with an open mouth, as if they out-shot Robin Hood, that Plato banished them (i.e. the Poets) out of his Commonwealth.
>
> Sidney, *Apologie for Poetrie*

***Robin Hood and Guy of Gisborne.*** Robin Hood and Little John, having had a tiff, part company, when Little John falls into the hands of the sheriff of Nottingham, who binds him to a tree. Meanwhile, Robin Hood meets with Guy of Gisborne, sworn to slay the 'bold forrester'.

The two bowmen struggle together, but Guy is slain, and Robin Hood rides till he comes to the tree where Little John is bound. The sheriff mistakes him for Guy of Gisborne, and gives him charge of the prisoner. Robin cuts the cord, hands Guy's bow to Little John, and the two soon put to flight the sheriff and his men. (Percy, *Reliques.*)

***Robin Hood's larder.*** *See* Oak.

***To go round Robin Hood's barn.*** To arrive at the right conclusion by very roundabout methods.

***To sell Robin Hood's pennyworth*** is to sell things at half their value. As Robin Hood stole his wares, he sold them, under their intrinsic value, for just what he could get on the nonce.

**Robin Redbreast.** The tradition is that when our Lord was on His way to Calvary, a robin picked a thorn out of His crown, and the blood which issued from the wound falling on the bird dyed its breast with red.

Another fable is that the robin covers dead bodies with leaves; this is referred to in Webster's *White Devil*, V, i (1612):

> Call for the robin-red-breast and the wren,
> Since o'er shady groves they hover,
> And with leaves and flowers do cover
> The friendless bodies of unburied men.

And in the ballad *The Babes in the Wood* –

> No burial this pretty pair
> From any man receives,
> Till Robin Redbreast piously
> Did cover them with leaves.

*Cp.* Ruddock.

***Robin Redbreasts.*** Bow Street runners were so called from their red waistcoats.

**Robin and Makyne.** An ancient Scottish pastoral. Robin is a shepherd for whom Makyne sighs. She goes to him and tells her love, but Robin turns a deaf ear, and the damsel goes home to weep. After a time the tables are turned, and Robin goes to Makyne to plead for her heart and hand; but the damsel replies –

> The man that will not when he may
> Sall have nocht when he wald.
>
> Percy, *Reliques*, etc., series ii

**Robin of Bagshot.** One of the highwaymen in Gay's *Beggar's Opera*, noted for the number of his aliases. *See* Alias.

**Robinson Crusoe.** Defoe's novel (1719) is founded on the adventures of Alexander Selkirk (1676–1723), a buccaneer who, at his own request, was, in 1704, marooned by himself on the uninhabited island of Juan Fernandez, off the coast of Chili, where he remained for over four years.

> The germ of *Robinson Crusoe*, the actual experience of Alexander Selkirk, went floating about for several years, and more than one artist dallied with it, till it finally settled and took root in the mind of the one man of his generation most capable of giving it a home and working out its artistic possibilities.
>
> Wm Minto, *Defoe*, ch. ix

**Robinsonians.** A 17th-century Independent sect of Puritans, followers of John Robinson (1575–1625), a Nottinghamshire clergyman who settled at Leyden in 1609 and became pastor of the English Separatist Church in the Netherlands.

**Roc.** A fabulous white bird of enormous size, and such strength that it can 'truss elephants in its talons', and carry them to its mountain nest, where it devours them. (*Arabian Nights*; *The Third Calender*, *and Sinbad the Sailor.*)

**Roch**, or **Roque, St.** Patron of those afflicted with the plague, because 'he worked miracles on the plague-stricken, while he was himself smitten with the same judgment'. He is depicted in a pilgrim's habit, lifting his dress to display a plague-spot on his thigh, which an angel is touching that he may cure it. Sometimes he is accompanied by a dog bringing bread in his mouth, in allusion to the legend that a hound brought him bread daily while he was perishing in a forest of pestilence.

His feast day, August 16th, was formerly celebrated in England as a general harvest-home, and styled 'the great August festival'.

***St Roch et son chien.*** Inseparables, Darby and Joan.

**Roche. *Sir Boyle Roche's bird.*** Sir Boyle Roche (1743–1807) was an Irish M.P., noted for his 'bulls'. On one occasion in the House, quoting from Jevon's play, *The Devil of a Wife*, he said, 'Mr Speaker, it is impossible I could have been in two places at once, unless I were a bird.'

> You may make a remark on the ubiquitous nature of certain cards, which, like Sir Boyle Roche's bird, are in two places at once.
>
> *Drawing-room Magic*

**Rochelle Salt.** A tartrate of sodium or potassium, so called because it was discovered by an apothecary of Rochelle, named Seignette, in 1672. In France it is called *sel de Seignette* or *sel des tombeaux*.

**Rochester,** according to Bede, derives its name from 'Hrof', a Saxon chieftain. (*Hrofs-ceaster*, Hrof's castle.)

**Rock.** 'The Rock', *par excellence*, is Gibraltar (*cp.* Rock English, *below*). As applied to pigeons – as in *Plymouth rock* and *blue rock* – the word is short for *rock-dove* or *rock-pigeon.* 'The Rock of Ages' (*see below*) is used of Jesus Christ as the unshakable and eternal foundation.

***A house builded upon a rock.*** Typical of a person or a thing whose foundations are sure. The allusion is to Matt. 7:24.

***Captain Rock.*** A fictitious name assumed by the leader of the Irish insurgents in 1822.

***On the rocks.*** 'Stony broke', having no money; a phrase from seafaring; a ship that is on the rocks will very quickly go to pieces unless she can be got off; so will a man.

***People of the Rock.*** The inhabitants of Hejaz or Arabia Petraea.

***Rock Day.*** The day after Twelfth-day, when, the Christmas holidays being over, women returned to their distaff, an old name for which was *rock*; the day is also called 'St Distaff's Day' – though, of course, there is no St Distaff. *Cp.* Plough Monday.

***Rock English.*** The mixed patois of Spanish and English spoken by natives at Gibraltar – 'The Rock'. Similarly, Malta or Mediterranean fever, which is common at Gibraltar, is also called *Rock fever*.

***Rock of Ages cleft for me.*** It is said that this well known hymn was written by Augustus Montague Toplady (1740–78) while seated by a great cleft rock near Cheddar, Somerset. Another story, which may belong to the realm of fable, has it that the first verse was written on the ten of diamonds in the interval between two rubbers of whist at Bath. Hence a *Toplady ring* is a ring set with ten stones in the form of the pips on a ten of diamonds. The phrase itself, as applied to Christ, is considerably older, and is traced to the marginal note to Is. 26:4, where the words 'everlasting strength' are stated to be, in the Hebrew, 'Rock of Ages'. In one of his hymns Wesley had written (1788) –

> Hell in vain against us rages;
> Can it shock
> Christ the Rock
> Of eternal Ages? *Praise by all to Christ be given*

Southey also has –

> These waters are the Well of Life, and lo!
> The Rock of Ages there, from whence they flow.
> *Pilgrimage to Waterloo*, pt ii, ca. iii

***That is the rock you'll split on.*** That is the danger, or the more or less hidden obstruction. Another seafaring phrase; there are rocks ahead in the path of the ship, and the helmsman must exercise the greatest caution.

***The Ladies' Rock.*** A crag under the castle rock of Stirling, where ladies used to witness tournaments.

***There are rocks ahead.*** *See* That is the rock above.

**Rocking Stones.** *See* Logan Stones.

**Rococo.** A term of uncertain origin, but probably from Fr. *rocaille*, pebble-work, applied to tastelessly florid and over-decorated architecture, furniture, jewellery, etc., especially the debased style of architecture that succeeded the Italian revival and was particularly prevalent in Germany, and Louis Quatorze and Louis Quinze furniture.

> The sacristy of St Lorenzo ... was the beginning of that wonderful mixture of antique regularity with the capricious bizarrerie of modern times, the last barren fruit of which was the rococo.
> H. Grimm, *Michel Angelo*, ch. xi

The word was regarded as a new coinage about 1836.

**Rod.** ***A rod in pickle.*** A scolding or punishment in store. Birch-rods used to be laid in brine to keep the twigs pliable.

***Spare the rod and spoil the child.*** An old saying drawing attention to the folly of allowing childish faults to go unreproved; founded on Prov. 13:24, 'He that spareth his rod hateth his child; but he that loveth him chasteneth him betimes.'

> Love is a boy, by poets styled,
> Then spare the rod, and spoil the child.
> Butler, *Hudibras*, II, i, 843

***To kiss the rod.*** To submit to punishment or misfortune meekly and without murmuring.

**Roderick** or **Rodrigo.** A Spanish hero round whom many legends have collected. He was the thirty-fourth and last of the Visigothic kings, came to the throne in 710, and was routed, and probably slain, by the Moors under Tarik in 711. Southey took him as the hero of his *Roderick, the last of the Goths* (1814), where he appears as the son of Theodofred, and grandson of King Chindasuintho. Witiza, the usurper, put out the eyes of Theodofred, and murdered Favila, a younger brother of Roderick; but Roderick, having recovered his father's throne, put out the eyes of the usurper. The sons of Witiza, joining with Count Julian, invited the aid of Muza ibn Nozeir, the Arab chief, who sent Tarik into Spain with a large army. Roderick was routed at the battle of Guadalete, near Xeres de la Frontera (711); he himself disappeared from the battlefield, and the Spaniards transformed him into a hero who would come again to save his country. One legend relates that he was befriended by a shepherd who was rewarded with the royal chain and ring. Roderick passed the night in the cell of a hermit, who told him that by way of penance he must pass certain days in a tomb full of snakes, toads, and lizards. After three days the hermit went to see him, and he was unhurt, 'because the Lord kept His anger against him'. The hermit went home, passed the night in prayer, and went again to the tomb, when Rodrigo said, 'They eat me now, they eat me now, I feel the adder's bite.' So his sin was atoned for, and he died.

**Roderigo.** A Venetian gentleman in Shakespeare's *Othello*. He was in love with Desdemona, and when the lady eloped with Othello, hated the 'noble Moor'. Iago took advantage of this temper for his own ends, told his dupe the Moor will change, therefore 'put money in thy purse'. The burden of his advice was always the same – 'Put money in thy purse'.

**Rodilardus.** A huge cat in Rabelais' *Gargantua* (iv, 67), which scared Panurge and which he declared to be a puny devil. The word means 'gnaw-bacon' (Lat. *rodo-lardum*).

**Rodomont** (in *Orlando Innamorato* and *Orlando Furioso*). King of Sarza or Algiers, Ulien's son, and called the 'Mars of Africa'. He was commander both of horse and foot in the Saracen army sent against Charlemagne, and may be termed the Achilles of the host. His lady-love was Doralis, Princess of Granada, who ran off with Mandricardo, King of Tartary. At Rogero's wedding-feast Rodomont rode up to the king of France in full armour, and accused Rogero (*q.v.*), who had turned Christian, of being a traitor to King Agramant, his master and a renegade; whereupon Rogero met him in single combat, and slew him.

> Who more brave than Rodomont?
>
> Cervantes, *Don Quixote*

**Rodomontade.** Bluster, brag, or a blustering and bragging speech; from Rodomont, the brave but braggart leader of the Saracens in Boiardo's *Orlando Innamorato* (*see above*).

**Rodrigo.** *See* Roderick.

**Roe, Richard.** *See* Doe.

**Rogation Days.** The Monday, Tuesday, and Wednesday before Ascension Day. Rogation is the Latin equivalent of the Greek word 'Litany', and on the three Rogation days 'the Litany of the Saints' is appointed to be sung by the clergy and people in public procession. ('Litany', Gr. *litaneia*, supplication. 'Rogation', Lat. *rogatio*, same meaning.)

The Rogation Days used to be called *Gang Days*, from the custom of *ganging* round the country parishes to beat the bounds (*see* Bounds) at this time. Similarly, the weed milkwort is still called *Rogation* or *Gangflower*, from the custom of decorating the pole (carried on such occasions by the charity children) with these flowers.

**Rogel** of Greece. A knight, whose exploits and adventures form a supplemental part of *Amadis of Gaul* (*q.v.*).

**Roger.** The cook in Chaucer's *Canterbury Tales*. 'He cowde roste, sethe, broille, and frie, make mortreux, and wel bake a pye'; but Harry Baily, the host, said to him –

> Now telle on Roger, and loke it be good;
> For many a Jakk of Dover hastow sold,
> That hath be twyës hoot and twyës cold.
>
> *Prologue to Cook's Tale*

***Roger Bontemps.*** *See* Bontemps.

***Sir Roger de Coverley.*** The simple, good, and altogether delightful country squire created by Steele as the chief character in the club that was supposed to write for the *Spectator*. He was developed by Addison, and it is to the latter that we are indebted for this perfect portrait of a perfect English gentleman. He has left his name to a popular country dance which, he tells us, was invented by his great-grandfather. Coverley is intended for Cowley, near Oxford.

***The Jolly Roger.*** The black flag with skull and cross-bones, the favourite ensign of pirates.

> Set all sail, clear the deck, stand to quarters, up with the Jolly Roger!
>
> Scott, *The Pirate*, ch. xxxi

**Rogero, Ruggiero,** or **Rizieri** of Risa (in *Orlando Furioso*), was brother of Marphisa, and son of Rogero and Galacella. His mother was slain by Agolant and his sons, and he was nursed by a lioness. He was brought up by Atlantes, a magician, who gave him a shield of such dazzling splendour that everyone quailed who set eyes on it, but, holding it unknightly to carry a charmed shield, he threw it into a well. He deserted from the Moorish army to Charlemagne, and was baptised, and his marriage with Bradamant, Charlemagne's niece, and election to the crown of Bulgaria conclude the poem.

Who more courteous than Rogero?

Cervantes, *Don Quixote*

In *Jerusalem Delivered* Rogero is brother of Boemond, and son of Roberto Guiscardo, of the Norman race. He was one of the band of adventurers in the crusading army, and was slain by Tisaphernes (bk xx).

**Rogue.** One of the 'canting' words used first in the 16th century to describe sturdy beggars and vagrants (perhaps from some outstanding member of the class named Roger). There is a good description of them in Harman's *Caveat for Common Cursitors vulgarly called Vagabones*, ch. iv. The expression *rogues and vagabonds* has since 1572 been applied in the Vagrancy Acts to all sorts of wandering, disorderly, or dissolute persons.

> It is Ordered and Ordained by the Lords and Commons in this present Parliament assembled and by Authority of the same, That all Stage-players and Players of Interludes and Common Plays are hereby declared to be, and are and shall be taken to be Rogues and punishable within the Statutes of the Thirty ninth year of the Reign of Queen Elizabeth and the seventh year of the Reign of King James ... whether they be wanderers or no.
>
> *Ordinance for Suppression of all Stage-Plays and Interludes*, Feb. 11th, 1647.

***Rogue in grain.*** *See* Grain.

***Rogue elephant.*** A savage and destructive elephant that lives apart from the herd, always vicious and dangerous.

***Rogue's badge.*** A race-horse or a hunter that becomes obstinate and refuses to do its work is known as a *rogue*, and the blinkers that it is made to wear are the *rogue's badge*.

***Rogues' gallery.*** The collection of portraits of criminals kept by the police.

***Rogues' Latin.*** The same as 'thieves' Latin'. *See* Latin.

***Rogues' March.*** The tune played when an undesirable soldier is drummed out of his regiment; hence, an ignominious dismissal.

**Roi Panade** (*King of Slops*). Louis XVIII was so nicknamed (1755, 1814–24).

**Roland** or (in Ital.) **Orlando.** The most famous of Charlemagne's paladins, slain at the battle of Roncesvalles (778), called 'The Christian Theseus' and 'the Achilles of the West'. He was Count of Mans and Knight of Blaives, and son of Duke Milo of Aiglant, his mother being Bertha, the sister of Charlemagne. Fable has it that he was eight feet high, and had an open countenance, which invited confidence, but inspired respect; and he is represented as brave, loyal, and simple-minded. On the return of Charlemagne from Spain Roland, who commanded the rearguard, fell into the ambuscade at Roncesvalles, in the Pyrenees, and perished with all the flower of the Frankish chivalry.

His achievements are recorded in the Chronicle attributed to Turpin (d.794), Archbishop of Rheims, which was not written till the 11th or 12th century, and he is the hero of the *Song of Roland* (*see below*), Boiardo's *Orlando Innamorato*, and Ariosto's *Orlando Furioso.* In Pulci's *Morgante Maggiore* he is also a principal character, and converts the giant Morgante to Christianity.

In *Orlando Furioso* (i.e. 'Orlando mad'), although married to Aldabella he fell in love with Angelica, daughter of the infidel king of Cathay; she married Medoro, a Moor, with whom she fled to India, whereupon Orlando went mad, or rather his wits were taken from him for three months by way of punishment, and deposited in the moon. Astolpho went to the moon in Elijah's chariot, and St John gave him an urn containing the lost wits. On reaching earth again, Astolpho first bound the madman, then, holding the urn to his nose, Orlando was cured of both his madness and his love.

***A Roland for an Oliver.*** A blow for a blow, tit for tat. The exploits of Roland and Oliver, another of the paladins of Charlemagne, are so similar that it is difficult to keep them distinct. What Roland did Oliver did, and what Oliver did Roland did. At length the two met in single combat, and fought for five consecutive days on an island in the Rhine, but neither gained the least advantage. Shakespeare alludes to the phrase: 'England all Olivers and Rolands bred' (*1 Henry VI*, 1, 2); and Edward Hall, the historian, almost a century before Shakespeare, writes:

> But to have a Roland to resist an Oliver, he sent solempne ambassadors to the Kyng of Englande, offeryng hym hys doughter in mariage.
>
> *Henry VI*

***Childe Roland.*** Youngest brother of the 'fair burd Helen' in the old Scottish ballad. Guided by Merlin, he undertook to bring back his sister from Elf-land, whither the fairies had carried her, and succeeded in his perilous exploit.

> Childe Roland to the dark tower came;
> His word was still 'Fie, foh, and fum,
> I smell the blood of a Britishman.'
>
> Shakespeare, *King Lear*, 3, 4

Browning's poem, *Child Roland to the Dark Tower Came*, is not connected in any way (except by the first line) with the old ballad.

***Like the blast of Roland's horn.*** Roland had a wonderful ivory horn, named 'Olivant', that he won from the giant Jutmundus. When he was set upon by the Gascons at Roncesvalles he sounded it to give Charlemagne notice of his danger. At the third blast it cracked in two, but it was so loud that birds fell dead and the whole Saracen army was panic-struck. Charlemagne heard the sound at St Jean Pied de Port, and rushed to the rescue, but arrived too late.

Oh, for one blast of that dread horn
On Fontarabian echoes borne,
That to King Charles did come.

Scott, *Marmion*, vi, 33

***Roland's sword.*** Durindana, or Durandal, which was fabled to have once belonged to Hector, and which – like the horn – Roland won from the giant Jutmundus. It had in its hilt a thread from the Virgin Mary's cloak, a tooth of St Peter, one of St Denis's hairs, and a drop of St Basil's blood. Legend relates that, to prevent Durandal falling into the hands of the Saracens, after he had received his death-wound he strove to break it on a rock; but as it was unbreakable he hurled it into a poisoned stream, where it remains for ever.

***The Song (Chanson) of Roland.*** The 11th-century *chanson de geste* ascribed to the Norman trouvère Théroulde, or Turoldus, which tells the story of the death of Roland and all the paladins at Roncesvalles, and of Charlemagne's vengeance. When Charlemagne had been six years in Spain he sent Ganelon on an embassy to Marsillus, the pagan king of Saragossa. Ganelon, out of jealousy, betrayed to Marsillus the route which the Christian army designed to take on its way home, and the pagan king arrived at Roncesvalles just as Roland was conducting through the pass a rearguard of 20,000 men; he fought till 100,000 Saracens lay slain, and only 50 of his own men survived. At this juncture another army, consisting of 50,000 men, poured from the mountains. Roland now blew his enchanted horn, and blew so loudly that the veins of his neck started. Charlemagne heard the blast, but Ganelon persuaded him that it was only his nephew hunting the deer. Roland died of his wounds.

The *Song* runs to 4,000 lines, and it was probably parts of this that – as we are told by Wace in the *Roman de Rou* – the Norman minstrel sang to encourage William's soldiers at the battle of Hastings:

Taillefer, the minstrel-knight, bestrode
A gallant steed, and swiftly rode
Before the Duke, and sang the song
Of Charlemagne, of Roland strong,
Of Oliver, and those beside
Brave knights at Roncevaux that died.

Arthur S. Way's rendering

***To die like Roland.*** To die of starvation or thirst. One legend has it that Roland escaped the general slaughter in the defile of Roncesvalles, and died of hunger and thirst in seeking to cross the Pyrenees. He was buried at Blayes, in the church of St Raymond; but his body was removed afterwards to Roncesvalles.

**Rolandseck Tower,** opposite the Drachenfels on the Rhine, 22 miles above Cologne. The legend is that when Roland went to the wars, a false report of his death was brought to his betrothed, who retired to a convent in the isle of Nonnewerth. When he returned home flushed with glory, and found that his lady-love had taken the veil, he built the castle which bears his name, and overlooks the nunnery, that he might at least see his heart-treasure, lost to him for ever.

**Roll.** ***The flying roll of Zechariah*** (5:1–5). 'Predictions of evils to come on a nation are like the flying roll of Zechariah.' This roll (twenty cubits long and ten wide) was full of maledictions, threats, and calamities about to befall the Jews. The parchment being unrolled fluttered in the air.

***A rolling stone.*** *See* Stone.

***Rolling stock.*** All the wheeled equipment of a railway that is fitted to run on rails; the locomotives, passenger coaches, vans, goods trucks, etc.

**Rolls, The.** The former building in Chancery Lane where the records in the custody of the Master of the Rolls were kept; now replaced by the Public Record Office; it included a court of justice and a chapel, and was originally built by Henry III as a *Domus Conversorum* (house for lay monks) for converted Jews. In the time of Edward III it was devoted to the purpose of storing records.

***The Master of the Rolls.*** The head of the Public Record Office, an ex-officio Judge of the Court of Appeal and a member of the Judicial Committee, ranking next after the Lord Chief Justice. His jurisdiction was formerly exercised in Chancery as the deputy of the Lord Chancellor, and he also sat independently in the Rolls Chapel.

The term has been punningly applied to a baker.

***To be struck off the rolls.*** To be removed from the official list of qualified solicitors, and so prohibited from practising. This is done in cases of professional misconduct.

**Rollrich** or **Rowldrich Stones,** near Chipping Norton (Oxfordshire). A number of large stones in a circle, which tradition says are *men* turned to stone. The highest of them is called *the King*, who 'would have been king of England if he could have caught sight of Long Compton', which may be seen a few steps farther on; five other large stones are called the knights, and the rest common soldiers.

**Roly-poly.** A crust with jam rolled up into a pudding; a little fat child. Roly is a thing rolled with the diminutive added. In some parts of Scotland the game of ninepins is called *rouly-pouly*.

**Romaic.** Modern or Romanised Greek.

**Roman.** Pertaining to Rome, especially ancient Rome, or to the Roman Catholic Church. As a surname or distinctive title the adjective has been applied to Giulio Pippi, *Giulio Romano* (1492–1546), the Italian artist.

Adrian van Roomen (1561–1615), the famous mathematician, *Adrianus Romanus*.

Stephen Picart (1631–1721), the French engraver, *le Romain*.

Jean Dumont (1700–81), the French painter, *le Romain*.

Marcus Terentius Varro (116–27 BC) was called the *Most Learned of the Romans*, and Rienzi (1313–54), the Italian patriot and 'last of the Tribunes', was known as *Ultimus Romanorum*, the Last of the Romans – an honorific title later applied to Horace Walpole, Charles James Fox, and others.

***King of the Romans.*** The title usually assumed by the sovereign of the Holy Roman Empire previous to his actual coronation in the Holy City. Napoleon's son, afterwards the Duke of Reichstadt, was styled the King of Rome at his birth in 1811.

***Roman architecture.*** A style of architecture, distinguished by its massive character and abundance of ornament, which combines the Greek orders with the use of the arch. It is largely a corruption of the Doric and Ionic.

***Roman birds.*** Eagles; so called because the ensign of the Roman legion was an eagle.

> Romanas aves propria legionum numina. Tacitus

***Roman figures.*** *See* Numerals.

***Roman roads in Britain.*** *See* Ermine, Fosse, Icknield, Watling.

> Fair weyes many on ther ben in Englond
> But four most of all ben zunderstond …
> Fram the south into the north takit *Erming-strete*;
> Fram the east into the west goeth *Ikeneld strete*;
> Fram south-est to North-west (that is sum deegrete)
> Fram Dover into Chester go'th *Watling-strete*;
> The forth is most of all that tills from Totëneys –
> Fram the one end of Cornwall anon to Catenays [Caithness] –
> Fram the south to North-est into Englondes end
> *Fosse* men callith thisk voix.
>
> Robert of Gloucester

The most remarkable of the numerous Roman remains in England are probably –

The pharos, church, and trenches in Dover. Chilham Castle, Richborough, and Reculver forts. The amphitheatres at Silchester (Berkshire), Dorchester, Nisconium (Salop), and Caerleon. Hadrian's wall (*q.v.*); the wall, baths, and Newport Gate of Lincoln. The earthworks at Verulam, near St Albans; York (Eboracum), where Severus and Constantius Chlorus died, and Constantine the Great was born; and the ancient parts of Bath.

***Roman type.*** Ordinary type, as distinguished from italic, clarendon, gothic or 'black letter', etc.; so called because founded on that used in ancient Roman inscriptions and manuscripts.

***The Holy Roman Empire.*** *See* Holy.

***The Last of the Romans.*** *See above, also* Last.

***The Roman Empire.*** The Empire established on the ruins of the Republic by Augustus in 27 BC, and lasting till AD 395, when it was divided into the Western or Latin Empire, and the Eastern or Greek.

> The Roman Empire was a power, and not a nation … The name *Roman*, in the use of Procopius, when it does not refer geographically to the elder Rome means any man, of whatever race, who is a subject of the Roman Empire or who serves in the Roman armies. His nationality may be not only Greek, Macedonian, or Thracian, but Gothic, Persian, or Hunnish.
>
> Freeman, *Historical Essays*, III, 246

***The Roman Republic*** was established about 509 BC after the overthrow of the last of the seven kings, Tarquinius Superbus, and survived till it was superseded in 27 BC by the Empire.

**Roman de la Rose.** *See* Rose, Romance of the.

**Roman des Romans.** A French version of *Amadis of Gaul* (*q.v.*), greatly extended by Gilbert Saunier and Sieur de Duverdier.

**Romance.** Applied in linguistics to the languages, especially Old French, sprung from the Latin spoken in the European provinces of the Roman Empire; hence, as a noun, the word came to mean a mediaeval tale in Old French or Provençal describing, usually in mixed prose and verse, the marvellous adventures of a hero of chivalry; the transition to the modern meanings – a work of fiction in which the scenes, incidents, etc., are more or less removed from common life and are surrounded by a halo of mystery – or the atmosphere of strangeness and imaginary adventure itself – is simple.

The mediaeval romances fall into three main groups or *cycles*, viz., the Arthurian, the Charlemagne cycle, and the cycle of Alexander the Great. Nearly, but not quite, all the romances are connected with one or other of these.

***Romance languages.*** Those languages which are the immediate offspring of Latin, as the Italian, Spanish, Portuguese, and French. Early French is emphatically so called; hence Bouillett says, '*Le roman était universellement parlé en Gaule au dixième siècle.*'

> Frankis speech is called Romance,
> So say clerks and men of France. *Robert le Brun*

**Romantic Revival, The.** The literary movement that began in Germany in the last quarter of the 18th century having for its object a return from the Augustan or classical formalism of the time to the freer fancies and methods of romance. It was led by Schiller, Goethe, Novalis, and Tieck; spread to England, where it affected the work of Collins and Gray and received an impetus from the publication of Percy's *Reliques* and Macpherson's *Ossian*; and, immensely stimulated by the French Revolution, effected a transformation of English literature through the writings of Keats, Byron, Wordsworth, Shelley, Coleridge, Scott, etc. In France its chief exponents were Chénier, de Musset, Victor Hugo, and Dumas.

**Romanus, St.** A Norman bishop of the 7th century; depicted fighting with a dragon, in allusion to the tale that he miraculously conquered a dragon which infested Normandy.

**Romany.** A gypsy; or the gypsy language, the speech of the Roma or Zincali. The word is from Gypsy *rom*, a man, or husband.

> A learned Sclavonian ... said of Rommany, that he found it interesting to be able to study a Hindu dialect in the heart of Europe.
>
> Leland, *English Gipsies*, ch. viii

***Romany rye.*** One who enters into the gypsy spirit, learns their language, lives with them as one of themselves, etc. *Rye* is gypsy for gentleman. Borrow's book with this title (a sequel to *Lavengro*) was published in 1857.

**Rome.** The greatest city of the antique world, according to legend founded (753 BC) by Romulus (*q.v.*) and named after him; but in all probability so called from Greek *rhoma* (strength), a suggestion confirmed by its other name Valentia, from *valens* (strong).

***Oh, that all Rome had but one head, that I might strike it off at a blow!*** Caligula, the Roman emperor, is said to have uttered this amiable sentiment.

***Rome penny, Rome scot.*** The same as Peter's penny (*q.v.*).

***Rome's best wealth is patriotism.*** So said Mettius Curtius, when he jumped into the chasm which the soothsayers gave out would never close till Rome threw therein 'its best wealth'.

***Rome was not built in a day.*** Achievements of great pith and moment are not accomplished without patient perseverance and a considerable interval of time. It is quite an old saying, and is to be found in Heywood's *Collection* (1562).

***'Tis ill sitting at Rome and striving with the Pope.*** Don't tread on a man's corns when you are living with him or are in close touch with him – especially if he's powerful.

> Mr Harrison the steward, and Gudyell the butler, are no very fond o' us, and it's ill sitting at Rome and striving with the pope, sae I thought it best to flit before ill came.
>
> Scott, *Old Mortality*, ch. viii

***When you go to Rome, do as Rome does.*** Conform to the manners and customs of those amongst whom you live; 'Don't wear a brown hat in Friesland.' St Monica and her son St Augustine said to St Ambrose: 'At Rome they fast on Saturday, but not so at Milan; which practice ought to be observed?' To which St Ambrose replied, 'When I am at Milan, I do as they do at Milan; but when I go to Rome, I do as Rome does!' (*Epistle* xxxvi). *Cp.* 2 Kings 5:18.

The saying is quite an old one, and is to be found in that great storehouse of proverbs, Porter's *Two Angry Women of Abingdon* (1599).

**Romeo and Juliet.** Shakespeare's tragedy (first published 1597) is founded on the story of the lovers of Verona as told in Arthur Brooke's poem, *The Tragicall Historye of Romeus and Juliet, containing a rare example of love constancie; with the subtill counsels and practices of an old Fryer* (1562), and a story in Painter's *Palace of Pleasure* (1567). Its earliest appearance in literature is in Masuccio's *Novelle* (Naples, 1476); next, as *La Giulietta*, by Luigi da Porta (1535); and then in Bandello's *Novella* (Lucca, 1554). It was the French translation of this latter by Pierre Boaisteau that was followed by Brooke and Painter.

Girolamo della Corte's *History of Verona to 1560* places the story in 1303, when a member of the Scala family (transformed by Shakespeare to *Escalus*) was ruling in Verona, and in Dante's *Divina Commedia* (about 1300–18) the Capulets and Montagues appear among the quarrelsome inhabitants of the town.

**Romulus.** With his twin brother, Remus, the legendary and eponymous founder of Rome. They were sons of Mars and Rhea Silvia, who, because she was a vestal virgin, was condemned to death while the sons were exposed. They were, however, suckled by a she-wolf, and eventually set about founding a city but quarrelled over the plans, and Remus was slain by his brother in anger. Romulus was later taken to the heavens by his father, Mars, in a fiery chariot, and was worshipped by the Romans under the name of Quirinus.

***The Second Romulus.*** Camillus was so called because he saved Rome from the Gauls, 365 BC.

***The Third Romulus.*** Caius Marius, who saved Rome from the Teutons and Cimbri in 101 BC.

***We need no Romulus to account for Rome.*** We require no hypothetical person to account for a plain fact.

**Ron** or **Rone.** The name of Prince Arthur's spear, made of ebony.

> His spere he nom [took] an honde, tha Ron was thaten [called].
>
> Layamon, *Brut* (twelfth century)

**Roncesvalles.** A defile in the Pyrenees, famous for the disaster which here befell the rear of Charlemagne's army, on the return march from Saragossa (778). Ganelon betrayed Roland (*q.v.*) to Marsillus, king of the Saracens, and an ambuscade attacking the Franks, killed every man of them, including Roland, Oliver, and all the paladins. *See* Song of Roland *under* Roland.

Roncesvalles is said to have left its name to *rouncival* peas, a large kind of garden pea. *See* Rouncival. In his *Glossographia* (1674) Blount has –

> *Rounceval Peas*, a sort of great Peas, well known, and took name from Ronceval, a place at the foot of the Pyrenean Mountains from whence they first came to us.

But there is no confirmation of this. *See also* Runcible Spoon.

**Rone.** *See* Ron.

**Ronyon** or **Runnion.** A term of contempt to a woman. It is probably the French *rogneux* (scabby, mangy).

> You hag, you baggage, you polecat, you ronyon! out, out!
>
> Shakespeare, *Merry Wives of Windsor*, 4, 2
>
> 'Aroint thee, witch!' the rump-fed ronyon cries.
>
> Shakespeare, *Macbeth*, 1, 3

**Rood** (connected with *rod*). The Cross of the Crucifixion; or a crucifix, especially the large one that was formerly set on the stone or timber *rood-screen*, that divides the nave from the choir in churches. This is usually richly decorated with statues and carvings of saints, emblems, etc., and frequently is surmounted by a gallery called the rood-loft.

> And then to zee the rood-loft,
> Zo bravely zet with zaints.
>
> Percy, *Ballad of Plain Truth*, ii, 292

***By the rood; by the holy rood.*** Old expletives used by way of asseveration. When the Queen asks Hamlet if he has forgotten her, he answers, 'No, by the rood, not so' (3, 4).

***Rood Day.*** Holy Rood Day (*q.v.*); September 14th (the Exaltation of the Cross), or May 3rd (the Invention of the Cross).

**Roodselken.** An old country name for vervain, or 'the herb of the cross'.

> Hallowed be thou, vervain, as thou growestin the ground,
> For in the Mount of Calvary thou wast found.
> Thou healedst Christ our Saviour, and staunchedst His bleeding wound:
> In the name of Father, Son and Holy Ghost, I take thee from the ground.
>
> Folkard, *Plant Lore*, p. 47

**Rook.** A cheat. 'To rook', to cheat; 'to rook a pigeon', to fleece a greenhorn. Sometimes it simply means to win from another at a game of chance or skill.

> 'My Lord Marquis,' said the king, 'you rooked me at piquet last night, for which disloyal deed thou shalt now atone, by giving a couple of pieces to this honest youth, and five to the girl.'
>
> Scott, *Peveril of the Peak*, ch. xxx

*Rook*, the castle in chess, is through French and Spanish from Persian *rukh*, which is said to have meant a warrior.

**Rookery.** Any low, densely populated neighbourhood, especially one frequented by thieves and vagabonds.

> The demolition of rookeries has not proved an efficient remedy for overcrowding.
>
> A. Egmont Hake, *Free Trade in Capital*, ch. xv

Of course, the allusion is to the way in which rooks build their nests clustered closely together. A colony of seals, and places where seals or sea-birds collect in the breeding season are also known as 'rookeries'.

**Room.** ***Your room is better than your company.*** Your absence is more to be wished than your presence. An old phrase; it occurs in Stanyhurst's *Description of Ireland* (1577), Greene's *Quip for an Upstart Courtier* (1592), etc.

**Roost.** A strong current or furious tide betwixt island groups, especially in the Orkneys and Shetlands.

> This lofty promontory is constantly exposed to the current of a strong and furious tide, which setting in betwixt the Orkney and Zetland islands and running with force only inferior to that of the Pentland Frith, ... is called the Roost of Sumburgh.
>
> Scott, *The Pirate*, ch. i

***To rule the roost.*** *See* Roast.

**Root.** ***Root and branch.*** The whole of it without any exceptions or omissions; 'lock, stock, and barrel'. The Puritans of about 1640 who wanted to extirpate the episcopacy altogether were known as 'Root-and-branch men', or 'Rooters', and the term has since been applied to other political factions who are anxious to 'go the whole hog'.

***The root of the matter.*** Its true inwardness, its actual base and foundation. The phrase comes from Job 19:28 –

> But ye should say, Why persecute we him, seeing the root of the matter is found in me?

***To take*** or ***strike root.*** To become permanently or firmly established.

**Rope.** ***A taste of the rope's end.*** A flogging – especially among seamen.

***Fought back to the ropes.*** Fought to the bitter end. A phrase from the prize-ring, the 'ropes' forming the boundary of the 'ring'.

> It is a battle that must be fought game, and right back to the ropes.
>
> Boldrewood, *Robbery Under Arms*, ch. xxxiii

***Ropes of sand.*** *See* Sand.

***She is on her high ropes.*** In a distant and haughty temper; 'high and mighty'. The allusion is to a rope-dancer, who looks down on the spectators. The French say, *Être monté sur ses grands chevaux* (to be on your high horse).

***The Rope-walk.*** Former barristers' slang for an Old Bailey practice. Thus, 'Gone into the rope-walk' means, he has taken up practice in the Old Bailey. The allusion is to the murder trials taking place there, a convicted murderer 'getting the rope', i.e. being hanged.

***To come to the end of one's rope*** or ***tether.*** *See* Tether.

***To fight with a rope round one's neck.*** To fight with a certainty of losing your life unless you conquer.

> You must send in a large force: ... for, as he fights with a rope round his neck, he will struggle to the last.
>
> Kingston, *The Three Admirals*, viii

***To give one rope enough.*** To permit a person to continue in wrongdoing, till he reaps the consequences. 'Give him rope enough and he'll hang himself' is a common saying of one addicted to evil courses.

***To know the ropes.*** To be up to all the tricks and dodges; to know exactly what is the proper thing to do.

> I am no longer the verdant country squire, the natural prey of swindlers, blacklegs, and sharks. No, sir, I 'know the ropes', and these gentry would find me but sorry sport.
>
> *Truth, Queer Story*, September 3rd, 1885

***To rope one in.*** To get him to take part in some scheme, enterprise, etc. An expression from the western states of America, where horses and cattle are roped in with a lasso.

***You carry a rope in your pocket*** (Fr.). Said of a person very lucky at cards, from the superstition that a bit of rope with which a man has been hanged, carried in the pocket, secures luck at cards.

> 'You have no occupation?' said the Bench, inquiringly, to a vagabond at the bar. 'Beg your worship's pardon,' was the rejoinder; 'I deal in bits of halter for the use of gentlemen as plays.'
>
> *The Times* (French correspondent)

**Roper.** ***Mistress Roper.*** A cant name given to the *Marines* by British sailors. The wit, of course, lies in the awkward way that marines handle the ship's ropes.

***To marry Mistress Roper*** is to enlist in the Marines.

**Roque, St.** *See* Roch.

**Roquelaure.** A cloak for men, reaching to the knees. It was worn in the 18th century, and is so named from Antoine-Gaston, Duke de Roquelaure (1656–1738), a Marshal of France.

> 'Your honour's roquelaure', replied the corporal, 'has not once been had on since the night before your honour received your wound.'
>
> Sterne, *Tristram Shandy*; *Story of Le Fevre*

**Rory O'More.** Slang for a *door*. *See* Rhyming Slang.

**Rosabelle.** The favourite palfrey of Mary Queen of Scots.

> I could almost swear I am at this moment mounted on my own favourite Rosabelle, who was never matched in Scotland for swiftness, for ease of motion, and for sureness of foot.
>
> Scott, *The Abbot*, ch. xxxvi

**Rosalia,** or **Rosalie, St.** The patron saint of Palermo, in art depicted in a cave with a cross and skull, or else in the act of receiving a rosary or chaplet of roses from the Virgin. She lived in the 12th century, and is said to have been carried by angels to an inaccessible mountain, where she dwelt for many years in the cleft of a rock, a part of which she wore away with her knees in her devotions. A chapel has been built there, with a marble statue, to commemorate the event.

> That grot where olives nod,
> Where, darling of each heart and eye.
> From all the youths of Sicily,
> St Rosalie retired to God.
>
> Sir Walter Scott, *Marmion*, i, 23

**Rosalind.** The anagrammatic name under which Spenser introduces his early love, Rosa Daniel (sister of Samuel Daniel, the poet), into the *Shepherd's Calendar*, he himself figuring as 'Colin Clout'. She was the wife of John Florio, the lexicographer who is caricatured in *Love's Labour's Lost* as 'Holofernes' (i.e. [Jo]h[an]nes Floreo).

In Shakespeare's *As You Like It* Rosalind is the daughter of the banished duke, brought up with Celia in the court of Frederick, the duke's brother, and usurper of his dominions. After sundry adventures, in the course of which she disguises herself as a youth and Celia as a peasant-girl, she obtains her father's consent to marry her lover, Orlando.

**Rosamond, The Fair.** Higden, monk of Chester, writing about 1350, says: 'She was the fayre daughter of Walter, Lord Clifford, concubine of Henry II, and poisoned by Queen Elianor, AD 1177. Henry made for her a house of wonderfull working, so that no man or woman might come to her. This house was named Labyrinthus, and was wrought like unto a knot in a garden called a maze. But the queen came to her by a clue of thredde, and so dealt with her that she lived not long after. She was buried at Godstow, in an house of nunnes, with these verses upon her tombe:

> Hic jacet in tumba Rosa mundi, non Rosa munda;
> Non redolet, sed olet, quae redole'rë solet.
> Here Rose the graced, not Rose the chaste, reposes;
> The smell that rises is no smell of roses.
>
> E. C. B.

This 'evidence', dating nearly 200 years after the supposed event, is all the substantiation we have for the popular legend about the labyrinth; and there is none for the stories that Rosamund Clifford was the mother of William Longsword and Geoffrey, Archbishop of York. She is introduced by Scott in two of his novels – *The Talisman* and *Woodstock*; and a subterranean labyrinth in Blenheim Park, near Woodstock, is still pointed out as 'Rosamond's Bower'.

> Jane Clifford was her name, as books aver
> Fair Rosamund was but her *nom de guerre*.
>
> Dryden, *Epilogue to Henry II*

**Rosana.** Daughter of the Queen of Armenia. She aided the three sons of St George to quench the seven lamps of the Knight of the Black Castle. (*The Seven Champions of Christendom*, ii, 8–9.) *See* Seven Champions.

**Rosary.** The bead-roll employed by Roman Catholics for keeping count of their repetitions of certain prayers; also, these prayers themselves. The rope of beads consists of three parts, each of which symbolises five mysteries connected with Christ or His virgin mother. The entire roll consists of 150 *Ave Marias*, 15 *Pater Nosters*, and 15 doxologies. The word is said by some to be derived from the chaplet of beads, perfumed with roses, given by the Virgin to St Dominic. (This cannot be correct, as it was in use AD 1100.) Others say the first chaplet of the kind was made of rosewood; others, again, maintain that it takes its name from the 'Mystical Rose', one of the titles of the Virgin. The set is sometimes called 'fifteens', from its containing 15 'doxologies', 15 'Our Fathers', and 10 times 15, or 150, 'Hail Marys'.

> The 'Devotion of the Rosary' takes different forms – (1) *the Greater Rosary*, or recitation of the whole fifteen mysteries; (2) *the Lesser Rosary*, or recitation of one of the mysteries; and (3) *the Living Rosary*, or the recitation of the fifteen mysteries by fifteen different persons in combination.

**Rosciad.** A satire by Charles Churchill, published in 1761; it canvasses the faults and merits of the metropolitan actors.

**Roscius.** A first-rate actor; so called from Quintus Roscius (d. about 62 BC), the Roman actor, unrivalled for his grace of action, melody of voice, conception of character, and delivery.

> What scene of death hath Roscius now to act?
>
> Shakespeare, *3 Henry VI*, 5, 6

***Another Roscius.*** So Camden terms Richard Burbage (d.1619).

***The British Roscius.*** Thomas Betterton (1635–1710), of whom Cibber says, 'He alone was born to speak what only Shakespeare knew to write.' The title was also accorded to Garrick.

***The Roscius of France.*** Michel Boyron (1653–1729), generally called Baron.

***The Young Roscius.*** William Henry West Betty (1791–1874). His first public appearance was in 1803 (as Oswyn, in *Zara*), and, after achieving astonishing success, he left the stage in 1824. It is said that in fifty-six nights he realised £34,000.

**Rose.** Mediaeval legend asserts that the first roses appeared miraculously at Bethlehem as the result of the prayers of a 'fayre Mayden' who had been falsely accused and was sentenced to death by burning. As Sir John Mandeville tells the tale (*Travels*, ch. vi), after her prayer

> sche entered into the Payer; and anon was the Fuyr quenched and oute; and the Brondes that weren brennynge, becomen red Roseres; and the Brondes that weren not kyndled, becomen white Roseres, fulle of Roses. And these weren the first Roseres and Roses, both white and rede, that evere any Man saughe. And thus was this Mayden saved be the Grace of God.

The *Rose* has been an emblem of England since the time of the Wars of the Roses (*see below*), when the Lancastrians adopted a *red* rose as their badge, and the Yorkists a *white.* When the parties were united in the person of Henry VII the united rose was taken as his device.

The *Red Rose* of Lancaster was, says Camden, the accepted badge of Edmund Plantagenet, second son of Henry III, and of the first Duke of Lancaster, surnamed Crouchback. It was also the cognisance of John of Gaunt, second Duke of Lancaster, in virtue of his wife, who was godchild of Edmund Crouchback, and his sole heir; and, in later times, of the Richmonds. Hence the rose in the mouth of one of the foxes which figure in the sign of the *Holland Arms*, Kensington. The daughter of the Duke of Richmond (Lady Caroline Lennox) ran away with Mr Henry Fox, afterwards Baron Holland of Foxley; the *Fox* ran off with the *Rose.*

The *White Rose* was not first adopted by the Yorkists during the contest for the crown, as Shakespeare says. It was an hereditary cognisance of the House of York, and had been borne by them ever since the title was first created. It was adopted by the Jacobites as an emblem of the Pretender, because his adherents were obliged to abet him *sub rosa* (in secret). Cecily Nevill, wife of Richard, Duke of York, and mother of Edward IV and Richard III, was known as *The White Rose of Raby.* She was a daughter of Ralph, Earl of Westmoreland, and granddaughter of John of Gaunt, and was the youngest of twenty-one children.

In heraldry the *Rose* is also used as the mark of cadency for a seventh son.

In Christian symbolism the *Rose*, as being emblematic of a paragon or one without peer, is peculiarly appropriated to the Virgin Mary, one of whose titles is 'The Mystical Rose'. It is also the attribute of St Dorothea, who carries roses in a basket, of St Casilda, St Elizabeth of Portugal, and St Rose of Viterbo, who carry roses either in their hands or caps; and of St Rosalie, St Angelus, St Rose of Lima, St Ascylus, and St Victoria, who wear crowns of roses.

In the language of flowers, different roses have a different signification. For example:

The Burgundy Rose signifies simplicity and beauty.

The China Rose, grace or beauty ever fresh.

The Daily Rose, a smile.

The Dog Rose, pleasure mixed with pain.

A Faded Rose, beauty is fleeting.

The Japan Rose, beauty your sole attraction.

The Moss Rose, voluptuous love.

The Musk Rose, capricious beauty.

The Provence Rose, my heart is in flames.

The White Rose Bud, too young to love.

The White Rose full of buds, secrecy.

A wreath of Roses, beauty and virtue rewarded.

The Yellow Rose, infidelity.

***A bed of roses.*** *See* Bed.

***No rose without a thorn.*** There is always something to detract from pleasure – 'every sweet has its sour', 'there is a crook in every lot'.

***Sing Old Rose and burn the bellows.*** 'Old Rose' was the title of a song now unknown; thus, Izaak Walton, in the *Compleat Angler* (1653) says, 'Let's sing *Old Rose.*' *Burn the bellows* may be a schoolboys' perversion of *burn libellos.* At breaking-up time the boys might say, 'Let's sing *Old Rose* and burn our schoolbooks' (*libellos*). This does not accord ill with the meaning of the well-known catch –

Now we're met like jovial fellows,
Let as do as wise men tell us,
Sing *Old Rose* and burn the bellows.

***Under the rose*** (Lat. *sub rosa*). In strict confidence. The origin of the phrase is wrapped in obscurity, but the story is that Cupid gave Harpocrates (the god of silence) a rose, to bribe him not to betray the amours of Venus. Hence the flower became the *emblem* of silence, and was sculptured on the ceilings of banquet-rooms, to remind the guests that what was spoken *sub vino* was not to be uttered *sub divo.* In 1526 it was placed over confessionals.

Est rosa flos Veneris, cujus quo furta laterent
Harpocrati matris dona dictavit amor.
Inde rosam mensis hospes suspendit amicis,
Convivae ut sub ea dicta tacenda sciant.

*Burmar's Anthologia*, v, 217 (1773)

**Rose Alley Ambuscade, The.** The attack on Dryden by masked ruffians, probably in the employ of Rochester and the Duchess of Portsmouth, on December 18th, 1679, in revenge for an anonymous *Essay on Satire* attacking the king, Rochester, and the Duchesses of Cleveland and Portsmouth, which was erroneously attributed to Dryden.

**Rose Coffee-house, The.** The tavern at the corner of Russell Street and Bow Street, Covent Garden, where Dryden presided over the genius of the town. Formerly known as 'The Red Cow', it was subsequently 'Will's'.

**Rose of Jericho, The.** The popular name of *Anastatica hierochuntina*, a small branching plant native to the sandy deserts of Arabia, Egypt, and Syria. When it is dry, if it is exposed to moisture, the branches uncurl. Also called the *rose of the Virgin,* or *Rosa Mariae.*

**Rose Noble.** A gold coin worth about 6*s.* 8*d.* current in the 15th and 16th centuries, so called because it was stamped with a rose. The value varied from time to time and place to place. *Cp.* Noble.

**Rose, The Romance of the.** An early French poem of over 20,000 lines; an elaborate allegory on the Art of Love beneath which can be seen a faithful picture of contemporary life. It was begun by Guillaume di Lorris in the latter half of the 13th century, and continued by Jean de Meung in the early part of the 14th. The poet is accosted by Dame Idleness, who conducts him to the Palace of Pleasure, where he meets Love, accompanied by Sweet-looks, Riches, Jollity, Courtesy, Liberality, and Youth, who spend their time in dancing, singing, and other amusements. By this retinue the poet is conducted to a bed of roses, where he singles out one and attempts to pluck it, when an arrow from Cupid's bow stretches him fainting on the ground, and he is carried far away from the flower of his choice. As soon as he recovers, he finds himself alone, and resolves to return to his rose. Welcome goes with him; but Danger, Shame-face, Fear, and Slander obstruct him at every turn. Reason advises him to abandon the pursuit, but this he will not do; whereupon Pity and Liberality aid him in reaching the rose of his choice, and Venus permits him to touch it with his lips. Meanwhile, slander rouses up Jealousy, who seizes Welcome, whom he casts into a strong castle, and gives the key of the castle door to an old hag. Here the poet is left to mourn over his fate, and the original poem ends.

In the second part – which is much the longer – the same characters appear, but the spirit of the poem is altogether different, the author being interested in life as a whole instead of solely in love; and directing his satire especially against women.

A 15th-century English version is often published with Chaucer's works, and it is probable that the first 1,700 lines or so are by Chaucer.

**Rose Sunday.** The fourth Sunday in Lent, when the Pope blesses the 'Golden Rose' (*q.v.*).

**Roses. *The Wars of the Roses.*** A civil contest that lasted thirty years, in which eighty princes of the blood, a large portion of the English nobility, and some 100,000 common soldiers were slain. It was a struggle for the crown between the houses of York (*White* rose) and Lancaster (*Red*), York (Edward IV and V and Richard III) deriving from Edmund of Langley, Duke of York, the youngest son of Edward III, and Lancaster (Henry IV, V, and VI) from John of Gaunt, Duke of Lancaster, an elder brother of Edmund. The wars started in the reign of Henry VI with a Yorkist victory at St Albans (1455) and ended with the defeat and death of the Yorkist Richard III at Bosworth (1485). His successor, Henry VII, was descended from John of Gaunt and married a descendant of Edmund of Langley, thus uniting the two houses.

**Rosemary** is *Ros-marinus* (sea-dew), and is said to be 'useful in love-making'. The reason is this:

Both Venus, the love goddess, and Rosemary or sea-dew, were offspring of the sea; and as Love is Beauty's son, Rosemary is his nearest relative.

The sea his mother Venus came on;
And hence some reverend men approve
Of rosemary in making love.

Butler, *Hudibras*, Pt ii, c.1

***Rosemary, an emblem of remembrance***. Thus Ophelia says, 'There's rosemary, that's for remembrance.' According to ancient tradition, this herb strengthens the memory. As Hungary water, it was once very extensively taken to quiet the nerves. It was much used in weddings, and to wear rosemary in ancient times was as significant of a wedding as to wear a white favour. When the Nurse in *Romeo and Juliet* asks, 'Doth not rosemary and Romeo begin both with a [i.e. one] letter?' she refers to these emblematical characteristics of the herb. In the language of flowers it means 'Fidelity in love'.

**Rosemordris Circle.** *See* Merry Maidens.

**Rosencrantz** and **Guildenstern.** Time-serving courtiers, willing to betray anyone, and do any 'genteel' dirty work to please a king. (Shakespeare, *Hamlet.*)

**Rosetta Stone, The.** A stone found in 1799 by M. Boussard, a French officer of engineers, in an excavation made at Fort St Julien, near Rosetta, in the Nile delta. It has an inscription in three different languages – the hieroglyphic, the demotic, and the Greek. It was erected 195 BC, in honour of Ptolemy Epiphanes, because he remitted the dues of the sacerdotal body. The great value of this stone is that it furnished the key whereby the Egyptian hieroglyphics have been deciphered.

**Rosicrucians.** A secret society of mystics and alchemists that is first heard of in 1614 (when was published at Cassel the anonymous *Fama fraternitatis des löblichen Ordens des Rosenkreuzes*), but that was reputed to have been founded by a certain Christian Rosenkreutz in the second half of the 15th century. Nothing is known of him or of the early history of this society, if, indeed, it ever really existed except as a kind of parody. In Freemasonry there is still an order or degree named the Rosy Cross.

It has been suggested that the title is neither from the founder nor from 'rose cross', but from *ros crux,* dew cross. Dew was considered the most powerful solvent of gold; and *cross* in alchemy is the symbol of light, because any figure of a cross contains the three letters L V X (light). 'Lux' is the menstruum of the red dragon (i.e. corporeal light), and this gross light properly digested produces gold, and dew is the digester. Hence the Rosicrucians are those who used dew for digesting lux or light, with the object of finding the philosopher's stone.

As for the Rosycross philosophers,
Whom you will have to be but sorcerers,
What they pretend to is no more
Than Trismegistus did before,
Pythagoras, old Zoroaster,
And Apollonius their master.

Butler, *Hudibras*, Pt ii, 3

**Rosin Bible. The.** *See* Bible, specially named.

**Rosinante.** *See* Rozinante.

**Ross** (Celtic). A headland; as Roslin, Culross, Rossberg, Montrose, Roxburgh, Ardrossan, etc.

*Ross*, from the Welsh *rhos* (a moor); found in Welsh and Cornish names, as Rossal Rusholme, etc.

***The Man of Ross***. A name given to John Kyrle (1637–1724), a native of Whitehouse, in Gloucestershire. He resided the greater part of his life in the village of Ross, Herefordshire, and was famous for his benevolence and for supplying needy parishes with churches. The Kyrle Society (*q.v.*) was named in his honour.

Who taught that heaven-directed spire to rise?
'The Man of Ross,' each lisping babe replies.

Pope, *Moral Essays*

**Rosse.** A famous sword which the dwarf Alberich gave to Otwit, King of Lombardy. It struck so fine a cut that it left no 'gap', shone like glass, and was adorned with gold.

This sword to thee I give: it is all bright of hue;
Whatever it may cleave, no gap will there ensue,
From Almari I brought it, and Rossë is its name;
Wherever swords are drawn, 'twill put them all to shame.

*The Heldenbuch*

**Rossel.** The second son of Reynard the Fox in the mediaeval beast-romance of that name. *Cp.* Russel.

**Rostrum.** A pulpit, or stand for public speakers, in Latin; the beak of a ship. In Rome, the platform in the Forum from which orators addressed the public was ornamented with the *rostra*, or ship-prows, taken from the Antiates in 338 BC.

**Rota.** A short-lived political club, founded in London in 1659 by James Harrington, author of *Oceana* (1656). Its objects were to introduce rotation in Government offices and voting by ballot. It met at the Turk's Head, in New Palace Yard, Westminster, and did not survive the

Restoration. Its republican principles are outlined in *Oceana*.

**Rota Romana.** A Roman Catholic ecclesiastical court composed of twelve auditors under the presidency of a dean, who hear appeals and adjudicate when a conflict of rights occurs. The name is said to allude to the wheel-like (Lat. *rota*, wheel) plan of the room in which the court used to sit.

**Rote.** ***To learn by rote*** is to learn by means of repetition, i.e. by going over the same beaten track or *route* again and again. *Rote* is really the same word as *route*.

> Take hackney'd jokes from Miller got by rote.
>
> Byron, *English Bards, etc.*

**Rotten Row.** Said to be so called from O.Fr. *route le roi* or *route du roi*, because it formed part of the old royal route from the palace of the Plantagenet kings at Westminster to the royal forests. Camden derives the word from *rotteran*, to muster, as the place where soldiers mustered. Another derivation is Norman *Ratten Row* (roundabout way), being the way corpses were carried to avoid the public thoroughfares. Others suggest A.S. *rot*, pleasant, cheerful; or simply *rotten*, referring to the soft material with which the road was covered.

**Roué.** The profligate Duke of Orleans, Regent of France, first used this word in its modern sense (about 1720). It was his ambition to collect round him companions as worthless as himself, and he used facetiously to boast that there was not one of them who did not deserve to be broken on the *wheel* – that being the most ordinary punishment for malefactors at the time; hence these profligates went by the name of Orleans' *roués* or wheels. The most notorious *roués* were the Dukes of Richelieu, Broglie, Biron, and Brancas, together with Canillac and Nocé; in England, the Dukes of Rochester and Buckingham.

**Rouen.** ***Aller à Rouen.*** To go to ruin. The French are full of these puns, and our merry forefathers indulged in them also, as, *You are on the highway to Needham* (a market town in Suffolk), i.e. your courses will lead you to poverty.

***The Bloody Feast of Rouen*** (1356). Charles the Dauphin gave a banquet to his private friends at Rouen, to which his brother-in-law Charles the Bad was invited. While the guests were at table King Jean entered the room with a numerous escort, exclaiming, 'Traitor, thou art not worthy to sit at table with my son!' Then, turning to his guards, he added, 'Take him hence! By holy Paul, I will neither eat nor drink till his head be brought me!' Then, seizing an iron maçe from one of the men at arms, he struck another of the guests between the shoulders, exclaiming, 'Out, proud traitor! by the soul of my father, thou shalt not live!' Four of the guests were beheaded on the spot.

**Rouge Croix.** One of the pursuivants of the Heralds' College (*q.v.*). So called from the red cross of St George, the patron saint of England.

**Rouge Dragon.** The pursuivant founded by Henry VII. The Red Dragon was the ensign of Cadwalader, the last Welsh king of the Britons, an ancestor of Henry VII, who employed it as the dexter supporter of his coat of arms.

**Rouge et Noir** (Fr. red and black). A game of chance; so called because of the red and black diamond-shaped compartments on the board. The dealer deals out to *noir* first till the sum of the pips exceeds thirty, then to *rouge* in the same manner. That packet which comes nearest to thirty-one is the winner of the stakes.

**Rough-hewn.** Shaped in the rough, not finished, unpolished, ill-mannered, raw; as a 'rough-hewn seaman' (Bacon); a 'rough-hewn discourse' (Howel).

> There's a divinity that shapes our ends,
> Rough-hew them how we will.
>
> Shakespeare, *Hamlet*, 5, 2

**Rough Music,** called in Somersetshire *skimmity-riding* (*cp.* Skimmington), and by the Basques *toberac*. A ceremony which takes place after sunset, when the performers, to show their indignation against some man or woman who has outraged propriety, assemble before the house, and make an appalling din with bells, horns, tin pans, and other noisy instruments.

**Rough-shod.** ***Riding rough-shod over one.*** Treating one without the least consideration. The shoes of a horse that is *rough-shod* have the nails projecting to prevent it slipping.

**Rough and Ready.** So General Zachary Taylor (1784–1850), twelfth president of the United States, was called.

There was a Colonel Rough in the battle of Waterloo; fable tells that the Duke of Wellington used to say 'Rough and ready, colonel', and that the family adopted the words as their motto.

**Rouncival.** Large; of gigantic size. Certain large bones of extinct animals were at one time said to be the bones of the heroes who fell with Roland in Roncesvalles (*q.v.*). 'Rounceval peas' are those large peas called 'marrowfats', and a very large woman is called a *rouncival*.

Hereof, I take it, it comes that seeing a great woman we say she is a *rouncival*. Mandeville

**Round.** There is an archaic verb *to round* (A.S. *rúnian*), meaning to whisper, or to communicate confidentially. Browning uses it more than once, e.g. –

First make a laughing-stock of me and mine,
Then round us in the ears from morn to night
(Because we show wry faces at your mirth)
That you are robbed, starved, beaten and what not!
*The Ring and the Book*, iv, 599

Bunyan, in the *Pilgrim's Progress,* speaks of 'that lesson which I will round you in the ear'. *Cp.* also –

France … rounded in the ear with [by] … commodity [self-interest] hath resolved to [on] a most base … peace.
Shakespeare, *King John*, 2, 1

And ner the feend he drough as nought ne were,
Ful privëly, and rounëd in his eere,
'Herkë, my brother, herkë, by thi faith … '
Chaucer, *Canterbury Tales*, 7132

***A good round sum.*** A large sum of money. Shakespeare says the Justice has a 'big round belly, with good capon lined'; and the notion of puffed out or bloated is evidently the idea of Shylock when he says to Bassanio, ''Tis a good round sum.'

***A round peg in a square hole.*** *See* Peg.

***A round robin.*** A petition or protest signed in a circular form, so that no name heads the list. The device is French, and the term seems to be a corruption of *rond* (round) *ruban* (a ribbon). It was first adopted by the officers of government as a means of making known their grievances.

***At a round pace*** or ***rate***. Briskly, rapidly, smartly.

He cried again,
'To the wilds!' and Enid leading down the tracks
…
Round was their pace at first, but slacken'd soon.
Tennyson, *Enid and Geraint*, 28

***In round numbers.*** In whole numbers, without regarding the fractions. Thus we say the population of the United Kingdom is forty-five millions and a half, in round numbers, and that of Greater London seven millions and a half. The idea is that what is round is whole or perfect, and, of course, fractions, being broken numbers, cannot belong thereto.

***Round dealing.*** Honest, straightforward dealing, without branching off into underhand tricks, or deviating from the straight path into the byways of finesse.

Round dealing is the honour of man's nature.
Bacon

***Sellinger's Round.*** *See* Sellinger.

***To get round one.*** To take advantage of him by cajoling or flattery; to have one's own way through deception.

***To round on one.*** To turn on him; to turn informer against him.

***To walk the Round.*** Lawyers used frequently to give interviews to their clients in the Round Church in the Temple; and 'walking the Round' meant loitering about the church, in the hope of being hired for a witness.

**Round Table, The.** The table fabled to have been made by Merlin at Carduel for Uther Pendragon. Uther gave it to King Leodegraunce, of Cameliard, who gave it to King Arthur when the latter married Guinever, his daughter. It was circular to prevent any jealousy on the score of precedency; it seated 150 knights, and a place was left in it for the San Graal. The first reference to it is in Wace's *Roman de Brut* (1155); these legendary details are from Malory's *Morte d' Arthur*, III, i and ii.

There Galaad sat with manly grace,
Yet maiden meekness in his face;
There Morolt of the iron mace,
And love-lorn Tristrem there;
And Dinadam with lively glance,
And Lanval with the fairy lance,
And Mordred with his looks askance,
Brunor and Bevidere.
Why should I tell of numbers more?
Sir Cay, Sir Banier, and Sir Bore,
Sir Caradoc the keen.
The gentle Gawain's courteous lore,
Hector de Mares, and Pellinore,
And Lancelot, that evermore
Looked stol'n-wise on the queen.
Scott, *Bridal of Triermain*, ii, 13

The table shown at Winchester was recognised as ancient in the time of Henry III, but its anterior history is unknown. It is of wedge-shaped oak planks, and is 17 ft in diameter and 2¾ in. thick. At the back are 12 mortice holes in which 12 legs probably used to fit. It was for the accommodation of twelve favourite knights. Henry VIII showed it to François I, telling him that it was the one used by the British king.

***The Round Table*** was not peculiar to the reign of King Arthur, but was common in all the ages of chivalry. Thus the King of Ireland, father of the fair Christabelle, says in the ballad –

Is there never a knighte of my round tablë
This matter will undergo? Sir Cauline

In the eighth year of Edward I, Roger de Mortimer established a Round Table at Kenilworth for 'the encouragement of military pastimes'. At this foundation 100 knights and as many ladies were entertained at the founder's expense. About seventy years later, Edward III erected a splendid table at Windsor. It was 200 feet in diameter, and the expense of entertaining the knights thereof amounted to £100 a week.

***Knights of the Round Table.*** According to Malory (*Morte d'Arthur*, III, i, ii) there were 150 knights who had 'sieges' at the table. King Leodegraunce brought 100 when, at the wedding of his daughter Guinever, he gave the table to King Arthur; Merlin filled up twenty-eight of the vacant seats, and the king elected Gawaine and Tor; the remaining twenty were left for those who might prove worthy.

A list of the knights and a description of their armour is given in the *Theatre of Honour* by Andrew Fairne (1622). According to this list, the number was 151; but in *Lancelot of the Lake* (vol. ii, p. 81), they are said to have amounted to 250.

The most celebrated of the Knights were Sirs Acolon, Agravain, Amoral of Wales, Ballamore, Banier, Beaumans, Beleobus, Bevidere, Belvour, Bersunt, Bliomberis, Bors (Arthur's natural son), Brandiles, Brunor, Caradoc, Colgrevance, Dinadan, Driam, Dodynas the Savage, Eric, Floll, Galahad, Gareth, Gaheris, Galohalt, Gawain (Arthur's nephew), Grislet, Ector of Maris, Kay, Ladynas, Lamerock, Launcelot du Lac (the seducer of Arthur's wife), Lanval, or Launfal, of the Fairy Lance, Lavain, Lionell, Lucan, Marhaus, Meliadus, Mordred the Traitor (Arthur's nephew), Morhault of the Iron Mace, Paginet, Palamedes, Pharamond, Pelleas, Pellinore, Persuant of Inde (meaning of the *indigo* or blue armour), Percivall, Peredur, Ryence, Sagramour le Desirus, Sagris, Superbilis, Tor, Tristram, Turquine, Wigalois, Wigamor, and Ywain. These knights went forth into all countries in quest of adventures, but their chief exploits occurred in quest of the San Graal (*q.v.*) or Holy Cup, brought to Britain by Joseph of Arimathea.

> Sir Lancelot is meant for a model of fidelity, bravery, frailty in love, and repentance; Sir Galahad of chastity; Sir Gawain of courtesy; Sir Kay of a rude, boastful knight; and Sir Modred of treachery.

There is still a 'Knights of the Round Table' Club, which claims to be the oldest social club in the world, having been founded in 1721. Garrick, Dickens, Toole, Sir Henry Irving, Tenniel, and Carl Rosa are among those who have been members.

***A Round Table Conference.*** A conference between political parties in which each has equal authority, and at which it is agreed that the questions in dispute shall be settled amicably and with the maximum amount of 'give and take' on each side.

The expression came into prominence in connection with a private conference in the house of Sir William Harcourt, January 14th, 1887, with the view of reuniting, if possible, the Liberal party, broken up by Gladstone's Irish policy.

**Roundabout**. Ancient circular encampments are so called.

> His desire of his companion a Pict's camp, or Roundabout. Scott, *The Antiquary*, ch. 1

***What you lose on the swings you make up on the roundabouts.*** *See* Swing.

**Roundheads.** Puritans of the Civil War period; especially Cromwell's soldiers. So called because they wore their hair short, while the Royalists wore long hair covering their shoulders.

> And ere their butter 'gan to coddle,
> A bullet churned i' th' Roundhead's noddle.
> *Men Miracles*, p. 43 (1656)

**Roundle,** in heraldry, is a charge of a circular form. There are a number of varieties, distinguished by their colours or tinctures, as – a *Bezant*, tincture 'or'; *Plate*, 'argent'; *Torteau*, 'gules'; *Hurt*, 'azure'; *Ogress* or *Pellet*, 'sable'; *Pomey* (because supposed to resemble an *apple*, Fr. *pomme*), 'vert'; G*olpe*, 'purpure'; *Guze*, 'sanguine'; *Orange*, 'tenney'.

**Roup.** The name by which an auction is called in Scotland. It is a Scandinavian word, and is connected with the M.Swed. *röpa*, to shout.

**Rouse.** A good, hearty bumper; a drinking bout. *See* Carouse.

**Rout.** A common term in the 18th century for a large evening party or fashionable assemblage. *Cp.* Drum, Hurricane, etc.

**Routiers,** or **Rutters.** Mediaeval adventurers who made war a trade and let themselves out to anyone who would pay them. So called because they were always on the *route* or moving from place to place.

**Rove.** The original meaning was to shoot with arrows at marks that were selected at haphazard, the distance being unknown, with the object of practising judging distance. Hence –

***To shoot at rovers.*** To shoot at random without any distinct aim.

> Unbelievers are said by Clobery to 'shoot at rovers'. *Divine Glimpses*, p. 4 (1659)

***Running at rovers.*** Running wild; being without restraint.

**Row.** A disturbance, noise, or tumult, is 18th-century slang, and is probably a contraction of *rouse* (*q.v.*).

***A row-de-dow.*** A hubbub, a din.

***To kick up a row.*** To make a disturbance or a noise; to cause a commotion.

**Rowan,** or **Mountain Ash,** called in Westmorland the 'Wiggentree'. It was greatly venerated by the Druids, and was known as the 'Witchen' by the early Britons, because it was supposed to ward off witches.

> Their spells were vain. The hags returned
> To their queen in sorrowful mood,
> Crying that witches have no power
> Where thrives the Rowan tree wood.
> *Laidley Worm of Spindleston Heughs* (a ballad)

Its scientific name is *Pyrus aucuparia,* and it is of the natural order *rosaceae*, while the common Ash is of the Natural Order *sepiariae*. The Mountain Ash is *icosandria*, but the common Ash is *diandria*; the former is *pentagynia*, but the latter is *monogynia*; yet the two trees resemble each other in many respects.

**Rowdy.** A ruffian brawler, a 'rough', a riotous or turbulent fellow, whose delight is to make a row or disturbance. Hence *rowdyism* and *rowdy-dowdy*. The term was originally American (early 19th cent.) and denoted a wild and lawless backwoodsman.

**Rowland.** *See* Roland.

**Rowley. *Old Rowley.*** Charles II was so called from his favourite racehorse. A portion of the Newmarket racecourse is still called Rowley Mile, from the same horse.

***The Rowley Poems.*** Certain poems written by Thomas Chatterton (1752–70), and said by him to be the work of a 15th-century priest of Bristol named Thomas Rowley, who, in fact, was purely fictitious. He began to write them before he was 15, and, after having been refused by Dodsley, they were published in 1769. Many prominent connoisseurs and *littérateurs*, including Walpole, were hoaxed by them.

**Roxburghe Club, The.** An association of bibliophiles founded in 1812 for the purpose of printing rare works or MSS. It was named after John, Duke of Roxburghe, a celebrated collector of ancient literature (d.1812), and was the forerunner of a number of similar printing clubs, as the Camden, Cheetham, Percy, Shakespeare, Surtees, and Wharton, in England; the Abbotsford, Bannatyne, Maitland, and Spalding, in Scotland; and the Celtic Society of Ireland.

**Roy, Le,** or **la Reine, s'avisera** (the *king*, or *queen, will consider it*). This is the royal veto, last put in force March 11th, 1707, when Queen Anne refused her assent to a Scotch Militia Bill.

During the agitation for Catholic emancipation, George III threatened a veto, but the matter was not brought to the test.

**Royal.** A standard size of writing papers measuring 19 x 24 in. In printings it is 20 x 25 in. or 20 x 25½ in.; hence a royal octavo book measures 10 x 6¼ in.

***Super royal*** in printing papers measures (with slight variations) 20 x 27 in., and in writing papers 19 x 27 in.

**Royal Merchants.** The wealthy Venetian merchants of the 13th century, such as the Sanudos, the Justiniani, the Grimaldi, and others, who erected principalities in divers places of the Archipelago. They and their descendants enjoyed almost royal rights in these districts for many centuries.

> Glancing an eye of pity on his losses,
> That have of late so huddled on his back,
> Enough to press a royal merchant down.
> Shakespeare, *Merchant of Venice*, 4, 1

Sir Thomas Gresham was called a 'royal merchant'; and in 1767 Fletcher's comedy, *The Beggar's Bush* (1622) was produced as an opera with the title *The Royal Merchant.*

**Royal Titles.** *See* Rulers, Titles of.

**Royston** (Herts) means king's town; so called in honour of King Stephen, who erected a cross there. (Fr. *roy*.)

***A Royston horse and Cambridge Master of Arts will give way to no one.*** A Cambridgeshire proverb. Royston was famous for malt, which was sent to London on horseback. These heavy-laden beasts never moved out of the way. The Masters of Arts, being the great dons of Cambridge, had the wall conceded to them by the inhabitants out of courtesy.

**Rozinante.** The wretched jade of a riding-horse belonging to Don Quixote (*q.v.*). Although it was nothing but skin and bone – and worn out at that – he regarded it as a priceless charger surpassing 'the Bucephalus of Alexander and the Babieca of the Cid'. The name, which is applied to similar hacks, is from Span. *rocin*, a jade, the *ante* (before) implying that once upon a time, perhaps, it *had* been a horse.

**Ruach.** The Isle of Winds, visited by Pantagruel and his fleet on their way to the Oracle of the Holy Bottle (Rabelais IV, xliii); the isle of windy hopes and unmeaning flattery. The people lived on nothing but wind, ate nothing but wind, and drank nothing but wind. They had no other houses but weathercocks, seeing everyone was obliged to shift his way of life to the ever-changing caprice of court fashion; and they sowed no other seeds but the wind-flowers of promise and flattery. The common people got only a fan-puff of food very occasionally, but the richer sort banqueted daily on huge draughts of the same unsubstantial stuff.

**Rub.** An impediment. The expression is taken from bowls, where 'rub' means that something hinders the free movement of your bowl.

> Without rub or interruption. Swift
>
> Like a bowle that runneth in a smooth allie without anie rub. Stanghurst, p. 10

***Don't rub it in, old man!*** Yes, I know I've made a fool of myself, but you really needn't go on emphasising the fact!

**Rubber.** In whist, bridge, and some other games, a set of three games, the best two out of three, or the third game of the set. The origin of the term is uncertain, but it may be a transference from bowls, in which the collision of two balls is a *rubber*, because they rub against each other.

***Those who play at bowls must look out for rubbers.*** There is always some risk in anything you undertake, and you've got to be prepared to meet it. You must take the rough with the smooth; 'you can't make omelettes without breaking eggs'.

**Rüberzahl.** A gnome or pixie of German folklore, also known as 'Number Nip'. He is a mountain spirit, and haunts the Riesengebirge in Silesia and Bohemia.

**Rubicon.** ***To pass the Rubicon.*** To take some step from which it is not possible to recede. Thus, when the Austrians, in 1859, passed the Ticino, the act was a declaration of war against Sardinia; and in 1866, when the Italians passed the Adige, it was a declaration of war against Austria; and in August, 1914, when the Germans crossed the frontier into Belgium it was utterly impossible to avoid the armed intervention of Great Britain.

The Rubicon was a small river separating ancient Italy from Cisalpine Gaul (the province allotted to Julius Caesar). When, in 49 BC, Caesar crossed this stream he passed beyond the limits of his own province and became an invader of Italy, thus precipitating the Civil War.

**Rubric** (Lat. *rubrica*, red ochre, or vermilion). An ordinance or law was by the Romans called a rubric, because it was written with vermilion, in contradistinction to praetorian edicts or rules of the court, which were posted on a *white* ground (Juvenal, xiv, 192).

> Rubrica vetavit = the law has forbidden it.
> (Persius, v, 99)
>
> Praetores edicta sua in albo proponebant, ac rubricas [i.e. jus civile] translaterunt.
> Quintilian, xii, 3, 11

The liturgical directions, titles, etc., in a Prayer Book are known as the *Rubric* because these were (and in many cases still are) printed in red. Milton has an allusion to the custom of printing the names of certain saints (*cp.* Red Letter Day) in red in the Prayer Book Calendar.

> No date prefix'd
> Directs me in the starry rubric set.
> *Paradise Regained*, iv, 392

**Ruby.** The ancients considered the ruby to be an antidote to poison, to preserve persons from plague, to banish grief, to repress the ill effects of luxuries, and to divert the mind from evil thoughts.

It has always been a very valuable stone, and even today a fine Burma ruby will cost more than a diamond of the same size.

> Who can finde a virtuous woman? for her price is far above rubies.
> Prov. 31:10; *cp.* also Job 23:18, and Ps. 8:11

Marco Polo said that the king of Ceylon had the finest ruby ever seen. 'It is a span long, as thick as a man's arm, and without a flaw.' Kublai Khan offered the value of a city for it, but the king would not part with it though all the treasures of the world were to be laid at his feet.

***The perfect ruby.*** An alchemist's term for the elixir, or philosopher's stone.

> He that once has the flower of the sun,
> The perfect ruby, which we call elixir, ...
> Can confer honour, love, respect, long life,
> Give safety, valour, yea, and victory,
> To whom he will.
> Ben Jonson, *The Alchemist*, II, i

**Rudder.** ***Who won't be ruled by the rudder must be ruled by the rock.*** Who won't listen to reason must bear the consequences, like a ship that runs upon a rock if it will not answer the helm.

**Ruddock.** The redbreast, 'sacred to the household gods'; *see* Robin Redbreast. Shakespeare makes Arviragus say over Imogen –

> Thou shalt not lack
> The flower that's like thy face, pale primrose: nor
> The azured harebell … the ruddock would
> With charitable bill … bring thee all these.
> *Cymbeline*, 4, 2

**Ruddymane.** The infant son of Sir Mordant, in Spenser's *Faërie Queene* (II, i, iii); so called because his hand was red with his mother's blood. She had stabbed herself because her husband had been paralysed by a draught from an enchanted stream.

**Rudiger.** Margrave of Bechelaren, a wealthy Hun, liegeman of King Etzel, one of the principal characters in the *Nibelungenlied.* He was sent to Burgundy by King Etzel, to conduct Kriemhild to Hungary if she would consent to marry the Hunnish king. When Gunther and his suite went to pay a visit to Kriemhild, he entertained them all most hospitably, and gave his daughter in marriage to Kriemhild's youngest brother, Giselher. When the broil broke out in the dining-hall of King Etzel, and Rudiger was compelled to take part against the Burgundians, he fought with Kriemhild's second brother, Gernot. Rudiger struck Gernot 'through his helmet', and the prince struck the margrave 'through shield and morion', and 'down dead dropped both together, each by the other slain'.

**Rudolphine Tables, The.** Astronomical calculations begun by Tycho Brahé, continued by Kepler, and published in 1627. They were named after Kepler's patron, Kaiser Rudolph II.

**Rudra.** Father of the tempest gods in the *Hindu mythology* of the Vedas. The word means 'run about crying' (Sansk. *rud*, weep; *dra*, run), and the legend says that the boy ran about weeping because he had no name, whereupon Brahma said, 'Let thy name be Rud-dra.'

**Rue,** called 'herb of grace' (*q.v.*), because it was employed for sprinkling holy water. *See also* Difference. Ophelia says –

> There's rue for you, and here's some for me! we may call it 'herb of grace' o' Sundays.
> Shakespeare, *Hamlet*, 4, 6

**Ruff.** An early forerunner of whist, very popular in the late 16th and early 17th centuries, later called *slamm*. The act of trumping at whist, etc., especially when one cannot follow suit, is still called 'the ruff'.

**Ruffian Hall.** That part of West Smithfield, later the horse-market, where in the 16th century 'tryals of skill were plaid by ordinary ruffianly people with sword and buckler' (Blount, p. 562).

> The field commonly called West-Smith field, was for many yeares called *Ruffians Hall*, by reason it was the usuall place of Frayes and common fighting, during the Time that Sword-and-Bocklers were in use.
> *Howes' continuation of Stow's 'Annals'* (1631), p. 1024

**Rufus.** (***The Red***). William II of England (1066, 1087–1100).

Otho II of Germany; also called *The Bloody* (955, 973–83).

Gilbert de Clare, Earl of Gloucester, son-in-law of Edward I (slain 1313).

**Ruggiero.** *See* Rogero.

**Rukenaw, Dame.** The ape's wife in *Reynard the Fox* (*q.v.*). The word means noisy insolence.

**Ruksh** or **Rakush.** The horse of the Persian hero Rustem (*q.v.*).

> And Ruksh, his horse,
> Followed him, like a faithful hound, at heel –
> Ruksh, whose renown was noised through all the earth.
> Matt. Arnold, *Sohrab and Rustem*

**Rule,** or **Regulus, St.** A priest of Patrae in Achaia, who is said to have come to Scotland in the 4th century, bringing with him relics of St Andrew, and to have founded the town and bishopric of St Andrews. The name Killrule (*Cella Reguli*) perpetuates his memory.

> But I have solemn vows to pay …
> To far St Andrew's bound,
> Within the ocean-cave to pray,
> Where good St Rule his holy lay
> Sung to the billow's sound.
> Scott, *Marmion*, i, 20

**Rule, Britannia.** Words by Thomson, author of *The Seasons*; music by Dr Arne (1740). It first appeared in a masque entitled *Alfred*, in which the name of David Mallett is associated with that of James Thomson, and some think he was the real author.

**Rule Nisi.** A 'rule' is an order from one of the superior courts, and a 'rule nisi' (*cp.* Nisi) is such an order 'to show cause'. That is, the rule is to be held absolute *unless* the party to whom it applies can 'show cause' why it should not be so.

**Rule of Thumb.** *See* Thumb.

***Rule of the road.*** *See under* Road.

***Rule the roost.*** *See* Roast.

**Rulers, Titles of.** Titles of sovereigns and other rulers may be divided into two classes, viz. (1) designations that correspond more or less to our *King* or *Emperor* (such as *Bey*, *Mikado*, *Sultan*), and (2) appellatives that were originally the proper name of some individual ruler (as *Caesar*).

*Akhoond*. King and high priest of the Swat (N.W. Provinces, India).

*Ameer, Amir*. Ruler of Afghanistan, Sind, etc.

*Archon*. Chief of the nine magistrates of ancient Athens. The next in rank was called *Basileus*, and the third *Polemarch* (field marshal).

*Beglerbeg*. *See* Bey.

*Begum*. A queen, princess, or lady of high rank in India.

*Bey* – of Tunis. In Turkey, a bey is usually a superior military officer, though the title is often assumed by those who hold no official position. The governor of a province is known as a *beglar-bey* or *beglerbeg* ('lord of lords').

*Brenn* or *Brenhin* (war-chief) of the ancient Gauls. A dictator appointed by the Druids in times of danger.

*Bretwalda* (wielder of Britain). A title of some of the Anglo-Saxon kings who held supremacy over the rest; a king of the Heptarchy (*q.v.*).

*Cacique*. *See* Cazique.

*Caliph* or *Calif* (successor). Successors of Mahomet in temporal and spiritual matters; the office is now claimed by the Sultan of Turkey, but a Shiite caliphate was instituted in Persia in 1502 and the succession to this is claimed by the Sophi.

*Cazique* or *Cacique*. A native prince of the ancient Peruvians, Cubans, Mexicans, etc.

*Chagan*. The chief of the Avars.

*Cham*. *See* Khan.

*Cral*. The despot of ancient Servia.

*Czar*. *See* Tsar.

*Dey*. In Algiers, before it was annexed to France in 1830; also the 16th century rulers of Tunis and Tripoli (Turk, *dāi*, uncle).

*Diwan*. The native chief of Palanpur, India.

*Doge*. The ruler of the old Venetian Republic (697–1797); also of that of Genoa (1339–1797).

*Duke*. The ruler of a duchy; formerly in many European countries of sovereign rank. (Lat. *Dux*, a leader).

*Elector*. A Prince of the Holy Roman Empire (of sovereign rank) entitled to take part in the election of the Emperor.

*Emir*. The independent chieftain of certain Arabian provinces, as Bokhara, Nejd, etc.; also given to Arab chiefs who claim descent from Mahomet.

*Emperor*. The paramount ruler of an empire (as India or Japan); especially, in mediaeval times, the Holy Roman Empire; from Lat. *Imperator*, one who commands.

*Exarch*. The title of a viceroy of the Byzantine Emperors, especially the *Exarch* of Ravenna, who was *de facto* governor of Italy.

*Gaekwar*. Formerly the title of the monarch of the Mahrattas; now that of the native ruler of Baroda (his son being the *Gaekwad*). The word is Marathi for a cowherd.

*Holkar*. The title of the Maharajah of Indore.

*Hospodar*. The title borne by the princes of Moldavia and Wallachia before the union of those countries with Roumania (Slavic, lord, master).

*Imam*. A title of the Sultan as spiritual successor of Mahomet; also of the ruler of Yemen, Arabia.

*Imperator*. *See* Emperor.

*Inca*. The title of the sovereigns of Peru up to the conquest by Pizarro (1531).

*Kabaka*. The native ruler of the Buganda province of the Uganda Protectorate.

*Kaiser*. The German form of Lat. *Caesar* (*see below, also* Tsar): the old title of the Emperor of the Holy Roman Empire, and of the Emperors of Germany and of Austria.

*Khan*. The chief rulers of Tartar, Mongol, and Turkish tribes, as successors of Genghis Khan (d.1227). The word means lord or prince.

*Khedive*. The title conferred in 1867 by the Sultan of Turkey on the viceroy or governor of Egypt. In November, 1914, the Khedive, who had declared himself an adherent of the Central Powers, was deposed and a British Protectorate declared, the new Khedive assuming the title of Sultan. *Cp*. Vali.

*King*. The Anglo-Saxon *cyning*, literally 'a man of good birth' (*cyn*, tribe, kin, or race, with the patronymic *-ing*).

*Lama*. The priest-ruler of Tibet. *See* Lama.

*Maharajah* (Hind. 'the great king'). The title of many of the native rulers of Indian States.

*Maharao*. The title of the native rulers of Cutch, Kotah, and Sirohi, India.

*Maharao Rajah*. The native ruler of Bundi, India.

*Maharawal*. The native rulers of Banswara, Dungarpur, Jaisalmer, and Partabgarh, India.

*Mikado*. The popular title of the hereditary ruler of Japan – officially styled 'Emperor'. The name (like the Turkish *Sublime Porte*) means 'The August Door'. *Cp*. Shogun.

*Mir*. The native ruler of Khairpur, India.

*Mogul* or *Great Mogul*. The Emperors of Delhi, and rulers of the greater part of India from 1526 to 1857, of the Mongol line founded by Baber.

*Mpret*. The old title of the Albanian rulers (from Lat. *imperator*), revived in 1913 in favour of Prince William of Wied, whose Mpretship, as a result of the outbreak of the Great War, lasted only a few months.

*Nawab*. The native rulers of Bhopal, Tonk, Jaora, and some other Indian States.

*Negus* (properly *Negus Negust*, meaning 'king of kings'). The native name of the sovereign of Abyssinia – officially styled 'Emperor'.

*Nizam*. The title of the native ruler of Hyderabad, Deccan, since 1713.

*Padishah* (Pers. protecting lord). A title of the Sultan of Turkey, the Shah of Persia, and of the former Great Moguls; also of the King of Great Britain as Emperor of India.

*Pendragon*. The title assumed by the ancient British overlord.

*Polemarch*. *See* Archon.

*Prince*. Formerly in common use as the title of a reigning sovereign, as it still is in a few cases, such as the Prince of Monaco and Prince of Liechtenstein.

*Rajah*. Hindustani for *king* (*cp*. Maharajah): specifically the title of the native rulers of Cochin, Ratlam, Tippera, Chamba, Faridkot, Mandi, Pudukota, Rajgarh, Rajpipla, Sailana, and Tehri (Garhwal). *Cp*. Rex.

*Rex* (*reg-em*). The Latin equivalent of our 'king', connected with *regere*, to rule, and with Sanskrit *rajan* (whence Rajah), a king.

*Sachem, Sagamore*. Chieftains of certain tribes of North American Indians.

*Satrap*. The governor of a province in ancient Persia.

*Shah* (Pers. king). The supreme ruler of Persia and of some other Eastern countries. *Cp*. Padishah.

*Sheik*. An Arab chief, or head man of a tribe.

*Shogun*. The title of the virtual rulers of Japan (representing usurping families who kept the true Emperor in perpetual imprisonment) from about the close of the 12th century to the revolution of 1867–68. It means 'leader of an army', and was originally the title of military governors. Also called the Tycoon.

*Sindhia*. The special title of the Maharajah of Gwalior.

*Sirdar*. The commander-in-chief of the Egyptian army and military governor of Egypt.

*Stadtholder*. Originally a viceroy in a province of the Netherlands, but later the chief executive officer of the United Provinces.

*Sultan* (formerly also *Soldan*). The title of the rulers of many Mohammedan States, especially Turkey.

*Tetrarch*. The governor of the fourth part of a province in the ancient Roman Empire.

*Thakur Sahib*. The title of the native ruler of Gondal, India.

*Tsar* (from Lat. *Caesar*; *cp*. Kaiser). The popular title of the former Emperors of Russia (assumed in 1547 by Ivan the Terrible), but officially his only as King of Poland and a few other parts of his Empire. His wife was the *Tsarina* or *Tsaritza*, his son the *Tsarevich*, and his daughter the *Tsarevna*. The sovereign of Bulgaria is still officially styled *Tsar*.

*Tuan Muda*. The title of the heir-presumptive to the Rajah of Sarawak.

*Tycoon*. An alternative title of the Japanese Shogun (*q.v.*). The word is from Chinese and means 'great sovereign'.

*Vali*. The title of the governors of Egypt prior to 1867, when the style *Khedive* (*q.v.*) was granted by the Sultan.

*Voivode*, or *Vaivode*. Properly (Russ.) 'the leader of an army', the word was for a time assumed as a title by the Princes of Moldavia and Wallachia, later called Hospodars (*q.v.*).

*Wali*. A title of the native ruler, or Khan, of Kalat, India.

(2) The following names have been adopted in varying degrees as royal titles among the peoples mentioned:

*Abgarus* (The Grand). So the kings of Edessa were styled.

*Abimelech* (my father the king). The chief ruler of the ancient Philistines.

*Attabeg* (father prince). Persia, 1118.

*Augustus*. The title of the reigning Emperor of Rome, when the heir presumptive was styled 'Caesar'.

*Caesar*. Proper name adopted by the Roman emperors. *See* Kaiser; Tsar.

*Candace*. Proper name adopted by the queens of Ethiopia.

*Cyrus* (mighty). Ancient Persia.

*Darius*, Latin form of *Darawesh* (king). Ancient Persia.

*Melech* (king). Ancient Semitic tribes.

*Pharaoh* (light of the world). Ancient Egypt.

*Ptolemy*. Proper name adopted by Egypt after the death of Alexander.

*Sophy* or *Sophi*. A former title of the kings of Persia, from Çafi-ud-din, the founder of the ancient dynasty of the Çafi or Çafavi.

**Ruminate.** To think, to meditate upon some subject; properly, 'to chew the cud' (Lat. *rumino*, from *rumen*, the throat).

> To chew the cud of sweet and bitter fancy.
> Milton
>
> On a flowery bank he chews the cud. Dryden

**Rump, The,** or **Rump Parliament.** The nickname given to the remnant of the Long Parliament that was left after Pride's Purge (*q.v.*) in 1648, and lasted till it was eventually ejected by Cromwell in April, 1653; also to the later remnant of the same Parliament that was restored in May, 1659, and dissolved by Monk in the following February. The 'Rump' was composed of those members who most strenuously opposed Charles I and the Restoration.

> The few,
> Because they're wasted to the stumps,
> Are represented best by rumps.
> Butler, *Hudibras*, Pt iii, 2

***Rump and dozen.*** A rump of beef and a dozen of claret; or a rump steak and a dozen oysters. A not uncommon wager among sportsmen of the late 18th and early 19th centuries.

**Rumpelstilzchen.** A passionate little deformed dwarf of German folktale. A miller's daughter was enjoined by a king to spin straw into gold, and the dwarf did it for her, on condition that she would give him her first child. The maiden married the king, and grieved so bitterly when the child was born that the dwarf promised to relent if within three days she could find out his name. Two days were spent in vain guesses, but the third day one of the queen's servants heard a strange voice singing –

> Little dreams my dainty dame
> Rumpelstilzchen is my name.

The child was saved, and the dwarf killed himself with rage.

**Run** (*see also* Running).

***A long run, a short run.*** We say of a drama, 'It had a long run', meaning it attracted the people to the house, and was represented over and over again for many nights. The allusion is to a runner who continues his race for a long way. The drama ran on night after night without change.

***He that runs may read.*** The Bible quotation in Hab. 2:2, is, 'Write the vision, and make it plain upon tables, that he may run that readeth it.' Cowper says –

> But truths, on which depends our main concern
> ...
> Shine by the side of every path we tread
> With such a lustre, he that runs may read.
> *Tirocinium*

***In the long run.*** In the final result. This allusion is to race-running: one may get the start for a time, but in the long run, or entire race, the result may be different. The hare got the start, but in the long run the patient perseverance of the tortoise won the race.

***On the run.*** Moving from place to place and hiding from the authorities; said specially of rebels.

***To be run in.*** To be arrested and taken to the lock-up.

***To go with a run.*** To go swimmingly; 'without a hitch'. A seaman's phrase. A rope goes with a run when it is let go entirely, instead of being slackened gradually.

***To have the run of the house.*** Free access to it, and free liberty to partake of whatever comes to table. A 'run of events' means a series of good, bad, and indifferent, as they may chance to succeed each other. And the 'run of the house' means the food and domestic arrangements as they ordinarily occur.

***To run a man down.*** To depreciate him, or to abuse him to a third party.

***To run a rig.*** *See* Rig.

***To run amuck.*** *See* Amuck.

***To run on,*** or ***on wheels.*** To be excessively voluble, to 'talk the hind-leg off a donkey'.

***To run through one's inheritance.*** To squander it at a rapid rate.

***To run riot.*** *See* Riot.

***To run the show.*** To take charge of it, generally with ostentation; to make oneself responsible for its success.

**Runcible Spoon.** A kind of fork used with pickles, etc., having three broad prongs curved like a spoon, one of which has a sharp cutting edge; said to be so called in humorous reference to the slaughter (with sharp swords) at Roncesvalles (*q.v.*). Also a horn spoon with a bowl at each end, one the size of a tablespoon and the other the size of a teaspoon. There is a joint midway between the two bowls by which they can be folded over.

> They dined on mince and slices of quince,
> Which they ate with a runcible spoon.
> Edw. Lear, *The Owl and the Pussy-cat*

**Rune.** A letter or character of the earliest alphabet in use among the Gothic tribes of Northern Europe. They were employed for purposes of secrecy or for divination; and the word is also applied to ancient lore or poetry expressed in runes. *Rune* is related to A.S. *rūn*, secret.

> There were several sorts of runes employed by the Celts, as (1) the *Evil Rune*, when evil was to be invoked; (2) the *Securable Rune*, to secure from misadventure; (3) the *Victorious Rune*, to procure victory over enemies; (4) *Medicinal Rune*, for restoring to health the indisposed, or for averting danger, etc.

**Runic Staff,** or **Wand.** *See* Clog Almanac.

**Runners.** *See* Redbreasts.

**Running.** ***His shoes are made of running leather.*** He is given to roving. There may be a pun between *roan* and *run*.

***Quite out of the running.*** Quite out of court, not worthy of consideration; like a horse which has been 'scratched' for some race and so is not 'in the running'.

***Running footmen.*** Servants of the 'upper ten' in the early part of the 18th century, when no great house was complete without some half-dozen of them. Their duty was to run beside the fat Flemish mares of the period, and advise the innkeeper of the coming guests. The pole which they carried was to help the cumbrous coach out of the numerous sloughs. It is said that the notorious 'Old Q' (*q.v.*) was the last to employ these menials.

***Running Thursday.*** December 13th, 1688, two days after the flight of James II. A rumour ran that the French and Irish Papists had landed; a terrible panic ensued, and the people betook themselves to the country, running for their lives.

***Running water.*** No enchantment can subsist in a living stream; if, therefore, a person can interpose a brook betwixt himself and the witches, sprites, or goblins chasing him, he is in perfect safety. Burns's tale of *Tom o' Shanter* turns upon this superstition.

***Running the Hood.*** It is said that an old lady was passing over Haxey Hill, when the wind blew away her hood. Some boys began tossing it from one to the other, and the old lady so enjoyed the fun that she bequeathed thirteen acres of land, that thirteen candidates might be induced to renew the sport on the 6th of every January.

**Rupert.** ***Prince Rupert's drops.*** Bubbles made by dropping molten glass into water. Their form is that of a tadpole, and if the smallest portion of the 'tail' is nipped off, the whole flies into fine dust with explosive violence. These toys were named after Prince Rupert (1619–82), grandson of our James I, who introduced them into England.

> The first production of an author … is usually esteemed as a sort of Prince Rupert's drop, which is destroyed entirely if a person make on it but a single scratch. *Household Words*

**Rupert of Debate.** Edward Geoffrey, fourteenth Earl of Derby (1799–1869). It was when he was Mr Stanley, and the opponent of the great O (i.e. O'Connell), that Lord Lytton so described him, in allusion to the brilliant Royalist cavalry leader in the Civil War, Prince Rupert. *See above.*

> The brilliant chief, irregularly great,
> Frank, haughty, bold – the Rupert of Debate.
> *New Timon*

**Rush.** ***Friar Rush.*** A name given to the will-o'-the-wisp; also to a strolling demon who, it is said, once on a time got admittance into a monastery as a scullion, and played the monks divers pranks. *See* Friar's Lanthorn.

***It's a regular rush.*** A barefaced swindle, an exorbitant charge. Said when one is 'rushed' into paying a good deal more for something than it is worth.

***Not worth a rush.*** Worthless, not worth a straw. Floors used to be strewn with rushes before carpets were invented. Distinguished guests had clean, fresh rushes, but those of inferior grade had either the rushes which had been already used by their superiors, or none at all.

> Strangers have green rushes when daily guests are not worth a rush.
> Lyly, *Sappho and Phaon* (1584)

***Rush-bearing Sunday.*** A Sunday, generally near the time of the festival of the saint to whom the church is dedicated, when anciently it was customary to renew the rushes with which the church floor was strewed. The festival is still observed at Ambleside, Westmorland, on the last Sunday in July, the church being dedicated to St Anne, whose day is July 26th. The present custom is to make the festival a flower Sunday, with rushes and flowers formed into fanciful devices. The preceding Saturday is a holiday, being the day when the old rushes were removed.

**Russel.** A common name given to a fox, from its russet colour. *Cp.* Rossel.

Daun Russel, the fox, stert up at oones,
And by the garget hente Chaunteclere
And on his bak toward the wood him bere.
Chaucer, *The Nonnes Prestes Tale*

**Rustam,** or **Rustem.** The Persian Hercules, the son of Zâl, prince of Sedjistan, famous for his victory over the white dragon Asdeev. His combat for two days with Prince Isfendiar is a favourite subject with the Persian poets. Matthew Arnold's poem *Sohrab and Rustam* gives an account of Rustam fighting with and killing his son Sohrab.

Let Zâl and Rustum bluster as they will,
Or Hatim call to Supper – heed not you.
Fitzgerald, *Rubaiyat of Omar Khayyam*, x

**Rusty.** ***He turns rusty.*** Like a rusty bolt, he sticks and will not move; he's obstinate.

**Rye-house Plot.** A conspiracy in 1683 in favour of Monmouth and for the assassination of Charles II and his brother James on their way from Newmarket, hatched at the Rye House Farm, in Hertfordshire. As the house in which the king was lodging accidentally caught fire, the royal party left eight days sooner than they had intended, and the plot miscarried. Lord William Russell and Sidney were among those executed for complicity.

**Ryence, King.** A Welsh king of the Arthurian romances, who sent a dwarf to King Arthur to say he had overcome eleven kings, all of whom gave him their beards to purfell his mantle. He now required King Arthur to do likewise. King Arthur returned answer, 'My beard is full young yet for a purfell, but before it is long enough for such a purpose, King Ryence shall do me homage on both his knees.' *See* Percy's *Reliques*, series iii, Bk 1.

Spenser tells a similar story in the *Faërie Queene* (vi, i), in which Crudor refused to marry the Lady Briana till she sent him a mantle lined with the beards of knights and locks of ladies. Briana appointed Maleffort, her seneschal, to divest every lady that drew near the castle of her locks, and every knight of his beard.

**Ryme.** A frost giant of *Scandinavian myth*, the enemy of the elves and fairies. At the end of the world he is to be the pilot of the ship *Naglefarë*.

**Rymenhild.** *See* King Horn.

**Ryot.** A tenant in India who pays a usufruct for his occupation. The Scripture parable of the husbandmen refers to such a tenure; the lord sent for his rent, which was not money but fruits, and the husbandmen stoned those who were sent, refusing to pay their 'lord'. Ryots have an hereditary and perpetual right of occupancy so long as they pay the usufruct, but if they refuse or neglect payment may be turned away.

**Ryparographer** (Gr. *ruparos*, foul, nasty). So Pliny calls Pyricus the painter, because he greatly excelled in the drawing of ridiculous and gross pictures. Rabelais might be called the ryparographer of wits.

**Rython.** A giant of Brittany, slain by King Arthur.

Rython, the mighty giant slain
By his good brand, relieved Bretagne.
Scott, *Bridal of Triermain*, ii, II

# S

**S.** The nineteenth letter of the English alphabet (eighteenth of the ancient Roman), representing the Phoenician and Hebrew *shin.*

***S*** in the nautical log-book signifies *smooth* (of the sea) or *snowy* (weather).

***Collar of S.S.*** or ***Esses.*** *See* Collar.

**'S.** A euphemistic abbreviation of *God's*, formerly much in use in common oaths and expletives; as, *'Sdeath* (God's death), *'Sblood*, *'Sdeins* (God's *dignes*, i.e. dignity), *'Sfoot*, etc.

> 'Sdeins, I know not what I should say to him, in the whole world! He values me at a crack'd three-farthings, for aught I see.
>
> Ben Jonson, *Every Man in his Humour*, *II*, i

> Why, 'sbuddikins, old Innocent himself
> May rub his eyes at the bustle!
>
> Browning, *Ring and the Book*, viii, 98

**$.** The typographical sign for dollars. It is thought to be a variation of the 8 with which 'pieces of eight' (*q.v.*) were stamped, and was in use in the United States before the adoption of the Federal currency.

**S.J.** The Society of Jesus; denoting that the priest after whose name they are placed is a Jesuit.

**SOS.** The arbitrary code signal used by Marconi wireless operators on board ship to summon the assistance of any vessels within call; hence, an urgent appeal for help.

The letters have been held to stand for *save our souls* or *save our ship*, but they were adopted merely for convenience, being 3 dots, 3 dashes, and 3 dots, ... — ...

During the Great War the school attached to headquarters for the training of snipers was known as *the SOS section.*

**S.P.Q.R.** Senatus Populus Que Romanus (the Roman Senate and People). Letters inscribed on the standards of ancient Rome.

**S.T.P.** ***Sanctae Theologias Professor.*** *Professor* is the Latin equivalent of the scholastic *Doctor.* 'D.D.' – i.e. Doctor of Divinity – is the English equivalent of 'S.T.P.'

**Saadia, Al.** A cuirass of silver which, according to Mohammedan tradition, belonged to King Saul and was lent to David for his encounter with Goliath. It was confiscated from the Jews on their expulsion from Medina, and fell into the hands of Mahomet.

**Sabaeans,** or **Sabeans.** The ancient people of Yemen, in south-western Arabia; from Arabic Saba', or Sheba, which was supposed to be the capital.

**Sabaism.** The worship of the stars, or the 'host of heaven' (from Heb. *Çābā*, host). The term is sometimes erroneously applied to the religion of the Sabians. *See* Sabianism.

**Sabaoth.** The Bible phrase *Lord God of Sabaoth* means *Lord God of Hosts*, not *of the Sabbath*, *Sabaoth* being Hebrew for 'armies' or 'hosts'. The epithaet has been frequently misunderstood; see, for instance, the last stanza of Spenser's *Faërie Queene* (VII, viii, 2):

> All that moveth doth in change delight:
> But thenceforth all shall rest eternally
> With Him that is the God of Sabaoth hight:
> O! that great Sabaoth God, grant me that Sabbath's sight!

**Sabbath** (Heb. *shābath*, to rest). Properly, the seventh day of the week, enjoined on the ancient Hebrews by the fourth Commandment (Exod. 20, 8–11) as a day of rest and worship; the Christian Sunday, 'the Lord's Day', the first day of the week, is often, wrongly, alluded to as 'the Sabbath'.

***A Sabbath Day's journey*** (Exod. 16:29; Acts 1:12), with the Jews was not to exceed the distance between the ark and the extreme end of the camp. This was 2,000 cubits, somewhat short of an English mile.

> Up to the hill by Hebron, seat of giants old,
> No journey of a Sabbath Day, and loaded so.
>
> Milton, *Samson Agonistes*

***Days set apart as Sabbaths.*** *Sunday* by Christians; *Monday* by the Greeks; *Tuesday* by the Persians; *Wednesday* by the Assyrians; *Thursday* by the Egyptians; *Friday* by the Mohammedans; *Saturday* by the Jews.

> Christians worship God on *Sunday*
> Grecian zealots hallow *Monday*,
> *Tuesday* Persians spend in prayer,
> Assyrians *Wednesday* revere,
> Egyptians *Thursday*, *Friday* Turks,
> On *Saturday* no Hebrew works. E. C. B.

***The Witches' Sabbath.*** *See* Witch.

**Sabbathians.** The disciples of Sabbathais Zwi, or Tsebhi of Smyrna (1626–76), perhaps the most remarkable 'Messiah' of modern times. At the age of fifteen he had mastered the Talmud, and at eighteen the Cabbala. When in a Turkish prison he embraced Mohammedanism, and later formed a half Mohammedan and half Jewish sect of Cabbalists.

**Sabbatical Year.** One year in seven, when all land with the ancient Jews was to lie fallow for twelve months. This law was founded on Exod. 23:10, etc.; Lev. 25:2–7; Deut. 15, 1–11.

**Sabean.** *See* Sabaeans.

**Sabellianism.** The tenets of the *Sabellians*, an obscure sect of Monarchians (*q.v.*) founded in the 3rd century by Sabellius, a Libyan priest. Little is known of their beliefs, but they were Unitarians and held that the Trinity merely expressed three relations or states of one and the same God. *See* Person (*Confounding the Persons*).

**Sabianism.** The religion of the *Sabians*, a sect mentioned in the Koran as being, with the Mohammedans, Jews, and Christians, believers in the true God.

> As to the true believers, and those who judaize, and the Sabians and the Christians, and the Magians, and the idolaters; verily God shall judge between them on the day of resurrection; for God is witness of all things. Koran, xxii

Some Arab commentators held that the Sabians professed to be Christians but were in reality star-worshippers; and they have been frequently confused with the adherents of Sabaism (*q.v.*).

**Sabines, The.** An ancient people of central Italy, living in the Apennines N. and N.E. of Rome, and subjugated by the Romans about 290 BC.

***The Rape of the Sabine Women.*** The legend connected with the founding of Rome is that as Romulus had difficulty in providing his followers with wives he invited the men of the neighbouring tribes to a celebration of games. In the absence of the menfolk the Roman youths raided the Sabine territory and carried off all the virgins they could find. The incident has frequently been treated in art; Rubens' canvas depicting the scene (now in the National Gallery, London) is one of the best known examples.

**Sable.** The heraldic term for *black*, shown in engraving by horizontal lines crossing perpendicular ones. The fur of the animal of this name is, of course, brown; but it is probable that in the 15th century, when the heraldic term was first used, the fur was dyed black, as seal fur is today

Sable fur was always much sought after, and very expensive.

By the Statute of Apparel (24 Henry VIII c. 13) it is ordained that none under the degree of an earl shall use sables. Bishop tells us that a thousand ducats were sometimes given for a 'face of sables' (*Blossoms*, 1577). Ben Jonson says, 'Would you not laugh to meet a great councillor of state in a flat cap, with trunk-hose … and yond haberdasher in a velvet gown trimmed with sables?' (*Discoveries*.)

***A suit of sables.*** A rich courtly dress.

> So long? Nay, then, let the devil wear black, for
> I'll have a suit of sables.
> Shakespeare, *Hamlet*, 3, 2

**Sabotage.** Wilful and malicious destruction of tools, plant, machinery, materials, etc., by discontented workmen or strikers. The term came into use after the great French railway strike of 1912, when the strikers cut the shoes (*sabots*) holding the railway lines.

**Sabra.** The legendary daughter of 'Ptolemy, King of Egypt', rescued by St George from the fangs of the dragon, and ultimately married to her deliverer. She is represented as pure in mind, saintly in character, a perfect citizen, daughter, and wife. Her three sons, born at a birth, were named Guy, Alexander, and David. Sabra died from the 'pricks of a thorny brake'.

**Sabreur. *Le beau sabreur*** (the handsome or famous swordsman). Joachim Murat (1771–1815).

**Sabrina.** The Latin name of the river Severn, but in British legend the name of the daughter of Locrine and his concubine Estrildis. Locrine's queen, Guendolen, vowed vengeance against Estrildis and her daughter, gathered an army together, and overthrew her husband. Sabrina fled and jumped into the Severn; Nereus took pity on her, and made her goddess of the river, which is hence poetically called Sabrina.

> There is a gentle nymph not far from hence,
> That with moist curb sways the smooth Severn stream,
> Sabrina is her name, a virgin pure.
> Milton, *Comus*, 840

**Saccharissa.** A name bestowed by Waller on Lady Dorothy Sidney (b.1617), eldest daughter of the Earl of Leicester, who, in 1639, married Lord Spencer of Wormleighton, afterwards Earl of Sunderland. Aubrey says that he was passionately in love with the lady, but the poems themselves give the impression that the affair was merely a poetical pose, which, at that period, was very fashionable.

**Sacco Benedetto** or **San Benito** (Span. the blessed sack or cloak). The yellow linen robe with two crosses on it, and painted over with flames and devils, in which persons condemned by the Spanish Inquisition were arrayed when they went to the stake. *See* Auto da fé. In the case of those who expressed repentance for their errors, the flames were directed downwards. Penitents who had been taken before the Inquisition had to wear this badge for a stated period. Those worn by Jews, sorcerers, and renegades bore a St Andrew's cross in red on back and front.

***Sack*** was used of any loose upper garment hanging down the back from the shoulders; hence 'sac-friars' or *fratres saccati*.

**Sachem.** A chief among some of the North American Indian tribes. *Sagamore* is a similar title.

**Sack.** A bag. According to tradition, it was the last word uttered before the tongues were confounded at Babel.

***To get the sack,*** or ***To be sacked.*** To get discharged by one's employer. The phrase was current in France in the 17th century (*On luy a donné son sac*); and the probable explanation of the term is that mechanics carried their implements in a bag or sack, and when discharged received it back so that they might replace in it their tools, and seek a job elsewhere. The Sultan used to put into a sack, and throw into the Bosporus, any one of his harem he wished out of the way; but there is no connection between this and our saying.

There are many cognate phrases, as *to get the bag*, *to receive the canvas*, etc. The French *trousser vos quilles* (pack up your ninepins *or* toys) is another idea, similar to 'Pack up your tatters and follow the drum.'

***A sack race.*** A village sport in which each runner is tied up to the neck in a sack. In some cases the candidates have to make short leaps, in other cases they are at liberty to run as well as the limits of the sack will allow them.

***Sack.*** Any dry wine, as sherry sack, Madeira sack, Canary sack, and Palm sack. (From Fr. *sec*, dry.)

**Sackerson.** The famous bear kept at Paris Garden (*q.v.*) in Shakespeare's time.

**Sacrament.** Originally 'a military oath' (Lat. *sacramentum*) taken by the Roman soldiers not to desert their standard, turn their back on the enemy, or abandon their general. We also, in the sacrament of baptism, take a military oath 'to fight manfully under the banner of Christ'. The early Christians used the word to signify 'a sacred mystery', and hence its application to baptism, the Eucharist, marriage, confirmation, etc.

***The five sacraments*** are Confirmation, Penance, Orders, Matrimony, and Extreme Unction. These are not counted 'Sacraments of the Gospel'. *See Thirty-nine Articles*, Article xxv.

***The seven sacraments*** are Baptism, Confirmation, the Eucharist, Penance, Orders, Matrimony, and Extreme Unction.

***The two sacraments*** of the Protestant Churches are Baptism and the Lord's Supper.

**Sacramentarians.** Those who believe that no change takes place in the eucharistic elements after consecration, but that the bread and wine are simply emblems of the body and blood of Christ. The name is applied specially to a party of 16th century German Reformers who separated from Luther.

**Sacred.** Applied to that which is consecrated (Lat. *sacrare*, to consecrate), or dedicated to, or set apart for, religious use.

***The Sacred Band.*** A body of 300 Theban 'Ironsides' who fought against Sparta in the 4th century BC. They specially distinguished themselves at Leuctra (371), and the Band was annihilated at Chaeronea (338).

***The Sacred City.*** *See* Holy City.

***The Sacred College.*** The College of Cardinals (*q.v.*) at Rome.

***The Sacred Heart.*** The 'Feast of the Sacred Heart of Jesus' owes its origin to a French nun of the 17th century, St Mary Margaret Alacoque, of Burgundy, who practised devotion to the Saviour's heart in consequence of a vision. The devotion was sanctioned by Pope Clement XII in 1732, and extended to the whole Church by Pius IX in 1856.

***The Sacred Isle,*** or ***Holy Island.*** An epithet used of Ireland because of its many saints, and of Guernsey for its many monks. The island referred to by Moore in his *Irish Melodies* is Scattery, to which St Senanus retired, and vowed that no woman should set foot thereon.

> Oh, haste and leave this sacred isle,
> Unholy bark, ere morning smile.
>
> *St Senanus and the Lady*

Enhallow (from the Norse *Eyinhalga*, holy isle) is the name of a small island in the Orkney group, where cells of the Irish anchorite fathers are said still to exist.

***The Sacred War.*** In Greek history, one of the wars waged by the Amphictyonic League in defence of the temple and oracle of Delphi.

(1) Against the Cirrhaeans (594–587 BC).

(2) For the restoration of Delphi to the Phocians, from whom it had been taken (448–447 BC).

(3) Against Philip of Macedon (346 BC).

***The Sacred Way.*** *See* Via Sacra.

***The Sacred Weed.*** Vervain (*see Herba Sacra*), or – humorously – tobacco.

**Sacring Bell.** The little bell rung to give notice that the 'Host' is approaching. Now called *Sanctus bell*, from the words *Sanctus, sanctus, sanctus, dominus, Deus Sabaoth*, pronounced by the priest. From the obsolete verb to *sacre*, to consecrate, used especially of sovereigns and bishops.

> He heard a little sacring bell ring to the elevation of a tomorrow mass.
>
> Reginald Scott, *Discovery of Witchcraft* (1584)
>
> The sacring of the kings of France. Temple

**Sacy's Bible.** *See* Bibles, specially named.

**Sad.** ***He's a sad dog. Un triste sujet.*** A playful way of saying a man is a debauchee.

***Sad bread*** (Lat. *panis gravis*). Heavy bread, bread that has not risen properly. Shakespeare calls it 'distressful bread' – not the bread of distress, but the *panis gravis* or ill-made bread eaten by those who can't get better. In America unleavened cakes are known as *sad cakes*.

**Sadah.** The tenth night of the month Bahman, when – according to tradition – the ancient Persian king Hushang discovered fire through a stone, that he had hurled at a demon, striking a spark out of flint. In memory of this a fire festival was long held in Persia on this date, at which the king freed birds with lighted wisps attached to their feet.

**Saddle.** ***A saddle of mutton.*** The two loins with the connecting vertebrae.

***Boot and saddle.*** *See* Boot.

***Lose the horse and win the saddle.*** *See* Lose.

***Saddle-bag furniture.*** Chairs and so on upholstered in a cheap kind of carpeting, the design of which is based on that of the saddle-bags carried by camels in the East.

***Set the saddle on the right horse.*** Lay the blame on those who deserve it.

***To be in the saddle.*** To be in a position of authority, in office; also to be ready for work and eager to get on with it.

**Sadducees.** A Jewish party which existed about the time of Christ, and denied the existence of spirits and angels, and, of course, disbelieved in the resurrection of the dead; said to be so called from Sadoc or Zadok (*see* 2 Sam. 8:17), who is thought to have been a priest or rabbi some three centuries before the birth of Christ. They were opposed to the Pharisees in that they did not accept the oral parts of the Law traditionally handed down from Moses, and as they did not believe in future punishments, they punished offences with the utmost severity.

**Sadler's Wells** (near Islington, London). There was a well at this place called *Holy Well*, once noted for 'its extraordinary cures'. The priests of Clerkenwell Priory used to boast of its virtues. At the Reformation it was stopped up, and was wholly forgotten till 1683, when a Mr Sadler, in digging gravel for his garden, accidentally discovered it again. Hence the name. In 1765 a Mr Rosoman converted Sadler's garden into a theatre.

**Sadlerian Lectures.** Lectures on Algebra delivered in the University of Cambridge, and founded in 1710 by Lady Sadler.

**Saehrimnir.** The boar of Scandinavian myth, which is served to the gods in Valhalla every evening; by next morning the part eaten is miraculously restored.

**Safa.** A mountain near Mecca where, according to Arabian legend, Adam and Eve came together, after having been parted for two hundred years, during which time they wandered homeless over the face of the earth.

**Safety Matches.** In 1847 Schrötter, an Austrian chemist, discovered that red phosphorus gives off no fumes, and is virtually inert; but being mixed with chlorate of potash under slight pressure it explodes with violence. In 1855 Herr Böttger, of Sweden, put the one on the *box* and the other on the *match*; and later improvements have resulted in the match being tipped with a mixture of chlorate of potash, sulphide of antimony, bichromate of potassium and red lead, while on the box is a mixture of non-poisonous amorphous phosphorus and black oxide of manganese, so that the match must be rubbed on the box to bring the two together. *Cp.* Prometheans, Lucifers.

**Saffron.** ***He hath slept in a bed of saffron*** (Lat. *dormivit in sacco croci*). He has a very light heart, in reference to the exhilarating effects of saffron.

> With genial joy to warm his soul,
> Helen mixed saffron in the bowl.

**Saga** (plural **Sagas**). The Teutonic and Scandinavian mythological and historical traditions, chiefly compiled in the 12th and three following centuries. The most remarkable are those of *Lodbrog*, *Hervara*, *Vilkina*, *Voluspa*, *Volsunga*, *Blomsturvalla*, *Ynglinga*, *Olaf Tryggva-Sonar*, with those of *Jomsvikingia* and of *Knytlinga* (which contain the legendary history of Norway and Denmark), those of *Sturlinga* and *Eryrbiggia* (which contain the legendary history of Iceland), and the collections, the *Heims-Kringla* and *New Edda*, due to Snorro-Sturleson. *Cp.* Edda.

**Sagamore.** *See* Sachem.

**Sagan of Jerusalem,** in Dryden's *Absalom and Achitophel*, is designed for Dr Compton, Bishop of London; he was son of the Earl of Northampton, who fell in the royal cause at the battle of Hopton Heath. The Jewish Sagan was the deputy of the high priest; according to tradition, Moses was Aaron's Sagan.

**Sages, The Seven.** *See* Wise Men.

**Sagittarius** (Lat. the archer). One of the old constellations, the ninth sign of the Zodiac, which the sun enters about November 22nd. It represents the centaur Chiron, who at death was converted into the constellation.

**Sagittary.** The name given in the mediaeval romances to the centaur, a mythical monster half horse and half man, whose eyes sparkled like fire and struck dead like lightning, fabled to have been introduced into the Trojan armies.

> The dreadful Sagittary
> Appals our numbers.
>
> Shakespeare, *Troilus and Cressida*, 5, 5

The 'Saggittary' referred to in *Othello* 1, 1:

> Lead to the Sagittary the raised search,
> And there will I be with him,

was probably an inn, but may have been the Arsenal, where, it is said, the statue of an archer is still to be seen.

**Sagramour le Desirus.** A knight of the Round Table, introduced in the *Morte d'Arthur*, *Lancelot du Lac*, etc.

**Sahib** (Urdu, *friend*). A respectful form of address used by Hindus to Europeans, about equivalent to our 'Sir' in 'Yes, sir', 'No, sir'. Also, an Englishman or European, a woman being *Mem-sahib*.

**Sail.** ***Sailing under false colours.*** Pretending to be what you are not with the object of personal advantage. The allusion is to pirate vessels, which hoist any colours to elude detection.

***To sail before the wind, close to the wind,*** etc. *See* Wind.

***To set sail.*** To start on a voyage.

***To strike sail.*** *See* Strike.

***You may hoist sail.*** Cut your stick, be off. Maria saucily says to Viola, dressed in man's apparel –

> Will you hoist sail, sir? Here lies your way.
>
> Shakespeare, *Twelfth Night*, 1, 5

**Sailor King, The.** William IV of England (1765, 1830–37), who entered the navy as midshipman in 1779, and was made Lord High Admiral in 1827.

**Saint.** *Note.* Individual saints who have a place in this *Dictionary of Phrase and Fable* will be found entered under their names.

Alexander III (1159–81) was the first Pope to restrict the right of canonisation (i.e. the making of a saint) to the Holy See; before his time it was performed by a synod of bishops and merely ratified by the Pope. It was not till the 4th century that persons other than martyrs were canonised, and none was inscribed on the Roll of the Saints until 608, when Boniface IV dedicated the Pantheon to St Mary of the Martyrs. The first saint to be made direct by a Pope was St Swidborg, canonised in 752 by Stephen II at the request of Pepin. St Alban, the English protomartyr, was canonised in 794 by Hadrian I, to please the Mercian King, Offa.

Popes who have been canonised. From the time of St Peter to the end of the 4th century all the Popes (with a few minor and doubtful exceptions) are popularly entitled 'Saint'; since then the following are the chief of those bearing the title:

Innocent I (402–17).
Leo the Great (440–61).
John I (523–26).
Gregory the Great (590–604).
Deusdedit I (615–19).
Martin I (649–54).
Leo II (682–84).
Sergius I (687–701).
Zacharias (741–52).
Paul I (757–67).
Leo III (795–816).
Paschal I (817–24).
Nicholas the Great (858–67).
Leo IX (1049–55).
Gregory VII, *Hildebrand* (1073–86).
Pius V (1566–72).

Among the kings and royalties so called are –

Edward the Martyr (961, 975–78).
Edward the Confessor (1004, 1042–66).
Eric IX of Sweden (1155–61).

Ethelred I, king of Wessex (866–871).

Ferdinand III of Castile and Leon (1200, 1217–52).

Irene (d.1124), the Empress; daughter of the king of Hungary and consort of John Comnenus, Byzantine Emperor.

Lawrence Justiniani, Patriarch of Venice (1380, 1451–55).

Louis IX of France (1215, 1226–70).

Margaret (d.1093), queen of Scotland, wife of William III.

Olaus II of Norway, brother of Harald III, called 'St Olaf the Double Beard' (984, 1026–30).

Stephen I of Hungary (979, 997–1038).

Theodora (d.867), Empress; consort of the Byzantine Emperor, Theophilus.

Wenceslaus (910, 928–936), king of Bohemia.

It is only on very rare occasions that persons are declared to be saints nowadays; but Joan of Arc, after being beatified by Leo XIII in 1894, was canonised by Pius X in 1909.

***The City of Saints.*** *See* City.

***The Island of Saints.*** So Ireland was called in the Middle Ages.

***The Latter-day Saints.*** The Mormons (*q.v.*).

***St Befana.*** There is no saint of this name, which is a corruption of *Epiphany*. *See* Befana.

**St Bernard Dog,** or **Great St Bernard.** A large and handsome breed of dog, so called because for many years they have been bred at the Hospice of St Bernard at the Great St Bernard Pass, Switzerland, and trained to track travellers lost in the snow.

**St Cloud.** A palace where many important events in French history took place, formerly standing about 1½ miles west of Paris, on the Seine. Built by Louis XIV (1658) on the site of an older castle, it was bought by Louis XVI for Marie Antoinette, and was later a favourite residence of Napoleon and of Napoleon III. It was badly damaged during the Franco-Prussian War, and afterwards demolished.

**St Cyr,** or **St-Cyr-l'École.** The famous French military school (about 14 miles south-west of Paris), transferred thither from Fontainebleau by Napoleon in 1806. The building was formerly occupied by the school for daughters of the nobility, founded by Mme de Maintenon.

**St Elian's Well.** A well that used to lie a mile or so south of Colwyn Bay, Denbighshire, but is long since dried up, and was famous as a 'cursing well'. The custom was to write the name of one's adversary on a pebble and drop it into the well; whereupon he was afflicted with cramp, ague, loss of cattle, etc., and would pine away and die.

**St Elmo,** or **St Elmo's Fire.** The corposant (Port. *corpo santo*, sacred body), or compozant, an electrical luminosity often seen on the masts and rigging of ships on dark, stormy nights. There is no saint of this name, and the suggestions are that 'Elmo' is a corruption of St *Anselm* (of Lucca), St *Erasmus* (the patron saint of Neapolitan sailors), or of *Helena*, sister of Castor and Pollux (*q.v.*), by which twin-name the St Elmo's Fire is also known.

> Sudden, breaking on their raptured sight,
> Appeared the splendour of St Elmo's light.
>
> *Orlando Furioso*, bk ix

**St Francis's Distemper.** Impecuniosity; being moneyless. Those of the Order of St Francis were not allowed to carry any money about them.

> I saw another case of gentlemen of St Francis's distemper. Rabelais, *Pantagruel*, v, 21

**St Germains, The Court of.** The intriguing circle of exiled English nobles and others that surrounded James II after his deposition, when he had settled at the château of St Germain-en-Laye (on the Seine, about 8 miles N.N.W. of Paris), a former residence of François I, Louis XIV, and others.

**St Giles's.** *See* Giles.

**St Grouse's Day.** A humorous name given to August 12th, when the grouse-shooting season commences in England.

**St James's, The Court of.** *See under* James.

**St John Lateran.** *See* Lateran.

**St Johnstone's Tippet.** A halter; so called from Johnstone the hangman.

> Sent to heaven wi' a St Johnstone's tippit about my hause. Scott, *Old Mortality*, ch. viii

**St Leger Sweepstakes.** A horse-race for three-year-olds, run at Doncaster early in September. It was instituted in 1776 by Colonel Anthony St Leger, of Park Hill, near Doncaster, but was not called the 'St Leger' (pron. silijer, or, popularly, ledger) till two years afterwards.

**St Martin's le Grand.** The familiar name for the postal system of Great Britain, because from 1825 its headquarters have been on and about the site of the ancient church and monastery of this name (dating from pre-Conquest times) at the south-east corner of Aldersgate Street, London.

**St Monday.** A facetious name sometimes given to Monday because many workmen and others who like an extended 'weekend' make it a holiday (*holy* day!). There is a story in the *Journal* of the Folk-lore Society (vol. i, p. 245) recording that –

> While Cromwell's army lay encamped at Perth, one of his zealous partisans, named Monday, died, and Cromwell offered a reward for the best lines on his death. A shoemaker of Perth brought the following:
> Blessed be the Sabbath Day,
> And cursed be worldly pelf;
> Tuesday will begin the week,
> Since Monday's hanged himself,
> which so pleased Cromwell that he not only gave the promised reward but made also a decree that shoemakers should be allowed to make Monday a standing holiday.

**St Partridge's Day.** A facetious name for September 1st, when partridge shooting becomes lawful in England.

**St Patrick's Purgatory.** *See* Patrick.

**St Petersburg.** The former name of the capital of the old Russian Empire, so called in honour of Peter the Great, who founded it in 1703. Soon after the outbreak of the Great War in 1914 it was changed by Imperial rescript to *Petrograd*, this being the Russian, while the other is a German, equivalent of *Peter's Town*.

**St Simonianism.** The social and political system of Count de St Simon (1760–1825), who proposed the institution of a European parliament to arbitrate in all matters affecting Europe, and the establishment of a social hierarchy based on capacity and labour. Fable says that he was led to his 'social system' by the apparition of Charlemagne, which appeared to him one night in the Luxembourg, where he was suffering a temporary imprisonment.

**St Stephen's.** The Houses of Parliament are so called, because, at one time, the Commons used to sit in St Stephen's Chapel.

***St Stephen's loaves.*** Stones; the allusion, of course, is to the stoning of St Stephen (Acts 7:54–60).

> Having said this, he took up one of St Stephen's loaves, and was going to hit him with it.
> Rabelais, *Pantagruel*, v, 8

**Sake.** A form of the obsolete word *sac* (A.S. *sacu*, a dispute or lawsuit), meaning some official right or privilege, such as that of holding a manorial court.

The common phrases *For God's sake, for conscience' sake, for goodness' sake*, etc., mean 'out of consideration for' God, conscience, etc.

***For old time's sake.*** For the sake of old acquaintance, past times.

***For one's name's sake.*** Out of regard for one's character or good name.

***Sakes!*** or ***Sakes alive!*** Low expressions of surprise, admiration, etc., commoner in the United States than in England.

**Saker.** A piece of light artillery, used, especially on board ship, in the 16th and 17th centuries. The word is borrowed from the saker hawk (falcon).

> The cannon, blunderbuss, and saker,
> He was the inventor of and maker.
> Butler, *Hudibras*, i, 2

**Sakhrat.** A sacred stone of Mohammedan fable, one grain of which endows the possessor with miraculous powers. It is of an emerald colour; its reflection makes the sky blue. *See* Kaf.

**Saktism.** A Hindu religious cult, originating about the 5th century AD, based on the worship of the active producing principle (Prakriti) as manifested in the goddess wives of Siva (Durga, Kali, and Parvati), the female energy, or *Sakti*, of the primordial male, Purusha or Siva. The rites of these worshippers of Sakti are, in many cases, mere orgies of lust.

**Sakuntala.** The heroine of Kalidasa's great Sanskrit drama, *Sakuntala*. She was the daughter of a sage, Viswamita, and Menakâ, a water-nymph, and was brought up by a hermit. One day King Dushyanta came to the hermitage during a hunt, and persuaded her to marry him; and later, giving her a ring, returned to his throne. In due course a son was born, and Sakuntala set out with him to find his father. On the way, while bathing, she lost the ring, and the king did not recognise her owing to enchantment. Subsequently it was found by a fisherman in a fish he had caught (*cp.* Kentigern), the king recognised his wife, she was publicly proclaimed his queen, and Bhârata, his son and heir, became the founder of the glorious race of the Bhâratas.

**Sakya-Muni.** One of the names of Gautama Siddartha, the Buddha (*q.v.*), founder of Buddhism.

**Salad.** ***A pen'orth of salad oil.*** A strapping; a castigation. It is a joke on All Fools' Day to send one to the saddler's for a 'pen'orth of salad oil'. The pun is between 'salad oil', as above, and the French *avoir de la salade*, 'to be flogged'. The French *salader* and *salade* are derived from the *salle* or saddle on which schoolboys were at one time birched. A block for the purpose is still kept in some of our public schools.

***Salad days.*** Days of inexperience, when persons are very green.

> My salad days.
> When I was green in judgment.
> Shakespeare, *Antony and Cleopatra*, 1, 5

**Salamander** (Gr. *salamandra*, a kind of lizard). The name is now given to a family of amphibious urodela (newts, etc.), but anciently to a mythical lizard-like monster that was supposed to be able to live in fire, which, however, it quenched by the chill of its body. Pliny tells us he tried the experiment once, but the creature was soon burnt to a powder (*Nat. Hist.* x, 67; xxix, 4). It was adopted by Paracelsus as the name of the elemental being inhabiting fire (*gnomes* being those of the earth, *sylphs* of the air, and *undines* of the water), and was hence taken over by the Rosicrucian system, from which source Pope introduced salamanders into his *Rape of the Lock*.

> When the Fair in all their Pride expire,
> To their first Elements the Souls retire:
> The Sprites of fiery Termagants in Flame
> Mount up, and take a *Salamander's* name
> *Rape of the Lock*, i, 57

François I of France adopted as his badge a lizard in the midst of flames, with the legend *Nutrisco et extinguo* (I nourish and extinguish). The Italian motto from which this legend was borrowed was *Nudrisco il buono e spengo il reo* (I nourish the good and extinguish the bad). Fire purifies good metal, but consumes rubbish.

Falstaff calls Bardolph's nose 'a burning lamp', 'a salamander', and the drink that made such 'a fiery meteor' he calls 'fire'.

> I have maintained that salamander of yours with fire any time this two-and-thirty years.
> Shakespeare, *1 Henry IV*, 4, 3

***Salamander's wool.*** Asbestos, a fibrous mineral, affirmed by the Tartars to be made 'of the root of a tree'. It is sometimes called 'mountain flax', and is not combustible.

**Salary.** Originally 'salt rations' (Lat. *salarium*, *sal*, salt). The ancient Romans served out rations of salt and other necessaries to their soldiers and civil servants. The rations altogether were called by the general name of *salt*, and when money was substituted for the rations the stipend went by the same name.

**Salic.** Pertaining to the Salian Franks, a tribe of Franks who, in the 4th century AD, established themselves on the banks of the Sala (now known as the Yssel), and became the ancestors of the Merovingian kings of France.

> Which Salique, as I said, 'twixt Elbe and Sala,
> Is at this day in Germany called Meisen.
> Shakespeare, *Henry V*, 1, 2

***Salic Code.*** A Frankish law-book, written in Latin, extant during the Merovingian and Carolingian periods.

***The Salic Law.*** A law derived from the Salic Code limiting succession to the throne, land, etc., to heirs male to the exclusion of females, chiefly because certain military duties were connected with the holding of lands. In the early 14th century it became the fundamental law of the French monarchy, and the claim of Edward III to the French throne, based on his interpretation of the law, resulted in the Hundred Years War. It was, also, through the operation of the Salic Law that the Crowns of Hanover and England were separated when Queen Victoria came to the throne in 1837.

**Saliens, The.** In ancient Rome, a college of twelve priests of Mars traditionally instituted by Numa. The tale is that a shield (*see* Ancile) fell from heaven, and the nymph Egeria predicted that wherever it was preserved the people would be the dominant people of the earth. To prevent its being surreptitiously taken away, Numa had eleven others made exactly like it, and appointed twelve priests as guardians. Every year these young patricians promenaded the city, singing and dancing, and they finished the day with a most sumptuous banquet, insomuch that *saliares caena* became proverbial for a most sumptuous feast. The word 'saliens' means dancing.

> Nunc est bibendum …
> … nunc Saliaribus
> Ornare pulvinar Deorum
> Tempus erat dapibus.
> Horace, *1 Odes*, xxxvii, 2–4

**Salisbury Crags.** These rocky hills, near Arthur's Seat just outside Edinburgh, are so called from the Earl of Salisbury who accompanied Edward III on an expedition against the Scots.

**Sallee-man,** or **Sallee rover.** A pirate-ship; so called from Sallee, a seaport on the west coast of Morocco, the inhabitants of which were formerly notorious for their piracy.

**Sally Lunn.** A tea-cake; so called from a woman pastrycook of that name in Bath, who used to cry them about in a basket at the close of the 18th century. Dalmer, the baker, bought her recipe, and made a song about the buns.

**Salmacis.** A fountain of Caria, which rendered effeminate all those who bathed therein. It was in this fountain that Hermaphroditus changed his sex. (Ovid, *Metamorphoses*, iv, 285, and xvi, 319).

> Thy moist limbs melted into Salmacis.
>
> Swinburne, *Hermaphroditus*

**Salmagundi.** A mixture of minced veal, chicken, or turkey, anchovies or pickled herrings, and onions, all chopped together, and served with lemon-juice and oil. The word appeared in the 17th century; its origin is unknown, but fable has it that it was the name of one of the ladies attached to the suite of Mary de Medicis, wife of Henri IV of France, who either invented or popularised the dish.

In 1807 Washington Irving published a humorous periodical with this as the title.

**Salmoneus.** A legendary king of Elis, noted for his arrogance and impiety. He wished to be called a god, and to receive divine honour from his subjects. To imitate Jove's thunder he used to drive his chariot over a brazen bridge, and darted burning torches on every side to imitate lightning, for which impiety the king of gods and men hurled a thunderbolt at him, and sent him to the infernal regions.

**Salop.** *See* Shropshire.

**Salsabil.** A fountain in the Mohammedan Paradise (Koran ch. lxxvi). The name signifies water that flows pleasantly and gently down the throat.

**Salt.** Flavour, smack. The salt of youth is that vigour and strong passion which then predominates.

> Though we are justices, and doctors, and churchmen, Master Page, we have some salt of our youth in us.
>
> *Merry Wives of Windsor*, 2, 3

Shakespeare uses the term on several occasions for strong amorous passion. Thus Iago refers to it as 'hot as monkeys, salt as wolves in pride' (*Othello*, 3, 3). The Duke calls Angelo's base passion his 'salt imagination', because he supposed his victim to be Isabella, and not his betrothed wife whom the Duke forced him to marry (*Measure for Measure*, 5, 1).

A sailor of large experience is often called an *old salt*, the reason is obvious – he has been well *salted* by the sea.

***Spilling salt*** was held to be an unlucky omen by the Romans, and the superstition remains to this day, though, with us, the evil may be averted if he who spills the salt throw a pinch of it over the *left* shoulder with the *right* hand. In Leonardo da Vinci's famous picture of the Lord's Supper, Judas Iscariot is known by the salt-cellar knocked over accidentally by his arm. Salt was used in sacrifice by the Jews, as well as by the Greeks and Romans; and it is still used in baptism by the Roman Catholic clergy. It was an emblem of purity and the sanctifying influence of a holy life on others. Hence our Lord tells His disciples they are 'the salt of the earth' (Matt 5:13). Spilling the salt after it was placed on the head of the victim was a bad omen, hence the superstition.

It is still not uncommon to put salt into a coffin; for it is said that Satan hates salt, because it is the symbol of incorruption and immortality; and in Scotland it was long customary to throw a handful of salt on the top of the mash when brewing, to keep the witches from it. Salt really has some effect in moderating the fermentation and fining the liquor.

***A covenant of salt*** (Numb. 18:19). A covenant which could not be broken.As salt was a symbol of incorruption, it, of course, symbolised perpetuity.

> The Lord God of Israel gave the kingdom … to David … by a covenant of salt.
>
> 2 Chron. 13:5

***Attic salt.*** *See* Attic.

***Cum grano salis.*** With a grain of salt (*see below*).

***He won't earn salt for his porridge.*** He will never earn a penny.

***If the salt have lost its savour, wherewith shall it be salted?*** (Matt. 5:13). If men fall from grace, how shall they be restored? The reference is to rock salt, which loses its saltness if exposed to the hot sun.

***Not worth your salt.*** Not worth your wages. The reference is to the *salary* (*q.v.*) composed of rations of salt and other necessaries served out by the Romans to their soldiers, etc.

***Put some salt on his tail.*** Catch or apprehend him. The phrase is based on the direction given to small children to lay salt on a bird's tail if they want to catch it; they don't as a rule realise that if they can do this they must have already caught the bird!

> His intelligence is so good, that were you to come near him with soldiers or constables, … I shall answer for it you will never lay salt on his tail.
>
> Scott, *Redgauntlet*, ch. xi

***The salt of the earth.*** Properly, the elect; the perfect, or those approaching perfection (*see* Matt. 5:13); now, however, often used of the high and mighty ones, those with great power or even merely great wealth.

***To eat a man's salt.*** To partake of his hospitality. Among the Arabs to eat a man's salt was a sacred bond between the host and guest. No one who has eaten of another's salt should speak ill of him or do him an ill turn.

> Why dost thou shun the salt? that sacred pledge,
> Which, once partaken, blunts the sabre's edge,
> Makes even contending tribes in peace unite,
> And hated hosts seem brethren to the sight!
>
> Byron, *The Corsair*, ii, iv

***To salt a mine.*** To introduce pieces of ore, etc., into the workings so as to delude prospective purchasers or shareholders into the idea that a worthless mine is in reality a profitable investment.

***To salt an account, invoice, etc.*** To put the extreme value upon each article, and even something more, to give it piquancy and raise its market value, according to the maxim, *sal sapit omnia*.

***To sit above the salt*** – in a place of distinction. Formerly the family *saler* (salt cellar) was of massive silver, and placed in the middle of the table. Persons of distinction sat *above* the 'saler' – i.e. between it and the head of the table; dependents and inferior guests sat below.

> We took him up above the salt and made much of him.
> Kingsley, *Westward Ho!* ch. xv

***True to his salt.*** Faithful to his employers. Here *salt* means salary (*q.v.*).

***With a grain of salt*** (Lat. *Cum grano salis*). With great reservations or limitation; allowing it merely a *grain* of truth. As salt is sparingly used in condiments, so is truth in remarks to which this phrase is applied.

**Salt Hill.** The mound at Eton where the Eton scholars used to collect money for the Captain at the Montem (*q.v.*). All the money collected was called *salt* (*cp.* Salary).

**Salute.** According to tradition, on the triumphant return of Maximilian to Germany, after his second campaign, the town of Augsburg ordered 100 rounds of cannon to be discharged. The officer on service, fearing to have fallen short of the number, caused an extra round to be added. The town of Nuremberg ordered a like salute, and the custom became established.

***Salute,*** in the British navy, between two ships of equal rank, is made by firing an equal number of guns. If the vessels are of unequal rank, the superior fires the fewer rounds.

***Royal salute,*** in the British navy, consists (1) in firing twenty-one great guns, (2) in the officers lowering their sword-points, and (3) in dipping the colours.

In India the native rulers are all entitled by law to certain salutes, these range from 21 guns in the cases of the Maharajahs of Baroda, Gwalior, and Mysore, and the Nizam of Hyderabad, down to 19, 17, 15, 13, and 11 guns to rulers of lesser States.

**Salutations.** *Shaking hands.* A relic of the ancient custom of adversaries, in treating of a truce, taking hold of the weapon-hand to ensure against treachery.

*Lady's curtsey.* A relic of the ancient custom of women going on the knee to men of rank and power, originally to beg mercy, afterwards to acknowledge superiority.

*Taking off the hat.* A relic of the ancient custom of taking off the helmet when no danger is nigh. A man takes off his hat to show that he dares stand unarmed in your presence.

*Discharging guns as a salute.* To show that no fear exists, and therefore no guns will be required. This is like 'burying the hatchet' (*q.v.*).

*Lowering swords.* To express a willingness to put yourself unarmed in the power of the person saluted, from a full persuasion of his friendly feeling.

*Presenting arms* – i.e. offering to give them up, from the full persuasion of the peaceful and friendly disposition of the person so honoured.

**Salve.** Latin 'hail', 'welcome'. The word is often woven on door-mats.

***Salve, Regina!*** An antiphonal hymn to the Virgin Mary sung in Roman Catholic churches from Trinity Sunday to Advent, after lauds and complin. So called from the opening words. *Salve, regina misericordiae!* (Hail, Queen of compassion!)

**Sam. *To stand Sam.*** To pay the reckoning. The phrase is said to be an Americanism, and to have arisen from the letters US on the knapsacks of the soldiers. The government of 'Uncle Sam' (*see below*) has to pay, or 'stand Sam' for all; hence also the phrase *Nunky pays for all.*

***Uncle Sam.*** The personification of the Government, or the people, of the United

States – a facetious adaptation of the initials. Fable has it that the inspectors of Elbert Anderson's store on the Hudson were Ebenezer Wilson and his uncle Samuel Wilson, who went by the name of 'Uncle Sam'. The stores were marked EA – US (*Elbert Anderson, United States*), and one of the employers, being asked the meaning, said US stood for 'Uncle Sam'. The joke took, and in the War of Independence the men carried it with them, and it became stereotyped. Another account places the store at Troy, N.Y., and dates the legend from the War of 1812.

***Upon my Sam!*** (or ***Sammy!***) A humorous form of asseveration; also, *'pon my sacred Sam!*

**Samael.** The prince of demons in Rabbinical legend, who, in the guise of a serpent, tempted Eve; also called the angel of death.

**Samaj.** *See* Brahmo Samaj.

**Samanides.** A dynasty of ten kings in western Persia (about 872 to 1004), founded by Ismail al Samani.

**Samaritan.** ***A good Samaritan***. A philanthropist, one who attends upon the poor to aid them and give them relief (Luke 10:30–37).

**Sambo.** A pet name given to anyone of negro race; properly applied to the male offspring of a negro and mulatto. (Span, *zambo*, bow-legged; Lat. *scambus*.)

**Samian.** ***The Samian letter.*** The letter Y, the Letter of Pythagoras (*q.v.*), employed by him as the emblem of the straight and narrow path of virtue, which is one, but, if once deviated from, the farther the lines are extended the wider becomes the breach.

> When reason doubtful, like the Samian letter,
> Pointe him two ways, the narrower the better.
>
> Pope, *Dunciad*, iv

***The Samian Poet.*** Simonides the satirist, born at Samos (about 556 BC).

***The Samian Sage***, or ***The Samian.*** Pythagoras born at Samos (6th cent. BC).

> 'Tis enough,
> In this late age, adventurous to have touched
> Light on the numbers of the Samian sage.
>
> Thomson

**Samiel.** The Turkish name of the simoom, a hot, suffocating wind that blows occasionally in the East (Arab. *samm*, poison, Turk, *yel*, wind).

> Burning and headlong as the Samiel wind.
>
> Moore, *Lalla Rookh*, Pt i

**Samite.** A rich silk fabric with a warp of six threads, generally interwoven with gold, held in high esteem in the Middle Ages. So called after the Gr. *hexamiton*, *hex*, six, *mitos*, a thread. *Cp.* Dimity.

**Sammael.** *See* Samael.

**Samosatenian.** A Paulian, or follower of Paul of Samosata, an heretical bishop of Antioch from 260 to 272, who denied the personality of the Logos and of the Holy Spirit.

**Samosatian Philosopher, The.** Lucian of Samosata, a Greek satirist of the 2nd century AD.

> Just such another feast as was that of the Lapithae
> described by the philosopher of Samosata.
>
> Rabelais, *Pantagruel*, iv, 15

**Sampford Ghost, The.** A kind of exaggerated 'Cock Lane ghost' (*q.v.*) or Poltergeist, which haunted Sampford Peverell for about three years in the first decade of the 19th century. Besides the usual knockings, the inmates were beaten; in one instance a powerful 'unattached arm' flung a folio Greek Testament from a bed into the middle of a room. The Rev. Charles Caled Colton (credited as the author of these freaks) offered £100 to anyone who could explain the matter except on supernatural grounds. No one, however, claimed the reward. Colton died 1832.

**Sampo.** *See* Kalevala.

**Sampson.** ***A dominie Sampson***. A humble pedantic scholar, awkward, irascible, and very old-fashioned. A character in Scott's *Guy Mannering*.

**Samson.** Any man of unusual strength; so called from the ancient Hebrew hero (Judges 13–16). The name has been specially applied to Thomas Topham (d.1753), the 'British Samson', son of a London carpenter. He lifted three hogsheads of water (1,836 lb) in the presence of thousands of spectators at Coldbath Fields, May 28th, 1741, and eventually committed suicide; and to Richard Joy, the 'Kentish Samson', who died 1742, at the age of 67. His tombstone is in St Peter's churchyard, Isle of Thanet.

**San Benito.** *See* Sacco Benedetto.

**Sance-bell.** Same as 'Sanctus bell'. *See* Sacring-bell.

**Sancho Panza.** The squire of Don Quixote (*q.v.*), in Cervantes' romance, who became governor of Barataria; a short, pot-bellied rustic, full of common sense, but without a grain of 'spirituality'. He rode upon an ass, Dapple, and was famous for his proverbs. Panza, in Spanish, means *paunch*.

***A Sancho Panza.*** A rough and ready, sharp and humorous justice of the peace. In allusion to Sancho, as judge in the isle of Barataria.

***Sancho Panza's wife,*** called Teresa, Pt ii, i, 5; Maria, Pt ii, iv, 7; Juana, Pt i, 7; and Joan, Pt i, 21.

**Sanchoniathon.** The *Fragments of Sanchoniathon* are the literary remains of a supposed ancient Phoenician philosopher (alleged to have lived before the Trojan War), which are incorporated in the Phoenician History by Philo of Byblos (1st and 2nd cents AD), which History was drawn upon by Eusebius (about AD 320), the 'Father of Church History'. The name is Greek and seems to mean 'the whole law of Chon'; whether this is the correct interpretation or whether Sanchoniathon is intended to be a personal name, it is probable that there was no such collection or author, and that the name was invented by Philo to give an air of authority and antiquity to his own teachings.

**Sanctum Sanctorum** (Lat. *Holy of Holies*). A private room into which no one uninvited enters; properly the Holy of Holies in the Jewish Temple, a small chamber into which none but the high priest might enter, and that only on the Great Day of Atonement. A man's private house is his sanctuary; his own special private room in that house is the sanctuary of the sanctuary, or the *sanctum sanctorum*.

**Sancy Diamond, The.** A famous historical diamond (53½ carats) said to have belonged at one time to Charles the Bold of Burgundy, and named after the French ambassador in Constantinople, Nicholas de Harlay, Sieur de Sancy, who, about 1575, bought it for 70,000 francs. Later it was owned by Henri III and Henri IV of France, then by Queen Elizabeth; James II carried it with him in his flight to France in 1688, when it was sold to Louis XIV for £25,000. Louis XV wore it at his coronation, but during the Revolution it was disposed of to Prince Paul Demidoff for £80,000. In 1865 the Demidoff family sold it to Sir Jamsetjee Jeejeebhoy; it was in the market again in 1889, and rumour has it that it was subsequently acquired by the Tsar of Russia. Its present whereabouts is unknown.

**Sand.** ***A rope of sand.*** Something nominally effective and strong, but in reality worthless and untrustworthy.

***The sand-man is about.*** A playful remark addressed to children who are tired and 'sleepy-eyed'. *Cp.* Dustman.

***The sands are running out.*** Time is getting short; there will be little opportunity for doing what you have to do unless you take advantage of *now*. Often used in reference to one who evidently has not much longer to live. The allusion is to the hour-glass.

> Alas! dread lord, you see the case wherein I stand, and how little sand is left to run in my poor glass. *Reynard the Fox*, iv

***To plough*** or ***to number the sands.*** To undertake an endless or impossible task.

> Alas! poor duke, the task he undertakes
> Is numbering sands and drinking oceans dry.
> Shakespeare, *Richard II*, 2, 2

**Sand-blind.** Dim-sighted; not exactly blind, but with eyes of very little use. *Sand-* is here a corruption of the obsolete prefix *sam-*, meaning 'half'. English used to have *sam-dead*, *sam-ripe*, etc., and *sam-sodden* still survives in some dialects. In the *Merchant of Venice* Launcelot Gobbo connects it with *sand*, the gritty earth.

> This is my true-begotten father, who, being more than sand-blind, high-gravel blind, knows me not. Shakespeare, *Merchant of Venice*, 2, 2

**Sandabar** or **Sindibad.** Names given to a mediaeval collection of tales that are very much the same as those in the Greek *Syntipas the Philosopher* and the Arabic *Romance of the Seven Viziers* (known in Western Europe as *The Seven Sages* (*Wise Masters*), and derived from the *Fables of Bidpai* (*q.v.*). These names do not, in all probability, stand for the author or compiler, but result from Hebrew mistransliterations of the Arabic equivalent of *Bidpai* or *Pilpay*.

**Sandal.** ***A man without sandals.*** A prodigal; so called by the ancient Jews, because the seller gave his sandals to the buyer as a ratification of his bargain (Ruth 4:7).

***He wears the sandals of Theramenes.*** Said of a trimmer, an opportunist. Theramenes (put to death 404 BC) was one of the Athenian oligarchy, and was nicknamed *cothurnus* (i.e. a sandal or boot which might be worn on either foot), because no dependence could be placed on him. He blew hot and cold with the same breath.

**Sandalphon.** One of the three angels of Rabbinical legend who receive the prayers of the faithful, and weave them into crowns.

> And he gathers the prayers as he stands,
> And they change into flowers in his hands,
> Into garlands of purple and red.
> Longfellow, *Sandalphon*

**Sandemanians** or **Glassites.** A religious party expelled from the Church of Scotland for maintaining that national churches, being 'kingdoms of this world', are unlawful. Called *Glassites* from John Glas (1695–1773), the founder (1728), and called *Sandemanians* from Robert Sandeman (1718–71), a disciple of his, who published a series of letters on the subject in 1755. Members are admitted by a 'holy kiss', and abstain from all animal food which has not been well drained of blood; they believe in the community of property, and hold weekly communions.

**Sandford and Merton.** The schoolboy heroes of Thomas Day's old-fashioned children's tale of this name (published in three parts, 1783–89). 'Master' Tommy Merton is rich, selfish, untruthful, and generally objectionable; Harry Sandford, the farmer's son, is depicted as being the reverse in every respect.

**Sandie.** *See* Alec.

**Sandschaki-sherif.** *See* Sinjaqu'sh-sharif.

**Sandwich.** A piece of meat between two slices of bread; so called from the fourth Earl of Sandwich (1718–92 – the noted 'Jemmy Twitcher'), who passed whole days in gambling, bidding the waiter bring him for refreshment a piece of meat between two pieces of bread, which he ate without stopping from play. This contrivance was not first hit upon by the earl in the reign of George III, as the Romans were very fond of 'sandwiches', called by them *offula*.

***Sandwichman.*** A perambulating advertisement displayer, with an advertisement board before and behind.

**Sang-de-boeuf** (Fr. bullock's blood). The deep red with which ancient Chinese porcelain is often coloured.

**Sang-froid** (Fr., cold blood). Freedom from excitement or agitation. One does a thing 'with perfect *sang-froid*' when one does it coolly and collectedly, without unnecessary display.

> … cross-legg'd, with great sang-froid
> Among the scorching ruins he sat smoking
> Tobacco on a little carpet.
>
> Byron, *Don Juan*, VIII, cxxi

**Sanglamort** ('blood and death'). The imaginary sword of Braggadocchio (*q.v.*). He had stolen Sir Guyon's horse and spear, but not his sword.

> That vile knight, whoever that he be,
> Which hath thy Lady reft and knighthood shent,
> By Sanglamort my sword, whose deadly dent
> The blood hath of so many thousands shed,
> I swear, ere long, shall dearly it repent.
>
> Spenser, *Faërie Queene*, III, x, 32

**Sanglier, Sir.** The evil knight in Spenser's *Faërie Queene* (V, i, 20), punished by Sir Artegall when he was on his quest to free the lady Ierna from the thraldom of Grantorto, is said to be intended for Shane O'Neill, leader of the Irish insurgents in 1567. The word is French for *boar*.

***Le Sanglier des Ardennes.*** Guillaume de la Marck (1446–85), driven from Liège, for the murder of the Bishop of Liège, and beheaded by the Archduke Maximilian.

**Sangrado, Dr.** A name often applied to an ignorant or 'fossilised' medical practitioner, from the humbug in Le Sage's *Gil Blas* (1715), a tall, meagre, pale man, of very solemn appearance, who weighed every word he uttered, and gave an emphasis to his sage dicta. 'His reasoning was geometrical, and his opinions angular.' He prescribed warm water and bleeding for every ailment, for his great theory was that 'It is a gross error to suppose that blood is necessary for life.'

**Sangrail** or **Sangreal.** The Holy Grail, *see* Grail. Popular etymology used to explain the word as meaning the *real blood* of Christ, *sang-real*, or the wine used in the last supper; and a tradition sprang up that part of this wine-blood was preserved by Joseph of Arimathaea, in the Saint, or Holy, Grail.

**Sanguine** (Lat., *sanguis, sanguinis*, blood). The term used in heraldry for the deep red or purplish colour usually known as *murrey* (from the mulberry). In engravings it is indicated by lines of vert and purpure crossed, that is, diagonals from right to left crossing diagonals from left to right.

**Sanguinary James, A.** Slang for a sheep's head not singed. *Jemmy*, a sheep's head, is so called from James I who introduced into England the national Scotch dish of 'singed sheep's head and trotters'. No real Scotch dinner is complete without a haggis, a sheep's head and trotters, and a hotch-potch (in summer), or cocky leekie (in winter).

**Sanhedrin** (Gr. *syn*, together; *hedra*, a seat; i.e. a sitting together). The supreme council of the Jews, consisting of seventy priests and elders, and a president who, under the Romans, was the high priest. It took its rise soon after the exile from the municipal council of Jerusalem, and was in existence till about AD 425, when Theodosius the Younger forbad the Jews to build synagogues. All questions of the 'Law' were dogmatically settled by the Sanhedrin, and those who refused obedience were excommunicated.

In Dryden's *Absalom and Achitophel* (*q.v.*), the *Sanhedrim* stands for the English Parliament.

> The Sanhedrim long time as chief he ruled,
> Their reason guided, and their passion cooled.

**Sanjaksherif.** *See* Sinjaqu 'sh-sharif.

**Sans Culottes** (Fr., *without knee-breeches*, perhaps because they wore *trousers* instead). A name given by the aristocratic section during the French Revolution to the extremists of the working-classes, the favourite leader of which was Henriot. Hence *Sansculottism*, the principles, etc., of 'red republicans'.

**Sans Culottides.** The five complementary days added to the twelve months of the Revolutionary Calendar. Each month being made to consist of thirty days, the 'riff-raff' days which would not conform to the law were named in honour of the *sans culottes*, and made idle days or holidays.

**Sans Gêne, Mme.** The nickname of the wife of Lefebvre, Duke of Dantzic (1755–1820), one of Napoleon's marshals. She was originally a washerwoman, and followed her husband–then in the ranks – as a vivandière. She was kind and pleasant, but her rough and ready ways and ignorance of etiquette soon made her the butt of the court, and earned her the nickname, which means 'without constraint' or 'free and easy'.

**Sans peur et sans reproche** (Fr., Without fear and without reproach). Pierre du Terrail, Chevalier de Bayard (1476–1524) was called *Le chevalier sans peur et sans reproche*.

**Sans Souci** (Fr.). Free and easy, void of care. It is the name given by him to the palace built by Frederick the Great near Potsdam (1747).

***Enfant Sans Souci.*** The mediaeval French Tradesmen's company of actors, as opposed to the Lawyers', the 'Basochians' (*q.v.*). It was organised in the reign of Charles VIII, for the performance of short comedies, in which public characters and the manners of the day were turned into ridicule; *Maitre Pathelin* (*see* Moutons), an immense favourite with the Parisians, was one of their pieces. The manager of the 'Care-for-Nothings' (*sans souci*) was called 'The Prince of Fools'.

***The Philosopher of Sans-Souci.*** Frederick the Great (1712,1740–86).

**Sanscara.** The ten essential rites of Hindus of the first three castes: (1) at the conception of a child; (2) at the quickening; (3) at birth; (4) at naming; (5) carrying the child out to see the moon; (6) giving him food to eat; (7) the ceremony of tonsure; (8) investiture with the string; (9) the close of his studies; (10) the ceremony of 'marriage', when he is qualified to perform the sacrifices ordained.

**Sansfoy, Sansjoy, Sansloy.** Three Saracen brothers in Spenser's *Faërie Queene* (Bks I and II), who cared for neither God nor man. The first (*Faithless*) typifies infidelity and unbelief, and was slain by the Red Cross Knight. The second (*Joyless*) typifies spiritual misery; he fought the Red Cross Knight but was saved by Duessa, and carried in the car of Night to the infernal regions, where he was healed of his wounds by Aesculapius. The third (*Lawless*), having torn off the disguise of Archimago and wounded the lion, carried off Una into the wilderness. Her shrieks aroused the fauns and satyrs, who came to her rescue, and Sansloy fled. The reference is to the reign of Queen Mary, when the Reformation was carried captive, and the lion was wounded by the 'False-law of God'.

The three were sons of Aveugle (*Spiritual blindness*).

**Santa Casa** (Ital., the holy house). The reputed house in which the Virgin Mary lived at Nazareth, miraculously translated to Dalmatia, and finally to Italy. *See* Loretto.

**Santa Claus** or **Santa Klaus.** A contraction of Santa Nikolaus (i.e. St Nicolas), the patron saint of children. His feast-day is December 6th, and the vigil is still held in some places, but for the most part his name is now associated with Christmastide. The old custom used to be for someone, on December 5th, to assume the costume of a bishop and distribute small gifts to 'good children'. The present custom is to put toys and other little presents into a stocking late on Christmas Eve, when the children are asleep, and when they wake on Christmas morn they find in the stocking at the bedside the gift sent by Santa Claus. *See* Nicholas: Kriss Kringle.

**Sapho.** Mdlle de Scudéry (1607–1701), the French novelist and poet, went by this name among her own circle.

**Sapphics.** A four-lined verse-form of classical lyric poetry, named after the Greek poetess Sappho, who employed it, the fourth line being an Adonic. There must be a caesura at the fifth foot of each of the first three lines, which run thus:

— ⏑ | — — | — ‖ ⏑ ⏑ | — ⏑ | — ⏑

The Adonic is –

— ⏑ ⏑ | — ⏑ *or* — —

The first and third stanzas of the famous *Ode* of Horace, *Integer vitae* (i, 22), may be translated thus, preserving the metre:

He of sound life, who ne'er with sinners wendeth,
Needs no Moorish bow, such as malice bendeth,
Nor with poisoned darts life from harm defendeth,
Fuscus believe me.
Once I, unarmed, was in a forest roaming,
Singing love lays, when i' the secret gloaming
Rushed a huge wolf, which though in fury foaming,
Did not aggrieve me. E. C. B.

Probably the best example of Sapphics in English is Canning's *Needy Knife-grinder*.

**Sappho.** The famous Greek poetess of Lesbos, known as 'the Tenth Muse'. She lived about 600 BC, and is fabled to have thrown herself into the sea from the Leucadian promontory in consequence of her advances having been rejected by the beautiful youth Phaon.

Pope used the name in his *Moral Essays* (II) for Lady Mary Wortley Montagu (*cp.* Atossa). *See also* Sapho, *above*.

***The Sappho of Toulouse.*** Clémence Isaure (about 1450–1500), a wealthy lady of Toulouse, who instituted in 1490 the 'Jeux Floraux', and left funds to defray their annual expenses. She composed a beautiful *Ode to Spring*.

**Saracen.** Ducange derives the word from *Sarah* (Abraham's wife); Hottinger from the Arabic *saraca* (to steal); Forster from *sahra* (a desert); but probably it is the Arabic *sharakyoun* or *sharkeyn* (the eastern people), as opposed to Magharibë (the western people – i.e. of Morocco). In mediaeval romance the term was applied to Moslems generally; but among the Romans it denoted any of the nomadic tribes that raided the Syrian borders of the Empire.

So the Arabs, or Saracens, as they are called ... gave men the choice of three things.
E. A. Freeman, *General Sketch*, ch. vi

**Saragossa.** ***The Maid of Saragossa.*** Augustina, a young Spanish girl (d.1857) noted for her bravery in the defence of Saragossa against the French, 1808. She was only twenty-two when, her lover being shot, she mounted the battery in his place.

**Sarasvati.** A sacred river in the Punjab, personified by the ancient Hindus as the wife of Brahma and goddess of the fine arts. The river loses itself in the sands, but was fabled to become united with the Ganges and Jumna.

**Sarcenet.** *See* Sarsenet.

**Sarcode.** *See* Protoplasm.

**Sarcophagus** (Gr. *sarx*, flesh, *phagein*, to eat). A stone coffin; so called because it was made of stone which, according to Pliny, consumed the flesh in a few weeks. The stone was sometimes called *lapis Assius*, because it was found at Assos of Lycia.

**Sardanapalus.** The Greek name of Asurbanipal (mentioned in Ezra 4:10, as *Asenappar*), king of Assyria in the 7th century BC. Byron, in his poetic drama of this name (1821), makes him a voluptuous tyrant whose effeminacy led Arbaces, the Mede, to conspire against him. Myrra, his favourite concubine, roused him to appear at the head of his armies. He won three successive battles, but was then defeated, and was induced by Myrra to place himself on a funeral pile. She set fire to it, and, jumping into the flames, perished with her master.

The name is applied to any luxurious, extravagant, self-willed tyrant.

**Sardonic Smile, Laughter.** A smile of contempt; bitter, mocking laughter: so used by Homer.

The Sardonic or Sardinian laugh. A laugh caused, it was supposed, by a plant growing in Sardinia, of which they who ate died laughing.
Trench, *Words*, lecture iv, p. 176

The *Herba Sardonia* (so called from Sardis, in Asia Minor) is so acrid that it produces a convulsive movement of the nerves of the face, resembling a painful grin. Byron says of the Corsair, *There was a laughing devil in his sneer.*

'Tis envy's safest, surest rule
To hide her rage in ridicule;
The vulgar eye the best beguiles
When all her snakes are decked with smiles,
Sardonic smiles by rancour raised.
Swift, *Pheasant and Lark*

**Sardonyx.** A precious stone composed of white chalcedony alternating with layers of sand, which is an orange-brown variety of cornelian. Pliny says it is called *sard* from Sardis, in Asia Minor, where it is found, and *onyx*, the nail, because its colour resembles that of the skin under the nail (*Nat. Hist.* xxxvii, 6).

**Sarpedon.** A favourite of the gods, who assisted Priam when Troy was besieged by the allied Greeks. When Achilles refused to fight, Sarpedon made great havoc in battle, but was slain by Patroclus. (Homer, *Iliad*.)

**Sarsen Stones.** The sandstone boulders of Wiltshire and Berkshire are so called. The early Christian Saxons used the word *Saresyn* (i.e. Saracen, *q.v.*) as a synonym of pagan or heathen, and as these stones were popularly associated with Druid worship, they were called *Saresyn* (or heathen) *stones*. Robert Ricart says of Duke

Rollo, 'He was a Saresyn come out of Denmark into France.'

**Sarsenet.** A very fine, soft, silk material, so called from its Saracenic or Oriental origin. The word is sometimes used adjectivally of soft and gentle speech:

> The child reddened … and hesitated, while the mother, with many a fye … and such sarsenet chidings, as tender mothers give to spoiled children. Scott, *The Monastery*, ii

**Sartor Resartus** (*The Tailor Patched*). A philosophical satire by Carlyle, first published in *Fraser's Magazine*, 1833–4.

*Diogenes Teufelsdröckh* is Carlyle himself, and *Entepfuhl* is his native village of Ecclefechan.

*The Rose Goddess*, according to Froude, is Margaret Gordon, but Strachey says it is *Blumine*, i.e. Kitty Kirkpatrick, daughter of Colonel Achilles Kirkpatrick. The *Rose Garden* is Strachey's garden at Shooter's Hill, and the *Duenna* is Mrs Strachey.

*The Zahdarms* are Mr and Mrs Buller, and *Toughgut* is Charles Buller.

*Philistine* is theRev. Edward Irving.

**Sassanides.** A powerful Persian dynasty, ruling from about AD 225–641; so named because Ardeshir, the founder, was son of Sassan, a lineal descendant of Xerxes.

**Sassenach.** The common form of *Sassunach*, Gaelic for English or an Englishman. It represents the Teutonic ethnic name, *Saxon*.

**Satan**, in Hebrew, means *adversary* or *enemy*.

> To whom the Arch-enemy
> (And hence in heaven called Satan).
> Milton, *Paradise Lost*, Bk i, 81, 82

In the Bible the term is usually applied to a human adversary or opposer, and only in three cases (Zech. 3, Job 1:2, and 1 Chron. 21:1) does it denote an evil spirit.

The name is often used of a person of whom one is expressing abhorrence. Thus, the Clown says to Malvolio –

> Fie, thou dishonest Satan! I call thee by the most modest terms; for I am one of those gentle ones that will use the devil himself with courtesy.
> Shakespeare, *Twelfth Night*, 4, 2

***The Satanic School.*** So Southey called Byron, Shelley, and those of their followers who set at defiance the generally received notions of religion. *See* the Preface to his *Vision of Judgment*.

**Satire.** Scaliger's derivation of this word from *satyr* is untenable. It is from *satura* (full of variety), *satura lanx*, a hotchpotch or olla podrida. The term originally denoted a medley or hotchpotch in verse; now it is applied to compositions in verse or prose in which folly, vice, or individuals are held up to ridicule. *See* Dryden's Dedication prefixed to his *Satires*.

***Father of satire.*** Archilochus of Paros, 7th century BC.

***Father of French satire.*** Mathurin Regnier (1573–1613).

***Father of Roman satire.*** Lucilius (175–103 BC).

> Lucillus was the man who, bravely bold,
> To Roman vices did the mirror hold;
> Protected humble goodness from reproach,
> Showed worth on foot, and rascals in a coach.
> Dryden, *Art of Poetry*, c. ii

**Saturday.** The seventh day of the week; called by the Anglo-Saxons Saeter-daeg, after the Latin Saturni dies, the day of Saturn. *See* Black Saturday.

**Saturn.** A Roman deity, identified with the Greek Kronos (*time*) (*q.v.*). He devoured all his children except Jupiter (*air*), Neptune (*water*), and Pluto (*the grave*). These Time cannot consume. The reign of Saturn was celebrated by the poets as a 'Golden Age'. According to the old alchemists and astrologers, Saturn typified lead, and was a very evil planet to be born under. 'The children of the sayd Saturne shall be great jangeleres and chyders … and they will never forgyve tyll they be revenged of theyr quarell.' (*Compost of Ptholomeus.*)

***Saturn's tree.*** An alchemist's name for the Tree of Diana, or Philosopher's Tree (*q.v.*).

**Saturnalia.** A time of unrestrained disorder and misrule. With the Romans it was the festival of Saturn, and was celebrated the 17th, 18th and 19th of December. During its continuance no public business could be transacted, the law courts were closed, the schools kept holiday, no war could be commenced, and no malefactor punished. Under the empire the festival was extended to seven days.

**Saturnian.** Pertaining to Saturn; with reference to the 'Golden Age', to the god's sluggishness, or to the baleful influence attributed to him by the astrologers.

> Then rose the seed of Chaos and of Night
> To blot out order and extinguish light,
> Of dull and venal a new world to mould,
> And bring Saturnian days of lead and gold.
> Pope, *Dunciad*, iv, 13

*Lead* to indicate dullness, and *gold* to indicate venality.

***Saturnian verses.*** A rude metre in use among the ancient Romans before the introduction of Greek metres. Also a peculiar metre, consisting of three iambics and a syllable over, joined to three trochees, like:

The queen was in the par-lour . . .
The maids were in the garden . . .

The Fescennine and Saturnian were the same, for as they were called Saturnian from their ancientness, when Saturn reigned in Italy, they were called Fescennine from Fescennina [*sic*] where they were first practised.
Dryden, *Dedication of Juvenal*

**Saturnine.** Grave, phlegmatic, dull and heavy. Astrologers affirm that such is the disposition of those who are born under the influence of the leaden planet Saturn.

**Satyr.** One of a body of forest gods or demons who, in *classical mythology*, were the attendants of Bacchus. Like the fauns (*q.v.*) they are represented as having the legs and hind-quarters of a goat, budding horns, and goat-like ears, and they were very lascivious.

Hence, the term is applied to a brutish or lustful man; and the psychological condition among males characterised by excessive venereal desire is known as *satyriasis*.

**Satyrane.** A blunt but noble knight in Spenser's *Faërie Queene*, son of Thyamis (Passion) and a satyr. He typifies natural chivalry, and has been taken as representing Sir John Perrot (d.1592), Lord Deputy of Ireland, in the political world, and as Luther in the religious. His deliverance of Una from the satyrs (I, vi) has been supposed to mean that Truth, being driven from the cities, took refuge in caves, where for a time it lay concealed. At length Sir Satyrane (Luther) rescues Una (Truth) from bondage; but no sooner is this the case than she falls in with Archimago, showing how very difficult it was at the Reformation to separate Truth from Error.

**Sauce** means 'salted food' (Lat. *salsus*), for giving a relish to meat, as pickled roots, herbs, and so on.

In familiar slang it means 'cheek', impertinence, the kind of remarks one may expect from a *saucebox* – an impudent youngster.

***The sauce was better than the fish.*** The accessories were better than the main part.

***To serve the same sauce.*** To retaliate; to give as good as you take; to serve in the same manner.

After him another came unto her, and served her with the same sauce; then a third.
Lyly, *The Man in the Moon* (1609)

***To sauce.*** To season, intermix.

Folly sauced with discretion.
Shakespeare, *Troilus and Cressida*, 1, 2

Also, to give cheek or impertinence to.

Don't sauce me in the wicious pride of your youth. Dickens, *Our Mutual Friend*, I, vii

***What's sauce for the goose is sauce for the gander.*** *See* Gander.

**Saucer.** Originally a dish for holding sauce, the Roman *salsarium*.

***Saucer eyes.*** Big, round, glaring eyes.

Yet when a child (bless me!) I thought
That thou a pair of horns had'st got,
With eyes like saucers staring.
Peter Pindar, *Ode to the Devil*

***Saucer oath.*** When a Chinese is put in the witness-box, he says: 'If I do not speak the truth may my soul be cracked and broken like this saucer.' So saying, he dashes the saucer on the ground. The Jewish marriage custom of breaking a wineglass is of a similar character.

**Saucy.** Cheeky, impertinent (*see* Sauce); *also* rakish, irresistible, that care-for-nobody, jaunty, daring behaviour which has won for many of our regiments and ships the term as a compliment.

How many saucy airs we meet,
From Temple Bar to Aldgate Street!
Gay, *The Barley-Mow and Dunghill*

But still the little petrel was saucy as the waves.
Eliza Cook, *The Young Mariners*, stanza 7

***The Saucy Greens.*** The 2nd Battn Worcestershire Regiment, the old 36th Foot.

***The Saucy Sixth.*** The Royal Warwickshires, formerly the 6th Foot.

***The Saucy Seventh.*** The 7th (Queen's Own) Hussars.

**Saul,** in Dryden's *Absalom and Achitophel*, is meant for Oliver Cromwell. As Saul persecuted David and drove him from his home, so Cromwell persecuted Charles II and drove him from England.

They who, when Saul was dead, without a blow
Made foolish Ishbosheth [Richard Cromwell] the crown forego. Pt i, 57, 58

***Is Saul also among the prophets?*** Said (from 1 Sam. 10:12) of one who unexpectedly bears tribute to a party or doctrine that he has hitherto vigorously assailed. The Jews said of our Lord, 'How knoweth this man letters, having never learned?' (John 7:15.) Similarly at the conversion of Saul, afterwards called Paul, the Jews said in substance, 'Is it possible that Saul can be a convert?' (Acts 9:21.)

**Sauve qui peut** (Fr.). Save (himself) who can. The cry of despair attributed to Napoleon when he realised that Waterloo was lost and all was over. Hence, a rout; Thackeray speaks of 'that general *sauve qui peut* among the Tory party'. (*The Four Georges*.)

**Save. *To save appearances.*** To do something to obviate or prevent exposure or embarrassment.

***To save one's bacon, skin, face.*** *See these words.*

***Save the mark!*** *See* Mark.

**Savoir-faire** (Fr.). Ready wit; skill in getting out of a scrape; hence *Vivre de son savoir-faire*, to live by one's wits; *Avoir du savoir-faire*, to be up to snuff, to know a thing or two.

> He had great confidence in his *savoir-faire*.
>
> Scott, *Guy Mannering*, ch. xxxiv

**Savoy, The.** A precinct off the Strand, London, noted for the palace built there by Peter of Savoy, who came to England about 1245 to visit his niece Eleanor, wife of Henry III. At his death the palace became the property of the queen, who gave it to her second son, Edmund Lancaster, whence it was attached to the Duchy of Lancaster. When the Black Prince brought Jean le Bon, King of France, captive to London (1356), he lodged him in the Savoy Palace, and there he died in 1364. The rebels under Wat Tyler burnt down the old palace in 1381; but it was rebuilt in 1505 by Henry VII, and converted into a hospital for the poor, under the name of St John's Hospital, which was used by Charles II for wounded soldiers and sailors.

Here, in 1552, was established the first flint-glass manufactory in England.

The *Chapel Royal* of the Savoy (first made a Chapel Royal by George III in 1773) was built about 1510 on the ruins of John of Gaunt's earlier chapel. This, largely rebuilt, is the only one of the old buildings remaining, the rest of the site being occupied by the Savoy Hotel and Savoy Theatre.

**Saw.** In Christian art an attribute of St Simon and St James the Less, in allusion to the tradition of their being sawn to death in martyrdom.

**Sawny** or **Sandy.** A Scotchman; a contraction of 'Alexander'.

**Saxifrage.** A member of a genus of small plants (*Saxifraga*) probably so called because they grow in the clefts of rocks (Lat. *saxum*, a rock, *frangere*, to break). Pliny, and later writers following him, held that the name was due to the supposed fact that the plant had a medicinal value in the breaking up and dispersal of stone in the bladder.

**Saxon Castles.** The principal ones remaining in England are:

Alnwick Castle, given to Ivo de Vesey by the Conqueror.

Bamborough Castle (Northumberland), the palace of the kings of Northumberland, and built by King Ida, who began to reign 559; now converted into charity schools and signal-stations.

Carisbrooke Castle, enlarged by Fitz-Osborne just after the Norman Conquest.

Conisborough Castle (Yorks).

Goodrich Castle (Herefordshire).

Kenilworth Castle. Kenil-worth means 'the farm of Cynehild' (a woman).

Richmond Castle (Yorks), belonging to the Saxon earl Edwin, given by the Conqueror to his nephew Alan, Earl of Bretagne; a ruin for three centuries. The keep remains.

Rochester Castle, given to Odo, natural brother of the Conquerer.

**Saxon Characteristics** (architectural).

(1) The quoining consists of a long stone set at the corner, and a short one lying on it and bonding into the wall.

(2) The use of large heavy blocks of stone in some parts, while the rest is built of Roman bricks.

(3) An arch with straight sides to the upper part instead of curves.

(4) The absence of buttresses.

(5) The use in windows of rude balusters.

(6) A rude round staircase west of the tower, for the purpose of access to the upper floors.

(7) Rude carvings in imitation of Roman work. (Rickman.)

**Saxon Shore.** The coast of Norfolk, Suffolk, Essex, Kent, Sussex, and Hampshire, where were castles and garrisons, under the charge of a count or military officer, called *Comes Littoris Saxonici per Britanniam*.

Branodunum (Brancaster) was on the Norfolk coast.

Gariannonum (Burgh) was on the Suffolk coast.

Othona (Ithanchester) was on the Essex coast.

Regulbium (Reculver), Rutupiae (Richborough), Dubris (Dover), P. Lemanis (Lyme), were on the Kentish coast.

Anderida (Hastings or Pevensey), Portus Adurni (Worthing), were on the Sussex coast.

**Say.** ***To take the say.*** To taste meat or wine before it is presented, in order to prove that it is not poisoned. *Say* is short for *assay*, a test; the phrase was common in the reign of Queen Elizabeth.

Nor deem it meet that you to him convey
The proffered bowl, unless you taste the say.
Rose, *Orlando Furioso*, xxi, 61

**Sbirri** (Ital. sing. *sbirro*). The Italian policemen, especially the force which existed in the pope's dominions.

Had I been silent, not a sbirro but
Had kept me in his eye, as meditating
A silent, solitary, deep revenge.
Byron, *Marino Falieri*, II, ii

**Scaevola** (i.e. *left-handed*). So Caius Mucius, a legendary hero of ancient Rome, was called, because, when he entered the camp of Lars Porsenna as a spy, and was taken before the king, he deliberately held his hand over the sacrificial fire at which he was to be burnt till it was burnt off, to show the Etruscan that he would not shrink from torture. This fortitude was so remarkable that Porsenna at once ordered his release.

**Scales.** From time immemorial the scales have been one of the principal attributes of Justice, it being impossible to out-weigh even a little Right with any quantity of Wrong.

... first the right he put into one scale,
And then the Giant strove with puissance strong
To fill the other scale with so much wrong.
But all the wrongs that he therein could lay,
Might not it peise.
Spenser, *Faërie Queene*, V, ii, 46

Call these foul offenders to their answers;
And poise the cause in justice' equal scales,
Whose beam stands sure, whose rightful cause prevails.
Shakespeare, *2 Henry VI*, 2, 1

The Koran says, at the judgment day everyone will be weighed in the scales of the archangel Gabriel. The good deeds will be put in the scale called 'Light', and the evil ones in the scale called 'Darkness'; after which they will have to cross the bridge Al Sīrát, not wider than the edge of a scimitar. The faithful will pass over in safety, but the rest will fall into the dreary realms of Jehennam.

***To hold the scales even*** or ***true.*** To judge impartially.

Kind Providence attends with gracious aid ...
And weighs the nations in an even scale.
Cowper, *Table Talk*, 251

***To turn the scale.*** Just to outweigh the other side.

Thy presence turns the scale of doubtful fight,
Tremendous God of battles, Lord of Hosts!
Wordsworth, *Ode* (1815), 112

**Scallop Shell.** The emblem of St James of Compostella (and hence of pilgrims to his shrine), adopted, says Erasmus, because the shore of the adjacent sea abounds in them. Pilgrims used them for cup, spoon, and dish; hence the punning crest of the Disington family is a scallop shell. On returning home, the pilgrim placed his scallop shell in his hat to command admiration, and adopted it in his coat-armour.

I will give thee a palmer's staff of ivory and a scallop-shell of beaten gold.
Peele, *Old Wives' Tale* (1590)

**Scambling Days.** *See* Skimble-skamble.

**Scammozzi's Rule.** The jointed two-foot rule used by builders, and said to have been invented by Vincenzio Scammozzi (1552–1616), the famous Italian architect.

**Scamp.** A deserter 'from the field', *ex campo*; one who *decamps* without paying his debts.

**Scandal** (Gr. *skandalon*) means properly a pitfall or snare laid for an enemy; hence a stumbling-block, and morally an aspersion.

In Matt. 13:41–2, we are told that the angels shall gather 'all things that offend ... and shall cast them into a furnace'; here the Greek word is *skandalon*, and *scandals* is given as an alternative in the margin; the Revised version renders the word 'all things that cause stumbling'. *Cp. also* 1 Cor. 1:23.

***The Hill of Scandal.*** So Milton calls the Mount of Olives, because King Solomon built thereon 'an high place for Chemosh, the abomination of Moab ... and for Molech, the abomination of the children of Ammon' (1 Kings 11:7).

His lustful orgies he [Chemosh] enlarged
Even to that hill of scandal by the grove
Of Moloch homicide, lust hard by hate,
Till good Josiah drove them thence to Hell.
*Paradise Lost*, I, 415

***Scandal broth.*** Tea. The reference is to the gossip held by some of the womenkind over their 'cups which cheer but do not inebriate'. Also called 'Chatter-broth'.

I proposed to my venerated visitor ... to summon my ... housekeeper ... with the tea-equipage; but he rejected my proposal with disdain ... 'No scandal-broth,' he exclaimed, 'No unidea'd woman's chatter for me.'
Scott, *Peveril of the Peak* (Prefatory letter)

**Scandalum Magnatum** (Lat. scandal of

magnates). Words in derogation of the Crown, peers, judges, and other great officers of the realm, made a legal offence in the time of Richard II. What St Paul calls 'speaking evil of dignities'; popularly contracted to *scanmag*.

**Scanderbeg.** A name given by the Turks to George Castriota (1403–68), the patriot chief of Epirus. The word is a corruption of *Iskander-beg*, Prince Alexander.

***Scanderbeg's sword must have Scanderbeg's arm.*** None but Ulysses can draw Ulysses' bow. Mohammed I wanted to see his scimitar, but when presented no one could draw it; whereupon the Turkish emperor, deeming himself imposed upon, sent it back; but Scanderbeg replied he had sent his majesty his sword, not the arm that drew it.

**Scant-of-grace.** A madcap; a wild, disorderly, graceless fellow.

> You, a gentleman of birth and breeding, ... associate yourself with a sort of scant-of-grace, as men call me. Scott, *Kenilworth*, iii

**Scantling,** a small quantity, is the French *échantillon*, a specimen or pattern.

> A scantling of wit. Dryden

**Scapegoat.** Part of the ancient ritual among the Hebrews for the Day of Atonement laid down by Mosaic law (*see* Lev. 16) was as follows: Two goats were brought to the altar of the tabernacle and the high priest cast lots, one for the Lord, and the other for Azazel (*q.v.*). The Lord's goat was sacrificed, the other was the *scapegoat*; and the high priest having, by confession, transferred his own sins and the sins of the people to it, it was taken to the wilderness and suffered to escape.

Similar rites are by no means uncommon among primitive peoples. The aborigines of Borneo, for instance, annually launch a small barque laden with all the sins and misfortunes of the nation, which they imagine will fall on the crew that first meets with it.

***The scapegoat of the family.*** One made to bear the blame of the rest of the family; one always chidden and found fault with, let who may be in the wrong.

**Scaphism** (Gr. *skaphe*, anything scooped out). A mode of torture formerly practised in Persia. The victim was enclosed in the hollowed trunk of a tree, the head, hands, and legs projecting. These were anointed with honey to invite the wasps. In this situation the sufferer might linger in the burning sun for several days.

**Scapin.** The knavish and intriguing valet, who makes his master his tool, in Molière's *Les Fourberies de Scapin* (1671).

**Scaramouch.** The English form of Ital. *Scaramuccia* (through Fr. *Scaramouche*) a stock character in Old Italian farce, introduced into England soon after 1670. He was a braggart and fool, very valiant in words, but a poltroon, and was usually dressed in a black Spanish costume caricaturing the dons. The Neapolitan actor, Tiberio Fiurelli (1608–94), was surnamed *Scaramouch Fiurelli*. He came to England in 1673, and astonished John Bull with feats of agility.

> Stout Scaramoucha with rush lance rode in,
> And ran a tilt with centaur Arlequin
> Dryden, *Epilogue to The Silent Woman*

**Scarborough Warning.** Blow first, warning after. In Scarborough robbers used to be dealt with in a very summary manner by a sort of Halifax gibbet-law, lynch-law, or an *à la lanterne*. Another origin is given of this phrase: It is said that Thomas Stafford, in 1557, seized the castle of Scarborough, not only without warning, but even before the townsfolk knew he was afoot.

> This term *Scarborrow warning*, grew, some say,
> By hasty hanging for rank robbery there.
> Who that was met, but suspect in that way,
> Straight he was trust up, whatever he were.
> J. Heywood

**Scarlet.** The colour of certain official costumes, as those of judges and cardinals; hence, sometimes applied to these dignitaries. The scarlet coat worn by foxhunters is not technically *scarlet*, but *pink* (*see* Pink).

***Dyeing scarlet.*** Heavy drinking, which in time will dye the face scarlet.

> They call drinking deep, dyeing scarlet.
> Shakespeare, *1 Henry IV*, 2, 4

***The Scarlet Lancers.*** The 16th Lancers, whose tunic is red.

***The Scarlet Woman,*** or ***Scarlet Whore.*** The woman seen by St John in his vision 'arrayed in purple and scarlet colour', sitting 'upon a scarlet coloured beast, full of names of blasphemy, having seven heads and ten horns', 'drunken with the blood of the saints, and with the blood of the martyrs', upon whose forehead was written 'Mystery, Babylon the Great, the Mother of Harlots and Abominations of the Earth' (Rev. 17:1–6).

St John was probably referring to Rome, which, at the time he was writing, was 'drunken with the blood of the saints'; some controversial

Protestants have applied the words to the Church of Rome, and some Roman Catholics with equal 'good taste', to the Protestant churches generally.

**Scarlet, Will.** One of the companions of Robin Hood (*q.v.*).

**Scavenger's Daughter.** An instrument of torture invented by Sir William *Skevington*, lieutenant of the Tower in the reign of Henry VIII. The machine compressed the body by bringing the head to the knees, and so forced blood out of the nose and ears.

**Scent.** ***We are not yet on the right scent.*** We have not yet got the right clue. The allusion is to dogs following game by the scent.

**Sceptic** literally means one who thinks for himself, and does not receive on another's testimony (from Gr. *skeptesthai*, to examine). Pyrrho founded the philosophic sect called 'Sceptics', and Epictetus combated their dogmas. In theology we apply the word to those who do not accept Revelation.

**Sceptre** (Gr. a staff). The gold and jewelled wand carried by a sovereign as emblem of his royalty; hence, royal authority and dignity.

> This hand was made to handle nought but gold:
> I cannot give due action to my words,
> Except a sword, or sceptre balance it.
> A sceptre shall it have, have I a soul,
> On which I'll toss the flower-de-luce of France.
>
> Shakespeare, *2 Henry VI*, 5, 1

The sceptre of the kings and emperors of Rome was of ivory, bound with gold and surmounted by a golden eagle; the British sceptre is of richly jewelled gold, and bears immediately beneath the cross and ball the great Cullinan diamond (*q.v.*).

Homer says that Agamemnon's sceptre was made by Vulcan, who gave it to the son of Saturn. It passed successively to Jupiter, Mercury, Pelops, Atreus, and Thyestes till it came to Agamemnon. It was looked on with great reverence, and several miracles were attributed to it.

**Scheherazade.** The mouthpiece of the tales related in the *Arabian Nights* (*q.v.*), daughter of the grand vizier of the Indies. The Sultan Schahriah, having discovered the infidelity of his sultana, resolved to have a fresh wife every night and have her strangled at daybreak. Scheherazade entreated to become his wife, and so amused him with tales for a thousand and one nights that he revoked his cruel decree, bestowed his affection on her, and called her 'the liberator of the sex'.

**Schelhorn's Bible.** *See* Bible, Specially named.

**Schiedam.** Hollands gin, so called from Schiedam, a town where it is principally manufactured.

**Schiites.** *See* Shiites.

**Schlemihl, Peter.** The man who sold his shadow to the devil, in Chamisso's tale so called (1814). The name is a synonym for any person who makes a desperate and silly bargain.

**Scholasticism.** The philosophy and doctrines of the 'Schoolmen' (*q.v.*) of the Middle Ages (9th to 16th cents) which were based on the logical works of Aristotle and the teachings of the Christian Fathers. It was an attempt to give a rational basis to Christianity, but the methods of the Scholastics degenerated into mere verbal subtleties, academic disputations, and quibblings, till, at the time of the Renaissance, the remnants were only fit to be swept away before the current of new learning that broke upon the world. *Cp.* Dialectics.

**Schoolmaster.** ***The schoolmaster is abroad.*** Education is spreading – and it will bear fruit. Lord Brougham said, in a speech (January 29th, 1828) on the general diffusion of education, and of intelligence arising therefrom, 'Let the soldier be abroad, if he will; he can do nothing in this age. There is another personage abroad … the schoolmaster is abroad; and I trust to him, armed with his primer, against the soldier in full military array.'

**Schoolmen.** The theologians of the Middle Ages, who lectured in the cloisters or cathedral schools founded by Charlemagne and his successors. They followed Aristotle and the Fathers (*see* Scholasticism), but attempted to reduce every subject to a system. They may be grouped under three periods –

***First Period.*** Platonists (from 9th to 12th cents).

Pierre Abélard (1079–1142).

Flacius Albinus Alcuin (735–804).

John Scotus Erigena (d.875).

Anselm (1030–1117). *Doctor Scholasticus.*

Berengarius of Tours (1000–88).

Gerbert of Aurillac (930–1003), afterwards Pope Sylvester II.

John of Salisbury (1115–80).

Lanfranc, Archbishop of Canterbury (1005–89).

Pierre Lombard (1100–64). *Master of the Sentences*, sometimes called the founder of school divinity.

Roscelinus of Compiègne (about 1050–1122).

***Second Period***, or ***Golden Age of Scholasticism***. Aristotelians (13th and 14th cents).

Alain de Lille (d.1203). *The Universal Doctor*.

Albertus Magnus (1206–80).

Thomas Aquinas (1224–74). *The Angelic Doctor*.

John Fidanza Bonaventure (1221–74). *The Seraphic Doctor*.

Alexander of Hales (d.1245). *The Irrefragable Doctor*.

John Duns Scotus (1265–1308), *The Subtle Doctor*.

***Third Period***. Nominalism Revived. (To the 16th cent.)

Thomas de Bradwardine, Archbishop of Canterbury (d.1349), *The Profound Doctor*.

Jean Buridan (about 1295–1360).

William Durandus de Pourçain (d. about 1333). *The Most Resolute Doctor*.

Gregory of Rimini (d.1358). *The Authentic Doctor*.

Robert Holcot (d.1349), an English Dominican and divine.

Raymond Lully (1234–1315). *The Illuminated Doctor*.

William Occam (d.1349), an English Franciscan. *The Singular* or *Invincible Doctor*.

François Suarez (1548–1617), the last of the schoolmen.

**Schoolmistress, The.** A quietly humorous poem in the Spenserian stanza by Shenstone (1742). The 'heroine' is designed for a 'portrait of Sarah Lloyd', the dame who first taught the poet himself.

**Science.** Literally 'knowledge', the Lat. *scientia* from the pres. part. of *scire*, to know. The old, wide meaning of the word is shown in this from Shakespeare:

> Plutus himself,
> That knows the tinct and multiplying medicine,
> Hath not in nature's mystery more science
> Than I have in this ring. *All's Well*, 5, 3

***The Dismal Science.*** Economics; a name given to it by Carlyle:

> The social science – not a 'gay science', but a rueful – which finds the secret of this Universe in 'supply and demand' ... what we might call, by way of eminence, the *dismal science*.
>
> Carlyle, *On the Nigger Question* (1849)

***The Gay Science.*** *See* Gay.

***The Noble Science.*** Boxing, or fencing; the 'noble art of self-defence'.

***The Seven Sciences.*** A mediaeval term for the whole group of studies, viz. Grammar, Logic, and Rhetoric (the *Trivium*), with Arithmetic, Music, Geometry, and Astronomy (the *Quadrivium*).

**Science Persecuted.** Anaxagoras of Clazomenae (d. about 430 BC) held opinions in natural science so far in advance of his age that he was accused of impiety, thrown into prison, and condemned to death. Pericles, with great difficulty, got his sentence commuted to fine and banishment.

Virgilius, Bishop of Salzburg (d.784), denounced as a heretic by St Boniface for asserting the existence of antipodes.

Galileo (1564–1642) was imprisoned by the Inquisition for maintaining that the earth moved. To get his liberty he abjured the heresy, but as he went his way is said to have whispered, '*E pur si muove*' (but nevertheless it does move).

Roger Bacon (1214–94) was excommunicated and imprisoned for diabolical knowledge, chiefly on account of his chemical researches. Dr Dee (*q.v.*) and Robert Grosseteste (d.1253), Bishop of Lincoln, were treated in much the same way. Of the latter it is said that as he was accused of dealings in the black arts the Pope sent a letter to the King of England ordering that his bones should be disinterred and burnt to powder.

Averroes, the Arabian philosopher, who flourished in the 12th century, was denounced as a heretic and degraded solely on account of his great eminence in natural philosophy and medicine.

Andrew Crosse (1784–1855), the electrician, was accused of impiety and shunned as a 'profane man' who wanted to arrogate to himself the creative power of God, because he asserted that he had seen certain animals of the genus *Acarus*, which had been developed by him out of inorganic matter.

**Scio's Blind Old Bard.** Homer. Scio is the modern name of Chios, in the Aegean Sea – one of the 'seven cities' that claimed the honour of being his birthplace.

> Smyrna, Chios, Colophon, Salamis, Rhodos, Argos, Athenae,
> Your just right to call Homer your son you must settle between ye.

**Scire facias** (Lat. make him to know). A judicial writ enforcing the execution or the annulment of judgments, etc.; so called from its opening words. These writs were formerly the common procedure, but they are now rarely issued except for the revocation of royal charters.

**Sciron.** A robber of Greek legend, slain by Theseus. He infested the parts about Megara, and forced travellers over the rocks into the sea, where they were devoured by a sea monster.

**Scissors.** The Latin *cisorium*, from *caedere*, to cut. In English the word was for centuries spelt without the *c*; the *sc-* spelling appeared in the 16th century, and seems to be due to confusion with Lat. *scissor*, the noun from *scindere*, to split or rend. *Scythe*, formerly *sithe*, has suffered in the same way.

In Johnson's *Dictionary* the word is entered in the singular; but the singular form has never been in common use, except in compounds such as *scissor-blade*, *scissor-tooth*, etc. (*cp. billiard-ball* from *billiards*, *trouser-button* from *trousers*, etc.).

***Scissors and paste.*** Compilation, as distinguished from original literary work. The allusion is obvious.

***Scissors to grind.*** Work to do; purpose to serve. *I have my own scissors to grind* is a way of saying, 'I've got my own work to do, or my own troubles, and can't be bothered with yours.'

**Scobellum.** A very fruitful land mentioned in the *Seven Champions of Christendom* (iii, 10), whose inhabitants 'exceeded the cannibals for cruelty, the Persians for pride, the Egyptians for luxury, the Cretans for lying, the Germans for drunkenness, and all nations together for a generality of vices'. To punish them the gods changed the drunkards into swine, the lecherous into goats, the proud into peacocks, scolds into magpies, idle women into milch-cows, jesters into monkeys, misers into moles, etc.; and eventually four of the Champions restored them to their normal forms by quenching the fire of the Golden Cave.

**Scogan's Jests.** A popular jest-book in the 16th century, said by Andrew Boorde (who published it) to be the work of one John Scogan, reputed to have been court fool to Edward IV. He is referred to (anachronously) by Justice Shallow in *2 Henry IV*, 3, 2, and must not be confused with Henry Scogan (d.1407), the poet-disciple of Chaucer to whom Ben Jonson alludes:

> Scogan? What was he?
> Oh, a fine gentleman, and a master of arts
> Of Henry the Fourth's times, that made disguises
> For the king's sons, and writ in ballad royal
> Daintily well.
>
> Ben Jonson, *The Fortunate Isles* (1624)

**Scone.** A parish about 2 miles north of Perth, the site of the castle where the ancient Scottish kings were crowned. It was from here that Edward I, in 1296, brought the great coronation stone on which the kings of Scotland used to be crowned, and which, ever since, has formed part of the Throne ('Edward the Confessor's Chair') in Westminster Abbey which British monarchs occupy at their coronation.

More than one fable has attached itself to this stone. The monks gave out that it was the very 'pillow' on which Jacob rested his head when he had the vision of angels ascending and descending between heaven and earth (Gen. 28:2); and it was also said to be the original 'Lia-faill' or 'Tanist Stone' (*q.v.*), brought from Ireland by Fergus, son of Eric, who led the Dalriads to Argyleshire, and removed thence by King Kenneth (in the 9th cent.) to Scone.

The tradition is that wherever the stone rests there will reign one of the royal line of Scotland –

> Unless the fates are faithless found
> And prophet's voice be vain,
> Where'er is placed this stone, e'en there
> The Scottish race shall reign.

**Score.** A reckoning; to make a reckoning; so called from the custom of marking off 'runs' or 'lengths', in games by the score feet.

***To pay off old scores.*** To settle accounts; used sometimes of money debts, but usually in the sense of revenging an injury, 'getting even' with one.

**Scorpion.** Fable has it that scorpions – like the toad – carry with them an oil which is a remedy against their stings.

> 'Tis true, a scorpion's oil is said
> To cure the wounds the venom made,
> And weapons dressed with salves restore
> And heal the hurts they gave before.
>
> Butler, *Hudibras*, iii, 2

This oil was extracted from the flesh and given to the sufferer as a medicine; it was also supposed to be 'very useful to bring away the descending stone of the kidneys' (Boyle, 1663).

Another mediaeval belief was that if a scorpion were surrounded by a circle of fire it would commit suicide by stinging itself with its own tail. Byron, in the *Giaour*, extracts a simile from the legend –

> The mind that broods o'er guilty woes
> Is like the Scorpion girt by fire; ...
> One sad and sole relief she knows,
> The sting she nourish'd for her foes,

Whose venom never yet was vain
Gives but one pang, and cures all pain.

***A lash*** or ***scourge of scorpions.*** A specially severe punishment, in allusion to the biblical passage –

My father hath chastised you with whips, but I will chastise you with scorpions.

1 Kings 12:11

In the Middle Ages a scourge of four or five thongs set with steel spikes and leaden weights was called a *scorpion*.

**Scot.** Payment, reckoning. The same word as *shot* (*q.v.*); we still speak of *paying one's shot*.

***Scot and lot.*** A municipal levy on all according to their ability to pay. *Scot* is the tax, and *lot* the allotment or portion allotted. *To pay scot and lot*, therefore, is to pay the ordinary tributes and also the personal tax allotted to you.

***To go scot-free.*** To be let off payment; to escape punishment or reprimand, etc.

**Scotch, Scots, Scottish.** These three adjectives all mean the same thing – belonging to, native of, or characteristic of, Scotland, but their application varies, and of late years their use has become something of a shibboleth among the more particular of the natives. *Scotch* is discarded as much as possible (though regularly used by Burns and Scott); this is a late 16th century contraction of the earlier *Scottish*, which was in use both in England and Scotland, while *Scots* was almost confined to native dialect writers and had become archaic (except in a few special cases, as, *a pound Scots*) by the 18th century. It is now used in the compound *Scotsman* (which is preferred to *Scot*, and much preferred to *Scotchman*), in speaking of the law of Scotland (*Scots law*), as qualifications to money, weights, and measures where these differ from English (*Scots acre*, *Scots pint*, etc.), and in the titles of certain regiments, as the *Scots Guards* and *Scots Greys* (*q.v.*).

***Scottish*** is more usual than *Scotch* in many connections, but can never altogether displace the latter; we speak of the *Scottish border*, *Scottish history*, and *Scottish literature*, but *Scottish terrier*, *Scottish cap*, *Scottish girl* would savour of affectation; while anyone asking for *a glass of Scottish* when he meant *a glass of Scotch* (whisky) would at once be told 'to take more water with it'.

***Broad Scotch*** (***Braid Scots***). The vernacular of the lowlands of Scotland; very different from the 'refined' enunciation of Edinburgh and from the Glasgow dialect.

I'll pledge my aith in guid braid Scotch,
He needna fear their foul reproach.

Burns, *Earnest Cry and Prayer*

***A Scotch breakfast.*** A substantial breakfast of sundry sorts of good things to eat and drink. The Scots are famous for their breakfast-tables and teas, and no people in the world are more hospitable.

***Scotch mist.*** The cloudy fog with drizzling rain, so common in Scotland.

*See also* Scots.

**Scotch.** To make a *scotch*, i.e. a score or incision, in, originally; but now the verb usually means to wound so that temporary disablement is caused, or to stamp out altogether. This application of the word arises from *Macbeth*, 3, 2, where Macbeth is made to say 'We have scotch'd the snake, not killed it.' *Macbeth* was not printed in Shakespeare's lifetime, and in the Folios the word appears as *scorch'd*; Theobald is responsible for the emendation (1726).

***Out of all scotch and notch.*** Beyond all bounds; *scotch* was the line marked upon the ground in certain games, as *Hopscotch*.

**Scotists.** Followers of the 13th-century scholastic philosopher, Duns Scotus, who maintained the doctrine of the Immaculate Conception in opposition to Thomas Aquinas.

Scotists and Thomists now in peace remain.

Pope, *Essay on Criticism*

**Scotland.** St Andrew is the patron saint of this country, and tradition says that his remains were brought by Regulus, a Greek monk, to the coast of Fife in 368 (*see* Rule, St).

The old royal arms of Scotland were – Or, a lion rampant gules, armed and langued azure, within a double tressure flory-counterflory of fleurs-de-lys of the second (this was quartered with the royal arms of the United Kingdom in 1603). *Supporters.* Two unicorns argent, imperially crowned, armed, crined, and unguled or, gorged with open crowns, with chains affixed thereto, and reflexed over the back, of the last. *Crest.* Upon the imperial crown proper, a lion sejant affrontée gules, crowned or, holding in the dexter paw a sword, and in the sinister a sceptre, both proper. *Mottoes*, 'Nemo me impune lacessit' (*q.v.*), and, over the crest, 'In Defence'.

In Scotland now the royal arms of Great Britain are used with certain alterations: the lion supporter is replaced by another unicorn (crowned), the Scottish crest takes the place of the English, and the collar of the Thistle encircles that of the Garter.

***Scotland a fief of England.*** Edward I founded his claim to the lordship of Scotland on four grounds, viz. – (l) the statement of certain ancient chroniclers that Scottish kings had occasionally paid homage to English sovereigns from time immemorial. (2) From charters of Scottish kings: as those of Edgar, son of Malcolm, William, and his son Alexander II. (3) From papal rescripts; as those of Honorius III, Gregory IX, and Clement IV. (4) From a passage in *The Life and Miracles of St John of Beverley* (*see* Rymer's *Faedera* I, Pt ii, p. 771), which relates how a miracle was performed in the reign of Athelstan, King of the West Saxons and Mercians, 925–940. The kins was repelling a band of marauding Scots and had reached the Tyne when he found that they had retreated. At midnight the spirit of St John of Beverley appeared to him and bade him cross the river at daybreak, for he 'should discomfit the foe'. Athelstan obeyed, and reduced the whole kingdom to subjection. On reaching Dunbar on his return march, he prayed that some sign might be vouchsafed to him to satisfy all ages that 'God, by the intercession of St John, had given him the kingdom of Scotland'. Then, striking the basaltic rocks with his sword, the blade sank into the solid flint 'as if it had been butter', cleaving it asunder for 'an ell or more', and the cleft remains to the present hour. This was taken as a sign from heaven that Athelstan was rightful lord of Scotland, and if Athelstan was, argued Edward, so was he, his successor.

**Scotland Yard.** The headquarters of the Metropolitan Police, whence all public orders to the force proceed. The original *Scotland Yard* was a short street near Trafalgar Square, so called from a palace on the spot, given by King Edgar (about 970) to Kenneth II of Scotland when he came to London to pay homage, and subsequently used by the Scottish kings when visiting England. *New Scotland Yard*, as it is officially called, is close by, on the Thames Embankment near Westminster Bridge.

**Scots.** *See* Scotch.

***A pound Scots*** was originally of the same value as an English pound, but after 1355 it gradually depreciated, until at the time of the Union of the Crowns (1603) it was but one-twelfth of the value of an English pound (1*s.* 8*d.*), which was divided into 20 *Scots shillings* each worth an English penny.

***A Scots pint*** was about equivalent to three imperial pints of the present day.

***The Scots Greys.*** The 2nd Dragoons, the colour of whose horses is grey.

**Scottish.** *See* Scotch.

**Scotus, Duns.** *See* Dunce.

**Scourers.** *See* Scowerers.

**Scourge.** A whip or lash; commonly applied to diseases that carry off great numbers, as *the scourge of influenza*, *the scourge of pneumonia*, etc., and to persons who seem to be the instruments of divine punishment. Raleigh, for instance, was called *the Scourge of Spain*, and Spenser, in his *Sonnet upon Scanderbeg*, calls him 'The scourge of Turkes and plague of infidels'.

***The Scourge of God*** (Lat. *flagellum Dei*). Attila (d.453), king of the Huns, so called by mediaeval writers because of the widespread havoc and destruction caused by his armies.

***The Scourge of Homer.*** The carping critic, Zoilus. *See* Zoilism.

***The Scourge of Princes.*** Pietro Aretino (1492–1556), the Italian satirist.

**Scowerers.** A set of rakes in the period about 1670 to 1720, who, with the Nickers and Mohocks, committed great annoyances in London and other large towns.

> Who has not heard the Scowerers' midnight
> fame?
> Who has not trembled at the Mohocks' name?
> Was there a watchman took his hourly rounds,
> Safe from their blows and new-invented wounds?
>
> Gay, *Trivia*, iii

**Scrap.** A thing (or person) is said to be *scrapped* when it is worn out and discarded, thrown away as useless.

***A scrap*** is a boxing bout, a set to at fisticuffs; hence almost any contest in war or peace that involves a scrimmage.

***On the scrap-heap.*** Thrown aside as worn out; said of one superannuated.

**Scrape.** Low slang for a shave, as 'You haven't had a scrape this morning.'

***Bread and scrape.*** Bread and butter, with the butter spread very thin.

***I've got into a sad scrape*** – an awkward predicament, an embarrassing difficulty. We use *rub*, *squeeze*, *pinch*, to express the same idea. Thus Shakespeare says, 'Ay, there's the rub'; 'I am come to a pinch' (difficulty).

***To scrape along.*** To get along in the world with difficulty, finding it hard to 'make both ends meet'.

***To scrape an acquaintance with.*** To get on terms of familiarity with by currying favour and by methods of insinuation. The *Gentleman's Magazine* (N. S. xxxix, 230) says that Hadrian went one day to the public baths and saw an old soldier, well known to him, scraping himself with a potsherd for want of a flesh-brush. The emperor sent him a sum of money. Next day Hadrian found the bath crowded with soldiers scraping themselves with potsherds, and said, 'Scrape on, gentlemen, but you'll not scrape acquaintance with me.'

***To scrape through.*** To pass an examination, etc., 'by the skin of one's teeth', just to escape failure.

**Scratch.** There are two colloquial 'sporting' uses of this word; a horse, or other entrant in a sporting event, is said to be *scratched* when its name is withdrawn (*scratched out*) from the list of competitors; the *scratch man* in a handicap is he who starts from *scratch*; i.e. the line marked out (originally *scratched*) to show the starting place.

***A scratch crew, eleven, etc.*** A team got together anyhow; not the regular team.

***A scratch race.*** A race of horses, men, boys, etc., without restrictions as to age, weight, previous winnings, etc., who all start from scratch.

***Old Scratch.*** Old Nick; the devil. From *skratta*, an old Scandinavian word for a goblin or monster (modern Icelandic *skratti*, a devil).

***Scratch cradle.*** Another form of 'cat's cradle' (*q.v.*).

***To come up to the scratch.*** To be ready when wanted; to fulfil expectations. In prize-fighting a line was scratched on the ground, and the toe of the fighter must come up to the scratch.

**Screw.** Slang for wages, salary; probably because in some industry the weekly wage was handed out in a 'screw of paper'.

***An old screw.*** A miser who has amassed wealth by 'putting on the screw' (*see below*), and who keeps his money tight, doling it out only in *screws*.

***He has a screw loose.*** He is not quite *compos mentis*, he's a little mad. His mind is like a piece of machinery that needs adjusting – it won't work properly.

***His head is screwed on the right way.*** He is clear-headed and right-thinking; he knows what he's about.

> His heart was in the right place ... and his head was screwed on right, too.
>
> Boldrewood, *Robbery under Arms*, xv

***Screwed.*** Intoxicated. A playful synonym of *tight*, which again is a playful synonym of *blown out*.

***The Screw Plot.*** The story is that when Queen Anne went to St Paul's in 1708 to offer thanksgivings for the victory of Oudenarde, disaffected conspirators removed certain screw-bolts from the beams of the cathedral, that the roof might fall on the queen and her suite and kill them.

> Some of your Machiavelian crew
> From heavy roof of Paul
> Most traitorously stole every screw,
> To make that fabric fall;
> And so to catch Her Majesty,
> And all her friends beguile.
>
> *Plot upon Plot* (about 1713)

***There's a screw loose somewhere.*** All is not right, there's something amiss. A figurative phrase from machinery, where one screw not tightened up may be the cause of a disaster.

***To put on the screw.*** To press for payment, as a screw presses by gradually increasing pressure. Hence *to apply the screw*, *to give the screw another turn*, to take steps (or additional steps) to enforce one's demands.

***To screw oneself up to it.*** To force oneself to face it, etc.; to get oneself into the right frame of mind for doing some unpleasant or difficult job.

**Scribe,** in the New Testament, means a doctor of the law. Thus, in Matt. 22:35, we read, 'Then one of them, which was a *lawyer*, asked Him ... Which is the great commandment of the law?' Mark (12:28) says, 'One of the *scribes* came ... and asked Him, Which is the first commandment of all?' They were generally coupled with the Pharisees (*q.v.*) as being upholders of the ancient ceremonial tradition.

In the Old Testament the word is used more widely. Thus Seraiah is called the *scribe* (secretary) of David (2 Sam. 8:17); 'Shebna the scribe' (2 Kings 18:18) was secretary to Hezekiah; and Jonathan, Baruch, Gemariah, etc., who were princes, were called scribes. Ezra, however, called 'a ready scribe in the law of Moses', accords with the New Testament usage of the word.

**Scriblerus, Martinus.** A merciless satire on the false taste in literature current in the time of Pope, for the most part written by Arbuthnot, and published in 1741. Cornelius Scriblerus, the father of Martin, was a pedant, who entertained all sorts of absurdities about the education of his son. Martin grew up a man of capacity; but though he had read everything, his judgment was vile and taste atrocious. Pope, Swift, and Arbuthnot founded a *Scriblerus Club* with the object of pillorying all literary incompetence.

**Scrimmage.** Originally, a *skirmish*, of which word this is a variant.

> Prince Ouffur at this skrymage, for all his pryde,
> Fled full fast and sought no guide.
>
> *MS Lansdowne*, 200, f. 10

*Scrummage* was another form of *scrimmage*; as *scrum* it still survives on the Rugby football field.

**Scriptores Decem.** A collection of ten ancient chronicles on English history, edited by Sir Roger Twysden and John Selden (1652). The ten chroniclers are Simeon of Durham, John of Hexham, Richard of Hexham, Ailred of Rieval, Ralph de Diceto (Archdeacon of London), John Brompton of Jorval, Gervase of Canterbury, Thomas Stubbs, William Thorn of Canterbury, and Henry Knighton of Leicester.

A similar collection of five chronicles was published by Thomas Gale (1691) as *Scriptores Quinque*.

**Scriptorium** (Lat., from *scriptus*, past part. of *scribere*, to write). A writing-room, especially the chamber set apart in the mediaeval monasteries for the copying of MSS, etc. Dr Murray gave the name to the corrugated iron outhouse in his garden at Mill Hill, in which he started the great *New English Dictionary*.

**Scripturalists.** Protestants who hold to the principle, 'the Bible, and the Bible only'.

**Scriptures, The,** or **Holy Scripture** (Lat. *scriptura*, a writing). The Bible; hence applied allusively to the sacred writings of other creeds, as the Koran, *the Scripture of the Mohammedans*, the Vedas and Zendavesta, of the Hindus and Persians, etc.

**Scripturists.** Another name for the Caraites (*q.v.*).

**Scrounge.** To purloin or annex something from nowhere particular or that has no obvious owner. A term much used in the army during the Great War.

**Scruple.** The name of the weight (20 grains, or 1/24 oz), and the term for doubt or hesitation (as in *a scruple of conscience*), both come from Lat. *scrupulus*, meaning a sharp little pebble, such as will cause great uneasiness if it gets into one's shoe. The second is the figurative use; with the name of the little weight compare that of the big one – *stone*.

**Scudamore, Sir.** The lover of Amoret in Spenser's *Faërie Queene* (Bk iv), and finally wedded to her. The name means 'Shield of Love'.

**Scullabogue Massacre.** In the Irish rebellion of 1798 Scullabogue House, Wexford, was seized by the rebels and used for a prison. Some thirty or forty prisoners confined in it were brought out and shot in cold blood, when the news of a repulse of the rebels at New Ross arrived (June 5th, 1798). The barn at the back of the house was filled with prisoners and set on fire, and Taylor, in his history, written at the time and almost on the spot, puts the number of victims at 184, and he gives the names of several of them.

**Scunner.** A Scotch term for a feeling of distaste amounting almost to loathing. *To take a scunner at one* is to conceive a violent dislike for him.

**Scurry.** A scratch race, or race without restrictions.

***Hurry-scurry.*** A confused bustle through lack of time; in a confused bustle. A 'ricochet' word.

**Scuttle.** ***To scuttle a ship*** is to bore a hole in it in order to make it sink. The word is from the Old French *escoutilles*, hatches, and was first applied to a hole in a roof with a door or lid, then to a hatchway in the deck of a ship with a lid, then to a hole in the bottom of a ship.

***Scuttle,*** for coals, is the A.S. *scutel*, a dish; from Lat. *scutella*, diminutive of *scutra*, a dish or platter.

***To scuttle off,*** to make off hurriedly, was originally *To scuddle off*, scuddle being a frequentative of *scud*.

**Scylla.** In Greek legend the name (1) of a daughter of King Nisus of Megara and (2) of a sea monster.

The daughter of Nisus promised to deliver Megara into the hands of her lover, Minos, and, to effect this, cut off a golden hair on her father's head, while he was asleep. Minos despised her for this treachery, and Scylla threw herself from a rock into the sea. At death she was changed into a lark, and Nisus into a hawk.

> Think of Scylla's fate.
> Changed to a bird, and sent to fly in air,
> She dearly pays tor Nisus' injured hair.
>
> Pope, *Rape of the Lock*, iii

The sea monster dwelt on the rock Scylla, opposite Charybdis (*q.v.*), on the Italian side of the Straits of Messina. Homer says that she had twelve feet, and six heads, each on a long neck and each armed with three rows of pointed teeth, and that she barked like a dog. He makes her a daughter of Crataeis; but later accounts say that she was a nymph who, because she was beloved by Glaucus (*q.v.*), was changed by the jealous Circe into a hideous monster.

> Glaucus, lost to joy,
> Curst in his love by vengeful Circe's hate,
> Attending wept his Scylla's hapless fate.
>
> Camoëns, *Lusiad*, bk vi

***Avoiding Scylla, he fell into Charybdis.*** *See* Charybdis.

***Between Scylla and Charybdis.*** Between two equal difficulties; between the devil and the deep sea.

***To fall from Scylla into Charybdis*** – out of the frying-pan into the fire.

**Scythian.** Pertaining to the peoples or region of Scythia, the ancient name of a great part of European and Asiatic Russia.

***Scythian defiance.*** When Darius approached Scythia, an ambassador was sent to his tent with a bird, a frog, a mouse, and five arrows, then left without uttering a word. Darius, wondering what was meant, was told by Gobrias it meant this: Either fly away like a bird, and hide your head in a hole like a mouse, or swim across the river, or in five days you will be laid prostrate by the Scythian arrows.

***The Scythian*** or ***Tartarian lamb.*** The Russian barometz, the creeping root-stock and frond-stalks of *Cibotium barometz*, a woolly fern, which, when inverted, was supposed to have some resemblance to a lamb. Mandeville in his *Travels* (ch. xxvi) gives a highly fanciful description of them.

**'Sdeath, 'Sdeins.** *See* 'S.

**Se non è vero,** etc. *See* Ben trovato.

**Sea.** Any large expanse of water, more or less enclosed; hence the expression 'molten sea', meaning the great brazen vessel which stood in Solomon's temple (2 Chron. 4:5, and 1 Kings 7:26); even the Nile, the Euphrates, and the Tigris are sometimes called seas by the prophets. The world of water is the *Ocean*.

***At sea,*** or ***all at sea.*** Wide of the mark; quite wrong; like a person in the open ocean without compass or chart.

***Half-seas over.*** *See* Half.

***The four seas.*** The seas surrounding Great Britain, on the north, south, east, and west.

***The high seas.*** The open sea, the 'main'; especially that part of the sea beyond 'the three-mile limit', which forms a free highway to all nations.

***The Old Man of the sea.*** A creature encountered by Sinbad the Sailor in his fifth voyage (*Arabian Nights*). This terrible Old Man got on Sinbad's back, and would neither dismount nor could be shaken off. At last Sinbad gave him some wine, which so intoxicated him that he relaxed his grip, and Sinbad made his escape. Hence the phrase is figuratively applied to bad habits, evil associates, etc., from which it is very difficult to free oneself.

***The king of the sea.*** The herring.

> The head of an average-sized whale is from fifteen to sixteen feet, and the lips open some six or eight feet; yet to such a mouth there is scarcely any throat, not sufficiently large to allow a herring to pass down it. This little scaly fellow [the herring], some fourteen inches in length, would choke a monster whale, and is hence called 'the king of the sea'.
>
> C. Thomson, *Autobiography*, p. 132

***The Seven Seas.*** *See* Seven.

**Sea Deities.** In classical myth, besides the fifty Nereids (*q.v.*), the Oceanides (daughters of Oceanus), the Sirens (*q.v.*), etc., there were a number of deities presiding over, or connected with, the sea. The chief of these are:

*Amphitrite*, wife of Poseidon, queen goddess of the sea.

*Glaucus*, a fisherman of Boeotia, afterwards a marine deity.

*Ino*, who threw herself from a rock into the sea, and was made a sea-goddess.

*Neptune*, king of the ocean.

*Nereus* and his wife *Doris*. Their palace was at the bottom of the Mediterranean; his hair was seaweeds.

*Oceanus* and his wife *Tethys* (daughter of Uranus and Ge). Oceanus was god of the *Ocean*, which formed a boundary round the world.

*Portumnus* (Gr.; Lat. *Palemon*), the protector of harbours.

*Poseidon*, the Greek Neptune.

*Proteus*, who assumed every variety of shape.

*Thetis*, a daughter of Nereus and mother of Achilles.

*Triton*, son of Poseidon.

**Sea-girt Isle, The.** England. So called because, as Shakespeare has it, it is 'hedged in with the main, that water-wallëd bulwark' (*King John*, 2, 1).

> This precious stone set in the silver sea,

Which serves it in the office of a wall,
Or as a moat defensive to a house,
Against the envy of less happier lands.
Shakespeare, *Richard II*, 2, 1

**Sea-green Incorruptible, The.** So Carlyle called Robespierre in his *French Revolution*.

The song is a short one, and may perhaps serve to qualify our judgment of the 'sea-green incorruptible'.
*Notes and Queries*, September 19th, 1891, p. 226

**Sea Lawyer.** A sailor (also applied to a soldier) who knows all about his rights, and is always arguing, criticising, raising objections to the orders of his superior officers, etc.

**Sea Legs. *He has got his sea legs*.** Is able to walk on deck when the ship is rolling; able to bear the motion of the ship without sea-sickness.

**Sea serpent.** A serpentine monster inhabiting the depths of the ocean, the existence – but not the *nature* – of which has been abundantly proved by the many indisputable accounts of its occasional appearances at the surface both in ancient and modern times. As stories of the 'Great Sea Serpent' are almost always received with smiles of incredulity, sailors are naturally rather shy of reporting its appearance; but, in spite of this, scarcely a year goes by without there being some additional and trustworthy evidence of its existence. To quote Mr Bartlett, Superintendent of the Zoo for many years –

I fully believe in the existence, in the deep, of animals at present unknown either by specimens or by perfect descriptions; not only do I accept as true the statements made to the best of the judgments and belief of the parties who have made them, but I do not doubt that from time to time those wonderful sights have presented themselves to the observer, and have remained unrecorded by him simply through fear of his statement being derided and discredited.

Pontoppidan, in his *Natural History of Norway* (Eng. tr., 1755), speaks of sea serpents 600 ft long.

**Seal.** The sire is called a *bull*, its females are *cows*, the offspring are called *pups*; the breeding-place is called a *rookery*, a group of young seals a *pod*, and a colony of seals a *herd*. The immature male is called a *bachelor*. A *sealer* is a seal-hunter, and seal-hunting is called *sealing*.

**Seamy Side.** The 'wrong' or worst side; as the 'seamy side of London', 'the seamy side of life'. In velvet, Brussels carpets, tapestry, etc., the 'wrong' side shows the seams or threads of the pattern exhibited on the right side.

My present purpose is to call attention to the seamy side of the Australian colonies. There is, as we know, such a thing as cotton-backed satin; but the colonists take care to show us only the face of the goods.
*Nineteenth Century*, April, 1891, p. 524

**Seasons, The Four.** Spring, Summer, Autumn, and Winter. *Spring* starts (officially) on March 21st, the Spring Equinox, when the sun enters Aries; *Summer* on June 22nd, the Summer Solstice, when the sun enters Cancer; *Autumn* on September 23rd, the Autumn Equinox, the sun entering Libra; and *winter* on December 22nd, when the sun enters Capricornus.

Autumn to winter, winter into spring,
Spring into summer, summer into fall, –
So rolls the changing year, and so we change
Motion so swift, we know not that we move.
D. M. Muloch, *Immutable*

The ancient Greeks characterised *Spring* by Mercury, *Summer* by Apollo, *Autumn* by Bacchus, and *Winter* by Hercules.

***The London Season.*** The part of the year when the Court and fashionable society generally is in town – May, June, and July.

***The silly season.*** *See* Silly.

***Season-ticket.*** A ticket giving the holder certain specified rights (in connection with travelling, entrance to an exhibition, etc.) for a certain specified period.

**Seat. *To take a back seat*.** *See* Back.

**Sebastian, St.** Patron saint of archers, because he was bound to a tree and shot at with arrows. As the arrows stuck in his body, thick as pins in a pincushion, he was also made patron saint of pinmakers. And as he was a centurion, he is patron saint of soldiers.

***The English St Sebastian.*** St Edmund, the martyr-king of East Anglia (855–70) has been so called. He gave himself up to the Danes in the hope of saving his people, but they scourged him, bound him to a tree, shot arrows at him, and finally cut off his head, which, legend relates, was guarded by a wolf till it was duly interred. The monastery and cathedral of St Edmundsbury (Bury St Edmunds) were erected on the place of his burial.

**Sebastianistes.** Persons who believed that Dom Sebastian (King of Portugal, 1557–78), who fell in the battle of Alcazarquebir in 1578, will return to earth, when Brazil will become the chief kingdom of the earth. He was very popular, and for twenty years and more after his death impostors were appearing and giving themselves out as him.

**Second.** The next after the first (Lat. *secundus*).

In duelling the *second* is the representative of the principal: he carries the challenge, selects the ground, sees that the weapons are in order, and is responsible for all the arrangements.

***A second of time*** is so called because the division of the minute into sixtieths is the *second* of the sexagesimal operations, the first being the division of the hour into minutes.

***To second an officer*** (accent on the second syllable) is, in military phraseology, to remove him temporarily from his regimental or military duties so that he may take up some other appointment.

***One's second self.*** His *alter ego* (*q.v.*); one whose tastes, opinions, habits, etc., correspond so entirely with one's own that there is practically no distinction.

***Second adventists.*** Those who believe that the Second Coming of Christ (*cp.* 1 Thess. 4:15) will precede the Millennium; hence sometimes also called *Premillenarians*.

***Second-hand.*** Not new or original; what has already been the property of another, as, 'second-hand' books, clothes, opinions, etc.

***Second nature.*** Said of a habit, way of looking at things, and so on, that has become so ingrained in one that it is next to impossible to shake it off.

***Second pair back.*** The back room on the floor two flights of stairs above the ground floor; similarly the front room is called the *second pair front*.

**Second Sight.** The power of seeing things invisible to others; the power of foreseeing future events by means of shadows thrown before them.

> Nor less availed his optic sleight,
> And Scottish gift of second sight.
>
> Trumbull

> These are Highland visions, Captain Campbell, as unsatisfactory and vain as those of the second sight.
> Scott, *The Highland Widow*, v

***Second wind.*** *See* Wind.

**Secondary Colours.** *See under* Colours (*Technical Terms*).

**Secret.** ***An open secret.*** A piece of information generally known, but not formally announced.

> It was an open secret that almost every one of Lord Palmerston's ecclesiastical appointments was virtually made by Lord Shaftesbury.
> *Leisure Hour*, 1887

***Un secret de polichinelle.*** No secret at all. A secret known to all the world; an open secret. Polichinelle is the Punch of the old French puppet-shows, and his secrets are 'stage whispers' told to all the audience.

> Entre nous, c'est qu'on appelle
> Le secret de polichinelle. *Le Mascotte*, ii, 12

**Secular.** From Lat. *saecularis*, pertaining to the *saeculum*, i.e., the age or generation; hence, pertaining to this world in contradistinction to the next.

***Secularism.*** The name given about 1851 by George Jacob Holyoake (d.1906) to an ethical system founded on natural morality, and opposed to the tenets of revealed religion and ecclesiasticism.

***Secular clergy.*** The parish clergy who live in daily contact with the world, in contradistinction to monks, etc., who live in monasteries.

***Secular games.*** In ancient Rome the public games lasting three days and three nights that took place only once in an age (*saeculum*), or period of 120 years.

They were instituted in obedience to the Sibylline verses, with the promise that 'the empire should remain in safety so long as this admonition was observed', and while the kings reigned were held in the Campus Martius, in honour of Pluto and Proserpine,

> Date, quae precamur
> Tempore sacro
> Quo Sibyllini monuere versus
> Horace, *Carmen Seculare*, AUC, 737

**Sedan Chair.** The covered seat so called, carried by two bearers on poles back and front, first appeared in Italy in the late 16th century, and was introduced into England by Prince Charles and the Duke of Buckingham on their return from Spain (1623).

The name *Sedan* was first used in England; it was probably coined from Lat. *sedere*, to sit, though it is just possible that Johnson's suggestion, viz., that it is connected with the French town, *Sedan*, has something in it.

**Sedan, the Man of.** Napoleon III was so called, because he surrendered his sword to William, King of Prussia, after the battle of Sedan (September 2, 1870).

**Sedrat.** The lotus tree which, according to Mohammedan legend, stands on the right-hand side of the invisible throne of Allah. Its branches extend wider than the distance between heaven and earth. Its leaves resemble the ears of an elephant. Each seed of its fruit encloses a houri; and two rivers issue from its roots. Numberless birds sing among its branches, and numberless angels rest beneath its shade.

**Sedulous.** ***To play the sedulous ape to.*** To study the style of another, and model one's own on his as faithfully and meticulously as possible: said, usually with more or less contempt, of literary men. The phrase is taken from R. L. Stevenson, who, in his essay, *A College Magazine* (*Memories and Portraits*), said that he had –

> played the sedulous ape to Hazlitt, to Lamb, to Wordsworth, to Sir Thomas Browne, to Defoe, to Hawthorne, to Montaigne, to Baudelaire, and to Obermann. ... That, like it or not, is the way to learn to write.

**See.** The diocese or jurisdiction of a bishop or archbishop, his *seat* (Lat. *sedes*, a *seat*, from *sedere*, to sit.)

***The Holy See.*** The Papacy, the papal jurisdiction and court.

**Seedy.** Weary, worn out, out of sorts; run to seed. A hat or coat is termed *seedy* when it has become shabby. A man is *seedy* after a debauch, when he looks and feels out of sorts.

**Seel.** To close the eyelids of a hawk by running a thread through them; to hoodwink. (Fr., *ciller*, *cil*, the eyelash).

> She that so young could give out such a seeming,
> To seel her father's eyes up, close as oak.
>
> Shakespeare, *Othello*, 3, 3

**Seian Horse, The.** A possession which invariably brought ill luck with it. Hence the Latin proverb *Ille homo habet equum Seianum*. Cneius Seius had an Argive horse, of the breed of Diomed, of a bay colour and surpassing beauty, but it was fatal to its possessor. Seius was put to death by Mark Antony. Its next owner, Cornelius Dolabella, who bought it for 100,000 sesterces, was killed in Syria during the civil wars. Caius Cassius, who next took possession of it, perished after the battle of Philippi by the very sword which stabbed Caesar. Antony had the horse next, and after the battle of Actium slew himself.

Like the gold of Tolosa and Hermione's necklace, the Seian or Sejan horse was a fatal possession.

**Selah.** A Hebrew word occurring often in the Psalms (and three times in Habakkuk, 3), indicating some musical or liturgical direction, such as a pause, a repetition, or the end of a section.

**Selene.** The moon goddess of *Greek mythology*, daughter of Hyperion and Thea, and roughly corresponding to the Roman Diana (*q.v.*), the chaste huntress. Selene had fifty daughters by Endymion, and several by Zeus, one of whom was called 'The Dew'. Diana is represented with bow and arrow running after the stag; but Selene in a chariot drawn by two white horses, with wings on her shoulders and a sceptre in her hand.

**Seleucidae.** The dynasty of Seleucus Nicator, one of Alexander's generals (about 358–280 BC), who in 312 conquered Babylon and succeeded to a part of Alexander's vast empire. The monarchy consisted of Syria, a part of Asia Minor, and all the eastern provinces, and the line of the Selucids reigned till about 64 BC.

**Self.** Used in combination for a variety of purposes, such as (1) to express direct or indirect reflexive action, as in *self-command*; (2) action performed independently, or without external agency, as in *self-acting*, *self-fertilisation*; (3) action or relation to the self, as in *self-conscious*, *self-suspicious*; (4) uniformity, naturalness, etc., as in *self-coloured, self-glazed*.

> Self-reverence, self-knowledge, self-control,
> These three alone lead life to sovereign power.
>
> Tennyson, *Oenone*

***A self-made man.*** One who has risen from poverty and obscurity to opulence and a position of importance by his own efforts. The phrase was originally American.

***The Self-denying Ordinance.*** The bill passed by the Long Parliament in 1645 ordering that Members of either House should give up their military commands and civil appointments within forty days; the reason being the suspicion that the Civil War was being prolonged for personal ends.

***Self-determination.*** The theory in political economy, that every nation, no matter how small or weak, has the right to decide upon its own form of government and to manage its own internal affairs. The phrase acquired its present significance during the attempts to resettle Europe after the Great War; but difficulties arose (as in the case of Ireland) when it was discovered that an exact and comprehensive definition of the word *Nation* could not be agreed upon.

**Seljuks.** A Perso-Turkish dynasty of eleven emperors over a large part of Asia, which lasted 138 years (1056–1194). It was founded by Togrul Beg, a descendant of Seljuk, chief of a small tribe which gained possession of Bokara.

**Sell.** Slang for a swindle, a hoax, a first-of-April trick; and the person hoaxed is said to be *sold*.

Street vendors who take in the unwary with catchpennies, chuckle like hens when they have laid an egg, 'Sold again, and got the money!'

***A selling race.*** One in which the horses that compete are sold after the race, the sale price being determined beforehand. The winner is generally sold by auction, and the owner gets both the selling price and the stakes. If at the auction a price is obtained above the ticketed price it is divided between the second best horse and the race fund. *See* Handicap.

> The owner of any of the horses may claim any horse in a selling race at the price ticketed.

***Selling the pass.*** Betraying one's own side. The phrase was originally Irish, and is applied to those who turn king's evidence, or who impeach their comrades for money. The tradition is that a regiment was sent by Crotha, 'lord of Atha', to hold a pass against the invading army of Trathal, 'King of Cael'. The pass was betrayed for money; the Fir-bolgs were subdued, and Trathal assumed the title of 'King of Ireland'.

***To sell a person up.*** To dispose of his goods by order of the court because he cannot pay his debts, the proceeds going to his creditors.

**Sellinger's Round.** An old country dance, very popular in Elizabethan times, in which –

> the dancers take hands, go round twice and back again; then all set, turn, and repeat; then lead all forward, and back, and repeat; two singles and back, set and turn single and repeat; arms all and repeat.
>
> John Playford, *The English Dancing Master* (1651)

It is said to be so called either from Sir Thomas Sellynger, buried in St George's Chapel, Windsor, about 1470, or from Sir Anthony St Leger, Lord Deputy of Ireland (d.1559).

**Semele.** In *Greek mythology*, the daughter of Cadmus and Harmonia. By Zeus she was the mother of Dionysus, and was slain by lightning when he granted her request to appear before her as the God of Thunder.

**Semidulites.** *See* Barsanians.

**Semiramis of the North, The.** Margaret of Denmark, Sweden, and Norway (1353–1412), and Catherine II of Russia (1729–96) have both been so called.

The original Semiramis was the half legendary wife of Ninus (founder of Nineveh), daughter of the Syrian goddess Derketo, and the possessor of unrivalled beauty and wisdom.

**Semitic.** Pertaining to the descendants of Shem (*see* Gen. 10), viz. the Hebrews, Arabs, Assyrians, Aramaeans, etc., nowadays applied in popular use to the Jews, who, when one means to be contemptuous, are often spoken of as *the Semites.*

***The Semitic languages*** are the ancient Assyrian and Chaldee, Aramaean, Syriac, Arabic, Hebrew, Samaritan, Ethiopic, and old Phoenician. The great characteristic of this family of languages is that the roots of words consist of three consonants.

**Senanus, St.** An Irish saint who, like St Kevin, fled to an island, Scattery, and resolved that no woman should ever visit it. An angel led St Canara to the island, but the recluse refused to admit her. *See* Moore's poem *St Senanus and the Lady* (*Irish Melodies*).

**Sennight.** A week; seven nights. *Fortnight*, fourteen nights. These words are relics of the ancient Celtic custom of beginning the day at sunset, a custom observed by the ancient Greeks, Babylonians, Persians, Syrians, and Jews, and by the modern representatives of these people. In Gen. 1 we always find the evening precedes the morning; as, 'The evening and the morning were the first day', etc.

**Sense. *Common sense.*** *See* Common.

***Scared out of my seven senses.*** According to ancient teaching the soul of man, or his 'inward holy body', is compounded of the seven properties which are under the influence of the seven planets. Fire animates, earth gives the sense of feeling, water gives speech, air gives taste, mist gives sight, flowers give hearing, the south wind gives smelling. Hence the seven senses are animation, feeling, speech, taste, sight, hearing, and smelling (*see* Ecclus. 17:5).

**Sentences, Master of the.** The Schoolman, Peter Lombard (d.1160), an Italian theologian and bishop of Paris, author of *The Four Books of Sentences* (*Sententiarum libri* iv), a compilation from the Fathers of the leading arguments pro and con., bearing on the hair-splitting theological questions of the Middle Ages.

The mediaeval graduates in theology, of the second order, whose duty it was to lecture on the *Sentences*, were called *Sententiatory Bachelors.*

**Separation, The.** The name given in the 17th century to the body of Independents and Protestant dissenters generally – called individually *Separatists.* Thus the Amsterdam parson, Tribulation Wholesome, says:

> These chastisements are common to the saints,
> And such rebukes, we of the Separation,

Must bear with willing shoulders, as the trials
Sent forth to tempt our frailties.

Ben Jonson, *The Alchemist*, III, i

**Sephardim.** The Jews of Spain and Portugal, so called from *Sepharad*, a district mentioned in Obad. 20, which was supposed by the rabbinical commentators to be intended for Spain. As Jews were evidently in captivity at Sepharad at the time the passage was written this cannot possibly be the correct interpretation.

**Sepoy.** The Anglicised form of Hindu and Persian *sipahi*, a soldier, from *sipah*, army, denoting a native East Indian soldier trained and disciplined in the British manner, especially one in the British Indian Army.

**September.** The seventh month from March, where the year used to commence.

The old Dutch name was *Herst-maand* (autumn-month); the old Saxon, *Gerst-monath* (barley-month), or *Haerfest-monath*; and after the introduction of Christianity *Halig-monath* (holy-month, the nativity of the Virgin Mary being on the 8th, the exaltation of the Cross on the 14th, Holy-Rood Day on the 26th and St Michael's Day on the 29th). In the French Republican calendar, it was called *Fructidor* (fruit-month, August 18th to September 21st).

***September Bible.*** *See* Bible, Specially named.

***September massacres.*** An indiscriminate slaughter, during the French Revolution, of Loyalists confined in the Abbaye and other prisons, lasting from September 2nd to 5th, 1792. Danton gave the order after the capture of Verdun by the allied Prussian army; as many as 8,000 persons fell, among whom was the Princess de Lamballe.

**Septentrional Signs.** The first six signs of the Zodiac, because they belong to the *northern* celestial hemisphere. The North was called the *septentrion* from the seven stars of the Great Bear (Lat. *septem*, seven, *triones*, plough oxen). *Cp.* Ursa Major.

**Septuagesima Sunday.** The third Sunday before Lent; in round numbers, seventy days (Lat. *septuagesima dies*) before Easter. Really only sixty-eight days before Easter.

**Septuagint.** A Greek version of the Old Testament and Apocrypha, so called because it was traditionally said to have been made by seventy-two Palestinian Jews in the 3rd century BC at the command of Ptolemy Philadelphus. They worked on the island of Pharos and completed the translation in seventy-two days.

This tradition applies, however, only to the Pentateuch; Greek translations of the other books were added by later writers, some, perhaps, being as late as the Christian era. The name Septuagint is frequently printed LXX – 'for short'.

**Sepulchre, The Holy.** The cave outside the walls of Jerusalem in which the body of Christ is believed to have lain between His burial and resurrection. From at least the 4th century (*see* Invention of the Cross, *under* Cross) the spot has been covered by a Christian church.

***Knights of the Holy Sepulchre.*** An order of military knights founded by Godfrey of Bouillon, in 1099, to guard the Holy Sepulchre. Since 1342 it has existed only as a religious body, the Latin Patriarch of Jerusalem being its Grand Master.

**Seraglio.** The palace of the Sultan of Turkey at Constantinople, situated on the Golden Horn, and enclosed by walls seven miles and a half in circuit. The chief entrance is *the Sublime Gate* (*cp.* Sublime Porte); and the chief of the large edifices is the *Harem*, or 'sacred spot', which contains numerous houses, one for each of the sultan's wives, and others for his concubines. The Seraglio may be visited by strangers; not so the Harem.

**Seraphic.** ***The Seraphic Doctor.*** The scholastic philosopher, St Bonaventura (1221–74).

***The Seraphic Father,*** or ***Saint.*** St Francis of Assisi (1182–1226); whence the Franciscans are sometimes called the *Seraphic Order*.

***The Seraphic Hymn.*** The Sanctus, 'Holy, holy, holy' (Is. 6:3), which was sung by the seraphim.

**Seraphim.** The highest order of angels in mediaeval angelology, so named from the seraphim of Is. 6:2. The word is probably the same as *saraph*, a serpent, from *saraph*, to burn (in allusion to its bite); and this connection with burning suggested to early Christian interpreters that the seraphim were specially distinguished by the ardency of their zeal and love.

***Seraphim*** is a plural form; the singular, *seraph*, was first used in English by Milton. Abdiel was

The flaming Seraph, fearless, though alone,
Encompassed round with foes.

*Paradise Lost*, v, 875

**Serapis.** The Ptolemaic form of Apis, an Egyptian deity who, when dead, was honoured under the attributes of Osiris (*q.v.*), and thus became 'osirified Apis' or [O]Sorapis. He was lord of the underworld, and was identified by the Greeks with Hades.

**Serat, Al.** *See* Al-Sirat.

**Serbonian Bog, The.** A great morass, now covered with shifting sand, between the isthmus of Suez, the Mediterranean, and the delta of the Nile, that in Strabo's time was a lake stated by him to be 200 stadia long and 50 broad, and by Pliny to be 150 miles in length. Typhon was said to dwell at the bottom of it, hence its other name, *Typhon's Breathing Hole*.

> A gulf profound as that Serbonian bog,
> Betwixt Damiata and Mount Cassius old,
> Where armies whole have sunk.
>
> Milton, *Paradise Lost*, ii, 592

The term is used figuratively of a mess from which there is no way of extricating oneself.

> Now, sir, I must say I know of no Serbonian bog deeper than a £5 rating would prove to be.
>
> Disraeli (Chanc. of the Exch.), March 19, 1867

**Serendipity.** A happy coinage by Horace Walpole to denote the faculty of making lucky and unexpected 'finds' by accident. In a letter to Mann (January 28th, 1754) he says that he formed it on the title of a fairy story, *The Three Princes of Serendip*, because the princes –

> were always making discoveries, by accidents and sagacity, of things they were not in quest of.

Serendip is an ancient name of Ceylon.

**Serene** (Lat. *serenus*, clear, calm). A title formerly given to certain German princes. Those who used to hold under the empire were entitled *Serene* or *Most Serene Highnesses*.

***It's all serene.*** All right (Span. *sereno*, all right – the sentinel's countersign).

> 'Let us clearly understand each other.' 'All serene,' responded Foster.
>
> Watson, *The Web of the Spider*, ch. viii

***The drop serene.*** *See* Drop.

**Sergeanty** or **Serjeanty.** A feudal tenure, the tenant rendering some specified personal service to the king.

***Petit sergeanty.*** Holding lands of the Crown by the service of rendering annually some small implement of war, as a bow, a sword, a lance, a flag, an arrow, and the like. Thus the Duke of Wellington holds Strathfieldsaye and Apsley House, London, by presenting a flag annually to the Crown on the anniversary of the battle of Waterloo, and the Duke of Marl-borough pays a similar 'peppercorn rent' on the anniversary of the battle of Blenheim for Blenheim Palace.

**Serif** and **Sanserif.** The former is a letter with the 'wings' or finishing strokes (as T); the latter is without the finishing strokes (as T); these strokes are the *serifs*.

**Serjeants-at-Law.** A superior order of barristers (*q.v.*) abolished in 1880. From the Low Latin *serviens ad legem*, one who serves (the king) in matters of law.

**Serpent.** *See also* Snake. The serpent is symbolical of –

(1) Deity, because, says Plutarch, 'it feeds upon its own body; even so all things spring from God, and will be resolved into deity again' (*De Iside et Osiride*, i, 2, p. 5; and *Philo Byblius*).

(2) Eternity, as a corollary of the former. It is represented as forming a circle, holding its tail in its mouth.

(3) Renovation and the healing art. It is said that when old it has the power of growing young again 'like the eagle', by casting its slough, which is done by squeezing itself between two rocks. It was sacred to Aesculapius (*q.v.*), the Greek god of medicine, as it was supposed to have the power of discovering healing herbs. Hence, two serpents still appear in the badge of the Royal Army Medical Corps. *See* Caduceus.

(4) Guardian spirits. It was thus employed by the ancient Greeks and Romans, and not unfrequently the figure of a serpent was depicted on their altars.

In the temple of Athena at Athens, a serpent, supposed to be animated by the soul of Ericthonius, was kept in a cage, and called 'the Guardian Spirit of the Temple'.

(5) Wisdom. 'Be ye therefore wise as serpents, and harmless as doves' (Matt.10:16).

(6) Subtilty. 'Now the serpent was more subtle than any beast of the field' (Gen. 3:1).

It is also symbolical of the devil, as the Tempter, and in early pictures is sometimes placed under the feet of the Virgin, in allusion to the promise made to Eve after the fall (Gen. 3:15).

In Christian art it is an attribute of St Cecilia, St Euphemia, St Patrick, and many other saints, either because they trampled on Satan, or because they miraculously cleared some country of snakes.

Fable has it that the cerastes hides in sand that it may bite the horse's foot and get the rider thrown. In allusion to this belief, Jacob says, 'Dan shall be ... an adder in the path, that biteth the horse heels, so that his rider shall fall backward' (Gen. 49:17). The Bible also tells us that the serpent stops up its ears that it may not be charmed by the charmers, 'charming never so wisely' (Ps. 58:4).

Another old idea about snakes was that when attacked they would swallow their young and not eject them until reaching a place of safety.

It was in the form of a serpent, says the legend, that Jupiter Ammon appeared to Olympia and became by her the father of Alexander the Great; hence the allusion –

When glides a silver serpent, treacherous guest!
And fair Olympia folds him to her breast.
Darwin, *Economy of Vegetation*, i, 2

***Pharaoh's serpent.*** *See* Pharaoh.

***Sea serpent.*** *See* Sea.

***The serpent of old Nile.*** Cleopatra, so called by Antony.

He's speaking now,
Or murmuring 'Where's my serpent of old Nile?'
For so he calls me.
Shakespeare, *Antony and Cleopatra*, 1, 5

***Their ears have been serpent-licked.*** They have the gift of foreseeing events, the power of seeing into futurity. This is a Greek superstition. It is said that Cassandra and Helenus were gifted with the power of prophecy, because serpents licked their ears while sleeping in the temple of Apollo.

***To cherish a serpent in your bosom.*** To show kindness to one who proves ungrateful. The Greeks say that a husbandman found a frozen serpent, which he put into his bosom. The snake was revived by the warmth, and stung its benefactor. Shakespeare applies the tale to a serpent's egg:

Therefore think him as a serpent's egg
Which, hatched, would (as his kind) grow dangerous.
*Julius Caesar*, 2, 1

**Serpentine Verses.** Such as end with the same word as they begin with. The following are examples:

Crescit amor nummi, quantum ipsa pecunia crescit.
(Greater grows the love of pelf, as pelf itself grows greater.)
Ambo florentes aetatibus, Arcades ambo.
(Both in the spring of life, Arcadians both.)

The allusion is to the old representations of snakes with their tails in their mouths, which was emblematic of eternity – no beginning and no end.

**Serve.** ***I'll serve him out*** – give him a *quid pro quo*. This is the French *desserver*, to do an ill turn to one.

***Serves you right!*** You've got just what you deserved (usually with the implication 'and a good job too!').

***To serve a rope.*** To lash or whip it with thin cord to prevent it fraying.

***To serve a sentence.*** To undergo the punishment awarded.

***To serve one's time.*** To hold an office or appointment for the full period allowed; to go through one's apprenticeship; also, to serve one's sentence in prison.

**Servus servorum** (Lat.). The slave of slaves, the drudge of a servant. *Servus servorum Dei* (the servant of the servants of God) is one of the honorific epithets of the Pope; it was first adopted by Gregory the Great (590–604).

Alexander episcopus, servus servorum Dei, Karissimo filio Willielmo salutem.
Rymer, *Faedera*, I, p. 1

**Sesame.** ***Open, Sesame.*** The 'password' at which the door of the robbers' cave flew open in the tale of *The Forty Thieves* (*Arabian Nights*); hence, a key to a mystery, or anything that acts like magic in obtaining a favour, admission, recognition, etc.

Genius was understood, and poetry a sort of 'open Sesame' to every noble door.
Mrs Oliphant, *Lit. Hist. of England*, I, p. 185

***Sesame*** is an East Indian annual herb, with an oily seed which is used as a food, a laxative, etc. In Egypt they eat sesame cakes, and the Jews frequently add the seed to their bread.

**Sesha, The.** King of the Serpents in *Hindu mythology*, on whom Vishnu reclines on the primeval waters. It has a thousand heads, on one of which the world rests.

**Session, Court of.** *See* Court.

**Set.** The Egyptian original of the Greek Typhon (*q.v.*), the god of evil, brother (or son) of Osiris, and his deadly enemy. He is represented as having the body of a man and the head of some unidentified mythological beast with pointed muzzle and high square ears.

**Set, To.** ***A set scene.*** In theatrical parlance, a scene built up by the stage carpenters, or a furnished interior, as a drawing-room, as distinguished from an ordinary or shifting scene.

***A set to.*** A boxing match, a pugilistic fight, a scolding. In pugilism the combatants were by their seconds 'set to the scratch' or line marked on the ground.

***Setting a hen.*** Giving her a certain number of eggs to hatch. The whole number for incubation is called a *setting*.

***Setting a saw.*** Bending the teeth alternately to the right or left in order to make it do its work properly.

***The setting of a jewel.*** The frame or bedding of gold or silver surrounding a jewel in a ring, brooch, etc.

> This precious stone set in the silver sea.
>
> Shakespeare, *Richard II*, 2, 1

***The setting of the sun, moon,*** or ***stars.*** Their sinking below the horizon. The saying, *The sun never sets on the British dominions* was used long ago of other Empires. Thus, in the *Pastor Fido* (1590) Guarini speaks of Philip II of Spain as –

> that proud monarch to whom, when it grows dark [elsewhere] the sun never sets:

Captain John Smith in his *Advertisements for the Unexperienced* notes that –

> the brave Spanish soldiers brag, The sunne never sets in the Spanish dominions, but ever shineth on one part or other we have conquered for our king:

and Thomas Gage in his *Epistle* Dedicatory to his *New Survey of the West Indies* (1648) writes –

> It may be said of them [the Dutch], as of the Spaniards, that the Sun never sets upon their Dominions.

***To set off to advantage.*** To display a thing in its best light, put the best construction on it. Perhaps a phrase from the jewellers' craft.

***To set the Thames on fire.*** *See* Thames.

**Setebos.** A god or devil worshipped by the Patagonians, and introduced by Shakespeare into his *Tempest* as the god of Sycorax, Caliban's mother.

> His art is of such power,
> It would control my dam's god, Setebos,
> And make a vassal of him.
>
> *Tempest*, 1, 2

**Sethians** or **Sethites.** A Gnostic sect of the 2nd century, who maintained that Seth, son of Adam, was the Messiah, and that Christ was a reincarnation of him.

**Seven.** A mystic or sacred number; it is composed of four and three, which, among the Pythagoreans, were, and from time immemorial have been, accounted lucky numbers. Among the Babylonians, Egyptians, and other ancient peoples there were seven sacred planets; and the Hebrew verb *to swear* means literally 'to come under the influence of seven things'; thus seven ewe lambs figure in the oath between Abraham and Abimelech at Beersheba (Gen. 21:28), and Herodotus (III, viii) describes an Arabian oath in which seven stones are smeared with blood.

There are seven days in creation, seven days in the week, seven graces, seven divisions in the Lord's Prayer, seven ages in the life of man, climacteric years are seven and nine with their multiples by odd numbers, and the seventh son of a seventh son was always held notable.

Among the Hebrews every seventh year was sabbatical, and seven times seven years was the jubilee. The three great Jewish feasts lasted seven days, and between the first and second were seven weeks. Levitical purifications lasted seven days; Baalam would have seven altars, and sacrificed on them seven bullocks and seven rams; Naaman was commanded to dip seven times in Jordan; Elijah sent his servant seven times to look out for rain; ten times seven Israelites go to Egypt, the exile lasts the same number of years, and there were ten times seven elders. Pharaoh in his dream saw seven kine and seven ears of corn; Jacob served seven years for each of his wives; seven priests with seven trumpets marched round Jericho once every day, but seven times on the seventh day; Samson's wedding feast lasted seven days, on the seventh he told his bride the riddle, he was bound with seven withes, and seven locks of his hair were shorn; Nebuchadnezzar was a beast for seven years; etc., etc.

In the Apocalypse we have seven churches of Asia, seven candlesticks, seven stars, seven trumpets, seven spirits before the throne of God, seven horns, seven vials, seven plagues, a seven-headed monster, and the Lamb with seven eyes.

The old astrologers and alchemists recognised seven planets, each having its own 'heaven' –

> The bodies seven, eek, lo hem heer anoon;
> Sol gold is, and Luna silver we threpe,
> Mars yren, Mercurie quyksilver we clepe;
> Saturnus leed, and Jubitur is tyn;
> And Venus coper, by my fader kyn.
>
> Chaucer, *Prol. of the Canon's Yeoman's Tale*

And from this very ancient belief sprang the theory that man was composed of seven substances, and has seven natures. *See under* Sense.

**Seven, The.** Used of groups of seven people, especially (1) the 'men of honest report' chosen by the Apostles to be the first Deacons (Acts 6:5), viz., Stephen, Philip, Prochorus, Nicanor, Timon, Parmenas, and Nicolas; (2) the Seven Bishops (*see below*); or (3) the Seven Sages of Greece (*see* Wise Men). *See also* Seven Names, *below*.

**Seven Against Thebes, The.** The seven Argive heroes (Adrastus, Polynices, Tydeus, Amphiaraus, Capaneus, Hippomedon and Parthenopaeus), who, according to Greek legend, made war on Thebes with the object of restoring Polynices (son of Oedipus), who had been expelled by his brother Eteocles. All perished except Adrastus (*q.v.*), and the brothers slew each other in single combat. The legend is the subject of one of the tragedies of Aeschylus. *See* Nemean Games.

**Seven Bishops, The.** Archbishop Sancroft, and Bishops Lloyd, Turner, Kew, White, Lake, and Trelawney, who refused to read James II's Declaration of Indulgence (1688), and were in consequence imprisoned for non-conforming. *Cp.* Nonjurors.

**Seven Champions, The.** The mediaeval designation of the national patron saints of England, Scotland, Wales, Ireland, France, Spain, and Italy. In 1596 Richard Johnson published a chap-book, *The Famous History of the Seven Champions of Christendom*. In this he relates that *St George* of England was seven years imprisoned by the Almidor, the black king of Morocco; *St Denys* of France lived seven years in the form of a hart; *St James* of Spain was seven years dumb out of love to a fair Jewess; *St Anthony* of Italy, with the other champions, was enchanted into a deep sleep in the Black Castle, and was released by St George's three sons, who quenched the seven lamps by water from the enchanted fountain; *St Andrew* of Scotland delivered six ladies who had lived seven years under the form of white swans; *St Patrick* of Ireland was immured in a cell where he scratched his grave with his own nails; and *St David* of Wales slept seven years in the enchanted garden of Ormandine, and was redeemed by St George.

**Seven Churches of Asia.** Those mentioned in Rev. 1:11, viz.:

(1) Ephesus, founded by St Paul, 57, in a ruinous state in the time of Justinian.

(2) Smyrna. Polycarp was its first bishop.

(3) Pergamos, renowned for its library.

(4) Thyatira, now called Ak-hissar (the *White Castle*).

(5) Sardis, now Sart, a small village.

(6) Philadelphia, now called Allah Shehr (*City of God*), a miserable town.

(7) Laodicea, now a deserted place called Eski-hissar (the *Old Castle*).

**Seven Cities.** ***Seven cities warred for Homer being dead.*** *See* Homer.

***The Island of the Seven Cities.*** A kind of 'Dixie land' of Spanish fable, where seven bishops, who quitted Spain during the dominion of the Moors, founded seven cities. The legend says that many have visited the island, but no one has ever quitted it.

**Seven Dials** (London). A column with seven dials formerly stood in St Giles, facing the seven streets which radiated therefrom.

> Where famed St Giles' ancient limits spread
> An in-railed column rears its lofty head,
> Here to seven streets seven dials count the day,
> And from each other catch the circling ray.
>
> Gay, *Trivia*, ii

The district has for long had an unenviable reputation for squalor (*cp.* Giles, St); hence Sir W. S. Gilbert's whimsical –

> Hearts just as pure and fair
> May beat in Belgrave Square,
> As in the lowly air
> Of Seven Dials.
>
> *Iolanthe*

**Seven Gifts of the Spirit, The.** Wisdom, Understanding, Counsel, Power or Fortitude, Knowledge, Righteousness, and Godly Fear.

**Seven Gods of Luck, The.** In Japanese folk-lore, Benten, goddess of love, Bishamon, god of war, Daikoku, of wealth, Ebisu, of self-effacement, Fukurokujin and Jurojin, gods of longevity, and Hstei, god of generosity. These are really popular conceptions of the seven Buddhist *devas* who preside over human happiness and welfare.

**Seven Heavens, The.** *See* Heaven.

**Seven Joys, The.** *See* Mary.

**Seven Names of God, The.** The ancient Hebrews had many names for the Deity (*see under* Name, *To take God's name in vain, and* Elohistic), and the Seven over which the scribes had to exercise particular care were – El, Elohim, Adonai, YHWH (i.e. our *Jehovah*), Ehyeh-Asher-Ehyeh, Shaddai, and Zebaot. In mediaeval times God was sometimes called simply, *The Seven.*

> Now lord, for thy naymes sevyn, that made both moyn and starnys,
> Well mo then I can neven thi will, lord, of me tharnys.
>
> *Towneley Mysteries*, xiii, 191 (about 1460)

**Seven Planets, Sacraments, The.** *See these headings.*

**Seven Sages of Greece, The.** *See* Wise Men.

**Seven Sciences, The.** *See* Science.

**Seven Seas, The.** The Arctic and Antarctic, North and South Pacific, North and South Atlantic, and the Indian Oceans.

**Seven Sisters, The.** An old name of the Pleiades; also given to a set of seven cannon, cast by one Robert Borthwick and used at Flodden (1513) –

> And these were Borthwick's 'Sisters Seven',
> And culverins which France had given;
> Ill-omened gift! The guns remain
> The conqueror's spoil on Flodden plain.
>
> Scott, *Marmion*, iv

**Seven Sleepers, The.** Seven noble youths of Ephesus, according to the legend, who fled in the Decian persecution (250) to a cave in Mount Celion. After 230 years they awoke, but soon died, and their bodies were taken to Marseilles in a large stone coffin, still shown in Victor's church. Their names are Constantine, Dionysius, John, Maximian, Malchus, Martinian, and Serapion. This fable took its rise from a misapprehension of the words, 'They fell asleep in the Lord' – i.e. died.

The mystic number is connected with other mediaeval 'Sleepers'; thus, Barbarossa turns himself once every seven years; once every seven years, also, Ogier the Dane thunders on the floor with his iron mace; and it was seven years that Tannhauser and Thomas of Ercildoune spent beneath the earth in magic enthralment.

**Seven Sorrows.** *See* Mary.

**Seven Stars, The.** Used formerly of the planets; also of the Pleiades and the Great Bear.

> *Fool:* The reason why the seven stars are no more than seven is a pretty reason.
> *Lear:* Because they are not eight?
> *Fool*: Yes, indeed; thou wouldst make a good fool.
>
> Shakespeare, *King Lear*, 1, 5

**Seven Virtues, The.** *See* Virtues.

**Seven Weeks War, The.** The war between Austria and Prussia in 1866 (June–July), ostensibly to settle the Schleswig-Holstein question, but in fact to end the long existing rivalry between the two countries and bring Austria to her knees. This was quickly done; the Austrians were decisively defeated at Sadowa (July 3rd), and her Italian allies on land at Custozza (June 24th) and at sea off Lissa (July 20th). Truce was declared on July 26th, and the Peace of Prague signed on August 23rd.

**Seven Wise Masters, The.** A collection of Oriental tales (*see* Sandabar) supposed to be told by his advisers to an Eastern king to show the evils of hasty punishment, with his answers to them. Lucien, the son of the king (who, in some versions, is named Dolopathos), was falsely accused to him by one of his queens. By consulting the stars the prince discovered that his life was in danger, but that all would be well if he remained silent for seven days. The 'Wise Masters' now take up the matter; each one in turn tells the king a tale to illustrate the evils of ill-considered punishments, and as the tale ends the king resolves to relent; but the queen at night persuades him to carry out his sentence. The seven days being passed, the prince tells a tale which embodies the whole truth, whereupon the king sentences the queen to death. The tales were immensely popular, and the germs of many later stories are to be found in this collection.

**Seven Wonders of the World, The.** *See* Wonders.

**Seven Works of Mercy, The.** *See* Mercy.

**Seven Years War, The.** The third period of the War of the Austrian Succession, between Maria Theresa of Austria and Friedrich II of Prussia. It began 1756, and terminated in 1763. At the close, Silesia was handed over to Prussia.

**Seventh.** ***In the seventh heaven.*** *See* Heaven.

***Seventh-day Adventists.*** A small sect of millenarians holding very strict Sabbatarian views.

***Seventh-day Baptists.*** Modern representatives of the Traskites (*q.v.*); more numerous in America than in England.

***The seventh son of a seventh son.*** *See* Seven, *above*.

**Several** (late Lat. *separate*, from *separare*, to separate). The English word used simply to denote which is severed or separate; each, as 'all and several'.

> Azariah was a leper, and dwelt in a several house.
>
> 2 Kings 15:5

And it is still used in this way, as –

> Three times slipping from the outer edge,
> I bump'd the ice into three several stars.
>
> Tennyson, *The Epic*, 12

**Severians.** *See* Corrupticolae.

**Severn.** *See* Sabrina.

**Severus, St.** Patron saint of fullers, being himself of the same craft.

***The Wall of Severus.*** A stone rampart, built in 208 by the Emperor Severus, between the Tyne and the Solway. It is to the north of Hadrian's wall, which was constructed in 120.

**Sèvres Ware.** Porcelain of fine quality, for ornament rather than use, made at the French government works at Sèvres, near Paris. The factory was first established at Vincennes in 1745; in 1756 it was removed to Sèvres, and three years later was acquired by the state.

**Sexagesima Sunday.** The second Sunday before Lent; so called because in round numbers it is sixty days (Lat. *sexagesima dies*) before Easter.

**Sextile.** The aspect of two planets when distant from each other sixty degrees or two signs. This position is marked by astrologers thus *.

In sextile, square, and trine, and opposite
Of noxious efficacy.

Milton, *Paradise Lost*, x, 659

At Eton a sixth-form boy is called a *Sextile*.

**Sexton.** A corruption of *sacristan*, a church official who has charge of the *sacra*, or things attached to a specific church, such as vestments, cushions, books, boxes, tools, vessels, and so on.

**Shaddock.** A large kind of orange, so called from Captain Shaddock (late 17th cent.), who first transplanted one in the West Indies. It is a native of China and Japan.

**Shade.** Wine vaults with a lounge attached are often known as *shades*. The term originated at Brighton, where the Old Bank, in 1819, was turned into a smoking-room and bar. There was an entrance by the Pavilion *Shades*, or Arcade, and the name was soon transferred to the drinking-bar. It was not inappropriate, as the room was in reality shaded by the opposite house, occupied by Mrs Fitzherbert.

***To put one in the shade.*** To out-do him, eclipse him; to attract to yourself all the applause and encomiums he had been enjoying.

**Shadow.** A word with a good many figurative and applied meanings, such as, a ghost; Macbeth says to the ghost of Banquo:

Hence, horrible shadow! unreal mockery, hence!

Shakespeare, *Macbeth*, 3, 4

An imperfect or faint representation, as 'I haven't the shadow of a doubt'; a constant attendant, as in Milton's 'Sin and her shadow Death' (*Paradise Lost*, ix, 12); moral darkness or gloom – 'He has outsoared the shadow of our night' (Shelley, *Adonais*, xl, 1); protecting influence –

Hither, like yon ancient Tower,
Watching o'er the River's bed,
Fling the shadow of Thy power,
Else we sleep among the dead.

Wordsworth, *Hymn* (*Jesu! bless*)

A prefiguring or promise – 'Coming events cast their shadows before' (Campbell); etc.

***Gone to the bad for the shadow of an ass.*** 'If you must quarrel, let it be for something better than the shadow of an ass.' Demosthenes says a young Athenian once hired an ass to Megara. The heat was so great at midday that he alighted to take shelter from the sun under the shadow of the poor beast. Scarcely was he seated when the owner came up and laid claim to the shadow, saying he let the ass to the traveller, but not the ass's shadow. After fighting for a time, they agreed to settle the matter in the law courts, and the suit lasted so long that both were ruined.

***He's afraid of his own shadow!*** He's awfully nervous, unreasonably timorous.

***He would quarrel with his own shadow.*** He is so irritable that he would lose his temper on the merest trifle for nothing at all.

***May your shadow never grow less!*** May your prosperity always continue and increase. The phrase is of Eastern origin. Fable has it that when those studying the black arts had made certain progress they were chased through a subterranean hall by the devil. If he caught only their shadow, or part of it, they became first-rate magicians, but lost either all or part of their shadow. This would make the expression mean, May you escape wholly and entirely from the clutches of the foul fiend. *See* Schlemihl.

***To be reduced to a shadow.*** Of people, to become thoroughly emaciated; of things, to become an empty form from which the substance has departed; the power of the Pope, for instance, is reduced to a mere shadow of what it was in the Middle Ages.

***To shadow.*** To follow about like a shadow, especially as a detective, or with the object of spying out all one's doings, and so on.

**Shady.** ***A shady character.*** A person of very doubtful reputation; one whose character would scarcely bear investigation in the light of day.

***On the shady side of forty*** – the wrong side, meaning more than forty. As evening approaches the shadows lengthen, and as man advances towards the evening of life he approaches the shady side thereof.

**Shafalus.** So Bottom the weaver and Francis Flute the bellows-mender, call Cephalus (*q.v.*).

*Pyramus:* Not Shafalus to Procrus was so true.
*Thisbe:* As Shafalus to Procrus, I to you.

Shakespeare, *Midsummer Night's Dream*, 5, 1

**Shaflites.** One of the four sects of the Sunnites (*q.v.*); so called from Al-Shafei (d.819), a descendant of Mahomet. *Cp.* Shiites.

**Shah.** The title of the king or emperor of Persia; that of his sons is *Shahzadah*.

**Shake.** ***A good shake up.*** Something sudden that startles one out of his lethargy and rouses him to action.

***A shake of the head.*** An indication of refusal, disapproval, annoyance, etc.

***I'll do it in a brace of shakes.*** Instantly, as soon as you can shake the dice-box twice.

***No great shakes.*** Nothing extraordinary; no such mighty bargain. The reference is probably to gambling with dice.

***Shake!*** An Americanism for 'Shake hands! let's be friends'; often said at an amicable ending to an acrimonious debate.

***To shake hands.*** A very old method of salutation and farewell; when one was shaking hands one could not get at one's sword to strike a treacherous blow. When Jehu asked Jehonadab if his 'heart was right' with him, he said, 'If it be, give me thine hand', and Jehonadab gave him his hand (2 Kings 10:15). Nestor shook hands with Ulysses on his return to the Grecian camp with the stolen horses of Rhesus; Aeneas, in the temple of Dido, sees his lost companions enter, and *avidi conjungere dextras ardebant* (*Aeneid*, i, 514); and Horace, strolling along the Via Sacra, shook hands with an acquaintance. *Arreptaque manu, 'Quid agis dulcissime rerum?*

***To shake in one's shoes.*** *See* Shoe.

***To shake one's sides.*** To be convulsed with laughter; *cp.* Milton's 'Laughter holding both his sides' (*L'Allegro*).

***To shake the dust from one's feet.*** *See* Dust.

**Shakedown.** ***Come and have a shakedown at my place*** – a bed for the night, especially a makeshift one. The allusion is to the time when men slept upon litter or clean straw.

**Shakers.** A sect of Second Adventists, founded in the 18th century in England by a secession from the Quakers, and transplanted in America by Ann Lee (1736–84), or 'Mother Ann', as she is generally known. She was an uneducated factory hand, daughter of a Manchester blacksmith. The sect has no creed; it repudiates the use of sacraments; is communistic and practises celibacy; and its sole ministry consists of two men and two women who are elected for life and act as the deputies of 'Mother Ann' who, the faithful allege, is still with them though invisible. Their official name is 'The United Society of Believers in Christ's Second Appearing' or 'The Millennial Church'; their popular name was given them in derision at their contortions during the religious dances of which their worship chiefly consists. They claim to be able to converse in Unknown Tongues, but the following extract from one of their hymns gives little reason to suppose that the Unknown Tongues are any advantage –

I love to dance and love to sing,
And, oh! I love my Maker:
I love to dance and love to sing,
And love to be a Shaker!

A sect of English Shakers, the 'People of God', was founded in Battersea about 1864 by Mary Anne Girling (1827–86), a farmer's daughter; its chief seat was in the New Forest, and it disappeared soon after her death.

**Shakespeare** (1564–1616). Was the greatest poet and dramatist of all time and all countries; born at Stratford-on-Avon, the third son of an alderman and bailiff of that town (variously described as a butcher, glover, and general trader), and Mary Arden, both of yeoman stock. What education he received is unknown; but it could not have been extensive, and Ben Jonson records that he had 'small Latin and less Greek'.

Ben Jonson calls him 'Sweet Swan of Avon', also 'The applause! delight! the wonder of our stage!' and says that 'He was not for an age, but for all time' (*To the Memory of Shakespeare*). Milton calls him 'Dear son of Memory, great heir of fame' (*An Epitaph*), and 'Sweetest Shakespeare, fancy's child' (*L'Allegro*); to Collins he was 'The perfect boast of Time' (*Epistle to Sir Thos Hanmer*); to Coleridge, 'Our myriad-minded Shakespeare' (*Biog. Lit.* xv); to Carlyle, 'the greatest of intellects' (*Characteristics of Shakespeare*); to Christopher North, 'the Poet Laureate of the Court of Faery'; to Landor, 'not our poet, but the world's'.

Dryden said of him –

Shakespeare's magic could not copied be;
Within that circle none durst walk but he.

*Prologue to the Tempest*

And that he 'was a man who of all modern and perhaps ancient poets, had the largest and most comprehensive soul'. Young says – 'He wrote the play the Almighty made'; (*Epistle to Lord Lansdowne*); Mallett – 'Great above rule. … Nature was his own' (*Verbal Criticism*); Dr Johnson –

Each change of many-colour'd life he drew;
Exhausted worlds, and then imagined new;
Existence saw him spurn her bounded reign,
And panting Time toiled after him in vain.

*Prologue*, 1747

Pope –

Shakespeare (whom you and every play-house bill
Style 'the divine', 'the matchless', what you will)
For gain, not glory, winged his roving flight,
And grew immortal in his own despite.

*Imitations of Horace, Ep. 1*

And Matthew Arnold –

Others abide our question. Thou art free.
We ask and ask – Thou smilest and art still,
Out-topping knowledge – *Shakespeare.*

There are thirty-seven plays credited wholly or in part to Shakespeare, and an enthusiast has discovered that they contain 106,007 lines and 814,780 words, *Hamlet* being the longest, with 3,930 lines, and *the Comedy of Errors*, with 1,777 lines, the shortest. The plays contain 1,277 speaking characters, of whom only 157 are females. The longest part is that of Hamlet, who has 11,610 words to deliver.

***Shakespeare's descendants***. Shakespeare married (1582 or 1583) Anne Hathaway, of Shottery, who was eight years his senior, and died in 1623. They had one son and two daughters – Susanna (b.1583), and the twins Hamnet and Judith (1585). Hamnet died at the age of 11; Judith married Thomas Quiney, had three sons, all of whom died young and unmarried, and died in 1662. Susanna married John Hall and died in 1649, leaving only one child, Elizabeth, the last descendant of the dramatist. She married twice, but had no children; and died as Lady Bernard, wife of Sir John Bernard, of Abington Manor, Northampton, in 1670.

***Shakespeare; the name.*** There is no way of spelling the dramatist's name that is *certainly* 'correct' (i.e. as he would himself have spelt it), because the six unquestionably genuine signatures of his that we possess (viz., three on the Will, two on the Blackfriars conveyance and mortgage, and one on his deposition in the suit brought by Stephen Bellott against Christopher Mountjoy) vary, and are very difficult to decipher. The most usual modern spelling – Shakespeare – is that used throughout the First and Second Folios (1623 and 1632), and in all the Quartos with the exception of the 1598 *Love's Labour's Lost* ('Shakespere') and the first 1608, *King Lear* ('Shakspeare'), in the dedicatory epistles to *Venus and Adonis* (1593) and *Lucrece* (1594), and though on his own monument the name is given as 'Shakspeare', on the tombs of his wife and daughter 'Shakespeare' is the spelling. Theobald (1733) used this spelling; Rowe (1709), Pope (1725), and Hanmer (1744) all followed the Third and Fourth Folios, which spelt the name 'Shakespear', Steevens and Malone (1778) preferred 'Shakspeare'.

The 'Shakspere' spelling was used in Bell's edition of the works (1788), and in Knight's various editions (1839), etc., but its more recent adoption in literary circles is due to Sir Frederick Madden, who advocated it on the ground that this was the spelling of the most legible of the signatures – that in the copy of Florio's *Montaigne* (1603) now in the British Museum – and to Furnivall having founded the 'New *Shakspere* Society' to take the place of the defunct 'Shakespeare Society'. This signature is now, however, generally taken to be a forgery. The most recently discovered autograph – in the Bellott-Mountjoy suit – does not help matters, as it is abbreviated to 'Willm Shak'p'' and on the bond that Shakespeare took out for his marriage licence the name appears as 'Shagspere'.

But there are more ways of spelling the name than there are 'of constructing tribal lays', and almost 'any single one of them' may be right. Anyone who wishes to decide for himself should consult J. R. Wise's *Autograph of William Shakespeare ... together with 4,000 ways of spelling the name*, published at Philadelphia in 1869.

***The Shakespeare of divines.*** Jeremy Taylor (1613–67).

***The Shakespeare of eloquence.*** So Barnave happily characterised the Comte de Mirabeau (1749–91).

***The German Shakespeare.*** Kotzebue (1761–1819) has been so styled.

***The Spanish Shakespeare.*** Calderon (1600–81).

***Le Shakespeare du boulevard.*** Guilbert de Pixérécourt (*see* Corneille).

**Shakuntala.** *See* Sakuntala.

**Shaky.** Not steady; not in good health; not strictly upright; not well prepared for examination; doubtfully solvent. The allusion is to a table or chair out of order and shaky.

**Shallott, The Lady of.** A maiden of the Arthurian legends, who fell in love with Sir Lancelot of the Lake, and died because her love was not returned. Tennyson has a poem on the subject; and the story of Elaine (*q.v.*), 'the lily maid of Astolat', is substantially the same.

**Shamanism.** A primitive form of religion, in which those who practise it believe that the world and all events are governed by good and evil spirits who can be propitiated or bought off only through the intervention of a witch-doctor, or *Shaman*. The word is Slavonic; it comes from the Samoyeds and other Siberian peoples, but is now applied to Red Indian and other primitive worship.

**Shamefast.** Bashful; awkward through shyness; sheepish. This is the old form of *shamefaced* (which is properly an error), the *-fast* meaning 'fimly fixed' or 'restrained' (by shame).

**Shamrock,** the symbol of Ireland, because it was selected by St Patrick to illustrate to the Irish the doctrine of the Trinity. According to the elder Pliny no serpent will touch this plant.

**Shan Van Voght.** This excellent song (composed 1798) has been called the Irish *Marseillaise*. The title of it is a corruption *of An t-sean bhean bhocht* (the poor old woman – i.e. Ireland). The last verse is –

> Will Ireland then be free?
> Said the Shan Van Voght. (repeat)
> Yes, Ireland shall be free
> From the centre to the sea,
> Hurrah for liberty!
> Said the Shan Van Voght.

**Shandean.** Characteristic of Tristram Shandy or the Shandy family in Sterne's famous novel, *Tristram Shandy* (9 vols, 1759–67). Tristram's father, Walter Shandy, is a metaphysical Don Quixote in his way, full of superstitious and idle conceits. He believes in long noses and propitious names, but his son's nose is crushed, and his name becomes *Tristram* instead of *Trismegistus*. His Uncle Toby was wounded at the siege of Namur, and is benevolent and generous, simple as a child, brave as a lion, and gallant as a courtier. His modesty with Widow Wadman and his military tastes are admirable. He is said to be drawn from Sterne's father. His mother was the *beau-ideal* of nonentity (described by Scott as a 'good lady of the poco-curante school'); and of Tristram himself, we hear almost more of him before he was born than after he had burst upon an astonished world.

> With a Shandean exactness ... Lady Anne begins her memoirs of herself nine months before her nativity, for the sake of introducing a beautiful quotation from the Psalms.
>
> *Biog. Borealis*, p. 269

**Shanks's Mare. *To ride Shanks's mare*** is to go on foot, the *shanks* being the legs. A similar phrase is 'Going by the marrow-bone stage' or 'by Walker's bus'.

**Shannon. *Dipped in the Shannon*.** One who has been dipped in the Shannon loses all bashfulness. At least, *sic aiunt*.

**Shanty Songs.** Songs sung by sailors at work, to ensure united action (Fr. *chanter*, to sing); also called *chanties*. They are in sets, each of which has a different cadence adapted to the work in hand. Thus, in sheeting topsails, weighing anchor, etc., one of the most popular of the shanty songs runs thus:

> I'm bound away, this very day,
> I'm bound for the Rio Grande.
> Ho, you, Rio!
> Then fare you well, my bonny blue bell,
> I'm bound for the Rio Grande.

**Shark.** A swindler, a pilferer, an extortionate boarding-house keeper or landlord, etc.: one who snaps up things like a shark, which eats almost anything, and seems to care little whether its food is alive or dead, fish, flesh, or human bodies.

> These thieves doe rob us with our owne good will,
> And have Dame Nature's warrant for it still;
> Sometimes these sharks doe worke each other's wrack,
> The ravening belly often robs the backe.
>
> *Taylor's Workes*, ii, 117

***To shark up.*** To get a number of people, etc., together promiscuously, without consideration of their fitness.

> Now, sir, young Fortinbras ...
> Hath in the skirts of Norway here and there
> Shark'd up a list of lawless resolutes,
> For food and diet, to some enterprise
> That hath a stomach in't.
>
> Shakespeare, *Hamlet*, 1, 1

**Sharp. *A regular Becky Sharp.*** An unprincipled, scheming young woman, who by cunning, hypocrisy, and low smartness raises herself from obscurity and poverty to some position in Society, and falls therefrom in due course after having maintained a more or less precarious foothold. Of course she is good-looking, and superficial amiability is a *sine qua non*. Becky Sharp, the original of this, and one of the finest creations in all fiction, is the principal character in Thackeray's *Vanity Fair* (1848).

***Sharp practice.*** Underhand or dishonourable dealing; low-down trickery intended to advantage oneself.

***Sharps and flats.*** *See* Flat.

***Sharp's the word!*** Look alive, there! no hanging about! The injunction is often completed with – 'and quick's the motion!'

**_Sharp-set._** Hungry; formerly used of hawks when eager for their food.

> If anie were so sharpe-set as to eat fried flies, buttered bees, stued snails, either on Fridaie or Sundaie, he could not be therefore indicted of haulte treason.
>
> Stanihurst, *Ireland*, p. 19 (1586)

**Sharpbeck** (*Sharp-beak*). The wife of Corbant, the Rook, in Caxton's version of *Reynard the Fox* (*q.v.*).

**Shave.** Just a grazing touch; *a near* or *close shave*, a narrow escape; *to shave through an examination*, only just to get through, narrowly to escape being 'plucked'. At Oxford a pass degree is sometimes called *a shave*.

**_A good lather is half the shave._** Your work is half done if you've laid your plans and made your preparations properly.

**_To shave a customer._** A draper's expression for charging more for an article than it is worth; because, so it is said, when the manager sees a chance of doing this he strokes his chin as a sign to the assistant that he may fleece the customer all he can.

**_To shave an egg._** To attempt to extort the uttermost farthing; to 'skin a flint'.

**Shaveling.** Used in contempt – especially after the Reformation – of a tonsured priest. We are told that in 1348 the clergy died so fast of the Black Death that youths were admitted to holy orders by being shaven.

> William Bateman, Bishop of Norwich, dispensed with sixty shavelings to hold rectories and other livings, that divine service might not cease in the parishes over which they were appointed.
>
> Blomfield, *History of Norfolk*, vol. iii

**She Bible. The.** *See* Bible, Specially named.

**She Stoops to Conquer.** Goldsmith's comedy (1773) owes its existence to an incident which actually occurred to its author. When he was sixteen years of age a wag residing at Ardagh directed him, when passing through that village, to Squire Fetherstone's house as the village inn. The mistake was not discovered for some time, and then no one enjoyed it more heartily than Oliver himself.

**She-wolf of France.** *See* Wolf.

**Shear. _God tempers the wind to the shorn lamb._** *See* God.

**_Ordeal by sieve and shears._** *See* Sieve.

**_Shear_** or **_Shere Thursday._** Maundy Thursday, the Thursday of Passion Week; so called, it is said, because in –

> old fadres dayes the people wolde that day shere theyr hedes, and clyppe theyr berdes, and poll theyr hedes, and so make them honest agenst Ester day.

**Sheathe. _To sheathe the sword._** To cease hostilities, make peace. In the early months of the Great War the phrase 'We will not sheathe the sword until the wrong done to Belgium has been righted' was on everybody's lips in the British Empire.

> England in those days gave a noble answer to his appeal and did not sheathe the sword until, after nearly twenty years of fighting, the freedom of Europe was secured. Let us go and do likewise.
>
> Mr Asquith, Speech at the Guildhall, Sept. 4th, 1914

**Sheba, The Queen of.** The queen who visited Solomon (1 Kings 10) is known to the Arabs as Balkis, Queen of Saba (Koran, ch. xxvii). Sheba was thought by the Greeks and Romans to have been the capital of what is now Yemen, S.W. Arabia; and the people over whom the queen reigned were the Sabaeans.

> There was never a Queen like Balkis,
> From here to the wide world's end; . . .
> There was never a King like Solomon,
> Not since the world began;
> *She* was Queen of Sabaea –
> And *he* was Asia's Lord –
> But they both of 'em talked to butterflies
> When they took their walks abroad.
>
> Kipling, *Just So Stories*

**Shebang. _Fed up with the whole shebang._** Tired of the whole concern and everything connected with it. *Shebang* is American slang for a hut or one's quarters; also for a cart; and also, in a humorously depreciatory way, for almost anything.

**Shebeen.** A place (originally only in Ireland) where liquor is sold without a licence; hence applied to any low-class public house.

> You've been takin' a dhrop o' the crathur' an'
> Danny says 'Troth, an' I been
> Dhrinking yer health wid Shamus O'Shea at
> Katty's shebeen.' Tennyson, *Tomorrow*

**Shedem.** *See* Mazikeen.

**Sheep.** *Ram* or *tup*, the sire; *ewe*, the dam; *lamb*, the young till weaned, when it is called a *tup-hogget* or *ewe-hogget*, as the case may be, or, if the tup is castrated, a *wether-hogget*.

After the removal of the *first* fleece, the tup-hogget becomes a *shearling*, the ewe-hogget a *grimmer*, and the wether-hogget a *dinmont*.

After the removal of the *second* fleece, the shearling becomes a *two-shear tup*, the grimmer a *ewe*, and the dinmont a *wether*.

After the removal of the *third* fleece, the ewe is called a *twinter-ewe*; and when it ceases to breed a *draft-ewe*.

***Sheepish.*** Awkward and shy; bashful through not knowing how to deport oneself in the circumstances. Scott (*Bride of Lammermoor*, xxix) speaks of 'the sheepish bashfulness common to those who have lived little in respectable society'.

***Sheep's head.*** A fool, a simpleton – a 'fat-head'.

> *Gostanzo*: What, sirrah, is that all?
> No entertainment to the gentlewoman?
> *Valerio*: Forsooth y'are welcome by my father's leave.
> *Gos.*: What, no more compliment? Kiss her, you sheep's head!
> Lady, you'll pardon our gross bringing up?
> We dwell far off from court, you may perceive.
> Chapman, *All Fools*, II, i

***The Black Sheep*** (Kârâ-koin-loo). A tribe which established a principality in Armenia that lasted 108 years (1360–1468); so called from the device of their standard.

***The White Sheep*** (Ak-koin-loo). A tribe which established a principality in Armenia, etc., on the ruin of the Black Sheep (1468–1508); so called from the device of their standard.

***There's a black sheep in every flock.*** In every club or party of persons there's sure to be at least one shady character.

***To cast a sheep's eye at one.*** To look askance, in a sheepish way, at a person to whom you feel lovingly inclined

> But he, the beast, was casting sheep's eyes at her.
> Colman, *Broad Grins*

***Vegetable sheep.*** *See* Scythian Lamb.

**Sheer Thursday.** *See* Shear.

**Sheet.** ***Three sheets in the wind.*** Very drunk; just about as drunk as one can be. The *sheet* is the rope attached to the lower end of a sail, used for shortening and extending sail; if quite free, the sheet is said to be 'in the wind' and the sail flaps and flutters without restraint. If all the three sails were so loosened, the ship would 'reel and stagger like a drunken man'.

> Captain Cuttle looking, candle in hand, at Bunsby more attentively, perceived that he was three sheets in the wind, or, in plain words, drunk. Dickens, *Dombey and Son*

***That was my sheet anchor.*** My best hope, chief stay, last refuge; if that fails me, then all is indeed lost. The *sheet anchor* is the largest anchor of a ship, which, in stress of weather, is the sailor's chief dependence. The Greeks and Romans said, 'my *sacred* anchor', because the sheet anchor was always dedicated to some god.

**Sheikh.** A title of respect among the Arabs (like the Ital. *signore*, Fr. *sieur*, Span. *señor*, etc.), but properly the head of a Bedouin clan, family, or tribe, or the headman of an Arab village.

***Sheikh-ul-Islam.*** The Grand Mufti, or supreme head of the Mohammedan hierarchy in Turkey.

**Shekels.** Colloquial for money – 'lots of shekels' = plenty of oof. The Hebrew shekel was a weight of about 250 grains troy, also a silver coin worth roughly 2*s.* 6*d.*

**Shekinah** (Heb. *shākan*, to reside). The visible glory of the Divine Presence in the shape of a cloud, which rested over the mercy-seat between the Cherubim, and in the Temple of Solomon (*see* Exod. 40:34–38). The word does not occur in the Bible, but is frequent in the Targums, and was employed by the Jews as a periphrasis for the Divine Name.

**Sheldonian Theatre.** The Senate House of Oxford; so called from Gilbert Sheldon (1598–1677), Archbishop of Canterbury, who built it.

**Shelf.** ***Laid on the shelft***, or ***shelved***. Put on one side as of no further use; superannuated. Said of officials and others no longer actively employed; an actor no longer assigned a part; a lady past the ordinary age of marriage; any 'has been'; also of a pawn at the broker's, a question started and set aside, etc.

**Shell** (A.S. *scell*). The hard outside covering of nuts, eggs, molluscs, tortoises, etc.; hence applied to other hollow coverings, as a light or inner coffin, and the hollow projectile filled with explosives and missiles which will explode on impact or at a set time.

***Eggshells.*** Many persons, after eating a boiled egg, break or crush the shell. This, according to Sir Thomas Browne –

> is but a superstitious relict ... and the intent thereof was to prevent witchcraft; for lest witches should draw or prick their names therein, and veneficiously mischief their persons, they broke the shell. *Pseudodoxia Epidemica*, V, xxii

***Scallop shells*** were the emblem of St James the Great (*q.v.*), and were hence carried by pilgrims, under whose special protection they were.

***Shell jacket.*** An undress military jacket, fatigue jacket.

***Shell shock.*** An acute neurasthenic condition, due to a shock to the system caused by the explosion of a shell or bomb at close quarters. We are indebted to the Great War both for the term and the terrible affliction it denotes.

***Shellback.*** Nautical slang for an old and seasoned sailor, an 'old salt'.

***To retire into one's shell.*** To become reticent and uncommunicative, to withdraw oneself from society in a forbidding way. The allusion is to the tortoise, which, once it has 'got into its shell', is quite unget-at-able.

*See also* Nutshell.

**Sheol.** *See* Hades.

**Shepherd. *The Shepherd Kings.*** *See* Hyksos.

***The Shepherd Lord.*** Henry, tenth Lord Clifford (d.1523), sent by his mother to be brought up by a shepherd, in order to save him from the fury of the Yorkists. At the accession of Henry VII he was restored to all his rights and seigniories. The story is told by Wordsworth in *The Song for the Feast of Brougham Castle.*

***The Shepherd of Banbury.*** The ostensible author of a Weather Guide (published 1744). He styles himself John Claridge, Shepherd; but is said to have been a Dr John Campbell.

***The Shepherd of the Ocean.*** So Sir Walter Raleigh is called by Spenser:

When I asked from what place he came,
And how he hight, himselfe he did ycleape
The Shepheard of the Ocean by name,
And said he came far from the main-sea deepe.
*Colin Clout's Come Home Again*, 64

***The Shepherd of Salisbury Plain.*** A famous religious tract by Mrs Hannah More, first published in *The Cheap Repository* (1795), a series of moral 'tales for the people'. It had enormous popularity; and the story is said to be founded on the life of one David Saunders, who was noted for his homely wisdom and practical piety, and whom she turns into a sort of Christian Arcadian.

***The Shepherd's Sundial.*** The scarlet pimpernel, which opens at a little past seven in the morning and closes at a little past two. When rain is at hand, or the weather is unfavourable, it does not open at all.

***The Shepherd's Warning.***

A red sky at night is the shepherd's delight,
But a red sky in the morning is the shepherd's warning.

The Italian saying is *Sera rosso et negro mattino allegra il pelligrino* (a red evening and a white morning rejoice the pilgrim).

***To shepherd.*** To guard and guide carefully as a shepherd does his flock; in colloquial use, to follow and spy on as a detective.

**Sheppard, Jack** (1701–24). A notorious highwayman, son of a carpenter in Smithfield, and noted for his two escapes from Newgate in 1724. He was hanged at Tyburn the same year.

**Sheraton,** or **Sheraton furniture.** A severe style of furniture, so called because it was designed and popularised towards the end of the 18th century by Thomas Sheraton (1751–1806).

**Shere Thursday.** *See* Shear.

**Sheriffmuir. *There was mair lost at the Shirramuir*.** Don't grieve for your losses, for worse have befallen others before now. The battle of Sheriffmuir, in 1715, between the Jacobites and Hanoverians was very bloody: both sides sustained heavy losses, and both sides claimed the victory.

**Sheva,** in Dryden's *Absalom and Achitophel*, Pt ii (*q.v.*), is designed for Sir Roger L'Estrange (1616–1704).

**Shewbread.** Food for show only, and not intended to be eaten except by certain privileged persons. The term is Jewish, and refers to the twelve loaves (one for each tribe; *see* Exod. 25:30, Lev. 24:5–8) which the priest 'showed' or exhibited to Jehovah, by placing them week by week on the sanctuary table. At the end of the week, the priest was allowed to take them home for his own eating; but no one else could partake of them.

**Shiahs.** *See* Shiites.

**Shibboleth.** The password of a secret society; the secret by which those of a party know each other; also a worn out or discredited doctrine. The Ephraimites could not pronounce *sh*, so when they were fleeing from Jephthah and the Gileadites (Judges 12:1–16) they were caught at the ford on the Jordan because Jephthah caused all the fugitives to say the word *Shibboleth* (which means 'a stream in flood'), which all the Ephraimites pronounced as *Sibboleth.*

Their foes a deadly shibboleth devise.
Dryden, *Hind and Panther*, Pt iii

**Shield.** The most famous in story are the *Shield of Achilles* described by Homer, of *Hercules* described by Hesiod, of *Aeneas* described by Virgil, and the *Aegis* (*q.v.*).

Others are that of:

*Agamemnon*, a gorgon.
*Amycos* (son of Poseidon), a crayfish, symbol of prudence.

*Cadmus* and his descendants, a dragon, to indicate their descent from the dragon's teeth.
*Eteocles*, one of the Seven Against Thebes, a man scaling a wall.
*Hector*, a lion.
*Idomeneus*, a cock.
*Menelaus*, a serpent at his heart; alluding to the elopement of his wife with Paris.
*Parthenopaeus*, one of the Seven Against Thebes, a sphinx holding a man in its claws.
*Ulysses*, a dolphin. Whence he is sometimes called Delphinosemos.

Servius says that the Greeks in the siege of Troy had, as a rule, Neptune on their bucklers, and the Trojans Minerva.

It was a common custom, after a great victory, for the victorious general to hang his shield on the wall of some temple.

***The clang of shields.*** When a chief doomed a man to death, he struck his shield with the blunt end of his spear by way of notice to the royal bard to begin the death-song.

Cairbar rises in his arms,
The clang of shields is heard.

Ossian, *Temora*, 1

***The Gold and Silver Shield.*** A mediaeval allegory tells how two knights coming from opposite directions stopped in sight of a shield suspended from a tree branch, one side of which was gold and the other silver, and disputed about its metal, proceeding from words to blows. Luckily a third knight came up: the point was referred to him, and the disputants were informed that the shield was silver on one side and gold on the other. Hence the sayings, *The other side of the shield*, *It depends on which side of the shield you are looking at*, etc.

***The Shield of Expectation.*** The perfectly plain shield given to a young warrior in his maiden campaign. As he achieved glory, his deeds were recorded or symbolised on it.

**Shi'ites** (Arab. *shi'ah*, a sect). Those Mohammedans who regard Ali as the first rightful Imam or Caliph (rejecting the three Sunni Caliphs), and do not consider the Sunna, or oral law, of any authority, but look upon it as apocryphal. They wear *red* turbans, and are sometimes called 'Red Heads'. *Cp.* Sunnites.

**Shillelagh** (Ir.). A cudgel of oak or blackthorn: so called from a village of this name in County Wicklow.

**Shilling** (A.S. *scilling*, which is connected either with O.Teut. *skel-*, to resound or ring, or *skil-*, to divide). The coin was originally made with a deeply indented cross, and could easily be divided into halves or quarters.

***Shilling shocker.*** *See* Penny Dreadful.

***To be cut off with a shilling.*** *See* Cut.

***To take the King's*** (or ***Queen's***) ***shilling.*** To enlist; in allusion to the former practice of giving each recruit a shilling when he was sworn in.

**Shilly shally.** To hesitate, act in an undecided, irresolute way; a corruption of 'Will I, shall I', or 'Shall I, shall I?'

There's no delay, they ne'er stand shall I, shall I,
Hermogenes with Dallila doth dally.

*Taylor's Workes*, iii, 3 (1630)

**Shimei**, in Dryden's *Absalom and Achitophel* (*q.v.*), is designed for Slingsby Bethel, the Lord Mayor.

Shimei, whose youth did early promise bring,
Of zeal to God and hatred to his king;
Did wisely from expensive sins refrain,
And never broke the Sabbath but for gain.

Pt i, 548–551

**Shindy.** A row, a disturbance. To *kick up a shindy*, to make a row. The word is probably connected with *shinty* or *shinny*, a primitive kind of hockey played in the north.

**Shine.** ***To take the shine out of one.*** To humiliate him, 'take him down a peg or two'; to outshine him.

**Ship.** In the printing-house the body of compositors engaged for the time being on one definite piece of work is known as a *ship*; this is said to be short for *companionship*, but it is worth noting that many printing-house terms (*cp.* Chapel, Friar, Monk) have an ecclesiastical origin, and *ship* was an old name for the nave of a church.

***Losing a ship for a ha'porth o' tar.*** Suffering a great loss out of stinginess. By mean savings, or from want of some necessary outlay, to lose the entire article. For example, to save the expense of a nail and lose the horseshoe as the first result, then to lame the horse, and finally perhaps kill it. The phrase was originally 'to lose the *sheep* for a ha'porth of tar' (tar being a remedy or preventive against certain diseases); but this form seems quite to have supplanted the earlier one.

***Ship-money.*** A tax formerly levied in time of war on ports and seaboard counties for the maintenance of the Navy. It was through Charles I levying this tax in 1634–7 without the consent of Parliament, and extending it to the inland counties illegally, that the Puritan party, led by Hampden, refused to pay and thus began the struggle which culminated in the Civil War.

***Shipshape.*** As methodically arranged as things in a ship; in good order. When a vessel is sent out temporarily rigged, it is termed 'jury-rigged', and when the jury rigging has been duly changed for ship rigging, the vessel is 'ship-shape', i.e. in due or regular order.

***Ship's husband.*** The agent on land who represents the owners and attends to the repairs, provisioning and other necessaries and expenses of the ship.

***Ships of the line.*** Men-of-war large enough to have a place in a line of battle.

***The ship of the desert.*** The camel.

> Three thousand camels his rank pastures fed,
> Arabia's wandering ships, for traffic bred.
>
> G. Sandys, *Paraphrase from Job* (1610)

***To take shipping.*** To set out on a voyage, to embark on board ship.

***When my ship comes home.*** When my fortune is made. The allusion is to the argosies returning from foreign parts laden with rich freights, and so enriching the merchants who sent them forth.

**Shipton, Mother.** This so-called prophetess is first heard of in a tract of 1641, in which she is said to have lived in the reign of Henry VIII, and to have foretold the death of Wolsey, Cromwell, Lord Percy, etc. In 1677 the pamphleteering publisher, Richard Head, brought out a *Life and Death of Mother Shipton*, and in 1862 Charles Hindley brought out a new edition in which she was credited with having predicted steam-engines, the telegraph, and other modern inventions, as well as the end of the world in 1881. Of course she, like the immortal Mrs Harris, is immortal only because 'there is no sich a person'.

**Shire.** When the Saxon kings created an earl, they gave him a *shire* (A.S. *scir*) or division of land to govern. *Scir* meant originally employment or government, and is connected with *scirian*, to appoint, allot. At the Norman Conquest *count* superseded the title *earl*, and the shire or earldom was called a *county*. Even to the present hour we call the wife of an earl a countess.

***Knight of the Shire.*** *See* Knight.

***The shires.*** The English counties whose names terminate in *-shire*; but, in a narrower sense, the Midland counties noted for fox-hunting, especially Leicestershire, Northamptonshire, and Rutland.

***Shire horses.*** The old breed of large, heavily-built English cart-horses, originally raised in the Midland shires. The term is applied to any draught horses of a certain character which can show a registered pedigree. The sire and dam, with a minute description of the horse itself, its age, marks and so on, must be shown in order to prove the claim of a 'shire horse'.

Clydesdale horses are Scotch draught horses, not equal to shire horses in size, but of great endurance.

**Shirt.** ***A boiled shirt.*** An Americanism for a stiff white shirt, as opposed to an unstarched coloured one.

***Close sits my shirt, but closer my skin.*** My property is dear to me, but dearer my life; my belongings sit close to my heart, but *Ego proximus mihi*.

***Not a shirt to one's name.*** Nothing at all; penniless and propertyless.

***The shirt of Nessus.*** *See* Nessus.

***To get one's shirt out.*** To lose one's temper, to get in a rage. A variant is *to get one's rag out*.

***To give the shirt off one's back.*** All one has.

***To put one's shirt on a horse.*** To back it with all the money one possesses.

**Shirty.** Bad-tempered; very cross and offended; in the state one is when somebody has 'got your shirt out' (*see* Shirt).

**Shiva.** *See* Siva.

**Shivering Mountain.** Mam Tor, a hill on the Peak of Derbyshire; so called from the waste of its mass by 'shivering' – that is, breaking away in 'shivers' or small pieces. This has been going on for ages, as the hill consists of alternate layers of shale and gritstone. The former, being soft, is easily reduced to powder, and, as it crumbles small 'shivers' of the gritstone break away from want of support.

**Shoddy.** Worthless stuff masquerading as something that is really good; from the cheap cloth called *shoddy* which is made up out of cloth from old garments torn to pieces and shredded, mixed with new wool.

***Shoddy characters.*** Persons of tarnished reputation, like cloth made of shoddy or refuse wool.

**Shoe.** It was at one time thought unlucky to put on the left shoe before the right, or to put either shoe on the wrong foot. It is said that Augustus Caesar was nearly assassinated by a mutiny one day when he put on his left shoe first.

> Auguste, cet empereur qui gouverna avec tant de sagesse, et dont le règne fut si florissant, restoit

> immobile et consterné lorsqu'il lui arrivoit par mégarde de mettre le soulier droit au pied gauche, et le soulier gauche au pied droit.
>
> St Foix

One of the auditions of Pythagoras was: 'When stretching forth your feet to have your sandals put on, first extend your right foot, but when about to step into a bath, let your left foot enter first.' Iamblichus says the hidden meaning is that worthy actions should be done heartily, but base ones should be avoided (*Protreptics*, symbol xii).

It has long been a custom to throw an old shoe, or several shoes, at the bride and bridegroom when they quit the bride's home, after the wedding breakfast, or when they go to church to get married.

> Now, for goode luck caste an old shoe after me.
>
> Haywood (1693–1756)
>
> Ay, with all my heart, there's an old shoe after you.
>
> *The Parson's Wedding* (Dodsley, vol. ix, p. 499)

In Anglo-Saxon marriages the father delivered the bride's shoe to the bridegroom, who touched her with it on the head to show his authority; and it is said that in Turkey the bridegroom is chased by the guests, who either administer blows by way of adieux, or pelt him with slippers.

Some think this shoe-throwing represents an assault and refers to the notion that the bridegroom carried off the bride with force and violence. Others look upon it as a relic of the ancient law of exchange, implying that the parents of the bride give up henceforth all right of dominion to their daughter. Luther told the bridegroom at a wedding that he had placed the husband's shoe on the head of the bed, *afin qu'il prît ainsi la domination et le gouvernement*.

Loosing the shoe (*cp*. Josh. 5:15) is a mark of respect in the East to the present hour. The Mussulman leaves his slippers at the door of the mosque, and when making a visit of ceremony to a European visitor, at the tent entrance.

In Deut. 25:5–10 we read that the widow refused by the surviving brother, asserted her independence by 'loosing his shoe'; and in the story of Ruth we are told 'that it was the custom' in exchange to deliver a shoe in token of renunciation. When Boaz, therefore, became possessed of his lot, the kinsman's kinsman indicated his assent by giving Boaz his shoe. 'A man without sandals' was a proverbial expression among the Jews for a prodigal, from the custom of giving one's sandals in confirmation of a bargain.

***Another man's shoes.*** 'To stand in another man's shoes' is to occupy the place or lay claim to the honours of another. Among the ancient Northmen, when a man adopted a son, the person adopted put on the shoes of the adopter.

In *Reynard the Fox* (*q.v.*) Reynard, having turned the tables on Sir Bruin the Bear, asked the queen to let him have the shoes of the disgraced minister; so Bruin's shoes were torn off and put upon the new favourite.

***Another pair of shoes.*** A different thing altogether; quite another matter.

***A shoe too large trips one up.*** A Latin proverb, *Calceus major subvertit*. An empire too large falls to pieces; a business too large comes to grief; an ambition too large fails altogether.

***No one knows where the shoe pinches like the wearer.*** This was said by a Roman sage who was blamed for divorcing his wife, with whom he seemed to live happily.

> For, God it wot, he sat ful still and song,
> When that his scho ful bitterly him wrong.
>
> Chaucer, *Canterbury Tales*, 6,074

The *fons et origo* of some trouble is called 'the place where the shoe pinches'.

***Over Edom will I cast my shoe*** (Ps. 60:8; 108:9). Will I march and triumph.

> Every member of the Travellers' Club who could pretend to have cast his shoe over Edom, was constituted a lawful critic.
>
> Sir W. Scott, *The Talisman* (*Intro.*)

***Over shoes, over boots.*** In for a penny, in for a pound.

> Where true courage roots,
> The proverb says, 'once over shoes, o'er boots'.
>
> *Taylor's Workes*, ii, 145 (1690)

***To die in one's shoes.*** To die a violent death, especially one on the scaffold.

> And there is M'Fuze, and Lieutenant Tregooze,
> And there is Sir Carnaby Jenks, of the Blues
> All come to see a man die in his shoes.
>
> *Ingoldsby Legends*, *The Execution*

***To shake in one's shoes.*** To be in a state of nervous terror.

***To shoe a goose.*** To engage in a silly and fruitless task.

***To shoe the anchor.*** To cover the flukes of an anchor with a broad triangular piece of plank, in order that the anchor may have a stronger hold in soft ground.

***To shoe the cobbler.*** To give a quick peculiar movement with the front foot in sliding.

***To shoe the wild colt.*** To exact a fine called 'footing' from a newcomer, who is called the 'colt'. Colt is a common synonym for a greenhorn, or a youth not broken in. Thus Shakespeare says – 'Ay, that's a colt indeed, for he doth nothing but talk of his horse' (*Merchant of Venice*, 1, 2).

***To step into another man's shoes.*** To take the office or position previously held by another.

> 'That will do, sir,' he thundered, 'that will do. It is very evident now what would happen if you stepped into my shoes.' *Good Words*, 1887

***Waiting for dead men's shoes.*** Looking out for legacies; looking to stand in the place of some moneyed man when he is dead and buried.

***Whose shoes I am not worthy to bear*** (Matt. 3:11). This means, 'I am not worthy to be his humblest slave.' It was the business of a slave recently purchased to loose and carry his master's sandals. When the Emperor Wladimir proposed marriage to the daughter of Reginald, she rejected him, saying, 'I will not take off my shoe to the son of a slave.'

**Shoemakers.** The patron saints of shoemakers are St Crispin and his brother Crispian, who supported themselves by making shoes while they preached to the people of Gaul and Britain. In compliment to these saints the trade of shoemaking is called 'the gentle craft'.

**Shogun.** The title of the actual ruler of Japan from the 12th century to the modernisation of the country in 1868. The Shoguns were hereditary commanders-in-chief (the word means 'army leader'), and took the place of the Mikados, whom they kept in a state of perpetual imprisonment. Also called the *Tycoon* (*q.v.*).

**Shoot.** *See also* Shot.

***Shooting-iron.*** Slang (originally American) for a firearm, especially a revolver.

***Shooting stars.*** Incandescent meteors shooting across the sky, formerly, like comets, fabled to presage disaster –

> A little ere the mightiest Julius fell,
> The graves stood tenantless, and the sheeted dead
> Did squeak and gibber in the Roman streets:
> As stars with trains of fire shed dews of blood,
> Disastering the sun ...
>
> Shakespeare, *Hamlet*, 1, 1

They were called in ancient legends the 'fiery tears of St Lawrence', because one of the periodic swarms of these meteors is between August 9th and 14th, about the time of St Lawrence's festival, which is on the 10th. Other periods are from November 12th to 14th, and from December 6th to 12th.

Shooting stars are said by the Arabs to be firebrands hurled by the angels against the inquisitive genii, who are for ever clambering up on the constellations to peep into heaven.

***To go the whole shoot.*** To do all there is to do, go the whole hog, run through the gamut.

***To shoot one's linen.*** To display an unnecessary amount of shirt-cuff.

***To shoot the cat.*** *See* Cat.

***To shoot the moon.*** To remove one's household goods by night to avoid distraint; to 'do a moonlight flit'.

***To shoot the sun.*** A sailor's expression for taking the sun's meridional altitude, which is done by aiming at the reflected sun through the telescope of the sextant.

**Shop.** ***The Shop,*** in military slang, is the Royal Military Academy, Woolwich; on the Stock Exchange it is the South African gold market.

***All over the shop.*** Scattered in every direction, all over the place; or pursuing an erratic course.

***To shop a person.*** To put him in prison, or to inform against him so that he is arrested; similarly, a billiard player will speak of 'shopping the white', i.e. putting his opponent's ball down in the pocket.

***To shut up shop.*** To retire from business, withdraw from participation in the undertaking, etc.

***To talk shop.*** To talk about one's affairs or business; to draw allusions from one's business, as when Ollapod, the apothecary in Colman's *Poor Gentleman*, talks of a uniform with rhubarb-coloured facings.

***You've come to the wrong shop.*** I can't help you, I can't give you the information, and so on, you require.

**Shopkeepers.** ***A nation of shopkeepers.*** This phrase, applied to Englishmen by Napoleon in contempt, comes from Adam Smith's *Wealth of Nations* (iv, 7), a book well known to the Emperor. He says –

> To found a great empire for the sole purpose of raising up a people of customers, may at first sight appear a project fit only for a nation of shopkeepers.

Ten years earlier, in 1766, J. Tucker had written in the third of his *Four Tracts*:

> A Shop-keeper will never get the more Custom

by beating his Customers; and what is true of a Shop-keeper, is true of a Shop-keeping Nation.

**Shoreditch,** according to tradition, is so called from Jane Shore, the mistress of Edward IV, who, it is said, died there in a ditch. This tale comes from a ballad in Pepys' collection –

I could not get one bit of bread
Whereby my hunger might be fed …
So, weary of my life, at length
I yielded up my vital strength
Within a ditch … which since that day
Is Shoreditch called, as writers say –

But the truth is, it appears in the Index to Kemble's *Codex Diplomaticus* as *Sordic*, in the 14th century as *Soerditch*, and Stow says that in the 12th century it was called *Soersditch*. It is probable that it is from a former Anglo-Saxon proprietor, *Soer*.

Jane Shore is supposed to have died about 1527, but the date and place are alike unknown.

***The Duke of Shoreditch.*** The most successful of the London archers received this playful title.

Good king, make not good Lord of Lincoln Duke of Shoreditch! *The Poore Man's Peticion to the Kinge* (1603)

**Shorne, John.** A rector of North Marston, Buckinghamshire, at the close of the 13th century. He is said to have blessed a well, which became the resort of multitudes and brought in a yearly revenue of some £500, and to have conjured the devil into a boot. After his death he was prayed to by sufferers from ague.

Maister John Shorne, that blessed man borne,
For the ague to him we apply,
Which juggleth with a bote; I beschrewe his herte rote
That will trust him, and it be I.

*Fantassie of Idolatrie*

**Short.** ***A drop of something short.*** A tot of whisky, gin, or other spirit, as opposed to a glass of beer.

***Cut it short!*** Don't be so prolix, come to the point; 'cut the cackle and come to the 'osses'. Said to a speaker who goes round and round his subject.

***My name is Short.*** I'm in a hurry and cannot wait.

Well, but let us hear the wishes (said the old man); my name is short, and I cannot stay much longer.

W. Yeats, *Fairy Tales of the Irish Peasantry*, p. 240

***Short commons.*** *See* Commons.

***Short thigh.*** *See* Curthose.

***The short cut is often the longest way round.*** It does not always pay to avoid taking a little trouble; e.g. there is no short cut to knowledge. Bacon has the same idea –

It is in life, as it is in ways, the shortest way is commonly the foulest, and surely the faire way is not much about.

*Advancement of Learning*, 66, ii

***To break off short.*** Abruptly, without warning, but completely. When a man breaks off short in the midst of a conversation it is not easy to get him to resume.

***To sell short.*** A Stock Exchange phrase meaning to sell stock that one does not at the moment possess on the chance that before the date of delivery the price will have fallen; the same as 'selling for a fall', or 'selling a bear'.

***To make short work of it.*** To dispose of it quickly, to deal summarily with it.

***To win by a short head.*** Only just to out-distance one's competitors, to win with practically nothing to spare. The phrase is from horse-racing.

**Shot.** ***A fool's bolt is soon shot.*** *See* Bolt.

***Down with your shot.*** Your reckoning or quota, your money. *See* Scot.

As the fund of our pleasure, let us each pay his shot. Ben Jonson

***He shot wide of the mark.*** He was altogether in error. The allusion is to shooting at the mark or bull's-eye of a target.

***I haven't a shot in the locker.*** A penny to bless myself with; my last resources are used up. A phrase from the days of the old men-of-war, when the ammunition was kept in lockers.

***Like a shot.*** With great rapidity; or, without hesitation, most willingly.

**Shotten herring.** A lean, spiritless creature, a Jack-o'-Lent, like a herring that has *shot*, or ejected, its spawn. Herrings gutted and dried are so called also.

Though they like shotten-herrings are to see,
Yet such tall souldiers of their teeth they be,
That two of them, like greedy cormorants,
Devour more then sixe honest Protestants.

*Taylor's Workes*, iii, 5

**Shoulder.** ***Showing the cold shoulder.*** Receiving without cordiality someone who was once on better terms with you. *See* Cold.

***Straight from the shoulder.*** With full force. A boxing term.

He was letting them have it straight from the shoulder. T. Tyrell, *Lady Delmar*, ch. v

***The government shall be upon his shoulder*** (Is. 9:6). The allusion is to the key slung on the shoulder of Jewish stewards on public occasions, and as a key is emblematic of government and power, the metaphor is very striking.

**Shovel Board.** A game in which three counters, or coins, were shoved or slid over a smooth board, very popular in the sixteenth and seventeenth centuries. The 'two Edward shovelboards' mentioned by Slender in the *Merry Wives of Windsor* (1, 1), were the broad shillings of Edward VI used in playing the game.

**Shrew-mouse.** A small insectivorous mammal, resembling a mouse, formerly supposed to have the power of poisoning cattle and young children by running over them. To provide a remedy our forefathers used to plug the creature into a hole made in an ash tree; then any branch from it would cure the mischief done.

**Shrieking Sisterhood, The.** A contemptuous epithet bestowed in less enlightened days on those women who battled for seats in Parliament and 'women's rights' generally.

> By Jove, I suppose my life wouldn't be worth a moment's purchase if I made public these sentiments of mine at a meeting of the Shrieking Sisterhood.
>
> *The World*, Feb. 24th, 1892

**Shrift.** The *shriving* of a person; i.e. his confession to a priest, and the penance and absolution arising therefrom.

***To give short shrift to.*** To make short work of. *Short shrift* was the few minutes in which a criminal about to be executed was allowed to make his confession.

> Tell my kind cousin [of Burgundy], if he loves such companions, he had best keep them in his own estates; for here they are like to meet short shrift and a tight cord
>
> Scott, *Quentin Durward*, viii

**Shrimp.** A child, a puny little fellow, in the same ratio to a man as a shrimp to a lobster. *Fry*, and *small fry*, are also used for children.

> It cannot be this weak and writhled shrimp
> Would strike such terror to his enemies.
>
> Shakespeare, *1 Henry VI*, 2, 3

**Shrivatsa.** *See* Vishnu.

**Shropshire.** The 'shire of shrubs'. The Anglo-Saxon name of Shrewsbury was *scrobbes byrg*, the burgh among the shrubs. The Normans could not pronounce *sc-*; so the A.S. name became *Salopesbury*, and for the name of the county the *-bury* (= town) was dropped, giving *Salop*, a name still used as an alternative for Shropshire; whence *Salopian*, a native of the county.

**Shrovetide.** The three days just before the opening of Lent, when people went to confession and afterwards indulged in all sorts of sports and merry-making.

***Shrove Tuesday.*** The day before Ash Wednesday; 'Pancake day'. It used to be the great 'Derby Day' of cock-fighting in England.

> Or martyr beat, like Shrovetide cocks, with bats.
>
> Peter Pindar, *Subjects for Painters*

**Shut up.** Hold your tongue. Shut up your mouth.

**Shutters.** ***To put up the shutters.*** To announce oneself a bankrupt.

> Do you think I am going to put up the shutters if we can manage to keep going?

**Shy.** ***To have a shy at anything.*** To fling at it, to try and shoot it.

**Shylock, A.** A grasping, stonyhearted Jewish moneylender; in allusion to the Jew in Shakespeare's *Merchant of Venice:*

> A stony adversary, an inhuman wretch
> Uncapable of pity, void and empty
> From any dram of mercy. 4, 1

> Those who had to borrow coin were obliged to submit to the expensive subterfuges of the Shylocks, from whose net, once caught, there was little chance of escape.
>
> A. Egmont-Hake, *Free Trade in Capital*, ch. vii

**Shyster.** A mean, tricky sort of person: originally American slang for a low-class lawyer hanging about the courts on the off-chance of exploiting petty criminals.

**Si**, the seventh note in music, was not introduced till the 17th century. Guido d'Arezzo's original scale consisted of only six notes. *See* Aretinian Syllables.

**Si Quis** (Lat., if anyone). A notice to all whom it may concern, given in the parish church before ordination, that a resident means to offer himself as a candidate for holy orders; and *if anyone* knows any just cause or impediment thereto, he is to declare the same to the bishop.

**Siamese Twins.** Yoke-fellows, inseparables; so called from the original pair, Eng and Chang, who were born of Chinese parents about 1814 and discovered at Mekong, Siam, in 1829, and were subsequently exhibited as freaks. Their bodies were united by a band of flesh, stretching from breast-bone to breast-bone. They married two sisters, had offspring, and died within three hours of each other on January 17th, 1874.

Other so-called Siamese twins were Barnum's 'Orissa twins', born at Orissa, Bengal, and joined by a band of cartilage at the waist only; 'Millie-Christine', two joined South Carolina negresses who appeared all over the world as the 'Two-headed Nightingale'; and Josepha and Roza Blazek, natives of Bohemia, who were joined by a cartilaginous ligament above the waist. They died practically simultaneously in Chicago (1922), Josepha leaving a son aged 12.

**Sibyl.** A prophetess of classical legend, who was supposed to prophesy under the inspiration of a deity; the name is now applied to any prophetess or woman fortune-teller. There were a number of sibyls, and they had their seats in widely separate parts of the word – Greece, Italy, Babylonia, Egypt, etc.

Plato mentions only one, viz., the *Erythraean* – identified with Amalthea, the *Cumaean Sibyl*, who was consulted by Aeneas before his descent into Hades and who sold the Sibylline books (*q.v.*) to Tarquin; Martian Capella speaks of two, the *Erythraean* and the *Phrygian*; Aelian of four, the *Erythraean*, *Samian*, *Egyptian*, and *Sardian*; Varro tells us there were *ten*, viz. the *Cumaean*, the *Delphic*, *Egyptian*, *Erythraean*, *Hellespontine*, *Libyan*, *Persian*, *Phrygian*, *Samian* and *Tiburtine*.

> How know we but that she may be an eleventh Sibyl or a second Cassandra?
>
> Rabelais, *Gargantua and Pantagruel*, 3, 16

The mediaeval monks 'adopted' the sibyls – as they did so much of pagan myth; they made them twelve, and gave to each a separate prophecy and distinct emblem:

(1) The *Libyan*: 'The day shall come when men shall see the King of all living things.' *Emblem*, a lighted taper.

(2) The *Samian*: 'The Rich One shall be born of a pure virgin.' *Emblem*, a rose.

(3) The *Cuman*: 'Jesus Christ shall come from heaven, and live and reign in poverty on earth.' *Emblem*, a crown.

(4) The *Cumaean*: 'God shall be born of a pure virgin, and hold converse with sinners.' *Emblem*, a cradle.

(5) The *Erythraean*: 'Jesus Christ, Son of God, the Saviour'. *Emblem*, a horn.

(6) The *Persian*: 'Satan shall be overcome by a true prophet.' *Emblem*, a dragon under the sibyl's feet, and a lantern.

(7) The *Tiburtine*: 'The Highest shall descend from heaven, and a virgin be shown in the valleys of the deserts.' *Emblem*, a dove.

(8) The *Delphic*: 'The Prophet born of the virgin shall be crowned with thorns.' *Emblem*, a crown of thorns.

(9) The *Phrygian*: 'Our Lord shall rise again.' *Emblem*, a banner and a cross.

(10) The *European*: 'A virgin and her Son shall flee into Egypt.' *Emblem*, a sword.

(11) The *Agrippine*: 'Jesus Christ shall be outraged and scourged.' *Emblem*, a whip.

(12) The *Hellespontic*: 'Jesus Christ shall suffer shame upon the cross.' *Emblem*, a T cross.

**Sibylline Books, The.** A collection of oracles of mysterious origin, preserved in ancient Rome, and consulted by the Senate in times of emergency or disaster. According to Livy there were originally nine: these were offered in sale by Amalthea, the Sibyl of Cumae, in Aeolia, to Tarquin, the offer was rejected, and she burnt three of them. After twelve months she offered the remaining six at the same price. Again being refused, she burnt three more, and after a similar interval asked the same price for the three left. The sum demanded was now given, and Amalthaea never appeared again.

The three books were preserved in a stone chest underground in the temple of Jupiter Capitolinus, and committed to the charge of custodians chosen in the same manner as the high priests. The number of custodians was at first two, then ten, and ultimately fifteen. Augustus had some 2,000 of the verses destroyed as spurious, and placed the rest in two gilt cases, under the base of the statue of Apollo, in the temple on the Palatine Hill; but the whole perished when the city was burnt in the reign of Nero.

A Greek collection in eight books of poetical utterances relating to Jesus Christ, compiled in the 2nd century, is entitled *Oracula Sibylina*, or the *Sibylline Books*.

**Sic** (Lat. thus, so). A word used by reviewers, quoters, etc., after a doubtful word or phrase, or a misspelling, to indicate that it is here printed exactly as in the original and to call attention to the fact that it is wrong in some way.

**Sicilian Vespers.** The massacre of the French in Sicily, which began at the hour of vespers on Easter Monday in 1282. The term is used proverbially of any treacherous and bloody attack.

**Sick Man, The.** So Nicholas of Russia (in 1844) called the Ottoman Empire, which had been declining ever since 1586.

> I repeat to you that the sick man is dying; and we must never allow such an event to take us by surprise.
>
> *Annual Register*, 1853

Don John, Governor-General of the Netherlands, writing in 1579 to Philip II of Spain, calls the Prince of Orange *the sick man*, because he was in the way, and he wanted him 'finished'.

> 'Money' (he says in his letter) 'is the gruel with which we must cure this sick man [for spies and assassins are expensive drugs].'
>
> Motley, *Dutch Republic*, Bk v, 2

**Side.** ***On the side of the angels.*** The famous phrase with which Disraeli thought he had settled the questions raised by Darwin's theory of the origin of species. It occurred in his speech at the Oxford Diocesan Conference in 1864:

> The question is this: Is man an ape or an angel? I, my lord, am on the side of the angels.

It was the same statesman who said in the House of Commons (May 14th, 1866), 'Ignorance never settles a question.'

***Putting on side.*** Giving oneself airs; being 'swanky' or bumptious. *To put on side* in billiards is to give your ball a twist or spin with the cue as you strike it.

***To side-track.*** Originally an American railroad term; hence, to get rid of, shelve, put on one side indefinitely.

**Sidney, Sir Philip** (1554–86), often taken as the type of the magnanimous and perfect soldier and statesman – the Happy Warrior. After he had received his death wound at the battle of Zutphen a soldier brought him some water, but as he was about to drink he observed a wounded man eye the draught with longing looks. Sir Philip gave up the water to him, saying, 'Poor fellow, thy necessity is greater than mine.' Spenser laments him in his *Astrophel* (*q.v.*), and largely modelled the Prince Arthur of the *Faërie Queene* on him.

***Sidney's sister, Pembroke's mother.*** Mary Herbert (*née* Sidney), Countess of Pembroke, poetess, etc. (Died 1621.) The line is from her *Epitaph*, which has been claimed both for Ben Jonson and for William Browne.

**Sidney-Sussex College,** Cambridge, founded by Lady Frances Sidney, Countess of Sussex, in 1598.

**Sidrac.** An old French romance which tells how Sidrac converted to Christianity Boccus, an idolatrous king and magician of India. Sidrac lived only 847 years after Noah, and became possessed of Noah's wonderful book on astronomy and the natural sciences. This passed through various hands, including those of a pious Chaldean, and Naaman the Syrian, until, as legend relates, Roger of Palermo translated it at Toledo into Spanish. The work is more a romance of Arabian philosophy than of chivalry. In Henry VI's reign an English metrical version was made by Hugh Campeden, and this was printed in 1510 as *The Historye of King Boccus and Sydracke*.

**Siegfried.** Hero of the first part of the *Nibelungenlied*. He was the youngest son of Siegmund and Sieglind, king and queen of the Netherlands, and was born in Rhinecastle called Xanton. He married Kriemhild, Princess of Burgundy, and sister of Gunther. Gunther craved his assistance in carrying off Brunhild from Issland, and Siegfried succeeded by taking away her talisman by main force. This excited the jealousy of Gunther, who induced Hagen, the Dane, to murder Siegfried. Hagen struck him with a spear in the only vulnerable part (between the shoulder-blades), while he stooped to quench his thirst at a fountain.

***Horny Siegfried.*** So called because when he slew the dragon he bathed in its blood, and became covered all over with a horny hide which was invulnerable, except in one spot between the shoulders, where a linden-leaf stuck.

***Siegfried's cloak of invisibility,*** called 'tarnkappe' (*tarnen*, to conceal; *kappe*, a cloak). It not only made the wearer invisible, but also gave him the strength of twelve men.

> The mighty dwarf successless strove with the mightier man:
> Like to wild mountain lions to the hollow hill they ran;
> He ravished there the tarnkappe from struggling Albric's hold,
> And then became the master of the hoarded gems and gold.
>
> Lettson, *Fall of the Nibelungers*, Lied iii

**Sieglind.** Mother of Siegfried, and Queen of the Netherlanders in the *Nibelungenlied* (*q.v.*).

**Sierra** (Span. a saw). A mountain whose top is indented like a saw; a range of mountains whose tops form a saw-like appearance; a line of craggy rocks; as *Sierra Morena* (where many of the incidents in *Don Quixote* are laid)', *Sierra Nevada* (the snowy range), *Sierra Leone* (in West Africa, where lions abound), etc.

**Siesta.** Spanish for 'the sixth hour' – i.e. noon (Lat. *sexta hora*). It is applied to the short sleep taken in Spain during the midday heat.

**Sieve and Shears.** ***The oracle of sieve and shears.*** This method of divination is mentioned by Theocritus. The *modus operandi* was as follows: The points of the shears were stuck in the rim of a sieve, and two persons supported them with their finger-tips. Then a verse of the Bible was read aloud, and St Peter and St Paul were asked if it was A, B, or C (naming the persons suspected). When the right person was named, the sieve would suddenly turn round.

> Searching for things lost with a sieve and shears.
>
> Ben Jonson, *Alchemist*, i, 1

**Sif.** Wife of the old Norse god, Thor (*q.v.*), famous for the beauty of her hair. Loki having cut it off while she was asleep, she obtained from the dwarfs a new fell of golden hair equal to that which he had taken.

**Sight,** for 'multitude', though now regarded as a colloquialism or as slang, is not an Americanism, but good old English, and was formerly in good literary use, the earlier significance being 'a show or display of something'. Thus, Juliana Berners, lady prioress in the 15th century of Sopwell nunnery, speaks of a *bomynable syght of monkes* (a large number of friars); and in one of the *Paston Letters* (May 25th, 1449) we read –

> ye sawe never suche a syght of schyppys take in to Englond thys c. [hundred] wynter.

***A sight for sore eyes.*** Something that it is very pleasurable to see or witness, especially something unexpected.

***Second sight.*** *See* Second.

***Though lost to sight, to memory dear.*** This occurs in a song by Geo. Linley (*c.*1835), but it is found as an 'axiom' in the *Monthly Magazine*, Jan., 1827, and is probably of much earlier date. Horace F. Cutter (*pseudonym* Ruthven Jenkyns) uses the expression in the *Greenwich Magazine for Mariners*, 1707, but this date is fictitious.

***To do a thing on sight.*** At once, without any hesitation.

**Significavit.** A writ of Chancery given by the ordinary to keep an excommunicate in prison till he submitted to the authority of the Church. The writ, which is now obsolete, used to begin with *Significavit nobis venerabilis pater*, etc. Chaucer says of his Sompnour –

> And also ware him of a significavit.
>
> *Canterbury Tales* (*Prologue*), 664

**Siguna.** Wife of Loki (*q.v.*) in old Norse myth. She nurses him in his cavern, but sometimes, as she carries off the poison which the serpents gorge, a portion drops on the god, and his writhings cause earthquakes.

**Sigurd.** The Siegfried (*q.v.*) of the *Volsunga Saga*, the Scandinavian version of the *Niebelungenlied* (*q.v.*). He falls in love with Brynhild, but, under the influence of a love-potion, marries Gudrun, a union which brings about a volume of mischief.

**Sikes, Bill.** The type of a ruffianly housebreaker of the lowest grade; from the brute of that name in Dickens's *Oliver Twist*. The only rudiment of a redeeming feature he possessed was a kind of affection for his dog.

**Sikh** (Hindu *sikh*, disciple). The Sikhs were originally a religious (monotheistic) body like the Mohammedans, founded in the Punjab in the 16th century. They soon became a military community, and in 1764 formally assumed national independence. Since 1849 the Sikhs have been ruled by the British.

**Silbury,** near Marlborough. A prehistoric artificial mound, 130 feet high, and covering seven acres of ground, said to be the largest in Europe, and to have been erected by the Celts about 1600 BC. Some say it is where 'King Sel' was buried; others, that it is a corruption of *Solis-bury* (mound of the sun); others, that it is Sel-barrow (great tumulus), in honour of some ancient prince of Britain.

**Silence. *Silence gives consent.*** A saying (common to many languages) founded on the old Latin law maxim – *Qui tacet consentire videtur* (who is silent is held to consent).

> But that you shall not say I yield, being silent,
> I would not speak.
>
> Shakespeare, *Cymbeline*, 2, 3

***Silence is golden.*** *See under* Speech.

***The rest is silence.*** The last words of the dying Hamlet (Shakespeare, *Hamlet*, 5, 2).

***Towers of Silence.*** The small towers on which the Parsees and Zoroastrians place their dead to be consumed by birds of prey. The bones are picked clean in the course of a day, and are then thrown into a receptacle and covered with charcoal.

> Parsees do not burn or bury their dead, because they consider a corpse impure, and they will not defile any of the elements. They carry it on a bier to the tower. At the entrance they look their last on the body, and the corpse-bearers carry it within the precincts and lay it down to be devoured by vultures which are constantly on the watch.

**Silent, The.** William I, Prince of Orange (1533–84), so called because when (1559) Henri II of France, thinking that he would be a ready accomplice, revealed to him the plans for a general massacre of Protestants in the Netherlands –

> the Prince, although horror-struck and indignant at the royal revelations, held his peace, and kept his countenance … without revealing to the monarch, by word or look, the enormous blunder which he had committed.
>
> Motley, *Dutch Republic*, II, 1

**Silenus.** The drunken companion of Dionysus (Bacchus) in *Greek mythology*; fond of music, and a prophet, but indomitably lazy, wanton, and given to debauch. He is described as a jovial old man, with bald head, pug nose, and face like Bardolph's.

> Within his car, aloft, young Bacchus stood,
> Trifling his ivy-dart, in dancing mood,
> With sidelong laughing; …
> And near him rode Silenus on his ass,
> Pelted with flowers as he on did pass
> Tipsily quaffing. Keats, *Endymion*, iv, 209

**Silhouette.** A black profile, so called from Étienne de Silhouette (1709–67), Contrôleur des Finances, 1759, who made great savings in the public expenditure of France. Some say the black portraits were called *Silhouettes* in ridicule of his petty economies; others assert that he devised this way of taking likenesses to save expense.

**Silk.** ***To take silk.*** Said of a barrister who has been appointed a King's Counsel (K.C.), because he then exchanges his stuff gown for a silk one.

***You cannot make a silk purse of a sow's ear.*** You must have the necessary materials or facilities before you can make or do what you are expected to. 'You cannot make a horn of a pig's tail.' A sow's ear may somewhat resemble a purse, and a curled pig's tail may somewhat resemble a twisted horn, but a sow's ear cannot be made into a silk purse, nor a pig's tail into a cow's horn.

> You cannot make, my lord, I fear,
> A velvet purse of a sow's ear.
>
> Peter Pindar, *Lord B. and His Motions*

**Silly** is the German *selig* (blessed) and used to mean in English 'happy through being innocent'; whence the infant Jesus was termed 'the harmless silly babe', and sheep were called 'silly'. As the 'innocent' are easily taken in by worldly cunning, the word came to signify 'gullible', 'foolish'.

***Silly-how.*** An old name – still used in Scotland – for a child's caul. It is a rough translation of the German term *glückshaube*, lucky cap. The caul (*q.v.*) has always been supposed to bring luck to its original possessor.

***The silly season.*** An obsolescent journalistic expression for the part of the year when Parliament and the Law Courts are not sitting (about August and September), when, through lack of news, the papers had to fill their columns with trivial items – such as news of giant gooseberries and sea serpents – and long correspondence on subjects of evanescent (if any) interest. The expression is obsolescent because later journalistic practice is to treat the whole year, from January to December, as a Silly Season.

**Silurian.** Of or pertaining to the ancient Silures or the district they inhabited, viz. Hereford, Monmouth, Radnor, Brecon, and Glamorgan. The 'sparkling wines of the Silurian vats' are cider and perry.

> From Silurian vats, high-sparkling wines
> Foam in transparent floods.
>
> Thomson, *Autumn*

***Silurian rocks.*** A name given by Sir R. Murchison to what miners call *gray-wacke*, and Werner termed *transition rocks*. Sir Roderick thus named them (1835) because it was in the region of the ancient Silures that he first investigated their structure.

**Silurist, The.** A surname adopted by the mystical poet Henry Vaughan (1621–95), who was born and died in Brecknockshire. *See* Silurian.

**Silver.** In England *standard silver* (i.e. that used for the coinage) formerly consisted of thirty-seven fortieths of fine silver and three fortieths of alloy (fineness, 925); but by an Act passed in 1920 the proportions, for reasons of economy, were changed to one half silver and one half alloy (fineness, 500).

***Silver*** is not legal tender for sums over £2.

***Silver articles*** are marked with five marks (*see* Hall mark): the maker's private mark, the standard or assay mark, the hall mark, the duty mark, and the date mark. The standard mark states the proportion of silver, to which figure is added a *lion passant* for England, a *harp* crowned for Ireland, a *thistle* for Edinburgh, and a *lion rampant* for Glasgow.

Among the ancient alchemists *silver* represented the Moon, or Diana; in heraldry it is known by its French name, *Argent* (which also gives its chemical symbol, 'Ag'), and is indicated in engravings by the silver (argent) portion being left blank.

***A silver lining.*** The prospect of better days, the promise of happier times. The saying, *Every cloud has a silver lining*, is quite an old one; thus in Milton's *Comus*, the Lady lost in the wood resolves to hope on, and sees a 'sable cloud turn forth its silver lining to the night'.

Though outwardly a gloomy shroud,
The inner half of every cloud
Is bright and shining:
I therefore turn my clouds about,
And always wear them inside out
To show the lining.
Ellen Thorneycroft Fowler, *The Wisdom of Folly*

***Born with a silver spoon in one's mouth.*** *See* Born.

***Silver of Guthrum.*** *See* Guthrum.

***Silver-tongued.*** An epithet bestowed on many persons famed for eloquence; especially William Bates, the Puritan divine (1625–99); Anthony Hammond, the poet (1668–1738); Henry Smith, preacher (1550–1600); and Joshua Sylvester (1563–1618), translator of Du Bartas.

***Silver Wedding.*** The twenty-fifth anniversary, when presents of silver plate (in Germany a silver wreath) are given to the happy pair.

***Speech is silver.*** *See* Speech.

***The Silver Age.*** The second of the Ages of the World (*q.v.*), according to Hesiod and the Greek and Roman poets; fabled as a period that was voluptuous and godless, and much inferior in simplicity and true happiness to the Golden Age.

***The silver cooper.*** A kidnapper. 'To play the silver cooper', to kidnap. A cooper is one who *coops up* another.

You rob and you murder, and you want me to ... play the silver cooper.
Sir W. Scott, *Guy Mannering*, ch. xxxiv

***The Silver-Fork School.*** A name given in amused contempt (about 1830) to the novelists who were sticklers for the etiquette and graces of the Upper Ten and showed great respect for the affectations of gentility. Theodore Hook, Lady Blessington, and Bulwer Lytton might be taken as representatives of it.

***The Silver Streak.*** The English Channel.

***Thirty pieces of silver.*** The sum of money that Judas Iscariot received from the chief priest for the betrayal of his Master (Matt. 26:15); hence used proverbially of a bribe or 'blood-money'.

***With silver weapons you may conquer the world.*** The Delphic oracle to Philip of Macedon, when he went to consult it. Philip, acting on this advice, sat down before a fortress which his staff pronounced to be impregnable. 'You shall see,' said the king, 'how an ass laden with gold will find an entrance.'

**Simeon, St,** is usually depicted as bearing in his arms the infant Jesus, or receiving Him in the Temple. His feast-day is February 18th.

***St Simeon Stylites.*** *See* Stylites.

**Similia similibus curantur** (Lat.) Like cures like; or, as we say, 'Take a hair of the dog that bit you.'

**Simkin.** Anglo-Indian for champagne – of which word it is an Urdu mispronunciation.

**Simnel Cakes.** Rich cakes formerly eaten (especially in Lancashire) on Mid-Lent Sunday ('Mothering Sunday'), Easter, and Christmas Day. They were ornamented with scallops, and were eaten at Mid-Lent in commemoration of the banquet given by Joseph to his brethren, which forms the first lesson of Mid-Lent Sunday, and the feeding of five thousand, which forms the Gospel of the day.

The word *simnel* is through O.Fr. from late Lat. *siminellus*, fine bread, Lat. *simila*, the finest wheat flour.

**Simon, St (Zelotes),** is represented with a saw in his hand, in allusion to the instrument of his martyrdom. He sometimes bears fish in the other hand, in allusion to his occupation as a fishmonger. His feast day is October 28th.

**Simon Magus.** Isidore tells us that Simon Magus died in the reign of Nero, and adds that he had proposed a dispute with Peter and Paul, and had promised to fly up to heaven. He succeeded in rising high into the air, but at the prayers of the two apostles he was cast down to earth by the evil spirits who had enabled him to rise.

Milman, in his *History of Christianity* (ii, p. 51) tells another story. He says that Simon offered to be buried alive, and declared that he would reappear on the third day. He was actually buried in a deep trench, 'but to this day', says Hippolytus, 'his disciples have failed to witness his resurrection'.

His followers were known as Simonians, and the sin of which he was guilty, viz. the trafficking in sacred things, the buying and selling of ecclesiastical offices (*see* Acts 8:18) is still called *simony*.

**Simon Pure.** The real man, the authentic article, etc. In Mrs Centlivre's *Bold Stroke for a Wife*, a Colonel Feignwell passes himself off for

Simon Pure, and wins the heart of Miss Lovely. No sooner does he get the assent of her guardian, than the Quaker shows himself, and proves, beyond a doubt, he is the 'real Simon Pure'.

**Simony.** *See* Simon Magus. The friar in the tale of *Reynard the Fox* (*q.v.*) is satirically so called.

**Simple, The.** Charles III of France (879, 893–929).

***The simple life.*** A mode of living in which the object is to eliminate as far as possible all luxuries and extraneous aids to happiness, etc., returning to the simplicity of life as imagined by the pastoral poets. The phrase was taken as the title of a book by Charles Wagner (1901), a Lutheran preacher in Paris who was brought up in the pastoral surroundings of the Vosges, and was much popularised by President Roosevelt, who publicly announced that the book contained 'such wholesome sound doctrine that I wish it could be used as a tract throughout our country'.

**Simple Simon.** A simpleton, a gullible booby; from the character in the well known anonymous nursery tale who 'met a pie-man'.

**Simplicity** is *sine plica*, without a fold; as duplicity is *duplex plica*, a double fold. Conduct 'without a fold' is *straightforward*, *simple*.

> The flat simplicity of that reply was admirable.
>
> Vanbrugh, *The Provoked Husband*, i

Disraeli spoke in the House of Commons (February 19th, 1850) of 'The sweet simplicity of the Three per Cents', plagiarising Lord Stowell, who had earlier spoken of their 'elegant simplicity' (*see* Campbell's *Lives of the Chancellors*, vol. x, 212).

**Sin,** according to Milton, is twin-keeper with Death of the gates of Hell. She sprang full-grown from the head of Satan.

> ... Woman to the waist, and fair,
> But ending foul in many a scaly fold
> Voluminous and vast, a serpent armed
> With mortal sting. *Paradise Lost*, ii, 650–653

***Original sin.*** That corruption which is born with us, and is the inheritance of all the offspring of Adam. As Adam was the federal head of his race, when Adam fell the taint and penalty of his disobedience passed to all his posterity.

***Sin-eaters.*** Persons hired at funerals in ancient times, to eat beside the corpse and so take upon themselves the sins of the deceased, that the soul might be delivered from purgatory.

> Notice was given to an old sire before the door of the house, when some of the family came out and furnished him with a cricket [low stool], on which he sat down facing the door; then they gave him a groat which he put in his pocket, a crust of bread which he ate, and a bowl of ale which he drank off at a draught. After this he got up from the cricket and pronounced *the ease and rest of the soul departed, for which he would pawn his own soul.*
>
> Bagford's letter on Leland's Collectanea, i, 76

***The Man of Sin*** (2 Thess. 2:3). Generally held to signify the Antichrist (*q.v.*), but applied by the old Puritans to the Pope of Rome, by the Fifth Monarchy men to Cromwell, and by many modern theologians to that 'wicked one' (identical with the 'last horn' of Dan. 7) who is immediately to precede the second advent.

***The seven deadly sins.*** Pride, Wrath, Envy, Lust, Gluttony, Avarice, and Sloth.

***To earn the wages of sin.*** To be hanged, or condemned to death.

> The wages of sin is death. Rom. 6:23
>
> I believe some of you will be hanged unless you change a good deal. It's cold blood and bad blood that runs in your veins, and you'll come to earn the wages of sin.
>
> Boldrewood, *Robbery under Arms*, ii

***To sin one's mercies.*** To be ungrateful for the gifts of Providence.

> I know your good father would term this 'sinning my mercies'. Scott, *Redgauntlet*

**Sine die** (Lat.). No time being fixed; indefinitely in regard to time. When a proposal is deferred *sine die*, it is deferred without fixing a day for its reconsideration, which is virtually 'for ever'.

**Sine qua non** (Lat.). An indispensable condition. Lat. *Sine qua non potest esse* or *fieri* (that without which [the thing] cannot be, *or* be done).

**Sinecure** (Lat. *sine cura*, without cure, or care). An enjoyment of the money attached to a benefice without having the trouble of the 'cure'; applied to any office to which a salary is attached without any duties to perform.

**Sinews of War.** Money, which buys the sinews, and makes them act vigorously. Men will not fight without wages, and the materials of war must be paid for.

The English phrase comes from Cicero's *Nervos belli pecuniam* (*Phil.* V. ii, 5), money makes the sinews of war. Rabelais (I, xlvi) uses the same idiom – *Les nerfs des batailles sont les pécunes*.

> Victuals and ammunition,
> And money too, the sinews of the war,
> Are stored up in the magazine.
>
> Beaumont and Fletcher, *Fair Maid of the Inn*, I, i

**Sing.** ***Singing bread*** (Fr. *pain à chanter*). An old term for the wafer used in celebration of the mass, because singing was in progress during its consecration. The reformers directed that the sacramental bread should be similar in fineness and fashion to the round bread and water *singing-cakes* used in private masses.

***Swans sing before they die.*** *See* Swan.

***To make one sing another tune.*** To make him change his behaviour altogether; make him recant what he has said.

***To sing in tribulation.*** Old slang for to confess when put to the torture. One who did this was termed in jail slang a 'canary bird'.

> 'This man, sir, is condemned to the galleys for being a canary-bird.' 'A canary-bird!' exclaimed the knight. 'Yes, sir,' added the arch-thief; 'I mean that he is very famous for his singing.' 'What!' said Don Quixote; 'are people to be sent to the galleys for singing?' 'Marry, that they are,' answered the slave; 'for there is nothing more dangerous than singing in tribulation.' Cervantes, *Don Quixote*, iii, 8

***To sing out.*** To cry or squall from chastisement; formerly said also of a prisoner who turned informer against his comrades. *See above*.

***To sing small.*** To cease boasting and assume a lower tone.

**Singapores.** Stock Exchange slang for 'British Indian Extension Telegraph Stock'.

**Single-Speech Hamilton.** William Gerard Hamilton (1729–96), who was Chancellor of the Exchequer in Ireland, 1763–84. So called from his maiden speech in Parliament (1755), a masterly torrent of eloquence which astounded everyone.

> Or is it he, the wordy youth,
> So early trained for statesman's part,
> Who talks of honour, faith, and truth,
> As themes that he has got by heart,
> Whose ethics Chesterfield can teach,
> Whose logic is from Single-speech?
> Scott, *Bridal of Triermain*, ii, 4

**Sinis.** A Corinthian robber of Greek legend, known as *the Pinebender*, because he used to fasten his victims to two pine trees bent towards the earth, and then leave them to be rent asunder by the rebound. He was eventually captured by Theseus and put to death in this same way.

**Sinister** (Lat. on the left hand). Foreboding of ill; ill-omened. According to augury, birds, etc. appearing on the left-hand side forbode ill-luck; but, on the right-hand side, good luck. Plutarch, following Plato and Aristotle, gives as the reason that the west (or left side of the augur) was towards the setting or departing sun.

***Corva sinistra*** (a crow on the left-hand) is a sign of ill-luck which belongs to English superstitions as much as to the ancient Roman or Etruscan. (Virgil, *Eclogues*, i, 18.)

> That raven on yon left-hand oak
> (Curse on his ill-betiding croak)
> Bodes me no good. Gay, *Fable* xxxvii

***Bar sinister.*** *See* Bar.

**Sinjaqu 'sh-sharif.** Mahomet's standard. *See* Banner of the Prophet.

**Sinon.** The Greek who induced the Trojans to receive the wooden horse. (Virgil, *Aeneid*, ii, 102, etc.) Anyone deceiving to betray is called 'a Sinon'.

> And now securely trusting to destroy,
> As erst false Sinon snared the sons of Troy.
> Camoëns, *Lusiad*, Bk i

**Sir.** Lat. *senex*, Span. *señor*, Ital. *signor*, Fr. *sieur*, *sire*. As a title of honour prefixed to the Christian name of baronets and knights, *Sir* is of great antiquity; and the clergy had at one time *Sir* prefixed to their name. This is merely a translation of the university word *dominus* given to graduates, as '*Dominus* Hugh Evans', etc. Spenser uses the title as a substantive, meaning a parson:

> But this, good Sir, did follow the plaine word.
> *Mother Hubberd's Tale*, 390

**Sirat, Al.** *See* Al-Sirat.

**Siren.** One of the mythical monsters, half woman and half bird, said by Greek poets (*see Odyssey*, xii) to entice seamen by the sweetness of their song to such a degree that the listeners forgot everything and died of hunger (Gr. *sirenes*, entanglers); hence applied to any dangerous, alluring woman.

In *Homeric mythology* there were but two sirens; later writers name three, viz. Parthenope, Ligea, and Leucosia; and the number was still further augmented by later writers.

Ulysses escaped their blandishments by filling his companions' ears with wax and lashing himself to the mast of his ship.

> What Song the Syrens sang, or what name Achilles assumed when he hid himself among women, though puzzling questions are not beyond all conjecture.
> Sir Thos Browne, *Urn Burial*, 7

Plato says there were three kinds of sirens – the *celestial*, the *generative*, and the *cathartic*. The first were under the government of Jupiter, the second under that of Neptune, and the third of

Pluto. When the soul is in heaven the sirens seek, by harmonic motion, to unite it to the divine life of the celestial host; and when in Hades, to conform them to the infernal regimen; but on earth they produce generation, of which the sea is emblematic. (Proclus, *On the Theology of Plato*, Bk vi.)

**Sirius.** The Dog-star; so called by the Greeks from the adjective *seirios*, hot and scorching. The Romans called it *canicula*, whence our Canicular days (*q.v.*), and the Egyptians *sept*, which gave the Greek alternative *sothis*. *See* Sothic Year.

**Sirloin.** Properly *surloin*, from Fr. *sur-longe*, above the loin. The mistaken spelling *sir-* has given rise to a number of stories of the joint having been 'knighted' because of its estimable qualities. Fuller tells us that Henry VIII did so –

> Dining with the Abbot of Reading, he [Henry VIII] ate so heartily of a loin of beef that the abbot said he would give 1,000 marks for such a stomach. 'Done!' said the king, and kept the abbot a prisoner in the Tower, won his 1,000 marks, and knighted the beef.
>
> *Church History*, vi, 2, p. 299 (1655)

Another tradition fathers the joke on James I:

> 'I vow, 'tis a noble sirloin!'
> 'Ay, here's cut and come again.'
> 'But pray, why is it called a sirloin?'
> 'Why you must know that our King James I, who loved good eating, being invited to dinner by one of his nobles, and seeing a large loin of beef at his table, he drew out his sword, and in a frolic knighted it. Few people know the secret of this.'
>
> Jonathan Swift, *Polite Conversation* ii

And yet another on Charles II.

In any case the joke is an old one; in Taylor the Water Poet's *Great Eater of Kent* (1680) we read of one who –

> should presently enter combate with a worthy knight, called Sir Loyne of Beefe, and overthrow him.

**Sirocco.** A wind from northern Africa that blows over Italy, Sicily, etc., producing extreme languor and mental debility.

**Sise Lane.** *See* Tooley Street.

**Sistine.** ***The Sistine Chapel.*** The private chapel of the Pope in the Vatican, so called because built by the Pope, Sixtus IV (1471–84). It is decorated with the frescoes of Michaelangelo and others.

***Sistine Madonna, The,*** or the *Madonna di San Sisto*. The Madonna painted by Raphael (about 1518) for the church of St Sixtus (San Sisto) at Piacenza; St Sixtus is shown kneeling at the right of the Virgin. The picture is in the Royal Gallery, Dresden.

**Sisyphus.** A legendary king of Corinth, crafty and avaricious, said to be the son of Aeolus, or – according to later legend, which also makes him the father of Ulysses – of Autolycus. His task in the world of shades is to roll a huge stone up a hill till it reaches the top; as the stone constantly rolls back his work is incessant; hence 'a labour of Sisyphus' or 'Sisyphean toil' is an endless, heart-breaking job.

> With useless endeavour,
> Forever, forever,
> Is Sisyphus rolling
> His stone up the mountain!
> Longfellow, *Masque of Pandora* (*Chorus of the Eumenides*)

**Sit.** ***To make one sit up.*** To astonish or disconcert him pretty considerably, to stir him up to action. *To make one sit up and snort* is an intensive implying that he is not only disconcerted but is inclined to protest about it.

***To sit on*** or ***upon.*** To snub, squash, smother, put in his place. *So-and-so wants sitting on* is said of a bumptious, 'uppish' individual.

***Sit on*** has other meanings also; thus *to sit on a corpse* is to hold a coroner's inquest on it; *to sit on the bench* is to occupy a seat as a judge or magistrate.

***To sit on the fence.*** *See* Fence.

***To sit tight.*** To keep your own counsel; to remain in or as in hiding. The phrase is from poker, where, if a player does not want to continue betting and at the same time does not wish to throw in his cards, he 'sits tight'.

***To sit under.*** A colloquialism for attending the ministrations of the clergyman named. The phrase was common three hundred years ago, and is still in use.

> There would then also appear in pulpits other visages, other gestures, and stuff otherwise wrought than what we now sit under, oft-times to as great a trial of our patience as any other that they preach to us.
>
> Milton, *Of Education* (1644)

**Sita.** Wife of Râma or Vishnu incarnate (of *Hindu Mythology*), carried off by the giant Ravana. She was not born, but arose from a furrow when her father Janaka, King of Mithila, was ploughing. The word means 'furrow'.

**Siva** or **Shiva.** The third person of the Hindu Trinity, or *Trimurti*, representing the destructive principle in life and also, as in Hindu philosophy restoration is involved in destruction, the reproductive or renovating power. He is a great worker of miracles through meditation and penance, and hence is a favourite deity with the ascetics. He is a god of the fine arts, and of dancing; and Siva, one only of his very many names, means 'the Blessed One'.

**Six. *At sixes and sevens.*** Higgledy-piggledy, in a state of confusion; or of persons, unable to come to an agreement. The phrase comes from dicing.

> The goddess would no longer wait;
> But rising from her chair of state,
> Left all below at six and seven,
> Harness'd her doves, and flew to heaven.
>
> Swift, *Cadenus and Vanessa* (closing lines)

***A six-hooped pot.*** A two-quart pot. Quart pots were bound with three hoops, and when three men joined in drinking each man drank his hoop. Mine host of the Black Bear (*Kenilworth*, ch. iii), calls Tressalian 'a six-hooped pot of a traveller', meaning a first-class guest, because he paid freely, and made no complaints.

***Six Principle Baptists.*** A sect of Arminian Baptists, founded about 1639, who based their creed on the six principles enunciated in Heb. 6:1, 2, viz., repentance, faith, baptism, the laying on of hands, resurrection of the dead, and eternal life.

***Six of one and half a dozen of the other.*** There is nothing to choose between them, they are both in the wrong – *Arcades ambo*.

***The Six Articles.*** An Act of Parliament passed in 1539 (repeated 1547) enjoining belief in (1) the real presence of Christ in the Eucharist; (2) the sufficiency of communion in one kind; (3) the celibacy of the priests; (4) the obligation of vows of chastity; (5) the expediency of private masses; and (6) the necessity of auricular confession, and decreeing death on those who denied the doctrine of Transubstantiation. It was also known as *The Bloody Bill*, and the *Six Stringed Whip*.

***The Six Clerks Office.*** An old name for the Court of Chancery (abolished in 1843) because there were six highly paid clerks connected with it.

***The six-foot way.*** The strip of ground between two parallel sets of railway lines.

***The Six Nations.*** The confederacy of North American Indian tribes consisting of the Five Nations (*q.v.*) and the Tuscaroras (formerly of North Carolina but now of New York and Ontario) who joined about 1715.

***The Six Points of Ritualism.*** Altar lights, eucharistic vestments, the eastward position, wafer bread, the mixed chalice, and incense. These were sanctioned in the Church of England in the time of Edward VI, and, it is held by many, were never forbidden by competent authority.

***The Six Stringed Whip.*** The Six Articles (*see above*).

**Sixteen-string Jack.** John Rann, a highwayman (hanged 1774), noted for his foppery. He wore sixteen tags, eight at each knee.

> Dr Johnson said that Gray's poetry towered above the ordinary run of verse as Sixteen-string Jack above the ordinary foot-pad.
>
> Boswell, *Life of Johnson*

**Sizar.** An undergraduate of Cambridge, or of Trinity College, Dublin, who receives a grant from his college to assist in paying his expenses. Formerly sizars were expected to undertake certain menial duties now performed by college servants; and the name is taken to show that one so assisted received his *sizes* or *sizings* (*q.v.*) free.

**Sizings.** At Cambridge, the allowance of food provided by the college for undergraduates at a meal; a pound loaf, two inches of butter, and a pot of milk used to be the 'sizings' for breakfast; meat was provided for dinner, but any extras had to be *sized* for. The word is a contraction of *assize*, a statute to regulate the size or weight of articles sold.

> A size is a portion of bread or drinke; it is a farthing which schollers in Cambridge have at the buttery. It is noted with the letter S.
>
> Minshien, *Ductor* (1617)

**Skadhi.** The wife of Niordhr (*q.v.*), the Scandinavian sea god. Her father was slain by the gods and, as an atonement, she was allowed to choose her husband from among them, but was obliged to do so seeing only their bare feet. She chose Niordhr thinking he was Balder, because he had the whitest feet.

**Skains-mate.**

> Scurvy knave! ... I am none of his skains-mates.
>
> Shakespeare, *Romeo and Juliet*, 2, 4

The meaning of the word is uncertain, but *skene* or *skean* is the long dagger formerly carried by the Irish and Scots (Gael. *scian*, *sgian*), so it may mean a dagger-comrade or fellow-cut-throat.

Swift, describing an Irish feast (1720), says, 'A cubit at least the length of their skains', and Greene, in his *Quip for an Upstart Courtier* (1592), speaks of 'an ill-favoured knave, who wore by his side a skane, like a brewer's bung-knife'.

**Skanda.** *See* Karttikeya.

**Skedaddle.** To run away hastily, make off in a hurry; to be scattered in rout. The Scotch apply the word to the milk spilt over the pail in carrying it. During the American Civil War the word came into prominence, and though its origin is 'wrapt in mystery', it is probably a fanciful Americanism.

**Skeleton.** ***The family skeleton,*** or ***the skeleton in the cupboard.*** Some domestic secret that the whole family conspires to keep to itself; every family is said to have at least one.

The story is that someone without a single care or trouble in the world had to be found. After long and unsuccessful search a lady was discovered whom all thought would 'fill the bill'; but to the great surprise of the enquirers, after she had satisfied them on all points and the quest seemed to be achieved, she took them upstairs and there opened a closet which contained a human skeleton. 'I try,' said she, 'to keep my trouble to myself, but every night my husband compels me to kiss that skeleton.' She then explained that the skeleton was once her husband's rival, killed in a duel.

***The skeleton at the feast.*** The thing or person that acts as a reminder that there are troubles as well as pleasures in life. Plutarch says in his *Moralia* that the Egyptians always had a skeleton placed in a prominent position at their banquets.

**Skevington's Daughter.** *See* Scavenger's.

**Skibbereen Eagle, The.** Sometimes still used as a type of newspaper that, without having any sort of influence, seeks by threats to direct political affairs; because an insignificant sheet of this name once solemnly warned Lord Palmerston that it had 'got its eye both on him and on the Emperor of Russia'.

**Skiddaw.** ***Whenever Skiddaw hath a cap, Scruffell wots full well of that*** (Fuller, *Worthies*). When my neighbour's house is on fire mine is threatened; when you are in misfortune I also am a sufferer; when you mourn I have cause also to lament. Skiddaw and Scruffell, or Scawfell, are neighbouring hills – about 15 miles apart in Cumberland. The saying signifies that when Skiddaw is capped with clouds, it will be sure to rain ere long at Scawfell.

**Skidhbladhnir.** In *Scandinavian mythology* the magic ship belonging to Freyr, but made by the sons of Ivaldi for Loki, which was large enough to hold all the gods but which could be folded together like a sheet of paper and put into a purse. It always commanded a prosperous gale. *Cp.* Ahmed, Carpet.

**Skill.** ***It skills not.*** It makes no difference; it doesn't matter one way or the other. The phrase was once very common, but is now looked upon as an archaism.

> Whether he [Callimachus] be now lyving I know not but whether he be or no, it skilleth not.
>
> Lyly, *Euphues and his England* (1580)

Similarly, *What skills talking?* What is the use of talking?

**Skimble-skamble.** Rambling, worthless. 'Skamble' is merely a variety of *scramble*, hence 'scambling days', those days in Lent when no regular meals are provided, but each person 'scrambles' or shifts for himself. 'Skimble' is added to give force.

> And such a deal of skimble-skamble stuff
> As put me from my faith.
>
> Shakespeare, *1 Henry IV*, 3, 1

> With such scamble-scemble, spitter-spatter,
> As puts me cleane beside the money-matter.
>
> Taylor, *The Water Poet*, ii, 39 (1630)

**Skimmington.** It was an old custom in rural England and Scotland to make an example of nagging wives and unfaithful husbands by forming a ludicrous procession through the village for the purpose of ridiculing the offender. In cases of hen-pecking Grose tells us that the man rode behind the woman, with his face to the horse's tail. The man held a distaff, and the woman beat him about the jowls with a ladle. As the procession passed a house where the woman was paramount, each gave the threshold a sweep. This performance was called *riding Skimmington* (also *riding the stang* – *see* Stang), and the husband or wife was, for the time, known as *Skimmington*. The origin of the name is uncertain, but in an illustration of the procession of 1639 the woman is shown belabouring her husband with a *skimming*-ladle.

The custom was not peculiar to Britain; it prevailed in Scandinavia, Spain, and elsewhere. The procession is described at length in *Hudibras* II, ii.

> 'Hark ye, Dame Ursley Suddlechop,' said Jenkin, starting up, his eyes flashing with anger; 'remember, I am none of your husband, and if I were you would do well not to forget whose threshold was swept when they last rode the skimmington upon such another scolding jade as yourself.' Scott, *Fortunes of Nigel*

**Skin.** ***By the skin of one's teeth.*** Only just, by a mere hair's breadth. The phrase comes from the book of Job (19:20):

> My bone cleaveth to my skin and to my flesh, and I am escaped with the skin of my teeth.

Coverdale's rendering of the passage is –

> My bone hangeth to my skynne, and the flesh is awaye only there is left me the skynne aboute my teth.

***To save one's shin.*** To get off with one's life.

***To sell the skin before you have caught the bear.*** To count your chickens before they are hatched. Shakespeare alludes to a similar practice:

> The man that once did sell the lion's skin
> While the beast lived, was killed with hunting him.
> *Henry V*, 4, 3

***To skin a flint.*** To be very exacting in making a bargain. The French say, *Tondre sur un oeüf.* The Latin *lana caprina* (goat's wool), means something as worthless as the skin of a flint or fleece of an eggshell. *Cp.* Skinflint.

**Skinfaxi,** in *Scandinavian mythology*, is the 'shining horse which draws Daylight over the earth'.

**Skinflint.** A pinch-farthing; a niggard. In the French *pince-maille. Maille* is an old copper coin.

**Skinners.** A predatory band in the American Revolutionary War which roamed over the neutral ground robbing and fleecing those who refused to take the oath of fidelity to the Republic.

**Skirt.** ***To sit upon one's skirt.*** To insult, or seek occasion of quarrel. Tarlton, the clown, told his audience the reason why he wore a jacket was that 'no one might sit upon his skirt'. Sitting on one's skirt is, like stamping on one's coat in Ireland, a fruitful source of quarrels, often provoked.

> Crosse me not, Liza, nether be so perte,
> For if thou dost, I'll sit upon thy skirte.
> *The Abortive of an Idle Howre* (1620)

**Skull.** ***Skull and crossbones.*** An emblem of mortality; specifically, the pirate's flag. The 'crossbones' are two human thigh-bones laid across one another.

> Half a score of us had been under the crossbones.
> Jas Runciman, *Skippers and Shellbacks*, p. 85

**Sky.** Rhyming slang for pocket, the missing word being *rocket. See* Rhyming Slang.

***If the sky falls we shall catch larks.*** A bantering reply to those who suggest some very improbable or wild scheme.

***Lauded to the skies.*** Extravagantly praised; praised to the heights.

**Sky-raker.** A nautical term for any topsail; strictly speaking, a sail above the fore-royal, the main-royal, or the mizzen-royal.

> We ... were upheaved upon the crown of some fantastic surge, peering our sky-rakers into the azure vault of heaven.
> C. Thomson, *Autobiography*, p. 120

**Skylark.** ***To skylark about.*** To amuse oneself in a frolicsome way, jump around and be merry, indulge in mild horseplay. The phrase was originally nautical and referred to the sports of the boys among the rigging after work was done.

**Skyscraper.** A very tall building, especially those of New York and other American cities. Some of them run to forty floors, and more. Also applied by sailors to a *sky-raker* (*q.v.*).

**Slam.** A term in card-playing denoting winning all the tricks in a deal. In Bridge this is called *Grand slam*, and winning all but one *Little slam. Cp.* Ruff.

**Slamecksan.** *See* Tramecksan.

**Slander.** Literally, a stumbling-block (*cp.* Scandal), or something which trips a person up (Gr. *skandalon*, through Fr. *esclandre*).

**Slang.** As denoting language or jargon of a low and colloquial type the word first appeared in the 18th century; its origin is not known, but it is probably connected with *sling* (*cp. mud-slinging*, for hurling abuse at one). Slang is of various sorts; most of it is introduced into the language from below, i.e. from the ranks of the thieves, rogues and vagabonds, and so on; but a good deal comes from above – from scientific and technical usage. *Phenomenal* is an instance of this, and such phrases as *the critical moment*, *out of commission*, which, in ordinary colloquial use, are true slang. But the greater part is simply metaphor, as *nut*, for head, *blind*, for intoxicated, *cat-lap*, for milk or any non-alcoholic drink, etc.

> All slang is metaphor, and all metaphor is poetry.
> G. K. Chesterton, *The Defendant*

*See also* Back-slang: Rhyming Slang.

***To slang a person.*** To abuse him, go for him 'like a Dutch uncle'; give him a piece of your mind.

**Slap-bang.** At once, without hesitation – done with a slap and a bang. The term was formerly applied to low eating-houses, where one slapped one's money down as the food was banged on the table.

They lived in the same street, walked to town every morning at the same hour, dined at the same slap-bang every day.

Dickens, *Sketches by Boz*, III, 36

**Slap-dash.** In an off-hand manner done hurriedly as with a slap and a dash. Rooms used to be decorated by slapping and dashing the walls so as to imitate paper, and at one time slap-dash walls were very common.

**Slap-up.** First-rate, grand, stylish.

[The] more slap-up still have the shields painted on the panels with the coronet over.

Thackeray

**Slate. *Slate club*.** A sick benefit club for working-men. Originally the names of the members and the money paid in were entered on a folding slate.

***To have a slate* or *tile loose*.** *See* Tile.

***To slate one*.** To reprove, abuse, or criticise him savagely. It is not known how the term arose, but perhaps it is because at school the names of bad boys were chalked up on the slate as an exposure.

The journalists there lead each other a dance.
If one man 'slates' another for what he has done,
It is pistols for two, and then coffin for one.

*Punch* (*The Pugnacious Penmen*), 1885

***To start with a clean slate*.** To be given another chance, one's past misdeeds having been forgiven and expunged, as writing is sponged from a slate.

**Slating, A.** A severe reprimand; a savage and devastating review; *see* To slate one, above.

He cut it up root and branch ... He gave it what he technically styled 'a slating', and as he threw down his pen ... he muttered, 'I think I've pretty well settled that dunce's business.'

*The World*, February 24th, 1892, p. 24

**Slave.** This is an example of the strange changes which come over some words. The *Slavi* were a tribe which once dwelt on the banks of the Dnieper, and were so called from *slav* (noble, illustrious); but as, in the later stages of the Roman Empire, vast multitudes of them were spread over Europe as captives, the word acquired its present meaning.

Similarly, *Goths* means the good or godlike men; but since the invasion of the Goths the word has become synonymous with barbarous, bad, ungodlike; and *cp*. Hun.

**Sleave. *The ravelled sleave of care*** (Shakespeare, *Macbeth*, 2, 2). The sleave is the knotted or entangled part of thread or silk, the raw, unwrought floss silk; hence, any tangle. Churton Collins (in *Studies in Shakespeare*) speaks of smoothing 'the tangled sleave of Shakespearean expression'.

**Sledge-hammer. *A sledge-hammer argument*.** A clincher; an argument which annihilates opposition at a blow. The sledge-hammer (A.S. *slecge*) is the largest hammer used by smiths, and is wielded by both hands.

**Sleep. *To sleep away*.** To pass away in sleep, to consume in sleeping; as, 'to sleep one's life away'.

***To sleep like a top*.** Excellently, go the night through without waking or discomfort. When peg-tops are at the acme of their gyration they become so steady and quiet that they do not seem to move; in this state they are said to 'sleep'. Congreve plays on the two meanings:

Hang him, no, he a dragon! If he be, 'tis a very peaceful one. I can ensure his anger dormant, or should he seem to rouse, 'tis but well lashing him and he will sleep like a top. *Old Bachelor*, I, v

***To sleep off*.** To get rid of by sleep.

***To sleep over a matter*.** To let a decision on it stand over till tomorrow.

**Sleeper, The.** Epimenides, the Greek poet, is said to have fallen asleep in a cave when a boy, and not to have waked for fifty-seven years, when he found himself possessed of all wisdom.

In mediaeval legend stories of those who have gone to sleep and have been – or are to be – awakened after many years are very numerous. Such legends hang round the names of King Arthur, Charlemagne, and Barbarossa. *Cp.* also the stories of the Seven Sleepers of Ephesus, Tannhauser, Ogier the Dane, Kilmeny, and Rip van Winkle.

***Sleeper Awakened, The*.** *See* Sly, Christopher.

**Sleeping Beauty, The.** This charming nursery tale comes from the French *La Belle au Bois Dormante*, by Charles Perrault (*Contes du Temps*). The Princess is shut up by enchantment in a castle, where she sleeps a hundred years, during which time an impenetrable wood springs up around. Ultimately she is disenchanted by a young Prince, who marries her.

***Sleeping partner*.** A partner in a business who takes no active share in running it beyond supplying capital.

***Sleeping sickness*.** A West African disease caused by a parasite, *Trypanosoma Gambiense*, characterised by fever and great sleepiness, and almost invariably terminating fatally. The disease known in England, which shows similar symptoms and the cause of which is unknown, is usually called *Sleeping illness* or *Sleepy sickness* as a means of distinction; its scientific name is *Encephalitis lethargica*.

**Sleepy.** Pears are said to be 'sleepy' when they are beginning to rot; and cream when, in the course of its making, the whole assumes a frothy appearance.

***Sleepy hollow.*** Any village far removed from the active concerns of the outside world. The name given in Washington Irving's *Sketch Book* to a quiet old-world village on the Hudson.

***Sleepy sickness.*** *See* Sleeping sickness, *above*.

**Sleeve. *To hang on one's sleeve.*** To listen devoutly to what one says: to surrender your freedom of thought and action to the judgment of another.

***To have up one's sleeve.*** To hold in reserve; to have it ready to bring out in a case of emergency. The allusion is to conjurers, who frequently conceal in the sleeve the means by which they do the trick.

***To laugh in one's sleeve.*** To ridicule a person not openly but in secret. At one time it was quite possible to conceal a laugh by hiding one's face in the large sleeves worn by men. The French say, *rire sous cape*.

***To pin to one's sleeve,*** as, 'I shan't pin my faith to your sleeve,' meaning, 'I shall not slavishly believe or follow you.' The allusion is to the practice of knights, in days of chivalry, pinning to their sleeve some token given them by their lady-love. This token was a pledge that he would do or die.

***To wear one's heart on one's sleeve,*** to expose all one's troubles to the eyes of the world.

**Sleeveless.** In the 16th century *sleeveless* was very commonly applied to *errand*, *answer*, *message*, etc., signifying that it was fruitless or futile, an errand, etc., that has no result. In *Eikonoclastes* Milton speaks of sleeveless reason, meaning reasoning that leads nowhere and proves nothing; and *a sleeveless message* was used of a kind of April fool trick – the messenger being dispatched merely so as to get rid of him for a time.

> If all these faile, a beggar-woman may
> A sweet love-letter to her hands convay,
> Or a neat laundresse or a hearb-wife can
> Carry a sleevelesse message now and than.
>
> *Taylor's Workes*, ii, 111 (1630)

**Sleipnir.** Odin's grey horse, which had eight legs, and could carry his master over sea as well as land. (*Scandinavian mythology*.)

**Sleuth-hound.** A blood-hound which follows the *sleuth* (old Norse *sloth*, our more modern *slot*) or track of an animal. Hence used, especially in America, of a detective.

> There is a law also among the Borderers in time of peace, that whoso denieth entrance or sute of a sleuth-hound in pursuit made after fellons and stolen goods, shall be holden as accessarie unto the theft.
>
> Holinshed, *Description of Scotland*, p. 14

**Slewed.** Intoxicated. When a vessel changes her tack, she staggers and gradually heels over. A drunken man moves like a ship changing her angle of sailing.

> Mr Hornby was just a bit slewed by the liquor he'd taken. W. C. Russell, *A Strange Voyage*

**Slick.** Adroit, dextrous, smart; the word is a variant of *sleek*.

***Hop off, and look slick about it!*** Clear out – and don't take long doing it.

**Sliding Scale.** A scale of duties, prices, payment, etc., which slides up and down as the article to which it refers becomes dearer or cheaper, or by which such payments accommodate themselves to the fluctuations in other conditions previously named. Thus, in the years following the Great War wages in many trades were governed by a *sliding scale* based on the cost of living.

**Slim.** A colloquialism, adopted from the Boers, for craftiness, cleverness in outwitting. President Kruger and his advisers were 'slim' in manoeuvring the British into a false position and then taking advantage of it.

**Slip. *Many a slip 'twixt the cup and the lip.*** Everything is uncertain till you possess it. *Cp.* Ancaeus.

> Multa cadunt inter calicem supremaque labra.
>
> Horace

***To give one the slip.*** To steal off unperceived; to elude pursuit. A sea phrase; a cable and buoy are fastened to the anchor-chain, which is let slip through the hawse-pipe. Done to save time in weighing anchor. The metaphor probably came originally from the action of 'slipping' a hound, i.e. allowing it to run free by slipping the lead from its collar. In coursing the official who releases the greyhounds is still called the *slipper*.

**Sloane MSS.** 3,560 MSS collected by Sir Hans Sloane (1660–1753), and left by him, together with his library (50,000 volumes) and other collections on condition that his heirs received £20,000, which was far less than their value.

These collections were bought and housed in Montague House, and formed the nucleus of the British Museum.

**Slogan.** The war-cry of the old Highland clans (Gael. *sluagh*, host, *ghairm*, outcry). Hence, any war-cry; and, in later use, a political party cry, an advertising catch-phrase, etc. 'Hang the Kaiser', for instance, was the principal *slogan* of the election of 1918. *Cp.* Slughorn.

**Slop, Dr.** The nickname given by Wm Hone to Sir John Stoddart (d.1856), a choleric physician who assailed Napoleon most virulently in *The Times* (1812–16). The allusion was to Sterne's famous Dr Slop in *Tristram Shandy*.

**Slops.** Police; originally 'ecilop'. *See* Back-slang.

I dragged you in here and saved you,
  And sent out a gal for the slops;
Ha! they're acomin', sir! Listen!
  The noise and the shoutin' stops.
  Sims, *Ballads of Babylon* (*The Matron's Story*)

**Slope.** To decamp; to run away. The term came from the United States, and may be a contraction of *let's lope*, *lope* being a dialect variation of *loup* (leap), to run or jump away.

***The slippery slope.*** The broad and easy way 'that leadeth to destruction'. *Facilis descensus Averno. See* Avernus.

**Slopecade.** The name given to the wife of the Badger (Grimbert) in Caxton's version of *Reynard the Fox*.

**Slough of Despond.** A period of, or fit of, great depression. In Bunyan's *Pilgrim's Progress*, Pt i, it is a deep bog which Christian has to cross in order to get to the Wicket Gate. Help comes to his aid, but Neighbour Pliable turned back.

**Slow. *Slow-coach.*** A dawdle. As a slow coach in the old coaching-days 'got on' slowly, so one that 'gets on' slowly is a slow coach.

***Slow-worm.*** *See* Misnomers.

**Slubberdegullion.** A nasty, paltry fellow. To *slubber* is to do things by halves, to perform a work carelessly; *degullion* is a fanciful addition (as in *rapscallion*).

Quoth she, 'Although thou hast deserved,
Base slubber-degullion, to be served
As thou didst vow to deal with me ...'
Butler, *Hudibras*, i, 3

**Slugabed.** A late riser. *To slug* used to be quite good English for to be thoroughly lazy. Sylvester has –

The Soldier, slugging long at home in Peace,
His wonted courage quickly doth decrease.
*Du Bartas*, I, vii, 340 (1591)

**Slug-horn.** A battle-trumpet; the word being the result of an erroneous reading by Chatterton of the Gaelic *slogan*. He thought the word sounded rather well; and, as he did not know what it meant, gave it a meaning that suited him:

Some caught a slughorne and an onsett wounde.
*The Battle of Hasting*, ii, 99

Browning adopted it in the last line but one of his *Childe Roland to the Dark Tower Came*, and thus this 'ghost-word' (*q.v.*) got a footing in the language.

**Sly, Christopher.** A keeper of bears and a tinker, son of a pedlar, and a sad, drunken sot in the Induction of Shakespeare's *Taming of the Shrew*. Shakespeare mentions him as a well known character of Wincot, a hamlet near Stratford-on-Avon, and it is more than probable that in him we have an actual portrait of a contemporary.

Sly is found dead drunk by a lord, who commands his servants to put him to bed, and on his waking to attend upon him like a lord and bamboozle him into the belief that he is a great man; the play is performed for his delectation. The same trick was played by the Caliph Haroun al-Raschid on Abou Hassan, the rich merchant, in *The Sleeper Awakened* (*Arabian Nights*), and by Philippe the Good, Duke of Burgundy, on his marriage with Eleanor, as given in Burton's *Anatomy of Melancholy* (Pt ii, sec. 2, num. 4).

**Sly-boots.** One who appears to be a dolt, but who is really wide awake; a cunning dolt.

The frog called the lazy one several times, but in vain; there was no such thing as stirring him, though the sly-boots heard well enough all the while. *Adventures of Abdalla*, p. 32 (1729)

**Sly Dog. *You're a sly dog.*** *Un fin matois.* A playful way of saying, You pretend to be disinterested, but I can read between the lines.

**Small. *A small and early.*** An evening party on a modest scale, with not a lot of guests, and not late hours.

***Small-back.*** Death. So called because he is usually drawn as a skeleton.

Small-back must lead down the dance with us all in out time.
Scott, *Quentin Durward*, ch. xxxvii

***Small beer.*** Properly, beer of only slight alcoholic strength; hence, trivialities, persons or things of small consequence.

*Iago*: She was a wight, if ever such wight were.
*Des.*: To do what?
*Iago*: To suckle fools and chronicle small beer.

> *Des.*: O most lame and impotent conclusion!
> Shakespeare, *Othello*, 2, 1

Hence, *he does not think small beer of himself*, he has a very good opinion of number one.

> To express her self-esteem [it might be said] that she did not think small beer of herself.
> De Quincey, *Historical Essays*

'Little potatoes' is a modern humorous variant of 'small beer' in this phrase.

***Small clothes.*** An obsolete term for breeches.

***Small-endians.*** *See* Little-endians.

***Small holding.*** A small plot of land (but larger than an allotment) let by a local or county council to a tenant for agricultural purposes. The Act of 1892 lays down that a small holding shall be not less than one acre nor more than fifty, and should not exceed £50 in annual value.

***Small talk.*** Chit-chat, trivial gossip.

***The small hours.*** The hours from 1 a.m. to 4 or 5 p.m., when you are still in the small, or low, numbers.

***The small of the back.*** The slenderer, narrower part, just above the buttocks.

***To feel small.*** To feel humiliated, 'taken down a peg or two'.

***To live in a small way.*** Keep a modest, unpretentious household; make both ends meet, but with little to spare and no ostentation.

> It was very right that he should take lodgings in his aunt's house, who lived in a very small way.
> Thackeray, *Pendennis*, ch. viii

***To sing small.*** To adopt a humble tone; to withdraw some sturdy assertion and apologise for having made it.

**Smalls.** The undergraduates' name at Oxford for Responsions, i.e. the first of the three examinations for the B.A. degree; about corresponding to the Cambridge Little-go.

**Smart Money.** Money paid by a person to obtain exemption from some disagreeable office or duty, or given to soldiers or sailors for injuries received in the service; in law it means a heavy fine. It either makes the person 'smart', i.e. suffer, or else the person who receives it is paid for smarting.

**Smash.** ***Come to smash*** – to ruin.

***Smashed to pieces,*** broken to atoms; bankrupt without a possibility of recovery.

> I have a great mind to … let social position go to smash. Eggleston, *Faith Doctor*, p. 63

**Smec.** A contraction of Smectymnuus (*q.v.*).

> The handkerchief about the neck,
> Canonical cravat of Smec
> Butler, *Hudibras*, Pt i, 5

**Smectymnuus.** The name under which was published (1641) an anti-episcopalian tract in answer to Bishop Hall's *Divine Right of Episcopacy*. The name is a sort of acrostic, composed of the initials of the authors, viz.:

*S*tephen *M*arshal, *E*dward *C*alamy, *T*homas *Y*oung, *M*atthew *N*ewcomen, and *W*illiam *S*purstow.

Milton published his *Apology for Smectymnuus*, another reply to Hall, in 1642.

**Smelfungus.** *See* Mundungus.

**Smell, To.** Often used figuratively for to suspect, to discern intuitively, as in *I smell a rat* (*see* Rat), *to smell treason*, to discern indications of treason, etc.

Shakespeare has, 'Do you smell a fault?' (*Lear*, 1, 1); and Iago says to Othello, 'One may smell in this a will most rank.' St Jerome says that St Hilarion had the gift of knowing what sins or vices anyone was inclined to by simply smelling either the person or his garments, and by the same faculty could discern good feelings and virtuous propensities.

***It smells of the lamp.*** *See* Lamp.

**Smiler.** Another name for shandy-gaff – a mixture of ale and lemonade or ginger-beer.

**Smith of Nottingham.** Applied to conceited persons who imagine that no one is able to compete with themselves. Ray, in his *Collection of Proverbs*, has the following couplet:

> The little Smith of Nottingham,
> Who doth the work that no man can.

**Smith's Prize-man.** One who has obtained the prize (£25), founded at Cambridge by Robert Smith, D.D. (Master of Trinity, 1742–68), for proficiency in mathematics and natural philosophy. There are annually two prizes, awarded to two commencing Bachelors of Arts.

**Smithfield.** The smooth field (A.S. *smethe*, smooth), called in Latin *Campus Planus*, and described by Fitz-Stephen in the 12th century as a 'plain field where every Friday there is a celebrated rendezvous of fine horses brought thither to be sold'. Bartholomew Fair was held here till 1855, at which date also the cattle-market was removed to Copenhagen Fields, Islington.

**Smoke.** To detect, or rather to get a scent of, some plot or scheme. The allusion may be to the detection of the enemy by smoke seen to issue from their place of concealment.

***Cape smoke.*** A cheap and villainous kind of whisky sold in South Africa.

***No smoke without fire.*** Every slander has some foundation. The reverse proverb, 'No fire without smoke', means no good without some drawback.

***Smoke-farthings, smoke-silver.*** An offering formerly given to the priest at Whitsuntide, according to the number of chimneys in his parish.

> The Bishop of Elie hath out of everie parish in Cambridgeshire a certain tribute called ... *smoke-farthings*, which the churchwardens do levie according to the number of ... chimneys that be in a parish. *MSS Baker*, xxxix, 326

***To end in smoke.*** To come to no practical result. The allusion is to kindling, which smokes, but will not light a fire.

***To smoke the pipe of peace.*** *See* Calumet.

**Snack** (a variant of *snatch*).

***To go snacks.*** To share and share alike.

***To take a snack.*** To take a morsel.

**Snag.** ***To come up against a snag.*** To encounter some obstacle in your progress. The phrase is from the American lumber camps, a *snag* being a tree-trunk fixed in the bottom of the river and reaching the surface, or near it.

**Snake.** Rhyming-slang (*q.v.*) for a looking-glass, the missing portion being 'in the grass'.

It was an old idea that snakes in casting their sloughs annually gained new vigour and fresh strength; hence Shakespeare's allusion –

> When the mind is quicken'd out of doubt,
> The organs, though defunct and dead before,
> Break up their drowsy grave, and newly move
> With casted slough and fresh legerity.
> *Henry V*, 2, 1

And another notion was that one could regain one's own youth by feeding on snakes.

> You have eat a snake
> And are grown young, gamesome, and rampant.
> Beaumont and Fletcher, *Elder Brother*, iv, 4

***A snake in the grass.*** A hidden or hypocritical enemy, a disguised danger. The phrase is from Virgil (*Ecl.* iii, 93), *Latet anguis in herba*, a snake is lurking in the grass.

***Great snakes!*** A common exclamation of surprise.

***To see snakes, to have snakes in one's boots, etc.*** To suffer from D.T.'s (delirium tremens). This is one of the delusions common to those so afflicted.

> He's been pretty high on whisky for two or three days, ... and they say he's got snakes in his boots now. *The Barton Experiment*, ch. ix

**Snap.** ***Not worth a snap of the fingers.*** Utterly worthless and negligible.

***Snapdragon.*** The same as '*flapdragon*' (*q.v.*); also, a plant of the genus *Antirrhinum* with a flower opening like a dragon's mouth.

***Snapshot.*** Formerly applied to a shot fired without taking aim, but now almost exclusively to an instantaneous photograph. Hence *to snapshot a person*, to take an instantaneous photograph of him.

***Snap vote.*** A vote taken unexpectedly, especially in Parliament. The result of a 'snap vote' has, before now, been the overthrow of the ministry.

***To snap one's nose off.*** *See* Nose.

**Snark.** The imaginary animal invented by 'Lewis Carroll' as the subject of his mock-heroic poem, *The Hunting of the Snark* (1876). It was most elusive and gave endless trouble, and when eventually the hunters thought they had tracked it down their quarry proved to be but a Boojum. The name (a 'portmanteau word' of *snake* and *shark*) has hence sometimes been given to the quests of dreamers and visionaries.

It was one of Rossetti's delusions that in *The Hunting of the Snark* 'Lewis Carroll' was caricaturing him and 'pulling his leg'.

**Snarling Letter** (Lat., *litera canina*). The letter *r*. *See* R.

**Sneck Posset.** To give one a sneck posset is to give him a cold reception, to slam the door in his face (Cumberland and Westmorland). The 'sneck' is the latch of a door, and to 'sneck the door in one's face' is to shut a person out.

**Sneeze.** St Gregory has been credited with originating the custom of saying 'God bless you' after sneezing, the story being that he enjoined its use during a pestilence in which sneezing was a mortal symptom. Aristotle, however, mentions a similar custom among the Greeks; and Thucydides tells us that sneezing was a crisis symptom of the great Athenian plague.

> Foote, in his farce *Dr Last in His Chariot*, makes one of the doctors ask why, when a person sneezes, all the company bow? and the answer given was that 'sneezing is a mortal symptom which once depopulated Athens'.

The Romans followed the same custom, their usual exclamation being *Absit omen!* The Parsees hold that sneezing indicates that evil spirits are abroad, and we find similar beliefs in India, Africa, ancient and modern Persia, among the North American Indian tribes, etc.

We are told that when the Spaniards arrived in Florida the Cazique sneezed, and all the court lifted up their hands and implored the sun to avert the evil omen.

***It is not to be sneezed at*** – not to be despised

**Snickersnee.** A large clasp-knife, or combat with clasp-knives. The word is a corruption of the old *snick and snee* or *snick or snee*, cut and thrust, from the Dutch. Thackeray, in his *Little Billee*, uses the term.

One man being busy in lighting his pipe, and another in sharpening his snickersnee.

Irving, *Bracebridge Hall*, p. 462

**Snob.** A vulgar person who apes the ways of gentlemen and truckles to those in a higher social position than himself; one who is *not* a gentleman but does what he can to palm himself off as such while having a contemptible respect for wealth.

Thackeray calls George IV a snob, because he assumed to be 'the first gentleman in Europe', but had not the genuine stamp of a gentleman's mind.

The word was originally applied to a journeyman cobbler or a shoemaker's apprentice; and at Cambridge it denotes a townsman as opposed to a gownsman.

**Snood.** ***The lassie lost her silken snood.*** The snood was a ribbon with which a Scotch lass braided her hair, and was the emblem of her maiden character. When she married she changed the snood for the curch or coif; but if she lost the name of virgin before she obtained that of wife, she 'lost her silken snood', and was not privileged to assume the curch.

**Snooks.** An exclamation of incredulity or derision. *To cock* or *pull a snook*, to make a gesture of contempt.

**Snotty.** Sailors' slang for a midshipman.

**Snow King, The.** So the Austrians called Gustavus Adolphus of Sweden (1594, 1611–32), because, said they, he 'was kept together by the cold, but would melt and disappear as he approached a warmer soil'.

**Snuff.** ***To be snuffed out*** – put down, eclipsed; killed. *To snuff it* is a euphemism for to die. The allusion is to a candle snuffed with snuffers.

'Tis strange the mind, that very fiery particle,
Should let itself be snuffed out by an article.

Byron, *Don Juan*, xi, 60

***Took it in snuff*** – in anger, in huff.

You'll mar the light by taking it in snuff.

Shakespeare, *Love's Labour's Lost*, 5, 2

Who … when it next came there, took it in snuff.

Shakespeare, *1 Henry IV*, 1, 3

***Up to snuff.*** Wide awake, knowing, sharp; not easily taken in or imposed upon; alive to scent.

**Soap,** or **Soft Soap.** Flattery especially of an oily, unctuous kind.

***How are you off for soap?*** A common street-saying of the mid-19th century, of indeterminate (or, sometimes, no) meaning. It may mean 'What are you good for?' in the way of cash, or anything else; and it was often just a general piece of cheek. *Cp.* 'What! No soap?' is Foote's nonsense passage (*see* Panjandrum).

***In soaped-pig fashion.*** Vague; a method of speaking or writing which always leaves a way of escape. The allusion is to the custom at fairs, etc., of soaping the tail of a pig before turning it out to be caught by the tail.

He is vague as may be; writing in what is called the 'soaped-pig' fashion.

Carlyle, *The Diamond Necklace*, ch. iv

**Soapy Sam.** Samuel Wilberforce (1805–73), Bishop of Oxford, and afterwards of Winchester; so called because of his persuasive and unctuous way of speaking in early life. It is somewhat remarkable that the floral decorations above the stall of the bishop and of the principal of Cuddesdon, were S. O. A. P., the initials of **S**am **O**xon and **A**lfred **P**ort.

Someone asking the bishop why he was so called, received the answer, 'Because I am often in hot water and always come out with clean hands.'

**Sob Stuff.** An expressive Americanism describing newspaper, film, or other stories of a highly sentimental kind.

**Sobersides.** A grave, steady-going, serious-minded person, called by some 'a stick-in-the-mud'; generally *Old Sobersides*.

**Social.** Pertaining to society, the community as a whole, or to the intercourse and mutual relationships of mankind at large.

***Social Democrat.*** A member of a political party aiming at a gradual improvement of society by the adoption of Socialist reforms.

***The social evil,*** or ***plague.*** Euphemisms for prostitution and venereal diseases.

**Socialism.** The political and social scheme foreshadowed by Robert Owen (1771–1858), from whose *New View of Society* (1813) has been developed the doctrine that the political and economic organisation of society should be based on the subordination of the individual to the interests of the community. It involves the collective ownership of the sources and instruments of production, democratic control of industries, co-operation instead of competition, state distribution of the products instead of payment by wages, free education, etc. *Cp.* Communist: Fourierist: Individualist: St Simonianism.

**Society.** The upper ten thousand, or 'the upper ten'. When persons are in 'society', they are on the visiting lists of the fashionable social leaders. The 'society' of a district are the great panjandrums thereof.

***Society of Friends.*** *See* Quakers.

***Society verse.*** *See* Vers de société.

**Socinianism.** A form of Unitarianism which, on the one hand, does not altogether deny the supernatural character of Christ, but, on the other, goes farther than Arianism, which, while upholding His divinity, denies that He is coequal with the Father. So called from the Italian theologian, Faustus Socinus (1539–1604), who, with his brother, Laelius (1525–62), propagated this doctrine.

**Sock.** The light shoe worn by the comic actors of Greece and Rome (Lat. *soccus*); hence applied to comedy itself.

> Then to the well-trod stage anon,
> If Jonson's learned sock be on.
>
> Milton, *L'Allegro*

The difference between the sock of comedy and the buskin (*q.v.*) of tragedy was that the sock reached only to the ankle, but the buskin extended to the knee.

**Socrates.** The great Greek philosopher, born and died at Athens (about 470–399 BC). He used to call himself 'the midwife of men's thoughts'; and out of his intellectual school sprang those of Plato and the Dialectic system, Euclid and the Megaric, Aristippus and the Cyrenaic, Antisthenes and the Cynic. Cicero said of him that 'he brought down philosophy from the heavens to earth'; and he was certainly the first to teach that 'the proper study of mankind is man'. He was condemned to death for the corruption of youth by introducing new gods (thus being guilty of impiety) and drank hemlock in prison, surrounded by his disciples. *See* Delias.

***Socratic irony.*** Leading on your opponent in an argument by simulating ignorance, so that he 'ties himself in knots' and eventually falls an easy prey – a form of procedure used with great effect by Socrates.

***The Socratic method.*** The method of conducting an argument, imparting information, etc., by means of question and answer.

**Sodom. *Apples of Sodom*.** *See* Apple.

**Soft,** or **softy.** A daft person, half an idiot; one whose brain shows signs of softening.

***A soft fire makes sweet malt.*** Too much hurry or precipitation spoils work, just as too fierce a fire would burn the malt and destroy its sweetness. 'Soft and fair goes far', 'the more haste the less speed' are sayings of similar meaning.

***Soft sawder.*** Flattery, adulation. Soft solder (pronounced *sawder*) is a composition of tin and lead, used for soldering zinc, lead, and tin; hard solder for brass, etc.

***Soft soap.*** *See* Soap.

***Soft words butter no parsnips.*** *See* Butter.

**Soho!** An exclamation used by huntsmen, especially in hare-coursing when a hare has been started. It is a very old call, dating from at least the 13th century, and corresponds to the 'Tally-ho!' of fox-hunters when the fox breaks cover.

***Soho,*** the district in London, is so called from a mansion which stood there in the time of Charles II, belonging to the Duke of Monmouth.

**Soi-disant** (Fr.). Self-styled, would-be; generally used of pretenders, as 'a *soi-disant* gentleman', i.e. a snob.

**Soil. *A son of the soil.*** One native to that particular place, whose family has been settled there for generations; especially if engaged in agriculture.

***To take soil.*** A hunting term, signifying that the deer has taken to the water. *Soil* here is the Fr. *souille*, mire in which a wild boar wallows.

> Fida went downe the dale to seeke the hinde,
> And founde her taking soyle within a flood.
>
> Browne, *Britannia's Pastorals*, i, 84

**Sol.** The Roman sun god; hence used for the sun itself.

> Sol through white curtains shot a timorous ray,
> And oped those eyes that must eclipse the day.
>
> Pope, *Rape of the Lock*, i, 13

The name was given by the old alchemists to gold, and in heraldry it represents *or* (gold).

In music *sol* is the name of the fifth note of the diatonic scale (*see* Doh).

**Solano. *Ask no favour during the Solano*.** A popular Spanish proverb, meaning – Ask no favour during a time of trouble or adversity.

The *solano* (*solanus*, sun, *see* Sol) of Spain is a south-east wind, extremely hot, and loaded with fine dust; it produces giddiness and irritation.

**Soldan** or **Sowdan.** A corruption of sultan, meaning in mediaeval romance the Saracen king; but, with the usual inaccuracy of these writers, we have the Soldan of Egypt, the Soudan of Persia, the Sowdan of Babylon, etc., all represented as accompanied by grim Saracens to torment Christians.

In Spenser's *Faërie Queene* (V, viii) the Soldan typifies Philip II of Spain who used all his power to bribe and seduce the subjects of Elizabeth, here figuring as Queen Mercilla.

Sir Artegal demands of the Soldan the release of the damsel 'held as wrongful prisoner', and the Soldan 'swearing and banning most blasphemously', mounts his 'high chariot', and prepares to maintain his cause. Prince Arthur encounters him 'on the green', and after a severe combat uncovers his shield, at sight of which the Soldan and all his followers take to flight. The 'swearing and banning' typify the excommunications thundered out against Elizabeth; the 'high chariot' is the Spanish Armada; the 'green' is the sea; the 'uncovering of the shield' indicates that the Armada was put to flight, not by man's might, but by the power of God.

**Soldier** originally meant a hireling or mercenary; one paid a *solidus*, or wage, for military service; but hireling and soldier convey now very different ideas.

***Soldiers' battles.*** Engagements which are more of the nature of hand to hand encounters than regular pitched battles; those that have to be fought by the soldiers themselves, their leaders not having been able to take up strategical positions. The principal 'Soldiers' Battles' of English history are Malplaquet, 1709, and Inkermann, 1854.

***Soldiers of fortune.*** Men who live by their wits; *chevaliers de l'industrie*. Referring to those men in mediaeval times who let themselves for hire into any army.

> His father was a soldier of fortune, as I am a sailor.
>
> Scott, *The Antiquary*, ch. xx

***To come the old soldier over one.*** To dictate peremptorily and profess superiority of knowledge and experience; also to impose on one.

> But you needn't try to come the old soldier over me. I'm not quite such a fool as that.
>
> Hughes, *Tom Brown at Oxford*, II, xvii

**Solecism.** A deviation from correct idiom or grammar; from the Greek *soloikos*, speaking incorrectly, so named from Soloi, a town in Cilicia, the Attic colonists of which spoke a debased form of Greek.

The word is also applied to any impropriety or breach of good manners.

**Solemn.** ***The Solemn League and Covenant.*** A league entered into by the General Assembly of the Church of Scotland, the Westminster Assembly of English Divines, and the English Parliament in 1643, for the establishment of Presbyterianism and suppression of Roman Catholicism in both countries. Charles II swore to the Scots that he would abide by it and therefore they crowned him in 1651 at Dunbar; but at the Restoration he not only rejected the Covenant, but had it burnt by the common hangman.

**Sol-fa.** *See* Tonic sol-fa.

**Solicitor.** *See* Attorney.

**Solid Doctor, The.** Richard Middleton, a Franciscan Schoolman of the late 13th century, author of works on theology and canon law.

**Solifidians** (Lat. *solus*, alone, *fides*, faith). Those who maintain the Lutheran doctrine that faith without works is sufficient for salvation. The doctrine is based on Rom. 3:28:

> Therefore we conclude that a man is justified by faith without the deeds of the law.

**Solipsism** (Lat. *solus*, alone, *ipse*, self). Absolute egoism; the metaphysical theory that the only knowledge possible is that of oneself.

**Solomon.** The famous king of Israel (d. about 930 BC). He was specially noted for his wisdom, hence his name has been used for wise men generally.

***The English Solomon.*** James I (1603–25), whom Sully called 'the wisest fool in Christendom'.

***The Solomon of France.*** Charles V (1364–80), *le Sage*.

***Solomon's Carpet.*** *See* Carpet, The Magic.

***Solomon's Ring.*** Rabbinical fable has it that Solomon wore a ring with a gem that told him all he desired to know.

***Solomon's Seal.*** *Polygonatum multiflorum*, a plant with drooping white flowers. As the stems decay the rootstalk becomes marked with scars that have some resemblance to seals; this, according to some, accounts for the name; but another explanation offered is that the root has medicinal value in *sealing* up and closing green wounds.

**Solon.** A wiseacre or sage; from the great lawgiver of ancient Athens (d. about 560 BC), one of the Seven Sages of Greece.

How legislated now, in this respect,
Solon and his Athenians? Quote the code
Of Romulus and Rome! Justinian speak!
Nor modern Baldo, Bartolo be dumb!
Browning, *The Ring and the Book*, I

***The Solon of Parnassus.*** So Voltaire called Boileau (1636–1711), in allusion to his *Art of Poetry*.

**Solstice.** The summer solstice is June 21st; the winter solstice is December 22nd; so called because on or about these dates the sun reaches its extreme northern and southern points in the ecliptic and appears to stand still (Lat. *sol*, sun, *sistit*, stands) before it turns back on its apparent course.

**Solyman.** King of the Turks (in *Jerusalem Delivered*), whose capital was Nice. Being driven from his kingdom, he fled to Egypt, and was there appointed leader of the Arabs (Bk ix). He and Argantes were by far the most doughty of the pagan knights. Solyman was slain by Rinaldo (Bk xx), and Argantes by Tancred.

**Soma.** An intoxicating drink anciently made, with mystic rites and incantations, from the juice of some Indian plant by the priests, and drunk by the Brahmins as well as offered as libations to their gods. It was fabled to have been brought from heaven by a falcon, or by the daughters of the Sun; and it was itself personified as a god, and represented the moon. The plant was probably a species of *Asclepias*.

***To drink the Soma.*** To become immortal, or as a god.

**Some.** Used – originally in America – with a certain emphasis as an adjective-adverb of all work, denoting some special excellence or high degree. 'This is *some* book,' for instance, means that it is a book that particularly fascinates, appeals to, or 'intrigues' the speaker; '*some* golfer', a super-excellent golfer; 'going *some*', going the pace pretty hot.

**Somerset House** occupies the site in the Strand, London, of a princely mansion built by Somerset the Protector, brother of Lady Jane Seymour, and uncle of Edward VI. At the death of Somerset on the scaffold it became the property of the Crown, and in the reign of James I was called Denmark House in honour of Anne of Denmark, his queen. Old Somerset House was pulled down in the 18th century, and the present structure was erected by Sir William Chambers in 1776.

**Somoreen.** *See* Zamorin.

**Song.** ***An old song.*** A mere trifle, something hardly worth reckoning, as 'It went for an old song', it was sold for practically nothing.

***Don't make such a song about it!*** Be a little more reasonable in your complaints; don't make such a fuss about it.

***The Songs of Degrees.*** Another name for the Gradual Psalms (*q.v.*).

***The Song of Roland.*** *See under* Roland.

***The Song of Songs.*** The *Canticles*, or the *Song of Solomon*, in the Old Testament.

**Sonnet.** ***Prince of the sonnet.*** Joachim du Bellay, a French sonneteer (1526–60); but Petrarch (1304–74) better deserves the title.

**Sooner.** Slang for a sponger, one who lives on his wits and will do anything *sooner* than work for his living.

In America the term is applied to settlers in the western districts who peg out their claims in the territory before the time appointed by the Government.

**Sooterkin.** A kind of after-birth fabled to be produced by Dutch women through sitting over their stoves; hence, an abortive proposal or scheme, and, as applied to literature, an imperfect or a supplementary work.

For knaves and fools being near of kin,
As Dutch boors are t'a sooterkin,
Both parties join'd to do their best.
To damn the public interest.
Butler, *Hudibras*, III, ii, 145

**Sop.** ***A sop in the pan.*** A tit-bit, dainty morsel; a piece of bread soaked in the dripping of meat caught in a dripping-pan; a bribe (*see below*).

***To give a sop to Cerberus.*** To give a bribe, to quiet a troublesome customer. Cerberus is Pluto's three-headed dog, stationed at the gates of the infernal regions. When persons died the Greeks and Romans used to put a cake in their hands as a sop to Cerberus, to allow them to pass without molestation.

**Soph.** A student at Cambridge is a Freshman for the first term, a Junior Soph for the second year, and a Senior Soph for the third year. The word Soph is a contraction of 'sophister', which is the Greek and Latin *sophistes* (a sophist). In former times these students had to maintain a given question in the schools by opposing the orthodox view of it. These opponencies are now limited to Law and Divinity degrees.

In American Universities *Soph* is an abbreviation of *Sophomore*, a term applied to students in their second year.

**Sophia, Santa.** The great metropolitan cathedral of the Orthodox Greek Church at Constantinople. It was built by Justinian (532–7), but since the capture of the city by the Turks (1453) has been used as a mosque. It was not dedicated to a saint named Sophia, but to the 'Logos', or Second Person of the Trinity, called *Hagia Sophia* (Sacred Wisdom).

**Sophist, Sophistry, Sophism, Sophisticator,** etc. These words have quite run from their legitimate meaning. Before the time of Pythagoras (586–506 BC) the sages of Greece were called *sophists* (wise men). Pythagoras out of modesty called himself a *philosopher* (a wisdom-lover). A century later Protagoras of Abdera resumed the title, and a set of quibblers appeared in Athens who professed to answer any question on any subject, and took up the title discarded by the Wise Samian. From this moment *sophos* and all its family of words were applied to 'wisdom falsely so called', and *philo-sophos* to the 'modest search after truth'.

**Sophy, The.** An old title of the rulers of Persia, first given to Sheik Juneyd u Dien, founder of the Safi dynasty (about 1500–1736), a Shiite who claimed descent, through Ali, from the twelve saints.

**Soppy.** Mawkish (of people), ultra-sentimental (of stories, etc.). *A soppy boy* is one who is 'tied to his mother's apron-strings' and 'can't say "Bo!" to a goose'.

**Sorbonne.** The institution of theology, science, and literature in Paris founded by Robert de Sorbon, Canon of Cambrai, in 1252. In 1808 the buildings, erected by Richelieu in the 17th century, were given to the University, and since 1821 have been the *Académie universitaire de Paris*.

**Sordello.** A Provençal troubadour (d. about 1255), mentioned a number of times by Dante in the *Purgatorio*, now remembered because of Browning's very obscure poem of this name (1840). It details, in a setting which shows the restless condition of northern Italy in the early 13th century, the conflict of a poet about the best way of making his influence felt, whether personally or by the power of song. Browning said of it:

> The historical decoration was purposely of no more importance than a background requires; and my stress lay on the incidents in the development of a soul; little else is worth study. I, at least, always thought so.

Tennyson's reference to *Sordello* is well known. He said he had done his best with it, but there were only two lines he understood – the first and the last – and they were both untrue. These are:

> Who will, may hear Sordello's story told.
> Who would has heard Sordello's story told.

**Sorites.** A 'heaped-up' (Gr. *soros* a heap) or cumulative syllogism, the predicate of one forming the subject of that which follows, the subject of the first being ultimately united with the predicate of the last. The following will serve as an example:

All men who believe shall be saved.

All who are saved must be free from sin.

All who are free from sin are innocent in the sight of God.

All who are innocent in the sight of God are meet for heaven.

All who are meet for heaven will be admitted into heaven.

Therefore all who believe will be admitted into heaven.

***The famous Sorites of Themistocles*** was: That his infant son commanded the whole world, proved thus:

My infant son rules his mother.
His mother rules me.
I rule the Athenians.
The Athenians rule the Greeks.
The Greeks rule Europe.
And Europe rules the world.

**Sorrow. *The Seven Sorrows of the Virgin*.** *See* Mary.

**Sort. *Out of sorts.*** Not in good health and spirits. The French *être dérangé* explains the metaphor. If cards are *out of sorts* they are *deranged*, and if a person is *out of sorts* the health or spirits are out of order.

In printers' language *sorts* is applied to particular pieces of type considered as part of the fount, and a printer is *out of sorts* when he has run short of some particular letters, figures, stops, etc.

***To run upon sorts.*** In printing, said of work which requires an unusual number of certain letters, etc.; as an index, which requires a disproportionate number of capitals.

**Sortes** (Lat. *sors, sortis*, chance, lot). A species of divination performed by selecting passages from a book haphazard. Virgil's *Aeneid* was anciently the favourite work for the purpose (*Sortes Virgilianae*), but the Bible (*Sortes Biblicae*) has also been in common use.

The method is to open the book at random, and the passage you touch by chance with your finger is the oracular response. Severus consulted Virgil, and read these words: 'Forget not thou, O Roman, to rule the people with royal sway.' Gordianus, who reigned only a few days, hit upon this verse: 'Fate only showed him on the earth, but suffered him not to tarry'; and Dr Wellwood gives an instance respecting King Charles I and Lord Falkland. Falkland, to amuse the king, suggested this kind of augury, and the king hit upon iv, 615–620, the gist of which is that 'evil wars would break out, and the king lose his life'. Falkland, to laugh the matter off, said he would show his Majesty how ridiculously the 'lot' would foretell the next fate, and he lighted on xi, 152–181, the lament of Evander for the untimely death of his son Pallas. King Charles soon after mourned over his noble friend who was slain at Newbury (1643).

In Rabelais (III, x) Panurge consults the *Sortes Virgilianae et Homericae* on the burning question, whether or not he should marry. In Cornelius Agrippa's *De Vanitate Scientiarum*, c. iv, there is a passage violently reprobating the *Sortes*.

**S O S.** *See under* S.

**Sotadic Verse.** *See* Palindrome.

**Soter.** Ptolemy I of Egypt (d.283 BC) was given this surname, meaning *the Preserver* by the Rhodians because he compelled Demetrius to raise the siege of Rhodes (304 BC).

**Sothic Period, Year.** The Persian year consists of 365 days, so that a day is lost in four years, amounting in the course of 1,460 years to a year. This period of 1,460 years is called a *sothic period* (Gr. *sothis*, the dog-star, at whose rising it commences), and the reclaimed year made up of the bits is called a *sothic year*. *See* Canicular Period.

**Soul.** Among the ancient Greeks the *soul* was the seat of the passions and desires, which animals have in common with man, and the *spirit* the highest and distinctive part of man. In 1 Thess. Paul says; 'I pray God your whole spirit, soul, and body be preserved blameless unto the coming of our Lord Jesus Christ.' *See also* Heb. 4:12; 1 Cor. 2:14 and 15; 15:45, 46.

Heraclitus held the soul to be a spark of the stellar essence: *scintilla stellaris essentiae* (Macrobius, *Somnium Scipionis*, i, 14).

> Vital spark of heavenly flame!
> Quit, oh quit this mortal frame.
>
> Pope, *The Dying Christian to his Soul*

Both the Greeks and Romans seemed to think that the soul made its escape with life out of the death-wound.

The Moslems say that the souls of the faithful assume the forms of snow-white birds, and nestle under the throne of Allah until the resurrection, and hold that it is necessary, when a man is bow-strung, to relax the rope a little before death occurs to let the soul escape.

In Egyptian hieroglyphics the soul is represented by several emblems, as a basket of fire, a heron, a hawk with a human face, and a ram.

***All Souls' Day.*** November 2nd, the day following All Saints' Day, set apart by the Roman Catholic Church for a solemn service for the repose of the departed. In England it was formerly observed by ringing the *Soul bell* (or passing-bell), by making and distributing *soul cakes*, blessing beans, etc.

***Soul cakes.*** Cakes formerly given in Staffordshire, Cheshire, and elsewhere on All Souls' Day, to the poor who go *a-souling*, i.e. begging for soul cakes. The words used were –

> Soul, soul, for soul-cake
> Pray you, good mistress, a soul cake.

**South-Sea Scheme** or **Bubble.** A stock-jobbing scheme devised by Sir John Blunt, a lawyer, in 1710, and floated by the Earl of Oxford in the following year. The object of the company was to buy up the National Debt, and to be allowed the sole privilege of trading in the South Seas. Spain refused to give trading facilities, so the money was used in other speculative ventures and, by careful 'rigging' of the market, £100 shares were run up to over ten times that sum. The bubble burst in 1720 and ruined thousands. The term is applied to any hollow scheme which has a splendid promise, but whose collapse will be sudden and ruinous. *Cp.* Mississippi Bubble.

**Southcottians.** The followers of Joanna Southcott (1750–1814), a domestic servant who became a religious fanatic and gave herself out as the

> woman clothed with the son, and the moon under her feet, and upon her head a crown of twelve stars. (Rev. 12:1)

Although 64 years old she was to be delivered of a son, the Shiloh of Gen. 49:10 –

> The sceptre shall not depart from Judah, nor a lawgiver from between his feet, until Shiloh come; and unto him shall the gathering of the people be.

October 19th, 1814, was the date fixed for the birthday; but no birth took place, and the expectant mother died of dropsy ten days later. Her rhymed and other prophecies were published in *A Book of Wonders* (1814), and it is said that the sect she founded still exists.

**Sovereign.** A strangely misspelled word (from Lat. *superanus*, supreme), the last syllable being assimilated to *reign*. French *souverain* is nearer the Latin; Ital., *sovrano*; Span, *soberano*.

A gold coin of this name, value 22*s*. 6*d*., was issued by Henry VIII, and so called because he was represented on it in royal robes; but the modern sovereign of 20*s*. value was not issued till 1817. Just a hundred years later, during the Great War, its issue was suspended in England (though not in the Dominions) and its place taken by paper Treasury Notes.

**Sow** (the female pig).

***A pig of my own sow.*** Said of that which is the result of one's own action.

***A still sow.*** A cunning and selfish man; one wise in his own interest; one who avoids talking at meals that he may enjoy his food the better. So called from the old proverb, 'The still sow eats the wash' or 'draff'.

> We do not act that often jest and laugh;
> 'Tis old, but true, 'Still swine eat all the draugh.'
> Shakespeare, *Merry Wives of Windsor*, 4, 2

***As drunk as David's sow.*** Very drunk indeed. *See* Davy.

***To get the wrong sow by the ear.*** To capture the wrong individual, to take the wrong end of the stick, hit upon the wrong thing.

***To send a sow to Minerva.*** To teach your grandmother how to suck eggs, to instruct one more learned in the subject than yourself. From the old Latin proverb, *Sus Minervam docet* (a pig teaching Minerva), which meant the same thing.

***You cannot make a silk purse out of a sow's ear.*** *See* Silk.

*See also* Pig-iron.

**Spade.** The spade of playing cards is so called from Span. *espada*, a sword, the suit in Spanish packs being marked with short swords; in French and British cards the mark – largely through the similarity in name – has been altered to something like the blade of a sharp-pointed spade.

***Spade guinea.*** An English gold coin value 21*s*., minted 1787–99, so called because it bears a shield like the 'spade' on playing cards on the reverse. The legend is M. B. F. et H. Rex F. D. B. L. D. S. R. I. A. T. et E. – Magnae Britanniae, Franciae, et Hiberniae Rex; Fidei Defensor; Brunsvicensis, Lunenburgensis Dux; Sacri Romani Imperii Archi Thesaurarius et Elector.

***To call a spade a spade.*** To be straightforward, outspoken, and blunt, even to the point of rudeness; to call things by their proper names without any beating about the bush.

> I have learned to call wickedness by its own terms: a fig a fig; and a spade a spade.
> John Knox

This is a translation of Erasmus's rendering of the old Latin proverb – *ficus ficus, ligonem ligonem vocat*.

> The world's too squeamish now to bear plain words
> Concerning deeds it acts with gust enough:
> But, thanks to wine-lees and democracy,
> We've still our stage where truth calls spade a spade!
> Browning, *Aristophanes' Apology*

**Spagyric.** Pertaining to alchemy; the term seems to have been invented by Paracelsus (*q.v.*). Alchemy is 'the spagyric art', and an alchemist a 'spagyrist'.

***Spagyric food.*** Cagliostro's name for the elixir of immortal youth.

**Spain.** *See* Hispania.

***Castles in Spain.*** *See* Castle.

***Patron saint of Spain.*** St James the Greater, who is said to have preached the Gospel in Spain, where what are called his relics are preserved.

**Span New.** *See* Spick.

**Spaniel.** The Spanish dog, from *español*, through the French.

**Spanish.** ***Spanish fly.*** The cantharis, a coleopterous insect used in medicine. Cantharides are dried and used externally as a blister and internally as a stimulant to the genito-urinary organs; they were formerly considered to act as an aphrodisiac.

***Spanish worm.*** An old name for a nail concealed in a piece of wood, against which a carpenter jars his saw or chisel.

***The Spanish Main.*** Properly, the northern coast of South America, going westward from the mouth of the Orinoco to the Isthmus of Panama, or a bit farther; the *main*-land bordering the Caribbean Sea, called by the Spanish conquerors *Tierra Firme*. The term is often applied, however, to the curving chain of islands forming the northern and eastern boundaries of the Caribbean Sea, beginning from Mosquito, near the isthmus, and including Jamaica, St Domingo, the Leeward Islands, and the Windward Islands, to the coast of Venezuela in South America.

**Spanker.** Used of a fast horse, also – colloquially – of something or someone that is an exceptionally fine specimen, a 'stunner'.

In nautical language the *spanker* is the fore-and-aft sail set upon the mizen-mast of a three-masted vessel, and the jigger-mast of a four-masted vessel. There is no spanker in a one- or two-masted vessel of any rig.

**Spare the rod, etc.** *See* Rod.

**Spartan.** The inhabitants of ancient Sparta, one of the leading city-states of Greece, were noted for their frugality, courage, and stern discipline; hence, one who can bear pain unflinchingly is termed 'a Spartan', a very frugal diet is 'Spartan fare', etc. It was a Spartan mother who, on handing her son the shield he was to carry into battle, said that he must come back either with it or on it.

She answer'd, 'Peace! and why should I not play
The Spartan Mother with emotion, be
The Lucius Junius Brutus of my kind?'
Tennyson, *The Princess*, ii, 282

***Spartan dog.*** A blood-hound; a bloodthirsty man.

O Spartan dog
More fell than anguish, hunger or the sea.
Shakespeare, *Othello*, 5, 2

**Spasmodic School, The.** A name applied by Professor Aytoun to certain authors of the 19th century, whose writings were distinguished by forced conceits and unnatural style. The most noted are Bailey (author of *Festus*), Gerald Massey, Alexander Smith, and Sydney Dobell.

**Speaker.** The title of the presiding officer and official spokesman of the British House of Commons, the United States House of Representatives, and of some other legislative assemblies.

In England the Speaker has autocratic and almost absolute power in the control of debates and internal arrangements of the House, etc.; he is elected by the members irrespective of party, and ceases to be a 'party man', having no vote – except in cases of a tie, when he can give a casting vote. He holds office for the duration of that Parliament, but by custom (not law) is invariably reappointed unless he wishes to resign (in which case he goes to the House of Lords); and custom has ordained that at a General Election he should be returned unopposed.

The Lord Chancellor is *ex officio* Speaker of the House of Lords.

***To catch the Speaker's eye.*** The rule in the House of Commons is that the member whose rising to address the House is first observed by the Speaker is allowed precedence.

**Speaking. *A speaking likeness.*** A very good and lifelike portrait; one that makes you imagine that the subject is just going to speak to you.

***Speaking heads.*** Fable and romance tell of a good many artificial heads that could speak (*cp.* Brazen head); among the best known are:

The statue of Memnon, in Egypt, which uttered musical sounds when the morning sun darted on it.

That of Orpheus, at Lesbos, which is said to have predicted the bloody death that terminated the expedition of Cyrus the Great into Scythia.

The head of Minos, fabled to have been brought by Odin to Scandinavia, and to have uttered responses.

The Brazen Head (*q.v.*) of Roger Bacon, and that of Gerbert, afterwards Pope Sylvester II (10th cent.).

An earthen head made by Albertus Magnus in the 13th century, which both spoke and moved. Thomas Aquinas broke it, whereupon the mechanist exclaimed: 'There goes the labour of thirty years!'

Alexander's statue of Esculapius; it was supposed to speak, but Lucian says the sounds were uttered by a man concealed, and conveyed by tubes to the statue.

The 'ear of Dionysius' communicated to Dionysius, Tyrant of Syracuse, whatever was uttered by suspected subjects shut up in a state prison. This 'ear' was a large black opening in a rock, about 50 ft high, and the sound was communicated by a series of channels not unlike those of the human ear.

***They are not on speaking terms.*** Said of friends who have fallen out; they do not even nod in the street or say 'How d'ye do?'

**Spear.** If a knight kept the point of his spear forward when he entered a strange land, it was a declaration of war; if he carried it on his shoulder with the point behind him, it was a token of friendship. In Ossian (*Temora*, i) Cairbar asks if Fingal comes in peace, to which Mor-annal replies: 'In peace he comes not, king of Erin, I have seen his forward spear.'

***The spear of Achilles.*** *See* Achilles' spear: Achillea.

***The spear of Ithuriel.*** *See* Ithuriel.

***The spear-side.*** The male line of descent, called by the Anglo-Saxons *spere-healfe*. *Cp.* Spindle-side.

***To break a spear.*** To fight in a tournament.

***To pass under the spear.*** To be sold by auction, sold 'under the hammer'. Writing to Pepys (Aug. 12th, 1689) Evelyn speaks of 'the noblest library that ever passed under the speare'. The phrase is from the Latin *sub hasta vendere*.

**Special Pleading.** Quibbling; making your own argument good by forcing certain words or phrases from their obvious and ordinary meaning. A pleading in law means a written statement of a cause *pro* and *con*, and 'special pleaders' are persons who have been called to the bar, but do not speak as advocates. They advise on evidence, draw up affidavits, state the merits and demerits of a cause, and so on. After a time most special pleaders go to the bar, and many get advanced to the bench.

**Specie, Species,** means literally 'what is visible' (Lat. *species*, appearance). As things are distinguished by their visible forms, it has come to mean *kind* or *class*. As drugs and condiments at one time formed the most important articles of merchandise, they were called *species* – still retained in the French *épices*, and English *spices*. Again, as bank-notes represent money, money itself is called *specie*, the thing represented.

**Spectacles.** In cricket, when a player scores a 'duck's egg' (i.e. nothing at all) in each of his two innings of one match, he is said to make 'a pair of spectacles'.

**Spectre of the Brocken.** An optical illusion, first observed on the Brocken (the highest peak of the Hartz range in Saxony), in which shadows of the spectators, greatly magnified, are projected on the mists about the summit of the mountain opposite. In one of De Quincey's opium-dreams there is a powerful description of the Brocken spectre.

**Spectrum, Spectra, Spectre** (Lat. *specto*, I behold). In optics a *spectrum* is the image of a sunbeam beheld on a screen, after refraction by one or more prisms. *Spectra* are the images of objects left on the eye after the objects themselves are removed from sight. A *spectre* is the apparition of a person no longer living or not bodily present.

**Speculate** means to look out of a watch-tower, to spy about (Lat. *speculari*). Metaphorically, to look at a subject with the mind's eye, to spy into it; in *commerce*, to purchase articles which your mind has speculated on, and has led you to expect will prove profitable.

***Specularis lapis,*** what we should now call window-glass, was some transparent stone or mineral, such as mica.

**Speculum Humanae Salvationis** (*The Mirror of Human Salvation*). A kind of extended *Biblia Pauperum* (*q.v.*) telling pictorially the Bible story from the fall of Lucifer to the Redemption of Man, with explanations of each picture in Latin rhymes. MS copies of the 12th century are known; but its chief interest is that it was one of the earliest of printed books, having been printed about 1467.

**Speech. *Parts of speech.*** *See* Part. *Speech is silver* (or *silvern*), *silence is golden*. An old proverb, said to be of oriental origin, pointing to the advantage of keeping one's own counsel. The Hebrew equivalent is 'If a word be worth one shekel, silence is worth two'.

***Speech was given to man to disguise his thoughts.*** This epigram was attributed to Talleyrand by Barrère in his *Memoirs*; but though Talleyrand no doubt used it he was not its author. Voltaire, in his XIVth Dialogue (*Le Chapon et la Poularde*), had said –

> Men use thought only as authority for their injustice, and employ speech only to conceal their thoughts.

Goldsmith, in *The Bee*, iii (1759), has –

> The true use of speech is not so much to express our wants as to conceal them.

And Bishop South, preaching on April 30th, 1676, said in his sermon –

> Speech was given to the ordinary sort of men, whereby to communicate their mind; but to wise men, whereby to conceal it.

**Spell.** A turn of work done by a man or group of men in relief of another man or group; hence, the period of one's turn of work. The word was formerly applied to the gang itself, and is probably the A.S. *spala*, a substitute.

***A pretty good spell.*** A long bout or pull, as a 'spell at the capstan', etc.

***Spell ho!*** An exclamation to signify that the allotted time has expired, and men are to be relieved by another set.

***To spell*** is to relieve another at his work.

**Spellbinders.** Orators who hold their audience *spellbound*, that is, fascinated, charmed, as though bound by a spell or magic incantation.

> Potent was the spell that bound thee
> Not unwilling to obey.
>
> Wordsworth, *Poems of the Imagination*, xxxv

The word came into use in America in the presidential election of 1888, and has been used of British political orators of persuasive eloquence – especially Mr Lloyd George.

> The Hon. Daniel Dougherty says: 'The proudest day of his life was when he beheld his name among the "spell-binders" who held the audience in rapture with their eloquence.'
>
> *Liberty Review*, July 7th, 1894, p. 13

**Spencer.** Now applied to a close-fitting bodice worn by women, but formerly the name of an outer coat without skirts worn by men; so named from the second Earl Spencer (1758–1834).

**Spenserian Metre.** The metre devised by Spenser (1592), founded on the Italian *ottava rima*, for his *Faërie Queene*. It is a stanza of nine iambic lines, all of ten syllables except the last, which is an Alexandrine. Only three different rhymes are admitted into a stanza, and these are disposed: a b a b b c b c c.

The stanza was used by Thomson (*Castle of Indolence*), Shenstone (*Schoolmistress*), Byron (*Childe Harold*), etc.

**Spheres.** In the Ptolemaic system of astronomy (*q.v.*) the earth, as the centre of the universe, was supposed to be surrounded by nine spheres of invisible space, the first seven carrying the 'planets' as then known, viz., (1) Diana or the Moon, (2) Mercury, (3) Venus, (4) Apollo or the Sun, (5) Mars, (6) Jupiter, and (7) Saturn; the eighth, the Starry Sphere, carrying the fixed stars, and the ninth, the Crystalline Sphere, added by Hipparchus in the 2nd century BC to account for the precession of the equinoxes. Finally, in the Middle Ages, was added a tenth sphere, the *Primum mobile* (*q.v.*), a solid barrier which enclosed the universe and shut it off from Nothingness and the Empyrean. These last two spheres carried neither star nor planet.

> They pass the planets seven, and pass the fixed [starry sphere],
> And that crystalline sphere … and that First-Moved.
>
> Milton, *Paradise Lost*, iii, 482

***The music,*** or ***harmony, of the spheres.*** Pythagoras, having ascertained that the pitch of notes depends on the rapidity of vibrations, and also that the planets move at different rates of motion, concluded that the planets must make sounds in their motion according to their different rates; and that, as all things in nature are harmoniously made, the different sounds must harmonise; whence the old theory of the 'harmony of the spheres'. Kepler has a treatise on the subject.

> There's not the smallest orb which thou behold'st
> But in his motion like an angel sings,
> Still quiring to the young-eyed cherubims.
>
> Shakespeare, *Merchant of Venice*, 5, 1

Plato says that a siren sits on each planet, who carols a most sweet song, agreeing to the motion of her own particular planet, but harmonising with all the others. Hence Milton speaks of the 'celestial syrens' harmony that sit upon the nine enfolded spheres'. (*Arcades.*)

**Sphinx.** A monster of ancient mythology; in Greece represented as having the head of a woman, the body of a lion, and winged; in Egypt as a wingless lion with the head and breast of a man.

The Grecian Sphinx was generally said to be a daughter of Typhon and Chimaera; she infested Thebes, setting the inhabitants a riddle and devouring all those who could not solve it. The riddle was –

> What goes on four feet, on two feet, and three,
> But the more feet it goes on the weaker it be?

and it was at length solved by Oedipus (*q.v.*) with the answer that it was a man, who as an infant crawls upon all-fours, in manhood goes erect on his two feet, and in old age supports his tottering legs with a staff. On hearing this correct answer the Sphinx slew herself, and Thebes was delivered.

The Egyptian sphinx is a typification of Ra, the sun god. The colossal statue of the reclining monster was old in the days of Cheops, when the Great Pyramid, near which it lies, was built. It is hewn out of the solid rock; its length is 140 ft, and its head 30 ft from crown to chin.

**Spick and Span New.** Quite and entirely new. A *spic* is a spike or nail, and a *span* is a chip. So that a spick and span new ship is one in which every nail and chip is new. According to Dr Johnson, who, in recording the term says it is one which he 'should not have expected to have found authorised by a polite writer', *span new* is from A.S. *spannan*, to stretch, and was originally used of cloth newly extended or dressed at the cloth-maker's, and *spick and span* is newly extended on the spikes or tenters. He gives quotations from Samuel Butler, Bishop Burnet, and Dean Swift, but cannot help adding 'it is however a low word'.

**Spider.** There are many old wives' fables about the spider, the most widespread being that they are venomous. Shakespeare alludes to this more than once –

> Let thy spiders, that suck up thy venom,
> And heavy-galted toads lie in their way.
>
> *Richard II*, 3, 2

There may be in the cup
A spider steeped, and one may drink, depart,
And yet partake no venom. *Winter's Tale*, 2, 1

and in the examination into the murder of Sir Thomas Overbury, one of the witnesses deposed 'that the countess wished him to get the strongest poison that he could ...' Accordingly he brought seven great spiders.

Other tales were that spiders would never spin a web on a cedar roof, and that fever could be cured by wearing a spider in a nutshell round the neck.

Cured by wearing a spider hung round one's neck
in a nutshell. Longfellow, *Exangeline*

Spiders were credited with other medicinal virtues. A common cure for jaundice in country parts of England was to swallow a large live house-spider rolled up in butter, while in the south of Ireland a similar 'remedy' was given for ague.

Yet another story was that spiders spin only on dark days:

The subtle spider never spins
But on dark days, his slimy gins.
S. Butler, *On a Nonconformist*, iv

***Bruce and the spider.*** In 1305 Robert Bruce was crowned at Scone king of Scotland, but, being attacked by the English, retreated to Ireland, and all supposed him to be dead. While lying *perdu* in the little island of Rathlin he one day noticed a spider try six times to fix its web on a beam in the ceiling. 'Now shall this spider (said Bruce) teach me what I am to do, for I also have failed six times.' The spider made a seventh effort and succeeded; whereupon Bruce left the island (1307), collected 300 followers, landed at Carrick, and at midnight surprised the English garrison in Turnberry Castle; he next overthrew the Earl of Gloucester, and in two years made himself master of well-nigh all Scotland, which Edward III declared in 1328 to be an independent kingdom. Scott tells us (*Tales of a Grandfather*) that in remembrance of this incident it has always been deemed a foul crime in Scotland for any of the name of Bruce to injure a spider.

I will grant you, my father, that this valiant burgess of Perth is one of the best-hearted men that draws breath ... He would be as loth, in wantonness, to kill a spider, as if he were a kinsman to King Robert of happy memory.
Scott, *Fair Maid of Perth*, ch. ii

***Frederick the Great and the spider.*** While Frederick II was at Sans Souci, he one day went into his anteroom, as usual, to drink a cup of chocolate, but set his cup down to fetch his handkerchief from his bedroom. On his return he found a great spider had fallen from the ceiling into his cup. He called for fresh chocolate, and next moment heard the report of a pistol. The cook had been suborned to poison the chocolate, and, supposing his treachery had been found out, shot himself. On the ceiling of the room in Sans Souci a spider has been painted (according to tradition) in remembrance of this story.

***Mahomet and the spider.*** When Mahomet fled from Mecca he hid in a certain cave, with the Koreishites close upon him. Suddenly an acacia in full leaf sprang up at the mouth of the cave, a wood-pigeon had its nest in the branches, and a spider had woven its net between the tree and the cave. When the Koreishites saw this, they felt persuaded that no one could have entered recently, and went on.

**Spidireen.** A sailors' name for an imaginary vessel. If a sailor is asked what ship he belongs to, and does not choose to tell, he will say, 'The spidireen frigate with nine decks.' Officers who do not want to tell their quarters, give B.K.S. (*q.v.*) as their address.

**Spigot.** ***Spare at the spigot and spill at the bung.*** To be parsimonious in trifles and wasteful in great matters, like a man who stops his beer-tub at the vent-hole and leaves it running at the bung-hole.

**Spike.** Slang for the workhouse; *to go on the spike* is to become a workhouse inmate.

***To get the spike.*** To get the needle. *See* Needle.

***To spike one's guns for him.*** To render his plans abortive, frustrate the scheme he has been laying, 'draw his teeth'. The allusion is to the old way of making a gun useless by driving a spike into the touch-hole.

**Spilt Milk.** *See* Cry.

**Spindle-side.** The female line of descent (*cp.* Spear-side). The spindle was the pin on which the thread was wound from the spinning-wheel.

**Spinning Jenny.** *See* Jenny.

**Spinster.** An unmarried woman.

The fleece which was brought home by the Anglo-Saxons in summer, was spun and woven into clothing by the female part of each family during the winter. King Edward *the Elder* commanded his daughters to be instructed in the use of the distaff. Alfred the Great, in his will, calls the female part of his family the *spindle side*; and it was a regularly received axiom with our frugal forefathers, that no young woman was fit to be a wife till she had spun for herself a set of body, table, and bed linen. Hence the maiden was termed a spinner or spinster, and the married woman a wife or 'one who has been a weaver'.

It is said that the heraldic *lozenge*, in which the armorial bearings of a woman are depicted instead of, in the case of a man, on a *shield*, originally represented a spindle. Among the Romans the bride carried a distaff, and Homer tells us that Kryseis was to spin and share the king's bed.

**Spirit.** Properly, the breath of life, from Lat. *spiritus* (*spirare*, to breathe, blow):

> And the Lord God formed man of the dust of the ground, and breathed into his nostrils the breath of life, and man became a living soul.
>
> Gen. 2:7

Hence, life or the life principle, the soul; a disembodied soul (a ghost or apparition), or an immaterial being that never was supposed to have had a body (sprite), as a gnome, elf, or fairy; also, the temper or disposition of mind as animated by the breath of life, as *in good spirits*, *high-spirited*, *a man of spirit*.

The mediaeval physiological notion (adopted from Galen) was that spirit existed in the body in three kinds, viz., (1) the *Natural spirit*, the principle of the 'natural functions' – growth, nutrition, and generation, said to be a vapour rising from the blood and having its seat in the liver: (2) the *Vital spirit*, which arose in the heart by mixture of the air breathed in with the natural spirit and supplied the body with heat and life: and (3) the *Animal spirit*, which was responsible for the power of motion and sensation, and for the rational principle generally; this was a modification of the vital spirit, effected in the brain.

*Spirit* also came to mean any volatile or airy agent of essence; and hence, through the old alchemists, is still used of solutions in alcohol of a volatile principle and of any strong distilled alcoholic liquor. The alchemists named four substances only as 'spirits', viz., mercury, arsenic, sal ammoniac, and sulphur:

> The first spirit quyksilver called is:
> The secound orpiment; the thrid I wis
> Sal armoniac; and the ferth bremstoon.
>
> Chaucer, *Canon's Yeoman's Prologue*

The *Elemental spirits* of Paracelsus and the Rosicrucians, i.e. those which presided over the four elements, were – the *Salamanders* (of fire), *Gnomes* (earth), *Sylphs* (air), and *Undines* (water).

***To spirit away.*** To kidnap, abduct; to make away with speedily and secretly. The phrase first came into use in the 17th century, in connection with kidnapping youths and transporting them to the West Indian plantations.

**Spiritualism.** The belief that communication between the living and the spirits of the departed can and does take place, usually through the agency of a specially qualified person (a 'medium') and often by means of rapping, table-turning, or automatic writing; the system, doctrines, practice, etc., arising from this belief. Hence, *Spiritualist*, one who maintains or practises this belief.

In Philosophy *Spiritualism* – the antithesis of *materialism* – is the doctrine that the spirit exists as distinct from matter, or as the only reality.

**Spit.** ***Spitting for luck***. Spitting was a charm against enchantment among the ancient Greeks and Romans. Pliny says it averted witchcraft, and availed in giving an enemy a shrewder blow.

> Thrice on my breast I spit to guard me safe
> From fascinating charms. Theocritus

Boys often spit for luck on a piece of money given to them; boxers spit on their hands, and costermongers on the first money they take in the day for the same reason.

**Spital** or **Spittle.** A hospital.

> A spittle or hospitall for poore folks diseased; a spittle hospitall, or lazarhouse for lepers.
>
> Baret, *Alveaire* (1580)

Hence *Spitalfields*, the site in London where, in 1197, a spital or almshouse was built in the fields by Walter Brune and his wife Rosia.

**Spitfire.** An irascible person, whose angry words are like fire spit from the mouth of a fire-eater.

**Spittle Sermons.** Sermons preached formerly on Easter Monday and Tuesday at St Mary Spital, Spitalfields, in a pulpit erected expressly for the purpose. Subsequently they were given at St Bride's, and later at Christchurch, Newgate Street. Ben Jonson alludes to them in his *Underwoods*, lx.

**Splay** is a contraction of *display* (to unfold; Lat. *dis-plico*). A *splay window* is one in a V-shape, the external opening being very wide, to admit as much light as possible, but the inner opening being very small. A *splay-foot* is a foot displayed or turned outward. A *splay-mouth* is a wide mouth, like that of a clown.

**Spleen,** the soft vascular organ placed to the left of the stomach and acting on the blood, was once believed to be the seat of melancholy and ill-humour. The fern *spleenwort* was supposed to remove splenic disorders.

**Splice.** To marry. Very strangely, 'splice' means to *split* or *divide* (Ger. *spleissen*, to split). The way it came to signify *unite* is this: Ropes' ends are first untwisted before the strands are interwoven. Joining two ropes together by interweaving their strands is 'splicing' them. Splicing wood is joining two boards together, the term being borrowed from the sailor.

***To splice the main brace.*** *See* Main Brace.

**Split.** To give away one's accomplices, betray secrets, 'peach'.

***To split hairs.*** *See* Hair.

***To split with laughter.*** To laugh uproariously or unrestrainedly; to 'split one's sides'.

***To split the infinitive.*** To interpose some word between *to* and the verb, as 'to thoroughly understand the subject'. This construction is branded as a solecism by stylists, but it is as old as the English language, and there are few of our best writers who have not employed it.

> Without permitting himself to actually mention the name.
>
> Matthew Arnold, *On Translating Homer*, iii
>
> It becomes a truth again, after all, as he happens to newly consider it.
>
> Browning, *A Soul's Tragedy*
>
> Implore them to partially enlighten her.
>
> Geo. Meredith, *The Egoist*

**Spoke.** ***To put a spoke in one's wheel.*** To interfere with his projects and frustrate them; to thwart him. When solid wheels were used, the driver was provided with a pin or spoke, which he thrust into one of the three holes made to receive it, to skid the cart when it went down-hill.

**Sponge.** ***Throw up the sponge.*** Give up; confess oneself beaten. The metaphor is from boxing matches, for when a second tossed a sponge into the air it was a sign that his man was beaten.

> We must stand up to our fight now, or throw up the sponge. There's no two ways about the matter.
>
> Boldrewood, *Robbery under Arms*, ch. xxxi

***To sponge on a man.*** To live on him like a parasite, sucking up all he has as a dry sponge will suck up water.

A *sponger* is a mean parasite who is always accepting the hospitality of those who will give it and never makes any adequate return.

**Sponging House.** A house where persons arrested for debt were kept for twenty-four hours, before being sent to prison. They were generally kept by a bailiff, and the person lodged was 'sponged' of all his money before leaving.

**Spoon.** A simpleton, a shallow prating duffer (*cp.* Wooden Spoon) used to be called a *spoon*, and hence the name came to be applied to one who indulged in foolish, sentimental love-making, and such a one is said to be *spoony*, and to be *spoons on* the girl.

In nautical phrase *to spoon* is to scud before the wind; and in sculling to dip the sculls so lightly in the water as to do little more than skim the surface.

***Apostle spoons.*** *See* Apostle.

***He hath need of a long spoon that eateth with the devil.*** You will want all your wits about you if you ally yourself with evil. Shakespeare alludes to this proverb in the *Comedy of Errors*, 4, 3; and again in the *Tempest*, 2, 2, where Stephano says: 'Mercy! mercy! this is a devil ... I will leave him, I have no long spoon.'

> Therefor behoveth hire a fol long spoon
> That schal ete with a feend.
>
> Chaucer, *Squire's Tale*, 594

***To be born with a silver spoon in one's mouth.*** *See* Silver.

**Spoonerism.** A ludicrous form of metathesis (*q.v.*) that consists of transposing the initial sounds of words so as to form some laughable combination; so called from the Rev. W. A. Spooner (1844–1930), Warden of New College, Oxford. Some of the best attributed to him are – 'We all know what it is to have a half-warmed fish within us' (for 'half-formed wish'); 'Yes, indeed; the Lord *is* a shoving leopard' ('loving Shepherd'); and 'Kingkering Kongs their titles take'. Sometimes the term is applied to the accidental transposition of whole words, as when the tea-shop waitress was asked for 'a glass bun and a bath of milk'.

**Sport.** ***To sport one's oak.*** *See* Oak.

The figurative meaning of *to sport* is to exhibit in public in a somewhat ostentatious way; the 'nut', for instance, will *sport* a highly coloured pair of socks, a new fashion in hats, or a monocle.

**Sporting Seasons in England.** The lawful season for venery, which began at Midsummer and lasted to Holy Rood Day, used to be called *the Time of Grace*. The fox and wolf might be hunted from the Nativity to the Annunciation; the roebuck from Easter to Michaelmas; the roe from Michaelmas to Candlemas; the hare from Michaelmas to Midsummer; and the boar from the Nativity to the Purification.

The modern times are as follows: those marked thus (*) are fixed by Act of Parliament.

*Black Game*,* from August 20th to December 10th; but in Somerset, Devon, and New Forest, from September 1st to December 10th.
*Blackcock*, August 20th to December 10th.
*Buck* hunting, August 20th to September 17th.
*Bustard*,* September 1st to March 1st.
*Red Deer* hunted, August 20th to September 30th.
*Eels*, (about) April 20th to October 28th.
*Fox* hunting, (about) October to Lady Day.
*Fox Cubs*, August 1st to the first Monday in November.
*Grouse* shooting,* August 12th to December 10th.
*Hares*, March 12th to August 12th.
*Hind*, hunted in October and again between April 10th and May 20th.
*Oyster* season, August 5th to May.
*Partridge* shooting.* September 1st to February 1st.
*Pheasant* shooting,* October 1st to February 1st
*Ptarmigan*, August 12th to December 10th.
*Quail*, August 12th to January 10th.
*Rabbits*, between October and March. Rabbits, as vermin, are shot at any time.
*Salmon*,* February 1st to September 1st.
*Salmon*, rod fishing,* November 1st to September 1st.
*Trout* fishing. May 1st to September 10th.
*Trout*, in the Thames, April 1st to September 10th.
*Woodcock*, (about) November to January.

For Ireland and Scotland there are special game-laws.

N.B. – Game in *England*: hare, pheasant, partridge, grouse, and moor-fowl; in *Scotland*, same as England, with the addition of ptarmigan; in *Ireland*, same as England, with the addition of deer, black-game, landrail, quail, and bustard.

**Sporus.** The name under which Pope satirised John, Lord Hervey (*see* **Fanny, Lord**) in his *Prologue to the Satires*:

Let Sporus tremble! What, that thing of silk?
Sporus! that mere white curd of ass's milk?
Satire or sense, alas! can Sporus feel?
Who breaks a butterfly upon a wheel?

The name, that of a favourite eunuch of Nero's, comes from Suetonius.

**Spot.** ***On the spot.*** At once; without having time to move away or do anything else; as – 'He answered on the spot', immediately, without hesitation.

***To knock spots off one.*** To excel him completely in something; originally an Americanism.

**Spouse** means one who has promised (Lat. *sponsus*, past part. of *spondere* to promise). In ancient Rome the friends of the parties about to be married met at the house of the woman's father to settle the marriage contract. This contract was called *sponsalia* (espousals); the man and woman were *spouses*.

***The spouse of Jesus.*** 'Our seraphic mother, the holy Teresa', born at Avila in 1515, is so called in the Roman Catholic Church.

All thy good works … shall
Weave a constellation
Of Crowns, with which the King thy spouse
Shall build up thy triumphant brows.

Crashaw, *Hymn to St Theresa* (1652)

**Spout.** ***To spout.*** To utter in a bombastic, declamatory manner; to declaim.

***Up the spout.*** At the pawnbroker's. In allusion to the 'spout' up which brokers send the articles ticketed. When redeemed they return down the spout – i.e. from the storeroom to the shop.

It's up the spout and Charley Wag
With wipes and tickers and what not
Until the squeezer nips your scrag,
Booze and the blowens cop the lot.

W. E. Henley, *Villon's Straight Tip*

**Sprat.** ***To throw a sprat to catch a mackerel.*** To give a small thing in the hope of getting something much more valuable. The French Say, 'A pea for a bean'.

**Spread-eagle.** The 'eagle displayed' of heraldry, i.e. an eagle with legs and wings extended, the wings being elevated. It is the device of the United States, and was hence humorously adopted as emblematic of bombast, hyperbole, and extravagant boasting. *Spread-eaglism* in a United States citizen is very much the counterpart of the more aggressive and bombastic forms of Jingoism (*q.v.*) in the Britisher.

***Spread-eagle oratory.*** 'A compound of exaggeration, effrontery, bombast, and extravagance, mixed with metaphors, platitudes, threats, and irreverent appeals flung at the Almighty.' (*North American Review*, November, 1858.)

In the navy a man was said to be *spread-eagled* when he was lashed to the rigging with outstretched arms and legs for flogging.

**Spring Tide.** The tide that springs or leaps or swells up. These full tides occur a day or two after the new and full moon, when the attraction of both sun and moon act in a direct line.

**Spruce.** Smart, dandified. The word is from the old Fr. *Pruce* (Ger. *Preussen*), Prussia, and was originally (16th cent.) applied to Prussian leather of which particularly neat and smart-looking jerkins were made.

> And after them, came, syr Edward Haward, then admyral, and with him sir Thomas Parre, in doblettes of Crimosin velvet, voyded lowe on the backe, and before to the cannell bone, laced on the breastes with chaynes of silver, and over that shorte clokes of Crimosyn satyne, and on their heades hattes after dauncers fashion, with fesauntes fethers in theim; They were appareyled after the fashion of Prusia or Spruce.
>
> *Hall's Chronicle*, *Henry VIII*, year 1 (1542)

***Spruce beer*** is made from the leaves of the *spruce fir*, this being a translation of the German name of the tree, *Sprossen-fichte*, literally 'sprouts-fir'.

**Sprung.** Slang for slightly intoxicated.

**Spunging House.** *See* Sponging.

**Spur.** ***On the spur of the moment.*** Instantly; without stopping to take thought.

***Spur money.*** A small fine formerly imposed on those who entered a church wearing spurs, because of the interruption caused to divine service by their ringing. It was collected by the choir-boys or the beadles.

***The Battle of Spurs.*** A name given to the battles of Guinegate (1513) and Courtrai (1302). The former, between Henry VIII and the Duc de Longueville, was so called because the French used their spurs in flight more than their swords in fight; and the battle of Courtrai because the victorious Flemings gathered from the field more than 700 gilt spurs, worn by French nobles slain in the fight.

***To dish up the spurs.*** In Scotland, during the times of the Border feuds, when any of the great families had come to the end of their provisions the lady of the house sent up a pair of spurs for the last course, to intimate that it was time to put spurs to the horses and make a raid upon England for more cattle.

***To ride whip*** (or ***witch***) ***and spur.*** To ride with all possible speed: to trample down obstacles ruthlessly.

***To win his spurs.*** To gain the rank of knighthood. When a man was knighted, the person who dubbed him presented him with a pair of gilt spurs.

**Spy Wednesday.** A name given in Ireland to the Wednesday before Good Friday, when Judas bargained to become the spy of the Jewish Sanhedrin (Matt. 26:3–5, 14–16).

**Squab.** Short and fat; plump: a person, cushion, etc., like this (a fat woman is *squabba* in Swedish). A young pigeon – especially an unfledged one – is called a *squab*, and a pie of mutton, apples, and onions is called a squab pie in some parts of the country.

> Cornwall squab-pie, and Devon white-pot brings,
> And Leicester beans and bacon, fit for kings.
>
> King, *Art of Cookery*

***Poet Squab.*** So Rochester called Dryden, who was very corpulent.

**Squad, Squadron.** *See* Awkward Squad.

**Squalls.** ***Look out for squalls.*** Expect to meet with difficulties. A nautical term, a squall being a succession of sudden and violent gusts of wind (Icel. *skvala*).

**Square.** ***On the square.*** Straight and above board, honest. Also said of a Freemason, with allusion to the mason's square.

***To square a person.*** To bribe him, or to pay him for some extra trouble he has taken.

***To square the circle.*** To attempt an impossibility. The allusion is to the impossibility of exactly determining the precise ratio between the diameter and the circumference of a circle, and thus constructing a circle of the same area as a given square. Popularly it is 3.14159 … the next decimals would be 26537, but the numbers would go on *ad infinitum*.

***To square up to a person.*** To put oneself in a fighting attitude.

> Are you such fools
> To square for this?
>
> Shakespeare, *Titus Andronicus*, 2, 1

**Squeers.** *See* Dotheboys Hall.

**Squib.** A political joke, printed and circulated at election times against a candidate, with intent to bring him into ridicule, and to influence votes.

> Parodies, lampoons, rightly named squibs, fire and brimstone, ending in smoke, with a villainous smell of saltpetre.
>
> Dean Hole, *Rose-garden and Pulpit*

**Squinancy.** *See* Quinsy.

**Squintum, Doctor.** George Whitefield (1714–70), so called by Foote in his farce *The Minor*.

Theodore Hook applied the sobriquet to Edward Irving (1792–1834), who had an obliquity of the eyes.

**Squire.** In mediaeval times a youth of gentle birth attendant on a knight (*see* Esquire); now a landed proprietor, the chief country gentleman of a place.

***Squire of dames.*** Any cavalier who is devoted to ladies. Spenser, in his *Faërie Queene*, introduces the 'squire', and records his adventures.

**Stabat Mater** (Lat. The Mother was standing). The celebrated Latin hymn reciting the Seven Sorrows of the Virgin at the Cross, so called from its opening words, forming part of the service during Passion week, in the Roman Catholic Church. It was composed by Jacobus de Benedictis, a Franciscan of the 13th century, and has been set to music by Pergolese, Rossini, Haydn, etc.

**Stable.** ***Locking the stable door after the horse is stolen.*** Taking precautions after the mischief is done.

**Staff.** ***I keep the staff in my own hand.*** I keep possession; I retain the right. The staff was the ancient sceptre, and therefore, figuratively, it means power, authority, dignity, etc.

> Give up your staff, sir, and the king his realm.
>
> Shakespeare, *2 Henry VI*, 2, 3

***The staff of life.*** Bread, which is the *support* of life. Shakespeare says, 'The boy was the very staff of my age'. The allusion is to a staff which supports the feeble in walking.

> 'Bread,' says he, 'dear brothers, is the staff of life.'
>
> Swift, *Tale of a Tub*, iv

***To put down one's staff in a place.*** To take up one's residence. The allusion is to the tent-staff: where the staff is placed, there the tent is stretched, and the nomad resides.

***To strike staff.*** To lodge for the time being.

> Thou mayst see me at thy pleasure, for I intend to
> strike my staff at yonder hostelry.
>
> Caesar Borgia, xv

**Stafford.** ***He has had a treat in Stafford Court.*** He has been thoroughly cudgelled. Of course, the pun is on the word *staff*, a stick. The French have a similar phrase: *Il a esté au festin de Martin Boston* (he has been to Jack Drum's entertainment).

Similarly, *Stafford law* is club law – a good beating.

**Stag.** The reason why a stag symbolises Christ is from the ancient idea that it draws serpents by its breath from their holes, and then tramples them to death. (Pliny, *Natural History*, viii, 50.)

***Stag in Christian art.*** The attribute of St Julian Hospitaller, St Felix of Valois, and St Aidan. When it has a crucifix between its horns it alludes to the legend of St Hubert. When luminous it belongs to St Eustachius.

***Stags.*** In Stock Exchange phraseology, are persons who apply for new shares, etc., on allotment, not because they wish to hold the shares, but because they hope to sell the allotment at a premium.

**Stagirite** or **Stagyrite.** Aristotle, who was born at Stagira, in Macedon (4th cent. BC).

> In one rich soul
> Plato, the Stagyrite, and Tully joined.
>
> Thomson, *Summer*, 1541
>
> And rules as strict his laboured work confine
> As if the Stagirite o'erlooked each line.
>
> Pope, *Essay on Criticism*
>
> And all the wisdom of the Stagirite.
> Enriched and beautified his studious mind.
>
> Wordsworth, *Epitaphs from Chiabresa*, ix

**Stalemate.** ***To stalemate a person.*** To bring him to a standstill, render his projects worthless or abortive. The phrase is from chess, *stalemate* being the position in which the king is the only movable piece and he, though not in check, cannot move without becoming so. *Stale* in this word is probably from O.Fr. *estal* (our *stall*), a fixed position.

**Stalking-horse.** A mask to conceal some design; a person put forward to mislead; a sham. Sportsmen often used to conceal themselves behind horses, and go on stalking step by step till they got within shot of the game.

> He uses his folly like a stalking-horse, and under
> the presentation of that he shoots his wit.
>
> Shakespeare, *As You Like It*, 5, 4

**Stammerer, The.** Louis II of France, *le Bégue* (846, 877–9).

Michael II, Emperor of the East (820, 829).

Notker of St Gall (830–912).

**Stamp.** ***'Tis of the right stamp*** – has the stamp of genuine merit. A metaphor taken from current coin, which is stamped with a recognised stamp and superscription.

> I weigh the man, not his title; 'tis not the king's
> stamp can make the metal heavier or better.
>
> Wycherley, *The Plain Dealer*, I, i (1677)
>
> The rank is but the guinea stamp;
> The man's the gowd for a' that!
>
> Burns, *Is There, for Honest Poverty?*

**Stand.** ***To be at a stand.*** To be in doubt as to further progress, perplexed at what to do next.

***To let a thing stand over.*** To defer consideration of it to a more favourable opportunity.

***To stand by.*** To be ready to give assistance in case of need. A *stand-by* is a person or thing on which one can confidently rely.

***To stand for a child.*** To be sponsor for it; to stand in its place and answer for it.

***To stand in with.*** To go shares; also, to have an understanding or community of interests with.

***To stand it out*** – persist in what one says. A translation of 'persist' (Lat. *per-sisto* or *per-sto*).

***To stand off and on.*** A nautical phrase for tacking in and out along the shore.

***To stand Sam, stand to reason, stand treat,*** etc. *See these words.*

***To stand to one's guns.*** To persist in a statement; not to give way. A military phrase.

> The Speaker said he hoped the gallant gentleman would try to modify his phrase; but Colonel Saunderson still stood to his guns.
>
> *Daily Graphic*, 3rd February, 1893

***To stand up for.*** Support, take his (or its) part.

***To stand upon one's privilege*** or ***on punctilios.*** Quietly to insist on one's position, etc., being recognised; this is the Latin *insisto*. In French, *Insister sur son privilège* or *sur des vétilles*.

**Standard.** A banner as the distinctive emblem of a Royal House, an army, or a nation, etc. The word first came into use in England in connection with the Battle of the Standard (*see below*), in telling of which Richard of Hexham (about 1139) says that the standard (a ship's mast with flags at the top) was so called because 'it was there that valour took its *stand* to conquer or die'. The word is, however, from Lat. *extendere*, to stretch out, through O.Fr. *estandard*.

Standards were formerly borne by others than royalties and nations, and varied in size according to the rank of the bearer. Thus, that of an *emperor* was 11 yards in length; of a *king*, 9 yards; of a *prince*, 7 yards; of a *marquis*, 6½ yards; of an *earl*, 6 yards; of a *viscount* or *baron*, 5 yards; of a *knight-banneret*, 4½ yards; of a *baronet*, 4 yards. They generally contained the arms of the bearer, his cognisance and crest, his motto or war-cry, and were fringed with his livery.

*Standard* is also applied to a measure of extent, weight, value, etc., which is established by law or custom as an example or criterion for others; and, in figurative use from this, to any criterion or principle, as 'The standard of an English gentleman'. The weights and measures were formerly known as 'the king's standard', and probably got the name in allusion to the king's standard being the central rallying point of an army, the point from which orders were issued.

In uses such as an *electric-light standard* (the lamp-post), *standard rose* (i.e. one that stands on its own stem and is not trained to a wall or espalier), etc., the word is the result of confusion with *stand*.

***The Battle of the Standard,*** between the English and the Scots, at Cuton Moor, near Northallerton, in 1138. Here David I, fighting on behalf of Matilda, was defeated by King Stephen's army under Raoul, Bishop of Durham, and Thurstan, Archbishop of York. It received its name from a ship's mast erected on a wagon, and placed in the centre of the English army; the mast displayed the standards of St Peter of York, St John of Beverley, and St Wilfred of Ripon. On the top was a little casket containing the consecrated host.

***The gold standard.*** A monetary standard based only on the value of gold.

***The standard of living,*** A conventional term to express the supposed degree of comfort or luxury usually enjoyed by a man, a family, or a nation: this may be *high* or *low* according to circumstances.

**Standing. *Standing orders.*** Rules or instructions constantly in force, especially those by-laws of the Houses of Parliament for the conduct of proceedings which stand in force till they are either rescinded or suspended. Their suspension is generally caused by a desire to hurry through a Bill with unusual expedition.

***The Standing Fishes Bible.*** *See* Bible, Specially named.

**Stand-offish.** Unsociable, rather contemptuously reserved.

**Stang. *To ride the stang.*** At one time a man who ill-treated his wife was made to sit on a *stang* (A.S. *staeng*, a pole) hoisted on men's shoulders. On this uneasy conveyance the 'stanger' was carried in procession amidst the hootings and jeerings of his neighbours. *Cp.* Skimmington.

**Stanhope.** The *Stanhope lens*, a cylindrical lens with spherical ends of different radii, and the *Stanhope press*, the first iron printing press to be used (1798), are so called from the noble inventor, Charles, 3rd Earl of Stanhope (1753–1816).

The light open one-seated carriage, with two or four wheels, called a *Stanhope*, gets its name from the Hon. and Rev. Fitzroy Stanhope (1787–1864), for whom the first of these conveyances was made.

**Stannaries, The.** The tin-mining districts of Cornwall and Devon (Lat. *stannum*, tin), which, from the earliest times to 1752 had their own parliament, consisting of twenty-four *stannators*, convened by the Lord Warden to the Duke of Cornwall. Until 1896 the administration of justice among the miners and others of these districts was in the hands of *Stannary Courts*, but at this date the business was transferred by Act of Parliament to the ordinary County Court.

**Star.** Figuratively applied to a specially prominent person on the stage, concert platform, etc., hence *star part*, the part taken by a leading actor, *star turn*, etc.

In ecclesiastical art a number of saints may be recognised by the star depicted with them; thus, St Bruno bears one on his breast; St Dominic, St Humbert, St Peter of Alcantare, one over their head, or on their forehead, etc.

A star of some form constitutes part of the insignia of every order of knighthood; the *Star and Garter*, a common inn sign, being in reference to the Most Noble Order of the Garter.

The stars were said by the old astrologers to have almost omnipotent influence on the lives and destinies of man (*cp.* Judges 5:20 – 'The stars in their courses fought against Sisera'), and to this old belief is due a number of phrases still common, as – *Bless my stars! You may thank your lucky stars*, *star-crossed* (not favoured by the stars, unfortunate), *to be born under an evil star*, etc.

> She made it plain, that Human Passion
> Was order'd by Predestination;
> That, if weak women went astray,
> Their Stars were more in Fault than They.
>
> Prior, *Hans Carvel*

***His star is in the ascendant.*** He is in luck's way; said of a person to whom some good fortune has fallen and who is very prosperous. According to astrology, those leading stars which are above the horizon at a person's birth influence his life and fortune; when those stars are in the ascendant, he is strong, healthy, and lucky; but when they are in the descendant below the horizon, his stars do not shine on him, he is in the shade and subject to ill-fortune. *Cp.* Houses, Astrological.

***I'll make you see stars!*** I'll 'put you through it'; literally, will give you such a blow in the eye with my fist that, when you are struck, you'll experience the optical illusion of seeing brilliant streaks, radiating and darting in all directions.

**Star Chamber.** A court of civil and criminal jurisdiction at Westminster, abolished in 1641, and notorious for its arbitrary proceedings, its chief activity being the punishment of such offences as the law had made no provision for.

So called either because the ceiling or roof was decorated with gilt stars, or because it was the chamber where the 'starrs' or Jewish documents were kept.

> It is well known that, before the banishment of the Jews by Edward I, their contracts and obligations were denominated ... starra or stars ... The room in the exchequer where the chests ... were kept was ... the starr-chamber.
>
> Blackstone, *Commentaries*, vol. ii, bk iv, p. 266

**Star of Bethlehem.** A bulbous plant of the lily family (*Ornithogallum umbellatum*), with star-shaped white flowers. The French peasants call it *La dame d'onze heures*, because it opens at eleven o'clock.

**Star of India.** A British order of knighthood, *The Most Exalted Order of the Star of India*, instituted in 1861 by Queen Victoria as a reward for services in and for India and a means of recognising the loyalty of native rulers. Its motto is 'Heaven's Light our Guide'.

**Starboard and Larboard.** Star- is the Anglo-Saxon *steor*, rudder, *bord*, side; meaning the right side of a ship (looking forwards). Larboard, for the left-hand side, is now obsolete, and 'port' is used instead. The word was earlier *leereboord* (A.S. *laere*, empty) that side being clear as the steersman stood on the star (*steer*) boord.

**Starry Sphere.** The eighth of the spheres (*q.v.*) of the Ptolemaic astronomers; also called the 'Firmament'.

> The Crystal Heaven is this, whose rigour guides
> And binds the starry sphere.
>
> Camoëns, *Lusiad*, Bk x

**Stars and Stripes** or the **Star-spangled Banner,** the flag of the United States of North America. The *stripes* are emblematic of the original thirteen States, and the *stars* – of which there are now forty-eight – of the States that have since been admitted into the Union.

> The first flag of the United States, raised by Washington June 2,1776, consisted of thirteen stripes, alternately red and white, with a blue canton emblazoned with the crosses of St George and St Andrew.
>
> In 1777 Congress ordered that the canton should have thirteen white stars in a blue field.
>
> In 1794 (after the admission of Vermont and Kentucky) the stripes and stars were each increased to fifteen.
>
> In 1818 S. R. Reid suggested that the original thirteen stripes should be restored, and stars added to signify the States in the union.
>
> The flag preceding 1776 represented a coiled rattlesnake with thirteen rattles, and the motto *Don't tread on me*. This was an imitation of the Scotch thistle and the motto *Nemo me impune lacessit*.

> Oh! say, does that star-spangled banner yet wave
> O'er the land of the free and the home of the brave?
>
> F. S. Key

**Starvation Dundas.** Henry Dundas, first Lord Melville (1740–1811) was so called by Walpole, because when the Opposition denounced the

Bill for restraining trade and commerce with the New England colonies (1775) on the ground that it would cause a famine in which the innocent would suffer with the guilty, he said that he was 'afraid' the Bill would not have this effect. It is in connection with this that the word first appears in English, but it is not clear that Dundas himself used it.

**Starved with Cold.** Half dead with cold (A.S. *steorfan*, to die). This used to be quite a common expression, but is now rarely heard except in the north.

**Stations. *The fourteen stations of the Catholic Church.*** These are generally called 'Stations of the Cross', and the whole series is known as the *via Calvaria* or *via Crucis*. Each station represents, by fresco, picture, or otherwise, some incident in the passage of Christ from the judgment hall to Calvary, and at each prayers are offered up in memory of the event represented. They are as follows:

(1) The condemnation to death.
(2) Christ is made to bear His cross.
(3) His first fall under the cross.
(4) The meeting with the Virgin.
(5) Simon the Cyrenean helps to carry the cross.
(6) Veronica wipes the sacred face.
(7) The second fall.
(8) Christ speaks to the daughters of Jerusalem.
(9) The third fall.
(10) Christ is stripped of His garments.
(11) The nailing to the cross.
(12) The giving up of the Spirit.
(13) Christ is taken down from the cross.
(14) The deposition in the sepulchre.

**Stator** (Lat. the stopper or arrestor). When the Romans fled from the Sabines, they stopped at a certain place and made terms with the victors. On this spot they afterwards built a temple to Jupiter, and called it the temple of Jupiter Stator or Jupiter who caused them to stop in their flight.

Here, Stator Jove and Phoebus, god of verse
The votive tablet I suspend. Prior

**Statute** (Lat. *statutum*, from *statuere*, to cause to stand; the same word, etymologically, as *statue*). A law enacted by a legislative body, an Act of Parliament; also laws enacted by the king and council before there were any regular parliaments. Hence, a *statute mile*, a *statute ton*, etc., is the measure as by law established and not according to local custom.

***On the statute book.*** Included among the laws of the nation: the *statute book* is the whole body of the laws.

***Statute fair.*** A mop fair. *See* Mop.

**Steaks, Sublime Society of the.** *See* Beefsteak Club, The.

**Steal. *One man may steal a horse, but another must not look over the hedge.*** *See* Horse.

***To steal a march on one.*** To come on one unexpectedly, to obain an advantage by stealth, as when an army appears unexpectedly before an enemy.

***Stolen sweets are always sweeter.*** Things procured by stealth, and game illicitly taken, have the charm of dexterity to make them the more palatable. Solomon says, 'Stolen waters are sweet, and bread eaten in secret is pleasant' (Prov. 9:17).

From busie cooks we love to steal a bit
Behind their backs and that in corners eat;
Nor need we here the reason why entreat;
All know the proverb, 'Stolen bread is sweet'.
*History of Joseph*, n.d.

In one of the songs in Act iii, sc. iv, of Randolph's *Amyntos* (1638) are the lines:

Furto cuncta magis bella,
Furto dulcior Puella,
Furto omnia decora,
Furto poma dulciora,

which were translated by Leigh Hunt as:

Stolen sweets are always sweeter,
Stolen kisses much completer,
Stolen looks are nice in chapels,
Stolen, stolen, be your apples.

**Steelyard.** A place (formerly a *yard* or enclosure) on the Thames just above London Bridge, where the Hanse merchants had their depot. The name is a mistranslation of Ger. *staalhof*, sample yard, *staal* meaning both *sample* and *steel*.

***Steelyard,*** the weighing machine with unequal arms, in which the article to be weighed is hung from the shorter arm and a weight moved along the other till they balance, is named from the metal and the measure (A.S. *gyrd, gerd*, a stick).

**Steenie.** A nickname given by James I to the handsome George Villiers, Duke of Buckingham. The half profane allusion is to Acts 6:15, where those who looked on Stephen the martyr 'saw his face as it had been the face of an angel'.

**Steeplechase.** A horse-race across fields, hedges, ditches, and other obstacles. The term arose in the late 18th cent. from a party of fox-hunters agreeing, on their return from an unsuccessful chase, to race in a direct line to the village church, the steeple of which was in sight, regardless of anything that happened to lie in the way.

For the principal English steeplechases, *see* Races.

**Stentor. *The voice of a Stentor*.** A very loud voice. Stentor was a Greek herald in the Trojan war. According to Homer, his voice was as loud as that of fifty men combined; hence *stentorian*, loud voiced.

**Stentorophonica.** The name given by Sir Samuel Morland to the speaking trumpet or megaphone invented by him (1670) for use at sea.

> I heard a formidable noise
> Loud as the stentorphonic voice
> That roared far off, 'Dispatch! and strip!'
>
> Butler, *Hudibras*, iii, 1

**Step-.** A prefix used before *father*, *mother*, *brother*, *sister*, *son*, *daughter*, etc., to indicate that the person spoken of is a relative only by the marriage of a parent, and not by blood (A.S. *stéop*, connected with *ástíeped*, bereaved). Thus, a man who marries a widow with children becomes *stepfather* to those children, and if he has children by her these and those of the widow's earlier marriage are *stepbrothers* or *stepsisters*. The latter are also called *half-brothers* and *half-sisters*; but some make a distinction between the terms, *half-brother* being kept for what we have already defined as a *stepbrother*, this term being applied only between the children of former marriages when both parents have been previously married. Thus, Mr X, a widower with two sons, A and B, marries Mrs Y, a widow with two sons, C and D. A and B then become *stepbrothers* to C and D. X and Y subsequently have a son, and he becomes a *half-brother* to the other children. Meanwhile, X is *stepfather* to C and D and Y *stepmother to* A and B.

***I feel like a stepchild.*** Said by one who is being left out of the fun or getting none of the titbits. Stepchildren are often (though by no means invariably) treated by the step-parent with somewhat less consideration than the others.

**Stephen, St.** The first Christian martyr – the 'protomartyr'. He was accused of blasphemy and stoned to death (Acts 7:58). He is commemorated on December 26th: the name means 'wreath' or 'crown' (Gr. *stephanos*).

***Fed with St Stephen's bread.*** Stoned. Of course, the allusion is to the stoning of Stephen.

***The Crown of St Stephen.*** The crown of Hungary, this St Stephen being the first king of Hungary (1000–38). He was a pagan, born at Gran about 969, and was converted to Christianity about 995. During his reign the faith became firmly established in his kingdom. He was canonised by Benedict IX shortly after his death, and is commemorated on September 2nd.

> If Hungarian independence should be secured through the help of Prince Napoleon, the Prince himself should receive the crown of St Stephen.
>
> Kossuth, *Memoirs of my Exile* (1880)

**Sterling,** when applied to coins and metal, denotes that they are of standard value, genuine; hence applied figuratively to anything of sound, intrinsic worth, as *A man of sterling qualities*. The word – first met with about the early 12th cent. – has been held to be a corruption of *Easterlings*, the Hanse merchants trading with England; but this is unlikely, and the suggestions are that it is either *steorling*, the coin with a star, some of the early Norman coins having a small star on them, or the bird *starling*, some of Edward the Confessor's coins bearing four martlets.

**Stern. *To sit at the stern; At the stern of public affairs*.** Having the management of public affairs. The stern is the *steorne*, or steering-place, hence the helm.

> Sit at chiefest stern of public weal.
>
> Shakespeare, *1 Henry VI*, 1, 1

**Sternhold and Hopkins.** The old metrical (largely doggerel) version of the Psalms that used to be bound up with the Book of Common Prayer and sung in churches. They were mainly the work of Thomas Sternhold (d.1549), and John Hopkins (d.1570). The completed version appeared in 1562.

> Mistaken choirs refuse the solemn strain
> Of ancient Sternhold. Crabbe, *Borough*

**Stet** (Lat. let it stand). An author's or editor's direction to the printer to cancel a correction previously made in a MS, proof, etc.

**Stew. *In a stew*.** In a fix, a flurry; in a state of mental agitation.

***Irish stew.*** A dish made by stewing together meat, onions, and potatoes. Called 'Irish' from the predominance of potatoes.

***To stew in one's own juice.*** To suffer the natural consequences of one's actions, to reap as you have sown. Chaucer has:

> In his own gress I made him frie,
> For anger and for verry jalousie.
>
> *Wife of Bath's Tale* (*Prologue*)

The Russian ambassador, when Louis Philippe fortified Paris, remarked, if ever again Paris is in insurrection, it 'can be made to stew in its own gravy (jus)'; and Bismarck, at the siege of Paris, in 1871, said, the Germans intend to leave the city 'to seethe in its own milk'.

**Stick.** *See also* Stuck.

***An old stick-in-the-mud.*** A dull, unprogressive old fogy.

***It sticks out a mile!*** Said to one who is trying to conceal some very obvious fault, disability, undesirable characteristic, etc., concerning that; as, 'Anyone can see he's a welsher – it sticks out a mile!'

***Over the sticks.*** Over the hurdles; hence, a hurdle-race, or steeplechase.

***The policy of the big stick.*** Threats, with some show of warlike attitude to back them up; and the same as 'rattling the sword in the scabbard'. The phrase was a favourite one with President Roosevelt.

***The sticking-place.*** The point at which a screw becomes tight; hence, the point aimed at. Shakespeare's use of the word is probably an allusion from the peg of a musical instrument, which is not much use unless it is actually at the 'sticking-place'.

> We fail!
> But screw your courage to the sticking-place,
> And we'll not fail. *Macbeth*, 1, 7

***The wrong end of the stick.*** Not the true facts; a distorted version. *To have got hold of the wrong end of the stick* is to have misunderstood the story.

***To cut one's stick.*** *See* Cut.

***To stick at nothing.*** To be heedless of all obstacles in accomplishing one's desire; to be utterly unscrupulous.

***To stick it up.*** Old slang for leaving one's 'score' at the tavern to be paid later; a note of it was stuck, or chalked up, at the back of the door.

***To stick up.*** Australian for to waylay and rob a coach, etc.; also in common use for raiding a bank and so on in daylight, the raiders closing the doors and covering all present with revolvers.

**Stickit.** A Scotticism for 'stuck (*stick-ed*) half-way', as a *stickit job*, one that is unfinished or unsatisfactory; hence, applied to persons who have given up their work through lack of means or capacity or some other reason, as a *stickit minister*, a retired minister.

**Stickler.** ***A stickler over trifles.*** One particular about things of no moment. *Sticklers* were the umpires in tournaments, or seconds in single combats, very punctilious about the minutest points of etiquette. The word is connected with A.S. *stihtan*, to arrange, regulate.

> I am willing ... to give thee precedence, and content myself with the humbler office of stickler. Scott, *Fair Maid of Perth*, ch. xvi

**Stiff.** Slang for a corpse; also for a horse that is sure to lose in a race: also (with reference to the stiff interest exacted by moneylenders) an I O U, a bill of acceptance. 'Did you get it stiff or hard?' means by an I O U or in hard cash.

> His 'stiff' was floating about in too many directions, at too many high figures.
> Ouida, *Under Two Flags*, ch. vii

**Stigmata.** Marks miraculously developed on the body of certain persons, which correspond to some or all of the wounds received by our Saviour in His trial and crucifixion. From Gr. *stigma*, the brand with which slaves and criminals in ancient Greece and Rome were marked; hence our verb stigmatise, to mark as with a brand of disgrace.

Among those who are said to have been marked with the stigmata are –

(1) *Men.* St Paul, who said 'I bear in my body the marks of the Lord Jesus' (Gal. 6:17); Angelo del Paz (all the marks); Benedict of Reggio (the crown of thorns), 1602; Carlo di Saeta (the lance-wound); Francis of Assisi (all the marks, which were impressed on him by a seraph with six wings), September 15th, 1224; and Nicholas of Ravenna.

(2) *Women.* Bianca de Gazeran; St Catharine of Sienna; Catharine di Raconisco (the crown of thorns), 1583; Cecilia di Nobili of Nocera, 1655; Clara di Pugny (mark of the spear), 1514; 'Estatica' of Caldaro (all the marks), 1842; Gabriella da Piezolo of Aquila (the spear-mark), 1472; Hieronyma Carvaglio (the spear-mark, which bled every Friday); Joanna Maria of the Cross; Maria Razzi of Chio (marks of the thorny crown); Maria Villani (ditto); Mary Magdalen di Pazzi; Mechtildis von Stanz; Ursula of Valencia; Veronica Giuliani (all the marks) 1694; Vincenza Ferreri of Valencia; Anna Emmerich, of Dülmen, Westphalia (d.1824); Maria von Mörl (in 1839); Louise Lateau (1860), and Anne Girling, the foundress of the English 'Shakers' (*q.v.*).

**Stilo Novo** (Lat. in the new style). Newfangled notions. When the calendar was reformed by Gregory XIII (1582), letters used to be dated *stilo novo*, which grew in time to be a cant phrase for any innovation.

> And so I leave you to your *stilo novo*.
> Beaumont and Fletcher, *Woman's Prize*, IV, iv

**Stinkomalee.** The name with which Theodore Hook sought to cover University College, London, with ridicule at its foundation in 1828; taken, at the time, for quite a good specimen of 'wit'. It was suggested by the facts that Trincomalee (Ceylon) was much in the public eye just then, and that the College buildings were erected on the site of a large rubbish store or sort of refuse field, into which were cast potsherds and all sorts of sweepings. As the non-religious education of the new college and its rivalry with Oxford and Cambridge gave for a time very great offence to the High Church and State party, the gibe seems to have attained a certain currency.

**Stir Up Sunday.** The last Sunday in Trinity. So called from the first two words of the collect. It announces to schoolboys the near approach of the Christmas holidays.

**Stirrup.** Literally, a rope to climb by (A.S. *stirap*, from *stigan*, to climb, and *rap*, a rope).

***Stirrup cup.*** A 'parting cup', given, especially in the Highlands, to guests on leaving when their feet are in the stirrups. *Cp.* Doch-an-doroch.

> Lord Marmion's bugles blew to horse;
> Then came the stirrup-cup in course;
> Between the baron and his host
> No point of courtesy was lost.
>
> Scott, *Marmion*, i, 21

Among the ancient Romans a 'parting cup' was drunk in honour of Mercury to insure sound sleep. *See* Ovid, *Fasti*, ii, 635.

***Stirrup oil.*** A beating; a variety of 'strap oil' (*q.v.*). The French *de l'huile de cotret* (faggot, *or* stick oil).

**Stiver. *Not a stiver*.** Not a penny, not a cent. The stiver (*stuiver*) was a Dutch coin, equal to about a penny.

**Stock.** Originally, a tree-trunk, or stem (connected with *stick*); hence, in figurative uses, something fixed, also something regarded as the origin of families, groups, etc.; as *He comes of a good stock*, from a good stem, of good line of descent, *Languages of Indo-Germanic stock*, etc. *To worship stocks and stones* is to worship idols, *stock* here being taken as a type of a motionless, fixed thing, like a tree-stump. The village *stocks*, in which petty offenders were confined by the wrists and ankles, are so called from the stakes or posts at the side; and *stock*, in the sense of fund, capital, is probably with reference to its being the stem from which a business is developed.

***It is on the stocks.*** It is in hand, but not yet finished. The stocks is the frame in which a ship is placed while building, and so long as it is in hand it is said to be or to lie on the stocks.

***Live stock.*** The cattle, sheep, pigs, horses, etc., belonging to a farmer; that part of his 'stock in trade' which is alive. In slang use, lice or other parasitical vermin.

***Lock, stock, and barrel.*** *See* Lock.

***Stock-broker, stock-jobber.*** The *broker* is engaged in the purchase of stocks and shares for clients on commission; the *jobber* speculates in stocks and shares so as to profit by market fluctuations, and acts as an intermediary between buying and selling brokers. The jobber must be a member of a Stock Exchange; but a broker need not necessarily be; if he is not he is known as an 'outside broker' or a 'kerbstone operator'. *Cp.* Bucket-shop.

***Stock in trade.*** The fixed capital of a business; the goods, tools, and other requisites of a trade or profession.

***Stock-rider.*** The Australian term for one in charge of cattle, i.e. stock. He uses a *stock-whip*, and herds his beasts in a *stock-yard*.

***To take stock.*** To ascertain how one's business stands by taking an inventory of all goods and so on in hand, balancing one's books, etc.; hence, to survey one's position and prospects.

**Stockdove.** The wild pigeon; so called because it nests in the stocks of hollow trees.

**Stockfish.** Dried cod, cured without salt. In Shakespeare's day the word was often used as a contemptuous epithet of abuse; thus Falstaff shouts at Prince Henry –

> Away, you starveling, you elf-skin, you dried neat's tongue, bull's pizzle, you stock-fish!
>
> *I Henry IV*, 2, 4

***I will beat thee like a stockfish.*** Moffat and Bennet, in their *Health's Improvement* (p. 262), inform us that dried cod, till it is beaten, is called *buckhorn*, because it is so tough; but after it has been beaten on the stock, it is termed stockfish.

> Peace! thou wilt be beaten like a stockfish else.
>
> Jonson, *Every Man in his Humour*, iii, 2

**Stocking.** Used of one's savings or 'nest-egg', because formerly money used to be hoarded up in an old stocking, which was frequently hung up the chimney for safety.

***Blue stocking.*** *See under* Blue.

**Stockwell Ghost.** A supposed ghost that created a great sensation in Stockwell, London, in 1772. The author of the strange noises was Anne Robinson, a servant. *Cp.* Cock Lane.

**Stoics.** A school of Greek philosophers (founded by Zeno, about 308 BC) who held that virtue was the highest good, and that the passions and appetites should be rigidly subdued. It was so called because Zeno gave his lectures in the *Stoa Poikile*, the Painted Porch (*see* Porch) of Athens.

Epictetus was the founder of the New Stoic school (1st cent. AD).

> The ancient Stoics in their porch
> With fierce dispute maintained their church,
> Beat out their brains in fight and study
> To prove that virtue is a body,
> That *bonum* is an animal,
> Made good with stout polemic bawl.
>
> Butler, *Hudibras*, ii, 2

**Stole** (Lat. *stola*). An ecclesiastical vestment, also called the Orarium. It indicates *Obedientiam fiilii Dei et jugum servitutis, quod pro salute hominum portavit*. Deacons wear the stole over the left shoulder, and loop the two parts together, that they may both hang on the right side. Priests wear it over both shoulders.

**Stole, Groom of the.** Formerly, the first lord of the bedchamber, a high officer of the Royal Household ranking next after the vice-chamberlain. The office was allowed to lapse on the accession of Queen Victoria; in the reign of Queen Anne it was held by a woman.

*Stole*, here, is not connected with Lat. *stola*, a robe, but refers to the king's *stool*, or privy. Lavatory accommodation was not always what it is today; and, certainly as late as the 16th century, when the king made a royal progress his close-stool formed part of the baggage and was in charge of a special officer or groom.

**Stolen Things.** *See under* Steal.

**Stomach.** Used figuratively of inclination, appetite, etc.

> He who hath no stomach for this fight.
>
> Shakespeare, *Henry V*, 4, 3
>
> Wolsey was a man of an unbounded stomach.
>
> *Henry VIII*, 4, 2
>
> Let me praise you while I have the stomach.
>
> *Merchant of Venice*, 3, 5

***To stomach an insult.*** To swallow it and not resent it.

> If you must believe, stomach not all.
>
> Shakespeare, *Antony and Cleopatra*, 3, 4

**Stone.** Used in a figurative sense in many ways when some characteristic of a stone is to be pointed out; as, *stone blind*, *stone cold*, *stone dead*, *stone still*, etc., as blind, cold, dead, or still as a stone.

> I will not struggle; I will stand stone still.
>
> Shakespeare, *King John*, 4, 1

In all ages stones, especially those of meteoric origin or those fabled to have 'fallen from heaven', have been set up and worshipped by primitive peoples, and the great stone circles of Stonehenge, Avebury, the Orkneys, Carnac, etc., are relics of religious rites. Anaxagoras mentions a stone that fell from Jupiter in Thrace, a description of which is given by Pliny. The Ephesians asserted that their image of Diana came from Jupiter. The stone at Emessa, in Syria, worshipped as a symbol of the sun, was a similar meteorite. At Abydos and Potidaea similar stones were preserved. At Corinth was one venerated as Zeus. At Cyprus was one dedicated to Venus, a description of which is given by Tacitus and Maximus Tyrius. Herodian describes one in Syria, and the famous 'black stone' (*see* Hajar al-Aswad), set in the Kaaba of the Moslems, is a similar meteor.

After the Moslem pilgrim has made his seven processions round the Kaaba, he repairs to Mount Arafat, and before sunrise enters the valley of Mena, where he throws seven stones at each of three pillars, in imitation of Abraham and Adam, who thus drove away the devil when he disturbed their devotions.

***A rolling stone gathers no moss.*** One who is always 'chopping and changing' and won't settle down will never become wealthy. So says the proverb (which is common to many languages), but it is not always borne out by facts – and its reverse does not hold true. Tusser, in his *Five Hundred Points of Good Husbandrie* (1573) has –

> The stone that is rolling can gather no moss,
> For master and servant oft changing is loss.

***Hag-stones.*** Flints naturally perforated, used in country places as charms against witches, the 'evil eye', etc. They are hung on the key of an outer door, round the neck 'for luck', on the bed-post to prevent nightmare, on a horse's collar to ward off disease, etc.

***Stone soup*** or ***St Bernard's soup.*** The story goes that a beggar asked alms at a lordly mansion, but was told by the servants they had nothing to give him. 'Sorry for it,' said the man, 'but will you let me boil a little water to make some soup of this stone?' This was so novel a proceeding, that the curiosity of the servants was aroused, and the man was readily furnished with saucepan, water, and a spoon. In he popped the stone, and begged for a little salt and pepper for flavouring. Stirring the water and tasting it, he said it would be the better for any fragments of meat and vegetables they might happen to have. These were supplied, and ultimately he asked for a little ketchup or other sauce. When ready the servants tasted it, and declared that 'stone soup' was excellent.

***Stone of stumbling.*** An obstacle, stumbling-block, or an occasion for being hindered. The phrase is from Isa. 8:14:

> He shall be ... for a stone of stumbling and for a rock of offence to both the houses of Israel.

***The Standing Stones of Stennis***, in the Orkneys, resemble Stonehenge, but are unlikely to have been Druidical. The custom of constructing these circles was prevalent in Scandinavia as well as in Gaul and Britain, and as common to the mythology of Odin as to Druidism. They were places of public assembly, and in the *Eyrbiggia Saga* is described the manner of setting apart the Helga Feli (Holy Rocks) by the pontiff Thorolf for solemn meetings.

***The Stone Age.*** The period when stone implements were used by primitive man. It preceded the Bronze Age; and some peoples, such as certain tribes in Papua, have not yet emerged from it. *See* Palaeolithic.

***The stone jug.*** Slang for prison. *See* Jug.

***To cast the first stone.*** To take the lead in criticising, fault-finding, quarrelling, etc. The phrase is from John 8:7:

> He that is without sin among you, let him first cast a stone at her.

***To kill two birds with one stone.*** *See* Bird.

***To leave no stone unturned.*** To spare no trouble, time, expense, etc., in endeavouring to accomplish your aim. After the defeat of Mardonius at Plataea (477 BC), a report was current that the Persian general had left great treasures in his tent. Polycrates the Theban sought long but found them not. The Oracle of Delphi, being consulted, told him 'to leave no stone unturned', and the treasures were discovered.

***You have stones in your mouth.*** Said to a person who stutters or speaks very indistinctly. The allusion is to Demosthenes, who cured himself of stuttering by putting pebbles in his mouth and declaiming on the seashore.

> The orator who once
> Did fill his mouth with pebble stones
> When he harangued. Butler, *Hudibras*, i, 1

*See also* Aetites, Philosophers' Stone, Precious Stones, Touchstone, etc.

**Stonebrash.** A name given in Wiltshire to the subsoil of the north-western border, which consists of a reddish calcareous loam, mingled with flat stones; a soil made of small stones or broken rock.

**Stonehenge.** The great prehistoric (Neolithic or early Bronze Age) monument on Salisbury Plain, originally consisting of two concentric circles of upright stones, enclosing two rows of smaller stones, and a central block of blue marble (18 ft by 4 ft), known as the Altar Stone. The Friar's Heel (*q.v.*) stands outside the circle to the N.E. Many theories as to its original purpose and original builders have been propounded. It was probably used (if not built) by the Druids, and from its plotting, which, it is certain, had an astronomical basis, it is thought to have been the temple of a sun god and to have been built about 1680 BC.

The *-henge* of the name seems to refer to something hanging (A.S. *hengen*) in, or supported in, the air, viz., the huge transverse stones; but Geoffrey of Monmouth connects it with Hengist, and says that Stonehenge was erected by Merlin to perpetuate the treachery of Hengist in falling upon Vortigern and putting him and his 400 attendants to the sword. Aurelius Ambrosius asked Merlin to devise a memento of this event, whereupon the magician transplanted from Killaraus, in Ireland, the 'Giant's Dance', stones which had been brought thither from Africa by a race of giants and all of which possessed magic properties.

**Stonewall, To.** A cricketers' term for adopting purely defensive measures when at the wicket, blocking every ball and not attempting to score. It was originally Australian political slang and was used of obstructing business.

**Stonewall Jackson.** Thomas J. Jackson (1824–63), one of the Confederate generals in the American civil war; so called because at the Battle of Bull Run (1861) General Bee, of South Carolina, observing his men waver, exclaimed, 'Look at Jackson's men; they stand like a stone wall!'

**Stony Arabia.** A mistranslation of *Arabia Petraea*, where Petraea is supposed to be an adjective formed from the Greek *petros* (a stone), and not, as it really is, from the city of Petra, the capital of the Nabathaeans. *Cp.* Yemen.

**Stool of Repentance.** The 'cutty stool', a low stool placed in front of the pulpit in Scottish churches, on which persons who had incurred ecclesiastical censure were placed during divine service. When the service was over the 'penitent' had to stand on the stool and receive the minister's rebuke.

**Store. *Store cattle.*** Beasts kept on a farm for breeding purposes, or thin cattle bought for fattening.

***Store is no sore.*** Things stored up for future use are no evil. *Sore* means grief as well as wound, our *sorrow*.

***To set store by.*** To value highly.

**Stork.** According to the Swedish legend, the stork received its name from flying round the cross of the crucified Redeemer, crying *Styrka! styrka!* (Strengthen! strengthen!).

Many fables and legends have grown up around this bird. Lyly refers to it more than once in his *Euphues* (1580), as –

> Ladies use their lovers as the stork doth her young ones, who pecketh them till they bleed with her bill, and then healeth them with her tongue.

And again –

> Constancy is like unto the stork, who wheresoever she fly cometh into no nest but her own.

And –

> It fareth with me … as with the stork, who, when she is least able carrieth the greatest burden.

Dutch and German mothers tell their children that babies are brought by storks; and another common belief was that the stork, like the secretary bird, will kill snakes 'on sight':

> 'Twill profit when the stork, sworn foe of snakes,
> Returns, to show compassion to thy plants.
>
> Philips, *Cyder*, Bk i

***King Stork.*** A tyrant that devours his subjects, and makes them submissive with fear and trembling. The allusion is to the fable of *The Frogs desiring a King*. *See* Log.

***Storks' law*** or ***Lex ciconaria***. A Roman law which obliged children to maintain their necessitous parents in old age, 'in imitation of the stork'. Also called 'Antipelargia'.

**Storm. *A brain-storm.*** A sudden and violent upheaval in the brain, causing temporary loss of control, or even madness. *Nerve-storm* is used in much the same way of the nerves.

***A storm in a teacup.*** A mighty to-do about a trifle; making a great fuss about nothing.

***Storm and stress.*** *See* Sturm und Drang.

***The Cape of Storms.*** So Bartholomew Diaz named the south cape of Africa in 1486, but John II of Portugal (d.1495) changed it to the *Cape of Good Hope*.

***To take by storm.*** To seize by a sudden and irresistible attack; a military term used figuratively, as of one who becomes suddenly famous or popular; an actor, suddenly springing to fame, 'takes the town by storm'.

**Stormy Petrel.** *See* Petrel.

**Stornello Verses** are those in which certain words are harped on and turned about and about. They are common among the Tuscan peasants. The word is from *tornare* (to return).

> I'll tell him the *white*, and the *green*, and the *red*,
> Mean our country has flung the vile yoke from her head;
> I'll tell him the *green*, and the *red*, and the *white*,
> Would look well by his side as a sword-knot so bright;
> I'll tell him the *red*, and the *white*, and the *green*,
> Is the prize that we play for, a prize we will win.
>
> *Notes and Queries*

**Storthing.** The Norwegian Parliament, elected every three years (*stor*, great; *thing*, assembly).

**Stovepipe Hat.** An old-fashioned tall silk hat, a chimney-pot hat (*q.v.*).

> High collars, tight coats, and tight sleeves were worn at home and abroad, and, as though that were not enough, a stovepipe hat.
>
> *Illustrated Sporting and Dramatic News*, Sept., 1891

**Strad.** A colloquial name for a violin made by the famous maker Antonio Stradivarius (1644–1737) of Cremona. His best period was about 1700 to 1725; he sold his violins for about £4 each; they have since realised as much as £3,000, and one of his 'cellos £4,000.

**Strafe** (Ger. *strafen*, to punish). A word borrowed in good-humoured contempt from the Germans during the Great War. One of their favourite 'slogans' was *Gott strafe England!* A punishment or 'wigging' is spoken of as a *good straffing*, but during the War this phrase meant a heavy bombardment, a sharp action, etc.

**Strain. *The quality of mercy is not strained*** (*Merchant of Venice*, 4, 1) – constrained or forced, but cometh down freely as the rain, which is God's gift.

***To strain a point.*** To go beyond one's usual, or the proper, limits; to give way a bit more than one has any right to.

***To strain at a gnat and swallow a camel.*** To make much fuss about little peccadilloes, but commit offences of real magnitude. The proverb comes from Matt. 23:24, which in Tyndale's, Coverdale's, and other early versions reads *to strain out*, etc., meaning to filter out a gnat before drinking the wine. The Revised Version also adopts this form, but the Authorised Version's rendering (*to strain at*) was in use well before the date of its issue (1611), so the *at* is not – as has been sometimes stated – a misprint or mistake for *out*. Greene in his *Mamillia* (1583) speaks of 'straining at a gnat and letting pass an elephant'. It means, to *strain* the wine *at* finding a gnat in it, but was early taken to stand for to swallow with considerable effort, imposing a strain on one's throat.

***To strain courtesy.*** To stand upon ceremony. Here, *strain* is *to stretch*, as parchment is strained on a drum-head.

**Stranger.** Originally, a foreigner; from O.Fr. *estrangier* (Mod. Fr. *étranger*), which is the Latin *extraneus*, one without (*extra*, without).

It is said that Busiris, King of Egypt, sacrificed to his gods all strangers who set foot on his territories. Diomed (*q.v.*) gave strangers to his horses for food.

> Oh fly, or here with strangers' blood imbrued
> Bursiris' altars thou shalt find renewed;
> Amidst his slaughtered guests his altars stood
> Obscene with gore, and baked with human blood.
>
> Camoëns, *Lusiad*, Bk ii

Floating tea-leaves in one's cup, charred pieces of wick that make the candle gutter, little bits of soot hanging from the bars of the grate, etc., are called 'strangers', because they are supposed to foretell the coming of visitors.

***I spy strangers!*** The recognised form of words by which a member of Parliament conveys to the Speaker the information that there is an unauthorised person in the House.

***The little stranger.*** A new born infant.

> We asked no social questions – we pumped no hidden shame –
> We never talked obstetrics when the Little Stranger came.
>
> Kipling, *The Three-Decker*

***The stranger that is within thy gates.*** *See* Proselytes.

**Strap.** ***A taste of the strap***, or ***a strapping*** is a flogging, properly with a leather strap.

***A strapping young fellow.*** A big, sturdy chap; a robust, vigorous young woman is similarly termed *a strapper*.

***Straphanger.*** An unfortunate person who can't get a seat in a suburban train, an omnibus, etc., and so has to do his journey standing on the floor and clinging to a strap – which is thoughtfully suspended from the roof for the purpose.

***Strap oil.*** Slang for a thrashing. *See above*.

**Strappado** (Ital. *strappare*, to pull). A mode of torture formerly practised for extracting confessions, retractions, etc. The hands were tied behind the back, and the victim was pulled up to a beam by a rope tied to them and then let down suddenly; by this means a limb was not unfrequently dislocated.

> Were I at the strappado or the rack, I'd give no man a reason on compulsion.
>
> Shakespeare, *1 Henry IV*, 2, 4

**Strassburg Goose.** A goose fattened, crammed, and confined in order to enlarge its liver.

**Straw.** As used in phrases *straw* is generally typical of that which is worthless, as *Not worth a straw*, quite valueless, not worth a rap, a fig, etc.; *to care not a straw*, not to care at all.

***A straw shows which way the wind blows.*** Mere trifles often indicate the coming on of momentous events. They are shadows cast before coming events.

***A man of straw.*** A man without means, with no more substance than a straw doll; also, an imaginary or fictitious person put forward for some reason, a male 'Mrs Harris'.

***I have a straw to break with you.*** I have something to quarrel with you about, or am displeased with you; I have a reproof to give you. In feudal times possession of a fief was conveyed by giving a straw to the new tenant. If the tenant misconducted himself, the lord dispossessed him by going to the threshold of his door and breaking a straw, saying as he did so, 'As I break this straw, so break I the contract made between us.' In allusion to this custom, it is said in *Reynard the Fox* –

> The kynge toke up a straw fro the ground and pardoned and forgaf the foxe alle the mysdedes and trespaces of his fader and of hym also.
>
> Ch. xvii

on condition that the Fox showed King Lion where the treasures were hid.

***In the straw.*** Applied to women in childbirth. The allusion is to the straw with which beds were at one time usually stuffed, and not to the litter laid before a house to break the noise of wheels passing by.

***The last straw.*** The only hope left; the last penny; in allusion to the old proverb, ' 'Tis the last straw that breaks the camel's back.' In weighing articles, as salt, tea, sugar, etc., it is the last pinch which turns the scale; and there is an ultimate point of endurance beyond which calamity breaks a man down.

***To catch at a straw.*** A forlorn hope. A drowning man will catch at a straw.

***To make bricks without straw.*** To attempt to do something without the proper and necessary materials. The allusion is to the exaction of the Egyptian taskmasters mentioned in Exod. 5:6–14.

***To pick straws.*** To show fatigue or weariness, as birds pick up straws to make their nests (or bed).

> Their eyelids did not once pick straws,
> And wink, and sink away;
> No, no; they were as brisk as bees,
> And loving things did say.
>
> Peter Pindar, *Orson and Ellen*, canto v

***To stumble at a straw.*** To be pulled up short by a trifle.

***To throw straws against the wind.*** To contend uselessly and feebly against what is irresistible; to sweep back the Atlantic with a besom.

**Strawberry.** So called from *straw*, probably because the achenes with which the surface is dotted somewhat resemble finely chopped straw.

> We may say of angling as Dr Boteler said of strawberries, 'Doubtless God could have make a better berry, but doubtless God never did.'
>
> Izaak Walton, *Compleat Angler*, ch. v

***Strawberry mark.*** A birthmark something like a strawberry. In Morton's *Box and Cox* the two heroes eventually recognise each other as long-lost brothers through one of them having a strawberry-mark on his left arm.

***Strawberry preachers.*** So Latimer called the non-resident country clergy, because they 'come but once a yeare and tarie not long' (*Sermon on the Plough*, 1549).

***The strawberry leaves.*** A dukedom; the honour, rank, etc., of a duke. The ducal coronet is ornamented with eight strawberry leaves.

**Street and Walker.** 'In the employ of Messrs Street and Walker'. Said of a person out of employment. A gentleman without means, whose employment is walking about the streets.

**Street Arab.** *See* Bedouin.

**Strenia.** The goddess who presided over the New Year festivities in ancient Rome. Tatius, the legendary Sabine king, entered Rome on New Year's Day, and received from some augurs palms cut from the sacred grove, dedicated to her. After his seizure of the city, he ordained that January 1st should be celebrated by gifts to be called *strenae*, consisting of figs, dates, and honey. The French *étrenne*, a New Year's gift, is from this goddess.

**Strephon.** A stock name for a rustic lover; from the languishing lover of that name in Sidney's *Arcadia*.

**Strike.** A cessation of work by a body of employees with the object of inducing the employers to grant some demand, such as one for higher wages, shorter hours, better working conditions, etc., or sometimes for no direct reason, but out of sympathy for other workers or for the furtherance of some political object. A *lightning strike* is one of which no notice has been given; and the converse of a strike, i.e. the refusal of the masters to allow the men to work until certain conditions are agreed upon or rules complied with, is termed a *lock-out*.

The word first appears in this sense in 1768, and seems to have had a nautical origin; sailors who refused to go to sea because of some grievance *struck* (lowered) the yards of their ship.

*Strike* is the name of an old grain measure, still unofficially used in some parts of England, and varying locally from half a bushel to four bushels. Probably so called because when filled the top of the measure was 'struck off' and so levelled instead of being left heaped up.

***It strikes me that*** ... It occurs to me that ..., it comes into my mind that ... Browning's poem, *How it Strikes a Contemporary*, tells how people can be altogether mistaken in their estimate of one (a poet, in this case) who lives among them.

***Strike-a-light.*** The flint formerly used with tinder-boxes for striking fire; also, the shaped piece of metal used to strike the flint.

The collar of the Order of the Golden Fleece is composed of linked pieces of metal of this shape, and so is sometimes called the 'collar of strike-a-lights'.

***Strike-breaker.*** A 'blackleg', a worker induced by the employer to carry on when the rest of the men have struck.

***Strike, but hear me!*** (Lat. *verbera, sed audi*). Carry out your threats – if you must – but at least hear what I have to say. The phrase comes from Plutarch's life of Themistocles. He strongly opposed the proposal of Eurybiades to quit the bay of Salamis. The hot-headed Spartan insultingly remarked that 'those who in the public games rise up before the proper signal are scourged'. 'True,' said Themistocles, 'but those who lag behind win no laurels.' On this, Eurybiades lifted up his staff to strike him, when Themistocles earnestly but proudly exclaimed, 'Strike, but hear me!'

Bacon (*Advancement of Learning*, ii) calls this 'that ancient and patient request'.

***Strike me dead! blind!*** etc. Vulgar expletives, or exclamations of surprise, dismay, wonder, and so on. *Strike-me-dead* is also sailor's slang for thin, wishy-washy beer.

***Strike while the iron is hot.*** Act while the impulse is still fervent, *or* do what you do at the right time. The metaphor is taken from the blacksmith's forge; a horse-shoe must be struck while the iron is red-hot or it cannot be moulded into shape. Similar proverbs are: 'Make hay while the sun shines', 'Take time by the forelock'.

***To be struck all of a heap.*** *See* Heap.

***To be struck on a person.*** A colloquialism for to be much interested in him (or her), to be 'nuts' on, or to have fallen in love with the person named.

***To strike an attitude.*** To pose; to assume an exaggerated or theatrical attitude.

***To strike a balance.*** *See* Balance.

***To strike a bargain*** (Lat. *faedus ferire*). To determine or settle it. The allusion is to the ancient custom of making sacrifice in concluding an agreement. After calling the gods to witness, they struck – i.e. slew – the victim which was offered in sacrifice. *Cp.* To strike hands *below*.

***To strike at the foundations.*** To attempt to undermine the whole thing, to overthrow it utterly; as 'Bolshevism strikes at the foundation of civilised society'.

***To strike camp.*** To lower the tents and move off; hence, to abandon one's position. A military phrase, adopted from the nautical phrase 'to strike colours'. *See* Flag.

***To strike hands upon a bargain.*** To confirm it by shaking or striking hands; to ratify it. *Cp.* To Strike a bargain *above*.

***To strike lucky.*** To have an unexpected piece of good fortune; a phrase from the miner's camps. *To strike oil* (*see* Oil) means much the same thing, and has a similar origin.

***To strike one's colours, or flag.*** *See* Flag.

***To strike out in another direction.*** To open up a new way for oneself, to start a new method, a fresh business.

***To strike sail.*** To acknowledge oneself beaten; to eat humble pie. A nautical expression. When a ship in fight or on meeting another ship, lets down her topsails at least half-mast high, she is said to *strike*, meaning that she submits or pays respect to the other.

> Now Margaret
> Must strike her sail, and learn awhile to serve
> When kings command.
>
> Shakespeare, *3 Henry VI*, 3, 3

***To strike up.*** To begin, start operations; as *to strike up an acquaintance*, to set it going. Originally of an orchestra or company of singers, who 'struck up' the music.

***Willing to wound, and yet afraid to strike.*** Said of one who dare not do the injury or take the revenge that he wishes. The 'tag' is from Pope's *Epistle to Dr Arbuthnot* (1.200).

**String. *Always harping on one string.*** Always talking on one subject; always repeating the same thing. The allusion is to the ancient harpers; some, like Paganini, played on one string to show their skill, but more would have endorsed the Apothecary's apology – 'My poverty, and not my will, consents'.

***To have two strings to one's bow.*** *See* Bow.

**Stroke.** The oarsman who sits on the bench next the coxswain, and sets the time of the stroke for the rest.

***To stroke one the wrong way.*** To vex him, ruffle his temper.

**Stromkarl.** A Norwegian musical spirit. Arndt informs us that the Stròmkarl has eleven different musical measures, to ten of which people may dance, but the eleventh belongs to the night spirit, his host. If anyone plays it, tables and benches, cups and cans, old men and women, blind and lame, babies in their cradles, and the sick in their beds, begin to dance.

**Strong.** A *strong verb* is one that forms inflexions by internal vowel-change (such as *bind, bound*; *speak, spoke*); *weak verbs* add a syllable, or letter (as *love, loved*, *refund, refunded*).

***Going strong.*** Prospering, getting on famously; in an excellent state of health.

***To come it strong.*** *See* Come.

**Strontium.** This element, a yellowish metal resembling calcium, receives its name from Strontian, in Argyleshire, where it was discovered by Dr Hope, in 1792.

**Struldbrugs.** Wretched inhabitants of Luggnagg (in Swift's *Gulliver's Travels*), who had the privilege of immortality without those of eternal vigour, strength, and intellect.

> Many persons think that the picture of the Stulbrugs (*sic*) was intended to wean us from a

love of life ... but I am certain that the dean never had any such thing in view.

*Paley's Natural Theology* (Lord Brougham's note, Bk i, p. 140).

**Stubble Geese.** The geese turned into the stubble-fields to pick up the corn left after harvest.

**Stuck.** ***Stuck up.*** Said of pretentious people who give themselves airs, nobodies who assume to be somebodies. The allusion is to the peacock, which sticks up its train to add to its 'importance' and 'awe down' antagonists. In Australia *to be stuck up* is to be waylaid and robbed on the highway.

***To stare like a stuck pig.*** *See* Pig.

**Stuff Gown.** A barrister (*q.v.*) who has not yet 'taken silk', i.e. become a K.C. *See* Silk.

**Stumer.** A swindle, or a swindler, a forged banknote or 'dud' cheque; a fictitious bet recorded by the bookmakers, and published in the papers, to deceive the public by running up the odds on a horse which is not expected to win.

**Stump.** ***A stump orator.*** A ranting, bombastic speaker, who harangues all who will listen to him from some point of vantage in the open air, such as the stump of a tree; a 'tub-thumper', mob orator. Hence such phrases as *to stump the country*, *to take to the stump*, to go from town to town making inflammatory speeches.

***Stumped out.*** Outwitted; put down. A term borrowed from the game of cricket.

***To stir one's stumps.*** To get on faster; to set upon something expeditiously.

This makes him stirre his stumps.

*The Two Lancashire Lovers* (1640)

The stumps are the legs, or wooden legs fastened to stumps of mutilated limbs.

For Witherington needs must I wayle,
As one in doleful dumpes;
For when his leggs were smitten off,
He fought upon his stumpes.

*Ballad of Chevy Chase*

***To stump up.*** To pay one's reckoning, pay what is due. Ready money is called *stumpy* or *stumps.* An Americanism, meaning money paid down on the spot – i.e. on the stump of a tree. *Cp.* On the Nail.

**Stunt.** A feat, performance; especially one of a startling or sensational nature. Hence, *to stunt*, to do something surprising or hazardous; *a newspaper stunt*, a movement, party cry, sensation, etc., worked by a newspaper and boomed by publicity men with the object rather of increasing 'net sales' than of championing the advertised cause or seeing that justice is done.

The word was originally American college slang for some exceptional athletic feat.

**Sturm und Drang** (Ger. storm and stress). The name given to the intellectual awakening of Germany towards the close of the 18th century. It had a considerable effect on our own 'Romantic Movement', and was so called from a drama of that name by Friedrich Maximilian von Klinger (1752–1831). Goethe and Schiller contributed to the movement.

**Sty,** an inflamed pimple on the eye-lid, is shortened from the earlier *styany* (taken as meaning *sty-on-eye*), which is from A.S. *stigend*, something that rises (*stigan*, to rise).

**Stygian.** Infernal, gloomy; pertaining to the river Styx (*q.v.*).

At that so sudden blaze the Stygian throng
Bent their aspect. Milton, *Paradise Lost*, x, 453

**Style** is from the Latin *stylus* (an Iron pencil for writing on waxen tablets, etc.). The characteristic of a person's writing is called his style. Metaphorically it is applied to composition and speech. Good writing is *stylish*, and, by extension, smartness of dress and deportment is so called.

Style is the dress of thought, and a well-dressed thought like a well-dressed man, appeals to great advantage. Chesterfield, *Letter* ccxl

***New style, Old style.*** *See* Calendar.

***To do a thing in style.*** To do it splendidly, regardless of expense.

**Styles**. *Tom Styles* or *John a Styles*, connected with *John-a-Nokes* (*q.v.*) in actions of ejectment; mythical gentlemen, like 'John Doe' and 'Richard Roe'.

And, like blind Fortune, with a sleight
Convey men's interest and right
From Stiles's pocket into Nokes's.

Butler, *Hudibras*, iii, 3

**Stylites** or **Pillar Saints.** A class of early and mediaeval ascetics, chiefly of Syria, who took up their abode on the top of a pillar, from which they never descended. The most celebrated are Simeon Stylites, of Syria, and Daniel the Stylite of Constantinople. Simeon (d.596) spent sixty-eight years on different pillars, each loftier and narrower than the preceding, the last being 66 feet high. Daniel (d.494) lived thirty-three years on a pillar, and was not unfrequently nearly blown from it by the storms from Thrace. This form of asceticism was still in vogue as late as the 12th century.

I, Simeon of the Pillar by surname,
Stylites among men – I, Simeon,
The watcher on the column till the end.
Tennyson, *St Simeon Stylites*

**Styx.** The river of Hate (Gr. *stugein*, to hate) – called by Milton 'abhorrëd Styx, the flood of burning hate' (*Paradise Lost*, ii, 577) – that, according to *classical mythology*, flowed nine times round the infernal regions.

The fables about the Styx are of Egyptian origin, and we are told that Isis collected the various parts of Osiris (murdered by Typhon) and buried them in secrecy on the banks of the Styx. Charon (*q.v.*), as Diodorus informs us, is an Egyptian word for a 'ferryman'.

By the black infernal Styx I swear
(That dreadful oath which binds the Thunderer)
'Tis fixed! Pope, *Thebais of Statius*, i

**Suaviter.** *Suaviter in modo, fortiter in re* (Lat.), gentle in manner, resolute in action. Said of one who does what is to be done with unflinching firmness, but in the most inoffensive manner possible.

**Sub hasta** (Lat.). By auction. When an auction took place among the Romans, it was customary to stick a spear in the ground to give notice of it to the public; literally, under the spear. *Cp.* Spear.

**Sub Jove** (Lat.). Under Jove; in the open air. Jupiter is the god of the upper regions of the air, as Juno is of the lower regions, Neptune of the waters of the sea, Vesta of the earth, Ceres of the surface soil, and Hades of the invisible or under-world.

**Sub rosa.** *See* Rose.

**Subject and Object.** In metaphysics the *Subject* is the ego, the mind, the conscious self, the substance or substratum to which attributes must be referred; the *Object* is an external as distinct from the ego, a thing or idea brought before the consciousness. Hence *subjective criticism*, *art*, etc., is that which proceeds from the individual mind and is consequently individualistic, fanciful, imaginative; while *objective criticism* is that which is based on knowledge of the externals.

***Subject-object.*** The immediate object of thought as distinguished from the material thing of which one is thinking.

The thought is necessarily and universally subject-object. Matter is necessarily, and to us universally, object-subject.
Lewes, *History of Philosophy*, II, 485

**Sublapsarian** (or **Infralapsarian**). A Calvinist who maintains that God devised His scheme of redemption *after* he had permitted the 'lapse' or fall of Adam, when He elected some to salvation and left others to run their course. The supralapsarian maintains that all this was ordained by God from the foundation of the world, and therefore *before* the 'lapse' or fall of Adam.

**Sublime.** From Lat. *sub*, up to, *limen*, the lintel; hence, lofty, elevated in thought or tone.

***From the sublime to the ridiculous is only one step.*** A favourite saying of Napoleon's; probably taken from Tom Paine, who has –

The sublime and the ridiculous are so often so nearly related that it is difficult to class them separately. One step above the sublime makes the ridiculous, and one step above the ridiculous makes the sublime again.
*Age of Reason*, Pt ii (note)

***The Sublime Porte.*** *See* Porte.

***The Sublime Society of Steaks.*** *See* Beefsteak Club.

**Submerged** or **Submerged Tenth, The.** The proletariat, sunk or submerged in poverty; the gutter-class; the waifs and strays of society.

All but the 'submerged' were bent upon merry-making. *Society*, Nov. 12th, 1892, p. 1273

**Subpoena** (Lat. under penalty) is a writ commanding a man to appear in court, to bear witness or give evidence on a certain trial named. It is so called because the party summoned is bound to appear *sub poena centum librorum* (under a penalty of £100). We have the verb to *subpoena*.

**Subsidy** (Lat. *sub-sedere*, to sit down). The *subsidii* of the Roman army were the troops held in reserve, the auxiliaries, supports; hence the word came to be applied to a support generally, and (in English) specially to financial support granted by Parliament to the king. It now usually means a contribution granted by the state in aid of some commercial venture of public importance.

***Subsidiary,*** auxiliary, supplemental, is, of course, from the same word.

**Subtle Doctor, The** (*Doctor Subtilis*). The Scottish schoolman and Franciscan friar, Duns Scotus (about 1265–1308).

**Succoth.** The Jewish name for the Feast of Tabernacles (Heb. *sukkoth*, booths). *See* Tabernacle.

**Suck,** or **Suck-in.** A swindle, hoax, deception; a fiasco.

*Sucking* is used (after *sucking-pig*) of a youth who is in training for something, as, *a sucking lawyer*, an articled clerk, *a sucking curate*, a student at a theological college who is trying his hand at parochial work, *a sucking patrician*, a younger son of the aristocracy, etc.

***To suck the monkey.*** *See* Monkey.

***To teach one's grandmother to suck eggs.*** *See* Eggs.

**Sudden Death.** In tossing, the decision arrived at as the result of the first toss; one generally tosses 'the best two out of three' or 'sudden death'.

**Suds, Mrs.** A facetious name for a washer-woman. Of course the allusion is to soap-suds.

***To be in the suds*** – in ill-temper. According to the song, 'Ne'er a bit of comfort is upon a washing day', all are put out of gear, and there-fore out of temper.

**Suède.** Undressed kid-skin; so called because the gloves made of this originally came from Sweden (Fr. *gants de Suède*).

**Suffering. *The Meeting for Sufferings*.** The standing representative Committee of the Yearly Meeting of the Society of Friends (i.e. the Quakers), which deals with any questions affecting the Society which may arise during the intervals of the Yearly Meetings; so called because when originally appointed in the 17th century their chief function was to relieve the sufferings caused to their members by distraint for tithes, persecution, etc.

**Suffragan.** An auxiliary bishop; one who has not a see of his own but is appointed to assist a bishop in a portion of his see. In relation to a metropolitan or archbishop all bishops are suf-fragans; and they were so called because they could be summoned to a synod to give their *suffrage*.

**Suffrage.** One's vote, approval, consent; or, one's right to vote, especially at parliamentary and municipal elections. The word is from Lat. *suffrago*, the hough or ankle-bone of a horse, which was used by the Romans for balloting with, whence the voting table came to be called *suffragium*.

Hence *Suffragette*, a woman (usually more or less 'militant') who in the ten years or so preceding the Great War 'agitated' for the parliamentary vote. The Suffragettes' cam-paigns of disturbance, violence, assault, wanton destruction of public property, arson, and attempted terrorism (for which many women were imprisoned and went on 'hunger-strike') reached alarming proportions; but it stopped dead on the outbreak of War, and in 1918 women of 30 were not only enfranchised but made eligible for seats in Parliament.

**Sui generis** (Lat. of its own kind.) Having a distinct character of its own; unlike anything else.

**Sui juris** (Lat.). Of one's own right; the state of being able to exercise one's legal rights – i.e. freedom from legal disability.

**Suicides** were formerly buried ignominiously on the high-road, with a stake thrust through their body, and without Christian rites. (Lat. *sui*, of oneself, *-cidium*, from *caedere*, to kill.)

> They buried Ben at four cross roads,
> With a stake in his inside.
>
> Hood, *Faithless Nelly Gray*

**Suisse. *Tu fais suisse*.** You live alone; you are a misanthrope. *Suisse* (i.e. Swiss) denotes in France a lodge-keeper or porter, hence *Parler au Suisse* is 'Inquire at the porter's lodge'. As he lived in a lodge near the main entrance he was cut off from the house and servants, and thus became a solitary.

**Suit. *A suit of dittoes*.** *See* Ditto.

***To follow suit.*** To follow the leader; to do as those do who are taken as your exemplars. The term is from games of cards.

**Sultan** (Arab., king, *cp.* Soldan). The chief ruler of Turkey, and of some other Mohammedan countries, as Oman, Zanzibar, and – since 1914 (*cp.* Khedive) – Egypt.

The wife (or sometimes the mother, sister, or concubine) of the Sultan is the *Sultana*, a name also given to a small, seedless raisin grown near Smyrna and to the purple gallinule (*Porphyrio coeruleus*), a beautiful bird allied to the moorhen.

> Some purple-wing'd Sultana sitting
> Upon a column, motionless
> And glittering, like an idol-bird.
>
> Moore, *Paradise and the Peri*

**Summer.** The second or autumnal summer, said to last thirty days, begins shortly before the sun enters Scorpio (Oct. 23rd). It is variously called –

St Martin's summer. St Martin's Day is Nov. 11th.

> Expect St Martin's summer, halcyon days.
>
> Shakespeare, *1 Henry VI*, 1, 2

All Saints' or All Hallows' summer (All Saints' is Nov. 1st).

> Then followed that beautiful season,
> Called by the pious Arcadian peasants the summer of All Saints.
>
> Longfellow, *Evangeline*

> Farewell, All Hallowen summer.
>
> Shakespeare, *1 Henry IV*, 1, 2

St Luke's little summer (St Luke's day is Oct. 18th); and – especially in the United States – the Indian summer.

***Summer Time.*** *See* Time.

**Summum bonum** (Lat. the highest good). The chief excellence; the highest attainable good.

*Socrates* said knowledge is virtue, and ignorance is vice.

*Aristotle* said that happiness is the greatest good.

*Bernard de Mandeville* and *Helvetius* contended that self-interest is the perfection of the ethical end.

*Bentham* and *Mill* were for the greatest happiness of the greatest number.

*Herbert Spencer* placed it in those actions which best tend to the survival of the individual and the race; and

*Robert Browning* (*see* his poem of this name) 'in the kiss of one girl'.

**Sumptuary Laws.** Laws to limit the expenses of food and dress, or any luxury. The Romans had their *leges sumptuarii*, and they have been enacted in many states at various times. Those of England were all repealed by 1 James 1, c. 25; but during the Great War, with the rationing of food, coals, etc., and the compulsory lowering of the strength of beer and whisky we had a temporary return to sumptuary legislation.

**Sun.** The source of light and heat, and consequently of life, to the whole world; hence, regarded as a deity and worshipped as such by all primitive peoples and having a leading place in all mythologies. *Shamash* was the principal sun god of the Assyrians, *Merodach* of the Chaldees, *Ormuzd* of the Persians, *Ra* of the Egyptians, *Tezcatlipoca* of the Mexicans, and *Helios* (known to the Romans as *Sol*) of the Greeks. Helios drove his chariot daily across the heavens, rising from the sea at dawn and sinking into it in the west at sunset; the names of his snow-white, fire-breathing coursers are given as Bronte (*thunder*), Eoos (*day-break*), Ethiops (*flashing*), Ethon (*fiery*), Erythreos (*red-producer*), Philogea (*earth-loving*), and Pyrois (*fiery*).

The Scandinavian sun god, *Sunna*, who was in constant dread of being devoured by the wolf Fenris (a symbolification of eclipses), was similarly borne through the sky by the horses Arvakur, Aslo, and Alsvidur.

*Apollo* was also a sun god of the Greeks, but he was the personification not of the sun itself but of its all-pervading light and life-giving qualities.

***A place in the sun.*** A favourable position that allows room for development; a share in what one has a natural right to. The phrase was popularised by William II of Germany during the crisis of 1911. In his speech at Hamburg (Aug. 27th) he spoke of the German nation taking steps that would make them –

> sure that no one can dispute with us the place in the sun that is our due.

It had been used by Pascal some two hundred years before.

***Heaven cannot support two suns, nor earth two masters.*** So said Alexander the Great when Darius (before the battle of Arbela) sent to offer terms of peace. *Cp.* Shakespeare:

> Two stars keep not their motion in one sphere;
> Nor can one England brook a double reign,
> Of Harry Percy and the Prince of Wales.
>
> *1 Henry IV*, 5, 4

***More worship the rising than the setting sun.*** More persons pay honour to ascendant than to fallen greatness. The saying is attributed to Pompey.

> I should fear those that dance before me now
> Would one day stamp upon me; it has been done;
> Men shut their doors against a setting sun.
>
> Shakespeare, *Timon of Athens*, 1, 2

***Out of God's blessing into the warm sun.*** One of Ray's proverbs, meaning from good to less good. When the king says to Hamlet 'How is it that the clouds still hang on you?' the prince answers, 'No, my lord, I am too much i' the sun,' meaning, 'I have lost God's blessing, for too much of the sun' – i.e. this far inferior state.

> Thou out of heaven's benediction comest
> To the warm sun.
>
> Shakespeare, *King Lear*, 2, 2

***The City of the Sun.*** *See* City.

***The empire on which the sun never sets.*** *See* Set (*The setting of the sun*).

***The Southern Gate of the Sun.*** The sign Capricornus or winter solstice. So called because it is the most southern limit of the sun's course in the ecliptic.

***The sun of Austerlitz.*** When Napoleon fought the Russians and Austrians at Austerlitz (Dec. 2nd, 1805), a brilliant sun suddenly burst through and scattered the mists, thus enabling him to gain an overwhelming victory. Napoleon ever after looked upon this as a special omen from heaven.

***The Sun of Righteousness.*** Jesus Christ. (Mal. 4:2.)

***To have been out in the sun,*** or ***to have the sun in one's eyes.*** To be slightly inebriated.

***To make hay while the sun shines.*** *See* Hay.

**Sunday** (A.S. *sunnendoeg*). The first day of the week, so called because anciently dedicated to the sun, as Monday was to the moon (*see* Week, Days of the). *See also* Sabbath.

***Not in a month of Sundays.*** Not in ever so long.

***One's Sunday best,*** or ***Sunday-go-to-meeting togs.*** One's best clothes, kept for wearing on Sundays.

***Sunday saint.*** One who observes the ordinances of religion, and goes to church on a Sunday, but is worldly, grasping, 'indifferent honest', the following six days.

***When three Sundays come together.*** Never.

**Sundew,** the *Drosera*, which is from the Greek *drosos*, dew. So called from the dew-like drops which rest on the hairy fringes of the leaves.

**Sundowner.** Australian slang for a tramp who times his arrival at the houses of the hospitable at sundown, so as to get a night's lodging.

**Sunflower.** What we know as the sunflower is the *Helianthus*, so called, not because it follows the sun, but because it resembles a conventional drawing of the sun. A bed of these flowers will turn in every direction, regardless of the sun. The *Turnsole* (*Heliotropium*), belonging to quite another order of plants, is the flower that turns to the sun.

> The sunflower turns on the god, when he sets,
> The same look which she turned when he rose.
>
> T. Moore (*Believe me if all those endearing young charms*)

**Sunna** (Arab. custom, divine law). Properly, the sayings and example of Mahomet and his immediate followers in so far as they conform to the Koran; hence applied to the collections of legal and moral traditions attributed to the Prophet, supplementary to the Koran as the Hebrew Mishna is to the Pentateuch.

**Sunnites.** The orthodox and conservative body of Moslems, who consider the Sunna (*see above*) as authentic as the Koran itself and acknowledge the first four caliphs to be the rightful successors of Mahomet. They form by far the largest section of Mohammedans, and are divided into four sects, viz., Hanbalites, Hanafites, Malikites, and Shafiites (*cp.* Shiites).

**Suo marte** (Lat.). By one's own strength or personal exertions.

**Super.** In theatrical parlance, 'supers' are supernumeraries, or persons employed to make up crowds, processions, dancing or singing choirs, messengers, etc., where little or no speaking is needed. (*See also* Superman *below*.)

**Supercilious.** Having an elevated eyebrow (Lat. *super*, over, *cilium*, eyebrow); hence contemptuous, haughty.

**Supererogation.** ***Works of supererogation.*** The term used by theologians for good works which are performed but are not actually enjoined on Christians (Lat. *super*, over, above, *erogare*, to pay out). In common use as a phrase.

**Superman.** A hypothetical superior human being of high intellectual and moral attainments, fancied as evolved from the normally existing type. The term (*übermensch*) was invented by the German philosopher Nietzsche (d.1900), and popularised in England by G. B. Shaw's play, *Man and Superman* (1903).

The wide popularity of the term gave rise to many compounds, such as *superwoman*, *super-critic*, *super-tramp*, *super-Dreadnought*, and *super-tax*.

**Supernaculum.** The very best wine. The word is Low Latin for 'upon the nail' (*super unguem*), meaning that the wine is so good the drinker leaves only enough in his glass to make a bead on his nail. The French say of first-class wine, 'It is fit to make a ruby on the nail' (*faire rubis sur l'ongle*). Nashe says that after a man had drunk his glass, it was usual, in the North, to turn the cup upside down, and let a drop fall upon the thumb-nail. If the drop rolled off, the drinker was obliged to fill and drink again (*Pierce Pennilesse*, 1592). Bishop Hall alludes to the same custom: 'The Duke Tenterbelly … exclaims … "Let never this goodly-formed goblet of wine go jovially through me;" and then he set it to his mouth, stole it off every drop, save a little remainder, which he was by custom to set upon his thumb-nail and lick off.'

> 'Tis here! the supernaculum! twenty years
> Of age, if 'tis a day. Byron, *Werner*, i, 1

Hence, *to drink supernaculum* is to leave no heel-taps; to leave just enough not to roll off one's thumb-nail if poured upon it.

> This is after the fashion of Switzerland, clear off neat, supernaculum.
>
> Rabelais, *Gargantua and Pantagruel*, Bk i, 5

> Their jests were supernaculum,
> I snatched the rubies from each thumb,
> And in this crystal have them here.
> Perhaps you'll like it more than beer.
>
> King, *Orpheus and Eurydice*

**Supply.** One who acts as a substitute, temporarily taking the place of another; used principally of clergymen, school teachers, and domestic servants.

In Parliamentary language *supplies* is used of money granted for the purposes of government which is not provided by the revenue. In England all money bills, i.e. those authorising expenditure, must originate in the House of Commons and must be based on resolutions passed by a *Committee of Supply*.

***The law of supply and demand.*** The economic statement that the competition of buyers and sellers tends to make such changes in price that the demand for any article in a given market will become equal to the supply. In other words, if the demand exceeds the supply the price rises, operating so as to reduce the demand and so enable the supply to meet it, and *vice versa*.

**Supralapsarian.** *See* Sublapsarian.

**Surgeon.** A contraction of the earlier *chirurgeon*, from Gr. *cheir*, hand, *ergein*, to work – one who works with his hands, or works by manual operations instead of through the agency of physic (as does the *physician*). The word is, etymologically, identical with *manufacturer* (Lat. *manus*, hand, *facere*, to work).

**Surloin.** *See* Sirloin.

**Surname.** The name added to, or given over and above, the Christian or personal name (O.Fr. *sur-*, from Lat. *super-*, over, above). English surnames (of which, it is said, there are some 30,000) came into use in the latter part of the 10th century, but were not widely used till much later. In origin they are for the most part appellations denoting a trade or occupation, the place of residence, or some peculiar characteristic.

**Surplice.** Over the *pelisse* or fur robe. (Lat. *super-pellicium*, from *pellis*, skin.) The clerical robe worn over the bachelor's ordinary dress, which was anciently made of sheepskin.

**Surt** or **Surtur.** The guardian of Muspelsheim, who keeps watch day and night with a flaming sword. At the end of the world he will hurl fire from his hand and burn up both heaven and earth. (*Scandinavian mythology*.)

**Susanna and the Elders.** A favourite subject among Renaissance and later artists. The *Story of Susanna*, one of the books of the Old Testament Apocrypha, tells how Susanna was accused of adultery by certain Jewish elders who had unsuccessfully attempted her chastity, how her innocence was proved by Daniel, and the Elders put to death.

**Sût.** One of the sons of Eblis (*q.v.*).

**Sutor.** *Ne sutor*, etc. *See* Cobbler.

**Sutras.** Ancient Hindu aphoristic manuals giving the rules of systems of philosophy, grammar, etc., and directions concerning religious ritual and ceremonial customs. They form a link between the Vedic and later Sanskrit literature, and are so called from Sansk. *sutra*, a thread, the aphorisms being, as it were, threaded together.

**Suttee.** The Hindu custom of burning the widow on the funeral pyre of her deceased husband; also, the widow so put to death (from Sansk. *sati*, a virtuous wife). In theory the practice, which lasted for some 2,000 years, was optional, but public opinion and the very severe form of ostracism the defaulting widow had to endure gave her practically no option. Women with child and mothers of children not yet of age could not perform suttee. The practice was declared illegal in British India in 1829, but even now it is probably not completely stamped out.

**Swaddler.** An early nickname for Wesleyan Methodists; applied later (by Roman Catholics) to Dissenters and Protestants generally. Cardinal Cullen, in 1869, gave notice that he would deprive of the sacrament all parents who sent their children to mixed Model schools, where they were associated with 'Presbyterians, Socinians, Arians, and Swaddlers' (*Times*, September 4th, 1869).

There is more than one explanation of the origin of the term. Southey's (*Life of Wesley*, ii, 153) is as follows:

> It happened that Cennick, preaching on Christmas Day, took for his text these words from St Luke's Gospel: 'And this shall be a sign unto you; ye shall find the babe wrapped in swaddling clothes lying in a manger.' A Catholic who was present, and to whom the language of Scripture was a novelty, thought this so ridiculous that he called the preacher a swaddler in derision, and this unmeaning word became a nickname for 'Protestant', and had all the effect of the most opprobrious appellation.

**Swag** (connected with Norwegian *svagga*, to sway from side to side). One's goods carried in a pack or bundle; hence, the booty obtained by a burglary – which is often carried away in a sack. *To get away with the swag* is used figuratively of profiting by one's cleverness or sharp practice.

***Swagman.*** The Australian term for a man who carries his *swag* about with him while on the search for work.

***Swag-shop.*** A place kept by a 'fence', where thieves can dispose of their 'swag'; also, a low-class shop where cheap and trashy articles are sold.

**Swagger** (frequentative of Swag). To strut about with a superior or defiant air; to bluster, make oneself out a very important person; hence, ostentatiously smart or 'swell'; as *a swagger dinner*, *a swagger car*, etc.

***Swagger-stick.*** The small cane carried by a soldier when walking out.

**Swainmote.** *See* Swanimote.

**Swallow.** According to Scandinavian tradition, this bird hovered over the cross of our Lord, crying '*Svala! svala!*' (Console! console!) whence it was called *svalow* (the bird of consolation).

Aelian says that the swallow was sacred to the Penates or household gods, and therefore to injure one would be to bring wrath upon your own house. It is still considered a sign of good luck if a swallow builds under the eaves of one's house.

> Perhaps you failed in your foreseeing skill,
> For swallows are unlucky birds to kill.
>
> Dryden, *Hind and Panther*, Pt iii

Longfellow refers to another old fable regarding this bird:

> Seeking with eager eyes that wondrous stone which the swallow
> Brings from the shore of the sea to restore the sight of its fledglings.
>
> *Evangeline*, Pt i

***One swallow does not make a summer.*** You are not to suppose summer has come to stay just because you have seen a swallow; nor that the troubles of life are over because you have surmounted one difficulty. The Greek proverb, 'One swallow does not make a spring' is to be found in Aristotle's *Nicomachaean Ethics* (I, vii, 16).

**Swan.** The fable that the swan sings beautifully just before it dies is very ancient, though baseless. Swans do not 'sing' at all, in the ordinary sense of the term, and the only one for which song of any kind can be claimed is the Whistling Swan (*Cygnus musicus*) of Iceland, of which it is reported –

> during the long dark nights their wild song is often heard resembling the tones of a violin, though somewhat higher and remarkably pleasant.
>
> Nicol, *Account of Iceland*

The superstition (which was credited by Plato, Aristotle, Euripides, Cicero, Seneca, Martial, etc., and doubted by Pliny and Aelian) probably arose from some such reasoning as – All birds sing; the swan is a bird; therefore it sings; and, as it has never been heard to sing it must do so at its last moment.

Shakespeare refers to it more than once. Emilia, just before she dies, says –

> I will play the swan,
> And die in music.
>
> *Othello*, 5, 2

In the *Merchant of Venice* (iii, 2) Portia says –

> He makes a swan-like end,
> Fading in music,

and Lucrece (*Rape of Lucrece*, l.1611) –

> And now this pale swan in her watery nest
> Begins the sad dirge of her certain ending.

Spenser speaks of the swan as though it sang quite regardless of death –

> He, were he not with love so ill bedight,
> Would mount as high and sing as soote [sweetly] as Swanne.
>
> *Shepheardes Calender*, *October*, 89

And Coleridge, referring to poetasters of the time, gives the old superstition an epigrammatic turn –

> Swans sing before they die; 'twere no bad thing
> Did certain persons die before they sing.

One Greek legend has it that the soul of Apollo, the god of music, passed into a swan, and in the *Phaedo* Plato makes Socrates say that at their death swans sing –

> not out of sorrow or distress, but because they are inspired of Apollo, and they sing as foreknowing the good things their god hath in store for them.

This idea made the Pythagorean fable that the souls of all good poets passed into swans, hence, the *Swan of Mantua*, etc. (*see below*).

*See also* Fionnuala; Leda; Lohengrin.

The male swan is called a *cob*, the female a *pen*; a young swan a *cygnet*.

***A black swan.*** A curiosity, a *rara avis* (*q.v.*).

***All your swans are geese.*** All your fine promises or expectations have proved fallacious. 'Hope told a flattering tale.' The converse, *All your geese are swans*, means all your children are paragons, and whatever you do is in your own eyes superlative work.

***Leda and the swan.*** *See* Leda.

***Swan-maidens.*** Fairies of northern folklore, who can become maidens or swans at will by means of the *swan shift*, a magic garment of swan's feathers. Many stories are told of how the swan shift was stolen, and the fairy was obliged to remain thrall to the thief until rescued by a knight.

***Swan song.*** The song fabled to be sung by swans at the point of death (*see above*); hence, the last work of a poet, composer, etc.

***Swan-upping.*** A taking up of swans and placing marks of ownership on their beaks. The term is specially applied to annual expeditions for this purpose up the Thames, when the marks of the owners (viz. the Crown and the Dyers' and Vintners' Companies) are made. The royal swans are marked with five nicks – two lengthwise, and three across the bill – and the Companies' swans with two nicks. Also called *Swan-hopping*.

***The Knight of the Swan.*** Lohengrin (*q.v.*).

***The Order of the Swan.*** An order of knighthood instituted by Frederick II of Brandenburg in 1440 (and shortly after in Cleves) in honour of the Lohengrin legend. It died out in the 16th century, but it is still commemorated in our *White Swan* public-house sign, which was first used in honour of Anne of Cleves, one of the wives of Henry VIII. The badge was a silver swan surmounted by an image of the Virgin.

***The Swan of Avon.*** Shakespeare; so called by Ben Jonson in allusion to his birthplace, Stratford-on-Avon. *Swan*, as applied to poets (because Apollo was fabled to have been changed into a swan), is of very old standing; thus, Virgil was known as *the Mantuan Swan*, Homer *the Swan of Meander*, etc.; and Anna Seward (1747–1809) was rather absurdly named *the Swan of Lichfield*.

***The Swan with Two Necks.*** The emblem of the Vintners' Company, and an old tavern sign. *Necks* is a corruption of *Nicks* (*see* Swan-upping, *above*).

**Swanhild.** An old Norse legendary heroine, daughter of Sigurd and Gudrun. She was falsely accused of adultery with the son of the king who was wooing her, and the king had him hanged and her trampled to death by horses.

**Swanimote.** A court held thrice a year before forest verderers by the steward of the court. So called from A.S. *swangemot*, a meeting of swineherds, because, under the *Charta de Foresta* (1217), it was a meeting of the keepers of the royal forests to arrange for the depasturing of pigs in autumn, the clearance of cattle during the deer's fawning season, etc.

**Swank.** To behave in an ostentatious manner, show off and 'cut a dash' to impress the observers with one's cleverness, smartness, or rank, etc. It is an old dialect word adopted as modern slang.

***He's a regular swanker.*** There's nothing in him – he just shows off for effect; his little game is merely bluff.

***It's all swank!*** All show, with little or nothing to back it up; often said of the 'new rich' who ape the ways of the old aristocracy.

**Swashbuckler.** A ruffian; a swaggerer. 'From swashing', says Fuller (*Worthies*; 1662), 'and making a noise on the buckler'. The sword-players used to 'swash' or tap their shield, as fencers tap their foot upon the ground when they attack. *Cp.* Swinge-buckler.

**Swastika.** The gammadion, or fylfot (*q.v.*), an elaborated cross-shaped design used as a charm to ward off evil and bring good luck. The word is Sanskrit, from *svasti*, good fortune.

**Swear, To.** Originally used only of solemnly affirming, by the invocation of God or some sacred person or object as witness to the pledge, to take an oath. Swearing came later to mean using bad language by way of expletives, intensives, and in moments of sudden anger through the sacred expressions being used in a profane way in lightly and irreverently taking oaths.

***Swearing on the horns.*** *See* Horn.

***Swear word.*** A profane or objectionable word used in swearing. Rudyard Kipling has been called 'the poet of the cuss-word and the swear' (Edgar Wallace; *Tommy to his Laureate*).

***To swear black is white.*** To swear to any falsehood.

***To swear like a trooper.*** To indulge in very strong blasphemy or profanity. – ' "Our armies swore terribly in Flanders," cried my Uncle Toby' (Sterne: *Tristram Shandy*, II, xi).

**Sweat.** ***To sweat a person*** is to exact the largest possible amount of labour from him at the lowest possible pay, to keep him working 'all out' at starvation wages. The term is also used of bleeding, or fleecing, a man; and of rubbing down coins so that one can obtain and use the gold or silver taken from them.

***Sweating sickness.*** A form of malaria epidemic, which appeared in England about a century and a half after the *Black Death* (1485). It broke out amongst the soldiers of Richmond's army as a violent inflammatory fever, without boils or ulcers, after the battle of Bosworth, and lasted five weeks. Between 1485 and 1529 there were five outbreaks, the first four being confined to England and France, the fifth spreading over Germany, Turkey, and Austria.

**Swedenborgians.** Followers of Emanuel Swedenborg (1688–1772), called by themselves 'the New Jerusalem Church' (Rev. 21:2). Their views of salvation, inspiration of Scripture, and a future state, differ widely from those of other Christians, and they believe the Trinity to be centred in the person of Jesus Christ (Col. 2:9).

**Sweep.** ***To sweep the threshold.*** To announce to all the world that the woman of the house is paramount. When the procession called 'Skimmington' (*q.v.*) passed a house where the woman 'wore the breeches' everyone gave the threshold a sweep with a broom or bunch of twigs.

**Sweepstakes.** A race in which stakes are made by the owners of horses engaged, to be awarded to the winner or other horse in the race. Entrance money has to be paid to the race fund.

> If the horse runs, the full stake must be paid; but if it is withdrawn, a forfeit only is imposed.

Also a gambling arrangement in which a number of persons stake money on some event (usually a horse-race), each of whom draws a lot for every share bought, the total sum deposited being divided among the drawers of winners (or sometimes of starters). Some 'sweeps' have very valuable prizes; as the 'Calcutta Sweep' on the Derby (organised by the Calcutta Club), the first prize of which comes to over £100,000.

**Sweet.** ***The sweet singer of Israel.*** King David (about 1074–1001 BC).

***To be sweet on.*** To be enamoured of, in love with.

***To have a sweet tooth.*** To be very fond of dainties and sweet things generally.

**Sweetness.** ***Sweetness and light.*** A favourite phrase with Matthew Arnold. 'Culture', he said, 'is the passion for sweetness and light, and (what is more) the passion for making them prevail' (*Preface* to *Literature and Dogma*). The phrase was used by Swift (*Battle of the Books*, 1697) in an imaginary fable by Aesop as to the merits of the bee (the ancients) and the spider (the moderns). It concludes:

> The difference is that instead of dirt and poison, we have rather chose to fill our hives with honey and wax, thus furnishing mankind with the two noblest of things, which are *sweetness* and *light*.

**Swell.** A person showily dressed; one who puffs himself out beyond his proper dimensions, like the frog in the fable; hence, a fashionable person, one of high standing or importance.

***Swell mob.*** The better-dressed thieves and pickpockets.

**Swelled Head.** An exaggerated sense of one's own dignity, usefulness, importance, etc.

**Swim.** ***In the swim.*** In a favourable position in society of any kind; a racing-man who is 'in the swim' is one who mixes with the class from which he can get the best 'tips'; and similarly with a diplomatist, a stockbroker, or a society lady. It is an angler's phrase. A lot of fish gathered together is called a *swim*, and when an angler can pitch his hook in such a place he is said to be 'in a good swim'.

***To do something – 'sink or swim'.*** To do it no matter what happens. In the good old times convicted witches were thrown into the water to 'sink or swim'; if they sank they were drowned; if they swam it was clear proof they were in league with the Evil One; so it did not much matter, one way or the other.

***To swim with the stream.*** To allow one's actions and principles to be guided solely by the force of public opinion.

**Swindle.** To cheat, defraud, gain a mean advantage by trickery. The verb is formed from the noun *swindler*, which was introduced into England by German Jews about 1760, from Ger. *schwindler*, a cheating company promoter (from *schwindeln*, to act heedlessly or extravagantly).

Tossing for drinks, etc., is sometimes called *having a swindle* for them.

**Swing.** ***Captain Swing.*** The name assumed by certain persons who, about 1830, sent threatening letters to farmers who employed mechanical means, such as threshing machines, to save labour. 'Captain Swing' was an entirely imaginary person – like the famous Mrs Harris – but three so-called *Lives* of him appeared in 1830 and 1831.

***I don't care if I swing for him!*** A remark of one very revengefully inclined; implying that the speaker will even go to the length of murdering the enemy, and getting hanged (swung) in consequence.

***In full swing.*** Going splendidly; everything prosperous and in perfect order.

***It went with a swing.*** Said of a ceremony, function, entertainment, etc., that passed off without a hitch and was a great success.

***What you lose on the swings you get back on the roundabouts.*** A rough way of stating the law of averages; if you have bad luck on one day you have good on another, if one venture results in loss try a fresh one – it may succeed. The phrase is, of course, from the showman's ground.

**Swinge-buckler.** A roisterer, a rake who went a bit farther than a swashbuckler (*q.v.*), in that he *swinged* (beat) his man, as well as *swashed* his buckler. The continuation of Stow's *Annals* tells us that in Elizabeth's time the 'blades' of London used to assemble in West Smithfield with sword and buckler for mock fights, called 'bragging' fights. They swashed and swinged their bucklers with much show of fury, 'but seldome was any man hurt'.

**Swiss.** The nickname of a Swiss is 'Colin Tampon'.

***No money – no Swiss*** – i.e. no assistance. The Swiss were for centuries the mercenaries of Europe – willing to serve anyone for pay – and were usually called in England *Switzers*, as in Shakespeare's 'Where are my Switzers? Let them guard the door' (*Hamlet*, 4, 5). In France an hotel-porter – also the beadle of a church – is called *un suisse*.

**Swithin, St.** ***If it rains on St Swithin's day*** (July 15th), *there will be rain for forty days.*

The legend is that St Swithin, Bishop of Winchester, who died 862, desired to be buried in the church*yard* of the minster, that the 'sweet rain of heaven might fall upon his grave'. At canonisation the monks thought to honour the saint by removing his body into the choir, and fixed July 15th for the ceremony; but it rained day after day for forty days, so that the monks saw the saint was averse to their project, and wisely abandoned it.

The St Swithin of France is St Gervais (*q.v.*; *and see* Médard). The rainy saint in Flanders is St Godelième; in Germany, the Seven Sleepers.

**Switzers.** *See* Swiss.

**Swollen Head.** *See* Swelled Head.

**Sword** (*Phrases and Proverbs*).

***At swords' point.*** In deadly hostility, ready to fight each other with swords.

***Fire and sword.*** Rapine and destruction perpetrated by an invading army.

***Poke not fire with a sword.*** This was a precept of Pythagoras, meaning add not fuel to fire, or do not irritate an angry man by sharp words which will only increase his rage. (*See* Iamblichus, *Protreptics*, symbol ix.)

***Sword and buckler.*** An old epithet for brag and bluster; as *a sword and buckler voice*, *sword and buckler men*, etc. Hotspur says of the future Henry V:

> And that same sword and buckler Prince of Wales,
> ...
> I'd have him poisoned with a pot of ale.
>
> Shakespeare, *1 Henry IV*, 1, 3

***Sword and Cloak Plays.*** *See* Cloak and Sword.

***Sword dance.*** A Scottish dance performed over two swords laid crosswise on the floor, or sometimes danced among swords placed point downwards in the ground: also a dance in which the men brandish swords and clash them together, the women passing under them when crossed.

***The sword of Damocles.*** *See* Damocles.

***The Sword of God.*** Khaled Ibn al Waled (d.642), the Mohammedan conqueror of Syria, was so called for his prowess at the battle of Muta.

***The Sword of Rome.*** Marcellus, who opposed Hannibal (216–14 BC).

***The Sword of the Spirit.*** The Word of God (Eph. 6:17).

***To put to the sword.*** To slay.

***Your tongue is a double-edged sword.*** You first say one thing and then the contrary; your argument cuts both ways. The allusion is to the double-edged sword out of the mouth of the Son of Man – one edge to condemn, and the other to save (Rev. 1:16).

***Yours is a Delphic sword – it cuts both ways.*** Erasmus says a Delphic sword is that which accommodates itself to the *pro* or *con* of a subject. The reference is to the double meanings of the Delphic oracles.

**Sybarite.** A self-indulgent person; a wanton. The inhabitants of Sybaris, in South Italy, were proverbial for their luxurious living and self-indulgence. A tale is told by Seneca of a Sybarite who complained that he could not rest comfortably at night, and being asked why, replied, 'He found a rose-leaf doubled under him, and it hurt him.'

Fable has it that the Sybarites taught their horses to dance to the pipe. When the Crotonians marched against Sybaris they played on their pipes, whereupon all the Sybarite horses began to dance; disorder soon prevailed in the ranks, and the victory was quick and easy.

**Sycamore and Sycomore.** The *Sycamore* is the common plane tree of the maple family (*Acer pseudo-platanus*, or greater maple); the *sycomore* is the Egyptian fig tree, and is the tree into which Zacchaeus climbed (Luke 19:1) to see Christ pass. Coverdale's, the Geneva, and other early English

Bibles, call it the 'wyld figge tre'. Both words are from Gr. *sukon*, fig, and *moron*, mulberry.

**Sycophant.** A sponger, parasite, or servile flatterer; the Greek *sukophantes* (*sukon*, fig, *phainein*, to show), which is said to have meant an informer against persons who exported figs or robbed the sacred fig trees. There is no corroboration of this, but the widely accepted story is that the Athenians passed a law forbidding the exportation of figs, and there were always found mean fellows who, for their own private ends, impeached those who violated it; hence *sycophantes* came to signify first a government toady, and then a toady generally.

**Sycorax.** A witch, mother of Caliban, in Shakespeare's *Tempest*.

**Syllogism.** A form of argument consisting of three propositions, a *major premise* or general statement, a *minor premise* or instance, and the *conclusion*, which is deduced from these.

The five hexameter verses which contain the symbolic names of all the different syllogistic figures are as follow:

Barbara, Celarent, Darii, Ferioque, *prioris*.
Cesare, Camestres, Festino, Baroko, *secundae*.
*Tertia*, Darapti, Disamis, Datisi, Felapton.
Bokardo, Ferison, *habet*. *Quarta insuper addit*
Bramantip, Camenes, Dimaris, Fesapo, Fresison.

The vowel.
*A* universal affirmative.
*E* universal negative.
*I* particular affirmative.
*O* particular negative.

Taking the first line as the standard, the initial letters of all the words below it show to which standard the syllogism is to be reduced; thus, Baroko is to be reduced to 'Barbara', Cesare to 'Celarent', and so on.

**Sylphs.** Elemental spirits of air; so named in the Middle Ages by the Rosicrucians and Cabalists, from the Greek *silphe*, some kind of beetle, or a grub that turns into a butterfly. *Cp.* Salamander.

Any mortal who has preserved inviolate chastity might enjoy intimate familiarity with these gentle spirits, and deceased coquettes were said to become sylphs, 'and sport and flutter in the fields of air'.

**Symmachians.** An ancient heretical sect of Ebionites (*q.v.*), said to have been founded by Symmachus, who translated the Old Testament into Greek in the 2nd or 3rd century.

**Symplegades, The.** *See* Cyanean Rocks.

**Symposium.** Properly, a drinking together (Gr. *syn*, together, *posis*, drink); hence, a convivial meeting for social and intellectual entertainment; hence, a discussion upon a subject, and the collected opinions of different authorities printed and published in a review, etc.

***The Symposium*** is the title given to a dialogue by Plato, and another by Xenophon, in which the conversation of Socrates and others is recorded.

**Syndicalism.** The doctrine in economics that all the workers in any industry should have a share in the control and in the profits arising from it, and that to compass this end the workers in the different trades should federate and enforce their demands by sympathetic strikes. The word was first used about 1907, and was coined from the French *chambre syndicale syndic*, a delegate), a trade union.

**Synecdoche.** The figure of speech which consists of putting a part for the whole, the whole for the part, a more comprehensive for a less comprehensive term, or *vice versa*. Thus, *a hundred bayonets* (for *a hundred soldiers*), *the town was starving* (for *the people in the town*).

**Synoptic Gospels, The.** Those of Matthew, Mark, and Luke; so called because, taken together and apart from that of John, they form a *synopsis* (Gr. a seeing together), i.e. a general view or conspectus, of the life and sayings of Christ.

Hence, the *Synoptic Problem*, the questions as to the origin and relationship of these three; *Mark* is generally supposed to be a source of *Matthew* and *Luke*, and *Luke* to have borrowed from *Matthew*.

**Syrinx.** An Arcadian nymph of Greek legend. On being pursued by Pan she took refuge in the river Ladon, and prayed to be changed into a reed; the prayer was granted, and of the reed Pan made his pipes. Hence the name is given to the *Pan-pipe*, or reed mouth-organ, and also to the vocal organ of birds.

**Syntax, Doctor.** The pious, hen-pecked clergyman, very simple-minded but of excellent taste and scholarship, created by William Combe (1741–1823) to accompany a series of coloured comic illustrations by Rowlandson. His adventures are told in eight-syllabled verse in the *Three Tours of Dr Syntax* (1812, 1820, and 1821).

# T

**T.** The twentieth letter of the alphabet, representing Semitic *taw* and Greek *tau*, which meant 'a mark'. Our T is a modification of the earlier form, X. *See also* Tau.

***It fits to a T.*** Exactly. The allusion is to work that mechanics square with a *T-square*, a ruler with a cross-piece at one end, especially useful in making right angles, and in obtaining perpendiculars and parallel lines.

***Marked with a T.*** Notified as a felon. Persons convicted of felony, and admitted to the benefit of clergy, were branded on the thumb with the letter T (*thief*). The law authorising this was abolished by 7 and 8 George IV, c. 27.

**Tabard.** A jacket with short pointed sleeves, whole before, open on both sides, with a square collar, winged at the shoulder like a cape, and worn by military nobles over their armour. It was generally emblazoned with heraldic devices. Heralds still wear a tabard.

***The Tabard Inn.*** The inn whence pilgrims from London used to set out on their journey to Canterbury; it was on the London estate of the abbots of Hyde, and lay in the Southwark (now Borough) High Street, a little to the south of London Bridge. It and its host, Harry Bailly, are immortalised in Chaucer's *Canterbury Tales.*

**Tabardar.** A scholar on the foundation of Queen's College, Oxford; so called because they used to wear a gown with tabard sleeves – that is, loose sleeves, terminating a little below the elbow in a point.

**Tabby.** Originally the name (from Arabic) of a silk material with a 'watered' surface, giving an effect of wavy lines; applied to the brownish cat with dark stripes, because its markings resembled this material.

> Demurest of the tabby kind,
> The pensive Selima reclined.
>
> Gray, *On the Death of a Favourite Cat*

**Tabernacles, Feast of.** A Jewish festival lasting eight days and beginning on the 15th Tisri (towards the end of September). Kept in remembrance of the sojourn in the wilderness, and was also the Feast of Ingathering. It was formerly a time of great rejoicing.

**Table. *Apelles table.*** A pictured board (Lat. *tabula*) or table, representing the excellency of sobriety on one side and the deformity of intemperance on the other.

***Table d'hôte*** (Fr., the host's table). The 'ordinary' at an hotel or restaurant; the meal for which one pays a fixed price whether one partakes of all the courses provided or not. In the Middle Ages, and even down to the reign of Louis XIV, the landlord's or host's table was the only public dining-place known in Germany and France.

***Table money.*** A small charge additional to that of the meal made at some clubs, restaurants, etc., towards the cost of attendance; also, in the Army, Navy, and Diplomatic Service, an allowance made to assist in meeting the expense of official entertaining.

***Table-talk.*** Small talk, chit-chat, familiar conversation.

***Table-turning.*** The turning of tables without the application of mechanical force, which in the early days of modern spiritualism was commonly practised at séances, and sank to the level of a parlour trick. It was said by some to be the work of departed spirits, and by others to be due to a force akin to mesmerism.

***Table of Pythagoras.*** The common multiplication table, carried up to ten. The table is parcelled off into a hundred little squares or cells. The name first appears in a corrupt text of Boethius, who was really referring to the abacus (*q.v.*).

***Tables of Cebes.*** Cebes was a Theban philosopher, a disciple of Socrates, and one of the interlocutors of Plato's *Phaedo*. His *Tables* or *Tableau* supposes him to be placed before a tableau or panorama representing the life of man, which the philosopher describes with great accuracy of judgment and splendour of sentiment. It is sometimes appended to the works of Epictetus.

***The Round Table,*** or ***Table Round.*** *See* Round.

***The Tables of Toledo.*** *See* Tabulae Toletanae.

***The Twelve Tables.*** The tables of the Roman laws engraved on brass, brought from Athens to Rome by the decemvirs.

***To lay on the table.*** The parliamentary phrase for postponing consideration of a motion, proposal, bill, etc., indefinitely. Hence, *to table a matter* is to defer it *sine die*.

***To turn the tables.*** To reverse the conditions or relations; as, for instance, to rebut a charge by bringing forth a counter-charge. Thus, if a husband accuses his wife of extravagance in dress, she 'turns the tables upon him' by accusing him of extravagance in his club. The phrase comes from the old custom of reversing the *table* or board, in games such as chess and draughts, so that the opponent's relative position is altogether changed.

**Tableaux vivants** (Fr., living pictures). Representations of statuary groups by living persons; said to have been invented by Madame de Genlis (1746–1830) while she had charge of the children of the Duc d'Orléans.

**Taboo** (Maori *tapu*). A custom among the South Sea Islanders of prohibiting the use of certain persons, places, animals, things, etc., or the utterance of certain names and words; it signifies that which is banned, interdicted, or 'devoted' in a religious sense. Thus, a temple is *taboo*, and so is he who violates a temple. Not only so, but everyone and everything connected with what is taboo becomes taboo also; Captain Cook was *taboo* because some of his sailors took rails from a Hawaiian temple to supply themselves with fuel, and, being 'devoted', he was slain.

With us, a person who is ostracised, or an action, custom, etc., that is altogether forbidden by Society, is said to be *taboo*, or *tabooed*.

> Women, up till this
> Cramped under worse than South-sea-isle taboo,
> Dwarfs of the gynaeceum, fail.
>
> Tennyson, *Princess*, iii, 278

**Taborites.** The extremists among the Hussites (*q.v.*); so called from the fortress Tabor, about fifty miles from Prague, from which Nicholas von Hussineez, one of the founders, expelled the Imperial army. They are now incorporated with the Bohemian Brethren.

**Tabouret** (Fr.). A low stool without back or arms. In the ancient French court certain ladies had the *droit de tabouret* (right of sitting on a tabouret in the presence of the queen). At first it was limited to princesses; but subsequently it was extended to all the chief ladies of the queen's household; and later still the wives of ambassadors, dukes, lord chancellors, and keepers of the seals, enjoyed the privilege. Gentlemen similarly privileged had the *droit de fauteuil*.

**Tabula rasa** (Lat., a scraped tablet). A clean slate – literally and figuratively – on which anything can be written. Thus, we say that the mind of a person who has been badly taught must become a *tabula rasa* before he can learn anything properly.

**Tabulae Toletanae.** The astronomical tables composed by order of Alphonso X of Castile, in the middle of the 13th century; so called because they were adapted to the city of Toledo.

> His Tables Tolletanes forth he brought,
> Ful wel corrected ne ther lakked nought.
>
> Chaucer, *Franklin's Tale*, 545

**Tace.** Latin for candle. Silence is most discreet. *Tace* is Latin for 'be silent', and candle is symbolical of *light*. The phrase means 'keep it dark', do not throw light upon it. Fielding, in his *Amelia* (ch. x), says, '*Tace*, madam, is Latin for candle.' There is an historical allusion worth remembering. It was customary at one time to express disapprobation of a play or actor by throwing a candle on the stage, and when this was done the curtain was immediately drawn down. Oultor (vol. i, p. 6), in his *History of the Theatres of London*, gives us an instance of this which occurred January 25th, 1772, at Covent Garden Theatre, when the piece before the public was *An Hour Before Marriage*. Someone threw a candle on the stage, and the curtain was dropped at once.

> There are some auld stories that cannot be ripped up again with entire safety to all concerned. *Tace* is Latin for candle.
>
> Scott, *Redgauntlet*, ch. xi (Sir Walter is rather fond of the phrase.)
>
> Mum. William mum. *Tace* is Latin for candle.
>
> W. B. Yeats, *Fairy Tales of the Irish Peasantry*, p. 250

We have several of these phrases; *see* **Brandy is Latin for Goose.**

**Tachebrune**, i.e. 'brown spot'. The horse of Ogier the Dane.

**Tages.** In *Etruscan mythology* a mysterious boy with the wisdom of an old man who was ploughed up, or who sprang from, the ground at Tarquinii. He is said to have been the grandson of Jupiter and to have instructed the Etruscans in the arts of augury. The latter wrote down his teaching in twelve books, which were known as 'the books of Tages', or 'the Acherontian books'.

**Taë-pings.** Chinese rebels of about 1850 to 1864. The word means *Universal Peace*, and arose thus; Hung-sew-tseuen, a man of humble birth, and an unsuccessful candidate for a government office, was induced by some missionary tracts to renounce idolatry, and founded the society of

Taëping, which came in to collision with the imperial authorities in 1850. Hung now gave out that he was the chosen instrument in God's hands to uproot idolatry and establish the dynasty of Universal Peace; he assumed the title of Taë-ping-wang (*Prince of Universal Peace*), and called his five chief officers princes. Nankin was made their capital in 1860, but Colonel Gordon ('Chinese' Gordon, afterwards General Gordon) in 1864 quelled the insurrection, and overthrew the armies of Hung.

**Taffeta** or **Taffety.** A material made of silk; at one time it was watered; hence Taylor says, 'No taffaty more changeable than they'. The word is from the Persian *taftan*, to twist or cure.

> The fabric has often changed its character. At one time it was silk and linen, at another silk and wool. In the eighteenth century it was lustrous silk sometimes striped with gold.

***Taffeta phrases.*** Smooth sleek phrases, euphemisms. We also use the words *fustian*, *stuff*, *silken*, *shoddy*, *buckram*, *velvet*, etc., to qualify phrases and literary compositions spoken or written.

> Taffata phrases, silken terms precise,
> Three-piled hyperboles.
> Shakespeare, *Love's Labour's Lost*, 5, 2

**Taffy.** A Welshman. So called from *David*, a very common name in Wales. Familiarly *Davy*, it becomes in Welsh *Taffid*, *Taffy*.

**Tag Rag, and Bobtail.** The *vulgus ignobile*; all sorts and conditions of riffraff. Shakespeare uses *tag* of the rabble –

> Will you hence
> Before the tag return? whose rage doth rend
> Like interrupted waters. *Coriolanus*, 3, 1

*Rag*, and *bobtail* were extensions.

> Midsummer's day moreover was the first of Bedford Fair;
> With Bedford Town's tag-rag and bobtail a-browsing there. Browning, *Ned Brats*

**Taghairm.** A form of divination anciently practised by the Scots. The seer, wrapped up in the hide of a fresh-slain bullock, was placed beside a waterfall, or at the foot of a precipice, and there left to meditate on the question propounded. Whatever his fancy suggested in this wild situation passed for inspiration of his disembodied spirit.

> Last evening-tide
> Brian an augury hath tried,
> Of that kind which must not be
> Unless in dread extremity,
> The Taghairm called.
> Scott, *The Lady of the Lake*, iv, 4

**Tail.** According to an old fable lions wipe out their footsteps with their tail, that they may not be tracked.

***Out of the tail of one's eye.*** With a sidelong glance; just to see a thing 'out of the corner of your eye'.

***To put salt on the tail.*** *See* Salt.

***To turn tail.*** To turn one's back and run away.

***Twisting the lion's tail.*** Seeing how far the 'Britishers' will bear provocation. 'To give the lion's tail another twist' is to tax the British forbearance a little further. The nation will put up with a deal rather than resort to the arbitration of arms.

***With his tail between his legs.*** Very dejected, quite downcast. The allusion is, of course, to dogs.

**Tailed men.** There are no such beings as tailed men, but fables of them are common, and even till recently reports every now and then cropped up of tribes with tails having been discovered in Central Africa, New Guinea, or other little known parts.

But in the early Middle Ages it was widely believed on the Continent, especially in France, that all Englishmen had tails, and it was for long a saying that the men of Kent (the part nearest to France) were born with tails, as a punishment for the murder of Thomas à Becket.

> For Becket's sake, Kent always shall have tails.
> Andrew Marvel

> A *Warwickshire* Man will be known by his Grinn, as Roman-Catholicks imagine a *Kentish* Man is by his Tail. Addison, *Spectator*, 172

One account fastens the legend or the town of Strode:

> As Becket, that good saint, sublimely rode,
> Thoughtless of insult, through the town of Strode,
> What did the mob? Attacked his horse's rump
> And cut the tail, so flowing, to the stump.
> What does the saint? Quoth he, 'For this vile trick
> The town of Strode shall heartily be sick.'
> And lo! by power divine, a curse prevails –
> The babes of Strode are born with horse's tails.
> Peter Pindar, *Epistle to the Pope*

But in Ray's time (early 17th cent.) St Augustine was generally credited with the miracle. He, it was said, was preaching to some pagan villagers when they, to make fun of him, fastened fish-tails to their posteriors, whereupon Augustine ordained that all the next generation should be born with tails; and it was so. This, moreover, was said to have taken place in Cerne, Dorsetshire, and not in Kent at all.

In the Middle Ages it was also popularly held that Jews were born with tails; this arose from a confusion of the word *rabbi* with *raboin* or *rabuino*, the devil, from Span. *rabo*, a tail.

**Tailor.** Nine tailors make a man. An old expression of contempt at the expense of tailors signifying that a tailor is so much more feeble than anyone else that it would take nine of them to make a man of average stature and strength. As a fact, the occupation of a tailor, and the cramped position in which he works, are not conducive to good physique; but *tailor* is probably a facetious transformation of *teller*, a *teller* being a stroke on the bell at a funeral, three being given for a child, six for a woman, and *nine* for a *man*.

The number mentioned is sometimes only three:

> Some foolish knave, I thinke, at first began
> The slander that three taylers are one man.
>
> Taylor, *Workes*, iii, 73 (1630)

Meredith, himself the son of a tailor, makes great play with the phrase in his *Evan Harrington*. The Countess de Saldar, for ever ashamed of her late father's occupation and terrified of its being known, at last announces that she is about to become a Roman Catholic:

> 'I renounce the world. I turn my sight to realms where caste is unknown. I feel no shame *there* of being a tailor's daughter.' … The Countess paused, and like a lady about to fire off a gun, appeared to tighten her nerves, crying out rapidly – 'Shop! Shears! Geese! Cabbage! Snip! Nine to a man!'
>
> Meredith, *Evan Harrington*, ch. xliv

***The three tailors of Tooley Street.*** Canning says that three tailors of Tooley Street, Southwark, addressed a petition of grievances to the House of Commons, beginning – 'We, the people of England'. Hence the phrase is used of any pettifogging coterie that fancies it represents the *vox populi*.

**Taiping.** *See* Taë-pings.

**Take. *To be taken aback.*** To be quite surprised for the moment, flabbergasted. From a nautical term, used when a ship's sails 'back-fill' and her 'way' is lost in consequence.

***To have a taking way with one.*** To be of an ingratiating disposition, able to make oneself liked at once; *fetching way*, *winning way*, mean the same thing.

***To take after.*** To have a strong resemblance to, physically, mentally, etc. 'Doesn't little Johnny take after his father?' 'Most of Lawrence's paintings seem to take after Romney.'

***To take back one's words.*** To withdraw them, to recant.

***To take down a peg.*** *See* Peg.

***To take in.*** To hocus somebody, gull him. Hence, *a regular take in*, a hoax, swindle.

***To take it into one's head.*** To conceive the notion that; to resolve to do so and so.

***To take it out of one.*** To 'give him beans', get one's own back; or, of oneself, to become thoroughly exhausted, as 'Working after midnight does take it out of me.'

***To take it upon oneself.*** To make oneself responsible, to assume control.

***To take off.*** To mimic or ridicule; also to start, especially in an athletic contest, as jumping or racing.

***To take on.*** To be upset or considerably affected; often said of a woman in hysterics; as, 'Come, don't take on so!'

> Lance, who … took upon himself the whole burden of Dame Debbitch's … 'taking on', as such fits of *passio hysterica* are usually termed.
>
> Scott, *Peveril of the Peak*, ch. xxvi

***To take over.*** To assume the management, control, or ownership of so and so.

***To take up.*** To take into custody, arrest; also used of patronising people and getting them introductions into good society, etc.

> 'Yes, Lady Rockminster has took us up,' said Lady Clavering.
>
> 'Taken us up, Mamma,' cried Blanche, in a shrill voice.
>
> 'Well, taken us up, then,' said my lady, 'it's very kind of her, and I dare say we shall like it when we git used to it, only at first one don't fancy being took – well, taken up, at all.'
>
> Thackeray, *Pendennis*, ch. xxxvii

**Tale.** A tally; a reckoning. In Exod. 5 we have *tale of bricks*. A measure by number, as of a shepherd counting his sheep:

> And every shepherd tells his tale
> Under the hawthorn in the dale.
>
> Milton, *L'Allegro*, 67

***An old wife's tale.*** Any marvellous legendary story. The phrase was used by George Peele as the title of a play (1595), and by Arnold Bennett as that of a novel (1908).

***A tale of a tub.*** *See* Tub.

***To tell tales out of school.*** To utter abroad affairs not meant for the public ear.

**Talent.** Ability, aptitude, a 'gift' for something or other. The word is borrowed from the parable in Matt. 25, and was originally the name of a weight and piece of money in Assyria, Greece, Rome, etc. (Gr. *talanton*, a balance). The value varied, the later Attic talent weighing nearly 57 lb troy, and being worth about £250.

***The Ministry of All the Talents.*** The name ironically given to Grenville's coalition of 1806. It included Fox, Erskine, Fitzwilliam, Ellenborough, and Sidmouth. The term has also been applied – ironically – to later coalitions.

**Tales.** Persons in the court from whom selection to supply the place of jurors who have been empanelled, but are not in attendance, is made. It is the first word of the Latin sentence providing for this contingency – *Tales de circumstantibus*, i.e. 'from such (persons) as are standing about'.

> To serve for jurymen or tales.
>
> Butler, *Hudibras*, Pt iii, 8

***To pray a tales.*** To pray that the number of jurymen may be completed.

> In the celebrated action Bardell *v.* Pickwick –
>
> It was discovered that only ten special jurymen were present. Upon this, Mr Serjeant Buzfuz prayed a *tales*; the gentleman in black then proceeded to press into the special jury, two of the common jurymen; and a greengrocer and a chemist were caught directly.
>
> Dickens, *Pickwick Papers*, ch. xxxiv

Those who supplement the jury are called *talesmen*, and their names are set down in the *talesbook*.

**Taliesin.** An ancient Welsh bard of whom very little is known. He is placed in the 6th century, is said to have been a schoolfellow of Gildas, and to have been buried at Aberystwith. The so-called *Book of Taliesin* (given in the *Mabinogion*) is not earlier than the 13th century.

Taliesin is said to have prophesied that his nation would once again rule over England – a 'prophecy' which was verified by the accession of Henry VII, son of Owen Tudor. Hence Gray's allusion to him –

> What strings symphonious tremble in the air,
> What strains of vocal transport round her play!
> Hear from the grave great Taliessin, hear;
> They breathe a soul to animate thy clay.
>
> *The Bard*

**Talisman.** A charm or magical figure or word, such as the Abraxas (*q.v.*), which is cut on metal or stone, under the influence of certain planets; it is supposed to be sympathetic, and to receive an influence from the planets which it communicates to the wearer.

In Arabia a talisman consisting of a piece of paper, on which are written the names of the Seven Sleepers and their dog, to protect a house from ghosts and demons, is still used; and in order to free any place of vermin a talisman consisting of the figure of the obnoxious animal is made in wax or consecrated metal, in a planetary hour.

> He swore that you had robbed his house,
> And stole his talismanic louse.
>
> Butler, *Hudibras*, pt iii, 1

The word is the Arabic *tilasmān*, from late Greek *telesma*, mystery.

**Talkee-talkee.** A copious effusion of talk with no valuable result; 'pi-jaw' (*q.v.*); also, any barbarous jargon, such as the broken English of negroes.

**Tall** anciently meant comely, fine, handsome; hence brave and valiant; and such phrases as *a tall and proper man*, *a tall ship* (i.e. one strong and well found in every respect) were used without any special reference to height.

> You were good soldiers, and tall fellows.
>
> Shakespeare, *Merry Wives of Windsor*, 2, 2
>
> The undaunted resolution and stubborn ferocity of Gwenwyn … had long made him beloved among the 'Tall Men' or champions of Wales.
>
> Scott, *The Betrothed*, ch. i
>
> Beyond the extreme sea-wall, and between the remote sea-gates,
> Waste water washes, and tall ships founder, and deep death waits.
>
> Swinburne, *Hymn to Proserpine*

**Tally.** To correspond. The tally used in the Exchequer was a rod of wood, marked on one face with notches (Fr. *taille*, a notch or incision) corresponding to the sum for which it was an acknowledgement. Two other sides contained the date, the name of the payer, and so on. The rod was then cleft in such a manner that each half contained one written side and half of every notch. One part was kept in the Exchequer, and the other was circulated. When payment was required the two parts were compared, and if they 'tallied', or made a tally, all was right; if not, there was some fraud, and payment was refused.

Tallies were not finally abandoned in the Exchequer till 1834, when orders were issued for their destruction. Two cartloads of them were lighted as a bonfire, and the conflagration set on fire the Houses of Parliament, which, with their offices and part of the Palace of Westminster, were burnt to the ground.

***Tallyman.*** A travelling hawker who calls at private houses to sell wares on the *tally system* – that is, part payment on account, and other parts when the man calls again; so called because he keeps a *tally* or score of his transactions.

***To live tally.*** Said of a couple who live together as man and wife without being married – presumably because they do so as their tastes *tally*, and not from any reason of compulsion.

**Tally-ho!** The cry of fox-hunters on catching sight of the fox. It is the English form of the old French *taïant*, which was similarly used in deer-hunting, and also as a cry to the hounds when their share of the disembowelled stag was thrown to them.

**Talmud, The** (Heb. instruction). The body of Jewish civil and religious law not contained in, but largely derived from, the Pentateuch. The name was originally applied only to the Gemara (*q.v.*), but it now usually includes also the Mishna (*q.v.*).

When the *Talmud* is spoken of without any qualification the reference is to the *Babylonian Talmud*, one of the two recensions of the Gemara, the other being the *Palestinian Talmud*, which is of only about a fourth the volume of the *Babylonian*, and is considered by Jews of less authority. The *Babylonian* codification dates from the 5th or 6th century, the *Palestinian* (or *Jerusalem*) from about a century earlier.

**Talus.** In *Greek mythology*, a man of brass, made by Hephaestus (Vulcan), the guardian of Crete. Whenever he caught a stranger on the island he made himself red-hot and embraced him to death.

He is introduced by Spenser into the *Faërie Queene* (Bk v) as the 'yron man' attendant upon Sir Artegal, and representing executive power – 'swift as a swallow, and as lion strong'.

> His name was Talus made of yron mould
> Immoveable, resistlesse, without end;
> Who in his hand an yron flale did hould,
> With which he thresht out falshood, and did truths unfould.
>
> *Faërie Queene*, V, i, 12

**Tamburlaine, Tamerlane.** Names under which the Tartar conqueror Timur, or Timur-leng, i.e. 'Timur the Lame' (1333–1405), is immortalised in Elizabethan drama. He had his capital at Samarkand, was ruler of vast territories in central Asia and a great part of India, and died while preparing to invade China. *Tamburlaine the Great* (acted in 1587), a blank verse tragedy, was Marlowe's first play. In Rowe's play, *Tamerlane* (1702), the warrior appears as a calm, philosophic prince – out of compliment to our William III.

**Taming of the Shrew, The.** Shakespeare's play (first printed in the 1623 Folio) was a re-writing of an anonymous comedy – *The Taming of A Shrew* – printed in 1594; its theme, a recipe for the management of wives, was very popular with contemporary audiences. *See* Sly.

**Tammany Hall.** The headquarters (in 14th Street, New York) of the controlling organisation of the Democratic Party in New York City and State; hence, the Party itself, and, as this has been so frequently prosecuted and exposed for, bribery and corruption, used figuratively for wholesale and systematic political or municipal malpractice.

*Tammany* was the name of a 17th century Delaware chief, and the patriotic, anti-British leagues of pre-Revolutionary days adopted the name 'St Tammany' to ridicule the titles of loyalist organisations – Societies of St George, St Andrew, and so on. After the Revolution these leagues became anti-aristocratic clubs, but all soon died a natural death except 'Tammany Society, No. 1', which was that of New York. This flourished, and was converted into a political machine by Aaron Burr in his conflict with Alexander Hamilton (about 1798), and in 1800 played a prominent part in the election of Jefferson to the Presidency.

**Tammuz.** *See* Thammuz.

**Tam-o'-Shanter.** The hero of Burns's poem of that name; the soft cloth cap is so called from him.

***Remember Tam-o'-Shanter's mare.*** You may pay too dear for your whistle, as Meg lost her tail, pulled off by Nannie of the 'Çutty-sark', in Burns's poem.

> Think, ye may buy the joys owre dear –
> Remember Tam-o'-Shanter'a mare.
>
> Burns, *Tam-o'-Shanter*

**Tancred** (d.1112). One of the chief heroes of the First Crusade, and a leading character in Tasso's *Jerusalem Delivered.* He was the son of Eudes (Otho) and Emma (sister of Robert Guiscard); Boemond or Bohemond was his cousin. In the epic he was the greatest of all the Christian warriors except Rinaldo, and showed a generous contempt of danger; his one fault was 'woman's love', and that woman Clorinda, a pagan (Bk i), whom he unwittingly slew in a night attack, and whose death he lamented with great lamentation (Bk xii). Being wounded, he was nursed by Erminia, who was in love with him (Bk xix).

Disraeli's novel, *Tancred* (1846), is a fantastic romance, telling how an early 19th century heir to a dukedom goes on a 'New Crusade' to the Holy Land.

**Tandem.** A pair of horses harnessed one behind the other; hence applied to a bicycle ridden by two persons in this position. The word is a punning use of the Latin *tandem*, at length, i.e. of time; the horses being 'lengthways' instead of side by side.

**Tangle.** A water sprite of the Orkneys; from Dan. *tang*, sea-weed, with which it is covered. It is fabled to appear sometimes in human form, and sometimes as a little apple-green horse.

**Tanist** (Gael. *tánaiste*). The elected heir presumptive to an ancient Irish chieftain, chosen generally from among the chief's relations. Hence, *tanistry*, the ancient Irish tenure of lands and chieftainship.

***Tanist stone.*** The monolith erected by the ancient Gaelic kings at their coronation; especially that called *Liafail*, which, according to tradition, is identical with the famous stone of Scone (*q.v.*), now forming part of the Coronation Chair in Westminster Abbey. It is said to have been set up at Icolmkil for the coronation of Fergus I of Scotland, a contemporary of Alexander the Great (about 300 BC), and son of Ferchard, King of Ireland.

**Tank.** The heavily armoured military motor fort, running on 'caterpillar' wheels, enclosed, and with room in the interior for quick-firing guns and several men, was so called by the War Office before it made its first appearance to prevent information as to its real nature leaking out to the enemy. Telegrams, etc., with enquiries about *tanks* would cause no suspicion if they fell into enemy hands. Tanks were invented during the Great War, and were first used in the British attack on the German lines at Flers, September 15th, 1916.

**Tanner.** Slang for a sixpenny piece; *why*, is not known. The term has been in use for over a hundred years.

**Tannhäuser.** A lyrical poet, or *minnesinger*, of Germany, who flourished in the second half of the 13th century. He led a wandering life, and is said even to have visited the Far East; this fact, together with his *Buszlied* (song of repentance), and the general character of his poems, probably gave rise to the legend about him – which first appeared in a 16th century German ballad. This relates how he spends a voluptuous year with Venus, in the Venusberg, a magic land reached through a subterranean cave; at last he obtains leave to visit the upper world, and goes to Pope Urban for absolution. 'No,' said His Holiness, 'you can no more hope for mercy than this dry staff can be expected to bud again.' Tannhäuser departs in despair; but on the third day the papal staff bursts into blossom; the Pope sends in every direction for Tannhäuser, but the knight is nowhere to be found, for, mercy having been refused, he has returned to end his days in the arms of Venus.

**Tansy.** A yellow-flowered perennial herb, so called from Gr. *athanasia*, immortality, because it is 'a sort of everlasting flower'.

**Tantalus.** In *Greek mythology*, the son of Zeus and Pluto (daughter of Himantes). He was a Lydian king, highly honoured and prosperous; but, because he divulged to mortals the secrets of the gods, he was plunged up to the chin in a river of Hades, a tree hung with clusters of fruit being just above his head. As every time he tried to drink the waters receded from him, and as the fruit was just out of reach, he suffered agony from thirst, hunger, and unfulfilled anticipation.

Hence our verb, *to tantalise*, to excite a hope and disappoint it; and hence the name *tantalus* applied to a lock-up spirit chest in which the bottles are quite visible but quite un-get-at-able without the key.

**Tantivy Men.** The High Churchmen and Tories of the post-Restoration period; so called because about 1680 they were caricatured as being mounted on the Church of England, 'riding tantivy' to Rome. *To ride tantivy* (a hunting term) is to ride at a rapid gallop.

> Those who took the king's side were Anti-Birminghams, abhorrers, and tantivies. These terms soon became obsolete.
>
> Macaulay, *History of England*, ch. ii

**Tantony Pig.** The smallest pig of a litter, which, according to the old proverb, will follow its owner anywhere. So called in honour of St Anthony, who was the patron saint of swineherds and is frequently represented with a little pig at his side.

*Tantony* is also applied to a small church bell – or to any hand-bell – for there is usually a bell round the neck of St Anthony's pig or attached to the Tau-cross he carries. *See* **Antony, St.**

**Tantras, The.** Sanskrit religious writings, forming the Bible of the Shaktas, a Hindu religion the adherents of which worship the divine power in its female aspect.

The Tantras consist of magical formulas for the most part in the form of dialogues between Shiva and his wife, and treat of the creation and ultimate destruction of the world, divine worship, the attainment of superhuman power, and final union with the Supreme Spirit. They are of comparatively recent date (6th or 7th cent. AD).

*Tantra* is Sanskrit for thread, or warp, and hence is used of groundwork, order, or doctrine of religion.

**Taoism.** One of the three great religious systems of China (Confucianism and Buddhism being the others), founded by the philosopher Lao-tsze (about 604–523 BC), and based on the *Tao-leh-king* (Book of Reason and Virtue), reputed to be by him.

**Tapis.** *On the tapis.* On the carpet; under consideration; now being ventilated. An English-French phrase, referring to the *tapis* or cloth with which the table of the council chamber is covered, and on which are laid the motions before the House.

> My business comes now upon the tapis.
>
> Farquhar, *The Beaux Stratagem*, iii, 3

**Tapley, Mark.** Martin's servant and companion in Dickens's *Martin Chuzzlewit*; often taken as the type of one who is jolly under all circumstances, never downhearted, and invariably cheerful.

**Tappit-hen.** A Scots term, properly for a hen with a crest or tuft on its head, but generally used for a large beer or wine measure. Readers of *Waverley* will remember (in ch. xi) the Baron Bradwardine's tappit-hen of claret 'containing at least three English quarts'.

***To have a tappit-hen under the belt*** is to have swallowed three quarts. *Cp.* Hen and Chickens; Jeroboam.

> Weel she lo'ed a Hawick gill
> And leugh to see a tappit-hen.

**Tap-up Sunday.** An old local name for the Sunday preceding October 2nd, when a fair was held on St Catherine's Hill, near Guildford. So called because any person, with or without a licence, might open a 'tap', or sell beer on the hill for that one day.

**Tar,** or **Jack Tar.** A sailor; probably an abbreviation of *tarpaulin*, of which sailors' caps and overalls are made. Tarpaulins are tarred cloths, and are commonly used on board ship to keep articles from the sea-spray, etc.

***To tar and feather.*** *See* Tarred.

**Tarakee.** A hero of Brahminical legend and miracle of ascetic devotion. He is fabled to have lived 1,100 years, and spent each century in some astounding mortification.

1st century. He held up his arms and one foot towards heaven, fixing his eyes on the sun the whole time.

2nd century. He stood on tiptoe the whole time.

8th century. He stood on his head, with his feet towards the sky.

9th century. He rested wholly on the palm of one hand.

11th century. He hung from a tree with his head downwards.

> One century he lived wholly on water, another wholly on air, another steeped to the neck in earth, and for another century he was always enveloped in fire. I don't know that the world has been benefited by such devotion.
>
> Maurice, *History of Hindostan*

**Tarantula.** A large and hairy venomous spider (so called from *Taranto*, Lat. *Tarentum*, a town in Apulia, Italy, where they abound), whose bite was formerly supposed to be the cause of the dancing mania hence known as *tarantism.* This was an hysterical disease, common, epidemically, in southern Europe from the 15th to the 17th centuries.

> At the close of the fifteenth century we find that Tarantism had spread beyond the boundaries of Apulia, and that the fear of being bitten by venomous spiders had increased. Nothing short of death itself was expected from the wound which these insects inflicted, and if those who were bitten escaped with their lives, they were said to be seen pining away in a desponding state of lassitude.
>
> Hecker, *Epidemics of the Middle Ages* (1859)

From the same insect the *tarantella* gets its name; this is a very quick Neapolitan dance (or its music) for one couple, and is said to have been based on the gyrations practised by those whom the tarantula had poisoned.

**Targums.** The name given to the various Aramaic (Chaldean) translations and interpretations of the Old Testament. They were transmitted orally from the period soon after the Captivity, and were not written down until about the close of the 1st century AD.

**Tariff.** A table of duties or customs, payable on the importation or exportation of goods; hence, a table of charges generally, as of those at an hotel or restaurant. The word is the Arabic *tarif,* information, which was adopted in Old French as *tariffe*, for arithmetic.

***Tariff reform.*** A political movement in Great Britain, inaugurated by Mr Joseph Chamberlain in 1903, for the extension of the tariff on imports, principally with the object of preventing 'dumping' (i.e. the disposal in our own country of surplus or unsaleable goods manufactured abroad at such a price that the home markets are cut out), and for the protection of home industries. Until the resettlement after the Great War the movement, though it made a great commotion, made little progress against the consensus of opinion, which held that – at all events in normal times – the prosperity of Great Britain was founded upon Free Trade.

**Tarot Cards.** Old Italian playing-cards, first used in the 14th century and still occasionally employed for fortune-telling. A pack contains 78 cards, 22 of which are trumps.

**Tarpaulin.** *See* Tar.

**Tarpeian Rock.** An ancient rock or peak (now no longer in existence) of the Capitoline Hill, Rome; so called from Tarpeia, a vestal virgin, the daughter of Spurius Tarpeius, governor of the citadel, who, according to the legend, agreed to open the gates to the Sabines if they would give her 'what they wore on their arms' (meaning their bracelets). The Sabines, 'keeping their promise to the ear', crushed her to death with their shields, and her body was hurled from the 'Tarpeian Rock'. Subsequently, traitors were cast down this rock and so killed.

> Bear him to the rock Tarpeian, and from thence
> Into destruction cast him.
>
> Shakespeare, *Coriolanus*, 3, 1

**Tarquin.** The family name of a legendary line of early Roman kings. Tarquinius Priscus, the fifth king of Rome, is dated 617–578 BC. His son, Tarquinius Superbus, was the seventh (and last) king of Rome, and it was his son, Tarquinius Sextus, who committed the rape on Lucrece, in revenge for which the Tarquins were expelled from Rome and a Republic established.

*Tarquin* is also the name of a 'recreant knight' figuring in the Arthurian cycle. A ballad given in Percy's *Reliques* tells how Sir Lancelot met a lady who requested him to deliver certain Knights of the Round Table from Tarquin's power. Coming to a river, he saw a copper basin suspended from a tree, and struck it so hard that it broke. This brought out Tarquin, when a furious encounter took place, in which the latter was slain, and Sir Lancelot liberated 'threescore knights and four, all of the Table Round'.

**Tarred.** ***All tarred with the same brush.*** All alike to blame; all sheep of the same flock. The allusion is to the custom of distinguishing the sheep of any given flock by a common mark with a brush dipped in tar.

***Tarred and feathered.*** Stripped to the skin, daubed with tar, and then rolled in feathers so that the feathers adhere; a common popular punishment in primitive communities, and still occasionally resorted to.

The first record of this punishment is in 1189 (1 Rich. I). A statute was made that any robber voyaging with the crusaders 'shall be first shaved, then boiling pitch shall be poured upon his head, and a cushion of feathers shook over it'. The wretch was then to be put on shore at the very first place the ship came to (Rymer, *Foedera*, i, 65).

**Tartan Plaid.** A plaid of a *tartan*, or chequered, pattern. A *plaid* is some twelve yards of narrow cloth wrapped round the waist, or over the chest and one shoulder, and reaching to the knees. It may be chequered or not; but the English use of the word in such a compound as *Scotch plaids*, meaning chequered cloth, is a blunder for *Scotch tartans*. The *tartan* is the chequered pattern, every clan having its own tartan. Though the thing is now typically Scotch, the word is from *Tartar* (Lat. *Tartenus*).

**Tartarian Lamb.** *See* Scythian.

**Tartarus.** The infernal regions of *classical mythology*; used as equivalent to Hades (*q.v.*) by later writers, but by Homer placed as far beneath Hades as Hades is beneath the earth. It was here that Zeus confined the Titans. *Cp.* Hell.

**Tartuffe.** The principal character of Molière's comedy so called; a pedantic, obscene, and hypocritical poltroon, said to be drawn from the Abbé de Roquette, a parasite of the Prince de Condé. The name is from the Italian *tartuffoli* (truffles), and was suggested to Molière on seeing the sudden animation which lighted up the faces of certain monks when they heard that a seller of truffles awaited their orders.

**Tassel-gentle.** The male goshawk trained for falconry; *tassel* being a corruption of *tiercel*, a male hawk, which is a third (*tierce*) less in size than the female, and called *gentle* because of its tractable disposition.

Shakespeare uses the term figuratively for a sweetheart:

> O for a falconer's voice
> To lure this tassel-gentle back again!
>
> Shakespeare, *Romeo and Juliet*, 2, 2

**Tatianists.** The disciples of Tatian, who, after the death of Justin Martyr,

> formed a new scheme of religion; for he advanced the notion of certain invisible aeons, branded marriage with the name of fornication, and denied the salvation of Adam.
>
> Irenaeus, *Adv. Hereses* (ed. Grabe), pp. 105, 106, 262

Tatian was a Greek Platonic philosopher, born in Mesopotamia in the 2nd century and converted to Christianity by Justin Martyr. He was the author of a *Discourse to the Greeks*, and composed the *Diatessaron* (Gr. through four), an uncritical combination of the four Gospels into a connected narrative, in which all that tended to relate Christ to human nature was as far as possible obliterated.

**Tattoo.** The beat of drum at night to recall soldiers to barracks is so called from Dutch *taptoe*, closed or put to. In the mid-17th century, when the word came into use, it was written *tap-too*, *tapp-too*, etc.

The other *tattoo*, to mark the skin by rubbing indelible pigments into small punctures, is one of our very few words from Polynesian. It is Tahitian (*tatau*, mark), and was introduced by Captain Cook (1769).

***The devil's tattoo.*** *See* Devil.

***Torchlight tattoo.*** A military entertainment, carried out at night in the open air with illuminations, evolutions, and a lot of music.

**Tau.** The letter T in Greek and the Semitic languages. Anciently it was the last letter of the Greek alphabet (as it still is of the Hebrew); and in Middle English literature the phrase *Alpha to Omega* was not unfrequently rendered *Alpha to Tau*.

*Tau cross.* A T-shaped cross, especially St Anthony's cross.

**Taurus** (Lat. the bull). The second zodiacal constellation, and the second sign of the Zodiac, which the sun enters about April 21st.

> As bees
> In spring-time, when the sun with Taurus rides,
> Put forth their populous youth about the hive
> In clusters. Milton, *Paradise Lost*, I, 768

**Taverner's Bible.** *See* Bible, the English.

**Tawdry.** A corruption of *St Audrey* (*Audrey* itself being a corruption of *Etheldrida*). At the annual fair of St Audrey, in the isle of Ely, cheap 'Brummagem' jewellery, and showy lace called *St Audrey's lace* was sold; hence *tawdry*, which is applied to anything gaudy, in bad taste, and of little value. *Cp.* Tantony.

> Come, you promised me a tawdry lace and a pair of sweet gloves.
>
> Shakespeare, *Winter's Tale*, 4, 4

**Taylor's Institute.** The University Museum at Oxford. So called from Sir Robert Taylor (1714–88), who made large bequests towards its erection.

**Te Deum, The.** This liturgical hymn, so called from the opening words of the Latin original, *Te Deum laudamus* ('Thee, God, we praise'), is usually ascribed to St Ambrose, but is probably of later date. It is said that St Ambrose improvised it while baptising St Augustine (386). In allusion to this tradition, it is sometimes called 'the Ambrosian Hymn', and in some of our early psalters it is entitled 'Canticum Ambrosii et Augustini'.

**Te Igitur.** One of the service-books of the Roman Catholic Church; so called from the first words of the canon of the Mass, *Te igitur* ('Thee, therefore') *clementissime Pater*.

***Oaths upon the Te Igitur.*** Oaths sworn on this service-book, which were regarded as especially sacred.

**Tea.** ***A nice old cup of tea.*** An ironical slang expression, which is applied to persons in much the same sense as *A nice old party*, and to awkward occurrences, unpleasant situations, or muddles.

***A tea-fight.*** A tea-party; especially a church or chapel gathering at which tea and buns, etc., are provided.

***Tea-kettle broth.*** 'Poor man's soup', consisting of hot water, bread, and a small lump of butter, with pepper and salt; the French *soup maigre*.

**Teague.** A contemptuous name for an Irishman (from the Irish personal name), rarely used nowadays but common in the 17th and 18th centuries.

> Was't Carwell, brother James, or Teague,
> That made thee break the Triple League?
>
> Rochester, *History of Insipids*

**Tear** (to rhyme with 'snare'). *To tear Christ's body*. To use imprecations. The common oaths of mediaeval times were by different parts of the Lord's body; hence the preachers used to talk of 'tearing God's body by imprecations'.

> Hir othës been so grete and so dampnable
> That it is grisly for to heere hem swere;
> Our blissed Lordës body thay to-tere.
>
> Chaucer, *Pardoner's Tale*, 144

**Tear** (to rhyme with 'fear').

***Tear-shell.*** A projectile which, on bursting, liberates gases which irritate the lachrymatory glands of all within range, causing the eyes to water and rendering them temporarily useless.

One of the novelties of the Great War – a German invention. Also called a 'lachrymatory shell'.

***Tears of Eos.*** The dewdrops of the morning were so called by the Greeks. Eos was the mother of Memnon (*q.v.*), and wept for him every morning.

***St Lawrence's tears.*** *See* Lawrence.

***The Vale of Tears.*** This world (*cp.* Baca).

**Tec, or 'Tec.** Slang for a de*tec*tive.

**Teeth** (*see also* Tooth).

***By the skin of one's teeth.*** *See* Skin.

***From the teeth outwards.*** Merely talk; without real significance.

***He has cut his eye-teeth.*** He is 'up to snuff'; he has 'his weather-eye open'. The eye-teeth (i.e. the upper canines) are cut late –

| | *Months.* | | | |
|---|---|---|---|---|
| *First set* – | 5 | to | 8, | the four central incisors. |
| | 7 | | 10 | lateral incisors. |
| | 12 | | 16 | anterior molars. |
| | 14 | | 20 | eye-teeth. |
| | *Years.* | | | |
| *Second set* – | 5 | to | 6, | the anterior molars. |
| | 7 | | 8 | incisors. |
| | 9 | | 10 | bicuspids |
| | 11 | | 12 | eye-teeth. |

*See also* Eye-teeth.

***His teeth are drawn.*** His power of doing mischief is taken from him. The phrase comes from the fable of the lion in love, who consented to have his teeth drawn and claws cut, in order that a fair damsel might marry him. When this was done the lady's father fell on the lion and slew him.

***In spite of his teeth.*** In opposition to his settled purpose or resolution; even though he snarl and show his teeth like an angry dog. Holinshed tells us of a Bristol Jew, who suffered a tooth to be drawn daily for seven days before he would submit to the extortion of King John.

> In despite of the teeth of all the rhyme and reason.
>
> Shakespeare, *Merry Wives*, 5, 4

***In the teeth of the wind.*** With the wind dead against one, blowing in or against the teeth.

> To strive with all the tempest in my teeth.
>
> Pope, *Epistles of Horace*, II, ii

***To cast into one's teeth.*** To utter reproaches.

> All his faults observed,
> Set in a note-book, learned, and conned by rote
> To cast into my teeth.
>
> Shakespeare, *Julius Caesar*, 4, 3

***To set one's teeth on edge.*** *See* Edge.

**Teetotal.** A word expressive of total abstinence from alcoholic liquors as beverages, coined about 1833 by Dick Turner, a plasterer or fish-hawker at Preston, Lancashire. The story that at a meeting he stammered forth, 'I'll have nowt to do with the moderation botheration pledge; I'll be reet down t–total, that or nowt', is not to be relied on.

Turner's tombstone contains the inscription; 'Beneath this stone are deposited the remains of Richard Turner, author of the word *Teetotal* as applied to abstinence from all intoxicating liquors, who departed this life on the 27th day of October, 1846, aged 56 years.'

**Teetotum.** A top for spinning with the fingers, having usually four or six flat sides each of which is marked with a letter, figure or other symbol. The top is spun, and the players follow the direction indicated by the side that is uppermost when it comes to rest. The modern 'Put and Take' (*q.v.*) is an adaptation of the teetotum, the early forms of which had four sides, marked 'T' (Lat. *totum*, all, meaning take all the stakes), 'P' (Lat. *pone*, put, i.e. put down, or pay in), 'N' (*nihil*, nothing), and 'H' (half), or sometimes 'A' (*aufer*, take away).

**Teian Muse, The.** Anacreon (about 563–478 BC), who was born at Teos, Asia Minor.

> The Scian and the Teian muse,
> The hero's heart, the lover's lute,
> Have found the fame your shores refuse.
>
> Byron, *The Isles of Greece*

**Telamones.** Large, sculptured male figures (*cp.* Atlantes, Caryatids) serving as architectural columns or pilasters. So called from the Greek legendary hero Telamon (father of Ajax), who took part in the Calydonian hunt and the expedition of the Argonauts.

**Telemachus.** Was the only son of Ulysses and Penelope. After the fall of Troy he went, attended by Athene in the guise of Mentor, in quest of his father. He ultimately found him, and the two returned to Ithaca and slew Penelope's suitors.

**Telephus.** *See* Achillea.

**Tell, William.** The legendary national hero of Switzerland, whose deeds are based on a Teutonic myth of widespread occurrence in northern Europe.

Fable has it that Tell was the champion of the Swiss in the War of Independence against the Emperor Albert I (slain 1308). Tell refused to salute the cap of Gessler, the imperial governor, and for this act of independence was sentenced to shoot with his bow and arrow an apple from the head of his own son. Tell succeeded in this dangerous skill-trial, but in his agitation dropped an arrow from his robe. The governor insolently demanded what the second arrow was for, and Tell fearlessly replied, 'To shoot you with, had I failed in the task imposed upon me.' Gessler now ordered him to be carried in chains across the lake, and cast into Küssnacht castle, a prey 'to the reptiles that lodged there'. He was, however, rescued by the peasantry, and, having shot Gessler, freed his country from the Austrian yoke.

The earliest form of the legend is found in the old Norse *Vilkina Saga* (based on Teutonic sources), which tells how King Nidung commanded Egil, the brother of Wayland Smith, to shoot an apple off the head of his son. Egil took two arrows from his quiver, the straightest and sharpest he could find, and when asked by the king why he did so, the god-archer replied, as the Swiss peasant to Gessler, 'To shoot thee, tyrant, with the second if the first fails.'

Saxo Grammaticus tells nearly the same story respecting Toki, who killed Harald, and similar tales are told of Adam Bell, Clym of the Clough, William of Cloudeslie and Henry IV, Olaf and Eindridi, etc.

Kissling's monument at Altorf (1892), has four reliefs on the pedestal: (1) Tell shooting the apple; (2) Tell's leap from the boat; (3) Gessler's death; and (4) Tell's death at Schachenbach.

**Teller.** Anciently, one who kept the Tallies (Anglo-Fr. *talier*) and counted the money; now, a bank-clerk who receives and pays out money at the counter.

Up to 1834 there were four officers of the Exchequer known as *Tellers of the Exchequer*, whose duty was to receive and pay out moneys. *See* Tally.

When shall our prayers end?
I tell thee (priest) ...
When proud surveyors take no parting pence,
When Silver sticks not on the Teller's fingers,
And when receivers pay as they receive.

Gascoigne, *The Steel Glass* (1576)

**Temora.** One of the principal poems of Ossian (*q.v.*), in eight books, so called from the royal residence of the kings of Connaught. Cairbar had usurped the throne, having killed Cormac, a distant relative of Fingal; and Fingal raised an army to dethrone the usurper. The poem begins from this point with an invitation from Cairbar to Oscar, son of Ossian, to a banquet. Oscar accepted the invitation, but during the feast a quarrel was vamped up, in which Cairbar and Oscar fell by each other's spears. When Fingal arrived a battle ensued, in which Fillan, son of Fingal, the Achilles of the Caledonian army, and Cathmor, brother of Cairbar, the bravest of the Irish army, were both slain. Victory crowned the army of Fingal, and Ferad-Artho, the rightful heir, was restored to the throne of Connaught.

**Templars** or **Knights Templars.** Nine French knights bound themselves, at the beginning of the 12th century, to protect pilgrims on their way to the Holy Land, and received the name of *Templars*, because their arms were kept in a building given to them for the purpose by the abbot of the convent on the site of the old Temple of Solomon, at Jerusalem. They used to call themselves the 'Poor Soldiers of the Holy City'.

Their habit was a long white mantle, to which subsequently was added a red cross on the left shoulder. Their war-cry was *Bauseant* (an old French name for a black and white horse), from their banner, which was striped black and white, and charged with a red cross. Their seal showed two knights riding on one horse, the story being that the first Master was so poor that he had to share a horse with one of his followers.

The Order afterwards became very wealthy and so powerful that its suppression (effected in 1312) was necessary for the peace of Europe.

In England the Order had its first house (built about 1121) near Holborn Bars, London, but a site between Fleet Street and the Thames was given to them by 1162, and here they were settled till Edward II suppressed the English branch and confiscated its possessions. The lands and buildings went to the Knights Hospitallers who, in the reign of Edward III, granted them to the 'students of the Common laws of England' (Stow). The Society of the Temple, a body of lawyers, was formed; in the reign of Henry VI this was split into two, viz. the *Inner Temple* and the *Middle Temple*, which still form two of the four Inns of Court (*q.v.*). Hence the term *Templar* is frequently applied to lawyers and law students.

**Temple.** The name of the place of worship is the Lat. *templum*, from Gr. *temenos*, a sacred enclosure, i.e. a space *cut off* from its surroundings (Gr. *temnein*, to cut). The Lat. *templum* originally denoted the space marked out by the augurs (*q.v.*) within which the sign was to occur.

The *temples* of the forehead represent Lat. *tempora*, the fatal spot, the temples (pl. of *tempus*, time).

**Temple, The.** The site between Fleet Street and the Thames formerly occupied by the buildings of the Knights Templars (*see* Templars *above*), of which the Temple Church (dating from 1185) is the only portion now remaining.

Since 1346 the Temple has been in the possession of doctors and students of the law, who, since 1609, have formed the two Inns of Court (*q.v.*) known as the *Inner* and *Middle Temples*. The badge of the former is the Winged Horse (*Pegasus*), that of the latter the Sacred Lamb (*Agnus Dei*). Fable has it that the horse typifies the expedition of the lawyers, the lamb their innocence!

The Inner Temple Hall is modern (1870), but that of the Middle Temple is one of the finest Elizabethan halls in existence. It was built in 1572, and Shakespeare's play of *Twelfth Night* was probably performed here in 1602.

**Temple Bar.** The old Fleet Street gateway into the City, formerly situated close to the entrance into the Temple, on the spot now marked by the monument known as the 'Griffin'. It was built by Wren in 1670, and was removed and re-erected in private grounds at Theobalds Park, Cheshunt, Herts, in 1878. It was long used for the exhibition of the heads of traitors and conspirators, and was hence sometimes called 'the City Golgotha'.

**Temple of Solomon, The.** The central place of Jewish worship, erected by Solomon and his Tyrian workmen (probably on Phoenician models) on Mount Moriah, Jerusalem, about 1006 BC. It was destroyed at the siege of Jerusalem by Nebuchadnezzar (588 BC), and some 70 years later the *Temple of Zerubbabel* was completed on its site. In 20 BC Herod the Great began the building of the last Temple – that of the New Testament – which was utterly destroyed during the siege of Jerusalem by Vespasian and Titus in AD 70. For many centuries the site has been covered by the splendid Mohammedan mosque, Haram esh Sherif.

The chief emblems of the Jewish Temple were:

The *golden candlestick*. The Church. Its seven lights, the seven spirits of God. (Rev. 4:6.)

The *shewbread*. The twelve loaves the twelve tribes of Israel. Represented in the Gospel by the twelve apostles.

The *incense* of sweet spices. Prayer, which rises to heaven as incense. (Rev. 8:3, 4.)

The *Holy of Holies*. The nation of the Jews as God's peculiar people. When the veil which separated it from the temple was 'rent in twain', it signified that thenceforth Jews and Gentiles all formed one people of God.

*See* Exod. 25:30–32; Rev. 1:12–20; *and see also* Jachin and Boaz.

**Tempora mutantur** (Lat. the times are changed). The tag is founded on the saying, *Omnia mutantur, nos et mutamur in illis* (all things are changed, and we with them), by Nicholas Borbonius, a Latin poet of the 16th century. Lothair, Emperor of the Holy Roman Empire, had, it is stated, already said, *Tempora mutantur, nos et mutamur in illis*.

**Ten.** ***Ten to one.*** Expressive of a very strong probability; as, 'It's ten to one that it will rain tonight', i.e. it's extremely likely to; *a ten to one chance*, one in which it is very much more likely that you will win than lose.

***The Council of Ten.*** A secret tribunal exercising unlimited powers in the old Venetian republic. Instituted in 1310 with ten members, it was later enlarged to 17, and continued in active existence till the abolition of the republic in 1797.

***The Ten Commandments.*** A humorous expression for the ten fingers, especially when used by an angry woman for scratching her opponent's face.

> Could I come near your beauty with my nails,
> I'd set my ten commandments in your face.
>
> Shakespeare, *2 Henry VI*, 1, 3

> 'I daur you to touch him,' spreading abroad her long and muscular fingers, garnished with claws, which a vulture might have envied. 'I'll set my ten commandments on the face of the first loon that lays a finger on him.'
>
> Scott, *Waverley*, ch. xxx

***The Upper Ten.*** The aristocracy, the cream of society. Short for *the upper ten thousand*. The term was first used by N. P. Willis, in speaking of the fashionables of New York, who at that time were not more than ten thousand in number.

**Tenant.** One who *holds* property – land, house, etc. – anciently by any kind of title, in modern use from the owner or landlord for payment; the French *tenant*, holding (*tenir*, to hold; Lat. *tenere*). Theoretically, all land in the United Kingdom belongs to the Crown, and all landholders are therefore tenants.

***Tenant at will.*** One who can at any moment be dispossessed of his tenancy at the will of the landlord or lessor.

***Tenant by frank-marriage.*** One holding lands or tenements by virtue of a gift thereof made to him upon his marriage.

***Tenant in chief.*** One who holds from the king direct.

***Tenant-right.*** The right of an outgoing tenant to claim from an incoming tenant compensation for the improvements he has made on the farm, etc., during his tenancy. In Elizabethan times the term denoted the right that certain tenants possessed of passing on the tenancy, at decease, to the eldest surviving issue; and it is now sometimes applied to the right of a well-behaved tenant to compensation if deprived of his tenancy.

**Tender.** *See* Legal tender.

**Tenner.** A ten-pound note; as *fiver* is a five-pound note.

**Tenpenny Nails.** Large-sized nails, originally so called because they were sold at 10*d.* a hundred. Similarly smaller sized nails used to be known as *eightpenny*, *sixpenny*, *fourpenny nails.*

**Tenson.** A contention in verse between rival troubadours; a metrical dialogue consisting of smart repartees, usually on women and love. A subdivision of the troubadours' love lyrics also had the same name.

**Tenterden. *Tenterden steeple was the cause of Goodwin Sands*.** A satirical remark made when some ridiculous reason is given for a thing. The story, according to one of Latimer's sermons, is that a Mr Moore, being sent into Kent to ascertain the cause of the Goodwin Sands, called together the oldest inhabitants to ask their opinion. A very old man said, 'I believe Tenterden steeple is the cause,' and went on to explain that in his early days there was no Tenterden steeple, and there were no complaints about the sands. This reason seemed ridiculous enough, but the fact seems to be that the Bishops of Rochester applied money that was raised in the county for the purpose of keeping Sandwich haven clear to the building of Tenterden steeple, so that when they found the harbour was getting blocked up there was no money for taking the necessary steps. *Cp.* Goodwin Sands.

**Tenterhooks. *I am on tenterhooks,*** or ***on tenterhooks of great expectation*.** My curiosity is on the full stretch, I am most curious or anxious to hear the issue. Cloth, after being woven, is stretched or 'tentered' on hooks passed through the selvedges. (Lat. *tentus*, stretched, hence 'tent', canvas stretched.)

> He was not kept an instant on the tenterhooks of impatience longer than the appointed moment.
>
> Scott, *Redgauntlet*, ch. xvi

**Tenth. *The submerged tenth*** (sometimes called *the Tenth Legion*). *See* Submerged.

***The Tenth Muse*.** A name given originally to Sappho (*q.v.*) there being *nine* true Muses (*see* Muse), and afterwards applied to various literary ladies, as Mme de la Garde Deshou-lières (d.1694), Mlle de Scudéry (d.1701), Queen Christina of Sweden (d.1689), and the English novelist and essay-writer, Hannah More (d.1833).

***The tenth wave.*** *See* Wave.

**Tercel.** *See* Tiercel.

**Term.** In schools and the universities, the period during which instruction is given; in the law courts, the period during which the courts are in session.

There are three terms at Cambridge in a year, viz., Lent, Easter, and Michaelmas, and four at Oxford, viz., Lent, Easter, Trinity, and Michaelmas, but the two middle Oxford terms are two only in name, as they run on without a break.

Lent –

*Cambridge*, begins January 13th, and ends on the Friday before Palm Sunday.

*Oxford*, begins January 14th, and ends on the Saturday before Palm Sunday.

Easter –

*Cambridge*, begins on the Friday of Easter-week, and ends Friday nearest June 20th.

*Oxford*, begins on the Wednesday of Easter-week, and ends Friday before Whit Sunday. The continuation, called 'Trinity term', runs on till the second Saturday of July.

Michaelmas –

*Cambridge*, begins October 1st, and ends December 16th.

*Oxford*, begins October 10th, and ends December 17th.

The lawyers' terms, called, since 1873, law sessions, are:

*Michaelmas Sessions* begin November 2nd, and end December 21st.

*Hilary Sessions* begin January 11th, and end the Wednesday before Easter.

*Easter Sessions* begin the Tuesday after Easter week, and end the Friday before Whit Sunday.

*Trinity Sessions* begin the Tuesday after Whit week, and end August 8th.

***To bring to terms*.** To force a person to accept one's conditions.

***To come to terms.*** To make an agreement with; decide the terms of a bargain.

**Termagant.** The name given by the Crusaders, and in mediaeval romances, to an idol or deity that the Saracens were popularly supposed to worship. He was introduced into the morality plays as a most violent and turbulent person in long, flowing Eastern robes, a dress that led to his acceptance as a woman, whence the name came to be applied to a shrewish, violently abusive virago.

In the Romances his name was usually joined with that of Mahomet, and the *-magaunt* of *Termagaunt* may represent *Mahound*, but as an early version of the name was *Tervagant* it has been suggested that perhaps the word is the Latin *ter vagantem*, the thrice wandering, with reference to Selene, or the Moon.

> 'Twas time to counterfeit, or that hot termagant
> Scot [Douglas] had paid me scot and lot too.
>
> Shakespeare, *1 Henry IV*, 5, 4

Thackeray's –

> Yonder is Sarah Marlborough's palace just as it stood when that termagant occupied it.
>
> *Four Georges*, iii

shows the modern use of the word.

***Outdoing Termagant*** (*Hamlet*, 3, 2). In old drama the degree of rant was the measure of villainy. Termagant and Herod, being considered the *beau-ideal* of all that is bad, were represented as settling everything by club law, and bawling so as to split the ears of the groundlings. *Cp.* Herod.

***That beats Termagant.*** Your ranting, raging pomposity, or exaggeration, surpasses that of Termagant of the old moralities.

**Terpsichore.** One of the nine Muses (*q.v.*) of ancient Greece, the Muse of dancing and the dramatic chorus, and later of lyric poetry. She is usually represented seated, and holding a lyre. Hence, *Terpsichorean*, pertaining to dancing.

**Terra damnata** (Lat. condemned or rejected earth). Another name for the Caput mortuum (*q.v.*) of the alchemists.

**Terra firma.** Dry land, in opposition to water; the continents as distinguished from islands. The Venetians so called the mainland of Italy under their sway, and the continental parts of America belonging to Spain were also called by the same term.

**Terrible, The.** Ivan IV (or II) of Russia. (1529, 1533–84.)

**Terrier.** A dog that 'takes the earth', or unearths his prey (Fr., from Lat. *terra*, earth); also formerly applied to the burrows of foxes, badgers, rabbits, and so on.

Also slang for a member of the Territorial Army.

A land-roll or description of estates is called a *terrier* from Fr. *papier terrier*, a register of land.

**Territorial Army.** The British home defence force which, in 1908, superseded the old Militia, Yeomanry, and Volunteers, and is on a territorial basis.

The infantry regiments of the line have been known as the *Territorial regiments* since 1881, when, following a new scheme of organisation, each became associated in name, depot, etc., with some particular county or district.

**Terror, The,** or the **Reign of Terror.** The period in the French Revolution between the fall of the Girondists and overthrow of Robespierre. It lasted 420 days, from May 31st, 1793, to July 27th, 1794. Also applied to similar cataclysms in the history of other nations, as the Russian Revolution (the *Red Terror*, March-Sept., 1917) when the worst excesses of the French Revolution were far surpassed.

**Terry Alts.** Insurgents of Clare, who appeared after the Union (1798) and committed numerous outrages. These rebels were similar to 'the Thrashers' of Connaught, 'the Carders', and the followers of 'Captain Rock' in 1822.

**Ter-Sanctus.** *See* Trisagion.

**Tertium Quid.** A third party which shall be nameless; a third thing resulting from the combination of two things, but different from both. Fable has it that the expression originated with Pythagoras, who, defining bipeds, said –

> Sunt *bipes* homo, et avis, et tertium quid.
>
> A man is a biped, so is a bird, and a third thing (which shall be nameless).

Iamblichus says this third thing was Pythagoras himself.

In chemistry, when two substances chemically unite, the new substance is called a *tertium quid*, as a neutral salt produced by the mixture of an acid and alkali.

**Terza Rima.** An Italian verse-form in triplets, the second line rhyming with the first and third of the succeeding triplet. In the first triplet lines 1 and 3 rhyme, and in the last there is an extra line, rhyming with its second.

Dante's *Divine Comedy* is in this metre; it was introduced into England by Sir Thomas Wyatt in the 16th century, and was largely employed by Shelley, as also by Byron in *The Prophecy of Dante*.

**Test Act.** An Act of Parliament directed against Roman Catholics and Nonconformists, especially that of 1673, which decreed that all holders of public offices must take the Oaths of Allegiance and Supremacy, receive the Church of England sacrament, renounce the doctrine of Transubstantiation, etc. It was repealed in 1828.

Hence, *to take the test*, to comply with the requirements of the Test Act.

**Test Match.** In cricket, one of the matches played in a series between two bodies of players (especially England and Australia) to decide which is the better.

**Tester.** A sixpenny piece; so-called from the *teston* of Henry VII, a coin which got its name from Ital. *testa*, head, because it was stamped on one side with the *head* of the reigning sovereign. Similarly, the head canopy of a bed is called its *tester*.

> Hold, there's a tester for thee.
>
> Shakespears, *2 Henry IV*, 3, 2

***Testers are gone to Oxford, to study at Brazenose.*** When Henry VIII debased the silver testers, the alloy broke out in red pimples through the silver, giving the royal likeness in the coin a blotchy appearance; hence the punning proverb.

**Testudo.** *See* Tortoise.

**Tête-à-tête** (Fr. head to head). A confidential conversation, a 'heart-to-heart talk'.

**Tête du Pont.** The barbican or watch-tower placed on the head of a drawbridge.

**Tether. *He has come to the end of his tether*.** He has outrun his fortune; he has exhausted all his resources. The reference is to an animal tied to a rope (he can graze only so far as his tether can be carried out), or to a cable run out to the 'bitter end' (*q.v.*).

Horace calls the end of life *ultima linea rerum*, the end of the goal, referring to the white chalk mark at the end of a racecourse.

**Tethys.** A sea goddess of the ancient Greeks, wife of Oceanus; hence, the sea itself.

> The golden sun, above the watery bed
> Of hoary Tethys raised bis beamy head.
>
> *Hoole's Ariosto*, Bk viii

**Tetragrammaton.** A word of four letters, especially the name of Deity, JHVH (*see* Jehovah), which the ancient Jews never pronounced. The word means 'I am', or 'I exist' (Exod. 3:14); but Rabbi Bechai says the letters include the three times – past, present, and future.

Pythagoras called Deity a Tetrad or Tetractys, meaning the 'four sacred letters', and it is curious that in so many languages the name of the Supreme Being should be composed of four letters; thus there are the Greek *Zeus* and θεος, in Latin *Jove* and *Deus*; Fr. *Dieu*, Dutch *Godt*, Ger. *Gott*, Dan. *Godh*, Swed. *Goth*, Arab. *Alla*, Sansk. *Deva*, Span. *Dios*, Ital. *Idio*, Scand. *Odin*, and our *Lord*.

> Such was the sacred Tetragrammaton. Things worthy silence must not be revealed.
>
> Dryden, *Britannia Rediviva*

**Tetrapla.** The Bible, disposed by Origen in four columns, each of which contained a different Greek version, viz. those of Aquila, Symmachus, Theodotion, and the Septuagint.

**Teucer.** In the *Iliad*, the son of Telamon, and step-brother of Ajax; he went with the allied Greeks to the siege of Troy, and on his return was banished by his father for not avenging on Ulysses the death of his brother.

**Teutons.** The Germans, and Germanic peoples; from the Latin name, *Teutones*, for an ancient northern tribe, their own name for themselves being *Thiudans*, i.e. kings or lords. *Cp.* A.S. *theoden*, a king. Our *Dutch* and the German *Deutsch* are variations of the same word, originally written *Theodisk*.

**Teutonic Cross.** A cross potent, the badge of the order of Teutonic Knights.

**Teutonic Knights.** An order which arose at the time of the Crusades. Originally only Germans of noble birth were admissible to the order. Abolished by Napoleon in 1809, and revived again in Austria in 1840.

**Th** (θ, *theta*). The sign given in the verdict of the Areopagus of condemnation to death (*thanatos*).

> Et polis es vitio nigrum praefigere theta.
>
> Persius

**Thais.** The Athenian courtesan who, it is said, induced Alexander the Great, when excited with wine, to set fire to the palace of the Persian kings at Persepolis.

> The king seized a flambeau with zeal to destroy;
> Thais led the way to light him to his prey,
> And, like another Helen, fired another Troy.
>
> Dryden, *Alexander's Feast*

**Thalaba.** The hero of Southey's long narrative poem, *Thalaba the Destroyer* (1800), son of Hodeirah and Zeinab (*Zenobia*).

> Thalaba, as Southey himself confessed, is a male Joan of Arc. Like her he goes forth a delegated servant of the Highest to war against the powers of evil; and, like her again, is sustained under the trials of the way by the sole Talisman of faith.
>
> Dowden, *Southey* (*English Men of Letters*, ch. vii)

**Thales.** *See* Seven Sages.

**Thalestris.** A queen of the Amazons, who went with 300 women to meet Alexander the Great, under the hope of raising a race of Alexanders.

> This was no Thalestris from the fields, but a quiet domestic character from the fireside
>
> C. Brontë, *Shirley*, ch. xxviii

**Thalia.** One of the Muses (*q.v.*), generally regarded as the patroness of comedy. She was supposed by some, also, to preside over husbandry and planting, and is represented holding a comic mask and a shepherd's crook.

**Thames.** The Latin *Thamesis* (the broad Isis, where *isis* is a mere variation of *esk*, *ouse*, *uisg*, etc., meaning water). It rises near Cirencester as the *Isis*, a name which has been applied to it as far as its junction with the *Thame*, near Dorchester.

> Around his throne the sea-born brothers stood;
> Who swell with tributary urns his flood:
> First the famed authors of his ancient name,
> The winding Isis and the fruitful Thame!
>
> Pope, *Windsor Forest*

***He'll never set the Thames on fire.*** He'll never make any figure in the world; never do anything wonderful and print his footsteps on the sands of time. The popular explanation is that the word *Thames* is a pun on the word *temse*, a corn-sieve; and that the parallel French locution *He will never set the Seine on fire* is a pun on *seine*, a drag-net; but these solutions are not tenable. There is a Latin saw, *Tiberim accendere nequaquam potest*, which is probably the *fons et origo* of other parallel sayings; and the Germans had *Den Rhein anzünden* (to set the Rhine on fire) as early as 1630.

> Of course water can, apparently, be set on fire but the scope of the proverb lies the other way, and it may take its place beside such sayings as 'If the sky falls we may catch larks.'

**Thammuz.** The Syrian and Phoenician name of Adonis (*q.v.*). His death happened on the banks of the river Adonis, and in summer-time the waters always became reddened with the hunter's blood. In Ezek. 8:14, reference is made to the heathen 'women weeping for Tammuz'.

> Thammuz came next behind,
> Whose annual wound on Lebanon allured
> The Syrian damsels to lament his fate
> In amorous ditties all a summer's day,
> While smooth Adonis from his native rock
> Ran purple to the sea, supposed with blood
> Of Thammus yearly wounded.
>
> Milton, *Paradise Lost*, iii, 446

**Thamyris.** A Thracian bard mentioned by Homer (*Iliad*, ii, 595). He challenged the Muses to a trial of skill, and, being overcome in the contest, was deprived by them of his sight and power of song. He is represented with a broken lyre in his hand.

> Blind Thamyris and blind Maeonides [Homer]
> And Tiresias and Phineus, prophets old.
>
> Milton, *Paradise Lost*, iii, 35

**That.** Seven 'thats' may follow each other, and make sense.

> For be it known that we may safely write
> Or say that 'that *that*' that that man wrote was right;
> Nay, e'en that that *that*, that 'that THAT' has followed.
> Through six repeats, the grammar's rule has hallowed;
> And that that *that* that *that* 'that THAT' began
> Repeated seven times is right, deny't who can.

> My lords, with humble submission *that* that I say is this: That that that 'that that' that that gentleman has advanced is not *that* that he should have proved to your lordships
>
> *Spectator*, No. 86

Another *that* catch is to make sense of the following by supplying the missing punctuation:

> that that is is that that is not is not is that it it is.

***And that's that!*** A colloquial way of emphatically and triumphantly making one's point, closing the argument, and so on.

**Thaumaturgus** (Gr. a conjurer, or wonder-worker). A miracle-worker; applied to saints and others who are reputed to have performed miracles, especially:

*Apollonius of Tyana*, Cappadocia (ad 3–98).

*St Bernard of Clairvaux*, 'the Thaumaturgus of the West' (1091–1153).

*St Filumena* (*q.v.*),

*St Francis of Assisi*, founder of the Franciscan order (1182–1226).

*Gregory*, Bishop of Neo-Caesarea, in Cappadocia, called emphatically 'Thaumaturgus', from the numerous miracles he is reported to have performed (died about 270).

*Plotinus* (died about 270), and several other Neoplatonists.

*Simon Magus*, of Samaria, called 'the Great Power of God' (Acts 8:10).

*St Vincent de Paul*, founder of the 'Sisters of Charity' (1576–1660).

**Theagenes and Chariclea.** The hero and heroine of an erotic romance in Greek by Heliodorus, Bishop of Trikka (4th century).

**Theban Bard or Eagle, The.** Pindar, born at Thebes (about 520–435 BC).

**Theban Legion, The.** Another name for the 'Thundering Legion' (*q.v.*), which was raised in the Thebaïd of Egypt, composed of Christian soldiers, and led by St Maurice.

**Thebes,** called *The Hundred-Gated*, was not Thebes of Boeotia, but the chief town of the Thebaïd, on the Nile in Upper Egypt, said to have extended over twenty-three miles of land. Homer says out of each gate the Thebans could send forth 200 war-chariots.

> The world's great empress on the Egyptian plain,
> That spreads her conquests o'er a thousand states,
> And pours her heroes through a hundred gates,
> Two hundred horsemen and two hundred cars
> From each wide portal issuing to the wars.
>
> Pope, *Iliad*, i

It is here that the vocal statue of Memnon stood, and here too are the tombs of the kings, the temple of Karnak, and large numbers of sculptures, sphinxes, etc. The village of Luxor now marks the spot.

***The Seven against Thebes.*** An expedition in Greek legend fabled to have taken place against Thebes, Boeotia before the Trojan War. The Seven were the Argive chiefs Adrastus, Polynices, Tydeus, Amphiaraus, Hippomedon, Capaneus, and Parthenopaeus.

When Oedipus abdicated his two sons agreed to reign alternate years; but at the expiration of the first year, the elder, Eteocles, refused to give up the throne, whereupon Polynices, the younger brother, induced the six chiefs to espouse his cause. The allied army laid siege to Thebes, but without success, and all the heroes perished except Adrastus. Subsequently, seven sons of the chiefs resolved to avenge their fathers' deaths, marched against the city, took it, and placed Terpander, one of their number, on the throne. These are known as the *Epigoni* (Gr. descendants). The Greek tragic poets Aeschylus and Euripides dramatised the legend.

**Thecla, St.** The *proto-martyress* of the Eastern martyrologies, as St Stephen is the *proto-martyr*. All that is known of her is from the *Acts of Paul and Thecla*, pronounced apocryphal by Pope Gelasius. According to the legend she was born of a noble family in Iconium, and was converted by the preaching of St Paul. Her day is 23rd September.

**Theist, Deist, Atheist, Agnostic.** *A theist* believes there is a God who made and governs all creation; but does not believe in the doctrine of the Trinity, nor in a divine revelation.

A *deist* believes there is a God who created all things, but does not believe in His superintendence and government. He thinks the Creator implanted in all things certain immutable laws, called the *Laws of Nature*, which act *per se*, as a watch acts without the supervision of its maker. Like the theist, he does not believe in the doctrine of the Trinity, nor in a divine revelation.

The *atheist* disbelieves even the existence of a God. He thinks matter is eternal, and what we call 'creation' is the result of natural laws.

The *agnostic* believes only what is knowable. He rejects revelation and the doctrine of the Trinity as 'past human understanding'. He is neither theist, deist, nor atheist, as all these subscribe to doctrines that are incapable of scientific proof.

**Thellusson Act.** The 39th and 40th George III, cap. 98. An Act (1800) to prevent testators from leaving their property to accumulate for more than twenty-one years. So called because it was passed in reference to the will of Peter Thellusson, a London banker who died in 1797 and left £600,000 and £4,500 a year to accumulate for the benefit of his eldest great-grandson after the death of all his sons and grandsons. The last grandson died in 1856, and the expense of the legal actions that followed swallowed up all the accumulated interest, so that Thellusson's eldest son's eldest grandson received barely the amount of the original legacy.

**Theodomas.** A famous trumpeter at the siege of Thebes.

> At every court ther cam loud menstralcye
> That never trompëd Joab for to heere,
> Ne he Theodomas yit half so cleere
> At Thebës, when the citë was in doute.
>
> Chaucer, *Canterbury Tales*, 9,592

**Theodoric.** A king of the East Goths (d.526), who became celebrated in German legend as Dietrich of Bern (*q.v.*), and also has a place in the Norse romances and the *Nibelungen Saga*. He invaded Italy about 490, and three years later slew Odoacer and became sole ruler.

**Theodoslan Table.** *See* Itinerary.

**Theon.** A satirical poet of ancient Rome, noted for his mordant writings. Hence, *Theon's tooth*, the bite of an ill-natured or carping critic.

*Dente Theonino circumrodi* (Horace, *Ep.* i, 18, 82) to be nastily aspersed.

**Theophany.** *See* Tiffany.

**Theosophy** (Gr. the wisdom of God). The name adopted by the *Theosophical Society* (founded in 1875 by Mme Blavatsky, Mrs Besant, Col. Olcott, and others) to define their religious or philosophical system, which aims at the knowledge of God by means of intuition and contemplative illumination, or by direct communion. *Esoteric Buddhism* is another name for it; and its adherents claim that the doctrines of the great world religions are merely the exoteric expression of their own esoteric traditions.

The name was formerly applied to the philosophical system of Boehme (d.1624).

> The Theosophist is a man who, whatever be his race, creed, or condition, aspires to reach this height of wisdom and beatitude by self-development.
>
> Olcott, *Theosophy*, p. 144 (1885)

**Theot, Catharine** (1725–95). A visionary born at Avranches, who gave herself out to be (like Joanna Southcott) the mother of God, and changed her name *Theot* into *Theos* (God). She preached in Paris in 1794, at the very time that the worship of the Supreme Being was instituted, and declared that Robespierre was the forerunner of the Word. The *Comité de la Sûreté Générale* had her arrested, and she was guillotined. Catharine Theot was called by Dom Gerle *la mère de dieu*, and she named Maximilien Robespierre 'her well-beloved son and chief prophet'.

**Theramanes.** *See* Sandal.

**Therapeutae** (Gr. servants, ministers). A sect of Jewish mystics described in a work attributed to Philo. They were a branch of the Essenes (*q.v.*) and were settled in Egypt in the 1st century AD.

**Thermidor.** The eleventh month of the French Republican calendar, containing thirty days from July 19th. So named from Gr. *therme* heat, *doron* a gift.

**Thermidorians.** The milder French Revolutionists, who took part in the *coup d'état* which effected the fall of Robespierre, on Thermidor 9th of the second Republican year (July 27th, 1794), thus bringing the Reign of Terror (*q.v.*) to a close.

**Thersites.** A deformed, scurrilous officer in the Greek army at the siege of Troy. He was always railing at the chiefs; hence the name is applied to any dastardly, malevolent, impudent railer against the powers that be. Achilles felled him to the earth with his fist and killed him.

> He squinted, halted, gibbous was behind,
> And pinched before, and on his tapering head
> Grew patches only of the flimsiest down.
> ... Him Greece had sent to Troy,
> The miscreant, who shamed his country most.
>
> *Homer's Iliad* (Cowper), Bk ii

In Shakespeare's *Troilus and Cressida* he is 'A slave whose gall coins slanders like a mint'.

**Theseus.** The chief hero of Attica in ancient Greek legend; son of Aegeus, and the centre of innumerable exploits. Among his deeds are the capture of the Marathonian bull, the slaying of the Minotaur (*q.v.*), his war against the Amazons, his part in the Argonautic expedition and the Calydonian hunt, and his desertion of Ariadne in Naxos. He was foully murdered by Lycomedes in Scyros. *See* Pirithous: Sinis.

*Theseus* is also the name of the Duke of Athens in Chaucer's *Knight's Tale*. He married Hippolita, and as he returned home with his bride, and Emily her sister, was accosted by a crowd of female suppliants who complained of Creon, king of Thebes. The duke forthwith set out for Thebes, slew Creon, and took the city by assault. Many captives fell into his hands, amongst whom were the two knights, Palamon and Arcite (*q.v.*).

Shakespeare gives the same name to the Duke of Athens in his *Midsummer Night's Dream*.

**Thespians.** Actors; so called from Thespis, an Attic poet of the 6th century BC, reputed to be the father of Greek tragedy.

> The race of learned men,
> ... oft they snatch the pen,
> As if inspired, and in a Thespian rage;
> Then write.
>
> Thomson, *Castle of Lndolence*, c. i, 52

> Thespis, the first professor of our art,
> At country wakes sang ballads from a cart.
>
> Dryden, *Prologus to Sophonisba*

**Thestylis.** A stock poetic name for a rustic maiden; from a young female slave of that name in the *Idylls* of Theocritus.

> And then in haste her bower she leaves,
> With Thestylis to bind the sheaves.
>
> Milton, *L'Allegro*

**Thetis.** The chief of the Nereids (*q.v.*) of Greek legend. By Peleus she was the mother of Achilles.

***Thetis's hair-stone.*** A fancy-name given to pieces of rock-crystal enclosing hair-like filaments.

**Thick.** ***It's a bit thick!*** A colloquial expression used to express annoyance, as when one has had a stroke of bad luck, when things have not come up to expectation, when one has been charged more than – or received less than – one thinks fair, etc.

***Those two are very thick.*** They are very good friends, on excellent terms with one another. *As thick as thieves* is a similar saying.

***Through thick and thin.*** Through evil and through good report; under any conditions; undauntedly.

> A griesly foster forth did rash …
> Through thick and thin, both over bank and bush
> In hope her to attain by hook or crook.
> Spenser, *Faërie Queene*, III, i, 17

***Thick and thin blocks*** are pulley-blocks with two sheaves of different thickness, to accommodate different sizes of ropes.

**Thick-skinned.** Not sensitive; not irritated by rebukes and slanders. *Thin-skinned*, on the contrary, means impatient of reproof or censure, having skin so thin that it is an annoyance to be touched.

**Thick'un.** Slang for a sovereign.

**Thief, The Penitent.** *See* Dysmas.

**Thieves' Latin.** Slang; gibberish.

> What did actually reach his ears was disguised so completely by the use of cant words and the thieves' Latin, called slang, that he … could make no sense of the conversation.
> Scott, *Redgauntlet*, ch. xiii

> He can vent Greek and Hebrew as fast as I can thieves' Latin. Scott, *Kenilworth*, ch. xxix

**Thimble.** From A.S. *thymel*, a thumb-stall; so called because it was originally worn on the thumb, as sailors still wear their thimbles.

***Just a thimbleful.*** A very little drop – usually of spirits. *Thimble* is sometimes used in place of *thimbleful* –

> 'Tis true to her cottage still they came …
> And never swallow'd a thimble the less
> Of something the Reader is left to guess.
> Hood, *A Tale of a Trumpet*

**Thimble-rigging.** A low-down form of cheating, carried on with three thimbles and a pea, principally on or about race courses. A pea is put on a table, and the swindler places three thimbles over it in succession, and then, setting them on the table, asks you to say under which thimble the pea is. You are sure to guess wrong.

The term *thimble-rigging* is used allusively of any kind of mean cheating or jiggery-pokery.

**Thin. *It's a lot too thin!*** Said of an excuse, explanation, story, etc. that sounds plausible but is quite unacceptable. The idea is that it is so thin as to be transparent – it is easily seen through.

***The thin red line.*** *See* Line.

***Thin-skinned.*** *See* Thick-skinned.

**Thing.** The Old Norse word for the assembly of the people, the legislature, 'parliament', court of law, etc. It is etymologically the same word as our *thing* (an object), the original meaning of which was a discussion (from *thingian*, to discuss), hence a cause, an object.

The great national diet of Norway is still called a *stor-thing* (great legislative assembly), and the two chambers which form it are the *lag-thing* (law assembly) and the *odels-thing* (freeholders' assembly).

***A poor thing.*** A person (or, sometimes, an inanimate object) that is regarded with pity or disparagement. Touchstone's remark about Audrey – 'An ill-favoured thing, sir, but mine own' (*As You Like It*, 5, 4) – is frequently misquoted, 'A *poor thing, but mine own*', when employed in half ironical disparagement of one's own work.

***Old thing.*** A familiar – very familiar – mode of address between friends. It is used by and to men and women, and the 'old' has, of course, no reference to age.

***One's things.*** One's minor belongings, especially clothes, or personal luggage.

***The thing.*** The proper thing to do; as, 'It's not the thing to play leapfrog down Bond Street in a top-hat and spats.'

***The very thing.*** Just what I was wanting; just what will meet the case.

***You can have too much of a good thing.*** 'Enough is as good as a feast.'

> People may have too much of a good thing –
> Full as an egg of wisdom thus I sing.
> Peter Pindar, *The Gentleman and his Wife*

**Thirteen.** It is said that the origin of sitting down thirteen at dinner being deemed unlucky is because, at a banquet in Valhalla, Loki once intruded, making thirteen guests, and Balder was slain.

In Christian countries the superstition was confirmed by the Last Supper of Christ and His twelve apostles, but the superstition itself is much anterior to Christianity.

The Italians never use the number in their lotteries; and in Paris no house bears it, and persons, called *Quartorzièmes*, are available to make a fourteenth at dinner parties. Sailors strongly object to leaving port on the 13th of the month – especially if it happens to be a Friday – and they always start on their thirteenth voyage with apprehension.

**Thirteenpence-halfpenny.** A hangman. So called because thirteenpence-halfpenny was at one time his wages for hanging a man.

**Thirty. *A man at thirty must be either a fool or a physician.*** A saying attributed by Tacitus (*Annals*, VI, xlvi) to the Emperor Tiberius, who died at the age of 77 in AD 37 (Plutarch gives the story, but changes the age to *sixty*). The idea seems to be that if a man has not learned to look after his health by the time he is thirty he must be a fool.

***The Thirty Tyrants.*** *See* Tyrant.

**Thirty-six Line Bible, The.** *See* Bible, Specially named.

**Thirty-nine Articles, The.** The articles of faith of the Church of England, the acceptance of which is obligatory on its clergy. They were originally issued in 1551 as forty-two, but in 1563 were modified and reduced to their present number. They received parliamentary authority in 1571.

**Thirty Years War.** A series of wars between the Catholics and Protestants of Germany in the 17th century, in which France, Sweden, and other peoples participated from time to time. It began in Bohemia in 1618, and ended in 1648 with the Peace of Westphalia.

**Thisbe.** *See* Pyramus.

**Thistle.** The heraldic emblem of Scotland; said to have been adopted at least as early as the 8th century in commemoration of an unsuccessful night attack by the Danes on Stirling Castle. Their presence was unsuspected, and was revealed through the barefooted scouts treading on thistles and suddenly crying out: the alarm was given, the Scots fell upon the party, and defeated them with terrible slaughter.

With the thistle was adopted the motto *Nemo me impune lacessit*, 'Nobody touches (or provokes) me with impunity'.

***The Most Ancient and Most Noble Order of the Thistle.*** The Scottish order of Knighthood (ranking only second to the Garter in the list of British Orders), traditionally said to have been founded in 787 by Achaius, king of the Scots, who, with Hungus, king of the Picts, was fighting an English king, in commemoration of a bright cross they saw in the heavens the night before the battle. It is said to have been refounded in 1540 by James V, and was certainly restored in 1687 by James VII and II, only to collapse in the Revolution of the following year and to be finally re-established by Queen Anne in 1703. Membership is confined to 16 Knights (beside Royalty), a Chancellor, Dean, Secretary, the Lyon King of Arms, and the Gentleman Usher of the Green Rod. Its insignia comprise the Badge (an elongated eight-pointed star with a figure of St Andrew and his cross), Star, Collar of golden thistles and sprigs of rue, Mantle, and dark green Ribbon.

***Thistles,*** especially 'Our Lady's Thistle', are said to be a cure for stitch in the side. According to the doctrine of signatures Nature has labelled every plant, and the prickles of the thistle tell us the plant is efficacious for *prickles* or the stitch. The species called *Silybum Marianum*, we are told, owes the white markings on its leaves to the milk of the Virgin Mary, some of which fell thereon and left a white mark behind.

**Thomas, St.** The Apostle who doubted (John 21:25); hence the phrase, *a doubting Thomas* applied to a sceptic.

The story told of him in the Apocryphal *Acts of St Thomas* is that he was deputed to go as a missionary to India, and, on refusing, Christ appeared and sold him as a slave to an Indian prince who was visiting Jerusalem. He was taken to India, where he baptised the prince and many others, and was finally martyred at Meliapore.

Another legend has it that Gondoforus, king of the Indies, gave him a large sum of money to build a palace. St Thomas spent it on the poor, 'thus erecting a superb palace in heaven'. On account of this he is the patron saint of masons and architects, and his symbol is a builder's square.

Another legend relates that he once saw a huge beam of timber floating on the sea near the coast, and the king unsuccessfully endeavouring, with men and elephants, to haul it ashore. St Thomas desired leave to use it in building a church, and, his request being granted, he dragged it easily ashore with a piece of packthread.

***St Thomas's Day.*** December 21st. *See* Thomasing.

***Christians of St Thomas.*** There are said to have been in the southern parts of Malabar some 200,000 persons who called themselves 'Christians of St Thomas' when Gama reached India in 1498. They had been 1,300 years under the jurisdiction of the patriarch of Babylon, who appointed their *Materene* (archbishop). In 1625 a stone was found near Siganfu with a cross on it, and containing a list of the *Materenes* of India and China.

***Thomas Atkins.*** *See* Tommy.

**Thomas the Rhymer.** *See* Rhymer.

**Thomasing.** Collecting small sums of money or obtaining drink from employers on St Thomas's Day, a custom that still exists in some districts. In London on December 21st every one of the Common Council has to be either elected or re-elected.

**Thomists.** Followers of St Thomas Aquinas (d.1274) – styled 'Doctor Angelicus' and, by Pius V, 'the Fifth Doctor of the Church' – and opponents of the *Scotists*, or followers of Duns Scotus.

Scotists and Thomists now in peace remain.
Pope, *Essay on Criticism*, 444

**Thone** or **Thonis.** In *Greek mythology* the governor of a province of Egypt to which, it is said by post-Homeric poets, Paris took Helen, who was given by Polydamnia, wife to Thone, the drug *nepenthes*, to make her forget her sorrows.

Not that nepenthes which the wife of Thone
In Egypt gave to love-lorn Helena,
Is of such power to stir up joy as this.
Milton, *Comus*, 695–697

**Thopas, Rime of Sir.** A burlesque on contemporary metrical romances, told as Chaucer's own tale in the *Canterbury Tales*. Sir Thopas was a native of Poperyng in Flanders, a capital sportsman, archer, wrestler, and runner. He resolved to marry no one but an elf queen, and set out for fairyland. On his way he met the three-headed giant Olifaunt, who challenged him to single combat. The knight got permission to go back for his armour, and promised to meet the giant next day. Here mine host interrupts the narrative as intolerable nonsense, and the 'rime' is left unfinished.

**Thor.** Son of Woden, god of war, and the second god in the pantheon of the ancient Scandinavians – their Vulcan, and god of thunder. He had three principal possessions; a Hammer (*Mjolnir*), typifying thunder and lightning, and having the virtue of returning to him after it was thrown; a Belt (*Meginjardir*) which doubled his power; and Iron Gloves to aid him in throwing his hammer.

He was god of the household, and of peasants, and was married to Sip, a typical peasant woman. His name is still perpetrated in our *Thursday*, and in a number of place-names, as *Thorsby* (Cumberland), *Torthorwoald* (Dumfries), and *Thurso* (Caithness).

**Thorn.** ***A thorn in the flesh.*** A source of constant irritation, annoyance, or affliction; said of objectionable and parasitical acquaintances, obnoxious conditions, of a 'skeleton in the cupboard', etc. There was a sect of the Pharisees (*q.v.*) which used to insert thorns in the borders of their gaberdines to prick their legs in walking and make them bleed.

***On thorns.*** In a state of painful anxiety and suspense; fearful that something is going wrong (*cp.* Tenterhooks).

***The Crown of Thorns.*** That with which our Saviour was crowned in mockery (Matt. 27:29); hence sometimes used of a very special affliction with which one is unjustly burdened.

Calvin (*Admonitio de Reliquiis*) gives a long list of places claiming to possess one or more of the thorns which composed the Saviour's crown. To his list may be added Glastonbury Abbey, where was also the spear of Longius or Longinus, and some of the Virgin's milk.

***The Glastonbury Thorn.*** *See* Glastonbury.

**Thorough.** The name given by the Earl of Strafford (executed 1641) to his uncompromising absolutist policy in favour of Charles I and against Parliament; especially to his harsh Irish policy, which he was determined to carry through regardless of all opposition and of all suffering.

**Thoth.** The Hermes of *Egyptian mythology*. He is represented with the head of an ibis on a human body. He is the inventor of the arts and sciences, music and astronomy, speech and letters. The name means 'Logos' or 'the Word'.

**Thousand.** ***He's one in a thousand.*** Said of a man who is specially distinguished by his excellent qualities; similarly, *a wife in a thousand*, a perfect wife, or one that exactly suits the speaker's ideas of what a wife should be.

*Thousand* is frequently used of large, indefinite numbers; as in Byron's

a small drop of ink,
Falling like dew, upon a thought, produces
That which makes thousands, perhaps millions, think.
*Don Juan*, III, lxxxviii

**Thread.** ***The thread of destiny.*** That on which destiny depends. According to *Greek mythology*, Clotho, one of the Fates (*q.v.*), spun from her distaff the destiny of man, and as she span her sister Lachesis worked out the events which were in store, and Atropos cut the thread at the point when death was to occur.

***The Triple Thread.*** Brahminism. The ancient Brahmins wore a symbol of three threads, reaching from the right shoulder to the left.

## Three

Faria says that their religion sprang from fishermen, who left the charge of the temples to their successors on the condition of their wearing some threads of their nets in remembrance of their vocation; but Osorius maintains that the triple thread symbolises the Trinity.

**Threadneedle Street.** The street in the City of London leading from Bishopsgate to the Bank of England. The name first appears – as *Three needle Street* – in 1598, and previously it seems to have been called *Broad Street*, as forming part of the present *Old Broad Street*. The name may have arisen from the sign of an inn, *The Three Needles* (though none of that name is recorded in the neighbourhood), or from some connection with the Needlemakers' Company, whose arms are 'three needles in fesse argent'.

***The Old Lady in Threadneedle Street.*** The Bank of England, which stands in this street. The term dates from the late 18th century, and there is a caricature by Gilray, dated May 22nd, 1797, entitled *The Old Lady in Threadneedle Street in Danger*, which refers to the temporary stopping of cash payments, February 26th, 1797, and to the issue of one pound banknotes on March 4th the same year.

The directors of the Bank of England were so called by William Cobbett, because, like Mrs Partington, they tried with their broom to sweep back the Atlantic waves of national progress.

> A silver curl-paper [i.e., a bank-note] that I myself took off the shining locks of the ever-beautiful old lady of Threadneedle Street.
>
> Dickens, *Dr Marigold*

**Three.** Pythagoras calls three the perfect number, expressive of 'beginning, middle, and end', wherefore he makes it a symbol of Deity.

A Trinity is by no means confined to the Christian creed. The Brahmins represent their god with three heads; the world was supposed by the ancients to be under the rule of three gods, viz. Jupiter (heaven), Neptune (sea), and Pluto (Hades). Jove is represented with three-forked lightning, Neptune with a trident, and Pluto with a three-headed dog. The Fates are three, the Furies three, the Graces three, the Harpies three, the Sibylline books three times three (of which only three survived); the fountain from which Hylas drew water was presided over by three nymphs; the Muses were three times three; the pythoness sat on a three-legged stool, or tripod; and in *Scandinavian mythology* we hear of 'the Mysterious Three', viz. 'Har' (the Mighty), the 'Like-Mighty', and the 'Third Person', who sat on three thrones above the rainbow.

Man is threefold (body, soul, and spirit); the world is threefold (earth, sea, and air); the enemies of man are threefold (the world, the flesh, and the devil); the Christian graces are threefold (Faith, Hope, and Charity); the kingdoms of Nature are threefold (mineral, vegetable, and animal); the cardinal colours are three in number (red, yellow, and blue), etc. *Cp.* Nine, which is three times three.

***A three-cornered fight.*** A parliamentary (or other) contest in which there are three competitors.

***A three-decker.*** Properly, a ship having three decks, a warship carrying guns on three decks, but applied to other triplicates, such as the old-fashioned pulpit, reading-desk, and clerk's desk arranged one above the other; and to the three-volume novel – the usual way of publishing fiction in most of the 19th century up to about 1895.

> In the midst of the church stands. . . the offensive structure of pulpit, reading-desk, and clerk's desk; in fact, a regular old three-decker in full sail westward.
>
> *The Christian Remembrancer*, July, 1852, p. 92

Kipling's poem, *The Three-Decker*, has as motto 'The three-volume novel is extinct'.

> Fair held the breeze behind us – 'twas warm with lovers' prayers,
> We'd stolen wills for ballast and a crew of missing heirs.
> They shipped as Able Bastards till the Wicked Nurse confessed,
> And they worked the old three-decker to the Islands of the Blest.
>
> Kipling, *The Three-Decker* (*Seven Seas*)

***Rule of Three.*** The rule of simple proportion; by which, given the relationship of two entities, the proportional relationship of a third can be ascertained.

***The Battle of the Three Emperors.*** The Battle of Austerlitz (December 2nd, 1805), when Napoleon inflicted a heavy defeat on the Russians and Austrians. The Emperors of the three Empires were all present in person.

***The Three Estates of the Realm.*** *See* Estates.

***The three-legged mare.*** An obsolete slang term for the gallows.

***The three R's.*** *See* R.

***The three tailors of Tooley Street.*** *See* Tailor.

***The three tongues.*** Those in which the inscription on the Cross were written, viz.

Hebrew, Greek, and Latin. In the Middle Ages it was considered that a thorough knowledge of these was necessary before one could begin to understand theology.

***Three Kings' Day.*** Epiphany or Twelfth Day, designed to commemorate the visit of the 'three kings' or Wise Men of the East to the infant Jesus. *See* Magi.

***Threescore years and ten.*** A ripe old age – not necessarily (in allusive use) exactly 70 years.

> Be merry, think upon the lives of men,
> And with what troubles three score years and ten
> Are crowded oft.
>
> Wm Morris, *Life and Death of Jason*, x, 101

The reference is to Ps. 90:10:

> The days of our years are threescore years and ten; and if by reason of strength they be fourscore years yet is their strength labour and sorrow; for it is soon cut off, and we fly away.

***Three sheets in the wind.*** *See* Sheet.

***Three-tailed bashaw.*** *See* Bashaw.

***To give one three times three.*** To give him a rousing ovation, cheer after cheer.

***We three.*** 'Did you never see the picture of *We Three*?' asks Sir Andrew Aguecheek (*Twelfth Night*, 2, 3) – not meaning himself, Sir Toby Belch, and the clown, but referring to a public-house sign of *Two Loggerheads*, with the inscription, 'We three loggerheads be', the third being the spectator.

***'When shall we three meet again?'*** – the title of a picture of *two* asses – is a similar 'joke'.

**Threshers.** Members of an Irish political organisation instituted in 1806 by Catholics in opposition to the Orangemen (*q.v.*). One object was to resist the payment of tithes. Their threats and warnings were signed 'Captain Thresher'.

**Thrimilce.** The Anglo-Saxon name for the month of May (*q.v.*).

**Throat. *Clergyman's throat.*** Chronic inflammation of the pharynx, to which clergymen and others who habitually overstrain the vocal organs are specially liable.

***To cut one's own throat.*** Figuratively, to adopt a policy, or take action that ruins one's own chances, plans, etc. Similarly, *to cut one another's throat* is to ruin one another by excessive competition.

***To jump down a person's throat.*** To interrupt and affront him, suddenly, sharply, and decisively.

***To lie in one's throat.*** To lie most outrageously, well knowing that you are lying, and meaning to.

**Throgmorton Street.** The financial world at large, or the Stock Exchange, which is situated in this narrow London street. So named from Sir Nicholas Throckmorton (d.1571), head of the ancient Warwickshire family, and ambassador to France in the reign of Queen Elizabeth.

**Through-stone.** A flat gravestone, a stone coffin or sarcophagus; also a bond stone which extends over the entire thickness of a wall.

> Od! he is not stirring yet, mair than he were a through-stane. Scott, *Monastery* (Introd.)

**Throw. *To throw away one's money.*** To spend it carelessly, recklessly, extravagantly.

***To throw back.*** To revert to ancestral traits; hence, *a throw-back* is one (human or animal) who does this.

***To throw oneself on someone.*** To commit oneself to his protection, favour, mercy, etc.

***To throw the helve after the hatchet.*** *See* Helve.

***To throw up one's hand.*** To abandon one's projects. A metaphor from card-playing.

**Thrums.** The fringe of warp threads left when the web has been cut off; weavers' ends and fag-ends of carpet, used for common rugs.

***Thread and thrum.*** Everything, good and bad together.

> Come, sisters, come, cut thread and thrum;
> Quail, crush, conclude, and quell!
>
> Shakespeare, *Midsummer Night's Dream*, 5, 1

The town immortalised by Sir James Barrie under this name in his *A Window in Thrums* (1889) is Kirriemuir, Forfarshire.

**Thug.** A member of a religious body of northern India, worshippers of Kali (*q.v.*), who could be propitiated only by human victims who had been strangled. Hence, the Thugs became a professional fraternity of stranglers, and supported themselves by the plunder obtained from those they strangled. Their native name is *P'hansigars* (stranglers); that of *Thug* (i.e. cheat) was given them in 1810. Their methods were rigorously suppressed under British rule, and were practically extinct by 1840.

**Thuggee.** The system of secret assassination preached by Thugs; the practice of Thugs.

**Thule.** The name given by the ancients to an island, or point of land, six days' sail north of Britain, and considered by them to be the extreme northern limit of the world. The name is first found in the account by Polybius (about 150 BC) of the voyage made by Pytheas in the late 4th century BC. Pliny says, 'It is an island in the

Northern Ocean discovered by Pytheas, after sailing six days from the Orcades.' Others, like Camden, consider it to be Shetland, in which opinion they agree with Marinus, and the descriptions of Ptolemy and Tacitus; and still others that it was some part of the coast of Norway. The etymology of the name is unknown.

> Where the Northern Ocean, in vast whirls,
> Boils round the naked melancholy isles
> Of farthest Thulë. Thomson, *Autumn*

***Ultima Thule.*** The end of the world; the last extremity.

Tibi serviat Ultima Thule.

Virgil, *Georgics*, i, 30

> Peshawar cantonment is the Ultima Thule of British India.
>
> *Nineteenth Century*, Oct. 1893, p. 533

**Thumb.** In the ancient Roman combats, when a gladiator was vanquished it rested with the spectators to decide whether he should be slain or not. If they wished him to live, they *shut up* their thumbs in their fists (*pollice compresso favor judicabatur*); if to be slain, they *turned out* their thumbs. *See* Pliny, xxviii, 2; Juvenal, iii, 36; Horace, *I Epist*. xviii, 66.

> Influenced by the rabble's bloody will,
> With thumbs bent back, they popularly kill.
> Dryden, *Third Satire*

Our popular saying, *Thumbs up!* expressive of pleasure or approval, is probably a survival from this custom.

***Every honest miller has a thumb of gold.*** Even an honest miller grows rich with what he prigs; for he simply can't help *some* of the flour that ought to go into the loaf sticking to his thumb! Chaucer says of his miller –

> Wel koude he stelen corn and tollen thriës,
> And yet he hadde a thombe of gold, pardee.
> *Canterbury Tales, Prologue*, 562

***Rule of thumb.*** A rough, guess-work measure; practice or experience, as distinguished from theory, as a guide in doing things. In some places the heat required in brewing is determined by dipping the thumb into the vat.

In the *Legend of Knockmany* Finn McCoul says:

> 'That baste Cucullin [is coming], ... for my thumb tells me so' [referring to the pricking of the thumb] (*see below*). To which his wife replies: 'Well, my Cully, don't be cast down ... Maybe I'll bring you better out of this scrape than ever you could bring yourself by your rule of thumb.'

W. B. Yeats, *Fairy Tales of the Irish Peasantry*, p. 270

***The pricking of one's thumb.*** In popular superstition, a portent of evil. The Second Witch in *Macbeth* (4, 1) Says –

> By the pricking of my thumbs,
> Something wicked this way comes.

And Macbeth enters.

Another proverb says, *My little finger told me that*. When your *ears tingle* it is to indicate that someone is speaking about you; when a sudden fit of *shivering* occurs, it is because someone is treading on the place which is to form your grave; when the *eye itches*, it indicates the visit of a friend; when the *palm itches* it shows that a present will shortly be received; and when the *bones ache* a storm is prognosticated. Sudden pains and prickings are the warnings of evil on the road; sudden glows and pleasurable sensations are the couriers to tell us of joy close at hand.

These and similar superstitions rest on the notion that 'coming events cast their shadows before', because our 'angel', ever watchful, forewarns us that we may be prepared.

> In ancient Rome the augurs took special notice of the palpitation of the heart, the flickering of the eye, and the pricking of the thumb. In regard to the last, if the pricking was on the left hand it was considered a very bad sign, indicating mischief at hand.

***Thumb-nail.*** Used attributively of various things, especially sketches, portraits, and so on, that are on a very small scale.

> 'Tis said, some men may make their wills
> On their thumb-nails, for aught they can bestow.
> Peter Pindar, *Lord B. and his Motions*

***Thumbs up!*** *See above*.

***To bite one's thumb at one.*** To insult him. Formerly a way of expressing defiance and contempt was by snapping the finger or putting the thumb in the mouth. Both these acts are termed a *fico*, whence 'I don't care a fig for you' (*see* Fig). Dekker, describing St Paul's Walk, speaks of the biting of thumbs, to beget quarrels, and biting one's glove (*see* Glove) was a similar token.

> I see Contempt marching forth, giving mee the fico with his thombe in his mouth.
>
> *Wits Miserie* (1596)

> I will bite my thumb at them; which is a disgrace to them, if they bear it.
>
> Shakespeare, *Romeo and Juliet*, 1, 1

***Tom Thumb.*** *See* Tom.

***Under one's thumb.*** Under the influence or power of the person named.

**Thumbikins** or **Thumbscrew.** An instrument of torture largely used by the Inquisition, compressing the thumb between two bars of iron by means of a screw. Principal Carstares (d.1715) was the last person put to this torture in Britain; he suffered for half an hour at Holyrood, by order of the Scotch Privy Council, because of his connection with the Rye House Plot (*q.v.*).

**Thunder.** Used figuratively of any loud noise, also of vehement denunciations or threats, as, the thunders of the Vatican, the anathemas and denunciations of the Pope, whose palace is the Vatican, at Rome.

Jupiter was the god of thunder in the *Roman mythology*; hence Dryden's allusion to the inactivity of Louis XIV –

> And threatening France, placed like a painted Jove,
> Kept idle thunder in his lifted hand.
>
> *Annus Mirabilis*, xxxix

***Sons of thunder.*** *See* Boanerges.

***To steal one's thunder.*** To forestall him; or to adopt his own special methods as one's own. The phrase comes from the anecdote of John Dennis (d.1734), the critic, who invented a very effective way of producing stage thunder for use in a play of his. The play was refused a hearing, but, to the author's extreme annoyance, they 'stole his thunder' for *Macbeth*.

**Thunderbolt.** A missile or mass of heated matter that was formerly supposed on occasion to be discharged from thunder-clouds during a storm; used figuratively of an irresistible blow, a sudden and overwhelming shock (*cp.* Bolt from the blue).

> Be ready, gods, with all your thunderbolts;
> Dash him to pieces!
>
> Shakespeare, *Julius Caesar*, 4, 3

Jupiter was depicted by the ancients as a man seated on a throne, holding a sceptre in his left hand and thunderbolts in his right.

***The Thunderbolt of Italy.*** Gaston de Foix, Duc de Nemours (1489–1512), nephew of Louis XII, was so called because of his brilliant campaign in Italy (1512).

**Thunderday.** *See* Thursday.

**Thunderer, The.** A name facetiously applied to *The Times* newspaper in the mid-19th century, in allusion to an article by the editor, Edward Sterling (d.1847), beginning:

> We thundered forth the other day an article on the subject of social and political reform.
>
> *The Times*

**Thundering Legion, The** (*Legio fulminans*). The XIIth Legion of the Roman army; probably so called because its ensign was a representation of Jupiter Tonans.

The name dates from much earlier times than those of Marcus Aurelius, but fable relates that it arose because in this Emperor's expedition against the Sarmatae, Marcomanni, etc., the XIIth Legion – stated for the purpose of the legend to have consisted of Christians – saved the whole army during a terrible drought by praying for rain. A terrible thunderstorm burst, and not only furnished a plentiful supply of water, but dispersed the enemy with lightning and thunderbolts.

> What wonders, yea, what apparent miracles did the prayers of former Christians procure! hence the Christian soldiers in their Army was called the Thundering Legion; they could do more by their prayers than the rest by their arms.
>
> Baxter, *Saints' Everlasting Rest*, II, vi, 6

The fable was long believed, but is none the less fictitious. In like manner a hailstorm was sent to the aid of Joshua, at the time when he commanded the sun to stay its course, and assisted the Israelites to their victory.

**Thursday.** The day of the god Thor (*q.v.*), called by the French *jeudi*, that is, Jove's day. Both Jove and Thor were gods of thunder, and formerly Thursday was sometimes called *Thunderday*. *See also* Black, Holy, Maundy Thursday.

***When three Thursdays come together.*** One of many circumlocutions for *Never*.

**Thyrsus.** *See* Torso.

**Tiara.** Anciently the name of the head-dress of the Persian kings; now applied to a coronet-like ornament, and especially to the triple crown of the Pope. This typifies the temporal claims of the papacy, and is composed of gold cloth encircled by three crowns and surmounted by a golden globe and cross.

Tradition has it that for the first five centuries the bishops of Rome wore a simple mitre like other bishops, and that Hormisdas (514–23) placed on his bonnet the crown sent him by Clovis. Boniface VIII (1294–1303) added a second crown during his struggles with Philip the Fair; and John XXII (1410–17) assumed the third.

There are other accounts of the original adoption of the crowns, and of their meanings; some say that the second was added in 1335 by Benedict XII, to indicate the prerogatives of spiritual and temporal power combined in the papacy; and that the third is indicative of the Trinity; and Pius IX, in 1871, spoke of it as –

> The symbol of my threefold dignity, in heaven, upon earth, and in purgatory.

Still another suggestion is that as the Pope claims to be (1) Head of the Catholic or Universal Church; (2) Sole Arbiter of its Rights; and (3) Sovereign Father of all the kings of the earth, he wears one crown as High Priest, one as Emperor, and one as King.

The tiara is very richly ornamented, and contains 146 jewels of all colours, 11 brilliants, and 540 pearls.

**Tib.** The ace of trumps in the game of Gleek. Tom is the knave.

> That gamester needs must overcome,
> That can play both Tib and Tom.
>
> Randolph, *Hermaphrodite*

***St Tib's Eve.*** Never. A corruption of St Ubes. There is no such saint in the calendar as St Ubes, and therefore her eve falls on the 'Greek Kalends' (*q.v.*) neither before Christmas Day nor after it.

**Tibert.** The name given to the Cat in Caxton's version of *Reynard the Fox*. *Cp.* Tybalt.

**Tick.** *To go on tick.* To owe for what one buys. In the 17th century *ticket* was the ordinary term for the written acknowledgement of a debt, and one living on credit was said to be *living on ticket*, or *tick*.

> If a servant usually buy for the master upon tick, and the servant buy some things without the master's order ... the master is liable.
>
> Chief Justice Holt (*Blackstone*, ch. xv, p. 468)

**Ticket.** *See* Etiquette.

***That's the ticket*** or ***That's the ticket for soup.*** That's the right thing. The ticket to be shown in order to obtain something.

***Ticket of leave.*** A warrant given to convicts to have their liberty on condition of good behaviour; hence, *Ticket-of-leave man*, a convict who is freed from prison and has to report himself to the police from time to time until his sentence is completed.

***To work one's ticket.*** An army expression for to get one's discharge before one's contract of service has expired.

**Tide.** Used figuratively of a tendency, a current or flow of events, etc., as in *a tide of feeling*, and in Shakespeare's –

> There is a tide in the affairs of men,
> Which, taken at the flood, leads on to fortune.
>
> *Julius Caesar*, 4, 3

***Lose not a tide.*** Waste no time; set off at once on the business.

***Tide-waiters.*** Custom-house officers who board ships entering ports and see that the customs regulations are carried out. The term has been figuratively applied to those who vote against their opinions.

***To tide over a difficulty, hard times,*** etc. Just to surmount the difficulty, just to come through the hard times, by force of circumstances and a little luck, rather than by one's own endeavours.

**Tidy** means in *tide*, in season, in time. We retain the word in eventide, springtide, and so on. Tusser has the phrase, 'If the weather be fair and tidy', meaning seasonable. Things done punctually and in their proper season are sure to be done orderly, and what is orderly done is neat and well arranged. Hence we get the notion of methodical, neat, well arranged, associated with tidy.

***A tidy fortune.*** A nice little bit of money. Tidy means neat, and neat means comfortable.

***How are you getting on? Oh! pretty tidily*** – favourably.

**Tied House.** A retail business, especially a public-house, that is obliged by a contract to obtain its supplies from some particular firm.

> There are tied houses in the drapery, grocery, dairy, boot and shoe, hardware, liquor, and book trades. *Liberty Review*, 14th April, 1894

**Tied up.** Married; 'spliced'; tied by the marriage-knot.

**Tiercel.** *See* Tassel-gentle.

**Tiffany.** A kind of thin silk-like gauze. The word is a corruption of *Theophany* (Gr. *theos*, god, *ephainein*, to show), the manifestation of God to man, the Epiphany; and the material was so called because it used to be worn at the Twelfth Night (Epiphany) revels.

**Tiffin.** An old Northern English dialect word for a small draught of liquor; it was introduced into India, where it acquired its modern meaning of a lunch, or light meal between breakfast and dinner. The word is almost solely used by Anglo-Indians, but it is in no way an Indian word.

**Tiger.** The nickname of the French statesman Georges Clemenceau (b.1841).

A liveried servant who rides out with his master used to be called a *tiger*, also a boy in buttons, a page; but the expression is now about obsolete. The same name is given in America to a final yell in a round of cheering.

**Tight.** Intoxicated.

***Blow me tight!*** A low expression of surprise, wonder, incredulity, etc.

> If there's a soul will give me food or find me in employ,
> By day or night, then blow me tight! (he was a vulgar boy).
> Barham, *Misadventures at Margate* (*Ingoldsby Legends*)

**Tike.** A provincial word (from Old Norse) for a dog or cur; hence used of a low fellow, as in the contemptuous insult, *You dirty tike*.

***A Yorkshire tike.*** A rustic of that county.

**Tilde.** The sign ~ placed over the letter *n* in Spanish words when this is to be pronounced like our *ni* in *bunion*, e.g. *cañon* (canyon). It is a relic of the small *n* placed over a word in Latin MSS to indicate a contraction, and the name is a variant of Span. *titulo*, title.

The tilde is also occasionally placed over an *l* to indicate the sound in *million*, and in Portuguese (called *til*) over the first vowel of a diphthong to show that the diphthong is to have a nasal pronunciation. In this language our *ni* of *bunion* is represented by *nh* not by *ñ*.

**Tile.** Low slang for a hat, this being to the head what the tiles are to a house.

***He has a tile loose.*** He is not quite *compos mentis*, not all there.

In Freemasonry, *to tile a lodge* means to close and guard the doors of a Masonic meeting, to prevent anyone uninitiated from entering, the officer who does this being called the *Tiler*. Of course, to tile a house means to finish building it, and to tile a lodge is to complete it.

**Timber Toe.** A wooden leg; one with a wooden leg is called *Timbertoes*.

**Time.** ***Summer time.*** The legal, as apart from actual, time during a certain portion of the year in Great Britain and some other countries. In the spring of 1916 the Summer Time Act was passed ordaining that –

> During the prescribed period in each year during which this Act is in force the time for general purposes in Great Britain shall be one hour in advance of Greenwich Mean Time.

The 'prescribed period' has varied, but in Great Britain is now (1922) fixed at from the 3rd Sunday in April to the day following the 3rd Saturday in September. The scheme had been proposed in 1906 by Mr William Willett, and it was adopted some few years after his death as a war measure, principally with the object of saving coal and light.

***Take time by the forelock.*** Seize the present moment; *Carpe diem*. Time called by Shakespeare 'that bald sexton' (*King John*, 3, 1), is represented with a lock of hair on his forehead but none on the rest of his head, to signify that time past cannot be used, but time present may be seized by the forelock. The saying is attributed to Pittacus of Mitylene, one of the Seven Sages of Greece.

***Time and tide wait for no man.*** One of many sayings pointing the folly of procrastination. It appears in Ray's *Scottish Proverbs* as 'Time bides na man'.

> For the next inn he spurs amain,
> In haste alights, and scuds away –
> But time and tide for no man stay.
> Somerville, *The Sweet-scented Miser*

***Time-expired.*** Applied to soldiers whose term of service is completed. Also used of freed convicts.

***Time-honoured Lancaster.*** Old John of Gaunt, Duke of Lancaster (about 1340–99), so called by Shakespeare (*Richard II*, 1, 1) because his memory had been honoured by Time. His father was Edward III, his son Henry IV, his nephew Richard II, and through his great granddaughter, Margaret Beaufort, he is the ancestor of all our sovereigns from Henry VII, Margaret's son. Shakespeare calls him 'old'; he was only fifty-nine at his death.

***Time is, Time was, Time's past.*** *See* Brazen Head.

***Time of Grace.*** *See* Sporting Seasons.

***To know the time o' day.*** To be smart, knowing, wide awake.

**Timeo Danaos.** *See* Greek Gift.

**Timias.** Prince Arthur's squire in Spenser's *Faërie Queene*, typifying Sir Walter Raleigh. *See* Amoret.

**Timoleon.** The Greek general and statesman (d. about 336 BC) who so hated tyranny that he voted for the death of his own brother Timophanes when he attempted to make himself absolute in Corinth.

> The fair Corinthian boast
> Timoleon, happy temper, mild and firm,
> Who wept the brother while the tyrant bled.
> Thomson, *Winter*

**Timon of Athens.** An Athenian misanthrope of the late 5th century BC, and the principal figure in Shakespeare's play so called. The play, which was acted about 1607 and printed in 1623, is not all Shakespeare's work.

Macaulay uses the expression to 'out-Timon Timon' – i.e. to be more misanthropical than even Timon.

**Timur.** *See* Tamburlaine.

**Tin.** Money. A depreciating synonym for silver, called by alchemists 'Jupiter'.

**Tine-man, The.** Archibald Douglas, 4th Earl of Douglas, who died 1424.

**Tintagel.** The castle on the north coast of Cornwall where, according to tradition, Uther died and King Arthur was born. Its ruins still exist, on a rocky headland jutting into the sea.

> Uther in his wrath and heat besieged
> Ygerne within Tintagil, where her men . . .
> Left her and fled, and Uther entered in.
>
> Tennyson, *The Coming of Arthur*, 198

**Tip.** A small present of money, such as that given to a waiter, porter, or schoolboy; from the cant verb (common in the 16th and 17th centuries) *to tip*, meaning to hand over, which also gives rise to the other signification of the verb, viz., private warning, such secret information as may guide the person *tipped* to make successful bets or gain some other advantage. A *straight tip* comes straight or direct from the owner or trainer of a horse, or from one in a position to know.

A man will sometimes give the police the *tip*, or hint where a gang of confederates lie concealed, or where lawbreakers may be found.

***Tip-top.*** First rate, capital, splendid.

***To have a thing on the tip of one's tongue.*** To have it so pat that it comes without thought; also, to have it on the verge of one's memory, but not quite perfectly remembered.

***To tip one the wink.*** To make a signal to another by a wink.

**Tiphany.** The name given in the old romances to the mother of the Magi. Of course it is a corruption of *Epiphany*. *See* Tiffany.

**Tiphys.** The pilot of the Argonauts (*q.v.*); hence a generic name for pilots.

> Many a Tiphys ocean's depths explore,
> To open wondrous ways untried before.
>
> *Hoole's Ariosto*, Bk viii

**Tipperary Rifle.** A shillelagh or stick made of blackthorn.

**Tippling House.** A contemptuous name for a tavern or public-house. A *tippler* was formerly a tavern-keeper or tapster, and the tavern was called a *tippling house*. At Boston, Lincolnshire, in 1577, five persons were appointed 'tipplers of Lincoln beer', and no 'other tippler [might] draw or sell beer' . . . under penalties.

**Tipstaff.** A constable, bailiff, or sheriff's officer: so called because he carried a staff tipped with a bull's horn or with metal. In the documents of Edward III allusion is often made to his staff.

**Tir.** One of the sons of Eblis (*q.v.*).

**Tiresias.** A Theban of Greek legend, who by accident saw Athena bathing, and was therefore struck with blindness by her splashing water in his face. She afterwards repented, and, as she could not restore his sight, conferred on him the power of soothsaying and of understanding the language of birds, and gave him a staff with which he could walk as safely as if he had his sight. He found death at last by drinking from the well of Tilphosa.

> Juno the truth of what was said denied,
> Tiresias, therefore, must the cause decide.
>
> Addison, *Transformation of Tiresias*

**Tirl.** A Scottish variant of *twirl*.

***He tirled at the pin.*** He twiddled or rattled with the latch before opening the door. The pin was not only the latch of chamber doors and cottages, but the 'rasp' of castles used instead of the modern knocker. It was attached to a ring, which produced a grating sound to give notice to the warder.

> Sae licht he jumpëd up the stair,
> And tirlëd at the pin;
> And wha sae ready as hersel'
> To let the laddie in. *Charlie is my Darling*

**Tironian.** Pertaining to a system of shorthand said to have been invented by Tiro, the freedman and amanuensis of Cicero. Our '&' (*see* Ampersand) is still sometimes called the *Tironian sign*, for it represents the contraction of Lat. *et* introduced by Tiro.

With regard to this Maunde Thompson (*Handbook to Greek and Latin Palaeography*, p. 84) says, 'Suetonius has it that "Vulgares notas *Ennius* primus mille et centum invenit,"' and adds that more generally the name of Cicero's freedman, Tiro, is associated with the invention, the signs being commonly named 'notae Tironianae'.

**Tirynthian.** Hercules is called by Spenser the *Tirynthian Swain* (*Faërie Queene*, VI, xii, 35), and the *Tirynthian Groom* (*Epithalamium*, 329), because he generally resided at Tiryns, an ancient city of Argolis in Greece, famous for its Cyclopean architecture, which is mentioned by

Homer, and the ruins of which are still magnificent.

**Tit for Tat.** Retaliation; probably representing *tip for tap*, i.e. blow for for blow. J. Bellenden Ker says this is the Dutch *dit vor dat* (this for that), Lat. *quid pro quo*. Heywood uses the phrase *tit for tat*, perhaps the French *tant pour tant*.

**Titans.** Primordial beings of *Greek mythology*, of enormous size and strength, and typical of lawlessness and the power of force. There were twelve, six male (Oceanus, Coeus, Crius, Hyperion, Japetus, and Cronus) and six female (Theia, Rhea, Themis, Mnemosyne, Phoebe, and Tethys), children of Uranus and Ge (Heaven and Earth). Legends vary, but one states that Cronus swallowed the rest of them, and that when liberated by Zeus (son of Cronus), they dethroned and emasculated their father, Uranus; whereupon they made war on Zeus, who, after defeating them, imprisoned them all – Oceanus alone excepted – in Tartarus.

By Virgil and Ovid the Sun was sometimes surnamed *Titan*; hence Shakespeare's:

> And fleckëd Darkness like a drunkard reels
> From forth Day's path and Titan's fiery wheels.
>
> *Romeo and Juliet*, 2, 3

**Titania.** Wife of Oberon (*q.v.*), and Queen of the Fairies in *A Midsummer Night's Dream*. Shakespeare was, apparently, the first to use this name.

**Tithonus.** A beautiful Trojan of Greek legend, brother to Laomedon, and beloved by Eos (Aurora). At his prayer the goddess granted him immortality, but as he had forgotten to ask for youth and vigour he grew old, and life became insupportable. He now prayed Eos to remove him from the world; this, however, she could not do, but she changed him into a grasshopper.

> An idle scene Tithonus acted
> When to a grasshopper contracted.
>
> Prior, *The Turtle and Sparrows*

**Titi, Prince.** The nickname of Frederick, Prince of Wales, eldest son of George II. Seward, a contemporary, tells us that he was a great reader of French memoirs, and wrote memoirs of his contemporaries under the pseudonym of 'Prince Titi'.

**Titles of Kings.** *See* Rulers; Religious.

**Titmouse.** *See* Misnomers.

**Titular Bishops.** The Roman Catholic dignitaries formerly known as bishops *in partibus*. *See* In partibus.

**Titus.** An alternative name of the Penitent Thief. *See* Dysmas.

***The Arch of Titus.*** The arch built in Rome in commemoration of the capture of Jerusalem by Titus and Vespasian (AD 70) shortly after that event. It is richly sculptured, and the trophies taken at the destruction of the temple are shown in relief.

**Tityre Tus.** Dissolute young scapegraces of the late 17th century (*cp.* Mohocks) whose delight was to annoy the watchmen, upset sedans, wrench knockers off doors, and insult pretty women. The name comes from the first line of Virgil's first *Eclogue*, *Tityre, tu patulae recubans sub tegmine fagi*, because the Tityre Tus loved to lurk in the dark night looking for mischief.

**Tityrus.** A poetical surname for a shepherd; from its use in Greek idylls and Virgil's first *Eclogue*. In the *Shepheardes Calendar* (*Feb.*, *June*, and *Dec.*) Spenser calls Chaucer by this name.

> Heroes and their feats
> Fatigue me, never weary of the pipe
> Of Tityrus, assembling as he sang
> The rustic throng beneath his favourite beech.
>
> Cowper, *The Winter Evening*, 750

**Tityus.** A gigantic son of Zeus and Ge in *Greek mythology* whose body covered nine acres of land. He tried to defile Latona, but Apollo cast him into Tartarus, where a vulture fed on his liver, which grew again as fast as it was devoured. (*Cp.* Prometheus.) He was the father of Europa.

**Tiu.** Son of Woden (*Scandinavian mythology*), and younger brother of Thor. The wolf Fenrir bit off his hand.

**Tizona.** One of the favourite swords of the Cid, taken by him from King Bucar. His other favourite sword was Colada. Tizona was buried with him.

**Tizzy.** A sixpenny-piece; a variant of *tester* (*q.v.*).

**To-do.** ***Here's a pretty to-do.*** Disturbance. The French *affaire* – i.e. *à faire* (to do).

**To-remain Bible.** *See* Bible, Specially named.

**Toads.** The device of Clovis was three toads (or *botes*, as they were called in O.Fr.); legend relates that after his conversion and baptism the Arians assembled a large army under King Candat against him. While on his way to meet the heretics Clovis saw in the heavens his device miraculously changed into three lilies *or* on a banner *azure*. He instantly had such a banner made, and called it his *liflambe*, and even before his army came in sight of King Candat, the host of the heretic lay dead, slain, like the army of Sennacherib, by a blast from the God of Battles (Raoul de Prèsles, *Grans Croniques de France*).

> It is wytnessyd of Maister Robert Gagwyne that before thyse dayes all French kynges used to bere in their armes iii Todys, but after this Clodoveus had recognised Cristes relygyon iii Floure de lys were sent to hym by diuyne power, sette in a shylde of azure, the whiche syns that been borne of all French kynges.
>
> *Fabian's Chronicle*

***The toad, ugly and venomous, wears yet a precious jewel in its head.*** Fenton says: 'There is to be found in the heads of old and great toads a stone they call borax or stelon, which, being used as rings, give forewarning against venom' (1569). These stones always beset a figure resembling a toad on their surface.

Lupton says: 'A toad-stone, called *crepaudia*, touching any part envenomed by the bite of a rat, wasp, spider, or other venomous beast, ceases the pain and swelling thereof.' In the Londesborough Collection is a silver ring of the 15th century, in which one of these toad-stones is set. The stone was supposed to sweat and change colour when poison was in its proximity. Technically called the *Batrachyte* or *Batrachos*, an antidote to all sorts of poison.

***Toads unknown in Ireland.*** It is said that St Patrick cleared the island of all 'varmint' by his malediction.

***Toad-eater*** or ***Toady.*** A cringing, obsequious parasite; probably so called because such a one is ready to do anything nauseating or revolting for his patron; *lickspittle* is a similar word.

Fable has, however, been busy on the word, and a false etymology of the past states that it represents Span. *mi todita* (my factotum), the story being that at the final overthrow of the Moors the Castilians made them their servants, and their active habits and officious manners greatly pleased the proud and lazy Spaniards, who addressed them thus.

***Toad-in-the-hole.*** A piece of beef baked in batter.

**Toast.** The person, cause, object, etc., to which guests are invited to drink in compliment. The word is taken from the toast which used at one time to be put into the tankard, and which still floats in the loving-cups at the Universities.

The story goes that in the reign of Charles II a certain beau pledged a noted beauty in a glass of water taken from her bath; whereupon another roysterer cried out he would have nothing to do with the liquor, but would have the toast – i.e. the lady herself. (*Rambler*, No. 24.)

> Let the toast pass, drink to the lass.
>
> Sheridan, *School for Scandal*

> Say, why are beauties praised and honoured most,
> The wise man's passion and the vain man's toast.
>
> Pope, *Rape of the Lock*, canto i

**Toaster, Toasting-iron.** *See* Cheese-toaster.

**Tobit.** The principal character of the *Book of Tobit*, a romance included in the Old Testament Apocrypha. While sleeping outside the wall of his courtyard he was blinded by sparrows 'muting warm dung into his eyes'. His son Tobias was attacked on the Tigris by a fish, which leapt out of the water and which he caught at the bidding of the angel Raphael, his mentor. Tobias afterwards married Sara, seven of whose betrothed lovers had been successively carried off by the evil spirit Asmodeus, who was driven by the angel Azarias to the extremity of Egypt, bound. Tobit was cured of his blindness by applying to his eyes the gall of the fish which had tried to devour his son.

**Toboso.** The village home of Don Quixote's lady-love, whom he renamed Dulcinea (*q.v.*). It is a few miles east of Ciudad Real.

**Toby.** The dog in the puppet-show of Punch and Judy (*q.v.*). He wears a frill garnished with bells, to frighten away the devil from his master.

***My Uncle Toby.*** Captain Shandon, the uncle of Tristram Shandy in Sterne's book of that name. He is the embodiment of the wisdom of love, as his brother is that of the love of wisdom.

***The high toby***, the high road; *the low toby*, the by-road. A highwayman is a 'high tobyman'; a mere footpad is a 'low tobyman'. This is probably from the Shelta (i.e. old tankers' jargon) word for road, *tobar*.

> So we can do a touch now … as well as you grand gentlemen on the high toby.
>
> Boldrewood, *Robbery under Arms*, ch. xxvi

**Toddy.** Properly the juice obtained by tapping certain palms, fermented so as to become intoxicating (Hindu *tãdi*, from *tãr*, a palm). It is also applied to a beverage compounded of spirits, hot water, and sugar, a kind of punch.

**Tofana.** An old woman of Naples (d.1730) immortalised by her invention of a tasteless and colourless poison, called by her the *Manna of St Nicola of Bari*, but better known as *Aqua Tofana*. Above 600 persons fell victims to this insidious drug.

**Toga.** The usual outer dress of a Roman citizen when appearing in public; the Romans were hence the *Gens togata* (*q.v.*), the 'togaed people'.

The toga consisted of a single piece of undyed woollen cloth, cut almost in a semicircle and worn in a flowing fashion round the shoulders and body.

***Toga picta.*** The toga embroidered with golden stars that was worn by the emperor on special occasions, by a victorious general at his 'triumph', etc.

***Toga praetexta.*** The toga with a purple border that was worn by children, by those engaged in sacred rites, magistrates, etc.

***Toga virilis.*** The toga worn by man (*virilis*, manly), assumed by boys when 15.

**Togs.** Slang for clothes; hence *togged out in his best*, dressed in his best clothes; *toggery*, finery. The word *may* be connected with *toga* (*see above*).

**Toledo.** A sword made at Toledo in Spain, which long before and after the Middle Ages was specially famous for them.

> I give him three years and a day to match my Toledo
> And then we'll fight like dragons.
>
> Massinger, *The Maid of Honour*, II, ii

**Tolosa. *He has got the gold of Tolosa.*** His ill-gotten wealth will do him no good. *See under* Gold.

**Tom.** Short for *Thomas*: used of the male of certain animals (especially the cat), and generically – like *Jack* (*q.v.*) – for a man. When contrasted, *Jack* is usually the sharp, shrewd, active fellow, and *Tom* the honest dullard. No one would think of calling the thick-headed male cat a *Jack*, nor the pert, dexterous, thieving daw a *Tom*. The former is almost instinctively called a *Tom-cat*, and the latter a *Jack-daw*.

> The man that hails you Tom or Jack,
> And proves by thumps upon your back
> How he esteems your merit,
> Is such a friend, that one had need
> Be very much his friend indeed
> To pardon or to bear it.
>
> Cowper, *Friendship*

***Great Tom of Lincoln.*** A bell at Lincoln Cathedral weighing 5 tons 8 cwt.

***Great Tom of Oxford.*** A bell in Tom Gate Tower (*see* Tom Gate) at Oxford, tolled every night at 9.10. It weighs 7 tons 12 cwt.

***Long Tom.*** A familiar name for any gun of great length; especially the naval 4.7's used on land in the second Boer War.

***Old Tom.*** A specially potent gin. The story goes that a Thomas Norris, employed in Messrs Hodges' distillery, opened a gin palace in Great Russell Street, Covent Garden, in the late 18th century, and called the gin concocted by Thomas Chamberlain, one of the firm of Hodges, 'Old Tom', in compliment to his former master.

***Tom and Jerry.*** Types of the roystering young man about town; from Pierce Egan's *Life in London; or, The Day and Night Scenes of Jerry Hawthorn, Esq., and his Elegant Friend Corinthian Tom* (1821). *Cp.* Jerry-shop.

***Tom, Dick, and Harry.*** A set of nobodies; persons of no note; persons unworthy notice. 'Brown, Jones, and Robinson' are far other men; they are the vulgar rich, who give themselves airs, especially abroad, and look with scorn on all foreign manners and customs which differ from their own.

***Tom Fool.*** A clumsy, witless fool, fond of stupid practical jokes; hence, *tomfoolery*.

***Tom Gate, The.*** The great gate of Christ Church, Oxford, begun by Wolsey and completed (1682) by Wren. In its tower is 'Great Tom' (*see above*).

***Tom Long.*** Any lazy, dilatory man. *To be kept waiting for Tom Long* is to be kept hanging about for a wearisome time.

***Tom Noddy.*** A puffing, fuming, stupid creature.

***Tom o' Bedlam.*** A mendicant who levies charity on the plea of insanity. In the 16th and 17th centuries applications for admission to Bedlam (*q.v.*) became so numerous that many inmates were dismissed half cured. These 'ticket-of-leave men' wandered about chanting mad songs, and dressed in fantastic dresses, to excite pity. Posing as these harmless 'innocents', a set of sturdy rogues appeared, called *Abram men* (*q.v.*), who shammed lunacy, and committed great depredations.

> With a sigh like Tom o' Bedlam.
>
> Shakespeare, *King Lear*, 1, 2

***Tom Quad.*** The great quadrangle of Christ Church, Oxford. *Cp.* Tom Gate.

***Tom Thumb.*** Any dwarfish or insignificant person is so called; from the pigmy hero of the old nursery tale, popular in the 16th century. *The History of Tom Thumb* was published by R. Johnson in 1621, and there is a similar tale by Perrault (*Le Petit Poucet*), in 1630.

The American dwarf Charles Sherwood Stratton (1838–83) was popularly called 'General

Tom Thumb' (*see* Dwarfs); and Fielding wrote a burlesque (acted 1730) entitled *Tom Thumb the Great*. *See also* Boast of England: Grumbo.

***Tom Tiddler's ground.*** A place where it is easy to pick up a fortune or make a place in the world for oneself; from the old children's game in which a base-keeper, who is called Tom Tiddler, tries to keep the other children, who sing –

> Here we are on Tom Tiddler's ground
> Picking up gold and silver

from crossing the boundary into his base.

***Tom Tiller.*** A hen-pecked husband.

**Tom's.** A noted coffee-house of the late 18th century, that was still in existence in Russell Street, Covent Garden, as late as 1865. It was owned by and named after Thomas West, and here in 1764 was founded *Tom's Club*, which included all the literary and social notabilities of the time.

**Tombland Fair.** *See* Maundy Thursday.

**Tomboy.** A romping girl, formerly used of a loose or immodest woman, whence the slang, *Tom*, applied to a prostitute.

> A lady
> So fair … to be partner'd
> With tomboys. Shakespeare, *Cymbeline*, 1, 6

**Tommy.** ***Tommy***, or ***Tommy Atkins***. A British private soldier, as a Jack Tar is a British sailor. At one time all recruits were served out with manuals in which were to be entered the name, age, date of enlistment, length of service, wounds, medals, and so on of the holder. With each book was sent a specimen form showing how the one in the manual should be filled in, and the hypothetical name selected, instead of the lawyers' *John Doe* or *Richard Roe*, was Thomas Atkins.

> For it's Tommy this, and Tommy that, and 'Tommy, wait outside';
> But it's 'Special train for Atkins' when the trooper's on the tide.
> Kipling, *Tommy* (*Barrack-Room Ballads*)

**Tommy Dodd.** The 'odd' man who, in tossing up, either wins or loses according to agreement with his confederate.

***To go Tommy Dodd*** for drinks, etc., is to toss 'odd man out', the odd man dropping out until there are only two left, who toss for who pays.

***Tommy rot.*** Utter nonsense, rubbish; a cock-and-bull story (*q.v.*).

***Tommy shop.*** A shop where vouchers, given by an employer in lieu of money, can be exchanged for goods; commonly run by large employers of labour before the truck system was made illegal.

**Tomorrow.** ***Tomorrow come never.*** Never at all – when two Sundays, or three Thursdays, meet.

> 'I shall acquaint your mother, Miss May, with your pretty behaviour tomorrow.' – 'I suppose you mean tomorrow come never,' answered Magnolia.
> Le Fanu, *The House in the Churchyard*

***Tomorrow never comes.*** Because, when it *does* come it ceases to be *tomorrow* and becomes *today*; a reproof to those who defer till tomorrow what should be done today.

A similar – though more caustic – saying is:

> Treason doth never prosper; what's the reason?
> For if it prosper, none dare call it treason.
> Sir John Harrington (d.1612)

**Tongue.** ***A lick with the rough side of the tongue.*** A severe reprimand, a good slating.

***The gift of tongues.*** Command of foreign languages; also the power claimed by the Early Church and by some later mystics (as the Irvingites) of conversing and understanding unknown tongues (from the miracle at Pentecost – Acts 2:4).

***The three tongues.*** *See* Three.

***The tongue of the trump.*** The spokesman or leader of a party.

> The tongue of the trump to them a'.
> Burns, *The Election Ballads*, III

***To give one the length of one's tongue.*** To talk to him 'like a Dutch uncle'; to tell him in unmeasured language what you really think of him; or to 'cheek' him.

***To give tongue.*** Properly used of a dog barking when on the scent; hence sometimes applied to people. Thus Polonius says to his son –

> Give thy thoughts no tongue,
> Nor any unproportioned thought his act.
> Shakespeare, *Hamlet*, 1, 3

***To hold one's tongue.*** To keep silent when one can speak; to keep a secret.

***To lose one's tongue.*** To become tongue-tied or speechless through shyness, fear, etc.

***To speak with one's tongue in one's cheek.*** Insincerely; saying one thing and meaning another.

***Tongue-tied.*** Speechless, usually through bashfulness or modesty; also (literally) having an impediment of the speech through shortness of the fraenum.

**Tonic Sol-fa.** A system of musical notation in which diatonic scales are written always in one way (the keynote being indicated), the tones being represented by syllables or initials, and time and accents by dashes and colons. *Tonic* is a musical term denoting pertaining to or founded on the keynote; *sol* and *fa* are two of the Aretinian Syllables (*q.v.*). *See also* Doh; Gamut.

**Tonquin Bean.** *See* Misnomers.

**Tonsure.** The sacerdotal custom among priests of wearing a tonsure or 'being tonsured', i.e. having the head, or part of it, shaved (Lat. *tonsura*, a shearing), dates from the 5th or 6th centuries, and signifies the renunciation of the world and its vanities. There are three forms, viz.:

***The tonsure of St Paul,*** which consists in shaving the whole head; the usual practice in the Eastern Church;

***The tonsure of St Peter,*** which may be the mere circular patch on the crown of the head (worn by secular priests), or the whole upper part of the head shaved, leaving only a fringe of hair (as in some monastic orders); and

***The tonsure of St John,*** the front of the head shaved on a line drawn from ear to ear. This was the method in the ancient Celtic Church, and is hence sometimes called the *Scottish*, or *Irish tonsure*.

**Tontine.** A form of annuity shared by several subscribers, in which the shares of those who die are added to the holdings of the survivors till the last survivor inherits all. So named from Lorenzo Tonti, a Neapolitan banker, who introduced the system into France in 1653.

**Tool.** ***To tool a coach.*** To drive one; generally applied to a gentleman Jehu, who undertook stage-coach driving for his own amusement.

***To tool*** is to use the tool as a workman, and a coachman's tools are the reins and whip.

**Tooley Street.** A corruption of St Olaf – i.e. 'T-olaf, Tolay, Tooley. Similarly, Sise Lane is St Osyth's Lane.

***The three tailors of Tooley Street.*** *See* Tailor.

**Toom Tabard** (Scot., empty jacket). A nickname given to John Baliol (1249–1315), because of his poor spirit, and sleeveless appointment to the throne of Scotland. The honour was an 'empty jacket', which he enjoyed only from 1292 to 1296. He died in Normandy.

**Tooth.** *See also* Teeth.

***Golden tooth.*** *See* Golden.

***Tooth and egg.*** An obsolete corruption of *tutenag* (from Arab. *tūtiyā*), an alloy rich in zinc, coming from China and the East Indies and largely used for lining tea-chests.

***With tooth and nail.*** In right good earnest, with one's utmost power; as though biting and scratching.

**Top.** *See also* Mizentop.

***A display of the top ropes.*** A show of gushing friendliness; great promise of help. The top rope is the rope used in hauling the topmast up or down.

> This display of the top-ropes was rather new to me, for time had blurred from my memory the 'General's' rhapsodies.
>
> C. Thomson, *Autobiography*, p. 189

***Over the top.*** One is said *to go over the top* when he takes the final plunge, or when he goes for a thing 'bald-headed'. A phrase from the Great War, recalling how, on a concerted attack, the soldiers in the trench would suddenly leap 'over the top' and rush the enemies' lines.

***The top o' the morning to ye!*** A cheery greeting on a fine day, especially in Ireland. It is about the same as 'The best of everything to you!'

***Top-heavy.*** Liable to tip over because the centre of gravity is too high; intoxicated.

***Top sawyer.*** A first-rate fellow, a 'high-flyer', a distinguished man. Literally, the sawyer who works the upper handle in a saw-pit; hence one who holds a superior position.

***To sleep like a top.*** *See* Sleep.

**Topham.** ***Take him, Topham.*** Catch him if you can; lay hold of him, tipstaff. Topham was the Black Rod of the House of Commons in the reign of Charles II, very active in apprehending 'suspects' during the supposed conspiracy revealed by Titus Oates. 'Take him, Topham', became a proverbial saying of the time, much the same as 'How are your poor feet?' 'There you are, then!' and so on.

> Till 'Take him, Topham' became a proverb, and a formidable one, in the mouth of the people.
>
> Sir Walter Scott, *Peveril of the Peak*, ch. xx

**Tophet.** A valley just to the south of Jerusalem, at the south-east of Gehenna (*q.v.*), where children were made to 'pass through the fire to Moloch'. Josiah threw dead bodies, ordure, and other unclean things there, to prevent all further application of the place to religious use (2 Kings 23:10), and here Sennacherib's army was destroyed (Is. 30:31–3). A perpetual fire was kept burning in it to consume the dead bodies, bones, filth, etc., deposited there, and hence it was taken as symbolical of Sheol or Hell. The name is Hebrew, and may mean 'a place to be spat upon', or it may be connected with *toph*, a drum, in allusion to the drowning of the murdered children's cries by the beating of drums.

**Topsy.** The little slave girl in Mrs Stowe's *Uncle Tom's Cabin* (1852); chiefly remembered because when asked by 'Aunt Ophelia' about her parents she maintained that she had had neither father nor mother, her solution of her existence being, 'I 'spects I growed.'

**Topsy-turvy.** Upside down; probably *top*, with *so* and obsolete *terve*, connected with A.S. *tearflian*, to turn or roll over. Shakespeare says, 'Turn it topsy-turvy down' (*1 Henry IV*, 4, 1). *Cp.* Half-seas Over.

**Toralva.** The licentiate In *Don Quixote* (II, iii, 5) who was conveyed on a cane through the air, with his eyes shut. In the space of twelve hours he arrived at Rome, and lighted on the tower of Nona, whence, looking down, he witnessed the death of the Constable de Bourbon. Next morning he arrived at Madrid, and related the whole affair. During his flight the devil bade him open his eyes, and he found himself so near the moon that he could have touched it with his finger.

**Torre, Sir.** One of the knights of the Round Table (*q.v.*), brother of Elaine, and son of the lord of Astolat. A kind blunt heart, brusque in manners, and but little of a knight.

**Torricelli.** An Italian mathematician (1608–47), noted for his explanation of the rise of water in a common barometer. Galileo explained the phenomenon by the *ipse dixit* of 'Nature abhors a vacuum.'

Hence *Torricellian tube*, the barometer, and *Torricellian vacuum*, the vacuum above the mercury in this.

**Torso.** A statue which has lost its head and limbs. The word is Ital. for a stump or stalk, from Lat. *thyrsus*, the attribute of Bacchus, consisting of a spear-shaft wreathed with ivy or vine branches and tipped with a fir-cone.

> The *Torso Belvedere*, the famous torso of Hercules, in the Vatican, was discovered in the fifteenth century. It is said that Michael Angelo greatly admired it.

**Tortoise.** The name is given to the ancient Roman *testudo*, i.e. the screen or penthouse formed by the overlapping shields held above their heads by soldiers when attacking a fort; and the animal is frequently taken as the type of plodding perseverance – 'slow but sure'.

The tortoise which, according to Hindu myth, supports Maha-pudma, the elephant which, in its turn, supports the world, is Chukwa.

***Achilles and the tortoise.*** *See* Achilles.

***Like the hare and the tortoise.*** *See* Hare.

**Tory.** The name given in the 17th century to the Irish who were turned out of their holdings by English settlers, and so took to the hills and bogs and developed into brigands and outlaws (from *toraidhe*, a pursued person). During the Revolution it was applied to the Catholics fighting for James II; hence to those in England who refused to concur in excluding James from the throne. Until the accession of George III the party had a Stuart bias, but it then decided vigorously to uphold the Crown, the Church as by law established, and all constituted authority. As the name of the political and parliamentary party it was gradually superseded after 1830, by 'Conservative' (*q.v.*), but it has been retained to denote the principles and policy of the party, especially those of its more 'unbending' wing. *Cp.* Die-hards: Liberal: Unionist.

**Totem.** A North American Indian (Algonkin) word for some natural object, usually an animal, taken as the emblem of a person or clan on account of a supposed relationship. Totemism, which is common among primitive peoples, has a distinct value in preventing intermarriage among near relations, for if persons bearing the same totem (as, for instance, in the case of brothers and sisters) intermarry the punishment is death. Another custom is that one is not allowed to kill or eat the animal borne as one's totem.

> This very extraordinary institution, whatever its origin, cannot have arisen except among men capable of conceiving kinship and all human relationships as existing between themselves and all animate and inanimate things. It is the rule and not the exception that all savage societies are founded open this belief.
>
> Andrew Lang, *Myth, Ritual, and Religion*

***Totem pole.*** The post standing before a dwelling on which grotesque and, frequently, brilliantly coloured representations of the totem were carved or hung. It is often of great size, and sometimes so broad at the base that an archway is cut through it.

**Toto caelo** (Lat.) (separated) by the whole sky; hence, diametrically opposite. Entirely. The allusion is to augurs (*q.v.*) who divided the heavens into four parts.

> Even when they are relaxing those general requirements ... the education differs *toto caelo* from instruction induced by the tests of an examining body.
>
> *Nineteen Century*, Jan., 1893, p. 23

**Touch and go.** A very narrow escape; a metaphor derived, perhaps, from driving when the wheel of one vehicle touches that of another passing vehicle without doing mischief. It was a *touch*, but neither vehicle was stopped, each could *go* on.

**Touchstone.** A dark flinty schist, jasper, or basanite (the *Lapis Lydius* of the ancients), so called because gold is tried by it. A series of needles are formed (1) of pure gold; (2) of 23 gold and 1 copper; (3) of 22 gold and 2 copper, and so on. The assayer selects one of these and rubs it on the touchstone, when it leaves a mark that is reddish in proportion to the quantity of alloy; the article to be tested is then similarly 'touched' and the marks compared. Hence the word is often used of any criterion or standard.

Fable has it that Battus saw Mercury steal Apollo's oxen, and Mercury gave him a cow to secure his silence, but, being distrustful of the man, changed himself into a peasant, and offered him a cow and an ox if he would tell him where he got the cow. Battus, caught in the trap, told the secret, and Mercury changed him into a touchstone (Ovid, *Metamorphoses*, ii).

> Men have a touchstone whereby to try gold; but gold is the touchstone whereby to try men.
>
> Fuller, *Holy and Profane State* (*The Good Judge*)

***Touchstone.*** A clown whose mouth is filled with quips and cranks and witty repartees, in Shakespeare's *As You Like It*. The original actor of the part was Tarlton.

**Touchy.** Apt to take offence on slight provocation. *Ne touchez pas*, *Noli me tangere*, one not to be touched.

**Tour.** *The Grand Tour.* Through France, Switzerland, Italy, and home by Germany. Before railways were laid down, this tour was made by most of the young aristocrats as the finish of their education. Those who went merely to France or Germany were simply tourists.

**Tour de force** (Fr.). A feat of strength or skill.

**Tournament** (O.Fr. *torneiement*, from Lat. *tornare*, to turn). A tilt of knights; the chief art of the game being so to manoeuvre or *turn* your horse as to avoid the adversary's blow.

***The Tournament of Tottenham.*** A comic romance, given in Percy's *Reliques*. A number of clowns are introduced, practising warlike games, and making vows like knights of high degree. They ride tilt on cart-horses, fight with ploughshares and flails, and wear for armour wooden bowls and saucepan-lids. It may be termed the 'high life below stairs' of chivalry.

**Tournemine.** *That's Tournemine.* Your wish was father to the thought. Tournemine was a Jesuit of the 18th century, of a very sanguine and dreamy temperament.

**Tours.** Geoffrey of Monmouth says: 'In the party of Brutus was one Turones, his nephew, inferior to none in courage and strength, from whom Tours derived its name, being the place of his sepulture.' Of course, this fable is wholly worthless historically. Tours is the city of the Turones, a people of Gallia Lugdunensis.

**Tout ensemble** (Fr.). The whole massed together; the general effect.

**Tout le monde.** Everyone who is anyone.

**Tow.** *To take in tow.* Take under guidance. A man who takes a lad in tow acts as his guide and director. To tow a ship or barge is to guide and draw it along by tow-lines.

> Too proud for bards to take in tow my name.
>
> *Peter Pindar*, *Future Laureate*, Pt ii

**Tower Liberty.** The Tower of London, with the fortifications and Tower Hill. This formed part of the ancient demesne of the Crown, with jurisdiction and privileges distinct from and independent of the City. *Cp. Liberty of the Fleet, under* Liberty.

**Tower of London.** The architect was Gundulphus, Bishop of Rochester, who also built or restored Rochester keep, in the time of William I. Tradition has it that the White Tower, the central and oldest portion, is on the site of a fort erected by Julius Caesar to awe the ancient inhabitants; hence Gray's well known allusion in *The Bard* –

> Ye Towers of Julius, London's lasting shame,
> With many a foul and midnight murther fed.

In the Tower lie buried Anne Boleyn and her brother; the guilty Catherine Howard, and Lady Rochford her associate; the venerable Lady Salisbury, and Cromwell the minister of Henry VIII; the two Seymours, the admiral and protector of Edward VI; the Duke of Norfolk and Earl of Sussex (Queen Elizabeth's reign); the Duke of Monmouth, son of Charles II; the Earls of Balmerino and Kilmarnock, and Lord Lovat; Bishop Fisher and his illustrious friend More. The bones of the 'little Princes', Edward

V and his brother the Duke of York, murdered there by order of Richard III in 1483, were discovered in 1674 and removed to Westminster Abbey.

**Towers of Silence.** *See* Silence.

**Town.** A.S. *tūn*, a plot of ground fenced round or enclosed by a hedge (connected with Ger. *zaun*, a hedge); a single dwelling; a number of dwelling-houses forming a village or burgh.

***A man about town.*** *See* Man.

***A woman of the town.*** A prostitute.

***The little stranger has come to town.*** The expected child is born.

***Town and Gown.*** The two sections of a university town; composed of those who are not attached to the university and those who are; hence, *a town and gown row*, a collision, often leading to a fight, between the students and non-gownsmen. *Cp.* Philistines.

***Town bull.*** A bull kept by the parish, in country places, for breeding purposes.

> And so, brother *Toby*, this poor Bull of mine … might have been driven into Doctors' Commons and lost his character – which to a Town Bull, brother *Toby*, is the very same thing as his life.
>
> Sterne, *Tristram Shandy*, IX, xxiii

***Town crier.*** A municipal official who goes about the streets, usually in a robe, ringing a bell and crying, *Oyez! Oyez!* (*q.v.*) to attract attention to his proclamations of notices, coming events, lost property, etc.

***Town house.*** One's residence in town as apart from that in the country.

***Town is empty.*** The season (*q.v.*) is over; society, everybody who is anybody, has left town for the country.

***Town planning.*** The regulating of the ground plan or extension of a town with a view to securing the greatest advantages from the point of view of health, public amenities, convenience in transport, etc. The Town Planning Act was passed in 1909 –

> to amend the Law relating to the Housing of the Working Classes, to provide for the making of Town Planning schemes, etc.

***The Town Planning Review,*** a quarterly, was first published in 1910.

**Toyshop of Europe, The.** So Burke called Birmingham. Here the word 'toy' does not refer to playthings for children, but to trinkets, knick-knacks, and similar articles.

**Tractarians.** The authors of the *Tracts for the Times* (*see below*), which enunciated the principles of the Oxford Movement (*q.v.*), also called the *Tractarian Movement*; also their followers. Hence applied to High Churchmen generally.

**Tracts for the Times.** A series of papers on theological and liturgical subjects, published at Oxford (hence sometimes called *The Oxford Tracts*) between 1833 and 1841. They were started by the Rev. J. H. Newman (afterwards Cardinal Newman) with the object of arresting 'the advance of Liberalism in religious thought', and reviving 'the true conception of the relation of the Church of England to the Catholic Church at large'. The authors, who used the first seven letters as signatures to their contributions, were:

A. Rev. John Keble, M.A., author of the *Christian Year,* fellow of Oriel, and Professor of Poetry at Oxford.
B. Rev. Isaac Williams, Fellow of Trinity; author of *The Cathedral, and other Poems.*
C. Rev. E. B. Posey, D.D., Regius Professor of Hebrew, and Canon of Christ Church.
D. Rev. John Henry Newman, D.D., Fellow of Oriel.
E. Rev. Thomas Keble.
F. Sir John Provost, Bart.
G. Rev. R. F. Wilson, of Oriel.

The series came to an end (at the request of the Bishop of Oxford) with Newman's *Tract No. xc*, 'On Certain Passages in the XXXIX Articles'; and later many of the Tractarians entered the Roman Catholic Church.

**Tracy.** *All the Tracys have the wind in their faces.* Those who do wrong will always meet with punishment. William de Traci was the most active of the four knights who slew Thomas à Becket, and for this misdeed all who bore the name were saddled by the Church with this ban:

> Wherever by sea or land they go
> For ever the wind in their face shall blow.

Fuller, with his usual *naïveté*, says, 'So much the better in hot weather, as it will save the need of a fan.'

**Trade.** ***Free Trade.*** *See* Free.

***The balance of trade.*** *See* Balance.

***The Board of Trade.*** A Government department – officially a Committee of the Privy Council – dealing with commercial and industrial affairs, such as bankruptcy, company matters, railways, weights and measures, harbours, patents, trade and merchandise marks, etc. Originally established by Oliver Cromwell, as at present constituted it dates from 1786.

***The trade.*** Usually the liquor trade, more particularly those engaged in the brewing and distilling industries; but applied also to the general body of persons engaged in the particular trade that is being spoken of.

***To blow trade.*** *See* Trade winds, *below*.

***To trade something off.*** To barter or exchange it; to sell it as a 'job lot'; an American expression.

***To trade upon.*** To make use of so as to obtain some advantage. Thus, blind men, cripples, and war-broken soldiers, will sometimes 'trade upon' their afflictions to get sympathy from strangers and extract money from their pockets.

***Trade board.*** An official council set up to regulate the conditions of labour in certain trades that otherwise might be 'sweated'.

***Trade dollar.*** A United States silver dollar formerly coined specially for Oriental trade. It weighed 420 grs, instead of the 412.5 grs of the ordinary dollar, and has not been coined since 1887.

***Trade follows the flag.*** Wherever the flag flies trade with the mother country springs up and prospers.

***Trade union.*** An association of employees in a trade, industry, or even a profession, formed for the promotion and protection of their common interests in regard to conditions of labour, wages, etc., and often for providing its members with payments during temporary unemployment, sickness, or strikes, and pensions in old age.

The earliest forerunner of the modern trade union was probably the combination of London cordwainers against their overseers in 1387; but until the passing of the first Trade Union Act (1871), all trade unions were, in so far as their objects could be held to be 'in restraint of trade', illegal associations.

> As early as the time of Henry V it was decided that a contract imposing a general restraint upon trade was void, and agreements between workmen not to take work except upon certain terms are at common law bad, and consequently any association which exists to promote such agreements or to enforce such terms is illegal ... By the Trade Union Act, 1871, it was declared that a Trade Union merely because its objects were in restraint of trade should not be held to be unlawful, and its agreements were made binding, so that they would be recognised in law.
>
> *The Labour Year Book*, 1916 (p. 174)

The modern trade union, and the name, came into being about 1830.

***Trade winds.*** Winds that *blow trade*, i.e. regularly in one track or direction (Low Ger. *trade*, track). In the northern hemisphere they blow from the *north-east*, and in the southern hemisphere from the *south-east*, about thirty degrees each side of the equator. In some places they blow six months in one direction, and six in the opposite. The term is sometimes applied to the Indian monsoons.

**Tragedy.** Literally, a goat-song (Gr. *tragos*, goat, *ode*, song), though why so called is not clear. Horace (*Ars Poetica*, 220) says, because the winner at choral competitions received a goat as a prize, but the explanation has no authority.

It was Aristotle (in his *Poetics*) who said that tragedy should move one 'by pity and terror':

> The plot ought to be so constructed that, even without the aid of the eye, he who hears the tale told will thrill with horror and melt to pity at what takes place.
>
> Aristotle, *Poetics*, xix (Butcher)

***The Father of Tragedy.*** A title given to Aeschylus (d.456 BC), author of the Orestean trilogy and many other tragedies, and to Thespis. *See* Thespians.

**Traitors' Gate, The.** The gloomy water-passage leading from the Tower of London to the Thames, by which persons accused of treason entered their prison. An old proverb says –

> A loyal heart may be landed at the Traitors' Gate.

**Trajan. *Trajan's Arch.*** There are two arches known by this name, commemorating the triumphs of Trajan. One, the finest ancient arch in existence, was erected in AD 114 over the Appian Way at Benevento, and the other in 112 at Ancona. Both are of white marble.

***Trajan's Column.*** The great monument in Rome (dedicated AD 114) commemorating Trajan's victories. It is a Roman Doric column of marble, 127½ ft high, covered with reliefs representing over 2,000 persons, besides many animals. It formed the model for the column in the Place Vendôme, Paris, and is now surmounted by a statue of St Peter.

***Trajan's Wall.*** A line of fortifications stretching across the Dobrudscha from Czernavoda to the Black Sea.

**Tram.** The old 'popular' derivation of this word from the name of Benjamin Ou*tram*, who ran vehicles on stone rails at Little Eaton, Derbyshire, in 1800, is absurd. The word is connected with Low Ger. *traam*, a balk or beam, and was applied as early as the 16th century to trucks used, in coal-mines, and run on long wooden beams as rails.

> Trams are a kind of sledge on which coals are brought from the place where they are hewn to the shaft. A tram has four wheels, but a sledge is without wheels.
>
> Brand, *History of Newcastle-upon-Tyne*, vol. ii, p. 681 (1789)

**Tramecksan and Slamecksan.** The High Heels and Low Heels, the two great political factions of Lilliput, in Swift's *Gulliver's Travels*. The High Heels are the Tories, and the Low Heels the Radicals, and 'the animosity of these two factions runs so high that they will neither eat, nor drink, nor speak to each other'. The king was a Tramecksan, but the heir-apparent a Slamecksan.

**Tramontane.** The north wind; so called by Italians because to them it comes from over the mountains (Lat. *trans*, across, *montem*, mountain). The Italians also apply the term to peoples, etc., north of the Alps. French lawyers, on the other hand, apply the word to Italian canonists, whom they consider too Romanistic. We in England generally call overstrained Roman Catholic notions 'Ultramontane' (*q.v.*).

**Translator-General.** So Fuller, in his *Worthies* (1662), calls Philemon Holland (1552–1637), who translated works by Pliny, Livy, Plutarch, and a large number of other Greek and Latin classics.

**Trap.** Slang for a policeman.

**Traps.** Luggage, one's personal belongings, and so on (as in, *Leave your traps at the station*), are called *traps* as short for *trappings*, bits of additional finery and decoration, properly ornamental harness or caparison for a horse.

**Trappistines.** An order of nuns affiliated with the Trappists; founded in 1692 by Princess Louise of Condé at Clacet, France.

**Trappists.** A religious order, so called from La Trappe, an abbey founded at Soligny la Trappe (Orne, France) in 1140, by Rotron, Count de Perche. It is a branch of the Cistercian order, and is noted for the extreme austerity of its rules.

**Traskites.** A sect of Puritan Sabbatarians founded by John Trask, a Somerset man, about 1620, which believed that the law as laid down for the ancient Hebrews was to be taken literally and applied to themselves and all men. Trask was brought before the Star Chamber and pilloried. He is said to have recanted later and to have become an Antinomian, and his followers became absorbed by the Seventh-day Baptists (*q.v.*).

**Travellers' Tales.** Tall yarns; exaggerated stories of wonderful adventures and sights told to impress the home birds. Telling such tales used to be called *tipping one the traveller*.

**Tre, Pol, Pen.** Very common prefixes for personal and place names in Cornwall –

> By their Tre, their Pol, and Pen,
> Ye shall know the Cornish men.

The extreme east of Cornwall is noted for *Tre* (old Cornish, or Welsh, for house), the extreme west for *Pol* (= pool), the centre for *Pen* (= height, peak).

On December 19th, 1891, the following residents are mentioned by the *Launceston Weekly News* as attending the funeral of a gentleman who lived at Tre-hummer House, Tresmere – Residents from Trevell, Tresmarrow, Treglith, Trebarrow, Treludick, etc., with Treleaven the Mayor of Launceston.

**Treacle** properly means an antidote against the bite of wild beasts (Gr. *theriake*, from *ther* a wild beast). The ancients gave the name to several sorts of antidotes, but ultimately it was applied chiefly to Venice treacle (*theriaca androchi*), a compound of some sixty-four drugs in honey.

Sir Thomas More speaks of 'a most strong treacle (i.e. antidote) against these venomous heresies'; and in the *Treacle Bible*, *see* Bible, Specially named, *balm* (Jer. 8:22) is translated *treacle* – 'Is there no treacle at Gilead? Is there no phisitian there?'

**Treason.** Betrayal of a trust or of a person. *High treason* is an act of treachery against the Sovereign or the State, a violation of one's allegiance; *petty treason* is the same against a subject, as the murder of a master by his servant.

***Treason doth never prosper.*** *See* Tomorrow (*Tomorrow never comes*).

**Treasures.** *These are my treasures*; meaning the sick and poor. So said St Lawrence (*q.v.*) when the Roman praetor commanded him to deliver up his treasures.

One day a lady from Campania called upon Cornelia, the mother of the Gracchi, and after showing her jewels, requested in return to see those belonging to the famous mother-in-law of Africanus. Cornelia sent for her two sons, and said to the lady, 'These are my jewels, in which alone I delight.'

**Treat.** *To stand treat.* To pay the expenses of some entertainment; especially to pay for drinks consumed by others.

**Trefa Meat.** Meat prohibited to the Jews as food because it has not been slaughtered in the orthodox manner; the opposite of *Kosher* meat. So called from a Hebrew word signifying 'that which is torn'.

**Tregeagle.** A fabulous giant of Dosmary Pool, Bodmin Downs (Cornwall), whose allotted task is to bale out the water with a limpet-shell. When the wintry blast howls over the downs, the people say it is the giant roaring.

**Tremont.** Boston, Massachusetts, was so called, from the three hills (Lat. *tres montes*) on which the city stands.

**Trencher.** ***A good trencher-man.*** A good eater. The trencher is the platter on which food is cut (Fr. *trancher*, to cut), by a figure of speech applied to food itself.

***He that waits for another's trencher eats many a late dinner.*** He who is dependent on others must wait, and wait, and wait, happy if after waiting he gets anything at all.

> Oh, how wretched
> Is that poor man that hangs on princes' favours!
> There is, betwixt that smile he would aspire to,
> That sweet aspect of princes, and their ruin,
> More pangs and fears than wars or women have.
>
> Shakespeare, *Henry VIII*, 3, 2

***Trencher cap.*** The mortar-board (*q.v.*) worn at college; so called from the *trenchered* or split boards which form the top.

***Trencher friends.*** Persons who cultivate the friendship of others for the sake of sitting at their board, and the good things they can get.

***Trencher knight.*** A table knight, a suitor from cupboard love.

**Trenchmore.** A popular dance in the 16th and 17th centuries.

> Nimble-heeled mariners ... capering ... sometimes a Morisco, or Trenchmore of forty miles long.
>
> Taylor, *The Water-Poet*

**Tressure.** A border within an heraldic shield and surrounding the bearings. The origin of the 'double treasure flory-counterflory gules' in the royal arms of Scotland is traced by old heralds to the 9th century. They assert that Charlemagne granted it to King Achaius of Scotland in token of alliance, and as an assurance that 'the lilies of France should be a defence to the lion of Scotland'.

**Trèves.** *The Holy Coat of Trèves.* A relic preserved in the cathedral of Trèves. It is said to be the seamless coat of our Saviour, which the soldiers would not rend, and therefore cast lots for (John 19:23, 25), which, according to tradition, was found and preserved by the Empress Helena in the 4th century.

**Tria Juncta in Uno** (Lat. three things combined in one). The motto of the Order of the Bath. It refers to the three classes of which the order consists, viz. Knights Grand Cross, Knights Commanders, and Companions.

**Triads.** Three subjects more or less connected treated as a group; as *the Creation, Redemption, and Resurrection*; *Brahma, Vishnu, and Siva*; *Alexander the Great, Julius Caesar, and Napoleon*; *Law, Physic, and Divinity*.

The Welsh *Triads* are collections of historic facts, mythological traditions, moral maxims, or rules of poetry disposed in groups of three for mnemonic purposes.

**Trials at Bar.** *See* Bar.

**Triamond.** Son of the fairy Agape, and brother to Diamond and Priamond in Spenser's *Faërie Queene* (Bk iv). He is a champion of friendship, and wins the prize on the second day of the tournament after being overcome by Satyrane (IV, iv). He was the husband of Canace.

**Tribune.** A chief magistrate, and very powerful official, among the ancient Romans. During the revolt of the plebs in 494 BC they appointed two of their number as protectors against the patricians' oppression; later the number was increased to ten and their office constitutionalised. They were personally inviolable, and could separately veto measures and proceedings.

As a military title *tribune* denoted the commander of a cohort.

***A tribune of the people.*** A democratic leader.

***The Last of the Tribunes.*** Cola di Rienzi (1313–54), who in 1347 led the revolt of the Romans against their aristocratic oppressors and was crowned tribune in the Lateran Church (Apr. 15th, 1348).

**Trice.** *In a trice.* In an instant; in a twinkling.

> To tell you what conceyte
> I had then in a tryce,
> The matter were too nyse.
>
> Skelton, *Phyllyp Sparowe* (*c.*1505)

*Trice* is probably the same word as *trice*, to haul, to tie up; the idea being 'at a single tug'; but other suggestions are that ours represents the Spanish phrase *en un tris*, *tris* meaning the crash of breaking glass, or that as *second* is the sixtieth part of a minute so *trice* (*third*) is the sixtieth part of a second.

**Tricoteuses.** Parisian women who, during the French Revolution, used to attend the meetings of the Convention and, while they went on with their *tricotant* (knitting), encouraged the leaders in their bloodthirsty excesses. They gained for themselves the additional title, *Furies of the Guillotine*, and never in any age or any country did women so disgrace their sex.

**Trilogy.** A group of three tragedies. Everyone in Greece who took part in the poetic contest had to produce a trilogy and a satyric drama. There is only one complete specimen extant, viz. that embracing the *Agamemnon*, the *Choephorae*, and the *Eumenides*, by Aeschylus.

**Trimalchio.** The vulgar and ostentatious multimillionaire of Petronius Arbiter's *Satyricon* (1st cent. AD); the subject of allusion on account of the colossal and extravagant banquet that he gave.

**Trimmer.** One who runs with the hare and holds with the hounds. George Savile, Marquis of Halifax, adopted the term in the reign of Charles II to signify that he was neither an extreme Whig nor an extreme Tory. Dryden was called a *trimmer*, because he professed attachment to the king, but was the avowed enemy of the Duke of York.

**Trinity.** The three Persons in one God – God the Father, God the Son, and God the Holy Ghost.

> And in this Trinity none is afore or after other; none is greater, or less than another; but the whole three Persons are co-eternal together and co-equal. *The Athanasian Creed*

*Cp.* Persons (*Confounding the Persons*).

Tertullian (about 160–240) introduced the word into Christian theology. Almost every mythology has a threefold deity. *See* Three.

***Trinity Sunday.*** The Sunday next after Whit Sunday. It has been observed in honour of the Trinity from very early times, but was first enjoined as a festival by the Synod of Arles in 1260. The Epistle and Gospel used in the Church of England on this day are the same as those in the Lectionary of St Jerome, and the Collect comes from the Sacramentary of St Gregory.

***Trinity Term.*** The period of law sittings in England from the first Tuesday after Trinity Sunday to the end of July.

**Trinobantes.** Inhabitants of Middlesex and Essex, referred to in Caesar's *Gallic Wars*. This word, converted into *Trinovantes*, gave rise to the myth that the people referred to came from Troy. *See* Troynovant.

**Tripe.** Journalists' slang for very second-rate 'copy' whose only use is as 'fill-ups'. *Cp.* Bilge-water.

**Tripitaka** (Pali *tipitaka*, the three baskets). The three classes into which the sacred writings of the Buddhists are divided – viz. the *Sutrapitaka* (Basket of Aphorisms or Discourses) or *Sutras*, the *Vinayapitaka* (Basket of Disciplinary Directions), and *Abidhammapitaka* (Basket of Metaphysics).

**Triple Alliance.** A treaty entered into by England, Sweden, and Holland against Louis XIV in 1668. It ended in the treaty of Aix-la-Chapelle.

A treaty between England, France, and Holland against Spain in 1717. In the following year it was joined by Austria, and became a *Quadruple Alliance*.

And that of 1883, between Germany, Italy, and Austria, against France and Russia.

**Tripos** (Gr. *treis*, three, *pous*, foot). A Cambridge term, meaning the *three* honour classes in which the best men are grouped at the final examination, whether of Mathematics, Law, Theology, or Natural Science, etc. The word is often emphatically applied to the voluntary classical examination. So called because the champion in the old university disputations held during the admission of graduates to their degrees used to sit on a *three-legged* stool.

**Triptolemus.** A Greek hero and demi-god, worshipped chiefly at Eleusis as the giver to man of grain and the first instructor in agriculture.

**Trisagion** (Gr. thrice holy). A hymn in the liturgies of the Greek and Eastern Churches in which (after Is. 6:3) a threefold invocation to the Deity is the burden – 'Holy God, Holy and Mighty, Holy and Immortal, have mercy upon us.'

The name is sometimes applied to Bishop Heber's hymn for Trinity Sunday –

> Holy, Holy, Holy! Lord God Almighty!
> Early in the morning our song shall rise to Thee –

which is more properly called the *Ter-Sanctus*.

**Triskelion** (Gr. three-legged). The emblem of the Isle of Man, and of Sicily; three human legs, bent at the knee, and joined at the thigh.

**Trismegistus** (Gr. thrice great). A name given to Hermes (*q.v.*), the Egyptian philosopher, or Thoth, councillor of Osiris, to whom is attributed a host of inventions – amongst others the art of writing in hieroglyphics, the first code of Egyptian laws, harmony, astrology, the lute and lyre, magic, and all mysterious sciences.

**Triton.** Son of Neptune, represented as a fish with a human head. It is this sea god that makes the roaring of the ocean by blowing through his shell.

***A Triton among the minnows.*** The sun among inferior lights. *Luna inter minores ignes.*

**Triumph.** A word formed from Gr. *thriambos*, the Dionysiac hymn, *Triumphe* being an exclamation used in the solemn processions of the Arval Brothers.

> Some … have assigned the origin of … triumphal processions to the mythic pomps of Dionysus, after his conquests in the East, the very word *triumph* being … the Dionysiac hymn.
>
> Pater, *Marius the Epicurean*, ch. xii

The old Roman *triumphus* was the solemn and magnificent entrance of a general into Rome after having obtained a great or decisive victory. *Cp.* Ovation.

**Trivet. *Right as a trivet*.** *See* Right.

**Trivia.** Gay's name for his invented goddess of streets and ways. His burlesque in three books so entitled (1716) is a mine of information on the outdoor life of Queen Anne's time.

> Thou, Trivia, aid my song.
> Through spacious streets conduct thy bard along
> …
> To pave thy realm, and smooth the broken ways,
> Earth from her womb a flinty tribute pays.
>
> Gay, *Trivia*, Bk i

*Trivia* is also the plural of *trivium* (*q.v.*).

**Trivial.** Commonplace, trifling, of little importance. From Lat. *trivialis* (*cp.* Trivium), belonging to the streets or cross-roads.

**Trivium.** The three roads (Lat. *tres*, three, *via*, a road) to learning in the Middle Ages, i.e. Grammar, Rhetoric, and Logic; forming the lower division of the seven liberal arts (*see* Quadrivium).

**Trochilus.** A small Egyptian bird fabled by the ancients to enter with impunity the mouth of the crocodile and to pick its teeth, especially of a leech which greatly tormented the creature. Allusions to it are common in 16th and 17th century authors.

> Not half so bold
> The puny bird that dares, with teasing hum,
> Within the crocodile's stretched jaws to come.
>
> Thomas Moore, *Lalla Rookh*, Pt i

**Troglodytes.** A people of Ethiopia, south-east of Egypt, so called from Gr. *trogle*, cave, *duein*, to go into, because they lived in cave dwellings, remains of which are still to be seen along the banks of the Nile. Hence applied to other cave-dwellers, and, figuratively to those who live in seclusion. There were troglodytes of Syria and Arabia also, according to Strabo, and Pliny (v, 8) asserts that they fed on serpents.

**Troilus.** The prince of chivalry, one of the sons of Priam, killed by Achilles in the siege of Troy (Homer's *Iliad*).

The loves of Troilus and Cressida, celebrated by Shakespeare and Chaucer, form no part of the old classic tale. It appears for the first time in the *Roman de Troie* by the 12 th century *trouvère* Benoît de Ste More. Guido delle Colonne included it in his *Historia Trojana* (about 1290), it thence passed to Boccaccio, whose *Il Filostrato* (1344) – where Pandarus first appears – was the basis of Chaucer's *Troilus and Criseyde*.

***As true as Troilus.*** Troilus is meant by Shakespeare to be the type of constancy, and Cressida the type of female inconstancy.

> After all comparisons of truth . . .
> 'As true as Troilus' shall crown up the verse,
> And sanctify the numbers.
>
> *Troilus and Cressida*, 3, 2

**Trojan. *He is a regular Trojan*.** A fine fellow, with good courage and plenty of spirit; what the French call a *brave homme*. The Trojans in Homer's *Iliad* and Virgil's *Aeneid* are described as truthful, brave, patriotic, and confiding.

> There they say right, and like true Trojans.
>
> Butler, *Hudibras*, i, 1

> In vain for a man you might seek
> Who could drink more like a Trojan,
> Or talk more like a Greek. Southey (on Porson)

**Trojan War.** The legendary war sung by Homer in the *Iliad* (*q.v.*) as having been waged for ten years by the confederated Greeks against the men of Troy and their allies, in consequence of Paris, son of Priam, the Trojan king, having carried off Helen, wife of Menelaus, king of Lacedemon (or of Sparta). The last year of the siege is the subject of the *Iliad*; the burning of Troy and the flight of Aeneas is told by Virgil in his *Aeneid*.

There is no doubt whatever that the story of the siege of Troy has some historical basis, but when it took place is purely a matter of conjecture. Many dates, ranging from the 11th to the 14th centuries BC have been assigned to it.

**Trolls.** Dwarfs of *Northern mythology*, living in hills, underground in caverns or beneath; they are represented as stumpy, misshapen, and humpbacked, inclined to thieving, and fond of carrying off children and substituting their own. These hill people, as they are called, are especially averse to noise, from a recollection of the time when Thor used to be for ever flinging his hammer after them.

> Out then spake the tiny Troll,
> No bigger than an emmet he.
>
> Danish ballad, *Etine of Villenskov*

**Troll-madam,** or **Troll-my-dames.** A popular indoor game in the 16th and 17th centuries (also known as *trunks*, *pigeon-holes*, or *nine-holes*), borrowed from the French and called by them *trou* (hole) *madame*. It resembled bagatelle, and was played on a board having at one end a number of arches, like pigeon-holes, into which balls were rolled. Shakespeare has a reference to it in *A Winter's Tale* (4, 2).

**Trooping.** ***The trooping season.*** The season when the annual reliefs of the British forces in India are made, usually commencing in late February or March.

***Trooping the colour.*** A military ceremonial parade in which the regimental flag, the *colour*, is carried between files of troops and received by the king or his representative.

The ceremony dates from the 18th century (probably from Marlborough's time), and was originally a guard-mounting ceremony, the battalion finding the guards for the day 'trooping' the colour to be carried on king's guard.

> Many years ago it became the custom to find the public guards on the King's birthday from the flank companies (picked companies) of the whole Brigade, instead of from one battalion, and it is from this custom that the ceremony of Trooping the Colour on his Majesty's birthday by detachments of the flank companies of all the battalions in London originates. The Field-Officer-in-Brigade-Waiting always commands the troops on this parade, irrespective of the regiment to which he belongs.
>
> *The Times*, 3 June, 1922

**Trophonius.** An architect, celebrated in Greek legend as the builder of the temple of Apollo at Delphi. After his death he was deified, and had an oracle in a cave near Lebadeia, Boeotia, which was so awe-inspiring that those who entered and consulted the oracle never smiled again. Hence a melancholy or habitually terrified man was said to have *visited the cave of Trophonius*.

> There is great danger that they who enter smiling into this Trophonian cave, will come out of it sad and serious conspirators.
>
> Burke, *Letters on a Regicide Peace*, i

**Troubadours.** Minstrels of the south of France in the 11th, 12th, and 13th centuries; so called from the Provençal verb *trobar*, to find or invent (*cp.* 'poet', which means 'a maker'). They wrote in the langue d'oc, principally on love and chivalry. *Cp.* Trouvères.

**Trouillogan's Advice.** None at all; 'yes and no'. When Pantagruel (Rabelais III, xxxv) asked the philosopher Trouillogan whether Panurge should marry or not, the reply was 'Yes'. 'What say you?' asked the prince. 'What you have heard,' answered Trouillogan. 'What have I heard,' said Pantagruel. 'What I have spoken,' rejoined the sage. 'Good,' said the prince; 'but tell me plainly, shall Panurge marry or let it alone?' 'Neither,' answered the oracle. 'How?' said the prince; 'that cannot be.' 'Then both,' said Trouillogan.

**Trouvères.** The troubadours of the *north* of France, in the 12th, 13th, and 14th centuries. So called from Fr. *trouver*, to find or invent (*cp.* Troubadours). Their work was chiefly narrative poems.

**Trows,** or **Drows.** Dwarfs of Orkney and Shetland mythology, similar to the Scandinavian Trolls. There are land-trows and sea-trows. 'Trow tak' thee' is a phrase still used by the island women when angry with their children.

> I hung about thy neck that gifted chain, which all in our isles know was wrought by no earthly artist, but by the Drows in the secret recesses of their caverns. Scott, *Pirate*, ch. x

**Troxartas** (Gr. bread-eater). King of the mice in *The Battle of the Frogs and Mice*, and father of Psycarpax, who was drowned.

> Fix their council . . .
> Where great Troxartas crowned in glory reigns . . .
> Psycarpax' father, father now no more!
>
> Parnell, *Battle of the Frogs and Mice*, Bk i

**Troy.** ***The Siege of Troy.*** *See* Iliad; Helen; Trojan War; etc.

***Troy Town.*** A Cornish expression for a labyrinth of streets, a regular maze. *Troy* was formerly used figuratively of any scene of disorder or confusion; a room with its furniture all higgledy-piggledy, for instance, would be called a *Troy fair*.

***Troy weight.*** The system of weights used in weighing precious metals and gems, the pound of 12 ounces weighing 5760 grains as compared with the pound avoirdupois which weighs 7000 grains and is divided into 16 ounces (*cp.* Avoirdupois). Why so called is not certainly known, but probably it was the system used at the great fairs at Troyes, in France. 1 lb troy = .822861 lb av., rather over four-fifths.

**Troynovant.** The name given by the early chroniclers to London, anciently the city of the Trinobantes (*q.v.*); a corruption of *Trinovant*. As *Troynovant* was assumed to mean *The New Troy*, the name gave rise to the tradition that Brute, a Trojan refugee (from whom they derived the name *Britain*), came to England and founded London.

> For noble Britons sprong from Trojans bold,
> And Troy-novant was built of old Troyes ashes cold.
> Spenser, *Faërie Queene*, iii, 9

**Truce of God.** In 1041 the Church attempted to limit private war, and decreed that there should be no hostilities between Lent and Advent or from the Thursday to the next Monday at the time of great festivals. This *Truce of God* was confirmed by the Lateran Council in 1179, and was agreed to by England, France, Italy, and other countries; but little attention was ever paid to it.

**Truck System, The.** The paying of employees otherwise than in current coin, or making it a condition that they shall buy food or other articles from some particular shop. In England this was made illegal by Acts passed in 1831, 1887, and 1896.

**True.** ***A true bill.*** *See* Bill.

***True blue.*** *See* Blue.

***True-lovers' knot.*** A complicated double knot with two interlacing bows on each side and two ends, used as a symbol of love.

> Three times a true-love's knot I tie secure;
> Firm be the knot, firm may his love endure.
> *Gay's Pastorals, The Spell*

***True Thomas.*** Thomas the Rhymer. *See* Rhymer.

**Truepenny.** Hamlet says to the Ghost, 'Art thou there, Truepenny?' Then to his comrades, 'You hear this fellow in the cellarage' (1, 5). And again, 'Well said, old mole; canst work?' The reference is, of course, to the sterling worth of his father – he was as honest and *true* as a genuine coin.

**Trump.** This word in such phrases as *a trumped up affair, trumpery,* etc., is the same word as *trumpet*; from Fr. *trompe*, a trumpet, whence *tromper* which, originally meaning 'to play on a trumpet', came to mean to beguile, deceive, impose upon.

*Trump* in cards, is from Fr. *triomphe* (triumph), the name of an old variant of écarté.

***The last trump.*** The final end of all things earthly; the Day of Judgment.

> We shall not all sleep, but we shall all be changed, in a moment, in the twinkling of an eye, at the last trump.
> 1 Cor. 15:51, 52

***To play one's last trump.*** To be reduced to one's last expedient; a phrase from card-playing.

**Trumpet.** *See* Trump *above*.

***The Feast of Trumpets.*** A Jewish festival, held on the first two days of Tisri (about mid Sept. to mid Oct.), the beginning of the ecclesiastical year, at which the blowing of trumpets formed a prominent part of the ritual. *See* Numb. 29:1.

***To blow one's own trumpet.*** To publish one's own praises, good deeds, etc. The allusion is to heralds, who used to announce with a flourish of trumpets the knights who entered a list. Similarly, *your trumpeter is dead* means that you are obliged to sound your own praises because no one will do it for you.

**Trust.** A combination of a number of companies or businesses doing similar trade to each other for the purpose of defeating competition or creating a monopoly, under one general control. So called because each member is on trust not to undersell the others, but to remain faithful to the terms agreed on.

**Truth.** Pilate said, '*What is truth*?' (John 18:38). This was the great question of the Platonists. Plato said we could know truth if we could sublimate our minds to their original purity. Arcesilaus said that man's understanding is not capable of knowing what truth is. Carneades maintained that not only our understanding could not comprehend it, but even our senses are wholly inadequate to help us in the investigation. Gorgias the Sophist said, 'What is right but what we prove to be right? and what is truth but what we believe to be truth?'

> Pilate asked, *Quid est veritas?* And then some other matter took him in the head, and so up he rose and went his way before he had his answer. He deserved never to find what truth was.
> Bp Andrewes, *Sermon on the Resurrection* (1613)

***Truth lies at the bottom of a well.*** This expression has been attributed to Heraclitus, Cleanthes, Democritus the Derider, and others.

> Naturam accusa, quae in profundo veritatem (ut ait Democritus) penitus abstruserit.
> Cicero, *Academies*, i, 10

> Let us seek the solution of these doubts at the bottom of the inexhaustible well, where Heraclitus says the truth is hidden.
> Rabelais, *Pantagruel*, xviii

**Tryanon.** Daughter of the fairy king who lived on the island of Oléron. 'She was as white as lily in May', and married Sir Launfal, King Arthur's steward, whom she carried off to 'Oliroun her jolif isle', and, as the romance says –

> Since saw him in this land no man,
> Ne no more of him tell I n'can
> For soothë without lie.
> Thomas Chester, *Sir Launfal* (15th cent.)

**Trygon.** The sting-ray, a fish with a sharp spine in its tail. It is said that Telegonus, son of Ulysses by Circe, coming to Ithaca to see his father was denied admission by the servants; whereupon a quarrel ensued, and his father, coming out to see what was the matter, was accidentally struck with his son's arrow, pointed with a trygon's spine, and died.

> The Lord of Ithaca,
> Struck by the poisonous trygon's bone, expired.
> West, *Triumphs of the Gout* (*Lucian*)

**Tsung-li Yamen.** The former department for foreign affairs in China, through which, from its establishment in 1861 until 1901, foreign ministers addressed their communications to the Emperor and the Government.

**Tu autem** (Lat. But thou). A hint to leave off; 'hurry up and come to the last clause'. In the long Latin grace at St John's College, Cambridge, the last clause used to be *Tu autem miserere mei, Domine. Amen*, and it was not unusual, when a scholar read slowly, for the senior Fellow to whisper *Tu autem* – i.e. Skip all the rest and give us only the last sentence.

**Tu quoque** (Lat. You too). A retort implying that the one addressed is in the same boat as the speaker – that his case is no better and no worse.

***The tu quoque style of argument.*** Personal invective; the argument of personal application; *argumentum ad hominem*.

**Tuatha De Danann.** A legendary race of superhuman heroes which invaded Ireland, overthrew the Firbolgs and Fomors, and were themselves overthrown by the Milesians, who later worshipped them as gods.

**Tub.** ***Tubs***, in rowing slang, are gig pairs of college boat clubs, who practise for the term's races. They are pulled on one side when a pair-oar boat in uniform makes its appearance. *Tubbing* is taking out pairs under the supervision of a coach to train men for taking part in the races.

***A tale of a tub.*** A cock-and-bull story; a rigmarole; nonsensical romance.

There is a comedy of this name by Ben Jonson (produced 1633), and a prose satire by Swift (1704) which portrays allegorically the failings of the English, Roman, and Presbyterian Churches.

***A tub of naked children.*** Emblematical in religious paintings of St Nicholas (*q.v.*), in allusion to the two boys murdered and placed in a pickling tub by a landlord, but raised to life again by this saint.

***To throw a tub to the whale.*** To create a diversion in order to avoid a real danger; to bamboozle or mislead an enemy. In whaling, according to Swift, when a ship was threatened by a school of whales, it was usual to throw a tub into the sea to divert their attention.

***Tub-thumper.*** A blustering, ranting public speaker; a 'stump-orator'. In allusion to the tub frequently used as a rostrum at open-air meetings.

**Tuba** (Arab. beatitude). A mythical tree of the Mohammedan Paradise, of gigantic proportions, whose branches stretch out to those who wish to gather their produce – luscious fruits, the flesh of birds already cooked, green garments, and even horses ready saddled and bridled. From its root spring the rivers of Paradise, flowing with milk and honey, wine and water, and on whose banks may be gathered inestimable gems.

**Tuck.** Schoolboy slang for extra food (that which can be *tucked* away inside), especially cakes, tarts, sweets, and so on. Hence *tuck-shop*, a shop where these can be procured.

***A good tuck in.*** A good feed – especially of the above.

***To tuck one up.*** To finish him, do for him. The allusion is probably to tucking children up in bed for the night – they are finished with till next morning; but there may be some reference to the long narrow duellist's rapier formerly called a *tuck* (Fr. *étoc*, stock).

**Tuck, Friar.** *See* Friar Tuck.

**Tucker.** The ornamental frill of lace or muslin worn by women in the 17th and 18th centuries round the top of their dresses to cover the neck and shoulders. Hence, *with clean bib and tucker*, nicely dressed, looking fresh and spruce.

Also slang for food (*cp.* Tuck):

> 'No,' said Palliser, 'we've no food.' 'By Jove!' said the other, 'I'll search creation for tucker tonight. Give me your gun.'
> Watson, *The Web of the Spider*, ch. xii

**Tuffet.** A dialect variant of *tuft*, which was formerly used of a small grassy mound or hillock.

Little Miss Muffet
Sat on a tuffet
Eating her curds and whey *Nursery Rhyme*

**Tuft.** A nobleman or fellow commoner at Oxford. So called because he wears a gold tuft or tassel on his college cap.

**Tuft-hunter.** A nobleman's toady (*see above*); one who tries to curry favour with the wealthy and great for the sake of feeding on the crumbs which fall from the rich man's table.

**Tug.** A name by which Collegers are known at Eton; from the *tog* (i.e. *toga*) worn by them to distinguish them from the rest of the school.

***Tug of war.*** A rural sport in which a number of men, divided into two bands, lay hold of a strong rope and pull against each other till one side has tugged the other over the dividing line.

***When Greek meets Greek then is the tug of war.*** *See* Greek.

**Tulchan Bishops.** Certain Scotch bishops appointed by the Regent, Morton, in 1572, with the distinct understanding that they were to hand over a fixed portion of the revenue to the patron. A *tulchan* is a stuffed calf-skin, placed under a cow that withholds her milk. The cow, thinking the 'tulcan' to be her calf, readily yields her milk to the milk-pail; the bishop was to have the empty title, and the Regent was to get the 'milk'.

**Tulip Mania.** A reckless mania for the purchase of tulip-bulbs that arose in Holland in the 17th century and was at its greatest height about 1634–37. A root of the species called *Viceroy* sold for £250; *Semper Augustus*, more than double that sum. The mania spread all over Europe, and became a mere stock-jobbing speculation.

**Tumbledown Dick.** Anything that will not stand firmly. 'Dick' is Richard Cromwell (1626–1712), the Protector's son, who was but a tottering wall at best.

**Tune. *The tune the old cow died of.*** Advice instead of relief; remonstrance instead of help. As St James says (2:15, 16), 'If a brother or sister be naked, and destitute of daily food, and one of you say to them, Depart in peace, be ye warmed and filled; notwithstanding ye give them not those things which are needful to the body; what doth it profit?' Your words are the tune the old cow died of. The reference is to the well-known song –

There was an old man, and he had an old cow,
But he had no fodder to give her,
So he took up his fiddle and played her the tune:
'Consider, good cow, consider,
This isn't the time for the grass to grow,
Consider, good cow, consider.'

***To change one's tune,*** or ***sing another tune.*** *See* Sing.

***To the tune of.*** To the amount of; as, 'I had to pay to the tune of £500.'

**Tuneful Nine, The.** The nine Muses (*q.v.*).

When thy young Muse invok'd the tuneful Nine,
To say how Louis did not pass the Rhine,
What Work had We with Wageninghen, Arnheim,
Places that could not be reduced to Rhime?
Prior, *Letter to Boileau Despreaux* (1704)

**Tunkers** or **Dunkers** (Ger. Dippers). A religious sect akin to the Baptists, founded in Germany in 1708 by Alexander Mack. In 1719 a party of them emigrated to Pennsylvania, and the sect has spread considerably in the Western States. They follow Bible teaching as closely as possible and adhere to the simplicity of the primitive Church.

**Turcaret.** One who has become rich by hook or by crook, and, having nothing else to show, makes a great display of his wealth. From the hero of Le Sage's comedy of the same name (1709).

**Turf, The.** The racecourse; the profession of horse-racing, which is done on turf or grass. A *turfite* is one who lives by the turf, either by running horses or betting.

All men are equal on the turf and under it.
Lord George Bentinck

**Turk.** Applied to barbarous, savage, cruel men, because these qualities have been for centuries attributed to Turks; also to mischievous and unruly children, as *You little Turk!*

***The Young Turks.*** The reforming party in the Ottoman Empire who, in the early part of the present century, tried to introduce the methods of modern Europe into the government.

***Turk Gregory.*** Falstaff's *ne plus ultra* of military valour – a humorous combination of the Sultan with Gregory VII (Hildebrand), probably the strongest of all the Popes.

Turk Gregory never did such deeds in arms as I have done this day. *1 Henry IV*, 5, 3

**Turkey: Turkey Rhubarb.** *See* Misnomers.

**Turn. *Done to a turn.*** Cooked exactly right; another turn on the gridiron would be one too much.

***He felt that the hour for the up-turning of his glass was at hand.*** He knew that the sand of life was nearly run out, and that death was about to turn his hourglass upside down.

***One good turn deserves another.*** A benefit received ought to be repaid.

***To serve its turn.*** To be appropriate – the right thing in the right place; often said of something that only barely meets its requirements.

***To turn down.*** To reject; a candidate at an examination, election, etc., who does not meet with success is said to be *turned down.*

In Eastern countries a glass is turned down at convivial gatherings as a memento of a recently departed companion:

And when like her, oh Sáki, you shall pass
Among the Guests Star-scatter'd on the Grass,
And in your joyous errand reach the spot
Where I made One – turn down an empty Glass!
Fitzgerald, *Rubáiyát of Omar Khayyám*, ci

***To turn the tables.*** *See* Table.

***To turn turtle.*** To turn completely over, upside down, topsy-turvy. Usually said of boats.

***Waiting for something to turn up.*** Expectant that the luck will change, that good fortune will arrive without much effort on one's own part. The principal characteristic of Mr Micawber in Dickens's *David Copperfield.* In Disraeli's *Popanilla* the national motto of Vraibleusia is *Something Will Turn Up.*

**Turncoat.** A renegade; one who deserts his principles or party.

Fable has it that a certain Duke of Saxony, whose dominions were bounded in part by France, hit upon the device of a coat *blue* one side, and *white* the other. When he wished to be thought in the French interest he wore the white outside; otherwise the blue. Whence a Saxon was nicknamed *Emmanuel Turncoat.*

**Turnip.** Common slang for a large, old-fashioned silver watch.

**Turnspit.** One who has all the work but none of the profit; he turns the spit but eats not of the roast. The allusion is to the *turnspit*, a small dog which was used to turn the roasting-spit by means of a kind of tread-wheel. Topsell says, 'They go into a wheel, which they turn round about with the weight of their bodies, so diligently ... that no drudge ... can do the feate more cunningly' (1607).

**Turpin.** A contemporary of Charlemagne, Archbishop of Rheims from 753 to 794, on whom has been fathered a French chronicle history, written in Latin in the first half of the 11th century. It purports to have been written at Vienne, in Dauphiny, whence it is addressed to Leoprandus, Dean of Aquisgranensis (Aix-la-Chapelle). The probable author was a canon of Barcelona.

It relates the expedition of Charlemagne to Spain in 777, and his return to France after subduing Navarre and Aragon. The chronicle says he invested Pampeluna for three months without being able to take it; he then tried what prayer could do, and the walls fell down of their own accord, like those of Jericho. Those Saracens who consented to become Christians were spared; the rest were put to the sword. Charlemagne then visited the sarcophagus of James, and Turpin baptised most of the neighbourhood. The king crossed the Pyrenees, but the rear commanded by Roland was attacked by 50,000 Saracens, and none escaped.

**Tut.** A word used in Lincolnshire for a phantom, as the *Spittal Hili Tut. Tom Tut will get you* is a threat to frighten children. *Tut-gotten* is panic-struck.

**Tutenag.** *See* Tooth (*Tooth and egg*).

**Tutivillus.** The demon of mediaeval legend who collects all the words skipped over or mutilated by priests in the performance of the services. These literary scraps or shreds he deposits in that pit which is said to be paved with 'good intentions' never brought to effect.

**Tweed.** The origin of this name of a woollen cloth used for garments is to be found in a blunder. It should have been *tweal*, the Scots form of *twill*; but when the Scotch manufacturer sent a consignment to James Locke, of London, in 1829, the name was badly written and misread; and as the cloth was made on the banks of the Tweed, *tweed* was accordingly adopted. *Twill*, like *dimity* (*q.v.*), means 'two-threaded'.

**Tweedledum and Tweedledee.** Names invented by John Byrom (d.1763) to satirise two quarrelling schools of musicians between whom the real difference was negligible. Hence used of people whose persons – or opinions – are 'as like as two peas'.

Some say compared to Bononcini
That mynheer Handel's but a ninny;
Others aver that he to Handel
Is scarcely fit to hold a candle.
Strange all this difference should be
'Twixt Tweedledum and Tweedledee.
J. Byrom

The Duke of Marlborough and most of the nobility took the side of G. B. Bononcini (d. about 1752), but the Prince of Wales,with Pope and Arbuthnot, was for Handel. *Cp.* Gluckists.

**Twelfth, The.** The 12th of August, 'St Grouse's Day'; the first day of grouse-shooting.

**Twelfth Night.** January 5th, the eve of Twelfth Day, or the Feast of the Epiphany, twelve days after Christmas, Jan. 6th. Formerly this was a time of great merrymaking, and the games that took place were, with little doubt, a survival of the old Roman *Saturnalia*, which was held at the same season.

Shakespeare's play of this name (produced in 1602) was so called because it was written for acting at the Twelfth Night festivities; the groundwork of the plot was ultimately drawn – through various sources – from the Italian of Bandello.

**Twelve. *Each English archer carries twelve Scotsmen under his girdle.*** This was a common saying at one time, because the English were unerring archers, and each carried twelve arrows in his belt.

***The Twelve.*** All the prelates of the Roman Catholic Church. Of course the allusion is to the Twelve Apostles.

> The Pope identifies himself with the 'Master', and addresses those 700 prelates as the 'Twelve'. *The Times*, December 11, 1869

***The twelve tables.*** The earliest code of Roman law, compiled by the Decemviri, and engraved on twelve bronze tablets (Livy, iii, 57; Diodorus, xii, 56).

**Twickenham. *The Bard of Twickenham.*** Alexander Pope (1688–1744), who lived there for thirty years.

**Twig.** *I twig you; do you twig my meaning?* I catch your meaning; I understand. (Irish *tuigim*, I understand.)

**Twinkling. *In a twinkling.*** In a second, in an instant of time; as *In the twinkling of an eye* (*see* 1 Cor. 15:52), *the twinkling of a bedpost* (*see* Bedpost).

**Twins, The.** A constellation and sign of the zodiac (May 21st to June 21st); representing Castor and Pollux (*q.v.*), the 'great twin brethren' of *classical mythology*.

> When now no more the alternate twins are fired,
> Short is the doubtful empire of the night.
> Thomson, *Summer*

**Twist. *Like Oliver Twist, asking for more.*** Oliver Twist, the workhouse-boy hero of Dickens's novel of that name (1838), greatly astonished the workhouse-master and caused general consternation by once actually asking for more gruel. The saying is sometimes used of a child who unexpectedly – or too frequently – asks for second helpings.

***To twist it on one.*** Slang for to swindle one or to bamboozle him to one's own advantage. Also (with allusion to giving the screw another twist), to extract from a person all one can – and a bit over.

**Twitcher, Jemmy.** A cunning, treacherous highwayman in Gay's *Beggar's Opera*. The name was given about 1765, in a poem by Gray, to John, Lord Sandwich (1718–92), noted for his *liaison* with Miss Ray, who was shot by the Rev. 'Captain' Hackman out of jealousy.

> See Jemmy Twitcher shambles – stop, stop thief!

**Two.** The evil principle of Pythagoras. Accordingly the second day of the second month of the year was sacred to Pluto, and was esteemed unlucky.

***The two eyes of Greece.*** Athens and Sparta.

***To have two strings to one's bow.*** *See* Bow.

***Two heads are better than one.*** Outside advice is often very useful. To the saying are sometimes added the words – *or why do folks marry?*

***Two is company, three is none.*** An old saying, much used by lovers; it is given in Heywood's collection of proverbs (1546).

***Two may keep counsel – if one of them's dead.*** A caustic saying expressive of the great difficulty of being *certain* that a secret is not told once it is imparted to someone else. Shakespeare has –

> Two may keep counsel when the third's away.
> *Titus Andronicus*, 4, 2

And in *The Testament of Love*, formerly attributed to Chaucer, is –

> For thre may kepe a counsel, if twain be awaie.

***Two of a trade did never agree.*** A very old proverb (it occurs in Hesiod's *Works and Days*), but one that is by no means of universal application.

> In every age and clime we see
> Two of a trade can ne'er agree.
> Gay, *Fables*, I, xxi

***Two wrongs cannot make a right.*** It's no use robbing Peter to pay Paul; figs will not come from thistles, nor good from evil.

***When two Fridays come together.*** One of a large number of circumlocutions for *Never!*

**Two Gentlemen of Verona, The.** Shakespeare's comedy (written certainly before 1598, but not printed till the Folio of 1623) is principally indebted for the story to the pastoral romance of

*Diana*, by George of Montemayor, a Spaniard, a translation of which by Bartholomew Yonge was in existence in 1582, but not printed till 1598. Other Italian stories, and perhaps Sidney's *Arcadia*, were drawn upon, and the love adventure of Julia resembles that of Viola in *Twelfth Night*.

**Twopenny.** Often used slightingly of things of very little value.

***Tuck in your twopenny!*** The schoolboy's warning to the boy over whose back the leap is to be made in leap-frog to keep his head down.

***Twopenny damn.*** *See* Damn.

***The Twopenny Tube.*** The Central London (Electric) Railway was so called, because for some years after its opening (1900) the fare for any distance was 2*d*.

**Tybalt.** Formerly a name commonly given to cats (*cp*. Tibert, in *Reynard the Fox*); hence the allusions to cats in connection with Tybalt, one of the Capulet family in Shakespeare's *Romeo and Juliet*. Mercutio says, 'Tybalt, you rat-catcher, will you walk?' (3, 1); and again, when Tybalt asks, 'What wouldst thou have with me?' Mercutio answers, 'Good king of cats! nothing but one of your nine lives' (3, 1).

**Tyburn.** A former tributary of the Thames rising at Hampstead (so called because composed of *two burns*, or rivulets), which gave its name to the district where now stands the Marble Arch, and where public executions formerly took place. Hence *Tyburn tree*, the gallows, *to take a ride to Tyburn*, to go to one's hanging, *Lord of the Manor of Tyburn*, the common hangman, etc.

The last criminal was hanged here in 1783, after which date the executions were carried out at Newgate.

**Tyburn Ticket.** A certificate which, under a statute of William III, was granted to prosecutors who had secured a capital conviction against a criminal exempting them from all parish and ward offices within the parish in which the felony had been committed. This, with the privilege it conferred, might be sold once, and once only, and the *Stamford Mercury* for March 27th, 1818, announced the sale of one for £280. The Act was repealed by 58 Geo. III, c. 70.

**Tyburnia.** The Portman and Grosvenor Squares district of London, described by Thackeray as 'the elegant, the prosperous, the polite Tyburnia, the most respectable district of the habitable globe'.

> On the Sunday evening the Temple is commonly calm. The chambers are for the most part vacant; the great lawyers are giving grand dinner parties at their houses in the Belgravian or Tyburnian districts.
>
> Thackeray, *Pendennis*, ch. xlix

**Tyke.** *See* Tike.

**Tyler's Insurrection.** An armed rebellion of peasants in southern England in 1381, led by Wat Tyler (an Essex man), in consequence of discontent aroused by the Statute of Labourers, and the heavy taxation, especially a poll-tax of three groats to defray the expenses of a war with France. Wat Tyler was slain by the Lord Mayor at Smithfield, the revolt was crushed, and many of the rebels executed.

**Tylwyth Teg** (Welsh, the Fair family). A sort of kobold family of Welsh folklore, but not of diminutive size. They lived in a lake near Brecknock.

**Tyndale's Bible.** *See* Bible, the English.

**Type.** Pica (*large type*), *litera picata*, the great black letter at the beginning of some new order in the liturgy.

Brevier (*small type*), used in printing the breviary.

Primer, now called 'long primer' (*small type*), used in printing small prayer-books called *primers*.

***A fount of type.*** *See* Letter.

In an ordinary fount the proportion of the various letters is usually as follows:

| | | | | | | | |
|---|---|---|---|---|---|---|---|
| a | 8,500 | i | 8,000 | q | 500 | y | 2,000 |
| b | 1,600 | j | 400 | r | 6,200 | z | 200 |
| c | 3,000 | k | 800 | s | 8,000 | , | 4,500 |
| d | 4,400 | l | 4,000 | t | 9,000 | . | 2,000 |
| e | 12,000 | m | 3,000 | u | 3,400 | ; | 800 |
| f | 2,500 | n | 8,000 | v | 1,200 | : | 600 |
| g | 1,700 | o | 8,000 | w | 2,000 | | |
| h | 6,400 | p | 1,700 | x | 400 | | |

**Typhoeus.** A giant of *Greek mythology*, with a hundred heads, fearful eyes, and a most terrible voice. He was the father of the Harpies. Zeus killed him with a thunderbolt, and he lies buried under Mount Etna.

**Typhon.** Son of Typhoeus. He was so tall that he touched the skies with his head. His offspring were Gorgon, Geryon, Cerberus, and the hydra of Lerne. Like his father, he lies buried under Etna. *See also* Set.

**Typographical Signs.** ´ An acute accent. In Greek it indicates a rise in the voice; in French vowel quality; in Spanish stress; in Bohemian and Hungarian a long vowel.

` A grave accent. In Greek indicating a fall of the voice; in French vowel quality, or sometimes a differentiation (as in *la*, *là*); and in English that the accented syllable is to be pronounced (as in *blessèd*),

^ A circumflex; in French usually indicating that an *s* has been dropped (as *être* for older *estre*), and that the marked vowel is long.

¸ under the letter *c* in French, is called a *cedilla*, and indicates that the *c* (ç) is to be pronounced as *s*. It represents the Greek *zeta* (*z*), which formerly followed the *c* to indicate an *s* sound.

¨ over the second of two vowels, as in *reëstablish*, denotes that each vowel is to be sounded and is called the *diaeresis*, in French, *trema*. In German it is the *umlaut* or *zweipunct* (*two dots*); and denotes a change in the vowel sound, a following vowel (usually *i*) having been dropped.

° over a vowel, is the Scandinavian form of the *umlaut* or *zweipunct* (*see above*).

~ The *tilde* (*q.v.*), used in Spanish, over the *n* (as *Oñoro*) to show that it is pronounced *ny*.

& And; the Tironian Sign, or Ampersand (*q.v.*).

? The note of interrogation, or query mark; said to have been formed from the first and last letters of Lat. *Quaestio* (question), which were contracted to $\overset{Q}{o}$

! The note of exclamation; representing the Latin *Io* (joy), written vertically $\overset{I}{o}$

' The apostrophe; indicating that a letter (or figure) has been omitted, as *don't*, *I'm*; *the rebellion of '98* (for 1798); also marking the possessive case (*John's book*), and plurals of letters and figures, as in *too many I's*, *half a dozen 8's*.

*, †, ‡ The asterisk, dagger (or obelisk), and double dagger; used as reference marks, etc. Another reference mark is

∴ or ∵ The asterism.

§ The section mark; said to represent the old long initial *s*'s (*ſſ*) of Lat. *signum sectionis*, sign of a section.

☞ An index-hand, to call attention to a statement.

¶ A blind p (a modification of the initial letter of *paragraph*), marks a new paragraph.

( ) Called parentheses, and

[ ] Called brackets, separate some explanatory or collateral matter from the real sequence.

**Tyrant.** In ancient Greece the *tyrant* was merely the absolute ruler, the *despot*, of a state, and at first the word had no implication of cruelty or what we call *tyranny*. Many of the Greek tyrants were pattern rulers, as Pisistratus and Pericles, of Athens; Periander, of Corinth; Dionysius the Younger, Gelon, and his brother Hiero of Syracuse; Phidion, of Argos, Polycrates, of Samos; etc. The word (*turannos*) soon, however, obtained much the same meaning as it has with us.

***A tyrant's vein.*** A ranting, bullying manner. In the old moralities the tyrants were made to rant, and the loudness of their rant was proportionate to the villainy of their dispositions.

***The Thirty Tyrants.*** The thirty magistrates appointed by Sparta over Athens, at the termination of the Peloponnesian war. This 'reign of terror', after one year's continuance, was overthrown by Thrasybulos (403 BC).

In the Roman empire those military usurpers who endeavoured, in the reigns of Valerian and Gallienus (253–268), to make themselves independent princes, are also called *the Thirty Tyrants*. The number must be taken with great latitude, as only nineteen are given, and their resemblance to those of Athens is extremely fanciful. They were –

| | *In the East.* | | *Illyricum.* |
|---|---|---|---|
| (1) | Cyriadës. | (11) | Ingenuus. |
| (2) | Macrianus. | (12) | Regillianus. |
| (3) | Balista. | (13) | Aureolus. |
| (4) | Odenathus. | | *Others.* |
| (5) | Zenobia. | (14) | Saturninus in Pontus. |
| | *In the West.* | | |
| (6) | Posthumus. | (15) | Trebellianus in Isauria. |
| (7) | Lollianus. | | |
| (8) | Victorinus and his mother Victoria. | (16) | Piso in Thessaly. |
| | | (17) | Valens in Achaia. |
| (9) | Marius. | (18) | Aemillianus in Egypt. |
| (10) | Tetricus. | (19) | Celsus in Africa. |

***The Tyrant of the Chersonese.*** Miltiades was so called, and yet was he, as Byron says (in *The Isles of Greece*), 'Freedom's best and bravest friend'.

**Tyre.** In Dryden's *Absalom and Achitophel* (*q.v.*) means Holland; Egypt means France.

I mourn, my countrymen, your lost estate …
Now all your liberties a spoil are made,
Egypt and Tyrus intercept your trade.

Pt i, 700–707

**Tyrtaeus.** A lame schoolmaster and elegiac poet of Athens who is said so to have inspired the Spartans by his songs that they defeated the Messenians (7th cent. BC). The name has hence been given to many martial poets who have urged on their countrymen to deeds of arms and victory.

**Tyselyn.** The name given to the Raven in Caxton's version of *Reynard the Fox* (*q.v.*).

# U

**U.** The twenty-first letter of the English alphabet; in form a modification of V with which for many centuries it was interchangeable. Words beginning with U and V were (like those in I and J) not separated in English dictionaries till about 1800, and in 16th and early 17th century books spellings such as *vpon* and *haue* are the rule rather than the exception. The following from the title-page of *Polymanteia* (Anon., 1595) is a good example of the confusion:

> Polimanteia, or, The meanes ... to ivdge of the fall of a Commonwealth, against the friuoulous and foolish coniectures of this age. Whereunto is added, a Letter ... perswading them to a constant vnitie ... for the defence of our ... natiue country ...

Printed by John Legate, Printer to the Vniversitie of Cambridge, 1595

**Ubiquitarians.** A school of Lutherans who maintained that as Christ is omnipresent His body is not only in the Eucharist but everywhere, a doctrine opposed by Zwingli, Calvin, Oecolampadius, and others.

**Udal Tenure.** The same as 'allodial tenure', the opposite of 'feudal tenure', which was the holding of a tenement under a feudal lord. Udal tenure is a sort of freehold, held by the right of long possession, and is obsolete, except in the Orkneys and Shetlands. The more correct spelling is *odal* (Icel. *ōthal*).

**Ugolino.** A Ghibelline (Ugolino della Gherardesca, Count of Pisa) who, about 1270, deserted his party and, with the hope of usurping supreme power in Pisa, formed an alliance with Giovanni Visconti, the head of the Guelphs. The plot failed; Giovanni died, and Ugolino joined the Florentines and forced the Pisans to restore his territories. In 1284 Genoa made war against Pisa, and the Count again treacherously deserted the Pisans, causing their total overthrow. At length a conspiracy was formed against him, and in 1288 he was cast with his two sons and two grandsons into the tower of Gualandi, where they were all starved to death. Dante, in his *Inferno*, has given the sad tale undying publicity.

**Uhlans.** The former Prussian light cavalry, which was chiefly employed in reconnoitring, skirmishing, and outpost duty.

**Ukase.** In the former Russian Empire, an edict either proceeding from the senate or direct from the emperor. Hence, a rigid order or official decree of any kind.

**Ul-Erin.** 'The Guide of Ireland'. A star supposed to be the guardian of that island (Ossian, *Temora* iv).

**Ulania.** In the Charlemagne romances, the queen of Perduta or Islanda. She sent a golden shield to Charlemagne, which he was to give to his bravest paladin, and whoever could win it from him was to claim the hand of Ulania in marriage. *See* *Orlando Furioso*, Bk xv.

**Ulema.** The learned classes in Mohammedan countries, interpreters of the Koran and the law, from whose numbers are chosen the mollahs, imaums, muftis, cadis, etc. (ministers of religion, doctors of law, and administrators of justice). *Ulema* is the plural of *ulim*, a wise man. The body is under the presidency of the Sheikh-ul-Islam.

> The Ulema is not an ecclesiastical body, except so far as law in Mahometan countries is based on the Koran.
>
> Creasy, *Ottoman Turks*, vi, 105

**Ullin.** Fingal's aged bard (*Ossian*).

**Ulster.** The northernmost province of Ireland, which was forfeited to the Crown in James I's reign in consequence of the rebellions of Tyrconnel and Tyrone, and colonised (1609–12) by English and Scottish settlers, who were forbidden to sell land to any Irishman. Since then the Ulstermen (*cp.* Orangemen) have been intensely English and anti-Irish in sentiment and action and have refused on any terms to coalesce with the original inhabitants, who have ever been anti-British.

The long loose overcoat known as an *ulster* is so called because originally made of Ulster frieze.

***The Red*, or *Bloody, Hand of Ulster.*** The badge of Ulster, a sinister hand, erect, open, and couped at the wrist, gules; also carried as a charge on the coat of arms of baronets of England, Great Britain, and the United Kingdom, in commemoration of the fact that this order was created by James I (1611) with the ostensible object of raising funds for the settlement of Ulster. *See* Baronet.

Legend has it that in an ancient expedition to Ireland, it was given out that whoever first touched the shore should possess the territory which he touched; O'Neill, seeing another boat likely to outstrip his own, cut off his left hand and threw it on the coast. From this O'Neill the princes of Ulster were descended, and the motto of the O'Neills is to this day *Lamh dearg Eirin*, 'red hand of Erin'.

**Ulster King of Arms.** Chief heraldic officer of Ireland, and Registrar to the Order of St Patrick. Created by Edward VI in 1552.

**Ultima Thule.** *See* Thule.

**Ultimus Romanorum** (Lat.). The Last of the Romans. *See* Last.

**Ultor** (Lat. the Avenger). A title given to Mars (*q.v.*) when, after defeating the murderers of Julius Caesar, Augustus built a temple to him in the Forum at Rome.

**Ultra vires** (Law Lat. *ultra*, beyond, *vires*, pl. of *vis*, strength). In excess of the power possessed; transcending authority. Used especially of a company; thus if a company which had obtained an Act of Parliament to construct a railway from London to Nottingham were to carry its rails to York, it would be acting *ultra vires*. If the Bank of England were to set up a mint on its premises, it would be acting *ultra vires*.

**Ultramontane Party.** The extreme Popish party in the Church of Rome. *Ultramontane* opinions or tendencies are those which favour the high 'Catholic' party. *Ultramontane* (beyond the mountains, i.e. the Alps) means Italy or the old Papal States. The term was first used by the French, to distinguish those who look upon the Pope as the fountain of all power in the Church, in contradistinction to the Gallican school, which maintained the right of self-government by national churches. *Cp.* Tramontane.

**Ulysses,** or **Odysseus** ('the hater'). A mythical king of Ithaca, a small rocky island of Greece, one of the leading chieftains of the Greeks in Homer's *Iliad*, and the hero of his *Odyssey* (*q.v.*), represented by Homer as wise, eloquent, and full of artifices.

According to Virgil it was he who suggested the device of the wooden horse through which Troy was ultimately taken.

***Ulysses' bow.*** Only Ulysses could draw his own bow, and he could shoot an arrow through twelve rings. By this sign Penelope recognised her husband after an absence of twenty years.

*Ulysses' bow* was prophetic. It belonged at one time to Eurytus of Oechalia.

> This bow of mine sang to me of present war …
> 'I have heard but once of such a weapon … the bow of Odysseus,' said the queen.
> Rider Haggard, *The World's Desire*, Bk ii, ch. i

**Uma.** The consort of Siva (*q.v.*) in the Hindu pantheon. She was famous for her defeat of the army of Chanda and Munda, two demons. She is represented as holding the head of Chanda in one of her four hands, and trampling on Munda, and the heads of their troops, strung into necklaces and girdles, adorn her body.

**Umble Pie.** A pie made of umbles – i.e. the liver, kidneys, etc., of a deer. These 'refuse' were the perquisites of the keeper, and umble pie was a dish for servants and inferiors.

> The keeper hath the skin, head, umbles, chine, and shoulder. Holinshed, *Chronicle*, i, 204

This is the origin of our phrase usually rendered 'to eat *humble* pie'.

**Umbrage.** ***To take umbrage.*** To take offence. Umbrage means shade (Lat. *umbra*), a gloomy view.

**Umbrella.** Used in China in the 11th century BC, in ancient Babylon and Egypt, and known in England in Anglo-Saxon times, though not commonly in use till the early 18th century, and, apparently, not introduced into Scotland till 1780. They are mentioned by Drayton in his *Muses Elizium* (1630) –

> And like umbrellas, with their feathers,
> Shield you in all sorts of weathers.

And Quarles in his *Emblems* (1635) uses the word to signify the Deity hidden in the manhood of Christ – 'Nature is made th' umbrella of the Deity' (iv, 14). Another mention is in Swift's *City Shower* (1710), in Gay's *Trivia* (1711), and *The Tatler*, in No. 238 (Oct. 17th, 1710), says:

> The young gentlemen belonging to the Custom House… borrowed the umbrella from Wilk's coffee-house.

Jonas Hanway (1712–86), the Persian traveller, seems to have popularised them, for his use of an umbrella in London to keep off the rain created a disturbance among the sedan porters and public coachmen, showing that they were not commonly used in the streets at the time.

***Under the umbrella of So-and-so.*** Under his dominion, regimen, influence. The allusion is to the umbrella which, as an emblem of sovereignty, is carried over certain African potentates as the Sultan of Morocco. In *Travels of Ali Bey* (*Penny Magazine*, Dec., 1835, vol. iv, 480), we are told, 'The retinue of the sultan was composed of a troop of from fifteen to twenty men on horseback. About 100 steps behind them came the sultan, mounted on a mule, with an officer bearing his umbrella, who rode beside him on a mule ... Nobody but the sultan himself [not even] his sons and brothers, dares to make use of it.'

> As a direct competitor for the throne – or, strictly speaking, for the shereeflan umbrella – he [Muley Abbas] could scarcely hope to escape.
> *Nineteenth Century*, August, 1892, p. 314

In 1874 the sacred umbrella of Koffee, King of the Ashantis, was captured. It was placed in the South Kensington Museum.

**Unam Sanctam** (Lat. one Holy, i.e. Church). A bull issued in 1302 by Boniface VIII during his quarrel with Philip IV of France, declaring that temporal power is inferior to spiritual, and that the Pope is a Sovereign over Sovereigns. So called – as is usual in bulls – from its opening words.

**Unaneled.** Unanointed; without having had extreme unction (A.S. *ele*, oil; Lat. *oleum*).

> Unhouseled, disappointed, unaneled.
> Shakespeare, *Hamlet*, 1, 5

*Unhouseled* is without having had the Eucharist, especially in the hour of death (A.S. *hūsel*, sacrifice, Eucharist).

**Uncials.** A kind of majuscule script used in MSS dating from about the 1st century BC to the 9th century AD; so called because they are about an inch (Lat. *uncia*) in height.

**Uncle.** Slang for a pawnbroker; an article that has *gone to my uncle's*, is pawned. Some wag has said that *Uncle* is a pun on Lat. *uncus*, a hook, because pawnbrokers used hooks to lift articles pawned before spouts were adopted, 'gone to the *uncus*' being equivalent to 'up the spout!' In French, however, the phrase is *C'est chez ma tante*.

***Don't come the uncle over me.*** In Latin, *Ne sis patruus mihi* (Horace, *2 Sat*. iii, 88) – i.e. do not overdo your privilege of reproving or castigating me. The Latin notion of a *patruus* or uncle left guardian was that of a severe castigator and reprover. Similarly, their idea of a stepmother was a woman of stern, unsympathetic nature, who was unjust to her stepchildren, and was generally disliked.

***Uncle Sam.*** *See* Sam.

**Unco.** A Scottish variant of *uncouth* (unknown; hence, strange, extraordinary). It has two meanings: As an *adjective* it means unknown, strange, unusual; but as an *adverb* it means very – as unco good, unco glad, etc. The 'unco guid' are the pinchbeck saints, too good by half.

> The race of the 'unco guid' is not yet quite extinct in Scotland. *A Daily Journal*

**Uncumber, St.** formerly calledSt Wilgefortis, a very mythical saint. 'Women changed her name' (says Sir Thomas More) 'because they reken that for a pecke of oats she will not faile to *uncumber* them of their husbondys.' The tradition says that she was one of seven beautiful daughters born at a birth to a queen of Portugal; wishing to lead a single life she prayed that she might have a beard. The prayer was granted; and she was no more cumbered with lovers; but one of them, a prince of Sicily, was so enraged that he had her crucified.

> If a wife were weary of a husband, she offered oats at Poules ... to St Uncumber.
> Michael Woode (1554)

**Underwriter.** One who engages to buy at a certain prearranged price all the stock in a new company, of a new issue, etc., that is not taken up by the public. *An underwriter at Lloyd's* is one who insures a ship or its merchandise to a stated amount. So called because he writes his name under the policy.

**Undine.** One of the elemental spirits of Paracelsus (*cp.* Sylph), the spirit of the waters. She was created without a soul; but had this privilege, that by marrying a mortal and bearing him a child she obtained a soul, and with it all the pains and penalties of the human race.

**Unguem.** *Ad unguem*. To the minutest point. To finish a statue *ad unguem* is to finish it so smoothly and perfectly that when the nail is run over the surface it can detect no imperfection. *See* Finger (*to have it at one's fingers 'ends*).

**Unhinged.** *I am quite unhinged*. My nerves are shaken, my equilibrium of mind is disturbed; I am like a door which has lost one of its hinges.

**Unhouseled.** *See* Unaneled.

**Unicorn** (Lat. *unum cornu*, one horn). A mythical and heraldic animal, represented by mediaeval writers as having the legs of a buck, the tail of a lion, the head and body of a horse, and a single horn, white at the base, black in the middle, and red at the tip, in the middle of its forehead. The body is white, the head red, and eyes blue. The oldest author that describes it is Ctesias (400 BC); the mediaeval notions concerning it are well summarised in the following extract:

> The unicorn has but one horn in the middle of its forehead. It is the only animal that ventures to attack the elephant; and so sharp is the nail of its foot, that with one blow it can rip the belly of that beast. Hunters can catch the unicorn only by placing a young virgin in his haunts. No sooner does he see the damsel, than he runs towards her,

> and lies down at her feet, and so suffers himself to be captured by the hunters. The unicorn represents Jesus Christ, who took on Him our nature in the virgin's womb, was betrayed to the Jews, and delivered into the hands of Pontius Pilate. Its one horn signifies the Gospel of Truth.
>
> *Le Bestiaire Divin de Guillaume, Clerc de Normandie* (13th century)

Another popular belief was that the unicorn by dipping its horn into a liquid could detect whether or not it contained poison. In the designs for gold and silver plate made for the Emperor Rudolph II by Ottavio Strada is a cup on which a unicorn stands as if to essay the liquid.

The supporters of the old royal arms of Scotland are two Unicorns; when James VI of Scotland came to reign over England (1603) he brought one of the Unicorns with him, and with it supplanted the Red Dragon which, as representing Wales, was one of the supporters of the English shield, the other being the Lion. Ariosto refers to the arms of Scotland thus:

> Yon lion placed two unicorns between
> That rampant with a silver sword is seen,
> Is for the king of Scotland's banner known.
>
> *Hoole's Translation*, Bk iii

The animosity which existed between the lion and the unicorn referred to by Spenser in his *Faërie Queene* (II, v)

> Like as a lyon, whose imperiall powre
> A prowd rebellious unicorn defyes –

is allegorical of that which once existed between England and Scotland.

***Driving unicorn.*** Two wheelers and one leader. The leader is the *one horn*.

**Unigenitus** (Lat. the Only-Begotten). A Papal bull, so called from its opening sentence, *Unigenitus Dei Filius*, issued in condemnation of *Quesnel's Réflexions Morales* which favoured Jansenism in 1713 by Clement XI; it was a *damnatio in globo* – i.e. a condemnation of the whole book without exception. It was confirmed in 1725, but in 1730 was condemned by the civil authorities of Paris and the controversy died out.

**Union. *The Union.*** A short term for *the United States of America*, and (in England) a familiar euphemism for the workhouse, i.e. the house maintained for the destitute by the Poor Law *Union*.

***The Act of Union.*** Specifically, the Act of 1706 declaring that on and after May 1st, 1707, England and Scotland should have a united Parliament. The two countries had, of course, been united under one sovereign since 1603.

The term is also applied to the Act of 1536 incorporating Wales with England; and to that of 1800, which united the kingdoms of Great Britain and Ireland on and after January 1st, 1801.

***The Union Rose.*** The combined emblematic rose of the Houses of York and Lancaster, the petals of which are white and red; white representing York, and red representing Lancaster. *See under* Ross.

***Union is strength.*** The wise saw of Periander, 'tyrant' of Corinth (665–585 BC).

***Union Jack.*** The national banner of Great Britain and Ireland. It consists of three united crosses – that of St George for England, the saltire of St Andrew for Scotland (added by James I), and the cross of St Patrick for Ireland (added at the Union in 1801).

The white edging of St George's cross shows the white field. In the saltire the cross is reversed on each side, showing that the other half of the cross is covered over. The broad white band is the St Andrew's cross; the narrow white edge is the white field of St Patrick's cross.

The Union Jack is technically described thus:

> The Union Flag shall be azure, the Crosses saltire of St Andrew and St Patrick quarterly per saltire, counter-changed, argent and gules, the latter fimbriated of the second, surmounted by the Cross of St George of the third, fimbriated as the saltire.
>
> *By order of the Council*

For the word 'Jack', *see* Jack.

**Unionists.** The Liberal and Radical party opposed to Home Rule in Ireland which was formed in 1886, and in 1895 joined the Conservative government; so named by Lord Randolph Churchill. After the formation of the Coalition Ministry in 1915 and, still more, after the granting of Home Rule to Ireland (1914 and 1920), the name tended to become obsolete though the party has never been formally dissolved.

**Unitarians.** Christians who deny the doctrine of the Trinity, maintaining that God exists in one Person only. Many of the early heretical sects were Unitarian in belief though not in name; and at the time of the Reformation Servetus, Hetzer (*Switzerland*), Palaeologus, Sega (*Italy*), Flekwyk (*Holland*), the 'Holy Maid of Kent' (*England*), Aikenhead (*Scotland*), Catherine Vogel (*Poland*), Dolet (*France*), and hundreds of others were put to death for holding this opinion.

The modern Unitarians in England ascribe

their foundation to John Biddle (1615–62), and among the famous men who have belonged to the body are Dr Samuel Clarke, Joseph Priestley, Dr Lardner, James Martineau, Sir Edward Bowring, and Joseph Chamberlain.

**United Kingdom.** The name adopted on January 1st, 1801, when Great Britain and Ireland were united.

**United States.** The forty-eight States, one Federal District, and two organised Territories of North America composing the Federal Republic. Thirteen of these are original States, and seven were admitted without previous organisation as Territories.

The nickname of a United States man is a *Yank*, or *Yankee* (*q.v.*); of the people in the aggregate *Brother Jonathan* (*q.v.*); and of the Government *Uncle Sam. See* Sam.

**Unities, The Dramatic.** *See* Dramatic.

**Universal Doctor.** Alain de Lille (1114–1203).

**University.** First applied to collegiate societies of learning in the 12th century, because the *universitas literarum* (entire range of literature) was taught in them – i.e. arts, theology, law, and physic, still called the 'learned' sciences. Greek, Latin grammar, rhetoric, and poetry are called *humanity studies*, or *humaniores literae*, meaning 'lay' studies in contradistinction to divinity, which is the study of *divine* things.

***The University Tests Act.*** An Act passed in 1871 abolishing in the Universities of Oxford, Cambridge, and Durham subscriptions to the XXXIX Articles, all declarations and oaths concerning religious belief, and all compulsory attendance at public worship.

**Unknown. *The Great Unknown*.** Sir Walter Scott. So called (first by his publisher, James Ballantyne) because the *Waverley Novels* were published anonymously.

**Unlearned Parliament, The.** Henry IV's Parliament, which met at Coventry in 1404; so called by Sir Edward Coke because it contained no lawyers; hence also sometimes spoken of as the *Lawless Parliament*.

**Unmentionables.** Breeches.

> Corinthians and exquisites from Bond Street, sporting an eye-glass, … waiting-men in laced coats and plush unmentionables of yellow, green, blue, red, and all the primary colours.
>
> Rev. N. S. Wheaton, *Journal* (1830)

**Unmerciful Parliament, The.** Another name for the Wonderful Parliament (*q.v.*).

**Unready, The.** Ethelred II, King of England 978–1016. So called because he was *redeless*, or deficient in counsel.

**Unrighteous Bible, The.** *See* Bible, Specially named.

**Unwashed.** The first application of the term, *the great unwashed*, to the mob has been attributed to Burke and also to Brougham – perhaps to others, too. Carlyle has, 'Man has been set against man, Washed against Unwashed' (*French Revolution*, II, ii, 4).

**Up. *The House is up.*** The business of the day is ended, and the members may rise up from their seats and go home.

***A.B. is up.*** A. B. is on his legs, in for a speech.

***'Up, Guards, and at them!'*** Creasy, in his *Fifteen Decisive Battles*, states that the Duke of Wellington gave this order in the final charge at the battle of Waterloo. It has, of course, been utterly denied, and we are informed that it was not the Guards, but the 52nd Light Infantry which broke the column of the French Imperial Guard in the final charge.

Wellington's other equally well known saying has met with a similar fate; for it has been shown that so far from the battle of Waterloo having been 'won on the playing fields of Eton' there were only a very small number of officers from Eton at the battle.

**Upanishads.** The oldest speculative literature of the Hindus, a collection of treatises on the nature of man and the universe, forming part of the Vedic writings, the earliest dating from about the 6th cent. BC. The name is Sanskrit, and means 'a sitting down (at another's feet)', hence 'a confidential talk', 'esoteric doctrine'.

**Upas Tree.** The Javanese tree, *Antiaris toxicaria*, the milky juice of which contains a virulent poison and is used for tipping arrows.

Fable has it that a putrid steam rises from it, and that whatever the vapour touches dies. This is chiefly due to Foersch, a Dutch physician, who published his narrative in 1783. 'Not a tree,' he says, 'nor blade of grass is to be found in the valley or surrounding mountains. Not a beast or bird, reptile or living thing, lives in the vicinity.' He adds that on 'one occasion 1,600 refugees encamped within fourteen miles of it, and all but 300 died within two months'. This 'traveller's tale' has given rise to the figurative use of *upas* for a corrupting or pernicious influence.

**Upper Ten, The.** *See* Ten.

**Upsee.** Used in combination with *Dutch*, *Freese*, *English*, as jesting terms for drunk or tippling. *Upsee Dutch* is 'in the manner of the Dutch', *upsee Freeze*, in the manner of a Frisian, etc.

**Upset Price.** The price at which goods sold by auction are first offered for competition. If no advance is made they fall to the person who made the upset price. *Reserved bid* is virtually the same thing.

**Urania.** The Muse of Astronomy in *Greek mythology*, usually represented pointing at a celestial globe with a staff. Milton (*Paradise Lost* vii, 1–20) makes her the spirit of the loftiest poetry, and calls her 'heavenly born' (the name means 'the heavenly one') and sister of Wisdom.

> Where was lorn Urania
> When Adonais died ? With veiled eyes,
> 'Mid listening Echoes, in her Paradise
> She sate — Shelly, *Adonais*, ii

**Uranus.** In *Greek mythology* the personification of Heaven; son and husband of Ge (the earth), and father of the Titans, the Cyclops, the Furies, etc. He hated his children and confined them in Tartarus; but they broke out (*see* Titans) and his son Cronus dethroned him.

The planet Uranus was discovered in 1781 by Herschell, and named by him *Georgium Sidus* in honour of George III. Its four satellites are named *Ariel*, *Umbriel*, *Titania*, and *Oberon*.

**Ur Hamlet.** *See* Hamlet.

**Urbanists.** *See* Franciscans.

**Urbi et Orbi** (Lat. *To Rome and the rest of the world*). A form used in the publication of Papal bulls.

**Urdar** or **the Urdan Fount.** In *Scandinavian mythology*, the sacred fount of light and heat, situated over the rainbow bridge Bifrost, where the gods sit in judgment. It is guarded by the three Norns (*q.v.*).

**Urdu.** One of the most important dialects of India, spoken by the Mohammedans; so named from Hindu *urdū-zabän*, the language of the camp.

**Urgan.** A mortal born and christened, but stolen by the king of the fairies and brought up in elf-land (Scott's *Lady of the Lake*, iv 12). It was decreed that if a woman signed his brow thrice with a cross he should recover his mortal form. Alice Brand did this, and the hideous elf became 'the fairest knight in all Scotland', in whom she recognised her brother Ethert.

**Urganda la Desconecida.** An enchantress or sort of Medea in the romances belonging to the Amadis and Palmerin cycles.

**Urgel.** One of Charlemagne's paladins, famous for his 'giant strength'.

**Uriah.** ***Letter of Uriah***, *see* 2 Sam. 11:15. A treacherous letter, importing friendship but in reality a death-warrant. *Cp.* Bellerophon.

**Uriel.** One of the seven archangels of rabbinical angelology, sent by God to answer the questions of Esdras (2 Esdras:4). In Milton's *Paradise Lost* (iii, 690) he is the 'Regent of the Sun', and 'sharpest-sighted spirit of all in heaven'. Longfellow, in the *Golden Legend*, makes Raphael (*q.v.*) the angel of the Sun, and Uriel the minister of Mars.

The name means 'Flame of God', or 'Angel of Light'.

**Urim and Thummim.** Two objects of uncertain form and material used in the early forms of ancient Hebrew worship, probably in connection with divination and obtaining oracular answers from Jehovah. They are mentioned in Ex. 28:30; 1 Sam. 28:6; Deut. 33:8; Ezra 2:63, etc., but fell out of use in post-exilic times, evidently through the Jews developing a higher conception of the Deity.

**Ursa Major.** The Great Bear, or Charles's Wain (*q.v.*), the most conspicuous of the northern constellations.

The legend is that Calisto, daughter of Lycaon, was violated by Jupiter. Juno changed her into a bear, and Jupiter placed her among the stars that she might be more under his protection. Homer calls it *Arktos*, the Bear, and *Hamaxa*, the Wagon. The Romans called it *Ursa*, the Bear, and *Septemtriones*, the Seven Ploughing Oxen; whence *Septentrionalis* came to signify the north.

Boswell's father used to call Dr Johnson *Ursa Major*.

**Ursa Minor.** The Little Bear; the northern constellation known also as *Cynosura*, or 'Dog's tail', from its circular sweep. The pole star is *a* in the tail. *See* Cynosure.

**Ursula, St.** ***St. Ursula and the eleven thousand virgins***. Ursula was a legendary Cornish princess, and, as the story says, was going to France with eleven thousand virgins in eleven galleys when they were driven by adverse winds to Cologne, where they were all massacred by the Huns.

This extravagant legend is said to have

originated in the discovery of an inscription to *Ursula et Undecimilla Virgines*, which could be rendered either 'the virgins Ursula and Undecimilla', or 'Ursula and her 11,000 (virgins)'. *Undecimilla* was probably the name of a handmaid or companion of Ursula. Visitors to Cologne are still shown piles of skulls and human bones heaped in the wall, faced with glass, which the verger asserts are the relics of the 11,000 martyred virgins. The bones exhibited were taken from an old Roman cemetery, across which the wall of Cologne ran, and which were exposed to view after the siege in 1106.

**Ursulines.** An order of nuns founded by St Angela Merici of Brescia about 1537, so called from their patron saint, St Ursula. The chief work of the order is the education of girls.

**Useless Parliament, The.** The Parliament convened by Charles I, on June 18th, 1625; adjourned to Oxford, August 1st; and dissolved August 12th; having done nothing but offend the king.

**Usher.** From Fr. *huissier*, a doorkeeper.

***Gentleman Usher of the Black Rod***, *See* Black Rod.

***Usher of the Green Rod.*** An officer in attendance on the Knights of the Thistle at their chapters.

**Usquebaugh.** Whisky (Ir. *uisgebeatha*, water of life). Similar to the Latin *aqua vitae*, and the French *eau de vie*.

**Ut Queant Laxis,** etc. This hymn (*see* Doh) was composed in 770. Dr Busby, in his *Musical Dictionary*, says it is ascribed to John the Baptist, but has omitted to inform us by whom.

**Ute.** Queen of Burgundy, mother of Kriemhild and Gunther in the *Nibelungenlied*.

**Utgard** (Old Norse, outer ward). The circle of rocks that hemmed in the ocean which was supposed by the ancient Scandinavians to encompass the world, and to be the haunt of the giants.

**Utgard-Lok.** The Scandinavian demon of the infernal regions.

**Uther.** A legendary king, or pendragon (*q.v.*), of the Britons; by an adulterous amour with Igerna (wife of Gorlois, Duke of Cornwall) he became the father of Arthur, who succeeded him.

**Uti possidetis** (Lat. as you at present possess them). The principle in international law that the belligerents are to retain possession of all the places taken by them before the treaty commenced.

**Uticensis.** Cato the Younger was so called from Utica, the place of his death.

**Utilitarianism.** The ethical doctrine that actions are right in proportion to their usefulness or as they tend to promote happiness; the doctrine that the end and criterion of public action is 'the greatest happiness of the greatest number'.

John Stuart Mill coined the word; but Jeremy Bentham, the official founder of the school, employed the word 'Utility' to signify the doctrine which makes 'the happiness of man' the one and only measure of right and wrong.

> Oh, happiness, our being's end and aim. ...
> For which we bear to live, or dare to die.
>
> Pope, *Essay on Man*, Epistle iv

**Utopia.** Nowhere (Gr. *ou*, not, *topos*, a place). The name given by Sir Thomas More to the imaginary island in his political romance of the same name (1516), where everything is perfect – the laws, the morals, the politics, etc., and in which the evils of existing laws, etc., are shown by contrast. *See* Commonwealths, Ideal; and *cp.* Weissnichtwo.

Rabelais (in Bk II, ch. xxiv) sends Pantagruel and his companions to Utopia, where they find the citizens of its capital, Amaurot, most hospitable. They reached the island by doubling the Cape of Good Hope, and sailing with a 'Tramontane Wind' past Meden, Uti, Uden, Gelasim, the Islands of the Fairies, and along the Kingdom of Achoria. *See* Queubus.

This fictional island has given us the adjective *Utopian*, applied to any highly desirable but quite impracticable scheme.

**Utraquists** (Lat. *utraque specie*, in both kinds). Another name for the Calixtines (*q.v.*), so called because they insisted that both the elements should be administered to all communicants in the Eucharist.

**Utter and Inner Barristers.** An *utter* or *outer barrister* means (in some cases at least) a full-fledged barrister, one licensed to practise. An *inner barrister* means a student.

**Uzziel.** One of the principal angels of rabbinical angelology, the name meaning 'Strength of God'. He was next in command to Gabriel, and in Milton's *Paradise Lost* (iv, 782) is commanded by Gabriel to 'coast the south with strictest watch'.

# V

**V.** The twenty-second letter of the alphabet, formerly sharing its form with U (*q.v.*).

In the Roman notation it stands for 5, and represents ideographically the four fingers and thumb with the latter extended.

**V. D. M. I. Ae.** Lat. *Verbum Dei manet in aeternum*, i.e. the word of God endureth for ever. The inscription on the liveries of the servants of the Duke of Saxony and Landgrave of Hesse, the Lutheran princes, at the Diet of Spires in 1526.

**Vacuum** (Lat. *vacare*, to be empty). A space from which air has been expelled. Descartes remarked, 'If a vacuum could be effected in a vessel, the sides would be pressed into contact.'

***Nature abhors a vacuum.*** Galileo's way of accounting for the rise of water in pumps. *See* Torricelli.

**Vade mecum** (a go-with-me). A pocket-book, memorandum-book, pocket cyclopaedia, lady's pocket companion, or anything else which contains many things of daily use in a small compass.

**Vae Victis!** (Lat.) Woe to the vanquished! So much the worse for the conquered! This was the exclamation of Brennus, the Gaulish chief, on throwing his sword into the balance as a make-weight, when determining the price of peace with Rome (390 BC).

**Vagabond.** An idle, disreputable person who wanders about from place to place without any settled home (late Lat. *vagabundus*, from *vagari*, to wander). Under the Vagrancy Act (1824) the term is applied to such as sleep out without visible means of subsistence. *Cp.* Rogue.

**Vail.** To lower; to cast down. From Fr. *avaler*, to descend.

> The time is come
> That France must vail her lofty plumed crest.
>
> Shakespeare, *1 Henry VI*, 5, 3

***Vails***, an obsolete term for a tip given to servants by visitors or for a bribe, is from Fr. *valoir*, Lat. *valere*, to be worth.

> *2 Fish.*: Ay, but hark you, my friend; 'twas we that made up this garment through the rough seams of the water; there are certain condolements, certain vails, I hope, sir, if you thrive, you'll remember from whence you had it.
> Per.: Believe it, I will – Shakespeare, *Pericles*, 2, 1

**Vaishnava.** One of the great sects of reformed Brahmins who worship Vishnu as supreme among the Hindu gods. Their sacred books are known as the *Vaiṣhnava Puranas*.

**Vaisya.** The third of the four chief Hindu castes, or a member of this. From a Sanskrit word meaning *a settler*.

**Vale!** Farewell! 2nd pers. sing. imp. of Lat. *valere*, to be worth, or to fare well.

> I thought once againe heare to have made an ende, with a heartie *Vale* of the best fashion.
>
> Spenser, *Letter to Gabriel Harvey* (1580)

***Ave atque vale!*** Hail and farewell; the words of Catullus at his brother's tomb.

> There beneath the Roman ruin where the purple flowers grow,
> Came that 'Ave atque Vale' of the poet's hopeless woe,
> Tenderest of Roman poets, nineteen hundred years ago.
>
> Tennyson, '*Frater, Ave Atque Vale*'

**Valentine, St.** A priest of Rome who was imprisoned for succouring persecuted Christians. He became a convert himself, and although he restored the sight of his gaoler's blind daughter he was martyred by being clubbed to death (February 14th, 269).

***St Valentine's Day.*** February 14th, the day when, according to every ancient tradition, the birds choose their mates for the year. Chaucer refers to this (*Parliament of Foules*, 309), as also does Shakespeare:

> Good morrow, friends! St Valentine is past;
> Begin these wood-birds but to couple now?
>
> *Midsummer Night's Dream*, 4, 1

It was an old custom in England to draw lots for lovers on this day, the person being drawn being the drawer's *valentine*, and being given a present, sometimes of an expensive kind, but oftener of a pair of gloves, and now frequently represented by a greeting card of a sentimental, humorous, or merely vulgar character.

> If I stood affected that way (i.e., to marriage) I would choose my wife as men do Valentines – blindfold, or draw cuts for them; for so I shall not be deceived in the choosing.
>
> Chapman, *Monsieur d'Olive*, I (1605)

This custom is said to have had its origin in a pagan practice connected with the worship of Juno on or about this day.

**Valentine and Orson.** An old French romance, connected with the Alexander cycle.

The heroes – from whom it is named – were the twin sons of Bellisant, sister of King Pepin and Alexander, and were born in a forest near Orleans. Orson (*q.v.*) was carried off by a bear, and became a wild man. While the mother was searching for him Valentine was carried off by his uncle, the king. Each had many adventures, but all ended happily, and Valentine married Clerimond, sister of the Green Knight, while Orson married a daughter of the Duke of Aquitaine.

**Valentinians.** An ancient sect of Gnostics. So called from their leader, Valentinus, an Egyptian Gnostic of the 2nd century AD.

**Valesians.** A sect of early Christians founded (according to Epiphanius) by a certain Valeus or Valesius in Arabia in the 3rd century AD. The chief fact recorded of them is that they regarded castration as essential to salvation.

**Valhalla.** In *Scandinavian mythology*, the hall in the celestial regions whither the souls of heroes slain in battle were borne by the Valkyries, and where they spent eternity in joy and feasting (*valr*, the slain, and *hall*).

Hence the name is applied to buildings, such as Westminster Abbey, used as the last resting-place of a nation's great men.

We both must pass from earth away,
  Valhalla's joys to see;
And if I wander there today,
  Tomorrow may fetch thee.

*Frithiof-Saga*, lay xi

**Vail.** The 'silent god' and guardian of justice among the ancient Scandinavians. He was the second son of Odin, and avenged the death of Balder by slaying his murderer, Hoder. He was one of the few who were to survive the catastrophe of the Twilight of the Gods, for Justice must not be banished from the earth.

**Valkyries, The** (Old Norse, The Choosers of the Slain). The twelve nymphs of Valhalla, who, mounted on swift horses, and holding drawn swords, rushed into the *mêlée* of battle and selected those destined to death. These heroes they conducted to Valhalla, where they waited upon them and served them with mead and ale in the skulls of the vanquished. The chief were Mista, Sangrida, and Hilda.

Mista black, terrific maid,
Sangrida and Hilda see.

Gray, *Fatal Sisters*

**Vallary Crown.** The same as a *mural crown* (*see under* Crown).

**Vallombrosa.** Milton says, 'Thick as autumnal leaves that strew the brooks in Vallombrosa' (*Paradise Lost* i, 302); but as the trees of Vallombrosa are chiefly pines, they do not strew the brooks with autumnal leaves. The beech and chestnut trees are by no means numerous.

**Vamana.** *See* Avatar.

**Vamp.** ***To vamp up an old story***, to refurbish it; *to vamp an accompaniment to a song*, to improvise it as one goes along.

***To vamp*** is properly to put new uppers to old boots; and *vamps* were short hose covering the feet and ankles (Fr. *avant-pied*, the forepart of the foot).

**Vampire.** A fabulous being, supposed to be the ghost of a heretic, excommunicated person, or criminal, that returns to the world at night in the guise of a monstrous bat and sucks the blood of sleeping persons who, usually, become vampires themselves.

But first on earth, as vampire sent,
Thy corse shall from the tomb be rent,
Then ghastly haunt thy native place
And suck the blood of all thy race.

Byron, *The Giaour*

The word is applied to one who preys upon his fellows – a 'bloodsucker'.

**Vandals.** A Teutonic race from the Baltic (allied to the *Wends*, i.e. *Wanderers*), which in the 5th century AD ravaged Gaul and, under Genseric, captured Rome and despoiled it of its treasures of art, literature, and civilisation generally.

The name is hence applied to those who wilfully or ignorantly destroy works of art, etc.

**Vandyke.** To scallop an edge after the fashion of the collars painted by Vandyck in the reign of Charles I. The scalloped edges are said to be *vandyked*.

***Vandyke beard.*** A pointed beard, such as those frequently shown in Vandyck's portraits, especially of Charles I.

**Vanessa.** Dean Swift's name for his friend and correspondent, Esther Vanhomrigh, made by compounding *Van*, the first syllable of her surname, with *Essa*, the pet form of Esther. Swift called himself *Cadenus*, an anagram on *Decanus* (Lat. for *Dean*).

**Vanguard.** *See* Avant-garde.

**Vanir.** The nature-gods of the old Scandinavians, who presided over the ocean, air, earth, streams, etc.; opposed to, and generally at war with, the Aesir (*q.v.*). Niörd, the water-god, was the chief; his son was Frey; his daughter Freyja (the Scandinavian Venus); his wife Skadi; and his home Noatun.

**Vanity Fair.** In Bunyan's *Pilgrim's Progress*, a fair established by Beelzebub, Apollyon, and Legion, in the town of Vanity, and lasting all the year round. Here were sold houses, lands, trades, places, honours, preferments, titles, countries, kingdoms, lusts, pleasures, and delights of all sorts.

Thackeray adopted the name for the title of his novel (1847) satirising the weaknesses and follies of human nature.

**Vanoc.** The son of Merlin, one of Arthur's Round Table Knights.

> Young Vanoc of the beardless face
> (Fame spoke the youth of Merlin's race),
> O'erpowered at Gyneth's footstool, bled,
> His heart's blood dyed her sandals red.
>
> Scott, *Bridal of Triermain*, ii, 25

**Vantage Loaf.** The thirteenth loaf of a baker's dozen.

**Varaha.** *See* Avatar.

**'Varsity.** A shortened form of *university*; but, in England, properly used only of Oxford or Cambridge.

**Varuna.** The Hindu Neptune. He is represented as an old man riding on a sea monster, with a club in one hand and a rope in the other. In the Vedic hymns he is the night sky, and Mitra the day sky. Varuna is said to set free the 'waters of the clouds'.

**Vathek.** The hero of Beckford's oriental romance of the same name (1784). The ninth caliph of the Abbasside dynasty, he is a haughty, effeminate monarch, induced by a malignant genius to commit all sorts of crimes. He abjures his faith, and offers allegiance to Eblis, under the hope of obtaining the throne of the pre-Adamite sultans. This he gained, only to find that it was a place of torture and that he was doomed to remain in it for ever.

**Vatican.** The palace of the Pope: so called because it stands on the *Vaticanus Mons* (Vatican Hill) of ancient Rome, which got its name through being the headquarters of the *vaticinatores*, or soothsayers.

Strictly speaking, the Vatican consists of the Papal palace, the court and garden of Belvidere, the library, and the museum.

***The Council of the Vatican.*** The twenty-first Oecumenical Council (*q.v.*), held at the Vatican, 1869–1870, under Pius IX. It promulgated the dogma of papal infallibility.

***The Thunders of the Vatican.*** *See* Thunder.

**Vaudeville.** A corruption of *Val de Vire*, or in O.Fr. *Vau de Vire*, the native valley of Oliver Basselin, a Norman poet (d.1418), author of convivial songs, which he called after the name of his birthplace.

**Vaudois.** *See* Waldensians (*cp.* Voodoo).

**Vauxhall.** A part of Lambeth, London; so called from *Falkes* (or *Fulkes*) de Breauté, who was lord of the manor in the early 13th century.

***Vauxhall Gardens.*** A very popular pleasure resort for Londoners, from 1661, when it was opened, till 1859. Pepys, who calls it Fox Hall, says the entertainments there are 'mighty divertising'; and nearly two centuries later, Thackeray, in *Vanity Fair* (ch. vi), sketches the loose character of these 'divertising' amusements.

**Ve.** Brother of Odin and Vili, in *Scandinavian mythology*. He was one of the three deities who took part in the creation of the world; and he and Vili slew Ymir and drowned the whole race of frost-giants in his blood.

**Vedas** or **Vedams.** The four sacred books of the Brahmans, comprising (1) the *Rig* or *Rish Veda*; (2) *Yajur Veda*; (3) the *Sama Veda*; and (4) the *Atharva Veda*. The first consists of prayers and hymns in verse, the second of prayers in prose, the third of prayers for chanting, and the fourth of formulas for consecration, imprecation, expiation, etc.

The word *Veda* means knowledge.

**Vehmgerichte.** Courts of justice, or tribunals, which were held in Germany (especially Westphalia) from about the 12th to the 16th centuries, for the preservation of public peace, suppression of crime, and maintenance of the Catholic religion. In all serious cases, such as charges of heresy, witchcraft, or murder, the sentence was death, and the proceedings were conducted in absolute secrecy; the judges were enveloped in profound mystery; they had their secret spies through all Germany; their judgments were certain, but no one could discover the executioner. Scott, in *Anne of Gierstein*, has given an account of the Westphalian Vehmgerichte.

**Velasquez.** ***Why drag in Velasquez?*** *See* Drag.

**Velvet.** ***On velvet.*** On a sure thing; certain of success. One who makes a bet that he is bound to win is said to be 'on velvet'.

***To prophesy upon velvet.*** To prophesy what is already a known fact. Thus, the issue of a battle flashed to an individual may, by some chance, get to the knowledge of a 'sibyl', who may securely prophesy the issue to others; but such a prediction would be a 'prophecy on velvet'; it goes on velvet slippers without fear of stumbling.

> If one of those three had spoken the news over again ... the old lady [or Sibyl] prophesies upon velvet. Scott, *The Pirate*, ch. xxi

**Vendée, War of La.** The rising of royalists against the French Republic in 1793–5 in La Vendée, a Department of western France, and Brittany. It was followed by the *War of the Chouans* (*see* Chouan), which was finally suppressed by Napoleon in 1800.

**Vendémiaire.** The first month in the French Republican calendar; from September 22nd to October 21st. The word means 'Vintage'.

**Vendetta** (Lat. *vindicta*, revenge). The blood-feud, or duty of the nearest kin of a murdered man to kill the murderer. It formerly prevailed in Corsica, Sicily, Sardinia, and Calabria, and is probably not yet extinct.

**Venerable** (Lat. *venerabilis*, worthy of honour). The title applied to archdeacons in formally addressing them ('The Venerable the Archdeacon of Barset', or 'The Venerable Archdeacon Brown'); and also in the Roman Catholic Church, the title of one who has attained the first of the three degrees of canonisation.

It specially belongs to Bede – the Venerable Bede – the monk of Jarrow, an English ecclesiastical historian (d.735), and to William of Champeaux (d.1121), the French scholastic philosopher and opponent of Abelard.

**Veneralia.** *See* Venus (*Venus Verticordia*).

**Veni, Creator Spiritus** (Lat., 'Come, Creator Spirit'). A hymn of the Roman Breviary used on the Feast of Pentecost. It has been ascribed to both Charlemagne and Pope Gregory I.

**Veni, Sancte Spiritus** (Lat., 'Come, Holy Spirit'). A mediaeval Latin hymn, used as a sequence in the Roman Church. It is ascribed to Robert II of France (d.1031).

**Veni, vidi, vici** (Lat., 'I came, I saw, I conquered'). According to Plutarch it was thus that Julius Caesar announced to his friend Amintius his victory at Zela (47 BC), in Asia Minor, over Pharnaces, son of Mithridates, who had rendered aid to Pompey.

Suetonius, however, says that the words were displayed before his title after his victories in Pontus, and does not ascribe them to Caesar himself.

They are often used as an example of laconism, extreme concision.

**Venial Sin.** One that may be pardoned; one that does not forfeit grace. In the Catholic Church sins are of two sorts, *mortal* and *venial* (Lat. *venia*, grace, pardon). *See* Matt. 12:31.

**Venice Glass.** The drinking-glasses of the Middle Ages, made at Venice, were said to break into shivers if poison were put into them.

> *Doge*: 'Tis said that our Venetian crystal has
> Such pure antipathy to poison, as
> To burst, if aught of venom touches it.
> Byron, *The Two Foscari*, v, i

Venice glass, from its excellency, became a synonym for *perfection*.

**Venire facias.** A writ directing the sheriff to assemble a jury. So called from its opening Latin words – 'Cause to come'.

**Venison.** Anything taken in hunting or by the chase. Hence Jacob bids Esau to go and get *venison* such as he loved (Gen. 27:3), meaning the wild kid. The word is simply the Latin *venatio*, hunting, but is now restricted to the flesh of deer.

**Venner's Plot.** A plot made by the Fifth Monarchy Men under Thomas Venner to seize Whitehall in 1661, during the absence of Charles II. The plot failed, and Venner and many of his followers were put to death.

**Venom.** ***The venom is in the tail.*** The real difficulty is the conclusion. The allusion is to the scorpion, which has a sting in its tail.

The French say *Il n'y a rien de plus difficile à écorcher que la queue* (it is always most difficult to flay the tail).

**Ventose** (Fr., windy). The sixth month of the French Revolutionary calender, February 19th to March 20th.

**Ventre-saint-Gris.** The usual oath of Henri IV of France, *Gris* being a euphemism for *Christ*, and *ventre*, stomach. Oaths not infrequently took this form of blasphemy – *God's nails*, *God's teeth*, etc., were common in England.

A similar juron is *Par le ventre de Dieu*. Rabelais has *Par sainct Gris*; and the suggestion has been made that the allusion was to Francis of Assisi, who was *ceint* (girdled) and clad in *gris* (grey).

**Ventriloquism.** The art of producing vocal sounds so that they appear to come, not from the person producing them, but from some other quarter. So called from Lat. *venter*, belly, *loqui*, to speak (speaking from the belly), with the erroneous notion that the voice of the *ventriloquist* proceeded from his stomach.

**Venus.** The Roman goddess of beauty and sensual love, indentified with the Aphrodite (*q.v.*) of the Greeks. She is said in some accounts to have sprung from the foam of the sea, but in others to have been the daughter of Jupiter and Dione. Vulcan was her husband, but she had amours with Mars and many other gods and demigods; by Mercury she was the mother of Cupid, and by the hero Anchises the mother of Aeneas, through whom she was regarded by the Romans as the foundress of their race. Her chief festival was April 1st (*see* Venus Verticordia, *below*).

Her name is given to the second planet from the sun, and in astrology 'signifiethe white men or browne … joyfull laughter, liberall, pleasers, dauncers, entertayners of women, players, perfumers, musitions, messengers of love,

> Venus loveth ryot and dispense.
>
> Chaucer, *Wife of Bath's Prol.*, 700

By the alchemists *copper* was designated *Venus*, probably because mirrors were anciently made of copper. A mirror is still the astronomical symbol of the planet Venus.

The best cast at dice (three sixes) used to be called *Venus*, and the worst (three aces) *Canis* (dog); hence the phrase, 'my Venus has turned out a whelp', equivalent to 'all my swans are geese'.

***Venus Anadyomene.*** Venus rising from the sea, accompanied by dolphins. The name is given to the famous lost painting by Apelles, and to that by Botticelli in the Accademia delle Belle Arti at Florence.

***Venus Callipyge*** (Gr., with the beautiful buttocks). The name given to a late Greek statue in the Museo Nazionale at Naples. There is no real ground for connecting the statue with Venus.

***Venus de Medici.*** A famous statue, since 1680 in the Uffizzi Gallery, Florence, ranking as a canon of female beauty. It is supposed to date from the time of Augustus, and was dug up in the 17th century in the villa of Hadrian, near Tivoli, in eleven pieces. It was kept in the Medici Palace at Rome till its removal to Florence by Cosmo III.

> So stands the statue that enchants the world,
> So bending tries to veil the matchless boast,
> The mingled beauties of exulting Greece.
>
> Thomson, *Summer*

***Venus Genetrix*** (Lat. she that produces). Venus worshipped as a symbol of marriage and motherhood. There are several statues of this name, she being represented as raising her light drapery and holding an apple – the emblem of fecundity.

***Venus of Cnidus.*** The nude statue of Praxiteles, purchased by the ancient Cnidians, who refused to part with it, although Nicomedes, king of Bithynia, offered to pay off their national debt as its price. It was subsequently removed to Constantinople, and perished in the great fire during the reign of Justinian (AD 532); but an ancient reproduction is in the Vatican.

***Venus of Milo***, or ***Melos.*** The statue, with three of Hermes, was discovered in 1820 by Admiral Dumont in Milo or Melos, one of the Greek islands. It dates from about 400 BC, and is probably the finest single work of ancient art extant. It now stands in the Louvre.

***Venus Verticordia.*** A temple was founded at Rome on April 1st, 114 BC, to Venus Verticordia as expiation for the loss of their chastity by three of the Vestal Virgins. April 1st thus became the *Veneralia*, or chief festival of Venus.

***Venus Victrix.*** Venus, as goddess of victory, represented on numerous Roman coins.

***Venus's hair-stone***, or ***pencil.*** Rock-crystal or quartz penetrated by acicular crystals of rutile which show through as hair-like filaments.

**Venusberg.** The Horselberg, or mountain of delight and love, situated between Eisenach and Gotha, in the caverns of which, according to mediaeval German legend, the Lady Venus held her court. Human beings were occasionally permitted to visit her, as Heinrich von Limburg did, and the noble Tannhäuser (*q.v.*); but as such persons ran the risk of eternal perdition, Eckhardt the Faithful, who sat before the gate, failed not to warn them against entering.

**Vera causa** (Lat., a true cause). A cause in harmony with other causes already known. A fairy godmother may be assigned in story as the cause of certain marvellous effects, but is not a *vera causa*. The revolution of the earth round the sun may be assigned as the cause of the four seasons, and is a *vera causa*.

**Verb. sap.** (Lat. *Verbum sapienti*, a word to the wise). A hint is sufficient to any wise man; a threat implying if the hint is not taken I will expose you.

**Verb. sat.** (Lat. *Verbum satienti*, a word is enough). Similar to the above. A word to the wise is enough.

**Verbatim et literatim** (Lat.). Accurately rendered, 'word for word and letter for letter'.

**Vere adeptus** (Lat., one who has truly attained). One admitted to the fraternity of the Rosicrucians.

In Rosycrucian lore as learned
As he the Vere-adeptns earned.

Butler, *Hudibras*

**Verger.** The officer in a church who carries the rod or staff, which was formerly called the *verge* (Lat. *virga*, a rod).

**Vergil.** *See* Virgil.

**Veronica, St.** A late mediaeval legend says that a maiden handed her handkerchief to our Lord on His way to Calvary. He wiped the sweat from His brow, returned the handkerchief to the owner, and went on. The handkerchief was found to bear a perfect likeness of the Saviour, and was called *Vera-Icon* (true likeness); the maiden became *St Veronica*, and is commemorated on Feb. 4th; and Milan Cathedral, St Sylvester's at Rome, and St Bartholomew's at Genoa all lay claim to the handkerchief.

The fact is that the name is a corruption of Gr. *Berenice*, and its similarity to *vera icon* gave rise to the legend.

**Vers de société** (Fr., Society verse). Light poetry of a witty or fanciful kind, generally with a slight vein of social satire running through it.

**Versi Berneschi.** *See* Bernesque.

**Vert.** The heraldic (from French) term for *green*, said to signify love, joy, and abundance; in engravings it is indicated by lines running diagonally across the shield from right to left. It is not considered a very 'honourable' tincture in English blazonry, and is scarce.

**Vertumnus.** The ancient Roman god of the seasons, and the deity presiding over gardens and orchards. He was the husband of Pomona. August 12th was his festival.

**Vervain.** Called 'holy herb', from its use in ancient sacred rites. Also called 'pigeons' grass', 'Juno's tears', and 'simpler's joy'. Supposed to cure scrofula, the bite of rabid animals, to arrest the diffusion of poison, to avert antipathies, to conciliate friendships, and to be a pledge of mutual good faith; hence it was anciently worn by heralds and ambassadors.

*Verbena* is its botanical name.

The term Verbena (quasi *herbena*) originally denoted all those herbs that were held sacred on account of their being employed in the rites of sacrifice. Mill, *Logic*, Bk iv, ch. v

**Vesica Piscis** (Lat., fish-bladder). The ovoidal frame or glory which, in the 12th century, was much used, especially in painted windows, to surround pictures of the virgin Mary and of our Lord. It is meant to represent a fish, from the anagram ichthus (*q.v.*).

**Vespers.** The sixth of the seven canonical hours in the Greek and Roman Churches; sometimes also used of the Evening Service in the English Church. From Lat. *vesperus*, the evening, cognate with *Hesperus* (*q.v.*), Gr. *Hesperos*, the evening star.

***The Fatal Vespers.*** October 26th, 1623. A congregation of some 300 had assembled in a small gallery over the gateway of the French ambassador, in Blackfriars, to hear Father Drury, a Jesuit, preach. The gallery gave way, and Drury with another priest and about 100 of the congregation were killed. This accident was, according to the bigotry of the times, attributed to God's judgment against the Jesuits.

***The Sicilian Vespers.*** *See* Sicilian.

**Vesta.** The virgin goddess of the hearth of *Roman mythology*, corresponding to the Greek *Hestia*, one of the twelve great Olympians. She was custodian of the sacred fire brought by Aeneas from Troy, which was never permitted to go out lest a national calamity should follow. *See* Vestals.

Wax matches that 'strike anywhere' are named from her.

**Vestals.** The six spotless virgins who tended the sacred fire brought by Aeneas from Troy and preserved by the state in a sanctuary in the Forum at Rome. They were subjected to very severe discipline, and in the event of losing their virginity were buried alive.

Other duties of the Vestal Virgins were to prepare from the first-fruits of the May harvest the sacrificial meal for the Lupercalia, the Vestalia, and the Ides of September.

The word *vestal* has been figuratively applied to any woman of spotless chastity. Thus, Shakespeare calls Queen Elizabeth –

A fair vestal, throned by the west.

*Midsummer Night's Dream*, 2, 1

**Veto** (Lat., I forbid). Louis XVI and Marie Antoinette were called *Monsieur* and *Madame Veto* by the Republicans, because the Constituent Assembly (1791) allowed the king to have the power of putting his veto upon any decree submitted to him.

**Via.** A way (Lat. *via*). Our use of the word, as in *I'll go via Chester*, i.e. 'by way of Chester', is *via*, the ablative of *via*.

***Via Appia.*** The Appian Way (*q.v.*).

***Via Dolorosa.*** The way our Lord went from the Mount of Olives to Golgotha, about a mile in length.

***Via Lactea.*** The Milky Way (*q.v.*).

***Via Sacra,*** the street in ancient Rome, was the street where Romulus and Tatius (the Sabine) swore mutual alliance. It does not mean the 'holy street', but the 'street of the oath'.

**Vial.** ***Vials of wrath.*** Vengeance, the execution of wrath on the wicked. The allusion is to the seven angels who pour out upon the earth their vials full of wrath (Rev. 16).

**Viaticum** (Lat.). The Eucharist administered to the dying. The word means 'money allowed for a journey', and the notion is that this sacrament will be the spirit's passport to Paradise.

**Vicar.** A parish priest who receives a stipend, the tithes belonging to a chapter, religious house, layman, or otherwise (*cp.* Rector). At the Reformation many livings which belonged to monasteries passed into the hands of noblemen, who, not being in holy orders, had to perform the sacred offices *vicar-iously*. The clergyman who officiated for them was called their *vicar* or representative, and the law enjoined that the lord should allow him to receive the use of the glebe and all tithes except those accruing from grain (such as corn, barley, oats, rye, etc.), hay, and wood.

***Lay vicar.*** A cathedral officer who sings those portions of the liturgy not reserved for the clergy. Formerly called a *clerk vicar*.

***Vicar apostolic.*** In the Roman Catholic Church, a titular bishop appointed to a place where no episcopate has been established, or where the succession has been interrupted. The term formerly denoted a bishop to whom the Pope delegated some part of his jurisdiction.

***Vicar choral.*** One of the minor clergy, or a layman, attached to a cathedral for singing certain portions of the service.

***Vicar forane.*** A priest appointed by a Roman Catholic bishop to exercise limited (usually disciplinary) jurisdiction in a particular part of his diocese.

***Vicar-General.*** An ecclesiastical functionary assisting a bishop or archbishop in his visitations, etc.

***The Vicar of Bray.*** A semi-legendary vicar of Bray, Berkshire, who, between 1520 and 1560, was twice a Papist and twice a Protestant in successive reigns. His name has been given as Symonds, Alleyne, and Pendleton, and his date transferred to the time of Charles II. Historically nothing is known of him; the well known song is said to have been written in Restoration times by an officer in Colonel Fuller's regiment.

> Brome says of Simon Alleyn that he 'lived in the reigns of Henry VIII, Edward VI, Mary, and Elizabeth. In the first two reigns he was Protestant, in Mary's reign he turned Papist, and in the next reign recanted – being resolved, whoever was king, to die Vicar of Bray.'

> Ray refers to Simon Symonds, a vicar who was Independent in the Protectorate, Churchman in the reign of Charles II, Papist under James II, and Moderate Protestant under William and Mary.

***The Vicar of Christ.*** A title given to the Pope, in allusion to his claim of being the representative of Christ on earth.

***The Vicar of Hell.*** A name playfully given by Henry VIII to John Skelton, his 'poet laureate', perhaps because Skelton was rector of Diss, in Norfolk, the pun being on Dis (*q.v.*). Milton refers to the story in his *Areopagitica*:

> I name not him for posterity's sake, whom Henry the Eighth named in merriment his vicar of hell.

**Vice.** The buffoon in the old English moralities. He wore a cap with ass's ears, and was generally named after some particular vice, as Gluttony, Pride, etc.

**Vice versa** (Lat., *vicis*, change, *versa*, turned). The reverse; the terms of the case being reversed.

**Vidar.** One of the Aesir of *Scandinavian mythology*, a son of Odin. He avenged his father's death by slaying the Fenris wolf at Ragnarok.

**View Holloa.** The shout of huntsmen when a fox breaks cover = 'Gone away!' *Cp.* Soho, Tally-ho.

**Vignette.** An engraving, especially on the title-page of a book, that is not enclosed within a border; properly, a likeness having a border of vine-leaves round it (Fr. little vine, tendril).

**Viking.** A Norse pirate of about the 8th to 10th centuries AD; probably so called from Icel. *vig*, war, cognate with Lat. *vincere*, to conquer. The word is not connected with *king*. There were *sea-kings*, sometimes, but erroneously, called 'vikings', connected with royal blood, and having small dominions on the coast, who were often *vikingr* or vikings, but the reverse is not true that every *viking* or pirate was a sea-king.

**Vili.** *See* Ve.

**Villain** means simply one attached to a villa or farm (late Lat. *villanus*, a farm-servant, from *villa*, a farm). In feudal times the lord was the great landowner, and under him were a host of tenants called *villains* (sometimes spelt *villein*, to differentiate this from the modern meaning). The highest class of villains were called *regardant*, and were annexed to the manor; then came the *Coliberti* or *Bures*, who were privileged vassals; then the *Bordarii* or cottagers (A.S. *bord*, a cottage), who rendered certain menial offices to their lord for rent; then the *Coscets*, *Cottarii*, and *Cotmanni*, who paid partly in produce and partly in menial service; and, lastly, the *villains in gross*, who were annexed to the person of the lord, and might be sold or transferred as chattels. The notion of wickedness and worthlessness associated with the word is simply the effect of aristocratic pride and exclusiveness.

> I am no villain; I am the youngest son of Sir Rowland de Boys; he was my father, and he is thrice a villain that says such a father begot villains. Shakespeare, *As You Like It*, 1, 1

**Vim.** University slang for energy, force, 'go'. The accusative of Lat. *vis*, strength.

**Vinayapitaka.** *See* Tripitaka.

**Vincent, St.** A deacon of Saragossa, martyred in the Dacian persecution, 304, and commemorated on January 22nd. He is a patron saint of drunkards, for no apparent reason; an old rhyme says:

> If on St Vincent's Day the sky is clear
> More wine than water will crown the year.

**Vincentian.** A Lazarist (*q.v.*), a member of the order of Lazarites, founded by St Vincent de Paul in the 17th century.

**Vine.** The Rabbis say that the fiend buried a lion, a lamb, and a hog at the foot of the first vine planted by Noah; and that hence men receive from wine ferocity, mildness, or wallowing in the mire.

**Vineam Domini** (Lat. The Vineyard of the Lord). The bull issued in 1705 against the Jansenists by Pope Clement XI. These words occur in the bull.

**Vinegar.** Livy tells us that when Hannibal led his army over the Alps to enter Rome he used vinegar to dissolve the snow, and make the march less slippery. Of course this tradition is fabulous. Where did the vinegar come from? Nepos has left a short memoir of Hannibal, but says nothing about the vinegar. (Livy, 59 BC to AD 17; Nepos about the same time; Hannibal, 247–183 BC).

***The Vinegar Bible.*** *See* Bible, Specially named.

**Vineyard Controversy.** A paper war provoked by the Hon. Daines Barrington (1727–1800), a well known lawyer, naturalist, and antiquary, who entered the lists to overthrow all chroniclers and antiquaries from William of Malmesbury to Samuel Pegge, respecting the vineyards of Domesday Book. He maintained that the vines were currants, and the vineyards currant gardens.

**Vinland.** The name given in the old Norse Sagas to a portion of the coast of North America discovered by wanderers from Denmark or Iceland about the opening of the 11th century. The tradition seems to have a solid foundation; the land touched at was probably New Jersey, and got its old name because of some small grapevines found growing there.

**Vino. *In vino veritas*** (Lat.). In wine is truth, meaning when persons are more or less intoxicated they utter many things they would at other times conceal or disguise.

**Vintry Ward** (London). So called from the site occupied by the *Vintners* or wine-merchants from Bordeaux, who anciently settled on this part of the Thames bank. They landed their wines here, and, till the 28th Edw. I, were obliged to sell what they landed within forty days.

**Vinum Theologicum.** An old term for the best wine obtainable. Holinshed (i, 282) says it was so called because religious men would be sure 'neither to drinke nor be served of the worst, or such as was anie waies vined by the vintner; naie, the merchant would have thought that his soule would have gone streightwaie to the devil if he would have served them with other than the best'.

**Violet.** A flower, nowadays usually taken as the type of modesty, but fabled by the ancients to have sprung from the blood of the boaster Ajax.

> As when stern Ajax poured a purple flood,
> The violet rose, fair daughter of his blood.
> Young, *The Instalment*

The colour indicates the *love of truth* and the *truth of love*. For ecclesiastical and symbolical uses, *see* Colours.

In 'flower language' the violet is emblematical of *innocence*, and Ophelia says in *Hamlet* that the King, the Queen, and even Hamlet himself now he has killed Polonius, are unworthy of this symbol.

***Corporal Violet.*** Napoleon Bonaparte; because when banished to Elba he told his friends he would return with the violets. 'Corporal Violet' became a favourite toast of his partisans, and when he reached Fréjus a gang of women assembled with violets, which were freely sold. The shibboleth was, 'Do you like violets?' If the answer given was '*Oui*', the person was known not to be a confederate; but if the answer was '*Eh bien*', the respondent was recognised as an adherent.

***The Violet-crowned City.*** *See* City.

***The violet on the tyrant's grave*** (Tennyson, *Aylmer's Field*). The reference is to Nero. It is said that some unknown hand went by night and strewed violets over his grave. Even Nero had one who loved him, and we are told that at his death his statues were 'crowned with garlands of flowers'.

**Violin.** *See* Amati; Cremona; Strad; Fiddle.

**Viper and File.** The biter bit. Aesop says a viper found a file, and tried to bite it, under the supposition that it was good food; but the file said that its province was to bite others, and not to be bitten.

> I fawned and smiled to plunder and betray,
> Myself betrayed and plundered all the while;
> So gnawed the viper the corroding file.
>
> Beattie, *Minstrel*

**Viraj.** *See* Menu.

**Virgate.** An early English measure of land; equal, sometimes to a quarter of a hide (i.e. about 30 acres), and sometimes to a quarter of an acre. So called from Lat. *virga*, a measuring rod.

**Virgil.** The greatest poet of ancient Rome, Publius Virgilius Maro (70–19 BC), born near Mantua (hence called *The Mantuan Swan*), a master of epic, didactic, and idyllic poetry. His chief works are the *Aeneid*, the *Eclogues* or *Bucolics*, and the *Georgics*. From the *Aeneid* grammarians illustrated their rules and rhetoricians selected the subjects of their declamations; and even Christians looked on the poet as half inspired; hence the use of his poems in divination. *See* Sortes.

In the Middle Ages Virgil came to be represented as a magician and enchanter, and it is this traditional character that furnishes Dante with his conception of making Virgil, as the personification of human wisdom, his guide through the infernal regions.

Virgil was wise, and as craft was considered a part of wisdom, especially over-reaching the spirits of evil, so he is represented by mediaeval writers as outwitting the demon. On one occasion, the legend says, he saw an imp in a hole of a mountain, and the imp promised to teach the poet the black art if he released him. Virgil did so, and after learning all the imp could teach him, expressed amazement that one of such imposing stature could be squeezed into so small a rift. The imp said, 'Oh, that is not wonderful', and crept into the hole to show Virgil how it was done, whereupon Virgil closed up the hole and kept the imp there. This tale is almost identical with that of the *Fisherman and the Genie* in the *Arabian Nights*, and most of the mediaeval stories that have crystallised round the name of the great Roman poet (*see*, for instance, those in the *Gesta Romanorum*) have a strong Oriental colouring.

***The Christian Virgil.*** Marco Girolamo Vida (d.1566), an Italian Latin poet, author of *Christias* in six books (1535), an imitation of the *Aeneid*.

***The Virgil and Horace of the Christians.*** So Bentley calls Aurelius Clemens Prudentius (fl. about AD 400). He was a native of Spain, and the author of several Latin hymns and religious poems.

**Virgin.** One of the ancient constellations (*Virgo*), and a sign of the Zodiac (Aug. 23rd to Sept. 23rd). The constellation is the metamorphosisation of Astraea (*q.v.*), goddess of justice, who was the last of the deities to quit our earth. *See* Icarius.

> When the bright Virgin gives the beauteous days.
>
> Thomson, *Autumn*

The word *virgin* is used as a prefix denoting that the article has never been used, tried, or brought into cultivation; as *paper of virgin whiteness*, paper that is unwritten, or unprinted, upon, a *virgin fortress*, one that has never been captured; a *virgin forest*, one that man has never attempted to tame or make use of.

***The Virgin Mary's Bodyguard.*** The name given to the old Scottish guard in France, organised in 1448 by Charles VII, because – it is said – Louis XI nominated the Blessed Virgin their colonel; also to the 7th Dragoon Guards, because in the time of George II they served under Maria Theresa of Austria.

***The Virgin Queen.*** Queen Elizabeth; also called (by Shakespeare) 'the fair Vestal'.

**Virginal.** A musical instrument of the 16th and 17th centuries, also called *a pair of virginals*. It has been suggested that it was so called because it was used in convents to lead the *virginals* or hymns to the Virgin, but it is more probable that it was simply because it was adapted to the use of young girls. It was a quilled keyboard instrument of two or three octaves.

**Virgo.** *See* Virgin.

**Virtues, The Seven.** Faith, Hope, Charity, Prudence, Justice, Fortitude, and Temperance. The first three are called the *supernatural*, *theological*, or *Christian* virtues; the remaining four are Plato's *Cardinal* virtues. *Cp.* Seven Deadly Sins.

**Vis inertiae** (Lat., the power of inactivity). That property of matter which makes it resist any change. Thus it is hard to set in motion what is still, or to stop what is in motion. Figuratively, it applies to that unwillingness of change which makes men 'rather bear the ills they have than fly to others they know not of'.

**Viscount.** A peer ranking next below an Earl (a *Vice-count*, or *Earl*) and above a Baron. As the Earl was often at Court he had to have a deputy, or *Vice*, to look after his affairs in his county, and in 1439 the title became a degree of honour and was made hereditary, the first Viscount in the modern sense being John, Lord Beaumont.

The *Coronet* of a Viscount bears 16 silver balls, and he is styled by the Sovereign 'Our right trusty and well-beloved Cousin'.

**Vishnu.** The Preserver; the second member of the Hindu trinity (*see* Trimurti), though worshipped by many Hindus as the supreme deity. He has had 9 incarnations, or *Avatars* (*q.v.*), and there is one – Kalki – still to come, during which Vishnu will at the end of four ages destroy sin, the sinful, and all the enemies of the world. He is usually represented as four-armed and carrying a club, a shell, a discus, and a lotus; a bow and sword are slung at his side, and on his breast is a peculiar mark called the *Shrivatsa*. He has millions of worshippers, especially under his Avatars as Rama and Krishna.

**Vitex.** The Latin name of the *Agnus Castus*, or *chaste tree*. In the language of flowers it means 'insensibility to love'. Dioscorides, Pliny, and Galen mention the plant, and say that the Athenian ladies, at the feast of Ceres, used to strew their couches with the leaves of *vitex* as a palladium of chastity. In France a beverage is made of them by distillation, and is (or was at one time) given to novitiates to wean their hearts from earthly affections. *Vitex*, from *vieo*, to bind with twigs; so called from the flexible nature of the twigs.

**Vitus, St.** A Sicilian youth who was martyred with Modestus, his tutor, and Crescentia, his nurse, during the Diocletian persecution, 303. All three are commemorated on June 15th.

***St Vitus's Dance.*** In Germany it was believed in the 16th century that good health for a year could be secured by anyone who danced before a statue of St Vitus on his feast day; this dancing developed almost into a mania, and came to be confused with chorea, which was subsequently known as *St Vitus's dance*, the saint being invoked against it.

**Viva**! An exclamation of applause or joy; Italian, meaning (long) live.

**Viva voce** (Latin, with the living voice). Orally; by word of mouth. A *viva voce* examination is one in which the respondent answers by word of mouth.

**Vivat rex!** (Lat.). Long live the King!

**Vivien.** An enchantress of the Arthurian romances, called also *Nimuë* and, because she lived in a palace in the middle of a magic lake, *The Lady of the Lake*. It was here that she brought up Launcelot, hence called *Launcelot of the Lake*.

She was Merlin's mistress, and at last caused his downfall by entrapping him in a hawthorn bush from which it was impossible for her to release him or for him to free himself.

In Tennyson's *Idylls* she appears as a wily wanton who 'hated all the knights'. She tried to seduce 'the blameless king', and did seduce Merlin, who, 'overtalked and overworn, told her his secret charm – '

Having obtained this secret, the wanton 'put forth the charm', and in the hollow oak lay Merlin as one dead, 'lost to life, and use and name, and fame'.

**Vixen** (A.S. *fyxen*). A female fox. Metaphorically, a shrewish woman, one of villainous and ungovernable temper.

**Vixere. *Vixere fortes ante Agamemnona*.** *See* Agamemnon.

**Viz.** A contraction of Lat. *videlicet*, meaning *namely*, *to wit*. The *z* represents ʒ, a common mark of contraction in the Middle Ages; as habʒ– *habet*, omnibʒ – *omnibus*.

**Vogue.** A French word. 'In vogue' means in repute, in the fashion. The verb *voguer* means to sail or move forwards. Hence the idea of sailing with the tide.

***Vogue la galère*** (Fr., lit. row the galley). Let the world go how it will; let us keep on, whatever happens; *arrive qui pourra*.

**Volapük.** A language intended for universal use, invented about 1879 by Johann Schleyer, a

German priest of Konstanz, Baden. So called from two of his manufactured words, *vol*, the world, *pük*, speech.

**Vole** (Fr. *voler*, to fly). *He has gone the vole*. He has been everything by turns. *Vole* is a deal at cards that draws the whole tricks. *To vole* is to win all the tricks.

> Who is he [Edie Ochiltree]? Why, he has gone the vole – has been soldier, ballad-singer, travelling tinker, and now a beggar.
>
> Scott, *The Antiquary*, ch. iv

**Voltaic Battery.** An apparatus for accumulating electricity. So called from the Italian physicist, Alessandro Volta (1745–1827), who first contrived it.

**Voltaire.** The assumed name of François Marie Arouet (1694–1778), the great French philosopher, poet, dramatist, and author, who, though an infidel, built the church at Ferney which has this inscription: *Deo erexit Voltaire*. Cowper alludes to this anomaly in the following lines:

> Nor his who, for the bane of thousands born,
> Built God a church, and laughed His Word to scorn *Retirement*, 687

Young said of him:

> Thou art so witty, profligate and thin,
> Thou seem'st a Milton, with his Death and Sin.

The name *Voltaire* is simply an anagram of Arouet L. I. (*le jeune*).

**Volume.** The *word* shows the ancestry of the *thing*; for it comes from Lat. *volvere*, to roll, and anciently books were written on sheets fastened together lengthwise and *rolled* on a pin or roller.

**Volund.** *See* Wayland.

**Voodoo,** or **Voodooism.** A degraded system of magic and witchcraft which includes snake-worship and, in its extreme forms, human sacrifices and cannibalism, said to be a relic of African barbarism and still practised by Creoles and negroes in Haiti and other parts of the West Indies and Southern American States.

The name is thought to have been first given to it by missionaries from Fr. *Vaudois*, a Waldensian, as these were accused of sorcery; but Sir Richard Burton derived it from *vodun*, a dialect form of Ashanti *obōsum*, a fetish or tutelary spirit.

**Votive Offerings.** *See* Anathema.

**Vox et praeterea nihil** (Lat. A voice, and nothing more). Empty words – 'full of sound and fury, signifying nothing'; a threat not followed out. When the Lacedemonian plucked the nightingale, on seeing so little substance he exclaimed, *Vox tu es, et nihil praeterea*. (Plutarch, *Apophthegmata Laconica*.)

**Vox populi vox Dei** (Lat. The voice of the people is the voice of God). This does not mean that the voice of the many is wise and good, but only that it is irresistible. You might as well try to stop the tide of the Atlantic as to resist the *vox populi*. After Edward II had been dethroned by the people in favour of his son (Edward III), Simon Mepham, Archbishop of Canterbury, preached from these words as his text.

**Vulcan.** A son of Jupiter and Juno, and god of fire, and the working of metals, and patron of handicraftsmen in *Roman mythology*, identified with the Gr. Hephaestus, and called also Mulciber, i.e. the softener.

His workshop was on Mount Etna, where the Cyclops assisted him in forging thunderbolts for Jove. It is said that he took the part of Juno against Jupiter, and Jupiter hurled him out of heaven. He was nine days in falling, and at last was picked up, half dead and with one leg broken, by the fishermen of the island of Lemnos. It was he who, with the stroke of an axe, delivered Minerva from the head of Jupiter; and he was the author of Pandora and the golden dogs of Alcinous, as he had the power of conferring life upon his creations. Venus was his wife, and in consequence of her amour with Mars he came to be regarded as the special patron of cuckolds.

**Vulcanist.** One who supports the Vulcanian or Plutonian theory, which ascribes the changes on the earth's surface to the agency of fire. These theorists say the earth was once in a state of igneous fusion, and that the crust has gradually cooled down to its present temperature. *Cp.* Neptunian.

**Vulgate, The.** The Latin translation of the Bible, made about 385–405 by St Jerome (*q.v.*), still used, with some modifications, as the authorised version by Roman Catholics.

**VXL.** A punning monogram on lockets, etc., standing for U XL (you excel). U and V were formerly interchangeable.

# W

**W.** The twenty-third letter of the English alphabet. The form is simply a ligature of two V's (VV); hence the name; for V was formerly the symbol of U (*q.v.*) as well as of V.

**Waac.** The familiar name of a member of the *W*omen's *A*rmy *A*uxiliary *C*orps, a body of women raised for non-combatant army service during the Great War. Many of these acrostic names came into use. *Cp.* **Anzac**: **Wrens**: **Wrafs**.

**Wabung Annung,** in *North American Indian mythology*, is the Morning Star. She was a country maiden wooed and won by Wabun, the Indian Apollo, who transplanted her to the skies. (Longfellow, *Hiawatha.*)

**Wade.** ***General Wade.*** The old rhyme –

> Had you seen but these roads before they were made,
> You would hold up your hands and bless General Wade,

refers to the Field-Marshal George Wade (1673–1748), famous for his military highways in the Highlands, which proceed in a straight line up and down hill like a Roman road, and were made about 1726–33.

***Wade's boat.***

> They can so mochë craft of Wadës boot,
> So mochë broken harm whan that hem list,
> That with hem schuld I never lyv in rest.
>
> Chaucer, *Merchant's Tale*, 180

Wade was a hero of mediaeval romance, whose adventures were a favourite theme in the 16th century. His famous boat was named *Guingelot*.

**Wadham College** (Oxford) was founded by a bequest from Nicholas Wadham (1532–1609) in 1613.

**Wage-slave.** The name by which any employee or person who works for wages is described by communists and extreme labour men.

**Wager.** Anything staked or hazarded on the event of a contest, etc. Connected with *gage* and *wage* (low Lat. *wadiare*, to pledge).

***Wager of battle.*** The decision of a contested claim by single combat – a common and legal method in Anglo-Saxon and early Norman times.

**Waggoner.** An old sailors' name for a book of sea-charts, Dalrymple's Charts being known as the *English Waggoner*. A corruption of Lukas *Waganaar*, a Dutch geographer whose charts were in use for long after their first appearance in the 16th century.

***Wagoner.*** *See* **Bootes**.

**Wahabites.** A Mohammedan sect, whose object is to bring back the doctrines and observances of Islam to the literal precepts of the *Koran*; so called from the founder, Ibn-abd-ul-Wahab (d.1787).

**Wainamoinen.** The hero of the Kalevala (*q.v.*).

**Waiters upon Providence.** Those who cling to the prosperous, but fall away from decaying fortunes.

> The side of the Puritans was deserted at this period by a numerous class of ... prudential persons, who never forsook them till they became unfortunate. These sagacious personages were called ... waiters upon Providence, and deemed it a high delinquency towards heaven to afford countenance to any cause longer than it was favoured by fortune.
>
> Scott, *Peveril of the Peak*, ch. iv

**Waiting.** ***Lords in Waiting, Gentlemen in Waiting, Grooms in Waiting,*** etc., are highly-placed functionaries in the Royal Household for personal attendance upon the King, the Prince of Wales, etc.

***Ladies in waiting*** (in the Queen's Household) are officially styled *Ladies of the Bedchamber*, *Bedchamber Women*, and *Maids of Honour*.

**Waits.** Street musicians, who serenade the principal inhabitants at Christmas-time, especially on Christmas Eve. From Rymer's *Foedera* we learn it was the duty of musical watchmen 'to pipe the watch' nightly in the king's court four times from Michaelmas to Shrove Thursday, and three times in the summer; and they had also to make 'the bon gate' at every door, to secure them against 'pyckeres and pillers'. They form a distinct class from both the watch and the minstrels. Oboes were at one time called 'waits'.

**Wake.** The feast of the dedication of a church, which was formerly kept by watching all night; also the merrymaking held in connection with this, hence merrymaking generally, a spree.

In Ireland the term denotes the watching of a dead body before the funeral by the friends and neighbours of the deceased, in which the lamentations were often followed by an orgy.

***Waking a witch.*** If a witch were obdurate, the most effectual way of obtaining a confession was by what was termed *waking* her. An iron bridle or hoop was bound across her face with prongs thrust into her mouth: this was fastened to the wall by a chain in such a manner that the victim was unable to lie down; and men were constantly by to keep her awake, sometimes for several days.

**Walcheren Expedition, The.** A disastrous undertaking during the French wars (1809) which, largely owing to the dilatoriness of the leaders, and to an outbreak of fever during which 7,000 British soldiers died, effected nothing, except the capture of Flushing. Lord Chatham and Sir Richard Strachan had been sent to the island of Walcheren to destroy the French fleet in the Scheldt and take Antwerp. The incident is commemorated in the following contemporary epigram:

Lord Chatham, with his sword undrawn,
Is waiting for Sir Richard Strachan;
Sir Richard, longing to be at 'em,
Is waiting for the Earl of Chatham.

**Waldemar's Way.** So the Milky Way is called in Denmark, the allusion being to Waldemar the Victorious, who substituted the Danebrog (*q.v.*) for the older banner of Denmark.

**Waldensians** or **Waldenses** (also called the *Vaudois*). Followers of Peter Waldo of Lyons, who began a reform movement in the Church about 1170. They threw off the authority of the Pope, bishops, and all clergy, appointed lay-preachers (women among them), rejected infant baptism and many other rites, and made themselves so obnoxious to the ecclesiastical powers that they met with considerable persecution. This they survived, and their descendants in doctrine still exist, principally in the Alpine valleys of Dauphiné, Provence, and Piedmont.

**Wales.** The older form is *Wealhas* (plural of *Wealh*), an Anglo-Saxon word denoting foreigners, and applied by them to the ancient Britons; hence, also, *Corn-wall*, the horn occupied by the same 'refugees'. The Welsh proper are *Cimbri*, and call their country Cymru; those driven thither by the Teutonic invaders were refugees or strangers. *Cp.* Walnut.

***The Prince of Wales.*** The popular story is that the title arose thus: When Edward I subdued Wales, he promised the Welsh, if they would lay down their arms, that he would give them a native prince who could not speak a word of English. His queen (Eleanor) having given birth to a son in Wales, the new-born child was entitled Edward, Prince of Wales; and ever since then the eldest son of the British sovereign has retained the title.

The facts, however, are that Edward I obtained the submission of the Welsh in 1276; his eldest son, afterwards Edward II, was born at Carnarvon in 1284, and it was not till 1301 that he was created Prince of Wales.

The male Heir Apparent is born *Duke of Cornwall*, but is not *Prince of Wales* until this title is conferred upon him, which it usually is. At death, or succession to the Throne, it lapses to the Crown and can only be renewed at the Sovereign's pleasure. Thus, when Edward VII became King his son did not become Prince of Wales; the title was conferred on him eight months later.

***The Prince of Wales's feathers.*** The tradition is, that the Black Prince, having slain John of Luxemburg, King of Bohemia, in the Battle of Cressy, assumed his crest and motto. The crest consisted of three ostrich feathers, and the motto was *Ich dien* (I serve). Much controversy has arisen on the question; the crest, for instance, has been stated to be a rebus of Queen Philippa's hereditary title – viz. Countess of *Ostre-vant* (ostrich-feather), and the motto a corruption of Welsh *Eich dyn*, behold the man. *See* Ich Dien.

It should be noted that *Prince of Wales's feathers* is technically a misnomer, for the plume does not belong to him *as* Prince of Wales, but is the badge of the Heir Apparent, whether he holds that title or not.

**Walhalla.** *See* Valhalla.

**Walk.** This is a remarkable word. It comes from the A.S. *wealcan*, to roll; whence we get *wealcere*, a fuller of cloth. In Percy's *Reliques* we read:

She cursed the weaver and the walker,
The cloth that they had wrought.

***A walk-over.*** A very easy victory; as in a running match when one's rivals could be beaten by walking.

***To make a man walk Spanish.*** To give him the sack; to give him his discharge.

***To walk into.*** To thrash, abuse, or 'make a mess of' a man; also, to partake heartily of, as 'to walk into an apple tart'.

***To walk off with.*** To steal and decamp with.

***To walk out with.*** A phrase used among servant-girls and the lower middle classes to denote a state of things approximately amounting to an engagement to marry. If a young man *walks out* with a girl her relations – and usually herself – quite expect a wedding will follow.

In America a workman's strike is called a *walk out*.

**To walk the chalk.** An ordeal used at police stations, in barracks, on board ship, etc., as a test of drunkenness. Two parallel lines are chalked on the floor and the delinquent must walk between them without stepping on either.

**To walk the hospitals.** To attend the hospitals as a medical student.

**To walk the plank.** *See* Plank.

**To walk through one's part.** To repeat one's part at rehearsal verbally, but without dressing for it or acting it; to do anything appointed you in a listless, indifferent manner.

> A fit of dulness, such as will at times creep over all the professors of the fine arts, arising either from fatigue or contempt of the present audience, or that caprice which tempts painters, musicians, and great actors ... to walk through their parts, instead of exerting themselves with the energy which acquired their fame. Scott, *Redgauntlet*, ch. xix

**Walk not in the public ways.** The fifth symbol of the *Protreptics* of Iamblichus, meaning follow not the multitude in their evil ways; or, wide is the path of sin and narrow the path of virtue, few being those who find it. The 'public way' is the way of the public or multitude, but the way of virtue is *personal* and separate. The arcana of Pythagoras were not for the common people, but only for his chosen or elect disciples.

> Broad is the way that leadeth to destruction.
>
> Matt. 7:13

**Walker. Hookey Walker!** A derisive exclamation meaning *Nonsense! Incredible!* used when hearing a 'tall story' or some statement that cannot be trusted. The legend is that John Walker was an outdoor clerk at Longman, Clementi and Co.'s, Cheapside, and was noted for his eagle nose, which gained him the nickname of *Old Hookey*. His office was to keep the workmen to their work, or report them to the principals. Of course it was the interest of the employees to throw discredit on Walker's reports, and the poor old man was so badgered and ridiculed that the firm found it politic to abolish the office.

**To go by Walker's bus.** To walk. Similar expressions are, 'To go by the Marrowbone stage', 'To ride Shanks's pony'.

**Walking Gentleman.** An actor who has little or nothing to say, but is expected to deport himself as a gentleman when before the lights. Similarly, *Walking lady*.

**Walkyries.** *See* Valkyries.

**Wall. To give the wall.** To allow another, as a matter of courtesy, to pass by on the pavement at the side farthest from the gutter; hence, to be courteous. At one time pedestrians *gave the wall* to persons of a higher grade in society than themselves.

Nathaniel Bailey's explanation of this phrase (1721) is worth perpetuating. He says it is –

> a compliment paid to the female sex, or those to whom one would show respect, by letting them go nearest the wall or houses, upon a supposition of its being the cleanest. This custom is chiefly peculiar to England, for in most parts abroad they will give them the right hand, though at the same time they thrust them into the kennel.

**To go to the wall.** To be put on one side; to be shelved. This is in allusion to another phrase, *Laid by the wall* – i.e. dead but not buried; put out of the way.

**To hang by the wall.** To hang up neglected; not to be made use of (Shakespeare, *Cymbeline*, 3, 4).

**To take the wall.** To take the place of honour, to choose 'the uppermost rooms at feasts' (Matt. 23:6).

> I will take the wall of any man or maid of Montague's.
>
> Shakespeare, *Romeo and Juliet*, 1, 1

**Walls have ears.** Things uttered in secret get rumoured abroad; there are listeners everywhere, and you'd better be careful. 'A bird of the air shall carry the voice' (Eccles. 10:20).

The Louvre was so constructed in the time of Catherine de Medicis, that what was said in one room could be distinctly heard in another. It was by this contrivance that the suspicious queen became acquainted with state secrets and plots. The tubes of communication were called the *auriculaires*. *Cp.* Dionysius's Ear *under* Ear.

**Wall, The Roman,** from the Tyne to Boulness, on the Solway Firth, a distance of 80 miles. Called –

> *The Roman Wall*, because it was the work of the Romans.
>
> *Agricola's Wall*, because Agricola made the south bank and ditch.
>
> *Hadrian's Wall*, because Hadrian added another vallum and mound parallel to Agricola's.
>
> *The Wall of Severus*, because Severus followed in the same line with a stone wall, having castles and turrets.
>
> *The Picts' Wall*, because its object was to prevent the incursions of the Picts.

**The Wall of Antoninus,** now called *Graeme's Dyke*, from Dunglass Castle on the Clyde to

Blackness Castle on the Forth, was made by Lollius Urbicus, legate of Antoninus Pius, AD 140. It was a turf wall.

**Wall-eyed.** The M.E. *wald-eyed*, a corruption of Icel. *vald eygthr*, having a beam in the eye (*vagl*, beam). Persons are wall-eyed when the white is unusually large, and the sight defective, due to opacity of the cornea, or strabismus. Shakespeare has *wall-eyed wrath or staring rage* (King John, 4, 3).

**Wallaby.** A small Australian kangaroo.

***On the wallaby,*** or ***on the wallaby track.*** On the tramp – usually because out of work.

**Wallace's Larder.** *See* Larder.

**Wallah.** Anglo-Indian for one who does something, as *Competition wallah*, the old nickname for a successful competitor in the Indian Civil Service exams., *bathroom wallah*, the man who looks after the bathrooms in an hotel, etc.

**Wallflower.** So called because it grows on old walls and ruined buildings. It is a native plant. Similarly, *wall cress*, *wall creeper*, etc., are plants which grow on dry, stony places, or on walls. *Wall fruit* is fruit trained against a wall. *Cp.* Walnut.

Herrick has a pretty fancy on the origin of this flower. A fair damsel was long kept in durance vile from her lover; but at last

> Up she got upon a wall
> 'Tempting down to slide withal;
> But the silken twist untied,
> So she fell, and, bruised, she died.
>
> Love, in pity of the deed,
> And her loving luckless speed,
> Turned her to this plant we call
> Now the 'Flower of the wall'.

Young ladies who sit out against the wall, not having partners during a dance, are called 'wallflowers'.

**Walloons.** A people of mixed Italic, Teutonic, and Celtic stock descended from the Belgae of ancient Gaul. They occupied the low track along the frontiers of the German-speaking territory, as Artois, Hainault, Namur, Liege, Luxemburg, with parts of Flanders and Brabant.

**Wallop.** To thrash; properly, to boil with a noisy bubbling sound. The word is the same as *gallop*; but fable derives it from a supposed Sir John Wallop, who, it is said, was sent in the reign of Henry VIII to Normandy to make reprisals, because the French fleet had burnt Brighton. Sir John burnt twenty-one towns and villages, demolished several harbours, and, in a word, *walloped* the foe to his heart's content.

**Walnut.** The foreign nut; called in M.E. *walnote*, from A.S. *wealh*, foreign. It came from Persia, and was so called to distinguish it from nuts native to Europe, as hazel, filbert, chestnut.

> Some difficulty there is in cracking the name thereof. Why walnuts, having no affinity to a wall, should be so called. The truth is, *gual* or *wall* in the old Dutch signifieth 'strange' or 'exotic' (whence *Welsh* foreigners); these nuts being no natives of England or Europe.
>
> Fuller, *Worthies of England*

It is said that the walnut tree thrives best if the nuts are beaten off with sticks, and not gathered. Hence Fuller says, 'Who, like a nut tree, must be manured by beating, or else would not bear fruit' (Bk ii, ch. 11). The saying is well known that –

> A woman, a dog, and a walnut tree.
> The more you beat them the better they be.

**Walpurgis Night.** The eve of May Day, when the witch-world was supposed to hold high revelry under its chief on certain high places, particularly the Brocken, in Germany.

Walpurgis was an English nun concerned in the introduction of Christianity into Germany. She died Feb. 25th, 779.

> He changed hands, and whisked and rioted like a dance of Walpurgis in his lonely brain.
>
> J. S. Le Fanu, *The House in the Churchyard*

**Walstan, St.** The patron saint in England of husbandmen. He was a rich Briton who gave up all his wealth, and supported himself by husbandry. He died mowing in 1016, and is usually depicted with a scythe in his hand, and cattle in the background.

**Watham Blacks.** *See* Black Act.

**Wand.** The long, slender rod used by magicians and conjurers; also by certain court functionaries as a staff of office, and by musical conductors as a baton.

In *Jerusalem Delivered* the Hermit gives Charles the Dane and Ubaldo a wand which, being shaken, infused terror into all who saw it; and in the *Faërie Queene*, the palmer who accompanies Sir Guyon has a wand of like virtue, made of the same wood as Mercury's caduceus.

**Wandering Jew, The.** The central figure of a very widespread mediaeval legend which tells how a Jew who refused to allow Christ to rest at his door while He was bearing his cross to Calvary, was condemned to wander over the face of the earth till the end of the world. The usual form of the legend says that he was Ahasuerus, a cobbler. The craftsman pushed him away, saying, 'Get off! Away with you, away!' Our

Lord replied, 'Truly I go away, and that quickly, but tarry thou till I come.'

Another tradition has it that the Wandering Jew was Kartaphilos, the door-keeper of the judgment hall in the service of Pontius Pilate. He struck our Lord as he led Him forth, saying, 'Go on faster, Jesus'; whereupon the Man of Sorrows replied, 'I am going, but thou shalt tarry till I come again' (*Chronicle of St Albans Abbey*; 1228).

The same *Chronicle*, continued by Matthew Paris, tells us that Kartaphilos was baptised by Ananias , and received the name of Joseph. At the end of every hundred years he falls into a trance, and wakes up a young man about thirty.

In German legend he is associated with John Buttadaeus, seen at Antwerp in the 13th century, again in the 15th, and a third time in the 16th. His last appearance was in 1774 at Brussels. In the French version he is named Isaac Laquedem, or Lakedion; another story has it that he was Salathiel ben Sadi, who appeared and disappeared towards the close of the 16th century, at Venice, in so sudden a manner as to attract the notice of all Europe; and another connects him with the Wild Huntsman (*q.v.*).

**Wandering Wood.** The wood in Bk i of Spenser's *Faërie Queene*, in which the Red Cross Knight and Una stray. Una tries to persuade him to leave the wood, but he is self-willed. Error, in the form of a serpent, attacks him, but the knight severs her head from her body. The idea is that when Piety will not listen to Una or Truth, it is sure to get into 'Wandering Wood', where Error will attack it; but if it then listens to Truth it will slay Error.

**Wangle.** To achieve some object by sly, roundabout, or underhand methods; to cook accounts (for instance), to manipulate. The word came into wide use during the Great War, but it was well known slang among printers from very early times.

**Wanion.** ***With a wanion***. An old imprecation; the word is pres. part of *wanion*, to wane, and meant misfortune, ill-luck.

> Look how thou stirrest now! come away, or I'll fetch thee with a wannion.
>
> Shakespeare, *Pericles*, 2, 1

**Wantley, The Dragon of.** An old story, preserved in Percy's *Reliques*, tells of this monster, which was slain by More, of More Hall. He procured a suit of armour studded with spikes, and kicked the Dragon in the mouth, where alone it was vulnerable. Percy says the Dragon was an overgrown, rascally attorney, who cheated some children of their estate, and was made to disgorge by one named More, who went against him, 'armed with the spikes of the law', after which the attorney died of vexation. Wantley is Wharncliffe in Yorkshire.

**Wapentake.** A division of Yorkshire and certain East Anglian counties, similar to that better known as a *hundred*. The word means 'touch-arms' (A.S. *waepengetaecke*, from Icel. *vapn*, weapon, *taka*, to touch or take), it being the custom of each vassal, when he attended the assemblies of the district, 'to touch the spear of his over-lord in token of homage'.

**Wapinshaw.** The Scottish name for a meeting for rifle-shooting, curling, or similar sport. Formerly, the periodical review of clansmen under arms, a *weapon-show*.

**War.** ***A holy war.*** War undertaken from religious motives, such as the Crusades; or in defence of a religion.

***In full war-paint.*** In full dress, 'full fig'. The allusion is to the paint, etc., put on the body by North American Indian and other savages before going into battle.

***On the war-path.*** Looking for one's adversary with every intention of catching him; thoroughly roused or incensed.

***War-horse.*** Used figuratively of a veteran who is overflowing with warlike memories; a 'fire-eater'.

**Ward.** A district under the charge of a *warden*. The word is applied to the subdivisions of Cumberland, Westmorland, and Durham, which, being contiguous to Scotland, were placed under the charge of lord wardens of the marches, whose duty it was to protect these counties from inroads. *See* Hundred.

**Warden Pie.** Pie made of the Warden pear. Warden pears are said to be so called from Warden, in Bedfordshire, but it is quite likely that the word is merely O.Fr. *wardant*, keeping, because they are good keeping pears.

> Myself with denial I mortify
> With a dainty bit of a Warden-pie.
>
> *The Friar of Orders Grey*

**Warlock.** An evil spirit; a wizard. A.S. *waerloga*, a traitor, one who breaks his word. Satan is called in Scripture 'the father of lies', the arch-warlock.

**Warm.** Used in slang with much the same force as *hot* (*q.v.*), as a *warm member*, said of a man who 'goes the pace', of a sharper, or of one who is particularly notable in connection with whatever happens to be the subject of discussion. *Warm thanks*, are hearty thanks; *he's in a warm corner* means he's in an awkward position.

***A house-warming.*** An entertainment given by new occupiers of a house; a first welcoming of friends to a fresh residence.

**Warming-pan.** One who holds a place temporarily for another; used specially of a clergyman who officiates while the actual holder of the living is qualifying. In public schools it used to be the custom to make a fag warm his 'superior's' bed by lying in it till the proper occupant was ready to turn him out.

Jacobites used to be nicknamed *Warming-pans*, because of the legend that the 'Old Pretender' was a child who was introduced into the queen's lying-in room in a warming-pan, her own child having been still-born.

**Warp.** The threads running the long way of a woven fabric, crossed by the *woof*, i.e. those running from selvedge to selvedge. *Warp* (A.S. *wearp*) is connected with Icel. *varpa*, to throw; *woof* with A.S. *wef*, web.

Weave the warp and weave the woof,
The winding-sheet of Edward's race;
Give ample room and verge enough
The characters of hell to trace. Gray, *The Bard*

*To warp* is a nautical term, meaning to shift the position of a vessel, which is done by means of a rope called a *warp*. *Kedging* is when the warp is bent to a kedge, which is let go, and the vessel is hove ahead by the capstan.

The potent rod
Of Amram's son in Egypt's evil day,
Waved round the coast, up-called a pitchy cloud
Of locusts warping in the eastern wind.
Milton, *Paradise Lost*, i, 338

In Lancashire, *warping* means laying eggs; and boys, on finding a bird's nest, will ask – 'And how many eggs has she warped?'

**Warrior Queen, The.** Boadicea, Queen of the Iceni, an ancient tribe of Eastern Britain subjugated by the Romans in AD 62.

When the British warrior queen,
Bleeding from the Roman rods,
Sought, with an indignant mien,
Counsel of her country's gods ...
Cowper, *Boadicea*

The Iceni were the faithful allies of Rome; but, on the death of Prasutagus, king of that tribe, the Roman procurator took possession of his kingdom, and when his widow Boadicea complained, the procurator had her beaten with rods like a slave.

**Wash. *It will all come out in the wash.*** Everything will turn out all right in the end; or, it's no use trying to cover up your misdeeds – they will be discovered in due season. The phrase is Spanish, and occurs in *Don Quixote*.

***Quite washed out.*** Thoroughly exhausted, done up, with no strength or spirit left.

***That story won't wash!*** It won't do at all; you'll have to think of something better than *that*! Said of an excuse or explanation that is palpably false, far-fetched, or exaggerated.

***The great unwashed.*** *See* Unwashed.

***To wash a brick.*** To engage in an utterly unprofitable enterprise; to do useless work. An old Latin proverbial expression (*laterem lavem*, Terence's *Phormio*, I, iv, 9).

***To wash one's dirty linen in public.*** To expose the family skeletons to the public gaze; openly to discuss private affairs that are more or less discreditable to one. The French say the English do not follow the advice of washing their dirty linen *en famille* – meaning that they talk openly and freely of the faults committed by ministers, corporations, and individuals. Horace (*2 Ep.* i, 220) says, *Vineta egomet caedam mea,* I do my own washing at home. Though the French assert that we disregard this advice, we have the proverb, 'It is an ill bird that fouls its own nest'.

***To wash one's hands of.*** *See* Hand.

***A regular wash out.*** A complete disappointment (of things), as of a picnic ruined by the rain; an utter failure (of persons).

**Wassail.** A carouse, drinking bout, or other festive occasion.

The king doth wake tonight and takes his rouse,
Keeps wassail. Shakespeare, *Hamlet*, 1, 4

Formerly a salutation used specially at the New Year over the spiced ale cup, hence called the 'wassail bowl' (A.S. *Waes hael*, be whole, be well).

An old story has it that when Vortigern was invited to dine at the house of Hengist, Rowena, the daughter of the host, brought a cup of wine which she presented to their royal guest, saying, '*Was hael, hlaford cyning*' (Your health, lord king). Robert de Brunne (late 13th cent.) refers to this custom:

This is ther custom and hev gest
When they are at the ale or fest:
Ilk man that levis gware him drink
Salle say 'Wosseillë' to him drink;
He that biddis sall say 'Wassaile',
The tother salle say again 'Drinkaille'.

That says 'Woisseille' drinks of the cup,
Kiss and his felaw he gives it up.

Hence *wassailers*, those who join a wassail; revellers, drunkards.

I should be loath
To meet the rudeness and swilled insolence
Of such late wassailers. Milton, *Comus*

**Waster.** A good-for-nothing fellow; a prodigal, spendthrift.

**Wastrel.** Diminutive of *waster*; used specially in municipal politics of spendthrift councillors who waste the ratepayers' money.

**Wat.** An old name for a hare, short for *Walter*. *Cp. Tom* for a cat, *Neddy* for a donkey, *Jenny* wren, etc.

By this, poor Wat, far off upon a hill,
Stands on his hinder legs, with listening ear.
Shakespeare, *Venus and Adonis*

**Watch.** In nautical use, the time during which each division of a ship's crew is alternately on duty (four hours except during the *dog-watches* of two hours by which the change from night to day duty is arranged); also, either half (*starboard* or *port watch* from the position of the sailors' bunks in the forecastle) into which the officers and crew are divided, taking duty alternately. In the merchant service the *starboard watch* is called the *captain's watch*; this is usually under the command of the second mate, the *port watch* under that of the first mate.

| | | | | |
|---|---|---|---|---|
| 12 | to | 4 | p.m. | Afternoon watch. |
| 4 | to | 6 | | First dog-watch. |
| 6 | to | 8 | | Second dog-watch. |
| 8 | to | 12 | | First night watch. |
| 12 | to | 4 | a.m. | Middle watch. |
| 4 | to | 8 | | Morning watch. |
| 8 | to | 12 | | Forenoon watch. |

***The Black Watch.*** *See* Black.

***The Watch on the Rhine.*** The national anthem of the old German Empire, sharing the place of honour with *Deutschland über Alles* (Germany over all).

***Watch and ward.*** Continuous vigilance; guard by night (*watch*) and by day (*ward*). In feudal times service 'by watch and ward' was due by certain tenants in towns; later the term was applied to the constabulary.

***Watch Night.*** December 31st, to see the Old Year out and the New Year in by a religious service. John Wesley grafted it on the religious system, and it has been adopted by most Christian communities.

**Watchword.** A word given to sentries as a signal that one has the right of admission, a password; hence, a motto, word, or phrase symbolising or epitomising the principles of a party, etc.

**Water. *Blood thicker than water.*** *See* Blood.

***Court holy water.*** Fair but empty words. In French, *eau bénite de cour*.

***I am for all waters*** (*Twelfth Night*, 4, 2). I am a Jack of all trades, can turn my hand to anything, a good all-round man. Like a fish which can live in salt or fresh water.

***In deep water.*** In difficulties; in great perplexity; similarly, *in smooth water* means all is plain sailing, one's troubles and anxieties are things of the past.

***In low water.*** Hard up; in a state of financial (or other) depression.

***It makes my mouth water.*** It is very alluring; it makes me long for it. Saliva is excited in the mouth by strong desire. The French have the same phrase: *Cela fait venir l'eau à la bouche*.

***More water glideth by the mill than wots the miller of*** (*Titus Andronicus*, 2, 1). The Scotch say, 'Mickle water goes by the miller when he sleeps'. *See* Miller.

***Of the first water.*** Of the highest type; very excellent. *See* Diamond.

***Smooth,*** or ***still, waters run deep.*** Deep thinkers are persons of few words; silent conspirators are the most dangerous; barking dogs do not bite. There are two or three French proverbs of somewhat similar meaning: *En eau endormie point ne se fie*; again, *L'eau qui dort est pire que celle qui court*. A calm exterior is far more to be feared than a tongue-doughty Bobadil.

Smooth runs the water where the brook is deep;
And in his simple show he harbours treason.
The fox barks not when he would steal the lamb;
No, no, my sovereign, Gloucester is a man
Unsounded yet, and full of deep deceit.
Shakespeare, *2 Henry VI*, 3, 1

***That won't hold water.*** That is not correct; it is not tenable. It is a vessel which leaks.

***The Father of Waters.*** The Mississippi, the chief river of North America. The Missouri is its child. The Irrawaddy is so called also.

***The water of jealousy.*** If a woman was known to commit adultery she was to be stoned to death, according to the Mosaic law (Deut. 22:22). If, however, the husband had no proof, but only suspected his wife of infidelity, he might take her before the Sanhedrin to be examined, and if she denied it, she was given the 'water of jealousy' to drink (Numb. 5:11–29). In this water some of the dust of the sanctuary was mixed, and the priest said to the woman, 'If thou hast gone aside may Jehovah make this water bitter to thee, and bring on thee all the curses written in this law.' The priest then wrote on a roll the curses, blotted the writing with the water, gave it to the woman, and then handed to her the 'water of jealousy' to drink.

***To back water.*** To row backwards in order to reverse the forward motion of a boat in rowing; hence, to go easy, to retrace one's steps, to retract.

***To carry water to the river.*** To carry coals to Newcastle. In Fr. *Porter de l'eau à la rivière.*

***To fish in troubled waters.*** To seek to turn a state of disturbance to one's own advantage; to 'profiteer' during a time of war, to seize power during a revolution, and so on. The French say *Pêcher en eau troublé.*

***To get into hot water.*** *See* Hot.

***To keep one's head above water.*** *See* Head.

***To throw cold water on a scheme.*** To discourage the proposal; to speak of it slightingly.

***To turn on the waterworks.*** To cry, blubber.

***To water stock.*** To add extra shares. Suppose a 'trust' (*q.v.*) consists of 1,000 shares of £50 each, and the profit available for dividend is 40 per cent., the managers 'water the stock', that is, add another 1,000 fully paid-up shares to the original 1,000. There are now 2,000 shares, and the dividend, instead of £40 per cent., is reduced to £20; but the shares are more easily sold, and the shareholders are increased in number.

**Water-gall.** The dark rim round the eyes after much weeping. A peculiar appearance in a rainbow which indicates more rain at hand.

> And round about her tear-distained eye
> Blue circles streamed, like rainbows in the sky;
> These watergalls ... foretell new storms.
>
> Shakespeare, *Rape of Lucrece*

**Watermark, A.** Designs impressed into paper while in course of manufacture. Watermarks were employed as early as 1282, and served to identify the product of each paper mill, the designs chosen (many of them extremely complicated) frequently also expressing emblematically the tenets of the manufacturers. The art of papermaking was almost entirely in the hands of the Huguenots and previous Protestants (Albigenses, Waldenses, Cathari, etc.), and the *Bull's head*, for instance, was an emblem of the Albigenses.

The watermark has in many cases been the origin of paper-trade terminology; thus the mark of the *cap and bells* gave us *Foolscap*, the *Post-horn*, *Post*, the *Pot*, *Pott*, and so on – all sizes of paper.

**Water Poet.** John Taylor (1580–1654), the humorous and sometimes scurrilous Thames waterman who confessed he never learnt so much as the accidence, and yet wrote fourscore books and verse pamphlets. In his closing days he opened an ale-house in Long Acre.

> Taylor, their better Charon, lends an oar,
> Once swan of Thames, though now he sings no more.
>
> *Dunciad*, iii

**Water-sky.** The term used by Arctic navigators to denote a dark or brown sky, indicating an open sea. An *ice-sky* is a white one, or a sky tinted with orange or rose-colour, indicative of a frozen sea (*cp.* Ice-blink).

**Waterloo. *He met his Waterloo.*** He had a final and crushing defeat; in allusion, of course, to the decisive defeat inflicted on Napoleon by Wellington at Waterloo in 1815.

***The Waterloo Cup.*** The 'Derby' of the coursing fraternity; the great dog-race held annually at Altcar during three days in February.

It was founded by a man named Lynn, the sporting owner of the Waterloo Hotel in Liverpool (whence its name) in 1836. Lynn was also the founder of the Grand National, run at Aintree.

**Watling Street.** The great Roman road extending east and west across Britain. Beginning at Dover, it ran through Canterbury to London, through St Albans, Dunstable, along the boundary of Leicester and Warwick to Wroxeter on the Severn, and so to Chester and Cardigan. *Watling* is said to be a corruption of *Vitellina strata*, the paved road of Vitellius, called by the Britons Guetalin.

**Wave. *The tenth wave*.** A notion prevails that the waves keep increasing in regular series till the maximum arrives, and then the series begins again. No doubt when two waves coalesce they form a large one, but this does not occur at fixed intervals.

> At length, tumbling from the Gallic coast, the victorious tenth wave shall ride, like the boar, over all the rest
>
> Burke

The most common theory is that the *tenth* wave is the largest, but Tennyson says the *ninth.*

> And then the two
> Dropt to the cove, and watch'd the great sea fall,
> Wave after wave, each mightier than the last,
> Till last, a ninth one, gathering half the deep
> And full of voices, slowly rose and plunged

Roaring, and all the wave was in a flame.

*The Holy Grail*

**Wax.** Slang for temper, anger; *he's in an awful wax*, he's in a regular rage. Hence *waxy*, irritated, vexed, angry.

***A man of wax.*** A model man; like one fashioned in wax. Horace speaks of the 'waxen arms of Telephus', meaning model arms, or of perfect shape and colour; and the nurse says of Romeo, 'Why, he's a man of wax' (1, 3), which she explains by saying, 'Nay, he's a flower, i' faith a very flower'.

***A nose of wax.*** Mutable and accommodating (faith). A waxen nose may be twisted any way.

**Way. *The way of all flesh.*** Death.

***The Way of the Cross.*** A series of pictures in a church (*see* Stations of the Cross) representing Christ's progress to Calvary; also the devotions suited to them.

***Under way.*** Said of a ship in motion; it is a mistake to take this as 'under *weigh*', and connect it with weighing the anchor.

**Way-bit. *A Yorkshire way-bit.*** A large overplus. Ask a Yorkshireman the distance of any place, and he will reply so many miles and a way-bit (*wee-bit*); but the way-bit will prove a frightful length to the traveller who imagines it means only a *little* bit over. The Highlanders say, 'A mile and a *bittock*', which means about two miles.

**Wayland.** A wonderful and invisible smith of English legend, the English form of Scandinavian Völund, a supernatural smith and King of the Elves, a kind of Vulcan. He was bound apprentice to Mimi the smith. King Nidung cut the sinews of his feet, and cast him into prison, but he escaped in a feather boat. He and Amilias had a contest of skill in their handicraft. Wayland's sword, Balmung, cleft his rival down to the thighs, but it was so sharp that Amilias was not aware of the cut till he attempted to stir, when he divided into two pieces.

Scott introduces Wayland, or Wayland Smith, into Kenilworth (ch. xiii), where we are told that he lived in a cromlech near Lambourn, Berks, (since called *Wayland Smith's Cave*), and that if a traveller tied up his horse there, left sixpence for a fee, and retired from sight, he would find the horse shod on his return.

**Wayleave.** Right of way through private property for the laying of water-pipes and making of sewers, etc., provided that only the surface-soil is utilised by the proprietor.

**Ways and Means.** A parliamentary term, meaning the method of raising the supply of money for the current requirements of the state.

**Wayzgoose.** An annual dinner, picnic, or 'beanfeast' given to, or held by, those employed in a printing-house. *Wayz* is an obsolete word for stubble, and a *wayzgoose* a 'stubble goose', properly the crowning dish of the entertainment. *See* Beanfeast, St Martin's Goose.

**We.** Used of himself by a Sovereign, as representing his subjects, by the editor of a newspaper, as the public representative of a certain body of opinion, and by a writer of an unsigned article, as representing the journal for which he is writing.

Coke, in the *Institutes*, says the first king that wrote *we* in his grants was King John. All the kings before him wrote *ego* (I). This is not correct, as Richard *Lion-heart* adopted the royal 'We'. *See* Rymer's *Foedera*.

**Weal.** A prosperous or sound state of affairs; the A.S. *wela*, cognate with *well*. Hence, the *common weal*, or the *public weal*, the welfare or prosperity of the community at large.

**Weapon Salve.** A salve said to cure wounds by sympathy; applied not to the wound, but to the instrument which gave the wound. The direction 'Bind the wound and grease the nail' is still common. Sir Kenelm Digby says the salve is sympathetic, and quotes several instances to prove that 'as the sword is treated the wound inflicted by it feels. Thus, if the instrument is kept wet, the wound will feel cool; if held to the fire, it will feel hot'; etc.

But she has ta'en the broken lance,
And washed it from the clotted gore,
And salved the splinter o'er and o'er.

Scott, *Lay of the Last Minstrel*, iii, 23

**Weapon-schaw.** *See* Wapinshaw.

**Weasel.** Weasels suck eggs; hence Shakespeare:

The weasel Scot
Comes sneaking, and so sucks the princely egg.

*Henry V*, 1, 2

I can suck melancholy out of a song, as a weazel sucks eggs. *As You Like It*, 2, 5

***To catch a weasel asleep.*** To expect to find a very vigilant person nodding, off his guard; to suppose that one who has his weather-eye open cannot see what is passing before him. The French say, *Croir avoir trouvé la pie au nid* (To expect to find the pie on its nest). The vigilant habits of these animals explain the allusions.

**Weather. *A weather breeder.*** A day of unusual fineness coming suddenly after a series of damp dull ones, especially at the time of the year when such a genial day is not looked for. Such a day is generally followed by foul weather.

***Fair-weather friends.*** Those that stick to you as long as all is going well, but desert you as soon as storms gather round your head and you look as though you might 'go under'. They are all right as long as they last, but not the slightest use in an emergency.

***I have my weather-eye open.*** I have my wits about me; I know what I am after. The weather-eye is towards the wind to forecast the weather.

***The peasant's weather-glass.*** A local name for the scarlet pimpernel, which closes its petals at the approach of rain. It is also called *the poor man's warning*.

Closed is the pink-eyed pimpernel;
'Twill sorely rain; I see with sorrow.
Our jaunt most be put off tomorrow.
Dr Jenner

***To get the weather-gage of a person.*** To get the advantage over him. A ship is said to have the weather-gage of another when it has got to the windward thereof.

Were the line
Of Rokeby once combined with mine,
I gain the weather-gage of fate. Scott, *Rokeby*

***To keep the weather of.*** To get round, or get the better of. A phrase from the seaman's vocabulary.

Mine honour keeps the weather of my fate:
Life every man holds dear; but the dear man
Holds honour far more precious dear than life.
Shakespeare, *Troilus and Cressida*, 5, 3

***To make fair weather.*** To flatter, conciliate, make the best of things.

But I most make fair weather yet awhile,
Till Henry be more weak, and I more strong.
Shakespeare, *2 Henry VI*, 5, 1

**Weathercock.** By a Papal enactment made in the middle of the 9th century, the figure of a cock was set up on every church steeple as the emblem of St Peter. The emblem is in allusion to his denial of our Lord thrice before the cock crew twice. On the second crowing of the cock the warning of his Master flashed across his memory, and the repentant apostle 'went out and wept bitterly'.

A person who is always changing his mind is, figuratively, a *weathercock*.

Ther is no feith that may your herte embrace;
But, as a wedercock, that turneth his face
With every wind, ye fare.
Chaucer(?), *Balade Against Woman Unconstant*

**Web.** *See* Warp.

***The web of life.*** The destiny of an individual from the cradle to the grave. The allusion is to the three Fates who, according to *Roman mythology*, spin the thread of life, the pattern being the events which are to occur.

***Web and pin.*** An old name for cataract, or a disease of the eye caused by some excrescence on the ball.

This is the foul fiend Flibbertigibbet ... he gives the web and pin, squints the eye, and makes the hare-lip. Shakespeare, *King Lear*, 3, 4

**Wed** is Anglo-Saxon, and means a *pledge*. The ring is the pledge given by the man to avouch that he will perform his part of the contract.

**Wedding Anniversaries.** Fanciful names have been given to many wedding anniversaries, the popular idea being that they designate the nature of the gifts suitable for the occasion. The following list is fairly complete, and of these very few except the twenty-fifth and fiftieth are ever noticed.

| | |
|---|---|
| First | Cotton Wedding. |
| Second | Paper Wedding. |
| Third | Leather Wedding. |
| Fifth | Wooden Wedding. |
| Seventh | Woollen Wedding. |
| Tenth | Tin Wedding. |
| Twelfth | Silk and Fine Linen Wedding. |
| Fifteenth | Crystal Wedding. |
| Twentieth | China Wedding. |
| Twenty-fifth | Silver Wedding. |
| Thirtieth | Pearl Wedding. |
| Fortieth | Ruby Wedding. |
| Fiftieth | Golden Wedding. |
| Seventy-fifth | Diamond Wedding. |

The *sixtieth* anniversary is often reckoned the 'Diamond Wedding' in place of the *seventy-fifth*; as the *sixtieth* year of Queen Victoria's reign was her 'Diamond Jubilee'.

**Wedding Finger.** The fourth finger of the left hand. Macrobius says the thumb is too busy to be set apart, the forefinger and little finger are only half protected, the middle finger is called *medicus*, and is too opprobrious for the purpose of honour, so the only finger left is the *pronubus*.

Aulus Gellius tells us that Appianus asserts in his Egyptian books that a very delicate nerve runs from the fourth finger of the left hand to the heart, on which account this finger is used for the marriage ring.

The finger on which this ring [the wedding-ring] is to be worn is the fourth finger of the left hand, next unto the little finger; because by the received opinion of the learned ... in ripping up and anatomising men's bodies, there is a vein of

> blood, called *vena amoris*, which passeth from that finger to the heart.
>
> Henry Swinburne, *Treatise of Spousals* (1680)

In the Roman Catholic Church, the thumb and first two fingers represent the Trinity; thus the bridegroom says, 'In the name of the Father', and touches the thumb; 'in the name of the Son', and touches the first finger; and 'in the name of the Holy Ghost' he touches the long or second finger. The next finger is the husband's, to whom the woman owes allegiance next to God; it represents the *humanity* of Christ, and is used in matrimony, because this is so largely concerned with humanity. The *left* hand is chosen to show that the woman is to be subject to the man.

In the Hereford, York, and Salisbury missals, the ring is directed to be put first on the thumb, then on the first finger, then on the long finger, and lastly on the ring-finger, *quia in illo digito est quaedam vena procedens usque ad cor*.

**Wednesday.** Woden-es or Odin-es Day, called by the French 'Mercredi' (Mercury's Day). The Persians regard it as a 'red-letter day', because the moon was created on the fourth day (Gen. 1:14–19).

**Weeds.** The mourning worn by a widow; from A.S. *waede*, a garment. Spenser speaks of –

> A goodly lady clad in hunter's weed.
>
> *Faërie Queene* II, iii, 21

Shakespeare has –

> And there the snake throws her enamell'd skin,
> Weed wide enough to wrap a fairy in.
>
> *Midsummer Night's Dream*, 2, 1

And in *Timon of Athens* (1, 1) we get the modern meaning –

> Hail, Rome, victorious in thy mourning weeds!

**Week, Days of the.** It is curious that while we owe the names of all the *months* to Rome, those of the *days* are Anglo-Saxon.

> Sunday (A.S. *Sunnandaeg*), day of the sun.
> Monday (A.S. *Monandaeg*), day of the moon.
> Tuesday (A.S. *Tiwesdaeg*), from Tiw, the god of war.
> Wednesday (A.S. *Wodnesdaeg*) from Odin, the god of storms.
> Thursday (A.S. *Thunresdaeg*), day of Thor, the god of thunder.
> Friday (A.S. *Frigedaeg*), day of Freya, goddess of marriage.
> Saturday (A.S. *Saterdaeg*: Lat. *Dies Saturnus*), day of Saturn, the god of time.

***A week of Sundays.*** A long time; a quite indefinite period, but longer than was anticipated.

**Weepers.** Slang for a widow's weeds, and for the black sash-like band that men used to wear flowing from their silk hats at funerals.

**Weeping.** A notion long prevailed in this country that it augured ill for a matrimonial alliance if the bride did not weep profusely at the wedding.

As no witch could shed more than three tears, and those from her left eye only, a copious flow of tears gave assurance to the husband that the lady had not 'plighted her troth' to Satan, and was no witch.

***The Weeping Philosopher.*** Heraclitus (d. about 475 BC), so called because he grieved at the folly of man.

***The Weeping Saint.*** St Swithin (*q.v.*), because of the tradition of forty days' rain if it rains on July 15th.

***To go by Weeping Cross.*** To suffer and repent of one's misdeeds. There are said to have been crosses called thus at Oxford, Shrewsbury, and Stafford.

> The tyme will come when comming home by weeping crosse, thou shalt confesse, that it is better to be at home in the cave of an Hermit than abroad in the court of an Emperor.
>
> Lyly, *Euphues and his England* (1580)

**Weigh** (A.S. *wegan*, to carry). ***To weigh anchor.*** To raise the anchor preparatory to sailing; hence, *Weigh anchor!* be off with you! get you gone.

> Get off with you; come, come! weigh anchor.
>
> Scott, *The Antiquary*

***Under weigh.*** A solecism for *under way*. *See* Way.

***Weighed in the balance and found wanting.*** Tested, and proved to be at fault, or a failure. The phrase is from Daniel's interpretation of the vision of Belshazzar (Dan. 5:27).

**Weight.** ***A dead weight.*** *See* Dead.

***A weight-for-age race.*** A sort of handicap (*q.v.*), in which the weights carried are apportioned according to certain conditions. Horses of the same age carry similar weights, *caeteris paribus*.

**Weissnichtwo** (Ger., I know not where). The imaginary city in Carlyle's *Sartor Resartus*; a sort of *Utopia*, *Erewhon*, or *Kennaquhair*.

**Welch.** An old spelling of *Welsh*; still retained in the names of certain Welsh regiments, as the *Welch Guards*, the *Welch Fusiliers*.

**Weliki Camenypoys.** *See* Riphaean Rocks.

**Well of Wisdom, The.** *See* Mimir.

**Well-beloved.** Charles VI of France, *le Bien-aimé* (1368, 1380–1422); also applied to Louis XV.

**Well-founded Doctor.** Aegidius de Columna. (d. 1316.)

**Wellington.** The Duke of Wellington (1769–1852) left his name to two kinds of boot, a tree (of the sequoia family – the *Wellingtonia*), and as a term in cards. Men's riding-boots with the front coming over the knee, and a shorter top-boot worn under the trousers are both called *Wellingtons*; and in 'Nap' a call of *Wellington* doubles *Napoleon* – i.e., the caller has to take all five tricks and wins (or loses) double stakes.

**Welsh**. Pertaining to Wales (*q.v.*), i.e. the country of foreigners (A.S. *waelse*, foreign).

*Welsch* is still the German for *foreign*, and the Germans call Italy *Welschland*.

It seems that from time immemorial Welshmen have been regarded as people not to be trusted. The reason is not known, and the modern Welshman is probably as trustworthy as any other national; but the fact is well authenticated, as the old rhyme –

Taffy was a Welshman, Taffy was a thief,
Taffy came to my house and stole a leg of beef –

and our words *Welsher* (*q.v.*) and *to welsh* testify.

*Taffy* is the generic name for a Welshman; from *David*, the patron saint.

***Welsh harp.*** The musical instrument of the ancient Welsh bards; a large harp with three rows of strings, two tuned diatonically in unison, the third supplying the chromatic sharps and flats.

***Welsh mortgage.*** A pledge of land in which no day is fixed for redemption.

***Welsh rabbit.*** Cheese melted and spread over buttered toast. *Rabbit* is sometimes taken to be a corruption of *rare-bit*, but it's not; the term is on a par with 'mock-*turtle*', 'Bombay *duck*', etc.

The Welshman he loved toasted cheese,
Which made his mouth like a mouse-trap.
*When Good King Arthur Ruled the Land*

**Welsher.** A race-course pest who sets up as a bookmaker, and, when he sees the 'book' is against him, makes off without paying out. Also applied to a punter who absconds without paying his losses. Hence, *to welsh*, to do this. The term is modern (though the practice is as old as horse-racing), and is probably connected with the popular notion that the Welsh (*see above*) are not to be trusted.

**Wen. *The Great Wen*.** So Cobbett called London, meaning that it was an abnormal growth, a blotch on the land. A wen is an encysted tumour, usually occurring on the neck.

**Wends.** Slavic people inhabiting Saxony, Prussia, and Eastern Germany generally. The word is probably connected with *wander*.

**Wergild.** The 'blood-money' (*wer*, man, *gild*, payment) paid in Anglo-Saxon times by the kindred of the slayer to the kindred of the slain to avoid a blood-feud in cases of murder or man-slaughter. There was a fixed scale – 1,200 shillings (about £24) for a freeman, 200 shillings for a villain, and 40 pence for a serf.

**Werther.** The sentimental hero of Goethe's romance, *The Sorrows of Werther* (1774), who was so overcome by his unrequited love for Lotte that he took his life – quite to the unconcern of the damsel. As Thackeray travestied the story –

Charlotte, having seen his body
Borne before her on a shutter,
Like a well-conducted person,
Went on cutting bread and butter.

**Werwolf.** A 'man-wolf' (A.S. *wer*, man), i.e. a man who, according to mediaeval superstition, was turned – or could at will turn himself – into a wolf (the *loup-garou* of France). It had the appetite of a wolf, and roamed about at night devouring infants and sometimes exhuming corpses. Its skin was proof against shot or steel, unless the weapon had been blessed in a chapel dedicated to St Hubert.

This superstition was once common to almost all Europe, and still lingers in Brittany, Limousin, Auvergne, Servia, Wallachia, and White Russia; while in the 15th century a council of theologians, convoked by the Emperor Sigismund, gravely decided that the werwulf was a reality.

Ovid tells the story of Lycaon, King of Arcadia, turned into a wolf because he tested the divinity of Jupiter by serving up to him a 'hash of human flesh'; Heredotus describes the Neuri as having the power of assuming once a year the shape of wolves; Pliny relates that one of the family of Antaeus was chosen annually, by lot, to be transformed into a wolf, in which shape he continued for nine years; and St Patrick, we are told, converted Vereticus, King of Wales, into a wolf.

**Wesleyan.** A member of the Nonconformist church founded by John Wesley (1703–91) about 1739.

**Wessex.** The ancient kingdom of the West Saxons; it included Hants, Dorset, Wilts, Somerset, Surrey, Gloucestershire, and Bucks.

***The Novelist of Wessex.*** Thomas Hardy (b.1840), the scenes of whose novels are laid in this country.

**West. *The West End.*** The fashionable quarter of London, lying between Charing Cross and the western boundary of Hyde Park. Hence *West-end style*, ultra-fashionable.

***To go west.*** Of persons, to die; of things, to be lost, rendered useless, never obtained, as *My chance of promotion has gone west*.

The phrase came into very wide use during the Great War, but is older than that, and originated in the United States, the reference being to the setting sun, which 'goes west', and then expires. The idea is very old; it occurs in a Greek proverb, and *cp*. Tennyson's –

> My purpose holds
> To sail beyond the sunset, and the baths
> Of all the western stars, until I die. *Ulysses*

**Western. *The Western Church.*** The Roman Catholic Church, which, after the Great Schism in the 9th century, acknowledged the headship of the Pope. *See* Eastern Church.

***The Western Empire.*** The western division of the Roman Empire having Rome as capital, after the division into an Eastern and Western Empire by Theodosius in 395.

**Wet.** Slang for a drink; hence, *to have a wet*, to have a drink, and *to wet one's whistle*, meaning the same thing. This last is a very old phrase; Chaucer has 'So was her joly whistle wel y-wet' (*Reeve's Tale*, 235), and in No. xiii of the *Towneley Plays* (about 1388) is

> Had she oones wett hyr Whystyll she could syng full clere
> Hyr pater noster.

***A wet blanket.*** *See* Blanket.

***Wet bob.*** At Eton a *wet bob* is a boy who goes in for boating; a *dry bob* one who goes in for cricket.

***Wet nurse.*** A woman employed to suckle children not her own.

**Whale. *Very like a whale.*** Very much like a cock-and-bull story; a fudge. Hamlet chaffs Polonius by comparing a cloud to a camel, and then to a weasel, and when the courtier assents Hamlet adds, 'Or like a whale'; to which Polonius answers, 'Very like a whale' (Act 3, 2).

**Whalebone.** *See* Misnomers.

***White as whalebone.*** An old simile; whalebone is far from white. Our forefathers seemed to confuse the walrus with the whale; and 'white as whalebone' is really a blunder for 'white as walrus-ivory'.

**What we Gave we Have.** The epitaph on 'the Good Earl of Courtenay' (*see* Gibbon's *Decline and Fall*, vol. vi, Ch. 61) –

> What wee gave, wee have;
> What wee spent, wee had;
> What wee left, wee lost

is a free rendering of Martial's –

> Extra fortunam est quidquid donatur amicis
> Quas dederis, solas semper habebis opes.

There are similar epitaphs in many churches; one in St George's, Doncaster, runs thus:

> How now, who is here?
> I, Robin of Doncastere
> And Margaret, my feere.
> That I spent, that I had;
> That I gave, that I have;
> That I left, that I lost.

**What's What. *He knows what's what.*** He is a shrewd fellow not to be imposed on. One of the senseless questions of logic was *Quid est quid?*

> He knew what's what, and that's as high
> As metaphysic wit can fly.
> Butler, *Hudibras*, Pt i, canto 1

**Wheatear.** The stonechat, a bird with a white tail. The name has no connection with either *wheat* or *ear*, but it is the A.S. *hwit*, white, *ears* – still in vulgar use as *arse* – the buttocks or rump. The French name of the bird, *culblanc*, signifies exactly the same thing.

**Wheel.** Emblematical of St Catharine (*q.v.*).

St Donatus bears a wheel set round with lights.

St Euphemia and St Willigis both carry wheels.

St Quintin is sometimes represented with a broken wheel at his feet.

***Broken on the wheel.*** *See* Break.

***The wheel is come full circle.*** Just retribution has followed. The line is from Shakespeare's *King Lear*, 5, 3.

***The wheel of Fortune.*** Fortuna, the goddess, is represented on ancient monuments with a wheel in her hand, emblematical of her inconstancy.

> Though Fortune's malice overthrow my state,
> My mind exceeds the compass of her wheel.
> Shakespeare, *3 Henry VI*, 4, 3

***To put a spoke in one's wheel.*** *See* Spoke.

**Whetstone.** *See* Accius Navius.

***Lying for the whetstone.*** Said of a person who is grossly exaggerating or falsifying a statement. One of the Whitsun amusements of our forefathers was the lie-wage or lie-match; he who could tell the greatest lie was rewarded with a whetstone to sharpen his wit. The nature of these contests may be illustrated by the following: one of the combatants declared he could see a fly on the top of a church steeple; the other replied, 'Oh, yes, I saw him wink his eye.'

When Sir R. Digby declared he had seen the 'philosopher's stone', Bacon quizzically replied, 'Perhaps it was a whetstone.'

***The whetstone of Witte.*** A famous treatise on algebra (1556) by Robert Recorde. The old name for algebra was the 'Cossic Art', and *Cos Ingenii* rendered into English is 'the Whetstone of Wit'. In Scott's *Fortunes of Nigel* the maid told the belated traveller that her master had 'no other books but her young mistress's Bible ... and her master's *Whetstone of Witte*, by Robert Recorde'.

**Whig.** The political party opposed to the Tories (*q.v.*); roughly speaking, the party in favour of gradual change towards more democratic government.

The name came into use in the later 17th century, and was supplanted by 'Liberal' (*q.v.*) in the early 19th. It is from obsolete *whiggamore*, a nickname for certain Scots who came to buy corn at Leith, from *whiggam*, an old Scottish equivalent to our *Gee up!* addressed to horses, and was originally applied to the Covenanters.

The south-west counties of Scotland have seldom corn enough to serve them all the year round, and, the northern parts producing more than they used, those in the west went in summer to buy at Leith the stores that came from the north. From the word *whiggam*, used in driving their horses, all that drove were called the *whiggamors*, contracted into *whigs*. Now, in the year before the news came down of Duke Hamilton's defeat, the ministers animated their people to rise and march to Edinburgh; and they came up, marching on the head of their parishes with an unheard-of fury, praying and preaching all the way as they came. The Marquis of Argyle and his party came and headed them, they being about 6,000. This was called the 'Whiggamors' Inroad'; and ever after that, all who opposed the court came in contempt to be called *whigs*. From Scotland the word was brought into England, where it is now one of our unhappy terms of disunion.

Bishop Burnet, *Own Times* (1723)

***The Whig Bible.*** *See* Bible, Specially named.

**Whip.** A member of Parliament appointed unofficially, and without salary (as such), whose duty is to see that the members of his party vote at important divisions, and to discipline them if they do not attend, or vote against the party. The Whips give notice to members that a motion is expected when their individual vote may be desirable. The circular, or *whip*, runs: 'A motion is expected when your vote is "earnestly" required.' If the word 'earnestly' has only one red-ink dash under it the receiver is *expected* to come, if it has two dashes it means that he *ought* to come, if it has three dashes it means that he *must* come, if four dashes it means 'stay away at your peril'. These notices are technically called *Red whips* (*Annual Register*, 1877, p. 86).

***A whip-round.*** An impromptu collection for some benevolent object.

***The whip with six strings.*** *See under* Six.

***Whip-dog Day.*** October 18th, St Luke's Day. Brand tells us (*Popular Antiquities*, ii, 273) that it is so called because a priest about to celebrate mass on St Luke's Day happened to drop the pyx, which was snatched up by a dog.

**Whipping Boy.** A boy kept to be whipped when a prince deserved chastisement. Mungo Murray stood for Charles I, Barnaby Fitzpatrick for Edward VI (Fuller, *Church History*, ii, 342). When Henri IV of France abjured Protestantism and was received into the Catholic Church in 1595, two ambassadors (D'Ossat and Du Perron, afterwards cardinals) were sent to Rome and knelt in the portico of St Peter, singing the *Miserere*. At each verse a blow with a switch was given on their shoulders.

**Whisky.** *See* Usquebaugh. The light one-horse gig of this name from *whisky*, to flourish a thing about with a quick movement.

**Whisper. *Angel's whisper.*** Army slang for the bugle call for defaulters' drill, or for fatigues.

***Pig's whisper.*** *See* Pig.

***To give the whisper.*** To give the tip, the warning; to pass some bit of secret information.

**Whist.** The card game originated in England (16th cent.) and was first called *Triumph* (whence *trump*), then *Ruff* or *Honours*, and then, early in the 17th century, *Whisk*, in allusion to the sweeping up of the cards. *Whist*, the later name, appears in Butler's *Hudibras* (1663), and was adopted through confusion with *Whist!* meaning Hush! Silence!

Let nice Piquette the boast of France remain,
And studious Ombre be the pride of Spain!
Invention's praise shall England yield to none,
While she can call delightful Whist her own.

Alexander Thomson, *Whist* (2nd edn, 1792)

**Whistle.** ***To whistle down the wind.*** To defame a person. The cognate phrase 'blown upon' is more familiar. The idea is to whistle down the wind that the reputation of the person may be blown upon.

***To whistle for a wind.*** It is a superstitious idea among old sailors that, in a calm, a wind may be obtained by whistling for it. Hence, a man who is trying to light a cigarette on a windy day in the open will sometimes remark to his companion, 'For goodness' sake don't whistle!' *Cp.* Capful.

What gales are sold on Lapland's shore!
How whistle rash bids tempests roar!

Scott, *Rokeby*, ii, 11

Only a little hour ago
I was whistling to St Antonio
For a capful of wind to fill our sail,
And instead of a breeze he has sent a gale.

Longfellow, *Golden Legend*, v

***Worth the whistle.*** Worth calling; worth inviting; worth notice. The dog is worth the pains of whistling for. Thus Heywood, in one of his dialogues consisting entirely of proverbs, says, 'It is a poor dog that is not worth the whistling.' Goneril says to Albany –

I have been worth the whistle.

Shakespeare, *King Lear*, 4, 2

***You may whistle for that.*** You must not expect it. The reference is to sailors whistling for the wind. They call the winds, but 'will they come when they do call them?'

***You paid too dearly for your whistle.*** You paid dearly for something you fancied, but found that it did not answer your expectation. The allusion is to a story told by Dr Franklin of his nephew, who set his mind on a common whistle, which he bought of a boy for four times its value. Franklin says the ambitious who dance attendance on court, the miser who gives this world and the next for gold, the libertine who ruins his health for pleasure, the girl who marries a brute for money, all pay 'too much for their whistle'.

**Whit Sunday.** White Sunday. The seventh Sunday after Easter, to commemorate the descent of the Holy Ghost on the day of Pentecost. In the primitive church the newly baptised wore *white* from Easter to Pentecost, and were called *albati* (white-robed). The last of the Sundays, which was also the chief festival, was called emphatically *Dominica in Albis* (Sunday in White).

An old idea is that it is the *Wit* or *Wisdom* Sunday, the day when the Apostles were filled with wisdom by the Holy Ghost.

This day Wit-sonday is cald,
For wisdom and wit sevene fald,
Was zonen to the Apostles as this day.

*Cambr. Univer. MSS*, Dd i, 1, p. 234

We ought to kepe this our Witsonday bicause the law of God was then of the Holy Wyght or Ghost deliured gostly vnto vs.

Taverner (1540)

This day is called Wytsonday because the Holy Ghost brought wytte and wysdom into Christis disciples ... and filled them full of ghostly wytte.

*In die Pentecostis* (printed by Wynkyn de Worde)

***Whitsun farthings.*** *See* Quadragesimals.

**White** denotes purity, simplicity, and candour; innocence, truth, and hope. *See* Colours, Symbolism of.

The ancient Druids, and indeed the priests generally of antiquity, used to wear white vestments, as do the clergy of the Established Church of England when they officiate in any sacred service. The magi also wore white robes.

The head of Osiris, in Egypt, was adorned with a white tiara; all his ornaments were white; and his priests were clad in white.

The priests of Jupiter, and the Flamen Dialis of Rome, were clothed in white, and wore white hats. The victims offered to Jupiter were white. The Roman festivals were marked with white chalk, and at the death of a Caesar the national mourning was white; white horses were sacrificed to the sun, white oxen were selected for sacrifice by the Druids, and white elephants are held sacred in Siam.

The Persians affirm that the divinities are habited in white.

***A white elephant.*** *See* Elephant.

***A white harvest.*** A late harvest, when the ground is white of a morning with a *white frost*, or hoarfrost.

***A white lie.*** An excusable or pardonable untruth; a misstatement made either with no ulterior motive or 'with the best intentions'.

***A white man.*** A thoroughly straightforward and honourable man, and who could never do a dirty action.

***A white night.*** A sleepless night; the French have the phrase *Passer une nuit blanche*.

***A white squall.*** One which produces no diminution of light, in contradistinction to a *black* squall, in which the clouds are black and heavy.

***A white witch.*** One who practised *white magic* (*q.v.*) only, and had no dealings with the devil.

Two or three years past there came to these parts one ... what the vulgar call a white witch, a cunning man, and such like.

Scott, *Kenilworth*, ch. ix

***Days marked with a white stone.*** Days of pleasure; days to be remembered with gratification. The Romans used a white stone or piece of chalk to mark their lucky days with on the calendar. Scott (in *The Antiquary*, ch. iii) calls such times the 'white moments of one's life'. Days that were unlucky they marked with black charcoal (*cp.* Red-letter Day).

***The white bird.*** Conscience, or the soul of man. The Mohammedans have preserved the old Roman idea in the doctrine that the souls of the just lie under the throne of God, like white birds, till the resurrection morn. *Cp.* Dove.

A white bird, she told him once ... he must carry on his bosom across a crowded public place – his own soul was like that.

Pater, *Marius the Epicurean*, ch. ii

***The White Brethren.*** A sect of Catholic reformers that appeared early in the 15th century. Mosheim says (Bk ii, p. 2, ch. v) a certain priest came from the Alps with an immense concourse of followers, all dressed in white linen. They marched through several provinces, following a cross borne by their leader. Boniface X ordered their leader to be burnt, and the multitude dispersed.

***The White Cockade.*** The badge worn by the followers of Charles Edward, the Pretender.

***The White Company.*** A band of French cut-throats organised by Bertrand du Guesclin in 1366, and led against Pedro the Cruel; so called because they wore a white cross on the shoulder. The name had previously (13th cent.) been given to a gang of assassins led by Folquet, the villainous Bishop of Toulouse, who massacred all suspected of heresy.

***The White Friars.*** The Carmelites (*q.v.*), so called because they dressed in white. Their monastery, founded in London on the south side of Fleet Street in 1241, gives the name to that district, and was for many centuries a sanctuary. *See* Alsatia.

***The White Horse.*** The standard of the ancient Saxons; hence the emblem of Kent. A galloping white horse is the device of the House of Hanover, and it is from this that many public houses bear the sign of 'The White Horse'.

On Uffington Hill, Berks, there is formed in the chalk an enormous white horse, supposed to have been cut there after the battle in which Ethelred and Alfred defeated the Danes (871). This rude ensign is about 374 ft long, and 1,000 ft above the sea-level. It may be seen twelve or fifteen miles off, and gives its name to the *Vale of White Horse*, west of Abingdon.

An annual ceremony was once held, called 'Scouring the White Horse'.

Foam-crested waves are popularly called *White horses*.

Now the great winds shoreward blow,
Now the salt tides seaward flow;
Now the wild white horses play,
Champ and chafe and toss in the spray.

Matthew Arnold, *The Forsaken Merman*

***White House.*** The presidential mansion in the United States, at Washington. It is a building of freestone, painted white. The cornerstone was laid by Washington, and the house was remodelled in 1902. Figuratively, it means the Presidency; as, 'He has his eye on the White House.'

***White Ladies.*** A species of *fée* in many countries, the appearance of whom generally forbodes death in the house. *Cp.* Banshee. A relic of old *Teutonic mythology*, representing Holda, or Berchta, the goddess who received the souls of maidens and young children.

German legend says that when the castle of Neuhaus, Bohemia, was being built she appeared to the workmen and promised them a sweet soup and carp on the completion of the castle. In remembrance thereof, these dainties were for long given to the poor of Bohemia on Maundy Thursday. She is also said to have been heard to speak on two occasions, once in December, 1628, when she said, 'I wait for judgment!' and once at Neuhaus, when she said to the princes, ''Tis ten o'clock.'

The first recorded instance of this apparition was in the 16th century, and the name given to the lady is Bertha von Rosenberg. She last appeared, it is said, in 1879, just prior to the death of Prince Waldemar. She carries a bunch of keys at her side, and is always dressed in white.

In Normandy the White Ladies lurk in ravines, fords, bridges, and other narrow passes, and ask the passenger to dance. If they receive a courteous answer, well; but if a refusal, they seize the churl and fling him into a ditch, where thorns and briers may serve to teach him gentleness of manners.

The most famous of these ladies is *La Dame d'Aprigny*, who used to occupy the site of the present Rue St Quentin, at Bayeux, and *La Dame Abonde*.

One kind of these the Italians *Fata* name;
The French call *Fée*; we *Sybils*; and the same
Others *White Dames*, and those that them have seen,
*Night Ladies* some, of which Habundia's queen.
*Hierarchie*, viii, p. 507

The most celebrated in Britain is the *White Lady of Avenel* (*q.v.*), introduced by Scott into *The Monastery*.

***The White League.*** A name of the Ku-Klux Klan (*q.v.*).

***The White Merle.*** A white fairy bird of old Basque folklore, whose singing would restore sight to the blind.

***The White Rose.*** The House of York, whose emblem it was (*see under* Rose).

***To hit the white.*** To be quite right, make a good shot. The phrase is from the old days of archery, the *white* being the inner circle of the target – the bull's eye.

***To show the white feather.*** To show cowardice. A phrase from the cockpit. No gamecock has a white feather; it indicates a cross-breed in birds.

***White-livered.*** Mean or cowardly; having 'no guts'. It was an old notion that the livers of cowards were bloodless.

How many cowards, whose hearts are all as false
As stairs of sand, wear yet upon their chins
The beards of Hercules and frowning Mars,
Who, inward search'd, have livers white as milk!
Shakespeare, *Merchant of Venice*, 3, 2

***White magic.*** Sorcery in which the devil was not invoked and played no part; opposed to black magic (*q.v.*).

***White rent.*** A duty of eightpence payable by every tin-miner in Devon and Cornwall to the Duke of Cornwall (the Prince of Wales), as lord of the soil.

***White satin.*** Old slang for gin.

***White tincture.*** The alchemist's name for a preparation that they believed would convert any base metal into silver. It was also called the Stone of the Second Order, the Little Elixir, and the Little Magisterium (*cp.* Red Tincture).

***The White Tsar.*** An epithet of the former Tsars of Russia, as Tsars of Muscovy; the King of Muscovy was called the White King from the robes which he wore. The King of Poland was called the Black King.

Sunt qui principem Moscoviae *Album Regem* nuncupant. Ego quidem causam diligenter quierebam, cur regis albi nomine appellaretur, cum nemo principum Moscoviae eo titulo antea [Ivan III] esset usus ... Credo autem ut Persam nunc propter *rubea* tegumenta capitis 'Kissilpassa' (i.e. rubeum caput) vocant; ita reges Moscoviae propter *alba* tegumenta 'Albos Reges' appellari. *Sigismund*

***White wine.*** Any wine of a light colour, not red; as champagne, hock, sauterne, moselle, etc.

**Whitebait Dinner.** A dinner of Cabinet Ministers and prominent politicians that, until the early '90's of last century was always held at Greenwich toward the close of the parliamentary session. Sir Robert Preston, M.P. for Dover, first invited his friend George Rose (Secretary of the Treasury) and an Elder Brother of the Trinity House to dine with him at his fishing cottage on the banks of Dagenham Lake. This was at the close of the session. Rose on one occasion proposed that Mr Pitt, their mutual friend, should be asked to join them; this was done, and Pitt agreed to repeat his visit the year following, when other members swelled the party. This went on for several years, when Pitt suggested that the muster should be in future nearer town, and Greenwich was selected, and the dinner became an annual event. The time of meeting was Trinity Monday, or as near Trinity Monday as circumstances would allow.

**Whiteboys.** A secret agrarian association organised in Ireland about the year 1760. So called because they wore white shirts in their nightly expeditions. In 1787 a new association appeared, the members of which called themselves 'Right-boys'. The Whiteboys were originally called Levellers (*q.v.*), from their throwing down fences and levelling enclosures.

**Whitechapel.** A quarter in the East End of London inhabited by the poorer classes, alien Jews, etc. *To play Whitechapel* (at cards) is to play in a mean, unsportsmanlike way; a *Whitechapel cart* is a light, two-wheeled spring cart, as used by small tradesmen for delivering goods; a *Whitechapel shave* is no shave at all, but rubbing powder over the bristles instead, 'for the sake of appearance'.

**Whitewash.** Excuses made in palliation of bad conduct; a false colouring given to a person's character or memory to counteract disreputable allegations. Thus, a politician or minister who has soiled his fingers with shady financial transactions is *whitewashed* if he or his leaders can show that what he did was done innocently – or that it wasn't he who did it at all, but someone else of the same name.

The term is also applied to the clearance by a bankrupt of his debts, not by paying them, but by judicial process.

**Whittington, Dick.** Sir Richard Whittington, 'thrice Lord Mayor of London', about whom the well known nursery story is told, was born about 1358, the son of Sir William de Whityngdon, lord of the manor of Pauntley, Gloucester. Being a younger son and unprovided for, he walked to London, was trained by a relative as a merchant, married his master's daughter and prospered to such an extent that he was able to lend Henry IV £1,000 – equal to over £10,000 in present money.

He was Lord Mayor of London in 1397, 1406, and 1419, besides being once named by Richard II to succeed a mayor who had died in office. He died in 1423.

> Beneath this stone lies Wittington,
> Sir Richard rightly named,
> Who three times Lord Mayor served in London,
> In which he ne'er was blamed.
> He rose from indigence to wealth
> By industry and that,
> For lo! he scorned to gain by stealth
> What he got by a cat.
>
> Epitaph (destroyed by the fire of London)

The legend that Whittington made his wealth largely through the agency of a cat seems to be founded on a confusion between Fr. *achat* and Eng. *a cat*. In the 14th and early 15th centuries trading, or buying and selling at a profit, was known among the educated classes as *achat* (still the French for 'purchase'), which was written – and probably pronounced – *acat* (*see* Riley's *Introduction* to the *Liber Albus*).

Another suggestion is that it arose through confusion with the *cat*, a ship on the Norwegian model, having a narrow stern, projecting quarters, and deep waist, and used in the coal trade. According to tradition, Sir Richard made his money by trading in coals, which he conveyed in his 'cat' from Newcastle to London. The black faces of his coalheavers gave rise to the tale about the Moors. But there are Eastern tales of the same kind, and it is probably one of these that became attached to the popular Lord Mayor.

**Wicked.** Connected with A.S. *wicca*, a wizard.

***The Wicked Bible.*** *See* Bible, Specially named.

***The Wicked Prayer Book.*** Printed 1686, octavo. In the Epistle for the Fourteenth Sunday after Trinity the following passage occurs:

> Now the works of the flesh are manifest, which are these; adultery, fornication, uncleanliness, idolatry ... they who do these things shall inherit the kingdom of God.

(Of course, 'shall inherit' should be 'shall *not* inherit'.)

**Wicket-gate.** The entrance to the road that leadeth to the Celestial City in Bunyan's *Pilgrim's Progress*. Over the portal is the inscription – Knock, and it shall be opened unto you.

**Wickliffe.** *See* Wyclif.

**Wide.** Slang for cunning, artful, or for one who is very wideawake.

**Wideawake.** Certain felt hats were so called by a pun, because they never had a *nap*. The term is now applied to any felt hat with a very wide brim.

**Widow, The.** Old slang for the gallows.

***Widow bench.*** An obsolete law term for the share of her husband's estate allowed to a widow over and above her jointure.

***The widow's cruse.*** A small supply of anything which, by good management, is made to go a long way and to be apparently inexhaustible. In allusion to the miracle of the cruse of oil in 2 Kings, 4.

***Widow's man.*** Old naval slang for a non-existent seaman whose name was borne on the ship's book, his pay, prize-money, etc., going to Greenwich Hospital or to a fund for widows.

***Widow's weeds.*** *See* Weeds.

**Wieland.** Another form of *Völund* (*see* Wayland), the wonder-working smith of *Norse mythology*.

**Wife.** A.S. *wif*, a woman. The ultimate root of the word is obscure; but it is 'certainly not allied to *weave* (A.S. *wefan*), as the fable runs' (Skeat).

The old meaning, *a woman*, still appears in such combinations as *fish-wife*, *housewife*, etc., and in the phrase *an old wife's tale* (*see* 1 Tim. 4:7) for an incoherent and unconvincing story.

***The Wife-hater Bible.*** *See* Bible, Specially named.

**Wig.** A shortened form of *periwig* (earlier, *perwig*), from Fr. *peruke*. In the middle of the 18th century we meet with thirty or forty different names for wigs: as the artichoke, bag, barrister's, bishop's, brush, bush (buzz), buckle, busby, chain, chancellor's, corded wolf's paw, Count Saxe's mode, the crutch, the cut bob, the detached buckle, the Dalmahoy (a bob wig worn by tradesmen), the drop, the Dutch, the full, the half natural, the Jansenist bob, the judge's, the ladder, the long bob, the Louis, the pigeon's wing, the rhinoceros, the rose, the scratch, the she-dragon, the small back, the spinach seed, the staircase, the Welsh, the wild boar's back.

***A bigwig.*** A magnate; in allusion to the large wigs that in the 17th and 18th centuries encumbered the head and shoulders of the aristocracy of England and France. They are still worn by the Lord Chancellor, judges, and barristers, and bishops used to wear them in the House of Lords till 1880.

> An ye fa' over the cleugh, there will be but ae wig left in the parish, and that's the minister's.
>
> Scott, *The Antiquary*

***Dash my wig!*** A mild imprecation, formerly very common.

> Fleas are not lobsters, dash my wig.
>
> Butler, *Hudibras*

***Scratch wig.*** A small one just large enough to cover the bald patch, as opposed to the full-bottomed wig.

***Wigs on the green.*** A serious disagreement likely to lead to a scrimmage; a rumpus.

**Wiggen tree.** *See* Rowan.

**Wigging.** A scolding, a reprimand. This word may be connected with *wig*, but it is not certain.

**Wild.** ***A wild-cat scheme.*** A rash and hazardous financial venture; a speculation in which one would have about as much chance of making a profit as of catching a wild-cat in the woods.

***The wild huntsman.*** A spectral hunter of mediaeval legend who, with a pack of spectral dogs, frequents certain forests and occasionally appears to mortals. One account has it that he was a Jew who would not suffer Jesus to drink out of a horse-trough, but pointed to some water in a hoof-print as good enough for 'such an enemy of Moses'.

The Germans locate him in the Black Forest; the French in the Forest of Fontainebleau – and confuse him with St Hubert; and in England he became Herne the Hunter (*q.v.*), once a keeper in Windsor Forest, who 'walks' in winter time, about midnight, and blasts trees and cattle. He wears horns, and rattles a chain in a 'most hideous manner' (*Merry Wives of Windsor*, 4, 4).

***To lead one a wild-goose chase.*** To beguile one with false hopes, or put one on an impracticable pursuit, or after something that is not worth the chase. A wild-goose is very hard to catch, and very little use when caught.

***To sow one's wild oats.*** *See* Oat.

***Wild men.*** A term often applied, in politics, to *intransigeants*, the extremists of either party who will not in any way accommodate their views and actions to changing conditions or public opinion.

Formerly women who took an active part in the movement for obtaining votes and political recognition were called *wild women*:

> Let anyone commend to these female runagates quietness, duty, home-staying, and the whole cohort of wild women is like an angry beehive, which a rough hand has disturbed.
>
> *Nineteenth Century*, March, 1892, p. 463

**Wilfrid, St.** A noble of Northumbria, who became Abbot of Ripon in 661, and in 705 Bishop of Hexham. It was he who at the Synod of Whitby (664) succeeded in substituting the Roman uses and their observation of Easter in England for the Celtic. For many centuries his banner was carried to the wars.

***St Wilfrid's Needle.*** A narrow passage in the crypt of Ripon cathedral, built by Odo, Archbishop of Canterbury, and said to have been used to try whether young women were virgins or not, none but virgins being able to squeeze through.

**Wilgefortis, St.** *See* Uncumber.

**Will o' the wisp.** *See* Friar's Lanthorn: Ignis Fatuus.

**William.** One of the most popular of Christian names; Fr. *Guillaume*, Ger. *Wilhelm*, it means *a protector*; literally, *a resolute helmet* – Ger. *wille helm*.

The *william pear* was originally the *William's pear*, named (like *greengage*) from the grower; *sweet william* is an old English name for an old English flower, *Dianthus barbatus*, a member of the pink family.

***William of Cloudeslie.*** A noted outlaw and famous archer of the 'north countrie'. *See* Clym of the Clough.

***William of Wykeham.*** *See* Wykehamist.

***William the Silent.*** *See* Silent.

Of the many saints of this name the following are perhaps the most noteworthy:

***St William of Aquitaine.*** A soldier of Charlemagne's, who helped to chase the Saracens from Languedoc. In 808 he renounced the world, and died 812. He is usually represented as a mailed soldier.

***St William of Maleval.*** A French nobleman of very abandoned life; but, being converted, he went as pilgrim to Jerusalem, and on his return retired to the desert of Maleval, where he died in 1157. The *Guillemites,* a branch of the

Benedictine order, was founded by Albert, one of his disciples, and named in his honour.

He is depicted in a Benedictine's habit, with armour lying beside him.

***St William of Montpelier*** is represented with a lily growing from his mouth, with the words *Ave Maria* in gold letters on the flower.

***St William of Monte Virgine*** (d.1142) is shown with a wolf by his side.

***St William of Norwich*** was the celebrated child said to have been crucified by the Jews in 1137 (*cp.* Hugh of Lincoln). He is represented crowned with thorns, or crucified, or holding a hammer and nails in his hands, or wounded in his side with a knife (*see* Drayton's *Polyolbion*, song xxiv).

In Percy's *Reliques* (Bk i, 3) there is a tale of a lad named Hew, son of Lady Helen, of Merryland town (Milan), who was allured by a Jew's daughter with an apple. She stuck him with a penknife, rolled him in lead, and cast him into a well. Lady Helen went in search of her boy, and the child's ghost cried out from the bottom of the well –

The lead is wondrous heavy, mither,
The well is wondrous deip;
A keen penknife sticks in my heirt, mither;
A word I dounae speik.

***St William of Roeschild*** (d.1203) is represented with a torch flaming on his grave.

***St William of York*** (d.1154) was a nephew of King Stephen, and became Archbishop of York in 1140. He was canonised by Honorius III about 1220 on account of the many miracles reported to have been performed at his tomb.

**Willie-Wastle.** This child's game is said to be named from William Wastle, governor of Hume Castle, Haddington. When Cromwell, so the story goes, sent a summons to him to surrender, he replied –

Here I, Willie Wastle,
Stand firm in my castle,
And all the dogs in the town
Shan't pull Willie Wastle down.

**Willis's Rooms.** *See* Almack's.

**Willow. *To handle the willow.*** To be a cricket-player. Cricket-bats are made of willow; hence the game is sometimes called *King Willow* (*see* the Harrow school song of this name).

***To wear the willow.*** To go into mourning, especially for a sweetheart or bride.

The willow, especially the *weeping willow*, has from time immemorial been associated with sorrow and taken as an emblem of desolation or desertion. Fuller says, 'The willow is a sad tree, whereof such as have lost their love make their mourning garlands', and the psalmist tells us that the Jews in captivity hanged their harps upon the willows in sign of mourning (cxxxvii).

Desdemona says in *Othello* (4, 3):

My mother had a maid call'd Barbara;
She was in love, and he she lov'd prov'd mad
And did forsake her; she had a song of 'willow';
An old thing 'twas, but it expressed her fortune,
And she died singing it.

And then comes the song –

The poor soul sat sighing by a sycamore tree,
Sing all a green willow;
Her hand on her bosom, her head on her knee,
Sing willow, willow, willow;
The fresh streams ran by her, and murmur'd her moans;
Sing willow, willow, willow:
Her salt tears fell from her, and soften'd the stones;
Sing willow, willow, willow;

***The Willow Pattern.*** A favourite design for blue china plates, imitating (but not copying) the Chinese style of porcelain decoration, introduced into England by Thomas Turner of Caughley about 1780, when the craze for things Chinese was at its height.

To the right is a mandarin's country seat, two stories high to show the rank and wealth of the possessor; in the foreground a pavilion, in the background an orange tree, and to the right of the pavilion a peach tree in full bearing. The estate is enclosed by a wooden fence, and a river crossed by a bridge, at one end of which is the famous willow tree and at the other the gardener's humble cottage. At the top of the pattern (left-hand side) is an island. The three figures on the bridge are the mandarin and the lovers, the latter also being shown in a boat on the river.

The willow pattern does not illustrate any Chinese story or legend, and is not Chinese in origin; but the following is the tale that has been built round it:

A wealthy mandarin had an only daughter named Li-chi, who fell in love with Chang, a young man living on the island shown, who had been her father's secretary. The father overheard them one day making vows of love under the orange tree, and sternly forbade the unequal match; but the lovers contrived to elope, lay concealed for a while in the gardener's cottage, and thence escaped in a boat to the island. The enraged mandarin pursued them with a whip, and would have beaten them to death had not the gods rewarded their fidelity by changing them both into turtle-doves. And all this occurred 'when the willow begins to shed its leaves'.

**Will's.** A famous coffee-house of Queen Anne's time that stood at the corner of Bow Street and Russell Street, Covent Garden, sometimes referred to as 'Russell Street Coffee House', and 'The Wits' Coffee House'. It was the meeting-place of the wits and literary men of the day, and was well known to Addison, who established his servant, Button, in another coffee-house, which eventually, as *Button's*, became the headquarters of the Whig *literati*, as Will's had been of the Tory.

**Willy-nilly.** *Nolens volens;* willing or not. Will-he, nill-he, *nill* being n' (negative), *will*, just as Lat. *nolens* is *n'-volens.*

**Willy-willy.** The Australian aboriginal term for the sudden whirlwinds which are common on the north-west coast. They can be seen approaching in a high circular column of leaves and dust from a great distance.

**Winchester.** Identified by Malory and other old writers with the *Camelot* of Arthurian romance.

> And Merlin let make by his subtility that Balin's sword was put in a marble stone standing upright as great as a mill stone, and the stone hoved always above the water and did many years, and so by adventure it swam down the stream to the City of Camelot, that is in English Winchester.
>
> Malory, *Morte d'Arthur*, II, xix

Hanmer, referring to *King Lear*, 2, 2, says Camelot is Queen Camel, Somersetshire, in the vicinity of which 'are many large moors where are bred great quantities of geese, so that many other places are from hence supplied with quills and feathers'. Kent says to the Duke of Cornwall:

> Goose, if I had you upon Sarum Plain,
> I'd drive ye cackling home to Camelot.

With all due respect to Hanmer, it seems far more probable that Kent refers to Camelford, in Cornwall, where the Duke of Cornwall resided, in his castle of Tintagel. He says, 'If I had you on Salisbury Plain [where geese abound], I would drive you home to Tintagel, on the river Camel.' Though the Camelot of Shakespeare is Tintagel or Camelford, yet the Camelot of King Arthur may be Queen Camel; and indeed visitors are still pointed to certain large entrenchments at South Cadbury (Cadbury Castle) called by the inhabitants 'King Arthur's Palace'.

**Wind.** According to *classical mythology*, the north, south, east, and west winds (*Boreas, Notus, Eurus*, and *Zephyrus*) were under the rule of Aeolus, who kept them confined in a cave on Mount Haemus, Thrace. Other strong winds of a more destructive nature were the brood of Typhoeus.

The story says that Aeolus gave Ulysses a bag, tied with a silver string, in which were all the hurtful and unfavourable winds, so that he might arrive home without being delayed by tempests. His crew, however, opened the bag in the belief that it contained treasure, the winds escaped, and a terrible storm at once arose, driving the vessel out of its course and back to the island it had left.

Latin names for other winds are: north-east, *Argestës*; north-west, *Corus*; south-east, *Volturnus*; south-west, *Afer ventus, Africus, Africanus*, or *Libs*. The *Thrascias* is a north wind, but not due north. *Aquilo* is another name for the north wind, as *Auster* is of the south and *Favonius* of the west.

> Boreas and Caecias, and Argestes loud,
> And Thrascias rend the woods, and seas upturn;
> Notus and Afer, black with thunderous clouds,
> From Serraliona. Thwart of these, as fierce,
> Forth rush ... Eurus and Zephyr ...
> Sirocco and Libecchio [Libycus].
>
> Milton, *Paradise Lost*, x, 699–706

For some specially named winds *see* Etesian, Harmattan, Kamsin, Mistral, Monsoon, Pampero, Puna, Samiel (or Simoom), Sirocco, Solano, Trade Winds, etc.

***A wind egg.*** An egg without a shell, or an unfertilised one; from the old superstition that the hen that lays it was impregnated, like the 'Thracian mares', by the wind.

***In the wind's eye.*** *See* Eye.

***One's second wind.*** Soon after the start in running, unless one is very fit one gets 'out of breath'; but, as the body becomes heated, breathing becomes more easy, and endures till fatigue produces exhaustion; this is called the *second wind.*

> That mysterious physical readjustment, known in animals as 'second breath', came to the rescue of his fainting frame.
>
> *The Barton Experiment*, ch. x

***There's something in the wind.*** There are signs that something is going to happen, some hitherto unanticipated development is about to take place.

***Three sheets in the wind.*** *See* Sheet.

***'Tis an ill wind that blows nobody any good.*** Someone profits by every loss; someone is benefited by every misfortune.

> Except wind stands as never it stood,
> It is an ill-wind turns none to good.
>
> Tusser, *Five Hundred Points of Good Husbandry*, xiii

***To get the wind up.*** To become thoroughly alarmed and, in consequence, nervous, over-anxious, 'funky'. *That'll put the wind up him* is a common saying of something that is calculated to frighten one or put him in a state of 'nerves'.

***To know which way the wind blows.*** To be aware of the true state of affairs.

***To raise the wind.*** To obtain ready money by hook or crook. A sea phrase; what wind is to a ship, money is to commerce. Also, to cause a commotion, to 'kick up a dust'.

***To sail before the wind.*** To prosper, to go on swimmingly, to meet with great success, to go as smoothly and rapidly as a ship before the wind.

***To sail close to the wind.*** In nautical use, to keep the vessel's head as near the quarter from which the wind is blowing as possible while keeping the sails filled; figuratively, to go to the very verge of what decency or propriety allow; to act so as just to escape the letter of the law.

> The jokes [of our predecessors] might have been broader than modern manners allow, ... but ... the masher sails nearer the wind than did his ruder forefathers.
>
> *Nineteenth Century*, Nov., 1892, p. 795

***To take*** **or** ***have the wind.*** To get or keep the upper hand. Bacon uses the phrase. *To have the wind of a ship* is to be to the windward of it.

***To take the wind out of one's sails.*** To forestall him, 'steal his thunder' (*see* Thunder), frustrate him by utilising his own material or methods. Literally, it is to sail to the windward of a ship and so rob its sails of the wind.

**Windbag.** A long-winded, bombastic speaker, who uses inflated phrases and promises far more than he can perform.

**Windfall.** An unexpected piece of good luck, especially an unexpected legacy; something worth having that comes to one without any personal exertion – like fruit which has fallen from the tree and so does not have to be picked.

**Windmills.** ***To fight with windmills.*** To face imaginary adversaries, combat chimeras. The allusion is to the adventure of Don Quixote who, when riding through the plains of Montiel, approached thirty or forty windmills, which he declared to Sancho Panza 'were giants, two leagues in length or more'. Striking his spurs into Rosinante, with his lance in rest, he drove at one of the 'monsters dreadful as Typhoeus' the lance lodged in the sail, and the latter lifted both man and beast into the air. When the valiant knight and his steed fell they were both much injured, and Don Quixote declared that the enchanter Freston, 'who carried off his library with all the books therein', had changed the giants into windmills 'out of malice' (Bk i, ch. viii).

***To have windmills in your head.*** To be full of fancies; to have 'bees in your bonnet' (*q.v.*). Sancho Panza says –

> Did I not tell your worship they were windmills? and who could have thought otherwise, except such as had windmills in their head?
>
> Cervantes, *Don Quixote*, Bk i, ch. viii

**Windsor.** ***The House of Windsor.*** The official title of the reigning dynasty of Great Britain and the British Dominions beyond the Seas since July 17th, 1917, when King George V signed a proclamation adopting this style for the Royal Family and declaring that –

> all the descendants in the male line of Queen Victoria who are subjects of these realms, other than female descendants who may marry or may have married, shall bear the name of Windsor.

From the time of George I to the death of Queen Victoria the dynasty was known as the *House of Hanover*; from the accession of Edward VII to the date of this proclamation it was the *House of Saxe-Coburg*, so named from Edward VII's father, Albert, Duke of Saxony, Prince of Coburg and Gotha.

***The Knights of Windsor.*** *See under* Knight.

***Windsor Herald.*** One of the six Heralds attached to the College of Arms (*see* Herald).

**Wine.** At the universities *a wine* is a convivial gathering at which wine, as a rule, is drunk.

***Win of ape*** (Chaucer). 'I trow that ye have drunken win of ape' – i.e. wine to make you drunk; in French, *vin de singe*. There is a Talmud parable which says that Satan came one day to drink with Noah, and slew a lamb, a lion, a pig, and an ape, to teach Noah that man before wine is in him is a *lamb*, when he drinks moderately, he is a *lion*, when like a sot he is a *swine*, but after, that any further excess makes him an *ape* that senselessly chatters and jabbers.

**Wing.** ***Don't try to fly without wings.*** Attempt nothing you are not fit for. A Latin saying,

Plautus has (*Poenulus* IV, ii, 47) *Sine pennis volare haud facile est*, It is by no means easy to fly without wings.

***On the wing.*** *Au vol*, about to leave. Young (*Night Thoughts*, vii) speaks of 'restless Hope, for ever on the wing'.

***The wings of Azrael.*** *See* Azrael.

***To clip one's wings.*** To take down one's conceit; to hamper one's freedom of action. In French, *Rogner les ailes* [*à quelqu'un*].

***To lend wings.*** To spur one's speed.

> This sound of danger lent me wings.
>
> R. L. Stevenson

***To take one under your wing.*** To patronise and protect. The allusion is to a hen gathering her chicks under her wing.

***To take wing.*** To fly away; to depart without warning (Fr. *s'envoler*).

> Oh, God! it is a fearful thing
> To see the human soul take wing.
>
> Byron, *Prisoner of Chillon*

**Winifred, St.** Patron saint of virgins, because she was beheaded by Prince Caradoc for refusing to marry him. She was Welsh by birth, and the legend says that her head falling on the ground originated the famous healing well of St Winifred in Flintshire. She is usually drawn like St Denis, carrying her head in her hand. Holywell, in Wales, is St Winifred's Well, celebrated for its 'miraculous' virtues.

**Wink.** ***A nod is as good as a wink to a blind horse.*** *See* Nod.

***Forty winks.*** A short nap, a doze.

***Like winking.*** Very quickly; as in 'to give an answer like winking'.

***To tip one the wink.*** To give him a hint privately; to 'put him wise'.

***To wink at.*** To connive at, or to affect not to notice.

> He knows not how to wink at human frailty
> Or pardon weakness that he never felt.
>
> Addison, *Cato*, v, iv

**Winkle, Rip van.** The creation of Washington Irving, hero of one of the stories in the *Sketch Book* (1810) which tells how he, a Dutch colonist of New York in pre-Revolutionary days, met with a strange man in a ravine of the Catskill Mountains. Rip helps him to carry a keg, and when they reach the destination he sees a number of odd creatures playing nine-pins, but no one utters a word. Master Winkle seizes the first opportunity to take a sip at the keg, falls into a stupor, and sleeps for twenty years. On waking, he finds that he is a tottering old man, his wife is dead and buried, his daughter is married, his native village has been remodelled, and America has become independent.

**Winter's Tale, The.** One of the last of Shakespeare's plays, acted in 1611 but not printed till 1623 (first Folio). It is founded on Greene's *Pandosto, The Triumph of Time* (1588), which was written round an actual incident that occurred in the Bohemian and Polish courts in the late 14th century.

In the play Polixenes, King of Bohemia, is invited to Sicily by King Leontes, and unwittingly excites the jealousy of his friend because he prolongs his stay at the entreaty of Queen Hermione. Leontes orders Camillo to poison the royal guest, but, instead of doing so, Camillo flees with him to Bohemia. In time Florizel, the son and heir of Polixenes, falls in love with Perdita, the lost daughter of Leontes. Polixenes forbids the match, and the young lovers, under the charge of Camillo, flee to Sicily. Polixenes follows the fugitives, the mystery of Perdita is cleared up, the lovers are married, and the two kings resume their friendship.

In Greene's romance Polixenes is *Pandosto*, Hermione *Bellaria*, Leontes *Egistus*, and Florizel and Perdita *Dorastus* and *Fawnia*.

**Wipe.** Old slang for a pocket-handkerchief.

***To wipe one's nose.*** To affront him; to give him a blow on the nose. Similarly, *to wipe a person's eye*, to steal a march on him, to *fetch one a wipe over the knuckles*, to give him a good rap.

***Wiped out.*** Destroyed, annihilated; quite obliterated.

**Wire.** Used as a verb, meaning *to telegraph to*. 'Wire me without delay', telegraph to me at once. An even more objectionable verb has been coined from *wireless* – 'I will wireless you from mid-Atlantic.'

***Wireless.*** Applied to telegraphic and telephonic communications sent through space instead of along a wire. The term is really a misnomer, for a great deal of wire is necessary even in 'wireless'.

***To pull the wires.*** To control events, politics, etc., clandestinely from behind the scenes, as the unseen operator manipulates the marionettes in a puppet-show.

**Wisdom Tooth.** The popular name for the third molar in each jaw. Wisdom teeth appear between 17 and 25.

***Cut your wisdom teeth.*** When persons say or do silly things, the remark is made to them that 'they have not yet cut their wisdom teeth', or reached the 'years of discretion'.

***The wisdom of many and the wit of one.*** Lord John Russell's definition of a proverb.

**Wise.** ***To put one wise.*** An Americanism, meaning to acquaint him with the facts, with the true position of affairs; to give him the necessary information.

The following have been surnamed *The Wise*:

Albert II, Duke of Austria, called *The Lame and Wise*. (1289, 1330–58.)

Alfonso X (or IX) of Leon, and IV of Castile, called *The Wise* and *The Astronomer*. (1203, 1252–85.)

Charles V of France, called *Le Sage*. (1337, regent 1358–60, king 1364–80.)

Frederick II, Elector of Saxony. (1482, 1544–56.)

John V of Brittany, called *The Good and Wise*. (1389, 1399–1442.)

***Wise Men of Greece, The;*** also known as *The Seven Sages*.

Solon of Athens (about 638–559 BC), whose motto was, 'Know thyself.'

Chilo of Sparta (d.597 BC) – 'Consider the end.' *See* De Mortuis.

Thales of Miletus (d.548 BC) – 'Who hateth suretyship is sure.'

Bias of Priene (fl. 6th cent. BC) – 'Most men are bad.'

Cleobulus of Lindos (d.564 BC) – 'The golden mean', or 'Avoid extremes.'

Pittacus of Mitylene (d.570 BC) – 'Seize Time by the forelock.'

Periander of Corinth (d.585 BC) – 'Nothing is impossible to industry.'

***The Wise Men of the East.*** *See* Magi.

**Wiseacre.** (Ger. *weissager*, a soothsayer or prophet. This word, like the Greek 'sophism', has quite lost its original meaning, and is applied to dunces, wise only 'in their own conceit'.

There is a story told that Ben Jonson, at the *Devil*, in Fleet Street, said to a country gentleman who boasted of his estates, 'What care we for your dirt and clods? Where you have an acre of land, I have ten acres of wit.' The landed gentleman retorted by calling Ben 'Good Mr Wiseacre'. The story may pass for what it is worth.

**Wisest Man of Greece, The.** So the Delphic oracle pronounced Socrates to be, and Socrates modestly made answer, ''Tis because I alone of all the Greeks know that I know nothing.'

**Wish.** ***The wish is father to the thought.*** We are always ready to believe what we most want to believe. When the Prince says to his dying father 'I never thought to hear you speak again,' Henry IV replies –

> Thy wish was father, Harry, to that thought!
> I stay too long for thee, I weary thee.
>
> Shakespeare, *2 Henry IV*, 4, 4

Young has:

> What most we wish, with ease we fancy near.
>
> *Love of Fame*, Sat. iii

***To wish one farther.*** To prefer his room to his company; to wish him gone.

***Wishing bone.*** *See* Merrythought.

***Wishing cap.*** Fortunatus (*q.v.*) had an inexhaustible purse and a wishing cap, but these gifts proved the ruin of himself and his sons. The object of the tale is to show the vanity of human prosperity.

**Wishy-washy.** A reduplication of *washy*. Very thin, weak, and poor; wanting in substance or body.

**Wit.** Understanding, intelligence (A.S. *witt*, knowledge); hence, the power of perceiving analogies and other relations between apparently incongruous ideas or of forming unexpected, striking, or ludicrous combinations of them; and so, a person distinguished for this power, a witty person.

***At one's wits' end.*** Quite at a loss as to what to say or what to do next; 'flummoxed'.

***Great wits jump.*** Great minds think alike, tally. Shakespeare says, 'It jumps with my humour' (*1 Henry IV*, 4, 2).

***The five wits.*** *See* Five.

***To have one's wits about one.*** To be wide awake; observant of all that is going on and prepared to take advantage of any opportunity that offers.

***To wit.*** Namely; that is to say.

**Witch** (A.S. *wiccian*, to practise sorcery). By drawing the blood of a witch you deprive her of her power of sorcery. Glanvil says that when Jane Brooks, the demon of Tedworth, bewitched a boy, his father scratched her face and drew blood, whereupon the boy instantly exclaimed that he was well.

> Blood will I draw on thee; thou art a witch.
>
> Shakespeare, *1 Henry VI*, 1, 5

Innocent VIII issued the celebrated bull *Summis Desiderantes* in 1484, directing inquisitors and others to put to death all practisers of witchcraft and other diabolical arts, and it has been computed that as many as nine millions of persons suffered death for witchcraft since that date.

John Fian, a schoolmaster at Saltpans, near Edinburgh, was tortured and then burnt at the stake on the Castle Hill of Edinburgh in 1591, because he refused to acknowledge that he had raised a storm at sea, to wreck James VI on his voyage to Denmark to visit his future queen. First, his head was crushed in upon his brain by means of a rope twisted tighter and tighter; then his two legs were jammed to a jelly in the wooden boots; then his nails were pulled out and pins inserted in the raw finger-tips; as he still remained silent, he was strangled, and his body burnt to ashes.

Matthew Hopkins, the notorious 'witch-finder', who, in the middle of the 17th century, travelled through the eastern counties to hunt out witches, is said to have hanged sixty in one year in Essex alone. At last he himself was tested by his own rule; when cast into a river he floated, and so was declared to be a wizard, and was put to death.

It is said that in England between three and four thousand persons suffered death for witchcraft between 1643 and 1661, and as late as 1705 two women were executed at Northampton for witchcraft.

***Witch hazel.*** *See* Wych.

***Witches' Sabbath.*** The muster at night-time of witches and demons to concoct mischief. The witch first anointed her feet and shoulders with the fat of a murdered babe, then mounting a broomstick, distaff, or rake, made her exit by the chimney, and rode through the air to the place of rendezvous. The assembled witches feasted together, and concluded with a dance, in which they all turned their backs to each other.

**Witchen.** *See* Rowan.

**Witenagemot.** The Anglo-Saxon parliament. *Witan* is A.S. for *wise men* (connected with *witt*, knowledge); *gemote* is *ge-*, together, *moot*, meet; hence 'an assembly of wise men'.

> The famous assembly of our forefathers was called by various names [as] *Mycel Gemot* (or great meeting); the Witenagemot (or meeting of the wise); and sometimes the Mycel Getheaht (or great thought).
>
> Freeman, *The Norman Conquest*, i, 3

**Witham. *You were born, I suppose, at Little Witham.*** A reproof to a noodle. The pun, of course, is on *little wit*. Witham is in Essex.

> I will be sworn she was not born at Witham, for Gaffer Stubbs … says she could not turn up a single lesson to be, a Christian.
>
> Scott, *Heart of Midlothian*, ch. xxxii

**Withers.** A horse's *withers* are the muscles uniting the neck and shoulders, or the ridge between the shoulder blades; so called from A.S. *wither*, against, because this part is *against* the collar or load. Hamlet says (3, 2):

> Let the galled jade wince, our withers are unwrung.

That is, let those wince who are galled; as for myself, my withers are not wrung. The skin of this part is often galled by the pommel of an ill-fitting saddle, and then the irritation of the saddle makes the horse wince. In *1 Henry IV*, 2, 1, one of the carriers gives direction to the ostler to ease the saddle of his horse, Cut. 'I prythee, Tom, beat Cut's saddle … the poor jade is wrung on the withers', that is, the muscles are wrung, and the skin galled by the saddle.

**Withershins.** An Anglo-Saxon word, still in use in Scotland and in north-country dialects, denoting a movement in a contrary direction to that of the sun – as of a clock whose hands are going backwards (Icel. *vithr*, against, *sinni*, movement). Hence, contrariwise, topsy-turvy.

The opposite of *withershins* is *deiseal*, a Gaelic word meaning 'righthandwise'.

**Wittelsbach, House of.** The former reigning dynasty in Bavaria.

**Wo,** or **Woe worth the day!** Cursed be the day! Evil betide it!

> Thus saith the Lord God: Howl ye, woe worth the day! — Ezek. 30:2
>
> Wo worth the chase ! wo worth the day
> That costs thy life, my gallant grey.
>
> Sir Walter Scott

*Worth* here is A.S. *weorthan*, to become.

**Woden.** The Anglo-Saxon form of *Odin*, the name of the supreme god of the later Scandinavian pantheon, he having supplanted Thor.

Odin was god of wisdom, poetry, war, and agriculture, and on this latter account Wednesday (*Woden's day*) was considered to be specially favourable for sowing. He was god of the dead also, and presided over the banquets of those slain in battle. *See* Valhalla. He became the *All-wise* by drinking from Mimir's fountain, but purchased the distinction at the cost of one eye, and is usually represented as a one-eyed man wearing a hat and carrying a staff. His remaining eye is the Sun.

The *father* of Odin was Bör.

His *brothers* are Vili and Ve.

His *wife* is Frigga.

His *sons*, Thor and Balder.

His *mansion* is Gladsheim.

His *court* as war-god, Valhalla.

His *two black ravens* are Hugin (thought) and Munin (memory).

His *steed*, Sleipnir.

His *ships*, Skidbladnir and Naglfar.

His *spear*, Gungnir, which never fails to hit the mark aimed at.

His *ring*, Draupnir, which every ninth night drops eight other rings of equal value.

His *throne* is Hlidskjalf.

His *wolves*, Geri and Freki.

He will be ultimately swallowed up by the Fenris wolf at Ragnarok.

***The promise of Odin.*** The most binding of all oaths to a Norseman. In making it the hand was passed through a massive silver ring kept for the purpose; or through a sacrificial stone, like that called the 'Circle of Stennis'.

> I will bind myself to you ... by the promise of Odin, the most sacred of our northern rites.
>
> Scott, *The Pirate*, ch. xxii

**Woeful. *The Knight of the Woeful Countenance*.** The title given by Sancho Panza to Don Quixote (Bk iii, ch. v).

**Wolf.** The tradition that wolves were extirpated from Great Britain in the reign of Edgar (959–975) is based upon the words of William of Malmesbury, who says (Bk ii, ch. viii) that the tribute paid by the King of Wales, consisting of 300 wolves, ceased after the third year, because *nullum se ulterius posse invenire professus* (because he could find no more); but in 1076 we find that Robert de Umfraville, knight, held his lordship of Riddlesdale in Northumberland by service of defending that part of the kingdom from 'wolves'. In 1369 Thomas Engarne held lands in Pitchley, Northamptonshire, by service of finding dogs at his own cost for the destruction of 'wolves' and foxes; and even as late as 1433 Sir Robert Plumpton held one bovate of land in the county of Notts by service of 'frighting the wolves' in Sherwood Forest.

*Wolf* has been applied as an epithet to many persons of savage and inhuman disposition, especially to Isabella, the *She-wolf of France*, the adulterous queen of Edward II. According to tradition, she murdered her royal husband by thrusting a hot iron into his bowels.

> She-wolf of France, with unrelenting fangs,
> That tear'st the bowels of thy mangled mate.
>
> Gray, *The Bard*

Dryden gave the name to the Presbytery in his *Hind and Panther*.

> Unkennelled range in thy Polonian plains,
> A fiercer foe the insatiate Wolf remains.

In music a discordant sound (occasioned by a faulty interval) in certain chords of the organ and stringed instruments such as the piano, violin, harp, etc. is called a *wolf*.

> Nature hath implanted so inveterate a hatred atweene the wolfe and the sheepe, that, being dead, yet in the operation of Nature appeareth there a sufficient trial of their discording nature; so that the enmity betweene them seemeth not to dye with their bodies; for if there be put upon a harpe ... strings made of the intralles of a sheepe, and amongst them ... one made of the intralles of a wolfe ... the musician ... cannot reconcile them to a unity and concord of sounds, so discording is that string of the wolfe.
>
> Ferne, *Blazon of Gentrie* (1586)

The squeak made in *reed* instruments by unskilful players is termed a 'goose'.

**Phrases.**

***Between dog and wolf.*** Neither daylight nor dark, the blind man's holiday. Generally applied to the evening dusk. In Latin, *Inter canem et lupum*; in French, *Entre chien et loup*.

***Dark as a wolf's mouth.*** Pitch dark.

***He has seen a wolf.*** Something or other has frightened him; formerly said of a person who has lost his voice. Our forefathers believed that if a man saw a wolf before the wolf saw him, he became dumb, at least for a time.

> Vox quoque Moerin
> Jam fugit ipsa; lupi Moerin videre priores.
>
> Virgil, *Bucolica*, eclogue ix

> 'Our young companion has seen a wolf,' said Lady Hameline, 'and has lost his tongue in consequence.'
>
> Scott, *Quentin Durward*, ch. xviii

To see a wolf is also a good sign, inasmuch as the wolf was dedicated to Odin, the giver of victory.

***He put his head into the wolf's mouth.*** He exposed himself to needless danger. The allusion is to Aesop's fable of the crane that put its head into a wolf's (or fox's) mouth in order to extract a bone.

***Holding a wolf by the ears.*** An old Greek saying; Augustus used it of his situation in Rome, meaning it was equally dangerous to keep hold or to let go.

He that goes to law (as the proverb is) holds a wolf by the ears.
Burton, *Anatomy of Melancholy* (*Democritus to the Reader*)

***To cry 'Wolf!'*** To give a false alarm. The allusion is to the well known fable of the shepherd lad who used to cry 'Wolf!' merely to make fun of the neighbours, but when at last the wolf came no one would believe him.

***To keep the wolf from the door.*** To ward off starvation. We say of a ravenous person 'He has a wolf in his stomach,' and one who eats voraciously is said *to wolf* his food. French *manger comme un loup* is to eat voraciously, and *wolfsmagen* is the German for a keen appetite.

***Wake not a sleeping wolf!*** (Shakespeare, *2 Henry IV*, 1, 2). A variant of 'Let sleeping dogs lie!' – let well alone.

**Wolf Men.** Giraldus Cambrensis tells us (*Opera*, vol. v, p. 119) that Irishmen can be 'changed into wolves'. Nennius asserts that the 'descendants of wolves are still in Ossory', and 'they retransform themselves into wolves when they bite' (*Wonders of Eri*, xiv). *See also* Werwolf.

**Wolf's-bane.** A species of aconite, *Aconitum lycoctonum.* The name is said to have arisen through a curious double etymological confusion. *Bane* is a common term for poisonous plants, and by some early botanist it was translated into Gr. *kuamos*, which means *bean*. The plant has a pale yellow flower, and was so called the *white-bane* to distinguish it from the *blue* aconite. The Greek for white is *leukos*, hence *leukos-kuamos*; but *lukos* is the Greek for wolf, and by a blunder *leukos-kuamos* (white-bean) got muddled into *lukos-kuamos* (wolf-bean). Botanists, seeing the absurdity of calling aconite a *bean*, restored the original word *bane* but retained the corrupt word *lukos* (a wolf), and hence we get the name wolf's-bane for white aconite.

This sounds rather far-fetched, and the true explanation would probably be that the plant is so called because meat saturated with its juice was supposed to be a wolf-poison.

**Wonder.** ***A nine days' wonder.*** Something that causes a sensational astonishment for a few days, and is then placed in the limbo of 'things forgot'. Three days' amazement, three days' discussion of details, and three days of subsidence.

For whan men han wel cried, than let hem roune!
For wonder last but nine night nevere in toune!
Chaucer, *Troilus and Criseyde*, iv, 587

***The Seven Wonders of the World.*** *Of Antiquity.*

The *Pyramids* first, which in Egypt were laid;
Then *Babylon's Gardens* for Amytis made:
Third, *Mausolus' Tomb* of affection and guilt;
Fourth, the *Temple of Dian*, in Ephesus built;
Fifth, *Colossus of Rhodes*, cast in brass, to the Sun;
Sixth, *Jupiter's Statue*, by Phidias done;
The *Pharos of Egypt*, last wonder of old,
Or the *Palace of Cyrus*, cemented with gold.
E.C.B.

*Of the Middle Ages.*

(1) The Coliseum of Rome.
(2) The Catacombs of Alexandria.
(3) The Great Wall of China.
(4) Stonehenge.
(5) The Leaning Tower of Pisa.
(6) The Porcelain Tower of Nankin.
(7) The Mosque of St Sophia at Constantinople.

The palace of the Escurial (*q.v.*) has sometimes been called the *Eighth Wonder*, a name which has also been given to a number of works of great mechanical ingenuity, such as the dome of Chosroes in Madain, St Peter's of Rome, the Menai suspension bridge, the Eddystone lighthouse, the Suez Canal, the railway over Mont Cenis, the Atlantic cable, etc.

***The Wonder of the World.*** The title given to Otto III, Emperor of the Holy Roman Empire, 983–1002, on account of his brilliant intellectual endowments. The Emperor Frederick II (1215–50) was also so called.

***The Wonderful,*** or ***Wondermaking, Parliament*** The same as 'The Unmerciful Parliament'; convened in the reign of Richard II (February 3rd, 1388). By playing into the hands of the Duke of Gloucester it checkmated the king.

**Wonder-worker.** St Gregory, Bishop of Neo-Caesarea, in Pontus, and one of the Fathers of the Eastern Church (d.270). So called because he 'recalled devils, stayed a river, killed a Jew by the mere effort of his will, changed a lake into solid earth, and did many other wonderful things'. *See* Thaumaturgus.

**Wood.** ***Drawn from the wood.*** Taken direct from the cask to the tankard or glass. Said of beer, wines, and spirits.

***Don't cry*** (or ***halloo***) ***till you are out of the wood.*** Do not rejoice for having escaped danger till the danger has passed away. 'Call no man happy till he is dead'; 'there's many a slip 'twixt the cup and the lip'.

**_One can't see the wood for the trees._** There is such a mass of detail that it is almost impossible to arrive at a true estimate of the thing as a whole.

**Woodbine.** A name given in different localities to many plants that bind or wind themselves around trees; especially the honeysuckle and the convolvulus. In the first quotation below probably the former is intended; in the second the latter.

> Where the bee
> Strays diligent, and with extracted balm
> Of fragrant woodbine loads his little thigh.
>
> Phillips

Shakespeare says –

> So doth the woodbine, the sweet honeysuckle
> Gently entwist.
>
> *Midsummer Night's Dream*, 4, 1

**Woodchuck.** A marmot (*Arctomys monax*) of North America, also called the *ground-hog*. Its name is a corruption of its North American Indian name, *wejack*, and has given rise to the punning conundrum –

> How much wood would a woodchuck chuck, if a woodchuck could chuck wood?

**Woodcock.** Old slang for a simpleton; from the supposition that woodcocks are without brains. Polonius tells his daughter that protestations of love are 'springes to catch woodcocks' (Shakespeare, *Hamlet*, 1, 3).

**Wooden.** Used of one who is awkward and ungainly, or of a spiritless, emotionless person.

**_The wooden horse._** An enchanted horse of the old romance that could be directed by a peg turned by the rider and could fly through the air. Cambuscan (*q.v.*) had such a horse, but his was of brass. *Cp*. Clavileno.

> This very day may be seen in the king's armoury the identical peg with which Peter of Provence turned his Wooden Horse, which carried him through the air. It is rather bigger than the pole of a coach, and stands near Babieca's saddle.
>
> *Don Quixote*, pt i, bk iv, 19

**_The wooden horse of Troy._** Virgil tells us that Ulysses had a monster wooden horse made after the death of Hector, and gave out that it was an offering to the gods to secure a prosperous voyage back to Greece. The Trojans dragged the horse within their city, but it was full of Grecian soldiers, who at night stole out of their place of concealment, slew the Trojan guards, opened the city gates, and set fire to Troy. Menelaus was one of the Greeks shut up in it. It was made by Epeios.

**_The wooden mare._** 'The mare foaled of an acorn'. An instrument of torture to enforce military discipline, used in the reign of Charles II and long after. The horse was made of oak, the back was a sharp ridge, and the four legs were like a high stool. The victim was seated on the ridge, with a firelock fastened to each foot.

> Here, Andrews, wrap a cloak round the prisoner, and do not mention his name ... unless you would have a trot on the wooden mare.
>
> Scott, *Old Mortality*, ch. ix

**_The wooden spoon._** The last of the honour men – i.e. of the Junior Optimes, at Cambridge. Sometimes two or more 'last' men are bracketed together, in which case the group is termed the *spoon bracket*. It is said that these men are so called because they used to be presented with a wooden spoon, while the other honour men had a silver or golden one, a spoon being the usual *prix de mérite* instead of a medal.

**_The wooden wedge._** Last in the classical tripos. When, in 1824, the classical tripos was instituted at Cambridge, it was debated by what name to call the last on the list. It so happened that the last on the list was Wedgewood, and the name was adopted to this slightly modified form.

**_Wooden walls._** Ships of war. Before the advent of ironclads England's defence literally were 'wooden walls'.

When the Greeks sent to Delphi to ask how they were to defend themselves against Xerxes, who had invaded their country, the evasive answer given was to this effect –

> Pallas hath urged, and Zeus, the sire of all,
> Hath safely promised in a wooden wall;
> Seed-time and harvest, weeping sires shall tell
> How thousands fought at Salamis and fell.

**Woodsear.** A local name for cuckoo spit (*q.v.*).

**Wood's Halfpence.** The copper coinage for which William Wood, a copper-founder of Wolverhampton, obtained from the Government the valuable privilege of supplying to Ireland, in 1722. The outcry against this was so great (*see* Drapier's Letters) that the patent was revoked in 1725.

**Woodwardian Professor.** The professor of geology at Cambridge. This professorship was founded in 1727 by Dr Woodward.

**Woof.** *See* Warp.

**Wookey Hole.** A noted cavern in Somersetshire, which has given birth to as many weird stories as the Sibyl's Cave in Italy. *Wicked as the Witch of Wookey* is an old local simile; and we read in Percy's *Reliques* that the witch was metamorphosed into stone by a 'lerned wight' from Gaston, but left her curse behind, so that the fair damsels of Wookey rarely find 'a gallant'.

**Wool.** ***Great cry and little wool.*** *See* Cry.

***Dyed in the wool.*** Said of a thorough sport, a hearty good fellow. Cloth which is wool-dyed (not piece-dyed) is true throughout 'and will wash'.

***No wool is so white that a dyer cannot blacken it.*** No one is so free from faults that slander can find nothing to say against him; no book is so perfect as to be free from adverse criticism.

***Your wits are gone wool-gathering.*** You are absent-minded; you're not thinking of the matter in hand. As children sent to gather wool from hedges are absent for a trivial purpose, so persons in a 'brown study' are absent on trivialities.

**Woollen.** In 1666 an Act of Parliament was passed for 'burying in woollen only', which was intended for 'the encouragement of the woollen manufactures of the kingdom, and prevention of the exportation of money for the buying and importing of linen'. Repealed in 1814.

'Odious! in woollen! 'twould a saint provoke!'
(Were the last words that poor Narcissa spoke).
'No! let a charming chintz and Brussels lace
Wrap my cold limbs, and shade my lifeless face.
One would not, sure, be frightful when one's dead;
And – Betty – give the cheeks a little red.'

Pope, *Moral Essays*, Ep. i

This was the ruling passion strong in death. At the time this was written it was compulsory to bury in woollen. Narcissa did not dread death half so much as being obliged to wear flannel next her skin!

**Woolsack, The.** The office of Lord Chancellor of England, whose seat in the House of Lords is called the *woolsack*. It is a large square bag of wool, without back or arms, and covered with red cloth. In the reign of Queen Elizabeth an Act of Parliament was passed to prevent the exportation of wool; and that this source of our national wealth might be kept constantly in mind woolsacks were placed in the House of Peers as seats for the judges. Hence the Lord Chancellor, who presides in the House of Lords, is said to 'sit on the woolsack', or to be 'appointed to the woolsack'.

**Word.** ***A man of his word.*** One whose word may be depended on; trustworthy; he is 'as good as his word', and 'his word is as good as his bond'.

***A word to the wise!*** Said when giving advice as a hint that it would be well for the recipient to follow it. The Latin *Verbum satis satienti*, a word is enough to the wise.

***By word of mouth.*** Orally. As 'he took it down by word of mouth' (as it was spoken by the speaker).

***I take you at your word.*** I will act in reliance of what you tell me.

***Many words will not fill a bushel.*** Mere promises will not help the needy. If we say to a beggar, 'Be thou filled', is he filled?

***Pray, make no words about it.*** In French, *N'en dites mot*. Don't mention it; make no fuss about it.

***Put in a good word for me, please!*** Do your best to get me some privilege or favour; put my claims, my deeds, etc., in the best light possible.

***Soft words butter no parsnips.*** *See* Butter.

***The Word.*** The Scriptures; Christ as the Logos (*see* John 1:1).

***The object of words is to conceal thoughts.*** *See* Speech.

***To give,*** or ***pass one's word.*** To give a definite undertaking, make a binding promise.

***To have words with one.*** To quarrel; to have an angry discussion. *To have a word with one*, is to have a brief conversation with him.

***Upon my word.*** Assuredly; by my troth.

***Upon my word and honour!*** A strong affirmation of the speaker as to the truth of what he has asserted.

**World.** ***A man*** or ***woman of the world.*** One who is acquainted with the ways of public and social life; not quite the same as a *worldly* man or woman, which expression would denote one that cares *only* for the things of this world.

In Shakespeare's time a *woman of the world* was merely a married woman:

*Touchstone*: Tomorrow will we be married.
*Audrey*: I do desire it with all my heart; and I hope it is no dishonest desire to be a woman of the world.

*As You Like It*, 5, 3

Celibacy was at one time exalted into 'a crown of glory', and mankind was divided into celibates and worldlings (or laity). The former were monks and nuns, and the latter were the *monde* (or people of the world).

Everyone goes to the world but I, and I may sit in a corner and cry heigho! for a husband.

*Much Ado about Nothing*, 2, 1

If I may have your ladyship's good will to go to the world, Isabel and I will do as we may.

*All's Well that Ends Well*, 1, 3

***All the world and his wife.*** Everyone without exception.

***The world, the flesh, and the devil.*** 'The world', i.e. the things of this world, in contradistinction to religious matters; 'the flesh', i.e. love of pleasure and sensual enjoyments; 'the devil', i.e. all temptations to evil of every kind, as theft, murder, lying, blasphemy, and so on.

> From all the deceits of the world, the flesh, and the devil, Good Lord, deliver us.
>
> *The Litany* (*Book of Common Prayer*)

**Worm.** The word was formerly used of dragons and great serpents, especially those of Teutonic and old Norse legend; and is now figuratively applied to miserable, grovelling creatures; also to the ligament under a dog's tongue.

***Idle worms.*** It was once supposed that little worms were bred in the fingers of idle servants. To this Shakespeare alludes –

> A round little worm
> Pricked from the lazy finger of a maid.
>
> *Romeo and Juliet*, 1, 4

***To be food for worms.*** To be dead.

> Your worm is your only emperor for diet: we fat all creatures else, to fat us; and we fat ourselves for maggots. Shakespeare, *Hamlet*, 4, 3

***To have a worm in one's tongue.*** To be cantankerous; to snarl and bite like a mad dog.

> There is one easy artifice
> That seldom has been known to miss –
> To snarl at all things right or wrong,
> Like a mad dog that has a worm in's tongue.
>
> Butler, *Upon Modern Critics*

***To satisfy the worm.*** To appease one's hunger.

***To worm out information.*** To elicit information indirectly and piecemeal.

***To worm oneself into another's favour.*** To insinuate oneself in an underhand manner into the good graces of another person.

**Worms,** in Germany, according to tradition, is so called from the Lindwurm or dragon slain by Siegfried under the linden tree.

> Yet more I know of Siegfried that well your ear may hold,
> Beneath the linden tree he slew the dragon bold;
> Then in its blood he bathed him, which turned to horn his skin
> So now no weapon harms him, as oft hath proven been. *Nibelungenlied*, st. 104

The place was called by the Romans Borbetomagus, and by the Germanic tribes Wormasza; the name is probably of Celtic origin.

**Wormwood.** Fable has it that this plant sprang up in the track of the serpent as it writhed along the ground when driven out of Paradise. Fact proclaims that it has nothing to do with *worms* or *wood*, but is the Anglo-Saxon *wer mod*, man-inspiriting, being a strong tonic.

**Worship** means state or condition of worth, hence the term 'his worship', meaning his *worthyship*. 'Thou shalt have *worship* in the presence of them that sit at meat with thee' (Luke 14:10) means 'Thou shalt have *worth-ship* – value or appreciation'. In the marriage service the man says to the woman, 'With my body I thee worship, and with all my worldly goods I thee endow' – that is, I confer on you my rank and dignities, and endow you with my wealth; the worthship attached to my person I share with you, and the wealth which is mine is thine also.

Magistrates and mayors are addressed as *Your Worship*, and in writing a mayor is *The Worshipful Mayor, Mr A.*

**Worst.** ***If the worst come to the worst.*** Even if the very worst occurs.

***To get the worst of it.*** To come off second best; to be defeated, worsted.

**Worsted.** Yarn or thread made of wool; so called from Worsted in Norfolk, now a village, but once a large market town with at least as many thousand inhabitants as it now contains hundreds.

**Worthies, the Nine.** Nine heroes – three from the Bible, three from the classics, and three from romance – who were frequently bracketed together, as in the burlesque Pageant of the Nine Worthies in Shakespeare's *Love's Labour's Lost*, They are – Joshua, David, and Judas Maccabaeus; Hector, Alexander, and Julius Caesar; Arthur, Charlemagne, and Godfrey of Bouillon.

> Nine worthies were they called, of different rites –
> Three Jews, three pagans, and three Christian knights. Dryden, *The Flower and the Leaf*

***The Nine Worthies of London.*** A kind of chronicle-history in mixed verse and prose of nine prominent citizens of London, published in 1592 by Richard Johnson, author also of *The Seven Champions of Christendom*. His 'Worthies' are –

*Sir William Walworth*, who stabbed Wat Tyler, the rebel, and was twice Lord Mayor (1374, 1380).

*Sir Henry Pritchard*, who (in 1356) feasted Edward III (with 5,000 followers), Edward the Black Prince, John, King of Austria, the King of Cyprus, and David, King of Scotland.

*Sir William Sevenoke*, who fought with the Dauphin of France, built twenty almshouses and a free school (1418).

*Sir Thomas White*, merchant tailor, who, in 1553, kept the citizens loyal to Queen Mary during Wyatt's rebellion.

*Sir John Bonham*, entrusted with a valuable cargo for the Danish market, and made commander of the army raised to stop the progress of the great Solyman.

*Christopher Croker*. Famous at the siege of Bordeaux, and companion of the Black Prince when he helped Don Pedro to the throne of Castile.

*Sir John Hawkwood*. One of the Black Prince's knights, and immortalised in Italian history as Giovanni Acuti Cavaliero.

*Sir Hugh Caverley*. Famous for ridding Poland of a monstrous bear.

*Sir Henry Maleverer*, generally called Henry of Cornhill, who lived in the reign of Henry IV. He was a crusader, and became the guardian of 'Jacob's well'.

The names of Sir Richard Whittington and Sir Thomas Gresham are 'conspicuous by their absence'.

**Wound.** *Bind the wound, and grease the weapon.* A Rosicrucian maxim. *See* Weapon-salve.

**Wove.** Applied to papers made on an ordinary dandy roll or mould in which the wires are woven, and used in contradistinction to *Laid* (*q.v.*).

**Wrafs.** Members of the *W*omen's *R*oyal *A*ir *F*orce; one of the acrostic names that sprang up in such profusion during the Great War. *Cp.* Waac; Wren.

**Wraith.** The phantom or spectral appearance of a still living person, usually taken as a warning that that person is very shortly going to die. It appears to persons at a distance, and forewarns them of the event.

**Wrangler.** The Cambridge term for one who has obtained a place in the highest class of the mathematical tripos. The first man used to be termed the *Senior Wrangler*, and the rest were arranged according to respective merit, but since 1909 this arrangement has been dropped and no one now can claim the title of *Senior Wrangler*.

In the Middle Ages college exercises were called *disputations*, and those who performed them *disputants*, because the main part consisted in pitting two men together, one to argue *pro* and the other *con*. In the law and theological 'schools' this is still done for the bachelor's and doctor's degrees.

**Wren.** A member of the *W*omen's *R*oyal *N*aval Division, an auxiliary force raised during the Great War. *Cp.* Waac; Wrafs.

***Wrenning Day.*** St Stephen's Day (Dec. 26th) used to be so called, because it was a custom among villagers to stone a wren to death on that day in commemoration of his martyrdom.

**Wright of Norwich.** ***Do you know Dr Wright of Norwich?*** A reproof given to a person who stops the decanter at dinner. Dr Wright, of Norwich, was a great diner-out and excellent talker. When a person stops the bottle and is asked this question, it is as much as to say, Dr Wright had the privilege of doing so because he entertained the table with his conversation, but you are no Dr Wright, except in stopping the circulation of the wine.

A similar reproof is given in the combination room of our universities in this way: The bottle-stopper is asked if he knows A or B (*any name*), and after several queries as to who A or B is, the questioner says, 'He was hanged,' and being asked what for, replies, 'For stopping the bottle.'

**Wrinkle.** Familiar slang for a useful bit of information, a 'tip' or a dodge. For instance, if a man were going to Paris for the first time he might go to a friend who was a frequent visitor *to get a wrinkle or two*, i.e. learn about the things to see, the way of living there, how to get through the Customs, etc.

**Write.** A.S. *writan*, connected with Icel, *rita*, to tear, cut, scratch out, etc.

***To write down***, besides meaning to commit to writing, means to criticise unfavourably, to depreciate. Contrariwise, *to write up* is to puff, to bring into public notice or estimation by favourable criticisms or accounts.

***To write off a debt.*** To cancel it.

***To write oneself out.*** To exhaust one's powers of literary production.

**Writer.** The Scottish term for a solicitor or attorney; in full a *Writer to the Signet*, the Signet being the smaller seal of the Sovereign.

In the navy a *writer* is a paymaster's non-commissioned assistant; a clerk to a paymaster, either afloat or ashore.

**Wrong.** ***The king can do no wrong.*** A legal maxim enshrining two truths; firstly, that as the king is – in theory – the creator of all law he cannot be subject to it; and, secondly, that the Sovereign, *as* Sovereign, does nothing except on the advice and with the consent of his ministers.

The Latin proverb – *Nihil potest rex nisi quod de jure potest* (the king can do nothing except what he can do by law) comes to the same thing.

***Wrong 'un.*** A swindler, a cheat, a palpably dishonest person; applied also to false coin and many things that are not what they purport to be; also to a horse which has run at any flat-race meeting not recognised by the Jockey Club, and so is boycotted by the Club.

**Wroth Money** or **Wroth Silver.** Money paid to the lord in lieu of castle guard for military service; a tribute paid for killing accidentally some person of note; a tribute paid in acknowledgement of the tenancy of unenclosed land. Dugdale, in his *History of Warwickshire*, says:

> There is a certain rent due unto the lord of this Hundred (i.e. of Knightlow, the property of the Duke of Buccleuch) called wroth money, or warth-money, or swarff-penny … *Denarii vicecomiti vel aliis castelanis persoluti ob castrorum praesidium vel excubias agendas* (*Sir Henry Spelman, Glossary*).

The rent must be paid on Martinmas Day (Nov. 11th), in the morning at Knightlow Cross, before sunrise. The party paying it must go thrice about the cross and say, 'The wrath-money,' and then lay it (varying from 1*d.* to 2*s.* 3*d.*) in a hole in the said cross before good witnesses, or forfeit a white bull with red nose and ears. The amount thus collected reached in 1892 to about 9*s.*, and all who complied with the custom were entertained at a substantial breakfast at the Duke's expense, and were toasted in a glass of rum and milk.

**Wulstan, St.** A Saxon Bishop of Worcester, who received his see from Edward the Confessor, and died in 1075. He fought against William the Conqueror, and when ordered to resign his see, he planted his crozier in the shrine of the Confessor, declaring if any of his accusers could draw it out he would resign; as no one could do so but St Wulstan himself, his innocence was admitted. This sort of 'miracle' is the commonest of legendary wonders. Arthur proved himself king by a similar 'miracle'.

**Wuyck's Bible.** *See* Bible, Specially named.

**Wych Hazel.** A North American shrub (*Hamamelis virginiana*) having several large branches. *Wych* is the A.S. *wyce* (connected with *wicker*), and means 'drooping'. The similarity of the prefix to *witch* led to the erroneous idea that it was so called because divining rods made from its twigs were efficacious in discovering witches.

**Wycliffite.** A Lollard (*q.v.*), a follower of John Wyclif (d.1384), the religious reformer, called 'The Morning Star of the Reformation'. He denied transubstantiation, condemned monasticism, and taught that all ecclesiastical and secular authority is derived from God and is forfeited by one who is living in mortal sin.

**Wyclif's Bible.** *See* Bible, the English.

**Wykehamist.** A member of Winchester College, past or present, which was founded in 1378 by William of Wykeham (1324–1404), Bishop of Winchester and Lord High Chancellor. Wykeham is a small place in Hampshire.

**Wynd.** ***Every man for his own hand, as Henry Wynd fought***. Every man for himself; every man seeks his own advantage. When the feud between Clan Chattan and Clan Kay was decided by deadly combat on the North Inch of Perth, one of the men of Clan Chattan deserted, and Henry Wynd, a bandy-legged smith, volunteered for half a crown to supply his place. After killing one man he relaxed in his efforts, and on being asked why, replied, 'I have done enough for half a crown.' He was promised wages according to his deserts, and fought bravely. After the battle he was asked what he fought for, and gave for answer that he fought 'for his own hand'; whence the proverb. (Scott, *Tales of a Grandfather*, xvii.)

**X.** The twenty-fourth letter of the alphabet, representing the fourteenth letter of the Greek alphabet (*ksi*), and denoting in Roman numeration 10, or, on its side (⋈) 1,000, and with a dash over it ($\bar{X}$) 10,000.

In algebra and mathematics generally *x* denotes an unknown quantity. The reason of this is that algebra came into use in Europe from Arabia, and that Arabic *shei*, a thing, a something (*cp. cosa* under Coss, Rule of) was used in the Middle Ages to designate the mathematically 'unknown', and that this was transcribed as *xei*.

X on beer casks formerly indicated beer which had paid the old 10*s*. duty, and hence it came to mean beer of a given quality. Two or three crosses are mere trade-marks, intended to convey the impression that the beer so marked was twice or thrice as strong as that which paid this duty.

**Xanthian Marbles, The.** A collection of ancient sculptures and friezes discovered by Sir Charles Fellows in 1838 at Xanthus, a Greek city of Lycia, Asia Minor, and now in the British Museum.

**Xanthippe** or **Xantippe.** Wife of the philosopher Socrates. Her bad temper shown towards her husband has rendered her name proverbial for a conjugal scold.

> Be she as foul as was Florentius' love,
> As old as Sibyl, and as curst and shrewd
> As Socrates' Xanthippe, or a worse,
> She moves me not.
>
> Shakespeare, *Taming of the Shrew*, 1, 2

**Xanthochroi.** The name given by ethnologists to the branch of the Caucasian race comprising the blonds or 'fair whites', persons with yellowish or reddish hair, blue eyes, and fair complexions (Gr. *Xanthos*, reddish yellow, *ochros*, pale).

**Xanthus** (Gr., reddish yellow). Achilles' wonderful horse, brother of Balios, Achilles' other horse, and offspring of Zephyrus and the harpy, Podarge. Being chid by his master for leaving Patroclus on the field of battle, Xanthus turned his head reproachfully, and told Achilles that he also would soon be numbered with the dead, not from any fault of his horse, but by the decree of inexorable destiny (*Iliad*, xix). (*Cp*. Numb. 22:28–30.)

*Xanthus* is also the ancient name of the Scamander and of a city on its banks. Elian and Pliny say that Homer called the Scamander 'Xanthos' or the 'Gold-red river', because it coloured with such a tinge the fleeces of sheep washed in its waters. Others maintain that it was so called because a Greek hero of this name defeated a body of Trojans on its banks, and pushed half of them into the stream.

**Xaverian Brothers, The.** A Roman Catholic congregation founded in Holland in 1846, and so named from St Francis Xavier (1506–52), one of the earliest of the Jesuit Order, and the great missionary to India and the Far East. It is concerned chiefly with the education of youth, and has branches in England and the United States.

**Xenocratic.** Pertaining to the doctrine of Xenocrates (396–314 BC), a disciple of Plato, noted for his continence and contempt of wealth. He combined Pythagoreanism with Platonism.

> Warmed by such youthful beauty, the severe
> Xenocrates would not have more been chaste.
>
> *Orlando Furioso*, xi, 8

**Xerxes.** A Greek way of writing the Persian *Ksathra* or *Kshatra*. Xerxes I, the great Xerxes, is identical with the Ahasuerus of the Bible.

When Xerxes invaded Greece he constructed a pontoon bridge across the Dardanelles, which was swept away by the force of the waves; this so enraged the Persian despot that he 'inflicted three hundred lashes on the rebellious sea, and cast chains of iron across it'. This story is probably a Greek myth, founded on the peculiar construction of Xerxes' second bridge, which consisted of three hundred boats, lashed by iron chains to two ships serving as supporters.

Another story told of him is that when he reviewed his enormous army before starting for Greece, he wept at the thought of slaughter about to take place. 'Of all this multitude, who shall say how many will return?' Similarly, it is said that Charlemagne viewed the fleet of the Norsemen in the Mediterranean with tears in his eyes, and remarked, 'There was reason for these Xerxes tears.'

Xerxes shed tears at the expected loss of his brave men, Charlemagne at the prospective disruption of his empire.

**Ximena.** The Cid's bride.

# Y

**Y.** The twenty-fifth letter of the alphabet, is a differentiation of the Greek γ (*see* Samian Letter) added by the Greeks to the Phoenician alphabet.

In Algebra it denotes the second unknown quantity (*cp.* X), and in the Middle Ages it was used in Roman numeration for 150. *See also* Ye.

**Yacu-mama** (mother of waters). A fabulous sea-snake, fifty paces long and twelve yards in girth, said to lurk in the lagoons of South America, and in the river Amazon. This monster draws into its mouth whatever passes within a hundred yards of it, and for this reason an Indian will not venture on an unknown lagoon till he has blown his horn, which the yacu-mama never fails to answer if it is within hearing. (Waterton.)

**Yahoo.** Swift's name, in *Gulliver's Travels*, for brutes with human forms and vicious propensities. They are subject to the *Houyhnhnms*, the horses with human reason. Hence applied to coarse, brutish, or degraded persons.

**Yahweh.** *See* Jehovah.

**Yama.** The god of the dead in *Hindu mythology*, the Hindu Pluto. The story is that he was the first mortal to die and so was made a god. He is of a green colour, four armed, with eyes inflamed, and sits on a buffalo.

**Yankee.** Properly a New Englander or one of New England stock; but extended to mean, first, an inhabitant of the Northern as apart from the Southern United States, and later to comprise all United States citizens.

It is generally taken to be a North American Indian corruption of *English* (or of Fr. *Anglais*). The story is that in 1713 one Jonathan Hastings, a farmer of Cambridge, Massachusetts, used the word as a puffing epithet, meaning genuine, what cannot be surpassed, etc.; as, a 'Yankee horse', 'Yankee cider', and so on. The students at Harvard catching up the term, called Hastings, 'Yankee Jonathan'. It soon spread, and became the jocose pet name of the New Englander.

**Yankee Doodle.** The quasi national air of the United States, the doggerel words of which are said to have been written by Dr Shuckburgh, a surgeon in Lord Amherst's army during the French and Indian war of 1755.

The origin of the tune is disputed; some say that it comes from a mediaeval church service, others that it was composed in England in Cromwell's time, others that it was played by the Hessian troops during the American Revolution and adopted by the revolutionaries in mockery. A Dutch origin has also been suggested.

**Yarborough.** A hand at bridge in which there is not a single trump (trumps having been called) is usually so named; but the term properly belongs to a hand in which there is no card higher than a nine. So called because the second Lord Yarborough (early 19th cent.) used to lay 1,000 to 1 against such an occurrence in any named hand. The actual mathematical odds are 1827 to 1 against.

**Ye.** An archaic way of writing *the*, the *y* representing A.S. ȝ (*ge*) which in Middle English became confused with þ, the character representing our *th* as in *then*. To pronounce the first word of *Ye Olde Cheshire Cheese* as though it were the same as the 2nd pers. pl. pronoun is a sign of ignorance, it never was pronounced other than *the*.

**Year** (connected with Gr. *horos*, a season, and Lat. *hora*, an hour). The period of time occupied by the revolution of the earth round the sun.

The Astronomical, Equinoctial, Natural, Solar, or Tropical year, is the time taken by the sun in returning to the same equinox, in mean length, 365 days, 5 hours, 48 min., and 46 sec.

The Astral or Sidereal year is the time in which the sun apparently returns to the same place in relation to the fixed stars: 365 days 6 hours 9 min. and 9 sec.

The Platonic, Great, or Perfect year (*Annus magnus*), was estimated by early Greek and Hindu astronomers at about 26,000 years, at the end of which all the heavenly bodies were imagined to return to the same places as they occupied at the Creation.

The Chaldean astronomers observed that the fixed stars shift their places at about the rate of a degree in seventy-two years, according to which calculation they will perform one revolution in 25,920 years, at the end of which time they will return to their 'as you were'. The Egyptians made it 30,000 years, and the Arabians 49,000.

***For a year and a day.*** In law many acts are determined by this period of time – e.g. if a person wounded does not die within a year and a day, the offender is not guilty of murder; if an owner does not claim an estray within the same length of time, it belongs to the lord of the manor; a year and a day is given to prosecute appeals, etc.

***Year of Grace.*** A year of the Christian era.

***Year in year out.*** All the year round, without cessation.

**Yellow** (A.S. *geolo*, connected with Gr. *chloros*, green, and with *gall*, the yellowish fluid secreted by the bile). Indicating in symbolism jealousy, inconstancy, and adultery. In France the doors of traitors used to be daubed with yellow. In some countries the law ordained that Jews must be clothed in yellow, because they betrayed our Lord, hence Judas, in mediaeval pictures, is arrayed in yellow. In Spain the vestments of the executioner are either red or yellow – the former to denote blood-shedding, the latter treason.

In heraldry and in ecclesiastical symbolism yellow is frequently used in place of gold.

***Yellow-back.*** A cheap novel, particularly one of a sensational kind. So called because of the yellow board bindings so well known on railway bookstalls up to about the early 'nineties of last century.

***Yellow-bellies.*** Slang for inhabitants of the fenlands of East Anglia and Lincolnshire; the allusion being to frogs. The Mexicans are also so called.

***Yellow Books.*** Official documents, Government reports, etc., in France; corresponding to our 'Blue Books' (*q.v.*); so called from the colour of their covers.

***Yellow boy.*** Slang for a golden sovereign, formerly fairly common in Great Britain.

> John did not starve the cause; there wanted not
> yellow-boys to fee counsel.
>
> Arbuthnot, *John Bull* (1712)

***Yellow-hammer.*** A bunting with yellowish head, neck, and breast (A.S. *amore*, Ger. *ammer*, a bunting). The tradition is that the bird fluttered about the Cross, and got stained with the Blood in its plumage, and by way of punishment its eggs were doomed ever after to bear marks of blood. Because the bird was 'cursed', boys were taught that it is as right and proper to destroy eggs of the bunting as to persecute a Jew.

***Yellow Jack.*** The yellow fever; also the flag displayed from lazarettos, naval hospitals, and vessels in quarantine.

***Yellow Peril, The.*** A scare, originally raised in Germany in the late 'nineties of last century, that the yellow races of China and Japan would in a very few years have increased in population to such an extent that incursions upon the territories occupied by the white races – followed by massacres and every conceivable horror – were inevitable.

***Yellow Press, The.*** Sensational and jingoist newspapers or journalism. The name arose in the United States about 1898 in consequence of scaring articles on the 'Yellow Peril'.

**Yemen.** The south-west corner of the Arabian peninsula, called by the ancients 'Arabia Felix'. *Felix* is a mistranslation by Ptolemy of *Yemen*, which means to the 'right' – i.e. of Mecca.

> Beautiful are the maids that glide
> On summer-eves through Yemen's dales.
>
> Thomas Moore, *Fire-worshippers*

**Yeoman.** Anciently, a forty-shilling freeholder, and as such qualified to vote and serve on juries, but not qualified to rank as one of the gentry. In more modern times it meant a farmer who cultivated his own freehold. Later still, an upper farmer, tenant, or otherwise, is often called a yeoman.

***Yeomen of the Guard.*** The beef-eaters (*q.v.*).

**Yeth-hounds.** Dogs without heads, of west country folklore; said to be the spirits of unbaptised children, which ramble among the woods at night, making wailing noises.

**Yew.** The yew is a British tree, and is commonly planted in churchyards because, as it is an evergreen, it is a symbol of immortality. It was planted by the Druids near their temples.

**Yiddish.** A Middle German dialect developed under Hebrew and Slavic influence, written in Hebrew characters, and used as a language by German and other Jews (Ger. *jüdisch*, Jewish).

Hence a Jew is sometimes called in contempt a *Yiddisher* or *Yid*.

**Yoke.** *To pass under the yoke.* To make a humiliating submission; to suffer the disgrace of a vanquished army. The Romans made a yoke of three spears – two upright and one resting on them. When an army was vanquished, the soldiers had to lay down their arms and pass under this archway of spears.

**Yorick.** The King of Denmark's deceased jester, 'a fellow of infinite jest and most excellent fancy', whose skull is apostrophised by Hamlet (Act 5, l). In *Tristram Shandy* Sterne introduces a clergyman of that name, meant for himself.

**York.** The Anglo-Saxon *Eure-wic* (pron. *Yorric*), the town on the Eure, now called the Ouse. The Romans Latinised the word *Eure* or *Evre* into 'Evora' or 'Ebora', and *wic* into 'vicum'; whence Ebora-vicum, contracted into *Eboracum*.

**Yorker.** A cricketing term for a ball bowled so as to pitch three or four feet from the wicket, immediately in front of the bat. Probably so called because first effectively used by a Yorkshire bowler.

**Yorkist.** A partisan of the White Rose in the Wars of the Roses. *See* **Rose**.

**Yorkshire.** ***I'se Yorkshire, too.*** I am as deep as you are, and am not to be bamboozled. The north countrymen are proverbially 'long-headed and cannie'.

***The Yorkshireman's toast.*** 'Here's tiv us, all on us; may we never want nowt, noan on us; nor me nawther.'

**Young.** Used as an epithet in the names of political parties who strive to sweep away abuses and introduce reforms. Thus, we have, or have had, *Young England*, *Young Italy*, the *Young Turks*, etc.

***Young Germany.*** A school headed by Heine in the mid 19th century, whose aim was to liberate politics, religion, and manners from the old conventional trammels.

***Young Ireland.*** The Irish politicians and agitators (at first led by O'Connell) who effected the rising of 1848.

***Young Italy.*** A league of Italian refugees, who associated themselves with the French republican party, called the *Charbonnerie Démocratique*. It was organised at Marseilles by Mazzini about 1834, and its chief object was to diffuse republican principles.

**Ysolde (Yseult, Isolde,** etc.). The name of two heroines of Arthurian romance, the more important *Ysolde the Fair*, King Mark's wife, being the lover of Tristram (*q.v.*), the other, *Ysolde of the White Hands*, or *Ysolde of Brittany*, being his wife, with whom he made a 'Maiden Marriage' (*see* Swinburne's *Tristram of Lyonesse*) after he had been discovered by King Mark and had been obliged to flee.

It was through the treachery of Ysolde of the White Hands that Sir Tristram died, and that Ysolde the Fair died in consequence. The story has it that King Mark buried the two in one grave, and planted over it a rose-bush and vine, which so intermingled their branches as they grew up that no man could separate them.

**Yule, Yuletide.** Christmas time. A.S. *geola*, from Icel. *jōl* (with which possibly our *jolly* is connected), the name of a heathen festival at the winter solstice.

***Yule log.*** A great log of wood laid in ancient times across the hearth-fire on Christmas Eve. This was done with certain ceremonies and much merrymaking.

> Ever at Yuletide, when the great log flamed
> In chimney corner, laugh and jest went round.
>
> Aldrich, *Wyndham Towers*, stanza 5

**Yves** or **Yvo, St.** Patron saint of lawyers, being himself a lawyer. He was an ecclesiastical judge at Rennes, was ordained priest in 1285, died in 1303, and was canonised in 1347. As he used his knowledge of the law in defending the oppressed, he is still called in Brittany (where his festival is kept on May 19th) 'the poor man's advocate'.

> Advocatus, sed non latro,
> Res miranda populo. *Hymn to St Yves*

**Ywain.** One of the Knights of the Round Table; identical with the Owain (or Owen) ap Urien of the Welsh bards and the *Mabinogion*. He is the hero of Chrestien de Troyes' *Le Chevalier au Lyon* (12th cent.), which appears as a 14th-century English metrical romance – *Ywain and Gawain*.

# Z

**Z.** The last letter of the alphabet, called *zed* in England, but in America *zee*. Its older English name was *izzard*.

In mathematics it denotes the third unknown quantity (*see* X); and in mediaeval times it was used as a Roman numeral for 2,000.

**Zadikim.** *See* Chasidim.

**Zadkiel.** In rabbinical angelology, the angel of the planet Jupiter.

The name was adopted as a pseudonym by the astrologer Lieutenant Morrison (1795–1874) of the Navy, author of the *Prophetic Almanac*, commonly called *Zadkiel's Almanac*.

**Zadoc,** in Dryden's satire of *Absalom and Achitophel*, is designed for Sancroft, Archbishop of Canterbury.

> Zadoc the priest, whom (shunning power and place)
> His lowly mind advanced to David's [Charles II] grace.
> Pt i, lines 801–2

**Zagtith.** *See* Jambuscha.

**Zakkum.** A tree growing in the Mohammedan hell, from which a food is prepared for the damned of inexpressible bitterness.

> How will it be for him whose food is Zakkum?
> *The Koran*

**Zal.** A semi-divinity of Persian myth, father of Rustem (*q.v.*), the Hercules of Persia. He was the son of Sâm Nerimân, and was exposed on Mount Elburz because he was born with white hair, and therefore supposed to be the offspring of a deer. He was brought up by the wonderful bird Seemurgh, and when claimed by his father, received from the foster-bird a feather to give him insight into futurity.

> Let Zal and Rustum bluster as they will.
> FitzGerald, *Rubáiyát of Omar Khayyām*

**Zalambur.** One of the sons of Eblis (*q.v.*).

**Zamorin.** The title of the native ruler of Calicut and the surrounding country.

**Zany.** The buffoon who mimicked the clown in the old theatrical entertainments; hence a simpleton, one who 'acts the goat'. The name is the Italian *zanni*, a buffoon, fem. of *Giovanni* (i.e. John), our *Jane*.

> For indeed,
> He's like the zani to a tumbler
> That tries tricks after him to make men laugh.
> B. Jonson, *Every Man out of his Humour*, iv, 2

> He belonged to one of those dramatic companies called *zanni*, who went about the country reciting and acting. *John Inglesant*, ch. xxvii

**Zarb.** *See* Bastinado.

**Zarps.** The policemen of Kruger's old Transvaal Republic were so called; from the initials on their buttons – standing for South (*Zuid*) African Republic Police. An acrostic word, like Anzac, Waac, etc.

**Zeitgeist** (Ger. *zeit*, time, *geist*, spirit). The spirit of the time; the moral or intellectual tendency characteristic of the period.

**Zemindar.** An Indian landowner holding direct from the Government and paying a fixed rent based on the revenue from his land.

**Zemire.** *See* Azor's Mirror: Beauty and the Beast.

**Zem Zem.** The sacred well near the Kaaba at Mecca. According to Arab tradition, this is the very well that was shown to Hagar when Ishmael was perishing of thirst

**Zend-Avesta.** The sacred writings of Zoroaster (or Zarathushtra) that formed the basis of the religion that prevailed in Persia from the 6th century BC to the 7th century AD. *Avesta* means the text, and *Zend* its interpretation into a more modern and intelligible language; hence the latter name has been given to the ancient Iranian language in which the *Zend-Avesta* is written.

> The sacred writings of the Parsees have usually been called *Zend-Avesta* by Europeans; but this is, without doubt, an inversion of the proper order of the words, as the Pahlavi books always style them 'Avisták-va-Zand' (text and commentary).
> Haug, *Essays on the Parsis*, Essay iii, p. 19

**Zenelophon.** A corruption of *Penelophon*. The beggar-maid loved by King Cophetua.

> The magnanimous and most illustrate king Cophetua set eye upon the pernicious and indubitate beggar Zenelophon.
> Shakespeare, *Love's Labour's Lost*, 4, 1

**Zenith, Nadir** (Arabic). *Zenith* is the point of the heavens immediately over the head of the spectator. *Nadir* is the opposite point, immediately beneath the spectator's feet. Hence, *to go from the zenith of prosperity to the nadir* is to fall from the height of fortune to the depths of poverty.

**Zephyr.** The west wind in *classical mythology*; son of Aeolus and Aurora, and lover of Flora; hence, any soft, gentle wind.

**Zero** (Arabic, a cipher). The figure 0; nothing; especially the point on a scale (such as that of a thermometer) from which positive and negative quantities are measured; on the Centigrade and Réaumur thermometers fixed at the freezing point of water, on the Fahrenheit 32° above this.

***Absolute zero*** is the point at which it would be impossible for a body to get any colder; i.e. that at which it is totally devoid of heat (estimated at about – 274° C).

***Zero point.*** In *Time*, 12 o'clock, midday; the time at which 24 hour clocks begin the day.

**Zeus.** The Grecian Jupiter (*q.v.*). The word means the 'living one' (Sanskrit, *Djaus*, heaven).

**Zincali** or **Zingari.** Gypsies; so called in Spain from *Sinte* or *Sind* (India) and *calo* (black), on the supposition that they came from India which no doubt is true. The Persian *Zangi* means an Ethiopian or Egyptian.

**Zion** (Heb. *Tsiyon*, a hill). *Daughter of Zion.* Jerusalem or its people. The city of David stood on Mount Zion.

In the *Pilgrim's Progress* Bunyan calls the Celestial City (i.e. Heaven) *Mount Zion.*

**Zionism.** The movement for colonising the Jews in their old home, Palestine, the Land of Zion.

**Zodiac** (Gr. *zodiakos*, pertaining to animals; from *zoon*, an animal). The imaginary belt or zone in the heavens, extending about eight degrees each side of the ecliptic, which the sun traverses every year.

***Signs of the Zodiac.*** The zodiac was divided by the ancients into twelve equal parts, proceeding from west to east; each part of thirty degrees, and distinguished by a sign; these originally corresponded to the zodiacal constellations bearing the same names, but now, through the precession of the equinoxes, they coincide with the constellations bearing the names next in order.

Beginning with 'Aries', we have first six on the north side and six on the south side of the equator; beginning with 'Capricornus', we have six *ascending* and then six *descending* signs – i.e. six which ascend higher and higher towards the north, and six which descend lower and lower towards the south. The six northern signs are: *Aries* (the ram), *Taurus* (the bull), *Gemini* (the twins), spring signs; *Cancer* (the crab), *Leo* (the lion), *Virgo* (the virgin), summer signs. The six southern are: *Libra* (the balance), *Scorpio* (the scorpion), *Sagittarius* (the archer), autumn signs; *Capricornus* (the goat), *Aquarius* (the water-bearer), and *Pisces* (the fishes), winter signs.

> Our vernal signs the Ram begins,
> Then comes the Bull, in May the Twins;
> The Crab in June, next Leo shines,
> And Virgo ends the northern signs.
>
> The Balance brings autumnal fruits,
> The Scorpion stings, the Archer shoots;
> December's Goat brings wintry blast,
> Aquarius rain, the Fish come last. E. C. B.

**Zohar.** The name of a Jewish book containing cabalistic expositions of the 'books of Moses'. Traditionally ascribed to Rabbi Simon ben Yochi, first century; but probably belonging to the 13th century.

> The renowned Zohar is written in Aramaic, and is a commentary on the Pentateuch, according to its divisions into fifty-two hebdomadal lessons.
> *Encyclopaedia Britannica*, vol. xii, p. 813

**Zoilism.** Harsh, ill-tempered criticism; so called from Zoilus (*q.v.*).

**Zoilus.** A Greek rhetorician of the 4th century BC, a literary Thersites, shrewd, witty, and spiteful, nicknamed *Homeromastix* (Homer's scourge), because he mercilessly assailed the epics of Homer, and called the companions of Ulysses in the island of Circe 'weeping porkers' ('*choiridia klaionta*'). He also flew at Plato, Isocrates, and other high game.

> Pendentem volo Zoilum videre. Martial

**Zollverein.** The customs union that existed from about 1820 between the States of the former German Empire for the purpose of establishing a uniform tariff of duties and maintaining Free Trade among themselves.

**Zophiel.** An angelic scout of 'swiftest wing' in Milton's *Paradise Lost* (vi, 355). The word means 'God's spy'.

**Zounds!** A minced oath; euphemistic for *God's wounds.*

**Zulal.** The stream of the Mohammedan Paradise, clear as crystal and delicious as nectar, of which the just drink.

**Zuleika.** The name traditionally ascribed to the wife of Joseph, and a very common name in Persian poetry.

**Zurich Bible, The.** *See* Bible, Specially named.

**Zwickau Prophets, The.** *See* Abecedarian.